THIRTY-SECOND EDITION

KOVELS'

ANTIQUES & COLLECTIBLES

PRICE LIST

FOR THE 2000 MARKET

ILLUSTRATED

D0061526

Three Rivers Press New York

Published by Three Rivers Press, 201 East 50th Street, New York, New York 10022.
Member of the Crown Publishing Group.

Random House, Inc. New York, Toronto, London, Sydney, Auckland

www.randomhouse.com

THREE RIVERS PRESS is a registered trademark of Random House, Inc.

Printed in the United States of America

Library of Congress Catalog Card Number: 83-643618
ISBN 0-609-80471-5 (pbk.)
10 9 8 7 6 5 4 3 2 1

Books by Ralph and Terry Kovel

American Country Furniture 1780–1875

A Directory of American Silver, Pewter, and Silver Plate

Kovels' Advertising Collectibles Price List

Kovels' American Art Pottery: The Collector's Guide to Makers,
Marks, and Factory Histories

Kovels' American Silver Marks: 1650 to the Present

Kovels' Antiques & Collectibles Fix-It Source Book

Kovels' Book of Antique Labels

Kovels' Bottles Price List

Kovels' Collector's Guide to American Art Pottery

Kovels' Collectors' Source Book

Kovels' Depression Glass & Dinnerware Price List

Kovels' Dictionary of Marks—Pottery & Porcelain

Kovels' Guide to Selling, Buying, and Fixing
Your Antiques and Collectibles

Kovels' Guide to Selling Your Antiques & Collectibles

Kovels' Illustrated Price Guide to Royal Doulton

Kovels' Know Your Antiques

Kovels' Know Your Collectibles

Kovels' New Dictionary of Marks—Pottery & Porcelain

Kovels' Organizer for Collectors

Kovels' Price Guide for Collector Plates, Figurines,
Paperweights, and Other Limited Editions

Kovels' Quick Tips—799 Helpful Hints on
How to Care for Your Collectibles

Kovels' Yellow Pages: A Collector's Directory

The Label Made Me Buy It: From Aunt Jemima to Zonkers—
The Best-Dressed Boxes, Bottles and Cans from the Past

It is hard to believe that this is the 32nd year we have compiled this price book. It has changed from a book with no illustrations and typewriter-style letters to this edition with hundreds of pictures and logos, about 50,000 prices, dozens of tips about care, and a special report, "Curious Collectibles," about objects that have not been used for years and are unfamiliar today. And the book is still being written by the original authors, Ralph and Terry Kovel.

READ THIS BEFORE YOU USE THIS BOOK—IT WILL HELP

This is a book for the average collector. All year we check prices, visit shops and shows, read our mail, check online computer services and the Internet, and decide what antiques and collectibles are of most interest. We concentrate on the average pieces in any category. We sometimes include one or two high-priced pieces in a category so you will realize that some of the rarities are quite valuable. For example, majolica listed this year includes a matchbox for $27 and a lobster-shaped dish for $9,200.

Examples of furniture, silver, Tiffany, or art pottery may sell for more than $50,000; we list few of those examples. The highest price in this book is $93,500 for a $22\frac{5}{8}$-inch-high Cherry and Cherry Blossom Tiffany lamp with a cat's-paw base. The lowest price is 30 cents for a Princess Brand butter wrapper with a cow picture from the 1940s. Most pieces we list cost less than $10,000. We even list the weird and the wonderful. This year you can find prices for a pair of 1920s driving goggles with amber glass lenses for $30, a metal gas nozzle for $65, a red gear-shift knob with white dots from the 1930s for $35, a Plains Indian skull cracker for $60, a 1925 license for dispensing opium for $55, and an old stick of Beeman's Pepsin gum for $45. The smallest object is a $\frac{3}{8}$-inch political button showing General Pershing for $22. The largest is a wrought iron garden gazebo, 12 feet by 12 feet, for $2,175.

Prices are up in some categories. Nippon and Noritake porcelains have become popular collectibles in Japan and the added interest has caused American prices to rise. Prices for studio jewelry from the 1950s, such as pieces by Sam Kramer and Arthur Smith, have been rising. Probably the most active area of collecting this year is again the furniture, glass, and lighting pieces made from the 1950s to the 1970s. European auction houses have started to hold 20th-century sales, and more than half a dozen specialized 20th-century shows are held annually. There is continued interest in garden antiques, art pottery, and tiles. The antiques malls that are springing up in all parts of the country and the auctions and sales found on the Internet are also influencing prices. Small pieces that are inexpensive and easy to identify sell quickly. It is said that about 20 percent of the buyers of antiques now use computers. This percent is increasing each year. The market online is getting larger and is international. Objects that are known in most of the world, like pens, cigarette lighters, Mickey Mouse toys, Royal Doulton pottery, majolica, and oak furniture, are selling well.

Each year categories are added or omitted to make it easier for you to find your antiques. New categories this year are Basalt, L.G. Wright glass, Malachite, Purinton pottery, Rorstrand pottery and porcelain, Rose Mandarin, and Science Fiction.

The book is kept at about 800 pages because it is written to go with you to sales. We try to have a balanced format—not too many glass, pottery, or collectible items, a variety of furniture from the 18th through the 20th centuries, not too many items that sell for over $5,000. The prices are *from* the American market *for* the American market. Few European sales are reported. We take the editorial privilege of not including any prices that seem to result from "auction fever." The computer-generated index is so complete it amazes us. Use it often. An internal alphabetical index is also included. For example, there is a category for Celluloid. Most items made of celluloid will be found there, but if there is a toy made of celluloid, it will be listed under Toy and also indexed under Celluloid. There are also cross-references in the listings and in the paragraphs. But some searching must be done. For example, Barbie dolls are found in the Doll category; there is no Barbie category. And when you look at "doll, Barbie" you will see a note that tells you that Barbie is under "doll, Mattel, Barbie" because most dolls are listed by maker. All pictures and prices are new every year, except pictures that are pattern examples shown in Depression Glass and Pressed Glass. The pictures have been computer-enhanced to make them as crisp as possible. Antiques pictured are not museum pieces but items offered for sale. We hate to waste space, so whenever computer-generated spaces appeared, we filled them with tips about care of collections, security, and other useful information. Leaf through the book and learn how to wash porcelains, store textiles, guard against theft, and much more. Don't discard this book when it is time to buy a new one next year. Old Kovels' price books should be saved for future reference, and for tax and appraisal information.

The prices in this book are reports of the general antiques market, not the record-setting examples. Each year, every price in the book is new. We do not estimate or "update" prices. Prices are actual asking prices, although a buyer may have negotiated a price to a lower figure. No price is an estimate. We do not ask dealers and writers to estimate prices. Experience has shown that a collector of one type of antique is prejudiced in favor of that item, and prices are usually high or low, but rarely a true report. If a price range is given, it is because at least two identical items were offered for sale at different times. The computer records prices and prints the high and low figures. Price ranges are found only in categories like Pressed Glass, where identical items can be identified. If the price is from an auction, it includes the buyer's premium, but like all of the prices, it does not include sales tax.

Some prices in *Kovels' Antiques & Collectibles Price List* may seem high and some may seem low because of regional variations. But each price is one you could have paid for the object.

If you are selling your collection, do not expect to get retail value unless you are a dealer. Wholesale prices for antiques are from 20 to 50 percent less than retail. Remember, the antiques dealer must make a profit or go out of business.

THE RECORD PRICES HYPE

The media loves to report record prices, amazing auctions, high-priced discoveries, and other events that really have little to do with the antiques and collectibles market of the average collector. A rare pickle bottle that was purchased at a tag sale for $3 was sold on the Internet for $44,000. A Rembrandt sketch was discovered inside the pages of an old book at a bookstore in Amsterdam. Great stories, but—like winning the lottery—not likely to happen to everyone. So study the records, but remember that these are the prices for the rarest and best.

BRONZE & OTHER SCULPTURES

- **James Earle Fraser bronze sculpture:** $277,500 for the bronze sculpture *The End of the Trail* by James Earle Fraser, cast number 4 at the Roman Bronze Works, 44½ inches. Seneca Chief John Big Tree modeled for the original in 1894.

CLOCKS & WATCHES

- **American tall-case clock:** $452,000 for a c. 1779 Delaware Chippendale tall-case walnut clock, made by Duncan Beard, with a rocking ship in the arch above the dial, 97 x 21 x 11 inches. The dial is signed by Duncan Beard, Appoquinimink, and the chalk inscription on the inside of the paneled pendulum door reads, "Made in Cantwell's Bridge/Delaware/1779."
- **Neoclassical ormolu mantel clock:** $156,500 for a Neoclassical ormolu mantel clock by Jean-Baptiste Dubuc, Paris, c. 1800. A figure of George Washington in military uniform leaning on a sword and a wingspread eagle on a globe are mounted above the clock, 19 x 14½ x 5½ inches.

FURNITURE

- **American 17th-century Southern armchair:** $288,500 for an American 17th-century Southern armchair, made of turned and joined cherry and ash.
- **Federal sideboard:** $255,500 for a Federal satinwood inlaid and figured mahogany sideboard bearing the label of William Lloyd, Springfield, Massachusetts, dated 1811.
- **Gustav Stickley armchair, no. 353A:** $4,675 for a Gustav Stickley armchair, with a three-vertical-slat back and original rush seat, 41 x 25 x 22 inches.
- **Gustav Stickley child's wardrobe:** $25,300 for a Gustav Stickley child's wardrobe, no. 920, with two paneled doors and copper V-pulls, an eight-drawer

one-shelf interior, marked with a red decal and a paper label, 60 x 33 x 16 inches.

- **Gustav Stickley china cabinet:** $187,000 for a c. 1901 Gustav Stickley china cabinet, trapezoid shaped, with nine glass panel doors of thin mitered and flared mullions above arched doors with ring-pull hardware, 66 x 57 x 13 inches.
- **Gustav Stickley Damascus plant stand with a Grueby tile:** $22,000 for a Gustav Stickley Damascus plant stand, no. 9, with eight angled legs and an inset green matte glazed octagonal Grueby tile, 18 x 18 x 21 inches.
- **Gustav Stickley library table:** $12,100 for a Gustav Stickley library table, no. 456, with a rectangular top, two hidden drawers, and a lower shelf, marked with a red decal, 36 x 24 x 29 inches.
- **Gustav Stickley Morris chair:** $46,750 for a Model 2342 slat-arm Morris chair by Gustav Stickley, c. 1901, with original finish and leather cushions, marked with an early red Stickley sticker under the arm.
- **Gustav Stickley plant stand:** $5,500 for a Gustav Stickley plant stand, with splayed legs, a keyed-tenon stretcher, and a notched rail, marked with a red decal, 14 x 14 x 26 inches.
- **Gustav Stickley table with twelve Grueby tiles:** $60,500 for a Gustav Stickley table with a top of twelve inset green matte glazed Grueby tiles, an arched apron, a lower shelf, and double keyed-tenon construction, marked with a red decal, 24 x 20 x 26 inches.
- **Gustav Stickley two-door bookcase:** $52,250 for a Gustav Stickley bookcase, no. 703, with double doors, each with three leaded panels above three vertical windows and an arched toe-board, marked with a red decal and a paper label, 60 x 14 x 58 inches.
- **Gustav Stickley umbrella stand:** $11,000 for a Gustav Stickley umbrella stand, marked with a red decal, 28½ inches.
- **Gustav Stickley wine cooler:** $9,350 for a Gustav Stickley wine cooler, no. 553, with tapered and slatted circular copper bands and copper hardware on a three-footed base, marked with a red box mark, 13 x 15 inches.
- **L. & J.G. Stickley bookstand:** $7,150 for a signed L. & J.G. Stickley bookstand with a slanted bookshelf above four shelves, 28 x 13 x 36 inches.

GLASS

- **Bellflower pattern pressed glass cake stand:** $4,600 for a Bellflower pattern pressed glass cake stand, 9¼ inches.
- **Bitters bottle:** $68,750 for a green, eight-sided "Bryant's Stomach Bitters" bottle made in 1857, cone shape, approximately 14 inches high. Bryant's of San Francisco produced this bottle for only one year.
- **Cassin's bitters bottle:** $44,000 for a "Cassin's Grape Brandy Bitters" bottle with an applied top and smooth base, 10 inches. This form was made from 1871 to 1875.
- **Cut glass decanter:** $30,000 for a turquoise cut-to-clear decanter in the Croesus pattern by J. Hoare, 13 inches.
- **Embossed "Sure Break" target ball:** $16,335 for an embossed yellow with amber tone "Sure Break" target ball, "Patent Apl'd for," with concave panels and a rough-sheared mouth, 2¼ inches.

- **"Free" set of miniature perfume samples:** $4,300 for a complete set of three Schiaparelli miniature samples, "Sleeping," "Shocking," and "Zut." This set was a free gift in the 1950s.
- **Julian Viard perfume flacon:** $12,875 for a Julian Viard flacon, "Parfum, les Trois Muses, La Danse," created by Charles Faÿ.
- **Non-flint pressed glass:** $5,100 for a piece of non-flint pressed glass—a hollow stem champagne glass in the Three Face pattern.
- **Perfume flacon:** $58,360 for a Coty "L'Idylle" flacon, created in 1911 by René Lalique.
- **Pressed glass goblet:** $10,500 for a Sandwich Vine pattern goblet with gilt highlights.
- **Pressed glass:** $14,000 for a Horn of Plenty pattern rectangular honey dish and cover with the original matching undertray.
- **Sandwich glass:** $52,900 for a mottled bright blue Sandwich glass inkstand set.
- **Triple Baccarat paperweight:** $45,100 for a triple Baccarat paperweight, formed by three sections fused together—half-inch millefioricanes in the bottom section, Macédoine in the middle, and a red-and-white clematis on top, $3\frac{1}{4}$ inches high.

LAMPS & LIGHTING

- **Handel lamp:** $82,500 for a Handel Aquarium lamp, 16 inches. The glass shade is a painted underwater scene of tropical fish swimming among plant life, signed by the artist, Bedigie. It has a bronzed base.
- **Pairpoint puffy apple tree lamp:** $32,450 for a Pairpoint puffy apple tree lamp with a 12-inch diameter shade.
- **Pairpoint puffy orange tree lamp:** $34,100 for a Pairpoint puffy orange tree table lamp with a 14-inch diameter shade.
- **Wall lights:** $1,817,500 for a set of four Louis XVI ormolu twin-branch wall lights made in 1781 for Marie-Antoinette's boudoir at Versailles.

METAL

- **Jarvie vase:** $28,600 for a swollen-form hammered-copper Jarvie vase with tapered body and original patina, 27 x $13\frac{1}{2}$ inches.

MISCELLANEOUS

- **Titanic boarding pass:** $110,000 for an original and intact immigrant inspection card that served as a boarding pass for third-class passenger Ana Sophia Sjoblom.
- **Leather Western saddle without silver:** $55,000 for a leather Western saddle without silver ornamentation, in a half seat design with tapaderos and raised floral carving, made by Main & Winchester of San Francisco, c. 1870.

MOVIE & CELEBRITY MEMORABILIA

- **One-sheet movie poster:** $60,555 for Karoly Grosz's 1933 one-sheet movie poster for the Universal film *The Invisible Man* by H.G. Wells, starring Claude Rains.
- **Three-sheet, style B poster:** $70,700 for a three-sheet, style B poster for the 1933 movie *King Kong,* starring Fay Wray, 41 x 81 inches, one of only four known to exist.

POTTERY & PORCELAIN

- **A pair of Charles Volkmar pastoral vases:** $5,500 for a pair of Charles Volkmar pastoral vases painted in the Barbizon style with scenes of horses pulling carts, sepia tones, and both signed "Chas. Volkmar," 12¼ x 7½ x 3¾ inches.
- **Chinese porcelain:** $3,764,360 for a doucai "chicken" cup with multicolored enamels and a soft blue underglaze, picturing two groups of cockerel, hen, and chicks, with rocks, red roses, and yellow daylilies in between, from the Chenghua period of the Ming Dynasty (1465–1487), 3¼ inches.
- **Clarice Cliff sugar sifter:** $9,775 for a Clarice Cliff, May Avenue pattern sugar sifter, cone shaped, 5½ inches.
- **Cowan figurine *Boy with Fawn*:** $4,840 for the Art Deco figure *Boy with Fawn* by artist Waylande Gregory, produced by Cowan in a limited edition, terra-cotta glaze, c. 1930, 16½ inches.
- **Grueby pottery and any piece of Arts & Crafts pottery:** $66,000 for a Grueby floor vase by Wilhemina Post with tooled and applied broad leaves, yellow buds, and leathery green matte glaze, 15½ x 10 inches.
- **Niloak, any piece:** $2,750 for a marbleized clay, handled jug, four-sided, 6 inches.
- **Niloak umbrella stand:** $2,310 for a brown-and-white marbleized umbrella stand, 20 inches.
- **Roseville Futura line vase:** $3,850 for an orange-and-brown Roseville Futura line vase, with a four-sided top section, two handles, and a stepped base, 14 inches.

SPORTS

- **Baseball board game:** $25,300 for Zimmer's Base Ball Game by McLoughlin Bros., New York, 1893–1895, with a brilliantly colored game board and gilt letters on a red ground on the box.
- **Baseball:** $3,005,000 for the 70th home-run ball hit by Mark McGwire.
- **Edward Vom Hofe reel:** $8,525 for an Edward Vom Hofe Perfection Trout reel, size 1, handmade German silver and hard rubber.
- **Foreign-made fishing tackle:** $10,450 for a brass trout click reel, engraced "Ustonson Makers To His Majesty Temple Bar Ld'n," England, c. 1830.
- **Royal Perth Putter:** $174,900 for a metal-head blade putter, from the Royal Perth Golfing Society, with a paper label, dating from the late 18th or early 19th century, 9¾ x 7½ inches.
- **Single baseball-related photograph:** $25,300 for a sepia-tone photograph of the 1911 All-Star team, with the photographer's stamp "Copyright 1911/by L. Van Oeyen/ Cleveland, Ohio" in raised silver lettering at the bottom left, 11 x 13½ inches.

TOOLS

- **18th-century wooden plane:** $15,300 for an 18th-century wooden, crown-molding plane, made and signed in Wrentham, Massachusetts, 13⅛ x 4⅜ inches.
- **Pincers:** $6,284 for an engraved and gilded farrier's pincers/pliers, dated 1706, with "DG" on the handle, 10 x 2 inches.

TOYS, DOLLS & GAMES

- **Barbie doll:** $13,500 for a 1959 Ponytail Barbie #1 in a rare Barbie-Q outfit, complete with accessories and original box.
- **China marble:** $6,925 for a Scenic Rose china marble, produced and hand-painted in Germany, with a blue pinwheel design on the top and bottom poles and six pink roses with green leaves around the diameter, and an opaque white base, 1¼ inches. There are only two other Scenic Rose china marbles known to exist.
- **Schoenhut circus:** $17,250 for Schoenhut Humpty Dumpty circus, c. 1928, oval tent with side panels, 30 x 45 x 17½ inches.
- **Schoenhut circus/safari animal:** $6,185 for a Schoenhut glass-eyed hyena with hand-shaped head.
- **Schoenhut Teddy Roosevelt set:** $19,500 for Teddy's Adventures in Africa set No. 2080, c. 1912, 17-piece set consisting of Teddy with camera, African man, animals, tent and camp accessories, original jungle printed background paper, and original box.
- **20th-century French doll:** $135,000 for a c. 1916 French bisque doll by Albert Marque, with a composition body, bisque socket head, blue glass inset eyes, closed mouth, and brunette human hair, in its original signed costume, 22 inches.

A NOTE TO COLLECTORS

You already know that this is a great overall price guide for all sorts of antiques and collectibles. Each entry is current, every picture is new, all prices are accurate.

But in the collecting world, things change quickly. Important sales produce new record prices. Rarities are discovered. Fakes appear. To keep up with these developments, you can read *Kovels on Antiques and Collectibles,* a monthly newsletter with up-to-date information on the world of collecting. It is filled with color photographs, about forty to an issue. The newsletter reports prices, trends, auction results, internet sales and other pertinent news for collectors *as it happens.* For a free sample of *Kovels on Antiques and Collectibles,* fill out and mail the postage-paid postcard at the back of this book. We now have an informational Web site. Visit www.kovelsprices.com to learn more.

KEEP READING—HOW TO USE THIS BOOK

There are a few rules for using this book. Each listing is arranged in the following manner: CATEGORY (such as Pressed Glass or Furniture), OBJECT (such as vase), DESCRIPTION (as much information as possible about size, age, color, and pattern). Some types of glass, pottery, and silver are exceptions to this rule. These are listed CATEGORY, PATTERN, OBJECT, DESCRIPTION. All items are presumed to be in good condition and undamaged, unless otherwise noted. If a maker's name is easily recognized, like Gustav Stickley, we try to include it near the beginning of the entry. If the maker is obscure, the name may be at the end. Because the descriptions are part of actual reports, we do not edit to make everything consistent in each entry. We try to edit enough to be sure that two items are not actually two descriptions of the same piece.

Several special categories were formed to make the most sensible listing possible. For instance, the Tool category includes special equipment because the casual collector might not know the proper name for an "adze." Many of the glass entries are in special categories: Glass-Art, Glass-Blown, Glass-Contemporary, Glass-Midcentury, and Glass-Venetian. Major glass factories are still listed under the factory names, and well-known types of glass, such as cut, pressed, Carnival, etc., can be found in their own categories. The silver listings are also a bit different. You will find silver flatware in either Silver Flatware Plated or Silver Flatware Sterling. You will also find a section for Silver Plate, which includes coffeepots, trays, and other plated pieces. Solid or sterling silver is listed by country, so look for Silver-American, Silver-English, etc. Pottery and porcelain are usually listed by factory name or item, but some are found in Art Pottery, Art Nouveau, Art Deco, Arts & Crafts, Dinnerware, Kitchen, Pottery, or Porcelain.

Sometimes we make arbitrary decisions based on the number of entries or interest in a subject. Fishing has its own category, but hunting is part of the larger category called Sports. We have eliminated all guns except toy types. It is not legal to sell weapons without a special license, and so guns are not part of the general antiques market. Airguns, BB guns, rocket guns, and others are listed in the Toy section. Several idiosyncrasies of style appear because the book is printed by computer. Everything is listed according to the computer alphabetizing system. This means words such as "Mt." are alphabetized as "M-T," not as "M-O-U-N-T." All numerals are before all letters; thus "2" comes before "A." A quick glance will make this clear, as it is consistent throughout the book.

We made several editorial decisions. A bowl is a "bowl" and not a "dish," unless it is a special dish, such as a pickle dish. A butter dish is a "butter." A salt dish is called a "salt" to differentiate it from a saltshaker. It is always "sugar and creamer," never "creamer and sugar." Political collectors often refer to "pinbacks," the round celluloid or tin pins that are decorated with candidates' names and faces. The word "button" is sometimes used in this book instead of the word "pinback." Of course, the word "button" is also used when referring to the fasteners used on clothing. Where one dimension is given, it is the height; or if the object is round, the dimension is the diameter. The height of a picture is listed before the width. Glass is clear unless a color is indicated.

Every entry is listed alphabetically, but the problem of language remains. Some antiques terms, such as "Sheffield" or "Pratt," have two meanings. Be sure to read the paragraph headings to know the meaning used. All category headings are based on the language of the average person at an average show, and we use terms like "mud figures" even if they are not technically correct.

This book does *not* include price listings of fine art paintings, antiquities, stamps, coins, or most types of books. *Big Little Books* and similar children's books *are* included. Comic books are *not* listed, but original comic art and cels *are* listed in their own categories.

All pictures in *Kovels' Antiques & Collectibles Price List* are listed with the prices asked by the seller. "Illus" (illustrated nearby) is part of the description if a picture is shown.

There have been misinformed comments about how this book is written. We *do* use the computer. It alphabetizes, ranges prices, sets type, and does other time-consuming jobs. Because of the computer, the book can be produced quickly. The last entries are added in June; the book is available in October. This is six months faster than would be possible any other way. But it is human help that finds prices and checks accuracy. We read everything at least three times, sometimes more. We edit from 80,000 entries to the 50,000 entries found here. We correct spelling, remove incorrect data, write category headings, and decide on new categories. We sometimes make errors. Information in the paragraphs is reviewed and updated each year. This year over fifty-five corrections and additions were made in the category headings.

Prices are reports from all parts of the United States and Canada (translated to U.S. dollars at the rate of $1.47 (U.S. to $1 Canadian) between June 1998 and June 1999. Prices are from auctions, shops, and shows. Every price is checked for accuracy, but we are not responsible for errors.

We cannot answer your letters asking for specific price information. But please write if you have any requests for categories to be included in future editions or any corrections to information in the paragraphs.

When you see us at the shows, stop and say hello. Don't be surprised if we ask for your suggestions for the next edition of *Kovels' Antiques & Collectibles Price List.* Or you can write us at P.O. Box 22200-K, Beachwood, Ohio 44122 or visit us at our Web site: www.kovelsprices.com.

RALPH & TERRY KOVEL
July 1999

DEDICATION

To Steve Magneson, advisor, knight in shining armor, trouble shooter, problem solver, business associate, and friend of many years. Good luck in your new career.

ACKNOWLEDGMENTS

Special thanks should go to those who helped us with pictures and deeds: Alderfer Auction Co.; Allard Auctions, Inc.; Auctions Unlimited Inc.; Bill Bertoia Auctions; Butterfields; Butterfield & Dunning; Charles G. Moore Americana; Christie's; Cincinnati Art Galleries; Collector's Auction Services; Conestoga Auction Co.; Copake Auction; Dan Ripley Antiques; David Rago Auction Inc.; DeFina Auctions; Fink's Off the Wall Auctions; Garth's Auctions, Inc.; Gary Kirsner Auctions; Gary Metz's Muddy River Trading Co.; Gene Harris Antique Auction Center, Inc.; Glass-Works Auctions; Jackson's Auctioneers & Appraisers; James D. Julia, Inc.; Lang's Sporting Collectables, Inc.; Los Angeles Modern Auctions; Manion's International Auction House, Inc.; McMasters; Michael Ivankovich Auction Co., Inc.; Michael A. Merrill; New Orleans Auction Galleries; Noel Barrett Antiques; Old Barn Auction; Pacific Glass Auctions; Phillips; Phillips-Selkirk's; Randy Inman Auctions, Inc.; Richard Opfer Auctioneering, Inc.; Robert C. Eldred Co., Inc.; Selman, Ltd.; Skinner, Inc.; Smith & Jones, Inc.; Sotheby's; Treadway Gallery, Inc.; William Doyle Galleries; and many anonymous collectors. An extra thank you for the special help given by Carmie Amata, Lee Markley, and James Measell.

To the others in the antiques trade who knowingly or unknowingly contributed to this book, we say "thank you": Afterwards Antiques; Al Zastrow; Andre Ammelounx; Antique Bottle Connection; Antiques & Elderly Things; Audrey Willmann; B & D Collectibles; Baker's International Antiques & Collectibles; Bea Gordon; Betty Parker; Big Beaver Antiques; Bill Smith; Block's Box; Bob & Helen Rarey; Bob Zajac; Brian Moran's; Buffalo Bay Auction Co.; Carl F. Gurley, Inc.; Carmel Doll Shop; Carolyn Kriner; Catherine & Bob Bohi; Cel-Ebration; Chagrin Antiques, Ltd.; Charles & Mildred Fisher; Charles E. Kirtley; Cheryl Leaf Antiques & Gifts; Cobweb Corner Antiques; The Collector's Stop; Craftsman Auctions; Crooked Stump Farm; Currier Antiques; Dialing for Dolls, Inc.; The Dancing Girl; Dave Martens; Dave & Penny Renner; David R. Geiger; Denise Scott; Dottie Noonan; Doug Wolk; DuMouchelle's Art Galleries; E & G Antiques; EAC Gallery; F. Fagan & Co., Inc.; Fern Martin; Fiesta Plus; Forever Heisey; Frank H. Boos Gallery; Frank Elske; Gene Howell; Gibb & Bev Green; Ginger Berry; Golf's Golden Years; Good Golly Ms Lolly; Grandma's Attic; Green Valley Auctions, Inc.; Greg & Barbara

Hall; Hake's Americana & Collectibles; Henry & Karen Johns; Hesson Collectables; Historic Originals Gifts & Collectibles; Ingrid O'Neil Sports & Oympic Memorabilia; J. C. Devine, Inc.; J.E. Porcelli; Jeff Hooven; Jerry's Antiques; Jim Reed; John J. McHugh; Joy Luke Auction Gallery; The Kentucky Sandpiper; Larry Gottheim; Leann Delange; Leland's Auctions; Linda Chadwick; LJ & JB Decker; Maritime Antiques & Auctions; Mary Tupta; Neil & Robert Ross; Nikel Enterprises, Inc.; Norma's Jeans; Norton's Auctions; Nostalgia Gallery; The Oriental Corner; Pat Austin; Paul Efron; Paul Irby; Perdue & Podner; Peter Vincent; Phil Mancini; Philip Norman; Phoenix Militaria Corporation; Pine Tree Antiques; Pook & Pook, Inc.; Postcards International; R & S Antiques; Ray Mortimeyer; Remmey Galleries; Replacements, Ltd.; Rex Stark; Richard Fitch Americana; Richard A. Powell; Robert W. Dyke; Roberta's Doll House; Paulene Seymour; Shelby Messinger; Sloan's; Snow Hill Antiques; Susan Blashford; Susan Levine; Susan's; Swann Galleries; Team's Tiffany Treasures; Ted Kromer; Theriault's; Thomas & Marcia Brown; Tim Gaudet; Timothy & Lillian Hart; Tom & Deena Caniff; Tom Polansky; Tom Waggoner; Tonquish Creek Fire Company; Toy Scouts Inc.; Treasure Trove; Turn of the Century Antiques; Vernon E. Spaulding; The Village Antiques; Virginia Kreutzer; Virginia Reece; Waverly Auctions, Inc.; Winter Brook Farm Antiques; Winter Associates; Wolf's; Woody Auction; Yankee Tools & Collectables; Yard's Antiques; and York Town Auction Inc.

Although the Kovel name is on the cover, this book is the work of many people. Their input, correcting, checking facts, reviewing art work, and other problem solving is what makes this the accurate, timely book it is. To Pam Stinson-Bell, who checks every word over and over and faces sleepless nights because of timing problems, our special gratitude. Merri Ann Morrell and Diane Dugal of Precision Graphics calmly corrected the computer problems. Chip Gibson, PJ Dempsey, Karen Minster, Elizabeth Bird, and John Sharp faced daily problems with the book in New York. Closer to home, Kitty Busher, Grace DeFrancisco, Marcia Goldberg, Harriet Goldner, Evelyn Hayes, Katie Karrick, Karen Kneisley, Benjamin Margalit, Eleanore Melzak, Gloria Pearlman, Nancy Saada, Cherrie Smrekar, Edie Smrekar, Virginia Warner, and Ann Wochner worked all year. But our biggest thank you is to Gay Hunter who coordinated the work in both cities and checked spelling, schedules, entries, paragraph updates, layout, and chased everyone to be accurate and on time.

A. WALTER made pate-de-verre glass under contract at the Daum glassworks from 1908 to 1914. He started his own firm in Nancy, France, in 1919. Pieces made before 1914 are signed *Daum, Nancy* with a cross. After 1919 the signature is *A. Walter Nancy*.

Bookends, 2 Nude Female Musicians, Standing At Each Bower, Green, Blue, Pair	5175.00
Bowl, Festoons, Crab & Seaweeds, Signed, c.1920, 9 3/4 In.	4025.00
Dish, Oval, Flared Quatrefoil, Hammered Motif, Yellow, Amber, Brown, 8 x 3 In.	760.00
Inkwell, Stag Beetle, Lemon Yellow, Ocher, Brown, Black, 1920, 6 1/2 In.	5175.00
Paperweight, Brown Swan On Green Opalescent Ground, 3 1/2 In.	173.00
Vase, Landscape, Brown, Olive, Yellow, Orange Sky, Green, Orange Foliage, 8 In.	605.00

ABC plates, or children's alphabet plates, were most popular from 1780 to 1860, but are still being made. The letters on the plate were meant as teaching aids for children learning to read. The plates were made of pottery, porcelain, metal, or glass. Mugs and other items were also made with alphabet decorations.

Cup, Pink Luster, Small	145.00
Plate, 2 Boys In Cart Pulled By Dog, Staffordshire, 1880, 7 In.	125.00
Plate, Aluminum, 7 In.	16.00
Plate, Base Ball, Running To First Base, American Sports, Staffordshire, 6 1/4 In.	345.00
Plate, Boy Giving Girl Flowers, Mary Gregory, 7 In.	50.00
Plate, Braille Symbol Inner Edge, German Shepherd Seeing-Eye Dog	22.00
Plate, Children Sledding, Gold Transfer Border, Burford Bros., c.1904, 6 1/8 In.	1135.00
Plate, Clockface Center, 7 In.	45.00
Plate, Franklin's Proverb, Make Hay While The Sun Shines, 6 In.	175.00
Plate, General Windfield Scott, Woman & Child, Soft Paste, 5 In., Pair	410.00
Plate, Gleaners, Glazed, 6 In.	80.00 to 115.00
Plate, Little Goose Box, Germany	45.00
Plate, Newspaper Boy, Malkin & Co., 6 In.	170.00
Plate, Punch & Judy, Dog Licking Punch, 7 1/2 In.	65.00
Plate, Punch & Judy, Judy Hitting Punch With Stick, 7 1/2 In.	155.00
Plate, Rugby Try, 7 1/4 In.	255.00
Plate, Stork Carrying Baby, Alphabet On Edge, Carnival Glass, 7 1/2 In.	26.00
Plate, Timely Rescue, 8 In.	165.00
Plate, Tin, Ohio Art, 6 1/4 In.	110.00
Plate, Woman, Carrying Bundle Of Twigs, 2 Children, Staffordshire, 6 In.	48.00
Plate, Women On Bridge, Brown Transfer, Edge Malkin & Co., 6 In.	110.00

ABINGDON POTTERY was established in 1908 by Raymond E. Bidwell as the Abingdon Sanitary Manufacturing Company. The company started making art pottery in 1934. The factory ceased production of art pottery in 1950.

Bookends, Horse, Pink	65.00
Cookie Jar, Bar Jar	525.00
Cookie Jar, Daisy, Blue	90.00
Cookie Jar, Little Bo Peep	400.00
Cookie Jar, Miss Muffet	400.00
Cookie Jar, Money Bag	100.00 to 125.00
Cornucopia, Triple, White, No. 583	30.00
Figurine, Goose, White	45.00
Urn, Pink Wreath, No. 538	20.00
Vase, Egert, Pink, Floor, 14 In.	225.00
Vase, Pearl Gray Rope, Floor, 18 In.	495.00
Window Box, No. 476	20.00

ADAMS china was made by William Adams and Sons of Staffordshire, England. The firm was founded in 1769 and is still working. All types of tablewares and useful wares have been made through the years. Other pieces of Adams will be found listed under Flow Blue.

Bowl, Hanover Terrace, Regents Park, 8 1/4 In.	385.00
Bowl, Serving, Kyber Pattern, Dark Blue Transfer, Octagonal, Handles	77.00
Chamber Pot, Cover, Columbia, 9 In.	66.00
Dish, Rose, Scalloped Border, Signed, 10 1/2 In.	192.00

Mug, Mush, Farmers Arms 90.00
Pitcher, Silver Cover, Brown Glaze, Neck, Foot, Early 19th Century, 9 In. 225.00
Pitcher & Bowl, Palestine, Turquoise Transfer 412.00
Plate, Oliver Twist, Orange Border 125.00
Plate, St. Paul's School, London, Dark Blue, 7 3/4 In. ....115.00 to 165.00
Platter, Blue Feather Edge, 15 1/2 In. 80.00
Platter, Feather Edge, Soft Paste, Signed, 15 1/2 x 19 1/2 In. 165.00
Platter, Jedburgh Abbey, Roxburghshire, Dark Blue Transfer, 17 In. 357.00
Platter, Mountain Scenery, Blue Transfer, 15 1/2 In. 192.00
Teapot, Floral Transfer, 6 1/2 In. 165.00

ADVERTISING containers and products sold in the old country store are now all collectibles. These stores, with the crackers in a barrel and a potbellied stove, are a symbol of an earlier, less hectic time. Listed here are many of the advertising items. Other similar pieces may be found under the product name, such as Planters Peanuts. We have tried to list items in the logical places, so large store fixtures will be found under the Architectural category, enameled tin dishes under Graniteware, paper items in the Paper category, etc. Store fixtures, cases, and other items that have no advertising as part of the decoration are listed in the Store category.

Anvil, Wincroft 100 Years, Cast Iron, 4 1/2 x 2 x 1 1/4 In. 55.00
Ashtray, Americana Hotel, Bal Harbor, Fla., Harker Pottery, Round, 5 In. 3.00
Ashtray, B-1 Lemon Lime Soda, Clear Glass, Red Logo, Pair 22.00
Ashtray, Bottle & Lampshade Type, Decal, 1930-1940, 6 In. 175.00
Ashtray, Commodore Hotel, Lenox 29.00
Ashtray, Electrolux, Sculptural Promotions, 1950s 125.00
Ashtray, Fisk Tires, Rubber & Glass, Fisk Glider 600/16, 6 1/2 In. 205.00
Ashtray, Green River Whiskey, Hotel Davenport, Horse In Relief, Copper, Post 50.00
Ashtray, Green River Whiskey, Metal, She Was Bred In Old Kentucky Logo, 1930 ...... 125.00
Ashtray, Hamburg American Line, Logo, Brass, 8 3/4 In. 95.00
Ashtray, K-Listo Kilovatio, 1950s, 4 x 1 In. 38.00
Ashtray, Kentucky Fried Chicken, Stamped Steel, Gray Finish 20.00
Ashtray, Lancer's Beer, Ceramic, 1950s 6.00
Ashtray, Michelin Man, Plastic, 4 3/4 x 5 x 5 1/2 In. 110.00
Ashtray, Playboy Club, Orange, Glass 25.00
Ashtray, Reddy Kilowatt, Glass, Red Reddy Character, 3 Cigarette Rests, 4 1/2 In. 35.00
Ashtray, Reddy Kilowatt, Red & White, 4 x 1 In. 95.00
Ashtray, White Owl Cigars, Glass, Blue & White Label, Square, 4 In. 100.00
Badge, Dr Pepper, Name, Safety Pin Type, Enamel Painted Base, 2 1/4 x 1 1/2 In. 440.00
Bag, Arrow Tobacco 15.00
Bag, Ole Virginia Hickory Chip, Paper & Grill, Paper, 6 x 14 In. 10.00
Banner, Aunt Jemima Pancakes, Cloth, Plate Of Pancakes In Corner, 34 x 58 In. 550.00
Banner, Dauntless Coffee And All Food Products, Cloth, 5 x 3 Ft. 220.00
Banner, Dean Martin, Jerry Lewis, Sound Off For Chesterfield, 60 x 29 In. 440.00
Banner, Rexall, The Original Rexall One Cent Sale, Cloth, 1923 .... 275.00
Banner, Texaco, Get The Jump On Spring, Canvas, 1954, 33 x 84 In. 230.00
Banner, Tuxedo Tobacco, You Should Worry!, It's Guaranteed, 119 x 44 In. 742.00
Banner, Veedol Motor Oil, Car & Road, Countryside Graphics, 36 x 82 In. 165.00
Bin, Beech-Nut Chewing Tobacco, Slanted Front, 10 x 8 x 9 In. 231.00
Bin, Blanke's Coffee, S-Curved Front, Text 3 Sides, 7 1/2 In. 225.00
Bin, Boye's Hand Sewing Needles, Tin, Counter, 18 x 19 x 9 In. 340.00
Bin, Capital Coffee, Sides & Front Panel, Pine, 32 1/3 x 21 In. 550.00
Bin, Cuba, Slant Front, Porcelain Knob, 18 x 14 x 12 In. 1065.00
Bin, Duke's Mixture Tobacco, All Around Graphics, Counter 770.00
Bin, Hickory Shoe Laces, Tin Lithograph, 12 Drawers, 11 x 12 1/2 In. 100.00
Bin, J.A. Folger & Co., Fine Young Hyusont, Ship, Rolled Front, 20 x 14 In. 2185.00
Bin, Jamo Coffee, Man, White Beard, Horse, Slant Top, 13 x 10 x 16 In. 12655.00
Bin, Loudon Johnson, Roasted Coffee, Gold Stencil, Painted Tin, 22 x 21 In. 695.00
Bin, Pastime Tobacco, John Finzer & Bros., Lithograph, 12 1/2 x 9 1/4 In. 145.00
Bin, Potato, Sioux City Garden Sees, Pine, Hinged Lid, Country, 29 In. 100.00
Bin, Shinkle, Wilson & Kreis Co. Coffee, Paper On Wood, 16 x 14 x 20 1/2 In. 175.00
Bin, Sure Shot Chewing Tobacco, Counter 700.00

Bin, Sweet Cuba Tobacco, 11 x 8 1/4 In. 95.00
Bin, Tiger Tobacco, Blue, Tiger On Front & Back, 8 1/2 x 11 1/2 In. 1610.00
Bin, Use Only Lion Coffee, Wooden Peg & Nail Construction, Pine, 31 1/4 x 20 In. 220.00
Bin, Wilbur's Seed Meal, Wooden, Lift Top, Mustard Paint, 36 1/2 x 18 x 20 In. 635.00
Blotter, Babes In Wood, C.M. Burd, 1913, 4 x 9 In. 9.00
Blotter, Camel Cigarettes, Man & Woman In Formal Clothes, 1930s, 3 1/2 x 6 In. 6.00
Blotter, Dewey Embossed Picture, Anti-Friction Metal Ad, 4 x 9 In. 85.00
Blotter, Dr Pepper, Plenty Good, 1930-1940 .... 125.00
Blotter, Edison Mazda Lightbulb, Valencia Plumbing & Electric Shop, 1922, 6 In. 15.00
Blotter, Green River Whiskey, Man, With Horse, Black Lettering, 9 1/2 x 4 In. 55.00
Blotter, Hercules Powder, 4 x 9 In. 75.00
Blotter, Ink, Franklin Duroil, Classic Auto, Logo, 6 x 3 1/2 In., 5 Piece 20.00
Blotter, Insurance Counselor, San Leandro, Cal., Unused, 1930s, 2 1/2 x 6 In. 2.00
Blotter, Merchant Of Venice, Broadway Play, Jos. DeGrasse, 1904, 9 x 4 In. 35.00
Blotter, Penn Securities, Lancaster, Penna., Girlie Type, Earl Moran, 1948, 4 x 9 In. 12.00
Blotter, Senex Insect Killer, Floral Design, Unused, 2 1/4 x 4 In. 4.00
Blotter, Weston Coal Co., Syracuse, N.Y., Unused, 1930s, 3 1/2 x 6 In. 3.00
Books may be included in the Paper category.
Booklet, Butterflies Of America, From Chase & Sandborn Coffee, 49 Pages, 1900 ...... 45.00
Booklet, Ceresota Flour, Painting Book In Story Form, 1912 .... 30.00
Booklet, Dutch Boy Paint, Copyright 1914 By John T. Lewis & Bros., 20 Pages 12.00
Booklet, G.E. Refrigerator, Big Top Circus, Unpunched, Envelope, 1950 .... 55.00
Booklet, Hendlers Ice Cream, Kewpie Eating Ice Cream, 4 Pages 6.00
Booklet, How To Be A Crack Shot, Remington Arms Co., 1973, 16 Pages, 8 x 11 In. 12.00
Booklet, Jell-O, Hungry King, 3-Way Fold, 1920s, 9 x 2 1/2 In. 11.00
Booklet, Jell-O, Hungry King, Child's Story, 3-Way Fold, 1920s, 9 x 2 1/2 In. 11.00
Booklet, Jell-O, Jack & Jill, Jell-O Ryme Only Story, 1920s, 9 x 2 1/2 In. 11.00
Booklet, Jell-O, King's Delight, 3-Way Fold, 1920s, 9 x 2 1/2 In. 12.00
Booklet, Jell-O, King's Delight, Child's Story, 1920s, 9 x 2 1/2 In. 12.00
Booklet, Jell-O, Mothers Of Whatsis Declare Independence, 1920s, 9 x 2 1/2 In. 15.00
Booklet, Jersey Gold Creameries Coupon, 1930s 4.00
Booklet, Kellogg's Funny Jungleland, Moving Pictures, 1932, 8 x 6 1/2 In. 55.00
Booklet, New Departure Coaster Brake Bicycle, 1914, 8 Pages, 3 x 6 In. 25.00
Booklet, Post Cereal Co., A Trip Through Posturnville, Hardcover, 1920 .... 45.00
Booklet, Story Of Heinz 57, 1930s 15.00
Booklet, The Adventures Of The Dutch Boy, Soft Cover, 1914, 20 Pages 12.00
Booklet, Western Holly Gas Range, Stove Care, Recipes, Linda Darnell Cover, 1940s ... 15.00
Bookmark, Comfort Soap, Baby, Paper 48.00
Bootjack, Lee Riders, Plywood, Rubber & Leather Trim, Mexico, 12 x 5 In. 45.00
Bootjack, Musselman's Plug Tobacco 125.00
Bootjack, Tony Lama, Wooden 25.00
Bottles are listed in their own category.
Bottle Openers are listed in their own category.
Bottle Topper, Whistle Soda, Girl's Head Sipping Straw, Oranges, Cardboard, 17 In. 85.00
Box, see also Box category.
Box, Carmen Complexion Powder, Stafford Miller Co., Cardboard, Round 22.00
Box, Carter's Inky Racer, 2 Bottles & Instruction Sheet, Cardboard, 2 3/4 x 3 In. 99.00
Box, Cereal, Blue Bell Rolled Oats, 3 Lb. 7 Oz. 170.00
Box, Cereal, Cream Of Wheat, Waiter With Bowl Of Cream Of Wheat, Cardboard, 13 In. . 55.00
Box, Cereal, Donald Duck 3 Minute Oats, 3 Lb. 210.00
Box, Cereal, Groub's Belle Rolled Oats, Woman In Hat, Cardboard, Round, 1 Lb. 4 Oz. .. 550.00
Box, Cereal, High Line Rolled Oats, Train On Bridge, Cardboard, Round, 3 Lb. 390.00
Box, Cereal, Home Brand Rolled Oats, Griggs, Cooper & Co., Early, 3 Lb. 7 Oz. 170.00
Box, Cereal, Kellogg's Corn Flakes, Free Sample, 1926, 5 1/4 x 8 3/4 In. .... *Illus* 48.00
Box, Cereal, Kellogg's Corn Flakes, Help Huck Rescue Yogi Bear Contest, 12 1/2 In. 68.00
Box, Cereal, Maltex, 1937, 6 Oz., Pair 55.00
Box, Cereal, Nicolet Rolled Oats, Frank C. Schilling Company, 3 Lb. 415.00
Box, Cereal, Peco Brand Quick Cook Rolled Oats, Cardboard, Round, 3 Lb. 7 Oz. 176.00
Box, Cereal, Post Toasties, Woman Cooking At Fireplace, Postum Cereal Co., Ltd., 9 Oz. . 232.00
Box, Cereal, Quaker Puffed Wheat, Shirley Temple, My Cereal, c.1937, 3 1/2 Oz. 220.00 to 248.00
Box, Cereal, Quick Draw McGraw, Sugar Smacks, 1962, 7 1/4 x 9 3/8 In. 125.00
Box, Cereal, Ralston Wheat Cereal, Sample, NRA Stamp, 1933-1935, 3 3/4 In. 55.00
Box, Ceresota Enriched Flour, Boy On Stool, Contents, 2 Lb. 100.00

Advertising, Box, Cereal,
Kellogg's Corn Flakes, Free Sample,
1926, 5 1/4 x 8 3/4 In.

Advertising, Matchbox,
Ogden's Cobnut, Sliced, Tin,
2 1/8 x 1 3/8 In.

Advertising, Matchbox,
Schinkenhager, Bottle,
Celluloid, 2 1/4 x 1 1/2 In.

Box, Cigar, Buck, Revenue Stamp, Inner Liner, Wooden, Virginia, 50 Count, c.1900 . . . . . 55.00
Box, Cigar, Exposition, Columbus, Miss Liberty, Administration Building 150.00
Box, Cigar, Forest King, Wooden, Iowa, 50 Count, c.1916 . . . . 175.00
Box, Cigar, Lead Mine, Revenue Stamp, Liner, Wooden, Illinois, 50 Count, c.1910 . . . . . . 77.00
Box, Cigar, Miss Detroit, Wooden, Michigan, 50 Count, c.1920 . . . . 88.00
Box, Cigar, Mon Amour, Wooden, Michigan, 50 Count, c.1915 . . . . 88.00
Box, Cigar, Old Columbia Cheroots, 200 Count, Patriotic Design, 1883 Tax Stamp 110.00
Box, Cigar, Old Judge, Wooden, Wisconsin, 100 Count, c.1916 . . . . 40.00
Box, Cigar, Pony Ranger, Wooden, New York, 50 Count, c.1900 . . . . 121.00
Box, Cigar, White Indian, Wooden, Michigan, 50 Count, c.1916 . . . . 204.00
Box, Cigar, Wide Open, Wooden, New York, 100 Count, c.1890 . . . . 33.00
Box, Cigar, Woodcraft, Wooden, Iowa, 50 Count, c.1916 . . . . 110.00
Box, Colman's Mustard, Wooden, London, England, 4 x 20 x 13 In. 110.00
Box, Cookie, Animal Crackers, Cardboard, Greyhound Shape, Blue, 1950s, 9 In. 55.00
Box, Display, Levi's Guys, Photos, Big E, 1960s, 8 x 8 x 12 In. 37.00
Box, Display, Nabisco Shredded Wheat, Factory, Niagara Falls, c.1932, 12 Oz. 150.00
Box, Display, Western Scout Toilet Soap, Buffalo Bill, Wooden, 17 x 8 x 2 In. 1250.00
Box, Dr. Blummers Maple Extract, Lincoln Chemical Works, Cardboard 100.00
Box, Duffy's Malt Whiskey, 1860, Rochester, N.Y., Wooden, 11 x 14 1/4 In. 65.00
Box, E.R. Durkee & Co.'s Select Spices, Wooden, Paper Label, 16 x 4 x 8 1/2 In. 110.00
Box, Egg, Rich's Poultry Farm, Red, Square, 12 In. 85.00
Box, Feed, Wilbur's Seed Meal, Top Lifts Out Exposing Stock Food, 36 x 20 In. 7700.00
Box, Gold Dust Washing Powder, Unopened, 8 1/2 In. 50.00
Box, Gold Dust, Twins Cleaning, Cardboard, 12 x 10 x 18 In. 120.00
Box, Gulf Wax, Logos 15.00
Box, Hires Root Beer, Wooden, Early 1900s, 5 Gal. 95.00
Box, Indian Herbs, Great American Herb Company, Cardboard, 150 Pills, 4 In. 72.00
Box, Jack & Jill Gelatin, Lemon Jell-O, 1940s 1.00
Box, Jonteel Cold Cream Face Powder, Long-Tailed Bird, 6 Sides, Inner Seal 25.00
Box, Kentucky Fried Chicken, Cardboard, Colonel Sanders On Lid, 1954 . . . . 75.00
Box, Knox Sparkling Gelatin, Cardboard, Charles B. Knox Gelatin Co., 1 Lb. 110.00
Box, Lakeland Rolled Oats, Moon On Water, 3 Lb. 185.00
Box, Mark Twain Cigars, Boy On River, Twain Inside Lid, 6 Cent Cigars 195.00
Box, Merlin Cleanser, Wizard, Crystal Ball, Paper On Cardboard, c.1929, 3 x 6 In. 83.00
Box, Mr. Dee-Lish Popcorn, 1950s 50
Box, Orange Fruit, Railroad, Unicorn Label, Original Lid, 1930s 95.00
Box, Pratt's Poultry Regulator, Cardboard, Unopened, 8 1/2 x 12 In. 33.00
Box, Pulver Chewing Gum, Cardboard 3300.00
Box, Remington, DuPont Blue Tablets, Cardboard, Shipping Type 195.00
Box, Robin Hood Ammunition Co., Wooden, Dovetailed, Load No. B-7 . . . . 305.00
Box, Schepp's Coconut 40.00
Box, Seed, Burt Seed Co., 9 Little Seed Boxes 50.00
Box, Seed, Card Seed Co., 1920s 1.00

Box, Seed, D.M. Ferry & Co. Seed, Choice Of Flower Seeds, Light Yellow, 9 In. 115.00
Box, Seed, D.M. Ferry & Co. Seed, Quartersawn Oak, Light Blue Ground, 11 In. 297.00
Box, Seed, D.M. Ferry & Co. Seed, Quartersawn Oak, Pink Ground, 16 x 8 x 4 In. 357.00
Box, Seed, D.M. Ferry, Label, 121 Packets At 5 Cents, 20 Cents & 15 Cents, 11 In. 88.00
Box, Seed, Webster's Mammoth Packet Seed, Green Ground, 1900, 29 x 15 In. 121.00
Box, Sensation Cut Plug Tobacco, Wooden Bail Handle, Dark Blue, 7 1/2 In. 120.00
Box, Shaker Salt, Wooden, Dovetailed Corners, 16 x 12 x 12 In. 27.00
Box, Shipping Crate, George J. Young, Utica, N.Y., Black, Wooden, 22 x 12 In. 115.00
Box, Toonerville Folks, Cookies, Shoelace Handle, Uneeda, Nabisco, c.1930 .... 210.00
Box, Yucatan Gum, Yellow, Red Accents, Square 200.00
Box, Zu Zu Ginger Snaps, Clown, Uneeda Bakers, Play Store Instructional Item 160.00
Broadside, Black Oil Liniment, 24 x 18 In. 325.00
Brochure, Around The World With The Graf Zeppelin, American Steel & Wire Co. 26.00
Brochure, Dr. David Roberts Veterinary, 48 Different Remedies For Cats & Dogs 30.00
Brochure, Krueger Beer In Cans, Fold-Out, Pop-Up Flattop Can 5.00
Buckle, Zippo, Submarine Squadron Sixteen Emblem, Box Bottom 25.00
Cabinet, De Laval Cream Separators, Oak, Drawers, Hooks, 26 x 17 1/2 x 11 In. 550.00
Cabinet, Diamond Dyes, Children Skipping Rope, Oak, Tin, 15 x 24 x 8 In. 770.00
Cabinet, Diamond Dyes, Evolution Of Women, Oak, Tin, 30 x 24 x 9 In. 890.00
Cabinet, Diamond Dyes, Maypole, 3 Shelves, 1915, 24 1/2 In. 1500.00
Cabinet, Diamond Dyes, Washer Woman, Mahogany, Green Background, 29 In. 1595.00
Cabinet, Hammermill Bond Examples Of Work We Do, Oak, Display, 41 x 2 In. 355.00
Cabinet, Hank-O-Chief, Men's Handkerchiefs, 2 For 25 Cents, Display 500.00
Cabinet, P. Lorillard Co., 2 Doors, 2 Drawers, Inlay, Display, 1883 .... 2500.00
Cabinet, Rainbow Dyes, Wooden, Contents, Display, Counter, 17 x 12 In. 825.00
Cabinet, Rit Dye, Tin Lithograph, 6 Wood & Tin Drawers, 14 1/4 x 16 1/4 In. 155.00
Cabinet, Spool, Brainard Armstrong & Co., Walnut, 4 Drawers, 20 x 16 x 9 In. 275.00
Cabinet, Spool, Cherry, Bird's-Eye Maple Veneer, Ring Pulls, 6 Drawers, 17 1/4 In. 605.00
Cabinet, Spool, Clark's Mile-End, Wooden, Reverse Painted, Drawers, 19 x 30 x 18 In. .. 495.00
Cabinet, Spool, Clark's O.N.T. Spool Cotton, 2 Drawers, 7 1/2 x 22 x 15 1/2 In. 172.00
Cabinet, Spool, Clark's O.N.T., Walnut, Ruby & Clear Glass Inserts, 23 x 9 1/2 In. 330.00
Cabinet, Spool, Clark's, Oak, Dress Braid In Roll Form 350.00
Cabinet, Spool, Clark's, Oak, Roll-Up Sides 1300.00
Cabinet, Spool, Corticelli Spool Silk, Walnut, Glass, 3 Drawers, 23 x 17 x 9 In. 195.00
Cabinet, Spool, Corticelli, Walnut, Bow Glass Door, 2 Drawers 1250.00
Cabinet, Spool, J.P. Coats, Mahogany, Eastlake Style, 29 x 25 x 18 In. 550.00
Cabinet, Spool, Lift Top, Oak, 4 Drawers, Vinyl Insert, 28 x 20 3/4 x 13 1/2 In. 305.00
Cabinet, Spool, Merrick's Dispenser, Oak, Oval, Curved Glass Ends, 32 x 23 In. 1980.00
Cabinet, Spool, Merrick's Standard Six Cord Spool Cotton, Walnut, 6 Drawers 825.00
Cabinet, Spool, Merrick's, Gold Stencil, Pat'd July 27, 1897, 18 x 22 In. 977.00
Cabinet, Spool, Merrick's, Oak, Curved Glass Ends, 32 x 23 In. ....*Illus* 1980.00
Cabinet, Spool, Oak, Pressed Stiles, 6 Drawers, Porcelain Pulls, 23 x 26 In. 605.00
Cabinet, Spool, Walnut, 6 Drawers, Paneled, Beaded Lines, 29 x 17 x 18 In. 330.00
Cabinet, Spool, Williamantic, 4 Drawers, Glass Pulls, 14 x 25 In. 1100.00
Cabinet, Star Braid, Walnut, Original Stenciling 1250.00
Cabinet, Veterinary Medicines, Pictures Doctor, Boxes, Tin & Wood 1200.00
Cabinet, We Sell Dy-O-La For Coloring At Home, Wooden, 13 1/2 x 17 x 8 1/2 In. 155.00

Advertising, Cabinet, Spool, Merrick's,
Oak, Curved Glass Ends, 32 x 23 In.

Tin signs and cans will fade from the
ultraviolet rays coming in a window
or from a fluorescent light. Plexiglass
UF-1 or UF-3 will cover the window
and keep the rays away from your
collection. There are also plastic
sleeves to cover fluorescent tubes.

Calendars are listed in their own category.
Can, Clabber Girl, 1940s, 4 Oz. 4.00
Can, Donald Duck Grapefruit Juice, Tin, Paper Label, Green Ground, 1 Qt. 14 Oz. 44.00
Can, Map-O-Spread, Ernest Carriere Inc., Montreal, Beaver 28.00
Can, Nabob Brand Baking Powder, Kelly, Doublas, Co., Strawberry Cake Label, 5 Lbs. ... 60.00
Can, Old Southern Molasses, Tin, Paper Label, J. Stromeyer Co., Philadelphia, 5 Gal. 110.00
Can, Pep Boys Lighter Fluid, Manny, Moe & Jack, Tin, 1934, 5 1/4 x 2 1/2 In. 205.00
Canisters, see introductory paragraph to Tins in this category.
Cards are listed in the Card category as card, advertising.
Carrier, Bottle, 7-Up, Family Pack, Cardboard, 10 x 15 x 7 In. 25.00
Carrier, Bottle, Moxie, Soda Clerk, 8 For 25¢, Cardboard, c.1940 .... 18.00
Carrier, Fresh Up With 7-Up, It Likes You, Aluminum, 24 Bottles, 17 x 12 In. 80.00
Carrier, Grapette, 6-Pack Aluminum, Logo Both Sides, 6 Oz. Bottles 210.00
Carton, Morton's Iodized Salt, It Pours, Classic Design, 1 Lb. 10 Oz. 30.00
Case, Banquet Cream Bread, 3 Glass Sides, Back Door, Shelf, 23 1/2 x 19 1/4 In. 275.00
Case, Case Knives, Oak, 5 Drawers In Back, 20 x 24 x 40 In. 550.00
Case, Cremo Export Cigar 1815.00
Case, Curtis Candies, Baby Ruth, Butterfinger, 2 Doors, 11 x 17 1/2 x 21 In. 330.00
Case, Garcia Grande Cigar, Tin, Lithograph, 13 x 9 x 13 In. 358.00
Case, Julius Schmid, Ramses, Sheik, Condom, XXXX, Decals, Wooden, 1931 .... 450.00
Case, Oak, 4 Glass Shelves, J. Riswig, Chicago, 14 x 21 x 9 In. 100.00
Case, Shiloh's Family Remedies, Wooden, Glass Door, 14 1/2 x 15 x 5 3/4 In. 85.00
Case, Squibb Vitamin Products, Wooden, Glass, 15 x 19 x 8 1/2 In. 65.00
Case, Storck's New Life Bread, Oak, Glass, Etched Label, 23 x 35 1/2 In. 230.00
Case, Waterman's Fountain Pens, Glass Front, Sides, Top, 17 1/4 x 16 In. 115.00
Case, Zeo Gum, Marquee Top, 3 Shelves, 10 x 18 In. 690.00
Case, Zippo, Tower Style, Light-Up, Rotates, 8 Sides, 23 In. 150.00
Case, Zippo, Tower Style, Light-Up, Rotates, 8 Sides, 41 In. 200.00
Chair, Smoke Piedmont, Cigarette Of Quality, Stadium, Porcelain Back, 1910 ....204.00 to 275.00
Chalkboard, Squirt Boy, Logo, 1950, 19 1/2 x 27 1/2 In. 100.00
Change Receiver, see also Tip Tray in this category.
Change Receiver, Fleer Bubble Gum, Piece Of Gum Picture 60.00
Change Receiver, Swastika Cigars, Glass, Cone Convex Top, 5 Cents, 1900, Large 295.00
Charm, Reddy Kilowatt, Figural, Brass, Red Enamel Paint, 1 In., Pair 60.00
Cigar Cutter, 2 Mechanical Handles, Round, Oval, Declarencia Havana Cigars, 9 In. 1025.00
Cigar Cutter, Clockwork, Wooden Base, Nickel Plated Cast Iron, 3 1/2 In. 475.00
Cigar Cutter, Figural, Nipper, RCA 880.00
Cigar Cutter, Reverse Painting, Favorita Cigars, Clockwork, Cast Iron, 3 3/4 In. 455.00
Cigar Cutter, Reverse Painting, Flor De Melba, Nickel Plated Iron, 3 In. 575.00
Cigarette Papers, Army Navy, 100 Leaves 14.00
Cigarette Papers, B & W, Red 8.00
Cigarette Papers, Big Ben 30.00
Cigarette Papers, Black Sea 11.00
Cigarette Papers, Bugler, 100 Leaves 5.00
Cigarette Papers, City Club, Name In Pencil On Front 53.00
Cigarette Papers, Country Gentleman 11.00
Cigarette Papers, Duke's Mixture, Gray 17.00
Cigarette Papers, Durham, 5 Cents 19.00
Cigarette Papers, Golden Grain, Not Gummed 12.00
Cigarette Papers, Great Puff 40.00
Cigarette Papers, Half And Half, Lucky Strike 12.00
Cigarette Papers, Himyar 11.00
Cigarette Papers, Orphan Boy 7.00
Cigarette Papers, Pride Of Reidsville 41.00
Cigarette Papers, Prince Albert, 15 Leaves 2.00
Cigarette Papers, Sir Walter Raleigh, Smoking Tobacco 20.00
Cigarette Papers, Targe, Long Cut 12.00
Cigarette Papers, Union Leader, Cut Plug 8.00
Cigarette Papers, Wheat Straw, The Only Genuine 15.00
Clocks are listed in their own category.
Coaster, Baltimore Brew, 1920s, 4 In. 27.00
Coaster, Beer That Made Milwaukee Famous, Paperboard, Square, 1940s, 4 1/4 In. 10.00
Coaster, Diamond Spring, Round, 1930s 16.00

To hang an old Coca-Cola tray use
a wire plate holder. The bent
parts that touch the tray should
be covered with plastic tubing.
Thin tubing is sold for use in
fish aquariums.

Advertising,
Dispenser, D.C.L.
Brand, Scotch Whiskey,
Edinburgh, 18 In.

Coaster, Pabst, Groucho Marx TV Show, Round, 1950s, 3 1/2 In.	3.00
Coaster, San Remo Restaurant, 2237 Mason St., San Francisco, 1940, 3 1/2 In.	5.00
Coaster, Schlitz, Beer That Made Milwaukee Famous, Square, 1940s, 4 1/4 In.	10.00
Coaster, Uhl's Beer, Round, 1930s	35.00
Container, Carnation Malted Milk, Aluminum Top, Porcelain, 8 1/2 x 6 In.	425.00
Cookbook Holder, Baker's Extracts, Tin, 7 1/2 x 5 1/2 x 3 In.	50.00
Cookie Cutter, Rumford	20.00
Cooler, Picnic, Vernor's Ginger Ale, Upholstered Top, In Store Carton	110.00
Counter Mat, Winston, Red & White, Rubber, 1950s, 9 1/2 x 8 In.	98.00
Creamer, Borden, Elsie, Individual	30.00
Crock, O.L. Gregory Vinegar Co., Elko County Pure Apple Juice Vinegar, Miniature	85.00
Cup, Dickinson's Pine Tree Timothy Seed, Porcelain, Handle, 2 3/4 In.	45.00
Cup, Hamm's Beer, Bear Relaxing In Backyard, Blue, Red, 1970, 5 In.	16.00
Cutout, De Laval Cow, Calf, Brown, White, Tin, 5 In. & 2 In., 2 Piece	205.00 to 220.00
Decal, Ballantine Ale & Beer, Cooler, 1950s, 17 x 15 In.	65.00
Decal, Salem Cigarettes, Window, Unused, 1950s, 8 1/2 x 8 3/4 In.	18.00
Dexterity Puzzle, Shell Thoro-Fast Service, 1930s Car, Cardboard, 2 1/4 In.	37.00
Dice Cup, Early Times Kentucky Bourbon, Red Leatherette, 5 Dice, Box, 4 In.	50.00
Dish, Elsie The Cow Ice Cream, Elsie Decals, Glass, 1940s, Set Of 4, 4 In.	100.00 to 110.00
Dispenser, Alka-Seltzer, Tin On Aluminum, Counter, 14 1/2 In.	265.00
Dispenser, Buckeye Root Beer	1725.00
Dispenser, Cannon's Orange Punch	8050.00
Dispenser, Cardinal Cherry Fizz	3737.00
Dispenser, Challenge Root Beer, Barrel, Wooden, Stainless Steel, 1950, 20 In.	345.00
Dispenser, Cherry Chic	5750.00
Dispenser, Cherry Smash	2250.00
Dispenser, Crawford's Cherry Fizz	4025.00
Dispenser, D.C.L. Brand, Scotch Whiskey, Edinburgh, 18 In. *Illus*	1115.00
Dispenser, Dixie Cups, Metal & Glass, Easton, Pa., Pat. Dec. 15, 1913, 32 In.	440.00
Dispenser, Dr. Swett's Root Beer	7762.00
Dispenser, Folger's, Red Metal Trim, Wall Mount, Glass	50.00
Dispenser, Fowler's Cherry Smash	2300.00
Dispenser, Fowler's Root Beer, Glass, Plated Lid & Base, 1930-1940	1205.00
Dispenser, Gillette Blades, Easel Back, Metal, Cardboard, Counter, 10 x 12 In.	30.00
Dispenser, Grape Crush, Glass	3162.00
Dispenser, Green River, Trophy Style, Glass, Chrome, 1930-1940	220.00
Dispenser, Hires Root Beer, Barrel, Oak, Stainless Banding, 1940s	375.00
Dispenser, Hires Root Beer, Drink Hires, Hourglass, 1920s	490.00
Dispenser, Hires, Marble, Copper, Brass & Glass, Victorian	4830.00
Dispenser, Hires, Porcelain Flavor Buttons, Pump, 4-In. Round Cover	135.00
Dispenser, Indian Rock Ginger Ale	4312.00
Dispenser, Lemon Crush	825.00
Dispenser, Liggett's Root Beer, Oak, Metal Bands, 3 Claw Foot Legs, 22 In.	715.00
Dispenser, Mint Julep, Stoneware, Glass, Brass Spigot, 18 1/2 In.	440.00
Dispenser, Mission, Real Fruit Juice, Mission Dry Corp., Ltd., Metal, Glass, 13 In.	415.00
Dispenser, Napkin, Plated, 1920s, 14 In.	200.00
Dispenser, Napkin, Swami, Stainless, Fortune, Penny	105.00

Dispenser, Necco Candy, Revolving, 4 Sides, 1930s, 18 In. 275.00
Dispenser, Orange Julep, 1920s 750.00
Dispenser, Queen Dairy Buttermilk, Porcelain, 1930, 15 x 34 In. 2415.00
Dispenser, Tea, Mirrored Front, Stenciled Design, Counter, 1880s, 15 x 20 In. 225.00
Dispenser, Van-Lansing Co. Lighter Fluid, 1 Cent Machine, Ellwood City, Pa., 19 In. 685.00
Dispenser, Ward's Orange Crush, 12 1/2 x 9 In. 1595.00
Dispenser, Ward's Orange Crush, 14 x 9 In. 1875.00
Display, Ballantine, Woman, Beer Glass, 1940s, 18 x 14 In. 45.00
Display, Beech-Nut Gum, Tin, 3 Tiers, 1950s, 27 1/2 x 15 1/2 In. 130.00
Display, Beech-Nut Mellor Fruit Chewing Gum, Woman, Gum, 1955, 10 x 12 In. 55.00
Display, Camel's Cigarettes, Jolly Santa, A Gift Sure To Please, 1940s, 9 x 11 In. 40.00
Display, Clinic Shoe, Figural Nurse, 1940-1950, 22 In. 245.00
Display, Dr. Grabow Pipes, 12 Pieces, 1950 . . . . 145.00
Display, Dr. Miles Laxative Tablets, Mabel, Girl, 3 Outfits, Cardboard, Stand-Up 230.00
Display, El Principal Cigars, Counter Stand-Up, Showing Open Box, 1920, 11 In. 60.00
Display, Elbeporo!, Cigars!, Gentleman, Holding Cigar, Die Cut, 13 x 21 In. 104.00
Display, Enjoy Grapette Cola, Easel Back, 1950s, 11 x 18 In. 92.00
Display, Fifty-Fifty Cigars, Counter Stand Up, 5 Cents Straight, 1940, 12 x 11 In. 60.00
Display, Gillette Blue Blade, Cardboard, Easel Back, 1930s, 30 x 22 In. 85.00
Display, Grapette, Pretty Woman & Bottle, Easel Back, 1950s 145.00
Display, Ice Cream, Soda Fountain Type, 1950, 5 1/2 x 11 In. 2.00
Display, Indian Maiden's Head, Tobacco, Plaster, Polychromed, Wall, 17 In. 175.00
Display, J.P. Wrigley's Chewing Gum, Reverse Etched Glass, 18 x 9 In. 75.00
Display, Joe Camel, Joe's Place, With Stand, 8 In. 35.00
Display, Kellogg's Cereals, Metal, Cardboard Back, 26 x 19 x 7 1/2 In. 385.00
Display, Kleenex, Little Lulu, Cardboard, Die Cut, 10 In., Pair 40.00
Display, M. Hohner, Finest Harmonica Made, 3-Tiered Wooden Box, Paper Label 40.00
Display, Man In Kilts, Usher's Scotch, Plaster, 17 In. 65.00
Display, Mobiloil, World's Best Known, Aluminum, Handle, 25 x 30 x 12 In. 445.00
Display, National's Eagle Whiskey, Light Blue, Papier-Mache, 1934, 15 x 24 In. 990.00
Display, Pelham Puppets, Pinocchio, Animals, Clown, Electric, England, 1960s, 21 In. . . . 385.00
Display, Pillsbury Doughboy, Figure, Styrofoam, Metal Stand, 54 In. 290.00
Display, Red Goose Shoes, Clown, Happy, Sad Face, Papier-Mache, Cardboard, 29 In. . . . 330.00
Display, Scoreze Golf Accessory, 2 Golfers, Plus Product, 1949, 10 x 13 In. 16.00
Display, Scripto, Vu-Lighter, Tower, Plastic, Acetate, Light-Up, Rotates, 23 In. 165.00
Display, Sharples Cream Separators, Woman Sitting, Cardboard, 52 x 40 In. 415.00
Display, Speedy Alka-Seltzer, Vinyl, Burnt Tan Patina, Small 250.00
Display, Store, Beech-Nut Mello Fruit Chewing Gum, Board, 1955, 10 x 12 In. 120.00
Display, Stork, Papier-Mache, Maternity Shop, c.1930, 34 In. 575.00
Display, Stroh's Beer, Plastic & Cardboard, 7 x 15 x 18 In., 3 Piece 66.00
Display, Sunbeam Bread, Look New Sunbeam Is Better, Little Girl With Bread, 26 In. . . . 632.00
Display, Sunshine Biscuits, Tin, Copper Front, Glass Window, 11 1/2 x 10 In. 230.00
Display, Tru Ade Bottle, Painted, Cardboard, 1950s, 5 1/2 x 22 1/2 In. 45.00
Display, Ullmann & Philpott Mfg. Co., Paintbrushes 575.00
Display, Waterman's Ideal Fountain Pen, Glass Sides, Tin Sign, 9 1/2 x 18 x 17 In. 770.00
Display, Whistle Orange Drink, Cute Girls Sipping Drink, 1950, 6 x 17 In. 35.00
Display, Winchester, Super Speed 22s, Crow Picture, Easel Back, 9 x 12 In. 90.00
Dolls are listed in their own category.
Door Knocker, Woody Woodpecker, Kellogg's Of Canada, Plastic, Die Cut, Box, 1966 . . . 48.00
Door Push, Chesterfield Cigarettes, 1930-1940, 4 x 9 In. 290.00
Door Push, Claussen's Bread, Metal, Red, White & Yellow Enamel, 6 x 3 In. 45.00
Door Push, Come In Drink Orange-Crush, Tin, 1920s, 3 x 12 In. 430.00
Door Push, Copenhagen Snuff, Celluloid Over Tin, Envelope, 3 x 8 In. 140.00
Door Push, Drink 2-1ay Beverage, Embossed, 4 x 10 In. 70.00
Door Push, King Cole Tea, Porcelain, Black, Yellow, Horizontal, 29 x 2 1/2 In. 25.00
Door Push, Kist, Aluminum, 1950s 145.00
Door Push, Munsing Wear, Brass, Embossed, 2 1/2 x 6 1/2 In. 260.00
Door Push, Squirt, Bottle Picture, Embossed, 1941, 3 1/2 x 9 In. 245.00
Door Push, Stegmaier's Gold Medal Beer, 1930s, 3 1/2 x 8 In. 75.00
Door Push, Tex Tobacco, Porcelain, 1920s, 4 x 6 1/2 In. 115.00
Envelope, Levi's, Advertising Display, Cowboys, 1956, 15 x 11 1/2 In. 55.00
Fans are listed in their own category.
Figure, Big Boy, Bobbing Head, 1950s, 7 1/2 In. 220.00

Figure, Big Boy, Holding Burger, Vinyl, Plastic, 1980s, 9 In. 35.00
Figure, Big Boy, Vinyl, Plastic, 1950s, Fat, 9 1/2 In. 55.00
Figure, Blatz Beer, Smiling Image Of Bartender Holding Mug, 1960, 10 1/2 In. 48.00
Figure, Boot, Pine Wooden, Gold, 19th Century, 11 3/4 x 10 3/4 In. 862.00
Figure, Campbell's Soup, Wizard Of O's, Soft Plastic, 7 In. 35.00
Figure, Cap'n Crunch, Stuffed Plush, Blue Felt Uniform, 17 In. 50.00
Figure, Count Chocula, Molded Plastic, Painted, Bag, 7 1/2 In. 30.00
Figure, Dr. Kool, Walking Along Carrying Satchel, Green Base, 1930, 4 1/2 In. 135.00
Figure, Falk's Milwaukee, Eagle On G Logo, 1866, 6 1/2 In. 50.00
Figure, Green Giant, Little Sprout, Soft Plastic, Painted, 1970s, 6 In. 25.00
Figure, Hamburger Helper Helping Hand, Gold, Plastic, 1 1/4 x 2 x 3 In. 18.00
Figure, Hamm's, Bear Cooking Dish, 1980s, 4 x 5 1/2 In. 77.00
Figure, Heinz Aristocat Tomato, Vinyl, Smiling, Monocle, Top Hat, 1950, 6 In. 240.00
Figure, Kellogg's Frosted Flakes, Tony The Tiger, Plush, Box, 8 In. 20.00
Figure, Labatt's Pilsner, Man In Alpine Garb By Barrel, Plastic, Hollow, 10 In. 25.00
Figure, Lamb Knit Sweaters, Lamb, 100% Pure Wool, Papier-Mache, 1920s, 15 In. 690.00
Figure, Lowenbrau Munchen, Lion, Sitting On Haunches, Drinking, 24 In. 200.00
Figure, Michelin Man, White Plastic, France, 1981, 12 In. 55.00
Figure, Mr. Clean, Bald Headed, Green Earring, Blue Dot Eyes, 1961, 8 In. 135.00
Figure, Mr. Pickwick, Chalk, 8 In. 110.00
Figure, Old Crow Whiskey, Hard Plastic, 9 1/2 In. 35.00
Figure, Old Crow, 14 In. 50.00
Figure, Pig, Avalon Arms Hog-Tone, Puts Kinks In Tails, Papier-Mache, 1920s 2500.00
Figure, Pillsbury Doughboy, Stuffed, Blue Silk-Screened Details, 13 In. 25.00
Figure, Pizza Inn, Telephone, Co. Name On Front, Red Lettering, Vinyl, 1970, 10 In. 28.00
Figure, RCA Victor, Nipper, Chalk, Cream, Painted Details, 4 In. 40.00
Figure, Reddy Kilowatt, Plastic, 1950s, 6 In. 198.00
Figure, Reddy Kilowatt, Translucent Pink Body, Plastic, 1930, 1/4 x 1 1/2 In. 290.00
Figure, Shoe Form, Lady's High Heeled Shoe, Pine, Brown, 7 1/2 x 3 1/4 In. 1380.00
Figure, Shoe, Elgin Watch Factory, Porcelain, 1900 .... 80.00
Figure, Shoe, Raised Buttons, Black, Pine, 19th Century, 9 3/4 In. 1380.00
Figure, Speedy Alka-Seltzer, Rubber, 1950-1960, 8 In. 405.00
Figure, Squirt, With Bottle, 1947, 13 In. 1150.00
Figure, Westinghouse Tuff Guy, Gold Paint, 1952, 5 In. 58.00
Foam Scraper, Ballantine's Ales & Beer, 1 Side, 1930s 28.00
Foam Scraper, Budweiser, 1950s, 1 Side 50.00
Foam Scraper, Hoffman, Bakelite, 1930s 45.00
Foam Scraper, Rheingold Beer & Ale 45.00
Foam Scraper, Tally Ho Beer, 1 Side, 1930s 26.00
Glass, Anthony & Kuhn XXX Brwg. Co., St. Louis, Embossed, 6 In. 40.00
Glass, Anton Mayer's, Lager Beer Terre Haute, Embossed, 1869, 7 1/4 In. 105.00
Glass, Cook & Rice's City Brewery, Evansville, Ind., 6 7/8 In. 40.00
Glass, Daisy Beer, Garden City Brewery, Chicago, 1907, 3 1/4 In. 105.00
Glass, E.T., Pizza Hut, 1982, 6 In., Pair 12.00
Glass, Excelsior Brewery Co., Pilsner Lager Beer, Embossed, 6 3/8 In. 105.00
Glass, F.W. Cook Brewing Co., Embossed, Star & Crescent Trademark, 6 In. 55.00
Glass, Great Falls Select Fine Beer, Red Enameled, 1950s, 5 1/2 In. 12.00
Glass, Indianapolis 500 Mile Speedway, 1960s, 6 In. 30.00
Glass, Kauffman Brewing Co., Cincinnati, Ohio, Embossed Lager Beer, 6 1/8 In. 105.00
Glass, Malto Dextrine, Non Alcoholic Moehn Beer, Iowa, 3 1/3 In. 40.00
Glass, McDonaldland, Big Mac & Captain Crook, 1977, 6 In. 8.00
Glass, Moxie, Licensed 45.00
Glass, Phoenix Brewing Co., Embossed Phoenix Bird, Barrel On Stem, 6 1/2 In. 230.00
Glass, San Antonio Brewing Ass'n., Etched Glass, Red XXX, City Factory, 3 In. 150.00
Glass, Stivioli, Embossed Diamond Shape, 6 1/2 In. 80.00
Glass, The American Brewing Co., St. Louis, Mo., Globe, Flag, 6 1/2 In. 50.00
Glass, The John Hauck Brewing Company, Golden Eagle, Cincinnati, Globe, 7 In. 45.00
Glass, The Straub Brewing Co., Pittsburgh, Color Label Applied To Glass, 4 In. 352.00
Glass, United Airlines, Clear, White Letters 25.00
Glass, United Airlines, White Embossed United 35.00
Glass Set, Phillips 66 Premium, Box, 5 In., Set Of 4 .... 20.00
Globe, Eyeball, Word Optician 1100.00
Goblet, Diehl's Extra Dry, Etched, 1910s, 5 1/4 In. 42.00

Grooming Kit, Gillette, Safety Razor, Shaving Cream, Deodorant, Case, 1950s	45.00
Gum, Beeman's Pepsin, Stick	45.00
Gum Wrapper, Baby Ruth, Curtiss, Real Pepsin Gum, Stick	40.00
Gum Wrapper, Beech-Nut, Peppermint Flavored Always Refreshing, Pack	23.00
Gum Wrapper, Black Jack Chewing Gum, Adams, Stick	4.00
Gum Wrapper, Blatz Grape Gum, Stick	72.00
Gum Wrapper, California Fruit Gum, Adams, Pack	39.00
Gum Wrapper, Everlasting Peppermint Chewing Gum, Stick	11.00
Gum Wrapper, Fan Tan, Royal Flavor, So Deliciously Different, Pack	3.00
Gum Wrapper, Florida Spearmint Chewing Gum, Pack, Tear On One Corner	55.00
Gum Wrapper, Goudey's Pick-A-Ninny Chewing Gum, Pack	460.00
Gum Wrapper, Goudey, Babe Ruth Swinging Silhouette, Ring Picture, 1935	125.00
Gum Wrapper, Hickman's Silver Birch Chewing Gum, Stick	3.00
Gum Wrapper, Kis-Me Gum, Imitation Grape Flavor, Stick	28.00
Gum Wrapper, Selby's Honolulu Fruit Chewing Gum, Stick	66.00
Gum Wrapper, Sen-Sen Gum, Adams, Peppermint Flavor, Multicolored, Stick	15.00
Gum Wrapper, Short's Skotchemint Chewing Gum, Stick	36.00
Gum Wrapper, Sterling Cinnamon Gum, Stick	50.00
Gum Wrapper, Yucatan Chewing Gum, Adams, Stick	2.00
Handbill, Imperial Grenade Fire Extinguisher, Newsprint, Red, Blue, England	45.00
Hat, Employee, McDonald's, 1960s, Adjustable Size	20.00
Hat, Fold-Out, Hometown Bread, Street Scene, Houses, Church	4.00
Hat, Kellogg's, Tony The Tiger, Yogi Bear, White Paper, 1960s	35.00
Hat, McDonald's Employee's, Paper, Red & Yellow, 1950s	65.00
Ice Bucket, Pabst Blue Ribbon, Waxed Paper, Lily	3.00
Jacket, McDonnell Douglas, MD-80 Aircraft, Black Satin, Zipper, Large	50.00
Jar, American Nut Company, Indianapolis, Ind., Embossed, 11 In.	240.00
Jar, Beater, Wesson Oil, Stoneware	65.00
Jar, Beich's, Candy, Barrel Shape, Embossed, 14 x 8 1/2 In.	88.00
Jar, Franklin Caro, Embossed Lid, Beveled Edges, c.1912, 10 1/2 In.	210.00
Jar, Ramon's Medicine, Metal Cover, 1930-1940	60.00
Jar, Smokey Bear, Candy Stick	600.00
Jar Ring, Bull Dog, Contents, Box	5.00
Jar Ring, ShurFine, Contents, Box	5.00
Jar Ring, Tite Rite, Contents, Box	5.00
Jug, Buckeye Distillery Co., Cincinnati, Oh., Miniature	165.00
Jug, Detrick, Tippecanoe City, Ohio, Pottery, Cream, Blue Transfer, 3 1/4 In.	175.00
Jug, Meredith's Diamond Club Rye, Ironstone, Emblem, Handle, 4 3/4 In.	55.00
Jug, Sweet Mash Corn, Atlantic Coast Distilling Co., Jacksonville, Fl., Miniature	185.00
Jug, W.W. Harper Whiskey, Blue On Tan, 3 1/4 In.	175.00
Key Chain, Texaco Blimp, 1963, 2 In.	85.00
Kick Plate, 7-Up, Fresh Up, 1951, 12 x 30 In.	1780.00
Kick Plate, Dr Pepper, 1930-1940, 10 x 24 In.	490.00
Kick Plate, Take Home A Handipack Orange-Crush, 6 Bottles, 1940s, 12 x 28 In.	1582.00
Kick Plate, Tip-Top Is Better Bread, 12 x 30 In.	150.00
Kick Plate & Door Push, Merita Bread	650.00
Label, Apples, K O, Boxing Glove, 1920s, Square, 10 In.	12.00
Label, Beer, Acme Beer, Die Cut, 8 Oz.	10.00
Label, Beer, Cascade Beer, Calif. Permit No. U-1103, 4% Alcohol, 11 Oz.	6.00
Label, Beer, Cascade Brew, Prohibition, 11 Oz.	22.00
Label, Beer, Golden Lion Lager Brew, Less Than 1/2 Of 1%, Prohibition	4.00
Label, Beer, Iroquois Bock Beer	24.00
Label, Beer, Lowenbrau Extra Beer, 4 1/2% Alcohol, Pre-Prohibition, 12 Oz.	75.00
Label, Beer, Pabst Milwaukee, Red Logo, 4 1/2 x 3 1/2 In.	8.00
Label, Beer, Stollo Temperance Beverage, Prohibition, 12 Oz.	13.00
Label, Bitters, Dr Bonker's Pepsin Stomach Bitters, Eagle Logo, 1890, 2 x 6 1/4 In.	5.00
Label, Cigar, Black Bass, Fish Theme, White Ground, Black Bass, 1910, 4 x 4 In.	10.00
Label, Cigar, Blue Bird, Embossed Bird, Blue Ground, 1917, 6 x 9 In.	10.00
Label, Cigar, Camel, Egyptian Desert Landscape, Pyramids, Man, 1930, 9 x 7 In.	14.00
Label, Cigar, Corona De Rosas, 2 Girls, Long Hair, By G.W. Chase, c.1910, 8 x 6 In.	12.00
Label, Cigar, Don Gudo, Spanish Don, Red Hat, 1919, 4 x 4 1/2 In.	9.00
Label, Cigar, Edmund Halley, Astronomical Instruments, Embossed, 1910, 6 x 9 In.	14.00
Label, Cigar, El Florio Aristocrats, Oval, Spanish Senorita, Veil, 1925, 10 x 6 In.	12.00

Label, Cigar, Elsie, Girl, Brick Wall, Eggs In Nest, 8 x 6 In. 15.00
Label, Cigar, Flyer, World's Greatest Flyer, Spirit Of St. Louis, 1920s, 8 x 19 In. 55.00
Label, Cigar, Francis Marbois, Frenchman, Pen, Quill, Bundle Of Facis, 1920, 4 x 4 In. . . 19.00
Label, Cigar, La Confederacion Suiza, Swiss Confederation Emblems, Cuba, 7 x 7 In. . . . 20.00
Label, Cigar, Lillian Ashley, Actress, Signature, 1910, 9 x 6 In. 10.00
Label, Cigar, Mark Twain, Pictorial, c.1930 . . . . 10.00
Label, Cigar, O'San, Egyptian Scene, Harem Girls, Embossed, 6 x 9 In. 12.00
Label, Cigar, Old Abe, Black On Gray Portrait Of Lincoln, c.1910, 2 1/2 x 6 1/2 In. 3.50
Label, Cigar, Peaceful Henry, Smiling Man, Cigar, Gray Smoke, Embossed, 6 x 9 In. 16.00
Label, Cigar, Primeros, Antique Ships, Gold Design, 1920s, 8 1/2 x 7 In. 9.00
Label, Cigar, Rigoletto, Opera Characters In Costume, 1910 . . . . 12.00
Label, Cigar, S.S. Pierce Overland, 2 Trains Crossing Mountains, 1930s, 7 x 9 In. 14.00
Label, Cigar, Sea Robin, Fish Theme, Riverbank, Fish Basket, Rod, 1920, 9 x 6 In. 22.00
Label, Cigar, Spanish Knight, Oval, Soldier, Tobacco Plantation, 1920, 6 x 9 In. . . . . .16.00 to 20.00
Label, Cigar, Spirit Of St. Louis, Flight Pattern To Paris, 1927, 8 x 6 In. 45.00
Label, Citrate Of Magnesia, RuMak Mfg. Co., Sacramento, 1930, 3 x 3 In. 3.00
Label, Food, Honey Buss Caddy, Women, Picking Flowers, 1900, 7 x 13 In. 88.00
Label, Food, Spring Creek, Tomatoes, J.H. Burley, Milan, Ohio, 13 3/4 x 4 1/2 In. . . .*Illus* 5.00
Label, Fruit, Pacific Fruit Product Co., Panama Pacific Expo., 1915, 5 x 8 1/2 In. 16.00
Label, Fruit, Panama Fruit Product Co., San Francisco, Expo, 1915, 8 In. 16.00
Label, Hotel Inverurie, Paget-West, Bermuda, Die Cut, 1940s, 3 In. 4.00
Label, Milk, Every Day Evaporated, Nestles Food Co. 8.00
Label, Peanut Butter, Frank's Jumbo, Black Background, 2 3/4 In. . . . . *Illus* 15.00
Label, Peanut Butter, Frank's Jumbo, Red Background, 2 3/4 In. . . . . *Illus* 15.00
Label, Sardines, Portola Brand, Monterey, Ca., 1916, 9 x 4 In. 8.00
Label, Syrup, Longwood Plantation Cane, Black Mammy, 1940, 3 1/4 x 11 In. 7.00
Label, Tobacco, Ebony, White Lettering, Black Ground, Frame, 1900, 10 1/2 In. 220.00
Label, Yellow Kid Ginger Wafer, 5 Images, 2 x 25 In. 105.00
Lamps are listed in the Lamp category.
Leaflet, Forest Giant Fine-Cut Chewing Tobacco, Scotten, Dillon Co., 1915, 3 x 8 In. 7.00
Leaflet, Keystone Cream Crackers, Marvin Biscuit Co., Paper, 1920s, 8 x 12 In. 200.00
Leaflet, Salesman's, Levi's Sta-Prest Sportswear, Question & Answer 20.00
Letter Opener, Phillips' Milk Of Magnesia 35.00
Light, Register, Ballantine Ale & Beer, Metal & Plastic, 1950s, 2 x 10 In. 55.00
Light, Rotating, Schlitz Beer, Plastic & Metal, 4 Sides, Logos, 1960s, 12 x 24 In. 105.00
Light, Spuds MacKenzie, Figural 175.00
Lipton Lunar Space Map, Commemorates 1969 Moon Landing, 1969 . . . . 8.00
Lunch Boxes are listed in their own category.
Marker, Sidewalk, 7-Up, Brass 44.00
Marker, Sidewalk, Grapette, 1940-1950 . . . . 50.00
Matchbook Cover, Glamour Girls, In Salesman Brochure 45.00
Matchbox, Ogden's Cobnut, Sliced, Tin, 2 1/8 x 1 3/8 In. . . . . *Illus* 5.50
Matchbox, Schinkenhager, Bottle, Celluloid, 2 1/4 x 1 1/2 In. . . . . *Illus* 3.30
Measuring Spoon, Sunbeam Bread, 1950s 10.00

Advertising, Label, Food,
Spring Creek, Tomatoes, J.H. Burley,
Milan, Ohio, 13 3/4 x 4 1/2 In.

Advertising, Label, Peanut Butter,
Frank's Jumbo, Black Background,
2 3/4 In.

Advertising, Label,
Peanut Butter, Frank's Jumbo,
Red Background, 2 3/4 In.

Medal, Admiral Byrd, American Guernsey Cattle Club, Brass, 1935, 2 1/2 In. 33.00
Medallion, NBC Radio Corporation, 10th Anniversary, 1936, 2 3/4 In. 50.00
Menu Board, 7-Up, Would You Like It, It Likes You, Wooden, Painted, 36 x 24 In. 110.00
Menu Board, Borden's Ice Cream, 9 Slots For Available Flavors, 12 x 24 In. 93.00
Menu Board, Campbell's Soups, 1950-1960, 11 x 17 In. 255.00
Menu Board, Campbell's Soups, Today's Specials, Good N' Hearty, 17 x 23 In. 44.00
Menu Board, Dr. Ross' Life Pills, Productos Populares At Base, 17 x 23 In. 1000.00
Menu Board, Squirt, Squirt Boy, Pointing To Today's Specials, Tin, 19 x 27 In. 93.00
Menu Board, Whistle Soda, Classic Elves At All 4 Corners Writing Area, 27 In. 385.00
Menu Sheet, Shows Kewpies On Ice Cream Mold, Signed O'Neill, 1930 .... 20.00

Advertising pocket mirrors range in size from 1 1/2 to 5 inches in
diameter. Most of these mirrors were given away as advertising pro-
motions and include the name of the company in the design.
Mirror, Angelus Marshmallows, Angelic Child, Celluloid, Pocket, 1 3/4 x 2 3/4 In. 120.00
Mirror, Angelus Marshmallows, Pocket 68.00
Mirror, Archias' Seed Store Corp., Sedalia, Mo., Foxed Top, Pocket 135.00
Mirror, Artesian Cream Co., Waco, Tx., Multicolored, Celluloid, Pocket 80.00
Mirror, Bell's Coffee, Pocket 20.00
Mirror, Bell's Mocha & Java Coffee, Chicago, Inscribed Bell, 2 1/8 In. 85.00
Mirror, Belle's Buffalo Soap, Blue & White Glass, Paper, Tin Frame, Pocket 44.00
Mirror, Berry Brothers' Toy Wagon-Taken From Life, Celluloid, Pocket 270.00
Mirror, Bluebonnet Glass & Mirror, Odessa, Texas, Celluloid, Green & Black, 2 In. 30.00
Mirror, Campbell's Soup, Just Add Hot Water & Serve, 10 Cents, Pocket, 1 1/4 In. 82.00
Mirror, Casino Rhodes On Pawtuxet, View Of Casino, Pocket 44.00
Mirror, Cooper Underwear Co., Buy White Cat Union Suits, Celluloid, Pocket 32.00
Mirror, Crescent Specialty Co., Brooklyn, N.Y., Tan Birthstone Border, Pocket 40.00
Mirror, Denver Dry Goods Co., Denver, Co., Multicolored, Celluloid, Oval, Pocket 70.00
Mirror, Did You Get Kist Today, Pocket 125.00
Mirror, Dr. Arthur Grimm, Dentist, New York, N.Y., Pretty Woman, Pocket 260.00
Mirror, Eat Hengratners' Ice Cream, Multicolored, Celluloid, 2 1/4 In. 400.00
Mirror, First National Bank, Pittsfield, Ill., Ecru, Red, Celluloid, 1910, 2 1/8 In. 125.00
Mirror, Genessee Coal & Ice Company, Hilo Coal, Flint, Mich., Old Face, Pocket 60.00
Mirror, George Brahm Sporting Goods, Indiana, Pocket 135.00
Mirror, Gillette Safety Razor, Baby Shaving, 1909 Calendar Around Edge, 2 1/4 In. 110.00
Mirror, Goodyear, Tire Around Globe, Multicolored Lithograph, Pocket 250.00
Mirror, Grapette, 1930-1940, 8 x 16 In. 195.00
Mirror, Gunther Beer, Gold Tone, 9 x 7 1/2 In. 55.00
Mirror, Hires Root Beer, Mug Version, Pocket, 1908, 2 3/4 In. 1300.00
Mirror, Home Of Wiehert Shoes, New York, Black Birthstone Border, Pocket 37.00
Mirror, Hope Rubber Co., Child On Blue Ground, Gold Lettering, Pocket, 2 1/8 In. 33.00
Mirror, Hope Rubbers, Girl, With Toy Camel, Pocket 52.00
Mirror, Horse Shoe Curve Beer, 2 Thermometers, 1940s, 15 x 23 In. 560.00
Mirror, Ilinoy Heaters Stoves & Ranges, Shield, White Lettering, Celluloid, 2 1/4 In. 70.00
Mirror, Imperial Golden Eagle Lager Beer, 1900, Pocket, 1 7/8 In. 76.00
Mirror, Kelly/Kendall/Prest-O-Lite, Lotta Miles Logo, Pocket, 3 1/2 In. 385.00
Mirror, Linwood Haines Limited Of America, Round, Multicolored, 2 3/16 In. 45.00
Mirror, Maxwell House Coffee, Reverse Decal On Glass, Frame, 30 x 26 In. 70.00
Mirror, Meet Me At The State Fair Pueblo, Woman, Celluloid, 1910, 2 3/4 In. 88.00
Mirror, Moreland Radio Co., Buckeye Road, Black On Green, Pocket, 2 x 2 5/8 In. 40.00
Mirror, Mortician, Globe Caskets, Pocket 30.00
Mirror, Morton's Salt, Pocket 35.00
Mirror, Nature's Remedy Tablets, Face, Tablet On Tongue, Multicolored, 2 1/8 In. 80.00
Mirror, New England Telephone & Telegraph Co., Boston, 2 In. 60.00
Mirror, Niagara Falls, Picturing Magnificence Of Niagara Falls, Celluloid, Pocket 45.00
Mirror, Old Colony Lemonade, Celluloid, Round, 9 In. 35.00
Mirror, Order Of Columbian Knights, Round, Multicolored On White, 2 3/16 In. 50.00
Mirror, Palm Gardens, Fairbanks, Alaska, Paper Backing, Rectangular, 2 x 2 In. 15.00
Mirror, Paul J. Clay, 905 N. Ninth St., Round, Birthstone Border, 2 1/2 In. 30.00
Mirror, People's Life Insurance Co., Chicago, Celluloid, Pocket, 1 3/4 x 2 3/4 In. 25.00
Mirror, Pyott Co., Chicago, Ill., Image Of Vase, Round, 1 1/2 In. 40.00
Mirror, Pyott Pulleys, Celluloid, Pocket, 2 3/4 In. 37.00
Mirror, Queen Quality Shoes, Alva, Ok., Multicolored, Oval, Celluloid, 2 x 1 In. 250.00

Mirror, Rausch's Cafe, Pottsville, Pa., Round, Clock Face, Red, White, 2 1/4 In. 105.00
Mirror, RCA Victor, Nipper, His Master's Voice, Celluloid, Pocket 495.00
Mirror, Samuel Colby & Co., Clothing Est., Embossed Shell, Brass, Pocket 80.00
Mirror, Sherman Williams Paints & Varnishes, Black Rim, Red, Celluloid, Pocket 50.00
Mirror, Shield Of Quality-Monogram-None Better, Celluloid, 2 1/4 In. 70.00
Mirror, Smith Premier, Syracuse, Round, Black & White, 2 1/8 In. 35.00
Mirror, Socony, 1920s, Pocket 135.00
Mirror, Sparrow's Chocolates, Empress Chocolates, Pocket, 1 1/4 x 2 1/4 In. 66.00
Mirror, St. Louis Button Company, Pocket 35.00
Mirror, Stroh's, GOP Convention, 1980, Wooden Frame, 14 x 21 In. 22.00
Mirror, Tainter's Music Pianos, Lewiston, Me., 2 Children, Gold Letters, Pocket 105.00
Mirror, Teho. J. Miller, Schaeffer Pianos, Dixon, Il., Color, Pocket 75.00
Mirror, Traveler's Insurance, Railroad Men's Reliance, Pocket, 2 1/4 x 1 1/2 In. 132.00
Mirror, Witherill's Ground Floor Stores, Syracuse, N.Y., Purple, White, Round, 2 In. 30.00
Mirror, Worley Hardware Co., Blue On White, Round, Pocket, 2 In. 55.00
Mirror, Worley Hardware Co., Reading, Pa., Blue On White, Round, 2 In. 55.00
Mug, Bartels Lager, Ceramic, c.1910, 5 In. 88.00
Mug, Berry's Famous Root Beer, Cobalt Blue Embossed Dragon, Salt Glaze, 4 In. 132.00
Mug, Bovril, Ceramic, White, Gold Trim, 3 1/2 In. 45.00
Mug, Hires, Child With Bib, White, Orange Letters, Pottery, Flared, England, 4 In. 145.00
Mug, Hires, Stoneware, Cream, Black Transfer, 6 1/4 In. 35.00
Mug, Iroquois Brewing, Indian's Head 150.00
Mug, Lash's 65.00
Mug, Nestle World 4.00
Mug, Ovaltine Golden Anniversary, Ceramic, Pictures Little Orphan Annie, 1981 .... 35.00
Mug, Playboy, Bunny Logo, Painted Glass, 1970s, Pair 18.00
Mug, Quaker Oats Man 20.00
Mug, Spuds MacKensie 40.00
Mug, Standard Cardinal Beer, Logo, Monk In Kitchen, Porcelain, Pre-Prohibition 10.00
Mug, Wieland's Extra Pale New Louvre, Painted Woman, Drinking Beer, 1 Pt. 185.00
Napkin Holder, Sprite Boy, Chrome Plated, 1950s 2300.00
Neckerchief, Hamilton Carhartt, Work Clothes, Red Cotton, Heart Designs, 26 In. 175.00
Notebook, D-A Lubricant, Celluloid Covers, 1931 Calendar, 3 3/4 x 2 1/4 In. 25.00
Pail, Armour's Veribest Peanut Butter, Tin, 1 Lb. ....110.00 to 165.00
Pail, Baker's Delight Baking Powder, Mammy With Rolls, Tin, 14 x 12 1/4 In. 365.00
Pail, Big Sister Brand Peanut Butter, Bail Handle, 1 Lb. 95.00
Pail, Buffalo Brand Peanut Butter, F.M. Hoyt & Co., Standing Buffalo, Tin, 10 Lb. 165.00
Pail, Dixie Maid Syrup, Child Pouring Syrup On Waffle, Tin, Label, 9 Lb. 63.00
Pail, Eight Brothers Tobacco, Tin Lithograph, 1920s Tax Stamp 55.00
Pail, Fanny Brice's Baby Snooks Pops, Lollipops, Tin, E. Rosen Co., c.1938, 3 In. 165.00
Pail, Hoody's Peanut Butter, Tin, 1 Lb. 195.00
Pail, Jack Sprat Coffee, Tin, Handle, 4 Lb. 715.00
Pail, Jackie Coogan Peanut Butter, Red Straight Sided, Tin, 12 Oz. 260.00
Pail, Jackie Coogan Salted Nut Meats, The Kelly Co, Jackie, Elephant, Tin, 7 In. 260.00
Pail, Lovell & Coval Candy, All Around Graphics & Text, 3 x 3 In. 275.00
Pail, Mammoth Peanut, Kelly Co., Tin, 10 Lb. 170.00
Pail, Merry Christmas & A Happy New Year Candy, Children Sledding, Tin, 4 In. 110.00
Pail, Monarch Teenie Weenie Peanut Butter, Embossed Top, Tin, 1 Lb. 100.00
Pail, Monarch Teenie Weenie Peanut Butter, Kids Chopping Peanuts, Tin, 10 Oz. 100.00
Pail, Monarch Teenie Weenie Peanut Butter, Kids Chopping Peanuts, Tin, 2 Lb. 120.00
Pail, Monarch Teenie Weenie Peanut Butter, Tin, 1 Lb. 65.00
Pail, Ontario Brand, Peanut Butter, Blue Ground, Oswego Candy Works, 3 1/2 In. 55.00
Pail, Pallas Peanut Butter, Ridenour-Baker Groc., Tin, 7 Oz. 205.00
Pail, Peter Pan Peanut Butter, Snap Top, E.K. Pond Co., Tin, 1 Lb. 65.00
Pail, Pickaninny Brand Peanut, F.M. Hoyt & Co., Tin, 10 Lb. 230.00
Pail, Pickwick Peanut Butter, Tin, 12 Oz. 30.00
Pail, R.B. Rice's Pure Country Lard, 50 Lb. 100.00
Pail, Riley's Rum & Butter Toffee, Children Playing, Handle, England, 4 Lb. 88.00
Pail, Roundy's Peanut Butter, Scene Of Children Playing At Beach, Tin, 14 Oz. 290.00
Pail, Scholl's Axle Grease, Handle, Wagon Scene, Independent Oil Co., Ohio, 6 1/2 In. .. 90.00
Pail, School Boy Peanut Butter, Tin, 1 Lb. 195.00
Pail, School Days Peanut Butter, Children, United Fig & Date Co., Tin, 14 Oz. 375.00
Pail, Scowcroft Peanut Butter, Children Picnicking, Tin, 1 Lb. 520.00

Pail, Squirrel Brand Peanut Butter 95.00
Pail, Sultana Peanut Butter, Boy & Girl, Lid, 1 Lb. .... .40.00 to 50.00
Pail, Sunny Boy Peanut Butter, Brundage Bros., Co., Tin, 25 Lb. 110.00
Pail, Teddie Peanut Butter, John W. Leavitt Co., Tin, 1 Lb. 90.00
Pail, Toyland Peanut Butter, E.K. Pond Co., Circus Scene, Tin, 1 Lb. ....110.00 to 170.00
Pail, Toyland Peanut Butter, Parade Scene, 3 1/2 x 4 In., 1 Lb. 127.00
Pencil Clip, Allentown Dairy Co., Inc., Drink More Milk, Green & White 24.00
Pencil Clip, Amsterdam Broom Co., Amsterdam, N.Y., Black On White Ground 25.00
Pencil Clip, Barreled Sunlight, Image Of Barrel, Black & White 24.00
Pencil Clip, Braender Ties, Image Of Dog & Girl, Red, White & Blue 40.00
Pencil Clip, Chevrolet, We Are Out To Beat Last Year's Record, White On Blue 17.00
Pencil Clip, Elsie The Cow, Tin Lithograph, 1950s 2.00
Pencil Clip, Habbersett's Quality Port Products, Red & Blue, Cream Ground 37.00
Pencil Clip, Home Kraft Fresh Bread, Red, Blue On White Ground 30.00
Pencil Clip, Merchant's Hotel, W.S. Bachamn, Reading, Red, Blue On White 33.00
Pencil Clip, Reddy Kilowatt, V For Victory, With Helmet & Rifle, Celluloid 40.00
Pencil Clip, Shapleigh Hardware Co., Diamond Edge, Black, Red, White 39.00
Pencil Clip, White House Coffee, Image Of White House, Black, Blue & White 33.00
Pennant, Buffalo Bill, Pawnee Bill, Profiles, Bamboo Cane, 1910, 7 1/2 In. 245.00
Pennant, La Flor De Ampere Cigars, H.L. Bowers Co., 26 1/4 x 11 In. ....*Illus* 10.00
Pennant, Pabst Blue Ribbon, The Beer Of Quality, Black Ground, Cloth, 30 In. 220.00
Pin, Buster Brown Shoes, Celluloid, Buster Brown & Tige, 1901-1910, 1 1/2 In........ 225.00
Pin, Capital Airlines, Half Wing, Pinback, 1948-1961, 2 1/2 In. 210.00
Pin, Dan Patch, With Buggy, Driver, World's Champion, Celluloid, Pinback, 1 In. 210.00
Pin, DuPont Smokeless Powder, Multicolored, Black Rim, Celluloid, Pinback 250.00
Pin, Favorite Stoves & Ranges, Sun Rising, Multicolored, Celluloid, c.1905, 7/8 In. 40.00
Pin, In The Night Kitchen, Maurice Sendak, Publisher's Promo, 1970s, 4 In........... 35.00
Pin, Kiddie Wings, Goodyear Blimp, Silver Plastic, 3 In. 22.00
Pin, Lobel's, For Christmas Gifts, Lithograph, Santa Claus, Celluloid, 1 3/4 In. 30.00
Pin, Lucas Paints, Man, Painting, Multicolored, Celluloid, Pinback, c.1905, 7/8 In. 65.00
Pin, Oscar Mayer Canned Wieners, Can Pictured, Red, Celluloid, 1930s, 1 1/4 In. 100.00
Pin, Reddy Kilowatt, Light's Diamond Jubilee, Celluloid, 1879-1954, 1 1/4 In. 155.00
Pin, Reddy Kilowatt, Red, Enamel, Die Cut, 1950s, 2 1/4 x 2 3/4 In. 48.00
Pin, This Du Pont Smokeless Powder, Celluloid, Multicolored, Grouse, 1 1/4 In. 250.00
Pin, Van Camp's Pork & Beans, Can Of Beans, Celluloid, Multicolored, c.1915, 7/8 In. ... 60.00
Pin, Worcester Salt, Black & White, World's Greatest Train, Celluloid, 1904, 1 1/4 In. ... 75.00
Place Mat, NASA, Kennedy Space Center, TWA Cafeteria, 1976, 10 x 14 In. 8.00
Plaque, Adams Chiclets, Yellow, Black Ground, Porcelain, 6 x 4 In. 100.00
Plaque, Bulova, Lindbergh Endorsement, Wooden, Metal, Brass, 9 x 12 In............ 148.00
Plaque, Standard Oil Company, Round 500.00
Plate, Huckleberry Hound Birthday Party, White, Red Border, 1959, 8 Piece 14.00
Plate, Reddy Kilowatt, Smiling Image Of Reddy, Dark Red Accent Rim, 1950, 9 In. 60.00
Potpourri Warmer, Pillsbury Doughboy, Pottery 140.00
Punch Bowl, Walker's Grape Juice, Porcelain, 1905-1915, 7 x 19 In................. 315.00
Puzzle, Cocomalt Boy & Dog, Envelope, 1930s 18.00
Rack, Wrigley's Gum, Tin Lithograph, 3 Shelves 45.00
Rain Gauge, John Deere, Tin, Glass Tube, 1940, 5 x 6 1/2 In. ....35.00 to 55.00
Recipe Box, Gold Medal Flour, Oak, Illustrated Card Dividers, 7 In. 27.00

Advertising, Pennant,
La Flor De Ampere Cigars,
H.L. Bowers Co., 26 1/4 x 11 In.

Advertising, Seed Packet,
R.H. Shumway Seedsman, Cactus,
Rockford, Ill., 5 x 3 1/4 In.

Ring, Marlin Guns, Eagle On Band, Gold Finish On Brass, Adjustable Band 248.00
Ring, Snap, Crackle, Pop, Kellogg's, Rubber Head, Brass Expandable Band, 1 In. 25.00
Rolling Pin, Krispy-Krust, Chrome, Red Handles, Original Box 65.00
Sack, Grain, E.R. Heller Milling Co., Rooster Pulling Boy In Cart, Paper, 10 Lb. 100.00
Sack, Potato, Mammy, Burlap, 2 x 3 Ft. 9.00
Salt & Pepper Shakers are listed in their own category.
Scales are listed in their own category.
Score Keeper, Celluloid, 2 Sides, 1910-1915, 2 1/2 x 3 1/4 In. 195.00
Scraper, Red Wing Flour, Metal 1155.00
Screen, Winchester Knives, Pipe Wrench, 5 Panels, Wooden, Paperboard, 53 x 101 In. . . . 495.00
Seed Packet, R.H. Shumway Seedsman, Cactus, Rockford, Ill., 5 x 3 1/4 In. . . . .*Illus* 5.00
Seeder, John Deere Type, Salesman's Sample 1450.00
Shelf, Bamby Bread Crest, Pine, Cleaned To Blue Paint, 37 x 11 x 50 In. 880.00
Shoe, Limbert's Holland Dutch Arts & Crafts Factory, Wooden, 3 3/4 In. 258.00
Shoehorn, Dorothy Dodd Shoes, Bakelite, Ivory, Gold, Green & Black Logo, 6 In. 25.00
Shoehorn, Montgomery Ward, Bakelite, Red 19.00
Shoehorn, Napoleon Shoe Store & Repair, Holyoke, Massachusetts, Metal 1.50
Shot Glass, J.W. Anderson, Rockville, Mo., The Druggist 45.00
Shot Glass, Red Snapper 25.00
Sign, 1st American Santa, With Soap Product, Printed Cloth, Frame, 32 x 24 In. 300.00
Sign, 7-Up, Bottle Shape, Tin, Die Cut, 45 In. 350.00
Sign, 7-Up, Bottle, Flange, 1950, 18 x 20 In. 920.00
Sign, 7-Up, Easel Back, Tin Over Cardboard, Debossed, 6 x 7 In. 150.00
Sign, 7-Up, Light-Up, Plastic, Tin, 1940-1950, 17 x 11 In. 290.00
Sign, 7-Up, Norman Rockwell Picture, Paper, 1950, 22 x 14 In. 17.00
Sign, 7-Up, We Proudly Serve, It Likes You, Embossed, 1940s, 10 x 30 In. 920.00
Sign, A.T. & T. Western Electric, Beginning 1876, 30 Pictures, Paper, 20 x 24 In. 9.00
Sign, Adam's Black Jack, Easel Back, Elephant Holding Chalkboard, 1916, 10 In. 1495.00
Sign, Admiration Cigars, Easel Back, 1910-1920, 5 1/2 x 7 1/2 In. 150.00
Sign, Admiration Coffee, Curved Porcelain, Brass Grommets, 4 1/2 x 5 In. 260.00
Sign, Airco Wielding & Cutting Products, Graphics, Porcelain, 26 1/4 x 18 In. 385.00
Sign, Alka-Seltzer, Be Wise, Alkalize, Reverse Foil On Glass, Wooden Frame, 21 x 9 In. . 100.00
Sign, Allen's Hosiery For Children, Cardboard, Original Frame, 13 x 17 In. 83.00
Sign, Allock's Porous Plasters, Paper Lithograph, c.1893, 15 x 30 In. 1925.00
Sign, An Orange Crush, Couple Sipping From 1 Glass, Norman Rockwell, 14 x 11 In. 15.00
Sign, Andy Pepsodent, Andy Holding Tube Of Pepsodent, Die Cut, 1930, 54 In. 915.00
Sign, Anheuser-Busch Malt Nutrine, Doctor, Crane As Shadow, Tin, Frame, 12 x 17 In. . . 110.00
Sign, Arden Milk, Aluminum, Die Cut, Arden Boy, 17 3/4 x 48 5/6 In. 1045.00
Sign, Arm & Hammer Soda, Cardboard, Horned Owl, Arnolt, 11 x 14 1/2 In. 65.00
Sign, Armour's Old Black Joe Fertilizer, Man, Banjo, Tin, Self-Framed, 17 x 36 In. 230.00
Sign, Ask For A Crush Carbonated Beverage, Crushy, 1940s, 10 x 28 In. 460.00
Sign, Augustiner-Brau, Munchen, Metal, Germany, 1930s, 23 1/2 x 8 In. 130.00
Sign, Auto-Lite, Cardboard, Die Cut, String Hung, 2 Sides, 6 x 12 1/2 In. 350.00
Sign, Avalon Cigarettes, Red, White, You'd Never Guess, They Cost Less, 1940 . . . . 40.00
Sign, Ayer's Cathartic Pills, J.C. Ayers Co., Lowell, Mass., Cardboard, 1883, 12 In. 550.00
Sign, Ayer's Hair Vigor, Girl Center, Reverse Glass, Frame, 18 x 20 In. 400.00
Sign, Ayer's Sarsaparilla, Piggyback Ride, Tin Lithograph, Self-Framed, 13 x 18 In. 825.00
Sign, B. Stuebner's Sons Decorated Shaving Cups, Mugs, Paper, 19 x 12 1/2 In. 35.00
Sign, Ballantine, Lady, With Beer Glass, Counter, 1940s, 18 x 14 In. 45.00
Sign, Ballantine, Reverse Painted Plastic, Bubbler, 9 x 12 In. 22.00
Sign, Banham's Keyno 5 Cents Cigar, Chas. Shonk Lithograph Co., Tin, 13 x 12 In. 137.00
Sign, Barber, Shave For A Penny, Let Blood Nothing, Teeth Drawn, Metal, 26 1/2 In. 690.00
Sign, Barumeister Pilsener Beer, Reverse Glass, 8 x 19 In. 93.00
Sign, Basement Store, Painted Wood, Self-Framed, Early 1930s, 58 x 32 In. 55.00
Sign, Bavisison Grocers & Dealers In West India Goods, 74 x 31 In. 8625.00
Sign, Beck Beer, Buffalo Best, Glass, Metal, Light-Up, 14 1/2 x 9 3/4 In. 195.00
Sign, Beeman's Pepsin Gum, Cardboard, Embossed, Die Cut, 17 3/4 x 13 1/2 In. 3960.00
Sign, Bell System, Public Telephone, Porcelain, 2 Sides, 11 x 11 In. 225.00
Sign, Ben-Hur Coffee, Porcelain, Die Cut, 1 Side, 21 x 18 1/2 In. 135.00
Sign, Bering, Havana Cigars, Paper On Paperboard, Gold Metal Frame, 29 x 38 In. 72.00
Sign, Betsy Ross Cigars, Holding Flag For 5 Cents Cigar, Frame, Tin, 10 x 15 In. 1430.00
Sign, Bilhorn & Schmidel Ice Co., Couple, Wood Scene, Oak Frame, 15 x 21 In. 770.00
Sign, Bireley's Happifies Thirst, Bottle Picture, 1950s, 18 x 54 In. 430.00

Sign, Blatz, Milwaukee's First Bottled Beer, Wooden, 6 1/2 x 6 1/2 In. 45.00
Sign, Bloodhound Chewing Tobacco, Embossed, 1940-1950, 12 x 18 In. 375.00
Sign, Bloodhound Chewing Tobacco, Red Bloodhound In Center, 1950, 27 In. 550.00
Sign, Blue Crown Husky Spark Plugs, Embossed Tin, 1946, 19 1/2 x 9 In. 310.00
Sign, Bock, Beck's Beer, Goat, Paper, Metal Strips, c.1900, 13 1/2 x 21 1/2 In. 95.00
Sign, Bond Bread, Easter Greetings, Girl, Paper, Textured, 13 x 38 In. 50.00
Sign, Book Bindery, Painted Tin, 19 1/4 x 15 In. 575.00
Sign, Boot & Shoemaker, Robin's-Egg Blue, 2 Sides, 19th Century, 19 In. 862.00
Sign, Bootmaker's, Solid Pine Boot, Red, Pine, 19th Century, 20 x 11 In. 920.00
Sign, Boots, Shoes, Leather, Salt & Lime, Wooden, Tan, Black, 1800s, 8 x 30 In. 3850.00
Sign, Borden's Farm Products Co., Cow, Pail, Children, Wagon, Horse, 14 x 11 In. 40.00
Sign, Borden's Ice Cream, Very Big On Flavor, Elsie, Tin, 24 x 44 1/2 In. 165.00
Sign, Borden's Pumpkin Center Ice Cream Brick, Elsie In Corner, 1950s, 14 x 11 In. 30.00
Sign, Borden, Ice Cream Cone, Elsie, Tin, 1 Side, 36 x 24 In. 125.00
Sign, Breyers Ice Cream, Plastic & Metal, 1960s, 24 1/2 x 12 1/2 In. 101.00
Sign, Budweiser, Electric Guitar, Neon, 41 In. 325.00
Sign, Budweiser, Indians Attack On Overland Stage, Frame, 1960s, 20 x 14 In. 295.00
Sign, Buffalo Bill's Wild West, Window Card, Cardboard, 22 x 14 In. 30.00
Sign, Buffalo Brewing Co., Bottles, Stein, Cigar, Tin, Self-Framed, 22 x 28 1/2 In. 990.00
Sign, Buffalo Pale Beer, Thrifty In Case Lots, Cardboard, 1930s, 13 1/4 x 34 In. 135.00
Sign, Bufferin, Twice As Fast As Aspirin!, Couple, Skating, Cardboard, 11 x 19 In. 38.00
Sign, Bull's Eye Beer, Golden West Brewing Co., Porcelain, Square, 18 In. 285.00
Sign, Busch Ginger Ale, 11 x 21 In. 545.00
Sign, C. Schiber, Pocket Watch Shape, Round, 14 In. 1210.00
Sign, C.E. Goddard, Optometrist, Brass Banded Spectacles, White Ground, 22 In. 3162.00
Sign, California Fruit Gum, Die Cut, Bear, Holding Gum Pack, Cardboard, 14 In. 4400.00
Sign, Call For Philip Morris, Red Lettering, Dark Yellow Ground, 27 x 14 1/2 In. 154.00
Sign, Camel Cigarettes, So Mild, Cardboard, Easel Back, 1950, 20 x 30 In. 105.00
Sign, Camel Cigarettes, We Sell 20 For 10 Cents, Prince Albert Tobacco, 10 In. 467.00
Sign, Canadian Club, 3 Men Enjoying Cigars, Paper, 1930s, 11 x 16 In. 24.00
Sign, Carling's Red Cap Ale, Plastic, Metal, 10 x 12 In. 5.00
Sign, Carnation Fresh Milk, Die Cut, 1940-1950, 14 x 15 In. 430.00
Sign, Carnation Hair Tonic, J. Sarubi Co., Metal, 2 Sides, 1920-1940, 18 1/2 x 7 In. 160.00
Sign, Carrol Rye, Triple A Whiskey, Young Girl, Frame, 27 x 21 In. 1650.00
Sign, Carta Blanca, Imported Beer, Plastic, Light-Up, Box, 9 1/2 x 11 1/4 In. 20.00
Sign, Cascade Lager Union Brewing & Malting Co., Tin, 13 1/4 x 19 In. 605.00
Sign, Cash Grocery, Painted Wood, 2 Sides, Frame, 60 x 20 In. 165.00
Sign, Cavalier Cigarettes, Musketeer Gentleman, Wearing Cap & Hat, 18 x 27 In. 49.00
Sign, Central Motor Co., Limited, See The New Chevrolet, Cardboard, 11 x 21 In. 200.00
Sign, Champion Mower, 2 Sides, Illustrations On Back, 19 1/2 x 15 1/2 In. 198.00
Sign, Chase & Sanborn, An Old-Fashioned New England Grocery, 13 1/2 x 17 In. 121.00
Sign, Chew Old Honesty Plug Tobacco, Elderly Gentlemen, Frame, 15 x 26 In. 1485.00
Sign, Chew Redman, Good Tasting Chewing Tobacco, Frame, 10 x 20 In. 60.00
Sign, Chew Smoke Mail Pouch, Porcelain, 1930s, 3 3/4 x 18 In. 245.00
Sign, Choice Of A Lifetime, Smoke Chesterfield, Matted, Frame, 20 x 9 In. 165.00
Sign, Clark's Teaberry, 1930-1940, 9 x 12 In. 520.00
Sign, Coal Coke Fuel Oils Co., Dayton, Wooden, 15 x 6 In. 120.00
Sign, Cognac Monnet, Woman, Kissing Sun In Her Glass, Cappiello, 1927, 77 x 50 In. . . . 3200.00
Sign, Cook's Beer, Preferred Since This Old Days, 1930s, 13 x 11 In. 105.00
Sign, Cook's Goldblume Beer, Red, Yellow, Tin, 28 x 14 In. 65.00
Sign, Copenhagen Castle, Tin Over Cardboard, Edelbrew Brewery, N.Y., 9 x 12 In. 40.00
Sign, Corgy's Whiskey, Tin Over Cardboard, String Hung, Easel Back, 12 x 9 In. 35.00
Sign, Cortez Cigars, Woman Holding Box, Kaeusermann M.M. Co., Tin, 1915 . . . . 1925.00
Sign, Cream Of Wheat Rastus, Cloth Doll On Wooden Frame, 25 x 33 1/3 In. 120.00
Sign, Crosley Coloradios, Motion, Light-Up, Glass, Metal Case, 1930-1940, Round 575.00
Sign, D.F. Waters & Sons, Germantown Dye Works, Factory, Paperboard, 14 x 11 In. 55.00
Sign, Dabrook's Perfumes, Bouquet Of Roses, 1905, 21 1/4 x 12 3/4 In. 420.00
Sign, Damona Perfume, Die Cut, Stand-Up, 14 Bottles, 14 3/4 x 9 3/4 In. 130.00
Sign, Dandro Solvent, Tin Over Cardboard, Bottle, Glass Stopper, 9 1/4 x 13 In. 300.00
Sign, Dawson's Ale & Beer, Royal Brews, Frame, Glass, 1930, 16 x 10 In. 150.00
Sign, De Laval Authorized Agency, Separator, Flange, Porcelain, 26 1/2 x 18 In. 715.00
Sign, De Laval Cream Separators, Bonneted Lass, Cow, Tin, Frame, 41 x 30 In. 2640.00
Sign, Deerfoot Farm Sausages, Made Of Little Pigs, Paperboard, 15 1/2 x 11 In. 220.00

Sign, Defiance SD-Spark Plugs, Slot, V-Shaped Support, Cardboard, 12 x 18 In. 30.00
Sign, DeSoto, 2-Color Neon, Bust Of DeSoto, Round, 36 In. 1100.00
Sign, Dial Smoking Tobacco 100% Burley, Red, Yellow Tin, 1930s, 12 x 18 In. 50.00
Sign, Diehl Beer, Cardboard, Die Cut, Waiter With Tray, 19 x 13 In. 220.00
Sign, Dingmans Soap, Baby, On Knees, Diaper, Die Cut, Frame, 13 x 15 In. 375.00
Sign, Dobler Beer-Ale, Color, Folded, 1954, 20 x 15 In. 9.00
Sign, Dodger Beverage, Bottle Shape, Die Cut, 1950s, 65 In. 375.00
Sign, Dolly Madison, Quality Checked Ice Cream, Metal Frame, 19 x 27 In. 187.00
Sign, Double Cola, Die Cut, 1930-1940, 12 x 36 In. 490.00
Sign, Double Cola, Kangaroo & Joeys, Cardboard, Die Cut, 12 1/4 x 11 1/4 In. 27.00
Sign, Dr Pepper, Celluloid Over Tin, 1930-1940, 8 x 11 In. 1210.00
Sign, Dr Pepper, Cheerleader, Plexiglas, Matted, Frame, 1940s, 13 x 21 1/2 In. 290.00
Sign, Dr Pepper, Good For Life!, 1930-1940, 8 x 36 In. 2530.00
Sign, Dr Pepper, Women In Car, Drinking Dr Pepper, Join Me!, 32 x 19 In. 82.00
Sign, Dr. A.C. Daniels, Embossed, Horse, Cat, Dog Medicines, 18 x 28 In. 90.00
Sign, Dr. Morse's Indian Root Pill, Cardboard, Die Cut, Easel Back, 9 1/2 x 19 1/2 In. . . . 130.00
Sign, Dr. Swett's Root Beer, The Great Health Beverage, Octagonal, 13 In. 495.00
Sign, Dr. Ward's Vegetable Asthmatic Pills, Thomas Hollis, Boston, 8 x 11 In. 95.00
Sign, Drink Anheuser-Busch, Grape Bouquet, Red Ground, Cardboard, 15 x 7 In. 330.00
Sign, Drink Barq's It's Good Ice Cold, Gas, Oil, 1930s, 11 x 35 In. 775.00
Sign, Drink Cheer Up, Chain Hanger, 9 1/2 x 11 In. 70.00
Sign, Drink Frostie Root Beer, Bottle Cap, 1940-1950, 28 In. 490.00
Sign, Drink Frostie Root Beer, Cap Type, Embossed, 1940s, 12 In. 415.00
Sign, Drink Goulding Springs Pale Dry Ginger Ale, Cardboard, 5 1/2 x 7 1/4 In. 25.00
Sign, Drink Grape Ola, Embossed, 1920-1930, 14 x 20 In. 150.00
Sign, Drink Hires, Die Cut, Embossed, 1950s, Oval, 20 x 30 In. 345.00
Sign, Drink Moxie, 1956, 44 x 34 In. 245.00
Sign, Drink Moxie, Tin On Cardboard, Wood Graining, H.D. Beach, 10 x 2 1/2 In. 90.00
Sign, Drink Nehi Beverages, Tin, By Donaldson Sign, Ky., 1940s, 11 x 30 In. 250.00
Sign, Drink Orange Blossoms, Bottle, Tin, Stout Sign Co., 27 1/2 x 12 1/2 In. 240.00
Sign, Drink Sambo, Carvin Bottle Cap Corp., Brooklyn, N.Y., Tin, 20 x 13 In. 330.00
Sign, Drink Smile, Orange-Headed Figure, Cardboard, 8 3/4 x 3 1/2 In. 35.00
Sign, Drink Vernor's, 4 Grommet Holes For Mounting, Tin, 25 x 19 In. 50.00
Sign, Duco Paint, Pinocchio, Cardboard, Double Easel Back, 1940s, 29 x 40 In. 200.00
Sign, DuPont Gun Powder, Tin Lithograph, Self-Framed, 23 x 32 1/2 In. 2200.00
Sign, Ebling Beer, Cardboard, Frame, 1950s, 10 x 25 In. 48.00
Sign, Eclipse Brand Oysters, Stone Lithograph, 1888s, 27 1/2 x 15 1/2 In. 150.00
Sign, Electric Tattooing Flash, 19th Century, 8 3/4 x 13 In. 1380.00
Sign, Enjoy Hires Root Beer, 1930s, 10 x 27 In. 290.00
Sign, Enjoy Ice Cream, Ice Cream Manufacturers, Diamond Shape, 1940s, 10 In. 290.00
Sign, Enjoy Orange Crush, Celluloid, Round, 1940s, 9 In. 65.00
Sign, Enjoy Orange Crush, Parents Magazine Seal, Round, 9 In. 220.00
Sign, Enjoy Red Rock Cola, Embossed, 1939, 8 x 32 In. 290.00
Sign, Enos Fruit Salt, Angelic Girl, Tray Of Fruit, Paperboard, Frame, 10 x 14 In. 190.00
Sign, Erb, That Perfect Cigar, Stamped Cardboard, Self-Framed, Oval, 9 1/2 x 15 In. 171.00
Sign, Ever Ready Light Company, Pictures Sultan, Metal, 1905, Round, 10 In. 650.00
Sign, Everybody Likes Popsicles Frozen Suckers, 1930-1940, 10 x 28 In. 490.00
Sign, Fabric, Burgess, Forbes & Co., Pure White Lead, c.1800, 9 x 10 In. 60.00
Sign, Fada Radio, Authorized Dealer, Tin, Self-Framed, 13 x 6 In. 80.00
Sign, Falstaff Beer, The Peacemaker, Tin, Self-Framed, 30 1/2 x 22 1/2 In. 1045.00
Sign, Famous Dukes Smoking Tobacco, Original Frame, 20 1/2 x 26 1/2 In. 1320.00
Sign, Fatima Cigarettes, Cardboard, Die Cut, 28 x 50 In. 5500.00
Sign, Fatima Cigarettes, Man & Woman In Canoe, Cardboard, Window, 28 x 50 In. 6050.00
Sign, Fatima Cigarettes, Nothing Else Will Do, Elegants, Paper, c.1920, 11 x 13 In. 125.00
Sign, Fatima Turkish Cigarettes, Portrait Of Veiled Women, Frame, 13 x 17 In. 181.00
Sign, Fatima Turkish Cigarettes, Red Ground, Frame, Cardboard, 13 x 17 In. 154.00
Sign, Fayette Street Shoe Store, Roses In Vase, Die Cut, 1880s, 8 3/4 x 5 3/4 In. 20.00
Sign, Federal Judge 5 Cent Cigar, Embossed, 1930s, 9 x 20 In. 70.00
Sign, Fehr's Malt Tonic, Seminude Lady In Center, Tin, Frame, 28 x 22 In. 1265.00
Sign, Fern Glen Rye, Tin, Man With Watermelon, Self-Framed, 33 x 23 In. 3300.00
Sign, Field's Bakery, Scrolling Design, Wooden, Late 19th Century, 7 3/4 x 65 In. 690.00
Sign, Fish Hook Chewing Tobacco, Quality Tobacco, Burnt Orange, 60 x 30 In. 77.00
Sign, Fitz Beer & Ale, Flavor Hits The Spot, Stand-Up, Cardboard, 15 x 18 1/4 In. 30.00

Sign, For A Treat Smoke Old Gold Cigarettes, Red Ground, 14 x 33 In. 231.00
Sign, Forthoffer's Creme De Menthe Cola, Man & Buxom Woman, 6 1/2 x 8 3/4 In. 50.00
Sign, Frand Ale, Metal, Stand-Up, 1940s, 6 x 8 In. 88.00
Sign, Frank Fehr Brewing Co., Try Our Bock Beer, 1880s, 34 x 23 1/2 In. 440.00
Sign, Franklin Fire Insurance Co., Porcelain, White, Green Letters, 18 x 12 In. 100.00
Sign, Free Land Union Made Guaranteed Overalls, 1930, 10 x 30 In. 315.00
Sign, French Corsets, Cardboard, 1875, 10 x 15 In. 660.00
Sign, Frigidaire, Blue Neon Tube, Yellow, White Lettering, Black, Metal, 16 x 4 In. 83.00
Sign, Friskies Dog Food For Your Dog, 2 Sides, Flange, 1950s, 17 x 18 In. 575.00
Sign, Friskies Dog Food, Tin, Die Cut, 27 3/4 x 17 1/2 In. 575.00
Sign, Fro-Joy Ice Cream, Sealtest, Porcelain, Die Cut, 2 Sides, 26 1/2 x 53 1/2 In. 360.00
Sign, Fro-Joy, Sealtest Ice Cream, 2 Sides, 1930-1940, 17 x 17 In. 315.00
Sign, Gedney King, Son, Chandlers & Instrument Makers, Boston, 24 x 36 In. 358.00
Sign, Gem City Ice Cream, Metal, 2 Sides, 20 x 28 In. 150.00
Sign, General Merchandise, Metal, 7 1/2 x 35 1/2 In. 50.00
Sign, Genesee Beer & Ale, Humphrey Bogart & Lauren Bacall, 1940s, 18 x 15 In. 155.00
Sign, Genesee, Plastic, Cardboard Back, 22 x 22 In. 10.00
Sign, Genessee Beer & Ale, Waitress Holding Beer On Tray, 2 Sides, Round, 11 In. 15.00
Sign, Globe Feed, Cameo Of Farm Scene On Flour Sack, Cardboard, 17 1/2 x 24 In. 82.00
Sign, Gold Dust Washing Powder, Twins Dusting, Baking Utensils, Frame, 12 x 22 In. . . .   165.00
Sign, Gold Dust, Embossed Tin, 2 Kids In Tub, 40 x 27 1/2 In. 2310.00
Sign, Gold Medal Flour, 1920, 10 x 60 In. 575.00
Sign, Golden Gate Brick Co., Woman, Red Dress, Plumed Hat, Paper, 15 x 18 In. 285.00
Sign, Goodrich Footwear, Flange, Tin, Die Cut, 2 Sides, 18 x 13 1/2 In. 550.00
Sign, Granpa's Wonder Soap, String Hung, Die Cut, 1894, 12 3/4 x 6 1/4 In. 9900.00
Sign, Grapette, Bottle Shape, Die Cut, 1930-1940, 41 In. 490.00
Sign, Grapette, Cap With Bottle, Foil Over Cardboard, 1940-1950, 8 In. 140.00
Sign, Grapette, Girl With Dog, Die Cut, 1940-1950, 14 x 16 In. 150.00
Sign, Greeley Horse Importing Estb., Paper, Stone Lithograph, 28 x 22 In. 495.00
Sign, Green River Whiskey, Frame, Dated 1919, 20 x 23 In. 100.00
Sign, Green River Whiskey, McCulloch The Distiller, Tin, Frame, 33 x 23 In. 1100.00
Sign, Green Spot, Real Orange-Ade 5 Cents, Tin, Mathews Co., Detroit, 12 x 36 In. 258.00
Sign, Greyhound Lines, 1940s, Oval, 36 x 24 In. 546.00
Sign, Greyhound Logo On Both Sides, Red, White, Blue, Gray, 40 x 24 In. 177.00
Sign, Gunpowder, Summer Shooting, 2 Quail, E.I. DuPont De Nemours, 6 x 4 In. 1050.00
Sign, H.T. Wolfe, Cigar Shape, Wooden, Painted, c.1930, 60 In.   3245.00
Sign, Hamborne Sweets Cigar Store, Die Cut, Black Man In Plane, 1927, 7 In. 40.00
Sign, Hamilton Brown Shoe Co., Flange, Porcelain, 2 Sides, 16 x 12 In. 210.00
Sign, Hamm's Beer, Tin, Self-Framed, 23 x 17 1/2 In. 45.00
Sign, Hampden Paint & Chemical Co., Tin, Embossed, 19 1/2 x 13 3/4 In. 275.00
Sign, Hand-Up Matches, First In Safety, Boy On Stool, Wooden, 89 x 42 In. 1265.00
Sign, Hard Water Soap, Oberne, Hosick & Co., Die Cut, 9 x 5 3/4 In. 45.00
Sign, Hem Stitching, 5 Cents Yard, Metal, 2 Sides, 13 1/2 x 20 In. 110.00
Sign, Hendlers Ice Cream, Cardboard, Die Cut, 36 x 23 In. 45.00
Sign, Hendlers Maple Walnut Crisp Ice Cream, Red, Blue, White, 1950s, 13 In. 10.00
Sign, Hills & Hills Law Office, Gold & Black, 18 x 24 In. 165.00
Sign, Hires Float, Since 1876, Root Beer With Roots, Paper, 22 x 7 In. 27.00
Sign, Hires To You, Large Bottle Featured, Tin, 13 1/2 x 41 1/2 In. 275.00
Sign, Hires, Bottle Shape, Die Cut, 1940s, 58 In. 375.00
Sign, Hires, For Pleasure & Thirst, Embossed, 1950s, 18 x 54 In. 575.00
Sign, Hires, Inset Girl, Glass & Bottle, Frame, Under Glass, 15 x 20 In. 1065.00
Sign, Hofbrauhaus, Wiesen-Marzen, Oktoberfest-Bier, Cardboard, 1950s, 16 x 23 In. 125.00
Sign, Hohenadel Beer, Frame, 1930, 14 3/4 x 8 3/4 In. 125.00
Sign, Holsum Bread Loaf, Die Cut, Wooden Frame, 1950-1960, 25 x 68 In. 200.00
Sign, Holsum Bread, Embossed, 13 x 27 In. 230.00
Sign, Hood's Ice Cream, Cow, Flange, Metal, Die Cut, 2 Sides, 19 In. 1485.00
Sign, Hope Rubber Co., Providence, R.I., Round, Black, White, Child, 2 1/8 In. 35.00
Sign, Horlacher Beer, Lithograph, Frame, 29 x 35 1/2 In. 155.00
Sign, Howel's Root Beer, Bottle Shape, Tin, Die Cut, 29 In. 400.00
Sign, Howel's Root Beer, Embossed, 1940s, 20 x 28 In. 575.00
Sign, Humer Bicycle, Premiere Marque Dumonde, Paper, 1920, 48 x 60 In. 2400.00
Sign, Hunt's Economy Ice Cream, Flange, 1940-1950, 9 x 15 In.   165.00
Sign, Hunt's Ice Cream, Marietta, Ga., Cone, Wood Grained, 1957, 18 x 54 In. 150.00

Sign, Hunter Whiskey, First Over The Bar, Jumping Horse, Frame, 36 x 26 In. 138.00
Sign, I.W. Harper Whiskey, Here's Happy Days, Vitrolite, Frame, 17 x 23 In. 825.00
Sign, I.W. Harper Whiskey, Log Cabin Interior, Print On Glass, 23 1/2 x 17 1/2 In. 345.00
Sign, Ice Cold Birch-O, Celluloid, Red, Yellow, Square, 8 3/4 In. 60.00
Sign, Ice Cold Bludwine For Your Healthy Sake, 5 Cents, Flange, 10 x 13 In. 125.00
Sign, Isaly's Milk Cream, Porcelain, 12 x 16 In. 50.00
Sign, It's Ideal Enriched Bread For Every Meal, 27 5/8 x 13 1/4 In. 121.00
Sign, Ithaca Featherlight Repeaters, Wild Turkey Flying, Die Cut, 21 x 14 In. 260.00
Sign, J.I. Case Threshing Machine Co., Eagle, Paper, c.1890, 19 1/2 x 25 In. 1045.00
Sign, Jacob Schmidt Brewing Co., Big Game, Tin, Self-Framed, 32 1/2 x 22 1/2 In. 1430.00
Sign, Japp's Rejuvenator, Tin Over Cardboard, String Hung, 13 1/4 x 9 1/4 In. 143.00
Sign, John W. Doe, Gold Lettering, Green, Black Ground, 8 3/4 x 47 In. 747.00
Sign, Johnson Sea Horse Outboard Motors, Woodcock, Lake, Cardboard, 9 x 8 In. 55.00
Sign, Johnston Hot Fudge, Milk Chocolate, Light-Up, 1930-1940, 13 1/2 In. 1265.00
Sign, Jolly Time Hullless, Tin, American Popcorn Co., 1927 . . . . 405.00
Sign, Julius C. Helb's High Grade Bottled Beer, York, Pa., Reverse Glass, 17 In. 635.00
Sign, Kayo Chocolate Soda, Tops In Taste, Tin, 1940, 14 x 27 1/4 In. 205.00
Sign, Keen Kutter, Embossed Tin Lithograph, Dealers Name & Location, 27 3/4 In. 80.00
Sign, Kellogg's Toasted Corn Flakes, Baby In Carriage, 2 Sides, c.1910, 19 In. 1250.00
Sign, Kemp's Balsam, Young Girl With Doll, Die Cut, 2 Sides, 13 x 13 In. 242.00
Sign, Kerr Views's Sweet Ice Cream, 2 Sides, 1930-1940, 24 x 54 In. 3680.00
Sign, King Drill Manufacturing, Girl & Dogs At Gate, Frame, c.1900, 16 x 20 In. 335.00
Sign, King Kard Overalls, Reverse Glass, Light-Up, 1920-1930, 16 In. 430.00
Sign, Kis-Me Gum, Red Riding Hood & Wolf, Cardboard, Die Cut, 5 x 7 1/2 In. 315.00
Sign, Knox's Gelatin, Harry Roseland Artwork, Paper, 1901, 26 x 20 In. 1430.00
Sign, Kodak, Vertical, Porcelain, Continental, 12 x 52 In. 265.00
Sign, Kool Cigarettes, Kool Penguin Posing As Army Sentry On Duty, 12 x 18 In. 135.00
Sign, Kool Cigarettes, Kool Penguin, Willy, Original Monocle, Black Hat, 1930, 14 In. . . . 660.00
Sign, Kool Cigarettes, Penguin Willy, Promoting B & W Coupons, 20 x 30 In. 210.00
Sign, Kool Coupon, Willy, Promoting B & W Coupons, U.S. War Stamps, 20 x 30 In. 192.00
Sign, Kramme's Full Flavored Beer & Ales, Tin, 9 x 20 In. 80.00
Sign, Kyanize Sanitary Floor Enamel, Enameloid, c.1914, 10 1/2 x 16 1/2 In. 50.00
Sign, L. Bauereis, Wooden, Gold, Black Repaint, 2 Sides, Steel Rods Base, 6 x 34 In. 275.00
Sign, Lakewood Pale Dry Ginger Ale, Cardboard, 1930s, 24 x 9 In. 35.00
Sign, Leiner Brau, Fortshendorf, Metal, Enamel, Germany, 1930s, 18 x 39 In. 300.00
Sign, Levi's Casuals, Smiling Sun Shape, Paper, Yellow, 10 In. 20.00
Sign, Lincoln Paints & Varnishes, Oakland, Cal., N.C. Hopkins, Metal, 20 x 9 In. 50.00
Sign, Lipton's Instant Cocoa, Tin Over Cardboard, 9 x 13 /4 In. 880.00
Sign, London Life, Elitist Enjoying Afternoon Smoke, Light Green, Frame, 20 In. 412.00
Sign, Love Nest Candy Bar, Best Eating Candy Bar In World, 1930, 10 x 28 In. 275.00
Sign, Lucas Carriage Gloss Paint, Celluloid, 9 x 13 In. 415.00
Sign, Lucky Strike & Tuxedo Tobacco, Best For The Pipe, Tin, 19 x 9 In. 715.00
Sign, Ludwigs Ice Cream, 1930-1940, 20 x 14 In. 125.00
Sign, M.W.W. Stone, Tailoress, Yellow Lettering, Black, Pine Panel, 33 In. 1035.00
Sign, Mack's Hit The Spot Coffees, Lancaster, Pa., Button, 8 3/4 In. 187.00
Sign, Madam X, Gypsy Fortune-Teller, 1950, 2 1/4 x 3 In. 4.00
Sign, Mann, Crossman & Paulin Ales & Stout, Logo Of Brewer, Metal, c.1920, 23 In. . . . 90.00
Sign, Marquette Club Pale Dry Ginger Ale, Cardboard, 1920-1930, 22 x 26 In. 195.00
Sign, Marvels, Cigarette Of Quality, Rooster, Tin, 13 1/2 x 9 3/4 In. 121.00
Sign, McCarty & Thompson, Warner's 1836 Hotel, Arched, Pine, 72 In. 2990.00
Sign, Mellin's Food, Cupid, Emile Munier Artwork, Paper, c.1894, 20 x 25 1/2 In. 315.00
Sign, Mellin's Food, Stand-Up Cardboard, Baby In High Chair 165.00
Sign, Mennen's Toilet Powder, Woman With Parasol, Paper, c.1910, 9 x 13 In. 175.00
Sign, Miles To, No. 7, Painted Cloth, 23 1/4 x 12 1/2 In. . . . . *Illus* 10.00
Sign, Miller High Life, Girl On Moon, Metal, 1940s, Round, 16 In. 50.00
Sign, Model's Tobacco, Model Logo Man Holding Tobacco, Tin, 6 x 15 In. 154.00
Sign, More Natural Goodness, It's Batter Whipped!, Sunbeam Bread, 19 x 12 In. 198.00
Sign, More Natural Goodness, Little Girl Pointing At Sunbeam Bread, 19 x 12 In. 203.00
Sign, Morris Evans' Renowned Remedies, Genie, Man, Cardboard, 10 x 14 3/4 In. 55.00
Sign, Moxie, Bottle Shape, Die Cut, 1920-1920, 11 x 28 In. 195.00
Sign, Moxie, Glass Bottle, 3-Dimensional, 14 In. 285.00
Sign, Mr. Boston Schnapps Stop, Light-Up, Plastic, Stop Sign Shape, 18 In. 25.00
Sign, Mr. Slushy Delicious Frozen Drink, 2 Sides, 1950-1960, 24 x 36 In. 80.00

Advertising, Sign, Miles
To, No. 7, Painted Cloth,
23 1/4 x 12 1/2 In.

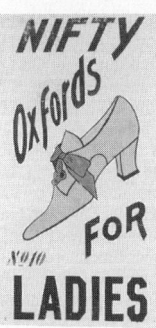

Advertising, Sign, Nifty
Oxfords For Ladies, No. 10,
23 1/4 x 12 1/2 In.

Advertising, Sign, Page's
Treasure Chest Ice Cream,
Cardboard, 21 1/2 x 10 In.

Sign, Mrs. Bard's Bread, Porcelain, 1940-1950, 9 x 19 In. 185.00
Sign, Munsing, Union Suits Of Young Child, Cardboard, Die Cut, 1905, 13 1/4 In. 340.00
Sign, Murad, Embossed Cardboard, Applied Cigarette Label, 20 1/2 x 2 3/4 In. 33.00
Sign, Murad, The Turkish Cigarette, 1920-1930, 3 1/2 x 22 In. 835.00
Sign, N.T. Swezey's Son & Co. Flour, Consolidated Milling Co., 1901, 15 x 23 In. 1540.00
Sign, Nabisco, Paper, Boy, Advertising On Reverse, c.1906, 6 1/2 x 9 1/2 In. 55.00
Sign, Narragansett Famous Lager & Ale, Mirrored, 10 x 18 In. 40.00
Sign, Neilson's Famous Ice Cream, Cloud Shape, Red, Porcelain, 23 x 36 In. 210.00
Sign, Neilson's Famous Ice Cream, Die Cut, 1940-1950, 24 x 36 In. 140.00
Sign, Nichol Kola, Embossed Tin, 20 x 27 3/4 In. 70.00
Sign, Nichol Kola, Embossed Tin, America Taste Sensation, 1930, 14 x 10 In. 55.00
Sign, Nichol Kola, Tin Lithograph, 1936, 8 x 24 In. 50.00
Sign, Nifty Oxfords For Ladies, No. 10, 23 1/4 x 12 1/2 In. . . . .*Illus* 35.00
Sign, Nigger Head...Fresh Oysters, Aughinbaugh Canning Co., Frame, 17 x 16 In. 605.00
Sign, Norseman Quality Sardines, Fisherman, Paperboard, c.1919, 13 x 10 In. 75.00
Sign, NuGrape Soda, Porcelain, 1940-1950, 6 x 12 In. 265.00
Sign, NuGrape Soda, Self-Framed Aluminum, 7 3/4 x 21 3/4 In. 175.00
Sign, NuGrape, Bottle Picture, Embossed, Glass, Frame, 1930s, 4 1/2 x 12 In. 175.00
Sign, NuGrape, Cardboard, Laminated, 6 x 11 In. 75.00
Sign, Oculist, Oval Spectacles Made, Wrought Iron, Tin, 23 x 43 In., Pair 10925.00
Sign, Oh Boy Gum, Tin Lithograph, Boy Fanning Sticks Of Gum, 7 1/4 x 15 In. 210.00
Sign, Ointment For Itch, Thomas Hollis, Boston, 6 1/2 x 11 In. 85.00
Sign, Old Boone Distillery, Thixton Millet & Co. Distillers, Tin, 26 x 18 In. 1100.00
Sign, Old Briar Tobacco, For Taste & Character, Tin, 14 x 5 1/2 In. 220.00
Sign, Old Crow Rye, Straight Hand Made Sour Mash, Monk, Tin, 29 x 22 In. 358.00
Sign, Old Crow, Those In The Know Ask For Old Crow, Composition, Round, 18 In. 88.00
Sign, Old Dutch Bock Beer, The Winah-H-H, 1950s, 20 x 13 In. 55.00
Sign, Old Dutch Cleanser, Porcelain, Black, White, 26 x 3 1/2 In. 205.00
Sign, Old Dutch Lager Beer, Ale & Porter, Tin, Round, 13 1/2 In. 22.00
Sign, Old Fort Feeds, Old Fort Mills Inc., Marion, Oh., Red Lettering, 40 x 48 In. 605.00
Sign, Old Gold Cigarettes, Pull For A Treat, Lady's Legs Dancing, Metal, 3 x 12 In. 146.00
Sign, Old Government, Perfection Of Whiskey, 25 Presidents, Frame, 27 x 22 In. 355.00
Sign, Old Harvest Corn Whiskey, Tin Lithograph, Daddy Holding Boy, 13 x 19 In. 825.00
Sign, Old Hillside Tobacco, Some Good Smoke, Believe Me, Frame, 16 x 21 In. 577.00
Sign, Old Overholt Rye Whiskey, Self-Framed, Tin, 1900, 28 x 38 In. 1200.00
Sign, Old Reliable Coffee, Always Good, Logo Gentlemen & Product Box, 9 In. 357.00
Sign, Old Style Lager, Girl In Kerchief, Cardboard, 23 x 28 In. 30.00
Sign, Old-Fashioned Brownie Camera, Yellow, Tin, 18 x 9 In. 2875.00
Sign, Optician, Applied Carved Lettering, Gilt, Black, 9 1/4 x 43 In. 345.00
Sign, Opticians, Gilded Zinc Spectacles, Eyes Painted On Lens, 19th Century, 48 In. 3250.00
Sign, Optometrist, C.F. Hussey, Polychrome & Gilt, 2 Sides, 1880s, 41 In. 2645.00
Sign, Orange Crush Carbonated Beverage, Crush Figure, Round, 9 In. 185.00
Sign, Orange Crush, Button & Bottle, Crushy, Celluloid, Rectangular, 9 In. 165.00

Sign, Orange Crush, Reverse On Glass, Crushy & Serving Cup, 14 1/4 x 11 1/4 In. 330.00
Sign, Orders For Painting & Glazing, Yellow, Red Ground, 16 x 42 In., Pair 3450.00
Sign, Pabst Blue Ribbon Beer, Cardboard, Frame, Copyright 1938, 39 x 30 In. 305.00
Sign, Pabst Malt Extract, Brings Roses To Your Cheeks, 1902, 9 1/2 x 8 In. 110.00
Sign, Pabst Old Tankard Ale, Cardboard, Frame, 1970, 18 1/2 x 14 1/2 In. 10.00
Sign, Packard, Caribbean Convertible, Celluloid Over Tin, 12 x 16 In. 200.00
Sign, Page's Treasure Chest Ice Cream, Cardboard, 21 1/2 x 10 In. ....*Illus* 8.00
Sign, Paints & Oil, Black Letters, White Ground, 19th Century, 7 x 48 In. 935.00
Sign, Parlin & Orendorff Plow, Gentleman On Clipper Tricycle Plow, c.1880, 11 In. 50.00
Sign, Paul Jones & Co. Whiskey, Temptation Of St. Anthony, Tin, 13 x 19 In. .....550.00 to 605.00
Sign, Pawn Shop, Iron, Tin, Fredericksburg, Va, 18th Century, 29 x 45 In. 785.00
Sign, Pears' Soap, Grandmother Scrubbing Boy's Ear, Cardboard, 1890, 12 In. 300.00
Sign, Penguin Ice Cream, Penguin On Iceberg, Tin, 2 Sides, 20 x 28 In. 440.00
Sign, People's Store, Dry Goods, Shoes, Groceries, Wooden, 55 x 36 In. 2640.00
Sign, Pet Dairy Division, Heavy Gauge, 1963, 16 x 20 In. 125.00
Sign, Pevely Super Test Ice Cream, 2 Sides, 1940-1950, 30 x 36 In. 175.00
Sign, Pewter Trade, Lion Supporting Center Crown, Germany, 1713, 16 In. 1840.00
Sign, Pfeiffer's Back Bar, Plastic, Light-Up, 1960s, 10 x 10 In. 63.00
Sign, Pfeiffer's Beer, War Admiral, 1930s Kentucky Derby Winner, 18 x 14 In. 220.00
Sign, Philadelphia Bayuk Cigar, Vivid Colors, Paper, 1930s, 9 x 14 In. 15.00
Sign, Philip Morris, Johnny, Promoting America's Favorite Cigarette, 15 x 43 In. 286.00
Sign, Phillies, Cigar, Enameled Tin, 20 1/4 x 13 1/4 In. 125.00
Sign, Phoenix Brewing Co., The Cockfight, Tin, Self-Framed, c.1912, 20 x 24 In. 110.00
Sign, Pick Up Purity Bread, The Softest Touch In Town, 27 1/2 x 11 1/4 In. 82.00
Sign, Piel's Beer, Showing Bert & Harry Welcome Sign Bar, 1960, 14 x 18 In. 65.00
Sign, Pig, Black, White, Suspended From 2 Hangers, Pine, 29 In. 9775.00
Sign, Piper Heidsieck Chewing Tobacco, Paper On Paperboard, Frame, 16 x 14 In. 260.00
Sign, Pocket Watch, Roman Numerals, Black, 2 Sides, 20 x 12 In. 862.00
Sign, Pocket Watch, Roman Numerals, Black, 2 Sides, 29 x 13 In. 1610.00
Sign, Pocket Watch, Roman Numerals, White, 2 Sides, 21 x 15 In. 1265.00
Sign, Pocket Watch, Roman Numerals, White, Black, 2 Sides, 17 In. 1725.00
Sign, Polk's Milk, Always Ahead, Cow, Porcelain, 2 Sides, Round, 1940, 22 In. 4715.00
Sign, Purebred Holstein Friesian, Parma, Idaho, Cow, Standing, 36 x 23 In. 355.00
Sign, Raleigh Cigarettes, Union Made, Sexy Girl With Puckered Lips, 11 x 15 In. 100.00
Sign, Raleigh, Pall Mall Cigarettes, Downright Smokeable!, Cardboard, 10 x 15 In. 55.00
Sign, RCA Victor Radio, Green Lettering, Black Ground, Red Trim, 17 x 71 1/2 In. 2640.00
Sign, Reach For Sunbeam Bread, At Its Best, Red Ground, 19 x 55 In. 795.00
Sign, Red Rock Cola, 1940-1950, 8 x 32 In. 195.00
Sign, Regatta Yacht Finishes, Boats, Tin, Embossed, 1960s, 35 1/2 x 23 1/2 In. 325.00
Sign, Reid's Quality Ice Cream Products, Tin, Frame, 10 1/2 x 44 3/4 In. 330.00
Sign, Reliable Watch Repairing At Moderate Prices, Black, Pine, 11 x 31 In. 345.00
Sign, Renault, Car Models, J. Minot, Paris, France, Paper, 45 1/4 x 61 In. 2070.00
Sign, Richardson Root Beer, Self-Framed, 1940-1950, 18 x 36 In. 140.00
Sign, Riley Bros., That's Oil, Tin Lithograph, 5 1/2 x 13 In. 60.00
Sign, Riverside Hotel, A. Fagan, Proprietor, Wooden, 43 x 3 In. 1870.00
Sign, Rockwell's Famous Pepsi Santa, Standing On Left Foot, 1960, 16 x 20 In. 95.00
Sign, Rolling Rock, Laminated Wood, 1940, 18 x 14 In. 20.00
Sign, Royal Baking Powder, Gingerbread Man Holding Book, 30 x 20 In. 125.00
Sign, Royal Crown Cola, Die Cut, 2 Sides, 1940, 16 x 24 In. 1670.00
Sign, Royal Crown Cola, Pick Of The Pack, Santa Claus, Paperboard, 28 x 11 In. 55.00
Sign, Royal Crown Cola, RC, Convex, 1960-1970, 32 x 48 In. 60.00
Sign, Royal Crown Cola, Wish Friends Merry Christmas, Santa, Paper, 28 x 11 In. 65.00
Sign, Rubifoam, For The Teeth, Girl Standing On Chair, Paper, 26 1/2 x 15 1/2 In. 1595.00
Sign, Russells' Ales, 29 x 20 3/4 In. 575.00
Sign, Ruud Storage System, Automatic Hot Water, Tin On Cardboard, 19 x 13 In. 65.00
Sign, S.B. Gasdaska Estate Insurance, Embossed, 12 1/2 x 22 1/2 In. 45.00
Sign, Salem Cigarettes Store Window Decal, White, 1950, 8 1/2 x 8 3/4 In. 18.00
Sign, Santa Ana Municipal Bowl BPO Elks Circus, Window Card, 22 x 14 In. 35.00
Sign, Sapolin Stove Pipe Enamel Paint, Cardboard, Die Cut, 1920s, 6 1/2 x 8 In. 90.00
Sign, Schaefer Beer, Tin & Cardboard, 1960s, 12 1/4 x 14 1/4 In. 22.00
Sign, Schlitz Beer, Cardboard, 19 x 16 In. 25.00
Sign, Schlitz Tonic, Bottle, Glass, Tin On Cardboard, 13 x 9 In. 65.00
Sign, Schlitz, Pride That Made Milwaukee Famous, Tin, 11 1/2 x 23 1/2 In. 305.00

Sign, Schmidt's Beer, City Club, Button, Tin On Cardboard, 9 In. 110.00
Sign, Seilheimer's Pale Dry Ginger Ale, Porcelain, 1930-1940, 10 x 18 In. 205.00
Sign, Shamrock Dairy, Elf Picture, 1940-1950, 22 x 66 In. 405.00
Sign, Sharples Tubular Cream Separators, Man & Girl, Tin, 2 Sides, 27 x 19 In. 605.00
Sign, Shea-Bocqueraz Company, Old Tea Cup Whiskey, 16 x 20 In. 120.00
Sign, Shoe Shape, Wooden, Post No Bill's, Number 49, 24 In. 465.00
Sign, Shoe Store, Boot Shape, Baueries Shoe Store, Delaware, Ohio, 1857, 27 In. 2200.00
Sign, Silverwood's DeLuxe Ice Cream, Tin, 2 Sides, 35 1/4 x 23 1/4 In. 105.00
Sign, Singer Sewing Machine, 2 Sides, 1920s, 12 x 20 In. 675.00
Sign, Singer, Large S, Woman At Sewing Machine, Enamel, 19 x 28 In. 520.00
Sign, Slick Black Hair Color, Cardboard, 11 x 16 In. 20.00
Sign, Smoke Kool Cigarettes, Penguin, Smoking, Green Ground, 10 1/2 x 13 In. 165.00
Sign, Smoke Piedmont, Porcelain, Blue, 11 1/4 x 11 1/4 In. 250.00
Sign, Snoboy, Snowman Picture, Porcelain, Round, 1940-1950, 36 In. 45.00
Sign, Sonny Sugar Cones, Smiling Man, Lithograph On Paper, 1910s, 19 x 8 In. 20.00
Sign, Specify Ward's Vitavim Bread, 1920-1930, Round, 30 x 28 In. 315.00
Sign, Sportsman's Game Guide, Winchester-Western, Tin, Self-Framed, 28 x 23 In. 75.00
Sign, Sprite Boy, 1955, 20 x 36 In. 245.00
Sign, Squire's Arlington, Hams, Bacon, Sausage, Pig With Medal, Tin, 20 x 24 In. 1815.00
Sign, Squirt, Bottle Of Squirt With Room To Write Specials, Frame, Tin, 28 In. 110.00
Sign, Stag Beer, Presents The St. Louis Blues, Cardboard, 18 x 24 In. 10.00
Sign, Standy Tomato Juice, Tin Picture, Porcelain, Round, 1940-1950, 36 In. 185.00
Sign, Star Brand Shoes, Embossed Tin, Glass Cover, 25 1/4 x 20 1/2 In. 120.00
Sign, Stillwell Ham, Paperboard, Grommet Hanger, 11 x 14 In. 50.00
Sign, Stroehmann Bread, Metal, 36 x 72 In. 85.00
Sign, Stroh's Light On Tap, Molded Plastic, Light-Up, 20 1/4 x 15 1/2 In. 20.00
Sign, Stroh's Light, Lion Logo, Molded Plastic, Light-Up, 16 x 20 1/5 In. 25.00
Sign, Stuebner's Phoamine Liquid Shampoo For Dandruff, 35 Center, 12 x 10 In. 10.00
Sign, Sun Cured Red Coon Chewing Tobacco, Raccoon, Holding Can, 12 x 18 In. 55.00
Sign, Sunbeam Bread, Embossed, 1959, 36 x 72 In. 690.00
Sign, Sunbeam Bread, It's Batter Whipped, 1973, 36 x 72 In. 490.00
Sign, Sunbeam Bread, Little Girl Holds Loaf, 1950s, 12 x 27 In. 1840.00
Sign, Sunbeam Rolls, Come In, Embossed, 1953, 18 x 54 In. 1553.00
Sign, Sunfreze Ice Cream By Arden, 2 Sides, 28 x 32 In. 865.00
Sign, Super Shell Gasoline, Busiest Line In Town, Paper, 1950s, 33 x 48 In. 100.00
Sign, Super-X Wildfowl Load, Western, Red, White & Black, Paper, 15 1/2 x 8 3/4 In. 115.00
Sign, Sweet, Orr & Co.'s Union Made Overalls & Pants, Embossed Tin, 10 x 7 In. 121.00
Sign, Tailor, C.T. Ingram, Family Crest, Between Banners, 1840-1860, 44 x 29 In. 2200.00
Sign, Target Cigarette Tobacco, Logo In Center, 1930s, 12 x 18 In. 45.00
Sign, Tastee-Freez, 50 Flavors, Shakes, Light-Up, Plastic, Metal, 10 1/2 x 24 In. 145.00
Sign, Tea Room, T Shape, Wooden, 33 x 28 In. 2645.00
Sign, Tellings Ice Cream, Sealtest, Porcelain, Die Cut, 2 Sides, 24 x 36 In. 230.00
Sign, There's Only One Orange Crush, Embossed, Round, 1939, 16 In. 195.00
Sign, They'll All Want Budweiser, Waiters, Paper On Cardboard, 32 x 14 In. 55.00
Sign, Thirsty? Just Whistle, Die Cut, 1938, 14 x 11 In. 205.00
Sign, Thirsty? Just Whistle, Embossed, Self-Framed, 1950s, 32 x 56 In. 220.00
Sign, Thirsty? Just Whistle, Embossed, Wood Graining, 1940s, 26 x 30 In. 920.00
Sign, This Farm Uses The Ferguson System, Showing Black Tractor, 22 x 11 In. 215.00
Sign, Time Out For Tom's Snacks, 1950s, 20 x 28 In. 290.00
Sign, Toledo Scales, No Springs, Honest Weight, Glass, Frame, 11 x 18 In. 85.00
Sign, Totem Cigars, Cardboard, 21 x 11 In. 155.00
Sign, Trolley, Cliquot Club Ginger Ale, 1920s, 11 x 21 In. 200.00
Sign, Trolley, Wrigley's Juicy Fruit Chewing Gum, Glass, Frame, 1930s, 11 x 21 In. 290.00
Sign, Twenty Grand Cigarettes, Horse's Head In Center & Logo, Frame, 10 x 5 In. 121.00
Sign, Uncle John's Syrup, Color, 1920s, 17 x 12 In. 40.00
Sign, Union Leader Cut Plug, Yellow Letter, Tin, 12 x 8 1/2 In. 99.00
Sign, Union Leader Smoking Tobacco, Eagle In Center, Frame, Tin, 10 x 15 In. 165.00
Sign, Uptown Cigarettes, 2 Young Black People, R.J. Reynolds, 1989, 18 x 25 In. 195.00
Sign, Valentine's Valspar Enamel, For Cards, Cardboard, Hanger, 12 x 16 In. 90.00
Sign, Valspar Enamel Paint, Celluloid Over Tin, Easel, 1920-1930, 11 x 14 In. 265.00
Sign, Valspar Paints & Stains, Celluloid Over Tin, Easel, 1930-1940, 11 x 14 In. 110.00
Sign, Vernor's Ginger Ale, Green & Red Lettering, Yellow Ground, Steel, 35 x 69 In. 488.00
Sign, Viceroy Cigarettes, Embossed, 1950-1960, 17 x 26 In. 105.00

Sign, Victor/Victoria Bicycles, Overman Wheel Co., Paper, c.1896, 9 x 13 In. 90.00
Sign, Vitralite Paints, Tin Over Cardboard, 1920-1930, 14 x 22 In. 430.00
Sign, Ward's Lemon Crush, Girl Silhouette, Cardboard, 18 x 8 In. 350.00
Sign, Way To Howdy, The Friendly Drink, Embossed, 1940s, 3 x 9 In. 205.00
Sign, Wayne Dog Food, Embossed, 1950s, 20 x 28 In. 430.00
Sign, We Give Eagle Stamps, Porcelain, 24 x 10 In. 215.00
Sign, We Serve Royal Crown Cola, Embossed, 1946, 20 x 28 In. 345.00
Sign, We Use The De Laval Cream Separator, Tin, Black, Yellow, 16 x 12 In. 33.00
Sign, Welch's Grape Juice, 1930-1940, 14 x 20 In. 690.00
Sign, Western Union Telegraph Here, Porcelain, 2 Sides, Split Flange, 11 x 17 In. 250.00
Sign, Western Union, Arrow Pointing Left, Black Lettering, Yellow, 30 x 9 In. 165.00
Sign, Western Union, Arrow Pointing Right, Purple Lettering, Purple, 30 x 7 In. 275.00
Sign, Western Union, Blue, White, Porcelain, 25 3/4 x 13 In. 220.00
Sign, Western Union, Telegraph Here, Flange, 1940s, 17 x 25 In. 195.00
Sign, Westinghouse Mazda Lamps, Jackie Cooper, Easel Back, 1930s, 30 x 40 In. 375.00
Sign, Wet Paint, Dutch Boy, Cardboard, 1920s, 10 3/4 x 7 In, Pair 27.00
Sign, White Eagle Beverages, Tin, 23 3/4 x 9 In. 42.00
Sign, White High Button Shoe, Scalloped Edge, Pine, 19th Century, 15 In. 575.00
Sign, White King Soap, Tin Lithograph, 9 3/4 x 14 In. 135.00
Sign, Whiting Adams Brushes, Clown, Tin On Cardboard, 18 1/2 x 26 1/2 In. 1870.00
Sign, Wiedemann's, Colonial Innkeeper, Cardboard, Frame, 1941, 24 x 22 In. 85.00
Sign, Willie Cool, Cigarette, 1941, 10 1/4 x 15 1/2 In. 25.00
Sign, Winchester Factory Loaded Shotgun Shells, Hanging, 112 1/2 x 8 1/2 In. 2750.00
Sign, Winchester Museum, Buffalo Bill Historical Center, Bicentennial, 1976, 28 In. 45.00
Sign, Winchester Western, Pony Express Rider, Tin, 36 In. 575.00
Sign, Winchester, Champion Shooter, Cardboard, Die Cut, Stand-Up, 22 In. 4290.00
Sign, Wings Cigarettes, Tobacco Workers Int'l Union, Color, 1930s, 12 x 18 In. 95.00
Sign, Wm. S. Kimball & Co, Cigarettes & Tobacco, Man & Woman, 1893, 7 x 10 In. 300.00
Sign, Wright & Taylor Distillers, Louisville, Factory Scene, Frame, 28 x 38 In. 2200.00
Sign, Wrigley's Delicious Lasting Flavors, Tin Over Cardboard, 1930s, 7 x 11 In. 750.00
Sign, Wrigley's, Girl With The Wrigley Eyes, 1911, 10 1/2 x 14 1/2 In. 125.00
Sign, Yeast Foam, Makes Delicious Buckwheat Cakes, Little Girl, 1970, 10 In. 45.00
Sign, Yeast Foam, Woman With Bread, Cardboard, Die Cut, Easel Back, 12 x 20 In. 360.00
Sign, Yellow Kid, Say! Get Hightoned 3 Cent Cigar, Brucker & Boghien, Phila. 2200.00
Sign, Zipp's Cherri-O, Glass, Frame, Glass, 1930s, 7 x 16 In. 120.00
Spice Container, Perfumed Cloves, Wm. Donaldson, Mpls., Wooden, Paper Label 30.00
Spinner, Kirkmans Borax Soap, Remember The Maine, Celluloid, Multicolored 75.00
Stein, Budweiser, Basketball, Box, 1991 .... 15.00
Stick, Ball Shape Top, Cotton Club Hot Sepian Revue, Wooden, 8 In. 20.00
String Holder, Cornell White Lead Paint, Dutch Boy, Bucket, 2 Sides 3100.00
String Holder, Lipton's Tea, Tin, Die Cut, 2 Sides, 13 3/4 x 19 1/2 In. 1485.00
String Holder, Red Goose Shoes, Cast Iron 6050.00
T-Shirt, Club Camel, Camel Cigarettes 5.00
T-Shirt, Shell Logo, Cotton & Polyester, Yellow, X-Large 25.00
Tag, Luggage, Celluloid, Tulsa, Ok., Hotel Mayo, Colored Picture 45.00
Tap Knob, Budweiser Beer, Ball, 1930s 38.00
Tap Knob, Frontenac Ale, Ball, 1930s 101.00
Tap Knob, Kaier's Special, Plastic, 1950s 25.00
Tap Knob, Old Shay Deluxe Beer, 1940s 22.00
Tap Knob, Utica Club XXX, Pale Cream Ale, Ball, 1930s 66.00
Thermometers are listed in their own category.
Tie Clip, Reddy Kilowatt 25.00
Timer, Eastman Kodak Co., Rochester, N.Y., Metal, Glass Face, 5 1/2 x 5 x 2 3/4 In. 110.00

Advertising tin cans or canisters were first used commercially in the United States in 1819 and were called *tins*. The English language is sometimes confusing. Today the word *tin* is used by most collectors to describe many types of containers, including food tins, biscuit boxes, roly poly tobacco containers, gunpowder cans, talcum powder sprinkle-top cans, cigarette flat-fifty tins, and more. Beer cans are listed in their own category. Things made of undecorated tin are listed under Tinware.

Tin, A & P Coffee, New York, 1 Lb. 39.00

Tin, Abbey Garden Brand Coffee, Mission Garden Co., 1 Lb., 6 1/4 In. 275.00
Tin, Adams Pepsin Tutti Frutti Gum, 6 In. 130.00
Tin, Airfloat Talcum, Lady & Claw Foot Tub Pictured 95.00
Tin, Alouette, Tobacco, Screw Top, Tax Stamp, Canada, 4 x 4 1/4 In. 28.00
Tin, American De Luxe Coffee, Red, White & Blue, Chicago, Illinois, 1 Lb. 28.00
Tin, American Eagle Tobacco Works, Gold, Blue Green, Pocket 1760.00
Tin, American Mills Samson Brand Coffee, J.S. Silvers & Bro., N.J., 1 Lb., 5 1/2 In. 688.00
Tin, Amocat Cloves, 2 Oz. 303.00
Tin, Angelus Marshmallows, Label, 1930-1940, Sample 220.00
Tin, Apex Coffee, Portland, Me., Paper Label, 1 Lb. 70.00
Tin, Aunt Nellie's Coffie, Harrisburg, Pa., 1 Lb. 220.00
Tin, Axle Grease, Stenciled On Cover, Bail Handle, 4 x 5 1/2 In. 110.00
Tin, Babcock's Coryopsis Talcum Powder, Japan, Colored Graphics, 4 1/2 In. 92.00
Tin, Bacon, Stickney, Eagle Brand Coffee, Albany, N.Y., Unopened, Key, 1 Lb. 110.00
Tin, Baker's Nursery Talcum Powder, Stork & Babies Both Sides, 6 In. 517.00
Tin, Baker's Talcum, Lady 135.00
Tin, Banner Boy Curry Powder, 2 Oz. 310.00
Tin, Ben-Hur Coffee, White Lettering, Red Ground, Chariot Pictured, 21 x 18 1/2 In. 935.00
Tin, Big Ben Tobacco, Horse, Sample 77.00
Tin, Biscuit, Huntley & Palmer, Stack Of Books In Strap Shape, 6 1/4 In. 330.00
Tin, Blue Bird Marshmallows, Blue Board, Triangular, Winter Scene, 3 3/4 x 7 In. 98.00
Tin, Blue Bonnet Coffee, Springfield Grocer Co., Mo., Dark Blue, Key, 1 Lb., 4 x 5 In. . . 298.00
Tin, Boot Jack Chewing Tobacco, 6 x 6 In. 70.00
Tin, Borden's Malted Milk, Small Top, 10 Lb. 45.00
Tin, Bouquet Talcum Powder 25.00
Tin, Bowers Bros. Coffee, Richmond, Virginia 50.00
Tin, Briardale Coffee, Des Moines, Ia., 1 Lb. 110.00
Tin, Brighton Blend Coffee, Girl Drinking Coffee, 1 Lb. 600.00
Tin, Brother Jonathan Chewing Tobacco, F.F. Adams, Milwaukee, 18 x 12 In. 8000.00
Tin, Buckingham Tobacco, Pocket 95.00
Tin, Bud Frozen Egg Products, Yellow A, Eagle, 12 1/2 x 9 3/4 In. 26.00
Tin, Buffalo Brand Fancy Salted Peanuts, Graphics, Large 165.00
Tin, Buffalo Brand Fancy Salted Peanuts, Pry Lid, Tin, 10 Lb. 209.00
Tin, Bunte Marshmallows, Pry Lid, Tin, 3 1/2 Oz. 204.00
Tin, California Nugget Chop Cut Tobacco, Flat, Yellow, Red, Green, 4 1/2 x 2 3/4 In. 65.00
Tin, Campbell Brand Coffee, Bale Handle, Camels & Desert Scene, Red, Yellow, 4 Lb. . . 100.00
Tin, Canco Candy, 5 Little Piggies 236.00
Tin, Cashmere Bouquet Talc Powder, Contents, c.1940, 4 3/4 x 2 1/2 In. 22.00
Tin, Catche's Tobacco, 6 x 3 In. 95.00
Tin, Chicago Cubs Chewing Tobacco, Round, Yellow, 1930s, 6 In. 75.00
Tin, Chocolate Cream Coffee, Chicago, Illinois, 1 Lb. 55.00
Tin, Chocolate Cream Coffee, Marshaltown, Ia., Bail Handle, 6 Lb. 260.00
Tin, Christy's Brand Coffee, Scene Of Plantation Workers, 1 Lb., 6 x 4 1/4 In. 385.00
Tin, Cliffs Siloam Tablets, Stomach Troubles, 2 Black Men, 2 x 1 1/2 In. 286.00
Tin, Coffee House, Bacon, Stickney & Co., N.Y., 1834 Scene Of Men Dining, 4 x 5 In. . . 231.00
Tin, Coleman's Mustard 10.00
Tin, Comfort Powder Talc, Nurse & Baby Picture, c.1915 . . . . 95.00
Tin, Comfort Talc Powder, Children, Lithograph, Error, 4 1/4 In. 205.00
Tin, Cookie, Drum Shape, Metal, Canada, 1930s, 8 1/2 In. 120.00
Tin, Cow Brand Baking Soda, 1/2 Lb. 100.00
Tin, Cowan's Perfection Coffee, Maple Leaf, Canada, Salesman's Sample 110.00
Tin, Daddy's Choice Coffee, Little Girl Picture, 1 Lb. 395.00
Tin, Daily Double Cigars, Slip Lid, Graphics Front & Back, Canister, 4 x 5 1/4 In. 93.00
Tin, Dead Shot Gun Powder, Picture Of Just-Shot Flying Duck, 5 3/4 In. . . . . 176.00 to 180.00
Tin, Deep-Rich Coffee, Red, Black & White, Key Wind, 5 x 4 In. 75.00
Tin, Del Monte Drip Grind Coffee, San Francisco, Green, 1 Lb. 30.00
Tin, Derby's Peter Pan Peanut Butter, Key Wind, Tin, 12 Oz. 55.00
Tin, Devotion Brand Coffee, Man & Woman, Coffee, Black, White, Yellow, 1 Lb. 135.00
Tin, Dill's Best Smoking Tobacco, Yellow, Pocket, 4 x 2 In. 55.00
Tin, Dixie Queen Tobacco, American Tobacco Co., 8 1/2 In. 200.00
Tin, Dixie Queen Tobacco, Lunch Box, 1930s-1940s 127.00
Tin, Dixie Queen Tobacco, Southern Belle Design, Knobbed Lid, Canister, 4 x 6 1/4 In. . . 200.00
Tin, Dr. Roberts Dog Remedy 1595.00

Advertising, Tin, Dry Stem Ginger,
Amoy Canning Corp, Ltd., Hong Kong,
5 1/2 x 3 1/2 In.

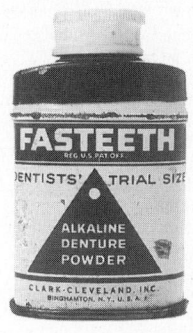

Advertising, Tin,
Fasteeth, Shaker, Plastic
Cap, Dentist's Trial Size,
Clark-Cleveland, Inc., 2 In.

Tin, Dr. Robinson, Condom 265.00
Tin, Dr. Scholl's Foot Powder 35.00
Tin, Dr. Scholl's Talcum Powder, Box 48.00
Tin, Dry Stem Ginger, Amoy Canning Corp, Ltd., Hong Kong, 5 1/2 x 3 1/2 In. . . . . . *Illus* 10.00
Tin, Duck Soup Automotive Cleaner, Cartoon, 1955 . . . . 5.00
Tin, Duck Soup Hand Cleaner, Yellow Duck, 1950s 5.00
Tin, Dunbar Cane & Maple Sugar Syrup, Pilgrims, Indians, Spout, Canister, 5 1/2 In. 94.00
Tin, Duncan Hines Coffee, Ithaca, N.Y., White, Red Letters, 1 Lb. 44.00
Tin, DuPont Superfine FFF Gunpowder, Red Paint, Oval, 1924, 6 x 4 In. . . . . .30.00 to 37.00
Tin, Durkee's Pepper 13.00
Tin, Durkee's Spice 7.00
Tin, Easy's Best Ribbon Can Syrup 22.00
Tin, Edgeworth Junior Tobacco, Striker, 4 1/2 x 3 In. 165.00
Tin, Eight Brothers Tobacco, Long Cut, Slip Lid, Tax Stamp, 5 1/2 In. 77.00
Tin, Elizabeth Park Brand Coffee, Vogel Bros., Garden Scene, 1 Lb., 4 x 5 In. 798.00
Tin, Empress Baking Powder, Ship In Oval 120.00
Tin, Empress Coffee, Maroon, Bail Handle, 5 Lb. 255.00
Tin, Fairy Dell Coffee, Peoria, Illinois, 1 Lb. 66.00
Tin, Fashion Tobacco, Lunch Box 178.00
Tin, Fasteeth, Shaker, Plastic Cap, Dentist's Trial Size, Clark-Cleveland, Inc., 2 In. . . *Illus* 10.00
Tin, Festival Coffee, Dubuque, Ia., Pry Lid, 1 Lb. 90.00
Tin, Fine Cup Coffee, Pittsburgh, Pa., 1 Lb. 121.00
Tin, Fireside Egg Coffee, Chicago, Il., Unopened, Key, 1 Lb. 182.00
Tin, Fisher Peanuts, Salted In The Shell, Pry Lid, 10 Lb. 105.00
Tin, Flying Dutchman Tobacco, 1 3/4 Oz. 3.00
Tin, Folger's Latona Coffee, Kansas City & San Francisco, Slip Lid, 1 Lb. 286.00
Tin, Forest & Stream 93.00
Tin, French's Spice 9.00
Tin, Fryer Clock Gum & Lozenge, Arrow Top Shape 1000.00
Tin, Gold Shield Coffee, Seattle, Wa., 1 Lb. 30.00
Tin, Golden Cup Coffee, Menominee, Mich., 1 Lb. 44.00
Tin, Grand Union Tea Company Baking Powder, Paper Label, Children, 1 Lb. 230.00
Tin, Grand Union Tea Company, Building On Back 260.00
Tin, H & K Coffee, Woman With Turbon, 3 Lb. 55.00
Tin, Hand Made Tobacco, Aqua Ground, Globe Tobacco Co., Detroit, 4 x 3 1/2 In. 165.00
Tin, Handsome Dan Tobacco, Mixture, Yale Bulldog Mascot, 1 5/8 x 4 1/2 x 3 In. 65.00
Tin, Hi-Plane Tobacco, Two Engine, Smooth Cut, Vertical, Pocket, Larus & Bros. 125.00
Tin, Hiawatha Tobacco, Green, 4 x 3 In. 235.00
Tin, High Art Brand Coffee, American Stores, Pastel Scene Of Fishing Village, 1 Lb. 253.00
Tin, Hills Bros. Blue Can Brand Coffee, c.1910, 1 Lb., 3 3/8 x 5 In. 523.00
Tin, Hills Bros. Blue Can Brand Coffee, Cardboard, Cardboard Inset Lid, 1 Lb. 385.00
Tin, Hills Bros. Coffee, No Finer Coffee Ever Passed Your Lips, Brown, 17 x 27 In. 198.00
Tin, Hills Bros. Coffee, Quality Quartet, White Lettering, Brown, 17 x 27 In. 220.00
Tin, Hills Bros. Fine Coffees, Dome Top 700.00
Tin, Home Brand Coffee, Paper Label, Bail Handle, 2 Lb. 60.00
Tin, Hoody's Famous Peanut Butter, Kids On Seesaw, Canister, 1 Lb. 198.00
Tin, Hoosier Poet Coffee, Indianapolis, In., 1 Lb. 495.00

Tin, Howard's Gun Oil, Tin Lithograph, Pour Spout, 3 1/4 In. 110.00
Tin, Indian Profile, Mohican Coffee, Mohican Co., Distributors, 4 1/4 x 5 3/4 In. 120.00
Tin, Iris Allspice, Flower, 2 Oz. 132.00
Tin, Jack Rose Pure Ginger, 2 Oz. 75.00
Tin, Jam-Boy Coffee, Picture Of Boy Eating Jam, 1 Lb. 650.00
Tin, Jolly Time Pop Corn, Guaranteed To Pop, Blue Ground, 8 1/2 In. 44.00
Tin, Just Suits Cut Plug, Buchanan & Lyall, Hinged, Red, Silver, Black Letters, 7 x 4 In. . 100.00
Tin, Kellogg's Kaffee Hag Coffee, Key, Instructions 88.00
Tin, Ken-More Gunpowder & Gold Cup Mixed, Maroon, 19th Century, Pair 650.00
Tin, King Othon Coffee, Union City, N.J., 1 Lb. 515.00
Tin, La Plata Tobacco, Black, Cream, 1880, 10 x 10 1/2 In. 30.00
Tin, La Touraine Coffee, N.Y., Chicago, Brown, Tan, Full Contents, 1 Lb. 40.00
Tin, Ladies' Home Journal, November 1913, Curtis Publishing Co., Philadelphia 50.00
Tin, Ladyette Coffee, Chicago & San Francisco, 1 Lb. 100.00
Tin, Lindy Hand Cleanser, Plane Flying Over Ocean, Red, White & Blue, 4 1/2 In. 125.00
Tin, Little Boy Blue Spice Ground Cloves, Lansing, Mi., 1 1/2 Oz. 55.00
Tin, Luzianne Coffee & Chicory, New Orleans, Black Woman, With Tray, Contents, 1 Lb. 145.00
Tin, Luzianne Coffee, Black Woman Holding Pot, 1928, 3 Lb. 85.00
Tin, Luzianne Coffee, Mammy With Tray, Variation, Pry Lid, Unopened, 1 Lb. 187.00
Tin, Magic Shaving Powder 25.00
Tin, Mammy Brand Salted Peanuts, Packed By Murray-Roll Co., 10 Lb. 4750.00
Tin, Mammy's Favorite Brand Coffee, Black Woman Serving, 4 Lbs., 11 x 6 In. 461.00
Tin, Mammy's Favorite Brand Coffee, Orange & Black Lithograph, Canister, 11 In. 192.00
Tin, Manhattan Coffee, St. Louis, Mo., City Skyline, 1 Lb. 250.00
Tin, Max-I-Mum Peanut Butter, Red Can, Los Angeles, Ca. 121.00
Tin, Maytag Fuel Mix, Trademark, 8 In. 70.00
Tin, Maytag Oil 30.00
Tin, Mazawattee Tea, Lithograph, 3 Boys, Empty Cups, 3 Lb., 6 x 8 1/2 x 5 1/2 In. 550.00
Tin, McLaughlin's Manor House Coffee, Green Trees, Contents, 1 Lb. 55.00
Tin, Melrose Marshmallows, Slip Lid, Canister, 5 Lb. 44.00
Tin, Mentholatum Ointment, Nurse, Contents, 1930s, 1 1/2 In. 22.00
Tin, Millar's Cocoa, Harvesting Scene Both Sides, 3 x 3 x 6 In. 105.00
Tin, Millar's Cocoa, Scenes On 4 Sides, 16 Oz. 121.00
Tin, Mohawk Chief Cigar, Liberty Can Co., Indian Wearing Headdress, 6 x 5 In. 550.00
Tin, Monarch Cocoa, Reid Murdoch & Co., Lion, Salesman's Sample 45.00
Tin, Monarch Coffee, Chicago, Il., 1 Lb. . . . . .33.00 to 35.00
Tin, Monarch Peanut Butter, 55 Lb. 950.00
Tin, Monell's Ointment, Train Engine, Paper Label, Contents, 1920s, 2 In. 33.00
Tin, Mosemann's Peanut Butter, 1 Lb. 115.00
Tin, Mount Cross Coffee, Milk Pail Shape, 5 Lb. 204.00
Tin, Nabob Brand, Baking Powder, Strawberry Cake, Red Lettering, 5 Lb., 7 1/2 In. 60.00
Tin, National Dairy Malted Milk, Aluminum, Cover With Knob, 8 1/2 x 6 In. 160.00
Tin, Negro Head Oysters, 1960s, 8 Oz. 27.00
Tin, Negro Pomade, Black Couple Picture, Free Sample, 1939 . . . . 4.00
Tin, New Bachelor Cigars, Man Smoking Cigar, Playing Solitaire, 4 x 2 In. 130.00
Tin, New Bachelor Cigars, Man Smoking Cigar, Playing Solitaire, 5 3/8 In. 132.00
Tin, New England Oyster Co., Haymarket, So. Boston, Tinsmith Made 100.00
Tin, Nigger Hair Smoking Tobacco, Brown, 7 x 5 In. 269.00
Tin, Nigger Hair Smoking Tobacco, Yellow, Tin Lithograph 660.00
Tin, Normandie, Ship Shape, Entire Deck Lifts Off, France, Biscuit, 1920 . . . . 1500.00
Tin, North Woods Egg Coffee, Chicago, 1 Lb. 65.00
Tin, Old Andy Brand Coffee, Paper Label Of Andrew Jackson, 1 Lb., 3 5/8 x 5 1/4 In. . . . 231.00
Tin, Old Manor Ground Savory, White Lettering, Red Ground, 1/4 Oz. 33.00
Tin, Old Master Coffee, Paper Label, Bearded Man Both Sides, 1 Lb., 6 x 4 In. 99.00
Tin, Old Partner Tobacco, Best Kentucky Smoking & Chewing, Tan, 8 x 12 In. 214.00
Tin, Oyster, Chas. Neubert & Co., Baltimore, Mermaid, Fish, Gallon 45.00
Tin, Parrot & Monkey Baking Powder, Red Can, 3 1/4 In. 99.00
Tin, Parrot & Monkey Baking Powder, Red Can, 5 In. 198.00
Tin, Peacock, Condom, Unused 18.00
Tin, Pedro Cut Plug, Lunch Box, Tin Lithograph 88.00
Tin, Pedro Tobacco, Royal Straight Flush On Side, Jack On Other, 6 1/2 In. 285.00
Tin, Pedro Tobacco, Royal Straight Flush, American Tobacco Co., Canister, 4 x 2 In. 285.00
Tin, Perique, Tobacco, Somer Bros. Tin, 3 1/2 x 2 In. . . . . *Illus* 15.00

Tin, Philip Morris Revelation Smoking Mixture, Hinged Lid, 1920s, 3 1/2 In., Pair 25.00
Tin, Pick Plug Cut Tobacco, Liggett & Myers Tobacco Co., Paper Label 160.00
Tin, Pioneer Brand Golden Flake Cavendish, Tobacco, Gold Flecks, 4 1/2 In. 27.00
Tin, Planters Hi-Hat Peanut Oil, 1 Gal. 55.00
Tin, Plaza Tobacco, Embossed, Canister, 5 x 4 1/2 In. 400.00
Tin, Plee-Zing Spice 7.00
Tin, Poppy Marshmallows, 4 Oz. 220.00
Tin, Postmaster Smokers, 50 Count, Canister 55.00
Tin, Postmaster Smokers, Cigar, Postmaster Smoking, Cigar, Red, 5 1/4 In. . . . . . . 137.00 to 140.00
Tin, Premier Cream Of Tarter 14.00
Tin, Punch Peanut Butter, With Handle, Kansas City, Mo., 12 Oz. 121.00
Tin, Radiant Roast Coffee, St. Paul, Minn. & Fargo, N.D., 1 Lb. 83.00
Tin, Rawleigh Pure Ground Mustard, Pure Food Act, Freeport, Illinois, 5 1/4 In. . . . . *Illus* 24.00
Tin, Rawleigh's Good Health Cocoa, Salesman's Sample 60.00
Tin, Red Belt Tobacco, No Striker, Pocket 95.00
Tin, Red Crown Tobacco, Lunch Box, Tin Lithograph 88.00
Tin, Revelation Smoking Mixture Pipe Tobacco, Philip Morris, 1926, 2 In. 60.00
Tin, Rexall, Contents, 1 Lb. 15.00
Tin, Rockwood's Pure Cocoa, Gentleman Drinking Cocoa, 2 Lbs. 35.00
Tin, Roly Poly, Coffee, Franklin 1380.00
Tin, Roly Poly, Dutchman, Dixie Queen 975.00
Tin, Roly Poly, Mayo's Cut Plug Tobacco, Mammy, 7 In. 750.00
Tin, Roly Poly, Mayo's Cut Plug Tobacco, Storekeeper 365.00
Tin, Rose Kist Popcorn 48.00
Tin, Rose-O-Cuba Cigar, Lithograph Of Senorita & Roses, 5 x 5 In. 90.00
Tin, Rosemary Coffee, Chicago, Il., Pry Lid, 1 Lb. 231.00
Tin, Roundup Coffee, Key Wind, Cowboy On Bucking Bronco, 3 1/2 x 5 In. 395.00
Tin, Royce Jamaica Ginger 25.00
Tin, Sally Clover Coffee, 1 Lb. 30.00
Tin, Sally Lee Coffee, Chicago, Il., Blue Figure Of Woman In Dress, 1 Lb. 187.00
Tin, Savoy Coffee, Chicago, Il., Unopened, Key, 1 Lb. 105.00
Tin, Saw Log Salmon, Light Blue Ground, 3 x 4 In. 38.00
Tin, Serv-Well Coffee, St. Paul & Minneapolis, Minn., 1 Lb. 264.00
Tin, Shelter Island Oyster Co., Greenport, N.Y., 1/2 Gal. 12.00
Tin, Shelter Island Oyster Co., Greenport, N.Y., Minced Clams, 16 Oz. 8.00
Tin, Silver Queen Coffee, Chicago, Il., Red, Cream, 1 Lb. 77.00
Tin, Simon's Roosevelt Cigar, Canada, Picture Of Teddy Roosevelt, 5 x 3 In. 165.00
Tin, Sir Walter Raleigh, For Pipe & Cigarettes, Orange Ground, Canister, 4 1/2 x 3 In. . . . 44.00
Tin, Sir Walter Raleigh, Smoking Tobacco, Orange & Black, 12 x 12 In. 12.00
Tin, Smith Brothers' Black Cough Drop, Hinged Cover, 4 x 10 In. 456.00
Tin, Societe Candies, Seattle 110.00
Tin, Society Brand Peanuts, Man Wooing Woman With Peanuts, 10 Lb. 230.00
Tin, Squadron Leader Tobacco, Airplane, 1920s 75.00
Tin, Stewarts Coffee, Chicago, Red Label, Contents, 1 Lb. 85.00
Tin, Sunset Trail Cigars, Scene Of Riders On Horses, Blue Ground, 4 x 6 In. 345.00
Tin, Sure Shot Tobacco, 8 x 14 In. 485.00
Tin, Sweet Georgia Brown, Picture, 1930-1940 . . . . 18.00

Advertising, Tin, Perique, Tobacco,
Somer Bros. Tin, 3 1/2 x 2 In.

Advertising, Tin,
Rawleigh Pure Ground
Mustard, Pure Food Act,
Freeport, Illinois, 5 1/4 In.

Tin, Thompson's Dandelion Coffee, Slip Lid, Unopened, 1/2 Lb. 66.00
Tin, Three Merry Widows, Condom 95.00
Tin, Tiger Tobacco, Double Handle, Rectangular, 6 1/4 In. 33.00
Tin, Tobacco, Union World, Globe Tobacco Co., 6 In. 230.00
Tin, Tole's Wigwam Syrup, Wigwam On Front, Key Wind, 1921, 6 x 8 1/2 In. 430.00
Tin, Torke Coffee, Hostess Blend, Sheboygan, Wis., 1 Lb. 175.00
Tin, Tube Rose Maple Syrup, Sacramento 40.00
Tin, Twin Oaks Tobacco Mixture, Gold Version 231.00
Tin, Twin Oaks Tobacco Mixture, Silver Version 110.00
Tin, Ultrex Platinum, Condom, Red, Silver 35.00
Tin, Uncle Sam Shoe Polish, Image Of Uncle Sam, Black Border, 3 3/4 In. 130.00
Tin, Union Club Cigars, Screw Lid, 1 Lb. 95.00
Tin, Union Leader Tobacco, Uncle Sam, Orange, Yellow, 4 1/2 x 3 1/2 In. 65.00
Tin, Union World Tobacco, Globe Tobacco Co., Canister, 6 1/4 In. 230.00
Tin, Velvet Tobacco, White Lettering, Red Ground, 4 In. 66.00
Tin, Violet Talc Powder, Colgate & Co., New York 95.00
Tin, Wabash Cocoa, Image Of Man & Cocoa Beans, White Lettering, Red Ground 220.00
Tin, Waldock Lard, Geese Flying Over Water, Heekin Can Co., 50 Lbs., 12 x 15 In. 175.00
Tin, Watkins Baking Powder, Trial Size, 2 1/2 In. 72.00
Tin, Wedding Breakfast Coffee, Denver, Co., People At Table, Pry Lid, 1 Lb. .....143.00 to 360.00
Tin, Weideman Cup Quality Coffee, Cleveland, Oh., Red Lettering, Tan, 10 1/4 In. 148.00
Tin, White Owl Cigars, Slip Lid, 50 Count, Tin Lithograph 200.00
Tin, White Plume Coffee, Louisville, Ky., Feather, Red Background, Contents, 1 Lb. 230.00
Tin, White Swan Talc, Swan In Lake, 8 In. 193.00
Tin, Winner Tobacco, Lunch Box, 1930s-1940s 230.00
Tin, World's Navy Tobacco, Canada, 8 x 8 x 3 In. 60.00
Tin, Yale Mocha & Java Coffee, Small Top, 2 Lb. 132.00
Tin, Yankee Boy S.D. Co., Union Made, Plug Cut, Baseball, 1910 .... 635.00
Tin, Yankee Peanut, 12 Oz. 140.00
Tin, Yucatan Gum, American Chicle Co. 130.00
Tin, Zenobia Pistachio Nut, Red Lettering, Dark Green Ground, Canister, 9 1/2 In. 33.00
Tin, Zig-Zag Tobacco, Canada, 4 x 4 1/2 In. 45.00

Advertising tip trays are decorated metal trays less than 5 inches in
diameter. They were placed on the table or counter to hold either the
bill or the coins that were left as a tip. Change receivers could be made
of glass, plastic, or metal. They were kept on the counter near the cash
register and held the money passed back and forth by the cashier.
Related items may be listed in the Advertising category under Change
Receivers.

Tip Tray, American Line, Ocean Liner Sailed To Philadelphia & Liverpool, 4 In. 130.00
Tip Tray, Angeles Brewing & Malting Co., Bottle Of Beer & Flag, 4 1/4 In. 220.00
Tip Tray, Ballantine's Ales & Beers, Pre-Prohibition, 4 In. 50.00
Tip Tray, Bartholomay Beers, Ales Importer, Winged Wheel, Maiden, 4 1/4 In. ....115.00 to 215.00
Tip Tray, Belmont Hotel & Bar, Vera Smart Owner, Dancing Girl, 4 1/4 In. 70.00
Tip Tray, Bettendorf Wagon, Horse Drawn, Lady Holding Bottle, 3 1/4 In. 340.00
Tip Tray, Beverwyck Lager, Where The Best Beer Is Brewed, Factory Scene, 4 In. 285.00
Tip Tray, Boston Herald, News Boy Running With Paper, H.D. Beach Co., 4 In. 160.00
Tip Tray, Buffalo Brewing Co., Children Of The World Paying Homage To Lady, 4 In. ... 190.00
Tip Tray, Buffalo's Best Bets Bottled Beer, Eagle, Red, White, Blue Shield, 4 In. 70.00
Tip Tray, C & B Line, The Great Ship Seeandbee, H.D. Beach Co., Lithograph, 4 In. 145.00
Tip Tray, Champagne Velvet Radijm, Terre Haute Brewing Co., People, Putti, 4 In. 110.00
Tip Tray, Christian Fiegenspan Breweries, Woman, Plunging Neckline, 4 1/4 In. 120.00
Tip Tray, Clysmic Mineral Water, Topless Girl, 4 In. 85.00
Tip Tray, Columbus Brewing Co., Christopher Columbus, 4 1/4 In. 80.00
Tip Tray, Corby's Old Rye Whiskey, Country Gentleman Reading Paper, Dog, 4 In. 65.00
Tip Tray, Cortez Cigars, Herman Cortez Himself, 6 In. 285.00
Tip Tray, Cottolene, Black Woman, Child Picking Cotton, 4 1/4 In. 85.00
Tip Tray, De Laval Cream Separators, Woman & Separator, Child, Tin, 4 1/4 In. 165.00
Tip Tray, Detroit Brewing Co., Eagle Amid Letter D, Chas. W. Shonk Co., 5 In. 95.00
Tip Tray, E. Robinsons & Sons Pilsner Beer, Emblem, Burgundy, Gold Border, 4 In. 85.00
Tip Tray, Edelbrau, Pre-Prohibition, 4 In. 72.00

Tip Tray, Evinrude, On A Crest Of The Wave, Woman In Boat, 4 In. 180.00
Tip Tray, Eye Fix, The Great Eye Remedy, Cherub, Eye Drops, H.D. Beach Co., 4 In. 125.00
Tip Tray, Fairy Soap, Girl Perched On Bar Of Soap, Tin Lithograph, 1900, 4 In. 75.00
Tip Tray, Goebel Beer, Bavarian Man, Enjoying His Mug, Meek Co., Lithograph, 4 In. ... 150.00
Tip Tray, Goebel Beer, c.1900, 4 1/2 In. 82.00
Tip Tray, Gold Seal Champagne, 8 1/4 In. 100.00
Tip Tray, Gottfried Krueger Brewing Co., Tin Lithograph, 4 1/4 In. 88.00
Tip Tray, Grain Belt Beers, A Barley Malt Product, Black Ground, 4 In. 38.00
Tip Tray, Grain Belt Beers, Aged The Natural Way, Black Ground, 4 In. 38.00
Tip Tray, Grand Old Party, Taft, Sherman Campaign, 1908 .... 330.00
Tip Tray, Gypsy Hosiery, Sultry Girl Dancing, Camp In Background, 6 In. 210.00
Tip Tray, H. Wagener Brewing Co., Bottle Beer, Kaufmann & Strauss Co., 5 In. 230.00
Tip Tray, Hamm's, Cudahy Packing Co., 4 1/4 In. 82.00
Tip Tray, Hires Baby With Mug 1380.00
Tip Tray, Incandescent Light & Stove Co., Home Lighting & Cooking Plant, 4 In. 110.00
Tip Tray, Indianapolis Brewing, The World's Standard Of Perfection, Bottle, 5 In. 60.00
Tip Tray, Iroquois Beer, Trademark Iroquois, Chas. W. Shonk Co., 4 1/4 In. 80.00
Tip Tray, King's Puremalt, Vintage Nurse Carrying Tray, 6 x 4 In. 80.00
Tip Tray, Laval Cream Separators, World's Standard, Victorian Lady, 1905, 5 In. 170.00
Tip Tray, Lehnert's Beer, Depicts Stock Stag, 5 In. 115.00
Tip Tray, Liberty Beer, 4 1/4 In. 65.00
Tip Tray, Lily-A Beverage, 1920s, 4 1/2 x 6 1/2 In. 100.00
Tip Tray, Lindquist's Crackers, 2 Bears Had A Home Out West, 1906, 5 In. 260.00
Tip Tray, Log Cabin Inn, I Won't Sleep Upstairs, Teddy Bear, 1906, 5 In. 375.00
Tip Tray, Los Angeles Brewing Co., Home Of East Side Beer, Factory Scene, 5 In. 90.00
Tip Tray, Louis World's Fair, Festival Hall & Cascades At 1904 St. Louis, 3 In. 60.00
Tip Tray, Luden's Cough Drop, 5 Cent, Menthol Cough Drops, 3 1/2 In. ....260.00 to 460.00
Tip Tray, Manure Spreader, Horse Drawn Manure Spreader, 3 1/2 In. 315.00
Tip Tray, Monticello Whiskey, Colonial Scene, Thomas Jefferson's Home, 4 In. 60.00
Tip Tray, Moxie, I Just Love Moxie Don't You, 6 In. 145.00
Tip Tray, Moxie, Lady Drinking From Soda, 6 In. 145.00
Tip Tray, N.K. Fairbank, Source Of Cottolene, Workers In Cotton Field, 4 1/4 In. 120.00
Tip Tray, National Beer, Race Horse, The Meek Company, 1908, 4 1/4 In. 115.00
Tip Tray, National Cigar Stand, Woman Pulling Petal Off Daisy, 6 In. 140.00
Tip Tray, Pacific Coast Steamship Co., Steamship Co. Flag, 3 3/4 In. 85.00
Tip Tray, Pennsy Select, Quick, A Glass Please For A Friend, 4 1/4 In. 345.00
Tip Tray, Pfeiffers, Bottle, Tin, 4 1/8 In. 77.00
Tip Tray, Pippins 5 Cent Cigar, Peach, Die Cut, c.1895, 5 x 5 1/4 In. 230.00
Tip Tray, President Suspenders, Grecian Lady, 4 1/4 In. 125.00
Tip Tray, Priscilla New England Furniture & Carpet Co., 4 1/4 In. 60.00
Tip Tray, Puremalt, Nurse Carrying Ray, 6 In. 90.00
Tip Tray, Red Raven, Ask The Man, Child, Finger In Mouth, 4 In. 357.00
Tip Tray, Red Raven, Ask The Man, Raven, Pouring For Suffering Mrs. Raven, 4 In. 192.00
Tip Tray, Red Raven, Bird, With Glass & Bottle, Green, Rectangular, 4 x 6 In. 187.00
Tip Tray, Roosevelt Bears, Compliments Of Oxford Bank, Bears At Edge, 1906 .... 245.00
Tip Tray, Ruhstaller's Lager, Best Beer Brewed, Kaufmann & Strauss Co., 4 In. 185.00
Tip Tray, Ruhstaller's, California Invites The World, Lady With Flowers, 4 1/4 In. 165.00
Tip Tray, Seitz Beer, Seitz Brewing Co., Easton, Pa., 1821, 4 1/4 In. 49.00
Tip Tray, Sheldon Optical, A Play That Caused The Biggest Laugh, Bears, 1906, 5 In. 260.00
Tip Tray, Silver Spire Ale & Lager, Tall Well By Woods, 4 3/4 In. 33.00
Tip Tray, Stegmaier Beer, Factory Scene, Chas. W. Shonk Co., Lithograph, 4 In. .....70.00 to 85.00
Tip Tray, Stewart Stoves & Ranges, Cupid & Woman By Fire, 3 1/4 In. 45.00
Tip Tray, Tivoli Brewing Co., Bottle Of Altes Lager Beer, 4 1/4 In. ....65.00 to 77.00
Tip Tray, Wagener Brewing Co., Bottle Of Imperial Export Beer, 5 In. 230.00
Tip Tray, Welsbach Lighting, Lady Reading In Wicker Chair, Child, 4 1/4 In. 115.00
Tip Tray, West End Brewing Co., Lady Liberty Draped In American Flag, 4 In. 170.00
Tip Tray, White Club Champagne, Red Ribbon Around Bottle, 4 In. 44.00
Tip Tray, Wrigley's Soap, Black Cat Sitting On Soap, Chas. W. Shonk Co., 4 In. 165.00
Tip Tray, Yuengling's Beer, Eagle Atop Keg, Char. W. Shonk Co., Lithograph, 4 In. 285.00
Tobacco Cutter, Brown's Mule 95.00
Tobacco Cutter, Dominion Tobacco 125.00
Tobacco Cutter, Star, By Enterprise Mfg. Co. 50.00

Advertising, Tray, Decorated
With Cuban Cigar Bands, Glass, Felt
Back, 5 x 9 In.

Advertising, Toy, McDonald's,
French Fry Guy, Fun With Food,
Happy Meal, 1989, 3 1/2 In.

Advertising, Toy, McDonald's,
Soft Drink Guy, Fun With Food,
Happy Meal, 1989, 3 1/4 In.

Token, Copa Cabana, Hat, $1.00, Brass, 1 1/2 In. 20.00
Token, Drink, Drink Jesse Moore Whiskey, Bonanza, 1 7/8 In. 230.00
Tote Bag, Jack In The Box, Take Life A Little Easier, Yellow Vinyl, 12 x 10 In. 30.00
Toy, Airplane, Fisk Tire, Windup, Ford Tri-Motor, Tin, Kingsbury, 21-In. Wingspan 5170.00
Toy, Burger Chef, Battery Operated, Box 145.00
Toy, McDonald's, French Fry Guy, Fun With Food, Happy Meal, 1989, 3 1/2 In. ....*Illus* 7.00
Toy, McDonald's, Soft Drink Guy, Fun With Food, Happy Meal, 1989, 3 1/4 In. .....*Illus* 7.00
Toy, Oscar Mayer Weinermobile, No. 2 .... 75.00
Toy, Roly Poly, Poll Parrot, Papier-Mache, 1930s, 3 1/2 In. 57.00
Toy, Truck, C.W. Brand Coffee, Read Tailgate, Metal Wheels, Metalcraft, 11 In. ...165.00 to 258.00
Tray, Tip, see Tip Trays in this category.
Tray, Apollo Beer, 1940s, 12 In. 41.00
Tray, Bartlett Spring Mineral Water, Mardi-Gras Types, 13 In. 120.00
Tray, Budweiser, Men At Table, 1930s, 13 1/4 x 10 1/2 In. 51.00
Tray, Cllysmic Table Water, 1960s, 13 In. 22.00
Tray, Corona Beer, Pretty Girl, Tin, 14 In. 50.00
Tray, Cunningham's Ice Cream, Factory Behind The Product, Oval, 18 1/2 x 15 In. 220.00
Tray, Decorated With Cuban Cigar Bands, Glass, Felt Back, 5 x 9 In. ....*Illus* 22.50
Tray, Dewar's Whiskey, 1910s, 12 1/2 x 16 In. 41.00
Tray, E. Robinson's Sons Pilsener Beer, Boat & People Scene, Round, 13 In. 750.00
Tray, Esslinger Premium Beer, 1950s, 13 In. 27.00
Tray, Fairy Soap, 13 In. 75.00
Tray, Falstaff Beer, Gentlemen, Being Served Beer By Barmaid, Tin, 24 In. 220.00
Tray, Fredicksburg Lager, Metal, Round, 13 In. 2420.00
Tray, Genesee Ale Beer, Red, Black, Yellow, Canco, 12 In. 22.00
Tray, Health Beverage Company, Prohibition, 12 In. 95.00
Tray, Hires Root Beer, Josh Slinger Soda Jerk, 13 In. 2300.00
Tray, Hoosier Cream, South Bend Brewing Assn., Woman, Tiger, 14 1/4 In. 230.00
Tray, Hull's Ale & Lager, 1930s, 13 In. 52.00
Tray, Humboldt Beer, 1930s, 10 1/2 x 13 In. 415.00
Tray, Imperial Whiskey, F. Zimmerman & Co., Portland, Ore., Octagonal, 13 In. 440.00
Tray, J.H. Cutter's Whiskey, Louisville, Ky., Sailing Ship, 16 1/2 x 13 1/2 In. 385.00
Tray, Koch's Beer, 1950s, 13 In. 35.00
Tray, National Brewing Co., Pastimes On Frontier, c.1910 .... 1750.00
Tray, Northern Beer, It's Superior, 1950s, 13 x 10 1 /2 In. 180.00
Tray, Rainier Beer, Beautiful Woman, Oval, 13 x 10 In. 375.00
Tray, Sparrow Chocolates, Girl Reaching For Candy, 6 1/2 x 8 In. 100.00
Tray, Swans Flour, Swans In Lake, Tin Lithograph, Oval, 17 In. 16.00
Tray, Virginia Dare, American Wines, Garrett & Co., Paul & Virginia, 12 In. 250.00
Tray, White Rock Bottled Beer, Image Of Woman Leaning On Tiger, 13 1/2 In. 165.00
Tray, White Rock, Metal, Octagonal, 13 In. 525.00
Tray, Zipp's Cherri-O, Bird & Soda Glass, 1920s, Round 575.00

Whistle, Good & Plenty Candy 10.00
Whistle, Hush Puppies, Dog-Shaped, Hush Puppies On Back, Molded Plastic, 2 In. 4.00
Wrapper, Bread, New Century Bread, Plastic, 1966 .... 20.00
Wrapper, Princess Brand Butter, Cow Picture, 1940s .... .30
Yardstick, Gulf Farm Products, Gulf Oil, Folding, Wooden, 1950s, Opens To 36 In. 14.00

AGATA glass was made by Joseph Locke of the New England Glass
Company of Cambridge, Massachusetts, after 1885. A metallic stain
was applied to New England Peachblow and the mottled design characteristic of agata appeared.

Creamer, Ribbed Handle, Square Mouth, 4 1/8 In. 1210.00
Tumbler, c.1887, 3 3/4 In. ....500.00 to 950.00
Tumbler, Rose To White, Blue Spots, 3 3/4 In., Pair 920.00
Vase, Lily, 6 In. 885.00

AKRO AGATE glass was made in Clarksburg, West Virginia, from 1932
to 1951. Before that time, the firm made children's glass marbles,
which are listed in this book in the Marble category. Most of the glass
is marked with a crow flying through the letter A.

Cigarette Lighter, From Smoking Stand, Gray & Blue 50.00
Cigarette Lighter, From Smoking Stand, Lemonade & Oxblood 65.00
Cup, Octagonal, Closed Handle, Green, 2 1/4 In. 6.00
Decanter, Liquor, Green, 13 1/4 In. 20.00
Dish, Child's, 7 Piece 35.00
Punch Cup, Gold Mottling, New England, 2 3/4 x 3 In. 230.00
Tea Set, Swirled, Cream, Brown, Puritan Shaped Honey Jug, 16 Piece 80.00
Tumbler, Green 18.00

ALABASTER is a very soft form of gypsum, a stone that resembles marble. It was often carved into vases or statues in Victorian times. There
are alabaster carvings being made even today. Because the alabaster is
very porous, it will dissolve if kept in water, so do not use alabaster
vases for flowers.

Bowl, Curved-In Edges, 14 In. 75.00
Bust, Diana, Carved, 24 In. 1265.00
Bust, Girl With Violin, Italy, 1900 .... 920.00
Bust, Marie Antoinette, Signed, A. Cipriani, Italy, 17 In. 475.00
Bust, Roman Senator, Raised On Circular Socle, Continental, 1824, 16 In. 690.00
Bust, Venus, Continental, 23 1/2 In. 1380.00
Bust, Victorian Woman, With Bonnet, 17 In. 145.00
Bust, Young Girl, Lace Edge Hat, Flower Corsage, Turned Base, 17 In. 575.00
Bust, Young Girl, Ruffled Hat, Bird On Shoulder, Pedestal, Wooden Base, 14 In. 405.00
Bust, Young Woman, Lace Hat, Pedestal, 26 In. 1785.00
Chandelier, Ceiling, Vine Carving, 18 1/2 In. 1320.00
Clock, Gothic Spire Shape, Gilt Metal, Glass Dome, Continental, 11 In. 375.00
Ewer, Roaring Dragon At Lip, Bird Of Paradise Handles, 75 In., Pair 8625.00
Figurine, Buddha, Seated In Lotus Posture, 11 1/2 In. 330.00
Figurine, Eagle, Standing, Rocky Base, 11 In. 770.00
Figurine, Greek Slave, Round Socle, Italy, 19th Century, 28 In. 1495.00
Figurine, Juliette, Rectangular Base, Continental, 14 In. 747.00
Figurine, Marguerite, Holding Daisy, Vichi-Firenze, 19th Century, 40 1/2 In. 3800.00
Figurine, Neoclassical Woman, Draped, Against Rock, A. Luchini, 1800, 21 In. 1090.00
Figurine, Semidraped Maiden, Beside Putto, A. DeCori 4312.00
Fruit, Painted 4 Peaches, 2 Pears, 6 Piece 132.00
Half Vase, Neoclassical, Acanthus Frieze, Mahogany Pedestal, 69 In., 4 Piece 12650.00
Lamp, Inverted Bell Form Shade, 4 Scrolled Feet, Bronze, Ruhlmann, 1927, 22 In. 26450.00
Lamp, Table, Italy, 1920, 28 1/2 In. 242.00
Lamp, Table, Neoclassical Style, 28 In., Pair 145.00
Lamp, Table, Neoclassical, White, Italy, 1927, 16 x 5 1/2 In. 212.00
Lamp, Vasiform, Slag Glass Pyramid Shade 55.00
Obelisk, Step Base, 14 1/2 In., Pair 670.00
Pedestal, Revolving Square Top, Octagonal Base, Reeded & Spiral Column, 36 In. 1610.00

ALEXANDRITE is a name with many meanings. It is a form of the mineral chrysoberyl that changes from green to red under artificial light. A man-made version of this mineral is sold in Mexico today. It changes from deep purple to aquamarine blue under artificial light. The Alexandrite listed here is glass made in the late nineteenth and twentieth centuries. Thomas Webb & Sons sold their transparent glass shaded from yellow to rose to blue under the name Alexandrite. Stevens and Williams had a cased Alexandrite of yellow, rose, and blue. A. Douglas Nash Corporation made an amethyst-colored Alexandrite. Several American glass companies of the 1920s made a glass that changed color under electric lights and this was also called Alexandrite.

Wine, Citron, Yellow To Fuchsia, Purple, 5 In.	863.00

ALUMINUM was more expensive than gold or silver until the 1850s. Chemists learned how to refine bauxite to get aluminum. Jewelry and other small objects were made of the valuable metal until 1914, when an inexpensive smelting process was invented. The aluminum collected today dates from the 1930s through the 1950s. Hand-hammered pieces are the most popular.

Ashtray, Picture Of House, Stanley Home Products, 3 1/4 In.	5.00
Ashtray, Whirlpool, October, 1954, 3/4 In.	8.00
Basket, Floral & Leaf Design, Cutouts, 5 1/4 x 8 In.	18.00
Bootjack, Bull's Head, Red Painted Eyes, Ricardo, 11 In.	25.00
Cake Plate, Leaves & Acorns, Wooden Acorn Knob, 10 In.	13.00
Canister Set, Jaan, 1950s, 4 Piece	30.00
Case, Cigar, World War II, Holds 3, Monogrammed	125.00
Chess Set, Machined Pieces, Laminated Metal Board, Case, Austin Cox	690.00
Chest, 7 Drawers, Aluminum Pulls, 42 x 27 1/2 In.	2660.00
Cocktail Set, Pitcher, Stirrer, Bronze Band, Leumas, 5 Glasses	80.00
Cocktail Shaker & 6 Doric Cups, Chase	77.00
Cookie Cutter, Cowboy, 6 In.	10.00
Cordial Set, Tray, 6 Cordials, Glass Inserts, 12 x 3 1/2 In.	95.00
Cup, Vietnam War Display, Made From Downed U.S. Helicopters, 3 x 4 In.	128.00
Ice Bucket, Bakelite Handles, Farberware	35.00
Ice Bucket, Cover, Wendell August Forge	140.00
Juice Extractor, Wear-Ever	20.00
Lamp, Floor, Kurt Versen, Flip-Up Light Source, Spun Shaft, 1950, 55 In.	287.00
Pitcher, Pine Needles & Cones, Hand Hammered, Wendell August Forge	150.00
Pitcher, Tulip, Signed, Rodney Kent, 10 In.	30.00
Pitcher, Water, Black Handle, Marked Gurdian, 10 3/4 x 6 In.	35.00
Plate, Flower Design, Handles, Marked, Hand Wrought, Federal S. Company, 18 In.	30.00
Scoop, 6 1/2 In.	6.00
Silent Butler, Moon & Star Design, 6 1/2 x 11 In.	25.00
Spoon, Embossed On Handle, Cream Top, 4 In.	12.00
Tea Strainer, Large	8.00
Tray, Everlast Metal, Signed, 14 x 9 1/2 In.	12.00
Tray, Fox Hunt, Engraved Horses & Hounds, Kensington, 23 x 14 In.	55.00
Tray, Hammered, Glass Insert, With Lid, 16 In.	14.00
Tray, Handles, Rodney Kent, 15 In.	28.00
Wastebasket, Pinecones, Wendell August Forge, 11 In.	165.00
Water Set, Pitcher, 6 Tumblers, Bamboo Pattern, Everlast	210.00

AMBER, see Jewelry category.

AMBER GLASS is the name of any glassware with the proper yellow-brown shading. It was a popular color just after the Civil War and many pressed glass pieces were made of amber glass. Depression glass of the 1930s–1950s was also made in shades of amber glass. Other pieces may be found in the Depression Glass, Pressed Glass, and other glass categories. All types are being reproduced.

Bowl, Golden, 2 x 5 In., Pair	25.00
Bowl, Pedestal, Underside Molded Ribs, 8 In.	40.00
Coaster, 4 In., 4 Piece	18.00
Cruet, Blue Salamander, Blue Handle & Stopper, 12 1/2 In.	195.00

Epergne, Enamel Flowers & Leaves, Blue Feet, 14 3/8 In. 395.00
Jar, Dresser, Floral & Scroll Design, 4 1/2 In. 25.00
Lamp, Fluid, Cruciform, 19th Century, 12 In. 92.00

AMBERETTE pieces are listed in the Pressed Glass category under the pattern name Amberette.

AMBERINA is a two-toned glassware made from 1883 to about 1900. It was patented by Joseph Locke of the New England Glass Company, but was also made by other companies. The glass shades from red to amber. Similar pieces of glass may be found in the Baccarat category. Glass shaded from blue to amber is called *Blue Amberina* or *Bluerina*.

Basket, Enamel Florals, Amber Feet & Handle, 4 In. 475.00
Bowl, Ruffled, Inverted Thumbprint, 2 1/2 x 4 1/2 In. 890.00
Celery Vase, Blue Opalescent, 4 1/4 In. 330.00
Celery Vase, Daisy & Button, Rowboat Shape, 14 x 5 In. 750.00
Cracker Barrel, Silver Plated Cover, Inverted Thumbprint, 7 1/2 In. 325.00
Creamer, Inverted Thumbprint, Handle, 2 1/2 In. 330.00
Cruet, Inverted Thumbprint, Cut Amber Handle, 6 1/4 In. 175.00
Cruet, Silver Plated, Amber Handle, 6 3/4 In. 6000.00
Finger Bowl, Diamond, Reverse, 2 3/4 In. 27.00
Finger Bowl, Fluted Rim, Fuchsia 345.00
Jug, Swirl Pattern, Amber Rope Handle, 9 In. 345.00
Pitcher, Enamel Flowers, Branches & Butterfly, Amber Handle, 10 In. 345.00
Pitcher, Hobnail, 7 3/4 In. 250.00
Pitcher, Inverted Thumbprint, Applied Amber Loop Handle, 7 x 6 In. 145.00
Pitcher, Square Rim, Inverted Thumbprint, Reeded Handle, 6 1/2 In. 125.00
Pitcher, Swirled Body, Applied Reeded Handle, Bulbous, 9 In. 259.00
Pitcher, Thumbprint, Amber Reeded Handle, Square Top, 7 1/2 In. 385.00
Pitcher, Water, Bulbous, Amber Reeded Handle, 9 In. 173.00
Punch Cup, Ribbed Panel, Clear Handle, Pear Shape 95.00
Syrup, Inverted Thumbprint, Ruby To Amber, New England, 5 3/4 x 3 1/2 In. 1495.00
Tankard, Twist Body, Gold Enamel Florals, Amber Twist Handle, 9 1/2 In. 450.00
Tumbler, Diamond-Quilted 130.00
Tumbler, Inverted Thumbprint, 3 3/4 In. 30.00
Tumbler, Paneled, 3 3/4 In. 36.00
Tumbler, Silver Plated, 3 3/4 In. 2400.00
Tumbler, Swirl, 3 3/4 In. 30.00
Tumbler Set, Swirl, 3 3/4 In., 6 Piece 315.00
Vase, Applied Rigaree, Venetian Diamond Pattern, Ruffled, 5 x 5 In. 460.00
Vase, Blown Ribbed Glass, Footed, 13 1/2 x 5 1/2 In. 2900.00
Vase, Dogwood, Applied Snake, Enamel, Rossler, 1920, 9 In. 400.00
Vase, Inverted Thumbprint, Footed, Pinched-In Top, 5 3/4 In., Pair 155.00
Vase, Jack-In-The-Pulpit Form, Swirl Pattern, Applied Amber Edge, 11 In. 345.00
Vase, Lily, 7 1/2 In. 60.00
Vase, Lily, Slight Ribbed, New England, 10 In. 260.00
Vase, Lily, Trumpet, 10 In. 475.00
Vase, Ruffled, 6 1/4 In. 125.00
Vase, Trumpet Shape, 10 In. 295.00
Water Set, Baby Thumbprint, 5 Piece 300.00
Water Set, Inverted Thumbprint, Cranberry To Amber, 7 Piece 230.00

AMERICAN DINNERWARE, see Dinnerware.

AMERICAN ENCAUSTIC TILING COMPANY was founded in Zanesville, Ohio, in 1875. The company planned to make a variety of tiles to compete with the English tiles that were selling in the United States for use in fireplaces and other architectural designs. The first glazed tiles were made in 1880, embossed tiles in 1881, faience tiles in the 1920s. The firm closed in 1935 and reopened in 1937 as the Shawnee Pottery.

Anthony & Cleopatra, Yellow, 18 x 6 In., Pair 1500.00
Sketch, American Indian Portrait, Green High Glaze, 9 x 8 In. 1035.00
Tile, Blue Ships 135.00
Tray, 4 Monks, Bright Green, 6 1/2 x 5 In. ....140.00 to 145.00

Insects like all sorts of natural specimens. Mothballs and insect sprays will help keep stuffed animal heads free of moths or carpet beetles. Stuffed animals or birds should be mothproofed regularly.

Animal Trophy, Robe, Buffalo

AMETHYST GLASS is any of the many glasswares made in the dark purple color of the gemstone called amethyst. Included in this category are many pieces made in the nineteenth and twentieth centuries. Very dark pieces are called *black amethyst* and are listed under that heading.

Basket, Fruit, Openwork, Sandwich Glass Co., Mid-19th Century, 8 x 8 In.	2415.00
Finger Bowl, Flint, 4 3/4 x 4 In.	22.00
Pitcher, 11 Vertical Ribs, Blown, Applied Handle, 4 5/8 In.	50.00
Vase, Applied Foot, Ruffled Rim, Bulbous, 10 5/8 In.	250.00

AMPHORA pieces are listed in the Teplitz category.

ANDIRONS and related fireplace items are included in the Fireplace category.

ANIMAL TROPHIES, such as stuffed animals, rugs made of animal skins, and other similar collectibles, are listed in this category. Collectors should be aware of the endangered species laws that make it illegal to buy and sell some of these items. Any eagle feathers, many types of pelts or rugs (such as leopard), ivory, and many forms of tortoiseshell can be confiscated by the government. Related trophies may be found in the Fishing category. Ivory items may be found in the Scrimshaw or Ivory categories.

Alligator Skull, Trophy Size, 25 In.	185.00
Bison Head, Mounted, 50 Lbs.	2700.00
Bobcat, Head Mount, Mouth Open, Claws	500.00
Buck Head, 10-Point, 48 In.	165.00
Buffalo Head, Shield Shape, Mahogany Backboard, 46 In.	583.00
Caribou Deer, Antlers, Carved, 1900	3300.00
Elk Head, Mounted, 5 Ft.	2700.00
Ostrich, African, Full Mount	440.00
Robe, Buffalo ....*Illus*	5500.00
Rug, Zebra, Lined, 113 x 71 In.	1275.00
Tusk, Narwhal, 86 1/2 In.	7000.00
Wild Boar Head, 22 1/2 In.	258.00

ANIMATION ART collectibles include cels that are painted drawings on celluloid needed to make animated cartoons shown in movie theaters or on TV. Hundreds of cels were made, then photographed in sequence to make a cartoon showing moving figures. Early examples made by the Walt Disney Studios are popular with collectors today. Original sketches used by the artists are also listed here. Modern animated cartoons are made using computer-generated pictures. Some of these are being produced as cels to be sold to collectors. Other cartoon art is listed in Comic Art and Disneyana.

Cel, 101 Dalmatians, Pongo's & Perdita's Puppies, Walt Disney, 1961, 5 x 11 In.	1265.00
Cel, Archie, Jughead, Sleeping On Bag, 1980s, 7 x 10 In.	50.00
Cel, Batman, Robin Running, Matted, 13 x 15 1/2 In.	45.00
Cel, Beauty & The Beast, Dancing, Hand Painted, Walt Disney, 11 x 18 1/2 In.	110.00

Cel, Bugs Bunny's Busting Out All Over, Warner Brothers Studio, 1980, 6 1/4 x 6 In. 345.00
Cel, Donald Duck, Orphan's Picnic, Donald Having Tantrum, Disney, 3 x 4 1/2 In. 414.00
Cel, Foghorn Leghorn, Friz Freleng, Warner Brothers, 1983, 7 x 7 1/2 In. 632.00
Cel, He-Man, One Hand Raised, Publicity Cel, Mattel Toys, 1983, 10 x 12 In. 35.00
Cel, Jungle Book, Baloo Holding Mowgli, Walt Disney, Frame, 12 x 16 In. 1092.00
Cel, Lion King, Simba, Narla, Baby & Rafiki, Hand Painted, Walt Disney, 10 x 16 In. ... 135.00
Cel, Peter Pan, Captain Hook's Pirate Ship 475.00
Cel, Peter Pan, Tinkerbell, Disney 1760.00
Cel, Pink Panther, Holding Snapshot Camera, Frame, c.1970, 16 x 19 1/2 In. 145.00
Cel, Pinocchio, Geppetto's Toy Shop 150.00
Cel, Raggedy Ann & Andy, Patchwork Dog, Frame, 1987-1988, 12 x 15 In. 68.00
Cel, Reluctant Dragon, Disney 695.00
Cel, Scooby Doo, Hulk-Type Monster, Wood Frame, Matted, 1970s, 18 1/2 x 21 In. 95.00
Cel, Scooby Doo, Smiling, Wood Frame, Matted, 1970s, 18 1/4 x 21 In. 115.00
Cel, Secret Of NIMH, Mr. Ages, 10 1/2 x 12 1/2 In. 115.00
Cel, Serigraph, Aladdin & Genie, Flying Carpet, Ed. 2500, 10 x 13 In. 55.00
Cel, Sleeping Beauty, Disney 1760.00
Cel, Smurf, 1974, 10 1/2 x 12 1/2 In. 55.00
Cel, Song Of The South, Scene Of Brer Fox, Rabbit & Bear 445.00
Cel, Sword In The Stone, Magical Merlin 925.00
Cel, Tri-Klops, Masters Of The Universe, Early 1980s, 10 x 12 In. 25.00
Cel, Wind In The Willows, Mr. Toad Rides Again 950.00
Cel, Witch Hazel, Disney 425.00
Cel, Yogi Bear & Boo Boo, Hanna-Barbera Studio, 1960, 7 x 9 In. 550.00
Drawing, Space Ghost, Co-Pilot, In Rocket, Pencil, Jack Kirby, c.1970, 8 1/2 x 11 In. 73.00

ANNA POTTERY was started in Anna, Illinois, in 1859 by Cornwall and
Wallace Kirkpatrick. They made many types of utilitarian wares,
bricks, drain tiles, and giftware. The most collectible pieces made by
the pottery are the pig-shaped bottles and jugs with special inscriptions, applied animals, and figures. The pottery closed in 1894.

Anna Pottery

Bottle, Latest & Only Reliable Railroad River Guide, 7 1/4 In. 4800.00
Jug, Albany Slip Glaze, Incised Little Brown Jug, Egg Shape, 4 In. 300.00
Jug, Temperance, Young Black Girl Hugging Neck Of Bottle, 1891, 7 In. 3300.00

APPLE PEELERS are listed in the Kitchen category under Peeler, Apple.

ARCHITECTURAL antiques include a variety of collectibles, usually
very large, that have been removed from buildings. Hardware, back-
bars, doors, paneling, and even old bathtubs are now wanted by collectors. Pieces of the Victorian, Art Nouveau, and Art Deco styles are
in greatest demand.

Backbar, Mirror, Lighted Base & Top, Brass Foot Rail & Gallery, 82 x 61 In. 990.00
Backbar, Mirror, Please Pay Cashier, Thank You, 1920s, Round, 11 In. 720.00
Bracket, Red Faux Marble Painted Top, Acanthus, Pearl Finial, Italy, 15 In., Pair 1380.00
Bracket, Wall, Black Walnut, Mahogany, Rectangular Top, Russia, 1840, Pair 4025.00
Brasses, Woman In Classical Clothes, Oval, Stamped HJ, 8 Piece 355.00
Cabinet, Post Office Box, 30 Bronze Eagle Fronts, No Locks, 23 x 45 x 14 In. 275.00
Column, Ionic, Early 20th Century, 9 In. 4600.00
Column, Light Green Onyx, Brass Banding, Rounded Column, 39 1/2 In. 430.00
Column, Molded Top, Tapered Shaft, Socle Base, Italy, 43 1/2 x 11 In. 460.00
Column, Neoclassical, Pine, Raised On Rectangular Plinth, 9 Ft. 1 In., Pair 4887.00
Column, Onyx, On Composite Order, Gilt Brass Capital, Stepped Plinth, 39 In. 805.00
D-Shaped Panel, Central Sunburst Design, Ocher, Gray, 23 In., Pair 805.00
Doghouse, House Shape, Shutters, Red, White & Green, England, 29 x 22 In. 1500.00
Door, Arched, Walnut, c.1880, 2 Pair 550.00
Door, Granary, Repeating Rows Of Raised Figures, 2 Flat Panels, Dogon, 32 In. 4315.00
Door, Kitchen, Hardwood, Paneled, Pebbled Glass Inserts, 54 x 26 In., Pair 55.00
Door Plates, Bronze, Louis Sullivan, 14 In., Pair 1650.00
Doorknob, Flying Crane, Russell & Erwin, Bronze Cast, c.1880 ....*Illus* 660.00
Doorknocker, Cat, Raised Back 95.00
Doorknocker, Colonial Man, Box 150.00
Dove Gate, Iron, Full-Bodied Figure, Wings Outspread, White, 9 1/2 In. 1955.00

Downspout, Griffin Shape, Zinc 1900.00
Drawer Pull, Canary Glass, No Post, 6 Piece 110.00
Eagle, Gold Leaf Surface, 46 x 54 In.. 6325.00
Eagle, Pediment, Copper, c.1880, 70 In...................................... 8500.00
Fan, Weathered, Wood, Black & Yellow Repaint, 36 x 18 In. 220.00
Fence, Iron, Pierced Panels, 2 Willow Gates, Victorian, 9 Sections, 107 In. 2070.00
Finial, Molded Zinc, Flame Form, Brown Paint, Black Base, c.1880, 21 In., Pair 675.00
Fireplace Surround, Empire, Pine, Worn Paint, Gray Marbleizing, 62 x 54 In. 220.00
Fireplace Surround, Foliate Tiles, Trent, 33 x 36 In., 45 Piece 890.00
Fireplace Surround, Gas Insert, Casting, 19th Century, 37 x 46 x 11 In. 975.00
Gate, Driveway, Iron, 112 x 48 In... 190.00
Gate, Garden, Wooden Plank, Scalloped Border, Weathered, Folk Art, 43 x 33 In. 880.00
Gate, Hispano Moor Design, Arched Crest, Radiating Rods, 59 x 46 In. 545.00
Gate, Iron, Bronze Grapes, Strapwork Frame, Edgar Brandt, Pair 25300.00
Gate, Iron, Late 19th Century, 84 x 69 In., Pair 2300.00
Gate, Iron, Openwork, Large Conforming Frame, 94 1/2 x 48 In. 1028.00
Gate, Iron, Vertical & Horizontal Rods, Fleur-De-Lis Finials, 57 x 45 In. 2662.00
Gate, Vestibule, Twin Scroll Cartouches, Iron, 56 In., Pair 1735.00
Handle, Bar Door, Bronze, 1930s, 34 1/2 In., Pair 1498.00
Handle, Iron, Leaf & Scroll Design, 14 1/2 In., Pair 35.00
Holder, Soap & Sponge, Hooks Over Side Of Bathtub, Solid Brass, 19th Century 325.00
Iron, Hinge, Ornate, Berks County, Pa., Pair 185.00
Knob Set, No Post, Opalescent Glass, 2 1/8 In., 10 Piece 135.00
Latch, Door, Pennsylvania, 18th Century, 15 In. 225.00
Lock, Door, Hand Wrought, Engraved Hearts & Scrolls, 18th Century, 5 1/2 x 7 In. 500.00
Lock, Iron, Square, Attached Strapping, Case, 18th Century, 8 x 5 3/4 In. 105.00
Mailbox, Glass, Box, Unused, May, 22, 1934 .... 185.00
Mantel, Apron Centered By Shell Carving, 47 1/2 x 57 1/2 In. 1100.00
Mantel, Basket Of Flowers, Carved Frieze, Fruit Flanked By Floral Swags, 57 In. 5175.00
Mantel, Carved Huntsman Matron, Center, Floral Medallions, 49 x 71 In. 605.00
Mantel, Cast Iron, Arched Opening, Molded Panels, 1840s, 56 x 45 In. 390.00
Mantel, Cherry, Raised Panels, Beveled Top Mirror, Bottom Mirror, 80 In. 1500.00
Mantel, Federal, Pine, Putty Color Repaint, Reeded, Moldings, 53 x 56 In. 685.00
Mantel, Fireplace, Yellow Pine, Reeded Frieze, Original Green Paint, 46 In. 980.00
Mantel, Free-Standing Marble Columns, Rouge Marble, c.1880, 50 x 72 In. 990.00
Mantel, Louis XVI Style, Black Veined White Marble, 1915, 43 1/2 x 62 In. 6600.00
Mantel, Mahogany, Carved, Fluted Pillars, Arched, 20th Century, 35 x 37 In. 525.00
Mantel, Mahogany, Victorian Style, Carved Fruit, Fluted Columns, 48 x 60 In. 440.00
Mantel, Marble, White, Floral Carved, 18th Century 9775.00
Mantel, Pine, Federal, Poplar, Natural Finish, 53 1/2 x 50 1/2 In. 165.00
Mantel, Pine, Flat Columns, Detachable Backsplash, Black, 53 x 63 In. 345.00
Mantel, Walnut, Free-Edge, George Nakashima, 1961, 124 x 13 In. 1100.00
Mantel, Yellow Pine, Oval Cartouches & Stiles, Half Columns, 91 x 60 1/2 In. 3410.00
Medallion, Buff Clay, Floral Circle, 4 Spandrels With Ivy, 33 In., 5 Piece 385.00
Medallion, Ceiling, Regency-Style, Silvered Bronze, 17 In. 135.00

If you clean brass plated
hardware too well and remove
some of the plating, try this first
aid suggestion. Get a gold or
brass wax at a craft shop. Rub a
little on the bad spot. Then seal
with clear lacquer. Don't use
brass-colored spray paint.

Architectural, Doorknob, Flying Crane,
Russell & Erwin, Bronze Cast, c.1880

Arita, Umbrella
Stand, 19 In.

Be careful about putting antique china or glass in the dishwasher. Glass will sometimes crack from the heat. Porcelains with gold overglaze decoration often lose the gold. Damaged or crazed glaze will sometimes pop off the plates in large pieces.

Mold, Plaster, Egg & Dart, 5 1/2 x 25 1/2 In.	95.00
Newel Post, Walnut, Carved & Turned, Paint Traces, Square, 1885, 53 x 7 In.	385.00
Newel Post Lamp, Iron, Hammered, Amber Glass, G. Stickley, 8 x 8 x 21 In.	4125.00
Ornament, Bow Of Viking Ship, Dragon, Shield, Cast Bronze, Germany, 35 In.	385.00
Ornament, Triangular Rays, 2 Painted, 1 Gilt, Metal, Bruce Goff, 10 1/2 In., 3 Piece	220.00
Roundel, Relief Plaster, Napoleon, Eagle, Ebonized Convex Frame, 7 x 7 1/2 In.	240.00
Safe, Label, Men Watching Safe In Furnace, S.C. Herring, 1852, 8 1/4 In.	250.00
Spandrel, Walnut, Baroque, St. Joseph, Carved, 1700, 12 1/2 x 9 1/2 In.	72.00
Spire, Gilt, Steel Blue, Iron Red, Mid-19th Century, 68 1/4 In.	5175.00
Toilet Liner, Porcelain, Man & Woman Type, Use Over Hole, Japan, 1880, Pair	1400.00

ARGY-ROUSSEAU, see G. Argy-Rousseau category.

ARITA is a port in Japan. Porcelain was made there from about 1616. Many types of decorations were used, including the popular Imari designs, which are listed under Imari in this book.

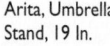

Bowl, Bamboo Branch & Flower Exterior, Tortoise Interior, 3 1/4 x 5 1/2 In.	330.00
Charger, Butterfly & Flowering Plants, Japan, Meiji, 1880, 15 1/4 In.	365.00
Charger, Flower-Basket Design, Japan, Meiji, 16 In.	120.00
Charger, Tree & Floral, Birds In Flight, Blue & White, 3 1/2 x 21 In.	605.00
Dish, Fish & Sea Grass, Oval, 7 In., 5 Piece	240.00
Umbrella Stand, 19 In. *Illus*	350.00
Vase, Alternating Blocks, Patterned Designs, Gilt Flowers, 9 1/2 In.	30.00

ART DECO, or Art Moderne, a style started at the Paris Exposition of 1925, is characterized by linear, geometric designs. All types of furniture and decorative arts, jewelry, book bindings, and even games were designed in this style. Additional items may be found in the Furniture category or in various glass and pottery categories, etc.

Figurine, Metal, Polychromed Red Dress & Hat, Marble Base, 19 In.	550.00
Powder Jar, Dolly Sisters, Frosted Green	135.00
Smokestand, Nude Emerging From Leaves, Nude Handle	350.00
Urn, Cast Stone, Circular Bowl & Pedestal Base, 21 In. Diam., Pair	165.00

ART GLASS, see Glass-Art category.

ART NOUVEAU is a style of design that was at its most popular from 1895 to 1905. Famous designers, including Rene Lalique and Emile Galle, produced furniture, glass, silver, metalwork, and buildings in the new style. Ladies with long flowing hair and elongated bodies were among the more easily recognized design elements. Copies of this style are being made today. Many modern pieces of jewelry can be found. Additional Art Nouveau pieces may be found in Furniture or in various glass categories.

Bust, Young Woman, Flowing Hair, White Marble, Gustave Obiols, 23 In.	7762.00
Coal Hod, Mahogany, Carved Panel Cover, Ornate Brass Hinges, 14 In.	120.00
Coal Hod, Nickel Plated, Reticulated Floral Design, Lift Lid, Liner, 13 1/2 In.	185.00
Figurine, Maiden In Evening Dress, Clutching A Fan, Ivory, R. Larche, 12 In.	2070.00

Transom, Stained Glass, Sunburst Design, Multicolored, Late 1800s, 52 x 24 In. 330.00
Vase, Pierced Band Of Trailing Pink, Lavender Peonies, Silver, Enameled, 6 In. 515.00

ART POTTERY was first made in America in Cincinnati, Ohio, during the 1870s. The pieces were hand thrown and hand decorated. The art pottery tradition continued until the 1920s when studio potters began making the more artistic wares. American, English, and Continental art pottery by less well-known makers is listed here. Most makers listed in *Kovels' American Art Pottery*, such as Arequipa, Ohr, Rookwood, Roseville, and Weller, are listed in their own categories in this book. More recent pottery is listed under the name of the maker or in the Pottery category.

Basket, Orange Red Glaze, 18 In. 55.00
Bottle, Mariposa RG, Blue, Green, Yellow, Squat, Signed, Natzler, 5 1/4 x 10 In. 4950.00
Pitcher, Incised Egyptian Design, Oriental Grasses, Light Blue-Gray Glaze, 8 In. 402.00
Umbrella Stand, Daffodil Design, Weller Type, 23 In. 440.00
Vase, Applied Vertical Leaves, Green, Brown Matte Glaze, Walley, 6 1/2 In. 3190.00
Vase, Frieze Of Nude Maidens, Pink, Brown, Yellow, J. Mayodon, 1925, 10 In. 5750.00
Vase, Green Iridescent Glaze, Purple, Gold, 2 Open Handles, Garzietta, 5 In. 231.00
Vase, Green, Blue, Taupe, Brown Glaze, Robineau, 5 1/2 In. 3850.00
Vase, Leaf Design, Multitoned Green Matte Glaze, 11 In. 605.00
Vase, Molded Leaves, Buds, Tobacco, Green Matte Glaze, 8 In. 330.00
Vase, Molded Vertical Leaves, Green, Brown Matte Glaze, 8 In. 286.00
Vase, Orange Red Glaze, Handle, 10 In. 100.00
Vase, Overall Purple, Green, Black Floral Design, Circular, 30 In. 604.00
Vase, Seed Form, Teal Blue Glaze, Early 20th Century, 6 1/8 In. 175.00
Vase, Stylized Buds, Leaves, White Outline, Deep Blue Ground, F. Rhead, 9 In. 550.00
Vase, Thick, Matte Green Glaze, Tapering, Signed, 9 1/2 In. 475.00

ARTS & CRAFTS was a design style popular in American decorative arts from 1894 to 1923. In the 1970s collectors began to rediscover Mission furniture, art pottery, metalwork, linens, and light fixtures from this period. The interest has continued. Today everything from this era is collectible, including jewelry, graphics, and silverware. Additional items may be found in the Furniture category, various glass categories, etc.

Box, Enameled Flowers, Cedar Lining, Peacock Feathers, Riveted Hinges, 7 x 5 In. 450.00
Plaque, Monk, Reading Book, Hand Tooled, 33 x 8 In. 990.00
Tray, Hammered Copper In Brass, Applied Cutout Handles, 23 x 10 In. 470.00
Tray, Raised Riveted Sides, 2 Handles, Wood & Iron, 22 x 13 In. 400.00

AURENE glass was made by Frederick Carder of New York about 1904. It is an iridescent gold, blue, green, or red glass, usually marked *Aurene* or *Steuben*.

AURENE

Basket, Blue, Coiled Prunt At Applied Handle, Ruffled Form, Carder, 7 In. 862.00
Bowl, Blue, 3 Applied Leaf Branches, Branch Feet, Pink Highlights, Carder, 6 In. 1150.00
Bowl, Blue, Flared, Circular Foot, Signed, 12 In. 920.00
Bowl, Blue, Scalloped Edge, Pink Highlights, Paper Label, 6 In. 495.00
Bowl, Gold, Bulb, 10 1/4 In. 430.00
Bowl, Gold, Calcite Exterior, Footed, 6 1/4 In. 287.00
Bowl, Gold, Calcite Exterior, Inverted Rim, 10 1/4 x 2 1/8 In. 230.00
Bowl, Gold, Closed Form, 8 x 4 In. 440.00
Bowl, Gold, Folded Over, 12 1/2 In. 345.00
Bowl, Underplate, Gold, Applied Ribbed Handle, Wavy Rim, 1920, 5 In. 431.00
Centerpiece, Flower, Gold Iridescent, Signed, 10 In. 350.00
Charger, Gold, Calcite Exterior, 12 In. 230.00
Dresser Bottle, Blue, Scrolled Feet, 4 In. 1500.00
Jar, Cover, Blue, Silver Designs, Purple Highlights, Signed, 5 x 3 1/2 In. 825.00
Lamp, Gold, Tubular Arm, Platinum Trim, Brass Base, 17 In. 2420.00
Lampshade, Gold, 5 In., Pair 330.00
Lampshade, Gold, Signed, 4 In., 4 Piece 770.00
Perfume Bottle, Gold, Engraved Floral & Crosshatching, Atomizer, 10 1/4 In. 1150.00
Perfume Bottle, Gold, Stopper, Steuben, 7 1/2 In. 660.00

Pitcher, Pink Highlights, Applied Handle, 10 In. 1265.00
Tumbler, Gold, Signed, 4 1/2 In. 132.00
Vase, Baluster, Gold, Marked, 8 3/4 In. 920.00
Vase, Blue, 3-Pronged Thorn, 7 3/8 In. 920.00
Vase, Blue, Bulbous, Signed, 8 1/2 In. 980.00
Vase, Blue, Fan, Knopped Stem, Spreading Foot, Signed, c.1900, 11 1/2 In. 287.00
Vase, Blue, Flared Neck, Steuben, 5 In. 715.00
Vase, Blue, Gold-Encrusted Bronze Holder, 11 In. 1200.00
Vase, Blue, Inverted Lip, 4 1/2 In. 935.00
Vase, Blue, Overall Blanket Of Flowers, Jade Yellow, Carder, 15 In. 9775.00
Vase, Blue, Stick, 6 In. 350.00
Vase, Blue, Stick, Flattened Disk Foot, Cylindrical, 7 3/4 In. 259.00
Vase, Bud, Gold, 3 Prongs, 1920, 6 1/4 In. 862.00
Vase, Everted Rim, Baluster, Gold, 9 In. 575.00
Vase, Gold, Blue & Green Sides, F. Carder, 1916, 10 In. 3737.00
Vase, Gold, Blue Everted Rim, Cylindrical, 1900, 8 In. 143.00
Vase, Gold, Chinese Shape, 1920-1925, 10 x 9 3/4 In. 845.00
Vase, Gold, Double Gourd, Green Loops On Top, Purple Highlights, 8 In. 1430.00
Vase, Gold, Fan, Green Trailings, Heart-Shape Leafage, F. Carder, 1925, 9 In. 2587.00
Vase, Gold, Overall Rainbow, 10 In. 231.00
Vase, Gold, Pulled Blue Peacock Feathers, Carder, 8 In. 4312.00
Vase, Gold, Rose, 12 x 11 In. 1650.00
Vase, Gold, Ruffled Rim, 2 1/2 In. 403.00
Vase, Gold, Ruffled Rim, Signed, 6 1/2 In. 690.00
Vase, Gold, Scrolled Foliate Design, Silver Rim, Pink Highlights, 3 In. 690.00
Vase, Gold, Tree Stump, Blue Highlights, 6 1/4 In. 550.00
Vase, Gold, Yellow, Signed, 11 In. 1495.00
Vase, Green & Gold, Blossoms, Heart & Vein Design, 10 In. 5175.00

AUSTRIA is a collecting term that covers pieces made by a wide variety of factories. They are listed in this book in categories such as Royal Dux, or Porcelain.

AUTO parts and accessories are collectors' items today. Gas pump globes and license plates are part of this specialty. Prices are determined by age, rarity, and condition. Signs and packaging related to automobiles may also be found in the Advertising category. Lalique hood ornaments will be listed in the Lalique category.

Ashtray, BF Goodrich, Black Rubber Tire-Shaped Rim, Glass Center, 6 In. 35.00
Ashtray, Goodyear Service Stores, Black Rubber Tire-Shaped Rim, Glass Center, 6 In. 23.00
Ashtray, Maybach, Lead Crystal, Frosted Detailing, Relief Design, 1930s, 5 x 5 x 2 In. ... 425.00
Booklet, Horses To Horse Power, Automobile Manufacturers Assn., 1955, 48 Pages 10.00
Bottle, Oil, Shell, Raised Logo, Ribbed, 1 Qt., 14 In. 95.00
Bottle, Oil, Socony Motor, Raised Letters Front & Back, Metal Spouts, 1 Qt., 16 In. 85.00
Bumper Plaque, Lincoln Auto Club, AAA, Map Of Neb., Capitol Building, 3 1/4 In. 35.00
Button, 38-Efficiency Dept., Across Center, White, Blue 1938 Chevrolet, Pinback, 2 In. .. 70.00
Button, Valve In Head—Motor Cars, Red, White, Blue, Pinback, 1910, 7/8 In. 34.00
Can, Sambo Axle Grease, Black Man With Oil Can, Missouri, 3 1/2 x 4 1/2 In. 195.00
Can, Simonize, Man Waxing Car, Orange, Red, Black, Late 1930s, 4 1/2 x 1 3/4 In. 15.00
Can, Texaco Home Lubricant 25.00
Car Robe, Cut Velvet, Wood Border, Backing, Soft Green, 48 1/4 x 67 1/4 In. 140.00
Catalog, Cadillac V-8, 7 Models, 1935, 12 Pages, 5 1/2 x 7 1/2 In. 28.00
Catalog, Pep Boys, New York World's Fair, Automotive Needs, 1940, 52 Pages 45.00
Catalog Sheet, Lafayette Motor Car, 4 Models, Full Color, 7 x 11 In. 28.00
Chauffeur Badge, Oregon, 1933, Hallmark Irwin Hudson, Co., Portland 40.00
Dispenser, Soap, Shell Gasoline, Cast Iron, Shell Logo, 5 In. 165.00
Display, Esso, Cardboard, Die Cut, Stand-Up, Sodico Paris, France, 15 1/2 In. 88.00
Display, Goodrich Silvertowns, Tin Tire, Color, Stand 45.00
Display, Super Shell, 2 Penguins On Ice Skates, Die Cut, 1930s, 5 x 4 In. 12.00
Driving Goggles, Amber Glass Lenses, Hinged Metal Frame, Elastic Strap, 1920s, Pair ... 30.00
Figure, Esso Gasoline Tiger, Service Station Clothes, 1960, 3 1/2 In. 6.00
Floor Mat, Quaker State Motor Oil, 1960, 17 x 24 In. 5.00
Fork, Pierce Petroleum Corp, Pennant 15.00
Gas Can, Datsun Saves A Gallon Of Gas A Day, Handle, Threaded Spout, 1970s, 1 Gal. ... 20.00

Gas Nozzle, K-721-1, Metal, 14 In. 65.00
Gas Pedal, Barefoot, Mounts Over Regular Pedal, Chrome Plated Metal, Package, 1960s . 20.00
Gas Pump, Bennett, Contains Lead Signs, Model 646, 73 x 29 x 18 In. 880.00
Gas Pump, Pennsylvania, Tydol Ethyl Signs, Model 52, 68 x 24 x 18 In. 1045.00
Gas Pump, Sharmeter, Neptune Meter Trademark, No. 132339, 68 x 25 x 22 In. 1210.00
Gas Pump, Wayne, Model 60, 75 x 27 x 18 In. 935.00
Gas Pump Globe, Ashland Kerosene Gas, Hull Body, 2 Lenses, 13 1/2 In. 605.00
Gas Pump Globe, Clock Face, Hays 1800.00
Gas Pump Globe, Gold Crown 600.00
Gas Pump Globe, Gulf No-Nox, Dark Blue, Porcelain 75.00
Gas Pump Globe, Holiday Regular 94 Octane, Glass, Metal Base, 2 Lenses, 13 1/2 In. 660.00
Gas Pump Globe, National White Rose Ethyl, Glass, 2 Lenses, 13 1/2 In. 415.00
Gas Pump Globe, Red Crown Ethyl, Embossed Lettering, 1 Piece, 17 1/2 In. 1210.00
Gas Pump Globe, Red Crown, Brass Nozzle 1300.00
Gas Pump Globe, Standard Oil, Milk Glass, King's Crown Shape, 16 In. 295.00
Gas Pump Globe, Standard Oil, Red 400.00
Gas Pump Globe, T & T Auto-Power Gasoline, 3-Piece Body, Glass, 13 1/2 In. 495.00
Gas Pump Globe, Tower, Air-Water 250.00
Gas Pump Sign, Jetrol Premium, Porcelain, Canada, 12 x 12 In. 248.00
Gas Pump Sign, Moore's Ethyl Supreme, Porcelain, 15 x 10 In. 385.00
Gas Pump Sign, Shell Gasoline, Paddle Sign, Porcelain, Die Cut, 2 Sides, 12 x 15 In. 770.00
Gas Pump Sign, Texaco Sky Chief, Made In U.S.A., 3-10-47, 18 x 12 In. 95.00
Gas Pump Sign, Texaco, Porcelain, Round, 8 In. 385.00
Gauge, Radiator, Boyce Motometer, Metal, Glass, Thermometer Style Indicator, 5 3/4 In. . 40.00
Gear Shift Knob, Die Shape, Red, White Dots, Plastic, Brass, 1930s-1940s, 1 3/8 In. 35.00
Hat, Attendant's, Mobil Service, Cloth, Plastic Rim, 5 x 10 In. 150.00
Hat, Attendant's, Phillips 66, Cloth, Embroidered Patch, Size 7 3/8 In. 230.00
Hood Ornament, 1957 Chevy, Finned, Chrome, Bullet, Pair 110.00
Hood Ornament, Checker Special, Crossed Flags Over North America, Aluminum 35.00
Hood Ornament, Felix, Showing Teeth, Threaded Base, Brass, 4 1/2 In. 154.00
Hood Ornament, Jockey & Horse, R. Men, Chrome, France, 7 3/8 In. 200.00
Hood Ornament, Mack, Bulldog, Chrome Plated, 1950s, 4 In. ....25.00 to 40.00
Hood Ornament, Packard, Winged Woman, Chrome 75.00
Horn, Bug Screen, Rubber Bulb 50.00
Hubcap, Cadillac, Early 1940s, Set Of 4 .... 125.00
Jack, Miniature Jack-In-The-Box, Salesman's Sample, Simplex, Box, Mailer, 3 In. 50.00
Lamp, Mazda, Westinghouse, Box, 10 Piece 10.00
Lamp, Neverout, Kerosene, Brass, Red & Clear Lenses, 9 x 4 In. 90.00
Lapel Pin, Citco Oil, 25 Year Service, 14K Gold, 3 White Stones, 1/2 In. 40.00
Letter Opener, Mobile Oil, Winged Horse, Copper, Tin Plated Handle, 9 In. 25.00
License Plate, Maine, 1914, Porcelain, 5 1/4 x 15 1/2 In., Pair 120.00
License Plate, Manitoba, Canada, 1950, Pair 25.00
License Plate, New Jersey, Porcelain, Horace E. Fine Co., Trenton, N.J., 6 x 13 In. 143.00
License Plate, Olympic Games, 1932, Los Angeles, Orange, Black, 4 1/2 x 11 1/2 In. 320.00
License Plate, Pennsylvania, 1913, Green & White 55.00
License Plate, Pennsylvania, 1915, Tractor, Porcelain, Brilliant Mfg. Co., 6 x 14 In. 132.00
License Plate, Pennsylvania, 1922, Stamped Metal, Cream, Maroon Keystones 20.00
License Plate, South Carolina, 1926 .... 15.00
License Plate, Texas, 1958, Pair 25.00
License Plate Attachment, C.S.E.A., Porcelain, Irvine & Jachens S.F. 6838, 5 x 3 In. ... 33.00
License Plate Attachment, Mobil, Winged Horse, Tin, Die Cut, Embossed, 4 x 5 In. 60.00
License Plate Ornament, Miami, The Magic City, Brushed Aluminum, 1940s 27.00
License Plate Ornament, Shell 40.00
License Plate Set, 48 States & DC, Cereal Premium, 1953, 49 Piece 175.00
Manual, De Soto, Fire Dome Eight, Dec. 1951, 52 Pages 10.00
Manual, Ford, 1920, 74 Pages 25.00
Mask, New Chevrolet 1938, Winking Figure In Top Hat, Stiff Paper, Die Cut 55.00
Measuring Stick, Wood, Paper Label, 5 x 35 1/2 In. 60.00
Notepad, Ford The Universal Car, Celluloid Cover, 1914, 2 1/2 x 4 1/2 In. 18.00
Oil Bottle, Master Manufacturing Co., Glass, Galvanized Tin Spout, 1920s-1930s, Qt. ... 20.00
Oil Can, Approved Red Hat, Independent Oil Men Of America, Chicago, Illinois, Gal. ... 2090.00
Oil Can, Atlantic Quality Lubricants, Atlantic Refining Company, 16 1/2 x 11 1/2 In. 65.00
Oil Can, Crown Premium Motor Oil, SAE 30, 1930s, 5 In. 25.00

Oil Can, Gas, Texaco 69.00
Oil Can, Gulfoil Household Lubricant, Metal, Spout, 5 3/4 In. 25.00
Oil Can, Handlin, Atchison, Topeka & Santa Fe, 5 Qt. 120.00
Oil Can, Hi-Val-Ue Motor Oil, 1 Qt. 60.00
Oil Can, Husky Motor Oil, Husky In Snow, Western Oil & Fuel Co., Qt. 770.00
Oil Can, Indian Motorcycle Oil, 1 Qt. 550.00
Oil Can, ISO-VIS Motor Oil, 1 Qt. 95.00
Oil Can, Monamobile Oil, Metal, Monarch Mfg. Co., Gal. 110.00
Oil Can, Oilzum Grease, 1930s, 5 Lbs. 125.00
Oil Can, Penn City Motor Oil, Tin, Qt. 132.00
Oil Can, Phillips 66, Metal, 5 Gal. 28.00
Oil Can, Phillips Trop-Artic Motor Oil, Igloo & Palm Trees, Qt. 715.00
Oil Can, Power Lube Motor Oil, The Powerine Company Denver, Colo., Gal. 2090.00
Oil Can, Red Giant Motor Oil, Text On Reverse With Logo At Top, 1 Qt. 90.00
Oil Can, Trop-Artic, Closed Touring Coupe, Manhattan Oil Co., Gal. 3520.00
Oil Can, Valvoline Motor Oil, Advertising On 4 Sides, Chicago, Gal. 205.00
Oil Can, Whippet Motor Oil, 1930s, 10 1/2 x 8 1/2 In. 440.00
Oil Globe, Martin's Kerosene, Metal, 1928, 15 In. 1200.00
Oil Jar, Standard Oil, Glass, Embossed, Metal Spout, 1 Qt., 15 In. 45.00
Penholder, Indianapolis Motor Speedway, Gold Metal Horseshoe, Racing Car, 2 1/2 In. .. 60.00
Pennant, Maxwell, Felt, 1920s, 13 In. 28.00
Pin, Chevrolet, White & Blue, 38-Efficiency Dept., Celluloid, 1938, 2 1/4 In. 70.00
Pitcher, Jaguar XK-150, Corvette, Austin Healy 100-Six, Glass, c.1958, 6 3/4 In. 15.00
Pitcher & Glass Set, Put A Tiger In Your Tank, 1960s-1970s, 9 & 5 1/2 In., Set Of 5 .... 40.00
Print, Pontiac, G.M. Corp, Indian Series, Indian Hunter, 16 1/2 x 11 In. 25.00
Print, Pontiac, G.M. Corp, Indian Series, Ottawa Chief, 16 1/2 x 11 In. 25.00
Sign, A.P.C Standard Motor Oil, Porcelain, Pillow, Round, 25 1/2 In. 120.00
Sign, Cadillac Certified Craftsman, Aluminum, 12 x 10 In. 198.00
Sign, Esso Heating Oil Authorized Dealer, Metal, 2 Sides 90.00
Sign, Ford, For Car Financing, Foil On Cardboard, 1950s, 9 x 12 In. 165.00
Sign, Goodyear Rubber Co., Rubber Heel, Man Walking, Pre-WWII, 18 x 7 1/2 In. 25.00
Sign, Goodyear Tires, Blue, Yellow, White Enamel, 23 1/4 x 66 In. 115.00
Sign, Goodyear Tires, Wooden Frame, 1 1/2 x 8 Ft. 490.00
Sign, Mobil Oil, Gargoyle Flange, Porcelain, 2 Sides, 1920s 650.00
Sign, Mobil Regular, Flying Horse, Blue, Red, Porcelain On Steel, 1940s, 12 x 14 In. 60.00
Sign, Mobil, Pegasus Horse, Porcelain, Die Cut, Frame, Toe To Wingtip 75 In. 1320.00
Sign, Mohawk Tires, Tin, Staggered, Self-Framed, 17 x 59 In. 260.00
Sign, Motor Penn All Pennsylvania Motor Oil, 2 Sides, 1930s, 8 1/2 x 6 In. 545.00
Sign, No Smoking, Texaco, Porcelain, Logo At Left Side, 4 x 23 In. 265.00
Sign, Phillips 66, Neon, Porcelain, Die Cut, Frame, Federal Electric Co., 48 x 46 In. 1760.00
Sign, Plymouth, Ed Wynn, Contest, Paper, 1936, 13 x 13 1/2 In. 20.00
Sign, Pump, Gulf No-Nox, Porcelain, 11 1/2 x 8 1/2 In. 55.00
Sign, Quaker State Oil, Arched Top, Farm Scene On Back, Porcelain, 29 x 26 1/2 In. 175.00
Sign, Regal, Leaded Glass, Crown Picture, Round, 22 In. 650.00
Sign, Shell Gas Station, Shell Logo Shape, Red, Yellow Enamel, Metal, 40 x 41 In. 175.00
Sign, Shell Motor Oil, Porcelain, Die Cut, 2 Sides, 25 x 25 1/2 In. 550.00
Sign, Shell Motor Oil, Porcelain, Self-Framed, 29 x 39 In. 192.00
Sign, Shell Oil Company, C. Perrier, ACB Lease, Porcelain, Steel, 1930-1950, 24 x 10 In. . 50.00
Sign, Sinclair Opaline Motor Oils, Porcelain, White, Red, 15 x 60 In. 270.00
Sign, Stop Here For Rayestos, Brake Service, Flange, 1920-1930, 14 x 18 In. 405.00
Sign, Super Chevrolet Service, Porcelain, 2 Sides, 48 1/2 x 41 1/2 In. 9600.00
Sign, Super Shell, 2 Penguins On Ice Skates, Die Cut, 1930s, 5 x 4 1/2 In. 12.00
Sign, Texaco Kerosene, Tin, 1 Side, 20 x 11 3/4 In. 70.00
Sign, Texaco Lubricants, Paper, Metal Strips, 43 1/2 x 38 In. 110.00
Sign, Veedol Motor Oil, Paper, Cloth Backing, Skater, Motor Oil Can, 32 x 24 In. 55.00
Spark Plug, AC, No. 2, 1/2 In. 15.00
Spark Plug, Affinity Baysdorfer, White Porcelain, 7/8 In. 40.00
Spark Plug, Auto, Spark Plug, Paf Non-Foul, No. 775, 1/2 In. 14.00
Spark Plug, Bethlehem, Mica, 3/4 In. 50.00
Spark Plug, Champion, No. 33, Gas Engine Special, 1/2 In. 30.00
Spark Plug, Diamond Reflex, 1/2 In. 20.00
Spark Plug, Excelsior, 1/2 In. 55.00
Spark Plug, Genuine Soot-Proof, Blue Logo, 7/8 In. 20.00

Spark Plug, Jewel, Brass, Mica, 1/2 In.	40.00
Spark Plug, Rentz, Lighthouse, 7/8 In.	20.00
Stand, Gulf Tire, 2 Sides, Wire, 8 1/2 x 14 x 10 In.	77.00
Tank, Gasoline Emergency, Wooden, Tin, 1920, 13 In.	33.00
Tin, Aero Eastern Motor Oil, 2 Gal.	58.00
Tin, Conoco Oil, 1 Gal.	40.00
Tin, Golden Shell Oil, Embossed, Tin, 13 3/4 In.	245.00
Tin, Goodyear Tire Accessories, Grain Painted, 20 x 23 x 13 In.	187.00
Tin, Hancock Motor Oil, For Car Models 1948-1951, 1 Qt.	350.00
Tin, Hancock Motor Oil, Lists 1948-51 Car Models, 1 Qt.	350.00
Tin, Maxoil, Gasoline Lubricant, Amarillo, Texas, Contents, 1 Pt.	12.00
Tin, Pep Boys Motor Oil, Manny, Noe & Jack On Bucking Bronco, 2 Gal.	161.00
Tin, Sliptivity Axle Grease, Canada	200.00
Tire Meter, Eco, Model 37, Clock Face, Metal, 17 x 10 x 10 In.	605.00
Vase, Vaseline Glass	55.00
Watch Fob, Dodge Brothers Motor Cars, Brass, Enamel, 1 1/4 In.	30.00
Window, Stained Glass, Texaco, Wire Frame, Texaco Letters Painted On, Round, 22 In.	1375.00

AUTUMN LEAF pattern china was made for the Jewel Tea Company beginning in 1933. Hall China Company of East Liverpool, Ohio, Crooksville China Company of Crooksville, Ohio, Harker Potteries of Chester, West Virginia, and Paden City Pottery, Paden City, West Virginia, made dishes with this design. Autumn Leaf has remained popular and was made by Hall China Company until 1978. Some other pieces in the Autumn Leaf pattern are still being made. For more information, see *Kovels' Depression Glass & Dinnerware Price List.*

Bowl, Cereal, 6 1/2 In.	14.50 to 25.00
Cake Plate, Metal Base	265.00
Clock, Electric, 9 1/2 In.	700.00
Coffeepot, Electric	435.00
Coffeepot, Rayed, 10 In.	44.00
Coffeepot, Sugar & Creamer	200.00
Cookie Jar, Big Ear	275.00
Cookie Jar, Tootsie	285.00
Cup & Saucer	12.50
Custard Cup	9.50
Jug, Ball, Hall, 7 1/2 In.	27.00
Jug, Ball, Ice Lip, 5 1/2 Pt.	35.00
Mixing Bowl, Nested, Set Of 3	50.00 to 75.00
Mug, Irish Coffee	110.00 to 130.00
Mustard Jar, 3 1/2 In.	40.00
Mustard Set, 3 Piece	85.00
Pie Lifter	45.00
Pitcher, Rayed, 6 In.	22.00
Plate, 6 In.	5.50
Plate, 7 In.	8.50
Plate, 9 In.	12.50
Salt & Pepper, Handle	50.00
Saucer, St. Denis	158.00
Sugar & Creamer, 1930s	65.00
Teapot, 11 In.	44.00
Teapot, Aladdin, 10 1/2 In.	27.00
Teapot, Newport, 1933	185.00 to 250.00
Tray, Glass, Wooden Handles	80.00
Tumbler, Frosted, 3 3/4 In.	40.00

AVON bottles are listed in the Bottle category under Avon.

AZALEA dinnerware was made for Larkin Company customers from 1918 to 1914. Larkin, the soap company, was in Buffalo, New York. The dishes were made by Noritake China Company of Japan. Each piece of the white china was decorated with pink azaleas.

NORITAKE
AZALEA PATT.
HANDPAINTED
JAPAN
NO. 19322
252627

Candy Jar, Cover, 5 In.	550.00

Celery Dish, Closed Handle, 10 In. 300.00
Coffeepot, After Dinner 550.00
Cup & Saucer 17.00
Dish, Lemon, 2 Handles, 5 1/2 In. 24.00
Gravy Boat, Attached Undertray 50.00
Grill Plate, 10 1/4 In. 175.00
Plate, 7 1/2 In., Set Of 12 .... 100.00
Platter, 12 In. 58.00
Soup, Dish, Cream, 6 In. 440.00
Sugar 25.00
Sugar & Creamer, Individual ....375.00 to 800.00
Teapot 95.00

BACCARAT

BACCARAT glass was made in France by La Compagnie des Cristalleries de Baccarat, located 150 miles from Paris. The factory was started in 1765. The firm went bankrupt and began operating again about 1822. Cane and millefiori paperweights were made during the 1860 to 1880 period. The firm is still working near Paris making paperweights and glasswares.

Ashtray, Square, c.1935, 2 1/2 x 2 1/2 In., 8 Piece 240.00
Candelabrum, 3-Light, Shading From Pink To Yellow, Prisms, Pair 1600.00
Candlestick, Cherubs, Holding Up Candle, Frosted Base, Signed, 12 1/2 In., Pair 450.00
Champagne, Sectioned Octagonal Form, Paper Label, 9 In. 345.00
Chandelier, 8-Light, Scrolled Arms, Allover Prisms & Chains, Electrified, 34 In. 4600.00
Clock, Interlacing Circles & Beads On Frame, Lion's-Mask Handles, 16 1/4 In. 8625.00
Decanter, Clear Cut, Stopper, Signed, 8 1/2 In. 110.00
Decanter, Clear Cut, Stopper, Signed, 9 3/4 In. 172.00
Decanter, Spike Sided, Blown Spiked Stopper, Taffeta-Covered Box 290.00
Decanter, Swirl, Stopper, 8 In. 65.00
Figurine, Lion's Head, Clear, 5 In. 258.00
Figurine, Owl, 4 1/2 In. 85.00
Figurine, Penguin, Blue, 15 1/4 In. 230.00
Figurine, Rabbit, Signed, 3 In. 95.00
Ice Bucket, Harmonie, Silver Handle 258.00
Lamp, Oil, Sunburst, Cranberry-Flashed Chimney 235.00
Obelisk, Clear Cut, Signed, 15 1/8 In. 300.00
Paperweight, Arrowhead & Star Canes, 3 Animal Silhouettes, 3 1/8 In. 1598.00
Paperweight, Butterfly, Millefiori Wings, Black Head, Turquoise Eyes, 2 3/8 In. 1900.00
Paperweight, Concentric Blue, Yellow, Red, & White Mushroom, 3 3/16 In. 700.00
Paperweight, Concentric, Arrowhead & Star Canes, Animal Silhouettes, 3 1/8 In. 1598.00
Paperweight, Double Clematis, Double Tier Of Petals, Bull's-Eye Cane, 2 1/2 In. 2500.00
Paperweight, Millefiori Garlands, Central Cane Of Arrowheads, 2 1/2 In. 265.00
Paperweight, Millefiori, Signed, 1846, 3 In. 2640.00
Paperweight, Pansy, Canes In Center, 3 In. 495.00
Paperweight, Pelican, Signed 225.00
Paperweight, Pompon, C-Shaped Petals, Stardust Stamens, 2 1/2 In. 1700.00
Paperweight, Pope John XXIII, Box 150.00

The best cleaner for your cut glass is a perfume-free, softener-free dishwasher detergent. Ammonia is too strong, and scented softeners sometimes leave an oily film.

Baccarat, Paperweight,
Triple, Millefiori, Macedoine,
Clematis, 3 1/4 In.

Paperweight, Primrose Garland, 6 Petals, Bull's-Eye & Star Canes, 2 3/4 In. 2250.00
Paperweight, Primrose, Ruby Petals, Stardust & Bull's-Eye Canes, 2 9/16 In. 2000.00
Paperweight, Red Dahlia, White Petals, Millefiori Cane Center, 1972, 2 15/16 In. 360.00
Paperweight, Rooster, Millefiori Base, Gridel, c.1970, 3 1/4 In. 430.00
Paperweight, Star Center, Striped Blossoms, Millefiori Cane, 2 1/2 In. 1610.00
Paperweight, Sulphide, Eleanor Roosevelt, Amethyst Star-Cut Base, 1971, 2 In. 65.00
Paperweight, Sulphide, James Monroe 75.00
Paperweight, Sulphide, Pope John XXIII, Box 150.00
Paperweight, Triple, Millefiori, Macedoine, Clematis,3 1/4 In. ....*Illus* 45100.00
Paperweight, Wall Flower, 5 Petals Outlined In Ruby, Millefiori Center, 2 7/16 In. 1000.00
Perfume Bottle, Djedi, Vertical Ridges, Flacon, Clear Rectangular Stopper, 8 In. 1285.00
Perfume Bottle, Emerald, Brass Cover, Green Enamel, Flacon, Rectangular, Stopper 730.00
Perfume Bottle, Guerlain Mitsouko, Clear 85.00
Perfume Bottle, Rue De La Paix, White Interior, Flacon, Laurel-Leaf Label, 1908, 4 In. . 1375.00
Perfume Bottle, Violets, Loup River, Diamond-Shape Stopper, 9 In. 600.00
Perfume Bottle, Woman Of The Day, Flacon, Clear Square Stopper, 3 1/2 In. 1545.00
Perfume Bottle, Zipper, Rose Teinte, Stopper, 5 In. 75.00
Sugar, Cover, Lacy, 7 1/4 In. 82.00
Vase, Clear, Blue Ground, 7 1/2 In. 303.00
Vase, Hexagon Form Body, 6 3/4 In. 115.00
Vase, Locust, Late 1800s, 8 1/2 In. 985.00
Vase, Rose, 13 In. 505.00
Vase, Serpentine, Clear, 12 In. 288.00
Vase, Tapering Octagonal Form, 10 In. 115.00
Vase, Urn Form, Squat, France, 10 1/4 In. 230.00
Wine, Cut To Clear, 8 In., 9 Piece 288.00

BADGES have been used since before the Civil War. Collectors search for examples of all types, including law enforcement and company identification badges. Well-known prison or law enforcement badges are most desirable. Most are made of nickel or brass. Many recent reproductions have been made.

Air Gunner, World War I, Austria 326.00
American Day Celebration, Eagle With Arrows, 1898 .... 67.00
Army, Canada, Cap, Royal Regiment Of Canadian Artillery 8.00
Army, Great Britain, Cloth, White On Khaki 4.00
Army, Infantry, Assault ....40.00 to 55.00
Army, Tyrolean Infantry Brigade 61.00
Aunt Jemima Breakfast Club, Stamped Tin, 1940s, 1 3/8 x 1 3/4 In. 8.00
Auto Racing, To Raise Funds For Olympic Village, Germany, Pre-1935 .... 225.00
Caddy, Elmhurst Country Club, Chicago, Class A, No. 1, Gold With Black Lettering 125.00
Chauffeur, Alabama, 1925, Hole At Top, Silver Metal 170.00
Chauffeur, Arizona, 1941 .... 45.00
Chauffeur, California, Silver Finish Brass, 1937 .... 70.00
Chauffeur, Illinois, 1939 .... 20.00
Chauffeur, Illinois, 1946 .... 20.00
Chauffeur, Illinois, Silver Finish Metal, 1927 .... 70.00
Chauffeur, Iowa, Silver Finish Metal, 1937 .... 50.00
Chauffeur, Kansas City, Mo., Nickel, Marked, 1923, 1 3/4 In. 43.00
Chauffeur, Maryland, Yellow, Black, Red Lettering, Celluloid, Pinback 150.00
Chauffeur, Michigan, 1934, 1 x 1 1/2 In. 10.00
Chauffeur, Missouri, 1924, Brass, Oval, 1 3/8 x 2 In. 22.00
Chauffeur, Missouri, 1941, Aluminum, 8 Sides, 1 1/2 In. 25.00
Chauffeur, New York, 1922 .... 18.00
Chauffeur, Ohio, 1944 .... 40.00
Chauffeur, Oregon, October 1926, 1 5/8 In. 33.00
Chevron, Assistant Manager, Cloisonne, Clasp Pin, 1 1/4 x 1 1/2 In. 245.00
Chicago Motor Club, School Safety Patrol, Wings, Cog Wheel, Pinback, 2 1/4 In. 20.00
Club, Leighton Round The World, Wings, Center Globe, Gold Tone, 1930-1950, 2 1/2 In. . 85.00
Colt Firearms, Employee, Nickel Plate, Color Enamel, 1930s 90.00
Delegate, 1892 National Democratic Convention, Union Shield, 5-Point Star In Center ... 37.00
Delegate, Central Pa. Volunteer Fireman's Assn., Tin, Celluloid, 1905, 5 1/2 In. 25.00
Delegate, Court, 37th District, Michigan, Blue Enamel Ring Center, Shiny White Metal .. 29.00

Deputy Constable, Bexar, Co., Eagle At Top, Star At Center, Nickel, Stamped, 2 In. 25.00
Deputy Sheriff, Arlington County, Va., 5-Pointed Star, Bronze Metal, 2 1/2 In. 40.00
Deputy Sheriff, Cheyenne, Wyoming, Shield, Nickel-Plated Copper, 2 In. 45.00
Deputy Sheriff, North Carolina, 5-Pointed Star, State Emblem, Silver Metal, 2 5/8 In. ... 50.00
Deputy U.S. Marshal, Colo., Star In Center, Sterling Silver, 2 In. 125.00
Engineer, All Out, Erin Go Bragh, Victory, 1942, Celluloid, 2 1/4 In. 75.00
Firefighter, 1921 Volunteer Firemen's Association, Delegate, Washington, 2 1/2 In. 22.00
Firefighter, Battalion Chief, Detroit Fire Dept., Eagle, Crossed Trumpets, City Seal, 2 In. . 40.00
Firefighter, Brunswick Fire Service 70.00
Firefighter, Cap, 5 Crossed Fire Horns, Stamped Gilt Metal, 1 1/2 In. 20.00
Firefighter, John Spohr, Hazleton, Pa., 1908 .... 25.00
Firefighter, Maine Firemen's Assn. Convention, Aug. 19-20, 1897, Celluloid, 4 1/2 In. ... 27.00
Firefighter, San Francisco Fire Dept., No. 67 .... 300.00
Firefighter, Sioux Falls Parade, Brass & Celluloid Bar, Ribbon, June 2-5, 1903, 2 x 6 In. . 48.00
Firefighter, Susquehanna Fire Co., Gold Ribbon, Brass & Celluloid Bar, 1910, 4 In. 15.00
Flying Tiger Line, Cap, White Wings, 2 1/2-In. Wingspan 602.00
Hat, Good Humor Ice Cream, Screw Back Mount, Cloisonne, 3 5/8 x 7/8 In. 355.00
Honor, Field, Hamburg, 1934 .... 50.00
Messenger, Soap Box Derby, Metal, 1949 .... 41.00
Motorman, New York City, Independent System, Nickel, 2 In. 20.00
Navy, Adcom Barracks, Master-At-Arms, 2 1/2 In. 20.00
Northwest Airlines, Cap, Wings, Blue Painted Center, Brass, 3 1/2-In. Wingspan 352.00
Northwest Airlines, Pilot Wings, Winged Globe, U.S. Air Mail, Gold Tone, 3 1/2 In. 80.00
Olympics, Rings, Enameled Brandenburg Gate, Germany, 1936 .... 200.00
Omaha, Hanging Medal Pictures Logo, Gilt, 1898, 1 5/8 In. 55.00
Pan-American World Airways, Cap, Globe With Logo In Center, Gold, Black Ground ... 163.00
Pan-American World Airways, Cap, Globe, Gold, Blue Enamel, 1945-1959, 1 1/2 In. 155.00
Pan-American World Airways, Half Wing, Gold Tone, Blue Enamel 350.00
Patriotic, Iron Cross 61.00
Pennsylvania Railroad, Veteran Employees, Brass & Celluloid Bar, Ribbon, 1916 ...... 20.00
Perry's Victory, Centennial, Erie, Pa., Brass, 1913 .... 40.00
Pilot, Austria, 1916 .... 280.00
Pilot, Imperial, Austro-Hungarian 275.00
Police, Buffalo Reserve, Eagle Top, Silver Metal 35.00
Police, Burley, Idaho, Blue Enamel Ring, White Metal, Gilt 27.00
Police, Cottonwood, Arizona, Eagle Top, State Seal Center, Gold Tone 160.00
Police, Dispatcher, Beatrice, Nebraska, Eagle Top, Gold Tone 90.00
Police, Erie County, N.Y., Captain, Civil Defense, Shield, Eagle, Gilt Metal 20.00
Police, Inauguration Of President, Smithsonian Institution, 1985, 3 In. 60.00
Police, Juvenile, Buffalo, Shield & Eagle, Silver Metal, 1 7/8 In. 20.00
Police, Lackawanna Township, Pa., Silver Finish, 2 1/2 In. 45.00
Police, Mishawaka, Indiana, No. 126, 2 1/2 x 1 1/2 In. 30.00
Police, New York City, Brooklyn, Brass, c.1910 .... 150.00
Police, North Carolina, State Seal, Cap, Gold Tone, Cadet Mfg. Co., Box, 2 1/2 In. 20.00
Police, Pawtucket, Wallet Clip Style, Shield Shape, Silver Metal, 2 3/4 In. 50.00
Police, Probation Officer, New Britain, Conn., Shield Shape, White Metal, 1 5/8 In. 50.00
Police, St. Louis Suburban Park, Gold Tone, E. Jaccard J. Co., 1896, 1 1/4 x 1 3/4 In. 180.00
Police, Villa Ricca, Georgia, State Seal, 2 1/2 x 1 3/4 In. 45.00
Police, Watertown Arsenal, Mass., Silver Finish, 1940, 3 In. 35.00
Post Office, Weatherford, Tex., Silver Tone 53.00
Post's JDC Detective, Cereal Premium, Nickel, Shield Shape, 1 1/2 In. 20.00
PWA Airlines, Half Wing, Stylized Wing & Logo, Brass, 1 1/4 In. 60.00
Skelly, Jimmie Allen, Airplane 25.00
Skelly, Jimmie Allen, Flying Cadet 35.00
Star Bus Lines, Cap, Polished Finish, Blue Bus In Circle, 2 1/2 In. 35.00
Sterling Southern Airways, Lapel Pin, Sterling Wing, Blue Enamel Center, 1 In. 50.00
Truant Officer, Long Beach School District, State Seal, Wallet Style, Gilded Brass, 3 In. . 55.00
Truck, Austin Powder Company, Red Shield, White Metal 91.00
Truck, Austrian Observer, 1917 .... 400.00
Union, Brotherhood Locomotive Firemen & Engineers, Golden State Lodge No. 633 .... 75.00
United Airlines, Lapel Pin, Gilt Wing, Map Of U.S., Green Enamel Ring 25.00
Veteran Association, With Ribbons 21.00
Warden, New Brunswick, 1939 .... 50.00

Watchman, Chrome 5.00
Wise Coal & Coke Co., Employee, White, Black, Metal, Celluloid Lens, 1 3/4 In. 30.00

BANKS of metal have been made since 1868. There are still banks,
mechanical banks, and registering banks (those that show the total
money deposited on the face of the bank). Many old iron or tin banks
have been reproduced since the 1950s in iron or plastic. Some old
reproductions marked Book of Knowledge or John Wright are listed.
Pottery, glass, and plastic banks are also listed here. Mickey Mouse
and other Disneyana banks are listed in Disneyana.

Airplane, Mustang, Air Force Logos, Silver Color 35.00
Airplane, Texaco, No. 1 . . . .   250.00
Airplane, Texaco, No. 3 . . . .   35.00
Airplane, Texaco, No. 5 . . . .   25.00
Amish Girl, Metal, Hand Painted, John Wright, 1960s, 5 In. 65.00
Apple, Cast Iron, Kyser & Rex, 1882, 3 x 5 1/4 x 5 In. 1870.00
Atlas Batteries, Save With Atlas, Tin Lithograph, 1950s 65.00
Aunt Jemima, Mammy With Spoon, A.C. Williams, 1905-1930s, 5 7/8 In. 275.00
Aunt Jemima, Porcelain, Hand Painted, 1970s 45.00
Aunt Jemima, With Spoon, Cast Iron, Hand Painted, A.C. Williams, 1905, 5 7/8 In. 425.00
Baby In Cradle, Cast Iron, John Wright Toys, 1960s, 3 1/4 x 4 In. 150.00
Baby In Egg, Japanned Egg, Lead, Key Locked Trap, 7 1/4 In. 460.00
Bailey's, Centennial Money Bank, Liberty Bell, Wooden Base, Cast Iron, 1876, 4 1/2 In. . .   66.00
Barney The Dinosaur, Plastic, Hand Painted, Lions Group Co., 1992 . . . .   48.00
Barrel, New Deal Bank, Prosperity, Wooden, Red, Brass Bands, 3 1/2 In. 125.00
Barrel, On Hand Cart, Metal, 1923, 4 1/4 x 3 In. 125.00
Battleship Maine, Cast Iron, Brown Patina, Grey Iron, 4 3/8 x 1 1/2 x 4 1/2 In. . . .115.00 to 350.00
Be Wise & Save Owl, Plastic, Hand Painted, 1960s, Box 75.00
Bear, Hand In Honey Pot, Metal, Silver Color, 1960s 75.00
Bell, German Olympics, White Pottery, Germany, 1936, 4 In. 175.00
Benjamin Franklin, Bust, Metal, Copper Tone, 1950s 95.00
Big Boy, Figural, Smiling, Checkered Overalls, Blue Lettering, 1960, 9 1/4 In. 85.00
Big Boy, Figural, Smiling, Checkered Overalls, Dark Blue Eyes, 1960, 8 In. 75.00
Big Boy, Figural, Smiling, Dark Brown Hair, Eyes, Checkered Overalls, 1973, 8 1/2 In. . .   48.00
Big Boy, Movable Head, Vinyl, Marriott Corp., 1973, 8 3/4 In. 25.00
Big Boy, Rubber, Vinyl, Coin Slot Back Of Head, 1973, 9 In. 25.00
Billiken, Cast Iron, A.C. Williams, 1909, 4 1/4 In. 85.00
Billy Possum, Cast Iron, J.M. Harper, 1909, 3 x 4 3/4 In. 3960.00
Bionic Man, Vinyl, Animals Plus, 1976, 10 1/2 In. 45.00
Bionic Woman, Vinyl, Animals Plus, 1976, 10 In. 40.00
Black Baker, Porcelain, Hand Painted, 1970s 45.00
Black Boy, 2 Faces, Cast Iron, Black & Gold, A.C. Williams, c.1910, 4 1/8 In. . . . .120.00 to 150.00
Black Clown, Animated, Musical 165.00
Black Man, Sitting On Cotton Bale, Cast Iron, 1970s 40.00
Black Woman, Sitting On Cotton Bale, Cast Iron, 1970s 40.00
Bob's Big Boy, With Hamburger, Plastic, Hand Painted, Package, 1960-1970 . . . .   75.00
Bokar Coffee Can, Tin Lithograph, 1940s 48.00
Boot, Western, Metal, Tin Turn Out Coin Trap, 1960s 95.00
Bosco The Clown Chocolate Syrup, Plastic Head, Glass Bottle, 1950s 65.00
Boston, Bull Terrier, Seated, Cast Iron, Hubley, 1930s, 4 3/8 x 5 5/8 In. 187.00
Bowery Savings Bank, Log Cabin, Pottery, Metal 85.00
Brewmaster Roly Poly, Tin Lithograph, Germany, 2 1/4 In. 155.00
Budget, Pressed Steel, Key Lock & Hinged Lid, Marx Toys, 1940-1950 . . . .   75.00
Budweiser Can 48.00
Buffalo, Cast Iron, A.C. Williams, 1920s, 3 1/8 x 4 3/8 In. 95.00
Bugs Bunny, Seated, Eating Carrot, Plaster, Warner Bros. Pictures Inc., c.1950, 20 In. 78.00
Building, Domed Bank, Cast Iron, A.C. Williams, 1899-1934, 4 1/2 x 3 1/4 In. 115.00
Building, Double Entry, Cast Iron, Painted, John Wright, 1960s, 5 3/4 x 5 1/2 In. 120.00
Building, State Bank, Cast Iron, Grey Iron Casting, 1889, 4 1/8 x 3 1/16 In. 375.00
Building, State Bank, Cast Iron, Kenton, c.1900, 8 3/4 In. 825.00
Building, Woolworth Building, Cast Iron, Kenton, 1915, 7 7/8 x 1 3/4 x 2 1/4 In. 140.00
Bulova Watch, In Case, Metal, 1930s 225.00
Burglar Proof House Safe, Cast Iron, Pat. Aug. 17, 1897, J. & E. Stevens 165.00

Bus, Model 1915 Ford, Cast Iron, 5 1/2 x 3 1/2 In. 75.00
Buster Brown & Tige, Cast Iron, A.C. Williams, 1920s, 7 In. 140.00
Cabin, Boy In Doorway, Cast Iron, By Book Of Knowledge, 3 1/2 In. 55.00
California Raisins, Figural, Sunmaid Brand Raisins, Plastic 65.00
Camel, Standing, With Saddle, A.C. Williams, 1920s, 7 In. 325.00
Campbell's Tomato Soup Can, 125th Anniversary, Tin 45.00
Can, Lasting Paints, Tin, 1940s 75.00
Capitalist, Man In Bowler Hat, Striped Pants, Cast Iron, c.1890, 5 In. 575.00
Car, Chevrolet, 1915 Model, Cast Iron, 5 1/2 x 3 1/2 In. 75.00
Car, Chevrolet Roadster, 1915 Model, Copper, Movable Wheels, 1974, Banthrico, 5 In. .. 65.00
Car, Chevy Corvette, 1953 Model, Metal, 1974, Banthrico, Box, 6 7/8 In. 75.00
Car, Ford, 1929 Model, 2-Seater Type, Metal, Banthrico, 6 In. 75.00
Car, Nash Rambler, 1902 Model, Metal, Copper, Movable Wheels, 1974, Banthrico, 5 In. .. 20.00
Car, Packard V-12, 1937 Model, Metal, Copper, Movable Wheels, 1974, Banthrico, 7 In. .. 30.00
Car, Rolls-Royce, 1937 Model, Metal, Banthrico, 7 In. 75.00
Car, Studebaker, 1904 Model, Cast Iron, 4 1/2 x 3 1/2 In. 75.00
Car, Yellow Cab, Cast Iron, Arcade, 1921, 4 1/4 x 7 7/8 In. 1035.00
Carnival Rocking Horse, Silver Plated, Leonard Silver Co., Italy, 1960s 65.00
Castle, With 2 Towers, Cast Iron, John Harper, 1908, 7 x 4 5/8 x 3 1/8 In. 1650.00
Cat With Bow, Sitting, Cast Iron, Hubley, 1930s, 4 3/4 In. 175.00
Century Of Progress, Tin 35.00
Charlie Brown, Porcelain, Italian, 7 In. 150.00
Church, God Loveth A Cheerful Giver, Tin Lithograph, Chein Toys, 1930s 95.00
Church, Tin Lithograph, U.S. Metal Co. 18.00
Church Window Safe, Cast Iron, Shimer Toy, 1890s, 3 1/16 x 2 1/4 x 2 3/16 In. 90.00
City Bank, Teller, Cast Iron, H.L. Judd, 5 1/2 x 3 1/4 x 4 3/8 In. 395.00
Clock, A Money Saver, Cast Iron & Steel, Arcade, c.1909, 3 1/2 x 2 15/16 In. 95.00
Clock, Time Is Money, Cast Iron & Tin, Movable Handles, H.C. Hart, c.1885, 5 In. 460.00
Clock, Time Is Money, Cast Iron, A.C. Williams, 1909-1931, 3 5/8 In. 95.00
Clock, World Time, Cast Iron & Paper, Arcade, 1910-1920, 4 1/8 In. 352.00
Clown, Del Monte 42.00
Clown, Tin, Chein 125.00
Coffee Money, Coffeepot, Pottery, Hand Painted, 1950-1960 .... 65.00
Conestoga Wagon, Metal, Premium For Independence, Mo., 5 In. 22.00
Cow, Holstein, Arcade, 1910-1920, 2 1/2 x 4 5/8 In. 215.00
Cow, Holstein, Cast Iron, Arcade, 1910-1920, 2 1/2 x 4 5/8 In. 200.00
Cow's Head, Chalkware, 1850, 5 x 3 In. 850.00
Crown Bank, Cast Iron, J. & E. Stevens, Grey Iron Casting Co., 1873-1907, 5 In. 285.00
Cup & Saucer, Brass, England, 1920, 1 3/4 x 4 1/2 In. 63.00
Cupola Bank, Cast Iron, J. & E. Stevens, 1872, 4 1/8 x 3 3/8 In. 190.00
Darkey, Black Sharecropper, Cast Iron, 1901, A.C. Williams, 5 1/4 In. 375.00
Darth Vader, Head, Pottery, Roman Ceramics, 20th Century Fox, 1977, 6 1/2 x 6 In. 55.00
Dime Savings, Brooklyn, New York, Porcelain, Painted, Tin Coin Trap, 1950-1960 ...... 75.00
Dog, Boxer, Cast Iron, A.C. Williams, 1920s, 4 1/2 x 3 7/8 In. 70.00
Dog, St. Bernard, With Pack, Cast Iron, A.C. Williams, 1901-1935, 5 1/2 x 7 3/4 In. 55.00
Donkey, I Made St. Louis Famous, Cast Iron, Made For Still Bank Collector's Club, 1991 65.00
Duck, Silver Plated, On Metal, Blue Eyes, Leonard Silverplate Co., 1960s 50.00
Egg Man, Wm. H. Taft, Cast Iron, Arcade, 1910-1913, 4 1/8 In. 2640.00
Eiffel Tower, Cast Iron, Sydenham & McOustra, 9 In. 1035.00
Eight O'Clock Coffee, Tin, Red, Gold & Black, 1940-1950 .... 45.00
Electric Railroad, Trolley Car, Cast Iron, 4 Wheels, Shimer Toy Co., 1893, 8 In. 977.00
Electrolux Vacuum Cleaner, Plastic, Push Button Coin Trap, Box, 1950-1960 .... 95.00
Elephant, Dewey, Florida, Pottery, 1948, 13 In. 350.00
Elephant, Howdah, Cast Iron, A.C. Williams, 1930s, 4 7/8 x 6 3/8 In. 275.00
Elephant, On Tub, Trunk Down, Cast Iron, Gold Paint, A.C. Williams, 1920, 5 3/8 In. 95.00
Elephant, Seated, Trumpeting, White Metal, Key Locked Trap, Vanio, 1936, 5 In. 70.00
Ever Ready Nine Lives, Cat, Plastic, 1970s 48.00
Felix Cat Food 9.00
Fire Alarm, Dan-Dee Imports, Japan, Box, 1950s, 6 x 5 In. 95.00
Flatiron Building, Cast Iron, Kenton, 1912-1926, 5 1/2 x 3 x 3 1/2 In. 215.00
Flintstones, Fred Loves Wilma, Pottery, Early 1960s, 7 1/2 In. 315.00
Florida Orange Bird, Vinyl, Orange, Smiling, Green Leaf Petal Hair, Yellow, 5 In. 38.00
Football Player, With Large Football, Cast Iron, Hubley, 1914, 5 1/8 x 3 1/4 In. 1760.00

Garfield Cat, Football Player, Ceramic, Enesco, 1981, 5 1/2 In. 85.00
GE Radio, Cast Iron, Green, Gold Dials, Arcade, 1932-1934, 3 7/8 In. 250.00
GE Refrigerator, Cast Iron, Hubley, 1930-1936, 3 3/4 x 2 In. 110.00
George Washington Bust, Preferred Bank Services Co., White Metal, 1920s, 5 7/8 In. ... 75.00
Give Me A Penny, Standing Black Man, Cast Iron, Hand Painted, 1960s Reproduction ... 95.00
Globe, Cast Iron, Red, Grey Iron Casting Co., 1903, 5 1/4 In. 295.00
Globe, Tin, Chein, Key Locked Trap, 1934-1977, 4 3/8 In. 40.00
Globe Savings Fund, Polychrome, Cast Iron, Kyser & Rex, 1889, 7 1/4 In. 685.00
Graf Zeppelin, On Wheels, Cast Iron, A.C. Williams, 1934, 2 1/4 x 7 13/15 In. 225.00
Grand Piano, Plastic, Turn Out Rear Leg Coin Tap, Plastic Masters Inc., 1950s 65.00
Hall Clock, Cast Face, Cast Iron, Hubley, 1920s, 5 13/16 x 2 3/16 In. 315.00
Hen On Nest, Cast Iron, Early 1900s, 3 x 3 3/8 In. 1560.00
Hershey Bar, Red Plastic 40.00
Hippopotamus, Cast Iron, 2 x 5 13/16 In. 5400.00
Horse, Thoroughbred, Cast Iron, Hubley, 1946, 5 1/4 x 6 7/8 In. ....40.00 to 110.00
House, Pittsburgh Paints, Natures Colors In Lasting Beauty, Glass 27.00
House, Victorian, Cast Iron, J. & E. Stevens, Patented 1892, 4 1/2 x 3 1/4 In. 190.00
Humpty Dumpty, Seated On Wall, Metal, 1960s 95.00
Hurdy Gurdy Monkey, Tin Lithograph, Chein 75.00
Hush Puppy, Vinyl, 8 In. 20.00
Ice Cream Cone, Safe-T-Cup, Plastic, Slot In Top, 27 In. 35.00
Immanuel Evangelical Lutheran Church, Cast Brass 28.00
Indian, Figural, Nodder 45.00
Indian Boy, With Rifle, Metal, Anco Toys, 1930s 75.00
Indian Chief, Bust, Cast Iron, 1978, 4 7/8 In. 65.00
Indian Chief, Terminal Tower, Cleveland, Bronzed, White Metal 65.00
Indian With Tomahawk, Cast Iron, 5 7/8 In. 135.00
Jerry Mouse, Tom & Jerry, Vinyl, MGM, 1978, Hong Kong, Box, 2 1/2 x 3 1/2 x 7 In. ... 50.00
Jimmy Durante, White Metal, Abbot Wares, 6 3/4 In. 110.00
Kentucky Fried Chicken, Col. Sanders, Full Figure, 1970, 12 1/2 In. 75.00
Kentucky Fried Chicken, Col. Sanders, Plastic, Black Glasses, 1970, 12 1/2 In. 75.00
Kitten, Playing With A Ball Of Yarn, Red Bow On His Neck, Ceramic 23.00
Kitty, White, Blue Bow, Cast Iron, Hubley, 1930s, 4 1/8 In. 198.00
Lamb, Cast Iron, Hand Painted, John Wright, 1960s 65.00
Li'l Abner, Tin, Multicolor, 1953, 4 1/2 In. 250.00
Liberty Bell, 1776-1976, Bicentennial, Aluminum, 4 1/2 x 4 1/4 In. 15.00
Liberty Bell, Carnival Glass, Amber, 1950s 48.00
Liberty Bell, Copper Color, Wooden Yoke, Metal, Banker's Savings, 1919, 4 x 3 3/4 In. ... 75.00
Liberty Bell, George Washington Cast On Front, Cast Iron, 1920s, 4 In. 125.00
Liberty Bell, Metal, Square Base, 1776-1976 .... 95.00
Lincoln, Bust, Lead, A.C. Rehberger, 1920s, 5 In. 18.00
Lion, Tail Between Legs, Cast Iron, 3 In. 70.00
Lion, Tail Right, Cast Iron, A.C. Williams, 1905-1931, 5 1/4 In. 85.00
Log Cabin Syrup, Glass, Tin Cap Coin Trap, 1950s 65.00
Lyndon B. Johnson, Molded Plastic, 1964, 3 In. 20.00
Mailbox, U.S. Mail, Cast Iron, Green Paint, Hubley, 1930s, 5 1/2 x 2 1/2 In. 95.00
Mailbox, U.S. Mail, Cast Iron, Kenton, Large Trap, 4 3/4 x 3 1/2 In. ....60.00 to 80.00
Mailbox, U.S. Mail, Cast Iron, Silver, Lift Lid For Coin, A.C. Williams, 1931, 4 3/8 In. .. 45.00
Mammy, Hands On Hips, Red Dress, Cast Iron, Hubley, 1914-1946, 5 1/4 In. .....175.00 to 275.00
Man, Sitting On Stump, Wooden, Chalkware, Head Nods, No Key, Germany, 8 1/2 In. ... 220.00
Mascot, Cast Iron, Hubley, 1914, 5 13/16 In. 3740.00

Mechanical banks were first made about 1870. Any bank with moving parts is considered mechanical. The metal banks made before World War I are the most desirable. Copies and new designs of mechanical banks have been made in metal or plastic since the 1920s. The condition of the paint on the old banks is important. Worn paint can lower a price by 90%.

Mechanical, Afghanistan, Cast Iron, 1880s 2587.00
Mechanical, Artillery, Cast Iron, 1960s 150.00
Mechanical, Bad Accident, Cast Iron, Hand Painted, Wood Base, James Capron, 1950s ... 1500.00
Mechanical, Bad Accident, Cast Iron, Painted, J. & E. Stevens, 10 In. 2090.00
Mechanical, Baseball, Cast Iron, Book Of Knowledge 225.00

Mechanical, Birdie Putt, 1950s, Richard Toys ....375.00 to 575.00
Mechanical, Boy Milking Cow, Cast Iron, Hand Painted, 1960s 150.00
Mechanical, Boy On Trapeze, Book Of Knowledge 975.00
Mechanical, Boy On Trapeze, J. Barton & Smith Co., 1891 .... 350.00
Mechanical, Boy Robbing Bird's Nest, Cast Iron, J. & E. Stevens, 1906 .... 8050.00
Mechanical, Boy Scout Camp, J. & E. Stevens, 1915 .... 6800.00
Mechanical, Boys Stealing Watermelons, Kyser & Rex, 1894 .... 4500.00
Mechanical, Butting Buffalo, Cast Iron, Book Of Knowledge 325.00
Mechanical, Butting Ram, Cast Iron, Ole O. Storle, 1895 .... 5600.00
Mechanical, Calamity, Football, Cast Iron, 1960s ....225.00 to 275.00
Mechanical, Cat & Mouse, Cast Iron, Book Of Knowledge 375.00
Mechanical, Cat & Mouse, Cast Iron, J. & E. Stevens, 1891 .... 4200.00
Mechanical, Chief Big Moon, Charles A. Bailey, Patent 1899, J. & E. Stevens, 10 In. 2875.00
Mechanical, Clown On Globe, Cast Iron, Hand Painted, 1960s 275.00
Mechanical, Clown On Globe, Cast Iron, Hand Painted, James Capron, 1950s 775.00
Mechanical, Clown On Globe, Cast Iron, J. & E. Stevens, 1890 ....2200.00 to 2750.00
Mechanical, Clown, Tin, Chein Toys, 1930s 225.00
Mechanical, Coffin, Tin, Windup, Yone Toys, Japan, 1960s 95.00
Mechanical, Coffin, Tin, Windup, Yone Toys, Japan, Box, 1960s 195.00
Mechanical, Creedmoor, Man Shooting, Tree, Iron, J. & E., Stevens, 1880, 6 In. . .805.00 to 1800.00
Mechanical, Darktown Battery, Baseball, Iron, J. & E. Stevens, 10 In. ....2420.00 to 5300.00
Mechanical, Dentist, Cast Iron, J & E. Stevens, c.1890, 9 In. ....3600.00 to 4950.00
Mechanical, Destination Moon Spaceship, Metal, Vacumet Co., Box, 1950-1960 .... 250.00
Mechanical, Dinah, Cast Iron, John Harper Co. Ltd., 6 1/2 In. 715.00
Mechanical, Dog On Turntable, Cast Iron, Judd Mfg. Co., 1870s 2400.00
Mechanical, Eagle & Eaglets, Cast Iron, Book Of Knowledge 425.00
Mechanical, Elephant, James Capron, 1950s 475.00
Mechanical, Empire Cinema, Tin, Germany, 1914 .... 15730.00
Mechanical, Fisherman's Luck, Cast Iron, Richards Toys 1275.00
Mechanical, Frog On Rock, Sitting, 1920, Kilgore Mfg. Co. 2420.00
Mechanical, Frog, 2 Frogs, Cast Iron, J. & E. Stevens, 1882 .... 1650.00
Mechanical, Gem, Cast Iron, c.1895, Paper Label, 5 In. 690.00
Mechanical, George Washington At Rappahannock, Cast Iron, John Wright 775.00
Mechanical, Girl Skipping Rope, Cast Iron, J. & E. Stevens, 1890 .... 1440.00
Mechanical, Hall's Excelsior, Cast Iron, Blue & Red, J. & E. Stevens, 1869 .....770.00 to 1250.00
Mechanical, Hall's Liliput, Cast Iron, J. & E. Stevens, 1877 ....1150.00 to 1200.00
Mechanical, Happy Hippo, Windup, Yone, Japan, Box, 1960s 100.00
Mechanical, Hell Master, Skull & Coffin, Plastic, Windup, Box 48.00
Mechanical, Home Town Battery, Baseball, Cast Iron, 1960s ....150.00 to 225.00
Mechanical, Humpty Dumpty, Cast Iron, Book Of Knowledge ....*Illus* 375.00
Mechanical, Humpty Dumpty, Cast Iron, Shepard Hardware, 1884 .... 2200.00
Mechanical, I Always Did 'Spise A Mule, Iron, J. & E. Stevens, 1897 ....1495.00 to 3200.00
Mechanical, Initiating Bank, First Degree, Goat, Frog, Man, Sept. 28, 1880, 11 1/2 In. 11000.00
Mechanical, Jolly Nigger, Aluminum, Starkie, 1920s 650.00
Mechanical, Jolly Nigger, Cast Iron, J. & E. Stevens, 19th Century, 6 3/4 In. 220.00
Mechanical, Jolly Nigger, Cast Iron, Shepard Hardware, 1883, 7 In. 330.00
Mechanical, Jolly Nigger, High Hat, Cast Iron, John Harper, 1880s ....675.00 to 950.00

Bank, Mechanical,
Humpty Dumpty,
Cast Iron, Book Of
Knowledge

Bank, Mechanical, Organ
Grinder & Performing Bear,
Cast Iron, Kyser & Rex

Bank, Mechanical, Stump
Speaker, Cast Iron,
Shepard Hardware, 1886

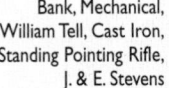

Bank, Mechanical,
William Tell, Cast Iron,
Standing Pointing Rifle,
J. & E. Stevens

Mechanical, Las Vegas Jackpot, Metal, Plastic Back, 1950s	50.00
Mechanical, Leap Frog, Cast Iron, Book Of Knowledge	375.00
Mechanical, Leap Frog, Cast Iron, Shepard Hardware	3165.00
Mechanical, Lion & Monkeys, Cast Iron, Kyser & Rex, c.1885, 9 1/2 In. . . . . . .920.00 to 1265.00
Mechanical, Little Moe, Wearing Straw Hat, Cast Iron, Chamberlin & Hill	2200.00
Mechanical, Log Cabin, Tin Lithograph, Couple Dancing, Chein, 3 x 3 1/2 In.	260.00
Mechanical, Log Cabin, Wooden Back & Base, Man Dances, Windup, 5 1/2 In.	935.00
Mechanical, Magic, Brown Painted Roof, Green Sides, Cast Iron, J. & E. Stevens	2587.00
Mechanical, Magician, Cast Iron, Book Of Knowledge	375.00
Mechanical, Mama Katzenjammer, Cast Iron, Kenton	5750.00
Mechanical, Mammy & Child, Cast Iron, Kyser & Rex, 7 3/4 In.	3025.00
Mechanical, Mason, Cast Iron, Shepard Hardware, 1887	15000.00
Mechanical, Monkey & Parrot, Red Monkey, Tin, Yellow, Selheimer & Strauss	825.00
Mechanical, Mule Entering Barn, J. & E. Stevens, c.1880 . . . . .920.00 to 1450.00
Mechanical, Organ Grinder & Performing Bear, Cast Iron, Kyser & Rex . . . .*Illus*	9775.00
Mechanical, Organ, Cat & Dog, Cast Iron, Musical, Kyser & Rex, 1882	1600.00
Mechanical, Owl, Head Turns, Pat. Sept. 28, 1880, J. & E. Stevens, 7 1/2 In. . .	495.00
Mechanical, Paddy & Pig, Cast Iron, 1885, J. & E. Stevens	1320.00
Mechanical, Paddy & Pig, Cast Iron, Book Of Knowledge, 1960s . . . . .155.00 to 375.00
Mechanical, Pelican, Cast Iron, Japanned, Paint Loss, Trenton Lock & Hardware, 8 In. . . .	1760.00
Mechanical, Penny Pineapple, Cast Iron, Hawaii As 50th State, 1960 . . . . .465.00 to 775.00
Mechanical, Planet, Metal, Plastic & Rubber Orbiting Planets, Vacumet Co., 1960	275.00
Mechanical, Professor Pug Frog's Great Bicycle Feat, Cast Iron, 1960s	275.00
Mechanical, Professor Pug Frog's Great Bicycle Feat, Cast Iron, J. & E. Stevens, 1886 . . .	2750.00
Mechanical, Professor Pug Frog's Great Bicycle Feat, Cast Iron, James Capron, 1950s . . .	950.00
Mechanical, Punch & Judy, Cast Iron, Book Of Knowledge, 1960s . . . . .225.00 to 350.00
Mechanical, Punch & Judy, Cast Iron, Shepard Hardware Co.	715.00
Mechanical, Rabbit In Cabbage, Cast Iron, Kilgore	675.00
Mechanical, Rabbit, Standing, Brushed Gold, Patent, Lockwood, 1882, 7 1/2 In.	2645.00
Mechanical, Race Horse, Cast Iron, Hand Painted, 1960s	425.00
Mechanical, Reaganomics, Cast Iron, A. America, 9 1/2 In.	75.00
Mechanical, Reclining Chinaman, Cast Iron, J. & E. Stevens, c.1890, 8 In. . . . . .1610.00 to 9300.00
Mechanical, Robotic Banker, Plastic, Large Box	65.00
Mechanical, Rocket Ship, Die Cast Metal, 4 Fins, Astro Mfg., 1950s, 11 1/2 In.	65.00
Mechanical, Rocket, Launches Coin Into Nose Cone, Metal, Astro Mfg., 1957, 11 1/4 In. . .	30.00
Mechanical, Saluting Sailor, Tin Lithographed, Germany, c.1910, 7 In.	1380.00
Mechanical, Santa Claus At Chimney, Cast Iron, John Wright	475.00
Mechanical, Santa Claus, Jolly Santa Seated On Small Home, Noel Decorations Inc.	242.00
Mechanical, Southern Comfort, Civil War Soldier, Metal, Hand Painted, 1950s	175.00
Mechanical, Speaking Dog, Cast Iron, Blue Dress, J. & E. Stevens, 1900s	2400.00
Mechanical, Speaking Dog, Cast Iron, Shepard Hardware, 1885	715.00
Mechanical, Springing Cat, Cast Lead, Charles A. Bailey	9775.00
Mechanical, Strike Bowling, Cast Iron, Hand Painted, Richards Toys	750.00
Mechanical, Stump Speaker, 1960s	650.00
Mechanical, Stump Speaker, Cast Iron, Shepard Hardware, 1886 . . . .*Illus*	2000.00
Mechanical, Tammany, Brown Pants, Cast Iron, J. & E. Stevens, 1873	950.00
Mechanical, Tammany, Cast Iron, 1970s	75.00

Mechanical, Tammany, Cast Iron, Book Of Knowledge .... 350.00 to 400.00
Mechanical, Tammany, Gray Pants, Cast Iron, J. & E. Stevens, 1873 .... 517.00 to 850.00
Mechanical, Teddy & The Bear, Cast Iron, J. & E. Stevens 1600.00
Mechanical, Thing, Battery Operated, Filmways, Japan, Box, 1964 .... 125.00
Mechanical, Trick Dog, Cast Iron, James Capron, 1950s 675.00
Mechanical, Trick Dog, Cast Iron, Yellow, Brown Base, Hubley, 1896 .... 385.00 to 595.00
Mechanical, Trick Pony, Cast Iron, Hand Painted, 1960s 225.00
Mechanical, Trick Pony, Cast Iron, Shepard Hardware, 1885 .... 1650.00 to 2400.00
Mechanical, Uncle Remus, Cast Iron, Book Of Knowledge 375.00
Mechanical, Uncle Remus, Iron, Patd. Feb. 2, 1876, Kyser & Rex, 5 In. .... 2200.00 to 3450.00
Mechanical, Uncle Sam, Cast Iron, Book Of Knowledge 550.00
Mechanical, Uncle Sam, Cast Iron, Shepard Hardware, 11 1/2 In. .... 715.00 to 2530.00
Mechanical, Wild West, Metal, 1950s 215.00
Mechanical, William Tell, Cast Iron, Standing Pointing Rifle, J. & E. Stevens ...... *Illus* 1045.00
Mechanical, World's Fair, Cast Iron, Indian Chief Leaps From Place, J. & E. Stevens 660.00
Metropolitan Refinery Co., Oil Drum, Tin 45.00
Milk Bottle, Glass, Tin Cap & Key Lock, 1940-1950, 1/2 Pt. 65.00
Mosque, 3 Story, Cast Iron, A.C. Williams, 1920s, 3 1/2 x 2 1/2 In. 185.00
Mosque, Domed, Cast Iron, Grey Iron Casting Co., 1903-1928, 4 1/4 x 4 1/8 In. 185.00
Mulligan The Cop, Cast Iron, A.C. Williams, 1905-1932, 5 3/4 In. .... 231.00 to 425.00
Mulligan The Cop, Cast Iron, SBCCA, 1986 .... 175.00
Multiplying, Cast Iron, J. & E. Stevens, 1883, 6 1/2 In. 2700.00
Mutt & Jeff, Cast Iron, A.C. Williams, 1930s .... 140.00 to 395.00
National Iron Safe, Cast Iron, 4 3/8 x 3 1/2 x 3 3/8 In. 60.00
Nipper, RCA Dealers Premium, Ceramic, Box 80.00
Nipper The Dog, RCA Victor, Cast Iron, 1970s 95.00
Old Homestead, Cast Iron 210.00
Oldenberg Brewery, Wooden, Inner Music Box, It's A Small World, 5 x 8 In. 22.00
Oregon Battleship, Cast Iron, J. & E. Stevens, 1898-1906 .... 275.00
Owl, Cast Iron, Gold, A.C. Williams, 1912-1920 .... 165.00
Owl, Metal, Green Glass Eyes, Napier, 4 In. 12.00
Pagoda, Cast Iron, England, 1889 .... 402.00
Patton's Sun Proof Paints, Can, Handle, Tin, 1920-1930 .... 95.00
Pay Coin Telephone, Ceramic, Hand Painted, Coin Return Cash Box Trap, 1960s 125.00
Penny, Dog Form, Stoneware 3850.00
Pig, Northwestern Savings & Loan, Mill Valley, Ca., Cardboard, 1959, 4 x 6 1/2 In. 13.00
Pig, People's Savings Banks In Benton Harbor, Pink, Plastic, 4 1/2 x 2 3/4 In. 8.00
Pig, Pottery, 2-Tone Brown Marbleized Glaze, 6 3/4 In. 20.00
Pig, Red Ribbon, Yellow Hair, Pottery, 12 In. 100.00
Pig, Seated, Cast Iron, A.C. Williams, 1910-1934, 3 x 4 1/2 In. 60.00
Pig, Sitting, Cast Iron, Hand Painted, John Wright, 10 x 6 In. 150.00
Pig, Sleeping, Composition, Love, Peace Dog Tag, Zodiac Emblem Button, Pink, 7 In. 20.00
Piggy, Pearl China 60.00
Pink Pig, Cast Iron, Hand Painted, John Wright, 1960s .... 65.00 to 75.00
Pistol Packing Pirate, On Chest, White Metal, 1950s 95.00
Policeman, Cast Iron, Arcade, 1920s, 5 1/2 In. 385.00
Policeman Safe, Cast Iron, J.M. Harper, 5 1/4 In. 2640.00
Pool Your Funds, Pool Table, Ceramic, Hand Painted, Ball & Cue Stick Top, 1950s 75.00
Poppin Fresh Pillsbury Doughboy, Porcelain, Painted Features, 1985, 8 1/2 In. 95.00
Postal Savings Truck, Friction, Coin Feeds Into Inside Safe, Tin, Japan, 1950s, 7 In. 150.00
Prairie Schooner, First National Bank Of Pittsburgh, Kans. On Base, 1960s, 4 1/2 In. 30.00
Prancing Horse, Cast Iron, Arcade Toys, 1910-1932, 7 3/16 x 6 9/16 In. 250.00
Prancing Horse, On Base, Cast Iron, Arcade, 1910, 7 3/16 In. 235.00
Prayer Lady, Pink, Ceramic 150.00
Prayer Lady, Pink, Pottery 275.00
Prudential, Glow-In-The-Dark, Green, Plastic, 1950s, 2 x 4 x 5 In. 18.00
R2-D2, Star Wars, Roman Ceramics, Box, 1978, 8 1/2 In. 65.00
Rabbit, Seated, Cast Iron, Dark Brown Paint, John Wright, 1960s 65.00
Raggedy Andy, Hard Vinyl, Yarn Hair, Clothes, Royalty Industries Of Fla., 1974, 9 In. 22.00
Raggedy Ann & Andy, Vinyl, 1972, 11 In., Pair 65.00
Red Goose Shoes, Cast Iron, Arcade, 1920s, 3 3/4 In. 175.00
Refrigerator, Electrolux, White Metal, Hand Painted, 1930s, 4 x 2 In. .... 75.00 to 95.00
Register, 2 Black Faces Form, Cast Iron, 3 In., Dime 66.00

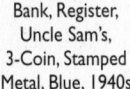

Bank, Register,
Uncle Sam's,
3-Coin, Stamped
Metal, Blue, 1940s

Bank, Rival Dog
Food, Removable
Bottom, Chicago,
Ill, 2 1/2 In.

Register, Benjamin Franklin Thrift, Tin, 1930s, 2 1/2 x 4 1/8 x 4 In.	175.00
Register, Elves Rolling Coins To Bank, Tin Lithograph, 1930s, Dime	175.00
Register, Uncle Sam's, 3-Coin, Stamped Metal, Blue, 1940s . . . .*Illus*	50.00
Register, Uncle Sam's, 3-Coin, Tin, 1960s	50.00
Register, Uncle Sam's, Metal, 6 1/4 x 4 1/2 x 5 1/4 In.	38.00
Reindeer, Cast Iron, A.C. Williams, 1910-1935, 6 1/4 In.	70.00
Republic Pig, Cast Iron, Wilton Products, 1970, 7 In.	115.00
Rival Dog Food, Removable Bottom, Chicago, Ill, 2 1/2 In. . . . .*Illus*	5.00
Rocket, Neil Armstrong, Wapakoneta, Ohio, 1969	30.00
Roller Safe, Cast Iron, Kyser & Rex, 1882, 3 11/16 In.	225.00
Roof Bank, Cast Iron, J. & E. Stevens, 1895-1906, 5 1/4 In.	260.00
Royal Safe Deposit, Cast Iron, Brass Combination Sides, 6 x 5 1/4 In.	110.00
Russel Stover's English Caramels, Tin	24.00
Safe, Old Style , Black, Gold, Metal, Henry C. Hart, Mfg., Co., Detroit, 1886, 5 In.	315.00
Safe, Pressed Steel, Combination Locking Door, 1960s, Large	95.00
Safe, Pressed Steel, Combination Locking Door, 1960s, Small	65.00
Safe, Security Safe Deposit, Cast Iron, Original Paint, 6 x 4 In. . . . . .155.00 to 185.00	
Safe, Young America, Cast Iron, Kyser & Rex, 1882, 4 3/8 x 3 1/8 In.	200.00
Sailboat, Cast Iron, Hand Painted, Duer & Wolery, 1988	95.00
Santa Claus, Cast Iron, Red Paint, Gold Trim, 5 7/8 In.	250.00
Santa Claus, Sleeping In Car, Cast Iron, Hand Painted, 1970s	65.00
Santa Claus, Sleeping, White Metal, Hand Painted, Banthrico, 1950s, 5 7/8 In.	125.00
Santa Claus, Standing With Tree, Wing, Cast Iron	2860.00
Santa Claus, Standing, With Christmas Tree, Hand Painted, 1960s, 5 3/4 In.	95.00
Santa Claus & Chimney, Cast Iron, Hand Painted, 5 x 8 In.	65.00
Savings Bank Safe, Cast Iron, Combination Lock, Kenton Toys, 1900s	225.00
Servel Electrolux, Refrigerator, White Metal, 4 x 1 7/8 In.	95.00
Shmoo, Li'l Abner, Plastic, On Card, 1948	85.00
Shmoo, Smiling, White, Dark Face, Plastic, 1948, 6 3/4 In.	70.00
Singer Sewing Machines Book, Brass, Leather Bound Cover, 1930s	95.00
Skyscraper, Cast Iron, A.C. Williams, 1900-1931, 4 3/8 x 2 1/8 In.	115.00
Smiley Face, Pottery, Yellow, Red & Black Details, 3 3/4 In.	22.00
Snoopy, Graduate, Vinyl, Coin Slot At Back Of Head, 6 1/2 In.	23.00
Snoopy, On Doghouse, Composition, 7 1/2 In.	45.00
Snoopy, On Doghouse, Plastic, 6 In. . . . . .7.50 to 8.00	
Snoopy, On Doghouse, Pottery, Hand Painted, United Features Syndicate, 1970s	95.00
Snoopy, Orange Collar, Coin Trap, Italy, Early 1960s, 6 1/2 In.	80.00
Space Rocket, Astro, Metal, 1957, 11 In.	45.00
Spaniel's Head, Pottery, Mottled Brown Glaze	22.00
Spirit Of '76, Banthrico, 6 x 5 In.	10.00
Statue Of Liberty, Cast Iron, A.C. Williams, 1910-1930s, 6 1/16 In. . . . . .95.00 to 140.00	
Statue Of Liberty, Metal, Copper Tone, 1960s	95.00
Steamboat, Cast Iron, Gold Traces, Arcade, 7 1/2 In.	220.00
Steamboat, Cast Iron, Red & Gold Paint, A.C. Williams, 1920, 7 5/8 In. . . . . .325.00 to 375.00	
Stork, Safe, Stork Standing Behind Safe, Cast Iron, J.M. Harper, 1907, 5 1/2 In.	977.00
Sylvester & Tweety Bird On Safe, Vinyl, 1972, 13 In.	30.00
Taft, Sherman, Politicians, Cast Iron, Copper Finish, J.M. Harper, 1908, 4 In.	2760.00
Tiger, Humble Oil & Refining Co., Orange, Black, Beige, 8 1/2 In.	30.00

Tootsie Roll, Candy Container, Large 24.00
Toy Soldier, Cast Iron, Painted, SBCCA, Laverne A. Worley, 1982, 7 1/2 In. 175.00
Treasure Safe, Cast Iron, Key & Combination, J. & E. Stevens, 5 1/8 x 3 1/4 In. 120.00
Truck, 1906 Mack Truck, Metal, Copper Finish, Movable Wheels, 5 In. 20.00
Truck, 7-Up Delivery, Metal, Ertl Toys, Box 50.00
Truck, Bell Telephone, Metal, Key, Lock & Coin Trap, Ertl Toys 95.00
Truck, Brinks Armored, Metal, Ertl Toys, Box 75.00
Truck, Dr Pepper Delivery, 1931 Model, Ertl Toys, Box 50.00
Truck, GMC Campbells Panel Delivery, 1951 Model, Metal, Ertl Toys, Box 50.00
Truck, Mack, Metal, Banthrico Co., 1970s 75.00
Turtle, Plastic, Dreamland Creations, 1965 .... 40.00
U.S. Mail, Cast Iron, Hand Painted, John Wright, 1960s 95.00
Wishing Well, Metal, Copper Tone, Round Coin Trap, 1960s 95.00

BANKO, Korean ware, and Sumida are terms that are often confusing. We use the names in the way most often used by antiques dealers and collectors. Korean ware is now called *Sumida Gawa* or *Sumida* and is listed in this book in the Sumida category. Banko is a group of rustic Japanese wares made in the nineteenth and twentieth centuries. Some pieces are made of mosaics of colored clay, some are fanciful teapots. Redware and other materials were also used.

Basin, Sloping Interior, Costumed Figures & Dragons, Meiji Period, 8 x 23 1/3 In. 975.00
Bowl, Blue & White Tapestry Design, Signed, 1930s, 3 In., Pair 30.00
Figurine, Shoki, Holding Sword, Rockery Base, 22 In. 390.00
Teapot, Lotus Leaf Form, Crab At Rim, Signed, 1930s, 4 1/2 In. 180.00

BARBED WIRE was first patented in 1867. Collectors want eighteen-inch samples.

10-Point Spur Rowel, C.A. Hodge, 1887, 18 In. 17.00
Allis' Ribbon, Small Sawtooth, 20 In. 5.00
Brink's Barb & Metallic Strip, 19 In. 10.00
Hallner's, Single Cut, Wraps Around Single Wire Strand, 25 In. 5.00
Reynolds Necktie, 1878, 18 In. 16.00
Stubbe's Formee Cross, 21 In. 10.00
Tack, Underwood, 1878, 18 In. 14.00

BARBER collectibles range from the popular red and white striped pole that used to be found in front of every shop to the small scissors and tools of the trade. Barber chairs are wanted, especially the older models with elaborate iron trim.

Chair, 1920 .... 650.00
Chair, Black Walnut, Congress, Patent October 30, 1880s, Burled Panels 3600.00
Chair, Child's, Horse Head 1650.00
Chair, Hydraulic Operated, Marble Base, Red, 1911 .... 4000.00
Chair, Kochs Columbia, Oak, Ornate 900.00
Chair, Koken Congress, Oak, 1901 .... 900.00
Chair, Koken, Embossed Filigree Sides, Imitation Leather, Wood, Headrest, 46 In. 920.00
Chair, Pedal Car, American National 6820.00
Chair, Porcelain Arms & Base, Leather Seat, Back & Headrest, Kochs, c.1920 .... 600.00
Chair, Porcelain, Carved Painted Horse Head 2760.00
Chair, Red Tufted Velour, Brass Plated Metal 1300.00
Pole, Porcelain, Beige Green, Red & White, White Globe, Rotating Cylinder, 91 In. 1150.00
Pole, Porcelain, Glass Cylinder, Red & White, 37 In. 425.00
Pole, Red, White & Blue Paint, Wood, 35 1/2 In. 895.00
Vase, Shaving Paper, Mary Gregory-Type Multicolored Boy & Girl, 5 3/4 In. 635.00

BAROMETERS are used to forecast the weather. Antique barometers with elaborate wooden cases and brass trim are the most desirable. Mercury column barometers are also popular with collectors. It is difficult to find someone to repair a broken one, so be sure your barometer is in working condition.

Allard Fils, Paris, White Enamel Dial, Chartreuse Rim, Numerals, 12 In. 431.00
Aneroid, A.W. Gamage, 34 1/2 In. 192.00

Aneroid, British Made, 31 1/2 In. 137.00
Aneroid, Leaf Accent Crest, Leaf Design At Base, Walnut, 34 In. 518.00
Ballard, Cranbrook, Mahogany Veneer, Inlaid, Silvered Dials, 37 1/2 In. 575.00
Banjo, A. Solca, Tunbridge Wells, Mahogany 495.00
Banjo, G. Soldini & Co., Mahogany, Silver Face, Engraved, 38 1/2 In. 1320.00
Banjo, Inlaid Mahogany, Acorn Finial Above Rosette, Inlaid Seashells, 38 1/2 In. 1380.00
Banjo, J. Abatte, Mahogany, Shell Inlay, Broken Classical Pediment, 38 In. 790.00
Banjo, J.J. Lockwood, Bolton, Inlaid Mother-Of-Pearl, 19th Century 220.00
Banjo, Mahogany & Walnut, Nautical, 40 In. 110.00
Banjo, Mahogany, Bonnet Top, Urn Finial, Bradford, England, 43 In. 605.00
Banjo, Regency, Mahogany, Pediment, Engraved Silver Dials & Gauge 825.00
Banjo, Regency, Mahogany, Pediment, Inlaid Edge, Engraved Silver Dials, Gauge 1210.00
Banjo, Walnut, Swan's-Neck Crest, Engraved Silver Dial, 19th Century, 38 In. 402.00
E. Bagues, Clock, Tortoiseshell Veneer, Winged Putti, Bronze Mounted, 37 In. 5750.00
Herman Miller Clock Co., Sheraton Style, Mahogany, 37 In. 275.00
P.F. Bellenbach, Chicago, Mahogany Veneer, Brass Trim, Labeled Dials, 40 In. 165.00
Pocket, Leather Outer Case, Eugene Dietzgen Co. 77.00
Pocket, Self-Recording, Stamped Brevette, 5 1/2 x 7 1/8 In. 105.00
Routledge, Carlisle, Mahogany Veneer, Silvered Dials, 37 3/4 In. 685.00
Stick, Broken Arch Crest, Ivory Finial, Rosettes, Pochaine, George III, 1870s, 40 In. ... 2530.00
Stick, Charles Wilder, Mahogany, Cock-Beaded Case, 1860, 35 3/4 In. 1725.00
Stick, G. Giobbio Moroni, Mahogany, 19th Century, 38 In. 402.00
Stick, Haggar & Brother, Mahogany, Cased Ivory Faces, 36 3/4 In. 3520.00
Stick, J. Bassnet 3700.00
Stick, Mahogany, Silver Scales, Bowfront Glass Door, 19th Century, 41 In. 10925.00
Stick, R. Spear, Dublin, Silvered Face, Mahogany, 39 In. 2200.00
Stick, Walnut, Timber, With Concave Sides, 1700, 37 In. 8050.00
Thermometer, Giltwood, Carved, Flower Basket, Louis XVI, 36 In. 2200.00
Thermometer, Mahogany, Wall Mounted, England, 19th Century, 37 1/4 In. 260.00
Thermometer, Mercury, Flanked By Columns, Floral, Shell Case, 33 3/4 In. 575.00
Thermometer, Oak, Wall Mounted, 42 1/2 In. 495.00
Thermometer, Painted Dial, Beveled Glass, Pinkham & Smith, 40 1/2 In. 1035.00
Thermometer, Ribbon Bow Crest, Bell Flower Swags, Louis XVI, 38 x 11 In. 184.00
Thermometer, W. Frasier, Molded Edge, White Printed Dial, Ohio, 1860, 40 In. 575.00
Thermometer, Walnut, Molded Cornice, Engraved Silver Dial, 35 In. 632.00
Thomas Taber, New York, Rosewood, 19th Century, 43 1/2 In. 1045.00
Wall, Neoclassical Floral & Scroll Design, Gilt, Continental, 43 In. 2530.00
Wheel, A. Gugeri, Swan's Neck Crest, Mahogany, 38 In. 747.00
Wheel, F. Amadio & Son, England, Satinwood, Signed, 19th Century, 42 In. 2070.00
Wheel, Oak, Foliate-Covered Pendant, 36 In. 172.00

BASEBALL collectibles are in the Sports category, except for baseball cards, which
are listed under Baseball in the Card category.

BASKETS of all types are popular with collectors. American Indian,
Japanese, African, Shaker, and many other kinds of baskets can be
found. Of course, baskets are still being made, so the collector must
learn to tell the age and style of the basket to determine the value.

Burl, Natural Growth, 4-Part Handle, 15 In. 300.00
Buttocks, Ash Splint, 28 Ribs, 1950s 70.00
Buttocks, Oak, Tight Weave, 12 1/2 x 10 In. 220.00
Buttocks, Splint, 12 x 20 In. 148.00
Buttocks, Splint, 22 Ribs, Bentwood Handle, 5 1/2 x 6 1/2 In. 245.00
Buttocks, Splint, 24 Ribs, Bentwood Handle, 4 3/4 x 5 x 2 1/2 In. 385.00
Buttocks, Splint, 30 Ribs, Bentwood Handle, 14 x 16 1/2 x 7 3/4 In. 220.00
Buttocks, Splint, Eye-Of-God Design, Bent Twig Handle, 12 x 15 In. 105.00
Buttocks, Splint, Handholds, Double Woven Handles, 20th Century, 19 x 27 In. 225.00
Buttocks, Splint, Plaited Medial Band, Bentwood Handle, 8 x 17 In. 1430.00
Buttocks, Splint, Ribbed Hickory, 1950, 17 In. 50.00
Egg, Ash Splint, Brown & Green Stain, New England, 1900s, 10 In. 95.00
Egg, Ash Splint, New England, 1900s, 12 In. 95.00
Egg, Chicken, Wire 28.00

Eskimo, Cover, Early 20th Century, 11 x 10 In. 745.00
Field, Oak Splint, Tennessee, 1900, 13 In. 80.00
Field, Oak Splint, Tennessee, 1930s, 18 In. 115.00
Fruit, Open Rim Handles, 11 x 16 1/2 In. 280.00
Grape Picker, Wooden, Cone Shape, France, 46 In. 1300.00
Market, Oak Splint, 1 Hinged Handle, 14 1/2 x 8 1/4 In. 275.00
Market, Oak Splint, Tennessee, 1930s, 16 In. 40.00
Market, Wicker, 1920, 13 In. 60.00
Nantucket, Early 19th Century, 13 3/4 x 9 7/8 In. 1265.00
Nantucket, Handle, 19th Century, 3 x 7 1/4 In. 1150.00
Nantucket, I Was Made On Nantucket Island, I Am Strong & Stout, Handle, 4 x 7 In. ... 2645.00
Nantucket, Made In Nantucket, Jose Formose Reyes, 4 x 8 In. 2070.00
Nantucket, Mitchell Ray, Paper Label On Base, 20th Century, 5 1/4 x 5 3/8 In. 747.00
Nantucket, Nailed Rim, Base, Handle, 19th Century, 5 1/4 x 8 In. 690.00
Nantucket, Oval, 3 1/2 x 9 3/4 In. 630.00
Nantucket, Paper Label, 20th Century, 4 3/8 x 8 3/8 In. 1265.00
Nantucket, R. Folger Maker, 6 3/4 x 10 In. 1380.00
Nantucket, R. Folger Maker, Nantucket, Mass. 1840.00
Nantucket, Swing Handle, 7 In. 2530.00
Nantucket, Turned Wooden Base, Splint & Cane, Swivel Bentwood Handle, 6 1/4 In. ... 220.00
Oak, Iron Belts, Stave Construction, Handle, 19th Century, 18 x 13 In. 85.00
Picket Fence, Galvanized Band At Base, Wire Ring At Top, 10 x 16 In. 247.00
Rye Straw, Bentwood Rim Handles, 9 3/4 x 20 In. 605.00
Rye Straw, Cover, 2 Handles, 10 1/2 x 14 In. 55.00
Rye Straw, Cover, 2 Handles, 13 x 18 In. 66.00
Rye Straw, Round, 6 1/4 x 12 In. 33.00
Sewing, Cover, Bamboo Splint, Glass Rings & Beads, Coins, Tassels, China, 10 In. 35.00
Sleigh, Longaberger, 1982 .... 800.00
Splint, 17 Ribs, Bentwood Handle, Woven, 5 1/2 x 4 1/2 In. 140.00
Splint, 33 Ribs, Bentwood Handle, Gray Patina, Round, 16 x 9 3/4 In. 190.00
Splint, 33 Ribs, Bentwood Handle, Round, 13 x 7 3/4 In. 135.00
Splint, 33 Ribs, Bentwood Handle, Round, 16 1/2 x 9 1/2 In. 165.00
Splint, 33 Ribs, Bentwood Handle, White Paint, Round, 13 x 8 In. 385.00
Splint, 33 Ribs, Bentwood Handles, Round, 12 x 7 1/2 In. 220.00
Splint, 64 Ribs, Bentwood Rim Handles, 5 3/4 x 15 In. 192.00
Splint, Bamboo For Flowers, Moon Shape, 21 1/2 In. 635.00
Splint, Bamboo, Irregular Egg Shape, 12 3/4 In. 680.00
Splint, Bamboo, Irregular Splinting Across Body, Ropework Handle, 20 1/2 In. 725.00
Splint, Bentwood End Handles, Bottom Of Handles Form Feet, 11 x 14 x 6 In. 358.00
Splint, Bentwood Handle, 5 3/4 x 7 In. 190.00
Splint, Bentwood Handle, Round, 16 x 8 In. 165.00
Splint, Blueberry Blue Paint, Maine, 19th Century, 13 1/2 x 14 In. 1850.00
Splint, Bulbous, Wood Bottom, 18 In. 385.00
Splint, Cheese, 21 In. 100.00
Splint, Copper Wire, Wrapped Around Rim, 22 In. 135.00
Splint, Egg, Oak, 19th Century, 12 x 11 In. 56.00
Splint, Gray Weathered, Rim Handles, 17 x 11 1/4 In. 170.00
Splint, Hanging Loom, Natural, Pink & Green, 9 1/2 x 8 3/4 In. 95.00
Splint, Oak, Arched Handle, Paper Tag, 13 x 21 1/2 In. 35.00
Splint, Oak, Carved Handle, 1920, 17 In. 65.00
Splint, Oak, Handle Continues To Bottom, Gizzard Shape, 8 1/2 x 10 1/2 In. 470.00
Splint, Openwork Handles, 20th Century, 9 1/2 x 17 1/4 In. 230.00
Splint, Peach, Diamond Design, 11 1/2 x 14 1/2 In. 192.00
Splint, Round, 15 1/2 x 9 1/2 In. 300.00
Splint, Scrubbed, Bentwood Handle, Oval, 10 1/2 x 12 1/2 x 6 In. 110.00
Splint, Straw & Oak, Coiled, 1900s, 11 In. 16.00
Storage, Bittersweet Bands, Round, 17 In. 950.00
Storage, Blue Bands, Round, 15 In. 850.00
Wash, Picket Fence, Red, Black & White, 10 1/2 In. 110.00
Wool Gathering, Oak Splint, 4 Short Legs, 1920s, 24 x 14 x 18 In. 75.00

BATCHELDER products are made from California clay. Ernest Batchelder established a tile studio in Pasadena, California, in 1909 and expanded until in 1916. Then he built a larger factory with a new partner. The Batchelder-Wilson Company made all types of architectural tiles, garden pots, and bookends. The plant closed in 1932. In 1936 Batchelder opened Batchelder Ceramics, also in Pasadena, and made bowls, vases, and earthenware pots. He retired in 1951 and died in 1957. Pieces are marked *Batchelder Pasadena* or *Batchelder Los Angeles*.

BATCHELDER
LOS ANGELES

Tile, Bird, Plumes & Feathers, Blue Patina Glaze, 4 In.	225.00
Tile, Cherub, Climbing Grapevine, Pale Yellow, Blue Patina Glaze, 3 x 6 In.	145.00
Tile, LaMayan, 3 1/2 In.	125.00
Tile, Medieval Man, Playing Guitar, 15 x 9 In.	750.00
Tile, Mythological Bird, Beast, Dark Gray, 6 In.	300.00

BATMAN and Robin are characters from a comic strip by Bob Kane that started in 1939. In 1966, the characters became part of a popular television series. There have been radio and movie serials that featured the pair. The first full-length movie was made in 1989. The third movie was made in 1995.

Bat Cave, Mego, For 3 3/4-In. Figures, Box	135.00
Batmobile, 2 Figures, Clear Plastic Dome, 12 In.	495.00
Batmobile, Plastic, Mexico, 8 In.	150.00
Batmobile, Plastic, Vinyl, Duncan, 8 1/2 In.	75.00
Bottle, Batmobile, Batman, Bubble Bath, Blue Plastic, Avon, Stickers, Box, 7 In.	30.00
Calendar, 1977, Figural, From Executive Set, Janex	175.00
Cookie Jar, Batmobile, Warner Brothers, Box	95.00
Cookie Jar, Ceramic, 1966	145.00
Doll, Mego, 1976, 12 In.	75.00
Figure, Batman With Flicker Ring, Ideal	175.00
Figure, Batman, Batman Forever, Resin, Hand Painted, Box	225.00
Figure, Robin, Batman Forever, Resin, 12 In.	175.00
Game, Batman & Robin, Hassenfeld, 1965	65.00 to 70.00
Game, Hasbro, Box, 1974	38.00
Game, University Games, 50th Anniversary Edition, 1989	25.00
Kit, Super Powers, Box	5.00
Lamp, Desk, Standing In Front Of Bat Cave, Brown, Black, Blue, 11 1/2 In.	50.00
Lunch Box, Aladdin Thermos	50.00
Magazine Cover, Life Magazine, 1966	30.00
Mask, Emblem, Perfect Features	100.00
Mug, Robin, Red Emblem, White Glass, Fire King, 3 1/2 In.	25.00
Paint Set Cartoonrama, Batman & Robin, Missing Paints, 1977	85.00
Postcard, Batman & Robin, Color, 1960s	25.00
Robot, Vinyl Head, Tin, Windup, Box	165.00
Toy, Batman Arkham Asylum, Sealed	15.00
View-Master Set, Unopened Card	20.00

BATTERSEA enamels, which are enamels painted on copper, were made in the Battersea district of London from about 1750 to 1756. Many similar enamels are mistakenly called *Battersea*.

Box, Bird On Nest, Yellow, Mirror Inside Top, 2 x 1 1/2 In.	345.00
Box, Patch, Biltone Enamel, Gilt Metal Frame, Motto On Lid, Oval, 1 1/2 In.	170.00
Box, Scene Of Boxers In Ring, Audience, Green Base, 2 In.	410.00
Box, Thimble, Enameled, Bilston	110.00
Box, Vicar & Moses, Pink Base, Stylized X Mark, 2 In.	465.00
Knob, Tieback, 1 3/4 In., Pair	520.00
Salt, Footed, Master	480.00

BAUER pottery is a California-made ware. J.A. Bauer moved his Kentucky pottery to Los Angeles, California, in 1909. The company made art pottery after 1912 and dinnerwares marked *Bauer* after 1929. The factory went out of business in 1962.

Ducks, Figurine, Head Up, 5 In.	45.00

Hand Thrown, Pitcher, Burnt Orange Glaze, 11 1/2 In. 375.00
Hand Thrown, Vase, Yellow, 8 In. 475.00
Monterey, Chop Plate, Green, 13 In. 175.00
Monterey, Chop Plate, White, 13 In. 150.00
Plainware, Butter Chip, 4 Piece 175.00
Plainware, Carafe, Jade Green 75.00
Plainware, Cookie Jar, White 3200.00
Ring, Bowl, Atlanta, Dark Blue, No. 12 .... 125.00
Ring, Bowl, Green, 4 In. 75.00
Ring, Bowl, Vegetable, Pumpkin, Footed, Green, Gold Overspray, 8 In. 75.00
Ring, Bowl, Yellow, 12 In. 125.00
Ring, Carafe, Burnt Orange, Metal Handle 100.00
Ring, Casserole, Burnt Orange, Holder, 7 1/2 In. 165.00
Ring, Chop Plate, Burnt Orange, 14 In. ....80.00 to 140.00
Ring, Chop Plate, Yellow, 17 In. 425.00
Ring, Cookie Jar, Yellow 995.00
Ring, Creamer, Burnt Orange, Low 60.00
Ring, Creamer, Yellow, Low 60.00
Ring, Creamer, Yellow, Tall 70.00
Ring, Cup & Saucer, Burnt Orange 25.00
Ring, Cup & Saucer, Dark Blue 85.00
Ring, Cup & Saucer, Light Blue 25.00
Ring, Cup & Saucer, Maroon 25.00
Ring, Cup & Saucer, Yellow 85.00
Ring, Jardiniere, Hi-Fire, Turquoise, 5 In. 65.00
Ring, Mixing Bowl, No. 9, Chartreuse 175.00
Ring, Mixing Bowl, No. 9, Gray 175.00
Ring, Mixing Bowl, No. 9, Yellow 165.00
Ring, Mixing Bowl, No. 12, Green 85.00
Ring, Mixing Bowl, No. 12, Yellow 85.00
Ring, Mixing Bowl, No. 30, Yellow 65.00
Ring, Mixing Bowl, No. 36, Yellow 85.00
Ring, Pitcher, Red, 3 Qt. 275.00
Ring, Plate, Burnt Orange, 7 In. 50.00
Ring, Plate, Burnt Orange, 9 In. 65.00
Ring, Plate, Green, 7 In. 50.00
Ring, Plate, Light Blue, 9 In. 65.00
Ring, Plate, Yellow, 9 In. 65.00
Ring, Platter, Yellow, 12 In. 65.00
Ring, Sugar & Creamer, Burnt Orange ....85.00 to 95.00
Ring, Sugar & Creamer, Yellow, Signed, 5 1/2 x 4 In. 175.00
Ring, Teapot, Cover, Burnt Orange, 6 Cup 95.00
Ring, Tumbler Set, Holder, Jade, Yellow, Orange, Blue, Black & White, 6 Piece 325.00
Ring, Vase, Cylinder, Green, 8 1/2 In. 80.00
Vase, Bulb, Dark Blue, No. 222 .... 30.00
Vase, Pillow, Green, 8 In. 35.00

BAVARIA is a region in Europe where many types of porcelain were made. In the nineteenth century, the mark often included the word *Bavaria.* After 1871, the words *Bavaria, Germany*, were used. Listed here are pieces that include the name *Bavaria* in some form, but major porcelain makers, such as Rosenthal, are listed in their own categories.

Bowl, Juvenile, Little Boy Using Camera, Picture Of Little Girl, 7 1/2 In. 65.00
Bowl, Sylvia, Pedestal, Flowers On Corners, Signed, 10 In. 45.00
Cake Plate, Red Roses, Green & Gold Ground, Marked, 11 In. 75.00
Chocolate Pot, Peaches, Green Ground, R & W, 10 1/2 In. 75.00
Creamer, Cow Form, 1930s, 7 1/4 In. 95.00
Cup & Saucer, Maria, Raised Flower, Rosenthal 18.00
Cup & Saucer, Richmond, 6 Piece 72.00
Dish, Hand Painted, Pink & Yellow Flowers, Gold Speckled, 2 Handles 65.00
Pitcher, Stylized Leaping Deer, Branches, Beige Gloss Ground, 5 3/4 x 7 1/2 In. 25.00
Plate, All Different Still Life Fruit, 7 3/4 In., 8 Piece 85.00
Plate, Empress, Schumann Bavaria, 10 1/4 In. 37.00

Plate, Floral, Blue, 7 1/2 In. 45.00
Plate, Fruit, Green Grapes, Leaves, Vines, Hutschenreuther, 8 3/8 In. 20.00

BEADED BAGS are included in the Purse category.

BEATLES collectors search for any items picturing the four members of
the famous music group or any of their recordings. Because these
items are so new, the condition is very important and top prices are
paid only for items in mint condition. The Beatles first appeared on
American network television in 1964. The group disbanded in 1971.
Ringo Starr, George Harrison, and Paul McCartney are still performing. John Lennon died in 1980.

Doll, Paul McCartney, Remco, Box 210.00
Doll Set, Paul, George, John, Ringo, Instruments, NEMS Ent. Ltd., 1964, 4 In., 4 Piece .. 410.00
Flicker Cake Decorations, Images Of George, John, Paul, Ringo, 1964, 3 In. 60.00
Floor Mat, 1960s 75.00
Fun Kit Magazine, Deidre Publications Inc., Copyright 1964, 52 Pages 35.00
Game, Flip Your Wig, Board, 1964 .... 115.00
Jigsaw Puzzle, With Poster, 1970 .... 50.00
Magazine, Beatles Are Back, July, 1964 .... 25.00
Postcard, 1964 .... 25.00
Poster, Beatlemania, 1980s, One Sheet 20.00
Poster, Beatles In Concert, Argentina, 1970s, One Sheet 60.00
Poster, Help, 1965, One Sheet 455.00
Poster, Let It Be, 1970, One Sheet 410.00
Poster, Let It Be, Concert, 1970, One Sheet 240.00
Poster, Yellow Submarine, 1968, Six Sheet 1090.00
Record, Abbey Road 45.00
Record, Document, Songs Recorded Live In 1963, Hamburg Beatles Convention, 1988 .. 20.00
Record, Hey Jude 45.00
Record, Let It Be 55.00
Record, Meet The Beatles, 1st Edition 55.00
Record, Sgt. Pepper, Limited Edition, 1978 .... 125.00
Record, Sgt. Pepper, Picture Disc, Limited Edition, 1978 .... 125.00
Suitcase, Overnight, Airflite, Black 575.00

BEEHIVE, Austria, or Beehive, Vienna, are terms used in English-
speaking countries to refer to the many types of decorated porcelain
bearing a mark that looks like a beehive. The mark is actually a shield,
viewed upside down. It was first used in 1744 by the Royal Porcelain
Manufactory of Vienna. The firm made porcelains, called *Royal Vienna*
by collectors, until it closed in 1864. Many other German, Austrian, and
Japanese factories have reproduced Royal Vienna wares, complete with
the original shield or *beehive* mark. This listing includes the expensive,
original Royal Vienna porcelains and many other types of beehive
porcelain. The Royal Vienna pieces include that name in the description.

Cachepot, Rococo Design, Porcelain, 1770, 4 x 6 1/2 x 5 In. 363.00
Chamberstick, Floral Cartouches, Molded Leaf Garlands, Checkerboard, 3 In. 115.00
Charger, Classical Scene, Beading, Gilt Borders, Handle, 12 1/2 In. 115.00
Charger, Cupid & Psyche, In Garden, Gilt Border Trim, 11 3/4 In. 115.00
Charger, Toilette Of Venus, Gilt, Blue Ground, Signed, 18 1/4 In. 1000.00
Dish, Arab Man & Lady Embracing, Navy, Gold Border, 9 1/2 In. 200.00
Figurine, Courting Couple, 18th-Century Costume, 6 1/2 In. 315.00
Figurine, Great Egret, No. 40221 .... 2200.00
Humidor, Dog, Begging, 1856, 12 In. 1250.00
Plate, Classical Figures, Gold Border, Blue Glaze, 8 In. 2990.00
Plate, Countess Gower & Child, Seated On Settee, Wearing Green Dress, 9 1/4 In. 805.00
Plate, Display, Landscape Scene, Woman With Young Girl, Cobalt Border, Blue, 12 In. .. 370.00
Plate, Gentleman In 17th Century Costume, 9 5/8 In. 115.00
Plate, Portrait, 2 Women In Water, Sailor, Gold, 9 1/2 In. 490.00
Plate, Portrait, Amors Songs, Elli Wieden, 10 1/2 In. 60.00
Plate, Portrait, Antoinette III, Flowers, Green Cartouches, Green Ground, 9 1/2 In. 460.00
Plate, Portrait, Dutch Woman & Children, Green Border, Gold Trim, 9 1/2 In. 85.00

Plate, Women, Gold Trim, Green Border, 9 3/4 In., Pair 600.00
Stein, Bearded Man With Stein In Hand, Inlaid Lid, 1/2 Liter 1955.00
Stein, Rinaldo & Armida, Inlaid Lid, 1/2 Liter 1785.00
Tray, Europa & The Bull, Red, Blue, Cream, Gilt, 19 1/2 In. 1725.00
Tray, Formal Garden Scene, Fountain In Center, 2 Handles, 16 In. 1495.00
Urn, Cover, Classical, Bands Of Floral, Scroll Design, Animal Paw Feet, 18 In., Pair 6900.00
Urn, Cover, Classical, Gilt Scroll, Foliate, 2 Gilt Handles, Cobalt Blue, 14 In., Pair 2300.00
Urn, Cover, Stylized Emblems, Gilt Scrolls, Red Ground, Applied Handles, 18 In., Pair . . 6900.00
Urn, Cover, Young Couple & 2 Putti, Gilt Trim, Signed, 12 In. 800.00
Urn, Leaf, Swag Design, Gilt, Amethyst, Pink, Pale Blue Ground, Handles, 24 In., Pair . . 13800.00
Urn, Stand, Campagna Form, Neoclassical Female Figures, Gilt Border, 16 In., Pair 400.00
Vase, Cobalt Blue, Gilt, Painted Polychrome Classical Scene, Royal Vienna, 6 1/2 In. 220.00
Vase, Domestic Scene, Everted Rim, Raised Gilt Highlights, Signed, 19 1/2 In., Pair 8050.00
Vase, Maiden & Attendant Scene, Ram's Head Handles, Flared Neck, 9 In. 920.00
Vase, Painted Romantic Scenes, Maiden & Cupids, 21 In. 6025.00
Vase, Palace, Floral, Woman Cartouche, Dark Green, Wagner, 26 x 11 1/2 In. 1380.00
Vase, Portrait, Cupid With Bow, Swan, Gold & Beading, 12 In. 125.00
Vase, Urn Shape, Jupiter & Calisto, Art & Music, Harp Handles, 13 1/2 In., Pair 2200.00

BEER BOTTLES are listed in the Bottle category under Beer.

BEER CANS are a twentieth-century idea. Beer was sold in kegs or returnable bottles until 1934. The first patent for a can was issued to the American Can Company in September of that year; and Gotfried Kruger Brewing Company, Newark, New Jersey, was the first to use the can. The cone-top can was first made in 1935, the aluminum pop-top in 1962. Collectors should look for cans in good condition, with no dents or rust. Serious collectors prefer cans that have been opened from the bottom.

Barbarossa, Cone Top, Ohio 80.00
Bluebonnet, Cone Top 178.00
Budweiser Bock Beer, Flat Top, 1950 . . . . 2165.00
Budweiser Double Bock Beer, 8 Oz. 135.00
Burger, Ohio 25.00
Burgermeister, California 40.00
Burgermeister Pale Beer, Flat Top, 1930s 10.00
Busch Bavarian, Missouri 10.00
Carling's, Ohio 30.00
Champagne Velvet, Cone Top, Indiana 75.00
Coors' Golden Brewery, 1940 . . . . 75.00
Croft Cream Ale, Cone Top 213.00
Ebling Beer, Cone Top 38.00
El Rancho Beer, Pull Tab, 1970s 25.00
Falstaff, Nevada 7.00
Fehr's, Red & White 31.00
Fidenbacha Beer, Flat Top, 1950s 62.00
Fitzgerald's, New York 22.00
Fox Deluxe, 8 Oz. 127.00
Frankenmuth Bock, Michigan 350.00
Georgia Tech Yellow Jacket Brew 20.00
Hans Leer, California 75.00
Happy Hops 31.00
Hof-Brau, California 15.00
Jacob Ruppert Ale, Flat Top, 1940s 170.00
Krueger Cream Ale, Cone Top, 1930s, 1 Qt. 183.00
Krueger Finest Beer, K-Man, Cone Top, 1 Qt. 2560.00
Olbrau, New Jersey 30.00
Old Georgetown, Washington, D.C. 60.00
Old Gibraltar, Maier Brewing Co. 34.00
Pearl, Texas 35.00
Progress, Oklahoma 110.00
Rainier Old Stock Ales, Low Profile Cone Top, 1930s 37.00
Red Fox Ale, Cone Top, Largay Brewing Co., Waterbury, Conn. 1616.00

Regal Bock Beer, Flat Top, 1950s	70.00
Regal Select Draft, Pull Tab, 1960s	60.00
Stag, Cone Top, Illinois	30.00
Standard Sparkling Ale, Cone Top, 12 Oz.	240.00
Stock Ale By Croft, Cone Top	300.00
Tam O'Shanter Ale, 1940s	70.00
Union Cream Ale, Roger Williams Brewing Corp	455.00
Waldorf Red Band	250.00
Worthington Pale Ale, Burton On Trent, England	120.00

BELL collectors collect all types of bells. Favorites include glass bells, figural bells, school bells, and cowbells. Bells have been made of porcelain, china, or metal through the centuries.

Abstract, Bronze, Soleri, 6 In.	260.00
Bronze, Carved Seal, Foo Dog Atop Bell, Horace Potter, 7 1/2 x 5 1/2 In.	75.00
Cow, Bronze, Embossed 1878 Chiantel Fondeur, Switzerland, 4 1/2 In.	25.00
Cow, Embossed Floral & Maker, Brass, Leather Collar, Switzerland, 7 In.	55.00
Cow, Floral, Saint & 1875 Viglino, Bronze, Leather Collar, Switzerland, 7 1/2 In.	70.00
Cow, Iron, Hand Folded & Riveted, Oval, 19th Century, 7 In.	27.00
Cow, Iron, Hand Forged, Riveted Seams, Rolled Corner, 19th Century, 6 In.	15.00
Cut Glass, Tyrone, Ireland, Box, 6 In.	20.00
Hand, Brass, Wooden Handle, 18th Century, c.1760, 8 In.	395.00
Jacobean Head Finial, Figures Around Side, Brass, 4 In.	110.00
Liberty, Brass, Black Metal Holding Bracket, 19 1/2 In.	460.00
Ox, 26 Bells, Brass, Figural Bull's Head Hanger, India, 32 In.	75.00
Prayer Lady, Pink, Pottery	90.00
Saddlebag, Brass, Turned Walnut Handle, Pendulum Clapper, 19th Century, 9 In.	120.00
Servant's, Brass & Iron, Wall Mount, Coiled Return Spring, 10 In.	90.00
Silver, Gorham, 1899, 4 x 2 1/2 In.	225.00
Sleigh, 5 Graduated Bells, Leather Hanger, 32 In.	145.00
Sleigh, 12 Bells, Brass, Leather Strap, 19th Century, 36 In.	95.00
Sleigh, 14 Graduated Bells, Bronze, Leather Strap, 40 In.	115.00
Sleigh, 16 Graduated Bells, Brass, Leather Strap	690.00
Sleigh, 24 Graduated Bells, Brass, Leather Strap, 70 In.	145.00
Teacher's, Brass	45.00
Town Crier, Brass, 6 3/4 In.	120.00
U.S. Navy, Harvard Lock Company, Cast Iron, 10 1/2 In.	45.00
Young Girl, Victorian Dress, Arms Out, Brass, 3 3/4 In.	65.00

BELLE WARE glass was made in 1903 by Carl V. Helmschmied. In 1904 he started a corporation known as the Helmschmied Manufacturing Company. His factory closed in 1908 and he worked on his own until his death in 1934.

Shaker, Blue Flowers, Frosted Finish, Signed, 3 5/8 In.	176.00

BELLEEK china was made in Ireland, other European countries, and the United States. The glaze is creamy yellow and appears wet. The first Belleek was made in 1857. All pieces listed here are Irish Belleek. The mark changed through the years. The first mark, black, dates from 1863 to 1890. The second mark, black, dates from 1891 to 1926 and includes the words *Co. Fermanagh, Ireland*. The third mark, black, dates from 1926 to 1946 and has the words *Deanta in Eirinn*. The fourth mark, same as the third mark but green, dates from 1946 to 1955. The fifth mark, green, dates from 1955 to 1965 and has an R in a circle added in the upper right. The sixth mark, green, dates after 1965 and the words *Co. Fermanagh* have been omitted. The seventh mark, gold, was used from 1980 to 1993 and omits the words *Deanta in Eirinn*. The eighth mark, introduced in 1993, is similar to the second mark but is printed in blue. The word *Belleek* is now used only on the pieces made in Ireland even though earlier pieces from other countries were sometimes marked *Belleek*. These early pieces are listed by manufacturer, such as Ceramic Art Co., Haviland, Lenox, Ott & Brewer, and Willets.

Ashtray, Shamrock, Boat, 4th Mark, Green, 4 1/2 In.	35.00

Basket, Shamrock, 3 Applied Rose Clusters, Basket Weave Bottom, 5 1/2 x 2 In. 275.00
Basket, Twig, Henshell's, 1955-1979, 6 x 8 In. 1150.00
Biscuit Jar, Shamrock Pattern, 6th Mark, Green, 6 3/4 In. 200.00
Breakfast Set, Pink Trim, c.1910, 2nd Mark, Black, 10 Piece 230.00
Cake Plate, Limpet, 6th Mark, Green, 9 3/4 In. 80.00
Cake Plate, Shamrock, Twig Handles, 4th Mark, Green 85.00
Coffeepot, Harp, 6th Mark, Green 185.00
Coffeepot, Limpet, 6th Mark, Green 335.00
Cup & Saucer, 5th Mark, Green, 1965 .... 125.00
Cup & Saucer, Neptune, 2nd Mark, Black, Demitasse 150.00
Cup & Saucer, Shamrock, 3rd Mark, Black 105.00
Cup & Saucer, Shamrock, 4th Mark, Green 60.00
Cup & Saucer, Shamrock, Harp Handle, 3rd Mark, Black 110.00
Eggcup, 6th Mark, Green 24.00
Ewer, Lid, Molded Leaf Design, Pink, Ivory, Gilt, 9 5/8 In. 440.00
Figurine, Pig, Seated, 2nd Mark, Black, 2 3/4 x 4 1/2 In. 300.00
Figurine, Swan, 6th Mark, Green 57.00
Lamp, Urn, Floral Applied, White Luster Glaze, Scalloped 545.00
Pitcher, Lemonade, Hand-Painted 135.00
Plate, Christmas, 1978 ....50.00 to 65.00
Plate, Cone, Pink Trim, 2nd Mark, Black, 6 1/2 In. 250.00
Plate, Shamrock, 4th Mark, Green, 6 1/2 In. 22.00
Sugar & Creamer, Shamrock, 3rd Mark, Black ....125.00 to 150.00
Sugar & Creamer, Shamrock, 4th Mark, Green 85.00
Sugar & Creamer, Underplate, Limpet, Black Mark, 7-In. Plate, 3 Piece 120.00
Teapot, Arched Handle 135.00
Teapot, Hexagonal, 2nd Mark, Black 635.00
Teapot, Limpet, 3rd Mark, Black 350.00
Teapot, Limpet, 5th Mark, Green 495.00
Teapot, Pink Trim, 2nd Mark, Black 750.00
Teapot, Shamrock, 3rd Mark, Black 285.00
Teapot, Shamrock, 5th Mark, Green 245.00
Vase, Shamrock, 5th Mark, Green, 7 1/2 In. 80.00
Vase, Stylized Flower, 7 1/2 In., Pair 58.00

BENNINGTON ware was the product of two factories working in
Bennington, Vermont. Both the Norton Company and the Lyman
Fenton Company were out of business by 1896. The wares include
brown and yellow mottled pottery, Parian, scroddled ware, stoneware,
graniteware, yellowware, and Staffordshire-type vases. The name is
also a generic term for mottled brownware of the type made in
Bennington.

Bottle, Coachman, Rockingham Glaze, 1849, 10 5/8 In. 390.00
Bottle, Coachman, Yellow, 9 1/2 In. 385.00
Bottle, Toby, Glazed, Marked 1847, 10 1/2 In. 460.00
Creamer, Cow, Flint Enamel, 19th Century, 5 1/4 x 7 In. 230.00
Crock, Bird, 2 Gal. ....475.00 to 695.00
Cuspidor, Brown Rockingham Glaze, Marked 1849, 9 In. 110.00
Flask, Book, Battle Of Bennington, 6 In. 385.00
Flask, Book, c.1849, 7 1/4 x 6 In. 1100.00
Flask, Book, Coachman, Signed & Dated 1849, 10 1/2 In. ....750.00 to 1000.00
Flask, Book, Departed Spirits, Flint, Mottled Brown, Yellow, Green, 5 1/2 In. .....374.00 to 467.00
Jug, Cobalt Blue Floral Spray, 4 Gal. 285.00
Jug, Toby, Light Green Sponging, Amber Interior, Marked 1849, 4 1/2 In. 660.00
Pie Plate, Yellow Highlights, Rockingham Glaze, 1849, 11 7/8 In. 962.00
Pipkin, Alternate Rib, 6 In. 350.00
Pitcher, Alternate Rib 350.00
Pitcher, Hanging Deer & Game Birds, Mottled Brown, 6 1/2 In. 295.00
Pitcher, Wild Rose, Parian, 9 3/4 In. 665.00
Tureen, Acanthus Leaf In Relief, 2 Handles, 13 1/2 x 10 In. 275.00
Vase, Tulip, Flint Enamel, 10 In. 110.00
Vase, Tulip, Mottled Brown Glaze, 1848, 10 In. 950.00

BERLIN, a German porcelain factory, was started in 1751 by Wilhelm Kaspar Wegely. In 1763, the factory was taken over by Frederick the Great and became the Royal Berlin Porcelain Manufactory. It is still in operation today. Pieces have been marked in a variety of ways.

Charger, Enamel Floral, Scrolled Gilt Rim, Signed, 15 3/4 In.	1725.00
Group, 3 Nude Children, Enameled, 19th Century, 13 3/4 In.	485.00
Plaque, 3 Muses Of Time, Signed, Early 20th Century, 7 1/2 x 9 7/8 In.	3225.00
Plaque, Annunciation, Rectangular Frame, 17 x 21 In.	8050.00
Plaque, Beautiful Woman, Shadow Box, Artist Signed	575.00
Plaque, Holy Family, Giltwood Frame, Late 19th Century, 7 1/2 In.	975.00
Plaque, Little Match Girl, Giltwood Oval Frame, c.1880, 15 1/2 x 10 1/4 In.	775.00
Plaque, Mignon, Peasant Maiden, Holding Lute, Giltwood Frame, 12 1/4 In.	368.00
Plaque, Porcelain, Woman & Child, Wood Frame, 9 1/2 x 7 In.	230.00
Plaque, Profile Of Woman Figure, Metal & Velvet Frame, 4 1/2 x 5 7/8 In.	690.00
Plaque, Ruth, Signed, Late 19th Century, 17 1/4 x 22 1/2 In.	4600.00
Plaque, Woman Warrior, Late 19th Century, 13 x 11 In.	3450.00
Plaque, Young Girl, Late 19th Century, 9 x 6 3/4 In.	1495.00
Plaque, Young Woman, Child Being Lifted Out Of Crib, Frame, Signed, 9 1/2 x 7 In.	2300.00
Plate, Courting Scene, New Family, Painted Central Design, 9 1/4 In., Pair	430.00

BESWICK started making earthenware in Staffordshire, England, in 1936. The company is now part of Royal Doulton Tableware, Ltd. Figurines of animals, especially dogs and horses, Beatrix Potter animals, and other wares are still being made.

Character Jug, Barnaby Rudge	60.00
Figurine, Amiable Guinea Pig, No. 2061	500.00 to 575.00
Figurine, Aunt Pettitoes, No. 2276	55.00
Figurine, Benjamin Bunny, No. 1105	40.00
Figurine, Burnham Beauty, Draft Horse, No. 2309	275.00
Figurine, Chickadee, Black Capped, No. 2189	95.00
Figurine, Cousin Ribby, No. 2284	38.00
Figurine, Eeyore, From Winnie The Pooh, No. 2196	100.00
Figurine, Flopsy, Mopsy & Cottontail, Brown	50.00
Figurine, Foxy Whiskered Gentleman, No. 1277	75.00
Figurine, Ginger Nutt, David Hand, No. 2559	600.00
Figurine, Goody Tiptoes, No. 1675	200.00
Figurine, Horse, Clydesdale, No. 2465	465.00
Figurine, Hunca Munca, Spills The Beads, No. 3288	60.00
Figurine, Jemima Puddleduck	150.00
Figurine, Jeremy Fisher, Gold	225.00
Figurine, Lady Mouse, No. 1183	50.00 to 130.00
Figurine, Little Pig Robinson Spying, No. 3031	70.00
Figurine, Little Pig Robinson, 1st Version, No. 1104/1	295.00
Figurine, Mare & Foal, Ceramic Base, No. 1811	325.00
Figurine, Miss Dormouse, No. 3251	60.00
Figurine, Miss Moppet, Gold	158.00
Figurine, Mr. Alderman, Ptolemy, No. 2424	90.00
Figurine, Mr. Toadflax, Brambly Hedge, No. DBH10	85.00
Figurine, Mr. Tod, No. 3091	275.00
Figurine, Mrs. Rabbit & Bunnies, No. 2543	75.00
Figurine, Mrs. Tiggy Winkle	50.00 to 55.00
Figurine, No More Twist, No. 3325	40.00
Figurine, Old Women Who Lived In A Shoe, No. 1545	150.00
Figurine, Oscar Ostrich, No. 1154	600.00
Figurine, Peter & Red Pocket Handkerchief	50.00
Figurine, Peter Ate A Radish, No. 3533	45.00
Figurine, Peter Rabbit, No. 1098	40.00
Figurine, Peter With Daffodils, No. 3597	45.00
Figurine, Peter With Postbag, No. 3591	45.00
Figurine, Pig-Wig, No. 2381	525.00
Figurine, Pigeon, No. 1383B	110.00
Figurine, Quarter Horse, Brown, No. 2186	250.00

Betty Boop, Figurine,
Chalkware, 15 In.

If you have a serious flood, be sure to have the power to the house turned off before you wade into the water. If you must turn off the power, wear rubber boots and dry rubber gloves. Stand on a wooden chair or ladder and use a broom handle to flip the main switch.

Figurine, Ribby, No. 1199	150.00
Figurine, Samuel Whiskers, Gold, No. 1106	130.00
Figurine, Timmy Tiptoes, Red Jacket	65.00 to 80.00
Figurine, Timmy Willie, No. 1109	50.00
Figurine, Tom Kitten & Butterfly, No. 3030	100.00 to 375.00
Figurine, Tom Kitten, No. 1100	145.00
Figurine, Tom Thumb, No. 2989	40.00
Figurine, Winnie The Pooh, No. 2193	100.00
Salt & Pepper, Sairey Gamp	65.00

BETTY BOOP, the cartoon figure, first appeared on the screen in 1931. Her face was modeled after the famous singer Helen Kane and her body after Mae West. In 1935, a comic strip was started. Her dog was named Bimbo. Although the Betty Boop cartoons ended by 1938, there was a revival of interest in the Betty Boop image in the 1980s and new pieces are being made.

Button, Betty Boop For President, 1980 National Convention, Tin, 1 1/4 In.	3.00
Clock, Quarter Moon, Shooting Stars	65.00
Cookie Jar, Boop Chef	45.00
Cookie Jar, Boop Holiday	45.00
Cookie Jar, Skyscraper	55.00
Doll, Cameo, Composition & Wood, Molded Clothes, 12 In.	1495.00
Doll, Composition, 12 In.	500.00
Doll, Splash Me, Composition, Gene George, Label, 1918	90.00
Doll, Wood Joints, 1931, 4 In.	39.00
Figurine, Chalkware, 15 In.	*Illus* 248.00
Figurine, Nurse, Dakin Company	8.00
Lunch Box, Tin	10.00
Marble	12.00
Perfume Bottle	35.00
Salt & Pepper	15.00
Spinner, Tin Lithograph, Tuxedo-Dressed Bimbo Top, Japan, 3 In.	110.00
Tambourine, Tin Lithograph, Dancing With Musical Notes, Japan, 6 In.	200.00
Tea Set, 4 Different Betty Pictures, Porcelain, Fleisher Studios, 10 Piece	810.00
Teapot	35.00
Tray, Betty As Santa Claus, Carrying Sack, White Rim, 1950, 6 1/4 x 3 /4 In.	55.00
Tray, Betty Gardening, Wearing Brown Outfit, White Rim, 1950, 6 1/4 In.	70.00
Tray, Betty In Maid's Outfit With Broom, Lulu, Purple, Spain, 1950s, 6 1/2 In.	48.00
Tray, Betty Swirling Around To Music, Light Pink, 1950, 6 1/8 x 1 1/2 In.	65.00
Wristwatch, Box	35.00

BICYCLES were invented in 1839. The first manufactured bicycle was made in 1861. Special ladies' bicycles were made after 1874. The modern safety bicycle was not produced until 1885. Collectors search for all types of bicycles and tricycles. Bicycle-related items are also listed here.

Bell, Chrome-Plated Iron, With Folding Cup	8.00

Bicycle, Boneshaker, Painted,
c.1860, 38 In.

Bicycle, Trigwell, Watson & Co., Regent
Kangaroo, England, c.1886, 36 In.

Boneshaker, Painted, c.1860, 38 In. . . . .*Illus* 1980.00
Columbia, High Wheel, Lakin's Cyclometer 5100.00
Columbia, Highway Patrol, Goodyear Balloon Tires, 1950s 500.00
Columbia, Hornet Speedo, Boy's, 3 Speeds, Maroon & Cream, 1952 . . . . 965.00
Columbia, Model 43, Tandem, Caliper Brakes, c.1900 . . . . 275.00
Columbia, Tandem, Green, Black Leather Seats, 90 In. 230.00
Dayton, Huffman Mfg. Co., Girl's, Blue Paint, Chrome, Balloon Tires 330.00
Elgin, Deluxe, Girl's, Horn Tank, Headlight, Skirt Guards, 1940 . . . . 220.00
Firestone, Streamline, Deep Fenders, 2 Silver Ray Lights, Crossbar, Spring Seat, 1937 . . . 149.00
Griffith's Corporation, Man's, Pneumatic Safety, Overland Roadster, 19th Century 250.00
High Wheel, Double-Spoked Front Wheels, Wood Grips, 1910, 29 In. 2070.00
Howe & Stainforth, Track Racer, Minute Man, c.1898 . . . . 550.00
Indian, Red & Gold, Indian Logos On Crossbar, Horn, Light, 1917, 76 In. 3410.00
Iver Johnson, Man's, Tool Pouch, Bell, Head Lamp, Pneumatic Tires, c.1915 . . . . 605.00
Lamp, Nickel, Magnifying Lens, Glass, Red & Green, Marked Solar, Scroll Top, 6 1/2 In. 231.00
Monark, Silver King, Girl's, Open Lug Frame, Stainless Fenders, 1936 . . . . 245.00
Pennant, Bendix Coaster Brake, Felt, Blue, Yellow, White, Late 1940s-1950s, 5 x 10 In. . 20.00
Poster, New Departure Coaster Brake, Cycle Queen Of Year, 1939-1940, 16 x 25 In. 20.00
R.H. Wolff, Pneumatic Safety, Matching Man's & Lady's, 19th Century, Pair 990.00
Rollfast, Hopalong Cassidy, 26 In. 6000.00
Rudge, High Wheel, Mustache Handlebars, Stirrup Handgrips, 19th Century, 52 In. 2530.00
Safety, Woman's, Hard Tires, 1891 . . . . 3200.00
Schwinn, Breeze, Girl's, Blue, Late 1960s 150.00
Schwinn, D97XE, Boy's, Horn Tank, Light, Red & Cream Paint, Whitewall Tires, 1939 . . 1155.00
Schwinn, Fiesta, Girl's, Pink & White, c.1960 . . . . 60.00
Schwinn, Jaguar Mark II, Phantom Rack, Taillight, Book Rack, 3 Speeds, 1955 . . . . 495.00
Schwinn, Pacemaker, Cantilever Frame, 24 In. 770.00
Schwinn, Panther, Balloon, Boy's, Blue & White, Spring Fork, 1960s 220.00
Schwinn, Stingray, Li'l Chik, Pink, Banana Seat, 1970s 143.00
Schwinn, Suburban, Boy's, Blue, Late 1960s 150.00
Schwinn, Town & Country, Tandem, Dealer Demo, Green, Child Carrier, 1952 . . . . 465.00
Schwinn, Wasp, Balloon Tires, 1950s 500.00
Shelby, Airflow, Cushioned Seat, Chrome, North Tonawanda License, 1950, 35 x 75 In. . . 660.00
Silver King, Model M137, Wing Bar, 1937 . . . . 3025.00
Silver King, Woman's, Aluminum, Lights, Horn, Chain Guard, Stand, 1938 . . . . 650.00
Spaceliner, Boy's, Red, Chrome, 26 In. 138.00
Spaceliner, Girl's, Chrome, 26 In. 28.00
Stand, Elmira, Red Paint & Pinstriping, Cast Iron 575.00
Star, Safety, High Wheel, c.1880 . . . . 1540.00
Swiss Army, 2 Parcel Bags, Tool Pouch, Air Pump, Generator, 1943 . . . . 1485.00
Tricycle, Kid Special, Boy In Knickers, Pull Toy, B. & R., 6 In. 415.00
Tricycle, Pierced Iron Seat, Victorian, 34 x 52 In. 450.00
Tricycle, Rambler, Red, Wire Spokes, Rambler, Steinfeld, Inc., New York 84.00
Trigwell, Watson & Co., Regent Kangaroo, England, c.1886, 36 In. . . . .*Illus* 18700.00
Velocipede, 19th Century 850.00
Waverly, Lady's, Head Lamp, Bell, Tool Pouch, Pneumatic Tires, Wooden Chair Guard . . 577.00

BING & GRONDAHL is a famous Danish factory making fine porcelains from 1853 to the present. Underglaze blue decoration was started in 1886. The annual Christmas plate series was introduced in 1895. Dinnerwares, stoneware, and figurines are still being made today. The firm has used the initials B & G and a stylized castle as part of the mark since 1898.

MADE IN DENMARK

Bowl, Figural, Pair Of Fish & Crab, 9 In.	315.00
Figurine, Baby Polar Bear	165.00
Figurine, Bird, No. 1852	35.00
Figurine, Boy & Girl, 4 1/2 In.	75.00
Figurine, Boy, Seated, Plays Flute, Signed, 1897, 11 In.	245.00
Figurine, Elephant, No. 1806	85.00
Figurine, Fox, Seated Position, Hand Painted, 4 x 5 In.	295.00
Figurine, Fox, Standing, Alert Position, Signed, 3 x 12 In.	295.00
Figurine, Girl, Seated Holding A Doll, No. 1526	38.00
Figurine, Kiss	85.00
Plate, Christmas, 1898, Roses & Star	950.00
Plate, Christmas, 1968, Christmas In Church	48.00
Plate, Christmas, 1969, Arrival Of Guests, 7 In.	12.00
Plate, Christmas, 1972, Christmas In Greenland	30.00
Plate, Mother's Day, 1970, Pheasants In The Snow, 6 In.	7.00
Plate, Mother's Day, 1975	125.00
Plate, World's Fair, 1904	300.00

BINOCULARS of all types are wanted by collectors. Those made in the eighteenth and nineteenth centuries are favored by serious collectors. The small, attractive binoculars called *opera glasses* are listed in their own category.

Auxiliary, Leather Strap	88.00
Binnacle, Cylindrical Brass Cover, Domed Cap, Ring Handle, 9 In.	130.00
Solid Brass, Hezzanith, c.1880	195.00

BIRDCAGES are collected for use as homes for pet birds and as decorative objects of folk art. Elaborate wooden cages of the past centuries can still be found. The brass or wicker cages of the 1930s are popular with bird owners.

Edwardian, 4 Hairy Paw Feet, Brass & Glass, c.1900, 34 1/2 x 18 1/2 In.	240.00
Fruitwood, Painted, Gilt, Lacquered, Birds, Landscape Scene, China, 16 1/2 In.	287.00
Hendy, Polychrome Design, Early 20th Century, Square, 13 x 15 In.	115.00
Tin, Decals, Stenciling, Hendryx, c.1870, 12 x 12 x 15 In.	550.00
Tole, White Paint, Black & Gold Highlights, Wrought Iron Floor Stand, 71 In.	250.00
Twisted Wire, Circular Domed Shape, Early 20th Century, 10 x 19 In.	85.00
Walnut, Wire, Dark Paint Traces, Crown Like Crest Top, Wooden Bird, 11 x 17 In.	605.00
Wire, Painted, Palais Du Trocadero Shape, Flags, France, 1880, 43 x 33 x 21 In.	5750.00
Wire, Pale Gray, Built For International Exhibition Of 1880, France, 43 3/4 In.	5750.00
Wooden, Domed Top, 3 Tiers, Painted Dark Green, Continental, 70 In. x 25 In.	4025.00
Wooden, Octagonal Cupola, Sloping Upper Section, Brown, Blue, Victorian, 33 In.	1150.00

BISQUE is an unglazed baked porcelain. Finished bisque has a slightly sandy texture with a dull finish. Some of it may be decorated with various colors. Bisque gained favor during the late Victorian era when thousands of bisque figurines were made. It is still being made. Additional bisque items may be listed under the factory name.

Bust, Young Girl & Boy, Intaglio Eyes, Germany, 8 1/2 In., Pair	120.00
Candlestick, Figural, Boy & Girl, Germany, 12 In., Pair	120.00
Figurine, Bathing Nude, Germany, 3 In.	50.00
Figurine, Boy & Girl With Dog, Napoleanic Clothes, Germany, 14 In., Pair	132.00
Figurine, Boy & Girl, 19th Century Blue Clothes, Germany, 16 In., Pair	165.00
Figurine, Boy & Girl, Gute Nacht & Gute Morgan, 10 In., Pair	75.00
Figurine, Cavalier & His Companion, Germany, 1910, 16 1/2 In.	73.00
Figurine, Child Pulling On Boot, Germany, 6 In.	65.00
Figurine, Child, Holding Baby, Other With Cat, Painted, 12 1/2 In., Pair	170.00
Figurine, Girl, Holding Flowers In Apron, Boy, With Wine Ball, Germany, 15 In., Pair	60.00

Figurine, Maiden & Her Beau, Both Wearing Floral Costume, 1910, 21 In., Pair 151.00
Figurine, Man & Woman, Harvester Type Clothes, Germany, 16 In., Pair 88.00
Figurine, Man & Woman, Intaglio Eyes, Germany, 11 In. 100.00
Figurine, Man & Woman, With Lutes, Japan, 6 In., Pair 35.00
Figurine, Moon Head, Holding Mandolin, White Outfit, Orange Shoes, 4 1/2 In. 145.00
Figurine, Noble Couple, Wearing Pale Blue Floral Costume, 1910, 18 In., Pair 180.00
Figurine, Young Boy & Girl, Badminton Rackets, Facing Pair, 9 1/4 In., Pair 225.00
Figurine, Young Man & Woman, 18th Century Clothes, Germany, 11 1/2 In., Pair 165.00
Figurine, Young Woman, Lace Edged Dress, 8 1/2 In. 22.00
Group, Man & Woman Singing, Germany, 14 In. 110.00
Group, Man & Woman, Napoleonic Clothes, Germany, 10 1/2 In. 75.00
Group, Man, Woman & Child, 19th Century Clothes, Germany, 14 1/2 In. 320.00
Group, Woman On Horse, Man Standing With Dachshund, Germany, 11 In. 230.00
Humidor, Young Dutch Boy, Green, Black Cap, 5 1/4 In. 275.00
Planter, Fox, Pastel, With Musket & Pipe On Branch, Germany, 10 In. 125.00
Planter, Man & Woman, With Lotus Flower Hats, Germany, 10 In., Pair 100.00
Planter, Ornate Scrolled Shell Sleigh, Cupid & Griffin, Germany, 8 In. 120.00
Planter, Scrolled & Floral Sleigh, Putti & Lion's Heads, Germany, 10 In. 200.00
Planter, Young Woman, Floral Boat, Wavy Sea, Germany, 8 1/2 In. 230.00
Planter, Young Woman, With Basket On Shell Base, Germany, 10 In. 275.00
Planter, Young Woman, With Lotus Flower, Handle, Germany, 8 In. 145.00
Plaque, Man & Woman, Japan, 6 In., Pair 15.00
Plaque, Young Couple Courting, Germany, 14 In., Pair 132.00
Toothbrush Holder, Uncle Walt & Skeezix, 4 In. 110.00
Toothbrush Holder, Young Girl, Near Basket, Germany, 6 1/2 In. 50.00
Vase, Ladies In Pastels, Under Flowering Trees, 9 1/2 In., Pair 105.00
Vase, Spill, Armchair Shape, With Girl & Kittens, Applied Floral, Germany, 8 1/2 In. 255.00
Vase, Spill, Girl Shape, With Lute, Germany, 9 In. 55.00
Vase, Winged Cherub, Flower Shape, 3 Openings, 7 1/4 In. 45.00

BLACK memorabilia has become an important area of collecting since the 1970s. The best material dates from past centuries, but many recent items are also of interest. F & F is the mark used on plastic made by Fiedler & Fiedler Mold & Die Works, Inc. in the 1930s and 1940s. Objects that picture a black person may also be listed in this book under Advertising, Tins; Banks; Bottle Openers; Cookie Jars; Salt & Pepper; Sheet Music; Toys; etc.

Ashtray, Coon Chicken Inn, Black Head, 1940-1951, 3 1/2 In. 20.00
Ashtray, Coon Chicken, Black Bellboy, Smiling Face 10.00
Ballot Box, State Of Georgia Supervisor, Wooden, Marked Blacks 395.00
Bellhop, Holding Shoe Brushes, Leather 225.00
Booklet, Buffalo Soldiers At Ft. Leavenworth In The 1930s & 40s, 54 Pages, 2 Piece 32.00
Booklet, Landon-Knox For Colored People, F. Douglass Quote, 80 Pages 75.00
Box, Coon Chicken Inn, Carry-Out, Tan, 1949 .... 95.00
Box, Soup, Aunt Jemima, Ready Mix For Yellow Pea Soup, Red, Cardboard, 4 Oz. 28.00
Boy, Dressed In Nightclothes, Brass, Incense Burner, Prospect Falls, Niagara, 4 1/2 In. .. 385.00
Button, Decatur Corn Carnival & Exposition, Boys Eating Corn On Cob, 1899, 1 3/4 In. . 60.00
Card, Boy & Girl, Holding Golliwog, Mechanical, 1920s, Germany, 2 x 4 In. 20.00
Carving, Buckboard, Pulled By 2 Mules, Black Man & Woman, Baby, 24 x 11 1/2 In. ... 2530.00
Coffee Tin, Mammy's Favorite Coffee, Metal Handle, C.D. Kenny Co., Baltimore, 10 In. . 240.00
Collar, Slave, HBM Engraved On Tag, HIATT On Clasp 2500.00
Cookie Jars are listed in the Cookie Jar category.
Display, Amos & Andy, Figural, Cardboard, Bent At Head, 1930s, 6 In. 200.00
Display, Amos & Andy, Stand-Up, Cardboard, Uncut Sheet Of 6, Pepsodent, 1931 ...... 230.00
Doll, Bellhop, Articulated, Original Paint, 11 1/2 In. 95.00
Doll, Bisque, Bare Feet, Swivel Neck, Braided Hair, 4 1/4 In. 950.00
Doll, Boy & Girl, Wooden, Painted Faces, Peg Jointed, c.1875, 5 1/2 In., Pair 550.00
Doll, Child, Wooden, Articulated, Composition Head & Arms, Painted Face, 7 In. 165.00
Doll, Cloth, Embroidered Face, Red Top 650.00
Doll, Cloth, Hooked Hair, Embroidered Face, Hand-Stitched Dress, Late 1800s, 32 In. ... 1380.00
Doll, Cream Of Wheat, Holding Cereal Bowl, Cloth, Stuffed, 18 In. 45.00
Doll, Dried Fruit Head, Handmade Costumes, 8 3/4 In. 110.00
Doll, Folk Art, Cloth, Embroidered Face, Wool Hair, 19th Century, 15 In. 165.00

Doll, Golliwog, Minstrel, Velveteen Bean Bear, Tag, England, 8 1/2 In. 40.00
Doll, Mammy, Red Dress, Blue, White Dust Cap, 18 In. 220.00
Doll, Muslin, Lithographed Face, Mitten Hands, Stitch Jointed Body, c.1900, 15 In. 2100.00
Doll, Striped Cotton Suit, Polka Dot Shirt, Folk Art, 16 1/4 In. 373.00
Doll, Stuffed, Black Composition Face, Straw Hat, Wood & Folks Company, 12 In. 25.00
Doll, Wearing Plaid Cotton Dress, Folk Art, Early 20th Century, 22 In. 172.00
Figurine, Black Boy On Watermelon, Bisque, Germany, 4 In. 33.00
Figurine, Boy With Cigar, Bronze, Painted, Austria, 1 3/8 In. 480.00
Figurine, Child Seated On Potty, Dime Coming Out Of Rear, Holding Watermelon, 5 In. . 225.00
Figurine, Uncle Tom's Cabin, Tom, Holding Eva, Hanging Wreath Of Roses, 7 In. 305.00
Game, Alabama Coon, Spears, Box, 11 x 6 In. 425.00
Game, Little Black Sambo, Board, Cadaco-Ellis, 1945 . . . . 75.00
Game, Target, Black Sambo, Original Box 135.00
Game, White-Eyed Coon, Rings, Spears, Complete, Box 300.00
Glass, Water, Coon Chicken Inn 10.00
Glass, Water, Coon Chicken Inn, Black Picture 30.00
Humidor, Black Woman With Painted-On Hoop Earrings, Straw Hat, 6 x 5 1/4 In. 305.00
Humidor, Blackamoor, Turban Holds Cover, Majolica, 11 x 8 In. 920.00
Inkwell, Boy Smoking Pipe, Lead, Germany 325.00
Key Ring, No Slavery, Black Painted Wooden Foot, 1830-1860, 2 1/4 In. 600.00
Lure, Fishing, Sambo 125.00
Mask, Mammy, Halloween 295.00
Menu, Coon Chicken Inn, Price Insert, 1949, 12 1/2 In. 295.00
Money Clip, Coon Chicken 75.00
Newspaper, Abolitionist, Herald Of Freedom, June 11, 1836, Concord, New Hampshire . . 44.00
Newspaper, Abolitionist, Liberator, May 11, 1838, Boston 75.00
Newspaper, Abolitionist, Liberator, May 17, 1844, Boston 80.00
Pencil Sharpener, Black Face, Germany 75.00
Photograph, Black Man Graduating, Formal, 1910 . . . . 45.00
Photograph, Black Swing-Era Woman Bandleader, Lil Armstrong, 1935, 8 x 10 In. 90.00
Photograph, Homestead Grays On Road, In Front Of Bus, Mar. 23, 1946, 8 x 10 In. 396.00
Photograph, Homestead Grays, Team Photo, 16 Players, 1934, 5 1/2 x 10 1/2 In. 605.00
Photograph, Kansas City Monarchs, In Uniforms, Rural Setting, 1950 . . . . 129.00
Photograph, Roberto Clemente, Suitcase In Hand, Stadium, 10/18/71, 8 x 10 In. 42.00
Photograph, Smiling Black Midget, Age 25 Years, Lyn Major White, 7 x 5 In. 40.00
Pitcher, Aunt Jemima, Black, White, Red Plastic, F & F Mold & Die Works, Dayton, Oh. 63.00
Plate, Coon Chicken, 10 In. 300.00
Platter, Steak, Coon Chicken Inn, Inca Ware 600.00
Postcard, 10th Black Cavalrymen, Captured, Carrizal Battle, Photograph, W.H. Horne . . . 425.00
Postcard, An Early Breakfast, Mammy Bottle Feeding White Baby, 1908 . . . . 35.00
Postcard, Black Boy, Asleep In Cotton, Memphis, Tenn., Dixieland, Unused 15.00
Postcard, Black Execution, Photograph, c.1910 . . . . 2500.00
Postcard, Black Jazz Cat, Banjo, Says Why Can't Every Man Have 3 Wives 40.00
Postcard, Black Sailor, From Shipmate D.L. Winfield, 1945 . . . . 50.00
Postcard, Black Take The Count, White Victor, Johnson & Jeffries, Faces On Roosters . . . 150.00
Postcard, Black Tennessee Miners, Work Gang At Opening 34.00
Postcard, Children, Beginners Southern Christian Institute, Edwards, Miss. 40.00
Postcard, Disturbing Piece, Boy With Bellyache, Eating Too Much Watermelon, 1908 . . . 35.00
Postcard, Golliwog, Steedman's Powder, For Fevers, England 50.00
Postcard, Little Alabama Coon, Black Baby In Chair, Poem, 1908 . . . . 20.00
Postcard, Man Pulling Another Man's Tooth With Block & Tackle, 1908 . . . . 45.00
Postcard, Negro Baptism, Boats & Shore Scene, Norfolk, Va., 1924 . . . . 30.00
Postcard, Prisoner Exchange, Mexican Revolution, Black Men Guarded By Soldiers 212.00
Postcard, Skinning A Coon, Red Neck Man, Picking Pocket Of Black Woman, 1908 . . . . 37.00
Postcard, Soldiers In Camp, At Mess, Pine Camp, New York 125.00
Postcard, Turpentine Industry In South, Men, Pine Trees, Unused, 1 Cent Stamp 15.00
Poster, Black Gold, Play, All Colored Cast, By Norman Studios, 1920s, 14 x 22 In. 185.00
Poster, Cab Calloway's Jumpin' Jive, 18 x 10 In. 118.00
Poster, Carrol County Fair, Black Boy & Donkey, Black & White 30.00
Poster, Hartley Toots & His Famous Orchestra, Yellow, Blue, Black, 1930s, 14 x 22 In. . . 157.00
Poster, Hercules Powder Co., Black Hunters, 1925, 20 x 14 1/2 In. 165.00
Poster, John Brown Still Lives, Dec. 30, 1859, Midwest Meeting, 8 1/4 x 12 In. 5365.00
Poster, Play, Without Pity, Mercury Theatre, Tues. May 9, 14 x 22 In. 133.00

Poster, Uncle Tom's Cabin, Black Man, Dancing With Child, 1890, 28 x 21 In. 300.00
Poster, Uncle Tom's Cabin, Paper, Wm. M. Donaldson & Co., 1883, 27 x 33 In. 195.00
Potholder, Mammy's Face, Chalkware 50.00
Potholder, Umbrella Girl 35.00
Puppet, Mammy, Ventriloquist, Glass Eyes, Wearing Red Gown, 62 In. 4125.00
Record, A Coon Wedding In Southern Georgia, Edison Cylinder Type, Box, 1905 .... 75.00
Ribbon, Colored Laundry Helpers Benevolent Asso., Mar. 1, 1917, Mobile, 5 1/2 In. 168.00
Shopping List, Pegboard, Mammy, We Needs, Wooden, 1940s 50.00
Sign, Smoking Sambo, Cardboard, Die Cut, Easel Back, Slit In Lips For Cigar, 5 x 10 In. . 88.00
Soap Dish, Aunt Jemima, Shape, Basket On Head, Cast Iron 305.00
Songbook, The Negro And The Flag, Photographs, Copyright 1917 .... 32.00
Table & Chair Set, Amos & Andy, Hand Carved Wood, 4 Chairs 7700.00
Toothpick Holder, African Native Next To Tree Trunk, Satirical, Pottery, Japan, 5 In. 22.00
Toy, Amos & Andy Fresh Air Taxi, Box, 1930, 8 In. ....950.00 to 1840.00
Toy, Amos & Andy, Walker, Wearing Hats, Marx, Box, 12 In. 3190.00
Toy, Strutting Sam, Black Tap Dancer, Tin, Battery Operated, Box, 11 In. 475.00
Toy, Turtle, Black Man, Riding, Windup, Tin, Chein 110.00
Toy, Washerwoman, Old Aunt Chloe, Clockwork, Woman Standing At Washtub, 10 In. 6325.00
Umbrella Stand, Ashtray, Original Paint, 35 In. 595.00
Valentine, Y'all Done Walked Right Into Mah Heart An' All Dat Ah Kin Say, Pair 55.00
Water Sprinkler, Cut-Out Boy, Rubber Hose, Metal Base, Metal, 36 In. 370.00
Wood Carving, Black Man Working With Hammer & Anvil, 1950s, 35 1/2 In. 250.00
Wooden Nickel, Sambo 8.00

BLACK AMETHYST glass appears black until it is held to the light, then
a dark purple can be seen. It has been made in many factories from
1860 to the present.

Box, White Enameled Leaf Sprays At Sides, Rose On Top, 2 3/8 x 2 3/8 In. 110.00
Cuspidor, Woman's 48.00
Shot Glass, Chicago, 2 3/8 In. 7.00

BLOWN GLASS, see Glass-Blown category.

BLUE GLASS, see Cobalt Blue category.

BLUE ONION, see Onion category.

BLUE WILLOW, see Willow category.

BOCH FRERES factory was founded in 1841 in La Louviere in eastern
Belgium. The wares resemble the work of Villeroy & Boch. The factory is still in business.

Lamp, Art Deco Design, Yellow & Green, Silvered Metal Mounts, 24 In. 900.00
Plate, Old Man & Old Woman, Pair 195.00
Vase, Animal, Gold Highlights, Orange Stamp, 7 In. 530.00
Vase, Art Deco, Fruit & Ribbons, Crackle Ware Ground, Signed, 15 5/8 In. 990.00
Vase, Floral, Interior Black Band, Mottled Brown Ground, Signed, 10 1/2 In. 560.00
Vase, Geometric Pattern, Brown & Sand, Charles Catteau, c.1925, 10 1/2 In. 35.00

BOEHM is the collector's name for the porcelains of Edward Marshall
Boehm. In 1953 the Osso China Company was reorganized as Edward
Marshall Boehm, Inc. The company is still working in England and
New Jersey. In the early days of the factory, dishes were made, but the
elaborate and lifelike bird figurines are the best-known ware. Edward
Marshall Boehm, the founder, died in 1961, but the firm has continued
to design and produce porcelain. Today, the firm makes both limited
and unlimited editions of figurines and plates.

Figurine, Alec's Red Rose, No. 132, 1980, 7 In. 430.00
Figurine, Arctic Tern, No. 331, 13 3/4 In. 405.00
Figurine, Arizona Queen Of The Night Cactus, No. 83, 1976, 10 In. 605.00
Figurine, Baby Blue Bird, 4 1/2 In. 138.00
Figurine, Baby Cardinal, 4 1/4 In. 120.00
Figurine, Blue Jay, 10 1/2 In. 517.00
Figurine, Cardinal, 11 3/4 In. 1035.00
Figurine, Fledgling Kingfisher, 6 1/4 In. 70.00

Figurine, Fledgling Magpie, 5 3/4 In. 58.00
Figurine, Goldfinch, 9 1/4 In. 488.00
Figurine, Gray Wagtail With Wild Arum, 10 3/4 In. 488.00
Figurine, Gull & Nest Of Eggs 747.00
Figurine, Hummingbird, No. 440, 10 In. . . . .\. 310.00
Figurine, Magnolia Warbler, 8 3/4 In. 632.00
Figurine, Marsh Harrier With Water Lilies, No. 53, 25 In. 1150.00
Figurine, Mockingbirds, No. 334, 10 1/4 In. 1095.00
Figurine, Parula Warblers, 14 1/4 In. 920.00
Figurine, Pascali Rose With Freesia, No. 102, 1978, 10 In. 490.00
Figurine, Prairie Chickens, 10 In. 345.00
Figurine, Rose, On Log, Yellow, 6 In. 175.00
Figurine, Royal Tern, 19 In. 920.00
Figurine, Sandpiper, 12 1/2 In. 920.00
Figurine, Scissor-Tailed Flycatcher, No. 11, 1977, 13 1/2 In. 1380.00
Figurine, Snow Buntings, 7 1/4 In. 862.00
Figurine, Supreme Orchid Cactus With Horned Toad, No. 69, 1976, 6 1/2 In. 405.00
Figurine, Tropicana Rose, No. 205, 1978, 4 In. 220.00
Figurine, Tufted Tit Mice, 10 In. 57.00
Figurine, Verdin, 8 1/2 In. 431.00
Figurine, Yellow-Throated Warbler, No. 431, 9 1/2 In. 310.00
Paperweight, Scarab, Commemorative, King Tut Exhibit, 1976 . . . .   95.00

BOHEMIAN GLASS, see Glass-Bohemian.

BONE DISHES were considered a necessary part of a table setting for the Victorian table. The crescent-shaped dish was kept at the edge of the dinner plate so the bones removed from the fish could be stored away from the uneaten food. Some bone dishes were made in more fanciful shapes and many resemble fish.

Orchard Gold, Aynsley, 10 x 8 3/4 In. 145.00
White, Dark Blue Pattern, J. & G. Meakin, 6 3/8 In. 15.00

BOOKENDS have probably been used since books became inexpensive. Early libraries kept books in cupboards, not on open shelves. By the 1870s bookends appeared, especially homemade fret-carved wooden examples. Most bookends listed in this book date from the twentieth century. Bookends are also listed in other categories by manufacturer or material.

Arts & Crafts, Daffodil Design, Square, 6 In. 385.00
Clowns On Back Of Bucking Donkey, Art Deco, Bronze 135.00
Copper, Hammered, Cleaned Patina, Impressed Mark, Dirk Van Erp, 5 In., Pair 330.00
Copper, Pierced Curved Row Rectangles Over Squares, Dirk Van Erp, 1915, 5 In. 1090.00
Cranes, Bronze, 7 3/4 In. 110.00
Dachshund, Adjustable, Bradley & Hubbard, 4 1/2 x 8 In. 22.00
Doe, Seated, Foliage, Wrought Iron, Edgar Brandt, 1925, 7 In. 5175.00
Doorway, Pingree House, Salem, Mass., Bronze, S. Symonds, 4 x 3 3/4 In. 770.00
Dutch Boy & Girl, Playing, Whimsical Style, Hubley, 4 1/2 x 4 1/2 In. 132.00
Elephants, Attacked By Crocodile, Bronze & Ivory, Mitsuyuki, 6 1/2 In. 970.00
Elk, Cast Iron, 4 In. 75.00
End Of Trail, By Pompeian, Bronze 185.00
End Of Trail, Indian On Horseback, Title On Front, 4 x 4 1/4 In.   125.00
Firemen, Holding Trumpet, Lantern In Other Hand, Wooden, 7 1/4 In. 110.00
Football Players, Running, Full Figure, Hubley, 5 3/4 x 5 1/2 In.   352.00
George III, Mahogany, Inlaid Satinwood 85.00
German Shepherd, Metal 46.00
Golfer, White Metal, Bronze Finish, 20th Century, 5 1/2 In. 125.00
Horses, Bronzed Cast Iron, Signed, Gregory S. Alen, Pair . . . .*Illus*   75.00
House, Trees, Gilded, Bradley & Hubbard . . . . .85.00 to 95.00
Indian, Seated, Bronze, Armor Bronze Company 715.00
Indian Chief, Adjustable, Bradley & Hubbard, 5 1/2 x 6 1/4 In.   88.00
Indian Chief, Adjustable, Bradley & Hubbard, 5 3/4 x 11 1/2 In.   110.00
John Alden & Priscilla, Colonial Style, Bradley & Hubbard, 6 x 3 3/4 In. 132.00
Krupka, Buffalo, Bronze, 1924 . . . .   220.00

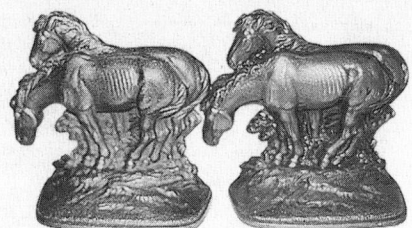

Bookends, Horses, Bronzed Cast Iron, Signed,
Gregory S. Alen, Pair

Need a quick measurement at an antiques show? A penny is 3/4 inch in diameter; a dollar bill is almost 6 inches long.

Lighthouse, Brass, 8 In.	220.00
Lion, Walking, Enamel Over Cast Iron	100.00
Lions, Reclining, Faux Marble Base, 5 x 7 1/4 In.	150.00
Mansion Door, Black, Bradley & Hubbard, 5 1/2 x 4 In.	132.00
Neoclassical Maiden, Bronze, Lyre, Seated On Column, Wooden Plinth, 14 3/4 In.	1035.00
Nude, Kneeling, Satin Glass, Marc Lalique, 1950, 9 In.	1573.00
Owl, Beige, Black Eyes, 6 x 5 1/2 In.	88.00
Pierced & Chased Silver Design, Birds In Flight, Copper, J.J. Brennan, 3 x 3 In.	295.00
Pierrette Design, Movable Hands, Stepped Onyx Base, Gilt, 9 In.	170.00
Praying Hands, Bronze Plated, 5 In.	70.00
Proud Peacock, Cobalt, Bradley & Hubbard, 6 1/4 x 5 In.	605.00
Ram's Head, Clear & Frosted Glass, 6 1/2 In.	35.00
Reclining Lion, On Wood Plinth, Ebonized Wood Base, Black Patina, 7 In.	170.00
Sailboat, Cast Iron, 20th Century, 8 In.	45.00
Sailboat, Label, Syroco	50.00
Spanish Galleon, Cast Iron, Gold Paint, 6 x 5 In.	20.00
Terrier, Standing On Grass, Hubley, 5 x 5 3/4 In.	110.00
Terrier, Standing, White Body, Black Ears, Spencer, Guilford, Conn., 5 x 5 In.	220.00
Woman, Flowing Gown, Harriet W. Frishmuth, Bronze, 9 1/2 In.	3520.00

BOOKMARKS were originally made of parchment, cloth, or leather. Soon woven silk ribbon, thin cardboard, celluloid, wood, silver, tortoiseshell, and metals were used. Examples made before 1850 are scarce, but there are many to be found dating before 1920.

1934 World's Fair, Federal Building Center, Orange Tassel, 4 3/4 In.	30.00
Butterfly Shape, View Of Treasure Island, Fair Logo, Plastic, Paper, Envelope	40.00
Christopher Robin Putting On Boots, Pewter	12.00
Cracker Jack, Tin, 2 3/4 In.	20.00
Presenting Philip Morris, Die Cut Of Johnny, Cardboard, 4 In.	95.00
Prevent Forest Fires, Hitler & Hirohito With Blazing Forest Fire, Orange, 2 x 7 In.	48.00
Red Silk Ribbon, Pierre, South Dakota, 1850s	65.00
Saratoga Springs, New York, 3 Horse Heads, 4 In.	4.00
Souvenir Of Panama-Pacific Exposition, Carnation Milk, 1915	50.00
Susan B. Anthony, Silk Ribbon, Gold Letters, How Beautiful It Is To Be With God	550.00
View Of Jerusalem, Holy Land On Reverse, Plastic Sleeve, 9 1/2 In.	10.00

BOSSONS character wall masks, plaques, figurines, and other decorative pieces are made by W.H. Bossons, Limited of Congleton, England. The company was founded in 1946 and is still working.

Geisha, Full Bodied, 13 In.	250.00
Indian Warrior Head	45.00
Midalo, Full Body, 14 In.	275.00
Pancho & Rawhide, Pair	45.00
Plaque, Woodpecker Feeding 2 Chicks In Tree Trunk, 11 1/2 In.	165.00
Romany, Green Scarf, 1970, 10 In.	185.00

BOSTON & SANDWICH CO. pieces may be found in the Lutz and Sandwich Glass categories.

BOTTLE collecting has become a major American hobby. There are several general categories of bottles, such as historic flasks, bitters, household, and figural. Pyro is the shortened form of the word *pyroglaze*, an enameled lettering used on bottles after the mid-1930s. For more bottle prices, see the book *Kovels' Bottles Price List* by Ralph and Terry Kovel.

Apothecary, TR: Lavand, Black Glass, Olive Amber, Painted Label, 12 1/2 In. 160.00

Avon started in 1886 as the California Perfume Company. It was not until 1929 that the name *Avon* was used. In 1939, it became Avon Products, Inc. Avon has made many figural bottles filled with cosmetic products. Ceramic, plastic, and glass bottles were made in limited editions.

Avon, Bay Rum, With Stopper, California Perfume Co., 1896, 4 Oz. 150.00
Avon, California Perfume Co. 30.00
Avon, Car, Volkswagen, Black, 1970 .... 12.00
Avon, Charlie Brown & Snoopy, Hugging, Non-Tear Shampoo, Box, 6 In. 25.00
Avon, Coleman Lantern, Green Paint Over Clear Glass, 1977, 5 Oz. 10.00
Avon, Decanter, Betsy Ross, White Paint Over Clear Glass, 1976, 4 Oz. 7.00
Avon, Decanter, President Lincoln, After Shave, Box, 1979 .... 25.00
Avon, Football, Box, 1984 .... 25.00
Avon, Goblet 10.00
Avon, Linus, Peanuts, Bubble Bath, White, Red, Black, Box, 5 In. 20.00
Avon, Lionel Classic Train Collection, 1995 .... 35.00
Avon, Lucy, Peanuts, Bubble Bath, Red, White, Black, Box, 6 In. 40.00
Avon, Snoopy & Doghouse, Shampoo, Red & White Plastic, Box, 5 In. 20.00
Avon, Snoopy As Flying Ace, Bubble Bath, Blue, White, Black, Doghouse Box, 6 In. 25.00
Avon, Snoopy's Snow Flyer, Bubble Bath, White & Red Plastic, Box, 6 In. 20.00
Avon, Stanley Steamer, 1978 .... 10.00
Avon, Stein, 1979 Car Classic & Western Roundup 20.00
Avon, Stein, Sporting, Box, 1978 .... 25.00
Barber, Amethyst, Bell Shape, Ribbed, Enamel Floral, Sheared Lip, Pontil, 7 5/8 In. 75.00
Barber, Amethyst, White, Yellow & Orange Enamel Floral, Flared Lip, Pontil, 7 1/2 In. .. 100.00
Barber, Bay Rum, Opalescent Milk Glass, Multicolored Floral, Pontil, 8 3/8 In. 3210.00
Barber, Clear, Cranberry Flashed Interior, Thumbprint, Rolled Lip, Pontil, 6 3/4 In. 145.00
Barber, Cobalt Blue, Rib Pattern, White Enamel Design, Sheared Lip, Pontil, 7 7/8 In. ... 75.00
Barber, Cranberry Opalescent, Seaweed, Teepee Shape 395.00
Barber, Frieze Of Muses, Border Of Oak Leaves, Wedgwood, 7 1/4 In. 285.00
Barber, Grass Green, Frosted, Ribbed, White, Gilt, Sheared Lip, Pontil, 7 3/4 In. 1155.00
Barber, Opalescent Cranberry, Daisy & Fern, Melon Sides, Rolled Lip, 7 1/8 In. 185.00
Barber, Opalescent Cranberry, Spanish Lace Design, Rolled Lip, Pontil, 8 3/8 In. 690.00
Barber, Opalescent Cranberry, White Stripes, Flared Lip, Pontil, 8 5/8 In. 360.00
Barber, Sapphire Blue, Ribbed, Enamel Art Nouveau Design, Rolled Lip, Pontil, 8 In. ... 635.00
Barber, Straw Yellow, Amber Tone, Hobnail, Rolled Lip, Pontil, 7 In. 110.00
Barber, Toilet Water, Opalescent Milk Glass, Corset Waist, Floral Design, Pontil, 9 In. ... 935.00

Beam bottles were made to hold Kentucky Straight Bourbon, made by the James B. Beam Distilling Company. The Beam series of ceramic bottles began in 1953.

Beam, Churchill Downs, 95th Kentucy Derby, 1970, 11 In. 45.00
Beam, Churchill Downs, 98th Kentucky Derby, Horse & Rider, 1972 .... 40.00
Beam, Corvette Stingray, 1963 Model 27.00
Beam, Cowboy, Houston, 1979 .... 35.00
Beam, Ford Phaeton, 1929 Model, 1982 .... 65.00
Beam, Grant Dining Car, 1982 .... 85.00
Beam, Indianapolis Speed Race, 1970, 2 x 8 x 8 In. 25.00
Beam, Northern Pike, 1978 .... 25.00
Beam, Opera, Aida, 1978 .... 95.00
Beam, Opera, Don Giovanni, 1980 .... 135.00
Beam, Opera, Madame Butterfly, 1977 .... 235.00
Beam, Rainbow Trout, 1975 .... 35.00
Beam, Saint Bernard, 1979 .... 35.00

Beam, Stutz Bearcat, 1914 Model, Yellow, 1977 .... 45.00
Beer, Anheuser-Busch Brewing Association, Embossed, Pre-Prohibition, 12 Oz. 40.00
Beer, Binder's Brewery Lager, 11 Oz. 12.00
Beer, Blue Crest Bock Beer, 1 Qt. 9.00
Beer, Grace Bros. Brewing Co., Santa Rosa, Calif., Amber, 1 Qt. 15.00
Beer, Hamm's Commemorative, Ceramic, 1972, 1 Qt. 21.00
Beer, Olive Green, Painted, 4 Monks At Table, Long Neck, Germany, 1880-1900 .... 90.00
Beer, Olive Green, Painted, Man With Stein, Long Neck, Germany, 1890-1920, 13 In. ... 65.00
Beer, Phoenix Brewery Co., Victoria B.C., Olive Green, Pontil 155.00
Bininger, A.M. & Co., 19 Broad St., N.Y., Cannon, Amber, Partial Label, 12 1/2 In. 605.00
Bitters, Baker's Orange Grove, Cherry Puce, Applied Sloping Collar, 9 1/2 In. 1265.00
Bitters, Bryant's Stomach, 8 Sides, Lady's Leg, Deep Olive Green, Pontil, 12 In. 7975.00
Bitters, Drake's Plantation, 6-Log, Cherry Puce, Sloping Collar, 9 3/4 In. 200.00
Bitters, Drake's Plantation, 6-Log, Grape Puce, Sloping Collar, Whittled, 10 In. 1650.00
Bitters, Lash's Kidney & Liver, Best Cathartic & Blood, 8 7/8 In. 35.00
Bitters, Old Sachem & Wigwam Tonic, Barrel, Amber, 9 1/2 In. 165.00
Bitters, Wait's Kidney & Liver, California's Own True Laxative, Amber, 8 3/4 In. 65.00
Black Glass, Mallet, Olive Amber, String Lip, Kick-Up, Pontil, 8 5/8 In. 185.00
Black Glass, Mallet, Olive Green, Wide Mouth, String Lip, Half-Size, Pontil, 1740, 6 In. . 855.00
Coca-Cola bottles are listed in the Coca-Cola category.
Cologne, 12 Sides, Teal Blue, Rolled Lip, 1860-1870, 4 3/4 In. 95.00
Cologne, Cut Glass, Hobstar, Stopper, 7 1/2 x 5 In. 450.00
Cologne, Diamond Cut, Stopper, Dorflinger, 6 3/4 x 4 In. 185.00
Cologne, Joy, Clear, 6 1/2 In. 350.00
Cologne, Standing Lion, Fancy Design, Tooled Mouth, Pontil, 1845-1855, 3 5/8 In. 105.00
Cordial, L.Q.C. Wishart's Pine Tree Tar, Phila., Patent 1859, Emerald Green, 9 1/2 In. ... 220.00
Cosmetic, Hyki Tonic, Dandruff Cure, Label Under Glass 195.00
Cosmetic, Melanine Hair Tonic, Dodge Brothers, Purple Amethyst, 7 3/8 In. 745.00
Cosmetic, Mrs. S.A. Allen's World's Hair Restorer, New York, Black Amethyst, 7 1/4 In. .. 405.00
Cure, Orcutt's Sure Rheumatic, Deep Cobalt Blue, Tooled Lip, 6 1/8 In. 635.00
Cure, Warner's Safe, Melbourne, London, Toronto, Rochester, Red Amber, 9 5/8 In. 100.00
Cyrus Noble, Buffalo Cow & Calf, 1977, 2nd Edition 85.00
Cyrus Noble, Burro, 1973 .... 60.00
Cyrus Noble, Carousel, Pipe Organ, 1980 .... 75.00
Cyrus Noble, Dolphin, 1979 .... 55.00
Cyrus Noble, Gold Miner, 1970 .... 175.00
Cyrus Noble, Miner's Daughter, 1975 .... 45.00
Cyrus Noble, Owl In Tree, 1980 .... 55.00
Decanter, Airplane, Winnie Mae, Balto Liquor Co., Porcelain, REM Originals, 1972 .... 100.00
Decanter, Blown, Gilt Holland Scenes, 2 Handles, Body Rigaree, Holland, 9 1/4 In. 175.00
Decanter, Emerald Green, Blue Coiled Snake & Stopper, 9 1/2 In. 45.00
Decanter, Pillar Molded, 8 Sides, Concave Panels, Cobalt Rib Ends, Pontil, 10 1/2 In. ... 580.00
Demijohn, Blown, Olive Amber, 13 In. 60.00
Demijohn, Blown, Olive Amber, Sloping Lip, Pontil, 18 1/2 In. 245.00
Demijohn, Olive Amber, Sloping Collar, Pontil, 1800-1830, 11 3/8 In. 155.00
Demijohn, Olive Green, Sloping Collar, Pontil, Bubbles, Swirl Lines, 12 5/8 In. 240.00
Demijohn, Red Amber, Tapered Collar, 14 In. 45.00
Demijohn, Tobacco Amber, Sloping Collar, Pontil, 1840-1860, 17 1/2 In. 385.00
Ezra Brooks, Asian Elephant, 1973 .... 20.00
Ezra Brooks, Auburn, U-War Eagle, 1982 .... 35.00
Ezra Brooks, Betsy Ross, 1975 .... 20.00
Ezra Brooks, Christmas Tree, 1980 .... 25.00
Ezra Brooks, Cigar Store Indian, 1968, 16 In. 40.00
Ezra Brooks, Horse, Man O' War, Horse, 1969 .... 35.00
Ezra Brooks, Indy Pace Car, Box, 1979, 10 1/2 In. 20.00
Ezra Brooks, Kachina, No. 1, Morning Singer, 1971 .... 85.00
Ezra Brooks, Kachina, No. 7, Mudhead, 1978 .... 55.00
Ezra Brooks, Keystone Cops, 1975 .... 35.00
Ezra Brooks, Pagliacci, 1979 .... 35.00
Ezra Brooks, Pontiac Pace Car, 1980 .... 25.00
Ezra Brooks, Trojan Horse, 1974 .... 55.00
Ezra Brooks, Whiskey, Cigar Store Indian, Ceramic, War Bonnet, 1968, 16 In. 40.00
Figural, Artichoke, Gesetzlich Geschutzt, Olive Green, Germany, 9 5/8 In. 275.00

When you open your windows in
warm weather, watch out for
blowing curtains. They may hit
glass or china displayed nearby
and cause damage.

Bottle, Flask, Heddon's
Of Dowagiac, 4th Of July
Derby 1925, Silver
Plated, 1 Pt.

Figural, Coachman, Holding Pipe & Glass, Milk Glass, 1880-1895, 10 1/4 In. 1650.00
Figural, Fish, W.H. Ware, Patented 1866, Amber, Applied Mouth, 11 1/2 In. 220.00
Figural, Hard Hat, Mannen, Man In Jacket, Orange Hat, c.1950, 9 In. 15.00
Figural, Lady Upside Down, France, 14 In. 55.00
Figural, Owl, Square, 8 In. 20.00
Figural, Roast Turkey, Amber, Embossed Monterey, 5 x 6 In. 100.00
Flask, Chestnut, 18 Ribs, Swirled Right, Green Aqua, Sheared Lip, Pontil, 6 1/4 In. 200.00
Flask, Chestnut, 18 Ribs, Swirled, Cobalt Blue, 6 In. 715.00
Flask, Chestnut, Citron, 15 Vertical Ribs, 1/2 Pt., 5 1/8 In. 605.00
Flask, Chestnut, Expanded Diamond, Citron, 6 In. 125.00
Flask, Chestnut, Olive Green, Applied Mouth, Pontil, 1780-1810, 7 1/4 In. 155.00
Flask, Chestnut, Yellow Olive, Amber Tone, Sloping Collar, Pontil, 8 5/8 In. 175.00
Flask, Chestnut, Yellow Olive, Sloping Collar Mouth, Pontil, 1780-1830, 8 1/2 In. 175.00
Flask, Clam, Amber, Ground Lip, Metal Screw Cap, 1885-1895, 5 1/4 In. 120.00
Flask, Eagle & Cornucopia, Yellow Olive Amber, Sheared Lip, Pontil, 1 Pt. 165.00
Flask, Eagle & Flag, Olive Amber, Semi-Open Pontil 715.00
Flask, Eagle & Willington, Forest Green, Sheared Mouth, Pontil, 1/2 Pt. 190.00
Flask, Heddon's Of Dowagiac, 4th Of July Derby 1925, Silver Plated, 1 Pt. . . . . *Illus* 1045.00
Flask, Horseman & Hound, Aqua, Double Collar Mouth, 1860-1870, 1 Pt. 105.00
Flask, Jenny Lind & Glasshouse, Calabash, Aqua, Sloping Collar, Pontil 85.00
Flask, John E. Rumsey, Cementon, Pa., Honest Measure, Aqua, 1 Qt. 80.00
Flask, Masonic Clasped Hands & Eagle, Aqua, 1 Qt. 132.00
Flask, Sheaf Of Wheat & Star, Calabash, Blue Aqua, Sloping Collar, Pontil 165.00
Flask, Success To The Railroad, Yellow Amber, Sheared Lip, OP, 1 Pt. 305.00
Flask, Sunburst, Pitkin Glass Works, Manchester, Ct., Yellow Olive, 1815-1830, 1 Pt. 2100.00
Flask, Union, Clasped Hands & Eagle, Amber, Applied Mouth, 1/2 Pt. 175.00
Flask, Washington & Taylor, Light Blue Green, Applied Mouth, Pontil, 1 Pt. 130.00
Food, Jumbo Brand Peanut Butter, Repro Cap, 3 1/2 Oz. 20.00
Food, Peerless Brand Mocha & Java Coffee, M.S. Ayer & Co., Amber, 1 Qt. 80.00
Food, Sunshine Brand Coffee, Springfield Grover Co., Springfield, Mo., 1 Qt. 18.00
Food, Tabasco Sauce, Original Stopper 225.00
Fruit Jar, A. Stone & Co., Philada, Cunninghams & Co., Aqua, Wax Sealer, IP, 1 Pt. 965.00
Fruit Jar, Atlas E-Z Seal, Apple Green, Stopper, 1 Pt. 22.00
Fruit Jar, Atlas Good Luck, Clover, 1/2 Gal. 22.00
Fruit Jar, Atlas Good Luck, Dimple Neck, 1/2 Pt. 18.00
Fruit Jar, Atlas Strong Shoulder Mason, Cornflower Blue, Metal Screw Lid, 1 Qt. 65.00
Fruit Jar, Ball Ideal, Bicentennial, Blue, 1/2 Pt. 24.00
Fruit Jar, Ball Ideal, Fisher Years, Square, 1986, 1 Qt. 35.00
Fruit Jar, Brockway Sur-Grip Square Mason, Band, 1/2 Gal. 15.00
Fruit Jar, Cohansey, Cover & Closure, 1 Pt. 65.00
Fruit Jar, Eagle, Aqua, Glass Lid, Iron Yoke, Applied Mouth, 1875-1885, 1 Qt. 120.00
Fruit Jar, Flaccus Bros. Steers Head, Milk Glass, Repro Screw Cap, 1 Pt. 175.00
Fruit Jar, Glenshaw G. Mason, Glenshaw Glass Lid, Band, 1 Qt. 9.00
Fruit Jar, Macomb Pottery Co., Stoneware, 1 Qt. 85.00
Fruit Jar, Mason's Patent Nov. 30th 1858, W C D, Aqua, Glass Cover, 1 Qt. 15.00
Fruit Jar, Mason's Patent Nov. 30th, 1858, Yellow Amber, Zinc Screw Lid, 1 Qt. 580.00

Fruit Jar, Petal, Blue Aqua, Applied Mouth, IP, 1855-1865, 1 Qt. 175.00
Fruit Jar, Protector, 1 Recessed Panel, Aqua, 1 Qt. 40.00
Fruit Jar, Triumph No. 1, Blue Aqua, Pressed Down Wax Seal Ring, 1 Qt. 715.00
Fruit Jar, Yeoman's, Aqua, Whittled, No Cork, 1/2 Gal. 54.00
Gemel, 2 Bands Of Applied Rigaree, Sheared Lips, Pontil, 9 1/4 In. 65.00
Gin, Case, Tappan Zee, Holland Gin, Fleischmann Co., Olive Green, Label, 10 1/8 In. ... 185.00
Ginger Beer, Clay, Gray Portobello 17.00
Ginger Beer, Crown, Cleveland, Ohio 35.00
Ginger Beer, Dr. J.A. Brown, Salt Glaze, Light Brown, Cobalt Slip, 6 7/8 In. 120.00
Ginger Beer, Ennis Bros., Utica, N.Y. 75.00
Ginger Beer, Freirs, Niagara Falls, N.Y. 75.00
Ginger Beer, John Halloran, Syracuse, N.Y. 65.00
Ginger Beer, Seneca Lake, N.Y. 40.00
Ginger Beer, Smiths Whiteroot F & D, Blue Gray, Cobalt, Stoneware, 1865, 9 7/8 In. 65.00
Grenadier, Fire Chief, 1973 .... 95.00
Grenadier, Horse, American, Thoroughbred, 1978 .... 60.00
Grenadier, Mr. Spock, Bust, 1979 .... 65.00
Grenadier, Santa Claus, Green Sack, 1978 .... 55.00
Grenadier, Soldier Mac Arthur, 1975 .... 35.00
Grenadier, Soldier, Continental Marines, 1969 .... 45.00
Grenadier, Soldier, Sergeant Major, Coldstream Guard, 1971 .... 45.00
Hoffman, Betsy Ross, 1974 .... 75.00
Hoffman, Lady Godiva, 1974 .... 45.00
Hoffman, Mrs. Lucky, 1974 .... 45.00
Hoffman, Rodeo, Steer Wrestler, 1978 .... 75.00
Household, Blacking, Olive Green, Oval, Rolled Lip, Pontil, 1835-1845, 4 3/4 In. 120.00
Ink, Carter's, Cathedral, Cobalt Blue, ABM Lip, Master, 9 3/4 In. 120.00
Ink, Harrison's Columbian, 8 Sides, Blue Green, Rolled Lip, Pontil, 1 7/8 In. 635.00
Ink, Jug, Keystone Jet Black Ink, Little Brown Jug, Pottery, Label, 2 3/4 In. 145.00
Ink, Pitkin Type, Broken Rib, Swirled Left, Olive Green, Tooled Disc, Pontil, 2 In. 690.00
Ink, Teakettle, 4 Sides, Cobalt Blue, Beveled Corners, Sheared Lip, 1 5/8 In. 360.00
Ink, Teakettle, Milk Glass, Embossed Flowers & Leaves, Silver Neck Ring, 2 1/2 In. 305.00
Ink, Umbrella, 8 Sides, Blue Aqua, Rolled Lip, Pontil, 3 1/8 In. 120.00
Ink, Water's, Troy, N.Y., Umbrella, 6 Sides, Aqua, Rolled Lip, OP, 2 7/8 In. 660.00
Jar, Battery, Pettingell Andrews Co., Aqua, Lead Core, Partial Label, 1900, 6 3/8 In. 185.00
Jar, Burma Shave 30.00
Jar, Food, G.A. Monogram, Barrel, Green, Wide Mouth, Folded Lip, Pontil, 8 3/4 In. 230.00
Jar, Tom's Roasted Peanut 15.00
Jar, Utility, Olive Green, Wide Mouth, Sheared & Tooled Lip, Pontil, 1780-1820, 12 In. .. 175.00
Jar, Utility, Pale Apple Green, Wide Mouth, Sheared & Tooled Lip, Pontil, 13 1/8 In. 165.00
Jug, O'Donnel's Old Irish Whisky, Belfast, Cream, Brown, Black Transfer, 7 5/8 In. 260.00
Jug, Paducah Club Kentucky Finest Whiskey, Pottery, Dark Blue, Beige, 3 1/4 In. 125.00
Jug, Whiskey, Finest Old Hollands Rotterdam, Canal Scene, Cream, Brown, 10 3/8 In. ... 385.00
Lewis & Clark, Charbonneau, 1973 .... 60.00
Lewis & Clark, Sacajawea, 1972 .... 75.00
Lewis & Clark, William Clark, 1971 .... 45.00
Lewis & Clark, York 125.00
Lionstone, Shoot Out OK Coral, 1971, Miniature 400.00
McCormick, Abe Lincoln, 1976 .... 75.00
McCormick, Centurion 55.00
McCormick, Charles Lindbergh, 1977, 1978 .... 125.00
McCormick, Christmas House, 1984 .... 75.00
McCormick, Daniel Boone, 1975 .... 35.00
McCormick, Elvis, Aloha, 1981 .... 350.00
McCormick, Elvis, Teddy Bear 700.00
McCormick, George Washington, 1975 .... 35.00
McCormick, Jesse James, 1973 .... 45.00
McCormick, Kit Carson, 1975 .... 35.00
McCormick, Louis Armstrong 125.00
McCormick, Michigan State Spartans 45.00
McCormick, Packard, Model 1937, Cream, 1980 .... 55.00
McCormick, Paul Bunyan, 1979 .... 55.00
McCormick, Pony Express, 1978 .... 55.00

McCormick, Queen Guinevere, 1979 .... 35.00
McCormick, Robert E. Lee, 1976 .... 75.00
McCormick, Spirit Of 76, 1976 .... 125.00
McCormick, Thomas Edison, 1977 .... 35.00
McCormick, Thomas Jefferson, 1975 .... 35.00
Medicine, Acid Nitric, Clear, Glass Stopper, 8 In. 20.00
Medicine, Alvas Brazilian Specific Company, Cactus Shape, Box, Pat'd 1890, 10 In. 110.00
Medicine, C. Heimstreet & Co., Troy, N.Y., 8 Sides, Sapphire Blue, Pontil, 7 1/8 In. 305.00
Medicine, Derwent Cough Balsam, Aqua, 5 In. 5.00
Medicine, Dr. Daniels Veterinary Colic Cure, 3 1/2 In. 4.00
Medicine, Dr. Jayne's Expectorant, Blue & Aqua 10.00
Medicine, Dr. S. Arnold's Balsam, 8 Sides, Pale Aqua, Flared Lip, Pontil, 2 3/8 In. 175.00
Medicine, Noxoff Corn Remedy, Foe To Corns, Amber, 4 In. 1.50
Medicine, Owl Drug Co., Owl On Mortar & Pestle, W.T. & Co., Cobalt Blue, 9 5/8 In. ... 255.00
Medicine, Peck Frisbie & Co., Great Magical Etherial Balm, New York, Blue, 5 1/2 In. .. 90.00
Milk, Alaska Dairy Products Corp., Anchorage, Ak., Red & Green, Square, 1 Qt. 175.00
Milk, Anchorage Dairy, Anchorage, Ak., Orange, 1 Qt. 165.00
Milk, Ashenhurst Dairy, Viola, Illinois, Cream Separator, Embossed, Round, 1 Qt. 125.00
Milk, Blairs Dairy Farm, Blairs, Va., Embossed, 1 Pt. 30.00
Milk, Brookfield Dairy, Hellertown, Pa., Baby Face, Mothers Who Care, Round, 1/2 Pt. .. 45.00
Milk, Brookfield Dairy, Hellertown, Pa., Double Babyface, Embossed, Square, 1 Qt. 150.00
Milk, Bryson's Farm Fresh Grade A, Augusta, Ga., Jack Is Nimble, Red, Square, 1 Qt. 25.00
Milk, Clearview Farm, Alvan E. Lippincott, Swedesboro, N.Y., Orange, Round, 1 Qt. 35.00
Milk, Cloverdale Farms, Binghamton, N.Y., Cream Top, 1 Qt. 32.00
Milk, Cloverleaf Dairy, Everett, Wash., Green, Poem On Back, 1 Qt. 30.00
Milk, Collier Bros. Creamery, Martinville, Ind., Embossed, 1 Qt. 30.00
Milk, Crater Lake Dairy Products, Klamath Falls, Orange, Round, 1 Qt. 48.00
Milk, Creamer, Cranford Dairy, New Jersey, Fan, Girl Talking To Scotty Dog, 1930s 28.00
Milk, Creamer, N.L. Mohegan Dairies, New London, Conn. 22.00
Milk, Creamer, New London & Mohegan Dairies, Conn. 18.00
Milk, Emmadine Dairy, Toothache Cream Top, Orange, Square, 1 Qt. 175.00
Milk, Farmers Dairy, Martinsburg, W.Va., Cream Top, Embossed, 1 Qt. 40.00
Milk, Forest Dairy Co., Kansas City, Mo., Remember They Need The Best, 1 Qt. 30.00
Milk, George Benedick's Jersey & Guernsey Milk, Mobile, Ala., Embossed, 1 Pt. 25.00
Milk, Guida's & Seibert Dairy, New Britain, Conn., Maroon, 1 Qt. 18.00
Milk, Gyan Creamery, Huntington, W.Va., Round, 1 Qt. 30.00
Milk, Hana Ranch Dairy, Hana, Maui, T.H., Green, 1 Pt. ....., ... 100.00
Milk, Hana Ranch Dairy, Maui T.H., Green, Squat, 1 Qt. 150.00
Milk, Hershey Estates Dairy, Orange, Square, 1 Qt. 22.00
Milk, Highland Dairy Co., Rochester, N.Y., Cop The Cream, Round, 1 Qt. 175.00
Milk, Hough's Dairy, Harpers Ferry, W.Va., Round, 1 Qt. 75.00
Milk, Independent Creamery, Los Gatos, California, 1 Pt. 25.00
Milk, Kendig Dairy, Millersville, Pa., Green, Square, 1 Qt. 40.00
Milk, Landgren's Dairy, Inc., Kenosha, Wis., Cream Top, Maroon, 1 Qt. 35.00
Milk, Lyon Brook Dairy, Aerated, El Haynes Milk, Metal Cap, Closure, 1 Pt. 100.00
Milk, Milk Protector, Absolutely Pure Milk, Glass Lid, Metal Closure, 1 Pt. 330.00
Milk, Palace Bekry, Quality Cottage Cheese, Kirksville, Missouri, Red, 1 Qt. 34.00
Milk, Peninsula Dairy, Va., Toothache, Cream Top, Square, 1 Qt. 125.00
Milk, Roper Dairy Farm, Trussville, Ala., Embossed, 1 Pt. 22.00
Milk, Rosedale Dairy, Silver City, New Mexico, Red, 1 Pt. 20.00
Milk, Sanitary Dairy Co., Waynesburg, Pa., Orange, Squat, 1 Qt. 25.00
Milk, Scotia Pure Milk Co. Limited, Halifax, Tooled Mouth, Cap Seat, 1/2 Gal. 35.00
Milk, Skyline Farms Co., Grade A Dairy Products, Lincoln, Neb., Red, Round, 1 Qt. 20.00
Milk, Slosek's Farm, Cow's Head, Orange, 1 Qt. 15.00
Milk, Smith Dairy, Boardman, Oh., Red, 1 Qt. 20.00
Milk, Sunrise Dairy, Lewiston, Me., Red, 1 Qt. 20.00
Milk, Sunshine Dairy, Multi-Vitamin, Paducah, Ky., Woman, Children, Amber, 1 Qt. 16.00
Milk, Sunshine Farms Branch Of Sherman White & Co., Lafayette, Red, Round, 1 Qt. ... 32.00
Milk, W.C. Coleman's Dairy, Little Rock, Ariz., Embossed, SP, Round, 1 Qt. 20.00
Milk, Wallis Case Dairy, Poplar Bluff, Mo., Red, Round, 1 Qt. 22.00
Milk, Wauregan Dairy, Cream Top, Red & Black, Poem On Back, 1 Pt. 75.00
Milk, Wells & Lassiter, Jackson, Tenn., Stork & Baby Picture, Green, Round, 1 Qt. 26.00
Milk, White Oak Dairy, Covington, Va., Embossed, 1 Qt. 22.00

Mineral Water, Eureka Spring Co., Saratoga, N.Y., Emerald Green, Torpedo, 8 7/8 In. ...   910.00
Mineral Water, Highrock Congress Spring, Rock, C & W, Yellow Olive Green, 1 Pt. 255.00
Mineral Water, Massena Spring Water, Monogram In Frame, Bird, Teal Blue, 1 Qt. 165.00
Mineral Water, Missisquoi A Springs, Yellow Amber, Sloping Double Collar, 1 Qt. 175.00
Nursing, Acme, W.T. & Co., Turtle, Cork, 8 Oz. 35.00
Nursing, Alexandra, SFG Co., Standing Turtle, 1880-1890 ....   38.00
Nursing, Allenbury's Double Ends, Bulbous Center, Box, England 46.00
Nursing, Baby Bunting, Wide Mouth, Cylinder, 1930-1940, 8 Oz. 30.00
Nursing, Baby Nurser, Flask, M.B.W., 8 Oz. 35.00
Nursing, Baby's Delight, Turtle, Wooden Cap & Cork, 1890-1900, 8 Oz. 143.00
Nursing, Beck's Security Nursing, Canada, Round, 1927-1937 ....   16.00
Nursing, Betsy Brown Sterilizer, Round, Pat. July 6th, '97, 8 Oz. 110.00
Nursing, Betty Jane Nurser, It Tilts, Sterilizer, 1934-1944, 8 Oz. 35.00
Nursing, Bostonia, Flask, SP, 16 Tbsp On Reverse, 8 Oz. 44.00
Nursing, Brecht Feeder, Marisco Infant Feeders, Nipple, Box, 1950-1960, Miniature 255.00
Nursing, Burr's Patent, Patd Nov. 26th 1872, Corset, 1872-1880, 8 Oz. 185.00
Nursing, Cimples Hygienic Feeding, Embossed Dimples, 16 Tbsp., England, 8 Oz. 88.00
Nursing, Clean-Well Sanitary Sterilizer, LWT CO, Round, 12 Oz. 25.00
Nursing, Cleaneasy Sanitary Sterlizer, Whitall Tatum Company, 1895-1910, 12 Oz. 22.00
Nursing, Cleanfont Vented, Fox, Fultz & Webster, Patented Oct. 25, '92, Turtle, 8 Oz. ...   120.00
Nursing, Cow & Gate, Sterilizer, Round, Box, 8 Oz. 1320.00
Nursing, Dog, Embossed Picture, Sterilizer, Oval, 1930-1944, 8 Oz. 14.00
Nursing, Dominion Glass Nursery Rhyme, Sterilizer, Canada, 8 Oz. ....40.00 to 88.00
Nursing, Nursery Rhymes, Old Mother Hubbard 35.00
Nursing, Stoneware, Mottled, Running Glaze, Brown, Green Amber, 6 In. 11.00
Oil, Dr. Sawen's Celebrated Oil Liniment, Watertown, N.Y., Blue, Rectangular, 6 1/4 In. . .   30.00
Oil, Gargling Oil, Lockport, N.Y., Yellow Green, 5 1/4 In. 30.00
Pepper Sauce, Cathedral, Light To Medium Green, 6 Sides, Double Collar, 10 1/2 In. ...   690.00
Perfume bottles are listed in their own category.
Pickle, Arrow Brand Pickles, J.J. Wilson, Chicago, Amber, Label, Indian, 8 5/8 In. 145.00
Pickle, Cathedral, 13 In. 450.00
Pickle, Cathedral, Aqua, 11 In. 450.00
Pickle, Cathedral, Blue Green, Applied Mouth, 1855-1865, 13 3/4 In. 935.00
Pickle, Cathedral, Green, 6 Sides, Applied Mouth, IP, 13 1/4 In. 1265.00
Pickle, R. & F. Atmore, Cathedral, Blue Aqua, Rolled Lip, IP, 11 1/2 In. 440.00
Pickle, Shaker Pickles, Aqua, Label, 6 7/8 In. 412.00
Poison, Carlton H. Lee, Boston, Skull Shape, Cobalt, Pat. June 26, 1894, 4 1/2 In. 935.00 to 1870.00
Poison, Lattice & Diamond, Cobalt Blue, Tooled Lip, Poison Stopper, 3 3/4 In. 145.00
Poison, Lattice & Diamond, Deep Cobalt Blue, Tooled Lip, 11 1/4 In. 405.00
Poison, Owl Drug Co., Owl On Mortar & Pestle, Cobalt Blue, Tooled Lip, 4 7/8 In. 90.00
Poison, Wyeth, Amber, ABM Lip, Labels, 2 1/4 In. 220.00
Sarsaparilla, Dr. Townsend's, Albany, N.Y., Emerald Green, IP, 9 5/8 In. 360.00
Sarsaparilla, John Bull Extract, Aqua, OP, 6 1/2 In. 230.00
Sarsaparilla, Log Cabin, Rochester, N.Y., Pat. Sept. 6 '87, Amber, 9 In. 105.00
Scent, 18 Vertical Ribs, Apple Green, Pinched Waist, Twisted Neck, Pontil, 3 In. 105.00
Scent, Grape Amethyst, Rigaree On Sides, Sheared Lip, Pontil, 1820-1850, 3 5/8 In. 690.00
Scent, Teal Green, Ground Lip, Pewter Screw Cap, 1850-1870, 3 1/8 In. 75.00
Seal, Geo. Willmott Axminster, Olive Amber, Sloping Double Collar, Pontil, 10 In. 360.00
Seal, GR, 1801, Olive Amber, Applied String Lip, Pontil, England, 8 3/4 In. 965.00
Seal, W.S., Deep Olive Amber, Applied Mouth, Pontil, England, 11 1/4 In. 230.00
Seltzer, Cooper Beverage, Pittsfield, Mass., Blue, Fluted 145.00
Seltzer, Mineral, New York, Aqua 30.00
Ski Country, Animal, Fox, 1 On A Log, 1981, 1.75 Liter 150.00
Ski Country, Animal, Koala Bear, 1973 ....   25.00
Ski Country, Bird, Peacock, 1973 ....   75.00
Ski Country, Bird, Peregrine Falcon, 1979, 1 Gal. 300.00
Ski Country, Eagle On The Water 135.00
Ski Country, Indian, Kachina Talavia 60.00
Ski Country, Indian, Rainbow Dancer 65.00
Snuff, 8 Hardstone Medallions, Red, 3 In. 258.00
Snuff, 14 Sides, Buddhist Symbols, Coral Stopper, 1 3/4 In. 2530.00
Snuff, Agate, Flask, Landscape, Calligraphy, Dragon Handles, Stopper, 1 3/4 In. ....*Illus*   1595.00
Snuff, Allover Prunus Design, Off-White Ground, Metal Stopper, 2 1/4 In. 115.00

Bottle, Snuff, Agate, Flask,
Landscape, Calligraphy, Dragon
Handles, Stopper, 1 3/4 In.

Bottle, Snuff, Horn, Thumbprint,
Mother-Of-Pearl Bottom, H.I.
Scratched On Bottom, 2 In.

Bottle, Snuff, Jade,
Pink Tourmaline Stopper,
2 1/4 In.

Snuff, Amethyst, Plum Blossoms, Branches, Amethyst Stopper, 19th Century, 2 In. 400.00
Snuff, Blue Overlay Of Figures & Trees, 3 In. 115.00
Snuff, Blue, 3 In. 105.00
Snuff, Carved Butterflies, Vines & Squirrel, Fruit Shape, Coral Stopper, 2 3/8 In. 715.00
Snuff, Carved Fishnet & Carp, Flattened Sides, Jade, China, 2 1/2 In. 85.00
Snuff, Chalcedony, Carved Floral Design, 2 1/4 In. 46.00
Snuff, Coconut Shell, Pilgrim Flask Shape, Horse Design, Hornbill Stopper, 2 1/4 In. 385.00
Snuff, Copper, Raised Dragon Medallions, 3 1/4 In. 100.00
Snuff, Double Interior Painted, Mountain Landscapes, Rose Quartz Stopper, 2 1/8 In. 247.00
Snuff, Figural Design, Rectangular Shape, China, 2 1/2 In. 50.00
Snuff, Glass, Fisherman, River Scene On 1 Side, Goldfish On Other Side, Chou Lo Yuan .   230.00
Snuff, Horn, Thumbprint, Mother-Of-Pearl Bottom, H.I. Scratched On Bottom, 2 In. *Illus*   22.50
Snuff, Ivory, Apple Shape, Branch Behind Stem Lifts, 2 In. 330.00
Snuff, Ivory, Maiden, Holding Peony & Fan, 4 In. 92.00
Snuff, Ivory, Squirrel Lying On Bunch Of Grapes, 2 3/4 In. 247.00
Snuff, Ivory, Youth Holding Lotus Leaf, Cap Shape Stopper, 3 1/4 In. 302.00
Snuff, Jade, 20-Character Inscription, Children, Playing, Pale Green, Yellow, 2 1/4 In. 345.00
Snuff, Jade, Birds In Flowering Trees, 1 1/2 In. 460.00
Snuff, Jade, Pebble Shape, Off White, Yellow, Brown, Peking Green Glass Top 285.00
Snuff, Jade, Pink Tourmaline Stopper, 2 1/4 In. . . . .*Illus*   3630.00
Snuff, Jade, White, Rabbit Shape, 2 3/4 In. 247.00
Snuff, Jade, White, Wave Design, Lapis Lazuli Stopper, 2 3/8 In. 1430.00
Snuff, Lapis Lazuli, Veins, Gold, White, Woman, Wearing Flowing Dress, Domed Stopper   460.00
Snuff, Macaroni Agate, 2 1/2 In. 103.00
Snuff, Mask, Mock Ring Handles, Spade Shape, Moss Agate Stopper, 2 In. 187.00
Snuff, Milk Glass, Woman In Garden, Dragonfly & Flowers On Reverse, 2 5/8 In. 247.00
Snuff, Multicolor Overlay, Yangzhou, 2 1/2 In. 103.00
Snuff, Nephrite Jade, Pebble Shape, Black & Gray Stopper, 3 3/4 In. 230.00
Snuff, Olive Amber, Sheared Flared Lip, Square, Pontil, 1825-1840, 4 1/4 In. 55.00
Snuff, Oriental Scene, Stopper, Marked, 2 3/4 In. 150.00
Snuff, Pine & Figures, Amber, 3 In. 103.00
Snuff, Porcelain, Celadon, Floral Carving, Pilgrim Flask Shape, Stone Stopper, 2 5/8 In. . .   55.00
Snuff, Porcelain, Figural Design, 2 3/4 In. 69.00
Snuff, Porcelain, Zodiac Figural Design, 3 1/2 In. 46.00
Snuff, Raised Floral & Landscape Panel, Demon Mask Handle, Pagtung, 2 1/8 In. 80.00
Snuff, Rose Quartz, Spade Shape, Pale Pink, Birds, Trees, Flowering Plants, 2 3/4 In. 400.00
Snuff, Tea Crystal, Chih Lung Dragon & Pagodas, 1 7/8 In. 137.00
Snuff, White Glass, Green Glaze, Pea Pod Shape, 3 In., 5 Piece 230.00
Snuff, Yellow Olive Amber, Sheared Flared Lip, Square, Pontil, 1790-1810, 5 In. 85.00
Soaky, Auggie Doggie 55.00
Soaky, Barney, Flintstones Fun Bath, Vinyl, Box, 1977, 2 1/2 x 8 In. 22.00
Soaky, Bozo The Clown 40.00
Soaky, Casper 35.00

Soaky, Frankenstein, 1960s ....40.00 to 65.00
Soaky, Huckleberry Hound 20.00
Soaky, Mr. Magoo, In Old-Fashioned Bathing Suit, 1960s, 10 In.................. 35.00
Soaky, Porky Pig 35.00
Soaky, Tennessee Tuxedo 40.00
Soaky, Tweety Bird 20.00
Soaky, Wolfman 80.00
Soda, Biedenharn Candy Company, Green, Hutchinson, 1900 .... 63.00
Soda, Big Chief Bottle Works, Green, Czechoslovakia, 11 In. 66.00
Soda, Donald Duck, Picture, 1951 .... 15.00
Soda, Dr Pepper, Green, With Bottle Topper Display, 1940s, 6 x 8 In. 1725.00
Soda, E.C. Eichelberg, York, Pa., Dark Amber, White Letters, Small 1210.00
Soda, Empire Soda Works, Vallejo, Eagle, Blue Green, Applied Mouth, 7 3/8 In. 110.00
Soda, EverVess, 12 Oz. 150.00
Soda, G. Upp, Jr., Aqua 200.00
Soda, Geo. Upp, Jr., York, Pa., Aqua, Tenpin 320.00
Soda, Geo. Upp, Jr., York, Pa., Cobalt Blue, Tenpin 550.00
Soda, J & B Jeuslury & Brown, Star Of David, Blue, 1880s 33.00
Soda, J. Seedorff, Charleston, S.C., Blue Green, Applied Blob Mouth, 7 In. 330.00
Soda, Kensington Glassworks, Emerald Green, Sloping Double Collar, IP, 7 1/4 In. 185.00
Soda, Lamb Bottling Works, Green, Orange Crush Dispenser, Austria, 11 In........... 55.00
Soda, Liggett's Cherriade Syrup, Backbar, Chrome Over Metal, 1920s 165.00
Soda, Orange Crush, Embossed, 1920 .... 35.00
Soda, Perko, Elyria, Ohio, Green, Jockey, Horse, Yellow, Red Painted Logo, 6 1/2 Oz. ... 85.00
Soda, Rocky Mountain Beverage Co., Czechoslovakia, 12 In. 16.00
Soda, Whippers Beverage, Green Glass, Painted Logo Of Wrestler, Toronto, 7 Oz. 350.00
Soda, William H. Baxter, Haslingden, Bird, Blue, Cod Stopper 44.00
Target Ball, Bogardus Glass Ball Patd. April 10 1877, Olive Green, 2 5/8 In. 1265.00
Target Ball, Bogardus, Blue 1400.00
Target Ball, C. Newman, Yellow Olive 3410.00
Target Ball, Hobnail Design Both Sides, Ribbing Along Mold Seams, Yellow Amber 1300.00
Target Ball, Liddle & Keating 7700.00
Target Ball, Man Shooting, Overall Diamond Design, Moss Green, 2 5/8 In. 635.00
Target Ball, N.B. Glass Works Perth, Blue Aqua, Diamond Design, England, 2 5/8 In. ... 95.00
Target Ball, W.W. Greener, Pink Amethyst, Diamond Pattern 450.00
Tonic, Abbot Spanish Wine, Baltimore, 10 1/2 In. 45.00
Tonic, Alexander's Sure Cure For Malaria, Elyria, Ohio, Amber, 7 3/4 In. 60.00
Tonic, Baldwin's Celery, Pepsin & Dandelion, Amber, 8 In. 75.00
Tonic, Dr. Mauro's Herb, Amber, 9 1/2 In. 40.00
Vinegar, H.H. Bailey, Pure Cider Vinegar, Jug, Brown Scratch, Miniature 295.00
Whiskey, Carhart & Brother, N.Y., Chestnut, Puce, Applied Mouth, Handle, Seal, 9 In. 1705.00
Whiskey, Casper's, Made By Honest North Carolina People, Cobalt Blue, 12 3/8 In. 525.00
Whiskey, Cream Of Irish Whiskey Shamrock, Stoneware, 1 Qt. 90.00
Whiskey, Duffy's Formula, Amber, Applied Mouth, Label, Contents, 9 7/8 In. 240.00
Whiskey, George Dickel, Commemorative, Amber, Curved Neck, Leather Handle, 14 In. . 30.00
Whiskey, Gray Beard Heather Dew Whiskey, Jug, Stoneware, 4 3/4 In. 140.00
Whiskey, Green River, Whiskey Without A Headache, Embossed, Label, Box, 8 1/2 In. ... 110.00
Whiskey, Griffith Hyatt & Co., Baltimore, Tobacco Amber, Applied Handle, Pontil, 7 In. . 525.00
Whiskey, Happy Days Famous Old Rye Whiskey, Stoneware, Jug, 1 Qt. 110.00
Whiskey, Overholt Pure Rye Blended, Flask, Aqua, 1/2 Pt. 45.00
Whiskey, S.T. Suit, Suitland, Mo., Little Brown Jug, Made 1869, Stencil, 7 In. 260.00
Whiskey, William Foust Rye, Glen Rock, Pa., Dark Amber 175.00
Wild Turkey, Series 1, No. 2, On Log, Female, 1972 .... 70.00
Wild Turkey, Series 1, No. 3, On The Wing, 1982 .... 40.00
Wild Turkey, Series 1, No. 5, With Flags, 1975 .... 30.00
Wild Turkey, Series 1, No. 7, Taking Off, 1977 .... 30.00
Wild Turkey, Series 2, No. 1, Lore, 1979 .... 45.00
Wild Turkey, Series 3, No. 3, Turkeys Fighting, 1983 .... 75.00
Wine, Black Glass, Olive Amber, Sloping Double Collar, Pontil, England, 11 5/8 In. 165.00
Wine, Black Glass, Sheared Top, Applied String Ring, Pontil, 1830-1850, 9 1/2 In. 30.00
Wine, Black Glass, Wide Mushroom Mouth, Magnum, Pontil, 13 3/8 In.............. 385.00
Wine, Duroy Blackberry Wine, Duroy & Haines Co., Stoneware, Jug, 1 Pt. 80.00
Zanesville, 24 Ribs Broken Swirl, Aqua, Club, 8 3/4 In......................... 137.00

BOTTLE CAP collectors search for the printed cardboard caps used during the past 80 years. Unusual mottoes, graphics, and caps from dairies that are out of business bring the highest prices.

Cherry, Grape & Grapefruit, Lined, 1950s, 4 Piece	3.00
Cork Lined, Soda Pop, 50 Piece	10.00
Donald Duck Cola, 1950	5.00
Lenny Lemonade, Cork	20.00
Mason, Zinc, 12 Piece	14.00

BOTTLE OPENERS are needed to open many bottles. As soon as the commercial bottle was invented, the opener to be used with the new types of closures became a necessity. Many types of bottle openers can be found, most dating from the twentieth century. Collectors prize advertising and comic openers.

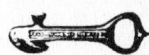

Amish Boy, Cast Iron	250.00 to 300.00
Baseball Cap, Cast Iron	40.00
Black Man's Face, Large Mouth, Cast Iron, 1950s, 4 In.	125.00
Black Man's Face, Winking, Cast Iron, 1950s	145.00
Calypso Guitar Player, Magnet, Japan, 6 In.	43.00
Chevrolet Logo, Dealer's Name, 1957, 4 1/2 In.	16.00
Donkey, Brass	40.00
Donkey, Cast Iron	40.00
Drunk, On Ashtray, Cast Iron	35.00
Elephant, Cast Iron	140.00
Frenchman, Cast Iron	45.00
Fresh Up With 7-Up, Die Cast Metal, 1960, 1 1/2 x 3 1/2 In.	14.00
Frog, Brass, Mounts On Wall, 3 In.	38.00
Horse, Hind Quarters, Cast Iron, 5 1/2 In.	55.00
Laughing Man's Head, Brass, 4 1/4 x 3 3/4 In.	95.00
Man's Face, Double Eyes, Cast Iron, 1940s, 3 3/4 x 3 1/2 In.	125.00
Pabst Blue Ribbon, 1950s	22.00
Pelican, Cast Iron	80.00
Skull, Cast Iron	1100.00

BOW is an English porcelain works started in 1744 in East London. Bow made decorated porcelains, often copies of Chinese blue and white patterns. The factory stopped working about 1776. Most items sold as Bow today were made after 1750.

Figurine, Lion, Recumbent On Yellow Washed Base, Head Turned Back, Brown, 4 In.	6325.00
Figurine, Pug Dog, Reclining On Tasseled Cushion, White, 1755, 5 1/2 In., Pair	3565.00
Figurine, Shepherdess Wearing Black Scarf, Puce Bodice, Standing Beside Lamb, 10 In.	690.00
Group, Allegorical Figure Of Liberty & Matrimony, Gallant Holding Basket, 1760, 8 In.	4890.00

BOXES of all kinds are collected. They were made of thin strips of inlaid wood, metal, tortoiseshell, embroidery, or other material. Additional boxes may be listed in other sections, such as Advertising, Battersea, Ivory, Shaker, Tinware, and various Porcelain categories. Tea Caddies are listed in their own category.

2 Tiers, Bobby R. Falwell, Zebrawood, Oval, 11 1/2 x 14 1/2 x 5 1/2 In.	920.00
2-Tone Orange Paint, Wire Bale, Wooden Handle, Round, 11 1/2 In.	465.00
Amber, Patch, Gold Bands, Yellow Scrolls, Enameled Flowers, 2 1/2 In.	135.00
Ammunition, U.M.C., Laflin & Rand Black Powder, 12 Gauge, 2 Piece	62.00
Baleen, 5-Finger, I.B. Initialed On Side, 3 3/4 x 5 1/2 x 7 In.	440.00
Band, Wallpaper Covered, Cardboard, Signed Joel Post	3300.00
Band, Wallpaper Covered, Floral Design, Blue Ground, Pine, 8 3/4 x 13 3/4 In.	220.00
Band, Wallpaper Covered, Geometric Floral Design, Black, White, Red, 9 1/2 x 15 In.	385.00
Band, Wallpaper Covered, Pine, Floral Design, 17 In.	440.00
Band, Wallpaper Covered, Red & Green Floral, Lined With 1845 Newspaper, 10 1/2 In.	395.00
Band, Wallpaper Covered, Round, Miniature	605.00
Beech, Blue Paint, White Striping, Floral, 5 1/2 In.	550.00
Bentwood, Ash, Poplar, Floral, White, Red, Black, Natural Ground, 14 In.	2090.00
Bentwood, Brown Repaint, Hersey Finger Type Construction, Copper Tacks, 6 1/2 In.	300.00

Bentwood, Cover, Swivel Handle, 11 x 8 1/4 In. 135.00
Bentwood, Finger Construction, Steel Tacks, Green Paint, Round, 5 1/8 In. 385.00
Bentwood, Green, Oval, 6 1/2 In. 300.00
Bentwood, J. Piper & Son, Variety Store, Augusta, Me., Round, 8 1/2 In. 220.00
Bentwood, Lapped Joint Sewn With Rawhide Thong, Dated 1832, 8 In. 1500.00
Bentwood, Spring Fastened Lid, Textured Paint, Oval, 10 1/2 In. 330.00
Bentwood, Stenciled & Freehand Foliage, Egg Shape, 8 In. 175.00
Bible, Dovetailed, Cotter Pin Hinged Lid, Walnut, 7 x 19 In. 1025.00
Bible, Floral & Figural Panels, Key, Flemish, 18th Century, 25 x 10 x 15 In. 1650.00
Bible, Foliate Carving Throughout, Dated, 1695, 12 x 24 3/4 In. 172.00
Bible, Hinged Slant Top, Cutout Feet, White Pine, 21 x 19 x 26 In. 425.00
Bible, Oak, On Stand, Relief Carved Front Panel, Strap Hinges On Lid, 25 1/2 x 26 In. 1320.00
Bible, Slide Cover, Breadboard, Wooden, Wallpaper Remnants, 12 x 9 3/4 x 3 In. 145.00
Black Japanned, Gilt, Cover, Continental, 5 1/2 x 9 In. 1090.00
Black Stenciled Eagle & Arrow, Lapped Seams, Green Paint, Cover, Round, 6 In. 275.00
Blanket, 6-Board, Turned Wood & Caster Feet, Dovetailed, 19 1/4 x 38 x 15 1/2 In. 230.00
Blanket, Applied Molded Lift Top, Dovetailed, Salmon Paint, 4 Feet, Penna., 22 x 36 In. . 230.00
Blue Paint, Lapped Seams, Cover, Round, 7 1/4 In. 605.00
Book Safe, Leatherbound, Hidden Drawer, Marbleized Paper 350.00
Book Shape, American Emblem On Cover, 6 American Flags, Wooden, 12 1/4 In. 690.00
Book Shape, Chippendale, Mahogany, Mariner's Society, R. Morwan, 1820, 20 x 14 In. .. 1155.00
Book Shape, Sliding Panels Conceal Key, 3 Compartments, Mahogany, 19th Century 375.00
Book Shape, Washington Portrait On Hinged Lid, 19th Century, 4 1/4 x 3 1/2 In. 110.00
Bottle Shape, Grained, Brass Bound, Inlaid Initials A.B. On Lid, Mahogany, 8 In. 195.00
Brass, Inset Miniature On Ivory, Man & Woman, 6 Sides, Signed, 3 3/8 In. 110.00
Brass, Panel Cover, Boar Fleeing Picture, 3 x 8 1/2 x 5 In. 230.00
Brass, Tiger-Eye Quartz Plaque Inset On Hinged Lid, Floral Bands, 5 7/8 x 4 3/8 In. 260.00
Brass Bail Handles At Sides & Top, Mahogany, 9 1/2 x 15 x 11 In. 110.00
Bride's, Bowl Of Fruit On Cover, Blue, Polychrome Flowers & Fruit, Pine, 18 1/2 In. ... 880.00
Bride's, Cover, Floral Design, Brown Ground, Pine, 10 1/4 x 16 3/4 In. 495.00
Bride's, Cover, Youth, Pushing Girl On A Swing, Blue Ground, Pine, 12 x 18 3/4 In. 2035.00
Bride's, Floral Painted Sides, Verse On Top, Pine, 9 x 19 In. 1870.00
Bride's, Geometric Designs, Carved, Revolving Lid, Wooden, Oval, 12 3/4 x 7 x 6 In. ... 230.00
Bride's, Hand Planed Shell, Fastened With Wood Splints, Pegs, Nails, Oval, 20 In. 575.00
Brown Graining, Sliding Lid, Pine, 9 1/4 In. 40.00
Brown Patina, White Ground, Dovetailed, Pine, 16 In. 192.00
Burl, Molded Edge Base & Lid, Dovetailed, Till, Brass Batwing Escutcheon, 14 In. 1705.00
Cake, Cover, Stylized Flowers, Leafage, Yellow Ground, Pa., Late 19th Century, 6 In. ... 2070.00
Candle, Dovetailed, Lock, Wrought Nails, Oak & Pine, 18th Century, 10 1/2 x 6 x 4 In. .. 445.00
Candle, Dovetailed, Sliding Cover, Walnut Finish, 14 x 5 1/2 x 2 1/2 In. 345.00
Candle, Hanging, Poplar, Dark Finish, Shelf, Peaked Crest, 12 x 6 x 17 In. 195.00
Candle, Natural, Molded Edge Sliding Lid, Poplar, 9 1/2 x 13 x 3 7/8 In. 80.00
Candle, Red Paint, Pine, 12 In. 220.00
Candle, Red Paint, Sliding Lid, 6 1/2 x 7 x 14 1/2 In. 330.00
Candle, Sliding Lid, Dovetailed, Cherry, Ebony Inlay, 11 In. 245.00
Candle, Wall, Double, Repaint Over Green, Pine, 14 1/4 x 7 1/4 x 23 1/2 In. 495.00
Candle, Wall, Dovetailed, Pine, Shaped Top & Crest, 12 x 5 1/2 x 8 3/4 In. 415.00
Candle, Wall, Dovetailed, Poplar, Maple Drawer, 12 x 9 x 12 1/2 In. 160.00
Candle, Wall, Nailed Drawer, Lift Lid, Crest, Walnut, 14 3/4 x 7 x 10 7/8 In. 355.00
Candle, Wall, Scalloped Crest, Slant Top, Staple Hinges, Poplar, 10 x 4 x 4 In. 198.00
Candle, Wall, Square Nail Construction, Curly Maple, 14 1/2 In. 230.00
Candle, Wall, Tin, Worn Japanning, 10 1/4 In. 115.00
Carved Designs On Scalloped Sides, Curly Maple, Poplar Bottom, 13 1/4 In. 1155.00
Carved Paterae Sides, Flower Heads On Lid, Scrolls, Walnut, Spain, 10 1/4 In. 1495.00
Cheroot, Varicolored Gold, Emblems Of Love, Foliage, Diamond, Mexico, 2 1/2 In. 3450.00
Chip Carved, Wall, 2 Sections, Initials RM, 7 1/2 x 9 1/2 In. 165.00
Cigarette, 24K Gold Inside, Platinum Medallion, Colonial Couple, Le Mieux, 5 x 4 In. .. 225.00
Cigarette, Marquetry Inlay, Cantilevered Interior 75.00
Cigarette, Transfer Printed Metal & Mahogany, Fornasetti, 2 x 7 3/8 In. 300.00
Coffer, Chip Carved, Hinged Lid, Scrubbed Finish, Hardwood, 12 3/4 x 9 x 10 1/2 In. ... 440.00
Compartments, Brass Carrying Handle, Mahogany, Early 19th Century, 9 3/4 In. 238.00
Compartments, Marbleized Paper Lining, Mid-18th Century, 17 1/2 In. 225.00

Copper Nail Design, Cherry, Brass, 18 1/2 x 13 x 9 1/4 In. 240.00
Cutlery, Covers, Dovetailed, Cutout Handle, Walnut 550.00
Cutlery, Open, Cutout, Dovetailed, Walnut 385.00
Cutlery, Serpentine, Hinged Lid, George III, Oval Medallion, Mahogany, 14 In., Pair 2645.00
Desk, Ebonized & Brass Inlay, Rosewood, c.1870, 2 1/4 x 8 In. 110.00
Desk, Florentine Carved, Chassis Shape, White & Gold, 1910, 11 1/2 x 7 1/4 In. 95.00
Desk, Oak, Relief Carved Flowers, Birds, 3 Inner Drawers, 25 x 16 In. 330.00
Desk, Pine, Gray Paint, 24 x 17 x 14 In. 165.00
Document, George Washington Medallion, Flowers, Gilt Shield, Mahogany, 9 x 13 In. 880.00
Document, Grain Painted, Flame Design, Pine, 6 1/4 x 18 x 16 In. 485.00
Document, Hinged Lid, Ivory, Bone Inlay, Diamond Border, Black, Red, Mahogany 2587.00
Document, Leather Covered Over Pine, Paper Lined, Bail Handle, 18th Century, 14 In. .. 476.00
Document, Leather Covered, Brass Studded, Washington Bank, Boston, 3 1/2 x 8 In. 242.00
Document, Leather Covered, Stenciled Dan'l Day, 5 3/4 x 12 In. 220.00
Document, Red, Yellow, White, Flowers, Black, I.C.H., Hinges, Clasp, 3 x 9 x 7 In. 6325.00
Dome Top, Adam & Eve In Garden Of Eden, Gate, Red Heart On Lid, 13 x 30 x 15 In. .. 1093.00
Dome Top, Black & Red Paint, 13 In. 1540.00
Dome Top, Brown Flame Graining, Dovetailed, Pine, 17 x 46 x 13 1/2 In. 355.00
Dome Top, Brown Vinegar Grained, White Ground, Pine, Poplar, 26 1/2 In. 445.00
Dome Top, Chinese Figures In Landscape, Green Japanned, Continental, 4 1/2 In. 1380.00
Dome Top, Chinoiseries, Foliage, Black, White, Regency, 1825, 5 x 7 3/4 In. 545.00
Dome Top, Dovetailed, Smoky Graining, Olive Ground, Pine, Wrought Iron Lock, 30 In. . 95.00
Dome Top, Floral Blue, White, Orange Design, Brown Ground, Pine, 6 In. 80.00
Dome Top, Floral, Bird, Red, White, Original Brown Paint, Hinged Lid, Pine, 10 In. 1980.00
Dome Top, Floral, Original Blue Paint, Black, White Strip, Hinged Lid, Blue, Pine, 8 In. . 605.00
Dome Top, Gray Green Paint, Dovetailed, Poplar, Sheet Metal Hasp, 17 x 17 x 14 In. 165.00
Dome Top, Old Red Paint, Pine, 21 3/4 In. 165.00
Dome Top, Original Blue Paint, Floral, White Stripe, Red, Yellow, Beech, 8 5/8 In. 1210.00
Dome Top, Original Brown Graining, Yellow, Poplar, 13 x 7 x 8 In. 1815.00
Dome Top, Polychrome Flowers, Design On Interior Of Lid, Inscription, 8 3/4 In. 192.00
Dome Top, Red Paint, Black Graining, Poplar, Wrought Iron Lock, 29 x 14 x 13 In. 275.00
Dome Top, Red Smoke Rings On Black Ground, 1825 Boston Newspaper Lined, 12 In. .. 750.00
Dome Top, Vaulted Lid, Painted Swags & Tassels, Blue & Black, Pine, 12 x 30 x 17 In. .. 3737.00
Dome Top, Worn Red Paint, Wrought Iron Lock & Hasp, Pine, 30 1/2 In. 190.00
Dome Top, Yellow Stripe Flowers, Red, White, Green, Hinged Lid, Pine, 9 3/8 In. 7700.00
Dresser, Sheraton, D-Front, Paneled Ends, Turned Feet, Cherry, Mahogany Veneer 935.00
Dresser, Victorian, Allover Gilt Floral, Pine, c.1840, 6 x 11 1/4 In. 330.00
Dresser, Woman's, Lacquer, Mother-Of-Pearl, 4 Perfume Bottles, 4 1/2 x 9 x 6 In. 300.00
Flowers & Ice Skater Scene, Bentwood, Pine, 17 In. 1073.00
Game, Black & Red Lacquer, Gilt Design, Chinese Export, 8 Trays, 1860s, 15 In. 862.00
Gilded Battle Scenes, Pewter Lined, Engraved Inner Lid, Lacquer, Oriental, 9 1/2 In. 275.00
Glove, 5 Long Drawers, Square Marble Top, Mahogany, 14 1/2 In. 865.00
Gray Paint, Lapped Seams, Cover, Round, 6 1/2 In. 275.00
Gray Paint, Lapped Seams, Cover, Round, 8 1/2 In. 275.00
Green Paint, Brass Handle, Poplar, 16 In. 70.00
Humidor, Mahogany, Old Finish, Metal Lined, 7 1/4 x 10 1/2 x 4 1/2 In. 95.00
Illuminating, Hinged, Rectangular, Silver Metal Disc, Black, Art Deco, 12 In. 4830.00
Inlaid, Straight Bracket Feet, Dovetailed, Mahogany, 6 1/2 x 12 x 6 1/2 In. 440.00
Jewelry, Black Forest, Carved, Silk Interior, c.1880 .... 695.00
Jewelry, Carved Ivory, Coral & Jade Design, Wooden, Mirror, China, 7 x 11 3/4 In. 45.00
Jewelry, Covered Jar Shape, Oriental 210.00
Jewelry, Fall Front, 7 Interior Drawers, Tortoiseshell & Ivory Veneer, Dutch, 10 1/4 In. 4370.00
Jewelry, Gilt Bronze, 18th Century Man Portrait, Continental, 19th Century, 3 x 6 In. 1610.00
Jewelry, Hardshell Case, Blue Opalescent Carving, Buxton, Box, 1960s, 15 x 8 x 5 In. ... 35.00
Jewelry, Inlaid Geometric Design, Domed Lid, Wooden, 8 1/2 x 15 1/2 In. 575.00
Jewelry, Inlaid Geometric Top, Fall Front, 7 Interior Drawers, Italy, 23 5/8 In. 4025.00
Jewelry, Inlaid Wood, Late 19th-Early 20th Century, 16 x 6 x 5 1/2 In. 140.00
Jewelry, Lacquered, Mother-Of-Pearl Top, Tray, 2 Compartments, 4 1/2 x 10 1/2 x 7 In. .. 145.00
Jewelry, Parquetry Brick Wall Shape, Fitted Interior Tray, Velvet Lined, 3 1/2 x 8 1/2 In. . 330.00
Jewelry, Royal Exchange Buildings, Papier-Mache & Mother-Of-Pearl, c.1850, 11 In. 675.00
Jewelry, Tooled Trim, Cameo Carving Lid Medallion & Escutcheon, Oak, 11 3/8 In. 110.00
Kindling, Pine, Continental, 28 x 30 1/2 x 18 3/4 In. 1840.00

Kindling, Tilt Out Bin, Shiplap Front, Iron Handle, Pine, 28 x 30 x 17 In. 60.00
Knife, Cutout Handle In Divider, Old Red Paint, Pine, 8 1/2 x 15 1/2 In. 110.00
Knife, Cutout Handle In Divider, Scalloped Edges, Original Red, Green Paint, Poplar 330.00
Knife, Dovetailed, Scroll Divider, Cutout Handle, Mahogany, 10 x 14 1/2 In. 360.00
Knife, George III, Inlaid Mahogany, Turned Finial, Domed Lid, 28 In. 8625.00
Knife, Georgian, Serpentine Front, Sheffield Escutcheon, Mahogany, c.1790 . . . .   370.00
Knife, Heart Shape Handle, Square Nail Construction, Pine, 19th Century 60.00
Knife, Hepplewhite, Inlaid Floral Bouquet, Basket, Mahogany, 10 1/2 x 7 1/2 x 18 In. . . .   345.00
Knife, Hepplewhite, Shell Inlay On Lid, Serpentine Front, Mahogany, 15 In., Pair . . .*Illus*   2200.00
Knife, High Sides, Scalloped Divider, Heart Cutout Handle, Walnut, 8 3/4 x 15 3/4 In. . . .   880.00
Knife, Ivory Inlay, Rosewood, 19th Century, 5 1/4 x 13 1/8 In. 1840.00
Knife, Mahogany Veneer Inlay, Incomplete Interior, 14 1/2 In. 220.00
Knife, Old Green Paint, Poplar, Walnut, 7 1/4 x 12 1/2 In. 80.00
Knife, Paint Traces, Dovetailed, Divider Handle, Pine, 9 1/2 x 14 In. 135.00
Knife, Serpentine & Block Front, Reeded Columns, Mahogany, 10 x 14 1/2 In., Pair 2875.00
Knife, Splayed Sides, Divider, Handle, Walnut, Worn Finish, 9 1/2 x 13 1/2 In. 90.00
Knife, Turned Handle, Bentwood, Ash & Chestnut, 13 x 8 1/2 In. 137.00
Lacquer, Brown Foo Dog Design, Black Ground, China, 2 x 12 1/4 x 7 In. 100.00
Lacquer, Gold Foliate Design, Shelf, 8 Sides, China, 11 1/2 In.   355.00
Lacquer, Papier-Mache, Oriental Figures & Animals, 10 x 12 In. 90.00
Lehnware, Black & Yellow Vines, Molded Base, Turned Feet, 6 x 11 x 6 In. 1980.00
Lift Lid, 1 Drawer, Label Dr. J.R. Freese's Family Medicine Chest, Walnut, 20 In. 190.00
Lift Lid, Grain Painted, Ditty Box Inside, 2 Drawers, Dovetailed, 19th Century, 19 1/2 In.   193.00
Lift Top, Carved Stylized Flowers, Pine, c.1840, 12 In. 154.00
Lift Top, Red Paint, Horace Hunt, Webster St., Rockland, Mass., 19th Century, 7 In. 110.00
Lollipop Top, Original Brown Paint, Butternut, 14 x 12 In. 1950.00
Mahogany Graining, Dovetailed, Poplar, 12 1/4 In. 95.00
Money, Cylindrical, Hinged Cover, Swags, Foliage, Steel, c.1830, 2 3/8 In. 1150.00
Mother-Of-Pearl, Hinged Top, Tortoiseshell, Fitted Interior, Italy, 6 x 9 1/2 In. 6325.00
Norwegian, Cover, Twisted Iron Handle, Paint Traces, Pine, Oval, 1820, 14 x 6 1/2 In. . . .   245.00
Ormolu, Copper, Tortoiseshell, Mother-Of-Pearl, 6 Bottles, Italy, 18th Century, 6 x 9 In. . .   6325.00
Painted, Lid Square Edge Molding, Pine & Poplar, 11 x 33 x 9 3/4 In. 55.00
Painted Plaid Pattern, Dovetailed, Cherry & Mahogany, 17 3/4 x 10 x 4 3/4 In. 1265.00
Pantry, 2-Finger, Green Paint, Round, 7 1/2 x 3 1/2 In. 290.00
Pantry, Bird's-Eye Maple Cover, Grain Painted, Tiger Maple Design On Side, 7 3/8 In. . .   325.00
Pantry, Wood Pegs, Hand-Cut Nails, Oak, Applied Handle, Round, 7 3/16 In. 125.00
Papier-Mache, English Interior Scene On Cover, Titled Life In London, 3 3/8 In. 50.00
Patch, Eglomise, Brass Frame, George Washington 660.00
Patch, Sulphide, General Lafayette, Glass, Swirl Pattern, Brass, Round, 2 1/2 In. 285.00
Pencil, Felix, Swing Time Felix, American Pencil Co., 1938 . . . .   75.00
Pencil, Reg'lar Fellers, Dark Blue, Eagle Pencil Co., c.1935, 3 1/2 x 8 1/4 In. 38.00
Pencil, Skippy, 1933 . . . .   49.00
Pencil, Spirit Of St. Louis, Tin Lithograph, 2 1/4 x 8 In. 88.00
Penwork, Chinoiseries, Foliage, Ebonized Bun Feet, Regency, 3 3/4 x 8 1/4 In. 1495.00
Perfume, Mother-Of-Pearl Inlay, Mahogany, 3 Gilt Bottles, Tahan Paris, 1800s 880.00
Pill, Oval Madonna Insert, Rhinestones 30.00
Pipe, Painted Red, Metal Lined Interior, Drawer, 19 1/2 x 8 3/8 In. 5750.00

Box, Knife, Hepplewhite, Shell Inlay On Lid,
Serpentine Front, Mahogany, 15 In., Pair

**Wooden boxes, toys, or decoys
should not be kept on the fireplace
mantel or nearby floor area when
the fire is burning. The heat dries
the wood and the paint. Unprotected
wooden items on warm TV sets and
stereos may also be damaged.**

Pipe, Scrollwork Edge, Carved Fan Drawer, Tiger Maple, Eldred Wheeler 130.00
Pipe, Tall Shaped Back, Hand Wrought Nails 695.00
Pipe, Wall, Compartment Base, Oak, Weathered, 24 1/2 In. 165.00
Polychrome Landscape All Sides, Cover, Pine, 7 1/2 x 8 1/2 x 11 1/4 In. 525.00
Potpourri, Red, Green & Gold Paint, Transfer Portrait, Figural Finial, Cast Iron, 7 1/2 In. 115.00
Powder Puff, Avocado Green, Pink, Chrome, Art Deco, 4 x 3 1/2 x 1 3/4 In. 55.00
Quail Form, Porcelain, 7 In., Pair 138.00
Red Lacquer, Cover, Rectangular, Italy, 6 x 8 1/2 In. 1495.00
Red Paint, Yellow Name On Lid, LePire, Brass Bail Handle, Poplar, 25 In. 110.00
Red Wash, Footed, Cotter Pin Hinges, Dovetailed, Wooden, 3 1/2 x 7 x 4 1/2 In. 385.00
Reticulated Mold, Applied Flower, Cover, Pine, Germany, 6 In. 38.00
Ribbon, Multicolored Floral, Green Ground, 1 1/2 x 2 x 3 3/4 In. 660.00
Saffron, Lehnware, Berry On Pink Ground, Red, Green, Blue Pedestal Base, 4 In. 300.00
Salt, Shaped Hanger Over Lift Lid, 1 Drawer, Walnut, c.1820, 16 x 11 In. 1150.00
Salt, Wall, Lift Top, 2 Sectional Drawer, Hardwood, Late 18th Century, 13 1/2 x 8 In. ... 465.00
Salt, Wall, Wire Nail Construction, Pine, 9 1/2 x 11 1/4 In. 190.00
Satinwood Veneer, Decoupage, Fitted, Paint Supplies, R. Peale, Aug., 1889, 9 x 10 In. ... 440.00
Scouring, Old Red Paint, 1820s, 11 In. 145.00
Scratch Carving, J.C. Wettenmann, Eagle, Upside Flags, Walnut, 1874, 13 In. 330.00
Shaving, Traveling, Federal, Bird's-Eye Maple, Lift Lid, Fold-Out Mirror, c.1820 .... 990.00
Ship With American Flag, Tray, Rosewood, Bird's-Eye Maple, 1800s, 5 x 12 x 10 In. ... 650.00
Sliding Cover, House Design, White Ground, Pine, Square, 3/4 In. 1100.00
Sliding Top, Painted, Carved Maple, 18th Century, 5 5/8 x 2 3/8 x 1 7/8 In. 110.00
Soap, Maple, Original Label, Massachusetts, Round, 19th Century 195.00
Specimen, Wooden, Parquetry, Continental, 19th Century, 10 x 16 x 12 In. 460.00
Spice, Brass, Early 19th Century, 3 x 2 In. 250.00
Spice, Mustard Paint, Handwritten Herb Names, Tin Scoop, 6 Tin Boxes, 1900, 10 x 7 In. 165.00
Spice, Walnut, Slide Lid, Late 18th Century, 1 3/4 x 8 In. 250.00
Sterling Silver, Enamel, Reversible Lid, Gold Washed, Potter Mellen, 1 x 2 In. 430.00
Storage, Paneled, Original Green Paint, Pine 275.00
Storage, Red Stippled Panels, Walnut Frame, Iron Strap Hinges, Poplar, 6 1/2 x 15 In. ... 1210.00
Storage, Staple Hinges Over Dovetailed Box, Pine, 18th Century, 10 x 22 3/4 In. 230.00
Swear, Heart Shape, Coin Slot, Painted Banner, Mahogany, Elm, 18th Century, 6 In. 3450.00
Tack, C. Vanderbilt, H. Bisel, Sons, Saddle, Harness, Trunk Makers, Pine, 40 In. 2650.00
Tea, Georgian, Greek Key, Sarcophagus Shape, Bowl, Satinwood, 1815, 6 x 12 In. 970.00
Tobacco, Boar Hunt Scenes On Lid & Bottom Panels, Inscriptions, Dutch, 5 3/8 In. 275.00
Tobacco, Brass, Engraved Lid, Dutch, 5 1/2 In. 355.00
Tobacco, Burl, Old Finish, Brass Hinge, 3 3/4 In. 135.00
Tobacco, Engraved Scenes, Crucifixion, Brass, Dutch, 17th Century, 5 1/4 In. 747.00
Tobacco, Engraved Tulip, Horn Of Plenty, Brass, Dutch, c.1700, 5 3/4 In. 335.00
Tobacco, Grass On Copper, c.1750, 7 7/8 x 5 1/4 In. 185.00
Tobacco, Pine & Split Hardwood, Oval, Reeded Container, c.19th Century 395.00
Tobacco, Smiling Cherub's Face On Lid, Cast Bell Metal, 1730-1760 .... 495.00
Tobacco, Tavern Scene, Late 17th Century, 5 In. 2530.00
Tobacco, William & Mary, Horn, Portrait In Profile Of Courtly Gentleman, 4 In. 862.00
Traveling, Cover, Mother-Of-Pearl Panel, Purple Velvet Interior, Victorian, 7 1/2 In. 1035.00
Traveling, Fall Front, Interior Sections & 1 Drawer, Red Lacquer, Wooden, Dutch, 7 In. .. 3220.00
Trinket, Exotic Wood Veneer, Inlaid Landscape, Ivory Foot, C.A Johnasson, 6 3/4 In. 165.00
Trinket, Lift Top, 9 Drawers, English Oak, Brass Knob, 19th Century, 4 1/4 x 9 1/2 In. ... 285.00
Trinket, Sliding Lid, Wooden, Whale Bone Shield Form Inlay, 19th Century, 8 1/2 In. 90.00
Utensil, Mahogany-Type Graining, Gold Pinstripes, Nail Construction, 7 x 14 In. 265.00
Valuables, Applied Molding Lid, Dovetailed, Till, Walnut, 5 1/2 x 14 1/2 In. 200.00
Vinaigrette, Gold, Enameled, Red Guilloche, Cocker Spaniel, France, c.1805, 1 1/8 In. .. 7475.00
Vinegar Grained, Dovetailed, Poplar, 10 1/4 In. 190.00
Wall, 3 Masted Ship, Under Sail Inscribed On Reverse, Pine, 18th Century, 17 3/4 In. 6900.00
Wall, Square Nail Construction, Light Brown Paint, Pine, 12 In. 350.00
Watch, Glass Front, Inner Hook For Watch, Red Paint, 9 1/4 In. 150.00
Wedding, Polychrome Painted, Couple By Trees Cover, Wooden, Oval, 18 1/4 In. 315.00
Work, Black & Gold, Octagonal, Lacquer, Chinese Export, 1830, 6 x 13 x 9 In. 120.00
Work, Inlaid Brass Lid Medallion, Fitted Interior, Base, Mahogany, England, 19 1/4 In. .. 415.00
Work, Inlaid, Mirror Interior Lid, Rosewood, 1850, 4 x 10 1/2 x 7 1/2 In. 150.00
Writing, Leather Writing Surface, Secret Drawer, Mahogany, Brass, 6 x 16 x 10 In. 750.00
Writing, Mahogany, Old Finish, 1 Dovetailed Drawer, 14 In. 495.00

Writing, Poplar, Inlaid Escutcheon, Fitted Interior, 19 1/2 In. 55.00
Yellow Paint, Red, Green, Oval, 9 3/4 In. 1760.00

BOY SCOUT collectibles include any material related to scouting, including patches, manuals, and uniforms. The Boy Scout movement in the United States started in 1910. The first Jamboree was held in 1937. Girl Scout items are listed under their own heading.

Ashtray, 1957 National Jamboree, Valley Forge, Spirit Of 76 Figures, Metal, 4 In. 35.00
Ax, 1910 . . . .   60.00
Ax, Bridgeport, Steel, Wooden Handle Covers, Engraved First Class Emblem, 13 In. 25.00
Backpack, Yucca Pack, Canvas, Khaki, Leather Straps, Brass Buckles, 1950s 30.00
Badge, Assistant Scoutmaster, Sterling Silver, Green Enamel, World War II Era 35.00
Badge, Palm Springs Cross Guard, 1961, Brass, Eagle At Top, 2 1/2 In. 50.00
Bank, Boy Scout Raises Flag As Coin Falls Into Bank, J. & E. Stevens, 1915 . . . .   3520.00
Bank, Cast Iron, Hubley, 6 In. 110.00
Belt & Buckle, Brown Leather, Bronze 2-Piece Buckle, Size 38 . . . .   25.00
Belt & Buckle, Brown Leather, Gilt Buckle, 1940s, Size 44 . . . .   25.00
Book, Handbook For Boys, 1958 . . . .   7.00
Calendar, 1954, C & F Motor Sales Montrose, Pa., 33 x 16 In. 50.00
Compass, Pathfinder, Original Box, Instruction Booklet, 1950 . . . .   60.00
Doll, Cub Scout, 11 1/2 In. 75.00
Game, Progress, 1926 . . . .   95.00
Hat, Campaign, Olive Drab Felt, Matching Band, Hat Cord, 1915-1920, Medium 30.00
Jacket, Philmont, Red Wool, Single Breasted Button Front, Size 38 . . . .   22.00
Knife, Pocket, Blade, Awl, Screwdriver, Plastic Grips, Camillus, 3 1/2 In. 20.00
Manual, Scouting For Rural Boys, Manual For Leaders, 1938, 453 Pages 45.00
Medal, Camping, Copper, Blue Satin Ribbon 65.00
Medal, Eagle Scout, Sterling Silver Eagle, Red, White & Blue Ribbon 155.00
Medal, Explorer Ranger Award, Compass & Powder Horn, 1945-1951 . . . .   460.00
Merit Badge Sash, Light Olive Green Twill, 27 Badges, Square Backgrounds, 29 In. 200.00
Painting, Oil, Baden Powell, Uniform, Frame, 15 1/2 x 19 In. 200.00
Patch, Last Ordeal, OA, Munhacke 88, June 1973, Arrowhead, Eagle, 3 1/2 In. 20.00
Playset, Steve Scout, Wilderness Base At Rocky Rapids, Plastic, Box 30.00
Postcard, Boy Scouts On The Trail, Bicycle, Signed Ella, Italy 40.00
Postcard, Encampment, Advertisement Bell Jardiniere Dept. Store, France 65.00
Postcard, Studio Portrait, Boys In Uniform, Photograph, England 50.00
Poster, Darnum & Gaily Scout Circus, Indian Chief's Head, 1928, 14 x 11 In. 30.00
Poster, Hope Of A Nation, Scout, Helping Man Across Street, 1929, 10 x 16 In. 51.00
Ring, Sterling Silver 35.00
Sheet Music, 1911 March Of Boy Scouts, Ella V. Herman, McKinley Music Co. 26.00
Sheet Music, 1912 March Of Boy Scouts, Julius Johnson, Koninsky Music Co. 26.00
Sheet Music, 1913 March Of Boy Scouts, For The Piano. 26.00
Shirt, 6 Merit Badges, Scouter Training Award Patch, Size 40 . . . .   50.00
Shirt, Explorer Scout, Valley Forge 1957 Jamboree Patch, Late 1950s, Size 13 1/2 . . . . . .   35.00
Signal Set, Box, 1948 . . . .   65.00
Statue, Mackenzie Scout, White Metal, Black Bakelite Base, 1930s, 10 1/2 In. 160.00
Tie Rack 35.00
Watch Fob, American Boy Scout, Kneeling Scout, Relief, Gilt Finish, 1 1/8 In. 90.00
Watch Fob, Salute The Flag, Scout & Flag, Bronze 90.00

BRADLEY & HUBBARD is a name found on many metal objects. Walter Hubbard and his brother-in-law, Nathaniel Lyman Bradley, started making cast iron clocks, tables, frames, andirons, lamps, chandeliers, sconces, and sewing birds in 1854 in Meriden, Connecticut. The company became Bradley & Hubbard Manufacturing Company in 1875. Charles Parker Company bought the firm in 1940. Their lamps are especially prized by collectors.

Andirons, Brass Washed, Ball Finials, Shovel, Pokers, Stand, 54 x 18 In. 935.00
Andirons, Griffin Disk, Curled Snakes, 23 In. 1400.00
Andirons, Spit Bar, Iron, Ball Finial, Scrolled Base 170.00
Chandelier, 6-Light, Floral Embossed Font & Scroll, 44 In. 550.00
Desk Set, Letter Holder, Blotter, Inkwell, Calendar, Blotter Edges 137.00

Lamp, 6-Panel Reverse-Painted Shade, Fleur-De-Lis, 22 In. 990.00
Lamp, Banquet, Brass, Marble, Milk Glass Globe, Scenes, Electrified 115.00
Lamp, Banquet, Hand-Painted Glass Shade, Chimney, Brass Bass, 23 In. 325.00
Lamp, Banquet, Reclining Male Figure, Red Shade, Griffin Design, 30 In. 490.00
Lamp, Bronzed Base, Reverse-Painted Glass Shade, Roses, 25 In. 3850.00
Lamp, Country Store 450.00
Lamp, Curved Green Slag Shade, Signed, 22 In. 1210.00
Lamp, Desk, Treasure Island 1320.00
Lamp, Emeralite Shade, Brass, Small 195.00
Lamp, Metal Figural Base, Brass Font, Signed, Lily Pattern Shade, 30 In. 850.00
Lamp, Oil, Hanging, Library Fixture 495.00
Lamp, Oil, Metal, White Blown-Out Globe Shade, Grapes, Electrified 250.00
Lamp, Panels Of Polychrome Slag Glass, Brass, Prairie School, 21 In. 1900.00
Lamp, Piano, Leaf Design, Bulbous, 2 Tiers, Scroll Handle, 24 In. 290.00
Lamp, School, Panels Of Polychromed Slag, Embossed, 21 In. 1430.00
Lamp, Student, Brass, Glass Shades, Floral, Duplex Chimney, Electrified, 21 In. 495.00
Lamp, Student, Melon Red Shade, Duplex Chimney, Signed, 22 In. 895.00
Lamp, Table, Bronze, Allover Geometric, Triangular-Shape Shade, 22 In. 1840.00
Letter Holder, Sections, Brass Plated, 6 x 10 In. 95.00
Screen, Fireplace, Woman With Torch 300.00

BRASS has been used for decorative pieces and useful tablewares since ancient times. It is an alloy of copper, zinc, and other metals. Additional brass items may be found under Bell, Candlestick, Tool, or Trivet.

Basin, On Pedestal, Flared Lip, Turned, Stepped Round Foot, Continental, 7 x 10 In. 490.00
Bed Warmer, Chased Floral Design, Turned Wooden Handle, c.1800, 47 1/2 In. 180.00
Bed Warmer, Engraved Copper Lid, Turned Wooden Handle, 43 In. 220.00
Bed Warmer, Engraved Design, 19th Century 176.00
Bed Warmer, Engraved Lid, Swan On Pond, Potted Flower, Early 19th Century 875.00
Bed Warmer, Engraved Lid, Turned Wooden Handle, 42 In. 275.00
Bed Warmer, Engraved Rooster & Sun Lid, Wooden Handle, 43 1/2 In. 660.00
Bed Warmer, Floral Engraved Lid, Wooden Handle, 40 In. 412.00
Bed Warmer, Pierced Box & Hinged Lid, 19th Century, 20 In. 110.00
Bed Warmer, Pierced, Engraved Design, Turned Wooden Handle, American 138.00
Bed Warmer, Pierced, Floral Engraved Lid, Turned Handle, 38 In. 165.00
Bowl, 2 Opium Pipes, Horace Potter, 2 1/2 x 7 1/2 In. 65.00
Bowl, Alms, Adam & Eve, Serpent-Entwined Tree, Germany, 16th Century, 10 In. 1265.00
Bowl, Alms, Center Encircled By Lions' Masks, Grapes, 16th Century, 14 3/8 In. 2530.00
Bucket, Handle, 16 1/4 x 6 1/4 In. 35.00
Calendar & Thermometer, Perpetual Calendar, 1880s, 4 x 4 In. 125.00
Can, Watering, Lid, Finial, Strap Handle, Early 19th Century, 16 In. 465.00
Candlesnuffer, Tray, Brass, c.1790 . . . . 185.00
Candlesnuffer, Trimmer, Ornate, 3-Footed, 6 1/2 In. 38.00
Case, Map, 18th Century, 30 In. 325.00
Chamber Set, Floral Arabesque, Animals, Dancers, India, 4 Piece 220.00
Chamberstick, Honeycomb Design, 19th Century, 6 1/2 In. 125.00
Chamberstick, Removable Bobeche, France, Early 18th Century 295.00
Chatelaine, Holds Tweezers, Measure Rule, Key, England, c.1400 . . . . 250.00
Compote, Applied Grape & Leaf Design, 8 In. 305.00
Compote, Griffins, Lions' Heads, Putti, Classical Figures, 19th Century, 12 In. 880.00
Compote, Lead Crystal Bowl, Marble Base, Prisms, 10 5/16 In. 90.00
Desk Set, Floral Inlay, Blotter, Tray, Renaissance Revival, Pietra Dura, 12 x 9 In. 690.00
Desk Set, Potter Bentley Studio, Cleveland, 1930s 690.00
Dispatch Case, Revolutionary War, Copper Trim, 17 In. 235.00
Door Knocker, Horseshoe Shape, Early 19th Century, 6 1/4 In. 150.00
Door Knocker, Lion, England 195.00
Dowry Bracelet, Carved, Yoruba Tribe, Africa, 1 1/4 Lb. 75.00
Easel, Rococo, 1900, 15 1/4 x 8 1/4 x 8 In. 210.00
Figurine, Cherub, Bonnet, Sitting On Base, 6 In. 300.00
Garniture, Nautilus-Shell Shape, Frosted Glass, Foliate Stand, Meriden, 7 1/2 In. 575.00
Gunpowder Measure, Adjustable, Octagonal Shape, Late 17th Century 295.00

Horn, Hunting, American, c.1850 .... 120.00
Humidor, Mahogany, Benson & Hedges, 12 1/2 In. 745.00
Humidor, Mahogany, Plum Pudding, Regency, 7 1/4 In. 690.00
Jardiniere, Ear Handles, Tooled, 16 x 12 In. 170.00
Jug, Cream, England, 1800-1830, 2 7/8 In. 95.00
Mirror Plateau, Round, Renaissance, Continental, 1880, 2 1/2 x 18 In. 395.00
Mold, Bullet, 10 In. 250.00
Mortar & Pestle, Eagle Head On Sides, 4 1/2 x 8 In. 100.00
Mortar & Pestle, Queen Anne, England, c.1710 .... 195.00
Padlock, Simmons Wireless, Embossed Ship Sending Distress Signal, Pre-1912 .... 40.00
Pail, Forged Iron Handle, Copper Rivets, 14 In. 50.00
Pail, Market, Face Of Devil, Flowers Trailing From Mouth, Reverse Flowers, c.1750 .... 250.00
Pan, Warming, Hammered, Wrought Iron Frame & Handle, Chase, c.1690, 40 x 11 In. ... 395.00
Pipe Tamper, Bust, Man, With Wreath, Mid-18th Century, England 175.00
Planter, Cover, Melon, Leaf, Turquoise Stone Finial, Signed, Horace Potter, 5 x 9 In. 200.00
Plaque, Eagle Flanked By Mermen, Ornate, 8 x 23 In. 330.00
Protractor, Hand-Engraved Numbers, Foliate Design, c.1720 .... 195.00
Punch Bowl, Footed, England, 1780, 13 1/2 In. 350.00
Samovar, Russia, 7 1/2 In. 16.00
Spurs, Horsehead, Marked N & J 225.00
Stand, Scrolled Lower Apron, Bulbous Knees, Cloven Feet, 12 x 17 x 17 In. 330.00
Sugar & Creamer, Tray, Salvador, Mexico, 3 Piece 75.00
Sugar Nips, Accordion Action, England, 18th Century, 4 1/2 In. 495.00
Sundial, Engraved, 18th Century, 4 In. 375.00
Teakettle, Porcelain Handle, Squat, Button Feet, 9 x 7 x 3 1/2 In. 150.00
Teapot, Aladdin Type, Curly Handle, England, 19th Century 195.00
Teapot, England, Early 19th Century, 6 1/4 In. 295.00
Tieback, Drapery, Fuchsia Garlands, c.1860, 9 1/2 x 4 1/2 In., Set Of 4 ... 154.00
Tray, Hammered, Snail Repousse Design, Arts & Crafts, Original Patina, 9 1/2 In. 400.00
Urn, Iron, Marked, Franklin Urn, Portland, Me., 22 In. 150.00
Urn, Mythological Beast Handles, Late 19th Century, 15 In. 395.00
Urn, Spelter Cover, Lion's Head, Drape & Floral Design, Medieval Scene, 24 In., Pair ... 633.00
Vase, 3 Handles, Stickley Bros., Impressed 8, Signed, 10 1/2 In. 385.00
Wall Pocket, Stylized Coronet, Foliate Design, England, 19th Century, 11 In. 150.00
Wall Pocket, Stylized Design, England, 19th Century, 7 1/4 In., Pair 200.00
Window, Bank Teller's, Bonds & Coupons Collections, Lighted, 36 1/2 In. 460.00

BRASTOFF, see Sascha Brastoff category.

BREAD PLATE, see various silver categories, porcelain factories, and pressed glass
patterns.

BRIDE'S BASKETS OR BRIDE'S BOWLS were usually one-of-a-kind
novelties made in American and European glass factories. They were
especially popular about 1880 when the decorated basket was often
given as a wedding gift. Cut glass baskets were popular after 1890. All
bride's baskets lost favor about 1905. Bride's baskets and bride's
bowls may also be found in other glass sections. Check the index at the
back of the book.

BRIDE'S BASKET, Blue, Leaves, Blossoms, Ruffled, Gold Frame 160.00
Peach, Ruffled Edge, Branch Form Handle, Victorian, 11 In. 230.00
Pink Interior, Fluffy Ruffles, Silver Plated Stand, Twist Bail 255.00
Silver Plate, Middletown Plate Co. Quadruple Plate 1857, Victorian, 9 x 5 In. 140.00
BRIDE'S BOWL, Cased, Deep Carmine To Green, Pedestal Stand, 9 x 7 In. 225.00
Cased, Pink, Polychrome Flowers & Fruit, Pink Scalloped Edge, 10 1/2 In. 330.00
Cased, Shading Red To Green, Silver Plated Stand, 7 x 9 In. 275.00
Cranberry, Gold Fleck, Silver Plated Holder, Pairpoint, 7 3/4 In. 275.00
Deep Pink, White & Gold Design, 5 In. 374.00
Enameled Bird, On Branch, Leaves At Edge, Ruffled, 8 1/2 x 6 1/2 In. 165.00
Grapes & Roses, Enameled Floral Allover, Silver Plated Holder, 14 x 12 1/2 In. 575.00
Hobnail, Opalescent, Pink, Aurora Silver Plate Holder, Mt. Washington, 12 In. 400.00
Ruffled, Embossed Lattice At Edge, Green Overlay, 3 5/8 x 11 1/2 In. 150.00
Ruffled Edge, 10 In. 125.00
Satin Glass, Swirl, Pink, Yellow & Blue, Pink Interior, 5 x 12 x 9 In. 1610.00

If you have a small-neck decanter or
bottle that doesn't seem to dry after
it is washed, try putting a small
amount of rubbing alcohol in the
bottle. Shake, pour out, and wait for
the remaining drops to evaporate.

Bristol,
Vase, Blue,
Enameled Child
With Book,
Flowers, Signed,
10 In.

BRISTOL glass was made in Bristol, England, after the 1700s. The
Bristol glass most often seen today is a Victorian, lightweight opaque
glass that is often blue. Some of the glass was decorated with enamels.

Dish, Flowers, Butterflies, Cut Glass Center, Blue, Gold, 10 1/2 In.	60.00
Lamp, Clambroth, Polychrome Floral Enameling, 29 In., Pair	165.00
Lamp, Greek Key, Black, Gray, White Opaque, Brass Collar, 12 1/2 In.	55.00
Lamp, Oil, Floral & Butterfly Enamel Design, Frosted Glass Shade, 19th Century	70.00
Rolling Pin, Opalescent, Anchor Design, 16 1/2 In.	130.00
Urn, Gilt & Blue Decoration, Rose Ground, 19th Century, 12 In.	145.00
Vase, 4 Narrow Gold Bands, Gold Rims At Top & Bottom, 10 In., Pair	170.00
Vase, Blue, Enameled Child With Book, Flowers, Signed, 10 In. . . . . *Illus*	125.00
Vase, Spring Flowers Design, Mahogany Base, 1870, 15 x 7 1/2 In.	91.00

BRITANNIA, see Pewter category.

BRONZE is an alloy of copper, tin, and other metals. It is used to make
figurines, lamps, and other decorative objects. Bronze lamps are listed
in the Lamp category. Pieces listed here date from the eighteenth, nineteenth, and twentieth centuries.

Basket, Bird Design, Woven, 3 x 5 In.	175.00
Bowl, Attached Sand Crab Design, Japan, 11 3/4 x 3 1/4 In.	175.00
Bowl, Everted Rim, Ribbed Frieze, Tripod Stand, 20 1/2 In.	2070.00
Bowl, Floral & Scroll Design, Leaf Handles, Curled Leaf Feet, Japan, 9 1/2 x 4 In.	115.00
Bowl, Ribbed Frieze, Tripod Stand, Thailand, 20 x 46 In., 3 Piece	2070.00
Bust, Antonius Pius, Hadrian, Neoclassical, Pair	17250.00
Bust, Barbedienne, Bacchus, Gilt Bronze, 30 1/4 In.	5520.00
Bust, Barbedienne, Hermes, 30 3/4 In.	3680.00
Bust, Barbedienne, Infant, Late 19th Century, 5 In., Pair	430.00
Bust, Barye, Louis, Fawn, Standing, Light Brown Patina, 4 1/2 In.	430.00
Bust, Buddha, China, 19th Century, 21 In.	1380.00
Bust, Buddha, Thailand, 6 1/2 In.	200.00
Bust, Caesar & Roman Senator, Neoclassical, Marble Plinth, Italy, 10 In., Pair	1150.00
Bust, Caesar, Roman Senator, Neoclassical, Italy, 10 In., Pair	1150.00
Bust, Clesinger, Jean Baptist, Woman, Italy, 1857, 10 1/2 In.	345.00
Bust, Dante, Cap & Laurel Wreath Around Head, Brown Patina, 18 In.	1725.00
Bust, Debut, Marcel, Hunter, Dark Brown Patina, 33 In.	1035.00
Bust, Dubois, Paul, Philosopher, 19th Century, 18 1/2 In.	2070.00
Bust, Dumaige, Etienne Henri, Daphne, Red Socle, 20 In.	2070.00
Bust, Fratin, Christophe, Lioness, Green Patina, 1864, 21 In.	1090.00
Bust, Goldscheider, Nude Woman, Forming Blossoming Flower, 26 In., Pair	9200.00
Bust, Kelety, Alexandre, Man, Black Stone Base, 15 In.	3220.00
Bust, Konti, Isidore, Pair Of Thinkers, 1914, 8 x 8 1/4 In.	1035.00
Bust, Marie Desire, Gentleman, Gilt Patina, 1870, 10 In.	115.00
Bust, Salmson, J., Bird Girl, 19th Century	230.00
Cigar Cutter, Nude Woman, Raised Leg Cuts Cigar, Marble Base, 8 1/2 x 7 x 5 In.	3500.00
Compote, Putti Astride Seahorses, Sea Monster Handle, Gilt, Pair	575.00

Dish, Cover, Sorensen, Bird Finial 110.00
Door Knocker, Lion's Head, Mask & Ring, 6 In. 517.00
Dresser Jar, Inlaid Woman's Portrait, Continental, Early 20th Century, 2 1/2 In. 260.00
Ewer, Allover Foliate, Scenic Designs, Brown Patina, 22 In., Pair 3680.00
Figurine, Aichele, P., Diana, Nude, Holding Her Bow, Signed, 32 In. 2300.00
Figurine, Anensch, G., Infantryman, World War I Uniform, 1923, 15 3/4 x 8 In. 665.00
Figurine, Atlas, Balancing Globe On Neck, White Marble Inverted Column, 16 In. 980.00
Figurine, Austrian Bird In Basket, Marked Geschutzt 2312.00
Figurine, Barye, Antoine Louis, Devouring A Hare, Dark Green, Brown, 5 x 13 3/4 In. 2185.00
Figurine, Barye, Antoine Louis, Elephant Of Senegal, F. Barbedienne Fondeur, 4 In. 1150.00
Figurine, Barye, Antoine Louis, Horse & Jockey, Green Marble Base, 17 x 18 x 6 In. 750.00
Figurine, Barye, Antoine Louis, Seated Hare, 1 7/16 x 2 7/8 In. 920.00
Figurine, Barye, Antoine Louis, Theseus Slaying The Centaur, Inscribed, 13 In. 4140.00
Figurine, Barye, Antoine Louis, Theseus Slaying The Minotaur, 14 In. ....*Illus* 12075.00
Figurine, Barye, Antoine Louis, Tiger, Attacking Stag, Patina, Inscribed, 6 In. 6325.00
Figurine, Bergman, Austrian Pheasant, No. 5724 .... 1320.00
Figurine, Bogucki, Edwin, Stallion, Red Brown Patina, 15 3/4 x 22 3/4 In. 745.00
Figurine, Bonheur, Isadore, Horse & Jockey, 28 3/4 In. 1430.00
Figurine, Booger, William, F. Jr., Shore Bird, 3 In. 350.00
Figurine, Boschetti, Dying Gaul, Rouge Marble Base, 19th Century, 16 In. 2200.00
Figurine, Bouraine, Marcel-Andre, Man Sitting On Horse, Horse Standing, 18 In. 5750.00
Figurine, Bouret, E., The Patriot, Light Brown Patina, 22 In. 1265.00
Figurine, Boy, Riding On Back Of St. Bernard, Brown Patina, 17 x 14 In. 1265.00
Figurine, Boyer, Daniel Webster, 1850s, 16 1/2 In. 2250.00
Figurine, Bronco Buster, 25 In. 330.00
Figurine, Buddha, Copper, Nepal, 15 3/4 In. 145.00
Figurine, Busch, L.C., Greek Athlete, Black Onyx Base, Berlin, 13 In. 825.00
Figurine, Cartier, Thomas-Francois, Panther, Snarling, On Rocky Crag, c.1920, 21 In. ... 1980.00
Figurine, Cartier, Thomas-Francois, Tiger, Brown Patina, 15 In. 520.00
Figurine, Chiparus, D.H., Girl In Clown Outfit, Gold Paint, Round Onyx Base, 9 In. 2015.00
Figurine, Classical Maiden, Standing In Classical Robes, Gilt, 12 In. 460.00
Figurine, Colinet, Claire J., Egyptian Dancer, Leaning Forward, Upraised Leg, 17 In. 3450.00
Figurine, Constant, Maurice, Field Hand, 17 3/4 In. 715.00
Figurine, Cosney, Charles, Patrician Man, Uniform, 1852, 14 1/4 x 9 In. 515.00
Figurine, De Blezer, Seated Maiden Reading Book, 13 1/2 In. 550.00
Figurine, Debut, Arab, Carrying Jug, 24 In. 2875.00
Figurine, Debut, Water Boy, 36 In. 4355.00
Figurine, Doe, Recumbent, White Marble Base, France, Late 19th Century, 7 1/2 In. 1095.00
Figurine, Drowsing Muse, Seated, 1870, 13 1/2 In. 1030.00
Figurine, Dubucand, Horse & Rider, 21 In. 4025.00
Figurine, Dumaige, Etienne Henri, Nude, Pair 8625.00
Figurine, Eagle Slayer, Art Union Of London, Brown Patina, 1898, 24 In. 1035.00
Figurine, Elischer, Hans, Fisherman & Mermaid, Slate Base, 1923, 13 1/8 In. 1150.00
Figurine, Ferrari, St. George & The Dragon, Riding Prancing Horse, Italy, 17 In. 1322.00
Figurine, Fratin, Europa & The Bull, 14 3/4 x 16 3/8 In. 2185.00
Figurine, Frink, Elizabeth, Birds, Fighting, Brown Patina, Black Base, 10 1/4 In., Pair ... 3450.00

Bronze, Figurine,
Barye, Antoine
Louis, Theseus
Slaying The
Minotaur, 14 In.

Bronze, Inkwell, Woman Holding Letter, Swinging
Covers, 2 Glass Inserts, 7 1/2 x 10 In.

Figurine, Frishmuth, Harriet, Nude, Gorham 2860.00
Figurine, Fritz, Hermann, Europa & Bull, Nude On Bull, Marble Base, 15 1/2 In. 2415.00
Figurine, Froman, Ann, Spring, Verde Patina, White Marble Plinth, 14 In. 515.00
Figurine, Fuller, Loie, Gilt Patina, 13 1/4 In. 12650.00
Figurine, Fuller, Loie, Gilt Patina, 18 In. 9200.00
Figurine, Gardet, Georges, Tiger, On Rock, About To Pounce Emerging Lizard, 10 In. ... 575.00
Figurine, Gaudez, A.E., David With Sling, Revolving Base, 32 In. 1955.00
Figurine, Gavdez, A.E., Female Figure, Dark Brown Patina, 40 In. 6900.00
Figurine, Gechter, Greyhound, Rectangular, Black Marble Base, 13 x 14 x 9 In. 990.00
Figurine, Gechter, Jean Francois Theodore, Hunter On Horse, Inscribed, 18 In. 4315.00
Figurine, Gemito, Vincenzo, Donna Diritta, Golden Brown Patina, 6 In. 170.00
Figurine, Gentlemen, Wearing Coat, Hat, Standing, Black Slate Base, 17 In., Pair 6325.00
Figurine, Gladenbeck, O., Woman, With Shield & Dagger, Deep Brown Patina, 11 In. ... 290.00
Figurine, God Mercury, Seated On Granite Rock, 20 In. 460.00
Figurine, Goodacre, G., Little Cowboy, 5 1/2 In. 258.00
Figurine, Greyhound, Lying On Marble Base, France, 6 In. 490.00
Figurine, Guiraud-Riviere, M., Maiden, Standing On 1 Leg, Ivory, 18 3/4 In. 5175.00
Figurine, Guyot, George, Panther, Standing, Looking Up, 13 1/4 x 19 1/2 In. 6900.00
Figurine, Hannaux, Emmanuel, Young Warrior, Marble Socle Base, c.1895, 23 In. 3105.00
Figurine, Hischinger, 4 Sparrows On Tree, Trunk, Small Branches, 12 1/4 In. 2695.00
Figurine, Hoffmann, Otto, Female Nude, On Tiptoes, Arms Out Wide, 8 3/4 In. 575.00
Figurine, Holweck, Louis, Le Vin, White Metal, c.1890, 29 1/2 In. 2850.00
Figurine, Hundriser, Emil, Baby Boy & Beetle, Marble Base, 11 In. 1092.00
Figurine, Kowalczewski, P., Woman Water Carrier, Dark Brown Patina, Marble Base 1035.00
Figurine, Lady & Dog, Gilt Bronze, Continental 375.00
Figurine, Lambert, Leon-Eugene, Urn Form, 2 Handles, 14 1/2 In. 6325.00
Figurine, Lanceray, N., Mounted Cossack, Wiping Sword On Mane Of Horse, 19 In. 6325.00
Figurine, Liberich, Mounted Cossack, 3 Hounds, Oval Base, 10 1/2 x 22 In. 2970.00
Figurine, Lions, Seated, Baring Teeth, Rectangular Plinths, 34 x 48 In. 17825.00
Figurine, Marcuse, Rudolf, Boy, Standing, Holding Teddy Bear, Marble Plinth, 6 3/4 In. ... 162.00
Figurine, Mene, Pierre Jules, Dog 230.00
Figurine, Mene, Pierre Jules, Hound, Oval Base, 6 1/2 In. 770.00
Figurine, Mene, Pierre Jules, Jockey On Horse, 16 1/2 x 16 In. 6040.00
Figurine, Mene, Pierre Jules, Lady On Horseback, Brown Patina, 10 1/4 x 8 3/4 In. 3450.00
Figurine, Mene, Pierre Jules, Pointer, Brown Patina, 4 5/8 x 9 1/16 In. 920.00
Figurine, Mene, Pierre Jules, Retriever, Signed, 6 7/8 x 12 5/16 In. 865.00
Figurine, Mene, Pierre Jules, Scottish Hunter With Fox, Inscribed, Patina, 19 In. 3737.00
Figurine, Mene, Pierre Jules, Setter Dog, Striding On Point, Bronze, Brown Patina 1265.00
Figurine, Mercury, Holding Staff, Circular Marble Pedestal, 33 In. 1035.00
Figurine, Meuller, Heinz, Girl, Reading, Gilt, Signed, 1930, 6 x 5 1/2 In. 375.00
Figurine, Moigniez, Jules, Hawk Taking Flight From Branch, Marble Base, 34 1/8 In. ... 2575.00
Figurine, Moigniez, Jules, Partridge With Rat, Dark Brown Patina, 7 1/2 In. 400.00
Figurine, Moigniez, Jules, Pointer With Rabbit, Signed, c.1890 .... 2875.00
Figurine, Moreau, Auguste, Iris, 19th Century 3250.00
Figurine, Moreau, Manthuin, Fountain Of Youth, 27 1/2 In. 2000.00
Figurine, Moreau, Manthuin, Peasant Girl, 27 In. 3162.00
Figurine, Morin, Georges, Hoop Girl, Marble Base, 17 3/4 In. 1955.00
Figurine, Muller, Hans, Muse Of Theater, 7 1/2 In. 264.00
Figurine, Muller, Hans, Neoclassical Woman With Mandolin, Signed, 7 1/2 In. 175.00
Figurine, Nagare, Masayuki, Standing Figure, Granite Base, Signed, Numbered, 7 1/4 In. . 1150.00
Figurine, Nude Maiden, Standing Up On Foot, Pointing Arm, 23 3/4 In. 2875.00
Figurine, Paris, Roland, Mephistopheles, Ivory, Gilt, Black Marble Base, 15 In. 4025.00
Figurine, Philippe, Paul, Flute Player, Standing, Ivory, Gilt, France, 21 In. 8050.00
Figurine, Picault, Emile-Louis, Man, Standing, Variegated Marble Base, 29 1/2 In. 2530.00
Figurine, Piccirilli, F., 2 Ostriches, Standing, Marble Base, Italy, 10 1/8 x 15 3/4 In. 4312.00
Figurine, Posoreck, S., Warrior, Bending His Bow, Brown Patina, 13 In. 575.00
Figurine, Potet, Loys, Youth & The Leopard, Sienna Marble Base, 22 In. 1984.00
Figurine, Pradier, Jean Jacques, Nude Female Figure, Bronze Base, 27 In. 3703.00
Figurine, Preiss, Fritz, Bather, Playing Flute, Standing, Onyx Base, 7 In. 8625.00
Figurine, Preiss, Fritz, Gamin, Ivory, Onyx Base, 9 5/8 In. 10350.00
Figurine, Preiss, Fritz, Partially Clad Figure Arched Backwards, Ivory Body, 11 In. 5750.00
Figurine, Preiss, Fritz, Tambourine Dancer, Onyx Base, 14 1/8 In. 9200.00
Figurine, Preiss, Fritz, Venus, Gilt, Onyx Base, 8 3/4 In. 9775.00

Figurine, Preiss, Fritz, Young Girl, Standing, Octagonal Black Marble Base 2300.00
Figurine, Puiforcat, Jean, Eagle, Sitting On Modern Pedestal, France, 8 x 11 1/2 In. 5750.00
Figurine, Remington, Frederic, Buffalo, Signed, c.1920 . . . . 1200.00
Figurine, Renda, Guiseppe, Blindfolded Woman, c.1870, 12 In. 920.00
Figurine, Rhind, William Birnie, Scottish Soldier, Standing, c.1920, 22 3/4 In. 1495.00
Figurine, Rigaud, Woman Figure, Kneeling, Gilt Floral Chain-Mail Bodice, 23 1/2 In. . . . 8625.00
Figurine, Robert, Seated Man Feeding Dog, Marble Base, 10 3/4 In. 515.00
Figurine, Russell, Cowboy & Horse, Marble Base 605.00
Figurine, Saint Cecilia, Veiled Head, Slate Base, 18th Century, 11 3/8 In. 5750.00
Figurine, Sandoz, E.M., Jumping Fish, France, 1921, 5 3/4 In. 3737.00
Figurine, Sandoz, E.M., Monkey Sitting, France, 1928, 7 In. 9200.00
Figurine, Sandoz, E.M., Parakeet, France, 1925, 7 5/8 In. 4600.00
Figurine, Sandoz, E.M., Small Eel, France, 1920, 7 1/2 In. 2875.00
Figurine, Saulo, Nude With Drape, Left Arm Extended, 28 In. 2055.00
Figurine, Schmidt, Hunter, Holding Bird & His Bow, 17 1/2 In. 460.00
Figurine, Siebern, E., Winged Nude Woman, Standing On Domed Base, 1920, 26 In. 3450.00
Figurine, Simard, Marie-Louis, Trojan Horse, Standing, 20 1/2 In. 12650.00
Figurine, Snake, Mother-Of-Pearl Inset Eyes, 23 In. 400.00
Figurine, Splieth, Heinrich, Standing Ewe, 9 1/2 In. 1250.00
Figurine, Steiner, Clement Leopold, Nymph, 19th Century, 37 In. 6900.00
Figurine, Tibetan Winged Deity, 12 3/4 In. 350.00
Figurine, Wayland, Paul, Eagle Astride Shield Draped Banner, 1916 . . . . 1430.00
Figurine, Wild Boar In Natural Surroundings, Brown Patina, 9 In. 230.00
Figurine, Winged Sphinx, Recumbent, c.1875, 3 3/4 x 8 1/8 In. 302.00
Figurine, Woodcutter & Bull, Firewood On Back, Removable Ax & Firewood, 32 In. 9500.00
Figurine, Zach, Bruno, Flapper, Standing, Leaning To Side, 26 In. 7475.00
Figurine, Zuniga, F., Woman, Seated, Wood Base, 1962, 6 1/2 In. 6900.00
Garniture, Grand Tour, Marble Socle, 2 Handles, Cup Shape, Pair 430.00
Group, Allegory Of Music, Onyx Pedestal, France, 19th Century, 7 3/8 In. 260.00
Group, Allouard, H., Faust & Marguerite, Embracing, 26 1/2 In. 3703.00
Group, Barye, Antoine Louis, Lion Attacking Eagle, Signed, 5 7/8 x 6 1/8 In. 1380.00
Group, Barye, Antoine Louis, Striped Tiger Wrestling Crocodile, Brown Patina, 8 In. 920.00
Group, Cartier, Thomas-Francois, 2 Setters, Gilt Patina, 18 x 21 In. 865.00
Group, Chotka, 2 Arabs, Bartering, Interior Setting, Cold Painted, 1920, 6 x 8 In. 805.00
Group, Classical Maidens, Standing, Draped In Veils With Flowers, 19 1/2 In. 1840.00
Group, Clodion, Bacchant, Gilt, 19th Century, 13 1/4 In. 575.00
Group, Clodion, Satyress With Girl Satyr & Putto, France, 12 1/2 In. 1005.00
Group, Cupid, Marble Plinth, France, 19th Century, 11 x 8 In. 315.00
Group, Fratin, 2 Dogs In Pursuit Of Stag, Golden Brown Patina, 16 In. 2300.00
Group, Gaudez, A., Man & Woman Dancing, 33 In. 2300.00
Group, Gratcheff, Troika, Man, Woman, Milepost, Marked, Woerffel, 17 In. 5750.00
Group, Handzaeme, 2 Soldiers Down & Firing Rifles, Brown, 1915, 4 x 10 In. 320.00
Group, Khodarovich, Peasant Oxen Cart, Russia, 14 1/4 x 23 In. 975.00
Group, Koch, Johann, Swinging Figures, Brown, Green Weathered Patina, 41 1/4 In. 5750.00
Group, Lanceray, Equestrian Cossack With Sweetheart, Marked, Chopin, 16 In. 4600.00
Group, Lavaysse, A., Man & Woman With Putto, Lying Down, 34 In. 5175.00
Group, LeFaguays, Pierre, Serpents, Supported By Seminude Women Figures 4600.00
Group, LeVerrie, 2 Deer, Patinated, Black Marble Base, Signed, 27 5/8 x 11 1/2 In. 1150.00
Group, Love, Maiden & Angel, 16 1/2 x 12 1/2 In. 575.00
Group, Manzu, Giacomo, Gli Amanti, Entwined Figures, Stamped, 14 x 12 In. 19550.00
Group, Mene, Pierre Jules, 3 Dogs Cornering Prey, 15 x 7 x 7 1/2 In. 1495.00
Group, Mercie, A., Gloria Victis, Standing, Arms Outstretched, France, 42 In. 16100.00
Group, Moigniez, Fox & Crane, Gilt Bronze Base, Signed, 4 x 5 7/16 In. 575.00
Group, Parsons, E.B., Puppies, 7 In. 1540.00
Group, Preiss, Fritz, Schoolboy & Hoop Girl, Onyx Base, 1943, 8 1/4 In. 3450.00
Group, Putti, Upward Gaze, Hand Held Up, Square Marble Base, 12 In. 230.00
Group, Roccamonte, A., Embracing Couple Upon Circular Base, Abstract, 14 In. 635.00
Group, Scholz, Heinrich K., Harlequin & Dancer, 1919, 14 In. 1610.00
Group, Steiner, Caught In The Vine, Signed, Fumiere Thiebaut Paris Seal, 25 In. 2015.00
Group, Woman On Camel, Holding Child, Man Standing Beside Her, 19 1/2 In. 1495.00
Hand, Gilt, China, 17th Century 3900.00
Hands, Bofill, Antoine, Marble Base, Signed, 37 1/2 In. 750.00
Hibachi, Landscape, Egg Shape, 14 1/2 In. 195.00

Inkwell, Woman Holding Letter, Swinging Covers, 2 Glass Inserts, 7 1/2 x 10 In. . . . .*Illus*   225.00
Jardiniere, Lion's Mask, Paw Design, England, 16 1/2 In. 255.00
Liqueur Set, Pumpkin, 4 Hinged Sections, Round Rocaille Base, Continental, 10 In. 8050.00
Mirror, Flower Shape, Round, 8 In. 605.00
Mirror, Raised Bird & Concentric Ring Design, 6 In. 330.00
Mold, Spoon, American, c.1825, 7 3/4 In. 325.00
Mold, Spoon, For Pewter Spoons, Rattail Bowl, Round Finial, 8 3/4 In., 2 Piece 460.00
Mortar, Acanthus Design Over Flower Heads, Horse-Head Handles, 1730s, 13 In. 5325.00
Mortar, Concentric Bands, Inscription, Germany, 1745, 13 1/2 In. 4025.00
Mortar, Dolphin Handles, c.1630, 4 3/4 In. 275.00
Obelisk, Continental, 1900-1915, 15 In. 100.00
Page Turner, Bird & Millet Design, Engraved Blade, Repousse Handle 105.00
Page Turner, Lotus & Frog Handle, Engraved Blade With Marsh Scene, 11 3/4 In. 105.00
Paquette, Adoration Of Shepherds, Silvered & Silver Studded, 1561, 7 x 5 In. 7474.00
Plaque, Colonial Washington, Society Of Colonial Wars, 1909, 3 1/2 x 5 In. 150.00
Plaque, Hobson, Langebahn, 7 x 9 1/2 In. 250.00
Plaque, St. Cecelia, After Donatello, Relief, Miccinglo, E., Walnut Frame, 14 x 12 In. . . .   440.00
Sculpture, Bertoia, Harry, Square Tree Form, Cast & Welded, 10 x 12 In. 4400.00
Stirrups, Built-In Spur Rowels, 5 1/2 In., Pair 400.00
Table Set, Barbedienne, F., 3 Roman Style Round Dishes, Oil Lamp, Vase, 6 Piece 3450.00
Tray, Calling Card, Art Nouveau Woman 125.00
Umbrella Stand, Birds & Vines, Engraved Greek Key Border, Japan 440.00
Urn, Bird & Tree Design, Carved Wooden Base, Japan, 20th Century, 22 In., Pair 880.00
Urn, Floral & Bird Relief Design, Stand, Japan, 13 In. 115.00
Urn, Phoenix Form Handles, 39 1/2 In. 1035.00
Vase, Chauchet-Guillere, Charlotte, Cast Bead Design, Fluted Paneling, 1922, 12 In. 1955.00
Vase, Dragon, Winding Around Body, Pear Shape, 19th Century, 11 1/2 In., Pair 460.00
Vase, Egg Shape, 19th Century, Japan, 12 1/2 In. 155.00
Vase, Figural, Head Of A Woman, Green, Black Patina, 9 In. 145.00
Vase, Gilt-Plumed Peacock, Draping Foliage On Rim, Art Nouveau, 12 1/4 In. 1150.00
Vase, Mandarin Duck Design, Late 19th Century, 13 In. 430.00
Vase, Meliodon, Jules Andre, Rapture Of Nymph & Satyr, 7 In. 1092.00
Vase, Morning Glories & Nymphs, Tin Liner, Grisard, c.1900, 16 1/2 In., Pair 3400.00
Vase, Raised Bird & Leaf Design, Egg Shape, Patinated, Japan, 18 In. 550.00
Vase, Silvercrest, Silver On Bronze, 6 In. 440.00
Vase, Trumpet-Shape Mouth, Shishi Handles, 19th Century, 11 In. 260.00
Vase, Villani, E., Figural, 2 Nude Female Figures, Vining Morning Glories, 35 In. 6900.00
Vase, Woman In Draped Garb, Art Nouveau, C.H. Korschann, 8 1/4 In. 405.00

BROWNIES were first drawn in 1883 by Palmer Cox. They are charac-
terized by large round eyes, downturned mouths, and skinny legs.
Toys, books, dinnerware, and other objects were made with the
Brownies as part of the design.

Figure, Policeman, Majolica . . . .*Illus*   375.00
Figure, Sailor, Majolica . . . .*Illus*   420.00

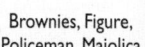
Brownies, Figure,
Policeman, Majolica

Brownies, Figure,
Uncle Sam, Majolica

Brownies, Figure, Sailor, Majolica

Figure, Uncle Sam, Majolica . . . .*Illus* 260.00
Game, Brownie Auto Race, Marble, Tin, Cars & Grandstand, Palmer Cox, 10 1/2 In. 225.00
Game, Tumbler, Hand Toys Of Canada, 1930s 250.00
Paper Doll, Palmer Cox, 2 Heads, 9 Outfits 125.00

BRUSH Pottery was started in 1925. George Brush first worked in 1901 in Zanesville, Ohio. He started his own pottery in 1907, but it burned to the ground soon after. In 1909 he became manager of the J.W. McCoy Pottery. In 1911, Brush and J.W. McCoy formed the Brush-McCoy Pottery Co. After a series of name changes, the company became The Brush Pottery in 1925. It closed in 1982. Collectors favor the figural cookie jars made by this company. Because there was a company named Brush-McCoy, there is great confusion between Brush and Nelson McCoy pieces. See McCoy category for more information.

MARK

Cookie Jar, Circus Horse 450.00
Cookie Jar, Clown Bust, Red Hair, Black Hat 295.00
Cookie Jar, Cow, Black & White, Cat Finial, Professionally Repaired Horn 950.00
Cookie Jar, Cow, Purple 1400.00
Cookie Jar, Elephant, With Ice Cream Cone . . . . .350.00 to 600.00
Cookie Jar, Formal Pig . . . . .200.00 to 250.00
Cookie Jar, Formal Pig, Black Coat 225.00
Cookie Jar, Happy Bunny 100.00
Cookie Jar, Humpty Dumpty, Sitting On Square Base, 10 In. 275.00
Cookie Jar, Humpty Dumpty, White 350.00
Cookie Jar, Puppy Police 495.00
Vase, Fan, Cream, 14 In. 40.00

BRUSH MCCOY, see Brush category and related pieces in McCoy category.

BUCK ROGERS was the first American science fiction comic strip. It started in 1929 and continued until 1965. Buck has also appeared in comic books, movies, and, in the 1980s, a television series. Any memorabilia connected with the character Buck Rogers is collectible.

Book, Big Big Book, Adventures Of Buck Rogers, 1934 . . . . 125.00
Book, Big Little Book, Buck Rogers & The Doom Comet, 1935 . . . . 68.00
Book, Big Little Book, Buck Rogers, Fiend Of Space, No. 1409 . . . . 65.00
Book, Big Little Book, Buck Rogers, Planetoid Plot, No. 1197, 1936 . . . . 40.00
Book, Color & Activity, Robert C. Dille, Whitman, 1979, 60 Pages 18.00
Bubble Blower, Plastic Bubb-A-Loons, Blister Card, Imperial Toy Corp., 1979 . . . . 10.00
Figure, With Flicker Ring, Ideal 400.00
Gun, Zoomerang, Sonic Ray & Tigrett 22.00
Helmet, Space, Cloth 350.00
Lunch Box, Metal 95.00
Matchbook Cover, Creamsicle, Buck Rogers On Radio, Starting May 4th, 1940 . . . . 35.00
Pistol, 25th Century, Daisy, c.1934, 9 1/2 In. 88.00
Pistol, Atomic, Daisy Mfg. 28.00
Pistol, Disintegrator, Model XZ-38, Metal, Daisy, 1935, 10 In. 235.00
Pop Gun, Copper Color 275.00
Ray Gun, Daisy, Pressed Metal, Engraved Picture Of Buck On Grip, 10 In. 100.00
Spaceship, Marx, 1930s 650.00
Spaceship, Tootsietoy 155.00
Spaceship, Windup, Lithographed, Marx, 12 In. 185.00
Starfighter, Corgi, Package, 1980 . . . . 35.00
Watch, Pocket 900.00

BUFFALO POTTERY was made in Buffalo, New York, after 1902. The company was established by the Larkin Company, famous manufacturers of soap. The wares are marked with a picture of a buffalo and the date of manufacture. Deldare ware is the most famous pottery made at the factory. It has either a khaki-colored or green background with hand painted transfer designs.

BUFFALO POTTERY, Bowl, Fruit, Willow, 1911, 4 3/4 In. 35.00
Bowl, Fruit, Willow, 1916, 4 3/4 In. 35.00

Bowl, Vegetable, Willow, Cover, Rectangular, 1908 .... 500.00
Bowl, Vegetable, Willow, No Cover, 1911 .... 350.00
Bowl, Vegetable, Willow, Oval, 1911, 9 5/8 In. 150.00
Bowl, Vegetable, Willow, Oval, 1916, 7 7/8 In. 130.00
Bowl, Vegetable, Willow, Oval, 1916, 8 1/2 In. 130.00
Bowl, Vegetable, Willow, Round, 1911, 9 1/4 In. 180.00
Bowl, Willow, 1911, 6 1/2 In. ....45.00 to 50.00
Bowl, Willow, 1911, 7 3/4 In. 60.00
Bowl, Willow, 1916, 7 3/4 In. 60.00
Bowl, Willow, 1917, 7 3/4 In. 60.00
Charger, Abino Ware, Country Scene Of Building, Trees, Pond, 1913, 12 In. 550.00
Creamer, Willow, 1911 .... 110.00
Cup, Willow, 1911, 2 1/8 In. 80.00
Cup, Willow, 1913, 2 1/8 In. 80.00
Cup & Saucer, Willow, 1916, 2 3/8 In. ....75.00 to 90.00
Cuspidor, Flower & Basket Weave 60.00
Fish Set, Platter & 6 Plates 475.00
Gravy Boat, Willow, 1909 .... 240.00
Gravy Boat, Willow, 1911 .... 240.00
Mug, Hoefler Ice Cream Co., 2-Tone Brown, c.1880, 4 1/4 In. 110.00
Pie Plate, Willow, 1911, 7 1/8 In. 35.00
Pie Plate, Willow, 1916, 7 1/2 In. 35.00
Pitcher, Chrysanthemum 165.00
Pitcher, Cinderella, 1907, 6 1/8 In. 440.00
Pitcher, Dutch Woman & Child, Lavender, Cerulean Blue, 1907, 6 In. 660.00
Pitcher, George Washington & Mt. Vernon, 1907, 7 1/4 In. ....440.00 to 575.00
Pitcher, Geranium, Floral, Blue Geraniums, Handle, 6 In. 522.00
Pitcher, Gloriana, 1908, 9 In. 550.00
Pitcher, Holland, 1908, 5 3/4 In. 467.00
Pitcher, Mason, European Lake Scene, Quaint Villages, Sailboats, 1907, 8 In. 880.00
Pitcher, Pilgrim At Plymouth Massachusetts, 1907, 9 1/4 In. 750.00
Pitcher, Rip Van Winkle, Handle, 1907, 6 1/4 x 6 In. 575.00
Pitcher, Robin Hood, Wearing Huntsman Attire, 1906, 8 In. 660.00
Pitcher, Roosevelt Bears, Activities, 10 1/4 In. 1495.00
Pitcher, Whirl Of The Town, 1908, 7 In. 450.00
Pitcher, Willow, Blue Transfer, Gold Trim Handle, 1908, 8 In. 605.00
Plate, Independence Hall, Blue-Green, 10 1/4 In. 35.00
Plate, Willow, 10 1/4 In. 95.00
Plate, Willow, 1909, 10 1/4 In. 100.00
Plate, Willow, 1911, 6 3/8 In. 30.00
Plate, Willow, 1911, 8 3/8 In. 45.00
Plate, Willow, 1911, 9 1/4 In. 40.00
Plate, Willow, 1914, 9 1/4 In. 40.00
Plate, Willow, 1916, 6 3/8 In. 30.00
Plate, Willow, 1916, 9 1/8 In. 40.00
Plate, Willow, 1916, 10 1/4 In. 100.00
Plate, Willow, 1916, 7 1/8 In. 35.00
Plate, Willow, 1917, 8 3/8 In. 45.00
Plate, Willow, 1918, 9 1/4 In. 40.00
Platter, Grand Review Army Of Potomac, By President Lincoln, 1863 .... 625.00
Platter, Oval, Willow, 9 5/8 In. 105.00
Platter, Oval, Willow, 10 3/4 In. 140.00
Platter, Willow, 1909, 9 5/8 In. 140.00
Platter, Willow, 1909, 14 1/8 In. 220.00
Platter, Willow, 1916, 10 3/4 In. 150.00
Soup, Cream, Willow 80.00
Soup, Cream, Willow, 1916 .... 110.00
Soup, Dish, Willow, 1911, 7 3/4 In. 44.00
Teapot, Argyle, 1914 .... 225.00
Teapot, Floral, Blue & White, 7 1/2 In. 115.00
Vase, Geranium, Blue, Closed Mouth, Contrasting White, 3 3/4 In. 165.00
BUFFALO POTTERY DELDARE, Bowl, Fallowfield Hunt, The Death, 3 1/2 x 9 In. 935.00
Bowl, Fallowfield Hunt, The Start, 1 3/4 x 6 In. 605.00

Bowl, Ye Olden Days, 5 1/2 In. 195.00
Bowl, Ye Village Tavern, 1908, 9 In. ....275.00 to 300.00
Bowl, Ye Village Tavern, 1924, 9 x 3 3/4 In. 400.00
Candlestick, Shield Back, Emerald, 7 In. ....*Illus* 2070.00
Candlestick, Village Street, 9 In., Pair 495.00
Chamberstick, White Flowers, Emerald, 7 In. 990.00
Chamberstick Holder, Scenes Of Village Life, 6 x 6 3/4 In. 1340.00
Charger, Evening At Ye Lion Inn, 14 In. 330.00
Charger, Fallowfield Hunt, 13 3/4 In. 428.00
Charger, Fallowfield, The Start, 14 In. ....450.00 to 550.00
Chop Plate, An Evening At Ye Lion Inn, 1908, 14 In. ....475.00 to 695.00
Chop Plate, Fallowfield Hunt, 14 In. 795.00
Creamer, Breaking Cover, 1908, 3 In. ....125.00 to 357.00
Creamer, Ye Olden Days, 1909, 2 3/4 In. 137.00
Cup & Saucer, Fallowfield Hunt 250.00
Dresser Tray, 12 x 9 In. 650.00
Eggcup, Emerald, 3 3/4 x 2 In. 1320.00
Hair Receiver, Ye Village Street, 2 3/4 x 4 In. 495.00
Humidor, Mariner, 1909 .... 850.00
Jardiniere, Ye Village Street, 9 In. 1760.00
Mug, Dr. Syntax Again Filled Up His Glass, Beer Scene, 1911, 4 In. 660.00
Mug, Fallowfield Hunt, 4 1/2 In. ....200.00 to 375.00
Mustard, Village Life In Ye Olden Days, 3 1/4 In. 910.00
Pitcher, Fallowfield Hunt, Breaking Cover, 7 x 5 In. 980.00
Pitcher, Fallowfield Hunt, The Dash, 6 In. 660.00
Pitcher, Their Manner Of Telling Stories, 6 x 5 1/4 In. 303.00
Pitcher, To Becky's Hand He Gave A Squeeze, Emerald, 1911, 12 In. 2090.00
Pitcher, To Demand My Annual Rent, Tahoy, 8 In. 515.00
Pitcher, To Spare An Old Broken Soldier, Handle, 7 In. 330.00
Pitcher, With A Cane Superior Air, Handle, GHJ, 9 1/2 In. 690.00
Pitcher, Ye Lion Inn, 10 In. 275.00
Plaque, Peacock, Balustrade With Pigeons, Emerald, 12 In. 2970.00
Plaque, Ye Lion Inn, M. Caird, 12 1/8 In. 357.00
Plate, Calendar, Elf At Various Seasons, 1910, 9 1/2 In. 2185.00
Plate, Dr. Syntax Lost, Emerald, 12 In. 1045.00
Plate, Dr. Syntax Making Discoveries, Emerald, 10 In. 1100.00
Plate, Dr. Syntax Soliloquizing, Emerald, 1911, 7 1/4 In. 300.00
Plate, Dr. Syntax To Becky's Hand, Emerald, 6 1/4 In. 550.00
Plate, Dr. Syntax, Disputing Bill, Emerald, 1909, 9 In. 200.00
Plate, Fallowfield Hunt, 10 In. 220.00
Plate, Fallowfield Hunt, 1908, 6 1/2 In. 130.00
Plate, Fallowfield Hunt, 8 1/4 In. 150.00
Plate, Fallowfield Hunt, 9 3/8 In. 150.00
Plate, Fallowfield Hunt, The Death, 8 1/2 In. 60.00
Plate, Garden Trio, Musicians, Floral, Emerald, 9 In. 935.00

Buffalo Pottery Deldare,
Candlestick, Shield Back, Emerald, 7 In.

Buffalo Pottery Deldare, Punch Set,
Fallowfield Hunt, 9-In. Bowl, 7 Piece

Plate, Misfortune At Tulip Hall, Emerald, 1911, 8 1/4 In. 605.00
Plate, Yankee Doodle, 2 Drummers, 1 Flutist, 1911, 10 In. 2860.00
Plate, Ye Olden Times, 9 1/2 In. 150.00
Plate, Ye Village Gossips, 1909, 10 In. ....125.00 to 225.00
Plate, Ye Village Street, 7 1/4 In. 100.00
Plate, Ye Village Street, N. Sheehan, 7 1/2 In. 630.00
Powder Jar, Cover, Stylized Heads Of Birds, Emerald, 4 In. 1210.00
Punch Set, Fallowfield Hunt, 9-In. Bowl, 7 Piece ....*Illus* 8625.00
Relish, Ye Olden Times, Scene, W. Fozler, 12 In. 495.00
Sugar, Cover, Ye Olden Days, 1908, 4 1/2 In. 545.00
Sugar & Creamer, Ye Olden Days, 4 In. ....137.00 to 355.00
Tankard, Fallowfield Hunt, 4 In. 495.00
Tankard, The Great Controversy, Stiner, 12 1/4 In. 795.00
Tankard, Ye Lion Inn, 4 In. 220.00
Teapot, Fallowfield Hunt, 6 Sides, 1908, 6 x 8 In. 575.00
Tile, Breaking Cover, 6 In. 247.00
Tile, Tea, Breaking Cover, 6 In. 660.00
Tray, Card, Fallowfield Hunt, Handles, 1908, 7 3/4 In. 357.00
Tray, Heirlooms, P. Hall, 13 3/4 x 10 3/8 In. 412.00
Trivet, Travelling In Ye Olden Days, S. Palmer, 6 1/4 In. 315.00
Vase, Butterflies, Stylized Floral, Emerald, 1911, 13 In. 115.00
Vase, Ye Village Schoolmaster, 8 1/4 In. 550.00

BUNNYKINS, see Royal Doulton category.

BURMESE GLASS was developed by Frederick Shirley at the Mt.
Washington Glass Works in New Bedford, Massachusetts, in 1885. It
is a two-toned glass, shading from peach to yellow. Some pieces have
a pattern mold design. A few Burmese pieces were decorated with pictures or applied glass flowers of colored Burmese glass. Other factories made similar glass also called *Burmese*. Related items may be
listed in the Fenton category and under Webb Burmese.

Bookends, Ivory 390.00
Bowl, 10 Fluted Edge, 19th Century, 12 In. 385.00
Bowl, Diamond-Quilted Pattern, Mt.Washington, 2 1/4 x 4 3/4 In. 144.00
Bowl, Floral, Albertine, Timothy Canty, Mt.Washington, 2 1/2 In. 260.00
Bowl, Queen's, Diamond-Quilted, Glossy Feet, 5 Brass Arms, 5 Vases, 8 In. 4180.00
Creamer, Floral, Melon Rib, Silver Plated, 3 1/2 In. 515.00
Cruet, Blown, Applied Handle, 1950, 7 In. 230.00
Cruet, Mt.Washington, 7 In. 1250.00
Cruet, Pastel Fernery, Orange Flowers, Gold Trim, Melon Stopper, Mt. Washington 2100.00
Cup & Saucer, Paper Label, Mt.Washington 585.00
Ewer, Tennyson Quotation, Mallard Ducks, Mt.Washington 5500.00
Lamp, Fairy, 2 3/4 In., Pair 385.00
Lamp, Fairy, Clear Base, Signed, 5 In. 200.00
Lamp, Kerosene, Mt.Washington, 15 In. 12250.00
Mug, Loop Handle, Mt.Washington, 2 3/4 In. 288.00
Mustard 300.00
Pitcher, Milk, Applied Loop Handle, 1880s, 7 1/4 In. 950.00
Punch Cup, Handle, Mt.Washington, 3 x 3 In. 200.00
Punch Cup, Mt.Washington, 2 3/4 x 3 In. 85.00
Rose Jar, Wild Rose, Petticoat Shape, Metal Insert, 5 In. 1610.00
Salt & Pepper, Satin, 4 1/4 In. 230.00
Sugar, Ruffled, Pink Satin, Mt. Washington, 3 x 4 In. 115.00
Sugar & Creamer, Berry Pontil, Wishbone Feet, 2 1/2 In. 1800.00
Syrup, Enameled Spider Mums, Silver Plate Cover, Egg Shape, 6 1/2 In. 4025.00
Taster, Whiskey, Diamond-Quilted, Satin, 2 3/4 In. 173.00
Toothpick, Diamond-Quilted, Tricornered, 2 1/4 In. 74.00
Tumbler, Glossy, Mt.Washington, 3 3/4 In. 290.00
Tumbler, Juice, Handle, Mt. Washington, 3 7/8 In. 170.00
Tumbler, Opaque Green, Mottled Blue Rim, New England Glass Co., 3 3/4 In. 415.00
Tumbler, Satin, Mt.Washington, 3 In. 115.00
Vase, Bow Knot, Applied Rigaree, Bulbous, Mt. Washington, 4 1/2 x 5 In. 860.00

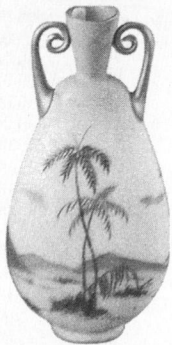

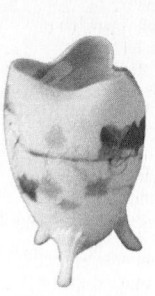

Burmese, Vase,
Egyptian, Palm Trees,
Ibis, 2 Gold Handles,
Mt. Washington, 11 In.

Burmese, Vase,
Enameled Monkey,
14 In.

Burmese, Vase,
Enameled, Ivy,
Tricornered Top,
3-Footed, 7 1/2 In.

Burmese, Vase,
Owls, 1 In Flight,
1 Perched, 13 In.

Vase, Egyptian, Palm Trees, Ibis, 2 Gold Handles, Mt. Washington, 11 In. . . . . *Illus* 8337.00
Vase, Enameled Bird Perched On Branch, 2 Milk Glass Handles, 11 1/2 In. 300.00
Vase, Enameled Monkey, 14 In. . . . . *Illus* 11212.00
Vase, Enameled, Ivy, Tricornered Top, 3-Footed, 7 1/2 In. . . . . *Illus* 1840.00
Vase, Frolicking Monkeys, 1 Large, 1 Small, Mt. Washington, 12 1/2 In. 9775.00
Vase, Gourd Shape, Green Leaves & Buds, Red, Yellow, 8 1/2 In. 400.00
Vase, Jack-In-The-Pulpit, 6 1/2 x 3 In. 230.00
Vase, Jack-In-The-Pulpit, Mt. Washington, 9 In. 316.00
Vase, Jack-In-The-Pulpit, Ruffled Edge, Mt. Washington, 7 1/2 In. 435.00
Vase, Lily, Matte, Mt. Washington, 12 1/2 In. 345.00
Vase, Lily, Salmon Pink To Yellow, 7 In. 170.00
Vase, Owl Decoration, Gold Highlights, 13 3/4 In. 10350.00
Vase, Owls, 1 In Flight, 1 Perched, 13 In. . . . . *Illus* 10350.00
Vase, Scattered Sprays Of Pansies, 10 In. 440.00

BUSTER BROWN, the comic strip, first appeared in color in 1902.
Buster and his dog, Tige, remained a popular comic and soon became
even more famous as the emblem for a shoe company, a textile firm,
and others. The strip was discontinued in 1920, but some of the adver-
tising is still in use.

Automaton, Buster & Tige, Animated, 1930s 2250.00
Bank, Buster & Tige, Iron, Moore No. 241 . . . . 125.00
Box, Allspice, Jas. H. Torbes Tea & Coffee Co., St. Louis, Mo., Cardboard, 1 1/2 Oz. 94.00
Box, Black Pepper, Jas. H. Forbes Tea & Coffee Co., Cardboard, 1 Lb. 35.00
Box, Buster Brown's Stocking, Gold Medal Award, 1905, 9 x 4 In. 33.00
Camera 62.00
Camera, Box 75.00
Clock, Light-Up, Buster & Tige, Pam Clock Co., N.Y., 15 In. 1030.00
Cup, Buster & Mary Jane Drinking Tea, Pottery, Germany, c.1908, 3 1/4 In. 68.00
Dictionary 30.00
Dish, Buster & Mary Jane Drinking Tea, Three Crown China, Germany, 5 1/4 In. 40.00
Display, Buster & Tige Swimming, Mechanical, 3-Dimensional, 50 x 53 In. 575.00
Display, Tige Pulling Buster In Shoemobile, Tin, Die Cut, 38 x 25 In. 8360.00
Figure, Inflator Head, Amusement Park Balloon, Cape & Pants 750.00
Figurine, Buster Brown Shoes, Red Outfit, Blue Tie, Bisque, c.1915, 2 3/4 In. 70.00
Game, Pin The Tie On Buster Brown, Selchow & Righter, Mailer, c.1910, 7 x 9 In. 95.00
Noisemaker, Harris Emery Co., Des Moines, Iowa, Pair 25.00
Postcard, Buster Brown Shoes, Cartoon, 1950s 3.00
Poster, Stage Play, Melville B. Raymond's Buster Brown, 1908, Three Sheet 2195.00
Ring, Whistle, Bigfoot, 1950s 20.00

Shoe Stand, Buster & Tige, Countertop, Tin, Die Cut, 8 x 13 In. 3300.00
Sign, B Stands For Buster, Buy Blue Ribbon Shoes, 1904, 7 x 5 In. 121.00
Sign, Buster Brown Bread, Head, Red Hat, 1907, 11 x 8 In. 110.00
Sign, Buster Brown Bread, Wooden Frame, Embossed, 1920-1930, 20 x 28 In. 1208.00
Sign, Buster Brown Shoes For Boys & Girls, Buster & Tige, Iron, 17 In. 5750.00
Sign, Buster Brown Shoes, Tin Over Cardboard, Easel, 1920s, 13 x 6 In. 140.00
Tin, Buster Brown Paprika, Buster & Tige 75.00
Watch, Pocket, Ansonia Clock Company 425.00
Whistle, Figural, Bisque 75.00

BUTTER CHIPS, or butter pats, were small individual dishes for butter. They were the height of fashion from 1880 to 1910. Earlier as well as later examples are known.

Floral Center, Blue Edge, J.H.W. & Sons, 3 1/8 In. 12.00
Grecian Statue, Flow Blue, Grindley 55.00
Green Leaf Surround, Limoges, 3 1/4 In. 15.00
Light Cream, Semivitreous, 3 In. 5.00
Lion Center, Sterling Silver, 2 3/4 In. 22.00
Porcelain, 18K Gold Trim, 3 In. 5.00

BUTTER MOLDS are listed in the Kitchen category under Mold, Butter.

BUTTON collecting has been popular since the nineteenth century. Buttons have been known throughout the centuries, and there are millions of styles. Gold, silver, or precious stones were used for the best buttons, but most were made of natural materials, like bone or shell, or from inexpensive metals. Only a few types are listed for comparison.

Brass, Henry Clay, Large 175.00
Bridle, Cleveland & Hendricks, 1 1/2 In., 2 Piece 305.00
Flasher, Plastic, Halley's Comet, Now You See It, Now You Don't, 2 In. 3.00
Folder, With 39 Buttons, Iowa Button Co., Lansing, 1952 . . . . 60.00

BUTTONHOOKS have been a popular collectible in England for many years but only recently have gained the attention of American collectors. The buttonhooks were made to help fasten the many buttons of the old-fashioned high-button shoes and other items of apparel.

Ivory Handle, Image Of Niagara Falls 102.00
Mixed Metal, Dauma Waking From Meditations, 3 1/2 In. 170.00
Sterling Silver, Ornate, 7 3/4 In. 40.00

BYBEE POTTERY was started in 1845 and is still working. The Lexington, Kentucky, firm makes pottery that is sold at the factory. Pieces are marked with the name or with the name enclosed by the outline of the state of Kentucky.

Bowl, Blue, Handle, 4 1/2 x 2 1/2 In. 13.00
Dish, Fluted, Blue, 10 x 1 1/2 In. 21.00
Jug, 100th B.J. Lunch, 2-21-85, Brown, Double B Mark, 3 3/4 In. 15.00
Pitcher, Light Brown, Marbleized, 6 In. 11.00
Pitcher, Maroon, 9 In. 21.00
Vase, Ruffled Top, Blue, 3 3/4 In. 26.00
Vase, Trees, Hanging Moss, Green, Tan, Mauve Overspray, Selden Bybee, 7 1/8 In. 56.00

CALENDARS made to hang on the wall or to be displayed on a desk top have been popular since the last quarter of the nineteenth century. Many were printed with advertising as part of the artwork and were given away as premiums. Calendars with guns, gunpowder, or Coca-Cola advertising are most prized.

1845, Sunup, First Savings Bank Of Colusa, Maxfield Parrish, 22 x 46 In. 350.00
1887, Lorillard's Old Reliable Mechanics Delight, 12 x 12 In. 175.00
1890, Ivory Soap, Lithographs, Beautiful Ladies 90.00
1891, Hood's Sarsaparilla, 3 Children, Musical Instruments 155.00
1894, Hood's Sarsaparilla, Die Cut, Full Pad 120.00
1895, Perpetual, Goodhart Bros. New Method Laundry, Paperboard, 10 In. 143.00

1897, Snag-Proof, Elves With Boot, Paperboard, 12-Month, 5 1/4 x 7 In. 121.00
1898, National Life Insurance 25.00
1900, Hood's Sarsaparilla, 2 Young Girls, Easel Back, Envelope & Pamphlet 175.00
1901, Quaker Oats, Fortune-Telling, 6 x 6 In. 175.00
1901, Rumford 145.00
1901, Will & Baumer Candle Manufacturers, Die Cut, Full Pad, 11 x 13 In. 110.00
1901, William Eichberg, Young Girl, Basket Of Flowers, Die Cut, 10 x 16 In. 190.00
1902, David Rohrer, Bourbon & Rye, Native Girl, Soldier, 18 x 27 In. 70.00
1902, Deering Harvester Co., Sign, Merged With International Harvester 950.00
1902, G. Scherling, Druggist, Wood Shoe, Flowers, Die Cut, Full Pad, 6 x 12 In. 70.00
1903, Pe-Ru-Na Cures Catarrh, Woman, With Large Bottle, Frame, 6 x 12 In. 375.00
1903, S. Mills, Young Girl, Flowers, Bows, Die Cut, 5 3/4 x 11 1/2 In. 138.00
1904, Metropolitan Life Insurance, Girl, Holly Leaves In Hair, 7 1/4 x 20 In. 45.00
1905, Great Atlantic & Pacific Tea Co., Young Girl Sipping Tea, 8 x 10 In. 72.00
1905, Harrington & Richardson Arms Co., Woman Ready To Shoot, 26 In. 1925.00
1906, St. Alban's Coffee Co., 2 Girls, 4-Leaf Clovers, Die Cut, 5 1/2 x 10 In. 205.00
1907, Daisy Soap, Oberne, Hosick & Co., Young Girl, Die Cut, 11 1/2 x 6 In. 285.00
1908, Celluloid, 3 x 2 In. 145.00
1908, Hampden 5 Cent Cigar, Gathering Wild Flowers, Frisky Bull, 9 x 7 In. 150.00
1908, Hood's Sarsaparilla, 2 Boys Training Dog 145.00
1908, Swift's Lowell Fertilizer Co., Mother & Daughter, Full Pad, 14 x 21 In. 100.00
1909, Fair Art Chocolate Co., Milwaukee, Woman Painting, Palette Shape 650.00
1909, Firemen's Insurance, Horses Pulling Steam Pumper, Full Pad, 11 In. 215.00
1910, Jack Sprat, Black Ground, Metal Easel Back, 2 1/4 x 3 1/5 In. 44.00
1910, L.L. Croner, Butcher & Grocer, Boy, Girl, Fountain, Full Pad, 12 x 17 In. 60.00
1910, Prudential Insurance Co., Girl Blowing Bubbles, Dog, 8 x 10 In. 145.00
1910, Robert Rankin, Western Dressed Beef, Butcher, Full Pad, 8 1/2 x 16 In. 242.00
1910, Singer Sewing Machine, Mother Giving Children First Lesson, 8 x 10 In. 77.00
1911, C.C. Morse & Co., San Francisco, July 1911 To June 1912, 5 x 5 3/4 In. 37.00
1912, Lowell Fertilizer Co., Woman With Roses, 9 In. 190.00
1912, Winchester, Matted, 15 1/2 x 30 In. 1450.00
1913, Hood's, Frame, 7 x 7 1/2 In. 180.00
1913, Iroquois Brewery, Indian Maiden, Oak Frame, 31 1/2 x 17 1/4 In. 1210.00
1914, Hiram Swank, Philadelphia Brick Mfg., Hounds & Fox Hunters, 35 In. 65.00
1918, Strange Bros. Hide Company, Sioux City, Iowa, 5 1/4 x 10 In. 72.00
1918, Watkin's Remedies, 2 Boys Fishing, Delivery Truck, 5 1/2 x 11 In. 110.00
1920, Bear Invading Campsite, 15 x 30 3/4 In. 550.00
1920, Pratt Food Company, Phila., Monthly Poultry, Folded, 18 x 26 In. 35.00
1920, Western Shotshells, Respecters Of Limits 450.00
1923, Meyer's Garage, Car With Flowers, Die Cut, Full Pad, 15 x 10 In. 275.00
1923, Wrigley's P.K. Chewing Sweet, 2 Children At Brook, 3 1/4 x 5 1/2 In. 40.00
1924, Mass & Steffen Furs 450.00
1924, Mazda, Maxfield Parrish, Full Pad 900.00
1926, Geo. Borgfeldt & Co., Celluloid, Listing Toys, Bye-Lo Dolls, 2 1/2 x 4 In. 110.00
1926, Peters Cartridge Company 700.00
1927, Peters Cartridge Company 600.00
1927, Sunshine Andy Gump Biscuits, Mother & Son, 9 1/2 x 13 1/2 In. 40.00
1927, Winchester Store 550.00
1928, Peters Cartridge Company, Marshall-Wells Company, Dog, 30 x 15 In. 160.00
1930, Mazda, Maxfield Parrish, Full Pad 650.00
1930, Ostendorf, Girl With Flowers On Balcony, Full Pad, 14 x 22 In. 155.00
1930, Winchester 1595.00
1931, Copps Coffee Co., Deerwood Coffee, Hard Board, Full Pad, 18 x 15 In. 105.00
1931, De Laval Separator Co., Indian Boy & Girl, Canoes, 4 Panels, 36 In. 66.00
1931, Liberty Hotel, Semi-Clothed Woman With Peacock Feather, 15 x 20 In. 220.00
1931, Mazda, Maxfield Parrish, Full Pad 600.00
1933, Mazda, Maxfield Parrish, Full Pad 700.00
1934, Diamond T Motor Car Co., Delivery Truck, Oct., Nov. & Dec., 8 x 16 In. 65.00
1934, Wrigley's, Matted, Frame, 8 1/2 x 15 In. 125.00
1936, Benny's Market, Bridgeport, Conn., Picture Of FDR, Cardboard, 10 In. 40.00
1936, Daniel Webster & Gold Coin Flours 70.00
1936, Goodwin, Cowboy On Horse, River, 8 x 16 In. 85.00

1936, Great Northern Railroad, Full Pad, 16 x 33 In. 175.00
1937, De Laval 45.00
1937, Dr Pepper, Earl Moran, Frame, Under Glass 2415.00
1937, Ford Motor Co., Thrifty Dogs In Front Of Auto, Full Pad, 15 x 23 In. 65.00
1937, Jack Sprat, Black Ground, Metal Easel Back, 2 1/4 x 3 1/4 In. 44.00
1938, De Laval 25.00
1938, Lucky Strike Green Pack, Pinup Girl, Color, 11 x 14 In. 8.00
1938, Pretty Girl, NeHi, Rolf Armstrong, Matted, Frame, 11 x 23 1/2 In. 375.00
1939, Sheer Beauty, Frame 175.00
1940, Greyhound Lines, Bus & Greyhound Dog, 20 x 32 In. 175.00
1940, Harvey's Cash Grocery, Will Rogers Beloved Philosopher, 21 x 45 In. 110.00
1940, Hercules Powder, Stagecoach Scene, N.C. Wyeth 175.00
1940, New York Central System, Speeding, Heart, Industrial America, 33 In. 300.00
1942, Royal Crown 190.00
1943, Hello Skipper, Moran, 11 x 23 In. 95.00
1943, Hercules Powder Co., Frame, 31 1/2 x 14 1/2 In. 253.00
1943, Hold Everything, Pinup, Armstrong, 11 x 23 In. 95.00
1944, Greyhound Lines, Futuristic Design Of Bus, 20 x 32 In. 165.00
1945, Borden's Ice Cream, Boy Scouts Of America, 33 x 16 In. 50.00
1946, Goebel, 8 Clydesdales Horses, Cubs, White Sox Schedule, 18 x 27 In. 35.00
1946, Sprite Boy 1450.00
1947, Petty, All Months 115.00
1947, Rock-Ola, Puget Sound Novelty, Patty Jenkins, 22 x 46 In. 575.00
1948, Jack Sprat, Black Ground, Metal Easel Back, 2 1/4 x 3 1/4 In. 44.00
1948, Squirt, Sweater Girl Holding Bottle, Little Squirt Looks Up, 16 x 23 In. 65.00
1948, Vargas, Pinup, All Months, 8 x 12 In. 48.00
1949, Dionne Quints, With Ads 30.00
1949, NuGrape Soda, Pretty Girl 80.00
1949, Squirt, Pretty Girls Each Page, 3 Months On 4 Pages 65.00
1950, Irresistible, Pinup, Armstrong, 11 x 23 In. 95.00
1952, Gay Products Co., If Its Gay, It's Ok, Grace Kelly Look-Alike 10.00
1953, Marilyn Monroe Nude, 9 x 11 In. 18.00
1954, Illinois Central Railroad, Couple Buying Pastries, 18 x 27 In. 75.00
1954, Marilyn Monroe, Nude 15.00
1954, Zoe Mozart Calendar 1, Green Ground, H.R. Mueller, Columbia, Mo. 110.00
1955, Jones Auto Supply, Marilyn Monroe Look-Alike Model, 33 x 16 In. 165.00
1955, Marilyn Monroe, Nude, 10 x 17 In. 20.00
1957, Jayne Mansfield, Original Wrapper 45.00
1958, American Beauty, Arthur E. Frahm, January, 11 x 23 In. 55.00
1958, Texaco 30.00
1958, Zoe Mozart Calendar 1, Pink Ground, H.R. Mueller, Columbia, Mo. 110.00
1960, Hummel, Colored Pictures Each Page 95.00
1960, Perpetual, Falstaff Beer, Metal, Cardboard, 17 x 9 In. 65.00
1982, Madame Alexander 20.00
Perpetual, Revolving Dial, Whitehead & Hoag, Celluloid, 6 x 7 In. 135.00

CALENDAR PLATES were very popular in the United States from 1906
to 1929. Since then, plates have been made every year. A calendar and
the name of a store, a picture of flowers, a girl, or a scene were featured on the plate.

1909, Bird 12.00
1909, Flowers & Fruit 35.00
1909, Scenic, Advertising 20.00
1910, Port Royal, Pennsylvania, Pastel Flowers 45.00
1913, Horseshoe 15.00
1919, American Flag 35.00
1920, Great World War, Victory, Peace 55.00
1928, To Old Orchard Beach, Maine, Deer Looking At Road Sign, 9 In. 60.00
1954, Fiesta, Ivory, 10 In. 38.00
1973, Currier & Ives 24.00
1980, Currier & Ives 24.00
1983, Currier & Ives 24.00

CAMARK POTTERY started in 1924 in Camden, Arkansas. Jack Carnes founded the firm and made many types of glazes and wares. The company was bought by Mary Daniel. Production was halted in 1983.

Candlestick, Double, 5 1/2 In., Pair	80.00
Candlestick, Hand Painted Rose	100.00
Vase, Blue & White Stipple, Art Deco, 8 In.	185.00
Vase, Green, 5 1/2 In.	35.00
Vase, Green, Blue & Yellow Glaze, 2 Handles, 10 1/2 In.	935.00
Vase, Green, High Glaze, 14 1/2 In.	125.00
Vase, Iris, Basket, 9 1/2 In.	75.00
Vase, Maroon, High Glaze, 12 In.	90.00 to 95.00
Vase, Ribbed, Blue, 5 In.	40.00
Wall Pocket, Painted Tree Along Riverbank, Metallic Purple & Red, Signed, 8 1/2 In.	465.00

CAMBRIDGE GLASS Company was founded in 1901 in Cambridge, Ohio. The company closed in 1954, reopened briefly, and closed again in 1958. The firm made all types of glass. Their early wares included heavy pressed glass with the mark *Near Cut.* Later wares included Crown Tuscan, etched stemware, and clear and colored glass. The firm used a C in a triangle mark after 1920. Some Cambridge patterns may be included in the Depression Glass category.

Alpine, Bowl, Footed, 4 3/4 x 10 1/2 In.	70.00
Apple Blossom, Bowl, 12 1/2 In.	40.00
Apple Blossom, Bowl, Gold Krystol, Gold Trim, 11 In.	125.00
Apple Blossom, Claret, 4 1/2 Oz.	65.00
Apple Blossom, Compote, 4 Footed, Gold Krystol	60.00
Apple Blossom, Compote, Cheese, Amber	49.00
Apple Blossom, Cordial, Gold Krystol	95.00
Apple Blossom, Jug, Pink, 80 Oz.	529.00
Apple Blossom, Pitcher, 80 Oz.	175.00
Apple Blossom, Plate, Gold Krystol, 8 1/2 In.	16.00
Apple Blossom, Relish, 5 Sections, Gold Krystol	89.00
Apple Blossom, Sherbet, Gold Krystol, 6 Oz.	20.00
Apple Blossom, Tray, Pickle, Gold Krystol, 9 In.	69.00
Apple Blossom, Vase, Pillow, Ebony, 9 In.	750.00
Azurite, Candlestick, 8 1/2 In., Pair	85.00
Bashful Charlotte, Flower Frog, 6 1/2 In.	195.00
Bashful Charlotte, Flower Frog, Satin, 11 1/2 In.	195.00
Caprice, Ashtray, Alpine	27.00
Caprice, Ashtray, Moonlight Blue, Triangular	12.00
Caprice, Bonbon, 2 Handles, Moonlight Blue, 4 1/2 In.	50.00
Caprice, Bowl, 2 Handles, Footed, 11 In.	115.00
Caprice, Bowl, 4-Footed, Moonlight Blue, 10 1/2 In.	80.00
Caprice, Bowl, Crimped, Alpine, Footed, 13 In.	175.00
Caprice, Bowl, Crimped, Emerald, 13 In.	110.00
Caprice, Bowl, Crimped, Moonlight Blue, 5 In.	1215.00
Caprice, Bowl, LaRosa, 11 In.	125.00
Caprice, Bowl, Moonlight Blue, 12 1/2 In.	125.00
Caprice, Bowl, Moonlight Blue, Oblong, 12 In.	125.00
Caprice, Candleholder, Moonlight Blue, Pair	135.00
Caprice, Candleholder, Moonlight Blue, With Prism, 7 In.	130.00
Caprice, Candlestick, 2-Light, Keyhole, Pair	125.00
Caprice, Candy Dish, Cover	20.00
Caprice, Candy Dish, Cover, Blue, 6 In.	110.00 to 150.00
Caprice, Candy Dish, Cover, Footed, Blue, 6 In.	225.00
Caprice, Celery Dish, 3 Sections, 8 1/2 In.	49.00
Caprice, Cheese Stand, Moonlight Blue	350.00
Caprice, Coaster	60.00
Caprice, Coaster, LaRosa	55.00
Caprice, Cocktail, Oyster, LaRosa	85.00
Caprice, Compote, Blue, 5 1/2 In.	75.00
Caprice, Cruet, Alpine	175.00

Caprice, Cruet, Moonlight Blue, 5 Oz. 350.00
Caprice, Cup & Saucer, Mocha 36.00
Caprice, Cup & Saucer, Moonlight Blue 50.00
Caprice, Finger Bowl, Underplate, Moonlight Blue ....60.00 to 110.00
Caprice, Goblet, Moonlight Blue, 9 Oz. 15.00
Caprice, Goblet, Water, Pressed, Amber, 10 Oz. 400.00
Caprice, Goblet, Water, Pressed, Amethyst, 10 Oz. 325.00
Caprice, Jug, Moonlight Blue, 32 Oz. 500.00
Caprice, Mustard, Moonlight Blue 175.00
Caprice, Parfait, LaRosa, 5 Oz. 169.00
Caprice, Plate, 2 Handles, Moonlight Blue, 8 In. 50.00
Caprice, Plate, 9 1/2 In. 45.00
Caprice, Plate, Handle, Moonlight Blue, 6 In. 35.00
Caprice, Plate, Mocha, 8 1/2 In. 29.00
Caprice, Plate, Moonlight Blue, 5 1/2 In. ....29.00 to 30.00
Caprice, Plate, Moonlight Blue, 8 1/2 In. 32.00
Caprice, Plate, Moonlight Blue, 11 In. 70.00
Caprice, Plate, Moonlight Blue, 15 In. 80.00
Caprice, Rose Bowl, Moonlight Blue, With Frog, 6 In. 450.00
Caprice, Saucer, Crimped, Blue, 5 In. 75.00
Caprice, Sherbet, Low, 5 Oz. 18.00
Caprice, Sugar & Creamer, Moonlight Blue, Individual 60.00
Caprice, Tray, Moonlight Blue, Oval, 9 In. 50.00
Caprice, Tumbler, Amber, 2 Oz. 35.00
Caprice, Tumbler, Footed, 5 Oz. 18.00
Caprice, Tumbler, Footed, 12 Oz. 22.00
Caprice, Tumbler, Footed, Moonlight Blue, 3 Oz. 95.00
Caprice, Tumbler, Footed, Moonlight Blue, 5 Oz. ....45.00 to 60.00
Caprice, Tumbler, Iced Tea, 12 Oz. 18.00
Caprice, Tumbler, Iced Tea, Moonlight Blue, 12 Oz. 137.00
Caprice, Tumbler, Moonlight Blue, 4 1/2 Oz. 45.00
Caprice, Tumbler, Moonlight Blue, 5 Oz. 80.00
Caprice, Tumbler, Moonlight Blue, 12 Oz. 150.00
Caprice, Tumbler, Mushroom, Moonlight Blue, 2 Oz. 60.00
Caprice, Tumbler, Mushroom, Moonlight Blue, 5 Oz. ....49.00 to 50.00
Caprice, Tumbler, Mushroom, Moonlight Blue, 12 Oz. 45.00
Caprice, Vase, Amber, 8 1/8 In. 189.00
Caprice, Vase, Cobalt Blue, 6 In. 250.00
Caprice, Vase, Cobalt Blue, 8 5/8 In. 289.00
Caprice, Vase, Moonlight Blue, 4 1/2 Oz. ....225.00 to 275.00
Caprice, Wine, Moonlight Blue, 2 1/2 Oz. 60.00
Caprice, Wine, Pressed, Moonlight Blue, 3 Oz. 195.00
Cascade, Goblet, Water, 10 Oz. 11.00
Chantilly, Candlestick, 5 In., Pair 200.00
Chantilly, Candy Dish, Cover 135.00
Chantilly, Relish, 3 Sections, 4 Handles 40.00
Chantilly, Salt & Pepper 15.00
Chantilly, Sugar & Creamer, Individual 65.00
Chantilly, Vase, 10 1/2 In. 125.00
Cleo, Compote, Pink, 5 1/2 In. 95.00
Cleo, Gravy Boat, Underplate, Pink 350.00
Cleo, Plate, Willow Blue, 8 1/4 In. 30.00
Colonial, Butter, Cover 42.00
Crown Tuscan, Ashtray, Seashell, 3-Footed, 4 In. 35.00
Crown Tuscan, Bowl, 4-Footed, 12 3/4 In. 195.00
Crown Tuscan, Candlestick, Keyhole, 2-Light, 6 In., Pair 250.00
Crown Tuscan, Candy Dish, Cover, 3 Sections, 8 In. 165.00
Crown Tuscan, Centerpiece, Flying Lady, Shell With Nude, 10 In. 650.00
Crown Tuscan, Vase, 6 1/2 In. 350.00
Crown Tuscan, Vase, 10 In. 185.00
Decagon, Bonbon, 2 Handles, Pink, 5 1/2 In. 27.00
Decagon, Bonbon, 2 Handles, Pink, 6 1/4 In. 24.00
Decagon, Bowl, 2 Handles, Emerald, 6 1/4 In. 15.00

Decagon, Bowl, Amethyst, 8 1/2 In. 65.00
Decagon, Bowl, Cupped, Emerald, 5 1/2 In. 55.00
Decagon, Bowl, Footed, Emerald, 6 In. 24.00
Decagon, Bread Plate, Pink, 6 1/4 In. 15.00
Decagon, Champagne, Moonlight Blue 24.00
Decagon, Creamer, Emerald 15.00
Decagon, Cup & Saucer, Moonlight Blue 28.00
Decagon, Cup & Saucer, Pink 20.00
Decagon, Decanter, Emerald, 9 1/4 In. 165.00
Decagon, Goblet, Water, Emerald, 9 Oz. 30.00
Decagon, Goblet, Water, Moonlight Blue 32.00
Decagon, Goblet, Water, Royal Blue, 9 Oz. 35.00
Decagon, Gravy Boat, Underplate, Emerald 125.00
Decagon, Ice Bucket, Pink 85.00
Decagon, Pitcher, Pink, 62 Oz. 125.00
Decagon, Plate, Emerald, 8 3/4 In. 18.00
Decagon, Plate, Pink, 6 In. 12.00
Decagon, Plate, Royal Blue, 6 In. 12.00
Decagon, Platter, Pink, 14 1/2 In. 75.00
Decagon, Relish, 2 Sections, Emerald, 8 1/2 In. 35.00
Decagon, Salt & Pepper, Royal Blue 125.00
Decagon, Saltshaker, Amber 22.00
Decagon, Sherbet, Royal Blue, 6 Oz. 24.00
Decagon, Sugar Shaker, Pink 165.00
Decagon, Sugar, Moonlight Blue 20.00
Decagon, Tray, Moonlight Blue 25.00
Decagon, Tumbler, Emerald, 8 Oz. 25.00
Decagon, Tumbler, Footed, Amethyst, 2 1/2 In. 25.00
Decagon, Tumbler, Juice, Footed, Pink, 5 Oz. 20.00
Decagon, Tumbler, Juice, Footed, Royal Blue, 5 Oz. 30.00
Decagon, Wine, Royal Blue 40.00
Diane, Compote, 5 1/2 In. 60.00
Diane, Cordial, 10 Oz. 75.00
Diane, Cup & Saucer 50.00
Diane, Vase, Keyhole, Footed, 12 In. 189.00
Draped Lady, Flower Frog, 9 In. . . . . .185.00 to 225.00
Elaine, Bonbon, 2 Handles, 5 1/4 In. 55.00
Elaine, Butter, Cover 229.00
Elaine, Cordial, 10 Oz. 95.00
Elaine, Cup & Saucer 50.00
Elaine, Plate, 8 1/2 In. 30.00
Elaine, Tumbler, 2 1/2 Oz. 77.00
Elaine, Tumbler, Iced Tea, 12 Oz. 45.00
Martha Washington, Candlestick, Diane Etch, 5 1/2 In., Pair 215.00
Martha Washington, Cup & Saucer 50.00
Martha Washington, Ice Bucket 145.00
Martha Washington, Plate, 7 1/2 In. 28.00
Martha Washington, Plate, 8 In. 23.00
Mt. Vernon, Plate, Amber, 11 1/2 In. 16.00
Pristine, Decanter, 32 Oz. 20.00
Pristine, Ice Bucket 26.00
Pristine, Relish, 3 Sections, 12 In. 16.00
Regency, Cocktail, 3 Oz. 75.00
Regency, Sherbet, Tall, 6 Oz. 50.00
Rose Point, Basket, Favor, 3 In. 850.00
Rose Point, Basket, Reeded Handle, 6 In. 550.00
Rose Point, Bonbon, Cupped, 3 1/2 In. 195.00
Rose Point, Bowl, 4-Footed, Sterling Overlay, 10 In. 295.00
Rose Point, Bowl, 9 1/2 In. . . . . .80.00 to 90.00
Rose Point, Bowl, 10 1/2 In. 125.00
Rose Point, Bowl, 12 In. 135.00
Rose Point, Bowl, Crimped, 10 1/2 In. 110.00
Rose Point, Butter, 1/4 Lb., 5 In. 495.00

Rose Point, Butter, Cover, 5 1/2 In. 200.00
Rose Point, Butter, Cover, Round 125.00
Rose Point, Candlestick, 5 In., Pair 85.00
Rose Point, Candy Dish, Cover 165.00
Rose Point, Celery Dish, 12 In. ....65.00 to 85.00
Rose Point, Cheese & Cracker Set 195.00
Rose Point, Claret, 4 1/2 Oz. 90.00
Rose Point, Compote, 2 Handles, 7 In. 100.00
Rose Point, Compote, 2 Handles, 8 In. 50.00
Rose Point, Compote, 5 1/2 In. ....87.00 to 125.00
Rose Point, Compote, 6 In. 135.00
Rose Point, Compote, 7 In. ....185.00 to 225.00
Rose Point, Cup & Saucer 40.00
Rose Point, Decanter, Keyhole Stopper 160.00
Rose Point, Dish, Corn Or Pickle, 9 1/2 In. 90.00
Rose Point, Finger Bowl, Underplate ....145.00 to 175.00
Rose Point, Goblet, Water, 10 Oz. 40.00
Rose Point, Ice Bucket 210.00
Rose Point, Ivy Ball, Footed, Ball Stem, 7 In. 585.00
Rose Point, Jug, 76 Oz. 450.00
Rose Point, Nappy, 6 In. 65.00
Rose Point, Pickle, 9 In. 65.00
Rose Point, Pitcher, 76 Oz. 350.00
Rose Point, Plate, 9 1/2 In. 65.00
Rose Point, Plate, 10 1/2 In. 225.00
Rose Point, Plate, Gadroon Edge, 7 1/2 In. 15.00
Rose Point, Platter, 12 1/2 In. 90.00
Rose Point, Platter, 2 Handles, 12 In. 60.00
Rose Point, Relish, 2 Sections, 7 In. 90.00
Rose Point, Relish, 3 Sections, 7 1/2 In. 175.00
Rose Point, Relish, 3 Sections, 9 In. 70.00
Rose Point, Relish, 3 Sections, 12 In. 70.00
Rose Point, Relish, 6 Sections, 12 In. 225.00
Rose Point, Salt & Pepper 185.00
Rose Point, Sherbet, 7 Oz. 22.00
Rose Point, Sugar & Creamer, Individual 40.00
Rose Point, Vase, Bud, 6 In. 95.00
Rose Point, Vase, Bud, 10 In. 105.00
Rose Point, Vase, Flared, 8 In. 260.00
Rose Point, Vase, Footed, 11 In. 155.00
Rose Point, Wine, 3 1/2 Oz. 50.00
Roselyn, Cordial 75.00
Scotty Dog, Bookends 125.00
Seagull, Flower Frog ....48.00 to 150.00
Square, Tumbler, 5 In. 15.00
Swan, Bowl, Peach-Blo, 10 In. 300.00
Swirl, Vase, Amber, 13 In. 170.00
Tally-Ho, Bowl, 3 Sections, 11 In. 169.00
Tally-Ho, Claret, Carmen, 4 1/2 Oz. 45.00
Tally-Ho, Cocktail, 3 1/2 Oz. 32.00
Tally-Ho, Cordial, Pressed, Carmen, 1 Oz. 65.00
Tally-Ho, Goblet, Water, Pressed, Carmen, 10 Oz. 35.00
Tally-Ho, Plate, 2 Handles, 11 1/2 In. 129.00
Tally-Ho, Plate, Carmen, 8 In. 20.00
Tally-Ho, Relish, 3 Sections, 8 In. 129.00
Tally-Ho, Sugar & Creamer 69.00
Trindle, Candlestick, Buttercup Etch, 8 In., Pair 225.00
Wildflower, Butter, Cover 195.00
Wildflower, Candlestick, Gold Trim, Pair 125.00
Wildflower, Candy Box, Cover 150.00
Wildflower, Candy Dish, Cover 100.00
Wildflower, Candy Dish, Cover, 3 Sections 125.00
Wildflower, Cheese & Cracker Set 135.00

Wildflower, Compote, Amber, Gold Trim	100.00
Wildflower, Compote, Cheese	50.00
Wildflower, Compote, Cover, Emerald	45.00
Wildflower, Dish, Mayonnaise, Underplate, Pink	165.00
Wildflower, Marmalade, Cover	175.00
Wildflower, Pitcher, Water, Emerald Green	165.00
Wildflower, Saltshaker	20.00
Wildflower, Sugar & Creamer, Cover, Moonlight Blue	50.00
Wildflower, Vase, Flared, 8 In.	110.00
Wildflower, Vase, Keyhole, Footed, 12 In.	150.00
Wildflower, Vase, Mandarin Gold, Globe, 5 In.	375.00
Wildflower, Vase, Sweet Pea, Emerald, 3 3/4 In.	295.00

CAMEO GLASS was made in much the same manner as a cameo in jewelry. Parts of the top layer of glass were cut away to reveal a different colored glass beneath. The most famous cameo glass was made during the nineteenth century. Signed cameo glass pieces are listed under the glasswork's name, such as Daum or Galle.

Bonbon, Morning Glory Blossoms, Sterling Silver Fittings, 3 x 5 In.	1950.00
Jar, Cover, Grapevine & Leaf Design, De Vez, France, 1900, 2 1/2 In.	660.00
Lamp Shade, Foliage, Flowers, Signed, 6 1/2 In., Pair	201.00
Vase, 12 Sailboats Around, Branches & Leaves Frame Border, Michel, 7 1/2 In.	825.00
Vase, Cherry, Red & White, Peking, 6 3/4 In., Pair	495.00
Vase, Flowers & Leaves, Shades Of Purple & Green, Signed, Arsall, 12 1/8 In.	975.00
Vase, Poppies, Orange, Brown, 2 Applied Handles, Charder, 10 1/4 In.	1840.00
Vase, Winter Landscape, Dominant Bare Trees, Le Gras, France, 1900, 4 1/2 In.	660.00

CAMPAIGN memorabilia is listed in the Political category.

CAMPBELL KIDS were first used as part of an advertisement for the Campbell Soup Company in 1906. The kids were created by Grace Drayton, a popular illustrator of the day. The kids were used in magazine and newspaper ads until about 1951. They were presented again in 1966; and in 1983, they were redesigned with a slimmer, more contemporary appearance.

Bowl, Winter Olympics, 1984, 8 1/2 In.	20.00
Cookbook, 1954	35.00
Growth Chart, Growing Up With Campbells, Measures To 2 Ft.	8.00
Postcard, 1910	15.00

CAMPHOR GLASS is a cloudy white glass that has been blown or pressed. It was made by many factories in the Midwest during the midnineteenth century.

Butter, Thistle, Red, 7 1/4 In.	26.00
Group, Boy Playing Flute, Girl With Bunnies, c.1900, 9 1/4 In.	65.00
Shade, Wall Sconce, Embossed Flower & Leaf, Pink, 9 In., Pair	97.00
Shoe, Baby's, Toe Covered With Daisies, 1930s, 4 In.	97.00
Vase, Butterfly, Late 1800s, 7 3/4 In., Pair	50.00

CANDELABRUM refers to a candleholder with more than one arm to hold many candles; a candlestick is designed to hold one candle. The eccentricity of the English language makes the plural of candelabrum into candelabra.

2-Light, Alabaster, Classically Clad Woman, Italy, 26 In., Pair	13800.00
2-Light, Brass, Figural, Medieval Men, Standing, 18th Century, 9 In., Pair	345.00
2-Light, Brass, Refractory, F.A. Walker & Co., Boston, 11 In.	93.00
2-Light, Empire, 2 Foliate Scrolled Branches, 19th Century, 24 In., Pair	6900.00
2-Light, Gilt Metal, Rococo, 1910, 8 1/2 In., Pair	151.00
2-Light, Old Williamsburg, Metal Screw	325.00
2-Light, Sterling Silver, Weighted, 15 In., Pair	315.00
3-Light, 2 Boys Playing Amidst Tree Branches, Floral Sprigs, Painted, 9 3/4 In.	143.00
3-Light, Brass, Arts & Crafts, Riveted Straps, Pierced Organic Pattern, 15 1/2 In.	550.00
3-Light, Brass, Central Bobeche, Scroll Arms, Hexagonal Post, 17 1/4 In., Pair	60.00

3-Light, Brass, Rampant Lions, 20th Century, 18 In., Pair 55.00
3-Light, Bronze, Empire, Round Leaf-Tip Cast Base, Bun Feet, 18 In., Pair 4600.00
3-Light, Bronze, Empire, Winged Figure, Converted, Tole Shade, 25 In., Pair 8625.00
3-Light, Bronze, Empire, Winged Woman, Square Plinth, 18 In., Pair 4600.00
3-Light, Girandole, Amethyst Prisms & Fleurettes, Louis XVI, 1920, 13 1/2 In. 305.00
3-Light, Pressed Glass, Scroll Arms, Baluster Shaft, Prisms, 1860, 21 In., Pair 935.00
3-Light, Sheffield, Fluted, Scroll Arms, Matthew Boulton, c.1830, 21 In. 2970.00
3-Light, Silver Plate, 2 Maidens, 3 Foliate Cups, Whip Arms, c.1900, 19 1/2 In. 1035.00
3-Light, Silver Plate, Convertible, Sheffield, 19th Century, 25 1/2 In. 3220.00
3-Light, Silver, Repousse, 4 Interchangeable Parts, Kirk, 14 1/2 In. 1925.00
3-Light, Sterling Silver, Baluster Stem, Domed Base, Mueck-Cary Co., Inc., 13 In. 115.00
3-Light, Sterling Silver, Gadroon Border, Foliate, John Roberts & Co., 19 In. 345.00
3-Light, Sterling Silver, Georgian, Arms Form Candlestick, Gorham, 11 In., Pair 150.00
3-Light, Sterling Silver, Hirsch, 16 In., Pair 475.00
3-Light, Sterling Silver, Randahl, 1920s, 7 In. 230.00
4-Light, Bronze, Figural, 3 Putti, Marble Base, Prisms 415.00
4-Light, Bronze, Rococo Revival, Cabochon, Scrollwork, 13 1/2 In., Pair 192.00
4-Light, Bronze, Winged Putti Standing On White Marble Column, 26 In. 3910.00
4-Light, Gilt Bronze, Empire, Winged Women Holding Arms, 27 In., Pair 6900.00
4-Light, Gilt Bronze, Foliate Scrolled, Porcelain, Floral Frame, Louis XV, Pair 1955.00
4-Light, Gilt Metal, 7 Scrolled Arms, Amethyst, Tear-Drop Prisms, 20 In., Pair 865.00
4-Light, Octagonal Standard, Faceted Bands, Star-Cut Base, Prisms, 23 3/4 In. 345.00
4-Light, Wrought Iron, Hanging, Adjustable Trammel, 27 In. 1760.00
5-Light, Brass, Glass, Prisms, 14 In., Pair 155.00
5-Light, Diamond Urn-Form Standard, Bobeches, Clarke's Cricklite, 29 In. 575.00
5-Light, Gilt Metal, Intertwining Flowering Vine, Louis XV, 20 In., Pair 1380.00
5-Light, Gilt Metal, Reeded Columns, Electrified, Pair 285.00
5-Light, Gilt Metal, Scroll Arms, Marble Base, Brass Feet, 19th Century, 16 In. 45.00
5-Light, Sheffield, Georgian, Acanthus Motif, Matt Boulton, c.1815, 24 In. 3300.00
5-Light, Sterling Silver, Reed & Barton, 16 In. 920.00
5-Light, Stylized Swan, 4 Scrolled Voluted Branches, Charles X, 23 In., Pair 7475.00
5-Light, Urn Pedestal, Weighted Base, 9 In. 115.00
6-Light, Gilt Bronze, Reeded Columnar Standard, Foliage, 3 Lion Feet, 32 In. 2185.00
6-Light, Gilt Metal, Cherub, Supporting Flowers, Foliage, 23 In., Pair 1725.00
6-Light, Metal, Scrolled Carved Stem, 2 Putti Figures, Wood Base, 17 1/2 In. 575.00
6-Light, Porcelain, Gilt, Painted Cherubs, Florals, Bronze Base, 21 In., Pair 1650.00
7-Light, Gilt Bronze, Elkington & Co., c.1885, 22 In., Pair 2420.00
8-Light, Brass, Hammered, Curved Arms, Round Foot, Josef Hoffmann, 8 In. 8050.00
8-Light, Bronze, Marble, Semi-Nude Men, Napoleon III, 1875, 35 x 15 In. 1210.00
9-Light, Cattails Flanked By Children Standard, Dolphins On Base, 34 1/4 In. 5175.00
9-Light, Indian Maiden, Foliate Scrolled Design, Louis XV Style, 32 In. 1265.00
Gilt, Foliate Scrolled Candle Branches, Porcelain Flower Heads, 16 In., Pair 4025.00
Girandole, 3-Light, Gilt Metal, On Stepped Gray, White Marble Plinth, Cobalt, Pair 8050.00
Girandole, 3-Light, Neoclassical, Gilt Metal, Cut Glass, Cobalt, Sweden, 27 In., Pair 8050.00
Girandole, Brass Figural Stem, Cut Prisms, Marble Base, 17 In., 3 Piece Set 440.00
Girandole, Brass, Victorian, 19th Century, Pair 200.00
Girandole, Clear-Cut Prisms, Stepped Marble Base, 15 1/2 x 17 1/2 In., 3 Piece 520.00
Girandole, Glass, Gilt Metal, Urn For Font, B. Gardiner, 19th Century, 20 In., Pair 4600.00
Girandole, Stags, Leaf Design, Prisms, Marble Base Plinth, Brass, 12 1/2 In., Pair 230.00
Metal, Floral Design, Verdigris Finish, 65 In. 110.00
Silver, 2 Arms, 3rd Socle In Removable Finial, Roger Evans, Georgian, 9 1/2 In. 880.00

CANDLESTICKS were made of brass, pewter, glass, sterling silver,
plated silver, and all types of pottery and porcelain. The earliest candlesticks, dating from the sixteenth century, held the candle on a
pricket (sharp pointed spike). These lost favor because in times of
strife the large church candlesticks with prickets became formidable
weapons, so the socket was mandated. Candlesticks changed in style
through the centuries, and designs range from classic to rococo to Art
Nouveau to Art Deco.

Bell Metal, Engraved Tapered Column, England, 9 3/8 In., Pair 1950.00
Bisque, Attached Pair Of Figures, 8 1/2 In. 325.00
Brass, 3 Fluted Rings, Oval Base, Push-Up, 7 In., Pair 140.00

Brass, Arts & Crafts, Applied Wire, Cast Flowers On Base, 10 1/2 x 5 3/4 In., Pair 168.00
Brass, Arts & Crafts, Theta Form, Double Gourd Shape, Jarvie, 6 x 13 In. 935.00
Brass, Band Of Chased Floral Design, Cut Glass Prisms, England, 16 In., Pair 345.00
Brass, Baroque, Round Drip Pan, Urn-Form Nozzle, Italy, 21 3/4 In., Pair 2070.00
Brass, Beehive & Diamond Design, Victorian, Push-Up, 13 1/2 In., Pair 165.00
Brass, Butterfly-Shape Flame Screen, Bobeches, India, 16 1/4 In., Pair 45.00
Brass, Diamond Prince, Victorian, Push-Up, 11 3/4 In., Pair 358.00
Brass, Diamond Prince, Victorian, Push-Up, 11 7/8 In. 305.00
Brass, Domed Base, Baluster Stem, 8 1/4 In. 355.00
Brass, Domed Base, Baluster Stem, Soldered Repairs, 8 In. 135.00
Brass, Empire, Push-Up, 12 In., Pair 155.00
Brass, Faceted Candle Cup, Stepped Octagonal Base, 1730s, 6 1/4 In. 3220.00
Brass, Federal, 5 3/4 In., Pair 38.00
Brass, Figural Stem, Clear Prisms, Stepped Marble Base, 18 In., Pair 430.00
Brass, Flared Candle Cup, Baluster Stem, Ejector Mechanism, 9 1/2 In., Pair 2645.00
Brass, Geometric, Inca Design, Original Patina, Apollo Studio, 8 In., Pair 440.00
Brass, Georgian, Footed, 1825-1830, 9 1/2 In., Pair 95.00
Brass, Girandole, Marble Base, Column Stem, Lovebird Prism Ring, 16 1/2 In., Pair 275.00
Brass, Good Luck Horseshoe, Concentric Rings, Victorian, Push-Up, 11 1/2 In., Pair 140.00
Brass, Hammered, Arts & Crafts, Rubbed Design Around Base, 9 x 8 1/2 In., Pair 250.00
Brass, Hexagonal, Georgian, 1775, 7 In., Pair 665.00
Brass, Hog Scraper, Early 19th Century 325.00
Brass, Hog Scraper, Finger Hook, Push-Up, 8 In. 385.00
Brass, King Of Diamonds, Victorian, Push-Up, 12 1/2 In., Pair ....415.00 to 440.00
Brass, King Of Diamonds, Victorian, Push-Up, 14 In., Pair 523.00
Brass, Knopped Baluster Stems, Domed Round Bases, 1880, 10 In., 3 Piece 430.00
Brass, Lip Hanger, Side Push-Up, 6 3/4 In. 478.00
Brass, Louis-Phillippe, Detachable Sockets, c.1835, 11 In., Pair 2200.00
Brass, Multitiered Dome, Turned Shaft, Drip Pan, 17th Century, 26 1/2 In., Pair 1668.00
Brass, Neo-Classical, 19th Century, 10 1/2 In., Pair 248.00
Brass, Octagonal Base, 5 3/8 In. 220.00
Brass, Original Glass Shade, Stamped Brass Ornaments, 1840, 15 1/2 In., Pair 275.00
Brass, Ostrich Shape, Bird, Standing, Holding Branch In Beak, 15 In., Pair 2300.00
Brass, Petal Base, Detachable Drip Pans, Georgian, 1745-1760, 10 In., Pair 365.00
Brass, Petal Base, Georgian, 1745-1760, 7 In., Pair 365.00
Brass, Picket, Stepped Round Base, 18 1/2 In., Pair 315.00
Brass, Pricket, Turned Stem, Mid-Drip Pan, Continental, 15 In., Pair 805.00
Brass, Queen Anne, Octagonal Shaft, Scalloped Base, 8 In., Pair 935.00
Brass, Queen Anne, Petal Base, Push-Up, Mid-18th Century, 8 3/8 In. 920.00
Brass, Queen Anne, Scalloped Base, Baluster Stem, 6 3/4 In., Pair 990.00
Brass, Queen Anne, Scalloped Foot, 8 1/4 In. 165.00
Brass, Queen Anne, Scalloped Lip & Foot, 8 1/8 In., Pair 330.00
Brass, Queen Anne, Scrolled Base, 7 3/8 In. 190.00
Brass, Queen Anne, Scrolled, Beaded Base, 8 1/8 In. 165.00
Brass, Queen Anne, Shaped Petal Base, 1720s, 5 In., Pair 2300.00
Brass, Queen Anne, Spiral, 5 3/4 In. 275.00
Brass, Queen Of Diamonds, Victorian, 11 1/2 In., Pair ....220.00 to 305.00
Brass, Removable Bobeches, England, c.1785, 10 5/8 In., Pair 385.00
Brass, Renaissance Revival, Pierced, Birds, 20th Century, 9 3/4 In., Pair 430.00
Brass, Ring-Turned Shaft, Continental, 17th Century, 11 In. 165.00
Brass, Scalloped Base, Drip Pan, 19th Century, 9 1/4 In., Pair 143.00
Brass, Semishell Base, England, c.1740, 7 1/2 In., Pair 1500.00
Brass, Supporting Glass Shade, Handles, Faux Marble, Continental, 19 In., Pair 4025.00
Brass, Tubular, Stepped Round Foot, Cobalt Rims, 21 In., Pair 35.00
Brass, Turned Stem, Chamfered Square Base, George III, 6 In., Pair 1725.00
Brass, Twisted Stem, 8 In., Pair 90.00
Brass, Victorian, Push-Up, 12 1/8 In., Pair 105.00
Brass, Woman Shape, Partially Clothed, Cornucopia, Continental, 14 In., 4 Piece 1265.00
Bronze, 3 Ormolu Sphinx Heads, Diamond Nozzle, Regency, 11 In., Pair 1440.00
Bronze, Altar, Renaissance Revival, 29 In., Pair 980.00
Bronze, Blackamoor Shape, Renaissance Clothes, 17 In., Pair 485.00
Bronze, Curled Feet, 10 1/2 In., Pair 518.00
Bronze, Empire, Egyptian Design, Tripod Lion-Paw Base, France, 14 1/2 In., Pair 1925.00

Bronze, Hexagonal Base, 7 1/4 In. 160.00
Bronze, Louis XVI, Shaft Chased With Laurel, Acanthus Leaves, Pair 6325.00
Bronze, Napoleon III, Electrified As Lamp, 1870, 17 In. 220.00
Bronze, Original Patina, Impressed Mark, Jesse Preston, 13 In. 3575.00
Bronze, Queen Anne, Scalloped, 8 1/4 In. 110.00
Bronze, Slender Organic Standard, Round Foliate Base, De Feure, 11 In., Pair 3680.00
Bronze, Winged Lion, Gilt Traces, 19th Century, 10 In. 100.00
Capstan, Brass, c.1650 . . . .   1100.00
Champleve, Blue Shades, Continental, 19th Century, 7 1/4 In., Pair 230.00
Copper, Arts & Crafts, Enameled Flowers, 3 Sides, 7 3/4 In. 350.00
Copper, Double Column Shape, Stepped Base, 11 1/8 In., Pair 150.00
Cut Glass, Large Prisms, 11 In., Pair 305.00
Enamel, White, Green Panels, Floral Spray, Fluted Bobeche, 18th Century, 11 In. 440.00
Gilt, Black Lacquer Tray, Foliate Sprays, Scrolled Supports, Steel Base, 42 In. 2300.00
Gilt, Red Enamel, Floral Design In Underglaze Blue, 6 5/8 In., Pair 187.00
Gilt, Rococo, Palm-Tree Shape, Surmounted By A Pineapple, Italy, 41 In., Pair 9775.00
Gilt Brass, Milk Glass Flowers, c.1905, 16 In., Pair 395.00
Gilt Silver, Prussian Eagle, Roses, Double Bells, Fraget W. Warszawie, Pair 385.00
Glass, Blown, Pillar Mold, 8 Ribs, Bulbous Socket, Pewter, Pittsburgh, 12 In., Pair 3685.00
Glass, Canary Yellow, 6 Sides, Wafered Base To Socket, 7 In. . . . . .110.00 to 135.00
Glass, Dolphin Base, Petal Socket, Flint, 9 7/8 In. 135.00
Glass, Green, Hexagonal, Pittsburgh, 9 3/8 In. 55.00
Glass, Lacy, Reed Stem, Square-Stepped Base, 6 In., Pair 440.00
Glass, Moonstone, 6 Sides, Wafered Stem To Font, 1835-1850, 9 1/2 In. 110.00
Iron, Openwork Cast Frieze Birds, Fruit, Round Base, Oscar Bach, Pair 1380.00
Iron, Pricket, Late 15th Century, 8 1/2 In. 845.00
Iron, Spiral, Brass Finials On 3 Legs, Late 17th Century, 13 1/2 In. 395.00
Iron, Spiral, Tripod Base, Penny Foot, No Push-Up, 6 1/2 In. 120.00
Iron, Sticking Tommy, Stamped D. Cleaves, 9 1/2 In. 145.00
Nickel Plated Base, Green Paint Reflector Hood, 2 Spring Loaded Sockets, 15 In. 305.00
Ormolu, Baroque, Winged Putto Shape, Italy, 19th Century, 13 In., Pair 9200.00
Ormolu, Louis XVI, Mounted As Lamp, Bellflowers, Leaf-Cast Socle, 28 In. 4600.00
Ormolu, Winged Putto Fitted With Round Nozzle, Italy, 13 1/4 In., Pair 9200.00
Pewter, Hammered, Bobeche Flowers, Leaves, Original Patina, Randahl, 13 In., Pair 175.00
Pewter, Hammered, Tudric, Impressed Mark, 6 1/2 In. 300.00
Porphyry, Neoclassical, Stepped Leaf-Tip Base, Domed Feet, Russia, 9 In., Pair 10925.00
Pottery, Bennington Type, Manganese Glaze Over Cream Ground, 9 In. 220.00
Pressed Glass, Cobalt Blue, 6 Sides, 9 1/4 In. 220.00
Pressed Glass, Flower Design, 1830s, 7 In., Pair 130.00
Silver Plate, Fluted Band, Coat Of Arms, Tapered Shaft, 11 In., 4 Piece 5750.00
Silver Plate, Push-Up Design, Sheffield, 4 1/2 In., Pair 176.00
Silver Plate, Repousse Border, 12 In., Pair 130.00
Silver Plate, Scrolled Foliage & Shell Border, Continental, 13 3/4 In., Pair 201.00
Silver Plate, Sheffield, Ribbed Shaft, Spreading Base, Telescoping, c.1840, 8 1/2 In. 137.00
Silver Plate, Short Narrow Stem, Tulip Form Holder, Derby Silver, 3 5/8 In., Pair 125.00
Silver Plate, Stepped Square Bases, Removable Nozzles, Sheffield, 11 In., Pair 1725.00
Silver Plate, Tapering Stem, Gadrooned Rim, Detachable Bobeche, 11 1/2 In. 230.00
Silver Plate, Weighted Base, Sheffield, 10 1/2 In., Pair 145.00
Sterling Silver, 4 Scrolling Stylized Dolphin Corners, Russia, 13 3/4 In., Pair 805.00
Sterling Silver, 8 Sides, Paneled, Scroll Engraving, Weighted Base, 16 In., Pair 440.00
Sterling Silver, Beaded Borders, Richard Rugg, 1811, 5 In., Pair 1725.00
Sterling Silver, Chamberstick, Beaded Border, Swag, Engraved Crest, 1800s, 3 In. 440.00
Sterling Silver, Chamberstick, Ribbed Border, AK, London, 1804, 2 1/8 In. 170.00
Sterling Silver, Chamberstick, Snuffer, Engraved Eagle Head, England, 19th Century 385.00
Sterling Silver, Chamberstick, Traveling, Studs Are Holder, Russia, 1870, 4 In., Pair 440.00
Sterling Silver, Chased, Engraved, International, 12 In., 2 Pair 880.00
Sterling Silver, Chased, Swags, Flowers, Square Base, Augsburg, 18th Century, 7 1/2 In. . .   863.00
Sterling Silver, Corinthian Column, c.1890, Mauser, 8 1/2 In., Pair 1298.00
Sterling Silver, Domed Base, Grapevine, Swans, Fishes, J. Ehrlich, Russia, 12 1/4 In. 1955.00
Sterling Silver, Elephant Head Shape, Marble Base, Gilt, Bronze, France, 8 In., Pair 1600.00
Sterling Silver, Flower Buds At Each Corner, Fluted Stem, Austria, 1865, 12 In., Pair 430.00
Sterling Silver, Fluted Shaft, Square Base, London, 1766, 13 1/4 In., 4 Piece 6050.00
Sterling Silver, Foliate & Fluted Design, Baluster Column, Germany, 6 1/2 In., Pair 138.00

Sterling Silver, Gadrooned Shell, Foliate Rim, Emes & Barnard, 1811, 6 In. 1495.00
Sterling Silver, George III, Banded Top & Base, Bailey, Banks & Biddle, 9 In., Pair 725.00
Sterling Silver, Georgian Style, 20th Century, 4 1/2-In. Base, 6 In., 4 Piece 1540.00
Sterling Silver, Incised Foliate, Arthur Stone, 4 1/2 In. 625.00
Sterling Silver, Molded Well Rest, Banded Waist, Cylindrical, Mexico, 4 In., Pair 285.00
Sterling Silver, Monogram, R. Makepeace & R. Carter, England, 1777, 9 1/2 In., Pair . . .   4887.00
Sterling Silver, Neoclassical, Chamfered Column, Oval Base, 10 In., Pair 1650.00
Sterling Silver, Overall Floral, Monogram, S. Kirk & Son, 10 In., Pair 1980.00
Sterling Silver, Removable Bobeche, Hexagonal, Arthur J. Stone, 4 1/2 In. 1850.00
Sterling Silver, Repousse, Kirk, 3 In. 395.00
Sterling Silver, Ribbed, Wood-Filled Bases, Sheffield, George III, 1807, 12 In. 2090.00
Sterling Silver, Rose, Stieff, 1945, 3 5/8 In. 300.00
Sterling Silver, Scrolled Foliate Rim, Bobeche, 5 1/2 In., Pair 330.00
Sterling Silver, Snuffer, Shell Thumb Rest, John Robertson, England, 4 1/4 In., Pair 1035.00
Sterling Silver, Square Base, Stylized Shell Design, Knopped Shaft, England, 1 In. 1760.00
Sterling Silver, Stepped Square Bases, George III, 1763, 11 In., 4 Piece 10925.00
Sterling Silver, Table, Banded Octagonal Stems, England, 1736, 26 Oz., Pair 4890.00
Sterling Silver, Table, Contemporary Crests, England, 1743, 27 Oz. 5405.00
Sterling Silver, Taperstick, Gold Washed, Foliate, Bobeche, Sheffield, 1832, 5 3/8 In. 345.00
Sterling Silver, Vase Shape, Gadroon Borders, Boulton & Co., 1802, 8 Piece 32200.00
Sterling Silver, Watson, 5 In., Pair 193.00
Tin, Porcelain Socket, 7 In. 38.00
Wooden, Turned, Hurricane Shade, Round Foot, 20th Century, 12 1/2 In., Pair 85.00

CANDLEWICK items may be listed in the Imperial and Pressed Glass categories.

CANDY CONTAINERS have been popular since the late Victorian era. Collectors have long favored the glass containers, but now all types, including tin and papier-mache, are collected. Probably the earliest glass container sold commercially was the Liberty Bell made in 1876 for sale at the Centennial Exposition. Thousands of designs were made until the cost became too high in the 1960s. By the late 1970s, reproductions were being made and sold without the candy. Containers listed here are glass unless otherwise described. A Belsnickle is a nineteenth-century figure of Father Christmas.

Airplane, Left Side Rear Door, Glass, Tin Propeller, 4 5/8 In. 550.00
Airplane, Liberty Motor, 6 1/4-In. Wingspan 2200.00
Airplane, Liberty Motor, Tin Wings, Glass, 4 5/8 In. 1430.00
Airplane, Musical Toy 66.00
Airplane, P-38 Lightning, Original Wire Clip, c.1942, 5 1/2 In. 190.00
Airplane, Spirit Of Goodwill, Metal Screw Cap & Propeller, 4 3/8 In. . . . . .175.00 to 220.00
Airplane, Spirit Of St. Louis, Blue Glass, Original Tin, 4 1/2 In. . . . . .358.00 to 520.00
Airplane, W. Glass Co., Green, Metal Wings, 4 1/2 In. 165.00
Ambulance, Ambulance Militaire, Service De Sante, Tin, 6 1/4 x 3 1/2 In. 275.00
Amos & Andy, Open Air Taxi, 4 1/2 In. 495.00
Bank, Candy Cigarette, Red Plastic, Miner Mfg. Corp., N.Y., 8 x 5 x 6 In. 240.00
Barney Google & Ball, King Features, Copyright 1927 . . . .   355.00
Baseball Player, On Base, Glass, Paint, Tin Lid, 5 In. . . . .*Illus*   687.00
Baseball Player With Bat, Raised P On Cap & Shirt, 3 1/4 In. 825.00
Basket, Boy With Valentine, Girl With Fan, Tin, Rectangular, 1930s, 5 In. 110.00
Bell, Liberty Bell With Hanger, Amber 28.00
Belsnickle, Papier-Mache, Mica, 12 In. 470.00
Boot, Papier-Mache, Pinecone Decoration, 5 In. . . . .*Illus*   20.00
Boy, Standing On Candy Box, Bisque Head, Spun Cotton Body, c.1910, 9 In. 795.00
Buddy, Bank Boy, Tin, Glass Jar, 4 1/8 In. . . . .*Illus*   330.00
Bulldog, Papier-Mache, Shaded Yellow, Germany, c.1900, 5 In. 500.00
Bus, Greyhound, Painted Blue, Victory Glass Co. 550.00
Bus, Jitney, Yellow, Black, No Driver's Seat, Tin Closure, West Bros. Co. 340.00
Bus, Victory Lines Special, Blue, Silver, Metal Snap-On Closure, c.1942 . . . .   55.00
Camel, Tin Base, Germany 85.00
Camera On Tripod, Painted Black, Red Bulb, Tin Closure, c.1913 . . . . .400.00 to 670.00
Candlestick, Colonial, 6 Sides, Tin Slide-On Closure, c.1913 . . . .   460.00
Cannon, 2-Wheel Mount #1, Glass Cannon, Tin Carriage, c.1930, 3 3/4 In. 220.00

Candy Container, Baseball
Player, On Base, Glass, Paint, Tin
Lid, 5 In.

Candy Container, Boot,
Papier-Mache, Pinecone
Decoration, 5 In.

Candy Container,
Buddy, Bank Boy, Tin,
Glass Jar, 4 1/8 In.

Cannon, Rapid Fire Gun, Glass Ammunition Compartment, Gray Carriage 210.00
Cannon, U.S. Defense Field Gun #17, Tin Cannon Barrel, Glass Base, 1940s 395.00
Car, Coupe, Long Hood, Original Tin Snap, Blade Fenders, Roof, Red Wheels 105.00
Car, Electric Coupe, Pat. Feb. 18, 1913, Marked Between Wheels, 1914, 3 In. 30.00
Car, Glass, Tin Cover 60.00
Car, Hearse No. 2, Tin Slide-On Closure, c.1920 .... 75.00
Car, Limousine With Rear Trunk & Tire 130.00
Car, Sedan With 6 Vents, Victory Glass Co., Jeanette, Pa. 65.00
Car, Sedan With 6 Vents, Yellow Paint, Victory Glass Co., Jeanette, Pa. 187.00
Car, Volkswagen, Plastic, Red Rubber Tires, 4 5/8 x 3 In. 25.00
Car, West Bros. Co. Limousine, Original Wheels & Candy, c.1912 .... 195.00
Careful Chubby D Cop, Original Box, Plastic, c.1950 .... 340.00
Carpet Sweeper, Dolly Sweeper, West Bros. Co., Grapeville, Pa., c.1914 .... 355.00
Cash Register, Tin Slide-On Closure, Dugan Glass Co., c.1913 .... 275.00
Cat, Felix On Pedestal, Original Top 2750.00
Cat, Felix, Next To Container 440.00
Cat, Gray, Black Stripes, Pink Nose, Red Ribbon, Papier-Mache, 8 1/4 In. 275.00
Cat, Gray, White Paint, Glass Eyes, Pink Mouth, Papier-Mache, 6 In. 190.00
Cat, In Shoe, Composition & Gesso, Cloth Flowers, 4 In. 138.00
Cat, In Shoe, Tan Shoe, Gray, White Cat, Papier-Mache, 4 In. 55.00
Cat, Seated, Gray & White, Glass Eyes, Pink Ribbon, Papier-Mache, 3 1/4 In. 275.00
Cat, Seated, Gray, Glass Eyes, Papier-Mache, 3 7/8 In. 55.00
Chick, In Shell Car, Red Tin Snap-On Closure, Victory Glass Co. 145.00
Chick, Standing, Painted Yellow, Black Beak, Eyes, Legs 60.00
Chicken, Crowing Rooster, Feathers, Tin Screw Closure, Marked V.G. Co. .... .350.00 to 520.00
Chicken, On Oblong Basket, Red Tin Snap-On Closure, Victory Glass Co. 55.00
Chicken, On Round Base, High Oval Basket, Gold Closure, Marked U.S.A. 360.00
Chicks, Papier-Mache 95.00
Chocolate Woman, Half Doll 995.00
Clock, Alarm, Amethyst, Incised Numerals, Metal Screw Lid, c.1916 .... 385.00
Clock, Mantel, Paper Dial, Pasted Inside, Bank Slot, Tin Slide-On Closure 60.00
Clock, Milk Glass, Marked Souvenir Grafton, N.D., c.1909, 3 1/4 In. 275.00
Coach, Esther, Overland Limited, Jeanette Glass Co., c.1916 .... 120.00
Coach, Interurban, Angeline, Wheels On Wire Axles, c.1916 .... 410.00
Coach, Parlor Car, New York Central R.R. 510.00
Coal Car, N.Y.C., Tin Slide-On Closure 220.00
Coal Car, Overland Limited, Jeanette Glass Co., c.1915 .... 355.00
Condiment Set, Vanstyle, Red Flashed Candles 45.00
Crystal Palace, 3 1/2 In. 130.00
Dirigible, Los Angeles, Painted Silver, Wheels On Sides, c.1930 .... 320.00
Dog, Bulldog, Gilt Collar, Marked 3/4 Oz., Avor., U.S.A. 45.00
Dog, Collie, Fabric Over Composition, Glass Eyes, Huyler's, 10 In. 385.00
Dog, Glass, 3 In. 10.00

You'll find the best selection at a weekend show on Friday, the biggest crowd on Saturday, and the best bargains on Sunday. Allow yourself plenty of time. Have a price range in mind. When you see it, buy it. And keep tabs on your wallet and purchases.

Candy Container, Duck, Large Bill, Glass, Paint, Tin Cover, 3 1/4 In.

Dog, Little Doggie In The Window 30.00
Dog, Scotty 30.00
Doll's Valise, Cardboard, Linen, Brass Lock, Leather Strap, France, c.1885, 6 In. 225.00
Dolly's Bathtub, Glass 3960.00
Don't Park Here, Blue-Green Top, Clear Standard, Marked U.S.A. 220.00
Duck, Large Bill, Glass, Paint, Tin Cover, 3 1/4 In. ....*Illus* 341.00
Duck, On Rope Top Basket, Green Glass, Tin Snap-On Closure 50.00
Duck, With Large Bill, Green Paint, Tin Slide-On Closure 340.00
Ear Of Corn, Cork, 5 1/4 In. 100.00
Elephant, G.O.P., Victory Glass Co., Marked U.S.A. 110.00
Elephant, Tin Base, Germany 85.00
Fat Boy On Drum, Closure Marked Happy Fat, Geo. Borgfeldt & Co. 440.00
Father Christmas, Black-Robe, Peering Through Yule Sprig, 20 In. 6050.00
Father Christmas, Woven Wicker, Open Sedan 2255.00
Fire Engine, Ladder Truck, Original Wheels, Victory Glass Co., 5 In. 190.00
Fire Truck, Hinged Top, Dunlop Tires, France 38.00
Fish Shape, Victorian, Glass Eyes, Dark Olive Back, Silver Side, 8 1/2 In. 410.00
Flossie Fisher's Chair, Silhouettes On Yellow Tin, Stamped, Borgfeldt & Co. 880.00
Flossie Fisher's China Closet, Silhouettes On Yellow Tin, Borgfeldt & Co. 935.00
Flossie Fisher's Dresser, Tin, Glass Pane Insert, Borgfeldt & Co., 3 In. 1430.00
Flossie Fisher's Sideboard, Tin, Mirror, Borgfeldt & Co. 990.00
Flossie Fisher's Table, Silhouettes On Yellow Tin, Borgfeldt & Co. ....1760.00 to 2640.00
Gas Pump, Gas 23 Cents Today, c.1928 .... 285.00
Gas Pump, Pump For Candy, Yellow, Both Labels, 6 1/8 In. 230.00
Gentleman, Papier-Mache, Painted Clothing, Germany, 10 In. 425.00
George Washington, 2 Cherry Trees 995.00
Girl, Ornament, Spun Cotton & Crepe Paper, Composition Face, Germany 375.00
Globe, Relief Of Continents, Glass, Nickel Plated Brass Screw Cap, 1 3/4 In. 25.00
Gun, Cambridge Automatic, 3 1/4 x 5 In. 65.00
Gun, Flint Lock Pistol, Green, Gilt Embossed Design, Glass, 16 In. 165.00
Gun, Stough's Whistling Jim, Straight Grip, With Tomahawk 70.00
Happy Hooligan, Composition, Felt & Cloth, 13 In. 190.00
Happy Hooligan, Wiggle Eyes, Composition, 4 1/2 In. 410.00
Hat, Uncle Sam 38.00
Hen, Painted Composition, Cardboard Base, 7 In. 350.00
Hen & Chicks, Molded Cardboard, Germany, 2 3/4 In. 35.00
Horn, Three Valve, Red, White & Blue Bands, Metal Screw Cap, c.1918 .... 210.00
Horse, Germany, 5 In. 250.00
Horse, Painted, 1920s, 7 1/2 x 7 1/2 In. 850.00
Horse, Trojan, Rosbro 25.00
House, All Glass, 2 3/8 x 2 3/4 x 2 1/8 In. 180.00
Independence Hall, 1876, 7 3/16 x 3 1/2 x 4 7/8 In. 250.00
Iron, Electric, Cord, Paper Plug 100.00
Iron, Flat, Ribbed Handle, Tin Sheet Bottom 440.00
Jackie Coogan, Metal Screw Cap, Copyright 1925 .... 550.00
Jeep, Belly Label 25.00

Jeep, J.H. Millstein & Co., Jeanette, Pa. 30.00
Kiddie Kar, Horse Head, Raised Figure Of Dog On Seat 145.00
Lady, Papier-Mache, Painted Clothing, Germany, 9 In. 425.00
Lady Turnip Head, Painted Composition, 4 3/4 In. 495.00
Lamp, Christmas, 3 1/2 In. 630.00
Lamp, Hobnail, Metal Screw Cap, T.H. Stough Co., Jeanette, Pa. 165.00
Lamp, Kerosene 55.00
Lamp, Miniature Hurricane, Red Tin Screw Cap, T.H. Stough Co., c.1950 .... 460.00
Lantern, Barn Type No. 1, Souvenir Of York, Pa., Wire Bail Handle 90.00
Lantern, Glass, Tin, Bail Handle, 4 In. 40.00
Lawn Swing, 2 Seats, Red & White Striped Canopy 330.00
Liberty Bell, Glass, Centennial Exposition, 1776-1876, 3 In. 250.00
Locomotive, Brainard's 1923, Tin Lithograph Closure, Cab's Interior 200.00
Locomotive, Little No. 23, Slide-On Closure 105.00
Locomotive, Silver Link, Screw Closure, 7 1/2 In. 1815.00
Mail Box, Souvenir, Dubua, Ia. 465.00
Man On Motorcycle With Side Car, Red Tin Snap-On Closure, 4 15/16 In. 520.00
Monkey Lamp, Glass Monkey, Red Plastic Shade 250.00
Nurser, Baby Nurser No. 2, Original Wooden Nipple, T.H. Stough Co., 1940s 90.00
Nurser, J.S. Co., Red Rubber Nipple, Original Sticker, 2 1/8 In. 35.00
Opera Glass, Victor, 2 Glass Containers, Brass Plated Tin Frame, Box 715.00
Petunia Pig 25.00
PEZ, Bride & Groom, Pair 4500.00
PEZ, Bullwinkle, Brown Stem 220.00
PEZ, Casper, Die Cut, Blue Stem 295.00
PEZ, Chick 70.00
PEZ, Donkey, Melody Maker 42.00
PEZ, Dumbo 25.00
PEZ, Easter Playworld Set 25.00
PEZ, Koala 25.00
PEZ, Lamb 25.00
PEZ, Octopus, Orange Head, Green Stem 85.00
PEZ, Parrot, Melody Maker 42.00
PEZ, Penguin, Melody Maker 42.00
PEZ, Pink Panther 5.00
PEZ, Psychedelic Eye ....460.00 to 995.00
PEZ, Rhino, Melody Maker 42.00
PEZ, Rudolph 65.00
PEZ, Thumper 85.00
PEZ, Uncle Sam 275.00
Phonograph, Glass Record Type, Tin Horn, Record Painted Black, 1 3/4 In. 300.00
Piano, Upright, Gilded, 7-Octave Keyboard, Bank, 2 13/16 x 2 7/8 x 2 In. 410.00
Policeman, Pumpkin Head 1439.00
Policeman's Nightstick, Amber, 10 1/2 In. 110.00
Pug Dog, Shoe In Mouth, Composition, Glass Eyes, 6 1/2 In. 495.00
Puppy, Glass 18.00
Purse, Souvenir Of Sunbury, Pa., Alligator Hide Design 465.00
Rabbit, Mother & Daughter, Red Apron, Gilt Baby, 9 1/8 In. 630.00
Rabbit, On Log, Glass 265.00
Rabbit, Papier-Mache, Germany 35.00
Rabbit, Pushing Chick In Shell Cart, Stippled, Gilt Rabbit, Victory Glass Co. .....495.00 to 605.00
Rabbit, Running On Log, Molded Flat, Gilt, 4 1/4 In. 330.00
Rabbit, Sitting On Hind Legs, Upright Ears, Glass Eyes, 1900, 25 In. 1725.00
Rabbit, Victorian, Glass Eyes, Serious Hare Face, 16 In. 1800.00
Rabbit, Wearing Hat 15.00
Rabbit, Wearing Red Fedora 1320.00
Rabbit, With Basket On Arm, Marked U.S.A., 4 3/8 In. 165.00
Rabbit Family 1485.00
Race Car, Pointed Nose, Tin Parts 3630.00
Reindeer, Standing, Germany 800.00
Rocking Horse, Clown Rider, c.1920, 3 5/8 x 4 5/16 x 1 7/16 In. 110.00
Rooster, Gray Wash, Black, Red, Yellow, Chalkware, 6 1/2 In. 130.00

Santa Claus, Ball Shape, Composition, Cardboard, Japan, 6 1/2 In. 450.00
Santa Claus, Germany, 21 In. 2300.00
Santa Claus, In Car, Celluloid, Cardboard, Japan, Prewar, 6 In.   500.00
Santa Claus, In Sleigh, Celluloid, Cardboard, Japan, Prewar, 5 3/4 In. 300.00
Santa Claus, Plaster Over Papier-Mache, Hand Painted, c.1915 . . . .   240.00
Santa Claus, Red Coat, Blue Pants, 10 In. 395.00
Santa Claus, Sack, Composition Hands, Chenille 125.00
Santa's Boot, Glass, 3 3/4 In. 10.00
Sheep, On Wheels, Removable Head, Wooden Legs, 4 Wheels, 1900, 10 In. 2300.00
Skookum, By Tree Stump, Bank, Borgfeldt & Co., c.1916 . . . .   440.00
Snowman, Chenille . . . . .85.00 to 95.00
Snowman Playing Accordion, U.S. Zone, Germany 95.00
Soldier, Next To Tent 2310.00
Soldier, With Sword, Red Tunic, Gray Pants, 5 1/8 In. 685.00
Spark Plug, Horse, Wrapped In Blanket, c.1925 . . . .   45.00
St. Patrick's Day Hat 95.00
Standing Boy Cat, Papier-Mache, Glass Eyes, 5 In. 275.00
Stop & Go, Signal Butterfly, Yellow Blade, Screw Cap 660.00
Stork, Pecking, Push-Rod Action, Feeds In Trough, Fisher, Germany, 3 In. 385.00
Striped Cat, Papier-Mache & Gesso, Gray Flocked, Black Stripes, 8 1/4 In. 275.00
Suitcase, Glass, Wire Handle, Tin Bottom, Pat Appl'd For, 3 3/4 x 2 1/2 In. 90.00
Suitcase, Pennant Design, Bear Decal, Milk Glass 50.00
Swan Boat, Rabbit & Chick, Stippled, Gilt Swan, Victory Glass Co. 685.00
Tank, World War I 143.00
Tom Turkey 225.00
Trunk, With Round Top, Milk Glass, 2 1/8 In. 100.00
Turkey, Gobbler, Stippled, 3 1/2 In. 100.00
U.S. Postal Mail Box, Glass 115.00
Uncle Sam, Glass, Partial Paint, Metal Screw Cap, 1915-1925, 3 3/4 In. 385.00
Vase, Hanging, 3 1/2 In. 40.00
Village, Bank, Log Cabin Roof, Tin Lithograph, Glass Liner, 3 In. 100.00
Village, Tudor House, Tin Lithograph, Glass Liner, 6 Cutout Windows 440.00
Wagon, U.S. Express, Pressed Glass Wagon Box On Tin Chassis, 4 In. 275.00
Watermelon 195.00
Wheelbarrow, Red Tin Closure 165.00
Windmill, 5 Windows, Ruby Flashed, 3 7/8 In. 465.00
Windmill, Dutch, 6-Sided Roof, Diamond Mark On Roof, 4 7/8 In. 220.00
Windmill, Teddy, Glass Container, Red Tin Housing, 1 1/2 Oz. 1155.00
World Globe On Stand, Our Country, Metal Screw Cap 440.00

CANES and walking sticks were used by every well-dressed man in the
nineteenth century, but by World War I the style had changed. Today
canes are used by few but the infirm. Collectors prize old canes made
with special features, like hidden swords, whiskey flasks, or risqué pictures seen through peepholes. Examples with solid gold heads or made
from exotic materials, such as walrus vertebrae, are among the higher
priced canes.

Alligator, Lobster, Serpent Design, 32 1/2 In. 1380.00
Amber, Twisted Shepherd's Crook Handle, Twisted Tip, 41 In. 132.00
Baleen, Turk's Head Knob Handle, Spiral Strips, 19th Century, 31 1/2 In. 1092.00
Ball-In-Box, Snake Intertwining Bottom, Ray Burrows, 20th Century, 35 In. 180.00
Bone, Carved Tassels & Ribbons, Bone Handle & Tip, 32 3/4 In.   77.00
Cap Firing, Metal Duck Handle, Firing Points On Bottom, 34 In.   105.00
Carrier, Cigars, 4 Stoppered Tubes In Shaft, Aluminum & Brass, c.1930 . . . .   295.00
Carved Effigy, Thomas Jefferson, c.1804 . . . . 1800.00
Carved Maple, Taloned Claw Gripping A Ball, Acorns & Oak Leaves, Folk Art, 35 In. . . .   700.00
Comical Horse's Head Handle, Man's Profile, Brass Ferule, KEPKVPA, 34 3/4 In. 115.00
Confederate, Sculptured Soldier's Head Handle, Twig Stem, 34 1/4 In. 485.00
Eagle Form Handle, 30 1/2 In. 60.00
Eagles, Black, Gold, American Shield, Alligator Decoration, 19th Century, 36 In. 149.00
Faberge, Gold, Imperial Russian Hallmark 56, c.1895, 2 1/4-In. Handle, 36 In. 12100.00
Face Of Black Figure, Yellow Shaft, Encircled By Serpent, 32 In. 605.00
Fishing Rod, Bone Handle, Metal Shaft, Brass Ferrule Unscrews, Reveals Rod, 35 In. . . . 1210.00

Glass, Blown, Continuous White Spiral Inner Shaft, 38 In. 110.00
Glass, Triple Swirl, Mahogany, 45 In. 220.00
Gold Filled, Presented By Employees Of U.S. Indian Warehouse 330.00
Hardwood, Dapple Stained, Enclosing Blown Glass Tumbler, Flask & Jigger, 36 In. 80.00
Hardwood, Rock Crystal Bird Head Top, Blue Guilloche Collar, 1910 . . . . 4070.00
Harmonica, Flat Knob Handle, Working Built-In Harmonica, 1920s, 35 1/4 In. 3410.00
Hercules, Holding Shield, c.1880, 4 In. 1500.00
Hickory, Odd Fellows Insignia, 4 Snakes, 35 1/4 In. 275.00
Hickory, Revolutionary War, Inscribed, Zachariah Powell, Massachusetts, 1777, 33 In. . . . 395.00
Ivory, Carved, Man's Fist Holding Baton, Incised Brass Ring, 33 1/2 In. 1380.00
Ivory, Elephant, Bear Attacked By Dogs, Malacca Shaft, Brass Ferule, 48 In. 6050.00
Ivory, Fist Handle Holding Truncheon, Wood Shaft, Brass Tip, J. Blish, 1900s, 36 In. 715.00
Ivory, Horn & Wood, Horn In Form Of Whale Lying Across Top Of Horn, 34 1/2 In. 4312.00
Ivory, L Form, Carved Face Of Woman, Ebony Shaft, 36 In. 220.00
Ivory, Phrenology Head 5500.00
Ivory, Pique, Pierced Open Dot, Brass Ferrule, Early 18th Century, 36 1/2 In. 5060.00
Ivory, Scrimshaw Engraved Whale On Handle, Handle & Tip, 32 3/4 In. 220.00
Ivory, Tiger Head 3000.00
Ivory Handle, Toiletry, Top Hinged Mirror, Lower Section Holds Toiletries, 35 1/2 In. . . . 5500.00
Ivory Top, Silver Plated Band, Engraved Y. Fisk, Brass Tip, 39 In. 175.00
Lady's Leg Handle 400.00
Lignum Vitae, One-Key Flute, David Caret, 35 1/2 In. 6600.00
Multipurpose, 3 Interchangeable Handles, Corkscrew, Carriage Key, Mahogany, 1880 . . . 4400.00
Narwhal, Silver-Capped, C Scrolls, Flower Blossoms, 38 In. 4510.00
Perfume Bottle, Malacca Shaft, Built-In Bottle, Ivory Handle, c.1900, 35 1/2 In. 1045.00
Pewter, Columbus' Head, Embossed Lettering Columbus 1792-1892 . . . . 275.00
Pine, Snake, Original Paint 800.00
Rock Crystal Bird Head, Sapphire Eyes, Enamel Collar, c.1910, 35 1/2 In. 4070.00
Serpent Form, 36 In. 405.00
Silver & Ivory, Tiffany, Art Nouveau, Flowers, Double Sawtooth Base, c.1900, 34 In. 4400.00
Silver Swirled Handle, Match Safe, Mahogany Shaft, 1900, 36 3/4 In. 577.00
Spotted Trout, Carved Salmon & Worms, Inscribed 1897, 34 1/2 In. 700.00
Sword, Presented To P.T. Barnum 18400.00
Telescope, Brass Instrument, Knob Handle, Brass Coat Of Arms, 39 In. 990.00
Vanity Case, Mirror, Bakelite Handle, Metal Ferrule, Woman's, 1920s, 39 1/2 In. 825.00
Walking Stick, 14K Gold Capped, Dr. Harrison, Ebonized Tapering Stick, 35 3/4 In. 345.00
Walking Stick, Alligator & Leaves, Hand Coming Out Of Leaf, M.R. Burrows, Child's . . 500.00
Walking Stick, Bamboo, Brass Tip, Lane Tremont, 31 7/8 In. 85.00
Walking Stick, Blow Gun Handle, Removable Ivory Tip & Handle, Asian Walnut, 33 In. . . 1000.00
Walking Stick, Carved Black Man's Head, Glass Eyes, Grained Shaft, 35 In. 330.00
Walking Stick, Carved Ivory Puzzle, Carved & Knopped Top, Baleen Spacers, 40 In. 1265.00
Walking Stick, Carved Snake & Alligator Encircling Wood Shaft, Folk Art, 35 In. 40.00
Walking Stick, Eagle Head , Macrame Handle, Carved Vine & Shield Shaft, 1890 . . . . . . 1250.00
Walking Stick, Engraved, U.S., 14K Gold Filled Knob, 1909 . . . . 275.00
Walking Stick, Fish, Over A Clenched Hand, Crosshatched Knob, 36 1/2 In. 1430.00
Walking Stick, Fluted & Faceted Ivory Handle, Carved Diamonds & Spirals, 32 1/4 In. . . 1092.00
Walking Stick, Fruitwood, Dog's Head Fitted With Glass Eyes, Boxer Top Grip, 34 In. . . . 272.00
Walking Stick, Goose Head, Black & Combed Finish, 37 In. 165.00
Walking Stick, Hardwood, Rabbit's Head Grip With Amber, Black Eyes, 1910, 38 In. 363.00
Walking Stick, Horse Handle 110.00
Walking Stick, Ivory, Hound & Fox 450.00
Walking Stick, Ivory, Silver Alloy, Hardwood, Toad Grip, 1900, 35 1/4 In. 272.00
Walking Stick, Ivory, Silver Mounted Malacca, Celestial Dragon Head Ivory Grip, 34 In. . . 393.00
Walking Stick, Rosewood, Greyhound Head, 1890-1895, 36 3/4 In. 333.00
Walking Stick, Rosewood, Ivory Afghan Head, Shortened, England, 1895, 9 1/2 In. 85.00
Walking Stick, Scrimshaw Hand Clasping Knop, 1851 . . . . 1600.00
Walking Stick, Scrimshaw, Wooden Shaft, Naughty Nellie Leg Handle, Whale Tooth 358.00
Walking Stick, Sitting Stag On Top Of Handle, Sterling Silver Band, 30 In. 200.00
Walking Stick, Snake & Lizards, Polychrome, 1914-1919, 39 In. 1430.00
Walking Stick, Spread Winged Eagle, Serpent Design, 35 In. 465.00
Walking Stick, Sterling Quill, Hardwood, Woman's, 1900-1910, 36 5/8 In. 363.00
Walking Stick, Sterling Silver Mounted Horn, 28 In. 230.00
Walking Stick, Walnut, Carved Head Of Eagle Handle, 19th Century, 37 1/12 In. 230.00

Walking Stick, Whale Bone, Ivory Handle Shaped As Clenched Fist, 37 In. 1705.00
Walking Stick, Wood, Ebonized, Small Faceted Diamond, Gold Head, 1895-1900, 36 In. . . 393.00
Whalebone, Clenched Hand, Holding Ebony Baton, 19th Century, 35 In. 1650.00
Whalebone, Turned Head, Ebony Shaft, 19th Century, 34 1/2 In. 220.00
White Metal, McKinley Bust, 3-Dimensional, 1896 . . . . 125.00
Wood, Antelope's Head Knob, Glass Eyes, 19th Century, 37 In. 230.00
Wood, Figure Of Snake, Faceted Glass Eyes, 23 1/2 In. 315.00
Wood, Rattlesnake, Painted Glass Eyes, Gold Collar, Whale Ivory Knob, c.1880 . . . . 885.00

CANEWARE is a tan-colored, unglazed stoneware that was first developed by Josiah Wedgwood about 1770. It has been made by many
companies since that time and is often used for cooking or serving
utensils.

Pie Dish, Cover, Acanthus Leaf, Crust Rim, Oval, Wedgwood, 9 1/8 In. 635.00
Pie Dish, Cover, Dead Game On Body, Rabbit Finial, Oval, Wedgwood, 9 In. 635.00
Pie Dish, Cover, Dead Game, Fruiting Grapevine, Oval, Wedgwood, 8 In. . . . . . . .375.00 to 545.00
Pie Dish, Cover, Pastry Strapwork, Twig Knop, Leaves, Berries, Wedgwood, 7 In. 375.00
Pie Dish, Dead Game Birds Surrounding Body, Wedgwood, 11 In. 750.00
Teapot, Cover, Arabesque, Scrolled Vinework, Floral, Wedgwood, 6 5/8 In. 545.00
Urn, Crater, Cover, Fruiting Grapevine Banding, Wedgwood, 10 3/8 In. 690.00

CANTON CHINA is a blue-and-white ware made near the city of Canton,
in China, from about 1785 to 1895. It is hand decorated with Chinese
scenes. Canton is part of the group of porcelains known today as
Chinese Export Porcelain.

Basket, Stand, Painted Pavilions & Pagodas, Pierced Border, 10 In. 805.00
Basket, Undertray, Reticulated, 8 3/4 In. 750.00
Bottle, Riverscape Design, Blue, White, 8 1/4 In. 260.00
Bowl, Blue, White, 4 1/4 x 4 3/4 In., 9 Piece 80.00
Bowl, Cover, 5 In. 460.00
Bowl, Cover, Pine Cone Finial, Orange Peel Glaze, 10 In. 330.00
Bowl, Cover, Pod Finial, Rectangular, 9 1/2 In. 120.00
Bowl, Cut Corners, 19th Century, 4 3/4 x 9 1/4 In. 431.00
Bowl, Cut Corners, Rectangular, 13 3/4 x 10 3/4 x 2 1/4 In. 290.00
Bowl, Scalloped Edge, Blue & White, 3 x 10 1/2 In. 430.00
Bowl, Scalloped, c.1820, 8 1/2 In. 330.00
Bowl, Scene In Center, 15 1/2 In. 2200.00
Bowl, Serving, 2 x 12 In. 490.00
Bowl, Vegetable, Cover, 9 1/2 In. 144.00
Bowl, Vegetable, Cover, Almond Shape, Blue, White, 10 1/2 In. 220.00
Bowl, Vegetable, Cover, Blue, White, 8 x 9 3/8 In. 190.00
Bowl, Vegetable, Cover, Cut Corners, Boar's Head Handles, Raised Base, 9 x 13 1/2 In. . . 980.00
Candlestick, Man On Bridge Design, Blue, White, 8 1/4 In., Pair 880.00
Charger, China, 16 1/2 In. 230.00
Chop Plate, Blue, White, 14 1/2 In. 165.00
Creamer, Almond Shape, Blue, White, 4 5/8 x 3 7/8 In., 2 Piece 220.00
Creamer, Boar's Head Handles, Blue, White, 4 x 7 In., 2 Piece 80.00
Creamer, Helmet Form, Blue, White, 4 1/4 In. 285.00
Creamer, Helmet Shape, Landscape Design, 3 In. 77.00
Creamer, Helmet, Blue, White, 4 In. 125.00
Creamer, Helmet, Leaf-Shaped Underliner, 4 1/4 In. 575.00
Cup, Blue, White, 9 Piece 55.00
Dish, Blue Flowering Design, Tapering Sides, 9 x 5 1/2 In. 177.00
Ginger Jar, Carved Wooden Cover, 7 In. . . . . .125.00 to 175.00
Jug, Cider, Cover, Twined Handle, Foo Dog Finial, 8 In. 1390.00
Mug, Landscape Design, Entwined Handle, c.1830, 4 In. 193.00
Planter, Footed Tray, Blue, White, Hexagonal Form, 20th Century, 10 x 13 In., Pair 285.00
Plate, Blue Design, Petal Border, Off-White Border, Round, 9 1/4 In. 287.00
Plate, Blue, White, 5 7/8 In. 80.00
Platter, 17 1/2 x 14 1/2 In. 825.00
Platter, 18 3/4 In. 920.00
Platter, 18 In. 490.00
Platter, 19th Century, 12 x 15 1/2 In. 300.00

Platter, 19th Century, 13 3/4 In. . . . . .375.00 to 385.00
Platter, Blue, White, 11 3/4 In. 220.00
Platter, Blue, White, 16 In. 440.00
Platter, Blue, White, 17 1/2 In. 247.00
Platter, Cut Corners, Blue & White, 17 3/4 x 15 In. 545.00
Platter, Octagonal, c.1825, 15 1/2 In. 468.00
Platter, Orange Peel Glaze, Blue, White, 14 3/4 In. . . . . .385.00 to 520.00
Platter, Pierced Inset, 19th Century, 17 1/4 In. 1035.00
Platter, Well & Tree, 19th Century, 18 In. 690.00
Platter, Well & Tree, White, Blue, Fitzhugh, Oval, 16 & 16 1/2 In. 980.00
Pot, Posset, Twined Handle, Fruit Finial, Blue & White, 3 1/2 In., Pair 240.00
Punch Bowl, 14 In. 2200.00
Sauceboat, Boar Head Handles, Blue, White, 7 1/2 In. 80.00
Sauceboat, Scalloped, Handle, 1840s, 8 In., Pair 785.00
Sauceboat, Underplate, 2 Handles, China, 8 In. 175.00
Sugar, Cover, Intertwined Strap Handles, 5 In. 175.00
Teapot, Cover, Barrel Form, Foo Dog Finial, 19th Century, 6 1/2 In. 690.00
Teapot, Twined Handle, 6 1/2 In. 412.00
Teapot, Twined Handle, Fruit Finial, 5 1/2 In. 845.00
Tile, Landscape Design, Round, 5 1/4 In. 220.00
Tureen, Boar's Head Handles, 12 3/4 In. 935.00
Tureen, Cover, 19th Century, 8 x 12 In. 990.00
Tureen, Cover, Bombe Form, Branch Form Handles, Blue, White, Fitzhugh, 13 In. 1610.00
Tureen, Cover, Green Band, 3 Fox Heads, Branch Form Handles, Blue, Fitzhugh, 12 In. . . . 1840.00
Tureen, Sauce, Cover, Undertray, Cut Corners, Boar's Head Handle, 7 In., Pair 1035.00
Tureen, Soup, 19th Century, 6 x 10 In. 862.00
Tureen, Soup, Cover, Boar's Head Handles, 12 In. 495.00
Warming Dish, 19th Century, 15 7/8 In. 402.00
Warming Dish, Landscape, Houses, Water, Oval, 14 1/4 x 10 In. 863.00

CAPO-DI-MONTE porcelain was first made in Naples, Italy, from 1743
to 1759. The factory moved near Madrid, Spain, reopened in 1771, and
worked to 1834. Since that time, the Doccia factory of Italy acquired
the molds and is using the crown and N mark. Societe Richard
Ceramica is a modern-day firm often referred to as Ginori or Capo-di-
Monte. This company uses the crown and N mark.

Bowl, Cherub & Woman, 20 In. 375.00
Bowl, Musicians, Continuous Scene, Twisted Brass Wire Handle, 9 In. 115.00
Box, Allegorical Design, Gilt Metal Frame, 19th Century, 3 x 7 In. 374.00
Box, Bronze Raised Allegorical Scenes On Cover, 15 x 12 1/2 In. 1725.00
Box, Cover, Couple, Romancing, Cupid Scenes, 3 x 3 1/2 In. 290.00
Box, Cover, Hunt & Gaming Scenes, 2 1/4 x 2 1/4 In. 175.00
Box, Hinged Lid, Satyrs, Putti In Relief, Brass Rim, Handle, 13 In. 980.00
Box, Putto Amidst Cloud Design, Oval, 5 In. 345.00
Casket, Paneled Sides, Gilt & Enamel Design, Pierced Trellis Edge, 13 1/4 In. 4025.00
Coffee Pot, Cover, Floral Sprigs, Wreath, Blossom, Crabstock Handle, 8 In. 2070.00
Compote, Armorial, Fish Scene, Coat Of Arms Plate, 6 3/4 In. 175.00
Dish, Classical Figures Among Clouds, High Relief, 19th Century, 18 In., Pair 1955.00
Ewer, Cherubs & Trees, Signed, 33 5/8 In. 165.00
Ewer, Neptune, Mermaids, Dolphins, Polychrome Enamel, Signed, 17 In. 440.00
Figurine, Dancing Woman, 18th-Century Dress, 11 In. 230.00
Figurine, Eagle, Outstretched Wings, Talons, Mounted Wooden Socle, 17 In. 60.00
Figurine, Pescatore Con Barca, Fisherman Hauling In Catch, 16 In. 230.00
Figurine, Rossina Va In Citta, Woman, Geese, Officer Regards Her, Signed, 16 In. 315.00
Group, Coach & Horses, Blue Crown & N, 14 In. 100.00
Group, Woman, Putto-Topped Sedan Chair, 16 In. 495.00
Jar, Ginger, Repetitive Mythological Figures, Pear Finial, 9 In., Pair 373.00
Plate, Border Of Classical Figures, Coat Of Arms Center, Signed, 11 1/2 In. 155.00
Plate, Christmas, 1974 . . . . 65.00
Plate, Putto At Play, Blue Cavetto, Gilt Foliate, 9 1/4 In. 90.00
Plate, Putto At Play, Blue Cavetto, Gilt Foliate, 10 In. 250.00
Plate Set, Classical Figures, Central Pseudo Crest, 10 1/2 In., 12 Piece 2185.00
Stein, Relief Children Around Body, Set-On Lid With Lion Finial, 1/5 Liter 82.00

Tureen, Cover, Cherubs, Fish Handles, Large 500.00
Urn, 4 Classical Female Mounts, Gilt Garlands, White, 19 1/2 In. 1495.00
Urn, Band Of Classical Sea Gods & Nymphs, 19th Century, 16 1/2 In., Pair 2300.00
Urn, Cover, Medieval Battle Scene, Tripod Support, Pair 1210.00
Urn, Cover, Neoclassical, Allover Foliate Design, 2 Scrolled Handles, 20 In. 1495.00
Urn, Cover, Putti As Musicians, Ram's Head Handles, 7 1/2 In., Pair 300.00
Urn, Cover, Satyrs & Putti, Ram's Head Handle, 15 1/2 In., Pair 805.00
Urn, Cover, Triumph Of Bacchus, Satyrs & Maenads, 1850s, 16 In., Pair 575.00
Vase, Classical Relief Scenes, Bacchic Mask Handles, 14 In. 345.00
Vase, Cover, Neoclassical Style, Figural Friezes, 15 1/4 In. 1540.00
Wall Bracket, Gilt, Pair 805.00
Wall Pocket, Portrait, Head Of Ram & Eagle On Either Side, 7 In., Pair 230.00

CAPTAIN MARVEL was introduced in February 1940 in Whiz comic
books. An orphan named Billy Batson met the wizard, Shazam, and
whenever he said the magic word he was transformed into a superhero.
A movie serial was released in 1940. The comic was discontinued in
1954. A second Captain Marvel appeared in 1966, a third in 1967.
Only the original was transformed by shouting *Shazam.*

Book, Punch Out, Samuel Lowe, Unused, 1942, 8 x 12 In. 265.00
Button, Pinback, 1941 . . . . 30.00
Code-O-Graph Decoder Pin, With Official Secret Code Book, 1941 . . . . .38.00 to 84.00
Magic Lightning Box 75.00

CAPTAIN MIDNIGHT began as a radio show in September 1940. The
first comic book appeared in July 1941. Captain Midnight was really
the aviator Captain Albright, who was to defeat the Nazis. A movie serial was made in 1942 and a comic strip was published for a short time.
The comic book Captain Midnight ended his career in 1948. The radio
premiums are the prized collector memorabilia today.

Badge, MagniMatic Decoder, Metal, 1945 . . . . 200.00
Book, Big Little Book, Moon Woman, No. 1452, 1943 . . . . 100.00
Book, Big Little Book, Secret Squadron vs. Orient, No. 1488, 1942 . . . . 75.00
Booklet, Heroes Stamp Album, Captain Midnight With Plane, 5 x 6 3/4 In. 85.00
Cup, Hot Ovaltine, Heart Of A Hearty Breakfast, Red Plastic, 3 1/8 In. 55.00
Cup, Ovaltine, Red Plastic 70.00
Decoder, Mirror, 1946 . . . . 75.00
Patch, Captain Midnight's 15th Anniversary Secret Squadron Emblem 35.00

CARAMEL SLAG, see Chocolate Glass category.

CARDS listed here include advertising cards (often called trade cards),
greeting cards, baseball cards, playing cards, and others. Color pictures
were rare in the nineteenth century, so companies gave away colorful
cards with pictures of children, flowers, products, or related scenes that
promoted the company name. These were often collected and stored in
albums. Baseball cards also date from the nineteenth century when
they were used by tobacco companies as giveaways. Gum cards were
started in 1933, but it was not until after World War II that the bubble
gum cards favored today were produced. Today over 1,000 cards are
issued each year by the gum companies. Related items may be found
in the Postcard and Movie categories.

Advertising, Acme Beer, 1940s 13.00
Advertising, Alden Fruit Vinegar, Bird Picture 4.00
Advertising, Armant's Lillita Perfume, Woman, Party Hat, Floral Ground, 3 x 4 1/4 In. . . . 17.00
Advertising, Baker, Umbrella Repair Man, Oriental Design, 1880, 2 1/4 x 4 In. 20.00
Advertising, Champion Wash Boiler, Woman, Nice Clothes, Standing 125.00
Advertising, Corticelli Spool Silk, Abraham Bros. Dry Goods, Oakland, Calif., 4 5/8 In. . . 22.00
Advertising, Croft Wilbur & Co., 5 Lbs. Pure Confections, 1 Dollar, 1885, 3 3/4 x 3 In. . . 45.00
Advertising, E.S. Harris, Agency For Sharps Rifle Co., Soldier, 3 Revolving Faces 250.00
Advertising, Equitable Life Insurance, Birds 55.00
Advertising, Groder's Syrup, Cure Sick Headache, Chicago World's Fair, 1893, 4 3/4 In. . 15.00
Advertising, H.J. Heinz Co., Pickle Girl Holding Tomato Soup Tin, Cardboard, 5 In. 100.00

Advertising, Hartford Sewing Machine Co., Child With Bird, 5 1/2 x 7 1/2 In. 55.00
Advertising, Joseph J. Byers Shoes, Brooklyn, N.Y., Birds At Beach, 1880s, 2 x 3 In. 6.00
Advertising, Keystone Wringer, Kennedy Spauling & Co., Syracuse, N.Y., 1870s 22.00
Advertising, Lautz, Bro's & Cos. Soaps, White Man Scrubbing Black Man's Face, 1880s . 40.00
Advertising, Lord & Taylor, New York, Best Alaskan Seal Fur Coat, 1880s, 3 x 5 In. 22.00
Advertising, McLaughlin's Coffee, 3 Children Scene 4.00
Advertising, Newsboy Tobacco, Agnes Reilly, 1893, 6 x 9 In. 28.00
Advertising, Parker's Ginger Tonic, Little Girl 1.00
Advertising, Red Rose Tea, Different Butterflies, 6 Piece 3.00
Advertising, Uncle Sam Mechanical Bank 500.00
Advertising, Union Evangelistic Campaign, Rev. Mark L. Scott, 1930, 6 x 6 In. 25.00
Advertising, Walter Baker & Co.'s Chocolate Broma & Cocoa, 1880 .... 65.00
Advertrising, Woman Suffrage Stove Polish, 2 Girls Fishing, 1880s 50.00
Baseball, Babe Ruth, Goudey, No. 53, 1933 .... 1750.00
Baseball, Ed Lopat, Topps, No. 57, 1952 .... 55.00
Baseball, Eddie Waitkus, Bowman, No. 142, 1949 .... 25.00
Baseball, Heine Manush, Topps, No. 187, 1954 .... 9.00
Baseball, Ken Henderson, Topps, No. 39, 1966 .... 1.00
Baseball, Luke Appling, Goudey, No. 27, 1934 .... 150.00
Baseball, Mike Thompson, Topps, No. 564, 1973 .... 2.00
Baseball, Norm Young, Bowman, No. 240, Error Card, 1949 .... 50.00
Baseball, Rabbit Maranville, Goudey, No. 117, 1933 .... 35.00
Baseball, Roy Campanella, 1949 .... 1040.00
Baseball, Travis Jackson, Goudey, No. 102, 1933 .... 135.00
Baseball, Willie Mays, Topps, All-Star, No. 579, 1961 .... 200.00
Basketball, Jerry West, Fleer, No. 43, 1961 .... 1100.00
Basketball, K.C. Jones, Fleer, No. 22, 1961 .... 225.00
Basketball, Walter Dukes, Fleer, No. 50, 1961 .... 300.00
Boxing, John L. Sullivan, Mecca Cigarettes 100.00
Business, Joe Cerruty & His Orchestra, Oakland, Calif., Musical Design, 1930s 4.00
Business, Larry Ryan, Radio Specialist, Oakland, Calif., 1930s 4.00
Football, Joe Perry, Topps, No. 110, 1956 .... 550.00
Football, Kenneth Snyder, Bowman, No. 55, 1953 .... 200.00
Football, Weldon Humble, Bowman, No. 1, 1951 .... 350.00
Golf, Fred Hershoff, American Tobacco Co., 1910 .... 12.00
Golf, Harry Vardon, Famous Golfers, No. 46, 1927 .... 15.00
Golf, Williams & Snead, Fleer, No. 67, 1963, Set 65.00
Greeting, Anniversary, To My Wife, Blondie & Dagwood, Folded, Hallmark, 1943 ...... 40.00
Greeting, Birthday, Dr. Who By TARDIS, In Original Bag, Denis Alan Print, 1970s 18.00
Greeting, Happy New Year, Dewey, Portrait, Ribbon 75.00
Greeting, Valentine, Baseball, Waiting To Be Called, 1930s, 6 x 4 1/2 In. 12.00
Greeting, Valentine, Boy & Girl, Heart Balloon, Mechanical, Germany, 1920s 10.00
Greeting, Valentine, Boy, Girl Holding Golliwog, Mechanical, Germany, 1920s, 2 x 4 In. . 20.00
Greeting, Valentine, Children, Locomotive Ground, 3-D, Germany, 7 x 4 In. 25.00
Greeting, Valentine, Foldover Card, Votes For Women, Die Cut, 4 x 4 In. 50.00
Greeting, Valentine, Girl With Phone Body, Mechanical, 1930s, 4 x 3 In. 13.00
Greeting, Valentine, Heart, Key, Verse, R.F. Outcault, Hanging, 8 1/2 x 9 In. 28.00
Greeting, Valentine, Jiggs, Be My Valentine Or The Jigg's Up, 1930s, 4 x 5 3/4 In. 10.00
Greeting, Valentine, Poem & Women On Knees, Suffrage 20.00
Greeting, Valentine, Snow White, 1938 .... 25.00
Greeting, Valentine, Votes For Women, Little Girl, Casting Her Vote, Embossed 150.00
Memorial, Enrico Caruso, Birth & Death Date, 2 Prayers, Black Border, 1921, 5 x 3 In. .. 50.00
Playing, Anheuser Busch, Mechanical Refrigeration Division, Felt Box, 1930s 45.00
Playing, Arrco Playing Card Co., Texas Size, 5 x 7 In. 25.00
Playing, Don't Hesitate, Woman Bather, Yellow Suit, Diving, Box, 2 1/2 x 3 1/2 In. 40.00
Playing, Edison Mazda Lamps, Maxfield Parrish, Waterfall, Box 250.00
Playing, Hamm's Beer 10.00
Playing, Marilyn Monroe, Unused, 1976 .... 15.00
Playing, Miller Beer, 1951 .... 35.00
Playing, Nord Deutscher Lloyd, Cruise Ships, Box, Germany, Early 1930s, 4 x 5 1/2 In. .. 42.00
Playing, Pinochle, Liberty Bell Oil Company, Girl Standing In Rigging Of Ship 30.00
Playing, Space Shuttle, Kennedy Space Center, Florida, Deck, In Cellophane, 1980 ..... 5.00

Playing, Tarot, Woodcuts, Issued In Genoa, Italy, 4 1/4 x 2 9/16 In.	1725.00
Playing, Vargas, 53 Pinups, Box	115.00
Trading, Addams Family, Black & White, 1964, 17 Piece	40.00
Trading, Lost In Space, Set	495.00
Trading, Man From Uncle, TV Series, Black & White, 1965, 20 Piece	25.00
Trading, Man On The Moon, Apollo 11 Moon Mission, Color, 1969, 42 Piece	35.00

CARDER, see Aurene and Steuben categories.

CARLSBAD is a mark found on china made by several factories in Germany, Austria, and Bavaria. Many pieces were exported to the United States. Most of the pieces available today were made after 1891.

Candleholder, Skull Shape, Porcelain, 3 1/2 In.	75.00
Vase, Floral, 5 In.	65.00
Vase, Hand Painted Dogwood, 5 In.	55.00
Vase, Hand Painted, 9 1/2 In.	350.00

CARLTON WARE was made at the Carlton Works of Stoke-on-Trent, England, beginning about 1890. The firm traded as Wiltshaw & Robinson until 1957. It was renamed Carlton Ware Ltd. in 1958. The company went bankrupt in 1995, but the name is still in use.

Ashtray, Dreamer	50.00
Biscuit Jar, Flow Blue Floral Design, Gilt, Silver Plated Fittings, 6 3/4 In.	210.00
Biscuit Jar, Hand Painted Floral	160.00
Bowl, Harebell, Pink Flowers, Green & Yellow Leaves, Gold Trim, Signed, 9 In.	495.00
Dish, Silver, Blue Ground, Diamond Shape, Wing Handles, 11 3/4 In.	44.00
Jar, Cover, Chinese Buildings & People, Gold Border, 9 3/4 In.	425.00
Nappy, Buttercup	38.00
Vase, Chinese Bird, Dark Blue Luster Ground, Drilled For Lamp, 8 In.	575.00
Vase, Parrots On Green, Black Interior, 8 In.	235.00

CARNIVAL GLASS was an inexpensive, iridescent, pressed glass made from about 1907 to about 1925. More than 1,000 different patterns are known. Carnival glass is currently being reproduced. Additional pieces may be found in the Northwood category.

Acanthus, Bowl, Green, 8 In.	75.00 to 80.00
Acorn, Bowl, Marigold, 7 In.	55.00
Acorn Burrs, Pitcher, Purple	495.00
Acorn Burrs, Punch Cup, Green	35.00
Acorn Burrs, Spooner, Amethyst	210.00
Acorn Burrs & Bark pattern is listed here as Acorn Burrs.	
Amaryllis pattern is listed here as Tiger Lily.	
April Showers, Vase, Amethyst, 12 In.	160.00
Basketweave, Basket, Marigold	95.00
Battenburg Lace No. 1 pattern is listed here as Hearts & Flowers.	
Beaded Shell, Mug, Purple	80.00
Broken Arches, Punch Cup, Marigold	26.00
Butterfly & Fern, Tumbler, Green	40.00
Butterfly & Fern, Water Set, Blue, 12 Piece	285.00
Butterfly & Plume pattern is listed here as Butterfly & Fern.	
Cattails & Water Lily pattern is listed here as Water Lily & Cattails.	
Cherry Wreathed pattern is listed here as Wreathed Cherry.	
Christmas Cactus pattern is listed here as Thistle.	
Chrysanthemum, Bowl, Blue, Footed	225.00
Coin Dot, Bowl, Green, 8 1/2 In.	170.00
Coin Dot, Bowl, Ruffled Edge, Peach Opalescent, 8 In.	85.00
Constitution pattern is listed here as God & Home.	
Daisy & Plume, Compote, Green	50.00
Diamond Point Columns, Vase, Green, 6 3/4 x 5 3/4 In.	200.00
Dragon & Lotus, Bowl, Amethyst, 8 In. *Illus*	105.00
Fan & Arch pattern is listed here as Persian Garden.	
Fantasy pattern is listed here as Question Marks.	

Feather & Hobstar pattern is listed here as Inverted Feather.
Feathers, Vase, Green, Marigold, 7 1/2 In. 80.00
Flowering Almonds pattern is listed here as Peacock Tail.
Fluffy Bird pattern is listed here as Peacock.
Four Pillars, Vase, Aqua Opalescent, 10 1/2 In. . . . . .180.00 to 200.00
God & Home, Tumbler, Blue 200.00
Good Luck, Bowl, Amethyst, 8 In. 360.00
Good Luck, Bowl, Electric Blue, Ruffled Edge . . . . .375.00 to 500.00
Grape & Cable, Banana Boat, Purple 360.00
Grape & Cable, Bowl, Blue, 7 In. 105.00
Grape & Cable, Bowl, Cobalt Blue, 6 In. 134.00
Grape & Cable, Bowl, Flat Ruffled Edge, Marigold, 7 In. 50.00
Grape & Cable, Bowl, Persian Medallion Interior, Ruffled Edge, 10 In. 150.00
Grape & Cable, Butter, Marigold 150.00
Grape & Cable, Cologne Bottle, Marigold 195.00
Grape & Cable, Perfume Bottle, Purple 335.00
Grape & Cable, Pin Tray, Marigold 150.00
Grape & Cable, Powder Jar, Green 200.00
Grape & Cable, Punch Bowl, Green 800.00
Grape & Cable, Tumbler, Amethyst . . . .*Illus* 65.00
Grape Delight pattern is listed here as Vintage.
Hearts & Flowers, Bowl, Ice Green, 8 1/2 In. 875.00
Hearts & Flowers, Bowl, Marigold, 9 In. 400.00
Heron & Rushes pattern is listed here as Stork & Rushes.
Hobnail pattern is listed in this book as its own category.
Holly, Bowl, Amethyst, 8 In. . . . . .65.00 to 75.00
Holly, Bowl, Blue, 9 In. 75.00
Holly, Bowl, Marigold, 8 In. . . . . .55.00 to 75.00
Holly, Bowl, Purple, 9 In., Pair 55.00
Holly, Bowl, Ruffled Edge, White, 9 In. 150.00
Holly, Plate, Marigold On Milk Glass 400.00
Horse Medallions pattern is listed here as Horses' Heads.
Horses' Heads, Bonbon, Marigold 175.00
Imperial Grape, Bowl, Amber, 9 In. 120.00
Imperial Grape, Goblet, Amethyst 225.00
Imperial Grape, Plate, Fluted, Marigold 104.00
Imperial Grape, Plate, Green, 9 In. 175.00
Inverted Feather, Bowl, Fruit, Marigold, Footed, 9 3/4 x 5 1/2 In. 175.00
Irish Lace pattern is listed here as Louisa.
Labelle Rose pattern is listed here as Rose Show.
Lattice & Points, Bowl, Marigold, 4 1/2 In. 75.00
Leaf Chain, Bowl, White, 9 In. 120.00
Leaf Chain, Plate, Blue, 7 1/2 In. 1300.00
Leaf Chain, Plate, White, 9 In. 290.00
Leaf Medallion pattern is listed here as Leaf Chain.

Carnival Glass, Dragon & Lotus,
Bowl, Amethyst, 8 In.

Carnival Glass,
Grape & Cable,
Tumbler, Amethyst

Carnival Glass, Peacock & Urn,
Compote, Marigold, Clear Stem

Lion, Bowl, Marigold, 8 In.	125.00
Louisa, Bowl, Footed, Marigold	85.00
Oak Leaf & Acorn pattern is listed here as Acorn.	
Orange Tree, Bowl, Footed, 4 In.	34.00
Orange Tree, Hatpin Holder, Blue	400.00
Orange Tree, Loving Cup, Blue	425.00
Orange Tree, Mug, Blue	115.00
Orange Tree, Mug, Marigold	58.00
Orange Tree, Orange Bowl, Marigold, 9 1/2 x 5 1/2 In.	195.00
Orange Tree, Powder Jar, Cover, Purple	145.00
Orange Tree, Punch Bowl, Blue, 5 Piece	195.00
Orange Tree, Punch Cup, Blue	32.00
Orange Tree, Tumbler, Amethyst	34.00
Orange Tree, Tumbler, Beaded, Blue	60.00
Orange Tree, Tumbler, Marigold	60.00
Pansy, Bowl, Purple, 9 In.	100.00
Pansy, Nappy, Green	25.00
Peacock, Bowl, Ruffled Edge, Ice Green	1100.00
Peacock & Grape, Bowl, Blue, 9 In.	195.00
Peacock & Grape, Bowl, Marigold, 9 In.	45.00 to 50.00
Peacock & Grape, Plate, Green	224.00
Peacock & Urn, Compote, Marigold, Clear Stem	*Illus* 104.00
Peacock & Urn, Compote, Ruffled Edge, Cobalt Blue	125.00
Peacock & Urn, Dish, Ice Cream, Amethyst	350.00
Peacock At The Fountain, Bowl, Marigold, 8 3/4 In.	235.00
Peacock At The Fountain, Butter, Marigold	124.00 to 250.00
Peacock At The Fountain, Pitcher, Blue	495.00
Peacock At The Fountain, Water Set, Marigold, 5 Piece	710.00
Peacock On Fence pattern is listed here as Peacock.	
Peacock Tail, Compote, Blue	85.00
Persian Garden, Plate, Marigold, 6 In.	100.00
Persian Medallion, Bonbon, Aqua	250.00
Persian Medallion, Bowl, Blue, 7 1/2 In.	125.00
Petal & Fan, Bowl, Peach Opalescent, 10 In.	185.00
Pine Cone, Plate, Blue, 6 In.	165.00
Pine Cone Wreath pattern is listed here as Pine Cone.	
Question Marks, Bonbon, Handle, Amethyst	75.00
Raindrops, Bowl, Fluted, 9 In.	175.00
Raspberries, Tumbler, Amethyst	75.00
Ripple, Vase, Amethyst, 11 In.	110.00
Ripple, Vase, Green, 8 7/8 In.	110.00
Ripple, Vase, Green, 12 1/4 In.	120.00
Ripple, Vase, Marigold, 12 In.	30.00
Rose Show, Bowl, Blue, 9 In.	2000.00
Rose Show, Bowl, Ice Blue, 9 In.	2300.00
Singing Birds, Berry Bowl, Green, 4 1/2 In.	33.00
Singing Birds, Mug, Blue	165.00
Singing Birds, Mug, Purple	90.00
Singing Birds, Water Set, 7 Piece	800.00
Stag & Holly, Bowl, Footed, Purple, Large	185.00
Star & File, Compote, Marigold	50.00
Star Of David & Bows, Bowl, Amethyst	79.00
Star Of David Medallion pattern is listed here as Star of David & Bows.	
Stippled Rays, Bowl, Amethyst, 8 In.	40.00
Stippled Rays, Compote, Celeste Blue	350.00
Stork & Rushes, Punch Bowl, Base, Marigold	195.00
Strawberry Wreath, Compote, Green	85.00
Target, Vase, Squat, Marigold, 4 1/2 In.	55.00
Teardrops pattern is listed here as Raindrops.	
Thistle, Vase, Amethyst, 10 In.	30.00
Three Fruits, Bonbon, Green	121.00
Three Fruits, Bowl, Footed, Green, 8 In.	595.00
Three Fruits, Plate, Amethyst, 8 1/2 In.	150.00

Three Fruits, Plate, Green, 8 1/2 In. 400.00
Three Fruits Medallion, Bowl, Footed, Aqua Opalescent 1100.00
Tiger Lily, Tumbler, Amethyst 95.00
Tree Trunk, Vase, Green, 8 In. 85.00
Tree Trunk, Vase, Ice Green, 11 In. 375.00
Vintage, Bowl, Marigold, 9 In. 35.00
Vintage, Plate, Blue, 7 In. 175.00
Vintage, Plate, Green, 7 In. 180.00
Vintage, Rose Bowl, White 85.00
Water Lily & Cattails, Butter, Cover, Marigold 195.00
Water Lily & Cattails, Pitcher, Water, Marigold 195.00
Windflower, Bowl, Marigold, 8 In. ....39.00 to 45.00
Windmill, Dish, Pickle, Purple 45.00
Wreathed Cherry, Banana Boat, Red Cherries, White 270.00

CAROUSEL or merry-go-round figures were first carved in the United
States in 1867 by Gustav Dentzel. Collectors discovered the charm of
the hand-carved figures in the 1970s, and they were soon classed as
folk art. Most desirable are the figures other than horses, such as pigs,
camels, lions, or dogs. A jumper is a figure that was made to move up
and down on a pole; a stander was placed in a stationary position.

Donkey, Nodding Head, Heyn 5290.00
Elephant, Round Seating On Back, Heyn, 1900s 9900.00
Fish, Gustave Bayol, c.1900 .... 5462.00
Giraffe, Painted Saddle & Details, Glass Eyes, 39 1/2 In. 460.00
Giraffe, Standing, 1900, 6 Ft. 16000.00
Goat, Polychrome Painted Saddle, Glass Eyes, 31 In. 575.00
Horse, Carved & Painted, 1890-1910, 45 In. 2700.00
Horse, Dapple Gray, 5 Suspended Chariots, Center Pole, Wood, Converse, 36 In. 1725.00
Horse, Front Legs Off Floor, Heyn 4025.00
Horse, Heyn, Long Hair Tail, 20th Century Reproduction 1250.00
Horse, Jumper, American Flag, Bird's Wing, Herschell-Spillman 8625.00
Horse, Jumper, Polychrome Painted, 56 In. 2500.00
Horse, Philadelphia Toboggan Co., c.1910 .... 7475.00
Horse, Running, Raised Head, Bridle, C.W. Parker Co., Abilene, Ks., 53 In. 3735.00
Horse, Standing, Heyn, 27 In. 4887.00
Horse, Tossed-Back Head, 7 Gold Rings On Breast Strap, Stein & Goldstein 6325.00
Horse, Trotting Position, Muller 8625.00
Lion, Jumper, Each Leg In Different Position, 30 x 33 In. 6900.00
Pig, Running, Bayol 5980.00
Rabbit, Bayol 8280.00
Rooster, Child Size, C.J. Spooner, c.1900, 34 x 34 In. 6900.00
Warthog, Bronze Casting, Child Size, Matthieu, 19 In. 6325.00

CARRIAGE means several things, so this category lists baby carriages,
buggies for adults, horse-drawn sleighs, and even strollers. Doll-sized
carriages are listed in the Toy category.

Baby Buggy, Victorian, 3 Wheels 435.00
Baby Buggy, Victorian, White 280.00
Baby Buggy, White Wicker, Wrought Iron Wheels, Brakes, Reverse Body, Full Size 1300.00
Baby Buggy, Wicker, Dapple Gray Horse, Wire Wheels, 70 In. 605.00
Baby Buggy, Wicker, Wooden Chassis & Wheels 302.00
Baby Buggy, Wooden Wheels, Upholstered Interior, Wakefield Reed Chair Co. 850.00
Baby Buggy, Wooden, Cane Seat, Wooden Spoke Wheels, Heywood 495.00
Cart, Child's, Pulled By Dog, Green Paint, Napoleon III, France 1500.00
Cart, Dog, Whitney Carriage Company, Maine 385.00
Child's, Dovetailed Pine, Orange & Black Paint, Canvas Top, Penna. 1650.00
Perambulator, Stick & Ball, 1860s 1200.00
Rickshaw, Tubular Steel Frame, Tufted Vinyl Cushion & Top, 20th Century, 80 In. 110.00
Sleigh, Cutter, Swell Body, Albany, 1850 .... 1250.00
Stroller, Rope Twist Sides, Cast Iron Parasol Holder, Heywood 800.00
Wagon, Farm, Mitchell, Professionally Repainted 1800.00

CASH REGISTERS were invented in 1884 because an eye on the cash was a necessity in stores of the nineteenth century, too. John and James Ritty invented a large model that resembled a clock and kept a record of the dollars and cents exchanged in the store. John Patterson improved the cash register with a paper roll to record the money. By the early 1900s, elaborate brass registers were made. About World War I, the fancy case was exchanged for the more modern types.

National, Candy Store, Milk Glass Shelf, Oak Base, 16 x 17 x 10 1/4 In.	715.00
National, Model 5, Bronze, 11-Key, Detail-Adder	1100.00
National, Model 129, Brass, Ornate, Plaque	550.00
National, Model 215, Candy Store, Brass	130.00
National, Model 313, Brass, 15-Key, 21 1/4 x 10 1/2 x 16 1/4 In.	475.00
National, Model 317, Brass, 15-Key, 21 1/4 x 10 1/2 x 16 1/4 In.	450.00
National, Model 332, 22-Key, 22 1/2 x 17 3/4 x 16 1/4 In.	425.00
National, Model 420, Brass, Marble Change Shelf, 31-Key, 26 x 18 3/4 x 15 In.	395.00
National, Model 572, Brass, Raised Paneled Oak Base	600.00
National, Nickel Plated, Ornate Cast Panels, Oak Trim, 22 1/2 x 17 1/2 x 17 In.	385.00
National, Oak, 4 Drawers, Filigree Design, Brass, 33 x 30 x 21 In.	460.00
National, Oak, 5 Drawers, Floor Model, Electric Or Manual	1800.00
National, Receipt Box, Gold-Painted Metal, Original Key, 6 3/4 x 6 In.	286.00

CASTOR JARS for pickles are glass jars about six inches in height, held in special metal holders. They became a popular dinner table accessory about 1890. Each jar had a top that was usually silver or silver plate. The frame, also of a silver metal, had a handle that arched above the jar and a hook that held a pair of tongs. By 1900, the pickle castor was out of fashion. Many examples found today have reproduced glass jars in old holders. Additional pickle castors may be found in the various Glass categories.

Pickle, Bulbous Thumbprint Insert, Cover & Tongs, Ball Footed, Silver Plated Frame	375.00
Pickle, Cobalt Blue Insert, Yellow Enamel, Frame, Tongs	425.00
Pickle, Cranberry Insert, Fork, Victorian, 11 In.	445.00
Pickle, Enameled Flowers, Cranberry Insert, Silver Plated Frame	395.00
Pickle, Silver Plate, Vaseline Glass Diamond Point Insert, 11 In.	165.00
Pickle, Tongs, Pressed Glass Insert	165.00

CASTOR SETS holding just salt and pepper castors were used in the seventeenth century. The sugar castor, mustard pot, spice dredger, bottles for vinegar and oil, and other spice holders became popular by the eighteenth century. These sets were usually made of sterling silver. The American Victorian castor set, the type most collected today, was made of silver plated Britannia metal. Colored glass bottles were introduced after the Civil War. The sets were out of fashion by World War I. Be careful when buying sets with colored bottles; many are reproductions. Other castor sets may be listed in various porcelain and glass categories in this book.

2 Bottles, Vaseline Glass, Silver Plated Holder	75.00

Castor Set,
6 Bottle, Silver,
Gothic Style, Pat
1857, 16 In., Pair

---

4 Bottles, Oil, Vinegar, Mustard, Pepper, Sterling Silver Holder 300.00
4 Bottles, Pewter Stand, Excelsior 425.00
5 Bottles, Cranberry Glass, Silver Plated Holder, Meriden 275.00
5 Bottles, Cut Glass, Acanthus Leaf Trim, Sterling Silver Holder 250.00
6 Bottles, Silver, Gothic Style, Pat 1857, 16 In., Pair .... *Illus* 1600.00

CATALOGS are listed in the Paper category.

CAUGHLEY porcelain was made in England from 1772 to 1814. Caughley porcelains are very similar in appearance to those made at the Worcester factory. See the Salopian category for related items.

Basket, Reticulated, 2 Handles, 1780, 3 3/4 x 7 3/4 x 9 1/2 In. 3920.00
Cup, Handless, With Worcester Saucer 110.00
Mug, Blue Design, Crescent Mark, Late 18th Century, 4 3/4 In. 172.00
Tankard, Blue Floral Design, Signed, 1880s, 4 3/4 In. 172.00
Teapot, Fisherman, c.1780 .... 7125.00
Waste Bowl, Pearlware, Blue & White Peony, Marked, 4 3/4 In. 165.00
Waste Bowl, Pearlware, Blue & White Peony, Marked, 6 1/8 In. 245.00

CAULDON Limited worked in Staffordshire, Great Britain, and went through many name changes. John Ridgway made porcelain at Cauldon Place, Hanley, until 1855. The firm of John Ridgway, Bates and Co. of Cauldon Place worked from 1856 to 1859. It became Bates, Brown-Westhead, Moore and Co. from 1859 to 1862. Brown-Westhead, Moore and Co. worked from 1862 to 1904. About 1890, this firm started using the words *Cauldon* or *Cauldon ware* as part of the mark. Cauldon Ltd. worked from 1905 to 1920, Cauldon Potteries from 1920 to 1962. Related items may be found in the Indian Tree category.

Plate, Dog, Large Bull Terrier, Gold Trim Edges, Signed, 10 1/2 In. 125.00
Punch Bowl, Flow Blue, Candia, 1870, 18 In. 2100.00
Teapot, Victorian Shape, Hand Painted Florals 70.00

CELADON is the name of a velvet-textured green-gray glaze used by Chinese, Japanese, Korean, and other factories. The name refers both to the glaze and to pieces covered with the glaze. It is still being made.

Bowl, Carved Fish & Waves, Brown-Black Glaze On White Ground, 16 1/2 In. 55.00
Bowl, Flared, Floral & Medallion, Pale Green & Beige, Ring Foot, Koru, 7 1/2 In. 290.00
Bowl, Lotus Petal Design, 6 1/2 In., Pair 290.00
Bowl, Pale Green, Beige Floral Medallions, Ring Foot, Koryo Dynasty, 7 x 2 3/4 In. 290.00
Bowl, Peony Design, 8 1/4 In. 440.00
Bowl, Scalloped Edge, Crackle Finish, Signed, 11 In. 22.00
Charger, Bouquet Of Flowers, Fruit, Flowering Band Interior, Sea Green, 18 In. 2990.00
Charger, Central Dragon Design, Lotus Leaves On Exterior, 22 3/4 In. 975.00
Cup, Libation, Scrolled Dragon Handle, 4 1/2 In. 385.00
Dish, Shrimp, c.1835, 10 1/4 In. 385.00
Falconer, Sea Green Cover, Duck Form, Dark Green Glaze, 6 x 12 In. 260.00
Figurine, Phoenix, Holding A Jui In Its Beak, 1800, 2 1/2 In. 110.00
Platter, Birds In Floral Garden, Blue & White, Rectangular, Cut Corners, China, 16 In. ... 170.00
Platter, Canton 1872, Oval, 19th Century, 19 1/2 In. 2090.00
Umbrella Stand, White Floral Design, 5 Holes Around Top, 22 1/2 In. 440.00
Vase, Birds In Garden Scene, Enameled, China, 19th Century, 17 1/4 In. 170.00
Vase, Birds, Flying, Flowering Prunus Tree Design, Blue, 18 In. 900.00
Vase, Bottle, Cover, Flowers, Birds, Butterflies, Chinese Export, 16 In. 355.00
Vase, Crackled, Foo Dog Mask Handles, 19th Century, 12 In. 259.00
Vase, Crackled, Hexagonal, Porcelain, 19th Century, 17 In. 316.00
Vase, Dragon Design, Porcelain, 19th Century, 9 In. 200.00
Vase, Incised Floral Design, Baluster, 11 In. 200.00
Vase, Landscape Design, Blue, White, 19th Century, 16 1/2 In. 302.00
Vase, Melon Ribbed, Teardrop Shape, 7 1/4 In. 467.00
Vase, Nature Scene, Finger Of A Buddha's Hand, Floral Shape, Knotty Branch, 5 In. 1840.00
Vase, Overall Underglaze Diamond & Spiral Design, 8 3/8 In. 1035.00
Vase, Peony & Vine Design, Egg Shape, 12 1/2 In. 4840.00

CELLULOID is a trademark for a plastic developed in 1868 by John W. Hyatt. Celluloid Manufacturing Company, the Celluloid Novelty Company, Celluloid Fancy Goods Company, and American Xylonite Company all used Celluloid to make jewelry, games, sewing equipment, false teeth, and piano keys. Eventually, the Hyatt Company became the American Celluloid and Chemical Manufacturing Company, the Celanese Corporation. The name *Celluloid* was often used to identify any similar plastic. Celluloid toys are listed under Toys.

Blotter, Indian Chief, Multicolored, Pittsburgh Jeweler	185.00
Book, Prayer, Floral Bronze, Art Nouveau, France	395.00
Brush, Compliments Of Consumers Builders Supply, Box, 1930s, 2 x 6 In.	25.00
Brush & Comb Set, Child's, Box	11.00
Dresser Set, Celery Green, 7 In., 17 Piece	60.00
Dresser Set, Pearlized, Honey-Amber, Early 1900s, 8 Piece	110.00
Fish, Brown, Yellow, Hollow, Steel Pin In Mouth, 2 1/2 In., Pair	40.00
Frame, Double Picture, Easel Stand, Hand Painted, Roses, c.1910, 4 1/2 x 3 1/2 In.	28.00
Pin, American Legion Convention, Cleveland, Ohio, Blue Lettering On White, 1 1/4 In.	45.00
Pin, Iceberg The Cow, Admiral Byrd's Antarctic Expedition, 1 1/4 In.	25.00
Shaving Mug, Mirror Under Lid, Storage Brush, Milk Glass Liner, 5 In.	27.00
Stamp Holder, Hamilton Watch, Railroad Timekeeper, Lancaster, Pa., 1 x 1 1/2 In.	44.00

CELS are listed in this book in the Animation Art category.

CERAMIC ART COMPANY of Trenton, New Jersey, was established in 1889 by J. Coxon and W. Lenox and was an early producer of American Belleek porcelain. It became Lenox, Inc. in 1906. Do not confuse this ware with the pottery made by the Ceramic Arts Studio of Madison, Wisconsin.

Vase, Bulbous, Purple, Green Leaves, Gold Rim, Nan D. Easton, 1900, 5 x 7 1/2 In.	300.00
Vase, Floral, Silver & Pink, Signed, 10 In.	375.00

CERAMIC ARTS STUDIO was founded about 1940 in Madison, Wisconsin, by Lawrence Rabbett and Ruben Sand. Their most popular products were expensive molded figurines. The pottery closed in 1955. Do not confuse these products with those of the Ceramic Art Co. of Trenton, New Jersey.

Bank, Razor, Tony The Barber, 4 3/4 In.	80.00 to 125.00
Bank, Skunky, 4 In.	230.00
Figurine, Accordion Boy, White & Blue, 5 In.	230.00
Figurine, Archibald Dragon, 6 1/4 In.	235.00
Figurine, Bear, Baby, Brown, 2 1/4 In.	50.00
Figurine, Billy Boxer & Butch Boxer, 2 & 3 In., Pair	185.00
Figurine, Colonel Jackson, 7 1/2 In.	50.00
Figurine, Comedy & Tragedy, Green, 10 3/8 & 10 In., Pair	120.00
Figurine, Dinky Skunk, 2 In.	45.00
Figurine, Ewe, Pink, 2 In.	50.00
Figurine, Fawn, 2 In.	65.00
Figurine, Giraffe Mother & Baby, 6 1/2 & 5 1/2 In., Pair	440.00
Figurine, Girl Praying, 3 In.	50.00
Figurine, Hansel & Gretel, 4 1/2 In.	90.00
Figurine, Jack Horner, 4 1/2 In.	30.00
Figurine, June, 4 1/2 In.	45.00
Figurine, Lillibeth, Brown Trim, 6 In.	40.00
Figurine, Lovebirds, 2 1/2 In.	45.00
Figurine, Madonna With Child, Blue, 6 1/2 In.	150.00
Figurine, Mary, 6 In.	65.00
Figurine, Miss Lucindy, Blue, 7 In.	45.00
Figurine, Mo-Pi & Smi-Li, 6 In., Pair	120.00
Figurine, Mother Bear & Baby, Snuggle, 4 1/2 & 2 1/4 In., Pair	65.00
Figurine, Mother Kangaroo & Joey, Snuggle, 4 3/4 & 2 3/8 In., Pair	140.00
Figurine, Mother Spaniel & Pup, 2 1/2 & 2 In., Pair	150.00
Figurine, Mouse & Cheese, Snuggle, 2 & 1 1/2 In., Pair	30.00

Figurine, Mr. Skunk, 2 7/8 In. 55.00
Figurine, Muff Kitten & Puff Kitten, 3 In., Pair 115.00
Figurine, Panda, With Hat, 2 3/4 In. 225.00
Figurine, Peek-A-Boo, Pixie, 2 3/4 In. 50.00
Figurine, Polish Girl, 6 1/4 In. 60.00
Figurine, Pom Standing, 2 3/4 In. 425.00
Figurine, Promenade Man, 7 3/4 In. 85.00
Figurine, Rhumba Dancers Man & Lady, 7 1/4 & 7 1/8 In., Pair . . . . .130.00 to 150.00
Figurine, Running Boy & Running Girl, 3 1/2 & 3 1/4 In., Pair 110.00
Figurine, Running Boy, 3 1/2 In. 50.00
Figurine, Skunk Family, 4 Piece 185.00
Figurine, Sooty & Taffy, Black & Tan, 3 In., Pair 105.00
Figurine, Spring Sue, Blue, 5 In. 50.00
Figurine, St. Francis Of Assisi, 7 In. 130.00
Figurine, St. George On Charger, 8 1/2 In. 190.00
Figurine, Tembino, 2 1/2 In. 110.00
Figurine, Ting-A-Ling & Sung-Tu, 5 1/2 & 4 In., Pair 85.00
Figurine, Young Love Boy & Young Love Girl, 4 1/2 In., Pair 110.00
Head Vase, Lotus & Manchu, 7 7/8 & 7 1/2 In., Pair 340.00
Jug, George Washington, 2 3/4 In. 40.00
Pitcher, Adam & Eve, 3 In. 65.00
Plaque, Attitude & Arabesque, 9 & 9 1/2 In., Pair 140.00
Plaque, Grace, 8 3/4 In. 60.00
Salt & Pepper, Bear Mother & Baby 65.00
Salt & Pepper, Blackamoor 80.00
Salt & Pepper, Bunny Mother & Baby Running 450.00
Salt & Pepper, Calico Cat & Gingham Dog 80.00
Salt & Pepper, Cat Mother & Kitten 225.00
Salt & Pepper, Circus Clown & Dog, Snuggle 165.00
Salt & Pepper, Cock Fighting, Right & Left 70.00
Salt & Pepper, Crocodile & Boy, Snuggle . . . . .195.00 to 350.00
Salt & Pepper, Dog & Dog House, Snuggle 90.00
Salt & Pepper, Elephant & Boy, Snuggle 230.00
Salt & Pepper, Frog, Singing & Toadstool 65.00
Salt & Pepper, Horse Heads . . . . .85.00 to 90.00
Salt & Pepper, Little Bo Peep & Lamb 55.00
Salt & Pepper, Monkey Mother & Baby, Snuggle 105.00
Salt & Pepper, Mother Bear & Baby, White, Snuggle . . . . .60.00 to 65.00
Salt & Pepper, Mother Cat & Kitten, Stylized, Brown 280.00
Salt & Pepper, Mouse & Cheese, Snuggle 40.00
Salt & Pepper, Mr. & Mrs. Penguin 60.00
Salt & Pepper, Paul Bunyan & Evergreen 280.00
Salt & Pepper, Sambo & Tiger 985.00
Salt & Pepper, Seahorse & Coral, Snuggle 95.00
Salt & Pepper, Siamese Mother & Kitten 90.00
Salt & Pepper, Straight Tail Fish . . . . .60.00 to 125.00
Salt & Pepper, Thai & Thai-Thai, Snuggle 115.00
Salt & Pepper, Twist Tail Fish 95.00
Salt & Pepper, Waldo Dachshund & Sassy Dachshund 605.00
Salt & Pepper, Wee Eskimo Boy & Girl 80.00
Saltshaker, Chinese Boy, Standing, 4 In. 20.00
Shelf Sitter, Ballet En Pose & En Repose, 5 1/4 In., Pair 170.00
Shelf Sitter, Birds, Pudgie Parakeet & Parakeet Budgie, Snuggle 125.00
Shelf Sitter, Chinese Boy & Girl, 4 In., Pair 40.00
Shelf Sitter, Grace & Greg, 6 1/4 & 7 In., Pair 90.00
Shelf Sitter, Harmonica Boy, 4 5/8 In. 70.00
Shelf Sitter, Jill, 4 3/4 In. 45.00
Shelf Sitter, Mexican Boy & Girl 440.00
Shelf Sitter, Nip & Tuck, 4 1/4 In., Pair 85.00
Shelf Sitter, Persian Cat, 4 1/2 In. 55.00
Shelf Sitter, Pierrot & Pierette, 6 3/4 In., Pair 295.00
Shelf Sitter, Su-Lin, 5 1/2 In. 60.00
Stein, Golfer, Painted, Silver Lid, 1/2 Liter 1725.00

CHALKWARE is really plaster of Paris decorated with watercolors. One type was molded from Staffordshire and other porcelain models and painted and sold as inexpensive decorations in the nineteenth century. Figures of plaster, made from about 1910 to 1940 for use as prizes at carnivals, are also known as chalkware. Kewpie dolls made of chalkware will be found in their own category.

Bank, Buffalo, 1950, 10 1/2 In.	28.00
Bank, Bull, Worn Brown & Amber, 15 1/4 In.	695.00
Bank, Clown, c.1950, 13 In.	38.00
Bank, Devil's Head, c.1950, 6 1/2 In.	71.00
Bank, Ferdinand The Bull, 1950, 9 In.	50.00
Bank, Owl, 6 1/2 In.	27.00
Bank, Porky Pig, c.1945, 12 In.	33.00
Bookends, Scotty Dog	25.00
Bust, Ulysses S. Grant, Brown-Haired Gentleman, Brown, Blue, Green, 9 1/4 In.	920.00
Figurine, Amos & Andy, Hand Painted, Statuary Co., Kansas City, Mo., 7 1/2 In.	385.00
Figurine, Antlered Deer, Recumbent, Black Plinth, 10 1/2 In., Pair	2420.00
Figurine, Betty Boop, 1930s, 15 In.	247.00
Figurine, Boy, Carrying Watermelon, 25 In.	715.00
Figurine, Cat, Gray Paint, Black Stripes, Ribbon, Pink Ears, 12 1/4 In.	440.00
Figurine, Cat, Seated, Red, Black, Yellow, c.1860, 9 7/8 In.	1430.00
Figurine, Cat, Sleeping, 12 In.	413.00
Figurine, Cat, Sleeping, White, Black, Yellow Ocher, 12 1/2 In.	80.00
Figurine, Cat, White Striped, Seated, Brown, Wearing, Red, Yellow Collar, 5 Piece	5460.00
Figurine, Compote Of Fruit, Filled With Fruits, Yellow, Brown, Red, Black, 12 In.	2300.00
Figurine, Compote Of Fruit, Filled With Grapes, Pears, Oranges, Bananas, 15 In.	1265.00
Figurine, Deer, Lying Down, On Base, 5 In.	495.00
Figurine, Deer, Red, Black, Yellow, 5 1/2 In., Pair	935.00
Figurine, Dog, Worn Red & Black Paint, 7 1/2 In.	192.00
Figurine, King Kong, 1930, 7 In.	33.00
Figurine, Man, Sowing Seeds, Painted, 16 1/2 In.	45.00
Figurine, Pig, Crying, 1950, 7 In.	11.00
Figurine, Poodle, Red, Yellow & Black Polychrome Finish, 7 1/2 In.	770.00
Figurine, Rooster, Crowing, Red & Green Feathers, Pinwheels, 9 In.	440.00
Figurine, Spaniel, Early 20th Century, 11 In.	55.00
Figurine, Still Life With Fruit, Red, Green, Yellow, Black Paint, 19th Century, 14 In.	3450.00
Figurine, Uncle Sam, c.1935, 15 In.	93.00
Watch Hutch, Green & Yellow Overpaint	425.00

CHARLIE CHAPLIN, the famous comic and actor, lived from 1889 to 1977. He made his first movie in 1913. He did the movie *The Tramp* in 1915. The character of the Tramp has remained famous, and in the 1980s appeared in a series of television commercials for computers. Dolls, candy containers, and all sorts of memorabilia picture Charlie Chaplin. Pieces are being made even today.

Candy Container, Barrel Container, Slotted, Tin Twist Closure, Borgfeldt	90.00
Candy Container, Straight-Sided Container, Metal Screw Cap, Smith	230.00
Doll, Composition Head, Hands, Shoes, Straw-Filled Body, 30 In.	120.00
Figurine, Charlie In Little Tramp Clothes, Shuffling, Key Wind, 1920, 6 In.	1770.00
Herald, Great Dictator, Die Cut Mask, Apollo Theatre Imprint, 1940	200.00
Lobby Card, City Lights, United Artists, 1931, 22 x 14 In.	1500.00
Lobby Card, The Circus, 1928	315.00
Poster, Laughing Gas, Movie, Keystone, 1914, Three Sheet	12650.00
Sheet Music, Charlie Chaplin Walk, New Fox Trot Song, 1915	75.00
Toy, Walker, Tin, Windup, Replaced Cane, Germany, 8 1/2 In.	550.00
Toy, Windup, Felt Over Tin, Shuffling Feet, Cane Spins, Schuco, 6 1/2 In.	495.00

CHARLIE MCCARTHY was the ventriloquist's dummy used by Edgar Bergen from the 1930s. He was famous for his work in radio, movies, and television. The act was retired in the 1970s.

Bank, Cast Metal, Hand Painted, Movable Mouth, Vanio, 1938	650.00
Bank, Charlie McCarthy, Standing, Composition, Key, Tag, 9 1/2 In.	300.00
Car, Mortimer Snerd Private Car, Duo Cruising, Red, Blue, 1939, 16 In.	4110.00

Doll, Composition Head, Cloth Body 295.00
Doll, Mortimer Snerd, Composition, Wire & Cloth Body, 1920s, 12 In. 350.00
Doll, Mortimer Snerd, Composition, Wire, N.M.T., 13 In. 545.00
Dummy, Cardboard, Chase & Sanborn Premium, Package, 1930s, 21 In. 100.00
Dummy, Composition, Lapel Pin, Hat, 1920s, 24 In. 565.00
Figurine, Chalkware, c.1938, 16 In. 60.00
Game, Charlie As George Washington, Green, White, 1940, 3 x 7 1/8 In. 6.00
Game, Put & Take Bingo, Whitman, McCarthy Inc., Box, 1938, 9 x 14 3/4 In. 52.00
Pencil Sharpener, Bakelite, 1930s 95.00
Salt & Pepper, Pottery, Davenport Japan, Late 1930s, 3 In. 115.00
Spoon, Silver Plate, Die Cut Charlie Portrait, Name On Handle, 1930s, 6 In. .... 5.00 to 14.00
Toy, Car, Benzine Buggy, Windup, Marx, 7 In. .... 305.00 to 675.00
Toy, Drummer, Marx, Box 1950.00
Toy, Walker, Windup, Tin Lithograph, Copyright 1930, Marx, 8 In. 155.00
Walker, Mortimer Snerd, Tin, Windup, Marx, 1939, 8 1/2 In. 220.00

CHELSEA porcelain was made in the Chelsea area of London from
about 1745 to 1784. Some pieces made from 1770 to 1784 may include
the letter *D* for *Derby* in the mark. Ceramic designs were borrowed
from the Meissen models of the day. Pieces were made of soft paste.
The gold anchor was used as the mark but it has been copied by many
other factories. Recent copies of Chelsea have been made from the
original molds. Do not confuse Chelsea porcelain with Chelsea Grape,
a white pottery with luster grape decoration.

Basket, Flower Filled, Foliate, White Blossoms, 1765, 7 1/4 In., Pair 1725.00
Box, Fashionable Lady, Wearing Puce Trimmed Lace Bonnet, Enamel, 3 In. 1955.00
Box, Head Of An Eastern Gentleman, Flower Sprays, Enamel, 1760, 3 In. 2070.00
Candlestick, Lady, Holding A Posy In 1 Hand, Gentleman, Holding Fife, 10 In., Pair 690.00
Dish, Cabbage Leaf, Green, Yellow, Puce Veining, 1755, 10 3/4 In. 1552.00
Dish, Leaf Shape, Flower Twig Handle, White, 1755, 10 7/8 In. 690.00
Dish, Sunflower, Open Yellow Sunflower, 2 Overlapping Green Leaves, 1755, 9 In. 8050.00
Dish, Sunflower, Open Yellow Sunflower, Stalk Handle, 1755, 8 In. 7475.00
Figurine, Cow, Lying Down In Field, 3 3/4 x 2 3/4 In. 425.00
Figurine, Shepherd & Shepherdess Standing Before A Floral Bocage, 8 In., Pair 1265.00
Plate, Dolphin & Baby, 10 1/4 In., 12 Piece 5500.00
Plate, Enamel Insects, Botanical Subject, 1755, 8 1/2 In. 3450.00
Plate, Floral Spray Design, 1752-1758, 8 1/2 In. 115.00
Plate, Floral Spray, Scalloped Edge, Gilt Border, 10 In., Pair 40.00
Sauceboat, Leaf Shape, Flower, Bud Terminals, Yellow, Red, Green Twig Handle, 7 In. .. 1035.00
Urn, Cover, Puce, White Alternating Ground, Ribbon, Floral Filled Basket, 12 In., Pair ... 400.00

CHELSEA GRAPE pattern was made before 1840. A small bunch of
grapes in a raised design, colored with purple or blue luster, is on the
border of the white plate. Most of the pieces are unmarked. The pattern
is sometimes called *Aynsley* or *Grandmother*. Chelsea Sprig is similar
but has a sprig of flowers instead of the bunch of grapes. Chelsea
Thistle has a raised thistle pattern. Do not confuse these Chelsea patterns with Chelsea Keramic Art Works, which can be found in the
Dedham category, or with Chelsea porcelain, the preceding category.

Cake Plate, Adderley, 9 3/4 In. 45.00
Cup & Saucer 40.00

CHINESE EXPORT porcelain comprises all the many kinds of porcelain
made in China for export to America and Europe in the eighteenth,
nineteenth, and twentieth centuries. Other pieces may be listed in this
book under Canton, Celadon, Nanking, and Rose Medallion.

Basin, Faux Wood Grain Glazing, Gilt Band, Grasshoppers Interior, 11 In. 880.00
Basket, Chestnut, Pagodas, Water Scenes, Zigzag Rim, 9 1/4 & 9 3/4 In. 1495.00
Bowl, Bird & Tree Interior, Orange Exterior, Famille Rose, Wood Stand, 10 In. 92.00
Bowl, Chrysanthemum Center, Red & Brown Ground, 3 1/2 x 9 1/2 In. 145.00
Bowl, Cover, Fu-Lion Finial, Floral Sprays, Ogee Mask Handles, 1770, 5 In. 1265.00
Bowl, Exterior Riverscape, Similar Interior, Square, c.1785, 9 5/8 In. 5175.00
Bowl, Famille Rose, 9 1/2 x 4 1/2 In. 110.00

Bowl, Figural Scene, Famille Rose, 15 3/8 In., Pair 400.00
Bowl, Figure Carrying Parasol, On Bridge, Trelliswork Edge, c.1790, 10 In. 920.00
Bowl, Floral Spray, 18th Century, 5 1/4 In. 90.00
Bowl, Lake Scene, Blue & White, Octagonal, 1790, 8 1/4 In., Pair 385.00
Bowl, Mandarin Pattern, Faux Bois Ground, 1800, 11 In. 1320.00
Bowl, Men Amid Bamboo Trees, 2 Storks, Scalloped Edge, 5 x 13 1/2 In. 690.00
Bowl, Polychrome Figures, Pink Flowers, 3 1/2 x 7 3/4 In. 440.00
Bowl, Polychrome Floral Design, c.1770, 5 3/4 In. 140.00
Bowl, Rose Mandarin, 18 1/4 In. 6050.00
Bowl, Rose Mandarin, Wooden Stand, 1840, 15 1/2 In. 2750.00
Box, Cover, Peach Design, Famille Rose, 6 1/2 In. 374.00
Brush Pot, Famille Rose, c.1800, 6 In. 2185.00
Candlestick, Painted In Iron Red, Flowers & Foliage Between Panels, 1740 .... 4600.00
Canister, Tea, Reserves Of Figures, Landscape, 19th Century, 4 1/8 In. 373.00
Casserole, Orange Foo Dog Finial & Handles, c.1775, 7 3/4 x 14 3/4 In. 4312.00
Charger, Center Reserve Of Precious Objects, Flower Head Ground, 10 In. 258.00
Charger, Peach Design, Famille Rose, 12 In. 230.00
Charger, Raised White Floral Design, Off-White Ground, Gilt, 15 In. 385.00
Chocolate Pot, Ribbon-Tied Bouquets, Spring Flowers, c.1765, 8 In. 460.00
Coffeepot, Domed Cover, Pagoda Scene, Trees, Strapwork Handle, 9 1/4 In. 860.00
Creamer, Floral, DM Monogram, Helmet Shape, 1800, 4 1/2 In. 240.00
Creamer, Pink & Gilt Design, Helmet Shape, 4 1/2 In. 120.00
Cup & Saucer, Burnt Orange Painted Floral Trim 100.00
Dish, Basket Weave Exterior, Colorful Flower Sprays Interior, 6 In., Pair 1150.00
Dish, Floral Spray Center, Lotus Petal Rim, Lotus Shape, Famille Rose, 10 In. 1495.00
Dish, Garden Scene, Floral Border, Famille Rose, 9 1/4 In. 172.00
Dish, Grisaille Design, Famille Rose, Green Lattice Ground, 18th Century, 10 In. 330.00
Dish, Pink, Yellow Flower, Scalloped Rim, Tobacco Leaf, Round, 9 In., Pair 4315.00
Dish, Tobacco Leaf, Scalloped Rim, Shallow, 1780, 6 1/2 In., 8 Piece 9200.00
Dish, Vegetable, Floral Sprigs, Pagodas, Blue, Lozenge Shape, 10 In., Pair 545.00
Figurine, Dove, Turned Head, 7 x 6 1/4 In., Pair 1725.00
Figurine, Scholar, Bearded, Robed Seated On Chair, Blue, White, 10 1/4 In. 290.00
Footbath, Blue & White, Oval, 1820, 16 x 11 In. 395.00
Garniture Set, Mandarin Design, Salmon Lattice Ground, 9 3/8 In., 3 Piece 935.00
Ginger Jar, Cover, Continuous Architectural Landscape, Famille Verte, 9 In. 865.00
Jar, Cover, Blue, White, 28 1/2 In. 575.00
Jar, Cover, Bulbous, Men & Women, 18th Century, 5 1/2 In. 230.00
Jar, Cover, Famille Verte, Baluster, 15 1/2 In. 290.00
Jar, Jade Inlaid Cover, Blue & White, Landscape Design, Round, 11 In. 1100.00
Jardiniere, Bird In Landscape, 12 1/4 In., Pair 410.00
Jardiniere, Calligraphic & Figural Design, Hexagonal, Late 1700s, 7 In. 577.00
Jug, European Style Clusters Of Spring Flowers, c.1805, 8 1/2 In. 805.00
Jug, Milk, Helmet Shape, 19th Century 110.00
Lamp, Cellwork Framed Birds & Floral Cartouches, Orange Ground, 16 In. 805.00
Lamp, Famille Verte, Figures In Landscapes, China, 18 1/2 In. 745.00
Mug, Central Urn Medallion, Twist Handle, 5 1/4 In. 605.00
Mug, People In Colorful Outfits, Flowers, 4 3/4 In. 635.00
Mug, Scenic View In Oval, Interlaced Strapped Handle, 5 1/4 In. 460.00
Pitcher, Cream, Salmon Pink & Gilt Design, Helmet Shape, 4 1/2 In. 120.00
Pitcher, Polychrome Floral, Insects & Butterflies, 5 1/2 In. 330.00
Plaque, 100 Bird, Famille Rose, Rosewood Frame, 53 1/4 x 31 In. 490.00
Plaque, Riverscape, Famille Rose, Teakwood Frame & Stand, 23 In. 160.00
Plate, Armorial, 9 3/4 In. 285.00
Plate, Armorial, Puce Floral Spray Border, Famille Rose, 9 In., Pair 1090.00
Plate, Central Dragons, Famille Rose, Yellow Ground, 8 In. 55.00
Plate, Crest & Monogram, Blue Border, 7 3/4 In. 55.00
Plate, Figural Scene, Famille Rose, 10 In., Pair 345.00
Plate, Figural Scene, Prunus Border, Famille Rose, 1840, 9 1/4 In. 260.00
Plate, Flower, Dragonfly Design, 10 1/4 In. 431.00
Plate, Landscape Center, Sepia, 10 In. 33.00
Plate, Landscape, Fish Scale Border Surround, Landscape Cartouche, 9 In. 143.00
Plate, Orange & White Dome Cover, Fitzhugh, 10 In., Pair 4600.00
Plate, Peacock, 2 Birds In Center, Pink Star Shape Floral Border, 8 In. 4890.00

Plate, Peacock, 2 Birds Perched On Orange, Gray Rock, 1770, 12 In., Pair 4025.00
Plate, Peony Sprays, Buds, Scatter Floral Sprigs, Barbed Rim, 15 In., Pair 4025.00
Plate, Raspberry Fitzhugh Pattern, 6 In. 4255.00
Plate, Rose Mandarin, Figural Design, 19th Century, 6 In., 4 Piece 55.00
Plate, Seated Man & Child, Figures On Cloud-Lined Ground, 10 3/4 In. 402.00
Plate, Soup, Tobacco Leaf, Floral, 1780, 8 3/4 In., 4 Piece 4600.00
Plate, Tobacco Leaf, Floral Sprays, Rounded Rectangular Shape, 13 In., Pair 8625.00
Plate, Vase & Garden Design, Famille Rose, 8 1/2 In., Pair 132.00
Platter, 6 Figures, Tobacco Brown & Gilt, 18 3/4 In. 2055.00
Platter, American Eagle, Blue, Salmon & Gilt Border, 14 1/2 In. 245.00
Platter, Armorial, Arms Of Chadwick, Gilt Husk Swag, c.1791, 16 In. 2760.00
Platter, Armorial, Blue Scroll Border, 18th Century, 14 1/2 In. 2300.00
Platter, Basket Weave, Figure Carrying Wood, River Scene, Blue, White, 14 In. 1610.00
Platter, Blue & White, Cut Corners, Oblong, 9 3/4 In. 220.00
Platter, Center Floral Spray, Rim Surround Of Floral Garlands, 14 1/2 In. 805.00
Platter, Center Scene, Blue & White, Octagonal, 19th Century, 13 In. 395.00
Platter, Chinese Pavilions, Reticulated, 1800, 11 1/2 x 8 3/4 In. 30.00
Platter, Grisaille, Iron Red, White, 16 In. 35.00
Platter, Pavilions & Pagodas In Landscape, Trelliswork Edge, 1790, 16 In. 977.00
Platter, Rose Mandarin, Central Figural Cartouche, Floral Rim, 14 In. 1035.00
Platter, Spray Of Flower Border, Famille Rose, 17 In. 575.00
Platter, Wood Of Copmanthorpe Armorial Design, 18th Century, 18 In. 715.00
Punch Bowl, Blue & Gold On White, Shield Design, 12 In. 935.00
Punch Bowl, Butterflies Exterior, Floral Sprays, Famille Rose, 9 1/2 In. 1495.00
Punch Bowl, Chinese Scene, Blue & White, 16 In. 8625.00
Punch Bowl, Country House, Gilt Floral Sprigs, c.1790, 11 1/4 In. 403.00
Punch Bowl, Dragon Design, 19th Century, 9 1/2 In. 110.00
Punch Bowl, Figural Scenes, Allover Gold Ground, Mandarin Palette, 10 In. 805.00
Punch Bowl, Floral, Blue & White, 1800, 16 1/4 In. 1100.00
Punch Bowl, Portrait, 2 Hong Merchants, 18th Century, 13 1/2 In. 18150.00
Salt, Floral Sprays, Scalloped Rim, Famille Rose, Rectangular, 3 In., Pair 1495.00
Salt, Tobacco Leaf, Scalloped Rim, Waisted Round Shape, 4 In., Pair 6325.00
Salt & Pepper, Flat Leaf Engraving, Foliate Landscape, 4 In. 5750.00
Sauceboat, Stand, Shell Form, Flowering Plants, Fishtail Handle, 1780, 7 In. 1035.00
Snuffbox, Painted Flower, 1765, 1 3/4 x 3 x 2 1/2 In. 1650.00
Sweetmeat Set, Floral, Butterfly Shape, 9 Sections, Stand, 19th Century, 17 In. 440.00
Teapot, American Eagle, Holding Shield, Entwined Handle, 4 1/2 In. 550.00
Teapot, Armorial, 4 1/4 In. 805.00
Teapot, Bird, Peonies, Rookery, Scrafiotto Ruby Ground, Famille Rose, 5 1/2 In. 515.00
Teapot, Domed Lid, 19th Century, 8 1/2 In. 220.00
Teapot, Drum, American Eagle Holding Shield, Entwined Handle, 4 In. 550.00
Teapot, Drum, Figural Design, Fruit Final, Entwined Handle, 1800s, 6 In. 165.00
Teapot, Drum, Masonic Design, Entwined Handle, 7 In. 165.00
Teapot, Drum, Pinecone Knop, Floral Terminals On Cover, 6 1/8 In. 575.00
Teapot, Famille Rose, Bamboo Design Handle & Spout, Rectangular, c.1780 . . . . 2640.00
Teapot, Famille Rose, c.1750, 6 In. 126.00
Teapot, Figural Design, Lattice Ground, Globular, 18th Century, 9 3/8 In. 1045.00
Teapot, Floral & Swag Enamel, Braided Handle, Cylindrical 440.00
Teapot, Floral, Qianlong, c.1760, 5 In. 260.00
Teapot, Hexagonal Cover, Bulbous, Flowering Branches, Blue, White, 10 In. 1725.00
Teapot, Persian Rose, Fruit Finial, Twined Handle, 6 In. 365.00
Teapot, Polychrome Fruit & Flowers, Twined Handle, Fruit Finial, 5 In. 300.00
Teapot, Twisted Handle, Late 18th Century, 5 3/4 In. 400.00
Teapot Stand, Lotus, Floral Design, Famille Rose, 1745, 5 In. 400.00
Tureen, Cover, Dog Form Finial, Handle, Hexagonal, 9 1/4 In. 1380.00
Tureen, Cover, Famille Verte, Panels Of Birds Amid Foliage, Gilt Rim, 11 In. 575.00
Tureen, Cover, Flowering Bushes, Birds, Handles, Blue, White, 13 1/2 In. 2530.00
Tureen, Cover, Overlapping Lotus Leaves, Floral Sprays, Orange, Gilt Rim, 12 In. 3160.00
Tureen, Cover, Pagodas, Trees, Floral Handles, Lobed Lozenge Shape, 13 In. 1610.00
Tureen, Cover, Trees, Pagodas, Blue Boar's Head Handles, Blue, White, 11 In. 1610.00
Tureen, Cover, Undertray, American Eagle, Salmon, 14 In. 495.00
Tureen, Orange Carp, Fitzhugh, 12 In., Pair 3450.00
Tureen, Sauce, Cover, Stand, Center Flower Spray, Gilt Edge, c.1780, 7 3/8 In. 5175.00

Tureen, Soup, Cover, Stand, Allover Floral, Rabbit's Head Handles, c.1780 .... 2300.00
Tureen, Soup, Cover, Stand, Pavilions & Pagodas, Celery Stalk Handles, 1790 .... 5750.00
Turen, Stand, Yellow, Pink Peonies Center, Famille Rose, 1755, 15 In. 2587.00
Urn, Palace, Floral Vinery, Cobalt Blue Ground, 53 1/2 In., Pair 4890.00
Vase, Applied Kylins, Foo Dogs, Famille Rose, Hardwood Stand, 24 In., Pair 2415.00
Vase, Bird, Floral Design, Famille Rose, Baluster, 17 1/2 In. 200.00
Vase, Birds Amidst Flowering Branches, Butterflies, Foliate, 8 & 7 In., Pair 460.00
Vase, Cover, Baluster, Wooden Base, China, 19th Century, 16 1/4 In., Pair 1610.00
Vase, Cover, Chicken Skin, Medallion, Dragon Handles, 13 In. 440.00
Vase, Cover, Mandarin Reserves, 1815-1820, 13 1/2 In. 968.00
Vase, Dragon, Fish Scale Molded Base, Pink & White Ground, 8 In. 200.00
Vase, Famille Rose, 19th Century, 24 In. 1100.00
Vase, Figural & Floral, Foo Dog Handles, Hexagonal, 1840, 24 In., Pair 3960.00
Vase, Figural Reserves, Kylin Form Handles, Famille Rose, 18 In. 805.00
Vase, Floor, Green, Red Figural Design, White Ground, 19th Century, 25 In. 920.00
Vase, Floor, Molded Flowering, Fruit Design, Famille Rose, 23 1/2 In. 1380.00
Vase, Floor, Peacock Perched On Rocks, Peonies, Famille Rose, 23 In., Pair 1035.00
Vase, Floral, Double Gourd Shape, 20th Century, 16 3/4 In., Pair 715.00
Vase, Foo Dogs, Celadon, Blue, Baluster, Handle, 1890, 23 3/4 In. 395.00
Vase, Garden Scene, Urns With Flowers, Handles, 11 & 11 3/4 In., Pair 1380.00
Vase, Mandarin Reserves, Turned Mahogany Base, 1830, 14 In. 1573.00
Vase, Painted Fruits & Flowers, Globular, 9 In. 125.00
Vase, Reserves Of Mandarin Scenes, Figural Handles, 9 1/2 In. 390.00
Vase, Rose Mandarin, Alternating Panels Of Floral Sprays, Bird, 18 In. 632.00
Vase, Rose Mandarin, Ring Handles, Baluster, 19th Century, 12 In., Pair 1210.00
Vase, Rouleau, Birds Perched On Tree, Famille Verte, c.1800, 10 1/2 In. 172.00
Wash Basin, Butterfly, Bird & Foliate Border, 19th Century, 5 x 16 In. 230.00
Water Dropper, Green Glaze, Yellow Stalk Handlepeony Shape, Box, 5 In. 230.00
Water Dropper, Overlapping Pink Petals, Stalk Handle, Lotus Shape, Pair 1150.00

CHINTZ is the name of a group of china patterns featuring an overall
design of flowers and leaves. The design became popular with English
makers about 1928. A few pieces are still being made. The best known
are designs by Royal Winton, James Kent Ltd., Crown Ducal, and Shelley.

Anemone, Ashtray, Square, Small 80.00
Anemone, Vase, Bud, 5 In. 265.00
Apple Blossom, Dish, Trefoil, James Kent 215.00
Balmoral, Bowl, Vegetable, Ascot Shape, Black Mark, Square, Royal Winton, 9 1/4 In. .. 255.00
Blue Chintz, Vase, 6 Sides, Trumpet Shape, Crown Ducal, 5 1/2 In. 255.00
Briar Rose, Cake Plate, Tab Handle, Lord Nelson 180.00
Cheadle, Bowl, Ascot Shape, Green Mark, Square, Royal Winton, 8 1/4 In. 255.00
Chelsea Rose, Bowl, Oval, Scalloped, James Kent, 12 x 10 In. 125.00
Clyde, Lamp, Green, Royal Winton, 9 1/2 In. 375.00
Clyde, Pitcher, Milk, Brown, Royal Winton, 5 1/2 In. 225.00
Country Lane, Jug, Tapered Sides, White Handle, Lord Nelson, 5 1/2 In. 207.00
Cranstone, Bowl, Salad, Silver Rim, Rheims Shape, Green Mark, Royal Winton, 8 In. ... 520.00
Crocus, Candy Dish, Cover, Gordon Shape, Green Mark, Royal Winton, 8 In. 720.00
DuBarry, Sugar & Creamer, James Kent 150.00
DuBarry, Teapot, Granville Shape, James Kent, 1938, 4 Cup 875.00
DuBarry, Tile, Tea, James Kent, c.1938 .... 210.00
Eleanor, Teapot, Albans Shape, Royal Winton 575.00
Estelle, Basket, Dudley Shape, Black Mark, Royal Winton, 4 1/2 In. 490.00
Estelle, Hot Water Pot, Albans Shape, Black Mark, Royal Winton, 7 In. 605.00
Estelle, Plate, Royal Winton, 7 In. 100.00
Esther, Teapot, Stacking, Colorful Flowers On Black, Royal Winton, Canada, 1952 ..... 1495.00
Evesham, Toast Rack, 2-Slice, Black Mark, Royal Winton, 2 1/2 x 4 1/2 In. 345.00
Fireglow, Toast Rack, 2-Slice, Queen Shape, Green Mark, Royal Winton, 2 1/2 x 4 In. ... 275.00
Floral Feast, Set, Tray, Toast Rack, Cup, Sugar, Creamer, Royal Winton, 5 Piece 545.00
Florida, Candlestick, Crown Ducal, 8 1/4 In. 545.00
Florida, Platter, Octagonal, Black Trim, Crown Ducal, 15 1/4 x 12 In. 2200.00
Florida, Sugar Shaker, Silver Plated Top, Crown Ducal 295.00
Gray Fruit, Tray, Crown Ducal, 10 1/2 x 8 In. 300.00
Hazel, Plate, Royal Winton, 7 In. 175.00

Hazel, Sugar & Creamer, Royal Winton 150.00
Julia, Sugar & Creamer, Royal Winton 195.00
Kew, Breakfast Set, Royal Winton, 1950s, 6 Piece 1850.00
Kew, Dish, Canoe Shape, Interior & Exterior Transfer, Royal Winton, 11 In. 445.00
Kew, Sugar & Creamer, Royal Winton 250.00
Kew, Teapot, Stacking, Delamere Shape, Royal Winton ....*Illus* 3740.00
Majestic, Gravy Boat, Stand, Royal Winton 275.00
Majestic, Jug, Globe Shape, Blue Mark, Royal Winton, 4 1/4 In. 430.00
Marguerite, Basket, Blue Trim, Hampton Shape, Green Mark, Royal Winton, 3 1/2 In. 175.00
Marguerite, Pitcher, Milk, Royal Winton, 5 In. 185.00
Marguerite, Pitcher, Royal Winton, Small 110.00
Marguerite, Plate, Royal Winton, 8 In. 100.00
Marguerite, Saltshaker, Metal Lid, Royal Winton 65.00
Marguerite, Sugar & Creamer, Royal Winton ....110.00 to 165.00
Marina, Cheese Keeper, Lord Nelson, 6 x 3 1/2 In. ....200.00 to 230.00
Marina, Cup, Lord Nelson, 2 In. 20.00
Marina, Jam Pot, Liner, Lord Nelson 205.00
Marina, Plate, Square, Lord Nelson, 7 1/2 In., 5 Piece 275.00
Marina, Teapot, Lord Nelson 595.00
Marina, Teapot, Stacking, Lord Nelson 925.00
Marion, Candy Box, Cover, Blue Mark, Royal Winton, 5 1/2 x 4 In. 240.00
May Festival, Candy Dish, Cover, Dark Blue, Gordon Shape, Black Mark, Royal Winton . 430.00
May Festival, Vase, Bud, Black Ground, Lune Shape, Black Mark, Royal Winton 105.00
Mayfair, Jam Pot, Liner, Lid, Chelsea Shape, Black Mark, Royal Winton, 4 In. 275.00
Maytime, Vase, Empire, Shelley, 8 1/2 In. 220.00
Nantwich, Plate, Ascot Shape, Royal Winton, 8 In. 165.00
Nantwich, Sandwich Tray, Ascot Shape, Green Mark, Royal Winton, 12 x 6 1/2 In. 300.00
Old Cottage, Biscuit Jar, Black Mark, Royal Winton, 5 3/4 In. 1093.00
Old Cottage, Bowl, Vegetable, Cover, Ascot Shape, Royal Winton, 10 In. 510.00
Old Cottage, Bread Tray, Royal Winton 195.00
Old Cottage, Coffeepot, Perth Shape, Green Mark, Royal Winton, 8 In. 775.00
Old Cottage, Compote, Footed, Royal Winton 125.00
Old Cottage, Jam Jar, Underplate, Metal Lid & Spoon, Royal Winton 225.00
Old Cottage, Plate, Round, Royal Winton, 8 In., 12 Piece 575.00
Old Cottage, Plate, Royal Winton, 9 In. 125.00
Old Cottage, Plate, Royal Winton, 10 In. 145.00
Old English Sampler, Creamer, Hollinsbead & Kirkham, Ltd. 40.00
Pekin, Biscuit Jar, Blue, Hand Painted, Rheims, Black Mark, Royal Winton, 6 1/2 In. 375.00
Pekin, Plate, Ivory, Royal Winton, 6 In. 35.00
Pelham, Jam Jar, Royal Winton 110.00
Primula, Strainer, 3-Footed, 7 Drain Holes, Crown Ducal, 8 x 3 In. 310.00
Purple Chintz, Cheese Keeper, Black Handle, Crown Ducal, 8 x 5 In. 375.00
Purple Chintz, Vase, 6 Sides, Crown Ducal, 9 3/4 In. 575.00
Queen Anne, Biscuit Jar, Royal Winton 425.00
Queen Anne, Bonbon, Metal Handle, Royal Winton 9.00
Queen Anne, Lamp, Royal Winton, 11 1/2 In. 460.00

Chintz, Sweet Pea, Teapot, Stacking,
Delamere Shape, Royal Winton, 3 Piece

Chintz, Royal Brocade, Teapot,
Stacking, Lord Nelson, 3 Piece

Chintz, Stratford, Tea Set, Ascot,
Raleigh Shape, Royal Winton, 17 Piece

Queen Anne, Relish, Canoe Shape, Green Mark, Royal Winton, 10 1/2 In.	140.00
Rapture, Dish, 2 Sections, James Kent	115.00
Richmond, Teapot, Royal Winton, 4 Cup	435.00
Rosalynde, Plate, James Kent, 7 1/2 In.	135.00
Rose Du Barry, Toast Rack, Flowers, Royal Winton, 4 Slice	195.00
Rosetime, Cup & Saucer, Lord Nelson	140.00
Rosetime, Vase, Lord Nelson, 5 In.	235.00
Rosina, Cup & Saucer, Royal Winton	110.00
Royal Brocade, Teapot, Stacking, Lord Nelson, 3 Piece *Illus*	413.00
Royal Tudor, Biscuit Barrel, Bluebirds	495.00
Rutland, Relish, 3 Sections, Gem Shape, Green Mark, Royal Winton, 8 In.	175.00
Skylark, Salt & Pepper, Lord Nelson	125.00
Somerset, Nut Dish, Bow Shape, Footed, White Interior, Royal Winton, 3 1/2 In.	240.00
Somerset, Pie Plate, Server, Black Mark, Royal Winton, 10 In., 2 Piece	230.00
Spring Blossom, Reamer, White Interior, Pour Spout	835.00
Stratford, Plate, Luncheon, Border, Ascot Shape, Black Mark, Royal Winton, 8 3/4 In.	105.00
Stratford, Tea Set, Ascot, Raleigh Shape, Royal Winton, 17 Piece *Illus*	4950.00
Summertime, Bread Tray, Royal Winton, 6 x 12 In.	295.00
Summertime, Cake Plate, Royal Winton	450.00
Summertime, Clock, Key Wind, Royal Winton	750.00
Summertime, Cup & Saucer, Royal Winton	95.00
Summertime, Hot Water Pot, Countess Shape, Green Mark, Royal Winton, 5 1/2 In.	660.00
Summertime, Jug, Duval Shape, Royal Winton, 5 In.	595.00
Summertime, Pitcher, Royal Winton, 3 In.	145.00
Summertime, Plate, Royal Winton, 9 3/4 In.	135.00
Summertime, Plate, Royal Winton, 11 1/2 In.	225.00
Summertime, Relish, Canoe Shape, Green Mark, Royal Winton, 10 1/2 In.	300.00
Summertime, Salt & Pepper, Square, Royal Winton	145.00
Summertime, Sugar & Creamer, Royal Winton	145.00
Summertime, Teapot, Ascot Shape, Blue Mark, Royal Winton, 4 Cup	805.00
Summertime, Teapot, Ascot Shape, Green Mark, Royal Winton, 6 Cup	865.00
Summertime, Teapot, Ascot, Royal Winton, 4 Cup	650.00
Summertime, Teapot, Elite Shape, Green Mark, Royal Winton, 6 Cup	920.00
Summertime, Teapot, Royal Winton	450.00
Summertime, Vase, Gem Shape, Green Trim, Green Mark, Royal Winton, 6 In.	520.00

Chintz, Kew, Teapot,
Stacking, Delamere Shape,
Royal Winton

Summertime, Vase, Royal Winton, 4 In. 165.00
Sunshine, Candy Box, Cover, Black Mark, Royal Winton, 2 x 4 x 3 1/2 In. 242.00
Sunshine, Teapot, Yellow Wash, Albans Shape, Green Mark, Royal Winton, 4 Cup 775.00
Sweet Pea, Butter Dish, Cover, Ascot Shape, Square, Royal Winton, 6 x 3 In. 430.00
Sweet Pea, Cup & Saucer, Royal Winton 190.00
Sweet Pea, Teapot, Stacking, Delamere Shape, Royal Winton, 3 Piece ....*Illus* 2530.00
Sweet Pea, Trivet, Ascot Shape, Green Mark, Square, Royal Winton, 5 3/4 In. 305.00
Victorian Rose, Salt & Pepper, Tray, Fife Shape, Royal Winton, 2 1/2 In., 3 Piece 245.00
Virginia Stock, Sugar & Creamer, Royal Winton 125.00
Welbeck, Bowl, Ascot, Royal Winton 225.00
Welbeck, Bowl, Salad, Silver Rim, Rheims Shape, Green Mark, Royal Winton, 8 In. 520.00
Welbeck, Jam Jar, Liner, Metal Lid, Rheims, Green Mark, Royal Winton, 4 In. 520.00
Welbeck, Muffineer, Silver Plated Lid, Ascot Shape, Blue Mark, Royal Winton, 7 x 3 In. . 430.00

CHOCOLATE GLASS, sometimes mistakenly called caramel slag, was made by the Indiana Tumbler and Goblet Company of Greentown, Indiana, from 1900 to 1903. It was also made at other National Glass Company factories. Fenton Art Glass Co. also made chocolate glass from about 1907 to 1915. More recent pieces have been made by Imperial and others.

Cactus, Butter, Cover ....150.00 to 275.00
Cactus, Compote, 8 In. ....150.00 to 225.00
Cactus, Cruet, Greentown 195.00
Cactus, Dish, Sweetmeat, Cover, Greentown 650.00
Cactus, Syrup, Greentown 210.00
Chrysanthemum Leaf, Cruet 2450.00
Dewey, Butter, Greentown 185.00
Dewey, Sugar, Cover, Greentown 70.00
Geneva, Pitcher, Greentown 890.00
Racing Deer & Doe, Pitcher, Greentown, 9 In. ....575.00 to 690.00
Ruffled Eye, Pitcher, Greentown ....550.00 to 700.00
Sawtooth, Tumbler, Greentown 95.00
Shuttle, Creamer, Greentown, 6 In. ....55.00 to 95.00
Shuttle, Tumbler ....60.00 to 85.00
Wild Rose With Bowknot, Toothpick 135.00
Wild Rose With Bowknot, Tumbler 165.00
Wild Rose With Scrolling, Toothpick 375.00

CHRISTMAS collectibles include not only Christmas trees and ornaments listed below, but also Santa Claus figures, special dishes, and even games and wrapping paper. A Belsnickle is a nineteenth-century figure of Father Christmas. A kugel is an early, heavy ornament made of thick blown glass, lined with zinc or lead, and often covered with colored wax. Christmas cards are listed in this section under Greeting Card. Christmas collectibles may also be listed in the Candy Container category. Christmas trees are listed in the section that follows.

Box, Puppy With Present, Cheerio, Cardboard, String Handle, 3 x 4 1/4 In. ....*Illus* 3.00

Christmas, Box, Puppy With Present, Cheerio,
Cardboard, String Handle, 3 x 4 1/4 In.

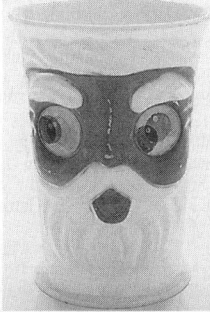

Christmas, Cup,
Santa Face, Magic
Eyes, Painted, Plastic,
3 3/4 In.

Creche, Paper, Die Cut, Folded, Germany, 1900	130.00
Cup, Santa Face, Magic Eyes, Painted, Plastic, 3 3/4 In. . . . . *Illus*	10.00
Decoration, Santa, Crepe Paper, Fold-Out, 3-D Effect, Box, 6 Ft.	250.00
Decoration, Village Set, Cardboard Buildings, Japan, 4 1/2 In., 12 Piece	135.00
Doll, Christmas Mouse, Annalee, Mobiltee, 1970, 16 In.	125.00
Doll, Santa Claus, Cloth, Composition Face & Feet, 4 In.	110.00
Doll, Santa Claus, Composition, Felt Clothes, 19th Century, 8 In.	330.00
Figure, Father Christmas, Papier-Mache, Russia, c.1930, 16 In.	100.00
Figure, Santa Claus, Bisque, Germany, 1908, 5 In.	150.00
Figure, Santa Claus, Celluloid, Composition, Cloth, Goose-Feather Tree, Japan, 15 In. . . .	325.00
Figure, Santa Claus, Composition Face, Straw Stuffed, Late 19th Century, 12 In.	440.00
Figure, Santa Claus, In Sled, Pulled By Reindeer, Bisque, Germany, 8 In.	125.00
Figure, Santa Claus, In Sleigh, Felt, Wicker, Pulled By Reindeer, Composition	7700.00
Figure, Santa Claus, On Sled, Waving, Bisque, Germany, 12 In.	175.00
Figure, Santa Claus, Riding Polar Bear, Bisque, Germany, 12 In.	225.00
Figure, Santa Claus, Toys Behind Back, Celluloid, Japan, Pre-World War II, 7 In.	75.00
Figure, Santa Claus, Waving, Holding Lantern, Celluloid, Japan, Pre-World War II, 6 In. .	85.00
Figure, Santa Claus, With Pack, Bisque, Hand Painted, 4 In.	44.00
Game, Santa Claus Ring Toss, Spears, Bavaria, Box, 9 x 14 In.	765.00
Game, Victorian Santa Claus, On Linen, Flames For Santa's Pipe, Paper Container	395.00
Greeting Card, Floral, Silk Fringe, 1880s, 4 Pages	60.00
Greeting Card, Fringed, Grain-Painted Frame	35.00
Greeting Card, Harold Teen, Here's Wishing You A Beaner Of A Christmas, 1924	55.00
Greeting Card, Nixon, 1973, Picture Of 1848 Kollner White House	30.00
Lantern, Dancing Santa, Battery Operated, Tin, Celluloid, Plastic, Japan, Box, 7 In.	75.00
Lantern, Santa's Head, Battery Operated, Tin, Milk Glass, Box, Japan, 5 In.	90.00
Lantern, Santa's Head, Blue Hood, Open Mouth, Composition, Germany, 5 1/4 In.	965.00
Lantern, Santa, Tree, Battery Operated, Tin, Milk Glass, Box, Japan, 5 1/2 In.	150.00
Pin, Santa Claus As Young Boy Picture, The Rike Kumler Co., Celluloid	30.00
Pin, Santa Claus Picture, Kindly Be Happy, Celluloid, Pinback, 1 1/4 In.	35.00
Pin, Santa, Kindly Be Happy, Celluloid, Artist Copyright, 1 1/4 In.	35.00
Plates that are limited editions are listed in the Collector Plate category or in the correct factory listing.	
Postcard, A Happy Christmas To You, Hold-To-Light	150.00
Postcard, Merry Christmas, Candles On Tree Scene, Germany	65.00
Postcard, Santa Claus Picture, Embossed, Twig Crown, Pine Tree Staff, Angel, P.F.B. . . .	45.00
Postcard, Santa Claus, Carrying 3 Dolls, Cloth Cap & Hair Beard	250.00
Postcard, Santa Claus, Cart Pulled By Bird, Mechanical	300.00
Postcard, Santa Claus, In Purple Suit With Packages, Embossed, Germany	30.00
Poster, Department Store, Maine, Frame, 3 1/2 x 4 1/2 Ft.	650.00
Record, Picture, Jingle Bells, We 3 Kings, Record Guild Of America, 1948, 6 1/2 In.	25.00
Santa Claus, Jack-In-The-Box, Red, White Wood, Brick Chimney, Box, 1938, 24 In.	1390.00
Sparkler, Santa Claus, Pops Out Chimney, Windows Light, Tin, Japan, 1950s, 5 In.	90.00
Stocking Holder, Pinocchio	95.00
Tin, Candy, Twas The Night Before Christmas, Art Deco	245.00
Toy, Blocks, Santa Claus, 6 Scenes, McLoughlin, 1897, 2 3/4 x 13 1/4 In.	2530.00
Toy, Rattle, Santa Claus, Celluloid, 5 1/2 In.	75.00
Toy, Santa Claus Cycle, Windup, Tin, Celluloid, Japan, Box, 3 1/2 x 5 x 3 In.	65.00
Toy, Santa Claus On Motor Scooter, Friction, Plastic, Box, Hong Kong, 4 In.	70.00
Toy, Santa Claus On Sled, Reindeer, Windup, Celluloid, Metal, Occupied Japan, 9 In.	40.00
Toy, Santa Claus Skier, Spins, Windup, Tin Lithograph, Vinyl Head, Japan, Box	130.00
Toy, Santa Claus, Driving Car, Passengers, Wicker Car, Cotton Batting Torso, 9 In.	630.00
Toy, Santa Claus, Holds Christmas Sign, Rings Bell, Tin, Japan, Box	175.00
Toy, Santa Claus, In Blue Sleigh, 4 Wheels, 1 White Reindeer, Hubley, 14 In.	2645.00
Toy, Santa Claus, In Sleigh With Reindeer, Windup, Tin, Strauss	1430.00
Toy, Santa Claus, Mechanical, Rings Bell, Alps, Japan, Box, 7 In.	90.00
Toy, Santa Claus, On Rotating Globe, Battery Operated, Box	2700.00
Toy, Santa Claus, Pip-Squeak, Germany, 19th Century	495.00
Toy, Santa Claus, Roly Poly, Composition, Germany, 1910, 4 1/4 In.	363.00
Toy, Santa Claus, Roly Poly, Schoenhut	1540.00
Toy, Santa Claus, Sled, 2 Reindeer, Tin Lithograph, Windup, Strauss, 11 1/2 In.	1320.00
Toy, Santa Claus, Sleigh, Reindeer, Windup, Tin Lithograph, Celluloid, Japan, 8 1/2 In. . . .	50.00
Toy, Santa Claus, Sleigh, Santa At Reins, 2 Reindeer, Wood, Bliss, 1900, 18 In.	4110.00

Toy, Santa Claus, Strolling, Holds Bell, Toy Sack, Windup, Celluloid, 7 In. 360.00
Toy, Santa Claus, Walking, Windup, Tin, 2 7/8 In. 32.00
Toy, Santa Claus, Windup, Alps, Box, 9 1/2 In. 215.00
Toy, Sleigh, Santa, Painted Cast Iron, Horse Pulling Sleigh, Hubley 2970.00

CHRISTMAS TREES made of feathers and Christmas tree decorations of
all types are popular with collectors. The first decorated Christmas tree
in America is claimed by many states, including Pennsylvania (1747),
Massachusetts (1832), Illinois (1833), Ohio (1838), and Iowa (1845).
The first glass ornaments were imported from Germany about 1860.
Dresden ornaments were made about 100 years ago of paper and tinsel. Manufacturers in the United States were making ornaments in the
early 1870s. Electric lights were first used on a Christmas tree in 1882.
Character light bulbs became popular in the 1920s, bubble lights in the
1940s, twinkle bulbs in the 1950s, plastic bulbs by 1955. In this book
a Christmas light is a holder for a candle used on the tree. Other forms
of lighting include light bulbs. Other Christmas memorabilia is listed
in the preceding section.

Aluminum, 8 Ft. 50.00
Aluminum, Storage Box, Late 1940s 28.00
Feather, Green, Red Berry Ends Of Limbs, 66 In. 560.00
Feather, Red & Gold Barrel, Red Berries, 4 Candle Clips, 27 In. 255.00
Feather, Walnut, Metal Cap, Japan, 1 In. 13.00
Fence, Cast Iron, Green & Gold Paint, 7 11-3/4 In. Sections, Gate 190.00
Fence, Picket, Green, Hinged Corners, 10 1/2 In. 60.00
Goose Feather, Victorian, With 9-Ft. Oak Carrying Case & Stand 1800.00
Light, Aqua, Fern Pattern, Ground Rim, England, 1880-1900, 3 3/8 In. 110.00
Light, Church Votive, Leaf Green, Conical, 3 In. 28.00
Light, Cluster Of Grapes, Purple Amethyst, Ground Rim, England, 3 7/8 In. 255.00
Light, Cobalt Blue, Diamond, Brass Lid, Hanger, Hochin, Mfg. Co., 3 5/8 In. 210.00
Light, Cobalt Blue, Diamond, Rough Sheared Lip, England, 1910, 4 In. 55.00
Light, Cranberry Flashed Interior, Diamond, Hochin, Mfg. Co., 3 5/8 In. 140.00
Light, Emerald Green, Starburst, G Inside Star, England, 1910, 3 7/8 In. 70.00
Light, Purple Amethyst, Diamond, JP Embossed Rim, England, 1900, 3 1/2 In. 85.00
Light, Sapphire, Diamond, JP Embossed Rim, England, 1900, 3 1/2 In. 95.00
Light, Twinkle, Changes Color, Box, 1950s 40.00
Light, Yellow Amber, Starburst, G Inside Star, England, 1910, 3 7/8 In. 105.00
Light, Yellow, Olive Tone, Diamond, JP Embossed Rim, England, 3 1/2 In. 95.00
Light Bulb, Andy Gump 45.00
Light Bulb, Cottage, Milk Glass 7.00
Light Bulb, G.E., Snowball Colored, 1960s, 9 Piece 15.00
Light Bulb, Globe, With Fish, Milk Glass 15.00
Light Bulb, Humpty Dumpty 25.00
Light Bulb, King Cole 22.00
Light Bulb, Santa Claus, 9 In. 110.00
Light Bulb, Sparkle Plenty, Box 75.00
Light Bulb, Star, Milk Glass 12.00
Light Bulb, Sylvania Fluorescent, String, Box, 7 Piece 65.00
Light Bulb, Wonder Star, Single Matchless, 5 Piece 100.00
Light Bulb Set, Figural, Japan, Box, 1926, 23 Piece 425.00
Light Bulb Set, Mickey Mouse, Noma, Box, 1935-1938 . . . . _Illus_ 150.00
Ornament, A Spot Of Christmas Cheer, Teapot, Hallmark, Box, 1980 . . . . 100.00
Ornament, Acorn, 3 Extended Arms Holding Smaller Ones, Glass 87.00
Ornament, Airplane, Blown Glass, Ink, Double Wings, Chalk Santa, 1915, 8 x 5 In. 275.00
Ornament, Amelia Earhart, White, Black & Blue, Blown Glass, 1930, 3 1/2 In. 275.00
Ornament, Baby In Bag, Glass, Germany, 1920s 95.00
Ornament, Bird, Blown Glass, Spun Glass Tail, Clip, 5 In. 10.00
Ornament, Bird, Hand Painted, Tail Feathers, Metal Clip, 1940s, 5 In. 25.00
Ornament, Blown Glass, Flapper Head, White Hat, Blue Brim, Gold Hair, 1920, 3 In. . . . 225.00
Ornament, Camel, 2-Sided, 3-D, Dresden, Pressed Paper, 1930s, 2 In. 170.00
Ornament, Candy Bag, Santa Claus, Clay Face, Chenille, Japan 148.00
Ornament, Cat In Car, Ceramic, Box, Kliban, 3 In. 152.00
Ornament, Classical Angel, Hallmark, Box, 1984, 5 In. 45.00

Christmas Tree, Light Bulb Set, Mickey Mouse,
Noma, Box, 1935-1938

Don't wrap Christmas ornaments in newspaper. The ink may rub off. Don't store them in plastic bags. Moisture may condense and cause problems.

Ornament, Clown Face, Blown Glass, Gold, Red & Black, Early 1900s, 4 In.	130.00
Ornament, Clown Head, Blown Glass, White, Red, Pink, & Green, 1910, 2 1/4 In.	145.00
Ornament, Cranberry, Brass Hanger, 3 1/4 In.	220.00
Ornament, Dino, Flintstones, Purple, Vinyl, Wire Hook, 1976, 4 In.	14.00
Ornament, Duck, Opalescence White, Red At Eyes & Bill, 3 3/4 In.	20.00
Ornament, Ear Of Corn, Blown Glass, Green & Yellow, 2 1/2 In.	53.00
Ornament, Egyptian Princess, Blown Glass, Russian, c.1950	13.00
Ornament, Elf, Hard Plastic, 3 1/2 In.	6.00
Ornament, Forest Frolics, Hallmark, 1990	25.00
Ornament, Foxy Grandpa Head, Blown Glass, White, Gold, Silver, 1920, 5 In.	110.00
Ornament, Frog, Blown Glass, Green & Red, 2 x 3 1/4 In.	23.00
Ornament, Frog, Blown Glass, White, Green Shading, Black Eyes, 1920, 3 1/4 In.	65.00
Ornament, Girl In Bag, Blow Glass, White Face, Red Bag, c.1920, 3 1/2 In.	95.00
Ornament, Glass Bead String, 36 In.	22.00
Ornament, Grapes, Cobalt Blue, 4 In.	495.00
Ornament, Grapes, Medium Green, Brass Hanger, 4 3/4 In.	580.00
Ornament, Grapes, Silver Green, Brass Hanger, 4 In.	440.00
Ornament, Green Grapes, 3 1/2 In.	375.00
Ornament, Guardian Angel, Berta Hummel, 1973	17.00
Ornament, Guitar, Tinsel Edge, Crepe Paper Covered Cardboard, 12 3/4 In.	48.00
Ornament, House, Blown Glass, Silver, Green Shading, Matte White, 1920, 2 3/4 In.	25.00
Ornament, Hulk With Santa Claus, Sun Catcher, 1970s	20.00
Ornament, Jester Bell, Blown Glass, Pink & White, Pearly White Face, 1920, 3 In.	95.00
Ornament, Jolly Trolley, Hallmark, Box, 1982	100.00
Ornament, King Of Edward Bust, Green Aqua, England, 1880-1900, 4 In.	330.00
Ornament, Kugel, Blue, Brass Hanger, 10 In.	1045.00
Ornament, Kugel, Brass Top, Cranberry Colored Glass, Melon Shape, 1890, 2 In.	130.00
Ornament, Kugel, Cobalt Blue, Brass Hanger, 5 3/4 In.	300.00
Ornament, Kugel, Cobalt, Czechoslovakia, 19th Century, 8 In.	365.00
Ornament, Kugel, Cranberry, Brass Hanger, 8 In.	990.00
Ornament, Kugel, Gold Grape Clusters, 4 In.	257.00
Ornament, Kugel, Silver, Brass Hanger, 8 In.	140.00
Ornament, Lady Slipper, Blown Glass, Silver, Gold Bow & Buttons, 1920, 3 In.	45.00
Ornament, Lemon, Blown Glass, Pale Yellow, 1910, 3 In.	30.00
Ornament, Old Lady, Glass, 1930s, 4 1/2 In.	48.00
Ornament, Peacock Green, Brass Hanger, 4 3/4 In.	635.00
Ornament, Peasant Girl, Blown Glass, Blond Ponytails, c.1945, 4 1/4 In.	36.00
Ornament, Penguin, Plastic, Opalescent White, Red, 1950s, 3 1/4 In.	18.00
Ornament, Pillsbury Doughboy, Piloting St. Nick's Sleigh	46.00
Ornament, Queen Victoria Bust, Cobalt Blue, Diamond Pattern, Pontil, 4 In.	360.00
Ornament, Rabbit, Clip-On, Purple & White, 4 1/4 In.	36.00
Ornament, Raggedy Ann, Ice Skating, Schmid, 1976	8.00
Ornament, Rocking Horse, Hallmark, Box, 1982	225.00
Ornament, Rocking Horse, Hand Painted Wax, 4 x 2 1/2 In.	20.00
Ornament, Sailboat, Blown Glass, Red, White & Blue, 5 In.	22.00
Ornament, Santa Claus, Holding Green Saw, 1950s, 3 3/4 In.	47.00
Ornament, Santa Claus, In Black 1956 Corvette, Enesco, Box	32.00
Ornament, Santa Claus, In Gondola Of Air Balloon, Glass	88.00

Ornament, Santa Claus, In Sleigh, 1 Reindeer, Plastic, Irwin, 1950s, 3 3/4 In. 23.00
Ornament, Santa Claus, On Donkey, Lithographed Paper On Cardboard 170.00
Ornament, Santa Claus, On Pig 495.00
Ornament, Santa, Red, Silver, Pink Face, Tree, Chenille Legs, Blown Glass, 1920, 5 In. . . 85.00
Ornament, Smurf, Looking Through Wreath, Gold Cord Hanger, Portugal, 1981 . . . . 114.00
Ornament, Snow Baby, Blown Glass, Hand Painted, 4 In. 40.00
Ornament, Snow White, Figural, 1960s, 7 Pieces 65.00
Ornament, Spaniel, Blown Glass, Seated, White Body, Black Eyes, 1930, 3 In. 45.00
Ornament, Spun Cotton Icicle, Silver Gray, 4 1/2 In. 16.00
Ornament, Squirrel, Paper, Dresden, 3 In. 198.00
Ornament, Star, Brass Bead 11.00
Ornament, Star, Cardboard & Foil, Dresden, Germany, c.1900, 4 In. 90.00
Ornament, Starship Enterprise, Hallmark, Box, 1991 . . . . 250.00
Ornament, Sun Face, Blown Glass, 2 Sides, White, Green Shading, c.1920, 3 In. 195.00
Ornament, Turkey, Blown Glass, Full Figure, White, Pink Shading, c.1910, 3 In. 145.00
Stand, Cast Iron, Acorns On 3 Upright Tree Stump Legs, Square, 10 In. 20.00
Stand, Cast Iron, Die Cast Acorns, Pinecones On Base, Square, 12 1/2 In. 22.00
Stand, Cast Iron, Die Cast Angels & Stars On Base, Square, 9 1/2 In. 44.00
Stand, Cast Iron, Embossed Acorns On Legs & Upright, Square, 10 In. 22.00
Stand, Santa & Poinsettia Decals, Green, Cone Base, Metal, 1915, 15 In. 90.00
Stand, Santa Claus Shape, Cast Iron, Square Forest Base, 8 3/4 In. 1210.00

CHROME items in the Art Deco style became popular in the 1930s. Collectors are most interested in high-style pieces made by the Connecticut firms of Chase Brass and Copper Company, and Manning Bowman.

Cocktail Set, Blue Moon, Chase, 6 Chrome Cobalt Glasses 300.00
Cocktail Set, Ribbed Shaker, Red Bakelite Handle, 5 Red Glass Goblets, Chrome Screw . 175.00
Cocktail Shaker, Chase, Black 35.00
Corn Set, Russel Wright, Chase, Tray, 4 Piece 695.00
Pitcher, Angular Design, Curved Handle, Peter Muller-Munk, 1935, 12 In. 1150.00
Tray, Geometric, Reverse-Painted Glass Over Foil, Art Deco, 16 x 10 In. 550.00

CIGAR STORE FIGURES of carved wood or cast iron were used as advertisements in front of the Victorian cigar store. The carved figures are now collected as folk art. They range in size from counter type, about three feet, to over eight feet high.

Indian, Brave, Headdress, Carved Wood, Jointed Arms, 1920, 32 In. 990.00
Indian, Chief, Leaf Headdress, Holding Cup, 1890-1910, 65 In. 3575.00
Indian, Headdress, Carved Wood, Square Base, Iron Wheels, 65 In. 2990.00
Indian, Princess, Braided Hair, Rosa Mora Cigars, Robb, 27 x 22 In. 41800.00
Indian, Princess, Red Dress, Green Leggings, 84 In. . . . . *Illus* 18700.00
William Penn, Displaying Cigar Box, Papier-Mache, 1919, 30 x 65 In. 3135.00

Be very careful if you're trying to clean a cigar box or other paper-labeled wooden box. First glue any loose spots on the label with diluted white glue, but be sure no glue seeps from under the paper to show on the wood. Never use liquid cleaners, not even water. A Pink Pearl eraser may be used on the wood and an art gum eraser on the paper. Always erase with the wood grain. Avoid any lettering.

Cigar Store Figures, Indian, Princess, Red Dress, Green Leggings, 84 In.

CINNABAR is a vermilion or red lacquer. Pieces are made with tens to hundreds of thicknesses of the lacquer that is later carved. Most cinnabar was made in the Orient.

Box, 3 Tiers, 6 1/2 x 6 x 6 In.	175.00
Box, Cover, Aquatic Floral, Removable Top, Gold, Black Metal Clasps, 15 1/2 In.	1265.00
Box, Cylindrical, Figural Landscape Design, China, c.1900, 2 7/8 x 4 3/4 In.	40.00
Box, Peach Shape, 15 In.	1035.00
Box, Round Cover, Slender Leafy Reed, Wave Ground, 17th Century, 2 In.	430.00
Ginger Jar, 11 x 6 In.	250.00
Lamp, Carved, Wood & Brass Base, 20th Century, 30 In., Pair	145.00
Lamp, Oriental Scene On Wood Base, Baluster, 16 In.	290.00
Pot, Cover, Continuous Band Of Various Figures Amidst Trees, 6 1/2 In.	40.00
Snuff Bottle, 2 Boys Playing, Reverse 2 Seated Scholars, 1830s, 3 In.	1250.00
Snuff Bottle, Cabochon Turquoise Stones, Egg Shape, Silver Frame, 4 In.	40.00
Snuff Bottle, Landscape, Chrysanthemum Borders, Black Ground, Cylindrical	230.00
Tray, Allover Black Floral, Figural & Landscape, Red Ground, 10 3/8 x 16 3/8 In.	230.00
Vase, Carved, 5 In.	65.00
Vase, Parcel Gilt, White Porcelain, Mounted As Lamp, 1920, 18 x 9 1/2 In.	150.00

CIVIL WAR mementos are important collectors' items. Most of the pieces are military items used from 1861 to 1865. Be sure to avoid any explosive munitions.

Bag, Carpet, Brass Clasp Lock, Key, 11 1/4 x 15 1/4 In.	290.00
Banner, Victory, Window, Yellow Fringe, 8 1/2 x 12 In.	38.00
Battle Alarm, Oak & Maple	215.00
Bayonet, Brass Guard, Leather Scabbard, 20-In. Blade	275.00
Bayonet, Leather Scabbard	150.00
Blotter, Getting A Kick Out Of Our Job, Tan, Red Lettering, 3 7/8 x 9 In.	38.00
Bore Gauges, Gunsmith's, Steel, C. Tollner, 4 3/16 In.	115.00
Box, Cartridge, Leather	80.00
Box, Cartridge, Marked	365.00
Buckle, Confederate, Brass, Embossed, 2 Men Standing	2240.00
Buckle, Lead Filled, Brass, 2 7/8 x 1 5/8 In.	120.00
Button, Confederate Veterans' Reunion, Poteau, I.T., Celluloid, 1906, 1 3/4 In.	135.00
Button, Military, West Point, 62 Piece	175.00
Canister, Cannonball, Canvas Cover, Old Red, 6 1/2 x 19 7/8 In.	185.00
Canteen, Cedarwood, Wooden & Metal Stopper, 1863, 7 x 2 3/8 In.	3220.00
Canteen, Wooden, 10 1/4 x 7 3/4 In.	100.00
Canteen, Wool Covering, Tin Spout, Ring & Cork Plug, Model 1858, 8 In.	275.00
Carbine Holder, Leather	35.00
Cartridge Box, Brass Us Buckle, Brass Eagle On Strap, Leather Strap	690.00
Cartridge Box, Leather, Marked, J.B. Dotti, 6 1/2 x 4 1/2 In.	120.00
Cartridge Pouch, Cap Box, Belt, U.S. Buckle	440.00
Chair, Camp, Folding, Maple, Sergt. Maj. Marshall, Folds To 26 3/4 In.	190.00
Chest, Lift Top, Pine, 4th Regt. Mass. Vol., Peter Chick, 16 x 31 1/2 In.	302.00
Coat, Pocket, 5 Large Eagle Buttons	40.00
Coat, Sack, Union, 5 Large Eagle Buttons	120.00
Cup, Collapsible, Pewter, Japanned Tin Case	65.00
Cutlass, Naval, Brass Hilt, Leather Grip, Ames, 1860	405.00
Discharge Certificate, 44th Regiment, Mass. Infantry, Wm. K. Millar, June, 1863	55.00
Discharge Certificate, Massachusetts, Joseph Donnelly, January 1, 1863, Frame	44.00
Drum, Boy's, Tin, Red Paint, Skin, Carved Design Rim, Whistle Drumstick, 10 In.	355.00
Drum, Boy's, Tin, Red Paint, Skin, Carved Design Rim, Wm. Boucher, 7 x 9 In.	145.00
Drum, Brass Stud Shield & Star, Odell M. Chaman, 17 3/4 x 16 1/2 In.	650.00
Drum, Eagle, Painted, Red Hoops, N.Y. Label, Stencil, Edward Baack	795.00
Drum, Snare, Band Of 5 Pointed Stars Metal Body, Wooden Rim, 12 1/2 x 17 In.	980.00
Epaulettes, Medical Staff Captain, Gilt Brass, Silk, Leather Lining, 9 3/4 In., Pair	1320.00
Flag, 37 States, Cloth, Frame, 31 x 22 In.	440.00
Flag, Stars & Stripes, General Christopher Colon Augur	3410.00
Flag, Union, Battle, 1 Center & 12 Stars In Circle	1870.00
Flask, Canteen, Gettysburg, Pa., July 1863, July 1913, Lee, Grant, Pottery, 5 1/4 In.	440.00
Flask, Pewter, Leather	80.00

Game, Dominoes, Bone & Ebony, Slide Top Box 130.00
Hat, Hardee, U.S. Army, Bugle 1 & 2, Brass Eagle, Shield Plate, 6 x 13 1/2 In. 1540.00
Ice Coffin, Wooden, Metal Ice Chamber, Meant To Be Reused 4500.00
Journal, William P. Woodlin, 8th Regt., Starts Nov. 1863 & Ends Oct. 31, 1864 .... 2200.00
Kepi, Cavalry, Original Label & Buttons 1675.00
Kepi, Eagle Buttons, Blue 30.00
Kepi, Eagle Buttons, Blue, Light Gray 200.00
Kepi, Leather Bill, Sweatband, Black Wool, Felt & Leather 2500.00
Kepi, Red Wool, White Piping, Black Band, Bent & Bush, Boston 605.00
Kit, Surgeon's, Folding, 10 Instruments, Leather, ID Stamp, St. Louis, Mo. 63, Pocket ... 575.00
Knife, Butcher, Camp, 16 In. 245.00
Knife, Massachusetts Volunteer Militia, Iron Bolsters, German Shield, 3 3/4 In. 85.00
Knife, Military Issue, Seaman's, Bone Handle 250.00
Knife/Spoon, Wooden Handle, Camillus Cutlery, N.Y. 120.00
Map, Battlefield Of Stone River, Troop Positions, Frame, 4 1/2 x 4 In. 60.00
Map, Peninsular Campaign, Chesapeake Bay, Potomac River 80.00
Mold, Shako Hat, White Plaster, Eagle, #78 & U.S.W. 145.00
Pin, United Confederate Veterans' Reunion, Multicolored, Celluloid, 2 In. 275.00
Pouch, Ammo, Embossed 30.00
Powder Horn, Inscribed Colt .36, 1863, 8 In. 295.00
Rosette, Horse, Brass, U.S. 25.00
Saber, Brass Guard, Wire Wrapped Handle, 36-In. Blade, Thomas Leech Co. 1320.00
Saber, Cavalry, Bright Original Blade, c.1840 .... 230.00
Saber, Cavalry, France 200.00
Saber, Cavalry, Iron Hilt, Bright Blade, Leather Grip, Scabbard 345.00
Saber, Iron Guard, Wood Handle, 31 1/4-In. Blade 165.00
Saber, Scabbard, 1859 .... 160.00
Shako, Strap & Button Marked Mass. Volunteer Militia, 1851 .... 1700.00
Shaving Cup, Soldier's, Tin, Gray Patina 110.00
Sheet Music, Liberty & Union, J.T. Wamelink, C.B. Bar, 1864, 10 1/4 x 13 1/4 In. 54.00
Sword, Brass Guard Handle, 29 7/8-In. Blade 90.00
Sword, Confederate, 36-In. Blade, Wm. Glaze & Co., Columbia, S.C., 1840 .... 3740.00
Sword, Fish Skin-Covered Handle, Brass Guard, 36-In. Blade 220.00
Sword, GAR, Wire Wrapped Leather Grip, Scabbard, 28 In. 250.00
Sword, Gold Sash With Ball, Brass Guard, Wire Wrapped Handle, 30-In. Blade 690.00
Sword, NCO, Brass Guard, 31 3/4-In. Blade, Horstmann, Philadelphia 210.00
Sword, NCO, Brass Guard, 32 1/8-In. Blade, Ames Mfg. Co., 1864 .... 175.00
Sword, Officer's, Dress, Blade Etched Eagle, Wire Wrapped Handle, 28-In. Blade 125.00
Sword, Officer's, Eagle On Hilt, American Spread Eagle, Floral, Black Scabbard 165.00
Sword, Officer's, Sharkskin Grip 260.00
Sword, Officer's, Springfield Armory, 1834 .... 385.00
Sword, Staff Officer's, Etched Blade With Eagles, Sharkskin Grip, Ames Mfg. Co. 575.00
Telescope, U.S. Signal Service, 4 Draw 2000.00
Tools, For Pistol, Polished Steel, Brass Ferrules, Ebony Handles, 6 Piece 155.00
Trousers, Light Blue, Metal Buttons 90.00
Whistle, Brass Steam Boat, 17 In. 210.00

CKAW, see Dedham category.

CLAMBROTH glass, popular in the Victorian era, is a grayish color and
is somewhat opaque, like clam broth. It was made by several factories
in the United States and England.

Bowl, Cornstarch Blue Trim, Applied Foot, Scalloped, 9 x 8 In. 110.00
Candlestick, Acanthus, Jadeite Socket, 7 3/4 In. 1705.00
Candlestick, Columnar Standard, Wafered Petal Socket, 1835-1850, 9 3/8 In. 120.00
Compote, Blue Bowl Cased In Clambroth, Cobalt Blue Base, 4 5/8 In. 550.00

CLARICE CLIFF was a designer who worked in several English factories
after the 1920s. She is best known for her brightly colored Art Deco
designs. She died in 1972.

Aurea, Bizarre, Sugar & Creamer, Flowers On Stems, Signed, 2 3/4 In. 200.00
Autumn, Vase, Oranges, Trees In Green Landscape, Red, Cylindrical, 9 In. 635.00
Avignon, Vase, Blue Bridge, Green, Lavender Trees, 8 In., Pair 2185.00

Bizarre, Bowl, Horizontal Band Of Blue, Lavender, Orange Triangles, Green, 7 In. 460.00
Bizarre, Vase, Crocuses, Colored Bands, Elongated Oval, Signed, 8 In., Pair 690.00
Bizarre, Vase, Landscape, Trees, Orange, Brown, Yellow, Black Outline, 1933, 9 In. 1092.00
Blue W, Jug, Lotus, Horizontal Ribbed Body, Sliced Orange, Lavender Circles 7820.00
Cafe-Au-Lait, Vase, Orange, Red Fruit, Black Leaves, Stippled Ground, 8 In. 805.00
Caprice Inspiration, Vase, Mauve, Lavender, Blue Fir Trees, 1930, 7 In. 1150.00
Caprice Inspiration, Vase, Trumpet, Mauve, Blue Stylized Fir Trees, 1930, 6 In. 690.00
Castellated Circle, Bowl, Bell Form, Border Orange, Black, Blue, 9 1/2 In. 635.00
Farmhouse, Bookends, Yellow Exterior, Orange Roof, 5 In. 920.00
Farmhouse, Tea Set, 13 Piece 1955.00
Forest Glen, Vase, Trumpet, Green Hillside, Cottage, 1937, 18 In. 575.00
Geometric Flowers, Jug, Lotus, Lemon, Orange, Green, Blue, Brown Triangles, 10 In. . . .   2070.00
Geometric Flowers, Vase, Orange Neck, Green, Olive Circles, Hexagonal, 15 In. 2185.00
Honolulu, Vase, Striped Green Trees, Orange, Yellow Leaves, 18 1/2 In. 865.00
Inspiration, Bowl, Green, Mauve, Lavender, Blue Fir Trees, 8 In. 460.00
Inspiration, Jug, Lotus, Isis Shape, Blue, Green, Lemon, Mauve Pulls, 12 In. 460.00
Limberlost, Vase, Orange Trees, Green Ground, 9 In. 3220.00
Lisbon, Vase, Trumpet, Green Crenellated Band, Orange, Green, 12 In. 140.00
Lucerne, Jar, Lotus, Castle, Mountains, Blue Sky, Horizontal Ribbed Body, 12 In. 7130.00
Lucerne, Vase, Castle, Blue, Yellow, Green Mountains, Blue Sky, 6 1/2 In. 7480.00
Melon, Bowl, Orange, Yellow, Blue Stylized Melons, 5 In. 690.00
Persian, Jug, Lotus, Isis Shape, Green, Blue, Mauve, 1930, 10 In. 690.00
Persian Inspiration, Bowl, Isis Shape, Bell Form, Green, Mauve Pulls, Turquoise 175.00
Rhodanthe, Vase, Orange, Yellow, Gray Flower Heads, 8 1/2 In.   490.00
Sliced Circle, Jug, Isis Shape, Sliced Lemons, Black Triangles, Orange Border, 10 In. 920.00
Summerhouse, Jug, Lotus, Orange Tree, Yellow Sky, 8 In. 575.00
Summerhouse Variant, Jar, Lotus, Orange Trees, Blue Blossoms, 1933, 12 In. 2070.00
Teepee, Teapot, Greetings From Canada, Newport Pottery Co. 578.00
Tulips, Dinner Service, Inset Panel, 29 Piece 635.00
Tulips, Vase, Summerhouse Amidst Blue, Pink Tulips, Green Border, 1934, 8 In. 805.00
Vine, Vase, Leaves & Clouds, Oval Form, Signed, 7 In. 230.00
Woman's Face, Plaque, Flowered Hair, Green, Red, Yellow, Orange, 1945, 6 In. 460.00

CLEWELL ware was made in limited quantities by Charles Walter
Clewell of Canton, Ohio, from 1902 to 1955. Pottery was covered with
a thin coating of bronze, then treated to make the bronze turn different
colors. Pieces covered with copper, brass, or silver were also made.
Mr. Clewell's secret formula for blue patinated bronze was burned
when he died in 1965.

Bookends, Candleholder Design, Brown, Green Patina, 6 1/2 In.   2310.00
Cider Set, Copper Clad, Embossed, 9-3/4 In. Pitcher, 5 Piece 1100.00
Jardiniere, Copper Clad, Green, Blue, Orange, Brown Patina, 7 1/2 x 10 1/2 In. 4125.00
Jardiniere, Copper Clad, Verdigris & Bronze Patina, 5 1/4 x 6 1/2 In. 1045.00
Mug, Copper Clad, Deer Head, Rivet Design, Brass, Original Brown Patina, 4 In., Pair . . .   165.00
Vase, Copper Clad, Brown To Verdigris Patina, 8 1/2 x 7 In. 1980.00
Vase, Copper Clad, Flared Shoulder, Green, Blue & Orange Patina, Signed, 6 In. 2200.00
Vase, Copper Clad, Green Patina, Drip Design, Signed, 4 1/2 In.   1210.00
Vase, Copper Clad, Green, Blue, Orange, Brown Patina, Footed, 6 1/2 In. 2530.00
Vase, Copper Clad, Green, Blue, Orange, Brown, Marked, 8 1/2 In. 2530.00
Vase, Copper Clad, Green, Brown, Blue Patina, 2 Handles, 4 1/2 In. 825.00
Vase, Copper Clad, Orange, Brown, Green, Blue Patina, Signed, 17 In. 9350.00
Vase, Copper Clad, Orange, Green, Blue Patina, 11 1/2 In. 1430.00
Vase, Copper Clad, Orange, Green, Blue Patina, Signed, 19 In. 6600.00
Vase, Copper Clad, Organic Shape, 2 Handles, Incised, 6 In. 1540.00
Vase, Copper Clad, Verdigris & Bronze Patina, 7 1/2 x 3 1/2 In.   2090.00
Vase, Copper Clad, Verdigris & Bronze Patina, 10 x 3 1/2 In. 2640.00
Vase, Copper Clad, Verdigris & Bronze Patina, Signed, 7 In. 1600.00
Vase, Copper Clad, Verdigris & Bronze Patina, Spherical, 5 x 4 1/4 In. 1200.00
Vase, Copper Clad, Verdigris Patina, 6 x 3 In. 522.00
Vase, Copper Clad, Verdigris Patina, 8 3/4 x 7 In. 1210.00
Vase, Copper Clad, Verdigris Patina, 10 x 5 In. 1100.00
Vase, Copper Clad, Verdigris Patina, Cupped Rim, Incised, 11 1/2 In. 1650.00
Vase, Copper Clad, Verdigris Patina, Signed, 9 In. 295.00

Vase, Copper Clad, Verdigris Patina, Squat, 10 1/4 x 4 1/2 In. 1870.00
Vase, Copper Clad, Verdigris, 3-Footed, Egg Shape, Incised, 6 1/2 In. 605.00
Vase, Incised Floral Design, Square, 5 1/2 In. 935.00

CLEWS pottery was made by George Clews & Co. of Brownhills
Pottery, Tunstall, England, from 1906 to 1961. Additional pieces may
be listed in the Flow Blue category.

Bowl, Landing Of General Lafayette, Blue, Signed, 9 3/4 In. 330.00
Bowl, Vegetable, States Pattern, Castle, Blue Transfer, 12 1/2 x 9 1/2 In. 5770.00
Bowl, Winter View Of Pittsfield, Mass., 12 1/2 In. 2055.00
Cup & Saucer, American Eagle On Urn, Blue, Handleless 3025.00
Cup & Saucer, Eagle On Urn, Blue Transfer, 6 Sets 1980.00
Cup & Saucer, Landing Of General Lafayette, Blue, Handleless 350.00
Cup Plate, Landing Of General Lafayette, 3 1/2 In. ....*Illus* 330.00
Cup Plate, States Pattern, Blue House Transfer, 4 1/2 In. 440.00
Plate, America & Independence, Dark Blue, 8 In. 330.00
Plate, City Hall, New York, Beauties Of America, Dark Blue Transfer, 10 In. ...... 135.00 to 345.00
Plate, Doctor Syntax Painting Portrait, 4 Piece 660.00
Plate, Dr. Syntax Turned Nurse, Dark Blue Transfer, 7 3/4 In. 460.00
Plate, Landing Of General Lafayette, Blue, 6 3/4 In. 187.00
Plate, Landing Of General Lafayette, Blue, 10 In. .... 300.00 to 330.00
Plate, Landing Of General Lafayette, Blue & White, 19th Century, 7 1/2 In. 247.00
Plate, Landing Of General Lafayette, Dark Blue, 9 In. 330.00
Plate, Landing Of General Lafayette, Dark Blue, 10 1/8 In. 450.00
Plate, Peace & Plenty, Dark Blue, 8 3/4 In. 220.00
Plate, Pittsfield Elm, Winter View, Dark Blue, 10 1/2 In. 345.00
Plate, State, Buildings, Trees, Blue, Scalloped Edge, 6 1/2 In. 165.00
Plate, States, 2-Story Building, Blue, 8 In. 190.00
Plate, States, 3-Story Building, Observatory, Blue, 10 1/2 In. 355.00
Plate, States, Blue Transfer, 8 In. ....*Illus* 192.00
Plate, The Valentine, Wilkie, Blue, 8 3/4 In. 190.00
Plate, Toddy, Landing Of General Lafayette, 5 1/2 In. 410.00
Plate, Winter View Of Pittsfield, Mass., Dark Blue Transfer, 6 In. 230.00
Plate, Winter View Of Pittsfield, Mass., Dark Blue Transfer, 8 5/8 In. 440.00
Platter, Dark Blue Transfer, Windsor Castle, 19 In. 412.00
Platter, English Castle, States, Blue, 12 3/4 In. 1375.00
Platter, Landing Of General Lafayette, 19th Century, 19 In. 880.00
Platter, Landing Of General Lafayette, Blue, 19 In. 1265.00
Platter, Landing Of General Lafayette, Dark Blue, 17 In. 1208.00
Platter, Little Falls At Luzerne, Hudson River, Black, 17 1/2 In. 440.00
Platter, Mansion, America & Independence, Dark Blue Transfer, 16 7/8 In. 660.00
Platter, Nottingham Scene, Dark Blue Transfer, 19 In. 715.00
Platter, Peace & Plenty, Dark Blue Transfer, 17 In. 715.00

Clews, Plate, States,
Blue Transfer, 8 In.

Clews, Cup Plate,
Landing Of General Lafayette, 3 1/2 In.

Platter, Pittsfield Elm, Scalloped, Dark Blue, 18 1/2 x 15 1/2 In. 3450.00
Platter, Sandusky, Dark Blue, 16 1/2 In. . . . . .5175.00 to 9075.00
Platter, Shepherd Boy Rescued, Dark Blue, 12 1/2 In. 115.00
Sauce, Cover, Underplate, Landing Of Lafayette, Blue, 4 1/2 x 8 3/4 In. 1375.00
Soup, Dish, Landing Of General Lafayette, Blue Transfer, 10 In. 330.00
Teapot, Eagle On Urn, Clear Transfer, 7 In. 1700.00
Teapot, Eagle On Urn, Dark Blue, 7 In. 1700.00
Toddy Plate, America & Independence, Dark Blue, 5 5/8 In. 110.00
Tray For Sauceboat, Landing Of General Lafayette, Dark Blue, 9 3/4 In. 960.00
Vase, Houses & Flowers, Chameleon Ware, Logo, 7 In. 110.00

CLIFTON POTTERY was founded by William Long in Clifton, New Jersey, in 1905. He worked there until 1908 making a line called *Crystal Patina*. Clifton Pottery made art pottery. Another firm, Chesapeake Pottery, sold majolica marked *Clifton ware*.

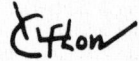

Jardiniere, Indian, 4 Mile Ruin, Arizona, Buff, Black, Brown Ground, 8 1/2 x 11 In. 440.00
Vase, Bottle Shape, Crystal Patina, 1906 & 1907, 8 1/2 x 5 In., Pair 495.00
Vase, Floral Design, Silver Overlay, Green, Tan Crystalline Glaze, 6 1/2 In. 1430.00

CLOCKS of all types have always been popular with collectors. The eighteenth-century tall case, or grandfather's clock, was designed to house a works with a long pendulum. In 1816, Eli Terry patented a new, smaller works for a clock, and the case became smaller. The clock could be kept on a shelf instead of on the floor. By 1840, coiled springs were used and even smaller clocks were made. Battery-powered electric clocks were made in the 1870s. A garniture set can include a clock and other objects displayed on a mantel.

2-Gong Strike, Mercury Pendulum, Floral Finials, Enameled Bronze, 1880, 14 In. 3450.00
Adams, Charles, E., Regulator, Wall, Calendar, 8-Day, Rosewood, Round Top, 24 In. 405.00
Advertising, 7-Up, Light-Up, Frosted Glass, Square, 16 In. 125.00
Advertising, 7-Up, Light-Up, Glass Face, Oak Frame, 1950s . . . . .150.00 to 195.00
Advertising, Alka-Seltzer, Electric, Round, 12 In. 305.00
Advertising, American Flyer, Die Cast, Locomotive, Cow Catcher On Base, 1927, 7 In. . . . 550.00
Advertising, Atlas Tires, Batteries & Accessories, Metal Body, Light-Up, 18 1/2 In. 770.00
Advertising, Aunt Jemima Buckwheat Pancakes, Plastic, Cardboard Face, 1956, 7 In. 550.00
Advertising, Ballantine Beer, Gold Trim On Face, Plastic, 12 x 10 In. 50.00
Advertising, Beverly Farms Milk, Metal, Glass, Light-Up, Pam Clock Co., Square, 14 In. . . 165.00
Advertising, Blue Crown Spark Plugs, Plastic, Metal, Light-Up, 25 1/2 x 15 In. 125.00
Advertising, Budweiser, Hand Painted, By Fenton Co. 105.00
Advertising, Busch Light 225.00
Advertising, Buy St. Joseph Aspirin, Metal, Light-Up, 1954, 14 1/2 In. 275.00
Advertising, Calumet Baking Powder, Regulator, Oak, Time To Buy, 38 x 16 In. 460.00
Advertising, Calumet Baking Powder, Waterbury, Reverse Painted, 1895, 38 x 15 In. 575.00
Advertising, Cat-Tex, Glass, Light-Up, Round 520.00
Advertising, Chewing Tobacco, Chew Friendship, Round Dial, Alarm, 1886, 4 1/4 In. . . . 3162.00
Advertising, Chico's Ice Cream, Plastic, Glass Front, Light-Up, Round, 16 In. 85.00
Advertising, Chocolat Revillion, Painted Metal, French 575.00
Advertising, Cities Services, Glass, Metal, Light-Up, Pam Clock, N.Y., 15 In. . . . .440.00 to 470.00
Advertising, Coors, Wall, Wooden Beer Barrel Head, Battery Operated, 10 1/2 In. 35.00
Advertising, Dayton Tires, Horse's Head Top Center, Light-Up, 15 In. 265.00
Advertising, Devil Brand Cigars, Devil Smoking Large Cigar, Cast Iron 4510.00
Advertising, Dick Smith Insurance Co., Metal, Light-Up, 21 1/2 x 24 1/2 In. 25.00
Advertising, Dr Pepper, Calendar, 7 1/2 Watt Bulb, 10 1/2 x 16 1/2 In. 50.00
Advertising, Dr Pepper, Drink A Bite To Eat, Fiberboard, Light-Up, 1940s, 15 In. 490.00
Advertising, Dr Pepper, Good For Life Logo, Metal Case, Round, 15 In. 145.00
Advertising, Dr Pepper, Light-Up, 1950-1960, 15 In. 315.00
Advertising, Dr Pepper, Metal, Light-Up, Plastic Face, 15 1/2 x 15 1/2 In. . . . . . . .135.00 to 145.00
Advertising, Dr Pepper, Reverse Glass, Electric Motor, 1930s 4485.00
Advertising, Dr Pepper, Wood Grain Ground, Gold V, Light-Up 275.00
Advertising, Drink Coca-Cola, Counter, Metal, Light-Up, Lunch With Us, 9 x 19 In. 1017.00
Advertising, Drink Squirt, Quality Soft Drink, Reverse Painted, Electric, Square, 15 In. . . 55.00
Advertising, Drink Topsy City Dairy, Tin, 14 x 14 In. 305.00
Advertising, Ever-Ready Safety Razor 3000.00

Advertising, Evervess Sparkling Water, Light-Up, 1940-1950, 15 In. 660.00
Advertising, Falstaff Beer, Plastic & Metal, Light-Up, 1960s, 11 1/2 x 8 1/2 In. 27.00
Advertising, Folger's Coffee, Reverse Painted, Neon, Octagonal, 1940s, 18 In. 260.00
Advertising, Frostie Root Beer, Plastic & Metal, 1960s, 15 x 15 In. 85.00
Advertising, Gold Dust Washing Powder, Windup, Plastic & Metal, Alarm, 3 1/4 In. 605.00
Advertising, Harley-Davidson, Neon, 15 1/2 In. 450.00
Advertising, Holland Ice Cream, Image Of Windmill On Left Side, 1950, 16 In. 495.00
Advertising, International Harvester, Neon, Square, 15 1/2 In. 295.00
Advertising, Joe Camel, 1989 .... 85.00
Advertising, Lee's Dairy, Double Bubble 425.00
Advertising, M&Ms, Wall, Red Plastic, Battery Operated, 15 x 10 In. 40.00
Advertising, Mayflower Movers, Truck Image, Light-Up, Round, 15 In. 365.00
Advertising, Meadow Gold Ice Cream, Neon, Octagonal, 16 1/2 In. 460.00
Advertising, Mobilgas Pegasus, Flying, Metal Housing, Light-Up, 15 In. 550.00
Advertising, Mobilgas Pegasus, Glass Face, Light-Up, Pam Clock Co., Inc., N.Y., 15 In. . 725.00
Advertising, Nash's Coffee, Light-Up, Telechron Works, Round, 15 In. 205.00
Advertising, O-So Grape, Bubble Glass, Light-Up, American Time, Round, 15 In. 130.00
Advertising, Old Mr. Boston, Fine Liquors, Bottle Shape, Embossed Metal, Key Wind ... 130.00
Advertising, Oldsmobile Service, Metal, Neon Lights, 21 x 6 In. 660.00
Advertising, Oldsmobile, Desk .... .85.00 to 95.00
Advertising, Orange Crush, 1950s 175.00
Advertising, Pabst Blue Ribbon, Digital, Plastic, Leaded Glass Style Sign, 13 x 9 1/2 In. . 35.00
Advertising, Pard Dog Food, Animated 300.00
Advertising, Pearl Lager Beer, Neon, Octagonal, 18 In. 240.00
Advertising, PEZ Logo On Face, Battery Operated, Round, Box 30.00
Advertising, Phillips 66, Double Bubble, Glass, Advertising Products, Ohio, 15 In. 990.00
Advertising, Phillips 66, Travel, Metal, Plastic, Seth Thomas, 1 x 2 1/4 In. 60.00
Advertising, Quaker State Motor Oil, Plastic, 1982, 4 x 16 In. 32.00
Advertising, Quaker State, Glass Face, Metal Housing, Light-Up, 15 In. 470.00
Advertising, Quaker State, Plastic, Metal Brackets, Light-Up, 16 x 16 In. 88.00
Advertising, Rambler, Glass Face, Metal, Light-Up, Pam Clock Co., N.Y., 16 In. 1030.00
Advertising, Rival Dog Good, Plate & Glass Cover, Wooden Frame, 15 1/2 In. .... 125.00 to 190.00
Advertising, Royal Crown Cola, Metal & Plastic, Insert At Top, Light-Up, 34 x 37 In. ... 1100.00
Advertising, Sauer's Flavoring Extracts, Pendulum, New Haven Clock Co., 42 x 15 In. .. 1650.00
Advertising, Schmidt's Beer, Light-Up, 14 x 12 In. 150.00
Advertising, Sealtest, Plastic, Light-Up 125.00
Advertising, Selmer Bank Instruments, Metal Case, Glass Face, Light-Up, 16 In. 825.00
Advertising, Sinclair HC Gasoline, White Neon, Metal, Light-Up, 21 In. 1540.00
Advertising, Snap-On Tools, Scantily Clad Woman, Battery Operated, 14 x 28 In. 105.00
Advertising, Sprite, Plastic, Light-Up .... .48.00 to 65.00
Advertising, Squirt, Metal Case, 1960s, 15 1/4 x 15 1/4 In. 380.00
Advertising, Sugardale Tender Meats, Neon Light-Up, 22 In. 460.00
Advertising, Swift's Ice Cream, Plastic, Metal, Light-Up, 1960s, Square, 16 In. 75.00
Advertising, U.S.G. Harness Oil, Papier-Mache, Tin, Oak Frame, 8-Day, Baird Clock Co. 3000.00
Advertising, Walter's Beer, Barrel Shape, Hand Painted, 1960s, 11 x 12 In. 71.00
Advertising, White King Soap, Die Cut, Neon, 26 x 36 In. 2070.00
Alarm, Billy The Kid 75.00
Alarm, C-3PO, R2-D2, Talking, Windup & Battery, Elgin, Box 75.00
Alarm, Elgin, World-Time Travel Alarm, Black Case, Brass Trim, Box, Round, 3 In. 45.00
Alarm, Enamel Dial, Round Brass Movement, Arabic Numerals, 1816, 6 1/4 In. 4890.00
Alarm, Garfield, Talking, Box 50.00
Alarm, Little Black Sambo, Boy Helping A Tiger, Wind-Up, Black Steel, Lux 150.00
Alarm, Roadrunner, Pocket, Box, 1970 .... 125.00
Alarm, Snow White, Bayard, 1950s 75.00
Alarm, Westclox, Big Ben, 1920s 50.00
Alarm, Woody Woodpecker, 1950s 375.00
Andrews, Terry, Double Steeple, Strawberries In Center, 2 Paneled Doors, 25 In. 1035.00
Animated, Amos & Andy, Alarm, Windup, Metal, Cardboard Face, 4 In. 990.00
Animated, Amos & Andy, Alarm, Windup, Paper Face, Copyright 1933, 3 3/4 In. 240.00
Animated, Black Child On Chamber Pot, I'm On The Go, Alarm, Windup, 5 x 6 In. 230.00
Animated, Hula Dancer, Self-Winding, Electric, United Novelty 100.00
Animated, Little Black Sambo, Alarm, Metal Body, Plastic Face, 3 1/4 x 2 3/4 In. 200.00
Animated, Little Black Sambo, Cardboard, Plastic, Metal, Copyright 1946, 3 1/2 In. 250.00

Animated, Shoe Shiner, Windup, Alarm, Cardboard Face, Lux Clock Mfg. Co., 3 3/4 In. . 935.00
Animated, Space Exploration, Warship Fires Light Beam At Planet, Westclox, 1970s 95.00
Animated, Swinging Playmates, Model 551, Bakelite Case, Mastercrafters 175.00
Anniversary, Brass Base, Glass Dome 140.00
Anniversary, Brass, Tin Face, Kieninger & Obergfell, West Germany, 12 1/4 In. 58.00
Ansonia, Blue Delft 495.00
Ansonia, China, Gilt, Floral, Mauve, Yellow, Green 1000.00
Ansonia, Delft 475.00
Ansonia, Hand Painted Pink Flowers, Mantel, 14 x 11 1/2 In. 550.00
Ansonia, Kitchen, Stenciled Silver On Glass Door, Paper Label, 22 1/2 In. 115.00
Ansonia, Kitchen, Walnut, 8-Day Time & Strike, Cutout Case 135.00
Ansonia, Mantel, Beveled Glass Sides, Scrolled Mounts, 18 1/2 In. 2055.00
Ansonia, Mantel, Black Iron, Gilt Ormolu, Porcelain Dial, 8-Day, Half-Hour Strike 330.00
Ansonia, Mantel, Gold & Faux Marble, Ebonized Finish, Time & Strike, 10 1/2 In....... 110.00
Ansonia, Mantel, Onyx, Gilt Metal Mounts, Time & Strike, Late 19th Century, 11 3/4 In. . 185.00
Ansonia, Mantel, Wautauga, Floral Design, Purple Ground 345.00
Ansonia, Regulator, Wall, Mahogany, Roman Numerals, Steel Spade Hands, 32 In. 201.00
Ansonia, Reverse Painted Red Rose Lower Panel, Gold Stenciling, Green 170.00
Ansonia, Shelf, Mahogany, Painted Metal Dial, Mirror Panel, Time & Strike, 18 1/2 In. .. 305.00
Ansonia, Shelf, Roman Chapters, Time & Strike, 11 3/4 In. 86.00
Ansonia, Shelf, Rosewood, Gothic, Time, Strike & Alarm, Replaced Paper Dial 105.00
Ansonia, The Huntress, c.1900 .... 3500.00
Ansonia, Wall, Cut Glass Throat & Base Panel, Westminster Chime 1595.00
Atkins, Wall, Mahogany, Rosewood, Drop, 30-Hour, Round, 24 In. 275.00
Atkins, Wall, Rosewood, Octagonal, Drop, Ripple Moldings, Metal Dial, 30-Hour, 25 In. . 990.00
Atkins & Downs, 8-Day, Triple Shelf, Reverse Glass, Columns, Eagle Crest, 38 In. 518.00
Atkins & Downs, Shelf, 8-Day, Wooden Works, Claw Feet, 39 1/4 In. 635.00
Atkins & Downs, Shelf, Reverse Painted Henry Clay Portrait, Stenciled Crest, 32 In. 920.00
Atmos, Perpetual Motion, Open Escapement, 9 3/4 In........................... 430.00
Automaton, Winged Putti Forging, Sharpening Arrows, Gilt, 25 In. 8050.00
Azura, Brass, Scroll Design, Weight Driven, Roman Chapters, Swiss, 9 3/4 x 18 3/4 In. ... 345.00
Bailey, Banks & Biddle, Empire, Gold Pillars, Gold Finials, 18 In. 1955.00
Bailey & Co., Mantel, Egyptian Revival, Round Marble, Bronze Dial, Pa., 19 In. 2415.00
Banjo, Federal, Brass Bezel, Convex Glass, Iron Dial, Brass Weights, c.1820, 30 In. 1782.00
Banjo, Howard Style, Grain-Painted Case, Black & Gold Glasses, 19th Century, 29 In. ... 660.00
Banjo, Ingraham, Mahogany, Nyanza, 38 In. 275.00
Banjo, Larkin, S., Mahogany, Painted Dial, Acorn Finial, Boston, 30 In. 522.00
Banjo, Mahogany Case, Brass Fittings, Brass Works, Reverse Painted Panels, 40 1/4 In. .. 820.00
Banjo, Mahogany Throat, Base Panels, Boston, 1830, 29 3/4 In. 825.00
Banjo, Mahogany, Acorn Finial, Painted Dial, Carved, Scrolled Wood Side Arms, 33 In. .. 550.00
Banjo, Mahogany, Brass Trim, Painted Metal Face, 33 1/4 In. 660.00
Banjo, Mahogany, Reverse Painted, Weight & Pendulum, Brass Trim, 33 1/2 In. 495.00
Banjo, New Haven, Mahogany, Brass Side Frets, Eagle Finial, 8-Day, 37 In. 250.00
Banjo, New Haven, Reverse Painting 350.00
Banjo, Noyes, L., Mahogany, Reverse Painted, Eagle Finial, Brass Works, 31 1/4 In. 1575.00
Banjo, Plymouth, Mahogany, Eagle Finial, 8-Day Half-Hour Strike, 30 In. ....135.00 to 150.00
Banjo, Waltham, Model 1525 .... 3950.00
Banjo, Willard Style, Mahogany & Giltwood, Castle, Eglomise Panel, c.1820, 33 In. 1265.00
Banjo, Willard, S., & Son, Mahogany, Eglomise Panel, Stylized Leaves, c.1820, 33 In. 8050.00
Banjo, Willard, S., Mahogany, Molded Brass Bezel, White Painted Dial, 1810, 29 In. 12650.00
Banjo, Willard, S., Patent, Federal, Eglomise, Beaded Wood, Eagle Finial, 44 In. 1725.00
Banjo, Willard, Simon, Ball & Steeple Finial, Enamel Dial, Naval Battle, 33 x 10 In. 4600.00
Banjo, Willard, Simon, Gilt Eagle Finial, Painted Dial, Naval Scene On Door, 32 1/2 In. .. 7280.00
Banjo, Willard, Simon, Reverse Painted, 41 1/2 x 10 1/4 x 3 1/2 In. 5775.00
Banjo, Wooden Bezel, Metal Dial, 8-Day, Mahogany, Mahogany Veneer, 1840, 34 In. 1150.00
Barnes Bartholomew, Shelf, Federal, Eagle Pediment, Eglomise Panels, 37 1/2 In. 605.00
Becker, Gustav, Regulator, Porcelain Dial, 8-Day, Weight Driven, Vienna, 1880, 55 In. ... 1995.00
Becker, Gustav, Walnut, Double Weight, Porcelain Dial, 52 In. 1650.00
Beech, Carved & Gilt, Louis XVI Style, Enameled Dial, Holland, c.1830, 16 1/2 In. 2860.00
Belle Epoch, Enamel Dial, Round, 22 x 13 x 5 1/2 In. 1150.00
Belle Epoch, Gilt Bronze, Enamel Dial, Swan Handles, Round 1035.00
Berthoud, Ferdinand, Wall, White Dial, Ormolu Flower Cornucopias, 13 x 11 In. 1150.00
Bigelow & Kennard, Bracket, Mahogany, Chiming, Ormolu Case 4255.00

Bigelow & Kennard, Mantel, Engraved Slate, Black, Gilt Dial, 8-Day, 1870s, 12 In. 660.00
Black, Starr & Frost, Repousse Case, Vine Design, Swiss Movement, Travel 138.00
Black Forest, 4 Trumpets, Black Lacquer, Brass Works, c.1875 . . . . *Illus* 5315.00
Black Forest, Figural, Girl, Sitting On Rock, Terra-Cotta, Continental, 1900, 26 In. 865.00
Black Forest, Wall, Walnut, Spread-Winged Eagle, Antelope, 8-Day, 47 x 27 In. 5610.00
Black Forest, Walnut, Carved Birds, 8-Day, 1850s, 33 x 35 1/2 In. 6600.00
Blinking Eye, Sambo, Cast Iron, 16 In. 1540.00
Bracket, Boulle, Empire, Gilt Bronze, Classical Women Base, 8-Day, 1820, 45 In. 3190.00
Bracket, Louis XV, Gilt Brass, Round Enamel Dial, Floral, Apple Green Ground 1725.00
Bracket, Mahogany, Arched Case, Round Enamel Dial, Bracket Feet, 12 In. 200.00
Bracket, Rosewood, Silver Metal, Japanese Numerals, Rosewood Case, Hinged Handle . . 6900.00
Brass Plated, Clear Cylinder, Celluloid Tablets, 6 1/2 In. 192.00
Brewster, Shelf, Gold-Painted Vine, Glass Door, Stenciled Border, 17 In. 430.00
Brewster & Ingrahams, Steeple, Mahogany Veneer, Brass, Pendulum, Key, 20 In. 82.00
Brewster & Ingrahams, Steeple, Rosewood Veneer Case, Brass Works, 19 1/4 In. 385.00
Bronze, Louis XV, White Enamel Dial, Black Roman & Arabic Numerals, 9 1/2 In. 6325.00
Bronze & Ivory, Classical Figure, Seated Beside Enamel Dial, Alabaster Plinth, 13 In. . . . 2600.00
Brown, C., Steeple, Walnut, Connecticut, 19th Century, 20 In. 358.00
Caldwell, J.E., Bracket, Carved Owl Peak, Musical, 8-Day, 1880, 45 x 23 In. 14300.00
Caldwell, J.E., White Onyx, Gilt Woman Bust, 8-Day Half-Hour Strike, Regilt, 15 1/2 In. . 495.00
Caldwell & Co., Wall, Brass, 8-Day 350.00
Carriage, Beveled Glass, Brass Case, Geometric, Floral Design, France, 5 1/2 In. 1380.00
Carriage, Beveled Glass, Enamel Dial, French, c.1900, 4 In. 330.00
Carriage, Blue Enamel, Sterling Silver, Swiss Movement, Leather Case, 1 3/4 In. 300.00
Carriage, Brass, c.1800, 5 1/4 In. . . . . *Illus* 1812.00
Carriage, Brass, Oval Beveled Glass Panels, Flowers, Woman, Cupid, France, 5 1/2 In. . . 1785.00
Carriage, Correll, A.B., White Dial, Gilt Face, 1911, Brass & Glass, 7 1/2 In. 805.00
Carriage, Edwardian, Bronze, Beveled Glass, 1900, 3 7/8 x 2 1/4 x 2 3/4 In. 150.00
Carriage, Half Strike, Repeat Button, Brass, Switzerland, 6 1/2 In. 460.00
Carriage, Porcelain Panel, Gilt Bronze, France, 1900, 2 In. 5750.00
Carriage, Repeater, Beveled Glass, Porcelain Dial 850.00
Carriage, Sterling Silver Case, Bail Handle, Bun Feet, 4 In. 517.00
Cartel, Louis XV, White Enamel Dial, Black Roman & Arabic Numerals, Scrolled Feet . . 1380.00
Character, C-3PO, R2-D2, Bradley, Elgin National, Battery Operated, Box, 1982 . . . . 60.00
Character, Cinderella, Carriage, Horses 135.00
Character, Flintstones, Wall, Battery Operated 15.00
Cheney, Martin, Tavern, Windsor, Vt. 4600.00
Cheuret, A., Mantel, Silver Plate, Diamond Face, Chevron Case, 13 Jewels, 5 x 16 In. . . . 39600.00
Cloisonne, Beveled Glass, 8-Day Time & Strike, France, 1890, 15 In. 4900.00
Cole, Thomas, Gilt Metal Tripod, Silver Dial, Round Stepped Plinth, 1865, 23 In. 10350.00
Cuckoo, Carved Walnut, Oak Branch With Leaves, Acorns, Continental, 19th Century . . . 287.00
Downes, Ephraim, Pillar & Scroll, Mahogany Veneer, Scroll, Brass Finials, 31 In. 825.00
Drum Dial, Putto Seated On Shell On Back Of Bull, Scrolled Feet, Bronze, 24 In. 4025.00
Drum Dial, Putto, Winged Griffins, 1870s, 23 In. 2875.00
Dufresne, Maurice, Mantel, Mahogany, Gilt Bronze Face, 1902, 15 1/4 In. 4025.00
Dungan & Klump, Hickory, Dickory, Dock, Mouse Goes Up Channel, Wood, 42 In. 1150.00

Clock, Black
Forest, 4 Trumpets,
Black Lacquer, Brass
Works, c.1875

Clock, Carriage,
Brass, c.1800,
5 1/4 In.

Federal, Cherry, Horizontal Cornice, Round Door, Roman Numerals, 1800, 42 In. 4025.00
Figural, Aesop, Seated On Tree Stump, Raised On Red Marble Base, Bronze, 25 In. 520.00
Figural, Asian Warrior On Horse, Bronze, Gilt Base, Dial & Bezel, France 1595.00
Figural, Birdcage & Bird, Brass, Cloisonne, 5 In. 170.00
Figural, Cherub In Chariot Pulled By Dog, Bronze, Roman Numerals, 7 1/2 In. 575.00
Figural, Cupid & Psyche, Marble, Round Bronze Dial, Paw Feet, 48 x 19 In. 5750.00
Figural, Elephant, Pendulum Clock Supported From Trunk, Brass, 10 In. 465.00
Figural, Man, Serenading Woman By Clock Tower, Bisque, Germany, 13 In............ 100.00
Figural, Phoebe, Marble Base, France, 24 x 8 x 11 In. 2250.00
Forestville Mfg. Co., Mantel, Mahogany, Ogee, Reverse Painted Door, 8-Day, 30 In. 195.00
Frankl, Paul, Telechron, Radiating Bands Of Silver & Gray, Electric, 8 x 5 In. 715.00
Gaudron, Pierre, Cartel, Repeater, Enameled Dial, Gilt Bronze, c.1725, 23 1/2 In........ 7150.00
Gilbert, Banjo, Mahogany, Rosewood Panel, Silver Dial, Brass Eagle Finial, 36 In. 195.00
Gilbert, Kitchen, Oak, Gingerbread, Applied Flowers, 8-Day Time & Strike, Alligatored . 145.00
Gilbert, M., & Co., Wall, Mahogany Veneer Case, Brass Movement 72.00
Gilbert, Mantel, Blackened Wood, Flat Top, 8-Day, Gilt Ormolu 85.00
Gilbert, Shelf, Brass Works, Pendulum, Key, Cast Metal, Bell, 17 1/2 In. 88.00
Gilbert, Shelf, Rosewood, Peaked Crest, Half Columns, 30-Hour Time & Strike, 27 In. .. 220.00
Gilbert, William, Floral, Lion's Heads, Scrolls, Porcelain, 11 In. 200.00
Gleichauf, B., Bracket, Partly Ebonized, Giltwood, Striking, Gilt Metal Finials, 18 In. 1495.00
Goodwin, J.N., Shelf, Finials 2300.00
Goujo, T., Swirling Clouds Against Starry Ground, Gilt Bronze, 1900, 19 In............ 6900.00
Grogan Co., Mantel, Chelsea Strike, Brass Footed Case, Pittsburgh, 11 x 21 In......... 1150.00
Hanging, Building, 3 Tiers, Galleries, Polychrome Paint, Brass Works, 36 1/2 In. 550.00
Heco, Mantel, Mahogany, Art Deco, 8-Day, Westminster Chimes, Germany 72.00
Herschede, Frank, Brass, Enamel Face, 10 In. 275.00
Howard & Co., Regulator, Railroad, Oak, Quarter-Sawed Figure, Brass Works, 65 x 19 In. 1760.00
Howard & Co., Wall, Key Shape, Oak, 31 In. 1265.00
Howard Miller, Asterisk, Avocado Paint, Black Hands, George Nelson, 10 In. 415.00
Howard Miller, Red Dial, Turquoise Pyramidal Base, George Nelson, 14 x 12 1/2 In. 440.00
Howard Miller, Starburst, White Spokes, Black Center, Red Hours, Nelson, 18 In. 605.00
Howard Miller, Sunburst, Black Painted Walnut Spikes, Brass, No. 2022-G, Nelson 403.00
Howard Miller, Triangular Black Face, Chrome Wire, George Nelson, 20 x 20 In. 3190.00
Howard Miller, Wall, Black Balls On Rays, Metal, George Nelson, 1970s 2600.00
Industrial, Swing, Figural Man 8500.00
Ingraham, Kitchen, Calendar, Pal 195.00
Ingraham, Kitchen, Oak 160.00
Ingraham, Kitchen, Oak, Gingerbread, 8-Day Time & Strike, Alligatored 105.00
Ingraham, Kitchen, Oak, Gingerbread, Calendar Dial, 8-Day Time & Strike, Refinished .. 185.00
Ingraham, Shelf, Grecian Mosaic, Maple & Mahogany, 8-Day Hour Strike, 1875 .... 895.00
Ingraham, Shelf, Grecian Mosaic, Maple & Mahogany, 8-Day, 8-Strike, 1875 .... 895.00
International, Master, Walnut Case, Victorian, 99 In. 2070.00
Ithaca, Calendar, Parlor, Walnut, Glass & Silver Dial, c.1875, 20 1/2 x 10 1/4 In. 2070.00
Ithaca, Calendar, Walnut, No. 2 Regulator, Double Dial, 8-Day, 46 x 19 In. 2415.00
Ithaca, Double Dial, Mahogany, Black Scroll Top, 31 In. 1725.00
Ives, Chauncey, Pillar & Scroll, Mahogany Veneer, 1 Day Wooden Works, c.1820 .... 2975.00
Japy, Mantel, Gothic Revival, Gilt Bronze, Porcelain Plaques, 12 In. 690.00
Jefferson, Wood, Brass Face, Nelson Style Hands, Rectangular, 1950, 5 1/2 In. 115.00
Jerome, Chauncey, Shelf, Mahogany, 30-Hour Time & Strike, Restored 200.00
Jerome, Shelf, Mahogany, Veneer, Metal Face, Floral, Gold, Alarm, 8-Day 82.00
Jerome & Darrow, Shelf, Carved Acanthus Pillars, Acanthus Scroll On Top, 31 In. 2645.00
Jerome & Darrow, Shelf, Mahogany, Column & Splat, 30-Hour, Wooden Works 220.00
Junghans, Bracket, Mahogany, Arched, Brass Dial, 8-Day Chime, Victorian 245.00
Kienzle, Regulator, Mahogany, Applied Scroll, Molded Case, 8-Day Time & Strike 220.00
Kingwood, Pedestal, Winged Cherubs In Clouds, Flowers, White Dial, 1880, 86 In. 16100.00
Kitchen, Walnut, Cutout Case, Silk-Screened Arch Door, 8-Day Time & Strike 95.00
Kitchen, Walnut, Reverse Painted Arch & Floral, Restored, 19th Century, 18 1/2 In. 95.00
Kroeber Clock Co., Shelf, Maid, Mandolin, 8-Day Strike, Metal Bombay Case, 18 In. 465.00
Leroy & Fils, Mantel, 2-Piece Enamel, Calendar Dial, Gilt Brass, France, 1880 .... 8050.00
Lescuyer, Louis XVI Style, Boulle, Paris, c.1819, 23 In. 4950.00
Lux, Bar Scene, Black Bartender, Windup, Metal, Glass Front, 3 3/4 In. 165.00
Lux, Cuckoo 95.00
Lyre Form, Enamel Dial, Putto Terms Holding Wreath, Floral Swags, 55 In. 2875.00

Malassine Trouay Vatan, Wall, Inlaid Brass, Mother-Of-Pearl, Glass, 24 In. 635.00
Manross, Elisha, Mahogany, Steeple, Gothic, Eglomise Panel, Time & Strike 135.00
Mantel, 4-Spiral Turned Columns, Round Enameled Dial, Continental, 17 In. 225.00
Mantel, Art Deco, Arched Gray Marble, Cream Alabaster Bronze, Ball Feet, 12 In. 520.00
Mantel, Art Deco, Black Marble Case, Brown, Green, 2 Large Spelter Dogs, 21 In. 690.00
Mantel, Art Deco, Red-Veined Marble Case, Woman, Seated, Parrot, 14 In. 635.00
Mantel, Art Deco, Tan, Gray Rectangular Case, Woman Playing With Fawn, 15 In. 430.00
Mantel, Art Deco, Taupe Marble Case, White, Spelter Bird On Left Side, 8 In. 520.00
Mantel, Belle Epoque, Bronze, Rectangular Marble Case, Round Enamel Dial, 20 In. 460.00
Mantel, Brass Urn Finial, Round Dial, Enameled Pendulum, Continental, 19 In. 400.00
Mantel, Brass, 2 Bells, Carrying Handle, Raised On Bracket Feet, 8 1/2 In. 100.00
Mantel, Brass, 4 Beveled Glass Panes, Gilt Bronze Face, 1900, 10 In. 316.00
Mantel, Brass, Porcelain Face, Lion's Head, Ring Handles, Claw Feet, France, 16 1/4 In. . . 150.00
Mantel, Brass, Swan's Neck Pediment, Round Dial, Scrolled Apron, Bracket Feet, 7 In. . . . 120.00
Mantel, Bronze, Marble Figural, 19th Century, 23 x 25 In. 575.00
Mantel, Bronze, Round Dial, Marble Case, Late 19th Century, 37 1/2 In. 1725.00
Mantel, Charles X, Bronze, Classically Clad Female Figure, White Enamel Dial, 15 In. . . 2300.00
Mantel, Charles X, Bronze, Ormolu, Classical Woman, Sitting On Clock, Plinth, 15 In. . . 2300.00
Mantel, Charles X, Sultana, Gilt Bronze, Mahogany Base, Glass Dome, 1825, 20 x 16 In. 1575.00
Mantel, Egyptian Revival, Bronze Bust, Alexander The Great, Sphinxes, c.1865, 15 In. . . 440.00
Mantel, Empire, Mahogany, Spike Finials, Glazed Door, Painted Tin Dial, 19 3/4 In. 60.00
Mantel, Federal, Mahogany, Painted Dial, Flanked By Columns, Bracket Feet, 30 In. 275.00
Mantel, Federal, Mahogany, Swan's-Neck Crest, Wooden Dial, Cutout Feet, 22 In. 7475.00
Mantel, Federal, Mahogany, Tri-Arched Pediment, Painted Dial, Plinth Base, 31 In. 550.00
Mantel, Figural, Woman Playing Violin, Cherub With Music, Marble Base, 16 1/2 In. 575.00
Mantel, Gilt Metal, Round Dial, Floral, Foliate Cast Case, Continental, 11 In. 250.00
Mantel, Gilt Metal, Scrolled Foliage, White Dial, Scroll Feet, 13 3/4 In. 144.00
Mantel, Giltwood, Patera Carved Base, Second Hand, France, 19th Century, 20 x 17 In. . . 2645.00
Mantel, Half-Hour Strike On Gong, Mercury-Filled Pendulum, Oval, Brass, 10 In. 402.00
Mantel, Louis Philippe, Bronze, Ormolu, Classical Man, Sitting On Clock, 20 x 14 In. . . . 4025.00
Mantel, Louis Philippe, Bronze, Steel Dial, Roman Numerals, Bun Feet, 20 1/4 In. 4025.00
Mantel, Louis Philippe, Chinoiserie Revival, Woman, Parasol, Chinese Base, 18 x 14 In. . 5175.00
Mantel, Louis Philippe, Woman, Sitting In Armchair, Steel Dial, Roman Numerals, 18 In. 5175.00
Mantel, Louis XV, Red, White Enamel Dial, Roman & Arabic Numerals, 21 1/2 In. 1725.00
Mantel, Louis XVI, Gilt, Round Dial, Lady, Wearing Period Costume, Roman Numerals . 230.00
Mantel, Lyre Shape, Louis XVI, Gilt Bronze, Blue Enamel Porcelain, 14 1/2 In. 2415.00
Mantel, Mahogany, Broken Arch Pediment, Pink Roses, Bracket Feet, 30 In. 2010.00
Mantel, Mahogany, Concave Sides, Round Enamel Dial, Turned Brass Feet, 11 In. 175.00
Mantel, Mahogany, Domed Top, Full Front Columns, Silver Dial, 8-Day Time & Strike . . 120.00
Mantel, Mahogany, Hexagonal Case, Round Tin Dial, Plinth Base, 14 In. 125.00
Mantel, Mahogany, Pagoda Top, Cast Putto, Enamel Dial, Bracket Feet, 18 In. 450.00
Mantel, Marble, 2 Bronze Female Figures On Marble Base, Turned Feet, 22 In. 2100.00
Mantel, Marble, Carved Mahogany, Rectangular Case, 18 x 13 x 8 In. 345.00
Mantel, Marble, Neoclassical, Man, On Horseback, Round Metal Dial 1100.00
Mantel, Marble, Pointed Arch Pediment, Round Glazed Door, Metal Dial, 13 In. 100.00
Mantel, Napoleon III, Cupid & Psyche, Enamel Dial, 1870, 18 1/2 x 17 1/2 In. 425.00
Mantel, Neoclassical, White Enamel Dial Raised On Elephant's Back, Italy, 26 In. 3910.00
Mantel, Organic Shape, 12-Petal Flower Face, Swirling Foliate, Wood, 17 In. 1725.00
Mantel, Red Paint, Silvered Columns, Reverse Painted Glass Door, 14 In. 105.00
Mantel, Regency, Mahogany, Inlaid Brass, 19 1/2 In. 5225.00
Mantel, Rococo Revival, St. George & Dragon, Gilt Bronze, 19th Century, 17 In. 990.00
Mantel, Rococo, Round Enamel Dial, Putto Figure, Pale Blue, Gilt, 17 1/2 In. 805.00
Mantel, Rosewood, Round Case, Painted Metal Dial, Plinth Base, 14 1/2 In. 300.00
Mantel, Round Molded Door, White Enameled Dial, Roman Numerals, Victorian, 16 In. . 690.00
Mantel, Walnut, Cathedral Top, Paper Dial, Glass Painted, c.1900, 18 x 4 x 11 In. 112.00
Mantel, Walnut, Octagonal, Alarm Dial, 19th Century, 14 In. 132.00
Mantel, Walnut, Victorian, Arched Cornice, Stepped Rectangular Plinth, 26 In. 1380.00
Mantel, Walnut, Victorian, Arched Molded Crest, 2 Dials, Roman Numeral Upper Dial . . . 920.00
Mantel, White Marble Top, Base, Gong Striking Movement, Rectangular, 1870 . . . . 6900.00
Mantel, White Marble, Architectural Shape, Brass Frieze, Split Columns, France 345.00
Mantel, White Marble, Brass Works, Trim, Enamel Face, Paris, 11 3/4 In. 275.00
Mantel, Woman, Opening Jewel Cask, Round Dial, Bronze, Gilt, 20 In. 1955.00
Mastercrafters, Ship 68.00

Mercier-Hupel, Hanging Case, Brass Face, Polychrome Japanning, Normandy, 55 In. 770.00
Mitchell, Shelf, Stenciled Column, Splat, Pillar, Gold Scroll Stencil, Lion's Feet, 29 In. . . 920.00
Motion, Waterfall 110.00
Moucin, Garniture, Regulator Clock, Marble Base, Ormolu, Brass Case, 3 Piece 1430.00
Muirhead & Arthur, Mahogany Veneer, Brass Trim & Inlay, Silvered Face, 16 1/4 In. . . . 220.00
Muller, Marble, Granite, Porphyry Columns, Sloped Plinth, 1900, 15 1/2 In. 8335.00
Nelson, G., Chronopak, Spherical Wood Case, Glass Face, Brass-Plated Steel Base 403.00
New England Clock Co., Steeple, Mahogany, Westminster Chimes, Contemporary 85.00
New Haven, Beveled Glass, Pendulum & Key, Gilded Brass Case, 11 1/2 In. 302.00
New Haven, Kitchen, Rhine, Walnut, Bust On Crest, 8-Day Time Strike, Alarm 195.00
New Haven, Mantel, 30-Hour, Weight Driven, Oak, Scenic Painting, 1890 . . . . 220.00
New Haven, Mantel, Iron, Red Marbleized, Waisted, Ormolu, 8-Day Half-Hour Strike . . . 246.00
New Haven, Paperweight, Mounted On Nude Male Figure, 9 In. 415.00
New Haven, Shelf, Guide, Gothic, Mahogany, Painted Metal Dial, Time, Strike & Alarm . 165.00
New Haven, Shelf, Walnut, Cutout Crest & Frets, 8-Day Time & Strike 250.00
Northrop & Smith, Sheraton, Pillar & Scroll Design, Painted Face, 30 In. 1380.00
Pewter, Arts & Crafts, Hammered, England, 14 x 6 1/2 In. 935.00
Pratt, Daniel, Jr., Mantel, Painted Wood Dial, Brass Alarm Ring, Reverse Painted, 32 In. . 357.00
Regulator, 2 Weights, Walnut, Columnar & Pedestal Design, Vienna, c.1885, 47 In. 550.00
Regulator, Jeweler's, Mahogany, Glass Pane Door, Brass Pendulum, 66 x 27 1/2 In. 2300.00
Regulator, Wall, Ebonized Case, Applied Moldings, Brass Works, Vienna, 50 In. 550.00
Regulator, Wall, Mahogany, Contemporary, Brass Dial, Westminster Chimes 110.00
Regulator, Wall, Simulated Rosewood, Round, Drop, Painted Metal Dial, 7 1/2 In. 195.00
Riley, Shelf, Reverse Painting Of A Ship, 30-Hour, 36 In. 1150.00
Sessions, Regulator, Calendar, Stenciled Door, Oak, c.1900, 40 x 18 In. 230.00
Sessions, Regulator, Oak, Brass Works, Calendar, Eglomise, Paper Face, 38 1/4 x 18 In. . . 275.00
Sessions, Regulator, Pressed Oak, Brass Works, Calendar Hand, 32 1/2 In. 250.00
Sessions, Wall, Aztec, Oak, Brass Numbers, Hands, Pendulum, 18 x 9 1/2 In. . . . . *Illus* 400.00
Seth Thomas, Beehive, 4 Jewel, Mahogany, 5 In. 55.00
Seth Thomas, Bell Ship's, Strikes Bells, Nickel-Plated Brass 275.00
Seth Thomas, Camel Back, Electric 150.00
Seth Thomas, Cottage, Time, Strike & Alarm, 19th Century, 10 1/2 In. 125.00
Seth Thomas, Empire, Rosewood Veneer, Ebonized, Brass Works, Key Wind, 16 In. 220.00
Seth Thomas, Kitchen, Walnut, Peaked Case, Painted Metal Dial, Time & Strike 110.00
Seth Thomas, Kitchen, Walnut, Silk Screened Door, Open Crest, 8-Day Strike & Alarm . . 330.00
Seth Thomas, Kitchen, Wooden Scrolled Top & Sides, Gold Glass Door, 21 In. 260.00
Seth Thomas, Mahogany, Brass Works, Reverse Painted Glass, 32 1/2 In. 137.00
Seth Thomas, Mantel, Adamantine, Faux Marble Wood Case, Brass Dial, 8-Day 148.00
Seth Thomas, Mantel, Beveled Glass, Gilt Metal, Leaf & Scroll, Enamel Dial, 6 x 12 In. . 575.00
Seth Thomas, Mantel, Black Enamel, Full Columns, Time & Strike, Gilt 255.00
Seth Thomas, Mantel, Brass, Glazed Sides, Back, Round Dial, Bracket Feet, 9 3/4 In. . . . 200.00
Seth Thomas, Mantel, Faux Slat & Marble, Time & Strike, Quarter Columns 110.00
Seth Thomas, Mantel, Figured Veneer, Lion's-Head Handles, Column Pilasters 138.00
Seth Thomas, Mantel, Mahogany Pillar & Scroll, Polychrome Dial, 1825, 31 In. 2415.00
Seth Thomas, Mantel, Mahogany, Art Deco, Cutout Brass, Hour Ring, Chime 120.00
Seth Thomas, Mantel, Open Escapement, 8-Day Half-Hour Strike, Black Marble 120.00
Seth Thomas, Mantel, Rosewood Veneer, Key & Lock, 27 x 5 x 14 In. 588.00
Seth Thomas, Mantel, Rosewood, Carved, Scene Transfer Panel, 1860, 14 1/2 In. 150.00
Seth Thomas, Mantel, Walnut, 8-Day, Paper Label, Eclipse Pendulum, 24 x 5 x 14 In. . . . 168.00
Seth Thomas, Pillar & Scroll, Reverse Painted Scene Of Monticello, 30 In. 1150.00
Seth Thomas, Postcard, European Cards, Go Up & Down, Oak Case, 72 In. 3500.00
Seth Thomas, Regulator, Crystal, 9 3/4 In. 28.00
Seth Thomas, Regulator, Empire, Crystal, Brass, Porcelain Dial, Garland Design 275.00
Seth Thomas, Regulator, Empire, No. 13, Verde Top, Lion, 8-Day Half-Hour Strike 715.00
Seth Thomas, Regulator, No. 2, Rosewood Veneer, 8-Day, Weight Driven, 1900 . . . . 1695.00
Seth Thomas, Regulator, Wall, Oak, Arched Pediment Top, 44 In. 880.00
Seth Thomas, Regulator, Walnut Veneer, Calendar, Patent March 4, 1862, 41 1/2 In. 2200.00
Seth Thomas, Shelf, Balloon Style, Mahogany Case, c.1905, 12 In. 895.00
Seth Thomas, Shelf, Curved Top, Chinese Red, Brass Columns, 19th Century, 18 In. 100.00
Seth Thomas, Shelf, Ebonized Trim, Alarm Movement, Pendulum & Key, 17 1/2 In. 165.00
Seth Thomas, Shelf, Mahogany, Empire, Eglomise, 25 In. 143.00
Seth Thomas, Shelf, Mahogany, Ogee, Gold Transfer Dog, Repainted Dial, 16 x 10 In. . . . 120.00
Seth Thomas, Shelf, Mahogany, Stenciled Cornucopia Crest, Gilt Dial, 29 x 17 x 5 In. . . . 1035.00

Tradition says the best place in a home for a grandfather clock is where it can be seen as soon as you enter the house.

Clock, Sessions,
Wall, Aztec, Oak,
Brass Numbers,
Hands, Pendulum,
18 x 9 1/2 In.

Seth Thomas, Shelf, Ogee, Mahogany, Reverse Painted Glass, 25 x 15 1/2 In.	200.00
Seth Thomas, Shelf, Parma Model, Balloon Style, Mahogany, c.1905, 12 x 7 x 5 In.	895.00
Seth Thomas, Shelf, Renaissance Revival, Walnut, Carved, Fluted Columns, 23 In.	220.00
Seth Thomas, Shelf, Rosewood Veneer, 8-Day, Pendulum, 16 In.	195.00
Seth Thomas, Shelf, Walnut, Curved Top, Applied Carvings, 19th Century, 22 In.	120.00
Seth Thomas, Ship's, Bells Chime During 4-Hour Watch, c.1900	875.00
Seth Thomas, Ship's, Outside Bell, Brass, Brass Works, 19th Century	650.00
Seth Thomas, Wall, Cast Plaster Sunburst, Brass Works, Painted Face, 1920s, 24 In.	192.00
Seth Thomas, Wall, Queen Anne, Cherry Case, 8-Day Time & Strike, 36 In.	660.00
Seth Thomas, Wall, Softwood, Octagonal, Drop, Painted Metal Dial, 24 In.	355.00
Seth Thomas, Wall, Union Pacific Railroad Case, Oak	125.00
Shelf, Brass Worked, Music Box, Junghous, Key, 20th Century, 12 3/4 In.	302.00
Shelf, Brass, Glass, Porcelain Face, Mercury-Filled Pendulum, France, 8 x 5 1/2 In.	242.00
Shelf, Chelsea Ship's Bell, Brass Face, Mounted On Wood, 1940	1150.00
Shelf, Empire, Mahogany Veneer, Ebonized Trim, 2-Part Glass Door, 33 1/4 In.	245.00
Shelf, Empire, Rosewood Veneer, Gilded Trim, Brass Works, 19 1/2 In.	165.00
Shelf, Federal, 8-Day Time & Strike, Mahogany, White Gilt Dial, Ball Feet, 36 In.	2990.00
Shelf, Figural, Marble & Bronze, France, 22 x 27 In.	5775.00
Shelf, Geometric, Light & Dark Arched Border, Gold Spiral Stencil, 15 In.	170.00
Shelf, Gothic Revival, Gilded Brass, Pendulum, 21 1/2 In.	495.00
Shelf, Rosewood, Gothic, Silk Screen Panel, Overpainted Dial	120.00
Shelf, Scroll & Leaf Design, Enamel Face, 4 Doric Pillars, Button Feet, France, 17 In.	330.00
Shelf, Walnut, Brass Works, Gold Transfer On Glass Front, Victorian, 20 1/4 In.	140.00
Shelf, Walnut, Dancing Children Panel, Octagonal, Time & Strike, 1870, 12 1/2 In.	95.00
Shelf, Walnut, Mirror Sides	650.00
Shelf, Walnut, Scroll Design, Brass Works, Alarm, Victorian, 21 In.	140.00
Shelf, Woman, Flanked By Black Stenciled Columns, White Dial, 1825, 23 In.	4887.00
Skeleton, Man & Dog, Metal, Marble & Wood Base, 19 In.	1035.00
Skeleton, Silver Regulator Dial, Scrollwork Frame, Turned Feet, 1840, 15 In.	12650.00
Skeleton, Victorian, Brass, Single Fusee, Scrolled Supports, 7 In.	430.00
Skeleton, Victorian, Brass, Steel Dial, Open Escapement, Quarter-Hour Strike, 21 In.	6325.00
Spencer & Wooster, Mantel, Architectural Landscape, 8-Day, Repeating, Brass, 1830	805.00
Speth, Andre, Wall, Rococo, Enamel, Brass Face, Frame, Pendulum, 19th Century	550.00
Spilhaus, 24-Hour World Time Dial, Mahogany, 1964, 16 In.	505.00
Tall Case, 8-Day, Connecticut, 1815, 87 In.	9250.00
Tall Case, A. Eares, George III, Inlaid Mahogany & Oak, Birmington, c.1850, 89 In.	8500.00
Tall Case, Ashton Tideswell, Free-Standing Columns, Gilt Metal Face, 81 In.	1955.00
Tall Case, Bonnet Top, Bracket Feet, Wood Dial, Apron, Late 18th Century, 83 In.	405.00
Tall Case, Brass-Capped Fluted Columns, Oak Case, England, 1710, 84 In.	2990.00
Tall Case, Chippendale, Mahogany, Painted Season Figures, Philadelphia	10350.00
Tall Case, Chippendale, Walnut, Floral Hands, Roman & Arabic Numerals, Brass Dial	18400.00
Tall Case, Chippendale, Walnut, Satinwood Inlay, Dial Repainted, Phila., 1770s, 93 In.	3680.00
Tall Case, Colonial Revival, Walnut, Swan's-Neck Crest, Glass Door, Moon Phases	2070.00
Tall Case, Coquillage Crest, Round Metal Face, 18th Century	3737.00
Tall Case, D. Peters, Quartersawn Oak, Chamfered Corners, Gooseneck Cornice, 85 In.	2200.00
Tall Case, Delicate Flower, Exotic Bird Hand Painted On Dial, 30-Hour, 82 1/2 In.	1725.00

Tall Case, Eli Bentley, Chippendale, Calendar Dial, Central Door, Ogee Feet, 88 In. 8800.00
Tall Case, Federal, Cherry, Enameled Dial, Quarter Columns, 95 In. 7000.00
Tall Case, Federal, Mahogany Inlaid, Tombstone Glazed Door, Iron Dial, 1810, 89 In. 14950.00
Tall Case, Federal, Walnut, Painted Metal Dial, Ogee Bracket Feet, 94 In. 10925.00
Tall Case, Federal, Walnut, Painted Metal Dial, Reeded Quarter Columns, 106 1/2 In. 14950.00
Tall Case, Flared, Keyed-Tenon Construction, Porcelain Face, Arts & Crafts, 80 In. 2420.00
Tall Case, Frederick Harrison, Arched Door, Brass Face, Rolling Moon Dial, 94 3/4 In. ... 5750.00
Tall Case, French Provincial, Oak, Cascading Flowers & Leaves, Enamel Dial 2070.00
Tall Case, G. Roberts, Pine, Minute Hand, Calendar, 30-Hour Wooden Works, 80 1/2 In. . 1960.00
Tall Case, George III, Black Japanned, 4 Brass Balls, Spire Finials, 18th Century, 78 In. .. 690.00
Tall Case, George III, Mahogany, Brass Finials, Brass Dial, 8-Day Movement, 93 In. 4025.00
Tall Case, George III, Mahogany, Painted Arched Dial, Inlaid Border, 97 In. 7475.00
Tall Case, Georgian, Oak, 8-Day, Woman Portrait, 1760-1780, 83 In. 1980.00
Tall Case, Grain-Painted Poplar, Wooden Dial, 30-Hour Movement, 19th Century 3200.00
Tall Case, Hand Painted Dial, Fluted Quarter Columns, Cherry Case, Bracket Feet, 97 In. . 3795.00
Tall Case, Henschel, Chippendale Style, Mahogany Case, Glass Door, 86 In. 315.00
Tall Case, Hepplewhite, Cherry, Musical, Flat-Top Bonnet, Scenic Face, 95 1/2 In. 4400.00
Tall Case, J.S. Krause, Walnut, 30-Hour Brass Works, Fluted Quarter Columns, 89 In. ... 4400.00
Tall Case, Jacob Hostetter, Walnut, 30-Hour, Barber Pole Inlaid, 1790, 98 In. 7700.00
Tall Case, James Willshire, George II, Calendar Aperture, Silent Lever, 101 In. 5175.00
Tall Case, John Everd, William & Mary Style, Marquetry, 86 1/2 In. 2300.00
Tall Case, Junghans Works, Rococo Style Case, Porcelain, Miniature, 12 In. 172.00
Tall Case, Louis XV, Mahogany, Rectangular Case, Gilt Metal Foliate, 83 In. 2530.00
Tall Case, M. Crosby, Engraved Face, Chapter Ring, Date, Seconds Dial, Moon, 95 In. ... 7190.00
Tall Case, Mahogany, Bonnet Top, 3 Brass Finials & Rosettes, Pedestal Base, 92 In. 2090.00
Tall Case, Mahogany, Bonnet Top, Oval Beveled Glass Door, 19th Century, 87 In. 660.00
Tall Case, Mahogany, Gooseneck Pediment, Fluted Columns, Painted Face, 91 In. 1495.00
Tall Case, Mahogany, Line Inlay, Urn, Birds, Corner Columns, Brass Works, 91 In. 2015.00
Tall Case, Mahogany, Moon Dial, Calendar Wheel, Metal Dial, Brass Works, 92 3/4 In. .. 2860.00
Tall Case, Mahogany, Moses On Face, Brass Finials, Inlaid Stringing, c.1840, 97 In. 2860.00
Tall Case, Mahogany, Pierced Fret Crown, Brass Columns, Arched, Beveled Door, 94 In. . 5060.00
Tall Case, Mahogany, Swan's-Neck Pediment, Brass Rosettes, Bracket Feet, 91 In. 2185.00
Tall Case, Mahogany, Urn Finials, Arched Pediment, Dome Door, 1800s, 93 In. 1430.00
Tall Case, Marquetry, 8-Day, Weight Driven, Moon Dial, Calendar, Holland, 1600s 14950.00
Tall Case, Meslin, Painted Flower & Leaf Design, Bombay Style Waist, 81 1/2 In. 2128.00
Tall Case, Nicolas Magnus, Carved Case, Raised Panels, Barley Sugar Twists, 90 1/2 In. . 1150.00
Tall Case, Oak, 30-Hour, Waist Door, Bracket Feet, 1770, 80 In. 815.00
Tall Case, Oak, Gilt Rooster Over Enamel Face, Scrolled, Beveled Door, 1700s, 84 In. ... 2200.00
Tall Case, Oak, Swan's-Neck Pediment Hood, Roman Numerals, Bracket Feet, 90 In. 2070.00
Tall Case, Original Copper Strap Hardware, Original Finish, Arts & Crafts, 76 In. 1650.00
Tall Case, Pine, Round Enamel Face, Foliage, Black Grapes, Continental, 89 In. 1380.00
Tall Case, Pine, Swan's-Neck Crest, White Wooden Dial, 1776 .... 12650.00
Tall Case, Poplar & Pine, 3 Finials, Arched Door, Lamb's-Tongue Molding, 1815, 94 In. . 3737.00
Tall Case, R. Whiting, Pillar & Scroll Top, Painted Clock Face, 90 In. 2530.00
Tall Case, Renaissance Revival, Walnut, Weights, Carved Faces, Germany, 1900, 79 In. .. 1955.00
Tall Case, Riley Whiting, Scrolled Fretwork, Brass Finials, Wooden Works, 87 In. 1150.00
Tall Case, River & Boat Sailing, Village Ground, Enamel Dial, Silver, 10 In. 460.00
Tall Case, S. Hoadley, Flat Cornice, Tombstone Panel, Wooden Dial, c.1820, 84 In. 2185.00
Tall Case, S. Willard, Federal, Mahogany Inlaid, Arched Cornice, Iron Dial, 89 In. 42550.00
Tall Case, Samuel Mulliken, Mahogany, Reeded Corner Columns, Glass Door, 90 In. 7475.00
Tall Case, Sheraton, Exotic Wood Veneer, Broken Arch Pediment, Brass Works, 97 In. ... 3300.00
Tall Case, Silvered Chapter Ring, Brass Spandrels, Miniature, 18 3/4 In. 1035.00
Tall Case, Straus Farringdon, Fox Hunting Scene, Inlaid Bird On Branch, 86 In. 2530.00
Tall Case, Thomas Read, Mahogany, Painted Moon & Globe, 18th Century, 86 In. 5225.00
Tall Case, Thomas Voight, Chippendale Style, Mahogany, Philadelphia, 94 In. 2300.00
Tall Case, Walnut, Bonnet Top, Brass Works, Weights & Pendulum, 19th Century, 85 In. . 440.00
Tall Case, Walter Burfee, Edwardian, Mahogany, Westminster Chime, Glass Door, 95 In. . 11500.00
Tall Case, Waltham, 9 Tubes, 3 Weights, 96 In. 8580.00
Tall Case, William & Phineas Quimby, Mahogany, Eagle Finial, Belfast, Maine, 95 In. ... 7475.00
Tall Case, William Maus, Cove Molding Between Sections, 1810, 90 In. 4950.00
Tall Case, William Young, Mahogany, Painted Pictorial Dial, 8-Day, 82 In. 4600.00
Teague, Walter Dorwin, Rectangular Glass Face, Metal Base, 1940, 7 In. 345.00
Terry, Eli & Sons, Pillar & Scroll Design, Stenciled Face, 30 In. 1065.00

Terry, Eli, Junior, Shelf, 8-Day, Wooden Works, Eagle Crest, Claw Feet, 37 x 18 In. 485.00
Terry, Eli, Pillar & Scroll, Mahogany Case, Eglomise Panel, 28 1/2 In. 1325.00
Terry, Eli, Pillar & Scroll, Wooden Works & Weights, Reverse Glass, 31 1/4 In. 1925.00
Terry, Eli, Pillar & Scroll, Wooden Works, Eglomise Panel, 31 In. 1375.00
Terry, Eli, Shelf, Mahogany Veneer, Wooden Works, Weights, Pendulum, 30 3/4 In. 137.00
Tiffany clocks are listed in the Tiffany category.
Tole, Brass Works, Key, France, 14 1/2 In. 220.00
Toyo, Wall, Brass, 8-Day Time & Strike, Wooden Bezel, Round 85.00
Urania, Year, Glass Dome, Germany, c.1910, 12 In. 165.00
Wag-On-Wall, Brass Works, Porcelain Face, Wooden Case, Miniature, 7 1/2 In. 110.00
Wag-On-Wall, Brass, Polychrome, Continental, 55 In. 315.00
Wag-On-Wall, Case, Floral Design, Brass, Wooden Face, 13 1/4 In. 170.00
Wall, Brass & Mother-Of-Pearl Inlay, Raised Enameled Chapters, 1860, 18 1/2 In. 300.00
Wall, Carved Oak, Rectangular Case, Round Steel Dial, Roman Numerals, 27 In. 172.00
Wall, French Ebonized, Tole Paint, Marble Dial, Roman Numerals, 22 3/4 x 19 In. 546.00
Wall, George I, Octagonal Molded Face, Arabic & Roman Numerals, Leaf Design, 68 In. .. 6900.00
Wall, Gilt Metal, Horse's Head, Leaf & Acorn Garlands, Round Inset Dial 600.00
Wall, Giltwood, Carved Ribbon, Garland Crest, Round Face, 37 In. 1265.00
Wall, Giltwood, Shadowbox Frame, Continental, Mid-19th Century 460.00
Wall, Louis XVI, Giltwood, Round Clock Face, Sunburst Border, 40 x 15 In. 3220.00
Wall, Mahogany, Swan's-Neck Pediment, Round Dial, Austria, 35 1/2 In. 275.00
Wall, Sheet Iron Case, Steel & Brass Works, Enamel Dial, France, 15 x 10 In. 165.00
Wall, Walnut, Brass & Porcelain Dial, 3-Finialed Crest, Germany, 37 x 12 1/2 In. 375.00
Wall, Walnut, Glass Front Door, Steeple Top, Key, Germany, 28 1/2 x 11 In. 460.00
Wall, Walnut, Porcelain, Brass, Glass Front, Carved Crest, Finials, Germany, 40 x 11 In. .. 460.00
Walnut, Bead, Reel Cornice, Fluted Columns, White Enamel Dial, Brass, 43 1/2 In. 545.00
Walnut, Celestial, Victorian, Swan's-Neck Pediment, Calendar Aperture, 1860, 27 In. 5175.00
Waterbury, Carriage, Brass Case, Beveled Glass, 3 In. 155.00
Waterbury, Gallery, Step-Down Case, Oak, Round, 26 In. 1000.00
Waterbury, Mahogany, Dome Top, 8-Day Quarter Hour Westminster Chime, 16 In. 195.00
Waterbury, Mantel, Mahogany Veneer, Painted Ship Scene On Reverse, 8-Day, 19 In. ... 165.00
Waterbury, Mantel, Rosewood Veneer, Alarm Dial, 19th Century, 14 In. 132.00
Waterbury, Rosewood, 8-Day Time & Strike, Painted Metal Dial, Eglomise 220.00
Waterbury, Walnut, Kitchen, Cutout Crest, 8-Day Time, Strike & Alarm, Pendulum 145.00
Webster, W., Arch Bracket, Carrying Handle, Brass Face, Strike, Repeat, 1735, 20 In. ... 3560.00
Wehrle, Daniel, Steeple, Mahogany Veneer, Brass Works & Pendulum, 19 3/4 In. 412.00
Welby, Tambour, Mahogany, Silvered Dial, 8-Day, Westminster Chime 50.00
Welch, E.M., Mantel, Elsa, Walnut, Cast Pendulum, 8-Day, Alarm, 21 x 5 x 13 In. 168.00
Welch, E.N., Shelf, Rosewood, Forestville, 8-Day Time & Strike, Frosted Panel 220.00
Welch, Shelf, Mahogany, Time & Strike, 30-Hour, Gilt Hourglass Door, 1870, 26 In. 150.00
Welch, Steeple, Rosewood Veneer Case, Courthouse Transfer, St. Louis, 19 1/2 In. 160.00
Welch Spring & Co., Shelf, Reverse Painted Nosegay, Black Bottom Door Panel, 16 In. .. 230.00
Welch Spring & Co., Shelf, Rosewood Veneer, Ebonized Trim, Brass Works, 13 5/8 In. .. 165.00
Willard, Simon, Shelf, Brass Bale Handle, Brass Acorn Finials, c.1800, 22 1/2 In. 3162.00
William Orion & Co., Shelf, Empire, Mahogany Veneer, Stencil, 32 In. 330.00

CLOISONNE enamel was developed during the tenth century. A glass
enamel was applied between small ribbons of metal on a metal base.
Most cloisonne is Chinese or Japanese. Pieces marked *China* are twentieth-century examples.

Basket, Cover, Brass Wire Mount, Round, France, 19th Century, 7 3/4 In. 690.00
Bowl, Multicolored Flowers, Gold Clouds, Black Ground, Blue Interior, 4 x 1 3/4 In. 45.00
Box, Allover Multicolored 5-Claw Dragon Design, Black Ground, 2 3/8 x 6 In. 46.00
Box, Allover Multicolored Dragon Design, Black Ground, Round, 4 3/4 In. 46.00
Box, Allover Multicolored Floral Design, Black Ground, 6 In. 34.00
Box, Allover Multicolored Floral Design, Yellow Ground, 5 1/2 In. 57.00
Box, Allover Multicolored Foliate Design, Black Ground, 4 1/2 In. 57.00
Cache Pot, Chrysanthemums, Lilies, Birds, Turquoise Ground, 8 x 14 In., Pair 545.00
Centerpiece, Gilt Bronze Mounted, Lion & Eagle Swags, 19th Century 4190.00
Charger, Birds, Flowers, Blue, 12 In. 315.00
Dish, Bird & Foliate Design, 12 In. 53.00
Ewer, Cover, Allover Lotus, Crouched Dragon Handles, Sky Blue, 15 In., Pair 1725.00
Figurine, Parrot, Green, Yellow, Carved Wood Base, 11 1/2 In., Pair 575.00

Ginger Jar, Cover, Allover Precious Objects Design, Turquoise, 10 In., Pair 260.00
Ginger Jar, Cover, Floral On Maroon Ground, 6 In. 115.00
Ginger Jar, Floral Design, 5 1/4 In. 44.00
Ginger Jar, Floral, Brick Red, Wooden Plinth, China, 5 In., Pair 130.00
Ginger Jar, Multicolored Dragon Design, Black Ground, 4 x 5 In. 69.00
Jar, Cover, Flowering Dogwoods, Butterflies, Blue Ground, 6 1/2 In., Pair 172.00
Jar, Dragon, Green, White, Red Ground, Blue Interior, 45 3/4 In. 1650.00
Jar, Dragons & Floral, White Ground, Wooden Stand, China, 8 1/4 In., Pair 770.00
Planter, Allover Multicolored Floral Design, Cartouche Shape, 6 3/4 x 8 5/8 In. 85.00
Plate, Flower Basket, Birds, Lotus Design On Other Plate, Blue Ground, 12 In., Pair 201.00
Salt & Pepper, Floral, Black 125.00
Snuff Bottle, Allover Bird & Foliage, Multicolored, Conforming Stopper, 4 In. 70.00
Snuff Bottle, Dragon On Front, Phoenix On Back, Metal Neck Rim, 1900, 2 1/8 In. 750.00
Tazza, Black, Brown & White Flowers, China, 19th Century, 7 x 7 In. 172.00
Teapot, Polychrome Lotus, Gilt Brass Handle, Turquoise Ground, 19th Century 920.00
Teapot, Varicolored Floral, Butterfly, Early 1900s, 3 In. 50.00
Tray, Bamboo Design, Central Panel Of Pavilions, Cranes, Lotus, 18 x 10 In. 1495.00
Tray, Birds In Flight, 19th Century, 15 In. 115.00
Tray, Pin, Butterfly & Flower, Blue Ground, 6 In. 60.00
Vase, Allover Black, 6 Sides, 4 3/4 In. 125.00
Vase, Allover Butterflies, Foliage & Fruit, Blue Ground, 12 1/4 In., Pair 115.00
Vase, Alternating Dragon & Peacock Panels, Meiji Period, 12 In., Pair 1380.00
Vase, Baluster, Bronze, Early 19th Century, 13 In. 1050.00
Vase, Bird & Flower, Midnight Blue Ground, Hexagonal, 9 1/2 In., Pair 665.00
Vase, Brass, Floral Design, 10 In. 100.00
Vase, Butterflies Amidst Peonies, Floral Design, 12 1/4 x 6 1/2 In., Pair 242.00
Vase, Cover, Double Gourd, Scrolled Crane Cartouche, 11 In., Pair 230.00
Vase, Crane & Colorful Lotus, Black Ground, Transparent, 5 1/8 In. 150.00
Vase, Cranes & Flowers, Blue Ground, 12 In. 180.00
Vase, Crow, Bamboo, With Seal, Cylindrical, 17 5/8 In. 12650.00
Vase, Dragon, Spiraling Around Body, Turquoise, 25 In., Pair 1495.00
Vase, Floral Design, Baluster, Early 20th Century, 21 1/2 In., Pair 632.00
Vase, Floral Design, Light Blue Ground, Enamel, 16 In. 80.00
Vase, Floral, 12 In. 275.00
Vase, Multicolored Floral Design, 10 In., Pair 180.00
Vase, Open White Flowers, Pink Buds, Leaves, Butterflies, Red Ground, 5 In. 65.00
Vase, Pair Of Egrets Among Water Lilies, Blue Ground, Japan, 6 1/2 In. 175.00
Vase, Palace, Peacock & Flower Design, Blue Ground, Mejii Period, 28 In. 905.00
Vase, Prunus Blossom Sprays, Bamboo Shoots, Green Ground, 6 In. 40.00
Vase, Roses, Pink & White Roses, Leaves, Red Foil Ground, Suzuki Mark, 7 1/2 In. 495.00
Vase, Scrolled Dragon, Bird Design, Multicolored Ground, Enamel, 9 5/8 In. 425.00
Vase, Sun, Crane, Hill Design, Japan, 12 In. 201.00

CLOTHING of all types is listed in this category. Dresses, hats, shoes, underwear, and more are found here. Other textiles are to be found in the Coverlet, Movie, Quilt, Textile, and World War I and II categories.

Apron, Child's, Pink, Lace & Silk Ribbons, 24 x 14 In. 68.00
Apron, Cook-Out, Snoopy Sitting On Hamburgers 28.00
Bandanna, Cotton, Red, Lee Work Clothes, White Factory Pictured, 1950s, 21 x 23 In. .. 110.00
Bandanna, Western, Red Cotton, Cowboy Hats, Horseshoes, Lariats, Boots, 20 In. 35.00
Belt, Beaded, Leather Back, 28 x 1 3/4 In. 85.00
Belt, Dress Sword, U.S. Navy Officer 93.00
Belt, Lebatt's Canada, 50 Years Of Brewing, Leather, 36 In. 27.00
Belt, Pink Suede, Box, Hickock, 1950s, Men's, Size 36 .... 22.00
Belt, Police, Dress, Brown Leather, Silver Toned Brass Buckle, Late 19th Century 85.00
Belt Buckle, 1910 .... 118.00
Belt Buckle, Woody Woodpecker, Brass, Plastic, Walter Lantz Prod., 1963, 2 3/4 In. 20.00
Bib, Baby's, Embroidered, 1930s 25.00
Bonnet, Homespun, Eyelet, New England, c.1810 .... 195.00
Bonnet, Mourning, Silk 38.00
Boots, Cavalry Officer, Pre-World War II 75.00
Boots, Combat, Black Leather, Toe Caps, BF Goodrich Heels, Box, Size 9 .... 45.00

Boots, Cowboy, Brown Leather, White Stitching, Tony Lama, 1960s, Size 11 1/2 A 20.00
Boots, Cowboy, Brown, Cutout Western Design, Poll Parrot, 1940-1960, Size 4 1/2 . . . . . 80.00
Boots, Cowboy, Brown, Leather, Box, 1950s 85.00
Boots, Cowboy, Child's, Russet Leather, Scroll & Pistol Design, 1940s, Size 8 . . . . 25.00
Boots, Rattlesnake, Brown Leather Tops, Tony Lama, Box, Size 9 1/2 D 70.00
Boots, Sport, Brown Leather, Calf Height, Irish Setter, Red Wing, Size 11 1/2 E 80.00
Boots, Sport, Brown Leather, Vibram Soles, Irish Setter, Red Wing, Box, Size 8 1/2 E . . . 300.00
Cap, Chauffeur's, Embossed 1915 Touring Car On Front, Leather & Tin 450.00
Cape, Silk, Green With Ivory Lining, c.1790 . . . . 495.00
Cape Coat, Movie Starlet Style, Tan, Brown Wiggly Design, 1940s, Medium 35.00
Capelet, Beaded, Long Bead Fringe, Victorian 75.00
Chaps, Play, Child's, Suede, Cowboy Silhouettes, 1940s, 22 x 15 In. 50.00
Chaps, Rodeo Cowboy's, Red Leather, Wide Brown Waist Belt, 1940-1960 . . . . 150.00
Coat, Bearskin, Black, Quilted Lining, Knot Button Fasteners, c.1900, Large 200.00
Coat, Car, Wool, Tan, Satin Lining, Pendleton, Size 42 . . . . 25.00
Coat, Chore, Denim, Blanket Lined, 4 Pockets, Button Front, Wrangler, Size 40 . . . . 35.00
Coat, Chore, Denim, Blanket Lined, Tan Corduroy Trim, Big Smith, Size 40 . . . . 130.00
Coat, Chore, Denim, White & Blue Stripes, Brass Buttons, OshKosh B'gosh, Large 95.00
Coat, Cotton, 1910 . . . . 55.00
Coat, Ermine, White, White Fox Collar, Silk Lining, Full Length, 1930s 1500.00
Coat, Evening, Black & Pink, Schiaparelli 515.00
Coat, Hunter's, Wool, Plaid, Red, Black, Button Front, Montgomery Ward, Large 40.00
Coat, Khaki Twill, Army Service 21.00
Coat, Lab, Gary Herringbone, Blue Trim, Detroit Overall Co., 1950s, Size 36 . . . . 35.00
Coat, Leather, Cowhide, Tan, Snap Front, 2 Pockets, Women's Size 14 . . . . 27.00
Coat, Rain, Detachable Hood, Metal Studs, White Courreges Lining 575.00
Coat, Tail, Formal, Black Wool, Vermont, 1911, Size 38 . . . . 50.00
Coat, Tiger Print, 1966, Size 9 . . . . 95.00
Coat, Velvet, Brown, Fur Trim On Sleeves, Brown Silk Lining, Franklin Simon, 1920s . . . 235.00
Coat, Winter, Corduroy, Black, Brown Plush Lining, Double Breasted, Large 75.00
Coat, Winter, Golden Suede, Fleece Lined, 2 Pockets, Berman Buckskin Co., Size 38 . . . . 65.00
Coat, Winter, Tan Suede, Fleece Lining, 2 Pockets, Button Front, Berman's, Size 40 . . . . . 100.00
Collar, Irish Lace 10.00
Cuff Set, Cowboy's, Brown Leather, Tooled Design, Lace Closure, Brass Stud, 6 In. 65.00
Dress, Battenberg Lace, Child's, c.1875, 23 In. 165.00
Dress, Beaded, Balenciaga, 1950s 1150.00
Dress, Campbell's Soup, Paper, Inspired By Andy Warhol 1840.00
Dress, Chemise, Pink Linen, Jeweled Neck, Christian Dior, 1950, Size 10 . . . . 210.00
Dress, Christening, White Lawn, Tucking, Applied Lace, 1800s, 36 In. 195.00
Dress, Christening, Tucked & Embroidered, 3 Piece 110.00
Dress, Cocktail, Black Lace Over Nude Silk Bodice, 1950s, Mainbocher, Size 12 . . . . 500.00
Dress, Cocktail, Black Satin, Schiaparelli, c.1940 . . . . 460.00
Dress, Cocktail, Black Taffeta, Hubert De Givenchy, 1950s . . . . .4312.00 to 4400.00
Dress, Cocktail, Blue, With Stole, Pauline Trigere, 1940s 1265.00
Dress, Cocktail, Velvet, Schiaparelli 630.00
Dress, Cotton, Black, White Polka Dots, Sleeveless, Pockets, Side Zipper, 1950s, Small . . 26.00
Dress, Cotton, Paisley & Floral, 1960s 898.00
Dress, Evening, Blue Pleated Silk, Tan, Black Stripe Beads, Gold Leaf Belt, Delphos 1495.00
Dress, Evening, Chanel, 1930s 1265.00
Dress, Evening, Chiffon, Peach, Callot Soeurs, 1905 . . . . 1700.00
Dress, Evening, Jacqueline, 1980s 8625.00
Dress, Evening, Strapless, Balmain, c.1960, Size 4 . . . . 977.00
Dress, Evening, Strapless, Ecru Silk, Beaded & Embroidered, Jean Dresses 220.00
Dress, Gold & Brown Silk, Empire Waist, Long Sleeves, 19th Century 220.00
Dress, Gold Silk & Bronze Satin, Bustle, 1880s 798.00
Dress, Green & Brown Plaid, c.1860, Child's 105.00
Dress, Ivory Silk, Lace Collar, Chiffon Flounces At Sleeves, Gathered Skirt, 2 Piece 155.00
Dress, Mourning, Cotton, Civil War Era 225.00
Dress, Sheath, Sequined, Hattie Carnegie, 1940s 977.00
Dress, Shirtwaist, Black Faille, Velvet Collar, Rhinestone Buttons, By Adrian, 1940s 2550.00
Dress, Short Sleeve, Cotton, Stripe, Square Neckline, Zipper Front, 1970s, Size 40 . . . . . . 175.00
Dress, Silk, Blue, Velvet Trim, 2 Piece, Victorian 595.00

Dress, Wedding, Chantilly Lace, Graduating Rows, Spaghetti Straps, Jacket, Train, 1939 .   375.00
Dress, Wedding, Nylon, Empire Waist, Short Sleeves, Lace Appliques, 1960s, Size 10 . . .   50.00
Dress, Wedding, Nylon, Rows Of Lace, Long Sleeve, Full Skirt, 1950s, Size 10 . . . .   120.00
Dress, Wedding, Silk Brocade, Mid-19th Century 485.00
Dungarees, Boss Of The Road, Denim, Zipper Fly, Tags, Lee, Size 42 x 32 . . . .   40.00
Dungarees, Denim, Plaid Flannel Lining, Zipper Fly, Tags, Maverick, Size 30 x 30 . . . . . .   65.00
Flight Helmet, Brown Leather, Eaglet, Metal Goggles, Fur Trim, 1920s 70.00
Gloves, Fur, Leather, Green Corduroy Lining, U.S. Frontier Period 35.00
Hat, Royal Canadian Mounted Police, Stetson, Tan & Brown Felt, 1960s, Size 6 3/4 . . . . .   85.00
Hat, Sombrero, Straw, Horseshoes, Sequins, Leather Applique, Mexico, 1950s, 22 In. . . .   20.00
Hat, Veterans Cab, Blue, Black Patent Leather Visor, Brass Letters, 1950s 58.00
Jacket, Air Jordan, Nylon, Black, Blue Accents, Winged Basketball, Nike, Child's XL . . .   30.00
Jacket, Chicago Special Police Duty, Black Nylon, Quilted Lining, Gerber, Size 46 . . . . .   55.00
Jacket, Cowboy, Denim, Pleated Front, Zipper, Wrangler, 3rd Model, 1960s, Size 36 . . . .   160.00
Jacket, Denim, 2 Pockets, Red Tab, Levi, Small E, 1970s, Size 36 . . . .   60.00
Jacket, Denim, Blanket Lined, Pleated Front, Copper Buttons, Child's Size 8 . . . .   80.00
Jacket, Denim, Blue Bell, Wrangler 103.00
Jacket, Denim, Pleated Front, Pocket, Foremost, JCPenney, 1940-1960, Medium 125.00
Jacket, Denim, Pleated Front, Talon Zipper, 4 Pockets, Wrangler, Size 38 . . . .   100.00
Jacket, Denim, Roebuck's Sanforized 31.00
Jacket, Denim, Stormrider 101-LJ, Blanket Lined, Tan Corduroy Collar, Lee, 1950s 150.00
Jacket, Evening, Woman's, Persian Lamb, Art Deco Buttons 250.00
Jacket, Farm, OshKosh B'gosh, Size 8 . . . .   20.00
Jacket, Flight Style, Suede, Olive Drab, Knit Collar, Cuffs, Zipper, 1940s, Size 46 . . . . . .   55.00
Jacket, Gabardine, Black, Germany, Jansen, 1930s, Woman's, Size Medium 40.00
Jacket, Gabardine, Blue, Rhinestone Accents, Single Breasted, 1940s, Small 20.00
Jacket, Letter, Brown Wool, Orange Leather Sleeves, Snap Front, Reed Sportswear, 38 . . .   160.00
Jacket, Letter, Orange Wool, White Leather Sleeves, Chenille Logo, 1980s 70.00
Jacket, Mink, Off-White, Dark Brown Accents, Bruno & Joseph Furs, Chicago 315.00
Jacket, Police, New Haven, Conn., Cloth, Black, Brass Buttons, Velcro, Size 34 . . . .   50.00
Jacket, Silk Brocade, Swirling Plume Pattern, Hot Pink Lining, Scaasi, 1960s 180.00
Jacket, Stadium, Blue Wool, Blue & Yellow Trim, Snap Front, 1960s, Size 38 . . . .   55.00
Jacket, Suede, Black Leather, Fringe, Flannel Lining, Canada, 1970s, Size 34 . . . .   55.00
Jacket, Ted Williams, Quilted, Nylon, Brown, Talon Zipper, Sears, XL 30.00
Jacket, Tour, Reversible, Black Velvet, Silk Dragons, White Satin, Tigers, Japan, 1950s . .   405.00
Jacket, University Of Notre Dame, Fighting Irish, Blue Wool, Leather Sleeves, Size 36 . .   50.00
Jacket, Warm-Up, Nylon, Orange, White Flannel Lining, Artex, Men's, Size Small 30.00
Jacket, Windbreaker, McDonald's Restaurant Employee, Nylon, Red, Pla-Jac, Medium . .   45.00
Jacket, Wool, Beige, Gray Accents, Plastic Buttons, Natalie Green, 1940s, Small 35.00
Jacket & Skirt, Silk, Flowers & Figures, Embroidered, China 385.00
Jeans, 501, Black Stitching, Button Fly, Levi's, Akamimi, Small E, Size 30 x 29 . . . .   45.00
Jeans, 501, Button Fly, Copper Rivets, Levi's, Akamimi, Small E, Size 29 x 34 . . . .   210.00
Jeans, 501, Dark Blue, Chopped Off At Ankles, Big E Levi's, Size 30 x 34 In. 98.00
Jeans, 501, Redline Jeans, Levi's 41.00
Jeans, 505, Levi's, Indigo Denim, Big E 67.00
Jeans, Denim, Dee Cee, Flare Leg, Zipper Fly, Tags, Washington, Size 29 x 34 . . . .   45.00
Jeans, Denim, Indigo, Dead Stock, Lee's Riders . . . . .26.00 to 30.00
Jeans, Denim, Indigo, Dead Stock, Western Pants, Lee's Riders 180.00
Jeans, Denim, Levi's, Big E 55.00
Jeans, Vintage Wrangler, 1960s . . . . .42.00 to 66.00
Jeans, Levi's, Flannel Lined, Zipper, Leather XX Tag, 1960s 85.00
Kimono, Black Crepe, Hand Embroidered Back & Front, 1930s 45.00
Kimono, Wedding, Embroidered Hand Driven Coach, Red Silk Lined, 37 1/2 In. 125.00
Kimono, Wedding, Gold Silk Brocade, Lattice Design 330.00
Kimono, Wedding, Silk, Embroidered Phoenix, Flowers, Gold Shades, White Ground 352.00
Overalls, Bib, Denim, Wrench Pocket, Hammer Loop, Tag, Lee R.M.R., Size 32 x 32 . . . .   50.00
Overalls, Blue & White Stripes, Union Made, Sanforized, Man's, Medium Size 98.00
Overcoat, Quilted, Light Gray, Zipper & Button Front, McGregor, Size 42 . . . .   30.00
Pants, Work, Dark Olive Drab, Sanforized, Tags, Washington Dee Cee, Size 40 x 34 . . . .   20.00
Petticoat, Blue & Brown, Original Suspenders 325.00
Petticoat, Quilted, Brown & Gray, c.1820 . . . .   285.00
Robe, Pink Silk, Blue Thread, Blossoming Tree, Grass & Figures, Japan, Woman's 70.00

Robe, Silk, Blue, Embroidered Floral Sprays & Clouds, Figures, Floral Trim 230.00
Robe, Silk, Dark Blue, Dragons, Gold Buttons, China, 19th Century, Man's, 64 In. 800.00
Robe, Silk, Red, Hand Embroidered Gold Butterflies, c.1880, Size Medium 330.00
Robe, Silk, Wine Red, Embroidered, 9-Dragon Clouds 660.00
Scarf, Black Ground, Gold, Raspberry & Cobalt Blue Design, Hermes, 34 In. 175.00
Scarf, Charmeuse, Leopard Print, Black, Brown Spots, Yves St. Laurent, 84 x 45 In. 230.00
Scarf, Charmeuse, Pink Pearl, Yellow Chain, Navy Background, Bottega Veneta 115.00
Scarf, Hot Pink Ground, Multicolored Floral Design, Gucci, 35 In. 60.00
Scarf, Knit, Red, Green & Yellow, Diamond & x Design, Ralph Lauren, 10 x 52 In. 20.00
Scarf, Saffron Yellow, Rose, Grape, Black, Trellis Check Design, Missoni 200.00
Scarf, Silk & Cashmere, Horses, Colored Stripes, Fringed, Hermes, 72 x 17 In. 230.00
Scarf, Silk Twill, Costumed Figure On Horse Within Red, White Square, Hermes 200.00
Scarf, Silk Twill, Floral, Pale Purple, White, Blue, Green Leaf Design, Hermes 201.00
Scarf, Silk Twill, Gold Coat Of Arms, Tassel, Pale Blue, White Ground, Hermes 144.00
Scarf, Silk Twill, Gold, White Perfume Bottles Against Black Ground, Hermes 144.00
Scarf, Silk Twill, Stylized Garden Scene, Lavender, Yellow, Pink, Fuchsia, Hermes 316.00
Scarf, Silk, Circle-In-A-Square Design, Pale Blue Ground, Fringe, Vasarely, 1969 .... 230.00
Scarf, Silk, Orange, Yellow, Green Floral, Pale Lavender, 1970 .... 85.00
Scarf, Silk, Paisley, Purple Center, Royal Blue, Turquoise, Red, Etro, 54 x 54 In. 201.00
Shako, West Point, The Cadet Store, West Point Label, c.1870, Size 7 1/8 In. 320.00
Shawl, Kashmir, Late 19th Century, 127 x 58 In. 345.00
Shawl, Paisley, Black Center, 68 x 69 In. 165.00
Shawl, Paisley, Grandma Johnston's, Black, Fringe Loss, 1840, 140 x 64 In. 135.00
Shawl, Paisley, Machine Woven, 72 x 72 In. 247.00
Shawl, Paisley, Sarah Johnston Allan, 1876, 70 x 68 In. 275.00
Shawl, Scottish Paisley, Green & Red, c.1850, 130 In. 275.00
Shawl, Silk, Bird & Flower, Red Ground, Needlework, China, 19th Century 175.00
Shirt, Black, Copper, Gold & Silver Accents, Gooden Snow Mount, Japan, Medium 25.00
Shirt, Blue Chambray, Long Sleeves, 2 Pockets, Four Kings, Tags, Boys, Size 13 .... 25.00
Shirt, Bowling, Blue Cotton, Goodyear Racing Division, Short Sleeve, Hilton, Large 40.00
Shirt, Bowling, Mint Green, Pasco Mortuary, Short Sleeves, Hilton, Size XL 45.00
Shirt, Chambray, Blue, Lavender Pearlescent Snaps, Big Smith, Size 38 .... 45.00
Shirt, Cowboy, Gray Plaid, Pearlized Snap Front, 2 Pockets, Roebucks, Medium 35.00
Shirt, Denim, Wrangler's, Blue Bell, Size 9 .... 252.00
Shirt, Gabardine, Beige, Silver Check Pattern, 2 Pockets, Campus, Men's, Medium 20.00
Shirt, Gabardine, Dark Blue, Mother-Of-Pearl Buttons, Riviera, 1940s 35.00
Shirt, Hawaiian, Rayon, Blue, Pineapples & Branches, Size XL 20.00
Shirt, Hawaiian, Rayon, Purple, Japanese Drums, Symbols, Coconut Buttons, 1950s 125.00
Shirt, Pullover, Light Brown, Talon Zipper, Gibralter, 1940s, Size 48-50 .... 40.00
Shirt, Wool, Plaid, Brown, Black, White, Pendleton, Medium 25.00
Shirt, Wool, Plaid, Red, Blue, Tan, 2 Pockets, Pendleton, Size XL 25.00
Shirt, Work, Black Twill, Big Yank Flyer, Size 14 1/2 .... 250.00
Shoes, Child's, Pied Piper, Brown Oxford, Size 10 1/2 B, Box, 8 3/4 x 4 3/4 In. ..... *Illus* 55.00
Shoes, Slip On, Beavees, Light Blue Canvas, Crepe Sole, B.F. Goodrich, Size 7 1/2 ..... 35.00
Shoes, Sport, Air Jordan Shoes, Nike, Size 8 .... 43.00

You may be able to rejuvenate dirty suede or cloth shoes with a light sanding with 000 sandpaper. Then rub with a cloth dampened with vinegar.

Clothing, Shoes, Child's, Pied Piper, Brown Oxford,
Size 10 1/2 B, Box, 8 3/4 x 4 3/4 In.

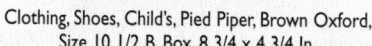

Shoes, Sport, All-Star, Black Canvas, White Rubber Soles, Box, Converse, Size 6 1/2 .... 47.00
Shoes, Sport, Basket, Oxford, White Leather, Yugoslavia, Puma, Box, Size 9 .... 100.00
Shoes, Sport, Basketball, High Top, Leather, Blue Swoosh, Box, Nike, Infant, Size 3 .... 70.00
Shoes, Sport, High Top Shoes, Nike, Size 8 ....24.00 to 40.00
Shoes, Sport, High Top, Air Jordan Shoes, First Edition, Nike, 1985, Size 8 .... 356.00
Shoes, Sport, High Top, Purple Canvas, Silver Swoosh, Nike, 1984, Size 10 .... 145.00
Shoes, Sport, High Top, University Of Oregon, Nike, 1984, Size 9 .... 300.00
Shoes, Sport, Lace-Up, Green Wool, Leather Soles, 1860s, 10 1/2 In. 345.00
Shoes, Sport, Leather, 6 Buttons, Child's, 6 In. 38.00
Shoes, Sport, Running Shoes, Nike, Size 7 .... 22.00
Shoes, Sport, Valkyrie, Nylon, Coral, Tan Swoosh, Waffle Soles, Nike, Size 8 1/2 ...... 35.00
Shoes, Woman's, Art Deco Design, Leather, High Heels, 11 In. 27.00
Shoes, Woman's, High Top, Leather, Black, Upper Laces, 1910, 10 In. 60.00
Shoes, Woman's, Lace Up, Leather, 1910, 8 In. 45.00
Shoes, Woman's, Victorian, Leather, Black, Upper Laces, 13 In. 70.00
Shoes, Work, Oxford, Brown Leather, Cord Heels & Soles, Size 8 1/2 .... 30.00
Slippers, Moccasins, Child's, Yogi Bear, Brown Vinyl, Fake Fur, Box, Early 1960s 45.00
Spats, Pair 12.00
Stockings, Crewel Work Embroidery, 1830s 225.00
Stockings, Infants, Knit, 19th Century, Pair 125.00
Suit, Amish, Black Twill, Jacket & Vest, Hooks & Eyes, Suspender Buttons On Pants 180.00
Suit, Blue Wool Blend, Double Breasted Jacket, Zipper Fly Trousers, Kensington 20.00
Suit, Pant, Knit, Hyperbole, White Zip, Enamel, Navy Blue, 1973 .... 460.00
Suit, Scottish, Child's, Green Plaid Skirt, Velvet Jacket, Vest & Hat, Size 8-Year 185.00
Suit, Tweed, Silk, 2-Tone Lavender, Goldtone Lion Buttons, 1960s 865.00
Suit, Wool Knit, Mink Collar & Cuffs, Brown, Holland, 1940s, 3 Piece 48.00
Sweater, Brown Wool, Green Accents, Taffeta Lined, Zipper, Large 70.00
Sweater, Knockabouts, Wool, Off-White, Blue, Red Geometric, Pendleton, 1940-1960 ... 70.00
Sweater, Pink Cashmere, White Chenille Poodles, Cat-Shaped Buttons, Small 32.00
Sweatshirt, California Raisins 10.00
Sweatshirt, Cotton, Gray, V-Neck, 1950s, Medium-Large 180.00
Sweatshirt, Hooded, Navy, Cream, Orange Swoosh On Label, Tags, Nike, Medium 60.00
Sweatshirt, U.S. Army Physical Training, Hooded, Light Gray, Talon Zipper, Small 25.00
Swim Suit, Topless, 1967, Rudi Gernreich, For Harmon Knitware 2875.00
Tuxedo, Cummerbund, Brooks Brothers, Size 46 .... 60.00
Uniform, 5th Marines, 2nd Division, Liberty Loan Patch 519.00
Uniform, Delivery Man, Gabardine, Cornflower Blue, Coat, Trousers, Tags, Size 34 ..... 20.00
Uniform, Dress, Red Cross Service, Light Blue Pinafore, White Shirt, 1940s, Size 36 .... 35.00
Uniform, Pre-World War II ROTC Cadet 57.00
Uniform, Royal Canadian Mounted Police, Wool Blouse, Hat, Belt, Boots, 1960s 385.00
Uniform, Station Master's, Kansas City Soughter Lines, Gray Wool, 1960 .... 175.00
Vest, Child's, Blue, Green & Orange Beaded, Yellow Wool 550.00
Waistcoat, Boy's, Cloth Covered Buttons, Yellow & Red Pattern, Small 795.00
Waistcoat, French Silk & Linen, 1760 .... 2200.00
Walking Suit, Wool, Gray & Black Check, 2 Piece, Victorian 698.00

CLUTHRA glass is a two-layered glass with small air pockets that form
white spots. The Steuben Glass Works of Corning, New York, made it
in 1920. Kimball Glass Company of Vineland, New Jersey, made
Cluthra from about 1925. Victor Durand signed some pieces with his
name. Related items are listed in the Steuben category.

Vase, Flared Rim, Amethyst, White, 10 1/2 In. 1380.00
Vase, Flared, Oval, Creamy White, Swirled & Bubbled, 10 1/2 In. 920.00
Vase, Internal Swirls, Bubbles & Splotches, Signed, Kimball, 1986, 6 In. 230.00
Vase, Swirled & Pulled Powders, Recessed Pontil, 17 1/2 In. 265.00

COALBROOKDALE was made by the Coalport porcelain factory of
England during the Victorian period. Pieces are decorated with floral
encrustations.

Melon Tureen, Cover, Yellow, Green, Flowering Stalk Handle, 1830, 10 In. 2590.00
Tray, Boudoir, Floral Design, Scrolled Rim, 2 Handles, 1830, 9 x 12 In. 200.00
Vase, Potpourri, Cover, Floral, Leaf Molded, Gilt, 2 Handles, 1840, 18 In. 230.00
Vase, Potpourri, Cover, Floral, Leaf Molded, Gilt, 2 Handles, 1875, 21 In. 115.00

COALPORT ware has been made by the Coalport Porcelain Works of England from 1795 to the present time. Early pieces were unmarked. About 1810–1825 the pieces were marked with the name *Coalport* in various forms. Later pieces also had the name *John Rose* in the mark. The crown mark has been used with variations since 1881. The date 1750 is printed in some marks but it is not the date the factory started.

Box, Trinket, Heart Shape, Pink, Yellow & Gold	195.00
Cup & Saucer, Beaded Enamel, White, Burgundy, Gold Handle, 4 3/4 x 2 1/4 In.	300.00
Cup & Saucer, Fluted, White Jewels, Gold Fleur De Lis, Cobalt Blue Ground, Demitasse	110.00
Cup & Saucer, Gold, Landscapes In Ovals, 4 5/8 x 2 1/4 In.	265.00
Cup & Saucer, White Roses Interior, Cobalt Blue Leaves, Demitasse	128.00
Dessert Service, Flower Wreaths, Fruit, Foliate C-Scrolls, 1825, 16 Piece	5750.00
Dessert Service, Flowering Oriental Plant, Blue Glaze, 1810, 16 Piece	2875.00
Dish, Dessert, Shell Shape, Large Moth In Center, Smaller Insects, Gilt Rim, 1810, 8 In.	1265.00
Dish, Shell Shape, Large Black Spider In Center, Numerous Smaller Insects, 8 In.	1495.00
Mug, Brightly Colored Bird Perched On Branch, 1840, 3 3/8 In.	92.00
Plate Set, Black & White Enamel Border, Apple Green Ground, 9 In., 16 Piece	805.00
Plate Set, Magenta Ground, Gilt Scrolls, Shaped Gilt Edge, 9 1/4 In., 8 Piece	430.00
Plate Set, Magenta Leaf & Gold Rim, 12 Piece	355.00
Platter, Floral, Gilt Borders, 14 3/4 x 17 In., Pair	1955.00
Tea & Coffee Service, Large Flowering Oriental Plant, Blue Glaze, 1810, 71 Piece	1725.00
Urn, Portrait Reserve, Gilt Rim, Interior Flecked Gold, 11 1/4 In.	1035.00
Vase, Floral Arrangement, Purple, Pink & Yellow Flowers, White Base, 4 1/2 In.	45.00

COBALT BLUE glass was made using oxide of cobalt. The characteristic bright dark blue identifies it for the collector. Most cobalt glass found today was made after the Civil War. There was renewed interest in the dark blue glass in the late 1930s and dinnerwares were made.

Bowl, Blown, 5 1/4 In.	245.00
Bowl, Blown, Applied Foot, 6 x 3 1/4 In.	275.00
Condiment Set, Ship Shape, Chrome, 3 x 8 In.	385.00
Creamer, 14 Vertical Ribs, Handle, 3 1/2 In.	247.00
Creamer, Blown, Applied Foot, Handle, 3 1/2 In.	165.00
Flower Frog, Cobalt Blue Rigaree, 5 1/4 x 4 3/8 In.	65.00
Goblet, Diamond, Cut To Clear, 9 In., 12 Piece	365.00
Pitcher, Flared Lip, Spout, Applied Foot, Handle, 7 1/8 In.	85.00
Plate, Enameled Floral, Metal Base, 19th Century, 6 In.	135.00
Wine, Cut To Clear, Vintage Stem, 9 In., 12 Piece	305.00

COCA-COLA was first served in 1886 in Atlanta, Georgia. It was advertised through signs, newspaper ads, coupons, bottles, trays, calendars, and even lamps and clocks. Collectors want anything with the word *Coca-Cola*, including a few rare products, like gum wrappers and cigar bands. The famous trademark was patented in 1893, the *Coke* mark in 1945. Many modern items and reproductions are being made.

Awning, Coca-Cola Refreshment Center, Canvas, 1950s, 24 x 60 In.	245.00
Bank, 1919 Lockheed Air Express, Metal, Ertl, Box	65.00
Bank, 1923 Chevy Delivery, Metal, Ertl, Box	50.00 to 75.00
Bank, 1932 Northrop Gamma, Metal, Box	65.00
Bank, Polar Bear, Mechanical, Ertl	75.00
Bank, Santa Claus, Mechanical, Metal, Ertl, 1st Series, Box	125.00
Bank, Santa Claus, Mechanical, Metal, Ertl, 2nd Series, Box	75.00
Bank, Santa Claus, Mechanical, Metal, Ertl, 3rd Series, Box	75.00
Banner, Coca-Cola Cartons, 1940s, 7 x 22 In.	125.00
Banner, Have A Coke, Compliments Of This Store, 1950s, 13 x 41 In.	105.00
Blotter, Bathing Girl, Frame, 1934	105.00
Blotter, Drink Coca-Cola, 1950s	7.00
Blotter, Elf Digging Bottle Of Coke Out Of Snowbank, 1953, 3 1/2 x 7 1/2 In.	10.00
Blotter, Good With Food, 1935	65.00
Blotter, Red Bottle & Printing On White Ground, Glass, Frame, 1926	70.00
Booklet, Know Your War Planes, 1943	35.00
Bookmark, Heart Shape, Celluloid, 1898, 2 x 2 1/4 In.	1035.00

Bottle, 6-Pack, 1950s, Miniature 200.00
Bottle, 6-Pack, Die-Cut, Wire Handle, 1950, 11 x 13 In. 1840.00
Bottle, 75th Anniversary, Macon, Ga., Metal Cap, Contents, 1977, 8 In. 30.00
Bottle, Binghamton, Yellow Olive, c.1900, 7 3/4 In. 105.00
Bottle, Georgia Tech, 75th Anniversary, Contents, 10 Oz. 15.00
Bottle, Pete Rose, Contents, 10 Oz. 100.00
Bottle, Seltzer, Coca-Cola Bottling Co., Cairo, Illinois 275.00
Bottle, Seltzer, Coca-Cola Bottling Co., Green, Illinois 143.00
Bottle, Syrup, Aluminum Jigger Cover, 1920s 545.00
Bottle, Trophy, 50th Anniversary, Gold Metal, Black Wood Stand, 1936, 3 1/3 In. 75.00
Bottle, Williamstown, N.J., Amber, Straight Sided, Salesman's Sample, 3 1/4 In. 2990.00
Bottle Opener, Starr X Stationary, Gray Metal, Wall Mount, Box 22.00
Calendar, 1913, Frame, Under Glass, 15 x 18 1/2 In. .... 990.00 to 10350.00
Calendar, 1914, December, Full Pad, Frame 2645.00
Calendar, 1918, 2 Women, Beach Scene, 13 Pages 7480.00
Calendar, 1937, Boy, Fishing, Frame, Under Glass 460.00
Calendar, 1942, Snowman Scene, Matted, Frame 125.00
Calendar, 1943, Girl With Bottle, 13 x 20 In. 315.00
Calendar, 1945, Girl With Scarf On Head .... 300.00 to 325.00
Calendar, 1954, Girl With Bottle 115.00
Calendar, 1958, Sign Of Good Taste, 2 Months Each Page 150.00
Calendar, 1959, Pause That Refreshes, 2 Months Each Page 200.00
Calendar, 1969, Man & Woman Sitting At Table 23.00
Calendar, 1976, Look Up America, It's The Real Thing, Bicentennial, 21 x 17 1/2 In. 15.00
Cap, Baseball, 1950s 5.00
Card, Playing, Airplane Spotters, Information, Box, 1943 .... 275.00
Card, Trade, 1893, 3 1/2 x 5 1/2 In. 2185.00
Carrier, 6-Bottle, Canada, 1924 .... 350.00
Carrier, 6-Bottle, Drink Coca-Cola Delicious & Refreshing, Metal Handle, 7 x 8 In. 70.00
Carrier, 6-Bottle, Enjoy Coca-Cola, Red, White, Wooden, 18 x 12 x 4 In. 25.00
Carrier, 6-Bottle, Wooden, Dovetailed, 1920s 400.00
Carrier, 12-Bottle, Delicious Coca-Cola Refreshing, Metal, 16 1/4 x 5 x 8 In. 40.00
Change Receiver, Ideal Brain Tonic, Ceramic, 1890s, 9 In. 5750.00
Clock, Coke, Light-Up, 1950s 110.00
Clock, Drink Coca-Cola, Light-Up, Glass, Metal, 1960s, 11 x 12 In. 165.00
Clock, Drink Coca-Cola, Sign Of Good Taste, Outdoor, Plastic, 1950s, 36 In. 720.00
Clock, Gilbert Style, 1970s, 3/4 Size, 12 x 27 In. 425.00
Clock, Green, Red & White, Electric, Shipping Box, 1960s 365.00
Clock, Ice Cold Coca-Cola, Light-Up, Girl, Drinking Coke, Glass, 15 In. 805.00
Clock, Light-Up, Fishtail Logo, 1950s, Small 150.00
Clock, Light-Up, Glass Front, Face, Metal Frame, 15 1/4 x 15 1/4 In. 440.00
Clock, Neon, 1940s, 15 1/2 In. 545.00
Clock, Red, Dark Brown, Gold Numbers, 1950s, Round, 18 In. 280.00
Clock, Wall, Wood Frame, Electric, 1939, 16 x 16 In. 458.00
Clock, With Wings, Telechron, 1948, 18 x 36 In. 1064.00
Coaster Set, Aluminum, Colored, Box, 1950s, 8 Piece 65.00
Coat Rack, Embossed Aluminum, 1930-1940, 7 1/2 x 10 In. 720.00
Cooler, Junior, Floor Model 1929, 18 x 25 x 34 In. 1150.00
Cooler, Picnic, Aluminum, Progressive Refrigerator Co., 1950s, 18 x 13 x 16 In. 75.00
Cooler, Red, White, Serve Yourself..., 4 Legs, 1920, 30 x 30 In. 1100.00
Cooler, Salesman's Sample, 1939, 8 1/2 x 11 x 9 In. 5500.00
Cooler, Swing Handle, 17 x 12 x 19 In. 125.00
Cooler, Wood, Lead Lined, 4 Legs, Gallery Back, Shelf, 1934, 32 x 20 x 38 In. 2012.00
Coupon Ad, Lillian Nordica, In Metropolitan Magazine, 1905, 6 1/2 x 9 3/4 In. 600.00
Crate, Wooden, Salesman Sample, 1920-1930, 5 1/2 x 8 1/4 In. 1740.00
Cup, Printing On Bottom Of Cup, Greencastle, Ind, 1930s 145.00
Dish, Pretzel, 3 Bottle Legs, Aluminum, Brunhoff Mfg. Co., 1935 .... 185.00 to 275.00
Dispenser, Spring Loaded, No Drip, 1940s, 7 1/2 In. 185.00
Dispenser, Syrup, 1950s, 1 Gal. 25.00
Dispenser, Syrup, Ceramic, No Spigot, 1896 .... 1898.00
Display, 6-Pack, Sign Of Good Taste, Die Cut, 1950s 295.00
Display, Counter, Bottle Shape, Celebrating Christmas, 1930, 20 In. 195.00
Display, Santa Claus, Easel, Die Cut, 1947-1950, 50 In. 405.00

Display, Santa Claus, Stand-Up, Die Cut, 1956, 28 In. 195.00
Doll, Santa Claus, Stuffed, 1950-1960, 18 In. . . . . .110.00 to 155.00
Door Bar, Adjustable, Wrought Iron Arms, 1930s, 7 x 32 In. 605.00
Door Bar, Tin, Adjustable, 1940s 175.00
Door Handle, Bakelite, Metal, 1930-1940, 12 In. 120.00
Door Push, Drink Coca-Cola, Be Really Refreshed, 4 x 8 In. 605.00
Door Push, Red & White, Porcelain, 1930s . . . . .300.00 to 350.00
Figurine, Polar Bear, Ceramic 15.00
Fishing Rod, Reel Combo, Johnson 30.00
Flyswatter, Wooden Handle, Wire Mesh, 1942 . . . . 10.00
Game, Ball Toss, Country Fair, 1940-1950, 72 In. 165.00
Game, Dominoes 15.00
Glass, Pewter, Leather Pouch, 1930s 1035.00
Glass, Wizard Of Oz 50th Anniversary, 1989, 6 Piece 20.00
Glass Set, Box, 1930s, 12 Piece 425.00
Hat, Driver's, 1950s 100.00
Ice Pick, Box, 9 In. 33.00
Jacket, Driver's, Dark Green Twill, Red Patch, 1950s 95.00
Jacket, Tan, Red & White Logo, Zipper Front, 2 Pockets, Swingster, Medium 35.00
Jar, Coca-Cola Chewing Gum, Thumbnail Cover, Green, 1903-1905 . . . . 635.00
Jug, Label, Box, 1930s, 1 Gal. 315.00
Jug, Syrup, Embossed Logo, 1900s, 1 Gal. 2530.00
Kickplate, Drink Coca-Cola, Porcelain, 1920s, 10 x 30 In. 690.00
Kite, Hi-Flyer, Paper, 1930s 550.00
Lamp, Lava, 19 x 7 x 9 In. 130.00
Lantern, Fishtail 150.00
Lighter, 1950s 35.00
Lighter, Coca-Cola Bottle, 2 1/2 In. 45.00
Lock, Kam-Indore Safety, Box, 1930-1940 . . . . 90.00
Machine, Automatic Cup Dispensing, Siphonmix, c.1923, 74 x 26 x 18 In. 17600.00
Magnet, Thermometer, Coke Bottle 2.50
Marker, Sidewalk, Brass, 1933, 3 1/2 In. 100.00
Match Holder, Metal, With Matches, 1959 . . . . 330.00
Match Holder, Wall Mount, Logos Each Side, 25 Full Matchbooks, Tin, 6 3/4 In. 300.00
Matchbook, A Distinctive Drink, 1922 . . . . 115.00
Menu Board, 1956, 20 x 28 In. 150.00
Menu Board, Black Cardboard, Red Button Logo, 6-Bottle Case, 1940s, 29 x 16 In. 215.00
Menu Board, Southwest Design 60.00
Mirror, Drink Coca-Cola, 5 Cents, Girl With Glass, Celluloid, 1914, Pocket 1962.00
Mirror, Young Lady With Large Hat, Oval, Pocket, 1910, 2 3/4 In. 305.00
Music Box, Plastic, 1950s 100.00
Napkin, Hot, Tired, Thirsty, Paper, Matted, Diamond Shape, 12 In. 105.00
Night-Light, Box, 1950s 50.00
Pants, It's The Real Thing & Enjoy Coca-Cola Logos, Cotton, Bell Bottoms, 1970s 20.00
Pencil, 1940s-1950, Set Of 12 In Original Sleeve 50.00
Pin, Coke Always Cool, Polar Bear Picture 2.00
Plate, Sandwich, Bottle & Glass Center, 1931, 7 3/8 In. .210.00 to 230.00
Postcard, Fill-In Message For Busy Soldier, France 125.00
Postcard, Take Home A Carton, 1930s, 5 1/2 x 6 1/2 In. 14.00
Poster, Easy To Take Home, 1941, 16 x 27 In. 1265.00
Poster, Goose Tatum, Globe Trotters, 1952, 26 x 27 In. 835.00
Poster, Lillian Nordica, Repainted Frame, 1939, 16 x 27 In. 205.00
Poster, Right Off The Ice, Trimmed Border, 1946, 16 x 27 In. 460.00
Poster, Skiers Skiing Around Coke Bottle, Cardboard, 1954, 29 x 50 In. 415.00
Poster, The Drink They All Expect, 1942, 16 x 27 In. 950.00
Poster, Waitress, They All Want Coke, 1941, 20 x 36 In. 460.00
Rack, Steel, Stamped Logo, Ardmore 7 57, 16 x 11 x 4 In. 40.00
Radio, Bottle, 1933, 24 In. 4620.00
Radio, Cooler Shape, AM Radio, 1950, 12 x 9 1/2 In. . . . . .490.00 to 905.00
Sheet Music, My Coca-Cola Bride, Juanita, 1906, 10 1/2 x 13 In. 720.00
Sheet Music, Old Folks At Home, Juanita, 10 1/2 x 13 In. 690.00
Sign, Arrow, 2 Colors, 1950s, 16 In. 1065.00
Sign, Attached Button Top, Pilaster, Hardware, 1953, 16 x 54 In. 1610.00

Sign, Bathing Girl On Rocks, Cardboard, 1938, 30 x 50 In. 805.00
Sign, Blue Lettering On Red Ground, Enameled Steel, 60 x 36 In. 175.00
Sign, Bobby Jones, Golfer, String Hanger, 13 x 15 In. 175.00
Sign, Bottle Shape, Die Cut, 1951, 16 In. 230.00
Sign, Bottle Shape, Die Cut, 1954, 72 In. 430.00
Sign, Button, Bottle, Porcelain, 24 In. 695.00
Sign, Button, Bottle, White Paint, Tin, 36 In. 660.00
Sign, Button, Porcelain, Drink Coca-Cola, 48 In. 1092.00
Sign, Button, Porcelain, Embossed Drink Coca-Cola, Mounted On Base, 62 x 30 In. 260.00
Sign, Button, Spite Boy Decal, 1950s, 16 In. 750.00
Sign, Button, With Bottle, Tin, Painted, 1964, 24 In. 950.00
Sign, Carrier, 6-Pack, Embossed, 1962, 30 x 36 In. 1495.00
Sign, Carrier, 6-Pack, King Size, Late 1950s, 30 x 36 In. 1670.00
Sign, Coca-Cola, Bottle, 2 Sides, 1940-1950, 36 x 72 In. 490.00
Sign, Coca-Cola, Friendly Pause, 3 Women Drinking Coke, Frame, 33 x 54 In. 480.00
Sign, Coke Toonerville City, Promotion Of Fontaine Fox' Town, 1930, 15 x 10 In. 93.00
Sign, Drink Coca-Cola Ice Cold, Red Dispenser, Porcelain, 2 Sides, 27 x 28 In. 3105.00
Sign, Drink Coca-Cola In Bottles, 2 Sides, Round, 1940-1950, 30 In. 430.00
Sign, Drink Coca-Cola, Dispenser, 2 Sides, 1940, 26 x 25 In. 1495.00
Sign, Drink Coca-Cola, Flange, 1946, 24 x 20 In. 490.00
Sign, Drink Coca-Cola, Metal, Plastic, Light-Up, 1950-1960, 12 x 24 In. 210.00
Sign, Drink Coca-Cola, Red Ground, Porcelain, 36 x 22 1/2 In. 203.00
Sign, Drink Coca-Cola, Script, Die Cut, 1930s, 5 1/2 x 18 In. 1840.00
Sign, Drink Coca-Cola, Wooden, Triangle, Kay, 1930s, 20 x 19 In. 1555.00
Sign, Enjoy Coca-Cola At Home, 2 Sides, 1930-1940, Canada, 11 x 16 In. 265.00
Sign, Figural, Baby, 6-Pack, Metal, 8 1/4 In. 750.00
Sign, Ice Cold Sold Here, Tin, Round, Red, Yellow & White, 1933, 20 In. 575.00
Sign, Indian Motorcycles Authorized Dealer, 2 Sides, 1940s, 58 x 51 In. 1210.00
Sign, Johnny Weissmuller & Marueen O'Sullivan, 1934 Movie, 13 1/2 x 19 In. 3680.00
Sign, Lillian Nordica, Cardboard, Reproduction Frame, 1939, 16 x 27 In. 575.00
Sign, Lillian Russell, Cardboard, 1904, 16 x 22 In. 2300.00
Sign, Lunch, 2 Sides, 1950s, 25 x 28 In. 980.00
Sign, Man & Woman With Bottle, 1941, 18 x 54 In. 890.00
Sign, McGuire Sisters, Hole To Hang, 16 x 27 In. 155.00
Sign, Party Pause, Gold Frame, 1947, 20 x 36 In. 545.00
Sign, Pause, Refreshed, Composition, Hollis Press, Round, 1940s, 8 3/4 In. 2415.00
Sign, Pick Up 6-Pack Carrier, 1954, 16 x 50 In. 1555.00
Sign, Picnic Grill, Cardboard, 1942, 27 x 56 In. 700.00
Sign, Plane, Martin PBM Mariner, Patrol Bomber, Cardboard, 1943, 13 x 15 In. 40.00
Sign, Please Pay When Served, Reverse On Glass, Round, 1920-1930, 11 1/4 In. 350.00
Sign, Policeman, Figural, 2 Sides, 72 In. 2250.00
Sign, Policeman, Logo On Back, Inner Frame, 1962 .... 4475.00
Sign, Refreshing, Wooden, Metal, Kay, 13 x 31 In. 275.00
Sign, Serve Yourself, Tin, 1920-1930, 6 x 3 1/4 In. 2875.00
Sign, Top Of The List...For Good, Couple Shopping, Paper, 1955, 20 1/4 x 14 1/4 In. 50.00
Sign, Waitress & Automobile, Silhouette, Porcelain, Outdoor, 2 Sides 2400.00
Sign, Wherever You Go, Coca-Cola, Tin, Wire Accents, Snow Scene, 14 x 18 In. 265.00
Sign, Woman, Bathing Suit, With Carrier, Cardboard, Frame, 1960s, 16 x 27 In. 45.00
Sign, Woman, With Wagon, Glass, Frame, Cardboard, Canada, 1944, 16 x 27 In. 140.00
Sign Set, Sports Series, Kay Display, Wooden, Wire, 1930-1940, 16 In., 4 Piece 2530.00
Thermometer, Bottle Shape, Embossed Die Cut, 1950s, 17 In. 105.00
Thermometer, Bottle Shape, Embossed, Hanger, 1950s, 17 In. 85.00
Thermometer, Bottles, Round, 1950s, 12 In. 165.00
Thermometer, Drink Coca-Cola In Bottles, Red, 1950s, Round, 12 In. 138.00
Thermometer, Drink Coca-Cola, 1941, 7 x 16 In. 775.00
Thermometer, Drink Coca-Cola, 1950s, 8 x 30 In. 865.00
Thermometer, Gold Bottle, 1937, 16 In. 155.00
Thermometer, Gold Bottle, 7 In. 25.00
Thermometer, Round, 1950s, 12 In. 225.00
Thermometer, Silhouette Girl, 1940, 16 In. 230.00
Thermometer, Silhouette Girl, Red, Canada, 1939, 18 In. 1955.00
Thermometer, Silhouette Girl, Red, Canada, 1940, 18 In. 2645.00
Thermometer, Tin, 16 In. 110.00

Thermometer, Wooden, 1905, 4 x 15 In. 690.00
Thimble, Coke, Plastic 1.25
Tip Tray, 1903, Hilda, Round, 4 In. 6565.00
Tip Tray, 1907, Relieves Fatigue, Oval, 4 1/4 x 6 In. 635.00
Tip Tray, 1909, Exhibition Girl, Oval, 6 1/4 In. ....218.00 to 440.00
Tip Tray, 1914, Betty, Bonnet, Shawl, Oval, 6 In. ....220.00 to 575.00
Tip Tray, 1920, Golfer Girl 160.00
Tip Tray, Coca-Cola Girl 150.00
Toy, Gas Station, Mission, Pumps, Signs, Unused 85.00
Toy, Roll, Metal, To Be Used With Stick, 1930s 145.00
Toy, Train Set, Lionel, Track, 1973-1974, Box 245.00
Toy, Truck, Delivery, Buddy L, Pressed Steel, Yellow, Box, 1960, 15 In. 575.00
Toy, Truck, Delivery, Every Bottle Sterilized, Red Cab, Metalcraft, 11 In. .... 935.00 to 990.00
Toy, Truck, Delivery, Goodrich Rubber Tires, Glass Coke Bottles, Metalcraft, 11 In. 963.00
Toy, Truck, Delivery, Metal Wheels, Radiator Marked White, Metalcraft, 11 In. 495.00
Toy, Truck, Delivery, Metal, Lithograph Front & Sides, Lumar Tires, Marx, 17 In. 330.00
Toy, Truck, Delivery, Yellow, Duel Bed Body, Pressed Steel, Marx, 12 1/2 In. 990.00
Toy, Truck, Drink Coca-Cola, Back Of Trailer, Yellow, Plastic, Marx, 1960s, 10 x 3 In. ... 350.00
Toy, Truck, Painted, Decals, Buddy L, Japan, 10 In. 80.00
Toy, Truck, Stake, 1 Dozen Cases, Hand Truck, Marx, 1940s, 17 1/2 In. 775.00
Toy, Truck, Tin Lithograph, Friction, Linemar, 3 In. 130.00
Toy, Yoyo, Red 4.00
Tray, 1904, Lillian Nordica, With Bottle, Oval, 10 5/8 x 12 7/8 In. 4180.00
Tray, 1910, Coca-Cola Girl, 10 1/2 x 13 1/4 In. 115.00
Tray, 1910, Hamilton King, Oval, 13 3/4 x 16 3/4 In. 1595.00
Tray, 1914, Betty, Oval, 12 5/8 x 13 3/8 In. 675.00
Tray, 1916, Elaine, Rectangular, 8 1/2 x 19 In. 225.00
Tray, 1921, Golfer Girl, Oval, 13 3/4 x 16 3/4 In. 775.00
Tray, 1924, Smiling Girl, 13 1/4 x 10 1/2 In. 800.00
Tray, 1927, Curb Service, 13 1/4 x 10 1/2 In. ....375.00 to 890.00
Tray, 1928, Girl With Bobbed Hair, 13 3/4 x 10 1/2 In. 980.00
Tray, 1928, Soda Jerk, Red Border ....375.00 to 900.00
Tray, 1929, Girl In Yellow Bathing Suit, 13 1/4 x 10 1/2 In. 600.00
Tray, 1931, Barefoot Boy, Norman Rockwell, 10 3/4 x 13 1/4 In. 1000.00
Tray, 1931, Menu Board, Specials To-Day, Tin, Embossed 138.00
Tray, 1934, Maureen O'Sullivan, Weismuller, Red Trim, 10 1/2 x 13 1/4 In. ....1450.00 to 1898.00
Tray, 1937, Running Girl, 13 1/4 x 10 1/2 In. ....165.00 to 520.00
Tray, 1938, Girl, In Yellow Hat, 13 1/4 x 10 1/2 In. ....200.00 to 605.00
Tray, 1939, Springboard Girl, 13 1/4 x 10 1/2 In. 105.00
Tray, 1940, Sailor Girl, 13 1/4 x 10 1/2 In. ....100.00 to 635.00
Tray, 1941, Skater Girl, 13 1/4 x 10 1/2 In. ....180.00 to 430.00
Tray, 1942, 2 Girls At Car, 13 1/4 x 10 1/2 In. ....120.00 to 490.00
Tray, 1948, Girl, With Red Hair, 13 1/4 x 10 1/2 In. 135.00
Tray, 1950, Menu Girl, 13 1/4 x 10 1/2 In. 65.00
Tray, 1961, Pansy Garden, 13 1/4 x 10 1/2 In. 35.00
Tray, 1971, Hamilton King Girl, 10 3/4 x 14 3/4 In. 10.00
Tray, 1976, 75th Anniversary, Hilda, Round, 12 In. 30.00
Trolley Sign, Girl, Matted, Glass, Frame, 1907, 11 x 20 1/2 In. 1265.00
Trolley Sign, Woman, Hat, Matted, Shrunk Wrapped, 1927, 9 1/2 x 20 In. 2070.00
Trophy, Coca-Cola Amateur Softball Assn., Newark, 1948, Gilt Metal, 30 In. 600.00
Umbrella, Beach, 1920s, 65 x 72 In. 405.00
Umbrella, The Pause That Refreshes, Canvas, Late 1930s 450.00
Window Shade, Bamboo, 1910-1920, 51 x 93 In. 460.00

COFFEE GRINDERS of home size were first made about 1894. They lost
favor by the 1930s. Large floor-standing or counter-model coffee
grinders were used in the nineteenth-century country store. The
renewed interest in fresh-ground coffee has produced many modern
electric and hand grinders, and reproductions of the old styles are
being made.

1 Wheel, Cast Iron 765.00
2 Wheels, Wrightsville Hardware 430.00
Bell Co., Model No. 3, C.S. Bell Co., Hillsboro, O., 21 x 17 1/2 x 19 1/2 In. 200.00

Don't try to remove dents in silver or pewter. This is a job for an expert.

Coffee Grinder,
Kitchen Aid, Electric,
Ivory Enamel

Coffee Grinder,
Lane Brothers,
Swift, 18 In.

Brass, Hand Stamped, 3-Piece, Folding Handle, Turkish, c.1830, 9 In.	30.00
Cast Iron, Franko American Logan & Sturbridge	50.00
Cast Iron, No. 1 1/2, 1 Wheel, Wooden Base	145.00
Cast Iron, Wood Base, Handle, Lid, Red Paint, No. 1 1/2 x 15 1/2 In.	195.00
Elgin National, 13 In.	688.00
Elgin National, No. 43, Metal, Brass Top, Eagle, Wood & Brass Scoop, 31 In.	1045.00
Enterprise, 2 Wheels On Base, Drawer, Stamped 123, Cast Iron, 12 In.	795.00
Enterprise, 2 Wheels, Drawer, Transfer, Cast Iron, Philadelphia, 22 1/2 In.	300.00
Enterprise, No. 100	120.00
Enterprise Mfg.Co., Philadelphia, Pat. Dec. 9, 1873, Cast Iron, 12 1/2 In.	1485.00
Golden Rule, Viewing Window, Iron, Wall Mount, 9 x 5 1/2 In.	440.00
Golden Rule Blend Coffee, Cast Iron, Wooden Base, Glass Bottle, 18 In.	200.00
Holwick, Electric, 12 1/2 x 13 x 28 In.	220.00
Kitchen Aid, Electric, Ivory Enamel ....*Illus*	50.00
Landers Frary & Clark, Red & Gold Trim, Decals, Cast Iron Drawer, 12 In.	660.00
Lane Brothers, Swift, 18 In. ....*Illus*	300.00
Magus, 7 1/2 x 4 1/2 In.	275.00
Maple, Dovetailed, Wrought Iron Top, 18th Century	410.00
Mokane, Brass, 8 1/2 x 5 1/4 In.	355.00
Poplar, Dovetailed, Pewter Hopper, Cast Iron Crank, Nailed Drawer, 9 1/4 In.	135.00
Poplar, Dovetailed, Pewter Top, Molded Base, Penna.	220.00

COIN SPOT is a glass pattern that was named by the collectors for the spots resembling coins, which are part of the glass. Colored, clear, and opalescent glass was made with the spots. Many companies used the design in the 1870–1890 period. It is so popular that reproductions are still being made.

Lamp, Cranberry Opalescent Font, Black Base, 9 In.	1350.00
Lamp, White Opalescent Foot, Clear Base, 8 In.	500.00
Salt & Pepper, Tall	345.00
Sugar Shaker, Cranberry Opalescent	295.00
Tankard, 3 Tiers, Cranberry	1375.00
Vase, Pink & Blue Stripes, Satin, Gourd Shape, 9 x 4 1/2 In.	115.00

COIN-OPERATED MACHINES of all types are collected. The vending machine is an ancient invention dating back to 200 B.C. when holy water was dispensed in a coin-operated vase. Smokers in seventeenth-century England could buy tobacco from a coin-operated box. It was not until after the Civil War that the technology made modern coin-operated games and vending machines plentiful. Slot machines, arcade games, and dispensers are all collected.

Automaton, Jolson Sings, 1920-1940 ....*Illus*	2090.00
Caille, Dictator, 1 Cent	2200.00
Caille, Dictator, 5 Cent	1750.00
Chrome Plated, Oak Base, 25 Cent, 25 1/2 In.	1100.00
Cigarette, Fortune Teller's Mouth, Art Deco, Indel & Graham, 1928, 8 In.	365.00
Cigarette, Rowe, Old Gold For A Treat, 69 In.	920.00

Cupid Nickelodeon, Walnut, Restored 12000.00
Fortune Teller, Gypsy 3300.00
Gambling, Lucky Lotto, Countertop, Metal, Cards, Keys, 25 Cent, 18 In. 90.00
Gum, Master, No. 2, Norn's Mfg. Co., Porcelain, c.1925, 16 In. 385.00
Gum, Pulver Chewing, Red Porcelain, With Cop 850.00
Gum, Pulver, Clown, Porcelain, 1 Cent, 20 1/2 In. 715.00
Gum, Pulver, Daffy Duck Figure, Walter Lutz, Box, 1 Cent, 20 In. 1760.00
Gumball, Acorn Penny, Glass Globe, Lock, Key, 1950 .... 75.00
Gumball, Hart 85.00
Gumball, Master Penny, 1920s 375.00
Jennings, Monte Carlo, Console, 25 Cent 5200.00
Kiss-O-Meter, 25 Cent 325.00
Matchbook, 1 Cent, c.1920 .... 885.00
Matches, Ohio Book Matches, 1 Cent 50.00
Negro Sport Machine, Ball Springs Forward, 1 Cent, Iron, Metal, 15 In. 770.00
Nickelodeon, Nelson-Wiggen, Mandolin, Drums, Bells, Coin Slot 6440.00
Peanut, Northwestern, Porcelain 190.00
Peanut, Topper, 1 Cent, 15 In. 55.00
Peanut, Victor, 1 Cent, 1940s 125.00
Rock-O-Plane, Amusement Park 8250.00
San Francisco World's Fair, 1933, Jigsaw, Rock-Ola, 38 In. 1320.00
Scale & Horoscope, American Scale Mfg. Co., 53 In. 280.00
Shooting Game, Challenger 400.00
Slot, Cigarette, Liberty, 1 Cent 350.00
Slot, Columbia, Deco Case, Mahogany Veneer, 5 Cent, 19 x 14 5/8 In. 1100.00
Slot, Jennings, Floor Model, Eagle & Flags, 5 & 25 Cent, 55 In. 495.00
Slot, Jennings, Indian Head On Front, Chrome Plated Case, 27 In. 1210.00
Slot, Jennings, Liberty Bell, Pays Out Nickels & Half Dollars, 5 Cent 950.00
Slot, Jennings, Little Duke, 1931, 25 1/2 In. ....*Illus* 1882.00
Slot, Jennings, Operator Bell, 25 Cent, 1920s 1435.00
Slot, Little Duke, O.D. Jennings & Co., 1931 .... 1882.00
Slot, Mills, Black Beauty, 1940 .... 1975.00
Slot, Mills, Blue Bell, 25 Cent 2000.00
Slot, Mills, Century Model, Burl Walnut Cabinet, 25 Cent, 1933 .... 3000.00 to 3500.00
Slot, Mills, Ferris Wheel 1200.00
Slot, Mills, Figural, One Arm Bandit, Cast Hand & Gun, 5 Cent, 70 In. 4070.00
Slot, Mills, Golden Falls, Embossed Cherries, 25 Cent, 1946, 26 In. 1205.00
Slot, Mills, Mystery, 1933 .... 2375.00
Slot, Mills, Pace, 1930 .... 1975.00
Slot, Mills, Walnut Cabinet, 25 Cent, 1933 .... 3000.00
Slot, O.D. Jennings, Deco, Chrome Plated Detail, 5 Cent, 27 3/4 In. 990.00
Slot, O.D. Jennings, Little Duke, Oak Case, 1 Cent, 22 1/2 In. 1650.00
Slot, Pace, Chrome, Silver Dollar, From Harrahs Casino, 24 In. 977.00
Slot, Rock-Ola, Series G, Model 1428 .... 3900.00
Slot, Tatling, Treasury 2600.00
Slot, Twin Jack Box, 24 x 15 In. 805.00
Stamp, Selector, 1940s 70.00
Strength, Mercury, 1 Cent 400.00

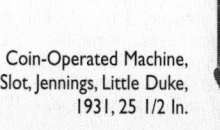

Coin-Operated
Machine, Automaton,
Jolson Sings, 1920-
1940

Coin-Operated Machine,
Slot, Jennings, Little Duke,
1931, 25 1/2 In.

Swami Fortune & Prediction, 1 Cent 165.00
Train, Entertain Waiting Travelers, Converted To Electricity, 50 In. 9200.00
Vending, Calex, Sports Card, 6 For 5 Cents, 56 In. 75.00
Vending, Dairy Maid Candies, Metal, 37 x 5 In. 230.00
Vending, Hot Nuts, Minneapolis, 15 In. 165.00
Vending, U.S. Postage Stamp 140.00
Viewer, Drop-Card, Cast Iron, Ball & Claw Legs, Girlie Cards 3600.00
Weighing, Red Over Iron, 1 Cent, 74 In. 165.00

COLLECTOR PLATES are modern plates produced in limited editions.
Some may be found listed under the factory name, such as Bing &
Grondahl, Royal Copenhagen, Royal Doulton, and Wedgwood.

Bareuther, Christmas, 1970 .... 25.00
Bradford, Rhett's Bright Promise 25.00
C.D. Kenney, Christmas, Tin Lithograph, Holding Wreath & Dog 145.00
Chambers, Annie & Sandy, 1982, 8 1/2 In. 40.00
Hamilton, Wizard Of Oz, 50th Anniversary, Box, 1989, 9 1/4 In. 20.00
Hibel, Mother & Daughter, Box, Set Of 6 .... 1550.00
Howard Rogers, Gone With The Wind, Home To Tara, No. 5927E, Box, Papers 70.00
S. Morton, Clark Gable, Hollywood Greats, 1982 .... 65.00
S. Morton, Gary Cooper, Hollywood Greats, 1981 .... 40.00
S. Morton, Henry Fonda, Hollywood Greats, 1981 .... 55.00
S. Morton, John Wayne, Hollywood Greats, 1981 .... 90.00
Schmid, Mother's Day, 1972, West Germany 25.00
Schmid, Mother's Day, 1976, Devotion For Mother, Sister Berta Hummel 35.00

COMIC ART, or cartoon art, is a relatively new field of collecting.
Original comic strips, magazine covers, and even printed strips are collected. The first daily comic strip was printed in 1907. The paintings
on celluloid used for movie cartoons are listed in this book under
Animation Art.

Banner, Snoopy, I Think I'm Allergic To Morning, Yellow Felt, 1968, 15 x 33 In. 40.00
Book, Charlie Brown Dictionary, Scholastic Book Services, 1975, 400 Pages 14.00
Book, Good Ol' Charlie Brown, Rinehart Co., 1957, 128 Pages, 5 x 8 In. 25.00
Book, I Go Pogo, Comic Strip Reprints, Paperback, First Edition, 1952, 190 Pages 22.00
Book, Pogo Stepmother Goose, First Edition, Softcover, 1954, 6 1/2 x 9 3/4 In. 20.00
Book, Pogo Sunday Book, Comic Strip Reprints, Simon & Schuster, 1956, 132 Pages ... 20.00
Book, Pogo, Comic Art Reprints, Simon & Schuster, 1951, 182 Pages, 5 1/4 x 8 In. 18.00
Book, Return Of Pogo, First Edition, Simon & Schuster, 1965, 192 Pages 20.00
Book, Suppertime! Suppertime!, Snoopy, Determined Productions, 1968, 68 Pages 14.00
Booklet, Joe Palooka, Red Cross, How Red Cross Helps Soldiers, 1949, 4 3/4 x 6 In. 45.00
Display, Snuffy Smith With Christmas Tree, Puck The Comic Weekly, 1948, 8 x 12 In. ... 60.00
Drawing, Moon Mullins, Portrait, Pencil, Signed Ferd Johnson, 1975, 5 3/4 x 7 1/2 In. ... 68.00
Strip, Blondie, Pen & Ink, Signed Chic Young, April 8, 1949 .... 358.00
Strip, Dennis The Menace, Pen & Ink, Signed Hank Ketcham, Aug. 17, 1951, 10 x 8 In. . 330.00
Strip, Dick Tracy, Pen & Ink, Signed Chester Gould, Jan. 8, 1947, 7 x 20 In. 990.00
Strip, Jiggs, Signed Kavanagh & Camp, March 20, 1975, 5 1/2 x 19 In. 60.00
Strip, Joe Palooka, Pen & Ink, Signed Ham Fisher, Dec. 6, 1940, 7 x 22 In. 358.00
Strip, Peanuts, Pen & Ink, Signed Schulz, Feb. 19, 1958, 6 3/4 x 29 In. 1430.00
Strip, Rip Kirby, Signed Alex Raymond 8-22 To George Geiger, 1950, 6 1/2 x 19 In. 358.00
Strip, Ripley's Believe It Or Not, Drawn For George Geiger, Signed, Feb. 12, 1941 ..... 330.00

COMMEMORATIVE items have been made to honor members of royalty
and those of great national fame. World's fairs and important historical
events are also remembered with commemorative pieces. Related collectibles are listed in the Coronation and World's Fair categories.

Apollo Moon Kit, Map, Compass, Flag, New York Toy Co., On Card, Late 1960s 34.00
Beaker, Imperial Eagle, Enameled, Nicholas II, Russia, 1896, 4 In. 2875.00
Button, North Pole Discovery, Explorers On Globe, Celluloid, 1910, 1 1/4 In. 70.00
Card, Memorial, Enrico Caruso, Birth, Napoli, Died Aug. 1, 1921, 5 x 3 In. 50.00
Figurine, Pony Express, Rider, Galloping Horse, Cast Metal, 1950s, 3 1/2 In. 100.00
Glass, Apollo 11, Man On The Moon, Lunar Module, 4 In. 8.00
Glass, Apollo 12, Return To The Moon, Red, White, Blue, 4 In. 10.00

Glass, Apollo 13, Red, White, Blue, 1970, 4 In., Set Of 4 .... 28.00
Key Holder, Apollo 11, Gold Metal, Eagle Landing On Moon, Box, 1969, 2 In. 25.00
Lighter, Moon Landing, Lunar Lander, Astronaut With Flag, Zippo, 1969 .... 135.00
Map, Lipton Lunar Space, Commemorates Moon Landing, 1969, 20 x 24 In. 8.00
Medallion, First Man On The Moon, Gold Colored Bracelet, Card, 4 x 6 In. 8.00
Mug, Neil Steps On Moon, Wapokoneta Daily News Headline, July 21, 1969 .... 20.00
Pen, First Man On The Moon, One Small Step, Plastic, Metal, On Card, 5 In. 20.00
Pennant, Apollo 11, Moon Landing Logo, Red, White, Blue, Felt, 29 In. 10.00
Photograph, Columbia, Space Shuttle, April 12, 1981, Envelope, 10 x 13 In. 14.00
Picture, Apollo 11, Astronauts Planting Flag, 3-D, Plastic, 1969, 11 x 14 In. 35.00
Picture, Astronauts Planting Flag On Moon, 3-D, Plastic, 1969, 17 x 22 In. 60.00
Plate, Alsatian Pioneer Batl. Nr. 15, White Ground 375.00
Plate, Pioneer Batl. Nr. 20, White Ground, 1893-1919 .... 375.00
Plate, Saxon Infantry, White Ground 375.00
Queen Victoria, Cherry Toothpaste, John Gosnell & Co., 3 1/2 In. 55.00
Tin, King George VI & Queen Elizabeth Marriage, 1923, 6 x 4 In. 40.00

COMPACTS hold face powder. A woman did not powder her face in
public until after World War I. By 1920, the beauty parlor, permanent
waves, and cosmetics had become acceptable. A few companies sold
cake face powder in a box with a mirror and a pad or puff. Soon the
compact was designed by jewelers and made of gold, silver, and pre-
cious materials. Cosmetic companies began to sell powder in attractive
compacts of less valuable metal or plastic. Collectors today search for
Art Deco designs, commemorative compacts from world's fairs or
political events, and unusual examples. Many were made with companion lipsticks and other fittings.

18K Gold Mesh, Yellow, White Gold, Blue, Enamel, Sapphire, Fitted Leather Case 880.00
Cartier, Gold Flowers, Sapphire Centers, Inside Mirror, Sterling Silver 575.00
Carven, Lipstick Case, Spool Shape, Enameled Ivory, Green, 1945, 2 In. 255.00
Celluloid, Butterflies 40.00
Ciner, Beaded Pearl Cover, Gold Metal, Lipstick Holder, Black Case ....*Illus* 200.00
Continental Silver, Courting Scene, Man & Woman, Gold Wash Interior, 3 In. 120.00
Coty, Goldtone Envelope, Puff With Logo, Mirror, 3 1/2 x 2 5/8 In. 70.00
Cub Scout Den Mother, 1950s 350.00
Elgin, Modern Design, Loose Powder Puff, Logo 85.00
Enamel, Locket, Silhouette Of Lady With Dog 95.00
Enamel, Man & Woman On Lid, Foliate Design On Reverse, 2 3/4 In. 275.00
Enamel, Woman & Child In Wooded Scene, Gold Wash Interior, 2 3/4 In. 330.00
Evans, Art Deco, Black Enameled Gazelle 175.00
Georg Jensen, Hammered, Embossed Flower, Sterling Silver, Signed, 2 In. 110.00
Georg Jensen, Sterling Silver 375.00
Green & Pink Rhinestones, Opens To Ashtray, Miniature 25.00
Gucci, Enamel, Red 125.00
Hingeco, Floral Engraving, Heart Shape, Sterling Silver ....'...... 65.00
J.E. Caldwell, Basket Weave, Cabochon Red Stone Closure, Leather Case 575.00

There are dozens of kinds of felt, cork, plastic, and
glass products made to protect tables from heavy
lamps, carpets from sofa-leg marks, or walls from
bumping mirrors. If you think an object is making a
mark or scratch on another piece or the wall or
floor, check at the store for the correct protector.

Compact, Ciner, Beaded
Pearl Cover, Gold Metal,
Lipstick Holder, Black Case

Lin Bren, Basket Of Flowers, Petit Point 40.00
Lipstick Case, Lipstick From Hell, Perfume Flacon, Brown Bakelite Case, 6 In. 860.00
Lucien LeLong, Round Lid, Light Green Enamel, Chrome Steel, Square, 2 1/2 In. 215.00
Marcella, Rouge 10.00
Massachusetts Institute Of Technology Logo, Ring Chain 100.00
Max Factor, Brass 20.00
Mother-Of-Pearl, Oval Shape 38.00
Porcelain, Metal, Cobalt Blue Enamel, Courting Couple Scene, Austria, 2 3/8 In. 105.00
Revlon, Goldtone, Demitasse Hand Mirror, Van Cleef & Arpels 50.00
Rhodium Plate, Buick Eight, Enameled Burgundy Panels, 1939 .... 200.00
Sterling Silver, Dancing Cherubs On Plaque, Floral Engraving On Base, 2 1/2 In. 300.00
Stratton, Cobalt, Pink & White Water Lilies 85.00
Stratton, Man Wearing Crown, Rhinestones 75.00
Textured Goldtone, Shape Of Cat, Faux Sapphire, Emerald & Diamond Eyes, Italy 300.00
Tobias, Fluted Cover Set With Diamonds & Sapphires, 14K Gold, 2 3/4 In. 1092.00
Volupte, Rhinestones 40.00
Volupte, Woman's Hand Shape, Black Lace Glove, Bracelet, 1940, 4 3/4 In. 275.00
Yardley, Goldtone, Embossed Design On Lid, Powder & Rouge Sections 70.00

CONSOLIDATED LAMP AND GLASS COMPANY of Coraopolis, Pennsylvania, was founded in 1894. The company made lamps, tablewares, and art glass. Collectors are particularly interested in the wares made after 1925, including black satin glass, Cosmos (listed in its own category in this book), Martele (which resembled Lalique), Ruba Rombic (1928–1932 Art Deco line), and colored glasswares. Some Consolidated pieces are very similar to those made by the Phoenix Glass Company. The colors are sometimes different. Consolidated made Martele glass in blue, crystal, green, pink, white, or custard glass with added fired-on color or a satin finish. The company closed for the final time in 1967.

Ashtray, Ruba Rombic, White Opalescent, 3 1/2 In. 1210.00
Bonbon, Ruba Rombic, Smoky Topaz, 3 Sections, 8 In. 250.00
Bonbon, Ruba Rombic, Sunshine, 3 Sections, 8 In. 880.00
Bottle, Ruba Rombic, Jungle Green, 7 1/2 In. 1800.00
Bowl, Almond, Ruba Rombic, Jungle Green, 3 In. 415.00
Bowl, Cupped, Ruba Rombic, Smokey Topaz, 8 In. 1200.00
Bowl, Ruba Rombic, Smoky Topaz, Cupped, 8 In. 1430.00
Celery Dish, Ruba Rombic, Jungle Green, 12 In. 880.00
Chandelier, 5-Light, Martele 650.00
Compote, Ruba Rombic, Jungle Green, 7 In. 990.00
Decanter, Ruba Rombic, Jungle Green, 9 In. 1200.00
Decanter Set, Ruba Rombic, Smoky Topaz, Tray, 9-In. Decanter, 8 Piece 4125.00
Plate, Ruba Rombic, Jungle Green, 8 In. 65.00
Sugar & Creamer, Ruba Rombic, Smoky Topaz, 8 In. 360.00
Toilet Set, Ruba Rombic, 2 Bottles, Tray, 3 Piece 5750.00
Tumbler, Ruba Rombic, Jungle Green, 9 Oz. 75.00
Vase, Blue Screech Owls, Salmon Reeds, Satin Custard, 5 3/4 In. 190.00
Vase, Fan, Bird Of Paradise, Pink Wash, 8 In. 89.00
Vase, Pine Cone, Brown On White Satin 295.00
Vase, Red Poppies, Satin Custard, 10 In. 275.00
Vase, Ruba Rhombic, Jade Satin, 9 x 7 1/2 In. 2750.00
Vase, Ruba Rombic, Jungle Green, 6 1/2 In. 990.00
Vase, Screech Owl, Gold On White Satin, Martele 250.00
Vase, Umbrella, Blackberry, Sepia Wash 1100.00

CONTEMPORARY GLASS, see Glass-Contemporary.

COOKBOOKS are collected for various reasons. Some are wanted for the recipes, some for investment, and some as examples of advertising. Cookbooks and recipe pamphlets are included in this category.

Better Homes & Garden, Loose-Leaf, 1937 .... 20.00
Betty Crocker, Dinner For Two, Hardcover, 204 Pages, 1958 .... 1.50
Beverly Hill Billies, Granny's 95.00

To remove the remains of sticky glue and tape from antiques, try rubbing peanut butter on the sticky area until the glue is gone. Do not use this method on porous materials where the oil from the peanut butter could leave a stain.

Cookbook, McCormick & Co., Selected Recipes That Keep The Family Happy, c.1928, 5 x 8 In.

Budweiser, How To Cook With, 1950s, 40 Pages	25.00
Campbell's Soup, c.1915	20.00
Cream Of Wheat, 1924	22.00
Creole, Picayne, Sesquicentennial Edition, 629 Pages	24.00
Davis Baking Powder, 1904	8.00
Fleischmann's, 1910	12.00
Gone With The Wind, Southern Recipes, Scarlett O'Hara At Tara On Cover, 48 Pages	65.00
Good Housekeeping, Good Meals & How To Prepare Them, 1927	30.00
Good Housekeeping Everyday Cookbook, Curtis, Springfield, 1903	11.00
Hyde Park Beer, Sportman's Way, 1940s, 100 Pages	25.00
Jell-O, 1932	12.00
Jell-O, Bride & Her Task	45.00
Loved Chicken & Turkey Recipes, Sue Swanson, 24 Pages, 1950	1.50
Magee Furnace Company, 1921	8.00
Mary Dunbar, Jewel Tea	15.00
McCormick & Co., Selected Recipes That Keep The Family Happy, c.1928, 5 x 8 In. *Illus*	12.00
Nat'l. Livestock Board, 1942	11.00
Pillsbury, Best 1000 Bake-Off Recipe Book, 1959	15.00
Southern, Black, Soft Cover, Illustrated	50.00

COOKIE JARS with brightly painted designs or amusing figural shapes became popular in the mid-1930s. Many companies made them and collectors search for cookie jars either by design or by maker's name. Listed here are examples by the less common makers. Major factories are listed under their own names in other categories of the book, such as Abingdon, Brush, Hull, McCoy, Red Wing, and Shawnee. See also the Black and Disneyana categories.

Aunt Jemima, Brown Face	695.00
Avon Bear, California Originals	115.00
Batmobile, Warner Brothers, Box	95.00
Bear, With Cookie, Marcia Of California	30.00
Bellhop, Clay Art	75.00
Ben Franklin, Treasure Craft	125.00
Beulah, Metlox	300.00
Big Bird, Chef, Muppet, California Original, Box	70.00
Blue Bonnet Sue, Nabisco	95.00
Bugs Bunny, Warner Brothers	60.00
Bus, Grateful Dead	100.00
Bus, Honeymooners, Ralph, Alice, Norton & Trixie, Vandor	120.00 to 140.00
Card King, California Cleminson	600.00
Casper Friendly Ghost	600.00
Cat In The Hat, Limited Edition	350.00
Century 21, Mouse, Box	495.00
Cheerleaders, Flasher, American Bisque	300.00 to 400.00
Churn Boy, American Bisque	200.00
Clock, Marshall Field	65.00

Clown On Stage, Flasher, American Bisque 225.00
Clown On Stage, Green Curtains, Flasher, American Bisque 375.00
Cookie Cop, Pfaltzgraff 500.00
Cookie Monster, California Originals, Box 70.00
Cow, Purple, Butterfly, White Flowers, Metlox 625.00
Cow, Purple, Metlox, Box 350.00
Cowboy Boots, Cookie In Raised Letters, American Bisque 65.00
Cream Of Wheat, Black Cook 825.00
Crocodile, Sun Glasses, Vandor 95.00
Daffy Duck, Warner Brothers 60.00
Derby Dan, Pfaltzgraff 95.00
Dog With Hawaiian Tie, Animals & Co. 225.00
Drum, Napco 25.00
Elephant, American Bisque 150.00
Elsie The Cow 350.00
Entenmann's Chef 400.00
Ernie, Keebler Elf, F & F 125.00
Ernie, Muppets, California Originals 70.00
Foghorn Leghorn, Warner Brothers 50.00
Frog Prince, Metlox 90.00
Funfetti, Pillsbury 45.00
Goldilocks, Regal China 395.00
Halloween Hoedown Witch, Fitz & Floyd 125.00
Harp, Regal China 750.00
Humpty Dumpty, Abington 175.00
I Love Lucy 100.00
James Dean, 16 In. 50.00
Jolly Chef, Metlox 350.00
Ken-L-Ration Dog, 1950s, F & F 245.00
Majorette, American Bisque 225.00
Mammy, Fitz & Floyd 795.00
Mammy, Hands On Hips, Wihoa, Rick Wisecarver's, 14 1/2 In. 210.00
Mammy, Yellow, Mosaic Tile ....*Illus* 550.00
Mammy Scrubbing Boys, Wihoa's Cookie Classic, 11 In. 215.00
Matilda, Brayton Laguna ....375.00 to 550.00
Miss Cutey Pie, Napco 275.00
Money Bag, Abingdon 55.00
Monkey, With Yellow Hat, DeForest 160.00
Mother Goose, Blue Bonnet, Twin Winton 50.00
Mother-In-The-Kitchen, Prayer Lady, Enesco ....350.00 to 395.00
Mrs. Fleck's Famous Oatmeal Cookies, Glass, Label 195.00
Nick At Nite, Nickelodeon On Reverse 425.00
Night Before Christmas, Franklin Mint 175.00
Noah's Ark, California Originals 70.00
Noah's Ark, Treasure Craft 70.00
Paddington, Eden, 1978 .... 700.00

Keep a few moth balls in the vacuum cleaner bag to kill moth larvae. Some new vacuum cleaners heat the bagged dirt at the end of the vacuuming. This kills dust mites and insect eggs.

Cookie Jar,
Mammy, Yellow,
Mosaic Tile

Panda Bear, Black & White, Cumberland Ware 125.00
Pennsylvania Dutch Girl, American Bisque 295.00
Pig, American Bisque, 11 1/2 In. 165.00
Pig, Sitting, F & F 90.00
Pig In Overalls, American Pottery 65.00
Pink Panther, Treasure Craft 150.00
Prayer Lady, Pink 450.00
Quaker Oats, Regal . . . . .70.00 to 90.00
Raccoon, Metlox 45.00
Red Baron & Airplane, California Originals 300.00
Rio Rita, Fitz & Floyd 130.00
Sadiron, American Bisque 85.00
Santa, White Face, Metlox 250.00
Santa Cycle, Fitz & Floyd 450.00
Sockhoppers Caddy, Fitz & Floyd 275.00
Southwest Santa Claus, Fitz & Floyd 550.00
Tony The Tiger, Head, Plastic, Kellogg Co. 225.00
Train, Sierra Vista 55.00
Tweety Bird, 12 In. 35.00
Umbrella Kids, American Bisque . . . . .150.00 to 160.00
Uncle Sam, American Cookie Jar Co. 150.00
Uncle Sam Bear, Metlox 750.00
Woody Woodpecker, On Stump, California Originals 600.00
Woody Woodpecker, William Correll, 1988 . . . . 850.00

COORS ware was made by a pottery in Golden, Colorado, owned by the
Coors Beverage Company. Dishes and decorative wares were produced from the turn of the century until the pottery was destroyed by
fire in the 1930s. The name *Coors* is marked on the back. For more
information, see *Kovels' Depression Glass & Dinnerware Price List.*

COORS
U.S.A.

Ashtray, Bull & Wheat 125.00
Baker, Rosebud, Green 100.00
Bean Pot, Rosebud, Rope Handles 70.00
Bowl, Batter, Rosebud Blue, Handle 120.00
Custard Cup, Rosebud 15.00
Pan, Baking, Rosebud, Green 100.00
Salt & Pepper, Red 50.00
Sugar Shaker, Off-White 250.00
Teapot, Rosebud, Individual 228.00
Tumbler, Rosebud, Footed 55.00
Vase, Blue, Ring Handles, 6 In. 45.00
Vase, Matte Peach, Turquoise Interior, 1930s, 6 In. 45.00
Vase, Yellow, 6 In. 40.00

COPELAND pieces listed here are those that have a mark including the
word Copeland used between 1847 and 1976. Marks include Copeland
Spode and Copeland & Garrett. See also Copeland Spode and Royal
Worcester.

Biscuit Barrel, Blue, White Body, Gilt, Silver Plated Top, Bamboo Handle, 5 In. 170.00
Bowl, Scalloped, Silver Plated Stand, 9 1/2 In., Pair 345.00
Charger, Enamel Landscape, Haunt Of Heron On Reverse, c.1880, 16 In. 690.00
Cup & Saucer, Floral Design, Gilt Trim, Enameled, Pink Ground Saucer, 6 Piece 690.00
Figurine, Garrett Monkey Band, Wearing Floral Sprigged Costume, 5 1/2 In., Pair 690.00
Figurine, Woman, Partially Nude, Standing By A Tree Trunk, Foley, 92 In. 2185.00
Inkstand, Multicolored Flowers, Bulbous Ink Pot, c.1895, 5 1/2 x 9 5/8 x 4 1/4 In. 430.00
Jug, Dragon Form Handle, England, 7 3/4 In. 375.00
Plate, Blooming Roses Border, Cobalt Blue Ground, 9 In., Pair 275.00
Plate, Gilt Foliate, Jeweled Design, 9 In., 12 Piece 115.00
Plate, New Bridge, Willow Variant, 1906, 9 3/4 In. 125.00
Plate, Scalloped Edge, Gilt Highlights, 1860s, 8 3/8 In., 5 Piece 172.00
Platter, Well & Tree, Imari Design, c.1840, 21 x 15 1/2 In. 520.00
Vase, Transfer Printed Figures & Animals, Arcadian Setting, 8 1/2 In., Pair 747.00

COPELAND SPODE appears on some pieces of nineteenth-century English porcelain. Josiah Spode established a pottery at Stoke-on-Trent, England, in 1770. In 1833, the firm was purchased by William Copeland and Thomas Garrett and the mark was changed. In 1847, Copeland became the sole owner and the mark changed again. W.T. Copeland & Sons continued until a 1976 merger when it became Royal Worcester Spode. Pieces are listed in this book under the name that appears in the mark. Copeland Spode, Copeland, and Royal Worcester have separate listings.

Breakfast Set, Chelsea Birds, 16 Piece	475.00
Cup, Bouillon, Fairy Dell, Underplate	40.00
Figurine, Cries Of London, 7 In.	70.00
Plate, Tower, Pink, Square, 8 1/2 In.	25.00
Service Set, Flowers, Floral Sprays, 20th Century, Platter, 12 Plates	1840.00
Toby Jug, Winston Churchill, 8 1/2 In.	160.00

COPPER has been used to make utilitarian items, such as teakettles and cooking pans, since the days of the early American colonists. Copper became a popular metal with the Arts & Crafts makers of the early 1900s, and decorative pieces, like bookends and desk sets, were made. Other pieces of copper may be found in the Arts & Crafts, Bradley & Hubbard, Kitchen, and Roycroft categories.

Basket, Cone Shape, Riveted, Strap Handle, Dirk Van Erp, Windmill Mark, 11 In.	900.00
Bed Warmer, Brass Fittings, Turned Wood Handle, 42 In.	85.00
Bed Warmer, Engraved Design, Turned Maple Handle	145.00
Bed Warmer, Punched Star Cover, Brass Ferrule, Turned Handle	165.00
Bed Warmer, Tooled Brass Cover, Flower Medallion, Turned Wooden Handle, 36 In.	165.00
Bed Warmer, Turned Ash, Continental, 1815-1825, 41 1/2 In.	120.00
Boiler, Coffee, Folded Seams, Brass Bail, 13 In.	132.00
Bottle, Storage, Dovetailed, 18th Century, 8 1/2 In.	195.00
Bowl, Hammered, Applied Brass Geometrics, Original Patina, 10 In.	140.00
Bowl, Hammered, Dirk Van Erp, Impressed Mark, 8 1/2 In.	660.00
Bowl, Hammered, Original Patina, Dirk Van Erp, 6 x 2 1/2 In.	550.00
Box, Arts & Crafts, Silvercrest, 6 x 3 2/3 In.	165.00
Box, Cigarette, Enamel Plaque Cover, Galleon Ship, Gertrude C. Twichell, 4 x 5 1/2 In.	2700.00
Box, Domed Cover, Finial On Leaves, Society Of Arts & Crafts Of Boston, 4 3/4 In.	295.00
Box, Hammered, Dirk Van Erp, Impressed Mark, 6 x 3 1/2 In.	1100.00
Box, Hammered, Gustav Stickley, 7 x 5 1/2 x 5 In.	2090.00
Box, Hammered, Peacock In Landscape Lid, Frank Marshall, 4 1/4 In.	2200.00
Box, Hammered, Straps & Rivets, 10 x 7 x 5 In.	495.00
Box, Hammered, Swirl Design Cover, Ivory Finial, Albert Berry, 7 In.	2900.00
Box, Spice, 5 Compartments, c.1800, 9 In.	550.00
Chamberstick, Arts & Crafts, Original Patina, Carl Deffiner, 10 In.	100.00
Coffeepot, Brass Lid, Pewter Spout & Finial, Wooden Handle, Hanning Bowman, 7 In.	50.00
Coffeepot, Georgian, Tapered, Apple Wood Handle, Lift Lid, Curved Spout, 11 In.	405.00
Coffeepot, Gooseneck Spout, Wooden Handle & Finial, 19th Century, 8 In.	55.00
Container, Cover, Dovetailed, Bail Handle, 19th Century, 4 1/2 x 4 1/4 In.	175.00
Cup, 3 Voluted Form Legs, Cylindrical, Maria Zimmerman, 5 1/2 In.	1265.00
Dinner Gong, G. Stickley, 5-Footed Base, 23 x 11 x 36 In.	6050.00
Dish, Sweetmeat, Hexa-Lobed, 2 Scrolling Handles, Herrengrund, 18th Century, 5 In.	1150.00
Figurine, Wasp, Articulated, Shakudo Eyes, Signed, 2 1/2 In.	2055.00
Flagon, Front Stamped Trinity College, Early 19th Century, 12 Gal.	495.00
Foot Warmer, Dovetailed, Lid Pierced With 10 Hearts, 18th Century	495.00
Glue Pot, Dovetailed, Penna. Co. Ally Shop, Early 19th Century	275.00
Humidor, Riveted Hammered Brass Strapped Edges, Arts & Crafts, 6 2/3 x 10 In.	425.00
Inkwell, Hammered, Original Patina, Dirk Van Erp, 4 1/2 x 2 1/2 In.	330.00
Jardiniere, Gustav Stickley, Applied Handles	6600.00
Jardiniere, Relief Design, Scalloped Rim, India, 9 1/4 x 5 1/4 In.	35.00
Kettle, Apple Butter, Dovetailed, Iron Bail Handle	195.00
Kettle, Dovetailed, W. Heiss, No. 213 North Street, 7 x 8 1/2 In.	1035.00
Kettle, Dovetailed, Wrought Iron Bail Handle, 20 x 14 In.	190.00
Kettle, Dovetailed, Wrought Iron Bar Handle, 19th Century, 17 In.	110.00
Kettle, Hammered, Flared Rim, Wrought Handles, 14 x 6 1/2 In.	70.00

Kettle, Hot Water, Oval, 19th Century, 13 In. 143.00
Kettle, Iron Bail, 17 In. 145.00
Kettle, Marked Rochester, N.Y., 13 1/2 x 12 In. 85.00
Kettle, Wrought Iron Rim, Bail Handle, 18 x 16 1/2 In. 165.00
Lantern, 19th Century, 9 x 6 In. 195.00
Letter Holder, Gustav Stickley, Signed, 5 x 8 In. 1100.00
Mask, Helmet, Old Man, Turtle Earrings, Painted Frog, Mexico, 13 1/2 x 9 1/2 In. 115.00
Measure, Hammermilled, Dovetailed, Boston Mark, c.1760, 8 1/2 In. 365.00
Molds are listed in the Kitchen category.
Mug, Ale, 18th Century, 5 In. 295.00
Mug, Ale, Hammered, America, 18th Century 295.00
Mug, Dovetailed, Scroll Handle, 19th Century, 3 7/8 In. 195.00
Pan, Double Boiler, Wooden Handles, 28 In. 45.00
Pan, Dovetailed, Handle, 19th Century, 10 In. 82.00
Planter, Bulging Bowl Shape, Inverted Rollover Rim, Dirk Van Erp, 1910, 8 1/2 In. 1265.00
Saucepan, Dovetailed, Handle, 19th Century, 6 1/2 In. 38.00
Saucepan, Iron Handle, Cover, Early 19th Century 295.00
Sconce, Arts & Crafts, Scalloped Edge, Marked Volk, c.1890, 7 1/2 x 11 In., Pair 210.00
Tankard, Ale, Hinged Lid, c.1800, 7 1/2 In. 395.00
Tea Set, Hammered, Silver, Large Handled Tray, Joseph Heinrichs, 12 Piece 1760.00
Teakettle, Gooseneck Spout, Swivel Handle, Wooden Lid Finial, W. Heyser, 7 In. 100.00
Teakettle, Hammered, Wrought Iron Bail, Late 18th Century, 5 1/4 x 5 1/4 In. 165.00
Teapot, Lid & Handle, Handmade, 19th Century, 9 x 9 1/2 In. 195.00
Tray, Arts & Crafts, Hammered, Original Patina, 19 In. 230.00
Tray, Hammered, Arts & Crafts, 20 In. 150.00
Tray, Hammered, Dirk Van Erp, 6 In. 300.00
Tray, Hammered, Raised Handles, Round, Dirk Van Erp, 15 In. 1320.00
Tray, Round, Signed, Gustav Stickley, 11 In. 630.00
Tray, Stand, Silvered Center Figure, Village Scene, 21 x 42 In. 690.00
Vase, Egg Shape, Dirk Van Erp, 1911, 6 1/2 In. 1495.00
Vase, Geometric Design, Arts & Crafts, Silvercrest, Signed, 9 1/4 In. 110.00
Vase, Geometric Floral Design, Arts & Crafts, Silvercrest, 6 In. 245.00
Vase, Hammered, Harry Dixon, 7 In. 990.00
Vase, Hammered, Original Patina, Dirk Van Erp, 4 1/2 x 3 1/2 In. 660.00
Vase, Hammered, Original Patina, Jarvie, 5 In. 385.00
Vase, Hammered, Original Patina, Red Tones, Dirk Van Erp, 4 1/2 In. 1540.00
Vase, Hammered, Red Patina, Bulbous, Dirk Van Erp, 5 x 5 3/4 In. 1540.00
Vase, Hammered, Rolled Rim, Original Patina, San Francisco School, 9 x 9 In. 880.00
Vase, Hammered, Rolled Rim, Original Patina, Spherical, Dirk Van Erp, 7 1/2 x 9 In. 4400.00
Vase, Hammered, Tapered, Jarvie, 27 x 13 1/2 In. 28600.00
Vase, Tooled & Hammered, Signed, Tookay Shop, 7 In. 4125.00

COPPER LUSTER items are listed in the Luster category.

CORALENE glass was made by firing many small colored beads on the outside of glassware. It was made in many patterns in the United States and Europe in the 1880s. Reproductions are made today. Coralene-decorated Japanese pottery is listed in the Japanese Coralene category.

Tumbler, Diamond-Quilted, Mother-Of-Pearl, Pink Satin, Blue Bugs 250.00

Mother was right: Have a place for everything and everything in its place. Don't stack old dishes or crowd vases on a shelf. Proper spacing prevents nicks and breaks in pottery and porcelain.

Coralene,
Vase, Cranberry,
Seaweed, 8 In.

Vase, Cranberry, Seaweed, 8 In. ....*Illus*	410.00
Vase, Floral, Japan, 4 In.	175.00
Vase, Shaded Blue To Yellow, Scalloped Rim, 3 5/8 In.	137.00
Vase, Snowflake, Golden Amber Blending To Pink, 4 1/2 In.	425.00
Vase, Yellow Green, White Shaded To Blue, 6 1/8 In.	137.00

CORDEY China Company was founded by Boleslaw Cybis in 1942 in Trenton, New Jersey. The firm produced gift shop items. In 1969 it was acquired by the Lightron Corp. and operated as the Schiller Cordey Co., manufacturers of lamps. About 1950 Boleslaw Cybis began making Cybis porcelains, which are listed in their own category in this book.

Figurine, Cat, Persian, Reclining, Gray, Allover Roses & Forget-Me-Nots, 10 In.	395.00
Figurine, Colonial Man, No. 4127, 11 In.	65.00
Figurine, Madonna, 1950s, 13 In.	48.00
Wall Pocket, Lady	175.00

CORKSCREWS have been needed since the first bottle was sealed with a cork, probably in the seventeenth century. Today collectors search for the early, unusual patented examples or the figural corkscrews of recent years.

Anheuser-Busch, Pre-Prohibition	18.00
Anheuser-Busch, Wooden Handle, 1890s	35.00
Golf Club	20.00
Horn, Crescent Shape, Silver Mount, Meriden Britannia Co., 6 In.	230.00
Ivory, 19th Century, 5 In.	275.00
Man, Wooden, In Top Hat, Handle	85.00
Montreal Brand Malt Rye, Metal, Wooden Tube, c.1910, 3 3/4 In.	22.00
Rainier, Drink The Famous, Wooden Handle, 1890s	18.00
Schlitz Beer, c.1900	22.00
Spigot, Silver, 1800s	125.00
Sterling Silver, Horn Handle	100.00

CORONATION souvenirs have been made since the 1800s. Pottery, glass, tin, silver, and paper objects with a picture of the monarchs and date have been sold at many coronations. The pieces that mention King Edward VIII, the king who was never crowned, are not rare; collectors should be sure to check values before buying. Related pieces are found in the Commemorative category.

Bowl, Edward VIII, Meakin, 5 In.	40.00
Coloring Book, 16 Pages, 1951, 14 x 10 1/2 In.	20.00
Medal, Silver Jubilee, George V & Mary, 1910-1935, Silver, 2 1/2 In.	50.00
Mug, Queen Elizabeth, 1953	24.00
Picture, Queen Elizabeth, Tin, 1953	40.00
Pin, Elizabeth II, 1953, Plastic, Hand Mirror Shape, 2 1/2 In.	40.00
Plate, George V & Mary, 1911	128.00

COSMOS is a pressed milk glass pattern with colored flowers made from 1894 to 1915 by the Consolidated Lamp and Glass Company. Tablewares and lamps were made in this pattern. A few pieces were also made of clear glass with painted decorations. Other glass patterns are listed under Consolidated Lamp and also in various glass categories.

Bowl, 10 In.	195.00
Lamp, Milk Glass, Small	95.00
Lamp, Oil, Opaque White Glass, Embossed Design, Taplin Hinged Burner, 14 1/2 In.	395.00
Lamp, Yellow & Blue Flowers, Shade, 9 1/2 In.	475.00

COVERLETS were made of linen or wool during the nineteenth century. Most of the coverlets date from 1800 to the 1880s. There was a revival of hand weaving in the 1920s and new coverlets, especially geometric patterns, were made. The earliest coverlets were made on narrow looms, so two woven strips were joined together and a seam can be found. The weave structures of coverlets can include summer and winter, double weave, overshot, and others. Jacquard coverlets have elaborate pictorial patterns that are made on a special loom or with the use of a special attachment. Quilts are listed in this book in their own category.

Double Weave, Blue & White Tile, Floral Border, Fringe, Dated 1841, 94 x 76 In.	375.00
Double Weave, Double Rose, Petals, Leaf Border, Red, White, Fringe, 89 x 71 In.	345.00
Double Weave, Floral Medallion, Long-Tailed Birds, Red, White, 1852, 89 x 98 In.	220.00
Double Weave, Geometric Design, Navy Blue, White, 70 x 84 In.	140.00
Double Weave, Mustard & Red Stripes, Double Grape & Leaf Border, 82 x 74 In.	375.00
Double Weave, Pine Tree, Plaid Snowflake, Red, Teal Blue, 64 x 79 In.	230.00
Double Weave, Tulips, Blue Double Tulip & Leaf Border, Ohio, 1847, 80 x 68 In.	290.00
Double Weave, Tulips, Snowflakes, Star Border, Red, Blue, Ohio, 1853, 89 x 72 In.	1093.00
Floral Designs, Diamond Border, Emanuel Meily, 1839, 93 x 82 In.	357.00
Floral Wreaths & Starburst, Floral Border, Emanuel Ettinger, 1837, 96 x 71 In.	605.00
Jacquard, 4 Rose Medallions Swag Border, Single Weave, 78 x 91 In.	1125.00
Jacquard, 4 Rose Medallions, Bird, Navy Blue, Single Weave, 70 x 82 In.	135.00
Jacquard, 4 Rose Medallions, Floral Border, Building Corners, 2 Piece, 68 x 86 In.	300.00
Jacquard, 4 Rose Medallions, Green, Red & Natural, G. Baer, 1856, 76 x 82 In.	275.00
Jacquard, 4 Rose Medallions, Vintage, Bird Border, Single Weave, 74 x 84 In.	715.00
Jacquard, Center Medallion With 4 Eagles, Floral Border, Single Weave, 74 x 90 In.	360.00
Jacquard, Center Star Medallion, Sun, Eagles, Wm. Ney, Pennsylvania, 89 x 82 In.	863.00
Jacquard, Center Wreath, Leaves, Scrolls, Urns, Red, Dated 1840, 89 x 79 In.	460.00
Jacquard, Central Floral Medallion, Eagle Spandrels, Floral Border, 76 x 80 In.	550.00
Jacquard, Central Floral Medallions, Birds, 1852 In Corners, 89 x 98 In.	220.00
Jacquard, Double Heart & Potted Plant Design, Eagle Border, 1840, 86 x 74 In.	373.00
Jacquard, Double Lily Pattern, Row Of Stars, Blue, Red, Green, 78 x 93 In.	525.00
Jacquard, Double Weave, Center Medallion, Angel, Floral Border, 72 x 80 In.	220.00
Jacquard, Double Weave, Floral Grid, Navy Blue & Natural, 2 Piece, 80 x 85 In.	245.00
Jacquard, Double Weave, Floral Medallions With Rose Wreaths, 73 x 82 In.	385.00
Jacquard, Double Weave, Floral Medallions, Tree Border, 74 x 92 In.	210.00
Jacquard, Double Weave, Floral, Bird Borders, Tomato Red, Navy Blue, 73 x 83 In.	440.00
Jacquard, Double Weave, Geometric Floral Medallion Center, 78 1/2 x 90 In.	575.00
Jacquard, Double Weave, Peacocks, Turkeys, Trees, Navy Blue, White, 68 x 84 In.	300.00
Jacquard, Double Weave, Star Medallion Center, Fruit Basket Border, 78 x 87 In.	355.00
Jacquard, Enter Medallion, Corner Eagles, Sarah Elizabeth Steuben, 93 x 80 In.	220.00
Jacquard, Floral & Eagle, Tree Border, 2 Lions, Blue & White, c.1840, 87 x 76 In.	1725.00
Jacquard, Floral Medallion, Red & Natural, 72 x 86 In.	440.00
Jacquard, Floral Medallions & Border, Stars, 4 Star Corners, J.B. 1857, 78 x 85 In.	385.00
Jacquard, Floral Medallions, Double Vintage Border, 76 x 84 In.	192.00
Jacquard, Floral Medallions, Floral & Vintage Borders, Made 1858, 66 x 80 In.	220.00
Jacquard, Floral Medallions, Labeled W. In Mt. Vernon, Ohio, 74 x 80 In.	357.00
Jacquard, Floral Medallions, Navy, Salmon, Olive, Natural, Some Fringe, 78 x 90 In.	180.00
Jacquard, Floral Medallions, Red, Blue, Single Weave, 75 x 82 In.	660.00
Jacquard, Floral Medallions, Scrolled Borders, Single Weave, 70 x 86 In.	410.00
Jacquard, Floral Medallions, Stars, Eagle & Tree Border, Single Weave, 70 x 80 In.	1595.00
Jacquard, Floral, Borders, Red, Blue & Natural, Fringe, 1868, 2 Piece, 68 x 85 In.	440.00
Jacquard, Floral, Eagle, Green, Red, H.F. Stager & Son, Single Weave, 76 x 80 In.	550.00
Jacquard, Floral, Red & Green, Wide Floral Border, Fringe, 79 x 83 In.	195.00
Jacquard, Floral, Vintage Border, Salmon Pink, Navy Blue, 72 x 86 In.	385.00
Jacquard, Large Floral Medallions, Vintage Border, Oh., Single Weave, 1848	465.00
Jacquard, Oak Leaf, Bellflower Design, J. Pearson, Oh., Single Weave, 76 x 82 In.	220.00
Jacquard, Peacock, Blue & White, Christain & Heathen Border, 1846, 68 x 84 In.	385.00
Jacquard, Peacocks Feeding Young, Navy Blue, White, Single Weave, 67 x 81 In.	330.00
Jacquard, Red, Blue, Green, Joshua Corick, Frederick County, Md., 1840s, 85 x 77 In. . . .	490.00
Jacquard, Rose With American Eagle, Eagle & Banner Border, 1852, 72 x 86 In.	460.00
Jacquard, Single Weave, Rose Medallions Borders, 63 x 80 In.	330.00
Jacquard, Star & Flower Medallions, E. Pluribus Unum, Peacocks Border, 60 x 88 In. . . .	715.00
Jacquard, Star Center, Deer Corners, Capital Building Borders, 1 Piece, 66 x 78 In.	275.00
Jacquard, Star Medallions, Floral Border, Corner Labels, Ohio, 1843, 64 x 90 In.	440.00
Jacquard, Star Medallions, Vintage Border, Trees & Birds, 1849, 76 x 85 In.	550.00
Jacquard, Tree & Sunburst, Red, Blue, Green & Yellow, J. Cleaver, 1842, 79 x 89 In.	355.00
Jacquard, Tulip Medallions, Bird Border, Single Weave, 72 x 81 In.	385.00
Jacquard, Urns Of Flowers, Navy Blue, Salmon Pink, Single Weave, 70 x 80 In.	355.00

Jacquard, Vintage Design, Tulip Border, Jacob Snyder, Ohio, 2 Piece, 1850, 74 x 82 In. ... 495.00
Overshot, Checkerboard Pattern, 19th Century, 94 x 70 1/2 In. 258.00
Overshot, Diamond Design, 78 x 96 In. 220.00
Overshot, Indigo, Orange Peel, White Wool, Linen, 19th Century, 79 x 77 In. 170.00
Overshot, Optical, Navy Blue, White, 72 x 106 In. 275.00
Overshot, Optical, Red, Navy Blue, Natural White, 68 x 98 In. 165.00
Overshot, Plaid, Red, Navy, Natural White, 2 Piece, 70 x 86 In. 355.00
Overshot Woven, Red, Navy Blue, Green, Natural White, Penna., 2 Piece, 71 x 82 In. ... 385.00
Star & Flower Medallions, Peacock Border, E. Pluribus Unum, 1842, 60 x 88 In. 715.00
Summer-Winter, Navy Blue, Red, Natural White, 72 x 83 In. 165.00

COWAN POTTERY made art pottery and wares for florists. Guy Cowan made pottery in Rocky River, Ohio, a suburb of Cleveland, from 1913 to 1931. A stylized mark with the word *Cowan* was used on most pieces. A commercial, mass-produced line was marked *Lakeware.* Collectors today search for the Art Deco pieces by Guy Cowan, Viktor Schreckengost, Waylande Gregory, or Thelma Frazier Winter.

Bookends, Elephant, Push-Me, Pull-Me, 1930, 4 3/4 In. 1100.00
Bookends, Sunbonnet Girl, Oriental Orange Color, 7 1/2 In. 1100.00
Bowl, Apple Blossom Pink, 4 In. 70.00
Bowl, Green Interior, Signed, 3 x 10 In. 80.00
Bowl, Mottled Green Glaze Over Turquoise, Scrolled Handles, Oblong, 15 1/4 In. 1100.00
Candlestick, Blue, 13 In., Pair 195.00
Candlestick, Etruscan, Variegated High Glaze, Signed, 4 3/4 In., Pair 82.00
Candlestick, Off-White, Incised Crown Mark, 4 In. 25.00
Compote, April Green, Ivory 40.00
Decanter, King & Queen, Orange Glaze, Waylande Gregory, 12 In., Pair 1045.00
Decanter, King Form, Old Ivory Glaze, Waylande Gregory, Signed, 10 In. 450.00
Decanter, Queen, Oriental Red, Waylande Gregory, 11 In. 625.00
Figurine, Elephant, Mottled Oriental Red, Signed, Margaret Postgate, 10 1/2 In. 4640.00
Figurine, Horse, Egyptian Blue, 9 In. 1500.00
Figurine, Pavlova, Nude, No. 698 ....270.00 to 275.00
Figurine, Russian Accordion Player, Alexander Blazys, 8 1/2 In. 1000.00
Figurine, Russian Balalaika Player, Alexander Blazys, 11 1/2 In. 1800.00
Figurine, Russian Drummer, Terra-Cotta, 8 In. 550.00
Figurine, Spanish Dancer, Woman, Ivory, Elizabeth Andersen, 8 3/4 In. 950.00
Flower Frog, Awakening, Ivory Glaze, Stamped, R. Guy Cowan, 9 In. 770.00
Flower Frog, Dancer, Twirling, Glossy White Glaze, Signed, 4 1/4 x 9 1/2 In. 1000.00
Flower Frog, Laurel, Ivory Glaze, Stamped, 10 In. 900.00
Lamp Base, Queen, Special Ivory 600.00
Nut Dish, April Green 120.00
Plate, Fish & Bubble, Clair De Lune, 10 In. 300.00
Plate, Fish & Seaweed, Clair De Lune, 10 In. 120.00
Plate Set, Luncheon, April Green, 6 Piece 170.00
Urn, Ribbed, 2 Handles, Peacock Glaze, Cover, Stamped, 9 1/2 In. 90.00
Vase, Allover Pink & Maroon High Glaze, Signed, 5 In. 77.00
Vase, Amaco, 8 In. 75.00
Vase, Arabian Night, Blue Glaze, Viktor Schreckengost, Impressed Cowan, 6 1/4 In. 550.00
Vase, Blue High Glaze, Drilled For Lamp, 12 1/2 In. 55.00
Vase, Blue Luster Glaze, 7 1/2 In. 85.00
Vase, Chinese Bird, Crystalline Glaze, Signed, 11 1/4 In. 880.00
Vase, Chinese Bird, Green, 11 In. 395.00
Vase, Chinese Orange, 8 In. 250.00
Vase, Fan, Sea Horse Base, April Green, 6 In. 60.00
Vase, Stylized Leaves, Persian Blue Crackled Glaze, Signed, 8 In. 800.00
Vase, Yellow To Green Glaze, c.1924, 8 1/4 In. 135.00

CRACKER JACK, the molasses-flavored popcorn mixture, was first made in 1896 in Chicago, Illinois. A prize was added to each box in 1912. Collectors search for the old boxes, toys, and advertising materials. Many of the toys are unmarked.

Booklet, In South Africa, Multicolor, 1 1/2 x 2 1/2 In. 220.00
Booklet, Riddles 38.00

Bottle Opener, Corkscrew	125.00
Game, Tic-Tac-Toe, Red, White & Blue, 1 1/2 x 2 1/2 In.	35.00
Lion Cage, Tin Lithograph, 1 1/4 In.	105.00
Postcard, Salesmen Behind Table, Large Cracker Jack Sign, Unused	78.00
Sign, For May Days & Every Day, Cracker Jack, Cardboard, 1919, 15 x 20 In.	176.00
Sled, Tin, Embossed Name, 1 In.	32.00
Toy, Clever Clown, Box	745.00
Truck, Marshmallows On 1 Side, Cracker Jack On Other Side, 1 x 1 In.	125.00
Wheelbarrow, Tin, Embossed Cracker Jack, 2 1/4 In.	25.00

CRACKLE GLASS was originally made by the Venetians, but most of the ware found today dates from the 1800s. The glass was heated, cooled, and refired so that many small lines appeared inside the glass. It was made in many factories in the United States and Europe.

Ginger Jar, Enameled Garden Scene, Bids, Dragonflies, China, 10 1/4 In., Pair	230.00
Pitcher, Amberina, 8 In.	35.00
Pitcher, Olive Green Handle, Pewter Hinged Top, 8 In.	145.00
Vase, Electric Blue, 9 x 7 In.	65.00
Vase, Light Green, Crimped Lip, 4 1/2 In.	15.00
Water Set, Emerald Green, Pinched Sides, 7 Piece	395.00

CRANBERRY GLASS is an almost transparent yellow-red glass. It resembles the color of cranberry juice. The glass has been made in Europe and America since the Civil War. It is still being made, and reproductions can fool the unwary. Related glass items may be listed in other categories, such as Northwood, Rubena Verde, etc.

Banana Bowl, Delaware	62.00
Bowl, Cut, Pedestal, 1880s, 6 In.	115.00
Bowl, Enamel Flowers, Wishbone Feet, 4 1/2 x 8 In.	175.00
Box, Cover, Crystal Rigaree, 4 1/2 In.	125.00
Cracker Jar, Silver Plated Cover, Bear Finial, c.1890, 10 In.	690.00
Creamer, Gold Enameed Grape, 3 3/4 In.	190.00
Creamer, Quilted Diamond, Applied Clear Handle & Foot, 5 In.	45.00
Decanter, c.1890, 7 1/2 In.	110.00
Jug, Claret, Hinged Top, Brass Rim & Handle, 9 1/2 In.	225.00
Lamp, Engraved, Camphored Shade, Pendant Prisms, Brass & Marble Base	715.00
Lamp, Hanging, Hobnail, Brass, Electrified, 8 1/2 x 8 In.	345.00
Salt, Enameled Floral	85.00
Salt, Silver Holder	75.00
Sugar Shaker, Silver Plated Cover, 19th Century	230.00
Sugar Shaker, Venetian Diamond	250.00
Tankard, Pitcher Shape, Clear Reeded Apple Handle, Hinged, 10 In.	175.00
Vase, Hobnail, Enameled Floral, Butterfly, 20th Century, 11 1/2 In., Pair	125.00

CREAMWARE, or queensware, was developed by Josiah Wedgwood about 1765. It is a cream-colored earthenware that has been copied by many factories. Similar wares may be listed under Pearlware and Wedgwood.

Beaker, Tea Party, Scrolled Foliate Border, Black Transfer, 1770, 3 In.	635.00
Bowl, Barber's, Entwined Grooved Strap Handle, Rim Cutout, Round, 10 In.	1495.00
Bowl, Cream, Cover, Pierced, Band Of Flutes On Lower Body, 1775, 7 In., Pair	1840.00
Cake Plate, Tea Party, Black Transfer, England, 1780, 6 In.	400.00
Charger, Blue Feather Edge, Band Of Onions, 18th Century, 15 In.	395.00
Coffeepot, Cover, Exotic Birds Perched Amongst Leafy Branches, 9 In.	5175.00
Coffeepot, Cover, Rose Spray, Entwined Grooved Strap Handle, 1780, 9 In.	1092.00
Coffeepot, Cover, Tea Party, Pear Shape, Black Transfer, Strap Handle, 9 In.	345.00
Coffeepot, Cover, Tea Party, Shepherd, Pear Shape, Strap Handle, 1780, 10 In.	345.00 to 460.00
Coffeepot, Pear Shape, Entwined Handle, Floral Finial, Staffordshire, 10 1/2 In.	690.00
Coffeepot, Reeded Spout, Leaf Handle, Floral Designs, c.1775, 8 3/4 In.	920.00
Coffeepot, Tea Party Side, Strap Handle, Leaf Spout, Floral Finial, 10 1/4 In.	862.00
Colander	160.00
Creamer, Cover, Tea Party, Shepherd, Entwined Strap Handles, Black Transfer	230.00
Cuspidor, Woman's, Polychrome Floral, Pink Luster, Leaf Handle, 4 1/4 In.	240.00

Dish, Feather-Molded Border, Round, 1770, 18 In. 690.00
Dish, Leaf, Bird Perched On Leaf & Berry, Staffordshire, c.1780, 11 In. 517.00
Dish, Ribbon-Tied Swags, Floral Lattice Work, Bellflower Garlands, 8 In., Pair 520.00
Figurine, Blackamoor, Enameled, Raised Round Plinth, Electrified, 9 1/2 In. 260.00
Jug, Captain Jones Of Macedonia, General Washington, Black, White, 6 1/2 In. 1850.00
Jug, Cover, Tea Party, Shepherd, Entwined Strap Handles, 1780, 5 In. 175.00
Mold, Gelatin, Pineapple, 2 Leaves In Scalloped Border, 4 Peg Feet, Oval, 10 In. 345.00
Mug, Bands Of Brown Slip, Scrolled Borders, 2 3/4 In. 345.00
Mug, Blue, White Bands, 19th Century, 5 1/2 x 6 In. 154.00
Mug, Blue, White, 19th Century, 4 1/4 x 4 1/2 In. 55.00
Plaque, Lafayette The Nation's Guest, Portrait Reserve, 1840s, 5 7/8 x 5 1/2 In. 287.00
Plate, 3-Masted Ship Flying American Flag, 15 Stars, England, 9 3/4 In. 144.00
Plate, Basket Weave, Reticulated Border, Pink & Green Luster Castle Tower, 8 In. 580.00
Plate, Brown Mottled Glaze, England, Late 18th Century, 8 In. 230.00
Platter, Blue Feather Edge, Onion Band, Oval, c.1785, 14 1/2 In. 395.00
Platter, Scrolled Border, 19 In. 192.00
Punch Bowl, Floral Cartouche, Black Exterior, Laurel, Trellis Border, 14 In. 4312.00
Stirrup Cup, Cow Shape, Late 18th Century, England, 4 7/8 In. 345.00
Stirrup Cup, Hound Head, Ocher, Brown Glaze, England, 5 In. 1380.00
Tea Canister, Cover, Tea Party, Shepherd, Black Transfer, 1780, 6 In. 460.00
Tea Canister, Cover, Tea Party, Shepherd, Black Transfer, Cylindrical, 4 7/8 In. 430.00
Tea Canister, Tea Party, Shepherd, Octagonal, 6 3/8 In., Pair 635.00
Tea Set, Tea Party, Chinese Trellis Chairs, Black Transfer, 1780, 6 In., 4 Piece 690.00
Tea Set, Vertical Bands Of Green Glaze, Everted Rim Teapot, 1780, 3 Piece 2875.00
Teapot, Cover, Crabstock Handle, Brown Mottled Glaze, England, 5 In. 230.00
Teapot, Cover, Death Pities None, Surrounded By Flower Sprays, 6 In. 1955.00
Teapot, Cover, Floral Sprigs, Green Glaze Crabstock Handle, 1770, 3 In. 860.00
Teapot, Cover, Miss Pitt, Seated At Table Making Tea, Scroll Handle, 1775, 5 In. 2875.00
Teapot, Domed Cover, Captain Cook, Red Flower Sprigs, Green Ovals, 6 In. 8050.00
Teapot, Harlequin & Columbine, William Greatbach, c.1780, 6 3/4 In. 402.00
Teapot, Oriental Figures, Strap Handle, Floral Finial, c.1795, 4 1/2 In. 1035.00
Teapot, Tea Party & Shepherds Transfers, Iron Red, 5 In. 545.00
Tureen, Cover, Domed, Entwined Grooved Strap Handle, 1770, 11 In. 1380.00
Tureen, Cover, Melon Shape, Curved Stalk, Looped Tendril Handle, 1770, 8 In. 2300.00
Tureen, Sauce, Cover, Ladle, Molded As Bunch Of Grapes, 8 In. 488.00

CREDIT CARDS, credit tokens, metal charge plates, phone cards, and
other similar collectibles that replace money are now part of the
numismatic collecting hobby.

Phillips 66, Paper, Green, White, Red Trim, 1940, 3 1/2 x 2 1/4 In. 50.00
Socony-Vacuum White Eagle Division, Paper, White, Red, 1940, 3 3/4 x 2 In. 35.00
Standard Oil Company Of California, Paper, Red, White & Blue, 1931, 3 x 2 In. 185.00
Texaco, Gray Ground, Black Lettering, Paper, 1947, 3 1/2 x 2 1/4 In. 50.00
Texaco, Texas Company, Paper, 1937, 3 1/2 x 2 1/4 In. 110.00
Texaco, Texas Company, Paper, White, Black Lettering, 1931, 3 3/4 x 2 In. 500.00

CROWN DERBY is the name given to porcelain made in Derby, England,
from the 1770s to 1935. Pieces are marked with a crown and the letter
D or the word *Derby*. The earliest pieces were made by the original
Derby factory, while later pieces were made by the King Street
Partnerships (1848–1935) or the Derby Crown Porcelain Co.
(1876–1890). Derby Crown Porcelain Co. became Royal Crown Derby
Co. Ltd. in 1890. It is now part of Royal Doulton Tableware Ltd.

Plate, Floral Bouquet Design, Foliate, Geometric, Gilt Rim, 9 In., 11 Piece 201.00

**When packing teapots to move, do not tape the lid to the pot.
The tape may leave a stain and the lid may chip if it is handled
roughly or just bumps around while being moved in a car.**

Tea Set, Imari Pattern, Box, 2 1/2-In. Plate, Miniature, 5 Piece 1265.00
Tray, Imari Pattern, Footed, Scalloped, Late 19th Century, 19 In. 545.00

CROWN DUCAL is the name used on some pieces of porcelain made by A. G. Richardson and Co., Ltd., of Tunstall and Cobridge, England. The name has been used since 1916.

Cake Plate, Chintz, Ivory 175.00
Demitasse Set 60.00
Plate, Scenes Of American History, 10 1/4 In., 8 Piece 115.00

CROWN MILANO glass was made by Frederick Shirley at the Mt. Washington Glass Works about 1890. It had a plain biscuit color with a satin finish. It was decorated with flowers and often had large gold scrolls.

Biscuit Jar, Enameled Flowers, Gold Trim, Silver Plated Lid & Fittings, 6 3/4 In. 770.00
Biscuit Jar, Starfish & Seaweed, White, Red, Green, 9 In. 978.00
Bride's Bowl, Pansies & Medallions, Ruffled Tricornered Edge, 10 1/2 In. 850.00
Candlestick, Maroon Ground, Woman, Silver Plated Base & Socket, 8 In. 1750.00
Jardiniere, Oak Leaves, Gold Berries, Light Brown Ground, 12 1/2 In. 863.00
Jardiniere, Rose Sprays, Allover Rose Tracery, 8 3/4 x 11 In. 1035.00
Lamp, Banquet, Garden Of Allah, Gold Wash Silver Base, 31 In. 10925.00
Rose Bowl, Yellow, Pink & White Chrysanthemum, 3 In. 370.00
Sugar & Creamer, Cover, Flowers, Gold Scrolls, Green Trim, 5 x 4 1/2 In. 2070.00
Vase, Cupid, Cherubs, Cartouches, Gold Trim, 2 Loop Handles, Signed, 9 x 7 In. 2645.00
Vase, Flared Neck, Rim Split Into 4 Points, Gold Leaves, Signed, 9 1/2 In. 862.00
Vase, Gold Enameled Foliage, Swirled Flutes, Scalloped Mouth, 5 In. 990.00
Vase, Guba Ducks, In Flight, 3 Ducks Reverse, Signed, 11 1/4 In. 4600.00
Vase, Peach, Yellow Ground, Gold Rose, Leaves, Buds, 5 In. 1200.00
Vase, Starling Perched Amidst Pine Branches, Foliage, Milk Glass, 18 In. 5750.00
Vase, Tulips, Morning Glories & Floral Sprays, Gold Trim, 9 In. 290.00
Vase, White, Tulips & Morning Glories, Gold Trim, 9 In. 290.00

CROWN TUSCAN pattern is included in the Cambridge glass category.

CRUETS of glass or porcelain were made to hold vinegar, oil, and other condiments. They were especially popular during Victorian times and have been made in a variety of styles since the eighteenth century. Additional cruets may be found in the Castor Set category and also in various glass categories.

Aqua Glass, 28 Vertical Ribs, Blown, Applied Handle, 5 7/8 In. 60.00
Aqua Glass, Blown, Applied Hollow Handle, Stopper, 6 In. 38.00
Blown Glass, Molded, Cut, Handle, Tole Frame, Ebonized Fittings, 11 In., 3 Piece 330.00
Blue Glass, Victorian, 4 Piece 225.00
Blue Opalescent Glass, Swirls, Hollow Stopper, Amber Handle, Blue, 7 1/4 In. 345.00
Cut Glass, Oregon Pattern, Ships Type, Stopper, 6 1/4 x 4 1/2 In., Pair 345.00
Cut Glass, Silver Stand, With Shell Style Handle, George III, London, 9 1/2 In., 5 Piece .. 745.00
Sterling Silver, England, Late 19th Century, 5 Piece 675.00

CUP PLATES are small glass or china plates that held the cup while a diner of the mid-nineteenth century drank coffee or tea from the saucer. The most famous cup plates were made of glass at the Boston and Sandwich factory located in Sandwich, Massachusetts. There have been many new glass cup plates made in recent years for sale to gift shops or limited edition collectors. These are similar to the old plates but can be recognized as new.

Anti-Slavery, Blue Transfer, 4 In. 250.00
Bird & Flower, Red Transfer, Staffordshire, 4 In., 4 Piece 192.00
Castle Garden Battery, Blue, Staffordshire, Wood & Sons, 3 5/8 In. 220.00
Columbus Georgia Scene, Light Blue, 3 7/8 In. 415.00
Corinth, Brown, James Edwards 55.00
Cottage In Woods, Staffordshire, Wood, 3 5/8 In. 165.00
LaFayette, Black Transfer, Staffordshire, 3 3/4 In. 630.00
Landing Of Founding Fathers, Pilgrim Scenes, Staffordshire, 6 Piece 150.00
Masted Ship & Sailor's Widow Design, Porcelain, 5 1/2 In. 350.00

New Orleans, Red Transfer, Red Rim, Staffordshire, 3 3/4 In. 137.00
Winter View Of Pittsfield, Massachusetts, Staffordshire, 4 5/8 In. 192.00
Woodlands Near Philadelphia, Blue, Staffordshire, 3 1/8 In. 300.00

CURRIER & IVES made the famous American lithographs marked with
their name from 1857 to 1907. The mark used on the print included the
street address in New York City, and it is possible to date the year of
the original issue from this information. Earlier prints were made by N.
Currier and use that name from 1835 to 1847. Many reprints of the
Currier or Currier & Ives prints have been made. Some collectors buy
the insurance calendars that were based on the old prints. The words
large, small, or *medium folio* refer to size. The original print sizes were
very small (up to about 7 x 9 in.), small (8.8 x 12.8 in.), medium (9 x
14 in. to 14 x 20 in.), large (larger than 14 x 20 in.). Other sizes are
probably later copies. Other prints by Currier & Ives may be listed in
the Card category under Advertising and in the Sheet Music category.
Currier & Ives dinnerware patterns may be found in the Adams or
Dinnerware categories.

Abraham Lincoln 16th President Of U.S., Frame 250.00
American Farm Yard, Evening, Shadowbox Frame, 20 3/8 x 27 1/8 In. 1815.00
American Homestead, Summer, Matted, Frame, 10 x 14 In. 110.00
American Homestead, Winter, Small Folio 220.00
American Privateer, Gen. Armstrong, 1812 War, Frame, 1830s, Medium Folio 600.00
American Winter Sports, Deer Shooting, Frame, Large Folio 2200.00
Battle At Cedar Mountain, 1862, Matted, Frame, 15 x 19 1/2 In. 165.00
Battle Of Antietam, Md., 1862, Matted, Frame, 13 1/2 x 17 3/4 In. 290.00
Battle Of Chancellorsville, Va., 1863, Frame, 13 1/2 x 17 3/4 In. 253.00
Battle Of Chancellorsville, Va., 1863, Matted, Frame, 14 3/4 x 19 1/4 In. 286.00
Battle Of Corinth, Miss., 1862, Frame, 13 1/2 x 17 5/8 In. 275.00
Battle Of Fair Oaks, Va., 1862, Matted, Frame, 15 x 19 1/2 In. 270.00
Battle Of Fair Oaks, Va., 1862, Matted, Frame, Large Folio 1045.00
Battle Of Fredericksburg, Va., 1862, Matted, Frame, 15 x 19 1/2 In. 286.00
Battle Of Mill Spring, Ky., 1862, Matted, Frame, 15 x 18 1/2 In. 165.00
Battle Of Pea Ridge, Ark., 1862, Matted, Frame, Large Folio 990.00
Battle Of Sharpsburg, Md., 1862, Matted, Frame, 13 3/4 x 17 1/4 In. 300.00
Brush For The Lead, 1867, 19 1/2 x 29 1/2 In. 680.00
Burning Of Steamship Golden Gate, July 27, 1862, Matted, Frame, 17 x 21 In. 220.00
Capture Of Andre, 1780, Matted, Frame, 12 1/4 x 16 1/4 In. 80.00
Clipper Ship Flying Cloud, Large Folio 275.00
Clipper Ship Ocean Express, Large Folio 185.00
Cottage Door Yard Evening, Hand Colored, Frame, 13 x 17 1/8 In. 110.00
Cottage Life, Summer, Frame, Medium Folio 195.00
Cutter Yacht Thistle, 1887, Small Folio 275.00
Ethan Allen & Mate & Dexter, Matted, Frame, Large Folio 770.00
First Ride, Small Folio 66.00
Frontier Lake, Frame, 9 7/8 x 14 In. 220.00
Frontier Lake, Frame, 12 1/2 x 16 1/2 In. 220.00
Frozen Up, 1872, Small Folio 1800.00
Fruits Of Season, Frame, Small Folio 110.00
General Meagher At Battle Of Fair Oaks, Va., 1862, Matted, Frame, 15 x 19 In. 245.00
General Shields At Battle Of Winchester, Va., 1862, Matted, Frame, 12 x 16 In. 245.00
Great West, Frame, Small Folio 577.00
Gunboat Candidate Battle Of Malvern Hill, Frame, Small Folio 200.00
Harvesting, Frame, Gilded Liner, 13 1/4 x 17 3/8 In. 220.00
Harvesting Last Load, Curly Maple Frame, 14 1/2 x 18 1/2 In. 220.00
Haunts Of Wild Swan, Maple Frame, 15 x 19 In. 302.00
Home In Wilderness, Frame, 13 3/8 x 17 3/8 In. 302.00
Home Of The Deer, Matted, Frame, 12 1/2 x 17 1/2 In. 355.00
James K. Polk, Matted, Frame, 19 x 15 In. 165.00
Jeff D. Hung On Sour Apple Tree, Greeley, Medium Folio 350.00
King Of House, Frame, 1875, 14 1/8 x 11 5/8 In. 140.00
Last Ditch Of Chivalry, Davis, Frame, Medium Folio 350.00
Last War-Whoop, Matted, Frame, 29 x 35 In. 4750.00

Lexington Of 1861, Frame, 14 1/2 x 19 In. 300.00
Lincoln, 3 In 1 Picture, Sherman & Grant, Shadowbox Frame, 17 x 20 In. 3250.00
Little Fireman, Frame, Large Folio 330.00
Mambrin, Painted Frame, 11 x 15 In. 550.00
New England Winter Scene, Frame, 26 x 31 1/2 In. 110.00
Off A Lee Shore, Conningham, No.4532, Frame, Small Folio 137.00
Old Weir Bridge, Lakes Of Killarney, Frame, 11 1/8 x 20 In. 285.00
On The Owago, 12 x 16 In. 165.00
Quail, Original Frame, Small Folio 110.00
Riverside, Matted, Frame, Medium Folio 330.00
Route To California, Frame, Small Folio 687.00
Saratoga Lake, Matted, Frame, 9 15/16 x 13 3/4 In. 82.00
Scenery Of The Catskills, Gilded Frame, 14 1/2 x 18 1/4 In. 385.00
Season Of Blossoms, Cross Corner Frame, 12 x 16 In. 245.00
Second Battle Of Bull Run, 1862, Matted, Frame, 14 3/4 x 19 1/4 In. ....245.00 to 275.00
Sheep Pasture, Frame, 12 1/4 x 15 5/8 In. 220.00
Soldier's Dream Of Home, Matted, Frame, 10 15/16 x 15 In. 74.00
Soldier's Home, The Vision, Matted, Frame, 10 x 14 1/16 In. 74.00
Steamboat Lexington, Jan. 13, 1840, N. Currier, Frame, 21 x 13 In. 3450.00
Strawberries, Black Beveled Frame, 11 3/4 x 15 3/4 In. 247.00
Summer In The Country, Frame, Small Folio 110.00
Summer In The Woods, Frame, Medium Folio 360.00
Summer Morning, Trimmed Margins, Frame, 9 7/8 x 13 7/8 In. 165.00
Surrender Of Port Hudson, La., July 8th, 1863, Frame 154.00
Through To The Pacific, Frame, Small Folio 192.00
Tomb Of Washington, Mount Vernon, Va., Frame, 11 1/4 x 14 1/2 In. 200.00
Tropical & Summer Fruits, 1867, 14 7/8 x 20 3/8 In. 110.00
Trotting Cracks On Snow, Figural Maple Frame, 25 1/4 x 33 1/2 In. 2905.00
Unconscious Sleeper, Black & White, Frame, 12 1/8 x 10 1/8 In. 125.00
United Americans, Patriotism, Charity & Harmony, Frame, 14 x 9 3/4 In. 220.00
Washington Family, Black & White, Frame, 1867, 11 1/8 x 15 In. 145.00
Washington's Reception On Bridge At Trenton, No. 6553, Frame, 14 x 10 In. 125.00
Western Farmer's Home, Mat, Beveled Frame, 12 1/2 x 16 1/2 In. ....341.00 to 357.00

CUSTARD GLASS is a slightly yellow opaque glass. It was first made in
England in the 1880s and was first made in the United States in the
1890s. It has been reproduced. Additional pieces may be found in the
Cambridge, Fenton, Heisey, and Northwood categories. Custard glass
is called Ivorina Verde by Heisey and other companies.

Argonaut Shell, Butter 150.00
Argonaut Shell, Compote, Jelly 145.00
Argonaut Shell, Creamer 159.00
Argonaut Shell, Cruet 895.00
Argonaut Shell, Sauce 65.00
Argonaut Shell, Spooner 159.00
Beaded Circle, Tumbler, Enameled Blossom In Circles 250.00
Chrysanthemum Sprig, Compote, Jelly, Gold Trim 85.00
Chrysanthemum Sprig, Creamer 145.00
Chrysanthemum Sprig, Jelly 115.00
Chrysanthemum Sprig, Toothpick 260.00
Chrysanthemum Sprig, Tumbler, Blue 225.00
Geneva, Sauce, Oval 45.00
Grape & Lattice, Vase, 3 1/2 In. 22.00
Intaglio, Berry Bowl 80.00
Intaglio, Berry Bowl, Blue Decoration, Master 365.00
Intaglio, Compote, Jelly, Blue Decoration 169.00
Intaglio, Creamer 70.00
Intaglio, Sauce, Footed 90.00
Intaglio, Sugar, Blue Decoration 195.00
Inverted Fan & Feather, Salt & Pepper 950.00
Louis XV, Berry Bowl, Master 195.00
Louis XV, Pitcher, Water 350.00
Louis XV, Spo0ner 100.00

Maize is its own category in this book.

Orange Tree, Sugar, Breakfast		100.00
Ring Band, Creamer, Roses		139.00
Ring Band, Cruet, Gold Trim		375.00
Ring Band, Pitcher, Water, Roses		395.00
Winged Scroll, Spooner, Gold Trim		115.00
Winged Scroll, Sugar & Creamer, Gold Trim, 4 1/2 In.		82.00
Winged Scroll, Syrup		550.00

CUT GLASS has been made since ancient times, but the large majority of the pieces now for sale date from the brilliant period of glass design, 1880 to 1905. These pieces have elaborate geometric designs with a deep miter cut. Modern cut glass with a similar appearance is being made in England, Ireland, and the Czech and Slovak republics. Chips and scratches are often difficult to notice but lower the value dramatically. A signature on the glass adds significantly to the value. Other cut glass pieces are listed under factory names.

Banana Bowl, Butterfly, Arcadia		300.00
Barrel, Whiskey, On Silver Plated Stand, 1890		2850.00
Basket, Braided Handle, 6 1/2 x 5 In.		475.00
Basket, Floral & Leaf, Double Notched Handle, 17 x 11 1/2 In.		745.00
Basket, Harvard, Etched Flowers, Cut Leaf & Vine, Thumbprint Handle, 21 In.		425.00
Basket, Rosebud, McKanna Cut Glass Co., 1915		295.00
Berry Bowl, Gooseberries & Leaves, 8 In.		495.00
Biscuit Jar, Cover, Diamond Fan, Brilliant, Facet Cut Finial		350.00
Bonbon, Notched Prism & Hobstar, 6 x 6 In.		175.00
Bottle, Bottle, Geometric & Rosette, Brilliant, 7 1/2 In.		220.00
Bottle, Honeycomb, Repousse Lid, Sterling Silver, 7 1/2 In.		180.00
Bottle, Strawberry-Diamond, Stopper, Case, England, 9 7/8 In.		170.00
Bottle, Water, Geometrics, Rosettes, Brilliant, c.1900, 7 1/2 In.		220.00
Bowl, 3 Flowers, Nailhead Center, Gowens, Kenty & Co., 8 In.		145.00
Bowl, 4 Hobstars, Brilliant, 4 x 10 1/4 In.		115.00
Bowl, 5 Hobstars, Brilliant, 3 3/4 x 9 In.		345.00
Bowl, 6 Hobstar Panels, Brilliant Cut, 8 In.		490.00
Bowl, 7 Hobstars, Brilliant, Clark, 3 x 8 3/4 In.		80.00
Bowl, 8 Hobstars, Brilliant, Flared, 6 1/2 x 9 1/2 In.		630.00
Bowl, Allover Foliate, Round, 8 In.		55.00
Bowl, Allover Hobstars, Clark, 2 1/4 x 9 In.		85.00
Bowl, Band Of Notched Diamonds & Fans, Scalloped Edge, Ireland, 10 In.		143.00
Bowl, Basketweave, Rolled Rim, 10 In.		400.00
Bowl, Brilliant, Hawkes, 7 x 3 1/4 In.		201.00
Bowl, Brilliant, Monogram LN, Sterling Mount, 4 1/4 x 8 In.		230.00
Bowl, Brilliant, Ruffled Edge, Square, 3 3/4 x 10 1/2 In.		145.00
Bowl, Center Hobstar, Radiates To Prism Edge, 9 x 2 In.		225.00
Bowl, Comet, Scalloped, 8 x 4 In.		325.00
Bowl, Crosshatch, Hobstars & Cane, 4 x 8 In.		375.00
Bowl, Egginton, Signed, 7 In.		175.00
Bowl, Elmira, Vertical Cut, 3 1/2 x 8 In.		350.00
Bowl, Essex, Dorflinger, Paper Label, 9 In.		595.00
Bowl, Expanding Star, 4 Sections, 9 In.		410.00
Bowl, Flared, Cross Cut Diamonds & Clear Tusks, 4 1/2 x 9 3/4 In.		425.00
Bowl, Harvard, Floral, Shallow, 8 1/2 In.		95.00
Bowl, Hobstar Base, Scalloped Edge, 8 1/2 In.		395.00
Bowl, Hobstar Border, Fern Leaves In Center, Hoare, 8 In.		500.00
Bowl, Hobstar, Geometrics & Flowers, Gowens, Kent & Co., 8 In.		150.00
Bowl, Hobstars, Brilliant, 2 1/2 x 9 In.		170.00
Bowl, Hobstars, Brilliant, 4 x 8 In.		60.00
Bowl, Hobstars, Fans & Cane, Sterling Silver Rim, Gorham, c.1900, 8 In.		375.00
Bowl, Holster Center, Square, Rolled Corners, Russia, 8 3/4 In., Pair		1000.00
Bowl, Rolled Corners, 9 1/2 In.		325.00
Bowl, Rose Design, c.1885, 4 1/4 In.		220.00
Bowl, Signed, Hoare, 8 x 3 3/4 In.		195.00
Bowl, Triple Miter Cut, Pineapple Shape, Russia		1595.00

Bowl, Tripod Base, Hawkes, 7 1/2 x 4 In. 55.00
Box, Handkerchief, Sterling Mounts, C.F. Monroe 675.00
Bread Tray, Allover Hobstars In Diamonds, Flower Buttonhole Center, 13 x 6 In. 165.00
Butter, Cover, Brilliant, Floral, Lapidary Knob, 6 1/2 x 7 In. 115.00
Candlestick, Brilliant, Teardrop Stem, Star Base, 6 In. 195.00
Candlestick, Teardrop Stem, 6 Sides, Hobstar Base, 9 1/2 In. 225.00
Candy Dish, Hobstars, 3-Footed, 8 x 3 In. 175.00
Carafe, Brilliant, Sterling Silver, 1900-1910, 7 1/2 In. 182.00
Carafe, Floral, Intaglio Foliate Design, Brilliant Cut, Circular Cut Band, 8 1/4 In. 80.00
Carafe, Hobstar, J. Hoare Co., 1853, 8 1/4 In. 100.00
Carafe, Jubilee, Clark, 8 /14 x 5 3/4 In. 260.00
Carafe, Marlboro, Dorflinger, 7 1/4 x 6 1/2 In. 305.00
Carafe, Sunburst & Hobstar, Hobstar Base, 8 1/4 x 6 In. 210.00
Carafe, Water, Sunburst, Brilliant, 7 1/2 In. 295.00
Celery Dish, 25 Hobstars, 13 1/2 In. 325.00
Celery Dish, Strawberry-Diamond, 11 1/4 In. 85.00
Celery Dish, Victoria, Hoare, 12 x 4 1/2 In. 215.00
Celery Vase, Hobstar & Notched Prism, Double Notched Handles, 6 1/4 In. 450.00
Celery Vase, Hobstars, Fans, Diamond Point, 12 In. 1250.00
Centerpiece, Baroque Revival, Gilt Bronze, Pheasant Base, 1875-1880, 20 x 13 In. 7475.00
Centerpiece, Diamond & Fan, Sawtooth Edge, Footed, 1825, 8 1/2 In. 440.00
Chalice, Wedding, Sweetheart, Brilliant, Kranz & Smith, 14 x 6 1/2 In. 860.00
Champagne, Kalana Lily, Hollow Stem, Dorflinger, 5 1/4 In. 75.00
Champagne Bucket, Hobstars 295.00
Cheese Dish, Cut Knob Cover, 4 Hobstars & Pinwheels, Brilliant, 7 1/2 x 9 1/2 In. 690.00
Cheese Dome, Quilted Diamond & Fan, c.1880, 8 1/2 In., 9 In. 88.00
Clock, Crosshatch Buttons, Original Works, Russian, 6 x 4 In. 385.00
Cocktail, Kalana Lily, Underplate, Dorflinger, 4 Piece 120.00
Compote, Brilliant, Stepped Base, 8 1/2 x 8 In. 245.00
Compote, Daisy & Hobstar, Brilliant, 11 3/4 In. 145.00
Compote, Floral Design, Scalloped Edge, Textured Pedestal, 8 1/2 In. 230.00
Compote, Goblet Shape, Cranberry To Clear, Fishing & Hunting Scenes, 9 1/2 In. 690.00
Compote, Graduated Hobstars, 7 1/2 x 9 In. 330.00
Compote, Hobstar & Strawberry-Diamond, Teardrop Stem, 7 1/2 In. 150.00
Compote, Hobstars, Fans, Crosshatch, Teardrop Stem, 8 1/2 x 6 In. 125.00
Compote, Hobstars, Sawtooth Rim, Square Pedestal, 8 1/2 x 6 1/2 In. 65.00
Compote, Jelly, Allover Hobstars & Crosshatch, Fans, Cut Sawtooth Rim, 4 In. 135.00
Compote, Leaf, Vine, Ruby Stain, Continental, 11 In. 374.00
Compote, Pinwheel, Brilliant, Notched Stem, Rayed Base, 9 x 6 In. 70.00
Compote, Ribbon & Star, 9 x 6 In. 175.00
Compote, Star Intersected By Hobstar, Handles, Hobstar Base, 10 1/2 In. 850.00
Compote, Sunburst, Geometric, Houndstooth Border, Brilliant, 6 1/2 x 7 1/2 In. 65.00
Compote, Teardrop Stem, 8 1/2 In. 395.00
Compote, Teardrop, Rolled Rim, Notched Stem, 9 x 6 In. 335.00
Cruet, Hobstar & Fan, Tricornered Spout, 6 1/4 In. 110.00
Cruet, Hobstar Diamond, Tricornered Spout, Stopper, Dorflinger, 7 1/4 In. 130.00
Cruet, Hobstar, Pinwheels 145.00
Cruet, Horizontal & Floral, Brilliant, 9 In. 160.00
Cruet, Pinwheel & Step, Hollow Cone Stopper, 10 In. 195.00
Cruet, Pinwheel, Single Star & Fan, 6 1/4 In. 80.00
Cruet, Renaissance, Stopper, Dorflinger 95.00
Decanter, 2 Chain Rings, 2 Neck Rings, Stopper, 8 1/4 In. 110.00
Decanter, Colonial, Cut Handle, Dorflinger, 12 1/4 In. 385.00
Decanter, Deep Pink To White To Clear, Stopper, 7 1/4 In. 165.00
Decanter, Elmira, Egg Shape, Stopper 725.00
Decanter, Fan & Star, Handle, Brilliant, c.1890, 10 In. 248.00
Decanter, Geometric, Triple Ring Necks, Round Shape, Stopper, 9 3/4 In., Pair 90.00
Decanter, Handle, Fan & Star, Brilliant, Oval, c.1890, 10 In. 248.00
Decanter, Hobstars, Double Lozenges, Bell, Gooseneck, Teardrop Stopper, 13 In. 450.00
Decanter, Sherry, Strawberry-Diamond & Fan, 8 In. 375.00
Decanter, Ship, Allover Geometric Design, Stopper, 10 In. 92.00
Decanter, Waterford Style, 10 1/2 In. 55.00
Decanter, Wedding Ring, Stopper 3500.00

Decanter, Wine, Allover Geometric Design, Curved Handle, Round, Squat, 6 1/4 In. 80.00
Dish, 4 Hobstars & Ovals, Brilliant, Double Handles, 13 3/4 x 10 In. 975.00
Dish, Clam Shell Shape, Prism, Brilliant 325.00
Dish, Mayonnaise, Cane & Hobstar, Underplate, 3 1/4 x 6 In. 345.00
Dish, Mayonnaise, Fairview, Hobstar Base, Quaker City, 7 x 4 1/2 In. 170.00
Dish, Mayonnaise, Spruce, Cut In Form Of 6 Scallops, Underplate, 6 1/2 In. 225.00
Dish, Meriden, Faceted Knob, Stick Handle, 4 1/2 x 6 In. 395.00
Dish, Quilted Square, Brilliant, Round, c.1885, 2 In. 275.00
Dish, Sweetmeat, Deer, Foliage, Navette Shape, Continental, 1900, 4 x 6 In., Pair 200.00
Dresser Jar, Woman's Portrait On Cover, Silver Mounted, 1 1/2 In. 85.00
Ewer, Floral, Stopper, Applied Handle, 13 In. 55.00
Fernery, Allover Geometric, 4 1/4 x 7 1/2 In. 235.00
Flask, Allover Ribs, Gorham Silver Top, Rectangular, 6 1/2 In. 115.00
Flask, Purse, Hexagonal Buttons & Stars, 4 x 2 1/2 In. 150.00
Girandole Set, Woman Kneeling Near Man, Gilt Metal, Prisms, 16 x 15 In., 3 Piece 545.00
Goblet, Golf, Bergen, 6 In. 65.00
Humidor, Art Nouveau, Sterling Silver Cover, International, c.1900, 6 1/2 In. 620.00
Humidor, Strawberry-Diamond & Fine Cut, Star Knob, Rayed Base, 9 In. 560.00
Ice Bowl, Vienna, Thumbprint, Hobstar, 7 1/2 x 4 In. 210.00
Ice Bucket, Brilliant, Hobstar Base, 8 1/2 In. 225.00
Ice Bucket, Geometric, Silver Plated Rim, Handle, Underplate, 5 1/2 x 4 7/8 In. 92.00
Ice Cream Set, Harvard, Brilliant, 16 1/2-In. Platter, 13 Piece 1725.00
Ice Cream Tray, Hobstar, Brilliant, 10 1/2 x 17 3/4 In. 1395.00
Ice Tub, Tab Handle, 7 1/2 In. 175.00
Jam Jar, Diamond, Berry Shape, 6 In. 225.00
Jar, Cover, Allover Mistletoe, 24 Point Hobstar Base, Clark, 7 In. 590.00
Jar, Cover, Cane & Hobstars, Meriden, 6 1/2 x 4 In. 285.00
Jar, Daisy & Button With Bar, Sterling Silver Floral Repousse Lid, 3 7/8 In. 360.00
Jug, Claret, Silver Plated Mount, Continental, 1910, 11 1/2 In. 330.00
Jug, Whiskey, Vertical Ribbed Panels, Notched Handle, Stopper, 4 3/4 In. 135.00
Knife Rest, Notched Prisms, 5 3/4 In. 85.00
Lamp, Baluster Shaft, Floral & Butterfly Shade, Brilliant, Prisms, c.1900, 18 In. 1210.00
Lamp, Cosmos, Mushroom Shape, American, 20 x 10 1/2 In. 345.00
Lamp, Dome Cut In Harvard Variation, 17 1/2 In. 2350.00
Lamp, Fan, Hobstar Shaft, Onion Shade, Brilliant, Cut Glass Prisms, 29 1/2 In. 3680.00
Lamp, Floral, Cosmos & Harvard, Mushroom Shade, 21 1/2 In. 575.00
Muffineer, Silver Sterling Top, Wilcox, 6 In. 100.00
Mug, Alhambra, Meriden 895.00
Napkin Ring, Cane, 8 Piece 275.00
Nappy, 2 Handles, 2 Sections, Hobstars, Brilliant, 3 1/4 x 8 In. 145.00
Nappy, Birds & Flowers, 4 Sections, Straus 175.00
Nappy, Floral Pinwheel, Intaglio, 2 Handles 255.00
Nappy, Pinwheel, 2 Handles, 4 Sections, Brilliant, 2 3/4 x 9 1/2 In. 170.00
Orange Bowl, 8 Hobstars, Brilliant, Hoare, 9 1/2 x 7 In. 1445.00
Orange Bowl, Allover Brilliant, Boat Shape, 4 1/2 x 11 1/2 In. 110.00
Pitcher, Cane, Silver Bamboo Mount & Handle, England, 10 3/4 x 4 In. 460.00
Pitcher, Champagne, Cane With Hobstars, 13 1/2 In. 600.00
Pitcher, Champagne, Feathered Pinwheel, Crosshatch, Scalloped Edge, 14 In. 675.00
Pitcher, Cranberry Cut To Clear, 9 In. 259.00
Pitcher, Desdemona, Cut Handle, Ruffled Base, Clark 2650.00
Pitcher, Harvard, Double Notched Handle, 11 1/2 In. 175.00
Pitcher, Hobstar, Double Notched Handle, Footed, 14 1/4 x 5 1/2 In. 1840.00
Pitcher, Hobstar, Triple Notched Handle, 11 1/2 x 4 In. 425.00
Pitcher, Juice, Hobstar & Cane, 6 1/4 In. 450.00
Pitcher, Juice, Hobstar & Strawberry-Diamond, Hoare, 5 3/4 In. 375.00
Pitcher, Lemonade, Daisy & Cosmos, Triple Notched Handle, 14 1/4 In. 575.00
Pitcher, Lemonade, Starling Bands, Horn Handle 950.00
Pitcher, Milk, Hobstars, Cane, Diamond Point 275.00
Pitcher, Otis, Higgins & Seiter, 8 1/2 In. 525.00
Pitcher, Panels Of Hobstars, Notched Prisms, Brilliant, Clark, 7 1/4 In. 200.00
Pitcher, Sherry, Strawberry-Diamond With Fan, Strap Handle, 8 In. 375.00
Pitcher, Sherwood, Hoare, 14 3/4 In. 1075.00
Pitcher, Sterling Silver Grape Leaf, Berry Rim, Brilliant, Dominick, Haff, 12 3/4 In. 1100.00

Pitcher, Sunburst, Triple Notched Handle, 12 In. 450.00
Pitcher, Water, Hobstar, Houndstooth Edge, Cylindrical, Tapered, 10 3/4 In. 85.00
Plate, 3-Leaf Clovers, 37 Hobstars, 7 In. 425.00
Plate, Allover Seneca, Empire Glass Co., 7 In. 295.00
Plate, Club Shape, 6 In. 95.00
Plate, Festoon, Silver Border, Square, 9 In. 185.00
Plate, Geometric & Intaglio, Monogram, 10 In. 350.00
Plate, Hobstar & Cane Design, Clark, 8 In. 245.00
Plate, Hobstars Between Points, Star Bottom, 8 In. 200.00
Plate, Ice Cream, Snowflake, 8 In., 9 Piece 165.00
Plate, Seneca, Fluted Edge, Empire, 10 In. 650.00
Plate, Zephyr, Blackmer, 7 In. 165.00
Powder Box, Diamond & Fan, Brilliant, Sterling Silver Cover, 4 1/2 x 6 1/2 In. 260.00
Powder Box, Thistle, Butterfly 375.00
Powder Jar, Hair Receiver, Engraved Floral, Sterling Silver Cover, 2 Piece 375.00
Powder Jar, Silver Enameled Foliate & Scroll Lid, Spaulding & Co., 2 x 3 1/2 In. 690.00
Punch Bowl, 6 Double Hobstar, Ruffled Edge, American Brilliant, 11 1/2 x 12 In. 745.00
Punch Bowl, Allover Cross-Hatched Star & Sunburst, Sawtooth Edge, 13 3/4 In. 430.00
Punch Bowl, Elmira, Brilliant, 14 x 13 In. 2587.00
Punch Bowl, Harvard, 15 x 13 1/2 In., 2 Piece 430.00
Punch Bowl, Hobstar & Cane, Brilliant, 10 x 10 In., 2 Piece 430.00
Punch Bowl, Hobstar & Fan, 10 1/2 x 12 In. 1595.00
Punch Bowl, Hobstar & Fan, Brilliant, 10 1/2 x 12 In. 1595.00
Punch Bowl, Pinwheels, Scalloped Sawtooth Edge, Brilliant, 16 In. 212.00
Punch Bowl, Sawtooth, England, 10 x 11 1/2 In. 470.00
Punch Bowl, Scalloped Edge Over Star, Footed Base, Brilliant, 14 In. 950.00
Punch Bowl, Strawberry-Diamond, Fans On Upper Edge, c.1880, 12 In. 935.00
Relish, Allover Geometric Cut Design, Houndstooth Border, 11 In. 80.00
Relish, Hobstar & Cane, Double Notched Handles, 4 Sections, 7 In. 125.00
Rose Bowl, 5 Large & 12 Small Hobstars, 5 x 7 1/2 In. 1475.00
Rose Bowl, Brilliant, Dorflinger, 6 In. 395.00
Rose Bowl, Hobstar & Swirls, 4 1/4 x 5 1/4 In. 375.00
Rose Bowl, Hobstars, Cane & Strawberry-Diamond, 4 3/4 x 6 1/2 In. 275.00
Rose Bowl, Teardrop Base, Scalloped Edge, Pedestal, 6 In. 495.00
Salt, Clover Shape 58.00
Scent Bottle, Cover, Cylinder, 12 In. 200.00
Spooner, Fans & Miters, 4 3/4 In. 115.00
Spooner, Geometric, Corset Waist Shape, Brilliant, Gold Scalloped, Handles, 5 In. 135.00
Spooner, Stars, Fans & Crosshatch, Sawtooth Edge, Cut Handles 150.00
Spooner, Strawberry-Diamond, Chaining Top & Base, Intaglio Flowers, 5 In. 110.00
Spooner, Tulip Shape, Hobstars On Sides 300.00
Stand, Figural, Putti, Square Onyx Base, 9 1/2 In. 115.00
Sugar & Creamer, Pinwheel, Brilliant, 1905-1910, 3 5/8 x 3 1/4 In. 212.00
Sugar & Creamer, Prism, Hoare 135.00
Sugar Shaker, Fan & Cane Design, Brass Cover, 5 3/4 In. 345.00
Tankard, 5 Pinwheels, Triple Notched Handle, 12 In. 145.00
Tankard, Floral & Harvard, Brilliant, 12 1/2 In. 200.00
Tankard, Floral, Daisy, Triple Notched Handle, 11 1/2 x 6 In. 115.00
Tankard, Harvard, Handle, 12 x 5 3/4 In. 170.00
Tankard, Panels, Engraved Lady On Horseback, Pewter Lid, 10 3/4 In. 470.00
Tray, Alternating Stars & Pinwheels, Brilliant, Round, c.1890, 12 In. 275.00
Tray, Brilliant, Scalloped Edge, Russia, 11 3/4 x 8 In. 330.00
Tray, Center Handle, Floral, 10 In. 195.00
Tray, Double Hobstars, Fans, Crosshatch & Strawberry-Diamond, 14 1/2 x 8 In. 475.00
Tray, Hobstar & Notched Prism, Oval, 10 1/2 In. 675.00
Tray, Hobstars & Crosshatch Buttons, 8 In. 295.00
Tray, Hobstars, Fans, Hobnail & Crosshatch, 12 3/4 x 8 In. 575.00
Tray, Ice Cream, Daisy, Brilliant Leaves, 14 x 7 3/4 In. 95.00
Tray, Ice Cream, Princeton, Brilliant, 13 1/2 x 8 1/2 In. 145.00
Tray, Sonoma, Dorflinger, 11 In. 975.00
Tray, Star, Strawberry-Diamond, Hobstars, Sawtooth Edge, 7 In., 2 Piece 80.00
Tray, Stars, Pinwheels, Brilliant, Round, c.1890, 12 In. 275.00
Vase, Allover Brilliant, Cylindrical, 12 x 3 In. 115.00

Vase, Amber Cut To Clear, Dorflinger, c.1905, 14 1/2 In. 1800.00
Vase, Baluster Stem, Pittsburgh, 10 1/4 In. 275.00
Vase, Blue Cut To Clear, New England, 8 1/4 In. 144.00
Vase, Brilliant, Everted Scalloped Sawtooth Rim, 17 x 9 1/2 In. 272.00
Vase, Brilliant, Hobstars, Puntees, Corset Waist, 10 1/2 x 4 1/4 In. 115.00
Vase, Brilliant, Pedestal, Notched Stem, Ruffled Edge, 12 x 5 3/4 In. 230.00
Vase, Bud, Victoria, Egginton, 14 In. 475.00
Vase, Center Star, Scalloped Edge, Brilliant, 2 Handles, 10 In. 1380.00
Vase, Chalice, Hobstar Base, 14 1/2 In. 1900.00
Vase, Comet, J. Hoare, 13 1/2 In. 3300.00
Vase, Fan, Hobstar, Footed, 12 x 7 1/2 In. 685.00
Vase, Hobstar & Crosshatch, 24 Point Base Star, Brilliant, 16 In. 950.00
Vase, Hobstars, Corset Waist, 8 In. 410.00
Vase, Leaf, Floral & Diamond Design, Corset Waist, Early 20th Century, 12 In. 60.00
Vase, Mantel, Hobstars In Vesicas, Sterling Rim, Gorham, 1903, 12 3/4 In., Pair 2275.00
Vase, Monarch, 2 Handles, J. Hoare, 12 In. 1950.00
Vase, Poinsettia, Hobstar, Serrated Edge, Flared, 13 1/4 In. 115.00
Vase, Strawberry-Diamond, Fans At Edge, Knop Stem, Pittsburgh, 8 In. 220.00
Vase, Strawberry-Diamond, Fans, Stars, Cylinder, 13 In. 30.00
Vase, Trumpet, Flowering Vines, Blue Enameled Silver, American, 12 1/2 In. 490.00
Vase, Trumpet, Hobstars, Fans, Cut Stem & Base, Dorflinger, 6 In. 195.00
Vase, Trumpet, Notched Stem, Ray Cut Base, Emerald Green, Dorflinger, 14 1/8 In. 1610.00
Vase, Trumpet, Star, Fan, Ruffled Notched Edges, Brilliant, 14 In. 460.00
Vase, Whirlwind, Brilliant, Bulbous, Quaker City, 12 1/2 x 10 In. 1435.00
Water Set, Harvard, American Brilliant, 1907, 7 Piece 1200.00
Water Set, Pinwheel, Brilliant, 8-1/2 In. Pitcher, 7 Piece 185.00

CUT VELVET is a special type of art glass, made with two layers of
blown glass, which shows a raised pattern. It usually had an acid finish or a texture like velvet. It was made by many glass factories during
the late Victorian years.

Bowl, Red Satin, Square, 2 1/2 x 3 5/8 In. 143.00
Lamp, Satin Ribbed Ball Shade, 17 In. 495.00
Vase, Blue, White Lining, 6 1/4 In. 80.00
Vase, Diamond-Quilted, Blue, Enameled, 10 3/4 In. 385.00
Vase, Diamond-Quilted, Ruffled Edge, 5 In. 110.00
Vase, Diamond-Quilted, Yellow, White Lining, Ruffled Edge, 7 In. 90.00

CYBIS porcelain is a twentieth-century product. Boleslaw Cybis came
to the United States from Poland in 1939. He started making porcelains
in Long Island, New York, in 1940. He moved to Trenton, New Jersey,
in 1942 as one of the founders of Cordey China Co. and started his
own Cybis Porcelains about 1950. The firm is still working. See also
Cordey.

CYBIS

Figurine, American Indian Brave, With Deer, Bisque, Wood Base, 10 1/4 In. 575.00
Figurine, American Indian Maiden, Bisque, Wood Base, 9 In. 345.00
Figurine, American Indian, Seated On Bear Rug, Pipe On Rug, 12 In. 345.00
Figurine, Beavers, Egbert & Brewster 400.00
Figurine, Boy's Head, Black Base, 30 In. 250.00
Figurine, Bunny, Mr. Snowball, 4 In. . . . . .35.00 to 70.00
Figurine, Bunny, Pat-A-Cake, 4 1/2 In. 165.00
Figurine, Burro, Fitzgerald, Retired, 7 In. 175.00
Figurine, Carousel Pony, Sugar Plum, 12 1/2 In. 875.00
Figurine, Donkey, 7 In. 880.00
Figurine, Elephant, Sitting 200.00
Figurine, Foal, Dapple Gray 275.00
Figurine, Funny Face, No. 34, 9 1/2 In. 205.00
Figurine, Funny Face, No. 488 . . . . 300.00
Figurine, Girl, Standing With Doll 150.00
Figurine, Great Horned Owl, Bisque, 17 1/2 In. 255.00
Figurine, Horse, Chestnut, Black, Standing Foursquare, Rectangular Base, 14 In. 450.00
Figurine, Lady Macbeth, No. 104, 13 In. 430.00
Figurine, Oceana, Sea King's Steed . . . . .975.00 to 1700.00

Figurine, Othello, No. 314, 15 In.	1006.00
Figurine, Pansies, Chi A Maid	250.00
Figurine, Prince & Princess, 8 1/4 & 7 1/2 In., Pair	195.00
Figurine, Raccoon, Eating Berries, 6 3/4 In.	138.00
Figurine, Sebastian, 5 1/2 In.	195.00
Figurine, Squirrel, Mr. Fluffy Tail, 8 In.	400.00
Figurine, Walrus	175.00
Figurine, Young Eskimo, No. 292, 9 1/2 In.	125.00

CZECHOSLOVAKIA is a popular term with collectors. The name, first used as a mark after the country was formed in 1918, appears on glass and porcelain and other decorative items. Although Czechoslovakia split into Slovakia and the Czech Republic on January 1, 1993, the name continues to be used in some trademarks.

CZECHOSLOVAKIA GLASS, Bowl, Blue, Black Enameled Floral, 3 Ball Feet, c.1920, 7 In.	430.00
Box, Rosary, Blue, With Sterling Rosary	125.00
Decanter, White Cut To Red, Enameled, 9 1/2 x 4 In., Pair	175.00
Dresser Set, Enameled Floral, Bottle & Box, 3 Piece	93.00
Figurine, Bowler, Multicolored, c.1950, 7 In.	115.00
Figurine, Doctor, Holding Needle, Multicolored, c.1950, 8 In.	185.00
Lamp, Blue Enameled Floral, 9 1/2 In.	45.00
Lamp, Enamel Design, Cut To Clear, Brass Base & Cap, 15 1/2 In.	90.00
Lamp, Metal Nude Woman Holding Hobstar Globe, 22 In.	110.00
Lamp, Mushroom Shade & Base, Windmill Scene, Marked, 9 In.	132.00
Lamp, Vanity, Mushroom Shade, Windmill Scene, 9 In. ....*Illus*	248.00
Lamp Shade, Windows Layered In Blue, Red & Green, Frame, 11 In.	44.00
Perfume Bottle, Cut Glass, Diamond Barrel, Nude Ball Stopper, 8 In.	140.00
Perfume Bottle, Lapis Lazuli, Leaves & Flowers, Ground Dabber, 6 3/8 In.	625.00
Powder Box, Mottled Orange & Yellow, Tripod, 7 In.	16.00
Vase, Black, Cane Design, Red Interior, 4 1/4 In.	110.00
Vase, Clear Over Browns, c.1920, 9 In.	140.00
Vase, Clear Over Multicolored, Luster, c.1920, 4 3/4 In.	80.00
Vase, Embossed Flowers, Ice Blue, Multicolored Mottled Base, 6 In.	38.00
Vase, Floral, Medallions, Thumbprint Rim, Cylinder Cut, 8 3/4 In.	115.00
Vase, Green & Red Tortoiseshell Finish, Bottle Shape, 13 1/2 In.	55.00
Vase, Orange Over White, Pinched Crystal Applied Snake, 12 In.	45.00
Vase, Red Cut To Clear, Deer & Castle Scene, Signed, 10 In.	525.00
Vase, Ruby Flashed, Mary Gregory Style Couple, 8 In.	415.00
Vase, Snake At Neck, Red & Blue Speckled Body, c.1930, 9 1/2 In.	120.00
Vase, Yellow Over White, Coiled Black Snake Middle, 6 In.	22.00
Vase, Yellow Wavy Lines, Hexagonal, 4 3/4 In.	38.00
Water Set, Red & Yellow Flowers, Green, 8-In. Pitcher, 3 Piece	210.00
CZECHOSLOVAKIA POTTERY, Bank, Piggy, 1890-1910	95.00
Figurine, Bride & Groom, Multicolored, c.1950, 8 1/4 x 7 1/4 In.	223.00
Figurine, Nude Woman Dancing, Drape & Ring, 5 1/2 In., Pair	110.00
Figurine, Nude Woman Snake Charmer, Gold Design, 10 In.	185.00
Lamp, Fruit Basket, Large	1350.00
Tea Set, Art Deco, Blue Band, Gilt Handle, Spout, 1930, 15 Piece	180.00

Czechoslovakia
Glass, Lamp, Vanity,
Mushroom Shade,
Windmill Scene, 9 In.

If you find an old lamp with part of a light bulb still in the socket, try this. Push a fresh potato or a wine cork down into the old socket. Turn it and it will probably unscrew the old light bulb base.

Vase, Forest Design, Molded, 10 In. 144.00
Wall Pocket, Bird, Fruit 60.00

D'ARGENTAL is a mark used in France by the Compagnie des
Cristalleries de St. Louis. The firm made multilayered, acid-cut cameo
glass in the late nineteenth and twentieth centuries. D'Argental is the
French name for the city of Munzthal, home of the glassworks. Later
they made enameled etched glass.

Box, Egg Shape, Yellow, Crimson, Azaleas, Butterflies, 1910, 6 In. 1150.00
Lamp, Domed Shade, Ripe Blackberries, Leaves, Thorny Branches, 1915, 22 In. 6325.00
Vase, Brown Berries, Leaves, Vines, Vivid Lime Green Ground, Signed, 8 In. 990.00
Vase, Etched Landscape & Riverside Scene, Bottle Form, Signed, 12 In. 990.00
Vase, Honeysuckle Vine, Umber, Yellow Ground, 9 1/2 In. 750.00
Vase, Landscape, Mediterranean Village Scene, Yellow, Maroon Overlaid, 8 In. 345.00
Vase, Mountains In Background, Castle On Hill, 10 1/2 In. 1500.00
Vase, Purple Wisteria, Frosted, Purple Ground, Signed, 13 In. 1320.00
Vase, Riverside Scene, Mountains, Signed, 8 In. 1220.00

DANIEL BOONE, a pre-Revolutionary War folk hero, was a surveyor,
trapper, and frontiersman. A television series, which ran from 1964 to
1970, was based on his life and starred Fess Parker. All types of Daniel
Boone memorabilia are collected.

Backpack, Fess Parker, 1964 .... 145.00
Play Set, Frontierland, Walt Disney, Box 95.00

DAUM, a glassworks in Nancy, France, was started by Jean Daum in
1875. The company, now called *Cristalleries de Nancy*, is still working. The *Daum Nancy* mark has been used in many variations. The
name of the city and the artist are usually both included.

Bowl, Boat Shape, Crystal, Signed, 20 In. 144.00
Bowl, Emerald Green, Wrought Iron Bands, Foliate Diamond Border, 10 In. 4370.00
Bowl, Gray, Blue & Rust Design, 1920s, 3 1/4 In. 632.00
Bowl, Rose, Yellow, Green, Enamel Design, 3 x 6 1/4 In. 1955.00
Box, Cover, Chrysanthemums, Gilt, Emerald Green Textured Ground, Etched, 5 In. 2300.00
Box, Cover, Geraniums, Leaves, White, Green, Red, Mottled Blue, Cameo, 1900, 3 In. 3162.00
Box, Cover, White Wheat Stalks, Pinwheels, Violet Base, White Wheat Stalks, 3-Footed .. 6900.00
Chandelier, 6 Central Round Shades, Frosted, Edgar Brandt, 40 In. 9200.00
Dish, Red, Green, Caramel Scarabs, Green, Blue, White, Yellow Ground, 5 1/4 In. 2185.00
Jug, Mottled Green & Gray, Snake Tail Handle, Drapes Around Jug, 12 x 14 In. 225.00
Lamp, Boudoir, Pink & Green, Peach Ground, Cameo, 13 1/2 In. ....*Illus* 8625.00
Lamp, Desk, 3-Light, Gray Glass, Wrought Iron Leaves, Insects, Cameo, 1925, 15 In. ... 4600.00
Lamp, Desk, Frosted Gray Glass, Broad Domed Shade, Cylindrical Base, Cameo, 15 In. .. 4600.00
Lamp, Desk, Striped Textured Pattern, Conical Shade, Stylized Star Base, 20 In. 2070.00
Lamp, Glass Body, Ribs On Etched Ground, 9 Balls On Iron Base, Signed, 12 3/4 In. 1265.00
Lamp, Gray Glass Shade, Etched, Wrought Iron Base, 1925, 16 1/4 In. 8050.00
Lamp, Hanging, Foliage, Dark Olive Green, Mottled Blue, Yellow Ground, Cameo, 13 In. 3450.00
Lamp, Hanging, Fruiting Vine, Brown, Mottled Orange, Yellow Ground, Cameo, 13 In. .. 3450.00
Lamp, Hanging, Fruiting Vine, Green, Mottled Yellow, Orange Ground, Cameo, 14 In. ... 6900.00
Lamp, Hanging, Gray, Orange, Yellow Rose, Wrought Iron, Stylized Leaf Mounts, 12 In. . 9200.00
Lamp, Orange Shade, Amber Flower Heads, Wrought Iron Base, Cameo, 10 1/2 In. 2300.00
Lamp, Spider Chrysanthemums, Leaves, Cameo, Conical, Bronze Base, 1900, 11 In. 12650.00
Lamp, Thistle Blossom, Pink, Green, Black Patina, Wrought Iron Base, Cameo, 21 In. 11500.00
Lamp, Yellow, Orange, Mottled Gray, Rose, Wrought Iron Base, Cameo, 1910, 19 In. 13800.00
Perfume Bottle, Red Trailing Thistle, Gilt, Textured Ground, Cylindrical, Stopper, 3 In. .. 977.00
Perfume Bottle, Windmill Scene, Boats, Black, Milky White Ground, Stopper, 3 1/2 In. . 575.00
Pitcher, Clover Blossoms, Leaves, Beaded Band At Neck, Cameo, Signed, c.1900, 3 In. .. 2415.00
Pitcher, Hops, Yellow Amber, Stylized Design, Black, Gold, Etched, 3 In. 1380.00
Pitcher, Yellow, Orange Powders, Gray Glass, Applied Handle, Flattened, 1920, 7 In. 345.00
Vase, Amber, Dark Orange, Flared Rim, Reticulated, Round Base, 12 1/2 In. 1610.00
Vase, Apple Blossoms, Seagull, Lake, Handles, White, Cameo, 1 1/2 In. 2300.00
Vase, Arboreal Design, Lime Green Ground, Etched, 3 1/4 In. 2300.00
Vase, Blossoms, Green Overlay, Rose, Tangerine Mottled, Cameo, 14 1/2 In. 2530.00

Daum, Lamp,
Boudoir, Pink &
Green, Peach
Ground, Cameo,
13 1/2 In.

Daum, Vase, Enamel
Winter Scene, Gold
Ground, 6 In.

Vase, Branching Roses, White, Pink, Green, Tapered, Oval, Cameo, 13 In. 11500.00
Vase, Burgundy Bean Plant, Spherical Base, Cameo, 11 1/2 In. 1935.00
Vase, Central Spiraling, Tiered Iron Foot, Edgar Brandt, 13 1/2 In. 5175.00
Vase, Colored Floral, Bulbous Upper Body, Green Base, Cameo, Signed, 16 In. 4180.00
Vase, Crowing Cock, Gray, Tomato Red, Yellow, Brown Overlay, Cameo, 1900, 5 In. 2300.00
Vase, Deep Orange Berries & Leaves, Green, Yellow, White, Orange, Cameo, 15 In. 3575.00
Vase, Deep Red Tobacco Flowers, Stems, Leaves, Yellow Hammered, Red, Cameo, 8 In. . 3575.00
Vase, Dutch Winter Scene, Cameo, Miniature, 2 1/4 In. 1495.00
Vase, Elongated Slender Neck, Specks Of Yellow, Signed, 7 In. 200.00
Vase, Enamel Bleeding Hearts & Leaves, Gray, 1900s, 9 3/4 In. 3450.00
Vase, Enamel Bleeding Hearts, Red, Blue Centers, Green, Purple Ground, Cameo, 3 In. . . 1430.00
Vase, Enamel Boats At Sea, Brown, Black Enamel, Yellow, Mustard Ground, 4 1/2 In. . . . 1430.00
Vase, Enamel Flowers, Gray, Wheel-Carved, Footed, Cameo, 1900s, 13 In. 2875.00
Vase, Enamel Flowers, Tangerine, Brown Textured Ground, Etched, 4 In. 1725.00
Vase, Enamel Heraldic Lion & Banner, Emerald Green Textured Ground, Baluster, 11 In. . 1380.00
Vase, Enamel Violets, Green, Purple, White Mottled Ground, Cameo, 5 In. 2310.00
Vase, Enamel Winter Scene, Gold Ground, 6 In. . . . . *Illus* 2300.00
Vase, Enamel Yellow Irises, Gray Mottled Glass, Tapered, 15 1/2 In. 3635.00
Vase, Fleshy Leaves, Vines, Caramel Overlay, Pale Blue Ground, Cameo, 1905, 10 In. . . . 5520.00
Vase, Flowers, Brown, Yellow Frosted Ground, Cameo, Signed, 8 1/2 In. 1760.00
Vase, Flowers, Gold Highlights, Purple Ground, Cameo, 4 Sides, 5 In. 1870.00
Vase, Flowers, Orange, Green, Yellow, Brown Mottled Ground, Cameo, 4 In. 1100.00
Vase, Flowers, Stems, Leaves, Gold Accents, Purple Ground, Cameo, 5 In. 1980.00
Vase, Foxgloves, Leaves, Orange, Red, Gray Highlights, Cameo, 1900, 31 In. 6900.00
Vase, Free-Form, Matte Finish, Orange, Green, Purple, 2 Handles, 6 1/2 In. 230.00
Vase, Fruiting Vine, Dark Olive, Mottled Glass, Orange Ground, Cameo, 24 In. 4370.00
Vase, Geometric Lozenge Design, Everted Rim, Spherical, 16 In. 6900.00
Vase, Grapes, Vines, Leaves, Gray, Yellow, Orange, Green, Cameo, 1900, 24 1/2 In. 7475.00
Vase, Gray, Tangerine, Roses, Leafy Stems, Tapering, Cameo, 1900, 5 In. 1610.00
Vase, Gray, White, Amber, Olive, Trumpet, 1900, 8 In. 1495.00
Vase, Green Flowers, Stems, Light Pink, Green Hammered Ground, Cameo, 11 In. 4400.00
Vase, Green, Yellow Foliage, Rolling Hills, Pale Blue Ground, Etched, 3 In. 1380.00
Vase, Grisaille Swamp Scene, Water Lilies, Dragonfly, Yellow, Green, Etched, 5 In. 1840.00
Vase, Intricate Floral Design, Tobacco Flowers, Orange, Black, Cameo, Signed, 12 In. . . . 1650.00
Vase, Lake Scene, Mountains Ground, Trees In Foreground, Signed, c.1910, 12 In. 2300.00
Vase, Lake Scene, Sailboats, Chocolate Brown, Yellow, Orange Ground, Cameo, 5 In. . . . 1150.00
Vase, Lake Surrounded By Trees, Gray, Black Enamel, White Ground, Cameo, 6 In. 605.00
Vase, Large Iris Blossoms, Leafage, Lavender, Lime Green, Cameo, 1900, 6 1/4 In. 3737.00
Vase, Lily & Foliage, Burnt Orange Overlay, Cameo, 13 In. 3450.00
Vase, Mauve Glass, Acid-Textured Ground, Inverted Cone, 8 1/2 In. 805.00
Vase, Mistletoe, Gold, White Enameled, Frosted Blue Ground, Cameo, Signed, 3 1/2 In. . . 522.00
Vase, Petunias, Yellow, Green Ground, Squared Rim, Etched, 4 3/4 In. 2530.00
Vase, Poppy Blossoms, Gray, Crimson, Cameo, 1900, 9 1/4 In. 3450.00
Vase, Poppy Blossoms, Leaves, Burnt Orange, Purple, Ocher, Cameo, 1900, 16 In. 11500.00
Vase, Prunus Blossoms, Leaves, White, Gray, Brown, Green, Cameo, 1900, 17 In. 4025.00
Vase, Rampant Lion, Mottled Red, Green Acid-Textured Ground, Etched, 9 1/2 In. 1955.00

Vase, Random Vertical Striations, Gray Glass, Wrought Iron Footed, 1910, 13 1/4 In. 6325.00
Vase, Red Thorn Apples, Mottled Green Leaves & Stems, Cameo, Signed, 8 In. 2090.00
Vase, Red Thorn Apples, Mottled Leaves, Cameo, Signed, 5 1/2 In. 970.00
Vase, Red, Purple Fuchsia, Green Stems, Gold Accents, Purple Ground, Cameo, 5 In. 2310.00
Vase, Red, Yellow, Green, Blue Mottled, 4 Sides, Signed, 19 1/2 In. 1100.00
Vase, Remote Winterscape Scene, Orange, Yellow Ground, Etched, 4 3/4 In. 2415.00
Vase, Ribs On Textured Ground, Yellow, Signed, c.1920, 8 1/2 In. 1725.00
Vase, River Scene, Tall Trees, Mottled Blue, Green Ground, Enameled, Etched, 9 3/4 In. . 6900.00
Vase, Sailboats On Lake, Trees In Foreground, Cameo, Signed, c.1910, 16 1/2 In. 2875.00
Vase, Thistle Blossoms, Leaves, Pale Blue, Green Mottled, Trumpet, Cameo, 19 In. 9200.00
Vase, Trees & Lake, Green, Rust, Pink, Yellow Mottled Opaque Ground, Cameo, 21 In. .. 5520.00
Vase, Trees, Brown, Green, Gray Highlights, Pink, Amber, Cameo, 1900, 22 In. 5462.00
Vase, Tulips & Leaves, Gray, Wheel-Carved, Cameo, 1900s, 13 1/2 In. 2070.00
Vase, Turk's-Cap Lilies, Orange Mottled, Mauve Overlay, Cameo, 13 In. 4025.00
Vase, Violets, Green Stems, Purple Ground, Cameo, 2 1/4 x 1/2 In. 935.00
Vase, Winter Landscape, Barren, Charcoal, Frosty White, Yellow, Orange, Cameo, 11 In. . 4025.00
Vase, Yellow With Pink & Green, Signed, 24 1/2 In. 1610.00

DAVENPORT pottery and porcelain were made at the Davenport factory in Longport, Staffordshire, England, from 1793 to 1887. Earthenwares, creamwares, porcelains, ironstone, and other ceramics were made. Most of the pieces are marked with a form of the word *Davenport*.

DAVENPORT
LONGPORT
STAFFORDSHRE

Bowl, Flow Blue, Octagonal, Pedestal, 11 1/2 In. 350.00
Bowl, Pink Luster, Wide Band Floral, Signed 545.00
Pitcher & Waste Bowl, Cypress, Mulberry 995.00
Plate, Friburg, 9 In. 60.00
Plate Set, Flow Blue, Amoy, 7 In., 4 Piece 130.00

DAVY CROCKETT, the American frontiersman, was born in 1786 and died in 1836. The historical character gained new fame in 1954 when the Walt Disney television show ran a series of episodes featuring Fess Parker as Davy Crockett. Coonskin caps and buckskins became popular and hundreds of different Davy Crockett items were made.

Bandanna, Black, Yellow, Name Repeated Around Border, 1950, 18 x 18 In. 45.00
Bandanna, Yellow, Red & Black Graphics Of Davy, Square, 17 In. 55.00
Cap Gun, Horsehead Grips 395.00
Cookie Jar, Boy, American Bisque 340.00
Cookie Jar, Coonskin Hat, Holding Rifle, Brush, 1950s, 10 1/2 In. 275.00
Cookie Jar, McCoy 495.00
Dinner Set, Plate, Bowl & Mug, Brown Graphics, Porcelain, 1940s, 3 Piece 40.00
Glass, Davy Crockett, 1955 .... 25.00
Glass, Indian Fighter, Red & Green 25.00
Gun, Clicker, Tin Lithograph, Multicolored Finish, 1952, 10 In. 275.00
Hat, Coonskin 50.00
Lamp, Plaster, Paper Shade, Remco Mfg., Chicago, 1950, 18 1/2 In. 360.00
Lunch Box 60.00
Night-Light, Davy's Face, Red Coonskin Hat, Porcelain 195.00
Pillow, Bean Bag, Davy Holding Rifle, Brown & Beige, Square, 15 In. 75.00
Plate, Indian Fighter Party, 2-Tone Brown, Tan Ground, 1955, 8 x 8 1/2 In. 25.00
Plate, Oxford China Co., 9 1/2 In. 35.00
Pouch, Storage, Yellow, Brown Borders, Davy, Holding Rifle, 12 x 28 In. 60.00
Record, Ballad Of Davy Crockett, Black Vinyl, 1953, 78 RPM 28.00
Ring, Portrait, Brass, Red Enameled, Box 135.00
Wallet 48.00

DE VEZ was a signature used on cameo glass after 1910. E. S. Monot founded the glass company near Paris in 1851. The company changed names many times. Mt. Joye, another glass by this factory, is listed in its own category.

Perfume Bottle, Black Landscape, Castle & Plant Life, Signed, 5 3/4 In. 95.00
Vase, Green Trees, Pink Mountains & Lake, 3 3/4 In. 550.00
Vase, Island Scene, House, Trees, Mountains In Background, Signed, 5 In. 695.00
Vase, Lake Scene, Blue, Yellow Frosted Glass, Cameo, Signed, 10 1/2 In. 825.00

Vase, Vines Hand From Top, Islands & Flowers Base, Signed, 4 1/8 In. 525.00
Vase, Wooded Mountainscape, Red, Forest Green, Tangerine Ground, Cameo, 17 In. 1725.00

DECOYS are carved or turned wooden copies of birds, fish, or animals.
The decoy was placed in the water or propped on the shore to lure flying birds to the pond for hunters. Some decoys are handmade; some
are commercial products. Today there is a group of artists making
modern decoys for display, not for use in a pond.

American Coot, Gus Nelo 450.00
Black Duck, Alma Fitchett 8250.00
Black Duck, Canvas Covered, George Boyd 1650.00
Black Duck, Dan English 8000.00
Black Duck, Hollow Carved, Daniel Lake Leeds 2200.00
Black Duck, Hollow Carved, Painted Eyes, Weighted, William Goffingon, 1930s 350.00
Black Duck, Ira Hudson 2530.00
Black Duck, Jim Pierce, Havre De Grace, Maryland, 16 1/4 In. 190.00
Black Duck, Mason Factory, c.1895 . . . . 3500.00
Black-Bellied Plover, c.1850 . . . . 275.00
Black-Bellied Plover, George Boyd 3740.00
Bluebill Drake, Carved Wings, Feather Stamping, Jim Nelson, 1930 . . . . 375.00
Bluebill Drake, Carved, Ken Hopkins, 1982, 12 In. 60.00
Bluebill Drake, Glass Eyes, Hand Carved, Lawrence Girard, 1969 . . . . 160.00
Bluebill Drake, Original Paint, Glass Eyes, Fred Plickta, Gibraltar, Michigan, 1930 . . . . . 55.00
Bluebill Drake & Hen, Ward Brothers, Pair 5200.00
Bobwhite Quail, A.J. King, Pair, Miniature 3025.00
Bufflehead, A.E. Crowell, 2 In. 410.00
Canada Goose, A.E. Crowell 3410.00
Canada Goose, Balsa Wood, Wildflower 120.00
Canada Goose, Capt. Clarence Bailey 2000.00
Canada Goose, Carved, Polychrome, Glass Eyes, David Lobbiestael, 1982, 13 In. 85.00
Canada Goose, Overpainted, Long Beach Island, New Jersey, 24 x 11 In. 345.00
Canada Goose, Primitive, White & Black Repaint, Glass Eyes, 21 In. 88.00
Canvasback Drake, Carved Bill Detail, Red Glass Eyes, Brown, Black, White 18400.00
Canvasback Drake, Carved, Polychrome, Glass Eyes, Tabler & Fairfield, 18 In. 145.00
Canvasback Drake, Glass Eyes, Hall, 15 1/2 In. 82.00
Canvasback Hen, Hollow, Bert Graves 2200.00
Canvasback Hen, Primitive, 17 3/4 In. 140.00
Common Tern, Glass Eyes, Driftwood Base, James Lapham 175.00
Crow, Hollow, Black Paint, Glass Eyes, Primitive, 14 1/4 In. 150.00
Curlew, Long-Billed, Shoebutton Eyes, Full-Carved, Original Paint, 6 In. 170.00
Duck, Papier-Mache, Glass Eyes, Wire Loop In Base, General Fibre Co., St. Louis, 15 In. 25.00
Fish, Spearing, Turtle Ice, Open Mouth, White Glass Eyes, Tin Legs, Tail, 4 1/2 In. 80.00
Fish, Spearing, Wooden, Frog-Shape Ice, Blue Glass Eyes, Green, White Belly, 7 In. 110.00
Fish, Trout, Painted, Tin Fins, Repaired Tail, 16 1/2 In. 2430.00
Fish, Wooden, Tin Fins, 9 1/2 In. 85.00
Gold-Crown Kinglet, Driftwood Base, James Lapham, Life Size 220.00
Golden Plover, Nantucket 2970.00
Golden Plover, Winter Plumage, A. Elmer Crowell 2585.00
Goldeneye Drake, Original Paint, J. Dodd Label, 1976 . . . . 40.00
Goldeneye Drake, Turned Head, Glass Eyes, J. Dodd, 1950s, 14 3/4 In. 145.00
Goose, Captain Clarence Bailey, Cape Cod, 15 x 29 In. 850.00
Goose, Oval Base, James Lapham, Miniature 247.00
Green-Winged Teal, Carved, Polychrome, Glass Eyes, 11 In. 45.00
Hooded Merganser, A.E. Crowell, 2 3/4 In. 520.00
Labrador Duck Hen, New England Area 3300.00
Loon, George Boyd, Miniature 1980.00
Mallard, Carved & Painted, Lead Weight, 16 In. 100.00
Mallard, Dodge 700.00
Mallard, Hollow, Glass Eyes, 16 In. 38.00
Mallard Drake, Applied Head, Lead Disc Counterweight, Painted, 12 In. 40.00
Mallard Drake & Hen, A.E. Crowell, Cape Cod 575.00
Mallard Duck, Carved Wingtips & Tail, A. Elmer Crowell 4950.00

Mallard Duck, Ward Brothers, Original Paint, Pair 880.00
Merganser Drake, Carved Full-Bodied, Black, White, Orange, Yellow Eyes 805.00
Merganser Drake, Glass Eyes, Original Paint, Sliced Tree Trunk Base, Bun Feet, 19 In. .. 138.00
Merganser Hen, Muckie Davis 800.00
Oldsquaw, Clinton Keith 770.00
Owl, White, Brown Paint, Early 20th Century, 19 In. 715.00
Pintail Drake, Carved, Polychrome, Glass Eyes, David Berard, 1982, 17 In. 85.00
Pintail Hen, Mason, Premier Grade 6160.00
Rainbow Trout, Ice Spearing, Minnesota 375.00
Red-Breasted Merganser, Brian Mitchell 187.00
Red-Breasted Merganser, Hollow Carved, 1900, Oversized 5775.00
Redhead Hen, Hollow Carved, Nate Quillen 2805.00
Ring-Necked Pheasant Drake, King, Under Glass, Miniature, Pair 2090.00
Ring-Necked Pheasant Hen, Black, White, Glass Eyes, Lead Weight, 10 In. 50.00
Shorebird, Gray Weathered, Black Paint, Tack Eyes, 12 1/2 In. 60.00
Shorebird, Mason Factory 1050.00
Shorebird, Pine, Worn Old Paint, Steel Stand, 9 1/4 In. 190.00
Shorebird, Root Head, Layers Of Paint, 11 In. 412.00
Snipe, Glass Eyes, Oval Base, James Lapham 247.00
Swan, Carved Bill Detail, Curved Neck, White, Black, 1941, 3 1/2 In. 1035.00
Swan, Carved, Painted, c.1910, 30 x 9 In. 2100.00
Swan, Horseshoe Weight, 18 1/2 x 25 In. 950.00
Swan, Madison Mitchell, 1961 .... 1450.00
Tern, Crowell 5280.00
Widgeon, A. Elmer Crowell 5280.00
Widgeon, Mason Factory 9075.00
Widgeon Drake, Made For 1939 World's Fair, George Boyd, Pair 1705.00
Widgeon Hen, Allover Feather, Benjamin Schmidt 3410.00
Wood Duck, Mason, 1896-1924 .... 600.00
Wood Duck Drake, Carved, Polychrome, Glass Eyes, David C. Berai, 1982, 14 In. 80.00
Yellow Throat, Carved, Round Pedestal, 4 x 6 In. 315.00
Yellowlegs, George Boyd 2475.00
Yellowlegs, Joseph Lincoln, c.1910 .... 1450.00
Yellowlegs, Original Paint & Bill, c.1900 .... 575.00
Yellowlegs, Papier-Mache, c.1900 .... 675.00

DEDHAM Pottery was started in 1895. Chelsea Keramic Art Works was established in 1872 in Chelsea, Massachusetts, by members of the Robertson family. The factory closed in 1889 and was reorganized as the Chelsea Pottery U.S. in 1891. The firm used the marks *CKAW* and *CPUS*. It became the Dedham Pottery of Dedham, Massachusetts. The factory closed in 1943. It was famous for its crackleware dishes, which picture blue outlines of animals, flowers, and other natural motifs.

Apple Tree, Plate, Orchard Scene, 8 1/2 In. 3190.00
Azalea, Charger, Floral Design, 12 In. 550.00
Birds In Potted Orange Tree, Plate, 8 In. 440.00
Butterfly & Flower, Plate, 9 3/4 In. 605.00
Cat, Plate, Child's, 7 1/2 In. 4950.00
Cherries, Plate, Signed, 6 In. 70.00
Chick, Pitcher, Signed, 6 x 6 1/4 In. 1090.00
Cosmos, Plate, 6 In. 1870.00
Crab, Plate, 6 1/4 In. 495.00
Crab, Plate, Blue Stamp, 7 1/2 In. ....316.00 to 575.00
Crab, Plate, Blue Stamp, 8 1/2 In. 374.00
Day Lily, Plate, 8 1/2 In. 1692.00
Day Lily, Plate, Crackle, Hugh Robertson, 8 3/4 In. 1210.00
Day Lily, Sugar, Cover, 3 x 4 In. 575.00
Dolphin, Plate, Upside Down Dolphins, 8 1/2 In. 935.00
Duck, Bacon Rasher, Blue Stamp, 6 x 9 1/2 In. 345.00
Duck, Plate, 8 1/2 In. ....230.00 to 412.00
Duck, Plate, Signed, 6 In. 355.00
Duck, Plate, Tufted Ducks, 10 In. 303.00

Elephant, Bowl, 2 x 5 In. 880.00
Elephant, Bowl, 3 x 7 In. 1870.00
Elephant, Candlestick, Signed, 2 x 4 In., Pair 1022.00
Elephant, Chop Plate, 12 In. 1650.00
Elephant, Cup & Saucer, 2 1/4 x 6 In. 770.00
Elephant, Eggcup, 2 1/2 x 2 In. 805.00
Elephant, Plate, 9 3/4 In. 585.00
Elephant, Platter, Oval, 8 1/4 x 14 In. 2090.00
Elephant, Salt & Pepper 852.00
Elephant, Saucer 535.00
Fairbanks House, Plate, Signed, 8 1/2 In. 1977.00
Floral, Toothpick, 2 3/4 x 2 3/4 In. 12222.00
Flower, Cup, Handleless, Signed, Demitasse, 2 3/4 In. 1222.00
Grape, Jam Jar, 5 1/4 x 4 1/2 In. 1265.00
Grape, Jam Jar, Cover, 5 x 4 1/4 In. 605.00
Grape, Pitcher, 4 3/4 x 6 1/4 In. 260.00
Grape, Pitcher, Signed, 4 3/4 x 6 1/4 In. 295.00
Grape, Plate, Maude Davenport, 6 In. 165.00
Horsechestnut, Cup & Saucer, 2 x 4 1/2 x 6 In. 357.00
Horsechestnut, Plate, Blue Stamp, 10 In. 86.00
Horsechestnut, Plate, Jagged Shells, CPUS, 8 In. 220.00
Horsechestnut, Plate, Signed, 6 In. 265.00
Horsechestnut, Salt & Pepper, Signed, 1 1/2 x 3/4 In. 530.00
Horsechestnut, Teapot, Cover, Spout, Handle, Bulbous, 7 x 7 1/4 In. 1650.00
Iris, Plate, Blue Stamp, 10 In. 60.00
Lion Tapestry, Plate, 9 3/4 In. 880.00
Lobster, Plate, 7 1/2 In. ....230.00 to 402.00
Lobster, Plate, Blue Stamp, 8 1/2 In. ....345.00 to 460.00
Magnolia, Plate, 6 In. ....110.00 to 192.00
Magnolia, Plate, 8 1/2 In. 110.00
Magnolia, Plate, Signed, 7 1/2 In. 330.00
Moth & Flower, Plate, 6 In. 935.00
Moth & Flower, Plate, Maud Davenport, 8 1/2 In. 450.00
Moth & Flower, Plate, Signed, Exhibition Sticker, 10 In. 5290.00
Mushroom, Plate, Dotted Mushrooms, 6 In. 880.00
Mushroom, Plate, Maude Davenport, 8 In. 605.00
Naughty Dutch Boy, Ashtray, Boy Figure, Wearing Blue Hat, 4 3/4 In. 825.00
Nut On Leaf, Salt & Pepper, 1 1/2 In., Pair 460.00
Pineapple, Plate, 9 3/4 In. 467.00
Polar Bear, Bowl, Lotus Edge, 5 3/4 In. 357.00
Polar Bear, Celery Dish, 9 3/4 In. 1220.00
Polar Bear, Plate, 8 In. 715.00
Pond Lily, Bowl, Maude Davenport, 6 In. 303.00
Pond Lily, Plate, Blue, Signed, 6 In. 70.00
Poppy, Bowl, 3 3/4 x 9 In. 2530.00
Poppy, Plate, Thistle Stem, 6 1/4 In. 1320.00
Prunus, Vase, Signed, 8 1/2 In. 3105.00
Rabbit, Bell, 4 In. 2200.00
Rabbit, Bouillon & Saucer, 2 Protruding Handles, 2 1/4 In. ......247.00 to 522.00
Rabbit, Bowl & Spoon, Porridge, Signed, 5 3/8 In. 192.00
Rabbit, Bowl, 2 x 5 1/2 In., Pair 330.00
Rabbit, Bowl, 8 In. 60.00
Rabbit, Bowl, 11 In. 145.00
Rabbit, Bowl, 12 In. 475.00
Rabbit, Bowl, 1905, 9 In. 145.00
Rabbit, Bowl, Flared Rim, 1 3/4 x 4 1/8 In. ....275.00 to 330.00
Rabbit, Bowl, Lotus Edge, 2 x 5 In. 715.00
Rabbit, Coffeepot, Cover, Underliner, 8 3/4 In. ....920.00 to 1650.00
Rabbit, Creamer, 5 In. 468.00
Rabbit, Creamer, Maude Davenport, 2 x 3 In. 660.00
Rabbit, Creamer, Signed, 4 1/2 x 3 1/2 In. 200.00
Rabbit, Cup & Saucer, Signed, 2 1/4 In. 190.00

Rabbit, Dish, Mayonnaise, 2 1/8 x 5 1/4 In. 385.00
Rabbit, Flower Holder, Signed, 6 1/4 x 4 1/4 In. 1820.00
Rabbit, Goblet, 5 1/8 x 3 In. 440.00
Rabbit, Pitcher, Maude Davenport, 5 3/4 x 3 1/2 In. 247.00
Rabbit, Pitcher, Maude Davenport, 5 x 4 1/4 In. 495.00
Rabbit, Pitcher, Signed, 5 In. 110.00
Rabbit, Pitcher, Water, 8 In. 880.00
Rabbit, Plate, 8 1/2 In. 125.00
Rabbit, Plate, CPUS Clover, 10 1/4 In. 275.00
Rabbit, Plate, Signed, 6 In. 110.00
Rabbit, Plate, Signed, 9 7/8 In. 322.00
Rabbit, Platter, Incised Rabbit, 12 x 7 3/4 In. 145.00
Rabbit, Platter, Oval, 14 In. 1100.00
Rabbit, Saltshaker, 2 1/2 In. 110.00
Rabbit, Sherbet, Handles, 3 In. 440.00
Rabbit, Spoon, Ladle Shape, Stamped, 4 In. 60.00
Rabbit, Tankard, Blue Stamp, 5 1/4 In. 230.00
Rabbit, Teapot, 7 1/2 In. 115.00
Rabbit, Tureen, Cover, 1931, 9 1/2 In. 260.00
Rabbit, Tureen, Cover, 7 In. 495.00
Rabbit, Tureen, Cover, 8 In. 145.00
Rabbit, Tureen, Cover, Flared Rim, Maude Davenport, 3 x 9 In. 715.00
Rabbit, Tureen, Cover, Signed, 8 x 11 In. 3040.00
Rabbit, Vase, 5 x 4 1/4 In. 605.00
Sailboat, Plate, Boat With Mast Sailing, Tranquil Waters, Blue, CPUS Clover, 8 In. 3410.00
Snowtree, Cup & Saucer, 6 In. 172.00
Snowtree, Plate, Blue Stamp, 10 In. 85.00
Strawberry, Plate, Deep Blue 2970.00
Swan, Bacon Rasher, 10 x 6 1/2 In. 695.00
Swan, Bowl, 3 1/2 In. 990.00
Swan, Coaster, Round, 4 In. 715.00
Swan, Cup & Saucer, 2 1/4 x 6 In. 357.00
Swan, Dish, Square, 8 1/4 x 8 1/4 In. 402.00
Swan, Plate, 8 1/2 In. 495.00
Swan, Plate, Maude Davenport, 6 In. 385.00
Swan, Sugar, Cover, 3 x 4 In. 575.00
Tapestry Lion, Plate, 8 1/2 In. 1150.00
Turkey, Bowl, 2 1/8 x 5 1/3 In. 275.00
Turkey, Pitcher, Signed, 3 1/2 x 6 In. 530.00
Turkey, Plate, 8 1/2 In. 247.00
Turkey, Plate, 10 In. 303.00
Turtle, Paperweight, Dome Shape, Protruding Feet, Tail, Head, 3 1/2 In. 715.00
Turtle, Paperweight, Signed, 3 1/4 x 2 1/4 In. 1190.00
Turtle, Soup, Dish, Cobalt Blue, 7 1/2 In. 600.00
Volcanic Ware, Colored Glaze Over Tan Glaze, Signed, 8 In. 1200.00

DEGUE is a signature acid-etched on pieces of French glass made in the
early 1900s. Cameo, mold blown, and smooth glass with contrasting
colored rims are the types most often found.

Bowl, Internal Swirls, Pedestal Footed, Signed, 17 In. 460.00
Bowl, Swirled Green Powders & Bubbles, Signed, 5 x 13 1/2 In. 285.00
Urn, Mottled Raspberry, Triple-Layer Handles, Cupped Foot, Signed, 8 In. 495.00
Urn, Triple Layer Handles, Goblet Form, Pedestal Foot, 8 In. 495.00
Vase, Orange Powdered Glass Overlay, Zigzag, Acid-Treated Ground, 1920, 13 In. 805.00
Vase, Triangle Design, Green Overlay, Flared, Oval, 18 In. 920.00

DELATTE glass is a French cameo glass made by Andre Delatte. It was
first made in Nancy, France, in 1921. Lighting fixtures and opaque
glassware in imitation of Bohemian opaline were made. There were
many French cameo glassmakers, so be sure to look in other appropriate categories.

Vase, Lavender Floral, Opalescent Frosted Ground, Signed, 7 1/2 In. 660.00

DELDARE, see Buffalo Pottery Deldare.

DELFT is a tin-glazed pottery that has been made since the seventeenth century. It is decorated with blue on white or with colored decorations. Most of the pieces sold today were made after 1891, and the name *Holland* appears with the Delft factory marks. The word *delft* also appears on pottery from other countries. Delft was made in England in the eighteenth century.

Bottle, Pewter Cover, Blue & White Flowers In Center Band, 7 1/4 In.	275.00
Bottle, Water, Bird In Tree Above Peonies, Everted Rim, Diaper Border, 1770, 9 In.	1035.00
Bowl, Blue Floral On White Reserve, Lobed, Scalloped Border, 8 1/2 In.	825.00
Bowl, Bristol, Manganese Powder Ground, c.1735	3250.00
Bowl, Butterfly, Polychrome Floral, 6 x 13 In.	1705.00
Bowl, Flowers, Blue, England, 1765, 9 In.	3162.00
Box, Dresser, Portrait Of Woman Cover, Scrolls, Flowers, 3 In.	403.00
Box, Dresser, Portrait Of Young Girl Cover, Satin Lining, 3 x 4 3/4 In.	750.00
Candlestick, White, Holland, c.1780, 8 In.	295.00
Charger, 3 Tulips, Amidst Flowers, Foliage, Blue, Green, Yellow, Blue Border, 13 In.	2875.00
Charger, 3 Tulips, Amidst Flowers, Foliage, Green, Blue, Yellow, Blue Dash Rim, 12 In.	4887.00
Charger, Adam & Eve, Either Side Of Serpent, Apple Tree, Brislington, 13 7/10 In.	4830.00
Charger, Adam & Eve, On Either Side Of Blue Sponge Tree, Yellow Fruit, 1710, 12 In.	4600.00
Charger, Bird In Still Life, Foliage, Floral Border, Blue, White, England, 13 3/8 In.	520.00
Charger, Bird, Floral Landscape, Holland, 18th Century, 13 In.	1265.00
Charger, Blue & White Floral, 14 1/2 In.	330.00
Charger, Bristol, Adam & Eve, Eve Offering Adam Apple, Serpent Around Tree, 13 In.	5520.00
Charger, Couple In 1-Horse Trap, Boch	85.00
Charger, Floral, Border	1045.00
Charger, Floral, Fern Design, Scrolled Vinework Border, Blue, White, Holland, 13 In.	635.00
Charger, Hand-Painted Towered Town, River, Trees, Scrolled Oval Shape, 16 1/2 x 13 In.	450.00
Charger, House, Tree, Birds, Blue & White, Liverpool, 18th Century, 13 1/2 In.	403.00
Charger, Man Astride Rearing Horse, Blue Trees, Blue, Green, 1700, 14 1/4 In.	8625.00
Charger, Man Rowing Skiff Down River, Germany, 13 1/2 In.	35.00
Charger, Man With Rifle & Dog In Woods, 2 Figures In Distance, Blue, Green, 13 In.	200.00
Charger, Oriental Plant & Building Border, Blue, 1742, 12 3/4 In.	2587.00
Charger, Puritan, Motto, Bristol, 1750	675.00
Charger, Riverscape Design, Blue, White, Signed, 15 1/2 In.	230.00
Cuspidor, Flaring Floral Lip, Hexagonal, Miniature, 4 x 5 In.	715.00
Dish, 2 Rows Of Convex Flutes, Peacock On Plateau, Scalloped Edge, 13 1/4 In.	1265.00
Dish, Continuous Band Of Slender Fish, Manganese, Green, Red, 1770, 8 In.	2990.00
Dish, Royal Portrait, Prince William III, Wreath Of Tulips, Tulip Edge, 13 5/8 In.	2070.00
Dish, Royal Portrait, Queen Anne, Blue, Zigzag Border, Round, 1705, 9 In.	10350.00
Dish, Stylized Floral Medallion, Spiral Center, Alternating Petal, Leaf Rim, 1760, 9 In.	805.00
Ewer, Polychrome, Pewter Mounts, 1800, 10 1/2 In.	1320.00
Ewer, Windmill, Lake, Sailboats, Flowers, c.1890, 10 In.	235.00
Figurine, Cat, Seated, Yellow Collar, Red Spots, Red, Blue, 1700, 4 In., Pair	3450.00
Jar, Chicken Shape, Pink & Green, Signed, 8 1/4 In.	395.00
Jug, White, Tapering Neck, Loop Handle, Early 18th Century, 8 5/8 In.	1725.00
Mug, Chinoiserie Seascape, Trellis Border, Late 18th Century, 6 1/8 In.	2070.00
Pill Slab, Apothecary's Guild Of London, Blue, 1720, 12 1/2 In.	14950.00
Pill Slab, Apothecary's Guild Of London, Blue, Rectangular, 1780, 12 In.	9200.00
Plaque, Bird, Theatrical Curtains On Sides, Birdcage Shape	3500.00
Plaque, Boat On Canal, Houses, Blue, White, Oval, 24 In.	360.00
Plate, 2 Oriental Scholars, Walking In Fenced Garden, Blue, 1749, 12 In.	2587.00
Plate, Allover Chinoiserie Design, Lobed, c.1740, 10 In.	990.00
Plate, Band Of Stylized Plants, Paneled Border Rim, Signed, 1736, 8 5/8 In.	2300.00
Plate, Blue & White Floral, England, Early 18th Century, 8 3/4 In.	165.00
Plate, Blue & White Landscape, Floral Border, 9 1/2 In.	100.00
Plate, Blue & White Oriental Design, 8 3/4 In.	55.00
Plate, Blue Floral, Border, 9 In.	165.00
Plate, Center Lion, Standing Near Cliff, Chinoiserie Figures In Landscape, 10 In.	1840.00
Plate, Center Stylized Plant, Flower Heads Edge, Late 18th Century, 9 3/8 In., Pair	1725.00
Plate, Central Medallion Design, 1793, 9 In., Pair	4312.00

Plate, Chinese Design, Dark Blue, 17th Century, Pair 2100.00
Plate, Flowers & Bird, England, 8 3/4 In. 385.00
Plate, Oriental Woman & Her Servant Beside Large Fish, Blue, 1750, 12 In. 1725.00
Plate, Polychrome, c.1780, 5 7/8 In. 250.00
Plate, Polychrome, Inscribed, 1785, France, 9 In. 325.00
Plate, Round Medallion, R * R Design Center, Blue, 1725 . . . . 2185.00
Plate, Royal Portrait, King William III, Holding Scepter, 9 In. 5750.00
Plate, Royal Portrait, Profiles Of Regal Couple, Polychrome, 8 7/8 In. 770.00
Plate Set, Oriental Woman, Seated Beneath Tree, Diaper Border, 1760, 8 Piece 2070.00
Posset Pot, Cover, c.1710 . . . . 3900.00
Posset Pot, Cover, Floral, Foliage, Red, Green, Blue, Bulbous, 1710, 9 1/4 In. 5750.00
Posset Pot, Cover, Red, Blue, Green Foliate Sprigs, Sprays, 2 Loop Handles, 1710, 9 In. . 10925.00
Punch Bowl, Basket Weave Border Above Trailing Flowers, 11 3/4 In. 605.00
Punch Bowl, Stylized Flower Sprigs, Florets, Sawtooth Border, Red, Green, Blue, 12 In. . 4887.00
Punch Bowl, Stylized Vases Of Flowers, Orange, Blue, Laurel-Wreath Borders, 5 1/2 In. . 2012.00
Punch Bowl, Success To Trade, 1770, England, 9 In. 1150.00
Salver, Oriental Woman & Servant In Garden, Raised Rim, 1750, 12 In. 3162.00
Stein, Blue & White Floral, Bird, Replaced Pewter Base & Cover, 5 1/2 In. 250.00
Stein, Windmill Scene, Cover, Silver Rim, Pottery, 1/2 Liter 255.00
Tile, Christmas, 1974 . . . . 20.00
Tile, Elephant, Standing Between Plants, Dotted Plateau, 5 In., 6 Piece 1610.00
Tile, Hand-Painted Church, Lake & Sailboats, 5 In. 50.00
Tile, Hannibal, Holding Frond, Seated On Elephant Warriors, 5 1/16 In., 4 Piece 517.00
Tile, Military Figure, Horizontal Mounted, Frame, 4 Piece 260.00
Tobacco Jar, Beehive Cover, Cartouche, Flanked By Tobacco Smoking Figures 2587.00
Tobacco Jar, Brass Cover, Painted Cartouche, Scrolls, Vase Of Flowers, 1740, 12 In. 7130.00
Tobacco Jar, Cover, 1730s 4800.00
Tray, Windmill & House By Water, Swaine & Co., Rectangular, 8 1/2 x 6 1/2 In. 115.00
Urn, Oriental Design, Bird Finials, Blue, White, 10 In., Pair 632.00
Vase, Bishop, Praying In Landscape, Blue, White, 1742, 8 1/2 In. 400.00
Vase, Couple Dancing Before House, Villagers Group Dancing, 17 x 16 In., Pair 1380.00
Vase, Cover, Peonies & Bamboo, Rocks, Flower Spray On Reverse, 13 1/8 In. 1610.00
Vase, Cover, Woman, Carrying Basket Of Flowers, Pastoral Setting, 14 In., Pair 1725.00
Vase, Floral, Oval Scene Of Youth In Landscape, Windmills, 8 1/4 In. 275.00
Vase, Gentleman Drinking Tea, Seated Before House, Scale Border, 13 In., Pair 1840.00
Vase, Rococo-Style Cartouche, Central Vase Of Flowers, Parrot Handles, 14 In. 575.00

DENTAL cabinets, chairs, equipment, and other related items are listed
here. Other objects may be found in the Medical category.

Cabinet, Mahogany, 3 Compartments, Marble At Bottom, 2 Drawers, 60 In. 2000.00
Cabinet, Mahogany, Milk Glass Top, Side Doors, Contents 2200.00
Cabinet, Oak, Eastlake, S.S. White Co., c.1880, 69 x 33 x 21 In. 4800.00
Cabinet, Roll Top, Burl Walnut, Marble Top, Victorian 7500.00
Case, Roll Top, Drawers, France, 12 1/2 x 12 1/2 In. 398.00
Case, Teeth Instruments, Home Care, Mirrored, Pocket Size 700.00
Drill, Buffalo Dental Mfg., Extra Heads, Foot Pedal, New Burrs & Tools 150.00
Forceps, Black Iron, Civil War 50.00
Kit, 11 Different Instruments, All-Purpose Handle, Original Case 185.00
Pin, American Dental Association, Celluloid 7.00

DEPRESSION GLASS was an inexpensive glass manufactured in large
quantities during the 1920s and early 1930s. It was made in many colors and patterns by dozens of factories in the United States. The name
Depression glass is a modern one. For more descriptions, history, pictures, and prices of Depression glass, see the book *Kovels' Depression
Glass & Dinnerware Price List*.

Adam, Ashtray, Green, 4 1/2 In. 25.00
Adam, Bowl, Cover, Pink, 9 In. . . . . .25.00 to 65.00
Adam, Bowl, Oval, Pink, 10 In. 30.00
Adam, Bowl, Pink, 7 3/4 In. 29.00
Adam, Cake Plate, Footed, Green, 10 In. 30.00
Adam, Cake Plate, Footed, Pink, 10 In. 28.00
Adam, Creamer, Pink . . . . .20.00 to 24.00

Adam, Cup & Saucer, Green 30.00
Adam, Grill Plate, Green, 9 In. ....18.00 to 22.00
Adam, Grill Plate, Pink, 9 In. 28.00
Adam, Plate, Green, 9 In. 30.00
Adam, Plate, Square, Green, 7 3/4 In. ....15.00 to 17.00
Adam, Plate, Square, Pink, 9 In. ....25.00 to 33.00
Adam, Platter, Oval, Pink, 11 3/4 In. 30.00
Adam, Sherbet, Green, 3 In. 37.00
Adam, Sherbet, Pink, 3 In. 30.00
Adam, Tumbler, Green, 4 1/2 In. 30.00
Adam, Tumbler, Pink, 4 1/2 In. ....30.00 to 32.00
Adam, Vase, Green, 7 1/2 In. 92.00
Alpine Caprice, Bowl, Blue, 13 In. 135.00
American Pioneer, Bowl, Handle, Pink, 9 In. 25.00
American Pioneer, Pitcher, Cover, Green, 7 In. 135.00
American Sweetheart, Bowl, 6 In. 17.00
American Sweetheart, Bowl, Monax, 6 In. 17.00
American Sweetheart, Bowl, Oval, Pink, 11 In. ....60.00 to 65.00
American Sweetheart, Bowl, Pink, 6 In. ....15.00 to 17.00
American Sweetheart, Bread Plate, Pink, 6 In. 5.00
American Sweetheart, Chop Plate, Monax, 11 In. 18.00
American Sweetheart, Creamer, Footed, Monax 10.00
American Sweetheart, Cup & Saucer, Pink ....22.00 to 24.00
American Sweetheart, Cup, Pink 18.00
American Sweetheart, Cup, Red 85.00
American Sweetheart, Plate, Monax, 8 In. 9.00
American Sweetheart, Plate, Monax, 9 3/4 In. 22.00
American Sweetheart, Plate, Pink, 8 In. 12.00
American Sweetheart, Plate, Pink, 9 3/4 In. 40.00
American Sweetheart, Platter, Oval, Pink, 13 In. 52.00
American Sweetheart, Salver, Monax, 12 In. 18.00
American Sweetheart, Salver, Pink, 12 In. ....17.00 to 22.00
American Sweetheart, Saucer, Monax 2.00
American Sweetheart, Sherbet, Footed, Monax, 4 1/4 In. 20.00
American Sweetheart, Sherbet, Footed, Pink, 4 1/4 In. 22.00
American Sweetheart, Tumbler, Pink, 5 Oz., 3 1/2 In. 95.00
American Sweetheart, Tumbler, Pink, 9 Oz., 4 1/2 In. 85.00
Anniversary, Berry Bowl, Pink, 4 7/8 In. 11.00
Anniversary, Bowl, Pink, 9 In. 35.00
Anniversary, Plate, Pink, 9 In. 18.00
Anniversary, Sandwich Server, Pink, 12 1/2 In. 25.00
Apple Blossom pattern is listed here as Dogwood.
Aurora, Bowl, Pink, 5 3/8 In. 14.00
Aurora, Cup, Pink 15.00
Avocado, Sugar & Creamer, Footed, Green 70.00
Ballerina pattern is listed here as Cameo.
Banded Rib pattern is listed here as Coronation.

Depression Glass,
Adam

Depression Glass,
Block Optic

Depression Glass,
Bubble

  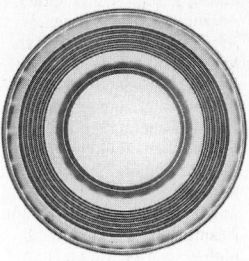

Depression Glass,
Cameo

Depression Glass,
Cherry Blossom

Depression Glass,
Circle

Beaded Block, Dish, Jelly, 2 Handles, Blue, 4 7/8 In.	20.00
Block pattern is listed here as Block Optic.	
Block Optic, Bowl, Green, 4 1/2 In.	6.00 to 7.00
Block Optic, Bowl, Green, 5 1/4 In.	12.00 to 15.00
Block Optic, Candlestick, Amber, 1 3/4 In., Pair	60.00
Block Optic, Cup & Saucer, Green	14.00 to 17.00
Block Optic, Cup, Pink	7.00
Block Optic, Goblet, Yellow, 9 Oz., 7 1/4 In.	15.00
Block Optic, Plate, Green, 6 In.	3.00
Block Optic, Sherbet, Pink, 5 1/2 Oz., 3 1/4 In.	8.00
Block Optic, Tumble-Up, Green	65.00
Block Optic, Tumbler, Footed, Pink, 9 Oz.	15.00
Bubble, Berry Bowl, Red, 8 3/8 In.	20.00
Bubble, Cup & Saucer, Green	16.00
Bubble, Tumbler, Green, 6 Oz.	16.00
Bubble, Tumbler, Green, 9 Oz.	15.00
Bubble, Tumbler, Red, 12 Oz.	12.00
Bubble, Tumbler, Red, 9 Oz.	9.00
Bullseye pattern is listed here as Bubble.	
Cabbage Rose pattern is listed here as Sharon.	
Cameo, Butter, Cover, Green	225.00
Cameo, Creamer, Green, 3 1/4 In.	23.00
Cameo, Cup & Saucer, Yellow	8.00 to 15.00
Cameo, Goblet, Green, 4 In.	75.00
Cameo, Goblet, Green, 6 In.	50.00
Cameo, Grill Plate, Green, 10 1/2 In.	9.00
Cameo, Grill Plate, Yellow, 10 1/2 In.	10.00 to 17.00
Cameo, Ice Bowl, 3 x 5 1/2 In.	190.00
Cameo, Plate, Green, 8 In.	10.00
Cameo, Salt & Pepper, Footed, Green	70.00
Cameo, Tumbler, Footed, Green, 3 Oz.	60.00
Cameo, Tumbler, Footed, Green, 9 Oz.	28.00
Cameo, Tumbler, Footed, Green, 11 Oz.	35.00 to 65.00
Cameo, Vase, Green, 8 In.	40.00 to 42.00
Candlewick pattern is listed in the Imperial Glass category.	
Cape Cod pattern is listed in the Imperial Glass category.	
Caprice pattern is included in the Cambridge Glass category.	
Cherry Blossom, Bowl, Green, 4 3/4 In.	18.00
Cherry Blossom, Bowl, Pink, 3-Footed, 10 1/2 In.	90.00
Cherry Blossom, Butter, Cover, Green	100.00
Cherry Blossom, Coaster, Green	13.00
Cherry Blossom, Cup & Saucer, Child's, Delphite	47.00
Cherry Blossom, Cup & Saucer, Green	26.00
Cherry Blossom, Grill Plate, Green, 9 In.	25.00
Cherry Blossom, Junior Dinner Set, Pink, 14 Piece	325.00
Cherry Blossom, Mug, Green, 7 Oz.	210.00

Cherry Blossom, Plate, Child's, Delphite, 6 In. 13.00
Cherry Blossom, Platter, Green, 13 In. 70.00
Cherry Blossom, Platter, Oval, Green, 11 In. 45.00
Cherry Blossom, Sandwich Server, Delphite, 10 1/2 In. 22.00
Cherry Blossom, Tumbler, Footed, Green, 3 3/4 In. 20.00
Cherry Blossom, Tumbler, Green, 3 1/2 In. 24.00
Circle, Tumbler, Green, 4 Oz., 3 1/2 In. 9.00
Cloverleaf, Candy Dish, Cover, Yellow 100.00
Cloverleaf, Creamer, Footed, Green, 3 5/8 In. 14.00
Cloverleaf, Cup, Green 8.00
Cloverleaf, Cup, Pink 7.00
Cloverleaf, Plate, Black, 8 In. 12.00
Cloverleaf, Sugar & Creamer, Black .... 30.00 to 45.00
Colonial, Butter, Cover 40.00
Colonial, Creamer, 5 In. 15.00
Colonial, Cup & Saucer, Green 20.00
Colonial, Cup, Pink 12.00
Colonial, Goblet, Cocktail, 3 Oz., 4 In. 14.00
Colonial, Goblet, Cordial, 1 Oz., 3 3/4 In. 18.00
Colonial, Goblet, Water, Green, 8 1/2 Oz., 5 3/4 In. 30.00
Colonial, Spooner, Green 100.00
Colonial, Tumbler, Footed, 3 Oz., 3 1/4 In. 12.00
Colonial, Tumbler, Footed, Pink, 10 Oz., 5 1/2 In. 34.00
Colonial, Tumbler, Pink, 9 Oz., 4 In. 20.00
Coronation, Bowl, 6 1/2 In. 20.00
Dancing Girl pattern is listed here as Cameo.
Della Robbia, Sherbet, 4 3/4 In. 15.00
Diamond Pattern is listed here as Miss America.
Dogwood, Berry Bowl, Pink, 8 1/2 In. 60.00
Dogwood, Bowl, Pink, 5 1/2 In. 30.00
Dogwood, Cake Plate, Green, 13 In. 120.00
Dogwood, Cup & Saucer, Pink .... 18.00 to 25.00
Dogwood, Sherbet, Footed, Pink 35.00
Doric & Pansy, Cup & Saucer 13.00
Double Shield pattern is listed here as Mt. Pleasant.
English Hobnail, Toilet Bottle, Ice Blue, 5 Oz. 60.00
English Hobnail, Tumbler, Amber, 10 Oz., 4 1/2 In. 50.00
Fire-King, Bowl, Nesting, Fruit 48.00
Fire-King, Casserole, Blue, 1 1/2 Qt. 15.00
Fire-King, Mixing Bowl, Ivory, Handle & Spout 30.00
Fire-King, Mixing Bowl, Spatter Proof, Distlefink, Red Bird, 9 In. 18.00
Fire-King, Pie Plate, Blue, 8 3/8 In. 6.00
Fire-King, Refrigerator Jar, Blue, 4 1/2 x 5 In. 10.00
Fleurette, Serva-Snack Set, 4 Trays & Cups, Box, 8 Piece 35.00
Floragold, Sugar & Creamer, Cover 25.00
Floral, Creamer 15.00

Depression Glass,
Cloverleaf

Depression Glass,
Colonial

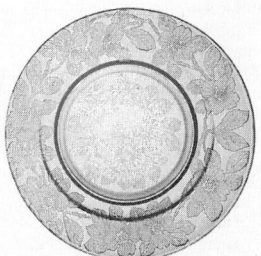

Depression Glass,
Dogwood

Depression Glass,
Doric & Pansy

Depression Glass,
Floral

Depression Glass,
Iris

Floral & Diamond Band, Butter, Cover, Green	130.00
Floral & Diamond Band, Compote, Green, 5 1/2 In.	18.00
Florentine No. 1, Soup, Cream, Pink, 5 In.	30.00
Florentine No. 2, Coaster, 3 3/4 In.	10.00
Forest Green, Bowl, 4 5/8 In.	7.00
Forest Green, Punch Set, 12 Cups, 14 Piece	95.00
Fortune, Bowl, Handle, Pink, 4 1/2 In.	7.00
Fruits, Cup & Saucer, Green	9.00
Georgian, Cup & Saucer, Green	13.00
Heritage, Bowl, 5 In.	7.00
Heritage, Bowl, 10 1/2 In.	13.00
Heritage, Cup & Saucer	8.00
Iris, Berry Bowl, Beaded, 4 1/2 In.	45.00
Iris, Goblet, 4 Oz., 5 3/4 In.	24.00
Iris, Goblet, Cocktail, 4 Oz., 4 1/4 In.	24.00
Iris, Goblet, Wine, 3 Oz., 4 In.	11.00
Iris, Pitcher, Footed, 9 1/2 In.	25.00 to 38.00
Iris, Sugar, Cover	24.00
Iris & Herringbone pattern is listed here as Iris.	
Jadite, Batter Bowl, Handle & Spout, 7 1/2 In.	45.00
Jadite, Cup & Saucer	15.00
Jadite, Mixing Bowl, Restaurant Ware, Handles, 11 In.	60.00
Jane-Ray, Plate, Salad, Jadite, 7 3/4 In.	15.00
Jubilee, Cake Plate, Handle, Pink, 11 In.	30.00
Jubilee, Cake Plate, Handle, Topaz, 11 In.	45.00
Jubilee, Creamer, Topaz	22.00
Jubilee, Cup & Saucer, Topaz	22.00
Jubilee, Goblet, Topaz, 10 Oz., 6 In.	33.00
Jubilee, Plate, Topaz, 7 In.	21.00
Jubilee, Plate, Topaz, 8 3/4 In.	24.00
Jubilee, Platter, Oval, Topaz, 11 In.	40.00
Jubilee, Saucer, Topaz	8.00
Jubilee, Sugar, Topaz	22.00
Knife & Fork pattern is listed here as Colonial.	
Lace Edge, Cup & Saucer, Pink	40.00
Lace Edge, Platter, Pink, 12 3/4 In.	37.00
Lace Edge, Relish, 3 Sections, Pink, 11 In.	25.00
Lace Edge, Relish, 4 Sections, Pink, 13 In.	69.00
Laurel, Bowl, French Ivory, 6 In.	10.00
Laurel, Cup & Saucer, French Ivory	10.00
Lincoln Inn, Sherbet, Red, 4 3/4 In.	14.00
Lincoln Inn, Tumbler, Water, Red, Footed, 9 Oz.	22.00
Lorna pattern is included in the Cambridge Glass category.	
Louisa pattern is listed here as Floragold.	
Lovebirds pattern is listed here as Georgian.	
Madrid, Cookie Jar, Cover, Amber	25.00

Depression Glass, Lace Edge   Depression Glass, Madrid

Madrid, Plate, Amber, 10 1/2 In. 45.00
Madrid, Soup, Cream, Amber, 7 1/2 In. 16.00
Madrid, Tumbler, Blue, 9 Oz., 4 1/4 In. 30.00
Manhattan, Bowl, Handle, 4 1/2 In. 6.00
Manhattan, Pitcher, Tilted, Pink, 80 Oz. ....65.00 to 75.00
Manhattan, Plate, 10 1/4 In. 16.00
Manhattan, Sherbet 7.00
Manhattan, Sugar, Pink 10.00
Manhattan, Tumbler, Footed, 10 Oz. 15.00
Martha Washington pattern is included in the Cambridge Glass category.
Mayfair Open Rose, Creamer, Pink 29.00
Miss America, Pitcher, Pink, 65 Oz., 8 1/2 In. 195.00
Miss America, Sherbet 6.00
Moderntone, Berry Bowl, Cobalt Blue, 5 In. 25.00
Moderntone, Creamer, Cobalt Blue ....10.00 to 12.00
Moderntone, Cup & Saucer, Cobalt Blue 15.00
Moderntone, Cup, Cobalt Blue 11.00
Moderntone, Custard, Amethyst 12.00
Moderntone, Plate, Cobalt Blue, 7 3/4 In. 12.00
Moderntone, Salt & Pepper, Cobalt Blue ....35.00 to 38.00
Moderntone, Sandwich Plate, Cobalt Blue, 10 In. 60.00
Moderntone, Sherbet, Cobalt Blue 12.00
Moderntone, Soup, Cream, Cobalt Blue, 4 3/4 In. ....20.00 to 22.00
Moderntone, Sugar, Cobalt Blue 12.00
Moondrops, Soup, Cream, Amethyst, 6 3/4 In. 70.00
Mt. Pleasant, Sherbet, Cobalt Blue 16.00
Mt. Vernon pattern is included in the Cambridge Glass category.
New Century, Tumbler, Cobalt Blue, 10 Oz., 5 In. 16.00
New Century, Tumbler, Cobalt Blue, 5 Oz., 3 1/2 In. ....12.00 to 18.00
No. 601 pattern is listed here as Avocado.
No. 618, Cup & Saucer 12.00
No. 618, Plate, 9 3/8 In. 13.00
No. 618, Plate, Indentation, 11 1/2 In. 20.00
Old Colony pattern is listed here as Lace Edge.
Old Florentine pattern is listed here as Florentine No. 1.
Open Lace pattern is listed here as Lace Edge.
Open Rose pattern is listed here as Mayfair Open Rose.

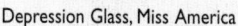

Depression Glass,
Mayfair Open Rose

Depression Glass, Miss America

Depression Glass,
Moderntone

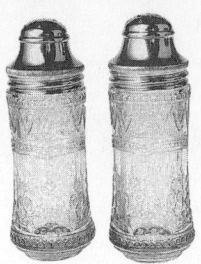

Depression Glass,
Mt. Pleasant

Depression Glass,
No. 618

Depression Glass,
Patrician

Optic Design pattern is listed here as Raindrops.
Patrician, Grill Plate, Amber 10.00
Patrician, Pitcher, Pink, 75 Oz., 8 In. 160.00
Petal Swirl pattern is listed here as Swirl.
Petalware, Candy, Cover, Pink 25.00
Pineapple & Floral pattern is listed here as No. 618.
Pinwheel pattern is listed here as Sierra.
Poinsettia pattern is listed here as Floral.
Poppy No. 1 pattern is listed here as Florentine No. 1.
Poppy No. 2 pattern is listed here as Florentine No. 2.
Pretty Polly Party Dishes, see also the related pattern Doric & Pansy.
Primrose, Sugar & Creamer, Cover 24.00
Princess, Cake Stand, Green, 10 In. 22.00
Princess, Cup & Saucer, Green 20.00
Princess, Cup, Pink 12.00
Princess, Plate, Green, 8 In. 14.00
Princess, Plate, Pink, 8 In. 14.00
Princess, Sugar, Green 10.00
Princess Feather, Goblet, 8 Oz., 6 In. 7.00
Prismatic Line pattern is listed here as Queen Mary.
Provincial pattern is listed here as Bubble.
Queen Mary, Bowl, Pink, 4 In. 6.00
Radiance, Sugar & Creamer, Red 45.00
Raindrops, Sherbet, Green 5.00
Raindrops, Tumbler, Green, 4 Oz., 3 In. 3.00
Royal Lace, Berry Bowl, Cobalt Blue, Round, 10 In. ....82.00 to 90.00
Royal Lace, Bowl, Ruffled, Cobalt Blue, 10 In. 400.00
Royal Lace, Bowl, Straight Edge, Footed, Cobalt Blue, 10 In. 80.00
Royal Lace, Cookie Jar, Cobalt Blue 415.00
Royal Lace, Creamer, Footed, Cobalt Blue ....54.00 to 55.00
Royal Lace, Pitcher, Ice Lip, Cobalt Blue, 68 Oz., 8 In. 175.00

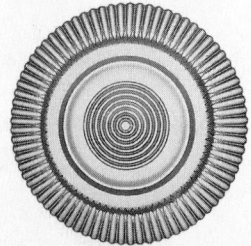

Depression Glass,
Petalware

Depression Glass,
Princess

Depression Glass,
Royal Lace

Royal Lace, Plate, Cobalt Blue, 8 1/2 In. 38.00
Royal Lace, Plate, Cobalt Blue, 9 7/8 In. 42.00
Royal Lace, Salt & Pepper, Cobalt Blue ....175.00 to 325.00
Royal Lace, Sherbet, Footed, Cobalt Blue 40.00
Royal Lace, Soup, Cream, Cobalt Blue, 4 3/4 In. 43.00
Royal Lace, Tumbler, Cobalt Blue, 5 Oz., 3 1/2 In. 54.00
Royal Lace, Tumbler, Cobalt Blue, 9 Oz., 4 1/8 In. 48.00
Royal Lace, Tumbler, Cobalt Blue, 12 Oz., 5 3/8 In. 110.00
Sail Boat pattern is listed here as Sportsman Series.
Saxon pattern is listed here as Coronation.
Sharon, Berry Bowl, Amber, 5 In. 7.50
Sharon, Berry Bowl, Green, 5 In. 12.00
Sharon, Bowl, Amber, 5 In. 8.50
Sharon, Bowl, Amber, 8 1/2 In. ....4.50 to 8.00
Sharon, Bowl, Amber, 10 1/2 In. ....16.00 to 20.00
Sharon, Bowl, Pink, 6 In. ....23.00 to 27.00
Sharon, Bowl, Pink, 10 1/2 In. 39.00
Sharon, Butter, Cover, Amber 46.00
Sharon, Creamer, Pink 16.00
Sharon, Cup & Saucer, Amber ....9.00 to 12.00
Sharon, Plate, Amber, 9 1/2 In. 12.00
Sharon, Plate, Green, 9 1/2 In. 20.00
Sharon, Plate, Pink, 6 In. ....6.50 to 7.50
Sharon, Plate, Pink, 7 1/2 In. 23.00
Sharon, Plate, Pink, 9 1/2 In. 20.00
Sharon, Platter, Oval, Pink, 12 1/2 In. 27.00
Sharon, Saucer, Amber 6.00
Sharon, Sherbet, Pink 10.00
Sharon, Sugar, Cover, Amber 45.00
Sharon, Tumbler, Footed, Pink, 15 Oz., 6 1/2 In. 52.00
Sharon, Tumbler, Pink, 12 Oz., 5 1/4 In. 40.00
Sharon, Tumbler, Pink, 4 1/8 In. 42.00
Sierra, Plate, Pink, 9 In. 22.00
Spoke pattern is listed here as Patrician.
Sportsman Series, Ice Bowl, Sail Boat, Blue 28.00
Sportsman Series, Tumbler, Sail Boat, Roly Poly, Blue, 6 Oz. 8.50
Sportsman Series, Tumbler, White Ship, Cobalt Blue, 9 Oz., 4 5/8 In. 8.00
Sunflower, Cake Plate, Footed, Pink, 10 In. 15.00
Sunflower, Plate, Green, 9 In. 16.00
Sunflower, Sugar, Green 16.00
Swirl, Sugar & Creamer, Delphite 32.00
Swirl, Sugar & Creamer, Ultramarine 22.00
Swirl, Ultramarine, Bowl, 5 1/4 In. 15.00
Swirl Fire-King, Cup & Saucer, Pink 10.00
Swirl Fire-King, Cup & Saucer, Sunrise 10.00
Swirl Fire-King, Plate, Sunrise, 9 1/8 In. 10.00

Depression Glass,
Sharon

Depression Glass,
Swirl

Depression Glass,
Windsor

Swirl Fire-King, Sugar, Cover, Sunrise 16.00
Swirl Fire-King, Sugar, Pink 10.00
Vertical Ribbed pattern is listed here as Queen Mary.
Waffle pattern is listed here as Waterford.
Waterford, Sugar & Creamer, Cover, Pink 42.00
White Ship pattern is listed here as Sportsman Series.
Wild Rose pattern is listed here as Dogwood.
Windsor, Plate, Green, 9 In. 20.00
Windsor, Salt & Pepper, Pink 30.00
Windsor, Saucer, Pink 5.00
Windsor, Tumbler, Pink, 5 Oz., 3 1/2 In. 20.00
Windsor Diamond pattern is listed here as Windsor.

DERBY has been marked on porcelain made in the city of Derby, England, since about 1748. The original Derby factory closed in 1848, but others opened there and continued to produce quality porcelain. The Crown Derby mark began appearing on Derby wares in the 1770s.

Bowl, Vegetable, Navette Shape, 1810-1825, 8 1/2 x 11 In., Pair 665.60
Compote, Column Shaped Pedestal, Round Foot, Square Base, 6 1/4 In. 12650.00
Creamer, Cover, Cow, Gilt, Early 19th Century, 4 In. 920.00
Desk Set, Tray On Paw Feet, Pen Tray, 3 Covered Pots, Signed, 8 1/2 In. 1035.00
Dinner Service, Ducks Swimming Among Oriental Foliage, 1820, 57 Piece 5750.00
Dish, Botanical, Red Plumeria Sprig, Scrolled Foliage Gilt Border, Oval, 1820, 11 In. 2990.00
Dish, Overlapping Lettuce Leaves, Bouquets, Butterfly, Leaf Shape, 1755, 10 1/4 In. 173.00
Dish, Shell Shape, Huntsman On Horseback & Hounds, Gilt Border, 1815, 10 In. 1150.00
Dish, Sunflower, Open Yellow Flower, Twig Handle, 1760, 4 1/4 In., 4 Piece 7475.00
Ewer, Kedleston Shape, Bloor, Exotic Birds On Branches, 2 Butterflies, 11 In. 368.00
Figurine, Cherubs, Standing, Holding A Basket Of Colorful Flowers, 5 & 5 3/4 In., Pair .. 635.00
Figurine, Squirrel, Seated On Grassy Oval Base, Holding A Nut, 3 1/4 In. 1265.00
Figurine, Stag & Doe, White Flowers On Rocky Base, 1765, 6 In., Pair 1725.00
Figurine, William Shakespeare & John Milton, Holding Corner Of Robe, 10 In., Pair 920.00
Fruit Cooler, Cover, 1810-1815, 11 x 9 1/2 In. 1936.00
Goblet, Deep Purple, Knopped Cup, Round Foot, 19th Century, 8 In. 5750.00
Ice Pail, Cover, Flower Sprays, Scattered Sprigs, 1790, 9 1/4 In. 1610.00
Ice Pail, Cover, Liner, Gilt Edged Medallion, Spray Of Roses, Apple Green, 9 In. 2530.00
Inkwell, Pen Holders, Side Pockets, Hand Painted, Red Crown & Cross Mark, 3 x 5 In. .. 336.00
Plate, Basket Overflowing With Ripe Fruits, Octagonal Gilt Border, 1820, 8 5/8 In. 517.00
Plate, Central Flower Spray, Round Gilt Dot Border, Salmon Pink Ground Rim, 1790 ... 460.00
Plate, Central Rose, Forget-Me-Not Spray, Round Gilt Dot Border, 1787, 9 In. 310.00
Plate, Floral Design, Imari Palette, 12 Piece 1090.00
Plate, Round Medallion Of Cherub, Birds Amongst Clouds, Blue, 1785, 9 3/16 In. 517.00
Plate, Spray Of Flowers, Blue, Gilt Line Rim, Oval, 1790, 12 1/2 In. 400.00
Potpourri, Cover, Stand, Reticulated Rim, River God Masque Design, 1825, 4 In., Pair .. 2057.00
Salt, Tapered Stem, Oval Foot, Oval, 2 1/4 x 4 In. 175.00
Stirrup Cup, Nature Scene, Rainbow Trout, Gilt Collar Rim, 1810, 5 1/4 In., Pair 3565.00
Tazza, Spar, Turned Out Rim, Columnar Black Marble Pedestal, Square Plinth, 8 In. 2587.00
Urn, Campagna, Horizontal Striations, Turned-Out Rim, Black Marble Square Base, 7 In. . 7475.00
Urn, Flower Filled, Gilt, Turquoise Borders, White Flowers, 1765, 7 1/4 In., Pair 920.00
Urn, Flower Vignettes, Puce Borders, 1765, 7 1/2 In., Pair 1035.00
Urn, Verde Antico Marble, Turned-Out Rim, Handles, Ormolu Borders, 5 In., Pair 10350.00
Urn, View Of Near Derby, Cobalt Blue Ground, Mask & Foliate Handles, 9 In. 172.00
Vase, Allover Floral, Gilt Design, 2 Handles, 10 In., Pair 1200.00

DICK TRACY, the comic strip, started in 1931. Tracy was also the hero of movies from 1937 to 1947 and again in 1990, and starred in a radio series in the 1940s and a television series in the 1950s. Memorabilia from all these activities are collected.

Book, Big Little Book, Bicycle Gang, No. 1445, 1948 .... 55.00
Book, Big Little Book, Boris Arson Gang, No. 1163, 1935 .... 45.00
Book, Big Little Book, Chains Of Crime, No. 1185, 1936 .... 35.00
Camera, Face & Name On Lens, Bakelite, 1940s, 5 x 2 1/4 In. 75.00
Camera, Leather Case 110.00
Car, Police, Box 350.00

Car, Police, Figure Inside, Friction, Siren Sound, Box, 10 In. 325.00
Car, Windup, Tin, Marx 245.00
Clock, Alarm, Box 25.00
Crime Stoppers Set, Nightstick, Cuffs & Badge, 1930s 125.00
Game, Cardboard Target, Pressed Steel Dart Gun, Box, Marx, Prewar, 21 In. 175.00
Model Kit, Box, Aurora 200.00
Police Car, Windup, Battery Operated, Tin, Characters Inside, Green, Box, 11 In. 110.00
Police Station, Friction Squad Car, Siren, Lithograph, 8 1/2 In. 550.00
Police Station, Tin, Marx, 1950, 8 In. 110.00
Poster, Register To Vote, Chester Gould, 1972, 8 1/2 x 17 In. 35.00
Salt & Pepper, Dick & Junior, Box, 1942, 2 1/2 In. 145.00
Toy, B.O. Plenty, Marx 210.00

DICKENS WARE pieces are listed in the Royal Doulton and Weller categories.

DINNERWARE used in the United States from the 1930s through the 1950s is listed here. Most was made in potteries in southern Ohio, West Virginia, and California. A few patterns were made in Japan, England, and other countries. Dishes were sold in gift shops and department stores, or were given away as premiums. Many of these patterns are listed in this book in their own categories, such as Autumn Leaf, Azalea, Coors, Fiesta, Franciscan, Hall, Harker, Red Wing, Riviera, Russel Wright, Vernon Kilns, Watt, and Willow. For more information, see *Kovels' Depression Glass & Dinnerware Price List.*

Apple Boot, Vase, Blue Ridge 180.00
Blue Heaven, Berry Bowl, Royal 6.00
Blue Heaven, Plate, Royal, 10 In. 8.00
Bluebird, Sugar & Creamer, Homer Laughlin 55.00
Boots & Saddle, Plate, Wallace China, 7 In. 50.00
Boots & Saddle, Plate, Wallace China, 10 1/2 In. 75.00
California Provincial, Casserole, Metlox, Individual 75.00
California Provincial, Platter, Turkey, Metlox, 13 1/2 In. 285.00
Caprice, Cup & Saucer, Castleton 13.00
Caprice, Plate, Castleton, 6 1/4 In. 10.00
Caprice, Plate, Castleton, 10 In. 15.00
Cattail, Cake Plate, Universal, 11 In. 40.00
Cattail, Cup & Saucer, Universal 11.00
Cattail, Plate, Universal, 7 1/4 In. 9.00
Cattail, Plate, Universal, 10 In. 20.00
Cattail, Platter, Universal, Round, 11 1/2 x 11 In. 40.00
Cattail, Salt & Pepper, Universal 28.00
Chanticleer, Pitcher, Rooster, Blue Ridge 110.00
Clover, Plate, Blue Ridge, 8 1/4 In. 12.00
Colonial Heritage, Gravy Boat, Metlox 40.00
Currier & Ives, Bowl, Blue, Royal, 9 In. 16.00
Currier & Ives, Calendar Plate, 1981, Royal 30.00
Currier & Ives, Casserole, Cover, Blue, White 90.00
Currier & Ives, Cup & Saucer, Royal 4.50
Currier & Ives, Gravy Boat, Blue, Royal 24.00
Currier & Ives, Mug, Coffee 25.00
Currier & Ives, Pie Baker 24.00
Currier & Ives, Plate, Royal, 6 In. 2.25
Currier & Ives, Plate, Royal, 9 In. 16.50
Currier & Ives, Platter, 13 In. 30.00
Currier & Ives, Sandwich Plate, Blue, Royal, 12 In. 15.00
Currier & Ives, Soup, Dish, Royal 10.00
Currier & Ives, Teapot, Cover 125.00
Currier & Ives, Tidbit, 3 Tier 80.00
George & Martha Washington, Salt & Pepper, W.S. George, 4 In. ....*Illus* 8.00
Grape Wine, Teapot, Snubnose, Blue Ridge 125.00
Homestead Provincial, Bowl, Vegetable, Metlox, 10 In. 25.00
Homestead Provincial, Canister Set, Metlox, 4 Piece 170.00
Homestead Provincial, Platter, Metlox, 13 1/2 x 10 In. 45.00

Dinnerware, Liberty Blue, Cup & Saucer,
Old North Church, 5 1/2-In. Saucer

Dinnerware,
George & Martha
Washington,
Salt & Pepper,
W.S. George, 4 In.

Homestead Provincial, Teapot, Metlox	80.00
Laurel Wreath, Plate, Blue Ridge, 9 1/2 In.	20.00
Liberty Blue, Cup & Saucer, Old North Church, 5 1/2-In. Saucer . . . . *Illus*	10.00
Log Cabin, Plate, Woodcrest, Blue Ridge, 10 In.	200.00
Organdie, Bowl, 2 Sections, Oval, Vernon Kilns, 11 1/2 In.	38.00
Organdie, Bowl, Cover, Vernon Kilns	30.00
Organdie, Butter, Cover, Vernon Kilns	25.00
Organdie, Salt & Pepper, Vernon Kilns	28.00
Provincial Flower, Dish, Divided, Metlox, 12 In.	45.00
Red Rooster, Coffeepot, Metlox	60.00
Red Rooster, Plate, Metlox, 6 1/4 In.	8.00
Red Rooster, Plate, Metlox, 9 3/4 In.	15.00
Sleepy Sam, Mug, Pfaltzgraff	19.00
Teapot, Mad Hatter, Regal China	3000.00
Tropicana, Vase, Metlox, 16 1/2 In.	65.00
Weather Vane, Plate, Blue Ridge, 10 In.	38.00
Wild Turkey, Platter, Johnson Bros., 21 In.	175.00

DIONNE QUINTUPLETS were born in Canada on May 28, 1934. The
publicity about their birth and their special status as wards of the
Canadian government made them famous throughout the world.
Visitors could watch the girls play; reporters interviewed the girls and
the staff. Thousands of special dolls and souvenirs were made picturing the quints at different ages. Emilie died in 1954, Marie in 1970.
Yvonne, Annette, and Cecile still live in Canada.

Book, We're Two Years Old, Black & White Photos, 1936	55.00
Bowl, Cereal, Metal	46.00
Doll, Composition, Replaced Shoes, 14 In.	450.00
Doll, Original Bed, Madame Alexander, 7 1/2 In.	950.00
Doll, Sitting, Wicker Basket, Wig, Madame Alexander, 7 1/2 In., 5 Piece	1495.00
Doll Set, Composition, With Pins, Madame Alexander, 8 In. . . . . *Illus*	825.00
Doll Set, In Chairs Or Cribs, Madame Alexander, 1935, 7 In., 5 Piece	3300.00
Game, Quints Dexterity, 1937	74.00
Pennant, Canada's Famous Five, Multicolor, Callander, 26 In.	100.00

Dionne Quintuplets, Doll Set,
Composition, With Pins,
Madame Alexander, 8 In.

DISNEYANA is a collector's term. Walt Disney and his company introduced many comic characters to the world. Collectors search for examples of the work of the Disney Studios and the many commercial products modeled after his characters, including Mickey Mouse, Donald Duck, and recent films, like *Beauty and the Beast* and *The Little Mermaid*.

Ashtray, Walt Disney World, Castle Logo, Pottery, White	30.00
Band, Mickey Mouse, 3 Horn Players, 1 Flute, Wood & Metal, 1920s, 2 3/4 In.	595.00
Bank, Donald Duck, Nabisco, 1966	45.00
Bank, Donald Duck, Orange Juice Can Shape, 3 7/8 In.	5.00
Bank, Donald Duck, Red Sock In Hand, Hard Vinyl, Hand Painted, 9 In.	55.00
Bank, Donald Duck, Suitcase, To Walt Disney World, Silver Plate, Leonard Co., 1970s	95.00
Bank, Humpty Dumpty, Alice In Philco Land, Leeds, 1940s	90.00
Bank, Mechanical, Goofy, Playing Soccer, Plastic, WDP, Reiss, Box, 8 In.	25.00
Bank, Mickey Mouse, Early Style, Pottery, Slot In Back Of Head, 6 In.	40.00
Bank, Mickey Mouse, Leeds China, Walt Disney Mark, 1940s, 6 In.	65.00
Bank, Mickey Mouse, Rubber, 1950s	25.00
Bank, Pinocchio, Trap Door Bottom, Key, Composition, Walt Disney, 5 1/4 In.	82.00
Bank, Snow White, Dime Register, $5, Dial On Front, Stamped Tin	135.00
Bank, Snow White, Leeds, 1938	150.00
Bank, Snow White, Shaw Pottery, c.1940, 7 In.	95.00
Bank, Uncle Scrooge, Squeeze Toy, Ducks Looking At Scrooge, Holding Key, Disney	33.00
Barrette, Mickey Mouse & Donald Duck, Brass, Enameled	40.00
Bell, Bicycle, Mickey Mouse, Germany	55.00
Biscuit Tin, Characters, Locking, c.1930, 13 x 8 x 2 1/2 In.	154.00
Blotter, Donald Duck, Sunoco, Walt Disney Enterprises, c.1938	150.00
Book, Bambi, Hardcover, 1944, 8 1/2 x 6 1/4 In.	22.00
Book, Big Little Book, Micky Mouse, 1934	40.00
Book, Coloring, Westward Ho The Wagons, Disneyland, 1956	25.00
Book, First Guide Book, 20 Pages, 1955, 6 x 8 3/4 In.	95.00
Book, Here They Are, Mickey, Minnie, Donald & Pluto In House, Hardcover, 1940	55.00
Book, Mickey Mouse Story Book, Hardcover, 1931, 8 3/4 x 6 In.	55.00
Book, Peculiar Penguins, Silly Symphony, 1934	65.00
Book, Playtime Set, Sleeping Beauty & Castle, Whitman, 1959, Pair	1100.00
Book, Walt Disney's Clock Cleaners, Donald & Mickey, Whitman, 1938, 10 Pages	50.00
Bowl, Cereal, Mickey Mouse, Beetleware, Plastic, Post Cereal Promotion, 5 In.	20.00
Bread Wrapper, Donald Duck, Color, Copyright WDP, 1940s, 16 x 16 In.	45.00
Buckle, Mickey Mouse, Pie-Eyes	45.00
Button, Mickey Mouse Club, c.1930	175.00
Cake Topper, Little Mermaid	30.00
Cake Topper, Mickey & Minnie Mouse, Pair	60.00
Camera, Ettleston	125.00
Camera, Mickey Mouse Head Shape, Plastic, Lens In Nose, WDP, 7 x 4 In.	22.00
Car, Disney Parade, Marx	675.00
Car, Mickey Mouse, Head Bobs From Spring Neck, Tin, Linemar, 5 1/4 In.	242.00
Cel, see Animation Art category.	
Charm, Donald Duck, Metal, Cracker Jack	10.00
Clock, Alarm, Mickey Mouse Face, Bell Ears, Red Metal, Bradley, West Germany, 1970s	95.00
Clock, Alarm, Mickey Mouse, Double Top Bell, Mickey & Pluto Face, Bradley	55.00
Clock, Alarm, Mickey Mouse, Pluto, Red Metal, Cream Face, WDP, Bradley, 4 1/4 In.	25.00
Clock, Alarm, Mickey Mouse, Wagging Head, Red, Round Metal Case, Ingersoll	193.00
Clock, Alarm, Mickey Mouse, Wagging Head, Topolino, Italy, 1930s	800.00
Clock, Electric, Mickey Mouse, Minnie & Friends, Green Metal Case, Ingersoll	352.00
Clock, Electric, Mickey Mouse, With Large Hand Dials, Cream Case, Ingersoll	132.00
Cookie Jar, Chief Mickey, White Bust	95.00
Cookie Jar, Donald Duck, Box, Hoan	70.00
Cookie Jar, Dumbo, Mouse On Lid	135.00
Cookie Jar, Ludwig Von Drake	800.00
Cookie Jar, Mickey & Minnie Mouse, Leeds	175.00
Cookie Jar, Mickey Mouse On Drum, California Originals	145.00
Cookie Jar, Mickey Mouse, Flower Sack, Box	70.00
Cookie Jar, Mickey Mouse, On Birthday Cake	375.00

Cookie Jar, Minnie Mouse, Treasure Craft 40.00
Cookie Jar, Mrs. Potts, Box 80.00
Cookie Jar, Pinocchio 250.00
Cookie Jar, Pinocchio, Doranne Of California 325.00
Cookie Jar, Pinocchio, Enesco 425.00
Cookie Jar, Pinocchio, Walt Disney Productions, Cuernavaca, Mexico 1000.00
Cookie Jar, School Bus 525.00
Cookie Jar, Simba, Lion King 75.00
Cookie Jar, Winnie The Pooh, Mexico 115.00
Creamer, Mickey Mouse, Fat Mickey Pours From Mouth, Japan, 1930s, 4 1/2 In. 65.00
Crib Toy, Minnie Mouse, Wooden, Bells For Hands, 1930s 100.00
Cup, Minnie Mouse 45.00
Cup & Plate, 3 Little Pigs, Patriot Chinaco, 2 Piece 40.00
Doll, Doc, Dwarf, Solid Rubber, 6 1/2 In. 68.00
Doll, Mickey & Minnie Mouse, Cloth, Stuffed, Pair 3450.00
Doll, Mickey Mouse, Cloth, Painted Face, Felt Ears, Knickerbocker, 1930s, 12 In. 517.00
Doll, Mickey Mouse, Plush, Label, California Stuffed Toys, 15 In. 22.00
Doll, Mickey Mouse, Rubber, France, 1930s 700.00
Doll, Pinocchio, Plush, Plastic Face, Brown Cloth Lederhosen, 1950s, 36 In. 30.00
Doll, Pinocchio, Wood-Jointed, 5 In. 28.00
Doll, Pinocchio, Wood-Jointed, Ideal Novelty Toy Co., 20 In. 385.00
Doll, Snow White, Madame Alexander, 14 In. 45.00
Doll, Snow White, Original Clothes, Walt Disney Enterprise, 15 1/2 In. 650.00
Fan, Snow White & Seven Dwarfs, Wood, Paper, 1950s, 7 1/2 In. 110.00
Figurine, Donald Duck, Chalkware, Spray Painted, Hollow, Carnival, 1940s, 14 In. 60.00
Figurine, Geppeto, Cast Carved Wood Type, Walt Disney Productions, 5 1/2 In. 30.00
Figurine, Mickey & Donald, Seated In Rowboat With Oars, Walt Disney, 2 x 6 In. 880.00
Figurine, Mickey & Minnie Mouse, Hand Painted, 1930s, 5 In., Pair 285.00
Figurine, Mickey Mouse, Black & White, Rosenthal, No. 550, 1930s, 3 1/4 In. 2070.00
Figurine, Mickey Mouse, Bust, Looking Up, Smiling, Tin 495.00
Figurine, Mickey Mouse, Santa, Wooden, Papier-Mache, 1930-1940, 8 1/2 In. 275.00
Figurine, Snow White & Seven Dwarfs, Royal Doulton 495.00
Game, Monorail, Disneyland, Box 20.00
Game, Peter Pan, Board, 1953 .... 65.00
Game, Pin The Tail On Mickey Mouse, Envelope, 1970s 25.00
Game, Snow White & Seven Dwarfs, Cadaco, 1977 .... 20.00
Game, Tiddlywinks, Mickey Mouse Club, 1963 .... 45.00
Game, Zorro, Board, 1964 .... 75.00
Go-Cart, Ludwig Von Drake, Friction 350.00
Gumball Machine, Mickey Mouse Head, WDP, Hasbro, 9 In. 25.00
Hurdy-Gurdy, Mickey Mouse, Pushing Tinplate Band Organ, Turning Crank 4600.00
Ironing Board, Snow White 25.00
Jump Rope, Mickey Mouse, Wooden Figural Handle, 1950s 95.00
Knife Rest, Mickey & Minnie Mouse, Continental, 1930s, 3 1/2 x 2 In. 325.00
Lamp, Mickey Mouse, Cloth Shade, Pie-Cut Eyes, Holding Book, 1936, 16 In. 1495.00
Letter & Envelope, Information On Mickey Mouse Club Magazine, WDP, 1956 .... 55.00
Light Bulb, Mickey Mouse, TV Bulb, Solar Electric, Box, 1950s, 6 1/2 In. 40.00
Lighter, Disney Castle, Logo, Enameled, Walt Disney Productions, 1971 .... 215.00
Lighter, Walt Disney World, Castle, Polished Finish, WDP, Zippo, 1977 .... 160.00
Lunch Box, Alice In Wonderland, Vinyl, Aladdin, 1974 .... 125.00
Lunch Box, Disney On Parade, Mickey In Balloon, Thermos, Aladdin 50.00
Lunch Box, Mickey Mouse Club, Metal, Aladdin, 1963 .... 75.00
Lunch Box, Mickey Mouse Club, Thermos, Steel 65.00
Lunch Box, Snow White & Seven Dwarfs, Animals, No Thermos, Aladdin, 1970s 65.00
Lunch Box, Snow White, Tin, Belgium, c.1930, 8 x 5 x 4 In. 275.00
Lunch Pail, Cover, Pictures Of Mickey & Minnie Mouse, Top Handles, Gray, Tin 935.00
Marionette, Mickey Mouse, Plastic, Cloth On Wood Body, Gund, Box, 11 In. 110.00
Marionette, Pinocchio, Composition, 1930s, 12 In. 125.00
Marionette, Pinocchio, Disney, Box, 1950s 350.00
Marionette, Pluto, Wooden, 10 In. 20.00
Mirror, Mickey Mouse, Birthday Greetings, WDE, 1930s, 2 1/2 x 3 1/2 In. 30.00
Mobile, 7 Disney Figures, Hostess Fruit Pie, Embossed, Celluloid, 1950s, 4 1/2 In. 66.00
Music Box, 3 Little Pigs, Pull Key, Disneyland 225.00

Music Box, TV, Snow White, Whistle While You Work, Hanscraft Co., 1950s 150.00
Napkin Ring, Mickey Mouse, Celluloid, Hand Painted, England, 1930s 315.00
Night-Light, Donald Duck, Molded Rubber, Plastic Base, Universal Lamp Co., 9 In. 45.00
Night-Light, Mickey Mouse, Plastic, Tan Shade With Characters, 16 In. 65.00
Night-Light, Minnie Mouse, Package, 1960s 25.00
Night-Light, Snow White, Package, 1960s 25.00
Nodder, Donald Duck, Celluloid, Supported On Tin Metal Base, Walt Disney, 6 In. 880.00
Pail, Snow White, Pictures All Around, Tin Lithograph, 1930s 150.00
Paper Doll, Snow White, Cut, 1930s 45.00
Paper Plate, Mickey Mouse Birthday 15.00
Pen, Fountain, Mickey Mouse & Minnie Mouse Figures, Bakelite, 1930s 195.00
Pencil, Mickey Mouse, Mechanical 225.00
Pencil Holder, Mickey Mouse, Composition, Papier-Mache, Dixon, 8 In. 440.00
Perfume Bottle, Mickey Mouse, Spring Legs, France, 5 1/4 In.   303.00
Picture, Donald Duck, Flocked, Frame, 13 x 9 In. 11.00
Pin, Mickey Mouse Good Teeth 125.00
Plant Stand, Wicker, Donald Duck, Painted Eyes, 26 In. 85.00
Plate, Cup & Bowl, Donald Duck, Daisy, Goofy, Artisan Melamine, WDP, Box, 3 Piece . .   25.00
Pog, Mickey Mouse 5.00
Pog, Snow White 5.00
Postcard, Donald Duck, Toothache, With Nephews & Dog, France 50.00
Postcard, Mickey Mouse, With Banjo, Singing, Germany 45.00
Poster, Election Day Gaieties, Movie, 1953, One Sheet 110.00
Poster, Fantasia, Dancing Hippos, Ostrich, Mickey Mouse, 1940, Half Sheet 2925.00
Poster, Flying Squirrel, Donald Duck, Movie, 1954, One Sheet 563.00
Poster, For Whom The Bulls Toil, Starring Goofy, 1954, One Sheet 535.00
Poster, In The Bag, Barney Bear, Movie, 1956, One Sheet 325.00
Poster, Jungle Book, Phil Harris, Sebastian Cabot Voices, Movie, 1967, One Sheet 160.00
Poster, Lady & The Tramp, Walt Disney, Movie, 1960s, 12 x 16 In. 10.00
Poster, Mickey Mouse Club, Mickey, Minnie, Donald, Goofy, Movie, 1958, 20 x 14 In. . .   410.00
Poster, Pluto's Christmas Tree, Movie, 1952, One Sheet 2055.00
Poster, Sword In The Stone, Movie, 1964, Six Sheet 110.00
Poster, Thanksgiving Day Mirthquakes, Movie, 1953, One Sheet 133.00
Powder Jar, Minnie Mouse, Art Deco 135.00
Print, Minnie Mouse, Donald Duck Peanut Butter 100.00
Program, Fantasia, 28 Pages, 1940, 12 1/2 x 9 1/2 In. 125.00
Puppet, String, Minnie Mouse, Wooden, England, 1930s, 6 In.   125.00
Puzzle, Disneyland Christmas, Whitman, 1956 . . . .   11.00
Rattle, Mickey & Minnie Playing, Celluloid, Rolling, 3 In. 88.00
Record Player, Alice & Wonderland, RCA, 1950s 200.00
Ring, Pluto, Sterling Silver, Child's, 1950s 75.00
Roly Poly, Mickey & Minnie Mouse, Pair 35.00
Rules Sheet, For Snow White Game, Board, 1937 . . . .   20.00
Salt & Pepper, Mickey Mouse & Piano 15.00
Salt & Pepper, Piglet & Eeyore, Large 38.00
Sheet Music, Bambi, 1941, Set Of 4 Booklets 50.00
Sheet Music, Bibbidi-Bobbodi-Boo, Cinderella, 1949 . . . .   15.00
Sheet Music, Der Fuehrer's Face, Donald Duck, World War II 80.00
Sheet Music, Mickey Mouse's Birthday Party, Irving Berlin, 1936 . . . .   80.00
Sheet Music, Pinocchio, When You Wish Upon A Star, 1939 . . . .   120.00
Soap, Mickey Mouse, Standing, Box 200.00
Stamp, Kit, Rubber, Carousel 25.00
Sweatshirt, Mickey Mouse, Cotton Blend, Gray, WDP, Medium 20.00
Tankard, Donald Duck, Ceramarte 60.00
Tankard, Mickey Mouse, Ceramarte 60.00
Tea Set, Horace, Clarabelle, Donald, Mickey, Minnie, Tin, Ohio Art, 1937, 8 Piece 330.00
Tea Set, Mickey & Minnie Mouse, Lusterware, Borgfeldt, Box, 21 Piece 660.00
Tea Set, Mickey Mouse, Porcelain, Japan, 1930s, 3 3/4-In. Teapot, 4 Piece 155.00
Tea Set, Mickey Mouse, Service For 6, Teapot, Creamer, Sugar, Luster, Japan, 1930s 715.00
Telephone, Mickey Mouse, Dial Tone, 1976 . . . . .140.00 to 150.00
Telephone, Mickey Mouse, Figural, Push Button, Plastic, AT&T, 14 1/2 In. 45.00
Telephone, Mickey Mouse, Western Electric, 1976 . . . .   125.00
Telephone, Winnie The Pooh, Holding Butterfly, Push Button Dial 300.00

Thermometer, Mickey Mouse, Standing On Pluto's House, Green, Walt Disney 88.00
Thermos, Mickey's Trip, Other Disney Characters, From Lunch Box, Metal, Japan 65.00
Tin, 3 Little Pigs, Europe, 1930s, 6 In. 33.00
Tin, Biscuit, Snow White & Seven Dwarfs, Forest Animals, Belgium, 1930s 225.00
Tin, Candy, Zorro, Lithographed, Round, WPD, France, 1950s, 4 1/2 In. 75.00
Tin, Mickey Mouse Pictures, With Younger Mouse, Red, Tin, Hexagonal 165.00
Toothbrush Holder, Donald Duck, Pottery, Walt E. Disney, Japan, 1930s, 5 1/2 In. 155.00
Toothbrush Holder, Mickey Mouse & Pluto, Bisque, Japan, 1930s 375.00
Toothbrush Holder, Mickey Mouse & Pluto, Ceramic, 3 1/2 x 4 1/2 In. 50.00
Toothbrush Holder, Mickey Mouse, Movable Arm, Painted, 1930s, 5 In. 325.00
Toothbrush Holder, Toothbrush, Mickey Mouse, Movable Arm, Bisque, 5 In. 350.00
Toy, Casey Jr., Train, Disneyland Express, Box, Marx 225.00
Toy, Disneyland Roller Coaster, With 1 Car, Chein 640.00
Toy, Donald Duck Duet, With Goofy, Windup, Tin, WDP, Marx, 1946, 10 1/2 In. 660.00
Toy, Donald Duck, Acrobat, Japan, Box 425.00
Toy, Donald Duck, Choo-Choo, Pull Toy, Donald Rings Bell, Fisher-Price, 8 1/2 In. . .75.00 to 83.00
Toy, Donald Duck, Drum Major, Pull Toy, Strutting, Pulling Cart, Fisher-Price, 10 In. 83.00
Toy, Donald Duck, Duckmobile, Tin, Celluloid, Friction, W. Toy, Japan, 1950s, 6 1/2 In. .. 165.00
Toy, Donald Duck, Fireman, Climbing, Linemar, Box 1150.00
Toy, Donald Duck, Hopper, Windup, Tin, WDP, Linemar, Japan, 4 In. 230.00
Toy, Donald Duck, In Red Wagon, Pull Toy, Twirling Baton, Wood, Fisher-Price 245.00
Toy, Donald Duck, Jack-In-The-Box, Spear, 1950s 250.00
Toy, Donald Duck, Nodder, Windup, Celluloid, Japan, Prewar 550.00
Toy, Donald Duck, On Skis, Windup, Metal, Mar Line Toys, Japan, 6 x 5 1/2 In. 105.00
Toy, Donald Duck, On Trike, Windup, Celluloid, Tin, Linemar, Japan, 4 In. 305.00
Toy, Donald Duck, Pulling Cart, Fisher-Price 110.00
Toy, Donald Duck, Race Car No. 5, Tin Lithograph, Orange, 4 In. 330.00
Toy, Donald Duck, Riding Tin Tricycle, Celluloid, Japan, 5 1/2 In. 715.00
Toy, Donald Duck, Standing, Long Billed, Celluloid, Walt Disney, 5 1/8 In. 495.00
Toy, Donald Duck, Waddler, Windup, Celluloid, Walt Disney, Prewar, 3 In. 305.00
Toy, Donald Duck, Xylophone Player, Fisher-Price 132.00
Toy, Dopey & Doc, Pull Toy, Tree Stump Drum, Fisher-Price, 1937, 11 1/2 In. 413.00
Toy, Dumbo The Elephant, Squeeze, Soft Vinyl, White, Dell, Walt Disney Prod. 30.00
Toy, Ferdinand The Bull & Matador, Bucking Bull, Marx, 1938, 7 3/4 x 5 In. 330.00
Toy, Ferdinand The Bull & Matador, Pull Toy 995.00
Toy, Ferdinand The Bull, Flower, Butterfly, Tin, Windup, Marx, Box, 6 In. ....121.00 to 255.00
Toy, Ferdinand The Bull, Matador, Holding Off Ferdinand, Windup, Marx, 1938, 7 1/2 In. 550.00
Toy, Ferdinand The Bull, Rubber, Seiberling, 1930s 150.00
Toy, Ferdinand The Bull, Squeak, Composition, Cloth, W.D.E., 1938, 8 In. 35.00
Toy, Ferdinand The Bull, Windup, Flower, Tail Spins, Tin, W.D.P., Linemar, Japan 150.00
Toy, Goofy, Gardener, Wheelbarrow, Windup, Tin Lithograph, Marx, 7 1/2 In. 633.00
Toy, Goofy, Tricycle, Windup, Tin, Ringing Bell On Back Wheels, Linemar, 7 In. 990.00
Toy, Jiminy Cricket, Walker, Pushing Violin, Plastic, WDP, 3 1/2 In. 25.00
Toy, Little Pig Playing Violin, Schuco, 1930s 275.00
Toy, Mary Poppins Dress-Up Kit, Colorforms 22.00
Toy, Mary Poppins, Windup, Plastic, WDP, Marx, Hong Kong, Box, 1964, 9 In. 75.00
Toy, Mickey & Minnie Mouse Tea Party, George Borgfeldt, Box 965.00
Toy, Mickey & Minnie Mouse, Acrobats, Holding Tin Bars, Celluloid, 11 In. 440.00
Toy, Mickey Mouse & Donald Duck, Dancing On Barrel, Windup, Celluloid, 7 In. 9020.00
Toy, Mickey Mouse & Minnie Mouse, Handcar, Lionel 1200.00
Toy, Mickey Mouse Express, Tin Lithograph, Windup, Walt Disney Prod., Marx 125.00
Toy, Mickey Mouse, Car, Tricky Rider, Pull String, Marked WDP, 4 1/4 x 3 In. 32.00
Toy, Mickey Mouse, Drummer, Pull Toy, Paper, Wood, Fisher-Price, 1950s, 7 1/4 In. 105.00
Toy, Mickey Mouse, Fire Truck, Sun Rubber 80.00
Toy, Mickey Mouse, Ice Skater, Pull Toy, Wooden, Metal Base With 2 Bells, 11 In. 355.00
Toy, Mickey Mouse, Locomotive, Bump & Go, Battery Operated, Tin Lithograph, 10 In. . 195.00
Toy, Mickey Mouse, Lying On Tin Sled, Minnie Mouse Seated On Back, 5 In. 550.00
Toy, Mickey Mouse, Pip-Squeak, Sun Rubber, 1950s, 10 In. 25.00
Toy, Mickey Mouse, Riding Tricycle, With Bell, Tin, Linemar, 3 5/8 In. 330.00
Toy, Mickey Mouse, Rollerskater, Yellow Cloth Pants, Tin, Linemar, 6 1/4 In. 495.00
Toy, Mickey Mouse, Saucer Spaceship, Flashing Lights, Lithograph, Japan, 8 In. 250.00
Toy, Mickey Mouse, Soldier Set, Inserts, Cork Gun, Walt E. Disney, Box, c.1935 .... 845.00
Toy, Mickey Mouse, Standing, Synthetic Rubber 90.00

Toy, Mickey Mouse, Train, Pull Toy, Fisher-Price, 1938 . . . . 895.00
Toy, Mickey Mouse, Train Set, Stoker, Engine, Coal Car, 3 Pullmans, Lionel, 29 In. 690.00
Toy, Mickey Mouse, Wooden, Wire Neck, Arms, Legs, Tail, 5 In. 40.00
Toy, Mickey Mouse, Xylophone, Linemar Toy Co., 5 3/4 x 6 1/2 In. 248.00
Toy, Mickey The Magician, Raises Top Hat, Chick Appears, Linemar, Japan, 10 In. 990.00
Toy, Mickey The Musician, Plays Xylophone, Battery, Plastic, Box, 1950s, 11 1/2 In. 525.00
Toy, Minnie Mouse Knitter, Sitting In Rocker, Windup, Tin, Linemar, 1950s, 7 In. 610.00
Toy, Pinnochio, Windup, Marx 550.00
Toy, Pinocchio Delivery Wagon, Windup, Tin, WDP, Marx, 1940, 9 In. . . . . .425.00 to 470.00
Toy, Pinocchio The Acrobat, Windup, Tin Lithograph, WDP, Marx, 1939, 19 1/2 In. 250.00
Toy, Pinocchio, On Donkey, Ringing Bell, Pull Toy, Fisher-Price, 1939, 6 1/2 In. 275.00
Toy, Plane, Air Mail, Pilot Mickey Mouse, Hard Rubber 125.00
Toy, Pluto, No-Fall, Windup, Tin Lithograph, WDP, Linemar, Japan, 6 1/2 In. 145.00
Toy, Pluto, Watch Me Roll Over!, Crouching, Windup, Tin, Marx, 1939, 9 In. . . . . . .77.00 to 140.00
Toy, Winnie The Poo & Friends, In Truck, Plastic, 1970s, WDP, 9 In. 35.00
Walker, Pinocchio, Windup, Copyright 1939, Marx, USA, 8 1/2 In. 225.00
Watch, Mickey Mouse, Ingersol, With Fob, Pocket, Box, 1935 . . . . 1250.00
Watch, Mickey Mouse, With Chain, Bradley, Pocket 475.00
Watch, Silver Toned Metal Case, Long Stem, Pocket, Ingersoll, 1933, 2 In. 375.00
Window Card, 3 Caballeros, 2 Latin Women, 3 Colors, 1944, 22 x 14 In. 460.00
Window Card, Saludos Amigos, Donald Duck, Joe Carioca, 1943, 22 x 14 In. 488.00
Wristwatch, Donald Duck, Leather Band, 1948 . . . . 225.00
Wristwatch, Dopey, Leather Band, 1948 . . . . 225.00
Wristwatch, Mickey Mouse, 3 Interchangeable Vinyl Bands, Bradley Time, 1970s 135.00
Wristwatch, Mickey Mouse, Bradley 60.00
Wristwatch, Mickey Mouse, First Version, 1930s 700.00
Wristwatch, Mickey Mouse, Leather Band, 1930s 550.00
Wristwatch, Pluto, Ingersoll 275.00
Wristwatch, Snow White, Gold Tone Case, Blue Leather Band, WDP, 1 In. 35.00

DOCTOR, see Dental; Medical

DOLL entries are listed by marks printed or incised on the doll, if possible. If there are no marks, the doll is listed by the name of the subject or country or maker. Notice that Barbie is listed under Mattel. G.I.
Joe figures are listed in the Toy section.

A.M., 11/0, Bisque, Open Mouth, Glass Eyes, Cloth Body, Dress, Bonnet, Cape, 11 In. . . . 412.00
A.M., 323, Bisque Head, Impish Mouth, Composition 5-Piece Body, 9 1/2 In. 1265.00
A.M., 323, Closed Mouth, Jointed Shoulders & Hips, Toddler, 1920s, 8 In. 862.00
A.M., 323, Googly, Papier-Mache, 6 In. 950.00
A.M., 390, Bisque Head, Blue Sleep Eyes, Open Mouth, Blond Wig, 23 In. 316.00
A.M., 400, Bisque, Flapper Body, Closed Mouth, 15 In. 2750.00
A.M., Florodora, Bisque Head, Brown Sleep Eyes, Open Mouth, 25 In. 201.00
A.M., Florodora, Bisque Head, Open Mouth, 4 Upper Teeth, Dress, Buckle Shoes, 18 In. . . 175.00
A.M., Just Me, Bisque, Sleep Eyes, Mohair Wig, Original Dress, 9 1/2 In. 2150.00
A.M., Our Pet, Character, Biscaloid Head, Sleep Eyes, Original Clothes, 15 In. 595.00
A.M., Queen Louise, Bisque Head Socket Head, Composition Body, 24 In. 650.00
Advertising, AT&T Telephone Repair Person, Black Woman, Box 85.00
Advertising, Brach's Candy, Frankenstein, Stuffed, 36 In. 75.00
Advertising, Burger King, Box 20.00
Advertising, Cadbury Bunny, Plush, Battery Operated, Clucks, Talks 295.00
Advertising, Campbell's Soup, Boy, Girl, Vinyl, Shipping Box, 1970s, Pair 165.00
Advertising, Checkerboard Square Scarecrow, Ralston Purina, 1965, 21 In. 40.00
Advertising, Cliquot Club, Eskimo Girl, Rag, Stuffed, 14 In. 20.00
Advertising, Gerber Baby, Rubber, Squeaks, Sun Rubber Co., 12 In. 30.00
Advertising, Green Sprout, Vinyl, 6 1/2 In. 30.00
Advertising, Jolly Green Giant, Dancing, Cloth Body, Tag, 36 In. 125.00
Advertising, Little Red Devil, The Devil's Fork, Cloth, Plastic Head, Kamar, Japan, 1969 . 30.00
Advertising, Milky Way, Character, Boy & Girl, Pair 945.00
Advertising, Pillsbury Doughboy, Poppin' Fresh On Hat, Stuffed, Blue, White, 14 In. 32.00
Advertising, Uneeda, Boy, Yellow Molded Hat, Cloth Body, 1930s 198.00
Alaskan, Native Style Sealskin Clothes, Wooden Carved Face, 1938, 9 In., Pair 245.00
Alexander dolls are listed in this category under Madame Alexander.

Doll, Alt Beck &
Gottschalck, Porcelain
Shoulder Head,
Boy, 24 In.

Doll, Alt Beck &
Gottschalck, Highland
May, Porcelain
Shoulder Head, 23 In.

Doll, Automaton, Monkey Band,
c.1930, 36 x 20 x 46 In.

Alt Beck & Gottschalck, 639, Closed Mouth, Blue Eyes, All Original, 13 In.	850.00
Alt Beck & Gottschalck, 698, Bisque Head Turned Right, Kid Body, c.1890, 18 In.	1000.00
Alt Beck & Gottschalck, Bisque Head, Sleep Eyes, Open Mouth, Auburn Wig, 28 In.	431.00
Alt Beck & Gottschalck, Highland May, Porcelain Shoulder Head, 23 In. . . . .*Illus*	700.00
Alt Beck & Gottschalck, Porcelain Shoulder Head, Boy, 24 In. . . . .*Illus*	450.00
Armand Marseille dolls are listed in this category under A.M.	
Arranbee, Bisque Head, Painted Hair, Sleep Eyes, Cloth Body, Infant, 13 In.	84.00
Arranbee, Cinderella, Plastic, Sleep Eyes, Floss Wig, Ball Gown, Tag, c.1952, 18 In.	750.00
Arranbee, Littlest Angel, Plastic Head, Sleep Eyes, Brunette Saran Wig, 1954, 10 In.	126.00
Arranbee, Nancy Lee, Composition, Shoes & Purse, 14 In.	495.00
Arranbee, Nancy Lee, Plastic, Sleep Eyes, Floss Wig, Floral Gown, Tag, c.1952, 14 In. . .	425.00
Arranbee, Nancy, All Original, 17 In.	300.00
Arranbee, Nanette, Walker, Blue Sleep Eyes, Formal Gown, Box, Early 1950s, 21 In.	650.00
Art Fabric Mills, Cloth, Ribbon Printed On Head, Plaid Dress, Slip, 26 In.	95.00
Arthur Gerling, Grumpy Baby, Pouty Mouth, Breather, Period Clothes, 16 In.	550.00
Arthur Schoenau, Princess Elizabeth, Bisque, Composition, Sleep Eyes, 2 Teeth, 21 In. . .	2000.00
Automaton, Bubble Blower, Music Plays, Girl Turns Head, France	2995.00
Automaton, Bubble Blower, Musical, Flowered Hat, France	2995.00
Automaton, Grandmother, Clockwork, Windup, Head Nods, Eyes Blink, 29 In.	1995.00
Automaton, Grandmother, Head Nods, Eyes Blink, Clockwork, 29 In.	1995.00
Automaton, Heubach, Boy, Shakes Rattles, Turns Head	1495.00
Automaton, Jumeau, Closed Mouth, Tree Base	4995.00
Automaton, Monkey Band, c.1930, 36 x 20 x 46 In. . . . .*Illus*	2090.00
Averill, Little Sister, 1927, 14 In.	495.00
Bahr & Proschild, 244, American Indian, Bisque, Mohair, Suede Outfit, c.1890, 12 In. . . .	1300.00
Bahr & Proschild, 277, Bisque Socket Head, Brown Inset Eyes, Open Mouth, 10 In.	800.00
Bahr & Proschild, 301, Bisque Socket Head, Child, Blue Sleep Eyes, 1898, 13 In.	425.00
Bahr & Proschild, 478, Bisque, Ball-Jointed Body, 42 In.	2495.00
Bahr & Proschild, Brown Bisque Socket Head, Open Mouth, Composition, 12 In.	1050.00
Barbie dolls are listed in this category under Mattel.	
Belton, Bisque, Brown Paperweight Eyes, 23 In.	1850.00
Belton, Bisque, Paperweight Eyes, Blond Mohair Wig, Antique Frock, 15 In.	2995.00
Belton, Composition, Blond Mohair, Closed Mouth, Straight Wrist, 12 In.	1995.00
Belton, Composition, Solid Dome, 5-Piece Body, Painted Socks, 11 1/2 In.	875.00
Belton Type, Bisque, Lamb's Wool Wig, Dressed, 12 In.	1750.00
Bergmann dolls are also in this category under S & H and Simon & Halbig.	
Bergmann, 1916, Bisque Head, Sleep Eyes, Fully Jointed, 23 In.	315.00
Bergmann, Bisque, Composition, Sleep Eyes, 4 Teeth, Human Hair, S & H 12, 28 In.	550.00
Bergmann, Queen Louise, Sitting, 24 In.	875.00
Bisque, Flapper Type, Movable Arms, Japan, 8 In.	22.00
Bisque, Kid Body, Bisque Arms, Sleep Eyes, Open Mouth, Germany, 13 In.	80.00
Bisque Head, Jointed, Wooden Body, Russian Costume, Germany, 12 In.	150.00
Bisque Head, Papier-Mache Body, Gauze Dress & Hat, Germany, 9 In.	60.00
Black dolls are included in the Black category.	

Bolland, Raggedy Ann, All Cloth, Jointed At Hips & Shoulders, Print Dress, 16 In. 565.00
Borgfeldt, Bisque, Girl, White Eyelet Dress, Pin Tucking Down Front, 25 In. 795.00
Borgfeldt, Blue Sleep Eyes, Lashes, Ball-Jointed Body, Long Curl Wig, Dressed, 24 In. .. 800.00
Bru Jne, Bisque Swivel Head, Narrow Blue Glass Eyes, Closed Mouth, Smiling, 14 In. .. 3400.00
Bru Jne, Bisque, Kid Body, Bebe Brevete, Label On Body, Original Clothes, 11 In. 9700.00
Bruckner, Topsy Turvy, Muslin, Brown & White Faces, Label, c.1900, 12 In. 800.00
Bruno Schmidt, 1072, Bisque, Pouty Girl, Blue Sleep Eyes, Toddler, 23 In. 5975.00
Bruno Schmidt, Bisque, Child, Sleep Eyes, Mohair Wig, Original Clothes, Shoes, 28 In. . 1375.00
Buddy Lee, Composition Head, Eyes To Side, Labeled Lee Bib Jeans, 13 In. 375.00
Buddy Lee, Plastic, Denim Jeans, Plaid Shirt, Cowboy Hat, Boots, 1959-1962, 14 In. 835.00
Bye-Lo, Bisque Head, Blue Sleep Glass Eyes, Baby, Grace Storey Putnam, 1920s, 13 In. . 375.00
Bye-Lo, Bisque, Domed Head, Flanged Neck, Brown Hair, Baby, Germany, 15 In. 550.00
Bye-Lo, Bisque, Pink Flannel Blanket, 14 In. 495.00
Bye-Lo, Painted Lashes, Molded & Painted Hair, Celluloid Hands, Baby, Dress, 11 In. ... 135.00
Cameo, Giggles, Composition Head, Smiling, Taffeta Underclothing, Box, 12 In. . .320.00 to 425.00
Celluloid, Baby, Painted Eyelashes, Movable Arms, 4 1/2 In. 25.00
Celluloid, Blue & White Lace Gown, Bonnet, Flower Bouquet, 5 In. 35.00
Celluloid, Glass Eyes, Original Wig, Soft Wool Dress, 20 In. 285.00
Chad Valley, Dopey, Louis Vuitton Label On Foot, 9 In. 275.00
Chad Valley, Pirate, Felt Body, Glass Eyes, Painted Features, 20 In. 1210.00
Character, Boy, Bisque Socket Head, Glass Sleep Eyes, Closed Mouth, Baby, 19 In. 750.00
Character, Boy, Domed Bisque Socket Head, Brown Hair, Baby, 1915, 15 In. 1300.00
Character, Girl, Bisque Socket Head, Glass Sleep Eyes, Closed Mouth, Baby, 16 In. 750.00
Chase, Gentleman, Velvet Suit, 40 In. 1495.00
Chase, Girl, Stockinet, Standing, Think Painted Hair, Painted Eyes, 17 In. 1400.00
Chase, Girl, Yellow Hair, Cotton Sateen Body, Trademark, Early 20th Century, 25 In. 207.00
China, Boy, Painted Hair, Gray Pants, White Shirt, Black Jacket, 1800s, 24 In. 180.00
China Head, Girl, Black Curly Hair, Germany, 12 In. 22.00
Chinese Boy, Bisque Face, Cloth Body, 14 3/4 In. 225.00
Cloth, Alabama Baby, Seated, Brown Curly Hair, Painted Blue Eyes, 1905, 19 In. 1900.00
Cloth, Black, Soldier's Uniform, Leather Hands, Straw Stuffed, 22 In. 1500.00
Cloth, Character, Girl, Standing, All Felt, Brown Eyes, Original Costume, 17 In., Pair ... 3400.00
Cloth, Girl, Brown Muslin, Stitch Jointed Limbs, Red Cotton Dress, Bandanna, 24 In. ... 400.00
Cloth, Jester Type, Hand Sewn, 19th Century, 24 In. 445.00
Cotton, Wearing Brown Calico Dress, Blue, White Striped Bonnet, Folk Art, 22 In. 805.00
Cramer & Heron, PM 914, Bisque, Baby, Sleep Eyes, Bent Limb, Jointed Body, 11 In. ... 200.00
DEP, 6, Paris Bebe, Bisque, Composition, Jointed, Sleep Eyes, 4 Teeth, Box, 17 In. 1100.00
DEP, 101, Boy, Original Wig, 8 1/2 In. 210.00
DEP, 719, Stiff Wrist, Open Mouth, 19 In. 1000.00
Dolly Varden, Dolly Jane, Printed Cloth, Uncut, 28 In. 90.00
Dressel, Bisque Socket Head, Blue Glass Sleep Eyes, Open Mouth, Straw Bonnet, 41 In. . 3100.00
Dressel, Bisque, Jutta Character Child, Blue Eyes, 25 In. 1795.00
Effanbee, Baby Dainty, Composition Head, Painted Teeth, Hair, Cloth Body, 14 In. 140.00
Effanbee, Boy, 185, With Goose, & Girl, With Bunny, Ecru & Blue, 17 In., Pair 22.00
Effanbee, Honey, Majorette, Plastic, 4 1/2 In. 550.00
Effanbee, Little Lady, Sleep Eyes, Human Hair, Trousseau, Box, c.1940, 18 In. 700.00
Effanbee, Sweetie Pie, Composition, 19 In. 225.00
Effanbee, Wee Patsy & Brother, Marked, Composition Heads, 5 1/2 In., Pair ......*Illus* 375.00
Erste Steinbacher, 500, Bisque, Composition, Wood, Blond Mohair, 1912, 15 In. 1700.00
Fashion, Bisque, Blue Paperweight Eyes, Original Dress, Shoes, France, 14 In. 2495.00
Fashion, Bisque, Gentleman's Ensemble, Top Hat, France, 14 In. 4550.00
Fashion, Porcelain, Kid Body, Human Hair, Folklore Dress, c.1865, France, 16 In. 1500.00
Fashion, Swivel Neck, Wooden Body, Dome Top Trunk, Clothes, France, 14 In. 6875.00
French, Bisque Swivel Head, Kid Body, Blue Eyes, Blond Mohair, c.1875, 14 In. 3400.00
French, Bisque Swivel Head, Kid Over Wood Body, Jointed, c.1867, 15 In. 3600.00
French, Bisque Swivel Head, Muslin Body, Blue Glass Eyes, c.1870, 24 In. 2300.00
French, Bisque, Baby, Socket Head, Blue Paperweight Eyes, Closed Mouth, 1890, 34 In. . 6000.00
French, Bisque, Baby, Socket Head, Brown Paperweight Eyes, Blond Mohair Wig, 15 In. . 2900.00
French, Bisque, Boy, Blue Eyes, Bisque Teeth, Blond Mohair, Ball-Jointed, 16 In. 1495.00
French, Bisque, Boy, Smile, Teeth, Blond Wig, Ball-Jointed Body, Purple Suit, 16 In. 1495.00
French, Bisque, Kid Body, Blue Glass Eyes, Blond Mohair, c.1860, 12 In. 1000.00
French, Bisque, Paris Baby, Socket Head, Blue Glass Paperweight Eyes, 1891, 32 In. 5250.00
French, Bisque, Swivel Head, Glass Eyes, 2-Strap Shoes, White Socks, 4 1/2 In. 900.00

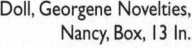

Doll, Effanbee, Wee Patsy
& Brother, Marked,
Composition Heads,
5 1/2 In., Pair

Doll, Georgene Novelties,
Nancy, Box, 13 In.

Doll, Georgene Novelties,
Sluggo, Box, 13 In.

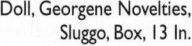

Fulper, Baby, Blue Eyes, Original Wig, Gowns, 21 In.	750.00
Fulper, Bisque Socket Head, Composition Body, 25 In.	950.00
G.I. Joe figures are listed in the Toy category.	
Gaultier, 9, Bisque, Kid Fashion Body, Paperweight Eyes, Human Hair, c.1875, 28 In.	3500.00
Gaultier, Bisque Swivel Head, Pale Blue Inset Eyes, Folklore Costume, 16 In.	3200.00
Gaultier, Fashion, Bisque Socket Head, Bisque Shoulder, Kid Body, 12 In.	2300.00
Gebruder Heubach dolls are also in this category under Heubach.	
Gebruder Heubach, 8192, Bisque Socket Head, Composition Flapper Body, 10 In.	700.00
Gebruder Heubach, 8413, Bisque Socket Head, Blue Glass Sleep Eyes, 1912, 8 In.	1150.00
Gebruder Heubach, 9573, Googly, Composition Body, 9 In.	1195.00
Gebruder Heubach, 10342, Googly, Bisque, Papier-Mache, Sleep Eyes, 7 In.	750.00
Gebruder Heubach, Bisque Socket Head, Deep Blue Intaglio Eyes, Pouty, 1915, 9 In.	325.00
Gebruder Heubach, Bisque, Baby, Lying On Back, Blond Sculpted Hair, Smock, 8 In.	350.00
Gebruder Heubach, Bisque, Baby, Lying On Stomach, Leg Kicking, Smock, 12 In.	700.00
Gebruder Heubach, Bisque, Baby, Seated, Feet Crossed, Blond Sculpted Hair, 9 In.	650.00
Gebruder Heubach, Bisque, Baby, Seated, Feet Crossed, Brown Sculpted Hair, 11 In.	925.00
Gebruder Heubach, Bisque, Crawling, Leg Kicking, Blond Hair, Open Back Smock, 6 In.	325.00
Gebruder Heubach, Bisque, Girl, Pirouette Position, Brown Curly Hair, 16 In.	1100.00
Gebruder Heubach, Bisque, My Coquette, Blue & White Frock, 14 In.	1195.00
Gebruder Heubach, Bisque, Seated, Clasping His Tummy, Crossed Ankles, 1920, 5 In.	425.00
Gebruder Heubach, Bisque, Seated, Clasping Toes, Blond Hair, Smock, 1910, 8 In.	375.00
Gebruder Heubach, Bisque, Seated, Coquettish Position, Side-Glancing Eyes, 5 In.	700.00
Gebruder Heubach, Bisque, Seated, Surprised Expression, Brown Painted Eyes, 5 In.	425.00
Gebruder Heubach, Bisque, Seated, With Fisticuffs, Side-Glancing Eyes, 1920, 5 In.	500.00
Gebruder Heubach, Bisque, Sunbonnet Girl, Seated, Sunbonnet, 1910, 8 In.	875.00
Gebruder Heubach, Boy, Solid Dome, Molded Hair, Jointed Composition Body, 10 In.	995.00
Gebruder Heubach, Character Child, Bisque Socket Head, Blue Sleep Eyes, 26 In.	4700.00
Gebruder Heubach, Character Child, Bisque, Standing, Brown Sculpted Hair, 9 In.	800.00
Gebruder Heubach, Child, Smiling, Extended Tongue, Composition Body, 15 In.	2450.00
Gebruder Heubach, Pink Bisque, Pouty, Glass Eyes, Ball-Jointed, Frilly Bonnet, 11 In.	1995.00
Gebruder Knoch, Bisque Socket Head, Blue Sleep Eyes, Blond Mohair Wig, 1910, 7 In.	225.00
Gebruder Kuhnlenz, Bisque, Closed Mouth, Blue Paperweight Eyes, 15 In.	1495.00
Gebruder Kuhnlenz, Bisque, Spiral Threaded Eyes, Blond Mohair Wig, 15 In.	1295.00
Georgene Novelties, Muslin Face, Twill Body, Painted Face, Yarn Pigtails, Label, 26 In.	225.00
Georgene Novelties, Nancy, Box, 13 In. ....*Illus*	850.00
Georgene Novelties, Raggedy Ann & Andy, Heart Tag, 15 In., Pair	950.00
Georgene Novelties, Sluggo, Box, 13 In. ....*Illus*	775.00
German, Bisque Socket Head, Child, Brown Glass Eyes, Closed Mouth, 1885, 15 In.	1300.00
German, Bisque Socket Head, Child, Large Brown Enamel Eyes, Blond Wig, 14 In.	1150.00
German, Bisque, Baby With Rattle, Seated, Blond Mohair, c.1900, 3 1/2 In.	200.00
German, Bisque, Blue Glass Inset Eyes, Open Mouth, Ball-Jointed Body, 1880, 14 In.	2500.00
German, Bisque, Boy, Muslin Body, Stitch-Jointed, Sculpted Hair, 1875, 22 In.	600.00
German, Bisque, Girl, Carrying Bouquet Of Roses, Blue Apron, 1880, 10 In.	100.00
German, Bisque, Girl, Papier-Mache 5-Piece Body, Sleep Eyes, 1920, 14 In.	375.00
German, Bisque, Nude Bathing Beauty, Seated, Blue Eyes, Brunette Mohair Wig, 2 In.	325.00
German, Bisque, Swivel Head, Sleep Eyes, Mohair, Black Stockings, c.1890, 5 1/2 In.	350.00

German, Black Girl, Porcelain, Muslin Body, Sculpted Hair, Bonnet, c.1880, 10 In. 2000.00
German, Boy, Molded Teeth, Intaglio Eyes, 18 In. 2150.00
German, Character, Bisque, Composition, Jointed, Painted Hair, Eyes, c.1920, 15 In. 1500.00
German, Character, Textured Composition Socket Head, Blue Eyes, 1908, 13 1/2 In. 1200.00
German, Character, Textured Composition Socket Head, Dark Blue Eyes, Kaulitz, 13 In. . 2000.00
German, Milliner's Model, Papier-Mache, Kid Body, Sculpted Hair, c.1860, 11 In. 400.00
German, Papier-Mache, Girl, Muslin Body, Glass Eyes, Sculpted Hair, c.1850, 16 In. 375.00
German, Porcelain, Girl, Muslin Body, Leather Arms, Black Painted Hair, c.1860, 16 In. . 350.00
German, Porcelain, Girl, Muslin Body, Sculpted Hair, Floral Coronet, c.1880, 21 In. 750.00
German, Shoulder Head, Black Painted Hair, Blue Eyes, Closed Mouth, Jointed, 12 In. .. 700.00
German, Wax Over Papier-Mache, Girl, Muslin, Papier-Mache Limbs, c.1870, 18 In. 500.00
Girl Boxer, Wax, Painted Molded Features, Curly Mohair Wig, 9 In. 100.00
Googly, Baby, 323, Sleep Eyes, Trunk, 7 In. 1475.00
Halbig, 149, Blue Eyes, 15 1/2 In. 975.00
Half Dolls are listed in the Pinchushion category.
Handwerck, 0 1/2, Bisque, Composition, Wood, Jointed, Flirty Sleep Eyes, Teeth, 17 In. .. 850.00
Handwerck, 4 1/2, Bisque, Composition, Wood, Jointed, Sleep Eyes, 4 Teeth, 24 In. 650.00
Handwerck, 69-12, Bisque, Composition, Jointed, Sleep Eyes, 4 Teeth, c.1900, 23 In. 600.00
Handwerck, 109, Bisque, Sleep Eyes, Human Hair Wig, Victorian Dress & Hat, 30 In. 1375.00
Handwerck, Bisque Head, Girl, Sleep Eyes, Open Mouth, Blond Wig, Clothes, 26 In. 575.00
Handwerck, Bisque Head, Girl, Sleep Eyes, Open Mouth, Pierced Ears, Blond, 18 In. 575.00
Handwerck, Bisque Socket Head, Baby, Blue Glass Sleep Eyes, Open Mouth, 1910, 18 In. 900.00
Handwerck, Bisque Socket Head, Child, Blue Sleep Eyes, Antique Costume, 25 In. 1050.00
Handwerck, Bisque Socket Head, Child, Blue Sleep Eyes, Open Mouth, 1900, 29 In. 775.00
Handwerck, Bisque Socket Head, Child, Blue Sleep Eyes, Open Mouth, Jointed, 24 In. .. 650.00
Handwerck, Bisque Socket Head, Child, Brown Sleep Eyes, Open Mouth, 1900, 25 In. .. 525.00
Handwerck, Bisque, Amber Sleep Eyes, Human Hair Wig, Signed, 25 In. 1175.00
Handwerck, Bisque, Composition, Jointed, Sleep Eyes, Open Mouth, c.1900, 29 In. 600.00
Handwerck, Bisque, Sleep Eyes, Open Mouth, Jointed Composition Body, 17 1/2 In. 517.00
Handwerck, Helmet Googly, Bisque Socket Head, Blue Googly Eyes, Jointed, 14 In. 1700.00
Handwerck-Halbig, Bisque, Sleep Eyes, Blond Human Hair, Dress, 24 In. 1085.00
Harold Lloyd, Walker, Tin Lithograph, Clockwork, Face & Arms Move, 11 In. 247.00
Hawaiian Girl, Brown Composition, Painted Eyes, Modeled Hair, Lei, c.1940, 17 In. 500.00
Hawaiian Girl, Celluloid, Windup, Tin, Grass Skirt, 6 1/2 In. 65.00
Hawaiian Girl, Souvenir, Molded Vinyl, Grass Skirt, Lei, 1960s, 15 In. 45.00
Helen Jensen, Gladdie, Terra-Cotta Head, Muslin, Modeled Hair, Glass Eyes, 20 In. 700.00
Hertel Schwab, 141, Bisque Socket Head, Brown Sleep Eyes, Closed Mouth, 18 In. 10200.00
Hertel Schwab, 1699, Bisque, Sleep Eyes, Strawberry Blond, Fully Jointed, 28 In. 920.00
Hertel Schwab, Bisque Head, Skippy Baby, All Original 995.00
Hertel Schwab, Bisque Socket Head, Blue Sleep Eyes, Composition, 1920, 16 In. 5750.00
Hertel Schwab, No. 151, Bisque Socket Head, Baby, Brown Eyes, Romper, 14 In. 300.00
Heubach dolls are also in this category under Gebruder Heubach.
Heubach, 17, Googly, Toddler, 12 In. 1495.00
Heubach, 200, Baby, 1910, 21 In. 550.00
Heubach, 250/3/0, Bisque Head, Sleep Eyes, Fully Jointed, 16 In. 230.00
Heubach, 267, Character, Sleep Eyes, Brown Mohair Wig, Baby, 18 In. 775.00
Heubach, 7604, Character, Pink Bisque Socket Head, Blond Hair, Composition, 12 In. ... 550.00
Heubach, 8191, Toddler, Jointed, Clothes, 16 In. 2350.00
Heubach, 8192, Bisque, Human Hair Eyelashes, Original Clothes, 21 In. 1395.00
Heubach, 8192, Boy, Brown Eyes, Green Wool Suit, 15 In. 995.00
Heubach, 8192, Pale Bisque, Braids, Straw Hat, Hair Eyelashes, 21 In. 1395.00
Heubach, Character, Girl, Pink Bisque Socket Head, Blond Hair, Intaglio Eyes, 18 In. ... 7000.00
Heubach, Character, Girl, Pink Bisque Socket Head, Intaglio Blue Eyes, 1910, 20 In. 1650.00
Heubach, Girl, Bisque, With Sunbonnet, Ruffled Bonnet, White Smock, Germany, 6 In. .. 850.00
Heubach, Laughing, Brown Sleep Eyes, Ball-Jointed Composition Body, 11 In. 1695.00
Heubach, Pouty Boy, 15 In. 750.00
Heubach Kopplesdorf, 250, Bisque, Blond Mohair, Sleep Eyes, Clothes, 14 In. 550.00
Horsman, Blue Bonnet Sue, 17 In. 75.00
Horsman, Bride & Groom, HEbee, SHEbee, Composition, 1925, 10 1/2 In., Pair 1600.00
Horsman, Ella Cinders, Book, 1925, 18 In. 795.00
Horsman, Ronald Reagan, Vinyl, 17 In. 70.00
Ideal, Baby Snooks, Fanny Brice, Composition, Poseable Arms, Legs, c.1938, 12 In. 35.00

Ideal, Bamm-Bamm & Pebbles, Movable Heads, Arms, Legs, 1964, 12 In., Pair 78.00
Ideal, Composition & Cloth, Baby, Flirting Steel Eyes, c.1933, 22 1/2 In. 230.00
Ideal, Composition, Sleep Eyes, Open Mouth, Cloth Body, Straight Legs, 18 In. 33.00
Ideal, Deanna Durbin, 1938, 21 In. 995.00
Ideal, Fanny Brice, Full Figure, Flex Spring Arms & Legs, Wooden Shoes, 12 In. 155.00
Ideal, Miss Ideal, Vinyl Head, Nylon Hair, Smiling Mouth, Original Dress, Shoes, 25 In. . 350.00
Ideal, Mortimer Snerd, Composition & Wire, 13 In. 545.00
Ideal, Nylon Hair, Sleep Eyes, Plastic Head & Body, Jointed Hips & Shoulders, 22 In. ... 50.00
Ideal, Peter Playpal, Walking, Vinyl Socket Head, Blue Eyes, Freckles, Shorts, 38 In. 550.00
Ideal, Thumbelina, Cloth, Painted Blue Eyes, Tosca Hair, 1961, 14 In. 425.00
Ideal, Toni Walker, Hard Plastic Body, Blue Dress, Organdy Bodice, Vinyl Shoes, 14 In. . 450.00
Indian dolls are listed in the Indian category.
Izannah Walker, Crazed Face, Clothes, 1868 .... 4000.00
J.D.K. dolls are also listed in this category under Kestner.
J.D.K., 211, Bisque, Sammy, Original Wig, Old Clothes, 19 In. 1550.00
J.D.K., 257, Toddler, Factory Fancy Clothes, Leather Shoes, 11 1/2 In. 650.00
J.D.K., Bisque Head, Molded Hair, Sleep Eyes, Bent Limb, Baby, 14 In. 345.00
Juillien, Bisque Socket Head, Brown Sleep Eyes, Brunette Mohair Wig, Baby, 19 In. 1000.00
Jules Steiner, French, Bisque, Open Mouth, Paperweight Eyes, Baby, 16 In. 2995.00
Jumeau, 5, Bisque Socket Head, Jointed, Paperweight Eyes, Depose, c.1885, 14 In. 6200.00
Jumeau, 5, Bisque, Composition, Jointed, Paperweight Eyes, 4 Teeth, Human Hair, 14 In. 1550.00
Jumeau, 5, Portrait, Bisque, Composition, Wood, Jointed, Glass Eyes, 16 In. 4600.00
Jumeau, 7, Bisque, Composition, Wood, Jointed, Paperweight Eyes, Depose, 1886, 17 In. . 4500.00
Jumeau, 7, Bisque, Paperweight Eyes, Blond Skin Wig, Straight Wristed, Clothes, 17 In. . 8200.00
Jumeau, 8, Bisque Socket Head, Blue Paperweight Eyes, Closed Mouth, 1890, 19 In. 3500.00
Jumeau, 8, Bisque, Composition, Jointed, Paperweight Eyes, Human Hair, 19 In. 3200.00
Jumeau, 10, Paperweight Eyes, Straight Wristed, Mohair Wig, 22 In. 9000.00
Jumeau, 11, Bisque, Composition, Jointed, Paperweight Eyes, c.1890, 24 In. 3300.00
Jumeau, 12, Bisque, Paperweight Eyes, French Mariners Clothes, 26 In. 7200.00
Jumeau, 12, Triste, Bisque, Composition, Jointed, Paperweight Eyes, c.1884, 26 In. 12500.00
Jumeau, 13, French Body, Open Mouth, Child, 25 In. ....*Illus* 3575.00
Jumeau, Bisque Socket Head, Bebe Triste, Brown Enamel Eyes, Blond Wig, 26 In. 15000.00
Jumeau, Bisque Socket Head, Bebe, Amber Brown Glass Paperweight Eyes, 21 In. 6200.00
Jumeau, Bisque Socket Head, Bebe, Blue Paperweight Eyes, Blond Mohair Wig, 12 In. .. 5100.00
Jumeau, Bisque Socket Head, Bebe, Blue Paperweight Eyes, Closed Mouth, 1885, 14 In. . 5600.00
Jumeau, Bisque Socket Head, Bebe, Blue Paperweight Eyes, Closed Mouth, 19 In. 5750.00
Jumeau, Bisque Socket Head, Bebe, Brown Enamel Eyes, Blond Mohair Wig, 16 In. 3800.00
Jumeau, Bisque Socket Head, Blue Enamel Inset Eyes, Closed Mouth, Jointed, 14 In. ... 5700.00
Jumeau, Bisque Socket Head, Blue Paperweight Eyes, Closed Mouth, Jointed, 17 In. 10000.00
Jumeau, Bisque Socket Head, Blue Paperweight Inset Eyes, Blond Mohair Wig, 22 In. ... 3800.00
Jumeau, Bisque Socket Head, Composition Body, 15 In. 4250.00
Jumeau, Bisque Swivel Head, Blue Paperweight Eyes, Closed Mouth, 1886, 17 In. 3100.00
Jumeau, Bisque Swivel Head, Pale Blue Enamel Eyes, Blond Mohair Pate, 1870, 15 In. .. 4200.00
Jumeau, Bisque, 8-Ball Body, Paperweight Eyes, Silk Dress, 15 In. 6500.00
Jumeau, Bisque, Paperweight Eyes, Blond Mohair Wig, Leather Shoes, 19 In. 7895.00
Jumeau, Bisque, Paperweight Eyes, Blond Mohair, Old Clothes, Extra Outfit, 19 In. 7895.00
Jumeau, Bisque, Sleep Eyes, Long Blond Human Hair Wig, Dressed, 24 In. 2975.00
Jumeau, Cork Pate, Wood & Composition Jointed Body, Dress, Shoes, 22 1/2 In. 4025.00
Jumeau, Opaque Bisque, Large Paperweight Eyes, Gibson Girl Type Dress, 22 In. 3995.00
Jumeau, Paperweight Eyes, Wool Sailor Dress, 13 In. 7300.00
Jumeau, Portrait, Bisque, 8-Ball Body, Almond Shaped Paperweight Eyes, Dress, 15 In. ... 8750.00
Jutta, Dressel, 1349, Bisque, Composition, Jointed, Sleep Eyes, Teeth, Nun's Habit, 27 In. 650.00
K * R, 65, Bisque, Composition, Jointed, Flapper-Era Body, Blue Eyes, c.1920, 26 In. ... 600.00
K * R, 100, Brown Bisque Socket Head, Brown Upper Glancing Eyes, 1909, 14 In. 1200.00
K * R, 100, Character, Bisque Socket Head, Painted Blond Hair, Blue Eyes, 1909, 11 In. . 1200.00
K * R, 100, Domed Bisque Socket Head, Azure Blue Painted Eyes, Closed Mouth, 16 In. . 650.00
K * R, 101, Bisque Head, Original Wig, Fully Jointed, Boy, Velveteen Costume, 10 In. ... 1150.00
K * R, 101/30, Marie, Bisque, Composition, Wood, Jointed, Folk Dress, c.1910, 12 In. ... 2500.00
K * R, 109, Bisque Socket Head, Blue Glancing Eyes, Closed Mouth, Ball-Jointed, 7 In. . 2500.00
K * R, 109/18, Bisque, Composition, Wood, Jointed, Blond Mohair Braids, c.1912, 7 In. . 2500.00
K * R, 114, Bisque Socket Head, Painted Blue Eyes, Brunette Mohair Wig, 1910, 15 In. .. 3800.00
K * R, 114, Boy, Sailor Suit, 21 In. ....*Illus* 6100.00
K * R, 115A, Bisque Socket Head, Blue Sleep Eyes, Brunette Mohair Wig, 1910, 13 In. ... 5000.00

Doll, Kestner, 171,
Daisy, Sleep Eyes,
Clothes, 18 In.

Doll, Jumeau, 13,
French Body, Open
Mouth, Child, 25 In.

Doll, K * R, 114, Boy,
Sailor Suit, 21 In.

K * R, 115A, Bisque Socket Head, Small Brown Sleep Eyes, Brunette Mohair Wig, 5 In. .   3700.00
K * R, 116A, Toddler, Jointed, 27 In. 5950.00
K * R, 117, Bisque Socket Head, Brown Sleep Eyes, Closed Mouth, 1912, 19 In. 5100.00
K * R, 117, Character, Bisque Socket Head, Small Blue Sleep Eyes, Closed Mouth, 18 In.   4300.00
K * R, 117, Mein Leibling, Bisque, Blue Sleep Eyes, 22 In. 8075.00
K * R, 117, Mein Liebling, Bisque, Clothes, 19 In. 2995.00
K * R, 117, Mein Liebling, Sleep Eyes, Auburn Wig, Antique Clothes & Shoes, 21 In. . . .   6985.00
K * R, 117N, Bisque, Composition, Jointed, Flapper, Flirty Eyes, 4 Teeth, c.1920, 25 In. .   1200.00
K * R, 117N, Bisque, Composition, Jointed, Flirty Eyes, 4 Teeth, c.1920, 22 In. . . .   1100.00
K * R, 121, Bisque, Composition, Gray Sleep Eyes, 2 Teeth, Mohair, c.1915, 11 In. 550.00
K * R, 121, Bisque, Dimpled Darling, Original Clothes, 17 In. 1495.00
K * R, 121/42, Bisque, Composition, Blue Sleep Eyes, Brunette Mohair, c.1915, 17 In. 800.00
K * R, 121/62, Bisque, Composition, Baby, Blue Sleep Eyes, 2 Teeth, Human Hair, 24 In.   1300.00
K * R, 122/42, Bisque, Composition, Brown Sleep Eyes, 2 Teeth, Mohair, c.1915, 17 In. .   750.00
K * R, 126, Bisque, Composition, Toddler, Blue Flirty Sleep Eyes, Mohair, 24 In. 1100.00
K * R, 126, Character, Bisque Socket Head, Glass Sleep Eyes, Composition, 29 In. 900.00
K * R, 171, Domed Bisque Head, Brown Baby Hair, Narrow Blue Sleep Eyes, 11 In. 1650.00
K * R, 192, Bisque Socket Head, Child, Blue Inset Eyes, Brunette Human Hair, 38 In. . . .   2100.00
K * R, 192, Bisque Socket Head, Child, Blue Sleep Eyes, Open Mouth, 1900, 27 In. 950.00
K * R, 403, Walker, Bisque, Composition, Wood, Sleep Eyes, 4 Teeth, c.1920, 18 In. 850.00
K * R, Bisque Head, Blue Sleep Eyes, Open Mouth, Blond Wig, 30 In. 633.00
K * R, Bisque Head, Intaglio Eyes, Pouty Mouth, Wood & Composition, 13 3/4 In. 3650.00
K * R, Bisque Head, Pouty Marie, Bisque, Painted Eyes & Mouth, 18 In. 44500.00
K * R, Bisque Socket Head, Child, Blue Sleep Flirty Eyes, Blond Human Hair, 30 In. 2050.00
K * R, Bisque Socket Head, Child, Brown Googly Sleep Eyes, Closed Mouth, 15 In. 12000.00
K * R, Bisque Socket Head, Child, Brown Sleep Eyes, Blue Mohair Bobbed Wig, 6 In. . .   425.00
K * R, Bisque Socket Head, Child, Brown Sleep Eyes, Open Mouth, 6 In. 400.00
K * R, Bisque Socket Head, Child, Gray Sleep Eyes, Blond Mohair Wig, 1915, 9 In. 600.00
K * R, Bisque Socket Head, Dark Blue Eyes, Closed Mouth, Ball-Jointed Body, 18 In. . . .   4000.00
K * R, Bisque, Auburn Human Hair Wig, Child, Antique White Dress, 29 In. 1650.00
K * R, Bisque, Flirty, Curls & Wavy Hair, Antique Clothes, 21 In.   895.00
K * R, Bisque, Girl, Sleep Eyes, Victorian White Dress, 29 In. 2250.00
K * R, Bisque, Pouty, Chubby Checks, Sleep Eyes, Child, Dressed, 30 In. 1350.00
K * R, Character, Bisque Socket Head, Painted Blue Eyes, Closed Mouth, 1910, 13 In. 8000.00
K * R, Gladdie, Biscaloid Head, Child, Open-Close Mouth, Teeth, Sleep Eyes, 18 In. 1950.00
K * R, Marie, Fully Jointed, Factory Original Clothes, 10 In. 2495.00
K * R, Sleep Eyes, Lashes, Auburn Mohair Wig, Baby Clothes, 21 In. 950.00
K * R, Walker, Bisque, Composition, Jointed, Blue Sleep Eyes, 4 Teeth, c.1920, 30 In. . . .   800.00
Kamar, E.T., Bean Bag, Leather-Like, Brown, Red On Chest & Finger, Label, 1982, 8 In.   28.00
Kathe Kruse, 162738, Girl, Cloth, Painted Face, Human Hair Braids, c.1935, 17 In. 1500.00
Kathe Kruse, Boy, Jointed, Lederhosen, Marked, 18 In. 825.00
Kathe Kruse, Boy, Painted Hair & Gray Eyes, Wool Coat, Smock, c.1916, 17 In. 2875.00
Kathe Kruse, Boy, Shaded Brown Eyes, Closed Mouth, Pouty Lips, 1935, 18 In. 5400.00
Kathe Kruse, Character, Brown Painted Eyes, Closed Mouth, Pouty, Frog Hand, 17 In. . .   5200.00
Kathe Kruse, Cloth, Boy, Hard Socket Head, Gray, Brown Eyes, Closed Mouth, 21 In. . . .   800.00
Kathe Kruse, Girl & Boy, Celluloid Body, Vinyl Heads, Rooted Hair, 16 In., Pair 795.00
Kathe Kruse, Girl, Brown Hair, Green Eyes, Closed Mouth, Pouty Lips, 1915, 17 In. 3400.00

Kathe Kruse, Girl, Cloth, Painted Face & Hair, Brown Hair, Brown Eyes, Series I, 17 In. . 2100.00
Kathe Kruse, Pouty, Child, Closed Mouth, Curly Hair, Brown Shaded Eyes, 17 In. 3700.00
Kathe Kruse, Rose Of Bertchen, 030047, Pressed Socket Head, Label, c.1947, 14 In. 1300.00
Kathe Kruse, Schildkrot, Completely Celluloid, Human Hair Wig, 17 In. 695.00
Kathe Kruse, Series 1, Girl, Cloth, Pouty, Blue Eyes, Dutch Costume, c.1915, 17 In. 2400.00
Kathe Kruse, Wide Hips, Sewn-On Thumb, Original Suit, 16 In. 3800.00
Kestner dolls are also in this category under J.D.K.
Kestner, 7, Bisque, Boy, Brown Sleep Eyes, Mohair Wig, 17 In. 1695.00
Kestner, 7, Bisque, Composition, Wood, Jointed, Brown Sleep Eyes, Blond, 13 In. 8500.00
Kestner, 8, White Bisque, Girl, Pouty, 12 In. 2800.00
Kestner, 10, Brown Bisque, Composition, Jointed, Sleep Eyes, Human Hair, 17 In. 850.00
Kestner, 11, Bisque, Composition, Wood, Sleep Eyes, Brunette Mohair, c.1890, 16 In. . . . 1400.00
Kestner, 13, Brown Bisque, Composition, Wood, Jointed, Black Eyes, c.1888, 19 In. 16500.00
Kestner, 14, Bisque, Composition, Baby, Blue Sleep Eyes, 2 Teeth, 1915, 20 In. 900.00
Kestner, 17, Bisque, Composition, Wood, Jointed, Human Hair, 4 Teeth, c.1895, 40 In. . . . 4300.00
Kestner, 60, Human Hair, Sleep Eyes, Ball-Jointed, 19 In. 850.00
Kestner, 143, Bisque, Composition, Jointed, Blue Sleep Eyes, 2 Teeth, c.1915, 27 In. 1400.00
Kestner, 143, Bisque, Sleep Eyes, Mohair Wig, Body Signed, 17 In. 1385.00
Kestner, 146, Bisque, Composition, Jointed, Brown Eyes, 4 Teeth, Mohair, c.1900, 32 In. . 800.00
Kestner, 149, Bisque Head, Blue Glass Eyes, Open Mouth, Brown Hair Wig, 17 1/4 In. . . . 403.00
Kestner, 150, All Bisque, Loop-Jointed, Brown Sleep Eyes, Mohair, c.1915, 10 In. 475.00
Kestner, 150, Bisque, Molded & Painted Socks & Shoes, 9 1/2 In. 875.00
Kestner, 154, Bisque, Pleated Jumper, Full Undies, 23 In. 595.00
Kestner, 156, Bisque, Child, Mohair Wig, Pink Silk Dress, Shoes, 26 In. 1875.00
Kestner, 160, Bisque Socket Head, Child, Blue Sleep Eyes, Blond Mohair Wig, 16 In. 750.00
Kestner, 160, Bisque Socket Head, Child, Brown Sleep Eyes, Open Mouth, 1900, 16 In. . 950.00
Kestner, 161, Bisque, Sleep Eyes, Blond Mohair, Plaster Pate, Old Dress, 18 1/2 In. 1475.00
Kestner, 162, Gibson Girl, Bisque, Composition, Wood, Sleep Eyes, Teeth, c.1910, 20 In. 1800.00
Kestner, 164, Bisque, Composition, Jointed, Sleep Eyes, Teeth, Human Hair, 28 In. 850.00
Kestner, 164, Sleep Eyes, Ball-Jointed, Long Auburn Wig, Old Outfit, 28 1/2 In. 1150.00
Kestner, 167, Bisque Head, 4 Upper Teeth, White Dress, Socks, Snap Shoes, 17 In. 470.00
Kestner, 168, Bisque, Composition, Jointed, Brown Sleep Eyes, 4 Teeth, c.1915, 20 In. . . 450.00
Kestner, 169, Bisque, Sleep Eyes, Jointed, Human Hair Wig, Plaid Outfit, 18 1/2 In. 1840.00
Kestner, 171, Bisque Head, Blue Sleep Eyes, Open Mouth, Blond Mohair Wig, 18 In. . . . 748.00
Kestner, 171, Bisque Head, Blue Sleep Eyes, Open Mouth, Blond Mohair Wig, 30 In. . . . 863.00
Kestner, 171, Bisque Head, Brown Sleep Eyes, 4 Upper Teeth, Wool Dress, 12 1/2 In. . . . 275.00
Kestner, 171, Bisque Socket Head, Child, Blue Glass Sleep Eyes, Jointed, 23 In. 800.00
Kestner, 171, Bisque Socket Head, Child, Blue Sleep Eyes, Blond Mohair Wig, 30 In. . . . 1000.00
Kestner, 171, Bisque Socket Head, Child, Brown Sleep Eyes, Open Mouth, 30 In. 1550.00
Kestner, 171, Bisque Socket Head, Composition, Ball-Jointed, Sleep Eyes, Teeth, 19 In. . . 1050.00
Kestner, 171, Bisque, Azure Eyes, Original Clothes, 33 In. 1495.00
Kestner, 171, Bisque, Composition, Jointed, Blue Sleep Eyes, 4 Teeth, c.1910, 30 In. 800.00
Kestner, 171, Daisy, Sky Blue Sleep Eyes, Dressed, 30 In. 1550.00
Kestner, 171, Daisy, Sleep Eyes, Clothes, 18 In. . . . .*Illus* 880.00
Kestner, 178, Bisque, Composition, Jointed, Sleep Eyes, Mohair, Sailor Dress, 11 In. 2800.00
Kestner, 186, Bisque, Composition, Jointed, Blue Eyes, Blond Mohair Braids, 19 In. 3000.00
Kestner, 187, Bisque Socket Head, Painted Blue Eyes, Wooden Ball-Jointed, 18 In. 5000.00
Kestner, 196, Bisque, Sleep Eyes, Open Mouth, Fur Eyebrows, Fully Jointed, 20 1/2 In. . . 373.00
Kestner, 208/3 1/2, Bisque Swivel Head, Brown Sleep Eyes, Mohair, c.1910, 5 1/2 In. . . . 300.00
Kestner, 211, Bisque Socket Head, Baby, Brown Glass Sleep Eyes, Open Mouth, 21 In. . . 800.00
Kestner, 211, Bisque Socket Head, Brown Sleep Eyes, Closed Mouth, 1915, 17 In. 700.00
Kestner, 215, Bisque Socket Head, Brown Glass Sleep Eyes, Open Mouth, 1915, 31 In. . . 950.00
Kestner, 220, Sleep Eyes, Open Mouth, Toddler, 11 In. 2200.00
Kestner, 221, Googly, Blond Mohair, Toddler, Clothes, 12 In. 6875.00
Kestner, 221, Googly, Blue Eyes, Original Wigs, Watermelon Mouth, 13 In. 6500.00
Kestner, 241, Girl, Bisque Head, Sleep Eyes, Painted Lashes, Pink Dress, Shoes, 18 In. . . . 5200.00
Kestner, 241, Young Girl, Bisque Socket Head, Brown Sleep Eyes, Open Mouth, 20 In. . . . 5700.00
Kestner, 243, Chinese Baby, Amber Tinted Bisque Socket Head, Open Mouth, 16 In. 6000.00
Kestner, 257, 2 Upper Teeth, Tremble Tongue, Baby, 23 In. 1650.00
Kestner, 260, Bisque, Child, Original Clothes & Wig, 35 In. 1995.00
Kestner, 260, Girl, Sleep Eyes, Blond Mohair Wig, Jointed Composition Body, 21 3/4 In. . 575.00
Kestner, American School Boy, Molded Hair, Brown Suit, 21 In. 995.00
Kestner, Bisque Head, Sleep Eyes, Closed Mouth, Pique Blouse, Blue Skirt, 15 In. 500.00

Kestner, Bisque Head, Torso, Brown Glass Sleep Eyes, Blond Mohair Wig, 1910, 11 In. . . 1600.00
Kestner, Bisque Socket Brown Sleep Eyes, Blond Mohair Wig, Ball-Jointed, 14 In. 1250.00
Kestner, Bisque Socket Head, Blue Glass Sleep Eyes, Open Mouth, Jointed, 1888, 21 In. . 1050.00
Kestner, Bisque Socket Head, Child, Blue Sleep Eyes, Mohair Wig, 1885, 15 In. 1700.00
Kestner, Bisque Socket Head, Child, Brown Glass Eyes, Open Mouth, 32 In. 1300.00
Kestner, Bisque Swivel Head, Blue Sleep Eyes, Closed Mouth, Germany, 1888, 27 In. . . . 1700.00
Kestner, Bisque, Azure Blue Eyes, Original Clothes, 33 In. 1495.00
Kestner, Bisque, Blond Mohair Wig, Wool Coat, Fur Hat, 34 In. 5300.00
Kestner, Bisque, Closed Mouth, Turned Head, Paperweight Eyes, 21 In. 1450.00
Kestner, Bisque, Composition, Ball-Jointed, Sleep Eyes, Brown Wig, Clothes, 27 In. 1200.00
Kestner, Bisque, Composition, Sleep Eyes, Blond Human Hair Wig, Jointed Body, 32 In. . 977.00
Kestner, Bisque, Turned Head, Individual Glass Teeth, 1880s, 28 In. 1095.00
Kestner, Bisque, Turned Shoulder Head, Cloth Body & Limbs, Kid Hands, 23 In. 488.00
Kestner, Brown Bisque Socket Head, Child, Brown Inset Eyes, Open Mouth, 13 In. 1250.00
Kestner, Character, Girl, Bisque Socket Head, Sleep Eyes, Open Mouth, 1912, 16 In. 1300.00
Kestner, Child, Closed Mouth, Turned Head, Old Clothes & Shoes, 23 In. 1450.00
Kestner, Closed Mouth, Straight Wrist, 8-Ball Body, Blond Wig, 21 1/2 In. 3200.00
Kestner, Daisy, Brown Mohair Wig, Sleep Eyes, Plaster Pate, Lace Dress, Shoes, 26 In. . . 1475.00
Kestner, Daisy, Composition, Sleep Eyes, Ball-Jointed Body, 18 1/2 In. 1485.00
Kestner, Hilda, Baby, Bisque Socket Head, Blue Sleep Eyes, Blond Mohair Wig, 13 In. . . 2400.00
Kestner, Hilda, Baby, Bisque Socket Head, Blue Sleep Eyes, Open Mouth, 1914, 22 In. . . 5000.00
Kestner, Hilda, Baby, Bisque, Open Mouth, Bent Limbs, Mohair Wig, 10 In. 2395.00
Kestner, IIX, Bisque, Brown Eyes, Hand Painted Smile, Ball-Jointed, Blue Frock, 12 In. . 2495.00
Kestner, Lady, Closed Mouth, 11 In. 495.00
Kestner, Turned Head, Antique Clothes & Shoes, 28 In. 850.00
Kestner, Turned Head, Closed Mouth, Wig, Antique Clothes, 27 In. 1850.00
Kewpie dolls are listed in the Kewpie category.
Kiddie Joy, Infant, Bisque Head, Painted Hair, Sleep Eyes, Cloth Body, Signed, 12 In. . . . 140.00
Kley & Hahn, 110, Toddler, Slant Hip, Blue Glass Sleep Eyes, Open-Close Mouth, 15 In. . 3250.00
Kley & Hahn, 546, Character, Bisque Socket Head, Blue Glass Sleep Eyes, 1910, 15 In. . . 3800.00
Kley & Hahn, 568, Toddler, Brown Eyes, 22 In. 3100.00
Kley & Hahn, 640, Fully Jointed, Toddler, 17 In. 2905.00
Kling, 131-8, Bisque, Muslin Body, Stitch-Jointed, Sculpted Hair, Blue Glass Eyes, 22 In. . 475.00
Kling, Bisque Head, Sleep Eyes, Hair Wig, Leather Body, K Inside Bell Mark, 21 In. 336.00
Kling, Bisque Shoulder Head, Child, Blue Threaded Eyes, Closed Mouth, 1885, 15 In. . . . 1850.00
Kling, Bisque, Blue Down-Glancing Eyes, Closed Mouth, Folklore Costume, 15 In., Pair . 1700.00
Knickerbocker, Laurel & Hardy, Bend 'em Doll, In Original Bags, 9 In., Pair 70.00
Knickerbocker, Raggedy Ann & Andy, 15 In., Pair 65.00
Knickerbocker, Raggedy Ann & Andy, Bean Bag, 1971, 10 In., Pair 390.00
Koenig & Wernicke, 1070, Bisque, Composition, Brown Sleep Eyes, 2 Teeth, 19 In. 1100.00
Koenig & Wernicke, Bisque, Composition, Wood, Toddler, Sleep Eyes, 2 Teeth, 16 In. . . . 850.00
Koppelsdorf, Character, Boy, Laughing, Pink Bisque Socket Head, Blond Hair, 16 In. . . . 800.00
KPM, Porcelain, Muslin Body, Leather Arms, Brown Painted Hair, c.1850, 22 In. 4600.00
Kuhnienz, Bisque Socket Head, Child, Blue Inset Eyes, Mohair Wig, 1888, 18 In. 5600.00
Lanternier, Black Bisque, Composition, Jointed, Glass Eyes, Teeth, c.1912, 20 In. 750.00
Lanternier, Toto, Bisque, Paperweight Eyes, 17 In. 995.00
Leibe & Hoffman, 9, Bisque, Fixed Eyes, Mohair Wig, Kid Body, Bisque Hands, 23 In. . . 143.00
Lenci, Bride, Blond Mohair Wig, Felt Costume, 9 In. 245.00
Lenci, Character, Boy, Standing, Felt Swivel Head, Blue Side-Glancing Eyes, 17 In. 4000.00
Lenci, Character, Girl, Standing, All Felt, Pale Blue Eyes, Closed Mouth, Pouty, 17 In. . . . 1400.00
Lenci, Dutch Child, Painted Features, Eyes Right, Felt Body, Wooden Shoes, 1925, 17 In. . 660.00
Lenci, Girl, Brown Side-Glancing Eyes, Mohair Wig, Jointed Body, 1930, 24 In. 1350.00
Lenci, Painted Features, Gray & Pink Dress, Matching Bonnet, Certificate, 26 In. 345.00
Lenci, Peasant, Child, Red Hair, Braid In Back, Babushka, 12 1/2 In. 695.00
Leon Casimir Bru, Poupee, Bisque Swivel Head, Wood Body, Jointed, 15 In. 4300.00
Levi's, Rag, Denim Jacket, Jeans, Yellow Yarn Hair, Big E Tag On Pocket, 1973, 16 In. . . 75.00
Little Lulu, Cowgirl, Oilcloth Face, Cloth Body, Metal Pistol, 1940s, 16 In. 515.00
Louis Wolf, 48, Bisque Head, Baby, Blue Eyes, Open Mouth, Bent Limb, 23 In. 374.00
Lucy, Peanuts, Cloth, Lavender Dress, Plastic Hook, Silgo International, 1980s, 20 In. . . . 14.00
Madame Alexander, Alexander-Kins, Parlor Maid, 8 In. . . . .*Illus* 550.00
Madame Alexander, Alice In Wonderland, Hard Plastic, Blond, Redressed, 17 In. 105.00
Madame Alexander, Alice In Wonderland, Maggie Head, Sleep Eyes, 1950-1952, 18 In. . . 475.00
Madame Alexander, Alice, Box, 14 In. 90.00

Madame Alexander, Alice, Plastic Head, Black Sleep Eyes, Tosca Wig, 1956, 8 In. 350.00
Madame Alexander, Alice, Vinyl, All Original, 1965, 13 1/2 In. 28.00
Madame Alexander, Amy, Plastic Head, Sleep Eyes, Blond, 7-Piece Walker, 1957, 8 In. . . . 655.00
Madame Alexander, Angel, Hard Plastic, 6 In. 85.00
Madame Alexander, Annabelle, All Original Clothes, 18 In. 700.00
Madame Alexander, Babs, Skater, 15 In. 750.00
Madame Alexander, Baby Jane, Original Clothes, Pin, 1935, 16 In. 995.00
Madame Alexander, Baby, Kathy, Box, 18 In. 200.00
Madame Alexander, Barbara Jane, All Original, 1952, 29 In. 450.00
Madame Alexander, Bride, Sleep Eyes, Mohair Wig, Bride Dress, Panties, Veil, 20 In. . . . 525.00
Madame Alexander, Bride, Walker, Hard Plastic, Auburn Hair, 17 In. 93.00
Madame Alexander, Caroline, Vinyl, Blue Sleep Eyes, Blond Wig, Box, 1961, 14 In. 200.00
Madame Alexander, Cinderella, Plastic, Sleep Eyes, Peasant Outfit, 1950-1952, 14 In. . . . 325.00
Madame Alexander, Cissy Bride, Plastic, Blue Sleep Eyes, Box, 1957, 20 In. 1000.00
Madame Alexander, Cleopatra, 12 In. 75.00
Madame Alexander, Cousin Karen, Plastic Head, Sleep Eyes, Brunette Saran Wig, 8 In. . . 425.00
Madame Alexander, Degas, Vinyl, All Original, 1965, 13 1/2 In. 28.00
Madame Alexander, Fischer Quintuplets, Vinyl, Box, 8 In., 5 Piece 360.00
Madame Alexander, Flora McFlimsey, Green Sleep Eyes, Label, c.1939, 13 In. 650.00
Madame Alexander, Flora McFlimsey, Green Sleep Eyes, Label, c.1939, 16 In. 550.00
Madame Alexander, Flower Girl, Plastic Head, Sleep Eyes, Blond, Walker, 1954, 18 In. . . 130.00
Madame Alexander, Glamour Girl No. 2001c, Plastic, Sleep Eyes, Hoop Slip, 18 In. 425.00
Madame Alexander, Juliet, Box, Portrait, 1976, 12 In. 55.00
Madame Alexander, Karen, Ballerina, Blue Sleep Eyes, Floss Hair, Tag, c.1946, 21 In. . . . 1100.00
Madame Alexander, Kathy, Skater, Auburn Braids, Blue Sleep Eyes, Tag, c.1951, 14 In. . . 575.00
Madame Alexander, Lady Windermere, Tagged, c.1946, 22 In. 2950.00
Madame Alexander, Laurie, Box, 12 In. 450.00
Madame Alexander, Lissy, Cinderella, Before The Ball, Tag, c.1966, 11 In. . . . . . .300.00 to 325.00
Madame Alexander, Little Genius, Blue Sleep Eyes, Organdy Dress, Tag, c.1949, 11 In. . . 550.00
Madame Alexander, Little Godey, Plastic Head, Blue Sleep Eyes, Saran Wig, 8 In. 1050.00
Madame Alexander, Little Women, Box, 8 In., 6 Piece 280.00
Madame Alexander, Madeline, Plastic Head, Blue Sleep Eyes, Red Hair, 1955, 15 In. 150.00
Madame Alexander, Maggie Mix-Up, Green Sleep Eyes, Blond Braided Wig, 8 In. 325.00
Madame Alexander, Maggie Mix-Up, Plastic Head, Green Sleep Eyes, Saran Wig, 8 In. . . 600.00
Madame Alexander, Maggie, Bridesmaid, Plastic, Yellow Tulle Dress, 17 In. 695.00
Madame Alexander, Maggie, Teenager, Plastic, Sleep Eyes, Skates, Tag, c.1951, 14 In. . . . 420.00
Madame Alexander, Margaret O'Brien, Green Sleep Eyes, Brown Braids, c.1948, 18 In. . . 850.00
Madame Alexander, Marmee, Little Women, Box, 1976, 11 1/2 In. 25.00
Madame Alexander, McGuffey Ana, Composition, Painted Blue Eyes, 9 In. 250.00
Madame Alexander, Meg, Hard Plastic, Hat Box, Brass Tag, 15 In. 165.00
Madame Alexander, Nina, Ballerina, 1950, 14 In. 245.00
Madame Alexander, Peter Pan, Plastic, Maggie Head, Sleep Eyes, Tag, c.1953, 14 In. 325.00
Madame Alexander, Plastic Head, Sleep Eyes, 5-Piece Walker Body, 1954, 8 In. 130.00
Madame Alexander, Prince Charming, Plastic, Sleep Eyes, Tag, c.1950, 18 In. 425.00
Madame Alexander, Prince Phillip, Green Sleep Eyes, Tuxedo, Tag, c.1953, 18 In. 400.00
Madame Alexander, Princess Elizabeth, Composition Head, Dressed, 17 In. 245.00
Madame Alexander, Princess Elizabeth, Green Sleep Eyes, Betty Face, c.1937, 13 In. 375.00
Madame Alexander, Princess Elizabeth, Original Clothes, Tag, 18 In. 695.00
Madame Alexander, Queen Elizabeth II, Walker, Blue Sleep Eyes, c.1953, 18 In. 1400.00
Madame Alexander, Renoir, Vinyl, Watering Can, All Original, 1965, 13 1/2 In. 28.00
Madame Alexander, Romeo, Portrait, Box, 1976, 12 In. 50.00
Madame Alexander, Rosamund Bridesmaid, Walker, Sleep Eyes, c.1953, 18 In. . . . . : . . . 750.00
Madame Alexander, Scarlett O'Hara, Original Clothes & Shoes, 18 In. 995.00
Madame Alexander, Scarlett O'Hara, Red & White Outfit, 12 In. 595.00
Madame Alexander, Scarlett O'Hara, Sleep Eyes, Flowered Dress, Label, c.1940, 11 In. . . 675.00
Madame Alexander, Scarlett, Composition, 18 In. 700.00
Madame Alexander, Shari Lewis, Box, 21 In. 975.00
Madame Alexander, Sir Winston Churchill, Sleep Eyes, Top Hat, c.1953, 18 In. 325.00
Madame Alexander, Sonja Henie, 17 In. 525.00
Madame Alexander, Sonja Henie, Brown Sleep Eyes, Human Hair, Label, 1939, 18 In. . . 750.00
Madame Alexander, Sonja Henie, c.1939, 15 1/4 In. 287.00
Madame Alexander, Sonja Henie, Composition Head, Sleep Eyes, Skating Dress, 20 In. . . 900.00
Madame Alexander, Story Princess, Plastic, Walker, Blue Sleep Eyes, c.1954, 14 In. 550.00

Use a feather duster to lightly clean your dolls.

Use Remove-Zit to remove the green discoloration from flesh-colored vinyl ears on dolls.

Doll, Madame Alexander,
Alexander-Kins,
Parlor Maid, 8 In.

Madame Alexander, Wendy Bride, Walker, Sleep Eyes, Blond Wig, Tag, c.1953, 18 In. . .	325.00
Madame Alexander, Wendy, Bridesmaid, Composition, Red Hair, Blue Dress, 21 In.	950.00
Madame Alexander, Wendy, Plastic Head, Black Sleep Eyes, Blond Saran Wig, 8 In.	300.00
Madame Alexander, Wendy, Plastic Head, Blue Sleep Eyes, Brunette Saran Wig, 8 In. . . .	375.00
Madame Alexander, Wendy, Plastic Head, Blue Sleep Eyes, Saran Hair, 1954, 8 In.	325.00
Mammy, Holding White Baby, Rag Stuffed, 8 In., With 3-In. Baby	950.00
Marcie, Cowboy, No. 042, Box, 7 In.	55.00
Marionette, Charlie Brown, Wood, Vinyl, Pelham Puppets, Box, 1970s, 5 x 10 In.	65.00
Marionette, Clown, Plaster Head, 14 1/2 In.	58.00
Marionette, Foxy Grandpa, Jointed, Sit & Dance, Tuck Engravers, 1890s, 6 x 14 In.	250.00
Marionette, Kokonut, Out Of The Inkwell, Vinyl, Cloth, Wood, Gund, 1962, 12 In.	63.00
Marseille, 253, Bisque Socket Head, Blue Sleep Googly Eyes, Papier-Mache Body, 7 In. .	550.00
Marseille, 323, Bisque Socket Head, Blue Sleep Googly Eyes, Closed Mouth, 1914, 8 In. .	850.00
Marseille, 323, Googly, Bisque, Papier-Mache Body, Impish Smile, Pug Nose, 7 In.	650.00
Marseille, 323, Googly, Sleep Eyes, Bisque, 5-Piece Papier-Mache, Mohair, c.1920, 7 In. .	400.00
Marseille, 353, Asian Baby, Bisque, Composition, Sleep Eyes, Baby Hair, c.1920, 12 In. .	725.00
Martha Chase, Cloth, Baby, Antique White Gown, c.1920, 16 In.	350.00
Martha Chase, Cloth, Stockinet, Painted Face, Brown Eyes, Closed Mouth, 21 In.	750.00
Mary Hoyer, Composition, Ball Gown, Gold Slippers, 14 In.	435.00
Mary Hoyer, Gigi, Plastic, Green Sleep Eyes, Gown, Mink Stole, Early 1950s, 18 In.	1500.00
Mary Hoyer, Green Sleep Eyes, Brown Mohair, White Negligee, Tag, Box, 1950s, 14 In. .	425.00
Mary Hoyer, Plastic, Blue Sleep Eyes, Red Mohair Wig, Jointed At Head, 1950s, 14 In. . .	259.00
Mattel, Barbie, American Girl, Blond Hair, Blue Eyes, 1965, 11 In.	2200.00
Mattel, Barbie, Blond Hair, Barbie-Q Outfit, Pink Dress, Silver Earrings, 1959, 11 In. . . .	13500.00
Mattel, Barbie, Brunette Hair, Blue-Eyes, Bendable Leg, 1964, 11 In.	3400.00
Mattel, Barbie, Bubble Cut, Blond, Blue Eyes, 1961, 11 In.	200.00
Mattel, Barbie, Bubble Cut, Blond, Blue Eyes, 1963, 11 In.	650.00
Mattel, Barbie, Bubble Cut, Side-Part, Blue Eyes, Auburn Hair, 1965, 11 In.	400.00
Mattel, Barbie, Career Girl, Brunette Hair, Blue Eyes, 1962, 11 In.	850.00
Mattel, Barbie, Empress Bride	1100.00
Mattel, Barbie, Enchanted Evening, Pink Satin Gown, Accessories, Box, 1963	1000.00
Mattel, Barbie, Evening Glamour, Rhinestone Jewelry, Box, 1963	1550.00
Mattel, Barbie, Happy Holiday, Box, 1988	1200.00
Mattel, Barbie, Holiday Princess	80.00
Mattel, Barbie, In Holland, Blue Eyes, Blond Ponytail, Dutch Girl Outfit, 1964, 11 In. . . .	475.00
Mattel, Barbie, Moon Goddess	200.00
Mattel, Barbie, Nighty Negligee, Auburn Hair, Bubble Cut, Pink Gown, 11 In.	375.00
Mattel, Barbie, No. 1, Blond, Black & White Swimsuit, Stand, 1959, 11 In.	1700.00
Mattel, Barbie, No. 3, Blond, Blue Eyes, Gold Dress & Coat, Fur Trim, 1960, 11 In.	4400.00
Mattel, Barbie, No. 3, Brunette, Side-Glancing Eyes, Sunglasses, 1960, 11 In.	650.00
Mattel, Barbie, No. 4, Blond, Blue Side-Glancing Eyes, Pearl Earrings, 1961, 11 In.	650.00
Mattel, Barbie, No. 5, Black Trunk, Accessories	550.00
Mattel, Barbie, Platinum Ponytail, Box	711.00
Mattel, Barbie, Ponytail, Titian Hair	375.00
Mattel, Barbie, Quick Curl, Original Box, 1972	45.00
Mattel, Barbie, Senior Prom, Brunette Ponytail, Blue Eyes, Aqua Gown, 1962, 11 In.	1250.00
Mattel, Barbie, Senior Prom, Satin, Tulle Formal, Shoes, Box, 1964	150.00

Mattel, Barbie, Side-Part, Bubble Cut, Bendable Legs, Blue Eyes, Blond, 1965, 11 In. ... 650.00
Mattel, Barbie, Silver Screen, Box 190.00
Mattel, Barbie, Solo In The Spotlight, Classic Black Gown, Accessories, Box, 1964 . . . . . 400.00
Mattel, Barbie, Special Expressions, Black, Made For Woolworth's, Box, 1989, 11 In. ... 25.00
Mattel, Barbie, Titian Swirl, Turquoise Side Glancing Eyes, Red Hair, 1964, 11 In. 500.00
Mattel, Charmin' Chatty, Plastic, 120 Different Phrases, 5 Mini Records, Box, 24 In. 180.00
Mattel, Christie, Talking, Brown Vinyl, Brown Eyes, Brown Wig, Box, c.1968, 11 In. ... 125.00
Mattel, Herman Munster, Talking, Stuffed, 1964 . . . . 400.00
Mattel, Holly Hobbie, Box 45.00
Mattel, Julia, Brown Vinyl, Twist & Turn Waist, TV Personality, Box, c.1969, 11 In. 125.00
Mattel, Ken, Bendable Legs, Turquoise Eyes, Brown Hair, 1985, 12 In. 300.00
Mattel, Ken, Doctor, Blue Eyes, Brown Hair, 1962, 12 In. 350.00
Mattel, Ken, In Holland, Blue Eyes, Blond Hair, Dutch Boy Outfit, 12 In. 350.00
Mattel, Ken, In Switzerland, Blue Eyes, Bond Hair, Dutch Outfit, 12 In. 300.00
Mattel, Ken, No. 1, Teal Eyes, Blond Flocked Hair, Sandals, 1961, 12 In. 170.00
Mattel, Ken, Ski Champion, Blue Eyes, Brown Hair, 1962, 12 In. 300.00
Mattel, Ken, Time For Tennis, Blue Eyes, Blond Hair, 1962, 12 In. 225.00
Mattel, Midge, Blue Eyes, Blond, Blue Suit, Shoes, 1963, 11 In. 175.00
Mattel, Midge, Blue Eyes, Freckles, Titian Wig, Chartreuse & Orange Suit, 1963, 11 In. . 200.00
Mattel, Midge, Straight Legs, 1963 . . . . 85.00
Mattel, Rickey, Blue Eyes, Freckles, Red Hair, Original Trunks, 1965, 9 In. 50.00
Mattel, Skipper, Bendable Legs, 1965 . . . . 20.00
Mattel, Skipper, Japanese, Blue Eyes, Blond Hair, 1963, 9 In. 500.00
Mattel, Skipper, Red Hair, Blue Eyes, 1964, 9 In. 125.00
Mattel, Skooter, Blond Hair, Brown Eyes, Freckles, Original Swim Suit, 1965, 9 In. 110.00
Mattel, Skooter, Titian Hair, Brown Eyes, Freckles, 1964, 9 In. 60.00
Mattel, Stacey, Talking, Red Hair, Blue Eyes, Box, c.1968, 11 In. 125.00
Mignonette, Bisque, Swivel Head, Blue Eyes, Closed Mouth, 1890, 2 In., Pair . . . .475.00 to 525.00
Mignonette, Bisque, Swivel Head, Blue Glass Eyes, Blond Mohair Wig, 4 1/2 In. 700.00
Mignonette, Bisque, Swivel Head, Blue Glass Eyes, Peg Jointed, Silk Dress, 4 1/2 In. ... 550.00
Mignonette, Bisque, Swivel Head, Blue Sleep Eyes, Closed Mouth, 1885, 5 1/2 In. 1050.00
Mignonette, Bisque, Swivel Head, Blue Sleep Eyes, Open Mouth, 1885, 6 In. 850.00
Mignonette, Brown Bisque, Swivel Head, Brown Sleep Eyes, Open Mouth, 1890, 7 In. . . 850.00
Milliner's Model, Papier-Mache, Kid Body, Wooden Arms & Legs, 10 In. 595.00
Monica, Composition, Painted Eyes, Blond Human Hair, Bridesmaid, c.1940, 21 In. 350.00
Morimura, Bisque, Composition Body, Ball-Jointed, 15 In. 260.00
Morimura, Bisque, Sleep Eyes, 12 In. 198.00
Mortimer Snerd, Walker, Windup, Tin Lithograph, Marx, 8 In. 220.00
Nancy Ann Storybook, Scotch, Bisque, Blond Mohair Wig, Jointed Body, 1939, 5 In. ... 950.00
Nancy Lee, Arranbee, Sleep Eyes, Long Polka Dot Dress, Socks & Shoes, 14 In. 250.00
Nippon, Baby Bud, Bisque, 4 1/2 In. 50.00
Nippon, Bisque, Baby, Movable Arms, 6 In. 22.00
Nippon, Googly Eyes, Ball-Jointed Composition Body, 15 In. 2495.00
Norah Wellings, Belinda, Black Wool Type Hair, 33 In. 850.00
Norah Wellings, Chad Valley Boy, Red Hair, 16 In. 750.00
Norah Wellings, Royal Canadian Mountie, Stuffed, Red Coat, 1920-1930, 14 In. 285.00
Norah Wellings, Violet, 17 1/2 In. 195.00
Notre Dame, Fighting Irish, Stuffed, Removable Hat, 1950s, 11 In. 65.00
Nursemaid & Child, Black Nurse Holding Bisque Baby, 1875, 9 In. 5375.00
Oriental, Kneeling Maiden Wearing Kimono, Ceramic, Rectangular Stand, 14 In. 173.00
Paper dolls are listed in their own category.
Papier-Mache, Baby, Painted Eyes & Hair, c.1880, 13 In. 460.00
Papier-Mache, Black Enamel Inset Eyes, Open Mouth, Original Costume, 1850, 32 In. . . . 2500.00
Papier-Mache, Black Painted Hair, Brown Eyes, Closed Mouth, Germany, 1830, 10 In. . . . 1150.00
Papier-Mache, Black Painted Pate, Black Enamel Inset Eyes, Jointed, 17 In. 750.00
Papier-Mache, Black Peddler, Penny Wooden Body, Hawk Type Face, 9 1/2 In. 1750.00
Papier-Mache, Braided Bun, Molded Comb, 20 In. 2600.00
Papier-Mache, Girl, Holz-Masse On Shoulderplate, 40 In. 1295.00
Papier-Mache, Original Clothes & Wig, 22 In. 1995.00
Papier-Mache, Peddler, Lady Book Seller, Glass Dome, c.1860, 9 1/2 In. 180.00
Papier-Mache, Peddler, Seller Of Religious Artifacts, Velvet Lined Base, 10 In. 150.00
Papier-Mache, Shoulder Head, Black Painted Pate, Black Enamel Inset Eyes, 17 In. 1150.00
Papier-Mache, Shoulder Head, Black Sculpted Hair, Painted Azure Eyes, 1840, 13 In. ... 11100.00

Papier-Mache, Shoulder-Length Curls, Painted Eyes, Kid Body & Upper Limbs, 17 In. . . . 2875.00
Parian, Glass Eyes, Pierced Ears, Bustle Dress, 17 In. 2495.00
Parian, Painted Eyes, Blond Molded Hair, 3 Painted Bands In Hair, 13 In. 795.00
Parian, Swivel Neck, Glass Eyes, Kintzbach Body, Sornheim & Fischer, 1870, 23 In. 1200.00
Parian, Woman, Blond Molded Fancy Hair, Blue & Gold Necklace, 13 In. 795.00
Pincushion dolls are listed in their own category.
Puddin Head, Metal & Composition, Ball-Jointed, Comic Strip, 8 In. 385.00
Puppet, Bamm-Bamm & Pebbles, Plush, Kohner Bros., N.Y., Early 1960s, 3 1/2 In., Pair   62.00
Puppet, Cat In The Hat, 1970, 18 In. 40.00
Puppet, Hand, Al Jolson, Vinyl & Cloth 50.00
Puppet, Hand, Beetle Bailey Sarge 45.00
Puppet, Hand, Felix, Plush, Felt Hand, Steiff, 9 In. 94.00
Puppet, Hand, Muppet, Cloth, 30 In. 45.00
Puppet, Hand, Nestle's Quik, Vinyl Head 100.00
Puppet, Hand, Red Barn Restaurant, Meet Big Barney At The Red Barn, 10 In. 40.00
Puppet, Punch & Judy Set, Wooden Framed Tent, England, 1908 . . . . 2475.00
Puppet, Punch, Judy, Policeman & Devil, Wooden Heads, Feet & Hands, 20 In. 488.00
Puppet, Sailor, Dances When Bar Is Moved, Paint & Wood Lithograph, 15 In. 690.00
Puppet, Spaniel, Sitting, Felt Nose, Tongue, Jointed Head, Knickerbocker, 1940s, 10 In. . 85.00
Puppet, Speedy Gonzalez, Vinyl, Warner Bros., Seven Arts, Japan, Late 1970s, 9 1/2 In. . 25.00
Puppet, Sweettooth Sam, Box 115.00
Rag, Black Girl, Embroidered Face, Plastic Earrings, White Dress, 7 In. 28.00
Ravca, Man & Woman, Marked . . . . *Illus* 265.00
Recknagle, Boy, Painted Googly Eyes, 8 In. 595.00
Revalo, Heubach Head, Blond Mohair Wig, Ball-Jointed Body, 25 In. 995.00
Rudolf Schneider, Wooden, Pin-Jointed, Swivel Head, Glass Eyes, Mohair, 1912, 15 In. . . 450.00
S & H dolls are also listed here as Bergmann and Simon & Halbig.
S & H, 939, Bisque, Closed Mouth, Mohair Wig, Straight Wrist, Ball-Jointed, 30 In. 6700.00
S & H, 949, Paperweight Eyes, Straight Wrist Body, Antique Dress & Shoes, 32 In. 4850.00
S & H, 1248, Santa Claus, Bisque, Brown Eyes, Clothes & Hat, 26 In. 1950.00
S.F.B.J., 8, Tete Jumeau, Bisque, Composition, Jointed, Sleep Eyes, 4 Teeth, Box, 20 In. . . 3100.00
S.F.B.J., 12, Bisque Head, Composition.Upper Teeth, Paperweight Eyes, 25 In. 1150.00
S.F.B.J., 60, Boy, Sleep Eyes, Human Hair, Ball-Jointed, 18 In. 650.00
S.F.B.J., 227, Bisque, Composition, Brown Glass Eyes, Painted Boy's Hair, Teeth, 21 In. . . 1000.00
S.F.B.J., 236, Bisque, Composition, Baby, Glass Eyes, 2 Teeth, Mohair, c.1915, 13 In. 700.00
S.F.B.J., 238, Bisque, Hazel Jewel Eyes, Blond Mohair Wig, Clothes, 18 1/2 In. 3950.00
S.F.B.J., 242, Baby, Nursing, Sleep Eyes, Jointed, 14 In. 2995.00
S.F.B.J., 247, Bisque, Toddler, 15 In. 2495.00
S.F.B.J., 247, Composition Head, Toddler, Open Closed Mouth, Sleep Eyes, 13 In. 595.00
S.F.B.J., 251, Slant Eyes, Dimples, Toddler, 20 In. 2450.00
S.F.B.J., 252, Bisque, Composition, Wood, Pouty Face, Sleep Eyes, Mohair, Label, 26 In. . 10750.00
S.F.B.J., Character, Bisque Socket Head, Composition Body, Jewel Eyes, 19 In. 3500.00
S.F.B.J., Kiss Throwing, Bisque Head, Flirty Eyes, Pierced Ears, Pull String, 22 In. 950.00
Scherf, Bisque Shoulder Head, Kid Body, Bisque Hands, 25 In. 800.00
Schmitt, Bisque, Parted Lips, Blond Wig, White & Lacy Clothes, Leather Shoes, 22 In. . . . 1150.00
Schmitt, Blond Mohair, Antique Clothes, 16 In. 8875.00

Doll, Ravca, Man &
Woman, Marked

**Keep dolls away from
direct sunlight to avoid
fading their hair and
clothes.**

Doll, Schoenhut, Maggie
& Jiggs, 8 & 7 1/2 In., Pair

Schmitt & Fils, Bisque Head, Child, Pale Blue Enamel Eyes, Closed Mouth, 12 In. 16500.00
Schoenau & Hoffmeister, 1906, Bisque Head, Painted Lashes, 4 Teeth, Dress, 26 In. 700.00
Schoenau & Hoffmeister, 1906, Bisque Socket Head, Child, Mohair Wig, 18 In. 325.00
Schoenau & Hoffmeister, 4990, Oriental Boy, 9 In. 795.00
Schoenau & Hoffmeister, Hanna, Bisque Socket Head, Hawaiian Outfit, 6 In. 105.00
Schoenau & Hoffmeister, Princess Elizabeth, Bisque, Jointed Body, Original Clothes 2995.00
Schoenhut, 101, Boy, Open-Close Mouth, Wig 995.00
Schoenhut, 101, Girl, Smiling, Carved Hair 1995.00
Schoenhut, 107, Wood, Socket Head, Pouty, Decal Eyes, Spring Jointed, c.1914, 14 In. .. 500.00
Schoenhut, 1417W, First Patented Walker, Wood, Socket Head, Mohair, 1918, 14 In. 650.00
Schoenhut, Maggie & Jiggs, 8 & 7 1/2 In., Pair ....*Illus* 525.00
Schoenhut, Wooden Head & Body, Toddler, Lower Tooth, Pink Romper, Socks, 16 In. 275.00
Schoenhut, Wooden, Jointed, Painted Eyes, Brown Wig, 23 In. 695.00
Shirley Temple dolls are included in the Shirley Temple category.
Simon & Halbig dolls are also listed here under Bergmann and S & H.
Simon & Halbig, 2 1/4, Bisque, Composition, Blue Sleep Eyes, 4 Teeth, c.1910, 21 In. ... 600.00
Simon & Halbig, 164, Burmese Lady, Bisque, Composition, Sleep Eyes, 4 Teeth, 18 In. .. 1300.00
Simon & Halbig, 719, Bisque Socket Head, Almond Brown Enamel Eyes, 24 In. 5000.00
Simon & Halbig, 719, Bisque Socket Head, Child, Blue Inset Eyes, Auburn Wig, 19 In. .. 4400.00
Simon & Halbig, 719, Bisque Socket Head, Child, Blue Inset Eyes, Open Mouth, 21 In. .. 2200.00
Simon & Halbig, 719, Bisque, Character, Closed Mouth, Blue Eyes, Mohair Wig, 22 In. .. 4495.00
Simon & Halbig, 719, Bisque, Fixed Open Eyes, Metal Body, Music Box, 22 In. 1150.00
Simon & Halbig, 905, Blond Mohair, Paperweight Eyes, 20 In. 1995.00
Simon & Halbig, 920, Fashion, Bisque Shoulder Head, Blond Mohair Wig, 1890, 18 In. .. 1800.00
Simon & Halbig, 927, Bisque Socket Head, Child, Sleep Eyes, Ball-Jointed, 26 In. 1700.00
Simon & Halbig, 929, Bisque Socket Head, Child, Sleep Eyes, Closed Mouth, 14 In. 2500.00
Simon & Halbig, 949, Bisque, Composition, Wood, Jointed, Pouty Face, Mohair, 26 In. .. 2300.00
Simon & Halbig, 949, Bisque, Paperweight Eyes, Ball-Jointed Body, 12 In. 1295.00
Simon & Halbig, 949, Hand Blown Paperweight Eyes, Belton Type Head, 14 In. 1995.00
Simon & Halbig, 1009, Bisque Socket Head, Blue Inset Glass Eyes, Open Mouth, 10 In. . 1000.00
Simon & Halbig, 1009, Bisque Socket Head, Child, Blue Glass Inset Eyes, 1890, 23 In. .. 1200.00
Simon & Halbig, 1009, Bisque Socket Head, Sleep Eyes, Eyelet Antique Dress, 27 In. ... 1500.00
Simon & Halbig, 1039, Bisque Socket Head, Brown Flirty Eyes, Open Mouth, 15 In. 950.00
Simon & Halbig, 1039, Bisque Socket Head, Child, Sleep Eyes, Open Mouth, 13 In. 850.00
Simon & Halbig, 1078, Bisque, Composition, Jointed, Sleep Eyes, Teeth, c.1900, 11 In. .. 600.00
Simon & Halbig, 1079, Bisque Head, Brown Sleep Eyes, Blond Wig, 29 In. 575.00
Simon & Halbig, 1079, Bisque Socket Head, Child, Brown Sleep Eyes, 1905, 32 In. 1500.00
Simon & Halbig, 1079, Bisque, Chunky Body, Original Dress, 37 In. 3350.00
Simon & Halbig, 1079, Bisque, Fixed Open Eyes, Mohair Wig, Fully Jointed, 17 1/2 In. .. 430.00
Simon & Halbig, 1079, Bisque, Sleep Eyes, Brown Mohair Wig, Original Dress, 11 In. ... 975.00
Simon & Halbig, 1079, Brown Bisque Socket Head, Brown Sleep Eyes, 1910, 19 In. 1250.00
Simon & Halbig, 1129, Boy, Bisque Head, Oriental, Human Hair Queue, 17 In. 1840.00
Simon & Halbig, 1159, Ball-Jointed, Antique Clothes, 28 In. 2995.00
Simon & Halbig, 1248, Bisque Socket Head, Child, Sleep Eyes, Ball-Jointed, 14 In. 950.00
Simon & Halbig, 1249, Bisque Socket Head, Child, Sleep Eyes, Open Mouth, 24 In. 1250.00
Simon & Halbig, 1249, Santa Claus, Bisque, Big Eyes, Red Hat, White Beard, 20 In. 1320.00
Simon & Halbig, 1279, Bisque Socket, Glass Sleep Eyes, Open Mouth, 1912, 23 In. 6200.00
Simon & Halbig, 1279, Composition, Toddler, Jointed, Blond Mohair Wig, 10 In. 2010.00
Simon & Halbig, 1299, Bisque, Blue Sleep Eyes, 2 Upper Teeth, Mohair Wig, 13 In. 1000.00
Simon & Halbig, 1299, Bisque, Composition, Wood, Jointed, Sleep Eyes, 2 Teeth, 18 In. . 950.00
Simon & Halbig, 1358, Bisque Socket Head, Large Brown Sleep Eyes, 20 In. 6500.00
Simon & Halbig, 1428, Bisque Head, Baby, Blue Eyes, Smiling, Blond Wig, 13 In. 1035.00
Simon & Halbig, 1428, Bisque, Blue Glass Sleep Eyes, Blond Wig, 11 In. 300.00
Simon & Halbig, 1428/9, Bisque, Composition, Wood, Blue Glass Eyes, c.1912, 15 In. ... 1700.00
Simon & Halbig, 1488, Bisque Socket Head, Baby, Sleep Eyes, Closed Mouth, 25 In. 5250.00
Simon & Halbig, Alabaster Bisque, Cocoa Brown Eyes, Auburn Human Hair Wig, 28 In. . 1250.00
Simon & Halbig, Bisque Head, Flirty Eyes, Teeth, Wood & Composition Jointed, 32 In. .. 1265.00
Simon & Halbig, Bisque Head, Flirty Eyes, Upper Teeth, Ball Jointed Body, 19 In. 1495.00
Simon & Halbig, Bisque Socket Head, Brown Sleep Eyes, Blond Mohair Wig, 24 In. 1050.00
Simon & Halbig, Bisque Socket Head, Child, Sleep Eyes, Blond Mohair Wig, 21 In. 700.00
Simon & Halbig, Bisque Socket Head, Composition, Human Hair Wig, 30 In. 1600.00
Simon & Halbig, Bisque Swivel Head, Blue Enamel Eyes, Wearing Costume, 12 In. 1200.00

Simon & Halbig, Bisque, Composition, Jointed, Sleep Eyes, 4 Teeth, Mohair, 22 In. 7250.00
Simon & Halbig, Fashion, Bisque, Twill Over Wood Body, Glass Eyes, c.1880, 15 In. 3500.00
Simon & Halbig, Swivel Head, Brown Sleep Eyes, Bisque Arms, Antique Clothes, 24 In. . 650.00
Skippy, Army Outfit, Pin On Hat, 14 In. 375.00
Skookum, Indian, 12 In. 135.00
Skookum, Indian, 14 In. 95.00
Skookum, Squaw, Composition, Box, 1930s, 9 1/2 In. 450.00
Soldier, Composition, Cloth Uniform, Black Leather Boots, 1945-1950, 10 In. 150.00
Sonja Henie, Composition, Tagged Clothes, 17 In. 995.00
Sonneberg, Bisque Socket Head, Composition, Wood, Blue Glass Eyes, Mohair, 15 In. .. 1300.00
Sonneberg, Bisque, Composition Body, Child, Original Dress, 10 In. 995.00
Squirt, Doll, Boy, Trademark, Blond Hair, Green Shirt, Red Pants, 17 In. 94.00
Steiff, Clownie, Vinyl Head, Glass Eyes, Painted Face, Hair, 16 In. 575.00
Steiff, Dutch Girl, Helen, Black Steel Eyes, c.1913, 13 3/4 In. 1150.00
Steiff, Tabby Cat, Glass Eyes, Felt Ears, Button, Jointed, 5 In. 65.00
Steiner, Baby Girl, Bisque Socket Head, Blue Paperweight Eyes, Closed Mouth, 18 In. .. 4700.00
Steiner, Bebe Gigoteur, Bisque, Composition, Waves Arms, Says Mama, c.1890, 17 In. .. 2000.00
Steiner, Bebe Mascotte, Bisque, Paperweight Eyes, Original Clothes, 28 In. 5995.00
Steiner, Bisque Head, Blue Paperweight Eyes, Blond Mohair Wig, Closed Mouth, 18 In. . 6000.00
Steiner, Bisque Socket Head, Blue Glass Sleep Eyes, Original Turkish Costume, 15 In. ... 2500.00
Steiner, Bisque Socket Head, Brown Glass Paperweight Eyes, Red Clown Wig, 15 In. ... 5400.00
Steiner, Bisque, Composition, Wood, Jointed, Paperweight Eyes, Auburn Mohair, 17 In. .. 5600.00
Steiner, Bisque, Composition, Wood, Jointed, Wire Lever Sleep Eyes, Mohair Wig, 23 In. 4500.00
Steiner, Bisque, Open Mouth, Paperweight Eyes, Antique Clothing, 16 In. 2995.00
Steiner, Blue Glass Enamel Inset Eyes, Blond Mohair Wig, Composition Body, 8 In. 3000.00
Steiner, Gigoteur, Kicking, Screaming, Key Wind Side, Cries Mama, 22 1/2 In. 3500.00
Steiner, Jointed Composition Body, Paperweight Eyes, Marked, 8 1/2 In. 3800.00
Steiner, Phenix, Socket Head, Composition, Metal Hands, Paperweight Eyes, 20 In. 2500.00
Stocking-Type, Girl, Stitched Blue Eyes, Nose & Ears, Original Clothes, 18 In. 850.00
Terri Lee, Jerri-Lee, Painted Eyes, Saran Wig, Hard Plastic Head, 1952, 16 In. ....620.00 to 625.00
Terri Lee, Patty Jo, Painted Brown Eyes, Black Lashes, Silky Long Wig, 1951, 16 In. 700.00
Terri Lee, Patty Jo, Painted Brown Eyes, Coarse Black Rolled Wig, Plastic Head, 16 In. .. 1150.00
Terri Lee, Tiny, Hard Plastic Head, Inset Eyes, Walking Mechanism, 10 In. 255.00
Tete Jumeau, 8, Bisque, Composition, Wood, Jointed, Paperweight Eyes, c.1890, 19 In. .. 4000.00
Tete Jumeau, 11, Bisque, Composition, Jointed, Paperweight Eyes, Mohair, 1888, 23 In. . 4000.00
Tete Jumeau, Bisque, Amber Paperweight Eyes, Long Blond Human Hair, 20 In. 5375.00
Tete Jumeau, Bisque, Long Blond Mohair Signed Head, 28 In. 6875.00
Tete Jumeau, Bisque, Paperweight Eyes, Artist Signed, Antique Clothes & Shoes, 32 In. . 6750.00
Tete Jumeau, Bisque, Paperweight Eyes, Chunky Body, Antique Costume, 31 In. 3975.00
Tete Jumeau, Bisque, Walker Body, Paperweight Eyes, Marked, 20 In. 5250.00
Tete Jumeau, Brown Paperweight Eyes, Lashes, Human Hair Wig, 24 In. 1800.00
Tete Jumeau, Closed Mouth, Blue Paperweight Eyes, French Style Dress, 21 In. 4750.00
Tete Jumeau, Girl, Blue Eyes, Original Long Tail Mohair Wig, Organdy Dress, 23 In. ... 550.00
Tete Jumeau, Painted Lashes, Long Chestnut Human Hair Wig, Silk Dress, Shoes, 14 In. . 3875.00
Tete Jumeau, Paperweight Eyes, Closed Mouth, Ball-Jointed Body, 22 In. 4000.00
Tete Jumeau, Paperweight Eyes, Closed Mouths, Antique Clothing, 17 In. 4495.00
Tete Jumeau, Sapphire Blue Eyes, Chemise, Signed Shoes, Extra Dress, 28 In. 6850.00
Thullier, A7T, Bisque, Composition, Jointed, Paperweight Eyes, Mohair, c.1888, 16 In. .. 11500.00
Tin Shoulder Head, Kid Body, Porcelain Forearms, Old Dress, Germany, 23 In. 40.00
Tubby Tom, Box, 13 In. 900.00
Turner, Dorothy, Wizard Of Oz, Toto In Basket, Soft Plastic, In Cardboard Sleeve, 14 In. . 30.00
Twin, In Bassinet, Mechanical, Wave When Wheels Turned, Germany, Pair 330.00
Unger, Cell-U-Pon, Female, Hollow Fiberboard, Pale Green, Flesh Tones, 13 In. 60.00
Unis, 60, Brown Bisque, Open Mouth, Glass Eyes, 5-Piece Composition Body, 10 In. 33.00
Ventriloquist Dummy, Danny O'day, Box, 22 In. 40.00
Ventriloquist Dummy, Farfel, Jimmy Nelson's TV Dog, With Record Box, 1950s 210.00
Ventriloquist Dummy, Jerry Mahoney, Original Clothing, Box, 1940s 420.00
Ventriloquist Dummy, Juro, Danny O'Day, Box, Booklet, Record, 1950s 155.00
Ventriloquist Dummy, Moe Howard, 3 Stooges, Vinyl Head, Hands, 36 In. 175.00
Vogue, Baby, Hard Plastic, 1976, 19 In. 75.00
Vogue, Brikette, Box, 22 In. 150.00
Vogue, Ginny, Clown Outfit, Satin Shoes & Hat, 1950s 30.00

Vogue, Ginny, Debs, Walker, Blue Sleep Eyes, Blond Wig, Formal, Box, c.1956, 8 In. ... 300.00
Vogue, Ginny, Kindergarten, Brown Sleep Eyes, Blond Pixie Wig, Tag, c.1952, 7 1/2 In. ... 400.00
Vogue, Ginny, Kindergarten, Sleep Eyes, Blond Dynel Wig, Plastic Head, 1952, 8 In. 450.00
Vogue, Ginny, Plastic Head, Brown Sleep Eyes, Auburn Poodle Wig, 1952, 8 In. 55.00
Vogue, Ginny, Ring Master, 8 In. 44.00
Vogue, Ginny, Scotch, Blue Sleep Eyes, Red Dynel Wig, Plastic Head, Box, 1952, 8 In. .. 400.00
Vogue, Ginny, Tightrope Walker, 8 In. 36.00
Vogue, Ginny, Walker, Blue Sleep Eyes, Brown Dynel Wig, Plastic Head, 1954, 8 In. 250.00
Vogue, Toddles, Bride, Composition Head, Bride Dress, Underclothing, Veil, 8 In. 185.00
Vogue, Toddles, Hansel & Gretel, Painted Eyes, Blond Mohair, c.1942, 7 1/2 In., Pair 450.00
Vogue, Toddles, Julie, Composition Head, Mohair Wig, Bib Pants, Knit Shirt, Shoes, 8 In. 155.00
Vogue, Toddles, Mistress Mary, Composition Head, Blue Eyes, 5-Piece Body, 7 In. 310.00
Vogue, Toddles, Red Riding Hood, Composition Head, Painted Eyes, 8 In. 275.00
Walkure, Bisque Head, Original Brown Human Hair Wig, Fully Jointed, 1920, 33 In. 920.00
Wax, Rooted Hair, Glass Eyes, Broidery Anglaise Gown, 17 In. 1100.00
Wooden, Clown, Red Suit, 8 In. 145.00
Wooden, Peddler, Painted Hair With Spit Curls, Original Costume, Wares, 9 In. 3700.00
Woodsy Owl, Teaches How To Dress, Cloth, Amway Corp., Box, 1973, 14 In. 38.00

DONALD DUCK items are included in the Disneyana category.

DOORSTOPS have been made in all types of designs. The vast majority of the doorstops sold today are cast iron and were made from about 1890 to 1930. Most of them are shaped like people, animals, flowers, or ships. Reproductions and newly designed examples are sold in gift shops.

Airplane, Spirit Of St. Louis, Cast Iron 165.00
Alpine Box, With Flower Basket, Iron, 7 1/4 In. 220.00
Aunt Jemima, Cast Iron, 9 In. ....55.00 to 75.00
Aunt Jemima, Wearing Brick Red Dress, White Apron, Littco Products, 13 x 8 In. ... 605.00
Basket Of Flowers, Bow On Handle, Cast Iron, Original Paint, 10 3/4 x 8 1/2 In. 80.00
Basket Of Flowers, Polychrome Paint, Cast Iron, 15 1/4 In. 140.00
Basket Of Fruit, Twisted Handle, Cherries At Base, Cast Iron, 12 x 10 In. 140.00
Black Bellhop, Original Paint, 8 In. 800.00
Bouquet, Lilies & Daisies In Urn, Triangular Base, Painted, Cast Iron, 10 x 8 In. 168.00
Bouquet, Poppies, Footed Vase, Painted, Cast Iron, 11 x 8 In. 168.00
Boy Blue With Bear, Albany Foundry, 5 1/4 x 3 1/2 In. 935.00
Boy With Fruit Basket, Cast Iron, 9 1/4 x 3 7/8 In. 300.00
Cat, Black, Cast Iron ....150.00 to 235.00
Cat, Halloween, Cast Iron ....*Illus* 935.00
Cat, Hunchback, Full Figure, 10 1/2 In. 330.00
Cat, Seated, Gray, White, Green, Cast Iron, 7 7/8 In. 214.00
Cat, Silhouette, Cast Iron ....*Illus* 138.00
Cat, Sitting, Cast Iron, 10 In. ....*Illus* 193.00
Cat, Standing, Open Mouth, Green Base, Hubley 1540.00
Charleston Dancers, Hubley, 8 7/8 x 5 3/8 In. ....935.00 to 1760.00
Clipper Ship, Cast Iron, 9 In. 120.00
Cockatoo, Marked DSS, Cast Iron, 11 3/4 In. 265.00
Cockatoo, White, 11 1/4 x 9 1/2 In. 1760.00
Conestoga Wagon, Cast Iron, 8 3/8 In. 240.00
Cosmos, Vase, Black-Eyed Susans, Iron, Hubley, 17 x 10 In. 1870.00
Cottage, Cape Cod, Light Green Roof, White House, Fence, Hubley, 5 1/2 x 7 3/4 In. ... 462.00
Cottage, Cape Cod, Medium Green Roof, Green Shutters, Eastern Specialty Mfg. Co. ... 352.00
Cottage, In The Woods, Red Roof, National Foundry, 4 5/8 x 10 In. 330.00
Cottage, Light Blue Shutters, Orange Roof, Red Chimney, Hubley, 5 3/4 x 7 1/2 In. 418.00
Cottage, Pastel Cream & Green, Yellow Flowers, Brick Chimney, Cast Iron, 6 x 7 In. 155.00
Cottage, With Fence, Thatched Room, Red Chimney, Hubley, 4 3/4 x 7 1/4 In. 935.00
Covered Wagon, Brass Finish, 1931 .... 45.00
Covered Wagon, Cast Iron, 6 1/4 x 3 5/8 In. ....135.00 to 150.00
Daisy Bowl, Hubley, 7 1/2 x 5 1/8 In. 418.00
Dog, Afghan, Standing, Full Figure, Red, Light Tan, 11 x 14 In. 825.00
Dog, Boston Terrier, Cast Iron, 9 1/2 In. 99.00
Dog, Boston Terrier, Original Paint, Cast Iron, 9 In. 200.00

Doorstop, Cat,
Halloween, Cast Iron

Doorstop, Cat,
Silhouette, Cast Iron

Doorstop,
Cat, Sitting,
Cast Iron, 10 In.

Dog, Boston, Terrier, Cast Iron, 8 x 10 In. 135.00
Dog, Boxer, Waynesburg, Virginia, 8 In. 240.00
Dog, Cocker Spaniel, Marked Va Metalcrafters, Waynesboro, Va., 1949, 9 In. 165.00
Dog, Dachshund, Sitting Up, Dark Brown, Dick Brothers, 1931, 11 1/8 x 5 In. 1325.00
Dog, Dachshund, Standing, Full Figure, Black, Short Haired, 5 1/2 x 9 1/2 In. 990.00
Dog, Fox Terrier, 8 1/2 x 8 1/4 In. 110.00
Dog, German Shepherd, Sitting, Ears Up, Bronze Patina, Cast Iron, 9 1/2 x 6 1/2 In. 90.00
Dog, Great Dane, Sitting, Red, 6 1/2 x 12 In. 1045.00
Dog, Malamute, Standing, Burnt Orange, Creation Co., 1930, 7 1/2 x 6 In. 660.00
Dog, Mutt, Pup, Yawning, Full Figure, 7 x 5 In. 605.00
Dog, Pekinese, Standing, Full Figure, Black Nose, Red, Hubley, 14 1/2 x 9 In. 1650.00
Dog, Pointer, Full Figure, Black & White Paint, Cast Iron, 15 1/2 In. ....220.00 to 250.00
Dog, Resting, Cast Iron, 8 1/2 In. 165.00
Dog, Russian Wolfhound, Standing, Full Figure, Black, Brown, 7 3/4 x 12 In. 352.00
Dog, Schnauzer, Cast Iron, 16 In. 75.00
Dog, Scottie, Marked Wilton Products Inc., Wrightsville, Pa., 7 3/4 x 4 1/2 In. 195.00
Dog, Sealyham, Hubley, 9 1/2 x 13 In. 660.00
Dog, Springer Spaniel, White Body, Black Markings, 6 3/4 x 7 In. 935.00
Dog, St. Bernard, Lying Down, White, Light Tan, Hubley, 3 1/2 x 10 1/2 In. 1100.00
Dog, Terrier, Black & Tan, Cast Iron 150.00
Dog, Terrier, Cast Iron, Hubley Sticker, 4 3/4 x 5 1/2 In. ....150.00 to 200.00
Dog, Welsh Corgi, Light Brown, Full Figure, 8 x 9 1/2 In. 308.00
Dog, Whippet, Light Brown, Tan, Full Figure, 8 x 9 1/2 In. 308.00
Dog, White Pug, Seated, Bone, Green Base, Cast Iron, 5 1/4 In. 230.00
Dolly Dimple, Cast Iron, 7 In. 165.00
Duck, Black, Signed, Large 395.00
Duck, Yellow, Orange Beak, Hubley, 5 x 3 3/4 In. 462.00
Ducks, Iron, Hubley 475.00
Dutch Boy, Wearing Black Pants, Hat, Judd Co., 7 1/2 x 6 In. 880.00
Dutch Girl, Holding Baskets, Judd Co., 7 1/8 x 5 3/4 In. 220.00
Dutch Girl, Red Skirt, Dark Green Apron, Full Figure, Judd Co., 6 x 3 3/4 In. 220.00
Elephant, Palm Tree, Cast Iron, 14 In. 265.00
Elephant, Trunk Up, 14 In. 350.00
English Coach, Horses, Cast Iron 150.00
Farm House, Brown, Green Shutter, Bradley & Hubbard, 6 x 8 In. 1760.00
Fireplace, Painted, Cast Iron, 7 7/8 x 5 7/8 In. 195.00
Fireside Cat, Gray & White, Hubley ....245.00 to 280.00
Flower Basket, Cast Iron, 7 1/2 In., Pair 242.00
Flower Basket, Cast Iron, 9 1/2 In. 90.00
Flower Basket, Lilies Of The Valley, Off-White Body, Pink Base, Hubley, 10 x 7 In. 308.00
Flower Basket, Petunias & Asters, Cream Body, Hubley, 9 1/2 x 5 1/2 In. 308.00
Flower Basket, Poppies & Cornflowers, Hubley, 7 1/4 x 6 In. 462.00
Flower Basket, Poppies & Snapdragons, Pink Base, Hubley, 7 1/2 x 5 In. 330.00
Flower Basket, Red Poppies, Black Center, Hubley 308.00

Flower Vase, Marked Hubley Made In U.S.A. 465, 10 3/4 x 6 1/2 In. 660.00
Flowerpot, Black Striped, Nasturtiums, Hubley, 7 1/4 x 6 1/2 In. 495.00
Flowerpot, Poppies, Red, Black Centers, Iron, Hubley, 7 x 6 In. 352.00
Flowers, Vase, Cast Iron, 3 7/8 x 7 1/8 In. 110.00
Fox, In Hollow, Vines, Leaves, Grapes, Polychrome Paint, 19th Century, 11 1/2 In. 358.00
Fruit Basket, Albany Foundry, 10 x 7 In. 275.00
Geisha, Cast Iron, Hubley, 7 In. 70.00
Girl With Bonnet, Standing, Waverly Studios, 8 x 5 1/4 In. 605.00
Girl With Dog, Standing, Wearing White Hat, 7 x 6 In. 1870.00
Gladiolus, Hubley, Marked 489, 10 x 8 In. 275.00
Gnome, The Warrior, Cast Iron, 13 1/2 In. 374.00
Golfer, Poised To Hit Ball, Cast Iron, 8 In. 415.00
Golfer, Putting, Iron, Worn Paint, Hubley, 8 In. ....695.00 to 770.00
Heron, Cast Iron, 7 1/2 x 5 1/8 In. 245.00
Horse, Full Figure, Palomino Painted, 8 In. 60.00
Horse, Iron, Repainted White 55.00
Horse, With Saddle & Bridle, Cast Iron 75.00
House, Judd Co., Marked, CJO 1288, 8 x 4 1/2 In. 275.00
House, With Woman, Embossed, Marked, Eastern Specialty Mfg.Co., 5 1/2 x 8 In. 715.00
Huckleberry Finn, Wearing Blue Overalls, Yellow Hat, Littco Products, 12 x 9 In. 1045.00
Indian, Cast Iron, 7 7/8 In. ....125.00 to 185.00
Indian Chief, Cast Iron, A.A. Richardson, Copyright 1927, 9 In. 980.00
Iris, Hubley ....295.00 to 585.00
Jiggs & Maggie, Wooden, Pair 65.00
Jill, Holding Flower Basket, Hubley, 8 3/4 x 5 3/4 In. 715.00
Kitten, Cast Iron, 8 In. 245.00
Lighthouse, Cast Iron 135.00
Little Colonial Lady, Cast Iron 100.00
Little Red Riding Hood & Wolf, Wearing Red Cape, National Foundry, 7 x 5 3/8 In. 462.00
London Royal Mail Coach, Cast Iron, 12 3/8 x 7 1/4 In. ....120.00 to 145.00
Lovebird, Cast Iron, 11 1/2 In. 1260.00
Mail Coach, Nuydea, Cast Iron, 8 x 7 In. 75.00
Mammy, Cast Iron, 13 1/2 x 8 In. 200.00
Mammy, Cast Iron, Painted, 9 In. 440.00
Mary Quite Contrary, Wearing Yellow Dress, Littco Products, 11 3/8 x 9 5/8 In. 1320.00
Monkey, Reading Book On Evolution, Marked 695.00
Old Salt, Cast Iron, 11 x 4 1/8 In. ....75.00 to 170.00
Olive Picker, Wearing Cape, Hat, Hubley, 7 3/4 x 8 3/4 In. 1320.00
Oriental Girl, Cast Iron, 8 In. 260.00
Owl, Cast Iron, 11 1/4 In. 485.00
Pansy Bowl, Light Blue Stripes On Body Of Bowl, Hubley, 7 x 6 1/2 In. 495.00
Parrot, Dark Brown, Olive Green Chest, 11 1/2 x 4 3/4 In. 88.00
Parrot, In A Ring, Cast Iron 195.00
Parrot, On Stump, Cast Iron, 6 1/2 In. 160.00
Pirate, With Sack On Back, Cast Iron, Paint Loss, 12 In. 695.00
Poppy Basket, Marked C.H. Co., E110, 10 1/2 x 8 In. 605.00
Prairie Schooner, Blue, Red & Cream Paint, Cast Iron, 8 1/2 x 11 1/2 In. 112.00
Punch & Judy, Punch, Holding Quill Pen, Cast Iron, 1900, 12 In., Pair 1495.00
Rabbit, By Fence, Dark Brown, Albany Foundry, 6 7/8 x 8 1/8 In. 440.00
Rabbit, Iron 165.00
Rabbit, Seated, Cast Iron 460.00
Rabbit, Standing, Cabbage, 8 1/8 x 4 7/8 In. 308.00
Race Horse, King's Genius, Cast Iron 90.00
Reading Girls, Sitting, 1 In Blue Dress & 1 In Red Dress, 5 x 8 5/8 In. 2200.00
Rooster, Cast Iron, 4 5/8 x 7 In. 165.00
Rooster, Standing, Green Base, 13 x 8 1/2 In. 990.00
Satyr Head Wearing Cornucopia Hat, Cast Iron, 11 1/4 In. 193.00
Scottish Highlander, With Staff, Cast Iron, 12 3/4 In. ....83.00 to 200.00
Soldier, In Revolutionary Era Uniform, Sword, Tiered Pedestal, Cast Iron, 13 x 6 In. 90.00
Southern Belle, Bonnet, Long Skirt, Shawl & Bouquet, Painted, Cast Iron, 12 x 6 In. 90.00
Stagecoach, 2 Horses, Cast Iron 150.00
Stork, Standing, Green Body, Dark Red Beak, Hubley, 5 1/2 x 3 1/2 In. 550.00

Sunbonnet Girl, Cast Iron 115.00
Swan, Marked, Spencer Guilford, Ct., 20 Sides, 8 x 13 In. 2970.00
Tulip Bouquet, Cast Iron ....150.00 to 295.00
Tulips, Soft Blue, Bronze 165.00
Turkey, Red Wattle, Black, 12 In. 1200.00
Turtle, Green, Cast Iron, 2 x 7 1/2 In. 160.00
Windmill, Burnt Orange, Embossed, A.M. Greenblatt Studios, Boston, 1926, 6 In. 2750.00
Witch, Cast Iron, Wooden Base, 15 In. 295.00
Woman, Sharp Profile, Yellow Paint, Bradley & Hubbard, 12 In. 1895.00
Woodsman With Pipe, Axe & Dog, Leading On Tree, Cast Iron, 15 1/2 x 4 1/2 In. 90.00
World War I Biplane, 19 1/2 In. 50.00
Zinnias, Hubley, 9 3/4 x 8 1/2 In. 115.00

DORCHESTER POTTERY was founded by George Henderson in 1895 in Dorchester, Massachusetts. At first, the firm made utilitarian stoneware, but collectors are most interested in the line of decorated blue and white pottery that Dorchester made from 1940 until it went out of business in 1979.

DORCHESTER POTTERY WORKS BOSTON, MASS.

Bowl, Blueberry, Blue Swirl Center, 6 1/2 In. 400.00
Bowl, Cereal, Good Morning, Pumpkin Center, Walking 220.00
Bowl, Cereal, Poinsettia Center, Blue Banded Floral Rim, 2 1/4 x 5 3/4 In. 192.00
Cruet, Stopper, Pussy Willow Design, White Buds, Deep Blue Ground, 4 1/2 In. 357.00
Cup, All Gone, Peter Pumpkin Eater, Wife In Pumpkin, Signed, 1951, 3 x 4 In. 247.00
Jam Jar, Cover, Stylized Strawberry, Blossoms, Blue, Knesseth Denisons, 3 1/4 In. 137.00
Mug, Anchors Aweigh, Anchor & Nautical, Handle, Knesseth Denisons, 5 In. 137.00
Mug, Captain, Deep Blue, White Ground, Handle, Knesseth Denisons, 4 3/4 In. 110.00
Mug, Harbor Lights, Lighthouse, Blue, White Ground, Knesseth Denisons, 4 3/4 In. 110.00
Mug, Rooster, Knesseth Denisons, 4 3/4 In. 137.00
Mug, Sailors' Horn Pipe, Sailor, Nautical, Handle, Knesseth Denisons, 4 3/4 In. ... 110.00
Mug, Whale In Water, Thar She Blows, Knesseth Denisons, Handle, 5 In. 137.00
Pitcher, Ship, Multi Blue Glaze, Reverse Anchor, Handle, K. Denisons, 7 x 8 In. 330.00
Plaque, Border, Stylized, Swirling Waves, Religious Motto Center, J.W.R., 12 In. 825.00

DOULTON pottery and porcelain were made by Doulton and Co. of Burslem, England, after 1882. The name *Royal Doulton* appeared on their wares after 1902. Other pottery by Doulton is listed under Royal Doulton.

Barrel, Spirit, 6 Cooper's Straps, Base Spigot, Lambeth, c.1880, 23 3/4 In. 402.00
Biscuit Jar, Blue & Tan Geometric, Stylized Flowers, Salt Glaze, Lambeth ....*Illus* 250.00
Bowl, Gold Overlay, Blue & White, Late 1800s, 11 3/4 In. 375.00
Cake Set, Watteau, Flow Blue, 8 Plates, c.1890, 9 Piece 850.00
Candlestick, Silicon, Lambeth 150.00
Dish, Gold, Pastel Water Lily, Scalloped Edge, Burslem, No. 71806, 7 In. ....*Illus* 95.00
Jardiniere, Blue Irises, Gold & White Ground, Burslem, 9 1/2 In. 220.00
Jug, Christmas, Brown, Tan, Lambeth, 2 In. 70.00
Jug, Special Highland Whiskey, Applied Ship Label, Brown, Olive, Cream, 7 1/8 In. 140.00

Doulton, Biscuit Jar, Blue & Tan Geometric, Stylized Flowers, Salt Glaze, Lambeth

Doulton, Dish, Gold, Pastel Water Lily, Scalloped Edge, Burslem, No. 71806, 7 In.

Lamp, Brass, Etched Shade, Stoneware, A.B. Barlow, c.1873, 21 In. 595.00
Pitcher, Blackberry & Blossom, Burslem, 8 1/2 In. 150.00
Pitcher, Salt Glaze, Brown Design, 1905, Lambeth, 2 1/4 In. 95.00
Pitcher, Watteau, Flow Blue, 10 1/2 In. 450.00
Pitcher & Bowl, Roses & Leaves, White To Golden Tan, Gold Trim, 17 x 13 3/4 In. 370.00
Plate, Child's, Peter Piper Nursery Rhyme, 8 In. 75.00
Plate, Henry VIII 135.00
Plate, Orchids 85.00
Plate, Persian Spray, Scroll Sunburst Design, Cobalt Blue, 1910, 10 3/8 In. 302.00
Plate, Rose & Thistle 50.00
Plate, Toxophilite 95.00
Umbrella Holder, Birds, Flowers, Blue, Ivory, Tapered Cylinder, Kensington, 24 In. 575.00
Umbrella Holder, Daffodil, Transfer & Hand Painting, Ivory Ground, 23 In. 550.00
Umbrella Holder, Floral & Bird Design, Blue, White, Gilt, Burslem, 23 1/2 In. 230.00
Vase, Brown Cover, Star & Bun Design, 1910, 2 1/2 In. 95.00
Vase, Bud, Stratford Church, Blue & White, Burslem 170.00
Vase, Mules, Grazing, Signed, Frank Butler, 1883, 8 1/4 In. 250.00
Vessel, Enamel Floral Design, Tooled Tan Band, 3 Handles, Lambeth, 6 1/8 In. 275.00

DRESDEN china is any china made in the town of Dresden, Germany.
The most famous factory in Dresden is the Meissen factory. Figurines
of eighteenth-century ladies and gentlemen, animal groups, or cherubs
and other mythological subjects were popular. One special type of figurine was made with skirts of porcelain-dipped lace. Do not make the
mistake of thinking that all pieces marked *Dresden* are from the
Meissen factory. The Meissen pieces usually have crossed swords
marks, and are listed under Meissen. Some recent porcelain from
Ireland, called *Irish Dresden*, is not included in this book.

Basket, Applied Flowers, White, Porcelain, 6 x 11 1/2 In. 290.00
Basket, Floral, Reticulated, 12 In. 175.00
Bowl, Drinking Cherub Finial, Scenes Of Excess & Debauchery, 13 In. 1870.00
Candelabrum, 5-Light, Woman Figure At Corners, 4 Arms, Pink & Blue, 20 In., Pair 517.00
Candy Dish, Reindeer Pulling Cart 500.00
Card Holder, Amethyst Zinnia 36.00
Card Holder, Flower Shape, Pink Carnation 36.00
Cup & Saucer, Plate, Scenes From Meistersinger & Tannhauser, Lamb, 3 Piece 405.00
Cup & Saucer, Polychrome Floral Design, Gilt, Demitasse, 6 Piece 85.00
Cup & Saucer, Scenes & Flowers In Panels, Scalloped Rim, Figural Handle, 3 1/8 In. 195.00
Dessert Service, Yellow Fish Scale, Floral Swags, Gilt, 6 Piece 405.00
Figurine, 2 Women Seated Before Mirrored Vanity, Signed, 1850s, 15 1/2 x 15 In. 258.00
Figurine, Cherub, Holding Floral Garland, 6 In. 200.00
Figurine, Child, Musician, Signed, 6 In. 300.00
Figurine, Each A Young Woman, Seated At A Table, Blue Glaze, 5 3/4 In., 3 Piece 920.00
Figurine, Gentleman, Standing, Gentleman's Woman, Signed, 13 In., Pair 1205.00
Figurine, Julianna, 8 1/2 In. 230.00
Figurine, Parrot, Perched On White Tree Trunk, Floral, Flowers, 14 In. 865.00
Group, 2 Couples Wearing Gilt Sprigged Costume, 12 x 17 In. 1840.00
Group, Dancing Couple In 18th Century Clothes, 1890, 11 1/2 x 9 1/2 In. 120.00
Group, Gentleman Delivering Basket Of Flowers & Letter, Blue, 7 1/2 In. 230.00
Lamp, Figural, 2 Couples, Dancing Around Tree, Lithophane Shade 575.00
Lamp, Figural, Cherub-Form Stem, Rocaille Base, Signed, 11 3/4 In. 85.00
Lamp, Floral Nosegays, White Ground, Clear Chimney, 11 In. 545.00
Lamp, Fluid, Baluster Stem, Cherubs, Overall Flowers, Ball Shade, 16 In. 373.00
Lamp, Table, Cherubim Design, Floral, Beaded Shade, 19 In. 345.00
Perfume Bottle, Floral Bouquets, Molded Flowers, 2 Handles, Blue, 9 3/4 In., Pair 60.00
Plaque, 2 Elegant Young Girls Eavesdropping Through Rosebush, 5 x 3 4/5 In. 460.00
Plaque, Mignon, Robed Beauty Holding A Lute, Venetian Gilt Frame, 6 x 4 1/2 In. 750.00
Plaque, Raphael, Hand Painted, Oval, 6 1/2 x 5 In. 100.00
Plaque, Ruth, 7 3/4 x 5 1/4 In. 920.00
Plaque, Woman, Partially Robed, With Flowing Brown Hair, 4 x 3 In. 405.00
Plaque, Young Man Trying To Interest A Young Woman, Frame, 6 x 3 In. 400.00
Plate, Dessert, Floral & Swag Design, 8 In., 12 Piece 220.00

Plate, Floral Rim, Green Cartouches, Pale Green Ground, 9 1/2 In. 345.00
Plate, Floral, Reticulated Rim, 7 1/2 In. 28.00
Plate, Grafin Dupari, Crimson Ground, Gilt Design, 10 1/4 In. 345.00
Plate, Hand Painted Floral, Reticulated, 6 In., 12 Piece 395.00
Tray, Mother Reading To Children, Seated On Sofa, 7 1/2 x 8 In. 690.00
Urn, Potpourri, Floral, 11 1/2 In., Pair 575.00
Vase, Applied Fruit & Flower Garland, Ormolu Foot, Floral Finial, 13 In. 345.00

DUNCAN & MILLER is a term used by collectors when referring to glass
made by the George A. Duncan and Sons Company or the Duncan and
Miller Glass Company. These companies worked from 1893 to 1955,
when the use of the name *Duncan* was discontinued and the firm
became part of the United States Glass Company. Early patterns may
be listed under Pressed Glass.

Adoration, Champagne, 6 Oz. 30.00
Adoration, Goblet, 10 Oz. 32.00
Adoration, Salt & Pepper 42.00
Block, Creamer, Ruby Stained, 3 In. 22.00
Canterbury, Ashtray, Rectangular 4.00
Canterbury, Bowl, 14 In. 30.00
Canterbury, Celery Dish, 11 In. 15.00
Canterbury, Cup & Saucer 15.00
Canterbury, Pitcher 80.00
Canterbury, Plate, 8 1/2 In. 6.00
Canterbury, Plate, Lily-Of-The-Valley Cutting, 8 In. 15.00
Canterbury, Salt & Pepper . . . . .20.00 to 23.00
Canterbury, Sugar & Creamer, Tray 10.00
Canterbury, Vase, 6 In. 8.00
Canterbury, Wine, 3 Oz. 3.00
Caribbean, Bowl, Sapphire Blue, 5 In. 19.00
Caribbean, Candelabrum, Sapphire Blue, Pair 300.00
Caribbean, Cup & Saucer, Sapphire Blue 68.00
Caribbean, Plate, Sapphire Blue, 7 1/2 In. 20.00
Caribbean, Punch Cup, Amber Handle 12.00
Caribbean, Punch Cup, Red Handle 12.00
Caribbean, Swan, Chartreuse, 7 In. 35.00
Caribbean, Vase, Sapphire Blue, 7 1/2 In. 60.00
Chanticleer, Cocktail Shaker, Green 140.00
Figurine, Swan, Green, Pair 275.00
Figurine, Swan, Pink, Pair 250.00
First Love, Bowl, 10 1/2 In. 65.00
First Love, Bowl, Scalloped Edge, 11 In. 71.00
First Love, Candlestick, 2-Light, Pair . . . . .129.00 to 150.00
First Love, Champagne, 5 Oz. 21.00
First Love, Cocktail, 3 Oz. 20.00
First Love, Compote, 5 1/2 In. 49.00
First Love, Goblet, Water, 10 Oz. . . . . .31.00 to 45.00
First Love, Plate, Square, 7 In. 20.00
First Love, Relish, 3 Sections, 8 In. . . . . .40.00 to 45.00
First Love, Sandwich Server, 2 Handles 34.00
First Love, Tumbler, Juice, Footed, 5 Oz. 21.00
First Love, Vase, Bud, 9 In. 65.00
Garland, Goblet 32.00
Garland, Plate, 7 1/2 In. 20.00
Hobnail, Basket, Handle, 7 In. 22.00
Hobnail, Bowl, Shallow, 12 In. 30.00
Hobnail, Cologne, Stopper, Blue Opalescent, 8 Oz. 119.00
Hobnail, Goblet, Blue Opalescent, 9 Oz. 39.00
Hobnail, Plate, 7 1/2 In. 7.00
Indian Tree, Rose Bowl, 5 In. 110.00
Language Of Flowers, Bowl, Flared, 12 In. 65.00
Mardi Gras, Goblet 25.00

Sandwich, Ashtray, Square 10.00
Sandwich, Bowl, Flared, 11 1/2 In. 40.00
Sandwich, Bowl, Flared, 12 In. 69.00
Sandwich, Cake Stand, Plain Pedestal, 13 In. 85.00
Sandwich, Candlestick, 4 In., Pair 25.00
Sandwich, Champagne, 5 Oz. 17.00
Sandwich, Coaster, 4 1/2 In. 12.00
Sandwich, Cocktail, 3 Oz. 10.00
Sandwich, Cup & Saucer 18.00
Sandwich, Goblet, 9 Oz. . . . . .14.00 to 18.00
Sandwich, Goblet, Ice Cream, 5 Oz. 12.00
Sandwich, Goblet, Wine, 3 Oz. 20.00
Sandwich, Plate, 6 In. 9.00
Sandwich, Plate, 8 In. 14.00
Sandwich, Plate, 12 In. 45.00
Sandwich, Plate, 14 In. 50.00
Sandwich, Plate, 16 In. . . . . .55.00 to 95.00
Sandwich, Plate, Deviled Egg . . . . .70.00 to 75.00
Sandwich, Plate, Handle, 7 In. 24.00
Sandwich, Torte Plate, 12 In. 49.00
Sandwich, Tumbler, Juice, Footed, 5 Oz. 9.00
Sandwich, Tumbler, Water, Footed, 9 Oz. . . . . .10.00 to 20.00
Sandwich, Vase, Footed, 10 In. 89.00
Teardrop, Ashtray, 3 In. 6.00
Teardrop, Bowl, Salad, Shallow, 12 In. 45.00
Teardrop, Plate, 6 1/4 In. 12.00
Teardrop, Plate, 8 1/2 In. 8.00
Teardrop, Salt & Pepper 25.00
Teardrop, Sherbet, Low, 5 Oz. 8.00
Teardrop, Sherbet, Tall, 5 Oz. 10.00
Teardrop, Tumbler, Footed, 8 Oz. 16.00
Teardrop, Wine, 3 Oz. 17.00

DURAND art glass was made from 1924 to 1931. The Vineland Flint Glass Works was established by Victor Durand and Victor Durand, Jr., in 1897. In 1924 Martin Bach, Jr., and other artisans from the Quezal glassworks joined them at the Vineland, New Jersey, plant to make Durand art glass.

Centerpiece, Pulled Feathers White On Red, Engraved Roses Rim, 14 In. 1840.00
Centerpiece, Swirling Blue, Gold Iridescent Interior & Ground, 10 In. 2070.00
Compote, King Tut, Cobalt Blue Ground, Clear Reeded Stem, 6 3/4 In. 520.00
Lamp, Gold Threading, 14 In. 1300.00
Vase, Blue Iridescent, Polished Pontil, Cylindrical, 1968, 8 In. 805.00
Vase, Blue, Flared Rim, Baluster Shape, 4 1/2 In. 575.00
Vase, Egyptian Crackle, Red, White, Iridescent, Everted Rim, 7 In. 1265.00
Vase, Genie, Silver Iridescent, Ribbed Body, 15 1/2 In. 2775.00
Vase, King Tut, Blue Green, Gold, 4 In. 1150.00
Vase, Pulled Feather, Blue, Yellow, Gold Iridescent Threads, 1910, 8 1/2 In. 546.00
Vase, Pulled Feather, Cobalt Blue Neck, Shoulder, Blue, Opaque White, 9 In. 290.00
Vase, Pulled Feathers, Red, White, Round Foot, Signed, 11 1/2 In. 920.00
Vase, Pulled Feathers, White, Pink Ground, Engraved Roses Rim, 13 In., Pair 3105.00
Vase, Trailing Hearts & Vines, Blue Iridescent, 18 1/2 In. 6900.00
Vase, Trailing Hearts & Vines, Peach Iridescent, Signed, 1924, 7 1/2 In. 920.00
Vase, Twist, Multicolored, Tan Interior, 6 1/2 In. 286.00

ELFINWARE is a mark found on Dresden-like porcelain that was sold in dime stores and gift shops. Many pieces were decorated with raised flowers. The mark was registered by Breslauer-Underberg, Inc., of New York City in 1947. Pieces marked *Elfinware Made in Germany* had been sold since 1945 by this importer.

Elfinware

Figurine, Swan 35.00
Furniture, Doll House, Chairs, Settee & Table, Moss & Flowers, Set 195.00

ELVIS PRESLEY, the well-known singer, lived from 1935 to 1977. He became famous by 1956. Elvis appeared on television, starred in twenty-seven movies, and performed in Las Vegas. Memorabilia from any of the Presley shows, his records, and even memorials made after his death are collected.

Booklet, 16 Pages Of Color Pictures, 1977	2.00
Bottle, McCormick, 1978	125.00
Bracelet, Identity, 445 Diamonds Spelling Name, 14K Gold Nugget	25300.00
Cookie Jar, Pink Cadillac, Elvis Playing Guitar, Porcelain	100.00 to 125.00
Giant Poster Book, Volume 1, 1977, 11 x 17 In.	25.00
Lighter, Zippo, 50 Years With Elvis, Painted Engraved Picture, Slim, 1989	60.00
Poster, Clambake, 1967, Six Sheet	100.00
Poster, Elvis On Tour, Documentary, 1972, One Sheet	230.00
Poster, Follow That Dream, 1962, One Sheet	85.00
Poster, King Creole, 1958, Heavy Stock Silkscreen, 40 x 60 In.	2645.00
Poster, Viva Las Vegas, 1964, Six Sheet	705.00
Radio, Battery Operated, Plastic, Cloth, Hong Kong, 1970s-1980s, 10 In.	55.00
Snowdome, Musical, Blue Suede Shoes	45.00

ENAMELS listed here are made of glass particles and other materials heated and fused to metal. In the eighteenth and nineteenth centuries, workmen from Russia, France, England, and other countries made small boxes and table pieces of enamel on metal. One form of English enamel is called *Battersea* and is listed under that name. There was a revival of interest in enameling in the 1930s and a new style evolved. There is now renewed interest in the artistic enameled plaques, vases, ashtrays, and jewelry. Enamels made since the 1930s are usually on copper or steel, although silver was often used for jewelry. Graniteware is a separate category, and enameled metal kitchen pieces may be included in the Kitchen category.

Bowl, Gilt, Silver, 2 Bear's-Head Handles, 3 1/2 x 8 In. ....*Illus*	9487.00
Box, Ship Design, Copper, Gertrude Twichell, 3 1/4 x 2 1/4 In.	920.00
Box, Sweetmeat, Bronze Mounted, Blue Bird, Seated Form, 1775-1790, 2 In.	514.00
Horn, Cherubs, Woman, Angels, Gilt Silver Knight, Dragon, Base, Vienna, 8 1/2 In.	2990.00
Inkwell, Sailing Ship, Copper, Gertrude Twichell, 2 1/2 x 2 1/2 In.	632.00
Jug, Cream, Women In Landscapes, Silver Handle, Winged Bust, Vienna, 5 1/4 In.	1095.00
Kovsh, Floral, Gold, Silver, TK 8 4 Mark, Russia, 8 1/2 x 5 x 3 In.	4025.00
Letter Holder, Hammered Copper, Sailing Ship Medallion, Gertrude Twichell, 4 3/4 In.	517.00
Pillbox, Multicolored Flowers On Blue Ground, Feodor Ruckert, Russia, c.1900, 2 1/8 In.	2300.00
Plaque, Crucifixion, Square, Brass Frame, Continental, 18th Century, 6 3/8 In.	1610.00
Plaque, Henricus II, Portrait, Gilt Trim, France, 19th Century, 6 x 7 1/4 In.	805.00
Teapot, European Figures, On Metal, Hexagonal, China, 18th Century, 6 In.	880.00
Tile, Wharf Scene, 5 Square Panels, Frame, 11 x 55 In.	287.00
Triptych, Crucifixion, White Design, Black Ground, France, 19th Century, 6 1/4 In.	490.00
Vase, Allover Multicolored Foliage, Gilt, Arabic Script, Germany, 10 1/4 In., Pair	6900.00
Vase, Entwined Gilt Foliage, Blue, Gilt Design, Marked, 1880, 12 1/2 In.	2530.00
Vase, Foil Under Opalescent Colors, C. Faure, 7 In.	3335.00

Enamel, Bowl, Gilt, Silver, 2 Bear's-Head
Handles, 3 1/2 x 8 In.

Moths seem to like to eat natural undyed horsehair but, strangely, do not eat dyed hair. Use moth balls and other deterrents to protect braided hair work and stuffed furniture.

ERPHILA is a mark found on Czechoslovakian and other pottery and porcelain made after the 1930s. The mark was used on items imported by Eberling & Reuss, Philadelphia, a giftware firm that is still operating in Pennsylvania. The mark is a combination of the letters *E* and *R* (Eberling & Reuss) and the first letters of the city, Phila(delphia). Many whimsical figural pitchers and creamers, figurines, platters, and other giftwares carry this mark.

Creamer, Mrs. Gamp	35.00
Figurine, Dog, Bulldog, Black, White, 6 1/2 x 3 1/4 In.	115.00
Figurine, Dog, Dalmatian, Sitting, Paws Crossed, 10 x 5 1/4 In.	200.00
Figurine, Dog, German Shepherd	45.00
Pitcher, Cat, Red, Cream, 9 In.	1000.00
Pitcher, Ram, Red, Cream, 9 In.	250.00
Planter, Oriental Man & Buckets, Germany	59.00
Sugar Shaker, Warwick	125.00
Teapot, Dog	98.00

ES GERMANY porcelain was made at the factory of Erdmann Schlegelmilch from 1861 to 1937 in Suhl, Germany. The porcelain, marked *ES Germany* or *ES Suhl*, was sold decorated or undecorated. Other pieces were made at a factory in Saxony, Prussia, and are marked *ES Prussia*. Reinhold Schlegelmilch made the famous wares marked *RS Germany*.

Relish, Bird Design, 8 In.	100.00
Vase, Leaves & Blossoms, 8 In.	65.00

ESKIMO artifacts of all types are collected. Carvings of whale or walrus teeth are listed under Scrimshaw. Baskets are in the Basket category. All other types of Eskimo art are listed here.

Ball, Game, Seal Skin, Dot Pattern, 8 In.	143.00
Canoe, Sealskin, Miniature, 3 Piece	192.00
Carving, 2 Walrus, 1 1/2 x 4 x 2 In.	65.00
Cribbage Board, Carved Ivory, Polar Bear Head Mounts, 15 1/2 In.	550.00
Cribbage Board, Inked Pinniped, Bear Form, Carved Walrus Tusk, Ivory, 13 In.	517.00
Cribbage Board, Walrus Tusk, Engraved Fish, Peg Section, 13 1/2 In.	275.00
Cribbage Board, Walrus Tusk, Walrus 1 End, Moose Other, Peg Section, 13 1/2 In.	220.00
Doll, Hooded Parka, 1 Arm Raised, Other At Side, Wood & Polychrome, 16 1/2 In.	105.00
Figurine, Blackbird, Sculptured, Black Stone, 5 1/2 In.	88.00
Figurine, Walrus, Reclining, Inuit, Stone, Noah Pe, 7 1/2 In.	58.00
Fish Hook, Mother-Of-Pearl & Bone, 3 1/2 In.	220.00
Lamp, Carved Stone, 19th Century, 13 x 6 x 3 In.	245.00
Letter Opener, Whalebone Handle, Eskimo In Kayak, 10 1/2 In.	90.00
Mat, 2-Masted Schooner, Grenfel, Frame, 13 1/2 x 16 In.	275.00
Model, Kayak, Hide-Covered, 26 1/2 In.	302.00
Model, Kayak, Sealskin, Seated Man, Ivory, 1900, 33 x 2 In.	605.00
Model, Kayak, Stretched Hide, Wood Frame, Ivory, Late 19th Century, 28 In.	230.00
Model, Kayak, Wooden Frame, Hide Covered, 2-Person, 19th Century, 27 In.	632.00
Tusk, Walrus, Uncarved, Early 20th Century, 18 In., Pair	132.00

FABERGE was a firm of jewelers and goldsmiths founded in St. Petersburg, Russia, in 1842, by Gustav Faberge. Peter Carl Faberge, his son, was jeweler to the Russian Imperial Court from about 1870 to 1914. The rare Imperial Easter eggs, jewelry, and decorative items are very expensive today.

Ashtray, Embossed Imperial Eagle, Inscribed War 1914, Copper, 4 1/4 In.	1150.00
Beaker, Silver, Repousse Swirls, Scrolls, Foliage, Gilt Interior, c.1890, 3 1/4 In.	4025.00
Box, Book Shape, Notepad Holder, Karelian Birch, Silver Scrolls, Flowers, 12 In.	9775.00
Cane, Dogwood Blossoms Top, Gold Over Dark Karelian Birch Wood, 1895	12100.00
Case, Tubular, Salmon Ground, Leaf-Tip Borders, Cover, Anna Ringe, c.1900, 2 In.	9200.00
Clock, Gilded Silver, Enamel Dial, Seed Pearls Border, M. Perchin, 1890, 5 1/2 In.	37950.00
Cuff Links, Enameled Translucent Pink, Oval, Pointed End, 5 5/8 In.	4887.00
Dish, Anthemion Border, Griffins On Each Handle, Oval, c.1910, 14 In.	5750.00

Figurine, Pig, Rhodonite, Blue Cabochon Eyes, c.1900, 1 1/4 In. 4025.00
Frame, Photograph, Silver, Enamel, Flaming Torches, Andre Gorianov, c.1900, 3 In. 5462.00
Hatpin, Gilt Silver, Translucent Lilac Enamel, Ribbons, Foliage, Silk Box, 11 In. 7475.00
Kovsh, Gilded Silver, Shaded Enamel, Stylized Foliage, Feodor Ruckert, 1 1/4 In........ 5462.00
Letter Opener, Gold Lily-Of-The-Valley Plant, Moonstones, c.1900, 6 1/4 In. 6900.00
Mirror, Table, Border Chased Scrolls, Flowers, Julius Rappoport, c.1890, 11 In. 2875.00
Pendant, Easter Egg, Gold & Enamel Cross, August Holmstrom, c.1914, 5/8 In......... 2530.00
Teapot, Engraved Strapwork, Stephan Wakeva, 1888, 7 In. 1380.00

FAIENCE refers to tin-glazed earthenware, especially the wares made in
France, Germany, and Scandinavia. It is also correct to say that faience
is the same as majolica or Delft, although usually the term refers only
to the tin-glazed pottery of the three regions mentioned.

Candlestick, Griffin Figure, Fish Handle, Blue, Yellow, Green, Umber, France, 11 In. 145.00
Charger, Stylized Foliage, Blossoms, Blue, Red, Yellow, Green, Round, 21 In. 345.00
Cruet Stand, Dog Heads Terminal, Blue, White, 1795, 8 x 8 1/4 In. 485.00
Dessert Service, Cabbage Leaf Shape, Green, Italy, 20th Century, 27 Piece 6900.00
Dinner & Dessert Service, Pink, Green Large Tulip, Narrow Pink Line Rim, 24 Piece ... 920.00
Dish, Elongated Quatrefoil Shape, 4 x 20 x 11 In. 385.00
Dish, Leaf, Green, Raised Veins, Pale Yellow, Continental, 1780, 14 In., Pair 2875.00
Garniture Set, Blue & White, Brass Mounted, Mantel Clock, 1840-1880, 3 Piece 968.00
Ginger Jar, Cover, Cupid In Cartouche Design, Blue, White, Continental, 14 In. 200.00
Inkstand, 3-Bay Country Mansion, 3 Faces Finial, Removable Drawers, 9 In........... 8050.00
Inkstand, Animals On Lobes, 5 1/4 In. 105.00
Inkwell, Hunters, 5 1/4 x 5 1/4 In. 137.00
Jar, Cover, Stalk Handle, Watermelon Shape, Yellow, Green Strips, 7 1/2 In., Pair 2875.00
Jardiniere, Art Nouveau Floral Design, Signed, Emaux Diapres, Round, 10 1/2 In. 259.00
Jug, Wine, Cityscape Design, Blue, White, Continental, 1737, 19 In., Pair 4315.00
Pitcher, Animals, Floral Design, Continental, 10 1/4 In. 109.00
Pitcher, Helmet Shape, Chinoiserie Design, 11 1/4 In. 115.00
Plate, Basket, Feather Design, Blue, White, Continental, 9 In., Pair 460.00
Plate, Cabinet, Floral Design, Cobalt, Green Floral Sprays, France, 8 In. 49.00
Plate, Creil Black & White, Marked, 1820, 9 1/4 In. 80.00
Plate, Creil Yellow, Black Transfer Design, 1820, 8 1/8 In. 121.00
Plate, Musical Verse Center, Paneled Floral Borders, France, 9 5/8 In., Pair 375.00
Platter, Basket, Blue & White, Flowers, Oval, Early 19th Century, France, 15 In. 193.00
Platter, Polychrome Floral Border, Pseudo Armorial Crest, 19th Century, 18 In. 373.00
Sauceboat, Curled Leaf With Stalk Handle, Flower Sprays, Brown Line Rim, 8 In., Pair .. 85.00
Tureen, Cover, Cabbage, Overlapping Leaves, Green Glaze, Continental, 4 3/8 In. 1440.00
Tureen, Cover, Cabbage, Overlapping Leaves, Green, 4 Twig Feet, 1769, 5 3/8 In. 6325.00
Tureen, Cover, Cabbage, Overlapping Leaves, Green, Yellow, 1755, 11 1/2 In. 8625.00
Tureen, Cover, Rooster Shape, Italy, 17 1/2 In. 170.00
Tureen, Melon, Cover, Green, Yellow Striped Fruit, Resting On Green Leaves, 9 In. 1150.00
Tureen, Undertray & Cover, Floral Design, Signed, 20th Century, 15 1/2 In. 137.00
Vase, Bird, Floral Design, France, 20 1/2 In. 980.00

FAIRINGS are small souvenir china boxes and figurines that were sold
at country fairs during the nineteenth century. Most were made in
Germany. Reproductions of fairings are being made, especially of the
famous *twelve months of marriage* series.

Box, Trinket, Child On Sideboard, With Cup & Pitcher, Conte & Boehme, 4 In. 50.00
Box, Trinket, Dog Finial, Yellowware, 3 x 3 1/2 In. 145.00
Box, Trinket, Dome Cover, Multicolored Castles, Buildings, Foliage, 3 x 4 1/4 x 3 In. 990.00
Box, Trinket, Dome Cover, Multicolored Floral & Foliage, Orange Ground, 4 x 3 In. 330.00
Box, Trinket, Figural, Baby In Bunting, Porcelain, 5 In. 110.00
Box, Trinket, Man On Recamier, 1 1/2 In. 27.00
Box, Trinket, Match, Working Carpenters, 4 x 4 In. 175.00
Box, Trinket, Reclining Mother & Baby, Coleslaw Border, 2 1/2 In. 45.00

FAIRYLAND LUSTER pieces are included in the Wedgwood category.

FAMILLE ROSE, see Chinese Export category.

FANS have been used for cooling since the days of the ancients. By the eighteenth century, the fan was an accessory for the lady of fashion, and very elaborate and expensive fans were made. Sticks were made of ivory or wood, set with jewels or carved. The fans were made of painted silk or paper. Inexpensive paper fans printed with advertising were giveaways in the late nineteenth and early twentieth centuries. Electric fans were introduced in 1882.

Advertising, Aux Galeries Lafayette, Palmate Shape, Wood Sticks, Gold, 1920, 9 In.	33.00
Advertising, Black Restaurant, 1930s	7.00
Advertising, Cafe Martin, New York, Wood Sticks, Double Paper Leaf, 1912, 8 1/2 In. . . .	60.00
Advertising, Garrett's Snuff, 1925 Calendar Pages, 7 3/4 x 9 In. . . . .*Illus*	15.00
Advertising, Hotel Crillon, White Paint, Wood Sticks, Paper, France, 1880, 8 1/2 In.	27.00
Advertising, M.J. Connell Company, Butte, Montana, Folding, Frame, 26 3/4 x 12 5/8 In. .	165.00
Advertising, Murrell Inn, Penn., 7 x 9 In. . . . .*Illus*	25.00
Advertising, Players Navy Cut Cigarettes, Paper & Wood, 16 In.	105.00
Advertising, Singer Sewing Machine, Floral Design, Tassel, Japan, 1910, 9 x 6 In.	35.00
Beechwood, Hand Painted, Celadon Satin, Velvet Lined Shadowbox, 14 x 25 In.	95.00
Bone Sticks, Bouquet Of Flowers Center, Velvet Lined Shadowbox, c.1870, 9 x 16 In. . . .	210.00
Bone Sticks, Flirting, Vine Design, Silver Inset, Pastoral Scene, 1800, 9 1/2 In.	66.00
Bone Sticks, Hand Painted Chiffon, Floral Design On Guard, Violet Bouquets, 12 In.	44.00
Bone Sticks, Hand Painted Chiffon, Floral Sprays, Pink, Yellow, Purple, 1880, 12 3/4 In. .	38.00
Bone Sticks, Hand Painted Floral Sprays, Colonial Courtship Scene, 1860, 8 1/4 In.	66.00
Bone Sticks, Jenny Lind, Pierced, Mother-Of-Pearl, 1870, 8 3/4 In.	33.00
Bone Sticks, Paper, Double Leaf, 2 Shepherdesses, Opens To 16 In.	145.00
Bone Sticks, Paper, Men & Women Drinking, Ship, Rowboat, c.1799, Frame, 14 x 23 In. .	460.00
Bone Sticks, Red, Pink Roses, Applied Ribbon Border, 1825, 7 1/2 In.	55.00
Calendar, 12 Sticks, Flower Garbed Fairies, January Through Dec., 1894, Cardboard	126.00
Cloth, Painted, Huntsmen, Maroon Ground, Hardwood Ribs, Shadowbox Frame, 25 In. . .	55.00
Electric, Ceiling, Emerson, 2 Blades, 1898	3000.00
Electric, Emerson, 5 Blades	4000.00
Electric, Emerson, Model 6250 K, Desk, Oscillating, Steel Housing, Stand	25.00
Electric, Eskimo, Desk, Wire Cage, Green Paint, Adjustable	20.00
Electric, General Electric, Desk, Oscillating, Model AOU No. 75423, 12 In. . . . .*Illus*	195.00
Electric, General Electric, Rotating, Brass & Iron, c.1920, 16 1/2 x 15 In.	88.00
Electric, Polar Club, Cast Iron Base	55.00
Electric, Rotobeam, Steel Wire Cage, Chrome-Plated, 5 Bakelite Blades & Base	374.00
Electric, Singer, Ribbonaire, Bakelite, Dark Brown Casing, Ribbon Blades, 10 In.	375.00
Feather, Brown & Tortoiseshell Handles, J. Duvelleroy, Box, 15 In.	55.00
Feather, Child's, Blue Forget-Me-Nots, Composition Loop, 6 In.	33.00
Feather, Child's, Brise, Painted, Green, Black Feathers, White Painted Wood, 5 In.	44.00
Feather, Ostrich, Black, Gold Painted Wood Sticks, Grosgrain Ribbon, 1890, 14 In.	66.00
Feather, Ostrich, Black, Tortoiseshell, 1890, 15 In.	77.00

Fan, Advertising, Garrett's Snuff, 1925 Calendar Pages, 7 3/4 x 9 In.

Fan, Advertising, Murrell Inn, Penn., 7 x 9 In.

Fan, Electric, General Electric, Desk, Oscillating, Model AOU No. 75423, 12 In.

Flirtation, Center Mirror, Victorian 175.00
Ivory, 4 Figures, Dragon, Surrounding A Central Medallion, 1820, 7 1/4 In. 1210.00
Ivory, Brise, Painted, Flowers & Paper Leaf, Shepherd, Shepherdess, 2 1/8 & 2 3/4 In. . . . 275.00
Ivory, Mandarin, Paper, Painted Pavilions Both Sides, Chinese Export, 1875, 11 In. 1045.00
Ivory Sticks, Carved, Painted Feather & Peacock-Eye, Shadowbox, 1855, 13 x 22 In. 240.00
Ivory Sticks, Carved, Shepherd & Shepherdess, Landscape On Reverse, 10 5/8 In. 250.00
Ivory Sticks, Child's, Brise, Painted, Floral Fabric Ribbon, 19th Century, 5 In. 88.00
Ivory Sticks, Hand Painted, Shepherd, Shepherdess, Landscape, Paper 250.00
Ivory Sticks, Satin, White, Wildflowers & Birds, Guards, 12 In. 22.00
Ivory Sticks, Silk Ribbon, Nude Woman, Sterling Silver Loop, Moorish, Box 450.00
Ivory Sticks, Silk, Embroidered, Figural Landscape & Flower Design 195.00
Lace, Applied Steels, Spangles, Black Corded Tassel, Ebony, 1860, 9 1/2 In. 80.00
Lace, Floral Design On Guards, Lace Leaf, 1870, 14 In. 44.00
Lace, Impressed Wavy Guards, Black, Ebony, 1890, 14 In. 27.00
Lace, Leaf With Sequins In Form Of Colonial Couple, Wood Sticks, 1850, 10 In. 33.00
Lace, Lower Lace Leaf, 3 Insets Of Cherubs Top Leaf, Gilt, Wood, 1865, 8 1/2 In. 105.00
Lace, Mother-Of-Pearl, Velvet Lined Shadowbox, 15 x 26 1/2 In. 210.00
Lace, Openwork Design, Applied Piques, 1810, 6 In. 55.00
Lace, Painted Forget-Me-Nots On Chiffon Leaf, 1890, 13 In. 27.00
Lace, Satin, Mother-Of-Pearl Sticks, Guards, 1870, 10 In. 27.00
Lace, Wedding, Mother-Of-Pearl, Brass Loop, 1890, 10 1/2 In. 88.00
Lace, White, Ivory, Frame, c.1900, 13 x 24 In. 145.00
Painted, Velvet Lined Shadowbox, c.1850, 11 x 20 In. 332.00
Paper, Double Sided, Figures, Ivory Faces, Carved Guards, Silk Tassel, 11 In. 1045.00
Paper, Figures, Ivory Faces, Silk Clothing, Sandalwood Sticks, 1875, 11 1/4 In. 110.00
Paper, Leaf, White Painted Wood, Bullfighting Scene, Cotton Tassel, 1880, 7 In. 22.00
Paper, Mother-Of-Pearl Guards, Peacock Shape, Life Of Don Quixote, 1870 . . . . 330.00
Paper, Napoleon & Josephine At Compeigne, Cafe Martin, Wood Sticks, 1900, 16 x 9 In. 60.00
Papier-Mache, Shaped Border, Wooden Handle, Allover Allegorical & Bird Design, 9 In. . 230.00
Sandalwood Sticks, Bone, Egyptian Pharaoh Shape, Bone Loop, 1850, 6 1/2 In. 143.00
Satin, Pink, Flared Sticks, Guards, Brass Loop, Pink Tassel, 1830, 8 In. 38.00
Silk, Black Lacquer, Cream Butterfly Design, Mother-Of-Pearl, 1900, 9 In. 27.00
Silk, Black, Gabardine Leaf, Mother-Of-Pearl, Black Cotton Tassel, 1860, 8 1/2 In. 38.00
Silk, Hand Painted Butterflies, Grasses, Black, Wood Sticks, Guards, 1880, 14 In. 22.00
Silver & Ivory Inlay, Classical Maidens With Attendants, 10 1/2 In. 70.00
Village Under Hillside, 3 Seals, Mounted, 17th Century 990.00
Wood Sticks, Cupid's Arrows, Silk Ribbon, Painted, France, c.1810, 11 1/4 In. . . .240.00 to 250.00
Wood Sticks, Hand Painted, Vignette Of Women In Courtyard, France, Box 165.00
Wood Sticks, Painted Floral & Birds, Mother-Of-Pearl, c.1890 . . . . 130.00

FAST FOOD COLLECTIBLES may be included in several categories, such as
Advertising, Coca-Cola, Toy, etc.

FEDERZEICHNUNG is the very strange German name for a pattern of
mother-of-pearl satin glass. The pattern had irregularly shaped sections
of brown glass covered with a pattern of gold squiggle lines. It was
first made in the late nineteenth century.

Vase, Pinched Ruffled Top, 6 In. 1265.00

FENTON Art Glass Company, founded in Martins Ferry, Ohio, by Frank
L. Fenton, is now located in Williamstown, West Virginia. It is noted
for early carnival glass produced between 1907 and 1920. Some of
these pieces are listed in the Carnival Glass category. Many other types
of glass were also made. Spanish Lace in this section refers to the pattern made by Fenton.

Animal, Bird, Purple Carnival, 4 In. 30.00
Animal, Cat, Custard Satin, Pink Blossom, 4 In. 50.00
Animal, Happiness Bird, Custard Satin, Pink Anemone, 6 1/2 In. 35.00
Animal, Happiness Bird, Rosalene, 6 1/2 In. 45.00
Aqua Crest, Basket, Aqua Ribbon Trim, Handle, 5 In. 119.00
Aqua Crest, Bonbon, 5 1/2 In. 20.00
Aqua Crest, Bowl, 13 In. 129.00
Aqua Crest, Compote, 6 In. 50.00

Aqua Crest, Vase, 4 1/2 In. 40.00
Aqua Crest, Vase, 6 In. 17.00
Aqua Crest, Vase, 10 1/2 In. 100.00
Aqua Crest, Vase, Footed, 4 In. 30.00
Aqua Crest, Vase, Square, 8 In. ....40.00 to 59.00
Basket Weave, Bowl, Lime Sherbet, 3 1/4 In. 20.00
Basket Weave, Plate, Ebony, 7 1/4 In. 25.00
Beaded Melon, Basket, Persian Blue, 10 1/2 x 9 1/2 In. 100.00
Bubble Optic, Vase, Coral, 11 1/2 In. 195.00
Burmese, Lamp, Paisley 300.00
Burmese, Vase, Cruet Form, Leaf Decorated, 6 1/2 In. 95.00
Burmese, Vase, Leaf Design, 7 In. 88.00
Burmese, Vase, Queen's Bird, 11 In. 250.00
Burmese, Vase, Roses, Signed, Sue Foster, 7 In. 120.00
Burmese, Vase, Violets, Levay, 1977, 7 In. 250.00
Buttons & Braids, Tumbler, Blue Opalescent, 6 Piece 185.00
Cactus, Bonbon, Topaz Opalescent, Handle 45.00
Cameo Opalescent, Vase, 5 1/2 In. 32.00
Clock, Copper Rose, 4 1/2 In. 75.00
Coin Dot, Basket, Cranberry, 1982, 8 In. 50.00
Coin Dot, Creamer, Cranberry Opalescent, 4 In. ....50.00 to 65.00
Coin Dot, Cruet, Cranberry 120.00
Coin Dot, Lamp, Cranberry Opalescent 80.00
Coin Dot, Pitcher, Water, Cranberry Opalescent, 9 In. 290.00
Coin Dot, Tumbler, Barrel, Blue Opalescent, 4 1/4 In. 40.00
Coin Dot, Tumbler, Cranberry Opalescent, 4 1/2 In. 40.00
Coin Dot, Vase, Blue Opalescent, 4 1/2 In. 55.00
Coin Dot, Vase, Cranberry Opalescent, 7 1/2 In. ....*Illus* 115.00
Coin Dot, Vase, Cranberry Opalescent, 11 In. 195.00
Coin Dot, Vase, Honeysuckle Opalescent, Tricornered, 7 In. 75.00
Cranberry Opalescent, Top Hat, Spiral Optic 118.00
Cranberry Opalescent, Vase, Tulip, 10 In. 40.00
Custard Satin, Fairy Light, Blue Birds 40.00
Custard Satin, Lamp, Student, Blue Birds, 20 In. 225.00
Daisy & Button, Ashtray, Slipper, Milk Glass 8.00
Diamond Lace, Epergne, French Opalescent, 2 Piece 55.00
Diamond Lace, Epergne, French Opalescent, 4 Piece 150.00
Diamond Lace, Vase, Fan, Blue Opalescent, 1948, 6 In. 40.00
Diamond Optic, Jug, Ruby, Handle, 6 In. 45.00
Diamond Optic, Plate, Ruby, Octagonal, 1920s, 8 In. 58.00
Diamond Optic, Vase, Jade Crest, Handle, 9 1/2 In. 75.00
Dot Optic, Pitcher, Green Opalescent, Black Handle, 70 Oz. 325.00
Drapery, Bowl, Aqua, Signed, 8 1/2 In. 95.00
Egg, Custard Satin, Orange Roses & Bands, 1972 .... 40.00
Egg, Lime Sherbet, Roses, 1973 .... 55.00
Egg, White Satin, Bluebells, Blue Bands, 1971 .... 45.00
Egg, White Satin, Snow Scene, 1991 .... 50.00
Elephant, Decanter, Sherry, Satin, 18 In. 200.00
Emerald Crest, Basket, 7 In. 72.00
Emerald Crest, Flowerpot, 4 1/2 In. 35.00
Emerald Crest, Tidbit, Handle, 10 In. 159.00
Emerald Crest, Vase, Fan, 4 1/2 In. 20.00
Figurine, Praying Boy & Girl, Peking Blue, Pair 30.00
French Opalescent, Top Hat, Swirl, 1922, 9 1/2 x 5 1/2 In. 165.00
Garland, Rose Bowl, Marigold 100.00
Gold Crest, Bowl, Ruffled Edge, 8 1/2 In. 35.00
Hanging Heart, Vase, Orange, Blue & Custard Ground, Robert Baker, Large 375.00
Hobnail, Apothecary Jar, Cover 82.00
Hobnail, Ashtray, Fan, Topaz Opalescent, 5 1/2 In. 29.00
Hobnail, Ashtray, Milk Glass 20.00
Hobnail, Basket, Blue Opalescent, 4 In. 40.00
Hobnail, Basket, Blue Opalescent, 5 1/2 In. 55.00
Hobnail, Basket, Blue Opalescent, 7 In. 50.00

**Never allow water to evaporate
in a glass vase. It will leave a
white residue that may be
impossible to remove.**

Fenton, Coin Dot,
Vase, Cranberry
Opalescent, 7 1/2 In.

Hobnail, Basket, Blue Opalescent, Footed, 6 1/4 In.	85.00
Hobnail, Basket, Cranberry Opalescent, 4 1/2 In.	150.00
Hobnail, Basket, French Opalescent, 5 1/2 In.	75.00
Hobnail, Basket, Oval, Milk Glass, 13 In.	89.00
Hobnail, Basket, Plum Opalescent, Oval, 12 In.	425.00
Hobnail, Basket, Topaz Opalescent, 4 1/2 In.	50.00
Hobnail, Bell, Milk Glass	10.00
Hobnail, Bonbon, Blue Opalescent, Handles, 5 1/4 In.	70.00
Hobnail, Bonbon, Cranberry Opalescent, 6 In.	26.00
Hobnail, Bonbon, Green Opalescent, Square, 6 In.	28.00
Hobnail, Bottle, Oil, Milk Glass	22.00
Hobnail, Bowl, Cranberry Opalescent, 9 In.	75.00
Hobnail, Candy Box, Blue Satin	55.00
Hobnail, Candy Dish, French Opalescent, Handle, 1953	26.00
Hobnail, Compote, Colonial Green	20.00
Hobnail, Compote, Topaz Opalescent	58.00
Hobnail, Condiment Set, Milk Glass, 7 Piece	110.00
Hobnail, Cruet, Stopper, Blue Opalescent	27.00
Hobnail, Dish, Mayonnaise, Blue Opalescent	35.00
Hobnail, Epergne, Milk Glass, 2 Piece	25.00
Hobnail, Epergne, Milk Glass, 4 Piece	65.00
Hobnail, Fairy Light, Milk Glass, Holly	40.00
Hobnail, Jug, Green Opalescent, 32 Oz.	220.00
Hobnail, Mustard, Cover, Blue Opalescent, Spoon	20.00
Hobnail, Mustard, Cover, Milk Glass, Spoon	42.00
Hobnail, Mustard, French Opalescent, Paddle	22.00
Hobnail, Pitcher, Cranberry Opalescent, 5 1/2 In.	65.00
Hobnail, Pitcher, Green Opalescent, 5 1/2 In.	40.00
Hobnail, Pitcher, Topaz Opalescent, 5 1/2 In.	65.00
Hobnail, Plate, Topaz Opalescent, 6 In.	20.00
Hobnail, Salt & Pepper, Blue Opalescent	48.00
Hobnail, Shrimp Set, 12-In. Tray, 5-In. Compote, 2 Piece	68.00
Hobnail, Slipper, Colonial Blue	25.00
Hobnail, Slipper, Ruby	24.00
Hobnail, Sugar & Creamer, Blue Opalescent	22.00
Hobnail, Syrup, 12 Oz.	175.00
Hobnail, Tray, Fan, Topaz Opalescent, 10 In.	33.00
Hobnail, Tray, Milk Glass, Chrome Handle	22.00
Hobnail, Tumbler, Blue Opalescent, Barrel	22.00
Hobnail, Tumbler, Cranberry Opalescent, Barrel	40.00
Hobnail, Tumbler, Topaz Opalescent, 4 1/4 In.	25.00
Hobnail, Vanity Set, Blue Opalescent, Pointed Stopper, 3 Piece	175.00
Hobnail, Vase, Blue Opalescent, 3 1/2 In.	15.00
Hobnail, Vase, Bud, Colonial Green, 10 In.	15.00
Hobnail, Vase, Bud, Topaz Opalescent, Footed, 8 In.	30.00
Hobnail, Vase, Cranberry Opalescent, 5 In.	80.00
Hobnail, Vase, Cranberry Opalescent, 8 In.	95.00

Hobnail, Vase, Fan, Blue Opalescent, 4 In. ....10.00 to 30.00
Hobnail, Vase, Fan, Green Opalescent, 3 1/2 In. ....16.00 to 29.00
Hobnail, Vase, Green Opalescent, 3 1/2 In. 17.00
Hobnail, Vase, Lime Green Opalescent, Crimped, 3 In. 40.00
Hobnail, Vase, Milk Glass, 5 1/2 In. 11.00
Hobnail, Vase, Topaz Opalescent, Flared, Crimped, 8 1/2 In. 175.00
Hobnail, Vase, Topaz Opalescent, Tricornered Rim, 4 In. 21.00
Hobnail, Vase, Tulip, Red Carnival, 8 In. 52.00
Jade, Console, 2 Handles, 4 5/8 In. 150.00
Jamestown Blue, Vase, 6 In. 65.00
Jamestown Blue, Vase, Pinch, 8 1/2 In. ....45.00 to 65.00
Jefferson, Compote, Opaque Patriot Red 98.00
Jefferson, Compote, White Satin 150.00
Lavender Satin, Fairy Light, Owl 65.00
Lily Of The Valley, Rose Bowl, Topaz Opalescent 65.00
Ming, Vase, Black Stand, 7 In. 60.00
Mountain Berry, Basket, Signed, Don Fenton, 8 In. 100.00
Mountain Reflection, Vase, Hand Painted, 10 In. 85.00
Owl, Ring Tree, Blue Satin 38.00
Paperweight, Fish, Lime Satin 38.00
Paperweight, Fish, Orange Carnival 38.00
Paperweight, Owl, Blue Satin 48.00
Peach Crest, Bowl, 8 Points, Crimped Edge, 1940 .... 300.00
Peach Crest, Bowl, Shell, 10 In. 75.00
Persian Medallion, Basket, Custard Satin 44.00
Pinwheel, Compote, Blue Satin 45.00
Plate, Mother's Day, 1976, 8 In. 50.00
Plate, Mother's Day, 1980, 8 In. 30.00
Polka Dot, Creamer, Cranberry Opalescent, 4 In. 90.00
Prayer Rug, Plate, Custard Glass, 7 1/2 In. 95.00
Ribbon Tie, Basket, Red Carnival 60.00
Rose Bowl, 90th Anniversary, Cranberry Opalescent, Large 47.00
Rose Butterfly, Candy Box, Heritage Green 38.00
Rubina Verde, Basket 100.00
Rubina Verde, Box, Melon 135.00
Ruby, Vase, Flared, 1934, 8 In. 70.00
Scroll & Eye, Nut Dish, Blue Satin 58.00
Silver Crest, Banana Boat, Footed ....50.00 to 60.00
Silver Crest, Basket, 6 In. 25.00
Silver Crest, Basket, 7 In. ....35.00 to 60.00
Silver Crest, Basket, 9 x 10 In. 50.00
Silver Crest, Basket, Painted Butterflies, 7 In. 40.00
Silver Crest, Bowl, 7 In. 18.00
Silver Crest, Bowl, 10 In. ....27.00 to 49.00
Silver Crest, Bowl, 13 In. ....37.00 to 55.00
Silver Crest, Bowl, Heart, Handle 27.00
Silver Crest, Bowl, Ruffled, 11 In. 38.00
Silver Crest, Cake Plate, 13 In. ....40.00 to 65.00
Silver Crest, Candy Dish, 7 In. 16.00
Silver Crest, Candy Dish, Cover, Footed, Spanish Lace 99.00
Silver Crest, Compote, 3 1/2 In. 21.00
Silver Crest, Compote, 7 In. 15.00
Silver Crest, Compote, Nut 29.00
Silver Crest, Cruet, Oil 80.00
Silver Crest, Epergne, 12 In., 4 Piece 100.00
Silver Crest, Plate, 7 In. 14.00
Silver Crest, Plate, 8 1/2 In. 27.00
Silver Crest, Relish, Divided 33.00
Silver Crest, Rose Bowl, Footed, 6 In. 55.00
Silver Crest, Tidbit, 2 Tiers 40.00
Silver Crest, Tidbit, 3 Tiers 55.00
Silver Crest, Top Hat, 4 x 4 In. 28.00
Silver Crest, Vase, 8 In. 45.00

Silver Crest, Vase, Fan, 12 In.	110.00
Silver Crest, Vase, Melon, 5 In.	25.00
Snow Crest, Bowl, Blue, 5 1/2 In.	25.00
Stiegel Blue Opalescent, Lamp, 1991, 15 In.	205.00
Three Fruit, Compote, Handle	55.00
Thumbprint, Decanter, Cranberry Opalescent, Stopper	175.00
Vasa Murrhina, Basket, Aventurine Green, Blue, 7 In.	75.00
Vasa Murrhina, Basket, Aventurine Green, Blue, 11 In.	125.00
Vasa Murrhina, Creamer, Autumn Orange, 4 In.	80.00
Vasa Murrhina, Pitcher, Aventurine Green, Blue, 14 In.	200.00
Vasa Murrhina, Vase, Autumn Orange, 4 In.	45.00
Vasa Murrhina, Vase, Autumn Orange, 8 In.	55.00
Vasa Murrhina, Vase, Aventurine Green, Blue, 4 In.	50.00
Vasa Murrhina, Vase, Aventurine Green, Rose, 4 In.	55.00
Vasa Murrhina, Vase, Aventurine Green, Rose, Square, 7 In.	95.00
Violets In The Snow, Bonbon, 6 In.	25.00
Violets In The Snow, Candy Dish	48.00
Violets In The Snow, Compote, Low	45.00
Water Lily, Basket, Lavender Satin, 7 In.	95.00
Water Lily, Basket, White Satin, 7 In.	40.00
Water Lily, Bowl, Blue Satin, 9 In.	45.00
Water Lily, Vase, Bud, Blue Satin	32.00

FIESTA, the colorful dinnerware, was introduced in 1936 by the Homer Laughlin China Co., redesigned in 1969, and withdrawn in 1973. It was reissued again in 1986 in different colors and is still being made. The simple design was characterized by a band of concentric circles, beginning at the rim. Cups had full-circle handles until 1969, when partial-circle handles were made. Harlequin and Riviera were related wares. For more information and prices of American dinnerware, see the book *Kovels' Depression Glass & Dinnerware Price List.*

Chartreuse, Ashtray, 5 1/2 In.	80.00 to 121.00
Chartreuse, Bowl, Dessert, 6 In.	72.00
Chartreuse, Chop Plate, 13 In.	75.00 to 125.00
Chartreuse, Chop Plate, 15 In.	145.00
Chartreuse, Coffeepot	550.00 to 585.00
Chartreuse, Cup & Saucer	45.00
Chartreuse, Cup & Saucer, After Dinner	625.00
Chartreuse, Eggcup	215.00
Chartreuse, Mug	90.00 to 95.00
Chartreuse, Mug, Tom & Jerry	70.00
Chartreuse, Nappy, 8 1/2 In.	83.00
Chartreuse, Pitcher, Disk	275.00
Chartreuse, Plate, 7 In.	13.00
Chartreuse, Plate, 9 In.	25.00
Chartreuse, Plate, 10 In.	48.00 to 50.00
Chartreuse, Plate, Deep, 8 1/4 In.	75.00
Chartreuse, Plate, Dessert, 6 In.	50.00
Chartreuse, Platter, 12 In.	65.00
Chartreuse, Sauceboat	90.00 to 95.00
Chartreuse, Saucer, After Dinner	110.00
Chartreuse, Soup, Cream	83.00 to 95.00
Chartreuse, Teapot, 6 Cup	250.00 to 395.00
Cobalt Blue, Ashtray, 5 1/2 In.	72.00
Cobalt Blue, Bowl, Fruit, 11 3/4 In.	350.00
Cobalt Blue, Cake Plate, Kitchen Kraft, 10 7/8 In.	83.00
Cobalt Blue, Casserole, Cover, Individual	75.00
Cobalt Blue, Casserole, Cover, Kitchen Kraft, 8 1/2 In.	110.00 to 150.00
Cobalt Blue, Coffeepot	275.00 to 355.00
Cobalt Blue, Coffeepot, After Dinner	395.00
Cobalt Blue, Cup	35.00
Cobalt Blue, Cup & Saucer, After Dinner	95.00
Cobalt Blue, Eggcup	75.00 to 105.00

Cobalt Blue, Jar, Large, Kitchen Kraft 435.00
Cobalt Blue, Jar, Medium, Kitchen Kraft 495.00
Cobalt Blue, Jug, Water, 2 Pt. 120.00
Cobalt Blue, Mixing Bowl, Kitchen Kraft, 6 In. 250.00
Cobalt Blue, Mixing Bowl, No. 1 . . . . .225.00 to 375.00
Cobalt Blue, Mixing Bowl, No. 2 . . . .   195.00
Cobalt Blue, Mixing Bowl, No. 2, Cover 1635.00
Cobalt Blue, Mixing Bowl, No. 4 . . . .   155.00
Cobalt Blue, Mixing Bowl, No. 5 . . . . .185.00 to 325.00
Cobalt Blue, Mixing Bowl, No. 7, Cover 725.10
Cobalt Blue, Mug 85.00
Cobalt Blue, Mustard . . . . .245.00 to 395.00
Cobalt Blue, Nappy, 8 1/2 In. 75.00
Cobalt Blue, Pitcher, 2 Pt. 120.00
Cobalt Blue, Plate, 10 In. 55.00
Cobalt Blue, Plate, Compartment, 12 In. 75.00
Cobalt Blue, Sauceboat 95.00
Cobalt Blue, Sugar 25.00
Cobalt Blue, Sugar & Creamer, After Dinner 125.00
Cobalt Blue, Sugar, Cover 40.00
Cobalt Blue, Teapot 125.00
Cobalt Blue, Teapot, 8 Cup 335.00
Cobalt Blue, Tumbler, Juice . . . . .40.00 to 55.00
Cobalt Blue, Tumbler, Water 85.00
Cobalt Blue, Vase, 8 In. 750.00
Cobalt Blue, Vase, 10 In. 950.00
Cobalt Blue, Vase, 12 In. 1500.00
Forest Green, Ashtray, 5 1/2 In. 99.00
Forest Green, Casserole, Cover . . . . .250.00 to 435.00
Forest Green, Chop Plate, 13 In. 80.00
Forest Green, Coffeepot . . . . .280.00 to 350.00
Forest Green, Cup & Saucer 45.00
Forest Green, Eggcup 160.00
Forest Green, Nappy, 8 1/2 In. 83.00
Forest Green, Pitcher, 2 Pt. 215.00
Forest Green, Pitcher, Disk 365.00
Forest Green, Plate, 6 In. 13.00
Forest Green, Plate, 10 In. . . . . .48.00 to 65.00
Forest Green, Plate, Compartment, 10 1/2 In. 95.00
Forest Green, Sauceboat 90.00
Forest Green, Saucer, After Dinner . . . . .185.00 to 225.00
Forest Green, Soup, Cream . . . . .83.00 to 95.00
Forest Green, Teapot, 6 Cup 250.00
Forest Green, Teapot, 8 Cup 395.00
Forest Green, Vase, 8 In. 750.00
Gray, Ashtray, 5 1/2 In. 105.00
Gray, Bowl, Dessert, 6 In. 55.00
Gray, Casserole, Cover 375.00
Gray, Chop Plate, 13 In. 95.00
Gray, Coffeepot . . . . .600.00 to 750.00
Gray, Eggcup . . . . .165.00 to 230.00
Gray, Mug . . . . .90.00 to 95.00
Gray, Pitcher, Disk 2900.00
Gray, Plate, 10 In. . . . . .48.00 to 70.00
Gray, Plate, Deep, 8 1/4 In. . . . . .50.00 to 65.00
Gray, Platter, 12 In. 60.00
Gray, Sauceboat 57.00
Gray, Saucer, After Dinner 195.00
Gray, Soup, Cream 83.00
Gray, Tumbler, Juice 450.00
Ivory, Bowl, Fruit, 11 3/4 In. 250.00
Ivory, Calendar Plate, 1954, 10 In. . . . . .40.00 to 45.00
Ivory, Calendar Plate, 1955, 9 In. 75.00

Ivory, Calendar Plate, 1955, 10 In. 55.00
Ivory, Candleholder, Bulb, Pair ....115.00 to 125.00
Ivory, Candleholder, Tripod, Pair 725.00
Ivory, Carafe 650.00
Ivory, Chop Plate, 13 In. 45.00
Ivory, Coffeepot 390.00
Ivory, Eggcup ....65.00 to 105.00
Ivory, Mixing Bowl, No. 1 .... 390.00
Ivory, Mixing Bowl, No. 2 .... 225.00
Ivory, Mixing Bowl, No. 2, Cover ....1300.00 to 1550.00
Ivory, Mixing Bowl, No. 3, Cover ....1330.00 to 1960.00
Ivory, Mixing Bowl, No. 4 .... 225.00
Ivory, Mixing Bowl, No. 5 .... 275.00
Ivory, Mixing Bowl, No. 7 .... 580.00
Ivory, Mug ....95.00 to 125.00
Ivory, Pitcher, Disk ....130.00 to 150.00
Ivory, Pitcher, Ice Lip 165.00
Ivory, Plate, 6 In. 7.00
Ivory, Plate, 7 In. 10.00
Ivory, Plate, 10 In. 40.00
Ivory, Plate, Turkey, 14 In. 115.00
Ivory, Soup, Onion, Cover 950.00
Ivory, Syrup 350.00
Ivory, Teapot, 6 Cup ....125.00 to 225.00
Ivory, Teapot, 8 Cup ....220.00 to 225.00
Ivory, Tom & Jerry 40.00
Ivory, Tumbler, Juice ....*Illus* 35.00
Ivory, Tumbler, Water 90.00
Ivory, Vase, 8 In. ....750.00 to 895.00
Ivory, Vase, 10 In. 650.00
Ivory, Vase, 12 In. 1500.00
Light Green, Ashtray, 5 1/2 In. ....50.00 to 72.00
Light Green, Calendar Plate, 1955, 10 In. 45.00
Light Green, Candleholder, Tripod, Pair 500.00
Light Green, Carafe ....225.00 to 325.00
Light Green, Casserole, Cover ....150.00 to 165.00
Light Green, Chop Plate, 13 In. 35.00
Light Green, Chop Plate, 15 In. 45.00
Light Green, Coffeepot ....180.00 to 225.00
Light Green, Coffeepot, After Dinner ....475.00 to 605.00
Light Green, Compote, 12 In. ....150.00 to 195.00
Light Green, Cup & Saucer 30.00
Light Green, Cup & Saucer, After Dinner ....85.00 to 100.00
Light Green, Eggcup ....50.00 to 83.00
Light Green, Mixing Bowl, No. 1, Cover 1150.00
Light Green, Mixing Bowl, No. 3 .... 225.00
Light Green, Mixing Bowl, No. 4 .... 195.00
Light Green, Mixing Bowl, No. 5 .... 225.00
Light Green, Mug 85.00
Light Green, Mustard 250.00
Light Green, Nappy, 8 1/2 In. 45.00
Light Green, Nappy, 9 1/2 In. 110.00
Light Green, Pie Plate, Concentric Rings Both Top & Bottom 650.00
Light Green, Pitcher, Disk ....90.00 to 145.00
Light Green, Plate, 7 In. 10.00
Light Green, Plate, 9 In. 12.00
Light Green, Plate, 10 In. ....28.00 to 30.00
Light Green, Relish 325.00
Light Green, Soup, Cream ....35.00 to 65.00
Light Green, Soup, Onion, Cover ....450.00 to 850.00
Light Green, Sugar & Creamer 85.00
Light Green, Teapot, 6 Cup 195.00
Light Green, Teapot, 8 Cup ....175.00 to 225.00

Fiesta, Yellow, Pitcher, Disk
Fiesta, Red, Tumbler, Juice
Fiesta, Ivory, Tumbler, Juice

Light Green, Tumbler, Juice . . . . .30.00 to 35.00
Light Green, Vase, 8 In. . . . . .650.00 to 785.00
Light Green, Vase, 12 In. . . . . .1095.00 to 1575.00
Medium Green, Ashtray, 5 1/2 In. 260.00
Medium Green, Bowl, 8 In. 125.00
Medium Green, Bowl, Cereal, 5 1/2 In. . . . . .50.00 to 65.00
Medium Green, Chop Plate, 13 In. . . . . .495.00 to 650.00
Medium Green, Creamer . . . . .80.00 to 125.00
Medium Green, Cup & Saucer 65.00
Medium Green, Mug . . . . .85.00 to 150.00
Medium Green, Nappy, 8 1/2 In. 215.00
Medium Green, Pitcher, Disk . . . . .1600.00 to 1900.00
Medium Green, Plate, 6 In. . . . . .20.00 to 35.00
Medium Green, Plate, 7 In. . . . . .30.00 to 45.00
Medium Green, Plate, 9 In. 65.00
Medium Green, Plate, 10 In. . . . . .100.00 to 195.00
Medium Green, Platter, 12 In. . . . . .75.00 to 182.00
Medium Green, Salt & Pepper . . . . .145.00 to 270.00
Medium Green, Sauceboat 195.00
Medium Green, Saucer 10.00
Medium Green, Soup, Cream . . . . .4000.00 to 8500.00
Medium Green, Sugar . . . . .300.00 to 330.00
Medium Green, Teapot, 6 Cup . . . . .870.00 to 1650.00
Red, Bowl, Fruit, 11 3/4 In. 420.00
Red, Cake Plate, Kitchen Kraft, 10 7/8 In. 75.00
Red, Candleholder, Tripod, Pair 845.00
Red, Carafe . . . . .125.00 to 475.00
Red, Casserole, Cover, Kitchen Kraft, Individual 175.00
Red, Coffeepot, After Dinner 725.00
Red, Compote, 12 In. . . . . .110.00 to 200.00
Red, Creamer 35.00
Red, Cup & Saucer 38.00
Red, Eggcup . . . . .65.00 to 125.00
Red, Jar, Marmalade 395.00
Red, Mixing Bowl Cover, No. 1 . . . . 1090.00
Red, Mixing Bowl, No. 1 . . . . 275.00
Red, Mixing Bowl, No. 3, Cover 1600.00
Red, Mixing Bowl, No. 7 . . . . 675.00
Red, Mug 110.00
Red, Mustard . . . . .235.00 to 395.00
Red, Nappy, 8 1/2 In. . . . . .31.00 to 45.00
Red, Pitcher, Disk . . . . .750.00 to 795.00
Red, Pitcher, Ice Lip 135.00
Red, Plate, 7 In. 10.00
Red, Plate, 10 In. . . . . .40.00 to 50.00
Red, Platter, 12 In. 75.00

Red, Sauceboat ....65.00 to 85.00
Red, Soup, Cream 75.00
Red, Teapot, 6 Cup ....125.00 to 225.00
Red, Tumbler, Juice ....*Illus*   50.00
Red, Vase, 8 In. ....750.00 to 1090.00
Red, Vase, 12 In. 2900.00
Rose, Ashtray, 5 1/2 In. 105.00
Rose, Bowl, Dessert, 6 In. 61.00
Rose, Bowl, Fruit, 4 3/4 In. ....25.00 to 28.00
Rose, Casserole, Cover 275.00
Rose, Cup & Saucer, After Dinner 790.00
Rose, Mug 95.00
Rose, Nappy, 8 1/2 In. 50.00
Rose, Pitcher, Disk ....210.00 to 275.00
Rose, Plate, 7 In. 14.00
Rose, Plate, Deep, 8 1/4 In. 55.00
Rose, Soup, Cream ....83.00 to 95.00
Rose, Teapot, 6 Cup ....185.00 to 450.00
Turquoise, Ashtray, 5 1/2 In. 40.00
Turquoise, Bowl, Salad, Individual, 7 1/2 In. 65.00
Turquoise, Carafe 380.00
Turquoise, Casserole, Cover ....135.00 to 145.00
Turquoise, Coffeepot 250.00
Turquoise, Coffeepot, After Dinner ....790.00 to 880.00
Turquoise, Compote, Sweets, 5 1/8 In. 125.00
Turquoise, Cup & Saucer 30.00
Turquoise, Cup & Saucer, After Dinner 115.00
Turquoise, Mixing Bowl, No. 4 .... 220.00
Turquoise, Mug 55.00
Turquoise, Pitcher, Disk ....100.00 to 120.00
Turquoise, Pitcher, Ice Lip 195.00
Turquoise, Plate, 6 In. 8.00
Turquoise, Plate, 10 In. 30.00
Turquoise, Salt & Pepper 135.00
Turquoise, Sugar & Creamer 85.00
Turquoise, Teapot, 6 Cup 150.00
Turquoise, Teapot, 8 Cup 280.00
Turquoise, Tray, Figure 8 .... 395.00
Turquoise, Tumbler, Juice ....35.00 to 40.00
Yellow, Bowl, Fruit, 11 3/4 In. 350.00
Yellow, Bowl, Kitchen Kraft, 8 In. 95.00
Yellow, Bowl, Salad, Footed, 11 1/4 In. 470.00
Yellow, Candleholder, Tripod, Pair 750.00
Yellow, Casserole, Cover ....130.00 to 250.00
Yellow, Casserole, Cover, Kitchen Kraft, 7 1/2 In. 60.00
Yellow, Casserole, French 450.00
Yellow, Coffeepot 150.00
Yellow, Coffeepot, After Dinner 515.00
Yellow, Creamer, Individual 75.00
Yellow, Cup & Saucer, After Dinner 95.00
Yellow, Eggcup ....60.00 to 65.00
Yellow, Jar, Marmalade 360.00
Yellow, Mixing Bowl Cover, No. 1 .... 1060.00
Yellow, Mixing Bowl, No. 1 ....225.00 to 325.00
Yellow, Mixing Bowl, No. 2 .... 140.00
Yellow, Mixing Bowl, No. 2, Cover 1375.00
Yellow, Mustard 125.00
Yellow, Pitcher, Disk ....*Illus*   125.00
Yellow, Pitcher, Juice 40.00
Yellow, Plate, 6 In. 5.00
Yellow, Plate, 7 In. 10.00
Yellow, Plate, 9 In. 12.00

Want to remove a bottle stopper that is stuck? Mix a teaspoon of rubbing alcohol with a half-teaspoon of glycerin and a half-teaspoon of salt. Pour the liquid around the stopper, let it seep in. Try removing the stopper after 24 hours.

Findlay Onyx,
Sugar, Cover,
5 5/8 In.

Yellow, Plate, 10 In.	.25.00 to 30.00
Yellow, Relish, Center	55.00
Yellow, Soup, Cream	35.00
Yellow, Teapot, 6 Cup	100.00
Yellow, Vase, 8 In.	.525.00 to 935.00
Yellow, Vase, 10 In.	860.00

FINCH, see Kay Finch category.

FINDLAY ONYX AND FLORADINE are two similar types of glass made by Dalzell, Gilmore and Leighton Co. of Findlay, Ohio, about 1889. Onyx is a patented yellowish white opaque glass with raised silver daisy decorations. A few rare pieces were made of rose, amber, orange, or purple glass. Floradine is made of cranberry-colored glass with an opalescent white raised floral pattern and a satin finish. The same molds were used for both types of glass.

Celery Vase, Gold Floral	395.00
Creamer	485.00
Sugar, Cover, 5 5/8 In. ....*Illus*	2007.00
Sugar, Platinum, 3 7/8 In.	275.00
Sugar Shaker	450.00
Sugar Shaker, Platinum	385.00

FIREFIGHTING equipment of all types is wanted, from fire marks to uniforms to toy fire trucks. It is said that every little boy wanted to be a fireman or a train engineer 75 years ago and the collectors today reflect this interest.

Alarm Box, Gamewell, 4 Circuit Register, Crank Wound, Brass	325.00
Alarm Box, Gamewell, Telegraph Station, Pull Hook Down Once & Let Go, 13 In.	35.00
Alarm Box, Gamewell, Wall Model, Beveled Glass, Brass Bell, Oak Case, 36 In.	4800.00
Alarm Box, Gamewell, Watchman Patrol Station, Key In Door, 11 x 15 In.	145.00
Alarm Box, Harrington, Flush Mount, 17 x 14 1/2 In.	160.00
Alarm Box, Iron, Milwaukee, 1916	1100.00
Alarm Box, Oakland Electrical Department	215.00
Banner, Wm. Penn, Hose Co. No. 18, Embroidered, Painted, 1890, 57 x 35 In.	2530.00
Belt, Leather, Brass, Old Town, Maine, Dirigo No. 1, 32 In.	175.00
Belt, Parade, Riveted Leather Fire Hose, Silvered Metal, Waterville On Back, 9 In.	350.00
Belt, Parade, Tooled Leather, Letters, Cumberland, 2-Piece Hose Buckle	100.00
Belt, Parade, White Lettering, American, Black	165.00
Beltplate, Brass, Sam F. Estabrook, Oregon Hose Co. No. 1, Shield Shape, 3 In.	975.00
Blotter, Fire Association Of Philadelphia, Fire Hose Logo, Unused, 1920s, 3 x 8 In.	5.00
Boot, Embossed Elephant, Woonsocket Rubber Company	65.00
Bucket, Chemical, Foamite Firefoam, Shield Label, Screw Cap In Bottom, 2 Gal.	55.00
Bucket, Green, Red Rim, Swing Handle, Leather, Signed, Israel Whiton, 1809	8050.00
Bucket, Handle, Black Rubber	440.00
Bucket, Leather, American Heraldic, Handle, Red Border, Columbian Eagle, 12 In.	6900.00

Bucket, Leather, F.F.D. 16, Iron Rings Hold Handle, Red Lettering Decals, 12 x 9 In. 220.00
Bucket, Leather, Green Ground, Handle, Marked, 19th Century, 12 In., Pair 2185.00
Bucket, Leather, Green Letters, Bowen, 1834 .... 860.00
Bucket, Leather, Handle, Dark Green Ground, Handle, Marked, 12 1/2 In. 6325.00
Bucket, Leather, Henry Wood, Quincy, No. 2, Handle, 14 x 8 1/2 In. 825.00
Bucket, Leather, Marked J.J. In Gilt Letters, 13 In., Pair 1320.00
Bucket, Leather, Painted Label, 13 1/2 In. 315.00
Bucket, Leather, Red, Gold Trim, Center Circle, Waltham, V.F.A. & C.L. 145.00
Bucket, Leather, Urban Fire Scene, Dark Green, Handle, Medford Co., 13 In. 14950.00
Bucket, Scrolling Banner, Black & Yellow, Benj. Pitman, 1830, 12 3/4 In. 460.00
Bucket, Wooden, Canvas, Leather, Red Paint, Coat Of Arms, England 66.00
Bucket, Wooden, Shaker, Metal Rings, Wood Handle, 9 x 10 1/2 In. 85.00
Cap, Visor, Hamburg, Germany, Blue Wool Crown, Silver Wire Chin Cord 25.00
Extinguisher, Dispenser, Refill, Minimax Refill, Wall 395.00
Extinguisher, Grenade, Alarm Bell, Patent 1932, Wooden Shipping Box 55.00
Fire Mark, Bird, Cast Iron, 5 1/2 x 7 In. 55.00
Gong, Brass, Painted White, Gamewell 110.00
Gong, Fire Engine, Foot Powered, 1920s 215.00
Gong, Wind Alert, Center Wind, Brass, 10 In. 360.00
Grenade, Cobalt Blue, Horizontal Rib Pattern, Tooled Mouth, 1 Pt., 6 1/8 In. 305.00
Grenade, H.N.S., Monogram, Yellow, Labels, Contents, 1875-1885 .... 175.00
Grenade, Harden's Fire Extinguisher, Blue, Cork Stopper Top, 6 1/2 In. 125.00
Grenade, Harden's Star, Blue, Contents 115.00
Grenade, Hayward, Amber Variation, Contents, 1875-1885 .... 265.00
Grenade, Hayward, Cobalt Blue, Patent 1871 .... 350.00
Grenade, Hayward, Lime Green, Contents, 1875-1885 .... 295.00
Grenade, Red Comet, Label, Box, 6 Piece 650.00
Grenade, S.F. Hayward, Cobalt Blue, 1875-1885 .... 265.00
Hat, Fire Chief, Box 250.00
Hat, Fire, Parade, Green, Spread Winged Eagle, Red, Gold, Leather, 15 In. 14950.00
Hat, Good Will 1802, Top Hat Style, Leather, Black Paint, Gold Letters, 6 x 13 In. 3163.00
Hatchet, Hand Forged Steel, Fitted Brass Sheath On Handle, 17 1/8 In. 320.00
Helmet, Aluminum, Leather Front, Abington Fire Company 230.00
Helmet, Brass, Georgian, Dragon Design, Crest, National Fire Brigades Union 220.00
Helmet, Brass, Plate Marked L.C.C.L.F.B., England, 19th Century, 10 In. 253.00
Helmet, Cairn's Model 770, Polycarbonate, Orange, Salesman's Sample 100.00
Helmet, Chief's, Cairn's Model 880, Polycarbonate, Yellow, Salesman's Sample 220.00
Helmet, Hoseman 4, RFD, Black Aluminum, Patent Leather Shield 220.00
Helmet, Leather Front, Black Aluminum, New Milford, Liner 120.00
Helmet, Leather, Eagle On Front Piece, America Hose, Liner 145.00
Helmet, Leather, Lobed Hat Surmounted By Gilt Metal Eagle's Head, 9 1/8 In. 115.00
Horn, Brass, 17 In. 520.00
Horn, Fireman's, Brass, Red Paint, Inscribed, 17 In. 575.00
Horn, Silver Plate, Inscribed, 18 In. 805.00
Horn, Silver Plate, Repousse Flowers, 23 In. 805.00
Hydrant, City, Red, Cast Iron, 20th Century, 16 1/4 In. 1955.00
Medal, Delegate, Fireman's Convention, Keystone Shape, Metal, Celluloid, 1909 .... 30.00
Mug, Glass, Royal Fire Co., York, Pa., 75th Anniversary, 1976, 5 1/2 In. 10.00
Nozzle, Brass, Leather Handles, New York Nozzle Company 110.00
Nozzle, Chief Model, 2 Man, Elkhart Brass Mfg. Co., 19 1/2 In. 170.00
Nozzle, Nickeled Brass, Haydenville Mfg. Company, 12 In. 120.00
Photograph, Chicago Co. Hose No. 21, Mounted, 19th Century, 10 x 12 In. 200.00
Ribbon, Fire Event, Blue Fabric, Silver Fire Wagon Design, 1906, 2 x 6 1/2 In. 24.00
Ribbon, Liberty Fire Engine Co., Red, Gold, July 4, 1891, Middletown, Pa., 2 x 6 In. 25.00
Ribbon, Reading Hose No. 1 Fire Co., Black, Silver, Late 1800s, 2 1/2 x 6 1/2 In. 18.00
Shot Glass, Silver Plate, Little Giant Engine Co., Chicago Fire Dept., 1871, 2 3/4 In. 175.00
Trumpet, Sheet Metal, Oval Mouthpiece, Tapered, Red Paint, Gold, 16 In. 980.00
Trumpet, Silver Plate, Columbia Club, Long Island City, Engraved, 16 3/4 In. 1265.00
Trumpet, Silver Plate, Fleur-De-Lis, Tassel, 19th Century, 18 3/4 In. 1090.00
Trumpet, Speaking, Fire Engine, Floral & Geometric, Presentation, 1887, 20 In. 300.00
Trumpet, Speaking, Nickel & Brass, Octagonal, Cairns 385.00
Trumpet, Speaking, Solid Brass, 14 In. 55.00

FIREPLACES were used to cook food and to heat the American home in past centuries. Many types of tools and equipment were used. Andirons held the logs in place, firebacks reflected the heat into the room, and tongs were used to move either fuel or food. Many types of spits and roasting jacks were made and may be listed in the Kitchen category.

Andirons, Brass & Iron, Claw Feet, Urn Top, 20th Century, 20 1/2 x 12 1/2 In.	196.00
Andirons, Brass, Ball Top Finial, Matching Back Firedog Finials, 15 In.	550.00
Andirons, Brass, Ball Top, 15 In.	220.00
Andirons, Brass, Ball Top, 16 1/2 In.	176.00
Andirons, Brass, Ball Top, 17 3/4 In.	137.00
Andirons, Brass, Ball Top, American, 17 In.	660.00
Andirons, Brass, Ball, Spur Legs, 16 In.	165.00
Andirons, Brass, Baluster Shape, 15 In.	154.00
Andirons, Brass, Baluster Shape, Ball Feet, 1810, 17 1/2 In.	275.00
Andirons, Brass, Cannonball Finals, Scrolled Legs, 20 In.	175.00
Andirons, Brass, Cannonball Top, Ball & Claw Feet, 28 In.	460.00
Andirons, Brass, Classical, Beaded Ball Top, Stepped Column, Hunneman, Boston, 11 In.	1100.00
Andirons, Brass, Clipper Ship Design, Square Arched Feet, Arts & Crafts, 25 In.	260.00
Andirons, Brass, Covered Urn Shape, Plinth Base, Claw, Ball Feet, 19 1/4 In.	70.00
Andirons, Brass, Double Lemon Top, 17 1/2 In.	385.00
Andirons, Brass, Double Lemon Top, Scrolled Base, Ball Footed, 25 In.	275.00
Andirons, Brass, Double Lemon Top, Spurred Cabriole Legs, Ball Footed, 22 In.	770.00
Andirons, Brass, England, 10 1/2 In.	345.00
Andirons, Brass, Flame Finial, Arched, Reeded Legs, Plinth Base, 29 In.	1150.00
Andirons, Brass, Hexagonal Column, Turned Baluster, Large Ball Finial, 22 In.	260.00
Andirons, Brass, Knife Blade, Flared Support, Arched Legs, Penny Feet, 20 In.	1955.00
Andirons, Brass, Large Spherical Finial, Arched, Spurred Feet, 19th Century, 21 In.	225.00
Andirons, Brass, Leaf-Capped Urn, Square Feet, 20 In.	980.00
Andirons, Brass, Lemon Top, Spurred Arch Supports, Ball Feet, 18th Century	425.00
Andirons, Brass, Napoleon III, Columns, Festooned Urn, 1870, 33 1/2 In.	605.00
Andirons, Brass, Rectangular Pedestal, Concave Sides, Urn Finial, 21 In.	1150.00
Andirons, Brass, Ring Turned, Spurred Legs, Ball Feet	260.00
Andirons, Brass, Santa Claus In Full Attire, Eastlake, 18 In.	4500.00
Andirons, Brass, Slipper Feet, Log Stops, Late 18th Century, 15 1/2 In.	900.00
Andirons, Brass, Steeple Top, 18 3/4 In. . . . . .385.00 to 990.00
Andirons, Brass, Steeple Top, Early 1800s	925.00
Andirons, Brass, Tapered Column Form, Claw, Ball Feet, 24 1/2 In.	290.00
Andirons, Brass, Tapered Column, Eagle Finial, Outstretched Wings, 22 In.	260.00
Andirons, Brass, Turned Type Post, Dome Top, Faceted Collar, 18 In.	575.00
Andirons, Brass, Turned, Tapered Column, Horizontal Fluted Sphere, Ball Feet	520.00
Andirons, Brass, Winged Female Terms, Raised On Paw Feet, 32 In.	1150.00
Andirons, Bronze & Nickel, Feather Shape, Iron Log Supports, 1930, 23 1/2 In.	1840.00
Andirons, Bronze, Balustrade Supporting Flame 1 End, Nude Children Other, 12 In.	2200.00
Andirons, Bronze, Dog & Cat, Seated On Cushion, Toupie Feet, Gilt, 13 1/2 In.	4312.00
Andirons, Bronze, Figural, Cherubs Sitting Stop Rococo Style Shell, 9 1/2 In.	400.00
Andirons, Bronze, Masks, Winged Beasts, Columns, Foliate Legs, 27 1/2 In.	1265.00
Andirons, Bronze, Putto Term Making Arrows, Urn On Hoof Supports, 17 12 In.	4600.00
Andirons, Bronze, Regency, Gilt, Recumbent Lion Shape, Plinth, 13 1/2 x 14 In.	2645.00
Andirons, Bronze, Renaissance Revival, Winged Putto On Plinth, Rams' Heads, 36 In. . . .	4887.00
Andirons, Bronze, Ribbon Tied Berried Laurel Leaf Garlands, Louis XVI, 33 In.	260.00
Andirons, Cast Iron, African-American Man & Woman, Hands On Knees, 15 1/2 In.	1150.00
Andirons, Cast Iron, Cat, Seated, Green Glass Eyes, Early 1900s, 16 In.	1495.00
Andirons, Cast Iron, Dolphin, Placed Face To Face, 14 x 16 1/2 In.	1210.00
Andirons, Cast Iron, Hessian Soldier, 17 In.	66.00
Andirons, Cast Iron, Hessian Soldier, 19th Century, 18 1/2 In.	230.00
Andirons, Cast Iron, Hessian Soldier, Black, 12 x 12 In.	135.00
Andirons, Cast Iron, Hessian Soldier, Log Supports, 19 x 9 1/2 x 29 In.	155.00
Andirons, Cast Iron, Hound, Half Round, 20th Century, 14 In.	2587.00
Andirons, Cast Iron, Open Scrollwork Design, 14 In.	25.00
Andirons, Cowboy, Orange Paint, 11 x 7 In.	1200.00
Andirons, Empire, Brass, Turned, Scrolled Legs, 19 In.	220.00
Andirons, Female Egyptian Bust, Egg Shape, Panther, Sleeping, 20 1/2 In.	2070.00

Andirons, Greek Woman, Classical Dress, Cornucopia Feet, 13 x 18 In. 395.00
Andirons, Indian Brave, Feathered Headdress, Tomahawk In Hand, 19 1/2 In. 1870.00
Andirons, Iron Scrollwork, Renaissance Style, Spiral Log Stops, 27 1/2 In. 200.00
Andirons, Iron, Brass Faceted Finial Knife Blade Upright, Arched Feet 230.00
Andirons, Iron, Brass Finial, Square Tapered Shafts, Arched Scrolled Footed, 25 In. 135.00
Andirons, Iron, Daisy Flower, Scroll Design Base, Arts & Crafts, 20 x 9 x 19 In. 335.00
Andirons, Knife Blade, Brass Urn Shape Finials, Penny Feet, J. Byers, 21 In. 770.00
Andirons, Knife Blade, Lemon Top, Penny Feet, 1790s, 15 In. 517.00
Andirons, Owl, Twig Base, Chrome Plate Co., 1890s 495.00
Andirons, Pewter, Lion Finial, 28 In. 345.00
Andirons, Rape Of Sabine Women, Grotesque Masks, Paw Feet, 34 In. 3450.00
Andirons, Steel & Brass, Penny Feet, Faceted Finials, 20 1/4 In. 360.00
Andirons, Steel, Knife Blade, Steeple, Urn Top Finials, 21 In. 575.00
Andirons, Triple Graduated Melon Ball, Flame Finial, Ball & Claw Feet, 26 1/2 In. 805.00
Andirons, Wrought Iron & Brass, Lemon Finial, Spurred Legs, Ball Feet, 25 In. 6325.00
Andirons, Wrought Iron, Partially Spirally Turned Standard, Bipod Legs, 42 In. 2300.00
Andirons, Wrought Iron, Penny Footed, Ring Top, 15 1/2 In. 185.00
Andirons, Wrought Iron, Ring Top, 15 In. 80.00
Andirons, Wrought Iron, Scrolled, 17 1/2 In. 55.00
Andirons, Wrought Iron, Snake Shape, Early 20th Century, 15 In. 1450.00
Andirons, Wrought Iron, Twist Forged Column, Ring Handles, 1900, 31 In. 200.00
Bellows, Design, Yellow Paint 245.00
Bellows, Leather & Walnut, Carved Flowers, Removable Brass Nozzle, 23 1/2 In. 5520.00
Bellows, Leather, Turtle Back, Cornucopia, Yellow Paint, Brass Nozzle, 18 1/4 In. 148.00
Bellows, Leather, Turtle Back, Red Paint, Cornucopia, Brass Nozzle, 18 In. 195.00
Bellows, Painted Design, Eckstein & Richardson, 16 In. 330.00
Bellows, Relief Eagle, Lions & Scrollwork, 25 In. 385.00
Bellows, Turtle Back, Fruit & Foliage Design, Brass Nozzle, Red Paint, 17 In. 120.00
Bellows, Turtle Back, Stenciled, Flowers & Foliage, Brass Nozzle, 17 1/2 In. 360.00
Bellows, Turtle Back, Yellow Paint, Freehand Fruit & Flowers, Brass Nozzle, 15 In. 355.00
Box, Coal, Metal Pull-Out Liner, Hammered, c.1910, 12 x 12 In. 85.00
Brass, George II, Tool Box, Bronze 170.00
Broiler, Rotating, Forged Iron 220.00
Broiler, Whirling, Wrought Iron, Late 18th Century 325.00
Broom, Oven & Hearth, Twist Wrapped Handle, 17 In. 160.00
Broom, Salmon Paint On Handle, Early 19th Century, 31 In. 350.00
Coal Scuttle, Copper, Hammered, Hand-Wrought Iron Handles, Arts & Crafts, 19 In. 605.00
Coal Scuttle, Hammered Brass, Relief Scenes, Knight's Helmet Crest, 17 x 15 In. 220.00
Coal Scuttle, Scoop, Brass, c.1890, 13 x 13 1/2 In. 180.00
Cover & Frame, Iron, Summer, Neoclassical, 1900, 30 x 31 x 3 1/2 In. 85.00
Dummy Board, Gardner, Resting On Shovel, Painted Wood, 18th Century, 66 5/8 In. 5750.00
Fender, Brass & Wire, D-Shape, 19th Century, 33 1/2 In. 175.00
Fender, Brass, 2 Pierced Bands Of Geometric Design, Lion Paw Feet, 43 1/2 In. 635.00
Fender, Brass, Art Deco, 9 In. 412.00
Fender, Brass, Bowed Ribbons & Medallion, Urn Finials, 12 1/2 x 53 x 14 1/2 In. 290.00
Fender, Brass, Copper, Pierced Looped Design, Rectangular Plinth, Victorian, 14 In. 100.00
Fender, Brass, Foliate, Floral Arabesques, Victorian, 68 In. 200.00
Fender, Brass, Gilt, Adjustable, Plinth At Each End, 43 In. 520.00
Fender, Brass, Leaf Swags Between Cast Posts, Leaf Finials, 54 x 15 In. 290.00
Fender, Brass, Paw Feet, England, 57 x 13 In. 460.00
Fender, Brass, Pierced Grill Work, 8 1/4 x 47 In. 115.00
Fender, Brass, Pierced, Adams Style, Late 19th Century, 63 In. 385.00
Fender, Brass, Pierced, Paw Feet, 19th Century, 9 1/2 x 47 x 14 In. 165.00
Fender, Brass, Reticulated Grill, Paw Feet, 49 1/2 In. 110.00
Fender, Brass, Scrolled Foliage, Lion Paw Feet, Regency, 7 1/2 x 54 1/4 x 15 In. 90.00
Fender, Brass, Spindle Gallery, Pierced Oval Foliate Design, 20th Century, 52 In. 230.00
Fender, Brass, Wire Mesh, Paw Feet, 19th Century, 9 x 48 x 10 In. 330.00
Fender, Bronze, Foliate, Hunting Scene Beneath Palm Tree, Gadroon Base, 23 In. 2875.00
Fender, Marble Inserts, Ribbon Design, Brass, 69 3/4 In. 385.00
Fender, Pierced Oriental Design, 53 In. 385.00
Fender, Wire, Crisscross Pattern, Brass Trim 115.00
Fender, Wire, Grass Top Rail, 24 x 35 1/2 In. 70.00
Fender, Wrought Iron, Wire Grill, Brass Top Rail, 42 1/2 x 12 In. 275.00

Fire Stand, Wrought Iron, 3 Footed, 19th Century, 8 1/2 In. 44.00
Fire Surround, Ornate Crest Top, Salesman's Sample, 1850 .... 650.00
Fireback, Hounds, Sleeping, Floral Border, 25 x 23 In. 470.00
Firedog, Dachshund, Iron, 21 3/4 x 7 1/8 In. 500.00
Firedog, Dachshund, Original Painted Surface, 12 x 32 In. 470.00
Flue Cover, Cowgirl With Rope, Tin, Stone Lithograph, Germany, c.1900, 9 1/2 In. 415.00
Footman, Iron & Brass, Quadrivet, Exaggerated Cabriole Front Legs, 12 In. 55.00
Fork, Wrought Iron, KEZ, 16 3/4 In. 145.00
Frying Pan, 3 Legs, Gate Case, 18th Century, 4 In. 135.00
Grate Cover, Cast Iron, Victorian Town House, Bay Windows, 19th Century, 17 In. 1995.00
Griddle, Wrought Iron, Hanging, 1830, 8 x 11 In. 175.00
Grill, Forged Iron, Rosehead Rivets, 1830-1850, 14 1/4 x 13 5/8 x 16 5/8 In. 235.00
Guard, Brass, Allover Lion Mask & Sea Serpents, 11 x 16 In. 97.00
Hook, Double Game, Toggle, Blacksmith Made, 18th Century, 11 In. 145.00
Inset, Cast Iron & Brass 1045.00
Iron, Wager, Hearts, Flourishes & Date, 1741 .... 750.00
Ladle, Drip Catcher, Hand Forged, Footed, c.1775, 16 In. 165.00
Mantel is listed in the Architectural category.
Oven, Sheet Iron, Reflecto, Spit, 1780 .... 450.00
Roaster, Hand Forged, Polished Ball Top, 18th Century 875.00
Roaster, Iron, Ball Finial, Double & Single Pronged Holders, Sliding Frame, 27 In. 460.00
Screen, 5-Panel, D-Shape, Brass Mounted Wirework, Early 19th Century, 30 In. 1725.00
Screen, Brass & Mesh, Louis XVI Style, Floral Design, Oval, 27 1/2 x 29 In. 1760.00
Screen, Brass, Fan Shape, Female Tambourine Player, Victorian, 33 In. 315.00
Screen, Brass, Fan Shape, Gadrooned, Strapwork Base, Belle Epoque, 1900, 27 In. 460.00
Screen, Brass, Fan Shape, Victorian 120.00
Screen, Brass, Stained Glass Panels, Multicolored, Center Top Handle, 26 x 20 In. 290.00
Screen, Giltwood, Velvet, Wreath & Torchere Crest, Scrolled Toes, 41 x 26 In. 330.00
Screen, Mahogany Frame, Mirror, Rectangular, Scroll Base, 19th Century, 46 In. 358.00
Screen, Pole, 19th Century 1875.00
Screen, Pole, Bargello Flame Stitch, Brocade Sampler, 55 In. 495.00
Screen, Pole, Chippendale, Mahogany, Urn Finial, Oval Needlepoint, Tripod 275.00
Screen, Pole, Hanging Embroidery, Red Felt, Oak, Adjustable, 44 In. 230.00
Screen, Pole, Mahogany, Carved Scroll Feet, Adjustable Frame, Needlepoint Insert 250.00
Screen, Pole, Mahogany, Needlepoint Inset, Retracting Into Base, 19th Century 200.00
Screen, Pole, Mahogany, Needlework Memorial, 1812, 67 x 21 In. 3737.00
Screen, Pole, Mahogany, Silk Embroidered Panel, Baluster Shaft, 58 In. 1320.00
Screen, Pole, Needlework Center Panel, Recumbent Dog, c.1860, 50 3/4 In. 1540.00
Screen, Pole, Sheraton, Satinwood Inlay, Tripod Base, 58 x 15 x 12 In. 725.00
Screen, Reticulated Brass, Belle Epoque, 1900-1915, 32 1/2 x 25 1/2 x 11 In. 665.00
Screen, Wire Mesh, Applied Floral Design, 44 In. 138.00
Screen, Wrought Iron, 40 3/4 In. 770.00
Screen, Wrought Iron, Schooner Beneath Billowing Clouds, France, 28 3/4 In. 5750.00
Shelf, Fireside, Wrought Iron, Penny Footed, 15 x 17 x 12 In. 330.00
Shovel, Smithed Steel, Ember, To Light Clay Pipes, Temper On End, 5 1/2 In. 295.00
Shovel & Tongs, Wrought Iron, Brass Ball Handles, 27 1/2 In., Pair 55.00
Shovel & Tongs, Wrought Iron, Steeple Top Handles, 33 In., Pair 525.00
Skimmer, Wrought Iron, Marked WH, 20 In. 145.00
Spatula, Wrought Iron, W.H. Kime, 13 1/4 In. 125.00
Spit, Clockwork, Brass, Salter & Col., 19th Century, 13 In. 77.00
Surround, Pine, Rectangular Stepped Mantle, Ocher, Backboard, 27x 34 In. 920.00
Surround, Walnut, Louis XV, Serpentine Top, Paneled Frieze, Flowers, 45 x 82 In. 1265.00
Toaster, 2 Strap Supports, Lower Ledge, Wrought Iron, Late 17th Century, 53 1/4 In. 1840.00
Toaster, Flip, Turned Handle, c.1800, 17 1/2 x 26 1/2 In. 195.00
Toaster, Rotating, Forged Iron 110.00
Toaster, Wrought Iron, 6 Fleurs-De-Lis, 1760-1820, 16 1/2 In. 375.00
Toaster, Wrought Iron, Hinged Handle 110.00
Toaster, Wrought Iron, New England, Early 19th Century 245.00
Tongs, Ember, Wrought Iron, 10 1/2 In. 210.00
Tongs, Ember, Wrought Iron, Spring Loaded, Attached Pipe Tamper, 17 1/4 In. 550.00
Tongs, Forged Iron, Scissor Action 190.00
Tongs, Wrought Iron, Ember 55.00
Tool Set, Cast Brass Handles, 1800, 28 In., Pair 225.00

Tool Set, Wrought Iron, Fork, Hook, Peel, 50 In. 145.00
Trammel, Ratchet, Brass, 19th Century, France 275.00
Wafer Iron, Eagle Design, Early 19th Century, 18 x 5 1/2 In. 632.00

FISCHER porcelain was made in Herend, Hungary, by Moritz Fischer. The factory was founded in 1839 and continued working into the twentieth century. The wares are sometimes referred to as *Herend* porcelain.   **MF**

After Dinner Set, Queen Victoria, 15 Piece 575.00
Bowl, Birds, Butterflies, Hand Painted, 9 3/4 In. 345.00
Box, Bird Finial, Floral & Gilt Design, Round, 4 1/2 In. 105.00
Box, Cover, Magenta Floral Design, Rose Finial, Round, 3 In. 60.00
Box, Cover, Reticulated, Round 160.00
Box, Leaf Shape, Applied Floral & Gilt Design, 5 In. 105.00
Box, Potpourri, Molded As Recamier, Reticulated Cover As Cushion, 11 In. 150.00
Breakfast Service, Floral & Gilt Design, 29 Piece 460.00
Breakfast Set, Fruits, Flowers, Vegetables, Teapot, Waste Bowl, Cream, Salt & Pepper ..   230.00
Candelabrum, 3-Light, Rothschild Bird, 9 7/8 In. 143.00
Candlestick, Floral & Gilt Design, 6 In., Pair 90.00
Charger, Floral Designs & Birds, 15 In. 250.00
Cider Set, Hand Painted Medallions, Serpent Handle, 12 1/2-In. Jug, 3 Piece 440.00
Cigarette Case, Bird Design, 4 1/4 x 3 1/2 In. 230.00
Dish, Floral & Butterfly Design, 11 In. 105.00
Figurine, Carp, Black, White Scales, Green Tail, Gold Fins, 5 1/2 In. 650.00
Figurine, Dolphin, Black, Blue Tail, Gold Fins, 1 1/2 In. 295.00
Figurine, Jesus, White Glazed Robe, Bisque Head, 11 1/2 In. 1100.00
Figurine, Kakiemon, Leaf Shape, 8 3/4 In. 375.00
Figurine, Man, Rearing Horse, 15 1/2 x 14 In. 1610.00
Figurine, Motherhood, 8 In. 200.00
Figurine, Mrs. Dery, 8 1/2 In. 115.00
Figurine, Nude, Looking In Hand Mirror 430.00
Figurine, Olympic Flame, White, Kneeling, Hand Outstretched, With Torch, 9 1/2 In. 1100.00
Figurine, Polar Bear, White, 7 3/4 x 9 In. 975.00
Figurine, Soldier, With Sword, No. 5505, 16 In. 1900.00
Figurine, Swan, White, Orange Beak, Black Brow, 4 1/4 In. 395.00
Figurine, Turkey, White, Burgundy Head, Neck, 4 3/4 In. 475.00
Figurine, Wine Drinker, 6 1/2 In. 315.00
Lamp, Rothschild Bird, Baluster, 12 1/2 In. 460.00
Plate, Pink, Yellow Carnations, Cream Ground, 1870, 11 1/2 x 1 3/4 In. 795.00
Sign, Tureen & Cover Shape, 6 x 8 1/2 In. 250.00
Tea Set, Applied Floral & Gilt Design, Teapot, Sugar, Creamer, 3 Piece 150.00
Tureen, Poisson, Miniature 155.00
Vase, Floral & Gilt Design, Flared Top, 7 In., Pair 175.00

FISHING reels of brass or nickel were made in the United States by 1810. Bamboo fly rods were sold by 1860, often marked with the maker's name. Lures made of metal, or metal and wood, were made in the nineteenth century. Plastic lures were made by the 1930s. All fishing material is collected today and even equipment of the past thirty years is of interest if in good condition with original box.

Booklet, Hardy's Anglers' Guide, Black & White Photos, England, 1938, 58 Pages 80.00
Box, Bait, Painted Star, Dots On Side, Bottom, Old Green Paint, Tin, Oval, Cover, 4 In. ..   465.00
Box, Bait, Pemberton's Busy Bait, Dealer's, Fishing Scene On Top, 12 Lures 1150.00
Box, Fly, 4 Hinged Lidded Trays, Canvas Straps, Aluminum, 5 1/2 x 6 x 4 In. 135.00
Box, Fly, Richardson, 4 Hinged Compartments, Web Harness 135.00
Box, Tackle, 4 Cantilever Aluminum Trays, Leather Handle, 9 x 9 x 16 In. 163.00
Box, Tackle, Ice Fishing, Filled With Rigs 110.00
Box, Tackle, Leather 330.00
Box, Tackle, Mahogany, 2 Brass Latches, 12 x 20 x 10 In. 355.00
Box, Tackle, Wood, 3 Lift Out Trays, Dovetailed, With Fish-Line Reels, 7 x 8 x 7 In. 245.00
Box, Trout, L.F. Grammes Sons, Wooden, Brook Trout Hatchery, 8 x 12 In. 305.00
Bucket, Minnow, Abbey & Imbrie, Image Of Largemouth Bass, Paper Label, 12 In. 395.00
Bucket, Minnow, Falls City Splendid Minnow, Black Fish, Gold Bands, Green Paint 105.00

Bucket, Minnow, Nu Air Flow, Brown, Tin 80.00
Bucket, Minnow, Perforated Lift Cover, Inverted, Original Green Paint, 9 x 12 In. 355.00
Bucket, Minnow, Torpedo Shape, Heavy Iron Ring, Conical Head, 7 x 19 In. 165.00
Creel, George Lawrence, Split Willow, Leather Strap, Buckle Lid Latch, 1857 .... 2860.00
Creel, Hardy Brothers Ltd., Twisted Reed Handle On Cover, Gold Brown Patina 330.00
Creel, Peg, Loop Latch, Twisted Reed Handle, Leather Harness 155.00
Creel, Peg, Loop Lid Latch, Twisted Reed Handle, Reed Hinges 70.00
Creel, Peg, Rawhide Thong Hinges, Leather Harness 70.00
Creel, Rattan Hinges, Intricate Edge Lacing, Wood Edges On Cover, 9 x 13 x 10 In. 300.00
Creel, Rattan, Leather Mount, 1900, 12 1/2 x 15 1/2 In. 110.00
Creel, Splint, Leather Trim 550.00
Creel, Split Willow, Center Hole, Wire Hinges, 8 x 11 x 9 In. 110.00
Creel, Split Willow, Concave Back, Leather Trim, Leather Hanging Strap 165.00
Creel, Split Willow, Embossed Leather Trim, Leather Hanging Strap 355.00
Creel, Split Willow, Leather Bound, George Lawrence, No. 4-A ....*Illus* 2860.00
Creel, Split Willow, Leather Latch, 5 1/2 x 10 1/2 x 7 In. 60.00
Creel, Split Willow, Metal, Leather Latch, Leather Harness 60.00
Creel, Split Willow, Rawhide Hinges, Harness 110.00
Creel, Wicker & Wood, Red, 1/2 Basket, 15 x 13 x 7 1/2 In. 138.00
Creel, Wicker, Leather & Canvas Strap, Leather Hasp, 13 1/2 In. 100.00
Creel, Wire Loop Latch, Wire Hinges, Twisted Reed Handle 60.00
Harpoon, Hand-Held, Macrame Handle, 9 In. 55.00
Harpoon, Whaling, New England, Forged Iron 45.00
License, Connecticut Angling License, Pink, White, Blue, 1926, 1 3/4 In. 50.00
License, Connecticut Hunting & Angling License, Blue, White, Black, 1 3/4 In. 50.00
License Application, Hennepin County, Minn., $1.00 Fee, Filled Out 4.00
Lure, Al Foss, Minnow, Port Rind, Box 95.00
Lure, Black Sambo 45.00
Lure, Bomber, Double Hooks, Paper Box, 3 1/2 In. 27.00
Lure, Boulton Bass Hog, White Body, Red Head, 3 Double Hooks, Style No. 1, 1911 .... 450.00
Lure, Cod Fish, Fish Shaped Lead Body, Eye, Fins, 2 Large Single Hooks 25.00
Lure, Dowagiac Crab Wiggler, Wood, Green & Yellow Scales, 2 Hooks, 3 1/4 In. 60.00
Lure, Gar Minnow, Special Color, Creek Chub Bait Co. ....*Illus* 990.00
Lure, Glass Squat, Cork Stopper, 6 In. 125.00
Lure, Heddon, Crazy Crawler, Bumble Bee, Double Hooks, Double Spoons, 2 1/2 In. 23.00
Lure, Heddon, Frog, 3 Hooks, Open Legs 400.00
Lure, Heddon, Minnow, Leaping Upward, Green Scale, 3 1/4 In. 425.00
Lure, Heddon, Minnow, No. 1400, 1913 .... 9900.00
Lure, Heddon, Minnow, Painted Gill Marks, Yellow, Red, Green, Black, 3 In. 150.00
Lure, Heddon, Minnow, Painted White, Red Eyes, No. 150 .... 95.00
Lure, Heddon, Minnow, Underwater, Red Scale Finish, Glass Eyes, No. 150, 4 In. 135.00
Lure, Heddon, River-Runt, Sinker, Double Hooks, Spoon, Box, 2 1/2 In. 25.00
Lure, Heddon, Surface Bait, Blue, White Head, Pin Collar, No. 200, 4 3/4 In. 135.00
Lure, Heddon, Wee Willie, Saltwater, Glass Eyes, 2 1/8 In. 355.00
Lure, Mermaid Shape 48.00
Lure, Neverfail Minnow, Glass Eyes, Green Crackle Back, Pflueger, 4 1/4 In. 3375.00

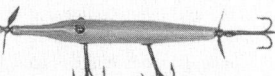

Fishing, Lure, Gar Minnow,
Special Color, Creek Chub Bait Co.

Fishing, Creel, Split Willow,
Leather Bound, George
Lawrence, No. 4-A

Fishing, Lure, Underwater Minnow,
Creek Chub Bait Co.

Fishing, Reel,
Edward Vom Hofe,
Fly, Fulton, N.Y.,
Jan. 23, 1883

Lure, Paul Bunyan Bait Co., Teardrop Spoon, Copper, 2-In. Hook, Box, 6 1/2 In. 30.00
Lure, Paw Paw Bait Co., Frog, No. 73 . . . . 200.00
Lure, Pflueger's Samuel Friend, Frog, Yellow Glass Eyes, 1 Hook, 1906 . . . . 715.00
Lure, Pflueger, Frog 400.00
Lure, Pflueger, Globe, Spinner, Wood, Bulldog Logo, 2 Hooks, 4 In. 40.00
Lure, Plunker, Wooden, Black, Glass Eyes 40.00
Lure, Underwater Minnow, Creek Chub Bait Co. . . . .*Illus* 990.00
Lure, Wilcox Wiggler, 1907 . . . . 3795.00
Lure, Wood Mfg. Co., Dipsy Doodle, Wooden, 1947, 1 1/2 In. 14.00
Motor, Outboard, Evinrude Big Twin, Blue Finish, Electric 300.00
Net, Aluminum, Rubber-Wrapped Wood Handle, 23 In. 60.00
Net, Folding, England 99.00
Net, Trout, Abercrombie & Fitch, Laminated Wood 132.00
Net, Trout, Wooden Frame, 22 3/4 In. 100.00
Net Float, S.H. Davis & Co., Pat. Jan. 16, 1877, Blue Aqua, 5 1/8 In. 285.00
Reel, A.L. Walker, Trout, Wide Spool, Roller Pillar Line Guide, 3 1/4 In. 1045.00
Reel, Abbey & Imbrie, Raised Pillar Hand, Beveled Edge, German Silver 1870.00
Reel, Ambassadeur De Luxe 5000C, Gold Plated Trim, Wooden Box 528.00
Reel, Billinghurst, Fixed Wooden Handle, 1859 . . . . 990.00
Reel, Chubb, Henshall-Van Antwerp, Bait Casting, Wide Spool, 2 1/2 x 1 3/8 In. 6600.00
Reel, Edward Vom Hofe, Bait, Cased, Patent Date Jan. 83, Fulton St., N.Y., 3 In. 770.00
Reel, Edward Vom Hofe, Fly, Cased, Marked Fulton St., N.Y., 3 In. 3300.00
Reel, Edward Vom Hofe, Fly, Fulton, N.Y., Jan. 23, 1883 . . . .*Illus* 4950.00
Reel, Edward Vom Hofe, Superfine Reel Oil, N.Y., 1880 . . . . 440.00
Reel, Edward Vom Hofe, Trout, Size 2 . . . . 4400.00
Reel, Edward Vom Hofe, Universal Star, Hard Rubber Reel, Model 621, 1902 . . . . 330.00
Reel, Edward Vom Hofe, Universal, Ocean, Wide Spool, German Silver, 3 5/8 x 2 In. 330.00
Reel, Fly, England, 1800s 95.00
Reel, Frank Fullilove, Bait Casting, Wide Spool, Ivory Handle Grasp, 2 1/8 x 1 3/8 In. . . . 3960.00
Reel, Gavin, Engraved Face Plate & Case 1430.00
Reel, George S. Gates, Trout, 1885 . . . . 2319.00
Reel, Horton Mfg. Co., No. 7, Bluegrass, Double Handle, German Silver With Nickel 825.00
Reel, Horton Mfg. Co., Tournament, Narrow Spool, German Silver 1320.00
Reel, Julius Vom Hofe, Bait, Patent Nov. 17, 1885 Oct. 8, 1899, 3 In. 165.00
Reel, Julius Vom Hofe, Wide Spool, Hard Rubber Plates, Nickel, 2 1/4 In. 250.00
Reel, Julius Vom Hofe, Wide Spool, Rubber Patina, Nickeled Brass, 2 1/8 In. 275.00
Reel, Leonard, Tapered Handle Grasp, German Silver 3575.00
Reel, Meek & Sons, Bait Casting, Bluegrass, Non-Level Wind, 1904 . . . . 220.00
Reel, Meek & Sons, Bait Casting, Bluegrass, Screw Slots, German Silver 385.00
Reel, Meek & Sons, Flat Raised Back Plate, No. 44, Louisville, Ky. 4510.00
Reel, Meek, Reel Oil, Cork Stopper 520.00
Reel, Milan, Counter-Balanced Handle, No. 3, Nickel Silver 962.00
Reel, Orvis, Trout, Riveted Construction, Narrow, Patent Spring, 2 3/4 In. 660.00
Rod, Orvis, Trout, Screw-Down Locking Reel Seat, Battenkill, 6 1/2 Ft., 2 Piece 550.00
Rod, Orvis, Trout, Walnut Spacer, Screw-Down Locking Reel, Battenkill, 4 1/2 Oz. 550.00
Reel, Orvis, Trout, Wide Spool, Riveted Construction, 1874, 2 7/8 In. 385.00
Reel, Pflueger, Bait Casting, Red Bearing Jewels, Click & Drag Switches 80.00
Reel, Pflueger, Bait Casting, Silver, Jeweled Bearing Caps, German Silver, 1907 . . . . 165.00
Reel, Pflueger, No. 1893L, White Metal . . . . .20.00 to 50.00
Reel, Pflueger, Skilfast, No. 1953, Chromed, Plastic Knobs, 2 In. 60.00
Reel, Philbrook & Paine, Orange, Black Pillar Crank Handle, German Silver 3850.00
Reel, Sea Wonder, Model FB 100.00
Reel, Sea, Mahogany & Brass, 5 In. 75.00
Reel, Shakespeare, Wonder Wheel, No. 1810 . . . . 50.00
Reel, Silver King, No. 250 . . . . 50.00
Reel, Talbot, Black Handle Grasp, Click Switch, Model 100 . . . . 4400.00
Reel, William Mills & Son, Trout, Wide Spool, Spiral Knurled Bearing Cap, No. 1, 3 In. . . 330.00
Rod, Atlantic Salmon, L.L. Bean, Extra Tip, Case, Cork Handle, 9 1/2 In. 109.00
Rod, Casting, Al Foss, True Temper 75.00
Rod, Casting, George A. Parker, Original Case, Silver Label, Lancaster, Mass. 65.00
Rod, Casting, Steel 75.00
Rod, Fly, Bamboo, Reel 95.00
Rod, Fly, F.E. Thomas, Special, Bangor, Maine, Extra Tip, Metal Case, 8 1/2 In., 3 Piece . 316.00

Rod, Fly, Leonard Rod Co., Split Bamboo, 4 Sections, 1936 .... 460.00
Rod, Fly, Leonard, Tournament, Extra Tip, Metal Case, 9 In. 345.00
Rod, Fly, Lyle Dickerson, 1948, 8 Ft. 2750.00
Rod, Fly, Salmon, Leonard, Green, Black Variegated Wraps, Red Tip, German Silver 300.00
Rod, Fly, Thomas & Thomas, Laminated Handle, Walnut, Silver Slide Band, 1983 ...... 3410.00
Rod, Fly, Thomas & Thomas, Walnut, Bamboo Spliced Butt, 1979 .... 2640.00
Rod, Fly, Thomas & Thomas, Walnut, Nickel Silver Butt Cap, Red Leather, 1985 .... 3850.00
Rod, Fly, Thomas & Thomas, Wide Slide Band, Ivory, Red Intermediate Wraps, 8 In. 2200.00
Rod, Fly, W.G. Scoffler, Black Flamed Rod, Burl Walnut Spacer, 9 Ft. 715.00
Rod, Heddon, Polin, Wood Supports, Salesman's Bag, 26 x 64 In. 275.00
Rod, Salmon, Hardy's Of England, Deluxe, Extra Tip, Aluminum Case, 9 In. 200.00
Rod, Salmon, Leonard, Black Oxidized Hardware, Dark Stained Cane, 10 1/2 Ft. 550.00
Rod, Salmon, Leonard, Invisible Wrap Near Butt End, 9 Ft., 3 Piece 330.00
Rod, Salmon, Leonard, Red Wraps, Down-Locking Reel Seat, 11 3/4 Ft. 440.00
Rod, Spinning, Orvis, Superlight, 6 1/2 Ft. 192.00
Rod, Trout, Garrison, Original Bag, Tube, German Silver Slide Band, 1962, 8 Ft. 3850.00
Rod, Trout, Gary Howells, 2 Tips, Line Rod, 8 Ft., 2 Piece 1925.00
Rod, Trout, Gooding, Golden Witch, Green Parrot Horns, Nickel Silver Frame, 9 Ft. 440.00
Rod, Trout, Leonard, Walnut Spacer, Original Handle, 7 1/2 Ft. 715.00
Rod, Trout, Paul H. Young, Screw-Down Locking Reel Seat, Spacer, Signed, 8 1/2 Ft. ... 580.00
Rod, Trout, Paul H. Young, Wood Spacer Reel Seat, 7 1/2 Ft. 770.00
Rod, Winchester 125.00
Rod & Reel, Hurd 150.00
Trap, Eel, Bamboo, Inward-Pointing Bamboo Cone, 30 x 10 In. 80.00
Trap, Minnow, 6-Sided Mason Jar, Green Glass, 4 x 7 In. 275.00
Trap, Minnow, Barrel Shape, Flint Glass, 6 x 11 In. 100.00
Trap, Minnow, Glass, Squat, 6 In. 125.00
Trap, Minnow, Orvis, Manchester, Vt., Glass, Screw-Cap Cover, Harness 130.00
Trap, Minnow, Orvis, Manchester, Vt., Hinged Cover, Wood 300.00

FLAGS are included in the Textile category.

FLASH GORDON appeared in the Sunday comics in 1934. The daily
strip started in 1940. The hero was also in comic books from 1930 to
1970, in books from 1936, in movies from 1938, on the radio in the
1930s and 1940s, and on television from 1953 to 1954. All sorts of
memorabilia are collected, but the ray guns and rocket ships are the
most popular.

Book, Big Little Book, Witch Queen Of Mongo, Whitman, 1936 .... 55.00
Box, Quick Kid's Meal, Belgium 10.00
Figure, With Flicker Ring, Ideal 220.00
Game, Bagatelle, Plastic, Cardboard, Nasta Industries Inc., Box, 1976, 6 x 11 In. 23.00
Gun, Click Ray, Marx, 1950s 250.00
Poster, Flash Gordon's Trip To Mars, Buster Crabbe, Serial, 1938, One Sheet 355.00
Rocket Gun, Plastic, Blister Card, Ja-Ru, King Features Syndicate, 1981, 6 x 9 In. 23.00

FLORENCE CERAMICS were made in Pasadena, California, from World
War II to 1977. Florence Ward created many colorful figurines, boxes,
candleholders, and other items for the gift shop trade. Each piece was
marked with an ink stamp that included the name *Florence Ceramics
Co.* The company was sold in 1964, and although the name remained
the same the products were very different. Mugs, cups, and trays were
made.

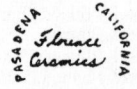

Bonbon 85.00
Dish, Serving, Cherub, Handles 95.00
Dish, Shell, 3 Center Roses, Triple, Pink & Gray 75.00
Figurine, Abigail, 8 In. 150.00
Figurine, Amelia, 15 In. 275.00
Figurine, Annabel, Pink, 8 In. 250.00
Figurine, Ava, 10 1/2 In. 250.00
Figurine, Betsy, Gray, 7 1/4 In. 115.00
Figurine, Camille, 8 1/2 In. ....200.00 to 245.00
Figurine, Camille, Green, 8 1/2 In. ....140.00 to 145.00

Figurine, Choir Boy, 6 In. 175.00
Figurine, Cindy, 8 In. 375.00
Figurine, Claudia, Gray Over Pink, 8 1/4 In. 195.00
Figurine, Cynthia, 9 1/4 In. 650.00
Figurine, Diane, 8 1/4 In. 225.00
Figurine, Edward, Seated, 7 In. ....250.00 to 525.00
Figurine, Elizabeth, On Sofa, 8 1/4 x 7 In. 500.00
Figurine, Eugenia, 9 In. 300.00
Figurine, Fall, Green, Gold, 6 1/2 In. 100.00
Figurine, Grace, Light Green, 7 3/4 In. 185.00
Figurine, Her Majesty, 7 In. 150.00
Figurine, Irene, 6 In. ....65.00 to 95.00
Figurine, Jenette, Olive, 7 3/4 In. ....140.00 to 200.00
Figurine, Joyce, 9 In. 290.00
Figurine, Kay, 7 In. 85.00
Figurine, Ku & She-Ti, 11 In., Pair 400.00
Figurine, Louis XVI & Marie Antoinette, White, 22K Gold Trim, 10 In., Pair .....750.00 to 800.00
Figurine, Matilda, 8 1/2 In. 150.00
Figurine, Melanie, Beige With Green, 7 1/2 In. 110.00
Figurine, Melanie, Pink Gown, White Bonnet, 7 1/2 In. 140.00
Figurine, Musette, 8 3/4 In. 265.00
Figurine, Musette, Blue, 8 3/4 In. 200.00
Figurine, Priscilla, Gray, 7 1/4 In. 155.00
Figurine, Rebecca, 7 In. ....110.00 to 200.00
Figurine, Rhett, 9 In. ....325.00 to 350.00
Figurine, Roberta, 8 1/2 In. 225.00
Figurine, Sarah, 7 1/2 In. 100.00
Figurine, Sarah, Pink Gown, Holding Purse, 7 1/2 In. 125.00
Figurine, Scarlett, 8 3/4 In. 850.00
Figurine, Scarlett, White Gown & Cape, 22K Gold Trim, 8 3/4 In. 200.00
Figurine, Shen & Yulan, 7 1/2 In., Pair 140.00
Figurine, Sue Ellen, 8 1/4 In. 145.00
Figurine, Sue Ellen, Gray With Maroon, 8 1/4 In. 150.00
Figurine, Sue Ellen, Pink Gown, Blue Balloon Cuffs, Blue Bonnet, 8 1/4 In. 175.00
Figurine, Victoria, Seated, 8 1/4 x 7 In. 450.00
Figurine, Wood Nymph 500.00
Figurine, Wynkin & Blynkin, 5 1/2 In., Pair 375.00
Flower Holder, Chinese Boy & Girl, Black & Chartreuse, 8 In., Pair 100.00
Flower Holder, Kay, 7 In. 60.00
Flower Holder, Wendy, 6 1/4 In. 80.00
Frame, Picture, White, Rose Buds, 5 x 3 3/4 In. 60.00
Plaque, Cameo, Woman, Beige Dress, Brown Trim, Oval 140.00
Wall Pocket, Young Man & Woman 128.00

FLOW BLUE, or flo blue, was made in England and other countries about 1830 to 1900. The plates were printed with designs using a cobalt blue coloring. The color flowed from the design to the white plate so that the finished plate has a smeared blue design. The plates were usually made of ironstone china.

Bone Dish, Ayr, W.T.E. Cord 30.00
Bone Dish, Burgess & Leigh, 12 Piece 385.00
Bowl, Conway, 9 In. 275.00
Bowl, Cover, Lonsdale, Rectangular, Loop Handles, Samuel Ford & Co. 275.00
Bowl, Cover, Nankin, Davenport 850.00
Bowl, European Buildings, K. & C.B. Late Mayer, 9 3/8 In. 145.00
Bowl, Florence, Thomas Till, 1891-1928, 10 In. 225.00
Bowl, Stanley Pottery 110.00
Bowl, Vegetable, Cover, Matlock, F. Winkle & Co., 11 1/2 x 7 In. 95.00
Bowl, Victoria, Wood & Sons, 10 1/4 In. 165.00
Bowl, Waldorf, 9 In. 275.00
Butter, Cover, Del Monte 295.00
Butter Chip, Ovando, Meakin 35.00
Butter Chip, Shanghai 60.00

Butter Chip, Yeddo, Arthur Wilkinson 60.00
Cake Plate, Pagoda, Gold Rim, 10 In. 85.00
Cake Stand, Whampoa 895.00
Chamber Pot, Oriental Scenery, Podmore, Walker 595.00
Coffeepot, Pelew, Challinor, 10 In. 600.00
Creamer, Amoy 450.00
Creamer, Conway 165.00
Creamer, Florida, Johnson Bros. 150.00
Creamer, Shell, Challinor 65.00
Creamer, Touraine 295.00
Creamer, Waldorf, New Wharf ....225.00 to 250.00
Cup, Touraine 50.00
Cup & Saucer, Arcadia 75.00
Cup & Saucer, Chen-Si, Handleless, John Meir 150.00
Cup & Saucer, Gothic, Handleless 195.00
Cup & Saucer, Litchfield, Ridgway 45.00
Cup & Saucer, Oriental 35.00
Cup & Saucer, Shanghae, Furnival 90.00
Cup & Saucer, Waldorf, New Wharf 115.00
Gravy Boat, Formosa, Mayer 120.00
Gravy Boat, Hong Kong, Charles Meigh 175.00
Gravy Boat, La Belle, Wheeling Potteries 375.00
Gravy Boat, Nonpareil, Burgess & Leigh 120.00
Gravy Boat, Undertray, Pekin, Dimmock 110.00
Pitcher, Cream, Wagon Wheel, Child's, 1840 .... 145.00
Pitcher, Ivy, 8 In. 250.00
Pitcher, Milk, La Belle, Wheeling Potteries 585.00
Pitcher, Milk, Touraine 425.00
Pitcher, Shanghae, J. Furnival, 7 In. 800.00
Plate, Amoy, 9 1/4 In. 110.00
Plate, Carlton, 7 1/4 In. 80.00
Plate, Chapoo, 9 In. 95.00
Plate, Chinese, 10 1/2 In. 65.00
Plate, Colonial, 9 1/2 In., Pair 130.00
Plate, Dessert, Shanghae, J. Furnival 40.00
Plate, Fleur-De-Lis, c.1860, 10 1/2 In. 225.00
Plate, Ivanhoe, 10 1/2 In. 40.00
Plate, Knox, New Wharf, 10 In. 125.00
Plate, Kyber, 10 In. 110.00
Plate, Luncheon, Shanghae, J. Furnival 110.00
Plate, Morning Glory, Copper Luster, 9 3/4 In. 55.00
Plate, Nonpareil, Burgess & Leigh, 9 3/4 In. 110.00
Plate, Oregon, 7 1/2 In. 95.00
Plate, Oregon, 8 1/2 In. 100.00
Plate, Salad, Shanghae, J. Furnival 88.00
Plate, Scinde, 7 In. 90.00
Plate, Scinde, 8 1/2 In. 80.00
Plate, Scinde, 9 1/2 In. 165.00
Plate, Scinde, Alcock, 7 1/2 In. 150.00
Plate, Shapoo, T. & R. Boote, 8 1/2 In. 100.00
Plate, State Border, WM In Gilt, Label, Shawmut Furniture Co., England, 9 In. 60.00
Plate, Temple, Podmore, Walker, 9 3/4 In. 110.00
Plate, Wagon Wheel, 8 In. 50.00
Plate, Watteau, New Wharf, 5 In. 40.00
Plate, Yedo, Ashworth, 10 1/4 In. ....65.00 to 155.00
Platter, Belfort, John Maddock & Sons Ltd., 17 In. 185.00
Platter, California, 1849 Mark, 16 In. 195.00
Platter, Chatsworth, 13 1/2 In. 250.00
Platter, Clover, 16 1/2 In. 50.00
Platter, Conway, 10 1/2 In. 125.00
Platter, Conway, New Wharf, 10 In. 75.00
Platter, Excelsior, 12 1/4 x 9 3/4 In. 375.00

Platter, Fairy Villas, 13 3/4 In. 303.00
Platter, Fairy Villas, 17 1/2 In. 330.00
Platter, Gotha, Joseph Heath, 13 1/2 x 10 In. 395.00
Platter, Grace, W.H. Grindley, 15 1/2 In. 275.00
Platter, Hamilton, John Maddock & Son, 16 In. 350.00
Platter, Hong Kong, 12 1/2 In. 250.00
Platter, Indian Stone, E. Walley, 13 3/4 In. 120.00
Platter, John Alcock, 21 1/4 x 17 1/4 In. 660.00
Platter, Lorne, W.H. Grindley, 15 In. 295.00
Platter, Lorne, W.H. Grindley, 16 In. 265.00
Platter, Manilla, Podmore, Walker, 12 1/2 In. 395.00
Platter, Marechal Niel, W.H. Grindley, 16 In. 250.00
Platter, Melbourne, W.H. Grindley, 16 In. 225.00
Platter, Nonpareil, Burgess & Leigh, 11 In. 135.00
Platter, Nonpareil, Burgess & Leigh, 12 In. 135.00
Platter, Nonpareil, Burgess & Leigh, 13 1/2 In. 245.00
Platter, Nonpareil, Burgess & Leigh, 16 In. 245.00
Platter, Oriental, 19th Century, 18 3/4 In. 385.00
Platter, Oriental, Alcock, 21 x 17 3/4 In. 550.00
Platter, Pekin, Albert Jones, c.1908, Oval, 16 x 12 1/2 In. 175.00
Platter, Rose, W.H. Grindley, 11 1/4 In. 55.00
Platter, Scinde Alcock, 16 In. ....595.00 to 650.00
Platter, Shanghae, J. Furnival, 16 In. 700.00
Platter, Waldorf, New Wharf, 10 3/4 In. 100.00
Relish, Shanghai, W.H. Grindley 50.00
Saucer, Baltic, W.H. Grindley 40.00
Saucer, Iris 50.00
Soup, Dish, Shanghae, J. Furnival 150.00
Soup, Dish, Waldorf, Flanged, New Wharf 110.00
Sugar, Cashmere 1095.00
Sugar, Cover, Chapoo 468.00
Sugar, Cover, Scinde, Thom. Walker 595.00
Sugar, Cover, Shanghae, J. Furnival 300.00
Syrup, Metal Lid, Underplate, La Belle, Wheeling Pottery 495.00
Teapot, Hamilton 695.00
Tray, Dresser, La Belle, Wheeling Pottery, 9 1/2 x 8 In. 225.00
Tray, Dresser, Pansy, Warwick, 11 x 8 In. 225.00
Tureen, Nonpareil, Burgess & Leigh, 11 1/2 In. 495.00
Tureen, Sauce, Cover, Sobraon 355.00
Tureen, Soup, Chrysanthemum, 6 Panels, Handle, 8 1/2 x 11 x 11 In. 210.00
Tureen, Soup, Hampton Spray, W.H. Grindley 795.00
Tureen, Soup, Marie, W.H. Grindley 475.00
Tureen, Soup, Shanghae, J. Furnival 1250.00
Tureen, Tedworth, Gold Highlights, 1891, 12 x 7 3/4 x 6 In. 340.00
Vase, Chrysanthemum, Bulbous Base, Medallions At Twisted Formed Neck, 16 In. 247.00
Vase, Lily, Gold Tapestry, Gold Sponge Work, Wm. Adderley, 5 1/2 In. 300.00
Waste Bowl, Oregon, T.J. & J. Mayer, 5 1/2 x 3 In. 120.00
Waste Bowl, Touraine 160.00
Waste Bowl, Wagon Wheel, 1840 .... 50.00
Waste Bowl, Waldorf, New Wharf 175.00

FLYING PHOENIX, see Phoenix Bird category.

FOLK ART is also listed in many categories of this book under the actual name of the object. See categories such as Box, Cigar Store Figure, Paper, Weather Vane, Wooden, etc.

Bank, Melancholy Black Man, Top Hat, Head Nods, Slot At Feet, 19th Century 950.00
Basket Of Flowers, Wax, Dust Dome, Victorian, 19 In. 345.00
Birdhouse, 2 Story House, Bow Windows, Iron, Red Paint, Gold Trim, 13 In. 2010.00
Block House & Building Set, White Paint, 1 2/3 x 7 1/4 In., 13 Piece 220.00
Box, Carved Smiling Man Bust 500.00
Box, Slide Lid, Chip Carved, Hardwood, Dark Brown Patina, Floral, 1 Piece, 7 In. 275.00

Busk, Maple Wood, Decorated Hearts & Dated 1790 .... 525.00
Cameo Shell, Carved, Woman Bust, Flowers, Wooden Stand 170.00
Chain, From Bottle Caps, 12 Caps, 24 In. 80.00
Chair, Crocheted, Multicolored, Albert Lohnes 3750.00
Chicken, Putty Feet & Comb, Canfield, Ravenna, Ohio, 18 In. 495.00
Cutout, Silhouette, Butler, Holding Ashtray, Wooden, 33 In. 66.00
Decoy, Diorama, Landscape Scene, Canvasback Drake, Victorian, 20 x 24 1/2 In. 230.00
Eagle, Carved Oak, Natural, Early 20th Century, 24 1/4-In. Wingspan 415.00
Fence Post Finial, Woodchuck Form, 19th Century, 16 3/4 In. 220.00
Figure, 7 Carved Dwarfs, Silvio Zoratti 660.00
Figure, Clown, Carved Wood, Polychrome, Late 19th-Early 20th Century, 42 1/2 In. 805.00
Figure, Dog, Spaniel, Reclining, Walnut, 9 In. 355.00
Figure, George Washington, Carved Feet & Legs, Papier-Mache Head, c.1800 .... 670.00
Figure, Laughing Sal, Fun House, Animated, Life Size 11000.00
Figure, Lion, Pine, 2-Sided, Seated, Red, Black Base, Cole Brothers, c.1930, 60 In. 1610.00
Figure, Man, Carved, Wearing A Cap, White Vest, Boots, Pine, Black, 9 1/2 In. 1840.00
Figure, Man, Dancing, Boxer, Rotating Head, Pine, Brown, 8 1/2 In. 1495.00
Figure, Old Black Man, With Cane, Georgia Cypress, 21 1/4 In. 220.00
Figure, Pair Of High Top Boots, Black & Red Paint, Bird's-Eye Base, 6 In. 195.00
Figure, Snake, Carved, 19th Century, 7 1/2 In. 325.00
Figure, Spinning Lady, Wearing A Bonnet, Prisoner Of War, Early 19th Century, 5 In. 3737.00
Figure, Tree, Owl & 4 Crows Perched On Branches, Painted, 20th Century, 52 In. 3737.00
Frame, Cherry, Eagle & Shield, Oval, 16 1/2 x 12 1/2 In. 715.00
Frame, Grain Painted, Yellows & Brown, York Co., Opening Is 11 3/4 x 8 3/4 In. 365.00
Mirror, Chip Carved, Walnut, Pilgrim Century, 17th Century, 10 3/4 In. 1450.00
Model, Church, Wooden, Original Paint 650.00
Ornament, Sphere, Circus Wagon, Laminated Wood, Geometric, Stand, 7 x 15 In. 245.00
Pig, Black & White, Rope Tail, Wooden, David Alvarez, 10 1/2 In. 55.00
Rooster, Crosshatched Carving, 20th Century, 13 In. 187.00
Rooster, Polychromed, Dated '74, Strausser, 17 1/2 In. 305.00
Rooster, Sheet Iron, 1890, 12 1/2 x 13 1/2 In. 895.00
Rooster, Wooden, Carved, Painted, Beveled Square Base, 17 1/4 x 11 1/2 In. 2473.00
Shelf, Blue Paint, Tiers Of Molding & Sawteeth, 12 x 26 In. 770.00
Shelf, Hanging, Beech, Cutout Double Shield, Chip Carved, Masonic Emblem, 24 In. 125.00
Shelf, Hanging, Walnut, Chip Carved, Hexagonal Containers, 18 x 14 In. 180.00
Stand, Jiggs, Comic Papers, Jigsaw Cut, Paint, 32 1/2 In. 50.00
Swordfish Bill Sword, Wood Design On Handle, Canada, 54 In. 300.00
Tobacco Caddy, Indian Figures, Smoking Scene, Walnut, 8 Drawers, 3 False, 1906 ...... 1200.00
Walking Stick, Carved Man's Head, 20th Century, 42 In. 165.00
Whiligig, Nantucket Sailor Boy, 1900s 750.00
Whirligig, Amish Man, Cutting Trees, Wooden 48.00
Whirligig, Black Man, Hand Carved, Metal Tacks, 17 In. 1210.00
Whirligig, Black Man, Watermelon Paddle Arms, 37 In. 165.00
Whirligig, Butter, Cover 12.00
Whirligig, Figure With Propeller Blades Supported By Rod, Tin, Germany, 3 1/2 In. 61.00
Whirligig, Happy Jack, Red, White & Blue Paint, 13 In. 605.00
Whirligig, Hussar, Wearing Full Uniform, Rotating Arms, Pine, Black, Blue, Gold, 13 In. .. 3450.00
Whirligig, Man Chopping Wood, 20th Century, 7 3/4 In. 220.00
Whirligig, Man Churning, Early 20th. Century, 17 In. 330.00
Whirligig, Man Dancing, Fiddle Player, Wood, Tin & Wire, Primitive, 35 In. 220.00
Whirligig, Man Standing, Green Hat, Paddle Arms, Late 19th Century, 29 In. 355.00
Whirligig, Man Wearing Cap, Baffle Arms, Pine Base, 1910s, 22 1/4 In. 3162.00
Whirligig, Man, Swivel Arms, 44 In. 1375.00
Whirligig, Nantucket Sailor, Blue, White, Black, 15 1/2 In. 575.00
Whirligig, Rattlesnake, Bucking Horse & Cowboy 1050.00
Whirligig, Sailor Boy, Bearded, Rotating Arms, White Trousers, Red Belt, 14 In. 517.00
Whirligig, Soldier, Hand Carved, Pine, Unpainted, For Indoors, 16 1/4 In. 975.00
Whirligig, Soldier, Northern Pine, Hand Carved, 16 1/4 In. 975.00
Whirligig, Spaceship, Swept Back Wings, Rocket Booster, c.1930, 15 In. 850.00
Whirligig, Uncle Sam, Wooden, Sheet Metal, Henry Sargent, 1900, 72 In. 12650.00
Whirligig, Washer Woman 155.00
Whirligig, Windmill, Green & White Paint, Iron Base, c.1910, 27 1/2 x 28 In. 595.00
Whirligig, Witch On Broomstick, Made From License Plates 575.00

FOOT WARMERS solved the problem of cold feet in past generations. Some warmers held charcoal, others held hot water. Pottery, tin, and soapstone were the favored materials to conduct the heat. The warmer was kept under the feet, then the legs and feet were tucked into a blanket, providing welcome warmth in a cold carriage or church.

Blue Enamel, Cast Iron, 1850s, 6 x 9 5/8 In.	290.00
Mahogany, Pierced Design, 8 x 11 x 6 3/4 In.	295.00
Punched Tin, Circle & Diamond Design, Wooden Frame, Turned Posts, 8 1/4 In.	220.00
Punched Tin, Wooden Frame, Bail Handle, 7 x 9 In.	225.00
Walnut Frame, Wire Bale Handle, Punched Circle Design, 1814, 6 1/2 x 8 1/2 In.	319.00

FOOTBALL collectibles may be found in the Card and the Sports categories.

FOSTORIA glass was made in Fostoria, Ohio, from 1887 to 1891. The factory was moved to Moundsville, West Virginia, and most of the glass seen in shops today is a twentieth-century product. The company was sold in 1983; new items will be easily identifiable, according to the new owner, Lancaster Colony Corporation. Additional Fostoria items may be listed in the Milk Glass category.

Alexis, Horseradish Jar, Cover	85.00
American, Ashtray, Oval	15.00 to 25.00
American, Ashtray, Square, 2 7/8 In.	7.00 to 10.00
American, Basket, Reed Handle	85.00 to 90.00
American, Biscuit Jar	800.00
American, Bottle, Water	550.00
American, Bowl, Oval, 10 In.	25.00
American, Bowl, Rolled Rim, 10 1/2 In.	30.00
American, Butter, Round	80.00 to 98.00
American, Cake Plate	40.00
American, Cake Stand, Round, 10 In.	100.00
American, Cake Stand, Square, 10 In.	125.00
American, Candlestick, 3 In., Pair	22.00
American, Cup	14.00
American, Decanter, Cordial	85.00
American, Decanter, Rye	100.00
American, Decanter, Whiskey	90.00
American, Goblet, 9 Oz.	10.00
American, Humidor, 6 In.	450.00
American, Hurricane Lamp	375.00
American, Ice Dish, Tomato Juice Insert, 5 Oz.	50.00
American, Ice Tub, Underplate, 9 1/2 In.	90.00
American, Pin Tray, Oval	105.00
American, Pitcher, 1/2 Gal.	130.00
American, Pitcher, Boudoir, 3 Pt.	50.00 to 58.00
American, Plate, 11 1/2 In.	20.00
American, Platter, 12 In.	60.00
American, Platter, Oval, 12 In.	55.00
American, Puff Box	2500.00
American, Punch Cup	14.00
American, Punch Set, 13 Piece	450.00
American, Ring Tree	750.00
American, Rose Bowl	39.00
American, Salt & Pepper, Tapered, Pair	25.00
American, Sauceboat, Underplate	48.00
American, Sherbet, Footed, 5 Oz.	8.00
American, Sugar & Creamer, Tray With Handles, 3 Piece	22.00
American, Torte Plate, 18 In.	105.00
American, Torte Plate, Oval, 13 1/2 In.	50.00
American, Tumbler, Water, 9 Oz.	14.00
American, Tumbler, Whiskey	11.00
American, Vase, 8 In.	55.00
American, Vase, Bud, 8 1/2 In.	20.00
American, Vase, Flared, 8 In.	80.00

American, Vase, Flared, 9 In. . . . . .93.00 to 110.00
American, Vase, Flared, 10 In. 55.00
American, Vase, Square Foot, 10 In. 40.00
American Lady, Cocktail, 3 1/2 Oz. 12.00
American Lady, Goblet, 10 Oz. 18.00
American Lady, Goblet, Amethyst 35.00
American Lady, Sherbet, 5 1/2 Oz. 10.00
American Lady, Tumbler, 10 Oz. . . . . .12.00 to 15.00
American Lady, Tumbler, 12 Oz. 15.00
Argus, Goblet, Water, Ruby, 10 1/2 Oz. 22.00
Argus, Wine, Ruby, 4 Oz. 21.00
Baroque, Candleholder, 2-Light, 8 1/4 x 10 In., Pair 375.00
Baroque, Candlestick, Blue, 4 In., Pair 35.00
Baroque, Candlestick, Topaz, 4 In., Pair 250.00
Baroque, Cocktail, Oyster, Azure 32.00
Baroque, Cup & Saucer, Topaz 24.00
Baroque, Cup, Azure, 8 Piece 30.00
Baroque, Goblet, Water, Azure, 9 Oz., Pair 30.00
Baroque, Ice Bucket, Topaz . . . . .75.00 to 125.00
Baroque, Pitcher, Azure 1395.00
Baroque, Plate, Azure, 9 In. 58.00
Baroque, Plate, Topaz, 6 In. 12.00
Baroque, Plate, Topaz, 7 In. 14.00
Baroque, Relish, 3 Sections, Oblong, Topaz . . . . .38.00 to 40.00
Baroque, Relish, 4 Sections, 10 In. 395.00
Baroque, Rose Bowl, Topaz 95.00
Baroque, Sauce, Oval, Topaz 50.00
Baroque, Sherbet, Low, Azure, 5 Oz. 28.00
Baroque, Sugar & Creamer, Azure, Individual 65.00
Baroque, Sugar & Creamer, Topaz 40.00
Baroque, Sugar & Creamer, Topaz, Individual 48.00
Baroque, Tumbler, Footed, Azure, 12 Oz. 40.00
Beverly, Berry Bowl, Green 20.00
Beverly, Candy Dish, Cover, 3 Sections, Amber 95.00
Beverly, Cup & Saucer, Footed, Green 20.00
Beverly, Plate, Green, 6 In. 5.00
Beverly, Plate, Green, 10 1/2 In. 35.00
Beverly, Salt & Pepper, Green 135.00
Beverly, Tumbler, Green, 5 Oz. 15.00
Beverly, Tumbler, Green, 12 Oz. 27.00
Brocaded Grapes, Bowl, Green, 12 In. 85.00
Buttercup, Candlestick, 4 In. 30.00
Buttercup, Plate, 7 1/2 In. 16.00
Buttercup, Plate, Dinner 50.00
Century, Bowl, 9 In. 30.00
Century, Compote 20.00
Century, Cup & Saucer 16.00
Century, Dish, Mayonnaise, Underplate, Ladle 40.00
Century, Salt & Pepper 25.00
Century, Sugar & Creamer 17.00
Century, Sugar & Creamer, Tray 25.00
Century, Vase, Bud 25.00
Chintz, Cake Plate, 2 Handles, 10 In. 40.00
Chintz, Compote, Cheese 50.00
Chintz, Goblet, Water, 9 Oz. 28.00
Chintz, Nappy, 3 Handles, 4 5/8 In. 24.00
Chintz, Plate, 7 In. . . . . .14.00 to 16.00
Chintz, Sherbet, Low, 5 Oz. 18.00
Chintz, Tumbler, 13 Oz. 30.00
Coin, Ashtray, Amber 10.00
Coin, Bowl, Fruit, Amber, 8 In. 35.00
Coin, Bowl, Oval, Amber, 9 In. 30.00
Coin, Bowl, Wedding, Cover, 8 1/4 In. 80.00

Coin, Candlestick, Ruby, 8 In. 53.00
Coin, Candy Box, Cover, Frosted, Azure 85.00
Coin, Lamp, Oil, Courting, 9 3/4 In. 110.00
Coin, Lamp, Patio, Electric, 16 1/2 In. 160.00
Coin, Nappy, Handle, Amber, 5 3/8 In. 15.00
Coin, Pitcher, Amber, 1 Qt. 50.00
Coin, Pitcher, Olive, 1 Qt. 50.00
Coin, Salt & Pepper, Amber 38.00
Coin, Vase, 6 Panels, Blue, 8 In. 30.00
Coin, Vase, Ruby, 8 In. 45.00
Colonial Dame, Cocktail, Oyster, 4 1/2 Oz. 5.00
Colony, Bowl, 10 In. 35.00
Colony, Bowl, 13 In. 40.00
Colony, Bowl, Azure, 9 In. 30.00
Colony, Compote, Cover, 6 In. 30.00
Colony, Plate, 7 In. 8.00
Colony, Plate, 8 In. 13.00
Colony, Tumbler, 12 Oz. 34.00
Colony, Vase, Bud, Topaz, 6 1/2 In. 50.00
Contour, Relish, 3 Sections 15.00
Corsage, Cordial 50.00
Fairfax, Butter, Cover, Topaz, Pair 90.00
Fairfax, Compote, Light Blue, 6 In. 45.00
Fairfax, Compote, Rose, 5 3/4 In. 75.00
Fairfax, Compote, Rose, 7 In. 28.00
Fairfax, Creamer, Rose, After Dinner 35.00
Fairfax, Cup & Saucer, Green 12.00
Fairfax, Cup, Green, After Dinner 10.00
Fairfax, Dish, Sweetmeat, Handle, Rose 24.00
Fairfax, Nut Dish, Amber 15.00
Fairfax, Nut Dish, Footed, Azure 18.00
Fairfax, Parfait, Rose 50.00
Fairfax, Salt & Pepper, Topaz 55.00
Fairfax, Sherbet, Low, Blue 22.00
Fairfax, Tumbler, Water, Footed, Blue 25.00
Fern, Tumbler, Footed, Ebony, 12 Oz. 15.00
Grape, Compote, Green 75.00
Hawaiian, Platter, Burgundy, 14 In. 220.00
Heather, Candy Dish, Cover, Footed 55.00
Heather, Champagne 18.00
Heather, Creamer, Footed 17.00
Heather, Sugar & Creamer, Tray, Individual 48.00
Heritage, Napkin Ring 25.00
Hermitage, Bowl, Low, Flared, Azure, 9 1/2 In. 95.00
Hermitage, Cocktail, Azure 95.00
Hermitage, Cocktail, Green, 3 1/2 In. 14.00
Hermitage, Goblet, Water, Azure 24.00
Hermitage, Ice Dish, Tomato Juice Insert, Topaz 20.00
Hermitage, Sherbet, Topaz 14.00
Hermitage, Wine, Amber 12.00
Holly, Goblet, Water, 10 Oz. 30.00
Holly, Sherbet, 4 1/4 In. 30.00
Holly, Sherbet, Low, 6 Oz. 30.00
Jamestown, Creamer, Azure 27.00
Jamestown, Goblet, Brown, 9 1/2 Oz. 8.00
Jamestown, Goblet, Smoke, 9 1/2 Oz. 8.00
Jamestown, Plate, Blue, 8 1/4 In. 24.00
Jamestown, Sherbet, Amethyst, 6 1/2 Oz. 20.00
Jamestown, Sherbet, Blue, 6 1/2 Oz. 15.00
Jamestown, Sherbet, Brown, 6 1/2 Oz. 5.00
Jamestown, Tumbler, Amber, 12 Oz. 15.00
June, Candlestick, Azure, Pair 110.00
June, Candlestick, Topaz, 3 In., Pair 75.00

June, Cup, Azure, 4 Piece 80.00
June, Cup, Rose 36.00
June, Goblet, Water, Azure, 9 Oz. 78.00
June, Ice Bucket 90.00
June, Sauceboat, Topaz 105.00
June, Tumbler, Water, Rose, 8 Oz. 48.00
Lafayette, Torte Plate, Ruby, 14 In. 40.00
Lido, Candy Dish, Cover, 3 Sections 65.00
Lido, Tumbler, Footed, 12 Oz. 22.00
Lotus, Vase, Cylindrical, Ebony, George Sakier, 5 x 13 In. 330.00
Lucerne, Toothpick 45.00
Mayfair, Relish, 5 Sections 40.00
Meadow Rose, Bowl, 3-Toed, 7 In. 32.00
Meadow Rose, Candleholder, 3-Light, Baroque, Pair 185.00
Meadow Rose, Candlestick, 3-Light, Blue, 6 x 8 1/2 In., Pair 275.00
Meadow Rose, Creamer, 3 3/4 In. 18.00
Meadow Rose, Sherbet, Low, 5 Oz. 20.00
Meadow Rose, Tumbler, Footed, 13 Oz. 35.00
Midnight Rose, Candlestick, 2-Light, Baroque, 4 7/8 In., Pair 145.00
Navarre, Bowl, 10 1/2 In. 75.00
Navarre, Bowl, Footed, 7 In. 40.00
Navarre, Bowl, Ruby, Footed, 9 In. 60.00
Navarre, Candleholder, 3-Light, Baroque, Pair 185.00
Navarre, Candlestick, 3-Light, Baroque, Pair 185.00
Navarre, Candlestick, 3-Light, Pair 135.00
Navarre, Candy Dish, Cover, Topaz 25.00
Navarre, Champagne, 5 1/2 In. 22.00
Navarre, Goblet, 10 Oz. 8.00
Navarre, Plate, Handle 28.00
Navarre, Sugar & Creamer 40.00
Priscilla, Butter, Green, Gold Trim 100.00
Priscilla, Syrup, Green, Gold Trim 495.00
Priscilla, Table Set, 4 Piece 250.00
Priscilla, Toothpick 45.00
Rivera, Compote, Candlesticks, Yellow, Gold Overlay, 12-In. Compote, 3 Piece 275.00
Robin Hood, Spooner 10.00
Romance, Salt & Pepper 52.00
Rose, Candlestick, Pair 50.00
Seville, Cup & Saucer, Amber 11.00
Seville, Plate, Amber, 8 1/2 In. 6.00
Trojan, Ice Bucket, Topaz 65.00
Trojan, Jug, Water, Footed, Low, Topaz 250.00
Trojan, Pitcher, Topaz 275.00
Versailles, Bowl, Whipped Cream, Topaz 15.00
Versailles, Claret, Topaz, 4 Oz. 85.00
Versailles, Cocktail, Topaz, 3 Oz. 25.00
Versailles, Cordial, Topaz, 3/4 Oz. 115.00
Versailles, Cup & Saucer, Footed, Topaz 22.00
Versailles, Cup & Saucer, Topaz, After Dinner 48.00
Versailles, Dish, Sweetmeat, Topaz 15.00
Versailles, Goblet, 10 Oz. 60.00
Versailles, Plate, Blue, 8 3/4 In. 25.00
Versailles, Sherbet, Tall, 6 Oz. 45.00
Vesper, Ice Bucket, Amber 80.00
Victoria, Rose Bowl, Frosted, 5 In. 145.00
Vintage, Candlestick, Baroque, 4 In., Pair 145.00
Willow, Champagne, 6 Oz. 12.00
Willow, Tumbler 12.00
Wreath & Shell, Rose Bowl, Opalescent 110.00

FOVAL, see Fry category.

FRAMES are included in the Furniture category under Frame.

FRANCISCAN is a trademark that appears on pottery. Gladding, McBean and Company started in 1875. The company grew and acquired other potteries. They made sewer pipes, floor tiles, dinnerwares, and art pottery with a variety of trademarks. In 1934, dinnerware and art pottery were sold under the name Franciscan Ware. They made china and cream-colored, decorated earthenware. Desert Rose, Apple, El Patio, and Coronado were best-sellers. The company became Interpace Corporation and in 1979 was purchased by Josiah Wedgwood & Sons. The plant was closed in 1984 but a few of the patterns are still being made. For more information, see *Kovels' Depression Glass & Dinnerware Price List*.

Apple, Batter Bowl, Early Mark, Original Sticker, 10 1/4 In.	385.00
Apple, Bowl, Vegetable, 7 3/4 In.	80.00
Apple, Bowl, Vegetable, Divided, 10 3/4 In.	45.00
Apple, Butter, 1/4 Lb.	50.00
Apple, Candleholder, 3 In., Pair	65.00
Apple, Casserole, Cover, 2 Qt.	45.00
Apple, Chop Plate, 12 In.	95.00
Apple, Chop Plate, 14 In.	95.00 to 125.00
Apple, Compote, 8 In.	80.00 to 95.00
Apple, Cookie Jar	295.00 to 375.00
Apple, Creamer, 3 In.	40.00
Apple, Cup & Saucer	110.00
Apple, Cup & Saucer, 3 3/4 In.	58.00
Apple, Grill Plate, 11 In.	115.00
Apple, Jam Jar, 3 1/2 In.	95.00
Apple, Mug, 7 Oz.	72.00
Apple, Mug, 12 Oz.	41.00
Apple, Pepper Mill Set	275.00
Apple, Pitcher, Syrup, 1 Pt.	82.00
Apple, Pitcher, Water, 2 Qt.	115.00 to 175.00
Apple, Plate, 6 1/4 In.	5.50
Apple, Plate, 9 1/2 In.	20.00
Apple, Plate, Child's, 7 1/4 In.	105.00
Apple, Platter, 14 In.	45.00 to 65.00
Apple, Platter, 19 In.	295.00
Apple, Relish, 3 Sections, 11 3/4 In.	75.00
Apple, Salt & Pepper	40.00
Apple, Soup, Dish, Footed, 5 1/2 In.	17.00 to 32.00
Apple, Tumbler, 6 Oz.	22.00
Apple, Tumbler, 10 Oz.	30.00
Apple, Tureen, 3-Footed, 5 1/4 In.	450.00
Apple, Tureen, Soup, 8 1/2 In.	450.00 to 895.00
Cafe Royal, Cup & Saucer	12.00
Cafe Royal, Tile, Square, 6 In.	39.00
Coronado, Chop Plate, Gray, 14 In.	35.00
Coronado, Creamer, Gray	35.00
Coronado, Cup & Saucer, Gray	45.00
Coronado, Plate, Coral, 10 1/2 In.	10.00
Coronado, Sugar, Cover, Coral	15.00
Daisy, Ashtray, 2 1/2 In.	30.00
Daisy, Bowl, 7 1/2 In.	19.00
Daisy, Creamer	15.00
Daisy, Cup	6.00
Daisy, Cup & Saucer	5.00
Daisy, Mug, 12 Oz.	40.00
Daisy, Plate, 6 1/2 In.	5.00
Daisy, Plate, 8 1/4 In.	10.00
Daisy, Plate, 9 1/2 In.	6.50 to 9.00
Daisy, Plate, 10 In.	14.00
Daisy, Platter, 19 In.	65.00
Daisy, Salt & Pepper	20.00

Daisy, Sugar & Creamer 16.00
Daisy, Teapot, 5 In. 75.00
Desert Rose, Ashtray, Individual 18.00
Desert Rose, Ashtray, Square 50.00
Desert Rose, Baking Dish, Square, 1 Qt. 175.00
Desert Rose, Bell, Danbury ....65.00 to 99.00
Desert Rose, Bowl, 5 1/4 In. ....5.00 to 8.00
Desert Rose, Bowl, 6 In. ....6.00 to 10.00
Desert Rose, Bowl, 8 In. 37.00
Desert Rose, Bowl, 9 In. ....22.00 to 33.00
Desert Rose, Bowl, 10 In. ....80.00 to 99.00
Desert Rose, Bowl, Vegetable, Divided, 10 3/4 In. ....35.00 to 50.00
Desert Rose, Butter ....20.00 to 45.00
Desert Rose, Candleholder, 3 In., Pair ....75.00 to 85.00
Desert Rose, Casserole, 1 1/2 Qt. ....75.00 to 95.00
Desert Rose, Chop Plate, 12 In. ....60.00 to 85.00
Desert Rose, Chop Plate, 14 In. ....95.00 to 145.00
Desert Rose, Cigarette Box, 3 1/2 x 4 1/2 In. 95.00
Desert Rose, Coffeepot, Cover, 9 In. ....55.00 to 100.00
Desert Rose, Compote, 8 In. ....60.00 to 75.00
Desert Rose, Cookie Jar, Cover ....125.00 to 350.00
Desert Rose, Cookie Jar, Open 95.00
Desert Rose, Cup & Saucer ....8.00 to 14.00
Desert Rose, Cup & Saucer, After Dinner 50.00
Desert Rose, Cup, Jumbo 45.00
Desert Rose, Dish, Pickle 42.00
Desert Rose, Gravy Boat ....22.00 to 25.00
Desert Rose, Grill Plate, 11 In. ....65.00 to 125.00
Desert Rose, Mug, 12 Oz. ....40.00 to 50.00
Desert Rose, Pepper Mill 80.00
Desert Rose, Pitcher, Milk, 1 Qt. ....78.00 to 90.00
Desert Rose, Pitcher, Water, 2 1/2 Qt. ....95.00 to 100.00
Desert Rose, Plate, 8 1/2 In. ....9.00 to 12.00
Desert Rose, Plate, 9 1/2 In. ....15.00 to 18.00
Desert Rose, Plate, 10 1/2 In. ....14.00 to 20.00
Desert Rose, Plate, Child's, Square ....125.00 to 135.00
Desert Rose, Platter, 12 1/2 In. ....25.00 to 42.00
Desert Rose, Platter, 14 In. ....35.00 to 65.00
Desert Rose, Platter, 19 In. ....185.00 to 275.00
Desert Rose, Relish, 11 In. 25.00
Desert Rose, Relish, 3 Sections, 12 In. ....70.00 to 90.00
Desert Rose, Salt & Pepper ....12.00 to 25.00
Desert Rose, Sherbet, 4 In. 20.00
Desert Rose, Sugar & Creamer, Tray 65.00
Desert Rose, Tea Jar, Cover 250.00
Desert Rose, Teapot ....50.00 to 135.00
Desert Rose, Tidbit, 2 Tiers 125.00
Desert Rose, Trivet ....95.00 to 195.00
Desert Rose, Tumbler, 10 Oz. 25.00
Desert Rose, Tumbler, 12 Oz. 25.00
Desert Rose, Water Set, 4 Tumblers, 5 Piece 310.00
Duet, Cup & Saucer 7.00
El Patio, Ashtray, Coral 8.00
El Patio, Carafe, Turquoise 40.00
El Patio, Casserole, Yellow 75.00
El Patio, Cup & Saucer, Yellow, After Dinner 12.00
El Patio, Pitcher, Turquoise 25.00
Forget-Me-Not, Baker, Square, 1 Qt. 125.00
Forget-Me-Not, Bowl, 5 1/4 In. 12.00
Forget-Me-Not, Butter, Cover 49.00
Forget-Me-Not, Plate, 6 1/2 In. 6.00
Forget-Me-Not, Sugar & Creamer ....38.00 to 45.00
Forget-Me-Not, Thimble, 1 In. 48.00

Fresh Fruit, Baking Dish, Square, 1 Qt. 195.00
Fresh Fruit, Bowl, 6 In. 18.00
Fresh Fruit, Casserole, 1 1/2 Qt. . . . . .195.00 to 225.00
Fresh Fruit, Mug, 7 Oz. 25.00
Fresh Fruit, Plate, 8 In. 22.00
Fresh Fruit, Plate, 10 In. 30.00
Fresh Fruit, Platter, 14 1/2 In. . . . . .65.00 to 85.00
Fresh Fruit, Teapot 295.00
Ivy, Ashtray, Leaf, 4 1/2 In. 22.00
Ivy, Bowl, 5 1/2 In. . . . . .14.00 to 15.00
Ivy, Bowl, 6 In. 20.00
Ivy, Bowl, 7 1/4 In. . . . . .40.00 to 50.00
Ivy, Bowl, 8 1/4 In. 60.00
Ivy, Bowl, Salad, 11 In. . . . . .120.00 to 125.00
Ivy, Bowl, Vegetable, Divided, 12 1/4 In. 65.00
Ivy, Butter, Cover, 1/4 Lb. 85.00
Ivy, Creamer 30.00
Ivy, Cup & Saucer . . . . .15.00 to 22.00
Ivy, Dish, Pickle, 11 In. . . . . .40.00 to 55.00
Ivy, Mug, 12 Oz. 80.00
Ivy, Pitcher, Green Trim, 8 In. 100.00
Ivy, Plate, 6 1/2 In. . . . . .8.00 to 12.00
Ivy, Plate, 10 1/2 In. . . . . .15.00 to 32.00
Ivy, Platter, 13 In. . . . . .70.00 to 85.00
Ivy, Platter, 19 In. 325.00
Ivy, Sherbet 38.00
Ivy, Sugar & Creamer 90.00
Ivy, Sugar, Cover 50.00
Ivy, Tray, TV, 13 1/2 In. 95.00
Meadow Rose, After Dinner 40.00
Meadow Rose, Bowl, 6 In. 10.00
Meadow Rose, Compote, 8 In. 95.00
Meadow Rose, Goblet, 6 1/2 In. 85.00
Meadow Rose, Pepper Mill Set 150.00
Meadow Rose, Plate, 8 1/2 In. 15.00
Meadow Rose, Plate, 10 1/2 In. 13.00
Meadow Rose, Platter, 14 In. 30.00
Meadow Rose, Platter, 19 In. 195.00
October, Bowl, 7 In. 18.00
October, Creamer 24.00
October, Cup & Saucer 25.00
October, Plate, 8 1/2 In. 18.00
October, Plate, 10 In. 28.00
October, Platter, 14 In. . . . . .45.00 to 65.00
October, Sugar, Cover 25.00
Poppy, Ashtray, 4 1/4 In. 60.00
Poppy, Bowl, 8 1/2 In. 125.00
Poppy, Butter, Cover 175.00
Poppy, Cup & Saucer 35.00
Poppy, Gravy Boat, Underplate 175.00
Poppy, Plate, 10 In. 45.00
Poppy, Platter, 13 In. 150.00
Poppy, Salt & Pepper 60.00
Poppy, Tumbler, Water, 10 Oz. 145.00
Starburst, Bowl, Vegetable, Oval 69.00
Starburst, Butter, Cover 45.00
Starburst, Coffeepot 195.00
Starburst, Creamer 29.00
Starburst, Pepper Mill Set 295.00
Wheat, Plate, 10 1/2 In. 45.00
Wildflower, Ashtray, Mariposa Lily 95.00
Wildflower, Bowl, 6 In. 145.00
Wildflower, Casserole, Cover 1195.00

Wildflower, Chop Plate, 14 In.	.500.00 to 700.00
Wildflower, Plate, 8 1/2 In.	120.00
Wildflower, Plate, 9 1/2 In.	125.00
Wildflower, Plate, 10 In.	145.00
Wildflower, Platter, 14 In.	500.00
Wildflower, Saucer	25.00
Wildflower, Tumbler, 10 Oz.	250.00
Willow, Chop Plate, 14 In.	225.00

FRANKART, Inc., New York, New York, mass-produced nude *dancing lady* lamps, ashtrays, and other decorative Art Deco items in the 1920s and 1930s. They were made of white lead composition and spray-painted. *Frankart Inc.* and the patent number and year were stamped on the base.

Ashtray, Nude On Copper Ball, 6 In.	700.00
Ashtray, Nude Standing On Tiptoes, 4 In.	450.00
Bookends, Airedale	95.00
Bookends, Antelope, Jumping	100.00
Bookends, Nude On Book, 10 In.	375.00
Bookends, Sailor Boy, 7 In.	75.00
Lamp, Nudes Kneeling Back To Back, Globe, 9 In.	750.00

FRANKOMA POTTERY was originally known as The Frank Potteries when John F. Frank opened shop in 1933. The factory is now working in Sapulpa, Oklahoma. Early wares were made from a light cream-colored clay from Ada, Oklahoma, but in 1956 the company switched to a red burning clay from Sapulpa. The firm makes dinnerwares, utilitarian and decorative kitchenwares, figurines, flowerpots, and limited edition and commemorative pieces.

Ashtray, Arrowhead	22.00
Ashtray, Golden Anniversary	25.00
Bookends, Irish Setter	260.00
Candleholder, Oral Roberts	13.00
Cup & Saucer, Plainsman, 6 Oz.	8.00
Ewer, Green & Black, Marked, V-6 Signed, Grace Lee Frank 2529, 13 x 4 In., Pair	100.00
Gravy Boat, Plainsman	10.00
Jug, Mayan-Aztec, 1951, Miniature	40.00
Lazy Susan, No. 818	75.00
Mug, Donkey, 1976	30.00
Mug, Elephant, 1968	50.00
Mug, Elephant, Nixon, Agnew, Red, 1969	68.00
Mug, Parts Is Parts	12.00
Mug, Wagon Wheel, Green, Handle, 5 In.	.6.00 to 10.00
Plate, Cherokee Alphabet	48.00
Plate, Christmas, 1971, No Room At The Inn	20.00
Plate, Christmas, 1975, Peace On Earth	20.00
Plate, Conestoga Wagon	.100.00 to 150.00
Plate, Mail Carrier	150.00
Plate, Wagon Wheel, Prairie Green, 10 In.	7.00
Platter, Plainsman, 13 In.	10.00
Platter, Wagon Wheel, Prairie Green, 15 In.	18.00
Platter, Westwind, 11 In.	8.00
Salt & Pepper, Indian Mask	60.00
Salt & Pepper, Mayan-Aztec	5.00
Salt & Pepper, Oil Derrick	40.00
Salt & Pepper, Teepee	40.00
Salt & Pepper, Turtle	15.00
Salt & Pepper, Wagon Wheel	20.00
Sign, Dealer	18.00
Teapot, Mayan-Aztec, 6 Cup	40.00
Teapot, Piano Player	200.00
Tile, Arced Corners, Blue, Ivory, White, Bruce Goff, 7 1/2 In., 3 Piece	355.00
Trivet, Good Luck	10.00

Trivet, Rooster 15.00
Vase, Flower Girl 130.00
Vase, Nude, 11 1/2 In. 175.00
Wall Pocket, Wagon Wheel 90.00

FRATERNAL objects that are related to the many different fraternal organizations in the United States are listed in this category. The Elks, Masons, Odd Fellows, and others are included. Furniture is listed in the Furniture category. Shaving mugs decorated with fraternal crests are included in the Shaving Mug category.

Eastern Star, Gavel, Gold, Enamels On Silver, 1938 . . . . 40.00
Elks, Badge, 67th Annual Reunion, Seattle, Washington, I.D. Pin, 4 3/8 In. 25.00
Elks, Badge, Atlantic City, Betty Bacharach Home, Afflicted Children, 3 1/2 In. 10.00
Elks, Badge, Grand Aerie Seattle, 1908, Washington Bust, 4 1/8 In. 52.00
Elks, BPOE Emblem, Line Design, Polished Finish, Zippo, 1959 . . . . 35.00
Elks, Mt. Ranier, Seattle, Washington, Fish Bar Center, Shield Shape Drop 25.00
Elks, Tankard, Brown, Warwick Logo, 10 1/2 In. 165.00
Improved Order Of Redmen, Shaving Mug, Emblem, H.W. Conner, c.1900, 3 5/8 In. . . . 175.00
Knights Of Columbus, Cuff Links & Tie Clip, Ruby Red 25.00
Knights Of Columbus, Sword & Sash, Stainless Steel, Composition, Cloth 65.00
Knights Of Columbus, Sword, Case, Enamel Handle, Admiral's Plumbed Hat 300.00
Knights Of Columbus, Sword, Engraved, Leather Scabbard, 1906 . . . . 90.00
Knights Of Knorason, Fez 20.00
Knights Of The Golden Eagle, Shaving Mug, G.W. Lewis, Emblem, 3 5/8 In. 230.00
Masonic, Apron 40.00
Masonic, Beaker, Bohemian Glass, Amber Cut To Clear, Octagonal Base, 5 1/2 In. 475.00
Masonic, Chalice, Glass, Cranberry Silver Sword Handles, 1908 . . . . 95.00
Masonic, Frock Coat, Knights Templar, Black Wool, Double Breasted, Buttons, 1954 . . . . 25.00
Masonic, Medal, 1882 . . . . 40.00
Masonic, Medal, Grand Lodge Of New York, Black Banner Across Shield 53.00
Masonic, Medal, Induction, Montefiore, Coat Of Arms, Motto, Silver, Enamel, 1894 . . . . . 55.00
Masonic, Medal, The Explorers Club, Metal Starburst In Center, White Metal, 1904 . . . . . 42.00
Masonic, Pin, 50 Year 8.00
Masonic, Plate, Shriner, Head Bandaged, Camel Caravans Edge, 11 In. 75.00
Masonic, Ring, Dividers, Square, Ruby 95.00
Masonic, Textile, Wool, Hand Loom Woven, Black & Red Design, 1800s, 8 x 8 Ft. 300.00
Masonic, Tray, Card, Bronze, Souvenir Of Valley Of Seattle 35.00
Masonic, Watch Fob, Masonic Symbols, Sterling Silver Interior, Rose Gold Wash 258.00
Masonic, Watch Fob, Multicolored, Enamel, 2 7/8 In. 79.00
Masonic, Watch Fob, Sterling & Ename Pocket Knife, 32nd Degree, 2 7/8 In. 80.00
Modern Woodmen Of America, Shaving Mug, Emblem, Limoges, 3 7/8 In. 95.00
Modern Woodmen Of America, Shaving Mug, J.E. Cook, c.1900, 3 5/8 In. 200.00
Odd Fellows, Pin, Odd Fellows 100th Anniversary, 1819-1919, Celluloid, Pinback 55.00
Odd Fellows, Secretary, Drop Front, Oak, Drawer, Fluted Legs, Crest, 31 x 24 x 81 In. . . . 660.00
Order Of Eagles, No. 293, Shaving Mug, Eagle, Bill Wagner, c.1900, 3 3/4 In. 210.00
Order Of Eagles, Shaving Mug, Emblem, Chiapas Bro., c.1900, 4 In. 175.00
Order Of Eagles & Shriners, Shaving Mug, Eagle Emblem, J.E. Henkel, 3 5/8 In. 110.00
Shriner, Cup, Atlantic City, 1904, 3 1/2 In. 85.00
Shriner, Postcard, Man, Shriner's Cap, Karom Sanctorum Lodge No. 195, 1922 . . . . 40.00
Shriner, Shriner Lapel Pins, 2 Point Diamond, Platinum 20.00
Shriner, Urn, Pittsburgh, 1908, 5 1/2 In. 75.00

FRY GLASS was made by the H. C. Fry Glass Company of Rochester, Pennsylvania. The company, founded in 1901, first made cut glass and other types of fine glasswares. In 1922, they patented a heat-resistant glass called *Pearl Ovenglass.* For two years, 1926–1927, the company made Fry Foval, an opal ware decorated with colored trim. Reproductions of this glass have been made. Depression glass patterns made by Fry may be listed in the Depression Glass category. Some pieces of cut glass may also be included in the Cut Glass category.

FRY, Aquarium, Golden Glow, 10 In. . . . . .95.00 to 100.00
Baker, Apple 30.00
Bowl, Blue Threaded, Sawtooth Cutting, Scalloped Edge, Pedestal, 1890, 9 3/4 In. 65.00

Bowl, Pinwheel Cutting, Signed, 8 In.	90.00
Bride's Basket, Signed At Handle, 12 x 16 In.	715.00
Candlestick, Emerald Green, Low	40.00
Candlestick, Golden Glow, Low, Pair	40.00
Compote, Golden Glow, Diamond-Optic, Twisted Stem, Black Threading	350.00
Dish, Pickle, Prince Cutting, Side Handle, Marked, 8 In.	195.00
Fernery, Footed, Signed	400.00
Goblet, Amethyst, Swirl Ball Stem	210.00
Goblet, Swirl Ball Stem	25.00
Perfume Bottle, Floral Cutting, Blue Stopper, 3 3/4 In.	357.00
Reamer, Emerald Green, Straight Sides	45.00
Vase, Controlled Bubbles, Gold Iridescent Threading, 6 In.	200.00
Vase, Controlled Bubbles, Green Threading, 8 In.	45.00
Vase, Trumpet, Yellow Opalescent, Blue Rim, 11 In.	60.00
FRY FOVAL, Candlestick, Jade & Opal, 12 In., Pair	1358.00
Coffeepot, Basket, Holder, White Handle & Cover	610.00
Compote, Cobalt Trim	150.00
Cup, White Opalescent, Jade Green Handle, 2 1/4 In.	31.00
Perfume Bottle, Pearl Base, Jade Stopper, 4 1/2 In.	228.00

FULPER Pottery Company was incorporated in 1899 in Flemington, New Jersey. They made art pottery from 1910 to 1929. The firm had been making bottles, jugs, and housewares from 1805. Doll heads were made about 1928. The firm became Stangl Pottery in 1929. Fulper art pottery is admired for its attractive glazes and simple shapes.

Barrel, Copper Dust Crystalline Glaze To Mirror Black Glaze, 4 3/4 x 4 In.	440.00
Bookends, Cat, Art Deco	450.00
Bookends, Kneeling Egyptians, Full Relief, Green, c.1910, 8 In.	373.00
Bookends, Roman Mausoleum, Ivory, White Matte Glaze, Mark	605.00
Bowl, Blue Green Drip Glaze, Shallow, c.1910, 3 1/2 In.	373.00
Bowl, Caramel Flambe Glaze, Closed-In Rim, Squat, 2 x 8 3/4 In.	144.00
Bowl, Cat's-Eye Flambe, Speckled Matte Glaze, Effigy, Signed, 7 1/2 x 10 1/2 In.	650.00
Bowl, Chinese Blue, Scalloped, 5 In.	220.00
Bowl, Green Over Gunmetal Glaze, Pale Green, Turquoise, 3-Footed, 3 x 18 In.	374.00
Bowl, Green, Effigy, 5 Figures, Signed, 10 x 7 In.	665.00
Bowl, Ibis, Flemington Green Flambe, Brown Exterior, Mark, 5 3/4 In.	935.00
Bowl, Pink & Cream Matte, Vertical Mark, 5 x 7 In.	195.00
Bowl, Seafoam Green Mottled, Gold, Blue Streaks, Closed-In Rim, 2 x 10 1/2 In.	144.00
Candlestick, Yellow Matte Glaze, Ink Racetrack Mark, 15 1/2 In., Pair	1320.00
Doorstop, Cat, Cat's-Eye Flambe Glaze, 6 x 9 In.	1045.00
Flask, Pilgrim, Flemington Green, White Frothy Flambe Glaze, 10 1/4 x 7 1/4 In.	495.00
Flower Frog, Frog On Lily Pad, Green, Ivory, Mahogany Glaze, Mark, 3 1/2 In.	165.00
Flower Frog, Frog Shape, Green, Mottled	175.00
Flower Frog, Frog Shape, Mirror Green & Caramel Flambe, 7 In.	220.00
Flower Frog, Indian Maiden, In Canoe, Green, Mahogany, Brown Glaze, 4 x 7 In.	550.00
Flower Frog, Mushroom, Brown Crystalline, Signed, 3 In.	59.00
Flower Frog, Penguin, White, Blue & Brown Glaze, Ink Mark, 7 In.	305.00
Flower Frog, Thick Famille Rose Matte Glaze, Ink Racetrack Mark, 2 x 6 1/2 In.	22.00
Jug, Flemington Green Flambe Glaze, 8 In.	65.00
Jug, Handle, 6 x 5 1/2 In.	125.00
Lamp, Blue Flambe Glaze, Mushroom Shade, Inset Leaded Glass, Signed, 24 In.	7500.00
Lamp, Cat's-Eye Flambe Glaze, Green, Ivory, Mushroom Shade, Leaded Glass Pieces	11000.00
Lamp, Cat's-Eye Flambe Glaze, Red Slag Glass, 18 1/2 In.	9455.00
Lamp, Dark & Light Blue Crystalline Glaze, Base, Signed, 10 In.	475.00
Lamp, Light Blue Flambe, Mushroom Shade, Amber Slag Glass, 20 In.	21850.00
Lamp, Matte Green Glaze, Drilled, 23 In.	360.00
Lamp, Olive Green Crystalline Glaze, Mushroom Shade, 17 x 16 In.	10350.00
Lamp, Perfume, Ballerina, Blue	425.00
Lamp, Perfume, Lavender, Ballerina Top	95.00
Lamp, Perfume, Tropical Colors, Cockatoo Shape, Yellow Ware, 12 1/2 In.	715.00
Lamp Base, Moth, Wisteria, Frothy White, Deep Blue Accents, Famille Rose, 8 1/2 In.	220.00
Teapot, Cat's-Eye Flambe Glaze, Signed, 5 1/8 In.	357.00
Urn, Blue, Green Crystalline Glaze, 2 Nubby Handles, 11 3/4 x 8 3/4 In.	1210.00

Urn, Mirror Black Glaze, Raised Racetrack Mark, 7 1/2 x 3 1/4 In. 275.00
Vase, 2-Tone Green Crystalline Glaze, Large Shouldered Shape, 12 In. 440.00
Vase, Black Crystalline Glaze, Bottle Shape, Incised Racetrack Mark, 8 x 6 In. 440.00
Vase, Black Glaze, Flattened Base, Stamped Vertical Mark, 5 1/2 In. 250.00
Vase, Black, Blue, Caramel Drip, 3 Handles, Vertical Mark, 7 In. 400.00
Vase, Blue Crystalline Glaze, Ink Racetrack Mark, 4 x 2 1/2 In. 245.00
Vase, Blue, Brown, Gunmetal Flambe, Vertical Mark, 7 In. 231.00
Vase, Blue, Caramel Flambe, Stamped Vertical Mark, 4 1/2 In. 319.00
Vase, Blue, Green Flambe Over Red Matte Glaze, Mission Shape, 2 Handles, 11 In. 1100.00
Vase, Blue, Purple, Stamp Vertical Mark, 3 In. 176.00
Vase, Blue, Red, Green Drip Glaze, 4 1/2 In. 176.00
Vase, Brown, Gold, Green, Blue Drip, 4 Buttressed Handles, 8 1/2 In. 825.00
Vase, Bud, Cobalt Crystalline Glaze, 4 Sides, 12 x 3 In. 825.00
Vase, Bud, Lavender, 8 In. 440.00
Vase, Bud, Speckled Brown Matte Glaze, 1915, 8 1/2 In. 220.00
Vase, Butterscotch Flambe, Mirrored Black To Mahogany, Ivory Glaze, Corset, 7 In. 357.00
Vase, Cafe-Au-Lait Glaze, Rectangular Ink Mark, 4 x 2 3/4 In. 357.50
Vase, Cat's-Eye & Mahogany Flambe Glaze, Signed, 7 1/4 In. 350.00
Vase, Cat's-Eye Flambe Glaze, Bullet, Handle, 7 x 5 In. 303.00
Vase, Cat's-Eye Flambe Glaze, Cobalt, Incised Racetrack Mark, 12 x 8 1/2 In. 1540.00
Vase, Cat's-Eye Flambe Glaze, Ink Racetrack Mark, 7 x 4 In. 303.00
Vase, Cat's-Eye Flambe Glaze, Racetrack Mark, 17 In. 1210.00
Vase, Cat's-Eye To Turquoise Flambe Glaze, Trumpet, 13 x 7 In. 1650.00
Vase, Chinese Blue High Glaze, Periwinkle Blue Matte, Beehive Shape, 6 1/2 In. 275.00
Vase, Chinese Blue, Periwinkle Blue Matte, Lavender Streaks, Ribbed, 8 1/2 In. 165.00
Vase, Cobalt Matte Glaze, Cylindrical Neck, 2 Handles, 9 x 6 In. 275.00
Vase, Copper Dust Crystalline Glaze, 2 Angular Handles, Ink Racetrack Mark, 5 x 6 In. . . .   660.00
Vase, Copper Dust Glaze, Shouldered, Vertical Mark, 5 1/2 In. 319.00
Vase, Copper Dust To Green Flambe Glaze, 2 Buttressed Handles, Mark, 9 In. 495.00
Vase, Cream Flambe Drip Over Orange, Brown, Ribbed, 2 Open Handles, 12 In. 1210.00
Vase, Cucumber Crystalline Glaze, 7 Sides, Ink Racetrack Mark, 10 x 5 3/4 In. 522.00
Vase, Cucumber Crystalline Glaze, Signed, 4 3/4 In. 220.00
Vase, Cucumber Green, Copper Dust Streaks, 6 In. 275.00
Vase, Cucumber Matte Glaze, Signed, 9 1/2 x 17 In. 1600.00
Vase, Dark Green Luster Glaze, Green Matte Ground, Ribbed, 3 Handles, 6 In. 192.00
Vase, Deep Olive Brown Luster, Metallic Black, Ribbed, Vessel Shape, 11 In. 330.00
Vase, Elephant's Breath Flambe Glaze, Corset, 1915, 7 1/2 x 4 1/2 In. 247.00
Vase, Elephant's Breath Glaze, Mauve Drip, 2 Buttressed Handles, 9 3/4 x 7 In. 935.00
Vase, Famille Rose Matte, Deep Burgundy, Baluster, 7 3/4 In. 192.00
Vase, Flemington Green, Black Flambe Glaze, Floor, 16 3/4 x 9 1/4 In. 3080.00
Vase, Frothy Ivory, Mustard Matte Glaze, Bottle Shape, Incised Racetrack Mark, 7 In. . . .   220.00
Vase, Glossy Lavender Crystalline Glaze, Bulbous Top, 2 Handles, 8 x 5 In. 385.00
Vase, Green & Blue Flambe, Signed, 6 In. 275.00
Vase, Green Crystalline Glaze, 2 Open Handles At Shoulder, 8 x 6 In. 440.00
Vase, Green Crystalline Glaze, 5 Looping Handles, Paper Label, 9 1/2 In. 770.00
Vase, Green Drip Over Red, Ribbed, Plugged In Base, 15 In. 305.00
Vase, Green, Blue, Charcoal Drip Over Red Matte, 3 Open Handles At Top, 6 1/2 In. 253.00
Vase, Green, Brown Glaze, 2 Handles, 8 1/2 x 6 1/2 In. 440.00
Vase, Gunmetal Matte Glaze, Green, 2 Handles, 6 1/2 x 5 In. 275.00
Vase, Gunmetal Over Caramel Crystalline Flambe, 2 Buttressed Handles, 3 In. 220.00
Vase, Ivory To Cat's-Eye Flambe Glaze, Signed, 3 1/4 x 4 3/4 In. 150.00
Vase, Khaki Flambe Glaze, Crystalline, Buttressed Handles, 11 1/4 In. 220.00
Vase, Leopard-Skin Crystalline Glaze, Cattail, Signed, 13 In. 650.00
Vase, Leopard-Skin Glaze, Green, Tan Crystals, Impressed Vertical Mark, 17 In. 2530.00
Vase, Light Blue & Green Matte Glaze, Dark Blue Highlights, Two Block Handles, 7 In. .   430.00
Vase, Light Blue To Elephant's Breath Flambe Glaze, 5 1/4 In. 350.00
Vase, Mirror Black To Amber Crystalline Glaze, 4 Buttressed Handles, 8 1/4 x 6 In. 522.00
Vase, Mirrored Blue Flambe, Signed, 4 3/4 In. 157.00
Vase, Mirrored Green, Twig Stick, 6 1/2 In. 200.00
Vase, Moss To Wisteria Flambe Glaze, 2 Handles, Raised Mark, 7 In. 495.00
Vase, Multicolored Drip Glaze, 2 Ring Handles, 12 In. 440.00
Vase, Olive Brown Flambe, Brown Streak Neck, Periwinkle Blue, Bottle Shape, 8 In. 247.00
Vase, Olive Flambe Glaze, Flowing Matte, Signed, 8 x 7 In. 450.00

Vase, Olive, White Flambe, Recessed Hammered, Ribbed Neck, Urn Shape, 13 In. 495.00
Vase, Pale Blue, Crystalline, Flambe, Pale Cucumber, Beehive Shape, Handles, 6 In. 220.00
Vase, Purple & Blue Crystalline Glaze, 2 Buttressed Handles, Signed, 8 x 6 1/2 In. 250.00
Vase, Purple Crystalline Glaze, Gray, Salmon, 7 1/2 In. 605.00
Vase, Purple, Blue Matte Glaze, 2 Square Handles, Vertical Mark, 5 In. 231.00
Vase, Rose Famille Over Gray Matte Glaze, 4 Buttressed Handles, 8 x 6 In. 385.00
Vase, Rose, Blue Flambe At Mid-Section, Bullet, 3 Buttressed Handles, 6 3/4 In. 275.00
Vase, Rust, Cream Drip Flambe Glaze, 2 Open Handles, 8 In. 522.00
Vase, Silver, Crystalline, Olive Finish Over Pale Green, Handles, 6 In. 165.00
Vase, Spherical, Chinese Blue Glaze, 3 Handles, Racetrack Mark, 6 In. 465.00
Vase, Thick Metallic Black Glaze, Cucumber Green Glaze, Ribbed, 3 Handles, 6 In. 165.00
Vase, Wisteria Drip To Famille Rose Flambe Glaze, 2 Handles, 8 x 6 In. 440.00
Vase, Wisteria Matte Glaze, Baluster, Incised Racetrack Mark, 10 1/2 x 4 In. 440.00
Vessel, Flemington Green Flambe Glaze, Barrel Shape, Ink Rectangular Mark, 5 x 4 In. . . 330.00
Wall Pocket, Brown & Caramel, Art Deco 850.00

FURNITURE of all types is listed in this category. Examples dating from the seventeenth century to the 1970s are included. Prices for furniture vary in different parts of the country. Oak furniture is most expensive in the West; large pieces over eight feet high are sold for the most money in the South, where high ceilings are found in the old homes. Condition is very important when determining prices. These are NOT average prices but rather reports of unique sales. If the description includes the word *style*, the piece resembles the old furniture style but was made at a later time. It is not a period piece. Garden furniture is listed in the Garden Furnishings category. Related items may be found in the Architectural, Brass, and Store categories.

Armchairs are listed under Chair in this category.
Armoire, 2 Carved Door Panels, Normandy, France, 1700, 70 x 56 x 18 In. 2900.00
Armoire, Chestnut, Molded Cornice, 2 Parquetry Doors, France, 1790, 91 In. 2662.00
Armoire, Chippendale, Cherry, Cornice, Blind Cabinet Doors, David T. Smith 1265.00
Armoire, Classical, Cherry, 2-Panel Door, Divided Interior, Bracket Feet, 86 In. 1980.00
Armoire, Edwardian, Walnut, Molded Cornice, Glass Panel, Fitted Interior, 85 x 49 In. . . . 920.00
Armoire, French Provincial, Fruitwood, 2 Doors, Block Feet, 1810, 88 In. 1936.00
Armoire, French Provincial, Fruitwood, 2 Paneled Doors, 1820, 103 x 55 x 24 In. 3630.00
Armoire, French Provincial, Oak, 2 Doors, Scalloped Apron, Cup Feet, 1810, 78 In. 1815.00
Armoire, French Provincial, Oak, Geometric Carving, Scalloped Apron, 1820, 89 In. 2662.00
Armoire, French Provincial, Pine, Crest, Carved Reserve Drawers, 19th Century 1380.00
Armoire, Louis XV, Fruitwood, 2 Doors, Paneled Frieze, Cabriole Legs, 89 x 62 In. 2530.00
Armoire, Mahogany, 2 Paneled Doors, Stepped Ogee Cornice, 1840s, 95 In. 2750.00
Armoire, Mahogany, Carved Crest, Bonnet Top, Paw Feet, 1900, 85 In. 705.00
Armoire, Mahogany, Parquetry, Center Door, Oval Mirror, Drawer, 81 In. 575.00
Armoire, Mahogany, Ribbon Bellflower & Urn Inlay, Mirror On Door, 77 x 47 In. 550.00
Armoire, Oak, Double Door, Rolling Pin Crest, 1910, 100 1/4 x 54 x 21 In. 1573.00
Armoire, Ogee Molded Cornice, Paneled Door, Bracket Feet, France, 1860, 80 In. 847.00
Armoire, Pine, 2 Glass Doors Over 2 Drawers, American, 1900, 80 x 48 x 18 In. 295.00
Armoire, Pine, Domed Crest, Paneled Door, Claw & Ball Feet, Casters, 80 1/2 In. 605.00
Armoire, Renaissance Revival, Mahogany, 2 Doors, Turned Pilasters, 1880, 79 In. 2300.00
Armoire, Rococo, Mahogany, Double Door, 1860, 75 x 69 x 20 In. 2057.00
Armoire, Rococo, Walnut, Fruit Crest, Arched Panel Doors, 2 Drawers, c.1860, 100 In. . . 1650.00
Armoire, Yew Wood, Cornice Over 2 Doors, Brass Escutcheons, Scroll Toes, 90 1/2 In. . . 266.00
Banquette, Regency, Walnut, Serpentine Top, Upholstered, Cabriole Legs, 45 In. 1840.00
Bar, Black Enameled Wire Frame, Rattan Screen, 4 Stools With Cushions, Weinberg 880.00
Bed, Aesthetic Movement, Mahogany, c.1880, Twin, 96 x 60 In. 690.00
Bed, Arts & Crafts, 5 Vertical Slats, Headboard & Footboard, 57 x 78 x 48 In. 935.00
Bed, Arts & Crafts, Oak, 3 Vertical Panels, 53 x 42-In. Headboard 430.00
Bed, Brass, 7 Ball Spindles At Headboard & Footboard, Fitted Spring 165.00
Bed, Brass, Egyptian Lily Design On Head & Footboard, Leaf & Ball Finials, 41 In. 400.00
Bed, Brass, Iron, Canopy, Casters, c.1880, 94 x 72 In. 850.00
Bed, Brass, Lacquered, Converted For Queen Mattress, 1900, 60-In. Headboard 3450.00
Bed, Brass, Scroll Design, 72 x 55 x 67 1/2 In. 1100.00
Bed, Campaign, Canopy, Reeded Posts, Acanthus Carved Borders, 18th Century 1725.00
Bed, Cannonball, Cherry, Poplar, Rope, Rolled Crest, 78 x 43 3/4 In. 275.00

Bed, Canopy, Federal, Reeded Foot Posts, Pine Headboard, Arched Frame, 75 In. 2645.00
Bed, Canopy, Georgian, Mahogany, Floral, Foliate Design, 1830, 88 In. 1694.00
Bed, Canopy, Maple, Pine, Octagonal Pencil Posts, New England, 87 x 46 x 70 In. 1870.00
Bed, Canopy, Sheraton, Mahogany, Spiral Turnings, Acanthus Leaf Bell, 88 In. 3680.00
Bed, Canopy, Sheraton, Reeded & Turned Posts, Red Paint, 68 x 52 x 76 In. 2243.00
Bed, Cherry, Turned Posts, Shaped Headboard, Victorian, 55 In. 385.00
Bed, Chestnut, Rope, Hired Man's, Square Posts, Turned Finials, 68 1/2 In. 110.00
Bed, Curly Maple Posts, Poplar Headboard, Acorn Finials, 89 In. 1650.00
Bed, E. Wheeler, Cherry, Sheraton Style, Flat Tester, Bulbous Posts 2420.00
Bed, E. Wormley, Tapered Black Lacquered Frame, Cane Panel, 38 x 41 In., Pair 403.00
Bed, Empire, Mahogany, Ormolu Mounted, Woman Mask, 42 x 73 x 48 In. 5175.00
Bed, Empire, Mahogany, Out-Scrolled Sides, Paw Feet, 43 x 67 x 50 In. 5460.00
Bed, Empire, Mahogany, Rectangular Headboard & Footboard, Paw Feet, 42 In. 5175.00
Bed, Federal, Curly Maple, Reeded Posts, Rope Rails, 19th Century, 52 x 70 x 82 In. 1380.00
Bed, Federal, Mahogany, Tall Post, Flame Finials, Reeded Posts, Carved Tassels 245.00
Bed, Federal, Maple, Low Baluster Posts, Ball Finials, Acanthus, 19th Century 260.00
Bed, Federal, Tiger Maple, Pencil Post, Straight Canopy, David T. Smith 1150.00
Bed, Figured Maple, Serpentine Tester Over Supports, Arched Headboard, c.1820 . . . . 4600.00
Bed, Four-Poster, Empire Gothic, Mahogany, 19th Century 4000.00
Bed, Four-Poster, Empire, Mahogany, Needlepoint Valance 4400.00
Bed, Four-Poster, Empire, Mahogany, Pineapple, Metal Bun Feet, American, 98 In. 2875.00
Bed, Four-Poster, Empire, Walnut, Canopy, American, Early 19th Century, 91 In. 2990.00
Bed, Four-Poster, Federal, Maple, Turned Posts, Scroll Headboard, c.1830, 52 In. 307.00
Bed, Four-Poster, Mahogany, Birch, Arched Headboard, 1800, 58 1/2 In. 2070.00
Bed, Four-Poster, Mahogany, Rope Twist Posts, Carved Flowers, 90 In. 1725.00
Bed, Four-Poster, Mahogany, Turned Leaf, Feather-Head Posts, 96 In. 2200.00
Bed, Four-Poster, Maple, Pine, Cannon Ball Finials, Baluster Posts, 19th Century 275.00
Bed, Four-Poster, Paneled Headboard, Victorian, 75 1/2 x 72 In. 302.00
Bed, Four-Poster, Rope, Maple, 76 x 45 In. 220.00
Bed, Four-Poster, Rope, Mixed Woods, Acorn Posts, 1840-1860, Pair 220.00
Bed, Four-Poster, Rope, Poplar, Goblet Finials, Bed Wrench, 52 1/2 In. 273.00
Bed, Four-Poster, Rope, Poplar, Round Rails, 55 x 72 x 43 In. 220.00
Bed, Four-Poster, Tiger Maple, Cannonball, Full Size 660.00
Bed, Four-Poster, Walnut, Arched Headboard, Turned Spools, Victorian, 82 x 60 In. 1810.00
Bed, Four-Poster, Walnut, Turned Lamb's-Tongue Chamfers, 19th Century, 86 In. 3520.00
Bed, French Provincial Style, Mahogany, Floral Design, 78 x 48 In. 155.00
Bed, G. Nelson, Birch, Cane Headboard, Metal Legs, Thin Edge, 38 x 77 In. 3850.00
Bed, G. Stickley, Mahogany, Inverted V-Top Rail, 59 x 48 x 78 In. 8800.00
Bed, G. Stickley, Maple, Inlaid Top, Paneled Headboard & Footboard, 50 In. 9900.00
Bed, Half Tester, Renaissance Revival, Walnut, Crest, Panels, 1860, 102 x 63 x 85 In. . . . 2180.00
Bed, L. & J.G. Stickley, Pencil Post, 54 x 58 In. 7155.00
Bed, Limbert, No. 471, Alternating Wide & Narrow Slats, 8 1/2 x 56 1/2 In. 3000.00
Bed, Louis XV, Curved Headboard, Polychrome, 19th Century, 49 x 80 x 57 In. 665.00
Bed, Louis XVI Style, Marquetry, Double, 51 x 53 In. 405.00
Bed, Louis XVI, Ivory, Rectangular Molded Top Rail, Acorn Finials, 41 In., Pair 920.00
Bed, Louis XVI, Kingwood, Gilt Bronze Relief Panel Of Cupids, 82 x 60 In. 1725.00
Bed, Low Posts, Rolling-Pin Headboard, Acorn Finial, 48 x 52 x 84 In. 330.00
Bed, Mahogany, Crest, Turned Finials, Cove Molded Panels, 19th Century 165.00
Bed, Mahogany, Pineapple Finials, Matching Headboard, Double, 56 In. 1100.00
Bed, Maple, Pine, Bell & Ball Design, Scroll Headboard, 43 x 75 1/2 In. 115.00
Bed, Maple, Poplar, Rope, Red Stain, Goblet Finial, 52 x 60 In. 360.00
Bed, Mission Style, Oak, 7 Square Spindles, Twin, 47 x 47 In. 2420.00
Bed, Napoleon III, Mahogany, Brass Mounts, Applied Finials, 58 x 56 In. 2178.00
Bed, Oak, Applied Carving, Headboard & Footboard, 1910, 61 x 58 In. 484.00
Bed, Oak, Turned Finials, Acorn & Flower Crest, Victorian 515.00
Bed, Pine, Maple, Folding, Flaring Posts, Hinged Rails, Three-Quarter, 95 In. 3450.00
Bed, Pine, Maple, Low Posts, Pitched Headboard, Painted, 19th Century, 52 x 80 In. 575.00
Bed, Queen Anne, Tiger Maple, Scroll Rectangular Head, 19th Century 431.00
Bed, Renaissance Revival, Walnut, Wraparound Footboard, Victorian, 54 x 67 In. 240.00
Bed, Rococo, Rosewood, Carved Female Face At Crest, Double 5280.00
Bed, Rococo, Walnut, Arched Head & Footboard, 19th Century, Child's 200.00
Bed, Rococo, Walnut, Arched Head & Footboard, Carved Crest, 19th Century 490.00
Bed, Rolling Pin Over Scroll Headboard, Country, Penna., 52 x 41 x 77 In. 440.00

Bed, Sleigh, Bird's-Eye Maple 535.00
Bed, Sleigh, Curved Top, Horizontal Panel, 42 1/2 x 73 In. 115.00
Bed, Sleigh, Empire, Mahogany Veneer, Gothic Trim, American, 19th Century 575.00
Bed, Sleigh, Mahogany, c.1859, 33 x 80 1/2 In. 455.00
Bed, T. Parzinger, White Lacquer, Square Posts, 1950, 84 In. 525.00
Bed, Tall Post, Federal, Mahogany, Acanthus Leaf Inlay, Canopy, 74 x 83 In. 2310.00
Bed, Tall Post, Federal, Maple, Scroll Headboard, New England, 1830s, 54 x 72 In. 1380.00
Bed, Tall Post, Sheraton, Maple, Birch, Curved Canopy Frame, 67 In. 1540.00
Bed, Tester, Chippendale, Walnut, Virginia, 18th Century 2990.00
Bed, Tester, Classical, Cherry, Scroll Crest Headboard, Pediment, 1820, Double 2415.00
Bed, Tester, Elizabethan Revival, Walnut, Gallery Headboard, 94 x 63 x 78 In. 2905.00
Bed, Victorian, Child's, 36 x 38 1/2 In. 90.00
Bed, Walnut, Turned & Faceted Posts, Paneled, Scroll Headboard, 1850s, 94 In. 4125.00
Bed Steps, George III, Mahogany, Hinged Top, Drawer, 1800, 25 x 19 In. 770.00
Bed Steps, Mahogany, Leather Inset Treads, Handholds, 1830s, 27 1/2 x 21 In. 8625.00
Bed Steps, Regency, Green Leather Inset, Commode, Sheraton Feet, 27 1/2 In. 1430.00
Bedroom Set, Cherry, 2 Single Beds, Stand, Oval Mirror, 2 Dressers, Kling, c.1938 ..... 345.00
Bedroom Set, Chest, Reeded Molding, Bracket Feet, Stand, Twin, Pair, 4 Piece 550.00
Bedroom Set, E. Wormley, 5 Drawers, 2-Door Chests, Twin Sleigh Beds, 4 Piece 2300.00
Bedroom Set, Eastlake Style, Cherry, Dresser, Washstand, 1905-1910, 3 Piece 2200.00
Bedroom Set, Federal Style, Mahogany, 5 Drawer Chest, Double Bed, 1930s 850.00
Bedroom Set, Light Wood, Vanity, Round Mirror, Wardrobe, 1930s, 4 Piece 5500.00
Bedroom Set, Metal, Red Trim, Twin Beds, Chest, Vanity, Stool, Stand, Child's 1500.00
Bedroom Set, Oak, Bowfront, Beveled Mirror, Victorian, 3 Piece 1595.00
Bedroom Set, Oak, Carved Rosettes, Marble Top, 19th Century, 3 Piece 290.00
Bedroom Set, Pine, Grain Painted, Cottage Style, 4 Piece 660.00
Bedroom Set, Renaissance Revival, Burl Walnut, American, 19th Century, 3 Piece 2300.00
Bedroom Set, Rohde, Ash Veneer, Leatherette Wrapped Pulls, 7 Piece 1320.00
Bedroom Set, Walnut, Carved, Burl Panel Bed, Marble-Top Dresser, 2 Piece 4140.00
Bedroom Set, Walnut, Carved, Marble Top, Victorian, 3 Piece 5200.00
Bedroom Set, White Paint, Blue & Red Trim, Polychrome Floral Design, 4 Piece 935.00
Bench, 3-Part Crest Rail, Gilt Spread-Wing Eagle, Downcurved Arms, Painted, 72 In. ... 373.00
Bench, Arts & Crafts, Chestnut Inglenook, Chamfered Back, Ebonized Finish, 57 In. 1100.00
Bench, Bucket, 3 Shelves, Red Paint, Scroll Plank Ends, 52 x 39 x 14 In. 990.00
Bench, Bucket, Cupboard Top 3300.00
Bench, Bucket, Open Back, 2 Shelves, Blue Over Red Paint, 43 x 38 x 14 In. 290.00
Bench, Bucket, Plank Ends, 2 Mortised Shelves, Pennsylvania, 31 1/2 In. 1045.00
Bench, Bucket, Red Paint, 2 Shelves, Cutout Ends 605.00
Bench, Bugatti, Wood, Brass, Vellum, Pewter Geometric Design, 1900, 58 1/2 In. 8625.00
Bench, Church, Oak, Acanthus Leaf Armrests, 48 In. 100.00
Bench, Church, Solid Ends, 61 In. 165.00
Bench, Cow Scene Painted On Top, Gray Paint, 11 x 48 x 19 In. 110.00
Bench, Curly Maple, Pennsylvania 3025.00
Bench, Deacon's, Painted, Half-Spindle Back, Fruit & Floral Gilt Stencil, c.1815, 71 In. ... 110.00
Bench, Dressing, Needlepoint, Tapered Rope Turned Legs, Victorian, 24 x 19 In. 115.00
Bench, E. Wormley, Mahogany, Brass, Upholstered, Cane Seat, 21 x 17 In., Pair 1980.00
Bench, E. Wormley, Orange Velvet, Bleached Mahogany Legs, 40 x 20 In. 770.00
Bench, E. Wormley, Square Brass Tubular Frame, Silk, 17 x 45 x 17 In. 920.00
Bench, Edwardian, Stained, Concave Back, Upholstered Seat, Arms, 29 In. 1150.00
Bench, Elm, Rectangular Seat, Splayed Cylindrical Legs, 19th Century, Pair 460.00
Bench, Fireside, Mahogany, Upholstered Seat, 6 Carved Legs, 18 x 23 x 43 In. 770.00
Bench, Frankl, Mahogany, Cream Lacquered Cork Top, Greek Key Base, 84 In. 2530.00
Bench, G. Nelson, Birch Slats, Ebonized Legs, 14 x 68 1/4 x 18 1/2 In. ....1100.00 to 1870.00
Bench, G. Nelson, Green Wool, Chrome Metal Base, Herman Miller, 60 x 15 In. 1320.00
Bench, G. Nelson, Light Wood Slats, Black Paint, 14 x 72 x 18 1/2 In. 1035.00
Bench, G. Nelson, Steel Frame, 4 Cushions, Upholstered, 80 x 20 x 15 In. 550.00
Bench, G. Stickley, No. 215, Child's, 30 x 38 In. 2420.00
Bench, G. Stickley, No. 224, Mahogany, Lift Seat, 48 x 22 x 42 In. 5500.00
Bench, George III, Damask, Square Legs, Out-Scrolled Arms, Pair 10350.00
Bench, George III, Saddle-Shaped Seat, Chamfered Legs, 18 In., Pair 13800.00
Bench, Georgian Style, Upholstered, Floral Needlework Panel, 40 x 17 x 14 In. 195.00
Bench, Gilt Metal, Upholstered Seat, Scroll & Floral Design, Paw Feet, 25 x 19 In. 290.00
Bench, Hitchcock, Grain Painted, Stenciled, Cane Seat, Arms 1380.00

Bench, Hitchcock, Triple Chairback, Stencil, Painted, Scroll Arms, 73 In. 805.00
Bench, Jacobean, Velvet Seat, 18 1/2 x 48 x 12 In. 151.00
Bench, Kneeling, French Provincial, Ladder Back, Rush Seat, 19th Century, 38 1/2 In. . . . 85.00
Bench, Kneeling, Poplar, Refinished, White Paint Traces 250.00
Bench, Kneeling, Prie Dieu, Elizabethan Revival, American, 1875, 35 x 18 x 19 In. 365.00
Bench, Kneeling, Prie Dieu, Gothic Revival, Mahogany, 19th Century, 35 x 20 In. 150.00
Bench, Kneeling, Walnut, Cut Velvet, France, 35 x 19 x 17 In. 272.00
Bench, Laverne, White Leather Straps, Chrome Frame, 1960, 48 x 21 x 14 In. 715.00
Bench, Lift Top, Needlework Seat, Late 19th Century, 22 x 10 1/2 In. 140.00
Bench, Louis XV, Fruitwood, Needlepoint Seat, 6 Cabriole Legs, 19th Century, 35 In. . . . 545.00
Bench, Louis XVI, Mahogany, Carved Rails, Tapered Legs, Upholstered, 23 1/2 In. 330.00
Bench, Louis XVI, Upholstered Seat Rail, Round Fluted Legs, 65 1/2 In. 920.00
Bench, Mahogany, Carved Paw Feet, Lions' Heads, Velvet Cushion, 23 x 29 1/4 In. . : . . . 577.00
Bench, Mahogany, Needlework, Carved Knees, 17 1/2 x 28 1/4 In. 690.00
Bench, Mahogany, Spindle Back, Square Tapered Legs, Shaped Arms, 50 In. 220.00
Bench, Mahogany, Upholstered Lift Seat, Cabriole Legs, Continental, 37 In. 500.00
Bench, Mammy's, Windsor, Black Over Red, Stenciled Flowers, 29 1/4 x 48 In. 1150.00
Bench, Matte Green-Blue Paint, c.1840, 70 3/4 In. 495.00
Bench, McCobb, Tapered Dowel Legs, Winchendon, 10 x 60 x 18 In. 460.00
Bench, Meetinghouse, Pine, Scalloped Legs, Blue Paint, 167 1/2 In. 373.00
Bench, Neoclassical, Gilt, Rectangular Upholstered Seat, Giltwood Scrolls, 20 In. 5750.00
Bench, Oak, Carved Panel Back, Lift Seat, Late 19th Century 400.00
Bench, Oak, Mortised & Pinned Construction, Leather Seat, 31 1/2 In. 907.00
Bench, Oak, Panel Back, Linenfold Carving, Lift Seat, 50 x 40 x 20 In. 465.00
Bench, Oak, Rectangular Seat, Trestle Ends, 19th Century 110.00
Bench, Oak, Regency, Roundels On Top, Tapering Legs, Part Ebonized, 1815, 23 3/4 In. . . 3737.00
Bench, Pine, Natural Finish, Shaped Cutout Ends, 11 x 61 x 18 In. 220.00
Bench, Pine, Oak, Red Stain, Arms, 48 x 18 x 40 In. 300.00
Bench, Pine, Salmon Paint, 5 Mortised Legs, Beaded Apron, 108 In. 245.00
Bench, Pine, Single Plank, 19th Century, 60 In. 92.00
Bench, Pine, Wire-Nail Construction, 13 1/2 x 31 x 17 3/4 In. 135.00
Bench, Pine, Yellow Comb Graining, 8 3/4 x 42 x 17 In. 190.00
Bench, Poplar, Brown Graining, 10 x 45 x 16 In. 55.00
Bench, Poplar, Gray Paint, 16 3/4 In. 215.00
Bench, Poplar, Oak Braces, Red Base, Varnished Top, Zoar, Ohio, 15 x 96 x 18 In. 300.00
Bench, Queen Anne Style, Mahogany, Padded Seat, Cabriole Legs, 41 x 13 x 17 In. 175.00
Bench, Robin's-Egg Blue Paint, Cutout Legs, Mortised, Pennsylvania, 84 In. 440.00
Bench, Shaker, Bucket 2000.00
Bench, Softwood, Tilt Top, Lift Seat, Octagonal Arms, 1810, 28 1/2 In. 4890.00
Bench, Spanish Colonial, Hardwood, 2 Spindles With Finials, 65 3/4 In. 1150.00
Bench, Tufted Leather Seat, Chrome Frame, Knoll, 62 x 18 x 17 In. 650.00
Bench, Walnut, Padded Back, Out-Scrolled Frame, Stylized Plant Shape, 70 In. 1495.00
Bench, Water, Federal, Pine, Painted, Shaped Apron, Shaped Ends, 20th Century 345.00
Bench, Water, Pine, Painted, 15 x 52 x 31 3/4 In. 365.00
Bench, Water, Pine, Shaped Cutout Feet, 33 x 11 x 34 In. 440.00
Bench, Water, Poplar, Gray Paint, Bootjack Feet, 14 x 34 x 25 In. 245.00
Bench, William & Mary, Walnut, 6 Turned Legs, Knurled Feet 550.00
Bench, William IV, Mahogany, Plank Seat, Inverted Lyre Supports, c.1835, 54 In. 370.00
Bench, Windsor, Pennsylvania Style, Half Spindle Back, Crest, Curved Arms, 70 In. 1380.00
Bench, Wood, Carved, Continental, 67 In. 1035.00
Bibliotheque, French Provincial, Fruitwood, 2 Doors, Block Feet, 1840, 78 In. 3630.00
Bibliotheque, Louis XVI, Veined Marble Top, Bombe Front, Tapered Legs, 59 In. 750.00
Bookcase, 4 Shelves, Lower Drawer, E.E. Hale Company, 61 x 35 In. 605.00
Bookcase, Bamboo, Sea Grass, 2 Doors, Ebonized Trim, Anglo-Indian, 1880, 34 In. 210.00
Bookcase, Biedermeier, Walnut Veneer, Glass Door, Scroll Feet, 69 In. 1100.00
Bookcase, Cherry, 2 Recessed Glazed Doors, 4 Shelves, Poplar Panels, 72 x 53 1/2 In. . . . 1725.00
Bookcase, Cherry, Revolving, Danner Company 550.00
Bookcase, Corner, Heywood-Wakefield Co., 2 Adjustable Shelves, c.1950, 40 In. 525.00
Bookcase, Eastlake, Walnut, 2 Drawers, Glass Doors, 64 x 53 In. 1375.00
Bookcase, Edwardian, Mahogany, Glass Door, Swan Top, 1910, 55 In., Pair 2055.00
Bookcase, Elm, 2 Pierced Cupboard Doors, 2 Shelves, Pierced Apron, 78 In. 1250.00
Bookcase, Empire Style, Mahogany, Cathedral Door Panels, 4 Drawers, 83 1/2 In. 1955.00
Bookcase, Empire, 2 Glass Doors, Cathedral Muttons, 1drawer In Base, 83 In. 6325.00

Bookcase, Empire, Mahogany, Glass Double Doors, 108 In. 2750.00
Bookcase, Frank Lloyd Wright, Mahogany, 3 Gilt-Edged Shelves, 1923, 48 In. 3420.00
Bookcase, G. Nelson, Primavera Birch, Door, Shelf, 30 x 52 x 12 In. 1150.00
Bookcase, G. Stickley, 2 Mitered Mullioned Doors, 8 Panes, Gallery Top, 56 In. 8800.00
Bookcase, G. Stickley, Adjustable Shelves, 2 Doors, Red Decal, 56 x 48 In. 3850.00
Bookcase, G. Stickley, Double Door, Gallery Top, 9 Panes, 44 3/4 In. 8250.00
Bookcase, G. Stickley, Double Door, Red Decal, 56 x 60 In. 7150.00
Bookcase, G. Stickley, No. 703, Leaded Panels, 3 Windows, 58 x 14 In. ....*Illus* 52250.00
Bookcase, G. Stickley, No. 717, Mahogany, 2 Doors, 8 Panes, 56 In. 5225.00
Bookcase, G. Stickley, No. 718, Mahogany, 2 Doors, Iron Hardware, 47 x 13 In. 6600.00
Bookcase, G. Stickley, Oak, 16 Pane Doors, Safecraft 13200.00
Bookcase, George II, Green Lacquer, Slant Front, 89 In. 8625.00
Bookcase, George III Style, Mahogany, Lattice Glazed Doors, 85 x 73 x 17 In. 3025.00
Bookcase, George III, Mahogany, 4 Adjustable Shelves, Molded Plinth Base, 84 In. 1035.00
Bookcase, George III, Mahogany, Arched Backboard, 2 Graduated Shelves, 59 In. 1955.00
Bookcase, George III, Mahogany, Glazed Mullioned Doors, 94 3/4 In. 4600.00
Bookcase, George III, Molded Dentil Cornice, 2 Drawers, Bracket Feet, 94 1/4 In. 2500.00
Bookcase, Georgian, Mahogany, 2 Short Drawers, Ogee Bracket Feet, 1840, 95 In. 2178.00
Bookcase, Georgian, Mahogany, 4 Cupboard Doors, 98 In. 690.00
Bookcase, Georgian, Mahogany, Arched Cornice, 2 Drawers, Bracket Feet, 78 In. 4600.00
Bookcase, Glazed Upper Doors, Short Lower Drawers, Animal-Paw Feet, c.1825 .... 4025.00
Bookcase, Globe-Wernicke, Oak, Lawyer's, 3 Stacks, Drawer Base, 52 1/2 In. 392.00
Bookcase, Globe-Wernicke, Oak, Stacking, 2 Units, 53 x 34 In. 250.00
Bookcase, Globe-Wernicke, Oak, Stacking, 6 Sections, Leaded Door 1320.00
Bookcase, Hepplewhite, Mahogany, Glass Mullioned Doors 3520.00
Bookcase, L. & J.G. Stickley, 3 Doors, 12 Panes, 73 x 12 x 55 In. 17600.00
Bookcase, L. & J.G. Stickley, 8 Panes, Gallery Top, Branded, 55 In. 4675.00
Bookcase, L. & J.G. Stickley, Double Door, Onondaga Shops, 49 x 54 In. 6050.00
Bookcase, L. & J.G. Stickley, No. 345, Oak, 4 Shelves On Stiles, c.1910, 45 x 19 In. 2875.00
Bookcase, L. & J.G. Stickley, No. 643, 2 Doors, 8 Panes, 39 x 55 In. 8250.00
Bookcase, L. & J.G. Stickley, No. 645, 2 Doors, Copper Pulls, Handcraft Decal 6325.00
Bookcase, L. & J.G. Stickley, Oak, Cupboard Door, 50 x 22 In. 4310.00
Bookcase, Lawyer's, Stacking, 3 Sections, 46 1/2 x 34 1/2 In. 145.00
Bookcase, Lifetime, Door, Small Panels At Top, Adjustable Shelves, 28 x 55 In. 1400.00
Bookcase, Louis XVI, Kingwood, Veined Marble Top, Cabriole Legs, 34 In. 1495.00
Bookcase, Mahogany, 3 Sections, Glass Doors, Mother-Of-Pearl Pulls 525.00
Bookcase, Mahogany, Revolving, Fan Inlay, 2 Open Shelves, Slatted Ends, 30 3/4 In. 600.00
Bookcase, Napoleon III, Mahogany, Marble Top, Drawer, Carved, 1870, 58 x 18 In. 1695.00
Bookcase, Oak, 4 Shelves, 2 Glass Doors 880.00
Bookcase, Oak, Carved Front & Side Pillars, 3 Glass Doors, Shoe Feet, 60 In. 1210.00
Bookcase, Oak, Egg-&-Dart Molding, 3 Masks On Frieze, 45 1/2 In. 460.00
Bookcase, Oak, Molded Top, 2 Tiers, Slatted Sides, Plinth Base, 26 In. 315.00
Bookcase, Oak, Stacking, Leaded Glass Fronts, 4 Tiers, Weiss 740.00
Bookcase, Oak, Stacking, Quartersawn, 3 Sections, Macey, 47 x 34 In. 330.00
Bookcase, Onondaga Shops, Chestnut, 5 Shelves, 48 x 36 In. 3255.00

Furniture, Bookcase,
G. Stickley, No. 703,
Leaded Panels,
3 Windows,
58 x 14 In.

Furniture,
Bookcase,
Renaissance
Revival, Walnut,
Carved, Incised,
114 x 101 In.

Bookcase, Pine, Continental, 108 In. 1840.00
Bookcase, Queen Anne, Oak, Double Dome, Fitted, Candleholders, 81 x 38 x 23 In. 5750.00
Bookcase, Queen Anne, Walnut, Molded Marble Top, 3 Drawers, 82 x 22 In. 8050.00
Bookcase, Regency, 2 Astragal Doors, 2 Paneled Cupboard Doors, 1820, 79 In. 2904.00
Bookcase, Regency, Mahogany, Arched Crest, 2 Pairs Of Drawers, Bun Feet, 47 In. 3565.00
Bookcase, Renaissance Revival, Walnut, Carved, Incised, 114 x 101 In. . . . .*Illus* 11500.00
Bookcase, Rosewood, Ogee Cornice Over 2 Glass Doors, Scrolling, 1800s, 90 In. 4400.00
Bookcase, Rosewood, Step Back, Glazed Doors, 2-Drawer Base, 98 3/4 In. 3740.00
Bookcase, Stacking, 3 Sections, Early 20th Century, 34 1/2 x 14 x 48 In. 405.00
Bookcase, Traveling, Regency, Oak, 2 Adjustable Shelves, Turned Legs, 47 3/4 In. 2750.00
Bookcase, Walnut, 2 Doors Over 2 Drawers, Mid-19th Century, 87 In. 1150.00
Bookcase, Walnut, Step Back, Cathedral Glass Panel Doors, 2 Drawers, 104 In. 3680.00
Bookcase-Secretary, Shaker, Maple, Fall Front, 2 Shelves, 4 Drawers, 87 x 33 In. 1610.00
Bookrack, Oak, Brass, Expandable, 1920s 60.00
Bookrack, Walnut, Revolving, Herringbone Bands, Star Inlay, 31 x 20 x 20 In. 545.00
Bookshelf, Pine, 4 Open Shelves Over 2 Short Drawers, Plinth Base, China, 71 In. 258.00
Bookshelf, Russel Wright, American Modern, Maple, 30 x 30 x 10 In. 690.00
Bookstand, Regency, Revolving, Gilt, Brass, Inlaid Top Over 2 Shelves, 31 In. 9200.00
Breakfront, Kittinger, Mahogany, Lion's-Head Knobs, Brass Mesh Openings, 78 1/4 In. . . . 880.00
Breakfront, Mahogany, Bull's-Eye Glass In Top 4 Doors, Mirrored Back, Desk 2310.00
Breakfront, Walnut, 2 Glazed Upper Doors, 2 Short Over 2 Long Drawers 3850.00
Breakfront-Bookcase, Chippendale, Mahogany, 2 Doors, Plinth Base 25300.00
Breakfront-Bookcase, George III, Mahogany, 2 Doors, Bracket Feet, 1775, 92 In. 15000.00
Breakfront-Bookcase, George III, Mahogany, 4 Glazed Doors, 96 In. 14950.00
Breakfront-Bookcase, Mahogany, 13 Panes In Upper Doors, Lower Doors, 80 In. 1035.00
Breakfront-Bookcase, Mahogany, 2 Drawers, Rectangular Marble Surface, 1840 . . . . 1500.00
Breakfront-Bookcase, Napoleon III, Brass Inlay, 2 Doors, 75 x 52 In. 8050.00
Breakfront-Bookcase, Neoclassical, Teakwood, 3 Shelves, Bracket Feet, Holland, 97 In. . . 3220.00
Buffet, Burl Elm, Banded Top, 2 Drawers, 2 Paneled Doors, Bracket Feet, 40 In. 2057.00
Buffet, Frank Lloyd Wright, Mahogany, Glass Door, 66 x 20 x 85 In., 2 Piece 4400.00
Buffet, Frankl, Black Limed Oak, Light Wood Base, Brass X-Handles, 33 x 58 In. 2013.00
Buffet, French Provincial, Cherry, 2 Drawers Over 2 Doors, 1790, 41 x 50 In. 2055.00
Buffet, French Provincial, Oak, 2 Drawers, Shaped Panel, 1790, 45 x 47 x 20 In. 2299.00
Buffet, French Provincial, Oak, Central Drawer, Floral Panel, 1820, 37 1/2 In. 3630.00
Buffet, Fruitwood, 2 Paneled Cupboard Doors, Molded Plinth Base, c.1790, 39 In. 2860.00
Buffet, Georgian Style, Molded Top, Panel Doors, Bracket Base, 62 x 19 x 31 In. 85.00
Buffet, Louis XV, Walnut, 2 Drawers Over Doors, 37 1/2 In. 2990.00
Buffet, Mahogany, 2 Drawers, Tambour Front Cupboard, 1840, 31 In. 1089.00
Buffet, Napoleon III, Mahogany, Gray, White Marble Top, Top Shaped Feet, 41 In. 1452.00
Buffet, Oak, 2 Drawers, Floral Carved Panel, France, 1860, 40 x 42 x 16 In. 2420.00
Buffet, Oak, Long Frieze Drawer Over 2 Cupboard Doors, Block Feet, 40 In. 1452.00
Buffet, Oak, Overhanging Top, Arcade Front, 2 Arched Doors, France, 53 x 67 In. 1035.00
Buffet, Walnut, 3 Doors, Scroll Toes, 35 x 57 3/4 In. 210.00
Buffet, Walnut, Marble Top, Drawer, 2 Doors, Inner Drawers, 47 1/4 In. 2530.00
Bureau, Chippendale, Birch, Serpentine Front, 4 Graduated Drawers, 1780, 37 In. 3737.00
Bureau, Edwardian, Mahogany, 3 Drawers, Tambour Doors, 46 x 23 x 35 In. 1380.00
Bureau, Empire, Mahogany, 2 Sections, 2 Small Over 4 Long Drawers, 50 In. 742.00
Bureau, Empire, Mahogany, 4 Drawers, Shaped Splashboard, Ogee Bracket Feet 315.00
Bureau, George II, Walnut, Rectangular Top, 2 Graduated Drawers, Bracket Feet 3335.00
Bureau, Louis XV, Beechwood, Arched Backrest, Down-Swept Padded Arms 3450.00
Bureau, Mahogany Veneer, 3 Short, 3 Long & 2 Half Drawers, c.1825, 45 In. 977.00
Bureau, Mahogany, 3 Drawers, Shaped Skirt, Paneled Sides, 17 x 14 1/2 In. 530.00
Bureau, Mahogany, Slant Front, Drawers, 1870s, 40 1/2 x 36 In. 1030.00
Bureau, Mahogany, Slant Front, Satinwood Interior Veneer, 18th Century, 43 In. 6250.00
Bureau, Pine, Attached Arched Mirror Frame, Glove Boxes, Wood Pulls 220.00
Bureau, Rococo, Marble Top, 3 Drawers, Blind Slipper Drawer 400.00
Bureau, Rosewood, Mirror, 2 Drawers Over 4 Graduated Drawers, Marble Top, 70 In. 330.00
Bureau, Sheraton, Mahogany, Bowfront, Cookie Corners, 39 x 40 In. 880.00
Bureau, Sheraton, Mahogany, Tiger Maple, Cookie Corners, Rope Turned Legs, 48 In. . . . 1155.00
Bureau, Walnut, 4 Drawers, Carved Pulls, Victorian 170.00
Cabinet, Art Deco, Black Lacquer, 3 Mirrored Doors, Astrological Motif, 30 x 62 In. 770.00
Cabinet, Art Deco, Ivory Lacquer, Rounded Front, Dolphin Legs, Italy, 66 x 73 In. 1100.00
Cabinet, Baroque Style, Fruitwood, Pullout Slides, Inset With Slate, 35 x 45 In. 140.00

Cabinet, Baroque, Oak, 2 Frieze Drawers, Portugal, 19th Century, 57 x 60 x 25 In. 3450.00
Cabinet, Baroque, Walnut, Cornice, 2 Pillars, Angle, Gargoyle Borders, Italy, 77 In. 5750.00
Cabinet, Beechwood, Upper Fitted Adjustable Shelves, Glazed Door, c.1900, 86 In. 485.00
Cabinet, Brown Saltman, 2 Doors, Shelf & 3 TV Trays, 19 x 27 x 27 In. 403.00
Cabinet, Brown Saltman, 3 Drawers, Light Wood Tops, 1950, 35 x 19 x 33 In. 880.00
Cabinet, Burl Veneer, 6 Drawers, Ebonized Ball Feet, Art Deco, 25 x 42 x 15 In. 132.00
Cabinet, Burl Walnut, Drop Front, 4 Foliate Legs, 1900, 51 In. 9775.00
Cabinet, China, Bowed Sides, Glazed Door, Rope Twist Columns, Bun Feet, 42 x 63 In. . 1035.00
Cabinet, China, Door, Side Shelves, Long Corbels, 3 Glass Panels, 57 In. 4125.00
Cabinet, China, Ebert, Oak, Curved Glass Sides, Glass Shelves, Label 630.00
Cabinet, China, Flemish Style, Mahogany, Drawer, Glass Doors, Stretcher Base, 65 In. .. 195.00
Cabinet, China, Frankl, Mahogany, 3 Glass Shelves, 7 Drawers, 72 x 21 In. 1100.00
Cabinet, China, G. Stickley, 1 Door, 12 Glass Panes, Overhanging Top, 63 In. 7150.00
Cabinet, China, G. Stickley, No. 803, Harvey Ellis Design, Glass Door, 33 x 60 In. 8800.00
Cabinet, China, G. Stickley, No. 820, Red Decal, Label, 63 x 36 In. 8250.00
Cabinet, China, L. & J.G. Stickley, No. 729, 16 Panes, 4 Doors ....*Illus* 19800.00
Cabinet, China, Leavens Co., 4 Shelves, 59 1/4 In. 625.00
Cabinet, China, Limbert, 2 Doors, Narrow, 56 x 31 In. 6600.00
Cabinet, China, Limbert, Double Door, Plate Rack, Glass Panes, 60 In. 4400.00
Cabinet, China, Limbert, No. 1466, 2 Doors, Through Tenon, 48 x 16 x 56 In. 7150.00
Cabinet, China, Limbert, Side Shelves, 3 Glass Panes, Single Door, 57 3/4 In. 4125.00
Cabinet, China, Mahogany Veneer, Bowfront, 40 x 61 1/2 In. 690.00
Cabinet, China, Mahogany, Veneer, Step Back, Double Diamond, 19th Century 1980.00
Cabinet, China, Oak, 4 Shelves, Curved Side Glass, Glass Door, 39 x 70 x 15 In. 995.00
Cabinet, China, Oak, Applied Pineapple Design, Paw Feet, 34 1/2 x 56 1/2 In. 405.00
Cabinet, China, Oak, Curved & Beveled Door, Mirrored Back, Square, 60 In. 1100.00
Cabinet, China, Oak, Curved Glass, 4 Shelves, Carved Acanthus, 40 x 61 x 16 In. 575.00
Cabinet, China, Oak, Curved Glass, Bowfront, Mirror Back, 1920, 62 x 39 In. 845.00
Cabinet, China, Oak, Serpentine Glass Front, Lion's Faces, 4 Shelves, 70 3/4 In. 2090.00
Cabinet, China, Rohde, 2 Doors, Brushed Steel Pulls, 36 x 17 x 58 In. ....825.00 to 880.00
Cabinet, China, Round Glass Ends, Bowed Door, Cabriole Legs, 52 x 34 In. 635.00
Cabinet, China, S. Marx, 8 Doors, Parchment Wrapped Front, 1940s, 87 In. 6050.00
Cabinet, China, S. Marx, Wood, 4 Doors, Glass Panes, 1940, 82 x 59 1/2 In. 9200.00
Cabinet, China, Walnut, Door, Drawer, 1930s 245.00
Cabinet, Chippendale, Mahogany, Pagoda, Side Glass Doors, China, 65 In. 1380.00
Cabinet, Corner, Cherry, 2 Doors, Glass Panes, Shaped Skirt, 80 1/2 In. 2300.00
Cabinet, Corner, Chippendale, Mahogany, Inlay, Broken-Arch Crest, Gothic Doors 975.00
Cabinet, Corner, Georgian, Mahogany, Mullioned Doors, 2 Middle Drawers, 90 In. 2135.00
Cabinet, Corner, Neoclassical, Triangular Top, Tapered Legs, Italy, Late 18th Century ... 1840.00
Cabinet, Corner, Pine, 2 Glazed Doors, Center Drawer, 19th Century 2200.00
Cabinet, Corner, Walnut, Arched Cornice, 2 Shelves, 18th Century, 72 x 20 In. 2300.00
Cabinet, Corner, Walnut, Paneled Frieze, Drawer, Shelved Interior, 30 1/2 In. 460.00
Cabinet, Curio, French Style, Ormolu Trim, 2 Glass Shelves, 20th Century, 53 In. 495.00
Cabinet, Curio, Golden Oak, Pilasters With Lions, Jeweled Eyes, Curved Glass, 65 In. ... 1072.00
Cabinet, Curio, Louis XV, Mahogany, Marble Top, Glass Door, Lighted Interior, 65 In. .. 3410.00
Cabinet, Curio, Mahogany, Square Tapered Legs With Brass Tips, 1900, 63 In. 303.00
Cabinet, Curio, Mirror Back, Curved Glass Door, Glass Shelf, 20th Century, 55 In. 345.00
Cabinet, Curio, Teakwood, Carved, Brass & Ivory Detail, China, 79 x 50 In. 880.00
Cabinet, Curio, Top Shelf Over Mirror, Carved Lion Base, 2 Curved Glass Doors 825.00
Cabinet, Display, Honduran Mahogany, Legs, Drawers, 120 In. 500.00
Cabinet, Display, Mahogany, Cherry, Velvet-Lining, Tripod Base, c.1830, 30 In. 275.00
Cabinet, E. Wormley, 2-Tone Mahogany, Walnut, 3 Drawers, 74 x 18 x 32 In. 825.00
Cabinet, E. Wormley, Mahogany, 2 Side Doors, Plinth Base, 80 x 18 x 31 In. 1980.00
Cabinet, Ebony, Inlay, Matching Base, 2 Paneled Doors, 19th Century, 44 In. 605.00
Cabinet, Edwardian, Mahogany, Rectangular Top, Mullioned Door, 56 In. 2760.00
Cabinet, Federal, Cherry, Shaped Backsplash, Drawer, Paneled Lower Drawer, 60 In. 1250.00
Cabinet, File, Charles Rohlfs, 3 Graduated Drawers 12650.00
Cabinet, File, French Provincial, 6 Drawers, 1880, 96 x 27 x 20 In. 3145.00
Cabinet, File, Oak, 35 Small Drawers 675.00
Cabinet, Flame Mahogany, 2 Doors, 3 Base Drawers, 1810, 88 x 66 In. 11000.00
Cabinet, Fornasetti, Wood, Stenciled Fruit, Brass Legs, Paper Labels, 1950s, 25 1/4 In. .. 6325.00
Cabinet, Frankl, Skyscraper, Silver & Black, 3 Drawers, 2 Doors, 86 x 33 x 15 In. 7700.00
Cabinet, G. Nakashima, Cherry, Pandanus Cloth, 27 In. 6325.00

Furniture, Cabinet, China,
L. & J.G. Stickley, No. 729,
16 Panes, 4 Doors

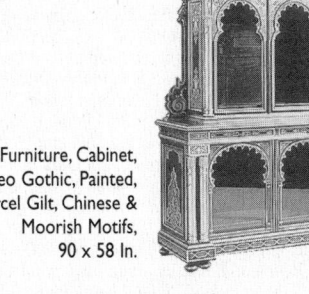

Furniture, Cabinet,
Neo Gothic, Painted,
Parcel Gilt, Chinese &
Moorish Motifs,
90 x 58 In.

Cabinet, G. Nelson, Birch Veneer, 4 Drawers, Plated Pulls, 36 x 19 x 30 In. 1650.00
Cabinet, G. Nelson, Birch Veneer, 5 Drawers, Plated Pulls, 24 x 19 x 46 In. 1430.00
Cabinet, G. Nelson, Birch Veneer, 5 Drawers, Plated Pulls, 40 x 19 x 40 In. 1540.00
Cabinet, G. Nelson, Rosewood Veneer, 3 Doors, Lift Top, Aluminum, 56 In. 7700.00
Cabinet, G. Nelson, Rosewood, 4 Drawers, Aluminum Legs, Herman Miller, 31 In. 4125.00
Cabinet, G. Nelson, Rosewood, 5 Drawers, Aluminum Legs, Herman Miller, 40 In. 4125.00
Cabinet, G. Nelson, Walnut Veneer, 2 Doors, Green Lacquer, 34 x 19 x 30 In. 1980.00
Cabinet, G. Nelson, Walnut Veneer, 4 Drawers, Green Lacquer, 34 x 19 In. 2090.00
Cabinet, G. Nelson, Walnut Veneer, Glass Shelves, Sliding Doors, 30 x 56 In. 1430.00
Cabinet, G. Nelson, Walnut Veneer, Sliding Glass Doors, 34 x 12 In. 475.00
Cabinet, George III, Black Japanned, 2 Doors, Brass Hinges, 52 In. 3450.00
Cabinet, George III, Black Japanned, Landscape, Frieze, 28 In. 3737.00
Cabinet, George IV, Rosewood, Marble Top, Silk-Lined Lower Doors, 34 In. 8625.00
Cabinet, Georgian, Hinged Doors, Scroll, Lattice Design, Cabriole Legs, 65 1/2 In. 1495.00
Cabinet, Georgian, Mahogany, Chinoiserie, Hinged Doors, Square Legs, 58 1/2 In. 920.00
Cabinet, Giltwood, Curved Glass Door, Mirrored Back, Glass Shelves 2200.00
Cabinet, Giltwood, Undulating Cornice, 2 Glazed Cabinet Doors, Bun Feet, 90 In. 8050.00
Cabinet, Golden Oak Era, China, Carved & Applied Designs, 4 Drawers, 58 x 75 In. 1515.00
Cabinet, Gun, Gallery Top, Glass Door, Drawer, Sliding Compartment, Yeager, 70 In. . . . 1650.00
Cabinet, Hoosier, Slag Glass Paneled Doors, Kutchins Furniture Co. 550.00
Cabinet, Inlaid Side, Rouge Marble Top, Hinged Door, Bun Feet, 44 1/2 In. 2530.00
Cabinet, Jacobean Style, Oak, Paneled Doors, Shelves, Drawer, On Stand, 65 x 40 In. . . . 430.00
Cabinet, Liquor, Louis XVI, Satinwood, Molded Bowfront Top, Top Shaped Feet, 55 In. . 750.00
Cabinet, Liquor, Napoleon III, Burl, Marquetry, Bottles & Goblets 8050.00
Cabinet, Louis XV Style, Open Shelves, Herringbone Inlay, Ormolu Trim, 39 In. 770.00
Cabinet, Louis XV, Variegated Marble Top, 2 Doors, Cabriole Legs 750.00
Cabinet, Louis XVI Style, Relief Floral & Figural Design, 27 x 33 In. 660.00
Cabinet, Mahogany, 20 Drawers, Bail Handles, Scalloped Base, Bracket Feet, 54 In. 1100.00
Cabinet, Mahogany, 3/4 Gallery, 2 Glazed Doors, Bronze Mounted, 60 In. 4837.00
Cabinet, Mahogany, Fruitwood, Rectangular Top, Round Tapered Legs, Pair 8050.00
Cabinet, Mahogany, Paneled Doors, Interior Shelves, Victorian, 58 1/2 In. 2990.00
Cabinet, Mahogany, Upper Mullioned Doors, Drawer, 68 1/2 In. 4125.00
Cabinet, McCobb, Bleached Mahogany, 4 Drawers, Brass Frame, 36 x 34 In. 1430.00
Cabinet, Mission, 3 Inlaid Doors, 3 Open Shelves, Shop-Of-The-Crafters, 63 In. 5500.00
Cabinet, Music, Mahogany, 2 Swing-Out Compartments, 18 1/2 x 15 1/2 x 40 In. 95.00
Cabinet, Music, Mahogany, Bowfront, Tapered Legs, 1890, 44 x 21 x 15 In. 180.00
Cabinet, Music, Mirror Backsplash, 6 Slide-Out Shelves, Brass Pulls 165.00
Cabinet, Music, Oak, 40 Drawers, Paneled Sides, Green Paint, 58 1/2 In. 385.00
Cabinet, Neo Gothic, Painted, Parcel Gilt, Chinese & Moorish Motifs, 90 x 58 In. . . . *Illus* 8050.00
Cabinet, Neoclassical, Mahogany, Fruitwood, Bowfront, Stepped Top, Pair 4600.00
Cabinet, Oak, 24 Drawers, Paneled Sides, Iron Pulls, 44 In. 740.00
Cabinet, Oak, 4 Fixed Shelves, Wainscoted Back, Panel Doors, 73 x 19 x 56 In. 1275.00
Cabinet, Oak, Bowfront, Carved Lion's Heads, Mirrored Backsplash, 72 5/8 In. 1045.00
Cabinet, Oak, Brass Mounted, 2 Frieze Drawers, Angular Doors, 19th Century 3450.00
Cabinet, Oak, China, Figural Cathedral Top, 82 x 53 1/2 In. 5000.00
Cabinet, Oak, Door, Stained & Leaded Glass, Carved Lion & Figural Masks, 91 In. 575.00

Cabinet, Oak, Incurved Cornice, Geometric Carved Paneled Door, Shelf, 59 In. 517.00
Cabinet, Phonograph, Oak, Bowfront, Cookie Corner, Turned Ball Feet, 33 In. 375.00
Cabinet, Pine, 8 Graduated Dovetailed Drawers, Paneled Ends, 15 x 11 x 25 1/2 In. 660.00
Cabinet, Pine, Folk Art Case, Rectangular Table, Turned Legs, 19th Century, 81 In. 825.00
Cabinet, Pine, Wire Mesh Inset Door, 3 Shelves, Arched Base, 30 x 33 In. 115.00
Cabinet, Print, Pine, 8 Long Drawers, Wood Pulls, Late 19th Century, 55 1/2 In. 905.00
Cabinet, Raymond Loewy, 8 Red Plastic Drawers, White Metal Frame, 1960s, 61 In. 1980.00
Cabinet, Raymond Loewy, Lacquered Wood, Metal Frame, Drawers, 29 x 80 x 19 In. ... 1265.00
Cabinet, Renaissance Revival, Burl Walnut, Mirror, Shelves, 2 Doors, 1880, 73 In. 575.00
Cabinet, Renaissance Revival, Burl Walnut, Parcel Gilt, Mirror, Shelf, 73 x 41 In. 575.00
Cabinet, Renaissance Revival, Pietra Dura Inlay, Early 19th Century, 40 x 23 In. 4675.00
Cabinet, Robsjohn-Gibbings, Walnut Veneer, 6 Drawers, 68 x 21 x 32 In. 825.00
Cabinet, Rohde, Light Walnut Veneer, Drop Front, 8 Shelves, 2 Doors, 42 x 46 x 17 In. .. 690.00
Cabinet, Rohde, Mahogany, 2 Doors, Carved Round Pulls, 29 1/2 x 33 x 14 In. 715.00
Cabinet, Rohde, Walnut, 2 Shelves Over 2 Doors, 62 x 36 x 17 In. .... .220.00 to 275.00
Cabinet, Rosewood, Kauang-Hsu, Mother-Of-Pearl Scenes, 1885, 53 x 48 In. 1030.00
Cabinet, S. Marx, Wood, Round Brass Pulls, 2 Slab Legs, 1940, 58 In. 9430.00
Cabinet, Satinwood, Outset Center Section, Fitted Interior, Sweden, 16 1/2 In. 2070.00
Cabinet, Shaker, Walnut, Paneled Doors, Interior Shelves, 77 x 37 In. 2750.00
Cabinet, Side, Georgian Style, Painted Neoclassical Design, Bun Feet, 50 x 67 In. 8050.00
Cabinet, Side, Louis XVI, Chinoiserie, Marble Top, Foliate Chutes, Cabriole Legs 2875.00
Cabinet, Side, Mahogany Veneer, 2 Glass Doors, 1830s, 90 x 55 1/2 In. 3680.00
Cabinet, Side, Mahogany, Beaded Edge Frieze, 2 Drawers, Wire Screen Door, 34 In. 150.00
Cabinet, Side, Mahogany, Mirror, Glass Panel, Scalloped Fluted Design, 41 1/2 In. 260.00
Cabinet, Smoking, G. Stickley, Drawer Over Door, Compartments, 29 In. 2970.00
Cabinet, Smoking, Limbert, Door, Copper Hardware, 12 x 36 In. 1100.00
Cabinet, Spice, 12 Drawers, Bird's-Eye Maple, Wire Nail Construction, 17 3/4 In. 385.00
Cabinet, Spice, 6 Drawers, Ash, Poplar, Labeled Drawers, Pure Food Co., 12 1/2 In. 192.00
Cabinet, Spice, 8 Drawers, Oak & Elm, Charles II, 13 x 14 In. 2185.00
Cabinet, Spice, Oak, 8 Drawers, Wall Mount, 18 In. 115.00
Cabinet, Spice, Wall, 6 Drawers, Birch, Wire Nail Construction, 12 3/4 x 12 3/4 In. 247.00
Cabinet, Spice, Walnut, Interior Divided Into Cubby Holes, Lower Drawer, 18 x 15 In. .. 880.00
Cabinet, Sue Et Mare, Mahogany, Ivory, Flame Grained, 3 Shelves, Ivory Pulls, 71 In. ... 8050.00
Cabinet, T. Parzinger, Light & Dark Mahogany, 2 Doors, 1940s, 25 In., Pair 770.00
Cabinet, Walnut, Paneled Door, 8 Interior Shelves, 31 In. 201.00
Cabinet, Walnut, Pierced, Carved, Fabric-Lined Door, Medallion Center, 25 In. 115.00
Cabinet, Walnut, Teakwood, 6 Drawers, Fluted Legs, Stretcher Shelf, 30 In. 690.00
Cabinet, Walnut, White Laminate Top, 3 Drawers, Black Metal Legs, Knoll, 28 In. 412.00
Cabinet, Yellow Molded Plastic, Cylindrical, 2 Sliding Doors, Anna Castelli, 26 In. 245.00
Candlestand, Ash, Round Top, Turned Shaft, Ball Feet 250.00
Candlestand, Birch, Maple, Shaped Shaft, Tripod Base, c.1800, 26 In. 335.00
Candlestand, Blackamoor, Tripod Base, Venetian, 28 3/4 x 14 In. 2675.00
Candlestand, Cherry, Dish Top, Birdcage Support, 3 Down-Swept Legs, c.1750 .... 4887.00
Candlestand, Cherry, Maple, Vase & Ring Post, Tripod Base, Green Paint, 25 In. 1035.00
Candlestand, Cherry, Oval Top, Baluster Pedestal, New England, 1790, 20 x 16 In. 690.00
Candlestand, Cherry, Round Top, Turned Pedestal, Cabriole Legs, Snake Feet, 28 In. 315.00
Candlestand, Cherry, Tiger Maple Post, Tilt Top, Tripod Base, 27 x 24 x 17 In. 345.00
Candlestand, Chippendale, Cherry, Tripod Base, Square 1-Board Top, 15 x 26 In. 440.00
Candlestand, Chippendale, Hardwood, Tripod, Round 1-Board Top, 15 x 24 3/4 In. 300.00
Candlestand, Dish Top, Double Edge, Urn-Shaped Standard, Slipper Feet, 28 1/2 In. 1100.00
Candlestand, Dish Top, Queen Anne, Mahogany, Round, 27 1/4 In. 6600.00
Candlestand, Dish Top, Snake Feet, Plum Pudding Striations, c.1775 .... 3200.00
Candlestand, Dish Top, Tiger Maple, Birdcage, Cabriole Legs, 21 1/2 In. 440.00
Candlestand, Dish Top, Tiger Maple, Birdcage, Turned Ball Pedestal, 22 In. 355.00
Candlestand, Dish Top, Tripod Base, Claw & Ball Feet, 19th Century, 31 In. 495.00
Candlestand, Dish Top, Walnut, 1-Board Top, Pedestal, Cabriole Legs, 19 x 27 In. 550.00
Candlestand, Dish Top, Walnut, Flame Grained, Snake Feet, Pennsylvania, 18 In. 1045.00
Candlestand, Federal Style, Oval Top, Turned Pedestal, Spider Legs, 26 In. 58.00
Candlestand, Federal, Cherry, Turned Pedestal, Tripod Base, 1800s, 27 1/2 In. 495.00
Candlestand, Federal, Mahogany, Rectangular Top, Pedestal, 1815, 27 x 20 x 26 In. 440.00
Candlestand, Federal, Maple, Fluted Standard, 3 Chip-Carved Legs, c.1810, 24 In. 1265.00
Candlestand, Figured Top, Turned Shaft 7500.00
Candlestand, Hepplewhite, Birch, Tripod Base, Spider Legs, 16 x 16 x 30 In. 550.00

Candlestand, Hepplewhite, Cherry, Maple, Tripod Base, Spider Legs, 16 x 18 x 28 In. ... 330.00
Candlestand, Hepplewhite, Cherry, Poplar, Tripod, 1-Board, 15 x 18 x 26 In. 275.00
Candlestand, Hepplewhite, Cherry, Vase Turned Pedestal, Splayed Feet, 25 1/2 In. 605.00
Candlestand, Mahogany, 28 In. 137.00
Candlestand, Mahogany, Octagonal, Tripod Base, England, 1790, 28 In. 715.00
Candlestand, Mahogany, Piecrust Top, Swirl Pedestal, Claw & Ball Feet, 26 1/2 In. 1870.00
Candlestand, Mahogany, Ring Turned Support, Tripod Base, 1800s, 28 In. 275.00
Candlestand, Maple, Turned Shaft, Cabriole Legs, Snake Feet, 27 In. 805.00
Candlestand, Queen Anne, Maple, Round Top, Vase-Form Standard, Cabriole Legs 170.00
Candlestand, Red Paint, Octagonal Top, 3 Feet, New Hampshire 8525.00
Candlestand, Round Top, Turned Standard, Cabriole Legs, Pad Feet, 18 x 26 In. 690.00
Candlestand, Scissor Arm Adjusts, Held By Wooden Pin, Iron Counterweight, 1840s 950.00
Candlestand, Shaker, Cherry, Tripod Base, Mt. Lebanon, 24 1/4 In. 3080.00
Candlestand, Shaker, Maple, Stationary Top, Cabriole Legs, Snake Feet 550.00
Candlestand, Tilt Top, Chippendale, Mahogany, Slipper Feet, 1780, 26 1/2 In. 1035.00
Candlestand, Tilt Top, Chippendale, Walnut, 21 1/2 x 29 1/4 In. 220.00
Candlestand, Tilt Top, Chippendale, Walnut, Snake's-Head Feet, 1800s, 29 x 19 3/4 In. .. 1345.00
Candlestand, Tilt Top, Federal, Canted Cut Corners, Urn Shaft, 3 Curved Legs, 27 In. ... 460.00
Candlestand, Tilt Top, Federal, Mahogany, Octagonal Top, 1800, 20 1/2 x 15 In. 990.00
Candlestand, Tilt Top, Federal, Mahogany, Octagonal, Banding, 3 Spider Legs 660.00
Candlestand, Tilt Top, Federal, Mahogany, Octagonal, Curved Legs, 19th Century 260.00
Candlestand, Tilt Top, Federal, Mahogany, Reeded, Tripod Base, Cut-Corner Top, 1810 .. 468.00
Candlestand, Tilt Top, Federal, Mahogany, Tripod Base, Splayed Feet, c.1810, 28 In. 880.00
Candlestand, Tilt Top, Federal, Urn-Shaped Support, New England, c.1800, 29 x 18 In. .. 1150.00
Candlestand, Tilt Top, Hepplewhite, Cherry, Mahogany, Spider Legs, 15 x 23 x 28 In. ... 415.00
Candlestand, Tilt Top, Hepplewhite, Curly Maple, Tripod, Rectangular Top, 14 x 21 In. .. 990.00
Candlestand, Tilt Top, Mahogany, American, 29 In. 330.00
Candlestand, Tilt Top, Mahogany, Birdcage, c.1790, 27 3/4 In. 7475.00
Candlestand, Tilt Top, Mahogany, Vase-Form, Pedestal, Arched Leg, 14 x 17 In. 635.00
Candlestand, Tilt Top, Maple, Square, Chip-Carved Plinth, 3 Legs, 27 1/2 In. 690.00
Candlestand, Tilt Top, Queen Anne, Mahogany, Center Turned Pedestal, 28 1/2 In. 315.00
Candlestand, Wallace Nutting, No. 17, Tripod 462.00
Candlestand, Walnut Top, Tiger Maple Shaft, Snake Feet, c.1820 .... 345.00
Candlestand, Walnut, Birdcage, Rim Pedestal, Snake Feet, 27 1/2 In. 1870.00
Candlestand, Walnut, Lift Top, Octagonal Top, Hexagonal Pedestal, 28 In. 6600.00
Candlestand, Walnut, Round Top, Pedestal Base, 3 Legs, Ball Pad Feet, 25 1/2 In. 290.00
Candlestand, Walnut, Stacked Baluster Standard, 3 Down-Swept Legs, c.1760 .... 3737.00
Candlestand, Wood, Adjustable Candle Arms, Early 19th Century, 40 In. 715.00
Canterbury, 2 Open Shelves Over Open Bottom, Ebonized, 34 In. 73.00
Canterbury, 4 Compartments, 2 Long Drawers, Top Shaped Feet, 21 x 19 3/4 In. 210.00
Canterbury, Divided By Supports, Pierced Handhold, Lower Shelf, 1880s, 17 1/2 In. 805.00
Canterbury, Federal, Mahogany, Divided Upper Section Over Drawer, 17 In. 2185.00
Canterbury, Federal, Rosewood, Arrow Supports, Ball Finials, c.1810, 18 1/4 In. 1725.00
Canterbury, Hardwood, 2 Dividers, Corner Finials, Handle, 18 3/4 In. 260.00
Canterbury, Mahogany, 2 Sections, Scrolling Divider, Bun Feet, Drawer, 21 In. 270.00
Canterbury, Mahogany, 4 Storage Compartments, 2 Drawers, Top Shaped Feet, 21 In. ... 270.00
Canterbury, Pine, Dark Varnish, Turned Spindles, 20th Century, 14 x 18 x 24 In. 165.00
Canterbury, Regency, Mahogany, 4 Open Shelves, 20 1/2 x 19 1/2 In. 180.00
Canterbury, Regency, Mahogany, 4 Slotted Sections Over 2 Drawers, 21 x 19 In. 220.00
Canterbury, Regency, Mahogany, X-Shaped Sides, Casters, 18 1/4 x 24 In. 3737.00
Canterbury, Regency, Rosewood, Divided Top Over Drawer, 20 3/4 In. 3737.00
Canterbury, Regency, Rosewood, Mahogany, Divided Top, Turned Legs, 19 In. 2070.00
Canterbury, Rosewood, Rectangular Dividers, Drawer, Casters, 20 1/4 In. 1955.00
Canterbury, Rosewood, X-Shaped Divided Top, Corner Finials, 21 1/4 In. 4025.00
Canterbury, Walnut, Burl Walnut, Long Drawer, Carved Top Shaped Feet, 35 x 30 In. ... 1725.00
Cart, Harvey Prober, Bleached Mahogany, White Pyrex Shelves, 32 x 37 In. 355.00
Cart, Mahogany, Collapsible Top, Square Shelved Legs, 28 x 27 In. 85.00
Cellarette, Crotch Mahogany Veneer, Dovetailed Drawer, Shaped Apron, c.1860 .... 450.00
Cellarette, G. Stickley, Drawer Over Cabinet Door, Hidden Compartment, 29 In. 3190.00
Cellarette, Galle, 2 Tier, Marquetry, Clematis, Leafage, Butterfly, 1900, 44 In. 5750.00
Cellarette, George III, Mahogany, Cavetto, Buckle Handles, Hinged Lid, 24 x 22 In. 2645.00
Cellarette, George III, Mahogany, Hinged Oval Top, Carrying Handles, Oval Stand 4312.00
Cellarette, L. & J.G. Stickley, Pullout Shelf, 2 Doors, Strap Hardware, 36 In. 5000.00

Cellarette, Mahogany, Domed Top, Metal Lining, Plinth Base, c.1840, 28 1/2 In. 1825.00
Cellarette, Mahogany, Hinged Top, Banded Stringing, Compartments, 1820, 22 In. 2925.00
Cellarette, Walnut, Hinged Top, Dovetailed, Drawer, 19th Century, 42 3/4 In. 1760.00
Chair, Aalto, Birch, Cantilevered Bentwood Frame, 1935, 30 1/2 In. 977.00
Chair, Aalto, C-Type, Cloth Seat & Back, Wood Arms, Artek, 1950s 2300.00
Chair, Acorn Finials, Rush Seat, Bulbous Front Stretcher, Child's, 18 In., Pair 3850.00
Chair, Adams, Female Portrait Medallion, Cane Seat, Block Feet, Arms 1600.00
Chair, Adirondack Style, Root & Burl, T.W. Quinn, Sulphur Springs, 1886 . . . . 4900.00
Chair, Adirondack Style, Root, T.W. Quinn, Sulphur Springs, Arms, 1887 . . . . 3080.00
Chair, Adirondack Style, Twig, Plank Seat, Arms 110.00
Chair, Adirondack Style, Twig, Round, Green Paint, Pair 920.00
Chair, Albini, Light Wood, Angular, Upholstered Seat & Back, Arms, Knoll, 17 x 16 In. . . 460.00
Chair, Andre Putnam, Curved Back, Rolled Arms, Upholstered, 32 x 28 x 31 In. 660.00
Chair, Arched Backrest, Upholstered Seat, Purple Velvet, Arms, Victorian, Pair 5060.00
Chair, Arrow Back, 17 1/2 x 33 In., Pair 110.00
Chair, Arrow Back, Brown Paint, Gold Stenciling, Bamboo Legs, Arms, 32 In. 130.00
Chair, Arrow Back, Painted, Canada 820.00
Chair, Ash, Maple, Pine, 9 Spindles, Saddle Seat, Continuous Arms, 1780, Pair 175.00
Chair, Ash, Teakwood, Peacock, Fan-Shaped Spindle Back, Cord Seat, Shaped Arms 3450.00
Chair, Augustus Eliaers, Lion's Heads Crest, Paw Feet, Cabriole Legs, Arms, 1853 . . . . . . 3410.00
Chair, Balloon Back, Button-Tufted Seat, Ram's-Head Knees, China 440.00
Chair, Balloon Back, Dark Brown Paint, Striping, Pennsylvania, 34 1/2 In., Pair 135.00
Chair, Balloon Back, Green Paint, Yellow Striping, Stencil, Pennsylvania, 33 1/4 In., Pair . 120.00
Chair, Balloon Back, Walnut, Tufted Back, Leaf Crested Frame, 1870s 125.00
Chair, Ballroom, Faux Bamboo, Rush Seats, Ebonized, 32 x 15 1/2 x 15 In. 212.00
Chair, Bamboo, Bow Back, Painted, Scroll Handhold, Plank Seat, 19th Century 345.00
Chair, Bamboo, Cross-Thatched Backrest, Vinyl Seat, Saber Legs, 20th Century, Pair 85.00
Chair, Bamboo, Horseshoe, Arched Top Rail, Box Stretcher, Pair 5175.00
Chair, Bamboo, Row Of Pole Splats, Solid Seat, Arms, China, Pair 520.00
Chair, Banister Back, Black Paint, Rush Seat, Turned Detail, 44 In. 495.00
Chair, Banister Back, Crest, Refinished, Bulbous, Half Arms, 44 3/4 In. 1100.00
Chair, Banister Back, Painted, Serpentine Crest Rail, Rush Seat, 18th Century 200.00
Chair, Barcelona, Knoll, Pair 1100.00
Chair, Baroque Style, Arched Crest, Carved Flower Heads, Upholstered Back & Arms . . . 1000.00
Chair, Baroque, Carved Shell Over Carved Back, Cane Seat, Arms, 51 x 25 In. 575.00
Chair, Baroque, Eagle, 2 Putti, Cane Seat 230.00
Chair, Baroque, Oak, Carved Griffin Back, Upholstered Seat, 19th Century, Pair 630.00
Chair, Baroque, Rectangular Backrest, Needlepoint, Pair 1265.00
Chair, Baroque, Scroll Crest, Raised On Turned Legs, Italy, Pair 2875.00
Chair, Baroque, Walnut, Rectangular Back, Petit Point, Arms 6325.00
Chair, Baroque, Walnut, Upholstered Seat, Square Legs, Arms, Italy 575.00
Chair, Beechwood, Cane Seat & Back, Arched Frame, Out-Scrolled Arms 1835.00
Chair, Beechwood, Carved Foliate Frame, 34 In. 287.00
Chair, Beechwood, Floral Carved Backrest, Cabriole Legs, Padded Arms, Pair 4600.00
Chair, Beechwood, Gros Point & Petit Point, Carved Foliate Frame, 20th Century 632.00
Chair, Beechwood, High Back, Carved, Upholstered, Scroll Arms, 45 In. 330.00
Chair, Belle Epoque, Rococo, Giltwood, Foliate, Cartouche Back, Cabriole Legs 660.00
Chair, Belter, Cornucopia 9680.00
Chair, Belter, Rococo, Laminated Rosewood, Cartouche Back, Pair 2185.00
Chair, Belter, Rococo, Laminated Rosewood, Needlepoint, Pair 1725.00
Chair, Belter, Rosalie Without Grapes, Laminated Rosewood, Upholstered, 37 1/2 In. 2935.00
Chair, Belter, Rosalie, Laminated Rosewood . . . .*Illus* 2200.00
Chair, Belter, Rosewood, Carved Fruit Crest, Floral Carving On Knees, 41 In. 2800.00
Chair, Belter, Rosewood, Slipper, Foliate Crest, Curved Splat, Upholstered Seat 1035.00
Chair, Bentwood, Curved Back, Arched Support, Splayed Legs, Arms, 1904 . . . . 1150.00
Chair, Bentwood, Stained Finish, Arms, Fischel, Paper Label 180.00
Chair, Biedermeier Style, Fruitwood, Ebonized Triple Splat, Taffeta, 38 In. 550.00
Chair, Biedermeier Style, Fruitwood, Ebony String Inlay, Upholstered Seat, Pair 415.00
Chair, Biedermeier, Finger Carved, Velvet, Scroll Arms, 38 In., Pair 405.00
Chair, Biedermeier, Mahogany, Arched Pierced Back, Upholstered Seat, Pair 2415.00
Chair, Biedermeier, Mahogany, Palm Backrest, Baluster Legs, Pair 2415.00
Chair, Biedermeier, Walnut, Shaped Back, Upholstered Demilune Seat, 37 In., Pair 1380.00
Chair, Black Leather, Casters, Open Arms . . . . .105.00 to 145.00

Chair, Black Paint, Gold & White Striping, Slip Seat, Upholstered, Baltimore, 30 In. 110.00
Chair, Black Pentagonal Tubular Frames, Calf-Hide Seat, 27 x 34 x 30 In. 1650.00
Chair, Bugatti, Brass, Oriental Design, Stepped Rectangular Back, Pewter, Ivory 3200.00
Chair, Bugatti, Chair, Corner, Ebonized Wood, Brass, Copper, Pewter Inlay, 29 In. 8000.00
Chair, Bugatti, Ebonized Wood, Brass, Ivory Geometric Design 2990.00
Chair, Bugatti, Ebonized Wood, Painted Parchment, Pewter, Brass Inlay, 63 In. 5175.00
Chair, Bugatti, Rosewood, Tooled Parchment, Pewter, Brass Inlay, 29 In. 4600.00
Chair, Bugatti, Tooled Parchment, Brass, Pewter Inlay, 1900, 31 3/4 In. 8050.00
Chair, Bugatti, Wood, Painted Parchment, Brass, Copper Inlay, Arms, 1900, 44 In. 11500.00
Chair, Bugatti, Wood, Painted Parchment, Brass, Cotton, 1900, 44 1/2 In. 6325.00
Chair, Bugatti, Wood, Painted Parchment, Silk, 1900, 59 In. 5460.00
Chair, Bugatti, Wood, Tooled Parchment, Pewter, Brass Inlay, 1900, 29 In. 3735.00
Chair, Burl Walnut, Veneer, Pierced Crest, Upholstered Rolled Arms, Victorian 220.00
Chair, Cabana, Adjustable Top, Upholstered, Vinyl Sides, 62 x 48 In., Pair 1200.00
Chair, Captain's, Swivel, Baluster Spindles, Plank Seat, Painted, 19th Century 145.00
Chair, Carved Dragons, Green Marble Insert, Damask Cushions, Arms, China, 34 In. 550.00
Chair, Cattle Horns, Red Crocodile Leather, 1920s 5800.00
Chair, Charles I, Walnut, Padded Back, Leaf-Capped Arms, Mid-19th Century, Pair 920.00
Chair, Charles II, Walnut, High Back, Crown Crest Rail, Foliate Carved, Arms, Pair 2400.00
Chair, Charles X, Fruitwood, Curved Crest, 2 Shaped Backrests, Scroll Arms 545.00
Chair, Cherry, Slip Seat, Turned Scroll Arms, Zoar, Ohio, 26 x 43 In. 3410.00
Chair, Chestnut, Cast-Metal Swivel Mechanism, Crocker Chair, c.1900, 39 1/2 In. 110.00
Chair, Chinese Export, Rosewood, Medallion Back, Cabriole Legs, Cane Seat, Pair 935.00
Chair, Chippendale Style, Brown & Red Paint, Slip Seat, China, 20th Century, 40 In. 140.00
Chair, Chippendale Style, Mahogany, Carved, S-Shaped Arms, 20th Century, 40 1/2 In. . . 165.00
Chair, Chippendale Style, Mahogany, Ladder Back, 20th Century, Pair 195.00
Chair, Chippendale Style, Mahogany, Upholstered Seat, Arms, Pair 520.00
Chair, Chippendale, Birch, Mahogany Finish, Square Legs, 17 x 37 3/4 In. 275.00
Chair, Chippendale, Carved Foliate Back, Arms, 20th Century, Pair 482.00
Chair, Chippendale, Chestnut, Rush Slip Seat, Pierced Splat, Crest, England, Pair 770.00
Chair, Chippendale, Crest Rail, Gothic Splat, Slip Seat, Trifid Feet, 1770, Pair 9900.00
Chair, Chippendale, Horizontal & Pierced Back Splats, Naugahyde Seat, Pair 130.00
Chair, Chippendale, Ladder Back, 4 Pierced Slats, Slip Seat, Serpentine Arms 220.00
Chair, Chippendale, Mahogany, Carved Back Splat, Upholstered Seat, 41 In. 2590.00
Chair, Chippendale, Mahogany, Carved Pagoda, Chinoiserie Fretwork, Cane Seat, Arms . . 550.00
Chair, Chippendale, Mahogany, Carved, Cabriole Legs, Upholstered Seat, 37 In. 4600.00
Chair, Chippendale, Mahogany, Claw & Ball Feet, 1760, Pair 1380.00
Chair, Chippendale, Mahogany, Crest, Leather Back & Arms, 39 In., Pair 605.00
Chair, Chippendale, Mahogany, Pierced Crest Over 3 Slats, Upholstered Seat 440.00
Chair, Chippendale, Mahogany, Pierced Crest Rail, 2 Horizontal Splats, Slip Seat 275.00
Chair, Chippendale, Mahogany, Pierced Splat Back, Upholstered Seat, c.1770, Pair 3300.00
Chair, Chippendale, Mahogany, Pierced Vase-Form, Upholstered Seat, 19th Century 375.00
Chair, Chippendale, Mahogany, Ribbonback, Pierced Crest, 3 Slats, Slip Seat 665.00
Chair, Chippendale, Mahogany, Ribbonback, Pierced Crest, Slip Seat, Pair 660.00
Chair, Chippendale, Mahogany, Serpentine Crest, Gothic Splat, Slip Seat, 1780 . . . . 2300.00
Chair, Chippendale, Mahogany, Serpentine Crest, Pierced Splat, Slip Seat 330.00
Chair, Chippendale, Mahogany, Upholstered Seat, 18 x 37 In. 275.00

Furniture, Chair,
Belter, Rosalie,
Laminated Rosewood

**If a chair rung is loose, try putting
a sliver of wood or a small wad of
steel wool into the hole, then put
glue in the hole and on the rung
and push the rung into the hole.**

Chair, Chippendale, Mahogany, Volute & Foliate Crest Rail, Trefoil Splat, 1760 . . . . 6900.00
Chair, Chippendale, Maple, Solid Splat, Rush Seat, Straight Legs 220.00
Chair, Chippendale, Maple, Square Legs, Woven Splint Seat, Pierced Splat 250.00
Chair, Chippendale, Martha Washington Type, Mahogany, Upholstered, 38 In. 275.00
Chair, Chippendale, Oak, Needlework Seat, Stretcher Base, 37 In. 405.00
Chair, Chippendale, Philadelphia Style, Carved Knees, Apron, Needlework Seat, 41 In. . . 260.00
Chair, Chippendale, Pierced Back, Reeded Legs, Upholstered Seat, 38 In., Pair 1035.00
Chair, Chippendale, Upholstered, Removable Cushions, 45 1/2 In., Pair 1150.00
Chair, Chippendale, Walnut, Shell Carved Crest, Vase-Form Splat, c.1760, 38 1/2 In. 5462.00
Chair, Chippendale, Walnut, Stepped Crest Rail, Solid Splat, c.1780 . . . . 440.00
Chair, Chippendale, Walnut, Upholstered Seat, Square Legs, 37 1/4 In., Pair 1980.00
Chair, Chippendale, Walnut, Vase-Form Splat, Drop-In Seat, Out-Curved Arms, Pair 1035.00
Chair, Colonial Revival, Stained Wood, Hinged Ladder Back, Flat Arms 3680.00
Chair, Corner, Beechwood, Rush Seat, Turned Legs, 1890, 26 x 16 x 16 3/4 In. 180.00
Chair, Corner, Chippendale, Carved Back Splats, Shaped Hand Rests, American, 31 In. . . 5040.00
Chair, Corner, Chippendale, Mahogany, Arms, 1750-1770 . . . . *Illus* 5175.00
Chair, Corner, Chippendale, Mahogany, Concave Arms, 1760 . . . . *Illus* 9200.00
Chair, Corner, Chippendale, Mahogany, Figured, Carved, 34 1/4 In. 40250.00
Chair, Corner, Eastlake, Walnut, Champagne Floral Brocade, 27 In. 195.00
Chair, Corner, Federal, Maple, Ash, Baluster-Shaped Stiles, Curved Slats, Rush Seat 375.00
Chair, Corner, Hardwood, Sausage Turning & Carved Arms Rail, Rush Seat, 31 1/2 In. . . . 605.00
Chair, Corner, Heywood Brothers & Co., Wicker, Upholstered Seat, Label, 1898 . . . . 165.00
Chair, Corner, Mahogany, 2 Splats, Balloon Seat, Pad Feet, Concave Arms, 32 1/2 In. 4887.00
Chair, Corner, Mahogany, Foliate Carved Crest Rail, Reeded Arms, Drop-In Seat 690.00
Chair, Corner, Mahogany, Reverse-Scroll Crest, Concave Arms, 1770, 30 In. 5175.00
Chair, Corner, Mahogany, Reverse-Scroll Crest, Concave Arms, 32 In. 9200.00
Chair, Corner, Mahogany, Slip Seat, Brocade, 33 1/2 In. 330.00
Chair, Corner, Maple, Vase-Form Supports, Rush Seat, Concave Arms, 1730s, 34 In. 1380.00
Chair, Corner, Modern Gothic, Ebonized, Parcel Gilt, Upholstered, 1870s, Pair 4485.00
Chair, Corner, Pennsylvania Style, Cherry, Bowed Crest Rail, Curved Arms 3025.00
Chair, Corner, Queen Anne Style, Urn-Shaped Splats, Upholstered Seat, 20th Century . . . 195.00
Chair, Corner, Queen Anne, Mahogany Concave Arms, 32 In. . . . . *Illus* 4887.00
Chair, Corner, Queen Anne, Painted, Splats, Baluster Arm Supports, Splint Seat 630.00
Chair, Corner, Queen Anne, Pillow Rail, Spanish Feet, Rolled Arms 1980.00
Chair, Corner, Queen Anne, Walnut, Comb Back, 46 In. 2750.00
Chair, Corner, Turned Spindles, Carved Seat Rails, Dark Stain, Upholstered 196.00
Chair, Corner, Windsor, Comb Back, Walnut, 7 Spindles, Flat Curved Arms, 45 In. 2310.00
Chair, Crest Rail Over Pierced Splat, Leaf & Vase In Medallion, Open Arms, China 247.00
Chair, Curly Maple, Saber Leg, Cane Seat, 32 1/4 In., Pair 300.00
Chair, Damask Back, Armrests & Seat, c.1890, 5 1/2 In., Pair 2090.00
Chair, Deck, Oak, Cane Back, Seat, c.1900 . . . . 175.00

Furniture, Chair, Corner,
Chippendale, Mahogany, Arms,
1750-1770

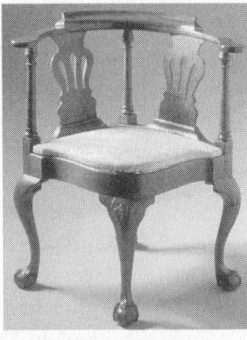

Furniture, Chair, Corner,
Chippendale, Mahogany,
Concave Arms, 1760

Furniture, Chair, Corner,
Queen Anne, Mahogany
Concave Arms, 32 In.

Chair, Donald Chadwick, Foam Filled, Plastic Base, Upholstered, Pair 460.00
Chair, Donald Knorr, Metal, Black Enamel, Conical, Cranbrook, 1956, 22 x 22 In. 2640.00
Chair, E. Wormley, Bent Ash, Upholstered Seat, Cane Back, Brass Feet, Arms, 25 x 25 In. 1380.00
Chair, Eames, Curved Seat & Back, Chrome Base, 1946, Pair 575.00
Chair, Eames, Curved Seat & Back, Chrome Frame, 1945, Pair 690.00
Chair, Eames, DCM, Molded Ash Plywood Seat & Back, Metal Frame, 29 In. 110.00
Chair, Eames, DCW, Molded Plywood & Frame, Black 403.00
Chair, Eames, Eiffel Tower, Metal Wire-Grid Seat, Upholstered 719.00
Chair, Eames, Eiffel Tower, Off-White Molded Fiberglass, Steel Wire Base, 31 x 18 In. .. 460.00
Chair, Eames, Eiffel Tower, Red Molded Fiberglass, Steel Wire Base, Arms 690.00
Chair, Eames, LCM, Walnut Veneer, Molded Plywood Seat & Back, Bent Steel 920.00
Chair, Eames, LCM, Walnut Veneer, Molded Plywood, Chrome Frame, 27 In., Pair 825.00
Chair, Eames, LCW, Birch, Molded Plywood, 22 x 22 x 27 In. 935.00
Chair, Eames, Molded Seat & Back, Chrome Base, 1946 .... 575.00
Chair, Eames, Red Aniline Plywood Seats, Chrome Frame, Herman Miller, 29 In., Pair ... 1045.00
Chair, Eames, Soft Pad, Aluminum Frame, Arms, 24 x 26 x 35 In. 275.00
Chair, Eames, Upholstered, Molded Fiberglass, 4-Point Aluminum Base, Pair 201.00
Chair, Eames, Wire Grid Seat, Dowel Legs With Wire Supports, Full Vinyl Pad 805.00
Chair, Eastlake, Walnut, Incised & Carved Design, Arms 75.00
Chair, Easy, Bun Feet, Leather, Waterfall Arms 920.00
Chair, Easy, Golden Brown Leather, Bun Feet, Waterfall Arms 1445.00
Chair, Easy, Mahogany, Barrel Back, Upholstered, Carved Apron & Legs 110.00
Chair, Ebonized, Copper & Mother-Of-Pearl Floral Inlay, c.1880 .... 412.00
Chair, Edwardian, Mahogany, Curved Crest Rail, 3 Vertical Slats, Arms, 1900 .... 2010.00
Chair, Elizabethan Style, Walnut, Carved, Upholstered Seat & Base, c.1850 .... 1210.00
Chair, Elizabethan, Carved, Leather Seat & Back, Caryatid Arm Supports 575.00
Chair, Elm, Hickory, 4 Splats, Rush Seat, Down-Swept Arms, 1740s 2645.00
Chair, Elm, Horseshoe Back, Curved Crest Rail Continuing To Arms, Plank Seat 258.00
Chair, Elm, Splat Back, Carved, Scroll Feet, Arms, China 287.00
Chair, Elm, Yoke Back, Plank Seat, Square Legs, Serpentine Arms, Pair 345.00
Chair, Elm, Yoke Back, Rattan Seat Over Seat Rail, Pierced Corners, Pair 575.00
Chair, Empire Style, Open Cane Back, Upholstered Seat, Arms 60.00
Chair, Empire, Bronze Griffins On Legs, Raised Paw Feet, 19th Century, 37 1/2 In. 1800.00
Chair, Empire, Mahogany, Carved Ormolu Crest, Paw Feet, Needlepoint Seat 345.00
Chair, Empire, Mahogany, Ormolu Mounted, Upholstered, 35 In., Pair 2300.00
Chair, Empire, Mahogany, Shaped Back Splat, Needlepoint Seat 50.00
Chair, Fan-Shaped Crest Tail, 11 Turned Spindles, Saddle Seat, c.1800 .... 4645.00
Chair, Fanback, Mahogany, Velour Seat, Pair 460.00
Chair, Fanback, Oak, Heart-Shaped Back, Upholstered Seat, Castors, Arms, 1900s 220.00
Chair, Federal, Mahogany, Slip Seat, Carved Crest, Scroll Arms, 32 1/2 In. 175.00
Chair, Federal, Mahogany, Square Back, Floral Crest Rail, Seat Rail, c.1810 .... 300.00
Chair, Federal, Mahogany, Upholstered Arms, Downswept Reeded Arms 140.00
Chair, Fleishman, Molded Plywood, Reticulated Back, Child's, 22 x 21 x 17 In. 440.00
Chair, Flemish, Carved Crest, Turned Stiles & Legs, Scroll Feet, Cane Back, Seat 330.00
Chair, Florence Knoll, Cube, Tufted, Chrome Legs, 32 In. 440.00
Chair, Florence Knoll, Walnut, Tufted Leather Seat, Back & Arms, 25 In., Pair 1430.00
Chair, Fluted Arm Supports, Green Paint, Loose Upholstered Seat, 33 1/2 In. 747.00
Chair, Folding, Cherry Red, Canvas Seat, Child's 85.00
Chair, Folding, Hunzinger, Walnut, Incised, Pat. May 18, 1873 .... 248.00
Chair, Folding, Mother-Of-Pearl Inlay, Persia 460.00
Chair, Frank Lloyd Wright, Aluminum, Leather Seat, Geometric Pedestal Base 1600.00
Chair, Frank Lloyd Wright, Birch, Oversized Tops, Slat Back, Child's, 1912 .... 9200.00
Chair, Frank Lloyd Wright, Geometric, Blue, Green, Pink, Aluminum, 1952 ....6900.00 to 8625.00
Chair, French Provincial, Fruitwood, Scalloped Crest, Rush Seat, Arms, 1860, 37 1/2 In. . 786.00
Chair, French Style, Mahogany, Marquetry, Needlework Slip Seat, 1920 .... 880.00
Chair, French Style, Open, Carved Frame, Upholstered, Early 20th Century, 40 In. 715.00
Chair, French Style, Upholstered Back, Seat & Arms, Carved Wreath Crest, 20 In. 805.00
Chair, G. Nakashima, Walnut, Spindle Back, 2 Paddle Arms, Loose Boucle Cushion 2200.00
Chair, G. Nakashima, Windsor Style, Walnut, Plank Seat, Arms, 27 In. 990.00
Chair, G. Nakashima, Windsor Style, Widdicomb, 29 x 23 x 18 In. 220.00
Chair, G. Nelson, Birch, Sculptural, Upholstered Seat & Back, 1954 .... 660.00
Chair, G. Nelson, Brown Leather, Swivel Base, De Padova, Arms, 27 x 23 In. 990.00

Chair, G. Nelson, Cantinary, Wool, Chrome Base, Herman Miller, 30 x 28 In. 2400.00
Chair, G. Nelson, Coconut, Triangular Metal Shell, Chrome Strut, 40 x 33 In. 9190.00
Chair, G. Nelson, Swag Leg, Flexible Fiberglass Back, Tubular Metal, 34 In. 1540.00
Chair, G. Nelson, Upholstered Seat, Black Steel Frame, Arms, 26 In. 385.00
Chair, G. Stickley, 5 Slats 7700.00
Chair, G. Stickley, Ladder Back, Leather Seats, Pyramidal Tacks, 36 In. 1870.00
Chair, G. Stickley, No. 310, 3 Horizontal Slats, Leather Seat, Red Decal, Arms, 36 In. . . . 2200.00
Chair, G. Stickley, No. 336, Mahogany, Bow Arms, Velvet Spring Cushion 13200.00
Chair, G. Stickley, No. 353a, Mahogany, Arched Seat Rail, Rush Seat, Arms, 41 In. 4675.00
Chair, G. Stickley, No. 398, Low H-Back, Leather Seat, 17 x 16 x 33 In. 1650.00
Chair, G. Stickley, No. 2340, 4 Horizontal Back Slats, Oak Frame, Red Decal 8625.00
Chair, G. Stickley, Swivel, Tacked-On Leather, Arms, 36 1/2 In. 1100.00
Chair, Gehry, Corrugated Cardboard, Masonite, 1972, 16 x 21 x 32 In. 935.00
Chair, George I Style, Shell Carved Knees, Needlepoint 1210.00
Chair, George I, Walnut, Shepherd's Crook, Shaped Crest, Needlework Seat, Arms 14950.00
Chair, George II, Elm, Curved Molded Back, Drop-In Seat, Out-Scrolled Arms 4312.00
Chair, George II, Mahogany, Arched, Padded Back, Cabriole Legs, Ball Feet, Arms 800.00
Chair, George II, Mahogany, Serpentine Crest, Foliage, Drop-In Seat, Pair 11500.00
Chair, George II, Mahogany, Shaped Scroll Crest Rail, Claw & Ball Feet, Arms 5175.00
Chair, George III Style, Curved Back, Foliate Carved Crest, Peg Feet, Padded Arms 1955.00
Chair, George III, Mahogany, Foliate Crest, Drop-In Seat, Straight Legs, Pair 3162.00
Chair, George III, Mahogany, Padded Backrest & Arms, c.1770 . . . . 3450.00
Chair, George III, Mahogany, Padded Backrest, Shell Apron, Scroll Feet, Pair 5175.00
Chair, George III, Mahogany, Painted Monogram & Crests, c.1775, Pair 6900.00
Chair, George III, Mahogany, Pierced Splat, Curved Rectangular Back, Tapered Legs 880.00
Chair, George III, Mahogany, Pierced Splat, Upholstered Seat, 18th Century, Pair 515.00
Chair, George III, Mahogany, Rectangular Back, 4 Stick Splats, Closed-Nail Seat 460.00
Chair, George III, Mahogany, Shaped Crest Rail, Drop-In Seat, 1780, Pair 4600.00
Chair, George III, Mahogany, Spoon-Shaped Pierced Back, Serpentine Seat 8625.00
Chair, George III, Mahogany, Young Girl Spinning, Flower Wreath 24150.00
Chair, George III, Shield-Shaped Back, Serpentine Seat, Splayed Feet, Arms, Pair 7475.00
Chair, Georgian Style, Cabriole Legs, Pad Feet, Ultra-Suede, Pair 440.00
Chair, Georgian, Mahogany, Arched Crest, Upholstered Seat, Cabriole Legs, Arms 575.00
Chair, Georgian, Mahogany, Crest Rail, Shell Apron, Claw Feet, Arms 6900.00
Chair, Giltwood, Square Back, Fluted Columns, Arms, Pair 5750.00
Chair, Gothic Revival, Walnut, Baluster Turned Stiles, 19th Century, Child's 60.00
Chair, Gothic Revival, Walnut, Upholstered, Turned Arms, 52 In. 415.00
Chair, Grain Painted, White Striping, Stencil, Plank Seat, 33 1/4 In., Pair 495.00
Chair, Grotesque Carved Crest, Upholstered Seat & Back, 1920s, 42 In., Pair 95.00
Chair, H. Bertoia, Bird, White Plastic-Coated Wire Grid, 38 x 38 x 25 In. 518.00
Chair, H. Bertoia, Black Wire, Child's, 20 x 12 x 10 In. 316.00
Chair, H. Bertoia, Chrome Wire Grid, 20 1/2 x 21 In., Pair 410.00
Chair, H. Bertoia, Diamond Back, Black Wire Base, Upholstered, 44 x 33 In. 660.00
Chair, H. Bertoia, Diamond Back, Coated Metal, Cushion Seat 172.00
Chair, H. Bertoia, Molded Fiberglass Shell, Chrome Wire Base, 20 1/2 x 21 In., Pair 110.00
Chair, H. Bertoia, Steel Grid Painted White, Upholstered, Pair 230.00
Chair, Hardwood, Carved, Shaped Apron, Square Carved Legs, Ball Feet 201.00
Chair, Hardwood, Foliate Scrollwork, Turned, Tapered Legs, England, Pair 144.00
Chair, Hardwood, Mother-Of-Pearl Inlay, Panel Seat, Round Tapered Legs 285.00
Chair, Hardwood, Yoke Back, Square Seat & Legs, China 240.00
Chair, Hepplewhite Style, Mahogany, Line Inlay, Gold Brocade, 48 In. 415.00
Chair, Hepplewhite, Hardwood, Light Natural Finish, Shield Back, Upholstered Seat 110.00
Chair, Hepplewhite, Mahogany, Pierced Back, Slip Seat, Serpentine Rail, Pair 1045.00
Chair, Hepplewhite, Oak, Pierced Splat, H-Stretcher, Curved Seat, England, 37 In. 220.00
Chair, Hepplewhite, Round Corner Blocks, Needlepoint Slip Seat, 18th Century 440.00
Chair, Hepplewhite, Yew Wood, Arms, c.1795 . . . . 575.00
Chair, Herman Miller, Office, Upholstered Seat & Back, Aluminum Base 86.00
Chair, Herman Miller, Walnut, Upholstered Seat & Back, Arms, Pair 175.00
Chair, Hickory Bark, Cane Seat, Arms, Dated 1854, Signed J.W.D., 55 In. 1900.00
Chair, Hitchcock, Floral Gilt, Horizontal Back Splat Of Eagle, Cane Seat 110.00
Chair, Hitchcock, Red & Black Graining, Stencil, Rush Seat, Varnished 55.00
Chair, Hitchcock, Stenciled, Painted, Plank Seat 125.00
Chair, Horseshoe Back, Crest Continuing To Arms, Paneled Seat, China, Pair 170.00

Chair, Horseshoe Back, Shandong Province, China, 19th Century, 35 x 27 In., Pair 295.00
Chair, Hunzinger Style, Folding, X-Frame, Upholstered, Fringed, Holmes, 1871, 42 In. .. 290.00
Chair, Hunzinger, Upholstered, Adjustable, Arms, 1866 .... 1995.00
Chair, Hunzinger, Walnut, Ebony, Incised, Upholstered, Fringe Seat, Pat. Feb. 6, 1866 ... 660.00
Chair, Hunzinger, Walnut, Folding, Velvet, c.1866 .... 230.00
Chair, Ice Cream, Iron, Wood Seat, White & Green Paint, 21 In., Pair 115.00
Chair, Iron, Neoclassical, Back, Rail & Lyre, Arms, Ram's Head, 19th Century 330.00
Chair, Iron, Regency, Back, Putti & Lyre Arms, Ram Feet, Ram's Head, Pair 1980.00
Chair, J. & J.W. Meeks, Rococo, Laminated Rosewood, Upholstered, Pair 2010.00
Chair, Jacobean Style, Cane Seat & Back, Carved Floral & Figural Design, Pair 1265.00
Chair, Jacobean Style, Open, Cane Seat, Back, Figural, Urn & Floral Design, Arms 1150.00
Chair, Jacobean Style, Walnut, Open, Rose Tapestry, Brass Tacks 405.00
Chair, Jacobean Style, Walnut, Rope Twisted Detail, Tapestry, Arms, 35 In. 715.00
Chair, Jacobean, Cane Seat & Back, Rope Twist Legs, Pair 110.00
Chair, Jacobean, Oak, Scrolls & Foliage, Shaped Arms, Plank Seat 1610.00
Chair, Jacobean, Walnut, Floral Cross-Stitched Back, Seat, Bun Feet 630.00
Chair, Jacobsen, Egg, Fritz Hansen, Denmark, 1957 .... 2760.00
Chair, Jacobsen, Swan, Leather, 1957 .... 4255.00
Chair, Katavolos, Littell, Kelley, Tufted Black Leather, Laverne, 28 In. 1430.00
Chair, Kem Weber, Airline, Arms 13200.00
Chair, Kem Weber, Mohair Cushions, Triple-Band Chrome Arms, 28 x 39 In. 1650.00
Chair, L. & J. Stickley, Windsor Style, Cherry, 43 1/2 In. 195.00
Chair, Lacquer & Floral Painted Crest, Gilt, Cane Seat, England, 19th Century, Pair 248.00
Chair, Ladder Back, Birch, Hickory, Arched Backrests, Rush Seat, c.1720, 41 In. 920.00
Chair, Ladder Back, Dark Finish Over Red, Splint Seat, 44 In. 385.00
Chair, Ladder Back, Elm, 4 Splats, Rush Seat, Down-Swept Arms, 18th Century 5750.00
Chair, Ladder Back, Fruitwood, Rush Seat, Round Legs, Cup Feet, 1860, 36 In. 303.00
Chair, Ladder Back, Hardwood, 3 Slats, Splint Seat, 41 In. 80.00
Chair, Ladder Back, Horse-Bone Legs, Maple, Brown Paint, 1730, 44 In., Pair 9200.00
Chair, Ladder Back, Mahogany, Rush Seat, Round Legs, 39 In. 42.00
Chair, Ladder Back, Maple, 5 Graduated Arched Slats, Rush Seat, 44 1/2 In. 3205.00
Chair, Ladder Back, Maple, 5 Graduated Arched Slats, Rush Seat, Pa., 43 3/4 In. 605.00
Chair, Ladder Back, Maple, Cherry, Hickory, 3 Splats, Mushroom Handholds 5750.00
Chair, Ladder Back, Maple, Chestnut, Rush Seat, Arms, 19th Century, Child's, 28 In. 920.00
Chair, Ladder Back, Oak, Rush Seat, McHugh, 24 x 23 x 40 In. 440.00
Chair, Ladder Back, Oak, Rush Seat, Round Turned Legs, Arms, France, 1880, 38 In. 242.00
Chair, Ladder Back, Painted, Shell Carved Slats, Rush Seats, Continental 145.00
Chair, Ladder Back, Red Paint, 3 Slats, Turned Finials, Splint Seat, 41 1/2 In. 55.00
Chair, Ladder Back, Rush Seat, 6 Graduated Arched Slats, Finials, Arms, 47 1/2 In. 1045.00
Chair, Ladder Back, Rush Seat, Splayed Legs, France, 19th Century, 38 1/2 In. 151.00
Chair, Ladder Back, Sausage Turned Stiles, Front Stretchers, Rush Seat 77.00
Chair, Ladder Back, Seascape Painted On Each Slat, 5 Slats, 19th Century 715.00
Chair, Ladder Back, Splint Seat, Box Stretcher, Scroll Arms, 30 3/4 In. 750.00
Chair, Ladder Back, Turned Posts, 4 Arched Slats, Finials, Rush Seat, 17 x 42 In., Pair ... 275.00
Chair, Ladder Back, Turned Spindles, Scroll Arms, Maple, Woven Paper Seat, 45 In. 65.00
Chair, Ladder Back, Walnut, Woven Rush Seat, Turned Legs, Bun Feet, Pair 200.00
Chair, Laminated Rosewood, Pierce-Carved Back, Rose At Crest, Upholstered, 36 In. ... 1120.00
Chair, Laverne, Invisible Group, Clear Molded Base & Back, Upholstered Seat, Arms ... 1725.00
Chair, Leleu, Aubusson Upholstery, Floral Sprays, Khaki Ground, Pair 6900.00
Chair, Limbert, No. 1935, 5 Vertical Slats Back, Wood Seat, 26 x 20 x 39 In. 605.00
Chair, Limbert, No. 8073, Mahogany, Horizontal Slats, Paper Label, 23 x 35 In. 231.00
Chair, Limbert, Oak, Leather Backrest, 42 In. 660.00
Chair, Lloyd, Chrome, Wood Arms, Cushions, 30 In. 135.00
Chair, Lolling, Chippendale, Mahogany, Arched Crest, Upholstered Arms, Pair 1760.00
Chair, Lolling, Chippendale, Mahogany, Square Reeded Legs, Serpentine Arms, Pair 745.00
Chair, Lolling, Mahogany, Serpentine Crest, Padded Seat & Back, Arms, c.1800, 43 In. .. 5462.00
Chair, Lolling, Upholstered, Late 18th Century 865.00
Chair, Louis Philippe, Mahogany, Undulating Foliate Scroll Top Rail, Arms, Pair 20700.00
Chair, Louis XIII, Walnut, Flowers, Down-Swept Arms 980.00
Chair, Louis XIII, Walnut, Landscape Needlework, Down-Swept Scroll Arms 1725.00
Chair, Louis XIV, Walnut, Arched Padded Backs, S-Scroll Legs, Pair 3162.00
Chair, Louis XIV, Walnut, Rectangular Backrest, Leaf Carved Arms 260.00
Chair, Louis XV Style, Cut Velvet, Button-Tufted Back, Arms, 20th Century 460.00

Chair, Louis XV Style, Polychrome Molded Crest, Cabriole Legs, Arms, 1870, 35 1/2 In. . 665.00
Chair, Louis XV Style, Walnut, Cabriole Scroll Legs, Down-Swept Arms, 1900 .... 402.00
Chair, Louis XV Style, Walnut, Cushioned Velvet Seat, Arms, 1860, 30 In. 786.00
Chair, Louis XV Style, Walnut, Floral Carving, Cabriole Legs, Arms, 1890, 33 In. 726.00
Chair, Louis XV Style, Walnut, Padded Back, Scroll Arms, Overstuffed Seat, Pair 1032.00
Chair, Louis XV Style, Walnut, Upholstered, Padded Arms, 1890, 33 1/2 In., Pair 970.00
Chair, Louis XV, Beechwood, Arched Back, Serpentine Loose-Cushion Seat, Arms, Pair .. 4025.00
Chair, Louis XV, Beechwood, Crested Frame, Serpentine Seat, Scroll Feet, Arms, Pair ... 3735.00
Chair, Louis XV, Beechwood, Floral Needlework, 35 3/4 In. 2420.00
Chair, Louis XV, Beechwood, Foliate Frame, Serpentine Seat, Arms, 34 In. 1150.00
Chair, Louis XV, Beechwood, Gros Point & Petit Point, Arms, 1880, 37 In. 1380.00
Chair, Louis XV, Beechwood, Serpentine Seat, Cabriole Legs 9200.00
Chair, Louis XV, Carved, Upholstered Back, Seat, Arms, 35 1/2 In., Pair 1035.00
Chair, Louis XV, Flower-Head Crest, Round Upholstered Seat, Cabriole Legs, Pair, Arms . 805.00
Chair, Louis XV, Giltwood, Molded Crest Rail, Shaped Seat Rail, Cabriole Legs, Arms .. 3735.00
Chair, Louis XV, Mahogany, Pierced Crest Rail, Foliate Legs, Padded Arms 980.00
Chair, Louis XVI Style, Belle Epoque, Aubusson, 1814, 39 3/4 In., Pair 2200.00
Chair, Louis XVI Style, Bow Carved Crest, Upholstered Seat & Back, 19th Century 250.00
Chair, Louis XVI Style, Bronze Acorn Finials, Serpentine Overstuffed Seat, 1900, Pair ... 575.00
Chair, Louis XVI Style, Giltwood, Carved, Embroidered On Silk, Child's, 23 In. 275.00
Chair, Louis XVI Style, Giltwood, Petit Point, Fluted Legs, Arms, 35 In., Pair 860.00
Chair, Louis XVI Style, Giltwood, Ribbon Carved Crest, Arms, 19th Century, 39 In., Pair . 2660.00
Chair, Louis XVI Style, Mahogany, Open Back, 4 Splayed Splats, Arms, Italy 865.00
Chair, Louis XVI Style, Open, Tapestry Seat & Back, Arms, People In Landscape 2300.00
Chair, Louis XVI Stiles, Walnut, Lyre Back, Fluted Stiles, Reeded Legs, Floral Design ... 250.00
Chair, Louis XVI, Beechwood, Carved Top Rail, Velvet, Arms, Pair 1090.00
Chair, Louis XVI, Giltwood, Bowfront Seat, Down-Swept Acanthus Leaf Arms, Pair 1610.00
Chair, Louis XVI, Giltwood, Serpentine Overstuffed Seat, Top Shaped Feet, Child's 400.00
Chair, Louis XVI, Giltwood, Top Shaped Feet, Out-Curved Scroll Arms, Pair 2300.00
Chair, Louis XVI, Padded Back, Serpentine Cushion Seat, Child's, Pair 1092.00
Chair, Louis XVI, Walnut, Rectangular Back, Bowfront Seat, Fluted Legs, Arms, Pair ... 2070.00
Chair, Lounge, Art Deco, U-Shaped Arm Supports, Wood Ball Feet, 1920, 22 In. 4312.00
Chair, Lounge, DiCarli, Lacquered Wood, Upholstered, 31 x 23 x 26 In., Pair 1035.00
Chair, Lounge, H. Bertoia, Bird, Chrome-Plated Wire, Upholstered, Stool 1150.00
Chair, Lounge, Heywood-Wakefield Co., Bentwood, Maple, Upholstered, 30 In. 330.00
Chair, Lounge, P. Paulin, Tubular Chromed Steel, Upholstered, Arms .... *Illus* 575.00
Chair, Mahogany, Cane Back, Cushioned Cane Seat, Arms, 1880, 41 In., Pair 2299.00
Chair, Mahogany, Carved Urn & Rosettes, c.1795 .... 1600.00
Chair, Mahogany, Cock Fighting, Carved Leaf On Back, Upholstered Seat, 33 In. 2185.00
Chair, Mahogany, Fruit, Foliate Carved Crest Rail, Cabriole Legs, Victorian 400.00
Chair, Mahogany, Giltood, Arched Curved Backrest, Claw & Ball Feet, Russia, Pair 9200.00
Chair, Mahogany, Molded Seat Rail, Turned Legs, Brass Casters, Scroll Arms, c.1835 ... 715.00
Chair, Mahogany, Open Back, Vase-Form Splat, Scroll Frame, Raised Seat On Rails 460.00
Chair, Mahogany, Pierced Splat, Prince Of Wales Plume, Upholstered Seat, 36 In. 2760.00
Chair, Mahogany, Rectangular Crest, Slip Seat, Upholstered, Arms, 19th Century 915.00

**Rattan and wicker furniture will
pick up the smell of cigarette
smoke. If you want to remove it,
put the piece outside to air. It
is also helpful to wash it with
Murphy's Oil Soap, rinse, then dry.**

Furniture, Chair, Lounge, P. Paulin,
Tubular Chromed Steel, Upholstered, Arms

Chair, Mahogany, Reeded Stiles, Drop-In Upholstered Seat, 18th Century 460.00
Chair, Mahogany, Rose Carving, Finger Carved Arms, Legs, Upholstered, 42 In. 259.00
Chair, Mahogany, Serpentine Crest, Padded Back, Seat & Arms, 43 In. 5462.00
Chair, Majorelle, Mahogany, Clematis Blossoms, Suede 7475.00
Chair, Majorelle, Mahogany, Stylized Foliage, Upholstered, Arms, 1920 . . . .   8625.00
Chair, Maple, Ash, Stiles Topped By Finials, 3 Shaped Slats, Rush Seat 6900.00
Chair, Maple, Pierced Foliate Scroll Design, Carved Lion's-Head Arms, Claw Feet 200.00
Chair, Maple, Roundabout, Horizontal Splats, Rush Seat, Scroll Arms, 28 In. 1092.00
Chair, Maple, Woven Splint Seat & Back, Arms, Late 19th Century, 34 In., Pair 805.00
Chair, Matta, Apple & Hat, Upholstered Foam, 1971, 36 x 28 In.   990.00
Chair, McCobb, Spindle Back, Dowel Legs, 31 x 17 x 17 1/2 In. . . . . .345.00 to 400.00
Chair, Medieval Style, Hardwood, Carved, Shield Back, 2-Headed Bird, 36 1/2 In. 140.00
Chair, Medieval Style, Oak, Triangular, Turned & Carved Detail, Velvet Cushion, 33 In. . .   550.00
Chair, Morris, G. Stickley, No. 336, Bow Arms 11000.00
Chair, Morris, G. Stickley, No. 3695, Bent Arms, 33 x 38 x 40 In. 8250.00
Chair, Morris, Hardin, Slats & Tenons, 39 x 35 In. 2310.00
Chair, Morris, J.M. Young, No. 186, 5 Slats Under Flat Arms, Cushion Seat, 40 In. 3850.00
Chair, Morris, J.M. Young, Prairie School, Flat Arms, Slats To Floor, Drop-In Seat, 36 In.   450.00
Chair, Morris, Knaus Mfg. Co., 5 Slats, Corbels Under Flat Arms, Leather, 38 In. 2970.00
Chair, Morris, L. & J.G. Stickley, Oak, 4 Vertical Slats, Oversize, Onondaga Shops 1870.00
Chair, Neoclassical, Arched Upholstered Backrest, Laurel & Berries, Saber Legs 8050.00
Chair, Neoclassical, Fruitwood, Scroll Back, Arms, Continental, Pair 3450.00
Chair, Neoclassical, Mahogany, Ebony, Gadrooned Backrest, Saber Legs, Arms 2645.00
Chair, Neoclassical, Mahogany, Foliate Scroll Top, Papyrus Wreath, Arms, Pair 10350.00
Chair, Neoclassical, Mahogany, Padded Armrests, Suede, 1835 . . . .   10350.00
Chair, Oak, Carved Dog's-Head Arms, Griffin Crest, Leather, 51 In. 230.00
Chair, Oak, Heraldic Crest Over Foliate, Paneled Back, Plank Seat, 1900s, Pair 495.00
Chair, Oak, High Back, Turned Stiles Support, Plank Seat, Leaf Carving 55.00
Chair, Oak, Hoop Back, Pierced Splats, Slab Seat, Splayed Legs, Arms 110.00
Chair, Oak, Spindle Back, England, 1880, Pair 300.00
Chair, Oak, Swivel, Curved Arms & Back, Leather, 36 In. 210.00
Chair, Oval Back, Loose Cushion, Molded Arms, Painted Cream, Early 20th Century 230.00
Chair, Ox-Yoke Crest, Pierced Back Splat With Bat, Jui & Round Mon, China 385.00
Chair, P. Evans, Sculptural Bronze, Abstract Upholstery, 1966, 28 x 24 In. 2530.00
Chair, P. Paulin, Ribbon, Sculptured, Upholstered, 30 x 26 x 26 In. 935.00
Chair, P. Paulin, Swan, Boucle, Aluminum Base, 30 x 30 x 26 In. 660.00
Chair, Papier-Mache, Arched Crest Rail, Painted Splat, Upholstered, Pair 400.00
Chair, Parcel Gilt, Painted, Carved Crest, Upholstered, Cabriole Legs, Italy, Pair 1725.00
Chair, Pine, Oak, Hickory, Maple, Sack Back, 7 Spindles, Arms, c.1780, 6 In. 1400.00
Chair, Pottier & Stymus, Rosewood, Gilt Incised, Bronze Mounts, Arms, c.1865 . . . .   3740.00
Chair, Potty, Moravian, Oak, Pine, Original Finish, 18th Century, 21 x 14 x 16 In. 375.00
Chair, Queen Anne Style, E. Wheeler, Mahogany, 20th Century, 40 In., Pair 400.00
Chair, Queen Anne Style, Mahogany Gooseneck Arms, Balloon Seat, Pair 175.00
Chair, Queen Anne Style, Red & Gold Chinoiserie Design, Slip Seat, 41 1/2 In. 330.00
Chair, Queen Anne, Cherry, Carved, Compass Seat, 39 In. 2587.00
Chair, Queen Anne, Cherry, Rush Seat, Bulbous Stretcher, Spanish Feet 770.00
Chair, Queen Anne, Curved Back Posts, Vase-Form, Spanish Feet, Rush Seat, 41 In. 880.00
Chair, Queen Anne, Dark Finish, Rush Seat, 18 x 44 1/4 In. 410.00
Chair, Queen Anne, Mahogany, Carved Crest & Legs, c.1750, 38 1/2 In. 4025.00
Chair, Queen Anne, Mahogany, Scalloped Crest, Pennsylvania, c.1780, 37 In., Pair 1960.00
Chair, Queen Anne, Maple, Cabriole Legs, Upholstered Seat, 41 In. 1815.00
Chair, Queen Anne, Maple, Spoon Back, Upholstered Balloon Seat, 18th Century 290.00
Chair, Queen Anne, Maple, Yoke Crest, Spanish Feet, Rush Seat, 1745, 42 In. 1840.00
Chair, Queen Anne, Walnut, Carved Yoke Crest, Solid Splat, Slip Seat, c.1740 . . . .   1700.00
Chair, Queen Anne, Walnut, Open, Rectangular Back, Cabriole Legs 900.00
Chair, Queen Anne, Walnut, Shell Carved Crest Rail, Philadelphia, c.1750 . . . .   3470.00
Chair, Queen Anne, Walnut, Upholstered, Cabriole Legs, Pad Feet, Pair 6325.00
Chair, Queen Anne, Walnut, Velvet, Compass-Shaped Seat, c.1730 . . . .   2300.00
Chair, Red Lacquer, Curved Crest Rail, Curved Splat, Plank Seat, Serpentine Arms 545.00
Chair, Reeded Leg, Splayed Feet, Carved Arms, Upholstered Seat, New York 1130.00
Chair, Regency, Beechwood, Arched Rail Continuing To Arms, Cane Back, Saber Legs . .   3450.00
Chair, Regency, Beechwood, Arched Top Rail, Cabriole Legs 920.00
Chair, Regency, Brass Inlay, Arched Top Rail, Scrolled, Tapered Legs, Pair 750.00

Chair, Regency, Cabriole Legs, Tufted Leather Seat & Back 690.00
Chair, Regency, Mahogany Veneer, Tablet Crest Rail, Spiral Legs 135.00
Chair, Regency, Mahogany, Scrolled Crest Rail, Turned Legs, Scroll Arms 2400.00
Chair, Regency, Round Back, Round Molded Seat, Round Front Rail 2320.00
Chair, Regency, Teakwood, Spindle Back, Cane Seat, Reeded, Tapered Legs, Arms, Pair .. 935.00
Chair, Regency, Walnut, Rectangular Cane Back, Cane Seat, Arms, 19th Century 3000.00
Chair, Renaissance Revival, Rosewood, Stepped Crest, Flowers, Foliage, Arms, Pair 2300.00
Chair, Renaissance Revival, Walnut, Cone Shaped Finials, Ring Stiles, Upholstered 1160.00
Chair, Restauration, Mahogany, Upholstered Seat, Scroll Arms, 1830, 35 1/2 In. 968.00
Chair, Rietveld, Zigzag, Bright Green Enamel, 30 1/4 x 14 x 18 In. 4125.00
Chair, Risom, Angular, Tapering Wood Frame, Webbing, Knoll 431.00
Chair, Rocker, is listed under Rocker in this category.
Chair, Rococo Style, Walnut, Button Tufted, Scroll Arms, Pair 745.00
Chair, Rococo, Laminated Rosewood, Carved Roses, Arms, Upholstered, Pair 6035.00
Chair, Rococo, Rosewood, Scroll Frame, Apron, Cabriole Legs, Arms, c.1860 .... 370.00
Chair, Rococo, Shell Medallion, Serpentine Seat, England, 1850, 37 In. 240.00
Chair, Rococo, Walnut, Arched Open Back, Overstuffed Seat, Foliage, Italy 290.00
Chair, Rococo, Walnut, Upholstered Seat & Back, Curved Legs, 19th Century 60.00
Chair, Rohlfs, Cutout Slats, Upholstered Seat, 35 In. 1980.00
Chair, Rosewood, Dolphin-Carved Crest, Conforming Arm Supports, c.1840s 4290.00
Chair, Rosewood, Floral Crest, Upholstered, Cabriole Legs, 1860 .... 305.00
Chair, Rosewood, Leather, Cushion Seat, Roundel Handholds, Pair 6325.00
Chair, Roundabout, Mahogany, Shaped Crest, Semicircular Arm Rail, 32 1/4 In. 2185.00
Chair, Roycroft, Meditation, Broad Flat Crest Rail, Tacked On Leather Seat, 34 In. 2640.00
Chair, Rush Seat, Pierced Back Splat, Light Green, Carved Arms, Continental, 33 In. ... 460.00
Chair, Saarinen, Grasshopper, Bent Laminate Legs, Arms, 36 x 24 In. ....850.00 to 1150.00
Chair, Saarinen, Pony, Polyurethane Foam, Upholstered, 1970, 24 x 42 x 36 In. 5500.00
Chair, Sausage Turned, Rush Seat, Child's, 25 1/2 In. 110.00
Chair, Savanarola, Walnut, Velvet Seat, Arms, Italy ....315.00 to 400.00
Chair, Savonarola, Damask, Victorian 595.00
Chair, Scholar's, Rosewood, Low Back, Marble Panels, China 1200.00
Chair, Scroll Arms, Gold-Decorated Gesso, Upholstered, c.1920, 39 x 34 In. 805.00
Chair, Sergio Mazza, Toga, Molded Red Fiberglass, 28 x 25 x 14 In., Pair 1320.00
Chair, Shaker, 3 Slats, Turned Finials, Taped Seat, 40 3/4 In. 770.00
Chair, Shaker, Ladder Back, 3 Arched Slats, Cloth Seat, Painted, New Hampshire 28.00
Chair, Shaker, Maple, Ladder Back, 3 Slats, Tilters In Back Feet, Taped Seat, 41 1/4 In. .. 1320.00
Chair, Shaker, Maple, Pine Revolving, Concave Crest, Spindles, Arched Legs, 19 x 30 In. 630.00
Chair, Shaker, No. 0, 3 Slats, Shaped Arms, Mushroom Caps, Taped Seat, 23 In. 770.00
Chair, Shaker, Splint Seat, 29 1/4 In., Pair 1265.00
Chair, Shaker, Tilter, Rush Seat, Mount Lebanon, c.1930 .... 995.00
Chair, Shaped Crest Over Vase-Form Splat, Spanish Feet, Rush Seat 165.00
Chair, Shaw-Walker, Aluminum, Wood, Rounded Backs, Upholstered Seat, Arms, Pair ... 520.00
Chair, Sheraton, Cane Seat & Back, England, Pair 198.00
Chair, Sheraton, Maple, Rush Seats, Arms, Pair 220.00
Chair, Shop Of The Crafters, No. 331, Inlay, Arms, 29 x 43 x 31 In. 4125.00
Chair, Slipper, Belter, Rosewood, Carved Grapes & Leaves Back, 43 In. 6440.00
Chair, Slipper, Floral Crest, Carved Gilt Bust, 19th Century, 51 3/4 In. 248.00
Chair, Slipper, Herter Type, Foliate Inlay On Skirt, Upholstered, 19th Century 440.00
Chair, Slipper, Queen Anne, Walnut, Bellflower Carved Crest, Compass Slip Seat 6900.00
Chair, Slipper, Queen Anne, Walnut, Figured Vase-Form Splat, Trifid Feet, c.1750, 37 In. .. 5462.00
Chair, Slipper, Victorian, Walnut, Round Turned Legs, Casters 172.00
Chair, Split Baluster Back, Black Paint, Rush Seat 275.00
Chair, Stag Horn, Carved Medallions, Dog's Head On Arms, Velvet Seat, 37 In. 1760.00
Chair, Stickley Brothers, Floral Inlay, Plank Seat, 21 x 40 In. 1320.00
Chair, Stickley Brothers, No. 312 1/2, Mahogany, 3-Slat Back, Plank Seat, 38 In. 330.00
Chair, Teakwood, Cane Seat Back, Arms, West Indies 605.00
Chair, Teakwood, Dowel Frame, Curved Back Slat, Arms, Denmark, 23 x 19 In. 230.00
Chair, Tiger & Bird's-Eye Maple, Rush Seat, Child's 330.00
Chair, Tiger, Curly Maple, Pillow Back, Rush Seat, c.1825, Child's, 15 In. 325.00
Chair, Tudor, High Back, Font Hill Foliate Tapestry, Arms 330.00
Chair, Urn Carved Crest Rail, Padded Arms, Foliate Carved Supports, Painted, Pair 3737.00
Chair, V. Panton, Cone, Chrome Wire, Round Upholstered Cushion, 1960, 30 In. 1650.00
Chair, V. Panton, Cone, Enameled Wire, Round Base, Cushion, 29 x 24 In., Pair 2420.00

Chair, V. Panton, Cone, Red Wool, Chrome Swivel Base, 1958, 21 x 33 In. 1045.00
Chair, Valet, Johannes Hansen, Oak, Sculpted Back, Hinged Storage Seat, 1953 . . . . 2070.00
Chair, Valet, Wegner, Ebonized Teakwood, Hinged Storage Seat 2588.00
Chair, Van Der Rohe, Barcelona, Leather Cushions, Steel Frame, Knoll, Pair 2200.00
Chair, Van Der Rohe, Brno, Chrome Frame, Blue Leather, 32 x 23 x 22 In. 190.00
Chair, Vase-Form Splat, Slip Seat, Saber Legs, 19th Century 105.00
Chair, Victorian, Hardwood, Mahogany Finish, Spindle, Cane Seat, Arms, 36 In. 220.00
Chair, Victorian, Mahogany, Carved Floral Design, Upholstered, 34 1/2 In. 205.00
Chair, Victorian, Mother-Of-Pearl Inlay, Papier-Mache, Pair 1090.00
Chair, Victorian, Walnut, Button-Tufted Back, Padded Arms 805.00
Chair, Victorian, Walnut, Button-Tufted Pinched-Waist Back, Serpentine, 44 In. 220.00
Chair, Victorian, Walnut, Floral Crest, Damask Corset Seat & Back 275.00
Chair, Victorian, Walnut, Rose Carved, Needlepoint Seat, Pair 220.00
Chair, Voltaire, Tufted Leather, c.1840, 35 1/2 In. 1100.00
Chair, W. Plattner, Bent Wire Base, Upholstered, Pair 460.00
Chair, Wallace Nutting, No. 311, Fanback 1073.00
Chair, Wallace Nutting, No. 402, Windsor, Continuous Arms, Script Brand 770.00
Chair, Wallace Nutting, No. 420, Knuckle Arms 660.00
Chair, Wallace Nutting, No. 437, Mahogany, Hepplewhite Type, Arms 743.00
Chair, Wallace Nutting, No. 442, Tenon Arms, Block Brand 1155.00
Chair, Wallace Nutting, Sack Back, Arms 825.00
Chair, Wallace Nutting, Windsor, Brace Back, 36 1/2 In. 550.00
Chair, Wallace Nutting, Windsor, Brace Back, 38 1/4 In. 550.00
Chair, Wallace Nutting, Windsor, Brace Back, Continuous Arms, 44 3/4 In. 825.00
Chair, Wallace Nutting, Windsor, Brace Back, Scroll Crest, Saddle Seat 1275.00
Chair, Walnut, Backrest, Ivory Inlay, Foliate Design 690.00
Chair, Walnut, Burl Walnut, Oval Medallion Carved Crest, Rolled Arms 305.00
Chair, Walnut, Button-Tufted Triple-Arched Back, Pierced Frame, Rails Into Legs 400.00
Chair, Walnut, Floral Carved Frame, Leaf Scroll Arms, Padded Seat, Arms, Pair 900.00
Chair, Walnut, Floral Crest, Tufted Corset Back, Castors, 1860 . . . . 330.00
Chair, Walnut, Padded Back, Upholstered Seat, H-Stretcher, Flemish, Pair 2587.00
Chair, Walnut, Patera Carving, Scroll Padded Back, Ball Feet, Arms, 1800, 36 x 24 In. . . . 1452.00
Chair, Walnut, Pierced Backrest, Shells, Urns, Upholstered, 1720s 2300.00
Chair, Walnut, Rattan Paneled Back, Scroll Crest & Legs, 17th Century 1840.00
Chair, Walnut, Scroll Arms, Upholstered Seat, Arms, 19th Century, 47 In. 2185.00
Chair, Walnut, Turned Spindle Back, Box Stretcher, Upholstered Seat, Arms, England . . . 110.00
Chair, Warren McArthur, Brushed Chrome, Textured Blue Vinyl, Folding, Arms, Pair 550.00
Chair, Warren McArthur, Threaded Aluminum, Loose Upholstered Seat & Back, Arms . . . 2588.00
Chair, Warren McArthur, Tubular Aluminum, Upholstered, Folding, Pair 460.00
Chair, Wavy Splat, Arms, 1770-1800 . . . . 7280.00
Chair, Wegner, Ash, Sloping Arms, Curved Back, Rope Seat, Arms, 25 x 20 In. 880.00
Chair, Wegner, Chrome Frame, Wool, Denmark, 38 x 34 In. 3575.00
Chair, Wegner, Flag Line, Metal Bar, Fabric Strands Form Seat, Arms, c.1950 . . . . 1400.00
Chair, Whalebone, Moose Antler, Cabriole Front Legs, c.1860 . . . . 2750.00
Chair, Wicker, Basket-Weave Rolled Edge, Coiled Design, Arms, 42 In. 100.00
Chair, Wicker, Square Back, Rolled Arms, Wood & Woven Seat, Basket-Weave Base 115.00
Chair, Wicker, Wood Frame, Cane Seat, Arms, Mid-1800s 175.00
Chair, William & Mary Style, Carved Floral & Scroll Design, Cane Seat, Back, Pair 805.00
Chair, William & Mary, Walnut, Crest Rail, Cane Seat & Back, Scroll Arms 715.00
Chair, William IV, Mahogany, Lotus Scroll Arms, Tapered, Reeded Legs, c.1835 . . . . 495.00
Chair, William IV, Rosewood, Upholstered Backrest, Padded Sides & Arms, c.1835 . . . . . 5750.00
Chair, William IV, Walnut, Turned Legs, Upholstered, 19th Century, 37 In., Pair 300.00
Chair, Windsor Hoop Back, 7 Spindles, Saddle Seat, Knuckle Arms 495.00
Chair, Windsor, 6 Spindles, Shaped Seat, White Paint, Arms 55.00
Chair, Windsor, 7 Spindles, Splayed Base, Saddle Seat, Black Paint, 17 1/2 In. 300.00
Chair, Windsor, 9 Spindles, Bamboo, Sage Green Paint, 35 1/2 In. 440.00
Chair, Windsor, Arrow Back, Bamboo, Painted, 34 1/4 In. 135.00
Chair, Windsor, Bamboo Turned, Birdcage, Arms, c.1910, Stamped G. Gaw 440.00
Chair, Windsor, Bamboo, 18 x 35 3/4 In. 165.00
Chair, Windsor, Bamboo, 6 Spindles, Medallion, Pair 355.00
Chair, Windsor, Bamboo, Black Paint, Step-Down Crest 165.00
Chair, Windsor, Bamboo, Brace Back, Sage Green Paint, Arms, 39 In. 740.00
Chair, Windsor, Bamboo, Flared Back, Shaped Spindles, Arms, 33 3/4 In. 240.00

Chair, Windsor, Bamboo, Green Paint, Child's, 21 1/2 In. 165.00
Chair, Windsor, Bamboo, Spindle Back, Arms, Child's, 27 In. 725.00
Chair, Windsor, Bamboo, Splayed, Continuous Arms 465.00
Chair, Windsor, Bow Back, 7 Spindles, Bamboo, Saddle Seat, 1810 . . . . 800.00
Chair, Windsor, Bow Back, 7 Spindles, Bamboo, Sage Green Paint, 36 3/4 In. 465.00
Chair, Windsor, Bow Back, 7 Spindles, Bamboo, Splayed Base, Saddle Seat, 34 In. 190.00
Chair, Windsor, Bow Back, 7 Spindles, Black Paint, Splayed Stretcher 355.00
Chair, Windsor, Bow Back, 9 Spindles, Saddle Seat, Dark Brown, 36 1/2 In. 260.00
Chair, Windsor, Bow Back, 9 Spindles, Upholstered Seat, Rhode Island, 36 1/4 In. 230.00
Chair, Windsor, Bow Back, Balloon Back, 7 Spindles, Bamboo Turned Legs, 37 1/2 In. . . 195.00
Chair, Windsor, Bow Back, Bamboo Turned Legs, Saddle Seat, 36 3/4 In. 250.00
Chair, Windsor, Bow Back, Bamboo Turnings, Scroll Arms, 16 x 37 In. 550.00
Chair, Windsor, Bow Back, Black Paint, Splayed, Saddle Seat, Arms, 41 3/4 In. 250.00
Chair, Windsor, Bow Back, Brown Finish, Saddle Seat, Spindle Back, Arms 745.00
Chair, Windsor, Bow Back, Dark Paint, Splayed Base, Saddle Seat, Arms, 37 In. 145.00
Chair, Windsor, Bow Back, Flared Spindles, Saddle Seat, Painted, 19th Century, Pair 2875.00
Chair, Windsor, Bow Back, Gray Paint, Saddle Seat, Shaped Arms, 39 In. 580.00
Chair, Windsor, Bow Back, Mixed Wood, Bulbous Bamboo Stretcher, 37 In. 245.00
Chair, Windsor, Bow Back, Oak, Child's, 22 3/4 In. 110.00
Chair, Windsor, Bow Back, Painted, Plank Seat, Baluster-Shaped Legs, 19th Century 290.00
Chair, Windsor, Bow Back, Pine, Ash, Maple 247.00
Chair, Windsor, Bow Back, Splayed Base, Black Paint, Turned Legs, Arms, 15 x 36 In. . . 660.00
Chair, Windsor, Bow Back, Tiger Maple, Arms 467.00
Chair, Windsor, Brace Back, 9 Spindles, Black Paint, Turned Legs, 35 In. 195.00
Chair, Windsor, Brace Back, Simonds Label, Early 20th Century, 44 3/4 In. 330.00
Chair, Windsor, Brace Back, Splayed Base, Saddle Seat, Arms, 18 x 37 In. 715.00
Chair, Windsor, Chicken Coop, 1800 . . . . 135.00
Chair, Windsor, Comb Back, 5 Spindles, Turned Finials, Arms 193.00
Chair, Windsor, Comb Back, 7 Spindles, Saddle Seat, Arms, c.1780, 45 In. 6900.00
Chair, Windsor, Comb Back, Splayed Base, Yoke Crest, Bulbous Legs, Arms, 40 In. 605.00
Chair, Windsor, Comb Back, U-Shaped Back Rail, Stamped I. Lambert, 17 In. 3450.00
Chair, Windsor, Continuous Arms, J. Bertine, N.Y. 6050.00
Chair, Windsor, Elm, Pierced Splat Back, Curved Stretcher 467.00
Chair, Windsor, Fanback, 5 Spindles, Shaped Crest With Ears 525.00
Chair, Windsor, Fanback, 7 Spindles, Red Brown Finish, Splayed Legs, Saddle Seat 1045.00
Chair, Windsor, Fanback, Bulbous Legs, Red Brown Finish, Saddle Seat, 39 In. 440.00
Chair, Windsor, Fanback, Oak, 38 In. 200.00
Chair, Windsor, Fanback, Painted, Serpentine Crest, Carved Handholds, Arms 1955.00
Chair, Windsor, Fanback, Shaped Crest, Splayed Base, Saddle Seat, Shaped Arms 520.00
Chair, Windsor, Fanback, Splayed Base, Turned Legs, Spindle Back, 20 x 41 In. 110.00
Chair, Windsor, Grain Painted, Striping & Stencil, Bamboo Legs, 34 In., Pair 385.00
Chair, Windsor, Hoop Back, 7 Spindles, H-Stretcher, Arms, Philadelphia 1980.00
Chair, Windsor, Hoop Back, 7 Spindles, Saddle Seat, H-Stretcher, Splayed Legs 220.00
Chair, Windsor, Hoop Back, Brace Back, 7 Spindles, Saddle Seat, Scroll Arms 275.00
Chair, Windsor, Looped Back, Elm Wood, Pierced Scroll Splat, Out-Curved Arms 170.00
Chair, Windsor, Oak, Vertical Slats, High Back, Bentwood Arms 150.00
Chair, Windsor, Sack Back, 7 Spindles, Maple, Ash, Arms, 38 In. 2155.00
Chair, Windsor, Sack Back, 7 Spindles, Saddle Seat, Splayed Legs, Black Paint 2300.00
Chair, Windsor, Sack Back, 9 Spindles, Saddle Seat, Black Paint, Late 1800s, Arms 715.00
Chair, Windsor, Sack Back, Black Paint, Early 19th Century 3737.00
Chair, Windsor, Sack Back, Green Paint, Arms, Late 18th Century 1150.00
Chair, Windsor, Sack Back, Knuckle Arms, Early 19th Century 990.00
Chair, Windsor, Sack Back, Tall Legs, Used In Counting House, 19th Century 660.00
Chair, Windsor, Saddle Seat, Continuous Arms 2185.00
Chair, Windsor, Spindle Back, Saddle Seat, Splayed Legs 895.00
Chair, Windsor, Turned, Plank Seat, Arms, 42 In. 220.00
Chair, Windsor, Writing Arm, Comb Back, 5 Spindles, 2 Drawers, Painted, 42 1/2 In. . . . 4025.00
Chair, Wing, Arched Back, Leather, Arms, Bun Feet 1610.00
Chair, Wing, Arched Crest Over Scroll Arms, Upholstered Seat & Back, 47 In. 1500.00
Chair, Wing, Chippendale, Mahogany, Claw & Ball Feet, Brocade, Arms, 41 In. 385.00
Chair, Wing, Chippendale, Mahogany, Straight Legs, 1780 . . . . 2400.00
Chair, Wing, Chippendale, Mahogany, Straight Legs, 43 x 32 In. 4070.00
Chair, Wing, George III, Mahogany, Barrel Back, Out Turned Arms, Cushion Seat 1955.00

Furniture, Chair &
Ottoman, Eames,
No. 670, Rosewood
Veneer, Upholstered

If you move a table, cabinet, or stand, take everything off it first. We once broke a Buffalo Pottery pitcher because we forgot it was out of sight on a shelf beneath a table we moved.

Chair, Wing, George III, Mahogany, Curved Back, Out-Scrolled Arms, 1800	8625.00
Chair, Wing, George III, Mahogany, Leather, 1780s	4025.00
Chair, Wing, Mahogany, Marlborough Legs, Needlepoint, 46 x 34 In.	2420.00
Chair, Wing, Maple, Birch, Ash, Arched Crest, Marlborough Legs, c.1790	2860.00
Chair, Wing, Oak, Down-Scrolled Arms, Upholstered, c.1730, 49 In.	990.00
Chair, Wing, Queen Anne, Out-Scrolled Arms & Seat, Upholstered Back, 46 In.	1300.00
Chair, Wing, Regency, Giltwood, Arched Padded Back, Seat, Pair	1495.00
Chair, Wing, Regency, Giltwood, Button-Tufted Back, Cabriole Legs, Pair	1265.00
Chair, Wing, Regency, Giltwood, Serpentine Carved Rails, Cabriole Legs, Pair	2645.00
Chair, Wing, Teakwood, Upholstered, Arms, Hans Olsen, 40 x 30 x 31 In.	880.00
Chair, Woven Rush Seat, Tubular Brass Frame, Arms, W. Lamb, 32 x 21 1/2 x 19 In. . . .	690.00
Chair, Writing Arm, Windsor, Bamboo, Turned Legs, Plank Seat, Desk Drawer, 37 In. . . .	555.00
Chair, Zigzag, White Enamel, Rietveld, 30 1/4 x 14 x 18 In.	5500.00
Chair & Footstool, Horn Frame, Button Tufted Seat & Back, American	1150.00
Chair & Footstool, Oak, Carved Back, Folding, Victorian, 35 In.	175.00
Chair & Ottoman, Bentwood, Tufted Brown Leather Cushions, Westnofa, Norway	140.00
Chair & Ottoman, Eames, Leather, Molded Rosewood Plywood Shell, Aluminum	3850.00
Chair & Ottoman, Eames, Naugahyde, Aluminum Frame, 26 x 26 x 37 In.	550.00
Chair & Ottoman, Eames, No. 670, Rosewood Veneer, Upholstered . . . .*Illus*	2990.00
Chair & Ottoman, H. Bertoia, Bird, Purple Boucle, Black Wire Base, 37 x 38 In.	1320.00
Chair & Ottoman, H. Bertoia, Bird, Wool, Black Wire Base, Knoll, 39 In.	950.00
Chair & Ottoman, H. Bertoia, Diamond, Welded Steel, Upholstered, Knoll	805.00
Chair & Ottoman, Jacobsen, Egg, Sculptural Fiberglass Shell, Aluminum	2970.00
Chair & Ottoman, P. Paulin, Ribbon, Sculptured, Wool, Wood Base, 1965	1980.00
Chair & Ottoman, Saarinen, Womb, Mauve Jersey, 36 x 39 x 34 In.	1320.00
Chair & Ottoman, Saarinen, Womb, Sculptural Fiberglass, Metal Frame	2200.00
Chair & Ottoman, Womb, Knoll, 1946	2875.00
Chair Set, 2-Tone Wood, Carved, Silk Damask Cushion, China, 38 In., 8 Piece	660.00
Chair Set, Adams Style, Shaped Splat, Cane Seat, 5	415.00
Chair Set, Adams, Mahogany, Padded Medallion Back, Upholstered, 2 Armchairs, 8	2055.00
Chair Set, Andre Arbus, Macassar Ebony, Arched Back, France, 1930, 4 Piece	5175.00
Chair Set, Arrow Back, J. Swint, c.1840, 5	360.00
Chair Set, Arrow Back, Stenciled Design, Leaves & Fruit, Plank Seat, 1830s, 5	1725.00
Chair Set, Art Deco, Rosewood, Upholstered Back, Sides & Seats, France, 3	2300.00
Chair Set, Arts & Crafts, Mission Oak, Folding, Adjustable, 1910, 4	795.00
Chair Set, Arts & Crafts, Vertical Slat Back, Arched Top Rail, 12	1100.00
Chair Set, Baroque Style, Walnut, Arched Padded Back, Upholstered Seat, 6	2875.00
Chair Set, Baroque, Oak, Nailed Leather, Rectangular Back, Continental, 6	3220.00
Chair Set, Baroque, Oak, Turned Legs, Leather, Nailheads, Continental, 6	3220.00
Chair Set, Beechwood, Arched & Padded Back, Saddle Seat, 6	1955.00
Chair Set, Belter, Oak, Shield Back, 2 Armchairs, 10	7475.00
Chair Set, Biedermeier, Flame Mahogany, Upholstered Seat, 1840, 36 In., 4	2000.00
Chair Set, Biedermeier, Fruitwood, Inlay, Slip Seat, Saber Legs, 33 In., 4	345.00
Chair Set, Birch, 3-Tier Spindles, Rush Seat, 2 Armchairs, 1900	2905.00
Chair Set, Blue Fiberglass Shell, Bright Chrome Legs, Ion, Gideon Kramer, 8	1430.00
Chair Set, Bow Back, Cherry, Painted Floral, Saddle Seat, Peter Kramer, 6	400.00
Chair Set, Brown Paint, Yellow & Brown Striping, Stenciled Fruit On Back, 4	875.00
Chair Set, Burl Panel Crest, Carved Borders, Cane Seat, 33 1/2 In., 6	230.00

Chair Set, Charles X, Mahogany, Pierced Trefoil Top Rail, Upholstered Seat, 4 .... 11500.00
Chair Set, Cherry, Saber Leg, 2 Armchairs, 8 .... 550.00
Chair Set, Child's, Table & Upholstered Armchairs, 3 Piece 210.00
Chair Set, Chippendale Style, Mahogany, Upholstered, 20th Century, 6 .... 890.00
Chair Set, Chippendale Style, Needlepoint, 37 In., 2 Armchairs, 8 .... 1144.00
Chair Set, Chippendale, Jas. A. Schoolbred, London, Label, 1920, 47 In., 6 .... 3500.00
Chair Set, Chippendale, Mahogany, Crest, Ribbon Splat, Slip-In Seat, 10 .... 3630.00
Chair Set, Chippendale, Mahogany, Pierced Ribbon Splat, 2 Armchairs, 12 .... 2904.00
Chair Set, Chippendale, Pierced Splat, Upholstered Spring Seat, Nailhead Trim, 3 ...... 330.00
Chair Set, Chippendale, Ribbonback, Upholstered Seat, Fluted Legs, 1 Armchair, 6 .... 528.00
Chair Set, Classical, Mahogany, Reeded Frame, Turned & Reeded Legs, 34 In., 8 ...... 3080.00
Chair Set, E. Wormley, Mahogany, Cane Back & Arms Supports, Dunbar, 6 .... 600.00
Chair Set, E. Wormley, Mahogany, Larsen Upholstery, 39 In., 6 .... 1870.00
Chair Set, E. Wormley, Walnut, Rattan Back, Vinyl Cushion, 8 .... 1430.00
Chair Set, Eames, DCM, Molded Walnut Plywood Seat & Back, Chrome Frame, 4 ...... 825.00
Chair Set, Eames, Eiffel Tower, Black Wire, Screw-On Footpads, Bikini Pads, 1951, 4 ... 1320.00
Chair Set, Eames, Eiffel Tower, Green Fiberglass, White Plastic-Coated Base, 4 .... 1553.00
Chair Set, Eames, Fiberglass, Aluminum, Upholstered, Wheels, Arms, 4 .... 345.00
Chair Set, Eames, Soft Pads, Aluminum Frame, Tilt & Swirl Mechanism, 32 In., 6 ...... 3080.00
Chair Set, Eames, White Molded Fiberglass, Upholstered, Steel, Arms, 4 .... 518.00
Chair Set, Eames, White Molded Fiberglass, Vinyl, Steel, Arms, 6 .... 575.00
Chair Set, Eastlake, Walnut, Spindles, Crest, c.1900, 2 Armchairs, 6 .... 847.00
Chair Set, Elm, Stylized Shell, Rush Seats, Turned Legs, Pad Feet, 1800, 6 .... 6900.00
Chair Set, Empire, Mahogany Veneer, Saber Legs, Slip Seat, Upholstered, 33 In., 6 ..... 495.00
Chair Set, Empire, Mahogany, Upholstered Seat, New York, c.1845, 6 .... 860.00
Chair Set, Empire, Open Carved Crest, Green Slip Seat, c.1850, 6 .... 990.00
Chair Set, Federal Style, Mahogany, Tablet Crest, Trapezoidal Slip Seat, 32 In., 6 ...... 3680.00
Chair Set, Federal, Mahogany, Shield Back, 6 .... 980.00
Chair Set, Federal, Mahogany, Shield Back, Upholstered Seat, 4 .... 1380.00
Chair Set, Federal, Paint & Stencil Design, Spindle Sides, c.1815, 2 Armchairs, 4 .... 805.00
Chair Set, Federal, Shield Back, Black Paint, Upholstered Seat, 4 .... 285.00
Chair Set, Florence Knoll, Swivel, Tufted Tan Leather, White Enamel Arms & Bases, 4 .. 990.00
Chair Set, Fornasetti, Molded Plastic Seat & Back, Metal Frame, 32 In., 6 .... 2090.00
Chair Set, Frankl, Light Oak, Upholstered, Curved X-Shaped Back, 2 Armchairs, 6 ..... 1955.00
Chair Set, French Provincial, Elm, Ladder Back, Rush Seat, 1890, 6 .... 785.00
Chair Set, French Provincial, Fruitwood, Crest, Scalloped Rails, Rush Seat, 1860, 6 ..... 1330.00
Chair Set, French Style, Carved Parcel Gilt Lyre Back, 6 .... 4600.00
Chair Set, Fruitwood, Curved Crest, 2 Rails To Rush Seat, Saber Legs, c.1880, 6 .... 845.00
Chair Set, Fruitwood, Ladder Back, Rush Seat, 1 Armchair, 4 .... 375.00
Chair Set, Fruitwood, Tablet Crest, Backrest Over Square Seat, Border, 6 .... 4025.00
Chair Set, G. Stickley, No. 384 & 386, Oak Spindle, Leather, 8 .... 6900.00
Chair Set, George I, Walnut, Shaped Crest Rail, Front Apron, Cabriole Legs, 5 .... 21850.00
Chair Set, George II, Mahogany, Undulating Ladder Back, Upholstered Seat, 8 .... 4885.00
Chair Set, George II, Walnut, Shell Crest, Shaped Rail, Cabriole Legs, Claw Feet, 6 ..... 14950.00
Chair Set, George III, Leather Slip Seat, 2 Armchairs, 6 .... 1100.00
Chair Set, George III, Mahogany, Carved Flower-Head Crest, Drop-In Seat, 6 .... 2300.00
Chair Set, George III, Mahogany, Stepped Crest, Horizontal Splats, 6 .... 2760.00
Chair Set, George IV, Painted, Concave Crest Rail, Cane Seat & Back, c.1825, 4 .... 2875.00
Chair Set, Georgian, Mahogany, Pierced Balloon Splat, Slip Seat, 2 Armchairs, 36 In., 7 . 1380.00
Chair Set, Giltwood, Rectangular Upholstered Backrest, Bowfront Seat, 4 .... 7475.00
Chair Set, Grain Painted, Stenciling, Curved Back, Center Splat, Zoar Ohio, 32 In., 6 .... 1568.00
Chair Set, Half Spindle, Fruit & Floral Crest, Plank Bottom, 1870s, 5 .... 440.00
Chair Set, Hepplewhite Style, Mahogany, Top Rail, Slat Back, Inlay, Rush Seat, 6 ...... 520.00
Chair Set, Hepplewhite, Mahogany, Pierced Back Splat, Slip Seat, 8 .... 7150.00
Chair Set, Hepplewhite, Mahogany, Shield Back, Needlepoint Slip Seat, 2 Armchairs, 4 .. 715.00
Chair Set, Hitchcock, Ring Turned Uprights, Stenciled Design, Rush Seat, 6 .... 3162.00
Chair Set, J. & J.W. Meeks, Rococo, Laminated Rosewood, Upholstered, 4 .... 8625.00
Chair Set, J. & J.W. Meeks, Rococo, Rosewood, Carved, Upholstered, 1850s, 4 .... 5225.00
Chair Set, Jacobsen, Molded Plywood, Tubular Steel, Nesting, 4 .... 546.00
Chair Set, Jacobsen, Oxford, Black Leather, Tall Back, Chrome Swivel Bases, 4 .... 1980.00
Chair Set, Jean Pascaud, Mahogany, Gray Floral Tapestry, 1930, 10 Piece 8280.00
Chair Set, Ladder Back, Rush Seat, Turned Legs, Stretcher, 1850, 4 .... 300.00
Chair Set, Landi, Perforated Stamped Aluminum, Bent Legs, Hans Coray, 2 .... 575.00

Chair Set, Limbert, No. 1711, 2-Slat Back, Leather Drop-In Seat, 1 Armchair, 10 . . . . 4400.00
Chair Set, Limbert, Single Slat Back, Drop-In Leather Cushion, 4 . . . . 1320.00
Chair Set, Loop Back, Urn Splat, Stenciled Fruit, Pennsylvania, 33 1/2 In., 6 . . . . 1610.00
Chair Set, Louis XIV, Oak, Cabriole Legs, Upholstered Seat, 4 . . . . 1610.00
Chair Set, Louis XV Style, Cane Bottom, 6 . . . . 2000.00
Chair Set, Louis XV, Silk, Cream Paint, Arms, 38 1/2 In., 4 . . . . 2645.00
Chair Set, Louis XVI, Molded Oval Backrest, 2 Back Splats, Upholstered Seat, 4 . . . . 4025.00
Chair Set, Mahogany, Carved Back, Cabriole Legs, China, 1925, 10 . . . . 1150.00
Chair Set, Mahogany, Crest Over Fan Splat, Scrolling Arms, Velvet Cushion, 34 In., 6 . . . 515.00
Chair Set, Mahogany, Ebonized Wood, Leaf Tips Over Back Splat, Upholstered, 6 . . . . . . 7187.00
Chair Set, Mahogany, Garland Carved Crest Rail, Upholstered Seat, 5 . . . . 1840.00
Chair Set, Mahogany, Oval Medallion Pierced Back, Upholstered Seat, 2 Armchairs, 8 . . . 1275.00
Chair Set, Mahogany, Ribbonback, Upholstered, 37 3/4 In., 2 Armchairs, 8 . . . . 2070.00
Chair Set, Mahogany, Shaped Crest Rail & Splat, Trapezoidal Seat, 6 . . . . 285.00
Chair Set, Mahogany, Shaped Crests, Center Splats, Needlepoint Seat, 5 . . . . 85.00
Chair Set, Mahogany, Shield Back, Cross-Stretcher Base, 8 . . . . 473.00
Chair Set, Mahogany, Shield Back, Pierced Splat, Drop-In Seat, 12 . . . . 4600.00
Chair Set, Mahogany, Shield Back, Tapered Grooved Legs, 38 In., 6 . . . . 2200.00
Chair Set, Mahogany, Trefoil Pierced Splats, Curving Rococo Legs, 1850s, 8 . . . . 6900.00
Chair Set, Mahogany, Upholstered Slip Seat, Scroll Carved Splat, 19th Century, 6 . . . . . . 920.00
Chair Set, Margolis, Mahogany, Pierced Splat, Naugahyde Seat, 2 Armchairs, 8 . . . . 6950.00
Chair Set, Masonic Designs, Plank Seat, Arms, 6 . . . . 4800.00
Chair Set, N. Cherner, Molded Walnut Plywood, Plycraft, 2 Armchairs, 6 . . . . 3000.00
Chair Set, Napoleon III, Ebony, Brass Inlay, Leather Backrest, Pilaster Legs, 6 . . . . 10925.00
Chair Set, Neoclassical, Birch, Incurved Backrest, Bowfront Seat, Saber Legs, 4 . . . . 10350.00
Chair Set, Neoclassical, Mahogany, Gilt, Arched Top Rail, Leafy Scrolls, 10 . . . . 36800.00
Chair Set, Oak, Brass Strapwork Mounts, Upholstered Trapezoidal Seat, 6 . . . . 975.00
Chair Set, Oak, Finials Over Padded Backrest, Upholstered Seat, 8 . . . . 2875.00
Chair Set, Oak, Pressed Oak, Slat Back, Cane Seat, 1 Armchair, 4 . . . . 545.00
Chair Set, Oak, Scalloped Crest Rail, Carved Shell Over Shaped Rails, Rush Seat, 6 . . . . 1090.00
Chair Set, Oak, T-Back, Vase-Form Back Slat, Plank Seat, Claw Feet, 6 . . . . 175.00
Chair Set, Painted & Parcel Gilt, Padded Backrest, Cushion Seat, Arms, 1780s, 4 . . . . 6325.00
Chair Set, Philippe Stark, Mahogany, 3 Legs, 1 Aluminum, 34 x 22 x 20 In., 8 . . . . 2310.00
Chair Set, Plank Bottom, Brown Paint, Rose Design Crest & Splat, 6 . . . . 1190.00
Chair Set, Plank Seat, Half Spindle Back, 33 1/2 In., 4 . . . . 110.00
Chair Set, Plank Seat, Stenciled Fruit On Taupe Ground, A. Spitler, 19th Century, 6 . . . . . 1210.00
Chair Set, Poplar, Black & Gold, Bands & Flowers, Pennsylvania, c.1870, 31 In., 6 . . . . . 1400.00
Chair Set, Queen Anne Style, Vase-Form Splat, Rush Seat, 41 1/2 In., 6 Piece 3105.00
Chair Set, Queen Anne, Vase-Form Splat, Knee & Back Shell Carving, 6 . . . . 2540.00
Chair Set, Queen Anne, Vase-Form Splat, Slip Seat, 1 Armchair, 8 . . . . 2145.00
Chair Set, Queen Anne, Vase-Form Splat, Slip Seat, Pad Feet, 4 . . . . 2760.00
Chair Set, Queen Anne, Walnut, 10 . . . . 6325.00
Chair Set, Queen Anne, Walnut, Drop-In Seat, Cabriole Legs, Splayed Feet, 8 . . . . 3450.00
Chair Set, Queen Anne, Walnut, Drop-In Upholstered Seat, 4 Armchairs, England, 7 . . . . 4800.00
Chair Set, Rabbit Ear, Tacked On Leather Seat, 41 In., 8 . . . . 6050.00
Chair Set, Regency, Mahogany, Scroll & Flower Pierced Back Splat, 34 In., 8 . . . . 6900.00
Chair Set, Regency, Mahogany, Troubadour Style, Silk, 34 1/4 In., 4 . . . . 1870.00
Chair Set, Renaissance Revival, Walnut, Arched Crest, Pierced Floral, 1860s, 4 . . . . 1980.00
Chair Set, Robin Day, Stacking, Orange Molded Plastic, Tubular Steel, 4 . . . . 115.00
Chair Set, Rococo, Balloon Back, Carved Crest, Splat, Upholstered Seat, 4 . . . . 400.00
Chair Set, Rococo, Fruitwood, Cartouche Back, Serpentine Seat, Holland, 4 . . . . 9200.00
Chair Set, Rococo, Fruitwood, Serpentine Fronted Upholstered Seat, 4 . . . . 9200.00
Chair Set, Rococo, Rosewood, Balloon, Serpentine Seat, Cabriole Legs, 4 . . . . 1330.00
Chair Set, Rococo, Rosewood, Upholstered Seat, 1 Armchair, 5 . . . . 1150.00
Chair Set, Rococo, Walnut, Balloon Back, Crest, Upholstered Slip Seat, 8 . . . . 745.00
Chair Set, Russel Wright, Folding, Molded Plywood, Metal Frame, Arms, 1940s, 4 . . . . . 2860.00
Chair Set, Sheraton, Curly Maple, Rush Set, 32 1/4 In., 5 . . . . 825.00
Chair Set, Sheraton, Grained, Stencil, Eagle Splat, Balloon Seat, 2 . . . . 1100.00
Chair Set, Sheraton, Pillow Back, Rush Seat, 1 Armchair, 5 . . . . 660.00
Chair Set, Sheraton, Tiger Maple, Cane Seat, 4 . . . . 1600.00
Chair Set, Thonet, Bentwood, Center Splat, Cane Seat, Curved Arms, 1910, 4 . . . . 220.00
Chair Set, Thonet, Bentwood, Vinyl, 33 In., 4 . . . . 95.00
Chair Set, Thumb Back, Bamboo Turnings, 6 . . . . 792.00

Chair Set, Thumb Back, Stencil, Paint, H-Stretcher, 6 . . . . 1430.00
Chair Set, V. Kagan, Chrome Wire Grip Seat, 3 Legs, 34 x 18 x 24 In., 4 . . . . 1320.00
Chair Set, Van Der Rohe, Brno, Chrome Cantilever, Upholstered, 4 . . . . 495.00
Chair Set, Van Der Rohe, Chrome-Plated Steel, Leather, 32 x 19 x 14 In., 6 . . . . 1150.00
Chair Set, Wallace Nutting, No. 393, Ladder Back, New England, Script Brand, 4 . . . . . . 1100.00
Chair Set, Walnut, 4 Pierced Arrow Splats, Woven Cane Seat, Victorian, 4 . . . . 110.00
Chair Set, Walnut, Carved Flower-Head Crest Rail, Square Seat, 6 . . . . 5750.00
Chair Set, Walnut, Spindle Back, Tied Spring Seat, Needlepoint & Fringe, 1900, 6 . . . . . . 2700.00
Chair Set, Walnut, Upholstered Seat, Victorian, 2 Armchairs, 6 . . . . 575.00
Chair Set, Warren McArthur, Tubular Aluminum, Velvet, 16 x 17 In., 4 . . . . 7475.00
Chair Set, Wegner, Teakwood, The Chair, Cane Seat & Back, 30 x 25 In., 6 . . . . 2310.00
Chair Set, Wegner, Y Chair, Bent Oak, Red Lacquer, Cord Seat, 6 . . . . 1380.00
Chair Set, William & Mary, Walnut, Acanthus, Scroll, Center Finial, 56 In., 4 . . . . 7475.00
Chair Set, William IV, Mahogany, Carved Back Rail, Loose Slip Seat, 6 . . . . 2360.00
Chair Set, Windsor, 6 Spindles, Gammon, 4 . . . . 2800.00
Chair Set, Windsor, Brace Back, Nova Scotia, 4 . . . . 3200.00
Chair Set, Windsor, Brace Back, W.D. Brandt, Elm Wood, Plank Seat, 19th Century, 6 . . . 315.00
Chair Set, Windsor, Elm, Turned Round Legs, 4 . . . . 288.00
Chair Set, Windsor, Low Back, Plank Seat, Brown, 4 . . . . 290.00
Chair Set, Windsor, Maple, 4 Arrow-Shaped Stiles, Saddle Seat, 4 . . . . 138.00
Chair Set, Windsor, Painted & Stenciled Leaf & Berry, 33 1/4 In., 4 . . . . 862.00
Chair Set, Windsor, Yew Wood, Ash, Spindled Hoop Back, 19th Century, 8 . . . . 6900.00
Chair-Table, David Blomberg, Satinwood, 5 Drawers, Upholstered Chair, 1929 . . . . 3220.00
Chair-Table, Green Over Red, Scrub Top, Mid-19th Century, 49 1/2 x 27 In. 4250.00
Chair-Table, Leather, Lift Top, Velvet-Lined Interior, Shaped Legs, 31 1/4 In. 2530.00
Chair-Table, Pine, 29 x 34 In. 325.00
Chair-Table, Telephone, Stickley Brothers, Paper Label 632.00
Chaise Longue, Bruno Mathesson, Bentwood Frame, Continuous Seat, 1936, 31 In. 2300.00
Chaise Longue, Chippendale, Mahogany, Canted Upholstered Back & Arms, 75 x 34 In. . 1265.00
Chaise Longue, E. Wormley, Listen-To-Me, Walnut, Upholstered, 72 In. 13200.00
Chaise Longue, E. Wormley, Mahogany, Curved Velvet Seat, 32 In., Pair 2310.00
Chaise Longue, E. Wormley, Mahogany, Tilt Back, Upholstered, 27 In., Pair 1320.00
Chaise Longue, Eames, Segmented Leather Cushions, Herman Miller, 1968, 29 In. 4125.00
Chaise Longue, Eames, Softpad, Leather, Aluminum Base 1380.00
Chaise Longue, Empire, Mahogany, Scroll Crest Rail, Padded Back, Arms, 84 In. 1150.00
Chaise Longue, Fabio Lenci, Glass Sides, Leather Roll Seat, 1970, 36 x 24 In., Pair 4400.00
Chaise Longue, Fabio Lenci, Leather Rolled Sling, Plate Glass, 48 x 28 In., Pair 4025.00
Chaise Longue, Frankl, Bamboo, Upholstered, Child's, 24 x 42 x 25 In. 1650.00
Chaise Longue, Frankl, Curved Lacquered Arms, Frame, Loose Cushions, 30 x 24 In. . . . 660.00
Chaise Longue, Frankl, Leather, Wool Seat & Back, 1930s, 28 In. 2200.00
Chaise Longue, Fritz Hansen, Arabesque, Wool, Folke Jansson, 33 x 27 In. 5500.00
Chaise Longue, G. Nakashima, Walnut, Webbed, Free-Edge Arms, 70 In. 13200.00
Chaise Longue, Girard, Aluminum Legs, U-Shaped Naugahyde Seat, 26 x 26 In., Pair . . . 2875.00
Chaise Longue, Joe Columbo, Plywood, 3 Interlocking Segments, 22 5/8 In., Pair 2760.00
Chaise Longue, Joe Columbo, Upholstered, Rectangular Cushions, 26 In. 6325.00
Chaise Longue, Kem Weber, Airline, Maple, Ash, Vinyl, 25 x 33 In. 13200.00
Chaise Longue, Kem Weber, Chrome Metal, Leather Cushions, Wood Arms, 1934 . . . . 4400.00
Chaise Longue, Kem Weber, Knockdown Construction, 1940s, 23 x 26 x 33 In., Pair 3300.00
Chaise Longue, Kem Weber, Tubular Chromed Metal, Leather Cushions, 28 In. 4000.00
Chaise Longue, L-Shaped Upholstered Back, Brass Scrolling, 56 1/4 In. 8050.00
Chaise Longue, Laverne, Tufted Leather, Chrome Base, X-Stretcher, 28 x 28 In., Pair 935.00
Chaise Longue, Louis XV Style, Upholstered, 62 In. 775.00
Chaise Longue, Marcel Breuer, Plywood Seat, Bentwood Frame, Cushion, 1937, 55 In. . . 6050.00
Chaise Longue, Mediterranean Style, Walnut Frame, Upholstered 155.00
Chaise Longue, P. Paulin, Upholstered, Tubular Steel, Chrome Base, Pivoting 575.00
Chaise Longue, Rattan, Multiple Bent Rattan Bands, 1940, 29 1/2 In. 1155.00
Chaise Longue, Risom, Birch Frame, Leather Strapping, 21 x 26 x 29 In. 1540.00
Chaise Longue, Risom, Wood, Angular Frame, Webbed 805.00
Chaise Longue, Rosewood, Brass Rosettes, 3 Bolsters, 3 Loose Cushions, 83 In. 2400.00
Chaise Longue, Russel Wright, American Modern, Maple, Slats, Vinyl 1380.00
Chaise Longue, Russel Wright, Solid Angular Wood Arms & Frame, Vinyl 748.00
Chaise Longue, Saarinen, Womb, Bent Chrome Base, Velvet 1035.00
Chaise Longue, V. Panton, Chrome Arms, Tufted, 28 x 36 In., Pair 770.00

Furniture, Chaise Longue,
Van Keppel & Green, Tubular Frame,
Upholstered, c.1954, 74 In.

Old finishes on furniture may dry out, and changes in temperature and humidity may cause fine hairline cracks in furniture finish. Paste wax can cover this checking or cracking. Use the paste wax as it suggests on the package, then rub with a soft cloth.

Chaise Longue, Van Keppel & Green, Enameled Tubular Steel Frame, 1947, 20 In. 2310.00
Chaise Longue, Van Keppel & Green, Sun-Lounge, Steel Base, Upholstered, 82 x 20 In. . 1380.00
Chaise Longue, Van Keppel & Green, Tubular Frame, Upholstered, c.1954, 74 In. . . .*Illus* 2875.00
Chaise Longue, W. Plattner, Black Wire Base, Mohair, Knoll, 39 x 40 In. 520.00
Chaise Longue, Walnut, Carved Acanthus Leaf, Upholstered, Victorian, 72 In. 275.00
Chaise Longue, Walnut, Upholstered Seat & Back, Panel Arms, Victorian, 35 In. 210.00
Chaise Longue, Warren McArthur, Tubular Aluminum, Channeled Sling Seat, 1930s 4950.00
Chaise Longue, Wegner, Sculptural Wood Frame, Upholstered, Arms, Pair 805.00
Chaise Longue, Wegner, Tubular Steel Legs, Upholstered, 23 1/2 x 18 In. 1035.00
Chaise Longue, Woodard, Aluminum Frame, Tufted, 55 x 24 x 28 In. 770.00
Chaise Longue & Ottoman, Eames, No. 670, Bent Laminated Rosewood, Leather 2990.00
Chaise Longue & Ottoman, Lloyd, Chromed Tubular Steel, Upholstered 1035.00
Chaise Longue & Ottoman, Saarinen, Womb, Wool, 34 x 38 x 36 In. 1650.00
Chest, 2 Small Back Drawers, 3 Reverse-Graduated Drawers, Child's, 15 1/2 In. 295.00
Chest, 3 Drawers, 2 Glove Drawers, Gallery, Painted, Quebec, Child's, 24 In. 1240.00
Chest, 3 Drawers, Marble Top, Carved Pulls, Victorian 275.00
Chest, 4 Drawers, Overhanging Top Drawer, Backsplash, Black & Red Paint, 42 In. 748.00
Chest, 4 Graduated Beaded-Edge Drawers, Columns, Cookie Corner Top, 41 In. 1670.00
Chest, 12 Drawers Side-By-Side, Red & Black Grain Painted, Putty Front, 34 In. 1320.00
Chest, Bachelor's, Burl Veneer, 5 Drawers, Pullout Shelf, Original Brasses, 35 In. 1980.00
Chest, Bachelor's, Chippendale, Mahogany, Crossbanded Burl Veneer, 26 x 16 In. 550.00
Chest, Bachelor's, Georgian, Walnut, Banded Folded Top, 4 Drawers, 28 x 25 In. 665.00
Chest, Bamboo, Allover Woven Bamboo Surface, Cracked Ice, 19th Century 8625.00
Chest, Biedermeier, Mahogany, Germany, 33 1/2 x 47 1/4 x 23 1/2 In. 3220.00
Chest, Biedermeier, Walnut, 2 Short Over 2 Long Drawers, Green Marble Top, 29 In. 1210.00
Chest, Biedermeier-Style, Cherry, 4 Graduated Drawers, Inlay, Ebonized, 42 In. 2080.00
Chest, Birch, Portsmouth, c.1800, 39 In. 4500.00
Chest, Bird's-Eye Maple, 2 Over 4 Drawers, Step-Down, 45 In. 2360.00
Chest, Blanket, 2 Drawers, Brasses, Handmade Iron Lock & Key, Iron Hinges, 1788 . . . . 7750.00
Chest, Blanket, 4 Drawers, Red Grain Painted, 19th Century 786.00
Chest, Blanket, 6-Board, Red, Black, Swirled Paint, Molded Top, 24 3/4 In. 805.00
Chest, Blanket, Camphorwood, Brassbound, Lift Top, 18 x 36 x 20 In. 1045.00
Chest, Blanket, Cherry, Inlay Medallions, 2 Pinwheels, Diamond Inlay, 1820s 1650.00
Chest, Blanket, Cherry, Turned Feet, Impressed Ash, Inscription, 17 x 10 x 11 In. 550.00
Chest, Blanket, Chippendale, Maple, 2 Drawers, Cotter Pins, 39 x 33 x 16 1/2 In. 1095.00
Chest, Blanket, Chippendale, Painted Design, Tulips, 1800, 23 x 51 x 22 In. 2750.00
Chest, Blanket, Chippendale, Pine, Poplar, Ogee Feet, Till & Lid, 45 x 18 x 26 In. 440.00
Chest, Blanket, Dovetailed Drawer, Blue Paint, 34 3/4 x 17 1/4 x 34 In. 2530.00
Chest, Blanket, Federal, Pine, Drawer, Turned Wood Pulls, Bracket Base 400.00
Chest, Blanket, Grain Painted, Panel Ends, 1840, 24 x 38 x 19 In. 2035.00
Chest, Blanket, Hepplewhite, Cherry, Inlay, 40 x 17 x 23 In. 1375.00
Chest, Blanket, Lift Top, 2 Drawers, Pine, Grain Painted, Scroll Apron, 42 x 41 x 18 In. . . 1540.00
Chest, Blanket, Lift Top, 3 Base Drawers, Till & Well, 19th Century, 51 1/4 In. 4205.00
Chest, Blanket, Lift Top, Paint Design, 2 False Lip Drawers Over 2 Drawers, 1820 . . . . . . 1100.00
Chest, Blanket, Lift Top, Pine, 2 Drawers, 18th Century, 44 3/4 x 36 1/2 x 19 In. 1495.00
Chest, Blanket, Lift Top, Pine, 2 Drawers, Turned Legs, 40 x 42 x 18 In. 355.00
Chest, Blanket, Lift Top, Walnut, 3 Drawers, Ogee Bracket Feet, c.1770, 31 x 48 In. 8800.00

Chest, Blanket, Line & Flowers, Tulips, Hanover, Pennsylvania, 1850, 49 x 27 x 22 In. . . 16500.00
Chest, Blanket, Oak, Mahogany Inlay Border On Top, 2 Drawers, 25 x 45 x 21 In. 690.00
Chest, Blanket, Oak, Relief-Carved Geometric Designs, Cutout Feet, England, 44 In. 360.00
Chest, Blanket, Painted Design, Straight Bracket Feet, John Shellenberger 1847 . . . . 1155.00
Chest, Blanket, Paul Kramer, Bird's-Eye Maple, Painted, Intaglio Arched Reserves 805.00
Chest, Blanket, Pine, 1-Board Top, Square Corner Post, Till, 39 x 19 x 24 In. 495.00
Chest, Blanket, Pine, 2 Drawers, Yellow & Brown Paint, 19th Century, 39 x 40 In. 2070.00
Chest, Blanket, Pine, 6-Board, Overlapping Drawer, Blue Paint, 36 x 15 x 31 In. 990.00
Chest, Blanket, Pine, 6-Board, Red Paint, Till With Lid, 42 In. 440.00
Chest, Blanket, Pine, Fishtail Strap Hinges, Till, Painted, Pennsylvania, 22 x 21 49 In. . . .   770.00
Chest, Blanket, Pine, Grain Painted, Interior Till, Bun Feet, 19th Century 440.00
Chest, Blanket, Pine, Grained, Bracket Feet, Dovetailed, Till, 48 5/8 x 22 1/2 In. 290.00
Chest, Blanket, Pine, Mahogany Graining, 2-Drawer Till, 37 5/8 x 21 x 24 In. 410.00
Chest, Blanket, Pine, Poplar, Dovetailed Case, Bracket Feet, Till, 18 3/4 In. 440.00
Chest, Blanket, Pine, Poplar, Grain Painted, Drawers, Till, Pa., 49 x 21 x 28 In. 440.00
Chest, Blanket, Pine, Poplar, Painted, Molded Edge Lid & Till, 48 x 20 x 26 In. 220.00
Chest, Blanket, Pine, Red Vinegar Paint, Yellow Ground, 24 1/2 In. 935.00
Chest, Blanket, Pine, Red, Dovetailed, Edge Moldings, Till, 48 3/4 x 20 x 29 In. 275.00
Chest, Blanket, Pine, Shaped Skirt, Rosehead Nails, Strap Hinges, c.1780, 25 x 49 In. . . . 2200.00
Chest, Blanket, Pine, Till & Secret Drawer, Painted Abstract Design, 17 x 43 In. 1380.00
Chest, Blanket, Pine, Till With Lid, Dovetailed Bracket Feet, 37 1/4 In. 275.00
Chest, Blanket, Pine, Till, Hinges, Bottom Board, 19th Century 110.00
Chest, Blanket, Pine, Wrought-Iron Lock, Bracket Feet 605.00
Chest, Blanket, Pine, Wrought-Iron Strap Hinges, End Handles, Continental, 37 1/2 In. . .   220.00
Chest, Blanket, Poplar, 2 Drawers, Red & Black Paint, Bracket Feet, 37 x 42 In. 1380.00
Chest, Blanket, Poplar, 6-Board, Red Paint, Cutout Feet, 42 x 17 x 24 In. 330.00
Chest, Blanket, Poplar, Bracket Feet, Dovetailed, Red Paint, Till, 50 x 23 x 23 In. 410.00
Chest, Blanket, Poplar, Dovetailed, Catharina Fidler, Pennsylvania, 44 x 20 x 27 In. 575.00
Chest, Blanket, Poplar, Dovetailed, Iron Lock & Strap Hinges, Till, 48 x 19 x 22 In. 165.00
Chest, Blanket, Poplar, Grain Painted, 1860, 23 x 40 x 19 In. 440.00
Chest, Blanket, Poplar, Red Paint, 30 3/4 x 17 1/4 x 19 In. 495.00
Chest, Blanket, Poplar, Red Paint, Pencil, Chalk Design On Lid, 20 3/4 In. 440.00
Chest, Blanket, Poplar, Red Paint, Till, Lid, 42 3/4 x 20 x 24 In.   330.00
Chest, Blanket, Queen Anne, 2 Lipped Drawers, Blue Paint, 1780, 28 x 50 x 24 In. 1540.00
Chest, Blanket, Shaker, Butternut, Painted, 43 x 42 x 18 In. . . . .*Illus* 1840.00
Chest, Blanket, Sheraton, Cherry, Paneled, Till, Lid, 44 x 18 x 28 In. 880.00
Chest, Blanket, Side Compartment Over Drawers, Ocher Paint, 27 x 37 x 22 In. 805.00
Chest, Blanket, Softwood, Bracket Feet, Red Wash, c.1810, 21 x 45 In. 345.00
Chest, Blanket, Sponge Design, Brown Over Yellow Paint 700.00
Chest, Blanket, Sponge Design, Molded Edge, Dovetailed Box, Mustard, Glen Rock 550.00
Chest, Blanket, Tulips Each End, Ocher Paint, Pennsylvania 16500.00
Chest, Blanket, Walnut, Dovetailed Bracket Feet, 43 x 19 x 82 In. 495.00
Chest, Blanket, Walnut, Initials & Date, Till, Lid, Pennsylvania, 56 x 24 x 26 In. 715.00
Chest, Blanket, Walnut, Square Corner Post, Paneled, 37 x 16 x 23 In. 425.00
Chest, Blanket, Walnut, Till, Lid, Wrought-Iron Strap Hinges, 29 x 14 x 14 In. 770.00
Chest, Bowfront, Chippendale Style, 4 Drawers, Bracket Base, 34 x 19 x 34 In. 490.00
Chest, Bowfront, Chippendale, Burl Walnut, 4 Graduated Drawers, 37 1/2 In. 4510.00
Chest, Bowfront, Federal, 2 Short, 3 Long Drawers, Beaded Edges, String Inlay 1210.00
Chest, Bowfront, Federal, Mahogany, 4 Drawers, Scalloped Apron, Turned Legs, 1830 . . . 1320.00
Chest, Bowfront, Federal, Mahogany, Four Cock-Beaded Drawers, 1795, 33 1/2 In. 3737.00
Chest, Bowfront, Mahogany Veneer, 4 Drawers, Edge Beading, 37 In. 2200.00
Chest, Bowfront, Mahogany, 2 Over 3 Drawers, Beaded Edge, Turned Legs, 42 In. 1035.00
Chest, Bowfront, Mahogany, 4 Cock-Beaded Graduated Drawers, 45 x 47 In. 1008.00
Chest, Burl Walnut Veneer, 3 Drawers 2 Sides, Side Lock, Hinged Door, 19th Century . . . 1045.00
Chest, Calamander, 2 Drawers Over 2 Doors, Indian Export, 41 1/2 In. 2300.00
Chest, Campaign, Brassbound, Oriental, 24 x 39 In. 172.00
Chest, Campaign, Camphorwood, Secretaire Drawer, 3 Drawers, Brassbound, 44 In. 3737.00
Chest, Campaign, Mahogany, 2 Short Over 3 Cock-Beaded Drawers, England, 40 In. 2860.00
Chest, Campaign, Mahogany, 2 Short Over 3 Long Drawers, England, 19th Century 825.00
Chest, Campaign, Mahogany, Drawer, Brass Trim, Lift-Out Tray, 31 x 18 x 19 In. 385.00
Chest, Campaign, Padouk, Upper 2 Short Over Deep Drawer, 2 Piece, 1860s, 41 In. 4312.00
Chest, Camphorwood, Brass Binding, China, 19th Century, 20 x 41 x 22 In. 525.00
Chest, Camphorwood, Brass Corner Plate & Handles, Teakwood Stand, 1850s, 28 In. 1900.00

Furniture, Chest,
Blanket, Shaker,
Butternut, Painted,
43 x 42 x 18 In.

Furniture, Chest,
Chippendale, Pine,
4 Drawers, Painted,
28 x 24 x 12 In.

Chest, Camphorwood, Floral Design, Leather Cover, Brassbound, 30 1/2 In. 550.00
Chest, Camphorwood, Lift Top, Brass Carrying Handles, China, 18 x 39 In. 1072.00
Chest, Camphorwood, Lift Top, Leather Cover, Brass Studs, China, 22 x 42 x 21 In. 330.00
Chest, Cedar, Lane, Mahogany, Shell Carvings Over Skirt 275.00
Chest, Cedar, Lift Top, Paneled, 24 3/4 x 49 x 27 1/4 In. 45.00
Chest, Cherry, 4 Dovetailed Drawers, Turned Feet, 20 x 21 x 25 In. 3520.00
Chest, Cherry, Walnut & Locust Inlay, Carl Stotts 8800.00
Chest, Chippendale, Birch, 6 Thumb-Molded Graduated Drawers, 1780, 51 In. 3105.00
Chest, Chippendale, Cherry, 4 Beaded Drawers, c.1790, 35 x 38 In. 2600.00
Chest, Chippendale, Cherry, 4 Graduated Drawers, 2-Board Top, 34 1/2 In. 2070.00
Chest, Chippendale, Cherry, 4 Graduated Drawers, Serpentine Top, c.1780, 38 x 41 In. 6325.00
Chest, Chippendale, Cherry, 4 Overlapping Dovetailed Drawers, Ogee Feet, 34 In. 3630.00
Chest, Chippendale, Cherry, 5 Graduated Drawers, Reeded Columns, 42 x 36 In. 1265.00
Chest, Chippendale, Curly Maple, 4 Graduated Drawers, 42 x 37 In. 2420.00
Chest, Chippendale, Mahogany, 2 Short & 3 Long Drawers, Cedar Lined, 1790, 34 In. 1936.00
Chest, Chippendale, Mahogany, 4 Drawers, Bracket Feet, 34 x 26 x 17 In. 220.00
Chest, Chippendale, Mahogany, 4 Drawers, Serpentine, 36 x 21 x 33 In. 770.00
Chest, Chippendale, Mahogany, 5 Lipped Drawers, Pierced Front Bracket Feet, 14 In. ... 875.00
Chest, Chippendale, Pine, 3 Graduated Drawers, Bracket Feet, 35 1/2 x 16 x 35 In. 230.00
Chest, Chippendale, Pine, 4 Drawers, Painted, 28 x 24 x 12 In. .... *Illus* 3540.00
Chest, Chippendale, Pine, 6 Graduated Drawers, Brown Paint, 73 In. 1725.00
Chest, Chippendale, Pine, Oak, Mahogany Facade, 4 Drawers, England, 29 x 36 In. 1540.00
Chest, Chippendale, Tiger Maple, 2-Drawer Base, 3 Recessed Panels 495.00
Chest, Chippendale, Tiger Maple, 4 Drawers, 30 x 36 x 16 In. 1430.00
Chest, Chippendale, Tiger Maple, 4 Graduated Drawers, New England, 19th Century 4887.00
Chest, Chippendale, Tiger Maple, 6 Graduated Drawers, Cornice, David T. Smith 2070.00
Chest, Chippendale, Walnut, 2 Short & 3 Long Drawers, c.1770, 37 1/2 x 39 In. 3450.00
Chest, Chippendale, Walnut, 3 Short & 5 Graduated Drawers, Pennsylvania, 56 x 62 In. ... 3025.00
Chest, Chippendale, Walnut, 4 Graduated Drawers, Ogee Bracket Feet, 34 3/4 In. 5000.00
Chest, Chippendale, Walnut, 5 Overlapping Drawers, 36 x 37 In. 3025.00
Chest, Classical, Mahogany, 5 Drawers, Acanthus & Reeded Stiles, Paw Feet, 45 In. 440.00
Chest, Cowry, Painted Design, Pennsylvania 3450.00
Chest, Crotch Mahogany, 4 Drawers, Glove Box 440.00
Chest, Cushion Frieze Drawer Over 2 Short & 3 Long Drawers, c.1840, 49 In. 1090.00
Chest, Dome Top, Wallpaper Lined, Iron Lock, Chip Carved, 1804, 6 In. 895.00
Chest, Dower, Eagle, Banner, Shield Front, Centre County, Pennsylvania, 1814 .... 12500.00
Chest, Dower, Pine, Lift Top, 3 Drawers, Ditty Box, Strap Hinges, 49 1/2 In. 990.00
Chest, Dowry, Samuel Grebiel, Pennsylvania, 1799, 23 1/2 x 48 1/2 In. 3450.00
Chest, E. Wheeler, Cherry, Graduated Tiger Maple Drawers, Bracket Feet 1760.00
Chest, E. Wormley, Chocolate Lacquer, 3 Light Veneer Drawers, 42 x 34 x 18 In. 1495.00
Chest, Eames, ESU 200, 3 Drawers, Black Laminate Top, Zinc Frame, 47 x 16 In. 11000.00
Chest, Empire Style, 3 Drawers, Marble Top, Bun Feet, 40 x 18 1/2 x 33 1/2 In. 115.00
Chest, Empire Style, Overlapping Drawers, Grain Painted, 48 In. 700.00
Chest, Empire, Cherry, 2 Over 3 Drawers, Ebonized, 21 x 39 x 47 In. 495.00
Chest, Empire, Cherry, 4 Dovetailed Drawers, Turned Feet, Pilasters, 22 x 42 x 47 In. ... 410.00
Chest, Empire, Cherry, Curly Maple Veneer Drawer Fronts, Step-Back Top, 50 In. 525.00
Chest, Empire, Cherry, Curly Maple, 3 Drawers, 11 x 21 x 19 In. 2090.00

Furniture, Chest,
Federal, Cherry,
4 Graduated Drawers,
String Inlay, 42 In.

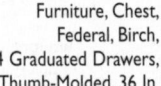

Furniture, Chest,
Federal, Birch,
4 Graduated Drawers,
Thumb-Molded, 36 In.

Chest, Empire, Cherry, Curly Maple, 4 Dovetailed Drawers, 47 3/4 In. 770.00
Chest, Empire, Cherry, Curly Maple, 4 Drawers, S-Pilasters, 43 x 47 In. 935.00
Chest, Empire, Cherry, Curly Maple, Bird's-Eye Maple, 6 Drawers, 49 In. 825.00
Chest, Empire, Cherry, Poplar, 4 Dovetailed Drawers, Swirled Knobs, 40 x 45 In. 495.00
Chest, Empire, Cherry, Poplar, 5 Dovetailed Drawers, 42 x 47 In. 605.00
Chest, Empire, Flame Mahogany Veneer, Dovetailed Drawers, c.1830, Miniature 1295.00
Chest, Empire, Mahogany, 5 Dovetailed Drawers, Acanthus Half Columns, 46 In. 495.00
Chest, Empire, Mahogany, 6 Drawers, Step Back, Carved Pineapple Columns 470.00
Chest, Empire, Poplar, Cherry, 3 Dovetailed Drawers, 43 x 19 x 34 In. 385.00
Chest, Empire, Rupp, 3 Graduated Drawers, Bonnet Drawer, Painted 935.00
Chest, Faux Bamboo, Tilt Mirror, Side Lock, c.1900 . . . . 7500.00
Chest, Federal, 4 Graduated Bird's-Eye Panel Drawers, Original Brasses, 1810 . . . . 1495.00
Chest, Federal, Birch, 2 Over 3 Drawers, Brasses, 19th Century 2070.00
Chest, Federal, Birch, 4 Graduated Drawers, Thumb-Molded, 36 In. . . . .*Illus* 1610.00
Chest, Federal, Bowfront, Cherry, 4 Graduated Drawers, 42 x 20 x 39 In. 1540.00
Chest, Federal, Bowfront, Mahogany Veneer, 4 Dovetailed Drawers, 41 x 24 x 39 In. 1265.00
Chest, Federal, Bowfront, Mahogany, 4 Drawers, Satinwood Inlay, 38 x 43 x 22 In. 2185.00
Chest, Federal, Bowfront, Mahogany, Walnut, Inlaid Drawers, 1780, 38 x 35 In. 2970.00
Chest, Federal, Cherry, 4 Graduated Drawers, String Inlay, 42 In. . . . .*Illus* 2900.00
Chest, Federal, Cherry, 5 Dovetailed Drawers, Inlay, 40 x 23 x 41 In. 1405.00
Chest, Federal, Figured Maple, 2 Over 3 Graduated Drawers, 41 x 42 x 19 In. 1650.00
Chest, Federal, Mahogany Veneer, 4 Dovetailed & 2 Step-Back Drawers, Crest, 47 In. . . . 550.00
Chest, Federal, Mahogany Veneer, 4 Drawers, D-Shape, J.U. Drew, Norwalk, O., 45 In. . . 1760.00
Chest, Federal, Mahogany, 4 Drawers, Turned Base, 19th Century 275.00
Chest, Federal, Mahogany, 4 Inlaid Graduated Drawers, Turned Legs, 43 3/4 In. 1150.00
Chest, Federal, Mahogany, Backsplash, Stylized Pineapple, Reeded Columns, 44 In. 880.00
Chest, Federal, Mahogany, Paw Feet, c.1815 . . . . 1092.00
Chest, Federal, Maple, Birch, 4 Drawers, Beading, 40 In. . . . .*Illus* 2185.00
Chest, Federal, Satinwood, 4 Drawers, Mahogany Inlay 2990.00
Chest, Federal, Tiger Maple, 4 Graduated Drawers, Rectangular Top, 1790, 37 In. 4880.00
Chest, Federal, Walnut, 4 Drawers, French Feet, c.1800, 39 1/2 In. 2310.00
Chest, G. Nakashima, 4 Drawers, Free-Edge, Dovetailed Top, 32 x 36 x 21 In. 7150.00
Chest, G. Nelson, Dark Walnut, 4 Drawers, White Door, No. 5211, 10 x 20 x 13 In. 5225.00
Chest, G. Nelson, Walnut, 3 Drawers, Door, Aluminum Pulls, 30 x 56 x 19 In. 2200.00
Chest, G. Nelson, Walnut, 4 Long Drawers, Herman Miller, 34 x 18 x 27 In., Pair 805.00
Chest, G. Stickley, 9 Drawers, Backsplash, Wood Pulls, Paper Label, 50 In. 8800.00
Chest, G. Stickley, Mahogany, Square Top Over Drawer, Shelf, 16 x 28 In. 7700.00
Chest, G. Stickley, No. 906, 2 Half Over 4 Full Drawers, Copper Straps, 48 In. 12100.00
Chest, G. Stickley, No. 913, Mahogany, 3 Drawers, Arched Toe Board, 47 In. 15400.00
Chest, George I, Walnut, 2 Short & 3 Long Crossbanded Drawers, Bracket Feet, 34 In. . . . 5462.00
Chest, George II, Mahogany, 2 Short Over 3 Long Drawers, 31 3/4 In. 3450.00
Chest, George II, Oak, Veneer, Brass Bail Handles, 35 1/2 x 35 1/2 x 20 1/2 In. 1345.00
Chest, George II, Walnut, Crossbanded Rectangular Top, 2 Drawers, 39 x 38 1/2 In. 3162.00
Chest, George III, Bowfront, Mahogany, 3 Graduated Cock-Beaded Drawers, 37 In. 750.00
Chest, George III, Mahogany, 2 Cock-Beaded Drawers, Ogee Bracket Feet, 47 In. 2415.00
Chest, George III, Mahogany, 2 Short & 3 Long Drawers, Ebony Inlay, 40 In. 1320.00
Chest, George III, Mahogany, 4 Drawers, Molded Top, Ogee Feet, 33 x 38 x 20 In. 1495.00
Chest, George III, Mahogany, Boxwood, 2 Over 3 Drawers, Inlay, 1800, 41 x 36 In. 1380.00
Chest, George III, Oak, 5 Graduated Drawers, Rectangular Top, 63 x 21 In. 4600.00

Chest, George IV, Veneer, Figured Calamander, Brass Mount, 1840, 33 x 39 x 19 In. 1815.00
Chest, Georgian Style, 4 Drawers, Reverse Serpentine Front, Plinth Base, 30 In. 115.00
Chest, Georgian, Mahogany, 2 Short Drawers & 3 Long Graduated Drawers, 53 In. 968.00
Chest, Georgian, Mahogany, 2 Short Drawers Over 2 Long Drawers, 1820, 31 In. 1028.00
Chest, Georgian, Pine, 3 Graduated Drawers, Bracket Feet, 1810, 31 x 34 x 19 In. 575.00
Chest, Hepplewhite Style, Bowfront, Mahogany Veneer, 4 Drawers, Mirror, 30 In. 550.00
Chest, Hepplewhite, Bowfront, Birch, Flame Veneer Drawers, 38 x 21 x 34 In. 2200.00
Chest, Hepplewhite, Bowfront, Cherry, 4 Dovetailed Drawers, 43 x 44 x 39 In. 3025.00
Chest, Hepplewhite, Bowfront, Rosewood, 5 Drawers, 41 1/2 In. 2588.00
Chest, Hepplewhite, Bowfront, Tiger Maple, 4 Cock-Beaded Drawers, 1800s, 39 In. 4830.00
Chest, Hepplewhite, Cherry, 2 Short Over 3 Long Drawers, Inlay, Tambour, 58 x 40 In. .. 6050.00
Chest, Hepplewhite, Cherry, 3 Dovetailed Drawers, 1-Board Top, 17 x 12 x 18 In. 4180.00
Chest, Hepplewhite, Cherry, 4 Drawers, Rope Banded, 18 x 38 x 42 In. 2255.00
Chest, Hepplewhite, Cherry, 4 Graduated Drawers, Inlay, 21 x 38 x 39 In. 2530.00
Chest, Hepplewhite, Cherry, Pine, 4 Drawers, Beaded, 41 1/2 In. 1935.00
Chest, Hepplewhite, Mahogany Veneer, 4 Beaded Drawers, Crossbanded, 40 In. 1100.00
Chest, Hepplewhite, Mahogany, 4 Cock-Beaded Drawers, French Feet, 38 x 37 In. 440.00
Chest, Hepplewhite, Mahogany, 4 Graduated Beaded Drawers, French Feet, 41 In. 2750.00
Chest, Hepplewhite, Walnut, 4 Drawers, Paneled Sides, Bracket Feet, 42 1/2 In. 605.00
Chest, Hepplewhite, Walnut, 4 Graduated Dovetailed Drawers, Pennsylvania, 53 x 38 In. .. 3300.00
Chest, Hinoki Wood, Stained Finish, 2 Drawers, Checkered Top, Handles, Japan, c.1890 . 330.00
Chest, Immigrant's, Pine, Dovetailed Brown Paint, R.A.P. 1866, 33 x 16 x 15 In. 235.00
Chest, Immigrant's, Pine, Red Paint, 2 Blue Panels, Tulip Design, 1849, 30 In. 165.00
Chest, Inlaid Whale Ivory, Lemon Wood, Inlaid Stars Doves On Hinged Lid, 72 In. 5750.00
Chest, Jacobean Style, Oak, 4 Drawers, Carved Frieze, Vase-Form Design, 45 x 39 In. ... 1150.00
Chest, Jewel, Mahogany, 4 Drawers, Side Lock, 13 1/2 x 15 1/2 In. 150.00
Chest, John Stuart, 2 Short Over 2 Long Drawers, 49 1/2 In. 460.00
Chest, Louis XV Style, Mahogany, 5 Drawers, Marquetry, Marble Top, 42 In. 770.00
Chest, Louis XV Style, Serpentine Front, Overall Gilt Design, 32 x 17 x 33 In., Pair 1095.00
Chest, Louis XV, Gilt Metal, Marble, Painted Reserve, 1860, 35 x 35 x 16 In. 1725.00
Chest, Louis XVI Style, Lift Top, Floral & Figural Design, On Stand, 35 In. 575.00
Chest, Mahogany, 2 Drawers Over Blind Drawer, John Webster, 1869, 12 1/4 In. 875.00
Chest, Mahogany, 3 Graduated Drawers, Bracket Feet, Victorian, 12 In. 374.00
Chest, Mahogany, 4 Drawers, Dovetailed Construction, c.1840, 13 1/2 x 12 3/8 In. 995.00
Chest, Mahogany, 4 Drawers, Shell Carved Block Front, Baker Co., 34 3/4 In. 805.00
Chest, Mahogany, 6 Drawers, Band Inlay, Ivory Pulls, Escutcheons, 11 x 12 In. 1495.00
Chest, Mahogany, Marble Top, Mid-19th Century, 39 1/2 x 44 x 22 In. 545.00
Chest, Mahogany, Reeded Top, 2 Short & 3 Long Beaded Drawers, Turned Legs, 50 In. .. 1320.00
Chest, Mahogany, Tiger Maple, 2 Over 3 Inset Drawers, Loop Handles, 55 x 43 In. 2070.00
Chest, Mahogany, Veneer, 3 Drawers, Wood Pulls, Bracket Feet, 19th Century 440.00
Chest, Map, 7 Long Between 6 Small Drawers 3190.00
Chest, Maple, Cherry, 5 Dovetailed Beaded Drawers, 41 x 42 x 18 In. 825.00
Chest, Marble Top, 2 Drawers, Gilt-Metal Mounted, Miniature, 10 x 11 In. 287.00
Chest, Mule, Charles II, Oak, Floral Carved Panel, Dated 1690, 32 x 54 In. 1380.00
Chest, Mule, Chippendale, Pine, 3 Overlapping Drawers, Painted, 37 x 48 In. 2035.00
Chest, Mule, Pine, 2 Drawers, Red Paint, Black Daubing, 6-Board, 43 In. 2530.00
Chest, Mule, Pine, Lift Top, 2 Drawers, Painted, Dovetailed, 41 x 44 In. 825.00

Furniture, Chest,
Federal, Maple,
Birch,
4 Drawers,
Beading, 40 In.

Furniture, Chest, Pine, Drawer, Grain
Painted, Hinged Top, 31 x 38 x 17 In.

Chest, Mule, Pine, Poplar, Dovetailed Drawer, Red, Brown Paint, 34 In. 660.00
Chest, Ollie Finley, 3 Drawers, Bun Feet, Nov. 26, 1860, 19th Century, Miniature 595.00
Chest, Parquetry, 6 Short Drawers, Canted Corners, Cast Sabots, 39 In. 2375.00
Chest, Pine, 2 Over 3 Graduated Drawers, Grain Painted, Rupp-Style Design 605.00
Chest, Pine, 2 Short Over 3 Long Drawers, Bulbous Top Shaped Feet, 1850, 41 x 43 In. . . . 665.00
Chest, Pine, 3 Drawers, Cutout Apron Base, Cream, Yellow & Brown, 17 x 13 In. 1100.00
Chest, Pine, 4 Drawers, Turned Feet, England, 31 1/2 x 17 x 35 3/4 In. 275.00
Chest, Pine, 4 Graduated Drawers, Hinged Top, Red Paint, 18th Century, 37 In. 5405.00
Chest, Pine, 4 Graduated Drawers, Paint, Beaded Frame, 27 x 36 x 42 In. 275.00
Chest, Pine, 6 Nailed Drawers, Quarter-Column Corners, 45 3/4 x 48 In. 550.00
Chest, Pine, 6-Board, Ripple Comb Painted, Hearts, Pennsylvania, 19 x 52 x 26 In. 1440.00
Chest, Pine, Birch, 4 Nailed Drawers, Daubs, Amber Varnish Wash, 36 In. 440.00
Chest, Pine, Bird's-Eye Maple, 5 Drawers, Brass Knobs, 35 x 43 x 37 In. 1100.00
Chest, Pine, Drawer, Grain Painted, Hinged Top, 31 x 38 x 17 In. ....*Illus* 920.00
Chest, Pine, Lift Top, 2 False Drawers, Shaped Apron, Bracket Base, 42 x 38 x 19 In. . . . 990.00
Chest, Pine, Lift Top, 6-Board, Interior Till, 19th Century, 26 x 48 x 24 In. 165.00
Chest, Pine, Mahogany, 3 Drawers, Shaped Backsplash, Early 19th Century, 46 In. 315.00
Chest, Pine, Poplar, 3 Drawers, Blue Paint, 36 x 18 x 29 In. 605.00
Chest, Pine, Poplar, 6 Drawers, Red Paint, Wood Knobs, 27 x 18 x 25 In. 550.00
Chest, Pine, Serpentine Top Drawer Over 3 Straight Drawers, 19th Century 248.00
Chest, Pine, Thumb-Molded Drawers, Continental, 29 1/2 x 40 x 22 1/2 In. 450.00
Chest, Queen Anne, 5 Long Drawers Upper, 3 Drawers Lower, Flat Top, 1750, 65 1/4 In. . 1380.00
Chest, Queen Anne, Burl Walnut, 2 Short & 3 Long Drawers, 1720, 33 x 40 In. 3267.00
Chest, Queen Anne, Cherry, 6 Drawers, Molded Fronts, Dutch Feet, 60 1/2 In. 2640.00
Chest, Queen Anne, Maple, 2 Short Over 4 Graduated Drawers, c.1750, 45 x 39 In. 2300.00
Chest, Queen Anne, Maple, 3 Short Over 8 Graduated Drawers, c.1740, 70 x 38 In. 9775.00
Chest, Queen Anne, Poplar, Lift Lid, Bracket Feet, New England, c.1750, 25 x 46 In. 575.00
Chest, Queen Anne, Walnut, 5 Dovetailed Drawers, Bandy Legs, 17 1/2 In. 495.00
Chest, Queen Anne, Walnut, 7 Dovetailed Drawers, Initials M.E., 58 x 40 In. 1650.00
Chest, Queen Anne, Walnut, Maple, 6 Long Thumb Drawers, Cabriole Legs, 71 In. 17250.00
Chest, Regency, 2 Short & 3 Long Graduated Drawers, 1820, 42 1/2 In. 1089.00
Chest, Regency, Pine, 4 Graduated Drawers, Bracket Feet, Red Paint, 1810, 37 In. 1089.00
Chest, Robsjohn-Gibbings, Mahogany, 6 Flush-Mounted Drawers, Dowel Details, 70 In. . 1100.00
Chest, Robsjohn-Gibbings, Pearwood, 4 Drawers, Contoured Front, Mirror, 43 x 36 In. . . 935.00
Chest, Rococo, 3 Short Drawers Over Cabinet, Grape Pulls, 19th Century 630.00
Chest, Roycroft, 3 Graduated Drawers, Rectangular Mirror, Child's 14300.00
Chest, Russel Wright, American Modern, 5 Drawers, Applied Cutout Handles, 47 x 34 In. 1093.00
Chest, Russel Wright, Blonde, 5 Drawers, 46 1/2 x 32 In. 440.00
Chest, Saarinen, Ash, 4 Drawers, Aluminum & Wood Pulls, 24 x 21 & 24 x 15 In., Pair . . 1045.00
Chest, Shaker, Cherry, 6-Board, 4 Recessed Panel Facades, Red Wash, 23 1/2 In. 575.00
Chest, Shaker, Cherry, 6-Board, Hinged Top, 4 Recessed Panels Facades, 24 In. 430.00
Chest, Sheraton, 2 Over 2 Graduated Drawers, Pennsylvania, 1840, 24 1/2 In. 2970.00
Chest, Sheraton, 2 Over 4 Scratch-Beaded Drawers, Painted, 1840, 52 x 41 In. 990.00
Chest, Sheraton, Bowfront, 2 Short Over 3 Long Drawers, 1800, 45 x 43 x 23 In. 1695.00
Chest, Sheraton, Cherry, 2 Over 3 Drawers, Ball Feet 525.00
Chest, Sheraton, Cherry, 2 Short Over 3 Long Drawers, Dark Frame, 40 x 45 In. 935.00
Chest, Sheraton, Cherry, 4 Drawers, Diamond Escutcheon Inlay, 35 x 18 x 43 In. 1095.00
Chest, Sheraton, Cherry, 4 Drawers, Inlaid Tiles, Eagle Brasses, 20 x 44 In. 685.00
Chest, Sheraton, Cherry, 4 Drawers, Turned Feet, Paneled Ends, 40 3/4 x 39 1/2 In. 495.00
Chest, Sheraton, Cherry, 4 Drawers, Turned Feet, Scroll Apron, 40 x 39 In. 770.00
Chest, Sheraton, Cherry, 4 Graduated Drawers, 39 x 20 x 40 In. 1210.00
Chest, Sheraton, Cherry, 4 Graduated Drawers, Beaded, 20 x 40 x 41 In. 990.00
Chest, Sheraton, Cherry, 7 Drawers, Rounded Top, Dovetailed, 41 x 69 In. 3025.00
Chest, Sheraton, Cherry, Maple, 4 Dovetailed Drawers, Turned Feet, 47 x 45 In. 715.00
Chest, Sheraton, Mahogany, 4 Drawers, Backsplash, Reeded Columns, 40 In. 1725.00
Chest, Sheraton, Walnut, 4 Dovetailed Drawers, Escutcheon Inlay, 20 x 42 x 43 In. 715.00
Chest, Sheraton, Walnut, 4 Dovetailed Drawers, Reeded Edge Top, 39 1/2 In. 770.00
Chest, Side Compartment, Ring Turned Bun Feet, Painted, 24 x 49 x 22 In. 975.00
Chest, Silver, Oak, Felt-Lined Interior, Fitted Lift-Out Tray 110.00
Chest, Spice, 14 Drawers, Walnut & Chestnut, Brass Pulls, 17 x 18 In. 412.00
Chest, Sponge Painted, Rope Beckets, Strap Hinges, China, 1875, 16 x 41 In. 770.00
Chest, Sugar, Cherry, Drawer, 3 Compartments, 40 x 27 3/4 In. 4675.00
Chest, Sugar, Cherry, Drawer, Divided Interior, 31 1/4 In. 1760.00

Chest, Sugar, Shaker, Maple, Cream Ground, Lift Lid, Ohio, 47 x 25 x 43 In. 1870.00
Chest, Tiger Maple, 5 Graduated Drawers, Daniel J. Hawkins, 51 In. 6900.00
Chest, Tiger Maple, 6 Graduated Drawers, Early 19th Century, 53 In. 2990.00
Chest, Wallace Nutting, No. 931, Oak, Sunflower, 2 Drawers 990.00
Chest, Walnut, 2 Short Over 5 Long Drawers, Ogee Bracket Feet, 5 3/4 In. 1610.00
Chest, Walnut, 3 Drawers, Applied Carvings, Porcelain Handles, 15 x 18 x 12 In. 490.00
Chest, Walnut, 3 Drawers, Marble Top, 35 x 38 x 17 In. 230.00
Chest, Walnut, 3 Graduated Drawers, Paneled, Pennsylvania, 1840, 27 x 33 x 18 In. 1320.00
Chest, Walnut, 4 Drawers, Racetrack Moldings, Victorian, 35 x 38 x 17 In. 365.00
Chest, Walnut, 4 Drawers, Scalloped Skirt, 26 x 18 In. 1045.00
Chest, Walnut, Mahogany Veneer, 3 Over 6 Long Drawers, Original Brasses 3500.00
Chest, Walnut, Nail Construction, Wood Hinges, c.1810, 18 x 17 x 25 In. 560.00
Chest, Walnut, Pine, 4 Drawers, Molded Feet, Chamfered Corners, 43 x 37 1/4 In. 1100.00
Chest, William & Mary, Oak, Lift Top, 3 Drawers, Turned Feet, 20 x 19 In. 710.00
Chest, William & Mary, Tiger Maple, 2 Over 4 Graduated Drawers, 48 In. 3393.00
Chest, William & Mary, Walnut, 3 Graduated Drawers, Rectangular Top, 36 In. 9775.00
Chest-On-Chest, 3 Short Over 3 Long Drawers, 3 Drawers In Lower Section, 72 In. 8050.00
Chest-On-Chest, Cherry, Applied Bracket Feet, 78 In. 7475.00
Chest-On-Chest, Cherry, Lower Drawer Over 3 Long Drawers, 1759, 81 In. 9775.00
Chest-On-Chest, Dutch Baroque Style, Shell Cornice, Astragal Glazed Doors, 91 In. 4600.00
Chest-On-Chest, George I, Walnut, 3 Long Drawers, Bracket Feet 9200.00
Chest-On-Chest, George III, Mahogany, 4 Drawers, Central Mirror Plate 7475.00
Chest-On-Chest, George III, Mahogany, 6 Drawers, Satinwood Inlay, 78 In. 9775.00
Chest-On-Chest, Georgian, Mahogany, 3 Graduated Drawers, Bracket Feet, 77 In. 5142.00
Chest-On-Chest, Georgian, Paneled Door Over 4 Long Drawers, 1840, 77 x 33 In. 1695.00
Chest-On-Chest, Mahogany, 3 Short Over 3 Long Drawers, Upper Frieze, 75 1/4 In. 5450.00
Chest-On-Chest, Mahogany, Molded Cornice, Corner Columns, Pa., 74 x 41 In. 11000.00
Chest-On-Chest, Maple, Tiger Maple, 10 Drawers, 76 x 38 In. 10925.00
Chest-On-Chest, Pair Of Doors, Raised Panels, Figural Narrative Scenes, 48 In. 575.00
Chest-On-Stand, Chippendale, Mahogany, Shell Carved Scroll Pediment, 86 In. 1540.00
Chest-On-Stand, E. Wheeler, Tiger Maple, 5 Drawers 2310.00
Chest-On-Stand, George I, Walnut, 3 Long Drawers, Molded Cornice, 61 In. 9200.00
Chest-On-Stand, Mahogany, 4 Graduated Drawers, Drop Pulls, 38 x 37 In. 1260.00
Chest-On-Stand, Maple, Cherry, Oak, 2 Drawers, Engraved Brasses, Painted, 54 1/2 In. . . 3220.00
Chest-On-Stand, Maple, Molded Cornice Over 4 Drawers, Scroll Apron, 41 In. 10450.00
Chest-On-Stand, Queen Anne, 6 Graduated Scratch-Beaded Drawers, 1760, 62 In. 5500.00
Chest-On-Stand, Queen Anne, Maple, 2 Over 4 Drawers, Scroll Apron, Cabriole Legs . . . 6930.00
Chest-On-Stand, Queen Anne, Maple, Pine, Cherry, 5 Graduated Drawers, 52 In. 1380.00
Chest-On-Stand, William & Mary, Oak, Lift Top, 3 Faux Drawers, 20 x 19 x 16 In. 630.00
Chiffonier, Empire, Mahogany, 5 Drawers, Rectangular Wood Top, 61 In. 7475.00
Chiffonier, L. & J.G. Stickley, No. 90, 2 Over 4 Drawers, 49 3/4 In. 4760.00
Chiffonier, L. & J.G. Stickley, No. 111, Fitted Interior, 48 x 40 In. 5775.00
Chiffonier, Regency, Mahogany, Ebonized, 19th Century, 55 1/2 In. 1840.00
Chiffonier, Regency, Mahogany, Gallery, 2 Doors, 1825, 52 x 30 In. 1800.00
Chiffonier, Walnut, Brass Rail, Doors, Interior Shelves, Peg Feet, Casters, 40 1/4 In. 1725.00
Chiffonnier, Louis XVI, White Marble Top, 3 Inlaid Drawers, 26 In., Pair 1725.00
Coat Rack, Arts & Crafts, Wood, Key Shape, Bronze Nail Hooks, 42 x 14 In. 259.00
Coat Rack, Baroque Revival, Oak, Strapwork, Cherub, 6 Iron Hooks, 20 x 60 x 9 In. 545.00
Coat Rack, Burl Walnut, Ebony Paint, Victorian, 33 x 9 x 12 In. 865.00
Coat Rack, Floral & Scroll, Cast Iron, Umbrella Holder, Late 19th Century, 75 In. 385.00
Coat Rack, G. Stickley, 70 3/4 In. 2875.00
Coat Rack, Propeller Shape, Metal, Fir, Glass & Copper, 78 In. 460.00
Commode, Biedermeier, Ash, Gray Marble Top, Stylized Ebonized Apron, 32 In. 2904.00
Commode, Bombe, Drawer Over 2 Doors, Bouquet Top, Continental, 34 x 41 In. 910.00
Commode, Bowfront, Walnut, Marble Top, Drawer Over 2 Doors, 29 In. 374.00
Commode, Burl Elm, Cushion-Frieze Drawer, Block Feet, c.1860, 28 1/2 In. 330.00
Commode, Charles X, Burl Walnut, 3 Long Drawers, Marble Top, 35 x 51 In. 2178.00
Commode, Charles X, Fruitwood, Marble Top, Brass Mount, France, 38 x 42 x 20 In. . . . 1575.00
Commode, Charles X, Mahogany, Marble Top, 3 Long Drawers, 1840, 38 1/2 In. 2420.00
Commode, Charles X, Walnut, Marble, Cushion Frieze Over 3 Drawers, 38 x 49 In. 2300.00
Commode, Corner, Mahogany, Broken Pediment, Marble Top, England, 32 x 51 In. 245.00
Commode, Federal, Pine, Painted, Backsplash, Drawer, 19th Century 430.00
Commode, Fruitwood, Marquetry, c.1790, 30 1/4 x 47 In. 8800.00

Commode, Herter Bros., Walnut, Drawer, Marble Top, c.1880, 31 In. 403.00
Commode, Lift Top, Empire Scrolls, Mustache Pulls, Yellow & Green, Quebec 578.00
Commode, Louis Philippe, Birch, Brown Marble Top, 3 Drawers, Bun Feet, 38 In. 4600.00
Commode, Louis Philippe, Mahogany, Black Marble Top, Ogee Feet, 1840, 39 In. 1694.00
Commode, Louis Philippe, Mahogany, Brass Mounted, 1835, 38 1/4 x 50 3/4 In. 4840.00
Commode, Louis Philippe, Mahogany, Gray Marble Top, 3 Drawers, 1850, 37 In. 1936.00
Commode, Louis Philippe, Walnut, Gray Marble Top, 3 Long Drawers, 1840, 39 In. 1331.00
Commode, Louis Philippe, Walnut, Marble, 2 Short Over 3 Long Drawers, 43 In. 2300.00
Commode, Louis XV Style, Gilt Metal Mounts, 14 3/4 x 27 x 29 1/4 In. 575.00
Commode, Louis XV, Black Lacquer, River Landscape Scene, Brown, Cream, 19 In. 5750.00
Commode, Louis XV, Gilt Chinoiserie Landscape Scene, Red Ground, Italy 575.00
Commode, Louis XV, Mahogany, Rouge Royal Marble Top, 2 Drawers, 31 x 49 In. 1955.00
Commode, Louis XV, Marble Top, Astragal Corners, 34 1/4 x 16 In. 3900.00
Commode, Louis XV, Rectangular Marble Top, 3 Drawers, 28 In. 745.00
Commode, Louis XV, Serpentine, Marquetry, Onyx Marble Top, Cabriole Legs, 31 In. ... 690.00
Commode, Louis XV, Tulipwood, Kingwood, Serpentine, Gray Marble Top, 33 In. 13800.00
Commode, Louis XV, Yellow, Gray Marble Top, 2 Long Drawers, 35 x 22 1/2 In. 5750.00
Commode, Louis XVI, Fruitwood, Block Front, Intertwined Banding 4950.00
Commode, Louis XVI, Gilt, Serpentine Top, 2 Drawers, Cabriole Legs, 36 In. 8625.00
Commode, Louis XVI, Mahogany, Marble Top, 3 Frieze Drawers, Top Shaped Feet 9775.00
Commode, Louis XVI, Mahogany, Rectangular Marble Top, Drawer, 24 In., Pair 635.00
Commode, Mahogany, Demilune, Chevron Inlay, 4 Long & 4 Side Drawers, 1800, 56 In. . 5462.00
Commode, Marble Top, Marquetry, 3 Drawers, France, 19th Century, 36 In. 3450.00
Commode, Napoleon III, Mahogany, Marble Top, 3 Drawers, Splayed Legs, 34 In. 2299.00
Commode, Napoleon III, Mahogany, Marble Top, 3 Long Drawers, 1890, 33 1/2 In. 1815.00
Commode, Neoclassical, Fruitwood, Inlay, 3 Drawers, Italy, 32 x 22 x 16 In. 1610.00
Commode, Neoclassical, Gilt, Figures In Period Costume, Green, Blue, Red, 37 In. 9200.00
Commode, Neoclassical, Mahogany, D-Shaped Top, 3 Drawers, Fluted Legs 8050.00
Commode, Neoclassical, Walnut, Fruitwood, Leaf Tip, Banded Borders, Italy 10350.00
Commode, Pine, Beechwood, Gray Paint, Ringed Brass Hardware, 1825, 50 1/2 In. 1540.00
Commode, Regency, Serpentine Marble Top, 3 Drawers, Bracket Feet 6325.00
Commode, Restauration, Walnut, White Marble Top, 3 Graduated Drawers, 37 In. 3520.00
Commode, Rococo, Serpentine Molded Top, 3 Serpentine Drawers, Italy, 35 In. 10925.00
Commode, Rococo, Walnut, Fruitwood, Serpentine Top, Handles, 34 In. 12650.00
Commode, Satinwood, 3 Drawers, Apron, Rectangular Top, 28 x 34 x 16 In. 1495.00
Commode, Satinwood, Brass, 3 Drawers, Brass Handles, Foliate Feet, 32 x 48 In. 2990.00
Commode, Walnut, Canted Corners, 4 Graduated Drawers, France, 38 In. 1540.00
Commode, Walnut, Gallery, Marble Top, Drawer, Cupboard Door, 1890, 39 1/2 In. 605.00
Commode, Walnut, Marble, Candlestands, Drawer, 2 Doors, 30 x 34 x 16 In. 220.00
Commode, Walnut, Serpentine, Italy, 27 x 19 1/2 In. 4025.00
Console, Art Deco, Wrought Iron, White Marble Top, Tripartite Curved Foot, 33 In. 6325.00
Console, Chinese Hardwood, Rouge-Variegated Marble Inset Top, 32 x 58 x 26 In. 895.00
Console, Empire, Mahogany, Marble Top, Elephant-Trunk Legs, Concave Base, 36 In. ... 880.00
Console, Frankl, Cream Lacquered Cork, Mahogany Shelf, 71 x 21 x 28 In. 3300.00
Console, Iron, Marble Top, Scroll, Foliate Bracket, 31 x 38 x 24 In., Pair 6900.00
Console, Louis XVI, Moroccan Onyx Top, Ogee Edge, Marble Plinth Base 2415.00
Console, Neoclassical, Giltwood, D-Shaped Marble Top, Tapered Fluted Legs, Italy 4600.00
Console, Neoclassical, Giltwood, Rectangular Marble Top, Leaf Carved Legs, Italy 5175.00
Console, Regency, Green Marble Top, Square Stepped Plinth, 36 In. 3737.00
Console, Regency, Oak, Serpentine Marble Top, Shell Carved Stretcher, 32 In. 4887.00
Console, Renaissance Revival, Mahogany, Inlay, Leon Marcotte, 46 x 58 x 17 In. 4370.00
Console, Rococo, Giltwood, Italy ....*Illus* 6900.00
Console, Rococo, Silvered Bronze, Serpentine Agate Top, Spain, 33 x 24 x 12 In. 3450.00
Cradle, Bentwood, Ivory Fittings, 39 x 41 In. 440.00
Cradle, Cast Iron, Wood Slat Bottom, Black, Victorian, 36 In. 230.00
Cradle, Cherry, Poplar, Brown Finish, Cutout Rockers, Scroll Crest, 44 In. 220.00
Cradle, Curly Maple, Cutout Hearts, 41 In. 550.00
Cradle, Iron & Wire Hood, Diamond Pattern, White Paint 415.00
Cradle, Pine, Shaped Headboard & Sides, Cutout Handles, Sponged, Pennsylvania 385.00
Cradle, Pine, Splayed Sides, Corner Posts, Turned Finials, 36 3/4 In. 170.00
Cradle, Pine, Whitewashed, 19th Century 115.00
Cradle, Spool Turned, 2-Tone Ebonized Finish, 39 1/2 In. 220.00
Cradle, Tiger Maple, Chestnut, Shoe Feet, Hanging, 30 x 41 1/2 In. 358.00

Furniture, Console, Rococo, Giltwood, Italy

If a screw that holds hardware on an old piece of furniture is loose, you should remove it. Insert a wooden matchstick in the hole, then put the screw back in the hole and tighten the screw.

Cradle, Tiger Maple, Scalloped Ends, Cheese Cutter Rockers, c.1800	165.00
Cradle, Walnut, Rockers, 38 1/2 In.	330.00
Cradle, Walnut, Shaped Top, Open Slats, Dovetailed, 19 x 16 x 38 In.	140.00
Cradle, White Wrought Iron, Bronze Finials, c.1920	495.00
Credenza, 2 Doors, Marble Top, Ormolu Mounted, 41 x 67 x 19 In.	9200.00
Credenza, Baroque, Walnut, Rectangular Top, Floral Urns On Side Panels, 50 In.	9200.00
Credenza, Beechwood, Still Life, Pendant Grape Clusters, Lower Shelf, 1825, 46 In.	3080.00
Credenza, Florence Knoll, Rosewood Veneer, Marble Top, 4 Drawers, Chrome, 75 In.	4675.00
Credenza, G. Nelson, Rosewood Veneer, Black Lacquer Drawers & Door, 56 x 19 In.	920.00
Credenza, Risom, Walnut, Aluminum Frame, 2 Drawers & Doors, 51 x 22 In.	605.00
Credenza, V. Kagan, Laminate, 2 Doors, 3 Drawers, Carved Handles, 32 x 78 x 20 In.	2300.00
Credenza, William IV, Burl Walnut, Tan Marble Top, 2 Cupboard Doors, 36 In.	2662.00
Crib, Tiger Maple, Mahogany, X-Latch On 1 Side, Turned Legs, Glass Casters, 48 In.	495.00
Crib, Tiger Maple, Turned Posts, Cheese-Cutter Rockers, c.1820, 35 x 35 1/2 In.	935.00
Crib, Walnut, Spindles, Arched Ends, Castors, 30 3/4 x 37 In.	230.00
Cupboard, Baroque, Walnut Chalice, Drawer, Caryatid Figures, 73 x 22 x 18 In.	3450.00
Cupboard, Bird's-Eye Maple, Cherry, 4 Top Doors, 65 x 92 x 18 In.	3450.00
Cupboard, Butternut, Step Back, 2 Doors & Drawers, Cornice, 44 x 80 In.	1980.00
Cupboard, Cherry, Step Back, Doors In Base, 8 Glass Panels In Top Doors, 52 3/4 In.	1515.00
Cupboard, Chestnut, 2 Glass Doors, Molded Cornice, Candle Drawers, 82 x 50 In.	1870.00
Cupboard, Chimney, 2-Board Door, Square Nails, Salmon Paint, 26 x 13 x 73 In.	575.00
Cupboard, Chimney, Shaker, Pine, Raised Panel Doors, 80 x 21 1/4 In.	5280.00
Cupboard, Cloak, Shaker, Walnut, Double Doors, Inner Rows Of Pegs, 77 3/4 In.	935.00
Cupboard, Corner, 2 Arched Doors, 10 Panes, Painted Design, Maryland, c.1825, 94 In.	5600.00
Cupboard, Corner, 2 Drawers Over 2 Raised Doors, 1800, 87 In.	2750.00
Cupboard, Corner, 2 Glazed Doors, Interior Butterfly Shelves, 1810, 94 In.	1760.00
Cupboard, Corner, 4 Glass Shelves, 3 Drawers, 19th Century, 87 x 19 In.	1440.00
Cupboard, Corner, Cherry, 2 Doors, 8 Panes, Barrel Back	3575.00
Cupboard, Corner, Cherry, 4 Raised Panel Doors, 2 Drawers, Cornice, 59 x 85 In.	2310.00
Cupboard, Corner, Cherry, Flat Top, 2 Hinged Drawers, 18th Century, 79 x 46 In.	2185.00
Cupboard, Corner, Cherry, Molded Cornice, 2 Doors, 46 x 48 x 90 3/4 In.	1485.00
Cupboard, Corner, Cherry, Poplar, Paneled Doors, Cornice, 41 x 44 x 79 In.	2200.00
Cupboard, Corner, Cherry, Poplar, Red Traces, Paneled Doors, 44 x 76 In.	1430.00
Cupboard, Corner, Chippendale, Mahogany, 19th Century, 96 x 49 In.	2415.00
Cupboard, Corner, Chippendale, Tiger Maple, Arched Door, 15 Panes, 2 Piece, 84 In.	9350.00
Cupboard, Corner, Curly Maple, Paneled Doors, 44 x 99 In.	10450.00
Cupboard, Corner, Door, 12 Panes, Yellow Tiger-Stripe Paint	8300.00
Cupboard, Corner, Drop Front, 6 Panes, 5 Drawers, 85 In.	4950.00
Cupboard, Corner, Federal, Cherry, Aqua Shelves, Pennsylvania, c.1815, 77 x 43 In.	2530.00
Cupboard, Corner, Federal, Mahogany, Swan's Neck Pediment, Door, 81 1/2 In.	2300.00
Cupboard, Corner, Federal, Poplar, Cornice Over Doors, Shelves, Lower Doors, 80 In.	2587.00
Cupboard, Corner, Hanging, Mahogany, Bowfront, Line & Shell Frieze, 1795, 46 In.	3162.00
Cupboard, Corner, Hanging, Mahogany, Open Shelves, Base Drawer, 39 x 22 3/4 In.	770.00
Cupboard, Corner, Hepplewhite, Cherry, 12 Panes, 90 In., 2 Piece	5225.00
Cupboard, Corner, Hepplewhite, Cherry, 3 Drawers, Glass Doors, 2 Piece, 86 In.	3850.00
Cupboard, Corner, Hepplewhite, Curly Maple, 4 Paneled Doors, 2 Piece, 83 In.	7920.00

Cupboard, Corner, Oak, Stylized Lion On Doors, Bracket Feet, 1630s, 44 1/2 In. 5175.00
Cupboard, Corner, Pine, 2 Doors, 11 Panes, Pennsylvania, 1840, 90 In. 4400.00
Cupboard, Corner, Pine, 2 Upper Doors, Single Panel Lower Door, c.1800, 81 In. 660.00
Cupboard, Corner, Pine, 6-Light Door, Paneled Lower Door, 79 1/2 In. 2750.00
Cupboard, Corner, Pine, Cornice, 2 Blind Panel Doors, 2 Lower Doors, 86 1/2 In. 825.00
Cupboard, Corner, Pine, Painted, Glass & Paneled Doors, 42 x 74 In. 880.00
Cupboard, Corner, Pine, Panel Doors, 29 x 72 In. 385.00
Cupboard, Corner, Pine, Panel Over Door, Lower Drawer, 2 Faux Drawers, 82 In. 2860.00
Cupboard, Corner, Pine, Poplar, Grain Painted, 8 Panes, 90 In., 2 Piece 2750.00
Cupboard, Corner, Poplar, 4 Doors, Inside Shelves, Blue Paint, c.1830, 79 x 43 In. 5175.00
Cupboard, Corner, Poplar, Carved Fan Detail, Paneled & Glass Doors, 84 3/4 In. 1530.00
Cupboard, Corner, Raised Panel Doors, 1800s, 84 x 48 In. 1845.00
Cupboard, Corner, Red Paint, Blue Interior, Pennsylvania, 2 Piece 6250.00
Cupboard, Corner, Walnut, 1-Piece Blind Door, Stepped-Out Base 1210.00
Cupboard, Corner, Walnut, 12 Panes, 1 Piece, 38 x 40 x 74 In. 1540.00
Cupboard, Corner, Walnut, Crown Cornice, 2-Door Top, Pennsylvania, 1 Piece, 78 In. ... 2310.00
Cupboard, Corner, Walnut, Paneled Doors, 4 Panes, 46 x 77 In. 1540.00
Cupboard, Corner, Walnut, Urn Finial, 2 Doors, Base Drawer, 92 In. 1485.00
Cupboard, Federal, Pine, Pewter, Cornice, Open Shelves, Scalloped, Paint Traces 2760.00
Cupboard, Gray Over Red Paint, 54 In. 6500.00
Cupboard, Hanging, Mahogany, 6 Drawers, 3 Step-Back Doors, 53 x 37 1/2 In. 550.00
Cupboard, Hanging, Oak Grained, Paneled Door, 28 x 8 1/2 x 38 In. 360.00
Cupboard, Hanging, Oak, Arched Stepped Pediment Top, Glass Door, 40 In. 1695.00
Cupboard, Hanging, Oak, Slant Front, Door, Iron Butterfly Hinges, England, 13 x 20 In. .. 300.00
Cupboard, Hanging, Pine, Glass Door, Scroll Design, Early 20th Century, 25 x 64 In. 115.00
Cupboard, Hanging, Pine, Oak-Grained Paint, Black Trim, 16 x 6 1/2 x 20 In. 300.00
Cupboard, Hanging, Pine, Poplar, Open Scalloped Shelves, 1 Piece, 49 x 21 x 77 In. 660.00
Cupboard, Hanging, Poplar, 4 Panes, 25 1/8 x 22 1/2 In. 385.00
Cupboard, Hanging, Step Back, Pine, Blue Over Light Blue Paint, 78 In. 6050.00
Cupboard, Hanging, Walnut, Drawer In Protruding Base, Double Doors, 25 3/4 In. 630.00
Cupboard, Hanging, Walnut, Raised Panel Door, Drawer, c.1790, 43 1/2 x 25 In. 1430.00
Cupboard, Hanging, Walnut, Stepped Cornice, Raised Panel Door, Shelves, 36 1/2 In. ... 1045.00
Cupboard, Hanging, Walnut, Tombstone Door, Lower Drawer & Shelf, 35 x 26 In. 6820.00
Cupboard, Jelly, 2 Drawers Over 2 Doors, June 1880 .... 330.00
Cupboard, Jelly, Braided Panel, Rattail Hinges, 18th Century, 67 x 42 In. 2950.00
Cupboard, Jelly, Pine, 2 Drawers Over 2 Doors, Bracket Feet, c.1840, 54 1/2 In. 880.00
Cupboard, Jelly, Pine, 3 Dovetailed Drawers, Cutout Feet, 53 In. 1705.00
Cupboard, Jelly, Pine, Poplar, 3 Drawers, 2 Paneled Doors, 46 x 20 x 48 In. 715.00
Cupboard, Jelly, Pine, Poplar, Grain Painted, 2 Overlapping Drawers, 47 x 59 In. 495.00
Cupboard, Jelly, Pine, Poplar, Yellow Brown Graining, 40 x 42 x 15 In. 550.00
Cupboard, Jelly, Pine, Scroll Backsplash, 2 Drawers, 2 Paneled Doors, 41 x 64 In. 630.00
Cupboard, Jelly, Plank Door, Gallery, Arched Cutout Feet, Red, 29 1/2 x 19 x 15 In. 935.00
Cupboard, Jelly, Poplar, Paneled Ends, 2 Drawers, 53 x 49 1/4 In. 605.00
Cupboard, Kitchen, Oak, Walnut, Pie Shelf, Porcelain Handles 675.00
Cupboard, Mennonite, Step Back, Frosted Glass Panes, Paneled Door, 80 In. 2300.00
Cupboard, Oak, Molded Stiles, 2 Drawers, Relief Carving, Pie Shelf, Victorian, 84 In. ... 770.00
Cupboard, Oak, Molded Top, Carved Base, Geometric Panels On Sides, 36 In. 2662.00
Cupboard, Oak, Pewter, Open Scalloped Top, 3 Shelves, 3 Drawers, 1740, 79 1/2 In. 5225.00
Cupboard, Oak, Scalloped Base, Paneled Doors, 2 Drawers, 2 Piece, 81 In. 385.00
Cupboard, Pale Blue Interior, Hinged Door, 60 In. 625.00
Cupboard, Pewter, Pine, 1-Board Doors, 2 Open Shelves, 73 x 49 In. 2200.00
Cupboard, Pewter, Pine, Red Paint, 1-Board Door, 30 x 19 x 71 In. 2090.00
Cupboard, Pine, 1-Board Door, Gray Paint, 19 x 9 x 27 In. 190.00
Cupboard, Pine, 1-Board Door, Green Over Gray Paint, Hanging, 25 x 20 In. 850.00
Cupboard, Pine, 2 Glass & 2 Paneled Doors, 3 Drawers, c.1830, 88 x 54 In. 7475.00
Cupboard, Pine, 12-Light Upper Door, Rattail Hinges, c.1750, 82 1/2 In. 5500.00
Cupboard, Pine, Hinged Door, Foliate Scroll Panels, 67 In. 530.00
Cupboard, Pine, Paneled Door, Interior Shelves, Bracket Feet, Continental, 71 x 40 In. ... 488.00
Cupboard, Pine, Pewter, Glass Doors, 2 Drawers, Pie Shelf, 2 Piece, 87 In. 2588.00
Cupboard, Pine, Poplar, 1-Board Doors, Gray & Olive Paint, 36 x 75 In. 1147.00
Cupboard, Pine, Poplar, Sliding Door, Crest, 10 1/2 x 10 x 20 1/2 In. 190.00
Cupboard, Pine, Step Back, 2 Interior Shelves, Iron Hinges, 18th Century, 66 1/2 In. ... 8050.00
Cupboard, Poplar, Paneled Doors, Punched-Tin Panels, Victorian, 75 In. 330.00

Cupboard, Poplar, Step-Back Open Top, Red Brown, 42 x 18 x 71 In. 1430.00
Cupboard, Poplar, Walnut, Glass & Paneled Doors, 3 Drawers, 81 1/2 In. 825.00
Cupboard, Red, White & Blue Paint, India, c.1920 . . . . 3800.00
Cupboard, Renaissance Revival, Olive Wood, Mahogany, Marble Top, 89 x 71 In. 2035.00
Cupboard, Renaissance Revival, Walnut, Oak, Carved, Marble, 95 x 61 In. 1265.00
Cupboard, Renaissance Revival, Walnut, Relief Carving, 91 x 63 In. 1595.00
Cupboard, Stand, Pine, Inlaid Facade, Brass Fittings, Center Doors, 31 1/4 In. 550.00
Cupboard, Step Back, 2 Base Doors, 3 Shelves, 75 x 35 In. 3300.00
Cupboard, Step Back, 2 Drawers, Doors, New England, 18th Century, 2 Piece, 81 In. 2070.00
Cupboard, Step Back, Blind Door, 2 Batten Doors Over Base, 2 Piece, 82 x 77 In. 825.00
Cupboard, Step Back, Cherry, Poplar, Glass Top Doors, Cutout Feet, 85 In. 1980.00
Cupboard, Step Back, Cherry, Scroll Cornice, 2 Glass & 2 Paneled Doors, 81 In. 2090.00
Cupboard, Step Back, Poplar, Steel Comb Graining, 2 Glass Doors, Cornice, 46 x 82 In. . . 1045.00
Cupboard, Step Back, Walnut, 4 Glass Over 2 Paneled Doors, 40 x 78 x 16 In. 575.00
Cupboard, Step Back, Walnut, 4 Paneled Drawers, Cornice, 50 x 81 In. 1210.00
Cupboard, Straight Front, 2 Doors, Reeded Panels, Molded Cornice, 87 In. 2530.00
Cupboard, Walnut, 6 Glass Doors, 2 Drawers, Canada, 64 1/2 x 85 1/4 In. 4400.00
Cupboard, Walnut, Cherry, 2 Doors, Pie Shelf, 53 x 83 x 18 In. 8800.00
Daybed, Charles X, Brass Mounted, Foliate Scroll Top Rail, Tapered Legs, 44 In. 8050.00
Daybed, Cherry, Paneled Sleigh Ends, Cushion & Bolsters, Ohio, 80 x 29 x 26 In. 605.00
Daybed, Cherry, Scroll Posts, Turned Spindles, Cushion, 30 x 84 In. 525.00
Daybed, Dunbar, Black Leather Cushion, Chrome Base, 75 In. 2760.00
Daybed, Empire, Curly Maple, Upholstered, Arms, 25 x 72 x 27 In. 660.00
Daybed, Empire, Mahogany, Hinged, Drawer, Rectangular Top, France, 34 In. 316.00
Daybed, Federal, Maple, Baluster-Shaped Posts & Legs, Early 19th Century 160.00
Daybed, Leleu, Rosewood, Scroll Sides, Upholstered Seat, 1935, 35 In. 8050.00
Daybed, Limbert, No. 651, Slanted Headrest, Drop-In Cushions, 23 x 26 x 74 In. 1900.00
Daybed, Louis XV, Fruitwood, Floral Carved Apron, 6 Cabriole Legs, 1900, 30 In. 786.00
Daybed, Louis XVI, Patera Carved Headboard & Footboard, Top Shaped Feet, 49 In. 1210.00
Daybed, Mahogany, Crest Over Pierced Strapwork Splat, Leather Slip Seat, 76 In. 1035.00
Daybed, Maloof, Mahogany, Canvas Inset, Dowel Legs, Leather Cushions, 68 x 30 In. 6600.00
Daybed, Napoleon III, Walnut, Paneled Headboard, Side Rail, 40 1/2 x 74 In. 745.00
Daybed, Pine, Fluted Corinthian Columns, Bulbous Top Shaped Feet, 1890, 38 1/2 In. . . . 847.00
Daybed, Pine, Round Panel, Shaped Feet, 1890, 41 x 77 x 35 1/2 In. 333.00
Daybed, Regency, Mahogany, Red Suede Rectangular Seat, Paw Feet, 75 In. 5462.00
Daybed, Wegner, Teakwood Veneer, Cane Backrest, 28 1/2 x 88 x 34 In. 1610.00
Desk, Art Deco, 4 Drawers, Chrome Handles, 1920, 40 x 35 x 24 In. 431.00
Desk, Art Deco, Faux Tortoiseshell, 6 Drawers & Compartments Over 9 Drawers, 38 In. . . 1045.00
Desk, Arts & Crafts, Drawer, Original Brass Hardware, Splayed Legs, 35 In. 297.00
Desk, Arts & Crafts, Walnut, Geometric & Foliage, Gallery, 25 x 20 x 37 In. 220.00
Desk, Bank, Walnut, Rotating Side Sections, Drawers, J.L. Shoemaker & Co., 60 In. 2530.00
Desk, Bird's-Eye Maple, Marble Top, 3 Drawers 1980.00
Desk, Burl Elm, Traveling, Painted Drawer Front, Brassbound, 1830s, 9 x 19 In. 1540.00
Desk, Burl Walnut, Hinged Lid, 3 Pigeonholes, 6 Drawers, Trumpet Legs, 34 1/2 In. . . . . : 3162.00
Desk, Butler's, Drop Front, Mahogany, 3 Drawers, Baltimore, 1810, 42 x 21 In. 7840.00
Desk, Butler's, Drop Front, Walnut, Drawer, Writing Surface, Fitted Interior 3160.00
Desk, Butler's, Drop Front, Walnut, Pigeonholes, Drawers, c.1850, 48 x 25 In. 1150.00
Desk, Butler's, Empire, Cherry, Curly Maple, 3 Drawers, Crest, 44 x 46 x 46 In. 1925.00
Desk, Butler's, Empire, Cherry, Maple, 3 Drawers, Pigeonholes, Carved, 44 x 57 In. 1950.00
Desk, Butler's, Empire, Cherry, Maple, Paw Feet, Pigeonholes, 44 x 57 In. 1950.00
Desk, Butler's, Federal, Cherry, 3 Cock-Beaded Drawers, Inlaid Apron, Splay Feet 4025.00
Desk, Butler's, Federal, Tiger Maple, Fitted Interior, 46 x 40 x 21 In. 3025.00
Desk, Butler's, George III, Mahogany, Leather Writing Surface, Bracket Feet, 41 In. 1700.00
Desk, Cherry, Contrasting Veneers, 2-Tier Interior, Drawers, 40 x 38 In. 2415.00
Desk, Cherry, Maple, Slant Front, 2-Tier Interior, 18th Century, 40 1/2 In. 2645.00
Desk, Chippendale Style, Slant Front, Mahogany, Serpentine Case, 41 1/2 x 36 In. 385.00
Desk, Chippendale, Drop Front, Mahogany, Serpentine, 2 Drawers, Pennsylvania, 39 In. . . 4400.00
Desk, Chippendale, Slant Front, 4 Serpentine Drawers, Stepped Interior, 42 1/2 In. 2530.00
Desk, Chippendale, Slant Front, Birch, 18th Century 3300.00
Desk, Chippendale, Slant Front, Cherry, 4 Drawers, Fitted Interior 2185.00
Desk, Chippendale, Slant Front, Cherry, 4 Drawers, Fitted Interior, 42 In. 1150.00
Desk, Chippendale, Slant Front, Cherry, 4 Drawers, Ogee Feet, c.1800, 42 In. 2100.00
Desk, Chippendale, Slant Front, Cherry, Pigeonholes, 18th Century 2590.00

Keep furniture away from a humidifier, especially the type that sprays vaporized water. The damp air will eventually cause the wooden parts of the furniture to mildew.

Furniture, Desk, G. Nelson, Action Office, Roll Top, Walnut, Tambour Top, 32 x 64 In.

Desk, Chippendale, Slant Front, Mahogany, Carved Kneehole, Claw & Ball Feet, 41 In. . . .	400.00
Desk, Chippendale, Slant Front, Serpentine Interior, Pennsylvania, c.1775	10725.00
Desk, Chippendale, Slant Front, Walnut, Interior Drawers & Pigeonholes, c.1770	2070.00
Desk, Cylinder, Eastlake, Cherry, Fitted, Casters, 70 x 43 x 24 In.	1955.00
Desk, Cylinder, Eastlake, Walnut, Burl Front, 45 x 32 In.	875.00
Desk, Cylinder, Renaissance Revival, Walnut, Late 19th Century, 63 In.	1495.00
Desk, Davenport, Rosewood, 4 Interior Drawers, Inkwell Drawer, 1850, 35 3/4 In.	3520.00
Desk, Davenport, Slant Front, Rosewood, Russet Leather, Fitted Interior, c.1840, 31 In. . .	1650.00
Desk, Davenport, Slant Front, Walnut, Leather Lined, 4 Drawers, 32 x 21 x 20 In.	2760.00
Desk, Drop Front, Walnut, Bombe, 3 Drawers, Holland, 18th Century	2600.00
Desk, Eastlake, Drop Front, Poplar, c.1890, 59 x 36 In.	390.00
Desk, Edwardian, Mahogany, 3 Drawers, Pedestal, Plinth Base, 1900, 28 x 48 In.	2185.00
Desk, Edwardian, Satinwood, 3 Drawers, 2 Doors, Painted, 47 1/4 In.	4600.00
Desk, Empire Style, Inlaid Leather Top, 3 Drawers, 56 x 28 x 30 In.	115.00
Desk, Empire Style, Mahogany, Ormolu Mounted, 30 1/2 x 51 x 27 In.	1790.00
Desk, Empire, Mahogany, 3 Drawers Each Side, Pedestal, Shelf, 1830, Woman's	80.00
Desk, Federal Style, Burl, Satinwood Inlay, Floral Medallion, 25 x 47 In.	460.00
Desk, Federal Style, Slant Front, Compartments, Woman's, 29 x 39 1/2 In.	200.00
Desk, Federal, Mahogany, Cove Top, 3 Doors, Turned Feet, Woman's, 54 In.	4312.00
Desk, Figured Maple, Interior Well, Pigeonholes, 3 Drawers, 34 In.	2185.00
Desk, Fletcher, Airline, Triangular, Rounded, Walnut Veneer, Painted Steel, 72 x 43 In. . . .	1955.00
Desk, Frankl, Combed Veneer, Double Pedestal, Bent Brass Handles, 29 1/2 x 50 In.	609.00
Desk, Frankl, Cream Lacquered Cork, 7 Drawers, Bookshelf, 60 x 25 In.	2420.00
Desk, Frankl, Light Mahogany, Combed Wood Cabinet, 3 Over 2 Drawers, 28 x 23 In. . . .	748.00
Desk, G. Nakashima, Black Walnut, Wall Mounted, 2 Drawers, 11 x 60 x 18 In.	3300.00
Desk, G. Nelson, Action Office, Roll Top, Walnut, Tambour Top, 32 x 64 In. . . . .*Illus*	3738.00
Desk, G. Nelson, Walnut, Laminate Top, 2 Drawers, Herman Miller, 22 In.	632.00
Desk, G. Nelson, Walnut, Walnut Top Over Nest Of 2 Drawers, Herman Miller	488.00
Desk, G. Nelson, Wood, Leather, Tubular Steel X-Stretcher, 54 x 42 In.	4600.00
Desk, G. Stickley, Drop Front, Full Gallery Interior, 2 Drawers, V-Pulls, 43 In.	2100.00
Desk, G. Stickley, No. 550, Slant Front, 2 Doors, Red Decal, 33 x 14 x 48 In.	9900.00
Desk, G. Stickley, No. 720, 2 Drawers, Pigeonholes, 38 x 23 x 73 In.	1375.00
Desk, G. Stickley, Postcard, Drawers, Letter Slots, 2 Drawers, 37 1/2 In.	1650.00
Desk, George III, Flame Mahogany, Leather Top, 9 Drawers, 1940s, 66 x 42 In.	3500.00
Desk, George III, Mahogany, Rectangular Thumb-Molded Top, 5 Drawers, 29 In.	1265.00
Desk, George III, Slant Front, Mahogany, 4 Graduated Drawers, 39 x 28 x 17 In.	975.00
Desk, George III, Slant Front, Mahogany, 42 1/2 x 35 1/2 x 19 In.	1955.00
Desk, George III, Slant Front, Mahogany, Fitted, 3 Graduated Drawers, 40 x 42 In.	2645.00
Desk, George IV, Pedestal, Mahogany, Leather Rectangular Top, 4 Drawers, 31 In.	10925.00
Desk, Georgian, Slant Front, Oak, Chamfered Legs, Early 20th Century, 40 1/2 In.	545.00
Desk, Gio Ponti, Walnut Veneer, 2 Floating Drawers, 65 x 23 x 30 In.	660.00
Desk, Gio Ponti, Walnut, 4 Tapered Legs, 4 Drawers, Bookshelf Back, 51 x 26 In.	3750.00
Desk, Hepplewhite, Drop Front, Cherry, Fitted, 3 Drawers, 41 x 19 x 46 In.	3025.00
Desk, Hepplewhite, Drop Front, Curly Maple, 4 Drawers, 42 x 19 x 42 In.	3300.00
Desk, Hepplewhite, Lift Top, Mahogany, 2 Doors, Glass Knobs, 45 1/2 In.	1760.00
Desk, Hepplewhite, Mahogany, Bombe, 3 Dovetailed Drawers, 41 x 21 x 31 In.	2200.00
Desk, Hepplewhite, Mahogany, Crossbanded Veneer, 4 Drawers, Woman's, 53 In.	3630.00

Desk, Herter Brothers, Drop Front, Mahogany, Marquetry, 53 x 20 x 30 In. 10350.00
Desk, Jacobean Style, Drop Front, Domed Top, Interior Compartments, 49 1/4 In. 1495.00
Desk, Jacobean Style, Oak, Pedestal, Leather Surface, 3 Drawers Each Side, 45 In. 895.00
Desk, Kneehole, Black Lacquer, Parcel Gilt, Top Drawer, 6 Side Drawers, 44 In. 6900.00
Desk, Kneehole, Chippendale, Mahogany, Center Drawer, 2 Pedestal, 50 x 20 In. 495.00
Desk, Kneehole, Leleu, Mahogany, Central Drawer, 1935, 30 In. 17250.00
Desk, Kneehole, Louis XV, Kingwood, 5 Drawers, Square Cabriole Legs, 31 In. 1610.00
Desk, Kneehole, Neoclassical, Frieze Drawer, Square Tapered Legs, 32 x 40 In. 9200.00
Desk, Kneehole, Regency, Bowfront, Mahogany, 3 Drawers Each Side, c.1800 . . . . 770.00
Desk, L. & J.G. Stickley, Drop Front, Oak, Drawer, 8 Pigeonholes, 39 In. 605.00
Desk, Lap, Bone Inlay, Paper Roller Baize Surface, Ink Bottles, c.1855, 16 In. 240.00
Desk, Lap, Book Form, Black Lacquer, Gold Designs, Inkwell, J. Pierce, 15 1/2 In. 230.00
Desk, Lap, Brassbound Opening, Leather Surface, Storage Compartment, 58 x 12 In. 605.00
Desk, Lap, Brassbound, Brass Inlaid Escutcheon & Lid, Fitted, Ink Bottles 220.00
Desk, Lap, Burl Walnut, Felt Writing Surface, Compartments, 7 1/2 x 19 1/4 In. 518.00
Desk, Lap, Hand Painted Maine Coastal Scene, Velvet Lined 495.00
Desk, Lap, Inset Brass Handles, China, 5 x 18 In. 120.00
Desk, Lap, Lacquer, Scene Design, Stand, Chinese Export, 19 1/2 In. 465.00
Desk, Lap, Mahogany, Brass Band, Fitted, England, 19th Century, 7 x 18 x 11 In. 460.00
Desk, Lap, Rosewood, Mother-Of-Pearl Escutcheon & Lid Medallion, Fitted 66.00
Desk, Lap, Tiger Maple, Tambour Roll Top, Line Inlay, c.1810, 51 1/2 x 11 In. 2300.00
Desk, Lap, Walnut, Veneer, John Castle, London, 7 x 20 x 11 In. 385.00
Desk, Lifetime, No. 8567, Drawer, Hammered-Copper Hardware, 33 x 45 In. 1320.00
Desk, Lift Top, Tapered Legs, Painted, 35 x 20 x 23 In. 935.00
Desk, Louis XV Style, 5 & 5 Faux Drawers, Cabriole Legs, 30 1/2 x 69 In. 2070.00
Desk, Louis XV Style, Inlay, Center Panel, Foliate Border, Drawer, 30 In. 2475.00
Desk, Louis XV, Walnut, Leather Top, Shaped Apron, Drawer, 29 x 37 In. 632.00
Desk, Mahogany Veneer, Brassbound, 3-Part Leather Top, 9 Drawers, Baker Co., 54 In. . . 357.00
Desk, Mahogany, Hinged Top, Interior Drawers, Retractable Surface, 36 x 32 In. 920.00
Desk, Mahogany, Lift Top, Carving, Floral, Animals, Bird Pilasters, India, 56 In. 2970.00
Desk, Mahogany, Slant Front, 4 Drawers, Fitted Interior, Grand Rapids, 39 1/2 In. 440.00
Desk, Mahogany, Slant Front, Cherry, Compartments, 4 Drawers, 42 3/4 In. 3630.00
Desk, Mahogany, Tambour, Inlay, Painted, England, 1800, Woman's 10890.00
Desk, Maple, Slant Front, Stepped Interior, Document Drawers, 18th Century, 40 In. 3450.00
Desk, McCobb, Mahogany Veneer, Box Drawers, Brass Stretcher, 29 x 54 x 26 In. 460.00
Desk, Mission Style, Oak, Quartersawn Veneer, Drawer, 29 1/4 x 30 3/4 In. 340.00
Desk, Mission Style, Slant Front, Quartersawn Oak, Open Base, 27 x 41 1/2 In. 330.00
Desk, Mission, Drop Front, Oak, Pigeonholes, Woman's, 40 x 28 x 13 In. 415.00
Desk, Mission, Quartersawn Figure, Drawer, 2 Hidden Compartments, 42 x 30 In. 220.00
Desk, P. Paulin, Black Laminate, 2 Walnut Veneer Drawers, H Supports, 51 x 24 In. 4025.00
Desk, Partner's, Bookshelf Sides, Drawer Each Side, Cherry Finish, Woman's 395.00
Desk, Partner's, Eastlake, Walnut, Paneled, 5 Drawers Each Side, 39 x 59 x 31 In. 1320.00
Desk, Partner's, Federal Style, Mahogany, Veneer, Leather Top, Drawers, 20th Century . . . 1380.00
Desk, Partner's, Georgian, Mahogany, Tooled Leather, 2 Pedestals, 60 x 46 In. 1694.00
Desk, Partner's, Mahogany, 4 Short & 1 Long Drawer, Victorian, 33 x 62 x 38 In. 4025.00
Desk, Partner's, Mahogany, Marquetry, Bombe Base, Multiple Drawers, 48 In. 3850.00
Desk, Partner's, Mahogany, Molded Frieze, 4 Drawers, Plinth Base, 1840, 30 In. 5000.00
Desk, Partner's, Mahogany, Rectangular Brass-Mounted Top, 31 In. 9775.00
Desk, Partner's, Oak, Carved, R.J. Horner & Co., c.1880 . . . . 5500.00
Desk, Partner's, Oak, Winged-Griffin Legs, R.J. Horner & Co., c.1880 . . . . 6875.00
Desk, Partner's, Walnut, Glass Top, Felt Liner, 2 Drawers, Victorian, 28 x 57 x 21 In. 952.00
Desk, Partner's, Walnut, Molded Rectangular Top, 3 Graduated Drawers, 30 In. 3600.00
Desk, Paul Sormani, Parquetry, Metal Mounts, Frieze Drawer, 30 x 45 1/2 In. 6900.00
Desk, Pedestal, Mahogany, 3 Center Drawers, Cabinet Each Side, Victorian 1610.00
Desk, Pedestal, William IV, Mahogany, Leather-Lined Top, 3 Drawers Each Side, 31 In. . . 7475.00
Desk, Plantation, Pine, 19th Century, 35 1/2 x 37 x 26 In. 430.00
Desk, Plantation, Walnut, Fitted Interior, Bird's-Eye Maple Drawers, 62 1/2 In. 935.00
Desk, Plantation, Walnut, Upper Bookcase, Kneehole Base, Mid-19th Century, 86 In. 1090.00
Desk, Queen Anne Style, Slant Front, Compartments, 2 Drawers, Baker Co., 38 1/2 In. . . . 1095.00
Desk, Queen Anne Style, Slant Front, Maple, Graduated Drawers, Child's 6900.00
Desk, Rectangular Writing Surface, Scroll Feet, Woman's, Victorian 440.00
Desk, Renaissance Revival, Slant Front, Walnut, 3 Drawers, Bookcase Top, 90 In. 1430.00
Desk, Renaissance Revival, Walnut, 2 Pedestals, Kneehole, 30 x 53 x 32 In. 1610.00

Desk, Robsjohn-Gibbings, Burl, Inlay, 2 Drawers, 1940s, 56 x 22 In. 3850.00
Desk, Robsjohn-Gibbings, Pearwood, Drawer, Contoured Front, Mirror, 40 x 20 1/2 In. . . 1210.00
Desk, Rococo, Slant Front, Jacaranda, Fitted, 18th Century, 43 x 47 x 21 In. 9200.00
Desk, Rococo, Slant Front, Mahogany, Leather, Serpentine, Portugal, 45 x 46 In. 7475.00
Desk, Rococo, Slant Front, Mahogany, Rectangular Top, 7 Drawers, Bracket Feet 7475.00
Desk, Rococo, Slant Front, Rectangular Top, Leather Writing Surface, 42 x 46 In. 9200.00
Desk, Rohde, Walnut Veneer, Freeform Top, 4 Drawers, Leatherette Skirting, 52 In. 2420.00
Desk, Roll Top, Calamander, 3 Drawers, Fitted, Indian Export 8625.00
Desk, Roll Top, G. Nelson, Action Office, Walnut, Laminate, Aluminum, 64 x 32 In. 3738.00
Desk, Roll Top, Oak, 1930, 44 x 54 In. 2000.00
Desk, Roll Top, S Roll, Ash, Drawers, Fitted Top, Cabinet Base, 19th Century 545.00
Desk, Roll Top, S Roll, Cherry, 8 Drawers, Fitted Interior, 45 x 48 In. 550.00
Desk, Roll Top, S Roll, Quartersawn Oak, Paneled, 9 Drawers, 48 x 47 x 27 In. 605.00
Desk, Roll Top, Tambour, Satinwood, Fitted Interior, Leather Surface, 1790, 40 In. 9200.00
Desk, Rosewood, Bird's-Eye Interior, 19th Century 4500.00
Desk, Ruhlmann, Oak, Leather Writing Surface, 1933, 30 In. 9200.00
Desk, Russel Wright, Ball, Pedestal, 3 Graduated Drawers, 29 x 40 In. 195.00
Desk, S. Marx, Wood, Ivory, 5 Drawers, 8 Tapered Block Legs, 1940 . . . . 7475.00
Desk, Schoolmaster's, Cherry, Maple, Lift Lid, 2 Drawers, Iron Pulls, 34 x 47 In. 550.00
Desk, Schoolmaster's, Slant Front, Birch, Poplar, 30 x 21 x 39 In. 220.00
Desk, Schoolmaster's, Slant Front, Drawer, Red Surface, Early 19th Century, 38 In. 1250.00
Desk, Schoolmaster's, Slant Front, Federal, Pine, Drawers, Fitted, 19th Century 575.00
Desk, Sea Captain's, Drawer, Turned Legs, Base, 36 1/2 In. 770.00
Desk, Sheraton, Drop Front, Cherry, Turned Legs 1870.00
Desk, Sheraton, Slant Front, Birch, 3 Drawers, Ridged Feet, Maine, 45 x 37 In. 1380.00
Desk, Sheraton, Slant Front, Maple, Interior, 8 Drawers, 6 Pigeonholes, 44 In. 1650.00
Desk, Sheraton, Slant Front, Walnut, Pigeonholes, 40 x 20 x 40 In. 2200.00
Desk, Slant Front, Allover Floral Inlay, Brass Gallery, 1900, Woman's 690.00
Desk, Slant Front, Cherry, Exposed Dovetailed Joints, 4 Drawers, 1780, 40 x 36 In. 3950.00
Desk, Slant Front, Cherry, Fitted Interior, 4 Drawers, Original Brasses, 41 1/2 In. 5775.00
Desk, Slant Front, Governor Winthrop, 4 Drawers, Claw & Ball Feet, 40 x 30 In. 303.00
Desk, Slant Front, Maple, Pine, Drawer, Turned Legs, H-Stretcher, 20th Century 83.00
Desk, Slant Front, Walnut, Fitted Interior, 3 Drawers, Victorian, 40 x 41 x 19 In. 605.00
Desk, Slant Front, Walnut, Fitted, Serpentine Drawer Fronts, c.1770, 43 1/2 In. 8050.00
Desk, Slant Front, Walnut, Gilt, Burl Veneer, Cherry, Cedar Interior, 1800s, 40 In. 2500.00
Desk, Slant Front, Walnut, Poplar, 5 Interior Drawers, 9 Pigeonholes, Turned Feet, Key . . 2860.00
Desk, Slant Front, Walnut, Rectangular, Shell Apron, Cabriole Legs, Trifid Feet, 32 In. . . . 374.00
Desk, Victorian, Walnut, 6 Drawers, Door, Hidden Compartment, 48 x 30 x 35 In. 950.00
Desk, Victorian, Walnut, Drop Front, Pigeonholes, Tiger Maple Interior Trim 1430.00
Desk, Victorian, Walnut, Lift Top, Spindle Back Gallery, Pillars, Woman's, 52 In. 460.00
Desk, Victorian, Walnut, Veneer, 2 Pedestals, Bowed Ends, Drawers, Baize Top 495.00
Desk, Wallace Nutting, No. 130, Child's 770.00
Desk, Wallace Nutting, No. 729, Slant Front, Mahogany 9900.00
Desk, Walnut, 4 Short Drawers, Drawer Under Writing Surface, 39 1/2 x 53 In. 4600.00
Desk, Walnut, Drop Front, Trestle, Fitted Interior, Arched Feet, 1900, 48 x 28 In. 150.00
Desk, Walnut, Slant Front, 2 Drawers, Double Doors, Turned Legs, 85 In. 1430.00
Desk, Walnut, Stand Type, Hinged Top, 18 1/4 x 20 3/4 x 28 In. 220.00
Desk, Warren McArthur, Aluminum Frame, Laminate Top, Gallery, 1930s, 50 x 37 In. 5500.00
Desk, Warren McArthur, Black Lacquer Top, Tubular Aluminum Frame, 1930, 29 In. 5225.00
Desk, Wooton, Cylinder, Leather Drop Front, 2 Paneled Doors, 56 x 42 x 32 In. 5750.00
Desk, Wooton, Oak, 2 Pedestals, Leather Inset, 3 Frieze Drawers, 31 x 60 x 72 In. 3450.00
Desk, Wooton, Walnut, c.1876, 66 x 37 x 25 In. 7280.00
Desk, Writing, Allover Dragon, Cloud, Wave Design, Rectangular Top, China, 45 In. 745.00
Dining Set, Art Deco, Breakfront, Marble-Top Server, Table, 6 Chairs, 9 Piece 1840.00
Dining Set, Art Deco, Mermaid Table Legs, Marble Base & Top, Gilt, Italy, 7 Piece 1100.00
Dining Set, Bamboo, 4 Upholstered Chairs, 6-Sided Glass-Top Table, 48 In., 5 Piece 290.00
Dining Set, Eero Aarnio, White Fiberglass, Upholstered, 1967, 5 Piece 2640.00
Dining Set, Frankl, Cream Cork Top, Y-Shaped Legs, 96-In. Table, 7 Piece 2750.00
Dining Set, G. Nakashima, Walnut, Widdicomb, 1959, 72 In., 7 Piece 4500.00
Dining Set, Jean Pascaud, Mahogany, 6 Chairs, White Leather, 56 In., 7 Piece 8050.00
Dining Set, N. Cherner, Walnut Veneer, Extension Table, 4 Triangular-Backed Chairs 1760.00
Dining Set, Rosewood, Round Table, Buffet, Sliding Doors, 6 Black Chairs, Denmark . . . 2300.00
Dining Set, Saarinen, Cast Metal, Pedestal Base, Formica Top, Knoll, 7 Piece 2875.00

Dining Set, Saarinen, Round Formica Top, Aluminum Base, 6 Tulip Chairs, 48 In. 2415.00
Dining Set, Sheraton, Cherry, Mahogany, Reeded Legs, 1830, 152 In., 3 Piece 3300.00
Dining Set, Wegner, Teakwood, 3-Legged Table, Six 3-Legged Chairs, 47 In. 3450.00
Dresser, Bird's-Eye Maple, Mirror, Serpentine, 2 Over 4 Drawers, 72 x 45 In. 440.00
Dresser, G. Stickley, Mirror, 4 Short Over 2 Long Drawers, Decal, 67 x 48 In. 6500.00
Dresser, G. Stickley, No. 911, 2 Half Over 2 Full Drawers, Mirror, 48 x 67 In. 7700.00
Dresser, G. Stickley, No. 913, Mahogany, 9 Drawers, Wood Knobs, 36 x 51 In. 7700.00
Dresser, Golden Oak Era, 5 Drawers, Door, Crest With Applied Carving, 49 x 33 In. 330.00
Dresser, Louis XVI, Mahogany, 3 Frieze Drawers, 1900, 66 x 50 x 22 In. 303.00
Dresser, Mahogany, Serpentine, Carved, Mirror, 3 Frieze Over 2 Drawers, 52 In. 395.00
Dresser, Oak, Quartersawn, Molded Drawers, Apron, 1910, 34 1/2 x 48 x 21 In. 514.00
Dresser, Pine, 3 Drawers, 3 Cupboard Doors, Block Feet, 33 x 65 x 20 In. 1573.00
Dresser, Queen Anne, Pine, 3 Frieze Drawers, Cabriole Legs, 33 x 60 x 17 In. 725.00
Dresser, Renaissance Revival, Mahogany, 3 Over 2 Wide Drawers, 1890, 38 x 55 In. 240.00
Dresser, Renaissance Revival, Walnut, Marble Top, Carved, 46 x 92 x 18 In. 495.00
Dresser, Rococo, Mahogany, Carved Crest Over Arched Mirror, Marble Top, 34 In. 786.00
Dresser, Victorian, Walnut, Mirror, Marble Top, 4 Drawers, 93 x 45 In. 615.00
Dresser, Walnut, 3 Drawers, Foliage Pulls, Adjustable Mirror, 77 In. 495.00
Dresser, Walnut, 3 Drawers, Inset Marble Top, Victorian, 45 1/2 x 32 In. 440.00
Dresser, Walnut, 5 Graduated Drawers, Door, Wood Feet, 40 x 56 1/2 In. 1265.00
Dresser, Walnut, 8 Drawers, Gilt Ceramic Pulls, Widdecomb, 1954, 69 1/2 In. 1840.00
Dresser, Walnut, Brown Marble Top, Serpentine, 1900, 32 x 48 x 24 In. 330.00
Dresser, Walnut, Marble Top, Mirror, Drop Pulls, 1890, 88 x 42 x 17 In. 465.00
Dry Sink, 1-Board Doors, Dovetailed Well, 28 1/2 x 47 3/4 In. 330.00
Dry Sink, 3 Paneled Drawers, Shelf, Stile Feet, 33 1/2 In. 975.00
Dry Sink, Cherry, Pine, Gallery Back, 2 Panel Doors, 19th Century, 42 In. 385.00
Dry Sink, Cupboard Top, Cornice, 2 Paneled Doors, 1880, 2 Piece 440.00
Dry Sink, Cupboard, Step Back, Raised Panel, Grain Painted, 76 In. 1895.00
Dry Sink, Pine, 2 Drawers, Door, 19th Century 595.00
Dry Sink, Pine, 4 Panel Doors, Drawer, Bracket Feet, 19th Century, 49 x 19 x 69 In. 288.00
Dry Sink, Pine, Poplar, Paint Layers, Paneled Doors, Drawer, 48 x 21 x 35 In. 795.00
Dry Sink, Pine, Raised Paneled Doors, Wood Pegs, 19th Century, 44 x 43 x 19 In. 375.00
Dry Sink, Poplar, Drawer Over 2 Paneled Doors, Pennsylvania, 1850 .... 605.00
Dry Sink, Poplar, Short Feet, 3 Dovetailed Drawers, Porcelain Knobs, 50 1/2 In. 1870.00
Dry Sink, Pump At Side, Blue Paint, 29 x 32 1/2 In. 925.00
Dry Sink, Scroll Backsplash, Covered Till, Drawer Over 2 Paneled Doors, 1860 .... 660.00
Dry Sink, White Paint, Zinc Lined, 47 1/2 In. 1850.00
Dumbwaiter, George III, Mahogany, 3 Tiers, String Inlay, Splayed Feet, 44 In. 825.00
Dumbwaiter, Revolving Dish Top, 2 Tiers, c.1760, 31 In. 450.00
Easel, Aesthetic Revival, Cutout Panel, Stiles, Adjustable Shelf, Oriental, 84 In. 275.00
Easel, Oriental-Style Carving, Stylized Dragons, Adjustable, 1880s, 70 1/2 In. 1250.00
Easel, Renaissance Revival, Giltwood, Walnut, Ebonized, Musical Design, c.1870, 78 In. . 2200.00
Easel, Stick & Ball, Arched Crest, Fretwork, Out Turned Scroll Legs 315.00
Easel, Victorian, Oak, Incised Spoon Carving, Brass Trim, Adjustable, 66 In. 175.00
Etagere, Aesthetic Movement, Rosewood, Brass, Staggered Shelves, 23 x 24 x 19 In. 1265.00
Etagere, Bamboo, Lacquer, 3/4 Gallery, Drawer, Anglo-Indian, 1880, 56 In. 1330.00
Etagere, Belle Epoque, Giltwood, Ribbon-Crested Frame, Cabriole Legs, 1900 .... 500.00
Etagere, Brass, 3 Onyx Shelves, Paw Feet, 60 x 26 In. 865.00
Etagere, Brass, Asymmetrical, 3 Onyx Shelves, Dolphin Feet, 46 x 28 In. 690.00
Etagere, Corner, Bamboo, Geometric Patterned Crest Rail, 3 Shelves, 26 3/4 In., Pair 805.00
Etagere, Corner, Bamboo, Sea Grass, 3 Shelves, Bamboo Supports, 1880, 50 In. 272.00
Etagere, Eastlake, Walnut, Scroll-Sawn Gallery Over 5 Shelves, 60 x 32 x 11 In. 210.00
Etagere, Federal, Mahogany, 3 Shelves, Lower Drawer, 1790-1810, 54 1/4 In. 6900.00
Etagere, Georgian, Mahogany, 3 Upper Shelves, 71 x 16 In., Pair 4830.00
Etagere, Mahogany, Broken Pediment Arch, Oval Mirror, Cabriole Legs, 68 1/2 In. 405.00
Etagere, Phoenix & Floral Scrolls, Black Lacquer Ground, 38 x 28 In. 275.00
Etagere, Rococo, Rosewood, Marble Top, Mirror, Pierced Foliage, c.1855, 68 In. 2200.00
Etagere, Rosewood, 5 Tiers, Dome Top, Urn Finials, Marble Shelf, Cabinet Base, 103 In. . 7500.00
Etagere, Rosewood, 5 Tiers, Raised On Turned Legs, Casters, 60 x 19 In. 2875.00
Etagere, Rosewood, Carved Crest, Center Mirror, Drawer, c.1855, 88 In. 3850.00
Etagere, Rosewood, Mirror Back, Marble Lower Shelf, 1860s 4400.00
Etagere, Rosewood, Scrolls, Foliage, Grapes, Central Mirror, Marble Top, 78 In. 7700.00
Etagere, Victorian, 5 Shaped Stepped Shelves, 58 3/4 x 30 3/4 In. 145.00

Etagere, Walnut, Half-Round, Mirror 4200.00
Etagere, Walnut, Spool Turnings, 7 Scalloped Front Shelves, Victorian, 77 1/2 In. 165.00
Fainting Couch, Carved Leaf Panels, Turned & Reeded Legs, 34 x 55 1/2 In. 165.00
Fainting Couch, Handcraft, Decal, 25 1/2 x 76 In. 1540.00
Footstool, Birch, Tapestry Cover, Summer Flowers On Black Ground, 3 Saber Legs 690.00
Footstool, Black & Brown Paint, White & Yellow Design Top, 7 x 14 x 7 In. 120.00
Footstool, Chippendale, Mahogany, Upholstered, Lyre & Foliate Design, Cabriole Legs . . 303.00
Footstool, Eagle & Shield Carved Skirt, 24 In. 2185.00
Footstool, Eagle & Stars Design On Top, Red, Yellow, Olive Green Stripes, 8 In. 253.00
Footstool, G. Stickley, No. 300, Green Finish, Arched Seat Rail, 4 Legs, 20 x 16 In. 1320.00
Footstool, Hickory, Woven Hickory Top, Square, 11 x 12 In. 55.00
Footstool, Louis XV Style, Upholstered, Carved Cabriole Legs, 12 x 18 x 10 In. 45.00
Footstool, Louis XV, Fruitwood, Floral Carved Scroll Feet, 11 x 14 x 12 1/2 In. 272.00
Footstool, Mahogany, Geometric Inlay, Relief Carving, Needlepoint Top, 8 1/2 In. 220.00
Footstool, Mahogany, Padded Top, Fretwork Carved Corners, 1830s, 17 1/2 In. 920.00
Footstool, Mahogany, Slip Seat, c.1790, Pair 412.00
Footstool, Mahogany, Stuffed Top, Serpentine Sides, Bracket Feet, 11 x 20 In. 160.00
Footstool, Oak, Needlepoint, Shaped Ball Feet, 1880, 6 x 19 In. 85.00
Footstool, Oriental, Lacquer, Incised Carved Flowers & Birds, 20th Century 127.00
Footstool, Pine, Fiddleback, 7 3/4 x 14 3/4 x 4 3/4 In. 330.00
Footstool, Pine, Green Paint, Yellow, 7 1/2 x 18 x 17 1/2 In. 165.00
Footstool, Pine, Scratch Carved, Compass & Star On Ends, 8 x 12 In. 220.00
Footstool, Pine, Walnut Inlay, Stylized Leaves, Stars, 8 x 16 In. 165.00
Footstool, Queen Anne, Mahogany, Needlepoint Slip Seat, Shell Knees, c.1720 . . . . 1650.00
Footstool, Rectangular, Beaded Edge Skirt, Upholstered, 16 x 20 x 14 In. 80.00
Footstool, Red Paint, 1830s, 18 In. 495.00
Footstool, Sheraton, Curly & Bird's-Eye Maple, Cane Top, 6 1/2 x 13 In. 440.00
Footstool, Victorian, Walnut, Floral Needlepoint Top, 14 x 17 3/4 In. 220.00
Footstool, Wallace Nutting, Branded 240.00
Footstool, Walnut, 4 Bun Feet 85.00
Footstool, Walnut, Finger Carved, Upholstered Top, 16 x 22 x 14 In. 173.00
Footstool, Wicker, Heart Shape 55.00
Footstool, Windsor, Bamboo, Painted, Yellow Striping, 5 1/4 x 11 3/4 In. 165.00
Footstool, Windsor, Pine, Painted, Oval Top, Splayed Legs, 19th Century, 10 x 15 In. . . . 287.00
Frame, Cherry, Eagle & Shield Top, Feathers On Sides & Bottom, 16 1/2 In. 715.00
Frame, Eagle & Shield, Black, Medallions, Oval, Iron, 1862, 20 x 11 3/4 In., Pair 550.00
Frame, Giltwood, Cavetto Molded, Petal Inner Edge, 19th Century, 44 x 29 In. 125.00
Frame, Giltwood, Ogee Molded, Foliate Scrollwork, 19th Century, 43 1/4 In. 175.00
Frame, Giltwood, Relief Bands Of Papyrus Heads, Beading, 19th Century, 26 In. 125.00
Frame, Grain Painted, Wood, Mustard, Red & Black, Penna., 17 x 13 In. 90.00
Frame, L. & J.G. Stickley, Mountain Landscape, 13 x 15 In. 1980.00
Frame, Majorelle, Mahogany, Whiplash Corners, Slight Arch, 16 In. 3580.00
Frame, Walnut, Maple, Swirled Design, Square Border, 10 x 8 1/2 In. 100.00
Frame, Wood, Gilt Gesso, Victorian, 16 x 18 In. 5.00
Hall Stand, Eastlake, Cherry, Spindles, Pierced Fretwork, c.1870, 81 1/2 In. 2500.00
Hall Stand, Eastlake, Walnut, Mirror, Drawer, 1885, 88 x 41 x 17 In. 970.00
Hall Stand, Golden Oak Era, Applied Foliage, Beveled Mirror, 83 In. 660.00
Hall Stand, Intertwined Serpents, Bronze, Rectangular Base, Art Deco, 25 In. 6900.00
Hall Stand, Marble Inset, Hat Rack, Beveled Mirror, Umbrella Stand, Iron, 1925, 74 In. . . 5750.00
Hall Stand, Mission Style, Beveled Mirror 77.00
Hall Stand, Oak, Umbrella Holder, Brass Hooks, Mirror, 1900, 77 In. 595.00
Hall Stand, Victorian, Ebony, Burl Walnut, Candleholders, Seat, Mirror 1540.00
Hall Tree, Belter, Oak, Marble Shelf 6050.00
Hall Tree, Burl Walnut 1800.00
Hall Tree, Golden Oak Era, Quartersawn, Cast-Iron Hooks, Porcelain Medallion, 79 In. . . 935.00
Hall Tree, Golden Oak Era, Umbrella Rack, Drawer, Brass Hooks, 72 3/4 x 33 In. 340.00
Hall Tree, Quartersawn Oak, 9 Hat Pegs, Umbrella Holder, Tin Tray, 80 x 38 In. 260.00
Hall Tree, Walnut, Cast-Iron Umbrella Stands, Marble Top, Carved Crest 1600.00
High Chair, Black, Gold Banding, Woven Cane Seat, American, 1800s, 33 In. 550.00
High Chair, Chippendale, Mahogany, Triple-Arch Crest, Solid Splat, c.1780 . . . . 2350.00
High Chair, French Provincial, Fruitwood, Ladder Back, Cane Seat, 1860, 33 1/2 In. 365.00
High Chair, Fruitwood, Rush Seat, Splayed Legs, c.1860, 38 In. 300.00
High Chair, Grain Painted, Plank Bottom, Turned Supports 130.00

High Chair, Ladder Back, 3 Arched Slats, Turned Finial, Rush Seat, Pennsylvania, 1800 . . 2860.00
High Chair, Ladder Back, Double Box Stretcher, Splint Seat, Carved Legs, 34 In. 1035.00
High Chair, Mahogany, Table Crest, Trailing Vines, Down-Scrolled Arms, Stand, 38 In. . . 978.00
High Chair, Oak, Pressed Back, Wide Crest Rail Over 4 Flattened Spindles 155.00
High Chair, Pine, Grain Painted, Brown Trim, Tan Ground, 19th Century, 35 x 17 In. 280.00
High Chair, Stenciled Fruit & Foliage, Red Striping, Black Paint, 35 3/4 In. 473.00
High Chair-Stroller, Oak 700.00
High Chair-Stroller, Oak, 1900 . . . . 495.00
Highboy, Cherry, 6 Long Over 3 Short Drawers, Fan Design, Flat Top, 18th Century 3300.00
Highboy, Chippendale Style, Mahogany, Carved, 10 Drawers, 2 Piece, 73 In. 1150.00
Highboy, Chippendale, Cherry, Pine, Chestnut, Apron, Cabriole Legs, 75 In. 4620.00
Highboy, Chippendale, Mahogany Veneer, Bonnet Top, Cabriole Legs, 20th Century 1265.00
Highboy, Chippendale, Mahogany, Bonnet Top, 12 Drawers, 35 x 22 x 39 In. 1980.00
Highboy, Chippendale, Walnut, Inlay, 7 Drawers, 24 x 42 x 65 In. 2145.00
Highboy, E. Wheeler, Queen Anne, Tiger Maple, 4 Drawers, Gallery 5175.00
Highboy, Hepplewhite, Cherry, 3 Over 5 Drawers, 3-Line Inlay, 1810, 65 x 40 In. 7925.00
Highboy, Mahogany, Wishbone Holder, Scroll Feet, c.1915, 47 In. . . . .*Illus* 1815.00
Highboy, Maple, 2 Short Over 4 Over 3 Short Drawers, Flat Top, 18th Century 2970.00
Highboy, Queen Anne Style, Mahogany, Drawer, Fan Carving, 79 x 39 In. 805.00
Highboy, Queen Anne, Curly Maple, 2 Piece 9200.00
Highboy, Queen Anne, Curly Maple, 9 Drawers, Fan Carving, 2 Piece, 73 In. 9200.00
Highboy, Queen Anne, Flat Top, 2 Short Over 3 Long Drawers 1045.00
Highboy, Queen Anne, Mahogany, 2 Small Over 1 Long Drawer, 81 1/2 In. 6600.00
Highboy, Queen Anne, Maple, 3 Graduated Drawers, Flat Top, Cabriole Legs, 69 In. 4025.00
Highboy, Queen Anne, Maple, 4 Overlapping Drawers, 73 x 35 1/2 In. 5500.00
Highboy, Queen Anne, Maple, 5 Dovetailed & 4 Small Drawers, 70 1/4 In. 7370.00
Highboy, Queen Anne, Maple, Bonnet Top, 1 Small Over 4 Graduated Drawers 1495.00
Highboy, Queen Anne, Maple, Curly Front, 21 x 39 x 70 In. 7370.00
Highboy, Queen Anne, Pine Cherry, 8 Drawers, Flat Molded Cornice 4950.00
Highboy, Queen Anne, Tiger Maple, Cornice, Shell Carved Drawer, 18th Century 2875.00
Highboy, Queen Anne, Walnut, 4 Graduated Drawers, Cabriole Legs, 54 In. 1694.00
Highboy, William & Mary, Curly Maple Veneer, 7 Dovetailed Drawers, 66 In. 5620.00
Huntboard, E. Wheeler, Federal, Tiger Maple, 2 Rows Of 3 Drawers 1955.00
Huntboard, Walnut, 3 Drawers, Edge Beading, 43 3/4 In. 2475.00
Huntboard, Walnut, 4 Drawers, Brown Marble Top, Carved Fish, Birds, Mirror, 93 In. . . . 8625.00
Hutch, 3 Leaded-Glass & 3 Paneled Doors, 3 Drawers, 2 Piece, 78 x 54 In. 140.00
Hutch, Bird's-Eye Maple, Leaded Glass Between Top & Base, 6 Drawers, 1900 . . . . 2200.00
Hutch, Harvest, 2-Board Top, Drawer, Tapered Square Legs, 30 x 38 x 82 In. 1210.00
Hutch, Harvest, Hardwood, Green Paint, 3-Board Poplar Varnished Top, 84 In. 1100.00
Hutch, Harvest, Walnut, Dark Finish, Turned Legs, 1-Board Top, 27 x 96 x 30 In. 2035.00
Hutch, Hepplewhite, Cherry, Inlay, Banding, Starburst & Paterae, 11 1/4 In. 3675.00
Hutch, Pine, 2-Board Top, 43 x 59 x 29 In. 1100.00
Hutch, Pine, Painted, Open Top Over 3 Drawers, Queen Rose, Yellow, Peter Hunt 920.00
Hutch, Pine, Red Paint, 36 1/2 x 50 x 28 1/2 In. 550.00
Hutch, Scotland, 1880s, 96 x 60 In. 3900.00
Hutch, Step Back, Pine, Painted, Base, 2 Glass Doors, Drawers, 19th Century 495.00
Ice Cream Set, 4 Heart-Shaped Wire Chairs, Round Walnut-Top Table, 5 Piece 220.00

Furniture, Highboy,
Mahogany, Wishbone
Holder, Scroll Feet,
c.1915, 47 In.

**Mahogany furniture can be cleaned
with a sponge dipped in equal
parts of warm water and white
vinegar. Dry with a soft cloth.**

Kas, Butternut, 2 Paneled Doors, Pennsylvania, 25 x 75 x 83 In. 2035.00
Kas, Cherry, 2 Drawers, Raised Paneled Doors, 49 x 20 x 52 In. 2805.00
Kas, Chippendale, Walnut, Stepped Cornice, Secret Drawers, Pennsylvania, 90 x 80 In. ... 1200.00
Kas, Paneled Doors, Red, Green, Yellow Floral, Birds, Blue Ground, 1820, 77 In. 5500.00
Lectern, Carved Eagle, Grain Painted, Gold Trim, 22 1/2 x 26 In. 4675.00
Lectern, Cast Iron, Adjustable, Cast-Iron Standard, Painted, 28 x 26 1/2 In. 575.00
Lectern, Mahogany, Pullout Writing Surface, 6 Drawers, Brass, Leather, Stool, 44 In. 575.00
Library Steps, French Provincial, Oak, 5 Steps, Arched Top Rail 1265.00
Library Steps, Georgian Style, Mahogany, 4 Steps, Brass Mounted, 47 In. 550.00
Library Steps, Georgian, Folding, Leather Cover, Nailhead Trim, 79 In. 1035.00
Library Steps, Mahogany, Folding, Round Bars, France, 10 Ft. 3 In. 2300.00
Library Steps, Pole, 6 Steps, Brass-Studded Leather, 80 In. 1840.00
Library Steps, Regency, 4 Steps, Casters, 35 x 35 1/2 x 18 In. 850.00
Linen Press, Cherry, 2 Arched Doors, Pennsylvania, 2 Piece, 76 x 40 x 20 In. 4400.00
Linen Press, Cherry, Drawer, Punched Design, 6 1/2 x 11 3/4 In. 605.00
Linen Press, Chippendale, Maple, 2 Doors, 2 Short Over 2 Long Drawers, 78 x 56 In. ... 9775.00
Linen Press, Double Paneled Doors, 2 Short & 2 Long Drawers 880.00
Linen Press, George III, Enameled Floral Blind Top Doors, 3 Drawers, 79 In. 1610.00
Linen Press, Mahogany, 2 Cock-Beaded Drawers, Bracket Feet, 92 3/4 x 55 In. 4000.00
Linen Press, Mahogany, 2 Paneled Doors, Sliding Shelves, Lower Doors, 91 In. 9200.00
Linen Press, Mahogany, Line & Band Inlay, Scalloped Skirt & Feet, 81 In. 770.00
Linen Press, Neoclassical Style, Mahogany, Ivory Paint, 83 1/2 In. 3520.00
Linen Press, Oak, Acorn Finial, Compressed Bun Feet, 19th Century, 86 x 23 In. 575.00
Love Seat, G. Nelson, Marshmallow, 18 Orange Vinyl Cushions, 30 x 52 x 33 In. 16500.00
Love Seat, Rococo, Black Walnut, Triple Back, Fruit & Grape Carved Crests, 1865 ..... 1900.00
Love Seat, Serpentine Front, Bun Feet, Upholstered, Early 20th Century, 66 In. 345.00
Love Seat, Triple Back, Fruit & Grape Carving, Button Tufted, c.1865 .... 2400.00
Love Seat, Walnut, Bowfront, Triple-Crested Rose Design, Yellow, Victorian, 55 In. 518.00
Love Seat, Walnut, Cameo Back, Carved Crest, Damask Tufted Back, Victorian 220.00
Love Seat, Wendell Castle, Double Molar, White Molded Fiberglass, 49 x 28 In. 220.00
Love Seat, Windsor, Maple, Thumb Back, Rush Seat, 1820, 31 x 51 In. 1845.00
Lowboy, 2 Drawers, Drop Bell Pendants, Japanned, 32 1/2 In. 1840.00
Lowboy, Chippendale, Mahogany, 3 Drawers, Geometric Carved Frieze, 31 In. 805.00
Lowboy, Chippendale, Mahogany, 4 Drawers, Shell, Cabriole Legs, 30 x 36 In. 605.00
Lowboy, Chippendale, Walnut, 4 Dovetailed Drawers, Scroll Apron, 29 In. 2695.00
Lowboy, Chippendale, Walnut, Philadelphia, Pennsylvania, 29 x 36 In. 1100.00
Lowboy, Drop Leaf, Walnut, 2 Graduated-Lip Drawers, York County, 32 x 28 In. 4290.00
Lowboy, E. Wheeler, Queen Anne, Tiger Maple, 1 Long Over 3 Short Drawers 1265.00
Lowboy, Mahogany, 1 Long Over 1 Short Drawer, Foliate Knees, 19th Century 488.00
Lowboy, Mahogany, 2 Bowfront Drawers, Cabriole Legs, Claw & Ball Feet, 28 1/2 In. ... 330.00
Lowboy, Mahogany, Chippendale, Notched Corner Top, Claw & Ball Feet, 29 In. 3300.00
Lowboy, Queen Anne, 3 Drawers, 2-Board Top, Center Drawer, Pad Feet, 31 In. 5462.00
Lowboy, Queen Anne, Burl Walnut, 3 Drawers, Molded Top, Cabriole Legs, 28 In. 3450.00
Lowboy, Queen Anne, Mahogany, 3 Drawers, Scalloped Apron, Duck Feet, 27 In. 1705.00
Lowboy, Queen Anne, Mahogany, Central Drawer, Cabriole Legs, Pad Feet, 28 In. 665.00
Lowboy, Wallace Nutting, No. 689, Mahogany 3630.00
Lowboy, Walnut, Scroll, Cabriole Legs, Trifid Feet, 29 1/2 In. 1495.00
Mirror, Adams, Giltwood, Oval, Urn Crest, Leafage, c.1920, 48 x 19 In. 605.00
Mirror, Aesthetic Movement, Giltwood, Scroll, Floral, Rectangular, 1880, 19 x 15 In. 210.00
Mirror, Architectural, Gold Paint, Primitive Oil Painting, 2 Piece, 32 x 20 In. 165.00
Mirror, Architectural, Maple, Geometric Curly Maple Strips, 21 x 14 In. 220.00
Mirror, Armorial, Beveled, Rectangular Frame, Floral Sprays, 44 x 28 3/4 In. 1150.00
Mirror, Art Deco, Beveled Mirror Plate, Hammered Metal Frame, 28 x 35 In. 212.00
Mirror, Art Deco, Bronze, Hexagonal, Fan, Sphere Design, 1920 .... 1380.00
Mirror, Art Deco, Wrought Iron, Hammered, Scalloped Frame, 1925, 26 In. 5750.00
Mirror, Arts & Crafts, Hammered Copper, 21 1/2 In. 1650.00
Mirror, Baroque Style, Giltwood, Beveled Glass, Arched Top, Scrolls, 50 In. 1092.00
Mirror, Baroque, Giltwood, Frame, Rectangular, Pierced Foliate, Bound Reeds 523.00
Mirror, Baroque, Giltwood, Stylized Guilloche Border, Italy, 37 3/4 x 21 In., Pair 4312.00
Mirror, Baroque, Molded Frame, Carved Leaf Pendant, Italy, 35 x 19 In. 490.00
Mirror, Beveled Glass, Molded Frame, 42 x 36 In. 25.00
Mirror, Bilbao, Marble, Giltwood, Urn With Leaves & Flowers, 29 x 14 In. 5462.00
Mirror, Brass Over Wood, Beveled Glass, Side Lights, Holland, 20 x 10 1/2 In., Pair 880.00

Mirror, Bugatti, Copper Inset, Round Wood Frame, Silk Tassel, 7 1/2 In. 2530.00
Mirror, Cheval, Leavens Co., 72 x 25 In. 880.00
Mirror, Cheval, Mahogany, Carved Floral Design, Reeded Columns, Claw Feet, 81 In. . . . 935.00
Mirror, Cheval, Mahogany, Footed Frame, Swivel, 19th Century, 32 x 61 x 22 In. 330.00
Mirror, Cheval, Mahogany, Swan's-Head Frame, Quervelle, 68 In. 1540.00
Mirror, Cheval, Walnut, Gold, R.J. Horner 18500.00
Mirror, Chinese Coromandel Style, 24 x 48 1/2 In. 85.00
Mirror, Chippendale Style, Mahogany, Composition Eagle, 36 1/2 In. 165.00
Mirror, Chippendale Style, Mahogany, Molded Frame, Glass, 19 1/2 x 12 1/2 In. 85.00
Mirror, Chippendale Style, Tiger Maple, Eagle Crest, 21 x 40 In. 230.00
Mirror, Chippendale, Gilt Phoenix In Crest, Giltwood Inner Rim, 36 x 20 In. 83.00
Mirror, Chippendale, Giltwood Interior Edge, 41 x 22 1/2 In. 110.00
Mirror, Chippendale, Giltwood, Shell & Scroll In Crest, 43 x 25 In. 138.00
Mirror, Chippendale, Giltwood, Urn & Flower Finial, Foliate Corners, 73 In. 650.00
Mirror, Chippendale, Mahogany Veneer, Gilt Phoenix Crest, Scroll, 32 x 18 In. 1760.00
Mirror, Chippendale, Mahogany Veneer, Molding, Old Paint, 54 x 29 In. 990.00
Mirror, Chippendale, Mahogany, 19th Century 275.00
Mirror, Chippendale, Mahogany, Carved Phoenix Crest, 1770, 52 x 52 In. 4000.00
Mirror, Chippendale, Mahogany, Crest, Gesso & Giltwood Shell, 24 x 13 1/2 In. 880.00
Mirror, Chippendale, Mahogany, Crossbanded Veneer, Scroll, 15 1/2 x 11 1/2 In. 325.00
Mirror, Chippendale, Mahogany, Giltwood Liner, 24 x 12 3/4 In. 345.00
Mirror, Chippendale, Mahogany, Giltwood, Scroll Frame, Late 18th Century, 39 In. 805.00
Mirror, Chippendale, Mahogany, Giltwood, Scroll, 29 x 17 In. 465.00
Mirror, Chippendale, Mahogany, Giltwood, Scroll, Crest, 40 1/2 x 19 3/4 In. 3575.00
Mirror, Chippendale, Mahogany, Giltwood, Scroll, Eagle Crest, 29 x 15 In. 550.00
Mirror, Chippendale, Mahogany, Giltwood, Tall Crest, Gesso Shell, 28 x 16 In. 660.00
Mirror, Chippendale, Mahogany, Scroll Crest, c.1780, 23 x 12 In. 475.00
Mirror, Chippendale, Mahogany, Scroll, Prince Of Wales Plumes, 29 x 17 In. 165.00
Mirror, Chippendale, Mahogany, Urn & String Inlay, 42 x 22 In. 165.00
Mirror, Chippendale, Pine, Mahogany Veneer, Dark Finish, Scroll, 22 3/4 In. 550.00
Mirror, Chippendale, Scroll, Pine, Mahogany Veneer, Crown Ornament, 31 3/4 In. 193.00
Mirror, Christian VII, Giltwood, Basket Top, Carved Panel Sides, 1785, 17 x 45 In. 1320.00
Mirror, Classic, Deep Cornice Over Split Columns, 3 Sections, Mantle 495.00
Mirror, Classical, Cheval, Mahogany, Satinwood Inlay, 20th Century, 68 x 32 In. 1090.00
Mirror, Classical, Giltwood, Pier, Inset Leafage Each Corner, c.1830, 49 x 26 In. 2200.00
Mirror, Cornice, Applied Half Columns, 3 Sections, Mantle, 24 x 58 In. 220.00
Mirror, Courting, Floral Pediment, Green Glass Border, 15 1/2 x 10 1/2 In. 330.00
Mirror, Courting, Stamped Brass, Continental, 26 x 15 In. 110.00
Mirror, Courting, Wood, Reverse-Painted Bird & Flowers, 16 1/2 In. 935.00
Mirror, Curly Maple, 25 1/4 x 37 1/4 In. 355.00
Mirror, Dressing, Louis XVI, Ribbon Carved Crest, 3 Sections, 28 x 65 In. 805.00
Mirror, Dressing, Mahogany, 3 Drawers, Reeded Supports, Brass Lions' Heads, 1800s . . . 550.00
Mirror, Eagle-Shaped Crest, Raised Floral & Scroll Design, 47 x 27 In. 405.00
Mirror, Eastlake, Walnut, 48 3/4 x 25 3/4 In. 250.00
Mirror, Eastlake, Walnut, Cove Molding, Mantle, 37 x 65 In. 272.00
Mirror, Edgar Brandt, Wrought Iron, Hammered Framework, Flower Heads, 33 In. 9200.00
Mirror, Edgar Brandt, Wrought Iron, Silver, Stylized Woman With Teapot, 26 In. 5750.00
Mirror, Eglomise Panel On Top, 1810s, 60 1/2 x 37 In. 2090.00
Mirror, Egyptian Revival, Walnut, Burl Walnut, Gilt, c.1875, 74 1/2 In. 1760.00
Mirror, Empire, Giltwood, American, Mantle, 24 x 84 In. 3025.00
Mirror, Empire, Giltwood, Divided Plate, 19th Century, Mantle, 26 x 68 In. 1380.00
Mirror, Empire, Giltwood, Gesso, Black Reeded Liner, 60 3/4 x 27 In. 770.00
Mirror, Empire, Giltwood, Rope Pilasters, Molded Cornice, 44 x 27 In. 1705.00
Mirror, Empire, Mahogany Veneer, Half Columns, Acorn Cornice, 36 x 20 In. 440.00
Mirror, Empire, Mahogany, 22 In. 143.00
Mirror, Empire, Mahogany, Ebonized Half Columns, Stencil, 2 Piece, 26 x 13 In. 220.00
Mirror, Empire, Mahogany, Giltwood, Gesso, 3 Sections, France, Mantle, 37 x 49 In. 210.00
Mirror, Federal Style, Walnut, Stand, Scroll Supports, 19th Century, 29 x 31 In. 252.00
Mirror, Federal, Convex, Eagle Finial, 32 1/2 In. 990.00
Mirror, Federal, Giltwood, Eglomise Landscape, Blue Ground, 32 x 18 1/2 In. 2090.00
Mirror, Federal, Giltwood, Eglomise Panel, Ivory Paint, 41 1/2 x 23 In. 2530.00
Mirror, Federal, Giltwood, Eglomise Pastoral Scene, 1800, 46 1/2 x 27 In. 4500.00
Mirror, Federal, Giltwood, Eglomise, 19th Century, 41 x 23 In. . . . . *Illus* 1265.00

Mirror, Federal, Giltwood, Gesso, Scalloped Design On Corners, 2 Piece, 39 x 20 In. 145.00
Mirror, Federal, Giltwood, Harbor Scene, Ornate Frame, 43 3/4 x 22 1/2 In. 4235.00
Mirror, Federal, Giltwood, Rectangular Plate, Gadrooned Frame, Foliate Skirt, 57 In. 630.00
Mirror, Federal, Giltwood, Rectangular Plate, Paterae Corners, Mantle, 27 In. 230.00
Mirror, Federal, Giltwood, Rectangular Plate, Trailing Husks, 52 x 34 In. 1265.00
Mirror, Federal, Giltwood, Tripartite, 19th Century, 27 x 66 In. 830.00
Mirror, Federal, Mahogany, Reeded Columns, Cavetto Cornice, 30 1/2 x 18 In. 200.00
Mirror, Federal, Rope Twist Frame, Ball Drops, Reverse Painted, 2 Piece, 31 x 18 In. 275.00
Mirror, G. Stickley, No. 918, Cheval, Peaked Full-Length, Dark Finish, 1904, 70 In. 18700.00
Mirror, George I, Walnut, Serpentine Crest, Molded Surround, 1720s, 25 1/2 x 13 In. 1265.00
Mirror, George II, Mahogany, Parcel Gilt, 39 1/2 In. 1380.00
Mirror, George II, Walnut, Rectangular Plate, Scroll Crest, 19th Century, 32 In. 100.00
Mirror, George III, Giltwood, Molded Frame, Floral Canopy, Mantle, 40 In. 19550.00
Mirror, George III, Giltwood, Oval, Gadrooning & Foliage, 1765, 3 In. 5750.00
Mirror, George III, Giltwood, Pierced Crest, Scroll Acanthus, 65 x 31 In. 2875.00
Mirror, George III, Palmette Border, Wedgwood Blue, White, Mantle 16100.00
Mirror, Giltwood, 2-Plate, Cavetto Frame, Leaf & Berry Design, 1865, 59 1/2 In. 726.00
Mirror, Giltwood, Arched, Molded Frame, Mid-19th Century, 41 x 28 In. 1155.00
Mirror, Giltwood, Arched, Rocaille Crest, Flowers, Ribboned Frame, 1850s, 75 In. 825.00
Mirror, Giltwood, Beveled Edge, Floral Garlands, Cupids, Belle Epoque, 61 In. 3750.00
Mirror, Giltwood, Bull's-Eye, c.1800, 27 1/2 In. 1575.00
Mirror, Giltwood, Bull's-Eye, Carved Eagle At Top, c.1830, 34 x 22 In. 7500.00
Mirror, Giltwood, Center Clock, Floral Sprays, G. Douglas, c.1830, Mantle, 38 In. 1725.00
Mirror, Giltwood, Conforming Frame, Floral Carved Corners, 25 1/2 x 22 In. 115.00
Mirror, Giltwood, Continental, 29 3/4 x 20 In. 290.00
Mirror, Giltwood, Convex, Ball Trim, 22 In. 715.00
Mirror, Giltwood, Convex, Eagle, Carved Foliage, 43 x 24 In. 5500.00
Mirror, Giltwood, Convex, Eagle, Cornucopias, c.1850, 46 x 39 In. 2310.00
Mirror, Giltwood, Eagle Finial, Tripartite Frame, Mantle, 56 In. 9200.00
Mirror, Giltwood, Eglomise Panel Of Perry's Victory, Gesso, 43 x 23 In. 1870.00
Mirror, Giltwood, Floral & Shell Design, 19 1/2 In. 80.00
Mirror, Giltwood, Foliate Carved Frame, 32 x 27 1/2 In. 660.00
Mirror, Giltwood, Foliate Scroll Frame, Molded Base, 1800s, Mantle, 57 x 104 In. 990.00
Mirror, Giltwood, Garland Carved Frieze, Reeded Half Columns, Mantle, 58 In. 400.00
Mirror, Giltwood, Gesso, Shell & Leaf Design, Victorian, 40 x 54 In. 390.00
Mirror, Giltwood, Gesso, Shield, Cut Glass Bull's-Eye, Floral, Victorian, 71 x 40 In. 1650.00
Mirror, Giltwood, Leaf Tip Border, Molded Border, Italy, 18th Century, 46 3/4 In. 8625.00
Mirror, Giltwood, Molded Frame, Fruit, Foliage Design, Victorian, 36 x 30 In. 125.00
Mirror, Giltwood, Oval, Cherubs, Fruit Basket, Beveled Edge, 41 x 27 In. 920.00
Mirror, Giltwood, Rectangular Plate, Arched Cornice, Cabochon, 53 x 32 In. 431.00
Mirror, Giltwood, Rectangular, Beveled Plate, Petal Molding, 40 1/4 In. 290.00
Mirror, Giltwood, Rectangular, Cherubs, Bellflowers, 36 x 20 In. 460.00
Mirror, Giltwood, Reeded Columns, Oleander Crest, Belle Epoque, Mantle, 60 In. 600.00
Mirror, Giltwood, Round Plate, Reeded Edge, Molded Cavetto Frame, 32 1/2 In. 1495.00
Mirror, Giltwood, Shaped Plate, Double Frame, Carved Shells & Leaf Tips, 62 In. 4887.00
Mirror, Giltwood, Split Baluster, 1830, 23 1/4 x 14 1/2 In. 465.00
Mirror, Girandole, Baroque, Gilt Metal, Stylized Guilloche, Italy, 37 3/4 In., Pair 4310.00

Large mirrors should not be taken down to be cleaned. Get an assistant to hold the mirror steady while it is being wiped.

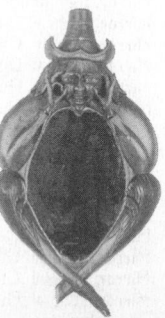

Furniture, Mirror,
Mahogany, Giltwood,
Gesso, Scroll, Phoenix
Crest, 37 x 23 In.

Furniture, Mirror,
Pine, Court Jester
Shape, Carved, 19th
Century, 21 x 12 In.

Mirror, Girandole, Giltwood, Bellflower Swag Drapes, 3 Candleholders, 51 x 26 In. 2310.00
Mirror, Hagenauer, Bronze, Ebonized Wood, Austria, 1920, 13 x 18 1/2 In. 3450.00
Mirror, Hagenauer, Stepped Chrome, Zigzag Design, 1925, 17 In. 4025.00
Mirror, Hepplewhite, Mahogany, Inlay, Gold Paint, 45 1/2 x 23 3/4 In. 2530.00
Mirror, Hepplewhite, Mahogany, Scroll, Crossbanded Veneer, 25 3/4 x 15 1/4 In. 440.00
Mirror, Herter Brothers, Rosewood, Portrait Bust Crest, Pilasters, 1870s, 71 In. 1100.00
Mirror, Italian Baroque, Parcel Gilt, Painted, Leaf Border, 4 Seasons, 46 x 52 In. 8625.00
Mirror, Italian Neoclassical, Walnut, Round, Everted Lip, 19th Century, 27 In. 3450.00
Mirror, Italian Rococo, Giltwood, Floral, Ear Corners, 18th Century, 47 x 33 In. 5750.00
Mirror, Louis XV, Giltwood, Dentil Cornice, Swag, Flower Basket Design, 52 In. 1089.00
Mirror, Louis XV, Pierced Foliate Scroll, Shell Cast Border, 17 x 12 1/4 In., Pair 2875.00
Mirror, Louis XVI Style, Carved Wood, Gold Leaf, Doves, Leaves, Torch, 22 x 12 In. ... 360.00
Mirror, Louis XVI, Giltwood, Acanthus & Shell Carving, Beaded Frame, 1890, 61 In. ... 1815.00
Mirror, Louis XVI, Giltwood, Gesso, Wreath & Garlands, Flowers, 76 In. 3000.00
Mirror, Louis XVI, Giltwood, Rectangular, Leaf Mold, Floral Garlands, 52 In. 545.00
Mirror, Louis XVI, Giltwood, Semi-Arched Frame, Twisted, Beaded, 20th Century 515.00
Mirror, Louis XVI, Gray Paint, Molded Frame, Festoons, Foliate, 42 x 61 In. 865.00
Mirror, Louis XVI, Parcel Gilt, Figural Pastoral Scene, Ribbon Crest, Sage Green 2070.00
Mirror, Mahogany Veneer, Ogee, 19th Century, 37 x 24 In. 77.00
Mirror, Mahogany Veneer, Reverse-Painted Sailboat, 22 x 11 5/8 In. 275.00
Mirror, Mahogany, Carved & Pierced Crest, Floral & Scroll, Beveled, 62 x 39 In. 245.00
Mirror, Mahogany, Eagle, Giltwood, Gesso, Gold Paint, 36 In. 550.00
Mirror, Mahogany, Giltwood Liner, Scroll, 35 x 18 In. 220.00
Mirror, Mahogany, Giltwood, Gesso, Scroll, Phoenix Crest, 37 x 23 In. ....*Illus* 1265.00
Mirror, Mahogany, Half Column, Black Panel, Stenciled, 37 x 17 In. 305.00
Mirror, Mahogany, House & Trees, Red, White, Green, Black, 19 x 11 In. 220.00
Mirror, Mahogany, Inlay, Painted, Floral Swag Frieze, c.1900, 49 x 32 In. 1100.00
Mirror, Mahogany, Line Inlay, Scroll Upper & Lower Crests, c.1780, 23 x 12 In. 300.00
Mirror, Mahogany, Molded Frame, Narrow Crest, Silvered, 20 x 11 5/8 In. 165.00
Mirror, Mahogany, Rectangular, Beveled, 1910, 25 x 33 In. 55.00
Mirror, Mahogany, Removable Urn Finial, Giltwood Inlay, c.1800, 50 x 22 In. 2300.00
Mirror, Mahogany, Rosettes, Giltwood Eagle At Top, Pendant Fruit, 1795, 46 In. 8050.00
Mirror, Mahogany, Scroll, 19th Century, 27 x 15 In. 195.00
Mirror, Napoleon III, Giltwood, Egg-And-Dart Cornice, Trailing Garlands, 84 x 54 In. ... 4600.00
Mirror, Napoleon III, Oriental Geometric Designs, Bamboo Trellis, Border 10350.00
Mirror, Neoclassical Style, Faux Malachite, Painted Border, 36 x 32 In. 1725.00
Mirror, Neoclassical Style, Giltwood, 33 x 27 In. 140.00
Mirror, Neoclassical Style, Giltwood, Figural, Urn, Scroll, Flowers, 24 x 51 1/2 In. 520.00
Mirror, Neoclassical, Faux Bois, Rectangular, Beveled, Italy, Pair 8050.00
Mirror, Neoclassical, Faux Malachite Border, Baltic, 36 x 32 In. 1725.00
Mirror, Neoclassical, Giltwood, 2 Reeded Columns, 3 Open Roundels, 39 In. 2300.00
Mirror, Neoclassical, Giltwood, Pearl Inner Frame, Floral, 62 In. 14950.00
Mirror, Neoclassical, Mahogany, Giltwood, Acanthus Capitals, Holland, Pair 10925.00
Mirror, Neoclassical, Silvered, Fluted Pilasters, Stepped Feet, 54 In., Pair 20700.00
Mirror, Neoclassical, Walnut, Everted Lip, Italy, 19th Century, 27 In. 3450.00
Mirror, Oak, Scroll Top, Shelf, Mantle, 56 x 31 1/2 In. 185.00
Mirror, Oval, Gesso, White Paint, 1890, Mantle, 38 x 33 In. 95.00
Mirror, Oval, Rectangular Walnut Frame, Easel Back, 19 1/2 x 16 In. 125.00
Mirror, Painted Panel, Gadrooned & Beaded Frame, Continental, 63 x 30 In. 920.00
Mirror, Pier, Eastlake, Carved Crest & Base, Marble Base Shelf, 92 In. 1155.00
Mirror, Pier, Eastlake, Walnut, Geometric Carved Crest, Marble Top, 102 x 29 In. 575.00
Mirror, Pier, Eastlake, Walnut, Marble Shelf, 94 x 33 1/2 In. 605.00
Mirror, Pier, Empire, Mahogany Veneer, Giltwood, Egg & Dart Cornice, Columns 1840.00
Mirror, Pier, Federal, Giltwood, Gesso, Eglomise Panel, 19th Century, 66 In. 4255.00
Mirror, Pier, Hairpin Arch, Carved Pendant Fruit & Leaves, c.1860, 86 1/2 In. 1030.00
Mirror, Pier, Mahogany, Inlay, c.1835, 97 3/4 In. 1870.00
Mirror, Pier, Napoleon III, Beveled Plate, Foliate Carved Frame, 84 x 54 In. 6325.00
Mirror, Pier, Neoclassical, Painted, Parcel Gilt, Sweden, 94 x 30 In. 7475.00
Mirror, Pier, Renaissance Revival, Burl Panels, Marble Top, 108 In. 2700.00
Mirror, Pier, Renaissance Revival, Walnut, Columns, 60 3/4 x 41 In. 415.00
Mirror, Pier, Rococo, 94 x 36 1/2 In. 1155.00
Mirror, Pier, Rococo, Mid-19th-Century, 92 x 37 In. 1680.00
Mirror, Pier, Walnut, Burl Panels, Diamond Dust Mirror, White Marble, 108 x 33 In. 2700.00

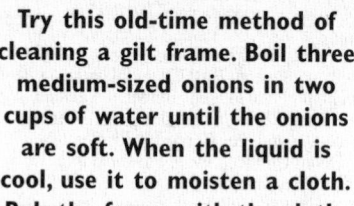

Try this old-time method of cleaning a gilt frame. Boil three medium-sized onions in two cups of water until the onions are soft. When the liquid is cool, use it to moisten a cloth. Rub the frame with the cloth.

Furniture, Mirror, Federal, Giltwood, Eglomise, 19th Century, 41 x 23 In.

Furniture, Mirror, Regency, Giltwood, Convex, Horse With Dragon Tail, 38 In.

Mirror, Pier, Walnut, Carved, Marble Inlay, 19th Century, 126 1/2 In. 3500.00
Mirror, Pine, Court Jester Shape, Carved, 19th Century, 21 x 12 In. . . . . *Illus* 3738.00
Mirror, Pine, Rectangular, Yellow, Ogee Frame, Late 19th Century, 31 In. 70.00
Mirror, Projecting Cornice, Acanthus Frieze, Center Ribbon Swags, 1900s, 37 In. 1430.00
Mirror, Queen Anne Style, Mahogany, Giltwood, Scroll & Shell Bottom, 53 x 17 In. 725.00
Mirror, Queen Anne, Figured Walnut Veneer, Scroll Crest, 20 1/2 x 11 In. 585.00
Mirror, Queen Anne, Giltwood, Beveled, Blue Glass Border 5750.00
Mirror, Queen Anne, Mahogany, Giltwood, Openwork Crest, Phoenix, 30 x 17 1/2 In. . . . 550.00
Mirror, Queen Anne, Pine, Walnut Veneer, Scroll Crest, 15 3/4 x 9 In. 770.00
Mirror, Queen Anne, Pine, Walnut Veneer, Scroll, England, 37 1/2 x 18 1/2 In. 605.00
Mirror, Queen Anne, Rectangular, Chinoiserie, 44 x 18 3/4 In. 690.00
Mirror, Queen Anne, Walnut, Double Glazed, 1720, 43 1/2 x 17 1/2 In. 4600.00
Mirror, Queen Anne, Walnut, Scroll Crest, England, 39 1/4 In. 4400.00
Mirror, Raymond Subes, Wrought Iron, Hammered Circles, 1924, 17 1/2 x 43 In. 4600.00
Mirror, Rectangular, Carved Leaf Design, 42 x 24 In. 60.00
Mirror, Rectangular, Petal Carved, Carved & Molded Surround, 19th Century 60.00
Mirror, Regency, Brass, Rectangular, Beveled, 24 x 14 In. 200.00
Mirror, Regency, Giltwood, Bull's-Eye, 1900, 16 1/4 In. 845.00
Mirror, Regency, Giltwood, Convex, Horse With Dragon Tail, 38 In. . . . . *Illus* 9200.00
Mirror, Regency, Giltwood, Gesso, Arched Rectangular Plate, Flowers, 56 1/2 In. 865.00
Mirror, Regency, Giltwood, Gesso, Scroll Molded Frame, Floral Crest, 53 x 36 In. 550.00
Mirror, Regency, Giltwood, Horse With Dragon's Tail, Lion's Head, 38 x 25 1/2 In. 9200.00
Mirror, Rococo Style, Giltwood, Gesso, Acanthus & Floral, France, 40 x 49 In. 60.00
Mirror, Rococo Style, Giltwood, Pierce Carved Flower, Foliate, 35 In. 345.00
Mirror, Rococo, Giltwood, Carved Flowers & Leaves, Continental, 39 x 21 In., Pair 2860.00
Mirror, Rococo, Giltwood, Carved Scrolls, Figural Landscapes, 50 In. 375.00
Mirror, Rococo, Giltwood, Cobalt Reserves, Flower Border, 58 x 38 In. 16100.00
Mirror, Rococo, Giltwood, Composition, Rope Twist, Mantle, 53 x 41 In. 690.00
Mirror, Rococo, Giltwood, Double-Faced Crest Rail, Gold Paint, 1820, 51 x 26 In. 545.00
Mirror, Rococo, Giltwood, Floral Molded Border, Italy, Mid-18th Century, 47 In. 5750.00
Mirror, Rococo, Giltwood, Rectangular Plate, Scrolls, Italy, 18th Century, 34 In. 1150.00
Mirror, Rococo, Pierced Frame, Flowers, Continental, 29 In. 300.00
Mirror, Shaving, 2 Candlesticks, Iron, Wilton 125.00
Mirror, Shaving, Cherry, Scroll Supports, Drawer Base, 26 x 32 In. 360.00
Mirror, Shaving, Curly Maple, Natural Finish, Turned Posts, 20 x 22 In. 135.00
Mirror, Shaving, Empire, Mahogany, Drawer, 19 1/4 x 10 1/2 x 19 3/8 In. 165.00
Mirror, Shaving, Federal, Mahogany Veneer, 4 Drawers, 25 In. 275.00
Mirror, Shaving, Federal, Mahogany Veneer, Bowfront, Inlay, 2 Drawers 170.00
Mirror, Shaving, Hardwood, Drawer In Base, Turned Frame, Oval, 19 1/4 In. 165.00
Mirror, Shaving, Hepplewhite, Bowfront, Mahogany, Drawer, Glass, 14 In. 165.00
Mirror, Shaving, Hepplewhite, Mahogany Veneer, Inlay, Drawer, 14 x 7 In. 190.00
Mirror, Shaving, Hepplewhite, Mahogany, Figured Veneer, 3 Drawers, 18 x 24 In. 245.00

Mirror, Shaving, Mahogany, Brass Mounted, c.1830, 18 x 21 1/2 In. 210.00
Mirror, Shaving, Mahogany, Hepplewhite, 2 Drawers, 17 3/4 In. 220.00
Mirror, Shaving, Mahogany, Hepplewhite, Shield Shape, 3 Drawers, 29 1/4 In. 360.00
Mirror, Shaving, Mahogany, Rope Columns, Serpentine Base, Late 19th Century 190.00
Mirror, Shaving, Mahogany, Shield Shape, Floral Inlay, 2 Drawers, 22 1/2 In. 575.00
Mirror, Shaving, Mahogany, Swan Arms, Continental 990.00
Mirror, Shaving, Mahogany, Turned Feet, Dovetailed Drawer, 14 x 6 x 16 In. 165.00
Mirror, Shaving, Regency, Mahogany, 3 Drawers, Turned Posts 300.00
Mirror, Shaving, Sheraton, Mahogany, Adjustable, Turned Posts, 15 1/4 x 7 x 20 In. 165.00
Mirror, Shaving, Silver-Plated, W.M.F. Gorman, Germany, 30 In. 5000.00
Mirror, Shaving, Swivel, 1 Long & 4 Short Drawers, 23 1/2 x 27 In. 285.00
Mirror, Sheraton, 2-Part Tabernacle, Reverse-Painted Landscape, 29 x 16 In. 467.00
Mirror, Sheraton, Mahogany, Reverse Painted, Rope-Turned Columns, 38 x 22 In. 220.00
Mirror, Sheraton, Mahogany, Rosewood & Cherry Panels, Spiral Columns, 47 In. 345.00
Mirror, Silvered Bronze, 2 Sloping Antelope Horn Legs, Ruhlmann, 1923, 17 In. 3737.00
Mirror, Tabernacle, Mahogany, Applied Carving, Water Scene, Peter Grinnel, 1815 . . . . . 315.00
Mirror, Tabernacle, Sheraton, Giltwood, 19th Century, 31 x 22 In. 275.00
Mirror, Teakwood, Carved Border, Battle Scenes, Ivory Bird Inlay, Oriental, 29 In. 1150.00
Mirror, Third Republic, Fruitwood, Ormolu Mounts, France, Mantle, 66 x 35 In. 382.00
Mirror, Triptych, Carved Flowers & Foliage, Coquillage Crests, 39 x 39 3/4 In. 1380.00
Mirror, Vanity, Distressed Wood, Triptych, 20th Century, 46 In. 230.00
Mirror, Vanity, Empire, Mahogany, Drawers, Split Columns, 19th Century 260.00
Mirror, Vanity, Federal, Mahogany, 3 Drawers, Turned Feet, 19 x 24 x 9 In. 86.00
Mirror, Vanity, Mahogany Veneer, 2 Drawers, Splashboard, 19th Century 1725.00
Mirror, Vanity, Mahogany, Inlay, Drawer, Ball Turned Feet, 20 1/2 x 12 1/2 In. 863.00
Mirror, Vanity, Mahogany, Line Inlay, Drawer, 17 x 14 1/4 x 6 1/4 In. 115.00
Mirror, Vanity, Neoclassical, Mahogany, Parcel Gilt, Drawer, Baltic, 36 x 21 In. 2875.00
Mirror, Venetian Glass, Amber, Beveled, 48 x 32 In. 431.00
Mirror, Venetian Glass, Amber, Etched Glass Basket Of Flowers 630.00
Mirror, Venetian Glass, Canted Rectangle, Scroll Ends, 39 x 18 In., Pair 345.00
Mirror, Wallace Nutting, No. 765, Mahogany, Eagle, Roses, Pair 3300.00
Mirror, Walnut, Arched Top, Finger Mold, Victorian, 39 x 24 In. 65.00
Mirror, Walnut, Giltwood, Pierced Foliate Crest, Trailing Floral Garlands, 53 In. 1400.00
Mirror, Walnut, Shadowbox, Giltwood Liner, Oval, 30 3/4 x 27 1/2 In. 247.00
Mirror, William & Mary, Eglomise Panel, Early 18th Century 4460.00
Mirror, William & Mary, Molded Arched Top, 33 x 16 In. 175.00
Mirror, William IV, Giltwood, Convex, Lion Atop Rocks Crest, 48 In. 4600.00
Mirror, William IV, Giltwood, Rectangular, Foliate, Black Velvet 7475.00
Ottoman, Bellini, Camaleonda, Dark Mohair, Welted & Tufted, 36 x 24 In. 805.00
Ottoman, Carved Wood, Reeded Legs, Velour, Beige Paint 357.00
Ottoman, Classical, Mahogany, Red Leather, Brass Nails, Ogee Bracket Feet, Pair 1210.00
Ottoman, Eames, Aluminum, Ribbed Vinyl Top, Pair 288.00
Ottoman, Regency, Walnut, Concave Body, Bun Feet, 1830, 15 1/2 x 21 In. 1694.00
Ottoman, Saarinen, Grasshopper, Birch, Molded Legs, Upholstered, 24 x 17 In. 825.00
Ottoman, W. Plattner, Steel Rods, Foam Cushion, Knoll, 24 x 15 In. 400.00
Ottoman, Wicker, Early 20th Century, 25 x 23 1/2 x 10 In. 145.00
Parlor Set, Eastlake, Walnut, 2 Chairs, c.1890, Armchair, 3 Piece 180.00
Parlor Set, Eastlake, Walnut, Upholstered, Settee, Rocker & Armchair, 3 Piece 330.00
Parlor Set, Hoffman, Settee, Chairs, Tea Table, Mahogany, Details, 6 Piece 1100.00
Parlor Set, Louis XV, Aubusson, France, 19th Century, 3 Piece 3250.00
Parlor Set, Louis XVI, Gilt, Crests, Upholstered, 1890, 5 Piece 1450.00
Parlor Set, Walnut, Applied Carvings, Upholstered, Armchair, 2 Side Chairs 1495.00
Parlor Set, Walnut, Carved, Upholstered, Chairs, Love Seat, 67 x 36 In., 7 Piece 890.00
Parlor Set, Wicker, Rolled Arms, Upholstered, Settee, 2 Chairs, 20th Century 175.00
Parlor Set, Wicker, Sofa, Rocker, Table, Green & White Paint, 6 Piece 440.00
Pedestal, Ebony, Incised, Gilt, c.1875, 13 x 13 x 42 In. 2530.00
Pedestal, Faux Grained, Square Top, Turned & Tapered Columns, 36 x 18 In., Pair 745.00
Pedestal, Federal, Mahogany, Tilt Top, Tripod Base, Down-Swept Legs, 28 In. 150.00
Pedestal, Louis XV, 2 Tiers, Marble Top, Ormolu, Painted Scenes, 41 x 11 1/2 In. 575.00
Pedestal, Louis XVI, Mahogany, Cane Top, Reeded Legs, 39 x 9 1/2, In., Pair 330.00
Pedestal, Mahogany, Marble Top, Central Medallion Of Louis XVI, 49 1/2 In. 9775.00
Pedestal, Mahogany, Rotating Top, Cylindrical, Square Base, 39 x 17 In. 1440.00

Pedestal, Neoclassical, Silver Gilt, Round, Greek Key Border, Italy, Pair 8050.00
Pedestal, Rope Twist, Glazed, Cast Stone, 17 1/2 x 15 In., Pair 240.00
Pedestal, Rosewood, Walnut, Lion Monopods, Butterfly Inlay, c.1870, 41 In. 3080.00
Pie Safe, 2 Tins Each Door & End, 2 Doors, 1870 .... 385.00
Pie Safe, 4 Punched Tin Panels, 3 Drawers 6250.00
Pie Safe, Cherry, 12 Punched Tin Panels, Mortised Frame, Drawer, 56 In. 1045.00
Pie Safe, Cherry, Poplar, 3 Punched Fork & Spoons Panels, c.1840, 51 x 45 In. 2200.00
Pie Safe, Cypress, Tin Panels, Mid-19th Century 770.00
Pie Safe, Door, 2 Shelves, Quarter Round Corners, Painted, 19th Century, 43 1/4 In. 330.00
Pie Safe, Pine, Punched Tin Panels, 57 x 32 x 14 In. 385.00
Pie Safe, Pine, Punched Tin Panels, Pegged Mortise & Tenon, c.1820, 66 In. 1650.00
Pie Safe, Poplar, 12 Punched Tin Panels, Green Paint, Drawer, 41 x 55 In. 715.00
Pie Safe, Poplar, 12 Punched Tin Panels, Painted, 40 x 17 1/2 x 59 In. 1540.00
Pie Safe, Poplar, 2 Punched Tin Panels, Star & Circles, 1-Board Ends, 41 x 15 x 49 In. ... 550.00
Pie Safe, Poplar, 3 Punched Tin Panels, Stars & Circles, Double Doors, 49 In. 1375.00
Pie Safe, Poplar, Gray Paint, High Feet, 57 3/4 In. 770.00
Pie Safe, Poplar, Punched Tin Panels, 2 Doors Over Drawer, 38 x 14 x 50 In. 855.00
Pie Safe, Punched Tin Compote Of Fruit, 48 In. 2400.00
Pie Safe, Punched Tin GA Seal, Green, White Wash, 19th Century 9500.00
Pie Safe, Punched Tin Panels, Drawer Below Doors, 58 x 40 1/2 In. 852.00
Pie Safe, Tin Panel, Love Birds In Foliage, 1868, 14 x 18 In. 110.00
Pie Safe, Tins All 4 Sides, Red Paint, c.1850 .... 2800.00
Pie Safe, Walnut, Cherry, Paneled Construction, Gallery, 41 x 17 x 52 In. 990.00
Pie Safe, Walnut, Punched Tin Panels, Pots Of Flowers, Stars, 2 Shelves, 49 x 53 In. 5750.00
Plant Stand, 4-Tiered, Wirework, White Caster, Victorian, 58 x 50 In. 575.00
Plant Stand, Reticulated Rococo Border, Hairy Paw Feet, Onyx Spire, Brass, 31 In. 220.00
Plant Stand, Square Top, Corbelled Pedestal Base, Arts & Crafts, 12 x 29 In. 275.00
Planter, Adirondack, Twig & Bark, Applied Pinecones, 1890-1910 .... 195.00
Planter, Regency, Mahogany, 3 Carved Legs, Pad Feet, 31 1/2 x 20 1/2 In. 180.00
Rack, Drying, Shaker, Walnut, Mortised Construction, Shoe Feet, 39 x 28 In. 165.00
Rack, Magazine, Art Deco, Cast Iron, Rooster & Sun Design 160.00
Rack, Magazine, Fornasetti, Brass, 1950s, 15 x 8 1/4 In. 3450.00
Rack, Magazine, Pine, Rustic, 1930, 15 In. 11.00
Rack, Magazine, Wrought Iron, Scroll & Floral Designs 82.00
Rack, Plate, Oak, 3 Shelves, Cornice Molding, Crest, 18th Century, 46 1/2 x 56 In. 1325.00
Rack, Plate, Oak, Elm, Hanging, 3 Shelves, Welsh, 43 1/4 x 44 In. 8050.00
Rack, Quilt, 5 Horizontal Slats, Tapered Stick, Shoe Feet, Wood Pins, 74 x 49 In. 290.00
Recamier, Belter, Rosewood, Finger Carved, Tufted Silk, Casters, 34 x 42 In., Pair 8340.00
Recamier, Carved Floral Design, Upholstered, Late 19th Century, 69 In. 175.00
Recamier, Eastlake, Overall Incised Design, 35 1/2 In. 260.00
Recamier, Ebonized Maple, Gilt, Cane Inset, Rooster Arms, Leather Casters, 1810 ...... 17500.00
Recamier, Empire, Rosewood, Parcel Gilt, Stencil, Out-Scrolled Arms, 85 In. 5750.00
Recamier, Mahogany, Undulating Backrest, Out-Scrolled Upholstered Sides, 72 In. 5750.00
Recamier, Scrolling Armrest, Lyre & Ball Support, Grain Painted, 78 In. 9775.00
Recamier, Walnut, Tufted Back, 39 x 28 x 58 In. 770.00
Rocker, Adirondack Style, Red Paint 195.00
Rocker, Adirondack, Tulip & Leaf Carved Design 1430.00
Rocker, Arrow Back, Wide Crest, Painted Design, Shaped Seat, 1820, Child's 230.00
Rocker, Arts & Crafts, Vertical Slats, Upholstered Cushion, J.M. Young, 32 x 30 In. 950.00
Rocker, Baluster Back, Rush Seat, Turned Stretchers, Black Paint, 18th Century 660.00
Rocker, Birch, Shaped Back & Sides, Pierced Handles, Trapezoidal Seat, Child's 373.00
Rocker, Boston Style, Spindle Back, Black Paint, Gold, Floral & Leaf, Cane Seat, 36 In. .. 58.00
Rocker, Brass, Polished Steel, Scroll Sides, Leather, Victorian 575.00
Rocker, Eames, Black Molded Fiberglass, Upholstered, Wood Runners 2128.00
Rocker, Eames, Fiberglass Shell, Orange, Seat Resting On Metal Supports 1092.00
Rocker, Eames, Fiberglass Shell, Orange, Zinc Struts, Birch Runner, Arms, 27 In. 1210.00
Rocker, Eames, Fiberglass Shell, Yellow, Herman Miller, 1950, 27 In. 575.00
Rocker, Eames, Fiberglass Shell, Zinc Struts, Birch Runner, Upholstered, 26 In. 770.00
Rocker, Eames, Zenith Shell, Gray, Birch Runner, 25 x 27 x 26 In. 1320.00
Rocker, Eames, Zenith Shell, Orange, Black Wire Struts, 1950, 27 In. 1540.00
Rocker, Eames, Zenith Shell, Yellow, Zinc Struts, Birch Runner, 25 x 27 x 26 In. 1430.00
Rocker, Floral Crest Over Spindles, Natural Arms & Plank Seat, Child's 316.00
Rocker, Fruitwood, Rush Seat, 19th Century, Child's, Arms 460.00

Rocker, G. Stickley, High Back, 34 1/2 In. 385.00
Rocker, G. Stickley, No. 309, 3 Horizontal Slats, Rush Seat, Red Decal, 32 In. 715.00
Rocker, G. Stickley, No. 313, H-Back, Leather Cushion, Decal, Arms, 37 In. 990.00
Rocker, G. Stickley, Thornden, 2 Horizontal Slats, Rattan Seat 605.00
Rocker, G. Stickley, Vertical Slats Under Arms, Leather Drop-In Seat, 41 In. 2090.00
Rocker, Gehry, Corrugated Cardboard, Masonite, 1972, 41 x 23 x 25 In. 4400.00
Rocker, Gold Cornucopia Stenciled On Crest Rail, Bent Back Spindles, Arms 450.00
Rocker, Gray Paint, Black & White Striping, Pennsylvania, 27 1/2 In. 275.00
Rocker, Harden, 32 In. 300.00
Rocker, Harden, Floral Carved Back & Front Legs, Rush Seat, Arms, 33 x 31 x 34 In. ... 2640.00
Rocker, Hardwood, Swan, Green Brocade, Arms, 30 1/2 In. 82.00
Rocker, Heywood Brothers & Co., Upholstered Seat 450.00
Rocker, Heywood-Wakefield Co., White, Pair 325.00
Rocker, Hitchcock, 7 Spindles, Grain Painted, Black & Gold, Arms, 1830 .... 795.00
Rocker, Hitchcock, Black & Gold Stenciled Fruit, Natural Seat 66.00
Rocker, Hitchcock, Black Paint, Gold Stenciled Fruit 82.00
Rocker, Horizontal Crest, 6 Spindles, Plank Seat, Painted & Smoke Design, 32 In. 8625.00
Rocker, House Painted On Crest, Baluster-Shaped Splat, Spindles, Curved Arms 373.00
Rocker, Hunzinger, Lollipop 1000.00
Rocker, Hunzinger, Platform, Oak 770.00
Rocker, Hunzinger, Woven Seat, Backrest, c.1876 .... 195.00
Rocker, J.M. Young, 3 Slats, Rush Seat, Curved Arms, Nova Scotia 411.00
Rocker, Jacaranda, Folding, Tall Back, Slung Fabric Seat, Pivoting Framework 805.00
Rocker, Karpen Furniture Co., 9 Square Cutouts Under Arms, Brown Leather 2640.00
Rocker, L. & J.G. Stickley, Chevron Crest Rail, Open Arms, Drop-In Seat 800.00
Rocker, L. & J.G. Stickley, Mahogany, 6 Vertical Slats, Drop-In Cushion, 35 In. 550.00
Rocker, L. & J.G. Stickley, No. 781, Leather Cushion & Back, Flat Arms, 38 In. 3300.00
Rocker, L. & J.G. Stickley, Open Arms, Horizontal Slats, Leather Seat, 38 In. 1100.00
Rocker, Ladder Back, Brown Paint, Splint Seat, Heavy Turned Front Stretcher 110.00
Rocker, Ladder Back, Hardwood, 4 Slats, Shaped Arms, Woven Splint Seat, 44 In. 110.00
Rocker, Ladder Back, Hardwood, Brown Finish, Rush Seat, Arms, 44 1/4 In. 300.00
Rocker, Ladder Back, Hardwood, Splint Seat, Arms, 39 In. 148.00
Rocker, Ladder Back, Knob Finials, Turned Arms, Splint Seat, 19th Century 110.00
Rocker, Ladder Back, Maple, 3 Graduated Arched Slats, Rush Seat, 41 In. 110.00
Rocker, Ladder Back, Maple, 5 Graduated Arched Slats, Rush Seat 105.00
Rocker, Ladder Back, Mixed Wood, Rush Seat, 19th Century 45.00
Rocker, Ladder Back, Pine, Cypress, Hide Seat, c.1850 .... 275.00
Rocker, Ladder Back, Spindles, Medallions, Brass Trim, Upholstered Seat, 44 3/4 In. 55.00
Rocker, Lifetime, Puritan Line, 6 Vertical Slats, 37 In. 165.00
Rocker, Light Green Paint, Child's 195.00
Rocker, Limbert, 5 Vertical Slats, Padded Seat, Arms, 38 In. 300.00
Rocker, Loop Back, Crest Rail Over 6 Stiles, Curved Arms, Saddle Seat 230.00
Rocker, Mahogany, Oval Backrest, Brass Tacks, Arms 110.00
Rocker, Mahogany, Upholstered, Arms, Victorian 395.00
Rocker, McHugh, Ladder Back, Oak, Rush Seat, Arms, 24 x 34 x 37 In. 990.00
Rocker, Morris, L. & J.G. Stickley, Stationary Back, 36 x 31 In. 3300.00
Rocker, Nursing, Spindles, Upholstered 125.00
Rocker, Oak, Maple Legs, Cane Seat, 1860-1870, Child's 110.00
Rocker, Oak, Pressed Back, Spindles, Cane Seat, Arms, 45 In. 100.00
Rocker, Oak, Shieldback, Upholstered Seat, Arms, 1880s 325.00
Rocker, Painted & Stenciled, Cane Seat, Child's, 28 In. 137.00
Rocker, Platform, Maple, Upholstered Seat & Back, Spool Turned, Arms, 19th Century .. 170.00
Rocker, Platform, Wicker, 1910, 34 1/2 x 21 x 23 In. 575.00
Rocker, Rectangular Crest, Spindle Back, Round Seat, Grain Painted, Woman's 57.00
Rocker, Red & Black Graining, Yellow Striping, Stenciled Floral Crest, 40 3/4 In. 145.00
Rocker, Red Paint, Boston, Child's 165.00
Rocker, Renaissance Revival, Walnut, Cane Seat & Back, 19th Century, Child's 165.00
Rocker, Rosewood Graining, Upholstered, Child's 350.00
Rocker, Sewing, Folding, Victorian 145.00
Rocker, Shaker, 2 Tapered Back Posts, Orange, Beige Tape Seat, Arms, 42 In. 805.00
Rocker, Shaker, 4 Graduated Back Slats, Curved Arms, Turned Supports, 45 In. 4313.00
Rocker, Shaker, 4 Slats, Shawl Bar, Taped Seat, Mt. Lebanon, 40 In. 330.00
Rocker, Shaker, 4 Slats, Upholstered Seat, Mt. Lebanon, 42 In. 410.00

Rocker, Shaker, Black Paint, Red & Black Taped Seat, Arms, Mt. Lebanon, 37 In. 165.00
Rocker, Shaker, Butternut, Open Back, 7 Rods, Woven Rush Seat, Box Stretcher 50.00
Rocker, Shaker, Maple, 3 Graduated Back Slats, Turned Post, Splint Seat, 41 In. 1093.00
Rocker, Shaker, Maple, 4 Arched Slats, Cane Seat, Mass., Arms, 1850, 49 x 16 In. 12650.00
Rocker, Shaker, No. 0, Taped Seat, Mt. Lebanon 770.00
Rocker, Shaker, No. 1, Taped Seat, Cushion Rail, Decal, Mt. Lebanon 330.00
Rocker, Shaker, No. 1, Woven Taped Seat, Stenciled Label, Mt. Lebanon, 28 1/2 In. 605.00
Rocker, Shaker, No. 3, Hardwood, Dark Brown Finish, Stencil, Mt. Lebanon, 34 In. 385.00
Rocker, Shaker, No. 3, Sewing, Taped Seat, Stenciled Label, Mt. Lebanon, 34 In. 357.00
Rocker, Shaker, No. 3, Taped Seat, Mt. Lebanon 413.00
Rocker, Shaker, No. 4, Woven Taped Seat, Stenciled Gold Label, Mt. Lebanon, 34 1/2 In. . 605.00
Rocker, Shaker, No. 7, Shaped Arms, Mushroom Caps, Shawl Bar, Mt. Lebanon, 40 In. ... 825.00
Rocker, Shaker, Splint Seat, 19th Century 220.00
Rocker, Shaker, Upholstered Seat & Back, Stenciled Label, Mt. Lebanon 165.00
Rocker, Sheraton, Painted, Stenciled, Boston, 1820-1850, 42 1/2 In. 180.00
Rocker, Slat Back, Webbed Seat, Arms, 19th Century, Canada 272.00
Rocker, Splint Seat, Stencil Design, Black Paint, Mid-19th Century 30.00
Rocker, Swan Arms, Blue Damask 275.00
Rocker, T-Back, Vertical Back Slat, Leather Seat, 31 In. 175.00
Rocker, Tapestry Seat & Back 225.00
Rocker, Thonet, Bentwood, Cane Seat & Back, Child's, 24 1/2 In. 385.00
Rocker, Twig, c.1900 .... 1900.00
Rocker, Walnut, Carved Grape Crest, Victorian 135.00
Rocker, Walnut, Finger Carved, Upholstered, Arms, Victorian 253.00
Rocker, Walnut, Leaf Carved Crest, Scroll Arms, Legs, c.1875 .... 225.00
Rocker, Walnut, Mahogany, Carved Flowers & Foliage, Velvet 357.00
Rocker, Walnut, Rose Carved Crest, Cane Seat & Back, Victorian, 34 In. 165.00
Rocker, Walnut, Rosewood Graining, Carved Frame, Silk Brocade, Victorian, 39 In. 250.00
Rocker, Walnut, Sleigh Runner, Finger-Molded Crest 165.00
Rocker, Walnut, Upholstered Seat & Back, Victorian 55.00
Rocker, Wavy Arms, Hardin, 36 In. 605.00
Rocker, Wicker, Barrel Shape, High Back, Early 20th Century, Child's 70.00
Rocker, Wicker, Dark Green, Cane Seat, Cortoy, Baltimore, Child's, 24 In. 110.00
Rocker, Wicker, Red Paint, Arms, Mid-1920s, Child's, 21 1/2 In. 135.00
Rocker, Windsor Style, Brace Back, Arms, Crocker Chair Co., 40 1/2 In. 250.00
Rocker, Windsor, 3 Spindles, Bamboo Turnings, Shaped Seat, Turned Arms, Child's 145.00
Rocker, Windsor, Comb Back, Bamboo, Narrow Slats, Arms, 42 In. 253.00
Rocker, Windsor, Comb Back, Black Paint, Step-Down Crest, Turned Legs, Arms, 44 In. . 193.00
Rocker, Windsor, Comb Back, Stenciled Grapevine Design, Black Ground 440.00
Rocker, Windsor, Crest, Plank Seat, Olive Green, Child's, 18 In. .... *Illus* 3540.00
Rocker, Windsor, Pine, Maple, Arrow Back, Painted, 19th Century, 33 x 24 In. 195.00
Rocker, Windsor, Tall Back, Bamboo Turnings, Shaped Seat, Brown Paint, 38 In. 230.00
Screen, 2-Panel, Black Lacquer Polychrome, Ivory Scenes Of Village Life, 72 x 36 In. ... 150.00
Screen, 2-Panel, Carved Walnut-Framed Panels, Embroidered Inserts, 72 x 21 In. 605.00
Screen, 2-Panel, Decoupage, Victorian, 60 x 25 In. 998.00
Screen, 2-Panel, Tosa Style, Landscape Scene, Sosho Calligraphy, 56 x 70 In. 1210.00
Screen, 3-Panel, Arts & Crafts, Oriental Painted Scene, 64 x 27 In. 1760.00
Screen, 3-Panel, Female Figures Carrying Water, Wading In Stream, 70 In. 3680.00

New research suggests that you should
never use silicone-based furniture
polish or feed the wood with oils.
Just dust with a soft cloth.

Furniture, Rocker, Windsor, Crest,
Plank Seat, Olive Green, Child's, 18 In.

Screen, 3-Panel, Folding, Floral Spray Design, Hand Painted, 68 x 60 In. 605.00
Screen, 3-Panel, Green Velvet Panels, Brass Hinges, 73 In. 115.00
Screen, 3-Panel, Hardwood, Silver Paint, Mirrors, Upholstered Panels, 20 x 57 In. 605.00
Screen, 3-Panel, Leather Panels, Floral Paint, 74 x 66 In. 3520.00
Screen, 3-Panel, Louis XV Style, Giltwood, Beveled Glass, 1895, 54 x 65 In. 1760.00
Screen, 3-Panel, Nobleman & Retainers In Landscape, Pine Trees, 18 x 47 In. 605.00
Screen, 3-Panel, Oak, Crewelwork, Foliate & Animals, 18 x 69 In. 230.00
Screen, 3-Panel, Paper, Bucolic Vignettes, Upper Swag, Foliage, c.1820, 63 In. 1495.00
Screen, 3-Panel, Scroll Foliate & Pinecone Finials, Glass Over Fabric, 60 1/2 In. 1035.00
Screen, 3-Panel, Scrolling, Arched Top, Casters, Gilt Iron, 77 x 62 In. 485.00
Screen, 3-Panel, Undulating Cresting, Upholstered Top, 47 1/2 x 15 3/4 In. 140.00
Screen, 3-Panel, Wood, Turned Spindles Over Vertical & Horizontal Panels, 75 In. 60.00
Screen, 4-Panel, Black Lacquer, Pair Of Scantily Draped Maidens, 72 x 16 In. 2875.00
Screen, 4-Panel, Black Lacquer, Polychrome, Figural Landscape, 72 x 16 In. 230.00
Screen, 4-Panel, Carved Wood Frame, Floral & Bird Panels, 35 1/2 x 10 3/4 In. 80.00
Screen, 4-Panel, Continuous Scene Of Turkish Characters, Charles X, 88 In. 12650.00
Screen, 4-Panel, Embroidered Dragon & Tiger, 1880, 67 x 21 1/2 In. 365.00
Screen, 4-Panel, Figure Painted On Silk, Velvet On Burlap, 68 3/4 x 23 In. 137.00
Screen, 4-Panel, Floral, 37 x 44 In. 805.00
Screen, 4-Panel, Fornasetti, Musical & Scientific Instruments, 1950s, 78 1/2 In. 14950.00
Screen, 4-Panel, Fornasetti, Pictorial Design 4025.00
Screen, 4-Panel, Full Length Robe, Scrolled Foliate Gold Silk, Victorian, 67 In. 980.00
Screen, 4-Panel, Leather, Floral, Urn & Scroll Design, Late 19th Century, 80 x 71 In. 2300.00
Screen, 4-Panel, Mahogany, Watercolors, Bronze Beaded Edges, 49 x 19 In. 745.00
Screen, 4-Panel, Needlepoint Brocade, 77 1/4 In. 6037.00
Screen, 4-Panel, Needlepoint, Silk Damask, Exotic Birds, 69 1/2 x 84 In. 3835.00
Screen, 4-Panel, Neoclassical, Birch, Folding, Mid-19th Century, 74 In. 4887.00
Screen, 4-Panel, Oriental Design, Hand Painted 550.00
Screen, 4-Panel, Oriental, Carved, 36 x 10 1/2 In. 220.00
Screen, 4-Panel, Silver Leaf, Arched Panels, Cornucopia Stencil, 64 x 85 In., Pair 1035.00
Screen, 4-Panel, Teakwood, Pierced Carving, Wildlife & Flowers, India, 74 x 20 In. 247.00
Screen, 4-Panel, Temple Landscape, 60 x 96 In. 815.00
Screen, 4-Panel, Vellum, Gilt, 38 x 48 1/2 In. 315.00
Screen, 4-Panel, Vintage Wallpaper, Winter Landscape, Ice Skaters, 22 x 77 In. 1320.00
Screen, 5-Panel, Directoire Style, Faux Bois, 94 x 93 In. 5635.00
Screen, 5-Panel, Genre Scene, Early 19th Century, 63 3/4 x 21 1/2 In. 1435.00
Screen, 6-Panel, Carved Teakwood, 2 Cloisonne Medallions Each Panel, 7 1/2 x 16 In. . . . 770.00
Screen, 6-Panel, Charles X, Papier-Mache, Sepia Italian Seaport Scene, 6 x 90 In. 4885.00
Screen, 6-Panel, Cranes & Pine Trees, Mountains, Peonies, c.1800, 142 In. 3365.00
Screen, 6-Panel, Cranes In River, Snow On Willow Tree, Gold Ground, 17 1/4 x 105 In. . . 1210.00
Screen, 6-Panel, Figures In Boats, River, Aquatic Plants, Chinese Export, 92 In. 6325.00
Screen, 6-Panel, Lacquered, Floral, Figural & Landscape, 72 1/4 x 16 In. 373.00
Screen, 6-Panel, Leather, Gold Ground, Flowers, Holland, 1750, 130 1/2 In. 9075.00
Screen, 6-Panel, Oriental Figural 1 Side, Birds & Flowers Other Side, 84 x 96 In. 465.00
Screen, 6-Panel, Painted Gothic Arched Windows 4885.00
Screen, 10-Panel, Eames, Birch Veneer, Bent Laminated Plywood, 68 In. 9200.00
Screen, 10-Panel, Eames, Molded Plywood, 68 In. 19250.00
Screen, 12-Panel, Black Lacquer, Elaborate Garden Scene, Pavilions, 107 In. 17250.00
Screen, Aubusson Tapestry Panel, Walnut, Metal Mounted, 42 x 23 1 1/2 In. 747.00
Screen, Brass, Bamboo, Floral Bouquet Panel, 1880, 37 x 18 1/2 In. 121.00
Screen, Floral & Shell Carving, Embroidered Silk Panel, Birds In Tree, 42 In. 110.00
Screen, Folding, Oak Veneer, Trompe L'oeil, Painted Library Shelves, 72 x 64 In. 415.00
Screen, Fox & Hounds, Arched Central Panel, Sloped Side Panels, 1920, 26 In. 6325.00
Screen, Louis XV, Giltwood, Gesso, Tapestry Center, 20th Century 400.00
Screen, Needlepoint Insert, Carved 245.00
Screen, Needlework, Chinese Pheasant Drinking From An Urn, Floral, 38 x 24 In. 1150.00
Screen, Teakwood, Porcelain, People, Camel, River, Oriental Writing, 19 1/2 x 34 In. 345.00
Screen, Walnut, Eastlake 395.00
Screen, Walnut, Eastlake Detail, Geometric Brocade, 28 1/2 x 31 1/2 In. 140.00
Seating Unit, Matta-Malitte, Foam, Stacking, Upholstered, Knoll, 62 x 64 In. 2530.00
Secretaire A Abattant, Painted, Gilt, Flat Front, Neoclassical Scenes, 56 In. 4887.00
Secretaire A Abattant, Rococo, Gilt Metal, Ebonized, 2 Doors, Germany, 15 x 10 In. 1150.00
Secretary, Aesthetic Movement, Mahogany, Inlay, England, 49 x 42 x 22 In. 6900.00

Secretary, Classical, Mahogany, Acanthus Columns, Flat Ball Feet, c.1825, 62 In. 3300.00
Secretary, Cylinder, Glass Doors, Late 19th Century, 85 In. 633.00
Secretary, Cylinder, Walnut, 3 Drawers, Glass Doors, Victorian, 86 In. 2130.00
Secretary, Cylinder, Walnut, Burl Veneer Panel 4125.00
Secretary, Drop Front, Mahogany, 2 Glass Doors, Block Front, Broken-Arch Top, 1950 .. 990.00
Secretary, Drop Front, Mahogany, 2 Glazed Doors, c.1790, 87 1/2 In. 6050.00
Secretary, Drop Front, Oriental Scene, 2 Doors, Shelved Interior 330.00
Secretary, Drop Front, Pine, Fitted Interior, Paneled Doors, 47 x 36 In. 490.00
Secretary, Drop Front, Rosewood, Maple Interior, Scroll Pierced Gallery, 63 In. 1100.00
Secretary, Drop Front, Walnut, Pigeonholes, Top Glass Doors, 43 x 19 x 82 In. 990.00
Secretary, E. Wheeler, Chippendale, Tiger Maple, Bonnet, Panel Doors 6325.00
Secretary, Eastlake, Cylinder, Walnut, 3 Drawers, Pullout Shelf, 2 Piece, 90 In. 1870.00
Secretary, Eastlake, Walnut, Cylinder, 3 Drawers, 2 Piece, 90 x 42 In. 1705.00
Secretary, Empire, Mahogany, Veneer, Glazed Doors, 1 Blind Over 2 Drawers 545.00
Secretary, Federal, Mahogany, 2 Diamond Mullioned Doors, 2 Drawers, 76 In. 3300.00
Secretary, Federal, Mahogany, Cornice, 2 Doors, Fitted, New England, 57 In. 2475.00
Secretary, Federal, Mahogany, Tambour Doors, Pigeonholes, 1800, 52 x 37 In. 4950.00
Secretary, Lacquer, Parcel Gilt, Scroll Pediment, Chinoiserie, 90 In. .... *Illus* 10350.00
Secretary, Mahogany, Glazed Doors, Figured Veneers, c.1830 .... 5500.00
Secretary, Mahogany, Mullioned Doors, Cupboard Base, 1870s, 6 In. 1755.00
Secretary, Mahogany, Tambour Doors, 7 Drawers, Inlaid Panels, 46 x 37 In. 920.00
Secretary, Napoleon III, Ormolu, Ebonized, Hardstone Inlay, 1870, 58 x 35 In. 5500.00
Secretary, Neoclassical, Mahogany, Fruitwood, Hidden Shelves, 93 In. .... *Illus* 17250.00
Secretary, Pine, Grain Painted, 75 1/4 In. 2200.00
Secretary, Queen Anne, Mahogany, Banded Inlay, 3 Piece 4000.00
Secretary, Rococo, Broken-Scroll Pediment, 3 Short Drawers, Green Lacquer 10350.00
Secretary, Rococo, Walnut, Etagere Top, 3 Drawer Base, 66 x 37 x 17 In. 515.00
Secretary, Rohde, Mahogany, 4 Doors, Herman Miller, 1940, 66 x 15 x 72 In. 2860.00
Secretary, Rosewood, Pewter Inlay, 10 Upper Drawers, 62 x 42 In. 8050.00
Secretary, Slant Front, Federal, Pine, Yellow Grain, Pigeonholes, 1820, 84 x 42 In. 4985.00
Secretary, Slant Front, Oak Veneer, Paw Feet, 3 Drawers, Curved Glass, Victorian, 78 In.. 1100.00
Secretary, Slant Front, Regency, Leather Writing Surface, Bracket Feet, 2 Piece 36800.00
Secretary, Slant Front, Rococo, Lacquer, Parcel Gilt, Glass Doors, Venetian, 90 In. 10350.00
Secretary, Slant Front, Walnut, 2 Doors Over 3 Drawers, 19th Century, 38 x 82 In. 795.00
Secretary, Upper Doors, Fitted Desk Drawer, 1800, 83 1/2 In. 2970.00
Secretary, Walnut, Chippendale, Blind Door, Ogee Bracket Feet 6270.00
Secretary-Bookcase, Cylinder, Eastlake, Oak, Griffin Gallery Crest, 88 x 39 x 22 In. 1815.00
Secretary-Bookcase, Drop Front, Biedermeier, Mahogany, Fitted Interior, 79 In. 2320.00
Secretary-Bookcase, Drop Front, Satinwood, Doors, 80 In. 2645.00
Secretary-Bookcase, Eastlake, Walnut, 3 Base Drawers, Pullout Writing Shelf, 81 In. 1870.00
Secretary-Bookcase, Edwardian, Mahogany, Upper Doors, Writing Surface, 90 In. 4600.00
Secretary-Bookcase, Empire, Mahogany, Glass Doors, Drawer, 19th Century, 83 In. 1090.00
Secretary-Bookcase, George III, Mahogany, 3 Drawers, 42 x 46 x 23 1/4 In. 4600.00
Secretary-Bookcase, George III, Mahogany, 4 Drawers, Greek Key Molding, 87 In. 10350.00
Secretary-Bookcase, George III, Mahogany, Fretwork Swan's Neck, 3 Piece, 84 In. 9775.00

Furniture, Secretary,
Lacquer, Parcel Gilt,
Scroll Pediment,
Chinoiserie, 90 In.

Furniture, Secretary,
Neoclassical, Mahogany,
Fruitwood, Hidden
Shelves, 93 In.

Furniture, Server,
Walnut, Carved Floral
Back, Turned Blocked
Posts, 63 x 36 In.

Furniture, Settee, Neoclassical, Painted,
Mythological Scene, Giltwood Paw Feet, 70 In.

Secretary-Bookcase, Glazed Doors, Hinged Writing Surface, 3 Drawers, 71 In. 1650.00
Secretary-Bookcase, Green Lacquer Chinoiserie, 4 Graduated Drawers, 91 In. 12650.00
Secretary-Bookcase, Mahogany Veneer, Drop Front, 2 Doors Over 2 Drawers 1210.00
Secretary-Bookcase, Mahogany, Adjustable Shelves, 4 Drawers, 90 In. 5750.00
Secretary-Bookcase, Mahogany, Adjustable Shelves, Lower Drawer, c.1780, 92 In. 8912.00
Secretary-Bookcase, Mahogany, Burl Veneer, 2 Piece 1210.00
Secretary-Bookcase, Mahogany, Satinwood Inlay, 18th Century, 91 x 50 In. 11500.00
Secretary-Bookcase, Roll Top, George III, Mahogany, Adjustable Shelves, 84 In. 9775.00
Secretary-Bookcase, Rosewood, 2 Glass Doors, Long Drawer, Victorian 220.00
Secretary-Bookcase, Rosewood, Silver-Plated Fire Station Plaque, 85 x 43 In. 9200.00
Secretary-Bookcase, Slant Front, George III, Mahogany, Mullioned Doors, 87 In. 5460.00
Secretary-Bookcase, Slant Front, Mahogany, 4 Drawers, Bracket Feet, 1800s, 86 In. 4840.00
Secretary-Bookcase, Slant Front, Oak, 2 Doors Over 4 Drawers, 37 x 79 x 18 In. 630.00
Secretary-Bookcase, Walnut, Drop Front, 3 Shelves Over 3 Drawers, Cameo Cornice . . . 1320.00
Server, Cherry, Gallery Top, Spindles, 1 Large Over 3 Graduated Drawers, 58 x 22 In. . . . 1680.00
Server, Empire Style, Foldover Top, Paneled Doors, Kindel, 40 x 31 1/2 In. 85.00
Server, Empire, Mahogany, Backsplash, Lower Drawer & Shelf, Paw Feet, 36 x 18 In. . . . 220.00
Server, Flame Veneer, Honeycomb Post Carving, 1810, 36 1/2 In. 3800.00
Server, G. Stickley, Plate Rack, 2 Small Drawers, Linen Drawer, 43 1/2 In. 2100.00
Server, Golden Oak Era, Applied & Relief Carved Designs, Beveled Glass, 78 In. 825.00
Server, Oak, 3 Short Over 1 Long Drawer, Stretcher Shelf, 1900 . . . . 275.00
Server, Queen Anne, Tiger Maple, Drawer, Straight Turned Legs, David T. Smith 690.00
Server, Renaissance Revival, Walnut, Drawer, Carving, Black Marble Top, 35 In. 440.00
Server, Walnut, Arched Panel Doors, Shelf, Carved Floral Backsplash, 63 x 37 In. 405.00
Server, Walnut, Carved Floral Back, Turned Blocked Posts, 63 x 36 In. . . . .*Illus* 403.00
Settee, Ash, Maple, Oak Splint Seat & Back, 1920s 1870.00
Settee, Baroque, Walnut, Figures In Wooded Landscape, Scroll Legs, 58 In. 17250.00
Settee, Barrister's, Reclining Back, Brass Pineapple Finials, Velvet, Pair 1100.00
Settee, Biedermeier, Maple, Stylized Foliate Design, Rectangular Seat, 34 x 73 In. 3335.00
Settee, Camelback, Padded Back, Out-Scrolled Arms, Upholstered Seat, 60 In. 1495.00
Settee, Camelback, Padded Seat & Back, Out-Scrolled Arms, Square Legs, 73 In. 660.00
Settee, Chippendale, Mahogany, Camelback, Square Tapered Legs, 54 In. 632.00
Settee, Chromed-Steel Tubular Frame, Olive Suede Cushions, 1930 . . . . 2875.00
Settee, Federal Style, Carved Mahogany, Reeded Column, Upholstered, c.1850 . . . . 1045.00
Settee, Fruitwood, Upholstered Back & Sides, Cushioned Seat, Brass Feet, 77 In. 4887.00
Settee, G. Stickley, Open Arms, Vertical Back Slats, 38 x 77 In. 2500.00
Settee, George III, Mahogany, Triple Padded Rectangular Chairback, 19th Century 1500.00
Settee, Georgian, Mahogany, Tapered Legs, Floral Brocade, 35 In. 847.00
Settee, Gilt Rounded Ends, Baluster Arms Supports, Upholstered, 19th Century, 62 In. . . 1725.00
Settee, Giltwood, Molded Crest Rail, Ribbon Carving Continues To Arms, 75 In. 460.00
Settee, Golden Oak Era, Lift Seat, Carved Serpents & Creatures, Arms, 1890 . . . . 10500.00
Settee, Gothic Revival, Crest Rail, Painted Design, Scroll Arms, Pa., 1850, 79 In. 5500.00
Settee, Half Spindle, Painted Grape Design, 20 1/2 x 71 In. 1755.00
Settee, Hardwood, Plank Seat, Scroll Arms, Spindle Back, Crest, 48 In. 305.00
Settee, Italian Provincial, Walnut, 3 Diamonds Centering Flowers, Rush Seat, 18 In. 575.00
Settee, Louis XV, Beechwood, Floral Carved Crest, Cabriole Legs, 46 x 30 In. 1495.00
Settee, Louis XV, Shell & Floral Crest, Upholstered, Padded Arms, 1890, 41 x 73 In. 970.00

Settee, Louis XVI, Cane Seat, Tapered Round Legs, Top Shaped Feet, 36 x 43 x 18 In. . . 545.00
Settee, Louis XVI, Fruitwood, Ribbon Carved Crest, Padded Medallion Back, 1880 . . . . . 665.00
Settee, Louis XVI, Giltwood, Down-Swept Elbow Armrests, Round Tapered Legs 2300.00
Settee, Louis XVI, Giltwood, Ribbon Carved Crest, Tapered Legs, 48 In. 8625.00
Settee, Louis XVI, Molded Top Rail, Upholstered Down-Swept Arms, Top Shaped Feet . . 1265.00
Settee, Mahogany, 2 Standing Griffins At Back, Tufted Back, Arms, 55 In. 405.00
Settee, Mahogany, Carved Eagle On Back, New York, 1825, 17 x 36 In. 6325.00
Settee, Mahogany, Chairback, Pierced Splat, Out-Scrolled Arms, 78 In. 5750.00
Settee, Mahogany, Double Chairback, Leaf Tablets Over Supports, Arms, 42 1/2 In. 9775.00
Settee, Mahogany, Mixed Wood, Pierced Slat Back, 6 Legs, Open Arms, 63 In. 2090.00
Settee, Mahogany, Triple Chairback, Radiating Splats, Out-Scrolled Arms, 69 In. 3737.00
Settee, Mahogany, Triple Chairback, Vertical Pierced Splat, Cushion Seat, 68 In. 575.00
Settee, Maple, Handmade, Leather Bottom, c.1930 . . . . 995.00
Settee, Napoleon III, Giltwood, Foliate Wreath, Tapered Legs, Top Shaped Feet, 44 In. . . 907.00
Settee, Neoclassical, Painted, Mythological Scene, Giltwood Paw Feet, 70 In. . . . . . . *Illus* 50600.00
Settee, Queen Anne, Mahogany, Triple Chairback, Cane, Out-Scrolled Arms, 84 In. 1815.00
Settee, Rattan, 2 Loose Cushions, Glen Plaid Wool, 45 In. 440.00
Settee, Regency, Beechwood, Foliate Crest, Serpentine Drop-In Seat, 70 In. 4025.00
Settee, Renaissance Revival, Rosewood, Floral, Stepped Crest, Overstuffed Seat 1495.00
Settee, Rococo, Rosewood, Carved, Button Tufted, 71 In., Pair 8050.00
Settee, Rococo, Walnut, Grape Carved Crest, Upholstered Arms, 19th Century 230.00
Settee, Rococo, Walnut, Rose Crest, Velvet 430.00
Settee, Rosewood, Double Padded Chairback, Pierced Crest, Overstuffed Seat, c.1870 . . . 975.00
Settee, Rosewood, Tripartite, Floral Carved Crest, Cabriole Legs, 65 3/4 In. 550.00
Settee, Saarinen, Womb, Molded Shell, Upholstered, Iron Frame, 32 x 60 x 24 In. 2530.00
Settee, Stickley Brothers, Oak, Slats, Notched Rail, Child's, 32 x 29 In. 1320.00
Settee, Triple Chairback, Crest, Scroll Arms, 1840, 37 x 79 x 27 In. 4950.00
Settee, W. Plattner, Wire Frame, Wraparound Wool Seat, Knoll, 68 In. 1200.00
Settee, Walnut, Arched & Padded Back, Foliate Garlands, Bolsters, 68 1/2 In. 2875.00
Settee, Walnut, Brocade, Victorian, 62 In. 385.00
Settee, Walnut, End Finials, Trumpet Feet, Velvet, 1870, 69 3/4 In. 2200.00
Settee, Walnut, Padded Back, Cushion Seat, Down-Swept Arms, 84 In. 510.00
Settee, Walnut, Padded Out-Scrolled Arms, Needlepoint Tapestry, 45 In. 9775.00
Settee, Walnut, Scroll Back, Fruit & Foliate, Carved Crest, Victorian, 57 In. 315.00
Settee, Walnut, Serpentine Carved Back, Upholstered, Victorian, 46 In. 255.00
Settee, Walnut, Triple Medallion Cane Back, c.1840 . . . . 1700.00
Settee, Walnut, Triple Padded Oval Chairback, Bowfront, Cabriole Legs, Victorian 460.00
Settee, Windsor, Bamboo, Red Paint, Arms, 19th Century, 74 In. 1000.00
Settee, Windsor, Comb Back, Carved Ears, Double Saddle Seat, Knuckle Arms 1045.00
Settee, Windsor, Fanback, Painted, Carved Handholds, David T. Smith 920.00
Settee, Windsor, Triple Serpentine Seat, 8 Legs, Knuckle Arms 1210.00
Settle, G. Stickley, No. 208, Even Arms, Rope-Seat, 29 x 76 x 32 In. 5500.00
Settle, G. Stickley, No. 219, Open Arms, Vertical Back Salts, 71 1/4 In. 2000.00
Settle, G. Stickley, Oak, Drop Arms, Plank Seat, 70 x 25 In. 3410.00
Settle, Gray Over White Paint, Turned Legs, Plank Seat, Arms, 99 In. 495.00
Settle, Hard & Soft Wood, Chair Base, Spindle Back, Plank Seat, 84 In. 220.00
Settle, J.M. Young, 14-Slat Back, Uneven Arms, 4 Side Slats, 81 1/2 In. 2512.00
Settle, L. & J.G. Stickley, 12-Slat Back, Drop-In Cushion, Brown Leather 3080.00
Settle, L. & J.G. Stickley, 15-Slat Back, Arched Rail, 70 x 27 x 38 In. 2530.00
Settle, L. & J.G. Stickley, 8-Slat Back, Cushion Seat, 38 x 42 In. 990.00
Settle, Lifetime, No. 614, Oak, Slat Back, Cushion Seat, 1905-1910, 36 x 73 In. 1150.00
Settle, Lifetime, Puritan, Mahogany, 10-Slat Back, Arched Rail, 74 x 37 In. 990.00
Settle, Limbert, Even Arms, 36 x 74 In. 5500.00
Settle, Mixed Woods, Plank Seat, Shaped Arms, Spindle Back, 84 In. 935.00
Settle, Oak, Paneled Back, Rope Seat, Loose Cushion, 38 1/2 x 74 1/2 In. 517.00
Settle, Olive Brown Paint, Cream Striping, Rose Design, Philadelphia, 73 1/2 In. 1430.00
Settle, Pine, Box Base, Plank Seat, Scroll Arms, Arrow Spindles, 74 3/4 In. 495.00
Settle, Pine, Concave Shape, Scroll Handholds, 1780, 63 x 43 In. 9200.00
Settle, Pine, Shaped Arms, Canted Back, 1-Board Seat, 35 3/4 x 43 1/2 x 19 In. 460.00
Settle, Poplar, Red Paint, Arms, 77 3/4 In. 520.00
Settle, Stickley Brothers, Oak, 76 1/2 In. 1155.00
Settle, Striping & Polychrome Floral, Plank Seat, Spindle Arms, 71 In. 1100.00
Settle, Vertical Slats At Back & Arms, 36 x 77 In. 1320.00

Shelf, Brass, Pierced Scroll, Wall Mount, Victorian, 10 In. 75.00
Shelf, Chippendale, Mahogany, Pagoda Top, Open Shelves, 30 x 33 In. 460.00
Shelf, Corner, Fretwork, Turned Finials, Mirrored Back, 27 1/4 In. 95.00
Shelf, Corner, Hardwood, Scroll Fretwork, 4 Shelves, 20th Century, 36 1/2 In. 220.00
Shelf, Corner, Teakwood, Carved, Elephant, Figures, India, 32 1/2 In. 305.00
Shelf, Corner, Walnut, Scroll Sawing, 4 Shelves, 1870, 44 x 18 x 13 In. 120.00
Shelf, Flower, Pine, Green Paint, 9 x 47 x 25 In. 470.00
Shelf, Fruitwood, Putti Holding Scallop Shell, Scroll Base, 1920, 26 In. 690.00
Shelf, Hanging, Pine, Cutout Sides, Drawer, 10 1/2 x 15 x 26 In. 45.00
Shelf, Hanging, Pine, Dark Brown Paint, Scalloped Sides, 25 x 9 1/2 x 30 In. 465.00
Shelf, Hanging, Pine, Red Paint, Primitive Molding, 31 x 6 x 31 In. 1128.00
Shelf, Hanging, Pine, Rose Mulled Design, 59 1/4 In. 495.00
Shelf, Hanging, Pine, Step Back, Black Paint, Scalloped Ends, 29 x 8 x 34 In. 1100.00
Shelf, Hanging, Poplar, Red Paint, 24 x 9 3/4 x 21 1/2 In. 740.00
Shelf, Hanging, Walnut, Red Finish, Scalloped Bracket, 2 Nailed Drawers, 32 In. 550.00
Shelf, Hanging, Walnut, Scrolled, Pierced Crest, Drawer, Victorian 330.00
Shelf, Mahogany, Carved 2-Masted Schooner, 19th Century, 17 x 12 x 6 In. 575.00
Shelf, Oak, Brass Coat Hooks, Oval Center Mirror, c.1930, 17 x 61 In. 485.00
Shelf, Pine, Green Paint, 17 1/4 x 14 3/4 x 60 In. 410.00
Shelf, Pine, Painted, 4 Shelves, 33 x 15 x 49 In. 550.00
Shelf, Pine, Painted, Cutout Feet, Square Nails, 2 Shelves, 35 x 35 In. 520.00
Shelf, Pine, Step Back, Red Paint, 3 Tiers, 1-Board Ends, Cutout Feet, 43 x 12 x 46 In. . . . 935.00
Shelf, Walnut, Natural Finish, 4 Graduated Shelves, 31 x 8 x 36 1/2 In. 165.00
Sideboard, Aesthetic Movement, Mahogany, Mirror, Shelves, 1870s, 97 x 58 In. 10925.00
Sideboard, Arts & Crafts, 2 Drawers, Lower Shelf, Iron Pulls, 48 x 20 In. 3300.00
Sideboard, Black Walnut, Hutch, Carved Rabbit, Fish, Berry, Victorian . . . . *Illus* 16100.00
Sideboard, Burl Walnut, Marble Top, Gilt-Incised Apron, 1875, 28 In. 660.00
Sideboard, Burl Walnut, Marquetry, 19th Century 1700.00
Sideboard, Carved Oak, Gargoyles Supporting The Upper Shelves 2420.00
Sideboard, Charles X, Mahogany, Brass Mounted, Frieze Drawers, Plinth Base 11500.00
Sideboard, Chippendale Style, Mahogany, Serpentine Top, 60 x 33 1/2 In. 575.00
Sideboard, E. Wormley, Woven Front Sliding Doors, 3 Drawers, 82 x 36 In. 1980.00
Sideboard, Empire, Mahogany, 3 Over 4 Drawers, Pullout Work Surface, 73 x 42 In. 865.00
Sideboard, Empire, Marble Top, Rectangular Green-Veined Marble Top, 36 In. 1955.00
Sideboard, Federal, Mahogany, 2 Central Drawers, Arched Apron, 1790, 38 In. 1840.00
Sideboard, Federal, Mahogany, 3 Inlaid Bowfront Drawers, 2 Doors, 41 In. 1045.00
Sideboard, Federal, Mahogany, Bowfront, Beading, c.1790, 64 In. . . . . *Illus* 5462.00
Sideboard, Federal, Mahogany, Cherry Inlay, Serpentine, 37 x 48 In. . . . . *Illus* 19550.00
Sideboard, Federal, Mahogany, Concave, Drawer, Inlay, 37 x 77 In. . . . . *Illus* 6900.00
Sideboard, Federal, Mahogany, Frieze Drawer, Square Tapered Legs, 39 x 65 In. 2100.00

Furniture, Sideboard,
Federal, Mahogany,
Bowfront, Beading,
c.1790, 64 In.

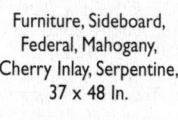

Furniture, Sideboard,
Federal, Mahogany,
Cherry Inlay, Serpentine,
37 x 48 In.

Furniture, Sideboard, Black
Walnut, Hutch, Carved Rabbit,
Fish, Berry, Victorian

Furniture, Sideboard,
Federal, Mahogany,
Concave, Drawer, Inlay,
37 x 77 In.

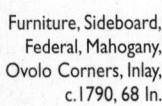

Furniture, Sideboard,
Federal, Mahogany,
Ovolo Corners, Inlay,
c.1790, 68 In.

Furniture, Sideboard, Marquetry,
Ebonized, Marble Top, Ormolu
Figures, 41 x 67 In.

Sideboard, Federal, Mahogany, New York, 1810-1815 . . . . 4370.00
Sideboard, Federal, Mahogany, Ovolo Corners, Inlay, c.1790, 68 In. . . . . *Illus* 1840.00
Sideboard, Figured Cherry, Center Drawers, 2 Cabinet Doors, Peter Kramer 460.00
Sideboard, Florence Knoll, Stained Ash Veneer, 4 Doors, Chrome Legs, Pulls, 75 In. 1210.00
Sideboard, G. Stickley, No. 814, Exposed Tenon, 48 x 66 In. . . . . .6900.00 to 7150.00
Sideboard, G. Stickley, No. 903, Chamfered Back, Arched Top, Plate Rail, 48 x 24 In. . . . 5500.00
Sideboard, G. Stickley, No. 961, 4 Central Drawers, Square Legs, Red Decal, 50 In. 8625.00
Sideboard, George III, Mahogany, 4 Drawers, Tapered Square Legs, 60 x 28 In. 4890.00
Sideboard, George III, Mahogany, 5 Drawers, Crossbanded, 1800, 35 x 54 In. 7500.00
Sideboard, George III, Mahogany, Crossbanded Top, Brass Rail, 6 Legs, 36 In. 10925.00
Sideboard, George III, Mahogany, Demilune Top, Cupboard Doors, 38 In. 6325.00
Sideboard, George III, Mahogany, Demilune, 4 Cock-Beaded Drawers, 36 1/2 In. 6900.00
Sideboard, Georgian Style, Mahogany, Serpentine Front, Inlay, 72 x 39 In. 1610.00
Sideboard, Georgian Style, Walnut, 2 Drawers Over 2 Doors, Paw Feet, 72 x 41 In. 460.00
Sideboard, Georgian Style, Walnut, Shaped Marble Top, Carved, 96 x 21 x 39 In. 6040.00
Sideboard, Georgian, Mahogany, Bowfront, Square Tapered Legs, 1840, 35 In. 2299.00
Sideboard, Georgian, Mahogany, Inlay, 2 Drawers, Hinged Cabinet Doors, 47 In. 6900.00
Sideboard, Georgian, Mahogany, Serpentine Top, 2 Graduated Drawers, 35 In. 1610.00
Sideboard, Hepplewhite, Mahogany Veneer, Bowfront, Drawer, Square Legs, 58 In. 2200.00
Sideboard, Hepplewhite, Mahogany Veneer, Serpentine, Inlay, 2 Drawers, 69 In. 3025.00
Sideboard, Hepplewhite, Mahogany, D-Shape, Fan Inlay, N.Y., 1800 . . . . 13200.00
Sideboard, Hepplewhite, Tiger Maple, Bowfront, 3 Drawers, 2 Doors, 39 1/2 In. 7425.00
Sideboard, Inlaid & Painted Splashboard, Carved Cutlery Drawer, c.1825 . . . . 8500.00
Sideboard, L. & J.G. Stickley, No. 734, 3 Center Drawers, Plate Rail, 44 In. 2310.00
Sideboard, Limbert, Gallery Top, 4 Small Drawers, 2 Panels, 49 In. 4950.00
Sideboard, Limbert, No. 1445, 2 Doors, Copper Strap Hinges, 60 x 23 x 46 In. 5500.00
Sideboard, Limbert, Oak, 2 Doors, Copper Hardware, 48 In. 2200.00
Sideboard, Louis XV, Fruitwood, Carved, Rectangular Top, 2 Drawers, 45 x 61 In. 5750.00
Sideboard, Louis XVI Style, Floral, Scroll & Grapevine Inlay, Gilt Metal Mounts, 29 In. . . 805.00
Sideboard, Mahogany Veneer, Serpentine, Square Legs, 18th Century, 41 x 73 In. 9350.00
Sideboard, Mahogany, 1 Long Over Recessed Drawer, Cellarette Drawer, 76 In. 3450.00
Sideboard, Mahogany, 2 Drawers, 3 Cupboard Doors, Columns, Paw Feet, 54 In. 2750.00
Sideboard, Mahogany, 2 Short Drawers, Splashboard, Bottle Drawers, c.1830, 55 In. 1100.00
Sideboard, Mahogany, 3 Drawers Over 3 Doors, Carved Gallery, China, 1925 . . . . 1090.00
Sideboard, Mahogany, A. McClellan, 1805, 53 x 42 In. 2990.00
Sideboard, Mahogany, Bowfront, 2 Long Drawers, Cupboard Doors, 39 1/2 In. 4888.00
Sideboard, Mahogany, Burl Veneer, Cornice, Animal-Mask Pulls, Victorian 1725.00
Sideboard, Mahogany, Center & Side Drawers, 3 Cabinet Doors, 1930, 38 x 68 In. 345.00
Sideboard, Mahogany, Maple Inlay, 3 Drawers, 2 Tiers, 1820, 74 1/2 In. 9200.00
Sideboard, Mahogany, Reverse Breakfront, 3 Drawers, Paw Feet, c.1820, 49 In. 9775.00
Sideboard, Mahogany, Serpentine Front, 6 Square Legs, Splayed Feet, 38 In. 1840.00
Sideboard, Mahogany, Serpentine, Inlay, Drawer Over 2 Doors, 1780, 70 In. 14850.00
Sideboard, Mahogany, Serpentine, Line Inlay, 18th Century, 41 x 73 x 27 In. 9350.00
Sideboard, Mahogany, Splashboard, 4 Center Drawers, Side Cabinets, c.1830, 55 In. 1430.00

Sideboard, Marquetry, Ebonized, Marble Top, Ormolu Figures, 41 x 67 In. . . . .*Illus* 9200.00
Sideboard, Oak, 2 Drawers Over 2 Doors, Turned Posts, Carving, Continental, 52 In. 173.00
Sideboard, Oak, Mirrored Backsplash, 2 Short Over 1 Long Drawer Over Doors 110.00
Sideboard, Oak, Stick & Ball, Mirror, 1880s 2090.00
Sideboard, Regency Style, Mahogany, Demilune Top, 4 Drawers, 37 x 68 x 19 1/4 In. . . . 1120.00
Sideboard, Regency, Gilt Brass, Rectangular Top, Bowfront Cupboards, 43 In. 4025.00
Sideboard, Regency, Mahogany Veneer, Paneled Doors, 66 x 21 x 36 In. 1375.00
Sideboard, Regency, Mahogany Veneer, Serpentine, 5 Drawers, Splayed Feet, 79 In. 6900.00
Sideboard, Regency, Rosewood, Rectangular Top, 2 Doors, Ball Feet, 1830, 45 1/2 In. . . . 1495.00
Sideboard, Sheraton, Mahogany, Scalloped Gallery, Rope & Star Frieze, 59 1/2 In. 4750.00
Sideboard, Sheraton, Walnut, Curly Maple, 4 Drawers, 69 x 70 x 43 In. 5500.00
Sideboard, Stickley Brothers, Mirror Back, Strap Hinges, 52 x 60 In. 4950.00
Sideboard, Tiger Oak, 4 Drawers, 2 Cabinets, Beveled Mirror, Carved Heads 1800.00
Sideboard, Walnut, 3 Frieze Drawers, Female Figures & Lion On Doors, 35 1/2 In. 1380.00
Sideboard, Walnut, 5 Drawers, 4 Doors, Scalloped Skirt Front, 19th Century 7700.00
Sideboard, Walnut, Inlay, 2 Short & 1 Long Drawer, 1850, 37 In. 3738.00
Sideboard, Walnut, Pine, Cock-Beaded Case, End Drawers, Central Cupboard, 39 In. 5520.00
Sofa, Alexander Girard, Black Naugahyde, 6 Aluminum Legs, Herman Miller, 26 In. 2530.00
Sofa, Art Deco, Walnut, Velvet, 1930, 98 x 29 x 33 In. 412.00
Sofa, Bamboo, Loose Cushions, Concentric Bands On Arms, 1940s, 78 In. 2070.00
Sofa, Beechwood, Regency Style, Gingham, c.1890, 62 3/4 In. 1650.00
Sofa, Belter, Rosalie With Grapes, Laminated Crest, 75 1/2 In. 7000.00
Sofa, Biedermeier, Birch, Ebonized, 19th Century, 88 1/2 In. 5200.00
Sofa, Biedermeier, Fruitwood, Beadwork Border, Scroll Feet, 86 1/2 In. 1380.00
Sofa, Birch, Camelback, Upholstered, 32 x 66 In. 1500.00
Sofa, Black Leather, Rolled Arms, 80 In. 545.00
Sofa, Camelback, Red Simulated Leather, Rolled Arms, Square Legs, 82 In. 405.00
Sofa, Chesterfield, Leather, Padded Back Continuing To Arms, 85 In. 2070.00
Sofa, Chesterfield, Light Brown Leather, Bun Feet On Casters, 67 In. 6325.00
Sofa, Chesterfield, Tufted Backrest, Sides & Seat, Black Leather, 84 In. 5750.00
Sofa, Chippendale Style, Camelback, Floral Brocade, 76 In. 495.00
Sofa, Chippendale Style, Walnut, Out-Scrolled Arms, Fretwork, Square Legs, 75 In. 430.00
Sofa, Chippendale, Bowfront Seat, Curved Back, Upholstered Shaped Arms 2860.00
Sofa, Chippendale, Camelback, Cream, Paine Furniture Co., 1937 . . . . 1995.00
Sofa, Chippendale, Camelback, Molded Legs, H-Stretchers, Upholstered 165.00
Sofa, Chippendale, Mahogany, Arched, Padded Back, 3 Seats, Claw & Ball Feet 1100.00
Sofa, Chippendale, Mahogany, Camelback, Out-Scrolled Arms, 33 1/4 x 82 In. 345.00
Sofa, Chippendale, Mahogany, Padded Back, Claw & Ball Feet, Arms, 81 In. 745.00
Sofa, Chippendale, Step-Down Back, Bowfront, 8 Carved Legs, Arms, 36 x 76 In. 3450.00
Sofa, Classical, Mahogany, Crest Rail, Volutes, Round Arms, Paw Feet, c.1825, 34 In. . . . 935.00
Sofa, Classical, Mahogany, Flared Crest Rail, Scroll Carving, Paw Feet, 1830, 89 In. 6600.00
Sofa, Classical, Mahogany, Scroll Arms, Upholstered, 1830, 92 In. 2080.00
Sofa, Classical, Mahogany, Scroll Crest, Upholstered, Arms, 1825, 80 In. 2090.00
Sofa, Curved Seat & Back, 4 Stainless Steel Legs, Marco Zanuso, Arflex, 1951, 34 In. . . . 2300.00
Sofa, E. Wormley, Faux Mink, Square Tuxedo Back, 37 x 86 x 35 In. 1150.00
Sofa, E. Wormley, Lacquered Wood, Angular, Upholstered, 31 x 97 x 29 In. 1035.00
Sofa, E. Wormley, Mahogany, Tufted Seat & Back, Dunbar, 39 x 28 x 28 In. 1100.00
Sofa, E. Wormley, Upholstered Angled Seat, L-Shaped Wood Supports, 89 x 30 In. 2875.00
Sofa, Eastlake, Shaped & Carved Walnut Frame, Victorian 85.00
Sofa, Ebonized, Triple-Panel Back, Leather Medallion, Scroll Arms, 85 In. 2420.00
Sofa, Empire, Claw Feet, Scroll Arms, Upholstered, New York 2365.00
Sofa, Empire, Figured Mahogany Veneer, S-Scroll Feet & Arms, Pillows, 81 3/4 In. 855.00
Sofa, Empire, Mahogany, Acanthus & Floral Carving, Paw Feet, Bolster Pillows, 75 In. . . 880.00
Sofa, Empire, Mahogany, Carved Fan, Upholstered, Scroll Arms, 83 In. 355.00
Sofa, Empire, Mahogany, Flame Grained, Early 19th Century, 79 In. 1495.00
Sofa, Empire, Mahogany, Leaf Capped, Turned Crest Bar, 3-Seat, Lion's-Paw Feet 4000.00
Sofa, Empire, Mahogany, Scrolled, Parcel Gilt Crest, Carved Lotus, Gilt Arms, 7 In. 3575.00
Sofa, Federal, Burl Walnut, Straight Sides, Padded Arms, Reeded Legs, 77 In. 3162.00
Sofa, Federal, Mahogany, Brocade, 76 In. 2970.00
Sofa, Federal, Mahogany, Carved Crest, Saber Legs, Brass Paw Feet, Rolled Arms 330.00
Sofa, Federal, Mahogany, Carved Legs, Upholstered, 19th Century 660.00
Sofa, Federal, Mahogany, Loose Cushion Bench Seat, 20th Century, 34 x 77 In. 201.00
Sofa, Federal, Mahogany, Out-Scrolled Arms, 4-Seat, Padded, Hairy Paw Feet 6000.00

Sofa, Federal, Mahogany, Paneled Top Crest, Rosette & Leaf, Paw Feet, 32 x 96 In. 1150.00
Sofa, Federal, Mahogany, Rectangular Upholstered Back, Scroll Arms, 76 In. 2185.00
Sofa, Federal, Painted, Upholstered Back & Arms, 19th Century 490.00
Sofa, Floral Upholstery, Rectangular Backrest, Bun Feet, 28 In. 4025.00
Sofa, Fornasetti, Faux Bamboo, Printed Metal, Faux Tiger Print, 70 In. 2990.00
Sofa, Frankl, Rattan, 3 Sections, 1940, 29 1/2 In. 977.00
Sofa, Fruitwood, Scroll Arms, Floral Tapestry, 2 Bolsters, 94 14 In. 2860.00
Sofa, G. Harcourt, Cleopatra, Wool, Metal Frame, 1973, 74 In. 3850.00
Sofa, G. Nakashima, Spindle Back, Flared Dowel Legs, Loose Cushion, 48 x 37 In., Pair . 4180.00
Sofa, G. Nakashima, Spindle Back, Paddle Arms, Dowel Legs, Loose Cushion, 78 In. 3575.00
Sofa, G. Nelson, Marshmallow, Round Cushions, Steel Frame, 1957, 52 In. 15400.00
Sofa, G. Nelson, Marshmallow, Round Magenta Cushions, Herman Miller, 1956, 31 In. . . 4675.00
Sofa, Giltwood, Painted Chinoiserie Tea Scene, Saber Legs, Gilt Paw Feet, 75 In. 8625.00
Sofa, Hepplewhite, Mahogany, Upholstered Back, Padded Sides, Arms, 84 In. 805.00
Sofa, Heywood-Wakefield Co., Bentwood, Maple, 3 Seats, Upholstered, 73 In. 715.00
Sofa, J. & J.W. Meeks, Rococo, Laminated Rosewood, Upholstered, 64 In. 5520.00
Sofa, J. & J.W. Meeks, Rococo, Rosewood, Silk Damask, Floral Sprays, 1850s, 65 In. . . . 6050.00
Sofa, Kem Weber, Triple-Band Chrome Arms, Orange Vinyl Cushions, 78 In. 3050.00
Sofa, Le Corbusier, Cube, 3 Seats, Tubular Chrome, Boucle, Matching Chair, 80 x 30 In. . 4400.00
Sofa, Louis XVI, Giltwood, Padded Armrests, 8 Round Fluted Legs, 69 In. 12650.00
Sofa, Louis XVI, Painted, Upholstered Seat & Back, Padded Arms, 65 In. 920.00
Sofa, Mahogany, Acanthus Design On Feet, Velvet, 91 In. 1100.00
Sofa, Mahogany, Camelback, 3 Seats, Out-Scrolled Arms 1725.00
Sofa, Mahogany, Tufted Seat & Back, Black & White Pattern, 28 x 39 In. 1100.00
Sofa, P. Evans, Sculptural Bronze Exterior, Abstract Upholstery, 1966, 60 x 36 In. 935.00
Sofa, Regency, Mahogany, Burl Veneer Crest, Fruit & Foliate Carvings, c.1865 . . . . 1008.00
Sofa, Regency, Mahogany, Carved, Ormolu Crest Rail, Scroll Arms, England, 86 In. 1320.00
Sofa, Rococo, Mahogany, Foliate Scrolls, Floral Crest On Back, 1850s, 43 In. 1430.00
Sofa, Saporiti Italia, 3 Seats, 86 In. 575.00
Sofa, Scalamandre, Trumpet Legs, 19th Century, 76 In. 920.00
Sofa, Sheraton, Birch, Upholstered, Arms, Pictou County 2200.00
Sofa, Sheraton, Mahogany, Camelback, Bellflower Arms, 37 x 76 x 30 In. 1380.00
Sofa, Sheraton, Mahogany, Reeded, Tapered Arms, Legs, Upholstered, 76 In. 1100.00
Sofa, Sheraton, Mahogany, Upholstered, Open Arms, Dark Finish, 78 In. 2200.00
Sofa, Sheraton, Open Back, Shaped Crest, Straight Apron, 2 Cushions, 31 x 79 In. 1670.00
Sofa, Steel Frame, Mueller Furniture Co., Grand Rapids, 100 In. 2875.00
Sofa, Teakwood, Cane, Down-Swept Legs, Brass Paw Casters, c.1840, 93 In. 9775.00
Sofa, Tubular Chrome, Vinyl 700.00
Sofa, V. Kagan, Walnut, Linen Biomorphic Cushions, 1950s, 96 x 44 In. 16500.00
Sofa, Walnut, Carved Grapes, Upholstered, Victorian, 67 In. 750.00
Sofa, Walnut, Medallion Back, Finger Carved, Fruit Carved Crest, Victorian, 59 In. 220.00
Sofa, Walnut, Triple Chairback, Carved Roses, Finger Carved Legs, Victorian, 63 In. 546.00
Sofa, Walnut, Veneer, Incised Gilt, Upholstered, Victorian, 1860s 275.00
Sofa, Wool, Dubar, 108 In. 6210.00
Stand, 2 Drawers, Red Wash, c.1800 . . . . 1420.00
Stand, Birch, Poplar, Cherry, Drawer, 4-Board Top, Brown Finish, 21 x 22 In. 250.00
Stand, Blue & White, Mason Drainer, 1820, 18 x 16 x 11 In. 395.00
Stand, Carved Prunus Blossoms, Marble Top, Carved Legs, 32 x 13 x 13 In. 635.00
Stand, Cherry, 1-Board Top, 2 Drawers, 19 x 21 x 29 In. 300.00
Stand, Cherry, 2 Drawers, Square Tapered Legs, 19 x 19 x 28 3/4 In. 245.00
Stand, Cherry, Drawer, 1-Board Diamond-Shaped Inlaid Top, 20 x 22 In. 520.00
Stand, Cherry, Drawer, 2-Board Top, 17 x 20 x 29 In. 330.00
Stand, Cherry, Drawer, 2-Board Top, Red, Turned Legs, 18 x 21 In. 300.00
Stand, Cherry, Drawer, Tapered Legs, Pennsylvania, 1830-1840, 29 In. 465.00
Stand, Cherry, Drawers, Turned Legs, 18 1/2 x 19 x 29 In. 240.00
Stand, Cherry, Mahogany Drawer Front, Turned Legs, Early 19th Century 275.00
Stand, Cherry, Maple Drawer Front, Scroll-Cut Backboard, Early 19th Century 522.00
Stand, Dressing, Painted, Stencil, 1820s, 40 x 34 x 17 In. . . . .*Illus* 460.00
Stand, Drop Leaf, Cherry, Drawer, Pullout Leaf Supports, 28 1/2 x 17 3/4 In. 330.00
Stand, Drop Leaf, Cherry, Mahogany Top, Drawer, Brass Pull, 19 x 20 x 20 In. 330.00
Stand, Drop Leaf, Cherry, Mahogany Veneer, 2 Drawers, 28 3/4 In. 275.00
Stand, Drop Leaf, Mahogany, 2 Drawers Each End, Tapered Legs 110.00
Stand, Drop Leaf, Pine, Poplar, Drawer, Grain Painted, 17 1/2 x 22 In. 330.00

Protect your antique tables with a piece of glass cut to fit the top. If you like flower arrangements, plants, perfume, or other liquids that might be used in a container on the tabletop, this is especially important. Put a few "spacers" under the glass to keep it from touching the top. If you ever write something while sitting at an antique table, a glass top will prevent you from making an indentation in the wood.

Furniture, Stand, Dressing, Painted, Stencil, 1820s, 40 x 34 x 17 In.

Stand, Drop Leaf, Sheraton, 2 Drawers, Beveled-Edge Door Fronts, 30 x 18 In.	315.00
Stand, Drop Leaf, Sheraton, Bird's-Eye Maple, 2 Dovetailed Drawers, 17 x 20 In.	770.00
Stand, Drop Leaf, Sheraton, Mahogany, 2 Dovetailed Drawers, 17 x 18 x 28 In.	355.00
Stand, Drop Leaf, Sheraton, Mahogany, Walnut, 2 Drawers, Turned Legs	100.00
Stand, Drop Leaf, Sheraton, Tiger Maple, Turned Legs, Drawer, 27 1/2 In.	1430.00
Stand, Drop Leaf, Walnut, 2 Drawers, Banded Inlay, Turned Legs, 28 1/2 x 23 In.	330.00
Stand, Drop Leaf, Walnut, 2 Drawers, Country, 19 3/4 x 22 x 9 3/4 In.	330.00
Stand, Drop Leaf, Walnut, Burl Veneer, Turned Legs, 2 Drawers, 28 3/4 x 21 3/4 In.	385.00
Stand, Drop Leaf, Walnut, Sausage Turned Legs, 2 Dovetailed Drawers, 12 x 29 In.	330.00
Stand, E. Wheeler, Federal Style, Tiger Maple Top, Painted Base, Drawer	165.00
Stand, E. Wormley, Lacquer, Drawer, 2 Doors, Brass & Rosewood Handles, 20 x 15 In. . .	575.00
Stand, Eastlake, Walnut, Marble Top, Rectangular	305.00
Stand, Egyptian Revival, Metal, 3 Figural Legs, Animal-Paw Feet, 36 x 18 In.	3162.00
Stand, Empire, Cherry, Curly Maple Drawer Front, 15 1/2 x 21 3/4 x 29 In.	300.00
Stand, Empire, Drawer, Cylindrical Pedestal, Quatrefoil Base, Turned Legs, 29 In.	1430.00
Stand, Empire, Mahogany, Square Top, Bancroft's Furniture, 1840, 28 x 34 x 17 In.	400.00
Stand, Empire, Walnut, Quatrefoil Base, Scroll Feet, Drawer, Columns, 29 1/2 In.	330.00
Stand, Federal Style, Bird's-Eye Maple, Brass Pulls, 19th Century, 29 x 26 x 17 In.	840.00
Stand, Federal Style, Mahogany, Corner, Backsplash, Drawer, Rope Inlay, 31 In.	322.00
Stand, Federal, Birch, Drawer, Square Tapered Legs, Early 19th Century	405.00
Stand, Federal, Cherry, Bird's-Eye Maple, 2 Drawers, 17 x 22 x 28 In.	1100.00
Stand, Federal, Cherry, Drawer, Inlaid Top, Frieze Drawer, c.1800, 28 x 20 In.	2300.00
Stand, Federal, Cherry, Figured Mahogany Veneer, 2 Drawers, 21 In.	440.00
Stand, Federal, Curly Maple, Rounded Front Drawers, 18 x 23 In.	825.00
Stand, Federal, Mahogany Top, Maple Column, Tilt Top, 17 x 23 x 26 In.	715.00
Stand, Federal, Pine, Drawer, Splayed Leg, Painted, c.1830, 28 x 22 x 21 In.	1955.00
Stand, Federal, Pine, Painted, Drawer, Baluster Legs, 19th Century	200.00
Stand, Fern, Fruiting Vine Design, Circular, Cast Iron, 24 3/4 x 51 1/2 In.	290.00
Stand, Flower, Mahogany, Flared Box, Copper Tray, Splayed Legs, Lower Shelf	475.00
Stand, Formica, White, Inlay, 3 Drawers, Door, Minoru Yamasaki, 16 x 36 In.	460.00
Stand, French Provincial, Mahogany, Gray Marble Top, Frieze Drawer, 27 In.	363.00
Stand, G. Nelson, Birch Veneer, 3 Sections, 17 x 14 x 40 In., Pair	1320.00
Stand, George III, Mahogany, Square Top, Inlay, Splayed Feet, 28 In.	5462.00
Stand, George III, Mahogany, Tripod, Spiral Twist Standard, Pad Feet, 28 In.	1725.00
Stand, Georgian, Round Frame, Lion Masks, Drum Base, Lion's-Paw Feet, 37 In., Pair . .	3450.00
Stand, Hepplewhite, Birch, Drawer, Serpentine Cut Edge, 26 3/4 In.	4180.00
Stand, Hepplewhite, Cherry, Banded Inlay, Drawer, Brass Knob, 26 In.	1150.00
Stand, Hepplewhite, Cherry, Dovetailed Drawer, 15 x 15 x 28 3/4 In.	440.00
Stand, Hepplewhite, Cherry, Inlay, Drawer, 1-Board, 17 x 28 In.	330.00
Stand, Hepplewhite, Cherry, Inlay, Drawer, Square Tapered Legs, 17 x 17 x 28 In.	440.00
Stand, Hepplewhite, Cherry, Pine, Dovetailed Drawer, 4 Legs, 26 In.	190.00
Stand, Hepplewhite, Cherry, Tripod Base, Spider Legs, Splayed Feet, 26 1/2 In.	220.00
Stand, Hepplewhite, Drawer, Early 19th Century	345.00
Stand, Hepplewhite, Mahogany, Drawer, c.1790, 28 1/2 In.	660.00
Stand, Hepplewhite, Pine, Dovetailed Drawer, 17 3/4 x 25 1/2 In.	440.00

Stand, Hepplewhite, Walnut, Splayed Base, Beaded Apron, 15 x 18 x 21 In. 190.00
Stand, Kidney Shape, Inlay, Drawer, Watson & Walton, 28 1/2 In. 412.00
Stand, Library, Walnut, Revolving, 2 Tiers, Victorian, 1870s 805.00
Stand, Lift Top, Mahogany, Turned Standard, 4 Reeded Legs, 55 x 29 In. 805.00
Stand, Magazine, G. Stickley, 3 Shelves, Beveled Top, Ebonized Finish, 35 In. 6600.00
Stand, Magazine, G. Stickley, 5 Shelves, 42 x 12 3/4 In. 2910.00
Stand, Magazine, G. Stickley, No. 79, 4 Shelves, Through Tenon, 14 x 10 x 40 In. 1760.00
Stand, Magazine, Heywood-Wakefield Co., Maple, Angled Shelf, 22 x 15 x 28 In. 374.00
Stand, Magazine, Knaus Mfg. Co., Vertical Slats, 42 1/4 x 12 In. 1100.00
Stand, Magazine, L. & J.G. Stickley, No. 46, 4 Shelves, 3 Slats To Each Side, 42 In. 2090.00
Stand, Magazine, Limbert, No. 300, Mahogany, 4 Shelves, Canted Sides, 37 In. 1210.00
Stand, Magazine, Limbert, No. 301, Mahogany, 2 Shelves, Arched Toe Board, 29 In. 1210.00
Stand, Magazine, Limbert, Oak, 4 Shelves, Cutout At Base, 37 x 20 In. 1540.00
Stand, Magazine, Robsjohn-Gibbings, Curly Birch, Walnut Top, X-Shaped Sides, 29 In. ... 355.00
Stand, Magazine, Velvet Covered, Shaped Platform Stretcher, Gold Braid, 30 1/2 In. 460.00
Stand, Magazine, Walnut Top, Black Lacquered Tripod, Laminate Holders, 22 x 25 In. ... 16380.00
Stand, Magazine, Walnut, 3 Shelves, Rope Twist & Turned Legs, Hathaway's 220.00
Stand, Mahogany Drawer, Turned Cherry Legs, Cookie Corner Top, 28 1/2 x 18 In. 520.00
Stand, Mahogany, Gallery Back, Ormolu Mount, Claw & Ball Feet 245.00
Stand, Mahogany, Mariner's-Star Inlay, Drawer, 1790, 28 In. 2990.00
Stand, Mahogany, Porringer Top Over 2 Cock-Beaded Drawers, Mass., 1810 .... 1210.00
Stand, Mahogany, Serpentine Top, Veneered Apron, 1810, 28 1/4 In. 6900.00
Stand, Maple, Curly Maple 2-Board Top, Cutout Ovolo Corners, 32 1/4 In. 165.00
Stand, Maple, Figured Birch Inlay, Stylized Floral, Drawers, c.1810, 27 1/2 In. 3450.00
Stand, Maroon Lacquer, Floral Sprays, Butterflies, Bird, 19 x 32 In. 3450.00
Stand, Marquetry, 2 Drawers, Square Tapered Legs, Italy, 29 x 20 x 19 In. 725.00
Stand, Music, Brass & Rosewood, Lyre Shape, Table Top, 22 x 14 1/2 In. 370.00
Stand, Music, Empire, Top Over Pullout Candlestands, 3 Saber Legs, 29 1/4 In. 862.00
Stand, Music, Lyre Design, c.1825 .... 2300.00
Stand, Music, Mahogany, Adjustable Column, c.1830, 37 1/2 In. 4312.00
Stand, Music, Mahogany, Ring Turned Column, Shoe Feet, 5 In. 2300.00
Stand, Music, Parcel Gilt, Lyre Section, Folio Rack, Lower Shelf, 54 1/2 In. 630.00
Stand, Neoclassical Style, Brass, Mask & Floral Design, Bird's-Leg Post, 28 1/2 In. 290.00
Stand, Neoclassical Style, Shelf Stretcher, Oval, 16 x 11 x 32 In. 80.00
Stand, Neoclassical, Mahogany, Parcel Gilt, Round Top, Continental, 34 In. 2185.00
Stand, Oriental, Bamboo, Lacquered, 2 Folding Shelves, Flowers, Birds, 41 1/2 In. 385.00
Stand, Pine, Mortise & Tenon Construction, c.1825, 24 x 31 1/2 In. 975.00
Stand, Pine, Tilt Top, Round Top, Central Wreath Of Flowers On Greens, 28 In. 2645.00
Stand, Plant, 3 Tiers, Twisted Wire, Victorian, 42 In. 300.00
Stand, Plant, 11 Graduated Arms, 4-Part Flowered Base, Cast Iron, 45 In. 425.00
Stand, Plant, 4 Tiers, Demilune, Blue Paint 775.00
Stand, Plant, Bamboo, Green Tile Inset, Splayed, Anglo-Indian, 1880, 31 x 14 In. 85.00
Stand, Plant, Brass, Iron, 3 Masks, Grape & Leaf Design, Iron Round Feet, 43 In. 170.00
Stand, Plant, Corner, 4 Curved Steps, Red Paint, 43 1/2 In. 345.00
Stand, Plant, Fruitwood, Late 19th Century, 48 In. 825.00
Stand, Plant, G. Stickley, Splayed Legs, Notched Rail, Decal, 14 x 14 x 26 In. 5500.00
Stand, Plant, Hardwood, Marble Inset Top, Square Legs, Ball Feet, 31 x 12 In., Pair 489.00
Stand, Plant, Hardwood, Mother-Of-Pearl Inlay, Cabriole Legs, 35 In. 150.00
Stand, Plant, Limbert, Square Top, Arched Apron, 12 x 27 In. 880.00
Stand, Plant, Mahogany, Brass Gallery, Pedestal, Reeded Legs, Paw Feet 70.00
Stand, Plant, Mahogany, Griffin Faces, Brass Claw & Ball Feet, c.1880 .... 995.00
Stand, Plant, Oak, 2 Tiers, Applied Carved Apron, Spool Legs 100.00
Stand, Plant, Stickley Brothers, Square Overhanging Top, Lower Shelf, 32 In. 900.00
Stand, Plant, Victorian, Mahogany, 49 In. 975.00
Stand, Plant, Victorian, Painted Wire, Metal, 2 Tiers, Gallery Rails, 31 1/2 In. 105.00
Stand, Plant, Wicker, Green 110.00
Stand, Regency, Rosewood, Drawers, Fluted Tapered Pedestal, Slipper Feet 1610.00
Stand, Renaissance Revival, Burl Veneer, Gilt, Revolving, 3 Tiers, 1870 .... 1150.00
Stand, Rococo, Pierced Brass, Onyx, 2 Tiers, Late 19th Century, 32 1/2 In. 413.00
Stand, Rosewood, 3 Tiers, Marble Inset Top, Claw Feet, China 245.00
Stand, Rosewood, Marble Top, Beaded Edge, Pink Marble Panel, 24 x 11 In., Pair 630.00
Stand, Sewing, Mahogany, Martha Washington, Queen Ann Style 450.00
Stand, Shaving, Adjustable Round Beveled Mirror, Cast Iron 275.00

Stand, Shaving, Mahogany, Carved, Double Oval Hinged Boxes, 31 x 27 x 9 In. 315.00
Stand, Shaving, Mahogany, Drawer, Turned Mirror Supports, 19th Century 193.00
Stand, Shaving, Mahogany, Rosewood, Horseshoe Mirror, Candle Arms, Victorian 745.00
Stand, Shaving, Mahogany, Velvet Lined Sections, Drawer, Fretwork, 31 1/4 In. 1150.00
Stand, Shaving, Nickel Plate, Beveled Mirror, Milk Glass Cup, 14 In. 22.00
Stand, Shaving, Sheraton, Mahogany, Pedestal, Adjustable Mirror, 1830 . . . . 1265.00
Stand, Sheraton, Cherry, 2 Drawers, 19 3/4 x 19 3/4 x 28 In. 410.00
Stand, Sheraton, Cherry, Bird's-Eye Maple Drawer Front, 29 x 18 1/2 x 19 In. 635.00
Stand, Sheraton, Cherry, Crossbanded Veneer Drawer, 17 x 18 x 29 In. 165.00
Stand, Sheraton, Cherry, Curly Maple, 2 Drawers, 1-Board Top, 18 x 21 In. 550.00
Stand, Sheraton, Cherry, Drawer, 2-Board Top, 12 x 21 In. 330.00
Stand, Sheraton, Cherry, Poplar, Curly Maple Top, Turned Legs, 19 x 21 x 28 In. 440.00
Stand, Sheraton, Cherry, Poplar, Yellow Paint, Orange Red Graining, 31 1/4 In. 1100.00
Stand, Sheraton, Curly & Bird's-Eye Maple, Drawer, 17 x 19 x 27 In. 715.00
Stand, Sheraton, Curly Maple, 2 Dovetailed Drawers, 18 x 22 x 29 In. 415.00
Stand, Sheraton, Curly Maple, Drawer, 2-Board Top, 18 x 19 x 29 In. 385.00
Stand, Sheraton, Curly Maple, Tilt Top, Tripod, Lobed Top, 15 3/4 x 21 3/4 In. 770.00
Stand, Sheraton, Curly Maple, Varnish, 2-Board Top, 19 1/4 x 21 x 29 In. 1345.00
Stand, Sheraton, Dovetailed Drawer, 1-Board Top, 18 3/4 x 21 x 29 In. 770.00
Stand, Sheraton, Drawer, D-Shaped Overhanging Top, Rim Turned Legs, 28 1/2 In. 290.00
Stand, Sheraton, Mahogany, Dark Finish, Reeded Seat Frame, 33 1/2 In. 440.00
Stand, Sheraton, Mahogany, Drawer, c.1780, 28 1/2 In. 1430.00
Stand, Sheraton, Maple, Bird's-Eye Veneer Drawer Front, Curly Top, 17 3/4 In. 905.00
Stand, Sheraton, Tiger Maple, 2 Curved Drawers, Glass Pulls, New York, 35 1/2 In. 865.00
Stand, Sheraton, Tiger Maple, Bowfront, 2 Drawers, 28 3/4 x 21 1/2 In. 835.00
Stand, Smoking, Art Deco, Cork, Chrome Base, 14 x 22 In. 220.00
Stand, Smoking, Metal, 2 Trays, Oscar Bach, 1920, 31 In. 230.00
Stand, Smoking, Mission Oak 210.00
Stand, Square Marble Top, Pierced Gallery Over Ormolu Mounts, 32 In. 415.00
Stand, Teakwood, Marble Inset, Floral Carved Apron, X-Stretcher, Round, 24 In. 305.00
Stand, Teakwood, Marble Top, Carved Apron, Square Feet, 32 1/2 In. 172.00
Stand, Teakwood, Soapstone Insert Top, China, 17 3/4 In. 247.00
Stand, Teakwood, Soapstone Insert Top, China, 35 1/2 In. 275.00
Stand, Tiger Maple Center Post, 2-Tier Revolving Top, 4 Spokes, Carved Feet, 31 In. 345.00
Stand, Trunk, Limbert, Mahogany, 6 Horizontal Slats, Rectangular Top, 18 In. 1100.00
Stand, Walnut, 1-Board Top, Dovetailed Drawer, Spool Turned Legs, 27 1/2 In. 181.00
Stand, Walnut, 1-Board Top, Drawer, Turned Legs, 18 x 22 5/8 x 29 In. 410.00
Stand, Walnut, 2 Drawers, Edge Beading, Pinwheel Knobs, 29 1/2 In. 412.00
Stand, Walnut, Drawer, Turned Legs, 18 3/4 x 28 1/2 In. 180.00
Stand, Walnut, Marble Top, Drawer, Ball Feet, France, 1860, 29 In. 363.00
Stand, Walnut, Poplar, 2 Dovetailed Drawers, Turned Legs, 19 x 21 x 27 In. 275.00
Stand, Walnut, Rouge Marble Inset Top, Tripod, Round, 16 x 28 1/2 In. 460.00
Stand, Walnut, Round Top, Turned Shaft, Tripod Base, France 20.00
Stand, Walnut, Tilt Top, Turned Birdcage Support, Cabriole Leg Base, 29 In. 2645.00
Stand, Writing, Mahogany, Interior Compartments, Baize Lined, Paw Feet, 31 In. 1265.00
Stool, Aalto, Round Laminate Top, 3 Bent Laminate Legs, 17 1/2 x 13 1/2 In., Pair 403.00
Stool, Bar, Louis Sognot, Chrome, S-Frame, Footrest, Metal, 35 1/2 In., 3 Piece 4830.00
Stool, Bar, Metal Mounts, Leather, Pair 115.00
Stool, Baroque, Giltwood, Red Velvet, Gold Fringe, Bun Feet, Italy, 22 In. 3450.00
Stool, Bentwood, Stacking, Seat Raised On 3 Flat Tapering Legs, Black, 4 Piece 805.00
Stool, Beveled Top, Wood Pegs, Turned Legs, Block Feet, England, 18 In., Pair 920.00
Stool, Birch, Mortise & Tenon Construction, Copper-Nail Design, c.1840 . . . . 295.00
Stool, Bugatti, Ebonized Wood, Brass, Pewter Inlay, 16 1/2 In. 6325.00
Stool, Burl Top, 3 Whittled Legs, 11 x 12 In. 245.00
Stool, Castiglioni, Plastic, Injection Molded, Upholstered Cushion, 16 1/2 x 16 In. 288.00
Stool, Chippendale Style, Claw & Ball Feet, Slip Seat, 15 x 26 x 20 In. 200.00
Stool, Dowel Legs, X-Stretcher, Upholstered, Gold Tag, 16 1/2 x 22 In., Pair 1380.00
Stool, Eames, Walnut, Concave Seat, Herman Miller, 13 x 15 In. 1100.00
Stool, Floral Upholstery, Cabriole Legs, Late 19th Century, 6 x 13 x 12 In. 132.00
Stool, Florence Knoll, Stacking, Light Wood, Steel Hairpin Legs, 18 x 13 In., Pair 403.00
Stool, G. Stickley, No. 301, Rush Seat, Branded, 20 x 16 x 18 In. 2860.00
Stool, George I, Mahogany, Slip Seat, Pendant Shells On Bellflower Legs, 15 In. 4600.00
Stool, George III, Mahogany, Drop-In Seat, Carved Legs, 12 1/2 In. 805.00

Stool, Gout, Mahogany, Adjustable, Upholstered Top, Ratchet Base, 1850s, 19 x 12 In. ...   172.00
Stool, Ice Cream Parlor, Child's, 24 In. 75.00
Stool, Italian Provincial, Upholstered Seat, Tapered Reeded Legs, 19 1/2 In. 1035.00
Stool, Jacobean, Hinged Top, 17th Century 975.00
Stool, Joint, Spiral Turned Legs, England, 19th Century 430.00
Stool, Kittinger, Expanding Top, Cubbyhole, Hinged Door Under Seat, 20 x 22 1/2 In. 110.00
Stool, Kittinger, Walnut, Ebonized Trim, Brass Label, 24 1/2 x 19 In. 82.00
Stool, L. & J.G. Stickley, No. 399, Folding, Leather Seat, 18 x 15 In. 2860.00
Stool, Mahogany, Acanthus Carved Cabriole Legs, Cushion, 16 x 21 In., Pair 1265.00
Stool, Mahogany, Accordion Action, Needlepoint Seat, c.1830 ....   385.00
Stool, Mahogany, Floral Carved Aprons, Cabriole Legs, Scroll Feet, 1930-1940 ....   220.00
Stool, Mahogany, Floral Needlepoint, Gadroon Molding, 10 x 15 In. 525.00
Stool, Mahogany, Marquetry, Curule, Padded Seat, Continental, 1830, 22 In. 1090.00
Stool, Mahogany, Padded Rectangular Top, Double-X Base, 13 In., Pair 1725.00
Stool, Mahogany, Scalloped Skirt, Tapered Legs, 19 x 19 1/2 In. 630.00
Stool, Mahogany, Serpentine Sides, Floral Carving, Velvet, 11 x 15 In. 247.00
Stool, Mahogany, Upholstered Top, Square Tapered & Reeded Legs, 17 x 17 In. 935.00
Stool, Maple, Upholstered Seat, X-Supports, 1830s 1265.00
Stool, McCobb, Square Vinyl Seat, Tubular Steel X-Stretcher, 15 x 20 In. 345.00
Stool, Neoclassical, Gilt, 1 Square Upholstered Seat, 1 Beaded Seat, 17 In., Pair 4600.00
Stool, Neoclassical, Walnut, Rectangular Upholstered Drop Seat, Saber Legs, 24 In. 2415.00
Stool, Oak, Carved Frieze, Turned & Blocked Legs, Rectangular Top, 21 x 12 x 17 In. ...   345.00
Stool, Oak, Lift Top, Carved Grapes & Leaves, Trestle Base, 19 In. 287.00
Stool, Oak, Rectangular Top, Turned & Blocked Legs, England, 18th Century, 24 In. 635.00
Stool, P. Paulin, Upholstered, Round, Tapers Toward Base, 14 x 20 In. 234.00
Stool, Piano, Classical, Rosewood, c.1840 ....   915.00
Stool, Piano, Mahogany, Adjustable Rotating Seat, Glass Ball Feet, 19 x 14 In. 150.00
Stool, Piano, Maple, Round Adjustable Top, Turned Pedestal, Glass Claw Feet 35.00
Stool, Piano, Oak, 6 Turned Spindle Back, Adjustable Round Seat, Brass Claw 175.00
Stool, Pierced Cusp Scrolling Stretchers, Upholstered, 1670s, 17 In. 2300.00
Stool, Poplar, Green Over Red Paint, 11 1/2 x 21 3/4 x 10 3/4 In. 180.00
Stool, Queen Anne, Mahogany, Oblong Slip Seat, Flat Stretcher, 17 x 20 x 15 In. 1320.00
Stool, Queen Anne, Walnut, Cushion Top, Cabriole Legs, John M. Pair 495.00
Stool, Queen Anne, Walnut, Slip Seat, Cabriole Legs, Shell Carving, 17 x 22 1/2 In. 2243.00
Stool, Regency Style, Painted & Parcel Gilt, Cane, Ball Feet, 16 1/2 In., Pair 2070.00
Stool, Renaissance Revival, Ebony, Adjustable, C. Cook & Co., c.1870, 18 In. 187.00
Stool, Rococo, Gilt, Square Upholstered Seat, Pale Orange Paint, 19 In., Pair 5462.00
Stool, Rococo, Serpentine Rails, Foliate, 4 Shell Cabriole Legs, Gray, 21 In., Pair 5750.00
Stool, Rush Seat, Scalloped Apron, Cabriole Legs, 18 x 26 In. 120.00
Stool, Saarinen, Round Upholstered Seat, White Enameled Base, 16 In., Pair 935.00
Stool, Saarinen, Tulip, Cast Aluminum, Upholstered, Knoll, 15 x 16 1/2 In., Pair 460.00
Stool, Saarinen, Tulip, Ivory Paint, Upholstered, 17 x 15 In., 4 Piece 660.00
Stool, Shaker, Cricket, Mt. Lebanon, 11 3/8 x 11 5/8 In. 247.00
Stool, Shaker, Revolving, Mt. Lebanon 5200.00
Stool, Spindled Seat Rail, Concave Slatted Seat, Liberty Thebes, 17 x 15 In. 1320.00
Stool, Victorian, Mahogany, Adjustable, Padded Base, Turned Feet 350.00
Stool, Walnut, 6-Pointed Star, 6 Crowned Birds, Vines, Mid-18th Century, 15 x 11 In. ...   517.00
Stool, Walnut, Hinged Embroidered Seat, Victorian 246.00
Stool, Wegner, Teakwood, Rattan, Bowed Sided, Upraised Handle, 26 In. 1265.00
Stool, William & Mary, Beechwood, Upholstered, Pierced Stretchers, c.1690, 19 In. 2587.00
Stool, Yew Wood, 3 Legs, England, c.1660 ....   495.00
Table, Aalto, Birch, Square Top, 4 Bent Rectangular Legs, 1935, 27 In. 575.00
Table, Alfons Bach, Chromed Tubular Steel, 2 Black Lacquer Shelves, 25 x 11 In., Pair ..   805.00
Table, Architect's, George III, Oak, Ratchet Support Over Drawer, 29 1/2 In. 1035.00
Table, Architect's, Neoclassical, Mahogany, Leather, 3 Shelves, Baltic, 46 x 32 In. 6325.00
Table, Art Deco, Faceted Top & Base, Square Pedestals, Steel & Bronze Accents, 60 In. ...   1320.00
Table, Art Deco, Galuchat-Veneered, Nesting, Green Stain, France, 1925 ....   5175.00
Table, Art Deco, Macassar Ebony, Round Top, Stepped Edge, 26 1/2 In. 1840.00
Table, Art Deco, Mahogany, Brass Mounted, Gold Lacquer, France, 1940s, 34 In. 3450.00
Table, Art Deco, X-Standard, Columns Continue To Base, 21 x 25 1/2 In. 2530.00
Table, Arts & Crafts, Round Top Over Shelf, 16 x 30 In. 286.00
Table, Bamboo, Embossed, 1880, 28 x 19 x 18 1/2 In. 180.00
Table, Bamboo, Sea Grass, Bamboo Supports, 1880, 26 x 24 1/2 In. 73.00

Table, Bamboo, Sea Grass, Octagonal Top, Bamboo Legs, 1880, 26 In. 96.00
Table, Bamboo, Sea Grass, Rectangular Top, Anglo-Indian, 1880, 20 x 14 In. 85.00
Table, Bamboo, Sea Grass, Square Top, Anglo-Indian, 26 x 14 In.   72.00
Table, Baroque, Mahogany, Rectangular Top, Lion's-Paw Feet, Pair 2530.00
Table, Baroque, Walnut, Italy, 31 x 35 In. 4600.00
Table, Biedermeier, Walnut, Rectangular Top, Frieze Drawer, Cabriole Legs, 27 3/4 In. 1265.00
Table, Bird's-Eye Maple, Marble Inset Top, Reeded Legs, 1840s, 29 1/2 In. 4312.00
Table, Black Marble Top, Gilt Metal Legs, Mario Villa, 22 1/2 x 36 In. 605.00
Table, Black Walnut, Pine, Removable Top, 2 Drawers, Pad Feet, Painted, 48 1/2 In. 2415.00
Table, Brass, Hammered, 2 Tiers, 4 Cylindrical Legs, 26 x 23 In.   1035.00
Table, Bronze & Marble Top, Floral Swags & Birds, Open Stretcher, 27 1/4 x 32 In. 775.00
Table, Bugatti, Ebonized Wood, Painted Parchment, Pierced Brass, 29 In. 8050.00
Table, Burgundy Lacquer, Spotted Bamboo, Corner Legs, 18 x 19 1/2 In. 5175.00
Table, Burl Walnut, Victorian, Marble Top, 29 1/2 x 31 1/2 x 22 In. 1785.00
Table, Butterfly, Cherry, 18th Century 1840.00
Table, Card, Biedermeier, Maple, Demilune, Ebonized Trim, Early 19th Century 1265.00
Table, Card, Chippendale, Tiger Maple, Scratch-Beaded Drawer, Pennsylvania, 38 In. . . .   5650.00
Table, Card, Empire, Mahogany, Mahogany Veneer, Lift Top, Lyre Standard 300.00
Table, Card, Empire, Mahogany, Rope Carved Legs, Swing Leg, 36 x 18 x 30 In. 1100.00
Table, Card, English Tudor Style, Oak, Square Herringbone Inlay, Bun Feet 115.00
Table, Card, Federal, Bird's-Eye Maple, Mahogany, Hinged, Rectangular Top, 30 In. 1610.00
Table, Card, Federal, Mahogany, Demilune, Urn Inlay 990.00
Table, Card, Federal, Mahogany, Drawer, Reeded Legs, 35 x 17 x 29 In. 990.00
Table, Card, Federal, Mahogany, Foldover Top, D Shape, Center Column, N.Y., 30 In. . . .   660.00
Table, Card, Federal, Mahogany, Hinged, Rectangular Top, Ring, Spiral Legs, 27 In. 172.00
Table, Card, Federal, Mahogany, Inlay, Demilune Top, Square Tapered Legs 375.00
Table, Card, Federal, Mahogany, Pine, Acanthus Leaf, 4 Scimitar Legs, 18 x 37 In. 2200.00
Table, Card, Federal, Mahogany, Serpentine Front, Medallion & Bellflower Inlay 605.00
Table, Card, Federal, Mahogany, Serpentine Front, Reeded, Swelled Legs, 30 In. 3737.00
Table, Card, George II, Walnut, Triple Top, Bowfront, Turned Legs, 1730, 29 In. 5175.00
Table, Card, George III, 2 Swing Legs, Block Feet, 36 x 38 In. 1840.00
Table, Card, George III, Mahogany, Crossbanded Serpentine Top, 1775, 28 3/4 In. 2875.00
Table, Card, George III, Mahogany, D-Shaped Top, Frieze Drawer, Block Feet, 29 In. 8050.00
Table, Card, George III, Mahogany, Foldover Top, Baize Surface, 28 3/4 In. 5750.00
Table, Card, Hepplewhite, Cherry, Swing Leg, String Inlay, 29 1/4 In. 2860.00
Table, Card, Hepplewhite, Foldover Top, Bowfront, Serpentine Sides, c.1800, 29 In. 6050.00
Table, Card, Hepplewhite, Mahogany, Demilune, 2 Swing Legs, 30 x 15 x 30 In. 2420.00
Table, Card, Hepplewhite, Mahogany, Demilune, Inlay, 31 x 36 x 18 In. 1495.00
Table, Card, Hepplewhite, Mahogany, Inlay, G. Parker, Newburyport, 28 1/2 In. 2013.00
Table, Card, Mahogany, Demilune, Folding, Diamond Inlay, Square Tapering Legs 530.00
Table, Card, Mahogany, Demilune, Inlay, Flap Leaves, 29 x 37 x 18 In. 17050.00
Table, Card, Mahogany, Hinged Top, Concertina Action, c.1840, 18 x 35 In. 695.00
Table, Card, Mahogany, Line Inlay, Baltimore, 29 x 35 3/4 In. 1330.00
Table, Card, Mahogany, Mahogany Veneer, Crossbanded, Spooner & Fitts, 1810 . . . .   4945.00
Table, Card, Mahogany, Serpentine Hinged Top, Veneered Apron, 1790, 29 1/2 In. 7475.00
Table, Card, Mahogany, Serpentine, Rose & Leaf, Reeded Legs, 29 x 36 In., Pair 8625.00
Table, Card, Mahogany, Swivel Top, Leaf Carved Knees, 30 1/2 In., Pair 9775.00
Table, Card, Regency, Mahogany, Swivel Top, Inset Leather Circle, 29 In. 715.00
Table, Card, Regency, Rosewood, Brass, Hinged Rectangular Top, Scroll Feet, 29 In. 747.00
Table, Card, Regency, Rosewood, Burl Inlay, Rectangular Top, 29 1/2 In. 6325.00
Table, Card, Rococo, Walnut, Serpentine Hinged, Cabriole Legs, 35 x 19 In. 545.00
Table, Card, Rosewood, Veneer, Shaped Top, Outset Corners, 19th Century 465.00
Table, Card, Sheraton, Mahogany, Bowfront, Turned & Reeded Legs, 29 1/2 In. 1005.00
Table, Card, Sheraton, Mahogany, Shaped Swivel Top, Apron, Reeded Legs 275.00
Table, Card, V. Kagan, Burl, Triangular Legs, High Gloss, 32 In.   1210.00
Table, Card, Victorian, Mahogany, Foldover Top, Telescopic Action, 29 In. 1265.00
Table, Cast Iron, Continental, 27 1/2 x 32 In. 750.00
Table, Center, Baroque, Jacaranda Wood, Brass, Rectangular Top, 3 Drawers 11500.00
Table, Center, Baroque, Mahogany, Rosewood, 3 Drawers, Portugal, 55 x 32 In. 3450.00
Table, Center, Baroque, Mahogany, Rosewood, 3 Short Drawers, Bun Feet, 35 In. 3450.00
Table, Center, Baroque, Rectangular Top, Wavy Border, Bun Feet, 19th Century 20700.00
Table, Center, Baroque, Satinwood, Kingwood, Fleur-De-Lis Border, Drawer 13800.00
Table, Center, Baroque, Winged Griffins, Triangular Base, Italy, 34 x 48 In. 4600.00

Table, Center, Biedermeier, Satinwood, Gray Variegated Marble Top, 30 x 48 In. 968.00
Table, Center, Charles X, Lemon, Amaranth, Rectangular Top, Frieze Drawer, 30 In. 9200.00
Table, Center, Chippendale, Marble Top, 19th Century, Ireland 6290.00
Table, Center, Classical, Mahogany, Faceted, Fluted, Scroll Legs, 1800s, 29 In. 4125.00
Table, Center, Eastlake, Walnut, Burl Veneer, Purple Gray Marble Top, 30 x 20 In. 385.00
Table, Center, Eastlake, Walnut, Round Top, 1880, 30 In. 300.00
Table, Center, Empire Style, Flower & Basket Inlay, Openwork, Century Co., 40 In. 2760.00
Table, Center, Empire, Mahogany, Marble Top, Pedestal, 3 Legs, 29 x 37 In. 2178.00
Table, Center, Empire, Mahogany, Pedestal, Concave Corners, Square, 36 x 36 In. 1330.00
Table, Center, George I, Faux Marble Top, Cabriole Legs, Hairy Paw Feet, 33 In. 290.00
Table, Center, George III, Elm, Rectangular Top, Chamfered Corners, 30 In. 1840.00
Table, Center, George IV, Rosewood, Round Top, Leaf Standard, Ball Feet, 28 In. 5750.00
Table, Center, J. & J.W. Meeks, Rococo, Marble Top, 28 x 44 x 29 In. 9775.00
Table, Center, Leon Marcotte, Renaissance Revival, Mahogany, Ebonized, 29 x 35 In. ... 8050.00
Table, Center, Louis XVI, Mahogany, White Marble Top, Fluted Legs, 26 x 27 1/2 In. ... 575.00
Table, Center, Louis XVI, Marble Top Painted Yellow, Fluted Legs, Oval, 29 In. 690.00
Table, Center, Louis XVI, Veined Marble Top, Floral, Berries, Acanthus Legs, 31 In. 2530.00
Table, Center, Mahogany, Faceted Bulbous Pedestal, Scroll Feet, 1830s, 29 In. 853.00
Table, Center, Mahogany, Parcel Gilt, Marble, 19th Century, Continental, 28 x 31 In. 4140.00
Table, Center, Mahogany, Round Marble Top, 3 Carved Legs, 19th Century, 29 In. 385.00
Table, Center, Mahogany, Tilt Top, Carved, Classical, Urn Base, 30 x 43 In. 2875.00
Table, Center, Napoleon III, Mahogany, Marble, Round, C-Scroll Legs, 1880, 38 In. 2660.00
Table, Center, Neoclassical, Ebony, Round Dark Gray Top, Paw Feet, 29 In., Pair 13800.00
Table, Center, Neoclassical, Elm, Round Pietra Dura Top, Geometric Border 9200.00
Table, Center, Neoclassical, Mahogany, Brass Mounted, 30 x 38 In. 9775.00
Table, Center, Neoclassical, Mahogany, Round Extension Top, 2 Leaves, 29 In. 10925.00
Table, Center, Neoclassical, Mahogany, Round Gray Fossilized Marble Top, 30 In. 5750.00
Table, Center, Neoclassical, Mahogany, Round Top, Gadroon Base, 29 In. 8050.00
Table, Center, Neoclassical, Rosewood, Marquetry, 3 Paw Feet, 29 x 39 In. 1725.00
Table, Center, Ormolu Beaded Top, X-Stretcher, 1890, 28 x 47 x 28 In. 425.00
Table, Center, Quartersawn Oak, Oval Top, 4 C-Scroll Feet, 1900, 30 x 44 In. 275.00
Table, Center, Regency, Mahogany, Brass Banding, 3 Gilt Hairy Paws 3740.00
Table, Center, Renaissance Revival, Walnut, Burl Veneer, Marble, 19th Century 1150.00
Table, Center, Rococo, Mahogany, Marble Top, Scrolled, Leaves, 29 In. 880.00
Table, Center, Rococo, Mahogany, Turtle-Shaped Top, 1860, 39 x 26 In. 665.00
Table, Center, Rococo, Walnut, Marble Top, Carved Apron, Cabriole Legs, 1800s, 30 In. . 1100.00
Table, Center, Rococo, Walnut, Marble Turtle-Shaped Top, 1865, 34 x 23 In. 1936.00
Table, Center, Rococo, Walnut, Scalloped Top, Bracketed Pedestal, 1870, 32 In. 330.00
Table, Center, Rococo, Walnut, Turtle-Shaped Top, Mid-19th Century, 30 1/2 x 26 1/4 In.. 1840.00
Table, Center, Rosewood, Carved Floral & Acanthus, Marble Turtle-Shaped Top, 30 In. .. 1760.00
Table, Center, Victorian, Rococo, Walnut, Ovolo Marble Top, 28 x 33 In. 660.00
Table, Center, Victorian, Walnut, Oval Pink Marble Top, Serpentine Legs, 28 In. 2200.00
Table, Center, Walnut Veneer, Marble Top, c.1880 .... 5225.00
Table, Center, Walnut, Drawer, Stretcher Base, Leather Top, Rounded Ends, 28 x 47 In. .. 660.00
Table, Center, Walnut, Marble Top, Carved, Scroll Supports, 31 x 37 1/2 In. 5750.00
Table, Center, Walnut, Marble Top, Oval, Center Pedestal, 33 x 24 x 30 1/2 In. 1095.00
Table, Center, Walnut, Marble Top, Scrolled Legs, Victorian, 30 x 37 x 28 In. 1265.00
Table, Center, Walnut, Oval Finger Molded, Incised Legs, 28 x 27 x 19 In. 100.00
Table, Center, Walnut, Oval Marble Top, Finger Carved Pedestal Base, 36 x 26 In. 545.00
Table, Cherry, Farmhouse, Plank Top, Over Frieze, Square Legs, 1860, 50 1/2 In. 1330.00
Table, Cherry, Poplar, Farmhouse, 2-Broad Top, 1850s, 30 x 57 In. 1344.00
Table, Chippendale, Mahogany, Tripod, 3 Acanthus Legs, Claw Feet, 29 1/2 In. 212.00
Table, Chippendale, Pine, Drawer, Thick 1-Board Top, 19 3/8 x 26 In. 110.00
Table, Chippendale, Walnut, Beaded Drawer, Pennsylvania, 1790 .... 330.00
Table, Cinnabar Red Lacquer, 11 1/2 x 18 1/2 x 14 In. 345.00
Table, Classical, Mahogany, Frieze Drawer, Rounded Leaves, 4 Paw Feet, 29 In. 1540.00
Table, Coffee, 4 Black & White Laminate Lift Tops, Walnut, Brown Saltman, 41 In. 550.00
Table, Coffee, Borge Mogensen, Teakwood, V-Legs, Tray Top, Cane Shelf, 60 x 21 In. ... 385.00
Table, Coffee, Chippendale, Mahogany, Pie-Crest Top, Reeded Splayed Legs, 18 In. 212.00
Table, Coffee, E. Wormley, Burl Veneer Pedestal, Round Glass Top, 42 In. 633.00
Table, Coffee, E. Wormley, Walnut, 3 Inset Natzler Tiles, Metal Tag, 18 x 30 x 22 In. 1495.00
Table, Coffee, Eames, CTW, Molded Plywood Top & Legs 1150.00
Table, Coffee, Eames, White Formica, Black Plastic Trim, Aluminum Base, Round, 36 In. . 230.00

Table, Coffee, Florence Knoll, Round Marble Top, Brushed Chrome Legs, 17 x 32 In. ... 275.00
Table, Coffee, Fornasetti, Round Floral Print Top, Neoclassical Base, 45 x 18 In. 880.00
Table, Coffee, Frankl, Combed Veneer, Black Lacquer Top, Curled Ends, 48 x 21 In. 863.00
Table, Coffee, Frankl, Contrasting Cork Veneer, Brass-Covered Feet, 54 x 27 In. 1035.00
Table, Coffee, Frankl, Mahogany, Cork Top, Greek Key Base, 1940s, 84 In. 1300.00
Table, Coffee, Frankl, Rattan, Round Wood Top, 1940, 16 1/2 x 43 In. 632.00
Table, Coffee, G. Nakashima, Walnut, Free-Edge, Cantilevered Base, 62 x 40 In. 8800.00
Table, Coffee, G. Nakashima, Walnut, Macassar Ebony, 22 1/2 In. 9775.00
Table, Coffee, G. Nelson, Walnut, Round, Steel Frame, Herman Miller, 41 In. 770.00
Table, Coffee, Georgian Style, Oak, Carved, Claw & Ball Feet, 54 x 30 x 17 1/2 In. ... 145.00
Table, Coffee, I. Noguchi, Ebonized Splayed Base, Glass Freeform Top, 50 x 36 In. 1210.00
Table, Coffee, I. Noguchi, Ebonized Wood, Triangular Glass Top, 50 x 36 x 16 In. 1430.00
Table, Coffee, I. Noguchi, Varnished Ash Splayed Base, Freeform Glass Top, 50 x 36 In. . 2310.00
Table, Coffee, Kem Weber, Rosewood Veneer, Square Legs, 21 x 28 x 28 In. 805.00
Table, Coffee, Louis XVI Style, Marble Top, 35 1/2 x 20 x 15 In. 85.00
Table, Coffee, Mahogany, Kidney Shape, Beveled Glass Lift Top, Lower Shelf, 30 In. ... 575.00
Table, Coffee, Mahogany, Leather Top, 4 Carved Legs, 40 x 16 x 22 In. 100.00
Table, Coffee, Mahogany, Tray Top, Shaped Gallery, Cabriole Legs, X-Stretcher 110.00
Table, Coffee, Marquetry, Ivory Marble Top, c.1920, 20 x 29 1/2 In. 935.00
Table, Coffee, McCobb, Brass Frame, 2 White Glass Shelves, 48 x 18 In., Pair 605.00
Table, Coffee, McCobb, Planner Group, Walnut, Flaring Dowel Legs, 15 x 48 x 18 In. ... 275.00
Table, Coffee, P. Evans, Gilt-Iron Swag Base, Round Slate Top, 11 1/2 x 38 In. 990.00
Table, Coffee, Robsjohn-Gibbings, Bent Bleached Walnut, Round Marble Top, 40 In. 1320.00
Table, Coffee, Robsjohn-Gibbings, Walnut, Glass Top, Brass Base, Square, 45 In. 2310.00
Table, Coffee, Rohde, Burl Veneer, Kidney Shape, 15 x 41 In. 1540.00
Table, Coffee, Rohde, Mahogany, Brushed Chrome Knobs, 42 x 17 x 17 In. 715.00
Table, Coffee, Saarinen, Round Laminate Top, Aluminum Pedestal Base, 15 x 36 In. 460.00
Table, Coffee, Saarinen, Walnut Veneer, Painted Aluminum Pedestal, 36 In. 633.00
Table, Coffee, Studio Tetrarch, Fiberglass Handkerchief, Square, 1960s, 36 x 16 In. 770.00
Table, Coffee, Tapio Wirkkala, Laminated Birch Inlay, Dowel Legs, 39 x 24 In. 3080.00
Table, Coffee, V. Kagan, 3-Sided Glass Top, Black Lacquered 3-Legged Base, 15 x 34 In. 550.00
Table, Coffee, Van Der Rohe, Square, Chrome X-Base, Plate-Glass Top, 42 In. 605.00
Table, Coffee, Widdicomb, Black Lacquer, Carved Floral Ends, 22 x 48 In. 920.00
Table, Coffee, Wood, Adjustable Slat Top, 4 Dowel Legs, 1950, 16 x 48 In. 28.00
Table, Conference, Teak, Elliptical, Chromed Steel Pedestal Base, Knoll, 1961, 96 In. 2185.00
Table, Console, E. Wormley, Mahogany, Black Lacquer Panels, Dunbar, 1950, 24 In. 825.00
Table, Console, Empire Style, Walnut Veneer, Stone Top, Brass Inlay, 32 x 54 In. 715.00
Table, Console, Empire, Mahogany, Acanthus Carved Pedestal, Legs, Paw Feet, 28 In. ... 495.00
Table, Console, Fan Carved Doors, Marble Top, 1820s 9800.00
Table, Console, George II, Giltwood, Marble Top, Eagle Base, 31 x 32 In. 6610.00
Table, Console, Giltwood, Marble Top, Fluted & Flat Leaf Legs, Italy, 32 x 35 In. 4025.00
Table, Console, Louis XV, Marble, 1850, 74 x 41 In. 6500.00
Table, Console, Louis XV, Wrought Iron, Marble Top, Cabriole Legs, 33 3/4 In. 2185.00
Table, Console, Mahogany, Curved Apron, Tapered Columns, Pilasters, Feet, 1800s 1100.00
Table, Console, Mahogany, Marble Top, Serpentine Front & Sides, c.1840, Pair 9200.00
Table, Console, Mahogany, Mirrored Back, Hairy Paw Feet, c.1820 .... 3162.00
Table, Console, Marble Top, Carved Front, Shells, Curved Legs, 29 1/2 x 31 In. 748.00
Table, Console, Painted, Castle Scene, Horses, Boats, Italy, 35 x 59 x 23 In., Pair 4600.00
Table, Console, Raymond Subes, Wrought Iron, Beveled Marble Top, 37 x 48 In. 3680.00
Table, Console, Rococo, Walnut, Serpentine, Marble, 19th Century, 40 In. 775.00
Table, Console, Rosewood, Relief Carved Frieze, Square Legs, China, 71 x 17 1/2 In. ... 245.00
Table, Console, Shaped Top, Painted Flora, Gold Trim, Italy, 34 x 60 x 17 In., Pair 3795.00
Table, Console, Sheraton, Reeded Legs, Cookie-Corner Top, Brass, c.1825, 29 x 37 In. ... 3750.00
Table, Console, Sheraton, Turned & Reeded Legs, c.1815-1830, 29 x 37 In. 3750.00
Table, Console, Walnut, Center Drawer, Wood Knobs 195.00
Table, Console, Walnut, Marble, Door, Side Mirrors, 32 3/4 x 54 x 15 In. 805.00
Table, Dinette, I. Noguchi, Round Laminate Top, Chrome Wire Struts, 36 In. 1200.00
Table, Dining, 2-Tone Wood, Plate-Glass Top, China, 42 x 66 x 31 In. 330.00
Table, Dining, Art Deco, Mahogany, Rectangular Top, Bronze Trim, 1928, 30 In. 6325.00
Table, Dining, Arts & Crafts, Extension Top, Apron, Leaves, Shoe Feet, 29 x 48 In. 500.00
Table, Dining, Ash, Trestle Feet, Oval, c.1820, 48 3/4 In. 1320.00
Table, Dining, Beechwood, Acanthus-Capped Legs, 4 Leaves, 50 3/4 In. 1840.00
Table, Dining, Drop Leaf, Federal, Rounded Corners, Turned Legs, 19th Century 490.00

Table, Dining, Drop Leaf, Fruitwood, Cabriole Legs, 66 1/2 In. 3450.00
Table, Dining, Drop Leaf, Georgian, Mahogany, Double Pedestal, 2 Leaves, 102 In. 4620.00
Table, Dining, Drop Leaf, Mahogany, D-Shaped Ends, Fluted Legs, 1810, 70 x 47 In. 1210.00
Table, Dining, Drop Leaf, Mahogany, String Inlay, c.1790, 89 1/2 In. 2750.00
Table, Dining, Drop Leaf, McCobb, Angled Tapered Legs, 57 x 36 In. 403.00
Table, Dining, Drop Leaf, Pine, Oval, Scalloped Apron, 30 x 90 In. 1090.00
Table, Dining, Drop Leaf, Queen Anne, Mahogany, Cabriole Legs, Splayed Feet, 48 In. ... 2070.00
Table, Dining, Drop Leaf, Tiger Maple, Cherry, c.1820, 78 In. Open 1380.00
Table, Dining, E. Wheeler, Tiger Maple Top, Painted Base, 2 Leaves 990.00
Table, Dining, E. Wormley, Maple Veneer Top, Mahogany Base, Dunbar, 66 In. 260.00
Table, Dining, E. Wormley, Walnut, Slab Legs, 3 Leaves, 72 x 42 x 29 In. 4125.00
Table, Dining, Eames, Aluminum & Chrome-Plated Steel, Oval Marble Top, 72 x 42 In. ... 1035.00
Table, Dining, Eames, Round White Laminate Top, Herman Miller, 48 x 29 In. 176.00
Table, Dining, Eames, Walnut Plywood, Folding Chrome Legs, 54 x 34 x 29 In. 1045.00
Table, Dining, Empire Style, Mahogany, X-Stretcher, 2 Leaves, 92 In. 2875.00
Table, Dining, Federal, Mahogany, Inlaid Aprons & Cuffs, 149 In. 2310.00
Table, Dining, Federal, Mid-Atlantic States, 1810, 2 Sections 700.00
Table, Dining, Frank Lloyd Wright, Mahogany, Rectangular Top, 64 x 42 x 29 In. 2750.00
Table, Dining, Frankl, Black Limed Oak, Light Wood Legs, 28 1/2 x 38 x 58 In. 2530.00
Table, Dining, Fruitwood, Farmhouse, Drawer Each End, c.1825, 29 1/4 x 98 1/2 In. 1875.00
Table, Dining, G. Nakashima, Rounded, Walnut, Free Edges, Butterfly Joints, 84 x 49 In. . 19800.00
Table, Dining, G. Nakashima, Walnut, Trestle, 28 3/4 In. 4600.00
Table, Dining, G. Nelson, Rosewood Veneer, Bowed Rectangle, Steel X-Legs, 78 x 42 In. 1553.00
Table, Dining, G. Stickley, No. 634 .... 7700.00
Table, Dining, Gateleg, Federal, Mahogany, c.1800, 28 1/2 x 54 x 41 1/2 In. 450.00
Table, Dining, Gateleg, Hepplewhite, Tiger Maple, 28 1/2 x 59 In. 1095.00
Table, Dining, Gateleg, Hepplewhite, Walnut, Demilune, Leaves, 83 In. Open 1210.00
Table, Dining, Gateleg, Maple, Vase-Form Turned Legs, 19th Century 440.00
Table, Dining, Gateleg, Pine, Compressed Bun Feet, 30 x 67 1/2 In. 1495.00
Table, Dining, Gateleg, Queen Anne, Cherry, 28 x 60 In. 1650.00
Table, Dining, Gateleg, Round Corners, 19th Century, 54 x 42 In. 165.00
Table, Dining, Gateleg, William & Mary, Walnut, c.1720, 50 1/2 In. 1675.00
Table, Dining, George II Style, Walnut, 19th Century, 29 x 45 x 34 1/2 In. 500.00
Table, Dining, George III, Mahogany, 3 Pedestals, D-Shaped Ends, 1810, 91 In. 8800.00
Table, Dining, George III, Mahogany, 3 Pedestals, Saber Legs, 80 x 47 In. 10925.00
Table, Dining, George III, Mahogany, Rectangular, 2 Pedestals, 2 Leaves, 107 In. 10350.00
Table, Dining, George IV, Mahogany, 3 Pedestals, 2 Leaves, Casters, 98 In. 9200.00
Table, Dining, Georgian Style, Floral & Scroll Frieze, Extension, 84 x 48 x 32 In. 5750.00
Table, Dining, Georgian Style, Mahogany, Pedestal, Extension, 29 1/2 x 98 x 48 In. 4590.00
Table, Dining, Georgian, Mahogany, Rectangular Top, Down-Swept Legs, 29 x 44 In. ... 1610.00
Table, Dining, Georgian, Mahogany, Rectangular Top, Reeded Edges, Legs, 29 In. 5175.00
Table, Dining, Hastings, Round, Decal, 48 In. 660.00
Table, Dining, Hepplewhite, Mahogany, Demilune, Pair, 91 1/2 In. 1760.00
Table, Dining, Heywood-Wakefield Co., Drop Leaf, Maple, Wishbone Legs, 58 x 40 In. ... 805.00
Table, Dining, Limbert, No. 1487, Prairie School Design, Round Top, 4 Leaves, 54 In. ... 8250.00
Table, Dining, Louis XV, Walnut, Foldover Top, 30 x 68 x 34 In. 517.00
Table, Dining, Louis XVI, Brass Mounted, Round Hinged Top, 4 Leaves, 30 In. 13800.00
Table, Dining, Louis XVI, Oak, Molded Top, Acanthus-Capped Legs, Apron, 30 In. 3160.00
Table, Dining, Magistretti, Molded Plastic, Cylinder & Cone Base, 26 x 46 In. 460.00
Table, Dining, Mahogany, 3 Fluted Pedestals, Paw Feet, Casters, 2 Leaves, 180 In. 5175.00
Table, Dining, Mahogany, 3 Pedestals, Extension, Gilt-Metal Paw Feet, 2 Leaves, 132 In. . 3220.00
Table, Dining, Mahogany, 6 Spool Turned Legs, 48 3/4 x 72 1/2 x 28 In. 550.00
Table, Dining, Mahogany, Canted Corners, Rope Turned Legs, 1 Leaf, 62 In. 175.00
Table, Dining, Mahogany, Fluted Column, Casters, Three 10-In. Leaves, 60 In. 2200.00
Table, Dining, Mahogany, Gadroon Top, Pedestal, 4 Down-Swept Legs, 30 In. 3300.00
Table, Dining, Mahogany, Oval, Scroll Legs, Pierced, 2 Leaves, 1860, 62 In. 1320.00
Table, Dining, Mahogany, Round, Pedestal, 4-Part Platform, Claw Feet, 1900, 48 In. 495.00
Table, Dining, Mahogany, Stepped Spreading Plinth, France, c.1930, 47 In. 1380.00
Table, Dining, Mahogany, Veneer, Round Top, Pedestal, 18-In. Leaf 1430.00
Table, Dining, Neoclassical, Fruitwood, Round Divided Top, Acanthus Paw Feet 6900.00
Table, Dining, Oak, Round Top, Square Pedestal, 4 Bracket Legs, 45 In. 135.00
Table, Dining, Oak, Round, Turned & Reeded Legs, Egg & Dart Skirt, 4 Leaves 1210.00
Table, Dining, Oak, Self-Storing Leaves, 30 x 114 In. 495.00

Table, Dining, Petal, Flower-Shaped Top, Black Enamel Branched Base, Knoll, 42 In. ... 770.00
Table, Dining, Peter E. Kramer, Cherry, Rectangular, Hollow Square Legs 865.00
Table, Dining, Prairie School, 4 Column Legs, Pedestal Base, Leaves, 60 In. 3500.00
Table, Dining, Queen Anne Style, Tripod Base, Baker Co., 60 x 46 x 30 In. 460.00
Table, Dining, Regency, Mahogany, 2 Leaves, Double Trestle Supports, 55 In. 8050.00
Table, Dining, Regency, Mahogany, 4 Splayed Legs, 5 Leaves, 31 In. 7260.00
Table, Dining, Regency, Mahogany, Brass Inlay 3090.00
Table, Dining, Renaissance Revival, Walnut, 46 x 30 1/4 In. 140.00
Table, Dining, S. Marx, Ebonized, 4 Lucite Slab Legs, 1940, 61 x 33 x 37 In. 3450.00
Table, Dining, Sheraton, Cherry, 1-Board, 68 x 42 In. 385.00
Table, Dining, Tulipwood, Marquetry, Foliate Swags, 83 In. 3335.00
Table, Dining, Walnut, Parquetry, Draw End, Scroll Toes, 29 1/2 x 70 In. 1755.00
Table, Dining, Walnut, Round, Pedestal, Carved & Scroll Feet, 6 Leaves, 52 In. 1555.00
Table, Dining, Walnut, Square Apron, Turned, Fluted Legs, Victorian, 41 x 29 In. 165.00
Table, Dining, Walnut, Trifid Feet, 52 1/2 x 48 In. 2587.00
Table, Dining, Walnut, Turned Fluted Legs, 3 Leaves, Early 20th Century, 28 x 48 In. 600.00
Table, Dining, Wegner, Recessed Leaves, Dowel Legs, Denmark, 28 1/2 x 55 x 35 In. ... 575.00
Table, Dining, Wegner, Teakwood, Flared Dowel Legs, 2 Leaves, 76 x 41 In. 2200.00
Table, Dining, Wrought Iron, Marble Top, 6 Tapered Legs, France, 1920, 31 In. 6325.00
Table, Dressing, Cherry, 2 Tiger Maple Drawers, Backsplash, Drawer In Base 715.00
Table, Dressing, Classical, Mahogany, Bronze-Mounted Columns, 3 Drawers, c.1820 .... 2640.00
Table, Dressing, Drawer, Carved Handle, Trestle Base, 29 1/2 In. 345.00
Table, Dressing, Drawer, Shaped Backsplash, Stenciled Design, 34 x 32 1/4 In. 1380.00
Table, Dressing, Federal, Mahogany, 5 Drawers, Rectangular Mirror, 1880, 33 In. 1955.00
Table, Dressing, Federal, Maple, Inlaid, Drawer, Scroll Backsplash, 19th Century 400.00
Table, Dressing, Federal, Pine, Drawer, Turned Legs, Mid-19th Century 115.00
Table, Dressing, Federal, Pine, Scrolled, 2 Glove Over Full Drawer, 19th Century 375.00
Table, Dressing, George III, Walnut, 3 Drawers, Rectangular Top, Square Legs, 30 In. ... 1495.00
Table, Dressing, Georgian, Mahogany, Rectangular Top, Tapered Legs, 36 x 16 In. 259.00
Table, Dressing, Grain Painted, Rosewood Type, 34 1/2 x 17 3/4 In. ....*Illus* 1150.00
Table, Dressing, Hepplewhite, Sponge Painted, Shaped Splashboard, Serpentine 3025.00
Table, Dressing, Inlaid Mahogany, Lift Top, Compartments, Bottle Well, 32 3/4 In. 3080.00
Table, Dressing, Louis XV Revival, Inlaid Mahogany, Frieze Drawers, 1900 .... 660.00
Table, Dressing, Mahogany, 2 Drawers, Cookie Corners, Reeded Legs, 28 1/2 In. 3410.00
Table, Dressing, Mahogany, 2 Short, 1 Long Drawer, Scroll, Foliate Supports, c.1830 .... 2200.00
Table, Dressing, Mahogany, 3 Drawers, Bowfront Case, Opalescent Pulls, 30 1/4 In. 1635.00
Table, Dressing, Mahogany, 3 Drawers, Inset Tiles, Leaves At Knees, 40 1/4 In. 1374.00
Table, Dressing, Mahogany, Satinwood Inlay, Drawers, Ivory Pulls, Foldover Top, 35 In. . 3220.00
Table, Dressing, New England, Gold, Green Stenciled Design, Drawer, 34 x 32 In. 1380.00
Table, Dressing, Queen Anne, Maple, Pine, 3 Drawers, c.1750, 29 x 34 x 18 In. 3737.00
Table, Dressing, Queen Anne, Walnut, 3 Side Drawers, Kneehole Over Door, 32 1/2 In. .. 5462.00
Table, Dressing, Renaissance Revival, Floral, Shell & Scroll Carving, Mirror, 99 In. 6040.00
Table, Dressing, Rohde, Rosewood Veneer, Semicircular Front, Glass Shelf, 22 x 52 In. .. 660.00
Table, Dressing, Sheraton, Mahogany, Hinged Writing Surface, Carved, 36 In. 750.00
Table, Dressing, Sheraton, Walnut, Oblong Top, 2 Drawers, 1840, Woman's, 26 1/2 In. ... 522.00
Table, Dressing, William & Mary, Walnut, 1 Short & 2 Deep Drawers, 30 1/2 In. 517.00
Table, Drop Leaf, Birch, Plain Frieze, Tapered Legs, 19th Century, 17 x 36 x 27 In. 200.00

If you spill water on a wooden table protected by a glass top, be sure to wipe it up quickly. If water gets below the glass, it will make white spots.

Furniture, Table, Dressing,
Grain Painted, Rosewood
Type, 34 1/2 x 17 3/4 In.

Table, Drop Leaf, Charles II Style, Oak, Round Supports, 18th Century, 57 In. 3220.00
Table, Drop Leaf, Cherry, Box Stretcher, Turned Legs, 25 x 30 In. 330.00
Table, Drop Leaf, Cherry, Hinged Leaves, Cabriole Legs, Pad Feet, 28 x 44 In. 1840.00
Table, Drop Leaf, Cherry, Rectangular, Rule-Jointed Drop Leaves, 28 x 37 1/4 In. 300.00
Table, Drop Leaf, Cherry, Spool Turned Legs, Dovetailed Drawer, Castors, 33 x 30 In. ... 385.00
Table, Drop Leaf, Chippendale, Mahogany, 8 Square Legs, Castors, 19 x 50 In. 990.00
Table, Drop Leaf, Chippendale, Mahogany, D-Shaped Leaves, 1770, 28 In. 9200.00
Table, Drop Leaf, Chippendale, Walnut, Drawer, 1780, 28 x 19 x 30 In. 2200.00
Table, Drop Leaf, Classical Revival, Mahogany, Rounded Corners, 19th Century 345.00
Table, Drop Leaf, Classical, Mahogany, Boston 4500.00
Table, Drop Leaf, Curly Maple, 2-Board Top, 6 Turned Legs, 23 x 42 In. 495.00
Table, Drop Leaf, Duncan Phyfe, Mahogany, Pedestal, 4 Claw Feet, 28 In. 805.00
Table, Drop Leaf, Empire, Dark Brown, Columnar Legs, 29 x 70 In. 980.00
Table, Drop Leaf, Empire, Mahogany, D-Shaped Leaf, Faux Drawer, 30 x 38 x 51 In. 545.00
Table, Drop Leaf, Federal, Birch, Round Corners, Baluster Turned Legs, 19th Century ... 230.00
Table, Drop Leaf, Federal, Mahogany, Drawer, Straight Tapered Legs 110.00
Table, Drop Leaf, Federal, Mahogany, Foliate Carved Turned Legs, Early 19th Century .. 248.00
Table, Drop Leaf, Federal, Mahogany, Scalloped Ends, Hairy Paw Feet, 29 In. 500.00
Table, Drop Leaf, Federal, Mahogany, Scalloped Leaves, Reeded Legs, 29 x 40 In. 800.00
Table, Drop Leaf, Federal, Mahogany, Square Corners, Baluster Turned Legs 345.00
Table, Drop Leaf, Federal, Maple, Reeded Top, Drawer, 19th Century, 27 x 45 In. 4887.00
Table, Drop Leaf, Federal, Pine, Rectangular Top, Plain Apron, New England, 29 In. 546.00
Table, Drop Leaf, French Provincial, Chestnut, Drawer, Square, Tapered Legs, 30 In. 660.00
Table, Drop Leaf, George II, Mahogany, Rectangular, Pad Feet, 28 1/2 In. 2300.00
Table, Drop Leaf, Hepplewhite Style, Mahogany, 2 Drawers, Splayed Feet, 30 x 42 In. ... 195.00
Table, Drop Leaf, Hepplewhite, Cherry, 1-Board Top, Cut Corners, 20 x 35 In. 495.00
Table, Drop Leaf, Hepplewhite, Cherry, Linenfold Tapered Legs, 28 In. 247.00
Table, Drop Leaf, Hepplewhite, Mahogany, Square Tapered Legs, Castors, 18 x 34 In. ... 880.00
Table, Drop Leaf, Hepplewhite, Walnut, Butternut, Square Tapered Legs, 2 Leaves 341.00
Table, Drop Leaf, Hepplewhite, Walnut, Drawer, Line Inlay, Tapered Legs 715.00
Table, Drop Leaf, Hepplewhite, Walnut, Rubbed, 1-Board Top, 15 x 47 In. 330.00
Table, Drop Leaf, L. & J.G. Stickley, Cutout Trestle, Shoe Feet, 24 In. 2200.00
Table, Drop Leaf, Library, Mahogany Veneer, Drawers, 1 False Drawer, c.1820 .... 275.00
Table, Drop Leaf, Mahogany, 6 Turned, Tapered, Reeded Legs, c.1820, 29 1/2 In. 1650.00
Table, Drop Leaf, Mahogany, Demilune Ends, c.1810, 102 In. 9200.00
Table, Drop Leaf, Mahogany, Double Elliptical Leaves, c.1815 .... 5175.00
Table, Drop Leaf, Mahogany, Drawer, Turned Legs, Early 19th Century 193.00
Table, Drop Leaf, Mahogany, Spider Legs, Pad Feet, 28 In. 880.00
Table, Drop Leaf, Mahogany, Tapered Legs, Pad Feet, 18th Century, 28 In. 1265.00
Table, Drop Leaf, Maple, Breadboard Ends, Turned Legs, Mid-1800s, 29 x 59 x 48 In. ... 2352.00
Table, Drop Leaf, Oak, Carved Wildflowers, 19th Century, 28 1/2 In. 800.00
Table, Drop Leaf, Oak, Expandable Top, Tapered Reeded Legs, Casters, 29 In. 145.00
Table, Drop Leaf, Pine, 72 x 38 In. 975.00
Table, Drop Leaf, Pine, Farmhouse, 30 x 90 1/4 In. 1045.00
Table, Drop Leaf, Poplar, Drawer, Turned Legs, American, 28 x 41 In. 357.00
Table, Drop Leaf, Queen Anne Style, Mahogany, Duck Feet, 20th Century, 29 x 41 In. ... 220.00
Table, Drop Leaf, Queen Anne, Mahogany, Drawer, 19th Century, 60 x 42 In. 2055.00
Table, Drop Leaf, Queen Anne, Mahogany, Duck Feet, England, 20 3/4 x 35 In. 605.00
Table, Drop Leaf, Queen Anne, Maple, Scroll Aprons, Cabriole Legs, 12 x 47 In. 1210.00
Table, Drop Leaf, Queen Anne, Tiger Maple, 2 Leaves, 18th Century, 26 x 47 x 16 In. ... 2750.00
Table, Drop Leaf, Queen Anne, Walnut, 2-Board Top, 6 Round Tapered Legs, 50 In. 2200.00
Table, Drop Leaf, Queen Anne, Walnut, Hinged Top, Scroll Cabriole Legs, Pad Feet 5750.00
Table, Drop Leaf, Sheraton, Birch, 1-Board Top, Red Paint, 21 x 42 In. 385.00
Table, Drop Leaf, Sheraton, Birch, 2-Board Top, Red Paint, 16 1/2 x 41 1/2 In. 330.00
Table, Drop Leaf, Sheraton, Cherry, Drawer, 20 x 42 x 28 In. 550.00
Table, Drop Leaf, Sheraton, Cherry, Drawer, Turned, Reeded Legs, 19 3/4 x 38 In. 330.00
Table, Drop Leaf, Sheraton, Curly Maple, Drawer, 3-Board Top, 22 x 35 In. 520.00
Table, Drop Leaf, Sheraton, Mahogany, Crossbanded Veneer, 20 x 42 In. 880.00
Table, Drop Leaf, Sheraton, Mahogany, Dovetailed Drawer, Reeded Legs, 28 In. 550.00
Table, Drop Leaf, Sheraton, Red & Yellow Flame, 1840s 495.00
Table, Drop Leaf, Walnut, 1-Board Top, 6 Legs, 21 x 46 x 29 In. 330.00
Table, Drop Leaf, Walnut, Turned Legs, 19th Century, 38 3/4 x 23 x 28 1/2 In. 250.00
Table, Drum, Classical Style, Multicolored Veneer, Burl Top, 20th Century, 28 3/4 In. 415.00

Table, Drum, Mahogany, Drawer, Leather Top, Duncan Phyfe Legs, 20th Century 195.00
Table, E. Wormley, Glass Mosaic Top, 3 Legs, Y-Stretcher, Gold Tag, 22 x 16 x 14 In. . . . 1840.00
Table, E. Wormley, Marble Top, Leather & Brass Base, Black Lacquered Column, 40 In. . 1150.00
Table, E. Wormley, Sheaf Of Wheat, Glass Top, Black Lacquer Round Base, 27 In. 575.00
Table, Eames, Birch Top, Rectangular, 4 Plywood Legs, 1945, 29 In. 3575.00
Table, Eames, CTW, Birch, Round, Bent Laminate Legs 1035.00
Table, Eames, Surfboard, Black Formica Top, Elliptical, Wire Strut Base, 89 x 29 In. 2530.00
Table, Eames, White Laminate, 4 Aluminum Feet, 25 x 30 In. 440.00
Table, Empire Style, Fruitwood, Octagonal Pedestal Base, 24 1/2 x 24 In. 250.00
Table, Empire, Mahogany, Gray Marble Top, 2 Frieze Drawers, 35 x 42 x 19 In. 151.00
Table, Empire, Mahogany, Molded Rectangular Top, Ormolu Mounted, 33 In. 4312.00
Table, Empire, Walnut, 2-Board Top, 6 Turned Legs, 21 x 44 In. 660.00
Table, English Regency, Mahogany, 2 Drawers, Inlaid, Saber Legs, 1820 . . . . 9020.00
Table, Extruded Aluminum Base, Round Glass Top, 1960s, 44 x 29 In. 550.00
Table, Federal, Mahogany, 2 Drawers, Carved Post, 28 3/4 x 41 In. 1035.00
Table, Federal, Mahogany, 2 Drawers, Writing Drawer, 16 x 21 In. 1540.00
Table, Federal, Mahogany, Demilune, c.1800 . . . . 6900.00
Table, Federal, Mahogany, Demilune, Felt-Lined Interior, Tapered Legs, 28 x 48 In. 750.00
Table, Federal, Mahogany, Inlay, New York, 19th Century 8050.00
Table, Federal, Mahogany, Rectangular Top, 3 Drawers, 38 x 61 x 24 In. 3737.00
Table, Federal, Mahogany, Satinwood Inlay, Faux Drawer, 39 x 41 x 36 In. 1495.00
Table, Florence Knoll, Marble, Square Top, Chrome Metal Base, 17 In., Pair 632.00
Table, Florence Knoll, Round, Walnut Veneer, Chrome Legs, 19 x 24 In. 440.00
Table, Florence Knoll, Square Top, Block Legs, 1960 . . . . 57.00
Table, Fornasetti, Transfer Printed Metal, Paper Label, 1950s, 16 In. 2530.00
Table, Frankl, Bent Rattan, Birch Top, 2 Tiers, 1940, 23 In. 201.00
Table, Frankl, Mahogany, Cork Top, 2 Tiers, Greek Key Base, 36 In. 325.00
Table, Frankl, Mahogany, Cream Lacquered Cork Top, 2 Tiers, 36 x 33 In. 715.00
Table, Frankl, Mahogany, Recessed Column, Attenuated Cabriole Legs, 32 x 21 In. 920.00
Table, French Provincial, Cherry, Drawer, Plank Top, 28 In. 1452.00
Table, French Provincial, Cherry, Plank Top, Drawer, 1860, 79 In. 1935.00
Table, French Provincial, Oak, Plank Top, 2 Drawers, Square Legs, 72 x 32 In. 2178.00
Table, French Provincial, Oak, Round Top, 3 Splayed Legs, 1860, 27 x 17 In. 363.00
Table, French Provincial, Pine, 2 Frieze Drawers, Cabriole Legs, 1880, 30 x 35 In. 152.00
Table, French Provincial, Pine, Plank Top, 2 Frieze Drawers, 1860, 63 In. 720.00
Table, French Provincial, Walnut, 2 Small Triangular Shelves, 1840, 25 x 12 In. 484.00
Table, French Provincial, Walnut, C-Scroll Legs, 1860, 30 x 55 x 39 In. 1452.00
Table, French Provincial, Walnut, Shaped-Apron Drawer, 1860, 27 In. 726.00
Table, French Provincial, Walnut, Shell Carved End, Cabriole Legs, 59 x 25 In. 485.00
Table, Fruitwood, 2 Tiers, Clematis Blossoms, Butterfly, 1900, Pair 5175.00
Table, Fruitwood, Bamboo Turned Legs, Baker Co., 22 1/2 x 30 In. 2300.00
Table, Fruitwood, Iron Trestle Base, Folding, 31 x 79 In. 1330.00
Table, Fruitwood, Oak, Drawer In Frieze, Baluster & Block Supports, 27 1/2 In. 8050.00
Table, G. Nelson, Bentwood Tray Top, Bright Chrome Stand, 19 x 15 In. . . . . .825.00 to 935.00
Table, G. Nelson, Rosewood Veneer, Cast Bronze 24 x 29 x 16 In. . . . .*Illus* 4888.00
Table, G. Nelson, Rosewood Veneer, Chrome-Plated Steel-Rod Base, 34 x 18 x 18 In. . . . 920.00
Table, G. Nelson, Walnut, Rectangular Metal Legs, 1952, 15 x 27 In. 373.00
Table, G. Stickley, 12 Grueby Tiles, 26 x 24 x 20 In. . . . .*Illus* 60500.00
Table, G. Stickley, Mahogany, Leather Top, Hexagonal, 48 x 30 In. 8250.00
Table, G. Stickley, Poppy, Base Shelf, 1901 . . . . 7475.00
Table, Game, Biedermeier, Walnut, Lotus Carved Legs, Claw & Ball Feet, 1890, 31 In. . . 1694.00
Table, Game, Chippendale, Mahogany, Leather Top, Concertina Extension, 38 x 19 In. . . . 1936.00
Table, Game, Classical, Mahogany, Lyre Pedestal, 4 Down-Swept Legs, 28 In., Pair 2640.00
Table, Game, Duncan Phyfe, Mahogany, Reeded Base, Drop Finials, Metal Paw Feet 165.00
Table, Game, Elm, Shaped & Pierced Apron, Cylindrical Legs, Stained, 33 1/2 In. 285.00
Table, Game, Elm, Square Top, Shaped Apron, Cylindrical Legs, 33 In. 230.00
Table, Game, Federal, Birch, Rectangular, Long Drawer, New England, 1810 . . . . 1045.00
Table, Game, Federal, Mahogany, Acanthus Leaves Leg, Lift Top, 29 x 35 In. 2185.00
Table, Game, Federal, Mahogany, Brass Ball Feet, 20th Century, 30 In. 1725.00
Table, Game, Federal, Mahogany, Carved, Rectangular, 1810, 29 1/2 In. 2587.00
Table, Game, Federal, Mahogany, Inlay, Serpentine, Phila., 1795, 28 x 36 x 17 In. 9800.00
Table, Game, Federal, Mahogany, Molded Frieze, Ring Turned Legs, 28 x 31 x 32 In. . . . 175.00
Table, Game, Frankl, Mahogany, Clover-Shaped Cork Top, 4 Armchairs, 5 Piece 385.00

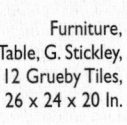

Furniture,
Table, G. Stickley,
12 Grueby Tiles,
26 x 24 x 20 In.

Furniture, Table, G. Nelson, Rosewood
Veneer, Cast Bronze 24 x 29 x 16 In.

Table, Game, Fruitwood, Inlaid Walnut, Frieze Drawer, Claw & Ball Feet, Holland, 34 In.	1725.00
Table, Game, G. Stickley, Turtle-Shaped Swivel Top, Wood Inlaid Border, 29 In.	8250.00
Table, Game, George II, Mahogany, Flower-Head Edge, Leaf Cabriole Legs, 28 1/2 In.	8625.00
Table, Game, Georgian, Rosewood, Pedestal, 4 Scrolled Feet, 36 x 28 In.	440.00
Table, Game, Hepplewhite, Mahogany, Folding, Hinged, Serpentine Frieze, Urn Inlay	522.00
Table, Game, Hepplewhite, Mahogany, Inlaid, Swing Leg	220.00
Table, Game, L. & J.G. Stickley, No. 563, Oak, Hexagonal	7700.00
Table, Game, Mahogany, Quadruped Base, Round Feet, Casters, Lift Top	330.00
Table, Game, Mahogany, Veneer, Rope Turned Legs	225.00
Table, Game, Marquetry, Checkerboard Top, Tripod Base, 1860s, 28 1/2 x 19 In.	545.00
Table, Game, Neoclassical, Mahogany, Lemon, Walnut, Square Top, Pad Feet, 30 In.	13800.00
Table, Game, Neoclassical, Parquetry, Continental, 30 1/2 x 33 1/2 x 33 1/2 In.	1000.00
Table, Game, Regency, Mahogany, Polished, Urn-Shape Base, Casters, 28 x 36 x 18 In.	630.00
Table, Game, Regency, Rosewood, Leather Top, Metal Paw Feet, 29 1/4 In.	6325.00
Table, Game, Renaissance Revival, Walnut, Demilune, Gilt Incised, 1870, 49 x 24 In.	1210.00
Table, Game, Rosewood, Fold Top, Carved, Pedestal, 1860, 29 x 36 x 35 In., Pair	6325.00
Table, Game, Rosewood, Piecrust Apron, Scroll Pedestal, 1800s	495.00
Table, Game, Sheraton, Mahogany, Serpentine Front, Reeded Edge, 1810-1820	1320.00
Table, Game, Stickley Brothers, No. 324, Hexagonal Top, 6 Chairs, 41 x 29 In.	3575.00
Table, Game, Stickley Brothers, Oak, Mortise & Tenon X-Stretcher, 36 In.	900.00
Table, Gateleg, Cherry, 20th Century, 68 x 48 In.	110.00
Table, Gateleg, Curly Maple, Drawer, Leaves, 30 x 48 In.	660.00
Table, Gateleg, Empire, Cherry, 6 Rope Carved Legs, 18 x 47 In.	560.00
Table, Gateleg, George II, Mahogany, Drawer, Claw & Ball Feet, 29 x 41 In.	5400.00
Table, Gateleg, Hepplewhite Style, Mahogany, Drawer, 16 x 35 x 15 In.	220.00
Table, Gateleg, Hepplewhite, Cherry, Square Tapered Legs, 17 x 46 In.	605.00
Table, Gateleg, Jacobean Style, Walnut, Bun Feet, 30 x 36 In.	172.00
Table, Gateleg, Mahogany, Satinwood, Continental, 23 3/4 In.	1035.00
Table, Gateleg, Maple, Breadboard Ends, Mid-1800s, 29 x 59 In.	2352.00
Table, Gateleg, Molded Frieze, Octagonal Legs, Casters, 46 x 21 x 29 In.	635.00
Table, Gateleg, Oak, Bobbin Turned Legs, Ditch Baroque, Oval Top, 29 x 32 In.	3737.00
Table, Gateleg, Oak, Dovetailed Drawer, Pinned Stretcher, 27 1/2 In.	990.00
Table, Gateleg, Pine, Drawer, Wrought-Iron Pull, 19th Century, 29 x 53 In.	230.00
Table, Gateleg, Queen Anne, Curly Maple, 13 x 41 3/4 In.	5500.00
Table, Gateleg, Queen Anne, Maple, Duck Feet, 1-Board Top, 27 1/2 In.	990.00
Table, Gateleg, Sheraton, Round Turned Legs, 20 x 47 x 29 In.	288.00
Table, Gateleg, Walnut, Dark Varnish, 2 Dovetailed Drawers, 17 x 48 x 21 In.	2580.00
Table, Gateleg, William & Mary, Maple, Frieze Drawer, Turned Legs, 28 x 19 In.	3737.00
Table, Gateleg, William & Mary, Oak, Maple	5175.00
Table, Gateleg, William & Mary, Walnut, D-Shaped Leaves, c.1700, 31 1/2 In.	10925.00
Table, Gateleg, William & Mary, Walnut, Trumpet Turnings	3630.00
Table, Gehry, Corrugated Cardboard, Inverted U-Shape, 20 x 25 x 17 In.	1100.00
Table, Gehry, Corrugated Cardboard, Open Cube, 16 x 16 x 18 In.	2640.00
Table, George I, Mahogany, Tilt Top, Round, Knop, Down-Swept Legs, 24 In.	600.00
Table, George III, Mahogany, 4 Curved Legs, 19th Century, 29 In.	1092.00
Table, George III, Mahogany, Bowfront, 2 Drawers, Light Wood Stringing, 31 In.	385.00
Table, George III, Mahogany, Central Column, Down-Swept Legs	12650.00
Table, George III, Mahogany, Crossbanded Border, Round, 28 In.	4025.00

Table, George III, Mahogany, Crossbanded, Reeded Legs, 28 1/2 In. 16100.00
Table, George III, Mahogany, Down-Swept Legs, c.1800, 59 In. 6900.00
Table, George III, Satinwood, Oval, 2 Tiers, Scalloped Gallery, 30 In. 3162.00
Table, George III, Turned Tapered Legs, 19th Century, 45 x 16 x 28 In. 1380.00
Table, George IV, Mahogany, Tilt Top, c.1825, 19 1/4 x 39 1/2 In. 665.00
Table, Georgian Style, Octagonal, Dolphin Supports, Floral Feet, 30 x 31 In. 1610.00
Table, Georgian, Mahogany, Square Top, Lower Shelf & Drawer, 31 x 14 1/4 In. 1045.00
Table, Gilt-Bronze Mounted Frieze, Female Caryatid Supports, 29 3/4 In. 5175.00
Table, Gilt-Metal Mounted, Ebonized & Parcel Gilt, Foliate Bands, 33 In. 4025.00
Table, Giltwood, Marble Top, Frieze Carved Corners, Floral Scroll Legs, 35 1/2 In. 3450.00
Table, Giltwood, Overall Geometric Design, Scagliola Top, Prussian Blue, 32 In. 4415.00
Table, Giraffe, Dark Ash, Wrought Iron Legs & Accents, Weinberg, 51 x 26 In. 1980.00
Table, Golden Oak Era, Pedestal Base, 4 Paw Feet, Quartersawn Veneer Top, 69 In. 440.00
Table, Gueridon, Greek Revival, Brass, Bronze, Marble, 27 x 12 In., Pair 5750.00
Table, Gueridon, Louis XV, Fruitwood, Marble Top, Cabriole Legs, 30 x 18 In. 455.00
Table, Gueridon, Mahogany, Cutout Top, 3 Drawers, France, 19th Century, 32 In. 485.00
Table, Gueridon, Oval Marble Top, Shaped Stretcher Shelf, 19th Century, 22 In. 400.00
Table, Hepplewhite, Drawer, Splayed Feet, Painted Design, 25 x 15 In. 965.00
Table, Hepplewhite, Mahogany, Tilt Top, Tripod Base, Spider Legs, 28 1/2 In. 550.00
Table, Ice Cream, Cast Iron, 4 Attached Seats, Display-Case Top, 32 x 24 x 24 In. 2070.00
Table, Ivory Inlaid, Foliate Scroll Borders, Tassel Feet, Anglo-Indian, 9 In. 2300.00
Table, Jacobean Revival, Oak, Rope Carved Legs, Cane Panels, 20th Century, 30 x 24 In. 175.00
Table, Kem Weber, Chromed Tubular Steel, 2 Black Lacquer Shelves, 22 x 20 x 20 In. ... 920.00
Table, Kittinger, Regency Style, Mahogany, Faceted Pedestal, Ball Feet, 17 In., Pair 287.00
Table, Leleu, Gilt Bronze, Tripod Base, 28 1/2 x 23 In. 5462.00
Table, Leleu, Mahogany, Columnar Standard, 1930, 22 In. 14950.00
Table, Leleu, Rosewood, Glass Tripod, Chrome Center, 3 Splayed Legs, 22 In. 3450.00
Table, Library, A.J. & J. Kohn, Mahogany, Bentwood Trestle, Bun Feet, 1910, 40 In. 690.00
Table, Library, Charles X, Mahogany, Brass Molding, Drawer, Compressed Bun Feet 4025.00
Table, Library, G. Stickley, No. 456, 2 Hidden Drawers, Shelf, 36 x 24 In. 12100.00
Table, Library, G. Stickley, No. 653, Drawer, Iron Hardware, 29 In. 1980.00
Table, Library, Georgian Style, Walnut, Floral Edge, Fluted Frieze, 72 x 39 x 32 In. 5750.00
Table, Library, Herter, Marquetry, Griffins & Columnar Trestles, 1870s 7150.00
Table, Library, Kittinger, Sheraton Style, Mahogany, Inlay, Leather Top, 29 x 46 In. 605.00
Table, Library, L. & J.G. Stickley, Blind Drawer, 29 x 54 In. 1540.00
Table, Library, Leavens Co., 29 3/4 In. 1255.00
Table, Library, Limbert, Bookcase Side, Cane Inserts, 29 x 42 In. 1200.00
Table, Library, Limbert, No. 1132, Mahogany, Lift Top Writing Surface, 29 In. 1760.00
Table, Library, Limbert, No. 1133, Pullout Desk, 29 x 48 In. 330.00
Table, Library, Limbert, Square Brass Pulls, Drawer, 29 x 42 In. 1300.00
Table, Library, Oak, Round Legs, Stretcher Base, Quartersawn Top, 84 x 44 1/2 In. 978.00
Table, Library, Regency, Mahogany, 2 Frieze Drawers, Down-Swept Legs, 29 In. 7475.00
Table, Library, Regency, Mahogany, 8 Drawers, Brass Pulls, Paw Feet 5460.00
Table, Library, Regency, Rosewood, Rectangular, Brass Inlay, 4 Legs, 28 x 39 In. 431.00
Table, Library, Rococo, Mahogany, 30 1/2 x 48 x 34 In. 920.00
Table, Library, Shop Of The Crafters, No. 335, Cross Stretcher, 36 x 29 In. 2860.00
Table, Library, Victorian, Mahogany, Trestle Base, Claw & Ball Feet, 36 In. 1150.00
Table, Library, Victorian, Oak, Leather-Lined Top, 120 In. 4600.00
Table, Library, Wallace Nutting, No. 637, Maple 1595.00
Table, Library, Walnut, Carved Flowers On Apron, Female Figures On Legs, 42 1/2 In. .. 1380.00
Table, Library, Walnut, Floral & Scroll Design, Removable Centerpiece, German 5635.00
Table, Library, Walnut, Shaped Leaf & Scroll Carved Apron, 30 3/4 x 34 1/2 x 22 In. 1960.00
Table, Library, Warren McArthur, Brushed Chrome Base, Black Lacquer Top, 60 In. 4675.00
Table, Limbert, No. 148, Round Top, Splayed Legs, 30 x 29 In. 5500.00
Table, Limbert, Octagonal Top, Splayed Cutouts & Legs, 45 x 29 In. 2860.00
Table, Louis XIV, Mahogany, 2 Carved Drawers, Apron, Cabriole Legs, 29 In. 230.00
Table, Louis XV Style, Wrought Iron, Marble Top, 66 1/2 In. 1650.00
Table, Louis XV, Giltwood, Oval, Green Onyx Top, Guilloche Apron 975.00
Table, Louis XV, Kingwood, Marquetry, Marble, Simulated Leather-Book Doors 1150.00
Table, Louis XV, Kingwood, Tulipwood, Oval Top, 2 Short Drawers, Cabriole Legs 5175.00
Table, Louis XV, Marble Top, 2 Serpentine Shelves, Tapered Legs, 27 x 38 x 19 In. 805.00
Table, Louis XV, Parcel Gilt, Painted Oriental People, Dish Top, 26 x 26 x 15 In. 9775.00
Table, Louis XV, Walnut, Shaped Apron, Cabriole Legs, France, 1920, 45 x 31 In. 970.00

Table, Louis XVI Style, Carved Wood, Gilt, White Onyx Top, Late 19th Century, 30 In. ..   525.00
Table, Louis XVI Style, Gilt Base, Ormolu & Onyx Top, 20th Century, 29 1/2 In. 295.00
Table, Louis XVI Style, Kingwood, Marble Top, Brass Gallery, 32 1/4 x 19 In. 1100.00
Table, Louis XVI, Mahogany, Rectangular, Veined White Marble Top, 4 Legs, 30 In. 8050.00
Table, Louis XVI, Marble Top, Milled Brass Edge, Crossbanded Apron, 28 3/4 In. 2185.00
Table, Louis XVI, Rectangular, Gray Veined Marble Top, Top Shaped Feet, 34 In. 1955.00
Table, Louis XVI, Variegated Marble Top, 2 Scroll Legs, 32 3/4 In. 1725.00
Table, Louis-Philippe, Rosewood, Tilt Top, c.1830, 54 1/4 In. 2200.00
Table, Macassar Ebony, Stepped-Edge Top, Round Stepped Base, 26 1/2 In. 1840.00
Table, Mahogany, 3 Legs Connected With Dimpled Polished Steel, Philippe Stark, Pair .. 2090.00
Table, Mahogany, Banded Top, Turned Vase-Form Splat, Brass Paws, 30 x 36 In. 425.00
Table, Mahogany, Black Marble Top, Ribbed Edge, Female Supports, 38 1/2 In. 8625.00
Table, Mahogany, Crossbanded Satinwood, Tilt Top, 48 In. 5462.00
Table, Mahogany, Crossbanded Top, Reeded Tripod Base, England, 103 x 30 In. 4500.00
Table, Mahogany, Ico Parisi, Stepped, Inverted V-Legs, Brass Caps & Balls, 26 x 20 In. ..   825.00
Table, Mahogany, Inlaid Zebrawood, Brass Castors, 27 x 58 In. 2990.00
Table, Mahogany, Leaf Over Bowed Frieze, Leaf Carved Pedestal, Paw Feet, c.1825 .... 1380.00
Table, Mahogany, Marble Top, Drawer, Columnar Supports, Paw Feet, 35 x 45 In. 2300.00
Table, Mahogany, Octagonal Top, Petal-Shaped Pedestal, Scroll Feet, 40-In. Top 550.00
Table, Mahogany, Oval Top, Brass Inlay, Platform Stretcher, Pad Feet, 27 In. 7475.00
Table, Mahogany, Paw Feet, 4 10-Inch Leaves, 1 6-Inch Leaf, Margolis, 63 1/2 In. 2860.00
Table, Mahogany, Piecrust, Tilt Top, 19th Century 1495.00
Table, Mahogany, Rectangular Top, Pedestal Feet, 23 x 28 x 13 In. 2070.00
Table, Mahogany, Rectangular Top, Spool Turned Legs, Victorian, 28 In. 220.00
Table, Mahogany, Reeded Edges, 5 Rope Turned Legs, Leaves, Victorian, 48 x 54 In. 825.00
Table, Mahogany, Shaped Gallery Top, 2 Drawers, Drop Pulls, Pair 125.00
Table, Mahogany, Spool Turnings, Serpentine Apron, Marble Top, Victorian, 27 In. 385.00
Table, Mahogany, Stenciled, Marble Top, Leaf & Rosette Legs, c.1825, 35 1/2 In. 8625.00
Table, Mahogany, Triangular Dish Top, Foliate Ormolu Feet, 1900, 30 1/2 In. 7475.00
Table, Marble Top, 3 Drawers, Brass Pulls, France, 30 x 14 x 10 In. 690.00
Table, Marble Top, 3 Drawers, Brass Pulls, France, 31 x 10 x 10 In. 865.00
Table, Marble Top, Pierced Gallery, Bronze Palmettes & Flower Heads, 32 In., Pair 6320.00
Table, Minoru Yamasaki, Inset White Formica, Shelf, Cupboard, 18 x 23 x 18 In. 315.00
Table, Mirror Top, Gilt Brass Apron, Quivers, Minerva Heads, Wood Legs, 29 1/2 In. 2640.00
Table, Mother-Of-Pearl Inlay, Rectangular Top, Prunus Blossom Branches, 11 In. 87.00
Table, Neoclassical, Bronze, Gilt, Green Faux Marble Top, 4 Ormolu Branches 11500.00
Table, Neoclassical, Demilune, Painted, Marble Top, Urn Feet, Italy, 37 x 16 In. 2300.00
Table, Neoclassical, Fruitwood, Parcel Gilt, Round, Frieze, Paw Feet, Austria, 38 In. 6900.00
Table, Neoclassical, Mahogany, Octagonal Top, Voluted Feet, Sweden 8625.00
Table, Nesting, Black Lacquer, Rectangular, Birds Of Paradise, Floral Sprays 315.00
Table, Nesting, Charreau, Pierre, Walnut, Recessed Shagreen Tops, 1920, 19 3/4 In. 5462.00
Table, Nesting, Floral Swag, Putti & Minerva Scenes., 24 x 22 1/2 In., 3 Piece 785.00
Table, Nesting, Galle, Fruitwood, Marquetry, Seashore Design, 28 In., 4 Piece 6900.00
Table, Nesting, Louis XV Style, Gilt & Floral Design, 24 1/2 In., 3 Piece 775.00
Table, Nesting, Risom, Round Blond Top, White Tubular Iron Base, 21 x 15 In., 4 Piece .. 1870.00
Table, Nesting, Sheraton Style, Mahogany, Satinwood, 28 x 20 In., 4 Piece 1210.00
Table, Oak, Baluster Turned Column, Quadruped Feet, 2 Leaves, 44 In. 58.00
Table, Oak, Cast-Iron Pedestal, Tripod Base, Round, Early 20th Century, 36 x 30 In. 115.00
Table, Oak, Drawer, Square Tapered Legs, France, 1860, 29 In. 514.00
Table, Oak, Frieze Drawer, Square Tapering Legs, c.1840, 32 x 29 3/4 In. 665.00
Table, Oak, Leaf Border Top, Long Frieze Drawer, 28 1/2 x 27 1/2 In. 1380.00
Table, Oak, Pine, 3 Chamfered Cleats, 2 Shaped Legs, Medial Stretcher, 92 1/2 In. 8625.00
Table, Octagonal Top, Round Stretcher, 26 1/4 In., Pair 8050.00
Table, Oval, Marble Top, Carved Quadruped Base, Victorian 250.00
Table, P. Evans, Sculptural Steel, 4 Triangular Wedges, Glass Top, 15 x 21 In. 825.00
Table, Papier-Mache, Tilt Top, c.1860, 27 1/2 x 18 1/2 In. 1500.00
Table, Parcel Gilt, Round, Rouge Royale Marble Top, 3 Supports, Paw Feet, 29 In. 8625.00
Table, Pembroke, Cherry, Eagle Escutcheon, c.1790, 28 3/4 x 19 x 33 In. 1230.00
Table, Pembroke, Cherry, Square Tapered Legs, Brass Bucket Casters, 28 In. 935.00
Table, Pembroke, Chippendale, Mahogany, Dovetailed Drawer, Leaves, 20 x 33 In. 1540.00
Table, Pembroke, Chippendale, Mahogany, Drawer, Fluted Legs, c.1780, 20 x 30 In. 8050.00
Table, Pembroke, Edwardian, Satinwood, Painted Musical Trophy, 27 1/2 In. 4600.00
Table, Pembroke, Federal, Mahogany, Hinged Leaves, Peg Feet, c.1810, 42 1/2 In. 2587.00

Table, Pembroke, Federal, Mahogany, Rectangular Top, Ring Turned Legs, 28 x 43 In. . . . 300.00
Table, Pembroke, George III, Mahogany, Frieze Drawer, 26 In. 2185.00
Table, Pembroke, George III, Mahogany, Hinged Rectangular Top, Drawer, 29 In. 920.00
Table, Pembroke, George III, Mahogany, Rectangular Top, 29 x 30 x 22 In. 1265.00
Table, Pembroke, George III, Mahogany, Rectangular Top, 4 Tapered Legs, 28 In. 5175.00
Table, Pembroke, George III, Mahogany, Rectangular Top, Marlborough Feet, 26 In. 980.00
Table, Pembroke, George III, Mahogany, Reeded Edges, Drawer, 1790, 27 In. 632.00
Table, Pembroke, George III, Mahogany, Tulipwood Top, Brass Feet, 1790, 28 In. 8625.00
Table, Pembroke, George III, Satinwood, Rectangular Top, Frieze Drawer, 28 In. 10925.00
Table, Pembroke, Georgian, Mahogany, 2 Drawers, Tapered Legs, 1790, 28 1/2 In. 1573.00
Table, Pembroke, Hepplewhite, Mahogany, 20 5/8 x 31 3/4 In. 245.00
Table, Pembroke, Hepplewhite, Mahogany, Drawer, 27 1/2 x 35 In. 405.00
Table, Pembroke, Hepplewhite, Mahogany, Square Tapered Legs, 28 x 31 x 19 In. 825.00
Table, Pembroke, Hepplewhite, Mahogany, Tapered Legs, 31 1/2 In. 2090.00
Table, Pembroke, Inlaid Satinwood, D-Shaped Leaves, Drawer, Casters, 28 3/4 In. 9200.00
Table, Pembroke, Mahogany, 2 Concave Drawers, New York, 29 x 42 In. 1325.00
Table, Pembroke, Mahogany, Base Drawer, Square Legs, c.1810, 29 In. 1210.00
Table, Pembroke, Mahogany, Drawer, Chamfered Square Legs, 27 3/8 In. 345.00
Table, Pembroke, Mahogany, Frieze Drawer, Brass Caps On Casters, 1780s, 28 In. 1610.00
Table, Pembroke, Mahogany, Hinged Leaves, Stringing On Square Legs, 28 1/2 In. 2990.00
Table, Pembroke, Mahogany, Inlaid Oval Top, 1775, 28 In. 8625.00
Table, Pembroke, Mahogany, Rib Edge, Brass Casters, 29 In. 2090.00
Table, Pembroke, Mahogany, Rosewood Banding On Top & Leaves, c.1820 . . . . 1495.00
Table, Pembroke, Mahogany, Satinwood, Crossbanded Rectangular Top, 1830 . . . . 1380.00
Table, Pembroke, Regency, Mahogany, Cylindrical Legs On Castors, 1830, 28 In. 520.00
Table, Pembroke, Sheraton, Mahogany, Drawer, Rope Turned Legs, 17 In. 935.00
Table, Pembroke, Sheraton, Mahogany, End Drawer, New York, 29 x 35 1/2 In. 2875.00
Table, Pier, Empire, Mahogany, Marble Top, Scroll Front & Legs, 3 Drawers, 54 In. 2530.00
Table, Pier, Mahogany, Marble Top, Inverted Ionic Columns, 18 x 41 x 35 1/2 In. 1760.00
Table, Pier, Mahogany, Marble Top, Mirror Inset Back, Convex Stretcher, 1825 . . . . 4025.00
Table, Pier, Mahogany, Rosewood, Stone Inlay, 19th Century, 35 x 36 x 18 In. 2090.00
Table, Pine, Farmhouse, Molded Edge, Turned Round Legs, 31 x 78 In. 785.00
Table, Pine, Maple, Beaded Stretcher, Blocked Legs, 27 5/8 x 42 5/8 In. 1495.00
Table, Pine, Poplar, Octagonal, Marbelized Top, Pedestal, Scalloped Feet, 19 x 25 In. 495.00
Table, Pine, Rectangular Top, Scroll Quadruped Base 82.00
Table, Poplar, Round 1-Board Top, Square Apron, 7-In. Overhang, 36 In. 82.00
Table, Queen Anne, 2-Board Top, 2 Drawers, 29 x 54 x 32 In. 1430.00
Table, Queen Anne, Cherry, Tilt Top, Cabriole Leg Base, Pad Feet, 28 x 21 3/4 In. 805.00
Table, Queen Anne, Mahogany, Scalloped Frieze, Cabriole Legs, 33 In. 6325.00
Table, Queen Anne, Pine, 2-Board Top, Breadboard Ends, Duck Feet, c.1770 . . . . 4000.00
Table, Queen Anne, Walnut, Oblong Top, 5 Leaves, Trifid Feet, c.1760, 41 1/2 In. 660.00
Table, Rectangular Marble Top, Winged Gilt Eagle, Wood Plinth, 31 x 45 In. 690.00
Table, Refectory, Cherry, Plank Top, Square Tapered Legs, 1890, 29 1/2 In. 1694.00
Table, Refectory, Jacobean Style, Carved Oak, 2 Drawers, 21 1/2 x 36 x 108 In. 1120.00
Table, Refectory, Jacobean, Oak, Carved Frieze, 8 Turned Legs, 31 x 69 x 25 In. 2645.00
Table, Refectory, Mahogany, Plank Top, Trestle End Supports, 110 In. 970.00
Table, Refractory, Oak, Arched Acanthus-Capped Feet, Platform Stretcher, 94 In. 3735.00
Table, Regency, Mahogany, 2 Tiers, 2 Round Graduated Trays, 1800, 34 In. 5462.00
Table, Regency, Mahogany, Brass Mounted, Turned Standard, Tripod, 28 In., Pair 4025.00
Table, Regency, Mahogany, Oval Top, 1840, 59 x 38 In. 2300.00
Table, Regency, Mahogany, Oval, Drawer, Line Inlay, Original Brasses, 45 x 36 In. 990.00
Table, Regency, Mahogany, Rosewood Banding, 4 Splayed Legs, 29 In. 1936.00
Table, Regency, Mahogany, Tilt Top, Round, Pedestal, Lotus Leaf Feet, 104 1/2 In. 2875.00
Table, Regency, Mahogany, Tilt Top, Turned Pedestal, 30 x 44 x 40 In. 1610.00
Table, Regency, Mahogany, Tulipwood Top, 4 Down-Swept Legs, 30 In. 1380.00
Table, Renaissance Revival, Ebonized, Marble, Pietra Dura Top 3735.00
Table, Renaissance Revival, Rosewood, Inlaid Design, Oval, Porcelain Casters 1000.00
Table, Renaissance Revival, Walnut, Molded Top, Dentil Frieze, 3 Bun Feet 690.00
Table, Renaissance Revival, Walnut, Rectangular, Marble, Putti, Italy, 23 In. 2875.00
Table, Robsjohn-Gibbings, Walnut Veneer, Round, 1955, 30 In. 990.00
Table, Robsjohn-Gibbings, Walnut Veneer, Square, Dowel Base, 30 In. 1045.00
Table, Rococo, Marble Top, Drawer, X-Stretcher 230.00
Table, Rococo, Parcel Gilt, Red Tortoiseshell, Barley Twist Legs, Bun Feet 28750.00

Table, Rohde, 2 Tiers, Burl Veneer, Rectangular, 22 x 28 x 16 In. 550.00
Table, Rohde, 2 Tiers, Burl Veneer, Round, 27 x 24 In. 715.00
Table, Rohde, Mahogany, Glass, Oval, Scalloped Sides, 27 1/2 x 47 In. 920.00
Table, Rohde, Walnut, Round Post, Herman Miller, 1940, 28 In., Pair 1150.00
Table, Rosewood, Gray Marble Top, Mirrored Back, 19th Century, 36 In.; Pair 11500.00
Table, Rosewood, Rectangular Top, Drawer, Shelf Stretcher, 19 1/2 x 28 1/2 In. 230.00
Table, Rosewood, Rectangular Top, Entwined Leaf Scrolls, 19th Century, 42 In. 5150.00
Table, Rosewood, Tilt Top, Foliate Carved Standard, Paw Feet, 48 In. 2415.00
Table, Rosewood, Tilt Top, Three Part Base, c.1845, 50 In. 4600.00
Table, Round Removable Top, 3 Pivoting Wood Legs, Bellman, 24 x 36 In. 1265.00
Table, Russel Wright, Black Lacquer, 3 Round Shelves, Flat Legs, 28 x 24 In. 440.00
Table, Saarinen, Cast Metal, Oval, Pedestal Base, Laminate Top, Knoll, 36 In. 920.00
Table, Saarinen, Marble Top, Pedestal Base, White Paint, 21 x 16 In. 345.00
Table, Satinwood, Mahogany Top, Serpentine Front, 19th Century, 28 x 38 3/4 In. 1840.00
Table, Sawbuck, Pine, Red Paint, Natural Breadboard Top, 24 x 49 x 28 In. 880.00
Table, Scagliola Top, Flower-Head Band, Bronze Band, Swan Supports, 39 1/2 In. 5750.00
Table, Schaefer, Rectangular Wood Top, Suspended Drawer, 24 x 20 x 18 In. 173.00
Table, Sewing, Biedermeier, Fruitwood, 2 Drawers, Pincushion Top, c.1825, 32 In. 2090.00
Table, Sewing, Biedermeier, Mahogany, Drum Shape, c.1820, 28 In. 5060.00
Table, Sewing, Black Lacquer, Trestle Supports, Carved Paw Feet, China, 28 1/4 In. 345.00
Table, Sewing, Cherry, Dark Stain, Ogee Drawer, Pincushion Top, 7 1/2 In. 110.00
Table, Sewing, Classical, Mahogany, Foldover Top, 2 Drawers, 4 Paw Feet, 31 In. 770.00
Table, Sewing, Classical, Rosewood, Hinged Lid, 2 Drawers, Scroll Supports, 32 In. 5060.00
Table, Sewing, Curly Maple, 6-Board Top, Folding, 20th Century, 22 x 34 x 27 In. 330.00
Table, Sewing, Drawer, Embroidered Bag, Brass Caps, 30 x 21 x 19 In. 860.00
Table, Sewing, Drop Leaf, 2 Drawers, Turned Legs, 19th Century, 22 1/2 x 29 In. 260.00
Table, Sewing, Drop Leaf, Birch, Mahogany Veneer, 2 Drawers, c.1830, 28 3/4 In. 747.00
Table, Sewing, Drop Leaf, Cherry, 2 Drawers, 1850, 28 x 21 x 24 In. 575.00
Table, Sewing, Drop Leaf, Hepplewhite, Mahogany, Drawer, England, 1780, 26 x 20 In. . . . 1320.00
Table, Sewing, Drop Leaf, Molded Edge, 2 Drawers, Silk Bag, c.1815, 28 In. 4620.00
Table, Sewing, Drop Leaf, Shaker, Maple, Pine, End Drawer, 28 3/4 x 49 In. 1925.00
Table, Sewing, Drop Leaf, Sheraton, Cherry Top, Tiger Maple Drawers, 26 1/2 In. 400.00
Table, Sewing, Drop Leaf, Sheraton, Mahogany, 3 Drawers, Spiral Legs, 28 1/2 In. 1380.00
Table, Sewing, Drop Leaf, Sheraton, Tiger Maple, Drawer, Turned Legs, 1800s, 28 In. 880.00
Table, Sewing, Drop Leaf, Tiger Maple Top, 2 Drawers, Convex Front, 1820s, 30 In. 1495.00
Table, Sewing, Drop Leaf, Walnut, Rectangular Top, 2 Drawers, Scroll Supports, 30 In. . . .   355.00
Table, Sewing, E. Wheeler, Federal, Tiger Maple, Crossbanded Veneer, Drawer 805.00
Table, Sewing, Edwardian, Satinwood, Lyre Shape, Scalloped Shelf Stretcher 862.00
Table, Sewing, Empire, Mahogany, 3 Drawers, Adjustable Writing Slide 430.00
Table, Sewing, Empire, Mahogany, Cylinder Pedestal, Carved Legs, Claw Feet, 31 In. 1320.00
Table, Sewing, Empire, Mahogany, Serpentine Front, Lyre Pedestal, Stepped Base, 29 In. . .   550.00
Table, Sewing, Federal, 2 Drawers, Turned Legs, 19th Century 290.00
Table, Sewing, Federal, Mahogany, 2 Drawers, 1-Board Top, 1820, 19 x 18 In. 935.00
Table, Sewing, Federal, Mahogany, 2 Drawers, Square Top, Inlaid Bands, 28 x 18 In. 550.00
Table, Sewing, Hepplewhite, Cherry, 4 Dovetailed Drawers, 41 x 56 1/2 x 28 In. 275.00
Table, Sewing, Hepplewhite, Cherry, Walnut, 1-Board Top, 42 x 28 In. 825.00
Table, Sewing, Hepplewhite, Maple, Drawer, 25 x 41 1/2 x 29 In.   385.00
Table, Sewing, Hepplewhite, Pine, Grain Painted, 3-Board Top, Nailed Drawer 715.00
Table, Sewing, Hepplewhite, Pine, Green Paint, 1-Board Top, 24 x 40 In. 220.00
Table, Sewing, Jenny Lind, Marble Top & Base, 1850, 28 x 23 x 18 In. 220.00
Table, Sewing, Lift Top, 2 Drawers, 1940s 95.00
Table, Sewing, Lift Top, Black Lacquer, Fitted Interior, Chinese Export, 28 In. . . . . , ...   825.00
Table, Sewing, Lift Top, Mahogany, 2 Drawers, 1920s 115.00
Table, Sewing, Lift Top, Marquetry, Victorian 3575.00
Table, Sewing, Lift Top, Rosewood, Mirror, Fitted, 2 Drawers, 1880s, 21 1/2 In. 770.00
Table, Sewing, Mahogany, 2 Drawers, Brass Pulls, Spiral-Reeded Legs, c.1840, 27 In. . . .   605.00
Table, Sewing, Mahogany, 3 Drawers, Fabric Basket, Rope Turned Legs, 28 In. 990.00
Table, Sewing, Mahogany, Lower Drawer With Basket Section, c.1800, 28 In. 660.00
Table, Sewing, Mahogany, Veneered Edge, Hanging Bag, Drawer, 1790, 27 1/2 In. 7475.00
Table, Sewing, Neoclassical, Walnut, Drawer, Austria, 19th Century, 21 x 15 In. 860.00
Table, Sewing, Papier-Mache, Fitted Interior, Mother-Of-Pearl Inlay, 1853, 27 1/2 In. . . .   920.00
Table, Sewing, Poplar, 2-Board Top, 2 Drawers 1500.00
Table, Sewing, Queen Anne, Walnut, Pincushion Top, Cabriole Legs, 1770, 28 x 56 In. . . . 5400.00

Table, Sewing, Regency, Mahogany, Crescent Support, 4 Down-Swept Legs, 17 In. 2070.00
Table, Sewing, Regency, Satinwood, Octagonal Hinged Top, Tapered Legs, 28 x 17 In. . . . 2185.00
Table, Sewing, Sheraton, Mahogany, Curly Maple Veneer, 2 Drawers, 15 x 20 x 27 In. . . . 2420.00
Table, Sewing, Sheraton, Walnut, 2 Dovetailed Drawers, 33 x 50 x 30 In. 1705.00
Table, Sewing, Softwood, 2-Board Top Over Apron, 2 Drawers, 69 x 34 x 29 In. 605.00
Table, Sewing, Tiger Maple, Cherry, Drawer, Hinged Pincushion, 1820, 29 x 25 x 19 In. . 1210.00
Table, Sewing, Walnut, 2 Drawers, Glass Pulls, c.1830 . . . . 415.00
Table, Sewing, Walnut, 4-Board Top, Drawer, Pennsylvania, 31 x 41 x 28 In. 990.00
Table, Sewing, Walnut, Chestnut, Poplar, Pincushion Top, Pennsylvania, 29 x 35 x 50 In. . 4400.00
Table, Sewing, Walnut, Drawer, Stretcher Base, Apron, 31 x 41 x 28 In. 990.00
Table, Sewing, Walnut, Maple, 2 Drawers, Tapered Turned Legs, 36 x 18 x 29 In. 285.00
Table, Sewing, William IV, Rosewood, Mother-Of-Pearl Inlay, Drawer, c.1835 . . . . 440.00
Table, Shaker, Maple, Hinged Leaf, 2 Short Drawers, 1820s, 28 x 48 1/4 In. 6900.00
Table, Sheraton, Cherry, Mahogany Veneer, Drawer, Ring Turned Legs, 14 x 39 In. 825.00
Table, Sheraton, Cherry, Poplar, Demilune, 1-Board Top, 48 x 27 x 29 In. 355.00
Table, Sheraton, Drawer, Turned Legs, Red Paint, c.1810, 30 1/2 In. 880.00
Table, Sheraton, Mahogany, Drawer, 22 3/4 x 36 1/2 x 28 1/2 In., 12-In. Leaves 1320.00
Table, Sheraton, Mahogany, Drawer, Figured Top, Leaves, Apron, 28 x 42 x 36 In. 495.00
Table, Side, Bombe Walnut, Stone Inset Top, 2 Drawers, Cabriole Legs, 26 x 22 1/2 In. . . 70.00
Table, Side, Brass, Round Marble Top, Cast Hoofed Feet, 25 1/4 In., Pair 1955.00
Table, Side, Bugatti, Brass, Oriental Design, Square Top, Ivory Inlay 2645.00
Table, Side, Bugatti, Fruitwood, Ivory, Arched Sides, Brass, Wood, 29 In. 2300.00
Table, Side, Chippendale, Mahogany, Tan Marble Top, Gadroon Apron, 30 In. 1089.00
Table, Side, Empire, Marble Top, Acanthus-Capped Term Legs, Italy, 34 3/4 In. 1800.00
Table, Side, French Provincial Style, Triangular, Marble Inserts, 26 x 28 In. 115.00
Table, Side, French Provincial, Marble Top, Drawer, Tapering Legs, 15 x 12 In. 375.00
Table, Side, Fruitwood, Rectangular Tray Top, Violin-Shaped Legs, 29 In. 3737.00
Table, Side, G. Nelson, Black Steel Frame, Drawer, 17 x 17 x 25 In. 605.00
Table, Side, George III, Mahogany, Pierced Brackets, Chamfered Legs, 35 In. 4887.00
Table, Side, Georgian, Mahogany, Frieze Drawer, Square Tapered Legs, 1860, 35 In. 786.00
Table, Side, Georgian, Mahogany, Frieze Drawer, Tapered Legs, 35 1/2 In. . . . . . . .425.00 to 726.00
Table, Side, Gothic Revival, Rosewood, Frieze Drawer, 19th Century, 27 x 17 In. 345.00
Table, Side, Gray Marble Top, Pierced Brass Gallery Rail, Oval Base, 22 x 20 x 14 In. . . . 1840.00
Table, Side, I. Noguchi, Round Laminate Top, Wire Struts, Wood Base, 24 In. 4400.00
Table, Side, Katona, Wrought Iron, Round, Black Stone Top, 23 In. 4600.00
Table, Side, Louis XV, Gilt, Rectangular Dish Top, Red, Cabriole Legs, 26 In. 9775.00
Table, Side, Louis XVI, Pierced Brass Gallery Rail, Turned Feet, 21 x 26 In. 374.00
Table, Side, Mahogany, Round Inlaid Top, Scroll Legs, Splay Feet, 29 x 22 In. 161.00
Table, Side, Majorelle, Mahogany, Fruitwood, Inlaid Maple Leaf Design, 27 1/2 In. 4600.00
Table, Side, Maple, Gray Marble Top, Drawer, Square Legs, Victorian 115.00
Table, Side, Mission Style, Oak, Barley Twist Legs, Drawer, Stretcher, 34 x 19 x 35 In. . . 200.00
Table, Side, Regency, Gray Marble Top, Guilloche Frieze, 1820, 34 x 72 x 30 In. 7139.00
Table, Side, Regency, Mahogany Banded, Inset Tooled Leather, 26 x 20 x 15 In. 840.00
Table, Side, Rococo, Gilt, 3 Short Drawers, Scallop Shell, Cabriole Legs, 30 In. 5750.00
Table, Side, Wallace Nutting, No. 614, Maple, Trestle, Block Brand 715.00
Table, Side, Walnut, Fluted, Vine Supports, Animal Heads On Legs, 28 In., 1870s 550.00
Table, Side, William & Mary, Rectangular, Crossbanded Border, 27 In. 2587.00
Table, Sorting, Pine, Red & Blue Paint, Removable Ball Finials, 26 x 35 x 34 In. 440.00
Table, Spanish Baroque, Walnut, Carved, 41 In. 4345.00
Table, Spanish Colonial Style, Oak, Ring & Baluster Turned Legs, 30 1/4 In. 4600.00
Table, Square Top, Tripod Base, Mid-20th Century, 27 x 12 In. 121.00
Table, Stickley Brothers, Oval, 28 1/2 x 36 x 28 In. 1925.00
Table, Tapio Wirkkala, Satinwood, Rectangular, Metal Tapered Legs 2300.00
Table, Tavern, Birch, Blue Paint, Turned Tapered Legs, 19th Century, 27 x 38 In. 920.00
Table, Tavern, Birch, Pine, Round Top, Turned Legs, Painted, c.1800, 26 x 27 In. 1035.00
Table, Tavern, Black Cherry, Hickory, Octagonal Batten Top, Slate Insert, 30 1/2 In. 6050.00
Table, Tavern, Cherry, 2 Drawers, Baluster Turned Legs, 29 1/2 x 60 In. 4025.00
Table, Tavern, Cherry, Pine, Cleated Top, Frieze Drawer, Disc Feet, 1780s, 28 1/2 In. 2587.00
Table, Tavern, Cherry, Turned Splayed Legs, Pegged, 1820s, 31 x 19 x 24 In. 895.00
Table, Tavern, Chippendale, Curly Maple, Breadboard Top, 26 x 36 In. 2530.00
Table, Tavern, Drawer, Scrub Top, Tapered Square Legs, Red Paint, 29 x 45 x 28 In. 690.00
Table, Tavern, Hepplewhite, Drawer, Breadboard Top, Square Legs, 28 x 42 In. 865.00
Table, Tavern, Maple, 2-Board Top, Disc Feet, Red, 18th Century 3737.00

Table, Tavern, Maple, Pine, Straight Skirt With Drawer, Square Stretchers, 27 In. 1610.00
Table, Tavern, Oak, Poplar, 2 Drawers, Pad Feet, Painted, 31 x 46 In. 2070.00
Table, Tavern, Poplar, Oblong Top, Drawer, Painted, c.1740, 26 x 19 In. 2300.00
Table, Tavern, Queen Anne, Birch, Painted, 3-Board Pine Top, 26 x 37 x 25 In. 2860.00
Table, Tavern, Queen Anne, Birch, Poplar, Drawer, Breadboard Top, 38 x 27 In. 880.00
Table, Tavern, Queen Anne, Cherry, Scalloped Apron, Drawer, 28 x 35 In. 1870.00
Table, Tavern, Queen Anne, Maple, Red Pine Top, Drawer, 28 x 39 In. 3520.00
Table, Tavern, Queen Anne, Maple, Splayed Base, 1-Board Top, 21 x 29 In. 880.00
Table, Tavern, Queen Anne, Poplar, Turned Maple, c.1740, 25 1/2 In. 2875.00
Table, Tavern, Wallace Nutting, No. 660, Maple, Pine Top, Block Brand 770.00
Table, Tavern, Walnut, Inverted Trumpet & Ball Turned Stretchers, c.1700, 28 In. 715.00
Table, Tavern, Walnut, Lift Top, 1 Long, 1 Short Drawer, Trifid Feet, c.1750, 29 1/2 In. . .   5500.00
Table, Tavern, Walnut, Lift Top, 2 Base Drawers, Bun Feet, c.1770, 29 1/2 In. 1045.00
Table, Tavern, Walnut, Red Paint, Drawer, 2-Board Top, Pennsylvania, 29 x 54 x 34 In. . .   920.00
Table, Tea, Biedermeier, Ash, Frieze Drawer, Ebonized Scroll Accents, 29 1/2 In. 726.00
Table, Tea, Cherry, Step-Down Top, Birdcage Support, Flaring Pedestal, 28 x 34 1/2 In. . .   518.00
Table, Tea, Cherry, Step-Down Top, Ring Turned Vase-Form Pedestal, 35 x 28 In. 825.00
Table, Tea, Chippendale, 3 Revolving Shelves, Tripod Base, Snake Feet, 47 In. 1045.00
Table, Tea, Chippendale, 3 Tiers, Mahogany, Tripod Snake Feet, 23 x 42 In. 990.00
Table, Tea, Chippendale, Mahogany, Birdcage Support, Claw & Ball Feet, 29 In. 2130.00
Table, Tea, Chippendale, Mahogany, Carved Apron, Cabriolet Legs, Paw Feet, 28 In. 4025.00
Table, Tea, Chippendale, Mahogany, Dish Top, Pedestal, Tripod, 26 x 27 1/2 In. 405.00
Table, Tea, Chippendale, Mahogany, Step-Down Top, Tripod Base, 26 x 28 In. 1045.00
Table, Tea, Chippendale, Step-Down Top, Mahogany, Snake Feet, Birdcage, 33 x 28 In. . .   1870.00
Table, Tea, Chippendale, Walnut, Birdcage, Pad Feet, 1780, 35 x 28 In. 2350.00
Table, Tea, E. Wheeler, Queen Anne, Tiger Maple, Rectangular Dish Top, Candle Slides . .   1495.00
Table, Tea, Empire, Cherry, Step-Down Top, Tripod Base, 4-Board Top, 34 x 28 In. 385.00
Table, Tea, George I, Walnut, Molded Tray, Drawers At Sides, Cabriole Legs, 28 In. 9775.00
Table, Tea, Georgian, Mahogany, Step-Down Top, Fluted Shaft, Claw & Ball Feet, 35 In. .   770.00
Table, Tea, Mahogany, 3 Tiers, Snake Feet, Early 20th Century, 41 1/2 In. 275.00
Table, Tea, Mahogany, Foldover Top, Square Legs, 28 1/4 x 35 In. 520.00
Table, Tea, Mahogany, Step-Down Top, Shell Carvings, Snake Pad Feet, 20th Century . . .   198.00
Table, Tea, Michael Camp, Queen Anne Style, Curly Maple, 16 x 26 x 24 In. 605.00
Table, Tea, Queen Anne, Cherry, Tilt Top, Round, c.1770, 27 1/2 In. 3300.00
Table, Tea, Queen Anne, Curly Maple, Tray Top, Duck Feet, 27 1/4 x 30 1/2 In. 3025.00
Table, Tea, Queen Anne, Mahogany, Tray Top, Cabriole Legs, Pad & Disc Feet, c.1720 . .   8625.00
Table, Tea, Queen Anne, Maple, Oval Top, Rectangular Apron, 32 x 24 In. 6600.00
Table, Tea, Queen Anne, Oak, Tray Top, Scroll Legs, Pad Feet, c.1790, 27 1/2 In. 6900.00
Table, Tea, Queen Anne, Walnut, Dish Top, 2 Short Drawers, Pad Feet, 28 3/4 In. 1610.00
Table, Tea, Rosewood, Rouge Marble Top, Carved Apron, China, 30 3/4 x 22 1/4 In. 880.00
Table, Tea, Shaker, Maple, Wrought-Iron Catch, Tripod Base, Watervliet, 26 3/4 In. 2310.00
Table, Tea, Single Tile Top, Birdcage, Dragon's Head Feet, Chinese Export, c.1830 . . . . . .   2400.00
Table, Tea, Walnut, Beaded Rim, Shell Carved Knees, Snake Feet, c.1790, 29 In. 1100.00
Table, Tea, Walnut, Dish Top, Birdcage Support, c.1770, 29 1/2 In. 3300.00
Table, Tea, Walnut, Molded Rim, Birdcage, Vase-Form Splat, 1790-1800, 34 1/2 In. 935.00
Table, Teakwood, 2 Drawers, Square Pedestal Base, Knoll, 17 x 29 In. 2185.00
Table, Teakwood, Floral Nacre Inlay, Scalloped Apron, 3 Drawers, China, 56 x 14 1/2 In. .   165.00
Table, Tiger Maple, Drawer, 1800, 30 x 20 x 20 In. 1575.00
Table, Tilt Top, Black Lacquer, Landscapes & Figures In Border, Gilt Design, 28 In. 4600.00
Table, Tilt Top, Cherry, Vase Turned Pedestal, Snake Feet, 29 In. 605.00
Table, Tilt Top, Chippendale, Hardwood Base, 5-Board Pine Top, 29 x 28 In. 465.00
Table, Tilt Top, Chippendale, Mahogany, 3 Cabriole Legs, Claw & Ball Feet, 28 In. 242.00
Table, Tilt Top, Chippendale, Mahogany, Carved Rim, Pedestal, Tripod, 29 In. 330.00
Table, Tilt Top, Chippendale, Mahogany, Tripod Snake Feet, England, 30 x 27 In. 800.00
Table, Tilt Top, Chippendale, Mahogany, Tripod, 2-Board Round Top, 21 1/2 In. 440.00
Table, Tilt Top, Chippendale, Mahogany, Tripod, Birdcage, England, 29 x 25 In. 440.00
Table, Tilt Top, Chippendale, Walnut, Round Top, Tripod, Pennsylvania, 36 x 29 In. 4235.00
Table, Tilt Top, Classical, Mahogany, Columnar Pedestal, 3 Carved Feet, 1820s, 28 In. . . .   1210.00
Table, Tilt Top, Cricket, 6-Board Top, Shoe Feet 600.00
Table, Tilt Top, E. Wormley, Mahogany, White Laminate Shelf, 40 x 26 In. 935.00
Table, Tilt Top, Ebony, Orange, Round Top With Star, 3 Legs, Jamaica, 31 In. 7475.00
Table, Tilt Top, George III, Mahogany, Piecrust, Foliate Pad Feet, Ireland, 37 In. 4025.00
Table, Tilt Top, Mahogany, Cabriole Legs, Carved, Turned Column, England, 27 In. 990.00

Table, Tilt Top, Mahogany, Columnar Pedestal, 4 Down-Swept Leg, 28 In. 865.00
Table, Tilt Top, Mahogany, Conch Shell, Band & String Inlay, Oblong, Tripod Base 660.00
Table, Tilt Top, Mahogany, Mother-Of-Pearl Inlay, 1910-1920 . . . . 495.00
Table, Tilt Top, Mahogany, Serpentine, Urn Post, 3 Cabriole Legs, 28 In. 2013.00
Table, Tilt Top, Mahogany, Veneer, Stringing, Baluster Standard, Ring Turned, Round . . . 330.00
Table, Tilt Top, Queen Anne, Mahogany, 28 x 33 1/2 In. 690.00
Table, Tilt Top, Regency, Papier-Mache, Lacquered, Mother-Of-Pearl, 1820, 27 In. 455.00
Table, Tilt Top, Wallace Nutting, No. 664, Mahogany, Piecrust, Block Brand 3410.00
Table, Tray, Chippendale, Mahogany, Hinged Ends, Rectangular Top, 16 In. 230.00
Table, Tray, Edwardian, Oval, Polychrome Painted Top, Gilt, Turned Legs, 19 x 19 In. . . . 285.00
Table, Tray, George III, Mahogany, Bowfront, Reeded Gallery, 29 In. 2875.00
Table, Tray, George III, Mahogany, Handholds, 28 1/4 In. 6325.00
Table, Tray, Georgian, Mahogany, Hinged Sides, 18 x 29 x 14 In. 440.00
Table, Tray, Jacobsen, Teakwood, Round, Folding, 17 x 20 In., Pair 403.00
Table, Tray, Mahogany, 3/4 Fretwork Gallery, X-Legs, Victorian, 35 x 33 In. 2585.00
Table, Tray, Mahogany, 4 Pierced Handle Drop Sides, Oval Top, Margolis 825.00
Table, Tray, Mahogany, Stand, Gallery, Pierced Handholds, 29 1/2 x 20 In. 1955.00
Table, Trestle, G. Stickley, Leather Top, Broad Lower Shelf, Paper Label, 28 In. 2530.00
Table, Trestle, Italian Baroque, Walnut, 2-Board Top, Stretcher, 90 1/2 In. 9200.00
Table, Trestle, L. & J.G. Stickley, 29 x 60 In. 2475.00
Table, Trestle, L. & J.G. Stickley, 29 x 72 x 45 In. 5500.00
Table, Trestle, Walnut, Iron Stretcher, Italy, 19th Century 825.00
Table, Tudor Style, 8-Sided Top, Floral & Gadroon Design, 38 1/2 x 24 1/2 In. 1035.00
Table, Tulip, Parquetry, Leather Surface, 3 Drawers, Female Busts On Legs, 69 In. 5750.00
Table, Victorian, Rattan, Octagonal, Fold-Down Trays, Medial Shelf, 27 x 22 In. 488.00
Table, Victorian, Walnut, Rectangular Marble Top, Serpentine Corners 395.00
Table, Victorian, Walnut, Round Marble Top, Pedestal, 3 Legs, 30 x 16 In. 100.00
Table, Walnut, 2-Board Scrubbed Top, Drawer, Pennsylvania, 28 x 31 x 22 In. 4125.00
Table, Walnut, Farmhouse, Plank Top, End Drawer, c.1860, 28 x 53 In. 485.00
Table, Walnut, Marble Top, Center Pedestal, 4 Carved Legs, 29 1/2 x 32 1/2 x 23 In. 635.00
Table, Walnut, Open Storage Compartment, Cabriole Legs, 1860, 28 In. 545.00
Table, Walnut, Rectangular Top, Frieze Drawer, Portugal, 33 1/2 In. 2415.00
Table, Walnut, Rope Twist & Ball Skirt, Rope Twist Legs, Wood Claw & Ball Feet 660.00
Table, Walnut, Splayed Leg, Overhanging Top, 19th Century 2530.00
Table, Walnut, White Marble Turtle-Shaped Top, Pedestal, Finger Carved Legs, 29 In. . . . 518.00
Table, Warren McArthur, Brushed Chrome, Flared Legs, Black Lacquer Top, 28 In. 3300.00
Table, Warren McArthur, Tubular Aluminum Frame, Lacquer Top, 1930s, 24 x 18 In. 4675.00
Table, Wicker, Hardwood Top, Oval, Turned Wood Legs, 20th Century, 32 x 21 In. 60.00
Table, Wiener Werkstatte, Mahogany, Brass, 4 Supports, Pyramid Base, 30 1/2 In. 630.00
Table, William & Mary Style, Oak, Expandable Leaves, Rope Twist Legs 200.00
Table, William & Mary, Japanned, Parcel Gilt, Frieze Drawers, 29 x 32 x 21 In. 1495.00
Table, William & Mary, Oak, Rectangular Top, Spindle Turned Legs, 21 In. 175.00
Table, William & Mary, Walnut, Ebonized Trim, 2-Board Top, Drawer, 23 x 34 In. 935.00
Table, William IV, Mahogany, Telescoping, Lifts To Form 3 Tiers, 45 x 43 In. 6325.00
Table, Windsor, Pine Top, Apron, Beaded Edge, Lancaster County, 27 x 22 In. 3025.00
Table, Wine Tasting, Federal, Mahogany, Tripod Base, Down-Swept Legs, 28 x 18 In. . . . 100.00
Table, Wine Tasting, Federal, Mahogany, Tripod Base, Down-Swept Legs, 28 x 20 In. . . . 550.00
Table, Wine Tasting, Fruitwood, Folding, Plank Top, Trestle Base, c.1820, 29 x 51 In. . . . 1450.00
Table, Wine Tasting, Fruitwood, Round Top, Folding, France, 1840, 28 x 39 In. 1150.00
Table, Wine Tasting, George III, Gallery Top, Candle Slide, Block Feet, c.1780, 25 In. . . . 660.00
Table, Wine Tasting, George III, Tilt Top, Mahogany, Scalloped, 28 In. 430.00
Table, Wine Tasting, Hardwood, Wide Grain, Brown Lacquer, 34 x 37 1/4 In. 385.00
Table, Wine Tasting, Mahogany, Molded Top, Tripod Base, 22 In., Pair 400.00
Table, Wine Tasting, William IV, Mahogany, Round Hinged Top, 24 In. 1955.00
Table, Wm. Adams & Co., Revolving, Walnut, Cast Iron, 19th Century, 30 In. 440.00
Table, Work, Empire, Mahogany, 2 Serpentine Drawers, 33 x 22 x 18 In. 630.00
Table, Writing, Bonheur Du Jour, Galle, Poppies, Leaves, 1900 . . . . 5750.00
Table, Writing, Bonheur Du Jour, Regency, Mahogany, Pierced Brass Gallery 3740.00
Table, Writing, Florence Knoll, Rosewood Top, Chrome-Plated Base, 29 x 72 x 30 In. . . . 2645.00
Table, Writing, French Provincial, Fruitwood, D Shape, Drawer, 1840, 53 x 27 In. 785.00
Table, Writing, Fruitwood, Butterfly And Blossoms, 1900, 31 In. 4312.00
Table, Writing, G. Stickley, No. 720, 2 Drawers, Divided, 38 x 22 x 37 In. 1650.00
Table, Writing, George III, Mahogany, Leather Writing Surface, 3 Drawers, 31 In. 690.00

Table, Writing, Georgian, Mahogany, 3 Drawers Each Side, 31 x 70 x 43 In. 1331.00
Table, Writing, Gilt, Tooled Leather, 4 Short & 1 Long Drawer, Fluted Legs, 31 In. 2640.00
Table, Writing, Inset Veneered Top, 2 Drawers, Cabriole Legs, 1910, 40 x 29 In. 385.00
Table, Writing, Mahogany, Marble Top, 2 Drawers, Female Supports, 44 1/2 In. 4887.00
Table, Writing, Neoclassical, Mahogany, Oval Top, 4 Tapered Legs, 28 x 30 In. 8050.00
Table, Writing, Walnut, Marquetry, Coaching Scene, Bookrest, 1780s, 30 In. 5750.00
Table, Writing, Walnut, Scroll Carved Serpentine Drawers, 31 1/2 x 39 x 25 In. 700.00
Table, Writing, William IV, Mahogany, 2 Drawers, Leather Top, 1830, 32 x 46 In. 2905.00
Tabouret, L. & J.G. Stickley, Decal, 20 x 18 x 18 In. 2580.00
Tabouret, L. & J.G. Stickley, No. 558, Octagonal Top, Post Legs, 15 x 17 In. 990.00
Tabouret, L. & J.G. Stickley, No. 560, Mahogany, Arched Stretchers, 16 x 18 In. 1540.00
Tabouret, Louis XVI, Rectangular Molded Frame, Floral, Cabriole Legs, 7 In., Pair 1150.00
Tabouret, Louis XVI, Wood, Carved Rails, Over-Stuffed Top, Fluted Legs, Pair 920.00
Tabouret, Rococo, Walnut, Parcel Gilt, Upholstered, Cabriole Legs, 17 x 25 x 25 In. 230.00
Tea Cart, Drop Leaf, Federal Style, Mahogany, Wagon-Style Wheels, 18 x 27 x 28 In. . . . 85.00
Tea Cart, Drop Leaf, Maple, Rectangular Top, Reeded Posts, Buggy Style Wheels 35.00
Tea Cart, Drop Leaf, Maple, Removable Tray 175.00
Tea Cart, Drop Leaf, Walnut, Removable Glass Tray, 31 x 19 x 29 In. 200.00
Tea Cart, Edwardian, Mahogany, Revolving Lift Top, 2 Shelves, 30 1/2 In. 882.00
Tea Cart, Mahogany, Drawer, Lower Glass Serving Tray 245.00
Tea Cart, McCobb, Brass Frame, Travertine Top, 2 Drawers, 3 Shelves 600.00
Tea Cart, Rattan, 1920s 220.00
Tea Cart, Silver-Plated Border, Glass Shelves, 3 Bottle Holders, 27 1/2 x 30 In. 975.00
Tea Cart, Teakwood, Dowel & Slat, Removable Tray, Denmark, 24 x 29 1/2 x 19 In. 288.00
Tea Cart, Victorian, Brass, 2 Plate-Glass Shelves, 41 x 23 x 32 In. 748.00
Umbrella Stand, Aesthetic, Cast Iron, Rotherham Registry Mark, June 6, 1882, 33 In. . . . 385.00
Umbrella Stand, Cast Iron, English Sailor On Crossed Anchor & Oar, 28 In. 825.00
Umbrella Stand, Castelli, Pluvium, Orange Plastic, Italy, 19 1/2 x 11 1/2 In. 165.00
Umbrella Stand, Faux Bamboo, Fitted To Hold 8 Umbrellas, 1890, 27 x 19 x 9 In. 85.00
Umbrella Stand, Fornasetti, Poodle Shape, Lithographic Metal, 1950s, 34 1/4 In. 1265.00
Umbrella Stand, G. Stickley, No. 55, 4 Tapered Posts, Divided Top, 20 x 12 x 34 In. 935.00
Umbrella Stand, G. Stickley, Triple, 33 x 20 In. 770.00
Umbrella Stand, Man With Bellows & Basket Of Grape Vines, Brass 110.00
Umbrella Stand, Octagonal, Slats, Leather Straps, Arts & Crafts, Lakeside Crafters 700.00
Umbrella Stand, Victorian, Bamboo, Tile Back 220.00
Vanity, Art Deco, 3 Drawers, Round Brass Pulls, Beveled Mirror, Red Lion 325.00
Vanity, Art Deco, Burl Veneer, 2 Nests Of Drawers Over Bottom, 1940, 58 In. 460.00
Vanity, Deskey, Burl, Ivory Enamel, Full Mirror, Glass Shelf, 1930s, 63 x 45 In. 165.00
Vanity, Federal, Mahogany, Removable Sectioned Tray, 29 x 22 3/4 In. 402.00
Vanity, Floral Etched Tri-Fold Mirror, 3 Drawers, Bench, 47 x 19 x 60 In. 805.00
Vanity, G. Nelson, Leather Cabinet, Mirror, Stool, Herman Miller, 57 In., 2 Piece 650.00
Vanity, G. Stickley, No. 919, Swivel Mirror, 2 Drawers, 36 x 18 x 55 In. 3850.00
Vanity, Louis XVI Style, Kidney Shape, Variegated Marble Top, 29 1/2 x 24 In. 450.00
Vanity, Raymond Loewy, Red Plastic, White Metal Frame, Sliding Top, 1960s, 40 In. 1650.00
Vanity, Rohde, Wood Veneer, Three Drawers, 1930s, 65 In. 610.00
Vitrine, Bamboo, Fitted Interiors, Asymmetrical Shelves, 79 x 30 x 13 In. 1840.00
Vitrine, Empire, Walnut, Swag Frieze, Palmetto Mounts, 19th Century, 31 In. 1936.00
Vitrine, French Provincial, Cherry, 2 Doors, Canted Corners, 1860, 86 x 50 In. 1450.00
Vitrine, Glass Lift Lid, Rose Ring Border, Workbasket On Shelf, France, 32 x 30 In. 5465.00
Vitrine, Louis XV Style, Bowfront, Ormolu, Mirror, Painted Scene, 58 x 29 In. 1785.00
Vitrine, Louis XV, Mahogany, Painted, Serpentine Frieze, 73 x 35 x 16 In. 975.00
Vitrine, Louis XV, Mahogany, Serpentine Top, Angel Figure, 4 Cabriole Legs, 68 In. 2185.00
Vitrine, Oak, Spray Of Water Leaves, Beveled Glass, Fluted Legs, 72 3/4 In. 4025.00
Vitrine, Regency, Mahogany, 2 Glazed Doors, Plinth Base, 85 x 53 In. 1936.00
Vitrine, Serpentine Faux Marble Top, Boulle Inlay, 19th Century, 41 x 43 In. 1035.00
Wardrobe, Eastlake, Walnut, Burl Veneer, 2 Drawers, 84 1/2 x 53 1/4 In. 990.00
Wardrobe, G. Stickley, No. 920, 8 Drawers, Red Decal, 60 In. 25300.00
Wardrobe, George IV, Mahogany, Paneled Doors, 76 In. 5750.00
Wardrobe, Georgian, Mahogany, 2 Doors, Bracket Feet, 1820, 81 x 46 In. 3146.00
Wardrobe, Louis XV Style, Crown Molding, Shell Relief Frieze, Paneled Doors 1380.00
Wardrobe, Oak, Paneled, Cameo Carved Scroll, 2 Doors, 27 x 73 x 17 In. 245.00
Wardrobe, Pine, 2 Raised Panel Doors, Canada, 87 x 57 In. . . . . *Illus* 1495.00
Wardrobe, Pine, Double Door, 1890s, 84 In. 1700.00

Mildew, fungus, stains, and odors can be removed from the wooden parts of furniture by using a commercial mildew remover found at the supermarket. Wipe the entire piece or it will have a lighter spot where it was cleaned.

Furniture,
Wardrobe, Pine,
2 Raised Panel
Doors, Canada,
87 x 57 In.

Wardrobe, Pine, Paint, Architectural Cornice, 2 Doors, Pilasters, 1820, 61 In.	550.00
Wardrobe, Satinwood, 2 Short, 1 Long Drawer, Trays, Panel Door, 1800s, 79 In.	990.00
Wardrobe, Victorian, Walnut, Breakdown Design, Paneled Ends & Door, 86 In.	1650.00
Wardrobe, Walnut, Paneled Door, Base Drawer, 30 x 17 3/4 x 73 In.	1650.00
Washstand, Cherry, Dovetailed Drawer, Gallery, 36 In.	495.00
Washstand, Cherry, Drawer, Basin & Accessory Wells, 33 1/4 In.	495.00
Washstand, Corner, Cherry, Tiger Maple, Gallery, Candle Shelf, Pennsylvania, 1820	1870.00
Washstand, Corner, Hepplewhite, Mahogany, Drawer, Gallery, 23 x 17 x 40 In.	990.00
Washstand, Corner, Hepplewhite, Pine, Drawer, Gallery, 22 x 15 x 32 In.	550.00
Washstand, Corner, Mahogany, Mahogany Veneer, Shelf, 1 Small & 2 False Drawers	1017.00
Washstand, Corner, Mahogany, Mid-Section Shelf, Basin Well, 46 In.	330.00
Washstand, Corner, Mahogany, Stepped Backsplash, Middle Shelf, Drawer, 39 1/2 In.	660.00
Washstand, Cottage, Pine, Paneled Doors, Drawer, Shelf Crest, 29 x 15 x 35 In.	245.00
Washstand, Empire, Pine, 2 Drawers, Scroll Splashboard, Mid-19th Century	375.00
Washstand, Federal, Mahogany, Arched Reeded Sides, Tambour Top, 1810, 36 In.	1495.00
Washstand, Federal, Mahogany, Square Top, Drawer, Square Tapered Legs, 31 In.	460.00
Washstand, French Provincial, Walnut, 4 Long Drawers, Block Feet, 1880, 39 In.	1331.00
Washstand, George III, Bowfront, Mahogany, Square Legs, Splayed Feet	700.00
Washstand, Golden Oak Era, 3 Drawers, Door, Towel Bar Back, 57 1/2 x 35 In.	305.00
Washstand, Grain Painted, Gallery, Center Drawer, Opalescent Pull, 19th Century	170.00
Washstand, Long Drawer Over 2 Doors, Towel Bar Each End	145.00
Washstand, Mahogany Veneer, 4 Drawers, Reeded Backsplash, Brass Pull	208.00
Washstand, Mahogany, Beveled Mirror, Serpentine Front, 1900, 30 In.	212.00
Washstand, Mahogany, Frieze Drawer, 2 Paneled Cupboard Doors, c.1910, 32 1/2 In.	210.00
Washstand, Oak, Bowfront, Mahogany, Marble Top, Drawer, Doors, 28 x 29 x 16 In.	150.00
Washstand, Oak, Demilune, Mirrored Backsplash, 3 Shelves, Cabriole Legs	550.00
Washstand, Pine, Art Nouveau Ceramic Tiles, Turned Legs, Drawer, 42 1/4 x 35 In.	415.00
Washstand, Pine, Shaped 3/4 Gallery, Basin Well, Platform Stretcher, 30 3/4 In.	375.00
Washstand, Sheraton, Mahogany, Dovetailed Drawer & Gallery, 20 x 30 In.	275.00
Washstand, Sheraton, Mahogany, Gallery, Drawer Over 2 Doors	880.00
Washstand, Sheraton, Pine, 3 Drawers, Backsplash, 39 In.	302.00
Washstand, Sheraton, Pine, Poplar, Drawer, Painted, Floral Design, 18 x 14 x 30 In.	190.00
Washstand, Sheraton, Poplar, Drawer, Scalloped Backsplash, 30 1/4 x 22 1/2 In.	412.00
Washstand, Sheraton, Tiger Maple, Scalloped Backsplash, 1815, 38 x 21 In.	1100.00
Washstand, Sheraton, Walnut, 2 Drawers, Backsplash, 39 In.	192.00
Washstand, Victorian, Cherry, Brown Marble Top, Paneled Door, 3 Drawers, 28 In.	195.00
Washstand, Victorian, Softwood, Candle Shelves, Drawer, 2 Doors	165.00
Washstand, Victorian, Walnut, Drawer, Applied Moldings, Pullout Shelf, 31 In.	525.00
Washstand, Walnut, Applied Moldings, Carving, Marble Top, 2 Shelves, 41 x 29 In.	550.00
Washstand, Walnut, Burl, Marble Top, Drawer, Paneled Doors, c.1870, 31 In.	825.00
Washstand, Walnut, Central Drawer, Shaped Cross Stretcher, 30 1/2 In.	465.00
Washstand, Yellow Paint, Stencil, Gallery, Candle Shelves, New England	605.00
Wastebasket, Arts & Crafts, 4 Slats Each Side, Arched Rail, 15 In.	660.00
Wastebasket, Arts & Crafts, Footed, Lakeside Craft Shops, Sheboygan, Mich., 15 In.	330.00
Wastebasket, Edwardian, Mahogany, Wicker Panels, Octagonal, 1900, 16 x 15 In.	430.00
Wastebasket, Fornasetti, Hand Painted, Transfer-Printed Metal, 1950s, 10 In.	3220.00

Wastebasket, Frankl, Combed Veneer, Tapering Square, 12 x 12 x 12 In. 288.00
Wastebasket, G. Stickley, 15 Slats, Iron Hoops, 12 x 15 In. 2090.00
Wastebasket, Stickley Brothers, No. 80 . . . . 1650.00
Whatnot Shelf, Chippendale, Mahogany, 4 Graduated Shelves, 3 Drawers, 36 In. 517.00
Whatnot Shelf, Corner, Gingerbread Design, Turned Columns & Finials, 50 x 29 In. 230.00
Whatnot Shelf, Mahogany, Drawer On Lowest Tier, 50 In. 8625.00
Whatnot Shelf, Walnut, 2 Drawers, 3 Shelves, Turned Posts, 47 x 16 1/2 In. 490.00
Whatnot Shelf, Walnut, Turned Posts, Fretwork, Molded Shelves, 47 1/4 In. 165.00
Window Seat, Carved Leaves, Rolled Arms 300.00
Window Seat, Mahogany Veneer, Curved Upholstered Seat, 1825, 39 1/2 In. 3450.00
Window Seat, Neoclassical, Gilt, Oval Upholstered Seat, 8 Fluted Legs 6900.00
Wine Cooler, George III, Mahogany, Brassbound, Tapered Legs, 24 In. 1725.00
Wine Safe, French Provincial, Holds 112 Bottles, Metal Doors, 1890, 64 x 40 In. 365.00

G. ARGY-ROUSSEAU is the impressed mark used on a variety of objects in the Art Deco style. Gabriel Argy-Rousseau, born in 1885, was a French glass artist.

G-ARGY-
ROUSSEAU

Butterflies, Outstretched Wings, Signed, c.1924, 5 1/2 In. 10350.00

GALLE was a designer who made glass, pottery, furniture, and other Art Nouveau items. Émile Galle founded his factory in France in 1874. After Galle's death in 1904, the firm continued to make glass and furniture until 1931. The name *Galle* was used as a mark, but it was often hidden in the design of the object. Galle glass is listed here. Pottery is in the next section. His furniture is listed in the Furniture category.

Galle

Atomizer, Blue Mountain Range Scene, Green Lake, Yellow Sky, Cameo, Signed, 7 In. . . 880.00
Base, Lamp, Baluster, Gray, Yellow, Blue Overlay, Trumpet Shape Flowers, 1900, 16 In. . 2070.00
Bottle, Amber, Engraved Lion, Applied Button Handles, Marked, 8 1/2 In. 660.00
Bottle, Dragonflies In Flight Over Pond, Light Green, Heart Shape, Stopper, 6 In. 5750.00
Bowl, Gray With White, Crimson Flowers Overlay, 1925, 2 1/2 In. 977.00
Bowl, Yellow Mottled, Etched, Maroon Flowers Overlay, Cameo, 5 In. 1610.00
Box, Cover, Cypress Lake Scene, Aubergine, Blue, Yellow Ground, Cameo, 5 3/4 In. 1150.00
Box, Cover, Landscape, Gray, Pale Pink, With Purplish Red, 1900, 7 1/4 In. 2300.00
Box, Cover, Poppies, Red Wine, Pale Pink Ground, Cameo, 6 In. 1150.00
Box, Cover, Trees On Cover, Leaves On Base, Brown, Green Ground, Cameo, 4 In. 1150.00
Box, Cover, Wildflowers, Grasses, Foliate Leaf, Berry Silver Mounts, 1900, 6 1/4 In. 7475.00
Chalice, Applied Dragons With Cabochons, Flared Bell Foot, Gilt, Ivy Figures, 5 In. 3450.00
Figurine, Owl, Perched On Russet Base, Gray, Amber, 1890, 13 In. 3740.00
Lamp, 2-Tone Red Grapes, Leaves, Yellow Ground, Cameo, 7 x 14 In. 5500.00
Lamp, Azalea Blossoms, Leafage, Gray, Lemon Yellow, Crimson Red, 1900, 21 In. 9775.00
Lamp, Blue Eagles, Deep Blue Evergreens, Light Blue Mountain On Base, 14 In. 1320.00
Lamp, Figural, Water Lily Shade, Bronze Base, Maiden, Outstretched Arms, 22 In. 10350.00
Lamp Base, Baluster, Gray, Russet Overlay, Prunus Branches, 1900, 17 In. 1610.00
Lamp Base, Stylized Foliate, Lavender To Green Layers, Etched, Cameo, 15 1/2 In. 402.00
Plafonnier, Ceiling Light, Vines, Pink, Green, White Mottled, Aubergine Overlay, 17 In. . 6670.00
Tray, Fish, Aquatic Plants, 2 Scalloped Handles, Pale Topaz, Rectangular, 2 3/4 In. 1150.00
Tumbler, Enameled, Amber, Blue Ribbons, Gold Banner, 1 3/4 In. 345.00
Vase, 2-Tone Green, Green Ground, Footed, Cameo, Signed, 16 In. 1650.00
Vase, 5 Butterflies, Wildflowers, Tapered Waist, Signed, c.1900, 22 1/4 In. 1070.00
Vase, Anemone Blossoms, Leaves, Yellow, Green, Periwinkle Blue, Cameo, 1900, 6 In. . . 3737.00
Vase, Apple Blossoms, Leaves, Gray, Pale Blue, Spring Green, Amber, 10 In. 5462.00
Vase, Apricot Flowers, Green & White Floral, Green Base, Cylindrical, Signed, 16 In. . . . 1540.00
Vase, Berry & Bee, Cut Thornbush Cameo, Signed, 24 1/2 In. 3160.00
Vase, Bleeding Hearts, Rose, Ivory, Green, Brown, Blue Leaves, Light Green, 15 1/2 In. . 3300.00
Vase, Blue, White Flowering Stems, Foliage, Etched, Cameo, 6 3/4 In. 1150.00
Vase, Brown Floral Over Green, Cameo, Marked, 8 In. 55.00
Vase, Brown Flowers, Transparent, Yellow Ground, Cameo, Signed, 8 In. 935.00
Vase, Brown Flowers, Vivid Yellow Ground, Cameo, Signed, 6 In. 880.00
Vase, Brown, Green Leaves, Satin, Yellow Ground, Cameo, Signed, 8 In. 1210.00
Vase, Bud, Flowers, Leaves, Brown Overlay, Satin Gray, Cameo, 1900, 7 In. 575.00
Vase, Bud, Slender Neck, Amber, Daisies, Yellow, Orange, Melon Shape, 1900, 9 In. 2585.00
Vase, Burgundy Floral, Yellow Ground, Signed, 4 1/2 In. 2540.00
Vase, Cabinet, Yellow, Purple Overlay, Fuchsia Blossoms, Inverted Baluster, 5 In. 1035.00

Vase, Carved Floral, Deep Red On Rose, Satin, Cameo, Signed, 5 In. 880.00
Vase, Carved Floral, Green, White, Purple, Peach, White Ground, Cameo, Signed, 10 In. . 1760.00
Vase, Carved Purple Flowers, Leaves, Purple, Satin, Cameo, Signed, 6 In. 605.00
Vase, Clematis, Deep Purple Cut To White Frost, Cameo, 1900, 7 In. 1495.00
Vase, Clusters Of Berries, Leaf Vines, Tendrils, Mottled Gray, Cameo, 1900, 18 In. 6785.00
Vase, Clusters Of Young Apples, Leafy Branches, Sunshine Yellow, Cherry Red, 23 In. ... 3737.00
Vase, Cut Leaves & Blossoms, Flattened Front & Back, Crimson Interior, Signed, 5 In. .. 1035.00
Vase, Delicate Purple Orchids, Deep Yellow Leaves, Cameo, Signed, 6 1/2 In. 385.00
Vase, Dragonfly Over Lotus, Overlaid In Orange, Green, Cameo, 6 3/4 In. 2300.00
Vase, Dragonfly, Yellow, Wisteria Blossoms, Green, Brown, Blue, Signed, 1900, 4 In. ... 1100.00
Vase, Etched Green & Blue Flowers, Yellow Ground, 8 In. 2860.00
Vase, Floral, Deep Purple, Green, Cameo, Signed, 5 In. 525.00
Vase, Floral, Deep Purple, Yellow, Deep Purple Ground, Cameo, 7 In. 715.00
Vase, Floral, Lavender, Aubergine Layers, Blossom Clusters, Pink, Cameo, 6 In. 690.00
Vase, Floral, Leaves, Green Ground, Cameo, Signed, 3 In. 180.00
Vase, Floral, Leaves, Pale Pink Layers, Purple, Amethyst, Cameo, 6 In. 805.00
Vase, Floral, Light Purple, Pink Ground, Cameo, Signed, 12 In. 1100.00
Vase, Floral, Purple, Pink Satin Ground, Cameo, Signed, 14 In. 990.00
Vase, Fuchsia Blossoms, Leaves, Plum, Magenta, Lavender, Red, Cameo, 1900, 13 In. ... 5750.00
Vase, Golden Amber, Layered Chartreuse, Maiden Hair Fern Fronds, Signed, 9 3/4 In. ... 2645.00
Vase, Gray With Peach & Green, Cylindrical, c.1910, 9 1/2 In. 1033.00
Vase, Gray, Crimson & Violet Overlay, Cut Clematis, Oval, 1900s, 17 In. 9775.00
Vase, Gray, Green, Brown Overlay, Cut Ferns, Barbell Shape, 1900, 11 In. 1265.00
Vase, Gray, Peach Overlay With Green, Cylindrical, Crimped Lip, 1920s, 13 1/2 In. 1610.00
Vase, Gray, Pink, Lime Green Overlay, Thistle Blossoms, 1904, 17 1/4 In. 2070.00
Vase, Green Fruiting Vine, Spherical, Cameo, 9 3/4 In. 3450.00
Vase, Green Horse Chestnut, Orange Ground, Etched, Cameo, 6 3/4 In. 1495.00
Vase, Green Leaves, Stems, Brown, Yellow Ground, Cameo, Signed, 8 In. 1100.00
Vase, Green Leaves, Tendrils, Clear-To-Salmon Ground, Cameo, Signed, c.1890, 6 3/4 In. 880.00
Vase, Green Nasturtium, Pink Ground, Etched, Cameo, 6 3/4 In. 1150.00
Vase, Green, Burgundy Fern, Everted Scalloped Rim, Tapered, Cameo, 19 In. 3220.00
Vase, Green, Lavender Flowering Branch Design, Pink, Gray Ground, Cameo, 4 1/8 In. .. 460.00
Vase, Green, Mauve Hydrangea, Pink Ground, Etched, Cameo, 6 3/4 In. 1725.00
Vase, Greenery Surrounding A Lake, Pale Yellow, Purple, Blue, Amber, 7 3/4 In. 2990.00
Vase, Hawthorn Berries, Leaves, Yellow, Orange, Brown, Pale Green Foot, 9 3/4 In. 4600.00
Vase, Hibiscus Blossoms, Leaves, Gray, Lemon Yellow, Crimson Red, 8 1/2 In. 3737.00
Vase, Hydrangea, Amber, Brown Layers, Blossoms Over Leafy Branches, 6 1/4 In. 862.00
Vase, Hydrangea, Lavender, Green, Opaque Ground, Cameo, 13 In. 4830.00
Vase, Hydrangea, Leaves, Gray, Pale Pink, White, Lavender, 20 In. 4600.00
Vase, Hydrangea, Olive Green, Lavender, Opaque Pink, White Ground, Cameo, 27 In. ... 3450.00
Vase, Hydrangea, Pink, Lavender, Globular, Signed, 1920, 5 1/2 In. 690.00
Vase, Intricate Limbs, Leaves, Berries, Red, Frosted Red, Yellow Ground, Cameo, 12 In. . 1650.00
Vase, Iris Blossoms, Leaves, Gray Opalescent, Cameo, Pilgrim Flask, 1900, 18 In. 9200.00
Vase, Irises, Crocuses, Gilt Leaves, Moss Green Ground, Applied Curved Handle, 5 In. .. 1495.00
Vase, Lakeside Landscape, Tall Trees, Mountains, Blue, Purple Layers, Cameo, 13 1/4 In. 4887.00
Vase, Landscape, Birds Flying Overhead, Brown, Yellow Ground, Cameo, 6 In. 715.00
Vase, Landscape, Brown Trees, Blue Mountains, Peach Ground, Cameo, 7 In. 660.00
Vase, Landscape, Forest, Lake, Gray, Brown Green, Bulbous, Cameo, 8 In. 1495.00
Vase, Landscape, Mountain, Trees, Lake, Purple, Green, Blue, Cameo, 6 In. 525.00
Vase, Landscape, Spring, Leafy Trees, Waving Grasses, Lime Green, Deep Umber, 21 In. . 7475.00
Vase, Landscape, Tropical, Rio De Janeiro, Palm Trees, Red, Orange, Cameo, 14 In. 4400.00
Vase, Lavender Poppy, Signed, 4 In. 750.00
Vase, Lavender To Clear, Satin, Cameo, Signed, 2 1/2 In. 510.00
Vase, Leaves & Berries, Green, Wine Enamel, Textured Pale Green Ground, 10 In. 2300.00
Vase, Lilies, Lily Pads, Gray Glass, Pale Yellow, Red, Cameo, 1900, 24 In., Pair 9200.00
Vase, Lotus, Snails, Mottled Yellow, Double Loop Handles, Everted Rim, 6 1/4 In. 3105.00
Vase, Mauve, Blue Clematis, Yellow Ground, Cameo, 8 1/4 In. 1725.00
Vase, Mountain Laurel Berries, Serrated Leafage, Gray, Lemon Yellow, Pale Blue, 12 In. . 5750.00
Vase, Olive, Pink Poppies, Opaque Ground, Cylindrical, 24 1/2 In. 3680.00
Vase, Opaque Iris, Cut Peach, Cameo, Signed, 4 In. 385.00
Vase, Orange Trailing Flower, Etched, Cameo, 6 3/4 In. 1265.00
Vase, Orchids, Leaves, Brown, Mottled Lemon Yellow, Gray, Cameo, 1900, 9 In. 2875.00
Vase, Peach Grape, Amethyst Cut, Long Neck, Cameo, 6 1/2 In. 660.00

Vase, Purple Flowers, Brown & Green, Signed, 9 In. 5750.00
Vase, Purple Flowers, Green Leaves, Purple, Peach Ground, Cameo, Signed, 17 1/2 In. . . .   2090.00
Vase, Purple Fuchsia, Yellow Ground, Cameo, Signed, 6 1/2 In.   605.00
Vase, Purple Irises, Lemon Yellow Ground, Cameo, 16 1/2 In. 2990.00
Vase, Purple Orchids, Purple Leaves, Stems, Yellow Ground, Cameo, Signed, 5 1/2 In. . . .   1100.00
Vase, Red Chrysanthemums, Yellow Ground, Flattened, Cameo, 13 In. 5750.00
Vase, Red Dicentra Spectabilis, Yellow Ground, Everted Rim, Cylindrical, Cameo, 9 In. . .   2185.00
Vase, Red Honeysuckle Vine, Yellow Ground, Inverted Cone, Cameo, 6 1/8 In. 1610.00
Vase, Ripe Grape Clusters, Leaves, Tendrils, Pale Amber, Peach, Dark Brown, 23 In. 4312.00
Vase, Sailing Ships, Purple Overlay, Blue, Yellow Ground, Pilgrim Flask, 5 In. 1495.00
Vase, Sang-De-Boef Overlay, Lilies, Red Opaque Ground, Squat, Cameo, 5 1/2 In. 1725.00
Vase, Squash, Blossoms, Leaves, Grass, Lime Green, Mustard, Yellow, Cameo, 14 In. . . .   5175.00
Vase, Stylized Fuchsia Blossoms, Lime Green, Pink, White Brown, Cameo, 10 In. 5775.00
Vase, Stylized Morning Blossoms & Vines, Signed, 8 In. 690.00
Vase, Swirling Vines, Grapes, Leaves, Opaque Aubergine, Yellow, White Mottled, 21 In. .   3220.00
Vase, Tall Trees Design, Brown, Green, Lake In Background, Cameo, Signed, 8 1/2 In. . .   1210.00
Vase, Tapering Cylindrical, Gray, Peach, Purple, Green, Hydrangea, 1900, 10 In. 1840.00
Vase, Trailing Florets, Overlaid In Green, Mauve, Etched, Cameo, 6 3/4 In. 920.00
Vase, Vine & Berry, Emerald Base, Clear & Emerald Ground, Signed, 14 In. 3960.00
Vase, Water Lilies & Lily Pads, Lime Green, Brown, White, Waterlily Shape, 10 In. 12650.00
Vase, Yellow Nasturtium, Etched, Cameo, 6 3/4 In. 1150.00
Wall, Pocket, Amethyst Poppies, Signed 795.00
Wall Pocket, Grasshopper, Signed, 9 1/2 In. 1100.00

GALLE POTTERY was made by Emile Galle, the famous French
designer, after 1874. The pieces were marked with the initials *E. G.*
impressed, *Em. Galle Faiencerie de Nancy,* or a version of his signature. Galle is best known for his glass, listed above.

Bowl, Peonies, Courtly Lady, Insect Finial, Lotus Shape, 6 1/2 In. 980.00
Coffeepot, Blue Faience, Rococo, Marked, 10 In. 908.00

GAME collectors like all types of games. Of special interest are any
board games or card games. Transogram and other company names are
included in the description when known. Other games may be found
listed under Card, Toy, or the name of the character or celebrity featured in the game.

12 O'Clock High, Milton Bradley, Card, 1965 . . . .   35.00
A-Team, Parker Brothers, Board, 1984 . . . .   20.00
ABC Monday Night Football, Computerized, Battery Operated, Aurora, Box, 1972 . . . . . .   23.00
Advance To Boardwalk, Parker Brothers, Board, 1985 . . . .   30.00
Adventures Of Robin Hood, Magic Windows, Bettye-B, Board, Box, 1956 . . . .   75.00
Adventures Of Sir Lancelot, Lisbeth Whiting, 1957 . . . .   130.00
Aero Flights Chad Valley, England, Kompactum Edition, Board 145.00
Alice & Wonderland, Cadaco, 1984 . . . .   25.00
All In The Family, Milton Bradley, Board, 1972 . . . .   35.00
All Star Baseball, Cadaco-Ellis, Board, 1962 . . . .   40.00
All-American Football, Cadaco, Board, 1969 . . . .   35.00
Alphabet Rolling A Barrel, A To Z Printed On Cloth, 2 x 3 1/4 In. 130.00
Animal Golf, Wagering Game Played On Golf Course 17.00
Annie, The Movie Game, Parker Brothers, Board, 1981 . . . .   20.00
Annie Oakley, Milton Bradley, Board, 1950s 50.00
Apple's Way, Milton Bradley, Board, 1974 . . . .   20.00
Arnold Palmer's Inside Golf, David Bremson Co., Board, 1961 . . . .   155.00
As The World Turns, Parker Brothers, Board, 1966 . . . .   40.00
Astronauts Action Marble Game, Wolverine Toy Co., Late 1960s, 5 x 9 x 1 In. 28.00
Authors, Russell Mfg. Co., Card, 1920s 40.00
Babar, Milton Bradley, Box, 1968, 8 1/2 x 16 1/2 In. 22.00
Backgammon, Ivory Dominoes, Pieces, Mahogany, Box, 1900, 15 x 9 In. 770.00
Ball Toss, Gondola Stage, Hand Painted Alpine Scene, 5 Figures, Le Dirigeable, 1910 . . .   2300.00
Bally Skill Derby, Horse Race, Electric, 72 In. 2070.00
Barbie, Queen Of The Prom, Mattel, Board, 1960 . . . .   10.00
Barbie's Keys To Fame, Mattel, Board, 1963 . . . .   40.00
Baretta, Milton Bradley, Board, 1976 . . . .   20.00

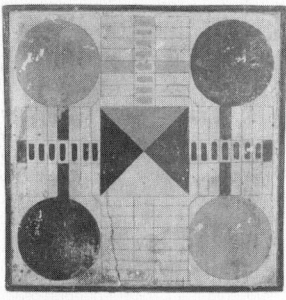

Game, Board, Parcheesi, Hand Painted, Wood

Coins must be stored properly. Do not put them in a sealed plastic or wooden container or loose in a box or envelope. Plastic, paper, cardboard, and wood give off chemical vapors that speed corrosion. Loose coins may be scratched. Buy archival coin holders, easily found at any coin shop.

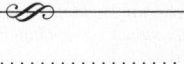

Barney Miller, Parker Brothers, Board, 1977	20.00
Baseball, Parker Brothers, Board, 1950	28.00 to 30.00
Baseball, Slugger, Animated Bat, Agate Marbles, Box, 1940s, 13 x 32 In.	143.00
Bat Masterson, Lowell, TV Show, Gene Barry, Board, 1958	38.00 to 70.00
Battle Cry, Milton Bradley, Board, 1962	40.00
Bazooka Bagatelle, Marx, Box	45.00
Beany & Cecil Jumping DJ Surprise Action, Mattel, Box, 1961, 9 x 11 In.	48.00
Beany & Cecil Skill Ball Game, Metal, 1961	50.00
Ben Hur Chariot Race, Loew's, Linen Box, 1959	150.00
Bermuda Triangle, Milton Bradley, Board, 1975	38.00 to 40.00
Beverly Hillbillies, Clampett Family On Box, Standard Toycraft, 1963	70.00
Beverly Hillbillies, Filmways, Card, Box, 1963	55.00
Bible Game Of New Testament Books, David C. Cook Publishing, 1930s	65.00
Bible Rhymes, Goodenough & Woglom, Card, 1930s	32.00
Bicycle Race, Milton Bradley, 1910, Square, 7 1/3 In.	175.00
Big Board, Dadem Inc., Watertown, N.Y., 1963	60.00
Big League Baseball, Electric, 1920s	225.00
Big League Spinner Baseball, Jacmar, 1950s	95.00
Bionic Crisis, Parker Brothers, Board, 1975	20.00
Bionic Woman, Parker Brothers, Jaime Sommers, TV Show, Board, 1976	22.00
Blockade, Corey Games, 1941	70.00
Board, 23 Clay Marbles, Side Trays, 1860s	115.00
Board, 44 Pine & Walnut Pegs, Birch & Walnut, 1760s	110.00
Board, Backgammon, Ebony, Ivory, Rectangular, Bun Feet, Late 18th Century, 23 In.	2990.00
Board, Colored Marquetry, Inlaid Horse & F.C.B. On Reverse, 1911, 16 5/8 x 17 1/4 In.	687.00
Board, Cribbage, Be-Speckled Trout, Copper Muskie	135.00
Board, Cribbage, Walrus Tusk, 23 In.	1000.00
Board, Depose, Round, 8 In.	225.00
Board, Faux Marble Paint, 2-Sided, Square, 20 1/2 In.	575.00
Board, Folding Box, Worn Black & Brown Paint, Yellow, Red & Blue, 24 x 24 In.	365.00
Board, Folding, 2-Sided, Red, White & Blue	4125.00
Board, Multicolored Florals, Quebec, c.1900	3700.00
Board, Parcheesi, Hand Painted, Wood	*Illus* 4675.00
Board, Parcheesi, Hearts, 2-Sided	4150.00
Board, Parcheesi, Orange, Black & Gray On Yellow	695.00
Board, Parcheesi, Red, Yellow, Black, Pine, 19th Century, 24 x 24 In.	3740.00
Board, Parcheesi, Red, Yellow, Brown, Black, Square, 27 x 37 In.	7475.00
Board, Pine, Yellow & Brown Paint, 18 x 25 In.	300.00
Board, Poplar, Black, Yellow & Red Paint, Natural Ground, Ohio, 25 x 25 In.	1265.00
Board, Wooden, Hand Painted, 19th Century	4950.00
Board, Yellow, Black & Green, Fox & Geese On Back	1210.00
Board & Box, Chess Outside & Backgammon Inside, Ebony, Ivory, 5 1/2 x 23 In.	2990.00
Bobbsey Twins, Twins On Farm, Milton Bradley, Board, 1957	75.00
Booby-Trap, Parker Brothers, 1965	55.00
Boxing, Electronic, Starting Bell, Knockout Buzzer, Flashing Light, Northwest Products	275.00
Bullwinkle Magnet Maze	440.00

Bullwinkle's Electric Quiz Fun Game, Cardboard, Battery Operated, c.1960, 11 In. 22.00
Careers, Parker Brothers, Board, 1971 .... 10.00
Carrier Strike, Milton Bradley, Board, 1977 .... 45.00
Casper & Company Lotto, Built-Rite Toys, Box, 1970s, 7 1/2 x 14 1/4 In. 22.00
Casper The Friendly Ghost, Milton Bradley, Board, 1959 .... 25.00
Casper The Friendly Ghost, Sliding Square Dial Game, By Roalez 275.00
Cattlemen, Selchow & Righter, 1977 .... 30.00
Charlie & Me, Robot Game, Box 135.00
Checkerboard, 2-Sided, Brown & Gold, Damier Francais & Canadien, 18 1/2 x 29 In. ... 495.00
Checkerboard, 2-Sided, Flag On Reverse, Wooden, Glass Beads, Folk Art, 30 x 15 In. ... 1785.00
Checkerboard, Box Type, Wooden, Backgammon Interior, 9 x 14 1/2 In. 135.00
Checkerboard, Folding, Wooden, Black & Red Wood Pieces, c.1840, 14 x 14 In. 425.00
Checkerboard, GAR, Post No. 146, Not To Be Taken From Hall On Reverse 935.00
Checkerboard, Hires Root Beer, Folding, 1900, Square, 12 In. 265.00
Checkerboard, Mahogany & Maple, 20th Century, 14 3/4 x 14 3/4 In. 110.00
Checkerboard, Painted Green, Brown, Black, Red, Yellow, 18 3/4 x 18 1/2 In. 1495.00
Checkerboard, Painted, Tan, Brown, Red Outlines, 19 1/2 x 33 In. 80.00
Checkerboard, Pine, Black Stained Squares, 13 x 23 3/4 In. 190.00
Checkerboard, Pine, Black, Mustard Yellow, Squares Numbered, 18 1/4 x 26 3/4 In. 605.00
Checkerboard, Pine, Mustard Yellow, Brown, Applied Edge, 17 x 16 1/2 In. 990.00
Checkerboard, Pine, Red Paint, Black Squares, Applied Gallery, 19 x 27 In. 440.00
Checkerboard, Poplar, Red & Black Paint, Stars, Gallery Edge, 19 x 27 1/2 In. 545.00
Checkerboard, Poplar, Red & Black Square, Applied Edge, 20 x 20 In. 1073.00
Checkerboard, Poplar, Red & Yellow, Black Border, Applied Edge, 16 3/4 x 16 1/4 In. ... 1430.00
Checkerboard On Front, Parcheesi On Back, c.1900, 20 x 16 1/2 In. 650.00
Chess Set, Alabaster, 32 Piece 100.00
Chessboard, Bone & Ebony, 1880, 4 3/4 x 4 3/4 In. 295.00
Chinese Checkers, Man-Dar-In, Baldwin Mfg. Co., Marbles 18.00
Ching Gong, Samuel Gabriel, Board, 1937 .... 65.00
CHIPS, Milton Bradley, 1977 ....28.00 to 30.00
Chiromagica, Case, Slide Cover, Answer Sheets, Question Disks, McLoughlin, 1870 .... 258.00
Chopper Strike, Milton Bradley, Board, 1976 .... 45.00
Christmas Dinner, Parker Brothers, 1897 .... 995.00
Chuggedy Chug Game, Milton Bradley, 1955 .... 95.00
Chutes & Ladders, Milton Bradley, Board, 1956 .... 20.00
Civil War Game 1863, Parker Brothers, Board, 1961 .... 65.00
Civil War Game Of Battlecry, Milton Bradley 350.00
Clown, France, 24 x 34 In. 325.00
Clue, Parker Brothers, Board, 1949 ....80.00 to 85.00
Colonel Jet Space Game, Silver Rich Corp., 1952, 9 x 10 1/2 In. 58.00
Combat Tank Game, Magic Wand Co., 1964 .... 35.00
Confucius Say, Milton Bradley, Card, 1937 .... 35.00
Countdown, Space Game, Transogram, Board, 1959 .... 85.00
Countdown To Space, E.S. Lowe Co., Board, 1967 .... 40.00
County Fair, Parker Brothers, Card, 1891 .... 133.00
Coup D'Etat, Parker Brothers, Board, 1966 .... 65.00
Creature Features, Athol Research, N.Y., Board, 1975 .... 110.00
Cribbage Board, 4 Round Feet, Late 18th Century, 9 1/2 In. 135.00
Cribbage Board, Carved Ivory 250.00
Cribbage Board, Continuous Track, Box 30.00
Cribbage Board, Red & Blue, Dovetailed Construction, 5 x 1 3/4 In. 247.00
Croquet, 4 Mallets, 4 Balls, Instructions, Box, 1936 .... 98.00
Croquet, Mallets, Balls & Wickets, 1940 .... 125.00
Crow Hunt, Parker Brothers, Target, 1930 .... 60.00
Dating Game, Hasbro, Board, 1967 .... 30.00
Dewey's Victory, Parker Brothers, Spinner, Box 600.00
Dexterity Puzzle, Beany & Cecil, Pressman, 1961 .... 85.00
Dexterity Puzzle, Boy On Sled, Metal Frame, Glass Front, Germany, 1930s, 1 1/4 In. ... 110.00
Dexterity Puzzle, Fox With Fishing Pole, Metal Frame, Glass Front, 1940s, 1 3/4 In. 77.00
Dexterity Puzzle, Girl With Dog, Metal Frame, Glass Front, Japan, 1950s, 1 1/2 In. 55.00
Dexterity Puzzle, Horace Horsecollar, Tiny Beads Form Image, France, 1930s, 2 1/2 In. .. 77.00
Dexterity Puzzle, Mice In Kitchen, Germany 55.00
Dexterity Puzzle, Zeppelin, Metal Frame, Glass Front, 1930s, 1 1/2 In. 33.00

Dino The Dinosaur, Transogram, Board, 1961 .... 45.00
District Messenger Boy, Lead Figures, McLoughlin, Board, Box 95.00
Dominoes, Black & White Paint, 2 3/4 x 5 1/2 In., 28 Piece 220.00
Dominoes, Bone, Ebony, 28 Tiles, Dice, Box, Sliding Lid, 1880s, 2 1/2 x 7 In. 747.00
Dominoes, Bone, Ebony, Wooden Box 78.00
Dominoes, Wooden, Box, c.1870 .... 375.00
Dr. Doolittle Picture Matching Game, Milton Bradley, Box, 1931, 9 x 11 In. 10.00
Dr. Jekyll & Mr. Hyde, Figural Box, England 150.00
Dream House, Milton Bradley, Board, 1968 .... 105.00
Dukes Of Hazzard, Ideal, Board, 1981 .... 20.00
E.T., Parker Brothers, Card, Box, Unopened, 1982, 4 x 6 In. 15.00
E.T., Transmitter Puzzle, Spaceship, Ghost Costume, Parker Bros., 1982, 9 x 17 In. 12.00
Ed Wynn, Fire Chief, Selchow & Righter, Board, 1937 .... 75.00
Electric Horserace, Pressman Toy Co., 1950s 95.00
Electric Whiz Raceway, Electric Game Co., Inc., Holyoke, Mass., 1950s 40.00
Electronic Radar Search, Ideal, Board, Box, 1967 .... 45.00
Elvis King Of Rock, Lee/Raymond, Board, Box, 1978 .... 25.00
Emergency, Milton Bradley, Parker Brothers, 1973 .... 20.00
Escape From Colditz, British, Parker Brothers, 1960s 135.00
Everest, J & L Randall, Ltd., England, 1961 .... 40.00
Family Ties, Applestreet, Board, 1986 .... 30.00
Fascination, Remco, Electric Maze, Battery Operated, Box, 1961 .... 80.00
Fast Mail Railroad Game, Milton Bradley, Board, 1930s 170.00
Figure, Shooting Gallery, Ram Running, Iron, White Paint, 9 In. 415.00
Figure, Shooting Gallery, Rooster, Iron, 4 5/8 In., Pair 55.00
Finance, Parker Brothers, Board, 1958 .... 30.00
Fireball XL5, Milton Bradley, Board, 1964 .... 30.00
Flip-A-Lid, Hassenfeld Bros., 1950s 30.00
Flying Aces, Selchow & Righter, Board, c.1940 .... 185.00
Flying Nun, Milton Bradley, Board, 1968 .... 40.00
Flying The Beam, Game Of Aerial Transport, Parker Brothers, Board, Box, 1940s 50.00
Forest Friends, Milton Bradley, 1956 .... 30.00
Funky Phantom, Hanna-Barbera, Milton Bradley, Board, Box, 1971, 8 x 16 In. 24.00
Game Box, Chess, Cribbage, Walnut, Maple, Drawer Holds Game Pieces, 3 5/8 x 15 In. .. 335.00
Game Of Base Ball, Spinning Wheels For Batter & Pitcher, McLoughlin, 1886 .... 1375.00
Game Of Chance, Monte Carlo, Reverse Painted Glass Top, 12 x 14 In. 308.00
Game Of The States, Milton Bradley, 1960 .... 40.00
Game Of The States, Milton Bradley, 2nd Edition, 1940 .... 55.00
Gang Busters, Target Game, Tin, Trap Doors, Original Gun, 1940 .... 180.00
Gee-Wiz Horse Race, Wood & Tin, 6 Horses, 10 x 29 In. 478.00
General Douglas MacArthur, 1974 .... 55.00
General Hospital, Cardinal Industries, Board, 1982 .... 40.00
Get The Message, Milton Bradley, Board, 1964 .... 30.00
Godfather, Family Games Inc., Board, 1971 .... 22.00
Going To Jerusalem, Parker Brothers, Board, 1955 .... 100.00
Gold Fever, Idea Makers, Inc., 1975 .... 40.00
Gracie Allen Murder Case, 1939 .... 1000.00
Grande Auto Race, Atkins & Co., Board, 1920s 65.00
Gray Ghost, Transogram, Board, 1958 .... 60.00
Great Family Amusement, Dart Gun, With Harmless Pistol, Elastic Tip Co., 1890s 130.00
Great Stampede West, Delight, Dallas, Texas, 1981 .... 35.00
Green Ghost, Transogram, Board, 1965 .... 40.00 to 65.00
Happy Days, Parker Brothers, Board, 1976 .... 20.00
Hardy Boys, Milton Bradley, Board, TV Show, Board, 1969 .... 65.00
Hats Off Bowling Game, Transogram, Box 75.00
Hey, Hey The Monkees, Board 115.00
Hi-Ho Cherry-O, Whiteman, 1960 .... 30.00
Hi-Seas, General Printing Corp., 1940 .... 45.00
Hialeah, Milton Bradley, 1930s 115.00
High Spirits With Calvin & Colonel, Milton Bradley, Board, 1962 .... 70.00
Hit The Beach, Milton Bradley, 1965 .... 50.00
Hokum, Parker Brothers, Card, 1927 .... 35.00
Hoop-O-Loop, Target Shooting, 6 Brass Rings, Tin Lithograph, Wolverine, 1925 .... 325.00

Horse Race, 9 Horses On Track, Hand Crank, Mahogany Case, 20th Century, 20 x 11 In. . . 1150.00
Horse Racing, 12 Painted Wood Horses, Double Track, Box, French, c.1900 . . . . 880.00
Horse Racing, 12 Wooden Horses, Painted, Double Track, Pine Box, Patented 1899 . . . . . 800.00
Horses, All Far, 1929 . . . . 55.00
Huckle-Chuck, 3 Carnival Games, Transogram, Box, 1961, 32 In. 150.00
Huckleberry Hound, Milton Bradley, Board, 1981 . . . . 20.00
Hunt For Red October, TSR, 1988 . . . . 20.00
Illya Kuryakin, Milton Bradley, Card, 1966 . . . . 20.00
International Derby Horserace Gambling, Gotham Pressed Steel Co., 1933 . . . . 125.00
Ipcress File, Milton Bradley, 1966 . . . . 70.00
Jack & The Beanstalk Adventure, Transogram, Board, 1957 . . . . 20.00
James Bond 007 Assault Game, Victory Games, 1961 . . . . .55.00 to 60.00
Jeu De Course, Horse Racing, Mechanical, Box, 1900, 7 3/4 x 21 In. 305.00
Jigsaw Puzzle, Blend Of Beauty, Elvgren, 1940, 400 Piece 30.00
Jigsaw Puzzle, Bugs Bunny Licking Lollipop, 63 Piece, Box, 1960, 7 x 9 1/2 In. 15.00
Jigsaw Puzzle, Charlie's Angels, Box 30.00
Jigsaw Puzzle, David Cassidy, Whitman, 224 Piece 50.00
Jigsaw Puzzle, Dennis The Menace, Box, 1960s 10.00
Jigsaw Puzzle, Evel Knievel 35.00
Jigsaw Puzzle, Flintstones, Pebbles Riding Dino, Frame Tray, 1963, 11 1/2 x 14 1/2 In. . . 18.00
Jigsaw Puzzle, Grim Outlook, Portrait Of Blackfoot Chief, Winold Reiss, Box 690.00
Jigsaw Puzzle, Huckleberry Hound, Painting Nautical Buoy, Whitman, 1960s, 7 x 9 In. . . 15.00
Jigsaw Puzzle, Hughes Oil Co., Paper Lithograph On Wood, Box, 11 x 3 1/4 In. 240.00
Jigsaw Puzzle, James Bond, Goldfinger, Box, 1965 . . . . 50.00
Jigsaw Puzzle, Journey To The Moon, Astronaut, Time, Inc., 1969, 500 Piece, 8 x 11 In. . . 8.00
Jigsaw Puzzle, King Leonardo & His Short Subjects, Frame Tray, Jaymar, 1961 . . . . 19.00
Jigsaw Puzzle, Marx Brothers, Can, Unopened 15.00
Jigsaw Puzzle, Michael Jackson, Colorforms, Shrink Wrap, 1984, 12 x 17 In. 25.00
Jigsaw Puzzle, Peanuts, Lucy & Charlie Brown With Football, 1978, 100 Piece 14.00
Jigsaw Puzzle, Peanuts, Lucy Jumping Rope, Wooden, Playschool, 1952, 11 1/2 x 9 In. . . 20.00
Jigsaw Puzzle, Punch & Judy, Frame, 1950 . . . . 15.00
Jigsaw Puzzle, Snoopy & Woodstock, Pressed Wood, Playskool, 11 1/2 x 9 1/2 In. 23.00
Jigsaw Puzzle, Super Six, Cartoon Crimefighters, Whitman, Box, 1969, 8 x 11 In. 12.00
Jimmy The Greek, Poker Dice Game, Aurora, Box, 1974 . . . . 40.00
Kentucky Derby, Whitman, Metal Pieces, Board, 1938 . . . . 25.00
Kicker & Catcher, Wooden Case, Cast & Painted Parts, 17 1/2 In. 690.00
King Kong, Ideal, Board, 1976 . . . . 32.00
Knight Rider, Parker Brothers, Board, 1983 . . . . 20.00
Krull, Parker Brothers, Board, 1983 . . . . 20.00
Lai-Shai, Karco, Inc., 1943 . . . . 50.00
Last Straw, Camel With Baskets Strapped On, Schaper, 1960s 35.00
Laugh-In's Squeeze Your Bippy, Hasbro, Board, 1968 . . . . 60.00
Lippy The Lion, Hanna-Barbera, Transogram, Box, Board, 1962, 8 x 15 In. . . . . .38.00 to 60.00
Love Boat, Unigame, 1980 . . . . 20.00
Luck, National Assoc. Service, Toledo, Ohio, 1943 . . . . 40.00
Mad Magazine, Parker Brothers, Board, Box, 1979, 9 x 18 In. 25.00
Mah-Jongg, Brass Fittings, Wooden Box 350.00
Mah-Jongg, Ivory & Bamboo Pieces, Dragon On Leatherette Case, 1920s, 9 x 6 1/2 In. . . . 88.00
Mah-Jongg, Ivory & Bamboo, Elaborate Case 500.00
Mail Express, McLoughlin, Box, 1890s 1100.00
Major League Indoor Base Ball, Philadelphia Game Manufacturing Co., Oak Case 1725.00
Man From U.N.C.L.E. Game, Napoleon Solo On Box, Card, 1965 . . . . 40.00
Mansion Of Happiness, Ives, Board, Lithographic Figures, Label, 1864 . . . . 259.00
Marathon Game, Sports Game Co., Lancaster, Pa., 1978 . . . . 20.00
Margie, Milton Bradley, Board, 1961 . . . . 20.00
Masterpiece, Art Auction Game, Parker Brothers, Board, 1970 . . . . 40.00
Meet The Missus, Sponsor, Fitzpatrick Bros., Radio Premium, 1937 . . . . 65.00
Miami Vice, Pepperlane, Board, 1984 . . . . 20.00
Mighty Mouse Playhouse Rescue, Harett-Gilman, Board, 1956 . . . . 75.00
Monopoly, John Waddinton Ltd., English Version, 1961 . . . . 55.00
Monster Squad, Milton Bradley, Board, 1977 . . . . 65.00
Mork & Mindy, Parker Brothers, Board, 1979 . . . . 30.00
Mother Hubbard's Party Game, Forbes Co., Boston 880.00

Movie Millions, Movie Stars On Box, Transogram, Board, 1938 .... 110.00
Mr. Magoo, Toykraft, UPA Pictures, Inc., Box, 1964, 9 1/2 x 18 1/2 In. 35.00
Mr. Ree, Selchow & Righter, Board, 1946 .... 25.00
Murder She Wrote, Jessica Fletcher On Cover, Warren, Board, 1985 .... 28.00
My Favorite Martian, Transogram, Bill Bixby & Ray Walston, Board, 1963 .... 50.00
National Base Ball Game, Marbles, 2-Level Field, Box, 19 x 23 In. 435.00
Newlywed Game, 3rd Edition, Hasbro Ind., Board, Box, 1969 .... 35.00
Nine-Pins, Grumpy Vegetable Figures, Live In Cabbage, Tomato Ball 2310.00
Nurses, Ideal, TV Show, 1963 .... 75.00
Official Baseball, Action Photographs, Box, Milton Bradley, 1969 .... 125.00
Old Maid, Built-Rite, No. 440, Card 20.00
Old Maid, Whitman, No. 4109, Card 18.00
Omnibus, Die Cut Inserts Of Interlocking Passengers, J. Pelling, c.1910, 35 x 25 In. 125.00
Pachinko, Electric, Wood, Chrome, Brass, Polychrome, Nishijin, Japan, 22 x 36 In. 230.00
Parcheesi, Selchow & Righter, Board, 1938 .... 35.00
Park & Shop, Traffic Game Co., Allentown, Pa., Board, 1952 .... 170.00
PDQ, Milton Bradley, TV Game Show, 1960s 50.00
Perry Mason Game, Transogram, Paisano Productions, Box, 1958 .... 45.00 to 75.00
Picture Lotto, McLaughlin Bros., 1888 .... 316.00
Pink Panther, Warren Paper Products Co., Board, Box, 1977, 9 x 17 In. 20.00
Pirate & Traveller, Milton Bradley, Board, 1936 .... 60.00
Pirate Plunder, All-Fair, 1950s 40.00
Pirates & Travelers, Board, Tri-Fold, Box, 1911 .... 120.00
Pitch-A-Ring, Milton Bradley, Box 50.00
Poison Ivy, Ideal, Board, 1969 .... 30.00
Poker Chip, Bakelite, Golfer Picture, Red 2.50
Poker Chips, Dogs Playing Cards, Wooden Holder 120.00
Poker Chips, Red, Blue & Butterscotch, Green Bakelite Case 80.00
Police Patrol Action Game, Hasbro, Board, 1950s 100.00
Pollyanna, Parker Bros., 1916 .... 95.00
Poosh-M-Up, Box 27.00
Pop-A-Part, Gun & Darts, Box 100.00
Pot O'Gold, All-Fair, 1950s 40.00
Prince Valiant, Transogram, Board, 1950s 60.00
Pro Football, Milton Bradley, Board, 1964 .... 35.00
Pursuit, Game Makers Inc., Board, 1940s 65.00
Puss In The Corner, Samuel Gabriel & Sons., 1940s 65.00
Quick Draw McGraw Private Eye, Milton Bradley, Box, 1960, 9 1/2 x 19 In. 120.00
Quiz Kids Own Game, Parker Brothers, 1940 .... 20.00
Rack-O, Milton Bradley, 1966 ....22.00 to 25.00
Radio Amateur Hour, Milton Bradley, Board, 1930s ....65.00 to 85.00
Raggedy Ann, Milton Bradley, Board, 1954 .... 55.00
Ranger Commandos, Parker Brothers, Board, 1944 ....40.00 to 70.00
Rifle Target, Dr Pepper, Electronic, Pictures Chuck Connors 35.00
Ring Toss, Folk Art, Carved, 13 x 15 In. 475.00
Ring Toss, Parker Brothers, Box, 1940s 48.00
Ring Toss, Ring-A-Clown, Board, Wood Clown, 4 Wood Rings, Parker, 1921 .... 193.00
Risk, Parker Brothers, Board, 1968 .... 20.00
Road Runner, Milton Bradley, Board, 1968 .... 28.00
Robin Hood, Parker Brothers, Board, 1973 .... 25.00
Robot Sam The Answer Man, Electric, Jacmar, Box, 8 x 10 In. 30.00
Roger Maris Action Baseball, Tin Lithograph, Box 149.00
Rook, Parker Brothers, Dixie Rook Edition, 1913 .... 20.00
Ropes & Ladders, Parker Brothers, Board, Box, 1954 ....25.00 to 28.00
Rumme, Milton Bradley, Card, 1914 .... 38.00
S.W.A.T. Target Set, Box 45.00
Sandlot Slugger, Milton Bradley, Board, 1968 ....30.00 to 32.00
Scoop, Publish Your Own Newspaper, Parker Brothers, Board, 1956 .... 75.00
Secret Of NIMH, Don Bluth Productions Art, Whitman, Board, Box, 1982, 8 x 16 In. ..8.00 to 20.00
Seduction, Createk, Board, 1966 .... 20.00
Sergeant Preston, Milton Bradley, Board, 1963 .... 130.00
Sherlock Holmes, Cadaco, 1982 .... 30.00
Shindig, Remco, Board, 1965 ....50.00 to 65.00

Siege Of Manila, Parker Brothers, Board, Spinner, 4 Metal Ships 288.00
Sinking Of The Titanic, Ideal, 3-Piece Game Board, Box, 1976 .... 30.00
Ski Shot Bagatelle, Model G79, Marx, Box, 1950s, 10 x 9 In. 35.00
Skirmish, Milton Bradley, Board, 1975 .... 25.00
Skittles Set, Figural, Soldier, Carved & Painted, Box, 3 3/8 In., 9 Piece 120.00
Skittles Set, Rabbit, Standing On Bright Blue Base, Wooden, Green Wagon, 1910, 6 In. . . 460.00
Smurf Chase, Gargamel & Trapped Smurf, Plastic, Galoob, Box, 1983, 3 3/4 x 4 x 10 In. . 40.00
Snagglepuss, Transogram, Board, 1961 .... 45.00
Snoopy & Red Baron, Skill & Action Game, Milton Bradley, Box, 1970 .... 25.00
Snow White & The Seven Dwarfs, Cadaco, Board, 1977 .... 20.00
Sonar Sub Hunt Naval Battle, Plastic, Battery Operated, Mattel, 1961 .... 50.00
Space Target, Tin Lithograph Board, Spring Loaded Gun, Box, 1950s, 23 1/4 x 15 In. ... 100.00
Spiderman, Web-Spinning Action, Box 75.00
Starsky & Hutch, Milton Bradley, Board, 1977 .... 38.00
State Fair, Bagatelle, Marx, Box 85.00
Steve Allen's Qubila, International Word Game, 1955 .... 45.00
Steve Canyon, Lowell, Board, 1959 .... 50.00
Stock Market Game, Avalon Hill, Bookcase, Sealed, 1970 .... 22.00
Strat-O-Matic Baseball, Board, 1988 ....30.00 to 32.00
Strategy, Game Of Armies, Corey Games, 1945 .... 150.00
Strategy, Milton Bradley, 1967 .... 40.00
Strength Tester, Uncle Same, Painted, Cast Iron, Oak, Chicago, Illinois, c.1915, 67 In. . . 16100.00
Superman Ii, Milton Bradley, Board, 1981 .... 20.00
Swayze, Milton Bradley, Board, 1955 .... 30.00
Tank Battle, Milton Bradley, Board, 1975 ....50.00 to 60.00
Tantalizer, Northern Signal Co., Board, 1965 .... 75.00
Target, Gallery, Rooster, Cast Iron, 4 1/2 In., Pair 75.00
Target, Shooting Gallery, Cast Iron, Bear, Marked H.C. Evans & Co., 5 1/4 In. 110.00
Target, Shooting Gallery, Cowboy, Steel, Cast Iron, 1930-1940, 53 In. 9725.00
Target, Shooting Gallery, Figural Donkey, Kicks When Hit, Steel, 24 x 30 In. 1760.00
Tarzan To The Rescue, Milton Bradley, Board, 1977 .... 20.00
Tee Off, New Parlor Game, Margal Co., Card, 1954 .... 45.00
Ten Little Niggers, Parker Brothers, 6 x 4 5/8 In. 175.00
Terrytoons Mighty Mouse, Milton Bradley, Box, 1978, 8 x 15 1/2 In. 20.00
Three Chipmunks Cross Country, Hassenfield Bros., 1960 .... 45.00
Time Tunnel, Ideal, Board, 1966 .... 125.00
Tom & Jerry, Milton Bradley, Board, 1977 .... 20.00
Touring, Milton Bradley 10.00
Tru-Action Electric Horse Race, Cardboard, Metal Playing Pieces, Model 525 .... 300.00
Tumble Bug, Racing Game, Schaper, Box 40.00
TV Guide TV Game, Trivia Inc., 1984 .... 30.00
Twilight Zone, Ideal, Board, 1964 .... 250.00
Uncle Jim's Question Bee, Toy Creations, Board, 1938 .... 70.00
Undersea World Of Jacques Cousteau, Parker Brothers, Board, 1968 .... 20.00
Up & Down Ladder, Spear Company 100.00
Visit Of Santa Claus, McLoughlin Brothers, Board, 1899 .... 1815.00
Wacky Races, Milton Bradley, 1969 .... 35.00
Waltons, Faces Of Family On Box Top, Milton Bradley, Board, 1974 ....20.00 to 38.00
Welcome Back Kotter, Milton Bradley, Card, 1976 .... 30.00
Wham-O! True Putt Trainer!, Plastic, Box, 1950-1960 .... 25.00
Wheel, Race-Horse Scenes, Reverse-Painted, Tripod Stand, 1880-1890 .... 5225.00
Whirling Jockey Race, 3 Lithographed Horses, Round Track, Box, McDowell, 9 3/4 In. . . 315.00
White Shadow Basketball, Cadaco, TV Show, Board, 1970s 90.00
Who Did It, Gardiner Games, Chicago, Ill., 1950s 30.00
Who's Afraid Of The Big Bad Wolf, Parker Brothers, 1933 .... 145.00
Wicket Golf, Box, 1930 .... 35.00
Wild Kingdom, Teaching Concepts, Board & Cards, TV Game, 1977 .... 22.00
Wings Air Mail, Parker Brothers, Card, 1920s 45.00
Wink Tennis, Tiddlywink Table Tennis, Transogram, Box, 1950s 40.00
Winnie-The-Pooh, Parker Brothers, 1933 .... 35.00
Wizard Of Oz, Cadaco, Board, 1974 .... 20.00
World Series Ball Game, Board, 1914-1915 .... 240.00
Wow-Pillow Fight Game For Girls, Milton Bradley, Board, 1964 .... 32.00

Game Plate, Birds Set,
Raspberries, Haviland, 2 Platters,
12 Plates, Plate 7 5/8 In.

Game Plate, Fish Set,
Orange & Gold Border,
Platter, Haviland,
6 Plates, Plate 9 In.

Yacht Race, J. Presman & Co., 1940s	95.00
Yacht Race, Parker Brothers, 1961	75.00
Yankee Trader, Corey Games, Board, 1941	120.00
Yoda The Jedi-Master Game, Kenner, 1981	40.00
Yogi Bear, Milton Bradley, Board, 1971	20.00
Yogi Bear Rummy, Ed-U-Cards, Card, Box, 1961, 2 x 3 In.	14.00

GAME PLATES are plates of any make decorated with pictures of birds, animals, or fish. The game plates usually came in sets consisting of twelve dishes and a serving platter. These sets were most popular during the 1880s.

Bird, Butterfly, Leaf & Blossom, Haviland, 7 1/2 x 7 1/2 In., Pair	100.00
Birds, Blue Border, Bavaria, 11 In., Pair	40.00
Birds, C.T., 8 1/2 In., 4 Piece	55.00
Birds Set, Raspberries, Haviland, 2 Platters, 12 Plates, Plate 7 5/8 In. ....*Illus*	2420.00
Deer, Rabbits & Fox, Pradet, Coronet, 10 In., Set Of 3	100.00
Elk, Magenta & Gold Border, STW Bavaria, 10 1/2 In.	65.00
Fish Set, Orange & Gold Border, Platter, Haviland, 6 Plates, Plate 9 In. ....*Illus*	495.00
Platter, 2 Pheasant, Carnation-McNicol, 15 In.	16.00
Platter, Pheasant, Z.S. & Co., 17 1/2 In.	100.00
Trout & Mallard, Germany, 8 In., Pair	27.00

GARDEN FURNISHINGS have been popular for centuries. The stone or metal statues, wire, iron, or rustic furniture, urns and fountains, sundials, and small figurines are included in this category. Many of the metal pieces have been made continuously for years.

Aquarium, Paneled Side, Central Spout, 3 Cranes Base, J.W. Fiske, 1880s, 44 1/2 In.	3450.00
Basket, Cast Stone, Flowers & Fruit, Neoclassical, Italy, 16 x 11 In., Pair	240.00
Bench, Angels Cutout On Back Rest	1540.00
Bench, Beaux Art Design, Heavy White Paint, Arms, Cast Iron, 46 In.	660.00
Bench, Cast Iron, Urn Shaped Sides, Early 20th Century, 24 x 19 1/2 In.	105.00
Bench, Double Arched Top, Down Swept Arms, Pierced & Arched Apron, Iron, 62 In.	1045.00
Bench, Double, Scrolled Arms, Woven Flat Iron Seat, 26 x 56 In.	715.00
Bench, Foliate, Curved Back, Cabriole Legs, Cast Iron, Late 19th Century, 36 3/4 In.	188.00
Bench, Foliate, Scrolled Carved Crest, Rectangular Seat, Marble, 31 In.	3450.00
Bench, Grape & Leaf Design, Iron, Pair	495.00
Bench, Iron, Wooden Slat Back, Seat, Scrolled Arms, 33 x 98 x 31 In.	2070.00
Bench, Out-Scrolled Slatted Construction, Splayed Legs, Iron, c.1850, 32 x 79 1/2 In.	1025.00
Bench, Painted Cast Iron, 43 In., Pair	3737.00
Bench, Reticulated, Marble, Italy, 1890-1910, 42 x 65 x 27 In.	11192.50
Bench, Serpentine Crest, Strapwork Seat, Leaf Form Legs, Cast Iron, 40 In., Pair	1955.00
Bench, Traces Of Red Lacquer, Chinese, Elm, 16 1/2 x 50 In.	770.00
Bench, White Paint, Stylized Panels, Dragon Legs, Semi-Circular, Cast Iron, 44 In.	1150.00
Birdbath, 4 Perched Marble Birds, Square Foot, Marble, 5 1/2 In., Pair	75.00
Birdbath, Egg & Dart Basin, Foliate & Floral Standard, Paw Feet, Plumbed, 65 In.	3450.00
Birdbath, Georgian, Dove On Edge Of Basin, England, Cast Lead, 4 x 14 1/2 In.	220.00

Birdbath, Iron, Piecrust Bowl, 2 Birds On Rim, Victorian, 38 x 22 In. 485.00
Boy, Holding Grapes, Girl, Holding Flowers, Bacchanalian, Cast Lead, 18 & 19 In., Pair . 490.00
Chair, Box Form, Crisscross Back, Painted, Iron, 31 x 24 1/2 In., Pair 275.00
Chair, Fern Design, Painted, Cast Iron, 19th Century, Arms 303.00
Chair, Floral Design, Painted White, Cast Aluminum, 20th Century 200.00
Chair, Richard Schultz, Woven Mesh Sling Seat, Painted Aluminum Frame, 4 Piece 805.00
Chair Set, Backrest Formed As Snail Shell, Scrolled Arms, Wrought Iron, Painted, 6 . . . . 9775.00
Chair Set, Shaped Back, Foliate Legs, Pierced Foliage & Scrolls, Cast Iron, Painted, 6 . . . 1495.00
Cistern, 12 Signs Of Zodiac, Lion Supports, Lead, 19th Century, 72 In. 4312.00
Fence, Victorian, Cast Metal, 20th Century, 35 1/2 x 61 x 21 In. 272.00
Figure, 3 Putti, Gamboling, Louis XVI, White Paint, Cast Stone, France, 22 In. 151.00
Figure, Beer-Making Elves, Germany, Cast Stone, 20 x 20 1/2 In., 4 Piece 780.00
Figure, Boy, Playing A Flute, Cast Lead, 24 1/2 In. 316.00
Figure, Boy, With Basket Of Fruit, Boy With Cinched Coat, Cast Stone, 28 In., Pair 1265.00
Figure, Child, Seated On Edge Of Shell, Bird Perched On Rim, Cast Lead, 16 In. 430.00
Figure, Child, Seated, Cast Stone, 20 In. 92.00
Figure, Child, Theatrical Costume, Plumed Headdress, Stone, 55 In. 8625.00
Figure, Child, With Grapes, Cast Lead, 29 1/2 In. 489.00
Figure, Diana De Versailles, Fiske, 60 In. 8625.00
Figure, Dog, Dalmatian, Cast Iron, Painted, 30 x 50 In., Pair 9775.00
Figure, Dragon Gargoyle, Limestone, 41 In. 6325.00
Figure, Eagle, Pedestal, Lead, c.1900, 52 In. 3162.00
Figure, Falcon, Lead, 22 1/2 In., Pair 5462.00
Figure, Frog, Leaping, Green Patina, Bronze, 28 1/2 In. 575.00
Figure, Frog, Stone, 20th Century, 21 In. 3162.00
Figure, Frontiersman, Antonio Bonazza, 18th Century, 58 In. 5750.00
Figure, Gnome, Seated On Turtle, 31 In. 4025.00
Figure, Greyhound, Lying, Ecru, Plinth Base, Cast Stone, 21 x 44 In., Pair 1570.00
Figure, Greyhound, Reclining, Iron, Painted White, Victorian, 17 3/4 In., Pair 3165.00
Figure, Greyhounds, Sitting, Cast Lead, 24 1/4 In., Pair 575.00
Figure, Lamb, Cast Lead, 18 1/2 In. 290.00
Figure, Lion, Gray, Carved, Sandstone, 13 1/2 In. 825.00
Figure, Pan, Concrete, 28 In. 82.00
Figure, Pan, Playing His Pipes, Cast Lead, 30 & 37 1/2 In., Pair 1090.00
Figure, Peacock, Standing, Feathers Spread, Lead, 24 In., Pair 2300.00
Figure, Putto, Winged Figure With Arms Upraised, Lead, 25 1/4 In. 920.00
Figure, Rabbit, Cast Iron, c.1900, 12 In. 365.00
Figure, Rabbit, Gray Paint, Pink Eyes, White Tail, Hubley, 1920, 11 5/8 In. 275.00
Figure, Rabbit, Sitting, White, Black Spots, Pink Ears, Iron 350.00
Figure, Sphinx, Reclining, Composition Stone, 20th Century, 45 In., Pair 4600.00
Figure, Stag, White Paint, Rectangular Base, White Paint, Iron, 62 1/4 In. 3850.00
Figure, Venus, Marble, 51 In. 6900.00
Figure, Woman, Stone, Mid 18th Century, Antonio Bonazza, 57 1/2 In. 3450.00
Figure, Young Bacchus, Seated On Urn, Lion's Mask, Early 20th Century, 56 In. 6700.00
Figure, Young Boy Riding Tortoise, Holding Conch Shell, Marble, 29 In. 4887.00
Figure, Young Child, Autumn, Holding Sheaf Of Wheat, Scythe, Lead, 30 In. 920.00
Finial, Gate Post, Cast Stone, c.1930, 15 x 16 In., Pair 895.00
Fountain, 2 Children Embracing Dolphin, Stone, Plumbed, 53 In. 2300.00
Fountain, 2 Putti, Bronze, F.A. Jelaco, Mid-1900s, 24 In. 7200.00
Fountain, Boy Holding Goose, Mouth Plumbed, Cast Iron, 30 In. 2070.00
Fountain, Boy, Holding Goose, White Paint, Iron, 33 In. 1695.00
Fountain, Boy, On Dolphin, Standing On Crab With A Turtle, Bronze, 54 1/2 In. 1650.00
Fountain, Boy, On Rocky Base, Holding Umbrella, Plumbed., Lead, 16 In. 2875.00
Fountain, Egg-And-Dart, Font, Cherub Embracing Dolphin, Marble, 1870s, 72 1/2 In. . . . 5750.00
Fountain, Foliate Column, Turtles, Frogs, Rocks On Base, Cast Iron, Fiske, 1850s, 44 In. . 2860.00
Fountain, Girl Partially Draped, Cast Iron, c.1850, 46 1/2 In. 2860.00
Fountain, Neoclassical, 4 Semicircular Leaf Bowls, Pedestal, White Marble, 38 In. 7560.00
Fountain, Putti, Holding Half Shell On Head, Grapevine Draped, Cast Stone, 49 In. 2057.00
Fountain, Renaissance, Verdigris Patina, Tripodal Dolphin Base, Bronze, 57 x 25 In. 1452.00
Fountain, Shell Top, Cherub, Basin & Column, 8 Sides, Cast Iron, 82 In., 3 Piece 495.00
Fountain, Wall, Lion's Head Spigot, Flat Sided Fluted Urn Basin, 54 x 27 x 14 In. 725.00
Fountain, Wall, Shell Flanked By Putti, Bronze, 28 x 51 In. 1610.00

Fountain, Young Boy Holding Goose, Painted White Iron, 19th Century, 33 In. 1090.00
Fountain, Young Boy, Crane On A Rock, Turtle, Large Fish Below, Bronze, 55 In. 1265.00
Furniture Set, Victorian, Wire Frame, Child's, 3 Piece 645.00
Gate, Cast Shield, Hinges & Latch, Shaped Label, Cincinnati Iron Fence Co., 46 x 31 In. . 365.00
Gate, Deco, Pierced Allover With Scrolls & Foliage, Wrought Iron, 1920s, 84 x 7 In. 3450.00
Gate, Fence, Cast Finials, Painted, Shield, Label Cincinnati Iron Fence Co., 46 x 31 In. . . 360.00
Gate, Leaded Glass & Jewel Center, Iron, Pair 1800.00
Gate Weight, Iron & Lead, Blacksmith Made, 18th Century 225.00
Gazebo, Supported By Classical Columns, Wrought Iron, 12 x 12 Ft. 2175.00
Hitching Post, Dog Head, Single Ring, Fluted Column, Iron, Square Base, 34 1/2 In. 825.00
Hitching Post, Gooseneck, Fluted Base, 3 Pear-Like Rings, Iron, 60 1/4 In. 1210.00
Hitching Post, Horse Head, 6-Sided Column, Black Flat Paint, Iron, 43 1/2 In. 440.00
Hitching Post, Horse Head, Iron, Mid-19th Century, 12 In. 220.00
Hitching Post, Horse Head, Lion Heads On Base, Cast Iron, J.W. Fiske, 44 In. 1210.00
Hitching Post, Horse Head, On Lion's Head Flute Column, 5 Rings, Iron, 54 In. 440.00
Hitching Post, Jockey, Black Child, Outstretched Arm, Ring In Hand, 37 In. . . . . .245.00 to 895.00
Hitching Post, Jockey, Black Man On Pedestal, Iron, 12 In. 33.00
Hitching Post, Jockey, From Admiral Perry's Front Yard, Iron, Fiske, 43 In. 1925.00
Hitching Post, Jockey, Green & Yellow, Iron, 46 1/2 In. 220.00
Hitching Post, Jockey, Lawn, Cast Iron, 27 x 18 In. 525.00
Hitching Post, Tree With Vines, White & Green Repaint, Iron, 64 In. 440.00
Jardiniere, Grape & Foliage Motif, Cast Iron, 20 In., Pair 77.00
Jardiniere, Neoclassical, Cover, Fluted, Swag Draped, 21 x 12 1/2 In., Pair 545.00
Jardiniere, Pierced Allover With Scrolls & Flower Heads, Scrolled Legs, Iron, 17 In. 3220.00
Lawnmower, Green Handle, Chrome Motor, Light At Tip, 1930s 775.00
Pagoda, 5 Tiers, Square Tapered Base, China, Carved Stone, 65 In. 575.00
Patio Set, Lily Pad Table, Iron, 7 Piece 440.00
Pedestal, Gnome, Cast Iron, 48 In. 385.00
Planter, Flower Basket Form, Black, Cast Iron, 15 In., Pair 220.00
Planter, Leaf & Grape Design, Rectangular, Cast Iron, 25 1/2 In., Pair 110.00
Planter, Lotus Form, Indian, Marble, 13 In., Pair 6900.00
Planter, Pierced Scrolled Frame, 4 Pots, Spiral Twist Arch, Hanging, Iron, 66 In. 2875.00
Planter, Tiered, 4 Graduated Baskets, Polychrome & Wirework, 65 x 38 In. 515.00
Seat, 5-Toed Dragon Design, Turquoise Ground, 18 1/2 In., Pair 430.00
Seat, Grape Leaf & Cluster Design, Cast Metal, Late 19th-Early 20th Century 45.00
Seat, Red Clay, Oriental Style, Mottled Blue & Black Glaze, 19 1/2 In. 160.00
Seat, Rose Medallion, Floral & Insect Design, 19 x 13 In. 200.00
Seat, Rose Medallion, Reticulated, c.1900, 19 1/2 In. 695.00
Set, Bench & Chair, Cast Iron, Scrolls, Portrait, Early 20th Century 1045.00
Set, Table & 4 Chairs, Rose Design, Plate Glass Table Top, Iron, 29 x 48 1/2 In. 192.00
Settee, Double Hooped Chair Back, Scalloped Apron, 41 x 54 In. 220.00
Settee, Fern Design, Wooden Slat Seat, Cast Iron, 59 x 35 x 23 In. 450.00
Settee, Grapevine Design, Pierced Seat, Cast Iron, Late 19th Century, 33 x 15 In. 230.00
Settee, Verdigris Finish, Openwork Panels, Suns, Wrought Iron, 38 In. 330.00
Settee, Victorian, Twisted Wire, 38 In. 495.00
Settee, White Paint, Steel, Wire, 37 In. 300.00
Settee & Chair Set, Grape Design, Cast Iron, 3 Piece 195.00
Sphere, Arrow Design, Turned Round Base, Wrought Iron, 33 1/4 x 23 1/8 In. 920.00
Spigot, Nozzle Formed As Dolphin, Pump Cast With Duck, Plaque, 66 In. 1265.00
Sprinkler, Black Boy, Brass Head, Hose, Metal Spike Base, 39 x 10 In. 260.00
Sprinkler, Little Girl, Holding Umbrella, W.D. Willen Mfg. Company, 51 In. 575.00
Sprinkler, Turtle Form 395.00
Sundial, Inlaid Granite, 1740s 950.00
Sundial, Inscribed Tell Ye Howres Amiddst Ye Flowrs, Bronze, Square, 1912, 14 x 7 In. . . 330.00
Table, 3 Dolphins Supporting Glass Top, Bronze, 29 x 50 In. 5462.00
Table, Dolphins, Flacons & Serpents, Terra-Cotta, 22 x 23 In. 1150.00
Table, Marble Top, Stamp Of Godin, Cast Iron, 28 x 20 In. 240.00
Table, Nesting, Lilypad Form, Scrolling Base, 22 In., Pair 165.00
Table, Pierced Foliate Top, Cabriole Legs, Cast Iron 440.00
Tree, Blossoming, Scrolled Branches, Lily Pad Base, Bulbs In Nozzles, Metal, 89 In. 9775.00
Urn, 2 Handles, Green, Iron, France, Late 19th Century, 17 3/4 x 24 x 19 In. 363.00
Urn, Campana, Cast Iron, 12 x 10 1/2 In., Pair 270.00

Urn, Campana, Cast Iron, 31 In., Pair	805.00
Urn, Campana, Grotesque Masks, Victorian, Cast Iron, 30 x 22 In.	970.00
Urn, Floral Design, Out-Turned Rim, 2 Handles, Terra-Cotta, Italy, 19th Century, 18 In.	175.00
Urn, Garland Design, Out-Turned Rim, Terra-Cotta, Italy, 19th Century, 19 1/2 In.	140.00
Urn, Griffins, 2 Handles, Out-Turned Rim, Terra-Cotta, Italy, 19th Century, 23 In.	175.00
Urn, Inverted Bell Form, Out Turned Rim, Meandering Floral Design, Marble, 23 In.	1380.00
Urn, Leaf Design, Scrolled Handles, Socle Base, Cast Iron, 19th Century, 35 In., Pair	2080.00
Urn, Leaf Edged Top, Cast Bases, J.W. Fiske, Cast Iron, 24 In., Pair	715.00
Urn, Leaf Relief Design, Lion's Head Handles, Cast Iron, 25 In., Pair	412.00
Urn, Lion Head Handle, Cast Iron, 24 In., Pair	385.00
Urn, Lion, Garland Design, Rectangular, Terra-Cotta, Italy, 19th Century, 9 1/2 In.	125.00
Urn, Marble, 23 1/2 x 21 In., Pair	975.00
Urn, Monument, Green Glaze, Footed, Mediterranean, 29 x 30 In., Pair	1210.00
Urn, Neoclassical, Fluted, Campana, 18 x 15 In., Pair	605.00
Urn, Relief Bands Of Geometric Motifs, Bracket Handles, Bronze, 22 x 21 In., Pair	1610.00
Urn, Relief Figural Design, Cast Iron, 20 In., Pair	245.00
Urn, Scalloped Edge, Black Paint, Cast Iron, 12 In., Pair	275.00
Urn, Stand, Scrolled Foliate Handles, White Paint, Iron, Victorian, 41 In.	345.00
Urn, Stand, Scrolled Handles, Floral Design, Iron, Late 19th Century, 30 x 25 In.	363.00
Urn, Stand, White Paint, Iron, 31 x 19 1/2 In.	665.00
Urn, Terrace, Everted Rim, Geometric Design, 2 Handles, Bronze, 20 In.	750.00
Urn, White Paint, Iron, 34 In.	330.00
Urn, White Paint, Iron, 37 In.	385.00
Urn, White, France, 13 x 18 In., Pair	605.00
Vase, 2 Handles, Terra-Cotta, England, Regency, 19 3/4 x 14 1/2 In., Pair	544.50
Vase, 2 Handles, Terra-Cotta, Regency, 20 x 14 1/2 In., Pair	968.00
Vase, Bacchic High Relief Friezes, 2 Handles, Terra-Cotta, Regency, 18 x 14 In., Pair	395.00
Vase, Campana Form, High Paneled Square Pedestal, Handles, Terra-Cotta, 54 In., Pair	970.00
Vase, Campana, Louis-Philippe, c.1835, 10 1/2 x 6 1/2 In., Pair	355.00
Vase, Iron, Georgian, England, 23 1/4 x 13 In., Pair	905.00
Vase, Louis XVI Style, Satyr Mask Handles, Terra-Cotta, 19 x 19 In., Pair	725.00
Vase, Terra-Cotta, England, Regency, 34 1/2 x 17 In., Pair	1815.00
Vase, Warwick Form, Double Entwined Vine Handles, Terra-Cotta, 20 x 32 In., Pair	968.00

GAUDY DUTCH pottery was made in England for America from about 1810 to 1820. It is a white earthenware with Imari-style decorations of red, blue, green, yellow, and black. Only sixteen patterns of Gaudy Dutch were made: Butterfly, Carnation, Dahlia, Double Rose, Dove, Grape, Leaf, Oyster, Primrose, Single Rose, Strawflower, Sunflower, Urn, War Bonnet, Zinnia, and No Name. Other similar wares are called *Gaudy Ironstone* and *Gaudy Welsh*.

Bowl, Sunflower, 6 1/2 In.	245.00
Coffeepot, Double Rose	2300.00
Coffeepot, Dove	1850.00
Coffeepot, War Bonnet, Red, Orange & Yellow Enamel, 10 In.	220.00
Creamer, Carnation, 4 1/2 In.	1375.00
Creamer, Dove, 4 1/4 In.	1650.00
Creamer, Single Rose, 4 1/2 In.	660.00
Cup & Saucer, Double Rose, Handleless	385.00 to 440.00
Cup & Saucer, Grape	410.00
Cup & Saucer, Grape, Handleless	575.00
Cup & Saucer, War Bonnet, Handleless	550.00 to 660.00
Cup Plate, Grape, 3 3/8 In.	1540.00
Cup Plate, War Bonnet, 3 7/8 In.	1540.00
Plate, Butterfly, 9 3/4 In.	4200.00 to 4300.00
Plate, Carnation, 6 1/4 In.	220.00
Plate, Carnation, 10 In.	1250.00
Plate, Carnation, Paneled, 8 1/4 In.	45.00
Plate, Double Rose, 4 3/8 In.	1210.00
Plate, Double Rose, 7 1/4 In.	440.00
Plate, Double Rose, 10 In.	935.00 to 1250.00
Plate, Dove, 10 In.	4500.00 to 4510.00
Plate, Grape, 5 5/8 In.	440.00

Plate, Grape, 6 In. 625.00
Plate, Grape, 7 1/4 In. 385.00
Plate, Grape, 8 1/4 In. . . . . .110.00 to 440.00
Plate, Grape, 9 3/4 In. 2310.00
Plate, Single Rose, 6 1/2 In. 440.00
Plate, Sunflower, 8 3/8 In. . . . . .785.00 to 950.00
Plate, Urn, 7 1/2 In. 1870.00
Plate, Urn, 9 3/4 In. 187.00
Plate, War Bonnet, 5 1/4 In. 300.00
Plate, War Bonnet, 7 In. 905.00
Plate, War Bonnet, 8 In. . . . . .495.00 to 1250.00
Plate, War Bonnet, 9 1/2 In. . . . . .1100.00 to 1125.00
Plate, Zinnia, 8 1/2 In. 2860.00
Soup, Dish, Butterfly, 8 In. 510.00
Soup, Dish, Single Rose, 10 In. 143.00
Teapot, Dahlia, 6 In. . . . . .12000.00 to 12100.00
Teapot, Single Rose 82.00
Teapot, War Bonnet, 6 In. 665.00
Waste Bowl, Butterfly, 3 3/4 x 6 1/2 In. 3080.00
Waste Bowl, Double Rose, 6 1/4 In. 935.00

GAUDY IRONSTONE is the collector's name for the ironstone wares with the bright patterns similar to Gaudy Dutch. It was made in England for the American market. There may be other examples found in the listing for Ironstone or under the name of the ceramic factory.

Bowl, Fruit, Half-Strawberry Embellished Design, Gilt Luster, 12 1/2 In. 1275.00
Bowl, Vegetable, Ashwood, Oval, 12 In., Pair 315.00
Cup & Saucer, Seaweed In Underglaze Blue 82.00
Dish, Cover, Imari Design, Stone China, 13 1/2 In. 347.00
Dish, Entree, Cover, Gilt Rope Handles, Pedestal, Ashworth 330.00
Plate, Blackberry, E. Walley, Niagara Shape, 9 5/8 In. 192.00
Plate, Carnation, 8 1/4 In. 80.00
Plate, Carnation, 9 1/4 In. 100.00
Plate, Fern & Flower, 8 1/4 In. 80.00
Plate, Fern & Flower, Swag, Walley, 6 Piece 230.00
Plate, Morning Glory, 9 1/4 In. 332.00
Plate, Rabbit, Cricket, 9 3/8 In. 400.00
Plate, Strawberry Panel, 7 1/2 In. 65.00
Plate, Strawberry, Pink & Green Enamel & Luster, 8 3/4 In. 137.00
Plate, Swag, Walley, 6 1/2 In. 10.00
Plate, Toddy, Florals With Eye, Impressed Pearl White, 6 3/8 In. 137.00
Plate, Urn, 8 1/2 In. 130.00
Platter, Floral, Purple, White, 19 5/8 In. 110.00
Platter, Morning Glory, 13 1/2 In. . . . . .413.00 to 605.00
Platter, Overall Floral, Fish-Eye Reserve, 19th Century, 21 In. 770.00
Platter, Polychrome Floral Enameled, Blue Underglaze, Staffordshire, 22 In. 770.00
Platter, Red Transfer, Blue, Derby, 17 1/4 In. 192.00
Platter, Strawberry, 10 1/4 x 13 1/4 In. 850.00
Platter, Strawberry, Red, Pink & Green Enamel & Luster, 13 1/2 In. 770.00
Saucer, Fern & Flower 10.00
Soup, Dish, Blackberry In Underglaze, Walley Paris White Ironstone, 9 5/8 In. 220.00
Soup, Dish, Seaweed, Underglaze, Blue & Red, Green Luster, 10 1/2 In., Pair 270.00
Sugar, Cover 500.00
Tea Set, Fern & Flower Swag, Corn Finial, Walley, 4 Piece 1000.00
Tureen, Sauce, Undertray, Ladle & Cover, 9 1/2 In. 505.00
Waste Bowl, Morning Glory, Copper Luster 55.00

GAUDY WELSH is an Imari-decorated earthenware with red, blue, green, and gold decorations. Most Gaudy Welsh was made in England for the American market. It was made after 1820.

Bowl, Blue Floral, 3 Large Flowers & Leaves, Red & Green Enamel, 10 In. 165.00
Bowl, Blue Transfer, Red Enameling, Transfer Label, 12 x 3 In. 220.00
Bowl, Junket, Grape Leaf Design, 8 1/2 x 5 In. 600.00

Bowl, Punch, Exterior Panels, Flower In Each, Yellow Edge, 10 In.	965.00
Bowl & Pitcher, Tulip Pattern, Miniature, 4 3/8 x 3 7/8 In.	330.00
Creamer, Translucent Porcelain, Gold Luster Over Glaze, 1840s, 4 In.	40.00
Cup, Floral, Oriental Pagoda, Blue With Red & Green Enameling, 3 1/8 In.	357.00
Jug, Faceted, Harlech, Handled, 7 1/4 In.	475.00
Jug, Pouch, Sunflower, Gargoyle Handle, 5 1/2 In.	400.00
Pitcher, Blue Transfer, Red & Green Enamel, Snake Handle, Marked, 9 3/4 In.	275.00
Pitcher, Floral Design, Blue, Red & Green Enamel, Molded, 9 In.	468.00
Pitcher, Floral Transfer, Blue Underglaze, Polychrome Enamel, Pewter Lid, 9 In.	110.00
Pitcher, Floral, 9 1/2 In.	90.00
Pitcher, Milk, Oyster, c.1910, Signed, 7 In.	140.00
Pitcher, Paneled, Dragon Handle, Blue, Red & Green Enamel, 6 1/2 In.	220.00
Pitcher, Paneled, Dragon Handle, Red & Green Enamel, Impressed, 8 In.	685.00
Pitcher, Rosebuds, 9 1/2 In.	110.00
Pitcher, Wash, Earthenware, Luster Trim, 10 1/2 In.	545.00
Platter, Amherst Japan, Blue Transfer, Red & Yellow Enamel, 16 1/2 In.	360.00
Punch Bowl, Balloon Pattern, Red & Green Enamel, Molded Scrolls, 11 x 6 In.	525.00
Punch Bowl, Large Interior Flowers, Footed, 4 1/2 x 9 In.	440.00
Punch Jug, Sunflower, Gargoyle Handle, 5 1/2 In.	400.00
Saucer, Urn, Floral	165.00
Sugar, Cover, Pinwheel, 6 1/2 x 7 In.	425.00
Teapot, Floral, Enamel & Pink Luster	845.00
Tureen, Blue Underglaze, Polychrome Enamel, Transfer Mark, Under Tray, 15 In.	1265.00
Wash Bowl, Floral, 12 In.	265.00

GEISHA GIRL porcelain was made for export in the late nineteenth century in Japan. It was an inexpensive porcelain often sold in dime stores or used as free premiums. Pieces are sometimes marked with the name of a store. Japanese ladies in kimonos are pictured on the dishes. There are over 125 recorded patterns. Borders of red, blue, green, gold, brown, or several of these colors were used. Modern reproductions are being made.

Cracker Jar, Gold & Enamel, Lavender Ground, 7 1/2 In.	115.00

GENE AUTRY was born in 1907. He began his career as the *Singing Cowboy* in 1928. His first movie appearance was in 1934, his last in 1958. His likeness and that of the Wonder Horse, Champion, were used on toys, books, lunch boxes, and advertisements.

Billfold	60.00
Book, 28 Songs, The Oklahoma Yodeling Cowboy, 1934	25.00
Book, Little Golden Book, First Edition, Gene Autry, Rearing Champion, 7 x 8 In.	18.00
Cap Gun	200.00
Chaps, Boys	250.00
Comic Book, Dell, No. 91, 1964	20.00
Game, Bandit Trail, Gene Autry, Smiling In Center Of Game, Kenton, 25 x 25 In.	198.00
Guitar, Case	185.00
Guitar, Guitar-Shaped Box, Raised Graphics, Chord Player Attachment, 33 In.	225.00
Guitar, Signature, All Wood, Box	200.00
Gun, Cast Iron, Holster	500.00
Gun Set, Double Holster, Lesley Henry	295.00
Lunch Box	325.00
Picture, Gene & Champion, Sunbeam Bread Handout, 1950s	10.00
Picture Puzzle, Box	45.00
Poster, Barbed Wire, 1952, One Sheet	55.00
Poster, Indian Territory, 1950, One Sheet	75.00
Poster, Sons Of New Mexico, 1950, Three Sheet	120.00
Program, Boston Garden Rodeo, Featuring Gene Autry, 1948	35.00
Program, Souvenir, Gene Riding His Horse, Champion, 1950s, 8 1/2 x 11 In.	35.00
Record, Album, Western Classics, Vol. 2, 78 RPM, 1949, Set Of 4	65.00
Ring, Brass	95.00
Song Book, Photos, 50 Pages, 1942	65.00
Wristwatch, Six Shooter, Animated Gun, Leather Band	175.00

GIBSON GIRL black-and-blue decorated plates were made in the early 1900s. Twenty-four different 10 1/2-inch plates were made by the Royal Doulton pottery at Lambeth, England. These pictured scenes from the book *A Widow and Her Friends* by Charles Dana Gibson. Another set of twelve 9-inch plates featuring pictures of the heads of Gibson Girls had all-blue decoration. Many other items also pictured the famous Gibson Girl.

Album, Celluloid, Musical, Old Man On The Moon, 1859	2250.00
Book, A Widow & Her Friends, Life Publishing Company	50.00
Plate, And Here Winning New Friends	105.00 to 195.00
Plate, Failing To Find Rest In The Country	228.00
Plate, Finds Exercise Does Not Improve Spirits, Royal Doulton, 1900, 10 1/2 In.	218.00
Plate, Message From The Outside World	153.00
Plate, Miss Babbles Brings A Copy Of The Morning Paper	113.00
Plate, Mr. Waddles Arrives Late & Finds Her Card Filled	195.00 to 203.00
Plate, She Contemplates The Cloister, c.1901, 10 In.	48.00
Plate, She Finds Some Consolation In Her Mirror	235.00
Plate, She Finds That Exercise Does Not Improve Her Spirits	218.00
Plate, They Go Fishing	262.00
Plate, Widow, Mr. Waddles Arrives Late, Finds Card Filled, 10 1/2 In.	205.00
Postcard, Why Do They Call Me A Gibson Girl, Postmark 1923	10.00
Print, Shadow Box Frame, 12 x 14 In.	65.00

GILLINDER pressed glass was first made by William T. Gillinder of Philadelphia in 1863. The company had a working factory on the grounds at the Centennial and made small, marked pieces of glass for sale as souvenirs. They made a variety of decorative glass pieces and tablewares.

GILLINDER

Lincoln, Frosted Glass, Philadelphia Centennial, 1876, 6 In.	155.00
Lion, Frosted Glass, Philadelphia Centennial, 1876, 5 1/2 In.	125.00
Shoe, Philadelphia Centennial, 1876, 6 14 In.	35.00

GIRL SCOUT collectors search for anything pertaining to the Girl Scouts, including uniforms, publications, and old cookie boxes. The Girl Scout movement started in 1912, two years after the Boy Scouts. It began under Juliette Gordon Low of Savannah, Georgia. The first Girl Scout cookies were sold in 1928.

Booklet, 3 Degrees In Hiking, 1920s	15.00
Booklet, Girl Scout Leader's Nature Guide, 1929	25.00
Booklet, Patrols & Their Court Of Honor In Girl Scout Troup, 1929	25.00
First Aid Kit, Wartime Container, Johnson & Johnson, 1942, 5 1/4 x 4 x 11 1/2 In.	40.00
Notebook, Field & Camp, Camp Harmony Notes, Illustrations, 1920s	35.00
Pamphlet, Girl Scout Hike Pack, 1920s	7.00
Pin, Junior Emblem, Gold Metal, 7/8 In. ....*Illus*	10.00
Postcard, British Troop, Girl In Uniform, 1910	100.00
Uniform, Leader's, Green Dress, Overseas Cap, Belt, Buckle, 1940s	50.00

Girl Scout, Pin, Junior Emblem,
Gold Metal, 7/8 In.

When moving, wrap dishes in bubble wrap and pack on edge. If you have no bubble wrap, put each dish in a plastic bag to keep it clean, then wrap in newspaper and pack on edge. Put about 3 inches of paper on the bottom of the carton.

GLASS-ART. Art glass means any of the many forms of glassware made during the late nineteenth or early twentieth century. These wares were expensive and production was limited. Art glass is not the typical commercial glass that was made in large quantities, and most of the art glass was produced by hand methods. Later twentieth-century glass is listed under Glass-Contemporary, Glass-Midcentury, or Glass-Venetian. Even more art glass may be found in categories such as Burmese, Cameo Glass, Tiffany, and other factory names.

Bowl, Fish, Yellow, Wrought Iron Stand, Floral, 43 1/2 In.	630.00
Bowl, Paperweight, Controlled Bubbles, 3 x 13 3/4 In.	30.00
Centerpiece, Pink, White Opalescent, 3 Prunties, Victorian, 20 In.	515.00
Compote, Opalescent, Cranberry Edge, Fluted, Spelter & Marble Base, 13 x 18 In.	28.00
Cup & Saucer, Cranberry Stained, Enamel, Lobmeyr, c.1890	345.00
Lamp Shade, Blue, Green Opalescent, Leaded, 5 1/2 In., 6 Piece	290.00
Pitcher, Pink Cased In Clear, Beaded Drape, Clear Handle, 9 1/4 In.	250.00
Pokal, Amber, Enameled Cavalier, Germany, c.1890, 13 In.	175.00
Tumbler, Agata, New England	650.00
Vase, Applied Green & Amber Drips, Ehrenfeld, c.1900, 8 In.	160.00
Vase, Blue Green Iridescent Botanical Design, Brown Edge, 6 1/2 In.	145.00
Vase, Bud, Cranberry Swirls, Asymmetrical Bands Interior, Elongated, 8 In.	86.00
Vase, Cranberry, Floral Design, Rippled Rim, Applied Feet, Victorian, 9 1/2 In.	230.00
Vase, Cut Cobalt Blue Panels, St. Louis, France, 11 In.	695.00
Vase, Dragonfly, Purple, Gold Enameled, Beaded Flowers, Victorian, 6 In., Pair	175.00
Vase, Elephant, Gilt, Light Caramel, 2 Elephant Head Handles, Rousseau, 14 In.	4500.00
Vase, Ice Blue, Spattered, Applied Flower, 10 1/2 In.	50.00
Vase, Iridescent Green, Bulbous, Austria, 7 3/4 In.	185.00
Vase, Leaf, Flower Design, Slender Neck, Bulbous, Yellow, Victorian, 7 In.	55.00
Vase, Sky & Cloud Design, Blue, Rose, Gilt Metal, France, 9 1/2 In.	489.00
Vase, White Iridescent, Allover Threading, Ruffled Edge, Red Interior, Europe, 7 x 5 In.	145.00
Vase, Woman, Thick Mold, Gilt, Green, 1920, 6 In.	121.00
Wine, Enameled, 1900, 7 1/4 In.	275.00

GLASS-BLOWN was formed by forcing air through a rod into molten glass. Early glass and some forms of art glass were hand blown. Other types of glass were molded or pressed.

Barrel, Raised Roses, Silver, Gold Molded Bands, Green Leaves, Wire, 1910, 2 In.	110.00
Bird Feeder, Applied Trough, Cobalt Blue Knob, 1890-1920, 5 7/8 In.	55.00
Bottle, Bar, Pillar Mold, Lavender Applied Rib Edge, 10 1/2 In.	660.00
Bottle, Stylized Tulip, Pewter Screw Top, 6 1/4 In.	130.00
Bowl, 16 Vertical Ribs, Cobalt Blue, Applied Foot, Continental, 1870, 4 3/8 In.	110.00
Bowl, Aqua, Rolled Rim, Midwestern, Open Pontil, 1830-1860, 7 3/4 x 5 1/2 In.	330.00
Bowl, Cranberry, 4 Sections, 1910, 4 In.	514.00
Bowl, Light Green, Footed, Rolled Rim, 8 1/4 x 2 7/8 In.	550.00
Bowl, Light Green, Rolled Rim, Midwestern, Open Pontil, 1830-1860, 10 x 3 1/4 In.	330.00
Bowl, Red, Green & White Over Gold, c.1750, 4 1/2 In.	295.00
Bowl, Topaz, Free-Form, Chalet, Canada, 10 In.	11.00
Candleholder, Pearly White, Red Flame & Trim, On Clip, 1920s, 4 In.	155.00
Canister, Cover, Clear, 2 Applied Sapphire Blue Rings, 9 1/2 In.	905.00
Compote, Cover, Wafer Stem, Rolled Rim, 8 x 11 3/4 In.	300.00
Compote, Cut Star, Applied Foot, Knop Stem, 10 1/4 x 6 1/2 In.	385.00
Cornucopia, Raised Flowers, Pearly Pink, Red & Green Flowers, 1920, 2 In.	35.00
Creamer, 16 Swirled Ribs, Amethyst, Handle, Folded Rim, 3 5/8 In.	145.00
Creamer, 3-Piece Mold, Rigaree Handle, 3 In.	192.00
Creamer, Crimped Handle, Folded Rim, Late 18th Century, 4 1/4 In.	175.00
Creamer, Folded Rim, Drawn Foot, England, 1880s, 4 3/4 In.	350.00
Decanter, 3 Applied Rings, Amethyst, 6 3/4 In.	55.00
Decanter, Cranberry, Floral, Facet Cut, Silver, England, 1900, 15 In.	483.00
Decanter, Rayed Sunburst On Body & Stopper, 9 In.	355.00
Dish, 3-Piece Mold, Folded Lip, 5 In.	50.00
Epergne, 3 Trumpets, Ruffled Edges, Graduated Colors, 15 In.	330.00
Fish Bowl, Pressed Flared Base, 16 3/8 In.	190.00
Hat, Amber, Tooled & Folded Rim, Pontil, 2 1/2 In.	105.00

Hat, Aqua, Made From Tumbler, Hexagonal 190.00
Hurricane Shade, c.1840, 21 In. ....495.00 to 770.00
Hurricane Shade, Etched, Wheel-Cut Eagles, Stars, 19th Century, 20 In., Pair 550.00
Hurricane Shade, Folded Rim, 13 3/4 In., Pair 245.00
Jar, Drug, De Porceleyne Schotel, 1750s, 8 1/2 In. 675.00
Pan, Cobalt Blue Lip, 6 1/4 In. 138.00
Pan, Folded Rim, Applied Sapphire Blue Ring, Ex Allan Hedges, 6 In. 138.00
Pig, Clover On Tummy, Pearly White, Red Ears, Black Eyes, 1920, 4 In. 195.00
Pitcher, Applied Foot & Handle, Squat, 5 3/4 In. 145.00
Pitcher, Applied Handle, 6 1/4 In. 28.00
Pitcher, Lily Pad, Aqua, Applied Strap Handle, Crimped Foot, Open Pontil, 1840s 4840.00
Pitcher, White Swag, Applied Handle, 13 1/2 In. 990.00
Salt, Amethyst, Applied Foot, 2 3/8 In. 275.00
Sugar, Cover, Purple, Applied Foot, Galleried Rim, 8 1/4 In. 275.00
Sugar, Lavender, Applied Flared Foot, Folded Rim, 4 1/4 x 3 7/8 In. 275.00
Sugar, Witch's Ball Cover, Aqua, 3 1/4 In. 3300.00
Sugar Shaker, Green, Silver Plated Cover, 19th Century 235.00
Tumbler, 3-Piece Mold, 5 3/4 In. 258.00
Tumbler, Flip, 3-Piece Mold, 5 1/4 In. 280.00
Vase, Gold Floral, Enameled, 8 1/2 In. 165.00
Vase, Hyacinth, Peacock Blue, Applied Foot, 8 3/8 In. 135.00
Vase, Pillar Mold, Baluster Stem, 8 Rib Bowl, Scalloped Edge, Pontil, 11 In. 193.00
Vase, Urn Shape, Amethyst, Clear Applied Foot, 13 In. 275.00
Walnut, Green, 1910, 1 3/4 In. 20.00
Wine, Red, Gold Design, Cut Ovals On Top, 8 1/2 In. 1430.00
Wine, Teal, Cut Panels, Flint, Pair 275.00
Witch's Ball, Chocolate Amber, Sheared, 4 1/8 In. 65.00
Witch's Ball, Clear, White Loopings, Sheared, 1860-1880, 3 3/4 In. 100.00
Witch's Ball, Cobalt Blue, Sheared, c.1875, 5 1/2 In. 100.00
Witch's Ball, Grape Amethyst, Sheared, 1865-1885, 3 3/4 In. 165.00
Witch's Ball, Medium Amber, Sheared, Stand, 1855-1885, 5 3/4 In. 160.00
Witch's Ball, Sapphire Blue, Sheared, 1865-1885, 5 1/4 In. 175.00

GLASS-BOHEMIAN Bohemian glass is an ornate overlay or flashed glass made during the Victorian era. It has been reproduced in Bohemia, which is now a part of the Czech Republic. Glass made from 1875 to 1900 is preferred by collectors.

Beaker, Amber Stain, Rheinstein Castle Scene, Fluted Body, c.1860, 5 In. 345.00
Beaker, Amber Stain, Wheel Cut Stag & Castle Scene, c.1900, 4 1/2 In. 80.00
Beaker, Amber, Enameled Knight & Diamond In Shield, Theresienthal, 6 1/2 In. 115.00
Beaker, Amethyst Over Clear, Amber Stain, Pasty Enamel, c.1860, 5 1/2 In. 320.00
Beaker, Circle Design, Cobalt, 1920, 5 In. 97.00
Beaker, Cobalt Blue Over Clear, Circle & Triangle, Facet Cut, 4 1/2 In. 160.00
Beaker, Cobalt Blue, Gilt Couple, Fluted Body, c.1860, 6 1/2 In. 230.00
Beaker, Cranberry & Amber Stain, Wheel Cut Floral Design, 4 1/2 In. 125.00
Beaker, Double Overlay, Pink Over White Over Clear, Floral, c.1860, 4 1/2 In. 220.00
Beaker, Facet Cut Design, Cobalt, 1860, 5 1/2 In. 271.00
Beaker, Facet Cut Design, White, 1875, 4 In. 190.00
Beaker, Facet Cut Design, White, 1875, 6 In. 179.00
Beaker, Floral, Horizontal & Wave Cut Design, Amber, 1890, 6 1/2 In. 270.00
Beaker, Friendship Scenes, Cut Floral, Amber, Cranberry, Blue, 1860, 6 In. 328.00
Beaker, Green, Enameled Cards, Germany, c.1890, 8 In., Pair 430.00
Beaker, Green, Enameled Sailing Ship, Knight's Armor, Egermann, 4 3/4 In. 125.00
Beaker, Harbor Scene, Wheel Cut, Facet Cut Body, 1840, 5 1/2 In. 151.00
Beaker, Overlay, White Over Green, Round Base, Flared Top, c.1860, 4 In. 160.00
Beaker, Pink Over White Over Clear, Facet Cut Design, c.1860, 5 3/4 In. 230.00
Beaker, Pocket, Eidelweiss Floral Design, Cranberry, 1890, 6 In. 156.00
Beaker, Pocket, Facet Cut Body, c.1860, 4 In. 170.00
Beaker, Ruby Stain, Facet Cut Design, Gold Tracery, c.1860, 5 In. 265.00
Beaker, Ruby Stained, Stag & Castle Scene, Fluted Body, c.1875, 5 In. 80.00
Beaker, Spa Scenes, Facet Cut, c.1850, 3 1/2 In. 160.00
Beaker, White Over Clear Over Blue, Facet Cut Design, Gold Tracery, 5 In. 375.00

Beaker, White Over Clear Over Cranberry, Facet Cut, Floral, c.1860, 5 In.	290.00
Bell, Clear, Transparent Enamel Floral Design, Haida, c.1930, 5 1/2 In.	115.00
Bottle, Bar, Blown, Engraved, 1900, 11 1/2 In., Pair	155.00
Bottle, Painted Floral, Gilt, Green, Bulbous, Gilt Stopper, 16 In., 2 Piece	110.00
Bottle, White Over Cranberry, Enamel Woman, 3 Ball Feet, c.1860, 8 In.	575.00
Bowl, Black Enameled, Cavaliers On Horseback, Steinschonau, c.1920, 4 x 8 In.	160.00
Box, Hinged Cover, Star, Cranberry To Clear, Rectangular, 3 1/4 x 3 1/2 In.	402.00
Decanter, Enameled Crest & Woman, Fritz Heckert, c.1875, 12 In.	345.00
Decanter, Gold, Green, Black, White, 8 In.	100.00
Decanter, Wheel Cut Floral Design, Facet Cut Body, Stopper, 1890, 13 In.	345.00
Flask, Uranium Yellow Green, Wheel Cut Stag Scene, c.1860, 6 1/2 In.	605.00
Girandole, Scrolls, Pendant Prisms, Ruby Flashed, 14 1/4 In., Pair	575.00
Goblet, Amber, Cut To Clear, Grape & Vine, Diamond, Crosshatch, 7 3/4 In.	172.00
Goblet, Amber, Enameled, Cavalier Drinking, Roemer Stem, Theresienthal, 12 In.	335.00
Goblet, Amber, Enameled, Floral & Verse, Germany, c.1890, 12 In.	105.00
Goblet, Amber, Enameled, Floral, Fritz Heckert, c.1890, 7 In.	115.00
Goblet, Amber, Silver & Gilt Enameled, Floral, Roemer Stem, Fritz Heckert, 9 In.	115.00
Goblet, Blue Stain, Enameled Woman, Gold Trim, c.1900, 6 In.	115.00
Goblet, Butterflies, Floral, Facet Cut Stem, Cranberry, 1890, 7 In.	133.00
Goblet, Cobalt Blue, Enamel Floral & Gold, Clear Ribbed Stem, 6 1/2 In.	125.00
Goblet, Cobalt Over Clear, Checkerboard, Floral, Prutzcher, Myer's Neffe, 8 In.	1785.00
Goblet, Cobalt To Clear, Trellis & Fan, 9 In., 12 Piece	330.00
Goblet, Cover, Deer, Standing In Forest, Scalloped Circular Foot, 19 3/4 In.	1380.00
Goblet, Cover, Stag In Landscape, Peach Ground, White Overlay, 9 In.	168.00
Goblet, Cranberry, Clear Stem, Wheel Cut Floral, Gold, K On Base, 6 1/2 In.	160.00
Goblet, Cut Floral, Boat Shaped Bowl, Lobmeyr, c.1875, 5 In.	430.00
Goblet, Enameled Art Nouveau Floral, Myer's Neffe, c.1900, 6 1/2 In.	195.00
Goblet, Enameled, Floral, Interior Fluted, Theresienthal, c.1910, 5 1/2 In.	115.00
Goblet, Floral Enamel, Art Nouveau, Myer's Neffe, c.1910, 6 In.	105.00
Goblet, Floral Enamel, Pink Stem, Art Nouveau, Myer's Neffe, c.1900, 5 3/4 In.	80.00
Goblet, Floral, 2-Tone, Diagonal Ribbed Roemer Stem, Myer's Neffe, 1900, 6 In.	181.00
Goblet, Floral, 2-Tone, Light Amber, Diagonal Ribbed Roemer Stem, 1900	133.00
Goblet, Floral, Green Stem, Myer's Neffe, 1910, 6 In.	181.00
Goblet, Floral, Green Stem, Theresienthal, 1900, 7 In.	403.00
Goblet, Floral, Prunted Bowl, Green, Myer's Neffe, 1890, 6 1/2 In.	144.00
Goblet, Floral, Prunts On Knopped Stem, Green, Theresienthal, 1890, 7 1/2 In.	141.00
Goblet, Floral, Theresienthal, 1900, 8 In.	302.00
Goblet, Gilt Floral, Cranberry, White Enameled Ground, 1900, 6 1/2 In.	374.00
Goblet, Green Over Clear, Checkerboard, Prutscher, Myer's Neffe, 8 3/4 In.	2875.00
Goblet, Green, Clear Ribbed Stem, Cut Gold Verse, Fritz Heckert, 6 3/4 In.	125.00
Goblet, Lion Beside Saxon Crest, Diagonal Ribbed Roemer Stem, Green, 7 In.	115.00
Goblet, Red Cut To Clear, Chapel To Our Lady At Coldspring, 7 In.	460.00
Goblet, Wheel Cut Floral Design, Facet Cut Stem, Green, 1890, 7 In.	121.00
Goblet, Wheel Cut Inset, Gold, Silver, Enamel, Fritz Heckert, 1900, 6 1/2 In.	362.00
Goblet, Wheel Cut Stag Scenes, Amber, 1900, 6 1/4 In.	115.00
Lamp, Tulip Top, White To Green, Enameled Pedestal, 30 In.	110.00
Mug, Amber Stained, Wheel Cut Spa Scene, Facet Cut, c.1850, 4 1/2 In.	220.00
Mug, Uranium Green, Horn Shape, Gilt Crest, Floral, Riedel, c.1890, 6 In.	605.00
Mustard, Cover, Mottled Green, Copper, 4 In.	33.00
Perfume Bottle, Gold Enamel Design, Sterling Silver Hinged Cap, 3 1/4 In.	200.00
Perfume Bottle, Gold Grapes & Leaves, Ruby, Enameled Stopper, 7 1/8 In.	110.00
Perfume Bottle, Red Over White, Ovals, Facet Cut, Silver Cap, Stopper, 4 1/2 In.	375.00
Pokal, Intaglio Cut Stags & Forest Scene, c.1875, 13 1/2 In.	720.00
Salt & Pepper, Cobalt Over Clear, Facet Cut, Floral, Ship Finials, 8 In.	835.00
Stein, Clear Over Ruby, Facet Cut, Relief, Pewter Lid, 1/2 Liter	545.00
Stein, Cobalt Blue Over Clear, Cut Deer In Forest, Karl Pohl, 1/2 Liter	2300.00
Stein, Cobalt Blue Over Clear, Cut Floral, Inlaid Porcelain Lid, 1/2 Liter	3105.00
Stein, Cover, Prism, Stag Scene, Wheel Cut, Facet Cut Body, 1875, 1/5 Liter	363.00
Stein, Pink Over White Over Clear, Facet Cut, Glass Inlaid Lid, 1/2 Liter	920.00
Stein, Ruby Stained, Wheel Cut, Walhalla & National Theater, 1/2 Liter	575.00
Stein, Wheel Cut Stag & Forest Scene, Prism Glass Inlaid Lid, 1/2 Liter	275.00
Tankard, Amber, Enameled, Cut Gold & Silver Inset, Fritz Heckert, 9 In.	775.00
Vase, Amber Cut To Clear, Stag Design, 8 In.	57.00

Vase, Amber, Gilt & White Enameled, Floral, Applied Beads, Fritz Heckert, 4 In. 80.00
Vase, Buttons & Spikes, Enamel, Luster, Bottle Form, Prisms, 10 In. 120.00
Vase, Cranberry, White Overlay, Floral, 1900, 14 1/2 In. 745.00
Vase, Deer & Forest Design, Amber, Etched, 6 3/4 In. 75.00
Vase, Embossed Threading, Panels, Gold & Purple Over Green, 4 1/2 In. 33.00
Vase, Floral Cutting Scene, Enameled, Theresienthal, 1900, 11 1/2 In. 288.00
Vase, Gold, Bronze Threading, 6 3/4 In. 275.00
Vase, Green, 4 Ormolu Griffin Form Handles, 4 Paw Feet, 17 In. 460.00
Vase, Green, Enameled, Floral, Butterfly, Man, Max Rade, Fritz Heckert, c.1900, 7 In. . . . 230.00
Vase, Green, Floral Enamel, c.1890, 14 In. 80.00
Vase, Iridized Texture Over Green, 8 In. 22.00
Vase, Luster, Ruby Flashing, Cut & Engraved, Clear Prisms, 12 1/2 In., Pair 330.00
Vase, Oil Spot, Green, Purple, Gold & Blue Over Black Amethyst, 5 In. 55.00
Vase, Oil Spot, Spattered Over Amethyst, Pinched Waist, 4 1/2 In. 33.00
Vase, Pull-Up, Frosted Handles, Butterscotch, Pink, White, 10 3/4 In. 440.00
Vase, Pull-Up, Green, Blue, Yellow, White, 1900, 8 1/4 In. 110.00
Vase, Pull-Up, Handle, Butterscotch, Pink, White, Pink Inner Lining, 7 In. 770.00
Vase, Ruby Cut To Clear, Acid Etched, Stag, Heart & Windmill, 12 1/4 x 5 In. 168.00
Vase, Snail Shape, Green, 1900, 8 In. 172.00
Vase, Uranium Yellow, Enameled, Floral, Rossler, c.1920, 7 1/2 In. 80.00
Vase, Vertical Stripes, Black Rim, Overlay, c.1930, 7 1/2 In. 85.00
Vase, Vines, Leaf Design, Raised On Circular Foot, 10 1/4 In. 60.00
Vase, White Leaf Design, 3 Enamel Medallions, Flared Neck, Gold, 7 In. 175.00
Vase, Yellow Overlay, Early 20th Century, 8 1/2 In., Pair 170.00
Vase, Yellow, White Layered Glass, Enameled, 8 1/2 In. 250.00
Water Set, Gold Enameling, 5 Piece 325.00

GLASS-CONTEMPORARY includes pieces by glass artists working after
1975. Many of these pieces are free-form, one-of-a-kind sculptures.
Paperweights by contemporary artists are listed in the Paperweight category. Earlier studio glass may be found listed under Glass-
Midcentury or Glass-Venetian.

Air Sculpture, Pink, Labino, 1983, 4 1/2 In. 450.00
Ewer, Amber To Opalescent Yellow, Erickson, 9 5/8 In. 55.00
Figurine, Bird, Rose, Cased Orange Glass Pedestal, Toikka, 17 In. 1495.00
Vase, Crimson, Orange Patches, Waisted, Fratelli Toso, 1965, 8 1/8 In. 460.00
Vase, Fossils, Ruby, Sandblasted, Mark Habus, '92, 7 1/2 x 9 In. 115.00
Vase, Multicolored Abstract Design, Kurt Jepsen, 1972, 7 1/2 x 10 1/2 In. 315.00
Vase, Pinched Vertical Lines, Labino, 1973, 6 1/2 In. 500.00
Vase, Tapering Cylindrical, Green, Blue, White, Signed Fellen, '87, 12 In. 55.00

GLASS-CUT, see Cut Glass category.

GLASS-DEPRESSION, see Depression Glass category.

GLASS-MIDCENTURY refers to art glass made from the 1950s to the
1980s. Some glass factories, such as Baccarat or Orrefors, are listed
under their own categories. Earlier glass may be listed in the Glass-Art
and Glass-Contemporary categories. Italian glass may be found under
Glass-Venetian.

Bottle, 5 Vertical Green, White Canes, Stopper, Morandiane, 1950, 14 In. 880.00
Bottle, Pinch, 1 Light, 1 Dark Amber, Stopper, Crackled, Blenko, 10 In., Pair 70.00
Bowl, Regalia, Crown, Gold Enamel Transfer, Georges Briard, Shallow, 5 1/4 In. . . . . *Illus* 15.00
Bowl, Smoky Gray, Free-Form, Lutkin, Signed, Holmegaard, 1961, 8 1/2 In. 86.00
Bowl, Smoky Gray, Spiral White Canes, Free-Form, 1950, 5 In. 517.00
Bowl, Vertical Rows Of Controlled Bubbles Exterior, Spiral Blue Interior, 1969 . . . . 230.00
Carafe, Red, Blue, Amber Spiraling Canes, Deep Amber, Kaj Franck, 1962 . . . . 154.00
Carafe, Stylized Cockerel, Multicolored, Blue Green, Kaj Franck, 12 In. 2275.00
Cocktail Shaker, Rooster, Cobalt Blue, Footed, Morgantown 395.00
Creamer, Amber, Applied Handle & Foot, Erickson, 3 3/4 In. 125.00
Decanter Set, Crackled Tangerine, Pitcher & Creamer, Pilgrim, 3 Piece 60.00
Ewer, Amber, Paneled Interior, Applied Handle, Morgantown, 9 1/2 In. 38.00
Figurine, Bird, Pointed Beak, Tail Feathers, Disk Eyes, A. Pianon, 1962, 9 1/2 In. 1610.00

~∽∾~

Glassware, old or new, requires careful
handling. Stand each piece upright, not
touching another. Never nest pieces. Wash
in moderately hot water and mild detergent. Avoid wiping gold- or platinum-
banded pieces while glasses are hot.
Never use scouring pads or silver polish
on glass. When using an automatic dishwasher, be sure the water temperature is
under 180 degrees.

Glass-Midcentury, Bowl, Regalia,
Crown, Gold Enamel Transfer,
Georges Briard, Shallow, 5 1/4 In.

~∽∾~

Figurine, Eve Holding Apple, Foliage, Edris Ekhardt, 1940s, 10 3/4 In.		2587.00
Figurine, Owl, Ruby Red, Viking, 5 & 4 1/2 In., Pair		33.00
Goblet, Wine, Instrument Form Handle, Amber, Fornasetti, c.1940, Pair		1150.00
Mobile, Orange, Blue, Green, Geometric, Clips, M. Higgins, 20 x 15 In.		1093.00
Pitcher, Amberina, Pinched, Blenko, 8 In.		33.00
Pitcher, Crinkle, Red, Clear Handle, Morgantown, 50 Oz.		150.00
Pitcher, Jonquil, Pinched Design, Clear Handles, Blenko, 6 In., Pair		44.00
Screen, 21 Layered Discs, Connected With Clips, M. Higgins, 54 x 30 In.		4600.00
Tray, Pigeon Blood, Swan Shape, Clear Neck & Head, Viking, 7 In.		27.00
Vase, Amberina, Handle, Morgantown, 8 1/2 In.		50.00
Vase, Controlled Bubbles, Tapered Cylinder, Flared Edge, Label, Blenko, 9 In.		58.00
Vase, Deep Amber, Morgantown, 11 1/2 In.		22.00
Vase, Green, Tan Bands, Internal Vertical, Medina, 5 1/2 In.		275.00
Vase, Lavender, Flared Edge, Signed, Blenko, 8 In.		52.00
Vase, Pillow, Light Green, Vertical Center Rib, Tan Interior, Medina, 6 1/2 In.		154.00
Vase, Purple, Green, Blue, Quadrilateral Prism Form, Kaj Franck, 1957		176.00
Vase, Ribbed, Clear, Spherical Shape, Walter Dorwin Teague, 8 x 7 In.		360.00
Vase, Smoky Gray, Tapio Wirkkala, 1960, 8 5/8 In.		862.00
Vase, Swollen Cylinder, Label, Signed, Holmegaard, P/15283, 5 In.		52.00
Vase, White, Caramel Aubergine Strips, Spiral Grid Of Squares, 9 In.		2875.00

GLASS-VENETIAN. Venetian glass has been made near Venice, Italy,
since the thirteenth century. Thin, colored glass with applied decoration is favored, although many other types have been made. Collectors
have recently become interested in the Art Deco and 1950s designs.
Glass was made on the Venetian island of Murano from 1291. The out-
put dwindled in the late seventeenth century but began to flourish
again in the 1850s. Some of the old techniques of glassmaking were
revived, and firms today make traditional designs and original modern
glass. Since 1981, the name *Murano* may only be used on glass made
on Murano Island. Other pieces of Italian glass may be found in the
Glass-Contemporary and Glass-Midcentury categories of this book.

Ashtray, Salmon, Gold, Murano		65.00
Basket, Amber, Green, Archimede Seguso, 1952, 9 3/4 In.		2875.00
Bottle, Cobalt Blue, Emerald Green Canes, Waisted, Stopper, Ponti, 15 In.		4025.00
Bottle, Inciso Sommerso, Turquoise Blue, Stopper, Paolo Venini, 15 In.		575.00
Bottle, Sommerso, Blue & Green Interior, Flattened, Etched, Medina, 9 In.		330.00
Bottle, Sommerso, Plum Iridescent, Frosted Stopper, Murano, 13 In.		99.00
Bowl, 2-Tone Opaline Patches, Amethyst, Barovier & Toso, 1950, 4 In.		1430.00
Bowl, A Canne, Red, Orange, Yellow, Amber, Blue, Barovier & Toso, 3 In.		10350.00
Bowl, Blue, Amber Ribs & Base, Free-Form, 11 In.		11.00
Bowl, Butterfly, Amber, Emerald Tips, 10 In.		33.00
Bowl, Inciso, Red, Orange Interior, Alfredo Barbini, 1960, 3 In.		1840.00

Bowl, Leaf Form, Filigrano, Alternating Pink, Blue, White, Toso, 1950, 11 In. 373.00
Bowl, Leaf Form, Segmented Interior, Iridescence, Barovier & Toso, 4 In. 230.00
Bowl, Leaf Form, White, Yellow Spiraling Canes, Dino Martens, 1954, 9 In. 172.00
Bowl, Shallow Blue Interior, Thick Satin Exterior, Conical, Barbini, 7 In. 805.00
Bowl, Sommerso, Red & Amber Swirls, Silver Leaf, Barovier, 3 x 6 3/4 In. 220.00
Bowl, Spicchi, Red & Green Bands, Tapering, Aureliano Toso, 4 In. 575.00
Bowl, Translucent Blue Body, Opaque White Rim, Prunts, Murano, 2 x 6 In. 66.00
Bowl, Violet, Random Hollow Cane Sections, Barovier & Toso, 1966 . . . . 1840.00
Bowl, White, Clear & Amber Retiuclated Pulled Edge, Free-Form, 16 In. 22.00
Box, Hinged Cover, Tortoiseshell Design, 4 1/2 In. 345.00
Candleholder, Deep Lavender, Plum, Alternating Disk, Barovier, 1930, 7 In. 120.00
Candlestick, Floral Design, Inverted Baluster Stems, Circular Bases, Pair 430.00
Champagne, Gold, Opal, Applied Dolphin Base, 7 3/4 In. 125.00
Chandelier, Molded Foliate, 5 Twisted Arms, Leaves On Edges, 1950, 15 In. 805.00
Compote, Swan Form Stem, Circular Cobalt Foot, 10 1/4 In. 285.00
Compote, White Over Red, Mottled Copper, Clear Petal Footed, 5 1/2 In. 33.00
Cornucopia, Fruit Design, Turquoise Glass Horns, Circular Bases, 6 In., Pair 460.00
Figurine, 2 Birds, In Tree, Murano 38.00
Figurine, Bird, Heavy Lime Green Body, Blue, Yellow Internal, Cenedese, 6 In. 198.00
Figurine, Birds, Long Tail Feathers, Purple, Gold, 10 1/2 In., Pair 175.00
Figurine, Birds, On A Branch, White, Gilt, 14 In., Pair 110.00
Figurine, Bull, Scavo, Textured Gray Surface, Alfredo Barbini, 1948, 7 In. 977.00
Figurine, Chicken, Opaque White, Fulvio Bianconi, 1950, 7 1/2 In., Pair 2860.00
Figurine, Clown, Multicolored, Murano, c.1960, 8 In. 150.00
Figurine, Clown, Multicolored, Murano, c.1960, 11 In. 175.00
Figurine, Cocks, Fighting, Perched Birds, Gold Fleck Highlights, 11 In., Pair 605.00
Figurine, Dog, Aqua, Multicolored, c.1950, 9 x 10 In. 150.00
Figurine, Elephant, Sommerso, Green & Blue, Salviati, 7 In. 173.00
Figurine, Fish, Ribbed, White, Yellow, Green Body, Amethyst Fins, Fratelli Toso 385.00
Figurine, Flamenco Dancers, Murano, Pair 45.00
Figurine, Harlequin, Cape, Murrine, Green, Amber, A. Da Ros, 29 In. 10350.00
Figurine, Jazz Musicians, Seated, Blue, Barovier & Toso, 1930, 6 1/2 In., Pair 2875.00
Figurine, Man & Woman, Skirt, Jacket Over Shoulders, Venini, c.1948, 12 In., Pair 1725.00
Figurine, Monkey, Seated, Dressed, Pearly Silver, Black Eyes, c.1900, 10 In. 225.00
Figurine, Owl, Clear, Controlled Bubbles, 12 1/4 In. 220.00
Figurine, Owl, Green, Painted Eyes, 5 In. 40.00
Figurine, Pear, Vaseline Over Amberina, Controlled Bubbles, Stem & Leaf, 6 In. 90.00
Figurine, Pigeon, White, Black Aventurine Trailings, Dino Martens, 1954 . . . . 747.00
Figurine, Polar Bear, Gray, Spotted Textured Surface, Alfredo Barbini, 6 In. 862.00
Figurine, Red Bird, Yellow Trim, Murano 45.00
Figurine, Rooster, Blue, 8 In., Pair 115.00
Figurine, Rooster, Blue, Red, White Strips, Gold Flecked Base, 10 In. 370.00
Figurine, Rooster, White, Red Spiraling Canes, Dino Martens, 1954, 10 In. 460.00
Figurine, Snail, Chartreuse, Spiral Design, Cordovan, 5 1/2 In. 60.00
Figurine, Swan, White Canes, Copper Aventurine Trailings, Dino Martens 575.00
Goblet, Green, Scratch Gilt Shield Design, Silver Stem Collar, c.1920, 6 1/4 In. 115.00
Lamp, Hanging, Mushroom, White & Clear Caning, Venini, 13 3/4 x 11 In. 495.00
Lamp, Metal, Rectangular Box, Colored Murrines, Italy 575.00
Lamp, Scavo Shade & Base, Blue & Purple, Chrome Shaft, Barbini, 24 x 16 In. 2640.00
Lamp Shade, Hanging, Bell Form, Vertical Turquoise, Opaque White Canes 935.00
Lamp Shade, Hanging, Bell Form, Vertical Turquoise, Red Canes, 1960, 11 In. 605.00
Lamp Shade, Hanging, Onion Form, Vertical Opaque White, Orange Bands 935.00
Lamp Shade, Hanging, Onion Form, White On Opaque White, 1960s, 12 In. 605.00
Lamp Shade, Hanging, Vertical Opaque White, Dark Amethyst Canes, 1960s 825.00
Lamp Shade, Hanging, White Opaque, 1960, 8 In. 385.00
Martini, Dog In Stem, Red Swirl, Stirrer, 4 1/2 In., Pair 450.00
Paperweight, Millefiori 30.00
Paperweight, White, Black, Gold, Yellow Spiraling Canes, Aurellilano Toso 33.00
Parfait, Underplate, White Threading, 6 Piece 230.00
Pitcher, Floreale, Murrine Flowers, Green, Opaque White, Green Handle, Toso 660.00
Pitcher, Multicolored Canes, Green, Red, Blue, Yellow, Lavender, Ponti, 9 In. 4025.00
Sculpture, Dolphin, White Streaks, Green Socle Base, Italy, 19 1/2 In. 276.00

Urn, Scavo, Blue-Green, Gold, 2 Satin Handles, Cendese, 18 x 7 In. 880.00
Vase, A Spina, Opaline Patches, Barovier & Toso, 1950, 9 In. 6600.00
Vase, Aboriginoe, Clear, Mustard, Avocado, Gray, Barovier & Toso, 1954, 11 In. 825.00
Vase, Amber, Female Torso With Out-Stretched Arms, 11 In. 6325.00
Vase, Amber, Green Interior, Burgundy Sommerso, Salviati, 14 In. 690.00
Vase, Applied Green Glass Drops, Teardrop Form, Fratelli Toso, 11 1/2 In. 1495.00
Vase, Aquarium, Fish, White, Maroon, Orange Canes, Cenedese, 11 In. 2760.00
Vase, Aubergine, Turquoise, Smoky Gray Patches, Fulvio Bianconi, 8 In. 7475.00
Vase, Blue, Dark Blue Cylindrical Neck, Tapio Wirkkala, 6 In., Pair 115.00
Vase, Bottle Form, Woman, Carrying Basket Of Fruit, N. Martinuzzi, 10 In. 3450.00
Vase, Bright Red Interior, White, Fulvio Bianconi, 1960s, 7 1/2 In. 175.00
Vase, Checkerboard, Blue Opalescent, Barovier & Toso, 1950, 9 In. 6600.00
Vase, Clear Edge, Deep Olive Green Center, Toni Zuccheri, 15 In. 2070.00
Vase, Clear, Orange & Red Thread Twist, Loop Handles, c.1950, 4 1/2 In. 80.00
Vase, Cobalt Blue Lower Section, Deep Green Upper Section, Licata, 10 In. 8625.00
Vase, Concentric Ribs, Red Orange, White, D'Arte, 1940, 11 1/2 In. 4600.00
Vase, Cranberry, Purple Spiral Ribs, Archimede Seguso, 1960, 7 In. 1265.00
Vase, Crepuscolo, Black, Square, Barovier & Toso, 1930, 13 In. 605.00
Vase, Deep Green Iridescent, Fulvio Bianconi, 1950, 7 1/2 In. 715.00
Vase, Deep Purple, Random Applied Spots, Fratelli Toso, 1950, 10 1/2 In. 2990.00
Vase, Fazzoletto Zanfirco, Venini, 3 In. 195.00
Vase, Fazzoletto, Deep Green Body, Fulvio Bianconi, 1950, 2 1/2 In. 121.00
Vase, Fazzoletto, Orange, Green Zanfirico Canes, Fulvio Bianconi, 1950, 3 In. 121.00
Vase, Gemmata, Gold Interior, Red Exterior, 1930, Barovier & Toso, 11 In. 1045.00
Vase, Green Neck, Large Black Basin, Black Canes, Basilissa, 1970, 9 In. 1320.00
Vase, Green, Black, Yellow, Straw Yellow Patches, F. Bianconi, 1950, 9 In. 6600.00
Vase, Gunmetal Blue, Candy Apple Red Exterior, Bianconi, 1950, 4 In. 770.00
Vase, Inciso, Light Yellow Interior, Incised Fine Lines, Paolo Venini, 10 In. 715.00
Vase, Inciso, Sommerso, Green, Cylindrical, Paolo Venini, 1956, 9 In. 690.00
Vase, Intarsia, Checkerboard, White, Barovier & Toso, 1970s, 12 In. 1540.00
Vase, Internal Red Casing, White Exterior, Fulvio Bianconi, 1950, 9 1/2 In. 825.00
Vase, Iridescent Multicolor On Red, Flowers, Ribbons, Ruffled Edge & Foot, 13 In. 440.00
Vase, Large Opaque White Design, Fulvio Bianconi, 1950, 11 In. 360.00
Vase, Latticinio, Swirled Blue, Gilt Handles, Footed, 8 1/4 In. 29.00
Vase, Light Amber Body, Applied Free-Form Band, Murano, 9 In. 55.00
Vase, Multicolored Swirled Threads, Gold Flecks, c.1950, 9 1/2 In., Pair 240.00
Vase, Orange Broad Trailings, Ludivico De Santillana, 4 3/4 x 7 1/8 In. 1035.00
Vase, Orange, Black, Teal, White, Royal, Light Blue, Dino Martens, 1948, 9 1/2 In. 9775.00
Vase, Orange, White, Dimpled Form, Cylindrical, Seguso, 1952, 11 1/4 In. 230.00
Vase, Pairs Of Opaline Patches, Amethyst Edge, Barovier & Toso, 10 In. 2310.00
Vase, Pale Orange, Textured Scavo Surface, Gino Cenedese, 1952, 5 In. 1035.00
Vase, Parabolici, Gray Strips, Amethyst, 1950s, Barovier & Toso, 5 In. 4400.00
Vase, Peach Cased, Teardrop Form, Filigree Feathers, Seguso, 11 In. 4025.00
Vase, Pezzato, Alternating Patches Of Blue, White, Barovier & Toso, 16 In. 1870.00
Vase, Pulled White, Lavender, Pale Amber Trails, Barovier & Toso, 1900, 3 In. 517.00
Vase, Red & Blue Angular Striping, Signed, Venini, 14 In. 920.00
Vase, Red, Amber, Pale Lavender, Cobalt Blue, Barovier, 1963, 6 3/4 In. 7187.00
Vase, Red, White, Green, Fulvio Bianconi, 1951, 11 In. 5750.00
Vase, Ribbon, Murano, 4 In. 38.00
Vase, Seguso, Overall Gold Leaf, Light Blue Body, Flavio Poli, 1940, 17 In. 231.00
Vase, Soffiati, 6 Applied Opaque White Loops, Green Body, Murano, 1920, 5 In. 357.00
Vase, Soffiati, Amber Lobed Body, Vertical Ribs, Square Handles, 1920, 7 In. 990.00
Vase, Soffiati, Amber Lobed Form, Looping Handles, Zecchin, 1920, 12 In. 1045.00
Vase, Soffiati, Amethyst Body, Vertical Ribs, Vertical Handles, 1920, 7 1/2 In. 140.00
Vase, Soffiati, Light Amethyst Body, Opaque Disk Stem, Cappellin, 1920, 8 In. 440.00
Vase, Soffiati, Translucent Royal Blue Body, Ribbon Handles, Cappellin, 6 In. 99.00
Vase, Soffiati, Yellow Cone Form, Vittorio Zecchin, 1920, 10 In. 660.00
Vase, Sommerso Ribbed, Pale Amber, Cranberry Spiral Ribs, 10 In. 460.00
Vase, Sommerso, Light Blue, Deep Blue, Murano, 12 1/2 In. 522.00
Vase, Striped Fish, Amber, Gray, Green, Barbini, 1955, 13 In. 2875.00
Vase, Turquoise Blue, Emerald Green, Teardrop Form, D'Arte, 1960, 10 In. 287.00
Vase, Vamsa Bollicine, Amber, Spiral Layer Of Dense Bubbles, Barbini, 1930, 8 In. 412.00
Vase, White & Burgundy Spirals, Clear Body, Cup-Shaped Mouth, 13 1/2 In. 173.00

Vase, White, Red, Green, Blue, Black, Bianconi, 1950, 9 In. 8250.00
Vase, Wisteria, Pale Amber & Brown Star Murrine, Murano, 7 In. 9775.00
Vase, Zanfirico, Orange, White Latticinio, Toso, 6 In. 373.00
Vase, Zigzag, Cobalt Blue, Emerald Green, Barovier & Toso, 6 4/5 In. 3220.00

GLASSES for the eyes, or spectacles, were mentioned in a manuscript in 1289 and have been used ever since. The first eyeglasses with rigid side pieces were made in London in 1727. Bifocals were invented by Benjamin Franklin in 1785. Lorgnettes were popular in late Victorian times. Opera glasses are listed in their own category.

Folding Into Case, Spring Loaded At Bridge, Engraved Landscape, Japan, 6 In. 50.00
Lorgnette, Floral & Scroll Design, Art Nouveau, 14K Yellow Gold 46000.00
Lorgnette, Tortoiseshell, Scroll Carved, Pierced Handle, Swiveling Eye Piece, 8 In. 220.00
Sharpshooter's, Amber Lens, Light Center, Silver Frame 130.00
Spectacles, 12K Gold Filled Frames, Bifocal Lenses, Salesman's Sample, c.1910, 2 In. .. 250.00
Spectacles, Blue Lens, Silver Frames, c.1800 .... 160.00
Spectacles, Brass Frames, Case, Benz, Early 19th Century, 5 1/8 In. 195.00
Spectacles, Brass, Round Lenses, Slide Adjustable 30.00
Spectacles, Green Lens, Steel Frame, 18th Century 265.00
Spectacles, Iron Frames, Steel Case, Purple Cloth Lining, Original Lenses, c.1760 ...... 310.00
Spectacles, Iron, Original Lenses, Iron Case, England, c.1765 .... 250.00
Spectacles, Round Lenses, Ribbon Loops, Iron, c.1750 .... 185.00
Spectacles, Steel Frames, Original Case, England, c.1750 .... 695.00
Spectacles, T.S. Curtis, 1840s 295.00

GOEBEL is the mark used by W. Goebel Porzellanfabrik of Oeslau, Germany, now Rodental, Germany. Many types of figurines and dishes have been made. The firm is still working. The pieces marked *Goebel Hummel* are listed under Hummel in this book.

Bank, Cat In Basket 95.00
Bank, Friar Tuck, Toes Showing 95.00
Bookends, Friar Tuck 495.00
Decanter, Friar Tuck, Full Bee Mark 85.00
Figurine, Angel Holding Candle, New Mark, 9 In. 35.00
Figurine, Cat, Sleeping, Ginger, Large 145.00
Figurine, Girl With Flowers & Knapsack, Three Line Mark, 8 In. 90.00
Figurine, Madonna Of The Doves, Three Line Mark, 10 In. 190.00
Figurine, Madonna Of The Doves, Vee Over Gee, 10 In. 110.00
Figurine, Madonna With Child, Full Bee, 14 In. 175.00
Figurine, Mother With Child, Vee Over Gee, 8 1/2 In. 50.00
Figurine, School Boys, No. 170/I, 7 1/2 In. 495.00
Figurine, Snow White & Seven Dwarfs 700.00
Figurine, Sparrow, Signed 275.00
Figurine, Titmouse, Blue, Vee Over Gee, 6 In. 27.00
Pendant, Necklace, What Now, Miniature 82.00
Salt & Pepper, Turkey On Nest 55.00

GOLDSCHEIDER has made porcelains in three places. The family left Vienna in 1938 and started factories in England and in Trenton, New Jersey. The New Jersey factory started in 1940 as Goldscheider-U.S.A. In 1941 it became Goldscheider-Everlast Corporation. From 1947 to 1953 it was Goldcrest Ceramics Corporation. In 1950 the Vienna plant was returned to Mr. Goldscheider, and the company continues in business. The Trenton, New Jersey, business, now called *Goldscheider of Vienna*, imports all of the pieces.

Bust, Girl, 8 1/4 In. 750.00
Figurine, Birds, Pink & Black Plumage, Molded Foot, 13 3/4 In. 485.00
Figurine, Marie Antoinette, Peggy Porscheer, 6 1/2 In. 85.00
Figurine, Standing Female Peasant, Signed, 42 In. 575.00
Lamp, Base, 1927, 18 1/2 In. 1610.00

GOLF, see Sports category.

GONDER Ceramic Arts, Inc., was opened by Lawton Gonder in 1941 in Zanesville, Ohio. Gonder made high-grade pottery decorated with flambe, drip, gold crackle, and Chinese crackle glazes. The factory closed in 1957. From 1946 to 1954, Gonder also operated the Elgee Pottery, which made ceramic lamp bases.

Figurine, Gazelle	45.00
Figurine, Panther, Green, 19 In.	200.00
Planter, Swan	65.00

GOOFUS GLASS was made from about 1900 to 1920 by many American factories. It was originally painted gold, red, green, bronze, pink, purple, or other bright colors. Many pieces are found today with flaking paint, and this lowers the value.

Compote, Cherries, 9 1/2 In.	55.00
Dish, Advertising, 15 In.	40.00

GOSS china has been made since 1858. English potter William Henry Goss first made it at the Falcon Pottery in Stoke-on-Trent. The factory name was changed to Goss China Company in 1934 when it was taken over by Cauldon Potteries. Production ceased in 1940. Goss china resembles Irish Belleek in both body and glaze. The company also made popular souvenir china, usually marked with local crests and names.

W.H.COSS

Beer Bowl, Dragon Shape, Crest, 6 1/4 x 2 1/2 In.	65.00
Bust, Shakespeare, Signed, Late 19th Century, 4 1/2 In.	105.00
Plate, Westminster Abbey, Black, White Ground, Gilt Edging, 8 In.	16.00
Pot, Rolan, Westminster Crest, 2 In.	12.00
Salt Pot, Isle Of Wight Crest, 2 3/4 In.	25.00
Vase, Crest Of King Edward VII, 4 1/2 In.	13.00

GOUDA, Holland, has been a pottery center since the seventeenth century. Two firms, the Zenith pottery, established in the eighteenth century, and the Zuid-Hollandsche pottery made the brightly colored wares marked Gouda from 1880 to about 1940. Many pieces featured Art Nouveau or Art Deco designs.

PLAZUID
GOUDA
HOLLAND

Ashtray, 8 In.	75.00
Bowl, Damascus, 4 In.	75.00
Candy Dish, Handle, 8 In.	110.00
Lamp, Encircled Rose, Rings At Neck, Gold Outlined, Gold Pedestal, 29 In.	188.00
Vase, Art Nouveau Flowers, 7 3/8 In.	770.00
Vase, Continuous Landscape Of Cottages, Windmill, Boats On Canal Scene, 7 1/2 In.	110.00
Vase, Floral Design, Multicolored, Green, White Ground, Signed, Made In Holland, 9 In.	176.00
Vase, Matte Florals, Black Borders, Signed, 4 In.	55.00
Vase, Multicolored Tulip Design, Green High Glaze Ground, 9 In.	412.00
Vase, Peasant Woman, Green, Marked, R.R. Holland, 4 1/4 x 12 1/5 In.	385.00
Vase, Trumpet, 12 In.	500.00

GRANITEWARE is an enameled tinware that has been used in the kitchen from the late nineteenth century to the present. Earlier graniteware was green or turquoise blue, with white spatters. The later ware was gray with white spatters. Reproductions are being made in all colors.

Basin, Blue & White Swirl, Applied Hanging Ring, 12 3/4 In.	120.00
Basin, Cobalt Blue, White Interior, Eyelet, 12 1/2 In.	55.00
Basin, Emerald Green, White Swirl, Blue Rim, White Interior, 11 x 3 In.	275.00
Bowl, Red, White Stripes, 8 x 3 1/4 In.	48.00 to 50.00
Bucket, Tin Cover & Finial, Bail Handle, 5 In.	50.00
Carrier, Dinner, Cover, Gray, Wooden Bail, Tab Handles, Oblong	105.00
Carrier, Dinner, White, Black Rim & Handles, Wooden Handle, 3-Stack	82.00
Carrier, Dinner, White, Cobalt Blue Rims, Wooden Handle, 5-Stack	95.00
Carrier, Lunch, Gray & White, Cast Handle, Swing Bail, 10 1/2 In.	93.00

Coffee Biggin, White, Black Rim & Knob, 5 Piece 95.00
Coffee Boiler, Black & White, Bail Handle, 11 In. 45.00
Coffee Boiler, Blue & White, Bail Handle 88.00
Coffee Server, Pink, French Type, 4 Handles, 18 In. 395.00
Coffeepot, Green, White, 10 In. 250.00
Coffeepot, Robin's-Egg Blue 95.00
Colander, Cream Interior, Green Exterior 20.00
Colander, White, Cobalt Blue Rim 20.00
Double Boiler, Cover, Blue & White Swirl, Black Rim & Handles 100.00
Funnel, Handle, Gray 28.00
Kettle, Preserve, Tin Cover, Gray, Mottled, Tipping Handle, 14 1/2 In. 22.00
Pail, Berry, Gray 35.00
Pail, Berry, Red & White, Wood Bail Handle, 6 1/8 x 4 3/4 In. 2420.00
Pail, Cover, Blue & White Swirl, Black Rim & Tab Handles, Wooden Bail, 7 1/2 In. 145.00
Pail, Milk, Cover, Brown & White, Speckle, Wire Bail Handle, 9 3/4 In. 22.00
Pan, End-Of-Day, White Interior, Rectangular, 12 x 7 1/2 x 2 1/8 In. 440.00
Pan, Frying, Blue Swirl, 7 In. 50.00
Pie Pan, Blue & White Swirl, 8 In. 40.00
Pie Plate, Brown & White Swirl, White Interior, 9 3/4 In. 72.00
Pie Plate, Chrystolite, Mottled Black Rim, White Interior, 9 3/4 In. 105.00
Pie Plate, Emerald Green, White Swirl, Blue Rim, 10 In. 90.00
Pitcher, Milk, Gray, 6 3/4 In. 55.00
Plate, Robin's-Egg Blue, White, 8 In. 11.00
Roaster, Cover, Blue & White, Mottled Black Rims & Handles, 17 1/2 In. 130.00
Sieve, Triangular, Blue Rim, Cream 28.00
Strainer, Robin's-Egg Blue & White, 12 In. 38.00
Syrup, Relish Pattern, Brown 225.00
Tea Strainer, Gray & White 55.00
Teakettle, Brown & White, Pewter Trim, Copper Base, 7 In. 165.00
Teapot, End-Of-Day, Red, Cobalt, Orange, Black, c.1900 .... 430.00
Teapot, Gooseneck Spout, Tin Lid, Wooden Finial, Black Painted Handle, 7 In. 155.00
Washbowl, Blue & White, 3 1/4 x 11 1/2 In. 55.00

GREENTOWN glass was made by the Indiana Tumbler and Goblet Company of Greentown, Indiana, from 1894 to 1903. In 1899, the factory became part of National Glass Company. A variety of pressed glass was made. Additional pieces may be found in other categories, such as Chocolate Glass, Holly Amber, Milk Glass, and Pressed Glass.

Austrian, Wine 40.00
Beaded Panel, Creamer 95.00
Brazen Shield, Tumbler, Blue 95.00
Cactus, Creamer, Cover ....95.00 to 110.00
Cord Drapery, Cruet, Stopper ....195.00 to 235.00
Cord Drapery, Tumbler 65.00
Cord Drapery, Wine, Amber 280.00
Cupid, Creamer, Cover, Nile Green 425.00
Cupid, Spooner 100.00
Dewey, Butter, Cover, Canary 80.00
Dewey, Creamer, Amber 30.00
Dewey, Parfait, Amber 70.00
Dewey, Spooner, Emerald Green 80.00
Dewey, Table Set, Canary, 4 Piece 435.00
Dog Head, Toothpick, Frosted 135.00
Early Diamond, Tumbler 65.00
Geneva, Creamer, Green 195.00
Leaf Bracket, Celery 95.00
Leaf Bracket, Creamer 90.00
Leaf Bracket, Spooner 50.00
Majestic, Compote, Jelly 625.00
Squirrel, Pitcher 145.00
Teardrop & Tassel, Spooner, Amber 150.00
Wild Rose With Scrolling Spooner, Child's Size 95.00

GRUEBY Faience Company of Boston, Massachusetts, was incorporated in 1897 by William H. Grueby. Garden statuary, art pottery, and architectural tiles were made until 1920. The company developed a matte green glaze that was so popular it was copied by many other factories making a less expensive type of pottery. This eventually led to the financial problems of the pottery.

Bowl, Carved Buds, Green Glaze, Flared Floriform, Stamp, 3 1/2 In.	2750.00
Bowl, Coupe, Green Glaze, Footed, Impressed Flower Mark, 3 3/4 In.	550.00
Bowl, Green Matte Glaze, Closed Form, Paper Label, 8 x 2 In.	495.00
Bowl, Raised Leaf & Bud Design, Signed, 8 1/2 In.	1455.00
Candlestick, Corseted, Applied Leaves, Tooled, Blue Green Matte Leathery Glaze, 8 In.	1980.00
Candlestick, Corseted, Tooled Leaves, Blue Green Glaze, Bulbous Top, Label, 8 In.	2530.00
Figurine, Scarab, Green Matte Glaze, 4 In.	1045.00
Humidor, Floral Band Rim, Sea Green Matte Glaze, Central Knob, Cylindrical, 8 In.	1092.00
Inkwell, Copper Cover, Hammered, Blue Matte Glaze, Vertical Panels, 5 x 5 1/2 In.	1870.00
Lamp, Vertical Leaves, Pinecones At Shoulder, Green Matte Glaze, Signed, 29 In.	16500.00
Paperweight, French Blue Glaze, Flower Stamp, 3 x 2 In.	660.00
Paperweight, Raised White Beetle, Sand Colored Glaze, Signed, 2 1/2 In.	316.00
Paperweight, Scarab, Cobalt Blue Glaze, Stamped, 2 1/4 In.	1045.00
Paperweight, Scarab, Green Matte Glaze, 3 7/8 In.	316.00
Paperweight, Scarab, Mustard Matte Leathery Glaze, Signed, 2 x 3 In.	700.00
Paperweight, Scarab, Pale Blue Matte Glaze, 4 In.	431.00
Table, 21 Tiles Top, Checkerboard Pattern, Geometric & Floral Corner Tiles, Iron Base	1265.00
Tile, Landscape, Pine Trees, Green, Blue, Brown, Cuenca, Arts & Crafts Frame, 6 In.	2310.00
Tile, Molded Bird Design, Brown, Blue Ground, Arts & Crafts Frame, 4 In.	550.00
Tile, Multicolored Ship At Sea, Green Water, Blue Sky, Arts & Crafts Frame, 4 In.	880.00
Tile, Oak Tree Against Cloud-Filled Sky, Green, Blue, White, Arts & Crafts Frame, 6 In.	1980.00
Tile, Scene, Green Shades, Blue & Brown, 6 x 6 In.	1430.00
Tile, Stylized Viking Ship On High Waves, Blue, Green, Brown, Arts Crafts Frame, 6 In.	2750.00
Tile, Tulip Design, Blue, Green, Dark Green Matte Ground, Square, 6 In.	990.00
Tile, Yellow, Black, Green, Dark Green Matte Ground, 4 1/2 x 6 In.	2860.00
Trivet, Landscape, Green Matte, Blue, Cream & Brown Glaze, 6 x 6 In.	2645.00
Vase, 3 Broad Leaf Blades, Green Matte Glaze, Bulbous, 7 1/4 In.	1380.00
Vase, 5 Broad Leaves, Mottled Green Matte Glaze, Signed, 2 3/4 In.	1585.00
Vase, 5 Vertical Leaves, Green Glaze, 2 3/4 x 4 1/4 In.	1585.00
Vase, Alternating Low Petals, Leaves, Mauve Matte Glaze, Squat, 7 3/8 x 4 3/4 In.	2300.00
Vase, Applied Double Overlapping Leaves, Green 2-Tone Matte Glaze, 8 x 7 1/2 In.	2860.00
Vase, Applied Leaves On Base, Stems, Buds, Green Matte Glaze, Signed, 8 In.	990.00
Vase, Applied Leaves, Alternating With Buds, Green Matte Organic Glaze, 7 x 4 In.	3575.00
Vase, Applied Leaves, Carved, Green Matte Leathery Glaze, 8 1/4 x 5 In.	2090.00
Vase, Applied Leaves, Divided By Carved Stems, Buds, Green Matte Glaze, 11 In.	2310.00
Vase, Applied Leaves, Divided By Vertical Stems, Brown, Dark Green, 8 1/2 In.	2310.00
Vase, Applied Leaves, Green Matte Glaze, Impressed Mark, Initials, 9 1/2 In.	4125.00
Vase, Applied Leaves, Long Stem Buds, Green Matte Glaze, 8 1/2 In.	4950.00
Vase, Applied Leaves, Tall Buds, Green Matte Glaze, Stamp, 7 1/2 In.	4400.00
Vase, Applied Rounded Leaves, Carved, Green Matte Leathery Glaze, Squat, 4 x 5 In.	2640.00
Vase, Applied Rounded Leaves, Light Green Glaze, Bottle Shape, 6 3/4 x 4 1/2 In.	1430.00
Vase, Applied Tendril Ribs, Green Matte Glaze, Bulbous, 5 7/8 In.	3737.00
Vase, Applied Vertical Leaves, Green Matte Glaze, Impressed Mark, 4 1/2 In.	1210.00
Vase, Applied Vertical Leaves, Green Matte Glaze, Ruth Erickson, 9 In.	2640.00
Vase, Applied Vertical Leaves, Light Green Matte Glaze, 5 In.	3575.00
Vase, Blue & Green Curdled Glaze, 6 1/2 In.	1200.00
Vase, Blue Matte Glaze, Cylindrical, Impressed Mark, 7 In.	605.00
Vase, Carved Applied Leaves At Base, Green Matte Enamel, Signed, 8 In.	2600.00
Vase, Carved Broad Leaves, Green Glaze, Floriform Rim, Stamped, 7 3/4 In.	2640.00
Vase, Carved Panels & Ribs, Green Matte Leathery Glaze, Squat, 3 x 3 3/4 In.	770.00
Vase, Carved Ribbed Panels, Green Matte Glaze, Bulbous, 3 3/4 x 5 In.	1320.00
Vase, Carved Vertical Leaves, Blue Matte Glaze, 7 x 8 In.	1760.00
Vase, Carved, Applied Leaves, Yellow Matte Glaze, White Buds, 6 1/2 In.	9350.00
Vase, Cucumber Matte Green, Signed, 9 In.	1400.00
Vase, Elongated Leafage & Flower Buds, Wilhelmina Post, c.1900, 10 In.	6325.00
Vase, Green Matte Glaze, 8 1/2 x 4 In.	880.00

Gustavsberg, Cigarette Box, Art Deco Reclining Nude, Green, Silver, Argenta, 5 5/8 x 4 In.

If it seems too good to be true, it usually is! Trust your instincts when buying antiques. Experienced collectors notice many little signs of repair or reproduction, often without realizing it.

Vase, Green Matte Glaze, Pinched, 8 In.	2550.00
Vase, Green Matte Glaze, Ribbed Body, Bulbous, 4 3/4 x 3 1/4 In.	825.00
Vase, Green, 5 Applied Handles, 11 In.	6325.00
Vase, Leaves, Green Matte Glaze, Mustard Yellow Ground, Impressed Mark, 8 3/4 In.	5500.00
Vase, Mottled Green Matte Glaze, Squat, 3 5/8 In.	1320.00
Vase, Oatmeal Glaze, Paper Label, Signed, Cylindrical, 11 1/4 In.	1060.00
Vase, Ribbed Body, Green Matte Leathery Glaze, Bottle Shape, 4 1/2 x 3 In.	770.00
Vase, Stylized Leaf Design, Flared Rim, Blue Matte Glaze, Signed, 3 3/4 In.	1800.00

GUNS that may be classed as toys, such as BB guns, air rifles, and cap guns, are listed in the Toy category.

GUSTAVSBERG ceramics factory was founded in 1827 near Stockholm, Sweden. It is best known to collectors for its twentieth-century art wares, especially a green stoneware with silver inlay called *Argenta*.   **Gustafsberg**

Cigarette Box, Art Deco Reclining Nude, Green, Silver, Argenta, 5 5/8 x 4 In. . . . . . .*Illus*	250.00
Dish, Argenta, Footed, Shallow	66.00
Jar, Cover, Stylized Blue & Green Flowers, Hammered Ground, Signed, 7 In.	450.00
Tray, Argenta, Round, 4 In.	45.00
Vase, Argenta, Fish & Bubbles, Flared, Marked, 8 x 6 3/4 In.	300.00
Vase, Bottle, White, Blue & Green Stripes, Marked, Sweden, 16 In.	230.00
Vase, Fish, 1950s, 6 In.	165.00
Vase, Nude Riding Fish, 7 1/2 x 6 In.	550.00
Vase, Turquoise Matte Glaze Body, Silver Overlay, Dragon Design, Signed, 7 In.	402.00

GUTTA-PERCHA was one of the first plastic materials. It was made from a mixture of resins from Malaysian trees. It was molded and used for daguerreotype cases, toilet articles, and picture frames in the nineteenth century.

Bracelet, Hand Carved Links On Elastic, Love Knot, Beaded Links, 1850s	140.00
Bracelet, Strips Of Gold, Hinged Bangle, Safety Chain, 7 1/4 In.	195.00
Earrings, Horseshoe Design, 1850s, 5/8 x 3/4 In.	185.00
Necklace, Teardrop Pendant, Interlocking Links, c.1850, 26 In.	155.00

HAEGER Potteries, Inc., Dundee, Illinois, started making commercial art wares in 1914. Early pieces were marked with the name *Haeger* written over an *H*. About 1938, the mark *Royal Haeger* was used. The firm is still making florist wares and lamp bases.

Ashtray, Gold Tweed, 8 x 4 1/4 In.	11.00
Bank, Owl, Turquoise, 7 1/2 In.	65.00
Basket, Hanging, Owl, 7 x 8 1/2 In.	50.00
Birdhouse, Wall Pocket, 2 Birds, 9 1/2 x 7 1/4 In.	31.00
Bookends, Puma	200.00
Bowl, Cutout Leaves, Mermaid Flower Frog, Pink & Blue, 16 In.	95.00
Candleholder, Mauve Agate, 4 1/2 In., Pair	45.00
Candy Jar, Peacock Glaze Over Black Matte Body, 1 x 7 In.	145.00

Figurine, Rooster, Gold Tweed Glaze, 22K Gold, 20 In. 500.00
Figurine, Swan, Uplifted Wings, Gray & Brown, 9 In. 45.00
Flower Frog, Lady, White 450.00
Flower Frog, Nude Woman, Art Deco, 7 In. 165.00
Pitcher, Ewer Shape, Yellow, 10 In. 85.00
Pitcher, Yellow, Chocolate, 16 In. 65.00
Vase, Black, Red & Orange Wrap, 15 1/4 In. 52.00
Vase, Double Conch Shell, Mallow Glaze, 10 In. 85.00
Vase, Swirled Feathers, Mauve, Agate, 10 In. 95.00

HALF-DOLL, see Pincushion Doll category.

HALL CHINA Company started in East Liverpool, Ohio, in 1903. The firm made many types of wares. Collectors search for the Hall teapots made from the 1920s to the 1950s. The dinnerwares of the same period, especially Autumn Leaf pattern, are also popular. The Hall China Company is still working. For more information, see *Kovels' Depression Glass & Dinnerware Price List.* Autumn Leaf pattern dishes are listed in their own category in this book.

HALL'S
SUPERIOR
QUALITY
KITCHENWARE

Blue, Pitcher, Water, Hercules, Peasant Ware, Westinghouse, 9 1/2 In. 85.00
Blue Blossom, Casserole, Cover 90.00
Blue Bouquet, Baker 22.00
Blue Bouquet, Bowl, Radiance, 7 In. 30.00
Blue Bouquet, Soup, Dish, 8 1/2 In. 20.00
Blue Bouquet, Gravy Boat 30.00
Blue Bouquet, Jug, No. 3 .... 125.00
Blue Bouquet, Mug, D-Style 22.00
Blue Bouquet, Platter, Oval, 11 In. ....25.00 to 30.00
Cameo Rose, Butter 50.00
Cameo Rose, Cup 8.00
Cameo Rose, Salt & Pepper 35.00
Crocus, Bowl, 6 1/8 x 3 In. 45.00
Crocus, Bowl, Radiance, 7 In. 30.00
Crocus, Gravy Boat 30.00
Crocus, Jug, Ball 200.00
Crocus, Jug, Ball, No. 3, 7 1/2 In. 178.00
Crocus, Mixing Bowl, 7 1/2 x 4 In. 55.00
Crocus, Plate, 10 In. 45.00
Crocus, Pretzel Jar 250.00
Gray & Yellow, Leftover, Refrigerator Ware, General Electric, 3 1/4 x 5 In. 17.00
Phoenix Blue, Butter, Cover, Westinghouse 55.00
Poppy, Baker, Round, 7 In. 9.00
Poppy, Bowl, 10 In. 50.00
Poppy, Plate, 9 In. 12.00
Poppy, Salt & Pepper, Teardrop 40.00
Poppy, Spoon 125.00
Red Poppy, Bowl, 9 In. 37.00
Red Poppy, Coffeepot, Daniel, Metal Dripper 46.00
Red Poppy, Cup 9.00
Red Poppy, Pitcher 35.00
Red Poppy, Plate, 10 In. 35.00
Red Poppy, Saucer 3.00
Red Poppy, Sugar & Creamer 45.00
Red Poppy, Sugar, Cover 20.00
Rose Parade, Bean Pot, 7 x 6 1/2 In. 90.00
Rose Parade, Casserole, Cover 5.00
Royal Rose, Casserole, Cover 45.00
Royal Rose, Salt & Pepper 23.00
Shaggy Tulip, Bean Pot 275.00
Silhouette, Bowl, Vegetable, Oval 30.00
Silhouette, Gravy Boat 25.00
Silhouette, Platter, Oval, 11 In. ....30.00 to 40.00

Mayonnaise can be used to
remove old masking tape,
stickers, or labels from glass
or china.

Hall, Teapot, Globe, No Drip,
Cobalt, Gold Trim

Silhouette, Tile, 6 In.	95.00
Teapot, Airflow, Canary Yellow	140.00
Teapot, Aladdin, Cobalt Blue, 11 In.	70.00
Teapot, Automobile	250.00 to 400.00
Teapot, Baltimore, Warm Yellow	50.00
Teapot, Boston, Poppy	350.00
Teapot, Bowling Ball	600.00
Teapot, Cleveland, Cobalt, Butterflies, Gold Trim	100.00
Teapot, Damascus, Blue	320.00
Teapot, Football, Chinese Red	750.00
Teapot, French, Black, Gold Daisies, 6 Cup	50.00
Teapot, Globe, No Drip, Cobalt, Gold Trim _Illus_	85.00
Teapot, Illinois, Pink, Gold Trim	248.00
Teapot, Los Angeles, Cobalt Blue, Gold Trim	75.00
Teapot, Los Angeles, Monterrey	65.00
Teapot, McCormick, Turquoise	50.00
Teapot, McCormick, Yellow	125.00
Teapot, Melody, Poppy	325.00
Teapot, New York, 4 Cup	25.00
Teapot, New York, Game Bird Decal	225.00
Teapot, New York, Gray, 1 Cup	12.00
Teapot, Parade, 4 Cup	45.00
Teapot, Parade, 6 Cup	55.00
Teapot, Parade, Canary Yellow, Gold Trim, 6 Cup	38.00
Teapot, Parade, Gold Squiggle, Gold Spout, Lid & Handle	45.00
Teapot, Poppy, Boston	250.00
Teapot, Rose Parade, Pert	77.00
Teapot, Rose White, 5 Cup	60.00
Teapot, Streamline, Chinese Red	300.00
Teapot, Victorian, Pink, Gold Plume	273.00
Teapot, Windshield, Camellia	40.00
Teapot, Yellow, Gold Trim	30.00
Teapot, Zeisel, Tomorrow's Classics, 6 Cup	160.00
Tulip, Bowl, 7 1/2 In.	35.00
Tulip, Bowl, 9 In.	30.00
Tulip, Creamer	12.00 to 15.00
Tulip, Plate, 10 In.	15.00 to 25.00
Wildfire, Bowl, Vegetable, 9 In.	28.00
Wildfire, Pitcher, Pert, 5 In.	75.00
Wildfire, Plate, 6 In.	3.00
Wildfire, Saucer	13.00
Wildfire, Sugar & Creamer	45.00
Zeisel, Bowl, Vegetable, Fern, Divided, 11 1/4 x 8 1/4 In.	40.00
Zeisel, Cookie Jar, Tritone	275.00
Zeisel, Sugar, Fern, Cover, 4 1/4 In.	25.00

HALLOWEEN is an ancient holiday that has changed in the last 200 years. The jack-o'-lantern, witches on broomsticks, and orange decorations seem to be twentieth-century creations. Collectors started to become serious about collecting Halloween-related items in the late 1970s. The papier-mache decorations, now replaced by plastic, and old costumes are in demand.

Apron, Dancing Witch & Cat, Crepe Paper, Cloth Ties, 18 x 21 In.	60.00
Apron, Jack-O'-Lantern, Black Cat Eyes, Bat Mouth, Crepe Paper, 18 x 21 In.	100.00
Arcade Machine, Haunted Mansion, Gottlieb, 1980	2500.00
Ashtray, Skull, Tan, Pottery, 5 In.	20.00
Banner, Black Cats, Owls, Bats, Pumpkins, Crepe Paper, Original Sleeve, 20 x 120 In.	85.00
Banner, Witches, Black Cats, Grinning Faces, Bats, Original Sleeve, 20 x 120 In.	90.00
Bookend, Arched Black Cat	85.00
Candleholder, Cat, Hunched Back, Pottery, Red, Germany, 4 1/4 In.	75.00
Candy Container, Black Cat In Shroud, Composition, Cloth, Germany, 5 3/4 In.	610.00
Candy Container, Black Cat, Accordion Head, Composition, Germany, 6 In.	535.00
Candy Container, Cat On Devil's Head, Composition, Germany, 6 In.	2300.00
Candy Container, Cat, Black, Wearing Apron	1320.00
Candy Container, Devil, Composition, Germany, 8 In.	1100.00
Candy Container, Devil, With Pitchfork	1045.00
Candy Container, Jack-O'-Lantern, Boy Riding Red Rooster, Germany, c.1910, 3 In.	1300.00
Candy Container, Jack-O'-Lantern, Riding Green Duck	1073.00
Candy Container, Orange Crepe Paper, Celluloid Clown's Head On Top	98.00
Candy Container, Pumpkin Boy, Removable Head, Composition, Germany, 3 In.	290.00
Candy Container, Pumpkin Man Admiral, Composition, Germany, 3 1/2 In.	555.00
Candy Container, Shrouded Skeleton, Composition, Cloth, Germany, 6 In.	610.00
Candy Container, Skull, Composition, Removable Bottom, Germany, 2 1/2 In.	335.00
Candy Container, Smiling Cat Pushing A Pumpkin, Wheels, 4 In.	198.00
Candy Container, Witch On Jack-O'-Lantern, Composition, Germany, 3 In.	815.00
Candy Container, Witch With Pumpkin Head, Composition, Germany, 3 3/4 In.	435.00
Candy Container, Witch With Pumpkin Head, Composition, Germany, 3 In.	690.00
Candy Container, Witch's Head, Composition, Germany, 3 1/2 In.	735.00
Candy Container, Witch, Crepe Paper & Composition, Germany, 4 1/2 In.	395.00
Candy Container, Witch, Germany, 6 1/2 In.	225.00
Candy Container, Witch, Papier Mache, Germany, 1950s, 8 In.	60.00
Candy Container, Witch, Wax	85.00
Costume, Barney Google, Tuxedo Jacket, Hat, 1936	45.00
Costume, Bat Masterson	40.00
Costume, Bullwinkle Moose, Ben Cooper, Box	125.00
Costume, Creature From The Black Lagoon, Cloth, Mask	95.00
Costume, E.T., Box	25.00
Costume, Evel Knievel, With Mask, Ben Cooper, Box, 1974	90.00
Costume, Ghost Busters	15.00
Costume, Goldilocks, Cloth, Mask	35.00
Costume, Hagar The Horrible, Box	45.00
Costume, Heckle & Jeckle, Terrytoons, Inc., Late 1950s, 36 In.	25.00
Costume, King Kong, Adult	25.00
Costume, Mary Hartline	45.00
Costume, Morticia, Addams Family	80.00
Costume, Mr. Spock, Star Trek, Ben Cooper, Paramount Pictures, Box, 1975, Child's	24.00
Costume, Planet Of The Apes, Full Head, Latex Mask, Real Hair, Adult	150.00
Costume, Planet Of The Apes, Lisa, Ben Cooper, Box, 1973	15.00
Costume, Raggedy Ann	15.00
Costume, Spiderman	15.00
Costume, Tom Corbett, Space Clothes, Yankiboy, Box	295.00
Costume, Top Cat, Black & Yellow Fabric, 1960s	25.00
Costume, Tweety	25.00
Costume, Witchie Poo, Plastic Mask, Dress, Sid & Marty Krofft TV Prod., 1970s	110.00
Costume, Zorro, Box	165.00
Figure, Cat Pushing Jack-O'-Lantern Cart, Plastic, Yellow Wheels, 6 1/2 In.	125.00
Figure, Crow, Papier-Mache, Glass Eyes, Large	75.00
Figure, Pumpkin Man, Jointed Arms & Legs, Composition, Germany, 3 1/4 In.	485.00
Figure, Scarecrow, Jack-O'-Lantern Head, Plastic, Wheels, Basket	50.00

 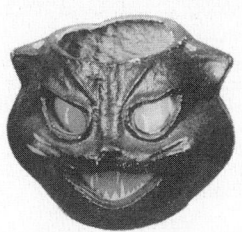 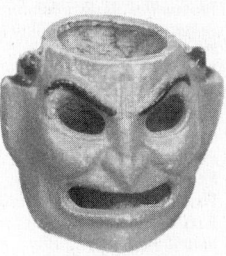

Halloween, Jack-O'-Lantern, Tissue
Paper Insert, Papier-Mache, Buffalo,
N.Y.

Halloween, Lantern, Cat,
Black, Tissue Paper Insert,
Orange Whisker, 5 1/4 In.

Halloween, Lantern,
Devil, Orange, Black,
7 3/4 In.

Figure, Witch Pulling Black Cat, Celluloid, Japan, Pre-World War II, 3 In.	830.00
Figure, Witch Sitting On Pumpkin, Celluloid, 5 3/4 In.	455.00
Game, Witch Of Endor, Box, 1929, 6 1/2 x 10 1/2 In.	105.00
Horn, Devil's Head, Open Mouth, Papier Mache, 5 3/4 In.	195.00
Jack-O'-Lantern, 2-Faced, Papier-Mache, Electric, 10 In.	395.00
Jack-O'-Lantern, Cat Face, Papier-Mache, Set Of 2	688.00
Jack-O'-Lantern, Cat, Full Body, Papier-Mache, 1940s	550.00
Jack-O'-Lantern, Composition, Tissue Paper Insert, 4 1/2 In.	200.00
Jack-O'-Lantern, Green & Orange Stripes, Papier-Mache	578.00
Jack-O'-Lantern, Hag Face, Papier-Mache	770.00
Jack-O'-Lantern, Metal, Hanging, Revolving Back For Candle	495.00
Jack-O'-Lantern, Paper Face, Papier-Mache, Orange, Green, 4 x 7 In., 5 Piece	605.00
Jack-O'-Lantern, Papier-Mache Cat, Cardboard, 4 Piece	495.00
Jack-O'-Lantern, Papier-Mache, Paper Insert, 6 In.	610.00
Jack-O'-Lantern, Pip-Squeak, 1920s, 6 In.	900.00
Jack-O'-Lantern, Pressed Cardboard, Mustache, Tissue Fringe Sideburns, 1930s	578.00
Jack-O'-Lantern, Tin Drum	688.00
Jack-O'-Lantern, Tissue Paper Insert, Papier-Mache, Buffalo, N.Y. *Illus*	308.00
Lantern, Black Cat Head, Molded Cardboard, Paper Insert, Germany, 4 In.	580.00
Lantern, Black Cat, Papier-Mache, Hand Made	29.00
Lantern, Cat, Black, Tissue Paper Insert, Orange Whisker, 5 1/4 In. *Illus*	238.00
Lantern, Devil's Head, Composition, Cut Out Eyes, Mouth, Germany, 3 1/2 In.	805.00
Lantern, Devil, Orange, Black, 7 3/4 In. *Illus*	220.00
Lantern, Devil, Papier-Mache, Hand Made	39.00
Lantern, Ghost Head, Molded Cardboard, Paper Insert, Germany, 4 1/2 In.	805.00
Lantern, Horned Devil's Head, Molded Cardboard, Germany, 3 3/4 In.	720.00
Lantern, Orange Cat, Papier-Mache, Hand Made	34.00
Lantern, Owl's Head, Molded Cardboard, Paper Insert Eyes, Germany, 4 3/4 In.	650.00
Lantern, Owl, Tin	75.00
Lantern, Pumpkin Head On Pumpkin Body, Squatty Legs, Paper Pulp, 9 1/2 In.	450.00
Lantern, Vegetable Man, Composition, Germany, 5 In.	880.00
Lantern, Watermelon, Composition, Paper Insert, Germany, 3 1/2 In.	1085.00
Mask, Batman, Heavy Rubber	45.00
Mask, Goliath, Odd Fellows Lodge, Full Horsehair Beard, Papier-Mache, 1890s	165.00
Mask, Jimmy Carter, Plastic	15.00
Mask, Ronald Reagan, Plastic	15.00
Mask, Yoda, Green Latex, Don Post, 1980, Adult	28.00
Milk Carton, UNICEF	38.00
Napkin, 1920s	4.00
New York Magazine, Halloween Cover, c.1940	10.00
Noisemaker, Harmonica Player, U.S. Metals	25.00
Noisemaker, Tin Bell, Wooden Handle, Lithograph	35.09
Ornament, Black Cat Playing Cymbals, Molded Cardboard, Germany, 7 1/2 In.	120.00
Ornament, Jack-O'-Lantern, Goofy Face, Molded Cardboard, Die Cut, Germany, 5 In.	40.00
Pinata, Witch, Blue Face, Original Candy Inside, 21 In.	45.00

Postcard, A Halloween Morning, Owl On Jack-O'-Lantern 600.00
Postcard, A Starry Hallowe'en, Girl, Witch, Jack-O'-Lantern 175.00
Postcard, Black Cat On Jack-O'-Lantern, 1909, 3 1/2 x 5 1/2 In. 35.00
Postcard, Bobbing For Apples, 1909, 3 1/2 x 5 1/2 In. 10.00
Postcard, Child & Jack-O'-Lantern, Embossed, Freixas, 1914 .... 125.00
Postcard, Child In Witch Costume, Photograph, 1908 .... 215.00
Postcard, Giant Bat & Jack-O'-Lantern, 1910, 3 1/2 x 5 1/2 In. 25.00
Postcard, Halloween Greetings, Children With Jack-O'-Lantern, Germany, 1909 .... 22.00
Postcard, Jolly Halloween, Witch, Cat, Cauldron, 1911, 3 1/2 x 5 1/2 In. 45.00
Postcard, Witches On Bats With Jack-O'-Lanterns, 1911, 3 1/2 x 5 1/2 In. 25.00
Rattle, Frying Pan, Goblins, Woman 50.00
Salt & Pepper, Big Boy 85.00
Sparkler, Black, Orange & Yellow 120.00
Sparkler, Cat, Sparkling Eyes 145.00
Sparkler, Space Ship, Germany 185.00
Tambourine, Black Cat, Tin, 6 In. 100.00
Tambourine, Orange & White, Metal, U.S.A. 35.00
Toy, Piano, Baby Grand, Tootsie, Iron, 3 1/2 x 3 x 2 In. 175.00
Toy, Roly Poly, 2 Embossed Owls In Tree, Celluloid, 3 1/4 In. 495.00

HAMPSHIRE pottery was made in Keene, New Hampshire, between
1871 and 1923. Hampshire developed a line of colored glazed wares
as early as 1883, including a Royal Worcester-type pink, olive green,
blue, and mahogany. Pieces are marked with the printed mark or the
impressed name *Hampshire Pottery* or *J.S.T. & Co., Keene, N.H.* Many
pieces were marked with city names and sold as souvenirs.

Bowl, Artichoke, Cucumber Green Matte Glaze, Leaf Rim, 3 x 4 In. 275.00
Bowl, Embossed Waterlily Pads, Buds, Brown & Green Matte Glaze, 3 x 10 In. 440.00
Bowl, Green Matte Glaze, Alternating Streak Panel Design, Flat Rim, 4 1/8 In. 440.00
Bowl, Indian, Maroon Red Light Luster, Mottled Red Brown Interior, 2 x 7 In. 1045.00
Bowl, Shrubbery Design, Repeating, Teal To Sea Foam Green Glaze, 2 x 5 1/2 In. 302.00
Bowl, Stylized Vine, Leaf, Repeating, Cerulean Blue Matte Glaze, 2 1/2 In. 247.00
Candleholder, Cucumber Green Matte Glaze, Rolled Lip, Round Base, 6 In. 165.00
Creamer, Volcanic Glaze, 3 x 5 In. 110.00
Ewer, Cucumber Green Matte Glaze, Mottled Dark Gray, Handle, 9 1/2 In. 605.00
Ewer, Flowing Green Glaze, Oval Body, 9 x 9 3/4 In. 400.00
Ewer, Green Matte Glaze, Arched Handle Resting On Squat Base, 6 1/2 In. 165.00
Ewer, Handle, Brown & Green High Glaze, Signed, 6 In. 100.00
Lamp, Floral Handel Shade, Pink Rose, Green Matte Glaze, 7 x 7 1/2 In. 1430.00
Lamp, Handel Shade, Embossed Flowers Top To Bottom, Signed, 21 5/8 In. 4400.00
Lamp, Tapering Form, 2 Handles, Green Glaze, Signed, 8 1/2 In. 1190.00
Lamp, Vertical Ribs, Geometric Leaded Glass Shade, Bulbous, 22 In. 1760.00
Lamp Base, Cucumber Green Matte Glaze, Hurricane Insert, Handle, 15 In. 1540.00
Lamp Base, Green Matte Glaze, Geometric Swirling Design, Electrified, 10 In. 715.00
Lamp Base, Rose Mauve Matte Glaze, Deep Mauve Veining, Dusty Rose, 11 In. 605.00
Lamp Base, Tricolored Cerulean Matte Glaze, 2 Handles, Electrified, 9 In. 1650.00
Pitcher, Cucumber Green Matte Glaze, Arched Handle, 11 1/4 x 4 In. 302.00
Stein, Holly Berry, Green Matte Glaze, 5 1/2 In. 192.00
Vase, Blue Green Matte Glaze, 5 x 6 In. 412.00
Vase, Blue Matte Glaze, Mottled Deep Chicory Blue Lip, Gray, Black, 12 In. 715.00
Vase, Bud, Mocha Brown Matte Glaze, Deep To Light Finish, 5 In. 220.00
Vase, Bud, Serpent, Serpent Head On Handle, Cucumber Green Matte Glaze, 6 In. 302.00
Vase, Bud, Serpent, Serpent Head On Handle, Olive Green Glaze, 6 In. 137.00
Vase, Cerulean Blue Matte Glaze, Lavender, Gray Base, Squat, 5 1/8 x 5 In. 495.00
Vase, Cobalt Blue Matte Glaze, Light Blue Flecks Throughout, 4 3/4 x 2 1/2 In. 165.00
Vase, Cucumber Green Matte Glaze, Closed-In Style Mouth, Baluster, 11 In. 770.00
Vase, Deep Cerulean Blue Matte Glaze, Gray Veining, 7 In. 605.00
Vase, Embossed Tulips, Arts & Crafts, Signed, 6 1/2 In. 605.00
Vase, Green Matte Glaze, 3 1/2 In. 308.00
Vase, Green Matte Glaze, Bulging Dandelion Buds Around Mouth, 6 x 5 In. 880.00
Vase, Green Matte Glaze, Dark Cucumber Green, 2 Buttressed Handles, 6 In. 330.00
Vase, Green Matte Glaze, Flared, Long Neck, 9 1/4 x 6 1/2 In. 440.00
Vase, Green Matte Glaze, Hand-Thrown, Soft Shoulders, 7 x 3 In. 247.00

Vase, Green Matte Glaze, Ribbed, Flared, Pinched Waist, 7 x 5 3/4 In. 825.00
Vase, Green Matte Glaze, Short Neck, Bulbous, 3 1/2 x 3 3/4 In. 302.00
Vase, Green Matte Glaze, Vivid Floral Rim, Large Arched Leaves, Tulip Shape, 8 In. 550.00
Vase, Green, 5 1/2 In. 440.00
Vase, Heart Shaped Leaves, Mottled Ocher Matte, Serrated Rim, 3 In. 990.00
Vase, Incised Design, Green Matte Glaze, C. Robertson, 2 1/2 x 5 1/2 In. 395.00
Vase, Matte Green Glaze, Broad, Soft Shoulder, Cylindrical Base, 8 x 5 In. 357.00
Vase, Melon, Ribbed Body, Feathered Mauve Glaze, Beige Ground, 3 1/8 In. 275.00
Vase, Molded Ear Of Corn, Vertical Leaves, Buds, Green Matte, Orange Glaze, 7 In. 357.00
Vase, Molded Ears Of Corn, Maize, Signed, 6 In. 1100.00
Vase, Molded Leaves & Stems, With Buds, Green Glaze, Signed, 7 In. 605.00
Vase, Molded Leaves, Blue Matte Glaze, 4 x 6 In. 550.00
Vase, Mottled Frothy Glaze, Veining, Steel Blue Neck, Gray, Pink, 9 In. 2750.00
Vase, Oatmeal Cream Beige Matte Glaze, Trumpet Shape, 9 3/4 x 6 3/4 In. 495.00
Vase, Open Tulip, Petal & Leaf Design, Green Matte Glaze, 9 x 6 In. 1320.00
Vase, Petals, Leaves, 2-Tone Blue Matte Glaze, Pale Blue, 3 x 6 In. 546.00
Vase, Raised Leaf, Tobacco Brown Glaze, Signed, 3 x 6 In. 530.00
Vase, Raspberry Curdled Matte Glaze, 6 x 3 3/4 In. 385.00
Vase, Stylized Floral Design, Cucumber Green Matte Glaze, 6 1/3 In. 467.00
Vase, Stylized Floral Design, Green Matte Glaze, Impressed Mark, 7 In. 715.00
Vase, Stylized Leaf Design, Blue Matte Glaze, Flared Rim, 9 1/2 In. 977.00
Vase, Teal Blue Glaze, Seed Shape, 6 3/4 In. 300.00

HANDEL glass was made by Philip Handel working in Meriden, Connecticut, from 1885 and in New York City from 1893 to 1933. The firm made art glass and other types of lamps. Handel shades were made not only of leaded glass in a style reminiscent of Tiffany but also of reverse painted glass. Handel also made vases and other glass objects.

Humidor, Cover, Painted Fisherman, Embossed Curlicues, Signed, 6 x 7 1/4 In. 275.00
Humidor, Cover, Spelter Pipe Shape, Can-Can Dancer Next To Thermometer, 6 x 7 In. 330.00
Humidor, Cover, Spelter Pipe Shape, Deer In The Mountains, Red, Green Ground, 7 In. ... 165.00
Lamp, 7 Amber Slag Panels, Field Flowers, Goldenrod, Bronze Base, 22 In. 3830.00
Lamp, 8 Bent Panels With Panel Borders, 19 1/4 In. 4125.00
Lamp, 8-Sided Slag Shade, Trees, Bronze, Signed, 28 x 24 In. 2860.00
Lamp, Boudoir, Reverse Painted Shade, Domed, Roses, Flowers, Black Leaves, 15 In. ... 2990.00
Lamp, Boudoir, Reverse Painted Shade, Parrots On Foliage, Tree Trunk, 6 Sides, 13 In. ... 3000.00
Lamp, Cutout Mushroom Design Base, Original Patina, 14 In. 2750.00
Lamp, Desk, Amber Shade, Pineneedle Design, Bronze, Stamped, 12 1/4 In. 1500.00
Lamp, Desk, Brown Glass Shade, White Interior, Bronze Metal Ribbed Base, 16 In. 977.00
Lamp, Desk, Caramel, Opal White, Adjustable, Bronze Metal Base, Glass, 15 In. 1495.00
Lamp, Desk, Green, Opal White, Adjustable, Leaf Design, 15 x 8 In. 1380.00
Lamp, Desk, Reverse Painted Shade, Autumn Landscape, Bronze, c.1915, 12 In. 1795.00
Lamp, Desk, Reverse Painted Shade, Mustard Ground, Bronze Metal Base, 14 In. 1650.00
Lamp, Glass Shade, No. 1851, Hampshire Base, Signed, 21 x 17 In. 4125.00
Lamp, Molded Leaf Shape Shade, Bronze, 1910-1920, 24 In. 920.00
Lamp, Overlay, Leaf Border, Signed Base & Shade, 24 In. 3850.00
Lamp, Piano, Acid Etched Geometric Shade, Bronze Base, 10 x 13 In. 1000.00
Lamp, Piano, Amber, Green, Leaf Border, Gilt Metal, Arched Tapered Arm, 19 In. 1495.00
Lamp, Reverse Painted Shade, Berry Vine, Black Stripe, Leaf Base, Signed, 6 3/4 In. 288.00
Lamp, Reverse Painted Shade, Connecticut River, Green, Blue, Purple, 18 3/4 In. 9200.00
Lamp, Reverse Painted Shade, Daffodil, Conical, 23 In. 10350.00
Lamp, Reverse Painted Shade, Dome, Textured Glass, 23 x 18 In. 6325.00
Lamp, Reverse Painted Shade, Domed, Allover Leaf, Green, Brown Patina, 1915, 17 In. ... 6900.00
Lamp, Reverse Painted Shade, Domed, Floral, Bell Shape, 20 1/2 In. 5750.00
Lamp, Reverse Painted Shade, Domed, Green, White Leaf Border, Signed, 18 In. 2530.00
Lamp, Reverse Painted Shade, Domed, Pink Band Of Tulips, Green, 1915, 22 x 16 In. ... 1035.00
Lamp, Reverse Painted Shade, Domed, Tropical Scene, Blue Interior, Bronze, 25 In. 7130.00
Lamp, Reverse Painted Shade, Domed, Winter Sunset Scene, Brown, Orange 4600.00
Lamp, Reverse Painted Shade, Intricate Flowers, Geometric Borders, 24 In. 3575.00
Lamp, Reverse Painted Shade, Landscape, Birch Trees, Bronze Metal, 24 In. 12100.00
Lamp, Reverse Painted Shade, Landscape, Mountains, Lake, Trees, 21 x 14 In. 5635.00
Lamp, Reverse Painted Shade, Nasturtiums, Decal On Base, Signed, 21 In. 2240.00

Lamp, Reverse Painted Shade, Nightscape, Signed, 18 x 16 In. 4000.00
Lamp, Reverse Painted Shade, Pink Dogwood, Bronze, Signed, Floor, 66 In. 12650.00
Lamp, Reverse Painted Shade, Pink Roses, Blue, Gray Leaves, Signed, 15 1/2 In. 3738.00
Lamp, Reverse Painted Shade, Red Flowers, Yellow Centers, 3 Butterflies, 24 In. 2970.00
Lamp, Reverse Painted Shade, Red, Yellow, Roses, Horizontal, Vertical Ribs, 26 In. 8250.00
Lamp, Reverse Painted Shade, Sailing Vessel, Moonlit Tropical Bay, 27 In. 16100.00
Lamp, Reverse Painted Shade, Signed On Shade & Base, 23 In. 3650.00
Lamp, Reverse Painted Shade, Spider Web Design, Harp Base, Signed, Floor, 10 In. 1650.00
Lamp, Reverse Painted Shade, Spring Scene, Trees & Birds, Bronzed Metal, 23 In. 9350.00
Lamp, Reverse Painted Shade, Sunset Scene, Floor, 24 In. 7700.00
Lamp, Reverse Painted Shade, Teroma, Trees, Birds 1760.00
Lamp, Reverse Painted Shade, Teroma, Wild Rose, 21 In. 7935.00
Lamp, Reverse Painted Shade, Treasure Island, Inverted Stem Base, Signed, 23 In. 10925.00
Lamp, Reverse Painted Shade, Trees, Sunset, Tam O'Shanter, 22 1/2 In. 1322.00
Lamp, Reverse Painted Shade, Woodland Scene, Bronze, Signed, 23 1/2 In. 8625.00
Lamp, Trapezoidal Leaded Shade, Caramel, Green, Red, Original Patina, 24 In. 17600.00
Lamp Base, Bronze, Broad Leaves, Vented Finial Top, 26 x 8 In. 1100.00
Shade, Domed, Lead, Open Floral Amber, Green Border, Geometric Ground, 1920 ...... 2530.00
Shade, Reverse Painted, Chipped Iced, Claret, Trees, Egg Shape, 1920 .... 385.00
Shade, Reverse Painted, Sunset, Metal Overlay, 22 1/2 In. 4750.00
Vase, Birch Trees & Flying Birds, Green, Yellow, Textured Ground, Urn Shape, 11 In. ... 1840.00
Vase, Birch Trees, Green, Blue, Brown, Everted Rim, Baluster, 8 In. 1265.00
Vase, Birch Trees, Leaves, Rose, Brown, Green, Flared Neck, 6 In. 1380.00
Vase, Red, Yellow Carnations, Green Ground, Metal Beaded Rim, 12 In. 460.00

HARDWARE, see Architectural category.

HARKER Pottery Company of East Liverpool, Ohio, was founded by Benjamin Harker in 1840. The company made many types of pottery but by the Civil War was making quantities of yellowware from native clays. They also made Rockingham-type brown-glazed pottery and whiteware. The plant was moved to Chester, West Virginia, in 1931. Dinnerwares were made and sold nationally. In 1971 the company was sold to Jeannette Glass Company and all operations ceased in 1972. For more information, see *Kovels' Depression Glass & Dinnerware Price List.*

Amy, Jug, Hi-Rise 150.00
Cameoware, Casserole, Blue, 7 3/4 In. 17.00
Morning Glory, Casserole, Cover 75.00
Shadow Rose, Rolling Pin 130.00

HATPIN collectors search for pins popular from 1860 to 1920. The long pin, often over four inches, was used to hold the hat in place on the hair. The tops of the pins were made of all materials, from solid gold and real gemstones to ceramics and glass. Be careful to buy original hatpins and not recent pieces made by altering old buttons.

Amethyst, 14K Gold, 6 1/2 In. 195.00
Art Nouveau, Woman, Reading Book, Silver Plated, 8 In. 95.00
Eastern Star, Enameled, 7 3/4 In. 70.00
Flower, Brass, 4 Cabochon Sapphires, 8 In. 110.00
Smiling Man, Wearing Derby, 6 3/4 In. 125.00

HATPIN HOLDERS were needed when hatpins were fashionable from 1860 to 1920. The large, heavy hat required special long-shanked pins to hold it in place. The hatpin holder resembles a large saltshaker, but it often has no opening at the bottom as a shaker does. Hatpin holders were made of all types of ceramics and metal. Look for other pieces under the names of specific manufacturers.

Enameled Lilies-Of-The-Valley, Gold Top, Signed 85.00
Mother Of Pearl, Initial R 50.00
Roses, Pink & Yellow, White Background, R.S. Germany 85.00
Violets, Gold Accents, 4 1/2 In. 300.00
Yellow Roses, Germany, 6 1/2 In. 90.00

HAVILAND china has been made in Limoges, France, since 1842. The factory was started by the Haviland Brothers of New York City. Pieces are marked *H & Co.*, *Haviland & Co.*, or *Theodore Haviland*. It is possible to match existing sets of dishes through dealers who specialize in Haviland china. Other factories worked in the town of Limoges making a similar chinaware. These porcelains are listed in this book under Limoges.

HAVILAND & CO.

Ashtray, Hotel Lotti, Paris	70.00
Basket, Gold Highlighted Floral, 1950s, 5 1/4 In.	45.00
Bonbon, Green Poppy, Pierced Border, Marked, 8 1/2 In.	45.00
Bone Dish, Baltimore Rose, Pink & Yellow, 6 Piece	275.00
Bowl, Broth, Louis XV, Allover Rose Blush & Gold Pattern, 3 Piece	145.00
Bowl, Meadow Visitors, Napkin Fold, 9 1/2 x 9 1/2 In.	140.00
Bowl, Salad, Marseille, 9 1/4 In.	70.00
Bowl, Vegetable, Hellebrorus Niger, Square, F & G Mark, 8 1/2 In.	72.00
Bowl, Vegetable, Marseille, Open	75.00
Cafe Filtre, Coffeepot, Cover, Filter, 2 Cups	*Illus* 577.00
Cake Plate, Baltimore Rose, Pink, Gold Marks, 10 1/2 In.	110.00
Cake Plate, Drop Rose, Fuchsia, 10 3/4 In.	132.00
Candlestick, Marseille, Floral, Hand Painted, 6 3/4 In., Pair	190.00 to 195.00
Celery Dish, Baltimore Rose, Pink & Yellow, 12 In.	195.00
Celery Dish, Her Majesty, Signed, 13 In.	66.00
Celery Dish, Musical Instrument Design, Cobalt Blue, Gold Trim, 12 1/8 x 5 7/8 In.	465.00
Chocolate Set, Hand Painted Floral, Pot, 6 Cups & Saucers	275.00
Chop Plate, Baltimore Rose, 12 1/2 In.	193.00
Chop Plate, Drop Rose Pink, Cobalt & Gold Marks, 12 3/4 In.	245.00
Chop Plate, Ranson, 13 In.	190.00
Coffee Set, Leaf Mold, Rose Final, Gold Trim, D & G Mark, 3 Piece	110.00
Coffee Set, Old Garden, Rope Shape, Triangular, 3 Piece	415.00
Coffeepot, Medallion Trim, Cover, Spout, Rope Handles, 8 Cup	95.00
Coffeepot, Moss Rose, Medallion Trim, Cover, Rope Handles, Spout, 8 Cup	95.00
Coffeepot, Ranson Blank, Allover Roses, Marked, 7 In.	60.00
Coffeepot, Sugar & Creamer, Floral Ranson Blank, 10-In. Pot, 3 Piece	110.00
Compote, Fruit, Old Pansy, 4 3/4 x 9 3/4 In.	185.00
Compote, Meadow Visitors, Napkin Fold, 5 1/4 x 8 1/2 In.	220.00
Cup & Saucer, Baltimore Rose, Pink & Yellow, Breakfast	85.00
Cup & Saucer, Blown Flowers, Gray Leaves, 4 & C Mark	30.00
Cup & Saucer, Breakfast, Baltimore Rose, Pink & Yellow	85.00
Cup & Saucer, Meadow Visitors, Papillon, Breakfast	105.00
Cuspidor, Moss Rose, 3 1/4 x 8 In.	250.00
Cuspidor, Rose Design, Double Circle Mark, 6 1/2 In.	190.00
Cuspidor, Rose Design, Smooth, 6 1/2 In.	192.50
Dinner Set, Leeds, Cream Ground, Gilt Edge, 119 Piece	405.00
Dish, Pickle, Leaf Mold, Shell Shape, Gold Trim, 8 3/4 In.	110.00
Eggcup, Moss Rose, Cream Trim, 3 5/8 In.	65.00

Haviland, Cafe
Filtre, Coffeepot,
Cover, Filter,
2 Cups

Haviland, Tea & Toast Set, Floral,
Gilt Trim, Marked D & A

Game Plate, Birds, Marked, 9 In., Pair 27.00
Invalid Feeder, Plain, Large Cup, Side Spout 120.00
Jar, Cover, Hand Painted, Indian Smoking Peace Pipe 150.00
Mustard Pot, Barrel, 3 1/4 In. 120.00
Olive Dish, Scattered Small Pink Roses 40.00
Oyster Plate, Fish & Floral, Sauce Center, 6 Sections, Star Shape 385.00
Oyster Plate, Marseille, Sauce Center, 4 Sections, 7 3/4 In. 105.00
Oyster Plate, Old Blackberry, Sauce Center, 6 Sections, Star Shape 220.00
Oyster Plate, President Hayes Service, Cobalt, Green & Gold, 8 3/4 In. 990.00
Pitcher, Allover Roses, Ranson Blank, Hand Painted, 9 In. 55.00
Pitcher, Grape & Vine Mold, Flowers, Embossed, Marked, 8 1/2 In. 120.00
Pitcher, Ivy, Gold Trim, Marked, 8 3/8 In. 120.00
Pitcher, Leaf Mold, Gold Trim, 8 3/8 In. 110.00
Plate, Baltimore Rose, Pink & Yellow, Heart Shape, 8 1/2 x 7 1/2 In. 275.00
Plate, Cabbage Rose, 9 3/4 In., 4 Piece ....250.00 to 280.00
Plate, Coromandel, 8 In. 13.00
Plate, Empress Marie-Louise & Caroline Bonaparte, c.1900, 9 In., Pair 150.00
Plate, Fruits & Berries, Berton, 8 1/2 In. 125.00
Plate, Osier, Fruit & Butterfly, Blue Center, 7 1/4 In. 50.00
Plate, Pallandre, Cobalt Blue & Gold, 8 1/2 In. 110.00
Plate, Parisian Flowers, Girardon, 8 1/2 In. 120.00
Plate, President Hayes Service, Grouse In Flight At Twilight, 1880, 9 In. 1100.00
Platter, Courting Couple, Outdoors Scene, Transfer & Hand Painted, 18 x 13 In. ...135.00 to 138.00
Platter, Fish, Marseille, 21 1/2 x 8 1/2 In. ....275.00 to 305.00
Platter, Memphis, Gravy Well, 14 x 11 In. 65.00
Platter, Moss Rose, Wild Flower, Blue Trim, Oval, 20 x 14 In. 50.00
Punch Bowl, Baltimore Rose, Pink, Scalloped, Footed, 7 1/4 x 14 1/2 In. 1210.00
Relish, Marseille, Marked, 8 1/4 x 5 1/2 In. 175.00
Soup Set, Tureen, Signed, Gold Trim, 13 Piece 550.00
Sugar, Moss Rose, Cover, Handles, 4 Cup 65.00
Sugar & Creamer, Baltimore Rose, Pink & Yellow 165.00
Sugar & Creamer, Mont Mery, c.1953 .... 95.00
Tankard, Saint Germain, Gold Trim, 10 1/4 In. 185.00
Tea & Toast Plate, Drop Rose, Pink, Gold Wreath Border, 2 Piece 165.00
Tea & Toast Plate, Violets & We, Hand Painted, Marked 65.00
Tea & Toast Set, Floral, Gilt Trim, Marked D & A ....*Illus* 95.00
Toothbrush Holder, Moss Rose, Gold Trim, 8 In. 110.00
Tureen, Soup, Drop Rose, Pink 385.00
Tureen, Soup, Floral, Braided Handles 190.00
Tureen, Soup, Meadow Visitors, Pink Ground, 13 In. 360.00
Tureen, Soup, Pompadour, Gold Marks, 12 1/4 In. 248.00

HAWKES cut glass was made by T. G. Hawkes & Company of Corning, New York, founded in 1880. The firm cut glass blanks made at other glassworks until 1962. Many pieces are marked with the trademark, a trefoil ring enclosing a fleur-de-lis and two hawks. Cut glass by other manufacturers is listed under either the factory name or in the general Cut Glass category.

Bowl, Allover Engraving, Flowers, Buds & Ferns, Signed, 8 In. 255.00
Bowl, Band Of 12 Hobstars, Star On Base, 8 1/4 In. 115.00
Bowl, Brilliant, 6 Hobstars, Notched Fan, Rayed Pedestal Base, Signed, 10 In. 920.00
Bowl, Fine Cut, Hobstars, 3 3/4 x 8 In. 475.00
Bowl, Fruit, Gladys, Brilliant, 10 x 4 1/2 In. 400.00
Bowl, Hobstar, Blown Out, Signed, 8 In. 585.00
Bowl, Hobstar, Scalloped Houndstooth Edge, Stylized Square Shape, 8 In. 145.00
Bowl, Intaglio, Berries & Leaves, 10 In. 775.00
Bowl, Kohinoor & Honeycomb, 3 1/2 x 8 In. 595.00
Bowl, Millicent, Engraved, Signed, 8 In. 1540.00
Bowl, Starburst, 19th Century, 11 x 7 1/4 In. 290.00
Butter Chip, Signed, 6 Piece 375.00
Candlestick, Floral & Leaf, Mushroom Shape, 3 1/4 x 5 In., Pair 60.00
Candlestick, Floral, 12 In., Pair 1100.00
Cocktail Shaker, Floral & Leaf, Sterling Silver Cover, 13 1/4 In. 265.00

Cologne Bottle, Diamond Cable, Signed, 8 In.	395.00
Cologne Bottle, Florence-Type, Marked	250.00
Cologne Bottle, Grecian, Stopper, 7 1/4 x 5 In.	635.00
Cruet, Oil, Hobstars, Marked	175.00
Fernery, Signed	700.00
Goblet, Gladys, 6 In., 8 Piece	750.00
Ice Bucket, Silver Plated Mount, Bale Handle, 6 1/2 In.	170.00
Juice Set, Russian, Rayed Button, Signed, 5 Piece	975.00
Martini Shaker, Checkerboard, Sterling Silver Lid, 12 In.	288.00
Pitcher, Cider, Brunswick, Triple Notched Handle, 6 1/2 In.	175.00
Pitcher, Martini, Club House & Golf Hole, Etched, 16 1/2 In.	200.00
Plate, Chrysanthemum, 7 In.	450.00
Plate, Queens, Signed, 7 In.	775.00
Powder Jar, Hair Receiver, Panel Cut, Sterling Silver Covers, 2 Piece	275.00
Salt, Leaf, Signed, 3 1/4 In.	30.00
Tray, Kohinoor, Petite Berries & Leaves, Signed	950.00
Tray, Portland, Signed, 13 In.	1850.00
Tray, Venetian, Oval, 9 x 7 In.	275.00
Tray, Venetian, Round, 12 In.	1400.00
Vase, Auto, Chain Of Hobstars, Prism Edge, Panels, Signed, 8 In.	395.00
Vase, Comet, Sterling Silver Overlay, 10 In.	425.00
Vase, Flowers, Swags, Tassels, Sterling Silver Band, Cylindrical, 9 3/4 x 3 3/4 In.	460.00
Vase, Hobstars, Urn Shape, 12 In.	416.00

HEAD VASES, generally showing a woman from the shoulders up, were used by florists primarily in the 1950s and 1960s. Made in a variety of sizes and often decorated with imitation jewelry and other lifelike accessories, the vases were manufactured in Japan and the U.S.A. Less elaborate examples were made as early as the 1930s. Religious themes, babies, and animals are also common subjects. Other head vases are listed under manufacturers' names and can be located through the index at the back of this book.

Barbie, Ceramic Arts Studio, 7 1/4 In.	24.00
Becky, Ceramic Arts Studio	78.00
Betty Lou Nichols, 11 x 7 In.	1650.00
Bonnie, Blond Hair, Ceramic Arts Studio, 7 In.	130.00
Clown, 6 In.	25.00
Flapper, 5 1/2 In.	20.00
Girl, Sun Glasses, Relpo, 5 1/2 In.	550.00
Girl, White Pottery, Large Hat	38.00
Jackie Kennedy, Inarco, 6 In.	350.00
Lotus, Ceramic Arts Studio, 7 3/4 In.	70.00
Mei-Ling, Blue, Ceramic Arts Studio, 5 In.	80.00
Raggedy Ann	35.00
Sven, Blonde Hair, Ceramic Arts Studio, 6 1/8 In.	100.00
Woman, Pearl Brooch & Earrings, Paper Label, Napcoware, 6 In.	45.00
Woman, Pearl Necklace, Pastel, Napco, 1960s, 6 In.	35.00
Young Woman, Earrings, Hand Painted, Napco	165.00
Young Woman, Hands Near Face, Foil Label, Napcoware, 5 3/4 In.	145.00
Young Woman, Long Eyelashes, Pearls, Napcoware, 3 3/4 In.	80.00
Young Woman, Pearls, Enesco Label, 5 3/4 In.	155.00
Young Woman, Plastic Flowers, Ardco Foil Label, 6 In.	175.00
Young Woman, Relpo, 7 In.	225.00

HEDI SCHOOP Art Creations, North Hollywood, California, started about 1945 and was working until 1954. Schoop made ceramic figurines, lamps, planters, and tablewares.

Hedi Schoop S

Ashtray, Figural, Bird, With Match Holder	50.00
Box, Raised Mask Face, 8 In.	48.00
Figurine, Cat, Sitting, Green & Blue, 7 1/2 In., Pair	140.00
Figurine, Couple With Baskets, 13 1/2 In.	165.00
Figurine, Lady, Dancing, Ruffled Skirt, 9 1/2 In.	65.00
Figurine, Oriental Girl, 11 1/2 In.	55.00

Flower Holder, Kneeling Girl, 8 In. 145.00
Planter, Bowing Debutante, Figural, 12 In. 85.00
Planter, Shell, Pink & Gold 50.00
Planter, Woman, Bowl On Head, 13 In. 75.00
Planter, Woman, Skirt, 12 In. 55.00
Vase, Butterfly, Brown, Lavender, Pink, Gold, 6 x 9 In. 50.00

HEINTZ ART Metal Shop made jewelry, copper, silver, and brass in
Buffalo, New York, from 1906 to 1935, when a new company name
was taken and the mark became *Silvercrest*. The most popular items
with collectors today are the copper desk sets and vases made with
applied silver designs.

Bookends, Pinecone Silver On Bronze, 5 x 3 In. 605.00
Bookends, Stylized Silver On Bronze, Verdigris Patina, 5 x 5 1/4 In. 125.00
Bowl, Floral Design, 2 Handles, Silver On Bronze, Original Patina, 11 1/2 In. 605.00
Candlestick, Silver On Bronze, Original Patina, Impressed Mark, 11 In., Pair 1210.00
Desk Set, Birds On Branches, Silver On Bronze, 4 Piece 850.00
Desk Set, Cattail Design, Silver On Bronze, 3 Piece 420.00
Desk Set, Silver Overlay Of Flowers, Sterling On Bronze, 10 Piece 373.00
Frame, Bronze, Applied Etched Design, Original Patina, 11 1/2 x 13 In. 357.00
Frame, Silver On Bronze, Original Patina, 5 x 3 1/2 In. 275.00
Lamp, Pinecone, Silver On Bronze, Original Verdigris, Cutout Shade, 11 In. 2530.00
Lamp, Silver Foliate, Linen Shade, Signed, 10 In. 1715.00
Lamp, Silver Foliate, Verdigris Patina, Linen Shade, Signed, 8 3/4 x 10 In. 1715.00
Lamp, Silver On Bronze, 10 1/2 In. 1650.00
Lamp, Stylized Floral Design, Silver On Bronze, Adjustable Shade, 9 x 13 In. 2850.00
Vase, 2 Open Buttresses, Silver On Bronze, Original Patina, 10 1/2 In. 1320.00
Vase, Bud, Primrose Over Green Patinated Ground, Silver On Bronze, 6 x 2 In. 247.00
Vase, Floral Design, Silver On Bronze, Impressed Mark, 15 In. 1320.00
Vase, Floral Design, Silver On Bronze, Original Patina, Impressed Mark, 9 In. 385.00
Vase, Green Patinated Ground, Silver On Bronze, Die Stamped Mark, 10 x 4 In. 770.00
Vase, Incised Lines Top To Bottom, 6 In. 250.00
Vase, Iris, Sterling Silver On Bronze, 9 In. 295.00
Vase, Orchid, Silver On Bronze, 8 In. 550.00
Vase, Silver Design On Verdigris Patina, Signed, 5 x 2 3/4 In. 285.00
Vase, Silvercrest, Silver On Bronze, 3 Thistles, 9 1/2 In. 495.00
Vase, Stylized Cherry Branches, Silver Overlay, 6 In. 85.00
Vase, Windmill, Sailboat Scene, Silver On Bronze, Original Patina, 1913, 12 In. 825.00

HEISEY glass was made from 1896 to 1957 in Newark, Ohio, by A. H.
Heisey and Co., Inc. The Imperial Glass Company of Bellaire, Ohio,
bought some of the molds and the rights to the trademark. Some
Heisey patterns have been made by Imperial since 1960. After 1968,
they stopped using the *H* trademark. Heisey used romantic names for
colors, such as *Sahara*. Do not confuse color and pattern names. The
Custard Glass and Ruby Glass categories may also include some
Heisey pieces.

Animal, Airedale 1400.00
Animal, Asiatic Pheasant 275.00
Animal, Colt, Balking 190.00
Animal, Colt, Kicking, Amber 250.00
Animal, Colt, Standing ....85.00 to 125.00
Animal, Colt, Standing, Amber 950.00
Animal, Donkey ....285.00 to 475.00
Animal, Elephant, Large 485.00
Animal, Elephant, Medium 425.00
Animal, Elephant, Small 225.00
Animal, Fighting Rooster 195.00
Animal, Giraffe, Head Back 295.00
Animal, Giraffe, Head Forward 195.00
Animal, Goose, Wings Half, Marked, 8 1/2 In. 85.00
Animal, Goose, Wings Up ....75.00 to 95.00
Animal, Plug Horse 145.00

Animal, Pouter Pigeon 1100.00
Animal, Ringneck Pheasant 160.00
Animal, Sow 1100.00
Banded Flute, Champagne, 4 1/2 Oz. 110.00
Bead Swag, Toothpick, Souvenir, Ruby Stain 40.00
Beaded Panel & Sunburst, Compote 130.00
Beehive, Plate, Moongleam, 14 In. 10.00
Bonnet, No. 463, Basket, Engraved Flowers & Stems, Marked, 16 In. 385.00
Bonnet, No. 463, Basket, Floral Engraving, 7 In. 160.00
Bookends, Fish 175.00
Bookends, Horse Head, 6 7/8 In., Pair 275.00
Cathedral, Vase, Flared, Cobalt Blue 395.00
Coarse Rib, Compote, High, 5 In. 25.00
Coarse Rib, Compote, Low, 5 In. 20.00
Coarse Rib, Plate, 7 3/4 In. 22.00
Coarse Rib, Plate, Flamingo, 7 In. 85.00
Coarse Rib, Plate, Moongleam, 7 3/4 In. 15.00
Colonial, Cocktail, 3 Oz. 15.00
Colonial, Jam Jar, Cover, Alexandrite 1500.00
Colonial, Pickle Jar, Cover 70.00
Colonial, Punch Bowl 135.00
Colonial, Punch Cup, Crystal 50.00
Colonial, Sherbet, Handle, 3 1/2 Oz. 5.00
Coronation, Tumbler, Bar, 1 Oz. 35.00
Criss-Cross, Berry Set, Gold Rims, Marked, 6 Sauces, 9 In. Bowl, 7 Piece 275.00
Crystolite, Bowl, Floral, 10 In. 25.00
Crystolite, Bowl, Shallow, 10 In. 50.00
Crystolite, Cake Stand, 11 In. 335.00
Crystolite, Candleholder, 4 In. 15.00
Crystolite, Candy Dish, Cover, Footed, 6 In. 95.00
Crystolite, Celery Dish, 12 In. 33.00
Crystolite, Coaster, 4 In., 4 Piece 20.00
Crystolite, Dish, Mayonnaise, Underplate, Ladle, 3 1/2 In. 44.00
Crystolite, Ice Jug, 1/2 Gal. 95.00
Crystolite, Jam Jar, Cover, Ladle 75.00
Crystolite, Nappy, 2 Sections, Handle, 8 In. 38.00
Crystolite, Plate, 8 In. 5.00
Crystolite, Platter, 14 In. 33.00
Crystolite, Punch Cup .... .5.00 to 6.00
Crystolite, Punch Set, 16 Cups 160.00
Crystolite, Relish, 3 Sections, 9 1/2 In. 32.00
Crystolite, Swan, Nut Set, Master & Individuals, 13 1/2 In., 8 Piece 900.00
Crystolite, Tumbler, Juice, Footed, 5 Oz. 21.00
Empress, Ashtray, Alexandrite 190.00
Empress, Bowl, Floral, Alexandrite, 11 In. 525.00
Empress, Bowl, Floral, Lion's Head Handles, 10 In. 550.00
Empress, Candlestick, Alexandrite, Pair 695.00
Empress, Candlestick, Flamingo, Pair 155.00
Empress, Candlestick, Sahara, 6 In., Pair 320.00
Empress, Compote, Oval, 6 In. 60.00
Empress, Creamer, Sahara 41.00
Empress, Cup & Saucer, Alexandrite 135.00
Empress, Cup & Saucer, Sahara 30.00
Empress, Dish, Mayonnaise, Underplate, Antarctic Etch 70.00
Empress, Ice Bucket, Tongs, Alexandrite 3255.00
Empress, Pitcher, 2 Tumblers, Dolphin Feet, Moongleam 550.00
Empress, Plate, Alexandrite, 7 1/2 In. 50.00
Empress, Plate, Alexandrite, Square, 7 In. .... .80.00 to 100.00
Empress, Plate, Cobalt Blue, Square, 8 In. 80.00
Empress, Plate, Sahara, Round, 8 In. 20.00
Empress, Plate, Sahara, Square, 6 In. 13.00
Empress, Plate, Sahara, Square, 8 In. 22.00
Empress, Relish, Moongleam, 3 Sections, 7 In. 40.00

Empress, Relish, Triplex, Moongleam, 7 In. 30.00
Empress, Sandwich Server, Center Handle, Square, 12 In. 48.00
Empress, Soup, Cream, Underplate, 7 In. 25.00
Fancy Loop, Potpourri Jar 195.00
Fancy Loop, Punch Cup 26.00
Fancy Loop, Spooner 95.00
Fancy Loop, Syrup 65.00
Fancy Loop, Toothpick, Gold Trim .... 50.00 to 60.00
Fancy Loop, Vase, Cylindrical, 8 In. 95.00
Fandango, Nappy 45.00
Fandango, Plate, 8 In. 45.00
Fandango, Toothpick .... 70.00 to 75.00
Fern, Sandwich Server, Center Handle, Dawn, 15 In. 250.00
Flat Panel, Jar, Cover, Crushed Fruit, 2 Qt. 225.00
Fleur-De-Lis, Plate, Signed, 8 In. 75.00
Greek Key, Compote, 5 In. 70.00
Greek Key, Cruet .... 70.00 to 75.00
Greek Key, Pitcher, Marked, 6 3/4 In. 220.00
Greek Key, Punch Bowl 950.00
Greek Key, Relish, Oval, 9 In. 55.00
Greek Key, Sherbet, Footed, 4 Piece 25.00
Greek Key, Spooner 10.00
Ipswich, Bowl, Floral, Footed, 11 In. 70.00
Ipswich, Centerpiece, Prisms, Footed, 2 Piece 120.00
Ipswich, Cocktail, Oyster, Footed, 4 Oz. 22.00
Ipswich, Plate, Square, 9 In. 35.00
Ipswich, Tumbler, Soda, Footed, 5 Oz. 30.00
Ipswich, Tumbler, Soda, Footed, 8 Oz. 30.00
Lariat, Bowl, Crimped, 12 In. 30.00
Lariat, Bowl, Floral, Oval, 13 In. 36.00
Lariat, Cheese Dish, Cover, Footed 40.00
Lariat, Cigarette Box, Cover 48.00
Lariat, Coaster, 4 In. 8.00
Lariat, Iced Tea 22.00
Lariat, Plate, 13 In. 45.00
Lariat, Punch Cup 10.00
Lariat, Punch Set, Bowl, Underplate, Ladle, 8 Cups 225.00
Lariat, Relish, 3 Sections, 10 1/2 In. 24.00
Lariat, Relish, 3 Sections, 12 In. 28.00
Lariat, Sugar & Creamer, Tray 57.00
Lariat, Tumbler, Water 22.00
McGrady, No. 372, Syrup, Sanitary, Moongleam, 7 Oz. 140.00
Minuet, Cocktail, 3 1/2 Oz. 35.00
Minuet, Iced Tea, 12 Oz. 60.00
Minuet, Plate, 8 In. 21.00
Narrow Flute, Bowl, Flamingo, 8 In. 95.00
Narrow Flute, Sugar & Creamer, Hotel 90.00
Narrow Flute, Tumbler, 12 Oz. 18.00
Octagon, Cup & Saucer, Empress 200.00
Octagon, Plate, Sandwich, 2 Handles, 10 In. 40.00
Old Sandwich, Mug, Cobalt Blue, Handle, 16 Oz. 360.00
Old Sandwich, Pitcher, Ice, Pressed Handle, 1/2 Gal. 120.00
Old Williamsburg, Candelabrum, 3-Light, Sahara, 15 1/2 In., Pair .... 1100.00 to 1325.00
Old Williamsburg, Candelabrum, Bobeches, Prisms 325.00
Old Williamsburg, Creamer, 4 1/2 In. .... 20.00 to 22.00
Orchid Etch, Ashtray, 3 In. .... 23.00 to 27.00
Orchid Etch, Basket, 10 In. 1100.00
Orchid Etch, Bowl, Salad, Waverly, 10 In. 225.00
Orchid Etch, Butter, Cover, Square, Waverly 95.00
Orchid Etch, Celery Dish, Waverly, 12 In. 40.00
Orchid Etch, Chocolate Dish, Cover 180.00
Orchid Etch, Compote, Low, Waverly, 6 1/2 In. 35.00
Orchid Etch, Cordial, Tyrolean, 1 Oz. 100.00

Orchid Etch, Creamer 35.00
Orchid Etch, Cruet, Waverly, 3 Oz. 120.00
Orchid Etch, Iced Tea, 12 Oz. 65.00
Orchid Etch, Relish, 3 Sections, Waverly, 11 In. 60.00
Orchid Etch, Salt & Pepper, Waverly 80.00
Orchid Etch, Sandwich Server, Center Handle, 14 In. 150.00
Orchid Etch, Sugar & Creamer, Tray, Waverly 85.00
Orchid Etch, Sugar & Creamer, Waverly 70.00
Orchid Etch, Torte Plate, Waverly, 14 In. 40.00
Orchid Etch, Wine, 3 Oz. 75.00
Paperweight, Rabbit ....185.00 to 225.00
Paperweight, Tiger 800.00
Picket, No. 458, Basket, Moongleam, 7 In. 430.00
Pineapple & Fan, Toothpick, Emerald, Gold Trim 150.00
Plantation, Candlestick, 2-Light, Pair 245.00
Plantation, Candy Dish, Cover, 5 In. 120.00
Plantation, Candy Dish, Cover, 8 In. 185.00
Plantation, Coaster 60.00
Plantation, Cruet 85.00
Plantation, Relish, 3 Sections, 11 In. 50.00
Plantation, Relish, 4 Sections, 8 In. 110.00
Plantation, Sherbet 38.00
Plantation, Sugar & Creamer, Footed 72.00
Plantation, Torte Plate, 10 1/2 In. 75.00
Plantation, Torte Plate, Ivy Etch, 14 In. 95.00
Plantation, Tumbler, Footed, 12 Oz. 80.00
Pleat & Panel, Candy Dish, Cover, Footed, Moongleam 95.00
Pleat & Panel, Champagne, Flamingo 24.00
Pleat & Panel, Compote, Cover, Moongleam, Pair 85.00
Pleat & Panel, Cruet, Flamingo 40.00
Pleat & Panel, Cruet, Moongleam 125.00
Priscilla, Toothpick 50.00
Priscilla, Vase, 8 In. 50.00
Prison Stripe, Toothpick 75.00
Provincial, Candlestick, Pair 65.00
Provincial, Sugar & Creamer, Footed 30.00
Punty Band, Bowl, 7 1/2 x 3 In. 110.00
Puritan, Cigarette Box, Cover, Horsehead Finial, 6 In. 100.00
Puritan, Compote, Footed, 7 In. 50.00
Puritan, Ice Tub, With Drain 95.00
Puritan, Jam Jar, Cover 110.00
Puritan, Punch Bowl, Base ....115.00 to 195.00
Queen Ann, Bowl, Floral, Footed, 11 In. 32.00
Queen Ann, Candlestick, 8 In., Pair 250.00
Queen Ann, Candlestick, Bobeche, Prism, 8 In., Pair 140.00
Queen Ann, Compote, Sterling Stem & Foot, Oval, 7 In. 50.00
Queen Ann, Plate, Cake, 10 In. 110.00
Queen Ann, Sugar & Creamer 65.00
Ridgeleigh, Candlestick, 2-Light, Bobeche, Prisms, Pair 225.00
Ridgeleigh, Dish, Jelly, 2 Sections, Handles, 6 In. 22.00
Ridgeleigh, Mustard, Cover 20.00
Ridgeleigh, Plate, Floral Etch, 9 1/2 In., 9 Piece 150.00
Ridgeleigh, Punch Cup 65.00
Ridgeleigh, Torte Plate, 13 In. 60.00
Ridgeleigh, Tumbler, 8 Piece 125.00
Ring Band, Toothpick, Covington, Oh. ....Illus   11.00
Ring Band, Toothpick, Enameled Gold ....Illus   55.00
Rooster, Stopper 40.00
Rose Etch, Bowl, 2 Sections, Oval 70.00
Rose Etch, Goblet 27.00
Rose Etch, Relish, 3 Sections, Round 70.00
Rose Etch, Torte Plate, Waverly, 14 In. 50.00
Spanish, Champagne, Cobalt Blue 85.00

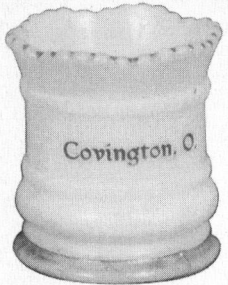

Heisey, Ring Band, Toothpick,
Covington, Oh.

Heisey, Winged Scroll,
Toothpick, Gold

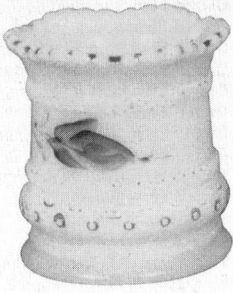

Heisey, Ring Band,
Toothpick, Enameled Gold

Spanish, Goblet, Cobalt Blue 145.00
Sussex, Goblet, Moongleam, 8 Oz. 55.00
Trident, Candlestick, 2-Light, Sahara, Pair 295.00
Trojan, Wine, Flamingo, 2 1/2 Oz. 40.00
Tudor, Dish, Mayonnaise, 2 Handles 65.00
Tudor, Goblet, 6 Oz. 45.00
Tudor, Punch Set, 13 Piece 500.00
Tudor, Sherbet, 5 1/2 Oz. 10.00
Twist, Bowl, Square Foot, Marigold, 8 In. 80.00
Twist, Plate, Moongleam, 7 In. 10.00
Twist, Plate, Moongleam, 11 In. 75.00
Twist, Tumbler, Moongleam, Footed, 9 Oz. 50.00
Victorian, Champagne, 5 Oz. 15.00
Victorian, Tumbler, 8 Oz., 8 Piece 150.00
Victorian, Tumbler, Bar, 2 Oz. 35.00
Victorian Girl, Bell, Frosted 85.00
Wabash, Candy Dish, Footed, Cover, 6 In. 100.00
Warwick, Candlestick, 2-Light, Pair . . . . .125.00 to 145.00
Warwick, Vase, Cornucopia, Sahara, 9 In. 35.00
Waverly, Bowl, Salad, 9 In. 210.00
Waverly, Candle Block, Pair 195.00
Waverly, Candlestick, 2-Light, Pair 195.00
Waverly, Dish, Jelly, Cover, Footed, 6 1/2 In. 35.00
Waverly, Relish, 2 Sections, Footed, 6 In. 20.00
Winged Scroll, Dish, Calling Card, Custard 65.00
Winged Scroll, Toothpick, Gold . . . .*Illus* 99.00
Yeoman, Cup & Saucer, Moongleam . . . . .22.00 to 25.00
Zodiac, Candy Dish, Cover, Footed, 10 In. 55.00

HEREND, see Fischer category.

HEUBACH is the collector's name for Gebruder Heubach, a firm working in Lichten, Germany, from 1840 to 1925. It is best known for
bisque dolls and doll heads, their principal products. They also manufactured bisque figurines, including piano babies, beginning in the
1880s, and glazed figurines in the 1900s. Piano babies are listed in
their own category. Dolls are included in the Doll category under
Gebruder Heubach and *Heubach.* Another factory, Ernst Heubach,
working in Koppelsdorf, Germany, also made porcelain and dolls.
These will also be found in the Doll category under Heubach
Koppelsdorf.

Figurine, Baby, Crawling, 4 1/2 In. 235.00
Figurine, Bunny Boy With Egg, Jointed Arms, Bisque, 5 1/2 In. 530.00
Figurine, Girl, Dancing, 11 1/2 In. 500.00
Figurine, Nanny, 12 1/2 In. 295.00

Figurine, Young Girl, Holding Her Skirt, Intaglio Eyes, Rising Sun Mark, 11 1/2 In. 275.00
Planter, Woman Seated On Shell Shape, Putti & Dove, Marked, 9 1/2 In. 60.00

HIGBEE glass was made by the J. B. Higbee Company of Bridgeville, Pennsylvania, about 1900. Tablewares were made, and it is possible to assemble a full set of dishes and goblets in some Higbee patterns. Most of the glass was clear, not colored. Additional pieces may be found in the Pressed Glass category by pattern name.

Bowl, 8 Feet, Fortuna, 7 In. 46.00
Bowl, Floral Oval, c.1910, 6 1/8 x 2 1/2 In. . . . . 30.00 to 31.00
Candy Dish, Bijou, 1900, 7 1/4 x 5 1/4 In. 27.00
Creamer, Footed, Paneled Thistle, 5 In. 53.00
Dish, Side Tree Design, 7 1/8 x 5 1/4 In. 30.00
Pitcher, Estelle, Ribbed Base, 7 1/2 In. 52.00
Plate, Thistle, c.1905, 9 In. 22.00
Relish, Thistle, c.1905, 9 x 4 In. 40.00
Spooner, Thistle, c.1900, 5 In. 77.00

HISTORIC BLUE, see factory names, such as Adams, Clews, Ridgway, and Staffordshire.

HOBNAIL glass is a style of glass with bumps all over. Dozens of hobnail patterns and variants have been made. Clear, colored, and opalescent hobnail have been made and are being reproduced. Other pieces of hobnail may also be listed in the Duncan & Miller and Fenton categories.

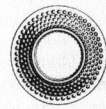

Basket, Blue, 8 In. 50.00
Basket, Cranberry, Clear Thorn Handle, 6 In. 55.00
Bowl, Ruffled, Blue, 7 In. 60.00
Bowl, Scalloped Edge, Oval, 9 x 5 1/2 In. 45.00
Lamp, Hanging, Cranberry Glass, Brass Fixture, Electrified, 8 1/2 x 8 In. 345.00
Lemonade Set, Pitcher, 6 Tumblers, Blue, 7 Piece 247.00
Tumbler, Blue 30.00
Water Set, Ruby 85.00

HOCHST, or Hoechst, porcelain was made in Germany from 1746 to 1796. It was marked with a six-spoke wheel. Be careful when buying Hochst; many other firms have used a very similar wheel-shaped mark.

Box, Trinket, Cover, Gentleman Standing Before A Stream, Trees, Blue, 1776, 4 In. 1035.00
Dessert Service, Roses, Summer Flowers, Gilt Rim, Puce, White Ground, 27 Piece 230.00
Figurine, Chinese Man With A Goat, Blue Glaze, Wheel Mark, 7 1/2 In. 115.00

HOLLY AMBER, or golden agate, glass was made by the Indiana Tumbler and Goblet Company of Greentown, Indiana, from January 1, 1903, to June 13, 1903. It is a pressed glass pattern featuring holly leaves in the amber-shaded glass. The glass was made with shadings that range from creamy opalescent to brown-amber.

Butter, Cover, Round, 6 x 7 1/2 In. 1265.00
Compote, 4 3/4 x 4 3/4 In. 375.00
Compote, Oval, 4 1/2 x 7 1/2 In. 125.00
Cruet . . . . 1700.00 to 1950.00
Pitcher 390.00
Spooner, 4 x 3 1/2 In. 258.00
Syrup, Amber . . . . 2150.00 to 2450.00

HOLT-HOWARD was an importer who started working in 1949 in Stamford, Connecticut. He sold many types of table accessories, such as condiment jars, decanters, spoon holders, and saltshakers. The figures shown on some of his pieces had a cartoon-like quality. The company was bought out by General Housewares Corporation in 1969. Holt-Howard pieces are often marked with the name and the year or HH and the year stamped in black. There was also a black and silver label.

Angel-Abra, Christmas Chimes, Brass, 12 1/2 In., Box . . . . *Illus*   50.00

Holt-Howard, Angel-
Abra, Christmas Chimes,
Brass, 12 1/2 In., Box

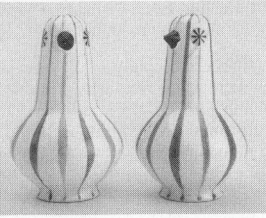

Holt-Howard, Salt & Pepper, Bird,
Green & White Stripe, 4 In., Pair

Holt-Howard, Mug, Clown,
White & Orange, Red Nose Handle,
1962, 2 3/4 In.

Holt-Howard, Salt & Pepper,
Cozy Kitten, White, Pink & Blue
Ribbon Collar, 4 1/2 In.

Candle Climber, Merry Mouse, Box, Pair	25.00
Candleholder, Angel, Pair	25.00
Candleholder, Christmas Angel, Pair	25.00
Candleholder, Cog Rouge, Rooster, Pair	30.00
Candleholder, Santa Claus	28.00
Candlestick, Pixie, Christmas	45.00
Cookie Jar, Pop-Up, Cozy Kitten, Just Take One, Attaches To Top Of Cookie Jar	25.00
Eggcup, Chick	25.00
Figurine, Christmas Angel, Pair	40.00
Figurine, Santa Claus, Box, 2 Piece	35.00
Jam Jar, Pixie	65.00
Jar, Mayonnaise, Pixie	40.00
Jar, Olive, Pixie	140.00 to 180.00
Letter Holder, Cozy Kitten	65.00
Mug, Clown, White & Orange, Red Nose Handle, 1962, 2 3/4 In. ....*Illus*	40.00
Mug, Cog Rouge, Rooster	10.00
Napkin Holder, Santa Claus	20.00
Planter, My Fair Lady, Christmas	125.00
Salt & Pepper, Bird, Green & White Stripe, 4 In., Pair ....*Illus*	25.00
Salt & Pepper, Cozy Kitten, White, Pink & Blue Ribbon Collar, 4 1/2 In. ....*Illus*	50.00
Salt & Pepper, Merry Mouse, Purple	45.00
Salt & Pepper, Santa Claus	35.00
Spoon Rest, Cog Rouge, Rooster	25.00
String Holder, Cozy Kitten	80.00 to 90.00
String Holder, White Cat, Box	110.00

HOPALONG CASSIDY was a character in a series of twenty-eight books
written by Clarence E. Milford, first published in 1907. Movies and
television shows were made based on the character. The best-known
actor playing Hopalong Cassidy was William Lawrence Boyd. His
first movie appearance was in 1919, but the first Hopalong Cassidy
film was not until 1934. Sixty-six films were made. In 1948, William
Boyd purchased the television rights to the movies, then later made
fifty-two new programs. In the 1950s, Hopalong Cassidy and his
horse, named *Topper*, were seen in comics, records, toys, and other
products. Boyd died in 1972.

Badge, 6-Pointed Star, Pewter Finish, Pinback	40.00
Badge, Sheriff, Bond Bread, Plastic, Pinback, Silver & Black	25.00
Binoculars	80.00
Bottle, Betsy Ross Grape Juice, Full Hopalong Cassidy Label	100.00

‒‒‒‒‒‒‒‒‒‒ ✐ ‒‒‒‒‒‒‒‒‒‒

If you use a roller to paint your walls, watch out for tiny droplets that spot furniture and collectibles nearby. The first few days you may be able to get rid of the drops by rubbing them with a cloth dampened with soap and water. Later you may have to use solvents or try to pop the drop off with a fingernail or razor blade.

‒‒‒‒‒‒‒‒‒‒ ✐ ‒‒‒‒‒‒‒‒‒‒

Hopalong Cassidy, Mug, Peanut Butter, White, Red Smiling Hoppy, 2 Guns, 2 x 3 In.

Button, Black, Yellow, Quality Dairy Co. Premium, 1950s 35.00
Button, Hopalong Cassidy Savings Club, Black, Red, White Ground, 1952 .... 45.00
Camera, Hoppy, Topper On Lens, Bakelite, 5 x 2 1/2 In. 250.00
Cap Gun, Black Plastic Grips, Bust Of Hoppy, Top Loading, 1950s 500.00
Card, Bond Bread, Hoppy Mounting Topper, White, 2 x 3 In. 10.00
Card, Bond Bread, Hoppy With Guns Drawn, 2 x 3 In. 10.00
Card Set, HC Chewing Gum, No. 187 To No. 208 .... 285.00
Clock, Alarm, Red Numerals & Hands, Black, U.S. Time 192.00
Coloring Book, 1951, 8 1/2 x 11 In. 55.00
Comic Strip, Pen & Ink, Signed Dan Spiegle, Jan. 6, 1951, 6 x 19 3/4 In. 330.00
Compass, Wrist 75.00
Container, Hopalong Cassidy Ice Cream, No Cover, 1951, Qt. 30.00
Earmuffs, Red 175.00
Game, Board, Milton Bradley 125.00
Game, Cowboy On Horses, Lead, Board, Box 95.00
Game, Target, Metal, 1950s, 16 x 27 In. ....190.00 to 200.00
Guitar 160.00
Kite, Sky Rider, Paper 40.00
Lamp, Motion, 9 1/2 In. 798.00
Laundry Bag, Original Shipping Envelope ....600.00 to 850.00
Linoleum, Hoppy, 30-In. Square 595.00
Lunch Box, Cloud Decal 150.00
Lunch Box Thermos, Aladdin 65.00
Magazine, WIBW Roundup, Hoppy & Topper On Cover, June 1948 .... 20.00
Mug, Peanut Butter, White, Dark Green Lettering, 1950, 3 In. 30.00
Mug, Peanut Butter, White, Red Smiling Hoppy, 2 Guns, 2 x 3 In. ....*Illus* 30.00
Mug, Red 32.00
Neckerchief, Hoppy Graphics, 14 x 14 In. 75.00
Place Mat, Hoppy Riding Topper, Plastic, 12 x 18 In. 95.00
Puzzle, Box 65.00
Radio, Red 900.00
Ring, Hoppy Portrait ....50.00 to 60.00
Rug, Hoppy & Topper, Chenille, 24 x 36 In. 175.00
Scrapbook, Leather, Embossed Hoppy On Topper, 12 x 14 In. 175.00
Skirt, Cowgirl's, Hoppy, Topper, Black Cotton Twill, 18-In. Waist 25.00
Spurs 100.00
Thermos, Aladdin, 1950 ....75.00 to 92.00
Toy, Projector Gun, Auto Magic, 1950s 75.00
Wristwatch, Band, Saddle & Paperwork, Ingersoll, Box 286.00
Wristwatch, Box ....400.00 to 425.00
Wristwatch, Girls, England 60.00

HOWARD PIERCE has been working in Southern California since 1936. In 1945, he opened a pottery in Claremont. His contemporary-looking figurines are popular with collectors. Pieces are marked with his name. He stopped making pottery in 1991.

Figurine, Bear & Cub 46.00

Figurine, Madonna & Child, White, 5 In.	48.00
Figurine, Polar Bear, White, 7 In.	175.00
Figurine, Roadrunner, 8 In.	95.00
Sign, Pottery Show, 1985	95.00

HOWDY DOODY and Buffalo Bob were the main characters in a children's series televised from 1947 to 1960. Howdy was a redheaded puppet. The series became popular with college students in the late 1970s when Buffalo Bob began to lecture on campuses.

Bag, Best Eating Apples, Images Of Show Characters, Vinyl, 6 x 17 1/2 In.	20.00
Bank, Howdy Standing, Plastic	65.00
Blue Bonnet Sue Doodyville Theater, Unpunched Sheet, Original Envelope	345.00
Book, Coloring, Howdy Doody's Clarabell, Funtime, 1955	33.00
Book, Little Golden Book, Howdy Doody & Clarabell, Simon & Schuster, 1951	18.00
Booklet, Jackpot Of Fun, Ice Cream Bars On Back Cover, 16 Pages, 6 x 10 In.	40.00
Booklet, Wonder Bread, History Album, 8 Pages, 1956, 8 x 8 1/4 In.	75.00
Box, Hand Puppet, Peter Puppet Playthings, 1950s	35.00
Cake Decorations, Howdy Characters, Plastic, Die Cut, Display Card, 7 x 8 In.	48.00
Chief Thunderhead, Peace Pipe, Wood, Feathers, Leather Thongs, 1950s, 26 In.	1035.00
Clarabell's Spray Bottle, Copper Colored, Black Top, 1950s, 13 In.	1825.00
Cookbook, Welch's Grape Juice, Recipes, Games, Pictures, 34 Pages, 1952	85.00
Cookie Jar, Purinton	325.00 to 550.00
Cookie Jar, Treasure Craft, 14 In.	250.00 to 275.00
Costume, Buffalo Bob, Yellow Jacket, Red Suede Fringe, Lee Carol, Miami	5510.00
Costume, Clarabell, Green & White Tiger Stripes, Fiddlers Costumes, Ca.	2680.00
Credits Crawl, Hand Painted, Paper, Photo Of Crew, 1956 Show, 90 x 11 In.	3465.00
Cufflinks, Gold, Shape Of TV Camera, Howdy On One & 10 Years On Other	1560.00
Cup, Be Keen, Drink Chocolate Flavored Ovaltine, Red Plastic, 3 1/4 In.	58.00
Display, Howdy Holding Wonder Bread, Heavy Paper, Die Cut, 13 x 6 In.	305.00
Doll, Cloth, Composition, Movable Mouth, Sleep Eyes, Ideal, 19 In.	135.00
Doll, Jointed Wood Arms, Legs, Molded Head, Copyright Bob Smith, 12 1/2 In.	1650.00
Doll, Marionette, Princess Summerfall-Winterspring	245.00 to 275.00
Doll, Plaster, Western Costume, Moving Glass Eyes, 22 In.	135.00
Doll, Plush Body, Rolling Eyes, Howdy Doody Neckerchief, Ideal, 1950s, 20 In.	665.00
Earmuffs, Composition Face	125.00
Embroidery Kit, Howdy & Princess, Milton Bradley, Box, 10 x 12 In.	38.00
Game, Bowling, Parker Brothers, Box	98.00
Game, Time Teacher, Pictorial, Package, 1960s, 10 x 20 In.	35.00
Glass, Circus Scene, Howdy, Princess, Seal, Welch's Grape Juice, 4 1/4 In.	21.00
Lunch Box, Candy Filled, Tin Lithograph	1200.00
Marionette, Dilly-Dally, Wood Hands, Head, Yellow Shag Hair, 1976, 29 In.	7235.00
Merchandising Catalog, Lunch Boxes, Food, Watches, Records, 22 Pages, 1955	75.00 to 90.00
Pencil, 3-D Plastic Head, Kagran, 1951-1956, 6 1/2 In.	35.00
Pin, I'm For Howdy Doody, TV Premium, Original NBC Card	575.00
Place Mat, Red, Pink, Blue Design, Howdy, Smiling At Characters, 9 x 13 In.	15.00
Plate, Howdy As Cowboy, Lariat, China, Taylor, Smith, Taylor, 1950s, 8 In.	370.00
Prize Catalog, 1954-1955	45.00
Puppet, Flub-A-Dub, Push, Kohner, Box	375.00
Puppet, Pop-Up, With Microphone	175.00
Puppet, Princess Summerfall-Winterspring	385.00
Purse	65.00
Puzzle, Clarabell, Whitman Publishing Co., 1954, 11 1/2 x 15 In.	25.00
Ranch House Tool Box, Steel, Wire Handle, Kagran, 1951-1956, 3 x 6 x 14 In.	68.00
RCA Party Promotion Kit, Pennant, Ad Mat, Balloon, Brochure	340.00
Record, Howdy Doody & Mother Goose, Kagran, 1951-1956, 45 RPM, 7 x 7 In.	35.00
Ring, Flasher, Premium Set, 8 Piece	145.00
Shopping Bag, Paper, Howdy Image, I've Been To The Howdy Doody Show	455.00
Sign, Clarabell Double Doody Bar, Ice Cream, Smiling Clarabell, 8 x 22 In.	58.00
Talkin' Tag, Face, Wheel Makes 4 Expressions, Cardboard, Kagran, 2 x 3 1/2 In.	28.00
Tie, Silk, Repeating Images Of Howdy, Howdy Doody Above	960.00
Toy, Band, Howdy Jigs, Bob Plays Piano, Windup, Tin, Unique Art, 9 In.	1100.00
Toy, Clock-A-Doodle, Box	2450.00
Toy, Flub-A-Dub Flip-A-Ring, Kagran, Unopened, In Bag, 6 1/2 x 12 In.	58.00

Washcloth, Mitt, Clarabell 45.00
Watch, Howdy & Buffalo Bob On Face, Leather Pouch 70.00
Wrapping Paper, It's Howdy Doody Time, Repeating Howdy Images 640.00
Wristwatch, Green Vinyl Straps, Chromed Metal Case, Girl's 95.00

HULL pottery was made in Crooksville, Ohio, from 1905. Addis E.
Hull bought the Acme Pottery Company and started making ceramic
wares. In 1917, A. E. Hull Pottery began making art pottery as well as
the commercial wares. For a short time, 1921 to 1929, the firm also
sold pottery imported from Europe. The dinnerwares of the 1940s,
including the Little Red Riding Hood line, the high gloss artwares of
the 1950s, and the matte wares of the 1940s, are all popular with collectors. The firm officially closed in March 1986.

Apple, Cookie Jar 65.00
Apple, Grease Jar 25.00
Apple, Salt & Pepper 20.00
Blossom, Pitcher, Ice Lip, Cinderella 125.00
Bluebird, Clock, Sessions Movement 375.00
Bow Knot, Cornucopia, Double, Pink, Blue, 13 1/2 In. 295.00
Bow Knot, Jardiniere, Pink, Blue, 9 3/8 In. 200.00
Bow Knot, Pitcher, 13 1/2 In. 125.00
Bow Knot, Vase, 8 1/2 In. 45.00
Bow Knot, Vase, 10 1/2 In. 300.00
Bow Knot, Wall Pocket, Cup & Saucer 225.00
Bow Knot, Wall Pocket, Iron 250.00
Bow Knot, Wall Pocket, Whisk Broom, Blue . . . . .225.00 to 265.00
Continental, Basket, 12 1/2 In. 190.00
Corky Pig, Bank, Pink & Blue . . . . .40.00 to 75.00
Dogwood, Pitcher, 4 3/4 In. 125.00
Ebb Tide, Pitcher, 13 In. 175.00
Ebb Tide, Vase, Fish, 11 In. 100.00
Gingerbread Man, Cookie Jar 450.00
Gingerbread Man, Plate 95.00
Gingerbread Man, Spoon Rest 20.00
Heritage Ware, Pitcher, 4 1/2 In. 22.00
Iris, Candlestick, Cream, Rose, 5 In. 55.00
Iris, Vase, Peach, Rose, 7 In. 125.00
Iris, Vase, Peach, Rose, 8 1/2 In. 100.00
Iris, Vase, Peach, Rose, 10 1/2 In. 255.00
Little Red Riding Hood, Bank, Standing 800.00
Little Red Riding Hood, Canister, Cereal . . . . .1200.00 to 1400.00
Little Red Riding Hood, Canister, Coffee 750.00
Little Red Riding Hood, Canister, Flour 810.00
Little Red Riding Hood, Canister, Pretzel 6000.00
Little Red Riding Hood, Canister, Sugar 600.00
Little Red Riding Hood, Canister, Tea 750.00
Little Red Riding Hood, Clock, Sessions Movement 850.00
Little Red Riding Hood, Cookie Jar, Orange End Basket, Orange Spray 395.00
Little Red Riding Hood, Cookie Jar, Orange End Basket, Poppy 325.00
Little Red Riding Hood, Cookie Jar, Poinsettia . . . . .400.00 to 650.00
Little Red Riding Hood, Cracker Jar . . . . .700.00 to 825.00
Little Red Riding Hood, Creamer, Pantaloons . . . . .335.00 to 400.00
Little Red Riding Hood, Creamer, Tab Handle . . . . .250.00 to 425.00
Little Red Riding Hood, Lamp 2100.00
Little Red Riding Hood, Matchbox, Wall, Hanging 1100.00
Little Red Riding Hood, Mustard, Spoon . . . . .200.00 to 500.00
Little Red Riding Hood, Pitcher, Milk . . . . .185.00 to 400.00
Little Red Riding Hood, Salt & Pepper, 3 1/2 In. . . . . .99.00 to 129.00
Little Red Riding Hood, Salt & Pepper, 5 1/2 In. 200.00
Little Red Riding Hood, Salt & Pepper, Gold Trim, 3 In. 145.00
Little Red Riding Hood, Spice Set, Pepper, Nutmeg, Cloves, Ginger, 4 Piece . . .3600.00 to 4900.00
Little Red Riding Hood, Stringholder 3000.00
Little Red Riding Hood, Sugar & Creamer, 5 In. 375.00

Little Red Riding Hood, Sugar & Creamer, Side Pour 925.00
Little Red Riding Hood, Sugar, Crawling 400.00
Little Red Riding Hood, Tea Set, Teapot, Sugar & Creamer, 3 Piece 750.00
Little Red Riding Hood, Teapot . . . . .175.00 to 375.00
Madonna, Planter, White . . . . .30.00 to 45.00
Magnolia, Sugar & Creamer, Gloss, 3 3/4 In. 125.00
Magnolia, Vase, Gloss, 6 1/2 In. 65.00
Magnolia, Vase, Gloss, 12 1/2 In. 380.00
Magnolia, Vase, Matte, 5 In. 35.00
Magnolia, Vase, Matte, 8 1/2 In. 135.00
Mammy, Cookie Jar 225.00
Mexican, Teapot, Porcelier, 4 Cup 65.00
Mexican, Teapot, Porcelier, 6 Cup 65.00
Open Rose, Basket, Hanging, Blue, Pink 140.00
Open Rose, Vase, Pink, Cream, 2 Handles, 6 1/4 In. 110.00
Open Rose, Vase, Swan, Rose, Cream, 6 1/2 In. 135.00
Parchment & Pine, Basket, 15 In. . . . . .140.00 to 150.00
Parchment & Pine, Console, 16 In. 60.00
Parchment & Pine, Cornucopia, 12 In. 60.00
Parchment & Pine, Pitcher, 13 1/2 In. 170.00
Parchment & Pine, Sugar & Creamer 125.00
Parchment & Pine, Teapot, 6 In. . . . . .95.00 to 125.00
Parchment & Pine, Vase, 7 In. 125.00
Rosella, Basket, Scalloped Rim, 7 In. 330.00
Rosella, Vase, 8 1/2 In. . . . . .75.00 to 87.00
Rosella, Vase, Label, 6 3/4 In. 95.00
Serenade, Basket, Yellow, 12 In. 250.00
Serenade, Cornucopia, Yellow, 11 In. 60.00
Serenade, Creamer, Pink, 3 1/2 In. 60.00
Sueno Tulip, Vase, Pastel Blue, Pink, 8 In. 195.00
Sunglow, Basket, Hanging, 6 1/2 In. 125.00
Sunglow, Wall Pocket, Cup & Saucer 50.00
Tokay, Basket, 8 In. 40.00
Tokay, Basket, Green, White, 10 1/2 In. 95.00
Tokay, Vase, 12 In. 95.00
Tuscany, Basket, 10 1/2 In. 95.00
Twin Geese, Planter 45.00
Water Lily, Basket, Tan, Brown, 10 1/2 In. . . . . .250.00 to 350.00
Water Lily, Candlestick, Pink, Turquoise, 4 In., Pair 150.00
Water Lily, Cornucopia, Double, Pink, Turquoise, 12 In. 225.00
Water Lily, Jardiniere, 5 1/2 In. . . . . .79.00 to 100.00
Water Lily, Pitcher, Pink, Turquoise, 5 1/2 In. 95.00
Water Lily, Vase, 5 1/2 In. 75.00
Water Lily, Vase, Pink, Turquoise, 10 1/2 In. 200.00
Wildflower, Basket, Yellow, Rose, 10 1/2 In. 250.00
Wildflower, Candleholder, Pink, Blue, Pair 120.00
Wildflower, Cornucopia, 7 1/2 In. 75.00
Wildflower, Ewer, 13 1/2 In. 650.00
Wildflower, Pitcher, Pink, Blue, 8 1/2 In. . . . . .145.00 to 165.00
Wildflower, Urn, Yellow, Brown, 15 In. . . . . .350.00 to 450.00
Wildflower, Vase, 8 1/2 In. 250.00
Wildflower, Vase, 12 1/2 In. 280.00
Woodland, Basket, Gloss, 10 1/2 In. 185.00
Woodland, Basket, Hanging, Cream, Blue, 7 1/2 In. 400.00
Woodland, Vase, 7 1/2 In. 110.00

HUMMEL figurines, based on the drawings of the nun M.I. Hummel
(Berta Hummel), are made by the W. Goebel Porzellanfabrik of
Oeslau, Germany, now Rodenthal, Germany. They were first made in
1934. The mark has changed through the years. The following are the
approximate dates for each of the marks: *Crown* mark, 1935 to 1949;
U.S. Zone, Germany, 1946 to 1948; *West Germany*, after 1949. The
company added the *bee* marks in 1950. The *full bee* with variations,

was used from 1950 to 1959; *stylized bee*, 1960 to 1972; *three line mark*, 1968 to 1972; *last bee*, sometimes called *vee over gee*, 1972 to 1979. In 1979 the V bee symbol was removed from the mark. The *Goebel, W. Germany* mark, called the *missing bee* mark, was used from 1979 to 1991; *Goebel, Germany*, originally called the *new mark*, was used from 1991 to the present. Porcelain figures inspired by Berta Hummel's drawings were introduced in 1997. These are marked BH followed by a number. They are made in the Far East, not Germany. Other decorative items and plates that feature Hummel drawings have been made by Schmid Brothers, Inc., since 1971.

Ashtray, No. 34, Singing Lesson, Stylized Bee	120.00
Ashtray, No. 34, Singing Lesson, Vee Over Gee	20.00
Ashtray, No. 114, Let's Sing, Stylized Bee	35.00
Bank, No. 118, Little Thrifty, Vee Over Gee	80.00
Bell, Christmas, No. 775, Ride Into Christmas, Boy Riding Sled, Box, First Edition, 1989	35.00
Bookends, No. 14/A & B, Bookworm, Stylized Bee	450.00
Bookends, No. 14/B, Book Worm Girl, Full Bee, 5 1/2 x 4 1/2 In.	300.00
Bookends, No. 250/A & B, Little Goat Herder & Feeding Time	145.00
Bust, HU3, M.I. Hummel, Vee Over Gee	70.00
Candy Box, No. III/53, Joyful, Full Bee, 6 1/2 In.	320.00
Figurine, No. 1, Puppy Love, Full Bee	143.00
Figurine, No. 1, Puppy Love, Vee Over Gee	105.00
Figurine, No. 2/III, Little Fiddler, Missing Bee	633.00
Figurine, No. 3/I, Bookworm, Vee Over Gee	150.00
Figurine, No. 9, Begging His Share, New Mark	105.00
Figurine, No. 11, Merry Wanderer, Crown Mark	345.00
Figurine, No. 11/0, Merry Wanderer, Full Bee	88.00
Figurine, No. 11/2/0, Merry Wanderer, Stylized Bee	55.00
Figurine, No. 12/2/0, Chimney Sweep, Full Bee	50.00
Figurine, No. 12/2/0, Chimney Sweep, Stylized Bee	44.00
Figurine, No. 13/2/0, Meditation, Vee Over Gee	50.00
Figurine, No. 15/0, Hear Ye, Hear Ye, New Mark	90.00
Figurine, No. 15/I, Hear Ye, Hear Ye, Vee Over Gee	195.00
Figurine, No. 16/2/0, Little Hiker, Full Bee	66.00
Figurine, No. 17/0, Congratulations, Full Bee	175.00
Figurine, No. 17/0, Congratulations, Stylized Bee	175.00
Figurine, No. 18, Christ Child, Full Bee	60.00
Figurine, No. 20, Prayer Before Battle, Stylized Bee	70.00
Figurine, No. 23/I, Adoration, Stylized Bee	175.00
Figurine, No. 28/II, Wayside Devotion, Full Bee	198.00
Figurine, No. 28/II, Wayside Devotion, Stylized Bee	110.00
Figurine, No. 32/0, Little Gabriel, Stylized Bee	66.00
Figurine, No. 43, March Winds, Full Bee	77.00
Figurine, No. 47/3/0, Goose Girl, Full Bee	60.00
Figurine, No. 47/3/0, Goose Girl, Stylized Bee	50.00
Figurine, No. 47/II, Goose Girl, Vee Over Gee	330.00
Figurine, No. 49/3/0, To Market, Full Bee	88.00
Figurine, No. 50/2/0, Volunteers, Stylized Bee	95.00
Figurine, No. 52/I, Going To Grandma's, Stylized Bee	198.00
Figurine, No. 53, Joyful, Stylized Bee	55.00 to 95.00
Figurine, No. 56/A, Culprits, Full Bee	245.00
Figurine, No. 56/A, Culprits, Stylized Bee	132.00 to 245.00
Figurine, No. 56/A, Culprits, Vee Over Gee	210.00
Figurine, No. 56/B, Out Of Danger, Full Bee	176.00
Figurine, No. 56/B, Out Of Danger, Vee Over Gee	150.00
Figurine, No. 57, Chick Girl, Vee Over Gee	195.00
Figurine, No. 57/0, Chick Girl, 2 Chicks In Basket, 1 On Ground, Full Bee	77.00
Figurine, No. 57/0, Chick Girl, 2 Chicks In Basket, 1 On Ground, Stylized Bee	50.00
Figurine, No. 58/0, Playmates, Full Bee	70.00 to 121.00
Figurine, No. 58/0, Playmates, New Mark	75.00
Figurine, No. 59, Skier, Crown Mark	430.00
Figurine, No. 59, Skier, Stylized Bee	121.00

Figurine, No. 63, Singing Lesson, Full Bee 66.00
Figurine, No. 64, Shepherd's Boy, Full Bee 121.00
Figurine, No. 64, Shepherd's Boy, Vee Over Gee 105.00
Figurine, No. 67, Doll Mother, Full Bee 99.00
Figurine, No. 67, Doll Mother, Stylized Bee 135.00
Figurine, No. 68/0, Lost Sheep, New Mark 165.00
Figurine, No. 68/2/0, Lost Sheep, Three Line Mark 55.00
Figurine, No. 71, Stormy Weather, Full Bee 253.00
Figurine, No. 71, Stormy Weather, Stylized Bee 165.00
Figurine, No. 71, Stormy Weather, Vee Over Gee ....230.00 to 300.00
Figurine, No. 73, Little Helper, Full Bee 70.00
Figurine, No. 74, Little Gardener, Stylized Bee 50.00
Figurine, No. 81/2/0, School Girl, Full Bee 70.00
Figurine, No. 81/2/0, School Girl, Stylized Bee 50.00
Figurine, No. 82/0, School Boy, Vee Over Gee 105.00
Figurine, No. 82/2/0, School Boy, Full Bee 70.00
Figurine, No. 82/2/0, School Boy, Stylized Bee 50.00
Figurine, No. 85/0, Serenade, All Fingers Down, Brown Coat, Blue Pants, Full Bee 66.00
Figurine, No. 85/0, Serenade, Stylized Bee 55.00
Figurine, No. 87, For Father, Full Bee 187.00
Figurine, No. 87, For Father, Orange Radishes, Stylized Bee 2100.00
Figurine, No. 88/I, Heavenly Protection, Three Line Mark 88.00
Figurine, No. 89/I, Little Cellist, Stylized Bee 82.00
Figurine, No. 89/II, Little Cellist, Full Bee 220.00
Figurine, No. 94/I, Surprise, New Mark ....82.00 to 110.00
Figurine, No. 95, Brother, Stylized Bee 60.00
Figurine, No. 97, Trumpet Boy, New Mark 90.00
Figurine, No. 99, Eventide, New Mark 135.00
Figurine, No. 109, Happy Traveller, Vee Over Gee 66.00
Figurine, No. 110/0, Let's Sing, Three Line Mark 140.00
Figurine, No. 111/I, Wayside Harmony, Full Bee ....132.00 to 160.00
Figurine, No. 112/3/0, Just Resting, Three Line Mark 44.00
Figurine, No. 112/I, Just Resting, Three Line Mark 190.00
Figurine, No. 119/0, Postman, Stylized Bee 90.00
Figurine, No. 123, Max & Moritz, Three Line Mark 82.00
Figurine, No. 124/0, Hello, Full Bee 41.00
Figurine, No. 124/0, Hello, Stylized Bee ....66.00 to 175.00
Figurine, No. 124/0, Hello, Vee Over Gee 82.00
Figurine, No. 127, Doctor, Stylized Bee ....50.00 to 159.00
Figurine, No. 128, Baker, Full Bee ....25.00 to 105.00
Figurine, No. 128, Baker, Vee Over Gee 100.00
Figurine, No. 135, Soloist, Full Bee 77.00
Figurine, No. 135, Soloist, Stylized Bee 44.00
Figurine, No. 136, Friends, Stylized Bee 935.00
Figurine, No. 136/I, Friends, Three Line Mark 55.00
Figurine, No. 141, Apple Tree Girl, Full Bee 60.00
Figurine, No. 141/3/0, Apple Tree Girl, Full Bee 55.00
Figurine, No. 141/I, Apple Tree Girl, Vee Over Gee 135.00
Figurine, No. 142/3/0, Apple Tree Boy, Full Bee 60.00
Figurine, No. 143/0, Boots, Full Bee 105.00
Figurine, No. 143/0, Boots, Last Bee 38.00
Figurine, No. 143/0, Boots, Stylized Bee 82.00
Figurine, No. 143/0, Boots, Vee Over Gee 105.00
Figurine, No. 144, Angelic Song, Vee Over Gee 100.00
Figurine, No. 150/0, Happy Days, Full Bee 77.00
Figurine, No. 152B, Umbrella Girl, Three Line Mark 1350.00
Figurine, No. 153/0, Auf Wiedersehen, Vee Over Gee 95.00
Figurine, No. 154/0, Waiter, Stylized Bee 90.00
Figurine, No. 163, Whitsuntide, Full Bee 430.00
Figurine, No. 169, Bird Duet, New Mark 60.00
Figurine, No. 171, Little Sweeper, Stylized Bee 55.00
Figurine, No. 171/4/0, Little Sweeper, New Mark 25.00
Figurine, No. 173/0, Festival Harmony, With Flute, Three Line Mark 121.00

Figurine, No. 174, She Loves Me, She Loves Me Not, Full Bee . . . . .88.00 to 137.00
Figurine, No. 175, Mother's Darling, Stylized Bee 120.00
Figurine, No. 178, The Photographer, Stylized Bee 55.00
Figurine, No. 178, The Photographer, Vee Over Gee 130.00
Figurine, No. 183, Forest Shrine, Full Bee 198.00
Figurine, No. 184, Latest News, Full Bee . . . . .35.00 to 88.00
Figurine, No. 184, Latest News, Vee Over Gee 135.00
Figurine, No. 186, Sweet Music, Full Bee 220.00
Figurine, No. 186, Sweet Music, New Mark 95.00
Figurine, No. 195/2/0, Barnyard Hero, Full Bee . . . . .60.00 to 105.00
Figurine, No. 195/2/0, Barnyard Hero, Stylized Bee 16.00
Figurine, No. 195/2/0, Barnyard Hero, Three Line Mark 165.00
Figurine, No. 195/I, Barnyard Hero, New Mark 60.00
Figurine, No. 196, Telling Her Secret, Full Bee 220.00
Figurine, No. 196/0, Telling Her Secret, Stylized Bee 260.00
Figurine, No. 196/I, Telling Her Secret, Vee Over Gee 245.00
Figurine, No. 197/2/0, Be Patient, Vee Over Gee 60.00
Figurine, No. 197/I, Be Patient, Vee Over Gee 125.00
Figurine, No. 198/I, Home From Market, Vee Over Gee 80.00
Figurine, No. 199, Feeding Time, Full Bee 192.00
Figurine, No. 200/0, Little Goat Herder, Three Line Mark 55.00
Figurine, No. 200/I, Little Goat Herder, Full Bee 143.00
Figurine, No. 201/2/0, Retreat To Safety, Full Bee 99.00
Figurine, No. 203, Signs Of Spring, Three Line Mark 70.00
Figurine, No. 203/2/0, Signs Of Spring, Full Bee 88.00
Figurine, No. 203/I, Signs Of Spring, Vee Over Gee 95.00
Figurine, No. 204, Weary Wanderer New Mark 95.00
Figurine, No. 204, Weary Wanderer, Full Bee 198.00
Figurine, No. 214A, Madonna & Jesus, Vee Over Gee 90.00
Figurine, No. 214F, Shepherd With Sheep, Vee Over Gee 100.00
Figurine, No. 217, Boy With Toothache, Stylized Bee 66.00
Figurine, No. 217, Boy With Toothache, Three Line Mark 190.00
Figurine, No. 217, Boy With Toothache, Vee Over Gee 190.00
Figurine, No. 218/2/0, Birthday Serenade, Three Line Mark 70.00
Figurine, No. 220, We Congratulate, Full Bee 93.00
Figurine, No. 226, The Mail Is Here, Full Bee 286.00
Figurine, No. 226, The Mail Is Here, Vee Over Gee 245.00
Figurine, No. 240, Little Drummer, Vee Over Gee 115.00
Figurine, No. 256, Knitting Lesson, Vee Over Gee 190.00
Figurine, No. 257, For Mother, Three Line Mark 125.00
Figurine, No. 304, The Artist, New Mark 132.00
Figurine, No. 306, Little Bookkeeper, New Mark 165.00
Figurine, No. 306, Little Bookkeeper, Three Line Mark 110.00
Figurine, No. 311, Kiss Me, New Mark 190.00
Figurine, No. 311, Kiss Me, Stylized Bee Mark 525.00
Figurine, No. 317, Not For You, New Mark 115.00
Figurine, No. 317, Not For You, Three Line Mark 66.00
Figurine, No. 319, Doll Bath, New Mark 165.00
Figurine, No. 322, Little Pharmacist, Vee Over Gee 135.00
Figurine, No. 328, Carnival, New Mark 105.00
Figurine, No. 328, Carnival, Three Line Mark 60.00
Figurine, No. 332, Soldier Boy, Muster Zimmer, Full Bee 3105.00
Figurine, No. 333, Blessed Event, Three Line Mark 275.00
Figurine, No. 334, Homeward Bound, Vee Over Gee 150.00
Figurine, No. 336, Close Harmony, Three Line Mark 110.00
Figurine, No. 336, Close Harmony, Vee Over Gee 115.00
Figurine, No. 337, Cinderella, New Mark 125.00
Figurine, No. 340, Letter To Santa Claus, Three Line Mark 305.00
Figurine, No. 341, Birthday Present, Full Bee 3565.00
Figurine, No. 342, Mischief Maker, Stylized Bee 1495.00
Figurine, No. 344, Feathered Friends, New Mark 125.00
Figurine, No. 345, A Fair Measure, Vee Over Gee 170.00
Figurine, No. 346, The Smart Little Sister, New Mark 110.00

Hummel, Figurine, No. 471,
Harmony In 4 Parts, Missing Bee

Hummel figurines should be cleaned by washing in liquid detergent and water, half and half. Never put them in the dishwasher.

Cleaning a lot of small figurines or other collectibles? Line the sink with a towel. Put the pieces in the sink. Spray them with window cleaner. Move them to another towel on the counter to air dry.

Figurine, No. 348, Ring Around The Rosie, Stylized Bee	1650.00
Figurine, No. 350, On Holiday, New Mark	60.00
Figurine, No. 352, Sweet Greetings, Without Fence, Three Line Mark	8625.00
Figurine, No. 355, Autumn Harvest, Vee Over Gee	110.00
Figurine, No. 367, Busy Student, New Mark	70.00
Figurine, No. 367, Busy Student, Three Line Mark	60.00
Figurine, No. 374, Lost Stocking, New Mark	66.00
Figurine, No. 374, Lost Stocking, Vee Over Gee	60.00
Figurine, No. 378, Easter Greetings, Vee Over Gee	110.00
Figurine, No. 387, Valentine Gift, Three Line Mark	345.00
Figurine, No. 394, Timid Little Sister, New Mark	300.00
Figurine, No. 403, An Apple A Day, New Mark	150.00
Figurine, No. 409, Coffee Break, New Mark	82.00
Figurine, No. 421, It's Cold, Missing Bee	125.00 to 150.00
Figurine, No. 422, What Now, Missing Bee	105.00
Figurine, No. 429, Hello World, Vee Over Gee	110.00
Figurine, No. 431, The Surprise, New Mark	105.00
Figurine, No. 447, Morning Concert, Missing Bee	80.00
Figurine, No. 449, The Little Pair, New Mark	145.00
Figurine, No. 463/0, My Wish Is Small, New Mark	95.00
Figurine, No. 471, Harmony In 4 Parts, Missing Bee	*Illus* 1155.00
Figurine, No. 487, Let's Tell The World, Missing Bee	465.00
Figurine, No. 495, Evening Prayer, New Mark	60.00
Figurine, No. 530, Land In Sight, New Mark	990.00
Figurine, No. 555, One, Two, Three, New Mark	70.00
Figurine, No. 626, I Didn't Do It, New Mark	80.00
Figurine, No. 760, Country Suitor, New Mark	120.00
Figurine, No. 825, Swedish International, Crown & Full Bee	4600.00
Figurine, No. 852, Hungarian International, Crown Mark	3450.00
Plaque, No. 187A, Dealer Display, Vee Over Gee	70.00 to 135.00
Plate, 1984, Little Helper, Box, Miniature	75.00
Plate, Annual, 1971, Heavenly Angel	295.00
Plate, Annual, 1971, Heavenly Angel, Box	425.00
Plate, Annual, 1973, Globe Trotter, Box	95.00
Plate, Annual, 1986, No. 738, Valentine Gift	40.00

HUTSCHENREUTHER Porcelain Company of Selb, Germany, was established in 1814 and is still working. The company makes fine quality porcelain dinnerwares and figurines. The mark has changed through the years, but the name and the lion insignia appear in most versions.

LORENZ
HUTSCHEN REUTER

GERMANY

Cup & Saucer, Demitasse, Silver Overlay	60.00
Figurine, Cat, Lying, With Ball	225.00
Figurine, Dachshund	190.00

Figurine, Doe, Lying, Small ....85.00 to 95.00
Figurine, Doe, Standing 235.00
Figurine, Elephant 169.00
Figurine, Goat, Frolicking 325.00
Figurine, Nude Woman, Kneeling, Feeding Fawn, Ivory 675.00
Figurine, Stag Deer, Lying, 4 In. 45.00
Figurine, Stag Deer, Lying, Large ....250.00 to 275.00
Figurine, Woman Dancer, Flowing Hair, Arms Out, On Knee, 1910, 11 In. 750.00
Plaque, Rebecca, Impressed Mark, Wood Frame, 5 x 3 1/2 In. 290.00
Plate, Service, Scrolled Floral Rim, Cobalt Blue Ground, Gilt, 10 3/4 In., 6 Piece 315.00
Plate, Service, Scrolled Leaf Border, 20th Century, 10 3/4 In., 8 Piece 430.00

ICONS, special, revered pictures of Jesus, Mary, or a saint, are usually
Russian or Byzantine. The small icons collected today are made of
wood and tin or precious metals. Many modern copies have been made
in the old style and are being sold to tourists in Russia and Europe.

Anastasis, Resurrection, 12 Feasts Around Border, Russia, 19th Century, 21 x 17 In. 4025.00
Annunciation, Gilt Silver Border, Enameled Halos, Russia, 18th Century, 12 x 10 In. 4312.00
Archangel Michael, Christ Pantocrator, Russia, 19th Century, 27 x 21 In. 4025.00
Burning Bush, Repousse Chased Gilt Silver Oklad, Russia, c.1830, 18 x 14 In. 5175.00
Chosen Saints For Month Of May, 4 Tiers, Russia, 13 3/4 In. 230.00
Christ Enthroned, Archangels, Mary, 3 Saints, Deesis, Metal Basma, 14 x 25 In. 5780.00
Christ Enthroned, Russia, 17th Century, 45 x 35 In. ....*Illus* 14950.00
Crucifixion, Corpus Christi, Flower Pattern, Brass, 18th Century, 15 In. 230.00
Descent Of Christ Into Purgatory, Christ Lifting Adam & Prophets, 12 x 10 1/2 In. 488.00
Dormition Of The Virgin, Christ, Apostles, Receiving Her Soul, Russia, 14 1/2 x 19 In. .. 575.00
Enthronement Of Virgin & Christ, Monk Saints, Russia, Early 19th Century, 8 7/8 In. ... 172.00
Feodorovskaya Mother Of God, Saints In Border, 12 x 10 In. 2070.00
Four Woman Saints, Enameled Border, Russia, Late 19th Century, 7 x 5 5/8 In. 260.00
Holy Trinity, Gilt Silver Border, Enameled Plaques, Russia, 19th Century, 12 x 10 In. 4025.00
Jesus, Enamel & Seed Pearls, Cyrillic Inscription On Frame, 2 1/2 x 3 In. 260.00
Jesus & Mary, Saints, Wooded Landscape, Russia, 14 x 12 In. 345.00
Kazan Mother Of God, Repousse Gilt Silver Oklad, Russia, c.1830, 12 x 11 In. 2587.00
Madonna & Child, Ornate Gilt, Oklad, 14 x 10 1/2 In. 805.00
Mary, Queen Of Heaven, Gilt & Polychrome, Greece, 19th Century 400.00
Mother Of God, Archangels, Russia, 18th Century, 20 x 15 In. 4025.00
Mother Of God, Enthroned, Gilt Silver Oklad, Russia, 19th Century, 13 x 10 In. 4600.00
Mother Of God, Metal Cover Riza, Russia, 12 x 8 1/2 In. 172.00
Mother Of God Of The Sign, Russia, 19th Century, 12 x 10 In. 2300.00
Peter & Paul, Holding Church, 3 Other Apostles, Gilt Carved Frame, 24 x 15 In. 4025.00
Pokrov, Hymn Of Exultation To Virgin Mary, Russia, 12 1/4 In. 632.00
Resurrection, Russia, 19th Century, 19 x 17 In. 2070.00
Resurrection & Cardinal Feasts, Late 19th Century, Russia, 14 x 12 In. 690.00
Sacred Heart Jesus, Oil On Gesso, Wood, 19th Century, 10 x 8 In. 460.00
Saint, Under Gilded Embossed Brass, Frame, Russia, 8 3/4 x 8 In. 275.00

We once pulled some of the silver plating
from a Sheffield candlestick when we
removed the cellophane tape that held a
Christmas decoration to the candlestick.
A friend pulled some of the glaze from a
plate when she pulled masking tape off
the plate. Don't use anything with a
strong glue on an antique surface.

Icon, Christ Enthroned, Russia,
17th Century, 45 x 35 In.

Savior Enthroned, Chased Foliage, Sterling Silver, Russia, 11 3/4 x 10 1/8 In. 2587.00
Shroud Of St. Veronica, Oil On Panel, 19th Century, 12 x 10 In. 175.00
St. George Slaying The Dragon, Silver Border, Russia, 19th Century, 12 x 10 In. 4887.00
St. Joachim The Patriarch, Greece, 8 1/8 x 5 3/4 In. 260.00
St. Joseph & St. Anna, Russia, 17th Century, 12 x 10 In. 6900.00
St. Marina, Martyr's Pose, Northern Greece, 17th Century, 38 x 24 In. 1955.00
St. Mark The Evangelist, On Wood Panel, Russia, 19th Century 345.00
St. Nicholas, Brass Faced Frame, Russia, 10 3/4 x 9 1/4 In. 275.00
St. Peter & St. John, Repousse Gilt Silver Oklad, Russia, 1829, 11 x 10 In. 2070.00
St. Phillipoes, Greece, Late 17th Century, 17 x 14 1/4 In. 2530.00
Virgin Enthroned, Tempera On Wood Panel, Greece, 19th Century, 13 3/4 x 8 1/2 In. 1035.00
Virgin Kazanskaya, Brass Riza, Mid 19th Century, Russia, 12 x 10 In. 258.00
Virgin Kazanskaya, Russia, 19th Century, 12 1/4 In. 172.00
Virgin With Saints, Holding Infant, Wood Panel, Gold Leaf, Greece, 15 x 10 1/2 In. 1380.00
Woman, Soul In Purgatory, Wooden, Gesso, Polychrome, 19th Century, 33 x 21 In. 4800.00

IMARI patterns are named for the Japanese ware characteristically decorated with orange, red, green, and blue stylized designs. The bamboo, floral, and geometric patterns on the Japanese ware became so familiar that the name *Imari* has come to mean any patterns of this type. It has been copied by Asian, European, and American factories since the eighteenth century. It is still being made.

Bottle, 6 In., Pair 220.00
Bowl, Allover Floral, Off-White Ground, 4 Character Mark, 11 1/4 In. 288.00
Bowl, Aristocratic Lady, Terraced Lakeside Garden, c.1890, 11 In. 150.00
Bowl, Blue, Red, Porcelain, 12 In. 575.00
Bowl, Brocade, Chrysanthemum Shape, c.1880, 9 1/2 In. 150.00
Bowl, Dutch Exploration Of Japan, Black Sailing Ship Center, 13 1/2 In. 3800.00
Bowl, Fisherman In Landscape, Polychromed Celestial Dragon, c.1890, 9 3/4 In. 357.00
Bowl, Flower Basket Design Interior, Bird & Flower Exterior, 11 In. 390.00
Bowl, Petal Shape, Scalloped Edge, Green, Blue, Rust, Ivory, 3 x 10 In. 405.00
Bowl, Shishi Center, Landscape Surround, Phoenix Panels, 10 In. 240.00
Charger, Blue Ground, 15 3/8 In. 245.00
Charger, Blue, White, Celadon Glaze, 18 In. 230.00
Charger, Center Fu Lions In Landscape, Floral & Foliage Border, 16 In. 210.00
Charger, Central Floral Medallion, Late 19th Century, 15 1/2 In. 200.00
Charger, Floral Center, Landscape Surround, 16 In. 205.00
Charger, Flower & Bird Design Panel, 1850, 12 1/4 In. 180.00
Charger, Green Dragon, 18 1/4 In. ....575.00 to 630.00
Charger, Landscape Scene, Iron Red, Green, Gold, Porcelain, 1890, 15 1/2 In. 242.00
Charger, Landscape Scene, Porcelain, 1900, 12 In. 85.00
Charger, Rockery, Pavilion, Flying Peacock On Wave, 18 1/2 In. 290.00
Charger, Rockery, Pavilion, Flying Peacock, Brocade Ground, 18 1/2 In. 485.00
Charger, Still Life Of Flowers, 19th Century, 18 In. 325.00
Charger, Warrior & Landscape Cartouches, 21 3/4 In. 225.00
Condiment Set, Sterling Silver Frame, Center Handle, c.1910 .... 155.00
Cup & Saucer, Gold Rim, Demitasse 25.00
Dish, 4-Masted Ship, Trellis Border, Porcelain, 8 1/2 In. 425.00
Dish, Bird, Flower & Book Design, Ginko Leaf Shape, 8 1/2 In. 215.00
Dish, Stag, Bamboo Design, Oval, 6 3/4 In., Pair 103.00
Figurine, Shishi, Crouched On Gilt Rockery Base, 7 In. 270.00
Fish Set, Late 19th Century, 17-In. Platter, 10-In. Plate, 7 Piece 4900.00
Hibachi, Scholars In Bamboo Grove, 10 In. 120.00
Jar, Cover, Floral Design, 7 5/8 In. 105.00
Jar, Rose Petal, 6 In. 120.00
Jardiniere, Bird & Floral Design, 19th Century, 16 1/4 In. 862.00
Jug, Cream, Cover, Prunus Design, Pear Shape, 5 In. 395.00
Lamp, Vase, Flowers, Blue, Gold, Rust, Green, 32 In. 230.00
Plate, Fan Designs & Phoenix Birds, 2 Piece 60.00
Plate, Floral Design, Porcelain, 8 1/2 In. 120.00
Plate, Oranges, Cobalt Blue, 8 1/2 In. 72.00
Platter, Garden Scene, Butterflies, Reverse Designs, 14 x 11 In. 390.00
Platter, Graduated Nest Of Four, 1820-1825, 10 1/4 x 13 x 15 1/4 In. 1573.00

Punch Bowl, Japanese Figures, Cobalt Blue & White 695.00
Vase, 4 Floral Reserved, Baluster, c.1900, 10 1/2 In. 220.00
Vase, Baluster, Porcelain, 1840-1860, 6 3/4 In., Pair 363.00
Vase, Flower Filled Basket, Leaf Design, Porcelain, 12 1/4 In. 287.00
Vase, Flowerhead Design, Baluster, Porcelain, 1880-1885, 9 1/2 In. 180.00
Vase, Palace, Ruffled Rim, Figures On Floral Ground, 37 1/2 In. 1030.00
Vase, Raised Floral Design, Double Gourd Shape, 6 1/2 In. 1210.00
Vase, Stick Neck, Bulbous, Blue Floral, Off-White Ground, 18th Century, 8 1/2 In. 175.00

IMPERIAL GLASS Corporation was founded in Bellaire, Ohio, in 1901.
It became a subsidiary of Lenox, Inc., in 1973 and was sold to Arthur
R. Lorch in 1981. It was sold again in 1982, and went bankrupt in 1984.
In 1985, the molds and some assets were sold. The Imperial glass preferred by the collector is freehand art glass, carnival glass, slag glass,
stretch glass, and other top-quality tablewares. Tablewares and animals
are listed here. The others may be found in the appropriate sections.

Animal, Bull, Nut Brown 1000.00
Animal, Colt, Balking, Ultra Blue 350.00
Animal, Colt, Standing, Amber 400.00
Animal, Elephant, Medium 250.00
Animal, Hen, Sunshine Yellow 600.00
Animal, Mallard, Wings Up, Amber 250.00
Animal, Plug Horse, Black, 1985 .... 250.00
Animal, Sow, Red 600.00
Animal, Wood Duck, Milk Glass 600.00
Art Glass, Vase, Mosaic, Cobalt, Opal, Orange, 6 1/2 In. 488.00
Art Glass, Vase, Trailing Hearts & Vines, Green, White, 8 3/4 In. 690.00
Art Glass, Vase, Yellow Green Hearts, Orange Iridescent, Everted Rim, 6 In. 750.00
Bookend, Fish, Amber 400.00
Candlewick, Ashtray Set, Nested, Round, 5 In., 3 Piece 30.00
Candlewick, Ashtray, 6 In. 225.00
Candlewick, Ashtray, Eagle, 6 1/2 In. 70.00
Candlewick, Ashtray, Heart, 4 1/2 In. 10.00
Candlewick, Basket, Beaded Handle, 5 In. 250.00
Candlewick, Bonbon, 7 1/2 In. 275.00
Candlewick, Bonbon, Heart, Handle, 6 In. 35.00
Candlewick, Bowl, 6 In. 60.00
Candlewick, Bowl, Gold Beads, Square, 5 In. 140.00
Candlewick, Bowl, Heart, Handle, 5 In. 35.00
Candlewick, Bowl, Square, 5 In. 150.00
Candlewick, Cake Plate, 11 In. 110.00
Candlewick, Cake Stand 95.00
Candlewick, Candleholder, Flower, 6 In. 60.00
Candlewick, Candleholder, Mushroom, Pair 50.00
Candlewick, Compote, 4-Bead Stem 98.00
Candlewick, Cup & Saucer 13.00
Candlewick, Egg Plate 110.00
Candlewick, Ice Tub 200.00
Candlewick, Pitcher, 80 Oz. ....215.00 to 325.00
Candlewick, Plate, Chip & Dip, 14 In. 795.00
Candlewick, Platter, Oval, 16 In. 185.00
Candlewick, Relish, 3 Sections 85.00
Candlewick, Relish, 3 Sections, 3-Toed, 10 In. 130.00
Candlewick, Relish, 4 Sections, Oblong, 12 In. 95.00
Candlewick, Salt & Pepper 20.00
Candlewick, Sugar & Creamer 22.00
Candlewick, Tray, Fruit, Center Handle, 10 1/2 In. 75.00
Candlewick, Tray, Lemon, Center Handle, 5 1/2 In. ....40.00 to 50.00
Candlewick, Tray, Pastry, Center Handle, 11 In. 40.00
Candlewick, Tumbler, 12 Oz. ....13.00 to 20.00
Candlewick, Vase, Bud, Footed, 5 3/4 In. 65.00
Candlewick, Vase, Crimped Edge, 8 In. ....125.00 to 135.00
Candlewick, Vase, Fan, Floral Cutting, 8 1/2 In. .... · 90.00

Cape Cod, Basket, 11 In. 300.00
Cape Cod, Bowl, 6 In. 15.00
Cape Cod, Bowl, 12 1/2 In. 125.00
Cape Cod, Bowl, Divided, 11 In. 60.00
Cape Cod, Bowl, Float, 8 In. 100.00
Cape Cod, Cake Plate, 4-Toed, 10 In. ....165.00 to 275.00
Cape Cod, Cake Plate, Birthday, 13 In. 300.00
Cape Cod, Cake Stand, 11 In. 75.00
Cape Cod, Candleholder, 5 In. 40.00
Cape Cod, Condiment Set, Square, 5 Piece 575.00
Cape Cod, Decanter 175.00
Cape Cod, Decanter, Red, 30 Oz. 275.00
Cape Cod, Goblet, 9 Oz. 10.00
Cape Cod, Goblet, Red, 9 Oz. 16.00
Cape Cod, Pitcher, Milk, 16 Oz. ....42.00 to 55.00
Cape Cod, Plate, 14 In. 35.00
Cape Cod, Plate, Cupped, 14 In. 35.00
Cape Cod, Plate, Cupped, 16 In. 65.00
Cape Cod, Plate, Salad, 8 In., 8 Piece 50.00
Cape Cod, Relish, 3 Sections, 11 1/4 In. 300.00
Cape Cod, Salt & Pepper, Fern Green 75.00
Cape Cod, Sugar & Creamer, Footed 35.00
Cape Cod, Tom & Jerry, Footed, 15 Piece 140.00
Cape Cod, Tumbler, 16 Oz. 45.00
Cape Cod, Tumbler, Old Fashioned, 7 Oz. 15.00
Cape Cod, Vase, Footed, 11 1/2 In. 135.00
Chrysanthemum, Cup Plate, Sample 1800.00
Dancing Nudes, Vase, Red Slag, 8 1/2 In. 120.00
Mt. Vernon, Cologne 40.00
Square, Creamer, Ruby 25.00
Tiger, Paperweight, Black 300.00
Windmill, Bowl, Milk Glass 25.00

INDIAN art from North America has attracted the collector for many
years. Each tribe has its own distinctive designs and techniques.
Baskets, jewelry, pottery, and leatherwork are of greatest collector
interest. Eskimo art is listed in another category in this book.

Bag, Ceremonial, Chippewa, Beaded, Floral, Wool Fringe, 1890, 39 x 14 In. 1760.00
Bag, Nez Perce, Corn Husk, Traditional Designs, Early 20th Century, 18 1/2 x 14 In. 1580.00
Bag, Parfleche, Crow, c.1900, Pair 3500.00
Bag, Pipe, Blackfoot, Beaded, 1920 .... 330.00
Bag, Pipe, Crow, Beaded, Quilled, Pre-1900 .... 3300.00
Bag, Plains, Christmas, Beaded, 1908 .... 125.00
Bag, Tobacco, Cheyenne, Antelope Hide, Sinew Sewn, Beaded, Fringed, 1880, 16 x 6 In. . 770.00
Bag, Yakima, Eagle On Shield, Beaded, Yellow Ground, Embroidered, 1930, 12 x 13 In. . . 750.00
Bandolier Bag, Chippewa, Beaded, Floral & Fruit Design, 43 x 14 In. 1880.00
Bandolier Bag, Great Lakes, Cloth, Beaded, 1880 .... 3738.00
Basket, Apache, Coiled, Black Devil's Claw, Band Of Figures, 3 x 11 In. 200.00
Basket, Apache, Coiled, People & Animal Figures, Round, 1920, 10 In. 1100.00
Basket, Apache, Jicarilla, 5 1/4 In. 250.00
Basket, Burden, Apache, Twined, Fringe & Tin Cones, 1930, 8 x 7 In. 465.00
Basket, Cherokee, Southeast, Handle, 1930 .... 165.00
Basket, Gathering, Woodland, Splint, Colored Stripes, 13 x 21 1/2 In. 275.00
Basket, Havasupai Coiled, 8 3/4 & 10 In., Pair 290.00
Basket, Micmac, Birchbark, Leather Strap, 12 1/2 x 14 In. 412.00
Basket, Pima, 12 Male Figures, Early 20th Century, 7 3/4 x 10 3/4 In. 1650.00
Basket, Pima, Coiled, Horsehair, Friendship Figures, 1975, 2 1/4 x 1/4 In. 440.00
Basket, Pima, Coiled, Horsehair, Rattlesnake Design, 1975, 2 1/2 x 1/2 In. 550.00
Basket, Pima, Geometric Design, 3 1/4 x 14 In. 260.00
Basket, Pima, Ollaswastikas, Women, 1920s, 8 1/4 In. 850.00
Basket, Pima, Stepped Geometric Designs, 8 x 10 In. 115.00
Basket, Pomo, Coiled, Beaded, White, Blue, Red Beads, Diamond Ground, 2 x 6 In. 575.00
Basket, Pomo, Feather, Alternating Bands Of Yellow, Brown Feathers, 2 x 3 3/4 In. 145.00

Basket, Salish, Red & Black Geometric Design, Round, 8 x 14 In. 175.00
Basket, Southwest, Brown Striped Design, Round, 11 1/4 x 10 7/8 In. 230.00
Basket, Storage, Tulare, Coiled, Hourglass, 1920, 19 x 10 In. 1870.00
Basket, Tlingit, Geometric Design, Tag, E.M. Rhodes & Co., Alaska, 8 x 10 1/2 In. 4600.00
Basket, Trinket, Pomo, Coiled Basket, Carved Shell Disks, Abalone Danglers, 3 In. 402.00
Basket, Washo, Sing Rod Construction, Finial Cover, Handles, 19th Century, 21 In. 800.00
Basket, Washo, Single Coil, Geometric Bands, Globular, 3 1/2 x 6 In. 85.00
Basket, Washo, Single Rod Construction, 19th Century, 21 In. 800.00
Belt, Beaded Panel, Red, White, Blue, Green, Orange, Loom Strings, 1 1/2 x 30 In. 20.00
Belt, Navajo, Concha, Silver 300.00
Bird House, Chippewa, Birchbark, Unused, 1940s 115.00
Blanket, Navajo, Geometric Forms, Outlined In Gray, 52 x 31 In. 460.00
Blanket, Navajo, Red, Gray, Black, Pink, 42 x 65 In. 495.00
Blanket, Navajo, Stylized Diamonds, Wool, Taupe Ground, 59 1/2 x 34 In. 265.00
Blanket, Oxaca, Bands Of Central Star, Brown, Tan, 48 x 84 In. 135.00
Blanket, Saddle, Navajo, Blue, Red, 31 x 61 In. 225.00
Blanket, Saddle, Navajo, Maroon, Brown & Blue, Cream Ground, 62 x 33 In. 200.00
Blanket, Saddle, Navajo, Small Geometric Stripes, Gray Ground, 1925, 33 x 30 In. 402.00
Bolo Tie, Navajo, Silver Set With Turquoise & Coral, Stamped Bison Head 86.00
Bonnet, Child's, Plains, Beaded, Geometric Design, Ribbon Tie, 20th Century 410.00
Bottle, Gila, Geometric, Black, White Slip, Pre-Historic, Bulbous, 5 1/2 In., 3 Piece 230.00
Bottle, Olla, Southwest, Black, White, Geometric, Flared Rim, Prehistoric, 5 In. 145.00
Bowl, Acoma, 2 Birds, 4 1/4 In. 85.00
Bowl, Acoma, Geometric Band, 5 In. 70.00
Bowl, Acoma, Geometric Design, Black Slip, Signed, Lucy M. Lewis Acoma, 3 In. 402.00
Bowl, Apache, 1900, 14 In. 990.00
Bowl, Apache, Coiled, Polychrome, Late 19th Century, 18 1/4 In. 2090.00
Bowl, Eastern Woodlands, Hand Holds Under Lip, Irregular Shape, 17 x 15 1/2 In. 7000.00
Bowl, Hopi, 4 Panels Of Black Slip, Hatched Bear Paw Design, Red Slip Collar, 5 In. . . . 862.00
Bowl, Hopi, Bird, Black Line Trim Edge, 3 1/2 x 8 1/2 In. 1000.00
Bowl, Hopi, Black Slip Interior With Central Rain Bird Design, Verna Nahee, 11 In. 149.00
Bowl, Hopi, Black Slip, Allover Repeated Abstracted Feather, Linear Design, 7 3/4 In. . . . 98.00
Bowl, Hopi, Crosshatched Geometric, Band Of Repeated Steppes, Cream, Orange, 8 In. . . 115.00
Bowl, Hopi, Geometric Design, 3 1/4 x 9 In. 4750.00
Bowl, Hopi, Kachina, Geometric Design, Black, Pale Red, Cream Slip Ground, 3 x 11 In. . 460.00
Bowl, Hopi, Stylized Bird Design, Black Slip Geometric Design, Cream, Orange, 6 In. . . . 230.00
Bowl, Jeddito, Geometric Black Interior, Linear Design Exterior, 2 3/4 x 7 In. 145.00
Bowl, Mesa Verde, Bulbous, Brown Geometric Design, Buff Ground, 4 3/4 x 4 1/4 In. . . . 45.00
Bowl, Santo Domingo Pueblo, Trading Post, Circle Design, 1930, 6 1/2 In. 95.00
Bowl, Zuni, Polychromed Umber, Cream & Black Floral, 8 1/4 In. 110.00
Box, Micmac, Birch Bark, Quills Woven In Concentric Zigzag, 4 In. 287.00
Box, Micmac, Original Green, Oval 2500.00
Box, Navajo, Sterling Silver, Turquoise Cabs, Stamped, 1955, 4 1/2 x 2 In. 990.00
Box, Storage, Micmac, Nova Scotia, 8 x 15 In. 1500.00
Bracelet, Navajo, Kingman Turquoise Stones, Large 165.00
Bracelet, Navajo, Lone Mountain Turquoise Stones 175.00
Bracelet, Navajo, Silver & Turquoise Stones, Stamped Design, c.1920 . . . . 402.00
Bracelet, Navajo, Silver & Turquoise, Round & Elliptical Stones, Twisted Silver, 1930s . . 575.00
Bracelet, Navajo, Silver, Turquoise, Coral 65.00
Bracelet, Navajo, Stamped & Twisted Silver, Elliptical Turquoise Stones, 1930s 575.00
Bracelet, Silver & Turquoise, 5 Silver Bands, Stamped Snake Design, 1 1/2 In. 747.00
Buckle, Navajo, Cluster, Silver, Turquoise 155.00
Buckle, Navajo, Silver, Coral, Signed 145.00
Canoe, Huron, Birchbark, 1900 . . . . 9800.00
Canoe, Northeast Woodlands, Birchbark, 19th Century, 11 Ft. 4025.00
Canteen, Acoma, Umber, Foliate Star, Scalloped Border, 4 1/2 x 5 1/4 In. 190.00
Canteen, Hopi, Abstract Rain Bird Design, Brown, Red Slip, Cream, Orange, 11 In. 460.00
Canteen, Hopi, Kachina Head Design, Marked From Hopi Villages, 4 1/2 In. 690.00
Canteen, Hopi, Kachina Head, Orange Ground, 4 1/2 In. 690.00
Cap, Iroquois, Black Velvet, Glen Gary, c.1900 . . . . 405.00
Case, Southern Plains, Beaded Awl, Navy Blue Hourglass, Pink, White Field, 16 In. 1092.00
Club, Plains, Leather Covered, Beadwork Handle, Horsehair At End, 19 In. 165.00
Club, War-Coup, Plains, Hide Wrapped, Sinew Sewn Shaft, Horse's Tail, 18 7/8 In. 345.00

Cradle, Sioux, Fully Beaded, Made On Pine Ridge Reservation 2750.00
Cradle Board, Apache, Gold, Red Stripes, 1920s, 37 x 14 In. 750.00
Cradle Board, Northern Plains, Doll Size 495.00
Cuffs, Sioux, Beaded, 1880s 795.00
Dance Wand, Plains, Carved Cottonwood, Painted Design, 15 In. 525.00
Diorama, Navajo, Weaver, Woman Working Loom, Baby On Cradleboard, 12 x 6 In. 22.00
Dish, Southwest, Gunmetal Finish, Signed, Carmelita Dunlap, 7 1/2 In. 172.00
Doll, Cherokee, Doll Cradle, 19th Century 330.00
Doll, Hopi, Kachina, Carved, Elaborate Headdress, Painted, 1940, 9 x 4 In. 175.00
Doll, Hopi, Kachina, Palik Mana, Signed 120.00
Doll, Hopi, Kachina, Priest In Felt Kilt & Tunic, Articulated Arms, c.1960, 10 In. 315.00
Doll, Hopi, Kachina, Small Ogre, Signed, 1940 .... 175.00
Doll, Hopi, Kachina, Snake Dancer Skirt, Long Hair, Painted, 1975, 18 In. 355.00
Doll, Iroquois, Male & Female, Stroud Cloth & Cotton, Edge Beaded Trim, 13 In., Pair .. 632.00
Doll, Navajo, Blanket, Sunday Saddle 360.00
Doll, Southwest, Kachina, c.1870, 14 In. 4200.00
Dress, Eastern Woodlands, Beaded 250.00
Dress, Sioux, Buckskin, Beaded Yoke, Tin Cones, Fringe, With Leggings, 1940, 49 In. 2310.00
Drum, Blackfoot, Beater, Beaded, 19th Century 220.00
Drum, Pine Log, Hollow, Skin, Wooden Splint, Red Stain, 6 x 7 1/8 In. 110.00
Drum, Sioux Buffalo, Ceremonial Hand, 1880 .... 330.00
Drum, Sioux Buffalo, Shield Medicine, 1880 .... 1650.00
Drum, Sioux, Beater, Beaded, 19th Century 250.00
Fan, Kiowa, Peyote Feather, Beaded Handle, Twisted Hide Fringe, 1900, 22 In. 715.00
Figurine, Owl, Black Slip Feather, Orange Slip Eye Rings, Cream Ground, 7 1/4 In. 98.00
Gauntlets, Lakota, Tan Hide, Fringe, Beaded Cuffs, 13 1/2 In. 490.00
Gauntlets, White Buckskin, Beaded Cuffs, 4-In. Fringe, 1920-1940, 5 1/2 In. 90.00
Hair Roach, Crow, Red Inner & Outer Rows, Brown Center, 1890s, 17 In. 450.00
Hat, Hupa, Twine Woven, 3 Color Twin Concentric Devises, 7 1/2 In. 230.00
Hat, Northwest, Cone Shape, Face, Painted, Yellow, Blue, Green, Red, Black, 6 x 15 In. ... 2990.00
Headdress, Iroquois, Turkey Feather 65.00
Jacket, Nez Perce, Buckskin, Fringe At Yoke, Rolled Buckskin Buttons, Fireside 395.00
Jacket, Northwest Territory, Moose Hide, Beadwork, c.1930, Small 445.00
Jacket, Sioux, Child's, Hide, Pictorial Beadwork 1210.00
Jar, Acoma, 8 Lizards At Shoulder, 20th Century, 7 1/2 x 10 1/2 In. 85.00
Jar, Acoma, Bulbous, Brown & Beige Geometric Design, c.1935, 11 1/2 x 10 In. 1670.00
Jar, Acoma, Bulbous, Geometric Design, Signed, D.H. Sanchez, c.1975, 5 1/2 x 3 3/4 In. .. 120.00
Jar, Acoma, Globular, Intricate Linear Star Design, Black Slip, 3 1/2 In. 287.00
Jar, Anasazi, Geometric, Black, White Slip, Handle, Pre-Historic, 8 1/4 In., 4 Piece 290.00
Jar, Hopi, Abstract Bear Paw Design, Red, Brown Slip, Cream, Orange Ground, 6 In. 1725.00
Jar, Hopi, Abstract Repeated Rain Bird Design, Scalloped Rim, Black, Red Slip, 7 In. ... 402.00
Jar, Hopi, Geometric & Scroll Design, Polychrome, 19th Century, 7 x 11 In. 1495.00
Jar, Hopi, Geometric Design, Soft Orange, Umber, Ocher, 6 1/2 x 6 In. 330.00
Jar, Hopi, Geometric Design, Tapered, Brown On Tan Ground, 3 1/2 In. 50.00
Jar, Hopi, Globular, Stylized Bird, Black, Maroon, White Slip, Strap Handle, 13 1/4 In. .. 575.00
Jar, Hopi, Red & Orange Neck, Bird Design, Garnet Pavatea, 5 1/2 In. 50.00
Jar, Hopi, Redware, Abstract Rain Bird Design, Black Slip, 7 1/2 In. 345.00
Jar, Hopi, Serpentine Crosshatch, Black Red, Cream Ground, 11 1/2 In. 374.00
Jar, Hopi, Stylized Bear Paw Design, Cream, Brown, Red, Square, 4 3/4 In. 1150.00
Jar, Hopi, Stylized Rain Bird, White Ground, 7 1/4 In. 1495.00
Jar, Mesa Verde, Bulbous, Allover Geometric Design, Buff & Brown Glaze, 7 1/2 x 6 In. . 175.00
Jar, Mesa Verde, Coil, Bulbous, Allover Buff Glaze, 4 1/2 x 4 5/8 In. 115.00
Jar, Mound Builder, Mississippi Area, Bulbous, Handle, Narrow Neck, Tan, 5 3/4 In. 115.00
Jar, Pueblo, Bulbous, Multicolored Geometric Design, 19th Century, 10 x 9 In. 575.00
Jar, San Ildefonso, Frieze Of Feathers, Black Slip Ground, Flared Sides, 4 x 4 3/4 In. 920.00
Jar, San Ildefonso, Globilar, Buffalo Below A Red Slip, Black Slip, Signed, 4 1/2 x 5 In. . 520.00
Jar, San Ildefonso, Narrow Hook Band, Black, Polished Ground, 3 x 4 1/4 In. 490.00
Jar, San Ildefonso, Stylized Feather Band, Black, Pale Red, Gray Slip Ground, 4 x 5 In. .. 145.00
Jar, Santa Clara, Stylized Avanyu Water Serpent, Black, Signed, 4 1/2 x 7 In. 575.00
Jar, Seed, Hopi, Painted Hatched Bear Paw, Fannie Nampayo, 7 1/2 In. 1437.00
Jar, Southwest, Blackware, Band Of Feather Design, Signed, Blue Corn, 7 In. 1495.00
Jar, Southwest, Gunmetal Finish, Signed, Rose, 5 1/2 In. 259.00
Jar, Zia, Fluttering Birds, Black, Pale Red, Floral, Geometric Ground, 12 x 11 In. 430.00

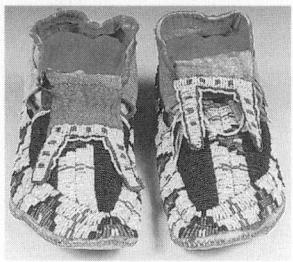

Leather needs care. Keep it in a room with high humidity. Leave tabs and other stress points unsnapped to lessen tearing. Don't hang leather saddles, holsters, etc., over sharp nails; use large diameter poles. Don't display near a heat source or in direct sunlight. Don't use neat's-foot oil, use an appropriate leather product.

Indian, Moccasins, Sioux, Beaded Hide,
Blue & White, c.1890, 10 In.

Jar, Zia, Stylized Arches, Cream Slip, Black, Red, Flared Sides, 8 x 7 3/4 In.	....	145.00
Jar, Zuni, Cream Slip, Black, Red, 4 Friezes, White Backed Deer, 9 x 10 In.	....	345.00
Ladle, Hopi, Pottery, 1890, 8 x 6 In.	....	880.00
Ladle, Pueblo, Mesa Verde, Geometric Design, Brown & Buff Glaze, 6 3/4 In.	....	120.00
Ladle, Pueblo, Mesa Verde, Geometric Design, Snake Handle, Brown & Buff Glaze, 7 In.		85.00
Leggings, Blackfoot, Buffalo Hide Beaded, 1880	....	2475.00
Leggings, Sioux, Mounted Figures, Wearing War Bonnets	....	8525.00
Leggings, Sioux, Pictorial, Geometric Designs	....	2310.00
Martingale, Nez Pierce, Tepees & A Horse, 1915	....	9500.00
Mask, Navajo, Ceremonial, Buckskin, Felt, Abalone & Horsehair, 21 x 11 1/2 In.	....	1150.00
Mask, Northwest Coast, Wolf, Articulated, Wolf's Teeth, Abalone Eyes, 8 1/2 x 14 In.	...	2760.00
Mask, Northwest, Carved, Crescent Eyes, Black, Red Nose, Lips, 11 1/2 x 7 1/2 In.	.....	2300.00
Mask, Northwest, Earthquake, Tom Patterson	....	1400.00
Mat, Brown & Beige Zigzag Design, 20th Century, 21 x 24 In.	....	35.00
Medal, Peace, Silver, Bronze Metal, Aug. 8, 1803	....	550.00
Mittens, Algonquin, Moosehide Body, Velvet Cuffs, Floral Beading, 1880s, 14 1/2 In.	...	825.00
Mittens, Naskapi, Caribou Hide, Linear Geometric Design, 1820s	....	8050.00
Moccasins, Blackfoot, Child's, Beaded	....	550.00
Moccasins, Blackfoot, Child's, Buffalo	....	330.00
Moccasins, Central Plains, Geometric Steppes, Crosses, Light, Medium Blue, Red, 9 In.	..	920.00
Moccasins, Central Plains, Woman's, High Top, Beaded, 1890	....	2990.00
Moccasins, Cheyenne, Lazy Stitch Beading, 1900, 9 In.	....	176.00
Moccasins, Cheyenne, Spot Stitch Beading, Concentric Medallions, 10 In.	....	605.00
Moccasins, Deer Fur, Beaded Trim, 1900, 3 In.	....	150.00
Moccasins, Kiowa, Blue, Red Beads, White Zigzagging, Buffalo Rawhide, 22 In.	....	2300.00
Moccasins, Northeast, Beaded Hide, Blue, Yellow, Red, White Ground, 10 In., Pair	......	10.00
Moccasins, Plains, Beaded, Diamond Design, White, Red, Blue, Orange, Green, 11 In.	...	1295.00
Moccasins, Plains, Buffalo Hide, Multicolored Beads, Fringed Top, 12 In.	....	980.00
Moccasins, Plains, Child's, Hide, Sinew Sewn Beadwork, Early 20th Century	....	247.00
Moccasins, Santee Sioux, Sinew, Hard Sole, Floral Quillwork, 1870, 10 In.	....	715.00
Moccasins, Sioux, Beaded Hide, Blue & White, c.1890, 10 In.	................*Illus*	1035.00
Moccasins, Sioux, Beaded, With Tongues, 1880	....	550.00
Moccasins, Sioux, Fully Quilled Fronts, White Beadwork, Quilled Tongue, 10 3/4 In.	....	1092.00
Moccasins, Sioux, Hightop, Buffalo Hide, 1880	....	250.00
Moccasins, Southern Plains, Single Lane Stitch Seed Beads, Black, White, 10 In.	....	8625.00
Moccasins, Woodlands, Floral Beaded, Beaver Fur Trim, Cloth Lining, 1920s, 12 In.	....	155.00
Mortar, Birch Log For Grinding Corn, Herbs, Dried Meats, 7 x 10 1/8 In.	....	90.00
Necklace, Acoma, Rosary, Blue Padre Beads, Silver Cross	....	190.00
Necklace, Navajo, Silver Beads, 30 In.	....	650.00
Necklace, Navajo, Squash Blossom, Dark Blue, Pyrite Turquoise, Clasp, 15 In.	....	525.00
Necklace, Navajo, Squash Blossom, Silver & Turquoise, 16 In.	....	385.00
Necklace, Navajo, Squash Blossom, Silver, Large Handmade Beads, 24 In.	....	65.00
Necklace, Navajo, Squash Blossom, Silver, Turquoise, Gold Matrix, 26 In.	....	410.00
Necklace, Osage, Beads, White, Blue & Salmon With Fringe, 1916	....	190.00
Necklace, Pueblo, 4-Strand Clamshell, Stone Nuggets, Cording, 1880s, 12 1/2 In.	....	326.00
Necklace, Santa Clara, Fetish, Black Pottery	....	550.00
Necklace, Silver, Squash Blossom, 1980s	....	250.00

Necklace, Zuni, Bone, Animal Fetishes 275.00
Necklace, Zuni, Fetish, Birds, 3 Strands Of Disk Carved Shells, 25 In. 287.00
Necklace, Zuni, Turtle Designs 90.00
Olla, 2 Spouts, Black Glaze, Double Arrowhead Design, Maria, 5 In. 132.00
Olla, Acoma, Geometric Feathers & Arrowheads, Black & White, 8 1/2 In. 520.00
Olla, Apache, Coiled, Early 20th Century, 9 1/2 In. 4310.00
Olla, Cover, Tesuque, Stylized Rain Cloud Design, Large 11500.00
Olla, Papago, Coiled, 8 In. 1350.00
Olla, Pueblo, Floral, Ocher, Umber, White Slip Ground, 6 1/4 In. 220.00
Olla, Zia, Pottery, Birds & Rainbows Around, 1975, 9 x 11 In. 465.00
Pillow Cover, Navajo, Striped, Red, Black, Brown, Early 20th Century, 23 x 41 In. 115.00
Pipe, Catlinite, Buffalo Effigy, Carved Twisted Stem, 1890, 28 In. 1045.00
Pipe, Catlinite, Lead Inlay, c.1840 .... 1550.00
Pipe, Sioux, Catlinite, Wooden Stem, Carved Horse Bowl, 30 In., 2 Piece 305.00
Pipe, Sioux, Inlaid Black, Original Stem, 1880 .... 40.00
Pipe Bag, Central Plains, Rows Of Lazy Stitch Single Lane Beadwork, Blue, Red, 36 In. . 4025.00
Pipe Bag, Crow, Hide, Fringe, Beaded Hourglass, 1880, 30 x 7 In. 275.00
Pipe Bag, Sioux, Beaded & Quilled 1980.00
Pipe Bag, Sioux, Beaded Top, Lower Panel Of Geometric Devises, Coup Feathers, 21 In. . 2415.00
Pipe-Tomahawk, Brass, Presentation, Inscribed U.S. 1775, 17 x 7 In. 1210.00
Pipe-Tomahawk, Bronze Head, Wooden Stem, Pewter Mouthpiece, 23 In. 90.00
Pot, Acoma, Clay, 10 1/4 In. 4600.00
Pot, Acoma, Geometric Design, 7 3/4 In. 345.00
Pot, Acoma, Stylized Horses, 10 In. 8050.00
Pouch, Sioux, Beaded, Buffalo Hide 90.00
Purse, Trading Post, Beaded, Floral, Green, Blue, Pink, White, 1900-1930, 6 1/2 In. 65.00
Ring, Navajo, Sterling Silver, Green Turquoise, 1930s 70.00
Robe, Mandan, Buffalo, South Dakota, 1860-1880 .... 5500.00
Rug, Navajo, 2 Gray Hills, Stylized Feather Border, Jenny Eetsitty, 54 x 88 In. 1100.00
Rug, Navajo, 3 Expanding Serrated Diamond, Black, Brown, Red, 43 x 60 In. 440.00
Rug, Navajo, 5 Female Figures, Tan Ground, Red & Black Borders, 43 x 62 In. 990.00
Rug, Navajo, Allover Diamond Pattern, Ivory Ground, 84 x 58 In. 220.00
Rug, Navajo, Allover Serrate Stripe, Double Dye Red, Gray, 27 x 57 In. 245.00
Rug, Navajo, Bands Of Cream, Brown, Rust, Yellow, Black, 20th Century, 47 x 82 In. ... 290.00
Rug, Navajo, Bands Of Serrate Diamonds, Black, Brown, 29 x 55 In. 165.00
Rug, Navajo, Bands, Black, Red, White, Gray, 20th Century, 25 x 39 In. 175.00
Rug, Navajo, Black, Gold, Gray & Brown, Cream Ground, 71 x 48 In. 900.00
Rug, Navajo, Brown, White, Sawtooth Border, Polygons, Mountain Peaks, 105 x 55 In. .. 1495.00
Rug, Navajo, Center Swastika, Brown & Orange, 31 x 53 In. 330.00
Rug, Navajo, Connected Stepped Triangles, Tan Ground, 51 x 76 In. 1100.00
Rug, Navajo, Diamond & Interlocking Bar H, Red, Dark Brown, 50 x 72 In. 275.00
Rug, Navajo, Diamond Design, Stepped Blocks, c.1945, 37 1/2 x 67 In. 522.00
Rug, Navajo, Diamond, Red, Dark Brown, Tan, 33 x 61 In. 330.00
Rug, Navajo, Diamond, Stepped Blocks, Natural, Gray Ground, 41 x 84 In. 355.00
Rug, Navajo, Diamond, Triangle Design, Soft Brown, Tan, Red, 54 x 79 In. 715.00
Rug, Navajo, Double Diamond, Black, White, Red, Tan, 96 x 59 In. 2530.00
Rug, Navajo, Eagles On Shields, Serrated Border, Gold, White, Gray, 85 x 50 In. 1265.00
Rug, Navajo, Earth Tones & Turquoise Figures, Cream Ground, 47 x 43 In. 450.00
Rug, Navajo, Natural Wool, Geometric, Diamonds, J.B. Moore, 1915, 91 x 66 In. 2475.00
Rug, Navajo, Pictorial, American Flag, 1960s, 24 x 41 In. 225.00
Rug, Navajo, Radiating Central Diamonds, Stepped Terrace Blocks, 1930, 42 x 78 In. 660.00
Rug, Navajo, Red Central Diamond, 4 Surrounding Diamonds, 38 x 48 In. 385.00
Rug, Navajo, Stripes, Brown, Beige, Rust, Black, 23 x 51 In. 175.00
Rug, Navajo, Stripes, Serrated Diamonds, 30 x 62 In. 165.00
Rug, Navajo, Sunrise Design, Elongated Diamonds, Zigzag Border, 36 x 62 1/2 In. 550.00
Rug, Navajo, Sunrise, Gray, Dark Brown Diamond, 31 x 54 In. 165.00
Rug, Navajo, Thunderbird Design, Hand Woven, 1930s, 27 x 32 In. 150.00
Rug, Navajo, Wool, Crystal, Waterbird Design, 1945, 44 x 76 In. 330.00
Rug, Yei, Brown Figures, Cream Ground, Mexico, 52 x 85 In. 275.00
Rug, Zigzag Design, Cream, Rust, Brown, Gray, Black, 20th Century, 42 x 46 In. 230.00
Saddle & Stirrups, Sioux, Zigzag Design Stirrups, Used By Elsie White Horse, 1870 .... 6600.00
Saddle Blanket, Geometric Multicolored Stripes, 1925 In Weave, 33 x 30 In. 402.00
Saddlebag, Plains, Woven Grass, Twisted Grass Strands, Braided Straps, 11 3/8 In. 285.00

Shield, Northern Plains, Hide Pierced & Leather Tied, Oak Frame, 13 In. 325.00
Shirt, Blackfoot, Toddler's, Felt With Straw Beads, Cowry Danglers At Sleeves, 9 In. 1092.00
Skull Cracker, Plains, Wood, Beaded Bands, Leather Covered Stone, 15 In. 60.00
Southwest, Knife & Sheath, Skin-Wrapped Haft, Fringe Loop, Mid-1800s, 5 In. 900.00
Spoon, Buffalo, Horn 200.00
Strike-A-Lite, Araphaho, Trade Beads, Tin Cones, 1880, 5 1/2 x 2 3/4 In. 525.00
Strike-A-Lite, Kiowa, Beaded Brick Stitch All Brass Beads, Fringe, 1870, 3 x 5 In. 660.00
Tomahawk, Pipe, Plains, Beaded Detail, Ash Stem, Pictograph Of Horse, 19 In. 2875.00
Tomahawk, Spiked, 1740-1770, 12 In. 195.00
Totem Pole, Carved & Painted, 20th Century, 60 In., Pair 302.00
Totem Pole, Carved, Unpainted, 27 In., Pair 358.00
Totem Pole, Northwest Coast, 4 Stylized Animals, Green, Black, Carved Cedar, 16 In. 1210.00
Totem Pole, Northwest Coast, Miniature 1595.00
Totem Pole, Northwest Coast, Wooden, 30 In. 875.00
Totem Pole, Northwest, Beaver On Bear Head, Carved, Painted, 17 1/2 In. 2300.00
Tray, Apache, Alternating & Repeating Stepped, Checkerboard Design, 15 In. 2530.00
Tray, Apache, Central Rosette Design, Repeated Steppes, Rhomboid, 8 1/2 In. 575.00
Tray, Apache, Human & Quadruped Figures, Coiled, 20th Century, 16 In. 1725.00
Tray, Basket, Pima, Geometric Pinwheel Design, 12 3/4 x 3 1/2 In. 750.00
Tray, Basket, Pima, Geometric Stepped Design, 15 1/2 x 4 In. 1440.00
Tray, Basket, Pima, Maze Design, Coiled Rim, Silver & Turquoise Button, 12 3/4 In. 690.00
Tray, Pima, 1900, 17 1/2 In. 385.00
Tray, Pima, Central Star Design, 5 Triangles At Braided Rim, 20th Century, 21 In. 1035.00
Tray, Pima, Devil's Claw Design, Natural, Brown, 14 In. 860.00
Tray, Pima, Maze Design, 1900, 16 1/2 In. 770.00
Vase, Santa Clara, 2 Handles, Pottery, Geometric Design, Polished Black Finish, 4 In. . . . 255.00
Vessel, Anasazi, Geometric Design, Black, White Slip Ground, 6 1/8 In., Pair 145.00
Vessel, Pueblo, Stylized Leaf Design, Black, White Slip, 4 3/4 x 6 1/2 In., 4 Piece 115.00
Vessel, Southwest, Black, White, Red Matte Slip, Geometric, 4 1/8 In., Pair 145.00
Vessel, Zuni, Stepped Geometric Devices, Corrugated Band, Coupling Frogs, 6 1/2 In. . . . 3105.00
Vest, Crow, Beaded, Floral, No. 16 . . . . 6050.00
Vest, Sioux, Fully Beaded, Sinew Sewn 2475.00
War Club, Sioux, Old Patina 600.00
Watch Band, Zuni, Silver, Turquoise 25.00
Weaving, Navajo, 2 Maltese Crosses, Hooked, Band Of Chevrons, 56 x 85 In. 1840.00
Weaving, Navajo, Band Of Horizontal, Wavy Stripes, Homespun Wool, 52 x 77 In. 460.00
Weaving, Navajo, Band Of Repeated Triangle, Striped Design, Homespun Wool, 69 In. . . . 1035.00
Weaving, Southwest, Allover Banded Design Of Stepped Rhomboid, 47 x 69 In. 517.00

INDIAN TREE is a china pattern that was popular during the last half of
the nineteenth century. It was copied from earlier Indian textile patterns that were very similar. The pattern includes the crooked branch
of a tree and a partial landscape with exotic flowers and leaves. Green,
blue, pink, and orange were the favored colors used in the design.

Bowl, Oval, Open, Johnson Brothers 30.00
Creamer, Johnson Brothers 70.00
Cup & Saucer, Johnson Brothers 60.00
Dinner Set, Cauldon, 42 Piece 125.00
Gravy Boat, Johnson Brothers 25.00
Jug, Milk, Johnson Brothers 135.00
Plate, Bread & Butter, Johnson Brothers, 6 1/4 In. 4.00
Plate, Johnson Brothers, 8 1/2 In. 9.00
Plate, Johnson Brothers, 9 3/4 In. 13.00
Soup, Cream, Johnson Brothers 70.00
Sugar, Cover, Johnson Brothers 35.00

INKSTANDS were made to be placed on a desk. They held some type of
container for ink, and possibly a sander, a pen tray, a pen, a holder for
pounce, and even a candle to melt the sealing wax. Inkstands date to
the eighteenth century and have been made of silver, copper, ceramics,
and glass. Additional inkstands may be found in these and other related
categories.

Brass, Bird Design, Japan, 9 1/2 In. 175.00

Brass, Indian Chief, Leaf & Acorn Design, 2 Wells 550.00
Bronze, 2 Putti Atop Mask, Scrolled Candle Branches, Base Drawer, 9 1/2 x 16 In. 1380.00
Bronze, Empire Revival, Gilt, 2 Flower Shaped Wells, 19th Century, 8 In. 200.00
Glass, Self-Closing, Sun-Colored Amethyst, Sengbusch 110.00
Iron, 2 Ribbed Glass Wells, Hinged Lid, With Letter Rack & Pen Rests, 8 In. 55.00
Iron, Ornate, 2 Swirled Glass Wells, Iron Cap, 10 In. 70.00
Mahogany, Silver Over Copper, Drawer, Pen Tray, Sander, Sheffield, 11 x 9 x 5 In. 690.00
Marble, Matching Egg-Form Lidded Wells, c.1900, 3/4 x 13 3/4 In. 138.00
Metal, 2 Milk Glass Revolving Bulldog Heads Well, 1860-1890, 4 1/2 In. 910.00
Metal Figure Of Cow, Pen Trays Over Drawer, Tortoiseshell Veneer, 6 1/2 x 12 In. 4600.00
Oak, 2 Cut Glass Wells, Cork Stopper, Nickel Handle, 11 In. 95.00
Pewter, Pottery Insert, Round, England, 19th Century 250.00
Silver, Glass, Applied Strapwork Rim, 4 Claw Feet, Henry Wilkinson & Co., 1852 ...... 1840.00
Tin Glazed Earthenware, White, Heart Shape, 3 Feet, Dutch, 18th Century 750.00
Wooden, Stenciled Eagle, 2 Glass Wells, Silliman & Co., Chester, Con., 4 3/4 In. 165.00

INKWELLS, of course, held ink. Ready-made ink was first made about
1836 and was sold in bottles. The desk inkwell had a narrow hole so
the pen would not slip inside. Inkwells were made of many materials,
such as pottery, glass, pewter, and silver. Look in these categories for
more listings of inkwells.

Black Lacquer, Louis XV, Chinese Figures In A Landscape, 5 1/2 x 18 In. 2300.00
Brass, Cherub On Lift Lid, 7 In. 300.00
Brass, Woman Bust Finial, 2 Locking Wells, Pen Holder, Paw Feet, 6 In. 385.00
Brass Fittings, Matching Finial On Hinged Top 235.00
Bronze & Ormolu Mounted, 4 Scrolled Mask Feet, France 488.00
Cut Glass, Ruby Cased, c.1890, 5 x 5 In. 240.00
Cut Glass, Silver Plated Top 50.00
Figural, Colonial Man, Goblet & Urn, Staffordshire, 3 1/4 In. 55.00
Fruitwood Barrel, Blown Glass Insert, Cover Seals Bottle, 2 3/8 In. 140.00
Glass, Blown Sawtooth Mold, 1 1/4 x 2 3/8 In. 176.00
Metal, Clown, Colored Outfit, Top Lifts Off, Cup Inside, Pen Place On Front, 5 x 3 In. 175.00
Metal, Devil's Face, Glass Insert, 3 x 2 In. 175.00
Painted Black Head, Numbered Section, Blue Scrolls, Staffordshire, F. Bridges, 5 In. ... 750.00
Paperweight, Clear, Multicolored Pebble Base, Stopper, Tooled Lip, Pontil, 2 7/8 In. 75.00
Pewter, Gourd, Embossed Lily Pads, Lily Pad Dish, Marked, Kayserzinn, 4 1/4 In. 55.00
Pewter, Original Patina, Tudric, 9 x 4 In. 310.00
Porcelain, 2 Sphinxes, Band Of Gilt Grapes & Leaves, Egyptian Revival Style, 7 In. 373.00
Porcelain, Blue Underglaze, Quill Pen, Chinese Export, 2 7/8 In. 135.00
Porcelain, Nautilus Shell, Helmet Shape, Covered Cut Glass Well, France 770.00
Silver, Enamel Flowers, Bulbous, 3 Legs, Flower Finial, China, 19th Century, 4 In. 690.00
Soapstone, Building With Columned Front, Applied Base, 1870-1900, 2 1/2 In. 130.00
Soapstone, Period Quill Pen, Square, 2 In. 120.00
Spatterware, Blue & White Sponge, Removable Insert, 2 5/8 In. 165.00
Spelter, Elephant's Head, Monkey Finial, Hinged Lid, Victorian, 6 1/2 In. 45.00
Wood, Carved, Grouse Head, Glass Eyes, Hinged Head, Clear Glass Well, c.1880, 5 In. .. 625.00
Wood, Chip Carved, Capstan Shape, England, 18th Century, 3 In. 200.00
Wood & Silver Owl, 6 1/2 In. 220.00

INSULATORS of glass or pottery have been made for use on telegraph
or telephone poles since 1844. Thousands of different styles of insulators have been made. Most common are those of clear or aqua glass;
most desirable are the threadless types made from 1850 to 1870.

American Telephone & Telegraph Co., Aqua, Micro Bubbles 50.00
American Telephone & Telegraph Co., Jade Milk 18.00
American Telephone & Telegraph Co., Purple 28.00
B.T. Co. Of Canada, Purple 23.00
Brookfield, X On Top, Threaded Inside 15.00
Canadian Pacific Railroad Co., Purple 50.00
Dominion, No. 42, Honey Amber 85.00
Dominion, No. 42, Orange Amber 65.00
H.G. Co., Jade Milk 20.00

H.G. Co., Patent May 2 1893, Petticoat, Dark Purple 450.00
H.G. Co., Petticoat, Sky Blue 10.00
Hemingray, No. 9, Jade Milk, Patent, May 2, 1893 .... 18.00
Hemingray, No. 19, Green 165.00
Hemingray, No. 19, Orange Amber 250.00
Hemingray, No. 25, Aqua 25.00
Hemingray, No. 660, Honey Amber 38.00
Hemingray, Patent May 2 1893, Petticoat, Cobalt Blue 375.00
Lynchburg, No. 30, Aqua 8.00
Lynchburg, No. 31, Aqua 15.00
Lynchburg, No. 36, Aqua 5.00
Lynchburg, No. 44, Pale Yellow 25.00
McLaughlin, No. 16, Apple Green 30.00
McLaughlin, No. 16, Emerald Green 12.00
McLaughlin, No. 16, Green 12.00
Pyrex, No. 63, Carnival 30.00
Pyrex, No. 662, Carnival 35.00
Telegraphos Nacionales, Medium Orange Amber 85.00
VTS Industrial Co., No. 8, Ruby Red 295.00
W.F.G. Co., No. 16, Blue 30.00
Whitall Tatum, No. 1, Purple 25.00
Whitall Tatum, No. 2, Olive Green 28.00

IRISH BELLEEK, see Belleek category.

IRON is a metal that has been used by man since prehistoric times. It is
a popular metal for tools and decorative items like doorstops that need
as much weight as possible. Items are listed here or under other appro-
priate headings, such as Bookends, Doorstop, Kitchen, Match Holder,
or Tool. The tool that is used for ironing clothes, an iron, is listed in the
Kitchen category under Iron and Sadiron.

Ashtray, Man, Leaning Against Lamp Post, Bourbon St. Bum, 4 1/2 In. 45.00
Ashtray Stand, Art Deco, 1920, 28 In. 36.00
Ashtray Stand, Black Butler Wearing Frock Coat, Bow-Tie, Box, 33 In. 550.00
Ashtray Stand, Black Butler Wearing Frock Coat, Bow-Tie, Holding Tray, 36 In. 660.00
Bed Warmer, Pierced Brass Cover, Starflower Design, Continental, 34 In. 55.00
Bell, Triangle & Clapper, Stamped G.B. Horr, Pennsylvania, 19th Century, 13 1/2 In. 695.00
Boot Scraper, 2 Stylized Dolphins, 1840, England, 21 1/2 x 18 x 6 1/2 In. 725.00
Boot Scraper, 2-Brush Form, Surmounted By 2 Black Stallions, Victorian, 11 x 14 In. ... 450.00
Boot Scraper, 2-Brush Form, Surmounted By White Horse, Victorian, 14 1/4 In. 475.00
Boot Scraper, Black Man, Sitting, Insert Boot & Brush On Either Side, 13 x 10 In. 245.00
Boot Scraper, German Shepherd, Old Paint, 17 x 12 x 14 In. 650.00
Boot Scraper, Griffons, Oval Dish Base, 9 1/2 x 14 x 10 In. 220.00
Boot Scraper, Limestone Block Base, 17 In. 245.00
Boot Scraper, Mammy & Shiner, Mammy, With Hands On Hips, 15 x 16 x 9 In. 465.00
Boot Scraper, Spaniel, Cast Zinc, Full Body, Black & White Paint, 19 x 11 x 15 In. 275.00

**Remove the rust from iron by soaking the piece
in kerosene for 24 hours, or use any one of
several commercial preparations made for the
removal of rust. Wash, dry, and coat the piece
with a light oil to protect it.**

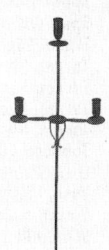

Iron, Candlestand,
3-Light, Wrought Iron,
Wallace Nutting

Brazier, 4 Large Flowers, Molded Handles, Italian, 17th Century, 23 In. 1840.00
Cachepot, Scalloped Crown Molded Top, Dolphin, Gilt, c.1929, 33 3/4 x 17 1/4 In. 615.00
Candlesnuffer, Original Red Paint, c.1750 .... 195.00
Candlestand, 2-Light, Floor, Adjustable, Pair 400.00
Candlestand, 3-Light, Wrought Iron, Wallace Nutting .... *Illus* 2970.00
Cannon, Model, Revolutionary War, Wooden, 15 1/4-In. Barrel, 27 In. 65.00
Canteen, Canvas Cover, US, Cuban Flags, Eagle, Spanish American War, 7 1/2 In. 275.00
Cauldron, S.S.S. For The Blood, Wire Handle, 1885-1900, 4 1/2 In. 330.00
Cigar Cutter, Betsy Ross 1035.00
Cigar Cutter, Griswold, No. 2494 .... 165.00
Cigar Cutter, Plug, Elf, On Wood Base, 7 3/8 x 13 In. 240.00
Cork Press, Leaf Designs, Bolts To Counter, 2 7/8 x 8 5/8 In. 125.00
Door Escutcheon, Round Knob, Organic Design, Louis Sullivan, 13 1/4 In., Pair 2990.00
Door Knocker, Cast Iron, Woodpecker, Green, Black, White & Red Paint, 4 In. 16.00
Door Knocker, Floral Basket, White, Pink, Blue, Yellow, Green, 4 x 3 1/2 In. 68.00
Door Knocker, Floral, 3 In. 55.00
Door Knocker, Woodpecker On Tree, Painted 145.00
Door Latch, Pennsylvania, Inscribed, I.W. 1788, 8 1/2 In. 495.00
Family Crest, Painted, 11 x 11 In. 60.00
Figure, Buddha Head, Elongated Ears, Oriental, 4 In. 175.00
Figure, Eagle, Wall Mounted, 20th Century, 41-In. Wingspan 275.00
Figurine, Dog, Painted, 9 In. 75.00
Figurine, Geisha, Traditional Costume, Hands Raised, 60 1/4 In. 8050.00
Figurine, Indian, Last Of Mohicans, Bow, Sheaf, Arrows, Club, 34 x 14 x 18 In. 2200.00
Flint Striker, 17th Century, 5 1/4 In. 495.00
Flint Striker, Serpent Shape, 18th Century, 3 1/2 In. 395.00
Frame, Gilt, Free Form Easel, Relief Cupids, 13 x 7 In. 100.00
Grill Section, Scrolled Overlapping Foliage, Green Patina, Metro, Guimard, 1904, 29 In. . 4600.00
Handcuffs, Old West, Hand Wrought, Pair 90.00
Hinge, Strap, Arrow Point, Late 18th Century, 31 1/2 In., Pair 90.00
Holder, Rush Light, Primitive, Candle Socket Counter Weight, Twisted, 12 1/2 In. 165.00
Holder, Rush Light, Wooden Base, 13 In. 165.00
Hook, Squirrel & Acorn, 6 3/4 In. 150.00
Jar, Figural, Man, Comical, Large Head, Hat Lid, Worn Black Paint, 4 1/4 In. 190.00
Jardiniere, Central Foliate Design, Hammered, Bale Handles, Angle Legs, 35 In., Pair ... 374.00
Jardiniere, Lily Pad Form, Green Patina, Rocaille Base, Continental, 15 In., Pair 2070.00
Kiln, Pipe, American, Penny Feet, 18th Century 395.00
Leg Shackle, Key, Blacksmith & Whitesmith Made, Late 17th Century 285.00
Padlock, U.S. Winall, Raised Lettering 30.00
Pipe Tongs, c.1770, 7 In. 1250.00
Pipe Tongs, Pocket, Engraved Initials & 1761, 6 1/4 In. 750.00
Planter, Flared Fluted Form, Victorian, 27 x 27 In. 489.00
Planter, William IV Style, England, 14 x 28 x 13 3/4 In., Pair 365.00
Rack, Coat, Adjustable Hooks, Hammered, Paul Kiss, 1925, 11 x 33 In. 1875.00
Salamander, Royal Crown Forged Handle, Engraved Leaves, c.1660, 22 1/2 In. 1500.00
Splint Holder, Candle Socket Counterweight, Wooden Base, 9 1/4 In. 270.00
Splint Holder, Knob Counterweight, Turned Wooden Base, 11 3/4 In. 195.00
Spur, Officer's, Revolutionary War, Extended Rowel, Pair 135.00
Stand, Lighting, Tripod, Tooled Stem, Candle Socket & Spring Clamp, 24 In. 575.00
Target, Shooting Gallery, Bird & Duck, Yellow & Orange Paint, 8 In. 150.00
Target, Shooting Gallery, Rooster, Black Paint, 8 In. 275.00
Target, Shooting Gallery, Star & Flying Bird, 8 In. 170.00
Target, Shooting Gallery, Turkey, Green Traces, H.C. Evans, 6 1/4 In. 115.00
Tobacco Cutter, Squirrel, Butternut Base 250.00
Urn, Scroll Handles, Pedestal, J.W. Fiske, Signed & Dated, 1875, Pair 2600.00
Vase, Village Scene, Flying Crane, Ribbed Basket Base, Japan, 12 1/2 In., Pair 211.00
Watch Holder, Man, With American Flag, Riding Dog Named Victory, 11 In. 251.00
Windmill Weight, Bird, 14 1/2 x 10 In. 2000.00
Windmill Weight, Bobtail Horse, Dempster On Horse's Side, No. 87J, 17 x 17 In. 375.00
Windmill Weight, Bull, Fairbury 600.00
Windmill Weight, Eclipse, A-13 .... 100.00
Windmill Weight, Eclipse, B-13 .... 200.00

Windmill Weight, Eclipse, Dry Moon 300.00
Windmill Weight, Horse, Standing On Plinth, White, Black Paint, 18 x 17 1/2 In. 345.00
Windmill Weight, Rooster, Elgin Wind, Power & Pump Co., 18 In. 1045.00
Windmill Weight, Rooster, Fantail 900.00
Windmill Weight, Rooster, Hummer E184, Elgin Wind, Power & Pump Co., 13 1/2 In. .. 330.00
Windmill Weight, Rooster, Rainbow-Tail, Red Comb, Wattle, Wooden Base, 19 x 17 In. . 1380.00
Windmill Weight, Rooster, Red, White Paint, Early 20th Century, 19 x 17 In. .....460.00 to 575.00
Windmill Weight, Rooster, White Paint, Red Comb, Wattle, Metal Base, 15 In. 745.00

IRONSTONE china was first made in 1813. It gained its greatest popularity during the mid-nineteenth century. The heavy, durable, off-white
pottery was made in white or was decorated with any of hundreds of
patterns. Much flow blue pottery was made of ironstone. Some of the
decorations were raised. Many pieces of ironstone are unmarked, but
some English and American factories included the word *Ironstone* in
their marks. Additional pieces may be listed in other categories, such
as Flow Blue, Gaudy Ironstone, Moss Rose, Staffordshire, and Tea
Leaf Ironstone.

Biscuit Jar, Cobalt Blue, Orange & Green, Barrel 125.00
Bowl, Vegetable, Cover, Hawthorn Transfer, 2 Handles, Finial, 7 1/2 x 9 1/4 In. 110.00
Bowl, Vegetable, Lake, Blue, White 192.00
Bowl, Vegetable, Square 20.00
Bowl, Zephyr, Polychrome, England, 19th Century, 9 1/2 x 5 In. 185.00
Cheese Dish, Dome Cover, 8 x 9 1/2 In. 125.00
Coffeepot, Cover, Floral Design, Polychrome, 10 In. 145.00
Coffeepot, Dora, Black Transfer, E. Challinor 247.00
Coffeepot, Vintage Finial, Black Transfer With Roses & Morning Glories, 9 In. 180.00
Compote, Cover, Fluted & Scalloped Design, T. & R. Boote, 8 In. 82.00
Creamer, Blue Snowflake Transfer, 4 1/2 In. 220.00
Creamer, Red & Yellow Sponge Design, Blue Bandings, 5 1/2 In. 275.00
Cup & Saucer, Blue Snowflake Transfer, Handleless, 4 Sets 330.00
Dish, Toothbrush, Ribbed Grape 125.00
Food Warmer, Clarke's Patent Pyramid, White, Black Transfer, Tin Stand, 10 1/2 In. 165.00
Mug, Child's, Dr. Franklin's Maxims, Plowing Scene, 2 3/4 In. 190.00
Pitcher, Blue Aurora Transfer, Paneled, 10 In. 250.00
Pitcher, Floral Transfer Ground, Painted Floral Bouquets, Bulbous, c.1875, 13 In. 132.00
Pitcher, Lucerne, Blue Transfer, A.W.P. & Company, 8 1/4 In. 165.00
Pitcher & Bowl, Snake Handle, c.1830, 11 In. 895.00
Plate, Peruvian Horse Hunt, Green, White Center, Brown Borders, 8 1/2 In. 75.00
Platter, American Marine, Transfer, Brown & White, 19th Century, 15 1/2 In. 209.00
Platter, Brown, White, Oval, 19th Century, 18 In. 77.00
Platter, Chinese Tree, Faux Bamboo Base, c.1850, 18 1/2 In. 300.00
Platter, Classical Figures, Cut Corners, Emile Lessore, 1855, 15 x 19 In. 805.00
Platter, Florentine, Mayer, 15 3/4 In. 192.00
Platter, Florentine, Mulberry & White, England, 19 In. 143.00
Platter, The Narrows, From Port Hamilton, Lion, Purple Transfer, 17 1/2 In. .....275.00 to 300.00
Punch Bowl, Multicolored Flowers, Fruit, Footed, 9 x 17 3/4 In. 750.00
Punch Bowl, Polychrome Enamel, Red Brown Floral Transfer, 12 3/4 In. 690.00
Punch Bowl, Rococo, Pink, Sepia Floral, Furnival, 9 1/2 x 17 1/2 In. 630.00
Tea Set, Black Transfer, Paneled, 8 3/4 In., 3 Piece 250.00
Teapot, Eagle, Blue, White, Hexagonal, England, 2 Piece 145.00
Tureen, Sauce, Polychrome, England, 19th Century, 9 In. 154.00
Tureen, Soup, 2 Handles, Octagonal, Blue, White, England 430.00
Tureen, Soup, Cover, Undertray, 2 Handles, Booth's, 19th Century 490.00
Tureen, Soup, Cover, Undertray, Ladle, Wheat, Berries, Leaves, J. & G. Meakin, 12 In. .. 200.00
Tureen, Soup, Fox Hunting Scenes, Blue, White, 16 In. 431.00
Tureen, Soup, Stand & Ladle, Meadow Flowers, John Maddock, c.1900, 7 x 14 In. 180.00
Tureen, Soup, Undertray, Gilt Floral Design, John Maddock & Sons, 17 In. 140.00
Tureen, Undertray, Pink Flowers, Green Foliage, Blue Handles, Fruit Finials, 15 In. 430.00
Vase, Royal Patriotic Fund, Black Transfer, January 1, 1855, 7 3/4 In. 165.00
Wash Set, Blue & White, England, Pre-1890s, 8 Piece 450.00
Wash Set, Enameled Floral, Real Ivory-Balt, Monogram, 19th Century, 7 Piece 265.00

IVORY from the tusk of an elephant is thought by many to be the only true ivory. To most collectors, the term *ivory* also includes such natural materials as walrus, hippopotamus, or whale teeth or tusks, and some of the vegetable materials that are of similar texture and density. Other ivory items may be found in the Scrimshaw and Netsuke categories. Collectors should be aware of the recent laws limiting the buying and selling of elephant ivory and scrimshaw.

Box, Figural Landscape Design, Cylinder, 1840, 1 1/2 In., Pair	231.00
Box, Panels Of Dragons, Bats, Foliage & Figures, China, 6 1/4 x 4 1/4 In.	1035.00
Box, Thread, Needle Case, Glove Stretchers, Chinese Export	143.00
Box, Tortoiseshell Portrait, Round	1250.00
Card Case, Figural Design, China, 19th Century, 4 x 2 x 5 In.	121.00
Card Case, Figural Landscape Design, Chinese Export, 1840, 3 7/8 In.	300.00
Card Case, Figural Landscape Reserve, Chinese Export, 19th Century, 4 1/2 In.	275.00
Cigarette Holder, Reclining Daruma, Signed, 5 In.	605.00
Cup, Cover, Bamboo & Bird Design, Oriental, Case, 19th Century, 5 In.	55.00
Cup, Oriental Courtyard Scene, 19th Century, 4 In., Pair	110.00
Doctor's Lady, Reclining, Wearing Shoes, Bracelets, Necklace, Wooden Stand, 18 1/2 In.	1980.00
Figurine, 7 Children Playing Blind Man's Bluff, Wooden Base, 4 In.	1320.00
Figurine, 8 Immortals, Inside Tree Trunk, Wooden Stand, 18 1/2 In.	1320.00
Figurine, Bacchante, Holding Grapes, Vine Entwined Rod, Wooden Stand, 7 1/2 In.	6325.00
Figurine, Celery, Radish Shape, 2 Grasshoppers, Snail, Late 19th Century, 11 1/2 In.	4600.00
Figurine, Child, Lying On Ground Holding Pearl, 19th Century, 5 3/4 In.	577.00
Figurine, Dragon Boat With 2 Sages Eating Peaches, 10 In.	192.00
Figurine, Dragon, Sections Pegged Together, Pearl Mouth, Wooden Stand, China, 72 In.	4310.00
Figurine, Emperor Riding In Cart, Attendants, 22 In.	6050.00
Figurine, Farmer, 7 In.	315.00
Figurine, Figure Among Trees & Rockery, 2 1/2 In.	258.00
Figurine, Fisherman, Lotus Leaf Hat, Bamboo Pole, Fish, China, 16 In.	975.00
Figurine, Foo Dog, Reclining, Raising Back Paw To Scratch Ear, Wooden Stand, 9 In.	920.00
Figurine, Goddess, Standing, Wooden Base, 7 1/2 In.	45.00
Figurine, Kwan Yin, Seated, Holding Lotus Flowers In Arms, c.1930, 7 In.	165.00
Figurine, Madonna & Child, Child Holding Orb, Flemish, 17th Century, 4 In.	862.00
Figurine, Man & Children Climbing Ladder, 10 In.	545.00
Figurine, Man & Woman, Ch'ing Dynasty Style Clothes, Rosewood Stand, 5 In., Pair	575.00
Figurine, Man, Standing String Of Coins, Wooden Stand, 6 In.	345.00
Figurine, Marine, Okimono, Oni Standing, Holding Club, Puppy At Feet, 2 3/4 In.	240.00
Figurine, Military Official, Sword, Yellow Patina, China, 18 In.	1495.00
Figurine, P'u Tai, Seated On Mat, Playing With Children, China, 19th Century, 3 1/2 In.	460.00
Figurine, Peasant Boy, Torn Shirt, Floppy Hat, Holding Rifle, On Pedestal, 3 7/8 In.	415.00
Figurine, Saint Sebastian, 18th Century, 8 3/4 In.	975.00
Figurine, Seated Buddha, Scene Around Base, Black Stain, Inscription, China, 5 1/4 In.	490.00
Figurine, Virgin Mary & Joseph, Embroidered Gowns, c.1700, 7 5/8 In.	9200.00
Figurine, Woman, Descending Stairs, Openwork Railings & Door, France, 5 x 5 In.	1610.00
Figurine, Woman, Dragon-Headed Staff, 11 3/4 In.	247.00
Figurine, Woman, On Antelope, Serpent Carved Stick, Wooden Base, 8 1/4 In., Pair	690.00
Figurine, Woman, Seated, Wearing Richly Ornamented Costume, 18th Century, 3 In.	330.00
Figurine, Woman, Standing, Holding Toy Horse Puppet, Signed, 9 1/2 In.	845.00
Figurine, Woman, With Guitar, 13 In.	630.00
Frame, 3 Pierced Doors, Figural Landscape, 19th Century, China, 4 3/4 In.	155.00
Group, Geese & Marsh Grass Scene, Early 19th Century, 3 3/4 In., Pair	852.00
Group, Sage, With A Peach & A Staff, Early 20th Century, 2 1/2 In.	77.00
Handle, Parasol, Polar Bear, Holding Seal, Walrus Ivory, Scrimshaw Tree, c.1900	495.00
Inro, Allover Travelers Landscape, 4-Case, Kagetoski, Mid-19th Century	3850.00
Jagging Wheel, Tear Drop Handle, Pierced Flower Head & Shield, 1860s, 6 In.	2185.00
Model, Steam Engine, Articulated, Shaped Gears & Beams, Walnut Base, 8 1/2 x 12 In.	5462.00
Napkin Ring, Figural, Nude Woman, Bent Backwards, Holding Toes, 2 In.	5750.00
Ojime, Ball Shape, Openwork 7 Theatrical Masks, Japan, 1900	300.00
Ojime, Daikoku's Head, Gold Patina, 18th Century, Japan	120.00
Okimono, Samurai, Annoyed With 3 Children, Shominsai Chikamasa, 3 1/2 In.	1540.00
Okimono, Skeleton, Seated, Lotus Blossom Skull, Signed Tadachika, 2 In.	385.00
Plaque, Taj Mahal Scene, Velvet Frame, 2 x 2 3/8 In.	230.00
Puzzle Ball, 3 Elephant Base, 5 In.	44.00

Puzzle Ball, Oriental Scholar Base, 8 In. 22.00
Puzzle Ball, Stand, 11 3/4 In. 385.00
Screen, Table, 5-Panel, Pouring Flowers From Basket, 5-Claw Dragons Cornice, 23 In. ... 2640.00
Shoehorn, Tapering Handle, Late 19th Century, 10 3/4 In. 38.00
Tankard, Battle Scene, Silver Mounts, 19th Century, 9 In. 5635.00
Tankard, Cherub Finial, Carved, Dionysian Revelry, Mermaid Handle, 9 3/8 In. 5280.00
Tusk, African, Carved, Totemic Male & Female Figures, Mask Design, 29 In. 460.00
Tusk, Allover Courtiers, Warriors, Horse, Gardens, Rosewood Base, China, 9 x 6 In. 1725.00
Tusk, Piety Finial, Amber Yellow Patina, Ch'ien Lung Mark Base, 15 In. 1725.00
Vase, Allover Fenestration & Floral, Wooden Base, China, 19th Century, 4 1/2 In. 120.00
Vase, Cover, Carved Dragons, Flaming Pearl, Loose Ring Handles, 20 3/4 In. 1650.00
Vase, Cover, Pagoda, Trees, Dragons Amidst Clouds, Mask Handles, Wood Base, 24 In. ... 2875.00
Vase, Dragon & Wave Reserves, China, 9 1/2 In., Pair 920.00
Vase, Men & Women Scenes, Iron Mask Handles, Yellow Patina, 18th Century, 12 In. ... 2760.00

JACK ARMSTRONG, the all-American boy, was the hero of a radio serial from 1933 to 1951. Premiums were offered to the listeners until the
mid-1940s. Jack Armstrong's best-known endorsement is for
Wheaties.

Book, Big Little Book, Ivory Treasure 20.00
Comic Book, No. 2 .... 95.00
First Aid Kit, Junior Ace, Tin 45.00
Game, Map, 1936 .... 100.00
Pedometer 85.00
Secret Bombsight, Unopened Mailer 425.00
Telescope, Jack Armstrong Explorer 30.00
Toy, Secret Bombsight, Bombs, Ships, Mailer 500.00
Toy, Shooting Plane, Mailer 175.00

JADE is the name for two different minerals, nephrite and jadeite.
Nephrite is the mineral used for most early Oriental carvings. Jade is a
very tough stone that is found in many colors from dark green to pale
lavender. Jade carvings are still being made in the old styles, so collectors must be careful not to be fooled by recent pieces. Jade jewelry
is found in this book under Jewelry.

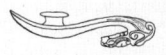

Bottle, Snuff, Kneeling Liiuhai, Smiling At Toad, 19th Century, 2 1/4 In. 2250.00
Ewer, Flowering Lotus Shape, Green, Gray, Black Veining, 6 x 3 1/2 In. 230.00
Figurine, 2 Children Playing With Bats & Lotus Blossoms, White, 5 1/4 In. 3300.00
Figurine, Emaciated Lohan, On Tree Stump, Frog Whispers In Ear, White, 5 1/2 In. 9250.00
Figurine, Water Buffalo, Reclining, Pale Green, 18th Century, 4 In. 440.00
Panel, Carved Bird & Branch, 8 1/2 x 4 3/4 In., Pair 805.00
Vase, Carp Shape, Spinach, China, 7 3/4 In. 865.00
Vase, Dragon, Passion Flower, Loose Ring Handles, Celadon Green, 4 1/2 In. 522.00
Vase, Relief Dragon About Neck, Pear Shape, Domed Cover, White, 9 3/4 In. 6600.00

JAPANESE CORALENE is a ceramic decorated with small raised beads
and dots. It was first made in the nineteenth century. Later wares made
to imitate coralene had dots of enamel. There is also another type of
coralene that is made with small glass beads on glass containers.

Orange, Ruffled Rim, Double Handles, 5 In. 92.00
Tankard, Nippon 7900.00
Vase, Floral, Pink, Green Ground, Gold Trim, Nippon, 8 5/8 In. 1100.00
Vase, Green Matte Ground, Gold Trim, 8 1/4 In. 495.00
Vase, Pink Shading To Pale Mint Beading, Signed, Nippon, 7 In. 425.00
Vase, Waterlily, Pad Design, Green Mark, Nippon, 6 7/8 In. 357.00

JAPANESE WOODBLOCK PRINTS are listed in this book in the Print category under
Japanese.

Check stored items once a year for infestation or deterioration.

JEWELRY, whether made from gold and precious gems or plastic and colored glass, is popular with collectors. Values are determined by the intrinsic value of the stones and metal and by the skill of the craftsmen and designers. Victorian and older jewelry have been collected since the 1950s. More recent interests are Art Deco and Edwardian styles, Mexican and Danish silver jewelry, and beads of all kinds. Copies of almost all styles are being made. American Indian jewelry is listed in the Indian category.

Belt, Christian Dior	100.00
Belt, Gold, Gucci	75.00
Belt, Rhinestone, Kenneth Jay Lane	125.00
Belt, Silver, Gucci	75.00
Bracelet, 3 Harlequin Masks, Blue Stone Eyes, Sterling Silver	430.00
Bracelet, 3 Rows Of Seed Pearls, Turquoise Spacers, Gilt Metal Mount	258.00
Bracelet, 5 Oval Plaques, Center Baroque Pearl, Black Onyx Ground, W.N. Brooks	395.00
Bracelet, 7 Slides, Tiger Head Clasp, Pears, Cameos, Colored Stones, 14K Gold	1495.00
Bracelet, Amethyst, Rainbow Design, Rectangular Gemstones, 14K Yellow Gold	374.00
Bracelet, Aurora Borealis Stones, Art Deco Links, Joseph Mazer	40.00
Bracelet, Bakelite, 2 Ivory Bands On Top, Thick Marbled Brown Clamp, 1 In.	360.00
Bracelet, Bakelite, Apple Juice, Rope Carved, 1 1/2 In.	357.00
Bracelet, Bakelite, Bangle, 3-Dimensional Seated Frog, Translucent Red, 1 In.	750.00
Bracelet, Bakelite, Bangle, Bowtie, Ivory, Multicolored Dots, Red, Green, Yellow, 1 In.	3250.00
Bracelet, Bakelite, Bangle, Dot, Red, Black Oval Dots, 5 In.	135.00
Bracelet, Bakelite, Bangle, Fish, 4 Red Fish, 4 Groups Of Seaweed, 1/4 In.	1210.00
Bracelet, Bakelite, Bangle, Fish, Reverse Carved, 1 In.	1430.00
Bracelet, Bakelite, Bangle, Green, Rhinestones, Orange Dots, 1/4 In.	121.00
Bracelet, Bakelite, Bangle, Ivory, Black Celluloid Loops, 5 In.	176.00
Bracelet, Bakelite, Bangle, Ivory, Black, Red Bands, Asymmetrically Carved, 1/4 In.	275.00
Bracelet, Bakelite, Bangle, Raised Dot, Orange, Ivory, 1 In.	605.00
Bracelet, Bakelite, Bangle, Stork In Flight Over Cattails, Lily Pads, Apple Juice, 1/4 In.	2310.00
Bracelet, Bakelite, Bangle, Yellow, Triangular Profile, Marbled Red Dots, 1 In.	120.00
Bracelet, Bakelite, Black Carved Sunflowers, 1 1/4 In.	231.00
Bracelet, Bakelite, Butterscotch Oval Dots, Red, Belle Kogan, 1/4 In.	605.00
Bracelet, Bakelite, Caramel, Brass Wire Segments, 1 In.	22.00
Bracelet, Bakelite, Carved Flower, Red Clamp Bracelet, Floral Mid-Section, 1 In.	525.00
Bracelet, Bakelite, End-Of-Day, Marbled Earthtones, Red, Black, Yellow, Floral	500.00
Bracelet, Bakelite, Faux Golden Pearl Cuff, Hinged, Abstract Leaves	2185.00
Bracelet, Bakelite, Green, Brown, Ivory Bands, Optic Carving, 1/4 In.	121.00
Bracelet, Bakelite, Hinged, Ivory, Rose Bushes, 1 1/2 In.	231.00
Bracelet, Bakelite, Hinged, Top Covered With Multicolored Stones, Weiss	48.00
Bracelet, Bakelite, Monopoly, Charms Of Ivory Bakelite Dice, Red Hotel, 6 1/2 In.	495.00
Bracelet, Bakelite, Multicolored Bands, Hinged Amber Section	3565.00
Bracelet, Bakelite, Philadelphia, Dark Blue Hinged Body, Black, Orange Fins, 1/2 In.	6050.00
Bracelet, Bakelite, Polka Dot, Ivory Injection Dots, 5 In.	3190.00
Bracelet, Bakelite, Ruby-Faceted Cut, 1 1/4 In.	150.00
Bracelet, Bakelite, Stretch, Lemon Slices & Brown Cylinder Shapes	95.00
Bracelet, Bakelite, Stretch, Yellow Lemon Slices, Brown Cylinder Shape	145.00
Bracelet, Bakelite, Zigzag, Ivory, Marbled Lime Green Interlocked Sections, 1 In.	495.00
Bracelet, Bakelite, Zigzag, Ivory, Marbled Red Interlocked Sections, 1 In.	525.00
Bracelet, Bangle, Cushion Sapphire, 14K Yellow Gold, c.1900	1725.00
Bracelet, Bangle, Floral & Vine Design, Buckle Design Closure, Yellow Gold	190.00
Bracelet, Bangle, Floral Design, 14K Yellow Gold, 1940s	125.00
Bracelet, Bangle, Hinged, 34 Diamond Melees, 2 Pearls, 14K Gold, Dresden Box	4715.00
Bracelet, Bangle, Hinged, Faceted Rows Of Garnets, Gilt Metal Mount	287.00
Bracelet, Bangle, Lattice Design, 14K Yellow Gold, 1940s	100.00
Bracelet, Bangle, Multicolored Gemstones, Cream Enamel, 18K Yellow Gold, 1940s	1090.00
Bracelet, Bangle, Raised Water Lily, Riker Bros., 14K Gold	1092.00
Bracelet, Bangle, Swirl Design, 14K Gold	185.00
Bracelet, Basket Weave Mesh Design, 14K Yellow Gold	325.00
Bracelet, Black Horn, Silver Bands, Vine & Floral Design, Green Stone	35.00
Bracelet, Bone Cuff, To Conform To Right Wrist, Sterling Silver, Tiffany	373.00
Bracelet, Braided Wire Design, Flexible Mesh Links, 18K Yellow Gold, Italy	1150.00
Bracelet, Brown & Yellow Cabochon, Sarah Coventry	30.00

Bracelet, Celluloid, Amber Scrolls, Red Rhinestones, 5 In. 295.00
Bracelet, Celluloid, Diamond, Amber, Lavender Rhinestones, Pink, 1/4 In. 285.00
Bracelet, Celluloid, Ivory, Green Band, Green Rhinestones, 5 In. 65.00
Bracelet, Chrysoprase, Green, Oval Onyx Links, 14K Yellow Gold, 1950s 920.00
Bracelet, Coral Beads, Carved Coral Silver Clasp 230.00
Bracelet, Cuff, Hinged, Horse & Rider Flanked By 6-Pointed Stars, Leaves 1150.00
Bracelet, Cuff, Silver Metal, Relief Floral Design, Safety Chain, Whiting Davis, 2 5/8 In.   20.00
Bracelet, Double Rows Of Gray Striated Agate, Silver Linked Marbles & Logs, Scotland .   435.00
Bracelet, Double Trace Link Design, Repousse Accents, 18K Yellow Gold 201.00
Bracelet, Filigree, Diamond, Peridot, 14K Gold, 1920s 390.00
Bracelet, Flexible, Art Deco, Swirl Motif, Platinum, Sapphire & Diamonds 3025.00
Bracelet, Geometric Form, Florentine Finish, 14K Yellow Gold 405.00
Bracelet, Gilt Metal, Topaz, Amber Rhinestones, Hobe, 7 x 1 In. . . . . .330.00 to 525.00
Bracelet, Gilt Metal, Zebra Heads, Rhinestones, Kenneth Jay Lane, 1 In. 90.00
Bracelet, Hair, Woven, Hinged, Rose-Cut Diamond Accents, 18K Gold, Victorian 1840.00
Bracelet, Harley-Davidson, Chrome 65.00
Bracelet, Hinged Bar Links, 14K Yellow & White Gold 520.00
Bracelet, Ivory, Double Dragons, Gold Dragons, China, 19th Century 860.00
Bracelet, Leaf Design, Silver Metal, Trifari 95.00
Bracelet, Linked Agate & Granite Barrels, Silver Ends, Scotland 550.00
Bracelet, Mourning, Daguerrean, Woven Human Hair, Brass & Enamel Shell 495.00
Bracelet, Navette Shape Platinum Links, 5 Small Pearls, 1910 . . . .   1265.00
Bracelet, Oval & Rectangular Peridots, Twisted Seed Pearl Links, Box, 18K Gold 1380.00
Bracelet, Pearl, Openwork Multicolored Enamel Plaques, 14K Yellow Gold 287.00
Bracelet, Pin & Earrings, Malachite, Silver, 1860 . . . .   85.00
Bracelet, Quatrefoil Slide, Seed Pearls, Black Enamel Tracery, 14K Yellow Gold 750.00
Bracelet, Quilted, Tapered Design, Rose-Cut Diamonds, 18K Yellow Gold 1725.00
Bracelet, Ram's Head, Open-Mouthed Ram's Head, Scroll, Gold, Victorian 690.00
Bracelet, Renaissance, Baroque Pearls, Multicolored, 14K Yellow Gold 1840.00
Bracelet, Row Of Polished Hearts, Rope Twist Edges, Heart Charm, 14K Gold, 7 1/2 In. .   545.00
Bracelet, Shakudo, Genre Scenes On Seven Plaques, Ivory Back, Silver & Gold 1840.00
Bracelet, Silver Ball Links, Chain Guard, Mexico 175.00
Bracelet, Silver Mounted & Linked Witch's Hearts, Malachite, Scotland 875.00
Bracelet, Silver, Pearl Cameo At Center, Braided Wire, Floral Overlays, 2 Clear Stones . .   20.00
Bracelet, Snake Design, 26 Mine Cut Diamonds, 2 Red Stones, 18K Yellow Gold 550.00
Bracelet, Snake, Coiled In Gold Wire, Red Stone Eyes, Flexible 402.00
Bracelet, Snake, Coiled, Ruby Eyes, Flexible, 18K Yellow Gold 1035.00
Bracelet, Snake, Overlapping Scales, Flexible, Green Stone Accents, White Gold 1150.00
Bracelet, Sterling Silver, 3 Blue Stones 70.00
Bracelet, Sterling Silver, 3 Floral Links, 3 Domed Links, Georg Jensen, No. 28 . . . .   632.00
Bracelet, Sterling Silver, Amethyst, Hammered Silver Knot, Silver Bead, T. Fahrner 745.00
Bracelet, Sterling Silver, Double Leaf, Toggle Clasp, Oval Links 86.00
Bracelet, Sterling Silver, Floral Links, Blue Rhinestones, Hobe, 6 1/2 In. 25.00
Bracelet, Sterling Silver, Floral, Domed Links, Georg Jensen, No. 16 . . . .   489.00
Bracelet, Sterling Silver, Wedge-Shaped Links, Georg Jensen 160.00
Bracelet, Tennis, Diamonds, Herringbone Design, 14K Gold, 1980s 495.00
Bracelet, Wedge Links, 5 Staggered Rows, 14K Gold, 1940 . . . .   1035.00
Bracelet, Wire Twist & Matte Gold Design, Prong-Set Rubies, Cartier 2300.00
Bracelet, Woven Gold, Braided Foxtail Chain, 18K Yellow Gold 690.00
Bracelet, Wrap-Around Snake, Spring-Loaded Body, Gold Metal, Whiting & Davis 25.00
Bracelet & Earrings, Silver Bangle, Whiting & Davis 95.00
Bracelet & Necklace, Blue Rhinestones, Barclay 85.00
Buckle, Dragon, Cloisonne, 3 1/4 In. 40.00
Buckle, Enameled Flowers, Liberty & Co., 1905 . . . .   1045.00
Buckle, Floral Design, Sterling Silver, India, 5 In. 65.00
Buckle, Shoe, Wrought Tines, Early 18th Century, Pair 250.00
Charm, Derringer Pistol, Polished Finish, Japan, 1 1/2 In. 20.00
Charm, Rotating Oval, Onyx, Carnelian, Scrollwork Design, 12K Gold 70.00
Charm, Tree-Of-Life, Happy Birthday, Gold & Pearl, Spinning Disc, 14K Yellow Gold . .   55.00
Chatelaine, 2 Ladies, Ball Fringe, Chain & Ring, German Silver 225.00
Chatelaine, Bracelet, 4 Drops, Memo Pad, Pencil, Compact, Sterling Silver 150.00
Choker, Bronze, 7 Shaped Triangular Links, Georg Jensen, 14 In. 350.00
Cigarette Holder, Dunhill, 3 Diamonds, 3 Cabochon Sapphires, Box, 18K Gold 264.00

Jewelry, Clip, Blackamoor,
Coral, Emeralds,
Turquoise, Gold, Silver,
c.1915, 2 x 1 1/8 In.

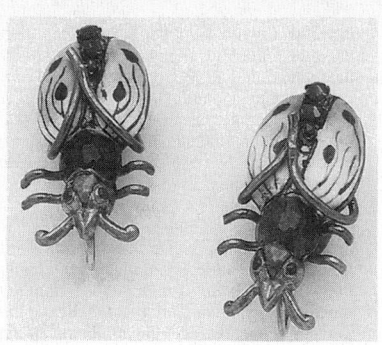

Jewelry,
Earrings, Beetle,
Enamel,
Semiprecious
Stones, Gold,
Victorian,
1 1/8 x 5/8 In.

Clip, Bakelite, Philadelphia	315.00
Clip, Bakelite, Vegetable, Green Leaves, 2 Asparagus Charms, 1 Squash, Carrot, 4 In.	1600.00
Clip, Bird, Silver Metal, Bird On Branch, Colorful Enameled, Trifari, 3 In.	240.00
Clip, Birdhouse, Silver Metal, Red, White, Blue, Black Birds, Tree, Trifari, 3 In.	1000.00
Clip, Blackamoor, Coral, Emeralds, Turquoise, Gold, Silver, c.1915, 2 x 1 1/8 In. ....*Illus*	1200.00
Clip, Elephant, Silver Metal, Gray Enameled, Clear Rhinestones, Trifari, 3 In.	350.00
Clip, Floral, Gilt Metal, Crystal Beads & Drops, Haskell, 4 In.	330.00
Clip, Flower, Silver Metal, Blue, Green, Brown Enameled, Topaz Stones, Trifari, 3 In.	375.00
Clip, Flower, Silver Metal, Red, Green Enameling, Clear Rhinestones, Trifari, 5 In.	550.00
Clip, Fruit Bowl, Jelly Belly, Lucite Body, Rhinestones, Corocraft, 2 In.	770.00
Clip, Money, Stirrup, 18K Yellow Gold	865.00
Clip, Spider, Jelly Belly, Lucite Abdomen, Rhinestones, Trifari, 2 In.	440.00
Cuff Links, Billiken, Goldtone	25.00
Cuff Links, Black Enameled Oriental Letters, 18K Yellow Gold	115.00
Cuff Links, Emerald, Ruby, Sapphire & Diamond, 18K Gold	2185.00
Cuff Links, Freeform, Gemstone Accents, Amethyst, Ruby & Sapphire, 18K Gold	747.00
Cuff Links, Golfer In Relief, Sterling Silver, Round, 1940s	175.00
Cuff Links, Green Enameled, Eagle Links, 14K Orange Gold	635.00
Cuff Links, Horse Head, Double-Sided Round Links, 14K Yellow Gold	460.00
Cuff Links, Intersecting Tricolor Bars, 18K Gold, Onyx, Hematite, Tiffany	575.00
Cuff Links, Mother-Of-Pearl, 1920s, 1 In.	25.00
Cuff Links, Napoleonic Button, Enamel, Brass, 1 1/8 In. ....*Illus*	75.00
Cuff Links, Oval Cabochon Ruby In Each Center, Diamond, 14K Yellow Gold	489.00
Cuff Links, Reeded Gold Discs, Blue Enameled, 18K Yellow Gold	315.00
Cuff Links, Row Of Round Sapphires, 18K Yellow Gold, Box	1380.00
Cuff Links, Sapphire, Cabochon Cut, Platinum Top, 14K Yellow Gold	460.00
Cuff Links, Scroll Design, Oval, 10K Yellow Gold	65.00
Cuff Links, Shell, Cameo, Man In Profile, Wearing Helmet, 18K Yellow Gold	175.00
Cuff Links, Viking Head, Swank	15.00
Earrings, 5 Rows Twisted Gold Wire, 4 Rows Bead Diamonds, 18K Yellow Gold	2530.00
Earrings, 5-Pointed Star In Brushed Gold, Barry Kieselstein, 18K Yellow Gold	575.00
Earrings, Asymmetrical Fan, Onyx Plaque, 18K Yellow Gold	259.00
Earrings, Bakelite, Butterscotch Disks, Red, Brown, Green, Yellow Wedges, 1 In.	175.00
Earrings, Bakelite, Hattie Carnegie	12.00
Earrings, Beetle, Enamel, Semiprecious Stones, Gold, Victorian, 1 1/8 x 5/8 In. .....*Illus*	250.00
Earrings, Bow Design, 10 Round-Cut Diamonds, 18K Yellow Gold	150.00
Earrings, Caliber-Cut Blue Sapphires, Square Shaped Frames, 18K Yellow Gold	201.00
Earrings, Diamond, 18K Yellow Gold, Jose Hess	745.00
Earrings, Diamond, Caliber-Cut Blue Sapphire, 18K Yellow Gold	920.00
Earrings, Drop, Double Ball, Black Enamel Tracery, Yellow Gold, 14K Gold	715.00
Earrings, Enameled Fruit, Colored Stones, Hollycraft	35.00
Earrings, Hardstone Flowers, Gold Drop, Leaf Border, Marie Zimmermann	4887.00
Earrings, Hoop, Tapered Spiral Design, 18K Yellow Gold	865.00
Earrings, Masquerade Face, Diamond Eyes, Limoges Enamel, Gold, Victorian	3500.00
Earrings, Onyx Cameo, Graduated Leaf Plaques, 18K Yellow Gold, Victorian	2530.00
Earrings, Pierced Navettes, 6 Pear-Shaped Diamonds, 1900	3162.00
Earrings, Rhodalite, 3 Pear-Shaped Faceted Garnets, Gold Leaf, Yellow Gold	632.00

Earrings, South Seas Pearl, Diamond-Set Platinum Hoops, Detachable Pearl Drop 4600.00
Earrings, Square-Cut Amethyst, 3 Diamond Accents, Yellow Gold, Honora 402.00
Earrings, Teardrop Pearl, Gilt-Metal Filigree Mount, Oversized, Stanley Hagler, 1967 ... 55.00
Earrings, Triangular Shape Frame, Cultured Pearl, 14K Yellow Gold 115.00
Earrings, Turquoise Bead, Curved Gold Bar, Ed Wiener, 10K Yellow Gold 345.00
Earrings, Twisted Wire Suspending A Hoop, Silver Bead Accents, Sterling Silver 977.00
Earrings, Wreath Beading, Wire Twist Detail, Victorian, 14K Yellow Gold 977.00
Earrngs, Coiled Design, Ram's Head, Ruby Eyes, Yellow Gold, Ilias Lalunis 1495.00
Hairpin, 6 Rose Diamonds, Collet-Set Emerald, 18K Gold, Early 19th Century 185.00
Hatpins are listed in this book in the Hatpin category.
Lavaliere, Suspended Pearl, Diamond & Pearl Terminal, Platinum & Pearl Charm 1380.00
Locket, Enamel, Gold Filled, Glass Insets, Mesh Chain, Victorian, 19-In. Chain 295.00
Locket, Pearls Accent, Interior Compartment With Photograph, Lock Of Hair 230.00
Locket, Portrait, Relief Floral Design, Gold Finish, Victorian, Oval, 1 5/8 x 2 1/4 In. 30.00
Lorgnette, Grillwork Handle, 14K Yellow Gold 315.00
Magnifier, Leaf Design, Rounded Corner Square, 14K Yellow Gold 290.00
Necklace, 15 Pale Blue Glass Beads, Bands Of Tiny Flower Heads, 1920, 18 1/2 In. 2300.00
Necklace, Abalone & Fresh Water Pearl Pendant, Foliate Design, Kalo, 14K Gold, 9 In. .. 3637.00
Necklace, Alternating 5 Round Blue Stones, Baroque Shaped Pearl, Chanel, 53 In. 230.00
Necklace, Amber Beads, Graduated, 18 In. 230.00
Necklace, Amethyst & Citrine Quarts Beads, 14K Yellow Gold 465.00
Necklace, Ancient Dancers, Enamel, Silver, Margot De Taxco, Mexico, 3 1/4 x 2 In. *Illus* 1500.00
Necklace, Archaeological Revival Style, Trace Link Chain, 14K Yellow Gold 1610.00
Necklace, Bakelite, Fruit, Peach, Cherry, Raspberry, Orange, Banana, Leaves, 17 In. 650.00
Necklace, Bib, Brass Filigree, Faux Pearl Strand, Seed Pearls, Miriam Haskell, 15 In. 1430.00
Necklace, Black Coral Beads, 14K Yellow Gold, 19 1/2 In. 201.00
Necklace, Black Glass Beads, Art Deco, 56 In. 25.00
Necklace, Black Onyx Bead, 14K Yellow Gold Filigree Catch 110.00
Necklace, Bracelet & Earrings, Bakelite, Red Berries, Green Gimp & Leaves 230.00
Necklace, Bracelet Set, Hand, Silver, Amethyst Stones, Spratling, 2 1/2 x 2 In. 1100.00
Necklace, Braided, Interwoven Foliate Circular Links, Joseff Of Hollywood, 16 1/2 In. 172.00
Necklace, Chain, Barrel Shape, Black Enamel, 14K Yellow Gold 1035.00
Necklace, Chain, Box Links, Leaves, Red Stone Accents, 18K Yellow Gold 400.00
Necklace, Chain, Double Curb Links, 26 In. 2070.00
Necklace, Chain, Double Square Links, 14K Yellow Gold, 30 In. 690.00
Necklace, Chain, Double Strand Trace Links, Collet-Set Round Amethyst, Gold, 54 In. 980.00
Necklace, Chain, Flat Circle Links, Oval, 14K Yellow Gold 400.00
Necklace, Chain, Link, Gold Peso, 1945, 30 In. 400.00
Necklace, Chain, Purple Glass Drop, Silver Foliate Cap, Hazel B. French, 25 In. 632.00
Necklace, Chain, Receded Oval Links, 18K Yellow Gold, Victorian 374.00
Necklace, Chain, Rose-Cut Diamond, Black Enamel Tracery, Victorian 865.00
Necklace, Charm, Enameled Fish, Sailboat, 4-Leaf Clover, Kitten, 14K Gold, 16 In. 315.00
Necklace, Choker, 3 Rows Of Clear Rhinestones, Blue Oval Rhinestone, Christian Dior .. 320.00
Necklace, Choker, Gold Mesh, Suspending Drops, 22K Yellow Gold 687.00
Necklace, Clear Rhinestone, Tie Shape, Large 45.00
Necklace, Collar Design, 14K Yellow Gold 400.00
Necklace, Coral Beads, 14K Yellow Gold 345.00
Necklace, Coral Beads, 18K White, Yellow Gold, 40 In. 161.00
Necklace, Cultured Pearls, Knotted, 14K Yellow Gold Filigree Clasp, 18 In. 103.00
Necklace, Edwardian Festoon, 4 Amethysts, 18K Gold, c.1895, 15 1/2 In. 825.00

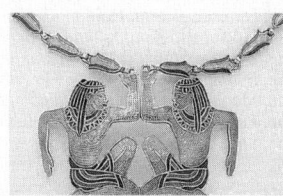

Jewelry, Cuff Links, Napoleonic Button,
Enamel, Brass, 1 1/8 In.

Jewelry, Necklace, Ancient
Dancers, Enamel, Silver, Margot De
Taxco, Mexico, 3 1/4 x 2 In.

Necklace, Edwardian, Filigree Tear-Shape Frame, Platinum, 18 In. 630.00
Necklace, Expandable Choker Style, 14K White & Yellow Gold 975.00
Necklace, Flower Head Links, Floral Pin, Diamond Pearl Pendant, Box 4890.00
Necklace, Garnet & Seed Pearl, 10K Yellow Gold, 1918 . . . . 1045.00
Necklace, Garnet Beads, Silk Cord, 26 In. 35.00
Necklace, Gold Bead, 14K Yellow Gold 546.00
Necklace, Gold Pearls, Freshwater, 14K Yellow Gold Clasp, 17 In. 175.00
Necklace, Goldtone Nuggets, Hattie Carnegie 95.00
Necklace, Graduated Discs, Flat Circular Plaques, Sterling Silver, Taxco 230.00
Necklace, Graduated Jadeite Beads, 32 In. 750.00
Necklace, Green Beads, 1920s, 5-In. Tassel, 32 In. Long 125.00
Necklace, Green Plastic, Hanging Bakelite Leaves 125.00
Necklace, Jadeite & Seed Pearl, 14K Yellow Gold 330.00
Necklace, Labradorite, Alternating Foliate, Flowerhead Links, Sterling Silver, 1933 . . . . . 2185.00
Necklace, Leaf Design, Platinum, 17 3/4 In. 575.00
Necklace, Link, Gilt Metal, Faux Pearls, Haskell, 19 In. 90.00
Necklace, Miriam Haskell, 22 In. 65.00
Necklace, Padlock, 940 Silver Links, Triple Band Rings, Mexico, Aguilar, 17 In. 1320.00
Necklace, Pearls & Silver Beads, Set With Simulated Diamonds, Lariat Style, 24 In. 230.00
Necklace, Pearls, Cultered, Semi-Baroque, 14K Yellow Gold Filigree Clasp, 18 In. 144.00
Necklace, Pearls, Cultured, 14K Gold Clasp, 24 In. 195.00
Necklace, Pearls, Cultured, 14K Gold Clasp, 52 In. 550.00
Necklace, Pearls, Cultured, 5 Gold Round Spacers, 14K Yellow Gold Clasp, 18 In. 115.00
Necklace, Pearls, Cultured, 6 Twisted Strands, 14K Gold Clasp 245.00
Necklace, Pearls, Cultured, Black & White, 14K Gold Beads, 50 In. 140.00
Necklace, Pearls, Cultured, Gold Coquiform Clasp, Semi-Baroque, 52 In. 3850.00
Necklace, Pearls, Cultured, Gold, 14K Yellow Gold Clasp, 23 In. 175.00
Necklace, Pearls, Cultured, Gray, White, 14K Yellow Gold & Clasp 575.00
Necklace, Pearls, Freshwater Pink, Gold, 17 1/2 In. 345.00
Necklace, Pearls, Freshwater, Black, Gold, 14K Yellow Gold Clasp, 17 1/2 In. 490.00
Necklace, Pearls, Freshwater, Bow Gold Clasp, 17 In. 865.00
Necklace, Pearls, Freshwater, Gold, 14K Yellow Gold Clasp, 18 In. 85.00
Necklace, Pearls, Freshwater, Knotted, 14K Yellow Gold Clasp, 18 1/2 In. . . . . .80.00 to 105.00
Necklace, Pearls, Off-Round & Ring Pearls, 14K Gold, 52 In. 405.00
Necklace, Pearls, Opera Length, 52 In. 460.00
Necklace, Rope Form, 18K Yellow Gold, 32 In. 630.00
Necklace, Scrolled Links, Moonstone Center, Mexico, Los Costillo, Sterling, 21 In. 500.00
Necklace, Seed Pearls, 3 Central Clusters, Mother-Of-Pearl Frames, 14K Yellow Gold . . . 402.00
Necklace, Snake, 18K Yellow Gold, Tiffany 575.00
Necklace, Spherical Amber Beads, Yellow Gold Rondels, Clasp, 21 In. 126.00
Necklace, Square Links, 14K Yellow Gold, 7 In. 545.00
Necklace, Tube Links, 18K White, Rose, Yellow Gold 150.00
Necklace, Wave Links, 14K Yellow Gold 250.00
Necklace, Woman In Profile, With Irises, 18K Yellow Gold, Signed, E. Dropsy 1725.00
Necklace, Yellow, Green Beads, Domed Silver Clasp, Sterling Silver, S. Wekstein 259.00
Necklace & Earrings, 3 Strands, Gaudy Red Glass, Vogue 50.00
Necklace & Earrings, Green, Blue, Pink Moon Shaped Cabochons, Haskell, 15 In. 935.00
Necklace & Pendant, Openwork, Blister Pearls, Sterling Silver Paper Clip Chain 2300.00
Ojime, Barber Pole-Like Design, Cylindrical, Silver, Copper & Shakudo 970.00
Ojime, Birds & Flowers, Hexagonal Panels, Red Lacquer 65.00
Ojime, Daikkoku Form, Holding His Hammer, Sterling Silver 365.00
Ojime, Flower Blossom, Relief Leaves & Stem, Silver & Brass 515.00
Ojime, Kakashi Form, Shakudo Hat, Copper & Shakudo 1390.00
Ojime, Marsh Scene, Grasses & Flowers, Cylindrical, Signed 455.00
Ojime, Monkey With Silver Gilt Face 455.00
Ojime, Pries, Seated With Compass In Belly, Bone 240.00
Ojime, Sake Barrel Form, Signed 300.00
Ojime, Seated Rabbit, Inlaid Eyes, Ivory 400.00
Ojime, Tree Stump Form, Coral 120.00
Pendant, Bakelite, Black, Round, Chain With Yellow Carved Flowers 38.00
Pendant, Biwa Baroque Pearls, Collet-Set Green Jade Beads, 18K Yellow Gold, Pair 1150.00
Pendant, Cabochon Garnet, Heart Shape, Diamonds & Seed Pearls In Frame 750.00
Pendant, Cameo, Woman In Profile, Agate, 18K Yellow Gold 750.00

Pendant, Carved Ram & Bird, Curved Linear Design, Mutton Fat Jade, 4 In. 165.00
Pendant, Chrysoprase, Green, Openwork Design, Silver Reeded Link Chain, 1920 ...... 230.00
Pendant, Coral, Head Of Bearded Mandarin, 14K Gold Mount 115.00
Pendant, Cross Design, 11 Emeralds, 18K Yellow Gold 275.00
Pendant, Flower Form, Pierced Floral Carving, White Jade, 2 1/8 In. 198.00
Pendant, Gold Coin, 1988 U.S. 50 Dollar Coin, 14K Gold Bezel 1035.00
Pendant, Gold Cross, 16 Collet Oval Rubies, Coiled Wire, 18K Yellow Gold 345.00
Pendant, Gold, Rose-Cut Diamonds, Crown, Flower, Cross 825.00
Pendant, Jesuit Crucifix, Bronze & Silver Metal, 2 1/4 x 1 3/4 In. 30.00
Pendant, Locket, Chalcedony Cameo, Enamel, Gold, Dec. 9, 1873, Art Nouveau 4850.00
Pendant, Moonstone Dragonfly, Crossed Bodies With Wings, Rene Leclerc, 7 In. 4945.00
Pendant, Oval Faceted Amethyst, Circular Leaf Frame, Sterling Silver, T. Fahrner 374.00
Pendant, Skull Form 120.00
Pendant, Tassel, Applied Beading, Black Enamel, 14K Yellow Gold 374.00
Pendant, Tiger's Head Design, Ruby Eyes, 18K Yellow Gold 175.00
Pendant, Topaz, Blue Pear-Shaped, 25 Carat 14K Gold 345.00
Pendant, Tourmaline, Tumble Green Center, Silver Curb Link Chain, 1950 .... 460.00
Pendant, Yellow Gold Fish, Black Cord, Sterling Silver, Georg Jensen, No. 5003 ...... 460.00
Pendant & Necklace, Graduated Openwork Platinum Circles, 3 Stones, 16 In. 920.00
Pendant & Pin, Cameo, Woman In Profile, Seed Pearls, Victorian, 14 Yellow Gold 1150.00
Pin, 4-Leaf Clover, 2-Color Gold, Diamond & Sapphire Center, Tiffany & Co., 1940s ... 1650.00
Pin, 14K Gold, Pearls, Thin Rope Twist Loops, Stylized Leaves 315.00
Pin, Amethyst, Openwork Design, 18K Yellow Gold, Georg Jensen 1725.00
Pin, Ax, Pearl Belly, Aqua Enamel, Faux Pearl Stones, Rhinestones, Trifari, 3 1/4 In. 495.00
Pin, Bakelite, 5 Strawberries, 6 Leaves, 3 1/2 In. 330.00
Pin, Bakelite, Abstract Butterscotch Pineapple, Faux Golden Pearls 345.00
Pin, Bakelite, Asian Man, Jointed Body, Ivory Pants, Red Coat, Yellow Hat, 3 1/5 In. 600.00
Pin, Bakelite, Black, Round, Several Red Attached Discs 38.00
Pin, Bakelite, Bulldog, Deeply Carved Head, Celluloid Teeth, Glass Eyes, 3 In. 990.00
Pin, Bakelite, Butterfly, 4 In. 250.00
Pin, Bakelite, Carved Basket, Reverse Carved, Apple Juice Oval Bar, Floral, 3 1/4 In. 360.00
Pin, Bakelite, Cigarette Charm 4675.00
Pin, Bakelite, Deeply Carved & Articulated With Birds Among Flowers, Red, 3 1/2 In. 660.00
Pin, Bakelite, Drum Major, Jointed, Ivory Pants, Red Coat, Hat, Brown Head, 4 In. 425.00
Pin, Bakelite, Gardening, Wood Trowel, Tomato, Turnip, Carrot, 4 In. 500.00
Pin, Bakelite, Native, Jointed, Gold Headdress, Black Body, Chocolate Legs, 4 In. 550.00
Pin, Bakelite, Open Rose, Carmel Color 25.00
Pin, Bakelite, Pear, Butterscotch, Leaf & Stem, Painted Details, 3 In. 1000.00
Pin, Bakelite, Portrait Of Josephine Baker, 4 In. 500.00
Pin, Bakelite, Scared Pup, Carved Red Running Dog, Painted Tongue, 3 In. 2420.00
Pin, Bakelite, Schoolboy, Carrying Red, White Schoolbook, Black Hair, Shoes 4485.00
Pin, Bakelite, Schoolhouse, Ruler Form, Suspending 2 Blue Pencils, Red Edge Slate 345.00
Pin, Bakelite, Ship In Bottle, Reverse Carved, Apple Juice, 3-Mast Sailing Ship, 3 In. 2090.00
Pin, Bakelite, Stork, Marbled Butterscotch, Ivory Baby Bootie Charms 1320.00
Pin, Bakelite, Sweater, 3 Flowers, Light Yellow Green, Hinged Metal Clip, 1 3/4 In. 20.00
Pin, Bakelite, Swordfish, Large Marbled Red Body, Applied Eyes, 4 In. 990.00
Pin, Bar, 14K Gold, 2 Seed Pearls, Dark Blue Stone, 1910 .... 50.00
Pin, Bar, Bakelite, Horizontal Rows Of Black, Brown Green, Vertical Green Ends, 2 In. .. 1320.00
Pin, Bar, Bakelite, Ivory Shaft, 4 Green, Orange, Yellow, Brown, Triangles, 4 In. 195.00
Pin, Bar, Citrine In Form Of Woman's Head, 14K Yellow Gold 375.00
Pin, Bar, Collet Set Cushion Shape Amethyst, White Enamel, 14K Yellow Gold 315.00
Pin, Bar, Diamond, Openwork, Square-Cut Sapphire, 14K Yellow Gold 345.00
Pin, Bar, Enamel Cherub, Gold Filled Setting, 2 In. 40.00
Pin, Bar, Engraved, 2 Mine-Cut Diamonds, 3 Rose-Cut Diamonds, 14K Yellow Gold 330.00
Pin, Bar, Etruscan Revival, Lion Head & Ball Drop, Yellow Gold, 19th Century 550.00
Pin, Bar, Gilt Metal, Blue, Green Rhinestones, Hobe, 2 1/5 In. 15.00
Pin, Bar, Thistle, Sapphire, Bezel-Set Oval, 18K Yellow Gold 335.00
Pin, Bar, Victorian, Crown Heart, Turquoise & Seed Pearls, Victorian, 15K Gold 325.00
Pin, Bar, Woman In Profile, Art Nouveau, 18K Yellow Gold 290.00
Pin, Barrel, Sterling Silver, Amethyst, Jugendstil 2185.00
Pin, Basket With Flowers, 5 Sapphires, 18K White Gold 635.00
Pin, Bee Shape, 19 Round-Cut Emeralds, 14K Yellow Gold 980.00
Pin, Bee, 5 Diamonds, 15 Rubies, 18K Yellow Gold 325.00

Pin, Bee, Baroque Pearl Body, Pave-Set Diamond Head, Emerald Eyes, Trio 2760.00
Pin, Bell Flowers, Lapis Lazuli Cabochon, Hammered, Silver, Georg Jensen, 1 In. 300.00
Pin, Bird Within Rectangular Foliate, Sterling Silver, Bead Frame, Georg Jensen 259.00
Pin, Bird's Nest, Silver Metal, Mother Bird Feeding Baby Birds, Boucher, 3 In. 1100.00
Pin, Bird, Blue Enameled Wings, Pave Rhinestones, Duette, Coro, 3 1/2 In. 80.00
Pin, Bird, Enamel Wings, Feathered Crown, 18K Yellow Gold 460.00
Pin, Bird, Gilt Sterling, Bird In Flight, Pave Rhinestones, Corocraft, 3 In. 220.00
Pin, Bird, Gilt Sterling, Enameled With Pave Rhinestone, Coro, 2 1/2 In. 80.00
Pin, Bird, Landing On Branch, Pave Rhinestones, Corocraft, 2 1/2 In. 165.00
Pin, Bird, Naturalistic Scene, Circular, Sterling Silver, Georg Jensen 259.00
Pin, Bird, Rectangular Naturalistic Scene, Sterling Silver, Georg Jensen, No. 204 . . . . . . 259.00
Pin, Bird, Round Frame With Flower & Berries, Pave Rhinestones, Corocraft, 3 In. 155.00
Pin, Bird, Silver Metal, Yellow Enameled Wings, Pave Rhinestone, Duette, Coro, 3 In. . . . 15.00
Pin, Bird, Sterling Silver, Collet-Set Coral Accents, Foliate Circular, Georg Jensen 805.00
Pin, Bird, Tin Gold, Stones, Rhinestones In Red Eye, Trifari 65.00
Pin, Bouquet Of Flowers, 14K Rose Gold Mount 1500.00
Pin, Bow Shape, Diamond & Emerald, Gold, Spain, 1760s, 3 3/8 In. 9200.00
Pin, Bracelet, Bakelite, Pirate, Charms, Parrot, Sword, Jug, Trunk, Chain, 7 In. 1300.00
Pin, Bracelet, Gilt Metal, Enameled Flowers, Blue Cabochons, Hobe, 7 In. 785.00
Pin, Bramble Form, Diamond, Emerald Ruby & Sapphire, 18K Yellow Gold 350.00
Pin, Bug, Gilt Sterling, Green, Red Rhinestones, Duette, Coro, 2 1/2 In. 415.00
Pin, Butterfly, Colored Semiprecious Gemstones, 10K Rose Gold Mount 373.00
Pin, Butterfly, Faux Seed Pearls, Crystal Beads, Miriam Haskell, 2 1/4 In. 231.00
Pin, Butterfly, Large Butterfly With Dangling Small Butterflies, Coral Beads, Haskell 230.00
Pin, Butterfly, Openwork Wings, Sterling Silver, Parenti 259.00
Pin, Butterfly, Rhinestone, 3 1/2 In. 25.00
Pin, Cabochon Citrine, Tourmaline, Peridot, 12 Diamonds, Onyx Inlay, 2 x 3 In. 1250.00
Pin, Cactus, Silver Metal, Red & Clear Rhinestone, Aqua & Topaz, Trifari, 23 1/2 In. 250.00
Pin, Cameo, Agate, Woman In Profile, Foliate Cap, Victorian, 18K Rose Gold 980.00
Pin, Cameo, Hard Stone, Pearls, 18K Gold, Italy, 1 3/4 x 1 1/2 In. . . . . *Illus* 2500.00
Pin, Cameo, Leaves, Multicolored Rhinestones, Sterling, 14K Gold Filled, Hobe 330.00
Pin, Cameo, Moonstone, Diamond & Burma Ruby In Gold Frame, Art Nouveau 3850.00
Pin, Cameo, Shell, Female Figure Riding A Horse-Drawn Chariot, 18K Yellow Gold 290.00
Pin, Cameo, Shell, Woman In Profile, Crowned With Grape Leaves, 14K Yellow Gold . . . 300.00
Pin, Cameo, Woman Shape, Simulated Pearl Border, Sterling Silver, 2 3/4 In. 258.00
Pin, Cat, Prong-Set Round Ruby Body, Gold Wire Face, Tail, 18K Yellow Gold 2530.00
Pin, Chalcedony, Bezel-Set Center, Blue, Blister Pearl, Jugendstil, 1920 . . . . 460.00
Pin, Christmas Tree, Blue Rhinestones, Weiss 65.00
Pin, Circle, 18K Yellow Gold, Signed, Tiffany & Co. 175.00
Pin, Circle, Oval Peridots, 14K Yellow Gold Leaves, Tiffany 1092.00
Pin, Circle, Prong-Set European-Cut Diamonds, Platinum Top, 18K Gold, Tiffany 3680.00
Pin, Circle, Rhodalite Garnet & Diamond, Interior Border Of Diamonds, 18K Gold 2185.00
Pin, Circle, Round Emerald, 4 Old Mine-Cut Diamonds, Yellow Gold 370.00
Pin, Circle, Textured Leaves, Sapphire Accents, 18K Gold, Tiffany 488.00
Pin, Citrine, Georgian Revival Design, Floral, Foliate Frame, 14K Yellow Gold 315.00

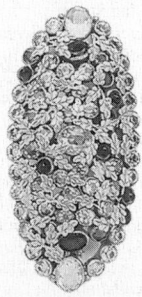
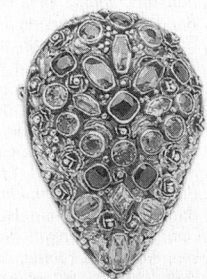

Jewelry, Pin, Cameo, Hard Stone, Pearls, 18K Gold, Italy, 1 3/4 x 1 1/2 In.

Jewelry, Pin, Cluster Of Leaves & Stones, Gold Metal, Hobe, 2 3/4 x 1 3/8 In.

Jewelry, Pin, Cluster Of Semiprecious Gemstones & Flowers, Sterling, Hobe, 2 x 2 3/4 In.

Pin, Classical Revival, Wirework, Porcelain Plaque Maiden Center, c.1880, 3 In. 1100.00
Pin, Clipper Ship Design, Blue, White Enamel, Red Bead Accent, 18K Gold 230.00
Pin, Cloak, Military Crossbow, Roman Legion, 3rd Century 195.00
Pin, Cluster Of Leaves & Stones, Gold Metal, Hobe, 2 3/4 x 1 3/8 In. ....*Illus* 75.00
Pin, Cluster Of Semiprecious Gemstones & Flowers, Sterling, Hobe, 2 x 2 3/4 In. ...*Illus* 85.00
Pin, Cockatoos, Flowers, Pave Clear Rhinestones, Enamel, Duette, 3 1/2 In., Pair 143.00
Pin, Coiled Emerald & Pearl Snake, Starburst, Rubies & Pearls, 18K Gold 1725.00
Pin, Collet-Set Demantoids, Beaded Accents, Openwork Frame, 15K Yellow Gold 517.00
Pin, Crescent Moon & Star, Rose-Cut Diamond, Pearl 440.00
Pin, Crystal Face, Emerald Eyes, Gold Wire Topknot, Collar, 18K Yellow Gold 2070.00
Pin, Cutout Design, Woman, Foliage, Cherub, Danecraft, 1 1/4 x 1 In. 40.00
Pin, Deer & Squirrel, Silver, Georg Jensen, Box 350.00
Pin, Dog, Sitting On Silk Pillow, Micromosaic, 14K Yellow Gold, 1890s 1600.00
Pin, Double Hearts, Palm Trees, Pink Lucite, N.G. 44, 1 1/2 In..................... 38.00
Pin, Dragon, Pearl, Ruby & Gold, Art Nouveau, 2 In. 950.00
Pin, Dragonfly, Art Nouveau, Enamel, Opals, Diamonds, Rubies, 18K Gold, 2 In. 6900.00
Pin, Dragonfly, Turquoise, Hattie Carnegie 45.00
Pin, Duck, 3-Dimensional, Lucite, 3 In. 176.00
Pin, Elephant & Palm Tree, Reverse Carved Elephant, Lucite, 3 1/2 In............... 165.00
Pin, Elephant, Pearl Belly, Gilt Metal, Faux Pearl Body, Black Enamel Stripes, Trifari ... 1430.00
Pin, Etched Brass, Pierced Surface Of Fish, Orange Bead, George W. Frost, 2 1/2 In. 350.00
Pin, Fairy, Plique-A-Jour, Polychromatic Wings, Round Diamond Accents, 14K Gold 4370.00
Pin, Fish, Diamond Eye, Sapphire Scales, 18K Gold, Italy, 2 In. 375.00
Pin, Fish, Floral Red, Blue Bouquet, Rhinestones, Corocraft, 2 In.................... 15.00
Pin, Fish, Jelly Belly, Rhinestones, Enameled, Coro, 2 1/2 In. 330.00
Pin, Fish, Pearl Belly, Gilt Metal, Faux Pearl Body, Red Rhinestones, Trifari, 2 1/2 In. ... 190.00
Pin, Floral Basket, Colored Stones, M.B. Boucher 302.00
Pin, Floral, Leaves, Hinged Drops, Blue, Clear Rhinestones, Silver Metal, Trifari, 4 In.... 1600.00
Pin, Floral, Potted Plant, Enameling, Red & Clear Rhinestones, Reja, 2 1/2 In. 850.00
Pin, Flower Head, Center Diamond, Surrounded By Enameled Petals, 18K Gold 460.00
Pin, Flower Shape, Dragon Design, Satsuma, 1 3/4 In............................. 72.00
Pin, Flower, Amethyst, Silver, Signed, Fred Davis 475.00
Pin, Flower, Enamel Centered By Pearl, 18K Yellow Gold, Tiffany 920.00
Pin, Flower, Gilt Metal, Blue Enamel, Blue Rhinestones, Coro, Duette, 2 1/2 In. 80.00
Pin, Flower, Gilt, Silver Metal, Trembler Petals, Green Rhinestones, Coro, Duette, 3 In. .. 110.00
Pin, Flower, Leaves, Sterling Silver, Hammered, Georg Jensen, No. 127 .... 259.00
Pin, Flower, Silver & Gilt Metal, Red Rhinestones, Boucher, 3 In.................... 60.00
Pin, Flower, Tanzanite & Moonstones, 14K Yellow Gold, Tiffany, 1937 .... 2800.00
Pin, Fox, Sapphire Eyes, Marquise Cut, 18K Yellow Gold 290.00
Pin, Fox, Swirl Pattern, Plastic, Lea Stein, Paris, Label 1950s 258.00
Pin, Free-Form Leaf Spray, 71 Full & Single Diamonds, 14K White Gold 1435.00
Pin, Frog, Allover Gold Beading, Lapis Eyes, 18K Yellow Gold 750.00
Pin, Frog, Gilt-Metal, Yellow Rhinestones, Nettie Rosenstein, 1950s 110.00
Pin, Fruit, Raspberries, Leaves, Clear Rhinestones, Boucher, 3 In. 425.00
Pin, Geometric Pierced & Interlocking Design, Agate, Carence Crafters, 1 5/8 In. 825.00
Pin, Gilt Metal, Red, Blue Rhinestones, Round, Hobe, 1 1/4 In..................... 90.00
Pin, Gold Link, 14K 2-Color Gold Links, 1940 .... 375.00
Pin, Hammered, Saw-Pierced Marine Design, Square, Leonore Doskow, 1 1/2 In. 165.00
Pin, Hand Painted Plaque, Maiden, Wirework, 17K Gold, c.1880, 3 In. 1100.00
Pin, Hat, Bird, Perched On A Foliate Spray, Diamond Accents, 18K Yellow Gold 201.00
Pin, Heart, Gilt Metal, Red, Pink Rhinestones, Hobe, 2 1/4 In..................... 300.00
Pin, Heart, Red Sparkle, Brushed Gold With Clear Baguettes, Trifari, 2 In. 30.00
Pin, Horse & Carriage, Gemstones Spray, 2-Color, 1945, 14K Gold 575.00
Pin, Horseshoe, Pearls Set In Gold, Edwardian 1250.00
Pin, Hourglass, Jelly Belly, Gilt Metal, Lucite Hourglass Form, Rhinestones, Trifari 660.00
Pin, Hummingbird, In Flight, Silver Metal, Clear Stones, Boucher, 4 1/5 In. 3250.00
Pin, Intertwined Feather Design, Pearl, Turquoise, 14K Yellow Gold 150.00
Pin, Jester, Gilt Metal, Clear Rhinestone, Stamped Staret, 3 In. 650.00
Pin, King & Queen, Faux Pearls, Green, Red Cabochons & Rhinestones, Duette, 2 In. ... 275.00
Pin, Kiss, Copper, Abstract Of Man & Woman Kiss, Stamped Rebajes, 2 1/4 In. 260.00
Pin, Koala, Ruby Eyes, Brushed 18K Yellow Gold, 1960s 460.00
Pin, Lapis Flower, Sterling Silver, Georg Jensen, No. 71 .... 402.00
Pin, Large Bow Knot, Aqua, Clear Crystals, Vogue, 5 In........................... 440.00

Pin, Large Rose, Vendome 45.00
Pin, Leaf Branch Design, Green Chalcedony Cabochon Buds, Silver, Denmark 259.00
Pin, Leaf Design, 1 Round-Cut Diamond, 14K Yellow Gold, Tiffany & Co. 175.00
Pin, Leaf Spray, Faceted Gemstones, Quartz, Topaz & Amethysts, 14K Gold 345.00
Pin, Leopard, Movable Wagging Tail, Rhinestone, Florenza ....35.00 to 40.00
Pin, Lily-Of-The-Valley, Pierced, Chased & Repousse, Kalo Shop, 2 1/4 In. 450.00
Pin, Lizard, Demantoid Garnet, Diamond, Gold & Platinum, Edwardian, 3 In. 12500.00
Pin, Love Birds, Flowers, Pave Clear Rhinestones, Enamel, Duette, 3 In., Pair 110.00
Pin, Lyre, Rose-Cut Diamonds, Rubies, Emeralds & Sapphires, 18K Gold Mount 1150.00
Pin, Malachite Stones, Micromosaic Of St. Peter's Square, 18K Gold 1100.00
Pin, Mallard Duck, In Flight, Reverse-Carved, Lucite, 4 In. 88.00
Pin, Maltese Cross, Retro Amethyst, Fred A Block, Large 125.00
Pin, Mermaid, Jelly Belly, Lucite Fish, Sterling Mermaid, Rhinestones, 3 In. 1320.00
Pin, Moor's Head, Man, In Turban, 18K Gold, 1920 .... 230.00
Pin, Moth, Diamond Wings, Pearl Body, Victorian 4750.00
Pin, Nude Maiden Amidst Stylized Branches, Green, Flesh Tones, 1900, 2 1/2 In. 13800.00
Pin, Opal Center, Surrounded By Diamond Scroll Frame, 14K Yellow Gold 1725.00
Pin, Openwork Design, 2 Acorns, Oak Leaf, Sterling Silver, Georg Jensen 430.00
Pin, Oriental Pagoda, Silver Metal, Glass Stones, Blue Glass Panel, Art Deco, 2 3/4 In. .. 25.00
Pin, Owl, Gilt Sterling, Green, Clear Rhinestones, Corocraft, Duette, 2 1/2 In. 230.00
Pin, Owl, Stylized, Amethyst Eyes, Silver, Spratling, 3 In. 880.00
Pin, Owls On Branches, Blue, Clear Rhinestones, Duette, 2 1/4 In. 220.00
Pin, Pansies, Vermeil Wire Twist Frame, Pietra Dura 287.00
Pin, Parrot, Pastel Flowers, Blue Enamel Wings, Pave Rhinestone, 1930 .... 145.00
Pin, Parrots, Rhinestone Bodies, Blue Enamel Wings, Duette, Signed Coro, 1930s 125.00
Pin, Pearl & Rhinestone, Sterling Silver, Trifari 50.00
Pin, Pearl Harbor, Eagle, Pearl, Red, White & Blue Enamel, Gilt Metal, Staret, 2 1/2 In. .. 770.00
Pin, Pearl, Ribbon & Bow Knot Shape, 5 Pearls, 14K Gold 430.00
Pin, Peasant Scene On Pottery Insert, Gold Finish Frame, Oval, 1 3/4 x 2 1/4 In. 25.00
Pin, Pink & Clear Faceted Stones, Gold Finish, Weiss, 1 1/2 In. 25.00
Pin, Pink Topaz, Cushion Shape, Openwork Foliate Frame, 1900 .... 1265.00
Pin, Poodle, Jelly Belly, Rhinestones, Lucite Body, Trifari, 2 In. 305.00
Pin, Praying Mantis, Silver Metal, 3 Dimensional, Boucher, 3 1/4 In. 1200.00
Pin, Prong-Set Zircons, Garnets, Peridot & Glass Doublets, 14K Gold Mount 287.00
Pin, Pumpkin Man, Googly Eyes, Green Celluloid Stem, Red Bakelite Nose, 5 In. 23100.00
Pin, Quatrefoil Design, Sterling Silver, Blue Enamel 575.00
Pin, Raised Cross & Leaves, Seed Pearl Center, Yellow Gold, 1890, 1 1/8 In. 120.00
Pin, Sailboat On Waves, Saw-Pierced, Panis Gallery, 1 3/4 In. 150.00
Pin, Salamander, Jelly Belly, Carved Lucite Body, Rhinestones, Trifari, 3 1/2 In. 470.00
Pin, Sardonyx Cameo, Bust Of Man In Profile, 18K Yellow Gold Frame 1725.00
Pin, Scarecrow, Bezel Square-Cut Sapphire, 18K Yellow Gold Hat, Coat 1495.00
Pin, Scarf, Purple, 15K Gold, Kreiseneide, 1860, 1 1/2 In. 200.00
Pin, Scroll & Leaf, 3 Oval Blue Topaz, 4 Cut Rubies, Swags, 18K Gold, Victorian 1265.00
Pin, Sea Serpent, Ruby, Emerald, Gold, Chaumet, 1940s 3000.00
Pin, Seal, Jelly Belly, Lucite Body, Red Rhinestones, Trifari, 2 1/2 In. 275.00
Pin, Seed Pearls, Prong-Set Diamond Accents, 14K Yellow Gold 260.00
Pin, Skeleton, Plastic Bones, Spring For Neck, Metal Ring, Japan, 1955, 5 1/2 In. 45.00
Pin, Smoky Quartz, 18K Gold Reticulated Mount 255.00
Pin, South Sea Pearl, 5 Round-Cut Diamonds, 3 Pearls, 18K Yellow Gold 150.00
Pin, Spider, Amethyst, Cultured Pearl, 14K Yellow Gold 230.00
Pin, Spider, Blue Enamel, 18K Orange Yellow Gold 2760.00
Pin, Spider, Crab, Spiral Design, Brass, Hammered Wire Twist, A. Calder 13800.00
Pin, Spiral Design, Seed Pearl, Hinged Bail, Hook, Catch, 14K Yellow Gold, Victorian ... 316.00
Pin, Squirrel, Holding Garnet, Diamond Eyes, 18K Yellow Gold, Tiffany 1840.00
Pin, Squirrel, Ruby & Gold, Tiffany & Co., France, 1940s 4500.00
Pin, Star, Moon, Onyx & Aqua, Mixed Metals, Silver, Copper, Mexico, Los Costillo, 2 In. 600.00
Pin, Stylized Boomerang, Spindle Support, Jade Stone, Silver, 2 3/4 In. 160.00
Pin, Stylized Leaf, 6 Round Emeralds, 13 Round Diamonds, 18K Yellow Gold 1265.00
Pin, Sunburst, 9 Old Mine-Cut Diamonds, 14K Yellow Gold 1100.00
Pin, Swan, Black Enameled Neck, Red, Green Cabochons, Red Rhinestones, Trifari 7150.00
Pin, Terrier, Seated, Gold, Ruby Eyes, Sapphire Nose, Diamonds On Collar, 2 1/4 In. 635.00
Pin, Thistle, Cairngorm, Sterling Silver, Victorian, England 115.00
Pin, Tiger's-Eye Shell, Gold Wings, Body, 18K Gold 287.00

Pin, Trembler Blossoms, Clear Rhinestones, Enamel, Duette, 3 In. 121.00
Pin, Trembling Flower, Jelly Belly, Gilt Metal, Enameled, Red Painted Nails, Trifari 1100.00
Pin, Turtle, Green Enamel Shell, 14K Yellow Gold 375.00
Pin, TWA Stewardess Wing, Gold Finish, Half-Wing, Red, White Enamel, 1960, 2 In. ... 125.00
Pin, Woman In Profile, Porcelain Disc, 18K Rose Gold, France 690.00
Pin, Woman On Stool With Terrier, Brass Tone, 2 1/4 x 1 3/4 In. 40.00
Pin, Woman's Head In Scrolls, Iris, Sterling Silver 82.00
Pin & Earrings, Bird, Jelly Belly, Lucite, Rhinestones, Corocraft, Duette, 2 & 1/4 In. 385.00
Pin & Earrings, Fly, Jelly Belly, Red Lucite Bodies, Blue Cabochon Eyes, 1 1/2 & 1 In. ... 230.00
Pin & Necklace, Lapis Beads, Yellow Gold Link Chain, 14K Yellow Gold 635.00
Ring, 2 1/2 Dollar Indian Head Coin, 14K Yellow Gold, Man's 250.00
Ring, 4 Montana Sapphires, 3 Diamonds, Leaves, 14K White Gold, Ziruth-Kaiser, Size 7 . 2450.00
Ring, Abstract Openwork, 3 Twisted Parallel Lines, 14K Yellow Gold, Jose Hess 144.00
Ring, Amethyst & Citrine, Art Deco, 14K Gold 150.00
Ring, Aquamarine, Clip-Corner, 14K Yellow Gold, 1940s 175.00
Ring, Aquamarine, Filigree, 14K White Gold 60.00
Ring, Aquamarine, Oval Shape, 14K Yellow Gold 138.00
Ring, Band, Topaz-Colored Stone In Center Of Star Design, Silver, Size 9 1/4 .... 100.00
Ring, Black Opal Doublet, Baguette-Cut Diamonds, 18K Yellow Gold 1380.00
Ring, Blue Topaz, 14K White Gold, 1980s 115.00
Ring, Ceylon Sapphire, Gold Leaves On Sides, 18K Gold, Lillian Foster, Size 5 3/4 ..... 2900.00
Ring, Class Of 1970, 10K Gold, Blue Stone, Panther, Book Of Knowledge, Size 9 3/4 ... 45.00
Ring, Class Of 1988, Gold Metal, Yellow Stone, Initials, Bird, Emblem, Size 7 1/4 ...... 40.00
Ring, Class, Mira Costa High School, Silver, Green Stone, Horse, Crest, 1971, Size 9 .... 35.00
Ring, Cluster, 11 Diamonds, Blue Enamel, 14K Gold 305.00
Ring, Cluster, Star Design, 14K Yellow Gold 920.00
Ring, Cluster, Stylized Flowers, Diamond, Emerald, Ruby, Sapphire, 14K Gold 145.00
Ring, Cocktail, Cluster, 34 Full-Cut Diamonds, 14K Gold 260.00
Ring, Cultured Pearl, Diamond, Dome Style Mount, Platinum 520.00
Ring, Diamond, 10 Graduated Square Emeralds, Platinum, Victorian 6875.00
Ring, Diamond, Art Deco, 18K White Gold 2012.00
Ring, Diamond, Butterfly, Blue Sapphire, Black Enamel Accents, 18K Yellow Gold 517.00
Ring, Diamond, Flower Design, 14K White Gold 460.00
Ring, Diamond, Pierced Platinum Mount, 1920 .... 1380.00
Ring, Diamond, Pink Sapphire, Emerald, 14K Rose Gold 431.00
Ring, Diamond, Sapphire, 18K Yellow Gold 1035.00
Ring, Diamond, Sapphire, Bypass, Edwardian, 18K Rose Gold 747.00
Ring, Diamonds, Platinum Mount, c.1915 .... 6900.00
Ring, Diamonds, Yellow Gold, Oval 5750.00
Ring, Emerald, Square Cut, 2 Round Diamonds, Platinum, Yellow Gold 1955.00
Ring, Entwined Snake Design, Sapphire, 18K Yellow Gold, Victorian 144.00
Ring, European-Cut Diamond, Flanked By 2 Baguette Diamonds, White Gold 6325.00
Ring, European-Cut Diamonds, Platinum, 1920 .... 6440.00
Ring, Georgian, Filigree, 5 Oval Ceylon Sapphires, 18K Yellow Gold 2500.00
Ring, Green Tourmaline, Diamonds 4 Corners, Art Deco, 14K White Gold 1400.00
Ring, Horseshoe Design, Diamonds, 14K White Gold, Man's 105.00
Ring, Hunter College, Cabochon Amethyst, Tiffany, 1928 .... 300.00
Ring, Lapis Lazuli, 14K Yellow Gold 150.00
Ring, Leaf Design, Silver & Moonstone, Georg Jensen 690.00
Ring, Leopard's Head Design, Marquise-Cut Emerald Eyes, 18K Yellow Gold 175.00
Ring, Marquise-Cut Diamond, 32 Diamond Melees, 14K White Gold 805.00
Ring, Masonic, 32nd Degree, Diamonds, 14K Gold 245.00
Ring, McDonald's Employee Merit, QSC, Silver Metal, Class Ring Style, Size 10 .... 65.00
Ring, Moonstone, Diamond Accents Set In Platinum, Yellow Gold Mount 430.00
Ring, Mother-Of-Pearl, White Sapphire, 18K Yellow Gold 80.00
Ring, Nugget, Tourmaline Stone, 14K Yellow Gold 175.00
Ring, Opal, Blue & Green Enamel, Custom Crafted, 14K Gold, Size 6 1/2 In. 1350.00
Ring, Oval Cabochon, Green, 14K Yellow Gold 45.00
Ring, Oval Cluster, 12 Old Mine Diamonds, Chrysoberyl Cat's Eye In Center, Gold 3080.00
Ring, Pear Shape Diamond & Sapphire, Baguette Diamond, Platinum, Art Deco 24000.00
Ring, Poison, Black Onyx, 10K Yellow Gold 105.00
Ring, Princess-Cut Diamonds, Flanked By Rubies, 18K Yellow Gold Mount 1150.00
Ring, Rectangular Pink Stone, 16 Round-Cut Diamonds, 18K Yellow Gold 100.00

Clean your hard stone jewelry, the diamonds and rubies, in a mixture of equal parts Wisk and water. Quickly swish dirty pearls, opals, or coral in a mixture of 1 teaspoon Ivory Liquid and 1 quart lukewarm water. Rinse, pat dry.

Jewelry, Stud Set, Agate, 18K Gold, Monogram,
Leather Case, c.1860, Tiffany & Co., 1 In.

Ring, Red Faceted Garnet, Baguette Diamond, 14K Yellow Gold, Man's	290.00
Ring, Retro, Step-Cut Amethyst, Scroll Design, Rectangular Rubies, 14K Yellow Gold	490.00
Ring, Rhodalite Garnet, Flanked By Square-Cut Garnets, Paloma Picasso	1092.00
Ring, Rose Gold, Brickwork Links, Buckle Clasp, 1940	315.00
Ring, Sapphire, Cabochon Cut, 14K Gold, Floral Engraved Shank	210.00
Ring, Sapphire, Diamond, Platinum, Art Deco, Tiffany & Co.	4250.00
Ring, Smoky Quartz, Oval, Yellow Gold	30.00
Ring, Snake, Silver, Tail Wraps Around Oval Jade, Blue Stone In Mouth	25.00
Ring, Solitaire, Prong-Set European-Cut Diamond, Platinum Mount	2875.00
Ring, Star Sapphire, Baguette & Round Diamond, Platinum, Shire & Strauss, Art Deco	4500.00
Ring, Star Sapphire, Gold, Egyptian Revival	350.00
Ring, Sterling Silver, Alternating Yellow Gold, Silver Graduated Inverted Discs	230.00
Ring, Swirl, 9 Opals, 14 Mine-Cut Diamonds, 14K Yellow Gold	495.00
Ring, Trinity, Tapered Band, Original Box, 18K White Gold	635.00
Stickpin, Black Opal, Diamond, Gold & Platinum, Edwardian	3650.00
Stickpin, Blue Opal, Surrounding Stones	20.00
Stickpin, Bust Of Woman In Enamel, Blue Guilloche Ground, 18K Yellow Gold	430.00
Stickpin, Cameo, Bouquet, Woman's Head, Coral Bow, 14K Yellow Gold	430.00
Stickpin, Center Oval Opal, Diamonds Surround, 14K Yellow Gold Mount, Box	460.00
Stickpin, Diamond, 4 Synthetic Sapphires, 14K White Gold	65.00
Stickpin, Faceted Green Tourmaline, 14K Green Gold, William Bramley, 7/8 In.	595.00
Stickpin, Gargoyle's Head, Diamond Center, Red Stone Eyes, 14K Yellow Gold	345.00
Stickpin, Gargoyle, Open Mouth Face With Ruby Eyes, 18K Yellow Gold	750.00
Stickpin, Moonstone, Man In The Moon & Stars, 4 Faceted Red Stones, Silver Mount	258.00
Stickpin, Opal, Man's Face In Black & White Headdress, 1900	805.00
Stickpin, Peridot, Oval, Yellow Gold	70.00
Stickpin, Round Diamond, Platinum Basket, 14K Yellow Gold	2875.00
Stickpin, Scarab, Yellow Gold Plated	25.00
Stickpin, Scotty, Black, Green Enamel Accents, Platinum	632.00
Stickpin, Wolf's Head, Sterling Silver, 2 3/4 In.	25.00
Stud Set, Agate, 18K Gold, Monogram, Leather Case, c.1860, Tiffany & Co., 1 In. ..*Illus*	2500.00
Tie Bar, Reddy Kilowatt, Gold, 1 In.	35.00
Tsuba, Iron, 2 Riobitsu, Metal Sea Shells, Irregular Hammer Rim, Japan, 2 7/8 In.	225.00
Tsuba, Iron, Crashing Waves, Waterfall, Gold Leaves, Oval, Japan, 2 7/8 In.	325.00
Tsuba, Iron, Mokko, Sage Rolling Out Scroll, Gold Inscribed, Textured, Japan, 3 3/8 In.	650.00
Tsuba, Iron, Namban, Beaded Rim, Demons Emerge From Clouds, Gold, Japan, 2 3/4 In.	350.00
Tsuba, Iron, Sukashi Riobitsu, Umbrellas, Round, Japan, 2 7/8 In.	250.00
Watches are listed in their own category.	
Watch, Diamonds, Half-Round Pearl Fob, Chain, 14K & 18K Yellow Gold, 1890	2800.00
Watch Chain, Braided Hair, Gold Filled Mount, Fob & Key, 19th Century, 11 In.	100.00
Watch Chain, Elongated Links, 14K Yellow & White Gold, 1930, 14 In.	150.00
Watch Chain, Gold Nuggets	625.00
Watch Chain, Mother-Of-Pearl Link, Horse Head Fob	295.00
Watch Chain, Rope Twist, Gold Filled, Pearl Slide, 10K Gold	55.00
Watch Chain, Rose & White Gold, c.1900, 14 1/2 In.	110.00

Watch Chain, Round Links, Swivel Hooks, Chalcedony Intaglio Fob, 14K Gold 805.00
Wristwatches are listed in their own category.

JOHN ROGERS statues were made from 1859 to 1892. The originals
were bronze, but the thousands of copies made by the Rogers factory
were of painted plaster. Eighty different figures were created. Similar
painted plaster figures were produced by some other factories. Rights
to the figures were sold in 1893 and they were manufactured for several more years by the Rogers Statuette Co. Never repaint a Rogers figure because this lowers the value to collectors.

Group, Charity Patient 475.00
Group, Fugitive's Story 475.00
Group, Going For The Cows, 1873 . . . . 225.00
Group, Matter Of Opinion, 1884 . . . . 350.00
Group, Taking The Oath, Drawing Rations, Soldier, Hat, Chalkware, 1899, 24 In. 440.00
Group, Wrestlers, 1881 . . . . 1025.00
Group, You Are A Spirit, I Know 475.00

JOSEF ORIGINALS ceramics were designed by Muriel Joseph George.
The first pieces were made in California from 1945 to 1962. They were
then manufactured in Japan. The company was sold to George Good in
1982 and he continued to make Josef Originals until 1985. The company was then sold to Southland Corporation. The name is now owned
by Applause.

Figurine, Astrological Girl 35.00
Figurine, Chick, With Hat, 5 In. 140.00
Figurine, Crol 35.00
Figurine, Down To Sleep 45.00
Figurine, Hedy, 6 In. 40.00
Figurine, Teddy 35.00
Night-Light, Mouse 45.00

JUDAICA is any memorabilia that refers to the Jews or the Jewish reli-
gion. Interests range from newspaper clippings that mention eigh-
teenth- and nineteenth-century Jewish Americans to religious objects,
such as menorahs or spice boxes. Age, condition, and the intrinsic
value of the material, as well as the historic and artistic importance,
determine the value.

Book, Prayer, High Holiday, Printed In Wilno, Leather Cover, 1829 . . . . 245.00
Candlestick, Sabbath, Leaf Feet, Inscribed For 75th Anniversary, Russia, 11 In., Pair 545.00
Case, Megillah, Reeded & Gadroon Spiraling, Finial Each End 375.00
Chandelier, 8-Light, Chains, Drip Pans, Hebrew On Pan, Sockets, Pendant Finial, 30 In. . 9200.00
Crown, Torah, 4 Tiers, Floral Overlay, Glass Jewels, Brass Bells 1000.00
Cup, Kiddush, 3 Oval Medallions, Sterling Silver, 3 3/8 In. 85.00
Cup, Kiddush, Center 3 Oval Medallions, Star Of David, Sterling Silver, 3 3/8 In. 85.00
Finial, Torah, Pierced 6-Sided Star, Hanging Bells, Silver Plate, 9 1/2 In., Pair 430.00
Knife, Sabbath, Challah, Folding, Mother-Of-Pearl, Engraved, German, 4 1/4 In. 275.00
Kovsch Cup, Floral, Gilt, Inscribed 1900, Maker HC, Russian Silver 895.00
Menorah, Oil Burning, Brass, Openwork, Beehive Shape, Birds, 8 Wells, 7 x 12 1/2 In. . . 100.00
Menorah, Trumpet-Form Base, 4 Branches, Sterling Silver, 10 1/2 In. 258.00
Plate, Seder, 6 Petals For Symbols, Star Of David Center, Karlsbad, 10 3/4 In. 460.00
Plate, Seder, Family Center, Gold Stars Of David Around Center, France, Limoges, 12 In. 368.00
Vase, Tapering Sides, Angled Shoulders, Egyptian, Alabaster, 3 3/8 In. 45.00

JUGTOWN Pottery refers to pottery made in North Carolina as far back
as the 1750s. In 1915, Juliana and Jacques Busbee set up a training and
sales organization for what they called *Jugtown Pottery.* In 1921, they
built a shop at Jugtown, North Carolina, and hired Ben Owen as a potter in 1923. The Busbees moved the village store where the pottery
was sold to New York City. Juliana Busbee sold the New York store in
1926 and moved into a log cabin near the Jugtown Pottery. The pottery
closed in 1959. It reopened in 1960 and is still working near Seagrove,
North Carolina.

Bowl, Chinese Blue Glaze, 4 x 7 1/4 In. 550.00

Bowl, Cover, Yellow Glaze, 5 3/4 In. 120.00
Pitcher, Pumpkin Orange Glaze, Impressed Mark, Redware, 10 1/2 In. 305.00
Urn, Chinese Blue Glaze, Bulbous, 7 x 5 1/4 In. 3850.00
Vase, Chinese Blue & Red Glaze, Incised Band On Top, 5 1/2 x 6 1/2 In. 2750.00
Vase, Chinese Blue Glaze, 11 x 7 3/4 In. 3850.00
Vase, Chinese Blue Glaze, 2 Handles, 8 3/4 x 8 In. 2420.00
Vase, Chinese Blue Glaze, 3 3/4 x 4 1/2 In., Pair 660.00
Vase, Chinese Blue Glaze, 4 x 3 In., Pair 412.00
Vase, Chinese Blue Glaze, Brown Clay Body, Bisque, Bulbous, 5 3/4 x 4 1/2 In. 1430.00
Vase, Chinese Blue Glaze, Classically Shaped, 9 1/2 x 7 In. 1320.00
Vase, Chinese Blue Glaze, Flared, 3 1/2 x 4 3/4 In. 275.00
Vase, Chinese Blue Glaze, Floral, Maroon, Blue Glaze, 4 In. 275.00
Vase, Chinese Blue Glaze, Oval, Signed, 4 1/2 x 5 In. 225.00
Vase, Chinese Blue Glaze, Signed, 9 1/4 In. 858.00
Vase, Chinese Blue Glaze, Tapered, Bulbous, 6 1/4 x 7 In. 770.00
Vase, Chinese Red Glaze, Pear Shape, 5 1/2 x 4 In. 1540.00
Vase, Chinese Red, Blue Glaze, 2 Applied Medallions, 7 1/2 x 4 In. 2640.00
Vase, Cream Glaze, Globular, Early 20th Century, 7 1/4 In. 220.00
Vase, Frothy Semimatte White Glaze, Oval, Signed, 3 x 4 1/4 In. 150.00
Vase, Purple, Green Dripping Glossy Glaze, 5 1/2 x 4 1/4 In. 1650.00
Vessel, Covered In Semimatte White Glaze, Signed, 3 1/2 x 5 In. 225.00

JUKEBOXES play records. The first coin-operated phonograph was
demonstrated in 1889. In 1906 the *Automatic Entertainer* appeared,
the first coin-operated phonograph to offer several different selections
of music. The first electrically powered jukebox was introduced in
1927. Collectors search for jukeboxes of all ages, especially those with
flashing lights and unusual design and graphics.

Electra, Holcomb & Hoke, Walnut Finish, Manuals, 1929 .... 2600.00
Rock-Ola, Model 1428, Plastic, Art Deco Grill, Etched Glass, c.1948, 60 In. 2587.00
Rock-Ola, Series G, Model 1428, c.1948 .... 3900.00
Seeburg, Consolette, Metal, Glass & Plastic, Type 5CI, Stereo, 15 x 6 1/2 x 13 In. 82.00
Seeburg, Model 100 B, 45 RPM Model, 100 Play Machine, c.1950, 54 In. 978.00
Seeburg, Wall, Model 200 .... 250.00
Wurlitzer, Model 1650, 1954 .... 2500.00
Wurlitzer, Model 1900, 1956 .... 3500.00
Wurlitzer, Model 42, 24 Tune, Walnut Case, Reverse Painted Mirror, 65 1/2 In. 4600.00

KAY FINCH Ceramics were made in Corona Del Mar, California, from
1935 to 1963. The hand-decorated pieces often depicted whimsical
animals and people. Pastel colors were used.

Kay Finch
CALIFORNIA

Charger, Santa Claus, Signed, No. 5680, 16 In. 400.00
Figurine, Bunny, Jacket, No. 5005 .... 145.00
Figurine, Chipmunk, Lying Flat On Belly, Brown 350.00
Figurine, Choir Boy 120.00
Figurine, Dove, Turquoise, Pair 450.00
Figurine, Draft Horse, Green, No. 130, 4 In. 145.00
Figurine, Draft Horse, No. 130 .... 125.00
Figurine, Fish, Green 95.00
Figurine, Grumpy Pig, Strawberries & White Flowers, No. 165, 6 x 8 In. 395.00
Figurine, Jezebel The Cat, No. 179, 7 In. 350.00
Figurine, Jocko, Monkey, No. 4842 .... 325.00
Figurine, Owl, 3 In. 42.00
Figurine, Owl, Brown Face, 6 In. 75.00
Figurine, Peasant Boy, Lavender Outfit, 7 In. 45.00
Figurine, Pig, Brown, 4 In. 100.00
Figurine, Pig, Smiley, No. 164 .... 275.00
Figurine, Rooster, Butch, No. 177 .... 125.00
Figurine, Terrier, No. 4832, 5 In. ....425.00 to 475.00
Planter, Bear, Block 50.00
Vase, Stylized Leaves, Holiday Green, 14 In. 95.00

KAYSERZINN, see Pewter category.

KELVA glassware was made by the C. F. Monroe Company of Meriden, Connecticut, about 1904. It is a pale, pastel-painted glass decorated with flowers, designs, or scenes. Kelva resembles Nakara and Wave Crest, two other glasswares made by the same company.

Box, Enameled Parrot Tulips, Leaves, Silver Plated Metal Collar, 3 1/2 x 6 In. 850.00
Box, Orange Floral Cover, Green, 3 3/4 In. 385.00
Toothpick, Enameled Flowers, Ormolu Handles, Octagonal, Pink & White 475.00
Tray, Blue, New Liner, 5 In. 72.00
Tray, Pink, Floral, Blue, New Liner, 6 In. 275.00

KEMPLE glass was made by John Kemple of East Palestine, Ohio, and Kenova, West Virginia, from 1945 to 1970. The glass was made from old molds. Many designs and colors were made. Kemple pieces are usually marked with a *K* on the bottom. Many milk glass pieces were made with or without the mark.

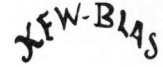

Box, Trinket, Amber, Label, 3 1/4 x 2 1/4 In. 30.00
Creamer, Rotec, Milk Glass, 4 In. 10.00
Dish, Oblong, Amberina, Sticker, Bontec, 3 1/2 x 4 3/4 In. 10.00
Plate, Cardinal On Wheat, Milk Glass, 6 In. 25.00
Sugar & Creamer, Lace & Dewdrop, Spatter Glass, Labels 168.00

KEW BLAS is the name used by the Union Glass Company of Somerville, Massachusetts. The name refers to an iridescent golden glass made from the 1890s to 1924. The iridescent glass was reminiscent of the Tiffany glass of the period.

Dish, Silver Plated Floral Handle, 5 1/2 In. 275.00
Jug, Pulled Over Green, Gold Luster, Polished Pontil, 3 In. 575.00
Vase, Pulled Feather, Mat-Su-Noke Around Neck, 7 3/4 In. 1450.00
Vase, Spiked Top Rim, Flared Amber Cylinder, Pulled Feather Design, Signed, 10 In. 595.00

KEWPIES, designed by Rose O'Neill, were first pictured in the *Ladies' Home Journal*. The figures, which are similar to pixies, were a success, and Kewpie dolls started appearing in 1911. Kewpie pictures and other items soon followed. Collectors search for all items that picture the little winged people.

Bank, Chalkware 42.00
Bank, Seated, Chalkware, Wire Spectacles, A.W. Brooks, Chicago, 1966, 11 In. 33.00
Bisque, Blunderboo, Arms Held To Head, 3 In. 1300.00
Bisque, Doodle Dog, Bathtub, Cameo Mark, 3 1/4 In. ....*Illus* 2970.00
Bisque, Doodle Dog, Kewpie With Umbrella, Heart Sticker, 2 1/2 In. ....*Illus* 138.00
Bisque, Feeding Doodle Dog, With Baby Bottle, Sitting On Bench, 3 1/2 In. 4800.00
Bisque, Grenadier 3800.00
Bisque, In Blue Blanket Swing, Black Stamp In Circle Mark, 2 3/4 In. 3100.00
Bisque, Jointed Arms, Bisque Head, Black Side-Glancing Googly Eyes, 8 In. 650.00
Bisque, Jointed, Signed, Rose O'Neill, Germany, 5 1/2 In. 185.00
Bisque, Prussian Helmet, Rifle, Saber 4300.00

Kewpie, Bisque, Doodle Dog, Bathtub, Cameo Mark, 3 1/4 In.

Kewpie, Bisque, Doodle Dog, Kewpie With Umbrella, Heart Sticker, 2 1/2 In.

Bisque, Riding Stork, Black Stamp In Circle Mark, 4 1/4 In. 4200.00
Bisque, Standing, Jointed Arms, Googly Side-Glancing Eyes, Germany, 6 In. 600.00
Bisque, Standing, Jointed Arms, Googly Side-Glancing Eyes, Germany, 12 In. 1050.00
Bisque, Standing, Movable Arms, Blue Wing, 7 In. 125.00
Bisque, With Brown Doodle Dog, 4 In. 4400.00
Black, Heart Chest Sticker, Rose O'Neill, 1930s 325.00
Bowl, Green Ground, Schafer & Vater, No. 9368, Signed Rose O'Neill, 2 1/4 In. 150.00
Candy Container, Kewpie By Barrel 95.00
Chalkware, Sitting, Elbows On Knees, Rose O'Neill, 4 In. 110.00
Clock, Bisque, Jasperware, Blue, Arched Case, Frolicking Kewpies, 1915, 5 1/2 In. 475.00
Coaster, Wag, Shaking Fist, Rose O'Neill, 3 In. 135.00
Composition, Chest Label, Rosie O'Neill, 9 In. 175.00
Composition, Factory Jacket, Heart Sticker, 12 In. 325.00
Composition, Jointed Arms, Kewpie Decal On Chest, 11 In. 110.00
Cup & Saucer, Blue & Green Ground 175.00
Hard Plastic, Pictures On Box Top, Rose O'Neill, Box, 8 In. 200.00
Jointed Shoulders & Hips, Cotton Sunsuit, Shoes, Socks, Cameo, 1930, 13 In. 145.00
Pie Plate, Green Trees, White, Marked 175.00
Plate, Green, Orange Luster, Scalloped, Rose O'Neill, Germany, 8 In. 200.00
Playing Mandolin, Menu Holder, Rose O'Neill 485.00
Postcard, Doll, Sitting On Golf Bag, Eating Ice Cream, Rose O'Neill, 1976 .... 4.00
Sign, Kewpie Pie, Hendler's Ice Cream, Cardboard, 8 1/2 x 17 1/2 In. 30.00
Sitting, O-Shape Mouth, Hands On Ears, Outstretched Legs, Rose O'Neill, 3 1/2 In. 1795.00
Soldier, Seated, German Helmet, Jointed Shoulders, 1913, 3 1/2 In. 1150.00
Tray, Purity Ice Cream, Kewpie Holding Tray With Strawberry Sundae On It, 17 In. 575.00
Valentine, Rose O'Neill 35.00
Vinyl, Cameo, 8 1/2 In. 75.00

KIMBALL, see Cluthra category.

KING'S ROSE, see Soft Paste category.

KITCHEN utensils of all types, from eggbeaters to bowls, are collected today. Handmade wooden and metal items, like ladles and apple peelers, were made in the early nineteenth century. Mass-produced pieces, like iron apple peelers and graniteware, were made in the nineteenth century. Other kitchen wares are listed under manufacturers' names or under Advertising, Iron, Tool, or Wooden.

Bathtub, Baby's, Oblong 195.00
Batter Bowl, Pouring Lip, Interior Gloss Cream, c.1900, 7 3/4 x 18 1/4 In. 110.00
Batter Set, Flowers, Century, Homer Laughlin, 3 Piece 250.00
Batter Set, Square Tray, Gold Trim, Homer Laughlin, 4 Piece 350.00
Beater, Aurelius, Triple 575.00
Beater, Minute Maid 345.00
Beater, Moore Patent, Ram 600.00
Beater, Rug, Wire 30.00
Beater, Side Handle, Holts 450.00
Biscuit Prick, Maple Handle, New England, 18th Century 350.00
Biscuit Prick, Walnut, Geometric Handle, Pennsylvania, Late 18th Century 250.00
Board, Cutting Cottage, Shape, Wrought Hanger, New England, 19th Century, 10 1/2 In. . 650.00
Board, Cutting, Butternut, Heart Handle, 27 In. 285.00
Board, Cutting, Lollipop Handle, New England, 19th Century, 15 In. 160.00
Board, Cutting, Mother's Helper, Tombstone, 14 In. 150.00
Bottle Drying Rack, Tapered Cylinder, Wire, Metal, Early 20th Century, 23 x 43 In. 125.00
Bowl, Chopping, Maple, Tiger Striping, Rectangular, 21 x 15 x 5 In. 490.00
Bowl, Chopping, Wooden, Hand Carved, Oval, 24 x 13 x 4 In. 115.00
Bowl, Chopping, Wooden, Red Paint, Round, 20 1/2 In. 1320.00
Bowl, Dough, France, c.1850, 17 3/4 In. 88.00
Bowl, Dough, French Provincial, Treen, Natural Waxed, Metal Repair, 1840, 33 In. 240.00
Bowl, Dough, Treen, French Provincial, Waxed, Wooden, Oval, 1840, 6 1/2 x 35 x 13 In. . 110.00
Bowl Set, Refrigerator, Stacking, Rectangular, Lids, Pyrex, 1950s, 4 Piece 30.00
Box, Spice, Oak, Double Slide, Chip Carved, Treen, Pilgrim Period, 13 x 9 x 3 1/2 In. ... 1895.00
Broiler, Open Grate, Wrought Iron, Handle, Filed Design, Late 18th Century, 24 In. 225.00
Brush, Crumb Pan, Prayer Lady 338.00

Butter Mold, look under Mold, Butter in this category.
Butter Paddle, Burl Wood, 8 In. 485.00
Butter Stamp, 4 Hearts, Crosshatching, Hardwood, Square Self Handle, 4 3/4 x 5 In. 440.00
Butter Stamp, Cow & Tree, Wooden, Turned 1 Piece Handle, Round, 4 1/4 In. 130.00
Butter Stamp, Eagle With Star, Hardwood, Round, 4 In. 305.00
Butter Stamp, Eagle, Filkksy 400.00
Butter Stamp, Sheaf Of Wheat 115.00
Butter Stamp, Sheaf Of Wheat, Rectangular 175.00
Butter Stamp, Stylized Heart 195.00
Butter Stamp, Stylized Pot Of Flowers, H.M., 1823, 2 5/8 x 4 In. 165.00
Butter Stamp, Stylized Tulip, Pine, Tin Hanger, 3 x 4 7/8 In. 247.00
Butter Stamp, Tulip & Leaves, Poplar, Primitive, Self Handle, 1796, 4 1/2 x 5 In. 550.00
Butter Stamp, Union, Heart & Stars, Butternut, 3 1/8 x 5 In. 357.00
Cabbage Cutter, Hardwood, Attached Box, Large 33.00
Cabbage Cutter, Walnut, Cutout Heart, Handle, 7 1/4 x 18 3/4 In. 300.00
Cake Board, Abraham & Isaac, HIW, Round, 5 7/8 In. 1600.00
Cake Board, Annunciation, HCE, Round, 8 3/4 In. 2600.00
Cake Board, Bird, Beeswax & Stone, C. Wiedemann, Hamburg, Round, 12 1/2 In. 700.00
Cake Board, Double Heart Handle, Walnut, Beveled Edge, 8 x 28 In. 1090.00
Cake Board, Heart, Carved Design, 2 Sides, 12 1/4 x 17 5/8 In. 1200.00
Cake Board, Mahogany, Carved, Double Signed, J. Conger, Football Shape 3850.00
Cake Decorator Set, Aluminum, 6 Tips, Box 35.00
Can Opener, Empress, Key Wind 7.00
Canister, Cinnamon, Red Paint, Gold Lettering, 1940s, 6 3/4 In. 185.00
Canister, Coffee, Delphite, Black Letters, Metal Lid, 40 Oz. 300.00
Canister, Spice, Nutmeg, Jadite, Square, 3 In. 130.00
Canister, Sugar, Delphite, Black Letters, Metal Lid, 40 Oz. 300.00
Canister Set, Enamel, Name, Floral Border, Blue, White & Pin, France, 6 Piece 500.00
Canister Set, Prayer Lady, Pink, Enesco 1900.00
Canister Set, Red Rooster, Metlox, 4 Piece 300.00
Canister Set, Veggie Design, Red Lids, Decoware, 4 Pieces 55.00
Casserole, Cover, Handles, Gingham, Vernonware, 4 x 10 1/2 In. 45.00
Chicken Fryer, Guardian Ware 45.00
Chopper, Herb, Wrought Iron Blade Curved Up To Hold Fruitwood Handle 138.00
Churn, Chestnut, Turned, Plunger, 14 x 10 In. 850.00
Churn, Dazey, 1 Qt. 1200.00
Churn, Dazey, Heavy Glass Jar, 2 Qt. 275.00
Churn, Dazey, No. 30 .... 175.00
Churn, Dazey, No. 60 .... 140.00
Churn, Hand Forged Iron Fittings, Robin's-Egg Blue 170.00
Churn, Original Old Red Cow Painting 250.00
Churn, Stave Construction, Brown Finish, Handle, Dasher, 22 In. 150.00
Churn, Stave Construction, Handle, Dasher, 24 In. 525.00
Churn, Wood, Iron Banding, Handles, 19th Century, 27 In. 193.00
Churn, Wooden, Cover & Dasher, Barrel Shape, 20 In. 120.00
Clock Jack, Brass, Cast Iron Wheel, Hooks, Iron, Trammel, Sawtooth, Adjustable, 39 In. . 520.00
Clothesline Reel, Lowell Ever Ready, Dustless 50.00
Coffee Grinders are listed in their own category.
Coffee Maker, Silex, Individual, Crystal, Box 30.00
Coffeepot, Metal, Meriden Homelectrics, Manning-Bowman Co., 1910-1925, 11 In. 22.00
Cooker, Copper, Tin, 2 Doors, Conservo, Toledo Cooker Co., Patd. 1907 .... 193.00
Cooker, Egg, Tin, 8 Egg Spaces, 10 1/2 In. 55.00
Cooker, Oak, Metal, 3 Sections, Toledo, Ohio, Ideal, Label, 19 x 15 x 15 In. 168.00
Cookie Board, 5 Carved Scenes, Woman With Baby In Crib, Man, Knotted Tree, 28 In. .. 220.00
Cookie Board, Beech, 16 Carved Designs, 4 3/4 x 26 3/4 In. 247.00
Cookie Board, Cherry, Bear, 7 7/8 x 5 In. 192.00
Cookie Board, Dog & Cat, Carved, 15 1/4 x 9 3/4 In. 305.00
Cookie Board, Man 1 Side, Woman On Other, Hardwood, 17 1/2 x 7 3/8 In. 275.00
Cookie Board, Pewter, 15 Sections, Animals, Flowers, Building, 3 7/8 x 7 In. 220.00
Cookie Cutter, Davis Baking Powder, Cat, Goose, Rabbit & Horse 10.00
Cookie Cutter, Embossed, Rumford 15.00
Cookie Cutter, Horse & Rider, Sheet Iron, 8 x 8 In. 407.00
Cookie Cutter, Man With Pipe, Hat, Frock Coat, Tin, 8 1/2 In. 522.00

Cookie Cutter, Pinwheel, Aluminum, Hand Made 14.00
Cookie Cutter, Rooster, Looking Right & Left, Sheet Iron, 6 1/2 x 7 1/2 In., Pair 175.00
Cookie Cutter, Snoopy, Charlie Brown, Linus, Lucy, Plastic, 4 In., 4 Piece 27.00
Cookie Cutter, Soldier, Detailed Buttons & Epaulets, Tin, 8 1/2 In. 635.00
Cookie Cutter, Woman, Hat, Long Dress, Tin, 9 In. 522.00
Corer, Apple, Ivory Handle, Silver, 6 In. 550.00
Creamer, Measuring, Post Cereal 35.00
Cup, Measuring, Brass, Turned Handle, Eyelet Holes, England, 17th Century, 1 Oz. 275.00
Curler, Butter, Hand Carved, Incised Handle 235.00
Cutter, Cheese, Tru-Cut, Enameled Green & White Base, Iron, Corcoran Mfg. 71.00
Damper, Stovepipe, Griswold, 3 In. 25.00
Damper, Stovepipe, Griswold, 4 In. 20.00
Damper, Stovepipe, Griswold, 6 In. 15.00
Dipper, Burl Ash, Varnish, Plain Handle, 11 3/4 In. 715.00
Dipper, Hard & Soft Woods, Copper Tacks, 7 1/2 x 8 In. 192.00
Dipper, Hardwood, Natural Burl Bowl, 12 1/2 In. 150.00
Dipper, Paddle, Curly Maple, Round Bowl, Worn Finish, 10 In. 95.00
Dipper, Wood, Burnt Sienna Patina, 4 3/4 x 7 1/4 In. 450.00
Dough Box, Pine, Red Paint, Cover, 1775, 29 x 16 x 11 In. 500.00
Dough Box, Poplar, Dark Worn Finish, Turned Legs, Dovetailed, Penna., 16 x 43 In. 330.00
Dough Box, Poplar, Repaint, Splayed, 2 Board Top, Penna., 19 x 39 x 28 In. 300.00
Dough Box, Poplar, Turned Splayed Legs, Button Feet, 21 x 36 x 27 In. 412.00
Dough Box, Red Paint, Slant Side, Stand, 27 x 36 x 15 1/4 In. 175.00
Dutch Oven, Griswold, No. 6, Tite-Top, Smooth Lid 180.00
Dutch Oven, Griswold, No. 7 .... 50.00
Dutch Oven, Griswold, No. 8, Tite-Top, Patented 2/10/20 .... 68.00
Dutch Oven, Tin, Iron Spit, 19 In. 55.00
Eggbeater, Holts Improved Dover, Cast Iron 30.00
Eggbeater, Taplin, 12 In. 45.00
Firkin, Cover, Bentwood Handle, Finger Lap, Blue Gray Paint, 5 1/4 x 7 1/2 In. 690.00
Firkin, Stave Construction, 1 Stave Extends To Form Handle, 13 In. 140.00
Flatiron, Rattle In Handle, Hand Forged, 18th Century 225.00
Flour Box, 4 Sections, 2 Cupboard Base Doors, Yellow Paint 2100.00
Flue Cover, Painted Reverse Of Pretty Lady, Birds 65.00
Food Chopper, A. Freeman, Thin Steel Blade, Brass, Wooden Handle, 6 In. 55.00
Food Chopper, Brass Handle, England, 6 x 5 In. 280.00
Food Chopper, Curly Maple Handle, 19th Century, 5 1/2 x 6 3/8 In. 150.00
Food Chopper, Griswold, No. 0 .... 50.00
Food Chopper, Griswold, No. 2 .... 30.00
Food Chopper, W. Blackmore, Wooden Handle, Brass Ferrule, 13 1/4 In. 150.00
Frying Pan, Brass, Copper Handles, Rivets, Handles, Footed, 17th Century, 10 In. 195.00
Funnel, Brass, Tinned Interior, American, Early 19th Century, 4 In. 150.00
Funnel, Pie, Blackbird, White, England, 4 1/2 In. 46.00
Grain Measure, Bentwood, Stenciled Shaker Society, Sabbathday Lake, Me., 7 1/2 In. ... 160.00
Grater, Nutmeg, Sliding Wooden Feeder, Blue Japanning, 5 1/2 In. 522.00
Grater, Nutmeg, Spring Compartment On Side 35.00
Grater, Nutmeg, Turned Mahogany, Brass Fittings, 7 5/8 In. 385.00
Grater, Nutmeg, Wood & Metal, 7 1/2 In. 120.00
Grater, Vegetable, Iron Back, Wooden Handle, Tin, Blue Paint 40.00
Griddle, Hanging, Wrought Iron, Early 19th Century, 9 1/2 x 9 3/4 In. 175.00
Grill, Aunt Jemima, Model PG 706B, Metal, Plastic Knobs, Instructions, 26 x 24 In. 3080.00
Grinder, Herb, Cast Iron, Boat Shape, Wheel Pestle, Wooden Handle, 16 In. 510.00
Grinder, Herb, Iron, Wooden Handle, 18th Century, 18 In. 1250.00
Grinder, Spice, Sheet Iron, Brass Funnel, 1790, 5 In. 550.00
Heater, Brass & Copper Scroll Design, 14 3/4 x 18 3/4 In. 60.00
Ice Chest, Eddy Refrigerator, Poplar, Metal Lined, Double Wooden Lid, Label, 30 1/4 In. .. 247.00
Ice Cream Freezer, Acme Jr. 25.00
Ice Crusher, Dazey, Triple, Box 25.00
Ice Shaver, Figural, Jerry Mouse, Plastic 45.00
Icebox, Flip Top, Grained Pine, 1880, 37 x 20 In. 775.00
Icebox, Halls, Salt Shelves, 3 Doors, 1897 .... 595.00
Icebox, Oak, 3 Doors, Original Hardware 412.00
Icebox, Oak, Paneled, 1 Door, Top Load, 22 x 36 x 14 In. 300.00

An iron frying pan should be washed with steel wool and soap. Food will stick and the pan will rust if you use detergent, not soap.

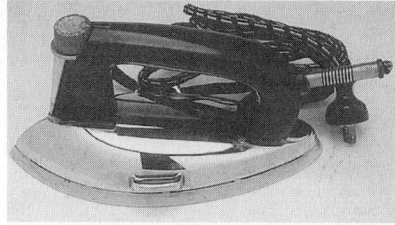

Kitchen, Iron, Electric, Sunbeam
Steam And Dry, No. S4, 9 x 4 In., Box

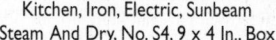

Icebox, Oak, Tin Lining, Lift Top, Chrome Plated Brass Hardware, Early 20th Century ...	385.00
Icebox, Pine, Paneled Doors, Lift Top For Ice, Metal Lined, 48 1/4 In.	440.00
Icebox, Polar Bear, Oak, Refinished, 47 x 32 x 18 In.	440.00
Iron, Electric, Sunbeam Steam And Dry, No. S4, 9 x 4 In., Box ....*Illus*	50.00
Iron, Fluting, Amer. Mach. Co., Cast Iron, Clamp, Marked Welcome	115.00
Iron, Goffering, Turned Steel, England, 19th Century	150.00
Iron, Steam, Monitor	60.00
Iron, Tailor's, Brass, Engraved Top, Boxwood Handle, 1785	595.00
Iron, Tailor's, Twist Handle, 1750	250.00
Jar, Instant Coffee, Prayer Lady	150.00
Kettle, Aluminum, Wagner	65.00
Kettle, Apple Butter, Copper	85.00
Kettle, Bean Hot Pot, Cover, Cast Iron, Salesman's Sample	125.00
Kettle, Brass, Cover, Handle, Covered Spout, Dovetailed Copper Insert Base, 20 In.	290.00
Kettle, Brass, Wrought Iron Tulip-Form Handle Attachments, 19th Century, 12 In.	225.00
Kettle, Copper, Iron Handle, 3-Legged Stand, J.P. Schaum, Lancaster, Pa., 29 In.	405.00
Kettle, Copper, Rochester, N.Y., 13 1/2 x 12 In.	85.00
Kettle, Elongated Gate, Cast Iron, c.1820, 5 3/4 In.	175.00
Kettle, Iron, Bail Handle, 19th Century, 10 In.	143.00
Kettle, Iron, Tripod Feet, 19th Century, 10 In.	303.00
Kettle, Maslin, Griswold, No. 4	75.00
Kettle Tilter, Iron, Long Monkey Tail Handle, 18th Century, 27 In.	695.00
Lemon Squeezer, Arcade, No. 2, Black, Porcelain Insert	60.00
Lemon Squeezer, Cherrywood, Late 18th Century, American	250.00
Lemon Squeezer, Wooden, Table Top, Turned Posts, Hinged	198.00
Masher, Burl, Bird's-Eye Figure, Amber Patina, 11 3/4 x 6 1/2 In.	295.00
Masher, Concave Body, 9 1/2 x 4 3/4 In.	195.00
Match Holders can be found in their own category.	
Match Safes can be found in their own category.	
Mixer, Bullet, Myers	165.00
Mixer, Hamilton Beach, No. 18	165.00
Mixer, Malt, Hamilton Beach, Singe-Head, Porcelain, Green	125.00
Mixer, Malt, Hamilton Beach, Triple-Head	250.00
Mixer, Milkshake, Hamilton Beach, Singe-Head, 2 Speed, Green Porcelain & Chrome ...	165.00
Mixer, Sunbeam Mixmaster, Juicer, Chrome	175.00
Mixing Bowl, Pouring Lip, Pierced Bottom, Ocher Interior, 10 x 21 5/8 In.	135.00
Molds may also be found in the Pewter and Tinware categories.	
Mold, Butter, Leaves & Acorns, Wooden, 1866	140.00
Mold, Butter, Pine, Pinned Tenon, Brown Patina, 20 In.	38.00
Mold, Cake, Deep Swirled Interior, Redware, Brown-Green Glaze, 9 1/2 In.	66.00
Mold, Cake, Lamb, Griswold, No. 888, 12 x 7 1/2 In.	130.00
Mold, Cake, Redware, Manganese Sponged & Rim, 7 1/2 In.	33.00
Mold, Cake, Redware, Swirl Interior, Manganese Splotches, Wide Rim, 9 In.	75.00
Mold, Cake, Redware, Swirled, Manganese Splotches, 7 1/2 In.	44.00
Mold, Cake, Santa Claus, Griswold	600.00
Mold, Candle, see Tinware category.	
Mold, Candle, 8-Tube, Copper, Late 18th Century	495.00
Mold, Candy, 3 Tiers Of 12 Soldiers, 6 x 10 1/2 In.	100.00

Mold, Candy, Heart Shape, Pine, House Type Design, 6 In.	140.00
Mold, Cheese, Interior Design With Date, 1792, Dovetail Construction, Rosehead Nails	495.00
Mold, Chocolate, 15 Santa Claus, Reindeer, Sleigh, Metal, Elsreimer & Co., 14 x 18 In.	110.00
Mold, Chocolate, Christmas Bells	65.00
Mold, Chocolate, Hen On Nest	65.00
Mold, Chocolate, Hen On Nest, Sitting On Bed Of Straw, Golden Eggs	4500.00
Mold, Chocolate, Hen On Nest, Tin, Removable Handled Base, Signed K & M, 7 In.	345.00
Mold, Chocolate, Rabbit	45.00
Mold, Chocolate, Rabbit In A Convertible	75.00
Mold, Chocolate, Racing Car, Metal, No. 108 Heille 80 Temple, 3 x 2 x 7 In.	185.00
Mold, Chocolate, Santa Claus	110.00
Mold, Chocolate, Zeppelin, Tin, c.1900, 12 1/2 In.	400.00
Mold, Confectionery, Floral Center, Beeswax & Plaster, 10 In.	495.00
Mold, Cornbread, Griswold, No. 262	65.00
Mold, Fish, Redware, Brown Glaze, 12 1/4 In.	220.00
Mold, Food, Redware, 11 1/4 In.	465.00
Mold, Food, Redware, Scalloped, Sponged Rim, 8 1/2 In.	165.00
Mold, Heart Shape, Pottery, Brown Slip Initials, Date 1853, 7 3/4 In.	440.00
Mold, Ice Cream, see Pewter category.	
Mold, Maple Sugar, Heart-Shape, Pine, 1830s, 3 In.	275.00
Mold, Sucker, Hen On Nest	35.00
Mold, Sucker, Rabbit	35.00
Mold, Sucker, Rabbit Riding Dog	35.00
Mold, Sugar, Carved Lamb, Cherry, c.1840, 5 1/4 x 6 3/4 In.	245.00
Mold, Turk's Head, Redware, 5 1/2 In.	160.00
Mold, Turk's Head, Redware, Mottled Green To Orange Glaze, 10 x 3 1/2 In.	275.00
Napkin Holder, Prayer Lady	25.00 to 45.00
Paddle, Butter, Bird's Head Handle, 8 1/2 In.	160.00
Paddle, Butter, Burl Maple, Chamfered Handle, 10 1/2 In.	165.00
Pan, Bread, Erie, No. 22	50.00
Pan, Breadstick, Griswold, No. 22, Iron, 1900	60.00
Pan, Corn Stick, Erie, No. 273	35.00
Pan, Corn Stick, Griswold, No. 273	40.00
Pan, Frying, Griswold, No. 3, Iron, 1900	15.00
Pan, Muffin, Cast Iron, 11 Sections, Pat. 1857, 9 x 13 In.	20.00
Pan, Muffin, G.F. Filley, No.'s 1 Through 12 Less No. 9, 11 Piece	3500.00
Pan, Popover, Griswold, No. 10	65.00
Pan, Popover, Griswold, No. 18	65.00
Pan, Pudding, Blue Swirl, Graniteware	40.00
Pan, Roaster, Guardian, Lid, 18 In.	45.00
Pan, Sauce, Cast Brass, Iron Handle, Copper Rivets, 1800s, 6 In.	45.00
Pantry, Box, Copper Tacks, Nutmeg Paint, 5 1/8 In To 9 3/4 In., 4 Piece	1095.00
Pastry Wheel, Wooden Handle, Brass Wheel Clock Gear, Red Paint, 1780s	195.00
Peel, Forged Iron, Heart Shape, 19 1/4 In.	155.00
Peel, Wrought Iron, Ram's Horn Handle, 37 3/4 In.	135.00

Clean your dishwasher regularly. Pour a cup of vinegar on the bottom shelf of an empty dishwasher. Run the wash and rinse cycles, but not the dry cycle. The vinegar will remove mineral buildups that may stain dishes later.

Kitchen, Potholder, Crocheted, 2 On Rollingpin Holder, 5 In. Diam.

CURIOUS COLLECTIBLES

"WHAT IS THIS?" asked the three-year-old looking at a picture book. It is a dial telephone from the 1950s. The twenty-first-century child lives with a push-button telephone—the old dial type is unknown. Other ordinary objects of the past have become unrecognizable today. The typewriter, finger bowl, razor strop, and smoking stand are often unfamiliar as well. Guests at a dinner party in the 1880s were served as many as twelve courses, each with the proper dishes and silverware. The rules of etiquette were so elaborate, there were at least 190 different serving pieces. There could be twenty different pieces of silver at each place. No diner in the year 2000 would know which piece to use. Most of us do not recognize a marrow scoop, a buckwheat cake server, asparagus tongs, or an ice-water pitcher. Household chores were also very different in the days before electricity. Just one chore, the laundry, required a day of boiling, bleaching, bluing, starching, drying, and ironing. Most of the equipment used then would be unfamiliar to a child or even to most adults today.

History can be studied through the unfamiliar changing forms of the everyday and decorative objects of the past. In the year 2100, will collectors recognize a PEZ® dispenser or a remote control for a television set? Will they understand the use of a pair of plastic shoes for a Barbie or a Teflon frying pan? Or will the obsolete objects of the twentieth century be mysteries?

There are many kinds of collectors. Some want to furnish a house. In the 1950s these collectors changed the use of many antiques. It was not uncommon to see a cobbler's bench used as a coffee table or a cranberry scoop used to hold magazines. Some collect items from a single industry and own hundreds of items related to cars or sewing. An unfamiliar item could be a rare spark plug or a sewing bird that would complete the collection. Others collect a particular type of collectible or things made by a particular manufacturer. Collectors of American art pottery, for example, may search for a Cowan pottery flower frog, and Heisey collectors may hunt for a Heisey glass mailbox.

But many collectors simply want objects of the past that appeal to them. They too must try to identify the unknown. A glass rolling pin is more interesting if you know it was filled with ice water when it was used to roll out a pie crust. A chair with a large hole in the seat is understandable when you learn that the lack of bathrooms forced people to use a chamber pot in the bedroom.

So expand your collection and your interests by taking the time to learn about the unfamiliar. You may find just the object you need.

KITCHEN MYSTERIES

This pottery boy's head can hold a towel if it is stuffed under his chin. The holder can be mounted to the wall with screws. It's 5¹/₂ inches long and is marked on the back with the letter "F." A pair cost $22 at a street fair.

Chinese laundries started by immigrant families were found in most big cities after 1900. The image of the Chinese man became a stereotype connected with wash days. Dry fabric is difficult to iron, so it was dampened with water from a pottery sprinkler bottle like this one (left) embossed with the words "Sprinkle Plenty." A matching figure (above) held measuring spoons in the kitchen. It is embossed "#1 measure boy." The 8-inch sprinkler ($60) and the 4¹/₄-inch holder ($40) made by the California pottery company Cleminson were found at a bottle show.

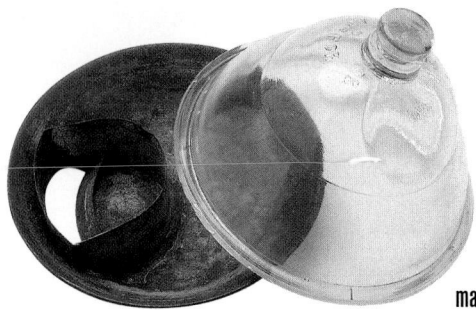

Insects presented a major dilemma before the invention of window screens. One solution was this fly catcher with a glass dome and 5¹/₂-inch tin bowl. Put sugar in the pan, cover, and wait for a fly to go inside and be trapped. It's marked "pat apd for" and was probably made in the 1880s. Today it's worth about $75.

Odors in the refrigerator are always a problem. An open box of baking soda is the cure. In the 1980s you could disguise baking soda in this ceramic polar bear made to be kept in the refrigerator. The 5¹/₂-by-4¹/₄-inch holder is signed "Lori, 78" on the bottom. It sold last year for $12 in a midwestern antiques mall.

Waste not, want not. Fats were among the most expensive ingredients in the home, so all types were saved to be reused. Small slivers of soap, which contained fat, could be reused by putting them in a soap saver and swishing it in the dishwater. This tin wire soap saver with a handle (left), used in the 1920s, is 10 inches long. It costs $15 today. From 1939 to 1945 cooking fat was saved for the war effort. In the 1950s and '60s it was saved to be recycled. The pottery grease holder shaped like a clown's head (right) is 4¹/₂ inches high. It has a twisted metal handle. The bottom is marked "Thames, Japan." The grease holder had matching teapot-shaped salt and pepper shakers (not pictured) meant to be kept as a set near the stove. The set is worth about $110.

DINNERWARE
DILEMMAS

In the nineteenth century, the best place to show off your family's prosperity was at the dinner table. Guests were invited not only to eat an elaborate meal but also to admire a table filled with expensive silver, glass, and porcelain. There was an elaborate centerpiece of figurines or flowers. In the early years of the century, the table was set with layers of tablecloths. At the end of some courses, the dishes, serving pieces, centerpiece, and dirty top tablecloth were removed. New dishes and a new centerpiece to match the food served during the next course were brought to the table. Part of the expensive display at the table was often a bowl of fruit used both as a centerpiece and as dessert at the end of the dinner. A pineapple cost so much that it was often displayed at the top of the fruit bowl. But it was there to admire, not to eat.

Table linens were always clean in the proper Victorian dining room. Because the layered tablecloth was no longer used, servants brushed crumbs and scraps from the table between courses to tidy up the cloth. The silver-plated blade of this 13-inch crumb scraper is engraved with a duck wounded by an arrow. It bears the hallmark "J. R. & S." with a crown. The handle is made of carved ivory. The Victorian crumber, which belonged to a silent-movie star, sold for $65 in an Orlando, Florida, movie memorabilia shop.

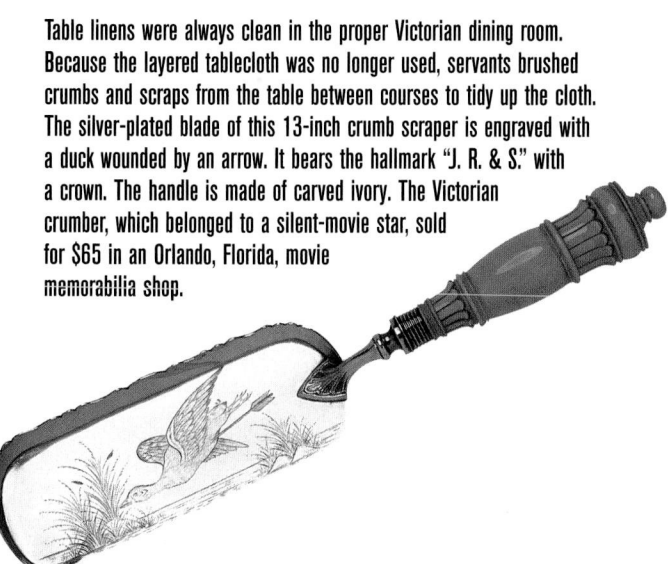

This is not a doll's dumbbell, but a knife rest. Rest the used blade of the knife on the knife rest instead of staining the tablecloth. This cut glass knife rest is 4¹/₄ inches long. It would sell for about $35. Others are made of porcelain or silver. A few are shaped like birds or animals.

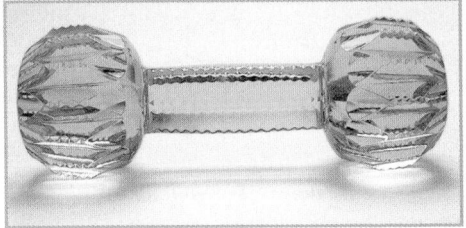

The early nineteenth-century table often had a huge pyramid of fruits and sweets as a centerpiece. There are reports of parties at which the table actually collapsed under the weight of the centerpiece. Good sense prevailed eventually, and these huge arrangements were out of style by Victorian times. But grapes and other fruit were still arranged in large bowls to be eaten for dessert. Notice the unusual blades of this pair of scissors. The scissors had to hold the stem and cut off a small bunch of grapes from the large bunch in the centerpiece. The silver-plated grape scissors are 7 inches long. The handles of grape scissors are often modeled to look like leaves or grapes. These handles are decorated with mythical beasts. Grape scissors sell today for $150 to $250.

Sometimes a form is unfamiliar because it had a different use in another country. This pot is based on a Chinese ceremonial wine ewer used before 1700. There is no lid on the pot—it is filled through an opening in the bottom. An early nineteenth-century English potter copied the shape to make a pot used to serve hot water with tea. Supposedly the shape is named for the Honorable Mrs. Cadogan, who brought back an example from China. This cadogan is shaped like a plum, suggesting that the Chinese would have used it for plum wine. It was made in China for export to England in the nineteenth century. Value, $200.

Tea was a very valuable product in the eighteenth century. It was kept in a locked box, and a teapot was usually small, holding about two cups of tea. The tea was carefully put into hot water in the pot. Additional hot water was added from another pot if the tea became too strong. By the nineteenth century, tea had become moderately priced. Sometimes loose tea leaves were steeped in the pot. Sometimes the tea leaves were put in an infuser—a small holder—and the infuser was dipped up and down in the water. Today many tea drinkers dip a teabag in a cup. Tea bags were introduced at the beginning of the twentieth century. Some say the tea bag was accidentally invented by a Chinese merchant who exported a small sample of tea in a silk bag. The London merchant who bought the tea didn't realize it should have been removed from the bag. Another story credits the invention to New York wholesaler Thomas Sullivan, who packed his tea in small muslin bags beginning in 1908. The unusual sterling silver tea infusers shaped like teapots (above) were made about 1930. Each is a little over an inch wide and sells for about $65.

This American-made glass dish with a silver-plated top was used to hold sardines, an expensive delicacy first sold commercially in England in the 1830s and first imported into New York City in the 1860s. Fancy sardine boxes were illustrated in silver catalogs as early as 1868. The 5¹/₄-inch box was designed so a tin of sardines could be emptied into it and fit exactly. It has cattails and a fish finial on the lid as a clue to the food being served. It is worth $110.

Not only is the shape of this server unfamiliar, the name of the food it served probably is too. This 13-inch Danish silver server is used to scoop up fried sprats, or sardines. The appropriately shaped fishnet spatula is marked "A. Bonebakker & Zoon" with a rampant lion. Carved elephant ivory was used for the handle. Cost, $125.

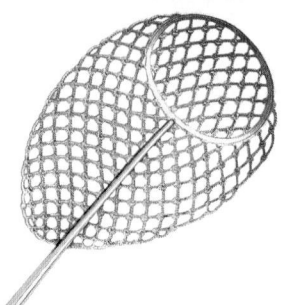

This rare 12-inch silver-plated contraption is hard to recognize. The engraved grapevines are a clue to its use. It is marked "Warwick's patent." The collar is put over the top of a wine bottle, and the bottom hook is forced over the edge of the base of the bottle so that it catches in the "push up." The large loop then forms a handle to use when serving the wine. If you can find one, expect to pay $100.

Shredded wheat breakfast biscuits were invented in 1892. By 1901 the cereal was a huge commercial success. Many new breakfast cereals were being manufactured and sold, often promoted as "health foods." This 7 1/4-by-6 1/2-inch Abbey pattern ironstone dish, made by George Jones & Sons of England, is just the size to hold two shredded wheat biscuits. It cost $45 at a California mall.

Honey was an alternative to sugar that deserved a place of honor on the table. By the early 1800s, removable wooden frames had been made for honey in domestic hives. The entire honeycomb could be slid from the frame and served at the table, or the honey could be extracted and served in a jar. This 5 1/2-inch-square honey server held a honeycomb. It is appropriately decorated with bees, skeps, and three-leaf clovers. Covered dishes with feet and finials intact are desirable pressed glass items. This one cost $165.

Butter was usually made at home in the nineteenth century. After the butter was churned, it was shaped with wooden paddles or squeezed so excess moisture was removed. The butter was then put into a mold or shaped into a mound with the paddles. The molds usually held a pound of butter. The housewife cut the butter into smaller pieces to serve at a party. Sometimes the small pats of butter were shaped into unusual forms to be even more attractive. These small (2 3/4-inch diameter) dishes are called butter chips. Each held a pat of butter. Both are French Haviland china. The one with a pink rim and blue flowers is marked "Haviland & Co. Limoges" in a blue circle (a mark used from 1864 to the present). The other, with a scalloped edge and floral design, is marked "Theodore Haviland, Limoges, France"(a mark used after 1893). Each butter chip is worth $20.

Sugar in the eighteenth century was purchased in a large cone wrapped in blue paper. The cook had to cut off large pieces using a special sugar nipper. By the 1830s granulated sugar was available. It was not as refined as modern sugar, so sugar bowls of the time were about three times as large as those used today. Henry Tate of London found a way to make a small cube of sugar by 1878. The perfect hostess would offer her guests sugar cubes neatly arranged in this holder. The Mission-style sterling server was made about 1915 by Marshall Field's and is marked "Colonial, MF & Co., 1171." It is 3 by 4 inches and cost $95 at a Florida Modernism show.

Red Cross brand condensed milk offered its customers this holder for the can. The slogan "Better than a cow" is printed on the inside. Condensed milk was used on cereal or fruit or as cream for coffee. The 4-inch-high holder is worth $50.

By the end of the nineteenth century, store-bought condiments were available. Companies responded by making attractive holders to disguise cans and jars on the table. A jam jar slides into this American Limoges holder with an underplate. A hole in the bottom of the holder made it possible to gently push the jam jar in and out. It is 4 inches high and appropriately decorated with red grapes, leaves, and gold handles. The holder sells for $95.

Pressed glass companies made full lines of table accessories. The most popular patterns had as many as one hundred different bowls, servers, plates, and stemware shapes. This odd-looking, 11-inch dish is a banana boat. Around 1870, improvements in transportation brought perishable fruit, like bananas, to the Victorian table. Such luxuries deserved a special place to be displayed. This banana boat is made of vaseline-colored glass in the Daisy & Button pattern. The color and pattern add to the value of this $175 boat.

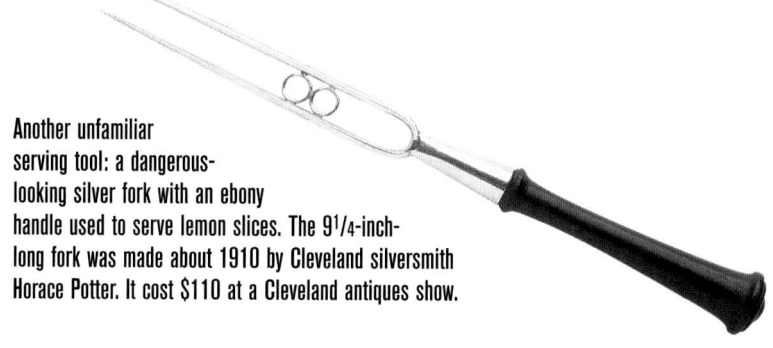

Another unfamiliar serving tool: a dangerous-looking silver fork with an ebony handle used to serve lemon slices. The 9¼-inch-long fork was made about 1910 by Cleveland silversmith Horace Potter. It cost $110 at a Cleveland antiques show.

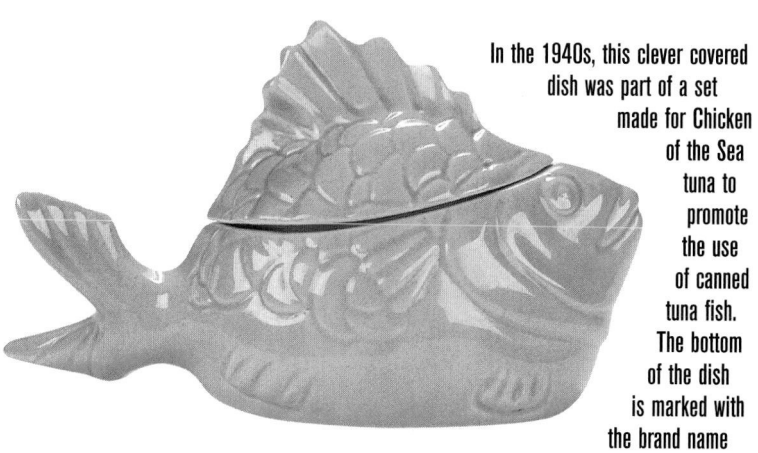

In the 1940s, this clever covered dish was part of a set made for Chicken of the Sea tuna to promote the use of canned tuna fish. The bottom of the dish is marked with the brand name and says "Tuna Baker/Salad Server, Made in California, Patent Applied For." It cost $45 several years ago in a California shop.

EVER~CHANGING FASHION

Hairstyles change with the times. Curls were popular in the 1930s and curling irons were used by women born with straight hair. The hot iron picked up strands of hair and wound them around the iron to form curls. Curling irons were heated on the stove or in the fireplace. This 9¹/₂-inch steel curling iron could be attached to a gas connection like those used for a gas stove or gas light. It dates from the 1930s, has painted wooden handles, and is marked on the heater with the brand name "Polly." It sells for $35.

Late nineteenth-century hairdos were puffed up with a "rat," a nest of hair that was positioned under long strands in the hairdo to add fullness. Women made rats from the hair that clung to a hairbrush. They would save the hair by stuffing it into the hole in the top of a hair receiver. This one is made of pressed glass with a silver-plated lid. Others were ceramic. This 4-inch hair receiver is worth $50.

There are all kinds of brushes. Sometimes they are hard to identify.
This brush came to us from a barber who used it in his shop in the 1920s.
After a haircut, he used it to whisk the bits of hair from a customer's neck and suit.
It has a turned wooden handle with hair bristles and is 9¹/₄ inches long.

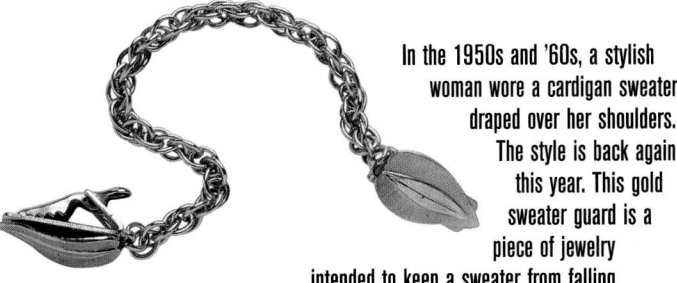

In the 1950s and '60s, a stylish woman wore a cardigan sweater draped over her shoulders. The style is back again this year. This gold sweater guard is a piece of jewelry intended to keep a sweater from falling. It has leaf clasps and a 6¹/₂-inch cable chain. We found it in a box marked "Anything, $2."

This looks like a bank, but it is not for money. It is a razor blade bank. Dull shaving blades could be safely deposited in the slot on the pottery man's head. Appropriately, he is perched on top of a 6-inch barber pole. We picked up this bank at a show for $22.50.

Laundering clothes was a major ordeal in the nineteenth century. A clever solution of that time is not used today. To minimize the need to wash whole garments, white collars, cuffs, and shirt fronts were removable. This box contains one dozen paper collars made by the Lynn Ladies Collar Co. The collars are made of embossed white paper that looks like lace. The collars kept the neckline of the dress clean and could be discarded when soiled. The set is worth $25 to $30.

Sewing was a proper and necessary pastime for women of previous centuries. This rare cardboard needle box of the 1830s is decorated with embossed metallic paper and has a mirrored lid. Fitted compartments inside that held needles or pins reveal its intended use. It is 2¹/₂ by 2 inches, and it sold for $50 at a shop in New York City.

This blue Jasperware-style oval box has two holes on the cover, a clue to its use. The 3¹/₂-inch-long holder dispenses thread stored inside. It sold for $10 at a house sale, although it is worth about $50.

This fashionable miniature shoe is made of leather trimmed with glass beads. The shoe is not meant for a doll because the inside is filled with padding. Although only 4³/₄ inches long, it is worth more than $125 to serious collectors. Why? Because it is a pincushion.

OTHER UNKNOWNS

This Sascha Brastoff item looks strange to collectors in "smoke-free" homes of the 1990s. It's a hooded ashtray designed to direct smoke up to the ceiling when a lit cigarette is put inside. Some collectors call it a "smoking ashtray." It is 7 inches high and has gold-on-gold decoration. The ashtray is signed with the commercial mark "Sascha B ® H6," indicating it was made after 1962. It sells for $65.

When cigarettes were still chic (before the Surgeon General's warnings), many household accessories were smoking related. These holders were for tiny match boxes used at the bridge or dinner table. This brass one, signed "Potter Studios," held a 2 1/4-inch matchbox. There is an opening on its side to make it possible to strike the match on the box. The elephant on top is jade. The holder is worth $65.

A well-organized desk was a symbol of a well-organized mind, especially in the age before telephones and e-mail messages. This bronze stamp holder with an art nouveau design is now one hundred years old. Like many pieces from the era, the 5-inch holder is decorated with a lady with flowing hair. There are three slanted wells inside sized to hold loose stamps. Value, $75.

Pictures were hung differently in the nineteenth century. Tacks were screwed or nailed into the wall and could be seen above the pictures. Ribbons were hung from the tacks to hold the picture frame. These brass tacks are about 2 inches long and have glass centers cut with stars or rosettes. Some are painted wtih enamel. They sell for $15 to $20 apiece.

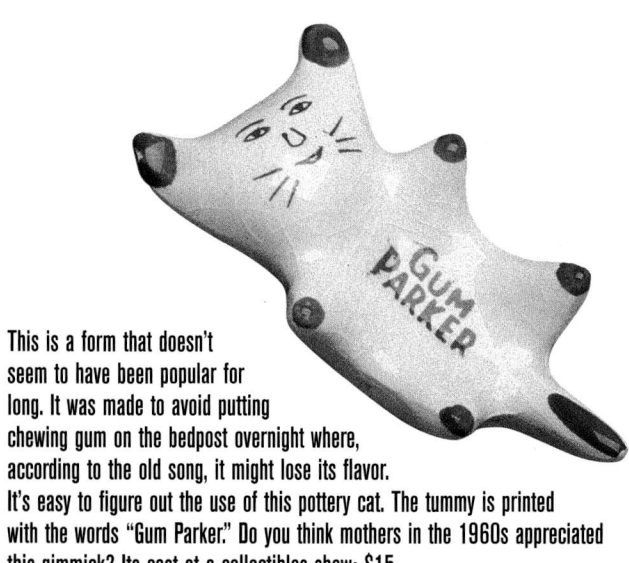

This is a form that doesn't seem to have been popular for long. It was made to avoid putting chewing gum on the bedpost overnight where, according to the old song, it might lose its flavor. It's easy to figure out the use of this pottery cat. The tummy is printed with the words "Gum Parker." Do you think mothers in the 1960s appreciated this gimmick? Its cost at a collectibles show: $15.

Peel, Wrought Iron, Ram's Horn Handle, 44 In. 55.00
Peeler, Apple, 19th Century, 22 In. 132.00
Peeler, Apple, Goodell, Cast Iron, Patent 1898 .... 75.00
Peeler, Apple, Goodell, Cast Iron, Turntable 65.00
Peeler, Apple, Quadrant 265.00
Pie Bird, Benny Baker 75.00
Pie Bird, Black Chef, All Red 750.00
Pie Crimper, 4-Pronged Pricker, Fluted Wheel, Turned Handle, Red, Green Rings 2587.00
Pie Crimper, Dolphin Shape Handle, 5 3/4 In. 302.00
Pie Lifter, Hand Wrought, 26 In. 395.00
Potato Masher, Wooden Handle, Heavy Gauge Wire, 1900s 20.00
Potholder, Crocheted, 2 On Rollingpin Holder, 5 In. Diam. ....*Illus* 7.00
Potholder, Patchwork, 18th Century, Pair 350.00
Press, Lard, Double Paddle 165.00
Rack, Utensil, 5 Hooks, 2 Birds, Wrought Iron, 14 1/2 In. 385.00
Rack, Utensil, 6 Hooks, 4 Chickens, Wrought Iron, 16 x 24 In. 110.00
Rack, Utensil, Pine Backboard, Scalloped, 7 Iron Hooks, Grained, 25 1/2 In. 220.00
Rack, Utensil, Pine, Hanging, 8 Various Kitchen Utensils, 41 1/2 In. 1150.00
Rack, Utensil, Wrought Iron, Scrolled Detail, 26 In. 248.00
Raisin Seeder, Everett, 1890s 85.00
Reamers are listed in their own category.
Roaster, Chestnut, c.1860 .... 185.00
Roasting Spit, Brass & Iron, Cylindrical, Windup, 19th Century, 15 1/2 In. 115.00
Rolling Pin, Advertising, Wildflower Design, Blue & White, 15 In. 400.00
Rolling Pin, Aqua Glass, 13 1/2 In. 50.00
Rolling Pin, Black Glass, White Splotches, Sheared & Pontiled End, 14 3/4 In. 240.00
Rolling Pin, Chrome, Red Handles, Krispy-Krust 65.00
Rolling Pin, Cobalt Glass, Gilded Transfer, Ships, Verse, Love & Live Happy, 27 In. 165.00
Rolling Pin, Ebony, Whale Ivory Handles, 19 In. 550.00
Rolling Pin, Milk Glass, House With Smoke, Union, To Bessie Dyer, 14 1/2 In. 695.00
Rolling Pin, Milk Glass, Wooden Handles 50.00
Rolling Pin, Olive Green Glass, 17 In. 115.00
Rolling Pin, Opaque White To Yellow Glass 175.00
Rolling Pin, Pumpkin Color Stripes, Blue Lettering, H.C. Pitney, Tampico, Ill. 550.00
Rolling Pin, Ruby Glass, White Looping, 12 In. 385.00
Rolling Pin, Stoneware, Boys Cash Store, Iowa 395.00
Rolling Pin, Turquoise Blue Glass, Tooled End, 15 1/4 In. 130.00
Sadiron, Monogram & Shield, 19th Century, 6 1/2 In. 33.00
Sadiron, Pluto, Electric, Leather Shot Bag, 1907 .... 38.00
Sadiron, Simmons Special 40.00
Salt & Pepper Shakers are listed in their own category.
Scoop, Cranberry, Tin & Wood, 19th Century 350.00
Scoop, Cranberry, Wood, Early 20th Century, 21 In. 412.00
Scoop, Ice Cream, Bakelite, Thick Red Handle 25.00
Scoop, Ice Cream, Benedict Indestructo No. 4, Size 30 .... 150.00
Scoop, Ice Cream, Canada Fisher Motor Co., Cold Dog, Short Barrel 2000.00
Scoop, Ice Cream, Clewell's Patent 1878 .... 75.00
Scoop, Ice Cream, Clipper, No. 16, 1915 .... 75.00
Scoop, Ice Cream, Cone Shape, Tin, Release Knob, 7 In. 22.00
Scoop, Ice Cream, Disher Co., Size 20 .... 1500.00
Scoop, Ice Cream, Dover 95.00
Scoop, Ice Cream, Dover Clipper No. 20, Pat'd. Feb. 1924, 7 1/2 In. 230.00
Scoop, Ice Cream, Erogs, No. 20, Squeeze, Round 45.00
Scoop, Ice Cream, Gem Spoon Co., Trojan Model 20 .... 120.00
Scoop, Ice Cream, Gilchrist No. 31, Banana Split 1000.00
Scoop, Ice Cream, Gilchrist, No. 33, Metal, Wood Handle, 10 In. 33.00
Scoop, Ice Cream, Hamilton Beach 20.00
Scoop, Ice Cream, Kingery, Double, 2 Handles 350.00
Scoop, Ice Cream, Maximillian Bach, Steel 2800.00
Scoop, Ice Cream, No-Pak 31, Pat. No. 1861655, Metal, Wood Handle, 9 3/4 In. 60.00
Scoop, Sandwich Ice Cream, Jiffy 525.00
Scraper, Dough, Heart Cut Out, Wrought Iron, 4 In. 247.00
Sifter, Flour, Bromwell 20.00

Sifter, Flour, Poplar, 8 x 10 1/4 In. 357.00
Skillet, Chrome, Griswold, No. 13, Oval 450.00
Skillet, Colonial Breakfast, Griswold, No. 566 .... 65.00
Skillet, Griswold, No. 0 .... 60.00
Skillet, Griswold, No. 4, Slant Letters 75.00
Skillet, Griswold, No. 7 .... 35.00
Skillet, Griswold, No. 8 .... 35.00
Skillet, Griswold, No. 10 .... 40.00
Skillet, Griswold, No. 12 .... 60.00
Skillet, Griswold, No. 14 .... 500.00
Skillet, Odorless, Griswold, No. 869 .... 150.00
Skillet, Queen Anne, Cast & Turned Brass, Iron Handle, c.1710, 16 In. 150.00
Skillet, Wagner, No. 14, Marked Lid 550.00
Skillet, Wrought Iron, Long Handle, 3-Footed 245.00
Skillet Set, Griswold, No. 3, 6 & 8, Square, 3 Piece 370.00
Skillet Set, Wagnerware, No. 3, 4, 5, 6, 7, 8, 9 & 10, 8 Piece 90.00
Skimmer, Brass, Rattail Handle, 6 1/2 x 16 In. 120.00
Slicer, Butter, Elgin, Green Enameled, Cast Iron Base, Chrome Top 60.00
Slicer, Cast Iron, Tin, Enterprise Mfg. Co. Phila., Pat. June 5, 1888, 16 1/2 In. 220.00
Slicer, String Bean, Metal & Wood, J. Deal 175.00
Slicer, Turnip, Hand Crank, Mechanical 100.00
Slicer, Vegetable, Walnut, Pennsylvania, 19th Century, 23 In. 195.00
Smoothing Board, Incised Pinwheel Design, Dated Anno 1705, 26 In. 605.00
Spice Crusher, Trough With Grinding Wheel, Oak, American, 19th Century, 16 1/4 In. 2070.00
Spice Mill, Brass, Iron, Kenrick & Sons, 6 In. 165.00
Spoon Holder, Prayer Lady 35.00
Spoon Rack, Charles II, Oak, Carved Flower Heads, Stylized Leaves, 1663, 17 1/2 In. ... 4600.00
Spoon Rack, Crowned Box Over Shelf, Tear Drops, Black Paint, Carved, 23 3/4 In. 302.00
Spoon Rack, Double Tier, Center Box On Top Shelf, Yellow Over Green, 21 x 24 In. 460.00
Sprinkler Bottle, Cat, Cardinal Marble Eyes 238.00
Sprinkler Bottle, Chinaman 65.00
Sprinkler Bottle, Cow 65.00
Sprinkler Bottle, Dearie Is Weary 425.00
Sprinkler Bottle, Dutch Boy ....135.00 to 195.00
Sprinkler Bottle, Elephant 55.00
Sprinkler Bottle, Elephant, Gray ....110.00 to 125.00
Sprinkler Bottle, Mammy 95.00
Sprinkler Bottle, Merry Maid, White, Red Apron 30.00
Sprinkler Bottle, Merry Maid, Yellow, Red Apron 32.00
Sprinkler Bottle, Poodle, Pink 115.00
Sprinkler Bottle, Santa Claus 65.00
Sprinkler Bottle, Siamese Cat 250.00
Sprinkler Bottle, Snowman 65.00
Sprinkler Bottle, Sprinkle Plenty Chinaman 236.00
Sprinkler Bottle, Woman Ironing 85.00
Stand, Pot, Swivel Grate Top On Handle, Iron, 24 In. 44.00
Steamer, Manning Bowman, Connecticut, Brass, Porcelain Insert, 1912, 3 Piece 120.00
Steamer, Steamro Hot Dog, Electric Bun Warmer, Aluminum, Porcelain, 1930s 545.00
Strainer, Cheese, Punched Tin, Heart Shape 143.00
Straw Holder, Colonial, Diamond Chain Around Base, Metal Lid 450.00
Straw Holder, Colonial, Metal Lid, Heisey 350.00
Straw Holder, Colonial, Tall 125.00
Straw Holder, Manhattan, Metal Lid, Bohemian Glass 625.00
Straw Holder, Toltec, Horizontal 500.00
String Holder, Balloon 105.00
String Holder, Beehive Shape, Pat. 1861, Cast Iron, Marked 85.00
String Holder, Cornell White Lead, Dutch Boy, 2 Sides, Die Cut, Tin, 20 x 14 In. 1150.00
String Holder, Dog 90.00
String Holder, Frog, Countertop 65.00
String Holder, Goose, Red Goose Shoes, Cast Iron, Red Paint, 15 x 11 In. 172.00
String Holder, Man With Sombrero 55.00
String Holder, Monkey On String Ball 200.00
String Holder, Orange Balloon, Ceramic 160.00

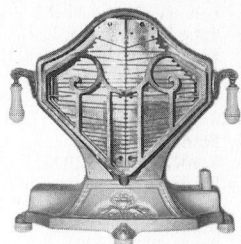

Shine the
chrome on your
1940s toaster
with baby oil,
club soda, or
lemon juice.

Kitchen, Toaster, Electric, Porcelier,
Basket Weave, Floral

Kitchen, Toaster, Electric,
Universal, Landers,
Fray & Clarke, c.1929

String Holder, Owl	60.00
String Holder, Prayer Lady, Pink	295.00 to 425.00
String Holder, S.S.S For The Blood, Cast Iron	500.00
String Holder, World War II Sailor	35.00
Sugar, Prayer Lady, Pink, Enesco	150.00
Sugar Nips, Iron, England, 9 1/2 In.	195.00
Taster, Dated On Handle, 1859, 10 1/2 In.	350.00
Teakettle, Cast Iron, Gooseneck Spout, 8 x 8 In.	275.00
Teakettle, Wagner Ware, Sidney, O., Cast Iron, Wire Handle, Swing Lid, 4 x 6 In.	115.00
Teapot, Prayer Lady, Pink, Enesco	395.00
Thermometer, Candy, 12 In.	80.00
Toast-O-Lator	300.00
Toaster, Electric, Porcelier, Basket Weave, Floral ....*Illus*	1400.00
Toaster, Electric, Universal, Landers, Fray & Clarke, c.1929 ....*Illus*	525.00
Toaster, Fitzgerald Mfg. Co. Star, Electric	85.00
Toaster, Lander's Frary & Clark Universal	50.00
Toaster, Sandwich, Round Type, 1930s	1725.00
Toaster, Toast Rite, Pink Willow, Pan Electric	3600.00
Toaster, Toastmaster, Model 1B18, 2-Slice, Chrome Finish, Bakelite Handles, Box, 1954 .	25.00
Toaster, Universal, 2-Slice, Hinged Doors, Steel, Chrome Finish, Royal Cord	20.00
Toaster, Universal, Model E9410	275.00
Toaster, Universal, Turned By Hand, Central Heat Coil	145.00
Toaster, Wrought Iron, Penny Footed, Twisted & Scrollwork, 16 1/2 x 19 In.	330.00
Wafer Iron, Eagle Design, Late 18th To Early 19th Century, 28 x 5 1/2 In.	633.00
Wafer Iron, Griswold	450.00
Waffle Iron, Art Deco, Chrome, Black Bakelite Handle	45.00
Waffle Iron, Griswold, No. 8, Hammered Finish	250.00
Waffle Iron, Griswold, No. 9, Iron, Pat'd Dec. 1, 1908, 2 Piece	100.00
Waffle Iron, Griswold, No. 12, Hotel, Cast Iron	110.00
Waffle Iron, Hall, Flowered Ceramic Top	265.00
Waffle Iron, Ray-O-Noc, Griswold, No. 8	50.00
Waffle Iron, Stover Junior, No. 8	160.00
Waffle Iron, Wagnerware, Signed, Pat. Feb. 22, Salesman's Sample, 1910, 3 x 4 In.	695.00
Washboard, Country Art, 14 1/2 x 7 In.	850.00
Washboard, Maple, Soap Box Carved Into Crest, 18th Century, 26 1/2 In.	525.00
Washtub, Galvanized Tin, 2 Handles, Salesman's Sample, Oval, 14 x 4 1/2 In.	45.00

KNIFE collectors usually specialize in a single type. In the 1960s, the
United States government passed a law that required knife manufacturers to mark their knives with the country of origin. This seemed to
encourage the collectors, and knife collecting became an interest of a
large group of people. All types of knives are collected, from top quality twentieth-century examples to old bone- or pearl-handled knives in
excellent condition.

Aluminum Handle, Bayonet Style Blade, Integral Cross Guard, Home Made, 7 1/2 In.	30.00
Bolo, Canvas, Leather Scabbard, Philadelphia, 1917	165.00

Bolo, Leather Scabbard, 1911 .... 240.00
Bone-Horn Handle, Joseph Rogers & Sons, 19th Century, 9 3/4 In., 5 Piece 175.00
Boot, Manhattan, Buffalo Horn Handle, Mother-Of-Pearl Inlay, Sheath 350.00
Boot, Sheffield, Mother-Of-Pearl Handle, 9 In. 300.00
Bowie, Brass Handle, 17 3/8 In. 910.00
Bowie, Confederate, D-Guard, Civil War, 16 1/4 In. 595.00
Bowie, D-Guard 750.00
Bowie, Fileguard Blade, Copper Butt, 18 1/2 In. 360.00
Bowie, Horn Handle, Star Cut In Butt, Hand Made Scabbard, 1900, 11 3/8 In. 220.00
Bowie, Knuckleduster, Liberty, Metal Grip, Eagle Head Pommel, Nylon Sheath, 9 1/2 In. .. 20.00
Bowie, Original Bowie Knife, Stag Grips, G.C. Co., Germany, 8-In. Blade 35.00
Bowie, Sheath, Etched Blade, Buffalo Horn Handle 375.00
Bowie, Walnut Grip, Brass Fittings, Leather Sheath, 1870s, 19 1/4 In. 650.00
California Style, Side, Double Edge Spear Point, Horn & Silver Scabbard, 9 1/2 In. 1200.00
Crooked, Chip Carved Diamonds & Hearts, Painted 1700.00
Dagger, Army Officer's Dagger With Name On Reverse Of Crossguard 400.00
Dagger, Croatian Air Force, Celluloid Grip, Nickered 2-Ring Scabbard 1010.00
Dagger, Ivory, Han-Style, Tao Tieh Mask, Pommel, Inscription, Box, 16 In. 575.00
Dagger, Luftwaffe, 1st Model 325.00
Dagger, Luftwaffe, 2nd Model 200.00
Dagger, Navy Officer Dagger, Silver 380.00
Dagger, Red Cross Hewer With Frog & Knot 460.00
Dagger, Steel Blade, Jade Grip, Foliage Ending In Ram's Head, Ruby Eyes, 18th Century 6900.00
Elkhorn Handle, Brass Cap, Belt, 4 1/8-In. Blade 170.00
Folding Blade, Maleham & Yeoman, Stag Grip, 4 5/8 In. 495.00
Ford, Nashville Dealer, Ornate Design Handle, Late 1920s 45.00
Hunting, Stag Handle 71.00
Hunting, Stag Handle, Leather Scabbard, Wm. Groaves, Hall Sheffield, 10 1/2 In. 175.00
Hunting, Stag Handle, Sheffield Blade, Brass Mount, 8 In. 135.00
Hunting, Stag Handle, Steel Blade, Brown Leather Sheath, Wilbert Cutlery, 8 3/4 In. 45.00
Hunting, Walnut Case, Signed, C.R. Sigman, Red House, W. Va., 9 1/2 In. 40.00
Jackknife, Horn Crosshatched Panels, Spanish, 18th Century 120.00
Jackknife, U.S. Navy, 5 Blades, Military Issue, Bone Grips 295.00
Long, Chip Carved Wood Scabbard, Brass Bands, Bolo Style Blade, Africa, 28 In. 175.00
Long, Varnished Wood Scabbard, Tin Bands, Stylized Animal Head, Africa, 25 In. 85.00
Machete, Engineer's, Walnut Handles, 15 In. 60.00
Penny, Wooden Handle, 19th Century 60.00
Plainsman, Flexible Steel, Iron Riveted Handle, 19th Century, 10 1/8 In. 315.00
Pocket, Anheuser-Busch, St. Louis, Brass, With Corkscrew, 3 1/4 In. 23.00
Pocket, Boker, Tree Brand, Lockback, Brown Plastic Handle, Tree Medallions, 3 1/4 In. . 20.00
Pocket, Cattaraugus, 3 Blades, Brown Bone Handles 30.00
Pocket, Hitler Youth Knife, With Motto 100.00
Red Ryder, Boy's First Knife, Steel Blade, Rubber Handle, Sheath, Box, 11 1/4 In. 22.00
Remington, 2 Blades, Pearl Handle 65.00
Remington, Deer Scene, Original Sheath, Etched Blade 145.00
Schrade, Kentucky Rifle 28.00
Sheath, Mother-Of-Pearl Handle, Signed, 8 In. 80.00
Skinning, Beaded, Blue, White, Red, Black 95.00
Skinning, Burl Handle, Engraved Floral, 4 1/4 In. 60.00
Skinning, Olsen, O.K., Stainless Steel Blade, Hardwood Grips, Leather Sheath, 3 3/4 In. .. 20.00
Skinning, Rawhide Sheath, Yellow, Green, Red, 1960, 9 1/2 In. 80.00
Skinning, Russell Green River Camp, 1870s, 6 1/4 In. 95.00
Stag Handle, Leather Sheath, Germany, 11 In. 60.00
Survival, Pilot's, Vietnam, Sheath 90.00
Trench, Marked, Eickhorn 182.00
U.S. Model 1909 Bolo, Springfield, Blade Dated 1910, 13 3/4 In. 60.00
Winchester, 3 Blades, Bone Handle, Pocket, 2 3/8 In. 111.00
Winchester, Black Bone Handles, 3 Blades, Pocket 110.00
Wostenholm, 3 Blades, Scissors, Rattlesnake Both Sides, 1890s 300.00

KNOWLES, TAYLOR & KNOWLES items may be found in the KTK and Lotus Ware categories.

KOREAN WARE, see Sumida.

KOSTA, the oldest Swedish glass factory, was founded in 1742. During the 1920s through the 1950s, many pieces of original design were made at the factory. The firm is still working.

LU
KOSTA

Bowl, Ice, 4 1/2 In.	30.00
Bowl, Lime Green Stripe, Blue Rim Wrap, Signed, 4 1/4 In.	57.00
Bowl, Radiating Leaf Design, Flared Rim, Signed, 12 1/2 In.	92.00
Candlestick, Teardrop, Lindstrom, 10 In., Pair	250.00
Carafe, Applied Arms, Stoppers, Press Molded Faces, Erik Hoglund, 1950, 11 In., Pair	385.00
Paperweight, Mushroom, Internal Bubbles Over Stem, Signed, 3 3/4 In.	287.00
Vase, Blue, Green Abstract, Cylindrical, 11 1/2 In.	690.00
Vase, Bud, Floating Bubbles, Foil Stamp, 7 3/4 In.	35.00
Vase, Rainbow, Signed, 11 1/2 In.	125.00
Vase, Triangular, Ribbed, 7 1/4 In.	140.00
Vase, White, Black Internal Canes, Vicke Lindstrand, 1950, 13 In.	330.00

KPM refers to Berlin porcelain, but the same initials were used alone and in combination with other symbols by several German porcelain makers. They include the Konigliche Porzellan Manufaktur of Berlin, initials used in mark, 1823–1847; Meissen, 1723–1724 only; Krister Porzellan Manufaktur in Waldenburg, after 1831; Kranichfelder Porzellan Manufaktur in Kranichfeld, after 1903; and the Kister Porzellan Manufaktur in Scheibe, after 1838.

K.P.M

Basket, Reticulated, Raised On 3 Gilt Paw Feet, 9 1/4 In.	920.00
Bowl, Painted Art Deco Style, Fish & Sea Grasses, 6 1/2 In.	345.00
Bowl, Undertray, Gilt Foliate, Blue Rims, Beaded Border, Signed, 4 3/4 x 9 In., Pair	460.00
Bust, Woman, White, Pastel, Gilt, 12 1/2 In.	250.00
Clock, Mantel, Penguin, Bird Perched On Case, Enamel Dial, c.1890, 23 In.	1495.00
Cup & Saucer, Landscape, Game Birds, 19th Century	245.00
Cup & Saucer, Stately Home Panel, Gilt Band, Marked, 6 In.	400.00
Figurine, Cat, White, 14 x 5 3/4 In.	90.00
Figurine, Europa & Bull, White, Lavender, Entering The Sea, Gilt, 1923, 15 1/2 In.	1725.00
Figurine, Mercury, 8 1/4 In.	460.00
Plaque, 3 Neoclassical Draped Female Figures In Moonlit Night Scene, 9 x 6 In.	1265.00
Plaque, Abraham Casting Out Hagar, Ehrhardt, Frame, 13 1/4 x 11 1/4 In.	4600.00
Plaque, Ascension Of The Virgin, Gazing Upward, Frame, 9 1/2 x 7 1/4 In.	3450.00
Plaque, Children Scene, Schoolgirl With Slate, Young Boy With Apple, 6 x 4 In.	4025.00
Plaque, Christ In The Temple, Blue, Green, Mauve, Yellow, Black, 12 x 15 In.	3450.00
Plaque, Clementine, Laurel Wreath In Hair, Von L. Schunzell, 11 1/2 x 8 7/8 In.	6900.00
Plaque, Goodnight Linette, No. 314, Signed, 8 1/8 x 6 1/4 In.	2200.00
Plaque, Gypsy, Velvet & Giltwood Frame, 10 3/4 x 8 7/8 In.	3680.00
Plaque, Lady Playing Organ, Bronze Frame, 5 In.	375.00
Plaque, Madonna & Child, Gilt Frame, 18 1/2 x 14 1/2 In.	3520.00
Plaque, Portrait, Madame Butterfly, Signed, 9 1/4 x 6 In.	2185.00
Plaque, Portrait, Rembrandt's Father, Giltwood Frame, 15 x 12 1/4 In.	3450.00
Plaque, Portrait, Rembrandt, Giltwood Fame, 15 x 12 1/2 In.	4875.00
Plaque, Seminude Woman, Reading Book, 19th Century	6050.00
Plaque, Three Fates, Wood Frame, 15 7/8 x 10 1/4 In.	6325.00
Plaque, Tooth Extractor, 1844, 8 3/4 x 10 7/8 In.	6900.00
Plaque, Vision, Woman, Signed Werner, Oval, Late 19th-Early 20th Century, 13 1/2 In.	2300.00
Plaque, Voluptuous Nudes Menaced By Armed Soldier, Frame, 9 1/2 x 12 In.	4600.00
Plate, Colorful Spray Of Autumnal Flowers, Gilt Rim, 10 1/4 In., 9 Piece	287.00
Plate, Multicolored Fruit, Off-White Ground, Gilt Border, Signed, 8 1/2 In., 4 Piece	258.00
Plate, Portrait, Frederick The Great, Reticulated, Octagonal, 9 1/8 In.	230.00
Salt, Cherub, Standing Between 2 Oval Bowls, Scrolled Feet	175.00
Tureen, Grapes & Leaves, Strawberry Finial, Figural Handles, 12 In.	1265.00
Tureen, Vegetable, Cover, Lavender, Green, Oval, 1850-1870, 14 In.	460.00
Vase, Double Gourd, Foliate Sprays, Turquoise, Late 19th Century, 14 In.	632.00
Vase, Figural, Cherub Pulling Shoe-Shaped Cart, 5 1/2 In.	90.00
Vase, Figural, Fairy With 2 Cornucopia Horns, Footed Base, 8 In.	35.00

If the glaze on your dishes is crazed, covered with small lines and cracks, don't use them to serve greasy food like butter or cream or bright-colored food like beets. The foods will stain the ceramic under the crazed glaze.

KTK, Platter, Blue Birds, 14 In.

KTK are the initials of the Knowles, Taylor & Knowles Company of East Liverpool, Ohio, founded by Isaac W. Knowles in 1853. The company made many types of utilitarian wares, hotel china, and dinnerwares. They made the fine bone china known as Lotus Ware from 1891 to 1896. The company merged with American Ceramic Corporation in 1928. It closed in 1934. Lotus Ware is listed in its own category in this book.

K.T.&K.
CHINA

Gravy Boat, Black Decal	20.00
Jug, Diamond Club Whiskey	110.00
Platter, Blue Birds, 14 In. ....*Illus*	100.00

KU KLUX KLAN items are now collected because of their historic importance. Literature, robes, and memorabilia are available. The Klan is still in existence, so new material is found.

Application Form, Gentile Or Jew, White Or Black, Questions, 8 1/2 x 11 In.	33.00
Book, Clansman, Historical Romance Of Ku Klux Klan, Thomas Dixon, 1905	16.00
Book, International Jew, World's Foremost Problem, Dearborn Pub. Co., 1920	25.00
Book, Songs About The Klan, Mary Goodwin, Major Kleagle Of Pa., 32 Pages	150.00
Book, Songs For Women Of The Ku Klux Klan, 31 Pages	250.00
Book, White, Kloran, Knights Of The Ku Klux Klan, K-UNO, 1916, 56 Pages	75.00
Button, Altoona, Pa., Konvention, Celluloid, 1 3/4 In.	112.00
Button, Fall Festivities, Oct. 4, 5, 6, Kansas City, 1898, 1 1/2 In.	135.00
Card, Identification, Invited Guest, Questions Other Side, 3 x 5 In.	18.00
Ceremonial Sash, Order Of The White Rose, Burgundy Silk, Fringe, 32 In.	57.00
Document, Kligrapp's Quarterly Report, Financial Statement, 1927	20.00
Handbook, Knight Of The Ku Klux Klan, David Duke, 1980	12.00
Hat, Felt, With Tassel	210.00
Knife, 3 Blades, Pocket	50.00
Knife, Loyal Order, 3 1/4 In.	155.00
Lantern, Front Opens To Light, 2 Red Glass Discs, 8 In.	440.00
Mirror, Today, Tomorrow & Forever, Sheet-Covered Horse, Rider, Pocket, 2 1/4 In.	1100.00
Photograph, Decorated Truck, Men, Hancock Klan 17, Frame, 9 x 11 In.	200.00
Plaque, Klan Symbols & Lettering, Plaster, Painted, 1920s, 8 x 9 In.	370.00
Plate, Burning Cross In Center, Edwin M. Knowles China Co., 6 In.	85.00
Plate, God Give Us Men, Scalloped Edge, China, 6 1/4 In.	85.00
Plate, Horse, Rider & Cross Burning, Yesterday To-Day & Forever, 1865, 6 In.	85.00
Postcard, Klan On Horses, Miami, Florida	75.00
Postcard, Pageant Day Parade, Flagler St., Miami, Florida, Unused	200.00
Record, A Victim Of The Big Mess, Pres. Johnson's Great Society Programs	44.00
Record, Flight NAACP 105, Voice Of Alabama, Rebel Label	44.00
Record, Looking For A Handout, Kajun Ku Klux Klan, 1960, 45 RPM	44.00
Robe, Brown, Pointed Hood, Skull & Crossbones On Hood, 19th Century	250.00
Stamp, Woman Of The Ku Klux Klan, Cast Iron, 8 1/2 In.	220.00
Statue, Kigy, Ku Klux Klan Member, Plaster, 16 1/4 In.	300.00
Statue, Man In Ku Klux Klan Uniform, Crossing Arms, Chalkware, 8 In.	260.00
Tag, Women, May 31, 1926, Dryden, 2 x 4 In.	27.50

Ticket, Barbecue & Naturalization Ceremony, Chattanooga, Tenn. 30.00
Token, I Was There, Illinois, 1928 . . . . 93.00

KUTANI ware is a Japanese porcelain made after the mid-seventeenth century. Most of the pieces found today are nineteenth-century. Collectors often use the term *kutani* to refer to just the later, colorful pieces decorated with red, gold, and black pictures of warriors, animals, and birds.

Bowl, Sauce, Spinach & Straw Glaze, Signed, 4 In. 70.00
Charger, Cartouche Of Warriors, Birds & Flowers, Snowy Landscape, 15 1/2 In. 390.00
Charger, Dragon, Phoenix Design, Blue, White, 18 In. 60.00
Lamp, Made From Vase, 12 Circles Showing Daily Life, Handles, Shade, 25 In. 405.00
Pitcher, Floral, Birds & Flying Storks, Gilt Rim, c.1875, 7 1/2 In. 395.00
Plate, Orange Dragon Interior, Gold Lined, Scalloped Edge, 7 1/4 In., 3 Piece 300.00
Plate, Pomegranate & Buddha's Hand Fruit, 7 In., 4 Piece 120.00
Umbrella Stand, Birds In Flight, Chrysanthemums, 19th Century, 25 In. 460.00
Vase, Dragon Handles At Neck, Views Interior, Figures Exterior, 12 In. 150.00
Vase, Eagles, Flowers, Birds, Blue, White Glaze, Arita Ware, 49 In., Pair 2875.00

L.G. WRIGHT Glass Company of New Martinsville, West Virginia, started selling glassware in 1937. Founder "Si" Wright contracted with Ohio and West Virginia glass factories to reproduce popular pressed glass patterns, like Rose & Snow, Baltimore Pear, and Three Face, and opalescent patterns, like Daisy & Fern and Swirl. Collectors can tell the difference between the original glasswares and L.G. Wright reproductions because of colors and differences in production techniques. Some L.G. Wright items are marked with an underlined W in a circle. Items that were made from old Northwood molds have an altered Northwood mark—an angled line was added to the N to make it look like a W. Collectors refer to this mark as "the wobbly W." The L.G. Wright factory was closed and the existing molds sold in 1999.

Coin Spot, Lamp, Cranberry Opalescent, 16 1/4 In. 250.00
Daisy & Fern, Basket, Loop Handle, Cranberry Opalescent, 12 x 7 In. 295.00
Daisy & Fern, Basket, Twist Handle, Topaz Opalescent 200.00
Daisy & Fern, Bottle, Barber, Blue Opalescent 95.00
Daisy & Fern, Pitcher, Water, Blue Opalescent 225.00
Daisy & Fern, Pitcher, Water, Topaz 195.00
Daisy & Fern, Pitcher, Water, Yellow Opalescent 290.00
Daisy & Fern, Rose Bowl, 4 In. 85.00
Daisy & Fern, Tumbler, Cranberry Opalescent, 3 3/4 In. 40.00
Peach Crest, Epergne, 16 In., 2 Piece 450.00

LACQUER is a type of varnish. Collectors are most interested in the Chinese and Japanese lacquer wares made from the Japanese varnish tree. Lacquer wares are made from wood with many coats of lacquer. Sometimes the piece is carved or decorated with ivory or metal inlay.

Box, Dresser, Mother-Of-Pearl, Gilt, Fitted Interior, Ivory Needle Case, c.1803, 3 1/2 In. . . 220.00
Box, Game, Gilt, Black, 5 1/2 x 14 In. 345.00
Butsudan, Figure Of Buddha, Flame Mandala, Brocade Exterior, 4 In. 725.00
Butsudan, Figure Of Fuo Mio, Seated, 9 1/2 In. 605.00
Comb, Rabbit & Wave Design, Gold, 5 In. 78.00
Cup, Sake, Crane & Pine Tree, Red & Gold 120.00
Desk, Lap, Painted Cover, Inset Velvet Writing Surface, Victorian, 4 x 13 x 9 1/2 In. 200.00
Panel, Mother-Of-Pearl, Eagles Perched On Branches, Wood, 23 In., Pair 690.00
Screen, Pole, Scalloped Panel, Chinoiserie Design, Tripod Base, Brass, c.1810, 59 1/2 In. . . 825.00
Tray, Artisans Making & Selling Wares, Black, Oriental, 9 1/2 x 12 1/2 In. 210.00
Tray, Bamboo & Chrysanthemum Design, Shinsaka Hosogawa Kaoku, 15 1/2 In. 60.00
Tray, Engraved Gyokusai, Geese & Rolling Waves, Black & Gold, Square, 13 In., Pair . . . 145.00
Tray, Pen, Black & Gold, Figural, China, 19th Century, 9 In. 75.00

LADY HEAD VASE, see Head Vase.

LALIQUE glass was made by Rene Lalique in Paris, France, between the 1890s and his death in 1945. The glass was molded, pressed, and engraved in Art Nouveau and Art Deco styles. Pieces were marked with the signature *R. Lalique*. Lalique glass is still being made. Pieces made after 1945 bear the mark *Lalique*. Jewelry made by Rene Lalique is listed in the Jewelry category.

LaLique

Ashtray, Leaf Design Edge, 5 1/8 In.	97.00
Ashtray, Overlapping Veined Leaves, 5 3/4 In.	85.00
Bowl, Bulbes, Central Flower, Bulb, Flared Rim, Circular, 10 In.	575.00
Bowl, Coquilles, 3 1/2 x 9 In.	1000.00
Bowl, Dahlias No. 1, Large Blossoms, Leaves, Blossom Feet, 9 1/4 x 3 5/8 In.	1093.00
Bowl, Gui, Berried Mistletoe Branches, Gray Enamel, 1921, 10 In.	260.00
Bowl, Nemours, Radiating Rings Of Flowers, Black Enameled Centers, 1929, 4 x 10 In.	632.00
Bowl, Ondes, Low Relief, Diminishing Elliptical Disks, Opalescent, 1934, 8 In.	488.00
Bowl, Ondines, Medium Relief, Nude Maidens, Floating, Opalescent, 1921, 8 In.	1610.00
Bowl, Perruches, Band Of 20 Molded Love Birds, Blossoms, 9 3/4 In.	2990.00
Bowl, Pinsons, Birds On Stylized Branches, 8 1/4 In.	690.00
Bowl, Sirene, Opalescent, Mermaid, Swirling Bubbles, 3 Conical Feet, 1920, 14 In.	4315.00
Bowl, Vernon, Large Sunflower Blossoms, Opalescent, 8 1/2 x 2 1/8 In.	690.00
Box, Cover, Amour Assis, Full Relief, Child, Seated Above Flowers, Coral Patina, 5 In.	3680.00
Box, Cover, Enfants, Bands Of Infants Supporting Tiers Of Roses, Coral Patina, 3 In.	1265.00
Box, Cover, Libellules, Medium Relief, 3 Dragonflies, Opalescent, 1921, 6 3/4 In.	805.00
Box, Cover, Quatre Papillons, 4 Butterflies Circling The Center, Floral Design, 3 x 2 In.	920.00
Box, Cover, Roger, Molded With Birds, Brown Patina, Marked, 5 1/4 In.	690.00
Box, Cover, Sultane, Seated Nude On Lid, Frosted, Square, 5 1/2 x 5 1/2 In.	8912.00
Box, Cover, Three Dahlias, Flowers Inside Cover, Satin Bottom, Signed, 1932, 8 1/2 In.	1000.00
Box, Emiliane, Floral, Colorless Molded, D'Orsay, 4 In.	260.00
Candlestick, Mesanges, 2 Birds, Encircled By Flowers, Signed, 6 1/2 In., Pair	675.00
Carafe, Sainte Odile, Profile Medallion Of Ste. Odile, Signed, 1927, 7 1/2 In.	805.00
Clock, Quatre Perruches, Birds, Perching Below Leafy Branches, Gray, 1920, 6 In.	1380.00
Decanter, Femmes Antiques, 8 Neoclassical Women, Oval, 9 1/2 In.	545.00
Figurine, Birds, Crystal, 5 1/2 In., Pair	92.00
Figurine, Chat Assis, Cat, Seated, Signed, 1932, 8 1/8 In.	1725.00
Figurine, Deux Danseuses, 2 Dancing Female Nudes, Frosted, Signed, 10 In.	550.00
Figurine, Deux Poissons, 2 Fish Encircling Each Other, Frosted, 12 In.	800.00
Figurine, Elephant, Standing, Upraised Curled Trunk, 1932, 13 1/4 In.	14950.00
Figurine, Longchamp, Full Relief, Stylized Head Of Horse, Gray Glass, 1929, 5 In.	2760.00
Figurine, Victoire, Full Relief, Female Head, Stylized Wind Blown Hair, Smoky Gray	8050.00
Hood Ornament, Grand Libellule, Frosted, Dragonfly, Wings Raised, 1928, 8 x 7 In.	7475.00
Hood Ornament, Libellule, Full Relief, Stylized Dragonfly, Gray, 1928, 8 1/2 In.	2760.00
Hood Ornament, Longchamp, Frosted, Horse's Head, Mane Streaming, 1929, 6 In.	4025.00
Hood Ornament, Perche, Perch Swimming Upward, 1929, 3 3/4 In.	5750.00
Hood Ornament, Saint-Christophe, Carrying The Christ Child, 1928, 4 1/2 In.	865.00
Lamp, Oil, Artichaut, Full Relief, Artichoke Leaves, Gray, 1927, 3 1/2 In.	1380.00
Lamp, Table, Suzanne, Frosted Amber, Nude Dancer, Outstretched Arms, 1925, 9 In.	6620.00
Oil & Vinegar Bottle, Bourgueil, Triangular Design, Flared Stoppers, 1933, 5 In., Pair	230.00
Paperweight, Bison, Buffalo, Frosted, 4 3/4 In.	410.00
Paperweight, Coq Nain, Head Lowered Tail Raised, Signed, 1928, 7 3/4 In.	1380.00
Paperweight, Coq Nain, Rooster, Crouching, Signed, 8 In.	750.00
Paperweight, Hibou, Owl, On Stump, Etched & Clear Glass, 3 1/2 In.	193.00
Paperweight, Perche, Frosted Fish, Signed, 4 x 6 In.	310.00
Perfume Bottle, Amelie, Medium Emerald Green, Tiers Of Leafage, Stopper, 3 In.	2300.00
Perfume Bottle, Anses Et Bouchon Marguerite, Thistle Side Handles, Stopper, 5 In.	3735.00
Perfume Bottle, Au Coeur Des Calices, Coty, Petals Interior, Honey Bee Stopper, 3 In.	9200.00
Perfume Bottle, Bobine, Worth, Coiled Rope Form, Clear Glass Stopper, 1944	5175.00
Perfume Bottle, Bouchon Cassis, Molded Berries, Blue Stripes, Blue Stopper, 4 1/2 In.	8050.00
Perfume Bottle, Bouchon Eucalyptus, Leafage, Berries, Gray, Green Patina, Stopper	20700.00
Perfume Bottle, Bouchon Fleurs De Pommier, Scallops, Tiara Stopper, 5 In.	16305.00
Perfume Bottle, Bouchon Mures, Mulberry Clusters, Ornate Stopper, 5 1/2 In.	9200.00
Perfume Bottle, Bouchon Papillon, Overlapping Butterflies, Stopper, 3 In.	2415.00
Perfume Bottle, Bouquet De Faunes, Guerlain, Low Relief, 4 Heads, Stopper, 4 In.	488.00
Perfume Bottle, Calendal, Molinard, Nude Female Dancers, Flowerhead Stopper, 5 In.	8050.00

Perfume Bottle, Camille, Medium Emerald Green, Twisted Fringe, Stopper, 3 In. 1840.00
Perfume Bottle, Capricorne, Scarabs, Spiral Design, Button Stopper, 3 1/2 In. 10300.00
Perfume Bottle, Carnette Fleur, Ribbed Body, Brown Patina, Pistil Stopper, 5 In. 4025.00
Perfume Bottle, Chypre, Wisteria, Ball Form Inner Stopper, Purple Patina, 4 In. 1610.00
Perfume Bottle, Cigales, Cicadas At Each Corner, Daisy Stopper, 1910, 5 In. 2415.00
Perfume Bottle, Cigalia, Roger & Gallet, Cicadas, Branch Stopper, 1925, 7 In. 1955.00
Perfume Bottle, Clamart, Berry Shape, Leaves, Blue, Gray Patina, Stopper, 4 1/2 In. 2745.00
Perfume Bottle, Coeur Joie, Nina Ricci, Heart Shape, Frosted, 4 In. 450.00
Perfume Bottle, Coeur Joie, Nina Ricci, Open Heart, Frosted, 4 In. 325.00
Perfume Bottle, Coeur Joie, Nina Ricci, Purse Flacon, Brass Screw Cap, 6 In. 815.00
Perfume Bottle, Dahlia, Stopper Forming Flower Center, 1 1/2 x 2 3/4 In. 1150.00
Perfume Bottle, Deux Fleurs, Signed, 3 3/4 In. 200.00
Perfume Bottle, Enfants, Domed Stopper, 1950, 4 x 3 5/8 In. 845.00
Perfume Bottle, Enfants, Medium Relief, Bands Of Infants, Tiers Of Roses, Stopper 460.00
Perfume Bottle, Epines, Molded With Thorny Branches, Blue Patina, Stopper, 5 In. 805.00
Perfume Bottle, Flausa, Roger & Gallet, Satin, Peach Stain, 4 3/4 In. ....*Illus* 6325.00
Perfume Bottle, Fleurs Concaves, Indented Flower Heads, Pale Blue Patina, 5 In. 2185.00
Perfume Bottle, Gri-Gri, Volnay, Brain Coral, Stopper, 1924, 3 3/4 In. 3335.00
Perfume Bottle, Gros Fruits, Volnay, Fruit Laden Branches, Leaf Stopper, 1919, 6 In. ... 5460.00
Perfume Bottle, Inalda, Delettrez, Band Of Black Dots On Stopper, 1930, 4 In. 3735.00
Perfume Bottle, Jardinee, Volney, Flowerhead Body, Stopper, 1922, 5 In. 2300.00
Perfume Bottle, Je Reviens, Worth, Signed, 1929, 11 1/4 In. 287.00
Perfume Bottle, Jeunesse, Cherub, On Block Of Ice, Stopper, 1933, 4 1/8 In. 13730.00
Perfume Bottle, Jeunesse, Cherub, Standing On Block Of Ice, Stopper, 1933, 4 1/8 In. .. 8625.00
Perfume Bottle, L'Air Du Temps, Nina Ricci, Double Dove, Box 265.00
Perfume Bottle, L'Elegance, D'Orsay, 2 Maidens, Patina, Flowerhead Stopper, 4 In. 2415.00
Perfume Bottle, L'Origan, Coty, Factice Flacon, Thorn, Ground Glass Stopper, Signed .. 690.00
Perfume Bottle, La Belle Saison, Leafy Branches, Centered By Maiden Figure, Stopper . 747.00
Perfume Bottle, Laurence, Masques, Blossoms, Original Tan Silk Cord, 1 1/2 In. 2630.00
Perfume Bottle, Le Jade, Roger Et Gallet, Jungle Bird Design, Green, Stopper, 3 1/4 In. . 2185.00
Perfume Bottle, Le Parfum Des Anges, Angels, X-Form Stopper, Oviatt, 1927, 3 In. 2645.00
Perfume Bottle, Le Parfum Des Anges, Facing Angels, Patina, Oviatt, 1927, 8 In. 7295.00
Perfume Bottle, Lentille, Rows Of Stylized Flowers, Brown, Glass Stopper, 2 In. ·..... 1890.00
Perfume Bottle, Lepage, Flower Heads, 2 Nude Female Figures, Stopper, 1920, 5 In. ... 5750.00
Perfume Bottle, Les Roses D'Orsay, D'Orsay, Chevrons, Arches, Female Stopper, 4 In. .. 2875.00
Perfume Bottle, Lezards, Frieze Of Lizards At Base, Stopper, 1911, 4 3/4 In. 3450.00
Perfume Bottle, Lunaria, Charcoal Gray Patina, Floriform Stopper, 1912, 2 7/8 In. 5175.00
Perfume Bottle, Muguet, Lily Of The Valley, Bouquet, Stopper, Blue Patina, 4 In. 13300.00
Perfume Bottle, Myosotis, Nude Female, Kneeling, Stopper, 1928, 10 In. 5175.00
Perfume Bottle, Nenuphar, Leaves, Pale Orange Patina, 1911, 4 7/8 In. 3735.00
Perfume Bottle, Olives, 8 Olives Protruding Around Base, Frosted Stopper, 4 1/2 In. 3950.00
Perfume Bottle, Olives, Stylized Olives, Stopper, 5 In. 1840.00

To loosen a perfume bottle stopper, put the bottle upside down in alcohol for a few days. It may help.

To dry a decanter or narrow-necked bottle or vase, try this method. Roll up a paper towel and insert it into the narrow neck until it is about an inch from the bottom of the bottle. The towel will absorb the moisture in the bottle in a day or so.

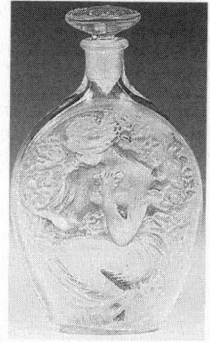

Lalique, Perfume Bottle, Flausa,
Roger & Gallet, Satin, Peach Stain, 4 3/4 In.

Perfume Bottle, Oree, Claire, Maidens, Flowers, Rectangular Stopper, 3 In. . . . . .545.00 to 2010.00
Perfume Bottle, Pan, Flower Heads, Masks Between Floral Festoons, Stopper, 5 In. 2875.00
Perfume Bottle, Panier De Roses, Roses, With Trellis, Gray Patina, Stopper, 4 In. 2585.00
Perfume Bottle, Pavot, Flowerhead, Leafage, Black Glass Stopper, 1910, 3 In. 5460.00
Perfume Bottle, Quatre Soleils, 4 Floral Roundels, Pale Brown Patina, 1912, 3 In. 4600.00
Perfume Bottle, Rien Que Du Bonheur, Arys, Beaded Edge, Stopper, 1920, 4 In. 1380.00
Perfume Bottle, Rosace Figurines, 4 Maidens, Moth Stopper, 4 1/2 In. . . . . . .3450.00 to 12015.00
Perfume Bottle, Salamandres, Salamanders, Fruit, Gray Green Patina, Stopper, 3 3/4 In. . 1495.00
Perfume Bottle, Salamandres, Salamanders, Fruit, Patina, Stopper, 1914, 3 7/8 In. 2530.00
Perfume Bottle, Sans Adieu, Green, Worth, Graduated Concentric Rings, Stopper, 5 In. . . 1150.00
Perfume Bottle, Satyr, Horned Faun Stopper, 1933, 3 5/8 In. 9200.00
Perfume Bottle, Serpent, Coiling Snake Skin Body, Snake Head Stopper, 1920, 4 In. . . . 1840.00
Perfume Bottle, Styx, Coty, Ribbed, Circle Of Wasps On Rim, Floriform Stopper, 5 In. . . 1495.00
Perfume Bottle, Tantot, Palmettes Design, Stopper, 1925, 5 7/8 In. 2990.00
Perfume Bottle, Vers Le Jour, Frosted Amber, Moon Shaped, 1926, 5 In. 805.00
Perfume Bottle, Vers Le Jour, Worth, Alternating Chevrons, Amber Triangles, 6 In. 1265.00
Perfume Bottle, Vinca, Coryse, Overlapping Black Mat Squared, White Stopper, 3 In. . . . 5175.00
Plafonnier, Provence, Molded With Leaves, Ceiling Fixture, Globular, 14 In. 2990.00
Plate, Ondines, Medium Relief, Female Nudes, Floating, Opalescent, 1929, 11 In. 1725.00
Vase, Actinia, Wavy Sawtooth Design, Frosted, 1934, 8 5/8 In. 460.00
Vase, Allover Leaf Design, Globular Form, Opalescent, Signed, 6 1/2 In. 1200.00
Vase, Archers, Nude Male Archers, Swooping Birds, Blue, 1921, 10 1/4 In. 15525.00
Vase, Archers, Nude Male Archers, Swooping Birds, Green Patina, 1921, 10 1/4 In. 5175.00
Vase, Avallon, Birds & Berries, Signed, 5 1/2 In. 1035.00
Vase, Bacchantes, Nudes Surround Vase, 1927, 10 In. 1950.00
Vase, Camaret, 4 Bands Of Fish, Gray Enamel, Globular, 1928, 5 3/8 In. 520.00
Vase, Camees, Everted Rim, Nude Maidens In Cameos, 1923, 10 In. 8050.00
Vase, Chamois, Stylized Gazelles, 2 Overlapping Tiers, Tan Patina, 1931, 5 In. 2300.00
Vase, Coqs Et Raisins, Long-Tailed Roosters, Beneath Grapevines, 1928, 6 In. 1150.00
Vase, Coqs Et Raisins, Long-Tailed Roosters, Grapevines, Red Patina, Gray, 1928, 6 In. . . 3162.00
Vase, Danaides, Nudes, Emptying Urns Of Water, Opalescent, Gray Patina, 7 In. 1840.00 to 2415.00
Vase, Davos, Opalescent Glass, 1932, 11 1/4 In. 2875.00
Vase, Druide, Overlapping Berried Branches, Opalescent, Footed, 1924, 6 3/4 In. 862.00
Vase, Eglantines, Thorny Branches, Rose Blossoms, 4 1/2 In. 403.00
Vase, Esterel, Molded With Leaves, Branches, Amber, 16 In. 1495.00
Vase, Eucalyptus, Vertical Overlapping Leaves, Knobby Feet, 1925, 6 1/2 In. 1380.00
Vase, Faune, Amidst Grape Vines, Black Patina, Gray, Handles, 1931, 12 1/2 In. 7187.00
Vase, Formose, Fish, Entwining, Opalescent, 1924, 6 3/4 In. . . . . .1150.00 to 2300.00
Vase, Formose, Overall Goldfish, Tails, Fins, White, Pale Blue, 1924, 6 3/4 In. 1610.00
Vase, Gros Scarabees, Large Scarab Beetles, White Patina, 1923, 11 3/8 In. 3737.00
Vase, Gui, Mistletoe, Interwoven Sprigs Of Mistletoe, Opalescent, 6 3/4 In. . . . .1035.00 to 1265.00
Vase, Laurier, Berried Laurel Branches, Signed, 1922, 7 5/8 In. 805.00
Vase, Lievres, Jack Rabbits, Leaping Amongst Spiraling Vine, Opalescent, 1923, 6 In. . . . 1840.00
Vase, Malaga, For Washing Grapes, Grape Bunch Design, 5 3/4 In. 575.00
Vase, Marisa, Trout, Spiral Design, Gray Frosted, Round, 9 1/2 In. 2990.00
Vase, Marquerites, Daisy, Blown, Floral, Blue Patina, 8 1/4 In. 1092.00
Vase, Moissac, Raised Leaf Form, Blue Patina, Flared, 5 1/4 x 6 In. 977.00
Vase, Mossi, Clear, Protruding Disks, Frosted Ground, Script Signature, 8 In. 231.00
Vase, Ormeaux, Elm Leaves, Overlapping, Gray, Spherical, 6 1/2 In. 920.00
Vase, Ormeaux, Elm Leaves, Overlapping, Red Amber, Spherical, 6 1/2 In. 2185.00
Vase, Ormeaux, Elm Leaves, Overlapping, White Patina, Amber, Spherical, 6 1/2 In. 1265.00
Vase, Perruches, Pairs Of Love Birds, Perched On Branches, Blue, 10 1/2 In. 9775.00
Vase, Poissons, Tropical Fish In Repeat Relief, Opalescent, 1921, 9 1/4 In. 1380.00
Vase, Poivre, Dense Clusters Of Berries, Frosted & Clear, Signed, 1921, 9 1/2 In. 1265.00
Vase, Ronces, Blackberry Brambles, Deep Amber, Frosted, 1930, 9 1/2 In. 2500.00
Vase, Ronces, Blackberry Brambles, Frosted, 9 1/2 In. 6900.00
Vase, Ronsard, Nude Woman, Seated, Ringed Shoulder Handles, Frosted, 1926, 8 In. 1610.00
Vase, Sauterelles, Ovoid, Grasshoppers On Blades Of Grass, Blue, Green, 1913, 10 In. . . . 3738.00
Vase, Six Figurines Et Masques, 6 Nude Female Figures, Opalescent, 1928, 9 1/2 In. 2875.00
Vase, Soucis, Stylized Flowers, Leaves, Frosted Blue, 1930, 7 1/8 In. 3220.00
Vase, Tulipes, Tulip Blossoms, Gray, 1927, 8 1/4 In. 2875.00
Veilleuse, Roses, Tiara Top, Full Roses, Gray, Tapered Base, 1921, 7 In. . . . . . . .6900.00 to 8050.00

LAMPS of every type, from the early oil-burning Betty and Phoebe lamps to the recent electric lamps with glass or beaded shades, interest collectors. Fuels used in lamps changed through the years; whale oil (1800–1840), camphene (1828), Argand (1830), lard (1833–1863), turpentine and alcohol (1840s), gas (1850–1879), kerosene (1860), and electricity (1879) are the most common. Other lamps are listed by manufacturer or type of material.

2-Candle, Tin, Center Post, Adjustable Shade, Weighted Base, Penna., 26 1/2 In.	1540.00
Advertising, Calvert Whiskey, Spinner	45.00
Aladdin, B-27, Simplicity Alacite, Gold Luster	120.00
Aladdin, B-30, Simplicity, White	175.00
Aladdin, B-52, Washington Drape, Amber	150.00
Aladdin, B-53, Washington Drape, Clear	70.00
Aladdin, B-53X, Washington Drape, Clear, No Oil Fill	100.00
Aladdin, B-54, Washington Drape, Green	175.00
Aladdin, B-60, Short Lincoln Drape, Alacite	585.00
Aladdin, B-60, Short Lincoln Drape, Ivory Alacite	325.00 to 600.00
Aladdin, B-62, Short Lincoln Drape, Ruby	1000.00
Aladdin, B-75, Tall Lincoln Drape, Alacite	150.00
Aladdin, B-75, Tall Lincoln Drape, Alacite, Scalloped	375.00
Aladdin, B-76, Tall Lincoln Drape, Cobalt Blue	1700.00
Aladdin, B-76, Tall Lincoln Drape, Cobalt, Scallop	1625.00
Aladdin, B-77, Tall Lincoln Drape, Rudy Crystal	750.00
Aladdin, B-81, Beehive, Green Crystal	135.00 to 160.00
Aladdin, B-82, Beehive, Amber Crystal	140.00 to 150.00
Aladdin, B-83, Beehive, Ruby	600.00
Aladdin, B-86, Diamond Quilt, Jade Green Moonstone	325.00
Aladdin, B-88, Vertique, Yellow Moonstone	650.00
Aladdin, B-90, Diamond Quilt, White Moonstone, Black Base	325.00
Aladdin, B-91, Diamond Quilt, White Moonstone Font, Rose Foot	300.00
Aladdin, B-97, Queen, Jade Green Moonstone	400.00
Aladdin, B-98, Queen, Rose Moonstone	450.00
Aladdin, B-100, Corinthian, Clear	80.00
Aladdin, B-101, Venetian, Green	150.00
Aladdin, B-102, Corinthian, Green Crystal	110.00
Aladdin, B-105, Colonial, Green	120.00
Aladdin, B-106, Colonial, Amber	175.00
Aladdin, B-110, Cathedral, White Moonstone	225.00
Aladdin, B-111, Cathedral, Green Moonstone	275.00
Aladdin, B-112, Cathedral, Rose Moonstone	225.00
Aladdin, B-115, Corinthian, Green Moonstone	190.00
Aladdin, B-116, Corinthian, Rose Moonstone	120.00 to 300.00
Aladdin, B-121, Majestic, Rose Moonstone, Plated Base	425.00
Aladdin, B-124, Corinthian, White	275.00
Aladdin, B-124, Corinthian, White Moonstone Font, Black Foot	225.00
Aladdin, B-125, Corinthian, White Moonstone Font, Green Moonstone Foot	225.00
Aladdin, B-126, Corinthian, White And Rose Moonstone	350.00
Aladdin, Caboose, Model B	357.00
Aladdin, G-18, Boudoir	91.00
Aladdin, G-41, Rose Gracette	405.00
Aladdin, G-375, Urn, Alacite, Dancing Ladies	940.00
Aladdin, No. 6, Oil, Milk Glass Shade, Hanging	165.00
Argand, 2 Branches, Brass Arms, Font, Prisms, Glass Shade, Electrified, England, Pair	1870.00
Argand, 2-Light, Gilt Metal, Frosted & Clear Glass Shades, B. Gardiner, 23 In.	1965.00
Argand, Brass, 1-Light, Classical, Mid-19th Century, 17 1/2 In., Pair	1980.00
Argand, Bronze, Molded Urn Form, Foliate Mounts, Gilt, Lewis Veron Co., 20 In., Pair	2185.00
Argand, Double, Opalescent Striped Shades, Brass & Marble, Electrified, 21 1/2 In.	785.00
Art Glass, Vase Shape, 40 In.	115.00
Astral, Banquet, Brass, Frosted Cut To Clear Shade, Marble Base, 27 1/4 In.	385.00
Astral, Blue Glass, Scroll Gilt Brass Base, Wheel Cut Shade, Faceted Prisms, 30 In.	3450.00
Astral, Brass Stem & Font, Pink Cased Glass Shade, Marble Base, 20 In.	687.00

Astral, Brass, Columnar, Glass Shade, Etched, Albert Prisms, Electrified, c.1845, 32 In. . . . 990.00
Astral, Brass, Cranberry Stem, Marble, J.G. Webb, Oct. 14, 1851, 13 1/2 In. 192.00
Astral, Brass, Opalescent Stem, Marble Base, Pat. J.G. Webb, Oct. 14, 1851, 13 In. 165.00
Astral, Brass, Wheel Cut Acid Finish, Corinthian Column, Swag Shade, 1843, 26 In. 1035.00
Astral, Bronze, Sinumbra, Gilt 3025.00
Astral, Classical Ormolu, Electrified, 1845, 17 3/4 In. 1090.00
Astral, Electric Insert, Ivory Glass Shade, Marble Base, Fluted Brass Stem, 23 In. 132.00
Astral, Frosted Cut To Clear Globe, Marble Base, 16 3/4 In. 105.00
Astral, Gilded Brass, Marble Base, Prisms, Frosted Shade, Flowers, Electrified, 21 In. . . . 248.00
Astral, Gilt, Frosted, Etched Tulip Glass Shade, Prisms, Mid-19th Century, 30 In. 1092.00
Astral, Glass Overlay, Red To White, Gilded Brass Base, Cut Shade, 33 In. 3450.00
Astral, Marble Base, Pierced & Ribbed Brass Collar, Red Glass Insert, Brass Font, 14 In. . 220.00
Astral, Reeded Column, Ionic Capital, Suspended Prisms, Shade, Electrified, 26 In. 488.00
Astral, Stepped Base, Gilded Brass Stem, Black Onyx Base, Mounted As Lamp, 22 In. . . . 137.00
Astral, Stepped Marble Base, Frosted Shade, Square & Rectangular Prisms, 29 1/2 In. . . . 805.00
Betty, Brass, Bird Finial Cover, Dated 1836 . . . . 45.00
Betty, Copper & Iron, Hinged Lid, Wrought Iron Hanger & Pick, 5 In. 135.00
Betty, Copper, Tin, Tall Base, 19th Century, 9 In. 100.00
Betty, Double, Copper Support, Pick & Hook Iron, 18th Century 350.00
Betty, Iron, Bail & Hook, 19th Century, 7 In. 33.00
Betty, Iron, Brass Rooster Finial, 19th Century, 9 In. 230.00
Betty, Tin, Saucer Stand, Base, Hanger, 13 In. 385.00
Betty, Tin, Shell Type, Twisted Wire Hanger, Chain, 10 1/2 In. 200.00
Betty, Tin, Stand, 13 In. 165.00
Betty, Wrought Copper, Double Wick, Primitive, 18th Century, 9 In. 295.00
Betty, Wrought Iron, Brass Heart Finial, Hinged Lid, Hanger, Chain, 4 In. 385.00
Betty, Wrought Iron, Hinged Lid, Hanger, 4 In. 135.00
Bouillotte, 2-Light, Brass, Circular Disk Form, Green Tole Shade, 18 3/4 In., Pair 2875.00
Bouillotte, 3-Light, Gilt Metal, 28 In., Pair 1085.00
Bouillotte, Empire, Brass, Adjustable Painted Metal Shade, Swan Candle Arms, 20 In. . . . 630.00
Bouillotte, Louis XVI, Brass, 3-Light Candle Shelf, Green Painted Metal Shade, 26 In. . . 630.00
Bradley & Hubbard lamps are included in the Bradley & Hubbard category.
Candelabrum, 2-Light, Brass, Amethyst Drops, Electrified, 1915, 13 In., Pair 423.00
Candelabrum, 2-Light, Bronze, Scroll Arms, F. Barbedienne, Electrified, 12 In., Pair 545.00
Candelabrum, 2-Light, Chinese Boy & Girl, Flowers, Rocaille Frame, 8 In., Pair 238.00
Candelabrum, 2-Light, Fawn, Cornucopia Branches, Clodion, Electrified, 17 In., Pair 4600.00
Candelabrum, 2-Light, Gilt, Electrified, 1915, 19 x 9 x 5 1/4 In. 363.00
Candelabrum, 2-Light, Harem Girl, Holding 2 Candle Nozzles, Electrified, 11 In. 460.00
Candelabrum, 2-Light, Louis XVI, Brass, Marble, Column, Leaves, Electrified, Pair 260.00
Candelabrum, 3-Light, Bobeches, Column, Raymond Lowey, Electrified, 6 1/2 In. 285.00
Candelabrum, 3-Light, Brass Arms, Amber, Amethyst Prisms, Electrified, 20 In., Pair . . . 805.00
Candelabrum, 3-Light, Chased Leaves, Fluted Nozzles, Electrified, Pair 11500.00
Candelabrum, 3-Light, White Metal, Undulating Leaf, Ornate, Electrified, 23 In., Pair . . . 345.00
Candelabrum, 4-Light, Black Cord Shades With Grilles, Electrified, 39 In., Pair 300.00
Candelabrum, 4-Light, Gadrooned Vase, Branches, Boulton Plate, Electrified, 27 In. 9779.00
Candelabrum, 4-Light, Rose Bouquet, White Marble, c.1890, 19 In. 2420.00
Candelabrum, 4-Light, Vase, Band Of Flutes, Boulton & Co., Electrified, 24 In. 19550.00
Candelabrum, 4-Light, Weighted Base, Center Socket, Sterling Silver, Alvin, Electrified . 80.00
Candelabrum, 5-Light, Branched Arms On Brass & Onyx Standard, Pad Feet, Electrified . 58.00
Candelabrum, 5-Light, Brass, Copper, Electrified, 9 1/2 In., Pair 258.00
Candelabrum, 5-Light, Empire, Gilt & Metal, Foliate Design, Electrified, 41 In., Pair 490.00
Candelabrum, 5-Light, Ram's Head Handles, Toupie Feet, Electrified, 22 1/4 In., Pair . . . 2530.00
Candelabrum, 5-Light, Urn Form Standard, Paw Foot Base, c.1890, 20 1/2 In., Pair 385.00
Candelabrum, 6-Light, Acanthus Branch, Charles X, Electrified, 37 1/4 In., Pair 13800.00
Candelabrum, 6-Light, Putto Reading Book, Bronze, Marble Base, Electrified, 26 1/2 In. . 700.00
Candelabrum, 6-Light, Seated Cherub, Spray Of Flowers, Electrified, 33 1/2 In., Pair 4025.00
Candelabrum, 7-Light, Acanthus Scroll Branches, Bronze, Electrified, 50 In., Pair 12650.00
Candelabrum, 7-Light, Bronze, Scrolls, Shells, Foliate Arms, Electrified, 24 In., Pair 3450.00
Candelabrum, 7-Light, Bronze, Vase Shape, Electrified, c.1885, 30 1/2 x 10 In., Pair 2904.00
Candlestick, Favrile, Oil Font, 15 In. 2200.00
Carriage, Beveled Glass Lenses, Tin & Brass, 19th Century, 14 1/2 In., Pair 330.00
Carriage, Brass Mounted, Sheet Iron, Bull's-Eye Lenses, Finial, France, 17 x 5 In., Pair . . 363.00
Carriage, Silver Plated, White Mfg. Co., 36 In. 860.00

Chandelier, 3-Light Tin Candle Branches, Glass Water Globe, Spun Glass Shade, 1800 . . 1950.00
Chandelier, 3-Light, Bronze, Bacchanalian Masks, Swags, Argand, 44 x 21 In., Pair 4830.00
Chandelier, 3-Light, Entwined Antlers, Electrified, 36 x 39 In. 2070.00
Chandelier, 3-Light, Hall, Cage Form, Leafy Foliage, Bronze, 22 1/2 In. 546.00
Chandelier, 3-Light, Majolica, Iron Suspension Chain, Electrified, Italy, 46 x 15 In. 395.00
Chandelier, 3-Light, Ormolu, Bronze, Vine Swags, Flower Shades, France, 40 x 18 In. . . . 1725.00
Chandelier, 3-Light, Wrought Iron, Floral Corona, Everted Base, Baluster, 29 1/2 In. 1265.00
Chandelier, 4-Light Scrolled Arms, Rococo, Bronze, Cherub, Glass Shades, 26 In. 975.00
Chandelier, 4-Light, Arts & Crafts, Brass, Electrified, 1910, 29 x 20 1/4 In. 363.00
Chandelier, 4-Light, Brass, Crystal, Scroll & Branch Arm, Teardrop & Fruit, 18 x 36 In. . 2185.00
Chandelier, 4-Light, Brass, Orange Iridescent Nuart Glass Shades 115.00
Chandelier, 4-Light, Bronze Dore Arms, Amethyst Hanging Crystals, Louis XVI 805.00
Chandelier, 4-Light, English Provincial, Ebonized Wood, Chain, 18th Century, 9 3/4 In. . . 6670.00
Chandelier, 4-Light, Frosted & Etched Glass, Victorian, Van Kirk, 22 x 24 1/2 In. 690.00
Chandelier, 4-Light, Gilt Bronze, Amber Glass Shades, 33 x 17 In. 690.00
Chandelier, 4-Light, Porcelain Figure Of Woman, Scrolled Branches, Metal Vines, 25 In. . 7475.00
Chandelier, 4-Light, Wood, Wire & Tin, 28 In. 1200.00
Chandelier, 5-Light, Arms Entwined With Multicolored Foliage, Painted Metal, 28 In. . . . 920.00
Chandelier, 5-Light, Art Deco, Cast Brass, Ceiling Rings, 12 1/2 x 21 1/4 In. 175.00
Chandelier, 5-Light, Brass, Glass, Foliate Design, Scroll Branch Arms, Prisms, 19 In. 175.00
Chandelier, 5-Light, Maple Shaft, Brass Candleholders & Cups, Maple, 12 1/2 In. 2185.00
Chandelier, 5-Light, Wrought Iron, 4 Serpents On Corona, Tray Form Basket, 26 In. 515.00
Chandelier, 6 Light, Brass, Electric Candles, Cloth Shades, 20th Century, 31 In. 155.00
Chandelier, 6-Light, Capo-Di-Monte Style, Pottery, Scroll Branch Arms, Bobeche, 24 In. . 605.00
Chandelier, 6-Light, Draped Chain, Electrified, c.1900, 30 1/2 x 19 In. 1320.00
Chandelier, 6-Light, Flower Heads, Gilt Brass, Beads, 36 x 38 In. 905.00
Chandelier, 6-Light, Georgian, Silvered Brass, 1935, 28 In. 850.00
Chandelier, 6-Light, Gilded Roses, Cranberry Glass Overlay Fitting, 20th Century 315.00
Chandelier, 6-Light, Gilt Metal, Cut Glass, Scroll Arms, Swags, Prism Drops, 13 In. 60.00
Chandelier, 6-Light, Ruby, Victorian, 1860, 28 x 15 In. 920.00
Chandelier, 6-Light, Scrolling Frame, Drops, Cut Glass Finial, Electrified, 44 In. 4025.00
Chandelier, 7-Light, Rope-Twist Iron Chain, Spike Arms, Wrought Iron, 39 In. 975.00
Chandelier, 8-Light, Cut Glass, Scroll Arms, Pearl Shape Prisms, Jeweled Chain, 32 In. . . 605.00
Chandelier, 8-Light, Gilt Metal, Cage Form, Leaves, Teardrop Prisms, Chains, 49 In. 4600.00
Chandelier, 8-Light, Louis XV, Brass, Marble, Scrolled Arms, Pink Marble, 32 x 30 In. . . 1815.00
Chandelier, 8-Light, Louis XVI, Cage Shape, Prisms, Chains, Maidenhead Stem, 24 In. . . 920.00
Chandelier, 8-Light, Rock Crystal, 2 Tiers Above Scrolled Arms, Prisms, 38 1/2 In. 6900.00
Chandelier, 8-Light, Scroll Brand Arms, Multicolored Grape, Fruit, Metal, Glass, 29 In. . . 1380.00
Chandelier, 8-Light, Venetian Glass, Floral, Foliate Plumes, 19th Century, 32 x 30 In. . . . 907.00
Chandelier, 9-Light, Louis XVI, Brass, 3 Putti Heads, Scrolled Arms, 27 x 30 In. 3630.00
Chandelier, 9-Light, Louis XVI, Brass, Foliate Draped Body, 3 Arms, 34 x 27 In. 726.00
Chandelier, 9-Light, Neoclassical, Gilt Metal & Marble, Foliate Scrolling Arms 880.00
Chandelier, 12-Light, Brass, 2 Tiers, Hanging, 20th Century, 26 x 26 In. 165.00
Chandelier, 12-Light, Brass, Candle, 18th Century, 27 In. 1760.00
Chandelier, 12-Light, Pendant Ring, Tiers Of Candlearms, Dutch, 18th Century, 30 In. . . . 4312.00
Chandelier, 12-Light, Restoration, Brass, Electrified, 1900, 25 x 23 In. 4598.00
Chandelier, 15-Light, Gilt, Bronze, 2-Tier Cage Form, Fruit Form Prisms, 43 x 39 In. . . . 4025.00
Chandelier, 16-Light, 2 Tiers Of Scrolled Branches, c.1900, 36 x 34 In. 5750.00
Chandelier, 16-Light, 6 Tiers, Scrolls Alternating With Rope Twist Arms, George III 2070.00
Chandelier, 16-Light, Neoclassical, Scrolled Pendant Sprays, Cobalt, 53 In. 25300.00
Chandelier, 18-Light, 5 Tiers, Cage Form, Beaded Chain, Prisms, Louis XVI, 48 x 36 In. . 2070.00
Chandelier, 18-Light, Beaded Chains, Fleurettes, Prisms, c.1890, 42 x 32 In. 6960.00
Chandelier, 18-Light, Central Stick, Porcelain Nozzles, Figural & Floral Panels, 23 In. . . . 3162.00
Chandelier, 18-Light, Louis XV, Cut Glass, Star Corona, Pendant Drops, 51 In. 23000.00
Chandelier, 18-Light, S-Scrolled Arms, Floral, Prisms, Beaded Chain, Victorian, 36 In. . . 3680.00
Chandelier, Beaded Crystal, Ball Form, Ball Pendant, Continental, 15 In. 690.00
Chandelier, Bronze, 4-Scrolled Arms, Foliate Scrolls, Fruit Swags, Gilt 3220.00
Chandelier, Corbeille Form, Brass, Gilt, Belle Epoque, Electrified, 1915, 22 x 14 In. 1089.00
Chandelier, Hanging, Brown Pinecones, Butterfly, Yellow, Brown, Green, Richard, 14 In. . . 3575.00
Chandelier, Mahogany, Carved, Polychromed, China, 1925, 11 x 20 x 28 In. 484.00
Chandelier, Radiating Rods, Lucite Crystal Bulbs, c.1960, 24 x 39 In. 410.00
Chandelier, Stained Glass, Brass Fittings, Prairie School, 5 1/2 x 30 In. 1540.00
Double Crusie, Iron, Rams Horn Finial, 5 1/4 In. 193.00

Electric, 8-Panel Shade, Green Slag Glass, Bronzed Metal Support, Arts & Crafts, 22 In. . 1320.00
Electric, Amber Cut Prisms, Chimney Shaped Globes, Feather Design, Piano, 15 In., Pair 715.00
Electric, American Victorian, Scrolls & Flower Heads Base, Amber Glass Shade, 32 In. . . 373.00
Electric, Angelo Monza, Saucer-Shaped Light On Brass Column, Black Base, 25 In. 1265.00
Electric, Arc, Contemporary, Tubular Column, Half-Sound Shade, Marble Base, 78 3/4 In. 115.00
Electric, Arco, Adjustable, Slate Base, Chrome Neck & Fixture, 84 In. 605.00
Electric, Art Deco, Arredolce, 3 Adjustable Chrome Arms, Shades, Marble Base, 60 In. . . 1760.00
Electric, Art Deco, Brass, Cylindrical, Round Glass Shades, 1930s, 12 x 78 In. 825.00
Electric, Art Deco, Donald Deskey, Copper, Glass, New Cylindrical Shade, 10 x 17 In. . . 2310.00
Electric, Art Deco, Half Oval Isinglass Shade, Black & Red Stylized Blossoms On Shade 950.00
Electric, Artichoke, P. Henningson, Copper, White Enameled Segments, Hanging, 32 In. . 5225.00
Electric, Arts & Crafts, Caramel Slag Glass Panels, Iron, Signed Success, 21 In. 270.00
Electric, Arts & Crafts, Wicker, Lined In Original Silk, 21 In. 200.00
Electric, Bambi, Figural, Ceramic, Illustrated Shade 80.00
Electric, Billy Haines, Green Patina Metal, Black Cubic Base, Linen Shade, 33 In. 690.00
Electric, Bisque, Cowboy, Horses On Shade, Occupied Japan 125.00
Electric, Black Hemisphere Shade, Brown Plastic Base, Martinelli Luce, 15 In., Pair 715.00
Electric, Bobrick, Controlamp, Fiberglass Reflector, Wood, Iron, Pottery, 35 In. 1035.00
Electric, Boudoir, Mica Panels, Arts & Crafts, Old Mission Kopperkraft, 12 In. 3500.00
Electric, Box Kite, Fabric Wrapped Plastic Shade, Wire Base, George Nelson, 28 In. 920.00
Electric, Brass, Blue Shaft, Marble Base, Prisms, Etched Glass Shade, c.1850, 27 In. 1045.00
Electric, Brass, Student, Double, Vasa Murrhina Shades, 20 In. 605.00
Electric, Brass, Student, Green Shade, 19th Century, 23 In. 165.00
Electric, Bristol, Enameled Maroon & Orange Flowers, Leaves, Spar Brenner, 8 5/8 In. . . 195.00
Electric, Bronze, Arab On Carpet, Cold Painted 660.00
Electric, Bronze, Classical Grecian God Figure, Cherubs Around Base, Floor, 59 In. 8625.00
Electric, Bronze, Coiled Dragon Body, Sea-Wave Base, 31 In., Pair 430.00
Electric, Bronze, Dancing Nymphs, Classical Garb, Carrying Grapes, 29 In., Pair 440.00
Electric, Bronze, Desk, Spherical Glass Shade, Faceted Foot, Genet & Michon, 15 In. . . . 5750.00
Electric, Bronze, Domed Shade, Emerald Green Geometric, Bronze Base, 1920, 20 In. . . . 1840.00
Electric, Bronze, Drunken Pierrot, Hand Blown Shades, Gold Flecks, Marked B, 15 In. . . 950.00
Electric, Bronze, Elephant, Jeweled Strappings, 9 In. 545.00
Electric, Bronze, Glass Overlay Cast Ribbons Shade, Garlands, Bronze Base, 12 In. 460.00
Electric, Bronze, Leaded Glass, Red, Green, Yellow Geometric Shade, 1910-1920, 16 In. . 2530.00
Electric, Bronze, Rug Merchant, Under Bamboo Trellis, Figural, Austria, 20th Century . . . 1725.00
Electric, Bronze, Young Boy At The Base Of A Tree, Gilt, Brown Patina, 11 In. 300.00
Electric, Candle, Bronze, Filigree, Verdigris, Green Glass, Apollo Studio, 15 3/4 In. 550.00
Electric, Caramel & Green Slag Leaded Shade, Cast Metal, Bronze Finish, 26 3/4 In. 770.00
Electric, Castiglioni, Arco, Cantilevered Aluminum Arm, Marble Base, 1960s, 96 In. 1320.00
Electric, Chandelier, Artichoke, Copper, Poul Henningson, 20 x 30 In. 4025.00
Electric, Classique, Reverse Painted Shade, Floral, Blue, Green, Butterflies, 13 In. 715.00
Electric, Copper, Hammered, 4-Panel Shade, 4-Light Base, Dirk Van Erp, 19 x 22 In. 9350.00
Electric, Copper, Hammered, 6 Panels, Mica Shade, Arts & Crafts, 15 x 17 In. 1650.00
Electric, Copper, Hammered, Brown Patina, Oak Pedestal, Canister Base, 15 x 22 In. 9300.00
Electric, Copper, Hammered, Green Slag Inserts, 4-Panel Shade, Arts & Crafts, 14 In. 6050.00
Electric, Copper, Hammered, Trumpet Base, Conical 4-Panel Shade, Dirk Van Erp, 18 In. 14000.00
Electric, D.I.M., Saucer Top, Frosted Spherical Diffuser, Disk Base, c.1930, 17 1/2 In. . . . 4600.00
Electric, Dazor Mfg., Model 1000, Mauve Metallic Paint, 1950s, Desk, 20 x 14 In. 60.00
Electric, Dirk Van Erp, Copper, Conical Mica Panels Shade, 3 Arms, Ovoid Base, 13 In. . 5460.00
Electric, Dirk Van Erp, Copper, Conical Mica Panels Shade, Bulging Foot, 1913, 20 In. . . 8625.00
Electric, Dirk Van Erp, Copper, Domed Mica Panels Shade, 4 Arms, 1911, 11 In. 19550.00
Electric, Domed Bronze, Glass Geometric Shade, Scalloped Rim, Green, Gorham, Table . 2300.00
Electric, Duffner Kimberly, Gold Dore Base, Leaded Shade, Geometric Design, 29 In. . . . 6325.00
Electric, Edouard-Wilfrid Buquet, Pivoting Conical Shade, Domed Base, Metal, 32 In. . . 3680.00
Electric, Emeralite, Green Cased Glass Shade, Desk, 50 In. 316.00
Electric, Empire Style, Griffin Base, Velvet Brocade Shade, Fringe, 73 1/2 In. 440.00
Electric, Fantoni, Scraffito Horses, Baluster Shape, Wood Base, Brass Fixture, 38 1/2 In. . 230.00
Electric, Figural, Boy & Girl, Bisque, Victorian Style, 24 In., Pair 90.00
Electric, Figural, Oriental Woman, Lotus Blossom, White Porcelain, 30 In. 115.00
Electric, Fornasetti, Screen-Printed Architectural Scene, Cylinder, Brass Plated, 36 In. . . . 805.00
Electric, Frederick Weinberg, Wrought Iron, Cylinder, Reed Mat Shade, 59 x 14 In. 770.00
Electric, Gae Aulenti, 2 Adjustable Shade, Green Metal, Art Deco, Label, 15 x 20 In. 1540.00
Electric, Gem City, Ice Cream Cone Shape, Pottery, Yellow Cone, Orange Top, 12 In. . . . 350.00

Electric, Georgian, Silver Plate Dish, Adjustable, 1900-1910, 4 x 13 In. 50.00
Electric, Giltwood, Porcelain, Baroque, Acanthus Supports, Beaded Border, 16 1/2 In. ... 290.00
Electric, Giltwood, Porcelain, Gesso Urn Form, Italy, 20th Century, 24 1/2 In., Pair 1725.00
Electric, Globe, Apothecary, Wooden Hand & Ball, Leaded Glass, 14 In. 1750.00
Electric, Globe, Handel Style, Parrot, Hanging, 11 In. 82.00
Electric, Green & Caramel Slag Glass Panels, Floral, Foliate Shade, 21 In. 201.00
Electric, Gretta Grossman, Bullet Shape Metal Shade, Tubular Tripod Base, 53 In. 978.00
Electric, Gustav Stickley, Copper, Mahogany, Oak Base, Glass Shade, 18 In. 11000.00
Electric, Gustav Stickley, Hammered Copper, Wicker Shade, 23 x 18 In. 4400.00
Electric, Gustav Stickley, No. 609, Oak Base, 4 Copper Straps, Wicker Shade, 12 x 20 In. 8800.00
Electric, Gustav Stickley, Oak Frame, 16 1/2 In. 3190.00
Electric, Gustav Stickley, Square Clip-Corner Top Over Lower Shelf, No. 611, 29 In. .. 1600.00
Electric, Gypsy Girl Standing By Flaming Urn, Marble & Alabaster, 31 In. 2300.00
Electric, Hall, Hanging, Cranberry Shade 550.00
Electric, Hammered, 4 Mica Sections, Riveted Copper Frame, Base, Dirk Van Erp, 14 In. . 7475.00
Electric, Hanging, Brass Frame, Cranberry Hobnail Shade, Clear Prisms, Rayo, 33 In. ... 825.00
Electric, Hanging, Conical, Corrugated Cardboard, 17 In. 110.00
Electric, Heifetz, Red & Gray Masonite Panels, Brass & Steel Frame, c.1951, 22 In. 3450.00
Electric, Homeric Bronze Works, Algerian Girl, Erotic Drapery Reveals Nude, 1915 ..... 515.00
Electric, Internally Lit White Glass Shades, Floor, Italy, 1960s, 16 x 49 In. 415.00
Electric, Jefferson, Reverse Painted Shade, Landscape Design, Brown, Orange, 23 In. ... 2920.00
Electric, Jefferson, Reverse Painted Shade, Landscape Design, Metal Base, 21 In. 1430.00
Electric, Jefferson, Reverse Painted Shade, Landscape, Yellow, Green, 18 x 22 In. 1980.00
Electric, Kurt Versen, Adjustable Tubular Metal, Black Shade, Floor, 20 x 54 In. 715.00
Electric, Kurt Versen, Tubular Chrome Frame, Black Enameled Shade, 1930s, 16 In. 825.00
Electric, Landscape Design, Trees, Riveted Bronze Shade, 4-Sides, 22 In. 1870.00
Electric, Laurel Lamp Co., Arched Chrome Base, White Sphere, 14 1/4 x 7 1/2 In. 245.00
Electric, Laurel Lamp Co., Brushed Chrome Base, White Sphere, 18 x 7 In., Pair 605.00
Electric, Laurel Lamp Co., Flattened Spherical Frosted Glass, Metallic Pedestal, 16 In. ... 403.00
Electric, Laurel Lamp Co., Frosted Mushroom Shade, Bright Brass Stem & Base, 56 In. . 465.00
Electric, Laurel Lamp Co., Frosted White Mushroom, Brushed Chrome Base, 56 In., Pair . 2750.00
Electric, Laurel Lamp Co., White Flattened Sphere, Pedestal Base, 16 In. 288.00
Electric, Laurel Lamp Co., White Glass Sphere, Pedestal Base, 12 In. 144.00
Electric, Lava, Gold Base, 1960s 70.00
Electric, Lava, Rod Flakes That Move When Heats Up 70.00
Electric, Leaded Glass Shade, Caramel, Blue & Pink, 29 In. 575.00
Electric, Leaded Glass Shade, Floral Design, Jagged Edge, Bronze Patina Base, 23 In. ... 1093.00
Electric, Light Bulb Shape, White Plastic, Pop Art Style, 40 x 15 In. 440.00
Electric, Lightolier, White Plastic, Tapering Base, 22 In., Pair 58.00
Electric, Louis Poulsen, Circular Turned Plastic Base, Lucite Dome Shade, 48 In. 345.00
Electric, Louis Poulsen, Plastic Base, Lucite Dome Shade, 27 In. 288.00
Electric, Louis XVI Style, Rock Crystal, Gilt Metal Mounted, 17 1/4 In., Pair 7475.00
Electric, Lucite, Circular Lampshade, Paper, Floor 93.00
Electric, Mahogany Base, Leaded Shade, Red & Green Flowers, Amber Ground, 71 In. .. 605.00
Electric, Martz, Brown Ceramic Base, Wood Chain, 24 In. 403.00
Electric, Metal, Bronze Finish, Glass Inserts In Shade, Enamel Flowers, Rainaud, 22 In. .. 880.00
Electric, Moe Bridges, Scenic, No. 192, 18 In. 4500.00
Electric, Motion, Antique Car, Econolite 195.00
Electric, Motion, Bar Is Open ....90.00 to 110.00
Electric, Motion, Econolite, Oval 250.00
Electric, Motion, Forest Fire, Bear 175.00
Electric, Motion, Goldfish, Green Glass 550.00
Electric, Motion, Goodman's Lighthouse & Ship 295.00
Electric, Motion, Mill Scene 195.00
Electric, Motion, Mountain Waterfall 195.00
Electric, Motion, Niagara Falls, Oval ....195.00 to 250.00
Electric, Motion, Train, Econolite, No. 763, 1956, 11 In. ....*Illus* 100.00
Electric, Motion, Yellowstone Falls 195.00
Electric, Mushroom Shape, Frosted White Glass, Internal Light, 1970s, 12 x 14 In. 165.00
Electric, Nessen Studios, Cylindrical Enamel Base, Linen Shade, 26 In., Pair 230.00
Electric, Nessen Studios, Domed White Plastic Shade, Chrome Base, 21 In. 173.00
Electric, Nessen Studios, Tubular Brass Rod, Tripod Legs, Linen Shade, 22 In., Pair 633.00
Electric, Night-Light, Willie-Wirehand, Plastic, Round, Sylvania, 1950s, 3 In. 50.00

To clean dirt and corrosion from lamps and lanterns, use brass polish and steel wool. Or, to avoid rubbing off the nickel plating, first clean the surface with Fantastik or 409. Then apply Naval jelly with a brush. Rub for several minutes with the brush. Let stand for 30 minutes and wash it off. Let dry, then polish gently with steel wool.

Lamp, Electric, Motion, Train, Econolite, No. 763, 1956, 11 In.

Electric, Oscar Bach, Domed Caramel Hide Shade, Faceted Metal Standard, 75 In., Pair . .	8625.00
Electric, Oscar Bach, Metal, Reticulated Crown Top, Column, Conical Shade, 30 In.	1610.00
Electric, Oscar Bach, Metal, Reticulated Metal Shade Case In Gold Glass Sphere, 26 In. .	2990.00
Electric, Pabst Blue Ribbon Beer, Electric, Boxer, Black & White Pants, Gloves, 18 In. . . .	110.00
Electric, Peter Pfisterer, Asymmetrical Design, Chrome Plate, 1935, 13 x 7 In.	5225.00
Electric, Pierre Cardin, Aluminum Spiral, Round Frosted Glass Shade, 1960s, 11 x 12 In. .	525.00
Electric, Pill Shape, Internal Lit Plastic, Design Studio, Italy, 5 x 20 In.	825.00
Electric, Porcelain Base, Green & White, Gilt, Cherub, Ram's Head Mounts, 18 In.	495.00
Electric, Porcelain, Blue, White Floral Design, 18 In., Pair	431.00
Electric, Porcelain, Floral Sprays, Gilt Metal Foliate Handles, Cobalt Blue, 17 In.	230.00
Electric, Poul Henningsen, PH-80, Aluminum, Ivory Enamel, White Saucer Shade, 53 In. .	495.00
Electric, Prairie School, Oak, Reverse Painted Sailboat Scene, Vented Shade, 19 In.	2200.00
Electric, President Wilson, Soldiers At Base, Slag Glass Shade, Small	375.00
Electric, Pttyn Product, Aluminum & Bakelite, Machine-Age Design, 8 x 20 In.	2530.00
Electric, Pulled Feather Glass, Brass Base, Iridescent Glass Shade, Boudoir, 1900, 22 In. .	2750.00
Electric, Raggedy Ann, Child Holding Ann Doll, Ceramic	95.00
Electric, Raggedy Ann, Matching Shade	65.00
Electric, Raggedy Ann, Pottery	75.00
Electric, Rectangular Shade, Raised On Tubular Lucite Base, 11 In.	285.00
Electric, Rock Shape Set, White Plastic, Internal Light, Singletron, Italy, 1960s, 4 Piece . .	1980.00
Electric, Rose Quartz, Carved, Flourite Base, China, 19th Century, 11 1/2 In.	385.00
Electric, Sandalwood, Walnut, Brass, Original Shade, Edward Wormley, 15 x 56 In.	1100.00
Electric, Sandstone Base, 4 Faces & Snake, E. Reed, 1980, 7 1/2 x 17 3/4 In.	495.00
Electric, Scara, White Glaze, Raised On Circular, Ceramic, Signed, 1928, 27 In.	3450.00
Electric, Scenic Over Slag Glass, Brass Base, Bradley & Hubbard, 12 In.	825.00
Electric, Sewer Pipe, Tree Trunk, Marked, 1927, 10 3/4 In.	330.00
Electric, Sewer Pipe, Tree Trunk, Marked, C.W. Meek, 1931, 8 1/2 In.	250.00
Electric, Sewer Pipe, Tree Trunk, Marked, Moore & Armstrong, Uhrichsville, Oh., 14 In. .	495.00
Electric, Spiral Twist Foliate Form, Turquoise, Gilt, Metal Mounted, 20 In., Pair	920.00
Electric, Stilnova, Chrome, White Enamel Tilted Shade, Italy, 1960s, 24 x 69 In.	770.00
Electric, Studio D.A., Pelota, Molded, Orange Painted Shade, Metal Diffuser, 13 1/2 In. . .	230.00
Electric, Table, Green Art Glass, Cut Back, Flowers, Leaves, Brass Mountings, 25 In. . . .	230.00
Electric, Television, 2 White Doves, California	28.00
Electric, Television, Panther, Green	35.00
Electric, Torchere, Aluminum, Bakelite, Etched Glass Shade, 56 In.	110.00
Electric, Tree Trunk Shape, Bronze, Full Relief, 1900-1920, 19 In.	517.00
Electric, Triple Cased Glass, Ruby Base, Pulled Feather Design, 10 1/2 In.	60.00
Electric, Urn Form, Marble, Gilt Bronze, Floral, Swag & Serpentine, France, 35 In.	2415.00
Electric, Urn Form, Onyx & Bronze, Neoclassical Style, Mask & Floral Design, 16 In.	405.00
Electric, Urn Shape, Greek God & Goddess, Bronzed, Vertical Scroll Handles, 28 In.	1035.00
Electric, V. Kagan, Wood Base, Cantilever Table, String Shade, 61 In.	2300.00
Electric, Virgin Mary, Light Bulb	20.00
Electric, Walnut, Adjustable Ratchet Support, Circular Base, England, Floor, 52 In., Pair .	1725.00
Electric, White Plastic Balls Shade, Chrome Frame, Hanging, 1960s, 19 x 16 In.	330.00
Electric, Wrought Iron, Brass Trim, Bridge, 55 In.	95.00

Electric, Yonel Lebovici, Fiche Male, Pop Art Form, Stainless Steel, 1978, 24 x 15 In. ... 3850.00
Fairy, Panels Of Hobs, Footed Base, Peaked Ruffles, Amber, 4 1/2 In. 150.00
Fairy, Yellow Nailsea, Clear Base, Signed, 4 1/2 In. 50.00
Fat, Hanging, Twisted Forged Hanger, Rooster Finial, Iron 65.00
Fluid, Brass, Opalescent Glass Font, Milky Coin Spot Design, Multicolored Base, 9 In. .. 550.00
Fluid, Cupid & Lamb Base, Clear Font, Metal, 11 In., Pair 82.00
Fluid, Drop Prisms, Cut Camphor Glass Shade, Marble & Brass Base, Electrified, 22 In. . 209.00
Fluid, Drop Prisms, Cut Camphor Glass Shade, Marble & Brass Base, Electrified, 23 In. . 468.00
Fluid, Etched Cranberry Font, Marble Vase, Metal Columns, Pair 105.00
Fluid, Hanging, Brass, Leaf Design, 2 Arms, Etched Glass Shade, Extra Shade, 25 In..... 200.00
Fluid, Milk Glass, Amethyst Top, 1860s, Pair 715.00
Fluid, Pewter, Candlestick Shape, Monogram, 1854, 10 In. 55.00
Fluid, Pressed Glass, Eye & Scale Pattern, Applied Collar, Boston & Sandwich, 8 1/4 In. . 130.00
Fluid, Pressed Glass, Flower & Vine Font, Brass Collar, 7 1/2 In. 110.00
Fluid, Pressed Sandwich Glass, Sweetheart, 8 1/2 In. 99.00
Gasolier, 12-Light, Cut Glass, Scrolled & Arched Frame, 6 Electric, 34 x 31 In. 1725.00
Gilt Metal, Porcelain, Courting Couple, Green Ground, Mask Mount, Sevres-Type, 19 In. 490.00
Grease, Brass, Drip Pan, 7 In. 75.00
Grease, Double Pan, Tin, 9 7/8 In. 165.00
Grease, Hanging, Twisted Post, Ratchet Trammel, Square Pan, Wrought Iron, 28 1/4 In. ... 302.00
Grease, Portable Chamber Type, 5 7/8 x 9 1/8 In. 180.00
Grease, Stoneware, Green Tan Glaze, Applied Handle, Saucer, Pan, Wick Spout, 5 3/4 In. 440.00
Grease, Tallgrass, Wrought Iron, Tripod, Adjustable Pan With Pick, 22 In. 230.00
Handel lamps are included in the Handel category.
Hanging, 7-Light, Gilt Bronze, Triangular Cage Form, Cut Crystal Sphere, 34 x 19 In. ... 1150.00
Hanging, Arts & Crafts, Wrought Copper, Glass Panels, Landscape Design, 16 1/2 In. ... 1380.00
Hanging, Brass Frame, Glass Jewels, Prisms, Caramel To Pink Ribbed Shade, 24 In...... 2310.00
Hanging, Cast Iron Frame, Milk Glass Shade, Clear Font, 14 In. 220.00
Hanging, Kerosene, Brass Font, Copper Reflector, Standard Lighting, Electrified .... *Illus* 175.00
Hanging, Leaded Glass Shade, Mushroom Shape, Floral Design, 7 x 28 In. 2875.00
Hanging, Nickel Plate Embossed Brass, Angle, 2 Burners, Electrified, 18 In. 245.00
Hanging, Poul Henningsen, Electric, PH-5, Persian Blue Enamel, 11 x 21 In. 445.00
Hanging, Victorian, Cranberry Hobnail Shade, Miller Lamp Co., 19 1/2 In. 1155.00
Kerosene, 2-Light, Angle Hanging, Early 20th Century, 16 x 23 In. 373.00
Kerosene, Aesthetic, Cut Glass, Silvered Metal, E.M. Duplex & Co., Victorian, 18 In. ... 545.00
Kerosene, Alabaster, Columns, Acanthus-Carved Bulbous Shaft, Stepped Plinth, 33 In. ... 330.00
Kerosene, Amber Swirled Stem & Base, Opalescent Ribbed, 9 In.................... 275.00
Kerosene, Band Of Thumbprints, Patent 11, 14, 1911 .... 65.00
Kerosene, Banquet, Cranberry Cut To White, Clear Stem & Font, Brass Collar, 17 In. 1180.00
Kerosene, Banquet, Cut Glass, Panel Cut Shade, Star Cut Base, Electrified, 28 In. 660.00
Kerosene, Banquet, Frosted Cut To Clear Shade, Brass Base, 28 1/2 In. 302.00
Kerosene, Banquet, Frosted, Etched Shade, Ruffled Top, Prisms, Large Stem, 37 In.. .... 230.00
Kerosene, Banquet, Gilded Brass Stem, Green To Clear Font, Collar, Marble Base, 21 In. . 385.00
Kerosene, Banquet, Sheffield Type, Silver Plate, Engraved Floral, Electrified, 33 In. 800.00
Kerosene, Brass Plate Stem, Cobalt To Clear Font, Black Stone Base, Victorian, 15 In. ... 495.00
Kerosene, Brass Shade, 6 Concave Sides, Bronze Base, 21 In. 575.00
Kerosene, Brass, Lime Green Opaque Font, Gilt, Stepped Marble Base, 11 3/8 In. 190.00
Kerosene, Brass, Student's, Milk Glass Shade, Electrified, 20 1/4 In. 245.00
Kerosene, Bronze, Blue & White Porcelain, China, 19th Century, 11 In. 745.00
Kerosene, Bronze, Cherub Holding Cornucopia, Black Onyx Base, France, 13 In........ 412.00
Kerosene, Cast Iron, Brass, Hoof Feet, Classical Scene Font, Satin Glass Globe, 16 In. ... 275.00
Kerosene, Embossed & Chased Brass, Mounted As Lamp, 31 In. 220.00
Kerosene, Finger, Swirl Design Chimney Font, Miniature 55.00
Kerosene, Gone With The Wind, Continental River Scene Transfer, Electrified, 21 In..... 165.00
Kerosene, Gone With The Wind, Green, White Floral Design, Ball Feet, Electrified, 27 In. 545.00
Kerosene, Gone With The Wind, Peach Blow, Fuchsia To Cream, Electrified, 15 3/8 In. .. 5175.00
Kerosene, Gone With The Wind, Puffy, Grape Design, Brass Base, Electrified, 22 In. 355.00
Kerosene, Gone With The Wind, Yellow Ground, Red Cabbage Rose, Electrified, 28 In. .. 577.00
Kerosene, Greek Key, 1911, Miniature 45.00
Kerosene, Hanging, Cranberry Hobnail, Brass, Nickel Plated Flowers, Prisms, 17 In. 1650.00
Kerosene, Hanging, Gilt Brass Frame, Prisms, Milk Glass Shade, Amber Font, 17 1/2 In. . 715.00
Kerosene, Milk Glass Shade, Brass Font & Base, Miller Lamp, Electrified, 12 3/4 In. 93.00
Kerosene, Milk Glass, Brass Collar & Connector, 20 1/4 In. 245.00

Parchment lampshades can
be cleaned with a cloth
soaked in milk. Then wipe
dry with a clean cloth.

Lamp, Hanging, Kerosene,
Brass Font, Copper Reflector,
Standard Lighting, Electrified

Lamp, Miner's, Tin, Long Spout,
Hook, 4 In.

Kerosene, Milk Glass, Cosmos Enamel Design, Clear Chimney, 8 In.	175.00
Kerosene, Milk Glass, Cut To Green, Hand Painted Floral, Table, Pair	275.00
Kerosene, Parlor, Claret Floral Ball Shade, Electrified, 1895, 36 1/2 In.	393.00
Kerosene, Parlor, Floral Design, Brass Mounted, 1890, 25 x 10 In.	303.00
Kerosene, Pink Shaded Glass Base, Shade, Floral Transfer, Cast Iron, Electrified, 16 In.	415.00
Kerosene, Polished Nickel, Brass Counted, Electrified, c.1890, 23 1/2 In.	275.00
Kerosene, Porcelain Insert Painted Winter Landscape, Acid Etched Floral Shade, 15 In.	192.00
Kerosene, Porcelain, Oriental Design, Carved Ivory Type, Electrified, 15 In.	120.00
Kerosene, Pressed Glass, Clear Font, Stepped Milk Glass Base, 13 In.	165.00
Kerosene, Purple & White Flowers, Gold Leaves, Miniature	285.00
Kerosene, Rayo, Brass, Glass Chimney, Late 19th Century, 21 In.	92.00
Kerosene, Rayo, Student, Electrified, Replaced Shade, 20 In.	305.00
Kerosene, Reticulated Floral Base, Globe, Milk Glass, Yellow, White, Electrified, 31 In.	154.00
Kerosene, Rubena Overshot Shade, Cranberry Font, White Metal Base, 19 1/2 In.	375.00
Kerosene, Student, Belgium Lamp, Brass, Green Shade, Chimney, Electrified, 23 In.	465.00
Kerosene, Student, Brass, 2-Font, Egg Shaped Font, Yellow, American, 24 x 32 In.	1610.00
Kerosene, Student, Brass, Green Cased Tam-O-Shanter Shade, E. Miller, 1880s, 22 In.	1395.00
Kerosene, Student, Colored Lithophane Shade, Electrified, Pair	3950.00
Kerosene, Student, Perfection, Brass, Green Shade, Pat. Nov. 22, '81, Electrified, 21 In.	440.00
Kerosene, Student, Spencer Lamp Co., Brass, 2 Milk Glass Shades, Horizontal Reservoir	900.00
Kerosene, White Onyx, Frosted Spherical Shade, Abco, Electrified, c.1885, 29 1/2 In.	245.00
Lace Maker's, Blown Glass	825.00
Lace Maker's, Lacy Base, Blown Font, Drip Pan, Spherical Font, 9 7/8 In.	430.00
Lard, Tin, Saucer Base, 9 In.	75.00
Love Filament, 1980s, 10 1/4 In.	10.00
Miner's, American Safety Lamp & Mine Supply, 9 1/2 In.	255.00
Miner's, Brass Carbide, Baldwin Lamp, 4 In.	50.00
Miner's, Brass Carbide, Guys Dropper, Shanklin Mfg. Co., 4 In.	33.00
Miner's, Carbide, With Cap	95.00
Miner's, Safety, White Metal, Glass Lens, Hook On Top, Koehler, 9 In.	120.00
Miner's, Sticker, Wrought Iron, Varney, 19th Century, 9 In., Pair	77.00
Miner's, Tin, Long Spout, Hook, 4 In. ....*Illus*	50.00
Miner's, With Candle Holder, Wisconsin, 10 1/2 x 6 3/4 In.	1300.00
Oil, Adjustable Horizontal Font, Pink Globe & Chimney, 15 1/2 In.	220.00
Oil, Allover Stars, Blue, Glass, 8 3/4 In.	460.00
Oil, Alternating Star & Chevron Design, 6 1/2 In.	385.00
Oil, Ambrose, Glass, 7 3/4 In.	60.00
Oil, Amethyst Font, Milk Glass Base, Ribbed Shoulder, Brass Connector, 9 1/2 In.	160.00
Oil, Atterbury Style, Pale Green Ribbed Shade	135.00
Oil, Banbury, Glass, 7 1/4 In.	40.00
Oil, Beaded Diamond & Rib, Glass, Finger, Applied Crimped Handle, 2 3/4 In.	60.00
Oil, Bell Form, Bands Of Summer Flowers, Electrified, Porcelain, France, 20 In., Pair	860.00
Oil, Bellflower, Coarse Rib, Pressed Glass, Flared	90.00
Oil, Blue Pressed Glass, Handle, Pair	330.00
Oil, Bradford, Glass, 9 1/2 In.	80.00
Oil, Brass, 1 Spout, Wick Advance Knob, France, 10 3/4 In.	95.00

Oil, Brass, Grecian Form, Electrified, 1 & W, 21 1/2 In. 595.00
Oil, Brass, Spout, Cone Shape Pedestal, Pick, 10 1/2 In. 90.00
Oil, Brewster, Glass, Footed, Finger, Plain Foot, 4 3/4 In. 50.00
Oil, Bronze, Trifid Form, Animal & Figural, 3 Paw Feet, Marble Plinth, 34 In. 405.00
Oil, Bull's-Eye Base, Heart & Sawtooth Font, Brass Collar, Flint, 9 5/8 In. 240.00
Oil, Bull's-Eye With Diamond Point, Pressed Glass, 6 7/8 In. 130.00
Oil, Bulls-Eye, Glass, Finger, Emerald Green, 3 In. 140.00
Oil, Cathedral, Glass, Blue Font, Amber Base, 13 In. 310.00
Oil, Center Medallion, Glass, 7 3/4 In. 200.00
Oil, Chamber, Tin, Center Wick Font, 7 In. 165.00
Oil, Cityscape Scenes, Yellow Painted, Cylindrical, Electrified, 19 In., Pair 2300.00
Oil, Classical Ormolu, Bronze, 1840s 430.00
Oil, Clear Pressed Glass Base, Light Blue Font, Opal Net, 9 In. 305.00
Oil, Clustered Fans, Glass, Finger, 3 In. 90.00
Oil, Columbian Coin, Glass, Footed Finger, Plain Font, 4 3/4 In. 80.00
Oil, Coolidge Drape, Glass, 9 In. 70.00
Oil, Crusie, Pre-1820, 9 3/4 In. 195.00
Oil, Cupid Supporting Pierced Font, Fern Fronds, Opaque Glass Shade, Electrified, 28 In. . 805.00
Oil, Daisy & Bowknot, Glass, Footed Finger, 5 In. 130.00
Oil, Diamond & Fan, Glass, Amber, 7 1/4 In. 150.00
Oil, Diamond Reversed, Glass, Finger, 3 In. 50.00
Oil, Diamond Thumbprint, Pressed Glass, 6 3/4 In. 700.00
Oil, Double Crusie, Hanging On Stand, Cast Iron Base, 19 1/2 In. 192.00
Oil, Double Crusie, Hanging, Wrought Iron, 6 In. 27.00
Oil, Duncan Ribbed Band, Glass, 8 In. 90.00
Oil, Eyewinker, Glass, 9 In. 180.00
Oil, Fine Rib With Bellflower Border, Pressed Glass, 5 1/2 In. 2050.00
Oil, Finger, Cup & Saucer 165.00
Oil, Finger, Custard Glass, Heart Design 310.00
Oil, Finger, Green Glass, Applied Handle, 3 3/4 In. 60.00
Oil, Finger, Peacock Feather, Footed, Blue . . . . .425.00 to 445.00
Oil, Finger, Seaweed Design, Blue Opalescent, No. 0, Burner & Chimney, 2 3/4 In. 1495.00
Oil, Fishscale With Cable Font, Glass, 9 1/2 In. 45.00
Oil, Fleur De Lis & Tassel, Glass, Footed Finger, 4 1/2 In. 130.00
Oil, Frosted Floral Band, Cranberry To Clear, Marble & Brass Base, Electrified, 24 In. . . . 770.00
Oil, Gilt Metal, Cut & Etched Grape & Scroll Shade, Prisms, Late 19th Century 415.00
Oil, Glass, Adams Panel & Rib, Finger, Applied Crimped Handle, 3 In. 40.00
Oil, Glass, Gilt Painted Design, Pink Ground, Milk Glass Shade, 32 1/4 In. 25.00
Oil, Gustav Stickley, Iron Scrolled Bands, Silk Lined Wicker Shade, No. 376, 13 In. 7000.00
Oil, Hanging, Scroll Leaf Design, Brass, Amber Glass, Cranberry Hobnail Shade, 14 In. . . 405.00
Oil, Harp, Pressed Glass, 6 In. 2750.00
Oil, Hobbs Snowflake, Glass, White Opalescent, 9 1/2 In. 475.00
Oil, Inverted Thumbprint, Glass, Finger, Blue, Applied Handle, 3 1/4 In. 230.00
Oil, James Hinks & Son, Clear Font, Brass Columnar Base, Electrified, 19th Century 135.00
Oil, Lattice & Oval Panels, Pressed Glass, 6 1/2 In. 210.00
Oil, Moon & Star, Clear & Frosted Font, Blue Stem & Foot, 11 In. 150.00
Oil, Morning Glory, Pressed Glass, 5 7/8 In. 1850.00
Oil, Opaque Cornstarch Blue Font, Painted Flowers, Baroque Base, 8 3/4 In. 325.00
Oil, Opaque White Base, Gilt, Cranberry Cut To Clear Font, Brass, 13 3/4 In. 275.00
Oil, Open Ended Ovoid Form, Cranberry Glass Shade, Brass, 19th Century, 16 3/4 In. . . . 315.00
Oil, Owl, Crescent Moon & Owls, Glass Eyes, Cast Metal Base, 21 In. 1750.00
Oil, Pan, Brass, Iron Trammel, Hanger, 19th Century, 6 In. 155.00
Oil, Peacock Feather, Pressed Glass, 10 1/2 In. 110.00
Oil, Peg, Gold & White Enameled Flowers On Ruffled Shade, 12 In. 295.00
Oil, Pigeon, Brass, France, 1895, 9 1/2 In. 125.00
Oil, Pressed Frosted Glass, Reverse Painted Landscapes, Yellow Ground, 13 1/4 In. 185.00
Oil, Princess Feather, Lemon Yellow Font, Clear Stem 450.00
Oil, Puffy Shade, Pressed Glass, Electrified 72.00
Oil, Sheldon Swirl, Vaseline Opalescent Font, Clear Base, 7 1/4 In. 375.00
Oil, Single Angle, Tin Body, Wick Adjuster, Milk Glass Shade 90.00
Oil, Stamped Fire Fly, Stars, 6 1/4 In. 440.00
Oil, Star East Industries, Tin Hanger & Reflector 135.00

Oil, Student, Brass, Burner, Green & White Overlay Shade, 20 1/2 In. 330.00
Oil, Student, Brass, Opaque White Shade, Electrified, 21 1/4 In. 275.00
Oil, Thousand Eye, Pressed Glass, Blue, 12 In. 170.00
Oil, Three Face, Pressed Glass, 8 3/4 In. 100.00
Oil, Tin, Pocket Type, Brass Top, 2 1/4 In. 120.00
Oil, Tin, Saucer Base, Handle, Removable Font, 7 1/4 In. 250.00
Oil, Tin, Standing, Weighted Base, Pick, 7 5/8 In. 190.00
Oil, Triple Angle, Brass Font, Wick Adjuster 1090.00
Pairpoint lamps are in the Pairpoint category.
Peace Filament, 1980s, 10 1/4 In. 10.00
Perfume, Glass Eyes, Germany, 10 In. 185.00
Rushlight, Blacksmith Made, Iron, England, 11 In. 495.00
Rushlight, Candle Socket, Counter Balance, Wrought Iron, 15 1/4 In. 247.00
Rushlight, Forged Iron, 24 In. 200.00
Rushlight, Iron, Candle Counter Weight, Wooden Base, 48 In. 770.00
Rushlight & Candleholder, Candle Socket 1 End, Save All Other, c.1750, 39 In. 1250.00
Rushlight & Candleholder, Wooden Base, 18th Century, 11 1/2 In. 495.00
Sconce, 2-Arm, Bronze, Gilt, France, 19th Century 1760.00
Sconce, 2-Light, Baroque, Brass, Urn Finial, S-Scroll Arms, 14 1/2 x 13 In. 220.00
Sconce, 2-Light, Brass, Hammered Anno 1698, 13 1/2 In., Pair 545.00
Sconce, 2-Light, Bronze, Pressed Glass, Angular Square Arms, Teardrop Prisms, Pair 630.00
Sconce, 2-Light, Candle, Round Mirror Reflector, 12 In. 286.00
Sconce, 2-Light, Candle, Tin, Crimped, Heart Reflector, 9 1/2 In., Pair 220.00
Sconce, 2-Light, Cloth Shade, Metal Frame, Glass Birds, Flowers, Electrified, 23 In., Pair 880.00
Sconce, 2-Light, Dutch Repousse, Flower & Fruit Design, Scrolled Arm, 19 1/2 In., Pair . 260.00
Sconce, 2-Light, Foliate Cape Scrolled Candle Arms, Corinthian Capital, George III, Pair . 1955.00
Sconce, 2-Light, Georgian Style, Eagle On Rock Shape, Giltwood, 43 In., Pair 2070.00
Sconce, 2-Light, Gilt Metal, Beaded, Floral, Leaf Crystal Prisms, Italy, 21 In., Pair 1610.00
Sconce, 2-Light, Glass Shade, Quezal, Signed, Rosewood, c.1910, 20 1/2 In., Pair 825.00
Sconce, 2-Light, Louis XV, Acanthus Leaf, Gilt Metal, 18 1/2 In., Pair 460.00
Sconce, 2-Light, Louis XV, Bronze, Foliate Standard, Foliage, Electrified, 22 In., Pair . . . 1495.00
Sconce, 2-Light, Louis XVI, Brass, Faceted Drops, Beads, Electrified, 1925, 20 In., Pair . . 1090.00
Sconce, 2-Light, Louis XVI, Floral Quiver, Ribbon Backplate, Electrified, 17 In., Pair . . . 1150.00
Sconce, 2-Light, Neoclassical Scene Cartouche, Applied Flowers, Porcelain, 16 1/2 In. . . . 630.00
Sconce, 2-Light, Scrolled Supports, Bell-Form Glass Shades, 8 1/2 x 10 1/2 In., 2 Pair . . . 4887.00
Sconce, 2-Light, Tropical Birds, Longwy Plaque, Bronze, 12 3/8 In. 287.00
Sconce, 3 Light, Brass, Milk Glass Flowers, c.1860, 11 x 12 In., Pair 750.00
Sconce, 3-Light, Acanthus Leaf, Fleur-De-Lis Design, Oval Wall Plate, Electrified, Pair . . 745.00
Sconce, 3-Light, Brass, Oval Floral Backplate 395.00
Sconce, 3-Light, Column Form Standard, S-Scrolled Arms, 16 In., Pair 200.00
Sconce, 3-Light, Louis XV, Scrolled Foliate Design, 19th Century, 16 1/2 In., Pair 430.00
Sconce, 3-Light, Round Backplate, Etched Shade, Electrified, 13 1/4 In., Pair 2875.00
Sconce, 3-Light, Tasseled Rib & Backplate, Electrified, Brass, 4 Piece 805.00
Sconce, 3-Light, Tin, 6 Point Star Back, Hanging Hole, Drip Pan, 10 1/4 In. 300.00
Sconce, 3-Light, Winged Female Figurine Holding Torch, Empire, 16 In., Pair 490.00
Sconce, 4-Light, Bronze, Ribbon Tied Wreaths Top, Electrified, 39 In., Pair 745.00
Sconce, 4-Light, Electric Candles, Porcelain Inserts, Gold Shade, Gilded Brass, Pair 275.00
Sconce, 4-Light, Urn With Flowers, Pendant Floral Drops, Pink, Blue Glass, 28 In. 2875.00
Sconce, 5-Light, Murano, Scalloped Shell Form Bracket, Mid-20th Century, 20 In. 5462.00
Sconce, 5-Light, Rosette Supporting Double Glass Back, Glass Beads, 11 1/4 In. 2875.00
Sconce, 7-Light, Floral & Foliate Standard, Foliate Bobeches, Prisms, 22 In. 1380.00
Sconce, Altar, Rococo, Gilt Metal, Wrought Iron, Germany, Pair 11000.00
Sconce, Bell & Plume, Latticinio, Blue 225.00
Sconce, Brass Arms, Stringed Graduated Glass Beads, Glass Bobeches, 22 In., Pair 259.00
Sconce, Brass, Pulled Feather Green, Gold Iridescent Glass, Signed, Pair 290.00
Sconce, Brass, Scrolled Foliage, Cornucopia, S-Scroll Arm, Removable, Dutch, 19 In. 2300.00
Sconce, Brass, White, Green Stripe Luster Shade, Glass, 11 In. 130.00
Sconce, Bronze, Female Tern Holding A Cornucopia, France, 28 In., Pair 3910.00
Sconce, Candle, Pine, Square Nails, 15 3/4 In. 160.00
Sconce, Crystal, Silver Plate, Scroll Arms, Osler, Victorian, England, 14 In., Pair 385.00
Sconce, Double Candle, Shell Crest, Lower Drip Pan, Brass, 1687, 13 1/2 In. 605.00
Sconce, Edgar Brandt, 2-Arm, Wrought Iron, Gray Glass, Orange On Curved Arm, Pair . . 10925.00
Sconce, Fluted, Curved Front, Shaped For 2 Candles, Tin, 1830s, 12 1/2 In., Pair 950.00

Sconce, G. Stickley, Brass, Opalescent Light Green Shade, 12 In., Pair 5500.00
Sconce, G. Stickley, No. 830, Iron, 6 Square Cutouts At Top, Amber Glass, 6 x 12 In. 4400.00
Sconce, George Nakashima, Walnut, Parchment, Semicylindrical, 17 x 9 3/4 x 5 In. 1540.00
Sconce, Louis XV, Bronze, 5 Scrolled Foliate, Phoenix Head Branches, 24 In., Pair 4600.00
Sconce, Louis XVI, Brass, Applied Magnifying Lenses, 14 In., Pair 980.00
Sconce, Mahogany, Brass, Twisted Glass Arm, Hurricane Globe, Prisms, Pair 305.00
Sconce, Punched Tin Star On Back, 6 3/4 In., Pair 495.00
Sconce, Silvered Metal, Diamond Shaped Plate, S-Shaped Arm, Louis XIV, 28 In., Pair .. 8625.00
Sconce, Tin, Oval Reflector, c.1800, Pair 950.00
Shade, Arts & Crafts, Green, Purple Corners, Caramel Glass Inserts, 18 In. 272.00
Shade, Hanging, Caramel & Green Slag Glass, Geometric Design, 17 1/2 x 22 In. 495.00
Silver Crest, Sterling On Bronze, 11 1/2 In. 995.00
Skater's, Green Globe, Brass & Tin, Wire Bale, 6 3/4 In. 60.00
Skater's, Perko Wonde, Tin, Clear Molded Globe, Jr. 66.00
Skater's, Tin, Clear Globe, Red Stain, 6 1/4 In. 110.00
Skater's, Tin, Cobalt Blue Globe, 6 3/4 In. 275.00
Skater's, Tin, Peacock Green Globe, Wire Bail, 7 3/8 In. 355.00
Student, 2 Green Cased Glass Shades, Manhattan Brass Co., 23 1/2 In. 403.00
Tiffany lamps are listed in the Tiffany category.
Torchere, 3-Winged Female Figures On Platform, Lion Paw Feet, 1850s, 56 In. 1090.00
Torchere, 6-Light, Faceted Dome, Down Scrolled Arms, Marble Plinth, 53 3/4 In., Pair .. 8050.00
Torchere, Beech, Blackamoor, Mother-Of-Pearl Eyes, c.1900, 48 1/2 In. 1760.00
Torchere, Blackamoor, Upside-Down Figure, Hands On Pillow, 36 1/2 In., Pair 8050.00
Torchere, Carved, Faux Marble, Robust Putti, Vases, On Heads, c.1875, 64 In., Pair 1030.00
Torchere, Chrome Metal Shade, Tapered Ring Standard, Jean Pascaud, 71 In. 2587.00
Torchere, Iridescent Patinated Metal, Art Deco, 62 3/4 In. 137.50
Torchere, Iron, Scroll Tripod Base, Floral Finial, 2-Candle, Iron, 20th Century, 68 In. 58.00
Torchere, Mahogany, William IV, Gadroon Carved Base, Paw Feet, c.1840, 48 1/2 In. ... 360.00
Torchere, Reeded Column Headed With Swags, Scrolled Base, 57 1/2 In., Pair 315.00
Torchere, Wheat Sheaf Carving, 3 Cabriole Legs, 19th Century, 60 In. 330.00
Torchere, Wrought Iron, Cobalt Blue Streak, Gray Shade, N. Daum, 69 1/2 In. 11500.00
Torchere, Wrought Metal, Tudor Style, 66 1/2 In., Pair 690.00
Whale Oil, 6-Sided, Pressed Glass, 1840s, 10 In. 120.00
Whale Oil, Baker's, Tin, Wooden Handle, 2-Spout Burner, 13 In. 165.00
Whale Oil, Bellflower, Glass, 7 1/2 In. 100.00
Whale Oil, Blown & Pressed Glass, Pewter Collar, 10 In. 170.00
Whale Oil, Blown Glass, Diamond, Knob Stem, Tin 2-Wick Burner, 7 1/2 In. 25.00
Whale Oil, Blown Glass, Finger, Waffles, Diamonds & Thumbprints, 3 In. 140.00
Whale Oil, Blown Glass, Octagonal Pressed Standard, Square Base, 8 1/4 In. 110.00
Whale Oil, Blown, Attached Stem & Foot, Open Pontil, 1830s, 5 In. 75.00
Whale Oil, Brass, Brass Burner, Pair 895.00
Whale Oil, Brass, Turned Bulges, 19th Century, Tall 195.00
Whale Oil, Brass, Turned, 19th Century, 9 In. 110.00
Whale Oil, Brass, Urn & Ring Shaft, 6 1/8 In., Pair 275.00
Whale Oil, Chamber, Brass, Hinged Snuffer, 6 1/2 In. 135.00
Whale Oil, Clear & Cobalt Blue, 5 In. 2950.00
Whale Oil, Gothic Arch, Glass, 10 In. 80.00
Whale Oil, Lace, Pressed Glass, Light Bulb Font, Pontil, 8 1/2 In. 145.00
Whale Oil, Moon & Star, Glass, Finger, 4 1/4 In. 100.00
Whale Oil, Onion Shape, Stepped Base, Double Wick, Tin Top, 10 In., Pair 316.00
Whale Oil, Peg, Tin, Dark Brown Japanning, 6 In. 90.00
Whale Oil, Pewter, Screw Top, 4 7/8 In. 195.00
Whale Oil, Pressed Glass, Ground Lip, 1830s, 6 In. 100.00
Whale Oil, Pressed Glass, Metal Wick Holder, 1830s, 8 1/2 In. 110.00
Whale Oil, Pressed Glass, Octagonal, Light Bulb Font, Metal Collar, 9 1/4 In. 195.00
Whale Oil, Pressed Glass, Square, Conical Font, Square, Knoft, 8 1/2 In. 110.00
Whale Oil, Punty & Ellipse, 19th Century, 7 In. 248.00
Whale Oil, Round Design, Open Pontil, 1830s, 6 1/4 In. 55.00
Whale Oil, Sandwich Glass, 19th Century, 10 1/2 In. 90.00
Whale Oil, Sandwich Heart, Glass, 10 In. 140.00
Whale Oil, Sandwich, Applied Pewter Collar, Base, 6 Sides, 11 In. 120.00
Whale Oil, Sandwich, Attached Wick Holder, 1830s, 10 In. 110.00
Whale Oil, Sandwich, Waterfall Base, 19th Century, 10 1/2 In. 175.00

Whale Oil, Waffle & Thumbprint, Glass, 9 5/8 In. 170.00
Whale Oil, Wall Hanging, Punched Design, Old Wick, 4 1/4 In. 170.00

LANTERNS are a special type of lighting device. They have a light
source, usually a candle, totally hidden inside the walls of the lantern.
Light is seen through holes or glass sections.

Apparatus, Ornamental, 4 Sides, Green & Red Glass, 1870, 15 In. 920.00
Barn, Painted Black, Tin, 19th Century, 23 In. 190.00
Barn, Poplar, 12 In. 220.00
Barn, Tin Heat Shield, Cherry, 11 In.. 330.00
Baroque, Painted, Parcel Gilt, Egg & Dart Top, Basket Weave, Italy, 25 x 21 In., Pair 3450.00
Brass, Centennial Lantern, Handle & Hook For Hanging, 1876, 3 x 10 1/2 In. 50.00
Brass, Mahogany, Pagoda Form, Fish Scale Concave-Sided Roof, Italy, 30 1/2 In. 2185.00
Brass, Onion-Domed Cover, Glass Sides, Pierced Band, Electrified, 13 In. 260.00
Brass, Regency, Portico, Cast Iron, 1900-1910, 28 x 25 In. 2904.00
Candle, Brown Japanning, Hinged Door, Glass 4 Sides, Wire Guards, Tin, 10 5/8 In. 303.00
Candle, Pyramid Top, Piercing & Tooling, Ring Handle, 10 In. 110.00
Candle, Tin, 4 Glass Panes, 19th Century, 11 In. 110.00
Candle, Tin, Cage, Original Except Glass, Square, 12 3/4 In. 280.00
Candle, Tin, Pierced, 19th Century, 17 x 6 In. 245.00
Candle, Tin, Pyramidal Top, Black Paint, Ring Handle, 11 1/2 In. 220.00
Candle, Tin, Universal Lantern, Philadelphia, 19th Century, 14 In. 82.00
Coleman, Green Porcelain, Large Bail, Black Plastic Carrier, Wichita, Kansas 40.00
Coleman, Model 200A, Red Porcelain, Bale Handle, Accessories, Box, 1962, 12 In. 105.00
Coleman, Model 220F, Green Enamel, Instructions, Brochure, Carton, 1964 .... 120.00
Coleman, Model 228F, Gas, Green Porcelain, Glass, Bale Handle, 1972, 15 In. 45.00
Copper, Hanging, Mica Panels, Arts & Crafts, 25 In. 950.00
Copper, Standard Navigation Lamps, Electrified, New Jersey, 23 In. 60.00
Dietz, New York Central, Bell Bottom 125.00
Dietz, Tin, Black Paint, Pressed Glass Globe, Dietz No. 3, 17 In. 55.00
Dietz, King, Seagrave On Water Shield, Tin Plate 450.00
Dietz, King Fire Dept. 25.00
Gilt Metal, Continental, Tole, Electrified, 19 1/4 In................................. 145.00
Hall, 18th Century Style, Open Scroll Work, Domed Top, Acanthus Finial, 37 1/2 In. 690.00
Hall, Pink Hobnail Glass, Scrolled Cast Iron Frame, Chains, 48 In., Pair 1150.00
Hanging, 4-Light, Sheraton Style, Urn Finials, 26 In. 190.00
Hanging, Baroque, Dart Top, Basket Weave Body, Italy, 25 1/2 x 21 In., Pair 3450.00
Hanging, Bronze, Mica Inserts, Flowers, Green, Blue, Red, Arts & Crafts, 25 In. 2200.00 to 2970.00
Hanging, Ceiling Hook, Foliate & Rosettes, Pine Cone Pendant, Bronze, 32 In. 1725.00
Hanging, Miner's, Metal, Glass, 10 3/4 In. 60.00
Hanging, Original Mild Glass Inserts, Pyramidal Vented Cap, G. Stickley, 30 In. 1320.00
Horn & Sheet Iron, American, 18th Century, Small 575.00
Iron & Tin, Painted, Hexagonal, Domed Roof, 25 1/4 In., Pair 2587.00
Kerosene, Brass, Bradley & Hubbard, Pressed Glass Globe, Tin Base, 9 1/2 In. 190.00
Kerosene, Tin, X-Wire Glass Guards, Cupola Vent, Handle, 18 1/2 In. 110.00
Mahogany, Italian Neoclassical, Pagoda Shape, Scalloped, Concave Roof, 30 x 18 In. 2185.00
Metal, Rococo, Surmounted By Foliate Scrolled Finial, Electricity, Italy, Pair 7475.00
Military Railroad, Adams & Westlake, Adlake Reliable, Pear Shape Globe, 1908 .... 250.00
Processional, 3 Sides, Rococo, Parcel Gilt, Painted, Venetian, 97 3/4 In., Pair 3450.00
Save All, Tin, Pierced, 24 In. 975.00
Scrolled Handled Door, Loop Handle, Punched Tin, 17 In. 253.00
Star & Diamond Design, Removable Font, Blown & Colorless Glass, 14 3/4 In. 1955.00
Tin, Curved Mica Panels, Gimbal, Ferule, Black Paint, 15 1/2 In. 55.00
Tin, Paul Revere, Pierced Wheel & Star Designs, 1800, 13 In. 120.00
Tin, Pierced, Paul Revere, Hinged Door, 1820, 15 In. 90.00
Tin, Police, Whale Oil, Dark Japanning, Bull's-Eye Lens, Shutter, 7 5/8 In. 82.00
Tin, Punched, Black Paint, 11 In. 77.00
Tin, Punched, Mexican, 1706, 18 In. 115.00
Tole, Parcel Gilt, Metal, Rococo, Hexagonal, Electrified, Italy, 89 In., Pair 7475.00
Traveling, Folding, 2 Figural Panels, Oriental, Tin Carrying Case, 6 In. 120.00
Wood & Paper, Relief Shishi & Peony Design, Brass & Copper, 14 1/2 In. 1210.00
Wrought Iron & Glass, 4 Sides, Wire Cage Around Glass, Oil, 19th Century, 14 In. 154.00

LE VERRE FRANCAIS is one of the many types of cameo glass made in France. The glass was made by the C. Schneider factory in Epinay-sur-Seine from 1920 to 1933. It is a mottled glass, usually decorated with floral designs, and bears the incised signature *Le Verre Francais.*

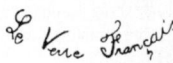

Bowl, Purple, Pink, White Mottled, Black Foot, 15 x 4 In. 303.00
Lamp, Butterflies, Orange, Purple, Domed Knop Shade, 18 In. 6670.00
Lamp, Deep Blue Cut Rondels, Flowers, Gray, Blue, 19 In. 2990.00
Lamp, Desk, Aubergine, Orange, Tapered, Circular Foot, 13 In. 3450.00
Lamp, Stylized Berried Foliage, Orange Ground, Wrought Iron, 20 In. 4600.00
Night-Light, Stylized Blossoms, Red, Yellow Tortoiseshell, 3 1/4 In. 374.00
Perfume Bottle, Purple, Rose Pink Etched, Yellow Pear Shape, Atomizer, 7 In. 374.00
Pitcher, Digitalis On Pink Ground, Orange, Deep Aubergine, Pad Foot, 11 In. 1380.00
Vase, 3 Large Upright Scarabs Around Body, Tapered Sides, 6 In. 880.00
Vase, 5-Petal Flowers, Border Of Grass, Signed, 1925, 15 1/2 In. 1380.00
Vase, Brown Tortoiseshell, Double Gourd Shape, 7 x 9 In. 920.00
Vase, Convoluted Leaf & Vine Designs, Mottled Aubergine, Blue, 22 In. 1380.00
Vase, Digitalis On Pink Mottled Ground, Orange, Aubergine, 14 3/4 In. 1840.00
Vase, Floral, Gray, White, Purple Ground, Signed, Charder, 11 In. 430.00
Vase, Grapevine, Orange, Red, Yellow, Maroon, Pedestal Foot, 16 In. 1495.00
Vase, Mottled Orange To Purple Shading, Pendent Clusters, 1900, 11 In. 632.00
Vase, Mushrooms Amidst Rushes, Aubergine, Pale Yellow, 32 In. 5750.00
Vase, Poppies On Yellow Ground, Brown, Pad Foot, 8 1/2 In. 1265.00
Vase, Salamanders Pursuing Dragonflies, Orange, Everted Rim, 11 In. 2415.00
Vase, Scarabs On Orange Ground, Pad Foot, 16 1/2 In. 1840.00
Vase, Stylized Art Deco Blossoms, Dots, Yellow, Orange Layers, 11 3/4 In. 1380.00
Vase, Stylized Art Deco Flowers, Leaves, Mottled Gray, Orange, Red, 28 In. 3737.00
Vase, Stylized Dahlia Blossoms, Mottled Purple, Gray, Orange, 11 3/4 In. 1035.00
Vase, Stylized Flower, Dark Aubergine Circular Foot, Orange, 7 In. 805.00
Vase, Stylized Flowering Trees, Orange, Yellow, Tango Red To Aubergine, 9 In. 1610.00
Vase, Stylized Leaves, Berries, 2 Purple Handles, Mottled Red, Yellow, 12 In. 1380.00
Vase, Stylized Orange Leaves, Berries, Deep Bell Form, Signed, 10 In. 1100.00
Vase, Stylized Pendent Flowers, Leaves, Mottled Orange, Red, Blue, 18 In. 4180.00
Vase, Stylized Roses, Orange, Moss Green, Cafe-Au-Lait Ground, 16 In. 1840.00
Vase, Stylized Sunflowers, Pink, Amethyst To Purple Shading, Etched, 4 In. 518.00
Vase, Trumpet, Cascading Flowers, Yellow To Red, Orange, 12 1/4 In. 977.00
Vase, Trumpet, Stylized Hollyhocks, Yellow, Cobalt, Orange Band, 19 In. 3737.00
Vase, Twisting Ribbons, Dots, Amber, Brown To Orange Cameo, 17 In. 920.00

LEATHER is tanned animal hide and it has been used to make decorative and useful objects for centuries. Leather objects must be carefully preserved with proper humidity and oiling or the leather will deteriorate and crack. This damage cannot be repaired.

Boots, Cowboy, Man's, Justin, Worn Soles, Size 9 . . . . 55.00
Box, Hat, Gentleman's, Early 19th Century 410.00
Box, Hat, Top Hat Inside, 19th Century 143.00
Case, Picnic, Ebonized Frame, England, 1900, 20 x 22 In. 825.00
Case, Picnic, Fully Fitted Interior, Frame, England, 1900 . . . . 357.00
Folio, Dark Blue, Gilt Embossed Foliate & Scroll Border, Blue Moire Lining, 16 In. 358.00
Frame, Picture, Alligator, Early 20th Century, 10 x 16 In. 303.00
Holster, Cowboy, Cross Draw, Brown, Slim, 9 1/4 In. 35.00
Money Belt, Kidskin, Blue Cloth Edge, Red Leather Fastenings, 19th Century 150.00
Pouch, Bullet & Shot, Sheet Brass Throat, 19th Century, 9 1/4 In. 125.00
Pouch, Bullet & Shot, Tin Throat, 8 1/4 In. 125.00
Pouch, Rifleman's, Hand Forged Iron Catch, 2 Compartments, 18th Century 295.00
Pouch, Tobacco, 2 Women Standing, 1 Woman Seated, Japan 95.00
Saddle, McClellan, Cavalry, 1904 . . . . 395.00
Saddle, Rifle Holder, Sword Hanger, Saddle Bags, Mexican, Pompom Rosettes 650.00
Saddle, Western, Deer Hide, Carved Antler Sash Buckle 88.00
Saddle Strap, 6 Horse Brasses, 1900s, Pair 330.00
Wallet, Raised Design, Marked, New Hampshire, 18th Century, 6 1/4 x 6 In. 1705.00

LEEDS pottery was made at Leeds, Yorkshire, England, from 1774 to 1878. Most Leeds ware was not marked. Early Leeds pieces had distinctive twisted handles with a greenish glaze on part of the creamy ware. Later ware often had blue borders on the creamy pottery. A Chicago company named Leeds made many Disney-inspired figurines. They are listed in the Disneyana category.

LEEDS POTTERY.

Bowl, Multicolored Floral, Bud, Leaf, 7 1/4 In.	198.00
Bowl, Multicolored Floral, Foliate, Geometric, Vine On Exterior, 10 3/4 In.	1650.00
Charger, Blue Feather, Yellow Urn, Multicolor Flowers, Scalloped Edge, 13 3/4 In.	1980.00
Coffeepot, Blue & Yellow Floral, 12 1/4 In.	740.00
Coffeepot, Dome Cover, Brown Orange Berries, Green Leaves, 12 In.	2090.00
Creamer, Blue Flower, Green & Tan Foliage, Bulbous, 3 3/4 In.	520.00
Creamer, Brown, Tan, Blue Running Vine, Blue & Brown Sprig, Bulbous, 4 1/2 In.	275.00
Creamer, Flora, Blue, Yellow, Green, Bulbous, 3 1/2 In.	355.00
Creamer, Stylized Running Acorn Design, 2 1/2 In.	1320.00
Cup & Saucer, Multicolored Floral & Leaf, Blue Border, Wood, Handleless	275.00
Cup & Saucer, Yellow, Blue, Tan, Green Leaves & Flowers, Handleless	495.00
Cup Plate, Multicolored Floral Vine, 3 5/8 In.	99.00
Mug, Lion, Blue Transfer, Child's, 2 1/4 In.	1540.00
Nut Set, Green Feather Edge, Bowl With Underplate, 4 Piece, 3 1/2 In.	1150.00
Plate, Blue & Yellow Floral Transfer, Embossed Multicolored Floral Border, 6 5/8 In.	99.00
Plate, Blue Design, Late 18th Century, 8 1/4 In.	395.00
Plate, Blue Feather, Urn, Pineapple, 5 1/2 In.	1045.00
Plate, Brown, Tan, Blue, American Eagle, Shield, 8 In.	1650.00
Plate, Floral, Blue Feather Rim, 8 In.	355.00
Plate, Green Feather Edge, Floral Bud, Leaves, Embossed Scalloped Border, 7 3/4 In.	577.00
Plate, Green Feather, Brown Basket, Zigzag, Dots, Flowers, Scalloped Edge, 9 5/8 In.	1100.00
Plate, Multicolored Flowers, Leaves, Acorn, Stubbs & Kent, 7 3/4 In.	605.00
Plate, Oriental Scene, 9 3/4 In.	165.00
Plate, Peacock On Branches, Octagonal, Cobalt Blue Trim, 7 1/2 In.	220.00
Plate, Peafowl On Branch, Tan, Blue, Green, 9 3/4 In.	825.00
Platter, Basketry Inner Border, Blue, White, 17 1/2 x 13 1/2 In.	210.00
Platter, Blue Feather, Oval, Molded Rim, Dixon, Austin & Co., 13 1/2 In.	83.00
Platter, Floral, Foliate Design, Cobalt, Floral Border, 17 x 13 3/4 In.	170.00
Sauceboat, Blue Feather Edge	70.00
Teapot, Blue & Yellow Flowers, Dome Top, 10 In.	770.00
Teapot, Blue, White Swirl Design, 4 In.	230.00
Tureen, Cover, Vegetable Supported On Leaf Stand, Stalk Handle, 10 In.	2185.00

LEFTON is a mark found on many pieces. The Geo. Zoltan Lefton Company has imported pottery, porcelain, glass, and other wares to be sold in America since 1940. The firm is still in business. The company mark has changed through the years; but because marks have been used for long periods of time, they are of little help in dating an object.

Bookends, Cats, H518	25.00
Bowl, With Cherub, No. 926	500.00
Bust, Bernard Shaw, 5 1/2 In.	35.00
Bust, Bloomer Girl, 4 1/2 In.	45.00
Bust, Brahms, 6 In.	35.00
Bust, Liszt, 7 In.	45.00
Candleholder, Holy, Climbers, Box	25.00
Candy Dish, Valentine Girl	15.00
Coffee Set, Pink & Yellow Roses, Gold Handles, 9 In., 3 Piece	130.00
Cookie Jar, Bluebird	375.00
Cookie Jar, Dainty Miss	195.00 to 275.00
Cookie Jar, Dutch Girl	250.00
Cookie Jar, Miss Priss	125.00
Cookie Jar, Mr. Toodles	300.00
Cookie Jar, Violets	75.00
Creamer, Miss Priss	35.00
Creamer, Mr. Toodles	45.00
Cup & Saucer, Reindeer, Box	45.00
Figurine, Bird Of Paradise, 6 3/4 In.	85.00

Figurine, Bird, Cardinal	20.00
Figurine, Chiropractor, Porcelain, 10 In.	15.00
Figurine, May Boy Playing Golf	70.00
Figurine, Pink Lady, 8 In.	95.00
Figurine, Snowbird	25.00
Figurine, Tiger, 8 1/2 In.	80.00
Head Vase, Ginger	50.00
Head Vase, Girl, Holding Candy Cane, 6 3/4 In.	48.00
Mug, Shamrock, Green, Pixie Handle, 5 1/2 In.	15.00
Pitcher & Bowl, Green, Heritage	65.00
Planter, Baby Chick, Hand Painted, 6 In.	45.00
Planter, Christmas, Girl, Carrying Lantern, 6 1/2 In.	30.00
Pocket Vase, Bluebird, 6 1/2 In.	100.00
Salt & Pepper, Bunny Girls	25.00
Salt & Pepper, Eastern Star, Gold Trim	12.00
Sugar, Cover, Bluebird	20.00
Sugar & Creamer, Dutch Girl	95.00
Sugar & Creamer, Rustic Daisy	35.00
Teapot, Dutch Girl	150.00
Teapot, Magnolia	185.00
Teapot, Miss Priss	85.00
Teapot, Violet Chintz	175.00 to 185.00
Vase, Forget-Me-Not, 7 In.	50.00 to 65.00

LEGRAS was founded in 1864 by Auguste Legras at St. Denis, France. It is best known for cameo glass and enamel-decorated glass with Art Nouveau designs. Legras merged with Pantin in 1920 and became the Verreries et Cristalleries de St. Denis et de Pantin Reunies.

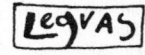

Bowl, Autumn Leaves, Silver Plated Stand, 3 x 9 3/4 In.	600.00
Bowl, Green Aubergine Leaves, Berries, Mustard Yellow Ground, 4 3/4 x 3 In.	173.00
Vase, Allover Enameled Pink, Maroon Flowering Branches, 8 1/2 In.	575.00
Vase, Allover Etching Of Waterfront Scene, Sailboats, Frosted, 3 1/2 In.	316.00
Vase, Autumn Green Holly Branches, Peach To Chartreuse Ground, 5 In.	1320.00
Vase, Burgundy Leaves, Shaded Peach, 15 3/4 In.	1150.00
Vase, Enameled Dark Branches Going Up Sides, Butterscotch Ground, 8 In.	385.00
Vase, Floral Design, Red, Enamel, Signed, 8 1/2 In.	275.00
Vase, Greyhounds, Rabbits, 9 In.	275.00
Vase, Landscape, Ebony Shepherd & Flock, Green Hillside, Cylindrical, 14 In.	660.00
Vase, Landscape, Enameled, Trees, Lake & Mountains In Distance, 8 1/2 In.	1485.00
Vase, Leafy Vine, Tendrils, Seed Pods, Enameled, Plum, Signed, 1910, 25 1/4 In.	2070.00
Vase, Orange Apples, Green Leaves, Clear Enameled Ground, Signed, 10 3/4 x 5 1/2 In.	60.00
Vase, Pendent Flowers, Purple, Flared Neck, Frosted Ground, 1900, 8 3/4 In.	345.00
Vase, Pendent Leafy Branches, Pod Clusters, Moss Green Ground, 8 1/4 In.	633.00
Vase, Pheasant In Trees, Red, Pink Design, Frosted Ground, Cameo, 7 In.	880.00
Vase, Scenic, Harbor Scene, People & Distant Buildings, Signed, 5 1/4 In.	850.00
Vase, Shaded Blue, Green & Rust Leaves, 11 1/2 In.	3500.00
Vase, Shepherd & Sheep Scene, Orange Woods, Gray, Green, Signed, 9 1/4 In.	800.00
Vase, Stylized Grape Arbor Border, Cameo, 6 In.	287.00
Vase, Swirls, 12 In., Pair	345.00
Vase, Thistles, Carmel Ground, Signed, 4 1/4 In.	850.00

LENOX is the name of a porcelain maker. Walter Scott Lenox and Jonathan Cox founded the Ceramic Art Company in Trenton, New Jersey, in 1889. In 1906, Lenox left and started his own company called *Lenox*. The company makes a porcelain that is similar to Irish Belleek. The marks used by the firm have changed through the years and collectors prefer the earlier examples. Related pieces may also be listed in the Ceramic Art Co. category.

Bowl, Water Lilies, Signed, 7 In.	95.00
Bust, Man & Woman, Ivory Glaze, Impressed, 8 3/4 In.	220.00
Centerpiece, Porcelain, Trumpet Shape, Reticulated, Silver, Gorham, 11 In.	1150.00
Dish, Leaf Design, Gilt Border, 2-Part Handles, 10 1/2 In.	20.00
Figurine, Girl, Flowing Gown, Ivory Glaze, Impressed, 13 In.	385.00

Figurine, Rapunzel	150.00
Figurine, Snow Queen	70.00
Figurine, Stardust	70.00
Nut Dish, Shell Shape, Green Mark	25.00
Pitcher, Face Under Spout, Signed, 1906	225.00
Pitcher, Ivory, Gold, 7 1/4 In.	40.00
Salt & Pepper, Robins & Jays, White	25.00
Salt & Pepper Mill, Lido	75.00
Server, 2 Tiers, Ivory, Gold, Center Handle, Round	40.00
Spooner, Waffle, Silver Plated Holder, c.1888	65.00
Toby Jug, William Penn, Blue Handle	175.00
Vase, Chinese Bird, Jade Green Glaze, Stamped, 11 In.	495.00
Vase, White, Green Mark, 8 In.	25.00

LETTER OPENERS have been used since the eighteenth century. Ivory and silver were favored by the well-to-do. In the late nineteenth century, the letter opener was popular as an advertising giveaway and many were made of metal or celluloid. Brass openers with figural handles were also popular.

Abraham Lincoln, Metal	35.00
Bayonet, Trench Art	183.00
Copper, Hammered, Nickel Finish, Carence Crafters, 8 In.	220.00
Elephants, Walking In Row, Carved Ivory, World War II, 9 1/4 In.	30.00
Excaliber, Sword Shape, Signed, 18K Gold	495.00
Gold, Nephrite, White Guilloche Enamel, Cabochon Sapphire, Gold Leaves, 5 In.	5175.00
Indian Chief, Cast Iron & Brass	65.00
Jack Sprat Food, Metal	75.00
Metal, Inscribed 1902	40.00
Mother-Of-Pearl, Napoleon 3-Dimensional Figure, Stanhope View, 5 1/2 In.	275.00
Nude Woman On Bearskin Rug, Ivory, Art Deco, Sterling Silver Handle, 15 In.	115.00

LIBBEY Glass Company has made many types of glass since 1888, including the cut glass and tablewares that are collected today. The stemwares of the 1930s and 1940s are once again in style. The Toledo, Ohio, firm was purchased by Owens-Illinois in 1935 and is still working under the name *Libbey* as a division of that company. Additional pieces may be listed under Amberina, Cut Glass, and Maize.

Bowl, 5 Large Hobstars, Strawberry-Diamond Fan, 4 1/2 x 9 In.	85.00
Bowl, Colonna, 8 x 1 3/4 In.	230.00
Bowl, Comet, 9 In.	925.00
Bowl, Ivernia, Signed, 2 3/4 x 9 In.	465.00
Bowl, Lovebird, Square Cut Corners, 8 x 8 x 3 In.	85.00
Candlestick, Floral Engraving, Blown Hollow Stem, Signed, 12 In., Pair	950.00
Cheese, Cover, Strawberry-Diamond & Fan, Faceted Knob, Rayed Base, 1896	495.00
Cruet, Kimberley, Cut Stopper, 7 In.	265.00
Cruet, Victoria, Tricorned Spout, 7 In.	210.00
Pitcher, Champagne, Hobstars & Cane, Handle, 14 In.	950.00
Pitcher, Large Hobstar With Strawberry-Diamond, Triple Notched Handle, 8 1/4 In.	175.00
Punch Bowl, Hobstar & Pineapple, Pedestal, Signed, c.1890	3500.00
Punch Cup, Diamond-Quilted, Ribbed Handle, Amberina, 2 3/4 In., Pair	170.00
Punch Cup, Hobstars, Notched Ladder, Fans, Signed, 8 Piece	245.00
Salad Set, Loretta, Signed	1950.00
Tumbler, Whiskey Sour, Nob Hill	11.00
Vase, Amberina, Deep Fuchsia Shading To Amber, Flaring Edge, 11 1/2 In.	950.00
Vase, Amberina, Signed, c.1917, 4 5/8 In.	1250.00
Vase, Folded Edge, Etched, 8 In.	75.00
Vase, Talisman, Flared Oval, Spiraled Green Interior, Crystal Foot, Signed, 14 In.	265.00

The best way to store plates is vertically in a rack.

LIGHTERS for cigarettes and cigars are collectible. Cigarettes became popular in the late nineteenth century, and with the cigarette came matches and cigarette lighters. All types of lighters are collected, from solid gold to the first of the recent disposable lighters. Most examples found were made after 1940. Some lighters may be found in the Jewelry category in this book.

A.S.R., Urn Style, Polished Finish, Table, Box, 3 In.	20.00
Alpha Company, 8th Cavalry, Crossed Sabers, Unit Crest, Brushed Finish, Vulcan, Japan	30.00
American General Life Insurance, George Washington, Horse, Brushed Finish, Box, 1972	85.00
Brass, Lift Arm, 2 In.	22.00
Brass, Polished, Round, Victorian, 1 1/2 In.	50.00
Budweiser, Anheuser-Busch Office Product Sleeve, Polished, Red, White & Blue	45.00
Bulldog, Austrian, 1900s	88.00
Cannon, Brass, Modern	45.00
Chevrolet Dealership, Box	45.00
Cigar, Black, Place Cigar In Mouth & Push Button, Electric, Cast Iron, 5 In.	1760.00
Cigar, Brass, Puck Figure On Pedestal, Circular Base, 7 1/2 In.	231.00
Cigar, Cast White Metal, Comic Figure, Burner In Top Hat, Bucket For Matches, 5 1/4 In.	412.00
Cigar, Falstaff, Top Hat Match Holder, Striker, Ash Receptacle, Marble Base	1500.00
Cigar, Metal, Figural, Gordon Highlander Officer, Enamel, 19th Century, 9 In.	950.00
Cigar, Store, Advertising, Cinco Cigars, 18 1/2 In.	1750.00
Cigar, Table, Brass, 3 Monkey Supports, Victorian, 6 x 6 x 6 In.	695.00
Cities Service, Logo	68.00
Colby, Silver Tone Finish, Textured Panels, Original Box	53.00
Dunhill, 18K Yellow Gold	440.00
Dunhill, Derringer	400.00
Dunhill, Lift Arm, Brass, Engraved, Switzerland, c.1925	180.00
Dunhill, Sally Rand	80.00
Evans, Triga-Lite, Cigarette Case, Polished Finish, Blue Enamel Panels, 5 In.	60.00
Florida, Sunshine State, Map, Palm Trees, Oranges, Stainless, Brushed, 1979	26.00
Golfer, Champion Of The World Golf, Brown Panel, Japan, 1 1/2 In.	20.00
Green Bay Packers, 1970s	79.00
Gun, Occupied Japan, Box	150.00
Hamms, Chrome & Anodized Metal, 1960s	30.00
Hinde & Dauch, Corrugated, Steel, Enameled Logo, Striped Box, 1953	110.00
James R. Hoffa, Yellow Gold Plated, Brushed Surface, 2 In.	62.00
Lighthouse Design, c.1924	295.00
Lockheed, Winged Star Emblem, Brushed Finish, 1964	70.00
M & R Pipeline Construction Co., Lima, Ohio, Logo, Brushed Finish, Box, 1965	45.00
Man Trout Fishing, Engraved, Enameled, 1980	95.00
Nasco, Lift Arm, 18K Gold Plated, 1 1/2 In.	25.00
Nimrod, Sportsman Pipeliter, Brown Leather, Cylinder, Original Box, 3 In.	29.00
Olympic, Discus Thrower, Brass, Bakelite, 1932	300.00
Parker, Watch Movement Inset, Dark Blue Enamel, 2 x 1 1/2 In.	865.00
Penguin, U.S.S. Lexington CVA-16, Aircraft Carrier, Brushed Finish, Slim, Japan	25.00
Penguin, U.S.S. Mackenzie, Asiatic Squadron, Des Ron Three, Box, Japan, 1964-1966	20.00
Phillips 66, Painted Logo, 1966	35.00
Pistol Grip, Wooden, Tinder, Flint Lock, Engraved, 7 In.	495.00
Plymouth Rapid Transit System, 5 Color Logo, Brushed, Box, 1970	118.00
Pontiac, Louis Frahm Pontiac Inc., Downey, Ca., Emblem, Brushed, Box, 1962	92.00
Purina Kitten Chow, Emblem, Brushed Finish, 1975	60.00
Richfield Products, Slim Style, 2 1/8 In.	145.00
Roland Viscount, Corsair II, Vought Aeronautics, Brushed Finish, Japan	20.00
Ronson, Adonis, Stainless Steel Finish, Line Engraving, Box	22.00
Ronson, Art Metal Works, Jumbo, Black Leatherette, 4 x 3 1/4 In.	80.00
Ronson, Canary, Singing, Plays Smoke Gets In Your Eyes, Box	25.00
Ronson, Penciliter, Tan Leather, Metal Case, Box, 14K Gold, 5 1/4 In.	35.00 to 70.00
Ronson, Penciliter, Teal Blue, Maroon Leatherette Case, 5 1/4 In.	50.00
Ronson, Princess, Silver Plated, Engraved Line Design, Box, Tag	35.00
Ronson, Standard, Golden Tan Enamel, Purple Felt Pouch, Original Box	25.00
Ronson, Touch-Tip, Brown Enamel, Table, Pre-World War II, 3 1/2 x 2 1/2 In.	75.00
Scripto, Vu-Lighter, Bruschi Bros. Inc., Bulldozer, Clear Plastic	25.00
Scripto, Vu-Lighter, Ford Farm-Industrial Equipment, Plastic, New Windguard Tin	40.00

Scripto, Vu-Lighter, Loyal Order Of Moose, Boy Praying, Clear Plastic 20.00
Scripto, Vu-Lighter, TC Transcon Lines, Truck, Clear Plastic, Polished Lid 30.00
Shell X-100, Shell Logo On Reverse, 2 1/8 In. 95.00
Socony Vacuum Oil, Catalin Plastic, 3 1/2 In. 120.00
Springvale Country Club, N. Olmsted, Ohio, Golfer, Enameled, Box, 1973 ...... 105.00
St. Louis To The Front, 35th Division, 1918 France, St. Louis On Horse, 3 1/4 In. 150.00
Texaco Marine Products, Marina Scene, 2 1/8 In. 605.00
Tobacconists, Gypsy, Half Length, Cigarette In Mouth, Gas Jet, Cast Metal, 31 In. 5175.00
Union 76, Station Scene, Logo, 2 1/8 In. 92.00
Whalen Erecting Co. Inc., Steel Erectors, Sterling, Slim, 1970s 175.00
Zippo, 50 Years & Glowing Stronger, Commemorative, Brass, Plastic Case, 1932-1982 .. 120.00
Zippo, 7-Up Logo, Polished Finish, Slim, 1968 .... 110.00
Zippo, ACA, 3rd Marine Division Logo, Brushed Finish 25.00
Zippo, Airplane, Beechcraft Model 76 Duchess, Polished Finish, Slim, Box, 1977 .... 30.00
Zippo, Airplane, Spirit Of St. Louis, Stylized Chrome, Table, 5-In. Wingspan 100.00
Zippo, Astronauts Edward White & James McDivitt Recovery, U.S.S. Wasp, June 7, 1965 70.00
Zippo, Barcroft, 2nd Model, Polished Finish, Plain Case, Table, 1947-1950, 4 1/4 In. 255.00
Zippo, Barcroft, 3rd Model, Polished Finish, Plain Case, Table, 1950-1952, 3 1/4 In. 290.00
Zippo, Barcroft, 4th Model, Brushed Finish, Inscribed, Table, Box, 1980, 3 1/4 In. .135.00 to 177.00
Zippo, Barcroft, 4th Model, Mack Truck Bulldog Logo, Table, 1954-1979, 3 1/4 In. 135.00
Zippo, Black Crackle Finish, World War II, 1943-1945 .... 165.00
Zippo, Bowler, Brushed Finish, Painted, Engraved, 1972 .... 50.00
Zippo, Buick Suggestion Winner 1953, Brushed Finish, Diagonal Striped Box 185.00
Zippo, Camel, Joe Camel On Motorcycle, Chrome, Box, 1991 .... 45.00
Zippo, Canon, Camera, Painted, Engraved, Brushed Finish, White & Gold Box, 1978 .... 85.00
Zippo, Castle Brand Meats Packers, Rose City Packing Co. Inc., Repair Box, 1965 ...... 50.00
Zippo, Charlie The Tuna, Think Safety, Cream Panels, Polished Finish, 1988 .... 180.00
Zippo, Chevron Supreme Gasoline, Cloisonne Emblem, 1 1/4 x 2 1/4 In. 120.00
Zippo, Detroit Diesel, Engraved, Polished Finish, Slim, 1967 .... 30.00
Zippo, Diagonal Lines At 2 Corners, 3 Barrel Hinge, Brushed Finish, 1933 ...... .560.00 to 605.00
Zippo, Diagonal Lines At 2 Corners, Polished Finish, 1936-1940 .... 210.00
Zippo, Diagonal Lines At 2 Corners, Polished Finish, 4 Barrel Hinge, 1936-1937 .... 450.00
Zippo, Eaton Truck Axles, Brushed Finish, White & Red Repair Box, 1975 .... 40.00
Zippo, Elsie The Cow Logo, Polished Finish, Slim, White & Gold Box, 1962 .... 80.00
Zippo, Engraved Initials, W.M.E., Brushed Chrome Sides, Steel Case, 1952 .... 23.00
Zippo, Ernie Pyle Memorial, Black Crackle Finish, Steel Case, Box, 1945 .... 1850.00
Zippo, Fisherman, Brushed Finish, Black Plastic Case, 1985 .... 35.00
Zippo, For Best Results Use Zippo Flint & Fluid, Zippo Mfg. Co., Bradford, Pa. 60.00
Zippo, Ford Steel Division Safety Award, 2nd Award, 1, 000, 000 Hours, 1953 .... 30.00
Zippo, Golfer, Advertising, Box 100.00
Zippo, H.C. Outzen Facsimile Signature, Brushed Finish, 3-Barrel Hinge, Late 1940s 75.00
Zippo, Harley Davidson, Black Crackle Finish, Boot Strap 30.00
Zippo, Hunter & Dog, Engraved, Brushed Finish, Box, 1970 .... 30.00
Zippo, Joe Camel .... .20.00 to 22.00
Zippo, Kendall Refining Co., 100th Anniversary, Polished Finish, 1981 .... 70.00
Zippo, Leather Wrapped, Steel Case, Brushed Finish, 1952 .... 90.00
Zippo, Lee Clothes Logo, Black Enamel, Engraved, Original Box 135.00
Zippo, Lincoln Foundry, Los Angeles, Brushed Finish, 5-Barrel Hinge 30.00
Zippo, Linde Union Carbide, Engraved, Brushed Finish, White & Gold Box, 1962 ...... 40.00
Zippo, Marine Corps Emblem, Black Crackle Finish, World War II 165.00
Zippo, Moderne, Cylinder, Polished Finish, Table, 1960s, 4 1/4 In. 110.00
Zippo, N.Y. State Electric & Gas Corp., Lancaster District, Safe Driving Awards, 1960 ... 55.00
Zippo, Naval Submarine Support Base, Kings Bay, Ga., Polished Finish, Brass, Box 25.00
Zippo, Navy Ship, Steel Case, Brushed Finish, 1952 .... 70.00
Zippo, Oscar Meyer, Box 35.00
Zippo, Phillips 66 Logo, K.S. Adams, Chairman, 10K Gold Filled 95.00
Zippo, Pittsburgh Paints, Brushed Finish, White & Gold Box, 1973 .... 50.00
Zippo, Prototype, Irregular Vertical Cuts, Gold Metal, 1978 .... 80.00
Zippo, Reddy Kilowatt, Brushed Finish, 1968 .... 185.00
Zippo, Reddy Kilowatt, Painted, Engraved, Polished Finish, Slim, Box, 1969 ..:...... 90.00
Zippo, Steel Case, Chromed Finish, 4 Barrel Hinge, 1942 .... 70.00
Zippo, Tampa Bay Buccaneers, Mascot, Polished Finish, Slim, 1975 .... 90.00

Zippo, Thompson Pumps, Precision Oil Well Pumps, Brushed Finish, Box, 1967 . . . . 65.00
Zippo, Town & Country, Deer Leaping, White Enamel, 1959 . . . . 72.00
Zippo, Town & Country, Horse Head On Lower Front, Engraved, Chrome Sides, 1950 . . . 65.00
Zippo, Town & Country, Mallard Duck, Hand Painted & Engraved, c.1949 . . . . 110.00
Zippo, TWA, Lockheed, Super G Constellation, Polished Finish, Plastic Case, 1953-55 . . . 95.00
Zippo, U.S. Army Lieutenant Colonel Rank Leaf, Brushed Finish, Late 1940s 75.00
Zippo, U.S. Navy Seabees Emblem, Brushed Finish, Late 1940s 80.00
Zippo, U.S.S. Bon Homme Richard, CVA-31, Polished Finish, Slim, 1969 . . . . 75.00
Zippo, U.S.S. Cacapon AO-52, Find 'em Forget 'em, 6 Colors, Slim, 1961 . . . . 130.00
Zippo, U.S.S. Denver LPD-9, Painted, Engraved, Polished Finish, 1989 . . . . 25.00
Zippo, U.S.S. Intrepid, CVS 11, Engraved Ship, 1967 . . . . 25.00
Zippo, U.S.S. Portland LSD-37, Ship, Polished Finish, Slim, 1977 . . . . 30.00
Zippo, U.S.S. Repose, Vietnam 1967-68, Polished Finish, Penguin, Japan 35.00
Zippo, U.S.S. Sam Rayburn SSBN-635, Brushed Finish, Black Plastic Case, 1984 . . . . . . 50.00
Zippo, U.S.S. Spruance DD-963, Engraved Ship, Polished Finish, 1979 . . . . 20.00
Zippo, U.S.S. Trout SS 566, Logo, Submarine, Brushed, 1955 . . . . 150.00
Zippo, United States Steel Logo, Brushed Finish, Diagonal Striped Box, 1955 . . . . 80.00
Zippo, Westinghouse Emblem On Lid, Polished Finish, Slim, 1966 . . . . 20.00
Zippo, Westinghouse Logo, Brushed Finish, 1958 . . . . 45.00
Zippo, Whirlpool Home Appliances, Silver 30.00

LIGHTNING ROD BALLS are collected for their variety of shapes and
colors. These glass balls were at the center of the rod that was attached
to the roof of a house or barn to avoid lightning damage.

Electra, Cobalt, 4 1/2 In. 175.00
Electra, Opaque Blue 35.00
Hawkeye 50.00
Moon & Star, Milk Glass 30.00
Schinn System, Amber 100.00
Swirl, Amber, 5 In. 100.00
Yellow Green, Sheared Ends, 1890-1935, 5 In. 120.00

LIMOGES porcelain has been made in Limoges, France, since the mid-
nineteenth century. Fine porcelains were made by many factories,
including Haviland, Ahrenfeldt, Guerin, Pouyat, Elite, and others.
Modern porcelains are being made at Limoges and the word *Limoges*
as part of the mark is not an indication of age. Haviland, one of the
Limoges factories, is listed as a separate category in this book.

Basket, Delicate Flowers, Rococo Gold Handle & Rim, 4 1/2 In. 48.00
Bowl, Center, Bird & Grapes Medallion, Scalloped, Relief Shells, Gilt Handles, 13 In. . . . 230.00
Bowl, Footed, 13 In. 100.00
Bowl, Vegetable, Cover, Gilt Edge, Handles, 12 In., Pair 80.00
Box, Cover, Egg Form, Hand Painted 85.00
Box, Cover, Enamel Floral, 19th Century, 3 1/2 In. 85.00
Box, Cover, Floral Spray Interior, Porcelain, 3 In. 46.00
Box, Jewelry, Cushion Shape, Violette Figure, 1900, Round, 4 1/4 x 8 In. 450.00
Cake Plate, Pink Roses, Green Foliage, Gold Trim, Pale Blue Ground, 10 In. . . . . . . .60.00 to 75.00
Cake Plate, Pink Roses, Green Leaves, Blue To Yellow Ground, Hand Painted, 10 In. . . . 75.00
Candy Dish, Colored Roses, Cover Scene, Boy Playing With Dog, 7 x 5 3/4 In. 103.00
Chamberstick, Enamel, Octagonal, Cartouches Between Foliate Design, 4 In. 490.00
Charger, Colonial Couple, At Bridge, Watching Swans, Hand Painted, 13 In. 275.00
Charger, Fruit Design Center, Pears, Blueberries, Blackberries, Blue, Gold Border 215.00
Charger, Yellow, Pink, Peach Flowers, Raised Gold Border, 12 In. 65.00
Chocolate Pot, Pink & White Roses, Shaded Blue Ground, T & V Mark, 9 1/2 In. 60.00
Clam Set, Shells, Gilt Ruffled Edge, Porcelain, 8 Plates, 1 Tray, 16 x 8 In. 520.00
Creamer, Child's, Pink, Yellow Flowers, 2 1/4 x 3 1/4 In. 45.00
Dessert Set, Floral, Gold Band Border 175.00
Dinner Set, Morning Glory, Blue, Green Foliage, White Ground, 34 Piece 115.00
Dresser Set, Powder Box, Pin Tray, Bottle, Hatpin Holder, Roses, 1909, 11 In. 495.00
Fernery, Violets, Gold Footed, Signed 500.00
Fish Set, Hand Painted, Gilt Borders, 6 Plates, Sauceboat, 23 x 9 In. 750.00
Fish Set, Pond Lilies Border, Art Nouveau, L. Martin, 23 1/2-In. Platter, 12 Piece 1090.00

Fish Set, Red Fish Design, Platter, Oval, 11 Piece	600.00
Game Plate, Fish, Cobalt Blue & Gold Border, M. Redon, 9 In.	60.00
Game Plate, Irregular Edge, Pheasants, Quail, 9 1/2 In., Pair	265.00
Game Set, Hand Painted, 18-In. Platter, 8 1/4-In. Plate, 8 Piece	430.00
Gravy Boat, Sea Shells, Scalloped Gold Rim, Handle	95.00
Hair Receiver, Pink & White Floral, Dark Green Ground, 2 1/4 x 4 In.	75.00
Jar, Cover, Overlapping Lozenges Panels, White, Black, Cobalt Blue, Faure, 17 In.	7475.00
Letter Holder, Large Pink Flowers, Dragonfly On Back, 2 Gold Handles, 8 In.	150.00
Oyster Plate, Pink, White, Gold Design	150.00
Oyster Plate, Tiny Sprigs Of Blue Flowers, Gold Highlights, 8 1/2 In.	210.00
Pitcher, Blue Flowers, Gilt Trim, G. Whitelaw, 1915	170.00
Pitcher, Cherries, Leaves, Gilt Border, Handle, 8 In.	115.00
Pitcher, Grape Leaf Design, Gilded Handles, 6 1/4 In.	200.00
Pitcher, Hand Painted Strawberries, Gold Trim	285.00
Pitcher, Ivory, Hand Painted, Vintage Borders, 6 1/4 In.	110.00
Plaque, 3 Game Birds, Dadat, FOC, 11 In.	130.00
Plaque, Cherubs, Gilt Metal Frame, 7 1/4 x 4 1/2 In., Pair	345.00
Plaque, Farmer & Wife In Field, Hanging, Signed Dubois, 13 In.	115.00
Plaque, Game Birds, Coronet, 10 In.	90.00 to 110.00
Plaque, Mallard, Coronet, A. Marty, 11 In.	155.00
Plaque, Mallard, Marked, 10 In.	33.00
Plaque, Pair Of Game Birds, Grosbaxs, 10 1/2 In.	100.00
Plaque, Pate-Sur-Pate, Woman, Blue Ground, France, 6 3/4 x 9 1/2 In., Pair	630.00
Plaque, Song Bird, Flambeau, 11 In.	55.00
Plaque, Underwater Scene, Opaque Enamels, Swimming Carp, F.G. Hale, 8 1/2 In.	2400.00
Plaque, Viking Ship, Full Sail, Oars Extended, F.G. Hale, 11 1/8 x 8 7/8 In.	2400.00
Plaque, Woman Portrait, Art Nouveau, Floral Frame, Dorval, 1900, 9 x 12 In., Pair	8050.00
Plaque, Young Girl, Long, Flowing Hair, Blue, Red Satin Dress, 6 x 4 In.	2070.00
Plate, Banding, Fruit & Gold Border, Purple Plumbs, Seed Pods, 12 1/4 In.	225.00
Plate, Bird Design, Gold Ruffled Edge, Signed, 8 1/2 In., 6 Piece	345.00
Plate, Bird Design, Hand Painted, Gilt Borders, Green Mark, 9 In., 6 Piece	290.00
Plate, Child's, Storybook, Counting Scenes, 6 Piece	750.00
Plate, Floral, Hand Painted, Gold	275.00
Plate, Flowers & Cherubs, Gilt Edge, White Ground, 12 In.	110.00
Plate, Flowers, Green, Purple, White, Green Border, Hand Painted, c.1912, 8 1/2 In.	133.00
Plate, Gilt Scroll & Leaf Border, 10 3/4 In., 12 Piece	275.00
Plate, Gilt, Bird On Cobalt Ground, Surrounding Reserve, 1870s, 9 1/2 In., 12 Piece	345.00
Plate, Oyster, Sprigs & Blue Flowers, 8 1/2 In.	210.00
Plate, Portrait, Long-Haired Maiden, With Flowers, Porcelain, Circular, 12 1/2 In.	150.00 to 161.00
Plate, Purple, White Flowers, Mint Green Border, Hand Painted, France, 8 1/2 In.	135.00
Plate, Village Scene, Church, River, Fisherman, Hand Painted, Gold Rim, Signed, 12 In.	285.00
Platter, Floral Border, Lobsters In Sea, Porcelain, Oval, 16 1/4 In.	121.00
Platter, Pinks, Oval, 1900, 14 x 20 1/4 In.	82.00
Platter, Trout Center, Fern Design, Gilt Edge, 24 x 10 In.	130.00
Platter, Trout, Artist, Rene, 16 In.	100.00
Powder Box, Hand Painted, Signed, 1920s	110.00
Punch Bowl, Hand Painted, 4 1/2 x 9 1/2 In.	395.00
Soup, Dish, Fluted Gilt Intaglio Rim, 7 1/2 In., 11 Piece	540.00
Sugar & Creamer, Pedestal	100.00
Tankard, Man With Beer Stein, Hand Painted, Gold Trimmed Base, Signed, 14 1/2 In.	550.00
Tea Set, Floral, Gilt Handles, Violet Design On Tray, 8 x 6 In., 3 Piece	145.00
Tile, Portrait, Dog, Gray & White, Green Ground, 6 x 6 In.	40.00
Tray, Butterflies, Pink, Gold Border, Signed, 13 1/4 x 9 In.	115.00
Tray, Dresser, Roses, Hand Painted, Dated 1902, 12 1/2 In.	425.00
Tray, Hand Painted, Fruit Design Center, Blue & Gold Border, Signed, 12 In.	214.00
Tray, Hand Painted, Lilacs, Green Ground & Trim, 12 In.	110.00
Turkey Set, Pink Peony Border, 5 Piece	220.00
Vase, Blossoms, Crimson, Rose, Shades Of Green, White, Faure, 1925, 11 1/2 In.	6325.00
Vase, Carved Medallion Relief, Seated Woman With Cupid, 9 1/2 In.	460.00
Vase, Geometric, Shades Of Green, Ovoid, Signed C. Faure, 6 3/4 In.	2530.00
Vase, Geometric, White, Aquamarine, Teal, Sky, Cobalt Blue, Faure, 10 In.	6900.00
Vase, Hand Painted Orchids, Ornate Gold Handles, 13 In.	1400.00
Vase, Mothers & Young Children, Landscape, Turquoise Blue, 16 In., Pair	1725.00

Vase, Overall Floral & Gilt Design, Ovoid, 8 1/4 In. 253.00
Vase, Stylized Flower Buds, Spiraling Leafage, Amethyst Interior, Faure, 8 In. 8050.00
Vase, Stylized Flowers, Enamel-On-Copper, c.1925, 11 1/2 In. 6325.00
Vase, Sunset Sky Scene, Enamel, 1900-1915, 5 In. 484.00
Vase, Victorian Woman Smelling Rose, Signed K. Ryboe, 13 1/2 In. 604.00
Vase, Winter Scenes, Hand Painted, Footed, 9 1/2 In., Pair 230.00

LINDBERGH was a national hero. In 1927, Charles Lindbergh, the aviator, became the first man to make a nonstop solo flight across the Atlantic Ocean. In 1932, his son was kidnapped and murdered, and Lindbergh was again the center of public interest. He died in 1974. All types of Lindbergh memorabilia are collected.

Bookends, Aviator, Iron, Bronze Finish 130.00
Fan, We, Lindbergh Portrait & Plane, Poem, 11 In. 135.00
Mirror, Boyhood Home, Little Falls, Minnesota, Inset Portrait, Pocket 350.00
Patch, Spirit Of St. Louis, NX211, Tan Twill, Embroidered Yellow Plane, 3 In. 20.00
Portrait, Photograph, Underwood, Description Of Lindbergh's Return Flight 40.00
Postcard, Lindbergh Photograph, Spirit Of St. Louis, France 100.00
Postcard, Lindbergh Portrait, Reverse Image, Jersey Supply Co., Atlantic City, N.J. 75.00
Spoon, Standing Figure Handle, Plane & Flight In Bowl 150.00
Stickpin, Spirit Of St. Louis, Celluloid, 3-D, 9 Separate Parts 85.00
Toy, Airplane, Lindy, Cast Iron, Animated Propeller, Hubley, 13-In. Wingspan 2860.00
Watch Fob, New York To Paris, Plane, Eiffel Tower, Statue Of Liberty, Metal, 1 1/2 In. ... 25.00

LITHOPHANES are porcelain pictures made by casting clay in layers of various thicknesses. When a piece is held to the light, a picture of light and shadow is seen through it. Most lithophanes date from the 1825–1875 period. A few are still being made. Many lithophanes sold today were originally panels for lampshades.

Lamp, 5 Colored Scenes Of People, Amethyst To Clear Font, 16 In. ....*Illus* 1045.00
Lamp, 5 Various Scenes, Ruby Enamel To Clear Font, Milk Glass Base, 16 In. 1015.00
Lamp, 5 Panels, White House, Western Scene, Boy & Girl With Goat, 15 In. 950.00
Lamp, 6 Panels With Women, Ruby Flashed Font, 18 In. ....*Illus* 1045.00
Lamp, Boy & Girl In Garden, Crystal Base, Clarke, Fairy, 4 1/4 In. 1750.00
Lamp, Student, Oil, 4 Panels With Children, Brass, 22 In. ....*Illus* 1650.00
Lantern, Tin, Pierced, 4 Square Landscape Panels, Burner, c.1870, 4 1/2 In. 250.00
Panel, 2 Maids, Pastoral Setting, Prancing Horse On Base, Metal Frame, 14 In. 2310.00
Panel, Moses Discovered In Bulrushes, Teakwood Frame, Lighted, c.1870, 13 In. 715.00
Panel, Women, Courtier, Classical Setting, Whippet On Base, Metal Frame, 14 In. 2640.00
Stein, Alemannia Sei's Pannier, Student Society, Pewter Lid, 1/2 Liter 230.00
Stein, Child, Munich, c.1896 .... 900.00
Stein, Student Fox, 1/2 Liter 660.00

Lithopane, Lamp, 5 Colored
Scenes Of People, Amethyst To
Clear Font, 16 In.

Lithopane, Lamp,
6 Panels With Women,
Ruby Flashed Font, 18 In.

Lithopane, Lamp, Student,
Oil, 4 Panels With Children,
Brass, 22 In.

LIVERPOOL, England, was the site of several pottery and porcelain factories from 1716 to 1785. Some earthenware was made with transfer decorations. Sadler and Green made print-decorated wares from 1756. Many of the pieces were made for the American market and feature patriotic emblems, such as eagles, flags, and other special-interest motifs. Liverpool pitchers are always called Liverpool jugs by collectors.

Charger, Trees, Flower, Cross-Banded Border, 18th Century, 13 1/2 In.	633.00
Coffeepot, Cover, White Floral Bouquet, Sprigs, Enameled, Scroll Handle, 1770, 11 In.	805.00
Figurine, Writing Hand, Designed For Circus Street School, 1812, 8 In.	2587.00
Jug, American Clipper Ship, 12 In.	1150.00
Jug, American Ship Independence, Washington, Liberty, 8 In.	1000.00
Jug, Map Of United States	1250.00
Jug, Masonic Symbols, Green, 12 In.	770.00
Jug, Masonic Symbols, Hunt Scene On Reverse, 8 In.	275.00
Jug, Poem About Washington On Reverse	1300.00
Jug, Portrait Of Commodore Preble, American Coat Of Arms, 1804	2090.00
Jug, Sailing Ship With Union Jack, Returning Sailor, 9 In.	635.00
Jug, Ship, Constitution, American Flag, Creamware, 19th Century, 12 In.	1840.00
Jug, Transfer Black, Washington, 15 Linked States, 11 In.	805.00
Jug, Transfer Of 3-Masted Ship, Under Sail, And Verse, Poor Jack, 6 7/8 In.	460.00
Jug, Transfer, Washington Ascending To Glory, Eagle Below Spout, 8 7/8 In.	2300.00
Jug, Underglaze Floral, Hound Head Spout, Creamware, c.1777, 7 1/2 In.	977.00
Jug, Washington Ascending Into Glory, Eagle Below Spout, Handle, 10 In.	1380.00
Jug, Washington Ascending Into Glory, Peace, Plenty & Independence, Eagle, 10 In.	1145.00
Jug, Washington Crowned With Laurels By Liberty, Border, 15 Linked States, 8 1/2 In.	1850.00
Plate, Lord Nelson, Creamware, Impressed Herculaneum, 10 In.	650.00
Plate, Mary Of Newbury Port, Moses Pearson, Creamware, 9 3/4 In.	3520.00
Plate, Polychrome Delft, c.1710	395.00
Plate, Ship, Transfer, Mary Of Newbury Port, Creamware, 9 3/4 In.	3520.00
Teapot, Pavilion On Rock, c.1760	695.00

LLADRO is a Spanish porcelain. Juan, Jose, and Vicente Lladro opened a ceramics workshop in Almacera in 1951. They soon began making figurines in a distinctive, elongated style. In 1958 the factory moved to Tabernes Blanques, Spain. The company makes stoneware and porcelain figurines and vases in limited and unlimited editions. Dates given are first and last years of production.

Figurine, Aggressive Duck, No. 1288, Retired	450.00
Figurine, Angel With Lyre, No. 1321, Retired	450.00
Figurine, Angela, No. 5211, 1984	235.00
Figurine, At Stroke Of Twelve, Signed, No. 1493, Retired	6500.00
Figurine, Barrister, No. 4908, Retired	425.00
Figurine, Belinda With Doll, No. 5045, Retired	230.00
Figurine, Bird Watcher, No. 4730, Retired	380.00
Figurine, Boy Pottery Seller, No. 5080, Retired	850.00
Figurine, Boy With Book, No. 1024, Retired	440.00
Figurine, Can I Play, No. 7610, Retired	495.00
Figurine, Cat & Mouse, No. 5236, 1984	95.00
Figurine, Cat Girl, No. 5164, Retired	630.00
Figurine, Centaur Boy, No. 1013, Retired	550.00
Figurine, Christmas Carols, No. 1239, Retired	880.00
Figurine, Cinderella, No. 4828, Retired	275.00
Figurine, Donkey In Love, No. 4524, Retired	400.00
Figurine, Dove, No. 1016, Retired	220.00
Figurine, Ducks In Flight, No. 4759, Retired	750.00
Figurine, Eskimo Boy & Girl, No. 2038.3, Retired	455.00
Figurine, Female Equestrian, No. 4516, 1969	500.00
Figurine, Flamenco Dancers, 1969-1993, 19 1/2 In.	155.00
Figurine, Flower Peddler, No. 5029, Retired	1270.00
Figurine, Flower Song, No. 7607, Retired	650.00
Figurine, Flowers In Pot, No. 5028, Retired	660.00
Figurine, Garden Classic, No. 7617, Retired	650.00

Figurine, Girl At Sink, No. 4838, Retired	255.00
Figurine, Girl Walking, No. 5040, Retired	550.00
Figurine, Girl With Bonnet, No. 1147, Retired	370.00
Figurine, Girl With Dice, No. 1176, Retired	255.00
Figurine, Girl With Doll, No. 1083, Retired	330.00
Figurine, Girl With Lamb, No. 1010, Retired	375.00
Figurine, Girl With Milk Pail, No. 4682, Retired	420.00
Figurine, Girl With Mother's Shoe, No. 1084, Retired	265.00
Figurine, Girl With Sheep, No. 4584, Retired	255.00
Figurine, Girl With Umbrella, No. 4510, 1969-1993, 10 1/2 In.	125.00
Figurine, Gypsy With Brother, No. 4800, Retired	400.00
Figurine, Hamlet, No. 4729, Retired	800.00
Figurine, Hebrew Student, No. 4684, Retired	880.00
Figurine, Hello Flowers, No. 5543, Retired	650.00
Figurine, Heron, 7 1/2 In.	120.00
Figurine, In The Gondola, No. 1350, 1978	1500.00
Figurine, Jazz Duo, No. 5930, 1992	550.00
Figurine, Little Eagle Owl, No. 1224, 1972-1978	95.00
Figurine, Little Girl With Cat, No. 1187, Retired	440.00
Figurine, Little Girl With Turkeys, No. 1180, Retired	250.00
Figurine, Little Traveler, No. 7602, 1986	1500.00
Figurine, Matrimony, No. 1404, Retired	585.00
Figurine, Mayumi, No. 1449, Retired	525.00
Figurine, Mimi, No. 4985, 1978-1980	375.00
Figurine, Missy, No. 4951, 1976-1985	650.00
Figurine, My Baby, No. 1331, Retired	995.00
Figurine, My Little Pet, No. 4994, Retired	250.00
Figurine, Oriental Girl, No. 4840, 1993-1997, 7 1/2 In.	175.00
Figurine, Pekingese, No. 4641, Retired	420.00
Figurine, Picture Perfect, No. 7612, Retired	650.00
Figurine, Pondering, No. 5173, Retired	650.00
Figurine, Purr-Fect, No. 1444, 1983	615.00
Figurine, Ride In The Country, No. 5354, Retired	550.00
Figurine, Seated Woman In Horse-Drawn Carriage, Driver, 11 1/2 x 21 1/2 In.	662.00
Figurine, Shepherdess With Basket, No. 4678, 1969	95.00
Figurine, Shepherdess With Rooster, No. 4677, 1969	90.00
Figurine, Sorrowful Mother, No. 5849, 1992, Retired	895.00
Figurine, Spring Bouquets, No. 7603, Retired	800.00
Figurine, Summer Stroll, No. 7611, Retired	550.00
Figurine, Swan, No. 4829, 1972-1983	90.00
Figurine, Sweet Harvest, No. 5380, Retired	1100.00
Figurine, Tinkerbell, No. 7518, Retired	1950.00
Figurine, Turtle Dove, No. 4550, 11 In., Retired	145.00
Figurine, Veterinarian, No. 4825, Retired	650.00
Figurine, Walk In Versailles, No. 5004, Retired	875.00
Figurine, Waltz Time, No. 4856, 1974-1985	300.00
Figurine, Young Mozart, No. 5915, Retired	5000.00
Figurine, Yuki, No. 1448, Retired	550.00
Group, Fishing With Gramps, No. 5215, 1984	400.00

LOCKE ART is a trademark found on glass of the early twentieth century. Joseph Locke worked at many English and American firms. He designed and etched his own glass in Pittsburgh, Pennsylvania, starting in the 1880s. Some pieces were marked *Joe Locke*, but most were marked with the words *Locke Art*. The mark is hidden in the pattern on the glass.

Cup & Saucer, Egyptian, 5 1/2 In.	22.00
Cuspidor, Woman's, Ferns, 3 x 5 In.	55.00
Goblet, Water, Poppies, 16-Panel Shape, Signed, 6 1/4 In.	110.00
Saucer, Cherries, 5 1/4 In.	44.00
Saucer, Poppies, 6 In.	5.50
Tankard, Floral, 11 3/4 In.	160.00
Tumbler, Cherries, 5 1/4 In.	105.00
Vase, Umbrella	200.00

LOETZ glass was made in many varieties. Johann Loetz bought a glassworks in Austria in 1840. He died in 1848 and his widow ran the company; then in 1879, his grandson took over. Most collectors recognize the iridescent gold glass similar to Tiffany, but many other types were made. The firm closed during World War II.

Basket, Amber Iridescent, Oil Spots, Handle, 1910, 12 In.	294.00
Bowl, Green Iridescent, Broad, Flaring Shape, Ruffled Edge, Signed, c.1900, 3 3/4 In.	220.00
Box, Purple Iridescent, Enameled Violets, Hinged	650.00
Candy Box, Amethyst, Signed, 5 1/2 In.	250.00
Inkwell, Leaf Design, Square, Bronze Hinged Cover, 5 In.	220.00
Inkwell, Purple Crisscross Threads, Brass Cap, Squat Form	450.00
Jar, Dresser, Gold Iridescent, Enameled, Brass Collar, Mark, 4 1/2 x 3 In.	230.00
Lamp, Blue, Iridescent Pulled Feather Design, Olive Shade, 18 1/2 In.	2300.00
Lamp, Desk, Sinuous Vine Standard, Shield Shape, Gilt Metal, Jeweled, 9 1/2 In.	1725.00
Lamp, Green, Platinum Iridescent, Floral Top, Ribbed Neck, Paperweight Shade, 15 In.	4675.00
Lamp, Iridescent Blue Oil Spots, Deep Red, Brown Patina, Holly Leaf Base, 18 In.	3450.00
Pitcher, Green Iridescent, Silver Plate Rim & Spout, Signed, c.1900, 8 1/2 In.	385.00
Vase, 6 Silver Iridescent Oil Spots, Foliate Overlay, Signed, c.1900, 3 In.	1150.00
Vase, Amber Iridescent, Gold Leaf, Wreath Around Warrior Medallion, c.1895, 8 1/2 In.	248.00
Vase, Amber, Silver Blue Random Trailings, Leafage, Silver Blossoms, Leafage, 7 In.	4025.00
Vase, Amethyst Eggshell Iridescent, Bulbous, Signed, 8 x 4 5/8 In.	235.00
Vase, Blue Cat Tail, Controlled Air Bubbles, Clear Body, 1920s, 8 In.	2535.00
Vase, Blue Iridescent Waves, Ruby Red Ground, Everted Rim, Squat, 5 1/2 In.	2070.00
Vase, Blue Iridescent, Amber, 1900, 7 In.	200.00
Vase, Blue, Green, Rose Iridescent, Dimpled, Flared Neck, 4 In.	275.00
Vase, Botanical, Bird Design, Concave Depression, Black, Enameled, 9 In.	345.00
Vase, Cranberry Iridescent, Fan & Swirl Optic, Bulbous, 6 3/4 x 4 3/4 In.	190.00
Vase, Gold Iridescent Concentric Trailings, Gray Ground, Peach, 18 1/2 In.	11500.00
Vase, Gold Iridescent, Applied Single Leaf, Jack-In-The-Pulpit, Pad Foot, 17 In.	2530.00
Vase, Gold Iridescent, Gold Oil Spots, Applied Silver Thistle, 10 In.	2185.00
Vase, Gray, Crimson, Chartreuse & Green, Ovoid, c.1904, 6 3/4 In.	1955.00
Vase, Green Iridescent, 1910, 11 In.	195.00
Vase, Green Leaves, Iridescent Gold Ground, Crimped, Signed, 7 1/4 In.	1800.00
Vase, Green Threading, 14 1/2 In.	385.00
Vase, Green, Blue, Rose Highlights, Dimpled Bottom, 4 1/2 In.	275.00
Vase, Green, Gold Iridescent, Ruffled Rim, 1900, 7 1/2 In.	173.00
Vase, Iridescent Body, Green, c.1900, 6 In.	102.00
Vase, Octopus, Deep Brown, Gold Decorations, Signed, 10 1/2 In.	1277.00
Vase, Oil Spot, Amber, Gray, Silver Blue Iridescent Waves, 1902, 6 3/4 In.	2875.00
Vase, Oil Spot, Copper, Silver Blue, Iridescent, 4 Applied Pulled Handles, Gray, 10 In.	1380.00
Vase, Oil Spot, Maroon, Pink, Platinum Iridescent, Crimped Top, 4 1/2 In.	286.00
Vase, Oil Spot, Purple, Green Iridescent, Bronze Mount At Top, 9 In.	825.00
Vase, Oil Spot, Purple, Green Iridescent, Original Patina To Metal, 9 In.	825.00
Vase, Oil Spot, Silver Blue, Wavy, Amber, Green, Scalloped Rim, 1900, 5 1/4 In.	287.00
Vase, Oil Spot, Yellow Iridescent, Baluster, 3 1/2 In.	60.00
Vase, Pale Amber Opalescent, Silver Pulled Trailings, 1900, 10 1/2 In.	2875.00
Vase, Pale Amber, Silver Blue Trailings, Purple Stringing At Base, 7 In.	5750.00
Vase, Papillon, Jack-In-The-Pulpit Rim, Spotted Gold Iridescent, Polished Pontil, 10 In.	690.00
Vase, Peacock Blue Iridescent, Green Ground, Double Gourd, 6 3/4 In.	1380.00
Vase, Peony, Mauve, Light Blue Ground, Etched, Cameo, 11 3/4 In.	1840.00
Vase, Pink Pulled Feathers, 4 Dimples, Everted Rim, Ovoid, Paper Label, c.1900, 5 In.	1265.00
Vase, Platinum On Orange, Green, 8 In.	2300.00
Vase, Purple Iridescent Streaks, Purple Ground, Shouldered Form, Metal Mount, 5 In.	2300.00
Vase, Purple, Brown Threaded Iridescent, Jack-In-The-Pulpit, 7 1/4 In.	230.00
Vase, Purple, Green Iridescent, Pale Green, 2 Applied Blue Handles, 6 In.	330.00
Vase, Purple, Green Iridescent, Pale Green, Blue Threading Around Neck, 8 In.	350.00
Vase, Quilted Green Glass, Applied Copper Collar, Original Patina, 6 1/2 In.	605.00
Vase, Red Iridescent, Cobalt, Gold, Heart & Trailing Vines, 1900, 7 1/4 In.	207.00
Vase, Red, Silver Blue Concentric Trailings, 1900, 7 1/8 In.	2875.00
Vase, Shaded Amber & Pink, Chain Of Looping, Signed, 1901, 11 3/8 In.	1725.00
Vase, Silver Strands, Bright Yellow, Waisted, Everted Rim, 11 In.	1380.00
Vase, Silver-Blue Middle, Concentric Lines Top, Deep Amber Glass, 1900, 6 3/4 In.	8050.00

Vase, Silver-Blue Oil Spots, Amber Glass, 2 Silver Loop Handles, 5 In. 2875.00
Vase, Silver-Blue Waves, Bands Of Salmon At Neck, Purple Base, Amber Glass, 4 In. . . . 4887.00
Vase, Silver-Blue, Iridescent, Yellow, 4 Spiraling Pulled Handles, 1900, 12 In. 1265.00
Vase, Silver-Blue, Pink Trailings, Gold Amber Iridescent, 1900, 4 3/4 In. 2300.00
Vase, Silvery Oil Spots On Amber, Gooseneck, 10 In. 750.00

LONE RANGER, a fictional character, was introduced on the radio in 1932. Over three thousand shows were produced before the series ended in 1954. In 1938, the first Lone Ranger movie was made. Television shows were started in 1949 and are still seen on some stations. The Lone Ranger appears on many products and was even the name of a restaurant chain for several years.

Badge, Lone Ranger Secret Compartment, Deputy 70.00
Badge, Safety Club, Butter-Nut Premium, Star Shape, Gold Metal, 1 1/2 In. 60.00
Blotter, Lone Ranger On Silver, Bond Bread, 1950s, 8 x 3 3/4 In. 50.00
Blotter, Premium Bond Bread, Red, Green, Yellow, Cardboard, 1940, 3 3/4 x 8 In. 30.00
Coaster, Lone Ranger Every Day, Ribbed Floral Border, Black Text, 1950, 5 In. 15.00
Comic Book, From Cheerios, 1954 . . . . 30.00
Comic Book, The Lone Ranger, No. 133, Dell 17.00
Figure, Blue Shirt, With Flicker Ring, Ideal 350.00
Figure, Red Shirt, Ideal 250.00
Figurine, Chalkware, 16 In. 85.00
Figurine, Horse, Saddle, Hat, 2 Pistols, Hartland, Original Box 325.00
Figurine, Lone Ranger On Silver, Tin, Louis Marx, 8 In. 220.00
Figurine, Tonto, Horse, Saddle, Pistol, Original Box, Hartland 275.00
First Aid Box, Tin Lithograph, Lone Ranger & Silver, 1938, 4 x 4 In. 60.00
Flashlight 150.00
Game, Board, Marx, 1938 . . . . 75.00
Game, Metal Horse Pieces, Parker Bros., 1938 . . . . 75.00
Kit, Model, No. 188 . . . . 85.00
Lantern, Box 300.00
Lunch Box 250.00
Photograph, Lone Ranger & Tonto Promoting Christmas Seals, Glossy, 8 x 10 In. 12.00
Pistol & Holster, Pony Boy, Black Leather, Pearl Handle, 1950s 522.00
Record, The Legend Of The Lone Ranger, Lone Ranger Looking At Bullet, 1981 . . . . 14.00
Ring, Atom Bomb, Kix Cereal, Metal, Plastic, c.1946 . . . . 33.00
Ring, Filmstrip 128.00
Silver Spoon, Hi-Yo, Image Of Long Ranger, Galloping Silver, 1938, 6 In. 50.00
Snowdome 165.00
Toy, Lone Ranger & Hi-Yo Silver, Windup, Missing Arm, Marx 33.00
Toy, On Silver, Spinning Lariat, Tin Lithograph, Windup, 1938 . . . . .375.00 to 465.00
Wristwatch, Band, New Haven Watch Co., Box, 1940 . . . . 132.00

LONGWY Workshop of Longwy, France, first made ceramic wares in 1798. The workshop is still in business. Most of the ceramic pieces found today are glazed with many colors to resemble cloisonne or other enameled metal. Many pieces were made with stylized figures and Art Deco designs. The factory used a variety of marks.

Ashtray, Liberation 150.00
Charger, Black Deer, Blue Glaze, Signed, Paper Label, 15 In. 715.00
Charger, Primavera, Enameled, 2 Women, Faun, Brown & Yellow, Signed, 14 1/4 In. 2310.00
Lamp, Oil Well, Floral Polychrome Enamel Design, Brass Fixtures, Electric, 12 In. 135.00
Plaque, Triangular Shape, Marked, Grand Feu, 10 1/2 In. 60.00
Tile, Birds, Geometric, Border, 8 x 8 In., 7 Piece 975.00
Vase, Incised Foliage, Crackle Ivory Ground, Signed, 8 3/4 In. 395.00

LONHUDA Pottery Company of Steubenville, Ohio, was organized in 1892 by William Long, W. H. Hunter, and Alfred Day. Brown underglaze slip-decorated pottery was made. The firm closed in 1896. The company used many marks; the earliest included the letters *LPCO*.

Vase, Apple Blossoms, Dark Glaze, Signed, 7 x 8 In. 265.00
Vase, Clover On Green & Brown Ground, 3 Handles, Signed, 4 In. 165.00
Vase, Floral Design, Brown Glaze, Signed, 8 1/2 In. 75.00

Vase, Yellow Roses, Brown Glaze, Mary Taylor, 4 x 5 In. 220.00

LOTUS WARE was made by the Knowles, Taylor & Knowles Company of East Liverpool, Ohio, from 1890 to 1900. Lotus Ware, a thin porcelain which resembles Belleek, was sometimes decorated outside the factory. Other types of ceramics that were made by the Knowles, Taylor & Knowles Company are listed under KTK.

Creamer, Fish Net Design, 5 1/4 In. 145.00
Rose Bowl, Leaf & Berry Design, Footed, 4 In. 410.00
Vase, Floral, Gold Beading & Reticulated Button Handles, 6 1/2 In. 470.00

LOW art tiles were made by the J. and J. G. Low Art Tile Works of Chelsea, Massachusetts, from 1877 to 1902. A variety of art and other tiles were made. Some of the tiles were made by a process called *natural*, some were hand modeled, and some were made mechanically.

J.&J.G.LOW

Tile, Street In Normandy, Shepherd Scene, Signed, 9 1/2 x 17 1/2 In. 920.00
Tile, Woman's Portrait, Mounted On Brass Box, Signed, 2 1/4 In. 230.00

LOY-NEL-ART, see McCoy category.

LUNCH BOXES and lunch pails have been used to carry lunches to school or work since the nineteenth century. Today, most collectors want either early tobacco advertising boxes or children's lunch boxes made since the 1930s. These boxes are made of metal or plastic. Boxes listed here include the original Thermos bottle inside the box unless otherwise indicated. Movie, television, and cartoon characters may be found in their own categories.

LUNCH BOX, Annie Oakley & Tagg, Metal, Aladdin, 1955 .... 300.00
  Barbie & Midge, Vinyl, Dome Top, King Seeley Thermos Co., 1965 .... 300.00
  Battle Star Galactica, Metal, Aladdin, 1978 .... 95.00
  Bionic Woman, Metal, Aladdin ....40.00 to 85.00
  Bobby Orr, Canadian Flag, Plastic, Aladdin, 1974 ....80.00 to 295.00
  Bobby Sherman, Meta, King Seeley Thermos, 1972 .... 20.00
  Bonanza, Metal, Aladdin 100.00
  Buccaneer, Pirate Scenes, Treasure Coins, Metal, Dome Top, Aladdin, 1957 .... 135.00
  Bullwinkle & Rocky, Metal, Universal, 1962 .... 750.00
  Casey Jones, Metal, Dome Top, Universal, 1960 .... 575.00
  Charlie's Angels, Metal, Aladdin, 1978 .... 20.00
  Chuck Wagon, Metal, Dome Top, Aladdin, 1958 ....278.00 to 280.00
  Circus, All Around Graphics Of Circus Troupe, 1930s 130.00
  Dark Crystal, Metal, King Seeley Thermos, 1982 ....22.00 to 50.00
  Donnie & Marie, Long Hair, Vinyl, Aladdin, 1976 ....90.00 to 120.00
  Dr. Seuss, Metal, Aladdin, 1970 .... 60.00
  Drag Strip, Metal, Aladdin, 1975 .... 55.00
  E.T., Metal, Aladdin, 1982 .... 125.00
  Empire Strikes Back, Metal, Thermos, 1980 .... 20.00
  Exciting World Of Metrics, Metal, King Seeley Thermos, 1976 ....20.00 to 30.00
  Fall Guy, Metal, Aladdin, 1981 .... 110.00
  Fireball XL5, Metal, King Seeley Thermos, 1964 .... 125.00
  Flintstones Bedrock Festival, Metal, No Thermos, Aladdin, 1971 .... 65.00
  Flying Nun, Metal, Aladdin, 1968 .... 98.00
  G.I. Joe Combat Soldier Lunch Kit, Vinyl, No Thermos 120.00
  Girl Scout, Vinyl, Aladdin, 1960 .... 175.00
  Green Hornet, Metal, King Seeley Thermos, 1967 .... 135.00
  Gunsmoke, Matt Dillon U.S. Marshall, With Double LLs, Metal, Aladdin, 1959 .... 395.00
  Gunsmoke, Thermos, Meal, Aladdin, 1972 .... 60.00
  Happy Days, American Thermos, 1977 .... 25.00
  Heathcliff, Metal, Aladdin, 1982 .... 85.00
  How The West Was Won, Metal, King Seeley Thermos, 1979 .... 65.00
  Huckleberry Hound, Metal, Aladdin, 1961 .... 200.00
  Hulk, Metal, Aladdin, 1978 .... 25.00
  Jet Patrol, Metal, Aladdin, 1957 .... 250.00

Jetsons, Metal, Dome Top, Aladdin, 1963 .... 400.00
Joe Palooka Lunch Kit, Metal, Continental Can, 1949, 4 3/4 x 7 x 4 In. 85.00
Johnny Lightning, Metal, Aladdin, 1970 ....20.00 to 32.00
Julia, Metal, King Seeley Thermos, 1969 .... 40.00
Jurassic Park, Warning Biological Material, Deep Red, Plastic, American Thermos 45.00
King Kong, Metal, American Thermos, 1977 .... 35.00
Knight Rider, Metal, King Seeley Thermos, 1984 .... 20.00
Land Of The Giants, Metal, Aladdin, 1968 .... 150.00
Partridge Family, Metal, King Seeley Thermos, 1971 .... 85.00
Peanuts, Charlie Brown At Pitcher's Mound, Red, Metal, King Seeley Thermos, 1976 ... 20.00
Peanuts, Snoopy & Gang Under Tree, Linus Band, Metal, King Seeley Thermos, 1973 .. 20.00
Pebble & Bamm Bamm, Metal, Aladdin, 1971 .... 65.00
Raggedy Ann & Andy, Ice Skating, Carrying Milk Pail, Plastic, Aladdin, 1973 .... 20.00
Robin Hood, Metal, Aladdin, 1956 .... 60.00
Ronald McDonald, Sheriff Of Cactus Canyon, Metal, Aladdin, 1982 ....27.00 to 95.00
Sesame Street, Metal, Aladdin, 1979 .... 20.00
Six Million Dollar Man, Metal, Aladdin, 1974 .... 65.00
Space 1999, Metal, King Seeley Thermos, 1976 .... 85.00
Spiderman & Hulk, Metal, Aladdin, 1980 .... 35.00
Strawberry Shortcake, Aladdin, 1980 .... 15.00
Strawberry Shortcake, Chein 25.00
Super Friends, Metal, Aladdin, 1976 .... 150.00
Thermos, Wild, Wild West, Aladdin, 1969 .... 75.00
Tiger Chewing Tobacco 50.00
Transformers, Aladdin, 1986 .... 15.00
Traveler, Transportation Graphics On Side Panels, Ohio Art, 1960s 78.00
Vinny Barbarino, John Travolta, Welcome Back Kotter, Vinyl, Aladdin, 1977 .... 450.00
Wayne Gretzky, Plastic, Aladdin, 1979 .... 40.00
Wild Bill Hickok, Metal, Aladdin, 1955 .... 100.00
Wild Wild West, Metal, Aladdin, 1969 .... 175.00
Woody Woodpecker, Metal, Aladdin, 1972 .... 125.00
LUNCH BOX THERMOS, Barbie & Midge, King Seeley Thermos, 1965 .... 20.00
Green Hornet, King Seeley Thermos, 1967 .... 175.00
Hector Heathcote, Hector Firing Cannonball, Metal, Aladdin, 1964 ....55.00 to 58.00
Linus The Lion Hearted, Aladdin, 1965 ....85.00 to 88.00
Munsters, King Seeley Thermos, 1965 .... 110.00
Pathfinder, Metal, Universal, 1959 .... 45.00
Peanuts, Snoopy & Gang, Metal, Tan Cup, King Seeley Thermos, 1966 .... 20.00
Robin Hood, Aladdin, 1965 .... 75.00
Tammy, Aladdin, 1964 .... 60.00
Tom Corbett Space Cadet, Aladdin, 1952 .... 13.00
U.S. Mail, Aladdin, 1969 .... 18.00
Wild Bill Hickock, Metal, Aladdin, 1955 .... 85.00
Yogi Bear, Aladdin 65.00
Yosemite Sam, Bugs Bunny, Elmer, Metal, Warner Bros., Inc., 1971 ....64.00 to 70.00
Zorro, Aladdin 65.00

LUSTER glaze was meant to resemble copper, silver, or gold. It has been used since the sixteenth century. Most of the luster found today was made during the nineteenth century. The metallic glazes are applied on pottery. The finished color depends on the combination of the clay color and the glaze. Blue and orange luster decorations were used in the early 1900s. Tea Leaf pieces have their own category.

Blue, Wall Pocket, Red Poppies, Yellow Butterflies, Japan 35.00
Copper, Creamer, White Reserves, Purple Transfer, Woman & Child, 4 1/8 In. 180.00
Copper, Pitcher, Basket Of Flowers, Animal Head Spout, Serpent Handle, 7 In. 755.00
Copper, Pitcher, Dancers Each Side, Green Foliage, 9 In. 22.00
Copper, Pitcher, England, 8 1/2 In., Pair 318.00
Copper, Pitcher, Floral Design, 7 1/4 In. 85.00
Copper, Pitcher, Old Foley, Small 45.00
Copper, Pitcher, Pink Luster Clock Face 1 Side, Medallion Other, W & J On Clock Face . 100.00
Copper, Pitcher, Scenes Of Lafayette & Cornwallis, Black Transfer, 6 3/8 In. 845.00

Copper, Pitcher, White Reserves, Transfer Scenes Of Woman & Children, Garden, 7 In. ... 192.00
Copper, Pitcher, Yellow Band, Reserves Of Badminton Players, 5 3/4 In. 340.00
Fairyland luster is included in the Wedgwood category.
Pink, Bowl, House Design, 5 In. 20.00
Pink, Bowl, Sailor's Farewell 1850.00
Pink, Coffeepot, Floral, Hand Painted, 19th Century, 8 In. 45.00
Pink, Cup & Saucer, Child & Cat, 1860 .... 75.00
Pink, Cup Plate, Rural Scenic Transfer 27.00
Pink, Flowerpot, Floral Band & Stripes, 5 3/8 In. 240.00
Pink, Mug, Present For Charles, Canary Luster Trim, Child's, 1 3/4 In. 720.00
Pink, Pitcher, Canary, Flowers, 6 1/2 In. 605.00
Pink, Pitcher, Country Lad & Lass, Sailor's Farewell Verse, Black Transfer, Pearlware ... 550.00
Pink, Pitcher, Eagle & Flowers, Pearlware, 5 5/8 In. 180.00
Pink, Pitcher, Gray Floral & Fruit, 6 1/2 In. 185.00
Pink, Pitcher, Stag, Enameled, Pearlware, 6 1/4 In. 425.00
Pink, Pitcher, Toby, Dark Blue Coat, Pink Lustre Trim, 5 1/2 In. 50.00
Pink, Pitcher, Wide Floral Band, Pearlware, 6 In. 485.00
Pink, Plate, 7 1/2 In. 20.00
Pink, Platter, Blue & Green Flowers, Sewell, 16 5/8 In. 545.00
Pink, Sugar, Cover, Schoolhouse 95.00
Pink, Tea Set, Strawberries, England, 10 Piece 275.00
Pink, Teapot 170.00
Pink & Copper, Jug, Spring-Langan, Boxing, England's Champion, 1824, 6 In. 950.00
Silver, Bank, Pig, Freehand Circle Design, England, 6 1/4 In. 165.00
Silver, Creamer, Canary, Floral, 3 3/4 In. 120.00
Silver, Mug, Canary, Running Vine, 2 In. 357.00
Silver, Pitcher, Ribbing, Purple Transfer Scenes, Pearlware, 5 3/4 In. 484.00
Silver, Pitcher, Top Border Of Grapes & Leaves, Paneled, Pale Blue, 7 x 8 In. 875.00
Silver, Sugar & Creamer, Lancaster 95.00
Silver, Waste Bowl, Floral Band, Pearlware, 6 3/8 In. 60.00
Sunderland luster pieces are listed in the Sunderland category.
Tea Leaf luster pieces are listed in the Tea Leaf Ironstone category.

LUSTRES are mantel decorations or pedestal vases with many hanging
glass prisms. The name really refers to the prisms, and it is proper to
refer to a single glass prism as a lustre. Either spelling, luster or lustre,
is correct.

Cranberry Glass, Floral Enameled, Tulip Top, 11 In., Pair 360.00
Crystal, Square Base, 2 Arms Supporting Candle Socket, Electric, 23 1/2 In. 300.00
Enamel & Gold Design, 10 Cut Glass Prisms, 13 In. 155.00
Enameled Pink Overlay, Double Row Of Prisms, 14 1/2 In., Pair 1100.00
Gold, Vase, Sisters Of Notre Dame, Bavarian, 11 1/2 In. 75.00
Green, Hand Painted, Pair 595.00
Green, White Overlay, Scalloped, Gilt Scrolls, Round Foot, 1880-1900, 12 1/2 In., Pair .. 2300.00

LUTZ glass was made by Nicolas Lutz working at the Boston and
Sandwich Glass Company from 1870 to 1888. He made delicate and
intricate threaded glass of several colors. Other similar wares made by
other makers are now known by the generic name *Lutz*.

Bowl, Threaded, Blue, 5 In. 150.00
Cup & Saucer, White, Gold Stripes 100.00
Goblet, Twelve Bands Of Green & Gold Aventurine, Hollow Stem, 6 1/2 In. 80.00

MAASTRICHT, Holland, was the city where Petrus Regout established
the De Sphinx pottery in 1836. The firm was noted for its transfer-
printed earthenware. Many factories in Maastricht are still making
ceramics.

Grill Plate, Abbey, 11 In. 75.00
Plate, Transfer, Red, 9 In. 15.00
Soup, Dish, Flow Blue 50.00
Vase, Signed, Max Verboeket, 8 In. 150.00

MAIZE glass was made by W.L. Libbey & Son Company of Toledo, Ohio, after 1889. The glass resembled an ear of corn. The leaves were usually green, but some pieces were made with blue or red leaves. The kernels of corn were light yellow, white, or light green.

Celery Vase, Blue Leaf, Amber, 6 1/2 In.	126.00
Cruet, Blue, 5 1/2 In.	852.00
Toothpick, Blue Leaf, 2 1/4 In.	247.00
Tumbler, Gold Leaf, 4 In.	88.00

MAJOLICA is a general term for any pottery glazed with an opaque tin enamel that conceals the color of the clay body. It has been made since the fourteenth century. Today's collector is most likely to find Victorian majolica. The heavy, colorful ware is rarely marked. Some famous makers include Wedgwood; Minton; Griffen, Smith and Hill (marked *Etruscan*); and Chesapeake Pottery (marked *Avalon* or *Clifton*).

Basin, Armorial, 20 1/4 In.	390.00
Basket, Asparagus, Underplate, Basket Weave	475.00 to 565.00
Basket, Joseph Holdcroft, 5 3/4 x 7 1/2 In.	355.00
Bowl, Bird & Fan, Footed, Wedgwood, 12 x 4 In.	275.00
Bowl, Lilies, Footed, Handles, 9 1/2 In.	115.00
Bowl, Renaissance, 3 Double Serpent Handles, Footed, 1890, 6 1/2 x 10 1/2 In.	545.00
Bowl, Sweetmeat, Italy, 2 1/2 x 7 In., Pair	35.00
Box, Cover, Young Boy, Lying, On Log, Continental, 6 In.	55.00
Box, Sardine, Attached Underplate, WS & S, 8 1/2 x 7 1/2 In.	275.00
Bread Tray, Oak Leaf	120.00
Butter, Cover, Bird, Fan, 9 1/2 In.	115.00
Cachepot, 3 Pots, Polychrome Flowers, c.1895, 14 1/4 In.	495.00
Cachepot, Vintage, England, c.1890, 11 3/4 In.	467.00
Cake Plate, Green Lily Pads, Central Flowers, 3 Raised Feet, 9 1/4 In.	110.00
Candleholder, Brownie, Figural, Germany, 7 1/2 In.	305.00
Centerpiece, Molded Acanthus, Scrolled, Beaded Rim, Green, Turquoise, 13 1/4 In.	747.00
Centerpiece, Rococo, 2 Putti Gamboling, Parcel Gilt, Continental, 1890, 15 3/4 In.	515.00
Centerpiece, Yellow & Pink Flowers, Pink Interior, c.1879, 9 In.	425.00
Charger, Allover Scrolling Vines, Lion & Armorial, 20th Century, 16 3/4 In.	172.00
Cheese Dish, Birds & Flowers, 7 In.	*Illus* 403.00
Cheese Dish, Leaves & Flowers, Wedge Shape, 9 In.	*Illus* 575.00
Cheese Dish, Strawberry Blossoms, George Jones, 5 In.	*Illus* 1380.00
Compote, 3 Winged Dragons, Jovial, Hand Painted, Italy, 14 x 17 In.	575.00
Compote, Maple Leaf, Yellow Basket Weave, Griffen, Smith & Hill, 4 3/4 x 9 In.	235.00
Compote, Palm Tree, Woman Goddess On Horseback, Man On Horseback, Pair	2750.00

Majolica, Cheese Dish,
Birds & Flowers, 7 In.

Majolica, Cheese Dish, Leaves & Flowers,
Wedge Shape, 9 In.

Majolica, Cheese Dish,
Strawberry Blossoms, George Jones, 5 In.

Majolica,
Humidor,
Defender,
Blue Hat

Compote, Putto On Bowl, 19th Century, 9 1/4 x 9 In.	230.00
Compote, Supported By 3 Girls In Yellow Dresses & Bonnets, 8 x 9 In.	345.00
Creamer, Branch Form Handle, c.1870, 2 1/4 In.	57.00
Dish, Flower Center, Fan Shape, c.1880, 6 1/2 In.	172.00
Dish, Lobster Shape, Minton	9200.00
Dish, Shell, 3 Dolphin Feet, Brown, Green & Yellow, 2 1/4 x 9 In.	45.00
Dresser Set, Basket Weave & Rose, 3 Piece	525.00
Eggcup Set, Basket Holder, 2-In. Cup, 5 x 7 x 5 In., 6 Piece	495.00
Ewer, Figures Slaying A Dragon To 1 Side, Cantigalli, Late 19th Century, 13 1/4 In.	575.00
Ewer, Mythological Figure, Cantigalli, Late 19th Century, 13 1/4 In.	575.00
Figurine, Central Figure Of Putti In Foliate, Volute Border, Bracket, 19 In.	400.00
Figurine, Cock, Fighting, Signed, 1870s, 15 1/2 In.	2200.00
Figurine, Hebe, Standing On Rocky Ground, Eagle At Her Feet, Italy, 28 1/4 In.	259.00
Figurine, Putti & Cart, Bird On Hand, R.M. Krause, 8 1/2 In.	110.00
Figurine, Rooster, Belgium, 24 In.	4900.00
Figurine, Sleeping Woman, Seated In Gilt Chair, Lace Scarf, Signed, 7 1/2 In.	632.00
Flask, Battle & Village Landscape Scene, Cantigalli, 19th Century, 11 In.	575.00
Humidor, Black Boy Sitting On Large Melon, Pipe, 10 1/2 In.	875.00
Humidor, Blackamoor Arab, Incised Mark, 7 1/2 In.	325.00
Humidor, Boy With Earflap Hat, 5 In.	125.00
Humidor, Defender, Blue Hat ....*Illus*	330.00
Humidor, Green, Purple, Black, Yellow, 6 In.	126.00
Humidor, Man, With Cigar Butt, Brown, Green, 5 1/4 In.	110.00
Humidor, Monk	395.00
Humidor, Offender, Palmer Cox Brownies	330.00
Humidor, Polychrome, Boy In Basket	302.00
Humidor, Skull, Striped Hat Lid, 4 1/2 In.	165.00
Jar, Druggist's, Mounted As Lamp, c.1920, 18 1/2 In.	250.00
Jardiniere, Acanthus Leaves, Flowers, Bull Heads, 23 3/4 In.	275.00
Jardiniere, George Jones & Sons, 9 1/2 In.	7600.00
Jardiniere, Leaf-Tip Edge, Winged Terms & Grotesque Masks, 11 1/4 In., Pair	6900.00
Jardiniere, Mocking Birds, Peonies, Footed, 8 In.	75.00
Jardiniere, Pedestal, 3 Harpies, Berries, Laurel Leaf Garlands, 4 Frogs, 1890, 57 In.	2070.00
Jardiniere, Yellow Foliate Design, Green Ground, Scrolled Handles, 12 In.	115.00
Jug, Cartouches With Squirrel, Birds, Stippled Ground, England, 1880, 9 In.	520.00
Jug, Puzzle, Honey Brown, Z.V. Pec, 7 In.	70.00
Jug, Water, Leaves, Geometric Bands, Green, Blue, Red, Open Mouth, 3 Handles, 13 In.	172.00
Lamp, Salon, Ribbed Gloss Brown, Slag Glass Domed Shade, Belle Epoque, 37 In.	1331.00
Match Box, Match, Squirrel On Top, WS & S, 5 3/8 In.	27.00
Nut Dish, Leaf Shape, Squirrel Handles, 10 In.	230.00
Oyster Plate, Lazy Susan, 27 Wells, 10 x 12 In.	14375.00
Oyster Platter, 12 Wells, Ivory, Turquoise Ground, Green Leaf, 14 3/4 In.	725.00
Pedestal, Orb & Lions' Heads, 29 3/4 In.	275.00
Pitcher, Basket & Flower, 9 1/2 In.	192.00
Pitcher, Bird, Blue & White, 10 In.	425.00
Pitcher, Bird, Fan Design, Wardle, 7 In.	85.00
Pitcher, Bird, Fan, Brownhill, 9 1/2 In.	175.00

Pitcher, Black Man's Head, Wearing Coronet, WS & S, 12 In. 2090.00
Pitcher, Corn, 4 1/2 In. 145.00
Pitcher, Corn, 9 1/2 In. 165.00
Pitcher, Embossed Flowers & Bird, Turquoise, 6 In. 93.00
Pitcher, Fence Shape With Flowers, Twig Handle, 4 Sides, 8 In. 115.00
Pitcher, Fence With Dogwood, 7 In. 105.00
Pitcher, Fish Shape, 9 In. 60.00
Pitcher, Floral, Signed, c.1880, 8 1/2 In. 395.00
Pitcher, Green Leaf Design, Brown & Yellow, 4 1/2 In. 110.00
Pitcher, Helmet, Wedgwood, 1875 .... 8775.00
Pitcher, Milk, Corn, 10 In. 80.00
Pitcher, Owl, 8 1/2 In. 650.00
Pitcher, Parrot, 14 In. 60.00
Pitcher, Peonies, 8 1/2 In. 85.00
Pitcher, Pineapple, 7 1/2 In. ....175.00 to 195.00
Pitcher, Polychrome Flowers, Blue Ground, Wedgwood, 5 3/4 In. 330.00
Pitcher, Scroll & Floral Mold, Under Brown & Lavender Glass, Erie-Onnainc, 7 In. 130.00
Pitcher, Shell & Seaweed, England, 7 1/2 In. 500.00
Pitcher, Wild Rose, 7 In. 155.00
Planter, Corn On The Cob Yellow Husk, Wardle, c.1890, 3 1/4 In. 115.00
Planter, Flamingo, 10 In. 150.00
Planter, Square Tree Trunk, Leaf, Footed, 10 In. 230.00
Planter, Wall, Cornucopia, 11 In. 60.00
Plaque, Profile Of Roman Emperor, Round, 18 In. 110.00
Plate, 2 Men In Dark Green, Bamboo Border, Light Green Ground, 8 1/2 In. 100.00
Plate, 2 Rabbits Carrying Rifles, Hunting, 9 In. 320.00
Plate, 6-Lobed Leaf Design, Brown, Green, 8 In., Pair 120.00
Plate, Blackberry, 9 1/4 In. 135.00
Plate, Deer, Hound, 11 In. 115.00
Plate, Grape Leaf, Fern, Floral, Greek Key Border, Hautin Boulanges, 1880s, 9 In., Pair . 275.00
Plate, Iris & Tulip, Celery Green, 10 In. 225.00
Plate, Leaf Shape, Deep Green, Brown, 8 x 6 In. 100.00
Plate, Neoclassical Figural Scene, 12 3/4 In. 520.00
Plate, Pink Berries, Blue, Green Leaves, Brown, Green, 8 In., Pair 65.00
Plate, Quatrefoil, Bird, 8 In. 105.00
Plate, Strawberries, Light Blue Ground, Germany, 11 1/4 In., Pair 55.00
Plate, Strawberries, Shell Shape, Leaves, Blossoms, England, 1867, 8 In., Pair 1725.00
Platter, Asparagus, Dressler, 16 1/4 x 10 3/4 In. 55.00
Platter, Basket Weave, Floral Border, Green Center, Wedgwood, 12 1/2 In. 522.00
Platter, Central Daisy, Floral, Leaf, Wheat, 14 In., Pair 115.00
Platter, Strawberries, Aqua, Cobalt Bows, 12 In. 350.00
Platter, Strawberries, Blue Ground, Staffordshire, 14 5/8 In. 522.00
Platter, Wine & Green Berries, Yellow Corners, Square, 9 In. 275.00
Powder Dish, Cover, Bloch, 2 1/4 x 4 In. 35.00
Seat, Garden, Raised Tower On Bottom, Dressler, 21 In. 325.00
Smoke Set, Removable Cover, Bloch, 5 x 9 3/4 In. 245.00
Stool, Barrel Seat, Irises In Relief, Green Glazes, Wardle, c.1895, 18 1/2 In., Pair 4600.00
Stove, Applied Anthemion, Floral Swags, White Crackle Glaze, Metal Doors, 78 In. 2000.00
Sugar & Creamer, Bird On Branch, Bamboo Trim 85.00
Tea Set, Blossoms, Black Berries, Wedgwood, 5 Piece 715.00
Teapot, Drum Shape, Cobalt Ground, Belt Form Finial & Handle, George Jones, 6 In. ... 5750.00
Teapot, Pineapple 210.00
Tobacco Jar, Young Girl, Majolica, 4 3/4 In. 60.00
Umbrella Stand, Oriental Polychrome Floral, Cobalt Blue Ground, 23 In. 468.00
Umbrella Stand, Reeds, Birds, 20 In. 895.00
Vase, Bird & Egg, c.1890, 5 In. 180.00
Vase, Brothers Urbach, Second Mark, 14 In. 120.00
Vase, Cover, Battle Scene, The Chariot Of Apollo, Double Serpent Handle, 34 1/2 In. 1815.00
Vase, Egyptian Revival, Dressler, 5 1/2 In. 70.00
Vase, Floral, Cobalt Scale Neck, Yellow Rings, 10 In., Pair 750.00
Vase, Jousting Frogs, Riding Seahorses, WS & S, 16 1/2 In. 45.00
Vase, Lovers In An Embrace, Scrolled, Italy, 19th Century, 14 1/2 In. 345.00
Vase, Man In 19th Century Musketeer Costume, On Rocky Crag, 11 1/2 In. 115.00

MALACHITE is a green stone with unusual layers or rings of darker green shades. It is often polished and used for decorative objects. Most malachite comes from Siberia or Australia.

Box, Jewelry, Veneered, Quilted Interior, c.1885, 5 1/4 In.	2300.00
Desk Weight, Silver Gilt, 4 Winged Putti Supporting Ball, Continental, 8 In.	690.00
Inkstand, Cut Glass Inkwell, Cover, Pen Well, 19th Century, 13 In.	3450.00
Obelisk, Gilt Metal Stars, Acanthus, Continental, 19th Century, 12 x 4 In., Pair	1955.00
Obelisk, Neoclassical, Ormolu Mounted, Laurel Wreath, Baltic, 28 In., Pair	4310.00
Snuff Bottle, Mask & Loose Ring Handles, Gold Etched Landscape, 2 3/4 In.	200.00
Urn, Campana Form, Everted Lip, Stepped Square Plinth, 10 1/4 In.	863.00

MAPS of all types have been collected for centuries. The earliest known printed maps were made in 1478. The first printed street map showed London in 1559. The first road map for use by drivers of automobiles were made in 1901. Collectors buy maps that were pages of old books, as well as the multifolded road maps popular in this century.

America, Petrus Kerius, Hand Colored, Engraved, 1646, 4 x 5 1/2 In.	242.00
Canada, Harbour Of Chebucto & Halifax, Family Crests, 1775, 10 1/2 x 8 1/2 In.	325.00
Carte Generale Des Royaume D' Angleterre, M. Sanson, 1658, 18 3/4 x 24 In.	209.00
Colorado, Denver & Rio Grande Railroad System, Lithographed, 17 1/2 x 14 1/2 In.	101.00
Diamond Motor Oil, 1936	12.00
Florida, Lewis & Clark, 17 3/4 x 21 1/2 In.	60.00
Florida Keys, J.H. Colton, 1855, 13 x 15 3/4 In.	125.00
Georgetown & Washington, Tidal Basin, T. Roosevelt Island, 1862, 15 x 12 1/2 In.	75.00
Gila National Forest, Southwestern New Mexico, Oversize, 38 x 48 In.	5.00
Globe, Celestial & Terrestrial, W. & S. Jones, Brass Meridian Circle, 18 In., Pair	5750.00
Globe, Celestial & Terrestrial, William Bardin, Table, 1782, 12 In., Pair	13800.00
Globe, Celestial, Mahogany Stand, Downswept Legs, Acorn Feet, Tripod Base, 40 In.	4890.00
Globe, Celestial, Newton, Mahogany Stand, Ebonized Border On Horizon Ring, 12 In.	1840.00
Globe, Terrestrial & Lunar, Story Of Moon, Replogle, Box, 1969, 10 x 16 In., Pair	38.00
Globe, Terrestrial, Lignum Vita Case, Pocket, 3 In.	1925.00
Globe, Terrestrial, Red Morocco Case, Celestial Map Inside Cover, Pocket, 3 In.	3025.00
Globe, Terrestrial, Rotating, Gessoed Rim, Tripod Stand, 39 x 15 In.	2185.00
Globe, Terrestrial, Wooden Base, 12 In.	467.00
Hawaiian Islands, Dole, 1937	250.00
Honolulu & Sandwich Island, Snydor, 1937	250.00
Idaho, Territory, 12 Counties, 1878, 10 1/2 x 14 1/2 In.	100.00
Kansas Cities, Pre-Civil War, 3 Sheets, 1858, 9 x 13 1/2 In.	135.00
Kentucky, Cumberland River From Falls To Nashville, 1834, 24 x 15 In.	200.00
Louisiana, Carte Geographique, Buchon, c.1825, 17 1/2 x 24 In.	440.00
Maine, Engraved, By Doolittle & Massachusetts, Matted, Frame, 18 x 28 In.	55.00
Maryland, Reconnaissance Between Baltimore & Philadelphia, 1827	325.00
Massachusetts, J. Reid, New York, Maple Frame, 16 x 19 In.	495.00
Massachusetts, Route Of Western Railroad, Connecticut River, 1837, 25 1/2 x 19 In.	175.00
Michigan, Canals, Roads & Distances, 16 1/8 x 13 In.	100.00
Middlesex County, England, Engraved, Hand Colored, Frame, 18th C., 7 1/2 x 5 In.	44.00
Minnesota, Counties, Colored, 16 x 13 In.	175.00
Minnesota, Road, Shell Gasoline, 1929, 12 x 9 In.	245.00
New Jersey, Road, Standard Oil Company, 1928, 11 x 8 In.	35.00
New Orleans & Adjacent Country, c.1815	660.00
New Orleans Plan, Capitol Of Louisiana, c.1720, M. De La Tour, 13 x 19 In.	1155.00
North America, California Gold Rush, J. Calvin Smith, 1852, 18 1/2 x 20 1/2 In.	1090.00
North America, European Settlements, West Indies, R.W. Seale, 8 1/2 x 14 1/2 In.	440.00
Ohio, Geographical, Statistical & Historical, Population, 581,434, 9 1/2 x 12 In.	225.00
Ohio, Scioto Valley, Twelve Mile Section, 7 1/2 x 10 In.	185.00
Ozark National Forest, Arkansas, 1971	5.00
Paris, Metro Map, Bus Routes & Subway Lines, 1982	2.00
Pennsylvania, Sinclair, Cartoon Style, Color, 1933	40.00
Santa Fe Trail, 16 In.	1100.00
Scotland, Rand McNally & Co., Frame, 26 x 19 In.	110.00
Siskiyou National Forest, Oregon & California, Photographs	12.00
Southern States, Capitals, Railroads, County Towns, Civil War, 1861, 20 x 30 In.	205.00

Staffordshire, England, Parks & Rivers, Hand Colored, Frame, 1788, 19 1/2 x 15 1/2 In. .   165.00
Terra Sancta, Hand Colored, Engraved, Petra Lacstan, Frame, 15 x 20 1/2 In. 220.00
Texaco, Road, Graphic Colors, 1928 . . . .   350.00
United States, Geological, March, 1842, 15 1/2 x 10 In. 175.00
United States, Greyhound Transcontinental Bus Time Tables, Pacific Greyhound, 1940 . .   12.00
United States Defense, Richfield Richlube, Statue Of Liberty, 1941 . . . .   20.00
Utah, Geological, Western Part Of Plateau Province, 1882, 18 x 29 1/2 In. 225.00
World, Globe, A.J. Johnson, 1867, 17 x 26 In. 160.00
World, Globe, J. Cary, 1811, 19 1/2 x 35 In. 260.00

MARBLE collectors pay highest prices for glass and sulphide marbles. The game of marbles has been popular since the days of the ancient Romans. American children were able to buy marbles by the mid-eighteenth century. Dutch glazed clay marbles were least expensive. Glazed pottery marbles, attributed to the Bennington potteries in Vermont, were of a better quality. Marbles made of pink marble were also available by the 1830s. Glass marbles seem to have been made later. By 1880, Samuel C. Dyke of South Akron, Ohio, was making clay marbles and The National Onyx Marble Company was making marbles of onyx. The Navarre Glass Marble Company of Navarre, Ohio, and M. B. Mishler of Ravenna, Ohio, made the glass marbles. Ohio remained the center of the marble industry, and the Akron-made Akro Agate brand became nationally known. Other pieces made by Akro Agate are listed in this book in the Akro Agate category. Sulphides are glass marbles with frosted white figures in the center.

Akro Agate, Box, 50 Piece 970.00
Buddy, 1920s, Box, With Contents, 1 x 3 x 4 In. 10.00
Carnelian, Akro Agate, No. 1, Box, 25 Piece 735.00
Clambroth, Caged White Base, Pink Strands, 2 3/4 In. 522.00
Cloud, Panel, Single Pontil, 2 1/4 In. 710.00
End-Of-Day, Blue, Green & Red, 2 In. 415.00
Green Brick, M.F. Christensen & Son Co. 580.00
Latticinio, Core Swirl, 1 1/2 In. 66.00
Latticinio, Core Swirl, 2 In. 93.00
Latticinio, Swirl, White Core, 16 Threads, Yellow, Red, Green & Blue Ribbons, 1 1/2 In. .   65.00
Lutz, Black Glass, 5/8 In. 325.00
Lutz, Blue, Copper Bands, 1 1/2 In. 357.00
Lutz, Mist, Ribbon, Yellow, Green, 3/4 In. 195.00
Lutz, Opaque White Base, 3/4 In. 330.00
Lutz, Ribbon Core, 3/4 In. 325.00
Lutz, Swirl, Gold, 3/4 In. 605.00
Mica Flakes, Blizzard Type Pattern, 1 13/16 In. 1522.00
Milky, National, No., Box, 25 Piece 2268.00
Miller Swirl, Christmas Tree, Peltier, 13/16 In. 950.00
Miller Swirl, Golden Rebel, Peltier Glass Co., 1927, Shooter Size 2993.00
Miller Swirl, Graycoat, Peltier, 7/8 In. 1020.00
Onionskin, End-Of-Day, 1 1/2 In. . . . . .77.00 to 165.00
Onionskin, End-Of-Day, 1 3/4 In. 132.00
Onionskin, End-Of-Day, 2 In. 385.00
Onionskin, Leaf-Hand Twist, Mica, 4 Panels, 2 1/4 In. 1428.00
Slag, Akro Agate, No. 3, 50 Piece, Box 1627.00
Sulphide, Bear In Brown Glass, 1 1/16 In. 1155.00
Sulphide, Bear, 1 1/2 In. 165.00
Sulphide, Cow, 2 In. 120.00
Sulphide, Dog, 1 1/2 In. 90.00
Sulphide, Dog, 2 3/4 In. 154.00
Sulphide, Elephant, 1 1/2 In. 121.00
Sulphide, Elephant, Green Glass, 1 3/4 In. 685.00
Sulphide, Horse, 1 1/2 In. 88.00
Sulphide, Lamb, 1 1/2 In. 143.00
Sulphide, Lion, 2 1/4 In. 220.00
Sulphide, Monkey, 1 1/2 In. 231.00

Sulphide, Owl, 1 3/4 In. 70.00
Sulphide, Reclining Cow, 1 1/2 In. 110.00
Sulphide, Reclining Lamb, 1 1/2 In. 82.00
Sulphide, Rooster, 1 3/4 In. 176.00
Sulphide, Standing Bear, Light Amethyst, 1 1/4 In. 90.00
Swirl, Open Core, 1 3/4 In. 121.00
Swirl, Solid Core, 1 3/4 In. 66.00

MARBLE CARVINGS, such as large or small figurines, groups of people or animals, and architectural decorations, have been a special art form since the time of the ancient Greeks. Reproductions, especially of large Victorian groups, are being made of a mixture using marble dust. These are very difficult to detect and collectors should be careful. Other carvings are listed under Alabaster.

Basin, Neoclassical, Fluted, Molded Lip, Waisted Socle, Italy, 16 x 23 In. 4600.00
Bath, Neoclassical Italian, White & Green Veined, Oval, Base, 7 x 18 In. 2415.00
Bath, Neoclassical, White & Green, Ring Handles, Black Base, 7 x 17 x 6 In. 2415.00
Bust, Augustus Caesar, Carrara Marble, Gilded Bronze, Pinedo, 24 In. 6325.00
Bust, Augustus Caesar, Draped, Italian, 24 1/2 In. 9200.00
Bust, Duke Of Wellington, White, Turned Base, Peter Turnerelli, 21 1/2 In. 990.00
Bust, Gentleman, Marked, C. Novanin, 1900-1920, 26 In. 725.00
Bust, Goddess Flora, Carved, 19 1/2 In. 2760.00
Bust, Hadrian, Neoclassical, Stepped Round Socle, Italy, 27 In. 9200.00
Bust, Man, Black Plinth, 19 1/4 In. 3450.00
Bust, Mussolini, Signed, Billotti, Italy, 18 In. 115.00
Bust, Roman Youth, Mahogany Stepped Base, 2nd Century A.D. 2990.00
Bust, Woman, Marked E. Dies, Roma 1898, 28 In. 1380.00
Bust, Young Boy, Contemplative Pose, 9 1/2 In. 175.00
Bust, Young Classical Woman, Chiton Lightly Draped, Socle Base, 25 In. 1150.00
Bust, Young Girl, Hair Tied Up With Ribbon, 9 In. 175.00
Bust, Young Woman, Feast Day Costume, Socle Base, Italy, 21 1/2 In. 290.00
Figurine, 5 Putti, Frolicking Amid Chair, Bronze, L. Gossin, 9 1/2 x 18 In. 4600.00
Figurine, Girl, Holding Bird, P. Barranti, 24 3/4 In. 935.00
Fountain, Courtyard, Renaissance, White Marble, Italy, 1900, 58 x 24 In. 2170.00
Garniture Set, Women In Landscape, Jeweled Cobalt Ground, 1875s, 19 In. 6325.00
Mortar, 19th Century, 9 3/4 x 18 In. 150.00
Pedestal, Column, Light Gray, Square Top, 40 x 12 x 12 In. 1030.00
Pedestal, Empire, 4 Corinthian Columns, Verde Antico Top, 43 In., Pair 865.00
Pedestal, Female Term, Rouge, White Marble Top, Bronze, 39 In., Pair 2760.00
Pedestal, Green Marble, Square Top, Raised On Square Base, 43 In., Pair 545.00
Pedestal, Green Mottled, Continental, 41 1/2 x 9 3/4 In. 460.00
Pedestal, Pink Marble Top, Brass, 19th Century, 11 1/2 x 38 In., Pair 250.00
Pedestal, Round Top, Ring-Turned Standard, 41 3/4 In. 230.00
Statue, 2 Semi-Draped Bacchic Youths, Rocky Base, 21 In. 6900.00
Statue, Asian Woman, On Rock Outcrop, 37 In. 230.00
Statue, Bacchante, 19th Century, 30 1/4 In. 1610.00
Statue, Capitolene Venus, Gray Marble Base, 24 In. 1495.00
Statue, Lioness & Cubs, Seated, Gray, Yellow Veined, 44 1/2 In. 2700.00
Statue, Lions, Reclining Pose, 1 Asleep, 1 Awake, 19th Century, 19 In., Pair 4500.00
Statue, Maiden, Seated, Pouring Milk, Round Pedestal Base, 25 In. 440.00
Statue, Nude Woman, Sitting, Marble Base, 15 1/2 x 17 In. 1870.00
Statue, Sarah Bernhardt, Ivory, 25 1/4 In. 13800.00
Statue, Seminude Classical Woman, Late 19th Century, 27 In. 2500.00
Statue, Young Cupid, In Hip-Shot Pose, With Full-Maned Lion, 24 In. 2000.00
Urn, Bronze Scrolled Arms, 14 In., Pair 1495.00
Urn, Classical Design, Carrara, Square Base, 15 1/2 In., Pair 440.00
Urn, Cover, Neoclassical, Oval, Waisted Socle, Italy, 11 1/2 In., Pair 3735.00
Urn, Cover, Neoclassical, White, Gray, Raised On Circular Stem, Italy, Pair 4600.00
Urn, Cover, Pierced Rim, Leaf-Tip Swags, Ram's-Mask Handles, 18 In., Pair 2875.00
Urn, Domed Stepped Cover, Neoclassical, Waisted Socle, 36 In., Pair 10925.00
Urn, Gilt Bronze, White Marble Columnar Bases, Louis XVI, 12 In., Pair 1725.00
Urn, Green Marble, Gilt Ram's-Head Handles, Floral Swags, 18 In., Pair 3162.00

Urn, Jasperware, Neoclassical, Lizard Handles, Russia, 10 1/2 x 9 1/2 In. 4600.00
Vase, Domed Lid, Acorn Finials, Ram's Masks, Signed AB, 17 1/2 In., Pair 4830.00

MARBLEHEAD Pottery was founded in 1905 by Dr. J. Hall as a rehabilitative program for the patients of a Marblehead, Massachusetts, sanitarium. Two years later it was separated from the sanitarium and it continued operations until 1936. Many of the pieces were decorated with marine motifs.

Bowl, Blue, Paper Label, 6 In. 247.00
Bowl, Blue, Signed, 2 x 8 3/4 In. 330.00
Bowl, Dark Blue Matte Glaze, Dark Brown Interior, Flat Rim, Spherical, 3 In. 275.00
Bowl, Flower Frog, Green Matte Glaze, Ship Mark, 1 1/2 x 3 1/4 In. 412.00
Bowl, Geometric Design, Brown, Olive Green Ground, 2 3/4 In. 900.00
Bowl, Lotus Leaf, Dark Blue Exterior, Light Blue Interior, Ship Mark, 3 x 8 In. 412.00
Bowl, Red Metallic Glaze, 6 x 3 In. 385.00
Bowl, Tan, Green, Interior Signed, 5 In. 385.00
Pitcher, Green Matte Glaze, Semigloss Blue, 3 Handles, 6 In. 192.00
Pitcher, Incised Ship At Sea, Blue High Glaze, Impressed Mark, 5 In. 330.00
Planter, Hanging, 4 x 6 In. 330.00
Planter, Hanging, Melon, Indigo Blue Matte Glaze, 3 Buttressed Handles 275.00
Plate, Frieze Of Camels & Nomads, White Ground, Signed, 7 1/2 In. 950.00
Tile, Deer & Trees, Square, 5 7/8 In. 1320.00
Tile, Floral Bouquet, Vine, Leaf Design, Sun Yellow, Cobalt Blue Petals, 6 1/8 In. 605.00
Tile, White Ship At Sea, Blue Sky Ground, Square, 4 In. 231.00
Vase, Alligator, Teal To Mint Green Matte Glaze, Aqua Blue Neck, 5 x 4 In. 302.00
Vase, Blue Matte Glaze, Closed Form, Impressed Mark, 3 1/2 In. 286.00
Vase, Blue Matte Glaze, Flared Rim, 6 1/4 x 5 1/4 In. 460.00
Vase, Blue Matte Glaze, Mottled Green, Brown, Tapered, 8 x 4 In. . . . . .825.00 to 1210.00
Vase, Blue Matte Glaze, Pear Shape, 6 x 5 In. 550.00
Vase, Blue Matte Glaze, Signed, 11 3/4 In. 660.00
Vase, Broad, Ribbed Body, Chicory Blue Interior, Olive Brown Glaze, 5 In. 137.00
Vase, Brown Glaze, Impressed Mark, 3 1/2 In. 385.00
Vase, Brown Matte Glaze, Paper Label, 3 1/2 In. 198.00
Vase, Bud, Gray Glaze, Squat, 6 x 3 In. 137.50
Vase, Cabinet, Chocolate Brown Specks, Mocha Brown Matte Glaze, 3 1/2 x 2 In. 220.00
Vase, Cabinet, Mottled Ocher, Light Beige Matte Glaze, Ivory Interior, 3 1/3 In. 247.00
Vase, Cabinet, Pink Matte Glaze, Ship Mark, 3 3/4 x 2 1/2 In. 137.00
Vase, Chocolate Brown Drip Glaze, Mocha Brown Matte Glaze, Speckled, 3 x 6 In. 330.00
Vase, Closed Mouth, Brown Flecks, Sage Green Matte Ground, 3 1/3 In. 192.00
Vase, Dark Green Matte Glaze, Cylindrical, 7 In. 517.00
Vase, Dove Gray Matte Glaze, Blue Specks, Chicory Blue Interior, Tapered, 9 In. 303.00
Vase, Dragonflies At Top, Blue, Brown, Green Matte Ground, Hannah Tutt, 6 In. 1760.00
Vase, Grape & Vine Design, Repeating, Blue Lavender Grapes, H. Tutt, 3 x 4 In. 2530.00
Vase, Grapevine, Gray, Indigo, Speckled Gray Matte Ground, Hannah Tutt, 6 In. 1430.00
Vase, Grapevine, Green, Brown, Blue, Mustard Matte Ground, Ship Mark, 5 In. 1430.00
Vase, Gray Blue Glaze, Shouldered Form, Impressed Mark, 3 1/2 In. 385.00
Vase, Green, Signed, 4 1/2 In. 303.00
Vase, Incised, Painted Geometric Design, Green Against Blue Matte, 4 1/2 In. 1760.00
Vase, Lavender Matte Glaze, Marked, 7 1/2 In. 715.00
Vase, Leaf Design, Speckled Blue Ground, Signed, 7 In. 2695.00
Vase, Leaf Design, Speckled Green Ground, Signed, 11 1/4 In. 2115.00
Vase, Mauve Glaze, Lavender Interior, Flaring, Signed, 7 1/2 In. 350.00
Vase, Painted, Carved Fruit, Floral Design, 2-Tone Brown, Blue, Gray Ground, 4 In. 825.00
Vase, Painted, Incised Geometric Design, Green Against Blue Ground, 6 In. 2750.00
Vase, Pink Matte Glaze, Impressed Mark, 3 1/2 In. 247.00
Vase, Purple Matte Glaze, Blue Highlights, 5 In. 385.00
Vase, Stylized Blossoming Standard Trees, Blue, Gray, Hannah Tutt, 5 x 3 In. 1760.00
Vase, Stylized Fish, Beige, Blue, Gray Ground, 4 1/2 x 4 In. 4950.00
Vase, Stylized Peacock Feathers, Dark Brown Matte, Dark Green Ground, 8 In. .4000.00 to 4125.00
Vase, Stylized Trees, Green & Brown, Mustard Ground, 14 In. 1850.00
Vase, Yellow Matte Glaze, Tapered, 5 1/2 x 3 1/2 In. 660.00
Vessel, Blue Matte Glaze, Light Blue Interior, Signed, 4 x 5 In. 400.00

MARTIN BROTHERS of Middlesex, England, made Martinware, a salt-glazed stoneware, between 1873 and 1915. Many figural jugs and vases were made by the three brothers. Of special interest are the fanciful birds, usually made with removable heads.

Jug, Grotesque, Devilish Bearded Smiling Face, Ocher, Brown, 1899, 8 In.	2675.00
Jug, Mythical Face, Swirling Foliage From Mouth, Ocher, Brown, 10 In.	1840.00
Vase, Crab, Lobster Design, Brown, Blue Ground, 1903, 9 In., Pair	1870.00
Vase, Red & Green Luster Glaze, Squat, 1900, Incised, 5 x 7 In.	525.00

MARY GREGORY is the name used for a type of glass that is easily identified. White figures were painted on clear or colored glass as the decoration. The figures chosen were usually children at play. The first glass known as Mary Gregory was made about 1870. Similar glass is made even today. The traditional story has been that the glass was made at the Sandwich Glass works in Boston by a woman named Mary Gregory. Recent research suggests that it is possible that none was made at Sandwich. In general, all-white figures were used in the United States, tinted faces were probably used in Bohemia, France, Italy, Germany, Switzerland, and England. Children standing, not playing, were pictured after the 1950s.

Bottle, Barber, Boy Tennis Player, Cobalt Blue, Pontil, 8 1/8 In.	210.00
Bottle, Barber, Gilt, Cobalt Blue	550.00
Bottle, Boy Holding Bird, Cobalt Blue, Clear Stopper, 9 1/2 In.	295.00
Bottle, Boy In White, Matching Sapphire Blue Stopper, 10 1/4 In.	195.00
Box, Cranberry, Gold Moser-Style	585.00
Box, Hinged Cover, Boy Holding Bird In Hand, Amber, 3 1/2 x 3 3/4 In.	245.00
Box, Hinged Cover, Sapphire Blue, 4 In.	365.00
Box, Souvenir, Atlantic City, Moss Green, c.1900, 2 1/2 In.	310.00
Creamer, Girl, Green	40.00
Dresser Set, Girl Standing In Leaves With Flowers, Steeple Stopper, 3 Piece	395.00
Goblet, Electric Blue, Pair	275.00
Goblet, Sapphire Blue, Pair	245.00
Lamp, Figure Both Sides, All Glass, Blue	945.00
Mug, Boy, Handle, Cranberry	100.00
Paperweight, Boy & Girl With Horns, Beveled Edge, Black Amethyst, 5 x 3 In.	195.00
Pitcher, Girl Walking With Staff, Olive Green, Pontil, 10 In.	165.00
Plate, Cupids, Cobalt Blue, 7 In.	175.00
Plate, Woman, Holding Fan, Man In Armor, Shield, 9 3/8 In., Pair	350.00
Shaving Bowl, Victorian Girl & Lilies-Of-The-Valley, Amethyst, Bulbous, 6 In.	595.00
Sugar & Creamer, Boy On Sugar, Girl On Creamer, Cranberry, 1920s	150.00
Tankard, Light Green, 11 In.	220.00
Tumbler, Gilt Children, Kite, Amethyst, c.1890, 4 In.	66.00
Vase, Boy & Lilies-Of-The-Valley, Crystal Shell Trim Sides, Blue, 7 In.	145.00
Vase, Boy Carries Tray Of Flowers, Green Opaque Bristol, 11 1/8 In.	225.00
Vase, Boy Facing Girl, Basket Of Flowers, Orange To Green, Pair	595.00
Vase, Boy, Walking, Cranberry, 4 1/2 In.	145.00
Vase, Couple, Amethyst, 8 1/4 In., Pair	425.00
Vase, Figures By Fence, Amber, 13 1/2 In.	395.00
Vase, Girl, Ruffled Edge, Amber, 8 In.	175.00
Vase, Girl, Seated In A Tree, 13 In., Pair	546.00
Vase, Profile Of Girl, Floral Sprigs, Green, Ruffled Edge, 1895, 7 1/2 In.	55.00
Vase, Young Boy With Ball On String, Black Amethyst, 8 In.	245.00
Water Set, Inverted Thumbprint, Girl, Leaves, Boy Tumblers, Cranberry, 5 Piece	430.00

MASON'S IRONSTONE was made by the English pottery of Charles J. Mason after 1813. Mason, of Lane Delph, was given a patent for this improved earthenware. He usually called it "Mason's Patent Ironstone China." It resisted chipping and breaking so it became popular for dinnerwares and other table service dishes. Vases and other decorative pieces were also made. The ironstone was decorated with orange, blue, gold, and other colors, often in Japanese inspired designs. The firm had financial difficulties but the molds and the name Mason were used by many owners through the years, including Francis Morley, Taylor

Ashworth, George L. Ashworth, and John Shaw. Mason's joined the
Wedgwood group in 1973 and the name is still found on dinnerwares.

Commode, Blue, White Country, Wick, Wood Handle, 11 1/2 In.	145.00
Pitcher, Basin, Chinoiserie Design, 16 1/4 In.	150.00
Pitcher, Milk, Oriental Transfer, Snake Handle, 5 1/4 In.	250.00
Plate, Cobalt & Coral Glaze, Hexagonal, 7 In.	145.00
Platter, Black Transfer, Oriental Scene, Signed, 16 In.	50.00
Platter, Floral Rim, Scalloped, Chinoiserie Interior, 15 x 12 In.	29.00
Platter, Imari Design, 22 3/4 In.	488.00
Tureen, Cover, Boar's-Head Handles	137.00
Tureen, Cover, Bowl Of Fruit On Stylized Rock, Goose, Green, Black, 12 In.	805.00
Tureen, Sauce, Undertray, Ladle, Chartreuse, Yellow, Green, Gold	130.00
Vase, Floral, Footed, 5 In.	175.00

MASONIC, see Fraternal category.

MASSIER, a French art pottery, was made by brothers Jerome, Delphin,
and Clement Massier in Vallauris and Golfe-Juan, France, in the late
nineteenth and early twentieth centuries. It has an iridescent metallic
luster glaze that resembles the Weller Sicardo pottery glaze. Most
pieces are marked *J. Massier*.

Vase, Arts & Crafts, Jerome Massier, 6 1/2 In.	375.00
Vase, Green Mistletoe, Lilac, 4 In.	350.00

MATCH HOLDERS were made to hold the large wooden matches that
were used in the nineteenth and twentieth centuries for a variety of pur-
poses. The kitchen stove and the fireplace or furnace had to be lit regularly. One type of match holder was made to hang on the wall, another
was designed to be kept on a tabletop. Of special interest today are
match holders that have advertisements as part of the design.

1876 Centennial, Hat, Musket, Sword, Ironstone, Glazed, 4 In.	275.00
American Brewing Company, Stoneware	165.00
Bell Shape, Moriage, 3 1/2 In.	125.00
Black Forest Bear, Wooden, Copper Insert On Back For Matches	44.00
Boy, Smoking Pipe, Sitting On Baskets, Corn Design, Cast Iron, 5 1/4 In.	220.00
Ceresota, Hanging, Die Cut Tin Lithograph, Box, 9 In.	660.00
Ceresota Prize Bread Flour, Barrel, Box	250.00
Conch Shell, Royal Bayreuth, Wall	325.00
Dog, Art Deco, Bisque, White	28.00
Earlville Hatchery, Earlville, Iowa, 5 In.	16.00
Farmers Co-Op, Anita, Iowa, Tin, Blue Enamel, 6 In.	33.00
Game Table, Bronze, 4 3/8 x 4 1/4 x 3 In. ....*Illus*	286.00
Gothic Revival, Brass, Interior Socket For Taper, 4 5/8 In.	60.00
Grape & Scroll, Cast Iron, Wall, 19th Century, 9 In.	90.00
Harlem Casino, New York, Copper, White Metal, Box, 1908, 5 x 3 In.	55.00
High-Top Shoe, Painted, 5 In. ....75.00 to 95.00	
Jenny Lind, Wall	85.00

**Don't store ivory, bone, horn, mother-of-
pearl, or wood handled tablewares near
heat sources like ovens or radiators.**

Match Holder,
Game Table, Bronze,
4 3/8 x 4 1/4 x 3 In.

Little Red Riding Hood, Striker, Staffordshire 75.00
Majolica, Brothers Urbach, 6 1/2 In. 85.00
Portly Man, With Suitcase, Starting On Long Journey, Porcelain, 6 In. 65.00
Redware, Green, Brown & Cream Glaze, Shenandoah Valley 415.00
Strike, Sharples Separator Co., Tin, Die Cut, 6 x 2 In. 315.00
Thermometer, Die Cut Brass, 2-Dimensional Head Of Black Boy, 7 1/4 In. 330.00
Winged Horse, Flour Sack Cameo, Always All Right, Tin, 3 x 5 3/4 In. 45.00
Young Boy With Bundle Of Wheat, Bisque, Gold Trim, Germany, 5 1/2 In. 45.00

MATCH SAFES were designed to be carried in the pocket. Early matches were made with phosphorus and could ignite unexpectedly. The matches were safely stored in the tightly closed container. Match safes were made in sterling silver, plated silver, or other metals. The English call these *vesta boxes.*

1895 Exposition, Atlanta, Ga., 2 Boys By Bale Of Cotton, 2 1/2 In. 465.00
Advance Thresher, Celluloid 185.00
Baby Head, In Collar Of Shirt, Brass 450.00
Basket Weave Pattern, 14K Gold, 2 1/4 x 1 3/4 In. 400.00
Black, Child's, Cast Iron, 4 1/2 In. 65.00
Black Band, Matching Striker On Top, Push-Button Opening, Agate, 2 3/4 In. 145.00
Boot, Hinged Cover, Striker Base, Tin, 2 1/2 In. 150.00
Boule, Brass, Red & Black Lacquer, 3 1/8 In. 250.00
Bowling Pins & Ball, Brass, Hinged Lid, 3 x 1 1/2 In. 45.00
Breakfast To Pres. Taft, Engraved, Sterling Silver, El Paso, Oct. 16, 1909 . . . . 225.00
Bullet, Screw Top, Blue, France, 3 1/8 In. 70.00
Canadian Pacific Steamship Lines, Post 210.00
Cavaliers All Around, Plated Metal, Stone Striker, Drawers, 2 3/8 x 1 5/8 In. 165.00
Cincinnati Zoo, Relief Horse Head, Aluminum, 2 3/8 In. 35.00
Civil War 175.00
Clamshell, Silvered, R. Wallace & Sons, 3 In. 275.00
Dog, Sterling Silver, 2 In. 60.00
Elk Medallion, Striker On Bottom, Stamped Jan. 12, 1904 . . . . 65.00
Floral, Inner Striker, Lacquer, Metal, Japan, 2 3/8 x 1 3/4 In. 10.00
H.C. Monogram, Enameled, Gorham, 1886 . . . . 350.00
Handmade Striker, Tin, 2 3/8 x 3 1/4 In. 115.00
Hercules Powder 195.00
Hudson-Fulton, 1909 . . . . 75.00
Hunter, 2 Hounds, Quail On 1 Side, Cattails 80.00
Indian Head 225.00
Inner Latch To Side Compartment For Photograph, Sterling Silver, 2 1/2 In. 87.00
John Feam Policeman, Engraved, No. 98A, Nickel Plated, 1850s, 1 3/4 x 2 1/2 In. 145.00
Kate Greenaway Style Figures, Oak Leaves, Copper, 3 In. 55.00
Keystone Grease Lubricant, Striker Bar, 1930s, 2 x 2 1/4 In. 38.00
Lima Clothing Co., Matchless Bargains, Hard Rubber, 2 3/4 In., 2 Piece 70.00
Owl, Head Flips Back To Open, Striker On Back, Plated Metal, 1 7/8 In. 240.00
Pabst, 1910s 67.00
Pan-American Exposition, Buffalo, New York, 1901, Celluloid Wrap 200.00
People, Horses & Buildings, Hinged Cover, Brass, 2 In. 175.00
Pillbox Style, Brass, Enamel, Propos Gallants . . . . *Illus* 385.00
Plaque, Classical Woman, Sterling Silver, Cauman, 1 7/8 x 1 1/8 In. 425.00
Raised Shamrocks, Signed 155.00
Safety Bicycle, Engraved, Relief Border, Sterling Silver, 19th Century 165.00
Scarab, Cold Paint, Bradley & Hubbard 750.00
Scroll & Floral, Whiting, Sterling Silver, 2 5/8 In. 220.00
Seminude Woman, Unger 245.00
Seminude Women, Cigar Cutter Base, Silver Plate, Victorian, 1 1/2 x 2 3/4 In. 165.00
Shield, Sterling Silver, Enamel, Codding Bros. & Heilborn, 1 1/4 In. 75.00
Shoe, Papier-Mache, Frog, Butterfly, 1 3/8 x 3 1/4 In. . . . . *Illus* 165.00
Shoe, Papier-Mache, Hinged Top, 1 1/2 x 3 1/4 In. . . . . *Illus* 165.00
Soldier, Cast Iron, E.G. Zimmerman, 4 3/4 In. 140.00
Standard Car Truck Company, Chicago, Celluloid, 2 5/8 In. 110.00
Sterling Silver, Hinged Compartment, Each End, England, 1908, 3 x 1 In. 88.00
Stone Striker, Inset On Top, Push-Button Opening, Blue, 2 3/4 In. 215.00

Match Safe, Pillbox Style, Brass, Enamel, Propos Gallants

Match Safe, Shoe, Papier-Mache, Hinged Top, 1 1/2 x 3 1/4 In.

Match Safe, Shoe, Papier-Mache, Frog, Butterfly, 1 3/8 x 3 1/4 In.

Use Ohio Blue Tips, For Safety, Foldover, Leather, 2 3/4 x 2 1/4 In.	75.00
Wilson Photograph, Celluloid, Metal	250.00
Woman, Riding Bicycle, Brass, Enamel, Pillbox Style, 1 7/8 In.	315.00
Woman, Smoking On 1 Side, Art Nouveau	130.00
Woman In Black, Removing Shoes, Fishing Creel & Rod Cover, 2 In.	880.00

MATT MORGAN, an English artist, was making pottery in Cincinnati, Ohio, by 1883. His pieces were decorated to resemble Moorish wares. Incised designs and colors were applied to raised panels on the pottery. Shiny or matte glazes were used. The company lasted less than two years.

MATT MORGAN —CIN. O— ART POTTERY CO

Urn, Birds On Dogwood Branch, Embossed Brown, Gold Band, 15 x 10 In. 1320.00

MCCOY pottery was made in Roseville, Ohio. Nelson McCoy and J.W. McCoy established the Nelson McCoy Sanitary and Stoneware Company in Roseville, Ohio, in 1910. The firm made art pottery after 1926. In 1933 it became the Nelson McCoy Pottery Company. Pieces marked *McCoy* were made by the Nelson McCoy Pottery Company. Cookie jars were made from about 1940 until December 1990, when the McCoy factory closed. In 1990 the McCoy mark was put back on pottery by a firm unrelated to the original company. Because there was a company named Brush-McCoy, there is great confusion between Brush and Nelson McCoy pieces. See Brush category for more information.

McCoy

Bank, Centennial Bear, Signed	110.00
Bank, Eagle	38.00 to 42.00
Bank, Woodsy Owl	120.00
Coffeepot, Barbecue	225.00
Cookie Jar, 101 Dalmations, 1961	450.00
Cookie Jar, Bean Pot	55.00
Cookie Jar, Bear, With Beehive	48.00
Cookie Jar, Black Engine	175.00
Cookie Jar, Boy On Baseball	225.00
Cookie Jar, Bugs Bunny, Cylinder	100.00
Cookie Jar, Chairman Of The Board, Burgundy Pants	550.00
Cookie Jar, Chilly Willy	55.00
Cookie Jar, Christmas Tree	775.00
Cookie Jar, Coalby Cat	150.00
Cookie Jar, Coffee Grinder	50.00
Cookie Jar, Cook Stove Shape, White, Gold Trim, 9 x 9 1/2 x 6 In.	50.00
Cookie Jar, Engine, Yellow	195.00
Cookie Jar, Frontier Family	60.00
Cookie Jar, Gleep	475.00
Cookie Jar, Globe	175.00 to 245.00
Cookie Jar, Have A Happy Day, Happy Face	75.00

Cookie Jar, Hobby Horse ....125.00 to 950.00
Cookie Jar, Hot Air Balloon 28.00
Cookie Jar, Indian 350.00
Cookie Jar, Leprechaun 1200.00
Cookie Jar, Mammy With Cauliflower ....330.00 to 1000.00
Cookie Jar, Mammy, White Dress, Green Trim 175.00
Cookie Jar, Monk, Thou Shall Not Steal 30.00
Cookie Jar, Mr. & Mrs. Owl 120.00
Cookie Jar, Owl 45.00
Cookie Jar, Owl, Brown, Marked 204 .... 40.00
Cookie Jar, Pineapple, Modern 125.00
Cookie Jar, Strawberry, 9 1/2 x 8 1/2 In. 85.00
Cookie Jar, Strawberry, Marked McCoy USA, 9 1/2 x 8 1/2 In. 52.00
Cookie Jar, Teepee, Slant Cover ....325.00 to 365.00
Cookie Jar, Touring Car ....110.00 to 130.00
Cookie Jar, Turkey 325.00
Cookie Jar, Wagon 110.00
Cookie Jar, Wren House 145.00
Cookie Jar, Yosemite Sam 375.00
Decanter, Apollo 45.00
Flower Frog, Bluebird, 4 In. 100.00
Jardiniere, Basketweave, White, Pedestal, 8 1/2 x 12 1/2 In. 395.00
Jardiniere, Diamond Quilt, White, Pedestal, 12 1/2 In. 250.00
Jardiniere, Quilted, Pedestal, Green ....*Illus* 125.00
Jardiniere, Springwood, Flowers, 8 In. 65.00
Jardiniere, Tulips, Loy-Nel-Art, 8 In. 230.00
Mug, Barrel, Brown, 5 In. 30.00
Mug, Barrel, Brown, Marked 4 Inside Shield, 5 In. 29.00
Mug, Green 224.00
Mug, Pirate, Green, Marked 6 Inside Shield, 4 3/4 In. ....29.00 to 30.00
Mug, Smiley Face, Yellow 14.00
Pitcher, Barrel, Green 90.00
Pitcher, Butterfly, Blue 235.00
Pitcher, Hobnail 160.00
Pitcher, Yellow, 6 In. 45.00
Planter, Alligator 58.00
Planter, Bird Dog, Gold Trim 395.00
Planter, Cat 20.00
Planter, Doe & Fawn 48.00
Planter, Dove & Turtle, Gold Trim 155.00
Planter, Dragonfly, Aqua, 5 1/2 In. 95.00
Planter, Hunting Dog 200.00
Planter, Pheasant 95.00
Planter, Rodeo Cowboy 130.00
Planter, Starburst, Emerald Green & White, 1968, 6 x 3 1/2 In. 35.00
Planter, Strawberry 15.00
Planter, Violin, Black 80.00

**Repairs on standing figures or pitchers should
be made from the bottom up.**

**Wash tea and coffee cups as
soon as possible to avoid stains.**

McCoy, Jardiniere,
Quilted, Pedestal, Green

Planter, Water Lily	95.00
Planter, Wishing Well, Brown, Green	45.00
Sugar & Creamer, Elsie & Elmer	155.00
Teapot, Daisy, 9 3/4 x 6 In.	75.00
Teapot, Sunburst, Sugar & Creamer	145.00
Tureen, Soup, El Rancho	395.00
Vase, Black Ram Head, 9 1/2 In.	250.00
Vase, Blue Glaze, 7 In.	65.00
Vase, Butterfly, Pink, 2 Handles, 10 In.	225.00
Vase, Castlegate, Butterfly, Yellow, 7 1/2 In.	185.00
Vase, Cherry, Yellow, Square, 10 In.	245.00
Vase, Cleo, c.1914, 11 In.	1498.00
Vase, Double Tulip, Yellow, 8 In.	95.00
Vase, Iris, 13 1/2 In.	30.00
Vase, Lily, White, 10 In.	175.00
Vase, Magnolia, 8 In.	225.00
Vase, Pansy, Loy-Nel-Art, 8 In.	250.00
Vase, Pillow, Orange & Yellow Floral, Signed, 5 x 5 In.	130.00
Vase, Poppies & Buds, Loy-Nel-Art, 12 1/4 In.	295.00
Vase, Swan, Yellow, Gold Trim, 9 In.	95.00
Wall Pocket, Apple	60.00
Wall Pocket, Basket Weave	80.00
Wall Pocket, Bird On Flower	60.00
Wall Pocket, Birdbath, Yellow	65.00
Wall Pocket, Clown Girl	138.00
Wall Pocket, Grape	65.00
Wall Pocket, Mexican	95.00
Wall Pocket, Violin	150.00
Wall Pocket, Yellow Lily	25.00

MCKEE is a name associated with various glass enterprises in the United States since 1836, including J. & F. McKee (1850), Bryce, McKee & Co. (1850 to 1854), McKee and Brothers (1865), and National Glass Co. (1899). In 1903, the McKee Glass Company was formed in Jeannette, Pennsylvania. It became McKee Division of the Thatcher Glass Co. in 1951 and was bought out by the Jeannette Corporation in 1961. Pressed glass, kitchenwares, and tablewares were produced. Jeannette Corporation closed in the early 1980s. Additional pieces may be included in the Custard Glass category.

Bowl, Laurel, Jade, 8 In.	45.00
Butter, Cover, Custard, 3 1/2 x 7 In.	45.00
Butter, Seville Yellow, 4 x 8 In.	50.00

MECHANICAL BANKS are listed in the Bank category.

MEDICAL office furniture, operating tools, microscopes, thermometers, and other paraphernalia used by doctors are included in this category. Medicine bottles are listed in the Bottle category. There are related collectibles listed under Dental.

Badge, 1st Annual Anthracite First Aid Contest, Kingston, Pa., 1940, 3 1/2 In.	5.00
Badge, 4th International Congress On School Hygiene, Buffalo, 1913, 3 1/2 In.	11.00
Bleeder, Mechanical, Civil War, Box, Large	330.00
Book, Humphrey's Homeopathic Manual, 1869, 138 Pages	20.00
Booklet, Johnson & Johnson First Aid, 1914	20.00
Bottle, Apothecary, Cover, Opium, Porcelain, Flower, 30 On Base, 2 In.	165.00
Bottle, Apothecary, Embossed, Ammonium Oxallate, Glass Stopper, Pat. May 1, 1883	9.00
Bottle, Hot Water, Copper	75.00
Bottle, Hot Water, Jane Mansfield, Figural, Plastic, Poynter Products, 22 x 7 x 4 In.	240.00
Bottle, Water, A.S. Campbell Co., Boston, 1912	100.00
Bowl, Bleeding, Brass, England, Mid 18th Century, 5 1/8 In.	225.00
Box, Medicine, Traveling, Pills, Instructions	175.00
Cabinet, Apothecary, 2 Large & 6 Small Drawers, Carved Pulls, c.1860, 10 x 13 In.	885.00
Cabinet, Apothecary, 7 Nailed Drawers, Poplar, Walnut, 15 1/2 x 7 x 14 3/4 In.	385.00

Cabinet, Apothecary, 9 Drawers, Pine, Wallpaper Interior, Porcelain Knobs, 23 In. 2400.00
Cabinet, Apothecary, 12 Drawers, Green Paint, c.1880, 24 1/2 In. 715.00
Cabinet, Apothecary, 12 Short Drawers, Cherry, 2 Doors, Sheraton, c.1810, 83 In. 3025.00
Cabinet, Apothecary, 20 Drawers, Hardwood, Chinese Characters On Drawers, 40 In. ... 770.00
Cabinet, Apothecary, 22 Drawers, Grained Door Fronts, Mustard Paint 400.00
Cabinet, Apothecary, 30 Drawers, Blue Paint, Labels, 19th Century, 36 x 62 In. 990.00
Cabinet, Apothecary, 42 Drawers, Blue Paint 1650.00
Cabinet, Apothecary, 50 Drawers, Blue Paint 1950.00
Cabinet, Apothecary, 96 Drawers 1285.00
Cabinet, Apothecary, Walnut, Painted Chinese Character, Brass Ring Pulls, 18 1/2 In. 145.00
Cabinet, Optometrist's, Roll Top, Oak, Lenses & Frames, 1900, 22 x 17 x 13 In. 675.00
Cabinet, Physicians Specialty Co., Ear, Nose, Throat, 5 Drawers, 1909, 17 x 22 In. 3500.00
Carrier, Leech, Pewter, 1 End Opens With Air Holes 110.00
Case, Doctor's, Mahogany, Lift Top, 1 Drawer, Brass Mounts, England, 25 In. 440.00
Case, Instrument & Accessories, Abraham Jacobi 500.00
Case, Vial, Leather Cover 200.00
Chest, Apothecary, Poplar, Worn Paint, 21 Drawers, Hinged Door, 35 x 9 3/4 x 26 In. ... 1045.00
Container, Berry's Barb Beater, Wooden Cylinder, Salesman's Sample 20.00
Cupboard, Apothecary, Table Top 495.00
Doctor's Model, Woman, Propped On Elbow, Carved Ivory, Ming Dynasty, 5 7/8 In. 700.00
Eyecup, Apple Green, Blown, Plinth On Narrow Stem, Victorian, 3 In. 90.00
Eyecup, Dark Blue Glass, Wyeth Gollyrium, 2 1/4 In. 20.00
Eyecup, John Bull, Dark Blue Glass, Pat'd Aug 13, 1917, 2 3/4 In. 20.00
Eyecup, Light Apple Green, Faceted Stem, Inverted Bowl, Machine Made 30.00
Fleam, 3 Blades, Horn Grips, Borwick, 3 1/16 In. 130.00
Fleam, 3 Blades, Knife, Leather Case, 5 x 1/2 In. 145.00
Fleam, Bone Handle, Cast Steel, Borwick, Early 19th Century 134.00
Fleam, Brass, 3 Blades 75.00
Hearing Trumpet, Tin Speaker, Black Paint, 1870s 160.00
Holder, Thermometer, Physician's, Sterling Silver 175.00
Inhaler, Shield Transfer, Ironstone, Glass Mouth Piece, Mawson & Thompson, 11 In. 275.00
Jar, Apothecary, High Domed Cover, Early 19th Century, 18 In. 200.00
Lancet, 3 Blades & Knife, Brass Side, Stamped How In London, 1690-1760 .... 285.00
Mortar, Ligum Vitae, Walnut Pestle, 18th Century 725.00
Mortar & Pestle, American, Birch & Maple, c.1780 .... 190.00
Mortar & Pestle, Black Paint, Gold Lettering, 1776, Tripod Stand, c.1890, 24 In. 132.00
Mortar & Pestle, Brass, Eagle Head On Each Side, 4 1/2 x 7 3/4 x 6 7/8 In. 100.00
Mortar & Pestle, Brass, Side Handles, 5 In. & 9 1/4 In. 40.00
Mortar & Pestle, Burl, Refinished, Brass Tip, 4 1/8 In. 120.00
Mortar & Pestle, Cast Iron, 19th Century, 6 7/8-In. Mortar, 10 5/8-In. Pestle 145.00
Mortar & Pestle, Gray Patina, 23 In. 85.00
Mortar & Pestle, Marble, 19th Century, 6 3/4-In. Mortar, 7 1/4-In. Pestle 125.00
Mortar & Pestle, Ring Turnings, Ivory, 2 In. 1495.00
Mortar & Pestle, Turned Wood, 19th Century, 8 In. 77.00
Mortar & Pestle, White Limestone, 17th Century, 3 1/2 In. 195.00
Operating Set, Surgeon's, Brass Bail Handle, Mahogany Case, c.1860, 6 Piece 2400.00
Ophthalmoscope, Iron Base, Electric Power, 22 1/2 x 25 In. 165.00
Paddle, Burl, Ash, Scrubbed Finish, 9 In. 368.00
Pattern For Fracture, Foot, Inventor James Wallace, MD, Pat. 1885 .... 12.00
Pill Roller, Walnut, Brass, Star Stamp, 12 In. 220.00
Pin, Norwood Schools Health Day, Celluloid, 1934 .... 6.00
Pin, Red Cross Christmas Roll Call, Celluloid, 1918 .... 25.00
Quack Device, Shock Producer, Battery, Metal Wands, Wooden Box, 5 1/4 x 8 3/4 In. 130.00
Saw, Amputation, For Fingers, 7 1/2 x 1 1/4 In. 98.00
Saw, Surgical, Sheffield, 3 x 18 In. 98.00
Scalpel, Horn Grip, 3 Blades 150.00
Splint, Bent Laminated Plywood, Charles Eames, Label, Evans, c.1940, 43 In. 110.00
Splint, Leg, Plywood, U.S. Navy, Charles Eames, Paper Wrapper ....175.00 to 242.00
Stethoscope, Plated Finish, Rubber Tubes, Goodman & Whurtleff, 17 In. 330.00
Stethoscope, Rosewood & Ivory, c.1865, 6 In. 375.00
Stethoscope, Woven Green & Rust Colored Covering On Tubes, 16 In. 330.00
Surgeon's Kit, Scalpel, Picks, Probe, Case, Pocket Size 150.00
Teether, Baby, Hand Chased, Gold Wash, Coral, 6 In. 1200.00

Tester, Vision, Cast Iron, Black Enamel Finish, 23 1/3 In.	82.00
Vaporizer, Cresolene	110.00
Wheelchair, Oak, Arms	320.00

MEERSCHAUM is a soft white, gray, or cream-colored mineral named magnesium silicate. The name comes from the German word for seafoam, because it was sometimes found floating in the Black Sea and people thought it was petrified seafoam. Pipes and other pieces of carved meerschaum listed here date from the nineteenth century to the present.

Pipe, Bearded Man's Head, Case, 1 1/4 In.	40.00
Pipe, Erotic, Leda & Swan, Case, 5 1/2 In.	110.00
Pipe, Man, Goatee, Yellow Straw Derby, Brown, White Stem, 4 1/2 In.	400.00
Pipe, Seminude Woman On Bowl, Floral Wreath, Amber Stem, 3 x 7 1/2 In.	310.00

MEISSEN is a town in Germany where porcelain has been made since 1710. Any china made in the town can be called Meissen, although the famous Meissen factory made the finest porcelains of the area. The crossed swords mark of the great Meissen factory has been copied by many other firms in Germany and other parts of the world. Pieces of Meissen dinnerware in the Onion pattern are listed in their own category in this book.

Bowl, Fruit, Blue & White, c.1890, 5 3/4 x 14 1/2 In.	150.00
Bowl, Leaf Design, Gilt, White, 11 In.	200.00
Bowl, Venus, Painted, 2 Handles, 14 In.	7920.00
Box, Artichoke, Cover, Overlapping Leaves, Green, Leaves On Lower Portion, 4 In.	3740.00
Box, Cover, Blue Underglaze, 7 1/2 x 7 3/4 In.	635.00
Box, Rose, Cover, Large Pink, White Cabbage Rose, Green Stem, Bud Handle, 5 In.	2300.00
Box, Rose, Cover, Overlapping Pink Petals, Curled Leafy Stalk Foot, 1760, 5 In.	5175.00
Box, Rose, Gilt Stalk Handle Cover, Overlapping Bright Pink Petals, 5 In.	1495.00
Box, Sweetmeat, Pocket Watch Shape, Gilt, Bronze, 1890, 3 7/8 In.	575.00
Cake Plate, Scalloped Latticed Rim, Gold Flower Design, 1830, 9 1/4 In.	385.00
Candlestick, Floral Encrusted, Pair	5175.00
Charger, Scallop Shell Design, Battle On Horses, Floral Border, 15 1/2 In.	290.00
Clock, 4 Figures, Applied Florals, 2 Part Case, 16 In.	2500.00
Clock, Figural, Flowering Branches, Gilt Metal Face, Enamel Numerals, 16 In.	4600.00
Clock, Figure Of Maiden Amongst Flowers, Leaves, Sprays, 4 Scroll Feet, 25 In.	7187.00
Clock, Mantel, Mounted With 4 Seasons, Gilt Metal Face, Late 19th Century, 22 In.	6900.00
Coffee Set, Figures Drinking Before A Tavern, Gilt Leaf Border, 6 Piece	805.00
Coffeepot, Cover, Chinoiserie Scene, Pair Of Figures Conversing, Pear Shape, 7 In.	6900.00
Coffeepot, Cover, Floral Sprigs, Insects Around Central Sprig, 20th Century, 17 In.	2530.00
Coffeepot, Cover, Overlapping Rose Petals, Green Stalk Handle, Pear Shape, 9 In.	5460.00
Compote, Allover Blue Bird, Pierced Latticework, Signed, 8 3/4 x 8 1/2 In.	460.00
Cup & Saucer, Applied Flowers, Leaves, Floral Sprays, 2 1/4 In.	92.00
Cup & Saucer, Applied Strawberries, Gooseberries, Blue Crossed Swords	170.00
Cup & Saucer, Cover, Figural Scenes Between Gilt Cartouches, Red Gilt Rim, 5 In.	143.00
Cup & Saucer, Fishing Village Scene, Turquoise, Black Fish Scale, Gilt, Blue	460.00
Cup & Saucer, Gray Rose, Green Leaves	170.00
Cup & Saucer, Rose Design, Dot Crossed With Swords	230.00
Dinner Service, Colorful Floral Sprigs Center, Gilt Rim, 1810, 40 Piece	4600.00
Dinner Service, Green Ivy Leaf Border, Part Service, 58 Piece	862.00
Dish, Cross, 4 Scrolled Flower Garlands, Puce Scale Border, 1755, 7 In., Pair	575.00
Dish, Floral Finial Cover, Floral Sprays, Cobalt Blue & Gilt Ground, Signed, 5 In.	100.00
Dish, Leaf Shape, Floral Design, 9 In., Pair	405.00
Dish, Leaf Shape, Overlapping Leaves, 1814, 12 1/8 In.	1092.00
Dish, Peony, Pink, 2 Green Leaves, Stalk Handle, 1765, 9 3/4 In.	3160.00
Dish, Raised Foliate, Floral Sprays, Scalloped Border, Early 19th Century, 15 In.	1265.00
Dish, Serving, Rose, 11 1/4 In.	201.00
Ewer, Green Leaf Scrolls, Blossoms, Gilt Scalework Border, Loop Handle, Pair	9775.00
Figurine, 19th Century Man & Woman, 14 1/2 In., Pair	2875.00
Figurine, Allegory Figure Of Cupid, Searching For Bird, 20th Century, 4 In., Pair	258.00
Figurine, Bacchante, Blue Underglaze, 19th Century, 8 In.	975.00
Figurine, Badger, Crouching, Snarling, Gray, White Body, Oval Grassy Base, 8 In.	1150.00

Figurine, Beggar Cherub, Standing With Crutches, Enamel, Gilt Trim, 8 1/4 In. 862.00
Figurine, Bird, Amidst Leaves & Branches With Insects, 6 1/4 In. 805.00
Figurine, Bird, Perched On Tree Stump, Acorn, Leaves & Beetle, Signed, 15 1/2 In. 1725.00
Figurine, Boy, 18th Century Dress, Floral Spray In Right Hand, Hoe In Other, 5 1/4 In. . . 630.00
Figurine, Boy, On A Sled, Girl, Warming Her Hands Over Brazier, 6 1/2 In., Pair 605.00
Figurine, Boy, Wearing A Pale Puce Coat, Girl, Seated On Stool, 6 In., Pair 1840.00
Figurine, Cherub, Enamel, Gilt Trim, Early 20th Century, 8 In. 1150.00
Figurine, Child Gardener With Basket Of Fruit, Flowers, Blue Glaze, 5 In. 230.00
Figurine, Children, Playing, 1 In Period Costume, Other Standing On Column, 7 In. 546.00
Figurine, Chinese Tailor, 20th Century, 8 In. 230.00
Figurine, Clown, Seated With Outstretched Legs, White Costume, 8 In. 3220.00
Figurine, Cupid, Seated Amidst Clouds, Gilt Base, Pink Oval Panel, 5 In., Pair 747.00
Figurine, Cupid, Thumbing Nose, 1920 . . . . 750.00
Figurine, Dandy, Purple Clothes, Late 19th Century, 6 1/2 In. 920.00
Figurine, Deer, Standing On Rectangular Base, Dark Brown, 1745, 5 In. 2415.00
Figurine, Dutch Peasant Bagpiper, Yellow Jacket, Dog, Lying At Side, 4 In. 1840.00
Figurine, Elephant, Seated On Round Disc, Signed, 4 In. 500.00
Figurine, Equestrian, Man In Gray Tricorner Hat, Fawn Jacket, Riding Pony, 9 In. 7762.00
Figurine, Freemason, Purple Coat, Hat, Standing On Gilt Column, 12 In. 1150.00
Figurine, Frightened Harlequin, Checkered Jacket, 1934, 7 In. 1495.00
Figurine, Frightened Harlequin, Seated On Tree Stump, 20th Century, 6 In. 1150.00
Figurine, Gentleman, Flying, Clasping Tricorner Hat To Head, 20th Century, 9 In. 2760.00
Figurine, Girl, Grapes In Apron, Polychrome & Gilt, Signed, 19th Century, 7 In. 412.00
Figurine, Greeting Harlequin, Checkered Jacket, 20th Century, 6 In. 2415.00
Figurine, Greeting Harlequin, Period Costume, Brown Shoes, 6 In. 1725.00
Figurine, Group Of Vintners, Late 19th Century, 8 1/4 In. 2645.00
Figurine, Harlequin, Playing Bagpipes, Blue, 1745, 5 1/4 In. 690.00
Figurine, Harlequin, Spectacles, Checkered Jacket, 1934, 9 In. 2530.00
Figurine, Hawk, Sitting On Square Base, With Extended Wings, 3 3/4 In. 316.00
Figurine, Lady Of Mopsorden, Wearing Voluminous Floral Crinoline Dress, 11 In. 9775.00
Figurine, Lady, Holding Cat, White Lace Dress, Gilt Round Base, 9 In. 1380.00
Figurine, Lady, Lacy Pale Blue Costume, Gentleman, Reading, 5 In., Pair 1725.00
Figurine, Lady, Playing A Spinet, 20th Century, 4 3/4 In. 230.00
Figurine, Lady, Seated Before Dressing Table, Lacy Dress, 5 1/4 In. 1265.00
Figurine, Lady, Sleeping, Lacy Dress, Rectangular Stone Base, 7 In. 690.00
Figurine, Lady, With Birdcage, Enamel, Gilt Design, Germany, 5 3/4 In. 632.00
Figurine, Man With Basket, Woman With Wreath, 19 In., Pair 3900.00
Figurine, Man, 18th Century Dress, Playing Cello, 4 3/4 In. 690.00
Figurine, Military Officer, 18th Century Costume, Signed, 3 In., Pair 488.00
Figurine, Officer, Teal Blue & Ivory Uniform, Standing On Mound Base, 9 In. 1035.00
Figurine, Owl, 2 In. 220.00
Figurine, Parrot, 6 In. 990.00
Figurine, People Gathering Flowers, Picking Fruit, Signed, 10 In. 1265.00
Figurine, Shepherd, Shepherdess, 18th Century, 10 In., Pair 7230.00
Figurine, Summer & Winter, Signed, 10 In., Pair 1265.00
Figurine, Woman & Man, Wine Barrels, 19th Century, 6 3/4 & 7 1/4 In., Pair 2185.00
Figurine, Woman Warrior, Standing, Multicolored, Blue Crossed Swords, 14 In. 200.00
Figurine, Woman, Playing Piano, Louis XVI Clothes, Signed, 4 3/4 In. 517.00
Figurine, Woman, Seated At A Table With Basket Of Flowers In Her Lap, 5 1/4 In. 517.00
Figurine, Young Girl, Holds Hat Filled With Flowers, 5 1/8 In. 630.00
Group, 3 Cherubs Surrounding An Easel, 1 Painting, 7 1/4 In. 2530.00
Group, 6 Bouquets Of Flowers, Scattered Flower Sprigs, Gilt Rim, 1755, 9 1/4 In. 8050.00
Group, Allegical, Figure Of Love, Courting Couple, Colorful Costumed, 17 1/2 In. 1725.00
Group, Allegical, Figure Of Sight & Smell, 5 Senses Set, Late 19th Century, 6 In. 2300.00
Group, Allegical, Figure Of Spring & Summer, Period Costumes, 6 In. 747.00
Group, Allegical, Figure Of Spring, 2 Children Playing, With Florals, 6 In. 632.00
Group, Allegical, Figure Of Taste & Hearing, 1 Seated At Spinet, 5 & 4 In., Pair 2760.00
Group, Allegorical, Gentleman Holding A Pocket Watch, 17 1/4 In. 2070.00
Group, Bacchantes & Donkey, Blue Underglaze, 19th Century, 8 In. 1300.00
Group, Boy & Girl Grape Gatherers In Wheelbarrow, 6 In. 220.00
Group, Boy, Playing French Horn, Girl, Playing Hurdy Gurdy, 1890, 10 In. 1380.00
Group, Children, Playing Ring-Around-The-Rosie, 2 Girls, 2 Boys, 6 In. 2185.00
Group, Children, Playing Ring-Around-The-Rosie, Blue Glaze, 20th Century, 5 In. 920.00

Group, Courting Couple, Woman, Flowered Costume, Oak Leaf Border, 9 In. 1610.00
Group, Courting Couple, Young Woman, Flowered Dress, 6 1/2 In. 862.00
Group, Discovered Lover, Seated In Her Bed, Eating, 20th Century, 4 x 2 x 7 In. 2760.00
Group, Europa & Bull, Attended By 2 Nymphs, Signed, 8 1/2 In. 2415.00
Group, Gardener & Companion, Both In Pastel Costume, 19th Century, 7 In. 862.00
Group, Gardener & Companion, Man, Wearing Lilac Coat, Holding Flowers, 7 In. 977.00
Group, Good Mother, Period Dress, Seated, Boy, Kneeling, 9 In. 1840.00
Group, Good Mother, Woman, Seated In An Armchair, 8 3/4 In. 2415.00
Group, Hounds, Attacking A Lion, Encrusted Flowers, Leaves, 1755, 8 1/4 In. 6612.00
Group, Man & Woman Embracing, Sheep & Dog By Their Feet, 8 1/4 In. 920.00
Group, Mother & Child, Lady, Wearing Colorful Period Dress, 1765, 8 In. 5750.00
Group, Musician & Dancer, Gentleman Playing Bagpipes, Leafy Base, 18 In. 2070.00
Group, Old Woman In Love, Sprigged Yellow Dress, Gilt Base, 5 In. 1265.00
Jar, Cover, Coastal Landscape, Figures, Footed Base, 19th Century, 6 1/2 In., Pair 6150.00
Plate, 1 Duck & 1 Chicken, 8 3/4 In., Pair 210.00
Plate, 2 Children, Playing A Ball Game, Laurel Swag Border, Blue, 1770, 18 In. 3450.00
Plate, Altenburger, Figural Frieze, Border Crest, c.1874, 8 3/4 In. 172.00
Plate, Bird, Shrub, Insect Borders, 19th Century, 9 In., Pair 275.00
Plate, Biscuit, Flower, Fruit, White, Variety Of Fruit, Roses, 19th Century, 9 1/2 In. 575.00
Plate, Exotic Birds Surrounded By Border Of 2 Dragons, Gilt, Blue, 10 In. 60.00
Plate, Famille Verte, 2 Birds, Perched On Flowering Prunus, Floral Border, 9 In. 1840.00
Plate, Fliegenderhund, Winged Beast, Pouncing Large Beetle, 1740, 12 In. 862.00
Plate, Teal Banded, c.1885, 7 In., 6 Piece 105.00
Plate Set, Alternating Floral & Courting Scene, 4 Panels, 8 1/4 In., 8 Piece 630.00
Plate Set, Central Floral Spray, Shell Form Rim, 9 In., 7 Piece 315.00
Plate Set, Scattered Flowers, Gilt Shell Borders, 1910, 8 1/2 In., 10 Piece 365.00
Platter, Central Floral Design, Floral Cartouche Border, 2 Handles, 16 In. 490.00
Potpourri Jar, Cover, Vignettes Of Fruit, Raised On 4 Scroll Feet, 8 3/8 In. 290.00
Salt, Open, Figural, Man & Woman, Basket Salt & Pepper, Signed, 4 3/4 In. 1265.00
Snuffbox, Cover, Allover Basketwork, Colorful Sprays & Sprigs, 1755, 3 In. 1035.00
Tankard, Scroll Design, Blue & White, Signed, 12 In. 650.00
Tea Caddy, Floral Design, Pomegranate Finial, 1775-1780, 4 7/8 In. 303.00
Tea Service, Floral Cartouche, Cobalt Blue, Gold Design, 39 Piece 1265.00
Tea Set, Floral, Blue, Gilt, Early 20th Century, 6 Piece 290.00
Tea Set, Gilt Rims & Borders, 9 1/2-In. Coffeepot, 6 Piece 345.00
Tea Set, Heavy Gilt, Signed, c.1900, 8 Piece 330.00
Tea Set, White Floral & Vine, Floral Finials, 3 Piece 275.00
Teapot, Bullet Shape, Pairs Of Putti, Puce Scale Border, 1760, 4 1/8 In. 1265.00
Teapot, Polychrome Floral Design, Early 19th Century, 7 1/2 In. 330.00
Teapot, Rose On Top Of Lid, Flower Design 600.00
Tray, Seated Lovers, Signed, 1910s, 6 1/2 x 7 1/2 In. 1265.00
Tray, Serving, Gold Scallop Shell, Scrolled Border, Handles, 16 1/4 In. 460.00
Tray, Serving, Laurel Leaves, Grape Border, Oval, Germany, 10 x 13 3/8 In. 1840.00
Tureen, Cover, Overlapping Leaves, Green, Puce Center Edge, 5 1/4 In. 3740.00
Tureen, Cover, Overlapping Leaves, Yellow, Green, 1 Leaf Curled Upwards, 5 In. 2875.00
Tureen, Cover, Putti Seated, Suspending Drapery Swags, Handles, 7 x 9 In., Pair 19500.00
Tureen, Maroon Berry Cluster On Cover, Figures Dancing, Gaming, 15 In. 1150.00
Tureen, Scroll Finial & Handles, 10 x 13 In. 350.00
Urn, Cover, Domed, Chrysanthemum Design, Inverted Body, Blue, 15 In. 125.00
Urn, Potpourri, Cover, Peasants, Near Inn, Floral Sprigs, Branch Handles, 13 In. 1380.00
Urn, Potpourri, Cover, Putti & Cupids Playing, White Shield Shape, 1800, 10 In. 1725.00
Urn, Twisted Snake Handle, Mounted As Lamp, 15 In. 465.00
Urn, White Glaze, Gilt, Double Snake Handles, 17 In. 690.00
Vase, Amorous Couple, Cobalt Blue Ground, 2 Handles, 8 1/2 In. 460.00
Vase, Colorful Floral Spray Scene, Snake Entwined Handles, Gilt Rim, 11 In., Pair 1035.00
Vase, Floral Design, Raised Gilt Highlights, Baluster, 13 In. 260.00

MERCURY GLASS, or silvered glass, was first made in the 1850s. It lost
favor for a while but became popular again about 1910. It looks like a
piece of silver.

Bowl, Fruit, 3 Applied Scroll Feet, 9 1/2 In. 275.00
Candlestick, Flowers On Green Band, Czechoslovakia, 13 In., 4 Piece 550.00
Candlestick, Paneled, 14 In., Pair 385.00

Mercury Glass,
Vase, White
Enameled Bird
& Floral,
10 1/2 In., Pair

Spray the inside of a glass flower vase with a non-stick product made to keep food from sticking to cooking pots. This will keep the vase from staining if water is left in it too long.

Cane, Yellow & Silver Swirls, 42 1/2 In.	180.00
Compote, Etched, Gilt, 8 1/2 x 9 In.	1550.00
Compote, Wide Flared Pedestal, Czechoslovakia, 9 In.	245.00
Figurine, Christ & Madonna, Painted Features, 7 1/2 In., Pair	300.00
Figurine, Mother & Child, Open Pontil, 7 x 3 In.	85.00
Goblet, Enameled Design, Satin Ground, 5 In., Pair	110.00
Pitcher, Clear Applied Handle, 6 1/4 In.	143.00
Salt, Cover, Footed	20.00
Tieback, Hand Cut Threads, Pewter Ferrules, N.E. Glass Co., 4 3/4 In., Pair	245.00
Tieback, Pressed Floral, Mid 19th Century, 3 1/2 In., Pair	110.00
Vase, 6 In.	45.00
Vase, 9 In., Pair	385.00
Vase, Amber, Stepped Art Deco Design, Germany, 7 In.	55.00
Vase, Bird & Floral, Gold Interior, 10 1/2 In., Pair	440.00
Vase, Enameled Flowers, 10 In., Pair	110.00
Vase, Ice Blue, 7 In.	65.00
Vase, Ice Blue, Czechoslovakia, 3 1/2 In.	80.00
Vase, White Enameled Bird & Floral, 10 1/2 In., Pair ....*Illus*	440.00
Vase, White Enameled Flowers, 9 In., Pair	330.00
Vase, White Enameled Grape & Leaf, 15 1/2 In., Pair	550.00
Wig Stand, Silver, Light Green, 11 In.	355.00
Witch's Ball, Tapered Base, 15 3/4 In.	415.00

MERRIMAC POTTERY Company was founded by Thomas Nickerson in Newburyport, Massachusetts, in 1902. The company made art pottery, garden pottery, and reproductions of Roman pottery. The pottery burned to the ground in 1908.

Vase, 3 Floral Forms, Dark Green Matte Glaze, 11 1/2 In.	1980.00
Vase, Gunmetal & Mauve Glaze, Bulbous, 10 In.	750.00
Vessel, Aquatic Plants, Green Matte Glaze, Signed, 8 In.	3250.00

METTLACH, Germany, is a city where the Villeroy and Boch factories worked. Steins from the firm are marked with the word *Mettlach* or the castle mark. They date from about 1842. *PUG* means painted under glaze. The steins can be dated from the marks on the bottom, which include a date-number code. Other pieces may be listed in the Villeroy & Boch category.

Bottle, No. 3507, Munich Child, Original Stopper, 1/2 Liter	360.00
Charger, Classical Figures Pate-Sur-Pate, Green, White, 18 1/2 In.	575.00
Charger, No. 2659, Fish & Seaweed, 17 1/2 In.	715.00
Charger, Troll, Sitting, Consuming His Porridge Beneath Toadstools, 1900, 17 In.	847.00
Cup & Saucer, Gold, Cream, Blue, 2 1/4 x 6 In.	175.00
Jardiniere, No. 2415, Leaf Design, Etched, 6 In.	750.00
Pitcher, No. 2085, Putty Applied Design, Pewter Lid, 15 3/4 In.	440.00
Pitcher, No. 3323, Art Nouveau Design, Etched, 5 1/4 In.	310.00
Plaque, No. 1044, Deer Grazing, PUG, 17 In.	375.00
Plaque, No. 1044, Lohengrin On Shore, Castle & People, PUG, 17 1/2 In.	633.00
Plaque, No. 1384, Knight Carrying Flag, Schultz, 14 1/2 In.	675.00

Plaque, No. 1385, Warrior Scene, Signed, Shultz, 1910, 14 1/2 In. 805.00
Plaque, No. 2079, 4 Dragoners On Horseback, Etched, 15 In. 1375.00
Plaque, No. 2081, 4 Husaren On Horseback, Etched, 15 In. 935.00
Plaque, No. 2113, Gnome In Tree, Drinking From Mug, Etched, 16 In. 1210.00
Plaque, No. 2146, Infantry Shooting Rifles, Etched, 15 In. 880.00
Plaque, No. 2147, Artillery Men Moving Cannons, Etched, 15 In. 1980.00
Plaque, No. 2322, Cavalier & Bar Maid, Blue Ground, 14 1/2 In. 795.00
Plaque, No. 2442, Trojan Warriors On Boat, Figures In White, 19 In. 950.00
Plaque, No. 2622, Man Making A Toast, 1910, 7 3/4 In. 235.00
Plaque, No. 2697, Dwarf Eating Porridge In Field Of Mushrooms, Etched, 17 In. 6615.00
Plaque, No. 2998, Young Woman In Snow-Covered Field, Etched, 18 In. 7190.00
Plaque, No. 7032, Cameo, Woman's Profile, Oval, 1900, 8 3/4 x 7 1/2 In. 345.00
Pokal, No. 1785, 4 Panels, Troubadour & Knights, Etched, Set-On Lid, 1 3/4 Liter 1900.00
Punch Bowl, No. 2339, Gnomes, Working At Wine Press, Drinking, 7 1/2 Liter . . .545.00 to 747.00
Punch Bowl, No. 2806, Bacchus, 2 Cameo Panels, 2 Handles, 7 1/4 Liter 403.00
Stein, No. 24, 1 Liter, 3 Hunting Scenes, Tan, Gray, Terra Cotta, Inlaid Lid 209.00
Stein, No. 32, 1/2 Liter, Gambrinus With Others, Tower Handle, Tan, Gray, Blue . .121.00 to 345.00
Stein, No. 63, 1 Liter, Sailboat 1065.00
Stein, No. 171, 1/2 Liter, 4 Seasons, Tan, Brown, Gray, Inlaid Lid 188.00
Stein, No. 171, 1/4 Liter, 4 Seasons, Tan, Cream, Blue, Inlaid Lid 146.00
Stein, No. 202, 1 Liter, Group Of Men Singing, Relief, Blue Ground, Inlaid Lid 320.00
Stein, No. 485, 1/2 Liter, Musicians In Vines, Green, Tan, Brown, Cream, Inlaid Lid 247.00
Stein, No. 967, 1/2 Liter, Gnomes Dancing, Clinking Mugs, PUG, Inlaid Lid 345.00
Stein, No. 1005, 1/2 Liter, 3 Tavern Scenes, Relief, Brown Ground, Inlaid Lid . . . .220.00 to 375.00
Stein, No. 1006, 4 1/2 Liter, Dancing Scene, Horned Face On Spout, Pewter Lid 525.00
Stein, No. 1037, 1/2 Liter, Hunter, PUG, Pewter Lid 545.00
Stein, No. 1038, 1/2 Liter, Frogs In Pond, PUG, Pewter Lid 520.00
Stein, No. 1121, 1/3 Liter, Geometric Design, Mosaic, Inlaid Lid 750.00
Stein, No. 1146, 1/2 Liter, Student Drinking In Tavern, Etched, Inlaid Lid . . . . . . .430.00 to 575.00
Stein, No. 1147, 5 Liter, Geometric & Medallions, Mosaic & Relief, Inlaid Lid 1325.00
Stein, No. 1154, 1 Liter, 4 Panel, Hunters, Pewter Lid 550.00
Stein, No. 1163, 1/2 Liter, Musicians, Etched, Inlaid Lid 430.00
Stein, No. 1164, 1/2 Liter, Musician & Girl, Etched, Pewter Lid 345.00
Stein, No. 1212, 1/2 Liter, Old Man Bowling, PUG, Pewter Lid 335.00
Stein, No. 1228, 1/2 Liter, Sailboats, Etched, Inlaid Lid Of Anchor 660.00
Stein, No. 1266, 1/4 Liter, 3 Drinking Scenes, Blue, Tan, Cream, Inlaid Lid 139.00
Stein, No. 1266, 4 Panels Figures, Terra-Cotta, Pewter Lid, 6 3/4 In. 165.00
Stein, No. 1282, 1/2 Liter, Hunter & Peasant, PUG, Pewter Lid 220.00
Stein, No. 1370, 1/2 Liter, Vine Design, Man & Woman With Verse, Pewter Lid 132.00
Stein, No. 1395, 1/2 Liter, French Card Scene, Etched, Inlaid Lid 560.00
Stein, No. 1397, 1/2 Liter, Man, With Hat, Inlaid Lid 605.00
Stein, No. 1453, 1/2 Liter, Hunters, Boars, & Dogs, Etched, Pewter Lid 430.00
Stein, No. 1471, 1/2 Liter, Musicians, Etched, Inlaid Lid 405.00
Stein, No. 1472, 1/2 Liter, Cattle In Pasture, Inlaid Lid 465.00
Stein, No. 1478, 1/2 Liter, Gnomes Making Barrels, Etched, Inlaid Lid 690.00
Stein, No. 1480, 1/2 Liter, Gnomes, Etched, Inlaid Lid 745.00
Stein, No. 1520, 1/2 Liter, Prussian Eagle, Cavaliers & Banner, Inlaid Lid 715.00
Stein, No. 1526, 1/2 Liter, Couple Holding Hands, Print Over Glaze, Pewter Lid 230.00
Stein, No. 1526, 1/2 Liter, Inft. Nr. 82, 1901 Shooting Prize, Pewter Lid 310.00
Stein, No. 1526, 1/2 Liter, Student Society, Pewter Lid, 1929 . . . . 1005.00
Stein, No. 1526, 1/4 Liter, Staten Island Quartette, Black 81.00
Stein, No. 1527, 1 Liter, Soldier Toasting Musical, Pewter Thumbrest 515.00
Stein, No. 1527, 1/2 Liter, Cavaliers Drinking, Inlaid Lid 395.00
Stein, No. 1566, 1/4 Liter, Man, Riding High-Wheel Bicycle, Inlaid Lid, 1891 . . . . 635.00
Stein, No. 1570, 1/2 Liter, Leaf Design, Mosaic, Inlaid Lid 520.00
Stein, No. 1641, 1 Liter, Cavalier With Pipe & Wine Jug, Tapestry, Pewter Lid 335.00
Stein, No. 1644, 1/2 Liter, Man Smoking, Tapestry, Relief Pewter Lid 255.00
Stein, No. 1655, 1/2 Liter, People Dancing, Inlaid Lid 415.00
Stein, No. 1675, 1/2 Liter, Heidelberg Scene, Etched, Inlaid Lid 405.00
Stein, No. 1724, 1/2 Liter, Fireman, Etched, Inlaid Lid 1495.00
Stein, No. 1725, 1/4 Liter, Lovers, Etched, Inlaid Lid 265.00
Stein, No. 1732, 1/2 Liter, Eagle With Crown, Soldiers With Flags, Inlaid Lid 1045.00
Stein, No. 1734, 2 Liter, Lovers, Man Holding Glass, Etched, Inlaid Lid 1210.00

Stein, No. 1757, 1 Liter, Man Smoking Cigar In Window, Inlaid Lid 690.00
Stein, No. 1786, 1 Liter, St. Florian, Dragon Handle, Etched, Glazed, Pewter Lid . .545.00 to 720.00
Stein, No. 1794, 1/2 Liter, Bismarck In Uniform, Etched, Inlaid Lid 345.00
Stein, No. 1797, 1/2 Liter, 4 Cards, Gold Coins On Lid, Etched, Inlaid Lid 605.00
Stein, No. 1802, 1/4 Liter, Floral Design, Mosaic, Inlaid Lid 405.00
Stein, No. 1863, 1/2 Liter, Stuttgart Scene, Etched, Inlaid Lid 633.00
Stein, No. 1901, 1/4 Liter, Floral Design, Mosaic, Inlaid Lid 430.00
Stein, No. 1909, 1/2 Liter, Old Man Bowling, Pewter Lid 346.00
Stein, No. 1914, 1/2 Liter, 4F, Man Holding Flag & Dumbbell, Etched, Inlaid Lid 545.00
Stein, No. 1932, 1/2 Liter, Cavaliers Toasting, Etched, Inlaid Lid 319.00
Stein, No. 1940, 3 Liter, Keeper Of Wine Cellar, Etched, Inlaid Lid 865.00
Stein, No. 1972, 1/4 Liter, 4 Seasons With Ladies, Inlaid Lid ....355.00 to 380.00
Stein, No. 1975, 1/4 Liter, Ram, Spotty Glaze, Inlaid Lid 525.00
Stein, No. 1987, 1/4 Liter, Wild Rose, Etched, Inlaid Lid 375.00
Stein, No. 1995, 1/2 Liter, Fat Man, Drinking, Inlaid Lid 525.00
Stein, No. 1997, 1/2 Liter, George Ehret Brewery, Etched & PUG, Inlaid Lid 320.00
Stein, No. 1998, 1/2 Liter, Trumpeter From Sackingen, Etched, Inlaid Lid 520.00
Stein, No. 1999, 1/2 Liter, Cavaliers & Vine, Inlaid Lid 117.00
Stein, No. 2001, 1/2 Liter, Scholars, Inlaid Lid 745.00
Stein, No. 2001A, 1/2 Liter, Book, Hand Painted Books Of Law, 1880s 575.00
Stein, No. 2002, 1/2 Liter, Town Of Munich, Verse, Etched, Inlaid Lid 290.00
Stein, No. 2003, 1/2 Liter, Troubador & Knights, Etched, Inlaid Lid 575.00
Stein, No. 2007, 1/2 Liter, Black Cat, Etched, Inlaid Lid 775.00
Stein, No. 2008, 1/2 Liter, Trumpeter On Black Horse, Etched, Inlaid Lid 635.00
Stein, No. 2025, 1/3 Liter, Cherubs Carousing, Inlaid Lid 288.00
Stein, No. 2029, 1/2 Liter, Military Scene, Original Pewter Lid 630.00
Stein, No. 2035, 1 Liter, Mythological Greek Figures Drinking Scene, Pewter Lid 248.00
Stein, No. 2035, 1/3 Liter, Bacchus Carousing, Etched, Inlaid Lid 205.00
Stein, No. 2038, 4 Liter, Town Of Rodenstein, Relief, Houses On Inlaid Lid 3105.00
Stein, No. 2052, 1/4 Liter, Munich Child With Children & Cherubs, Inlaid Lid 320.00
Stein, No. 2057, 1/2 Liter, Festive Scene, Peasants Dancing, Inlaid Lid ....266.00 to 300.00
Stein, No. 2075, 1/2 Liter, Telegrapher, Stylized Eagle, Etched, Inlaid Lid 1380.00
Stein, No. 2082, 1/2 Liter, William Tell, Shooting Apple, Etched, Inlaid Lid .....750.00 to 975.00
Stein, No. 2083, 1/2 Liter, Boar Hunt, Inlay 920.00
Stein, No. 2090, 1/3 Liter, Man, Sitting At Table, Etched, Inlaid Lid ....230.00 to 415.00
Stein, No. 2091, 1/2 Liter, St. Florian Pouring Water On Head, Etched, Inlaid Lid 805.00
Stein, No. 2092, 1/2 Liter, Owl By Clock, Gnome On Ladder, Etched, Inlaid Lid 890.00
Stein, No. 2093, 1/2 Liter, Card Panels, Etched, Inlaid Lid 330.00
Stein, No. 2106, 1/4 Liter, Monkeys In Cage, Monkey Handle, Inlaid Lid 2750.00
Stein, No. 2133, 1/2 Liter, Gnome In Tree, Drinking, Inlaid Lid ....2420.00 to 3105.00
Stein, No. 2134, 1/2 Liter, Gnome Sitting In Nest, Etched, Inlaid Lid 1980.00
Stein, No. 2140, 1/2 Liter, Boat, S.M.Y Hohenzollern, PUG, Inlaid Lid 1955.00
Stein, No. 2182, 1/2 Liter, Bowling Scene, Tan & Blue, Inlaid Lid 248.00
Stein, No. 2184, 1/3 Liter, Gnomes Drinking, PUG, Inlaid Lid ....260.00 to 275.00
Stein, No. 2190, 1/2 Liter, Bicycle Scene, Etched, Inlaid Lid ....550.00 to 890.00
Stein, No. 2192, 1/2 Liter, Student Joke, Etched, Inlaid Lid 520.00
Stein, No. 2204, 1 Liter, Black Prussian Eagle, Tan, Inlaid Lid 750.00
Stein, No. 2204, 1 Liter, Prussian Eagle, Black, Tan Ground, Etched, Inlaid Lid . .690.00 to 1100.00
Stein, No. 2211, 1/3 Liter, Outdoor Bowling Scene, Terra-Cotta 155.00
Stein, No. 2231, 1/2 Liter, Tavern Scene, Etched, Inlaid Lid 490.00
Stein, No. 2235, 1/2 Liter, Barmaid, Holding Steins, Etched, Pewter Lid 460.00
Stein, No. 2238, 1/2 Liter, 7th Regiment Armory, Eagle, Flags, Etched, Inlaid Lid 1265.00
Stein, No. 2255, 1 Liter, Etruscan Wedding Scene, Etched, Pewter Lid 635.00
Stein, No. 2277, 1/4 Liter, Heidelberg, Etched, Inlaid Lid ....415.00 to 484.00
Stein, No. 2282, 1/2 Liter, Man In Wine Cellar, Inlaid Lid 605.00
Stein, No. 2286, 3 Liter, Tavern Scene, Etched, Inlaid Lid 1095.00
Stein, No. 2324, 1/2 Liter, Rugby Football Game, Football Scene, Inlaid Lid 1870.00
Stein, No. 2358, 1/2 Liter, Drinking Scene, Blue, Cream, Tan, Inlaid Lid 346.00
Stein, No. 2373, 1/2 Liter, St. Augustine, Florida, Alligator Handle, Etched, Inlaid Lid ... 605.00
Stein, No. 2382, 1 Liter, Thirsty Rider, Body Forms Tower, Inlaid Lid ....575.00 to 1155.00
Stein, No. 2391, 1 Liter, Wedding March Of Swan Knight, Inlaid Lid 1955.00
Stein, No. 2391, 1/2 Liter, Lohengrin Wedding Scene, Inlaid Lid 715.00
Stein, No. 2394, 1/2 Liter, Scenes From Siegfried's Youth, Etched, Inlaid Lid .....460.00 to 575.00

Stein, No. 2401, 1/2 Liter, Tannhauser In The Venusberg, Etched, Inlaid Lid 546.00
Stein, No. 2402, 1/2 Liter, Courting Of Siegfried, Pewter Lid & Thumb Rest 625.00
Stein, No. 2403, 1/2 Liter, Wartburg, Etched, Inlaid Lid 635.00
Stein, No. 2430, 3 Liter, Tavern Scene, Rust Field 880.00
Stein, No. 2440, 1/2 Liter, Classical Figures, Relief, Light Blue Ground, Inlaid Lid 490.00
Stein, No. 2520, 1 Liter, Man, At Table With Bar Maid, Pewter Lid 525.00
Stein, No. 2524, 4 1/2 Liter, Scene At Castle, Body Forms Tower, Pewter Lid 4620.00
Stein, No. 2532, 1/2 Liter, Drunken Scene, Inlaid Lid 550.00
Stein, No. 2572, 1/2 Liter, Art Nouveau, Blue, Red Ribbons, Painted, Pewter Lid 490.00
Stein, No. 2580, 1 Liter, Festive Scene At Castle, Inlaid Lid 965.00
Stein, No. 2582, 1/2 Liter, Jester On Table In Front Of Tavern, Etched, Inlaid Lid 690.00
Stein, No. 2583, 1/2 Liter, Egyptian, Etched, Inlaid Lid 1265.00
Stein, No. 2632, 1/2 Liter, Bowling & Tavern Scene, Etched, Inlaid Lid 460.00
Stein, No. 2635, 1/2 Liter, Woman With Bicycle, Inlaid Lid, Bicycle Thumblift 965.00
Stein, No. 2639, 1/2 Liter, Blacksmith & Cavalier, Drinking, Inlaid Lid 660.00
Stein, No. 2690, 1/2 Liter, Drunken Cavaliers, Singing, Etched, Inlaid Lid 745.00
Stein, No. 2752, 1/2 Liter, Cavaliers Sitting At Table, Tricorner Hats, Inlaid Lid 550.00
Stein, No. 2765, 1 Liter, Knight Riding White Horse, Inlaid Lid . . . . .2860.00 to 3105.00
Stein, No. 2766, 1/2 Liter, Man, With Fur Hat, Sitting At Table, Inlaid Lid 685.00
Stein, No. 2776, 1/2 Liter, Keeper Of The Wine Cellar, Inlaid Lid . . . . .605.00 to 660.00
Stein, No. 2782, 4 1/2 Liter, Man Drinking, Pewter Lid 880.00
Stein, No. 2788, 1/2 Liter, Gentleman With Pipe, Pewter Lid 490.00
Stein, No. 2807, 1/2 Liter, Tavern Scene, Etched, Inlaid Lid 460.00
Stein, No. 2833D, 1/3 Liter, Man & Woman Sitting At Table, Etched, Inlaid Lid 330.00
Stein, No. 2836, 1/4 Liter, 3 Women Scenes, Inlaid Lid 525.00
Stein, No. 2880, 1 Liter, Tavern Scene, Etched, Inlaid Lid 430.00
Stein, No. 2886, 1/2 Liter, Politicians Talking At Table, Inlaid Lid 550.00
Stein, No. 2936, 1/2 Liter, Elk's Club, Etched, Inlaid Lid 460.00
Stein, No. 2950, 1/2 Liter, Bavarian Coat Of Arms, Cameo, Pewter Lid 605.00
Stein, No. 2951, 1 Liter, Prussian Eagle, Cameo, Pewter Lid 690.00
Stein, No. 2957, 1/2 Liter, Bowling Scene, Inlaid Lid 360.00
Stein, No. 3003, 1/2 Liter, Man Reading Music, Pewter Lid 550.00
Stein, No. 3004, 1 Liter, Man With Drink, Etched, Pewter Lid 635.00
Stein, No. 3085, 1/2 Liter, Postman, Tapestry, Etched, Relief Pewter Lid 462.00
Stein, No. 3089, 1/2 Liter, Diogenes, Etched, Inlaid Lid 865.00
Stein, No. 3091, 1 Liter, Knight Drinking, Etched, Inlaid Lid 1073.00
Stein, No. 3091, 1/2 Liter, Knight Drinking, Etched, Inlaid Lid 880.00
Stein, No. 3170, 1/2 Liter, People Walking In Falling Snow, Inlaid Lid 910.00
Stein, No. 3200, 1/2 Liter, Heidelberg Scene, Etched, Inlaid Lid 605.00
Stein, No. 5006, 1/2 Liter, Nurnberg, Faience Type, Pewter Lid 255.00
Stein, No. 5022, 1 Liter, Rural Scene, Harbor Scene On Reverse, Pewter Base, Lid 1760.00
Stein, No. 5024, 1 Liter, Floral Design, Pewter Top Ring, Lid 1595.00
Stein, No. 5188, 1/2 Liter, Delft Type, Gentleman, Pewter Lid 405.00
Stein, No. 5393, 1 Liter, Diana The Huntress, Pewter Base, Lid 1980.00
Stein, No. 5442, 1 Liter, Cavalier Leaning Against Barrel, Pewter Lid 2530.00
Vase, Floral Design, Red, Turquoise, Blue Ground, 9 1/2 In. 330.00
Vase, Geometric Design, Red, Green, Cream Ground, 10 In. 550.00

MILK GLASS was named for its milky white color. It was first made in
England during the 1700s. The height of its popularity in the United
States was from 1870 to 1880. It is now correct to refer to some colored glass as blue milk glass, black milk glass, etc. Reproductions of
milk glass are being made and sold in many stores. Related pieces may
be listed in the Cosmos, Vallerysthal, and Westmoreland categories.

Biscuit Jar, Hand Painted Floral 70.00
Compote, Square, Diamond Pattern, Turned Pink, 4 1/4 In. . . . .*Illus* 25.00
Cup & Saucer, Enameled Oriental Style, Germany, c.1780, 1 1/2 x 3 1/4 In. 724.00
Dish, Admiral Dewey Cover, 4 1/4 In. 30.00
Dish, Cannon Cover, Drum Base, 4 1/4 In. 75.00
Dish, Deer Cover, Fallen Tree Base, E.W. Flaccus Co., Wheeling, W. Virginia, 7 In. 410.00
Jar, Cover, Owl 45.00
Mustard, Bull's Head, Tongue Spoon, Alterbury, 4 1/4 In. 120.00
Pitcher, Jenny Lind, Pink 195.00

If you receive a package of glass antiques during cold weather, let it sit inside for a few hours before you unpack it. The glass must return to room temperature slowly or it may crack.

Milk Glass,
Compote,
Square, Diamond
Pattern, Turned
Pink, 4 1/4 In.

Pitcher, Water, Thumbprint, Rabbit, Opalescent	120.00
Plate, Admiral Sampson, 7 1/4 In.	115.00
Plate, Major General Fitzhugh Lee, 5 1/2 In.	60.00
Plate, Remember The Maine, 7 1/4 In.	25.00
Shade, Aladdin, Curtain Drapery	80.00
Sugar, Cover, Opalescent, 3 Opalescent Blue Feet, Pontil, 20th Century, 4 In.	65.00
Syrup, Bulbous	55.00
Syrup, Orange Flowers, Green Leaves, Pewter Top, Green, 8 1/2 In.	135.00
Syrup, Stars & Stripes, Pewter Lid	110.00
Toothpick, Tramp's Shoe, 1895 Patent	125.00
Vase, Bud, Indian Design, 7 In.	75.00
Vase, Flame, Blue, 9 In.	25.00

MILLEFIORI means, literally, a thousand flowers. Many small pieces of glass resembling flowers are grouped together to form a design. It is a type of glasswork popular in paperweights and some are listed in that category.

Bottle, Close Pack, White, Yellow Clover, Dome Shaped, Stopper	546.00
Decanter, Paperweight, Clear, 7 In.	375.00

MINTON china has been made in the Staffordshire region of England from 1793 to the present. The firm became part of the Royal Doulton Tableware Group in 1968, but the wares continued to be marked *Minton*. Many marks have been used. The one shown dates from about 1873 to 1891, when the word *England* was added.

Biscuit Dish, Domed Latticework Cover, Flower Knop, Porcelain, 1869, 6 1/2 In.	290.00
Cup & Saucer, Cranes & Plants, Red Ground, Gold & Silver, 4 5/8 x 2 1/2 In.	255.00
Figurine, Classical Nude Woman, 14 1/2 In.	115.00
Figurine, Clorinda, Woman Warrior, Wearing Armor, c.1848, 13 1/2 In.	460.00
Figurine, Una & Lion, John Bell, 14 3/4 In.	1840.00
Fish Set, Fish Pictures, 23-In. Platter, 9-In. Plate, 11 Piece	1200.00
Jardiniere, Multicolored Floral Design, 2 Figural Handles, Navy Blue Ground, 22 In.	1430.00
Jardiniere, Scenes From Sir Walter Scott, Black, Gold Design, Square, 10 1/2 In.	340.00
Plate, Bellflowers, Swags, Cobalt Blue Band, Cream Gilt Rim, 10 In., 12 Piece	460.00
Plate, Portrait, Various Women, Reticulated Border, A. Boullen, 9 1/2 In., 7 Piece	3045.00
Plate, Service, Stylized Tulips Band, White Reserve, Red Poppies, 9 In., 12 Piece	545.00
Plate, Tea, Ardmore, Floral, 1920, Marked, 6 1/4 In., 10 Piece	60.00
Platter, Dragon & Scroll Design, Oval, Blue & White, 10 1/2 In.	85.00
Tile, Eagle, With Banner, Brown, Cream, 1776-1876, Square	350.00
Tile, Floral & Geometric Design, Arts & Crafts, Square, c.1900	38.00
Tile, Portrait, Hollins	34.00
Tureen, Sauce, Cover, Undertray, Floral & Ribbon, Flow Blue	200.00
Vase, 2 Colorful Exotic Birds, Perched On Tree, Cobalt Blue, 8 1/2 In.	575.00
Vase, Flowers, Applied Handles, Cobalt Blue Ground, 9 In., Pair	700.00
Vase, Transfer-Printed Flowers, Blue, Yellow, Aesthetic Movement, 25 x 12 In.	550.00
Wash Set, Ovals, Flower Heads, Beaded Ropes, Swags, Gilt Borders, 5 Piece, 9 1/2 In.	230.00

MIRRORS are listed in the Furniture category under Mirror.

MOCHA pottery is an English-made product that was sold in America during the early 1800s. It is a heavy pottery with pale coffee-and-cream coloring. Designs of blue, brown, green, orange, black, or white were added to the pottery and given fanciful names, such as *Tree*, *Snail Trail*, or *Moss*.

Bowl, Brown & White Design, Dark & Light Brown Bands, 5 In.	215.00
Bowl, Seaweed, Green, 12 1/4 x 5 3/4 In.	495.00
Bowl, Seaweed, Yellow, Blue, White, 6 1/2 x 3 In.	175.00
Bowl, Zigzag Earthworm, Dark Brown, Blue, White, Orange Ground, 4 1/2 In.	770.00
Mug, Brown Stripes & Bands, Blue & Chocolate Brown, 5 1/8 In.	715.00
Mug, Cat's Eye & Dots, Shades Of Blue Stripes, Leaf Handle, 6 7/8 In.	1100.00
Mug, Cat's Eye, Blue, Brown, Alternating Thin Brown Lines, Reeded Handle, 4 In.	805.00
Mug, Earthworm, Geometric Border, 19th Century, 5 1/2 In.	517.00
Mug, Earthworm, Looping, Dark Brown, Blue, White, Straight Sides, 3 1/4 In.	522.00
Mug, Seaweed, Blue & Gray Bands, Applied Handle, 6 1/4 In.	288.00
Mug, Seaweed, Yellow, Blue, White, 3 In.	300.00
Mug, Tree, Blue, Green, Black On White Ground, Black & Green Bands, 5 1/2 In.	440.00
Mustard, Blue & Brown Band, Ear Handle, 2 1/4 x 3 In.	220.00
Mustard, Seaweed, Brown, White, 3 1/2 In.	415.00
Pepper Pot, Blue Cover, Blue & White Stripes, Brown Band, 4 3/4 In.	715.00
Pepper Pot, Dome Cover, Coggled, Dot Bands, Brown, Cream Ground, 4 In.	797.00
Pepper Pot, Dome Cover, Zigzag Earthworm & Cat's Eye, Orange, White, Brown, 4 In.	1100.00
Pepper Pot, Earthworm, Dome Cover, Brown, Blue Gray Ground, Feather Edge, 5 In.	1320.00
Pepper Shaker, Seaweed, 4 In.	1210.00
Pitcher, Cat's Eye, Incised Green Band, Black Ground, Gray Handle, 7 1/2 In.	2013.00
Pitcher, Cat's Eye, White With Brown & Blue Bands, Dark Brown Stripes, 8 In.	1210.00
Pitcher, Earthworm & Bands, White Stripes, Leaf Handle, 6 1/2 In.	1265.00
Pitcher, Earthworm & Cat's Eye, 8 In.	3400.00
Pitcher, Earthworm & Polka Dots, Blue, Tooled Band & Stripes, 8 In.	880.00
Pitcher, Earthworm, Blue, Dark Brown, White, Alternating Thin Blue Lines, 5 In.	690.00
Pitcher, Earthworm, Stripes, Yellow Ocher Band, Leaf End Handle, 6 1/2 In.	687.00
Pitcher, Seaweed, Blue, Pumpkin, Brown, c.1840, 6 In.	900.00
Pitcher, Seaweed, Brown & Blue Bands, Applied Seashell In Front, 10 In.	935.00
Pitcher, Washing, Seaweed, 1 Wide Band, Blue, White Design, Yellow Ground, 8 1/2 In.	1265.00
Salt, Master, Cat's Eye, Green, Gray Ground, Brown Bands, 2 3/4 In.	605.00
Salt, Master, Seaweed, Brown, Gray Ground, Dark Brown Bands, Bulbous, Footed, 2 In.	355.00
Sugar, Cover, Brown, White Checkered Bands, Blue Agate Ground, 4 x 5 In.	465.00

MONMOUTH Pottery Company started working in Monmouth, Illinois, in 1892. The pottery made a variety of utilitarian wares. It became part of Western Stoneware Company in 1906. The maple leaf mark was used until 1930. If *Co.* appears as part of the mark, the piece was made before 1906.

Bowl, Batter, Pouring Spout, Handle, Cobalt Blue, Maple Leaf Mark, 7 3/4 In.	45.00
Cooler, Water, Tan Salt Glaze, Black Lettering, Spongeware, 13 In.	195.00
Creamer, Speckled Brown Glaze, Maple Leaf Mark, 2 3/4 In.	11.00
Lamp, Matte Orange & Yellow Rust Glaze, 22 In.	75.00

MONT JOYE, see Mt. Joye category.

MOORCROFT pottery was first made in Burslem, England, in 1913. William Moorcroft had managed the art pottery department for James MacIntyre & Company of England from 1898 to 1913. The Moorcroft pottery continues today, although William Moorcroft died in 1945. The earlier wares are similar to the modern ones, but color and marking will help indicate the age.

Bonbon, Pomegranate, Silver Plate, Duchess, 5 In.	595.00
Bowl, Clematis, Red, Yellow, Olive Green Ground, Flattened, 6 3/4 In.	575.00
Bowl, Cover, Anemone, Dark Blue Ground, Signed, 5 1/2 In.	385.00
Bowl, Floral, 5 1/2 In.	200.00
Bowl, Floral, Green Ground, Marked, 6 1/4 In.	275.00
Bowl, Moonlit Blue, Landscape Scene, 3 1/2 x 7 1/2 In.	800.00
Bowl, Orchid, Polychrome, Signed, 4 1/2 In.	193.00

Bowl, Pomegranate, Red, Deep Maroon, Blue, Green, Marked, 1921, 3 3/4 In. 920.00
Candlestick, Leaf & Fruit, Blue Ground, Tapered Pewter Base, 3 3/4 In., Pair 460.00
Charger, Rose Garland 500.00
Coffee Set, Pomegranate, Painted Fruit & Leaves, 1910, 3 Piece 9460.00
Jam Jar, Pomegranate, Silver Plated Top, Duchess 475.00
Jar, Cover, Frieze Of Cranes & Flowers, Flowers & Leaf Panels, Signed, 10 In. 345.00
Jar, Cover, Leaf & Fruit, Pink, Yellow, Green, Blue, 10 1/2 In. 719.00
Lamp, Iris, c.1918, 11 In. 2000.00
Lamp, Leaf & Fruit, Flame, c.1920, 11 In. 2200.00
Mug, Flamminian Ware, Signed, 3 3/4 In. 357.00
Sugar & Creamer, Pomegranate, Celadon Ground, Signed, 5 1/2 x 4 1/2 In. 2090.00
Vase, Blue & Pink Flowers, White Ground, Signed, 6 3/4 In. 1980.00
Vase, Claremont, Red, Green, Yellow Mushrooms, Blue Ground, Marked, 8 1/2 In. 2640.00
Vase, Eventide, Squeezebag, Green Trees, Cobalt Blue Sky, 19 1/2 x 8 In. 7700.00
Vase, Flambe, Deep Red, Black, Gold Highlights, 1929, 15 3/4 In. 3450.00
Vase, Floral, c.1930, 5 In. 395.00
Vase, Floral, Multicolored, Green, Blue Ground, Impressed Marks, 6 In. 357.00
Vase, Floral, Pear Shape, Blue Ground, 10 In. 685.00
Vase, Florian Ware, Anemones, Blue, Yellow, 2 Handles, White Ground, 10 x 7 In. 3190.00
Vase, Leaf & Fruit, Flambe Glaze, Signed, 3 1/4 In. 495.00
Vase, Orchid, Dark Flowers, Teal Green Ground, Marked, 7 x 5 In. 2530.00
Vase, Orchid, Original Label, 3 1/2 In. 412.00
Vase, Pansy, 2 In. 295.00
Vase, Pansy, Cobalt Blue Ground, c.1918, 7 1/8 In. 605.00
Vase, Pansy, Large Flowers, Pink, Purple, Cobalt Blue Ground, Baluster, 13 x 7 In. 1870.00
Vase, Pansy, Liberty Tudric Hammered Pewter Base, Stamped, 6 1/4 In. 880.00
Vase, Pomegranate, Blue, 7 x 5 3/4 In. 895.00
Vase, Pomegranate, Red, Deep Maroon, Blue, Green, Marked, 1930, 9 1/4 In. 747.00
Vase, Pomegranate, Rose, Peach, Green, Deep Blue Ground, 5 3/4 In. 635.00
Vase, Pomegranate, Signed, 10 1/2 In. 695.00
Vase, Pomegranate, Signed, 5 In. 695.00
Vase, Pomegranate, Swelling Body, c.1918, 9 1/8 In. 715.00
Vase, Waving Corn, Wine Color Ground, Marked, 27 In. 374.00
Vase, Wisteria, Bulbous Bottom, Cobalt Blue Ground, c.1918, 8 In. 550.00

MORIAGE is a special type of raised decoration used on some Japanese pottery. Sometimes pieces of clay were shaped by hand and applied to the item; sometimes the clay was squeezed from a tube in the way we apply cake frosting. One type of moriage is called *Dragonware* and is listed under that name.

Candlestick, Butterflies, Flowers, Blue Edge, Cream Colored Base, 8 In, Pair 500.00
Humidor, Clover, Butterfly Design, 5 1/2 In. 247.00
Pitcher, Tan, Green & White Beading, Maple Leaf Mark, 6 1/2 In. 58.00
Pitcher & Mug Set, Monkey, Red, Brown, Off-White Ground, 5 Piece 205.00
Vase, Roses, 2 Handles, 6 In. 130.00

MOSAIC TILE COMPANY of Zanesville, Ohio, was started by Karl Langerbeck and Herman Mueller in 1894. Many types of plain and ornamental tiles were made until 1959. The company closed in 1967. The company also made some ashtrays, bookends, and related giftwares. Most pieces are marked with the entwined *MTC* monogram.

Desk Box, Hound Dog On Cover, Dark Bronze Glaze, 8 3/8 In. 85.00
Figurine, Black Bear 125.00
Tile, Mammy, Yellow 495.00
Tile, Ship At Sea, Yellow Sail, Blue Water, Square, 6 In. 286.00

MOSER glass is made by Ludwig Moser und Sohne, a Bohemian (Czech) glasshouse founded in 1857. Art Nouveau-type glassware and iridescent glassware were made. The most famous Moser glass is decorated with heavy enameling in gold and bright colors. The firm, Moser Glassworks, is still working in Karlsbad, West Czech Republic. Few pieces of Moser glass are marked.

Bowl, Intaglio Florals, Oval, Signed, 2 1/2 x 7 1/2 In. 480.00

Ceiling Light, Amber Glass Balls, 2 Silk Cords, Metal Mount, Koloman, 41 In. 8280.00
Cologne Bottle, Stick, Floral, Amber Luster, Bulbous, Stopper, 5 1/2 In. 495.00
Compote, Enameled Leaves, Pink Opaline, Pinched Rim, Amber Tree Stem, 7 1/2 In. ... 1725.00
Cup, Applied Acorns, Lime Green, Paris 350.00
Cup, Enameled, Acorns, Green 100.00
Decanter, Brandy, Gold Gilt Wreaths Top & Bottom, White Letters, 14 In. 500.00
Decanter, Enameled Floral Design, Layered, Cranberry, 1900, 15 In. 345.00
Decanter, Enameled Oak Leaves, Acorns, Cranberry, c.1890, 9 In. 4830.00
Goblet, Clear, Green Stained, Fluted Interior, Scalloped Foot, 8 3/4 In., 6 Piece 490.00
Goblet, Cobalt Blue Cut To Clear, Gilt Rim, c.1930, 7 1/4 In., Pair 300.00
Goblet, Cranberry Stained Bowl, Gilt, c.1890, 5 In. 125.00
Goblet, Enameled Floral, Fluted Interior, Green, Amber Stem, c.1890, 7 In. 115.00
Goblet, Enameled Floral, Gilt Threaded, Ruby, 1890, 6 1/2 In. 362.00
Goblet, Enameled Floral, Gilt, Blue, 1890, 8 In. 423.00
Goblet, Enameled Floral, Gilt, Cranberry, 1890, 6 1/4 In. 211.00
Goblet, Enameled Floral, Gilt, Fluted, Cranberry, c.1900, 5 3/4 In. 375.00
Goblet, Enameled Floral, Gilt, Prunts On Bowl, Green, 1890, 7 In. 167.00
Goblet, Enameled Floral, Green, c.1890, 12 1/2 In. 218.00
Goblet, Gilt Floral, Pulled Foot, Cranberry, c.1890, 4 3/4 In. 150.00
Goblet, Gilt Floral, Ruby, c.1890, 5 1/2 In. 185.00
Goblet, Gilt Oak Leaves, Acorns, Rolled Foot, Cranberry, c.1890, 5 In. 603.00
Goblet, Green, Gilt & Silver Oak Leaves, Acorns, Roemer Stem, 7 3/4 In., 4 Piece 2070.00
Goblet, Venetian Style, Floral Enamel, Leaping Deer, Flat 8-Sided Bowl, c.1900, 7 In. ... 140.00
Goblet, White Enameled Floral, Amber, 1900, 6 1/2 In. 145.00
Juice, Silver & Gilt Floral & Butterfly, Fluted Interior, c.1890, 3 1/4 In. 172.00
Perfume Bottle, Egyptian Man, Headdress & Staff, 11 In. 805.00
Perfume Bottle, Heavy Gold Leaves, Blue Forget-Me-Nots, Cranberry, Atomizer 195.00
Pitcher, Egyptian, Cranberry, Frosted Handle, Signed, 10 In. 1955.00
Pitcher, Enameled Blue, Yellow Pineapple, Applied Handle, 11 In. 2530.00
Pitcher, Enameled Floral Design, Orange Amber, 4 3/4 In. 260.00
Pitcher, Floral, Pink, Gold, Fluted, 13 In. 665.00
Rose Bowl, Fish & Plants, Puffy, 3 1/2 In. 365.00
Sherbet, Underplate, Enameled Gold & White, Green Cut To Clear, Signed 250.00
Toothpick, Gold Acorns & Leaves, Frosted, 1 3/4 In. 200.00
Tray, Enamel Leaves, Cranberry, 2 Handles, 12 7/8 In. 1265.00
Tumbler, Allover Gold Scroll, Signed, 3 3/4 In. 200.00
Tumbler, Central Band Of Scrolled Leaf Design, Blue, Enamel, 3 7/8 In. 230.00
Tumbler, Gold, 3 Silver Panels, Multicolored Birds, Cranberry, 3 7/8 In. 300.00
Tumbler, Rainbow, Dogwood, Diagonal Ribbed Body, 1890, 4 1/2 In. 575.00
Vase, Allover Heavy Gilt, Vaseline Green Foot, 14 In. 350.00
Vase, Amber, Elephants Under Palm Tree, Inverted Baluster, 1925, 8 In. 1720.00
Vase, Cut Amethyst, 2 Handles, 1910, 11 1/2 In. 460.00
Vase, Enameled & Gilt Floral, c.1890, 12 1/2 In. 332.00
Vase, Enameled Floral, Leaves, Green Flared Rim, 17 1/2 In. 325.00
Vase, Enameled Oak Leaves, Pink, Opalized, Applied Acorns, Amber Rolled Feet, 6 In. .. 1035.00
Vase, Enameled Snake, Insect & Fern, Gilt, 10 1/2 In. 2990.00
Vase, Floral Carving, Green, 3 3/4 In. 230.00
Vase, Floral, Gilt, Cranberry, 1890, 13 1/2 In. 604.00
Vase, Floral, Variegated Yellow, Ruby Band, 1890, 16 In. 288.00
Vase, Leaves & Insects, Amberina, 1900s, 12 1/2 In., Pair 6500.00
Vase, Paneled Form, Amber, Flared Top, 6 1/4 In. 55.00
Vase, Red, Gold Enamel, 2 Handles, 4 1/2 In. 145.00
Vase, Shaded Dark Green To Clear, Vaseline Foot, Gold Trim, 14 In. 300.00
Vase, Swimming Fish, Sapphire Blue, Flowers, 8 1/2 In. 317.00

MOSS ROSE china was made by many firms from 1808 to 1900. It has
a typical moss rose pictured as the design. The plant is not as popular
now as it was in Victorian gardens, so the fuzz-covered bud is unfamiliar to most collectors. The dishes were usually decorated with pink
and green flowers.

Tureen, Oval, Haviland 33.00

MOTHER-OF-PEARL GLASS, or pearl satin glass, was first made in the 1850s in England and in Massachusetts. It was a special type of mold-blown satin glass with air bubbles in the glass, giving it a pearlized color. It has been reproduced. Mother-of-pearl shell objects are listed under Pearl.

Cigarette Case, Applied Turtle, Gold Leaves	85.00
Cup & Saucer	385.00
Ewer, Herringbone, Deep Pink To White, Applied Handle, 9 In.	115.00
Ewer, Herringbone, Ruffled Edge, Handle, Satin, 8 1/2 x 4 In.	200.00
Pitcher, Water, Coin Spot, Deep Rose, Applied Pattern, 8 3/4 In.	518.00
Pitcher, Water, Red To Pink To White, Ruffled Edge, Handle, 9 In.	460.00
Rose Bowl, Diamond-Quilted, Rainbow, 2 1/2 In.	600.00
Shade, Yellow Swirl, White Interior, 5 In.	295.00
Tumbler, Diamond-Quilted, Apricot To White Satin	125.00
Tumbler, Diamond-Quilted, Bird, Leaves, Pink Satin	235.00
Tumbler, Diamond-Quilted, Leaves, Flowers, Blue Bugs	250.00
Tumbler, Diamond-Quilted, Leaves, Flowers, Blue Satin	225.00
Tumbler, Diamond-Quilted, Pink Satin To White	125.00
Tumbler, Herringbone, Pink Satin To White	125.00
Vase, Blue Lattice, Ground Pontil, 6 1/2 In.	90.00
Vase, Diamond-Quilted, Ruffled Lip, Peach Shaded, 14 In.	265.00
Vase, Dotted Swiss, Melon Rib, Blue To Bluish White, 7 1/2 In.	288.00
Vase, Gold Over Red, Herringbone, White Lining, Gourd Shape, 12 x 4 1/2 In.	230.00
Vase, Ribbed Melon, Deep Rose, 11 1/2 In.	230.00
Vase, Ribbed Melon, Ruffled Edge, White Lining, 7 7/8 In.	225.00

MOTORCYCLES and motorcycle accessories of all types are being collected today. Examples can be found that date back to the early years of the twentieth century. Toy motorcycles are listed in the Toy category.

Bracelet, Harley-Davidson, Wing Logo, Chain Link Sides, Silver, Mexico, 3 In.	32.00
Cap, Buco Products, Black Twill, White Visor, 1950s, Size 6 7/8	120.00
Card, Harley-Davidson Dealers, Motorcycle With Sidecar, 1920s, 2 3/4 x 4 3/4 In.	35.00
Catalog, Sears De Luxe Motorcycles, 36 Pages, 1914	115.00
Catalog, Triumph, Descriptions Of 4 Models, 1953, 8 1/2 x 11 In.	45.00
Folder, Indian Motorcycle, How To Ride, Bill Stern On Cycle, Late 1940s	48.00
Hat, Harley-Davidson, Brando Style, Black Cloth Top, Cord Chinstrap, 1960s	85.00
Helmet, Blue Knights Logo, Blue Molded Plastic, Premier Crown Corp., Medium	32.00
Jacket, Black Leather, Zip-In Plush Lining, Epaulets, Talon Zipper, Brooks, Size 44	120.00
Jacket, Harley-Davidson, Black Leather, Zipper Front, Quilt Lining, 1950s, Size 34	615.00
Jacket, Horsehide, Black, Zipper Front, 2 Zippered Pockets, Satin Lining	360.00
Mailer, Harley-Davidson Christmas Gifts, Paper, 1954, 12 x 18 In.	48.00
Manual, Owner's, Harley-Davidson, 44 Pages, 1929, 6 3/4 x 4 3/4 In.	60.00
Oil Can, Bardahl 2-Stroke Injection Motorcycle Oil, Contents, 1 Qt.	35.00
Oil Can, Indian Motorcycle Oil, Contents, 1940s, 1 Qt.	250.00
Patch, Harley-Davidson Motorcycles, Wings, 1950s, 7 1/2 In.	75.00
Pin, M & M Motorcycle, American Motor Co., Multicolored, Celluloid, Pinback	230.00
Pin, Take A Joy Ride-Flying Merkel, Multicolored, Celluloid, Pinback, 7/8 In.	240.00
Stickpin, Indian Motorcycle, Indian With Swastika, Stamped, 5/8 In.	110.00
Tool Pouch, Harley-Davidson, Black Leather, Belt, Buckle Fastener, 10 x 6 x 4 In.	60.00
Watch Fob, Harley-Davidson National Championship, 1900s, 1 1/2 x 1 1/4 In.	205.00

MOUNT WASHINGTON, see Mt. Washington category.

MOVIE memorabilia of all types is collected. Animation cels, games, sheet music, toys, and some celebrity items are listed in their own section. Listed here are costumes and paper collectibles. A lobby card is 11 by 14 inches. A set of lobby cards includes seven scene cards and one title card. A one sheet, the standard movie poster, is 27 by 41 inches. A three sheet is 81 by 40 inches. A half sheet is 22 by 28 inches. A window card, made of cardboard, is 14 by 22 inches. An insert is 14 by 36 inches. A herald is a promotional item handed out to patrons. A press book was sent to newspapers and magazines to promote a pic-

TAKE 1

ture. Press books and/or press kits (with photos) were sent to the media
to promote a movie.

Autograph, Barbra Striesand, Photograph 75.00
Autograph, Bette Davis, Kid Galahad, Title Lobby Card, 1937 .... 750.00
Autograph, Bette Davis, Signed Photograph, Black & White, 8 x 10 In. 45.00
Autograph, Charles Bronson, As Wild Bill Hickok, Signed Photograph, 8 x 10 In. 35.00
Autograph, Chuck Connors, Signed Photograph, Black & White, 8 x 10 In. 75.00
Autograph, Humphrey Bogart, Invasion Currency, Lire, Note, 1943 .... 995.00
Autograph, John Travolta, Photograph, 8 x 10 In. 10.00
Autograph, Judy Garland, Signed Check, Dated October 20, 1966 .... 750.00
Autograph, Mary Pickford, Signed Photograph, Very Sincerely, 11 x 14 In. 75.00
Autograph, Stan Laurel, Signed Photograph 375.00
Autograph, Sunset Carson & Cactus, Signed Photograph, Black & White, 8 x 10 In. 20.00
Badge, Junior G-Men Club, Universal Serial, Celluloid, Pinback, 1 1/2 In. 25.00
Banner, House Of Frankenstein, Boris Karloff, 1944, 24 x 82 In. 1495.00
Battery Tester, W.C. Fields, Red Nose, Full Figure On Card, 11 1/2 x 5 In. 15.00
Bookmark, Things To Come, Raymond Massey, Ralph Richardson, 1936, 3 x 8 In. 100.00
Bust, Marilyn Monroe, Flesh Tones, Ruby Lips, Inscribed, 1954-1957, 20 1/2 In. 375.00
Contract, Fred Astaire, Signed, Bing Crosby Enterprises, December 13, 1951 .... 115.00
Doorknob Hanger, Flirtation Walk, Dick Powell & Ruby Keeler, Alabama Theatre 50.00
Dress, Fatal Instinct, Matching Bolero Style Jacket, Green & White Silk 350.00
Dress, Female Animal, White Chiffon, Silver Sequins, Hedy Lamarr, 1958 .... 650.00
Figure, Clark Gable, Plaster, 1974, 18 In. 100.00
Figure, Groucho Marx, Plaster, 16 In. 90.00
Film, Bugs Bunny, Super 8, 1940 .... 15.00
Harem Costume, Road To Morocco, Yvonne De Carlo, 1942 .... 800.00
Herald, Birth Of A Nation, D.W. Griffith, Silent Film, Foldout, 8 Pages 275.00
Jacket, Great Race, Blue Velvet, Jack Lemmon, 1965 .... 700.00
Jersey, Baseball, Pride Of Yankees, Gary Cooper 8250.00
Knickers, Navy Wool, Personal, Ava Gardner 125.00
Lobby Card, Across The Pacific, Humphrey Bogart, Mary Astor, Warner Bros., 1942 .... 295.00
Lobby Card, African Queen, Katharine Hepburn, Humphrey Bogart, 1951 .... 140.00
Lobby Card, All About Eve, Marilyn Monroe, Fox, 1950 .... 785.00
Lobby Card, Amazing Dr. Clitterhouse, E.G. Robinson, Bogart, Warner Brothers, 1938 .. 615.00
Lobby Card, Andy Hardy Meets Debutante, Mickey Rooney, Judy Garland, 1940 ...... 105.00
Lobby Card, Before I Hang, Boris Karloff, Columbia, 1940 .... 260.00
Lobby Card, Big Shot, Humphrey Bogart, 1942 .... 85.00
Lobby Card, Black Friday, Boris Karloff, Bela Lugosi, Universal, 1940 .... 230.00
Lobby Card, Boy Meets Girl, James Cagney, Pat O'Brien, In Sleeve, 1938 .... 485.00
Lobby Card, Brother Orchid, Bogart & Robinson, Warner Brothers, 1940 .... 242.00
Lobby Card, Camille, Greta Garbo, Robert Taylor, MGM, 1937 .... 220.00
Lobby Card, Captives Of The Zero Hour, Commando Cody, Orange Lettering, 1953 ..... 115.00
Lobby Card, Creature From The Black Lagoon, 1954 .... 250.00
Lobby Card, Dark Passage, Humphrey Bogart, Lauren Bacall, Warner Brothers, 1947 .... 485.00
Lobby Card, Dr. Zhivago, Geraldine Chaplin, Julie Christie, Omar Sharif, 1965, 5 Piece .. 66.00
Lobby Card, Dracula, David Manners, Helen Chandler, 1931 .... 845.00
Lobby Card, Dracula, Greatest Horror Show Of All Time, Orange Ground, Reissue, 1951 . 210.00
Lobby Card, Frankenstein Meets The Wolf Man, 1943 .... 759.00
Lobby Card, Frankenstein, Monster Science Created, Reissue, 1951 .... 645.00
Lobby Card, Gone With The Wind, Clark Gable & Vivian Leigh, MGM, 1939 .... 1200.00
Lobby Card, Headin' Home, Babe Ruth, 1921 .... 990.00
Lobby Card, Hold Your Man, Jean Harlow, Clark Gable, 1933 .... 487.00
Lobby Card, House On Haunted Hill, 1958 .... 100.00
Lobby Card, Invisible Man's Revenge, Universal, 1944, 4 Piece 33.00
Lobby Card, King Kong, Eighth Wonder Of The World, 1933 .... 3600.00
Lobby Card, King Kong, Fay Wray Is On Bough Of Tree Looking On, Reissue, 1942 .... 460.00
Lobby Card, La Casa El Cafe, Laurel & Hardy, Heads & Hats Move, Die Cut, 9 1/2 In. .. 50.00
Lobby Card, Life Begins For Andy Hardy, Mickey Rooney, Signed, 1941 .... 110.00
Lobby Card, Little Women, Katherine Hepburn, 1933 .... 160.00
Lobby Card, Misfits, Marilyn Monroe, No. 5, 1961 .... 65.00
Lobby Card, Missile Monsters, Walter Reed, Lois Collier, 8 Piece 105.00
Lobby Card, Mr. Smith Goes To Washington, James Stewart, Columbia, 1939 .... 1330.00

Lobby Card, Mummy's Curse, Lon Chaney, Signed By Actor Martin Kosleck, 1944 ..... 66.00
Lobby Card, My Man Godfrey, William Powell, 1936 .... 860.00
Lobby Card, Niagara, Marilyn Monroe, Joseph Cotten, Jean Peters, 1953 .... 242.00
Lobby Card, Phantom Of The Opera, 1925 .... 315.00
Lobby Card, Philadelphia Story, Katherine Hepburn, Cary Grant, MGM, 1940 ....110.00 to 545.00
Lobby Card, Private Lives Of Elizabeth & Essex, Warner Brothers, 1939 .... 605.00
Lobby Card, Radar Men From The Moon, Commando Cody, Black Lettering, 1953 ..... 90.00
Lobby Card, San Quentin, Humphrey Bogart As Convict, Warner Brothers, 1937 .... 265.00
Lobby Card, Sit Tight, Joe E. Brown, 1931 .... 515.00
Lobby Card, Snow White & The Seven Dwarfs, Blue Ground, Border, Reissue, 1937 ... 290.00
Lobby Card, Son Of The Sheik, Rudolph Valentino, United Artists, 1926 .... 212.00
Lobby Card, Talk Of The Town, Cary Grant, Jean Arthur, Ronald Colman, 1942, 8 Piece . 143.00
Lobby Card, The Cameraman, Buster Keaton, 1928 .... 920.00
Lobby Card, To Have & Have Not, Bogart, Bacall, Walter Brennan, Warner Bros., 1945 .. 220.00
Lobby Card, Two Mrs. Carrols, Bogart, Stanwyck, Alexis Smith, Title Card, 1947 ...... 133.00
Lobby Card, Wizard Of Oz, Judy Garland, Frank Morgan, Ray Bolger, Bert Lahr, 1939 .. 1035.00
Lobby Card, Wizard Of Oz, MGM, 1939 .... 4285.00
Lobby Card, Wizard Of Oz, Ray Bolger, Bert Lahr, Jack Haley, Soldiers, 1939 .... 1330.00
Lobby Card, Wizard Of Oz, Wicked Witch Of The West Scene, MGM, Reissue, 1949 .... 440.00
Lobby Card, Zombies Of The Stratosphere, Leonard Nimoy, Republic Serial, 1952 ...... 95.00
Photograph, Charles Laughton, 8 x 5 In. 5.00
Photograph, Gone With The Wind, Scarlet, Wounded, On Ground, Reissue, 10 x 8 In. 35.00
Photograph, Group Of Men Stars, Anthony Quinn, Donald Sutherland, 8 x 10 In. 40.00
Photograph, Ingrid Bergman, Beaded Gown, Color, 14 x 11 In. 195.00
Photograph, Lillian Gish, 1932, 2 7/8 x 1 1/8 In. 10.00
Photograph, Marilyn Monroe, Black Lacy Slip, Milton H. Greene, 1956, 11 x 14 In. 215.00
Photograph, Marilyn Monroe, Full Length, Color, Milton H. Greene, 11 x 14 In. 285.00
Photograph, Marilyn Monroe, Portrait, Milton H. Greene, 1956, 11 x 14 In. 515.00
Photograph, Ramon Novarro, 1932, 2 7/8 x 1 1/8 In. 10.00
Photograph, Ronald Coleman, 1932, 2 7/8 x 1 1/8 In. 10.00
Photograph, Wizard Of Oz, Dorothy, Scarecrow, Tin Man, Wizard, & Lion, 11 x 14 In. .. 195.00
Poster, 7th Voyage Of Sinbad, Ray Harryhausen, 1958, Insert 100.00
Poster, Abbot & Costello Meet The Invisible Man, 1951, Insert 195.00
Poster, Alamo, John Wayne, Richard Widmark, 1960, One Sheet 240.00
Poster, Alphaville, 1965, France Or Belgian, 47 x 63 In. 690.00
Poster, An American In Paris, 1951, Three Sheet 1380.00
Poster, Anastasia, Ingrid Bergman, 1956, One Sheet 16.50
Poster, And Then There Were None, Barry Fitzgerald, Walter Huston, 1945, One Sheet .. 198.00
Poster, Apocalypse Now, Bob Peak Artwork, 1979, One Sheet 50.00
Poster, Attack Of The 50 Ft. Woman, Reynold Brown Artwork, 1958, Insert 2725.00
Poster, Babes In Arms, Al Hirschfeld Artwork, Style D, 1939, One Sheet 530.00
Poster, Babes In Arms, Mickey Rooney, Judy Garland, Style C, 1939, One Sheet 443.00
Poster, Beau Geste, Gary Cooper, Ray Milland, Robert Preston, 1939, Half Sheet 138.00
Poster, Bedlam, Boris Karloff, 1946, One Sheet 690.00
Poster, Birdman Of Alcatraz, Burt Lancaster, Bob Peak Artwork, 1962, Three Sheet 182.00
Poster, Bold Caballero, Bob Livingston, Heather Angel, Linen, 1936, One Sheet 413.00
Poster, Breakfast At Tiffany's, Audrey Hepburn, 1961, One Sheet 2415.00
Poster, Bride Of Frankenstein, 1935, One Sheet 35.00
Poster, Bride Of Frankenstein, Universal, 1935, Argentine, One Sheet 7475.00
Poster, Brides Of Dracula, Peter Cushing, 1960, One Sheet 180.00
Poster, Bridge On The River Kwai, Style B, 1957, Half Sheet 295.00
Poster, Bullitt, Steve McQueen, 1968, Heavy Stock Silkscreen, 39 x 55 In. 400.00
Poster, Bus Stop, Marilyn Monroe, 1956, One Sheet 485.00
Poster, Bye Bye Birdie, Janet Leigh, Dick Van Dyke, Ann-Margret, 1963, One Sheet ... 120.00
Poster, Camille, Greta Garbo, Robert Taylor, Linen Back, Style D, 1936, One Sheet 2330.00
Poster, Captain America, Chapter 11, Republic Serial, 1944, One Sheet 490.00
Poster, Chinatown, Jack Nicholson, 1974, One Sheet 180.00
Poster, Cleopatra, Cecil B. DeMille, Paramount, 1934, One Sheet 6325.00
Poster, Cleopatra, Elizabeth Taylor, Richard Burton, 1963, One Sheet 195.00
Poster, Clown, Red Skelton, MGM, 1953, One Sheet 550.00
Poster, Creature With The Atom Brain, Richard Denning, 1955, One Sheet 55.00
Poster, Daddy, Jackie Coogan, 1923, One Sheet 920.00
Poster, Deadline U.S.A., Humphrey Bogart, 1952, Three Sheet 150.00

Poster, Dirty Harry, Clint Eastwood, 1971, One Sheet 375.00
Poster, Don't Bother To Knock, Richard Widmark, Marilyn Monroe, 1952, Insert 485.00
Poster, Dr. Strangelove, 1964, One Sheet 690.00
Poster, Father's Little Dividend, Spencer Tracy, Elizabeth Taylor, 1951, One Sheet 150.00
Poster, Fighting O'Flynn, Douglas Fairbanks, Jr., 1949, One Sheet 33.00
Poster, From Here To Eternity, Burt Lancaster, 1953, One Sheet 575.00
Poster, From Russia With Love, James Bond Is Back, 1963, One Sheet 200.00
Poster, Funny Face, Audrey Hepburn, Fred Astaire, 1957, One Sheet 430.00
Poster, Funny Girl, 1968, Half Sheet 230.00
Poster, Galloping Ghost, Red Grange, 1938, One Sheet 365.00
Poster, Geisha Boy, Jerry Lewis, 1958, One Sheet 48.00
Poster, Gentlemen Prefer Blondes, Jane Russell, Marilyn Monroe, 1953, Half Sheet 515.00
Poster, Ghost Of Slumber Mountain, Dinosaurs Fighting, 1919, Three Sheet 4390.00
Poster, Godfather, Marlon Brando, 1972, One Sheet 145.00
Poster, Godzilla, Raymond Burr, 1956, Three Sheet 1265.00
Poster, Great Impersonation, Ralph Bellamy, 1942, One Sheet 250.00
Poster, Guys & Dolls, 1955, Half Sheet 230.00
Poster, Guys & Dolls, Marlon Brando, Frank Sinatra, 1955, Three Sheet 240.00
Poster, Hell's Hole, Charles Jones, 1924, One Sheet 1035.00
Poster, High School Big Shot, Tom Pitman, 1959, One Sheet 25.00
Poster, His Girl Friday, Cary Grant, Rosalind Russell, 1949, Half Sheet 231.00
Poster, His Girl Friday, Cary Grant, Rosalind Russell, 1949, Insert 231.00
Poster, Horse Feathers, Marx Brothers, Paramount, 1932, One Sheet 9775.00
Poster, How To Marry A Millionaire, Betty Grable, Marilyn Monroe, 1953 .... 575.00
Poster, I'll Never Forget You, Tyrone Power, Ann Blyth, M. Rennie, 1951, One Sheet ... 33.00
Poster, I'll Take Sweden, Bob Hope, Tuesday Weld, Frankie Avalon, 1965, One Sheet ... 28.00
Poster, Incredible Shrinking Man, Grant Williams, 1957, One Sheet 550.00
Poster, Jason & The Argonauts, 1963, Three Sheet 152.00
Poster, Jaws, Richard Dreyfuss, Heavy Stock Silkscreen, 1975, 40 x 60 In. 315.00
Poster, Jesse James, Tyrone Power, Henry Fonda, Nancy Kelly, 1938, Insert 303.00
Poster, King Kong, Fay Wray, Reissue, 1952, One Sheet 375.00
Poster, Kismet, Ronald Colman, Marlene Dietrich, MGM, 1944, One Sheet 176.00
Poster, Ladies In Retirement, Ida Lupino, Louis Hayward, 1941, One Sheet 44.00
Poster, Lifeboat, Tallulah Bankhead, William Bendix, 1944, One Sheet 2185.00
Poster, Lion In Winter, Peter O'Toole, Katherine Hepburn, 1968, One Sheet 140.00
Poster, Little Foxes, Bette Davis, 1941, One Sheet 1100.00
Poster, Little Old New York, Alice Faye, Fred MacMurray, 1940, One Sheet 400.00
Poster, Little Shop Of Horrors, Jack Nicholson, 1960, Half Sheet 65.00
Poster, Love In The Afternoon, Gary Cooper, Audrey Hepburn, 1957, One Sheet 200.00
Poster, Lucky Partners, Ronald Colman, Ginger Rogers, RKO, 1940, Insert 50.00
Poster, Magic Carpet, Lucille Ball, John Agar, Columbia Pictures, 1951, One Sheet 77.00
Poster, Man Of La Mancha, Peter O'Toole, Heavy Stock Silkscreen, 1972, 40 x 60 In. ... 90.00
Poster, Man On Eiffel Tower, Charles Laughton, 1949, One Sheet 230.00
Poster, Man Who Lived Again, Boris Karloff, 1936, One Sheet 805.00
Poster, Man Who Reclaimed His Head, Claude Rains, 1934, One Sheet 2990.00
Poster, Mary Poppins, Julie Andrews, Dick Van Dyke, 1964, Six Sheet 180.00
Poster, Masquerader, Ronald Colman, United Artists, 1933, One Sheet 297.00
Poster, Merrie Melodies, Bugs Bunny At Cartoonist's Easel, 1948, One Sheet 585.00
Poster, Merry Widow, Lana Turner, 1952, One Sheet 36.00
Poster, Mighty Joe Young, 1949, 24 Sheet For Billboard 2125.00
Poster, Misfits, Clark Gable, Marilyn Monroe, Montgomery Cliff, 1961, One Sheet 460.00
Poster, Missile Monsters, Walter Reed, Lois Collier, 1958, One Sheet 99.00
Poster, Mississippi, Bing Crosby, W.C. Fields, Joan Bennett, 1935, One Sheet 932.00
Poster, Mothra, 1962, Three Sheet 245.00
Poster, My Life With Caroline, Ronald Colman, Anna Lee, RKO, 1941, One Sheet 28.00
Poster, Nothing But Trouble, Laurel & Hardy, 1944, One Sheet 305.00
Poster, O'Henry's Full House, Fred Allen, Anne Baxter, 1952, Three Sheet 100.00
Poster, O.S.S., Alan Ladd, Geraldine Fitzgerald, Paramount, 1946, One Sheet 55.00
Poster, Old Oaken Bucket, Terry-Toons Cartoon, 1941, One Sheet 110.00
Poster, Once Upon A Time, Cary Grant, Janet Blair, 1944, One Sheet 28.00
Poster, One Million Years B.C., Raquel Welch, 1966, Three Sheet 240.00
Poster, Picnic, William Holden, Kim Novak, 1955, One Sheet 345.00
Poster, Porgy & Bess, Saul Bass Logo Art, 1959, One Sheet 345.00

Poster, Postman Always Rings Twice, Lana Turner, John Garfield, 1946, One Sheet 1265.00
Poster, Prince & The Showgirl, Monroe, Laurence Olivier, 1957, One Sheet 690.00
Poster, Private Lives Of Elizabeth & Essex, Bette Davis, Errol Flynn, 1939, One Sheet .. 1815.00
Poster, Psycho, Janet Leigh, Anthony Perkins, 1960, One Sheet 1035.00
Poster, Queen Of Outer Space, Zsa Zsa Gabor, 1958, Six Sheet 880.00
Poster, Rebel Without A Cause, James Dean, Warner Bros., 1955, Six Sheet 6900.00
Poster, Red Dust, Clark Gable, Jean Harlow, 1932, One Sheet 2475.00
Poster, Red Shoes, 1949, One Sheet 560.00
Poster, Rio Bravo, John Wayne, Dean Martin, 1959, One Sheet 920.00
Poster, River Of No Return, Robert Mitchum, Marilyn Monroe, 1954, One Sheet 460.00
Poster, Romeo & Juliet, Norma Shearer, Leslie Howard, 1936, One Sheet 520.00
Poster, Sabrina, Humphrey Bogart, Audrey Hepburn, 1954, Insert 385.00
Poster, Sandpiper, Elizabeth Taylor, Richard Burton, 1965, Half Sheet 52.00
Poster, Sands Of Iwo Jima, John Wayne, 1949, One Sheet 1610.00
Poster, Sea Wife, Joan Collins, Richard Burton, 1957, One Sheet 45.00
Poster, Sinbad The Sailor, Douglas Fairbanks, Jr., Maureen O'Hara, 1946, One Sheet 132.00
Poster, Some Like It Hot, Marilyn Monroe, Tony Curtis, Jack Lemmon, 1959, One Sheet . 315.00
Poster, Song Of Bernadette, Norman Rockwell Artwork, 1943, One Sheet 710.00
Poster, South Pacific, Mitzi Gaynor, 1958, Half Sheet 60.00
Poster, Sting, Paul Newman, Robert Redford, 1973, One Sheet 265.00
Poster, Street Of Chance, Burgess Meredith, Claire Trevor, Frames, 1942, One Sheet 230.00
Poster, Suddenly Last Summer, Elizabeth Taylor, Katherine Hepburn, 1959, One Sheet .. 575.00
Poster, Sunset Boulevard, Gloria Swanson, William Holden, 1950, One Sheet 2100.00
Poster, Talk Of The Town, Cary Grant, Jean Arthur, Ronald Colman, 1942, Half Sheet ... 88.00
Poster, Ten Commandments, Charlton Heston, 1956, Six Sheet 485.00
Poster, Terry-Toons Cartoon, Frame-Up, Gandy Goose, 1938, One Sheet 133.00
Poster, The Birds, Alfred Hitchcock, 1963, One Sheet 430.00
Poster, Under Two Flags, Ronald Colman, Claudette Colbert, 1936, One Sheet 550.00
Poster, Valley Of The Sun, Lucille Ball, James Craig, 1942, One Sheet 145.00
Poster, West Side Story, 1961, One Sheet 630.00
Poster, White Christmas, 1954, Half Sheet 230.00
Poster, World Without End, Hugh Marlowe, 1956, Six Sheet. 750.00
Press Book, Producers, 1988 .... 20.00
Press Book, Towering Inferno, 1974 .... 35.00
Press Kit, Coal Miner's Daughter, 21 Photographs, 1980 .... 20.00
Press Kit, Death On The Nile, 7 Photographs, 1978 .... 20.00
Program, Black Pirate, Douglas Fairbanks, 1926 .... 135.00
Program, Can Can, Frank Sinatra, Shirley MacLaine, 16 Pages 22.00
Program, Covered Wagon, Lois Wilson, Warren Kerrigan, 1923, 20 Pages 45.00
Program, Double Or Nothing, Bing Crosby, Martha Raye, Andy Devine, 1936, 42 Pages . 22.00
Program, Gigi, Leslie Caron, Cecil Beaton Designed Top, 16 Pages 35.00
Program, In Old Chicago, Tyrone Power, Alice Faye, 1938, 10 Pages 30.00
Program, Rio Rita, Bebe Daniels, John Doles, 1929, 4 Pages 55.00
Program, Romeo & Juliet, Norma Shearer, Leslie Howard, 1936, 20 Pages 45.00
Purse, Evening, Loaded Weapon, Kathy Ireland, 1993 .... 135.00
Script, Double Or Nothing, Bing Crosby, Martha Raye, 42 Pages, 1936, 8 x 11 In. 22.00
Shorts, Mighty Barnum, Gold Stars & Tassels, Adolph Menjou, 1932 .... 395.00
Sign, Buffalo Bill, Linda Darnell, R.C. Cola, Cardboard, 1940, 11 x 28 In. 150.00
Sign, Happy Go Lucky, Mary Martin, R.C. Cola, Cardboard, 1940, 11 x 28 In. 125.00
Sign, Pinup Girl, Betty Grable, R.C. Cola, Cardboard, 1940, 11 x 28 In. 125.00
Skirt, Boy On A Dolphin, Green Velvet, Sophia Loren, 1957 .... 475.00
Stickpin, Master Key, Commemorating Universal First Movie 65.00
Suit, 3 Piece, Hawaii Five-O, 1980 .... 210.00
Wastebasket, Planet Of The Apes, Characters 65.00
Window Card, 42nd Street, Busby Berkeley, 1933 .... 1770.00
Window Card, Body & Soul, Fox, 1931 .... 242.00
Window Card, Crime School, Humphrey Bogart, Dead End Kids, 1938 .... 363.00
Window Card, Footlight Parade, James Cagney, Joan Blondell, Art Deco Design, 1933 ... 2750.00
Window Card, Gaucho, Douglas Fairbanks Sr., 1928 .... 805.00
Window Card, Gone With The Wind, Rhett Holding Scarlett, 1939 .... 885.00
Window Card, Jezebel, Bette Davis, 1938 .... 1100.00
Window Card, One Hundred & One Dalmations, 1961 .... 175.00
Window Card, Wings, Clara Bow, 1927 .... 990.00

MT. JOYE is an enameled cameo glass made in the late nineteenth and twentieth centuries by Saint-Hilaire Touvier de Varraux and Co. of Pantin, France. This same company made De Vez glass. Pieces were usually decorated with enameling. Most pieces are not marked.

Vase, Enameled Bean Vine, Pods & Leaves, 6 3/4 In.	395.00
Vase, Enameled Floral, Spider & Web, Satin Cameo, 9 In.	605.00
Vase, Enameled Flowers, Mitered Bishop Mark, 14 In.	895.00
Vase, Enameled Poppies, 4 1/4 In.	154.00
Vase, Gold Enameled Thistles, Textured Green, Tapered, 13 1/2 In.	165.00

MT. WASHINGTON Glass Works started in 1837 in South Boston, Massachusetts. In 1870 the company moved to New Bedford, Massachusetts. Many types of art glass were made there until 1894, when the company merged with Pairpoint Manufacturing Co. Amberina, Burmese, Crown Milano, Cut Glass, Peachblow, and Royal Flemish are each listed in their own category.

Beverage Set, Mother-Of-Pearl, Diamond-Quilted, Rose To White, 7 Piece	585.00
Bowl, Enameled Yellow Daisies, Blue To Pink, 2 3/8 In.	2530.00
Bride's Basket, Pigeon Blood, Silver Plated Holder	695.00
Bride's Bowl, Mother-Of-Pearl, Raspberry, Gold Design, Plated Holder, 13 In.	490.00
Bride's Bowl, Opalescent Pink To White, Diamond-Quilted, 8 x 4 1/2 In.	515.00
Bride's Bowl, Swirl, Pink Interior, Satin, Plated Holder, 9 x 11 In.	205.00
Decanter, Triple Miter Trellis, Handle, 12 In.	1095.00
Ewer, Herringbone, Clear Satin Handle, 7 In.	600.00
Flower Frog, Mushroom Shape, Wild Rose, Yellow To White, 3 1/2 x 5 In.	255.00
Lamp, Fluid, Burmese, Egyptian Design, Ibis Birds Oasis Scene, 20 x 10 In.	10350.00
Mustard, Pink Wild Roses, Yellow To White Ground, Handle, 2 3/4 In.	375.00
Relish, Pillar Ribbed, Enameled, Silver Top	135.00
Salt & Pepper, Egg Shape, Apple Blossom, 2 3/4 In.	200.00
Salt & Pepper, Fig Shape, Enameled Floral, 2 1/2 In.	258.00
Salt & Pepper, Little Apple, Blue & White Enameled Forget-Me-Nots	125.00
Saltshaker, Egg Shape, Blue Floral	55.00
Saltshaker, Floral, Soft Pink	55.00
Sugar & Creamer, Fern Design	290.00
Sugar & Creamer, Fern Design, Lusterless White, Silver Plated Mounting	275.00
Sugar Shaker, Egg Shape, Apple Blossom, Blue To Cream, Metal Cover, 4 In.	375.00
Sugar Shaker, Egg Shape, Blue & White Enameled Flowers, 4 3/4 In.	217.00
Sugar Shaker, Egg Shape, Enameled Flowers, White Shaded To Pink, 4 1/4 In.	715.00
Sugar Shaker, Egg Shape, Floral Branches, 4 1/2 In.	345.00
Sugar Shaker, Egg Shape, Pink Flowers, Leaves, Cream, 4 1/2 In.	450.00
Sugar Shaker, Fig Shape, Pansies On Cream Ground, 4 In.	1320.00
Sugar Shaker, Tomato Shape, Blue & Cream, Silver Top, 3 In.	460.00
Sugar Shaker, Tomato Shape, Enameled Flowers, 2 3/4 x 3 7/8 In.	440.00
Sugar Shaker, Tomato Shape, White & Blue Enamel Design, Silver Plated Top	460.00
Syrup, Enameled Design, Silver Plated Top, 5 1/2 In.	245.00
Syrup, Garden Of Violets, Opaque White, 7 1/2 In.	1250.00
Toothpick, Diamond-Quilted, Fuchsia, 2 1/2 In.	285.00
Toothpick, Parallel Greek Key, Enameled Daisies, 2 3/4 In.	715.00
Vase, Allover Coraline Wheat, Blue, 12 In.	1250.00
Vase, Allover Violet Design, Satin, 2 Leaf Handles, 6 In.	575.00
Vase, Colonial Ware, Raised Gold Scrolls, Enameled Floral, Leaf Handles, 9 1/2 In.	975.00
Vase, Egyptian, Ethnic Costumed Man With Camel, Gilt Borders, 12 In.	6900.00
Vase, Lava, 6 3/8 In.	35.00
Vase, Mother-Of-Pearl, Diamond-Quilted, Ruffled Edge, Camphor Rim, 9 1/2 In.	230.00
Vase, Mother-Of-Pearl, Herringbone, Tricornered, 8 x 5 In.	650.00
Vase, Roses & Forget-Me-Nots, Entwining Flowers, 8 In.	1250.00
Vase, Swirl Ribbed, White Satin, Cylinder, 17 1/2 In.	395.00

MULBERRY ware was made in the Staffordshire district of England from about 1850 to 1860. The dishes were decorated with a reddish brown transfer design, now called *mulberry*. Many of the patterns are similar to those used for flow blue and other Staffordshire transfer wares.

Bowl, Bird, Flowers, Scalloped Border, Ashworth, 9 3/4 In.	35.00

Bowl, Cover, Dresden, Challinor 80.00
Creamer, Corean 225.00
Creamer, Cyprus, Davenport, 5 1/4 In. 100.00
Cup, Rose, Handleless, Challinor 10.00
Cup & Saucer, Corean, Handleless, Podmore, Walker 120.00
Cup & Saucer, Handle, Ning Po 45.00
Cup & Saucer, Washington Vase 110.00
Cup & Saucer, Whampoa 45.00
Gravy Boat, Corean, Podmore, Walker, 4 3/4 In. 55.00
Pitcher, Calcutta, Large 145.00
Pitcher, Corean, Podmore, Walker, 8 1/2 In. 130.00
Pitcher, Corean, Podmore, Walker, 11 In. 200.00
Pitcher, Cyprus, Davenport, 8 3/4 In. 65.00
Plate, Corean, 7 3/4 In. 45.00
Plate, Corean, 10 1/2 In. 65.00
Plate, Pelew, Rectangular, Challinor, 9 1/4 x 6 3/4 In. 145.00
Platter, Abbey, W. Adams & Sons, 12 1/2 In. 185.00
Platter, Antiquarian, Pink Transfer, Staffordshire, 17 x 14 In. 295.00
Platter, Caledonia, Adams, 19 1/2 In. 770.00
Platter, Chinese Fountains, 13 1/4 x 11 3/4 In. 242.00
Platter, Corean, 9 7/8 x 7 1/4 In. 90.00
Platter, Corean, Podmore, Walker, 15 3/4 In. ....165.00 to 245.00
Platter, Cyprus, Davenport, 16 x 12 1/4 In. 155.00
Platter, Cyprus, Davenport, 20 1/4 x 15 3/4 In. 255.00
Platter, Drainer, Ribbons & Roses, 13 5/8 In. 265.00
Platter, Jeddo, 15 3/4 In. 225.00
Posset Cup, Corean 125.00
Posset Cup, Jeddo, Adams, 3 3/4 In. 35.00
Sugar, Child's, Berries & Vine, Charles Meigh 55.00
Sugar, Child's, Berries & Vine, Gold Trim, Charles Meigh 80.00
Sugar, Corean, Gothic Shape, Podmore, Walker, 7 3/4 In. 120.00
Sugar, Corean, Lion Head Handles, Podmore, Walker 145.00
Sugar, Cover, Corean, Lion Head Handles, Podmore, Walker, 6 1/2 In. 255.00
Sugar, Cover, Cyprus, 8 Sides, Handle 110.00
Teapot, Corean, 6 Sides, Podmore, Walker 330.00
Teapot, Corean, Podmore, Walker 65.00
Teapot, Cyprus, Gothic Shape, Davenport, 10 In. 20.00
Teapot, Rhone Scenery, T. & J. Mayer, 9 In. 295.00
Teapot, Stylized Floral Design, Magenta, White, Staffordshire, 11 1/2 In. ... 155.00
Tureen, Pink & White, Field Dove Cover, Base Nest Shape, Staffordshire, 8 1/2 In. 1840.00
Tureen, Soup, Corean, 8 Sides, Clemenson, 12 In. 715.00
Tureen, Soup, U & C, Handle, 11 1/2 In. 165.00
Waste Bowl, Cyprus, Davenport, 5 3/4 x 3 In. ....100.00 to 130.00

MULLER FRERES, French for Muller Brothers, made cameo and other glass from about 1895 to 1933. Their factory was first located in Luneville, then in nearby Croismare, France. Pieces were usually marked with the company name.

Chandelier, Central Shade, Gray Glass, Brown, Wrought Iron, 1920, 32 In. 13800.00
Chandelier, Large Central Sphere, 6 Central Shades, 35 In. 1495.00
Lamp, Desk, Arctic Landscape, Opaque Mottled Peach, Conical Shade, 13 In. 5900.00
Lamp, Figural, Peacock, Strutting, Silver Foil Internal Inclusions, 1925, 13 In. 5175.00
Lamp, Leaves, Cobalt Blue, Orange, Tapered Shade, 18 3/4 In. 2875.00
Lamp, Poppy Blossoms, Leaves, Ocher Yellow, Blue, Wrought Iron, 14 In. 10925.00
Lamp, Stylized Hemisphere, Beadwork, Wrought Iron, Hammered, 74 In. 6900.00
Vase, Gold Inclusions, Yellow, Blue Ground, Wrought Iron Armature, 17 In. 2300.00
Vase, Landscape, Island, Mountains, Hut, Cameo, 12 In. 2875.00
Vase, Landscape, River, Leafy Trees, Orange, Brown, Cameo, 1900, 13 In. 3450.00
Vase, Landscape, Trees & Lake, Trumpet Shape, Pinched Neck, 11 In. 2310.00
Vase, Poppy Blossoms, Leaves, Yellow, Ocher, Blue, 1925, 18 In. 5462.00
Vase, Red Chrysanthemums, Acid-Textured Yellow, Red Ground, Cameo, 17 In. 1840.00
Vase, Red, Deep Blue, 9 In., Pair 374.00
Vase, Stylized Blossoms, Leaves, Gray, Turquoise, Deep Cobalt Blue, 11 In. 3450.00

MUNCIE Clay Products Company was established by Charles Benham in Muncie, Indiana, in 1922. The company made pottery for the florist and giftshop trade. The company closed by 1939. Pieces are marked with the name *Muncie* or just with a system of numbers and letters, like *1A*.

Muncie

Lamp Base, Matte Green, 10 In.	250.00
Vase, Black, Bulbous Base, 6 In.	68.00
Vase, Fan, Ruba Rombic, Green Drip Over Lavender, 6 In.	550.00
Vase, Orange Peel Glaze, 6 In.	90.00

MURANO, see Glass-Venetian category.

MUSIC boxes and musical instruments are listed here. Phonograph records, jukeboxes, phonographs, and sheet music are listed in other categories in this book.

Accordion, Hohner, 1950	300.00
Autoharp, 12 Bars, Tuning Wrench, Picks, Oscar Schmidt, 21 3/4 x 11 3/4 In.	85.00
Autoharp, Zimmerman, Wooden Box, Sheet Music, 14 In.	125.00
Banjo, G.S. Locke, 5 Strings, Laminated Maple Neck, Dowel Stick, 1880, 10 15/16 In.	315.00
Banjo, George Dobson, 5 Strings, Rosewood Inlay, Walnut Neck, 1875, 11-In. Body	230.00
Banjo, James A. Morrison, 5 Strings, Laminated Maple Body, Mahogany Neck, 11 In.	460.00
Banjo, John C. Haynes Co., 5 Strings, Laminated Maple Neck, Body, Boston, 9 7/8 In.	150.00
Banjo, Ludwig, Stratford, No. 8650, Pearl Inlay, 1931, Case, 10 3/4-In. Body	460.00
Banjo, Tenor, Epiphone, Laminated Walnut Neck, Pearl Inlay, N.Y., 1927, 11-In. Body	690.00
Banjo, Thompson & Odell, 5 Strings, Laminated Mahogany Neck, 1885, 10-In. Body	200.00
Banjo, Vega, Model Vegavox II, Laminated Maple, 1932, Case, 10 7/8-In. Body	1380.00
Banjo-Mandolin, Tieri, Spruce Wood, Label, Case, 10-In. Body	86.00
Bassoon, Antler & Bone Mouthpiece, Leather Covered Body, Russia	3520.00
Bow, Violin, Albert Nurnberger, Ebony Frog With Parisian Eye, Silver Adjuster	1090.00
Bow, Violin, Albert Nurnberger, Ebony Frog, Nickel Adjuster, Silver Mounted	805.00
Bow, Violin, Chadwick, Ebony Frog With Pearl Eye, Round Stick, Nickel Mounted	85.00
Bow, Violin, Dodd, Ebony Frog, Nickel, Ebony Adjuster, Nickel Mounted	115.00
Bow, Violin, E. Sartory, Ebony Frog With Parisian Eye, Silver Adjuster, France	2645.00
Bow, Violin, Ebony Frog With Pearl Eye, Silver & Ebony Adjuster, France	2070.00
Bow, Violin, Emile A. Ouchard, Ebony Frog With Parisian Eye, Silver Mounted	6035.00
Bow, Violin, Frank J. Callier, Ebony Frog, Silver Adjuster, Tinsel Wrap	345.00
Bow, Violin, Jacques Francais, Ebony Frog With Pearl Eye, Silver, Ebony Adjuster	980.00
Bow, Violin, Joseph Arthur Vigneron, Ebony Frog With Pearl Eye, France	2415.00
Bow, Violin, Leipzig School, Ebony Frog With Pearl Eye, Tinsel Wrap	2070.00
Bow, Violin, Leon Pique, Ebony Frog, Silver & Ebony Adjuster, Tinsel Wrap	575.00
Bow, Violin, Marc Laberte, Ebony Frog With Parisian Eye, Nickel Mounted, France	260.00
Bow, Violin, Marcel Lapierre, Ebony Frog With Parisian Eye, Octagonal Stick, France	1265.00
Bow, Violin, Victor S. Fletcher, Ebony Frog With Pearl Eye, Silver Mounted, N.Y.	430.00
Bow, Violin, Wm. E. Hill & Sons, Ebony Frog With Pearl Eye, Silver Adjuster	1610.00
Bow, Violin, Wm. E. Hill & Sons, Ebony Frog, Silver Adjuster, England	1380.00
Bow, Violin, Wm. E. Hill & Sons, Ivory Frog With Parisian Eye, Octagonal Stick	2530.00
Bow, Violoncello, Ebony Frog With Pearl Eye, Silver & Ebony Adjuster, Silver Mounted	635.00
Bow, Violoncello, Ebony Frog With Pearl Eye, Silver Adjuster, 1840	1610.00
Bow, Violoncello, Roger Gerome, Ebony Frog With Parisian Eye, Silver Mounted	1725.00
Box, 12 Tunes, Walnut Case, 20 1/2 x 9 In.	1150.00
Box, A. Maliginon, Cylinder, Inlaid Rosewood, 8 Tunes, Label, 20 1/4 x 6 1/2 In.	1900.00
Box, Baker-Troll, 8 Tune Card, Switzerland, 18 1/4 In.	1150.00
Box, Bells In Vue, 10 Tunes, Mahogany Veneer Case, Clock In Crest, 25 1/2 In.	2860.00
Box, Birdcage, Singing Bird, Automaton, Brass, 11 In.	290.00
Box, Cylinder, Inlaid Rosewood, 8 Tunes, Label, Switzerland, 20 x 9 1/4 In.	1035.00
Box, Excelsior, Interchangeable Cylinder, 6 Tunes, Tune Card, Crank Wind, 23 In.	1725.00
Box, Grand Piano, Speidel Wristwatch Co., Wooden, 10 x 10 x 6 In.	25.00
Box, Inlaid Rosewood, Flowers, 8 Classical Songs, France, c.1860, 24 x 10 x 10 In.	2500.00
Box, Jacot, 10 Tunes, Bracket Feet, Switzerland, c.1875, 7 7/8 x 9 5/8 x 21 In.	1850.00
Box, Kalliope, 10 Bells, 18 In.	7800.00
Box, Mermod Freres, Mira, Walnut, 20 Metal Discs	1925.00
Box, Mermod Freres, Stella, Mahogany, Step Top, 12 Records, 12 x 19 x 25 In.	2760.00
Box, Nicole Freres, 10 1/4 Inch Cylinder, 6 Tunes, Tune Sheet, Key Wind, 18 In.	1035.00

Box, Polyphon, 13 Discs, Coin Operated 6600.00
Box, Polyphon, Mahogany, Upper Section Above Gadroon Frieze, 13 1/4-In. Disc 2300.00
Box, Regina, 11-In. Disc, Single Comb, Carved Case, 15 In. 1840.00
Box, Regina, Spiral Turned Columns, Shell, Scroll Top, Oak Case, Cabriole Legs, 67 In. . 21850.00
Box, Regina, Walnut, 9 Discs, Floral Inlaid Top, 21 x 18 1/2 In. 2990.00
Box, Rosewood Case, Inlaid Musical Instruments, Stringing, 10 Tunes 990.00
Box, Singing Bird, Automaton, 3 Feathered Birds, Birdcage, Brass, 10 x 21 In. 3960.00
Box, Singing Bird, Automaton, Molded Foliage, Birdcage, Gilt Metal, France, 11 In. 517.00
Box, Singing Bird, Bird Moves & Sings, Birdcage, Germany, 11 In. 690.00
Box, Singing Bird, Birdcage, Brass, Moves To Music 95.00
Box, Singing Bird, Birdcage, Brass, Victorian, 11 x 6 In. 750.00
Box, Singing Bird, Birdcage, Ornate Embossed Brass, Germany 675.00
Box, Singing Bird, Domed Pierced Top, Birdcage, Continental Silver, 8 1/2 In. 4025.00
Box, Singing Bird, Feathered, Birdcage, Brass, Victorian, 12 x 6 1/2 In. 450.00
Box, Sublime Harmonie & Orpheus, Oak Case, 3 Cylinders, 1885-1890, 20 1/2 In. 5225.00
Box, Sublime Harmonie, Oak Case, Metal Ornaments, 2 Cylinders, 30 1/2 In. 2750.00
Box, Swiss, Victorian, Interchangeable Cylinder 6000.00
Box, Symphonion, Label, Germany, 8 Discs, 9 1/2 x 14 1/4 In. 1375.00
Box, Teddy Bear, White Mohair, Stuffed, Missing Eyes, 1920s, 12 In. 825.00
Box, Thorens, 6 Classical Tunes, Cylinder, 5 x 9 In. 650.00
Check, Enrico Caruso, Mishkin Photograph, Signed, 1913 .... 625.00
Clarinet, Signet, Selmer, Case 425.00
Concertina, Globe, 21 Key, Case, c.1930 .... 500.00
Dulcimer, Hammer, Mahogany, 19th Century, 54 x 32 In. 275.00
Dulcimer, Stylized Urn With Flowers, Blue Velvet, Black Painted Case, 14 x 22 In. 560.00
Flute, W. Schaper, Ivory Fittings, Pin Mounted Keys 525.00
Guitar, C.F. Martin, Inlaid Rosewood Veneer, Spruce Top, Pearl Inlay, 1865, 18 In. 1610.00
Guitar, C.F. Martin, Mahogany, Faux Tortoiseshell, Spruce Top, 1936, 16 x 15 In. 6210.00
Guitar, C.F. Martin, Mahogany, Spruce Top, Pearl Position Dots, 1944, 16 In. 2300.00
Guitar, C.F. Martin, Rosewood Back, Herringbone Center Strip, Cedar Neck, 12 In. 1495.00
Guitar, C.F. Martin, Rosewood Veneer, Spruce Top, Pearl, Ivory, 1904, 19 x 14 In. 5750.00
Guitar, C.F. Martin, Rosewood, Spruce Top, Pearl, Inlay, Ivory, 1927 .... 16100.00
Guitar, Elmer Stromberg, Arch Top, Maple Sides & Back, Sunburst Finish, 1953 .... 18400.00
Guitar, Gibson Epiphone, Signed By B.B. King, On Body Of Instrument 1035.00
Guitar, Gibson, Super 400 CESN, 1991 .... 9000.00
Guitar, J. Berwind, Rosewood Veneer, Spruce Top, Cedar Neck, 1880, 12 7/8 In. 1380.00
Guitar, National Style 2, Resonator, Rose Floral Design, Pearl Eyes, 1928, 14 3/16 In. ... 2300.00
Guitar, National Style 3, Resonator, Lily Of The Valley Design, Pearl Inlay, 1928, 14 In. . 3450.00
Guitar, Stella, Sunburst Finish, Case, 1940s, 36 1/4 In. 95.00
Guitar, Vega Co., Broad Curl Sides, Mahogany Neck, Pearl Inlay, 1935, 17 3/16 In. 2990.00
Harmonica, Chromonica, No. 64, Hohner, Germany, 7 x 2 In. 75.00
Harmonica, Hohner, Exposition Band, 1915, Box, 4 In. 100.00
Harmonica, Weiss, With Bell, 1891, 5 x 1 In. 44.00
Harmonicon, Francis Hopkinson Smith, 24 Graduated Glasses, 1826, 31 x 38 x 22 In. ... 4830.00
Hurdy-Gurdy, A. Martin, Madrid, 23 1/2 In. 3500.00
Mandolin, C.F. Martin & Co., Rosewood, Ebony Fingerboard, Case, 1914, 12 In. 400.00
Mandolin, Gibson Style A-1, Spruce, Mahogany Neck, Case, 1917, 13 3/4 In. 545.00
Mandolin, Roger H. Hildreth, '30, Hanover, N.H., 1930s 140.00
Melodeon, Carhart & Needham, Ivory & Ebony Keyboard, Rosewood Veneer, 28 In. 165.00
Melodeon, Carhart & Needham, Rosewood, Fold-Up Scrolled Legs 330.00
Melodeon, Victorian, Rosewood 395.00
Metronome, Mahogany, Brass Label For Maelzel Paquet, c.1900, 8 1/2 In. 70.00
Nickelodeon, J.P. Seeburg Piano Co., Chicago, Leaded Glass Front, 64 x 58 In. 2300.00
Nickelodeon, Link, Art Glass Front Panels, Coin-Operated, NY, 77 x 64 In. 4025.00
Nickelodeon, Link, Style C, Coin-Operated Corner Lamps, 1915-1920 .... 9500.00
Nickelodeon, Nelson-Wiggen, Cabinet Style, Art Glass Panels, Xylophone & Bells 7500.00
Nickelodeon, Regal, 6 Tunes, 44 Note, Stained Glass 4800.00
Nickelodeon, Seeburg, A Style, Art & Clear Glass, Mandolin, Restored 7500.00
Nickelodeon, Wurlitzer, Style I, Oak, 3 Art Glass Panels 3500.00
Organ, Barrel, Chamber, Mahogany, Josephus Fuzelli, London, 1799, 63 1/4 In. ..... *Illus* 5925.00
Organ, Barrel, Monkey, 39 Keys 5000.00
Organ, Barrel, Monkey, Yager & Brummer, 2 Stops, 8 Rolls 7300.00
Organ, Belly, Folding Stand, 3 Rolls 5400.00

Music, Organ, Barrel,
Chamber, Mahogany,
Josephus Fuzelli, London,
1799, 63 1/4 In.

**Be very careful if you try to oil
the mechanism of a music box.
Too much oil will cause damage.**

**Piano keys can be cleaned
with yogurt.**

Organ, Hammond, 2 Keyboards, Rhythm, 1950	1500.00
Organ, Packard, Fold-Down Candleholders, Fort Wayne Argan Co., 1890s, 53 x 46 In.	750.00
Organ, Pump, Child's, 21 Pipes, Stool, 23 x 30 1/2 x 11 3/4 In.	650.00
Organ, Pump, Cornwall & Co., Stool, 81 x 53 In.	1500.00
Organ, Pump, Estey, c.1935, Miniature	300.00
Organ, Pump, Mason & Hamlin, 5 Stop, Early 1900s, 41 In.	1200.00
Organ, Pump, Oak, Hand Rubbed Oil Finish, Beveled Mirror, 80 In.	1800.00
Organette, Japanned Ebony, Mother-Of-Pearl Keys, Design On Bellows, 12 1/8 In.	160.00
Organette, Mahogany & Bird's-Eye Maple, Ebony Keys, Green Bellows, 11 In.	190.00
Organette, Mahogany, Mother-Of-Pearl Keys, Brass Fittings, Bellows, 9 1/2 In.	180.00
Phonograph, Victor, Music Cabinet, Oak Veneer, Oak Case, 34 1/2 x 19 1/2 In.	275.00
Piano, Baby Grand, Chickering & Sons, Walnut, 1958	1955.00
Piano, Baby Grand, Decker Bros., Cabriole Legs, 1863	1000.00
Piano, Baby Grand, Monington & Weston, Black Lacquer Bench, White Trim, 39 In.	20700.00
Piano, Baby Grand, Steinway, Walnut, Plain Case, Cabriole Legs, Bench, 70 In.	9200.00
Piano, Coin-Operated, Seeburg, Beveled Glass Front	4500.00
Piano, Coin-Operated, Wurlitzer, Model IX, Egyptian Design Case, Roll Changer	2500.00
Piano, Grand, Bosendorfer, Ivory Keys, 90 In.	4800.00
Piano, Grand, Chickering, Mahogany, Tapered Square Legs, Brass Castors, 66 In.	2300.00
Piano, Grand, Hazelton Brothers, Rosewood, Square	2500.00
Piano, Grand, John Broadwood & Sons, Rosewood, Faceted Tapered Legs, 1884	1725.00
Piano, Grand, John Broadwood & Sons, Rosewood, Signed, c.1850, 82 1/2 In.	3520.00
Piano, Grand, Keppler, Burl Walnut, c.1880, 37 x 54 1/4 x 74 In.	3520.00
Piano, Grand, Kimball, Mahogany, 57 In.	865.00
Piano, Grand, Marshall & Wendell, Square Back, 1885	3500.00
Piano, Grand, Steinway & Sons, Oak	10400.00
Piano, Grand, Steinway, Model A, Mahogany, 1912	13000.00
Piano, Player, Aeolian, Upright, Mahogany, Bench & Rolls	8500.00
Piano, Player, Aeolian, Upright, Walnut, Bench, Restored, 1920s	3500.00
Piano, Player, Grand, Upright, Windsor, 10 Rolls, 1912	2300.00
Piano, Player, Grand, William Knabe, Mahogany, Ivory Keys, Bench, 31 x 68 In.	1840.00
Piano, Player, Lyon & Healy, Electrified, 30 Rolls	3000.00
Piano, Player, Upright, Stroud	1500.00
Piano, Player, Walnut, Bench, 100 Rolls	3500.00
Piano, Player, Waltham, New Mechanism & Keys, 1921	6000.00
Piano, Reproducing, Baby Grand, Chickering, Mahogany, Ampico, 210 Rolls, Bench	5225.00
Piano, Reproducing, Grand, Chickering, Ampico Mechanism, 68 In. ....6800.00 to	7500.00
Piano, Reproducing, Grand, Welte-Mignon Mechanism, Mahogany, Bench	8500.00
Piano, Reproducing, Pianola, George Steck, Mahogany, Duo Art, Bench, 54 In.	345.00
Piano, Reproducing, Upright, Ampico Mechanism, Burled Walnut Case	4500.00
Piano, Reproducing, Upright, Steinway, Duo Art, Mahogany, Steamboat Ump, 1914	2000.00
Piano, Upright, Steinway, Carved Rosewood, Matching Bench	7500.00
Pianoforte, H. & W. Gelb, 7 Rope Twist Legs, Mahogany Veneer, 34 3/4 x 67 1/2 In.	577.00
Pianoforte, Thomas Geib, Rosewood, Gilt Metal Banded, Stencil, 1826, 35 x 67 In.	3450.00
Saxophone, King Cleveland G13, Polished Brass, King Musical Instruments, Case	110.00
Saxophone, Silvertone, C.G. Conn	140.00
Score, Gregorian Chants, Spanish, Frame, c.1750	575.00
Stand, Oak & Iron, Adjustable Height, c.1900, 39 1/2 In.	275.00

Trumpet, Brass, Nickel Mouthpiece, Velvet-Lined Case, Grand Rapids 60.00
Ukulele, Duke Kahanamoku, Hawaii 125.00
Ukulele, Martin, Tenor, 1930s 550.00
Viola, Broad Curl, Scroll, Orange, Brown Finish, England, 1900, 16 7/16 In. 5750.00
Viola, Jean Coplere, Medium Curl, Scroll, Fine To Medium Grain, Red Finish, 1969 ..... 1495.00
Viola, Norman Pickering, Narrow Curl, Scroll, Fine Grain, Orange, Brown Finish, 1953 .. 805.00
Viola, Wm. Lewis & Son, Light Narrow Curl, Medium Grain, Gold, Red Finish, 1930 ... 635.00
Violin, Artistique & Leblanc, Strong Irregular Curl, Orange Finish, Case, 2 Bows 1380.00
Violin, Carlo Gebonzi, Bow, Case, 23 1/2 In. 1100.00
Violin, E. Reinhold Schmidt, Mother-Of-Pearl Bow & Case, Copy Of Josef Guanerius ... 305.00
Violin, Ernst Heinrich Roth, Narrow Curl, Orange Finish, Bow, Case, 1929, 14 3/16 In. .. 2415.00
Violin, Gaetano Sgarabotto, Light Medium Curl, Medium Grain, Red Finish, 14 In. 26450.00
Violin, George Craske, Narrow Curl, Red Brown Finish, England, 13 13/16 In. 5460.00
Violin, Henry Richard Knopf, Medium Curl, Orange Red Finish, N.Y., 1917, 14 1/16 In. .. 2875.00
Violin, J.B. Guadagnini, Medium Curl, Orange, Brown Finish, Vienna, 1850, 14 In. 3450.00
Violin, John Friedrich, Strong Narrow Curl, Red Finish, N.Y., 1928, 13 15/16 In. 2300.00
Violin, Plinio Michetti, Narrow Curl, Orange Red Top Finish, Italy, 1926, 13 13/16 In. ... 7475.00
Violin, Shroetor, Case & Bow 170.00
Violin, Vincent Panormo Rue, Irregular Narrow Curl, Gold Brown Patina, 1800, 14 In. ... 5400.00
Zither, E. Link, Silver & Ivory Mounted, Case, Manual 193.00

MUSTACHE CUPS were popular from 1850 to 1900 when the large, flowing mustache was in style. A ledge of china or silver held the hair out of the liquid in the cup. This kept the mustache tidy and also kept the mustache wax from melting. Left-handed mustache cups are rare but are being reproduced.

Embossed Floral, Pink & Gold Luster, Saucer, Germany, 3 1/2 In. 50.00
UN, Saucer, Haviland 100.00

MZ AUSTRIA is the wording on a mark used by Moritz Zdekauer on porcelains made at his works in Altrolau, Austria, from 1884 to 1909. The mark was changed to MZ Altrolau in 1909, when the firm was purchased by C.M. Hutschenreuther. The firm operated under the name Altrolau Porcelain Factories from 1909 to 1945. It was nationalized after World War II. The pieces were decorated with lavish floral patterns and overglaze gold decoration. Full sets of dishes were made as well as vases, toilet sets, and other wares.

Cake Plate, Grapes, 10 In. 50.00
Hair Receiver, Footed, Pink Flowers, Green Leaves, Gold Trim, 3 3/4 x 4 3/4 In. 79.00
Plate, Pink Flowers, Scalloped Rim, Marked Habsburg China Norma, 8 3/4 In. 26.00
Salt, Basket, Blue Flowers, Gold Trim, Scalloped Rim, Pierced Handles, 3 In. 37.00

NAILSEA glass was made in the Bristol district in England from 1788 to 1873. It was made by many different factories, not just the Nailsea Glass House. Many pieces were made with loopings of either white or colored glass as decoration.

Creamer, Aqua, White & Red Spatter, 4 In. 110.00
Flask, Clear, Pink & White Loopings, 8 3/4 In. 220.00
Flask, Clear, Red Looping & White Herringbone, Sheared Lip, Pontil, 8 5/8 In. 240.00
Flask, Clear, White Looping, Sheared Lip, Pontil, 8 In. 120.00
Flask, Clear, White Looping, Tooled Lip, Pontil, 6 1/4 In. 85.00
Flask, Gemel, Clear, White Looping, Sheared Lip, Pontil, 7 7/8 In. 175.00
Flask, Gemel, Milk Glass, Red Looping, Sheared Lips, Pontil, Applied Foot, 8 3/4 In. 210.00
Flask, Milk Glass, Red Herringbone, Tooled Lip, Pontil, 8 In. 230.00
Flask, Olive Green, White Looping, Sheared Lip, Pontil, 6 1/2 In. 440.00
Flask, Opalescent Cranberry, White Swirls, Tooled Lip, Pontil, 7 3/8 In. 415.00
Flask, Red, Blue & White Loopings, 8 3/4 In. 192.00
Flask, White & Pink Loopings, 7 3/4 In. 192.00
Lamp, Fairy, Clear Base, 5 In. 295.00
Rolling Pin, Clear, Cobalt Looping, Plaster Inside, Sheared & Tooled Ends, 13 1/4 In. ... 360.00
Rolling Pin, Clear, Pink & White Loopings, Sheared Ends, 16 1/4 In. 220.00
Rolling Pin, Clear, White & Red Loopings, Sheared Ends, 13 In. 155.00
Rolling Pin, Red, White & Blue Loopings 255.00

NAKARA is a trade name for a white glassware made about 1900 by the
C. F. Monroe Company of Meriden, Connecticut. It was decorated in
pastel colors. The glass was very similar to another glass made by the
company called *Wave Crest*. The company closed in 1916. Boxes for
use on a dressing table are the most commonly found Nakara pieces.
The mark is not found on every piece.

NAKARA

Box, Lining In Cover, Shaped Shield, Woman's Portrait, Signed, 3 x 5 In. 900.00
Box, Opaque Milk Glass, 2 Transfer Cherubs On Lid, Hinged Collar, 2 1/2 x 3 3/4 In. . . . 435.00

NANKING is a type of blue-and-white porcelain made in Canton, China,
since the late eighteenth century. It is very similar to Canton, which is
listed under its own name in this book. Both Nanking and Canton are
part of a larger group now called *Chinese Export* porcelain. Nanking
has a spear-and-post border and may have gold decoration.

Coffeepot, Fruit Finial, Twined Handle, Gold Trim, 9 1/8 In. 1150.00
Dish, 6 In., Pair 86.00
Dish, Cover, Twined Handles, Pinecone Finial, 11 1/8 In. 820.00
Dish, Twined Handles With Berries, 12 3/4 In. 210.00
Plate, Soup, Chinese Pavilions, 1820, 9 5/8 In., Pair 242.00
Plate, Warming 300.00
Platter, 16 In. 400.00
Platter, 18 In. 400.00
Platter, Chinese Pavilions, Oblong, c.1810, 14 1/2 In. 137.00
Platter, Drainer, Pagodas, Water Scenes In Center, Lattice Work Borders, 17 In. 805.00
Platter, Orange Peel Glaze, 13 7/8 In. 845.00
Tea Canister, Circular Cover, Landscape, Water Setting, Animals, Boats, 9 3/4 In. 860.00
Tureen, Cover, Bombe Form, Pagodas, Water Scene, Handles, 13 In. 1725.00
Tureen, Cover, Pagodas, Water Scene, 2-Branch Form Handles, 13 In. 890.00
Warming Dish, Pagodas, Water Scenes, 10 In. 290.00
Warming Dish, Pagodas, Water Scenes, 10 In., Pair 690.00

NAPKIN RINGS were in fashion from 1869 to about 1900. They were
made of silver, porcelain, wood, and other materials. They are still
being made today. The most popular rings with collectors are the silver plated figural examples. Small, realistic figures were made to hold
the ring. Good and poor reproductions of the more expensive rings are
now being made and collectors must be very careful.

Enamel, Triangular, 2 1/4 In., 6 Piece 860.00
Figural, 2 Rose Buds On Branches, Silver Plate 85.00
Figural, Bird On Leaf, Silver Plated, Meriden Co., 3 1/4 In. 300.00
Figural, Boy & Dog, Silver Plate, Meriden 245.00
Figural, Boy Pulling Sled, Silver Plate 1200.00
Figural, Boy, Rolling Hoop, Silver Plate 100.00
Figural, Cherries, Silver Plate 175.00
Figural, Cherub, Holding Bud Vase, Silver Plate 695.00
Figural, Chick, Eggshell, Derby 99.00
Figural, Dog & Bird, Silver Plate, Aurora 185.00
Figural, Girl In Bonnet, Talking To Dog, Silver Plate 1250.00
Figural, Horse Drawn Sleigh, Red Ground, Sterling, Russia, 2 1/8 In. 302.00
Figural, Ladder Back Chair, Victorian, Silver Plate, 4 1/2 In. 80.00
Figural, Lion, Silver Plate 195.00
Figural, Mother & Daddy, Octagonal, Pair 150.00
Figural, Squirrel, Silver Plate 150.00
Fruit & Leaf Design, Hartford Silver Co., Silver Plate, Victorian, Pair 110.00
Sterling Silver, Monogram, Kalo Shop, Chicago, 3 1/4 In., Pair 75.00
Sterling Silver, Scotland, Case, Brook & Son, 1883, Pair 950.00

NASH glass was made in Corona, New York, from about 1928 to 1931.
A. Douglas Nash bought the Corona glassworks from Louis C. Tiffany
in 1928 and founded the A. Douglas Nash Corporation with support
from his father, Arthur J. Nash. Arthur had worked at the Webb factory
in England and for the Tiffany Glassworks in Corona.

NASH

Bowl, Controlled Bubbles Interior, Pale Green Powders, Marked, Libby, 9 In. 86.00

Dish, Sherbet, Pale Amethyst, Amber, 2 3/8 In. 11.00
Vase, Amber, Pink & Blue Iridescent, Tapering, Ovoid, Signed, 1928, 4 In., Pair 287.00
Vase, Chintz, Interior Orange Stripes, Yellow Amber Pulled Threading 5 1/4 In. 195.00
Vase, Gold Stripes, Blue, Green, 8 In. 650.00
Vase, Green Design, Blue Pinstripes, 5 1/2 In. 170.00
Vase, Trumpet, Zipper, Seafoam Green Design, 12 In. 345.00

NAUTICAL antiques are listed in this category. Any of the many objects that were made or used by the seafaring trade, including ship parts, models, and tools, are included. Other pieces may be found listed under Scrimshaw.

Ax, Boarding, Long Handle, 26 1/2 In. 630.00
Baggage Sticker, United States Lines, Ship Design, Red, White & Blue, 1950, 3 In. 8.00
Bandanna, Naval Battle, War Against Britain, June 18, 1812, Frame, 21 x 24 In. 4250.00
Bell, Polished Metal, Bracket, 9 In. 250.00
Binnacle, Brass, Iron Compensating Balls, Wooden Base, Illuminated, 49 x 25 In. 1925.00
Binnacle, Marine, Brass, Gimbaled Compass, 43 1/2 In. 385.00
Block, Double, Whale Ivory, 1870s, 1 1/4 x 2 3/4 In. 3450.00
Boat, Tinplate, Soldered Joints, Yellow, Blue, Early 20th Century, 14 In. 245.00
Box, Ditty, Fitted Mahogany Lid, 4 Fingers Bottom, 2 5/8 x 7 5/8 In. 4312.00
Box, Document, Whaleship Midas, Dovetail Construction, 9 1/2 x 16 In. 605.00
Box, Oak, Polychrome Sailors' Compasses All Sides, 6 1/2 In. 150.00
Broom, Baleen Bristles, Turned Bone Handle, 15 In. 1380.00
Bucket, Iron Bound, Whalebone Pins, 11 x 12 1/2 In. 495.00
Caliper, Brass, Stylus Holder, Undivided Arc, 20 1/2 In. 115.00
Candle Lamp, Brass, Gimbaled, Dolphin Support 176.00
Chest, Camphor Wood, Hinged Lid, Till, 1 Drawer, 17 x 39 In. 2070.00
Chest, Chart, Oak & Pine, Door At Both Ends, Charts, 19th Century, 42 x 18 x 17 In. 357.00
Chest, Lift Top, Dovetailed, Canted Front, Back, Ditty Box Inside, 38 x 19 x 17 In. 286.00
Chest, Lift Top, Seaman's, 42 x 18 x 17 In. 121.00
Chest, Rose Inlay Of Sailor's Compass, Divided Inner Chambers, 1870s 1175.00
Chest, Sea, Lift Top, 4-Masted Ship Painting On Interior Lid, Gray, 33 In. 302.00
Chest, Seaman's, Hinged Top, Rope Handles, 19th Century, 13 x 62 In. 1150.00
Chronometer, Hamilton, Model 22, 21 Jewel Movement, Mahogany Case, 6 In. 400.00
Chronometer, Hamilton, Silver Dial, Roman Numerals, Mahogany Case, 7 1/2 In. 145.00
Chronometer, Marine, 2-Day, Silver Dial, Black Roman Numerals 2300.00
Chronometer, Thomas Mercer, Marine, 2-Day, Silver Matte Dial, Roman Numerals 1495.00
Chronometer, Thomas Mercer, Silver Matte Dial, 2-Tier Mahogany Box, 1963, 8 In. 2875.00
Chronometer, Ulysse Nardin, 2 Day, Up-Down Indicator, 3-Tier Box, Signed, 7 1/2 In. .. 2530.00
Chronometer, Ulysse Nardin, Gilt 2-Tier Movement, Brass Mounted Box, 1944, 7 In. ... 4310.00
Chronometer, Wempe, 2-Day Marine, Silver Matte Dial, 2-Tier Wood Box, 7 x 5 In. 1955.00
Clock, Marine, Chelsea Co., Nickel Plated, Black Face, Windup, Boston, 1917, 4 1/4 In. .. 130.00
Clock, Marine, Chelsea, Bronze, Wheel Shape, Bell, 17 1/2 x 5 1/2 In. 1760.00
Clock, Marine, Whitfield & Hakes, Brass, Polished Steel, Key, Hull, 7 1/4 In. 275.00
Clock, Wall, Nickel Plated, Outside Bell, 11 In. 460.00
Clock, Waterbury Ship's Bell, No. 10, Silver Dial, Arabic Numerals, 1910, 8 1/4 In. 290.00
Compass, Boxed, Brass, 9 In. 175.00
Compass, Brinton, Marked, C.A.S., MKI 1862, Thos. J. Evans, Esq., London, 3 5/8 In. .. 175.00
Compass, C. Galbraith & Son, New York, Wooden Box, 2 1/2 In. 120.00
Compass, Dry, John J. Murray, 6 1/2 In. 385.00
Compass, Gimbal, Mahogany, 19th Century, 6 x 10 x 9 3/4 In. 365.00
Compass, Harris Co., Me., Monochrome Rose Brass Case, Gimbal, 8 1/2 In. 230.00
Compass, Marine, D. Baker, Melrose, Ma., Cased, 4 In. 100.00
Compass, Sighting, Stanley, London, Brass, c.1900 .... 165.00
Compass, Whaleboat, Chamfered Sliding Lid, Finger Holes, 5 1/2 x 7 In. 517.00
Deck Blanket, Steamship, Cunard, Blue, Red 75.00
Dinghy, Luan Plywood, Oak Stringers, Seth Persson Boatbuilding, 1968, 50 In. 1485.00
Diorama, Rescue At Sea, Atlantic Tramp Steamer, Case, 1920, 10 x 14 x 9 1/2 In. 1100.00
Dirk, British Naval, Ivory Handle, Double Edge Blade, Leather Scabbard, 1800s, 15 In. .. 440.00
Document, SS Harry Luckenbach, Steamship To Los Angeles Port, 1924, 8 x 14 In. 5.00
Epaulet Set, Eagle & Anchor, 19th Century, Case 220.00
Fid, Sailor's, Bone, Macrame Turk's Head Belt Sheath, 19th Century, 16 In. 400.00
Figurehead, Dark Haired Woman, Yellow Robes, Painted Support, c.1850, 12 In. 4600.00

Figurehead, Mermaid, Carved Scales, Flowing Hair, Arms Crossed, 18th Century, 32 In. .   5175.00
Figurehead, Woman, Standing, Arm Across Chest, Green Dress, 48 In. 13750.00
Flare Gun, Fox Gun Company, Brass 165.00
Fog Horn, Brass, 14 1/2 In. 100.00
Gun, Darting, Whaling Sunbeam, 2 Bomb Lances, 28 In., 5 Piece 3162.00
Gyroscope, Brass, Wooden Base, Gyro Sperry, 56 In. 550.00
Harpoon, Double Flue, Iron Shaft Marked L.B. & Co., 39 1/2 In. 1265.00
Harpoon, Iron, Hand Held Type, Macrame Handle, 9 In. 55.00
Harpoon, Whale, Double Flue, Wood Pole, Roping, 1852, 100 In. 5462.00
Instrument, Trim Gauge, No. 2, Brass Case, Boston, Mass., 6-In. Diam. 176.00
Jackknife, Sailor's, Whale Bone Handle, 19th Century, 5 1/2 In.   75.00
Lamp, Gimbal, P. & A. Mfg. Co., Conn., Brass, Smoke Shade, 9 In., Pair 285.00
Lamp, Lighthouse, Aluminum 395.00
Lamp, Lighthouse, Brass, c.1930 . . . .   450.00
Lamp, Marine, Blue Glass 475.00
Lamp, Pewter, Dunham & Sons, Whale Oil 517.00
Lantern, Brass, Port & Starboard, Bail Handle, Early 20th Century, 10 In., Pair 375.00
Lantern, H.M.S. Queen Mary, Red Ball Globe, 18 In. 345.00
Lantern, Marine, Perkins, Galvanized Steel & Brass, Spherical Globe, 14 1/2 In. 110.00
Lantern, Wilcox, Crittendan & Co., Brass, 360 Degree Lens, 10 In. 100.00
Life Ring, U.S. Navy, Guantanamo Bay, Cuba 20.00
Liquor Set, Captain's, Oak & Iron Bound Case, 10 1/2 x 15 x 11 In. 935.00
Log Box, Taffrail, Grain Painted, Red & Black, 10 x 10 3/8 x 30 1/4 In. 135.00
Menu, SS Lurline Matson Lines, Beachcomber Night Dinner, Nov. 28, 1966, 12 In. 14.00
Model, 2-Masted Schooner Polly, Billet Carving, 27 x 33 In. 605.00
Model, 3-Masted 22-Gun Warship, Carved & Painted, Primitive, 37 x 26 In. 245.00
Model, 3-Masted Augusta, Full Sail, Decoupage Ground, Shadowbox, 24 3/8 In. 575.00
Model, 3-Masted Clipper Ship, Fully Rigged, Black Hull, Cased, Late 1800s, 30 In. 1320.00
Model, 3-Masted Sailing Ship, Whalebone & Wood, 19th Century, 25 x 15 In. 1650.00
Model, 3-Masted, Full Sail, Shadowbox, 19th Century, 29 1/2 In. 632.00
Model, 3-Masted, Ivory, On Wooden Stand, 19th Century, 9 1/2 x 13 In. 1090.00
Model, 3-Masted, Rigging, Black Hull, Oval Wooden Stand, 27 x 34 In. 635.00
Model, America's Cup Yacht, America, Case, 31 x 12 In. 2310.00
Model, American Frigate, Essex, Case, 23 x 32 In. 1430.00
Model, American Steam Yacht, Corsair, Basswood Deck, Cabins, Case, 56 x 48 In. 275.00
Model, American Whaleship, Calendar, Whaleboats, Hatches, Cabin, 42 x 49 In. 2640.00
Model, Bark, Black & White Paint, 19 x 21 In. 275.00
Model, Boat, Turtle, Korean, Glass Case 8050.00
Model, Boston Clipper Ship, Flying Cloud, Boathouses, Hatchways, 45 x 58 In. 1430.00
Model, Brig, Venus, Plank On Frame, Case, 39 x 46 In. 1265.00
Model, British Man Of War, Half-Hull, Laminated, Jane On Hull, 2 x 27 In. 1375.00
Model, Carnegie, Wooden, Nonmagnetic Survey Ship, 50 x 69 In. 2200.00
Model, Chinese Junk, Wooden, 15 1/4 In. 60.00
Model, Clipper Ship, Ebony Case, Young America, 20th Century, 11 x 16 x 6 In. 1090.00
Model, Clipper Ship, Rigged With Canvas Sails, Painted Wood, 50 In. 1090.00
Model, Clipper Ship, Sovereign Of The Seas, Late 18th Century, 28 x 29 1/2 In. 305.00
Model, Clipper Ship, Wooden, 19th Century, 7 x 5 In. 465.00
Model, Constitution, 2 Sailors On Deck, Wood, Metal, Cloth & String, 25 1/2 In. 577.00
Model, Cruise Ship, Conti Di Savoia, Metal & Wood, 51 In. 800.00
Model, Cutty Sark, 3-Masted Tall Ship, 1869 Replica, Wooden 170.00
Model, Dolphin, Gilt Details, Late 19th Century, 72 x 54 In. 2800.00
Model, Dory, Dory Men, 26 1/3 In. 242.00
Model, Eastport Pinky, Deck House, Pump, Stovepipe, Mahogany Base, 22 x 17 In. 605.00
Model, Freighter, Cotolene, Green & Black, White Bridge, Cased, 36 x 12 x 22 In. 880.00
Model, Full-Hull, Flying Cloud, Mahogany Case, 24 x 36 In. 1035.00
Model, Full-Rigged, Wooden Sails, Hollow Carved, Early 20th Century, 32 x 40 In. 1100.00
Model, Galleon, 4-Masted, Wood, Sheet Metal & Canvas, 33 In.   110.00
Model, Half-Hull, Mounted, Schooner, Hustler, T.D. Conlon, Boston, 1889, 10 x 45 In. . .   468.00
Model, Half-Hull, Pilot Boat, America, Mounted, T.D. Conlon, Boston, 1896, 9 x 32 In. . .   495.00
Model, Half-Hull, Schooner, Actress, Mounted, T.D. Conlon, Boston, 1871, 11 x 44 In. . .   550.00
Model, Half-Hull, Yacht, Rainbow, America's Cup, Skylights, Brass Winches 440.00
Model, Half-Moon, Wooden, 28 x 24 In. 190.00
Model, Lightship, Nantucket, Wm. Hitchcock, Builder, Cased, 7 x 9 x 2 In. 825.00

Model, Monitor, Match Stick, Removable Gun Turret Top, 1870, 45 In. 245.00
Model, New Bedford Whaleboat, Sails & Equipment, 18 In. 2035.00
Model, Ohio Riverboat, Full-Hull, Paddlewheel, Lifeboats, People, c.1930, 50 In. 1250.00
Model, Opium Clipper, Rose, Swansea, Mass., 1836, 32 x 44 x 17 In. 1955.00
Model, Paddlewheel Steamboat, Mount Washington 1870.00
Model, Pond Boat, With Sails, England 1500.00
Model, Sailing, Fair Wind, Glass Case, Painted Back Scene, 1920s, 44 x 34 In. 2185.00
Model, Schooner, 2-Masted, Canvas Sails, Red & Black Paint, 18 In. 300.00
Model, Schooner, Builder's Laminated Half, 19th Century, 46 1/2 In. 2185.00
Model, Ship, Aquitania, In Light Bulb 550.00
Model, Ship, Half-Model, Black Ground, 19th Century, 10 x 49 In. 1320.00
Model, SS Carolina, Passenger Liner, Accompanied By 2 Tug Boats, 66 In. 515.00
Model, Steam Launch, Columbia, Mahogany Deck Cabin, Bronze Propeller, Rudder 1430.00
Model, Sterling Silver, Japanese War Ship, Wood Box, 12 5/8 x 10 In. 1035.00
Model, Towboat, Freedom, Wood, Metal, Glass, Glass Case, Stand, 29 In. 1725.00
Model, Tugboat, Steam, Brooklyn, Mahogany Wheelhouse, Cased, 13 x 25 x 5 In. 1650.00
Model, Tugboat, Steam, Hercules, Green, Maroon, Red Deckhouse, Cased, 6 x 12 x 3 In. . . 1045.00
Model, Tugboat, Wooden, 25 1/4 In. 140.00
Model, U.S. Constitution, Carved, Wooden, 20th Century, 34 x 38 In. 805.00
Model, Whaling, 3-Masted, Painted Black & White, Wooden Stand, 26 3/4 x 38 In. 1380.00
Model, Whaling, New Bedford, Rigged, Sails, Case, 18 In. 2035.00
Model, Whippet, Single Masted, Sailing, Fully Rigged, 25 3/4 x 20 1/4 In. 355.00
Needle Case, Bone & Rubber, Incised Handle, Third Quarter 19th Century, 3 1/8 In. 747.00
Oar, Corner-Tipped With Leather Grips, c.1920, Pair 75.00
Octant, Spencer Browning & Company, Ebony & Ivory, Brass Hardware 410.00
Quadrant, Spencer, Browning & Rust, Brass, Ebony, Ivory Scales 950.00
Sailboat, Pond, 62 x 48 In. 1840.00
Sailor's Valentine, Central Heart, Flowers & Geometric Shapes, Shells, 9 x 9 In. 1610.00
Sailor's Valentine, Double Octagonal Wooden Case, 9 x 18 In. 2310.00
Sailor's Valentine, For My Sister, Mollusk Shells, Octagonal Wooden Box, 9 1/4 In. 1265.00
Sailor's Valentine, Heart Shape Box, Pink Paper Lining, 7 1/2 x 5 1/4 In. 175.00
Sailor's Valentine, Heart, Forget-Me-Knot Other Side, 9 x 18 In. 2200.00
Sailor's Valentine, Love To The Receiver For The Giver, Shells, 1820s, 9 x 18 In. 2100.00
Sailor's Valentine, Octagonal Segmented Case, Exotic Shells, To One I Love, 9 x 9 In. . . . 2185.00
Sailor's Valentine, Pinwheel Design, Shells, 9 x 9 In. 747.00
Sailor's Valentine, Shellwork, Heart Shape, Glass Enclosed Diorama, 1895, 8 1/4 In. 1380.00
Sailor's Valentine, Star Design, Shells, 10 x 19 1/2 In. 3737.00
Sailor's Valentine, Yours Truly, Geometric & Floral Design, Shells, 9 x 9 In. 1725.00
Sea Bag, Knot Work Carrying Handle, Canvas, Hand Sewn, Turk's Head Slide 495.00
Sea Captain, Carved, Standing, Hat & Officer's Coat, New England, 19th C., 21 In. 728.00
Sea Chest, Hinged Cover, Portrait Of A Ship On Interior, 17 x 36 x 18 In. 690.00
Searchlight, Marine, Brass Bracket & Base, Pre-1950, 10 In. 200.00
Sextant, A. Hobbs, London, Brass, Pocket, 3 1/16 In. 215.00
Sextant, Alexander Cairns, Liverpool, Lacquered Arc, Oxidized Lattice Frame, 12 In. . . . 920.00
Sextant, C. Plath, Ladder Frame, Black Lacquer, Silvered Scale Divided, 12 In. 295.00
Sextant, Footed Case 450.00
Sextant, J. Good, Ebony, Brass & Ivory Trim, 13 In. 440.00
Sextant, Kelvin White, N.Y., Black Lacquer, Silvered Scale, Mahogany Case, 1918 . . . . . 345.00
Sextant, U.S. Navy, Mark II, Cased 135.00
Sextant, W.C. Mann, Paper Label In Mahogany Case, 2 Lenses, 10 In. 385.00
Shears, Sail Maker's, Newark, N.J., 13 1/4 In. 77.00
Ship Model, see Nautical, Model.
Sign, Trade, Painted Sperm Whale, Open Mouth, Nail Teeth, 41 In. 3450.00
Skiff, Rowing, Mahogany, Thames River, 12 Ft. 3 In. x 4 Ft. 5 In. 1100.00
Speaker, Ship's, Brass 1250.00
Spotting Scope, Bronze, Steel Mount, Flip-In Amber Filter, 24 3/4 In. 300.00
Statue, Stone, Figure, Standing, Safe Harbor, Scotland, 19th Century 9500.00
Sundial, Silver Pocket, Butterfield A Paris, Bird Pointer, Velvet Lined Leather Box 1955.00
Sundial Compass, Cherry, Plumb Line, Inscribed J.L. 7 77, 2 1/2 x 2 In. 355.00
Sundial Compass, Compass In Base & On Interior Of Lid, Brass, 3 1/4 In. 357.00
Sundial Compass, Mahogany, Folding, Plumb Line, 19th Century, 2 1/2 x 3 In. 110.00
Table, Ship's Wheel, Oak, Mahogany, Sits On Hub, Handles, 19 x 60 In. 660.00
Telegraph, Chas. Cory & Sons, Brass, 44 1/2 In. 605.00

Telescope, 1-Draw, Spencer Browning & Co., Leather Case, Open, 38 1/8 In. 310.00
Telescope, 1-Draw, Thos. J. Evans, Esq., London, Tripod, Brass, 13 13/16 In. 190.00
Telescope, 2-Draw, Wooden Barrel, Messer London Day Or Night, Brass, 36 In. 550.00
Telescope, 4-Draw, Andrew J. Lloyd, Boston, Brass, Dust-Slide, Lens Cap, 11 In. 230.00
Telescope, 5-Draw, Imperial, A. Clarkson & Co., Ltd., Leather Cover, 1890, 42 In. 1430.00
Telescope, 5-Draw, Sun Shade Over Scope, Leather Case, Opens To 45 In. 600.00
Telescope, Brass, Leather Cover, 46 In. 220.00
Telescope, Gilbert & Sons 495.00
Thermometer & Hygrometer, G.F. Hausmann, Brass & Steel, 6 1/2 In. 632.00
Trumpet, Speaking, Communicate Between Ships, Brass, 19 In. 528.00
Whale's Tooth, Lacquer, Peacock & Peony, Chinoiserie, 19th Century, 7 1/4 In. 385.00
Wheel, Ship's, 19th Century, 72 x 18 In. 895.00
Whistle, Bosun's, Dragon Design, China, 19th Century, 5 1/2 In. 355.00
Whistle, Bosun's, Sterling Silver, England, 4 1/4 In. 247.00

NETSUKES are small ivory, wood, metal, or porcelain pieces used as toggles on the end of the cord that held a Japanese money pouch. The earliest date from the sixteenth century. Many are miniature, carved works of art.

Bamboo, Tree Stump, Jui Fungus, Lengthy Inscription Carved In Trunk, Kyuchikasai 365.00
Bone, Folded Straw Hat 540.00
Bone, Rat, Inlaid Horn Eyes, Seated On Awabi Shell 455.00
Boxwood, Actor Kneeling, Wearing Ivory Mask, Signed 490.00
Boxwood, Hanasaka Jihii, Seated On Tree Stump, Lacquered, 19th Century 430.00
Boxwood, Onagadori, Long-Tailed Rooster, 3 Leaves, Ryusa Type, 2 1/2 In. 1320.00
Boxwood, Sennin On Tortoise, 19th Century, 1 1/4 In. 430.00
Boxwood, Woman With Basket Of Grain, Horse, Lacquered, 1 1/2 x 1 1/2 In. 480.00
Brass, Manju Shape, Opens To Reveal Compass, Engraved, 19th Century 605.00
Ebony, Elderly Aino Man, Abstract Form, 5 1/4 In. 665.00
Ebony, Swimming Duck, Inlaid Eyes, Mitshiro Style 550.00
Ivory, 2 Men Dancing, Drum Bucket, Flowers Around Rim, 19th Century 400.00
Ivory, 3 Men Fighting, Comic Expressions, Signed Masatsugu 515.00
Ivory, 4 Rabbits, 19th Century, 2 In. 630.00
Ivory, 4 Samurai, Searching Horizon, Signed Shousai 770.00
Ivory, 7 Arhats, Dragon, Cinnabar Seal, 19th Century, 1 3/4 In. 860.00
Ivory, 8 Figures In Boat, Waves Around Base, Signed Tomochika, 19th Century 430.00
Ivory, Archer, Arrow Pierces Rock, Seal Shape, Signed 550.00
Ivory, Ashinaga & Octopus, Inlaid Eyes, 19th Century, 2 3/4 In.   920.00
Ivory, Benki Blowing Conch Shell Trumpet, Boy, Signed Tomogi, 19th Century 400.00
Ivory, Blind Leading The Blind, Story Illustration, Signed, 19th Century 630.00
Ivory, Boat Carrying 3 People, Signed Shin, Cinnabar Seal, 2 1/4 In. 345.00
Ivory, Boat, With Buddhist Divinities, Demons, Tengu At Tiller, 2 1/2 In. 315.00
Ivory, Boy Holding Mask, 1 In. 85.00
Ivory, Boy On Water Buffalo, 1 3/4 In. 345.00
Ivory, Daikoku & Hoteh, Guarding Treasure Sack, Signed 695.00
Ivory, Daikoku, Carrying Hammer, Rat Hitched Ride, Meiji Period 220.00
Ivory, Dancing Octopus, With Inro & Manju, Signed Hakusan 300.00
Ivory, Daruma, Standing, Humorous Expression, Hosso On Back, Signed Dosho 2310.00
Ivory, Dog, With Her Puppies, Inlaid Eyes, Dyed Horn, 19th Century, 1 1/2 In. 1380.00
Ivory, Dutchman, Seated In Bow, 18th Century 1980.00
Ivory, Ebisu, Large Fish, Delicate Fishing Pole, 19th Century 230.00
Ivory, Fisherwoman, Eating Grilled Rice Cakes, Signed Sukeyuki, 19th Century 285.00
Ivory, Flute Player, Seated On Geta, Mother-Of-Pearl Inset Plaque, Yoshimin 220.00
Ivory, Grazing Horse, Brocade Cloth Back Cover, 19th Century 690.00
Ivory, Herdsman & Water Buffalo 135.00
Ivory, Jurojin, With Youthful Attendant, Signed Tomomasa 520.00
Ivory, Kaikoku, Sleeping On Treasure Bag, Mice, Signed Kogyoku, 1 1/2 In. 690.00
Ivory, Karako Beating Drum, Holding Shishi Puppet, 18th Century 660.00
Ivory, Legendary Toad-Turtle, On Nutshell, Meiji, 1870 . . . .   110.00
Ivory, Lion, Resting In Rockery, 18th Century 330.00
Ivory, Long-Haired Dog, Paw Raised To Face, Seated, 18th Century, 1 1/2 In. 7000.00
Ivory, Man & Fish, 19th Century 115.00
Ivory, Man In Boat, 19th Century 175.00

Ivory, Man On Barrel, 19th Century 115.00
Ivory, Man Riding Fish, 1 1/2 In. 315.00
Ivory, Man, With 3 Boys, Signed Masatomo, 19th Century 374.00
Ivory, Mask, Man, Laughing, Gyokuzan 135.00
Ivory, Monkey Trainer, With Monkey & Puppy, 19th Century, 2 1/2 In. 690.00
Ivory, Monkey, Clinging To Gnarled Tree, 2 In. 95.00
Ivory, Monkey, Dressed As Nobleman, Riding Horse 755.00
Ivory, Monkey, Perched On Bamboo Stalk, Fly Below, Hiroaki 440.00
Ivory, Nitta No Shiro, Armored Warrior, In Combat With Boar, 19th Century 630.00
Ivory, Okame Startled By Mouse, 19th Century, 1 1/2 In. 460.00
Ivory, Old Man, Signed, 19th Century 115.00
Ivory, Oni Crying, Demon's Arm, Rashomon Shrine, Wood, 19th Century, 2 3/4 In. 1265.00
Ivory, Ox & Calf, 18th Century, 2 In. 1380.00
Ivory, Puppy, Tiny Monkey Clinging To Neck, 19th Century 690.00
Ivory, Rat, Climbing Back Of Smiling Sennin, 19th Century 660.00
Ivory, Samurai, Dog, Cat, Pheasant, Signed Mitsuo, Late 19th Century 1320.00
Ivory, Samurai, Sharing Fruit Bag With Monkey, Taisho Period 605.00
Ivory, Scholar With Book, 1 1/2 In. 180.00
Ivory, Sciobo, Elaborate Costume, Ornate Hair Dressing, Basket, Soken Kisho, 1781 .... 5175.00
Ivory, Sennin, In Mugwort Cape, Holding Staff, Inlaid Eyes, 19th Century 745.00
Ivory, Sennin, Long Hair, Hat, Long Stick, 18th Century, 3 In. 920.00
Ivory, Sennin, Moving Double Gourd With Movable Horse, Late 19th Century 605.00
Ivory, Sennin, Peach & Branch, 19th Century, 2 1/2 In. 258.00
Ivory, Shishi Lion, With Its Cubs, Oval Base, 1 1/2 In. 1650.00
Ivory, Shishi Nibbling His Leg, Inlaid Eyes, 18th Century 2640.00
Ivory, Small Boy, Helping Dancer With Fox Mask, 19th Century 345.00
Ivory, Sugawara Michizama, Holding Calligraphic Scroll 515.00
Ivory, Sumo Wrestler, 1 1/2 In. 287.00
Ivory, Tiger, Seated, Tail Curled Over Back, Head Looking Back, Black Eyes, 1 In. 5750.00
Ivory, Tortoise, Curling Waves, 5 1/4 In. 1118.00
Ivory, Traveler, Holding Basket Of Flowers, With Large Backpack, 19th Century 690.00
Ivory, Water Buffalo & Calf, Inlaid Eyes, Signed Tomotada, 3 In. 5060.00
Red Coral, Monkey, Holding Turtle, Tomokazu 390.00
Rock Crystal, Rabbit, Coral Eyes 665.00
Staghorn, Box, Engraved Calligraphy, 19th Century 245.00
Staghorn, Dragon Lying On Leaf, Crystal Inlay On Head, Kokusai 1025.00
Staghorn, God Of Longevity, Signed, Fukurokuju, 19th Century, 3 1/2 In. 230.00
Staghorn, Tongue-Cut Sparrow, Inlaid Horn Eyes, Masayuki, 19th Century 2250.00
Walnut Shell, Man In Boat 1 Side, Water Plants Other, 19th Century 115.00
Walnut Shell, Rooster In Landscape, Shozan, 19th Century, 1 7/8 In. 900.00
Wood, Boat, 2 1/2 In. 58.00
Wood, Daruma, Signed, 1 1/2 In. 230.00
Wood, Disappointed Rat Catcher, Cat On Back, Shunkosai, 1800 .... 605.00
Wood, Earthquake Fish, Inlaid Eyes, Suigetsu, 4 In. 495.00
Wood, Elderly Woman, Resting On Dog, Sosho Inscription, 19th Century 550.00
Wood, Gods Of Good Fortune, Stacks In Form Of Sparrow, Masanao 513.00
Wood, Group Of Nuts, Japan 55.00
Wood, Man, Seated, Holding Open Fan, Mid-19th Century 165.00
Wood, Mask Of O-Beshimi, Green & Gold, Damon, 19th Century, 7/8 In. 700.00
Wood, Otter, Waiting For Eel To Emerge From Rock 2420.00
Wood, Paper Knife, Sashi, Body Separates To Reveal Blade, Yoshiyama, 8 In. 665.00
Wood, Rat, Holding Chestnut, Inlaid Eyes, 1800 .... 935.00
Wood, Snail, Emerging From His Shell, Tadatsugu 1030.00
Wood, Snake 125.00
Wood, South Seas Islander, Holding Jar, Branch Of Coral, Lacquered 515.00
Wood, Tian, Sitting On Clamshell, Signed, Early 19th Century 770.00

NEW MARTINSVILLE Glass Manufacturing Company was established in 1901 in New Martinsville, West Virginia. It was bought and renamed the Viking Glass Company in 1944. In 1987 Kenneth Dalzell, former president of Fostoria Glass Company, purchased the factory and renamed it Dalzell-Viking. Production ceased in 1998.

Amy, Tumbler, Footed 22.00

Figurine, Bear, Pair 440.00
Janice, Basket, Light Blue, 11 In. 295.00
Janice, Bowl, Light Blue, Cupped, 3-Toed, 10 1/2 In. 85.00
Janice, Creamer, Light Blue, Footed, Tall 32.00
Janice, Cup & Saucer, Light Blue 32.00
Janice, Plate, Light Blue, 2 Handles, 11 In. 55.00
Janice, Plate, Light Blue, 8 1/2 In. 20.00
Janice, Tumbler, Ruby, Footed, 10 Oz. 35.00
Janice, Tumbler, Water, Light Blue, Footed 35.00
Janice, Vase, Tripod, Cupped, Ruby, 8 In. 100.00
Judy, Vanity Set, Cologne, Green, 3 Piece 95.00
Judy, Vanity Set, Cologne, Pink, 3 Piece 95.00
Moondrops, Ashtray, Ruby 32.50
Moondrops, Bowl, 3-Footed, Ruby, 10 In. 65.00
Moondrops, Bowl, Amber, 8 In. 22.00
Moondrops, Bowl, Ruby, Footed, 8 1/4 In. 45.00
Moondrops, Butter, Cover 225.00
Moondrops, Candlestick, Amber, 5 In., Pair 300.00
Moondrops, Candlestick, Ruffled Edge, Ritz Blue, 2 In. 35.00
Moondrops, Cordial, Red, 2 7/8 In. 48.00
Moondrops, Decanter, Pink, Stopper 25.00
Moondrops, Mug, Lemonade, Green 12.00
Moondrops, Tumbler, Ruby, 3 5/8 In. 15.00
Moondrops, Tumbler, Whiskey, Green, 2 3/4 In. 10.00
Moondrops, Vase, Ruffled Edge, Green, 7 3/4 In. 60.00
Octagon, Puff Box, Green 50.00
Oscar, Pitcher, Red 95.00
Prelude, Candlestick, 2-Light, Pair 150.00
Prelude, Candlestick, Pair 129.00
Prelude, Relish, 3 Sections, Oval 5.00
Radiance, Basket, Metal Handle, Ruby, 8 In. 85.00
Radiance, Bonbon, Light Blue, Footed, 6 In. 32.00
Radiance, Cordial, Ruby, Silver Trim 37.50
Radiance, Punch Bowl, Ruby, 9 In. 200.00
Radiance, Punch Cup, Light Blue 15.00
Radiance, Relish, 2 Sections, Light Blue 47.00
Radiance, Tray For Sugar & Creamer, Light Blue 30.00
Radiance, Vase, Crimped, 10 In. 139.00

NEWCOMB Pottery was founded by Ellsworth and William Woodward at Sophie Newcomb College, New Orleans, Louisiana, in 1895. The work continued through the 1940s. Pieces of this art pottery are marked with the printed letters *NC* and often have the incised initials of the artist as well. Most pieces have a matte glaze and incised decoration.

Bowl, Black Swirls, Green & Brown Ground, Stamped, 1940, 3 In. 5500.00
Bowl, Floral Design, Green, Blue, Ivory High Glaze, 6 1/2 x 3 In. 2750.00
Bowl, Floral Design, Pink, Green Leaves, Yellow Centers, Blue Matte Ground, 9 In. 1000.00
Bowl, Low, Blue, Pink & Green Flowers, Blue Ground, 2 3/4 In. 1000.00
Bowl, Pink Flowers, Yellow Centers, Blue Matte Ground, H. Bailey, 7 x 2 1/2 In. 1000.00
Bowl, Red Violets, Yellow Centers, Green, Blue Matte Ground, Littlejohn, 8 1/2 In. 1000.00
Bowl, White Flowers, Green Leaves, Blue Matte Ground, A.F. Simpson, 7 In. 1760.00
Bowl, With Flower Frog, Green, Blue High Glaze, 3-Sided Rim, 7 In. 665.00
Candlestick, Freesia Blossoms, Blue Matte Glaze, Joseph Meyer, 1919, 7 In. .. 7150.00
Candlestick, Low Relief Blossoms, Blue Matte Glaze, Sadie Irvine, 1919, 7 In. 4400.00
Cup & Saucer, Floral, Blue High Glaze, Light Blue Ground, C. Luria, 3 x 5 1/2 In. 2100.00
Cup & Saucer, Stylized Wild Rose & Vines, Blue Matte Glaze, J. Meyer, c.1920 .... 3520.00
Mug, Landscape, Blue-Green Overglaze, Impressed, 1901, 4 x 5 In. 3575.00
Pitcher, Green Berries, Leaves, Ivory, Blue Ground, R. Kennon, 8 In. 7150.00
Pitcher, Incised Yellow Daffodils, Green Stems, Pale Blue, Harriet Joor, 1905 9350.00
Pitcher, Landscape, Blue, Green Trees, Yellow High Glaze Ground, 3 1/2 In. ... 3850.00
Pitcher, Pink Morning Glories, Green Leaves, 1924, Incised, 8 x 6 In. 3850.00
Pitcher, Pink Nasturtium, Green Leaves, 1924, Incised, 8 x 6 In. 2310.00

Plaque, Landscape, Fishing Boat, River, Oak Tree, 1922, 6 In. 13200.00
Plaque, Satyrs Playing Musical Instruments Below Moon, Frame, 8 x 7 In. 2200.00
Plaque, Statue, White Chapel, Multitone Blue Matte Ground, 1918, 6 x 10 In. 17600.00
Plate, Clover Leaf Design, Green, Ivory Ground, Harriet Joor, 1898, 10 In. 1760.00
Plate, Intertwined Flowers, Green Stems, Blue-Green Glaze, Sadie Irvine, 1910, 7 In. .. 2400.00
Plate, White, Yellow Chrysanthemum Blossoms, Green Leaves, Simpson, 1913, 10 In. ... 1760.00
Teapot, Ivory Flowers Outlined In Blue, Stems & Buds, M.T. Ryan, 1904, 5 In. 4400.00
Tile, 3-Masted Ship, Turquoise Glaze, Incised, 5 1/2 In. 1045.00
Tile, Band Of Trees Inside Rim, Mary Louise Dunn, 1910, 6 1/8 In. 550.00
Tile, Incised Freesia & Vine, Blue Semimatte Glaze, M. L. Dunn, c.1911, 3/4 In. 523.00
Vase, 6 Geese, Cream & Green On Dark Blue, High Glaze, M.W. Richardson, 6 1/2 In. .. 13200.00
Vase, Abstract Vertical Design, Blue Matte Glaze, K. Smith, 1932, 3 5/8 In. 1870.00
Vase, Alternating Stylized Pine Needle Spray, Cream, Pale Green, 1915, 4 x 5 In. 635.00
Vase, Band Of Flowers, Margaret Sterling Lea, 1907, 5 3/4 In. 6875.00
Vase, Band Of Lilies, Carved, 8 1/4 In. 18150.00
Vase, Band Of Painted Daisies, Yellow Centers, Leaves, H. Bailey, 1914, 6 1/2 In. 1100.00
Vase, Band Of Repeating Crocus, Incised, Cream, Yellow, Pale Blue, 1905, 4 x 5 In...... 4025.00
Vase, Bell-Shaped Flowers, Blue-Green Ground, Impressed, 5 1/2 In. 1980.00
Vase, Blue, Red High Glaze, L. Nicholson, 3 1/2 In. 550.00
Vase, Bud, White Flowers, Dark Blue Green Glossy Ground, LeBlanc, 9 x 3 In. 6600.00
Vase, Camellias, Incised, Blue Matte Glaze, J. Meyer, C. Littlejohn, c.1914, 2 3/4 In. 935.00
Vase, Dark Blue Matte Glaze, Signed, 3 1/2 x 3 3/4 In. 400.00
Vase, Floral Design, Blue, Brown & Cream High Glaze, J. Meyer, 5 1/2 In. 1000.00
Vase, Floral Design, Green, Blue, Light Blue, Dark Blue Ground, Urquhart, 3 In. 2970.00
Vase, Floral Design, Ivory, Green, Blue, C. Payne, 9 1/2 In. 6050.00
Vase, Floral Design, Matte Glaze, Carved, 4 Handles, Irvine, 6 1/2 In. 4400.00
Vase, Floral Design, White Flowers, Green Leaves, Vines, Blue Ground, 5 1/2 In. 1320.00
Vase, Freesia Blossoms, Incised, Light Blue, Blue, Yellow, Leona Nicholson, 8 In. 26400.00
Vase, Grape Vines, Incised, Cobalt, Blue Green, Glossy Blue Ground, Kennon, 6 In. 8250.00
Vase, Green Over Natural Glaze, Signed, 3 In. 2750.00
Vase, Green, Blue Bats On Shoulder, Yellow Band Neck, Green, Blue Border, 6 In. 9900.00
Vase, Green, Blue Thistles, Cream, Dark Blue Ground, Mary Butler, 4 In. 5225.00
Vase, Horizontal Bands, Turquoise, Cranberry, Mushroom Glaze, J. Meyer, 3 1/2 In. 385.00
Vase, Incised Lines Under Semimatte Gold Glaze, Juanita Gonzales, 1931, 7 1/2 In. 1100.00
Vase, Incised Stylized White Lilies, Light Blue, Yellow, Denim Blue Ground, 4 In. 7150.00
Vase, Ivory, Yellow Blossoms Outlined In Blue, Green Ground, 9 In. 6600.00
Vase, Landscape, Anna Frances Simpson, 1913, 12 5/8 In. 2750.00
Vase, Landscape, Green Live Oak Trees, Spanish Moss, Pink Sky, 6 1/2 x 8 In. 1980.00
Vase, Landscape, Moonlit, Blue, Green, Live Oaks, Spanish Moss, Sadie Irvine, 8 In. 2860.00
Vase, Landscape, Moonlit, Spanish Moss, Oak Trees, Sadie Irvine, 1923, 11 x 6 In. 6050.00
Vase, Landscape, Moss-Laden Cypress Trees, 10 In. 3575.00
Vase, Landscape, Moss-Laden Oak Trees, Pink Ground, Simpson, 8 1/2 In. 4950.00
Vase, Landscape, Moss-Laden Oaks, A.F. Simpson, 6 1/2 In. 2530.00
Vase, Landscape, Moss-Laden Oaks, Green, Blue, Pale Yellow Moon, 4 In. 1870.00
Vase, Landscape, Moss-Laden Oaks, Green, Blue, Simpson, 3 In. 2200.00
Vase, Landscape, Moss-Laden Oaks, Soft Pink Sky, Sadie Irvine, 5 In. 2640.00
Vase, Landscape, Moss-Laden Oaks, Yellow Moon Matte Glaze, Sadie Irvine, 6 In. 3575.00
Vase, Landscape, Moss-Laden Oaks, Yellow Moon, A.F. Simpson, 5 1/2 In. 2750.00
Vase, Landscape, Oak Trees, Spanish Moss, Full Moon, 1932, 6 In. 1900.00
Vase, Landscape, Spanish Moss Trees, Simpson, 5 In. 3200.00
Vase, Landscape, Trees, Anna Frances Simpson, 1930, 4 1/2 In. 4200.00
Vase, Lavender Roses, Green Stems, Leaves, Blue, Green Matte Ground, 6 1/2 In. 4675.00
Vase, Leaves Covered In Mottled Green Glaze, Signed, 6 1/4 In. 1600.00
Vase, Light Blue Band, Yellow Flowers, Denim Blue Ground, Sadie Irvine, 6 x 3 In. 1540.00
Vase, Light Blue Flowers, Ivory, Green Centers, Blue Matte Ground, Irvine, 6 In. 1320.00
Vase, Live Oak Trees, Spanish Moss, Moon, Paper Label, 1932, 3 1/2 In. 3190.00
Vase, Live Oaks, Spanish Moss, Denim Blue, Sadie Irvine, 2 1/4 In. 1430.00
Vase, Magnolias, Incised, Bands, Oxblood, Blue Underglaze, Joseph Meyer, 8 In. 6050.00
Vase, Moon & Moss, Blue Matte Glaze, Kenneth Eugene Smith, 1932, 5 1/2 In. 2750.00
Vase, Moss & Cypress Trees, Blue Matte Glaze, Joseph Meyer, c.1912, 8 1/2 In. 5775.00
Vase, Moss-Laden Oaks, Trees In Background, Blue Matte Glaze, 1923, 6 In. 5500.00
Vase, Mottled Green High Glaze Over Neutral Opaque Glaze, J. Meyer, 1907, 4 In. 385.00
Vase, Multicolored Green Crystalline Glaze, Gunmetal Highlights, Handles, 6 In. 935.00

Vase, Nighttime Scene, Live Oak Trees, Spanish Moss, Full Moon, Signed, 6 1/2 In. 4500.00
Vase, Oak Trees, Spanish Moss, Egg Shape, Impressed, 1930, 6 x 3 1/2 In. 4000.00
Vase, Overlapping Leaves, Blue, Green Ivory Matte Glaze, 6 1/2 In. 1650.00
Vase, Painted Roses & Leaves, Carved, Matte Glaze, S. Irvine, 10 1/2 In. 6600.00
Vase, Pink Blossoms, Green Leaves, Purple Ground, Henrietta Bailey, 1918, 4 In. 1980.00
Vase, Pink Chrysanthemums, Blue Ground, Stamped, 1926, 5 3/4 In. 1320.00
Vase, Pink, Narcissus, Yellow Centers, Blue Matte Ground, A.F. Simpson, 7 x 6 In. 1980.00
Vase, Purple Flowers, Green Stems, Blue Green Ground, Sadie Irvine, 1915, 11 In. 3575.00
Vase, Purple Narcissus, Purple Ground, Impressed, 1917, 6 In. 2200.00
Vase, Raspberry Matte Glaze, Bulbous, 4 x 3 1/4 In. 495.00
Vase, Red, Green, Blue On Blue Ground, Matte Glaze, Irvine, 3 In. 1000.00
Vase, Ridged Body, Flaring, Semimatte Glaze, Kenneth Smith, 7 1/2 In. 550.00
Vase, Rose Blossoms, Green Stems, Blue Ground, Sadie Irvine, 6 In. 2860.00
Vase, Scenic, Oaks & Spanish Moss, Full Moon, Sadie Irvine, 1922, 8 In. 2900.00
Vase, Vertical Carved Ribs, Brown Clay Body, White Thick Glaze, 6 In. 880.00
Vase, White Flowers, Dark Blue Band, Squat, Impressed, 1926, 3 x 4 In. 1870.00
Vase, White Irises, Green Stems, Blue Green Ground, A.F. Simpson, 1910, 8 1/2 In. 7700.00
Vase, White Lilies, Green Stems, Blue Ground, 4 Handles, A.F. Simpson, 1916, 4 In. 3080.00
Vase, Yellow Sunflower Petals, Blue Seed, Ivory Ground, Squat, 4 In. 4950.00
Vase, Yellow, Pale Blue, Purple Irises, Green Leaves, Light Blue Ground, 12 x 5 In. 4400.00
Vessel, Landscape, Live Oak, Spanish Moss, Full Moon, Sadie Irvine, 5 1/2 In. 1900.00
Vessel, Magnolia Blossoms, Light Blue, Cream, Blue Ground, Kennon, 4 1/2 In. 2640.00
Wall Pocket, Stylized Cockatoos, Blue Matte Glaze, Sadie Irvine, c.1930, 8 In. 7480.00

NILOAK Pottery (Kaolin spelled backward) was made at the Hyten
Brothers Pottery in Benton, Arkansas, between 1909 and 1947.
Although the factory did make cast and molded wares, collectors are
most interested in the marbleized art pottery line made of colored
swirls of clay. It was called *Mission Ware.* By 1931 the company made   NILOAK
castware, and many of these pieces were marked with the name
Hywood.

Ashtray 95.00
Candlestick, Marbleized, Handle, Signed, 4 7/8 In. 247.00
Figurine, Duck, Red Matte, 4 In. 12.00
Figurine, Frog, Pink & Green Matte, Label, 5 In. 45.00
Flowerpot, Underplate, Hole For Drainage, 10 x 9 In. 1045.00
Jar, Marbleized, Blue, Brown, Terra-Cotta, Cream, 3 3/4 In. 110.00
Pitcher, Floral Geometric Design, Signed 35.00
Powder Jar, 6 In. 520.00
Tumbler, Marbleized, Blue & Brown, 4 In. 35.00
Umbrella Stand, 20 In. 2310.00
Vase, Hywood, Dark Pink, 11 In. 50.00
Vase, Marbleized, 4 In. 95.00
Vase, Marbleized, Brown & Tan, 3 3/4 In. 30.00
Vase, Marbleized, Corset Shape, Brown, Blue & Terra-Cotta, Stamped, 10 In. 360.00
Vase, Marbleized, Cream, Brown, Blue, Red Clay, Cylindrical, 3 In. 154.00
Vase, Marbleized, Waisted Form, Blue, Red, Brown, Cream, Impressed Mark, 10 In. 275.00

NIPPON porcelain was made in Japan from 1891 to 1921. *Nippon* is the
Japanese word for *Japan.* A few firms continued to use the word
Nippon on ceramics after 1921 as a part of the company name more
than as an identification of the country of origin. More pieces marked
Nippon will be found in the Dragonware, Moriage, and Noritake
categories.

Bowl, Geometric Art Deco Design, Green Field, 4 x 10 In. 325.00
Bowl, Green Mark, 7 3/4 In. 110.00
Bowl, Kingfisher, Green Mark, 3 5/8 x 7 1/4 In. 935.00
Bowl, Nut Interior, Green Mark, 2 3/4 x 7 In. 27.00
Bowl, Phoenix Bird, Crowsfoot On Base, Green Mark, 2 1/2 x 7 1/2 In. 55.00
Bowl, Purple & White Grapes, Gold Ground, Footed, Signed, 6 1/2 In. 87.00
Bowl, Purple, White Grapes, Gold Ground, Footed, 6 1/2 In. 90.00
Bowl, Roses, Green Ground, Gold Trim, 2 Closed Handles, Maple Leaf Mark, 10 In. 115.00
Bowl, Ruffled Rings, Opalescent, 9 In. 35.00

Bowl, Tan, Chestnuts, Leaves & Gold Beading, 3 Legs, Maple Leaf Mark, 7 1/4 In. 115.00
Box, Dresser, Portrait Cover, Enamel & Gilt Beading, Tall Footed, 4 In. 230.00
Cake Plate, Gaudy, Red Roses, Gold, Large, 9 In. 175.00
Cake Plate, Yellow & Red Roses, Ornate Gold Border, Maple Leaf Mark, 11 In. 90.00
Candlestick, Landscape Columns, Floral, Spider Web Design, 8 1/2 In., Pair 325.00
Candlestick, Light Green, Gold Highlights, Pedestal Base, Maple Leaf Mark, 11 In. 132.00
Carafe, Cranberry, Etched, 12 In. 30.00
Celery Dish, Violet, Green & Gold Ground, 12 In. 38.00
Celery Tray, Plush Roses, Cobalt Blue, Gold, Maple Leaf Mark, 11 1/2 In. 110.00
Chocolate Pot, Poppies, Gold Trim, Green Mark, 8 1/2 In. 165.00
Chocolate Pot, Scene, Vining Flowers Design, Gold, 9 In. 105.00
Chocolate Pot, Swan Medallions, Cobalt Blue, Gold, Green Mark, 9 1/2 In. 220.00
Cologne Bottle, Enameled Grapes & Leaves, White Ground, Stopper 125.00
Creamer, Child's, Floral 20.00
Creamer, Cover, Underplate, Roses On White 35.00
Dish, Leaf Shape, Cobalt, 7 1/2 In. 65.00
Dresser Set, Violets, Maple Leaf Mark, 6 Piece 575.00
Egg Caddy, Landscape, Handle Over Stopper, Holds 4 Eggs, M In Wreath, 6 x 4 In. 85.00
Hair Receiver, Raised Gilt & Colored Slip, 3 1/2 x 2 In. 80.00
Hatpin Holder, Medallion Front & Back, Roses, Gold Beaded, Signed, 2 1/2 x 3 In. 125.00
Hatpin Holder, Open Top, Gold Trim 55.00
Hatpin Holder, Violets, Gold Accents, 4 1/2 In. 300.00
Humidor, Blown Out, No. 539 .... 825.00
Humidor, Cover, Cottage Landscape, Green M In Wreath, 6 1/2 In. 316.00
Humidor, Cover, Indian Portrait, Arrows On Border, Signed, 8 x 5 1/2 In. 850.00
Humidor, Man Smoking Pipe, Marbleized Ground, Green Mark, 8 In. 165.00
Humidor, Outdoor Scene, Ducks, Flying, Green Mark, 4 In. 330.00
Humidor, Portrait, Red Ace Design, Green Mark, 5 1/2 In. 2145.00
Humidor, Scene, Green Mark, 5 1/2 In. 176.00
Jug, Whiskey, Pine Cone, No. 863 .... 525.00
Mayonnaise Set, Floral Gilt, Cobalt, 3 Piece 195.00
Muffineer, Flowers, 2 Oval Panels, Gold Trim, Handle, Blue Maple Leaf Mark, 5 In. 80.00
Mug, Windmill Scene, Scrolled Cobalt Blue Border, Green M In Wreath, 5 In. 75.00
Nappy, Woodland, Shield, Lion Border, Green Mark, 7 In. 275.00
Nut Bowl, Folded-Down Rims, 6 1/2 In. 55.00
Pitcher, Green, 1891, 10 x 5 In. 775.00
Pitcher, Milk, Cover, Egyptian Style Boats, Lavender Ground, Maple Leaf Mark, 7 In. ... 213.00
Pitcher, Purple Flowers, Dark Green Ground, c.1890, 6 1/2 In. 90.00
Pitcher, Sailboats, Island, Lavender Ground, Blue Maple Leaf Mark, 6 In. 167.00
Plaque, 2 Indian Warriors, Green M In Wreath, Round, 10 1/2 In. 748.00
Plaque, Dutch Mother & Children, Waiting By Shore, Blue M In Wreath, Round, 10 In. .. 115.00
Plaque, Egyptian Boat, Sphinx Head Type, Blue, Lavender, 10 In. 185.00
Plaque, Fishermen In Boat, Hand Painted, Gold Rim, M In Wreath, Round, 11 In. 173.00
Plaque, Horses, Fence & Trees, In Relief, Tan, Brown, M In Wreath, Round, 10 3/4 In. .. 633.00
Plaque, Monk In Red, Scrolled, Medallions, Green Maple Leaf, 9 1/2 In. ....*Illus* 660.00
Plate, River Scene Palms, 10 In. 95.00

Nippon, Plaque, Monk In Red, Scrolled,
Medallions, Green Maple Leaf, 9 1/2 In.

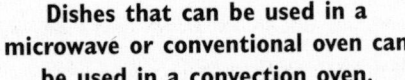

**Dishes that can be used in a
microwave or conventional oven can
be used in a convection oven.**

Plate, Violets, 2 Handles, 6 1/2 In. 16.00
Plate, Water, Trees, Mountain, Birds, Gold Border, Maple Leaf Mark, 9 1/2 In. 81.00
Platter, Dogwood Floral, Gilt, 10 In. 70.00
Powder Dish, Blackberries, Gold 45.00
Spooner, Floral, 2 Handles, Green M In Wreath, 8 In. 38.00
Spooner, Scenic, Orange, Purple & Teal, 8 In. 142.00
Sugar & Creamer, Cobalt Floral, Gilt Beading, 4-Footed 165.00
Sugar Shaker 65.00
Tankard, Floral Medallion, Raised Gold Enamel Design, Maple Leaf Mark, 10 In. 259.00
Tankard, Monk Portrait, 10 In. 5200.00
Tea Set, Service For 3, 1900, 9 Piece 120.00
Tea Set, Swans In Pond, Gold Highlights, M In Wreath, 6-In. Teapot, 9 Piece 173.00
Teapot, Child's, Floral 25.00
Tray, Dresser, Raised Floral Slip, 11 In. 105.00
Trivet, Stag Leaping, Brown Highlights, 6 Legs, Green M In Wreath, 6 In. 81.00
Urn, Cover, 8 In., Pair 750.00
Vase, 2 Storks Flying Over An Island At Sunset, Gold Handles, Coralene Border, 12 In. . . 160.00
Vase, 4 Flying Geese, Gilt & Turquoise, Handles, 9 In. 425.00
Vase, Acorn & Oak Leaf Moriaga, Beaded Top & Base, 5 1/2 In. 265.00
Vase, Birds, Blossoms, Black Ground, Brown Mark, 8 3/4 In. 38.00
Vase, Brown, Gold Leaf Design, Bulbous, 2 Open Handles, Maple Leaf Mark, 7 1/4 In. . . 155.00
Vase, Cabin By Stream In Forest, Green & Brown, Hand Painted, Signed, c.1892, 12 In. . . 215.00
Vase, Fishing Boat, Handles, 12 In. 195.00
Vase, Floral & Lattice, Ribbed Panels, Handles, Blue Cherry Blossom Mark, 9 1/2 In. . . . 75.00
Vase, Floral Design, 5 1/2 In. 95.00
Vase, Floral, Gold, Tan Ground, Green Mark, 6 In. 110.00
Vase, Grape Clusters & Leaves, 6-Sided Handles, Gold Beading, Signed, 14 1/2 In. 645.00
Vase, Grape Vines, Gold Trim, Bulbous, Green Maple Leaf Mark, 6 1/2 In. 81.00
Vase, Green, Yellow, Magenta, Gold Accents, Gold Rim, Handles, Marked, 12 In. 260.00
Vase, Medallions, Floral Band, Roses, Green Mark, 7 1/2 In. 121.00
Vase, Owl On Branch, Gold Trim, Green Mark, 8 1/2 In. 880.00
Vase, Pansy, Gold, Bulbous, 7 In. 125.00
Vase, Phoenix Bird In Gold Medallion Design, Blue Ground, Green Mark, 8 3/4 In. 247.00
Vase, Pink Flowers, Green Leaves, White, 8 In. 75.00
Vase, Purple & White Flowering Branches, Purple, Blue & Black, Hexagonal 145.00
Vase, Raised Gold Beading, 11 1/2 In. 45.00
Vase, Rose, Gold, Multicolored Ground, Kinran Mark, 8 3/4 In. 297.00
Vase, Scene, Enamel Trim, 12 In. 165.00
Vase, Scene, Gold, Green Mark, 10 1/8 In. 550.00
Vase, Scene, Woman, On Path To Cottage, Green Mark, 9 1/4 In. 209.00
Vase, Storks Flying, Lavender Into Golden Sunset, Camellia Flower Mark, 12 In. 160.00
Vase, Tapestry, Gold Royal, Rising Sun Mark, 3 1/2 In. 187.00
Vase, White & Red Roses, Gold Highlights, Maple Leaf Mark, Hand Painted, 14 In. 230.00
Vase, Young Woman, Floral Scene, Ruffled Top, Open Handles, Squat, 5 In. 375.00

NODDERS, also called nodding figures or pagods, are figures with heads and hands that are attached to wires. Any slight movement causes the parts to move up and down. They were made in many countries during the eighteenth, nineteenth, and twentieth centuries. A few Art Deco designs are also known. Copies are being made. A more recent type of nodder is made of papier-mache or plastic. These often represent sports figures or comic characters.

Armadillo, Spring Mounted Head, Tail, Plastier, 5 In. 45.00
Bear, Standing, Brown Wool Fur, Button Eyes, Composition, 6 In. 185.00
Bisque, Moving Arms, Head, Pink, Gold Highlights, 7 x 6 1/2 In. 303.00
Bisque, Woman, Man, Green Design, 7 1/8 In., Pair 303.00
Black Girl, Porcelain, Hand Painted, Japan, 6 In. 295.00
Black Man, Cigar In Mouth, Porcelain, 5 In. 100.00
Bonzo, Head Mounted On Spring, Papier-Mache, Composition, Germany, 5 1/2 In. 230.00
Cat, Gray Stripes, Black, Yellow, Green, Papier-Mache, 5 1/2 In. 145.00
Cat, Gray, Glass Eyes, Papier-Mache, 9 In. 300.00
Cow, Cow Hide Cover, Natural Horns, Glass Eyes, Composition, 12 In. 192.00
Donkey, Celluloid, Painted, Occupied Japan, 7 In. 80.00

Nodder, Dutch Boy
& Girl, Bisque
Heads, 6 In., Pair

Nodder, Hula Girl,
Aloha, Fringe Skirt
& Lei, Hips Swing,
Magnet Bottom,
Japan, 6 1/2 In.

**Windows in outside
doors should be
covered with
grillwork or made of
unbreakable glass.**

Dutch Boy & Girl, Bisque Heads, 6 In., Pair ....*Illus*	205.00
Hawaiian Hula Dance, Marked Lensille China, Ardalt, Japan, 2 Piece	395.00
Hula Girl, Aloha, Fringe Skirt & Lei, Hips Swing, Magnet Bottom, Japan, 6 1/2 In. ..*Illus*	175.00
Keystone Kop, Movieland, 1930s	100.00
Man, Porcelain, Oscillating Tongue, Hands Counter Weighted, 12 1/2 In.	2090.00
Mandarin Man & Woman, Gilt & Enamel, German, 1900s, 6 3/4 In, Pair	632.00
Mice & Cheese, Fitz & Floyd	200.00
Our Gang, Original Sticker, Hal Roach Studios, Bisque, Germany, 1930, 6 Piece	850.00
Roy Rogers, Composition, Smiling, White Hat, Square Base, 1962, 7 In.	143.00
Salt & Pepper shakers are listed in the Salt & Pepper category.	
Ventriloquist, Composition, Carnival Novelty Co.	100.00
Woman, Persian, Hold Fan, Gold Trim, Bisque, 5 x 3 In.	165.00

NORITAKE porcelain was made in Japan after 1904 by Nippon Toki
Kaisha. The best-known Noritake pieces are marked with the M in a
wreath for the Morimura Brothers, a New York City distributing company. This mark was used until 1941. There may be some helpful price
information in the Nippon category, since prices are comparable.
Noritake Azalea is listed in the Azalea category in this book.

Bowl, Gold Handle, Blue, Gold, Orange & Black Peacock Feathers Inside, 10 In.	110.00
Bowl, Tree In Meadow, Open Handles, 10 In.	60.00
Cake Plate, Tree In Meadow, Open Handles	38.00
Candy Dish, Scene Of Ribbed Bank, House Along Stream On Bowl, 9 In.	85.00
Celery Dish, Swan Scene	48.00
Chocolate Set, Orange & Tan Floral, White Ground, Gold Highlights, 5 Piece	115.00
Compote, Blue, White, Landscape In Center, Gold Trim, Signed, 8 3/4 In.	40.00
Demitasse Set, 16 Piece	310.00
Nut Dish, Painted, 7 In.	48.00
Plate, Cookie, Orange Luster, Sunflowers, Handles, 10 1/2 In.	125.00
Plate, Tree In Meadow, 9 3/4 In.	125.00
Plate, Tree In Meadow, Lemon Slice, 9 In.	30.00
Plate, Tree, Water, Cabin Scene, Signed, 5 3/4 In.	10.00
Platter, 2 Game Birds, Dolson, 16 In.	50.00
Pot, Tree In Meadow, Demitasse	225.00
Salt & Pepper, Woman, With Bouquet Of Flowers	250.00
Snack Set, Blue Luster, Betty Boop Like Face In Cup	95.00
Sugar, Cover, Gaylord	18.00
Sugar & Creamer, Tree In Meadow	55.00
Toast Rack, 4 Slice, Blue, Gray, Green M In Wreath, 3 1/2 x 5 1/2 In.	135.00
Toothpick, Tree In Meadow	45.00
Vase, Allover Black, White Cherry Blossoms, 10 In.	80.00
Vase, Low Cherry Blossoms, Yellow, Black, White, 10 In.	75.00
Vase, Raised Multicolored Pheasant, Peach Luster, Red Mark, 5 1/4 In.	95.00
Vase, Tree In Meadow, 2 Handles, Green M In Wreath, 13 In.	144.00
Vase, Tree In Meadow, 8 1/2 In.	98.00
Vase, Water Scenes In Oval Panels, 4-Sided, Gold Beading, M In Wreath, 8 1/2 In.	173.00
Vase, White & Pink Flowers, Gold Birds, Ruffled Top, 2 Handles, M In Wreath, 13 In.	288.00

NORSE Pottery Company started in Edgerton, Wisconsin, in 1903. In 1904 the company moved to Rockford, Illinois. The company made a black pottery, which resembled early bronze relics of the Scandinavian countries. The firm went out of business in 1913.

Bowl, Repeating Borders On Body, Snake Head Feet, Signed, 2 1/2 In.	247.00
Candlestick, Incised Shields & Ribbons On Shoulder, Signed, 3 1/4 In.	300.00
Vase, Incised Designs At Shoulder, Signed, 9 1/4 In.	550.00
Vessel, Salamander Handles, Incised Designs, Animal Head-Feet, Signed, 3 3/4 In.	357.00

NORTH DAKOTA SCHOOL OF MINES was established in 1892 at the University of North Dakota. A ceramic course was included and pieces were made from the clays found in the region. Students at the university made pieces from 1909 to 1949. Although very early pieces were marked *U.N.D.*, most pieces were stamped with the full name of the university.

Bottle, Water, Stopper, Signed	650.00
Bowl, Red River Ox Cart, Brown, Green Matte Glaze, Cable	1540.00
Charger, Dark Brown Flowers, Burnt Sienna, M. Cable, 9 In.	990.00
Humidor, Brown, Green Berries, Mustard Ground, Cable	5225.00
Pitcher, Squat, Red River Ox Carts, Embossed, Buff, 5 In.	990.00
Trivet, Fish, Green, Ocher, Light Ground, Mattson, 5 In.	275.00
Trivet, Stylized Eagle, Black, Brick Ground, Mattson, 4 3/4 In.	275.00
Vase, Azure Blue, Bud, M. Cable, Julia Mattson	214.00
Vase, Bison, Brown, Ochre Matte Glaze, 5 1/4 In.	1980.00
Vase, Blue At Rim, Rose At Base, March 1927, 5 1/2 In.	220.00
Vase, Carved Viking Ships, Blue, Green, Light Blue, 4 In.	770.00
Vase, Carved, Prairie Roses, Glossy Pink Glaze, Mattson, 8 In.	660.00
Vase, Cowboys, Embossed, Brown, Green Ground, 7 In.	440.00
Vase, Cowboys, In Chaps, Arm-In-Arm, Brown, Green, 5 In.	1430.00
Vase, Daffodils, Light Green Semimatte Glaze, Cable, 7 In.	2860.00
Vase, Evergreens & Deer, Brown, Yellow, Red Ground, 3 In.	825.00
Vase, Excised Daffodils, 1950, 8 3/4 In.	1700.00
Vase, Floral Design, Red Clay Body, Light Cream, Blue, 8 In.	605.00
Vase, Glossy Azure Blue Glaze, M. Cable, 7 1/2 In.	215.00
Vase, Green High-Glaze, Charcoaling, Signed, 6 In.	130.00
Vase, Green Stripes, Julia Mattson, Signed, 3 1/4 In.	325.00
Vase, Haystacks, Green Matte Ground, Bulbous, 4 x 3 In.	605.00
Vase, Incised Trees, Green Matte Glaze, F. Huckfield, 11 In.	4950.00
Vase, Oak Trees Under Green Glaze, Huckfield, 10 3/4 In.	4000.00
Vase, Plowman, Field Plowing Scenes, Brown, 5 In.	1870.00
Vase, Prairie Rose, Freida Hammers, 3 3/8 In.	440.00
Vase, Prairie Rose, Green Matte Ground, Spherical, 3 In.	495.00
Vase, Prairie Rose, Rose Glaze, Flora C. Huckfield, 1951, 3 In.	47.00
Vase, Sioux, Warriors, Horse, Brown Matte, 6 In.	1980.00
Vase, Spherical, Covered Wagon, Brown Glaze, 6 1/4 In.	2530.00
Vase, Stylized Mushrooms, Blue, Turquoise, White, 6 In.	1650.00
Vase, Stylized Red, Blue Flowers, Blue Ground, 7 In.	1980.00
Vase, Turkeys, Green Matte Glaze, Squat, 3 1/4 x 3 3/4 In.	550.00

NORTHWOOD Glass Company was founded by Harry Northwood, a glassmaker who worked for Hobbs, Brockunier and Company, La Belle Glass Company, and Buckeye Glass Company before founding his own firm. He opened one factory in Indiana, Pennsylvania, in 1896, and another in Wheeling, West Virginia, in 1902. Northwood closed when Mr. Northwood died in 1923. Many types of glass were made, including carnival, custard, goofus, and pressed. The underlined N mark was used on some pieces.

Beads & Bark, Vase, Blue Opalescent, c.1903	75.00
Blown Twist, Tumbler, White, Opalescent, 1903	95.00
Bluebird & Strawberry, Tumbler	60.00
Bushel Basket, Bowl, Green	260.00
Cherries, Tumbler, Blue	35.00

Cherry & Lattice, Spooner	75.00
Cherry & Lattice, Sugar, Cover	75.00
Cherry & Plum, Compote, Cover, Collared Base, 6 1/2 In.	225.00
Cherry Thumbprint, Sugar, Cover	90.00
Chrysanthemum Sprig, Toothpick, Blue	350.00
Chrysanthemum Sprig, Tumbler, Blue, Gold Trim	225.00
Chrysanthemum Sprig, Tumbler, Custard	95.00
Daisy & Fern, Toothpick, Cranberry Opalescent, Swirl Mold, 1895	475.00
Grape & Cable, Berry Set, 7 Piece	140.00
Grape & Cable, Punch Bowl, Base, Amethyst, Small	650.00
Grape & Cable, Tankard Pitcher, Amethyst	800.00
Grape & Cable, Tumbler, Amethyst	35.00
Grape & Gothic Arches, Butter, Cover, Green	95.00
Grape & Gothic Arches, Goblet	45.00
Hobnail, Creamer, Small	50.00
Maple Leaf, Butter, Cover, Custard	235.00
Maple Leaf, Creamer	150.00
Memphis, Table Set, Green, Gold Trim, 4 Piece	300.00 to 350.00
Oriental Poppy, Tumbler, Green, Gold Trim	50.00
Osiris, Vase, 5 1/2 In.	220.00
Peach, Table Set, Green, Gold Trim, 4 Piece	350.00
Peach, Water Set, Green, 6 Piece	300.00
Posies & Pods, Bowl, Ruffled, Green, 8 In.	40.00
Regent, Creamer, Green, Gold Trim	60.00 to 125.00
Singing Birds, Bowl, Cover, Marked, 7 In.	180.00
Star Of David, Nappy, Gold Handle	145.00

NU-ART see Imperial category.

NUTCRACKERS of many types have been used through the centuries. At first the nutcracker was probably strong teeth or a hammer. But by the nineteenth century, many elaborate and ingenious types were made. Levers, screws, and hammer adaptations were the most popular. Because nutcrackers are still useful, they are still being made, some in the old styles.

Bearded Man Head, Pointed Cap, Carved Wood, 19th Century, 9 1/2 In.	325.00
Chinese Man, Full-Bodied, Sitting, Orange Carved, 19th Century, 6 1/2 In.	395.00
Donkey, Hand Wrought Iron, Painted Black, 6 x 11 In.	145.00
Eagle Head, Cast Iron, Pat'd. 1860, 10 1/4 In.	310.00
Elephant, Cast Iron, Worn Red Paint, 9 3/4 In.	135.00
Peasant Woman, Full-Bodied, Wooden, 7 3/4 In.	285.00
Soldier On Rocking Horse, Germany, 10 1/4 x 9 1/2 In.	95.00
Squirrel, Cast Iron, Painted	175.00

NYMPHENBURG, see Royal Nymphenburg.

OCCUPIED JAPAN was printed on pottery, porcelain, toys, and other goods made during the American occupation of Japan after World War II, from 1945 to 1952. Collectors now search for these pieces. The items were made for export.

Cup & Saucer, Flowers	14.00
Doll, Crocheted Dress, Celluloid	55.00
Figurine, Black Cat, 3 In.	10.00
Figurine, Dutch Girl, 5 In.	20.00
Figurine, Oriental Couple Kissing, 5 In., Pair	35.00
Lighter, Camera Shape, On Tripod, Brushed Finish, 2 1/2 x 1 1/2 x 1/4 In.	30.00
Lighter, Cigarette Dispenser, Leader, Radio Shape, Stainless Steel, 4 x 2 In.	65.00
Salt & Pepper, East Indian, Seated	13.00
Salt & Pepper, Gondola	35.00
Salt & Pepper, Strawberry, Tray	20.00
Salt & Pepper Condiment Set, Red Plastic Handles, Chrome, 6 1/2 x 2 In.	35.00
Sugar & Creamer, Tomato	25.00
Toy, Boy On 3-Wheeled Scooter, Celluloid, Painted, 4 1/2 In.	110.00
Toy, Cowboy & Bucking Bronco, Key Wind, Celluloid, 5 In.	110.00 to 115.00

Outdoor lights help prevent crimes, but install them high enough so they are difficult to unscrew.

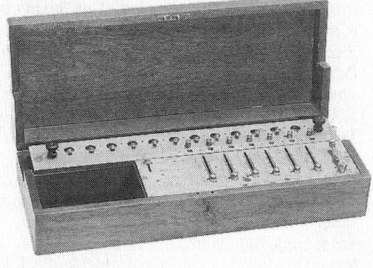

Office, Adding Machine, Arithmometre,
Brass, Colmar, No. 936, c.1870

Toy, Crazy Car, Dagwood, Windup, Tin, Celluloid, 4 1/2 In. 215.00
Toy, Fancy Dan The Juggling Man, Key Wind, Celluloid, Modern Toys, Box, 5 In. 200.00
Toy, Funny Man, Clown, Windup, Celluloid, Hand Painted, Alps, Box, 6 1/2 In. 305.00
Toy, Gray Bear With Fish, Key Wind, Tin, Gray Fur, Paper Tag, 5 1/2 In. 75.00
Toy, Hawaiian Dancer, Celluloid, Silk Grass Skirt, S.S.S., Box, 6 1/2 In. 175.00

OFFICE TECHNOLOGY includes office equipment and related products, such as adding machines, calculators, and check-writing machines. Typewriters are in their own category in this book.

Addiator Duplex Calculator, Brass 25.00
Adding Machine, Arithmometre, Brass, Colmar, No. 936, c.1870 .... *Illus* 4530.00
Adding Machine, Burk's Kollector, 1910 .... 4673.00
Adding Machine, Burk, c.1910 .... 4673.00
Adding Machine, E.M., Oak Case, Pat. Mar. 19, 1907 .... 72.00
Adding Machine, Paper Roll, Burrough, 20th Century, 12 x 10 x 15 In. 11.00
Adding Machine, Resulta-9, Deluxe Quiet Model, Metal Housing, Germany 20.00
Book Press, Cast Iron, 2 3/4 x 3 3/4 In. 1200.00
Calculator, Conversion, Cleveland Twist Drill Co., Mechanical, 79 mm 25.00
Dictaphone, Victor Talking Machine, 1904 .... 1000.00
Holder, Rubber Stamp, 4 Tiers, Cast Iron, 1880s, 18 In. 900.00
Ink, Peacock, Blue, Glass Bottle, Tin Lithograph Container 225.00
Paper Clip, Victorian, Tin, 3 3/4 In. 450.00
Paper Clip, Wizard, Hinged & Spring-Loaded Clips, Pat. 1899, 2 1/2 In. 20.00
Puncher, Top Of Pages, Marvel, Wilson-Jones, Cast Iron, 1920s 190.00
Stamp, Lead Lettering Set, Cast Iron, 1890 .... 190.00
Staple Gun, Advertising Plumbing & Heating Supply 140.00
Staple Gun, Bates, Endless Brass Wire, Extra Spool, 8 In. 155.00
Stapler, Acme, No. 1, Cat Iron, 1880s 560.00
Typewriter, Rem-Blick, Letters On Ball 275.00

OHR pottery was made in Biloxi, Mississippi, from 1883 to 1918 by George E. Ohr, a true eccentric. The pottery was made of very thin clay that was twisted, folded, and dented into odd, graceful shapes. Some pieces were lifelike models of hats, animal heads, or even a potato. Others were decorated with folded clay *snakes*. Reproductions and reworked pieces are appearing on the market. These have been reglazed, or snakes and other embellishments have been added.

Bowl, Dimpled Body, Black Exterior, Speckled Brown, Black Interior, Folded Rim, 4 In. . 1320.00
Bowl, Free-Form, Glossy Dripping Green, Purple, Ocher Interior, Collapsed Rim, 4 In. ... 1210.00
Bowl, Free-Form, Gunmetal Glaze Exterior, Green, Ocher Interior, Signed, 2 x 5 In. 4675.00
Bowl, Free-Form, Gunmetal, 2 x 5 In. 4200.00
Bowl, Horizontally Dimpled, Folded Sides, Coppery Glaze, Impressed Mark, 3 x 4 In. .. 3210.00
Bowl, Twisted Body, Folded Rim, Glossy Dark Green, Raspberry Glaze, 1903, 4 x 6 In. .. 3850.00
Chamber Pot, Mottled Ocher, Olive Green & Brown, 2 x 3 1/2 In. 450.00
Chamberstick, Frothy Raspberry, Green Matte Glaze, Ribbon Handle, Squat, 6 x 4 In. ... 2860.00
Chamberstick, Twisted Body, Ribbon Handle, Gunmetal, Green Glaze, Incised, 4 In. 2310.00
Cup, Flaring, Vertical Dimples, Green, Purple Glaze, Matte Red, 3 x 4 1/2 In. 2860.00
Mug, Joe Jefferson, Toast Written On Side, Pink & Green Glaze, Signed, 1896, 3 x 4 In. .. 1100.00
Pitcher, Angular Ribbon Handle, Applied Rosette, Umber, Clay Price Tag, 4 In. 2970.00
Pitcher, Asymmetrical, Pinched Rim, Gunmetal Black Glaze, Signed, 3 3/4 x 3 1/4 In. ... 1760.00

Pitcher, Gourd Shape, Ribbed, Blue & Green Glaze, Impressed, 6 In. 1320.00
Pitcher, Ribbon Handle, Applied Rosettes, Umber & Gunmetal Glaze, Marked, 4 In. 2700.00
Pitcher, Ribbon Handle, Pink, Green, Red, White Glaze, Impressed Mark, 6 1/2 In. 7700.00
Puzzle Jug, Landscape Design, Incised Wheat Sheaf, Brown, Green Glaze, 1899, 8 In. ... 1540.00
Puzzle Mug, Twisted Body, Rabbit Handle, Brown Glaze, 1895, Stamped, 4 In. 2420.00
Teapot, Cadogan, Hammered Texture, Ear-Shaped Handle, Long Spout, Brown, 7 1/2 In. . 2420.00
Teapot, Snake Spout, Speckled Glossy Glaze, Signed, 6 1/2 In. 2000.00
Teapot, Speckled Teal Green Glaze, Snake Spout, Bulbous, Marked, 3 1/4 x 6 In. 2000.00
Vase, Bisque, Bulbous, Deep Twisted Body & Folds, Unglazed, Script Signature, 6 In. ... 1650.00
Vase, Bottle Shape, Gunmetal, Raspberry, Green Frothy Glaze, Squat, 4 x 3 3/4 In. 2750.00
Vase, Corseted, Pinched Rim, Twisted Body, Dark Brown Exterior, Ocher Interior, 3 In. .. 1210.00
Vase, Dark Blue Glaze, Pinched Twisted Neck, Folded Rim, 9 3/4 In. 2530.00
Vase, Dimpled Middle, Aventurine & Black Glaze, Folded Rim, Signed, 4 3/4 In. 2500.00
Vase, Folded Middle, Flared Bottom, Signed, 5 In. 1760.00
Vase, Free-Form, Gunmetal, Ocher Glaze, Signed, 3 x 6 In. 3850.00
Vase, Free-Form, Pinched, Folded, Incised Script, 4 In. 3190.00
Vase, Glossy Deep Purple Glaze, Folded Rim, Signed, 3 3/4 x 5 1/2 In. 5225.00
Vase, Glossy Dripping Dark Blue Glaze, Twist Top, Signed, 4 1/2 x 4 1/2 In. 2200.00
Vase, Green & Blue Spotted Interior, Signed, 3 1/2 In. 410.00
Vase, Green, Gunmetal Glaze, Exaggerated Labial Rim, Script Signature, 5 1/2 In. 1650.00
Vase, Gunmetal, Brown Glaze, 2 Handles, 5 In. 1980.00
Vase, Incised Lucy On Front, Double-Gourd Form, Gunmetal Matte, Signed, 5 In. 935.00
Vase, Khaki To Brown Glaze, Pinched Twisted Band, Scalloped Piecrust Rim, 4 1/4 In. .. 1725.00
Vase, Marbleized Glossy Glaze, Scalloped Rim, Signed, 6 1/4 In. 2000.00
Vase, Ocher, Red, Gunmetal Brown, Baluster Shape, Impressed Mark, 6 1/2 In. 1980.00
Vase, Pear Shape, Twisted Body, Speckled Ocher, Brown Glaze, Impressed Mark, 6 In. .. 4400.00
Vase, Pinched, Cutout Handle, Brown Gunmetal Glaze, Impressed Mark, 3 1/2 In. 2090.00
Vase, Pinched, Folded, Scroddled Clay, Unglazed, Incised Script, 3 x 5 In. 3570.00
Vase, Pinched, Scrolled Handle, Mirror Black Glaze, Folded Rim, Impressed Mark, 5 In. . 1100.00
Vase, Raspberry, Green, Blue & Gray Glaze, Folded Rim, Stamped, 6 In. 4400.00
Vase, Red Mottled Glaze, Pinched, Flared Body, Handle, 3 3/4 In. 374.00
Vase, Scroddled Clay, Free Form, Unglazed, Signed, 4 x 5 1/2 In. 4675.00
Vase, Speckled Glossy Glaze, Collapsed & Folding Rim, Signed, 4 1/2 In. 3500.00
Vase, Speckled Ocher & Green Glaze, Folded Rim, Impressed Mark, 4 3/4 In. 2640.00
Vase, Sponged Glossy Glaze, Folded Rim, Signed, 3 1/4 x 4 In. 2700.00
Vase, Sponged Matte & Glossy Glaze, Signed, 4 In. 1900.00
Vase, Squat, Pinched & Folded Rim, Aventurine Glaze, Impressed, 3 1/2 In. 1980.00
Vase, Torn Rim, Collapsed Shoulder, Green, Brown, Gunmetal, Ocher, Impressed, 5 In. .. 5500.00
Vase, Twist Near Rim, Speckled Gunmetal & Khaki Glaze, Signed, 6 1/4 In. 1800.00
Vase, Twisted Body, Speckled Umber & Gunmetal Glaze, Folded Rim, Impressed, 4 In. .. 2090.00
Vessel, Asymmetrical, Green Mottled Glaze, Folded & Twisted Rim, 3 3/4 x 4 1/2 In. 2530.00
Vessel, Blue, Green, Black, Buff Clay Body, Folded Rim, 3 x 4 In. 2530.00
Vessel, Granular Dark Brown Luster Glaze, Folded Rim, Tapered, 3 3/4 x 3 3/4 In. 770.00
Vessel, Green Glossy Glaze, Folded Rim, 4 1/2 x 4 3/4 In. 3300.00
Vessel, Green Speckled Matte Purple Glaze, Squat, 3 1/2 x 4 1/4 In. 880.00
Vessel, Red Clay, Folded & Collapsed In 3 Lobes, Unglazed, 5 x 5 1/2 In. 1980.00
Vessel, Scroddled Clay, Brown Red, Folded Rim, Unglazed, 4 3/4 x 3 1/2 In. 825.00
Vessel, Scroddled Clay, Brown, Red, Unglazed, Folded Pinched Rim, 3 1/4 x 3 3/4 In. ... 605.00

OLD IVORY china was made by the Ohme Porcelain Works in Silesia,
Germany, a factory working from 1882 to 1928. The china had an
ivory matte background and was usually decorated with flowers or
fruit. Dinner sets, fish sets, mustache cups, and souvenir pieces were   OLDIVORY
also made. Pieces were marked with a crown, the cipher OH, and the   84
word *Silesia*. Some pieces are also marked with the words *Old Ivory*.
The pattern numbers appear on the base of many pieces.

Biscuit Barrel, Rose, 8 1/2 In. 495.00
Bowl, No. 16, 9 1/2 In. 140.00
Bowl, Oatmeal, Clarion 130.00
Bowl, Rose, 9 1/2 In. 225.00
Cake Plate, Clarion, 13 In. ....158.00 to 173.00
Cake Plate, No. 75, Open Handled, 12 In. 195.00
Cake Plate, Open Handles, 10 In. 125.00

Celery Dish, Signed	50.00
Chocolate Pot, No. 11	410.00
Chocolate Set, Clarion, No. 16, 13 Piece	800.00
Cup & Saucer, Clarion	75.00
Cup & Saucer, No. 75	95.00
Plate, Clarion, 6 In.	85.00
Plate, Clarion, 8 1/2 In.	75.00
Plate, Dessert, Clarion, 5 Piece	25.00
Plate, Dessert, Empire	40.00
Plate, Floral, Scalloped Edge, Ohme, 8 In.	75.00
Plate, No. 10, 6 1/3 In.	32.00
Plate, No. 82, Large Yellow Tea Rose In Center, Old Ivory Border, 8 In.	155.00
Plate, No. 84, 8 In.	40.00 to 75.00
Plate, Open Handle, Ohme, 11 1/2 In.	75.00
Plate, Rose, 7 1/2 In., 6 Piece	75.00
Plate, Rose, 8 1/2 In., 6 Piece	400.00
Plate, Scalloped, No. 75	75.00
Platter, Clarion, 11 1/2 In.	155.00
Platter, Clarion, 13 1/2 In.	200.00
Relish, Empire, 8 In.	30.00
Sugar & Creamer, No. 16	182.00
Tray, Dresser, No. 82, Scalloped Rim, 12 x 7 In.	225.00
Tray, Open Handles, No. 75, 11 1/2 In.	225.00

OLD PARIS, see Paris category.

OLD SLEEPY EYE, see Sleepy Eye category.

OLYMPIC, see Souvenir category.

ONION PATTERN, originally named *bulb pattern*, is a white ware decorated with cobalt blue or pink. Although it is commonly associated with Meissen, other companies made the pattern in the late nineteenth and the twentieth centuries. A rare type is called *red bud* because there are added red accents on the blue-and-white dishes.

Bowl, Blue, Square, Incut Corners, Meissen, 8 In.	165.00
Bowl, Porcelain, Shallow, Meissen Type, 19th Century, 14 In.	275.00
Cake Plate, Footed, Meissen, 5 1/4 In.	60.00
Chocolate Pot, Cover, Blue, Meissen, 20th Century, 10 In.	316.00
Coffeepot, Blue, Bud Finial, Meissen, 9 1/2 In.	350.00
Compote, Reticulated, Meissen, 9 In., Pair	345.00
Dish, Blue, 3-Lobed, Meissen, 12 In.	860.00
Plate, Leaf & Scroll Pierced Border, Blue, Meissen, Signed, 8 In., Pair	210.00
Plate, Reticulated, Meissen, 19th Century, 9 1/4 In.	295.00
Platter, Blue, Meissen, 21 1/2 In.	475.00
Platter, Blue, Meissen, Oval, 14 In.	65.00
Platter, Blue, White, Rust, Gilt Edges, Meissen, 12 x 17 In.	260.00
Rolling Pin, Blue & White, G.M.I. Stamped On Edge, No Handles, 7 In.	75.00
Rolling Pin, Cobalt Blue Floral Design, Milk Glass, Wooden Handles, 15 In.	330.00
Salt Box, Wooden Lid, 6 1/4 x 6 1/2 In.	245.00
Tea Caddy, Blue, Meissen, Porcelain, 5 1/2 In.	170.00
Tea Set, Blue, Teapot, Sugar, Creamer, Cup & Saucer, Tray, Meissen, 12 Piece	460.00
Tureen, Leaf Knop On Cover, Blue, Scrolled Leaf Handles, Meissen, 10 In.	190.00

OPALESCENT GLASS is translucent glass that has the tones of the opal gemstone. It originated in England in the 1870s and is often found in pressed glassware made in Victorian times. Opalescent glass was first made in America in 1897 at the Northwood glassworks in Indiana, Pennsylvania. Some dealers use the terms *opaline* and *opalescent* for any of these translucent wares. More opalescent pieces may be listed in Hobnail, Northwood, Pressed Glass, Spanish Lace, and other glass categories.

Acorn, Plate, Leaf Border, Lacy, 7 In.	270.00
Beatty Rib, Celery Dish, Blue	87.00

Beatty Rib, Creamer, Blue 35.00
Beatty Rib, Finger Bowl, Blue 48.00
Beatty Rib, Mug, Blue 58.00
Beatty Rib, Spooner, Blue 67.00
Beatty Rib, Sugar Shaker, White 275.00
Beatty Swirl, Celery 90.00
Big Windows, Syrup, White 385.00
Bubble Lattice, Syrup, Blue 495.00
Buttons & Braids, Pitcher, Cranberry 1850.00
Buttons & Braids, Pitcher, Green 285.00
Buttons & Braids, Pitcher, White 100.00
Chippendale, Compote, Vaseline, 8 1/2 x 10 In. 245.00
Christmas Snowflake, Pitcher, Ribbed, Cranberry 2100.00
Chrysanthemum Swirl, Celery Dish 140.00
Chrysanthemum Swirl, Salt & Pepper, Cranberry 595.00
Chrysanthemum Swirl, Sugar Shaker, Blue 345.00
Chrysanthemum Swirl, Tankard, Cranberry 2250.00
Coinspot, Pitcher, Cranberry 300.00
Coinspot, Pitcher, Green, 9 1/4 In. 250.00
Coinspot, Syrup, Paneled, Pewter Flip Top, Spout, White 75.00
Coinspot, Tumbler, Cranberry, 3 3/4 In. 48.00
Coinspot, Water Set, Green, 5 Piece 215.00
Coinspot & Swirl, Syrup, Blue 185.00
Colonial Stairsteps, Toothpick, Blue 45.00
Crackled Diamonds, Creamer, Bulbous, Cranberry 475.00
Criss-Cross, Berry Bowl, Cranberry 100.00
Criss-Cross, Creamer, White . . . . .255.00 to 285.00
Criss-Cross, Syrup, White 545.00
Daisy & Fern, Pitcher, Blue 250.00
Daisy & Fern, Syrup, Blue 275.00
Daisy & Fern, Tumbler, Cranberry 110.00
Daisy & Plume, Bowl, Ruffled Edge, Blue, 10 In. 50.00
Daisy In Criss-Cross, Syrup, White 545.00
Diamond Spearhead, Sugar, Vaseline 230.00
Drapery, Water Set, Blue, Gold Trim, 7 Piece 520.00
Hilltop Vines, Dish, Aqua 75.00
Hobb's Optic, Syrup, Cranberry 280.00
Hobnail, Cruet, Cranberry 85.00
Hobnail, Pitcher, Clear Ribbed Handle, Square Mouth, 6 5/8 In. 330.00
Hobnail, Toothpick, Blue 75.00
Hobnail, Toothpick, White 35.00
Hobnail, Vase, Cranberry, 5 1/2 x 6 In. 60.00
Honeycomb & Clover, Pitcher, Green 325.00
Idyll, Spooner, Blue 95.00
Iris With Meander, Butter, Cover 225.00
Iris With Meander, Saltshaker, Blue, Pair 225.00
Iris With Meander, Toothpick, Blue 95.00
Iris With Meander, Toothpick, White 35.00
Jewel & Flower, Creamer, Blue 55.00
Jewel & Flower, Tumbler, Blue 25.00
Jewelled Heart, Berry Set, White, 7 Piece 285.00
Palm Beach, Creamer, Blue 150.00
Palm Beach, Spooner, Blue 150.00
Palm Beach, Sugar, Cover, Blue 225.00
Polka Dot, Syrup, Blue 345.00
Reverse Swirl, Carafe, Cranberry 545.00
Reverse Swirl, Pitcher, Blue 425.00
Reverse Swirl, Pitcher, Cranberry 495.00
Reverse Swirl, Syrup, Blue 345.00
Reverse Swirl, Syrup, Cranberry 1145.00
Reverse Swirl, Syrup, Vaseline 395.00
Ribbed Opal Lattice, Bowl, Crimped Edge, Cranberry, 10 In. 135.00
Ribbed Opal Lattice, Pitcher, Cranberry 1800.00

Ribbed Opal Lattice, Sugar Shaker, Cranberry 750.00
Ribbed Opal Lattice, Sugar Shaker, Cranberry, 4 1/2 In. 195.00
Ribbed Opal Lattice, Syrup, Blue 335.00
Ribbed Opal Lattice, Tankard, Cranberry 2100.00
Stars & Stripes, Cruet, Cranberry ....565.00 to 575.00
Swag With Brackets, Sugar, Green 135.00
Swirl, Lamp Shade, Ruffled Edge, Vaseline, 3 3/4 In., Pair 195.00
Swirl, Lamp, Brass Plated, Vase Stem, Acorn Finial, Cranberry, 24 In. 55.00
Swirl, Pitcher, Blue, 8 1/2 In. 225.00
Tokyo, Pitcher, Green 245.00
Toothpicks are listed in the Toothpick category.
Wild Bouquet, Creamer, Blue 125.00
Windows, Bottle, Barber, Cranberry, Stopper, 9 In. 173.00
Windows, Pitcher, Blue 425.00
Windows, Pitcher, Cranberry 675.00
Windows, Salt & Pepper, Blue, Swirled 150.00
Windows, Salt & Pepper, Cranberry, Swirled 215.00
Wreath & Shell, Butter, Cover, Vaseline 165.00
Wreath & Shell, Spooner, Vaseline 85.00
Wreath & Shell, Sugar, Cover, Vaseline 195.00
Wreath & Shell, Tumbler, Vaseline 90.00

OPALINE, or opal glass, was made in white, green, and other colors.
The glass had a matte surface and a lack of transparency. It was often
gilded or painted. It was a popular mid-nineteenth-century European
glassware.

Box, Cover, Gilt Metal Mounts, Blue, 3 1/4 x 4 In. 402.00
Candy Dish, Strawberries & Flowers, 3 Amber Feet 545.00
Dresser Set, Brass Foliate Overlay On Bottle, Brass Lid, Brass Collars, 2 Piece 145.00
Eggcup, Pink Looping, Hollow Stem, 3 7/8 In. 165.00
Lamp, Pink, Gilt Bands, 33 In., Pair 145.00
Vase, Blue Looping, Applied Foot, Ruffled Edge, 15 In. 770.00
Vase, Blue, Brass Scrolled Handles & Base, 19 In. 315.00
Vase, Blue, Gilt, France, 19th Century, 4 1/4 In., Pair 165.00
Vase, Polychrome Printed Amorous Children, Greek Key Border, 13 1/2 In., Pair 143.00
Vase, Ruffled Edge, 28 1/2 In. 115.00
Vase, Trumpet, 10 1/2 In. 40.00

OPERA GLASSES are needed because the stage is a long way from some
of the seats at a play or an opera. Mother-of-pearl was a popular decoration on many French glasses.

C.D. Peacock, Tortoiseshell, Metal, Black Leather Fitted Case 80.00
Chevalier Paris, Mother-Of-Pearl, Brass, Handle 105.00
Duval, Mother-Of-Pearl Panels, Leather Case, 3 7/8 In. 50.00
Enamel, Cobalt Ground, Cartouche Rim, 4 In., Pair 260.00
Enamel, Ruby Ground, Floral, Continental, 4 1/2 In. 488.00
Lemaire, Enamel, Floral, 3 1/2 In. 330.00
Lemaire, Enamel, Garnet Ground, Brass, Case 138.00
Lemaire, Gold Mother-Of-Pearl, Gilt Bronze, Marked, 1850 .... 120.00
Reichsparteitag, Souvenir 150.00
Tortoiseshell, Brass, Hinged Arm, France, Late 19th Century, 4 1/2 In. 400.00

ORPHAN ANNIE first appeared in the comics in 1924. The redheaded
girl and her friends have been on the radio and are still on the comic
pages. A Broadway musical show and a movie in the 1980s made
Annie popular again and many toys, dishes, and other memorabilia are
being made.

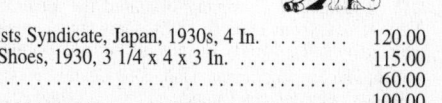

Ashtray, Annie & Sandy, Figural, Famous Artists Syndicate, Japan, 1930s, 4 In. 120.00
Ashtray, Annie Wearing Orange Dress, Black Shoes, 1930, 3 1/4 x 4 x 3 In. 115.00
Badge, Decoder, Mysto-Matic, Brass, 1939 .... 60.00
Badge, Radio, Mysto Magic Decoder, 1939 .... 100.00
Bank, Dime Register, Annie On Stool & Sandy, Tin Lithograph, 1936, 3 In. 440.00
Book, Little Orphan Annie At The Circus, Cupple & Leon, 1927 .... 33.00

Book, Little Orphan Annie Saves Sandy, Whitman, 1938, 32 Pages	25.00
Book, Radio Premium, Secret Society Manual, 1937	80.00
Bubble Set, Pipe, Tray, Box, Pressman, Harold Gray	60.00
Comic Book, Adventures Of Little Orphan Annie Comics, Radio Premium	100.00
Comic Book, The Adventures Of Little Orphan Annie, Quaker Puffed Wheat, 1941	65.00
Cup, Ovaltine	45.00
Decoder, Radio Premium, 1935	85.00
Decoder, Rotating Disk, Radio Premium, 1937	40.00
Decoder, Rotating Disk, Radio Premium, 1939	85.00
Decoder, Secret Compartment, Radio Premium, Brass, 1936	55.00 to 70.00
Decoder, Speedomatic, Manual, Radio, 1940	22.00
Decoder Ring, Secret Compartment, 1936	35.00
Doll, Annie, Extra Clothes, Knickerbocker, Box, 1982, 10 In.	20.00
Doll, Oilcloth, 13 In.	125.00
Doll, Wearing Dress With Her Name On It, Red Mohair Wig, 1930s, 17 In.	175.00
Figure, Wood, Jointed, 5 1/2 In.	44.00
Game, Treasure Hunt, Board	30.00
Game, Treasure Hunt, Playing Pieces	55.00
Mug, Cold Ovaltine, Ivory White Beetleware, Orange Lid, 1935, 4 3/4 In.	65.00
Pastry Set, Orphan Annie, Transogram, Box, 1930s	125.00
Sheet Music, Little Orphan Annie's Song, Wander Co., 1931, 8 3/4 x 11 In.	28.00
Stove, Tin	85.00
Toy, Tin, Windup, Harold Gray, Marx, 5 In.	275.00
Watch, Round Face, Chrome Cased	275.00
Watch, Sun, Brass, 1930s, 1 1/2 In.	22.00

ORREFORS Glassworks, located in the Swedish province of Smaaland, was established in 1898. The company is still making glass for use on the table or as decorations. There is renewed interest in the glass made in the modern styles of the 1940s and 1950s. Most vases and decorative pieces are signed with the etched name.

Orrefors

Bowl, Corona, Large	70.00
Bowl, Deep Burgundy, Pale Amber, Sven Palmquist, 1945, 11 3/4 In.	460.00
Bowl, Geometric Grid Of Graduated Rectangles, Mossy Gray, Green, 1954, 4 In.	2070.00
Bowl, Irregular Rim, Rust Inclusions, Sven Palmquist, 2 5/8 x 5 1/8 In.	1150.00
Bowl, Stylized Leaves, Sectioned Sides, Circular, 10 1/8 In.	69.00
Decanter, Romeo & Juliet, Juliet On Balcony On Reverse, Signed, 12 1/2 In.	395.00
Vase, Apple Shape, Green, Spherical, Ingeborg Lundin, 1957, 15 1/8 In.	6037.00
Vase, Ariel, Vertical Controlled Air Bubbles, Blood Red, Etched, 3 1/2 In.	308.00
Vase, Controlled Bubbles, Ariel Ingeborg Lundin, 8 1/2 In.	1750.00
Vase, Dancing Nude Woman, Snake, Engraved, 7 In.	374.00
Vase, Deep Burgundy Spiraling Threads, Teardrop Shape, Edward Hald, 1953, 14 1/4 In.	920.00
Vase, Deep Cobalt Blue, Amber, Teardrop Shape, Sven Palmquist, 1954, 8 1/2 In.	1150.00
Vase, Deep Cobalt Blue, Aubergine, Edvin Ohrstrom, 1950, 6 In.	17250.00
Vase, Deer, Tree, Bird, Signed, 7 3/4 In.	55.00
Vase, Engraved Woman With Basket, Signed, 1953, 5 x 7 In.	445.00
Vase, Etched Figures Of Standing Maidens, Flowers, Oval, 11 1/2 In.	77.00
Vase, Fish Graal, Clear, Green, Black, Interior Aquatic Scene, Signed, Hald, 6 1/2 In.	460.00
Vase, Gondolier, Clear, Blue, Amber, Internal Design, Signed, Ohrstrom, 7 In.	4025.00
Vase, Graal, Camels & Oasis Design, Bulbous, Edward Hald, 6 In.	1265.00
Vase, Nude Dancing Woman & Musicians, 2 Handles, 9 In.	2070.00
Vase, Nude Woman, In Garden, Holding Flowers, Signed, 1920s, 11 7/8 In.	1150.00
Vase, Oriental Princess, Profile Of Aiden, Florals, Dove Within Frame, 1937, 7 3/4 In.	4025.00
Vase, Red Over Blue, Heavy Blue Rim, 1957, 5 x 8 1/2 In.	2200.00
Vase, Swollen Cylinder, Acid Etch, Signed, S/3534, CJH, 9 In.	58.00

OTT & BREWER Company operated the Etruria Pottery at Trenton, New Jersey, from 1863 to 1893. They started making belleek in 1882. The firm used a variety of marks that incorporated the initials *O & B*.

Dish, The Singing Lesson, Dark Blue Center, Ivory, Saunders, 1876, 9 In.	18400.00
Soup, Cream, Saucer, Limpet	162.00
Vessel, Forget-Me-Nots, 3 Scalloped Openings, Signed, 5 3/4 In.	750.00

OVERBECK pottery was made by four sisters named Overbeck at a pottery in Cambridge City, Indiana. They started in 1911. They made all types of vases, each one-of-a-kind. Small, hand-modeled figurines are the most popular pieces with today's collectors. The factory continued until 1955, when the last of the four sisters died.

Figurine, Chick, Yellow, Impressed, 1 In.	550.00
Figurine, Old Man With Can, Woman With Frying Pan, Marked, 5 In.	700.00
Figurine, Spaniel Dog, Impressed, 1 1/2 In.	250.00
Figurine, Woodpecker, Impressed, 2 1/2 In.	385.00
Vase, 16 Hummingbirds, Brown, Green Matte Glaze, Open Handles, 6 In.	6050.00
Vase, 3 Panels Of Women, Japanese Style, Pastel Shades, 3 In.	1100.00
Vase, 5 Sets Of Love Birds, Semigloss Glazes, Logo, E. & M., Frances, 7 3/8 In.	8800.00
Vessel, 3 Excised Panels Of Stylized Birds, Mauve Ground, Signed, 5 1/2 In.	2800.00

OWENS Pottery was made in Zanesville, Ohio, from 1891 to 1928. The first art pottery was made after 1896. Utopian Ware, Cyrano, Navarre, Feroza, and Henri Deux were made. Pieces were usually marked with a form of the name *Owens*. About 1907, the firm began to make tile and discontinued the art pottery wares.

Ewer, Nasturtium, Helen Smith, Signed, 5 1/2 In.	136.00
Ewer, Utopia, Yellow Roses, Brown, Green, Amber, Sarah Timberlake, 9 3/8 In.	305.00
Jug, Brown Glaze, 7 In.	435.00
Pitcher, Crane Standing Beside Lotus Blossom, 5 7/8 In.	357.00
Tankard, Wheat, Utopian, 12 In.	350.00 to 385.00
Tile, Acorns & Oak Leaves, Tan Ground, Signed, 5 3/8 x 5 7/8 In.	247.00
Vase, Corn, Black Stenciling, Matte Green, 8 In.	695.00
Vase, Daffodil Design, Tan, Brown Ground, Elongated Neck, Bulbous, 13 1/4 In.	172.00
Vase, Feroza, Metallic Glaze, 9 In.	175.00
Vase, Floral, Aqua, Brown Ground, 10 3/4 In.	185.00
Vase, Incised Woman, Red Hair Encircling Vase & Handles, Gold Outline, 9 In.	440.00
Vase, Pillow, Indian Portrait, Cream & Red Vest, Signed, 8 x 8 1/2 In.	1210.00
Vase, Pillow, Utopian, 5 In.	175.00
Vase, Pink Flowers, Green Leaves, White Ground, 6 In.	395.00
Vase, Tulip, Green Leaves On Brown Ground, Signed, 10 In.	275.00
Vase, Utopian, 6 1/2 In.	170.00
Vase, Utopian, 11 In.	395.00
Vase, Utopian, Artist Signed, 5 In.	250.00
Vase, Utopian, Floral Design, Signed, 4 1/2 x 7 In.	130.00
Vase, Utopian, Floral, Signed, 4 1/2 x 7 In.	130.00
Vase, White & Green Grapes, Vines & Leaves, Signed, 7 1/2 In.	245.00

OYSTER PLATES were popular from the 1880s. Each course at dinner was served in a special dish. The oyster plate had indentations shaped like oysters. Usually six oysters were held on a plate. There is no greater value to a plate with more oysters, although that myth continues to haunt antiques dealers. There are other plates for shellfish, including cockle plates and whelk plates. The appropriately shaped indentations are part of the design of these dishes.

4 Wells, All White Relief Design, Haviland, 7 1/2 In.	130.00
4 Wells, Leaf Mold, Gold Trim, Haviland, 7 1/2 In.	110.00
4 Wells, Marseilles, Sauce Center, Marked I, 7 3/4 In.	105.00
4 Wells, Turquoise With Pink & White, Fan Shape, Majolica, G. Jones, 9 1/4 In.	4115.00
5 Wells, Cobalt Blue, Gold, Haviland, 7 3/4 In.	200.00
5 Wells, Floral Sprig On White, Gilt Border, Limoges, 9 In., 6 Piece	580.00
5 Wells, Gold Trim, Limoges, 1891-1900, 7 3/8 In.	130.00
5 Wells, Pink Floral, Carlsbad, 8 1/4 In., 7 Piece	465.00
5 Wells, Pink Floral, Haviland	415.00
5 Wells, Presidential Seal, President Hays Service	900.00
5 Wells, Ranson, Sauce Center, Marked L, 9 In.	105.00
6 Wells, Brown & Green Seaweed, Majolica, George Jones, 10 1/2 In.	3145.00
6 Wells, Enameled Women Between Shell Dishes, Sitzendorf Style, 6 1/2 x 9 In.	1610.00
6 Wells, Fish & Floral, Sauce Center, Star Shape	88.00

Be careful about putting antique china or glass in the dishwasher. Glass will sometimes crack from the heat. Porcelains with gold overglaze decoration often lose the gold. Damaged or crazed glaze will sometimes pop off the plates in large pieces.

Oyster Plate, 6 Wells, Shellfish & Birds,
Sauce Center, 9 In., 8 Piece

6 Wells, Floral Design, Green Ground, Carlsbad, 9 In., 5 Piece	4535.00
6 Wells, Green & Pink Highlights, Blue Dividers, Gold Edge, 8 3/4 In., 10 Piece	920.00
6 Wells, Hand-Painted Oysters, France, 9 In.	115.00
6 Wells, Painted Oysters, 9 In., 5 Piece	575.00
6 Wells, Seaweed & Snails, 9 In., 3 Piece	288.00
6 Wells, Shellfish & Birds, Sauce Center, 9 In., 8 Piece ....*Illus*	700.00
6 Wells, Shells & Seaweed, Mauve, Majolica, 9 In., 3 Piece	1028.00
6 Wells, White Seaweed, Gilt Trim, Brownfields, Signed, 9 1/4 In., 5 Piece	845.00
6 Wells, White To Pink, Sauce Center, 8 3/4 In., 6 Piece	380.00
7 Wells, White, Hall China Co., East Liverpool, Ohio, 10 5/8 In.	130.00
Blue Cornflower Design, Carlsbad, 8 1/2 In., 6 Piece	460.00
Enamel, Gilt Design, Limoges, 9 1/4 In., 4 Piece	258.00
Flowers, Pale Gray & Pink, Haviland, 6 In., 8 Piece	860.00
Gilt, Scalloped Rim, Gold Trim, Germany, 6 Piece	275.00
Scalloped, Gold Trim, Germany, 6 Piece	300.00
Stangl, 9 In.	450.00
Turquoise, Pink, Black, Majolica	325.00
White, Pillivuyt Factory, 1910-1920, 9 1/4 In., 3 Piece	240.00

PADEN CITY Glass Manufacturing Company was established in 1916 at Paden City, West Virginia. The company made more than seventy different colors of glass. The firm closed in 1951.

Ardith, Cake Plate, Footed, 10 In.	145.00
Ardith, Dish, Mayonnaise, Underplate, Yellow	95.00
Black Forest, Berry Bowl, Black	125.00
Black Forest, Cake Plate, Green, Footed, 10 In.	125.00
Black Forest, Vase, Black, 10 In.	250.00
Black Forest, Vase, Black, Squat, 6 1/2 In.	175.00
Black Forest, Vase, Green, 6 1/2 In.	150.00
Crow's Foot, Candlestick, Red, Square Base, 5 1/4 In., Pair	125.00
Crow's Foot, Cup & Saucer, Red	18.00 to 22.00
Figurine, Pelican, Barth Art	295.00
Figurine, Pony, Blue, 12 In.	185.00
Gazebo, Dish, Mayonnaise	25.00
Gothic Garden, Cake Plate, Yellow, Footed, 10 In.	100.00
Largo, Cup & Saucer, Blue	25.00
Largo, Plate, Underplate, Chrome Handle, 13 1/2 In.	40.00
Lela Bird, Cake Plate, Green, 10 In.	125.00
Lela Bird, Vase, Black, Etched, 12 In.	225.00
Lela Bird, Vase, Ebony, 10 In.	195.00
Orchid, Vase, Red, 10 In.	395.00
Party, Dish, Banana Split, Green	20.00
Penny, Iced Tea, Red, 12 Oz.	23.00
Pouter Pigeon, Bookends	185.00
Utopia, Vase, Black, 10 In.	195.00

PAINTINGS listed in this book are not works by major artists but rather decorative paintings on ivory, board, or glass that would be of interest to the average collector. Watercolors on paper are listed under Picture. To learn the value of an oil painting by a listed artist you must contact an expert in that area.

Acrylic On Canvas, Cotton Pickers Down South, Almarie Little, 5 x 7 In.	120.00
Acrylic On Canvas Board, Key West, Dean Close, Frame, 1977, 26 x 30 In.	165.00
Enamel, Lady, C. Hatson, On Copper, Brass Frame, 3 In.	265.00
Enamel, Woman, On Copper, Signed, Brass Frame, 3 1/2 x 3 1/4 In.	360.00 to 410.00
Graphite On Paper, Wrestlers, George Dureau, 16 1/2 x 14 In.	210.00
Ink & Oil On Parchment, Dodge Family Coat Of Arms, Image, 17 x 10 1/4 In.	370.00
Ink & Oil On Parchment, Stone Family Coat Of Arms, Sight, 13 1/4 x 9 1/4 In.	370.00
Oil On Board, 2 Cats In Sailboat, 6 x 8 In.	467.00
Oil On Board, 3-Masted Ship, Gilt Frame, 17 1/4 x 19 1/2 In.	495.00
Oil On Board, A Cloudy Afternoon, Frame, 8 x 9 In.	300.00
Oil On Board, A Courtier With Pet Bird, Frame, 14 x 10 In.	287.00
Oil On Board, A Cropper, Along The Furrow, Thomas Ivester Lloyd, Pair, 10 x 14 In.	1980.00
Oil On Board, Basket Of Flowers With Butterfly, Gilt Frame, 3 1/4 x 5 3/8 In., Pair	305.00
Oil On Board, Bayou, Cypress, Oak Trees, Alexander J. Drysdale, 1916, 20 x 29 In.	2310.00
Oil On Board, Boy Fishing Landscape, 16 5/8 x 11 3/4 In.	220.00
Oil On Board, California Mountain Landscape, T. Douglas, Frame, 11 1/2 In.	100.00
Oil On Board, Deer Family In Landscape, Burl Frame, 16 1/2 x 21 1/2 In.	260.00
Oil On Board, Desert Scene, Watson Barratt, Frame, 1911, 10 1/2 x 11 In.	770.00
Oil On Board, Fall Scene, Barn, 23 x 17 In.	55.00
Oil On Board, Forest Path, 2 Women & Man, 18th Century Clothes, 12 x 9 In.	245.00
Oil On Board, Gentleman, Gilt Frame, 11 x 10 1/2 In.	165.00
Oil On Board, Girl In Nautical Hat, Howard Chandler Christy, 11 1/2 x 7 1/2 In.	1035.00
Oil On Board, Girl Skaters, Mildred C. Jones, Carved Frame, 24 1/2 x 29 1/2 In.	1610.00
Oil On Board, Indians, On Horses In Desert, E.R. McAnelly, c.1890, 7 x 10 In.	145.00
Oil On Board, Landscape, C.W. Knapp, Ornate Gilt Frame, 9 7/8 x 13 1/2 In.	770.00
Oil On Board, Landscape, Trees, Barn, H.R. Kenyon, Frame, 9 1/2 x 11 1/4 In.	405.00
Oil On Board, Lobster Traps, Rockport, James K. Bonnar, 19 1/2 x 23 1/2 In.	920.00
Oil On Board, Louisiana Live Oak, Alexander J. Drysdale, 9 1/2 x 29 1/2 In.	1980.00
Oil On Board, Morning At W. Chatham, H. Dunbar, Frame, 11 x 16 In.	55.00
Oil On Board, Motorboats At Dock, Trees, Ken Gore, Frame, 11 3/4 x 13 1/2 In.	345.00
Oil On Board, Mountain Landscape, Village, Demes Csanky, 7 3/8 x 10 1/2 In.	140.00
Oil On Board, O Sleep Darling, Sleep O Rest, Frame, 12 5/8 x 16 5/8 In.	440.00
Oil On Board, Patria, Landscape With Mountains, Richard Kozlow, 25 x 46 In.	460.00
Oil On Board, Portland Harbor, G.W. Hathaway, Gold Gesso Frame, 6 x 10 In.	2530.00
Oil On Board, Road In Nova Scotia, Charles Gruppe, Gold Frame, 7 3/4 x 11 1/4 In.	920.00
Oil On Board, Rockport Bass Rocks, Emile A. Gruppe, 1960, 15 1/2 x 19 1/2 In.	1150.00
Oil On Board, Rocky Coastline, G.M. Hathaway, Gilt Gesso Frame, 9 x 12 1/2 In.	1035.00
Oil On Board, School Approaching Lighthouse, Frame, 19th Century, 14 x 24 In.	410.00
Oil On Board, Still Life, Basket Of Cherries, Gilt Frame, 12 1/4 x 16 1/2 In.	300.00
Oil On Board, Still Life, Fruit In Bowl, Gold Painted Frame, 17 1/2 x 24 In.	275.00
Oil On Board, Titanic, April 13, 1912, O. Plant, Frame, 14 1/2 x 35 1/2 In.	575.00
Oil On Board, Urban Landscape, Man On Sidewalk, T. Harta Becket, Frame, 21 x 13 In.	95.00
Oil On Board, Wharf Scene, Gerrit Hondius, 13 3/4 x 21 1/2 In.	135.00
Oil On Board, Winter Landscape, Walter Emerson Baum, Frame, 13 1/2 x 9 1/2 In.	865.00
Oil On Board, Young Girl With Bowl, Man In Chair, Frame, 14 x 10 1/2 In.	375.00
Oil On Canvas, 2 Cats On Rug, Percy Sanborn, Gold Gesso Frame, 12 1/2 x 14 1/2 In.	865.00
Oil On Canvas, 2 Cowboys Fording Stream, H.S.S. Burg, Gilt Frame, 16 3/4 x 22 In.	192.00
Oil On Canvas, 3 Young Women, Dancing In Wooded Setting, Frame, 19 x 43 In.	27.00
Oil On Canvas, 3-Masted Sailing Ship, V.F. Porter, 1925, 22 x 34 In.	1265.00
Oil On Canvas, 3-Masted Ship, On Rocks, Stormy Sea, Frame, 22 x 34 In.	440.00
Oil On Canvas, 7 Black Men Gambling, Frame, 8 x 11 In.	770.00
Oil On Canvas, A Rest Outside Of The Village, H. Nichols, Frame, 1877, 12 x 22 In.	517.00
Oil On Canvas, A Stitch In Time, Signed, David Fulton, England, Frame, 20 x 16 In.	2070.00
Oil On Canvas, After The Ball Is Over, John C. Wittmenn, 1936, 30 1/2 x 40 1/2 In.	1095.00
Oil On Canvas, Alaskan Landscape, Steamship, Audrey Roth, Gesso Frame, 30 x 45 In.	750.00
Oil On Canvas, Allegorical Figure Of A Woman With Fruits, Almonds, 25 x 19 In.	575.00
Oil On Canvas, Alpine Scene, Pines & River, F. Kammeyer, Frame, 23 x 31 In.	80.00

Oil On Canvas, Approaching Storm, Frame, 26 x 32 In. 1380.00
Oil On Canvas, Approaching Storm, John J. Enneking, Frame, 11 1/2 x 17 1/2 In. 865.00
Oil On Canvas, Autumn Days, Sheep Grazing, Thomas Craig Ana, Frame, 12 x 16 In. ... 575.00
Oil On Canvas, Autumn Landscape, Harold C. Dunbar, Frame, 32 x 37 x 42 In. 990.00
Oil On Canvas, Barn Interior, Horses, Dog, F. Selzer, 1878, 10 x 15 In. 345.00
Oil On Canvas, Bayou Shack, M. Coltraro, 8 1/4 x 10 1/4 In. 70.00
Oil On Canvas, Beached, Signed, Hubert Thornley, England, Frame, 19 x 28 In. 3680.00
Oil On Canvas, Black Youth, Birds In Straw Hat, Frame, 13 x 10 In. 412.00
Oil On Canvas, Boats In Mexican Harbor, Jeb Bjorkegran, 49 3/4 x 49 3/4 In. 165.00
Oil On Canvas, Boy Going Over Fence, Dog, Gilt Frame, 24 1/4 x 14 In. 355.00
Oil On Canvas, Boys & Dog At Beach, J. Sutcliffe, Gesso Frame, 11 1/2 x 8 1/2 In. 2990.00
Oil On Canvas, Brook, Pool, Forest, A. Thieme, Frame, 1941, 19 1/2 x 27 1/2 In. 1150.00
Oil On Canvas, Chickens In Hay Pile, Howard Hill, Frame, 1874, 8 3/4 x 6 3/4 In. 865.00
Oil On Canvas, Church Interior, Worshipers, E.V. Simonson, 1890, 34 x 26 In. 1150.00
Oil On Canvas, Civil War Cavalry, Union Soldiers, Gesso Frame, 25 1/2 x 41 1/2 In. 1955.00
Oil On Canvas, Clipper Ship At Sea, Frame, 1934, 24 x 34 In. 400.00
Oil On Canvas, Clipper Ship, Royal Dane, R. MacGregor, Frame, 19 1/2 x 29 1/2 In. 690.00
Oil On Canvas, Coaching Scene, Signed, England, Frame, 24 x 36 In. 1955.00
Oil On Canvas, Coastal Scene, Ogunquit, Me., Frame, 25 x 30 In. 1035.00
Oil On Canvas, Courting Lovers, 19th Century, 23 1/4 x 31 1/4 In. 1587.00
Oil On Canvas, Cows At Water, Farmhouse, Gold Decorated Frame, 12 x 16 In. 1725.00
Oil On Canvas, Cows Watering At The River, J. Braithwaite, 1800s, 20 x 30 In. 660.00
Oil On Canvas, Daisies In Field, Frame, Late 19th Century, 19 1/2 x 9 1/2 In. 165.00
Oil On Canvas, English Landscape, Abbey & Cows, Lillian Alsdorf, Frame, 20 x 30 In. .. 935.00
Oil On Canvas, European Genre Scene, A. Berger, Gilt Frame, 26 x 36 In. 195.00
Oil On Canvas, European Harbor Scene, Ships At Dock, Monogram H, 17 x 31 In. 880.00
Oil On Canvas, European Landscape, Gothic Ruins, Frame, 22 1/2 x 26 3/4 In. 365.00
Oil On Canvas, European Scene, Palace, Wood Mounted, Frame, 31 x 45 In. 355.00
Oil On Canvas, Farm Landscape, Haystacks, Nicholas Richard Brewer, 15 x 23 In. 1495.00
Oil On Canvas, Farmer & Horses Plowing, Walter Goltz, 22 1/2 x 27 1/2 In. 1610.00
Oil On Canvas, Farmyard Scene, Horses & Chickens, Frame, 14 x 16 In. 1955.00
Oil On Canvas, Forest Scene With Stream, Ernest Fredericks, Frame, 20 1/2 x 25 In. 195.00
Oil On Canvas, French Cavalier, 20th Century, 32 1/4 x 26 1/4 In. 200.00
Oil On Canvas, Fruit Still Life, M. Campbell, Signed, 1905, 20 x 30 In. 72.00
Oil On Canvas, Garden & Pavilion Scene, Chinese Export, 1820, 18 x 22 In. 990.00
Oil On Canvas, Gentleman With Book, England, 18th Century, 29 1/4 x 22 1/4 In. 805.00
Oil On Canvas, Gentleman, 19th Century, 28 x 22 1/2 In. 1035.00
Oil On Canvas, Gentleman, John Smibert, Oval, Giltwood Frame, 13 x 11 In. 300.00
Oil On Canvas, Gentleman, Lemuel Sherwood, 19th Century, 36 x 29 In. 825.00
Oil On Canvas, Gentleman, Red Chair, Gilt Frame, 35 1/2 x 30 1/2 In. 220.00
Oil On Canvas, Girl With Black & White Dog, Framed, 16 x 13 In. 302.00
Oil On Canvas, Girl, Brown Hair, S.B. Waugh, 1854, Gilt Frame, 24 x 20 In. 410.00
Oil On Canvas, Gloucester Fishing, T.V.C. Valenkamph, Frame, 1902, 20 x 28 In. 1438.00
Oil On Canvas, Golden Autumn, Lake, Cottage, Frederick D. Ogden, Frame, 24 x 36 In. .. 302.00
Oil On Canvas, Gray Jungle Fowls, Edwin Megargee, 1910, 13 1/2 x 21 1/2 In. 345.00
Oil On Canvas, Gypsy Encampment, Leslie Cope, Frame, 1956, 24 1/2 x 28 3/4 In. 1375.00
Oil On Canvas, Gypsy Girl, A. Ricio, Europe, Late 19th-Early 20th Century, 12 x 9 In. ... 290.00
Oil On Canvas, Harbor Scene, Windmill, George Herbert McCord, 8 1/4 x 10 1/4 In. 375.00
Oil On Canvas, Harbor Scene, With Sailboats, Signed, A. Martens, Frame, 7 x 10 In. 345.00
Oil On Canvas, Hay Wagon Crossing A Bridge, Frame, 19 3/4 x 23 1/2 In. 546.00
Oil On Canvas, Head Of Young Woman, Harry Mills Walcott, 12 3/4 x 9 1/2 In. 575.00
Oil On Canvas, Highland Sheep, Mountain Landscape, Wm. Watson, Jr., 21 x 32 In. 1100.00
Oil On Canvas, Horse & Rider On Ridge, Bill L. Hill, Frame, 19 1/4 x 29 1/4 In. 1725.00
Oil On Canvas, Hudson River Valley Landscape, Frame, 18 x 24 In. 135.00
Oil On Canvas, Indian Couple At Lily Pond, 1900, 19 x 23 1/2 In. 950.00
Oil On Canvas, Interior Scene Of Elderly Musician, Signed, Frame, 19 x 12 1/2 In. 770.00
Oil On Canvas, Lady With Horse, Henry R. Poore, 24 x 38 1/2 In. 920.00
Oil On Canvas, Lake & Mountains, Lily Meyer, Gilt Frame, 15 1/2 x 11 1/2 In. 70.00
Oil On Canvas, Landscape Scene, Farmer Beside Thatch Roof Cottage, 20 x 30 In. 805.00
Oil On Canvas, Landscape With People, Village, Frame, 19 1/4 x 24 1/4 In. 345.00
Oil On Canvas, Landscape, A. De Beul, Gilt Frame, 19 x 23 1/4 In. 110.00
Oil On Canvas, Landscape, Cows, Carl Wilhelm Malchin, 1898, 11 x 19 1/4 In. 1540.00
Oil On Canvas, Landscape, Deer, Stream, Waterfall, G.F. Keil, 25 1/2 x 41 1/2 In. 520.00

Oil On Canvas, Landscape, El Burkhart, Frame, 22 x 26 In. 715.00
Oil On Canvas, Landscape, Fall, Signed Greta Strom, 1918, 25 x 36 In. 412.00
Oil On Canvas, Landscape, Figures On Path, Know, Frame, 19th Century, 15 x 25 In. 250.00
Oil On Canvas, Landscape, Hudson River, 19th Century, 22 x 30 In. 1650.00
Oil On Canvas, Landscape, J.W. Spelman, Gilt Frame, 15 1/2 x 19 1/2 In. 110.00
Oil On Canvas, Landscape, Man, Horse & Cart, Continental, 19th Century, 20 x 30 In. ... 920.00
Oil On Canvas, Landscape, Mountains & Cows, Gilt Frame, 23 3/4 x 30 3/4 In. 55.00
Oil On Canvas, Landscape, Schoen, Frame, 1898, 26 1/2 x 38 1/4 In. 55.00
Oil On Canvas, Lighthouse, Fishing Boats, A. Van Beest, 1860, 11 1/2 x 19 1/2 In. 3163.00
Oil On Canvas, Lobster Boat At Dock, Wm. Lester Stevens, Frame, 24 x 29 1/2 In. 3105.00
Oil On Canvas, Madonna, Child, European School, Carved Gilt Frame, 24 5/8 x 20 In. 3165.00
Oil On Canvas, Maine Cottage, Signed, F.H. McKay, Frame, c.1930, 16 x 20 In. 248.00
Oil On Canvas, Man & Woman, Primitive, Masonite Back, Frame, 29 x 24 In., Pair 1100.00
Oil On Canvas, Man With Cane & Bible, Adelheid Dietrich, Frame, 8 x 10 1/2 In. 2070.00
Oil On Canvas, Man Working In Flower Garden, R. Hargrove, Frame, 26 x 28 In. 110.00
Oil On Canvas, Man, Black Frock Coat, Walking Stick, Frame, 41 x 35 In. 990.00
Oil On Canvas, Man, Blue Coat, Frame, 21 1/2 x 18 In. 880.00
Oil On Canvas, Man, Plaid Coat, Harry Farlow, 29 3/4 x 24 1/2 In. 135.00
Oil On Canvas, Man, Signed Legal, Frame, 28 3/4 x 23 1/2 In. 550.00
Oil On Canvas, Marsh On Stormy Day, Alexander Helwig Wyant, 15 1/2 x 19 1/2 In. 990.00
Oil On Canvas, Monhegan, Maine Shore, Harry Pierce, Frame, 20 x 17 In. 247.00
Oil On Canvas, Moonlit Lake, Man In Canoe, Joseph B. Kahill, Frame, 27 x 17 In. 575.00
Oil On Canvas, Moonlit Sea, Crashing Waves, Robert Wood, Gilt Frame, 20 x 24 In. 290.00
Oil On Canvas, Morning Light, Harbor Scene, Anthony Thieme, 24 1/2 x 29 1/2 In. 9775.00
Oil On Canvas, Mountain Landscape, Lake, Dixon, Gilt Frame, 21 1/2 x 31 3/4 In. 220.00
Oil On Canvas, Munchen, Mountain Landscape, Pond, Albert Gos, 22 x 24 In. 635.00
Oil On Canvas, Muskingham River Lock, A. Tallmadge, Frame, 23 3/4 x 27 3/4 In. 72.00
Oil On Canvas, North African Bazaar, Marino Passini, 30 x 40 In. 80.00
Oil On Canvas, Old Woman, Bonnet, Grandmother Died 1842, Frame, 14 x 11 In. 300.00
Oil On Canvas, Older Gentleman, Ornate Frame, 17 x 21 3/4 In. 80.00
Oil On Canvas, On The River Meuse Holland, Walter F. Lansil, Frame, 1899, 9 x 12 In. .. 460.00
Oil On Canvas, People Haying, Horses & Wagon, Gustave Purcha, Frame, 23 x 31 In. 520.00
Oil On Canvas, Peter Minuit, Indian Chiefs, Buy Manhattan Island, 29 x 36 In. 8050.00
Oil On Canvas, Place Blanche, Paris, Antoine Blanchard, Frame, 19 1/2 x 23 1/2 In. 1150.00
Oil On Canvas, Pond & Birch Trees, Gilbert O. Roy, Frame, 1920, 42 3/4 x 30 1/2 In. ... 260.00
Oil On Canvas, Portrait, John H. Waymire & Wife, Gilt Frame, 27 x 22 In., Pair 660.00
Oil On Canvas, Portrait, Man & Woman, 1800, 26 x 25 In., Pair 1650.00
Oil On Canvas, Portrait, Oriental, E. Burkhart, Brass Strip Frame, 18 1/4 x 21 1/4 In. 360.00
Oil On Canvas, Portrait, Ruth Blake Lovering, Gilt Frame, 1820s, 20 x 15 1/2 In. 1438.00
Oil On Canvas, Portrait, Willam Stowe, Signed, Titled, J.G. Chandler, 1847, 36 x 29 In. .. 550.00
Oil On Canvas, River In October, Thos. Patten, Frame, 36 1/2 x 32 1/2 In. 305.00
Oil On Canvas, Road To Hope, 2 Farmers, Country Road, K. Sato, 21 x 17 1/2 In. 370.00
Oil On Canvas, Rocky Landscape, Sailing Ship, C. Howard, 16 x 24 In. 290.00
Oil On Canvas, Rural Cottage, E. Cole, England, Early 1900s, 16 x 20 In. 495.00
Oil On Canvas, Sagamore Porch Window, View, E.C. Clark, Frame, 1930, 15 x 12 In. 231.00
Oil On Canvas, Sailboats In Bay, American, Signed L.R., Frame, 20 x 24 In. 145.00
Oil On Canvas, Sailing Ship, A.W. Johnston, Gilt Frame, 30 x 24 1/2 In. 110.00
Oil On Canvas, Sea Captain, Board Mounted, Frame, 13 3/4 x 10 3/4 In. 515.00
Oil On Canvas, Seascape, Gaday, Gilt Frame, 17 1/2 x 26 1/4 In. 110.00
Oil On Canvas, Seascape, Rocky Shore At Sunrise, Geo. F. Schultz, 12 x 24 In. 165.00
Oil On Canvas, Seated Gentleman, Walter I. Cox, Ornate Gilt Frame, 36 x 28 In. 460.00
Oil On Canvas, Seated Woman, 43 x 32 In. 575.00
Oil On Canvas, Sheep In Pen, F. Stewart, Gesso Gilt Frame, 23 1/2 x 36 1/2 In. 460.00
Oil On Canvas, Ship At Sunset, M.F.H. De Haas, Gesso Frame, 12 1/4 x 22 3/4 In. 805.00
Oil On Canvas, Ship On The High Seas, England, 19th Century, 12 x 18 In. 715.00
Oil On Canvas, Shipwrecked Steamer, Crowd On Shore, Lighthouse, 20 x 30 In. 690.00
Oil On Canvas, Shore Whaling Scene, Palm Tree, 12 x 16 In. 245.00
Oil On Canvas, Skaters On River, Houses, Continental, Frame, 26 1/2 x 33 1/2 In. 1610.00
Oil On Canvas, Still Life With Bird, Phillipe Moyen, Gilt Frame, 1957, 5 1/4 In. 30.00
Oil On Canvas, Still Life With Wine Decanter, Irving Patterson, 1910, 18 x 14 In. 550.00
Oil On Canvas, Still Life, Flowers & Vase, G. Ames Aldrich, Frame, 29 1/2 x 15 1/2 In. .. 980.00
Oil On Canvas, Still Life, Flowers, Brown Vase, Van Horn, Frame, 18 x 21 In. 110.00
Oil On Canvas, Still Life, Flowers, Gilt Frame, 24 x 19 In. 385.00

Oil On Canvas, Still Life, Fruit Basket, F.W. Butler, Frame, 1880, 7 1/2 x 9 1/2 In. 405.00
Oil On Canvas, Still Life, Grapes & Orange, Gilt Frame, 10 x 11 5/8 In. 440.00
Oil On Canvas, Still Life, Sunflowers, Cory Bernsen, Frame, 1952, 23 1/4 x 29 1/2 In. ... 250.00
Oil On Canvas, Stormy Seascape, Sailing Vessel, Kenneth Carter, 41 1/2 x 71 1/2 In. 55.00
Oil On Canvas, Street Scene, Horses & Carriage, Brissong, Frame, 23 1/2 x 35 1/2 In. ... 290.00
Oil On Canvas, Summer Landscape, Gustave Wigand, Frame, 15 1/2 x 11 1/2 In. 1095.00
Oil On Canvas, Sunflowers In Vase, Clara L. Deike, Early 1900s, 23 x 19 3/4 In. 1650.00
Oil On Canvas, Tavern Scene, Frame, 20 x 17 In. 575.00
Oil On Canvas, Trees In Autumn, C.W. Dickinson, Art Nouveau Gilt Frame, 46 x 33 In. ... 770.00
Oil On Canvas, Venetian Scene, George Bogert, 19 1/2 x 29 1/4 In. 660.00
Oil On Canvas, Victorian Woman, Black Dress, White Lace Collar, Frame, 43 x 36 In. ... 495.00
Oil On Canvas, Waiting, Anne Allen, 19th Century, Frame, 18 x 24 In. 467.00
Oil On Canvas, Western Landscape, Rafael Guzman, Gilt Frame, 19 x 23 In. 55.00
Oil On Canvas, Winter Scene With Skaters, Signed Edward Gay, Frame, 15 x 25 In. 1210.00
Oil On Canvas, Winter Scene, Frank Louville Bowie, Frame, 16 1/2 x 20 1/2 In. 980.00
Oil On Canvas, Woman In Evening Dress, P. Perkins, 20th Century, 20 x 30 In. 250.00
Oil On Canvas, Woman With Letter, Red Cape, Gilt Frame, 29 x 24 1/2 In. 715.00
Oil On Canvas, Woman, 19th Century, 23 x 19 In. 205.00
Oil On Canvas, Woman, England, 19th Century, 50 x 40 In. 1150.00
Oil On Canvas, Woman, Francis DeErdely, 1941, 20 x 16 In. 230.00
Oil On Canvas, Woman, Green Dress, Red Drape, Gilt Frame, 34 x 29 In. 1320.00
Oil On Canvas, Woman, Kneeling, Near Girl In Bed, Miniature, 7 3/8 x 6 1/4 In. 495.00
Oil On Canvas, Woman, Lace Cap, Frame, 29 x 24 In. 145.00
Oil On Canvas, Woman, Oliver Dennett Grover, 30 x 24 In. 770.00
Oil On Canvas, Woman, White Dress, Frame, 27 x 22 3/4 In. 1320.00
Oil On Canvas, Young Woman Holding A Bluebird, Signed, 16 x 10 In. 720.00
Oil On Canvas, Young Woman With Green Shawl, Frame, 28 x 21 In. 690.00
Oil On Canvas, Young Woman With Rose, C. Burdick, Gesso Frame, 1893, 20 x 16 In. 200.00
Oil On Canvas, Young Woman, Black Dress, Gilt Frame, 30 x 25 In. 385.00
Oil On Canvas, Young Woman, Blue Scarf, Gilt Frame, 30 x 25 In. 135.00
Oil On Canvas, Young Woman, Pink Dress, Frame, 29 x 24 In. 1760.00
Oil On Cardboard, Bearded Man Husking Corn, Gilt Frame, 13 x 9 1/2 In. 85.00
Oil On Masonite, Clown, Pastel Colors, Leonore C. Antheil, Frame, 35 3/4 x 28 In. 55.00
Oil On Masonite, Composition With Goldfishes, Jim Harmon, '49, 24 x 20 In. 70.00
Oil On Masonite, Round Up On The Desert, Dean Close, Frame, 27 x 31 In. 55.00
Oil On Masonite, Water Stop On The Prairie, Dean Close, Frame, 31 1/4 x 43 1/4 In. 140.00
Oil On Masonite, Wharf Scene, Boats, Nets, Leslie Cope, Frame, 1978, 33 x 45 In. 1430.00
Oil On Masonite, Winter Landscape, K. Lundborg, Frame, 1935, 11 x 15 1/4 In. 165.00
Oil On Panel, Admiration, Men On Bridge, Folk Art, Burl Frame, 16 x 21 1/2 In. 460.00
Oil On Panel, Boy Blue, Richard Howard, Frame, 5 1/4 x 3 3/4 In. 357.00
Oil On Panel, English Landscape, Brick Bridge, J. Singer, Frame, 20 x 26 1/4 In. 82.00
Oil On Panel, Farmyard Scene, Horses & Livestock, Signed, Frame, 1846, 13 x 19 In. ... 1955.00
Oil On Panel, Indian Soldier Scout, Frame, 19th Century, 6 3/4 x 7 In. 3450.00
Oil On Panel, Kitten In Compote, Initialed, 13 x 9 In. 245.00
Oil On Panel, Landscape With River, CNM, 19th Century, 9 3/4 x 7 1/4 In. 220.00
Oil On Panel, Landscape With Sheep, Amy Beck, Gilt Frame, 12 1/2 x 20 1/2 In. 165.00
Oil On Panel, Landscape, Julie Hart Kempson, Frame, 19th Century, 15 x 10 In. 275.00
Oil On Panel, Landscape, Trees & Poultry, I.S. Verheygen, Gilt Frame, 25 x 27 In. 880.00
Oil On Panel, Man, Black Coat, Gilt Frame, 24 x 20 In. 440.00
Oil On Panel, Man, Black Frock Coat, Frame, 32 x 19 In. 550.00
Oil On Panel, Portrait, Duke Of Wellington, Alexandre De Latour, 4 1/2 x 3 1/2 In. 1210.00
Oil On Panel, Rev. Richard, Man In Red Chair, Frame, 18th Century, 9 x 6 3/4 In. 345.00
Oil On Panel, River Scene, People On Horseback, England, 18th Century, 21 x 29 In. 2200.00
Oil On Panel, Still Life, Morning Glories, Geo. Cochran Lambdin, 1870, 20 x 7 In. 1760.00
Oil On Panel, Swan Flights, Frame, 1980, 11 1/2 x 15 1/2 In. 200.00
Oil On Panel, Village Scene, Tavern, William Collins, 11 3/4 x 9 1/2 In. 1100.00
Oil On Panel, Wheat Field & Landscape, Frame, 14 x 21 1/4 In. 405.00
Oil On Panel, Woman At Table With Book, Folk Art, Frame, c.1810, 30 x 24 1/2 In. 520.00
Oil On Panel, Woman, Dark Hair, Rose, Gilt Frame, 35 x 30 In. 990.00
Oil On Panel, Young Man, Bird's Eye Veneer & Walnut Frame, 11 x 9 In. 330.00
Oil On Paper, Fox Hunting & Hounds, Mounted On Board, Frame, 16 3/4 x 22 In. 220.00
Oil On Paper, Zacharis Family, N. Orleans, Marion Beasley, 1844, 7 5/8 x 11 5/8 In. 1320.00
Oil On Tin, Barnyard Scene, Frame, 16 x 23 1/8 In., Pair 935.00

Oil On Tin, Gentleman & Woman, Brass On Wood Frame, 15 x 13 In., Pair 550.00
Oil On Tin, Landscape, Train Crossing Bridge, 19th Century, 23 3/4 x 33 1/2 In. 490.00
Oil On Wood, 3-Masted Ship, American Flag, W.H. Brunnings, Frame, 13 x 15 3/4 In. ... 220.00
Oil On Wood, Indian, George W. Maher, Frame, 14 & 20 In., Pair 1980.00
Oil On Wood, Landscape, Pine Tree, Gilt Frame, 17 1/2 x 13 3/4 In. 82.00
Oil On Wood, Woman Spinning, Moorish Window, Ornate Frame, 21 1/2 x 19 1/2 In. 220.00
On Celluloid, Napoleon By Andree Bigol, Metal Frame, 4 x 3 1/2 In. 550.00
On Ivory, 2 Distinguished Gentlemen, Diagonal, England, 4 Piece 1150.00
On Ivory, An Elegant Gentleman, Yew Wood Frame, 5 7/8 x 7 1/8 In. 315.00
On Ivory, Gentleman, Frock Coat, White Hair, Lacquered Frame, Brass Trim, 5 3/4 In. ... 330.00
On Ivory, Gentleman, Gilt Frame, Brooch Back, 1 11/16 In. 138.00
On Ivory, Gentleman, Sir Bevil Grensil, Frame, 5 1/2 x 5 In. 270.00
On Ivory, Infant, Wearing White Gown, Cap, Oval, England, 2 x 1 1/2 In. 545.00
On Ivory, Lady With Pearls, Filigree Brass Frame, 3 1/4 x 2 1/2 In. 300.00
On Ivory, Lady, Gilt Brass Frame, 19th Century, 2 1/2 x 2 1/8 In. 180.00
On Ivory, Madonna & Child, Gilt Filigree Frame, 4 x 3 3/4 In. 900.00
On Ivory, Man, Black Coat, Gold Case, Woven Hair On Reverse, 2 1/4 x 2 3/4 In. 465.00
On Ivory, Marie De Medicis, Gilt Metal Frame, Dieugaat, 4 1/2 In. 275.00
On Ivory, Matron, Lace Bonnet, Gilt Insert, Leatherized Case, Marked, 1778, 3 x 4 In. ... 468.00
On Ivory, Military Man, Red Uniform, Lacquered Frame, Brass Trim, 6 1/4 In. 220.00
On Ivory, Portrait, Colonial Sibthorpe, Presentation 1875, 6 1/2 x 5 1/2 In. 165.00
On Ivory, Portrait, Lady Wearing Ribbons, Pearls In Hair, Continental, 6 x 4 1/2 In. 690.00
On Ivory, Portrait, Man & Woman, Blue Ground, Frame, 3 1/4 x 2 1/2 In., Pair 495.00
On Ivory, Portrait, Young Man, Frock Coat, Lacquered Frame, Brass Trim, 4 3/8 In. 165.00
On Ivory, Sarah Johnson Livingston, 1745, 1 3/4 x 1 1/2 In. 863.00
On Ivory, White Haired Man, Gray Waist Coat, Frock Coat, Frame, 4 1/2 x 4 In. 545.00
On Ivory, Woman, Bonnet With Flowers, Black Dress, Marie Marcellas, Frame, 5 1/4 In. . 755.00
On Ivory, Woman, Elaborate Coiffure, Playing Instrument, Bouillard, 7 1/4 In. 852.00
On Ivory, Woman, Facing 3/4 Left, Late 19th-Early 20th Century, 4 1/4 In. 265.00
On Ivory, Woman, High Collar, Mary Augusta, Albany, August 1825, Frame, 4 5/8 In. ... 355.00
On Ivory, Woman, In Elizabethan Dress, Late 19th-Early 20th Century, 3 1/4 In. 195.00
On Ivory, Woman, Lace Bonnet & Collar, Black Dress, Lacquered Frame, 5 1/4 In. 357.00
On Ivory, Woman, Red Shawl, White Dress, Gold Frame, Locks Of Hair, 2 3/4 In. 3220.00
On Ivory, Woman, Seated, Draped Interior, Wooden Frame, 6 1/2 x 5 1/4 In. 260.00
On Ivory, Woman, With Fan, Leather Booklet Holder, 6 x 4 1/2 In. 290.00
On Ivory, Young Child, Blond Hair, Blue Eyes, Oval, Frame, 4 1/4 x 3 5/8 In. 385.00
On Ivory, Young Indian Woman, With Jewels, Bender, Frame, 8 x 7 1/4 In. 325.00
On Ivory, Young Lady, Lace Bonnet, Versehinden 1839, Brass Frame, Round, 2 1/4 In. .. 230.00
On Ivory, Young Man, Blue Background, Gilt Frame, 4 3/4 x 4 1/4 In. 247.00
On Ivory, Young Woman, Black Dress, Necklace, Sky, Buildings, Frame, 4 x 3 1/2 In. ... 605.00
On Ivory, Young Woman, Bonnet, Lavender Sash, Brass Oval Frame, 3 7/8 In. 755.00
On Ivory, Young Woman, Dog, Romney, Gilded Frame, Easel Back, 4 1/8 x 3 3/8 In. 440.00
On Metal, Village, Windmill, Mechanical, Electric Motor, Frame, 25 x 31 x 8 In. 2300.00
On Panel, Woman, White Bonnet, Primitive, Varnished, 20 x 16 In. 72.00
On Paper, Woman, Black Dress, White Bonnet, Leatherized Case, 4 7/8 x 4 1/4 In. 248.00
On Porcelain, Genre Scene, Ebonized Wooden Frame, 10 1/4 x 12 5/8 In., Pair 490.00
On Porcelain, Gentleman, Handlebar Mustache, Oval Frame, 3 5/8 In. 110.00
On Porcelain, Likeness Of Daphne, Laurel Wreath, Florentine Frame, Signed, 3 1/4 In. .. 247.00
On Porcelain, Young Girl, Frame, Circular, 2 In. 550.00
On Velvet, Basket, Of Strawberries, Shadow Box Frame, 16 x 21 In. 1725.00
On Velvet, Eagle Flag, Rose, 3 American Beauties, Glitter, Modern Frame, 23 x 26 In. ... 330.00
On Velvet, Landscape, Castle, People, 19th Century, 19 1/2 x 25 1/2 In. 460.00
On Velvet, Rooster & 2 Hens, Frame, 24 1/4 x 27 In. 385.00
On Velvet, Stag, Palm Trees, Primitive, Gilt Frame, 29 1/2 x 20 In. 220.00
On Wood, Flying Amazing Circus, Silver, Gold Frame, 1920s, 60 In. 400.00
Reverse On Glass, Napoleon, 12 x 9 In. 575.00
Reverse On Glass, Sinking Of Titanic, Frame, 20th Century, 13 1/2 x 27 1/2 In. 75.00
Reverse On Glass, Titanic Sinking, Life Rafts In Water, Frame, 15 1/2 x 19 1/2 In. 86.00
Reverse On Glass, Water & Pavilions, Mountains, China, 19th Century, 20 x 29 In. 770.00
Reverse On Glass, Young Man, Alexander Hamilton, Frame, 1757-1804, 7 x 5 In. 575.00
Reverse On Glass, Young Woman Interior, Blue Border, China, 20 x 14 In., Pair 990.00
Theorem, Bluebirds & Red Roses, Cream Velvet, Frame, 24 x 18 In. 385.00
Whaling Scene, American & British Ships, 36 x 48 In. 880.00

PAIRPOINT Manufacturing Company started in 1880 in New Bedford, Massachusetts. It soon joined with the glassworks nearby and made glass, silver-plated pieces, and lamps. Reverse-painted glass shades and molded shades known as *puffies* were part of the production until the 1930s. The company reorganized and changed its name several times but is still working today. Items listed here are glass or glass and metal. Silver-plated pieces are listed under Silver Plate.

Banana Boat, Myrtle, 11 x 5 In. 780.00
Basket, Green, 8 In. 85.00
Bowl, Bishop's Hat, Thistle, 3 x 10 In. 410.00
Bowl, Blackberry, Amber, Cuspidor Shape, 10 In. 125.00
Bowl, Light Green, Flared, Controlled Bubble Ball Connector, 10 In. 200.00
Bowl, Myrtle, 9 In. 730.00
Box, Cover, Green To White, Gold, Signed, PMC, 3 In. 403.00
Box, Dresser, Pansy Blossoms On Cover, 2 1/2 x 6 In. 485.00
Carafe, Beatrice 250.00
Centerpiece, Allover Diamond Point, Silver Plated Putto, Holding Flower, 9 1/4 In. 230.00
Centerpiece, Stag Heads Hold Oval, Brass, Crystal Bowl, c.1920, 10 x 14 x 11 In. 550.00
Chalice, Bryden Burmese, Satin, 10 1/4 In. 345.00
Cologne Bottle, Nevada, 5 In. 225.00
Cologne Bottle, Nevada, Sterling Silver Stopper, 5 In. 295.00
Compote, Blueberry, 8 1/4 x 7 In. 200.00
Compote, Hobstar Foot, Teardrop Stem, 9 3/4 In. 650.00
Cracker Jar, 16 Panels, Gold, Pink Roses, Green Leaves, Bryden Custard, Signed, 6 In. .. 595.00
Cup & Saucer, Repousse Panels, Exotic Florals, c.1885, 3 x 9 1/2 In. 55.00
Figurine, Swan, Spray Of 6 Enameled Flowers, 1970s, 7 x 6 1/2 In. 145.00
Goblet, Cobalt Blue Twist, Floral, 6 1/2 In. 160.00
Goblet, Floral Body, Cobalt Blue Twist, Stem, 6 1/2 In. 115.00
Goblet, Tassel Body, White Twist Stem, Swag, Star, 6 1/4 In. 140.00
Goblet, Yellow, White Twist Stem, 7 1/2 In. 175.00
Humidor, Nevada, Cutting, 9 1/2 In. 1325.00
Lamp, Cut Shade, 2-Light, Prisms, 15 1/2 In. 895.00
Lamp, Devonshire Shade, Silver Garland, 21 In. 11500.00
Lamp, Directoire Shade, Landscape, Towns, Castles, 24 In. 5460.00
Lamp, Exeter Shade, Scenic, 19 1/2 In. 3100.00
Lamp, Floral, 8 Panel, Brass Mesh Shade, Applied Reeds, 18 x 22 In. 550.00
Lamp, Landsdown Shade, Nautical Design, Dolphin Base, 15 1/2 In. 2300.00
Lamp, Mold Blown Shade, Blooms, Hummingbirds, White Metal Base, 13 1/2 In. 5750.00
Lamp, Papillion Shade, Silver Metal Butterfly, Roses, 20 In. 9200.00
Lamp, Puffy, Deep Pink Roses With Butterflies, Art Nouveau Base, 13 1/2 In. 7475.00
Lamp, Puffy, Grape, Multicolored, 19 In. 20700.00
Lamp, Puffy, Grapes, 2 Butterflies, Goblet Form Base, 8 In., Pair 3100.00
Lamp, Reverse Painted, Butterflies, Multicolored Trees, Flowers, 14 In. 1045.00
Lamp, Reverse Painted, Fishing Scene, Fishing Ships In Port, 18 In. 3850.00
Lamp, Reverse Painted, Gladioli, 1915, 21 In. 9775.00
Lamp, Reverse Painted, Landscape, G. Morley, 14-In. Shade 1665.00
Lamp, Reverse Painted, Landscape, Patinated Base, 23 In. 4025.00
Lamp, Reverse Painted, Metal, Stylized Floral, Red, Yellow, Green, Black, 15 In. 3450.00
Lamp, Reverse Painted, Onyx & Silver Plate Base, 14 In. 1610.00
Lamp, Reverse Painted, Orange Flowers, Green Centers, Ivory Ground, 13 In. 1045.00
Lamp, Reverse Painted, Rose Interior, Red, Pink, Yellow, Green Patina, 1915, 11 In. 5175.00
Lamp, Reverse Painted, Serene Landscape, Cottage, 15 In. 1150.00
Lamp, Reverse Painted, Ships At Sea, Stippled Conical Shade, C. Durand, 22 1/2 In. 4620.00
Lamp, Reverse Painted, Sunset Scene With Trees, Signed, 8 x 13 In. 330.00
Lamp, Reverse Painted, Tapestry, Etched Panels, 3 Light, Gilt Metal, 27 In. 2415.00
Lamp, Reverse Painted, Windmill, People, Animal Scene, 18 x 26 In. 10450.00
Lamp, Rose Tree Shade, 2 Butterflies Above Pink, Yellow Roses, 14 In. 4140.00
Lamp, Seville Shade, River Scene, Bronze, Gray Interior, 21 In. 6325.00
Lamp, Silvertone Panther & Cornucopia, Matching Shade & Base 2970.00
Lamp, Stratford Shade, Apple Blossoms, Roses, 15 x 8 In. .... 2875.00 to 3335.00
Lamp, Stratford Shade, Blue, Yellow Dogwood Blossoms, 15 x 8 In. 3450.00
Pitcher, Exotic Flora & Fauna, c.1885, 14 1/2 In. 240.00

Tray, Floral & Leaf Border, Scrolling Foliate Handles, 30 In. 5445.00
Urn, Rosario, Quilted, Footed, 1930, 11 In. 300.00
Vase, Auroria, Rock Crystal Cut, Urn Shape, 12 x 5 In. 425.00
Vase, Canaria Yellow, Floral Engraving, 8 In. 173.00
Vase, Cobalt Blue, Controlled Bubble Ball Connector Stem, 12 In. 170.00
Vase, Cornucopia, Clear Bubble Balls, 7 In. 250.00
Vase, Green, Leaf, Controlled Bubble Ball Connector Stem, 12 In. 115.00
Vase, Green, Quadruple Plate Holder, 12 In. 295.00
Vase, Mayfair, 13 In. 345.00
Vase, Ruby, Circular Knop, Everted Sloping Rim, 10 1/4 In. 690.00
Vase, Stick, Green, 12 In. 100.00

PALMER COX, BROWNIES, see Brownies category.

PAPER collectibles, including almanacs, catalogs, children's books, some greeting cards, stock certificates, and other paper ephemera, are listed here. Paper calendars are listed separately in the Calendar category. Paper items may be found in many other sections, such as Christmas and Movie.

Almanac, Ayer's American, Lowell, Massachusetts, 1879 .... 8.00
Almanac, B.F. Goodrich Farmer's Handbook & Almanac, 1948 .... 3.00
Almanac, Capital Almanac, 1890, 44 Pages, 8 1/2 x 8 In. 21.00
Almanac, Dr. Morse's Indian Rot Pills Almanac & Weather Forecaster, 1935 .... 4.00
Almanac, Dr. Mul-Cee's Family Practice Of Medicine & Almanac, Louisville, Ky., 1881 . 10.00
Almanac, Farmer's, 1820s 150.00
Almanac, Kate Greenaway, 1887 .... 120.00
Almanac, Lum & Abner's Family Almanac & Helpful Hints, Radio Premium, 1936 . .18.00 to 30.00
Almanac, Montgomery's Tippecanoe, 1841 .... 605.00
Almanac, Rhode Island, Stafford, 1738 .... 1650.00
Almanac, Telephone, American Telephone & Telegraph Co., 1937 .... 10.00
Almanac, Uncle Sam's, F.J. Haskin, 1941 .... 25.00
Almanac, Vinegar Bitters, New York City, 1874 .... 15.00
Almanac, War, Military Data, Dell Publishing, 1942 .... 50.00
Almanac, Warner's Safe Cure Company, Woman, Helm Of Boat, 1895 .... 18.00
Bond, Mortgage, South Mountain Railroad Co., $500, Due Feb. 1, 1903, 11 x 27 In. 8.00
Book, Better Little Book, Lone Star Martin Of The Texas Rangers, Whitman, 425 Pages .. 25.00
Book, Big Little Book, Air Fighters Of America, No. 1448, 1941 .... 50.00
Book, Big Little Book, Barney Baxter, In Air With The Eagle Squadron, No. 1459, 1938 . 45.00
Book, Big Little Book, Blondie, Count Cookie In Too, No. 1430, 1947 .... 30.00
Book, Big Little Book, Blondie, Everybody's Happy, No. 1438, 1948 .... 50.00
Book, Big Little Book, Buck Jones, Killers Crooked Butte, No. 1451 .... 55.00
Book, Big Little Book, Buck Jones, Roughriders In Forbidden Trails, No. 1486, 1943 .... 80.00
Book, Big Little Book, Buck Jones, Two-Gun Kid, No. 1404, 1937 .... 33.00
Book, Big Little Book, Bugs Bunny In Double Trouble On Diamond Island, 1967 . .12.00 to 18.00
Book, Big Little Book, Buz Sawyer And Bomber 13, No. 1415, 1946 .... 35.00
Book, Big Little Book, Captain Easy, Soldier Of Fortune, No. 1128, 1934 .... 30.00
Book, Big Little Book, Charlie Chan, Honolulu Police, No. 1478 .... 80.00
Book, Big Little Book, Chester Gump, Silver Creek, Ranch, No. 734, 1933 .... 35.00
Book, Big Little Book, Dan Dunn, Trail Of Wu Fang, No. 1454, 1938 .... 25.00
Book, Big Little Book, Tailspin Tommy, Dirigible Flight To N. Pole, No. 1124, 1934 .... 55.00
Book, Big Little Book, Tailspin Tommy, Hooded Flyer, No. 1423, 1937 .... 50.00
Book, Big Little Book, Tarzan, Beasts Of Tarzan, No. 1410, 1937 .... 37.00
Book, Big Little Book, Tarzan, Of The Apes, No. 744, 1933 .... 60.00
Book, Big Little Book, Tarzan, Of The Screen, No. 778, 1934 .... 35.00
Book, Big Little Book, Tarzan, Terrible, No. 1453, 1942 .... 95.00
Book, Big Little Book, Terry And The Pirates, Giants Vengeance, No. 1446, 1939 .... 30.00
Book, Big Little Book, Terry And The Pirates, Shipwrecked, Island, No. 1412, 1938 .... 50.00
Book, Big Little Book, Texas Ranger, Trail Of The Dog Town Rustlers, No. 1135, 1936 .. 35.00
Book, Big Little Book, The Texas Ranger, No. 1135, 1936 .... 25.00
Book, Big Little Book, Tim McCoy, Sandy Gulch Stampede, No. 1490, 1939 .... 60.00
Book, Big Little Book, Tim McCoy, Westerner, No. 1193, 1936 .... 25.00
Book, Big Little Book, Tim Tyler, Plot Exiled King, No. 1479, 1939 .... 65.00
Book, Big Little Book, Tiny Tim, Adventures Of, No. 7767, 1935 .... 25.00

Book, Big Little Book, Tiny Tim, Big, Big World, No. 1472, 1945 .... 65.00
Book, Big Little Book, Tiny Tim, Mechanical Men, No. 1172, 1937 .... 39.00
Book, Big Little Book, Tom Beatty, Ace Of Service, No. 723, 1934 .... 35.00
Book, Coloring, Ballerina Barbie, Mattel, Inc., 1977 .... 10.00
Book, Coloring, Bewitched, Samantha & Darrin, Treasure Books, 1965 .... 35.00
Book, Coloring, Dudley Do-Right Fun Book, Merrigold Press, 1972, 128 Pages 23.00
Book, Coloring, Follow The Stars, Saalfield, 1950s, 20 Pages, 11 x 12 In. 8.00
Book, Coloring, Funky Phantom, Whitman, 1972, 128 Pages 18.00
Book, Coloring, Gabby Hayes, Gabby Graphic On Cover, 1954, 10 x 14 In. 95.00
Book, Coloring, Harold Teen Color & Paint, McLaughlin Brothers, 1932, 24 Pages 30.00
Book, Coloring, Heckle & Jeckle, Treasure Book, 1957, 64 Pages, 8 x 11 In. 18.00
Book, Coloring, Jetsons, George & Jane In Spacecraft, Whitman, 1963, 124 Pages 25.00
Book, Coloring, Linus The Lionhearted, So-Hi, Whitman, General Foods Corp., 1965 ... 40.00
Book, Coloring, Marty Mouse, Waldman Publishing Corp., 1964, 96 Pages 15.00
Book, Coloring, Pink Panther, Painting Self-Portrait, Whitman, 1975, 8 x 11 In. 19.00
Book, Coloring, Planes & Jets, Whitman, 1952, 11 x 15 In. 10.00
Book, Coloring, Rivets, Comic Strip Dog, Saalfield, 1961, 96 Pages, 8 x 11 In. 14.00
Book, Coloring, Smokey Bear Push Out, Stick On, Whitman, 1970, 10 x 12 In. 14.00
Book, Coloring, Space Mouse, Saalfield, 1966, 96 Pages 25.00
Book, Coloring, Underdog, Whitman, 1972, 8 x 11 In. 25.00
Book, Coloring, Yakky Doodle & Chopper, Yogi Bear, 1962, 8 x 11 In. 19.00
Book, Little Golden Book, Bozo & The Hide 'n' Seek Elephant, 1968, 24 Pages, 6 x 8 In. 14.00
Book, Little Golden Book, Bugs Bunny, 3rd Printing, Simon & Schuster, 1949, 42 Pages . 14.00
Book, Little Golden Book, Madeline, 1954, 28 Pages, 6 3/4 x 8 In. 20.00
Book, Little Golden Book, Woody Woodpecker, Simon & Schuster, First Printing, 1952 .. 14.00
Booklet, American Model Builder, Instruction Manual For Kit, Contest, April, 1914 ..... 45.00
Booklet, Omaha, Aluminum Cover, Omaha TMIE, 1898, 2 1/2 x 4 1/4 In. 110.00
Bookplate, Fish, Coryphaena Hippurus, Frame, A.F. Schmidt 145.00
Bookplate, Trumpeting Angels, Bird In Tree, Hallelujah, Watercolor, 1810, 6 1/2 In. 9350.00
Catalog, A.J. Gammeyer, 1908-1909, Shoe & Hosier, 40 Pages, 7 x 9 In. 10.00
Catalog, Aldens, 1931, Spring & Summer 85.00
Catalog, American Bicycle Company, 1902, 53 Pages, 6 x 8 In. 24.00
Catalog, Atwater Kent Radio, 1927, 28 Pages 25.00
Catalog, Baird-North Co., 1918, Silverware, Watches, Jewelry, 190 Pages, 7 x 10 In. 10.00
Catalog, Bob Sleighs, Picturing Sleighs & Prices, c.1900, 12 Pages 28.00
Catalog, Boyertown Burial Casket Co., 1902, Hardbound, 12 x 14 In. 165.00
Catalog, Chicago Apparatus Co., 1929, Scientific Supplies, 499 Pages 25.00
Catalog, Eaton's, 1974, Christmas, Canada, 474 Pages 75.00
Catalog, Edison Blue Amberol Record, 82 Pages 25.00
Catalog, Ertl, 1983, Toy Model Kits, 44 Pages 20.00
Catalog, FAO Schwartz, 1962, Christmas, Centennial Celebration, 102 Pages 90.00
Catalog, Fisher-Price Toys, Dealer, 1956, 16 Pages 100.00
Catalog, Franklin Simon Fashion, 1923 .... 11.00
Catalog, G.A. Soden & Co., Wholesale Jewelers, Chicago, 280 Pages, c.1910, 9 x 12 In. . 10.00
Catalog, Hasbro Bradley Inc., 1985, Mr. Potato Head, My Little Pony, 104 Pages 100.00
Catalog, Higbee's, 1970, Christmas, Cleveland, 32 Pages 25.00
Catalog, Illinois State Fair, Sept. 18-26, 1914, 100 Pages, 6 x 9 In. 30.00
Catalog, J.C. Penney, 1966, Spring & Summer 40.00
Catalog, J.C. Penney, 1976, Fall & Winter 30.00
Catalog, Kellog Selections For 1945, Toys, Gadgets, Puzzles, Illustrated, 9 x 6 In. 16.00
Catalog, Larkin Soap Company, Premium, Palmer Cox Brownies On Cover, c.1885 ...... 45.00
Catalog, Lionel Train, 1956, Full Color, 8 x 11 In. 35.00
Catalog, Lionel Train, 1971 .... 20.00
Catalog, Marshall Field & Co., 1900, Women's Wear, Chicago 25.00
Catalog, Marshall Field, 1946, Christmas, 14 Pages 25.00
Catalog, Marshall Field, 1976, Gifts For Children, Toys, 48 Pages 20.00
Catalog, Mattel, 1969, Christmas & Hobby Book, Toys, 16 Pages 40.00
Catalog, Merricks Spool Cotton Cabinets 30.00
Catalog, Military Goods From Gov't. Auction, 1907 .... 115.00
Catalog, Monnitor Drill Co., 1906, 31 Pages, Color Cover 40.00
Catalog, Montgomery Ward, 1920, Fall & Winter, 1038 Pages 150.00
Catalog, Montgomery Ward, 1935, Christmas Sale, 80 Pages 35.00
Catalog, Murphy, In-A-Door Beds, 1920s, 48 Pages 90.00

Catalog, Neiman Marcus, 1971, Christmas 30.00
Catalog, Rawling Farm Implement, Supply House Of The South, 5 1/2 x 8 In. 50.00
Catalog, Sears Roebuck, 1911, Fall & Winter, 1364 Pages 225.00
Catalog, Sears Roebuck, 1933, Spring & Summer 35.00
Catalog, Sears Roebuck, 1938, Spring & Summer, 786 Pages 25.00
Catalog, Sears Roebuck, 1939-1940, Fall & Winter, 1114 Pages 25.00
Catalog, Standard Mail Order, 1915, 377 Pages 35.00
Catalog, Superior Match Co., 1952, Salesman's 45.00
Catalog, True Value, 1972, Christmas, Toys, Gifts, Kitchen Items, 48 Pages 25.00
Catalog, Walgreen Agency Drug Stores, 1960, Christmas, 244 Pages 100.00
Catalog, Western Auto, 1964, Spring & Summer, 320 Pages 35.00
Catalog, Western Auto, 1968, Christmas, Gifts, Appliances, 72 Pages 40.00
Certificate, Baptismal, Hand Colored, 1830, 16 x 13 In. 27.00
Certificate, Birth & Baptismal, Elizabeth, J. Harrold & Elizabeth Daughter, 15 1/2 In. 3155.00
Check, Carson City Savings Band, Carson, Nev., Ornate, Canceled, 1878 . . . .   10.00
Check, Orville Wright, Winters Nat. Bank & Trust Co., Dayton, Ohio 595.00
Check, Peoples National Bank, Rock Island, Ill., Eagle, Ornate Design, Canceled, 1903 . .   6.00
Dance Card, Dated 1888, For Journeymen & Plasterers, Tiny Pencil Attached 60.00
Dance Card, Journeymen & Plasters, Dated 1888, Attached Pencil 80.00
Deed, Indiana Land, Martin Van Buren, 1840, Seal, Frame, 13 1/4 x 19 In. 60.00
Deed, On Parchment, Red Wax Seal, Framed Between Glass, England, 1668, 20 x 16 In. .   127.00
Fraktur, Angels, Birds On Lower Panel, Red, Blue, Frame, J. Ritter, Reading, Pa., 18 In. .   330.00
Fraktur, Anna Aingrich, Dated Feb. 18, 1850, Frame, 16 x 11 1/4 In. 330.00
Fraktur, Baptismal, Mariann Of David Lautenseblager & Lydia, 1856, 19 x 16 In. 220.00
Fraktur, Bible Exodus, Pen & Ink, Watercolor, 1889 Inscription, Frame, 15 x 12 In. 2860.00
Fraktur, Birth & Baptism, Pickaway County, Ohio, 1829, Angels, Frame, 13 x 12 In. 55.00
Fraktur, Birth & Baptismal, Joseph & Elizabeth Lang, Dated 1799 & 1801, 13 x 16 In. . .   4025.00
Fraktur, Birth Certificate, Bethlehem Township, Pa., 1803, 13 x 8 In. 1100.00
Fraktur, Birth Record Of Conrat, December 10, 1793, Birds, Flowers, Heart, 15 3/4 In. . .   495.00
Fraktur, Birth, 1801, Carl Bruckman, Heinrich Keyfer, Frame, 16 1/4 x 13 1/8 In. 275.00
Fraktur, Birth, Abraham & Jacob Lang, Twins, June 8, 1811, Frame, 16 x 13 In., Pair 2200.00
Fraktur, Birth, John Son, Jacob Eichelberger, April 24, 1775, Verse, Frame, 12 x 8 In. . . .   3850.00
Fraktur, Birth, Juliana Fahrne, Sept. 18, 1794, Frame, 15 1/2 x 12 3/4 In. 2255.00
Fraktur, Birth, Northampton County, German Text, Martin Brechell, Frame, 16 x 12 In. . .   1100.00
Fraktur, Birth, Weyenburg Township, Flying Angel, Ink, Watercolor, Frame, 13 x 16 In. .   3410.00
Fraktur, Excerpt From Chapter 20, Book Of Exodus, 1889 . . . .   2860.00
Fraktur, Floral, Red, Yellow, Blue, Green, Frame, 1782, 17 x 20 1/2 In. 385.00
Fraktur, Flowers & Heart, Frame, 12 3/4 x 10 5/8 In. 165.00
Fraktur, Name With Flowers, German, Watercolor, Frame, 7 1/2 x 12 1/4 In. 1210.00
Fraktur, Pen & Ink, Watercolor, Wayne County, Ohio, October 11th A.D. 1854, 9 x 11 In.   580.00
Fraktur, Vorschrift, German Text, Red & Black Ink, Frame, 5 3/4 x 8 In. 685.00
Fraktur, Watercolor, Eagle With Ribbon, German Text, Frame, 12 1/2 x 10 3/8 In. 275.00
Guide, Union Pacific Travel, The Overland Route, Colorado Mountain, 48 Pages, 1928 . .   22.00
Hand Book, Panama Pacific Line California, 30 Pages 30.00
Label, Mark Twain Cigar, Pictorial, c.1930 . . . .   10.00
Land Grant, Columbiana County, Ohio, Thomas Jefferson, 1806, Seal, 17 x 27 In. 5390.00
Land Grant, Parchment, Inscription, Marietta, Ohio, 1837, Signed, Frame, 12 x 17 In. . . .   25.00
Land Grant, Several Ohio Plots, James Monroe, 1822, Gilt Frame, 25 x 19 In. 605.00
License, Opium Dispensing, 1925 . . . .   55.00
Magazine, Aviation Week & Space Technology, Apollo 11 Article, July 7, 1969 . . . .   14.00
Magazine, Jack & Jill, Walt Kelly Article, Pogo & Churchy On Cover, May 1969 . . . .   44.00
Magazine, Life, Astronaut Glenn Flight Return, March 9, 1962 . . . .   10.00
Magazine, Life, Free Balloonist, December, 1940 . . . .   10.00
Magazine, Life, Michigan's Great Harmon, November, 1940 . . . .   12.00
Magazine, Life, Peanuts Cover, March 17, 1967 . . . .   14.00
Magazine, Life, Planes Over England, November, 1939 . . . .   10.00
Magazine, Mad, 1955 . . . .   300.00
Magazine, McClure's, September 1909, 190 Pages 20.00
Magazine, Red Is Right, April, 1941 . . . .   10.00
Magazine, Scribner's Monthly, Leather Bound, Volume 1, Number 1, 1872 . . . .   75.00
Manual, 1955 Chevrolet Corvette All-American Sports Car 70.00
Manual, Owners, Pontiac, 1948 . . . .   40.00
Matchbook Cover, Englishtown Clothes, Frederick, Md., Man, Top Hat 5.00

Matchbook Cover, San Francisco Municipal Airport Skyway Cafe, Airplane, 1939 ...... 5.00
Menu, Empire State Building, New York, 1930s 22.00
Menu, Exposition Fish Grotto, Fisherman's Wharf, 1939 .... 30.00
Menu, Fairmont Hotel Tonga Room, San Francisco, 1950 .... 20.00
Menu, Hotel Whitcomb Coffee Shop, 1941 .... 20.00
Menu, Joe Di Maggio's Grotto, San Francisco, Fisherman's Wharf, 1940s 55.00
Menu, Lido Cafe, San Francisco, 1930s 30.00
Menu, Lucca In San Francisco, 1952 .... 23.00
Menu, Mayflower Hotel Coffee Shop, 1941 .... 20.00
Menu, Metropolitan Life Insurance Co., Anniversary Dinner, History, 1946, 32 Pages 20.00
Menu, New Amsterdam Bar, 1949 .... 20.00
Menu, New Year's Eve In The Mural Room, St., Francis Hotel, 1946 .... 18.00
Menu, Pig'n Whistle, Los Angeles, 1940 .... 30.00
Menu, Pioneer Inn, Lahaina Maui, 1950 .... 15.00
Menu, Riviera Restaurant, San Francisco, 1939 .... 15.00
Menu, The Nut Tree, Vacaville, Ca., 1960s 40.00
Menu, Tiki Bob's, San Francisco, 1950 .... 16.00
Passport, Turkish, Gilt Calligraphy, 30 1/2 x 40 In............................. 125.00
Program, America's Top Jazz Concert, Benny Goodman Tour, 1958, 14 Pages, 12 In..... 37.00
Program, Buffalo Bill's Wild West, 64 Pages, Advertising, 1894 Ambrose Park Map 745.00
Program, Cleveland National Air Race, Autographed, Jimmy Doolittle, 1929 .... 120.00
Program, Los Angeles Memorial Sports Arena, July 4, 1959, Colored Covers, 20 Pages .. 13.00
Program, Lou Walters, Latin Quarter, New-Miami, Girls, Girls, 1942 .... 20.00
Program, Orpheum Theatre, Houdini In Chinese Water Torture Cell, Frame, 1922 ...... 405.00
Program, The Daisies, Women's Baseball Team, Fort Wayne, Ind., 1950s 10.00
Sticker, Baggage, United States Lines, Ship Design, 1950, 3 In. 8.00
Stock Certificate, Eagle Lock, Tarryville, Ct., 1880s 15.00
Stock Certificate, Hygienic Health Food Co., Oakland, Cal., 1919, Canceled 13.00
Stock Certificate, North American Light & Power Co., 1930s 3.00
Stock Certificate, Palmer Union Oil Co., California Corp, Oil Wells, 1928, Canceled 11.00
Stock Certificate, Philip Best, 1870s, Were $1, 000 A Share 60.00
Stock Certificate, Tobacco Products Corp, Black Family Picking Tobacco, 1925 .... 19.00
Stock Certificate, Transcontinental Railroad, 1880s 18.00
Ticket, Hard Time Dinner & Dance, Code Of Ethics Club Hospital Fund, 1939, 2 x 3 In. . 5.00
Ticket, Mutt & Jeff Stage Play, Princess Theater, Wed., Nov. 13, c.1907, 2 3/4 x 5 1/2 In. . 12.00
Timetable, TWA Airline, Radio City, New York, 1947, 16 Pages, 8 x 9 In. 25.00
Voucher, Salary, Southern Express Co., Illiterate Black Porter, X For Signature, 8 In. 12.00
Yearbook, Hollywood Park, 1964, Silver Anniversary, 8 1/2 x 9 In.................. 20.00

PAPER DOLLS were probably inspired by the pantins, or jumping jacks, made in eighteenth-century Europe. By the 1880s, sheets of printed paper dolls and clothes were being made. The first paper doll books were made in the 1920s. Collectors prefer uncut sheets or books or boxed sets of paper dolls. Prices are about half as much if the pages have been cut.

Annette Funicello, 1956, Cut ....60.00 to 65.00
Annie Oakley, 1956, Uncut 65.00
Barbie, Christie & Stacey, Whitman, Book, 1968, 10 x 13 In. 45.00
Barbie & Ken, All Sports Tournament, Whitman, Box, 1976, 27 Piece Wardrobe 15.00
Barbie & Ken, Whitman, Box, 1976 .... 15.00
Big & Little Sister, 1945 .... 45.00
Blondie & Friends, Saalfield, No. 1334, Book, 1968, 8 1/4 x 12 1/2 In. 30.00
Children From Other Lands, Costumes For Each Child, Whitman, 1961, Uncut 20.00
Cindy & Mindy, Twins, Book Form, 2 Pockets Inside, Whitman, 1960, Uncut 35.00
Eskimo Twins, Ladies Home Journal, April, 1922, 1 Uncut Page 7.00
Gone With The Wind, 1929, Uncut 600.00
Gone With The Wind, Merrill Pub., Book, 1940, 10 1/4 x 17 1/4 In., Uncut 650.00
Grace Kelly 4.95
Historic Costumes, 1934 .... 35.00
Janet Leigh, 1958, Cut 45.00
Ladies Home Journal, December 15, 1910, Paper Doll Page 20.00
Little Lulu, Figural Book, Whitman, 1971, 7 1/4 x 15 1/2 In. 45.00
Little Women, Artcraft, No. 1527, Book 20.00

Mary Poppins, Julie Andrews, Whitman, No. 1967, 1973, 7 1/4 x 15 1/2 In. 40.00
Mrs. Beasley, Coloring Book, Cutout Clothes, Uncut 45.00
Nancy & Sluggo, 1974, Cut 12.00
Partridge Family, Artcraft Color Covers, Book, 1971, 10 x 13 In. 45.00
Pebbles & Bamm Bamm, Hanna-Barbera, Book, 1964, 10 x 13 In. 45.00
Polly & Peter Perkins, 1933, Uncut 20.00
Princess Diana, Golden Book, Punch-Out, 1985, 10 x 13 In. 50.00
Princess Diana & Prince Charles, Full Color, Tom Tierney, 1985, Uncut 15.00
Princess Elizabeth & Margaret 145.00
Raggedy Ann & Andy, Whitman, Book, 1972, 10 x 13 In. 30.00
Raggedy Ann & Raggedy Andy, Saalfield, 1944, Uncut 125.00
Schiaparelli Fashion Review 4.95
Snow White, Whitman, 1970s, Unpunched 25.00
Stage Door Canteen, 1943 . . . . 45.00
Star Princess & Pluta At North Star Space Base, Whitman, 1979, 10 x 13 In. 25.00
Susan Dey, Laurie Of The Partridge Family, Artcraft Corp., 1971 . . . . 90.00
Trisha Nixon, W.H.S., Uncut 25.00
Waltons 25.00
World Of Barbie, Whitman, No. 1987-69, Book, 1971, 10 x 13 In. 45.00

PAPERWEIGHTS must have first appeared along with paper in ancient Egypt. Today's collectors search for every type, from the very expensive French weights of the nineteenth century to the modern artist weights or advertising pieces. The glass tops of the paperweights sometimes have been nicked or scratched, and this type of damage can be removed by polishing. Some serious collectors think this type of repair is an alteration and will not buy a repolished weight; others think it is an acceptable technique of restoration that does not change the value. Baccarat paperweights are listed separately under Baccarat.

Advertising, A.T.A. Nelson Co., Naked Woman Behind Hide, 2 1/2 x 4 In. 145.00
Advertising, Buckeye Harvesting Machinery & Binder Twine 350.00
Advertising, Chief Red Cloud's Snake Oil Remedy, Glass, 1910, 3 1/8 In. 660.00
Advertising, Donnelly Machine Co., Vintage Factory, Scalloped Edge, 3 x 4 1/2 In. 55.00
Advertising, Embossed Car, Packard Motor Car Co., Detroit, Mich., Brass, 3 1/2 In. 355.00
Advertising, Franklin Fire Insurance Co., 90th Anniversary, Bronze, 1919, 3 In. 35.00
Advertising, Hance Brothers & White, Phila., Medal In Glass, 1 1/4 In. 130.00
Advertising, Heywood Hoe Inside, Vintage Shoe, 2 1/2 x 4 In. 45.00
Advertising, J.H. Starin-Glen Island, Multicolored, White Ground, 3 In. 125.00
Advertising, Master Safe Company, Movable Combination Lock, Lucite Base 50.00
Advertising, McDonnell Logo, Gemini VII Heat Shield, Lucite, 1965 . . . . 150.00
Advertising, New England Glass Co., 2 1/2 x 3 1/4 In. 489.00
Advertising, Oscar R. Hoehne & Co., Gold Scale, 2 1/2 x 4 In. 70.00
Advertising, St. Louis Pumps, Cast Iron, Copper Hose & Nozzle, Embossed, 7 3/4 In. 550.00
Alexander, 3 White Iris, Blue Iridescent Blue, Orient & Flume 55.00
Ayotte, Bird, Blossoming Branches, 3 1/2 In. 575.00
Banford, Aquarium, 3 Exotic Fish, Sea Plants & Shells, 3 3/8 In. 345.00
Banford, Black Snake, Yellow, Orange Spots, 3 1/4 In. 715.00
Banford, Pink Rose, Blue Opaque Base, Signed, 3 1/8 In. 330.00
Banford, Red Flower Bouquet, 5 Blossoms, Diamond Cut Base, 3 1/4 In. 460.00
Banford, Rose Bouquet, 5 Orange & Amber Roses, Opaque Sky Blue Ground, 3 In. 558.00
Banford, Snake, Spotted Black & Yellow, Tadpoles On Cullet Base 710.00
Bridgeton Studio, Butterfly & Flowers, Iridescent Blue Ground 72.00
Bronze, Reclining Nude, 2 x 8 x 3 1/2 In. 155.00
Clichy, Clusters Around Central Red On White Cane, 2 1/2 In. 530.00
Clichy, Panel Design, White & Red Clusters, Central Cane, 2 1/2 In. 530.00
Clichy, Pinwheel Swirl, Pink Center, Turquoise, 3 In. 1190.00
Correin, Blue, Heart Shaped Vine, Signed, V.2.88.6, Paper Label 242.00
Cristal D'Albert, Franklin Roosevelt 98.00
Cuda, Lily, Blue, White, Green Base, 1989, 3 In. 65.00
Figural, Snoopy On Doghouse, Box 45.00
Figural, Stag, Amber Base, Bohemian, 3 In. 143.00
Figural, Turtle, Opalescent, 6 1/4 In. 45.00

Flower, 3 Cane Cut 28.00
Flower, 8-Petal Red Poinsettia, Green Base, 3 7/8 In.. .... 155.00
Flower, Cane Scramble, Animals, People, 1848, 2 1/2 In.. .... 1320.00
Flower, Cobalt, Green Leaves, Applied Foot, 3 1/2 In. 85.00
Flower, Red, Rabbit Under Leaf, Green Leaves On Blue, 4 x 3 1/2 In. 90.00
Hamon, Pull-Up Flowers, Red, White, Blue, White Base, 2 1/2 In. 65.00
Hansen, 10-Petal Blue Flower, Millefiori Cane Center, Blue Base, Signed, 2 In. 100.00
Hansen, Pink Flowers, Green Leaves, Buds, Blue Opalescent Cushion, 2 In. 120.00
Hansen, White Poinsettia, Blue, White Millefiori Canes, Star Cut Base, 3 In. 120.00
Kaziun, White Spider Lily, Gold Bee, Red Center, Cobalt Blue Ground, 1 5/8 In. 230.00
Lotton, Orange Flowers, Green Leaves, 1984, 2 3/4 In.. .... 75.00
Millefiori, Pink, Green Canes, 6 Concentric Circles, Purple Base, 2 In. 65.00
Millefiori, Spoke, Yellow Latticinio Twists, Yellow Opaque Base, 2 9/16 In. 20.00
Millefiori, White To Clear 70.00
Millville, Dark Pink Rose, Green Leaves, Clear Dome, c.1900, 3 1/2 In. 88.00
New England Glass Co., Pears, 4 Cherries & Leaves, White Lattice, Conical, 2 1/2 In. ... 362.00
Olma, 3 Slag Glass Flowers, Blue Centers, Green Leaves On A Vine, 1986, 4 In. 80.00
Olma, Cobalt Flowers, Orange Centers, Green Leaves, 1984, 3 3/4 In.. .... 90.00
Perthshire, Concentric Circle Millefiori, Cobalt Base, Signed, 2 1/4 In. 80.00
Perthshire, Flower Branch, Canes, Cobalt Ground, Label, Box, 2 5/8 In. 93.00
Perthshire, Goldstone Dragonfly, Complex Millefiori Canes, 1970, 2 In. 285.00
Perthshire, Penguin In Interior, Blue Overlay, 3 1/8 x 2 11/16 In. 120.00
Perthshire, Princess Diana Commemorative, 4 Forget-Me-Nots, 1961, 3 In. 380.00
Salazar, Compound Floral, Poinsettia Star Blossom, White Ground, 3 1/4 In. 200.00
Smith, 3 Strawberries, 2 Red & 1 Green, Cobalt Base, Signed, 1984, 3 3/16 In. 230.00
Snowdome, Beautiful Dreamer, Willitts, 1965, Box 35.00
Snowdome, Betty Boop, Red Roses For A Blue Lady, Box 30.00
Snowdome, Bullwinkle & Rocky 48.00
Snowdome, Creature From The Black Lagoon, Box 35.00
Snowdome, Dutch Girl 125.00
Snowdome, Felix The Cat, Musical, Plays Memory 30.00
St. Clair, Caramel, White Ribbon, Signed, 4 x 3 In. 10.00
St. Clair, Green, White Ribbon, Signed, 4 x 3 In. 35.00
St. Clair, White Coral, Yellow Base, 3 5/16 In. 70.00
St. Louis, 3 Cherries, Pear, Latticinio Base, 1980, 1 15/16 In. 395.00
St. Louis, Alternating Ribbons Of White Latticinio, Red, Blue, 3 1/4 In. 3105.00
St. Louis, Blue Over White Over Clear, Mushroom Overlay, c.1970, 3 In. 575.00
St. Louis, Clematis, Overlay Coral, Blue Blossoms, Millefiori Cane Centers, 3 In. 230.00
St. Louis, Clematis, Pink, 3 Tiers Of Petals, Swirling Latticinio Ground, 2 7/8 In. 1000.00
St. Louis, Fuchsia, 2 Closed Buds, Double Swirl Latticinio Ground 1800.00
St. Louis, Gilded Salamander On Pink, Star Cut Base 660.00
St. Louis, Latticinio Twists, Complex Millefiori Canes, Blue Base, 1972, 3 5/16 In. 465.00
St. Louis, Magnum, Pink, Blue, White Spiral Latticinio, 1977, 4 In.. .... 230.00
St. Louis, Millefiori In Star Shape, c.1970, 3 In. 185.00
St. Louis, Mushroom, Overlay, Multicolored Concentric Millefiori Cane, 3 In. ....345.00 to 431.00
St. Louis, Nosegay, 4 Millefiori Cane Flowers, Pink, Blue, White, 3 In. 287.00
St. Louis, Persian Double Clematis, Ridged Petals, Swirling Latticinio, 3 1/16 In. 1200.00
St. Louis, Pink Crocus With Stamen Center, Green Leaves, Signed 385.00
St. Louis, Pink, White Salamander, Star Cut Base, 1980, 3 1/4 In. 660.00
St. Louis, Pompoms, Squashed Tubes, Star Of David, Canes, 3 1/8 In.. .... 3000.00
St. Louis, Pompon On Latticinio, C-Shaped Petals, Ruby Bud, 2 7/8 In. 1600.00
St. Louis, Red Poinsettia On Green Leaves, Cobalt Base, 1980 .... 285.00
St. Louis, Spotted Greyhound, Lace Filigree Torsade, 3 1/8 In. 3500.00
St. Louis, White, Blue Fluted Canes, White Cross, 8 Red, Blue Florets, 2 3/4 In. 259.00
St. Louis, White, Green Cog Canes, 5 Silhouette Canes, 3 In. 6325.00
Stankard, Ants & Indian Pipes, White Blossoms, Tan Buds, Signed, 3 In. 1247.00
Sulphide, Admiral Neslon, 3 1/4 In. 375.00
Sulphide, Buck Deer, Lying Down 1350.00
Sulphide, Carp, Nibbling At Bait, 2 7/8 In. 600.00
Sulphide, Easter Bunny With Egg 1175.00
Sulphide, Lion On Red Glass Bed, Pontil, 1890-1920, 3 1/4 In. 110.00
Sulphide, Lion, Crossed Paws, On Crushed Glass, Czechoslovakian, 4 1/8 In. 600.00
Sulphide, Moon Astronauts, Gilbert Poillerat, c.1970, 3 1/2 In. 150.00

Sulphide, Pug Dog, With Hat 1650.00
Sulphide, Tom Turkey 1475.00
Tarsitano, Berry Bouquet, Columbine Flowers, Multicolored Berries, 3 1/4 In. 920.00
Tarsitano, Bouquet In Basket, 5 Purple, Pink Flowers, Cobalt Blue Berries, 3 In. 920.00
Tarsitano, Bouquet, Spotted Bug, Dahlia & Blossoms, 3 1/4 In. 1120.00
Tarsitano, Floral, 5-Petal Blossom, Scrambled Cane Ground, 3 1/2 In. 530.00
Tarsitano, Floral, Center 6-Petal Blossom, 2 1/2 In. 330.00
Trabucco, White Flower, Black Leaves, Complex Stamen Center, 2 1/16 In. 240.00
Vandermark, Cut Butterfly, Iridescent Orange, 1980 . . . .   50.00
Whitefriars, Cane Design, Paper Label, 3 1/8 In. 82.00
Whittemore, 3-Flower Bouquet, Pink, Blue, Cobalt Base, Signed, 2 1/2 In. 285.00
Whittemore, Cobalt Cased Rose, 4 Green Leaves, Footed, Signed, 2 3/8 x 4 In. 200.00
Zimmerman, Morning Glory, Pink, White, Pink Base, 3 7/16 In. 100.00
Zimmerman, White Over Pink Lily, Green Base, 3 3/4 In. 65.00

PAPIER-MACHE is made from paper mixed with glue, chalk, and other
ingredients, then molded and baked. It becomes very hard and can be
painted. Boxes, trays, and furniture were made of papier-mache. Some
of the nineteenth-century pieces were decorated with mother-of-pearl.
Furniture made of papier-mache is listed in the Furniture category.

Box, Bird, Floral, Allover Gilt, Rectangular, 15 In. 305.00
Box, Work, Black Lacquered, c.1825, 6 x 12 1/2 In. 605.00
Egg, Anastasis, St. Feodor, Lacquered, Gilt Borders, Russia, c.1875, 3 3/4 In. 1380.00
Figurine, Hen, On Nest, Brown, Beige, Red, Green, F.N. Burt Co., 1924, 7 In. 165.00
Form, Military Jacket, Tripod Mahogany Base, 42 x 13 x 8 1/2 In. 210.00
Hurstmonceux Castle, Black, Gold, 29 1/4 In. 315.00
Stand, Mother-Of-Pearl Inlay, Checkerboard Top, Tilt Top, Wood Post, 29 In. 175.00
Tray, Black Lacquer, Gold Flowers, Butterflies, H. Clay, 23 x 31 In. 605.00
Tray, Center Painted Spaniel's Head, Faux Bamboo Stand, 21 x 28 1/2 In. 825.00
Tray, Floral Bouquet, Faux Bamboo Stand, Jennens & Bettridge, c.1880, 30 In. 1020.00
Tray, Gilt Leaf Border, Central Scene Of Parrot & Fruit, Stand, c.1820, 29 In. 1330.00
Tray, Lacquered, Geometric Design, On Stand, 1850, 21 x 25 x 20 In. 725.00
Tray, Mother-Of-Pearl Inlay, Castle Scene, Horace Potter, 23 1/4 x 29 1/2 In. 515.00
Tray, Regency, Lacquer, Chinoiserie, Faux Bamboo Stand, 1820, 21 x 24 In. 665.00
Tray, Stand, Harvesting Scene, Mother-Of-Pearl Inlay, c.1820, 30 x 24 In. 495.00

PARASOL, see Umbrella category.

PARIAN is a fine-grained, hard-paste porcelain named for the marble it
resembles. It was first made in England in 1846 and gained in favor in
the United States about 1860. Figures, tea sets, vases, and other items
were made of Parian at many English and American factories.

Bust, Charles Sumner, 7 1/2 In. 125.00
Bust, General Lee, Signed J & TB, 7 3/4 In. 400.00
Bust, Grant, Lt. General Uniform, 7 In. 375.00
Bust, Mozart, Germany, Late 19th Century, 14 1/4 In. 230.00
Bust, Robert Burns, 15 1/2 In. 190.00
Bust, Slave, Collar & Chain On Neck, Glazed, 10 In. 2350.00
Bust, Woman, Classical Beauty, Socle, Ebonized Wood Base 200.00
Figurine, Ariadne On Panther, Johan-Heinrich Von Dannecker, 14 In. 1725.00
Figurine, Cupid, Leaning On Tree Trunk, Jean-Marie Pigalle, 17 In. 1495.00
Figurine, Diana, Nude, Wrist Shackles 295.00
Pitcher, Milk, Wheat & Leaf Design, Twig Formed Handle, Signed, 9 1/4 In. 65.00
Pitcher, Soldier With Gun, Volunteer, Rifle Corp., Blue & White, 8 In. 305.00

PARIS, Vieux Paris, or Old Paris, is porcelain ware that is known to
have been made in Paris in the eighteenth or early nineteenth century.
These porcelains have no identifying mark but can be recognized by
the whiteness of the porcelain and the lines and decorations. Gold decoration is often used.

Basin, Sugar, Cover, Floral Reserves, Gilt Vermicelli Ground, 1815-1820, 6 7/8 In. 1694.00
Basket, Anneau D'or, 19th Century, 8 In. 735.00
Basket, Centerpiece, Navette Form, Reticulated, 1835, 10 x 12 3/8 In. 1028.50

Bowl, Centerpiece, Stand, Overall Gilt Script, 1815, 8 1/2 x 11 In. 2057.00
Bowl, Condiment, Neoclassical, Signed, 1825, 1 7/8 x 10 1/4 In., Pair 726.00
Box, Cover, Napoleonic Design In Cartouche, Royal Blue Ground 575.00
Cabaret Service, Geometric Design Exterior, Green Enamel, Flower Sprigs, 8 Piece 6900.00
Cachepot, Children In Landscape, Green Ground, 7 1/2 In., Pair 805.00
Candelabrum, 6-Light, Floral Panels, Gilt Scrolled Handles, Lily-Form Branches, 28 In. . 4600.00
Clock, Stand, Flower Heads, Enamel Dial, Jacob Petit, c.1845, 17 x 11 1/2 In. 1870.00
Compote, Central Russian Imperial Crest, Foliate Border, Gilt Ground, 8 3/4 In., Pair . . . 745.00
Compote, Cut-Out Rim, Peach Bands, Gilt Highlight, Shell Feet, 19th Century, 8 1/2 In. . 303.00
Compote, Fruit Design, Cherub On Triangular Base, Gilt, Enamel, 10 5/8 In., Pair 10925.00
Cup & Saucer, Coffee, Magenta Ground Reserves, Emerald Green, 2 x 5 In. 514.00
Cup & Saucer, Crossed American Flags, 15 Stars, Fuchsia Rim, 1820s 875.00
Cup & Saucer, Demitasse, Floral Motif, Gilt Border, 10 Sets 440.00
Dessert Set, Polychrome Painted, Floral Spray, Gilt Scrolling, 43 Piece 258.00
Dish, 4 Sections, Scallop Shells, 2 Entwined Sea Snakes On Handle, 12 In. 35.00
Figurine, Lady & Gentleman, Polychrome, Scrolling On Base, c.1850, 9 In., Pair 248.00
Figurine, Spaniel, Seated On Oval Base, Green, Puce, Blue Collar, 8 1/4 In. 920.00
Garniture, Corbeille, Rococo, Flowers, Women Skating On Reverse, 1850, 12 x 18 In. . . . 485.00
Gravy Boat, Cover, Gilt Finial, Scrolled Lobed Handles, Attached Base, 19th Century . . . 523.00
Group, Classically Draped Maiden, Seated Beside Tree Stump, Signed, Nast 345.00
Jar, Pharmacy, Cover, 9 1/2 In., Pair 315.00
Lamp, Campagna Urn Base, Green Ground, Polychrome Floral & Gilt, 21 In., Pair 440.00
Plate, Crossed American Flags, 15 Stars, Gilt Trim, Fuchsia Rim, 1820s, 7 In. 875.00
Plate, Lovers Visiting Future Mother-In-Law, Lovers & Eros In Garden, 1815, Pair 302.00
Platter, Tureen, Double-Leaf Handles, Blue Banded, c.1860, 15 1/4 x 10 1/4 In. 95.00
Sauceboat, Underplate, Polychrome Floral Sprays, Gilt Highlights 248.00
Tea Set, Magenta, Green Floral Sprays, Gilt Design, 7 Piece 125.00
Urn, Campagna, Green, Gilt, Polychrome Floral Sprays, Peach Ground, 1800s, 9 In., Pair . 248.00
Urn, Campagna, Royal Couple, Courting, Gilt Rim, 11 In., Pair 690.00
Urn, Campagna, Scene, Oriental, Polychrome, Gilt Floral Garland On Reverse, c.1850, 10 In. . 550.00
Urn, Couple Scene, Gilt, 19th Century, 10 1/2 In., Pair 900.00
Urn, Floral Panel, 2 Swan Handles, Gilt Ground, Signed, 12 1/2 In., Pair 1610.00
Urn, Gilt Design, Gilt Mask Handles, 10 3/4 In., Pair 1840.00
Vase, 2 Women In Landscape, Flower & Leaf Handles, Gilt Trim, 22 In., Pair 4600.00
Vase, 2 Women In Landscape, Ruffle Top, Vine Handles, 19 1/2 In., Pair 1380.00
Vase, Arab Lady & Man On 1 Side, Flowers On Reverse, Gilt Handle, Cobalt 230.00
Vase, Bospherus & Grand Canal, Views, Painted & Stylized, 1870s, 17 1/2 In., Pair 6325.00
Vase, Central Floral Spray, Gilt Highlight, 8 3/4 In. 17.00
Vase, Colorful Chinoiserie Figures, Gold Scaly Dragons On Sides, 17 3/4 In., Pair 37375.00
Vase, Exotic Landscape, Giant Moths, Ducks, Caterpillars, Floral, 18 In., Pair 4140.00
Vase, Foliate Form Mouth & Handles, Allover Floral, 16 1/2 In., Pair 805.00
Vase, Gilt & White, Polychrome Floral Reserves, 19th Century, 13 In., Pair 880.00
Vase, Landscape, 1810-1815, 14 1/4 In., Pair 6352.50
Vase, Large Polychrome Flowers, Leaves, Pink Neck, Gilt, Everted Neck, 18 In. 460.00
Vase, Leaf Handles, Central Floral Design, Fan Form, 14 In. 173.00
Vase, Potpourri, Relief Floral Spray Panel, Apple Green Ground, 8 x 5 1/4 x 5 1/4 In. 1815.00
Vase, Rococo, Floral Reserves, Ice Blue, Mulberry Ground, 2 Handles, 1860, 14 In., Pair . 1210.00
Vase, Scottish Highlands & Figures, Floral Reserve On Reverse, Blue Ground, 13 In. 545.00

PATE-DE-VERRE is an ancient technique in which glass is made by blending and refining powdered glass of different colors into molds. The process was revived by French glassmakers, especially Galle, around the end of the nineteenth century.

Bowl, 3 Swallowtail Butterflies, Deep Blue, Green, 1915, 3 1/8 In. 7475.00
Dish, Cicadas On Each End, Seafoam Green, Blue Mottled Ground, 11 In. 2760.00
Lamp, Stylized Aquatic Foliage, Purple, Red, Wrought Iron, 1924, 13 In. 9200.00
Plaque, Classical Style Woman, Basket Of Putti Watching 1 Fly Away, 5 In. 290.00
Vase, 2 Rows Of Flower Heads, Orange, Charcoal, Yellow, Purple, 1924, 12 In. 10350.00
Vase, Aubergine Design, Smoky, Hexagonal, A. Francois, Decorchemont, 8 In. 5520.00
Vase, Low Relief Upper, Ribbed Lower Section, Olive Green, Brown, 1925, 4 In. 2875.00
Vase, Papyrus Fronds, Turquoise, Blue, Scalloped Borders, 1924, 10 In. 11500.00
Vase, Stylized Wave, Gray, Green, Turquoise, Side Handles, 1909, 5 In. 11500.00

PATE-SUR-PATE means paste on paste. The design was made by painting layers of slip on the ceramic piece until a relief decoration was formed. The method was developed at the Sevres factory in France about 1850. It became even more famous at the English Minton factory about 1870. It has since been used by many potters to make both pottery and porcelain wares.

Decanter, Maiden Sleeping On Hammock, Floral Bands At Foot, 14 1/4 In.	1380.00
Pitcher, Man Seated On Bench, Floral At Base, Bands Of Flowers, 7 1/2 In.	488.00
Plaque, Classical Maiden Seated On Bench, White, Black Ground, Cope, 7 In.	920.00
Plate, Interior Scene Of 2 Maidens, Gilt Border, Blue Ground, 8 1/2 In., Pair	230.00
Stein, Woman, With Elk & Dog In Waves, Tree Branches In Sky, 1 Liter	1100.00
Vase, Cherub, Gilt Banded Border, Teal Blue Ground, 9 1/2 In.	460.00
Vase, Landscape Scene, Central Relief Of Birds, Foliate Border, 13 In., Pair	920.00
Vase, White Cranes, Bamboo, Gilt, Tapered, Flared Mouths, 13 In., Pair	2760.00

PAUL REVERE POTTERY was made at several locations in and around Boston, Massachusetts, between 1906 and 1942. The pottery was operated as a settlement house program for teenage girls. Many pieces were signed *S.E.G.* for Saturday Evening Girls. The artists concentrated on children's dishes and tiles. Decorations were outlined in black and filled with color.

Ashtray, 1897 Commemorative, Navy Blue Edge, Luster, 1937, 5 1/4 In.	110.00
Bowl, Buttercup Yellow, Deep Chicory Blue Drip, Midnight Blue, 3 x 7 1/2 In.	247.00
Bowl, Chirping Trio Of Chicks, Black Lined, 1934, 2 x 4 1/4 In.	605.00
Bowl, Crystalline Cloud Bursts, Orange Flambe Interior, 12 In.	275.00
Bowl, Geese In Cuerda Seca, Green Exterior, Label, 1912, 11 3/4 In.	4500.00
Bowl, Geometric Border, Blue Ground, Tillie Block, 1911, 4 x 10 In.	550.00
Bowl, Green Glaze, 8 1/4 In.	130.00
Bowl, Landscape Scene, Blue Ground, Paper Label, 6 1/4 In.	1190.00
Bowl, Landscape, Brown Trees, Yellow Ground, 5 x 2 In.	495.00
Bowl, Landscape, Tall Scrub Pine, Overlooks Hills, 6 In.	412.00
Bowl, Maroon & Mauve Interior, Steel Blue Exterior, Flared Mouth, 3 x 5 3/4 In.	165.00
Bowl, Porridge, Stylized Dancing Rabbits, Tillie Block, 1911, 2 1/2 x 5 In.	2640.00
Bowl, Stylized Geometric Border, Blue Ground, 4 x 10 In.	550.00
Bowl, Swollen Form, Red Tinted Rim, Signed, 3 3/8 x 4 1/2 In.	172.00
Bowl, White Lotus Flowers, Buttercup Yellow, T. Molinari, 2 x 5 In.	247.00
Bowl, White Lotus Flowers, Incised Broad Band, Rose Bacchini, 1926, 3 x 9 In.	412.00
Bowl, White Rabbits, Yellow Ground, Cuerda Seca, 1911, 2 x 5 In.	770.00
Bowl, Yellow Hens, Yellow, White Chicks, Cuerda Seca, 1909	825.00
Bowl, Yellow Interior, Flared, 1937, 12 In.	275.00
Breakfast Set, Landscape, Sage Green Hills, White Rabbit, 1922, 3 Piece	1210.00
Breakfast Set, Rabbits, Running, White, Cuerda Seca, Blue Ground, 3 Piece	1430.00
Charger, Band Of Green Trees, Blue Sky, Ivory Ground, 1917, 12 In.	660.00
Cup & Saucer, Sage Green Tree, Chicory Blue Skyline, Geneco, 1919, 2 x 5 3/4 In.	220.00
Inkwell, Brown Glaze, Signed, 2 1/2 x 2 3/4 In.	130.00
Inkwell, Ships, Sage Green Sails, White Sky, Blue Water, Square, 2 x 4 In.	1760.00
Jug, Cream, Incised Windmills, Signed, 23 1/4 In.	402.00
Mug, Juvenile, Benjamin, His Mug, Smiling Child, 1934, 3 1/8 In.	467.00
Nut Dish, Landscape, Sage Green Trees, Cerulean Blue Sky, JG, 3 In.	275.00
Paperweight, Blue Skyline, 1914, 3 In.	990.00
Paperweight, Paul Revere, Midnight Ride, Blue, Green, Fannie Levine, 1914, 3 In.	990.00
Paperweight Tile, Image Of Swan, 2 1/2 In.	275.00
Pitcher, Chirping Chicks, Handle, 3 1/8 x 3 3/4 In.	605.00
Plate, 3 Ivory Chicks, Powder Blue Band, 5 1/2 In.	220.00
Plate, Band Of Lotus Flowers, Yellow Glaze, 1913, 6 1/3 In.	192.00
Plate, Camel Design, 8 1/2 In.	1870.00
Plate, Chirping Chicks, Yellow, 1921, 7 In.	665.00
Plate, Circle Center, Yellow, Signed, 7 3/4 In.	467.00
Plate, Goose, White With Orange Beak, Green Hills, 1914, 7 1/2 In.	1450.00
Plate, Green, Brown Trees, Cuerda Seca Design, Dark Blue Ground, 1914, 8 In.	385.00
Plate, Ivory Ducks, Peering Upwards, Deep Chicory Blue, 6 In.	550.00
Plate, Landscape Design, House In Center, Light Blue Borders, 8 In.	470.00

Plate, Large Goose, Incised White, Orange Beak, Feet, H.O.S., 7 In. 1430.00
Plate, Lotus Flowers, Yellow Glaze, Bacchini & Geneco, 6 In. 195.00
Plate, Pigs, Trotting, Ivory, Yellow, Ocher, Ivory Ground, 1910, 8 1/2 In. 2970.00
Plate, Pinecones, Light Brown, Green Pine Needles, Geneco, 1917, 7 3/4 In. 248.00
Plate, Rabbit, Fully Clothed In Little Girl's Dress, Sage Green Field, 6 1/3 In. 1760.00
Plate, Trio Of Chicks, Ivory Ground, 6 1/2 In. 660.00
Plate, Whimsical Chick, Cream, Yellow, 6 In. 715.00
Plate, White Cottage, Blue Water, Trees, Grass, Yellow Sky, 1922, 6 1/2 In. 550.00
Plate, White Lotus Flowers, Black, Buttercup Yellow Glaze, 1913, 7 In. 210.00
Porringer & Bowl, Medallion, Stylized Landscape, E. Brown, 4 In. 900.00
Tea Caddy, Indigo Irises, Cuerda Seca, Brown, Green Ground, 4 x 3 In. 1320.00
Tile, Badger House, Corner Prince & Thatcher Street, 3 3/4 In. 860.00
Tile, Geometric On Blue, Outlined In Black, S.E.G., Signed, Frame, 5 In. 275.00
Tile, Large Ship, Sage Green Sail, Chicory Blue Water, E. Brown, 5 In. 165.00
Tile, Mother Hen, Chick, Yellow, Don't Bother Me, Round, 6 In. 2000.00
Tile, Mother Hen, Ivory Chick, Pale Yellow Glaze, Levine, 5 In. 2090.00
Tile, Windmill, Sage Green, Steel Blue Sky, Octagonal, 1914, 3 In. 990.00
Tray, Incised & Painted Tree, Signed, 7 In. 310.00
Trivet, Ship, Signed, 9 1/4 x 5 3/4 In. 430.00
Vase, Blue Glaze, 4 x 4 In. 165.00
Vase, Blue Semigloss Glaze, 4 1/2 In. 130.00
Vase, Drip Design, Runs Over Mouth, Tapering, 10 1/8 In. 220.00
Vase, Robin's Egg Blue Matte Glaze, 1920, 8 3/4 x 7 1/4 In. ....440.00 to 750.00
Vase, Tulip, Floral, Buttercup Yellow, Cerulean Blue, Edith Brown, 4 In. 110.00
Vase, Yellow Floral Band, Cream, Green, Blue Ground, Signed, 5 In. 1840.00

PEACHBLOW glass originated about 1883 at Hobbs, Brockunier and
Company of Wheeling, West Virginia. It shades from yellow to peach
and is lined with white glass. New England peachblow is a one-layer
glass shading from red to white. Mt. Washington peachblow shades
from pink to blue. Reproductions of all types of peachblow have been
made. Some are poor and easy to identify as copies, others are very
accurate reproductions and could fool the unwary. Related pieces may
be listed under Gunderson and Webb Peachblow.

Bell, Yellow Top, Clear Handle, Custard Finial, Rolled Rim, 11 3/4 In. 415.00
Bowl, Floral Decoration, Yellow, White Green, Ruffled Edge, 2 1/4 In. 2013.00
Celery Vase, New England, 6 1/8 In. ....303.00 to 685.00
Celery Vase, Square Top, 5 In. 300.00
Cruet, Enameled Floral, Dragonfly, New England, 5 1/2 In. 660.00
Cruet, Petticoat, Amber Handle, Cut Amber Stopper, Wheeling 1400.00
Cruet, Wheeling 1100.00
Decanter, Pilgrim, Amber Rope Handle, Cut Amber Stopper, Wheeling, 9 1/2 In. 1895.00
Finger Bowl, New England, Satin, 2 1/2 x 5 1/4 In. 385.00
Finger Bowl, Wheeling 200.00
Pitcher, Milk, c.1890, 7 1/2 In. 1000.00
Pitcher, Satin Cloverleaf Top, Extended Handle, Mt.Washington, 8 In. 750.00
Rose Bowl, 4 In. ....*Illus* 225.00
Salt & Pepper, Sterling Tops, Wheeling 1100.00

**Don't hide keys in the obvious places:
over the door, under the mat,
under the steps, in the mailbox.
There are several types of key holders
that will let you hide a key in better
ways. Some are magnetic, some look
like stones or garden figures.**

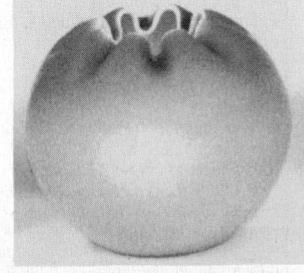

Peachblow, Rose Bowl, 4 In.

Toothpick, Tricornered, New England 95.00
Toothpick, Wild Rose, New England, 2 1/4 In. 485.00
Tumbler, New England .... .225.00 to 410.00
Tumbler, Satin, New England 415.00
Tumbler, Wheeling .... .300.00 to 425.00
Vase, Frosted Wishbone Feet, 4 1/2 x 3 In. 115.00
Vase, Jack-In-The-Pulpit, New England 60.00
Vase, Lily, New England, 7 7/8 In. 522.00
Vase, Lily, New England, 12 1/2 In. 460.00
Vase, Lily, Opaque Base, New England, 8 1/4 In. 230.00
Vase, Lily, Wild Rose, New England, 12 In. 515.00
Vase, Painted Flowers, Handle, 6 x 4 1/2 In. 60.00
Vase, Stick, Amber Rigaree, Wheeling, 8 1/4 In. 770.00
Vase, Stick, Wheeling, 10 In. 1100.00
Vase, Swirled, Ribbon Edge, Satin, 7 1/4 In. 187.00
Vase, Wheeling, 8 In. 550.00
Vase, Wheeling, 10 In. 1500.00
Vase, White Enameled, 5 1/2 In. 165.00

PEARL items listed here are made of the natural mother-of-pearl from shells. Such natural pearl has been used to decorate furniture and small utilitarian objects for centuries. The glassware known as mother-of-pearl is listed by that name. Opera glasses made with natural pearl shell are listed under Opera Glasses.

Knife & Fork Set, Service For 6, Green Satin Lining Case, 11 In. 38.00
Mirror, Bone Inlaid, Ebony Floral Inlaid Frame, 69 1/2 x 43 In. 5750.00
Tea Caddy, Bow Front, Divided Lidded Compartment, Regency, 5 1/2 In. 1150.00

PEARLWARE is an earthenware made by Josiah Wedgwood in 1779. It was copied by other potters in England. Pearlware is only slightly different in color from creamware and for many years collectors have confused the terms. Wedgwood pieces are listed in the Wedgwood category in this book.

Pearl

Basket, Canton Style, Reticulated, 10 3/4 In., Pair 750.00
Bowl, Blue & White, Oriental Transfer, Yellow Rim, 8 3/4 x 3 7/8 In. 145.00
Bowl, Floral, Enameled Rim, Pink, Red, Green, Black, Mahogany Stripes, 10 3/8 In. 248.00
Bowl, Rural Farm Scene, Floral Border, Staffordshire, 9 In. 210.00
Bowl, Strawberries, 6 1/4 In. 100.00
Chop Plate, Blue & White Floral, Blue Feather Edge, 14 1/4 In. 220.00
Chop Plate, Strawberry, Blue Feather Edge, Leeds, 13 1/4 In. 2420.00
Coffeepot, Blue Florals, Pedestal Base, 10 1/2 In. 77.00
Coffeepot, Delft Type, c.1820 .... 675.00
Cup, Floral & Foliage, Gold, Green, Yellow & Brown, No Handle, 6 In. 100.00
Cup & Saucer, Handleless, Gaudy Floral, Wood & Sons 270.00
Figurine, 2 Falconers, Fish Monger, Gardener, Staffordshire, 4 Piece 2530.00
Figurine, Eagle, Perched On Rocky Base, c.1800, 6 1/2 In. 1035.00
Jug, Chinoiserie Figure Groups, Swansea, 1804, 6 7/8 In. 713.00
Loving Cup, 3 Interior Frogs, Floral Transfer, Initialed JTG 247.00
Mug, Blue Oasis, Yellow, Black Frog, Pink Luster, 4 In. 245.00
Mug, Red & Green Design, William Street, Dewsbury Moor, 4 1/4 In. 395.00
Pitcher, Chinoiserie Design, Polychrome, 6 In. 660.00
Pitcher, Classical Scenes, Pink & Copper Luster, 5 1/2 In. 80.00
Pitcher, Milk, Floral, 6 1/2 In. 155.00
Plate, Chinoiserie Pagoda, 9 3/4 In., Pair 290.00
Plate, Floral & Strawberries, 9 1/2 In. 440.00
Plate, General Lafayette, Red Striping, Floral Rim, Brown, Red Transfer, 7 5/8 In. 465.00
Plate, Line Border, Feathered Rim, Blue Underglaze, Swansea, 1788, 9 In. 8662.00
Plate, Pavonian Porch, Blue Transfer, Reticulated, 7 3/8 In., Pair 320.00
Plate, Queen's Rose, Stawberries, 10 In. 385.00
Platter, Chinoiserie, Blue Transfer, Mid-19th Century, 20 1/2 In. 85.00
Platter, Gaudy Blue & White, Floral, Molded Feather Edge, 16 1/4 In. 968.00
Platter, Octagonal, Canton, England, 12 3/4 In., Pair 172.00
Punch Bowl, Continuous Landscape, Road To London, 3 Carriages, 1800, 17 In. 12650.00

Teapot, Brown Floral Transfer, Orange Enamel Trim, 5 1/2 In. 270.00
Teapot, Cover, Tea Party, Pink Luster, Blue Transfer, Globular, England, 5 In. 230.00
Tureen, Sauce, Molded Green Feather Edge, 7 1/4 In. 280.00
Waste Bowl, City Hall, New York Scene, Rose Border, Light Blue Transfer, 7 In. 110.00

PEKING GLASS is a Chinese cameo glass first made popular in the eighteenth century. The Chinese have continued to make this layered glass
in the old manner, and many new pieces are now available that could
confuse the average buyer.

Bowl, Bird On White Ground, Blue Floral, 2 1/2 x 6 1/4 In. 192.00
Bowl, Blue Landscape, Horse Design, White, Bell Shape, 19th Century, 6 1/4 In. 550.00
Bowl, Butterfly, Flower Design, Blue, White, 1900, 7 In. 192.00
Bowl, Deep Turquoise, Foliate Shape, Flared Mouth, 7 1/4 x 6 1/4 In. 690.00
Jar, Cover, Squirrel, Grapevine, Globular, 1900, 6 3/4 In. 330.00
Jar, Red Floral, Milk White Ground, 19th Century, 5 1/2 In. 412.00
Jar, Shou Designs, Yellow, Globular, 1840, 5 5/8 In. 660.00
Snuff Bottle, 5 Colors, 9 Buddhist Lions, Playing Over Rock, 1950s, 2 7/8 In. 2750.00
Snuff Bottle, Blue To White, Ovoid, 3 In. 85.00
Snuff Bottle, Carp, Crashing Waves, Coral, Dyed Ivory Top, 19th Century, 2 In. 172.00
Snuff Bottle, Cranberry Overlay, Snowflake, Scrolled Chih Lung Dragons, 2 In. 172.00
Snuff Bottle, Dragons, Ovoid, 19th Century, 3 In. 1760.00
Snuff Bottle, Lotus, Peony & Other Flowers, Opalescent, 3 In. 1500.00
Snuff Bottle, Overall Raised Bird & Floral, Ovoid, 3 1/8 In. 170.00
Snuff Bottle, Red Overlay, Snowflake, Boy In A Boat, Holding Lotus, Stopper 287.00
Snuff Bottle, Red, Green, Yellow, Blue Overlay, Pumpkin Shape, 2 1/2 In. 345.00
Snuff Bottle, Ribbed Handles, Ovoid, 1780s, 3 In. 975.00
Snuff Bottle, Scholars In Landscape, Snowflake Ground, 1820s, 2 3/4 In. 1850.00
Snuff Bottle, Simulated Goldstone, Flattened Disk Shape, 2 1/2 In. 173.00
Snuff Bottle, Wreathes Of Chih Lung Dragons, Tortoiseshell, Pear Shape, 3 In. 431.00
Vase, Bird & Florals, Red Cut To White, 12 In., Pair 345.00
Vase, Blue Cut To White, Lotus Meanders, 19th Century, 5 1/2 In. 690.00
Vase, Cranes, Flying Over Rocks, Chih Mushrooms, Lemon Yellow, 12 In., Pair 1092.00
Vase, Emerald Green, Club Shape, 19th Century, 8 1/8 In. 825.00
Vase, Landscape, Flowering Vines, Puce, Green Ground, 8 In., Pair 1090.00
Vase, Peony, Prunus, Forest Green Ground, 19th Century, 8 In., Pair 1210.00
Vase, Red Landscape Design, White Ground, Pear Shape, 19th Century, 7 In. 715.00
Vase, Red Phoenix On Rock, Floral, Yellow Ground, 5 3/8 In. 3740.00
Vase, Ruby, Faceted Base, Club Shape, 1800, 7 In. 1540.00
Vase, Yellow Cut To White, Bird & Floral, China, 20th Century, 10 3/4 In., Pair 260.00
Vase, Yellow Overlay, White, Iris Flowers, Flared, 20th Century, 9 1/4 In. 230.00

PELOTON glass is a European glass with small threads of colored glass
rolled onto the surface of clear or colored glass. It is sometimes called
spaghetti, or shredded coconut, glass. Most pieces found today were
made in the nineteenth century.

Vase, Pink, White Enameled Flowers, Green Shredded Coconut, 6 In. 220.00
Vase, Tricornered Rolled Rim, 4 In. 275.00

PENS replaced hand-cut quills as writing instruments in 1780 when the
first steel pen point was made in England. But it was 100 years before
the commercial pen was a common item. The fountain pen was
invented in the 1830s but was not made in quantity until the 1880s. All
types of old pens are collected.

PEN, Conklin, Desk Set, Lapis Blue, Bronze Dog, 1926 .... 175.00
Conklin, Fountain, Black, Incised Wavy Design, Gold Band, 1903 .... 60.00
Cross, Tiffany Sterling Silver 45.00
Eversharp, Desk Set, Red, Gold Seal, 2 Pens, 1942 .... 125.00
Fountain, Carved Relief Dragon Images, Spring Loaded Plunger 115.00
Glass, Cobalt Blue, Sterling Silver & 14K Gold, c.1920, 6 1/4 In. 265.00
Glass, Light Blue Aquamarine, Sterling Silver & 14K Gold, c.1920, 7 3/4 In. 325.00
Parker, Orange, Box 40.00
Parker, Vacumatic, Green Stripe 65.00
Sheaffer, 14K Gold Top, Box 25.00

Sheaffer, Green, Gold Caps, Box, 1945	85.00
Tiffany, Ballpoint, Silver, Man's, Box	110.00
Tiffany, Fountain, Silver, Musical Note, Box & Carrying Case	90.00
Waterman, Ideal, 14K Overlay Gold, 1920s	750.00
Waterman, Ideal, Sterling Overlay Vine, 1920s, 5 1/4 In.	800.00
PEN & PENCIL, Cross, Centennial, Silver Colored, Checkerboard Design, Red Case, Box	20.00
Dr Pepper, Celluloid, Over Metal	1150.00
Parker, Ballpoint, Sterling Silver	110.00
Parker, Maroon Plastic, Stainless Metal, Plunger Fill Type Pen	35.00
Sheaffer, Snorkel, Light Blue, Gold & Silver Finish Caps, Satin Lined Case	50.00
Tiffany, Sterling Silver, Foam-Lined Plastic Tray, 4 In.	110.00
Waterman, Black, Gold Caps, Box, 1954	70.00
Waterman, Graduation Gift, 14K Gold Filled, Box, 1918	225.00

PENCILS were invented, so it is said, in 1565. The eraser was not added to the pencil until 1858. The automatic pencil was invented in 1863. Collectors today want advertising pencils or automatic pencils of unusual design. Boxes and sharpeners for pencils are also collected.

PENCIL, Aspre, Gold, London	115.00
Bullet, Advertising	10.00
Mechanical, L.B.K. & I. Transit Co., Plastic, Late 1930s, 5 1/2 In.	18.00
Mechanical, Mr. Peanut, Planters, Plastic, 5 1/2 In., Pair	30.00
Shelter Island Oyster Co.	3.00
PENCIL SHARPENER, Alligator, Hasbro, 1976	50.00
Black Face	75.00
Dandy, Automatic, c.1900	150.00
Dandy, Cast Iron, Patent 1900	360.00
Dexter, No. 3 Improved, Metal, Celluloid, 1940s, 3 1/2 x 2 1/2 x 4 In.	55.00
Donald Duck, Decal On Bakelite, 1940s, 1 3/8 In.	35.00
Electric, Swingline, Electro-Pointer, Gray Plastic	330.00
Globe, Lithographed Tin, Die Cast Base, Prewar, Germany	35.00
Lion, Crown On Head, Hasbro, 1976	50.00
Navy Airplane, Green, Bakelite	60.00
Popeye, Decal On Bakelite, 1929, 2 1/4 In.	35.00
Sedan, Tinplate, Japan, 3 1/2 In.	290.00
Sparky, Photograph Insert, Square	95.00
US Army Tank, Red Bakelite	25.00
Mr. Puffin, White	10.00

PENNSBURY Pottery worked in Morrisville, Pennsylvania, from 1950 to 1971. Full sets of dinnerware as well as many decorative items were made. Pieces are marked with the name of the factory.

Pennsbury Pottery

Amish, Cake Stand, Pedestal, Couple, Children & Trees, 11 1/2 x 4 1/2 In.	125.00
Amish, Pitcher, Couple, 6 In.	40.00
Ashtray, Signed, 5 In.	12.00
Figurine, Bird, Rooster & Hen, Multicolored, Pair	285.00
Lamp, Magnolia Warbler	250.00
Red Rooster, Coffeepot, 8 In.	110.00
Red Rooster, Mug, Beer	28.00
Sweet Adeline, Bowl, Pretzel	60.00

PEPSI-COLA, the drink and the name, was invented in 1898 but was not trademarked until 1903. The logo was changed from an elaborate script to the modern block letters on the 1970 Pepsi label. Several different logos have been used. Until 1951, the words *Pepsi* and *Cola* were separated by 2 dashes. These bottles are called *double dash.* In 1951 the modern logo with a single hyphen was introduced. All types of advertising memorabilia are collected, and reproductions are being made.

PEPSI-COLA

Ashtray, Pepsi's Got Your Taste For Life, Black Plastic, Memphis, Mo. Bottling Co.	30.00
Bank, Delivery Syrup Truck, Metal, Plastic, Box	48.00
Bank, Die Cast Metal, Stand	18.00
Bank, Hot Air Balloon, Stand	25.00
Bank, Truck, Metal, Plastic, Box	48.00

Bank, Vending Machine 15.00
Blotter, Pepsi & Pete The Pepsi-Cola Cops, Red, White, Blue 80.00
Blotter, Pepsi & Pete, Bottle, 1930s 65.00
Bottle, Limited Edition, 1940, 12 Oz. 3.00
Bottle, Richmond, Green, Embossed, Octagonal, 1920s, 6 1/2 In. 46.00
Bottle Opener, Chrome 5.00
Bottle Opener, Drink Pepsi-Cola, Die Cast, 1950, 4 1/8 In. 18.00
Can, Cone Top, 1951 .... 450.00
Can, Syrup, Bottle Cap Logo, Tin, 1950s, Gallon 35.00
Clock, Double Bubble, 1950s, 15 In. 2070.00
Clock, Double Bubble, Be Sociable, Have A Pepsi, Round 1150.00
Clock, Double Bubble, Say Pepsi Please, Stripes, Round 750.00
Clock, Say Pepsi Please, Plastic, Light-Up, Square, 1960s, 16 In. 85.00
Clock, Tastee-Freeze Refreshment Bar, Light-Up, Motion, 1950s, 20 x 20 In. 2185.00
Clock, Teardrop, Metal 250.00
Cooler, Aluminum, Salesman's Sample, 1940s, 12 x 7 1/2 x 11 1/2 In. 2990.00
Crate, Wooden, 1930s, 91 x 12 x 10 In. 35.00
Display, Santa Claus, On Left Foot, Holds 1960s Bottle, Rockwell, 16 x 20 In. 95.00
Door Push, Porcelain, 37 1/2 x 3 In. 300.00
Glass, Daffy Duck, Warner Bros., 1973 .... 5.00
Glass, Henry Hawk, 1973 .... 35.00
Glass, Yosemite Sam, Warner Bros., 1973 .... 5.00
Kick Plate, Embossed, 1940s, 10 x 30 In. 635.00
Machine, Model 27, Light Blue Paint, Pepsi Bottle Cap, Vendorlator Mfg. Co., 52 In. 575.00
Poster, Indiana Jones, Color, Original Tube, 25 x 35 In. 1.00
Pushbar, Enjoy Pepsi-Cola Iced, Porcelain 120.00
Sign, 5 Cents, Bottle Picture, Metal, 1930s, 16 x 48 In. 575.00
Sign, Bottle Cap Logo, Dormeyer # 5, Seldon Jaycees, Wooden, 1950s, 24 x 8 In. 55.00
Sign, Bottle Cap, Light-Up, Wheel Spins, 3-D Effect, Electric, 12 1/2 In. 1210.00
Sign, Bottle Shape, 5 Cents, 1940s, 45 In. 720.00
Sign, Bottle Shape, 5 Cents, Arrow, 1936, 45 In. 1265.00
Sign, Bottle Shape, Tin, Die Cut, 45 In. 625.00
Sign, Button, Courtesy Panel, 1940s, 50 x 42 In. 400.00
Sign, Couple Drinking Pepsi, More Bounce To The Ounce & Bottle Cap, 28 In. 192.00
Sign, Curb Service Pepsi-Cola Ice Cold, Bigger-Better, Light Blue Ground, 15 In. 440.00
Sign, Drink Pepsi-Cola, Under Glass, Frame, 1920, 3 1/2 x 9 1/2 In. 265.00
Sign, Light-Up, Polar Bear, Plastic, Wooden Frame, 1950s, 14 x 24 In. 1095.00
Sign, More Bounce To The Ounce, Porcelain, 1940s, 18 x 48 In. 4715.00
Sign, Patrol Boy, School Crossing, Figural, 1950s, 30 x 64 In. 690.00
Sign, Pepsi-Cola Bottle Cap, 2 Sides, 1950s, 29 x 35 In. 215.00
Thermometer, Buy Pepsi-Cola, Box, 1940s, 7 x 27 In. 1670.00
Thermometer, Diet Pepsi, Outdoor, 1960-1970, 32 x 46 x 3 In. 100.00
Thermometer, Drink Pepsi-Cola Ice Cold, Pam, Round, 12 In. 1120.00
Thermometer, Girl With Straw, 1941, 7 x 27 In. 1064.00
Thermometer, The Light Refreshment, Tin, Embossed, 1950s, 7 x 27 In. 230.00
Toy, Truck, Balsa Wood, Box, 1940s, 5 1/4 In. 230.00
Toy, Truck, Delivery, Red, Blue Cab, Open Side Body, Compartments, Box, 16 In. 770.00
Toy, Truck, Metal, 1940s, 6 In. 215.00
Tumbler Set, Robin The Boy Wonder, 1979, Pair 15.00
Whistle, Bakelite, 2 Bottles With Pepsi Decal, 1950s, 3 In. 85.00

PERFUME BOTTLES are made of cut glass, pressed glass, art glass, silver, metal, enamel, and even plastic or porcelain. Although the small bottle to hold perfume was first made before the time of ancient Egypt, it is the nineteenth- and twentieth-century examples that interest today's collector. DeVilbiss Company has made atomizers of all types since 1888 but no longer makes the perfume bottle tops so popular with collectors. These were made from 1920 to 1968. The glass bottle may be by any of many manufacturers even if the atomizer is marked *DeVilbiss*. The word *factice*, which often appears in ads, refers to store display bottles. Glass or porcelain examples may be found under the appropriate name such as Lalique, Czechoslovakia, Glass-Bohemian, etc.

2 Bears, Clear & Frosted, Art Deco Stopper, Ingrid, Czechoslovakia, 5 1/2 In. 800.00

Atomizer, Gold Iridescent Glass, 8 1/2 In. 288.00
Bell Shape, Enamel Flowers & Leaves 875.00
Bourjois, Courage, Red, Yellow Silk Tassel, White Bakelite Screw Cap, 6 In. 645.00
Bourjois, Evening In Paris, Dancing Couple Under Lamppost, Blue, 2 Piece 345.00
Bourjois, Evening In Paris, Oyster Shape, Light Green Bakelite Box, 5 In. 990.00
Bourjois, Glamour, Sample Inside Cigarette Case, Tortoiseshell, 5 1/2 In. 515.00
Bourjois, Lavender, Purse Flacon, Blue Bakelite Screw Cap, Blue Tassel 95.00
Bourjois, Springtime In Paris, Electric Blue Glass Flacon, Brass Screw Cap 240.00
Caron, Bellodgia, Red Interior, Black Cap, Pink, Black Label, 3 In. 300.00
Chanel, Jasmin, Tester, White Paper Label, Black Lettering, 6 In. 385.00
Chanel, No. 5, Classic Shape, Black Cap, White & Black Box, 3 1/2 In. 345.00
Cinderella, France, 5 In. 70.00
Clear, Facet Cut Body, Stopper, c.1840, 3 1/2 In. 160.00
Cobalt Blue, 8 Ribs, Applied Rings, Flared Lip, Mushroom Stopper, 5 5/8 In. 355.00
Colonial Man, Blue Coat, Head Is Stopper, Porcelain, 3 1/4 In. 55.00
Coty, Complice, Raised Leaves, Frosted Tiara Stopper, 4 In. 265.00
Cut Glass, Lay-Down, Cane, Brilliant, Brass Hinged Lid, 9 x 1 3/4 In. 170.00
Cut Glass, Lay-Down, Cane, Sterling Silver Cover, Round, 7 x 1 1/4 In. 200.00
Cut Glass, Ruby Cut To Clear, Original Atomizer, 1880, 8 In. 450.00
Dark Green Glass, Sterling Silver Overlay, Stopper, 6 In. 1210.00
DeVilbiss, Art Deco, Black, Gold Trim, 7 In., Pair 175.00
DeVilbiss, Atomizer, White Feather Design 35.00
DeVilbiss, Milk Glass, Roses 15.00
Diamond-Quilted, Mother-Of-Pearl Satin Glass, Faceted Stopper, 8 In. 175.00
Dior, Miss Dior, White, Gold Label, White Screw Cap, 3 In. 275.00
Elizabeth Arden, Blue Grass, Gold, Black Label, Gilded Cap, Blue Box, 3 In. 190.00
Elizabeth Arden, Memoire Cherie, Woman Figure, Draped, Glass Stopper 815.00
Fath, Fath De Fath, 8-Point Star Shape, Brass Pointed Screw Cap, 4 1/2 In. 240.00
Figural, Frosted Nude, Perido Green Base, Czechoslovakia, 5 1/2 In. 298.00
Figural, Violin, Gold, Shagreen Case, c.1740, 2 5/8 In. 13800.00
Googly, Germany 95.00
Goya, Black Rose, 3-Tiered, Red Rose In Front, Burgundy Bakelite Screw Cap 175.00
Guerlain, Mitsouko, Cube Shape, Green Plastic Screw Cap, 4 In. 475.00
Guerlain, Vol De Nuit, Flacon Shape, Smoky, Gray, Brown, Square Stopper 515.00
Hattie Carnegie, Flacon, Woman Figure, Draped, Gilded Stopper, 1935, 4 In. 945.00
Helena Rubinstein, Heaven Sent, Poems, Bakelite Screw Cap, 3 1/2 In., Pair 1890.00
Helena Rubinstein, Town, Serigraphed Skyscraper, Copper Screw Cap, Box 190.00
Houbigant, Quelques Fleurs, White Bakelite Ribbed Ball Screw Cap, Box, 5 In. 170.00
Jockey Club, Rectangular, Reverse Glass, Milk Glass, Pat'd. Apr. 2, 1889, 7 In. 225.00
Jovoy, Allez Hop, Figural, Small Dog, Paris, 1924, 11 In. 1585.00
Lancome, Cuir De Lancome, Flacon, 8-Pointed Star Stopper, Box, 1947, 12 In. 2230.00
Lucien LeLong, Cachet, Purse Flacon Shape, Gilded Brass Casing, 6 In. 255.00
Lucien LeLong, Mon Image, Flacon, Brass Ball Screw Cap, 4 1/2 In. 385.00
Lucien LeLong, Tailspin, Purse Flacon Shape, Brass Casing Openwork, 6 In. 470.00
Lucien LeLong, To My Valentine, Red, White Paper Label, Brass Screw Cap 1030.00
Marquay, Coup De Feu, Salvador Dali, Tiered Red & Black Box 132.00
Maurice Marinot, Controlled Air Bubbles, Acid-Etched, Ball Stopper, 8 In. 6900.00
Maurice Marinot, Controlled Air Bubbles, Amber, Ball Stopper, 1925, 7 In. 4600.00
Maurice Marinot, Controlled Air Bubbles, Teal, Pink, Ball Stopper, 1925, 5 In. 8050.00
Maurice Marinot, Watermelon Design, Diamonds, Ball Stopper, 1925, 5 In. 9200.00
Molinard, Christmas Bells, Flacon, Bell Shape, Red, Gold Label, Stopper, 8 In. 1030.00
Mottled Blue Waves Over Orange, No Bulb, Czechoslovakia, 3 1/2 In. 27.00
Paperweight, Red, Light Blue, Yellow Swirled Glass, Hinged Metal Stopper 1725.00
Pleville, Flamme De Gloire, Flacon, Pyramid, 3 Faces, Crystal Stopper, 9 In. 1030.00
Prince Matchabelli, Windsong, Advertising Premium For 1955 Chevrolet, Box 25.00
Scent, Porcelain, Enamel, Floral, Winter Scene, Brass Cap, 3 1/2 In. 140.00
Scent, Silver Snake Foliate Hinged Lid, Ruby Glass, Cylindrical, I.W. Ltd., 3 In. 345.00
Schiaparelli, Sleeping, Candle Flacon, Blue Neck, Ground Glass Stopper 2060.00
Schiaparelli, Succes Fou, Glass Cube Stopper 45.00
Sterle, Amphora Shape, White, Black Label, Black Screw Cap, Gray, White Box 240.00
Stevens & Williams, Pompeian Swirl, Mother-Of-Pearl, 7 3/4 In. 1265.00
Vigny, Golliwogg, 2 3/8 In. 44.00
Vigny, Golliwogg, Paper Label, 2 5/8 In. 180.00

Vigny, Incised Vertical Stringing, Stopper, 1925, 5 In. 2585.00
Vigny, Vertical Striations, Molded Stopper, 1925, 10 In. 6325.00
Yellow, Pulled Red Design, Maroon Satin Atomizer, Czechoslovakia, 6 In. 45.00

PETERS & REED Pottery Company of Zanesville, Ohio, was founded
by John D. Peters and Adam Reed in 1897. Chromal, Landsun,
Montene, Pereco, and Persian are some of the art lines that were made.
The company, which became Zane Pottery in 1920 and Gonder Pottery
in 1941, closed in 1957. Peters & Reed pottery was unmarked.

Bowl, Branch Design, Green Matte Glaze, 3 x 8 In. 295.00
Bowl, Horizontal Stripes Inside & Out, 11 1/2 In. 175.00
Flower Frog, Green Flower, Black, 3 1/2 In. 25.00
Pitcher, Brown, Bulbous 75.00
Planter, Aztec, Hanging 95.00
Planter, Moss Aztec, Hanging 85.00
Vase, Abstract Painted Design, Black, Turquoise & Yellow, Signed, 12 x 7 In. 100.00
Vase, Landscape, Blue, Rust, Cream, Green & Cobalt, 8 3/8 In. 440.00
Vase, Molded Floral Design, Cream Matte Glaze, Brown Highlights, 18 In. 385.00
Vase, Moss Aztec, 3-Dimensional Pine Cones, 9 3/4 In. 330.00
Vase, Moss Aztec, Floral Design, Green, Red Glaze, 10 In. 385.00
Vase, Zaneware, Drip Glaze, Signed, 8 3/4 In. 137.00
Wall Pocket, Egyptian, Matte Green 250.00

PETRUS REGOUT, see Maastricht category.

PEWABIC POTTERY was founded by Mary Chase Perry Stratton in
1903 in Detroit, Michigan. The company made many types of art pottery, including pieces with matte green glaze and an iridescent crystalline glaze. The company continued working until the death of Mary
Stratton in 1961. It was reactivated by Michigan State University in
1968.

Ashtray, Egyptian Blue, Gold, Small 115.00
Bowl, Embossed Lily Pads, Forming Ring Handles, Green Glaze, Signed, 8 1/2 In. 3000.00
Box, Antelope On Cover, Signed, 1 7/8 x 4 3/4 In. 355.00
Tile, Candle In Wreath, Iridescent Gold & Blue, Square, 2 1/4 In. 82.00
Tile, Overall Geometric Design, Iridescent Glaze, Square, 8 In. 125.00
Vase, Black, Green & Lavender Glaze, Squat, Impressed, 3 1/2 In. 495.00
Vase, Blue Metallic Glaze, Iridescent, Bulbous Form, 10 x 9 In. 2530.00
Vase, Blue, Green Gunmetal Glaze, 8 In. 605.00
Vase, Flecks Of Light Green, Green Rim, 10 1/4 In. 1320.00
Vase, Iridescent Cobalt Glaze, Signed, 3 3/4 In. 350.00
Vase, Leaves Under Flowing Matte Green Glaze, Signed, 6 x 8 In. 5750.00
Vase, Turquoise & Taupe Glaze, Impressed, 5 1/2 In. 715.00

PEWTER is a metal alloy of tin and lead. Some of the pewter made after
1840 has a slightly different composition and is called *Britannia metal*.
This later type of pewter was worked by machine; the earlier pieces
were made by hand. In the 1920s pewter came back into fashion and
pieces were often marked *Genuine Pewter*. Eighteenth-, nineteenth-,
and twentieth-century examples are listed here.

Basin, Francis Piggott, England, 18th Century, 13 In. 145.00
Basin, Samuel Hamlin, 2 x 5 3/4 In. 522.00
Biscuit Jar, Archibald Knox, Stylized Foliage, 5 1/2 In. 977.00
Bottle, Feeding, Henry Joseph, London, c.1750 . . . . 1350.00
Bowl, Samuel Ellis, Plug Hole In Rim, 13 1/4 In. 165.00
Cake Plate, Deer Eating Leaves From Tree Center, Marked, Hanging Hole, 10 1/2 In. . . . 750.00
Candlestick, Baroque, Pricket, Germany, c.1680, 9 In., Pair 900.00
Candlestick, Bobeche, 8 1/2 In., Pair 190.00
Candlestick, Capstan Base, 4 3/4 In., Pair 715.00
Candlestick, Henry Hopper, Removable Bobeches, 1840s, 10 In., Pair 990.00
Candlestick, Louis XIV Style, Foliate Design, 9 1/2 In., Pair 345.00
Candlestick, Pricket, Baroque, Turned Stem, 3-Footed Base, 23 In., Pair 440.00
Chamber Pot, 2 Handles, Touchmarks Of Bush & Perkins, Longon, 1770 . . . . 395.00

Chamberstick, Push-Up, Dark Patina, 19th Century, EWN, 4 In. 38.00
Charger, Eagle Touch, Thomas Badger, 13 1/4 In. 468.00
Charger, England, 13 1/2 In. 90.00
Charger, England, 15 In. 120.00
Charger, Engraved Angel Rim, I.C. VP, Richard Bache, 16 1/2 In. 275.00
Charger, John Townsend, London, 1748, 16 1/2 In. 250.00
Charger, Multiple-Reeded Rim, Engraved, Hallmark, c.1680, 18 1/4 In. 950.00
Charger, Wavy Edge, England, c.1750, 18 3/4 In. 850.00
Clock, Hammered, Tudric, Original Patina, 4 x 3 In. 935.00
Coffeepot, Domed Lid, Lighthouse Shape 550.00
Coffeepot, Dunham, Flower Finial, 8 1/4 In. 165.00
Coffeepot, Freeman Porter, Pear Shape, Footed Base, 12 In. 330.00
Coffeepot, Gray Graniteware, Hinged Lid, Wooden Finial, 10 In. 120.00
Coffeepot, Homan & Co., Flower Finial, Cincinnati, 8 3/4 In. 75.00
Coffeepot, Lighthouse Shape, F. Porter, 11 In. 935.00
Coffeepot, Plymouth Pewter, 7 In. 16.00
Coffeepot, Rufus Dunham, c.1761, 11 1/2 In. 990.00
Coffeepot, Sellew & Co., 10 3/4 In. 245.00
Creamer, Ear Handle, Hinged Hid, 6 1/4 In. 110.00
Crumber Set, Hammered, Arts & Crafts Design, Signed, 10 x 5 In. 90.00
Dish, Deep, Samuel Ellis, Early 19th Century, 14 In. 155.00
Dish, John Townsend, Wavy Edge Design, London, c.1750, 15 In. 495.00
Dish, Luke Porter, Narrow Rim, London, c.1680, 13 In. 495.00
Dish, Thomas Alderson, Royal Cipher Of King George IV On Edge, 1820, 16 In. 750.00
Flagon, Communion, Ear Handle, 10 1/2 In. 135.00
Flagon, Communion, Smith & Feltman, Albany, 12 In. 190.00
Flagon, Engraved Inscription, Switzerland, 1739, 10 In. 850.00
Flagon, Kayserzinn, Embossed Florals, Horse On Side, Dog On Other, 1910, 12 3/4 In. .. 395.00
Flagon, Spread Eagle Applied To Front, Fluted Body, Lion Mask Feet, 1760s, 19 1/4 In. ... 750.00
Flagon, Stylized Wheat Stalks & Hops, Kayserzinn, Signed, 15 7/8 In. 200.00
Ice Bucket, Tudric, Foliate Design, 6 x 8 In. 855.00
Inkpot, Isaac Holt, Engraved 1803 I.H., Canaan, Maine, 2 In. 395.00
Inkwell, Clear Glass Insert, 3 1/4 In. 82.00
Ladle, Ashberry Best Metal Warranted For Use, 13 1/2 In. 11.00
Ladle, J. Weeks, 13 1/4 In. 165.00
Lamp, Fluid Burner, 5 3/4 In. 125.00
Lamp, Fluid, Brass, Acorn Font, 7 7/8 In. 55.00
Lamp, Fluid, Hand, Petticoat, Snuffer Caps, 3 1/4 In. 70.00
Lamp, Fluid, Hand, Snuffer Caps, 5 In. 165.00
Lamp, Hinged Lid With Pick, Flared Base, Ring Handle, 9 In. 120.00
Lamp, Lace Maker's, Roswell Gleason, Bull's-Eye 550.00
Lamp, Lard Oil, Flat, 6 3/8 In. 105.00
Lamp, Spout, Hinged Lid, Flared Base, Ring Handle, 9 In. 105.00
Lamp, Spout, Wrought Iron Pick, Hinged Lid, 19th Century, 6 In. 130.00
Lamp, Table, 38 In., Pair 85.00
Lamp, Whale Oil, 6 In. 165.00
Lamp, Whale Oil, 7 5/8 In. 138.00
Lamp, Whale Oil, 8 1/4 In. 55.00
Lamp, Whale Oil, Acorn Font, 8 5/8 In. 220.00
Lamp, Whale Oil, Barrel Shaped Containers, Baluster Base, Pair 375.00
Lamp, Whale Oil, Mounted On Wooden Base, 11 1/2 In. 120.00
Match Safe, Woman's Shoe, Hinged Cover, Striker Base, Pewter, 1 x 3 1/2 In. 170.00
Mayonnaise Set, Bowl, Ladle, Underplate, Karl Kipp, Signed, 5 1/4 In. 300.00
Measure, Gill, 1/4, 1/2 & Cup, England, 19th Century, 3 Piece 35.00
Measuring Cup, 1/4 Gill, 1/2 Gill, 1 Gill, 1/2 Pt., 1 Pt., 1 Qt., 6 Piece 245.00
Measuring Set, Georgian, Graduated, 1 To 1/4 Gill, 1830, 6 Piece 210.00
Measuring Set, Graduated, Cylinder, Liter To Centiliter, France, 1830, 6 Piece 150.00
Mold, Confection, 3 Piece, England, 19th Century, 6 1/2 In. 325.00
Mold, Ice Cream, Duck 55.00
Mold, Ice Cream, E & Co., No. 1160 .... 60.00
Mold, Ice Cream, Fruit, Fluted Sides, 1920s 45.00
Mold, Ice Cream, Lemon 25.00
Mold, Ice Cream, Rabbit, Basket On Back, 16 In. 120.00

Mold, Knights Of Columbus Seal 50.00
Mug, Handle, James Yates, England, 19th Century, 4 3/8 x 3 3/8 In. 195.00
Mug, Tavern, Heart-Shaped Terminal To The Handle, Crowned Mark, 1790, Qt. 250.00
Mug, Tavern, Inscribed WR, 18th Century, England, Pair 325.00
Mug, Tavern, John Townsend, London, 1 Pt. 495.00
Mug, U-Shaped, Hallmarks, WR Crowned Excise Mark, Handle, 1/2 Pt. 95.00
Pepper Pot, 4 3/4 In. 27.00
Pitcher, Cover, Thomas Boardman, 10 1/2 In. 385.00
Pitcher, Hammered, Nekrassoff, Scroll Handle, 6 In. 350.00
Pitcher, Water, 7 1/2 In. 165.00
Plate, Continental, 9 5/8 In. 95.00
Plate, Eagle Touch, Thomas D. Boardman, 7 5/8 In. 190.00
Plate, Griffith, London, 9 1/4 In., 4 Piece 110.00
Plate, Harbeson, Phila., 7 7/8 In. 275.00
Plate, T. Danforth, 7 3/4 In. ....165.00 to 190.00
Plate, Thomas Badger, 7 3/4 In. 385.00
Plate, Townsend & Compton, 7 5/8 In. 55.00
Platter, Deer Head, Vine, Leaf Border, Repose, 16 1/2 x 12 1/2 In. 115.00
Platter, Kayserzinn, Art Nouveau, 16 1/2 x 10 1/4 In. 25.00
Platter, Kayserzinn, Domed Cover, Scrolling Lobes, c.1900, 21 1/2 In. 860.00
Platter, Nekrassoff, Art Nouveau, 10 In. 80.00
Pokal, Ostrich Egg, Ostrich Finial, c.1880, 21 1/2 In. 1150.00
Porringer, Calder, Cast Flowered Handle, 5 1/4 In. 660.00
Porringer, Cast Handle, England, 4 1/4 In. 190.00
Porringer, Flowered Handle, Samuel E. Hamlin, Jr., 5 1/2 In. 720.00
Porringer, Flowered Handle, William Billings, 5 In. ....270.00 to 330.00
Porringer, Hamlin, Handle, Eagle Touch, 4 1/4 In. 190.00
Porringer, Heart & Crescent Handle, New England, c.1800 .... 250.00
Porringer, R.G. Under Handle, 4 In. 375.00
Porringer, R.G., Cast Crown Handle, 4 3/8 In. 205.00
Porringer, T.D & S.B., Crown Handle, 5 In. 520.00
Porringer, Taster, Relief Cast Handle, c.1800, 2 1/8-In. Bowl 210.00
Pot, Tall, Urn Shape, Dixon & Son, Wooden Finial Wafer, 12 1/2 In. 220.00
Pot, Whitlock, Troy, N.Y., 10 3/4 In. 240.00
Sign, Trade, Cooper, Engraved Name, Tools & Date, 1759 .... 495.00
Snuff Spoon, Pipe Tamper, 18th Century, 2 3/8 In. 185.00
Soup, Dish, Feld Marschall Von Blucher, Incised Portrait, 10 1/2 In. 400.00
Tankard, Boardman & Co., 7 5/8 In. 660.00
Tankard, Green Marble, Mounted In Pewter, 19th Century, 6 In. 195.00
Tankard, Hammered, Whiplash Handle, Original Patina, Tudric, 4 1/2 In. 90.00
Tankard, Hinged Lid, Coin, Wood, Pierced Strapwork, F. Santesson, Sweden 238.00
Tankard, Lid, Side Spout, 8 1/8 In. 38.00
Tankard, Vaer Beredt, Glass Bottom, Hinged Lid, Reed & Barton, Pat. 1898, 6 In. 35.00
Tankard, William Charlesley, London, c.1740, 1 Qt. 1950.00
Tea Caddy, Flat Hinged Lid, Bombay Shaped Sides, c.1850, 4 1/2 x 4 1/2 In. 275.00
Teapot, B & P Touch, Individual, 6 1/2 In. 410.00
Teapot, G. Richardson Warranted, 7 1/2 In. 205.00
Teapot, George Richardson, Pear Shape, Domed Lid, Black Handle, 11 In. 405.00
Teapot, Griswold, 6 1/2 In. 85.00
Teapot, McQuilkin, 8 7/8 In. 220.00
Teapot, Pear Shape, Eben Smith 1430.00
Teapot, Pear Shape, Samuel Pierce, 7 In. 815.00
Teapot, Putnam, 8 3/4 In. 245.00
Teapot, Queen Anne, c.1825 .... 325.00
Teapot, Ribbed Body, Wooden Handle, Dixon, England, 8 1/2 In. 75.00
Teapot, Roswell Gleason, 19th Century, 10 1/2 In. 155.00
Teapot, Roswell Gleason, Painted Metal Handle, Turned Wood Finial, 8 In. 290.00
Teapot, Sellew & Co., Cincinnati, Ohio, 7 3/8 In. ....115.00 to 220.00
Teapot, Trask, 9 1/4 In. 190.00
Teapot, Wooden Finial, American, 6 1/2 In. 44.00
Tobacco Jar, Acorn Finial, Lid, 18th Century, England, 5 1/2 In. 225.00
Tray, Bowl, Clovers, Hammered, Handle, Liberty Tudric, 11 x 7 In. 225.00
Tray, Continental, Art Nouveau, Standing Female, Holding Cup, On Lily Pad Form, 8 In. .. 200.00

Tray, Lady With Flowing Hair, Art Nouveau, 6 x 5 In. 195.00
Tray, Stingrays, Oval, Art Nouveau, 16 1/2 x 11 In. 207.00
Tureen, Soup, Cover, Ladle, Pierced Foliate Handles, John Yates, 10 1/4 x 13 1/2 In. 230.00
Urn, Hot Water, Gold Chinoiserie, Cabriole Legs, Ball Feet, 18 In. 460.00
Urn, Scroll Legs, Wood Handle, Finial, Buckeye Brass Works, Dayton, O. 195.00
Vase, Hammered, Whiplash Design, 2 Open Handles, Tudric, 7 1/2 In. 385.00
Water Bottle, England, Mid-18th Century, 7 1/2 In. 295.00

PHOENIX BIRD, or Flying Phoenix, is the name given to a blue-and-white kitchenware popular between 1900 and World War II. A variant is known as Flying Turkey. Most of this dinnerware was made in Japan for sale in the dime stores in America. It is still being made.

Butter, Cover 90.00
Butter Chip 15.00
Creamer, Blue 15.00
Cup & Saucer ....10.00 to 15.00
Eggcup, Blue 12.00
Gravy Boat 40.00
Mug 18.00
Sugar, Cover, Blue 15.00
Teapot, Japan, 5 In. 75.00

PHOENIX GLASS Company was founded in 1880 in Pennsylvania. The firm made commercial products, such as lampshades, bottles, and glassware. Collectors today are interested in the "Sculptured Artware" made by the company from the 1930s until the mid-1950s. Some pieces of Phoenix glass are very similar to those made by the Consolidated Lamp and Glass Company. Phoenix made Reuben Blue, lavender, and yellow pieces. These colors were not used by Consolidated. In 1970 Phoenix became a division of Anchor Hocking, then was sold to the Newell Group in 1987. The company is still working.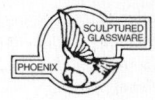

Pitcher, Green 295.00
Plate, Dancing Nymphs, 8 1/2 In. 60.00
Vase, Bittersweet, 10 In. 250.00
Vase, Bluebells, Pink & Green, On White Satin 80.00
Vase, Crystal, Molded Putto, 9 1/4 In. 316.00
Vase, Daisy, Aqua On Clear, White Ceramic Pattern, S.A. Label 375.00
Vase, Daisy, Pearlized Flower, Burgundy Ground 425.00
Vase, Dancing Girls, Coral On White Satin, 12 In. 450.00
Vase, Dancing Girls, Pearlized, Brown Ground, Label, 11 1/2 In. 385.00
Vase, Dancing Girls, Tan On White Satin, Label, 11 1/2 In. 675.00
Vase, Dancing Nymphs, Gilt, Red Frosted, 12 In. 400.00
Vase, Madonna, Pearlized, Burgundy Ground, 10 In. 177.00
Vase, Screech Owls, 7 In. 175.00
Vase, Wild Rose, Pink On White Satin 350.00

PHONOGRAPHS, invented by Thomas Edison in 1877, have been made by many firms. This category also includes other items associated with the phonograph. Jukeboxes and records are listed in their own categories.

Brunswick, Chinoiserie Design All Sides, Grill, 42 1/2 In. 440.00
Columbia, Gramophone, Tin Trumpet, Wooden Carrying Case, 20th Century 920.00
Columbia Grafanola, Mahogany Case 231.00
Columbia Gramophone Co., Dictaphone, 1915 .... 150.00
Edison, Crank, Floral Painted Horn, Oak Case, 11 Cylinders, c.1905 .... 625.00
Edison, Home, Horn, Crank, Oak Case, 11 Cylinders, c.1905 .... 745.00
Edison, Home, Metal Trademark Plate, Early 20th Century 175.00
Edison, Home, With Cylinders 490.00
Edison, Model C Reproducer, Oak Case, Horn, 10 Cylinders, 10 x 12 1/2 In. 375.00
Edison, Model H, 4 Minute Reproducer, Oak Case, Horn, 10 Cylinders, 20 In. 375.00
Edison, Morning Glory Horn, 2 & 4 Minute Reproducer 750.00
Edison, Oak Case, Crank, Horn, 10 Cylinders, 16 x 8 1/2 x 10 In. 345.00

Dust your antiques regularly but carefully. Dust leads to mold growth and attracts insects.

Phonograph, Pathe Le
Gaulois, Glass Horn,
8 x 8 1/2 x 6 3/4 In.

Edison, Standard, Oak, Cylinder, Black Horn, Crank, Label, 31 In. Horn, 12 x 8 In. 575.00
Edison, Triumph, Large Brass Horn, Oak Case, 28 Cylinders, Signed, 16 x 17 In. 880.00
Edison, Triumph, Music Master Horn, Matching Base Cabinet, Oak 4850.00
Emile Berlineer Improved Model, Gramophone, 1898 .... 4473.00
Gramophone, Windup, Birch, Portable, 1940 .... 135.00
Imperial Symphonion, Disk Player, Mahogany, 14 Disks 1610.00
Pathe Le Gaulois, Glass Horn, 8 x 8 1/2 x 6 3/4 In. ....*Illus* 5228.00
Player, Record, Palm Beach, Portable, Electric, 3-Speed 100.00
Record Rack, Gold Tone Wire Rack, Slots For 40 Records, Wood Handles, 13 x 5 In. 30.00
Reginaphone, Double Comb, Plated Morning Glory Horn, 15 Discs 5500.00
Reginaphone, With Gramophone, 21 1/2-In. Discs, Interchangeable Disc 7130.00
Silvertone Super Deluxe, Crank Style, Wood & Leatherette Case, 17 x 14 x 7 In. 35.00
Victor, Flat Top, Oak, Crank, 14 1/2 x 15 x 9 In. 115.00
Victor, Model VV-VIII, Interior Horn, Oak Case 165.00
Victor, Model VVXIV, Floor Model 140.00
Victor, Talking Machine, Type VICIV 4800.00
Victrola, Mahogany Veneer, 10 Portfolios With 156 Records, 22 x 23 x 48 In. 550.00

PHOTOGRAPHY items are listed here. The first photograph was a view from a window in France taken in 1826. The commercially successful photograph started with the daguerreotype introduced in 1839. Today all sorts of photographs and photographic equipment are collected. Albums were popular in Victorian times. Cartes de visite, popular after 1854, were mounted on 2 1/2-by-4-inch cardboard. Cabinet cards were introduced in 1866. These were mounted on 4 1/4-by-6 1/2-inch cards. Stereo views are listed under Stereo Card. The cases for daguerreotypes are listed in the Gutta-Percha category. Stereoscopes are listed in their own section.

Album, Chromolithograph Pages, Leather, Beveled Glass Cover, 9 1/2 x 8 In. 330.00
Album, Class Book, 68 Oval Albumen Portraits Of Men, 1860 .... 165.00
Album, Red Mohair, Ornate Brass Corners, Liberty Bell, Mirror, 11 x 19 In. 70.00
Albumen, Abraham Lincoln As Father, White Card Mount, 6 x 8 In. 675.00
Albumen, Butler, Standing With Cap & Sword, N.C. Sanborn, Lowell 125.00
Albumen, Execution Of Lincoln Conspirators, Gallows, 5 1/2 x 5 1/2 In. 1200.00
Albumen, Robt. E. Lee & 8 Confederate Generals, Mounted, 1869 .... 5940.00
Albumen, Steamer On Wisconsin River, Dells, Wild Bill Cody, 8 x 10 In. 1500.00
Albumen, Street & Boardwalk Colorado Scene, Warnky, 4 1/4 x 6 1/2 In. 275.00
Ambrotype, 2 Children, Sitting, J.D. Fowler, 1/6 Plate 125.00
Ambrotype, 2 Union Riflemen, 1/4 Plate 425.00
Ambrotype, 6 Men, 4 In Uniforms, Niagara Falls, Full Plate, Wooden Frame 1100.00
Ambrotype, Boy On Rocking Horse, Tassel Hat, Cloth Backdrop, 1/6 Plate 300.00
Ambrotype, Buildings, Farm Type, 1/6 Plate, Case 600.00
Ambrotype, Civil War Officer, Full Dress Militia Uniform, 1/6 Plate 450.00
Ambrotype, Confederate Private, Seated, Signed, 6th Plate, Case, 3 x 3 5/8 In. 275.00
Ambrotype, Confederate Soldier, Seated, Revolver, 8th Plate, Case, 2 1/2 x 3 In. 660.00
Ambrotype, Confederate Soldier, Standing, 1/4 Plate, Case, 3 x 5 In. 550.00
Ambrotype, Confederate, Holding Musket, 1/9 Plate, Case, 2 x 3 In. 275.00
Ambrotype, Gentleman With Fire Helmet, Franklin 2, Center Eagle 85.00

Ambrotype, Horn Of Plenty, Gutta-Percha Case 125.00
Ambrotype, House, Landscape, 5 People On Porches & Lawn, 1/2 Plate 1300.00
Ambrotype, Lincoln, Beardless, Joseph Baker, June 1860, 2 x 2 1/2 In............... 5500.00
Ambrotype, Man Standing, Beside Horse, 1/2 Plate............................. 1600.00
Ambrotype, Officer, Smoking Pipe, Uniform, Floral Mat, 1/6 Plate 710.00
Ambrotype, William T. Biedler, Member Of Mosby's Rangers 2970.00
Cabinet Card, 2 Sisters, Youngest With Doll Carriage, Garlock, Cattaraugus, N.Y. 65.00
Cabinet Card, 3 Girls, Violinists, Ethnic Clothes, J.N. Choate, Carlisle, Pa. 120.00
Cabinet Card, Alaska, Indian Family, Dog, Otter Bay 100.00
Cabinet Card, Annie Oakley, Chest Full Of Medals, Stacy 1975.00
Cabinet Card, Annie Oakley, Facsimile Signature 3080.00
Cabinet Card, Arizona Territory Indian, Breechcloth & Belt 330.00
Cabinet Card, Black Boy, With Ox-Drawn Sled, Reed & Wallace, Alabama 175.00
Cabinet Card, Black Kids Eating Watermelon On Fence, C.H. Gallup & Co............ 85.00
Cabinet Card, Black Lady From Philadelphia, Lottie Cooper, Crier, Arch St. 40.00
Cabinet Card, Bride & Groom, Edourt & Cobb, San Francisco, 1877, 7 x 11 In. 17.00
Cabinet Card, Buffalo Bill, Mounted, c.1900.................................. 399.00
Cabinet Card, Buffalo Bill, Portrait, 1900 .... 400.00
Cabinet Card, Buffalo Bill, Signed Breisbois 550.00
Cabinet Card, Calamity Jane, Ge. Crooks Scout, H.R. Locke, 1895, 5 1/2 x 6 1/2 In. 1600.00
Cabinet Card, Cowgirl.. 425.00
Cabinet Card, Crow, Chief Spotted Horse, Standing, O.S. Goff, Dickinson 450.00
Cabinet Card, Crow, Dancer, Standing, O.S. Goff, Dickinson, 1884-1888 .... 450.00
Cabinet Card, Dakota, Indian, Young Woman, 1870s, 6 1/2 x 4 1/4 In. 345.00
Cabinet Card, Dolly Varden Mine, Miner & Shack, Saxon Mt. Georgetown, Colo. 150.00
Cabinet Card, Duck Hunter In Boat With Gun, Dog, Dead Birds 50.00
Cabinet Card, Formal Portrait Of 3 Yuma Warriors, 7 1/4 x 4 1/2 In. 690.00
Cabinet Card, Geronimo, Standing, With Gun, C.S. Fly, 1886, 5 x 8 1/2 In. 900.00
Cabinet Card, Henry Ward Beecher, Sister Harriet Beecher Stowe, Gurney 175.00
Cabinet Card, Indian In Winnipeg Street Scene, Hall & Lowe 250.00
Cabinet Card, Indiana Photographer, With Camera, J.W. Edwards, Rosedale 175.00
Cabinet Card, Isadora Duncan, Metropolitan Opera, Schloss, N.Y., 1899 .... 255.00
Cabinet Card, Japanese Princess, Group Of Ladies, Elaborate Dress 80.00
Cabinet Card, Jefferson Davis, President, Confederate, 1864, 6 x 4 In. ....*Illus* 2530.00
Cabinet Card, Joe Jefferson, Actor, Sarony, Autographed 75.00
Cabinet Card, John M. Ward, Capt. New York B.B. Club, Newsboy, N.Y. 620.00
Cabinet Card, Kiowa, Indian, Sitting, Moccasins, Holding Quirt 600.00
Cabinet Card, Laguna Pueblo Children From New Mexico, 6 1/2 x 4 1/4 In. 258.00
Cabinet Card, Lillian Russell, Elite Studio, Jones & Lutz, San Francisco, 1880s 25.00
Cabinet Card, Lone Star Harry, Champion 6 Shooter Manipulater 935.00
Cabinet Card, Louis Agassiz & Wife, Bradley & Rufofson, Pair 300.00
Cabinet Card, Man, Beard, Crawford, Brooklyn, 1880s 5.00
Cabinet Card, Mendicant, Skull, Patch Over Eye, Maximilian Taubles 410.00
Cabinet Card, Nevada Indians & Family, Dog, Wash., Cann, 7 x 9 In. 225.00
Cabinet Card, Newsboy, Lillian Russell, 1890s 25.00
Cabinet Card, Newsboy, Modjeska, 1890s 20.00
Cabinet Card, Off For Klondike, 4 Men, Winchester Rifles, 5 x 8 In. 425.00
Cabinet Card, Officer, Indian Wars Era 105.00
Cabinet Card, Ossified Black Man, Lying On Bed, Medical Condition, 1847 .... 225.00
Cabinet Card, Paiute, Portrait, Sitting, C. W. Carter, 1868 .... 750.00
Cabinet Card, Patriotic Girl In Striped Dress, Holding American Flag 32.00
Cabinet Card, Phoenix, AZ, Bank, Hotel, Liquor Store, Bicycle Store, 1903 .... 67.00
Cabinet Card, Portrait Of Tightly Cradled Indian Infant, 8 1/2 x 5 1/4 In. 143.00
Cabinet Card, Primrose & West, With Canes, Vaudeville, 1890s 20.00
Cabinet Card, Professor E. Leon, Aerialist Performer, Standing, Arms Crossed 100.00
Cabinet Card, Sauk & Fox, War Chief, Ma-Tan-E-Qua, Seated, Died Oct. 1897 .... 400.00
Cabinet Card, Sherphard The Sharpshooter 363.00
Cabinet Card, Siamese Twins, Chinese Boys, Joined At Chest, 1903 .... 200.00
Cabinet Card, Sitting Bull, Palmquist & Jurgens, History Back, 1884, 6 x 4 In. 825.00
Cabinet Card, Susan B. Anthony & Anna Shaw, Marceau, 8 x 10 1/2 In.............. 1100.00
Cabinet Card, Twin Girls, Pulling Necklace, Bairston, Warren, Pa. 65.00
Cabinet Card, Ute Chief, Ouray, Wife, Chipeta, Carlisle Indian School, 1880 .... 977.00
Cabinet Card, Ute, Women & Children Group, 3 Generations 225.00

Photography, Cabinet Card,
Jefferson Davis, President,
Confederate, 1864, 6 x 4 In.

Daguerreotype cases can be polished with liquid shoe wax (not polish).

Photography, Camera,
Kodak, Brownie, Starflex
Outfit, Box, c.1960

Cabinet Card, Veteran Soldier Holding Flag, Sumner & Son	88.00
Cabinet Card, Warrior, Skull, Large Hat & Blanket, Maximilian Taubles	380.00
Cabinet Card, Wedding, Edourt, & Cobb, San Francisco, Marked Married 1877	25.00
Cabinet Card, Well-Dressed Black Man, Goatee, Top Hat, Holding Book	48.00
Cabinet Card, White Cycling Academy, c.1890, 6 x 8 In.	65.00
Cabinet Card, Wild Bill Cody, Stacy	875.00
Cabinet Card, Wild Bill Cody, Union View Co., Rochester, Hand Tinted, 1870s	1500.00
Cabinet Card, Wild Bill Hickok, Tinted Background, 8 x 10 In.	6750.00
Camera, Argus, Anastigmat, 50 mm	35.00
Camera, Argus, Argoflex Seventy-Five, Shutter, Black Bakelite Case	20.00
Camera, Bell & Howell, Movie, 16 mm, Leather Carrying Case	45.00
Camera, Brownie, Special 616	15.00
Camera, Charlie Tuna, Plastic, Aqua, Flash, Cartridge Type Film, 1971, 10 In.	56.00
Camera, Eastman Kodak, Cartridge, 8 1/2 In.	95.00
Camera, Ensign Midget, Model 22, Instructions, Box	88.00
Camera, Graflex Ciro 35, Aluminum, 50 mm Lens, Leather Carrying Case, 5 x 3 In.	30.00
Camera, ICA, Sirene, Model 135, Folding Plate, 1914-1926	35.00
Camera, Kodak, Boy Scout, Leather Case, c.1930	250.00
Camera, Kodak, Brownie, Brown Textured Metal, Plastic	29.00
Camera, Kodak, Brownie, Holiday Flash, Brown Bakelite, Dakon Lens	20.00
Camera, Kodak, Brownie, Reflex Synchro Model, Original Box	21.00
Camera, Kodak, Brownie, Starflex Outfit, Box, c.1960 ....*Illus*	75.00
Camera, Kodak, Vest Pocket, Folding, 1902	25.00
Camera, Kodak, Vigiland Six-20, Black Leatherette, 105 mm Lens, 7 x 5 1/2 In.	40.00
Camera, Movie, Keystone, Leather Case, 2 1/2 In.	28.00
Camera, Movie, Mansfield Holiday II, 8 mm, Spring Wind Motor, 3 Lenses	22.00
Camera, Movie, Spirit Of Hollywood, Box	605.00
Camera, Nikon, Nikkormat, Plus 3 Lenses	330.00
Camera, Photosphere, 1 Dark Side, Viewfinder, c.1888	1995.00
Camera, Polaroid 430, Flash Adapter, Folding Bellows Style, Case	30.00
Camera, Polaroid, Land, Model 95, Metal, Leather Cover, Instructions, Box	22.00
Camera, Polaroid, Swinger Model, Black Plastic, White Plastic, Pair	26.00
Camera, Polaroid, SX-70 Land, Model 2, Tan, Brown, Vinyl Strap, 7 x 4 x 6 In.	75.00
Camera, Realist 35, Aluminum, Black Case, 50 mm Lens, Germany, 5 x 3 In.	30.00
Camera, Ricoh Auto 66, Look-Down Viewfinder, Japan	35.00
Camera, Rolliflex, 2.8F, Assorted Lenses & Attachments	975.00
Camera, Sears, Roebuck & Co., Marvel S-16, Art Deco, Box, 5 1/2 x 3 1/2 In.	30.00
Camera, Thagee, Zenith, 1940, 6 1/2 In.	45.00
Camera, Thornton Pickard, Roller Blind, String Set Shutter	175.00
Camera, Voigtlander Bessa II, Leather Case, 120 mm, 3.5 Lens	145.00
Carte De Visite, 1st Lt. Merrill Savage, Standing, Brooks & Blauvelt, Trimmed	300.00
Carte De Visite, 2 Acrobats, Standing, Hand On Hips, Curly Hair, Wood, N.Y.C.	50.00
Carte De Visite, 6 Men In Uniform, Drummer, Rifles, Sashes, Swords, Scabbards	345.00
Carte De Visite, Aged Indian, Sitting, Ragged Coat, Holds Staff	225.00
Carte De Visite, Black Ga. Nursemaid, Holding White Infant, J.N. Wilson	212.00
Carte De Visite, Bridge, Suspension, Ohio River, Cincinnati & Covington	91.00

Carte De Visite, Brown's Marble Works, Horses, Wagon, Schoharie, NY 69.00
Carte De Visite, Fletcher Webster, 12th Mass., KIA, 2nd Bull Run 157.00
Carte De Visite, General George Stoneman, Cavalry, Brady-Anthony 145.00
Carte De Visite, General John Buford, Died Of Typhoid 1863 . . . .   880.00
Carte De Visite, General John G. Barnard, Autograph, Anthony 400.00
Carte De Visite, General Marcy & Friends, Tent, Alexander Gardner, 1862 . . . .   500.00
Carte De Visite, Gregory, Co, Mine Buildings, Gregory Store, c.1860 . . . .   586.00
Carte De Visite, Interracial Street Vendors, Man With Wagon, Saratoga, N.Y. 430.00
Carte De Visite, John Sutter, Uniform, Stinson 325.00
Carte De Visite, Johnson, First Sanctum Our President, Schleier, 1865 . . . .   400.00
Carte De Visite, Kiowa, Woman, Sitting, A. D. Trott, Junction City, Kansas 135.00
Carte De Visite, Locomotive, Wood Car, B.B. & St. Louis RR 272.00
Carte De Visite, Mine Buildings & Stores Scene, Gregory, Colo, 1860s, 2 3/4 In. 585.00
Carte De Visite, Mother & Daughter With White Sewing Machine, L.W. Thornton 125.00
Carte De Visite, Nadar's 2 Balloons, People, Nadar, Paris, Trimmed 500.00
Carte De Visite, Navy Officer, Cap On Table, Wenderoth & Taylor, Trimmed 60.00
Carte De Visite, Officer, Portrait, Arms Crossed, Oval, Webster & Bro. 150.00
Carte De Visite, Old Bob, Lincoln's Horse, Funeral Blanket 1540.00
Carte De Visite, Overland In Mexico, Clarence Dresser, Phila. Press, 1883 . . . .   300.00
Carte De Visite, Pauline Cushman, Union Spy, Uniform, Sword 330.00
Carte De Visite, Puma, Resting, A.S. Hayward, Chester, Vt. 161.00
Carte De Visite, Ragged Old Black Man, Boy & Girl Each Side, W. Oglivie, Va. 605.00
Carte De Visite, Rear Admiral Joseph Smith, Autograph, Brady ID On Reverse 181.00
Carte De Visite, Robert E. Lee, Lumpkin & Co., 3 Stars On Collar 750.00
Carte De Visite, Safford A La Rebel, Confederate, Pencil Inscription Back 1380.00
Carte De Visite, Sam Houston, Anthony 450.00
Carte De Visite, Sojourner Truth 2310.00
Carte De Visite, Soldier Buddies, Sitting, Geo. B. Wood 100.00
Carte De Visite, St. Peter's Church, Yorktown, 1862 . . . .   125.00
Carte De Visite, Street Vendors, Saratoga Springs, NY, P.H. McPhernon 432.00
Carte De Visite, Virginia Baseball Player, With Bat, C.R. Rees, Richmond, 1880 . . . .   390.00
Carte De Visite, Westtown Boarding School, Boys, Buildings, Chester, PA, 1864 . . . .   42.00
Carte De Visite, Work Gang, Pittsburgh Railroad, 10 Men, Shovels, Pick, Dabbs 125.00
Daguerreotype, 2 Men, Logging Tools, Snow & Sled, 1/6 Plate 7250.00
Daguerreotype, 3 Children, Boy Leaning Against Older Girl, 1/6 Plate 145.00
Daguerreotype, Baby, Swathed, Arms Out, Scalloped Mat, 1/9 Plate 225.00
Daguerreotype, Black Woman, Seated, Dark Shawl, 1/6 Plate 825.00
Daguerreotype, Boxer, 1/6 Plate 9900.00
Daguerreotype, Boy, With Closed Jackknife In Hand, 1/6 Plate 425.00
Daguerreotype, Child, Postmortem, Resting On Pillow, 1/6 Plate 450.00
Daguerreotype, Daniel Webster, Full Leather Case, Full Plate 7500.00
Daguerreotype, Distinguished Looking Gentleman, 1/5 Plate 100.00
Daguerreotype, Ellen Windale In Coffin, 1/6 Plate 385.00
Daguerreotype, Family Group, England, 1/4 Plate 200.00
Daguerreotype, Gentleman, Huges Bros., Hinged Frame, 3 x 3 1/4 In., Pair 550.00
Daguerreotype, Girl Post Mortem, On Bier, Virginia, 1/6 Plate 1180.00
Daguerreotype, Girl Under Tree, Gutta-Percha Case, Oval 38.00
Daguerreotype, Man & Woman, Anthony, Clarke & Co., 1843, 1/6 Plate 225.00
Daguerreotype, Man, Militia, Shako On Table, 1/4 Plate 1500.00
Daguerreotype, Man, On White Horse, Girl At Horse's Head, 1/6 Plate 1850.00
Daguerreotype, Man, Playing Flute, 1/6 Plate 1100.00
Daguerreotype, Miner, With Coins In Hands, Blue Shirt, Full Case, 1/6 Plate 5100.00
Daguerreotype, Mother & Daughter, Cooley, 1/2 Plate 900.00
Daguerreotype, Older Woman, Langenheim Bros., 1/6 Plate 500.00
Daguerreotype, Portrait Of Young Boy, Case, c.1860, 2 x 2 1/2 In. 63.00
Daguerreotype, Portrait, Man, Leather Case, Urn & Floral Design, 4 3/4 x 3 3/4 In. 60.00
Daguerreotype, Portrait, Young Girl With Basket Of Roses, 3 5/8 x 3 1/8 In. 862.00
Daguerreotype, Sailor, Middy Blouse, Straw Hat, 1/9 Plate 900.00
Daguerreotype, Susan L. Ware & Ware, Wares Lotion, 1889, 1/4 Plate, Pair 2250.00
Daguerreotype, Woman, Standing Beside Horse, Servant, 3 1/4 x 4 1/2 In. 26400.00
Daguerreotype, Woman, With Fan, Octagonal Mat, 1/6 Plate 225.00
Daguerreotype, Young Girl With Basket Of Flowers, Oval, 4 1/2 x 3 1/4 In. 1815.00
Daguerreotype, Young Girl, Blue Dress, Oval, Full Case, 1/6 Plate 500.00

Magic Lantern, Nickel Plated, T.H. McAllister, 1886, 19 x 16 In.	665.00
Magic Lantern, Stromberg-Carlson, 3 Slides, Wood Case	275.00
Photograph, 2 Women In Car, Dirt Road, Citrus Grove, 1910, 3 1/2 x 5 1/2 In.	12.00
Photograph, Ahwahnee Hotel View, Stetson Hindes, 1930s, 8 x 10 In.	20.00
Photograph, Bathers At Lakeside Park, Ill., Couples Dancing, Sepia	20.00
Photograph, Black Man Execution, Columbus, Miss. Prison, 1930s, 8 x 10 In.	1210.00
Photograph, Buffalo Bill Cody, Pearson, Indians, Chicago, 1912, 11 x 14 In.	1600.00
Photograph, Cadillac Testers, H.N. Nelson, Detroit, 1912, 7 1/2 x 43 1/2 In.	175.00
Photograph, Camping, Man With Tent, Mount Shasta, Cal., 1919, 5 x 4 In.	13.00
Photograph, Chas. Mitchel, Lynched, Urbana, Ohio, Black Man, June, 1897, 4 In.	620.00
Photograph, Chicago & Northwestern Trains Collision, 1920s, 8 x 10 In.	25.00
Photograph, Civil War Camp, Cavalry Men, Frame, c.1870, 16 x 14 In.	125.00
Photograph, Civil War Statue, Evans, 10 x 8 In.	360.00
Photograph, Civil War, Napolean Ruff, Confederate, Lane's Rangers, 1/9 Plate	1650.00
Photograph, Clarence Chamberline Inset Portrait, AMOCO Biplane, 6 x 8 In.	250.00
Photograph, Cliff House, Playland At Beach, San Francisco, 1915, 4 x 6 1/2 In.	22.00
Photograph, Comanche Quannah Parker, Chief, Traditional Dress, c.1890, 5 1/2 In.	1150.00
Photograph, Doug Marsden, Standing, Hands On Hips, 1940s, 5 x 3 1/4 In.	85.00
Photograph, Flathead, Indian Chief Charlie, Haynes, St. Paul, Grainy Toned, 16 x 12 In.	125.00
Photograph, Girl, Charcoal Hand Colored, Brass & Copper Frame, 25 x 15 In.	100.00
Photograph, Groucho Marx & Cigar Over Old NBC Microphone, 8 x 10 In.	95.00
Photograph, Hunter With Dogs, Tinted, Victorian Walnut Frame, 20 x 25 In.	230.00
Photograph, Indian Papoose Carrier, Buckskin, Hand Colored, 7 1/4 x 4 1/4 In.	250.00
Photograph, Iwo Jima, Flag, Feb. 23, 1945, Autograph, Lou Lowery, 8 x 10 In.	605.00
Photograph, Lace Galleries, 20th Century	165.00
Photograph, Little Girl, Huge Ribbon, Lace Dress, 1914, 3 1/2 x 5 1/2 In.	8.00
Photograph, Man, Period Clothing, Working As Weaver, 11 x 14 In.	20.00
Photograph, Mark Twain & Jim, Runaway Slave, 9 x 7 In.	300.00
Photograph, Musicians, Silver, Signed Farrel, 12 1/2 x 9 1/2 In.	1600.00
Photograph, Our Catch At Catalona Island, 6 x 8 1/2 In.	100.00
Photograph, Passengers On Pacific Electric R.R., Mt. Lowe, Cal., 1910, 6 1/2 In.	22.00
Photograph, Philadelphia Expo., Old High Street Of 1776, 1926, 3 1/2 x 5 1/2 In.	9.00
Photograph, President Dwight Eisenhower, Seated At Desk, Signed, 15 x 12 In.	335.00
Photograph, Shephard, Sharpshooter, Dude Outfit, Swords Bro's., York, Pa.	363.00
Photograph, Steamship, City Of Rockland, Tinted, Frame, 15 1/2 x 23 1/2 In.	115.00
Photograph, Steve Reeves, Mr. Universe, 10 x 8 In.	135.00
Photograph, Sweetwater Dam, San Diego, 1910, 4 1/2 x 6 1/2 In.	19.00
Photograph, Titanic, 2 Ocean Liners & Tugboat In Harbor, 8 x 10 In.	242.00
Photograph, Titanic, Leaving Southampton Dock, Tugboat, 8 x 10 In.	292.00
Photograph, Tsar Nicholas & Family, 5 1/2 x 3 1/2 In.	330.00
Photograph, Woman, Fish In 1 Hand, Rod In Other, San Francisco, 1915, 5 x 7 In.	19.00
Photograph, Wright Flier, Le Mans, France, Autographed, 11 1/2 x 17 3/4 In.	5390.00
Photogravure, Winter, Absaroke, Indian, Wood Bundle, Sepia, Curtis, 17 x 22 In.	400.00
Rack, Storage, For Stereo Views, Walnut Fretwork, c.1880	220.00
Tintype, 2 Young Men, Unidentified Uniform Jacket, 1/6 Plate	200.00
Tintype, 3 Naval Officers, Standing, 6th Plate, Thermoplastic Case, 3 x 4 In.	330.00
Tintype, Black & White Boxers Squaring Off, Bare Knuckled Boxing Stance	72.00
Tintype, Black Rebel Soldier, In Uniform, Richmond Dixie Regiment, 1865, 2 x 2 In.	1176.00
Tintype, Boy & Girl, Oval Mat, Frame, 1915, 2 x 3 In.	15.00
Tintype, Cadet, Seated, Forage Cap, A Insignia, Tinted Face, 2 3/4 x 3 1/4 In.	55.00
Tintype, Civil War Enlisted Man, Revolver In Belt, Cased	250.00
Tintype, Civil War Infantryman, Musket, Bayonet, 1/4 Plate	600.00
Tintype, Civil War Soldier, Inscription, c.1865, 1/4 Plate	332.00
Tintype, Civil War, Corporal, Camp Scene, 1/4 Plate	302.00
Tintype, Civil War, Soldier Sitting, Bedroll, Knapsack, Hat, 1/4 Plate	425.00
Tintype, Civil War, Soldier, Rifle, Bayonet, Full Dress, Knapsack, 1/6 Plate	335.00
Tintype, Civil War, Soldier, Rifle, Knife In Belt, Painted Background, 1/4 Plate	636.00
Tintype, Civil War, Soldier, Sitting, Rifle, Bayonet, Belt Buckle, U.S., 1/9 Plate	215.00
Tintype, Civil War, Union Officer, Standing, Arms Folded, Sash, Sword, 1/6 Plate	325.00
Tintype, Civil War, Union, Sgt., Nonregulation Uniform, 1/6 Plate, Oval	200.00
Tintype, Colonel Michael Corcoran, Abbott	150.00
Tintype, Family Of 5, Full Plate, Walnut Frame, 1875, 12 x 14 In.	40.00
Tintype, House, 8 People, Dog, Tribes Hill, N.Y., 7 1/8 x 10 In.	200.00

Tintype, Infantry Man, Civil War Gun Boat, Black, Gutta-Percha Case, 2 1/2 x 3 In.	425.00
Tintype, Portrait Of Soldier, Holding Trumpet & Sword	495.00
Tintype, Rural Scene, Family & Children, 6 1/4 x 9 1/4 In.	330.00
Tintype, Sergeant, Seated, Patriotic Liner, 1/6 Plate	245.00
Tintype, Smiling Woman, Wrapped In American Flag, Holding 2 Flags, 2 x 3 In.	110.00
Tintype, Soldier Wearing Kepi, Telescope, Cased, 2 3/8 x 2 7/8 In., 1/6 Plate	245.00
Tintype, Soldier, Musket, Bayonet, Bowie In Belt, 1/6 Plate	600.00
Tintype, Stagecoach, Full View, Indians, W. Guire, Rushville, 1/2 Plate	975.00
Tintype, Union Soldier, Rain Gear, Standing, Case, 3 1/4 x 3 5/8 In.	165.00
Tintype, Union Soldier, Rifle, Bayonet, 1/4 Plate	1831.00
Tintype, Union Soldier, Seated, Flag Backdrop, Cased, 3 x 3 1/2 In., 1/6 Plate	220.00
Tintype, Woman, Reading, Cloth Over Head, Uncased, 2 x 4 In.	50.00
Tintype, Young Gentleman, Original Morocco Case, c.1860	112.00
Tintype, Young Man With Hat, Bee Skep, Brown, Gutta-Percha Case, 2 1/2 x 3 In.	120.00

PIANO BABY is a collector's term. About 1880, the well-decorated home had a shawl on the piano. Bisque figures of babies were designed to help hold the shawl in place. They range in size from 6 to 18 inches. Most of the figures were made in Germany. Reproductions are being made. Other piano babies may be listed under manufacturers' names.

Boy, Sitting, Molded & Painted Hair, Feet Crossed At Ankles, 8 1/2 In.	350.00
Holding 2 Dogs	290.00
Sitting, On Brick Wall, Smiling, Side-Glancing Eyes, Beaded Smock, 6 In.	225.00
Sitting & Crawling, Ruffled White Gown, 6 1/4 & 7 1/4 In., Pair	55.00

PICKARD China Company was started in 1898 by Wilder Pickard. Hand-painted designs were used on china purchased from other sources. In the 1930s, the company began to make its own china wares in Chicago, Illinois. The company now makes many types of porcelains, including a successful line of limited edition collector plates.

Bowl, Brown Nuts & Leaves, Brown Ground, Challinor, 1912-1918 Mark, 8 3/4 In.	330.00
Bowl, Jade With Leaves, Open Handles, 1930s, 9 In.	65.00
Bowl, Strawberries, C. Hahn, 1903, 3 1/4 In.	330.00
Bowl, Violet Supreme, Fisher, 1912, 9 3/4 In.	385.00
Bread Tray, Cornflower, Signed AC	195.00
Cake Plate, Allover Gold, Central Handle, 9 3/4 In.	80.00
Candlestick, Basket Of Flowers, Oval Panel, Pink Ground, 1922, 8 1/4 In., Pair	410.00
Candlestick, Rose & Daisy, Allover Gold, 1925-1930 Mark, 2 3/4 In.	33.00
Candlestick, Rose & Daisy, Rolled Over Rim, 1925, 2 3/4 In.	35.00
Candy Dish, Gold Etched, 1919-1922	25.00
Chalice, Plain Hops & Matte Green, Signed Hessler, 1905-1910, 11 1/4 In. ....*Illus*	1430.00
Charger, Golden Pheasant, Challinor, 1919-1922 Mark, 12 1/2 In.	550.00
Chocolate Pot, Carnations & Matte Green, Rean, 1910	770.00

Pickard, Chalice, Plain Hops &
Matte Green, Signed Hessler,
1905-1910, 11 1/4 In.

Pickard, Pitcher, Cider,
Arabian, Marked,
1903-1905, 8 In.

Pickard, Tankard, Grapes,
Leaves, Signed Coufall,
1905-1910, 14 1/4 In.

Pickard, Tankard, Monk
Peeling Turnip, Signed P. Gasper,
1905-1910, 13 3/4 In.

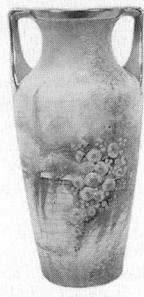

Pickard, Vase, Garden Wall,
Flowers, 2 Gilt Handles, Signed
E. Challinor, 10 1/4 In.

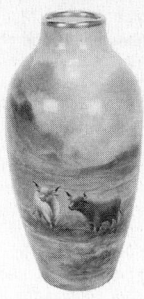

Pickard, Vase, Landscape,
Cattle, Signed Kubash,
1903-1905, 7 1/4 In.

Chocolate Pot, Raided Gold Daisy, 1905-1910 Mark, 10 3/4 In.	330.00
Chocolate Set, Platinum Overlay Design, 1918, 3 Piece	300.00
Coffeepot, Pheasant Medallion On White, Challinor, 1912, 7 1/4 In.	690.00
Creamer, Encrusted Linear, 1912	445.00
Cup & Saucer, Demitasse, 4 Piece	95.00
Hatpin Holder, Moorish Design, Wagner, 1905-1910 Mark, 5 In.	385.00
Jam Jar, Deserted Garden, Handles, J. Nessy, 1912-1918 Mark	55.00
Jam Jar, Deserted Garden, Nessy, 1912	350.00
Pitcher, Antique Chinese Enamels, E. Tolpin, 1912-1918 Mark, 10 In.	410.00
Pitcher, Bordure Antique, Coufall, 1910-1912 Mark, 6 3/4 In.	165.00
Pitcher, Cider, Arabian, Marked, 1903-1905, 8 In. *Illus*	1760.00
Pitcher, Easter Lily, Schoner, 1903, 7 1/2 In.	770.00
Pitcher, Lemonade, Bordure Antique, Coufall, 1910, 6 3/4 In.	990.00
Pitcher, Lemonade, Hops In Lustre & Matte Green, Lind, 1905, 6 1/2 In.	605.00
Pitcher, Lemonade, Purple Grapes, LeRoy, 1903, 6 1/2 In.	715.00
Pitcher, Metallic Grapes, Hanisch, 1905, 10 3/4 In.	605.00
Pitcher, Morning Glories, Gilded Band, 1912-1918 Mark, 6 1/2 In.	100.00
Pitcher, Morning Glory, Gilded Band, 1912, 6 1/2 In.	105.00
Plate, Cherries & Gold Web, Breidel, 1903-1905 Mark, 7 1/2 In.	77.00
Plate, Dogwood Flowers, Marker, 1905-1910 Mark, 6 1/4 In.	75.00
Plate, Florida Moonlight, Arler, 1912-1928 Mark, 8 3/4 In.	110.00
Plate, Scenic, Trees & Lade, W. Rawlins, 8 1/4 In.	195.00
Plate, Strawberries & Leaves, Fisher, 1903-1915 Mark, 7 1/2 In.	75.00
Plate, Walled Garden, 2 Handles, Challinor, 1912, 7 1/2 In.	275.00
Punch Bowl, Red Currants & Leaves, Maroon To Yellow Ground, Vokral, 6 x 13 In.	3960.00
Sugar & Creamer, Gold	55.00
Sugar & Creamer, Pink & White Deco Styling, Efdon	150.00
Sugar & Creamer, Rose & Daisy, Allover Platinum & Gold, 1925-1930 Mark	85.00
Syrup, Underplate, Easter Lily, O. Schoner, 1903, 5 1/2 In.	630.00
Tankard, Grapes, Leaves, Signed Coufall, 1905-1910, 14 1/4 In. *Illus*	2475.00
Tankard, Monk Peeling Turnip, Signed P. Gasper, 1905-1910, 13 3/4 In. *Illus*	3190.00
Tea Set, Tulip Conventional, F. Lind, 3 Piece	385.00
Teapot, Classic Ruins By Moonlight, Marker, 1912, 6 1/2 In.	410.00
Tray, Dresser, Italian Garden, Landscape & Lake, Gasper, 1912, 15 1/2 In.	165.00
Tray, Hunting Dog In Meadow, Signed Farrington, Round, 16 In.	1995.00
Tray, Pin, Yellow Flowers, Green Leaves, 5 3/4 In.	35.00
Vase, Allover Gold, Pale Green Ground, 6 In.	135.00
Vase, Aura Mosaic, Hess, 1905, 6 In.	300.00
Vase, Courting Couple, In Garden, Gold Trim, 7 1/2 In.	195.00
Vase, Encrusted Fruit, Gold Ground, Rean, 1912-1918 Mark, 8 In.	275.00
Vase, Encrusted Linear, 1912, 6 1/2 In.	150.00
Vase, Floral Design, Art Deco, Colored Bands On Gilt Ground, Signed Ross, 10 1/2 In.	115.00
Vase, Floral Geometric, Purple Lilies, 1905-1910 Mark, 11 3/4 In.	990.00
Vase, Fruits Linear, Tolpin, 1912, 10 1/4 In.	495.00
Vase, Garden Wall, Flowers, 2 Gilt Handles, Signed E. Challinor, 10 1/4 In. *Illus*	1980.00

Vase, Landscape, Cattle, Signed Kubash, 1903-1905, 7 1/4 In. . . . .*Illus*   3850.00
Vase, Locust, 3 1/4 In. 45.00
Vase, Pale Green, 6 In. 135.00
Vase, Palm Tree, Scenic, 1918, 8 1/4 In. 440.00
Vase, Peacock Design, Gold & Black Ground, Challinor, 1925-1930, 14 In. 1870.00
Vase, Peacock On Gold & Black, E. Challinor, 1925-1930 Mark, 14 In. 1870.00
Vase, Pine Trees By Moonlight, E. Challinor, 1912-1918 Mark, 7 In. 935.00
Vase, Poppy & Black, 1903-1905 Mark, 13 1/2 In. 935.00
Vase, Rose Gilt, Signed, 19th Century, 10 1/8 In. 750.00
Vase, Roses, 10 In. 195.00
Vase, Scenic, Signed, 7 1/4 In. 495.00
Vase, Waterfall Scene, Marker, 10 In. 695.00
Vase, White Poppy & Daisy, Gasper, 1905, 9 3/4 In. 770.00

PICTURE FRAMES are listed in this book in the Furniture category under Frame.

PICTURES, silhouettes, and other small decorative objects framed to
hang on the wall are listed here. Sandpaper pictures are black and
white charcoal drawings done on a special sanded paper. Some other
types of pictures are listed in the Print and Painting categories.

Beadwork, Man Fishing, Woman & Child, 12 1/2 x 13 1/2 In. 275.00
Charcoal, Moonlight On The Shenandoah, 19th Century, 13 x 19 In. 176.00
Charcoal & Crayon, Standing Nude, Moses Soyer, 16 1/4 x 9 In. 315.00
Charcoal On Paper, Mount Vernon, Ship In Ground, Grained Frame, 10 x 14 In. 440.00
Crayon On Paper, 3 Women, Robert Henri, 10 5/8 x 8 1/2 In. 345.00
Crewelwork, Flowers, Flying Songbirds, Velvet Ground, Frame, 37 x 36 1/2 In. 523.00
Cut Paper Design, Hearts & Lover's Knot, Folded, Frame, 16 1/4 x 16 1/4 In. 165.00
Diorama, 2-Masted Sailboat, Painted Lighthouse, Waves, 14 1/2 x 20 In. 575.00
Diorama, Cottage Scene, Mossy Vegetation, Shadowbox Frame, 12 x 17 1/2 In. 55.00
Diorama, Sloop, 1 Mast, Wood, Painted Background, Lighthouse, Trees, 24 x 26 In. 748.00
Engraving, Boston Massacre, 19th Century, Frame, 11 3/4 x 13 In. 358.00
Engraving, Botanical, S. Curtis Walworth, Matted, Frame, 1829, 13 1/2 x 10 1/2 In. 55.00
Engraving, Carte Du Cours Du Fleuve De Saint Laurent, Bellin, 1761, 27 x 39 1/2 In. . . .   138.00
Engraving, Carte Reduite De L'Isle De La Martinique, Bellin, 1758, 26 3/4 x 39 1/4 In. . . .   110.00
Engraving, Cityscape, Richard Aberle Florsheim, 18 x 13 3/4 In.   45.00
Engraving, Gen. R.E. Lee, Stonewall Jackson, A.B. Walter, Frame, 9 3/4 x 8 In., Pair 210.00
Engraving, Grant & Colfax, Liberty & Loyalty, Justice & Public Safety, Frame, 21 In. . . .   80.00
Engraving, Horse Soldier, Tissue Paper, Frank French, Matted, Frame, 15 x 16 In. 90.00
Engraving, Libby Prison, August 23, 1863, Frame, 1882, 7 x 8 1/2 In. 110.00
Engraving, Moths & Caterpillars, Hand Colored, Continental, Frame, 15 x 11 In. 315.00
Engraving, Specious Orator & View Near Hyde Park, England, 1794, 10 x 8 In., Pair 55.00
Engraving, The Summer Duck, Color, Frame, 12 x 16 In. 176.00
Engraving, Town Of Forfar, I. Clarke, England, 18 x 24 In. 275.00
Engraving, Town Of Peterhead, Whales In Harbor, London, Frame, 1824, 18 x 23 In. 176.00
Engraving, View In Smithfield, Hand Colored, J. Moore, London, Frame, 32 x 36 In. 220.00
Etching, 3 Ducks In Flight, Pencil, Signed, Roland Clark, Frame, 9 x 11 3/4 In. 99.00
Etching, Cavaliers Enjoying Music, V. Courtin, 1883, 16 1/2 x 13 In. 458.00
Etching, Children Of King Charles, LaGuillermine, Late 19th Century, 24 1/4 x 31 In. . . .   230.00
Etching, City Gate, Alfred Heber Hutty, American, Early 1900s, 7 1/2 x 8 3/4 In. 880.00
Etching, Duck Hunter, Ogden Pleissner, 20th Century, Frame, 10 3/4 x 15 In. 3630.00
Etching, Duck Shooting, Ogden Pleissner, 20th Century, Frame, 7 3/4 x 11 3/4 In. 1430.00
Etching, In A Southern City, Alfred Heber Hutty, American, 1929, 7 3/8 x 9 1/4 In. 90.00
Etching, L'enfant De La Montagne, Arthur W. Heintzelman, 1927, 7 1/2 x 9 1/2 In. 138.00
Etching, Little Girl With St. Bernard, Thomas Kelly, Frame, 7 x 12 In. 380.00
Etching, Momba's Cabin, Charleston, Elizabeth O. Verner, 1900s, 5 x 7 In. 1265.00
Etching, Philadelphia St. Charleston, Elizabeth O. Verner, 1924, 7 x 10 In. 770.00
Etching, Pineapple Gates, Charleston, Alfred Heber Hutty, American, 7 1/2 x 8 3/4 In. . . .   1045.00
Etching, Pond, Gabriele Dev. Clemens, Dated '83, 6 3/8 x 11 1/2 In. 110.00
Etching, St. Michael's Spire, Alfred Heber Hutty, American, Early 1900s, 11 x 8 In. 605.00
Etching, Woman Flirting With Bust Of Satyr, Olga Gert, Matted, Frame, 24 1/2 x 19 In. . . .   160.00
Etching, Woman, Gerald Leslie Brockhurst, 5 1/2 x 6 1/2 In. 165.00
Etching & Collage, Fidelio, Mikulas Kravjansky, 26 x 19 3/4 In. 35.00
Gouache, Path Leading To The Lake, Jane Peterson, Frame, 11 1/2 x 17 1/2 In. 2750.00

Gouache, Watercolor & India Ink, Matador & Bull, Jean Jansem, 15 x 22 1/4 In. 865.00
Gouache On Masonite, London Dieppe, P. Dessau, Gilt Frame, Linen Liner, 7 x 9 In. 115.00
Hair Wreath, Woven, Walnut Shadowbox 310.00
Ink, Leaping Lion, A.E. Dealer, Frame, 19th Century, 22 x 28 In. 1380.00
Lithograph, Burlington, Formerly County Seat Lawrence Co. Ohio, Frame, 18 x 23 In. ... 50.00
Marquetry, Indian In Canoe, Gun At Moose, Oak Frame, 22 x 41 3/4 In. 495.00
Needlework, Anne Rowe Smith, 11 Years, June 18th, 1847, Florals, 21 1/4 x 18 3/4 In. .. 460.00
Needlework, Biblical Narrative, Woman & 2 Children, Parrot, Frame, 1680s, 41 x 28 In. . 3737.00
Needlework, Birds Panel, Trees, Flowers, Frame, 11 1/2 x 8 3/4 In. 690.00
Needlework, Bowditch Family Coat Of Arms, Blues, 18th Century, 25 1/2 x 25 In. 4025.00
Needlework, Cattle, Tree & Shepherd, Wool On Linen, Gilt Frame, 17 3/8 x 16 1/4 In. ... 385.00
Needlework, Couple In Landscape, Church & House, Windmill, 14 x 16 1/4 In. 4887.00
Needlework, Dog, Isabella C. Miller, Newton, Mass., 1833, 12 x 14 In. 165.00
Needlework, Eagle Over Draped Flags, Banner, Pluribus Unum, Frame, 13 x 16 In. 460.00
Needlework, Elderly Couple Flanked By Trees, Plants, Green, Ocher, Red, 19 x 23 In. ... 690.00
Needlework, Embroidered, Basket Of Flowers, On Paper, Cherry Frame, 16 x 19 In. 235.00
Needlework, Hooked Wool, Couple In Sleigh, Frame, Dated '66, 17 x 25 In. 165.00
Needlework, In Memory Of Deceased Friends, Revolutionary War, Silk, 17 x 24 In. 2250.00
Needlework, La Fontaine's Fables, Gilt Frame, 15 x 19 In., Pair 4600.00
Needlework, Moses In Bulrushes, Pharaoh's Daughter, 19 x 17 1/2 In. 4600.00
Needlework, Narrative Of Christ & Woman At Well, 1670s, 24 x 19 1/2 In. 1725.00
Needlework, Panel, 2 Saints, Red Velvet Border, Continental, 38 x 12 In., Pair 690.00
Needlework, Parting Of Hector & Romanche, Mary Allen, Age 15, c.1790, 20 x 24 In. ... 863.00
Needlework, Sailing Ship, British Flag, 19th Century, 16 x 22 1/2 In. 1150.00
Needlework, Shepherd & Shepherdess, Floral Sprays At Corners, Frame, 32 x 32 In. 125.00
Needlework, Silk, Eagle With Flags In Claw, Shield, Banner, Frame, 19 x 20 In. 805.00
Needlework, Silk, Flower Filled Basket, Silk Ground, Gilt Frame, Victorian, 25 x 26 In. .. 2185.00
Needlework, Silk, George Washington, Beneath Large Willow Tree, 1814, 16 In. 1955.00
Needlework, Silk, Mother & Child Seated In Tree-Lined Landscape, 10 1/2 x 9 In. 920.00
Needlework, Silk, Pink, Green, Ocher, Cream, Floral Wreath, England, 8 1/2 x 11 In. 345.00
Needlework, Silk, Pink, Green, Ocher, Tan, Cream, Black Thread, Floral, 7 x 9 In., Pair ... 1035.00
Needlework, Silkwork, Eagle, American Shield, Philippines, 19th Century, 18 x 20 In. ... 605.00
Needlework, Stylized Flower, Birds, Basket Of Fruit, Miriam Smith, 10 1/2 x 8 In. 145.00
Needlework, Stylized Flowering Tree, Crocheted, Appliqued, Linen, Frame, 16 x 12 In. .. 55.00
Needlework, Sympathy, Alphabet Pans, Band Of Geometric Design, 19 x 16 1/2 In. 4890.00
Needlework, Trees, Bird Panel, Floral, Sawtooth, Stylized Flowers Border, 18 In. 1955.00
Needlework, View Of Somersetshire, England, Frame, Late 1800s, 7 x 9 In. 330.00
Needlework, Woman Reading, Buildings, Silk, England, 19th Century, 16 x 22 In. 770.00
Needlework, Young Gentleman Carrying Bundle, Maiden Gathering Wheat, 13 In. 750.00
Pastel, Landscape, Pond, Shrubs, Trees, Thomas B. Craig, Matted, Frame, 10 x 12 In. ... 115.00
Pastel, Still Life, Vase & Flowers, Sailuzza, Pierced Wood & Gesso Frame, 22 x 17 In. .. 115.00
Pen & Ink, Birds & Nest, W.W. Spitler, Center, Ohio, Frame, 1903, 19 x 26 In. 220.00
Pen & Ink, Birds Nest, W.W. Spitler, Frame, 1904, 22 5/8 x 30 1/2 In. 275.00
Pen & Ink, Calligraphy, George Washington On Horse, Samuel G. Hayes, 19 x 15 In. 1725.00
Pen & Ink, Surveyor's Map, Knox County, Ohio, Frame, 1842, 14 x 9 In. 55.00
Pen & Ink, Waiting Room, Bernstein, Matted, Frame, 18 3/4 x 22 3/4 In. 110.00
Pen & Watercolor, Fisher Building, Grand Blvd. At Second, Detroit, 32 1/2 x 23 In. 690.00
Pencil, Country Home, Eliz. A. White, American, 19th Century, 11 1/2 x 14 In. 220.00
Pencil, Girl With Dove, In Floral Garland, Frame, 15 x 12 In. 40.00
Pencil, Ink & Crayon On Paper, Woman, Outsider, Frame, 25 x 19 In. 110.00
Petit Point, Cat On Pillow, Wool, Pink Ground, Walnut Shadowbox Frame, 16 x 20 In. .. 135.00
Reverse Decoupage On Glass, George II & Duke Of Brunswick, Glass, 18 x 14 In., Pair . 440.00
Reverse Decoupage On Glass, The Quarrel, London, Frame, 1804, 15 3/4 x 11 3/4 In. ... 250.00
Reverse Decoupage On Glass, This Happy Couple, Frame, 11 3/4 x 16 In. 150.00
Sandpaper, Pleasure & Cargo Boats, Black & White, 27 3/4 x 37 In. 110.00
Silhouette, Benjamin Franklin, Frame, 12 x 10 In. 395.00
Silhouette, George & Martha Washington, Wax, Shadowbox Frame, 1840, 3 x 6 In., Pair . 220.00
Silhouette, George Washington, Eglomise, S. Folwell, Frame, 5 1/8 x 3 3/8 In. 165.00
Silhouette, George Washington, Frame, Initial, Dated 1779, 8 x 6 In. 495.00
Silhouette, John Randolph, Roanoke, Statesman & Orator, 5 1/2 x 7 In. 285.00
Silhouette, Man & Woman, Black & Gold Frame, 4 x 2 1/2 In., Pair 132.00
Silhouette, Man & Woman, Full-Length, J. Wood, Frame, 11 3/4 x 9 3/4 In., Pair 660.00
Silhouette, Man & Woman, Hollow Cut, Brass Frame, 8 1/2 x 7 1/4 In., Pair 165.00

Silhouette, Man, Gilt Trim, College Friend, G.H. Nuses, Matted, Frame, 1858, 6 x 5 In. . . .   80.00
Silhouette, Samuel Findlay, Full-Length, 1840, 12 In. 210.00
Silhouette, Standing Gentleman, Mahogany Frame, 1802, 5 1/4 x 3 1/4 In. 120.00
Silhouette, Woman, Pencil Hair, Oval, Brass & Wood Frame, 3 1/2 x 2 3/4 In. 115.00
Silhouette, Young Man, J.I. Magin Artist, Oval Frame, 4 3/4 x 3 1/2 In. 110.00
Silhouette, Young Man, Sponge Painted Frame, Central Mass., 4 x 3 1/4 In. 2185.00
Theorem, Basket Full Of Flowers, Period Gold Leaf Frame, 18 x 20 In. 1650.00
Theorem, Basket Of Flowers, Watercolor On Paper, Frame, 1843, 14 x 16 In. 1650.00
Theorem, Basket Of Fruit, Watercolor, Frame, 14 x 18 In. 715.00
Theorem, Basket Of Fruit, White Velvet, Wm. Rank, Frame, Square, 6 In. 105.00
Theorem, Basket Of Strawberries, Vine Border, Velvet, Wm. Rank, Frame, 23 x 21 In. . . . 495.00
Theorem, Bird, Perched On Fruit Basket, Frame, 19th Century, 16 1/4 x 18 1/4 In. 1980.00
Theorem, Bowl & Compote Of Stylized Flowers & Fruit, Gilt Frame, 25 1/2 x 31 1/4 In. . 385.00
Theorem, Flowers, Green, Blue, White & Pink, Shadowbox Frame, 9 x 10 In., Pair 83.00
Theorem, Fruit & Foliage, Gold Painted Frame, 19 x 16 In. 358.00
Theorem, On Paper, Butterfly & 2 Birds, Graphite Wash, Signed, 9 x 8 1/2 In. 71.00
Theorem, On Paper, Flowers, Reverse Painted Glass, Frame, c.1820, 10 x 13 In. 403.00
Theorem, On Paper, Flowers, Uneven Brown Ground, Matted, Frame, 16 1/2 x 20 In. 660.00
Theorem, On Paper, Red Tulip, Purple Flower, Leaves, Frame, Gilded Liner, 12 3/8 In. . . 247.00
Theorem, On Silk, Trapunto Basket Of Flowers, 16 1/2 x 19 In. 470.00
Theorem, On Velvet, Basket Of Flowers, Butterfly, 1840, 13 1/2 x 19 In. 2400.00
Theorem, On Velvet, Basket Of Fruit, Bee, D.Y. Ellinger, Frame, Gilt, 27 3/4 x 22 In. . . . 880.00
Theorem, On Velvet, Basket Of Fruit, Ellinger, Gilt Frame, 21 3/4 x 27 3/4 In. 1870.00
Theorem, On Velvet, Basket Of Strawberries, Fruit & Bird, Frame, 13 3/4 x 16 1/2 In. . . . 1705.00
Theorem, On Velvet, Blue Fluted Bowl, Grained Frame, 15 1/2 x 18 1/2 In. 2700.00
Theorem, On Velvet, Bowl Of Flowers, Frame, 20 3/4 x 24 1/4 In. 165.00
Theorem, On Velvet, Roses, Leaves, Yellow, Green, Brown, Black, 12 1/2 x 16 1/2 In. . . . 85.00
Theorem, On Velvet, Urn Of Flowers, Gilt Frame, 17 x 14 3/4 In. 725.00
Theorem, Still Life, Basket Of Fruit, On Velvet, Frame, 19 x 15 1/2 In. 1725.00
Theorem, Still Life, Basket Of Fruit, Yellow Painted Period Frame, 16 1/4 x 15 In. 4025.00
Theorem, Still Life, Of Fruit Spilling From A Canton Porcelain Bowl, On Velvet, 17 In. . . 1840.00
Tinsel, 4 Parrots, Foliage, Black Ground, Reverse Painted, Frame, 10 x 16 In. 190.00
Tinsel, Bird, Flowers, Anna Jane Flickinger, 1862, 14 x 17 In. 130.00
Watercolor, 2 European Ships, Sailors In Rigging, 5 1/2 x 8 In. 110.00
Watercolor, Arched Doorway By Canal, H.A. Dyer, 15 1/2 x 11 1/2 In. 550.00
Watercolor, Autumn Landscape, E. Burkhart, Frame, 1950, 16 3/8 x 19 3/8 In. 330.00
Watercolor, Autumn Road In Tennessee, Frederick Tanqueray Anderson, '07, 12 x 16 In. . 193.00
Watercolor, Baby In High Chair, White Dress, Glass, Frame, 1820, 8 1/2 In. 825.00
Watercolor, Basket Of Flowers, Inscription, Maple Frame, 11 x 13 In. 405.00
Watercolor, Beached Boats Scene, J. Kauffman, Matted, Frame, 31 x 23 In. 72.00
Watercolor, Black Men In Forest, Daniel Rhodes, 12 3/4 x 17 1/4 In. 230.00
Watercolor, Black Poodle, Will Rannells, Frame, 25 x 21 In. 82.00
Watercolor, Black Woman With Cauldron, Allen Huntington, 1921, 5 1/2 x 3 1/2 In. 90.00
Watercolor, Blessing Of Shrimp Fleet, Noel Rockmore, 24 x 18 In. 242.00
Watercolor, Cows In Field, William Henry Howe, Matted, Gilt Frame, 20 x 13 1/4 In. . . . 440.00
Watercolor, Drawing, Man Seated At Desk, F.F. Ottey, Frame, 10 x 9 In. 110.00
Watercolor, Dutch Man Milking Cow, H.G. Wolters, Frame, 13 x 20 1/2 In. 1035.00
Watercolor, Equestrian Figure, Frame, 24 3/4 x 19 3/4 In. 125.00
Watercolor, European Harbor Scene, Wm. Paskell, Frame, 1930s, 7 1/4 x 11 In. 143.00
Watercolor, Fishing Schooners Racing To Lighthouse, Matted, Frame, 13 x 20 1/2 In. . . . 575.00
Watercolor, Gathering, 19th Century, 6 1/4 x 9 1/4 In. 78.00
Watercolor, Girl With Drum, Black Hat, Red Striped Dress, 8 1/4 x 5 In. 260.00
Watercolor, Grand Canyon, Gunnar Mauritz Widforss, 24 1/2 x 19 1/2 In. 9775.00
Watercolor, Homestead, Fence, Geo. Hecht, 16 1/4 x 22 1/8 In. 27.00
Watercolor, In The Barnyard, W. Savery Bucklin, Frame, 1897, 21 x 26 1/2 In. 1725.00
Watercolor, Italian Scene, Matted, Frame, 21 1/2 x 17 1/2 In. 110.00
Watercolor, Landscape Of Bayou, C.J. Mason, 12 x 19 In. 135.00
Watercolor, Landscape, Birch Trees & House, J.J. Francis, Frame, 5 1/2 x 10 1/2 In. 143.00
Watercolor, Lobster Shacks, Rocky Harbor, H.I. Shumway, 10 1/4 x 15 In. 115.00
Watercolor, Lumber Schooners, Calais, Me., G.M. Hathaway, Frame, 10 3/4 x 7 1/2 In. . . 690.00
Watercolor, Magician No. 5, Robert Andrew Parker, 32 x 28 1/2 In. 690.00
Watercolor, Mallard, Frame, Signed, 1976, 9 x 10 1/2 In. 35.00
Watercolor, Man, James E. Ellsworth, Frame, 3 x 8 In. 1495.00

Watercolor, Man, Portrait, Mahogany Frame, 5 1/2 x 4 3/4 In. 330.00
Watercolor, Man, Top Hat, Eglomise Mat, Frame, 12 x 9 In. 385.00
Watercolor, Mourning, Man At Tomb, Pencil & Crayon, Veneer Frame, 8 x 7 1/8 In. 410.00
Watercolor, Naval Battle, Constitution & Guerriere, J.O. Davidson, 20 1/2 x 24 In. 385.00
Watercolor, Night At Boothbay, Store Fronts, Ken Olsen, Frame, 17 1/2 x 23 In. 750.00
Watercolor, Nina, Pinta & Santa Maria At Port, Richard Turner Shewcraft, 9 5/8 x 20 In. . 405.00
Watercolor, Old Man, White Goatee, Lowell E. Smith, 10 7/8 x 7 1/2 In. 110.00
Watercolor, Path To The Shanty, M. Brooks, American, Late 19th Century, 7 x 10 In. 193.00
Watercolor, People Returning From Rice Paddies, Tadashi Nakayama, 15 x 21 1/4 In. ... 550.00
Watercolor, Primitive, Black Woman, Cabin, Jennie Lancaster, Frame, 1911, 10 x 14 In. . 250.00
Watercolor, River, Houses On Bluff, Trees, Frame, 9 1/2 x 11 1/2 In. 230.00
Watercolor, Roman Ruins, Martin, 22 x 15 In. 60.00
Watercolor, Roses, Mahogany Veneer Frame, 17 x 14 3/8 In. 137.00
Watercolor, Roses, Pink & Yellow, Gilt Frame, 13 x 11 1/8 In. 110.00
Watercolor, Ship In Harbor, A. Martina, 10 x 22 In. 145.00
Watercolor, Street Scene, Signed, 12 1/4 x 8 1/2 In. 330.00
Watercolor, Sylvan Landscape, Cattle & Man, England, 19th Century, 18 x 25 In. 385.00
Watercolor, Terries, Will Rannells, Frame, 25 x 21 In. 55.00
Watercolor, View From Mount Ida, Frame, 11 x 18 In. 1100.00
Watercolor, Wellfleet Harbor, Reynolds Beal, 10 1/2 x 12 1/2 In. 660.00
Watercolor, White Egret, Dolores Witt, 9 3/4 x 7 In. 260.00
Watercolor, Winter Landscape, J. Crosby, 17 1/4 x 23 1/4 In. 25.00
Watercolor, Young Girl With Pet Bird, Franz Gory Romo, Oval Mat, Frame, 11 x 9 In. .. 520.00
Watercolor, Young Man, Brown Coat, Round Frame, 4 5/8 In. 330.00
Watercolor & Gouache, Breaking Cover, Cecil Charles Windsor Aldin, 13 1/2 x 23 In. ... 920.00
Watercolor & Gouache, Civil War Battle, F.X. Chamberlain, Frame, 14 1/2 x 25 In. 575.00
Watercolor & Gouache, Coastal Landscape, China, 19th Century, 17 1/2 x 25 1/4 In. 805.00
Watercolor & Ink, 3 Plagues Of Life, Jackson Lindon, Frame, 10 5/8 x 17 In. 440.00
Watercolor & Ink, Silhouette, Woman, Marked, Frame, 9 x 8 In. .. 415.00
Watercolor & Pastel, Forest Stream, G.H. Flavelle, Matted, Frame, 32 1/4 x 42 1/4 In. .. 385.00
Watercolor & Pastel On Cardboard, Still Life In Silence, R.M. Gatrell, 32 x 38 In. 250.00
Watercolor & Pencil, Le Congre Der Vint, Emile Dupont, Frame, 1818, 10 3/4 x 17 In. .. 290.00
Watercolor & Pencil On Paper, Drawing, 2 Children, Matted, Framed, 17 x 15 In. 248.00

PIERCE, see Howard Pierce category.

PIGEON FORGE Pottery was started in Pigeon Forge, Tennessee, in 1946. Red clay found near the pottery was used to make the pieces. Molded or thrown pottery with matte glaze and slip decoration was made. The pottery is still working.

The Pigeon Forge Pottery Pigeon Forge Tenn

Tile, Exotic Flowers, Douglas Ferguson, Signed, 6 1/8 x 6 1/8 In. 247.00

PILKINGTON Tile and Pottery Company was established in 1892 in England. The company made small pottery wares, like buttons and hatpins, but soon started decorating vases purchased from other potteries. By 1903, the company had discovered an opalescent glaze that became popular on the Lancastrian pottery line. The manufacture of pottery ended in 1937. Pilkington's Tiles Ltd. has worked from 1938 to the present.

Bowl, Green, Art Nouveau, 8 x 4 3/4 In. 165.00
Vase, Gold Underwater Scene, Bubbles, c.1919, 7 1/4 In. 1650.00

PINCUSHION DOLLS are not really dolls and often were not even pincushions. Some collectors use the term *half-doll*. The top half of each doll was made of porcelain. The edge of the half-doll was made with several small holes for thread, and the doll was stitched to a fabric body with a voluminous skirt. The finished figure was used to cover a hot pot of tea, powder box, pincushion, whisk broom, or lamp. They were made in sizes from less than an inch to over 9 inches high. Most date from the early 1900s to the 1950s. Collectors often find just the porcelain doll without the fabric skirt.

Arms Away, No Pincushion, Goebel, 6 1/2 In. 295.00
Arms Away, Sitting, Legs Kicking 250.00
Pink Dress, Japan, 3 In. 38.00

Woman, Hat, Arms Out To Waist, Full Dress 100.00
Young Woman, Original Wig, 5 1/2 In. 850.00

PINK SLAG pieces are listed in this book in the Slag category.

PIPES have been popular since tobacco was introduced to Europe by
Sir Walter Raleigh. Carved wooden, porcelain, ivory, and glass pipes
may be listed here. Meerschaum pipes are listed under Meerschaum.

Black Boy, Clinging To Bowl, Fending Off Alligator With Stick, 1920s, 12 3/4 In. .330.00 to 385.00
Black Man, At End Of Log, Alligator Behind Him, Biting His Posterior, Wood, Green ... 440.00
Box, Walnut, Heart On Crest, Brass Pull, 18th Century, 14 1/8 In. 145.00
Briar, Kentucky Club Tobacco, Derby Day Contest, 1955, 6 In. 45.00
Burl, Grinning Man's Head, Hollow Root Stem, Spiraling Band, 21 In. 1380.00
Busts, 2 Bearded Men, Wood, Painted, Plastic Stem, 15 In. 20.00
Gold Banded End, Leatherette Satin Lined Case, Cigar Holder, Continental 85.00
Hunter & Dog, White, Pottery, Wooden & Plastic Stem, Tin Bowl Cover, Bavaria, 9 In. .. 75.00
Kay Woodie, Sherlock Holmes Style, 3Y3 On Bowl Front 30.00
Man, Drinking From Barrel, Porcelain, 4 In. 300.00
Man, Playing Mandolin, Yellowware Bowl, 13 In. 80.00
Napoleon's Head, Chalkware 395.00
Opium, Carved Yin-Yang Symbol Underside, 17 In. 467.00
Opium, Paktong & Ivory Mount, Russet, Lacquer Tube, China, 23 In. 170.00
Owl, Porcelain, E. Bohne Sohne, 2 3/4 In. 520.00
Pistol Shape, Bowl Is Pistol Grip, Composition, 5 In. 30.00
Sea Captain, Porcelain, E. Bohne Sohne, 2 1/2 In. 320.00
Tongs, Iron, Pocket Size, c.1750 .... 310.00
Woman's Head, Whale Ivory, Carved Bowl, 20th Century, 7 In. 402.00

PISGAH FOREST pottery was made in North Carolina beginning in
1926. The pottery was started by Walter R. Stephen in 1914, and after
his death in 1961, the pottery continued in operation. The most famous
kinds of Pisgah Forest ware are the cameo type with designs made of
raised glaze and the turquoise crackle glaze wares.

Creamer, Covered Wagon Pulled By Oxen, W. Stephen, 1953, 3 1/8 In. 220.00
Ginger Jar, Turquoise, 3 In. 115.00
Teapot, Pioneer Family, Covered Wagon, W. Stephen, 1953, 5 In. 320.00
Vase, Blue Crystalline Glaze, Mustard Ground, Tapered To Base, 7 In. 546.00
Vase, Blue High Glaze, Signed, 9 1/2 In. 230.00
Vase, Celadon & Caramel Crystalline Glaze, Signed, 8 In. 750.00
Vase, Covered Wagon Scene, Green Cameo, Green Glossy Base, Signed, 4 1/2 In. 200.00
Vase, French Blue & Bone Crystalline Glaze, Corseted, 1944, 6 In. 300.00
Vase, Green Crystalline Glaze On Speckled Oatmeal, Signed, 1935, 5 1/2 In. 775.00
Vase, Green Exterior, Pink Interior, 20th Century, Signed, 6 1/4 In. 112.00
Vase, Light Blue Glaze, Raised Rim, Squat, 1934, 4 In. 115.00
Vase, Metallic Brown & Cream, Crystalline, 8 In. 165.00
Vase, Turquoise Crackle, Pink Interior, 6 1/2 In., Pair 125.00

PLANTERS PEANUTS memorabilia is collected. Planters Nut and
Chocolate Company was started in Wilkes-Barre, Pennsylvania, in
1906. The Mr. Peanut figure was adopted as a trademark in 1916.
National advertising for Planters Peanuts started in 1918. The company was acquired by Standard Brands, Inc., in 1961. Standard Brands
merged with Nabisco in 1981. Some of the Mr. Peanut jars and other
memorabilia have been reproduced and, of course, new items are being
made.

Ashtray, Mr. Peanut, Brass 35.00
Bank, Mr. Peanut, Cast Iron, 1970s 95.00
Blotter, Truck With Mr. Peanut On Side, 1930 .... 10.00
Box, Counter Display, Holds 24 5-Cent Packs, Die Cut, 9 x 9 In. 1100.00
Canister, Enameled, Peanut Finial Cover, 10 In. 27.00
Cookie Cutter, Mr. Peanut, 5 In. 11.00
Cruet, Oil & Vinegar, 1960s, Pair 125.00
Dispenser, Tarco, 1960s, 3 x 6 x 12 In. 60.00
Figure, Mr. Peanut, Pip-Squeak, Rubber 1870.00

There is special polish for Lucite and
other plastics. Novus Plastic Polish
can be found in lamp shops.

Remove stains from plastic dishes
with paste silver polish.

Plastic, Charm, Scotty Dog, 7/8 In.

Figure, Mr. Peanut, Wood, Jointed	325.00
Jar, 6 Sides, Yellow Mr. Peanut Label, Peanut Finial, 7 1/4 In.	145.00
Jar, Blown-Out Peanut Each Corner	245.00
Jar, Embossed Planters, Mr. Peanut, Peanut Finial On Lid, Barrel Shape, 12 In.	115.00
Jar, Embossed Planters, Tin Lid, Pat. For Clipper Jar, 8 1/2 x 5 1/4 x 10 In.	300.00
Jar, Figural Peanuts On Corners, Planters, Peanut Finial, 11 3/4 In.	305.00
Jar, Planters Pennant, Mr. Peanut, 5-Cent Salted Peanuts, 10 1/4 In.	230.00
Jar, Slanted Fishbowl Shape, Peanuts Embossed On Front, Tin Lid, 9 In.	80.00
Knife, Peanut Butter, 7 In.	15.00
Letter Opener, Mr. Peanut At Top, Metal	1650.00
Marble Bag, Mr. Peanut, Contents, 1950s	7.00
Peanut Butter Maker, Mr. Peanut, Box	55.00 to 70.00
Pencil, Mechanical, Mr. Peanut, 1940, Package	14.00
Salt & Pepper, Red	30.00

PLASTIC objects of all types are being collected. Some pieces are listed
in other categories; gutta-percha cases are listed in photography, celluloid in its own category.

Case, Cigarette, Lucite, Black & Pearl Chips	38.00
Charm, Scotty Dog, 7/8 In.	*Illus* 8.00
Clock, Bakelite, Marbled Butterscotch Case, Black Dots, Wind Up Mechanism, 3 In.	230.00
Crib Toy, Bakelite, 2 Elephants On String, Bells, 8 In.	150.00
Lamp, Bakelite, Red, Black & Apple Juice With Gold Leaf, Round, Disk Foot, 9 In.	1000.00
Poker Chip Set, Bakelite, Red, Green & Yellow Marbled Chips, Holder, 100 Chips	70.00
Sailboat, Bakelite, Peach, Fabric Leaves, Sails, Seagulls, 8 1/2 In.	210.00
Trinket Box, Bakelite, Raised Knickered Golfer On Top, Beetleware, 1930, 4 In.	85.00

PLIQUE-A-JOUR is an enameling process. The enamel is laid between
thin raised metal lines and heated. The finished piece has transparent
enamel held between the thin metal wires. It is different from cloisonne because it is translucent.

Beaker, Birds, Flowers, Man, Geometric Cable Edges, Domed Foot, Russia, 5 In.	7475.00
Bowl, Made In Peoples Republic Of China, 6 In.	82.00
Box, Floral Design, 4 1/4 x 8 In.	165.00
Scoop, Enamel & Silver, Monogrammed A.V.P., 5 In.	220.00
Spoon, Sterling Silver, 5 In.	192.00
Spoon, Viking Ship Shape, 2 x 3 3/4 In.	1320.00 to 2310.00
Spoon, Viking Ship Shape, 4 3/4 x 8 1/4 In.	5775.00
Tumbler, Red, Blue Floral, 2 1/2 In.	33.00

POLITICAL memorabilia of all types, from buttons to banners, is collected. Items related to presidential candidates are the most popular, but
collectors also search for material related to state and local offices. Many
reproductions have been made. A jugate is a button with photographs of
both the presidential and vice presidential candidates. In this list a button is round, usually with a straight pin or metal tab to secure it to a shirt.
A pin is brass, often figural, sometimes attached to a ribbon.

Armband, Votes For Women, Felt, Black On Yellow, 1 1/2 x 24 In.	50.00

Ashtray, Nixon, Vice Presidential Seal 125.00
Autograph, Frederick Douglass, 1876 .... 333.00
Autograph, William Jennings Bryan, 11 x 14 In. 72.00
Autographs, Aaron Burr, Alexander Hamilton, Burr's 1792, Hamilton Receipt, 1800 .... 1995.00
Ax, Carrie Nation Prohibition, All Nation, Metal, Caricature Of Carrie, 1901, 4 In. 80.00
Ax, Prohibition, Blade, Carrie Nation, Caricature, Art Stove Co., Detroit, 1901, 4 In. 67.00
Badge, Bryan, Stevenson, Madison Square Garden, October 18, 1900 .... 200.00
Badge, Photographer's, Taft's Inauguration, Police Permit For Parade Route, 1909 ...... 100.00
Badge, Photographer's, Truman's Inauguration, To Cross Police Lines 85.00
Badge, Ulysses S. Grant, Center Ferrotype Image, Image Of Grant, Grass, 1 3/8 In. 500.00
Bandanna, Democratic Tariff Reform, Red, Eagle & Shield, 1892-1896 .... 44.00
Bandanna, Garfield Portrait, Mauve Border, Eagle Corners, Frame, 16 x 16 In. 375.00
Bandanna, Harrison, Morton, Red, White & Blue, 24 x 23 In. 200.00
Bandanna, Teddy Roosevelt, Delegate, First Convention Iowa Progressives, Linen 300.00
Bank, Franklin Delano Roosevelt, Metal, 1930s 95.00
Bank, John F. Kennedy, Bust, Banthrico Toys, 1960s 95.00
Banner, Benjamin Harrison, Levi P. Morton, Portraits, Frame, 22 1/2 x 23 1/2 In. 173.00
Banner, G. Washington & B. Harrison, Inauguration, Linen, 1779-1889, 60 x 30 In. 550.00
Baseball, Autographed, Harry Truman 1775.00
Bill Hook, Daily & Sunday Times, Celluloid, 8 In. 125.00
Blotter, Dewey, Sampson, Other Portraits, Sample Shoe Co., Piqua, Oh., 3 x 8 In. 50.00
Book, Coloring, Spiro Agnew, 1969 .... 14.00
Bottle, Franklin D. Roosevelt, Above Eagle, TVA, Aqua, 1936, 10 In. 125.00
Box, Abraham Lincoln, Black & Blue Image On Cover Under Glass, 1 x 4 In. 3500.00
Bubble Gum Cigar, Mondale, Fight For Fritz, 3 Cigars In Box 20.00
Bumper Sticker, Grits, Fritz & Metz, Ohio, 4 x 14 1/2 In. 5.00
Bumper Sticker, Mondale, Ferraro, Autographed, 1984, 3 x 12 In. 40.00
Bumper Sticker, Nixon's, The One 1.50
Bumper Sticker, Signed By George McGovern & Sargent Shriver, 3 x 12 In. 28.00
Bumper Sticker, Wallace For President 5.00
Bumper Sticker, Wallace For President, Autograph 23.00
Bust, Abraham Lincoln, Plaster, L.W. Volk Sculptor 1860, 13 In. 700.00
Bust, Dewey, Bisque, 4 In. 125.00
Bust, President McKinley, Hanging Loop, 4 1/2 x 6 1/2 In. 265.00
Bust, Schley, White Glass, Polished, 5 In. 85.00
Bust, Willkie, Plaster, Sally Clark, 1940, 6 In. 125.00
Button, 21 & Voting, Willkie, Green, White, 1 In. 12.00
Button, Adlai & Estes Are The Bestes, Vote Democratic, 1 1/4 In. 35.00
Button, Alfred E. Smith For President, Celluloid, 6 In. 450.00
Button, American Legion Convention, Cleveland, Oh., White, Celluloid, Pinback, 1 In. .. 45.00
Button, AuH2O, Goldwater, 1964, Black, Gold, 1 1/4 In. 5.00
Button, Black Is Beautiful, Black Panther Party, Panther In Center, 1 1/2 In. 18.00
Button, Burn, Baby, Burn, Celluloid, Neon Pink On Black, 1960s, 1 In. 30.00
Button, Calvin Coolidge Around Image, Silver Metal, Stud Back, 5/8 In. 30.00
Button, Carter, Mondale, Inaugural, 1977, 3 1/2 In. 3.00
Button, CIO, On Strike, Don't Buy Phila. Record, Newspaper Guild, Red, White, 3 In. .. 97.00
Button, Clean House With Dewey, Broom, 1 In. 5.00
Button, Cleveland, Bust, Engraved, Celluloid, Brass Frame, Baldwin & Gleason, 7/8 In. . 67.00
Button, Defend Black Rights, Stop Racist Violence, 1 1/2 In. 6.00
Button, Draft Eisenhower For President, 1 1/4 In. 9.00
Button, Dump Nixon, 1 1/4 In. 4.00
Button, Edith Willkie, For First Lady, Picture, 1 1/4 In. 30.00
Button, Elect Clinton & Gore, 3/4 In. 5.00
Button, Every Buddy For Willkie, In Uniform, Celluloid, 1 In. 120.00
Button, Farraro, Celluloid, 1984, 2 1/2 In. 3.00
Button, Fight To Save Democracy, Victory With Justice For All, 1 In. 181.00
Button, Flasher, Goldwater, 3/4 In. 9.00
Button, Flasher, Humphrey For President, 1 In. 7.00
Button, Franklin Delaware Roosevelt, Black & White, 3 1/2 In. 65.00
Button, G, Wear A G For Goldwater For President 1964, White Enamel, On Card 8.00
Button, General George Patton, Striped Edge, 1 1/4 In. 9.00
Button, General Pershing, 3/8 In. 22.00
Button, George Washington, 1732-1799, 7 In. 10.00

Button, Goldwater In '64, Face, Celluloid, Red, Blue, Gold, 1 In. 4.00
Button, Harding & Coolidge, 1 1/4 In. 7.00
Button, Harrison Inauguration, Picture, Capitol On Reverse, White Metal, 1899 .... 85.00
Button, Harry S. Truman, For President, Picture, Donkeys, 1 1/2 In. 60.00
Button, Help Fight Discrimination, Manhattan Citizens Comm., Blue, White, 3/4 In. 34.00
Button, How Many More?, Anti-Vietnam, Blue & White, 1969, 2 1/2 In. 25.00
Button, Huckleberry Hound For President, Red, White, Blue, Yellow, Tin, 1960, 7/8 In. ... 6.00
Button, Hughes, Centered, 1 1/4 In. 7.00
Button, Humphrey For President, Face, Red Letters, Tinted Picture, 1 1/4 In. 5.00
Button, I Was There, King's Dream, Celluloid, Blue, White, 1963, 3 In. 130.00
Button, Iron County, Landon Elephant, Black & White, 1936, 3/4 In. 47.00
Button, J. Stitt Wilson, Socialist For Gov., Berkeley Minister, Red, Blue, White, 7/8 In. ... 170.00
Button, James M. Cox, Stud Back, 5/8 In. 85.00
Button, Jesse Jackson For President '88, Celluloid, 6 In. 6.00
Button, Jewelry, John Fitzgerald Kennedy, Map Shape, 3/4 In. 20.00
Button, JFK, 1960, 3 1/2 In. 15.00
Button, Job Harriman, Socialist Candidate For Mayor, Red, White, Blue, 1 1/4 In. 98.00
Button, Keep Our Boys Over Here, America Wants Peace, 7 In. 9.00
Button, Kent State, Anti-Vietnam, Pulitzer Prize Image Of Girl Kneeling, 2 1/4 In. 65.00
Button, Lady Bird Special, Whistlestop Tour, 1964, Cello, 3 In. 30.00
Button, LBJ For The USA, Picture On Map Of U.S., Red, White, Blue, 3 1/2 In. 6.00
Button, Make Love, Not War, Anti-Vietnam, Red, White, Blue, 3/4 In. 28.00
Button, March On Washington For Jobs & Freedom, Aug. 28, 1 3/4 In. 78.00
Button, March On Washington For Jobs & Freedom, King March, 1963, 1 3/4 In. 80.00
Button, McGovern For The Love Generation, Peace Symbol, Black, Green, 1 1/2 In. 11.00
Button, McKinley & Roosevelt, Presidential Campaign, Celluloid, 1900, 3/4 In. 30.00
Button, McKinley, Presidential Campaign, Stamped Brass, Enamel Shield, 1 1/2 In. 20.00
Button, Memory Of Harry S. Truman, 1972, 3 In. 10.00
Button, Mondale, Ferraro, Jugate, '84, Pictures, 3 1/2 In. 3.00
Button, Montana Silver Dollar, FDR, Wheeler, Murray, Ayers, Monaghan, 1 In. 1017.00
Button, Nat'l. Unity Conference, Seamen & Longshoremen, Red, Cream, 1934, 1 In. 75.00
Button, National Freedom March, I Was There, Aug. 28, 1963, Washington DC, 3 In. ... 127.00
Button, Nixon & Lodge, Winning Team, 3/4 In. 32.00
Button, Nixon, Lodge, Stars In Band, Lithographed Metal, Red, White, Blue, 1 In. 25.00
Button, People's Congress, Pittsburgh, Pa., Blue On White Ground, 1937, 1 1/2 In. 103.00
Button, Perot, By The People, Red White & Blue, 3/4 In. 2.00
Button, Poor People's Campaign, 1968, 2 In. 20.00
Button, Portrait, President Abraham Lincoln, V. P. Andrew Johnson, 1 In. 220.00
Button, Presidential Campaign, Temperance, Mrs. Swallow & Carrol, 1904 .... 125.00
Button, Reagan & Bush, America's New Dawn, Sun Over Mountains, Celluloid, 2 In. ... 45.00
Button, Remember The Main, Pictures The Ship Underway, Celluloid, Pinback, 1 In. 40.00
Button, Robert Kennedy, Vote For Our Next President, Celluloid, 1968, 4 In. 20.00
Button, Ronald Reagan, For President, Picture, '80, 1 In. 3.00
Button, Rosalyn Carter For First Lady, 1980, 3 In. 3.00
Button, Row Of Democrats, Roosevelt, Osborn, Wallace, St. Louis Button, 1 1/4 In. 935.00
Button, Security & Freedom Through World Wide Disarmament, 1960s, 1 3/4 In. 15.00
Button, Socialist Party, Arm Holding Torch, Red, 1 1/4 In. 227.00
Button, Stevenson, In Script, 1 1/4 In. 15.00
Button, Stop Graft, Elect Taft, 1 1/4 In. 6.00
Button, Stop The Bombing! Out Now!, Anti-Vietnam, Bomber & Faces, 3 1/4 In. 30.00
Button, Stop The Draft, Anti-Vietnam, White, Green Ground, 1 1/2 In. 31.00
Button, Strom Thurmond For President, Picture, 1 1/4 In. 3000.00
Button, Taft, Inset Of Head In Iron Elephant, GOP, 6 In. 300.00
Button, Teddy Roosevelt, Portrait, Shield, Stars, Ribbon, Whitehead & Hoag, 1 1/4 In. .. 49.00
Button, Tennesseans For Dole, 1996, Oval, 2 In. 5.00
Button, Texans For McGovern, Map Of Texas, 1 1/4 In. 8.00
Button, Theodore Roosevelt, Picture, 1 1/2 In. 20.00
Button, Thomas E. Dewey, For President, Head Shown, 3/4 In. 8.00
Button, U.S. Grant, Your Credit Is Good At The New England, Celluloid, 1 In. 50.00
Button, Uncle Sam Pointing Finger, Join, 1 1/2 In. 31.00
Button, Union Party, Lemke, O'Brian, 1936 Campaign, Tin Lithograph, 3/4 In. 35.00
Button, United Women's Committee, Soldier Kissing Child, 3/4 In. 130.00
Button, Village Improvement Society, So. Shaftsbury, Vt., Uncle Sam, 1 1/4 In. 50.00

Button, Vote Communist, Gus Hall, Jarvis Tyner For Vice President, 3 In. 6.00
Button, Votes For Women, 10 Stars, Blue On Gold, 7/8 In. 100.00
Button, Votes For Women, Patriotism, Center Eagle & Flags, 3/4 In. 73.00
Button, War Is Not Healthy For Children & Other Living Things, Flower, 3 In. 12.00
Button, War Is Not Healthy For Children, Other Living Things, Anti-Vietnam, 2 In. 51.00
Button, Watts Cooking, We Want Work, Black On Cream, Flames, 1965 Riot, 1 In. 40.00
Button, We Salute Taft-Hartley Law, Red, White, Blue, Center, Bronx Cheer, 1 1/4 In. ... 91.00
Button, We Shall Overcome, Blue & White, 1 1/4 In. 30.00
Button, We Want Mamie, 1 1/4 In. 7.00
Button, William Jennings Bryan, William Sulzer, Stars & Stripes Motif, 1 1/4 In. 85.00
Button, Willkie, Shield, 1 In. 27.00
Button, Wilson & Marshall, Jugate, Blue Ribbon, 1 3/4 In. 1800.00
Button, Wilson Inauguration, Brass, Pinback, 1913 .... 55.00
Button, Wilson, Sepia Picture, Tin Stud, 7/8 In. 55.00
Button, Woodrow Wilson, Sepia Bust, Celluloid, 1910s, 3/4 In. 25.00
Button, Your Credit Is Good At The New England, Picturing Grant, Celluloid 50.00
Cabinet Card, Giant Campaign Ball, Civil War Slogans, President Harrison, 1888 ...... 266.00
Cabinet Card, McKinley & Wife, House, Sepia, 1896, 4 x 7 In. 40.00
Cabinet Card, Mrs. Cleveland, Side View, Currans Rheumatic Remedy, Holyoke, Mass. ... 85.00
Candle, Nixon 75.00
Candy Dish, Presidents Of The U.S. To T. Roosevelt, Glass, Heart Shape, 1900s, 6 In. ... 20.00
Card, Hayes Elected In A Pig's Ass, Pig Picture, 6 In. 175.00
Card, Ronald Reagan, America Needs Reagan, 1980, Black & White, 4 x 9 In. 1.00
Card, Souvenir Inauguration Of Pres. Taft, Washington, Photograph, Mar. 4, 1909 ...... 40.00
Card, Stereo, Justice Parker, His Dog Senator 35.00
Card, Volunteer Sign-Up, Reagan Texas Campaign, 1984 .... 2.50
Cartoon, Teddy Roosevelt, Autograph, W.L. Evans, 1909, 8 x 10 In. 440.00
Certificate, Contributor's, Communist Election Campaign, Browder, Ford, 1936 .... 60.00
Charm, Adlai, Metal, Hole At Top 15.00
Charm, Souvenir, JFK, LBJ Inaugural Ball, Pewter, 1961 .... 25.00
Cigar, Bubble Gum, Nixon's The One, Picture 7.00
Cigar Case, William Henry Harrison, Papier-Mache 9075.00
Cigar Label, Franklin Roosevelt Picture 15.00
Cigarette Lighter, LBJ Senate Majority Leader, 1956 .... 40.00
Cloth, American Eagle Medallion, Flag Border, Linen, Painted, 1840s, 6 x 4 In. 330.00
Costume, Halloween, Brain Twister, N.R.A., C.C.C., I.W.W., P.W.A., FDR Programs 100.00
Decal, Nixon & Nimtz, Red, White, Blue, 1968, 4 In. 30.00
Document, Naval, Franklin Delano Roosevelt, Signed, Frame 750.00
Doll, Goldwater, Box 26.00
Envelope, Lincoln, The Nation Mourns, April 15, 1865 .... 35.00
Fan, Black Lawmakers In Congress, Frame, 1970s 60.00
Fan, Votes For Women, Keep Cool!, Election Day, Mass., November 2, Map Reverse 400.00
Figurine, Hat, Straw Boater, McKinley Decal Inside Crown, Milk Glass, 4 In. 250.00
Figurine, Ronald Reagan, Plaster, 1981, 18 In. 125.00
Flag, Let Iowa Women Vote, Add Another Star To Flag Of Free States, 3 x 6 1/2 In. 500.00
Flag, Progressive Party, Prosperity, Roosevelt, Bullmoose, 1912, 11 x 18 In. 3025.00
Flag, Promoting Clay, Frelinghuysen Ticket, 20 1/4 x 27 1/4 In. 5775.00
Flag, Teddy Roosevelt Center, 16 Ships, Naval Commanders, Frame, 13 x 18 In. 2500.00
Flag, U.S., Ulysses S. Grant Portrait Center, Silk, 1868 .... 8900.00
Flier, Reagan, The Time Is Now, Full Color, 1980 .... 2.00
Flyer, Committee Against Racism, Smash Racism, Stop Nazis, San Jose, 1970s, 11 In. ... 20.00
Flyer, Nixon, Made For College Campus, Tear Off For Volunteering, 1972, 8 x 11 In. 9.00
Flyer, Wm. J. Bryan, Adlai E. Stevenson, Open Work Net Banner, 1900, 14 x 17 In. 333.00
Fob, Bryan, Blue & White, 3/4 In. 75.00
Game, Nose Around, Ring The Nose, Nixon 25.00
Glass, Antiprohibition, Elephant, Donkey Leaning On Beer Barrel, 1932, 3 3/4 In. 50.00
Glass, Nixon, Union County Republican Victory Banquet, 1973, 6 In. 30.00
Gloves, Woman's, White, Carry On With Roosevelt Design, Red, White & Blue 185.00
Goblet, End Of Prohibition, 7 Scenes Of Happy Days, 1933 .... 150.00
Hand Puppet, Nixon, Agnew, Pair 75.00
Handbill, Regular Democratic Ticket, Cleveland & Stevenson, 1892, 4 In. 75.00
Handkerchief, Bryan & Sewall, White 33.00
Handkerchief, Dewey, Flags Border, Cotton, Multicolored, 11 In. 125.00

Handkerchief, George Washington, Effect Of Principle, Frame 750.00
Hanger, Door, Reagan, Bush, Anti-Mondale, 1984 .... 2.00
Hat, Paper, Folding, Experience Counts, Vote Nixon, Lodge, Elephant, Red, White, Blue . 12.00
Invitation, Lincoln, Johnson, Inaugural Ball 1200.00
Invitation, Lincoln, Johnson, Inaugural Ball, All Filled In, 7 1/2 x 10 1/2 In. 1600.00
Jewelry, Charm, Jack Kennedy, Silver Color, 3/8 In. 8.50
Jug, Metal, Cox, F.D.R, Solid Back 95.00
Kerchief, Roosevelt & Fairbanks, Prosperity, Red, White, 17 In. 30.00
Kerchief, We Want Roosevelt, Blue Letters, Blue Outer Border, Cotton, 11 3/4 In. 30.00
Kerchief, We Want Roosevelt, Red Letters, Red Outer Border, Cotton, 11 3/4 In. 30.00
Key, Democratic National Convention, Atlantic City, 1964 .... 12.50
Key Chain, Reagan, Bush, Inaugural Ball, 1985 .... 10.00
Key Ring, Landon Portrait, Brown Bakelite, Under Glass 200.00
Knife, George Wallace, 2 1/4 In. 20.00
Knife, Pocket, Carter, Mondale, Pictures, 1980 .... 20.00
Label, Vote For Barry Goldwater, 1964 Presidential Campaign, Caterer, Los Angeles 200.00
Lantern, Dinner Pail Shape, McKinley & Roosevelt, 4 More Years, Tin 1100.00
Letter, Fellow Campaigner, Dick Nixon Autograph, 1952 .... 275.00
Letterhead, Frankin D. Roosevelt, Signed Executive Mansion, 1932 .... 595.00
Letterhead, Willkie For President Club, 1940 .... 2.00
License Plate, Wallace For President, '68, Red, White & Blue 120.00
License Plate, Wallace For President, Picture, Metal, 1968 .... 14.00
License Plate Attachment, Landon For President 150.00
License Plate Attachment, Perot, 1992 .... 3.00
License Plate Attachment, We Want Willkie, Tin, Image At Top, 6 1/4 x 5 3/4 In. 135.00
Lighter, Goldwater For President, Edwin Steers For Attorney General, Elephant 48.00
Log Cabin & Hard Cider, Campaign, Printed Cotton, 27 x 22 1/2 In. 385.00
Magazine Cover, John F. Kennedy, S.E.P., Dec. 14, 1963, Rockwell 20.00
Magnet, Nixon, Metal 8.00
Mask, Nixon 22.00
Match Pack, Air Force One Plane, Lyndon B. Johnson 11.00
Matchbook, Betty Ford, 1976 .... 2.50
Matchbox, Roosevelt, Churchill, Stalin, Celluloid, 2 1/8 x 1 1/2 In. ...._Illus_ 88.00
Medal, Inauguration, Truman, Bust, Goddess, 51 mm 60.00
Medal, Official 1949 Truman Inaugural, 2 In. 150.00
Medal, Official 1961 John F. Kennedy Inaugural, Bronze, 2 3/4 In. 35.00
Mirror, Eisenhower Portrait, Pocket, 2 x 3 In. 30.00
Mirror, Re-Election Of Wm. V. Pacelli As Alderman, Wheat, Celluloid, Pocket 80.00
Mirror, Wm. McKinley Memorial Picturing The Memorial, Celluloid, Pocket 45.00
Oyster Plate, Artist's Studio On Beach, Hayes Presidential China, Haviland, 9 In. ..._Illus_ 1925.00
Oyster Plate, Swells, Blue & Green, Hayes Presidential China, Haviland, 8 1/4 In. ..._Illus_ 990.00
Paperweight, Dwight D. Eisenhower, Mirrored, Facsimile Signature, 1953, 4 x 3 In. 20.00
Paperweight, Grover Cleveland, White Back 250.00
Paperweight, LBJ, Crystal, Bing & Grondahl, Norway, 1964, 3 1/2 x 1 1/2 In. 120.00
Paperweight, Parker, Davis, Milk Glass, Red, White & Blue 600.00
Paperweight, Teddy Roosevelt & Fairbanks, Milk Glass, Red, White & Blue 475.00

Political, Matchbox, Roosevelt, Churchill, Stalin,
Celluloid, 2 1/8 x 1 1/2 In.

Political, Oyster Plate, Artist's Studio
On Beach, Hayes Presidential China,
Haviland, 9 In.

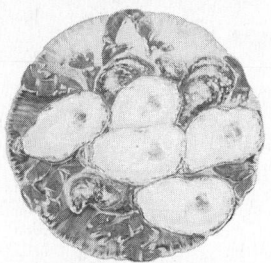

Political, Oyster Plate, Swells,
Blue & Green, Hayes Presidential
China, Haviland, 8 1/4 In.

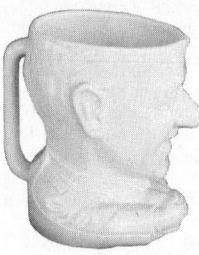

Political, Pitcher, Beer,
Alfred Smith,
Patriotic Products

Political, Plate, Grouse In Flight
At Twilight, Hayes Presidential
China, Haviland, 9 In.

Paperweight, U.S. Grant, Glass, Bronzed Plaster Bust Interior	275.00
Pen, Ballpoint, Figural, Charles DeGaulle, Ivory Plastic, Military Uniform, France, 6 In.	30.00
Pen, Hoover	10.00
Pen, Willkie	28.00
Pennant, First Men On The Moon, Commemorative, 1969, 5 x 10 1/2 In.	30.00
Pennant, Goldwater, 1964	10.00
Pennant, Hoover For President, West Branch, Red, Yellow, Black, 11 In.	65.00
Pennant, President Wilson, Blue, White, 21 In.	150.00
Pennant, Votes For Women, Button Attached, Black On Yellow, Felt, 17 In.	200.00
Photograph, Autograph, Candidate Harold Stassen, Frame, 10 x 8 In.	38.00
Photograph, Autograph, Dan Quayle, Color, Frame, 10 x 8 In.	22.00
Photograph, Autograph, Harry S. Truman, Omar M. Bradley, Oval Office, 7 x 9 In.	385.00
Photograph, Autograph, Herbert Hoover, 3 x 5 In.	100.00
Photograph, Autograph, Werner Von Braun To Gen. Matt. Ridgway, 7 x 9 In.	303.00
Photograph, Franklin D. Roosevelt, Portrait, Otto Hagel, 13 1/2 x 10 1/2 In.	350.00
Photograph, Harry S. Truman & Lee Marshall, Sepia, Signed, 1949, 15 x 14 In.	245.00
Photograph, Harry Truman & Gen, Omar Bradley, Oval Office, Color, 6 3/4 x 9 In.	385.00
Photograph, John F. Kennedy & Jacqueline, Seated, Color, 14 x 11 In.	90.00
Photograph, President John F. Kennedy, Inscription, Frame, Fabrian Bachrach	1980.00
Pitcher, Beer, Alfred Smith, Patriotic Products *Illus*	350.00
Place Mat, Cafeteria, Kennedy Space Center Tours, 1976, 9 1/2 x 14 In.	20.00
Plaque, Lincoln, With Malice Toward None, Bronze, Shield, 12 x 12 In.	55.00
Plate, Franklin D. Roosevelt, Center Picture, Blue & White, 10 In.	55.00
Plate, Grouse In Flight At Twilight, Hayes Presidential China, Haviland, 9 In. *Illus*	1100.00
Plate, McKinley, Center Picture, Staffordshire, 10 In.	35.00
Plate, Nixon, Republican Centennial, Stars Around Inner Circle, 10 In.	55.00
Plate, Pres. Wilson, Seal Top, Sebring Pottery Co., 9 In.	90.00
Plate, President William McKinley, Memorial, Pressed Glass, 10 In.	55.00
Plate, Townsend Plan, Pottery, Children Transfer, Gold Letters, 6 1/2 In.	32.00
Plate, W.H. Harrison In Uniform, Surrounded By Hero Of The Thames, 8 1/2 In.	3630.00
Postcard, 1908 Presidential Campaign, Evolution Of Big Stick, T. Roosevelt, 1908	150.00
Postcard, Cartoon Of Soldier Kicking Hitler, He Has A Kick Coming	18.00
Postcard, Dukakis, Bentsen, 1988	2.00
Postcard, Dwight D. Eisenhower, Photograph On Front, Text On Back, 1948	21.00
Postcard, Hoover & Lindbergh	125.00
Postcard, Indiana Nixon For President Campaign, Pat & Dick On Front, 6 x 9 In.	17.00
Postcard, Iowa Governor Harold Hughes, Autographed, 1960s	18.00
Postcard, Jim Sherman, Our Jim Is It, Sepia, June 26, 1908	50.00
Postcard, Kindred Spirits In Cause Of Liberty, Wilson, Lincoln & Washington, 1917	15.00
Postcard, Let's Send George To Washington, Wallace Pictured, Outline Of State	38.00
Postcard, President Lincoln, Bust Photograph, Soldiers' National Cemetery, 1909	45.00
Postcard, President McKinley, Photograph, Inset With American Flag, Memorial	100.00
Postcard, President Roosevelt, American Flag, Photograph	50.00
Postcard, President Wilson, Hand Drawn Caricature, Black & White, Garrity, 1915	40.00
Postcard, Robert F. Kennedy, Pose By Fabian Bacharach, 7 x 9 In.	18.00
Postcard, Submission Never! Message Of Woodrow Wilson, 1917	18.00

Postcard, Suffrage, I Believe In Equal Rights For Women 40.00
Postcard, Suffragette, Parade, Washington, Horse Drawn Floats, March, 1913 .... 60.00
Postcard, Taft & Sherman Campaign, 1908 .... 20.00
Postcard, Teddy Roosevelt & Asian, Caricature 100.00
Postcard, Teddy Roosevelt, 3rd Term, Oyster Bay Umbrella, On Leather, 1907 .... 120.00
Postcard, Theodore Roosevelt, Jamestown Exposition, 1907 .... 45.00
Postcard, U.S. Presidents, Portrait, Washington To Teddy Roosevelt, 1911 .... 85.00
Postcard, Vote For Women, Merry Christmas To All, Pixie Santa, Dec. 19, '15 .... 275.00
Postcard, Votes For Women, No Taxation Without Representation, Wall 50.00
Poster, America, Roosevelt, Portrait, Red, White, Blue, 1940, 9 x 12 In. 60.00
Poster, Blaine, Logan, 24 x 18 In. 300.00
Poster, Democratic Candidates & Party Chieftains, F. Witte, 27 x 21 In. 110.00
Poster, Franklin D. Roosevelt, 1944, 11 x 15 In. 25.00
Poster, Goldwater For President, Indiana State Rally, Red, White & Blue, 22 x 14 In. 38.00
Poster, Harry S. Truman, President, Alben W. Barkley, Vice President 350.00
Poster, J.F. Kennedy, Color, 16 x 12 In. 12.00
Poster, Mandela, Color Picture, 1994, 30 x 20 In. 40.00
Poster, Nixon, The Nation Needs Coolness, 1972, 17 x 22 In. 10.00
Poster, Peter Camejo For President, 1968, 12 x 18 In. 5.00
Poster, Stevenson, We Must Look Forward To Great Tomorrow, 28 x 40 In. 50.00
Poster, Time Has Come To Conquer Or Submit, Woodrow Wilson Portrait, 20 x 30 In. 115.00
Poster, Truman, Barkley, Forrest Smith, Vote Democratic, Nov. 2, 1948, 14 x 22 In. 250.00
Poster, Vote For Landon & Knox, Sepia, 21 x 15 1/2 In. 50.00
Print, Dewey, Olympia By Statue Of Liberty, Naugatuck, Ct., Cafe, Frame, 12 x 15 In. .. 100.00
Print, Washington Closing The Grant Lodge Of Virginia, Frame, 22 x 16 In. 245.00
Program, FDR Rally, Charlotte, N.C., Sept. 10, 20 Pages, 8 x 10 1/2 In. 23.00
Program, Souvenir, Nixon, Agnew Inaugural Invitation, 1969 .... 20.00
Rain Cap, Goldwater In '64 .... 12.00
Rain Cap, Goldwater, Elephant 3.00
Rattle, Parades & Rallies, Copper & Tin 1050.00
Record, Wake Up America, By Sharon Connally, John Connally For President, 1980 .... 3.00
Ribbon, Against The Combine, Black, White 12.00
Ribbon, Bartender's Union Local 175, Black, White 13.00
Ribbon, Buy Bonds, Member Minnesota Police & Peace Officers, 1943, 1 3/4 In. 20.00
Ribbon, California Presidential Postmaster's Association, Brown, Yellow, 1910 .... 30.00
Ribbon, Campaign, Seymour & Blair, Lost To Grant, 1868 .... 500.00
Ribbon, Celebration Bunker Hill, Philadelphia, 1908 .... 20.00
Ribbon, Cloth, Pat For 1st Lady, Nixon, 1968 .... 1.00
Ribbon, Delegate, Am Clothing Workers, Cleveland, 1950 .... 17.00
Ribbon, Delegate, Clothing Workers, 1964 .... 18.00
Ribbon, Delegate, Democratic National Convention, Chicago, 1952 .... 40.00
Ribbon, Delegate, Democratic National Convention, Truman, 1948 .... 55.00
Ribbon, Delegate, Federation Of Labor, Pa., 1941 .... 20.00
Ribbon, Delegate, NSA, Atlantic City, N.J., 1925 .... 13.00
Ribbon, Delegate, Republican National Convention, 1944 .... 60.00
Ribbon, Delegate, Republican National Convention, Chicago, 1956 .... 42.00
Ribbon, Delegate, Steel Workers Conference, 1949 .... 32.00
Ribbon, Delegate, Union Council, Hagerstown, Md., 1949 .... 16.00
Ribbon, Delegate, United Steelworkers, Atlantic City, 1946 .... 17.00
Ribbon, Dewey, Did I Remember The Maine, Silk, Red White & Blue 125.00
Ribbon, Firemen's Assoc., Philadelphia 25.00
Ribbon, For President, Sam'l J. Tilden, Picture, 1876, 1 1/2 x 4 1/4 In. 80.00
Ribbon, Funeral, We Mourn Our Loss, Dr. Martin Luther King, 1 1/2 In. 55.00
Ribbon, Garden Place Lodge, M.B.A., Globeville, Colorado 35.00
Ribbon, In Commemoration Of 100th Anniversary Of Birth Of Abraham Lincoln 30.00
Ribbon, Island Park, Winfield Kansas, Old Soldiers, 8th Reunion, 1913 .... 30.00
Ribbon, Labor Day, Penna Rural Letter Carriers' Convention, Reading, 1906, 7 In. 75.00
Ribbon, Ladies Benevolent Asso., Gold Letters & Fringe, July 18, 1917, 3 x 8 In. 43.00
Ribbon, McKinley & Roosevelt, Club, 1 3/4 In. 20.00
Ribbon, McKinley, Hobart, Illinois Day, October 21, 1896, Black, Gold 30.00
Ribbon, Ohio Stands By Blaine, Dayton, Silk, Blue, Black, 3 x 6 In. 80.00
Ribbon, Ohio, Y.P.B., McKinley Birthplace, 1921 .... 20.00
Ribbon, Our New President, Nixon, Red, White & Blue 9.00

Ribbon, Perry's Victory Centennial, 1913 .... 12.00
Ribbon, Silk, Red Cross, Public Order, Inauguration, 1901, 2 1/2 x 6 1/2 In. 50.00
Ribbon, Wallace In '72, Gold, Purple 9.00
Ribbon, Wallace, Stand Up For America, Pictures Wallace & Wife, 2 1/4 In. 95.00
Ribbon, Wide Awake, Sound Money Parade, Hartford Veterans, 1900, Pair 135.00
Ribbon, Willkie War Veteran 25.00
Ribbon, Win Willkie With No Third Term, Vote Republican, 1940 .... 25.00
Ribbon, Worker's Hospitality, California, 1956 Republican National Convention 10.00
Ribbon, Young Democratic Clubs Of America, 1936 .... 25.00
Salt & Pepper, Jimmy Carter, Plains, Ga. Home Of Jimmy Carter, Peanut Man, 5 In. 26.00
Salt & Pepper, John F. Kennedy In Rocker 65.00
Sash, Votes For Women, Linen, Blue, Yellow, 6 x 29 In. 303.00
Sewing Kit, Teddy Roosevelt 15.00
Sheet Music, Douglas Funeral March, H. Grante, Chicago, 1861 .... 55.00
Sheet Music, March & Quick Step, President Pierce's, Capitol Behind Portrait 300.00
Sheet Music, President Garfield's Funeral March, 1881, 10 1/2 x 14 In. 25.00
Sheet Music, President Kennedy March, 1964 .... 48.00
Sheet Music, Thomas E. Dewey March, 1952 .... 10.00
Sheet Music, Tippecanoe Or Log Cabin Quick Step, 1840, 10 x 13, 2 Pages 110.00
Sheet Music, Women Forever, E.T. Paull, Frame, 15 x 18 In...................... 50.00
Shower Head, Nixon 75.00
Sign, Peace, Hand In V, Flowers, Molded Plastic, c.1969, 15 x 6 In. 25.00
Snuffbox, Zachary Taylor's Campaign, 1848 .... 3520.00
Soap Doll, McKinley, Original Tag, 1896, 4 1/2 In. 150.00
Song Sheet, Know-Nothings, Anti-Catholic Sentiment, 9 x 13 In. 300.00
Song Sheet, McClellan Will Be President, Women Holding Portrait, Full Color 275.00
Spoon, Sterling Silver, Andrew Jackson, CSA Battle Flag, Enameled Bowl 150.00
Spoon, Sterling Silver, Susan B. Anthony, Wreath Political Equality 750.00
Stereo Card, Cleveland, Thurman 2.00
Sticker, Wallace, Stylized Bird, 1 1/2 x 4 In. 1.00
Sticker, Window, Wallace For President, Stand Up For America, 1968 .... 2.00
Stickpin, Benjamin Harrison, Bust, Presidential Campaign, Copper, 1880s, 2 In. 25.00
Stickpin, Benjamin Harrison, Picture, Shell, Broom Shape 110.00
Stickpin, Bull Moose, 1912 .... 18.00
Stickpin, Calvin Coolidge, Around Image, Metal, 5/8 In. 40.00
Stickpin, Dewey, Tinted Face, Yellow Ground, Red, White & Blue, 5/8 In. 50.00
Stickpin, Jas. G. Blaine, Picture, Cardboard In Brass 130.00
Stickpin, Socialist Unity Party, Enamel, Germany 5.00
Stoneware, Mug, McKinley Inaugural, For Gold & Our Country's Honor, 1897 .... 350.00
Stud, Harrison, Morton, Moonstone 400.00
Studs, Silk, Cleveland, Thurman, 1888 .... 30.00
Tab Button, Democrats For Nixon, 3/8 In. 6.00
Tab Button, LBJ, Hat Shape, Blue White, 3/8 In. 8.50
Tab Button, Roosevelt, Blue & White, 3/4 In. 2.00
Thimble, Just So You'll Remember C.C. Lillibridge For State Senator, Plastic 5.00
Ticket, Garfield & Arthur Inauguration Reception Concert, 5 3/4 x 9 3/4 In. 350.00
Ticket, Press, Republican State Convention, Boston Theater, Oct. 3, 1901, Signed 10.00
Tie, Re-Elect Pres. Roosevelt, Picture 75.00
Tie Clasp, Landon, 1 1/2 In. 20.00
Tie Clasp, Landon, White Enamel 25.00
Tie Clasp, Roosevelt, Enamel, Red Donkey, Blue Letters 35.00
Tie Clip, Flasher, Elephant, Vote Republican, 1 1/4 x 7/8 In. 5.00
Tintype, Cleveland & Thurman, Name Below Pictures 75.00
Tip Tray, Center Taft & Sherman, White House Background, Republic Presidents Edge ... 55.00
Tip Tray, Grand Old Party 1856-1908, Taft & Sherman, White House, 4 In. 80.00
Token, Cleveland, Cand. For President, Picture 15.00
Torch, Campaign, Ax Form, Hollow Tin, 14 x 16 In. 1540.00
Torch, Campaign, Star Shape, Hollow Tin 660.00
Torch, Double Swing, Mahogany Pole, 6 Wick Holders, Brass, 1860, 53 In. 440.00
Towel, Linen Damask, Independence Of U.S. Of America, July 4th, 1776, Red Borders ... 22.00
Toy, Spinner, Votes For Women, Yellow & White 200.00
Toy, U.S. Capitol, Paper Spool Display Of Presidents, Reed Toy Co., Pat. 1884 .... 495.00
Trash Can, Spiro Agnew, Golfing & Playing Tennis, Comic Slogans, 1970 .... 38.00

Tray, McKinley	45.00
Tray, Parker, Multicolored, Oval, 13 1/2 x 16 1/2 In.	750.00
Tray, William Henry Harrison, Behind Plow, North Bend Log Cabin, 18 1/4 x 25 1/2 In.	5775.00
Tumbler, Bryan & Sewall, Jugate, 16 To 1, Free Coinage Of Silver, Etched	100.00
Union Charter, AFL, Signed Gompers, Frame, 1917, 19 x 27 In.	433.00
Wallet, Jackson, Portrait, New Orleans Jan. 8, 1815, Leather, Burr Beham	1650.00
Watch Fob, Fairbanks	70.00
Watch Fob, Ford, Reagan	2.00
Watch Fob, Hoover, Celluloid Insert	40.00
Watch Fob, Parker, Davis, 1904	35.00
Watch Fob, Robert Taft	26.00
Watch Fob, Taft & Sherman 1908, Campaign, Brass, Leather Strap, 1 1/2 In.	30.00
Watch Fob, Taft, Our Next President	20.00
Watch Fob, Woodrow Wilson, Relief Picture, Stamped Metal, 1 3/8 In.	20.00
Window Decal, Eisenhower, Young Republican, 1956	3.00
Window Sticker, Goldwater, 1964	2.00
Wooden Nickel, Anti-John F. Kennedy, 1962	3.00
Wristwatch, Spiro Agnew, Box	55.00

POMONA glass is a clear glass with a soft amber border decorated with pale blue or rose-colored flowers and leaves. The colors are very, very pale. The background of the glass is covered with a network of fine lines. It was made from 1885 to 1888 by the New England Glass Company. First grind was made from April 1885 to June 1886. It was made by cutting a wax surface on the glass, then dipping it in acid. Second grind was a less expensive method of acid etching that was developed later.

Celery Vase, Floral Band, 1st Grind, 6 1/2 In.	176.00
Celery Vase, Floral, Butterfly, 2nd Grind, 6 1/4 In.	121.00
Finger Bowl, 2 1/2 x 5 In.	55.00
Finger Bowl, Inverted Thumbprint, Rolled Rim, 2nd Grind, 2 1/4 x 4 1/2 In.	16.00 to 22.00
Mustard, Hinged Metal Cover, Scalloped Border, New England Glass Co., 3 x 2 In.	230.00
Pitcher, Enameled Floral, 2nd Grind, 7 1/2 In.	66.00
Pitcher, Honeycomb, Twisted Rope Band, Floral, 7 1/2 In.	795.00
Punch Cup, Bayberry, 2nd Grind, 3 3/4 In.	27.00
Ramekin, Underplate, Blueberry, 2 1/4 x 4 1/2 In.	85.00
Sugar, Floral Handle, Crimped Edge, 2 3/4 x 5 1/2 In.	70.00
Sugar & Creamer, Blueberry, Footed, 2nd Grind	220.00
Toothpick	150.00
Tumbler, Acorn & Leaves	85.00
Tumbler, Bayberry, 1st Grind, 3 5/8 In.	115.00
Tumbler, Corn Flower, 1st Grind, 3 5/8 In.	50.00
Tumbler, Cornflower Design, 2nd Grind, New England	90.00
Tumbler, Pansy & Butterfly Design, 2nd Grind, New England	120.00
Vase, Draped Medallion, Scalloped Edge, Footed, 6 1/2 In.	65.00
Vase, Planter Form, Blue Cornflower, Gold Leaf Border, Crimped Edge, 5 In.	546.00

PONTYPOOL, see Tole category.

POPEYE was introduced to the Thimble Theater comic strip in 1929. The character became a favorite of readers. In 1932, an animated cartoon featuring Popeye was made by Paramount Studios. The cartoon series continued and became even more popular when it was shown on television starting in the 1950s. The full-length movie with Robin Williams as Popeye was made in 1980.

Bank, Bust, Vinyl	115.00
Bank, Dime Register, Cast Iron, 7 In.	121.00
Bank, Dime Register, Metal	65.00
Bank, Dime Register, Tin Lithograph, 1929	175.00
Book, Big Big Book, Black Spine, Whitman, 1935, 9 1/2 x 7 In.	16.00
Book, Popeye And The Pirates Animated, Red Lettering, Yellow, 1945, 8 x 9 In.	33.00
Book, Popeye In Rowboat, 3 Pop-Up Pictures, 1935, 9 x 8 In.	340.00
Bottle, Soaky	25.00

Don't turn on the porch light if you will be gone for a long time. It tells everyone that you are away. Install a photocell light that automatically turns on at dusk, off at daylight, or install a gas light.

Popeye, Doll,
Composition,
King Features,
1935, 17 In.

Bubble Blower, Box	3600.00
Card, Olive Oyl's Ponytail Hair Holder, Popeye Racing On Back Of Horse, 5 x 9 In.	38.00
Clock, Alarm, Britain, Windup, 1967	160.00
Coaster, Bringing Up Father, Brown Popeye Against White Ground, Yellow, 1950, 5 In.	10.00
Cookie Jar, ABC	550.00
Doll, Cloth, 24 In.	25.00
Doll, Composition, King Features, 1935, 17 In. ....*Illus*	500.00
Eggcup	160.00
Figure, Olive Oyl, Wooden, Jointed, Hand Painted Face, KFS, 5 In.	85.00
Figure, Popeye, 2-Part Mold, Closure Clamp, Tin, 7 1/2 In.	143.00
Figure, Popeye, Bendy, Lakeside, 1968	40.00
Figure, Popeye, Soap, Smiling, With Hands At Sides, Tan, Mid-1930s, 3 3/4 In.	18.00
Figure, Popeye, Walking, With 2 Parrots In Cages, Chein, 8 1/2 In.	193.00
Figure, Popeye, Wooden, Jointed, Smoking Pipe, Hand-Painted Face, KFS, 5 In. ...55.00 to 145.00	
Game, Paint-O-Graf, Easy As Pie, Milton Bradley, 1935, 18 x 17 In. ....345.00 to 430.00	
Game, Shipwreck, Popeye & His Friends Shipwrecked On Island, King Features	132.00
Lamp, Boat, White Metal, Filament Bulb, 7 1/2 In.	385.00
Lamp, Figural, No Pipe Or Shade, Metal, 1930s	275.00
Lunch Box, Thermos	25.00
Marble, Red Akro Agate, Box Says I Yam Wat I Yam, I Yam A Marble Shooter, Arf, Bag	1260.00
Marionette, Rubber, Plastic, Fabric Body, Gund Mfg. Co., 1950s, 11 1/2 In.	40.00
Mug, Olive Oyl, Vandor, 1980	25.00
Mug, Popeye Eating Spinach	45.00
Napkin Holder, Ceramic	15.00
Pencil Sharpener, Bakelite ....90.00 to 95.00	
Pin, Popeye, 1930s	20.00
Plate, Popeye & Friends Party, Bud Sagendorf, 1978, 9 In., 8 Piece	10.00
Puppet, Popeye, Talking, Mattel, Box, 1967	115.00
Puppet, Swee'pea, Vinyl Face, Gund, Box	82.00
Ring, Popeye, Buck-Tooth Nephew, Flicker	16.00
Salt & Pepper, Ceramic, Japan, 1930s, 3 3/4 In.	295.00
Sand Pail, Under The Sea, Handle, 9 In.	385.00
Sand Pail, Wimpy, In Strong Man Garb, Tin, 1933, 12 In.	330.00
Sparkler, Celluloid, Tin, Chein, 1959, 5 1/4 In.	154.00
Thimble Theater, Stage, Composition Figures, Harding Products, King Features, 1939	195.00
Toy, Acrobat, Windup, Tin Lithograph, Rocking Base, Linemar, 12 In.	2090.00
Toy, Boxers, Popeye & Brutus, Linemar	1760.00
Toy, Bubble Blowing Popeye, Battery Operated, Tin, Linemar, Japan, 13 In. .....950.00 to 1035.00	
Toy, Car, Olive Oyl On Roof, Tin Lithograph	908.00
Toy, Express, Popeye With Wheelbarrow, Trunk, Parrot, Marx, c.1930, 8 In.	610.00
Toy, Floor Puncher, Windup, Tin, Celluloid Punch Bag, Chein, Prewar, 7 1/2 In. ..690.00 to 1100.00	
Toy, Handcar, Popeye & Olive Oyl, Linemar, Japan, 1950s, 6 1/2 In.	1320.00
Toy, Handcar, Popeye & Olive Oyl, Windup, Tin, Rubber, Marx, Box, 1935, 7 1/2 In.	440.00
Toy, Jack-In-The-Box, Popeye's Head, Spinach Can, Mattel, 1957 ....125.00 to 195.00	
Toy, Lantern, Linemar	550.00
Toy, Motorcycle, Hubley, 8 1/2 In.	1900.00

Toy, Motorcycle, Spinach Patrol, 3-Wheel, King Features Copyright, Hubley USA, 6 In. ... 725.00
Toy, Olive Oyl On Tricycle 2200.00
Toy, Pirate Gun, Clicker, Tin Lithograph, Characters On Barrel, Box, 1935, 10 In. 825.00
Toy, Popeye & Olive On Roof, Windup, 9 In. 1075.00
Toy, Popeye Basketball Player, Linemar 2750.00
Toy, Popeye Carrying Parrots In Cages, Tin, Windup, Marx, 1935, 7 3/4 In. 385.00
Toy, Popeye Flyer, Planes Fly Around Pole, Windup, Tin Lithograph, Marx 440.00
Toy, Popeye On Motorcycle, Hubley 4400.00
Toy, Popeye On Tricycle, Tin, Celluloid, Windup, Linemar, Japan, 4 1/4 In. ......580.00 to 715.00
Toy, Popeye Shadow Boxer, Chein, 1930s ....715.00 to 995.00
Toy, Popeye The Pilot, Marx 1320.00
Toy, Popeye The Sailor, In Rowboat, Hoge, 1930s 9900.00
Toy, Popeye, Dancer, Windup, Lakeside, Box, 1967 .... 125.00
Toy, Popeye, Ramp Walker, Celluloid, Cardboard Ramp, Irwin, 1948 .... 275.00
Toy, Popeye, Tumbling Tin Lithograph 1870.00
Toy, Popeye, Walker, Ramp, Blue Sailor Outfit, Pushing Wheelbarrow, 3 In. 38.00
Toy, Smoking Popeye, Linemar 4400.00
Toy, Squeeze, Bluto, Rubber, Hand Painted, KFS, 1940-1950, 8 In. 115.00
Toy, Squeeze, Olive Oyl, Hand Painted, 1940-1950, Italy, 7 In. 85.00
Toy, Submarine, Popeye Racing On Giant Black Whale, Green Submarine, 5 x 8 In. 18.00
Toy, Tank, Windup, Tin Lithograph, Tank Rolls Over Flattened Popeye, 4 In. 275.00
Toy, Wimpy On Tricycle 1045.00

PORCELAIN factories that are well known are listed in this book under
the factory name. This category lists pieces made by the less well-
known factories.

Asparagus Box, Cover, Bundle Of Asparagus, Blue Ribbon, 5 In. 1725.00
Bowl, Blue & White, Japan, 15 1/2 x 3 3/4 In. 50.00
Bowl, Blue Chrysanthemum Transfer, Maddock, 11 1/2 In. 135.00
Bowl, Fish, Landscape & Animals, China, 18 x 21 In., Pair 665.00
Bowl, Flowering Prunus Branch Design, Japan, Meiji Period, 5 In. 400.00
Bowl, Footed, Blue & White Ground, Japan, 7 3/4 In. 45.00
Bowl, Ship Design, Blue, White, 19th Century, 6 1/2 In. 137.00
Bowl, Yellow Glaze, 19th Century, 6 1/4 In. 55.00
Box, Cover, Leafy & Floral Vines, Scrolled Cartouches, Germany, 4 1/2 x 7 In. 230.00
Box, Cover, Lettuce, Overlapping Leaves, Green, Yellow, Continental, 4 1/4 In. 1440.00
Box, Egg Form, Bird Design, Gilt Ground, France, 5 In. 375.00
Bust, Lady, Renaissance Attire, Cobalt Blue Glaze, Circular Pedestal, 16 In. 345.00
Cache Pot, Birds, Flowers, Twig Handles, Meissen Style, Carl Thieme, 5 x 7 In., Pair ... 290.00
Cache Pot, Lily-Of-The-Valley 50.00
Cache Pot, Mythological Beast Head, Foliate, Gilt, 10 1/2 In. 350.00
Cake Stand, Apples, Strawberries, Cherries, Green, Gilt Borders, England, 9 In. 145.00
Cake Stand, Floral, Pink, Gold Border, Daniel London, 9 In., Pair 515.00
Charger, Central Peony Design, Blue, White, Late 18th Century, 14 In. 115.00
Charger, Floral Design, Gold, Burnt Orange, Germany, 1880, 12 1/4 In. 109.00
Charger, Summer Scene, Parasol Over Tables, Squeezebag, Crown Devon, 12 In. 135.00
Cheese Dish, Cover, Imari, England, 9 1/2 In. 635.00
Cocoa Pot Set, Floral, Hand Painted, Germany, 5 Piece 195.00
Compote, 2 Women Harvesting Grapes & Grain, Austria, 1900, 8 In. 50.00
Compote, 3 Cherubs Supporting Openwork Basket, Roses, Meissen Style, 12 In. 330.00
Desk Set, 2 Inkwells, Tray, Floral Reserves, Cobalt Blue Ground, France, 1880, 11 In. ... 145.00
Dish, Chinoiserie Design, Orange, White Ground, Continental, 9 1/2 In. 200.00
Dish, Cover, Yellow, Cobalt, On White, Gilt, Cupid Finial, Fraureuth, 8 In. 440.00
Dish, Yellow Disk Supported By 2 Putti With Garlands, Wiener Werkstatte, 8 x 10 In. ... 880.00
Ewer, Wild Flowers, Royal Winchester, 1880, 8 In., Pair 650.00
Figurine, American Eagle In Flight, Wolfgang Gawantka, Kaiser, 11 In. 165.00
Figurine, Cassin's Kingbird, Burgues, 9 In. 220.00
Figurine, Chipping Sparrow, Fitted Wood Stand, Giuseppe Tagliariol, Kaiser, 5 In. 65.00
Figurine, Clown, Outstretched White Figure, Knitted Brows, Vera Bartels, 15 In. 690.00
Figurine, Cockatoo, Perched On Branch, 19 1/2 In. 65.00
Figurine, Colonial Gardener, Japan, 10 x 4 In. 10.00
Figurine, Country Girl & Gentleman, Louis XV Clothes, Biscuit, 19 x 8 In., Pair 240.00
Figurine, Dancer, Gold Costume, Flowing Scarf, Art Deco, Gallura & Holmann, 8 In. 55.00

Figurine, Drum Set, Red, White & Blue, Germany, 1920s, 2 In. 22.00
Figurine, Hummingbird, Ruby Throated, Burgues, 8 In. 575.00
Figurine, Jeanne D'arc, White Biscuit, c.1850, 11 1/4 In. 95.00
Figurine, Kingfisher, Kaiser, 9 1/2 In. 65.00
Figurine, Kwan Ti, Seated On Lion, 11 1/2 In. 192.00
Figurine, Levade With Rider, Lippizzan Stallion, Front Legs Lifted High, 10 1/2 In. 78.00
Figurine, Lulu, Nude, Cat By Feet, Artist, Germany, 20th Century, 14 In. 375.00
Figurine, Oriental Man & Woman, In Native Attire, Polychrome, 10 In., Pair 415.00
Figurine, Owl, Long-Eared, Giuseppe Tagliariol, Kaiser, 9 In. 65.00
Figurine, Prairie Dog, Blacktailed, Burgues, 7 In. 175.00
Figurine, Pug Dog, Seated, Gilt Collar, Tag, 4 1/4 In., Pair 290.00
Figurine, Putti Astride Dove, Rococo, Germany, 1900-1910, 3 1/4 In., Pair 121.00
Figurine, Roadrunner, Fitted Wood Stand, Wolfgang Gawantka, Kaiser, 7 In. 65.00
Figurine, Sparrow, White-Throated, With Eggs On Mountain, Burgues, 7 1/4 In. 130.00
Figurine, Woman With Wings, Tyrolean Dress, 3 1/4 In. 85.00
Flower Basket, Cover, Flowers, Leaves, Handle, Beige Ground, 1835, Pair 290.00
Garniture, Fruit Pickers, Rococo, Schierholtz, 1900 . . . .   85.00
Garniture Set, Fruit, White, Blue, Egyptian Revival Handles, Gilt Edge, c.1830, 3 Piece .   715.00
Garniture Set & Clock, Louis XVI, Gilt Metal, Putti & Foliate Scrolls, 1900, 3 Piece 805.00
Ginger Jar, Hawthorn Design, Blue, White, Globular, Late 19th Century, 10 1/2 In. 176.00
Group, 4 Figures Of The Seasons, Early 20th Century, Germany, 5 1/2 In. 259.00
Group, Gypsy With Children, Man With Child, Sitzendorf, 7 In., Pair 405.00
Group, Musicians & Child, Polychrome Enamel, Gilt, 10 In. 660.00
Group, Young Man & Woman, 18th Century Clothes, Dresden Style, 12 1/2 In. 130.00
Jar, 3 Ram's-Head Handles, White Glaze, 20 1/2 In. 467.00
Jar, Bird & Flower, Globular Form, 5 1/4 In. 192.00
Jar, Cover, Phoenix Design, Teal, Mauve, 1930s, Pair 115.00
Jar, Overall Multicolored Floral, Mounted As Lamp, 25 1/2 In. 50.00
Jar, Passion Flower Design, Blue & White, 12 1/2 In. 522.00
Jar, Prunus, Crackled Ice Ground, Blue, White, Qing Dynasty, 19th Century, 10 In. 259.00
Jardiniere, French Aesthetic Movement, Dogwood, Insects & Fans, 7 1/2 In., Pair 490.00
Jardiniere, Undertray, Floral Design, Green Ground, China, 15 3/4 x 14 1/4 In. 145.00
Jewelry Casket, Gilt Rocaille, Cobalt Blue Ground, Serpentine, 15 x 5 x 10 In. 5175.00
Loving Cup, Dutch Harbor Scene, Wardle, c.1880, 6 In., Pair 750.00
Mirror, Heart Shape, Applied Flowers & Putti, Germany, c.1870, 14 x 11 In. 850.00
Mug, Puzzle, Hunting Scene With Trees & Animals, Gold, 1860, 6 In. 197.00
Pitcher, Gilt & Painted Floral Design, Green & White Ground, 9 In. 25.00
Pitcher, Gilt Bands & Sprigs, 2 Bouquets, Tucker & Hemphill, 1826, 7 1/2 In. 8625.00
Pitcher, Gilt Bands, Flowering Vine, Tucker & Hemphill, 1832, 9 1/4 In. 6900.00
Pitcher, Lemonade, Lemons, Green Ground, Hand Painted, 6 In. 38.00
Pitcher, Polychrome Design, Foliate Reserves, William Tucker, 1860s, 9 1/4 In. 172.00
Pitcher, White, Applied Lavender Classical Figures, Lion & Unicorn Mark, 11 In. 320.00
Plaque, Cherubs Playing Allegorical Scene, Volkstedt, 1900, 13 x 16 In., Pair 1500.00
Plaque, City Square Scene In Vienna, Squadron Of Soldiers, 6 x 7 In. 7035.00
Plaque, Coastal Landscape Scene, Ebonized Frame, Rudhardt, 6 x 9 3/4 In. 375.00
Plaque, Hound At Hearth, A.J. Keene, 12 x 14 In. 200.00
Plaque, Madonna & Child, Carved & Gilded Florentine Frame, 14 x 7 1/2 In. 385.00
Plaque, Neopolitan Boy, Gilt Scrolled Frame, Oval, Italy, 13 3/4 x 20 1/2 In. 315.00
Plaque, Old Sailor With Pipe, Victorian Frame, 5 In. 115.00
Plaque, Palace & Garden Scene, Figures Strolling Amidst Fountains, 6 x 7 1/2 In. 6040.00
Plaque, Sprite, Hand Painted, Gilt Trim, Frame, 17 x 12 3/4 In., Pair 770.00
Plaque, Virgin Mary, Blue Velvet, Gold Ground, Gilded Frame, 6 x 3 In. 85.00
Plaque, Young Girl Before A Courtyard Wall, Frame, 3 1/2 x 4 1/2 In. 460.00
Plate, Cabinet, Gilt, Woodland Nymphs, Vienna, 1890, 9 3/4 In. 200.00
Plate, Eva, Each Representing Part Of Body, Fornasetti, 12 Piece 4830.00
Plate, Floral & Pictorial Scenes, Blue Crossed Swords, 9 1/2 In. 525.00
Plate, Foliate Scroll Design, Gilt & Green Borders, England, 10 In. 470.00
Plate, Grapes, Gold Border, Artist Georges, Austria, 8 In. 27.00
Plate, Imperial Double-Headed Eagle, Inscription, 1825-1855, Russia, 8 5/8 In. 1035.00
Plate, Mountain Landscape, Blue, White, Kondo USO, Japan, c.1962, 9 1/4 In. 1840.00
Plate, Multicolored Floral Design, Off-White Ground, 8 In., Pair 86.00
Plate, Pink, Orange, Cobalt Blue & Gold, Imari, Samuel Radford, 1890-1910 . . . .   68.00
Plate, Polychrome Floral Design, Gilt, Crossed Swords Mark, 7 3/4 In., 6 Piece 270.00

Plate, Portrait, Ariadne, Signed, Wagner 1495.00
Plate, Wild Turkey, Johnson Bros., 12 Plates, 12 Cups, England 515.00
Platter, Flowers, Basket-Weave Border, Enamel, Austria, 19th Century, 15 In. 345.00
Quill Holder, Overall Multicolored Floral, Yellow Edges, 4 1/8 In. 258.00
Rice Bowl, Blue Fish Design, Brown Glaze, Off-White Ground, 4 1/2 In., 8 Piece 115.00
Sconce, Blue, Gilt, Scrolls, Leaves, Kornilov, Russia, Late 19th Century, 8 In., Pair 3737.00
Sconce, Mirror, 3 Candle Arms, Sitzendorf Mark, Germany, c.1900, 18 In., Pair 1500.00
Tea Set, Red Oriental Transfer, Polychrome Enamel, Child's, 7 Piece 275.00
Tea Set, Sprays Of Flowers, White Reserves, Gilded Border, Gardner, 15 Piece 1725.00
Tea Set, Tete-A-Tete, Painted Flowers, Raised Fruit Reserves, Jacob Petit, 10 Piece 1850.00
Teapot, Allover Landscape Design, Blue, White, 5 1/4 In. 230.00
Teapot, Blue & White, Raised American Eagle, Castleford, England, 5 1/2 In. 385.00
Teapot, Gold Over Cobalt Blue Glaze, Arthur Wood, Boston, 6 1/2 In. 55.00
Teapot, Green, White, Polychrome Flowers, Gilt, 7 3/8 In. 120.00
Teapot, Head With Elephant Nose, Shield-Form Base, Warmer, 9 1/2 In. 1265.00
Teapot, Monkey Form, Monkey Spout, Monkey Handle, Germany, 6 3/4 In. 977.00
Tureen, Sauce, Cover, Polychrome & Gilt, France, 19th Century 358.00
Tureen, Soup, Bombe Shape, Austria, 12 1/2 In. 60.00
Tureen, Soup, Transfer Design, Applied Handles, Large 55.00
Urn, Allegorical Scene, Cobalt & Gilt Ground, Austria, 10 1/2 In. 345.00
Urn, Battle Scenes On Both Sides, Magenta Ground, Germany, 13 In., Pair 1725.00
Urn, Cover, Harbor Scene Front, Floral Spray On Verso, Angular Handles, 16 In., Pair ... 3220.00
Urn, Figural Allegorical Band, Scroll Handles, Jeweled Gilt, Austria, 10 In., Pair 1150.00
Urn, Swirl Design, Multicolored Floral, Bronze, Cobalt Blue Top, France, 16 In., Pair ... 1095.00
Urn, White, Snake Handles, Gilt Trim, Crossed Swords Mark, 11 In., Pair 305.00
Vase, Art Deco, Flowers, Yellow Ground, Gilt Handles, Caroline Yeargain, 7/12/24 ...... 145.00
Vase, Beauty Reserve, Brass Mount, Vienna, 1895-1900, Mounted As Lamp, 12 1/4 In. .. 242.00
Vase, Bee & Dragonfly Design, Faux Wood Brown, Ring Handles, Bretby, 10 In. 110.00
Vase, Birds, Foliage, Blue, White, Continental, 19th Century, 6 In., Pair 140.00
Vase, Blue & White, Floral & Leaf, 14 In. 22.00
Vase, Club Form, Dragon Pursuing Flaming Pearl, Blue, White, 8 3/4 In. 230.00
Vase, Cover, Scenes Of Couples Courting, France, 17 In., Pair 5175.00
Vase, Different Songbirds Amidst Colorful Flowers, Gilt Ball Feet, 5 In., Pair 430.00
Vase, Everted Rim, Lilac Flowers, Leaves, 2 Gilt Handles, 12 In. 60.00
Vase, Floral Garden Scene, Bamboo, Japan, 12 In., Pair 1035.00
Vase, Flower Design, Baluster, Late 19th Century, 14 1/2 In. 132.00
Vase, Meiping Form, Carved Dragon, Flower Design, Blue, Green, 9 1/4 In. 198.00
Vase, Noble Woman In Living Room, Coat Of Arms, Foliate Handles, Yellow, Gilt, 18 In. . 745.00
Vase, Onion Shape, Leaf Design, Locust & Butterfly, Japan, 14 In. 35.00
Vase, Pale Yellow Crackle Glaze, Adelaide Robineau, 1914, 5 In. 4025.00
Vase, Phoenix Design, Black Ground, Baluster, 10 In. 50.00
Vase, Pilgrim Flask Form, Cartouches, Floral Ground, Blue, White, 18 In. 121.00
Vase, Portrait, Brunette Woman, Royal Schwartzberg, 3 In. 150.00
Vase, Rose Celadon, Scholars, Foo Dog Handles, 19th Century, 16 1/2 In. 632.00
Vase, Spill, Flower Shape, With Winged Putti, 9 1/2 In., Pair 155.00
Vase, Spill, Stylized Foliage, Molded Beaded Borders, Puce Ground, England, 6 In. 316.00
Wall Pocket, Dragon's Head, c.1825, 6 x 7 x 8 In. 2500.00
Woodpecker, Pileated, Burgues, 7 1/2 In. 80.00

POSTCARDS were first legally permitted in Austria on October 1, 1869.
The United States passed postal regulations allowing the card in 1872.
Most of the picture postcards collected today date after 1910. The
amount of postage can help to date a card. The rates are: 1872 (1 cent),
1917 (2 cents), 1919 (1 cent), 1925 (2 cents), 1928 (1 cent), 1952 (2
cents), 1959 (3 cents), 1963 (4 cents), 1968 (5 cents), 1973 (8 cents),
1975 (7 cents), 1976 (9 cents), 1978 (10 cents), 1981 (12 cents), 1981
(13 cents), 1985 (14 cents), 1988 (15 cents), 1991 (19 cents), 1995 (20
cents).

3 Telephone Linemen, On Cables Above Street, 2 Smoking, 1 Working, 1911 .... 33.00
4th Of July, Boy With Firecracker, Girl With Flag, Dog Watching 40.00
4th Of July, Miss Columbia, On Liberty Bell, Firecrackers, Embossed 40.00
A Sure Bet, Jeff Jeffries & Jack Johnson, Boxing 220.00
Airship, York Fairgrounds, Photograph, Early 1900s, 3 1/2 x 5 1/2 In. 33.00

Album, Classic Works Of Art, European & American, 240 Piece 16.00
All Lifers, Iowa State Prison, 9 Prisoners, Photograph, 1910 .... 130.00
Allan Lums New Grand East Cafe, Los Angeles, Uncut, 1950s, 8 1/2 x 11 1/2 In. 38.00
American Life & Acc. Ins. Co., Match Cover, 1939 .... 10.00
Apollo 11, Planting Flag On Moon, Color, 3-D, 4 x 6 In. 18.00
Appalachian Exp. Street Scene, Pepsi-Cola Sign 28.00
Appalachian Expo, Pepsi & Expo Signs, Crowd, Horses & Buggies In Street 29.00
Athletic Sports Meet, Old Man, Carrying Torch, Earth, Japan, 1914 .... 100.00
Atomic Bomb Explodes, Mushroom Cloud Yucca Flats, Nev., 1949 .... 17.00
Atoms For Peace Stamp, J.R. Oppenheimer Autograph, 1935 .... 125.00
Auto, Plymouth, 1939, 3 1/2 x 5 1/2 In., 3 Piece 18.00
Ballerina, Charter Yacht, New York Area, Waters Off E. Hampton, L.I., 1950 .... 6.00
Baptist Church, Perry, N.Y., Black & White, 1910 .... 4.00
Barnum & Bailey Circus Fire, Collapsed Tent, Smoke, 1913, H. Berne 68.00
Barnum & Bailey Commissary Wagon, Mailbox On Side, Mailman At Post, c.1912 ..... 67.00
Barometer, Weather-Nose, Novelty, Caricature, Black Boy, Die-Cut Paper 175.00
Belief Me, Jewish Man, Large Diamond, c.1907 .... 45.00
Blatz Beer, Factory Scene, 1920s 18.00
Bonzo, Every Dog Has His Day, With Cigar, Golf Bag, Floating Celluloid Eyes, 1928 ... 27.00
Boy & Girl Dressed U.S. Patriotic Costume, Photograph, John Fasnacht, 1908 .... 300.00
Buffalo Bill, Photograph, Hon. W.F. Cody, Elaborate Saddle, Lariat On Floor 145.00
Buffalo Bill, William F. Cody, Portrait 100.00
Buffalo Courier-Express, Comic Strip Promo, Jolly Junior Sunshine Club, 1934 .... 60.00
Buick Special Sedan, Model 41, Sepia, Linen Paper, c.1938 .... 25.00
Busch Extra Dry Ginger Ale, Horse & Man, Bottle 100.00
C.A. & C. Railroad Depot, Landscape, Howard, Ohio, 1913 .... 30.00
C.A. & C. Railroad Station, Track, Wagons, Mt. Vernon, Ohio 32.00
Canadian Red Cross, They Never Fail You, France 85.00
Cape Cod Canal Dredger, Photograph 35.00
Cherry Smash, Heavily Embossed, 1910-1915 .... 315.00
Christmas Fashions, Purple Design Coat, M. Koehler 175.00
Cleveland & Harrison, GOP Hats, C.H. Tenny, N.Y. City, Order Form Printed Below 125.00
Coke Pepsin Gum, Washington Monument, Richmond, Va., 1908 .... 375.00
Consumers Glue Co, St. Louis, 1927 .... .50
Cracker Jack, Slogan On Banner, Salesmen In Tent, Table With Soda & Ice Blocks 78.00
Dr Pepper Soda Pop, Penny 9.00
Earth From Apollo 8, 5 x 7 1/8 In. 5.00
Easter, Chicks, Embossed, 1908 .... 5.00
Ettor & Giovannitti, Lawrence Textile Strike, IWW Union, Blue & White 325.00
Fashionable Woman, Blue Dress, M. Likure 600.00
Felix The Cat, Outside Window, Ever Heard This One Felix, England, 1924 .... 20.00
Folder, Denver, Colorado, Color Views, 1908, 22 Piece 50.00
Forest Of Kolodesy, Russian Forest, Wrecked Artillery Gun, Germany 5.00
Fredericksburg Brewery Views, San Francisco, California 125.00
Furniture Store Exterior, Owner In Delivery Wagon 44.00
Girl, Holding Teddy Bear Book, Christmas Tree, Photograph, Cushing, Maine, 1908 ..... 125.00
Glenn H. Curtiss & Wm. A. Sunday, Winona Lake, Ind., Photograph 240.00
Golf Scenes, Scotsmen In Kilts, Arbuckle Coffee Co., No. 3, Scotland 43.00
Gordo, Dancing Senorita, Dog & Cat, Gus Arriola, Signed, 1983 .... 41.00
Graham All Steel Lawn Mower, Woman, Pushes Mower, Manad On Back 65.00
Great White Fleet, Flying Homeward-Bound Pennant, Middlesex Co. 45.00
Happy Easter, Gnome & Rabbit, Paint Easter Eggs, Germany 40.00
Head Of Schroon Lake, N.Y., Photography, 1922 .... 6.00
Heart Of Ireland, Embossed, Gold Trim 7.50
Hermann Goering, General Marshall Uniform 10.00
Hold-To-Light, Christmas Angels & Stars, England, 1905 .... 60.00
Hold-To-Light, Dressed Rabbit Family, Painting Easter Eggs 75.00
Hold-To-Light, Happy New Year To You, Boy Making Snowball, 1909 .... 85.00
Hold-To-Light, Lincoln Park Boat Station, Chicago 35.00
Horse Show, Camden, So. Carolina, Woman With Horse 100.00
Ice Cream Wagon, Horse & Driver, W.B. Smith Ice Cream Cones Sign 209.00
Ice Delivery Wagon, Horses, Geo. O. Dilling, Hughesville, Pa., Photograph, 1908 ...... 300.00
Indian, Cowboy Attire, Overalls, Bull Whip, Spurs, 6 Gun 133.00

Indian, John Smith, Age 127, Photograph	45.00
Indian Chief White Dog, Photograph, Glacier National Park	75.00
Indian Cowboy, Bib Overalls, 6-Gun, Bull Whip, Spurs	133.00
Indian Crazy Snake, Assembling His Warriors, Photograph, W.H. Martin, 1909	85.00
Indian Maiden, Ah-Wen-Eyu, J.L. Blessing, Salmanaca, N.Y., 1908	50.00
Is A Caddy Always Necessary, Golfing, T. Earl Christy, 1907	25.00
Italian Pasta Factory, Mickey Mouse	240.00
Jolly Joker's Club, Indigestion, Massachusetts, 1906	75.00
Josephine Baker, Portrait Photograph, D'Ora, Paris	325.00
Judge Roy Bean's Place At Langtry, Tx., The Lippe Studio, Del Rio, Tx., 1900	15.00
Kansas State Capital, Topeka, 1935	.50
King Edward VII, Portrait, On Silk Patch, Sealable Double Fold Letter Card	65.00
Labor Day, Brick Cleaner, Workman, Chipping Bricks, Photo, 1907	35.00
Labor Day, Child Coal Mines Working, Carbon, Pa., Photo, 1907	60.00
Labor Day, Dubols, Pa., Horse Drawn Wagon, Large Lump Of Coal, Photo, 1908	45.00
Labor Day, Model Cigar Factory, Tampa Series, Colorized Photo, Raphel Tuck, 1907	60.00
Labor Day, Reading Pa., People On Street Scene, Photo, 1907	45.00
Labor Day, U.S. Bureau Of Engraving & Print, Photo, 1907	40.00
Labor Day Parade, Sept. 4, 1911, Jackson, Mich., Photo, Color	15.00
Labor Day Souvenir, Man In Overalls, Holding Flag, Holding Sledge Handle, 1907	100.00
Lafayette Square, New Orleans, 1908	.75
Largest Resort Hotel In World, Traymore Hotel, Atlantic City	.75
Leda & Swan, R. Kirchner	175.00
Main Street, Perry, N.Y., Unpaved Street, Autos, Wagons, 1920	3.00
Mauritania	6.00
Mechanical, Beer Stein	100.00
Mechanical, Falstaff Beer, Bottle & Glass	600.00
Michelin Tires, Semelle Michelin, Bibendum Man	100.00
Miss Liberty, Wrapped In Stars & Stripes, Photograph, Rock Island Plow Co.	120.00
Motorcycle Riders, Indian & Harley-Davidson, Photograph, 1920s, 3 1/4 x 5 1/4 In.	35.00
Motorcycle Riders, Man & Woman, European	28.00
Mountain Troops, Austria, 1916	25.00
My Business Is Picking U, Ragpicker, Going Through Trash, Lather	17.00
National Apple Show, Spokane, Washington, Nov. 14 To 19, 1910	65.00
Navajo, Boy, Photograph, E.S. Curtis, Brown & White, 1904	100.00
Navajo, Trading For Indian Blankets, G.M. Harris Curio Co., Denver, Colo.	40.00
New Departure Coaster Brake, Bears Chase Scots Scientist, Bristol, Connecticut	85.00
New East Side Market, Cleveland, Ohio, Trolley Car, 1917	.75
New York City, Skyline, Statue Of Liberty, C.G. Frey, Newark, N.J., 1900	65.00
Newark Pool Table Mfg., Billiard Table, Multicolored	45.00
Night View Of Liberty Bell, Official, 1920s	5.00
Nude Portrait, Silver Bromide Print, Photographer's Name	1312.00
Our Tanks Cross Shisdra, Panzers Fording Soviet River	5.00
Pan American World Airways, Preview Of Tomorrow's Flying Clippers	250.00
Pat Ryan, With 2 Sioux Indians, Studio Pose	100.00
Peerless Steam Plow, Marshal Rask, Snow, Photograph, 1909	100.00

Postcard, Sarah Bernhardt,
A. Mucha

**Never store paper items
with any metal staples or
paper clips. They may rust.**

Postcard, Votes For
Women, L.H. Chamberlin

Postcard, Titanic, White Star Line

Postage stamps or produce seals or other gummed paper pieces that have stuck together can be separated with this simple trick: Put them in a freezer overnight. The glue will loosen.

Promoting Women's Suffrage In Ohio, Poster Style, 1915	900.00
Removing The Hump, Pittsburgh, Pa. Construction Area, 1910-1920	5.00
Santa Claus, Green Robe, Tucks	25.00
Santa Claus, With Tree & Gifts, Pullout Accordion Of Broughty Ferry, England	85.00
Sarah Bernhardt, A. Mucha ....*Illus*	600.00
Shopping Woman, Man, Trottin' Flirt, England	40.00
Signed By Rolling Stones, November 22, 1963, 4 1/2 x 5 1/2 In.	690.00
Sioux, Chief Blackhorn, American Indian Villages, 1935	40.00
Son Lights Candles, Father, Hanukkah Lights, Block Pub. Co., N.Y., Black & White	60.00
Special Thanksgiving Greeting, Woman, Pumpkin Patch, S. Schmucker	100.00
St. Valentine's Greeting, Victorian Woman, Tray Of Fruit, Silk, Winsch	40.00
Steam Shovel, 5 Workers, Posed, Marion Shovel, Model 36	25.00
Sultry Woman Portrait, Rompard, Italy	40.00
Temple EmanuEl, San Francisco, California, Photograph, 1945	35.00
Texaco Station, Mission, 3 Coca-Cola Signs, 2 Gas Pumps, Texaco Star On Post, 1920s	86.00
Thanksgiving, Woman, In Pumpkin Patch, Gold Frame, Embossed, S. Schmucker	100.00
The Sioux, Mother & Child, Photograph, 1930	50.00
Thos. E. Drake Furniture Store, Horse & Wagon, Driver, Drake, Prospect, Oh., 1907	44.00
Thy Will Be Done On Earth As It Is Heaven, Lord's Prayer Series	11.00
Titanic, Black & White, Mailed From Rhode Island June 20, 1912	132.00
Titanic, England	250.00
Titanic, Largest Ship In The World Remembrance, 1912	520.00
Titanic, Successfully Launched May 31st, 1911, Photograph, 1912	800.00
Titanic, White Star Line ....*Illus*	850.00
Tlingit, Man, Portrait, Wearing Fur, Winter A. Pond, Alaska, Mailer Back	120.00
To My Valentine, Victorian Woman, Printed On Silk, Winsch	40.00
Tobacco, Harvesting, Planting, Selling, Tobacco Farm, 1909, 64 Piece	38.00
Tommy Dorsey, Photograph, King Liberty Trombone, H.N. White Company, Cleveland	45.00
TWA Superjet, Plane In Flight, Color, 1960s, 3 1/2 x 5 1/2 In.	5.00
U.S. Post Office Department, Train Picture, 1887, 2 Sides	200.00
Uncle Sam, With Child, Photograph	150.00
Valentine, Woman Swinging Golf Club, 1911 Postmark	17.00
Varga Girl, Esquire Pilgrim & Senorita, 1941, 4 1/2 x 7 In.	25.00
Veterans, Massacre Canyon Battle, Sioux Chiefs, Others, 1 Child, August 5, 1873	91.00
Votes For Women, L.H. Chamberlain ....*Illus*	125.00
Wagon, W.B. Smith Ice Cream Cones	209.00
Wall Street, New York City, Photograph, Thaddeus Wilkerson	75.00
Warrior & Squaw, Chilkat, Alaska, Photograph, Shortridges, 1912	60.00
Waverly Cycles, Artist Mucha	8500.00
Weber Spittoon, Office Girl Likes New Model, Photograph, Lee S. Smith, 1910	195.00
White Star Line	12.00
Wilbur Wright, In His Aeroplane	563.00
Wild Bill Hickok's Tombstone & Grave, Tombstone Of Calamity Jane	15.00
Woman, Large Hat, Sepia, Otto Schilbad, Germany	25.00
Woman & Cat, A. Munzer	200.00
Woodland Lodge No. 496, Boiler Makers Inter. Soc. Of America, Photo, 1907	60.00
Yankee Clipper Takeoff, LaGuardia Field, New York City, Photograph, 1942	75.00
Young Woman Answers Telephone, Seattle Commercial School, Photograph	40.00
Yukon Prospector, Young Man, Pipe & Backpack, Winchester Rifle	82.00

POSTERS have informed the public about news and entertainment events since ancient times. Nineteenth-century advertising or theatrical posters and twentieth-century movie and war posters are of special interest today. The price is determined by the artist, the condition, and the rarity. Other posters may be listed under Movie, Political, and World War I and II.

2 Children Observing Toy Parade With Lunch, France, 1900, 51 x 38 In.	2070.00
Air France, West Africa, Elephants, 1930, 24 1/2 x 39 1/4 In.	975.00
Alexander, The Man Who Knows, Man In Turban, 1915-1920, 41 x 24 In.	335.00
Alexander Magic, The Man Who Knows, c.1915, Three Sheet, 41 x 81 In.	523.00
Annie Oakley, Swinging Lasso, Cloth, Full Color, 1920s, 20 1/2 x 21 In.	60.00
Anti-Semitic, When Jews Laugh, People Laughing Montage, 12 x 17 In.	645.00
Apollo, NASA, Man On The Moon, 1969, 17 x 23 In.	10.00
Are Ghosts Real, Thurston Mysteries, Performed By Will Rock, 41 x 27 In.	880.00
Beach Boys, Endless Summer, Capitol Records, 1974, 26 1/2 x 36 1/2 In.	125.00
Bernardi Greater Shows, Trained Wild Animal Exhibition, Color, 1920s, 28 x 41 In.	600.00
Billy Rice & Hooley's Minstrels, Chatterton Opera House, Stone Litho, 15 x 18 In.	70.00
Billy Rose's Aquacade, Great Lakes Exposition, Cleveland, Fanny Brice, 40 x 28 In.	2600.00
Buffalo Bill Original Wild West, Circus, Indian Shooting, 40 x 28 In.	10925.00
Buffalo Bill's Wild West, Rough Riders, 23 1/2 x 19 In.	2200.00
Buffalo Ranch Real Wild West Show, Stone Lithograph, 1910, 24 x 56 In.	2000.00
Cacao Lacter, L. Lafevre, Unframed, c.1890, 48 1/4 x 34 1/4 In.	1035.00
Carter The Great, Carter Rides A Camel, Stone Lithograph, 1926-1928, 41 x 27 In.	1610.00
Carter The Great, Magician & Devil Playing Cards, c.1920, 13 1/2 x 21 1/4 In.	100.00
Carter The Great, Modern Priestess Of Delphi, Stone Litho, 1926-1928, Three Sheet	1120.00
Chained For Life, Hilton Sisters, Siamese Twins, Color, 1950, 40 x 60 In.	400.00
Chap-Book, Woman, Walking Woods, Ice Skates, Will H. Bradley, 19 3/4 x 14 In.	2185.00
Cheating The Gallows, Mirgil Magic, 1940s, 41 x 28 In.	280.00
Christiani Bros., 3-Ring Circus, Wild Animal, Dogs, Horses, Wilmington, 1950s	80.00
Circus Scene, Equestrian Performance, Creber, Unframed, c.1890, 42 x 28 In.	1380.00
Cole Bros. Big RR Circus, Color, 1930s, 16 x 28 In.	250.00
Cole Bros. Circus, Full Color, 1930s, 22 x 28 In.	200.00
Cycles & Automobiles Clement, R. Leverd, c.1905, 46 x 62 In.	1840.00
Cycles La Francaise, Paul Dupont, Unframed, 1900, 55 1/2 x 39 1/2 In.	745.00
Cycles Roachet, Chaix, Unframed, c.1890, 48 1/2 x 34 3/4 In.	517.00
Dejeuner Sur L'Yerbe, Paul Wunderlich, Signed, 1977, 26 x 36 1/2 In.	230.00
Delahaye, Les Qualites De Le Race, Lithograph, Black & Red, c.1925, 63 x 47 In.	2530.00
Deuxieme Salon Du Cycle, Jules Forain, 1894, 38 1/2 x 78 In.	3737.00
Elks Circus, B.P.O. Elks Lodge No. 794, Majestic Poster Press, 42 x 28 In.	35.00
ES Cycles Olympique, Rene Walch, Unframed, 1924, 61 1/2 x 45 In.	2195.00
Folies-Bergere, Phryne, Ballet, Charles Lucas, 24 x 63 In.	805.00
Folies-Bergere, Tous Les Soirs, La Cavalier, Jean De Paleologue, 34 x 48 In.	1725.00
Frank Buck In Jungle Terror, Tigers, Backed, 1940s, 28 x 41 In.	300.00
G.I., Modern Joe & Scenes, Hasbro, 1988, 23 1/2 x 35 In.	40.00
George, Supreme Master Of Magic, Car Load Of Scenic Effects, 41 x 27 In.	440.00
George Supreme Master Of Magic, Stone Lithograph, Backed, 1917, 28 x 41 In.	550.00
Gondoliers, Theater, Woman & Flowers, 1920s, 20 x 30 In.	125.00
Great Chang & Fak-Hong's Oriental Review, 1925-1929, 28 x 22 In.	205.00
Great Levante, Bats, Devils, Owls & Witches, England, 28 x 18 5/8 In.	460.00
Grosser Festzug, Night Cityscape, 1912, 18 x 25 In.	375.00
Grow Your Own, Can Your Own, Office Of War, 1943, 22 1/2 x 16 In.	49.00
International Air Races, St. Louis, 4-Color, Paper, 1923, 14 x 22 In.	350.00
International Air Races, St. Louis, Bi-Planes, 1923, 14 x 12 In.	400.00
Ireland Welcomes You, Ireland's Transport Co., Smiling Sun, c.1958, 24 x 39 In.	150.00
Irish Airlines, Ireland, Horse, Wagon Rural Scene, 25 x 39 3/4 In.	575.00
Join The United States School Garden Army, Girl Behind Tiller	2070.00
Joseph Beuys, In Memoriam, Andy Warhol, Silkscreen Colors, Signed, 32 x 24 In.	175.00
Jungle Terror, Frank Buck, 1940s, 41 x 28 In.	200.00
Kar-Mi, Buried Alive For 32 Days, Lithograph On Linen, 78 1/2 x 41 In.	1380.00
Kar-Mi, Performing The Most Startling Mystery Of All India, c.1914, 41 x 27 In.	275.00
Kar-Mi, Selma, Performing Most Startling Mystery Of All India, 1914, One Sheet	970.00
Kar-Mi, Swallows A Loaded Gun Barrel, c.1914, 41 x 27 In.	303.00

Karl, Magician, Stone Lithograph, Backed, 1910, 20 x 30 In. 750.00
Kodak, R. Lelong, 57 1/2 x 37 1/2 In. 1610.00
La Fiesta De Los Angeles, Early Street Fair, 3-Color, Cardboard, 1930s, 22 x 26 In. 175.00
La Moto Peugeot, C. Faire, Unframed, c.1928, 47 1/4 x 31 1/2 In. 557.00
Lectures On Phrenology From Phrenological Magazine, 19th Century, 29 x 19 In. 805.00
Leland McNamee's Minstrels, Cardboard, 80 x 41 In. 330.00
Les Lions Du Nouveau Cirque, Canvas, France, 27 x 41 In. 275.00
Man On Highwheeler, Boy On Bike, Girl On Scooter, 1940, 30 x 20 In. 120.00
Martha's Vineyard, Cottage City, Oak Bluffs, Summer, 1887, Frame, 27 1/2 x 17 In. 448.00
Maserati, Showroom, 1972, 1973, 37 x 24 In. 95.00
Meeting D'Aviation, Nice, Man In Plane, Over Cote D'Azur, 42 x 30 In. 3910.00
Mexico, Volcan Paricutin, Volcano, 1945, 27 x 37 In. 1495.00
Minnesota State Fair & Expo, Red, Black, 1915, 28 x 41 In. 250.00
Montana Frank And His Famous Miles City Roundup, Cowgirl, Steer, 28 x 42 In. 1210.00
Narragansett Park, Horse Racing 250.00
New York Journal, Colored Comic Supplement, Oct. 18th, 1894, Yellow Kid 1035.00
Norway, Land Of Midnight Sun, Puffins & Dolphins Cavort, c.1948, 24 x 37 In. 110.00
Olson Shows, Carnival, 1950s, 28 x 41 In. 150.00
On The Stroke Of Twelve, Matted, Frame, U.S. Printing Co., 1899, 32 x 24 1/2 In. 205.00
Orient Line Cruises, Venice, San Marco Piazza, 25 x 40 In. 450.00
Pan American Glasgow By Clipper, Irish Dancer, 1951, 28 x 42 In. 375.00
Pan American World Airways, Fly To Mexico By Clipper, 28 x 42 In. 460.00
Pantomomes Lumineuses, Theatre Optique De E. Reynaud, Jules Cheret, 33 x 37 In. 1150.00
Peace Sign, Psychedelic Pink, Blue, Silk Screen, Gemini Rising Inc., 23 x 35 In. . . . .55.00 to 60.00
Playbill, Blacksom & Burns, Stone Lithograph, 1880s, 50 x 30 In. 605.00
Plaza De Acho, Monumental, Bullfighting, Canvas, Spain, 1928, 96 x 47 In. 358.00
Polack Bros. Circus, Clown & Horse Act, 1940s, 28 x 41 In. 150.00
Ringling Bros. & Barnum & Bailey Circus, Celebrated Repenski Family, Frame, 17 x 9 Ft.   385.00
Ringling Bros. & Barnum & Bailey Circus, Clown, 20 1/2 x 28 In. 35.00
Ringling Bros. & Barnum & Bailey, Gargantua The Great Ape, 17 x 24 In. 65.00
Ringling Bros. & Barnum & Bailey, Lion Tamer, Erie Lithograph, 17 x 24 In. 195.00
Ringling-Barnum-Bailey Circus, Charging Lion & Tiger, 1940s, 28 x 41 In. 175.00
Sells-Floto Circus, Buffalo Bill Wild West, 1914, 26 x 38 3/4 In.   3910.00
Sesquicentennial Expo, Philadelphia, 1926, Voice Of Liberty Bell, Linen 450.00
Sinatra, Nat King Cole, Judy Garland, Tennessee Ernie, Old Capitol Record, 41 x 57 In. .   145.00
Smokey Bear, 1950s, 26 x 20 In. 65.00
Smokey Bear, South Carolina State Commission Of Forestry, 1948, 11 x 21 In. 45.00
Smokey's Rules, Fire Prevention, Paper, 1961, 13 x 18 In. 35.00
Steamboat, Hudson River, Albany, Ohio, North America, 19th Century, 12 x 8 In., Pair . .   935.00
Telephone Evolution, 30 Pictures, Beginning 1876, Updates, Innovation, 20 x 24 In. 8.95
Territ & Co., Cycles-Motorcyclettes, Tamagno, Unframed, c.1890, 55 1/4 x 39 1/2 In. . . .   1380.00
The Great Virgil, Magician, 3 Sheets, Color, 1940s, 40 x 80 In., 2 Pieces 375.00
Thurston, Great Magician, Do The Spirits Come Back, 41 x 27 In. 5315.00
Thurston, World's Famous Magician, Portrait, Devils On Shoulders, 28 x 22 In. 2015.00
Toros En Sevilla, Bullfighting, Canvas, Spain, 95 x 46 In. 385.00
Travel, Cannes, c.1925, 33 1/2 x 46 In. 1500.00
TWA Hostesses, Flown Over 1/4 Million Miles, Timely Events, June 10, 1938, 17 In. 28.00
U.S. Army Builds Men, Musicians, Red, White, Black, 1924, 24 x 29 In. 175.00
Uncle Tom's Cabin, Black Man With White Hair, Plastic Frame, 89 1/2 x 41 In. 825.00
Vermont Ski Area, Flexible Flyer Skis, 37 1/4 x 23 3/4 In. 4140.00
Viola Clifton's Female Minstrels, Matted, 19th Century, 21 x 16 In. 88.00
Virgil, 5 Year World Tour, Evening Of Enchantment, Panel, Frame, 15 x 33 In. 220.00
Virgil, World Famous Magician, Indian Rope Trick, Panel 180.00
Virgil, World Famous Magician, Mystery Of The Jungle, 41 x 27 In. 465.00
Visit India, W.W. Byltylis, c.1920, 39 1/4 x 24 3/4 In. 400.00
Wanted, John Herbert Dillinger, 1934, 16 x 9 In. 695.00
Wanted By FBI, John Edward Summers, Murderer & Auto Thief, 1949 . . . .   35.00
We Want Your Kitchen Waste, Pig Food, British, Unframed, 22 1/4 x 14 3/4 In. 230.00
White Star To New York, Olympic, Red, White & Blue, 1920, 40 x 25 In. 3910.00
You Can Help, Red Cross, W.T. Benda, Unframed, 29 3/4 x 20 In. 115.00
Zamloch, Most Marvelous Of Conjurers, Broadside, Mid To Late 1800s 145.00

POTLIDS are just that, lids for pots. Transfer-printed potlids had their heyday from the 1840s to the early 1900s. The English Staffordshire potteries made ceramic containers with decorative lids for bear's grease, shrimp or meat paste, cold cream, and toothpaste. Printed advertising and pictures of historical events, portraits of famous people, or scenic views were designed in black and white or color. Reproductions have been made.

American Dentifrice, C.R. Coffin, Stencil, With Base	70.00
Bear Climbing Pole, Circus, England	130.00
Cold Cream Of Roses, Caswell Massey & Co., White, Red Transfer, 2 1/2 In.	170.00
Crystal Palace, New York, England, 1853, 5 1/8 In.	1045.00
Danson's Eye Salve, London, Stenciled, Monochrome, 2 1/4 In.	90.00
Eugene Roussel Odontine Or Rose Tooth Paste, Black Transfer, Square, 2 3/4 In.	90.00
French Street Scene, 4 In.	130.00
Genuine Beef Marrow, Pomatum, X. Bazin, White, Black Transfer, 3 1/8 In.	145.00
H.P. Wakelee Druggist, Genuine Bear's Grease, White, Multicolored Transfer, 3 In.	1540.00
Hill's Horehound & Irish Moss For Coughs & Colds, Green Transfer, 2 1/8 In.	35.00
Landing The Fare Pegwell Bay, Man Carrying Woman From Ship, Wood Frame, 4 In.	120.00
Peace, 4 In.	130.00
Taylor's Saponaceous Compound, Man Shaving, Black Transfer, 3 3/4 In.	305.00 to 415.00
The Enthusiast, 4 In.	130.00
Village Wedding, 4 In.	187.00
Woods Areca Nut Toothpaste, Plymouth, Black & White Stencil	25.00
Worsley, Wholesale Perfumer, Philadelphia, Capitol At Washington, 3 1/2 In.	605.00

POTTERY and porcelain are different. Pottery is opaque; you can't see through it. Porcelain is translucent. If you hold a porcelain dish in front of a strong light, you will see the light through the dish. Porcelain is colder to the touch. Pottery is softer and easier to break and will stain more easily because it is porous. Porcelain is thinner, lighter, and more durable. Majolica, faience, and stoneware are all pottery. Additional pieces of pottery are listed in this book in the Art Pottery category and under the factory name. For information about pottery makers and marks, see *Kovels' Dictionary of Marks—Pottery & Porcelain: 1650–1850* and *Kovels' New Dictionary of Marks—Pottery & Porcelain: 1850 to the Present.*

Ashtray, Yantra, Geometric, Mauve Glaze, Ettore Sottsass, 6 x 4 x 3 In.	220.00
Beaker, Band Of Flowers, Leaves, Brown, Blue Ground, Marked, Swansea, 1809, 5 In.	862.00
Beaker, Flower Spray, Lace Pattern Border, Footed, Swansea, 1840, 4 3/8 In.	241.00
Bottle, Brown & Beige Mottled, Iga Ware, Flared Neck, Edo Period, Japan, 5 7/8 In.	230.00
Bottle, Buff, Tan, Brown, Square, Shoji Hamada, Japan, c.1961, 3 7/8 x 9 In.	5175.00
Bottle, Bulbous, Incised Banded Design, Brown & Black Mottled, Koishibara, 9 3/8 In.	175.00
Bottle, Figural, Pig With Pipe, 7 In.	835.00
Bottle, Saki, Tamba Ware, Bulbous, Narrow Neck, Brown, Beige, Japan, 9 3/4 In.	145.00
Bottle, Turquoise, Mottled, Semicrystalline Glaze, Flared Lip, Signed, Natzler, 8 1/2 In.	2640.00
Bottle, Volcanic Green, Mauve Luster, Signed, Beato, 16 In.	5225.00
Bottle, Yellow, Orange, Ivory Volcanic Glaze, Signed, Fantoni For Raymor, 12 1/2 In.	247.00
Bowl, Abstract Design Center, Oatmeal Glaze, Green, Black, Peter Voulkos, 8 In.	1100.00
Bowl, Abstract Design, Brown, Black, Flared, Square, Shoji Hamada, 11 1/2 x 2 1/2 In.	2300.00
Bowl, Abstract Woman, Leather Back, Free-Form, Illegible Inscription, Fantoni, 9 In.	115.00
Bowl, Apple Blossom & Branch Design, Square, Sakura, Japan, c.1961, 9 3/4 x 1 In.	345.00
Bowl, Beige Glaze, Flared, Round, Yi Dynasty, Korea, 5 3/4 x 3 1/4 In.	230.00
Bowl, Blue & White Drip, Scroll Handles, Betty Woodman, 7 x 12 In.	190.00
Bowl, Bright Yellow Hare's Fur Glaze, 4 Sides, Dimpled, Signed, Natzler, 4 x 5 In.	2860.00
Bowl, Broad, Metallic Silver Finish, Tan, Khaki Ground, Scheier, 3 x 5 1/2 In.	220.00
Bowl, Brown & Pale Green Glaze, Flared, Ring Foot, Yi Dynasty, Korea, 8 x 3 1/2 In.	145.00
Bowl, Candy Apple Green Glaze, Folded Form, Signed, Natzler, 5 1/2 x 2 In.	1100.00
Bowl, Cereal, Snoopy, Dancing, White, Yellow Ground, Iroquois, 1968, 7 In.	25.00
Bowl, Chartreuse Glaze, Shallow, Flared, Signed, Natzler, 8 1/2 In.	3850.00
Bowl, Cover, 2 Figures Of Cupid, Puce Brown, Footed, Swansea, 1819, 4 In.	529.00
Bowl, Cover, Brown, Tan, Pierced Pedestal Base, Round, Silla Dynasty, Korea, 6 In.	115.00
Bowl, Cover, Footed, Bulbous, Pierced Pedestal Base, Korea, Silla Dynasty, 4 3/8 In.	160.00

Bowl, Deep Blue Nocturne Glaze, Black, Blue, Signed, Natzler, 6 x 2 In. 1760.00
Bowl, Floral Design, Turquoise Glaze, Fish Interior, Persia, 8 1/2 In. 259.00
Bowl, Flower & Leaf, Cream Ground, Box, Kensan, 18th Century, 10 In. 480.00
Bowl, Footed, Pierced Pedestal Base, Korea, Silla Dynasty, Round, 5 In. 105.00
Bowl, Geometric & Dot Design, Bulbous, Ring Foot, Yi Dynasty, Korea, 6 x 4 In. 375.00
Bowl, Glazes In Black, Tan & Iron Red, Cream Ground, Picasso, 1955, 10 In. 2300.00
Bowl, Gold & Platinum Metallic Glaze Over Yellow, Beatrice Wood, 9 In. 1650.00
Bowl, Green, Brown Crystalline Matte Glaze, Natzler, 5 1/2 x 2 1/2 In. 1760.00
Bowl, Incised Floral Design, Buff Clay, George & Mary Edington, 1756, 10 3/4 In. 300.00
Bowl, Mahogany Flambe, Ocher, Swirled Interior, Open Flared, Scheier, 3 x 7 In. 275.00
Bowl, Mauve, Gilt Rim, White, Swansea, 1809, 7 1/4 In. 632.00
Bowl, Mottled Beige Glaze, Flared, Ring Foot, Yi Dynasty, Korea, 7 1/4 x 3 1/4 In. 175.00
Bowl, Multicolored Geometric & Floral, Beige Ground, Flared, Morocco, 10 3/4 In. 230.00
Bowl, Orange, Red, Black Glaze, Footed, Natzler, 6 1/2 x 2 1/2 In. 1980.00
Bowl, Pebbled Celadon, Irregular Rim, 6 1/4 In. 390.00
Bowl, Periwinkle Blue, Lavender Glaze, Deep Brown, Footed, Scheier, 4 1/2 x 6 In. 220.00
Bowl, Red Brown Glaze, Handles, North Carolina, 13 x 18 In. 55.00
Bowl, Screen Printed Face & Hand, Cylindrical, Shallow, Signed, Fornasetti, Milan, 5 In. .   288.00
Bowl, Sgraffito Woman, Leather Backed, Fantoni, Shallow, 10 3/4 In. . . . .*Illus*   10.00
Bowl, Verdigris & Purple Volcanic Glaze, Footed, Signed, Natzler, 6 1/2 In. 3575.00
Bowl, White, Arabia, Square, 4 Inverted Pyramids, Kaj Franck, Finland, 1966, 9 1/2 In. . .   230.00
Bowl, Yellow High Glaze, Charcoal Highlights, Natzler, 4 1/2 x 2 In. 660.00
Box, Cover, Floral Design Around Box, Turquoise Glaze, Persia, 4 3/4 In. 144.00
Breakfast Set, Mottled Yellow, Teapot, Signed, Beato, 1950s, 9 Piece 4400.00
Bulb Pot, Square Tapering Form, Painted Rose Spray, Gilt Foliage, 4 1/2 In., Pair 115.00
Butter Pot, Celadon Style Alkaline Glaze, T.M. Chandler, 1850s 6160.00
Charger, Glazed, Blue, Green, White, Middle Eastern, 12 1/2 In.   250.00
Charger, Man & Plow, Verse, 4 Colors, Hendrick Murmans, 1716, 18 In. 7700.00
Charger, People In Blue Design, Salvador Meli, 1950, 21 In. 2530.00
Clock, Mantel, 2 Vases, Airbrushed Geometric, Black, Brown, Ivory, Germany, 9 In. 550.00
Compote, Pine Needles, Pinecones Interior, G. Stickley, Onandaga, 9 x 4 1/2 In. 1760.00
Cookie Jar, Cottage, Swing Handle, Pottery, England, 6 1/2 In. 50.00
Cradle, Deep Yellow Glaze, 4 5/8 In. 300.00
Creamer, Raised Animal Design, White, Blue, 3 1/2 In. 30.00
Crock, Cobalt Blue Stylized Flower, Pfaltzgraff, 2 Gal. 84.00
Cup, Bullwinkle & Rocky, White, Brown, Yellow, P.A.T. Ward Prod. Inc., 1960s, 3 In. . . .   55.00
Cup & Saucer, Cabinet, Blue Bell Flowers, Green, Gilt Foliate, Serpent Handle, Swansea .   287.00
Dinner Service, Silver Luster Band, Round Well, Rectangular, Jean Luce, 14 Piece 690.00
Dish, Altar, Off-White, Hexagonal Pedestal Base, Round, Korea, Yi Dynasty, 7 In. 220.00
Dish, Brown, Fruiting Vine Border, Enamel, Shell Shape, Swansea, 1806, 8 1/4 In. . . . . . :   575.00
Dish, Buff, Brown & Tan Geometric Glaze, Shoji Hamada, Japan, 7 1/4 In. 1440.00
Dish, Dresser, Rose On Cover, Black, Chartreuse, California, 4 1/2 x 3 1/2 In. . . . . . .*Illus*   30.00
Dish, Floral, Geometric, Brown, Buff, Round, Mino District, Momoyama Period, 4 3/4 In.   315.00
Dish, Purple, White, Gilt Rim, Swansea, 1809, 10 5/8 In. 598.00
Dish, Screen Printed Woman, Rectangular, Shallow, Signed, Fornasetti, Milan, 5 1/2 In. . .   115.00
Figurine, Bird, Green Glaze, 8 3/4 In. 86.00

Pottery, Bowl,
Sgraffito Woman,
Leather Backed,
Fantoni, Shallow,
10 3/4 In.

Pottery, Dish, Dresser, Rose On Cover,
Black, Chartreuse, California, 4 1/2 x 3 1/2 In.

Figurine, Cat, Black & White, Italy, 14 1/4 In. 50.00
Figurine, Dog, Seated, Buff Clay, Variegated Brown Glaze, Black Highlights, 8 In. 495.00
Figurine, Emma, Reclining Woman, Blue Dress, Lisa Larsen, Sweden, 6 In. 86.00
Figurine, Fish, Teal Blue, Green Black, On Iron Stand, Carl Walters, 1930, 24 In. 4600.00
Figurine, Flamingo, Pink, Green, 8 In. 25.00
Figurine, Lion, Buff Color, Green White Glaze, Rectangular Base, Ohio, 9 1/2 In. 710.00
Figurine, Lion, Oval Base, Amber Glaze, Ohio White Clay, 6 In., Pair 715.00
Figurine, Man, Dancing, Han Dynasty, 14 1/2 In. 690.00
Figurine, Snoopy On Doghouse, I'm Allergic To Morning, 4 1/2 x 3 In. 40.00
Figurine, Squirrel, Standing, Nut, Santa Clara, 3 3/4 In. 125.00
Figurine, Woman Equestrienne, Seated, Rearing Horse, Rectangular Base, 2 Piece 2590.00
Figurine, Woman With Sunhat, Sweeping Skirt, White, Art Deco, Japan, 7 1/4 In. 45.00
Flowerpot, Saucer, Manganese Splotches, Yellow Glaze, 7 x 7 In. 275.00
Humidor, Cover, Cafe-Au-Lait Crystalline Glaze, California, 6 1/4 x 5 3/4 In. 990.00
Humidor, Drinking Man, On Lid, Barrel Shape, Molded, 8 In. 55.00
Humidor, Head, Black Man With Pipe, 4 3/4 In. 350.00
Humidor, Owl, Cobalt Blue, Yellow & Brown, High Glaze, 7 In. 350.00
Jar, Cover, Brown & Tan Glaze, Bulbous, Koishibara, Japan, c.1960, 6 1/2 In. 275.00
Jar, Cover, Painted Blue Flowers, Chinese-Style, Gilt Edge, Charlotte Rhead, 6 3/4 In. ... 110.00
Jar, Cover, Pierced Ring Foot, Brown, Buff, Bulbous, Korea, Silla Dynasty, 3 1/2 In. 115.00
Jar, Cover, Tobacco, Backer & Kern, Winchester 1500.00
Jar, Incised Wavy Banded Design, Bulbous, Round, Silla Dynasty, Korea, 5 x 6 In. 145.00 to 205.00
Jar, Multicolored Floral Glaze, Rectangular, Kawai Takaichi, Japan, 6 3/4 In. 315.00
Jar, Round, Brown & Tan Glaze, Loop Handles, Sawankalok, Siam, 4 3/8 x 2 1/2 In. 80.00
Jar, Storage, French Provincial, Ribbed Design, 1880, 36 1/2 In. 305.00
Jar, Storage, French Provincial, Ribbed Design, 3 Handles, 1880, 38 1/2 In. 575.00
Jar, Water, Stylized View Of Mount Fuji, Gray Ground, 7 1/4 In. 362.00
Jardiniere, Sponged Brown & Green On Ivory, Pierced Ovals, Woodman, 7 1/2 In. 605.00
Jug, Faint Leaf Design, Blue Slip, Pfaltzgraff, 12 In. 132.00
Jug, Grotesque, Blue & White Eyes, Green Ash Glaze, B.B.C., 12 1/2 In. 385.00
Jug, Grotesque, Bulging Eyes, Green Ash Glaze, Steve Abee, Lenoir, N.C., 12 1/2 In. 220.00
Jug, Grotesque, Double-Faced Devil, Horns, Green Ash Glaze, Lanier Meaders, 8 1/2 In. . 4180.00
Jug, Grotesque, Green Ash Glaze, A.G. Meaders, 6 1/4 In. 165.00
Jug, Grotesque, Stone Teeth, Green Ash Glaze, Lanier Meaders, 10 In. 1980.00
Jug, Red Clay, Brown Slip, Stenciled Label, Little Brown Jug, 1860, 7 1/2 In. 165.00
Jug, Rolled Clay Eyes & Teeth, Lanier Meaders, 1977, 10 1/4 In. 1155.00
Jug, Santa Claus Face, Incised Eyebrows, Beard & Moustache, Jerry Brown 192.00
Lamp Base, Peering Faces, Repeating, Deep Brown, Chartreuse, Scheier, 19 In. 770.00
Pan, Milk, Slipware, 3-Color Design, Brown, Green & White, 4 x 13 In. 275.00
Pitcher, Blue Embossed Flower, Gray & Brown Salt Glaze, Crolius Pottery, 6 3/4 In. 30.00
Pitcher, Blue Floral Design, Gray Ground, Continental, 7 1/2 In. 55.00
Pitcher, Design, Sonner Strasburg 2000.00
Pitcher, Floral, Military Man Portrait, White Ship, Continental, 12 1/4 In. 250.00
Pitcher, Japonesque, Painted Gold Bamboo & Birds, 6 x 8 In. 25.00
Pitcher, Milk, Figural, Mutt From Mutt & Jeff Comic Strip, 1930s, 6 In. 165.00
Pitcher, Multiglaze, Straight Sides, Strasburg 1750.00
Planter, Fawn, Figural, 5 1/2 In. 11.00
Planter, Prayer Lady, Yellow, Enesco 225.00
Planter, Rabbit Peering Over Tree Stump, Green, 6 x 5 In. 25.00
Planter, Relief Floral & Fruit Design, Oval, Italy, 15 x 6 In. 35.00
Plaque, Allegorical, Figures Of Day & Night, Frame, 6 In., Pair 175.00
Plaque, Gazelles, Mongooses, Floral Design, Turquoise Ground, Oval, Persia, 9 1/2 In. .. 201.00
Plaque, Screen Printed Changing Faces, Signed, Fornasetti, Milan, 5 1/2 In., Pair 230.00
Plate, Abstract Image Of Woman, Blue & Brown, Rectangular, Fantoni, 8 x 4 In. 58.00
Plate, Botanical Speciman Figure, Chocolate Brown Line Rim, White, Swansea, 7 In. ... 391.00
Plate, Bouquet Of Flowers, Gilt Rim, Swansea, 1926, 8 In. 322.00
Plate, Brown, Buff & Tan Glaze, Round, Flared, Shima Oka, Japan, 8 In. 405.00
Plate, Crest Of Bull's Head, Narrow Blue Ground Border, Swansea, 1805, 8 1/4 In. 299.00
Plate, Dessert, Country House, Fruiting Vine Border, Brown Enamel, Swansea, 1806 .... 598.00
Plate, Gilt Peonies Amongst Foliage, Pink, Seeded Green Ground, Swansea, 9 In. 310.00
Plate, Horse Eye Design, Brown & Buff Glaze, Japan, 10 In. 430.00
Plate, Incised White Cottage, Yellow Skyline, 1922, 6 1/2 In. 550.00
Plate, Screen Printed Chess Pieces, Signed, Fornasetti, Milan, 6 In. 173.00

Never put a collector plate in a
dishwasher or microwave oven. The
glaze may be damaged.

Silver and gold trim will wash off
dishes in time. Do not unload any
dishes with metallic trim until they
have completely cooled.

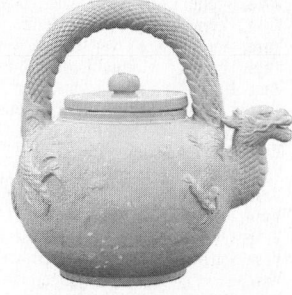

Pottery, Teapot, Figural Dragon Handle
& Spout, Unglazed, Yixing Type

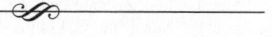

Plate, Screen Printed Currency Notes, Signed, Fornasetti, Milan, 5 1/2 In., Pair	288.00
Plate, Screen Printed Stylized Sun, Square, Signed, Fornasetti, Milan, 5 In.	230.00
Plate, Yellow, White, Gilt Rim, Swansea, 1809, 7 1/4 In.	253.00
Pot, Buff Clay, Light Green, Brown Sponging, Handle & Spout, Virginia, 4 3/4 In.	165.00
Sugar & Creamer, Handle, Red Brown, Ocher Ground, Scheier, 4 x 3 1/2 In.	110.00
Tankard, Vine, Pink Roses, Oval Portrait, Gentleman, Carousing, Swansea, 1809, 6 In. ...	414.00
Tea Bowl, Brown & Tan Glaze, Footed, Shoji Hamada, Japan, 5 1/8 x 3 5/8 In.	2070.00
Tea Bowl, Buff Glaze, Flared, Ring Foot, Round, Rakusan Yaki, c.1962, 5 3/4 In.	230.00
Tea Bowl, Mottled Buff Brown, Flared, Ring Foot, Round, Japan, c.1900, 5 3/4 In.	200.00
Teapot, Cover, Acanthus Everted Rim, Rural Landscape, London Shape, Swansea, 1817 .	460.00
Teapot, Cover, Bamboo Shape, Branch Handle, Late 19th Century, 5 In.	165.00
Teapot, Cover, Red, Brown, Peach Shape, Branch Handle, 19th Century, 6 In.	220.00
Teapot, Cover, Red, Brown, Peach Shape, Leaf Branch Handle, 19th Century, 4 3/4 In. ..	220.00
Teapot, Figural Dragon Handle & Spout, Unglazed, Yixing Type ....*Illus*	95.00
Teapot, Mandarin, Oriental Figures Meeting Beside A Lake, Black, Swansea, 6 In.	2760.00
Teapot, Peacock Design, Fireproof Made In Germany, 6 1/2 In.	120.00
Teapot, Red, Bamboo Shape, Branch Handle, 1900, 4 In.	110.00
Teapot, Red, Brown, Melon Shape, Vine Spout, Handle, Late 19th Century, 5 1/2 In.	220.00
Teapot, Scoddleware, 2 Spout, Metal Lid, Ettle From M.S. Sept 5, 1903, 7 1/2 In.	90.00
Teapot, Tree Trunk Shape, Branch Handle, 19th Century, 7 1/2 In.	154.00
Tray, Enameled, George Briard	60.00
Tureen, Cauliflower, Cover, White Cauliflower Head, Green Leaves, 6 In.	3162.00
Tureen, Cover, Mottled Brown, Handled Metal Cover, Scrolled Handles, 9 x 14 1/2 In. ...	258.00
Tureen, Lettuce, Cover, Green Enamel, England, 7 1/2 In., Pair	4890.00
Tureen, Stand, Fruiting Vine Border, Brown Enamel, White, Swansea, 1809, 8 5/8 In. ...	690.00
Urn, Fruit Cover, Garlands Of Fruit Around Body, Everted Round Neck, White	1495.00
Urn, Fruit Cover, Neoclassical, White, Fruit Garlands, Ribbons, Continental, 48 x 18 In. ..	1495.00
Vase, 4 Incised Hummingbirds, Green Ash Glaze, Blue, Lanier Meaders, 17 1/2 In.	4620.00
Vase, Abstract Deep Red Design, Blue, Oatmeal Ground, Round, Peter Voulkos, 8 In.	2530.00
Vase, Black Geometric, Cylindrical Shape, Bitossi, Ettore Sottsass, 6 x 18 In.	550.00
Vase, Blue & Green Hare's Fur Glaze, Bottle Shape, Incised, Friberg, 12 1/2 In.	1430.00
Vase, Blue Multitones, Black Crater Glaze, Scheier, 17 In.	1320.00
Vase, Blue, Brown, Camel Design, Cream Ground, 10 In.	330.00
Vase, Blue, Rose Glaze, Footed, Signed, Natzler, 5 1/2 In.	2640.00
Vase, Blue, White Figure, Orange Mouth & Fish, Signed, Gravern, Norway, 17 In.	46.00
Vase, Blue, White Incised Lines, Waisted, Upsala Eckeby, Signed, Ue, Sweden, 12 In. ...	144.00
Vase, Brown Matte Glaze, Green Highlights, Laura Andreson, 3 1/2 In.	138.00
Vase, Brown, Diamond Texture, Impressed, Soholm, Denmark, 17 In.	86.00
Vase, Bulbous, Incised Wavy Banded Design, Tan, Buff, Korea, Silla Dynasty, 9 In.	230.00
Vase, Calligraphy Design, Brown, Meiping Shape, 19th Century, 9 1/2 In.	137.00
Vase, Cartouche With Fruit, Leather, Illegible Inscription, Fantoni, 20 In.	690.00
Vase, Carved, Black Glazed, 2 Spouts, Puebro, Maria Adelicia, 1949, 4 x 4 3/4 In.	120.00
Vase, Deep Yellow High Glaze, Rose Highlights, Natzler, 6 1/2 x 4 1/2 In.	2310.00
Vase, Dripped Green Glaze, Conical, Signed, P W Pillin, 12 In.	288.00
Vase, Feelie, Gray, Purple, Black Matte Glaze, Rose Cabat, 3 In.	253.00

Vase, Feelie, Lime Green Matte Glaze, Rose Cabat, 3 1/2 In. 247.00
Vase, Feelie, Yellow, Green, Purple Matte Glaze, Rose Cabat, 3 In. 220.00
Vase, Green Matte Over Blue Velvet Glaze, Brown Clay Body, Rose Cabat, 3 1/2 In. 360.00
Vase, Hanging, Mottled Brown & Beige, Metal Ring Handle, Shigaraki Ware, 6 In. 185.00
Vase, Lavender Crystals On Green Matte Glaze, Brown Clay Body, Rose Cabat, 3 In. 385.00
Vase, Light Blue High Glaze, Natzler, 2 1/2 In. 1045.00
Vase, Moon Pot, Dripping Cobalt, Ochre, Gun Metal, Toshiko Takaezu, 7 1/2 In. 2310.00
Vase, Mother Design, Turquoise, Gold, Metallic Lustre Glaze, Signed, D. Balon, 4 In. ... 176.00
Vase, Multicolored, Abstract Sgraffito Forms, Pillow, Signed, Fantoni, Italy, 10 x 8 In. ... 300.00
Vase, Orange Matte Glaze, Lane, Incised Mark, 2 In. 65.00
Vase, Oribe Design, Buff, Brown, Green, Cylindrical, Kato Tokuro, 1960, 4 3/8 In. 1725.00
Vase, Owl, Painted & Incised, Black, Brown On White, Signed, Picasso, 11 1/2 In. 2860.00
Vase, Periwinkle Matte Over Brown Clay Body, Blue, Lavender, Natzler, 5 x 4 In. 2310.00
Vase, Pinched, Tan Glaze, Deep Brown Accents, Scheier, 5 1/4 x 7 1/4 In. 275.00
Vase, Polychrome Floral Design, Continental, 18 1/2 In. 45.00
Vase, Primitive Figures In Medallions, Gun Metal, Chalice Shape, Scheier, 8 3/4 In. 605.00
Vase, Pulled Platinum Design, Rose, Gold Accents, Dark Blue, C. Lotton, 1982, 4 In. 132.00
Vase, Red, Green, Black Glaze, White, Gray Free Form Design, Peter Volkous, 12 In. .. 4125.00
Vase, Red, Turquoise Metallic Spots, Cream Glaze, Gourd Shape, Beatrice Wood, 5 In. .. 1650.00
Vase, Relief Floral, Gilt & Figural Design, Earthenware, Japan, 23 1/2 In. 290.00
Vase, Sepia Blossoms, Buff Ground, Yuan Dynasty, 8 1/2 In. 400.00
Vase, Squat, Blue Glaze, Stylized Flowers, Gray Interior, Lucie Rie, c.1980, 7 x 9 In. 560.00
Vase, Storage, French Provincial, Partially Ochre Glazed, Handles, 1895, 8 1/2 In. 180.00
Vase, Tan, Brown, Blue Matte Glaze, Brown Clay Ground, Rose Cabat, 4 1/2 In. 440.00
Vase, Tan, Yellow, Green Matte Glaze, 2-Tone Brown Clay Ground, Rose Cabat, 5 In. ... 495.00
Vase, Volcanic Blue, Green Luster, Bulbous, Bottle Shape, Signed, Beato, 5 In. 1980.00
Vase, Woman Holding Flowers, Young Lady & Horse On Reverse, Pillin, 20 In. 825.00
Vessel, Cobalt Matte Glaze, Aqua Blue, Ocher, Scheier, 4 x 5 In. 220.00
Vessel, Multi-Brown Glaze, Deep Chocolate Brown, Ocher Accents, Scheier, 4 x 5 In. ... 137.00
Wall Pocket, Pixie, With Grapes, Gilner 45.00
Wash Set, Bowl, Pitcher, Slop Jar, Green Floral Design, White & Blue Ground, 7 Piece ... 280.00
Water Dropper, Blue Floral & Characters, Off-White Ground, Square, Yi Dynasty, 3 In. . 1150.00

POWDER HORNS and powder flasks were made to hold the gunpowder
used in antique firearms. The early examples were made of horn or
wood; later ones were of copper or brass.

POWDER HORN, 2 Sailing Ships Cut Into Horn, Floral, Flower Design Cap, 12 1/2 In. 275.00
2 Sailing Ships Cut Into Horn, Floral, Vine, Wooden Cap, 16 1/2 In. 175.00
Animal Scene, Dogs Chasing Fox, Wooden End, 11 1/2 In. 90.00
Artillery Priming Type, Black & Ivory, Wooden Plug, Spring Door, 13 1/2 In. 275.00
Banner Inscribed Christ Rideth Into Jerusalem, 1841 .... 1250.00
Birds, Vessels & Men Fishing, Thomas Stead, Canada, 1864 .... 950.00
Blown, Amber, Drawn Knob On End, Ring 2 1/2 In. Below Lip, c.1840, 13 In. 190.00
Brass Bound Cap, Manasseth Emanuel His Horn AD 1761, 11 In. 700.00
Carved, Christ Astride A Donkey, Timothy Tansel, Hendricks Cty., Ind., 1841 .... 7500.00
Carved Wooden Plug, Cork, Cap, Marked, A.A. Clark, 17 In. 385.00
Conception Bay, Luke Long, 1879 .... 750.00
Early Hunting Pouch, Powder Measure, Shot Flask, 6 1/2 x 9 In. 155.00
Encircled By Carved Serpent, Clark Little Made For Att. Chester 395.00
Engraved, Cornelius Gerner His Horn Anno 1759, Pre-Revolutionary War 4400.00
Engraved, Stylized Figures, Indian Brave, Holding Spear, Signed, A. Coth 1495.00
French & Indian War, New York Map Engraved, 1760s 7800.00
Hunt Scene, Mounted Huntsman, Dogs, Vine Border, T. Norton, 1796, 24 In. 2875.00
Inscribed Moses Gordon, Vignette Of Colonial Buildings, Tavern, 16 1/2 In. 2128.00
Ivory Patina, Brass, Flattened Style, Hunters, Soldiers, Game, Russia, 1867 .... 660.00
Made From Burnside Cartridge, Engraved Eagle, Brass Fittings, 1777, 13 In. 190.00
Mother-Of-Pearl Star Cap, Me Cut Into Horn, Wooden Cap, 14 In. 90.00
Pewter Spout, Wood End, 11 1/2 In. 100.00
Scrimshaw, Puma & Indian On Horseback, Carved Wooden End, 12 In. 65.00
Ship, Hearts, Jeremiah Donohue, Age 21, 1871, Patrick Donohue, 1866, 9 In. 137.00
Teepees Around Cap, Fish, Turtle, Snake, Bird, 10 1/2 In. 2310.00
With Sailing Ship, Snake, Star, Fish, Wooden End Cap, 1771, 11 1/2 In. 305.00
Woman's Face In Half Moon, Dog's Head, Star, Metal End Cap, 8 In. 110.00

Wooden End Cap, Brass Spout, 7 In. 120.00
Wooden End Cap, Horn Stopper, Light Brown, 10 1/2 In. 135.00
Wooden End Cap, Rings, 3 In. 140.00

PRATT ware means two different things. It was an early Staffordshire
pottery, cream-colored with colored decorations, made by Felix Pratt
during the late eighteenth century. There was also Pratt ware made
with transfer designs during the mid-nineteenth century in Fenton,
England. Reproductions of the transfer-printed Pratt are being made.

PRATT FENTON

Cradle, 11 1/2 In. 2415.00
Figurine, Sheep, Reclining, Grassy Domed Base, Ocher Coat, 1800, 1 7/8 In. 201.00
Jar, Abolition, Polychrome Scene, Beating Of Uncle Tom, England, 4 In. 220.00
Jar, Early Boar Hunt Scene, Blue Glaze, 4 In. 11.00
Jug, Triple Face 850.00
Mustard Jar, Uncle Tom & Eva, Arbor By Lake, Multicolored 600.00
Pitcher, 2 Hunters Accompanied By Black, White Spotted Dogs, Green, Blue, 7 In. 635.00
Pitcher, Embossed Grape, Leaf & Fish Scale, 5 1/2 In. 410.00
Pitcher, Portraits Of Men, Molded Pearlware, 7 1/2 In. 110.00
Plaque, 2 Lions, Reclining, Ocher Manes, Spotted Coats, Manganese, Ocher, Oval, 11 In.   2587.00

PRESSED GLASS was first made in the United States in the 1820s after
the invention of glass pressing machines. Hundreds of patterns of
pressed glass were made in complete table settings. Although the
Boston and Sandwich Works was the most famous of the pressed glass
factories, there were about sixteen other factories making pressed glass
from 1830 to 1850, and still more from 1850 to 1900, when pressed
glass reached its greatest popularity. It is now being widely reproduced. The pattern names used in this listing are based on the information in the book *Pressed Glass in America* by John and Elizabeth
Welker. There may be pieces of pressed glass listed in this book in
other categories, such as Lamp, Ruby, Sandwich, and Souvenir.

1000-Eye, Pattern Is Listed Here As Thousand Eye. . . . .
Acanthus pattern is listed here as Ribbed Palm.
Actress, Bread Tray 130.00
Actress, Champagne, 5 In. 425.00
Actress, Cheese Dish, Cover, 6 1/2 In. 210.00
Actress, Goblet, 6 1/4 In. 140.00
Actress, Jam Jar, Cover, 6 1/2 In. 160.00
Actress, Pitcher, Water, 9 1/4 In. 350.00
Actress, Salt & Pepper, 3 In. 90.00
Alabama, Compote, Cover, 5 In. 125.00
Alabama, Creamer 22.00
Alaska, Berry Set, Blue Opalescent, 7 Piece 495.00
Alaska, Creamer, White 65.00
Alaska, Pitcher 375.00

Pressed Glass, Actress

Pressed Glass, Austrian

Pressed Glass, Barberry

Alaska, Sauce, Vaseline Opalescent 45.00
Alaska, Sugar, Cover, Vaseline Opalescent 55.00
Alaska, Table Set, Blue Opalescent, 4 Piece 795.00
Alaska, Water Set, Blue Opalescent, 7 Piece 895.00
Amberette, Bowl, Amber, Frosted, 6 In. 250.00
Amberette, Creamer, Amber 255.00
Amberette, Punch Cup, Frosted Amber Cross, 2 1/2 In. 145.00
Argus, Goblet 25.00
Argus, Mug 15.00
Artichoke, Spooner, Frosted 90.00
Ashburton, Celery Vase, 9 In. ....90.00 to 100.00
Ashburton, Eggcup, Flint 22.00
Ashburton, Goblet, Flint ....42.00 to 47.00
Ashburton, Vase, Scalloped Rim, 10 1/2 In. 170.00
Atlanta, Cake Stand, 5 3/4 In. 320.00
Atlanta, Compote, Cover, 9 In. 100.00
Atlanta, Compote, Etched, Square, 6 In. 110.00
Atlanta, Cruet, Stopper 290.00
Atlas, Goblet 35.00
Austrian, Tumbler, Canary 165.00
Baby Face, Celery Vase, 7 3/4 In. 70.00
Baby Face, Goblet 325.00
Baby Thumbprint pattern is listed here as Dakota.
Balder pattern is listed here as Pennsylvania.
Balky Mule pattern is listed here as Currier & Ives.
Baltimore Pear, Berry Bowl, Master, 8 In. 75.00
Baltimore Pear, Butter, Cover 85.00
Banded Buckle, Sugar, Cover 80.00
Banded Portland, Goblet 40.00
Banded Portland, Wine 40.00
Bar & Flute, Compote, Jelly, Ruby Stain 95.00
Barberry, Sauce 20.00
Barberry, Sugar, Cover 85.00
Barley, Creamer 25.00
Barley, Pitcher, Water, Applied Handle 110.00
Barley & Oats pattern is listed here as Wheat & Barley.
Barley & Wheat pattern is listed here as Wheat & Barley.
Barred Forget-Me-Not, Creamer 22.00
Barrel Excelsior, Goblet, Flint 40.00
Barreled Block pattern is listed here as Red Block.
Basket Weave, Goblet, Canary 30.00
Basket Weave, Pitcher, Blue, Tall 79.00
Basket Weave, Spooner, Yellow 35.00
Beaded Bull's-Eye & Drape pattern is listed here as Alabama.
Beaded Dewdrop pattern is listed here as Wisconsin.
Beaded Grape, Cake Stand, Square, 9 In. 125.00
Beaded Grape, Compote, Large 55.00
Beaded Grape, Creamer 45.00
Beaded Grape, Dish, Tab Handle 22.00
Beaded Grape, Sugar, Cover 48.00
Beaded Grape Medallion, Celery Tray 25.00
Beaded Grape Medallion, Pitcher, Water, Emerald 120.00
Beaded Grape Medallion, Spooner, Emerald Green 45.00
Beaded Grape Medallion, Tankard, Emerald Green 125.00
Beaded Mirror, Goblet 25.00
Beaded Mirror, Goblet, Grape & Fern Etch, 5 3/4 In. 100.00
Beaded Rosette, Goblet 25.00
Bearded Head pattern is listed here as Viking.
Bellflower, Cake Stand, 9 1/4 x 3 3/4 In. 4600.00
Bellflower, Castor Set, Five Bottles, 1857 Patent, 9 1/4 In. 750.00
Bellflower, Celery Vase, 8 1/4 In. 325.00
Bellflower, Creamer, 6 In. 275.00
Bellflower, Decanter, Cut Ovals On Neck, Stopper, Pint, 11 3/4 In. 750.00

Bellflower, Goblet, Blue 40.00
Bellflower, Goblet, Cut, 6 1/4 In. 400.00
Bellflower, Goblet, Flared Rim 90.00
Bellflower, Honey, Scalloped & Pointed Rim, Star Base, 3 In. 100.00
Bellflower, Lamp, Oil, Scalloped Base, 9 In. 650.00
Bellflower, Pitcher, Milk, 7 1/2 In. 1800.00
Bellflower, Plate, Flint 60.00
Bellflower, Sugar, Cover, 8 1/2 In. 80.00
Bellflower, Sugar, Octagonal, Cover, 8 In. 1550.00
Bellflower, Syrup, 6 In. 500.00
Bellflower, Syrup, 7 1/2 In. 600.00
Bellflower, Tumbler, Whiskey, 2 7/8 In. 230.00
Bellflower Double Vine, Champagne, Cut, 5 In. 450.00
Bellflower Double Vine, Creamer, 6 3/4 In. 210.00
Bellflower Double Vine, Goblet, Cut, 6 1/4 In. 425.00
Bellflower Double Vine, Pitcher, Milk, 7 In. 550.00
Bellflower Double Vine, Pitcher, Pint, 6 1/4 In. 1800.00
Bellflower Double Vine, Pitcher, Water, 8 1/4 In. 450.00
Bellflower Double Vine, Sugar, Cover, 8 3/4 In. 230.00
Bellflower Double Vine, Syrup, 7 1/4 In. 1300.00
Bellflower Double Vine, Tumbler, Footed, 4 7/8 In. 275.00
Bellflower Double Vine, Tumbler, Water, Cut, 3 1/2 In. 400.00
Bellflower Double Vine, Wine, Cut, 4 In. 250.00
Bellflower With Loops, Goblet, 5 1/2 In. 210.00
Bent Buckle pattern is listed here as New Hampshire.
Bird & Strawberry, Cake Stand, 9 In. 75.00
Bird & Strawberry, Compote, Cover, 6 In. 165.00
Bird & Strawberry, Goblet 675.00
Bird & Strawberry, Nappy, Footed, 5 1/2 In. 55.00
Bird & Strawberry, Tumbler 55.00
Bird & Strawberry, Wine 70.00
Birds At Fountain, Goblet 42.00
Blaze, Goblet 50.00
Bleeding Heart, Cake Stand, 9 In. 85.00
Bleeding Heart, Compote, Cover, 8 In. 125.00
Block & Star pattern is listed here as Valencia Waffle.
Block & Thumbprint, Water Set, 5 Piece 395.00
Bluebird pattern is listed here as Bird & Strawberry.
Bowtie, Compote, 10 1/2 x 10 In. 200.00
Bradford Blackberry, Goblet 60.00
Bradford Grape pattern is listed here as Bradford Blackberry.
Bringing Home The Cows, Pitcher, Water 525.00
Broken Column, Banana Stand 175.00
Broken Column, Celery Vase 65.00
Broken Column, Compote, 6 In. 40.00
Broken Column, Compote, Cover, 8 In. 195.00

Pressed Glass,
Beaded Grape Medallion

Pressed Glass,
Bellflower

Pressed Glass,
Bird & Strawberry

Broken Column, Cracker Jar, Cover 165.00
Broken Column, Creamer 125.00
Broken Column, Pitcher, Water, Ruby Stain 345.00
Broken Column, Plate, 7 In. 40.00
Broken Column, Salt & Pepper, Ruby Stain 345.00
Broken Column, Sugar & Creamer 45.00
Bryce pattern is listed here as Ribbon Candy.
Bucket pattern is listed here as Oaken Bucket.
Buckle, Goblet 25.00
Buckle, Goblet, Flint 55.00
Buckle, Lamp, Oil, Opalescent Base, 10 1/2 In. 75.00
Bulging Loops, Toothpick 85.00
Bull's-Eye, Eggcup, 4 In. 60.00
Bull's-Eye, Eggcup, Cover, 5 1/4 In. 250.00
Bull's-Eye, Goblet, Amethyst 26.00
Bull's-Eye, Goblet, Flint, 6 5/8 In. 100.00
Bull's-Eye & Fleur-De-Lis, Ale, 6 1/4 In. 650.00
Bull's-Eye & Fleur-De-Lis, Goblet, 6 3/8 In. 90.00
Bull's-Eye With Diamond Point, Eggcup, 4 In. 180.00
Bull's-Eye With Diamond Point, Goblet, 6 7/8 In. 130.00
Bullet Emblem, Butter Dish, 5 In. 425.00
Bullet Emblem, Sugar, Cover 160.00
Cable, Goblet, 5 1/2 In. 210.00
Cable With Ring, Creamer 250.00
California pattern is listed here as Beaded Grape.
Candlewick as a pressed glass pattern is properly named *Banded Raindrop*. There is also a pat-
tern called *Candlewick*, which has been made by Imperial Glass Corporation since 1936. It is
listed in this book in the Imperial Glass category.
Candy Ribbon pattern is listed here as Ribbon Candy.
Cane, Plate, Amber, 4 1/2 In. 20.00
Cane, Plate, Blue, 4 1/2 In. 20.00
Cane, Plate, Green, 4 1/2 In. 20.00
Cardinal pattern is listed here as Cardinal Bird.
Cardinal Bird, Creamer 22.00
Cat Up A Tree, Dog, Pitcher, Water 450.00
Cathedral, Bowl, Amber, 9 In. 45.00
Centennial, see also the related patterns Liberty Bell, Viking, and Washington Centennial.
Chain, Goblet 25.00
Chain & Shield, Goblet, Blue 30.00
Chain With Diamonds pattern is listed here as Washington Centennial.
Chain With Star, Compote, Cover, 8 In. 55.00
Chain With Star, Goblet 25.00
Chain With Star, Plate, Handle, 11 In. 30.00
Chicken, Frosted, Jam Jar, 6 1/8 In. 120.00
Chrysanthemum Leaf, Toothpick 85.00

Pressed Glass,
Cable With Ring

Pressed Glass,
Columbian Coin

Pressed Glass,
Croesus

Classic, Compote, Cover, 8 In. 295.00
Classic, Plate, Warrior, 11 1/2 In. 120.00
Cleopatra, Bread Plate 60.00
Coin Spot pattern is listed in this book in its own category.
Colorado, Bowl, Ruffled Edge, Green, Gold Trim, 8 In. 48.00
Colorado, Butter, Cover, Green, Gold Trim 125.00
Colorado, Toothpick, Floral Design 50.00
Columbian Coin, Wine, Frosted Coins 60.00
Comet, Goblet, Flint ....120.00 to 140.00
Comet, Tumbler, Whiskey, 3 In. 180.00
Compact pattern is listed here as Snail.
Cone, Syrup, Pink 165.00
Cord & Tassel, Goblet 28.00
Cosmos pattern is listed in this book as its own category.
Cottage, Plate, Ruby Stained, 5 In. 15.00
Croesus, Cake Stand, 9 3/4 In. 495.00
Croesus, Celery Vase, Amethyst, Gold Trim 425.00
Croesus, Compote, Jelly, Amethyst, Gold Trim 245.00
Croesus, Compote, Jelly, Green, Gold Trim 225.00
Croesus, Creamer, Amethyst, Gold Trim 150.00
Croesus, Cruet, Green, Gold 165.00
Croesus, Cruet, Green, Gold Trim 380.00
Croesus, Plate, 7 In. 135.00
Croesus, Spooner, Amethyst, Gold Trim 150.00
Croesus, Sugar, Amethyst, Gold Trim 170.00
Croesus, Sugar, Cover, Green, Gold Trim 175.00
Crosby, Mug 25.00
Crystal Wedding, Pitcher, Water, Tankard Shape 185.00
Cupid & Venus, Bread Plate 54.00
Cupid & Venus, Champagne, 5 In. 70.00
Cupid & Venus, Compote, 8 1/2 In. 185.00
Cupid & Venus, Goblet 75.00
Cupid & Venus, Wine, 3 3/4 In. 80.00
Currant, Bowl, Oval 20.00
Currant, Creamer, Applied Handle 20.00
Currier & Ives, Decanter 45.00
Currier & Ives, Platter, Oval 40.00
Cut Log, Cruet, Stopper 75.00
Cut Log, Mug 25.00
Cut Log, Pitcher, Water ....85.00 to 145.00
Cut Log, Sauce, Footed 32.00
Cut Log, Sugar, Cover 60.00
Daisy & Button, Berry Bowl, Amber, 8 In. 85.00
Daisy & Button, Goblet, Amber 30.00
Daisy & Button, Pitcher, Water, Amber 95.00
Daisy & Button With Finecut Panels, Creamer 30.00
Daisy & Button With Thumbprint, Cake Stand, Amber 65.00
Dakota, Butter Dish, Etched 77.00
Dakota, Cake Stand, Cover, 9 3/4 In. 425.00
Dakota, Sauce, Cobalt Blue, 4 In. 55.00
Deer & Doe With Lily-Of-The-Valley, Cheese Dish 135.00
Deer & Dog, Champagne, 5 3/8 In. 280.00
Deer & Dog, Compote, Cover, Etched, 7 In. 395.00
Deer & Dog, Compote, Cover, Etched, 8 In. 375.00
Deer & Oak Tree, Pitcher, Water 175.00
Deer & Pine Tree, Pitcher, Water 75.00
Delaware, Banana Boat, Emerald, Gold Trim 65.00
Delaware, Banana Boat, Green, Gold Trim ....55.00 to 77.00
Delaware, Bowl, Emerald, Gold Trim, Oval, 11 1/2 In. 150.00
Delaware, Bowl, Green, Oval 65.00
Delaware, Lemonade Set, 7 Piece 275.00
Delaware, Salt & Pepper, Green, Gold Trim, Pair 395.00
Delaware, Tankard, Green, Gold Trim 115.00

Pressed Glass,
Excelsior

Pressed Glass,
Deer & Dog

Pressed Glass, Frosted Circle

Delaware, Tumbler, Green, Gold Trim 40.00
Delaware, Vase, Green, Gold Trim, 6 In. 95.00
Dewdrop In Points, Bread Plate 25.00
Dewey, Butter, Cover, Amber 110.00
Diamond, Sugar, Swan Finial Cover, Handles, Footed 1100.00
Diamond Medallion pattern is listed here as Grand.
Diamond Point, Cake Stand, Flint, 14 In. 675.00
Diamond Point, Claret, 5 1/2 In. 60.00
Diamond Point, Compote, Flint, 8 x 8 1/2 In. 137.00
Diamond Point, Goblet, Flint 26.00
Diamond Point, Goblet, Knob Stem 120.00
Diamond Point With Panels, Bowl, 4 1/8 x 6 3/8 In. 19.00
Diamond Point With Panels, Goblet, Flint 70.00
Diamond Point With Panels, Pitcher, Cream, Applied Handle, 6 3/4 In. 55.00
Diamond Point With Panels, Sugar, Cover, 8 3/4 In. 38.00
Diamond Point With Panels, Tumbler, Flint, 3 5/8 In. 100.00
Diamond Thumbprint, Champagne, 5 1/4 In. 425.00
Diamond Thumbprint, Compote, Flint, 7 1/4 In. 60.00
Diamond Thumbprint, Goblet 6 3/4 In. 700.00
Diamond Thumbprint, Wine, 4 1/4 In. 150.00
Doric pattern is listed here as Feather.
Double Daisy pattern is listed here as Rosette Band.
Double Loop pattern is listed here as Ribbon Candy.
Double Vine pattern is listed here as Bellflower Double Vine.
Double Wedding Ring pattern is listed here as Wedding Ring.
Drapery, Spooner 18.00
Early Thumbprint, Cordial, 3 1/4 In. 200.00
Early Thumbprint, Goblet, 5 3/4 In. 200.00
Early Thumbprint, Goblet, 6 1/2 In. 80.00
Early Thumbprint, Salt, Cover, Donut Shape Finial, 3 7/8 In. 375.00
Egyptian, Pitcher, Water . . . . .275.00 to 325.00
Egyptian, Platter, Cleopatra Center, Motto 50.00
Egyptian, Sauce, 3 1/2 In. 15.00
Empress, Berry Bowl, Master, Green, Gold Trim 395.00
Empress, Sugar, Cover, Gold Trim 110.00
English Hobnail Cross pattern is listed here as Amberette.
Esther, Compote, Flared, 9 In. 95.00
Esther, Compote, Jelly, Amber 85.00
Esther, Cruet, Green 165.00
Esther, Cruet, Green, Gold Trim 325.00
Etched Dakota pattern is listed here as Dakota.
Everglades, Berry Set, Vaseline Opalescent, 7 Piece 695.00
Everglades, Sugar, Cover, Vaseline Opalescent 200.00
Excelsior, Carafe, Bar Lip 150.00
Excelsior With Maltese Cross, Goblet 80.00
Feather, Butter, Cover, Flanged Rim 65.00

Feather, Butter, Cover, Vaseline 115.00
Feather, Compote, Cover 75.00
Feather, Cordial, 3 1/8 In. 180.00
Feather, Creamer 28.00
Feather, Cruet 38.00
Feather, Pitcher, Milk 125.00
Feather, Plate, Amber, 6 In. 15.00
Feather, Plate, Blue, 7 In. 22.00
Feather, Spooner 38.00
Feather, Wine 15.00
Festoon, Cake Stand ....45.00 to 95.00
Filley, Spooner 25.00
Fine Cut & Feather pattern is listed here as Feather.
Fine Rib, Eggcup, Custard, Handle, 3 7/8 In. 325.00
Fine Rib, Goblet, Bellflower Border, 5 1/2 In. 2050.00
Fine Rib, Tumbler, Whiskey, Handle, 3 In. 300.00
Flat Diamond & Panel, Eggcup, 4 In. 45.00
Flat Diamond & Panel, Goblet, 6 1/8 In. 210.00
Flat Diamond & Panel, Goblet, 6 3/8 In. 350.00
Flora, Salt & Pepper, Green, Gold Trim, Pair 160.00
Flower Flange pattern is listed here as Dewey.
Flying Robin pattern is listed here as Hummingbird.
Forget-Me-Not In Scroll, Cake Stand, Paneled 75.00
Forget-Me-Not In Scroll, Goblet 25.00
Frosted patterns may also be listed under name of main pattern.
Frosted Circle, Creamer 30.00
Frosted Eagle, Butter, Cover, Etched 225.00
Frosted Leaf, Champagne, Flint, 5 In. 275.00
Frosted Leaf, Goblet 90.00
Frosted Roman Key pattern is listed here as Roman Key, Frosted.
Galloway, Creamer 75.00
Garfield Drape, Goblet 42.00
Garfield Drape, Spooner 25.00
Girl With Fan, Goblet 42.00
Good Luck pattern is listed here as Horseshoe.
Gooseberry, Creamer 40.00
Gooseberry, Mug 30.00
Gothic, Eggcup 45.00
Grand, Goblet 20.00
Grape, see also the related patterns Beaded Grape, Beaded Grape Medallion, Magnet & Grape
with Frosted Leaf, and Paneled Grape.
Grape & Cable pattern is listed in this book in the Northwood category.
Grape Band, Goblet 40.00
Grasshopper, Creamer, Etched 85.00
Grasshopper, Sugar, Cover, Etched 40.00
Grooved Bigler, Compote, Flint, 8 In. 45.00
Hamilton, Compote, Flint, Pair, 8 In. 60.00
Hamilton, Eggcup 45.00
Hamilton With Frosted Leaf, Champagne, 4 7/8 In. 275.00
Hawaiian Lei, Butter, Cover 52.00
Hawaiian Pineapple, Goblet 90.00
Hawaiian Pineapple, Goblet, Flint 190.00
Heart Band, Mug, Green 30.00
Heart With Thumbprint, Bowl, Crimped Edge, Gold Trim, 9 In. 45.00
Heart With Thumbprint, Goblet 75.00
Heart With Thumbprint, Ice Bucket ....120.00 to 125.00
Heart With Thumbprint, Lamp, Finger 195.00
Heart With Thumbprint, Lamp, Green 225.00
Heart With Thumbprint, Rose Bowl, 2 1/4 In. 30.00
Heart With Thumbprint, Tray, Card, Folded, Gold Trim 30.00
Hearts Of Loch Laven pattern is listed here as Shuttle.
Hinoto pattern is listed here as Diamond Point with Panels.
Hobnail pattern is in this book as its own category.

Pressed Glass,
Horseshoe

Pressed Glass,
Inverted Fan

Pressed Glass,
Inverted Thumbprint

Holly, Bowl, Oval, 9 In. 65.00
Honeycomb With Diamond, Eggcup 35.00
Horizontal Oval Frames, Goblet 160.00
Horn Of Plenty, Butter, Cover, Washington Head, 5 In. 500.00
Horn Of Plenty, Cake Stand, 4 1/4 In. 1800.00
Horn Of Plenty, Champagne 190.00
Horn Of Plenty, Compote, Oval, 6 In. 1500.00
Horn Of Plenty, Creamer, 5 1/4 In. 250.00
Horn Of Plenty, Eggcup 50.00
Horn Of Plenty, Eggcup, Flint 65.00
Horn Of Plenty, Goblet, Flint . . . . .75.00 to 85.00
Horn Of Plenty, Sugar, Domed Cover, Flint 120.00
Horseshoe, Butter, Cover 85.00
Horseshoe, Cake Stand, 7 1/2 In. 130.00
Horseshoe, Cake Stand, 10 In. 145.00
Horseshoe, Creamer . . . . .22.00 to 48.00
Horseshoe, Goblet 40.00
Horseshoe, Pitcher, Milk 135.00
Horseshoe, Pitcher, Water 135.00
Horseshoe, Spooner 40.00
Hummingbird, Creamer, Sapphire Blue 75.00
Ida pattern is listed here as Sheraton.
Idyll, Spooner, Blue Opalescent 110.00
Illinois, Plate, Square 65.00
Illinois, Tumbler 55.00
Indiana Swirl pattern is listed here as Feather.
Inverted Fan & Feather, Tumbler 40.00
Inverted Fan & Feather, Water Set, Custard, Gold Trim, 7 Piece 1195.00
Inverted Fern, Champagne, 5 In. 140.00
Inverted Fern, Eggcup 45.00
Inverted Fern, Sugar, Cover, 8 1/2 In. 60.00
Inverted Strawberry, Berry Bowl, Scalloped Rim, 9 1/2 In. 65.00
Inverted Strawberry, Wine 85.00
Inverted Thumbprint, Ewer, Green, Ruffled Edge, Applied Handle, 13 In. 27.00
Inverted Thumbprint, Sugar, Pewter Hinged Lid, Albert Pick Co., Chicago, 4 In. 20.00
Iris With Meander, Compote, Vaseline Opalescent 80.00
Ivanhoe, Salt 35.00
Jacob's Ladder, Cake Stand, Large 125.00
Jacob's Ladder, Celery Vase 45.00
Jacob's Ladder, Creamer 35.00
Jacob's Ladder, Salt Dip, Footed, Master 30.00
Jefferson's Optic, Punch Cup, Enameled, Floral 125.00
Jefferson's Optic, Tumbler, Enameled, Floral 125.00
Jewel Band, Creamer . . . . .22.00 to 25.00
Jewel Band, Eggcup 30.00
Jeweled Moon & Star pattern is listed here as Moon & Star.

Jumbo, Creamer 295.00
Kamoni pattern is listed here as Pennsylvania.
King's Crown, see also the related pattern Ruby Thumbprint.
King's Crown, Berry Set, Boat Shape, 7 Piece 140.00
King's Crown, Bowl, 7 1/2 In. 65.00
King's Crown, Bowl, Orange 300.00
King's Crown, Cake Plate, 10 1/2 In. 55.00
King's Crown, Compote, 8 1/2 In. 50.00
King's Crown, Pitcher, Cream 45.00
King's Crown, Pitcher, Water, Etched Bird 225.00
Klondike pattern is listed here as Amberette.
Late Georgian, Finger Bowl, Blue, c.1820 . . . . 258.00
Lattice & Oval Panels pattern is listed here as Flat Diamond & Panel.
Lattice Leaf, Toothpick 65.00
Liberty Bell, Butter, Cover 145.00
Liberty Bell, Compote, 6 3/4 In. 75.00
Liberty Bell, Compote, 8 In. 85.00
Liberty Bell, Goblet, Blue 30.00
Liberty Bell, Mug, Snake Handle, 3 1/2 In. 250.00
Liberty Bell, Wine, Pair 60.00
Lily-Of-The-Valley, Champagne 165.00
Lily-Of-The-Valley, Relish, Oval 35.00
Lily-Of-The-Valley, Wine 175.00
Lincoln Drape, Bowl, Flint, 5 3/8 x 8 1/4 In. 125.00
Lincoln Drape, Compote, Flint, 5 1/4 In. 50.00
Lincoln Drape, Compote, Wafer Joining Bowl & Base, Flint, 5 3/8 x 8 1/4 In. 125.00
Lincoln Drape With Tassel, Goblet, 6 In. 375.00
Lion, Frosted, Creamer 70.00
Lion, Frosted, Goblet 65.00
Lion, Frosted, Spooner 50.00
Lion's Leg pattern is listed here as Alaska.
Locket On Chain, Cake Stand 120.00
Loop, see also the related pattern Seneca Loop.
Loop, Compote, 9 1/2 x 9 In. 100.00
Loop, Compote, Wafer Connector, Flint, 11 1/4 In. 225.00
Loops & Drops pattern is listed here as New Jersey.
Lotus, Bread Plate 35.00
Lotus, Plate, Cleopatra 50.00
Magnet & Grape With American Shield & Frosted Leaf, Champagne, 5 1/8 In. 180.00
Magnet & Grape With American Shield & Frosted Leaf, Goblet, 6 1/2 In. 300.00
Manhattan, Straw Holder, Metal Lid, 12 In. 415.00
Maple Leaf, Bowl, Green, Oval, 10 In. 50.00
Maple Leaf, Goblet, 6 In. 170.00
Maple Leaf, Plate, 6 In. 45.00

The early 1840s were the time of pressed-glass table settings. Early patterns were simple, with heavy loops or ribbed effects. The 1870s brought more elaborate naturalistic patterns. Clear and frosted patterns with figures were in style during the 1870s. Overall patterns that were slightly geometric in feeling were in style by 1880, and patterns such as Daisy & Button and Hobnail came into vogue. Colored pressed-glass patterns became popular after the Civil War.

Pressed Glass, Jumbo

Pressed Glass, Liberty Bell   Pressed Glass, Moon & Star   Pressed Glass, Pleat and Panel

Marquisette, Goblet	25.00
Maryland, Creamer	18.00
Maryland, Goblet	30.00
Mascotte, Wine	15.00
Masonic, Tumbler	25.00
Mellon, Eggcup, Blue	145.00
Memphis, Decanter	95.00
Michigan, Butter, Cover	95.00
Michigan, Goblet	35.00
Michigan, Spooner	65.00
Michigan, Sugar, Cover	95.00
Minerva, Champagne, 5 In.	600.00
Minerva, Compote, 8 In.	185.00
Minerva, Pickle	15.00
Minerva, Pitcher, Water	145.00
Minerva, Sugar, Cover	115.00
Minnesota, Basket	135.00
Minnesota, Cruet	55.00
Minnesota, Toothpick, Green	165.00
Missouri is listed here as Palm & Scroll.	
Moon & Star, Cake Stand	95.00
Moon & Star, Compote, Cover, 16 In.	410.00
Moon & Star, Sugar, Cover	65.00
Moon & Star, Wine, Frosted	95.00
Morning Glory, Champagne, 5 In.	210.00
Morning Glory, Goblet, 5 7/8 In.	185.00
Nail, Pitcher, Water, Etched	125.00
Nailhead, Goblet	30.00
Nestor, Berry Set, Amethyst, 7 Piece	110.00
New England Pineapple, Champagne, 5 1/4 In.	210.00
New England Pineapple, Compote, Flint, 8 x 5 In.	40.00
New England Pineapple, Goblet	75.00
New England Pineapple, Wine, 4 In.	90.00
New Hampshire, Mug	25.00
New Hampshire, Syrup	145.00
New Jersey, Creamer, Ruby	125.00
Nursery Tales, Butter Bottom	45.00
Nursery Tales, Tumbler	35.00
Oaken Bucket, Creamer	25.00
Old Abe pattern is listed here as Frosted Eagle.	
One-Thousand Eye pattern is listed here as Thousand Eye.	
Orion pattern is listed here as Cathedral.	
Oval Star, Creamer	14.00
Oval Star, Sugar, Cover	30.00
Owl pattern is listed here as Bull's-Eye with Diamond Point.	
Owl In Fan pattern is listed here as Parrot.	

Palm & Scroll, Cake Stand, 9 In. 85.00
Palm & Scroll, Compote, Flint 110.00
Palm Leaf Fan, Compote, 7 In. 45.00
Palm Leaf Fan, Plate, Square 45.00
Palmette, Lamp 195.00
Paneled 44, Champagne 125.00
Paneled 44, Pitcher, Water 225.00
Paneled Daisy, Spooner 25.00
Paneled Dewdrop, Creamer 30.00
Paneled Forget-Me-Not, Goblet 40.00
Paneled Grape, Goblet 25.00
Paneled Holly, Berry Bowl, Gold Leaves, Holly, Dots, Opalescent, 8 In. 125.00
Parrot, Goblet 42.00
Pavonia, Compote, Open, Etched 58.00
Pavonia, Creamer, Apple Handle, Footed 30.00
Pavonia, Decanter, Whiskey, Stopper 65.00
Pavonia, Goblet, Etched 45.00
Pavonia, Tankard, Etched 65.00
Pavonia, Tumbler, Etched 30.00
Pennsylvania, Goblet . . . . .20.00 to 30.00
Pennsylvania, Spooner, Gold Trim 48.00
Persian Spear, Goblet, Flint 85.00
Pillar & Bull's-Eye pattern is listed here as Thistle.
Pinafore pattern is listed here as Actress.
Pineapple, Goblet, Flint 95.00
Pittsburgh Daisy, Tumbler 25.00
Pittsburgh Pillar, Candlestick, 11 3/4 In. 3600.00
Pleat & Panel, Butter Chip 85.00
Pleat & Panel, Goblet . . . . .30.00 to 35.00
Pleat & Panel, Platter, Open Handles 5.00
Plume, Goblet 35.00
Portland With Diamond Point Band pattern is listed here as Banded Portland.
Powder & Shot, Cake Stand, Flint, 4 1/2 In. 600.00
Powder & Shot, Eggcup 45.00
Powder & Shot, Eggcup, Flint 55.00
Powder & Shot, Goblet 65.00
Prayer Rug pattern is listed here as Horseshoe.
Pressed Leaf, Creamer 35.00
Queen, Pitcher, Water, Amber 85.00
Queen, Spooner, Blue 45.00
Red Block, Goblet 34.00
Reverse 44 pattern is listed here as Paneled 44.
Ribbed Ivy, Decanter, Cordial, Hollow Stopper, 7 In. 400.00
Ribbed Ivy, Goblet, Flint 60.00
Ribbed Ivy, Salt, Cover, 4 1/2 In. 190.00
Ribbed Ivy, Tumbler, Whiskey, Handle, 2 3/4 In. 230.00
Ribbed Palm, Bowl, Footed, Flint, 4 1/4 In. 45.00
Ribbed Palm, Champagne, 5 1/2 In. 120.00
Ribbed Palm, Eggcup 50.00
Ribbed Palm, Goblet, Flint 65.00
Ribbon Candy, Donut Stand, 3 In. 150.00
Roanoke, Compote, Cover, 8 In. 125.00
Roman Key, Frosted, Tumbler, Flint 65.00
Roman Key, Sugar & Creamer 55.00
Roman Rosette, Bread Plate 35.00
Roman Rosette, Goblet 40.00
Roman Rosette, Platter 35.00
Roman Rosette, Spooner 30.00
Rose In Snow, Creamer 22.00
Rose In Snow, Goblet 35.00
Rose In Snow, Mug 40.00
Rose Sprig, Butter, Cover 165.00
Rose Sprig, Creamer 75.00

Pressed Glass,
Ribbon Candy

Pressed Glass,
Rose In Snow

Pressed Glass,
Sandwich Star

Rose Sprig, Plate, Amber, 6 1/2 In. 40.00
Rose Sprig, Plate, Square, 6 1/2 In. 45.00
Rose Sprig, Tumbler, Vaseline 95.00
Rosette & Palms, Goblet 25.00
Rosette Band, Compote Cover, 6 In. 45.00
Rosette Band, Compote, Cover, 8 1/2 In. ....45.00 to 48.00
Rosette Band, Compote, Cover, Etched, 7 1/2 In. 95.00
Rosette Band, Goblet, Etched 35.00
Royal Ivy, Pitcher 250.00
Ruby Thumbprint, see also the related pattern King's Crown.
Sandwich, Sugar, Flint 38.00
Sandwich Overshot, Pitcher, Bulbous, Cranberry Stained, Clear Handle, 7 In. 900.00
Sandwich Star, Goblet, 6 1/2 In. 1500.00
Sandwich Star, Wine, 4 1/2 In. 325.00
Sawtooth, Compote, Cover, Flint, 12 In. 60.00
Sawtooth, Compote, Cover, Flint, 9 1/2 x 8 1/4 In. 148.00
Sawtooth, Eggcup, Cover, 5 1/4 In. 70.00
Sawtooth, Pitcher, Milk, Bulbous, Handle, Flint, 7 3/8 In. 70.00
Scalloped Tape pattern is listed here as Jewel Band.
Scroll, Goblet, Blue 30.00
Scroll With Cane Band, Toothpick, Ruby Stained 65.00
Seneca Loop, Goblet, Flint 30.00
Shell & Jewel, Compote, 19 In. 45.00
Shell & Jewel, Creamer 25.00
Shell & Jewel, Mug 45.00
Shell & Jewel, Pitcher Set, Blue, 7 Piece 275.00
Shell & Jewel, Tumbler 45.00
Shell & Jewel, Tumbler, Amber 35.00
Shell & Jewel, Water Set, 7 Piece 33.00
Sheraton, Butter, Cover, Blue 90.00
Sheridan & Stippled Double Loop, Creamer 30.00
Shoshone pattern is listed here as Victor.
Shrine, Toothpick, Cranberry, Souvenir 225.00
Shuttle, Cake Stand, 10 In. 145.00
Snail, Butter, Cover 90.00
Snail, Compote, Cover, 8 In. 245.00
Snail, Goblet, Flower & Leaves Etched 115.00
Snail, Rose Bowl, 6 1/2 In. 80.00
Snail, Salt 30.00
Snail, Spooner ....30.00 to 35.00
Spanish Coin pattern is listed here as Columbian Coin.
Square Fuchsia, Compote, Cover, 7 In. 85.00
Square Fuchsia, Goblet, Etched 35.00
Square Fuchsia, Mug, Blue, Large 65.00
Square Fuchsia, Mug, Large 25.00
Square Fuchsia, Mug, Small ....25.00 to 45.00

Star & Punty pattern is listed here as Moon & Star.
Star Rosetted, Goblet . . . . .25.00 to 50.00
States pattern is listed here as The States.
Stippled Chain, Creamer, Applied Handle 30.00
Stippled Dahlia pattern is listed here as Square Fuchsia.
Stippled Forget-Me-Not, Cake Stand 45.00
Stippled Medallion, Eggcup 55.00
Stippled Medallion, Goblet, Flint 120.00
Stippled Scroll pattern is listed here as Scroll.
Stippled Star, Eggcup 40.00
Strawberry & Currant, Goblet 40.00
Tacoma, Table Set, 4 Piece 325.00
Teardrop pattern is listed here as Teardrop & Thumbprint.
Teardrop & Thumbprint, Cruet 95.00
Tennessee, Bowl, Cover 65.00
Tennessee, Pitcher, Milk 85.00
Tennessee, Platter 75.00
Tennessee, Wine 135.00
Texas, Cake Stand 125.00
Texas, Wine 95.00
Texas Star, Toothpick 70.00
The States, Goblet, Wine, 4 Piece 100.00
Thistle, Cake Stand, 10 In. 85.00
Thistle, Compote, 8 In. 195.00
Thistle, Dish, Pickle 55.00
Thousand Eye, Butter, Cover, Yellow 125.00
Thousand Eye, Cruet 110.00
Thousand Eye, Cruet Stand, Blue, Double 150.00
Thousand Eye, Goblet, Blue . . . . .30.00 to 45.00
Thousand Eye, Mug 20.00
Thousand Eye, Pitcher, Pink, 7 3/4 In. . . . . .88.00 to 90.00
Thousand Eye, Syrup, Blue 225.00
Thousand Eye, Toothpick, Amber 35.00
Three Face, Biscuit Jar, 9 1/2 In. 1700.00
Three Face, Butter, Cover, 8 In. 20.00
Three Face, Champagne, Hollow Stem, 4 1/4 In. 5100.00
Three Face, Compote, Cover 185.00
Three Face, Creamer, Frosted Base 165.00
Three Face, Wine, 4 3/4 In. 190.00
Three Graces, see also the related pattern Three Face.
Three Sisters pattern is listed here as Three Face.
Torpedo, Goblet 55.00
Torpedo, Pitcher, Milk, Ruby Stained 95.00
Tree Of Life, Portland, Goblet, Marked, 6 1/2 In. 50.00
Tree Of Life With Hand, Cake Stand 130.00
Trilby, Goblet 160.00

Pressed Glass,
Shell & Jewel

Pressed Glass,
Square Fuchsia

Pressed Glass,
Tree of Life

Truncated Cube, Wine, Ruby Stained 40.00
Two Panel, Compote, Cover, Blue, 7 1/4 x 9 In. 295.00
Two Panel, Creamer 40.00
Valencia Waffle, Berry Set, Cranberry Stained, 7 Piece 295.00
Valencia Waffle, Compote, Cover, Blue, 8 In. 165.00
Valencia Waffle, Goblet 25.00
Valentine pattern is listed here as Trilby.
Victor, Compote, Green, 8 In. 42.00
Victoria & Albert, Butter, Cover, Opal, 5 1/4 x 7 In. 175.00
Viking, Bowl, Cover, 7 In. 125.00
Viking, Butter, Cover 105.00
Viking, Celery Dish 85.00
Viking, Creamer 65.00
Viking, Dish, Pickle 75.00
Viking, Eggcup 40.00
Viking, Sugar, Cover 95.00
Waffle & Thumbprint, Champagne, 5 1/2 In. 110.00
Waffle & Thumbprint, Goblet, 6 5/8 In. 60.00
Washington, Goblet, 6 In. 120.00
Washington Centennial, Bread Tray 130.00
Washington Centennial, Bread Tray, Frosted Center 145.00
Washington Centennial, Cake Stand 55.00
Water Lily & Cattails, Pitcher, Water, Frosted 175.00
Wedding Ring, Goblet, Flint 110.00
Westward Ho, Bowl, Cover 245.00
Westward Ho, Bread Tray, Oval 125.00
Westward Ho, Compote, Cover, 6 In. 40.00
Westward Ho, Compote, Cover, 7 In. 550.00
Westward Ho, Compote, Cover, 11 1/2 x 6 In. 475.00
Westward Ho, Compote, Cover, Oval, 11 In. 125.00
Westward Ho, Creamer 195.00
Westward Ho, Spooner 90.00
Wheat & Barley, Goblet, Amber 38.00
Wheat & Barley, Mug, Amber 55.00
Wheat & Barley, Plate, 7 In. 42.00
Wheat & Barley, Plate, Blue, 7 In. 35.00
Wheat & Barley, Sugar, Cover, Blue 95.00
Wild Rose With Bow Knot, Butter, Cover, Green 150.00
Wildflower, Creamer, Amber 40.00
Wildflower, Goblet, Blue .... .30.00 to 40.00
Wildflower, Tray, Water, Blue 145.00
Willow Oak, Compote, Large 35.00
Willow Oak, Tray, Water 35.00
Willow Oak, Tumbler 55.00
Windflower, Goblet 34.00
Wisconsin, Salt & Pepper 95.00
Wooden Pail pattern is listed here as Oaken Bucket.
Wreath & Shell, Butter, Cover, Blue Opalescent, Gold Trim 40.00
Wreath & Shell, Creamer, Vaseline Opalescent 145.00
Wreath & Shell, Salt, Vaseline, Opalescent 165.00
Wreath & Shell, Toothpick 225.00
X-Ray, Butter, Cover, Green, Gold 110.00
X-Ray, Cruet Holder, Green, Gold Trim 75.00
Zipper Slash, Toothpick, Souvenir 40.00
Zippered Block, Toothpick 45.00

PRINT, in this listing, means any of many printed images produced on paper by one of the more common methods, such as lithography. The prints listed here are of interest primarily to the antiques collector, not the fine arts collector. Many of these prints were originally part of books. Other prints will be found in the Advertising, Currier & Ives, Movie, and Poster categories.

Alken, Henry, Pike Fishing, Flacker Shooting, Pheasant Shooting, 8 x 11 1/2 In. 90.00

Alvar, Sonol, Young Girl In Bonnet, Beneath Window, Lithograph, 30 x 23 In.	200.00
Ansdell, Richard, The Scotch Gamekeeper, England, 26 x 20 In.	140.00
Appel, Karel, Stylized Face, HC, Serigraph, 1971, 23 x 33 In.	375.00
Arts & Crafts, Stylized Geometric Design, Green Trees, Brown, Oak Frame, 5 x 6 In.	230.00

Audubon bird prints were originally issued as part of books printed from 1826 to 1854. They were issued in two sizes, 26 1/2 inches by 39 1/2 inches and 11 inches by 7 inches. The quadrupeds were issued in 28-by-22-inch prints. Later editions of the Audubon books were done in many sizes, and reprints of the books in the original size were also made. The bird pictures have been so popular they have been copied in myriad sizes by both old and new printing methods. This list includes originals and later copies because Audubon prints of all ages are sold in antiques shops.

J.W.Audubon

Audubon, Common American Deer, Frame, 1845, 19 x 26 In.	5405.00
Audubon, Common Grackle, 1858, 27 x 21 In.	345.00
Audubon, Common Pine Finch, 1893, 28 1/2 x 20 In.	357.00
Audubon, Esquimaux Dog, Frame, 1847, 19 x 25 In.	977.00
Audubon, Long Haired Squirrel, Frame, 1844, 26 x 21 In.	747.00
Audubon, Long Tailed Deer, Frame, 1847, 19 x 26 In.	2415.00
Audubon, Olive Sided Flycatcher, Frame, 1833, 24 x 17 In.	230.00
Audubon, Orange-Crowned Swamp Warbler, Frame, 25 x 17 In.	460.00
Audubon, Orchard Oriole, 25 x 20 In.	660.00
Audubon, Red Texan Wolf, Male, 1845, 19 x 26 In.	2645.00
Audubon, Say's Marmot-Squirrel, Frame, 1847, 19 x 26 In.	230.00 to 345.00
Audubon, Small Green-Crested, Flycatcher, 1832, 17 1/4 In.	517.00
Audubon, Summer Wood Duck, 38 x 24 In.	345.00
Audubon, Texan Lynx, Female, Frame, 1846, 19 x 26 In.	977.00
Audubon, Townsend's Ground Squirrel, Frame, 1843, 16 x 23 In.	374.00
Barnet, Will, Silent Seasons, Autumn, Lithograph, 26 x 20 In.	260.00
Beck & Pauli, View Of Millbury, Mass., Black, White, Frame, 1880, 23 x 28 In.	213.00
Black Soldiers Assaulting Fort At San Juan, 1907, 16 x 20 In.	205.00
Blome, Richard, Deer Hunting, Frame, 1686, 17 x 12 In., Pair	950.00
Boston Steel Loop De Loop Railway, Roller Coaster, Coumiem, 16 x 19 In.	990.00
Coignard, James, Composition, Signed, 1925, 25 1/2 x 39 1/4 In.	275.00
Currier, Extraordinary Express Across Atlantic, 1846, Small Folio	132.00
Flint, Sir William Russell, The Secret Retreat, 1964, 16 7/8 x 22 7/8 In.	125.00
Gould, Euphema Bourkii, Parakeets, Lithograph, Hand Colored, Frame, 34 x 28 In.	360.00
Gutmann, Home Builders, 7 1/2 x 9 1/2 In.	145.00
Hodgkin, Howard, Blue Venetian Glass, Lithograph, 27 3/4 x 33 3/4 In.	290.00
Hohlwein, Ludwig, Race Horse, Lithograph, 19 1/2 x 19 1/2 In.	405.00
Hoyuvson, 6 Horse Drawn Fire Vehicles, Frame, 12 x 32 In.	120.00
Huggins, South Sea Whale Fishery, Trimmed, Glued, Matted, Frame, 23 x 27 In.	465.00
Hutty, Alfred, Southern Street, Signed, 7 7/8 x 8 7/8 In.	300.00
Hutty, Alfred, Street Scene, Signed, 10 1/2 x 8 3/4 In.	300.00

Icart prints were made by Louis Icart, who worked in Paris from 1907 as an employee of a postcard company. He then started printing magazines and fashion brochures. About 1910 he created a series of etchings of fashionably dressed women and he continued to make similar etchings until he died in 1950. He is well known as a printmaker, painter, and illustrator. Original etchings are much more expensive than the later photographic copies.

Icart, Attic Room, Signed, 1940, 14 5/8 x 17 1/8 In.	3160.00
Icart, Autumn Leaves, Signed, 20 7/8 x 16 3/4 In.	1265.00
Icart, Bacchus & Nymphs, Signed, 8 x 5 3/4 In.	485.00
Icart, Backstage, 1926, 11 x 7 1/2 In.	980.00
Icart, Beauty And The Beast, Bears Signature, 8 7/8 x 6 3/8 In.	690.00
Icart, Blue Buddha, Frame, Signed, In Pencil, 18 x 22 In.	805.00
Icart, Celebration, Signed, 1928, 11 1/2 x 52 1/4 In.	2415.00
Icart, Chronicles Of Women, 1917, 10 1/4 x 7 In.	1095.00
Icart, Doves, Signed, 15 1/2 x 14 In.	1035.00
Icart, En Caleche, Frame, 13 x 16 1/8 In.	5750.00

Icart, Fair Dancer, 1937, 18 x 11 In. 2070.00
Icart, French Doll, 1926, 14 1/2 x 19 1/4 In. 545.00
Icart, Frolicking, Pub Scene, 1920, 14 3/4 x 18 7/8 In. 1095.00
Icart, Gay Trio, 1936, 11 x 19 In. 4830.00
Icart, Hiding Place, 1927, 14 1/2 x 14 1/2 In. 920.00
Icart, Hortensias, Etching, Signed, Matted, Frame, Oval, 1929, 26 1/4 x 29 1/4 In. 660.00
Icart, Lady Of Camelias, Signed, 1927, 16 1/4 x 20 1/4 In. 865.00
Icart, Love Birds, Signed, 18 3/4 x 13 5/8 In. 1095.00
Icart, Loves Blossom, 1937, 16 1/2 x 24 1/2 In. 1840.00
Icart, Madame Bovary, 1929, 20 1/2 x 16 In. 920.00
Icart, Martini Cocktail, 1932, 12 1/2 x 16 1/2 In. 5750.00
Icart, Miss America, Signed, 20 3/4 x 16 5/8 In. 1495.00
Icart, New Grapes, Etched, 1922, 19 1/4 x 13 In. 980.00
Icart, Nurse, Matted, Frame, Signed, In Pencil, 1917, 20 x 16 In. 400.00
Icart, Repose, 1934, 18 5/8 x 45 1/2 In. 10350.00
Icart, Russian Dancers, On Metal, 19 x 18 1/2 In. 160.00
Icart, Scene From Faust, Frame, Signed, 20 x 12 1/2 In. 1840.00
Icart, Sleeping Beauty, 1927, 14 3/4 x 18 1/2 In. 1265.00 to 1840.00
Icart, Smoke, 1926, 14 1/8 x 19 3/8 In. 1035.00
Icart, Speed, 1933, 15 x 24 In. 2530.00
Icart, Spilled Apples, Signed, 19 1/2 x 12 1/2 In. 1495.00
Icart, Summer Dreams, 1934, 19 5/8 x 17 1/2 In. 6325.00
Icart, Symphony In Blue, 1936, 20 x 24 In. 2300.00
Icart, Thoroughbreds, 13 1/2 x 24 1/2 In. 70.00
Icart, Two Beauties, 1931, 16 3/4 x 24 1/2 In. 19550.00
Icart, White Underwear, Signed, 15 5/8 x 19 3/4 In. 1725.00
Icart, Winter, 1928, 8 1/2 x 6 1/2 In. 1955.00
Icart, Wistfulness, Matted, Frame, Signed, In Pencil, 1924, 13 x 18 In. 805.00
Jacoulet, Fleurs Du Soir, Evening Flowers, 1941, 15 1/2 x 11 7/8 In. 1650.00
Jacoulet, La Lettre Du Fils, Son's Letter, Tea Jar Seal, 1938 . . . . 550.00
Jacoulet, La Mariee, The Bride, 1948 . . . . 1045.00
Jacoulet, Le Nid, The Nest, 1941 . . . . 2200.00
Jacoulet, Le Repas Des Mendiants, Beggar's Meal, Tea Jar Seal 1210.00
Jacoulet, Le Tresor, The Treasure, 1940 . . . . 825.00
Jacoulet, Les Deux Freres, Two Brothers, Good Luck Hammer Seal, 1936 . . . . 550.00
Jacoulet, Les Papillons, Butterflies Of Tropics 1540.00
Jacoulet, Les Paradisiers, Birds Of Paradise, Tea Jar Seal, 1937 . . . . 880.00
Jacoulet, Marchande De Carpes, Old Carp Seller, Fan Seal, 1934 . . . . 165.00
Jacoulet, Marionettes Chinoises, Chinese Puppets, Mandarin Duck Seal, 1935 . . . . 275.00
Jacoulet, Nuit De Neige, Christmas Card 132.00
Jacoulet, Nuit De Neige, Snowy Night, 1939 . . . . 990.00
Jacoulet, Orchidees Blanches, Christmas Card 467.00
Jacoulet, Premier Mour, First Love, Good Luck Hammer Seal, 1937 . . . . 1650.00
Jacoulet, Retour De La Jungle, Return From Jungle, 1948 . . . . 1320.00

Japanese woodblock prints are listed as follows: Print, Japanese, name of artist, title or description, type, and size. Dealers use the following terms: Tate-e is a vertical composition. Yoko-e is a horizontal composition. The words Aiban (13 by 9 inches), Chuban (10 by 7 1/2 inches), Hosoban (12 by 6 inches), Oban (15 by 10 inches), and Koban (7 by 4 inches) denote size. Modern versions of some of these prints have been made.

Japanese, Hiroshi Yoshida, Sleigh, 9 3/4 x 14 3/4 In. 175.00
Japanese, Kaiko Moti, Sunset Flight, Signed, 15 3/4 x 24 1/5 In. 170.00
Japanese, Kawase Hasue, Lake Matsubara At Morning, Signed, 9 1/2 x 14 3/8 In. 230.00
Japanese, Kawase Hasue, Night Scene At Soemoncho, Signed, 14 1/2 x 9 1/2 In. 230.00
Japanese, Kawase Hasui, Mount Fuji Seen From Narusawa, Oban, 9 1/4 x 14 1/4 In. 230.00
Japanese, Kawase Hasui, Snow At Hinuma Swamp, Mito, Oban, 9 1/2 x 14 1/4 In. 405.00
Japanese, Kawase Hasui, Tengu Rock, Shiobara, Oban, 14 1/2 x 9 1/4 In. 316.00
Japanese, Sasjima, Temple Through The Trees, Signed, 1962, 16 3/4 x 11 5/8 In. 15.00
Japanese, Toyokuni III, Courtesan, Landscape, 14 x 10 In., Pair 85.00
Japanese, Tsukioka Yoshitoshi, Moon Of The Enemies' Lair, Oban, 13 x 8 3/4 In. 230.00
Japanese, Tsukioka Yoshitoshi, Moon's Invention, Hozo Temple, Oban, 13 1/8 x 8 3/4 In. . . . 230.00

Japanese, Wrestler, Wearing Robe, Holding Bell In Teeth, Signed, 14 x 9 5//8 In. 60.00
Japanese, Yoshida, Young Girl, Signed, 5 7/8 x 4 In. 110.00
Kasimir, Hamburg, Germany, Signed, 11 7/8 x 8 In. 175.00
Kasimir, Street Scene, 9 1/4 x 12 1/4 In. 200.00
Kellogg, Brave At Home, Family Farewell To Officer, 11 x 8 In. 50.00
Kellogg, DeWitt Clinton & Henry Clay, Black & White, Frame, 20 1/2 x 17 1/2 In., Pair . . 120.00
Kellogg & Comstock, Washington, 11 7/8 x 8 5/8 In. 80.00
Kurz & Allison, Battle Of Fort Donelson, Frame, 21 7/8 x 27 In. 355.00
Lindner, Richard, Room For Rent, AP, Serigraph, 40 1/2 x 29 In. 460.00
Marvin, Frederick, Processional, Signed, 7 3/4 x 14 1/8 In. 70.00
Max, Peter, Angel, HC, Serigraph, 22 x 29 1/2 In. 290.00
Max, Peter, Liberty, Signed, 1988, 23 3/4 x 19 3/4 In. 150.00
McCrady, John, Wreck Of The Old, Signed, 10 1/4 x 14 In. 800.00
McKenney & Hall, Wa-Em-Boesh-Kaa, Chippeway Chief, 19th Century, 20 x 14 1/2 In. . . 665.00
McKenney & Hall, Wesh Cubb, Chippeway Chief, 19th Century, 20 1/8 x 14 3/8 In. 605.00
McKenney & Hall, Young Ma-Hus-Kah-Chief Of Ioways, 20 1/8 x 14 3/8 In. 665.00
Mountain Scene, American Indian, Horses, Arts & Crafts, Frame, 8 x 14 In. . . . . .385.00 to 440.00
Never Too Young To Learn, Woman, Pin-Up Type, Brown & Bigelow, 1940s, 10 x 12 In. . 50.00

Nutting prints are now popular with collectors. Wallace Nutting is
known for his pictures, furniture, and books. Nutting *prints* are actually hand-colored photographs issued from 1900 to 1941. There are *Wallace Nutting*
over 10, 000 different titles. Wallace Nutting furniture is listed in the
Furniture category.

Nutting, A Century Of Age, 13 x 17 In. 105.00
Nutting, A Sip Of Tea, Signed, 1861, 7 1/4 x 9 1/2 In. 144.00
Nutting, A Stitch In Time, Signed, 1861, 11 x 14 In. 115.00
Nutting, Coming Out Of Rosa, Signed, 1861, 10 x 13 In. 259.00
Nutting, Goose Chase Pattern, Signed, 1861, 4 x 9 1/2 In. 43.00
Nutting, Guardian Mother, Frame, 11 x 17 In. 2970.00
Nutting, Hope, Flowering Tree, Stone Fence & Stream, 13 x 16 In. 146.00
Nutting, Jersey Blossoms, Frame, 1915, 24 1/2 x 20 3/4 In. 85.00
Nutting, Landscape Photograph, Pastel Crayon, Carved Oak Frame, 13 x 7 In. 135.00
Nutting, Memory Of Childhood, Hand Colored, Signed, 5 3/4 x 9 In. 77.00
Nutting, On The Slope, 13 x 6 1/2 In. 475.00
Nutting, Thanksgiving Goodies, Signed, 1861, 7 1/4 x 9 1/2 In. 144.00
Nutting, To Meet Me, Signed, 1861, 4 x 9 1/2 In. 43.00
Nutting, Tranquil Vale, Signed, 1861, 5 1/4 x 13 In. 80.00
Nutting, Yosemite, Water, 13 x 16 In. 94.00
O'Neill, Elizabeth Verner, Side Entrance, Signed, 5 1/8 x 3 3/8 In. 300.00
Orozco, Jose Clemente, The Masses, Signed, 1935, 13 1/4 x 16 7/8 In. 1600.00

Parrish prints are wanted by collectors. Maxfield Frederick Parrish
was an illustrator who lived from 1870 to 1966. He is best known as a *Maxfield Parrish*
designer of magazine covers, posters, calendars, and advertisements.

Parrish, Air Castles, Frame, 1904, 14 x 18 In. 225.00
Parrish, Daybreak, Frame, 1928, 14 x 18 In. 200.00
Parrish, Jester Playing Mandolin, New Frame, 1920s, 11 x 9 In. 195.00
Parrish, The End, Actress Taking Bow, Swiveling Art Deco Frame, 14 3/4 x 14 1/4 In. . . . 425.00
Phillips, Gordon, Tracks, Snowed Under, Signed In Pencil, 30 x 23 In. 45.00
Picasso, Charger, Green, Blue, Yellow, Brown, 15 1/4 In. 4600.00
Union Straw Works, Foxboro, Mass, Carpenter & Co., Frame, 19th Century, 21 x 27 In. . 220.00
Vargas, Huntress, With Dog, Lithograph, 20 3/4 x 15 7/8 In. 980.00
Vargas, Woman In Floral & Pearl Headdress, Holding Ship, 22 3/4 x 16 In. 345.00
Ward, James, Outside Of A Country Ale House, March, 1797, 17 5/8 x 23 3/4 In. 80.00
Weiss, St. Jame's Park, Black & Gold Reverse Painted On Glass, 19 x 22 1/2 In. 495.00
Woodblock, Elizabeth Norton, Tree In Foreground, Arts & Crafts Oak Frame, 3 x 4 In. . . 360.00
Woodblock, Hood For Sea Voyage, Black & White, 1870s, 6 x 8 In. 7.00
Woodblock, Hopkins, Edna Boise, Cornflower, Frame, c.1911, 11 x 7 1/4 In. 2600.00
Woodblock, Hopkins, Edna Boise, Datura, Frame, c.1910, 11 x 7 1/4 In. 2100.00
Woodblock, Hyde, Helen, A Day In June, Woman, Baby, Iris Field, Frame, 8 x 16 In. 715.00
Woodblock, Lemos, Pedro, Sunset Mountain, Tree-Lined Lagoon, Oak Frame, 10 x 9 In. . 1320.00
Woodblock, Lemos, Pedro, Trees On Hillside, Boats, Matted, Frame, 8 x 10 In. 605.00

Woodblock, Lum, Bertha, Birds In Tree, Swirling Female Figure, Matted, Frame, 16 In. ... 1210.00
Woodblock, Old Woman Walking In Graveyard, For Charity's Sake, 1870s, 6 x 9 In. 7.00
Woodblock, Orchids, Purple, Red, Blue, Green, Arts & Crafts, Oak Frame, 5 x 7 In. 285.00
Woodblock, Patterson, Margaret J., On The Canal, Frame, c.1920, 8 1/2 x 6 In. 1300.00
Woodblock, Patterson, Margaret, Mountains Above Village, Oak Frame, 10 x 7 In. 400.00
Woodblock, Rocks In Water, Gray, Black, Green, Gold, Arts & Crafts, Oak Frame, 12 In. .. 400.00
Woodblock, Ships Of Yesterday, Arts & Crafts Frame, Signed, 11 x 8 1/2 In. 1400.00
Woodblock, Swans, 2 Yellow, Ivory, Blue Body Of Water, Arts & Crafts, 14 x 12 In. 1320.00
Woodcut, Baumann, Gustave, October Night, Farmhouse Scene, 1916, 9 x 11 1/4 In. 4370.00
Woodcut, Cook, Howard, Boat Builders, Signed, Pencil, 1926, 16 3/4 x 8 3/8 In. 920.00
Woodcut, Cook, Howard, Rubber Center, Signed, Pencil, 1928, 10 x 12 1/2 In. 2990.00
Woodcut, Dow, Arthur W., Ipswich Waterfront, 1895, 5 x 2 3/8 In. 3450.00
Woodcut, Dow, Arthur W., Waterfront Shanties, Ipswich, Signed, Pencil, 1895, 5 x 2 In. . 3680.00
Woodcut, Gat, Moshe, Boy Cleaning Fish, Israel, 35 1/4 x 22 1/2 In. 90.00
Woodcut, Heckel, Erich, Bildnis, Ocher, Brown, Black, Cream, Signed, 20 x 15 In. 1092.00
Woodcut, Heckel, Erich, Die Tote, Signed, 1912, 9 3/4 x 11 5/8 In. 2070.00
Woodward, Ellsworth, The Oaks In Audubon Park, Moss-Laden Trees, Frame, 5 x 4 In. .. 330.00

PURINTON POTTERY COMPANY was incorporated in Wellsville, Ohio, in 1936. The company moved to Shippenville, Pennsylvania, in 1941 and made a variety of hand-painted ceramic wares. By the 1950s Purinton was making dinnerware, souvenirs, cookie jars, and florist wares. The pottery closed in 1959.

Purinton Pottery

Apple, Creamer ....22.00 to 25.00
Apple, Mug, Beer 115.00
Apple, Water Set, Purinton, 7 Piece 180.00
Brown, Candy Dish, Ring Handle 60.00
Chartreuse, Candy Dish, Ring Handle 90.00
Chartreuse, Sugar & Creamer 445.00
Cookie Jar, Apple 68.00
Cookie Jar, Humpty Dumpty 425.00
Cruet, Oil & Vinegar 75.00
Heather Plaid, Chop Plate 55.00
Intaglio, Coffeepot, 8 Cup 45.00
Normandy Plaid, Jam Jar 65.00
Normandy Plaid, Platter, 11 In. 45.00
Palm Tree, Plate, 9 3/4 In. 375.00
Petals, Bowl, 5 1/2 In. 15.00
Red Ivy, Cookie Jar 40.00
Red Ivy, Teapot, 6 Cup 15.00

PURSES have been recognizable since the eighteenth century, when leather and needlework purses were preferred. Beaded purses became popular in the nineteenth century, went out of style, but are again in use. Mesh purses date from the 1880s and are still being made. How to carry a handkerchief and lipstick is a problem today for every woman, including the Queen of England.

Art Nouveau, Black, Yellow, & Pale Green, Zigzag Bottom, Whiting & Davis 95.00
Beaded, 3 Children Design, 11 x 7 1/4 In. 425.00
Beaded, Bird On Branch, 4 x 4 1/4 In. 75.00
Beaded, Bird On Branch, Enameled Frame, 6 x 5 In. 175.00
Beaded, Blue & White Check, Polychrome Floral Center, Lined, Drawstring, c.1840 .... 375.00
Beaded, Clutch, White Beads, Geometrically Across Entire Purse, 6 x 9 In. 68.00
Beaded, Clutch, White Seed Beads, Green Beaded Leaves, Japan, 8 1/2 x 4 1/2 In. 35.00
Beaded, Drawstring, Linen Lining, Lower Tassel 70.00
Beaded, Floral & Butterfly, Multicolored, Black, Red, White, Green, Judith Leiber, 6 In. . 1495.00
Beaded, Floral Pattern, Both Sides, Cotton Liner, Silk Drawstring, 19th Century, 8 5/8 In. 185.00
Beaded, Flower & Geometric Design, Zipper Closure, Czechoslovakia 55.00
Beaded, Flower Vase, Multicolored, 10 1/2 x 7 In. 275.00
Beaded, Metallic Medallion Design, Fringed, France, 13 x 7 In. 100.00
Beaded, Metallic Silver Swan Scroll Border, Beaded Fringe, Flap Closure, 5 1/2 In. 90.00
Beaded, Metallic, Geometric Bands, Silver Filigree Frame, Beaded Fringe, 7 1/2 x 6 In. .. 50.00
Beaded, Owl's Eye, Judith Leiber 660.00

Use Simichrome polish to clean metal mesh bags. Unpainted, unlined mesh bags can be cleaned in a solution of equal parts ammonia and liquid laundry detergent. Swish the bag up and down in the mixture. Rinse, then dry with a hair dryer to keep rust from forming.

Purse, Leather, Tooled, Black & Brown,
1960s, 10 1/2 x 10 In.

Beaded, Palm Tree Design	75.00
Beaded, Peacock & Florals, 7 x 12 In.	345.00
Beaded, Pearl Clasp, Josef	45.00
Beaded, Pearls, Occupied Japan	65.00
Beaded, Pearls, White & Gray, Chain Handle, 7 x 6 In.	50.00
Beaded, Roses, Red, Green & White, Silk Lining, Cord Handle, Victorian, 6 x 12 In.	225.00
Beaded, Scenic, Ornate Silver Frame, Fringe, Maroon, Orange, Green, Blue	325.00
Beaded, Silver, Crochet Chatelaine, Lion's Head, Art Nouveau Frame, 8 1/2 x 5 In.	295.00
Beaded, Venetian Canal Scene, Micromosaic Frame, Italian, 13 12 x 8 In.	160.00
Beaded, White & Crystal Beads, 6 x 9 In.	68.00
Beaded, White, Gold Tone Frame, Chain Handle, Dormer, Paris, Belgium, N.Y., 7 x 5 In.	75.00
Coin, Double, Chatelaine, Teal	110.00
Coin, Mesh, Chatelaine, Silver, Gold Plate, 4 Dolphins, Teardrop Fringe, Germany	198.00
Coin, Mesh, Garnets, Simons Brothers, Philadelphia, 2 5/8 x 2 3/4 x 3/4 In.	295.00
Crochet, Clutch, Orange, Pink, Gold, Rhinestone Circle Pin On Flap, 7 x 4 In.	10.00
Fruiting Branches Front & Back, Leather Interior, Sterling Silver, c.1890, 4 3/4 In.	135.00
Fur, Navy, Square, Bamboo Handle, Leather Shoulder Strap, Gucci	632.00
Ivory, Choriao Offering Shoe To Kosekiko, Kosekiko On Reverse, 18th Century, 2 7/8 In.	5250.00
Ivory, Floral Carving, Shishi Finial, Barrel Form	605.00
Ivory, Inlaid Butterfly Dancer, 4-Case, Shokasai, Gold Lacquer	665.00
Ivory, Sleeve, Woman Carrying Basket, Boy Feeding Fowl, 2 Inside Sections, 3 1/2 In.	6750.00
Leather, Black Calf, Baguette Shape, Gilt Metal, Silver Clasp, Hermes, 1960s	635.00
Leather, Courchevel, Gilt Metal Lock, Key Sheath, Brown, Hermes, 1990	2070.00
Leather, Embossed, Art Nouveau, Bronze Mount	135.00
Leather, Gray, Channeled Stitching, Gold Link Strap, Rectangular, Chanel, 5 In.	115.00
Leather, Peacock Design, Meeker, 6 x 6 1/2 In.	125.00
Leather, Satchel Shape, Louis Vuitton	100.00
Leather, Tooled, Black & Brown, 1960s, 10 1/2 x 10 In. ....*Illus*	75.00
Lucite, Amber Tortoiseshell, Llewellyn	395.00
Lucite, Clear & White, 2 Handles, 4 Footed, 6 x 3 3/4 x 5 In.	125.00
Lucite, Clutch, Blue, Silver Sparkles, Gold Plated Clasp, 9 1/4 x 1 3/8 x 4 1/2 In.	75.00
Lucite, Egg Shape, Faberge Style, Judith Leiber	1430.00
Lucite, Gray Marbleized, Etched Flowers, Metal Grill	75.00
Lucite, Tortoise, Ribbed, Swing Handles, Carved Lid	60.00
Mahogany, Swing Handle, Expanding Square Case, 9 x 8 In.	105.00
Mesh, 14K Gold, Compact	550.00
Mesh, 14K Yellow Gold, Cabochon Sapphire Clasp, Chain, 1930, 5 x 8 1/4 In.	665.00
Mesh, Art Deco, Enameled Chain, Whiting & Davis, 1940, 7 x 7 In.	85.00
Mesh, Art Deco, Geometric, Red, Yellow, White, Scalloped Edge, Whiting & Davis	110.00
Mesh, Art Deco, Multicolored, Zigzag Bottom Edge, Whiting & Davis	165.00
Mesh, Art Deco, Swirl, Pink, Blue, Yellow & Brown, Zigzag Bottom, Whiting & Davis	105.00
Mesh, Black & White Enamel Design, Silver Top, Chain, 1920s-1930s, 4 1/2 x 6 In.	85.00
Mesh, Central Cartouche, Line Border, Black, Pink, Zigzag Bottom, Whiting & Davis	95.00
Mesh, Central Floral Medallion, Black, White & Yellow, Zigzag Bottom, Signed, El-Sah	75.00
Mesh, Chatelaine, Engraved Handle, Sterling Silver, 4 x 5 In.	200.00
Mesh, Chrome, Whiting & Davis, 4 x 5 1/2 In.	125.00
Mesh, Diamond Grid Pattern, Cream & Browns, Zigzag Bottom, Whiting & Davis	85.00

Mesh, Diamond Inside Square, Overlapping Arches, Blue, Green, Pink, Whiting & Davis . 140.00
Mesh, Diamond Pattern, Multicolored, Zigzag Bottom, Edge, Whiting & Davis 85.00
Mesh, Enamel, Gold Plated Frame, Wire Handle, Whiting & Davis 55.00
Mesh, Fancy Floral Spray, Yellow, Orange, Black, Gray, Zigzag Edge, Whiting & Davis . . 110.00
Mesh, Floral Design On Frame, Silver, 6 x 6 3/4 In. 143.00
Mesh, Floral Design, Pink & Black On Cream Ground, V-Shaped Fringe, Mandalian 165.00
Mesh, Floral Repousse Frame & Hanger, Silver, Germany, 1901 . . . . 145.00
Mesh, Geometric Design, Greens, Brown, Blue, Zigzag Bottom, Whiting & Davis 110.00
Mesh, Geometric Design, Red & Black On Yellow, Blue Ground, Whiting & Davis 145.00
Mesh, Geometric Diamond Bands, Blue, White & Gold, Zigzag Bottom, Whiting & Davis 100.00
Mesh, Gold, Rhinestone Frame, Whiting & Davis 55.00
Mesh, Gold, Snap Top, Whiting & Davis 65.00
Mesh, Link Chain Over Floraform Handle, Monogrammed, Sterling Silver 105.00
Mesh, Rhinestone Clasp, Whiting & Davis, 5 x 7 In. 98.00
Mesh, Snakeskin Pattern, Green & Yellow, Straight Bottom Edge, Whiting & Davis 65.00
Mesh, Vanity, Chasing Both Sides, Leather Compartments, Sterling Silver 250.00
Mesh, Wrist Chain, Whiting & Davis, 5 x 7 In. 98.00
Needlepoint, Flamestitch, 18th Century, Opens To 9 x 9 In. 1595.00
Needlepoint, Scenic, 4 Couples In Brook, Scalloped, 8 x 6 In. 265.00
Needlepoint & Silk, c.1900 . . . . 20.00
Needlework, Knapsack Form, 19th Century, 4 x 3/4 In. 44.00
Patent Leather, Black, Gold Shoulder Chain, Colored Stones, Judith Leiber, 7 x 2 In. . . . 200.00
Rhinestones, Aurora Borealis, Beaded Trim, LeLill, 4 3/8 x 8 1/2 In. 150.00
Satin, Khaki, Gold Shoulder Chain, Tiger-Eye Latch, Judith Leiber, 7 In. 70.00
Shoulder, Gilt Metal Hands Clasping Flowers, Gold Chains, Judith Leiber, 1972 . . . . 345.00
Sterling Silver, Hinged Engraved Sleigh Scene, Divided Interior, 7 3/4 In. 200.00
Suede, Brown, Foldover Style, Metal Pivot Clasp, Gucci, 1978 . . . . 430.00
Suede, Navy, Goldtone, Leather Buckle & Strap, Gucci 172.00

QUEZAL glass was made from 1901 to 1924 by Martin Bach, Sr., in Queens, New York. Other glassware by other firms, such as Loetz, Steuben, and Tiffany, resembles this gold-colored iridescent glass. Martin Bach died in 1921. His son-in-law, Conrad Vahlsing, Jr., went to work at the Lustre Art Company about 1920 and his son, Martin Bach, Jr., worked at the Durand Art Glass division of the Vineland Flint Glass Works after 1924.

Quezal

Bowl, Gold Luster, Footed, c.1905, Signed, 5 1/2 In. 572.00
Lamp, Base, Pulled Feathers, Gold, Green, Gold Lining, Cream Ground, 12 In. 825.00
Lamp, Pulled Feathers Shade, Bronze Reclining Lion Base, Weight Balance, 13 In. 1190.00
Lamp, Zipper, Green, 18 3/4 In. 35.00
Salt, Iridescent Gold, 2 1/2 In. 230.00
Salt, Paneled Ribs, Flared Rim, Gold Aurene, 1 7/8 In. 357.00
Shade, Green & Gold Pulled Feathers, Gold Interior, Signed F, 4 1/2 In. 200.00
Shade, Ivory, Gold Looping, Gold Aurene Interior, 5 In., Pair 605.00
Shade, Pulled Feathers, Blue, 6 In., Pair 450.00
Shade, Pulled Feathers, Gold Opalescent, Green Glass, 5 In., 7 Piece 1150.00
Shade, Pulled Feathers, Gold To White Opalescent, Green Feather Edge, 5 1/4 In., Pair . . 403.00
Shade, Pulled Feathers, Green Outline, Gold Interior, Ivory, 5 In. 137.00
Shade, Ribbed, Gold Iridescent, Signed, 6 In. 286.00
Shade, Tulip, Iridescent White, Green Designs, Gold String Overlay, 4 Piece, 5 3/4 In. . . . 468.00
Shade, White Calcite, Signed, 4 3/4 In., Pair 46.00
Shade, White Iridescent, Green Trailing Hearts, Gold Stringing, c.1905, Pair 220.00
Vase, Amber, Gold, Crimson Iridescent, 1900-1920, 9 1/2 In. 546.00
Vase, Deep Amber Striated Pulled Feathers, Blue Iridescent, Tomato Red Sides, 12 In. . . . 4887.00
Vase, Flower Form, Pulled Feathers, Green, Gold, Scalloped Edge, Pad Foot, 7 In. 1610.00
Vase, Gold Iridescent, 4-Crimped Top, Inscribed Mark, 5 In. 605.00
Vase, Gold, Rose, Blue Iridescent Highlights, Flared, 5 1/2 In. 412.00
Vase, Green Pulled Leaves, Gold Trailings, Tricornered, Signed, 1901, 8 In. 1035.00
Vase, Green Trailings, Ribbed, Tricornered, Signed, 1925, 4 1/4 In. 920.00
Vase, Interior & Exterior Golden Orange Luster, Signed, 8 In. 530.00
Vase, Iridescent Opalescent, Green, Amber Striated Feathering, Amber Interior, 7 In. 1840.00
Vase, Iridescent Yellow, Blue Swirls, 7 1/4 In. 1100.00
Vase, Jack-In-The-Pulpit, Gold Amber Interior, Emerald Green Exterior, 1920, 9 In. 3737.00

Vase, Pulled Feathers, Green, Gold Border, White Ground, Pedestal, 5 In. 1100.00
Vase, Rainbow Gold Iridescent, Scrolled Trailings, Baluster, 6 In. 1265.00
Vase, Silver Iridescent Trailing Hearts & Vines, Blue Iridescent, 5 1/2 In. 3335.00
Vase, Silver Overlay, Deep Amber, Red, Silver Blue, Gold Iridescent, 1900, 5 1/8 In. 1380.00
Vase, Sweet Pea, Gold On Oyster White With Green, Fluted, 7 3/4 In. 2300.00
Vase, Threaded, White Trailing Heart, Deep Blue, Signed, 7 In. 1100.00
Vase, Trumpet, Iridescent Gold, Serpent Bronze Base, Griffoul, 1916, 20 x 5 In. 2000.00
Vase, White Ground, Yellow Trailings, Flared, Scalloped, Pedestal Footed Base, 9 1/2 In. . . 770.00

QUILTS have been made since the seventeenth century. Early textiles were very precious and every scrap was saved to be reused. A quilt is a combination of fabrics joined to a filler and a backing by small stitched designs known as quilting. An appliqued quilt has pieces stitched to the top of a large piece of background fabric. A patchwork, or pieced, quilt is made of many small pieces stitched together. Embroidery can be added to either type.

Album, Diamond In Square, Pieced, Dated 1849, Medford, N.J. 825.00
Amish, Diamond In Square, Feather Quilting, 1920s, 78 x 76 In. 1725.00
Amish, Patchwork, Black, Faded Wine Stripe, Blue Alternating With Khaki, 66 x 82 In. . . 385.00
Amish, Patchwork, Black, Light Blue, Beige, Brown, 1946, 72 x 84 In. 550.00
Amish, Patchwork, Blue, Brown, Black, Gray Tan, Cotton, Crib, 30 1/2 x 38 1/2 In. 330.00
Appliqued, 4 Floral Medallions, White Ground, Serpentine Border, 86 x 82 In. 385.00
Appliqued, 4 Red Baskets, White Ground, 74 x 74 In. 495.00
Appliqued, 6 Floral Medallions, Calico, 20th Century, 80 x 96 In. 605.00
Appliqued, 9 Different Designs, Sampler, Red, Green & Yellow, White, 66 x 72 In. 440.00
Appliqued, 9 Floral Medallions, Red, Pink, Green, Vine Border, 74 1/2 x 76 In. 960.00
Appliqued, 9 Patch, Blue & White Calico, 76 x 84 In. 245.00
Appliqued, 9 Star Medallions, Red, Yellow & Brown Calico, 88 x 88 In. 220.00
Appliqued, 16 Baskets Of Flowers, Vining Floral Border, Red, Green, 87 x 89 In. 835.00
Appliqued, 25 Squares, Floral Wreaths & Sprays, Red Borders, 19th Century, 99 x 99 In. . 8625.00
Appliqued, 25 Squares, Florals, Eagle Center, Vine Border, c.1860, 60 x 60 In. 8050.00
Appliqued, 49 Squares, Friendship, Odd Fellow Insignia, 80 x 80 In. 520.00
Appliqued, Bear Paw, Pink & Green Calico, 90 x 90 In. 440.00
Appliqued, Blossoms, Buds & Leaves, Hawaiian, 1925, 71 1/2 x 85 1/2 In. 690.00
Appliqued, Blossoms, Pink Calico, Green Leaves, Scalloped, 72 x 88 In. 190.00
Appliqued, Brown Tulips, Hearts & Scallops, Vine Border, 19th Century, 82 x 84 In. . . . 895.00
Appliqued, Compass Rose Design, 19th Century, 98 x 98 In. 457.00
Appliqued, Floral Medallions, Red, Green, Goldenrod, 71 x 82 In. 190.00
Appliqued, Floral, White Field, Running Vine Border, 1950, 94 x 81 In. 330.00
Appliqued, Flying Geese, White, Red, 74 x 80 In. 330.00
Appliqued, Log Cabin, Sawtooth Border, 70 x 80 In. 465.00
Appliqued, Pinwheels & Miniature 9 Block, 72 x 64 In. 165.00
Appliqued, Red Calico, Solid Green, 91 x 91 In. 495.00
Appliqued, Red Flowers, White Squares, 88 x 70 In. 315.00
Appliqued, Rose & Bud, Pink Calico, Green, Red, White Ground, 90 x 73 In. 460.00
Appliqued, Rose Wreath, Cut Corners, Red, Teal Green, Mid-19th Century, 84 x 82 In. . . 230.00
Appliqued, School House, All Green Border, Crib, 50 x 47 In. 95.00
Appliqued, Star Medallions, Red & Green Calico, 84 x 84 In. 1210.00
Appliqued, Star Of Bethlehem, Red, Green & Yellow Star, White Field, Crib, 19 x 28 In. . 300.00
Appliqued, Star, Red, White & Blue, 82 x 68 In. 495.00
Appliqued, Stars, Red & Brown Calico & Yellow, White Ground, 74 x 88 In. 275.00
Appliqued, Stylized Floral Medallions & Border, Trapunto, 87 x 87 In. 2420.00
Appliqued, Stylized Floral Medallions, Swag & Flower Border, 83 x 86 In. 495.00
Appliqued, Stylized Floral Medallions, Teal Blue, Red & Burnt Orange, 86 x 90 In. 687.00
Appliqued, Stylized Poinsettia, Red, Yellow & Green, Machine Binding, 88 x 90 In. 275.00
Appliqued, Sunburst & Eagle, Green, Terra-Cotta, Red, White Field, 88 x 90 In. 230.00
Appliqued, Sunflower, 4 Concentric Circles, Feathered Chain Border, All White, 1910 . . . 165.00
Appliqued, Tulip Medallions, Vining Border, Pink Fabric, 78 x 90 In. 275.00
Appliqued, Tulip, Yellow, Green & Red, 20th Century, 66 x 89 In. 450.00
Embroidered, 42 Blocks, Flowers, Animals, Civil War Soldier, 1864, 68 x 78 In. 9200.00
Embroidered, Cross-Stitch, Sunflower & Pineapple-Border, 1930, 91 x 76 In. 55.00
Embroidered, Parrots In Square On Men's Suiting Fabric, c.1920, 64 x 74 In. 2800.00
Patchwork, 4 Oak Leaf Pinwheels, Stripes & Star Grid, 75 x 82 In. 302.00

Patchwork, 9 Patch Variation, Calicos, Shirting Fabric, Square, 78 In. 135.00
Patchwork, 9 Patch, Green Floral & Pink Calico, 76 x 88 In. 330.00
Patchwork, 9 Patch, Pink & Green Calico, Navy Blue Print Ground, 64 x 64 In. 355.00
Patchwork, 9 Patch, Prints, 81 x 81 In. 440.00
Patchwork, 9 Star Medallions, 75 x 75 In. 435.00
Patchwork, 12 Stars In Grid, Red & White, 64 x 81 In. 300.00
Patchwork, 12 Stars, Blue, Apricot & Turquoise, White Ground, 73 x 84 In. 465.00
Patchwork, 16 Patch, Blue & White, 74 x 74 In. 250.00
Patchwork, 20 Lyres Hearts, Green & Goldenrod, 80 x 86 In. 1155.00
Patchwork, 21 Ice Cream Cone Medallions, 3 Sides Sawtooth Border, 72 x 81 In. 195.00
Patchwork, American Pillar, Pieced Postage Stamp Diamonds, 92 1/2 x 91 1/4 In. 1495.00
Patchwork, Baby Block, Child's, Herringbone Field, Spruce Green, Blue, Brown, 35 In. . . 170.00
Patchwork, Barn Raising, Solids & Plaids, Gray & Turquoise Center, 73 x 73 In. 660.00
Patchwork, Bars Variation, Blue Printed Shirting, Hired Man's Bed, 39 x 76 In. 95.00
Patchwork, Basket, Red & White, 64 x 76 In. 435.00
Patchwork, Bowtie, Multicolored Prints & Calico, 65 x 71 In. 357.00
Patchwork, Bowtie, Navy Blue Print & White, 77 x 77 In. 495.00
Patchwork, Buggy, Corduroy Velvet & Wool, c.1890, 68 1/2 x 56 In. 110.00
Patchwork, Checkerboard Corner Blocks, Blue & White, 1920s, 78 x 84 In. 410.00
Patchwork, Crazy, Birds & Flowers, Silk, Cotton, Embroidered, Cut Velvet, 69 x 57 In. . . 3680.00
Patchwork, Crazy, Embroidered, Unbound, 62 x 74 In. 165.00
Patchwork, Crazy, Silk & Velvet, Red Chintz, Ruffle, Embroidered, 1800s, 81 x 84 In. . . 193.00
Patchwork, Crazy, Triangle & Log Cabin, Knotted, 70 x 92 In. 110.00
Patchwork, Crown Of Thorns, Blue & Black Calico On White, 74 x 88 In. 220.00
Patchwork, Delectable Mountains, Blue, Brown & Gray, 56 x 70 In. 165.00
Patchwork, Documents & Parishioners Of Zion Missionary Baptist Church, 102 x 84 In. . . 230.00
Patchwork, Double Irish Chain, Blue & Pink Calico, Sawtooth Border, 71 x 80 In. 495.00
Patchwork, Embroidered Blue Flowers, Blue & White, 1940, 80 x 80 In. 305.00
Patchwork, Embroidered Flower Blocks, Quilter Betty Sans Barrows, 1929, 92 x 74 In. . . 220.00
Patchwork, Embroidered, Rhymes, People, Animals, Flag, Border, c.1920, 66 x 76 In. . . . 825.00
Patchwork, Fence Around Field, Green & Goldenrod, Brown Center, 81 x 82 In. 300.00
Patchwork, Floral, Swag & Tassel Border, 80 x 82 In. 285.00
Patchwork, Flying Geese, Red Calico Border, Sawtooth Stripe, 68 x 82 In. 330.00
Patchwork, Flying Geese, Triple Border, Reversible, Bars Back, 30 x 31 In. 190.00
Patchwork, Geometric, Salmon & Royal Blue, White Ground, 80 x 102 In. 440.00
Patchwork, Grandmother's Flower Garden, Prints & Solids, 71 x 80 In. 165.00
Patchwork, House, Several Blue Prints, 66 x 88 In. 905.00
Patchwork, Irish Chain, Blue White & Red Calico, Rebound, 82 x 82 In. 220.00
Patchwork, Irish Chain, Green Calico, Red, 63 x 79 1/2 In. 440.00
Patchwork, Irish Chain, Red & Green Calico, Pink Binding, 80 x 80 In. 465.00
Patchwork, Irish Chain, Red, White, Purple, Green, White Ground, 96 x 79 In. 1610.00
Patchwork, Le Moyne Star, Dark Solids & Prints, 74 x 90 In. 220.00
Patchwork, Lightning, 22 x 24 In. 110.00
Patchwork, Log Cabin, Barn Raising, Burgundy, Blue, Brown, 62 x 68 In. 650.00
Patchwork, Log Cabin, Courthouse Steps, Pale Pink Logs, Green, Gold, 36 x 34 In. 805.00
Patchwork, Log Cabin, Multicolored, Various Fabrics, 68 x 90 In. 440.00
Patchwork, Lone Star, Machine Sewn Binding, 80 x 82 In. 385.00
Patchwork, Medallion With Sawtooth Edge, Feather Stitching, 76 x 78 In. 355.00
Patchwork, Monkey Wrench, Multicolored, Machine Stitched Binding, 72 x 84 In. 195.00
Patchwork, Multicolored Squares, Maroon Border, 73 x 61 In. 200.00
Patchwork, Multicolored Stars, White Ground, 19th Century, 70 x 74 In. 275.00
Patchwork, Ocean Waves, Chintz Border & Back, 84 x 84 In. 1045.00
Patchwork, Ocean Waves, Small Print Blue Ground, 87 x 86 In. 770.00
Patchwork, Patriotic Starburst, c.1910, 65 x 73 In. 550.00
Patchwork, People & Dogs, Silk, Velvet & Mixed Fabric, 76 x 56 1/2 In. 1320.00
Patchwork, Pine Tree, Blue, Green, Black, Lavender, Machine Binding, 72 x 72 In. 300.00
Patchwork, Princess Feather, Pink, Green & White, 94 x 94 In. 950.00
Patchwork, Quaker, Made By Caroline Coles Shinn, c.1865, 100 x 104 In. 2185.00
Patchwork, Raspberry & White Triple Border, 85 x 87 In. 175.00
Patchwork, Robbing Peter To Pay Paul, Blue & White, 82 x 86 In. 560.00
Patchwork, Rolling Stone, Red & White, 88 x 90 In. 145.00
Patchwork, Sawtooth Border, White Ground, Unwashed Condition, 101 x 99 In. 965.00
Patchwork, Spider Web & Ocean Waves Quilting, Prints, Red Calico, 82 x 102 In. 440.00

Patchwork, Star Of Bethlehem, White Ground, Green, Pink, Blue, Yellow, 98 x 96 In. ... 2300.00
Patchwork, Star, Multicolored Prints & Calico, 80 x 83 In. 440.00
Patchwork, Star, Red, White, 64 x 74 In. 135.00
Patchwork, Star, White Ground, 20th Century, 114 x 112 In. 745.00
Patchwork, Stylized Floral Medallions, Pink Calico, Red, Green, 67 x 82 In. 770.00
Patchwork, Sunbursts, Gold & Red 1 Side, Green Medallions Other Side, 76 x 78 In. 490.00
Patchwork, Sunflower, Orange, Multicolored Print, Pink Grid, 66 x 82 In. 165.00
Patchwork, Sunshine & Shadow, 64 x 82 In. 270.00
Patchwork, Sunshine & Shadow, Prints & Solids, Sawtooth Border, 68 x 82 In. 275.00
Patchwork, Trees In Green, Alternate With White Quilted Pinwheels, 76 x 100 In. 495.00
Patchwork, Tumbling Star Blocks, Triple Border, Southern York Co., 96 x 90 In. 330.00
Patchwork, White Squares With Blue Patches, Red Ground, 75 x 67 In. 205.00
Patchwork, Wrench Pattern, Homespun Backing & Binding, 72 x 72 In. 247.00
Patchwork, Yellow, Red & Green Calico Triangles, Yellow Ground, 82 x 82 In. 195.00
Patchwork & Appliqued, Floral, Embroidered, Yellow, White, 1940, 80 x 96 In. 245.00
Patchwork & Appliqued, Goose Foot, Red & Green, Print Ground, 1900, 42 x 42 In. 395.00
Patchwork & Appliqued, Patches Arranged In Princess Feather Design, 78 x 68 In. 1150.00
Trapunto, White Floral, White Cotton Homespun Panels, 86 x 88 In. 3520.00

QUIMPER pottery has a long history. Tin-glazed, hand-painted pottery has been made in Quimper, France, since the late seventeenth century. The earliest firm, founded in 1685 by Jean Baptiste Bousquet, was known as HB Quimper. Another firm, founded in 1772 by Francois Eloury, was known as Porquier. The third firm, founded by Guillaume Dumaine in 1778, was known as HR or Henriot Quimper. All three firms made similar pottery decorated with designs of Breton peasants and sea and flower motifs. The Eloury (Porquier) and Dumaine (Henriot) firms merged in 1913. Bousquet (HB) merged with the others in 1968. The group was sold to a United States family in 1984. The American holding company is Quimper Faience Inc., located in Stonington, Connecticut. The French firm has been called Societe Nouvelle des Faienceries de Quimper HB Henriot since March 1984.

Bowl, Peasant, Yellow, With Double Handles 25.00
Bowl, Windmills & Sailboats, Flowering Foliage, Handles, Oval, 7 1/4 In. 727.00
Bowl, Woman, Wearing Colorful Costume, Blue Border, Yellow, Green, Henriot, 8 In. ... 860.00
Bust, Woman In Black, Orange, White Dress, Man In Orange Shirt, Wood Pedestal, Pair . 145.00
Charger, 2 Gentlemen On Horseback, Trees, Windmills In Background, Henriot, 12 In. .. 594.00
Charger, Landscape Scene, Figures, Playing Bocce, Floral Borders, 1930, 18 In. 1035.00
Cup & Saucer, Heart Shape, Peasant Man, Flower Sprays, Blue Dot, 5 In. 165.00
Cup & Saucer, Scalloped Rim, 6 Sets 165.00
Dish, Kitchen Scene, Mother & Father, Blue, Dark Green Border, Henriot, Oval, 10 In. .. 1256.00
Dish, Naive Couple, 4 Sections, Center Handle, Square, 8 1/2 In. 115.00
Eggcup, Figural Swan, Speckled Breast & Neck, Blue Wings & Feathers, Marked, 3 In. .. 185.00
Figurine, Elderly Woman, Wearing Orange, Black Sprigged Bodice, Henriot, 14 In. 529.00
Fish Set, Blue & Black Trim, Molded Fish Head, Opposing Tail, 8 Piece 115.00
Plaque, Coat Of Arms, Dancing Couple, 19 x 13 1/2 In. 1500.00
Plate, Floral Design, Henriot, 8 In. 35.00
Plate, Standing Figures, 9 1/2 In., 6 Piece 165.00
Platter, Fisherman Returning, Basket Of Fish, c.1905, 17 x 12 In. 3000.00
Platter, Fisherman's Wife & Child Bidding Farewell, c.1905, 17 x 12 In. 3000.00
Platter, Man, Holding Walking Stick, Dark Blue Dot Rim, Henriot, Oval, 24 In. 991.00
Platter, Peacock, Polychrome Border, 14 3/4 In. 275.00
Porringer, Star Design, Small 90.00
Salt, Flowers 40.00
Snuff Bottle, Shoe Shape, Blue & Yellow Blossoms, Red Ground, Dot Design, 4 In. 440.00
Teapot, Double Chamber, Signed, 5 1/2 In. 385.00
Tray, Man With Bagpipes, Signed, 10 1/2 In. 385.00
Tureen, Biniou Player, Seated Beside A Woman, Yellow Foliate Border, Henriot, 7 In. .. 529.00
Vase, 2 Biniou Players Above Odet River, Floral Sprays, Dragon Handles, Henriot, 14 In. . 1587.00
Vase, 2 Biniou Players, Seated On Cask, Dark Blue Ground, 14 In. 1322.00
Vase, 3 Trumpet Vases, Portrait Of Man, Orange Flowers, 15 In. 315.00
Vase, Man & Woman, Tricorned, Flowers, Foliage, Henriot, 20th Century, 11 1/4 In., Pair 594.00
Vase, Man Smoking, Seated, Yellow C-Scroll Handles, Blue Border, Henriot, 15 In. 462.00

Vase, Tulip, 5 Apertures, Raised On Dolphin Feet, Seated, Henriot, 7 1/4 & 11 3/4 In. ... 926.00
Vase, Wedding Scene, Yellow, Green Flower Head Rim, Blue Ground, Henriot, 25 In. ... 1190.00
Vase, Woman, Carrying A Basket, Gentleman, Tricorned, Henriot, 12 1/2 & 11 3/4 In. ... 594.00
Vase, Woman, Carrying Jug, Dark Blue Borders, Foliate Handles, Henriot, 12 In., Pair ... 792.00
Wall Pocket, 2 Figures Standing Beside Floral Design, Henriot, 7 In., Pair 165.00
Wall Pocket, Gentleman, Walking, In Colorful Costume, Blue, Henriot, 10 In., Pair 400.00

RADIO broadcast receiving sets were first sold in New York City in 1910. They were used to pick up the experimental broadcasts of the day. The first commercial radios were made by Westinghouse Company for listeners of the experimental shows on KDKA Pittsburgh in 1920. Collectors today are interested in all early radios, especially those made of Bakelite plastic or decorated with blue mirrors. Figural advertising radios and transistor radios are also collected.

1980 Winter Olympics, Lake Placid Logos, Transistor, White Plastic, Vinyl Handle 33.00
Admiral, AM Clock, White, 4 Plastic Case, 1950s, 11 x 6 x 4 In. 70.00
Advertising, Hawaiian Punch, Punchy, Plastic, Battery Operated, Box, 1970s, 7 x 6 In. ... 60.00
Advertising, Pillsbury Doughboy, Figural, Clock, Alarm, AM/FM, 1986, 5 1/4 x 9 5/8 In. . 195.00
Advertising, Snoopy, Figural, Plastic, Determined Products, Box, 1974, 5 x 7 In. ....35.00 to 40.00
Advertising, Winston Cigarettes, Cooler Bag, 8 x 9 In. 15.00
Aeriola St., 11 Tubes 360.00
Air Castle, Tombstone, Wood, Cloth Grill, 6 Buttons 50.00
Airline, Model 62-131, Tombstone, Wood, Airplane Dial, 4 Knobs, 1935 .... 50.00
Airline, Model 62-177, Tombstone, Wood, Cloth Grill, 4 Knobs 60.00
American Bosch, Model 575-F, Tombstone, Wood, Airplane Dial, 2 Tubes, 1935 .... 45.00
Arvin Industries, Inc., Model 852P, AC Or DC, Tubes, 1956, 11 x 8 In. ....*Illus* 75.00
Atwater Kent, Model 20, Big Boy, Wood, Battery, 1924, Table Model 100.00
Atwater Kent, Model 33, Wood, Battery, 1927, Table Model 220.00
Atwater Kent, Model 40, Metal, Lift-Off Top, Gold Logo, 1928, Table Model 25.00
Atwater Kent, Model 45, Metal, Lift-Off Top, 1929, Table Model 475.00
Bendix, Model 636D, Wood, Slide Rule Dial, 1947, Table Model 25.00
Catalin, AMC, Model 126, Rounded Brown Body, Orange Circular Grill Handle, 7 In. ... 805.00
Catalin, Bendix, Model 526, Dark Green, Jade Green Knobs, Ribbed Grill, Bakelite, 7 In. 430.00
Catalin, Emerson, Model 564, Series A, Brown Handle, 1940 .... 550.00
Catalin, Emerson, Tombstone Shape, Amber, 3 Rows Of Cream Vents, Bakelite, 10 In. ... 1150.00
Catalin, Emerson, Vertical Grill Openings, Handle, Amber Case, Bakelite, 7 In. ...275.00 to 575.00
Catalin, Fada, Bullet Shape, Butterscotch Case, Knobs, Bakelite, 7 In. ....375.00 to 660.00
Catalin, Fada, Model 115, Bullet Shape, Orange, Cream, Bakelite, 6 1/2 In. .....505.00 to 1380.00
Catalin, Fada, Model 252, Temple, Green Body, Amber Border, Bakelite, 7 In. 370.00
Catalin, Fada, Model 845, Rounded Arch, Green, Cream Handle, Bakelite, 6 In. ...585.00 to 690.00
Catalin, Fada, Orange Case, Browning Green Grill, Bakelite, 6 In. 520.00
Catalin, Fada, Rounded Arch Form, Orange, Red Border, Bakelite, 6 1/2 In. .....750.00 to 1265.00
Catalin, Garod, Model 6AV, Red Body, Orange Grill, Rectangular, Bakelite, 7 In. ..405.00 to 520.00
Catalin, Motorola, Butterscotch Case, Green Handle, Bakelite, 6 1/2 In. 2415.00
Catalin, Sentinel, Model 248, Yellow Body, Amber Grill, Bakelite, 7 In. ....865.00 to 1380.00

Radio, Arvin Industries, Inc., Model 852P,
AC Or DC, Tubes, 1956, 11 x 8 In.

**Plastic should be cleaned gently.
Wipe with a damp cloth, then dry.
Do not use an abrasive cleaner.
Soapy water can be used.**

Catalin, Stewart-Warner, Shortwave, Green Mottled, Amber Grill, Bakelite, 8 In. 405.00
Crosley, Model 11AB, Bakelite, Wrap-Around Louvers, 2 Knobs 15.00
Crosley, Model 124, Cathedral, Woos, 10 Tubes, 1931 .... 180.00
Crystal, Philmore, Box 105.00
Emerson, Tombstone, Model AU-190, Green Finish, 1938 .... 7700.00
Emerson 888 Explorer Nevabreak, Pocket, Black Plastic, 6 1/2 x 2 In. 20.00
Emud, Rekord Senior 60, Wood Case, Push Buttons, West Germany, 20 x 10 x 13 In. 150.00
Everyman Radiophone Receiver Type, Brown Wooden Case, 9 1/2 x 7 In. 363.00
General Electric, Model 678, Transistor, 1956 .... 125.00
General Electric, Model C437A, Pink Plastic Cabinet, Rotary Tuner, AM, Table Model .. 21.00
Heathkit, Ham Transceiver, HW-101, SSB, All Band 200.00
K-Mart, Model 30-62, AM Rotary Tuner, Ivory Colored Cabinet, Table Model 20.00
Majestic, Model 71, Highboy, Walnut, 1928 .... 35.00
Majestic, Model 90, Console, Walnut Over Oak Cabinet, Brass Hardware, 1929 .... 225.00
Motorola, Model 51X16, S-Grill, Bakelite, Black & Red, 1939, 6 1/2 x 10 In. ..3500.00 to 7150.00
Packette, Crystal Type, Black Plastic, Box, 1950s, 3 1/2 x 2 In. 25.00
Panasonic, Transistor Ball & Chain, Green Plastic Ball, Key Ring, 4 1/4 In. 23.00
Peerless, Cathedral, Speaker, S. Radio Corp 95.00
Philco, 1930s, Floor Model 165.00
Philco, Brown Plastic, Table Model, 2 Knobs 20.00
Philco, Brown Plastic, Table Model, 5 Knobs, 1950s 18.00
Philco, Cathedral Style, Wood Veneer, Tube Type, Rotary Tuner 95.00
Philco, Portable, Tambour Front, Wood, Leather 50.00
Radiomatic, 25 Cents, Coin-Operated, Wooden Case 285.00
RCA Victor, Levermatic, Clock, Beige, 1950s 60.00
RCA Victor, Model 86T1, 3-Band, Wood Case, Glass Dial Front, Table Model, 16 x 11 In. 25.00
Receiver, Aircraft, CRV-46151, 195 MHz To 9.05 MHz 100.00
Receiver, Shortwave, National, SW-54 .... 125.00
San Francisco Cable Car, Bay & Taylor, Green & Orange, Battery Operated, Box, 8 In. .. 45.00
Sparton, Model 500, Cloisonne, Enamel & Chrome, 1939, Table Model 3520.00
Speaker, Atwater-Kent, Type E3, Metal, Gold Fabric Cover, Round, c.1928, 13 In. 35.00
Stromberg-Carlson, Bakelite Case, Black, Red & White, Gold Numerals, 10 1/2 In. 58.00
Stromberg-Carlson, Tube, Brown Bakelite, Horizontal AM Tuner 55.00
Transistor, Captain 335.00
Transistor, Overland Mail Stagecoach 75.00
Transistor, Regency, Black Case, 1954 .... 295.00
Transistor, Sinclair Gasoline, Gas Pump Shape, Plastic, Box, 4 1/2 In. ....16.00 to 25.00
Tube, De Forest, 1906 .... 1335.00
Western Auto, Model D-3614A, Transistor, Peach & Gray Plastic, 1950-70, 6 x 2 In. 45.00
Winnie The Pooh, Figural, Philgee 150.00
Wrist, Superiorsonic, AM Transistor, Black Leather Band, Battery Operated 25.00
Zenith, Model 600, Trans-Oceanic, Portable, 1953 .... 65.00
Zenith, Model A600L, Trans-Oceanic, Wave Magnet 130.00
Zenith, Model H500, Trans-Oceanic ....50.00 to 110.00
Zenith, Royal 90, Transistor, Orange, Box 43.00
Zenith, Standard Broadcast Shortwave, Mediumwave, Wood, Upright 350.00

RAILROAD enthusiasts collect any train memorabilia. Everything is
wanted, from oilcans to whole train cars. The Chessie system has a
store that sells many reproductions of their old dinnerware and uniforms.

Ad, Northern Pacific RR, Yellowstone Park, Lewis & Clark Expo., 1905, 4 1/2 x 6 In. ... 4.00
Badge, Guard, Union Pacific Railroad, Brass, c.1899 .... 150.00
Badge, Police, B C & M Railroad 225.00
Badge, Police, Erie Railroad Co. 150.00
Badge, Police, Norfolk & Western Railway 150.00
Badge, Police, Pennsylvania Police 150.00
Barrel, Water, Caboose 60.00
Beer Can, Rushton Railroad 15.00
Bell, Steam Locomotive, Bronze, Yoke & Cradle, NYC RR 995.00
Berry Bowl, Missouri Pacific, The Eagle 42.00
Book, B & O, World's Fair, 1893 .... 35.00
Book, Rules, C & O Railway Co., Black Leather, Jan. 1899, Pages 7 Through 68 .... 25.00

Book, Southern Pacific, The Shasta Route, San Francisco To Portland, 1916	45.00
Booklet, California Limited, Santa Fe, 1927	60.00
Booklet, California Zephyr, 1949	75.00
Booklet, Grand Canyon, Santa Fe Railroad, Photographs, Map, 1902, 9 1/2 x 7 1/2 In.	50.00
Booklet, Pullman's Diamond Jubilee, 1934	40.00
Booklet, Railway Guide, Atlantic & Pacific Railroad, 4 Pages, 1871, 5 3/4 x 9 In.	137.00
Booklet, Santa Fe Scout, 1934	45.00
Booklet, Santa Fe's Golden State, 1938	45.00
Booklet, Southern Pacific Proudly Presents The Sunset Limited, 1952	25.00
Booklet, Streamliner, City Of Los Angeles, 1930s	40.00
Booklet, Union Pacific Railroad Timetables, Jan. 10, 1954, 48 Pages	7.00
Bottle, Whiskey, N.Y.C., Seagrams Centennial	15.00
Cabinet, First Aid, British, Early 20th Century, 61 x 20 In.	2898.00
Calendar, 1938, Great Northern Railway, Blackfoot Medicine Man, 16 x 34 In.	185.00
Calendar, 1939, Pennsylvania Railroad, Engine & Cars At Night, Grif Teller, 28 1/2 In.	35.00
Cap, Conductor, Pillbox Style, Netherlands National Railways	125.00
Cap, Trainman's, CPR	40.00
Card, Playing, Chessie System Railroads, Cats, In Case, Shrink-Wrapped, 2 Decks	40.00
Card, Playing, Frisco, In Sealed Package	22.00
Card, Playing, Olympian, 1940	30.00
Card, Playing, Union Pacific	27.00
Carte De Visite, Smith, Dawson & Baily Locomotives, BB & S RR, Newton	270.00
Clipboard, Cotton Belt Railroad, Brass, 1920, 5 3/4 x 4 In.	46.00
Desk Pad Holder, Reading Railway, Copper Metal, Purple Felt Pad, 8 1/2 x 5 1/4 In.	30.00
Hat, Brakeman's, With Badge, Santa Fe	125.00
Jacket, Union Pacific, Black Polyester & Cotton, Zipper, Dunbrooke, Size 40-42	25.00
Lamp, Aladdin, Caboose, Paper Shade, Wall Mount, 1940s	225.00
Lantern, Amber Globe, Dietz Number 900, AA RR Specifications	120.00
Lantern, Chicago & Northwestern Railway, Tin, Adlake, 9 In.	75.00
Lantern, Clear Globe, Gray Metal, Marked, 9 1/2 x 3 1/4 In.	56.00
Lantern, Dietz Acme Inspector Lamp, Stenciled NYC, 15 In.	95.00
Lantern, Dietz Fitzal Globe, C.I. Ham Mfg., Co., Tin, 15 In.	105.00
Lantern, Dietz, Swing Handle, Red Globe, Steel Clad, c.1920, 10 In.	40.00
Lantern, Inspection, Dietz, Pennsylvania Railroad	80.00
Lantern, Red Globe, Black Metal, Marked, 9 1/2 x 3 1/4 In.	70.00
Lantern, Star Headlight & Lantern Co., Tin, 15 In.	95.00
Luggage Tag, Canadian National Steamship To Alaska, 1930s, Round, 3 In.	15.00
Luggage Tag, Panama Pacific Link, Lithographed Steamer Trunk, c.1913, 6 x 7 In.	35.00
Map, Commuter Rail, Metropolitan Transportation Authority, 1981	1.00
Map, Cram's Township, Alabama, Foldout, Post Office, 22 Railroads, 4 x 6 In.	65.00
Map, New York Central Lines, American Express, 1934, 32 x 18 In.	15.00
Map, United States Great Northern Railway, 1959	12.00
Matchbook Cover, Fred Harvey Food Services, Los Angeles Union Station, 1940	4.00
Model, Steam Engine, Stationary	250.00
Paperweight, Largest Locomotive In The World, Canadian National, Figural, 1924	95.00
Pass, Housatonic Railroad Company, Chicago & Northwestern RR, Signed, 1882	75.00
Pass, New York, Lake Erie & Western Railroad, Signed By First VP, 1889, 2 1/2 x 4 In.	30.00
Pass, Press, Chicago Railroad Fair, Train At Station, 1949, 2 1/2 x 4 In.	25.00
Pass, Railroad Officer, South Carolina Railway Co., Signed By General Manager, 1889	18.00
Pennant, Chicago Railroad Fair, Green, White, Pink, Yellow, Felt, 1949, 5 1/2 x 15 In.	18.00
Photograph, Collision Of 2 Trains, Chicago & Northwestern, 1920s, 8 x 10 In.	25.00
Photograph, Mt. Lowe, Railroad Track, Tourists On Rocks, 1910, 5 3/4 x 6 1/2 In.	20.00
Photograph, People, Chicago & Northwestern & L & N, 1920s, 8 x 10 In.	25.00
Pin, Brotherhood Of Locomotive Engineers, Green Rim, Celluloid, 7/8 In.	90.00
Pin, Lapel, Burlington Route, 40 Years Service, 10K Gold, Enamel Logo	85.00
Pin, Lapel, Frisco, Quarter Century Service, 14K Karat, Red Enamel Logo	70.00
Pin, Lapel, Union Pacific, Shield, Safety First, Overland Route, Red, White, Blue, 1930s	100.00
Pin, Pacific Electric Railway, Los Angeles, Celluloid, 1 1/4 In.	90.00
Pitcher, New York, DeWitt Clinton, Marked Syracuse, 1942, 4 3/4 In.	65.00
Plate, B & O, Commemorative, Harper's Ferry, Wooden Frame, 10 1/2 In.	165.00
Plate, Gulf Mobile & Ohio, White, Pink Border, Syracuse China, 6 1/2 In.	60.00
Plate, New York City, Pacemaker, Green, 9 1/2 In.	80.00
Postcard, Erie Air-Conditioned Diner Lounge Car, Black Waiter, Linen	40.00

Poster, American Railway Express, Express Moves, Fast Trains, 1927, 36 x 56 In. 3450.00
Poster, New 20th Century Limited, NY Central System, 1938, 40 3/4 x 27 In. 6900.00
Rack, Luggage, Brass 250.00
Safety Glasses, Pullman Car Co., Blue Gray Tint, Nickel Frame, Case, 1920-1940 ...... 50.00
Saucer, Coffee, Missouri Pacific, Eagle 35.00
Sign, Rock Island Line, Streamlined Train, Paper On Cardboard, Frame, 22 x 16 In. 145.00
Signal, Kerosene, Cast Iron 250.00
Stamper, Ticket Ink, Pullman, Metal Frame, Wooden Knob, 7 In. 45.00
Stereo Card, Construction Workers Outside Tunnel No. 4, Union Pacific RR 102.00
Stereo Card, Railroad War, Pittsburgh, View Of Aftermath Of Strike, July, 1877 .... 100.00
Stereo Card, Train In Grand Canyon, Clear Creek, Canyon & Colorado Central RR 140.00
Stereo Card, Wood Train & Chinamen, San Fran., Central Pacific RR, T. Houseworth ... 137.00
Stock Certificate, Cleveland & Pittsburgh Railroad Co., 100 Shares, Issued 1925 .... 15.00
Stock Certificate, Erie RR, 1940-1950 .... 2.00
Stock Certificate, New York Central RR, 1950-1960 .... 2.00
Stock Certificate, Pennsylvania RR, 1910-1920 .... 3.00
Tablecloth, California Zephyr Dining Car, Cotton Damask, Logo In Center, 45 x 42 In. ... 95.00
Teapot, Canadian Pacific Railway 40.00
Tie Tack, Service, Union Pacific, Shield Shape, 10K Gold, Silver Tone 35.00
Timetable, Boston & Main RR 12.00
Timetable, Burlington Route, 1911 .... 15.00
Timetable, Illinois Central, 1950-1960 .... 6.00
Towel, Pullman Company, White Cotton, Blue Stripe, 24 x 16 In. 35.00
Whistle, Steam, Brass, Pull Arm Mechanism, 13 In. 120.00

RAZORS were used in ancient Egypt and subsequently wherever shaving was in fashion. The metal razor used in America until about 1870 was made in Sheffield, England. After 1870, machine-made hollow-ground razors were made in Germany or America. Plastic or bone handles were popular. The razor was often sold in a set of seven, one for each day of the week. The set was often kept by the barber who shaved the well-to-do man each day in the shop.

Clark, Walnut Handle, 18th-19th Century, 6 In. Closed 145.00
Durham, Duplex, Tooth Guard, Case 25.00
Ever-Ready, Safety, 1930 .... 35.00
Fasan, Safety, With Blades, Leather Case 20.00
Independent Tobacco Company, Straight 40.00
Joseph Elliot, Straight, Horn Handle, Inlaid Mother-Of-Pearl 75.00
Keen Kutter, Straight, Nude Woman Handle 85.00
Valet Autostrop, Detachable Handle, Leather Strap, Velvet-Lined Metal Case 20.00
W. Greaves, Etched Blade, Old Rough & Ready 475.00
Winchester, Safety 35.00
Winchester, Straight 75.00

REAMERS, or juice squeezers, have been known since 1767, although most of those collected today date from the twentieth century. Figural reamers are among the most prized.

Boat, Clambroth 165.00
Cambridge, Green 200.00
Cat, Stylized, Yellow Pearlized, Japan 290.00
Clown, 2 Piece 55.00
Clown, 6 Matching Clown Tumblers 4460.00
Clown, 8 1/4 In. 145.00
Clown, Orange Textured Body, Hands On Stomach 240.00
Crisscross, Green 375.00
Crisscross, Orange 250.00
Crisscross, Pink 325.00
Fry, Amber 375.00
Fry, Opalescent, Large 35.00
Grapefruit, GMG 145.00
Grapefruit, Yellow 275.00
Greyline 1400.00
Jeanette, Pink 175.00

Old Charley	175.00
Pear, Ceramic, 3 Piece	65.00
Pig, White, Japan	140.00
Radiant, Pink	400.00
Sairey Gamp	185.00
Speakeasy, Green	40.00
Sunkist, Black	675.00 to 800.00
Sunkist, Caramel	375.00
Sunkist, Chalaine Blue	275.00 to 295.00
Sunkist, Crown Tuscan	375.00
Sunkist, Custard	35.00 to 65.00
Sunkist, Opalescent	200.00
Sunkist, Opalescent White	45.00
Sunkist, White	25.00

RECORDS have changed size and shape through the years. The cylinder-shaped phonograph record for use with the early Edison models was made about 1889. Disc records were first made by 1894, the double-sided disc by 1904. High-fidelity records were first issued in 1944, the first vinyl disc in 1946, the first stereo record in 1958. The 78 RPM became the standard in 1926 but was discontinued in 1957. In 1932, the first 33 1/3 RPM was made but was not sold commercially until 1948. In 1949, the 45 RPM was introduced. Compact discs became available in the U.S. in 1982 and many companies began phasing out the production of phonograph records.

Album, Archy & Mehitabel, C. Channing, E. Bracken, Columbia, 33 1/3 RPM, 1950s	20.00
Album, Barbie Sings, Mattel, 45 RPM, 1961, 3 Records	21.00
Album, Bing Crosby, 78 RPM	30.00
Album, First Anniversary Of 45 RPM Records, RCA, Box, 1949, 12 Records	20.00
Album, Huckleberry Hound With Stories & Songs Of Uncle Remus, 33 1/3 RPM, 1977	14.00
Album, Richard Diamond, TV Detective Series, Mercury Records, 33 1/3 RPM, 1959	40.00
Album, Rocky & Friends	295.00
Album, Yogi Bear & Huckleberry Hound, Fairy Tales, Wrapped, 33 1/3 RPM, 1977	7.00
Ballad For Americans, Paul Robeson, 78 RPM, 2 Records	75.00
Bill Cosby, When I Was A Kid, With Fat Albert, 1971	25.00
Bonanza Christmas On The Ponderosa, RCA Victor, 33 1/3 RPM, 1963	35.00
Charlie Brown Christmas, With 12-Page Read-Along Book, 33 1/3 RPM	45.00
Deputy Dawg, T.V. Show, Blue Label, Sleeve, Terrytoons, 45 RPM, 1962	18.00
Dinah Shore, Season's Best From Your Chevrolet Dealer, 4 Songs, 45 RPM	25.00
Donny & Marie Osmond, Vinyl, Cardboard Box, 45 RPM, 1977	75.00
Down Homers, Bill Haley, Vogue Picture	200.00
First Man On The Moon, MGM, 45 RPM, 1969	30.00
Hey There It's Yogi Bear, Paper Sleeve, Columbia Pictures, 45 RPM, 1960s	14.00
NASA Radio Presentation, Oct. 18, 1976, Oblique Wing, 3 Other Programs	5.00
Only The Lonely, Frank Sinatra, Capitol, 33 1/3 RPM, 1958	25.00
Paint Your Wagon, Movie Soundtrack, Paramount, 33 1/3 RPM, 2 Records	11.00
Snoopy & His Friends The Royal Guardsmen, Laurie Records, 33 1/3 RPM, 1967	60.00
The 5000 Fingers Of Dr. T, Lyrics By Dr. Seuss, 33 1/3 RPM, 1950s	45.00

RED WING Pottery of Red Wing, Minnesota, was a firm started in 1878. The company first made utilitarian pottery. In the 1920s art pottery was made. Many dinner sets and vases were made before the company closed in 1967. Rumrill pottery was made for George Rumrill by the Red Wing Pottery and other firms. It was sold in the 1930s. For more information, see *Kovels' Depression Glass & Dinnerware Price List*.

Art Pottery, Figurine, School Girl, No. 1121, 8 3/4 In.	650.00
Art Pottery, Figurine, Tambourine Girl, No. 1178, 13 In.	195.00
Art Pottery, Figurine, Wren, Ivory, No. 1036, 6 In.	130.00
Art Pottery, Lamp, Elephant Handles, Black	45.00
Art Pottery, Lamp, Elephant Handles, Yellow	125.00
Art Pottery, Planter, Banjo	80.00

Modern bleach can damage 18th-century and some 19th-century dishes. To clean old dishes, try hydrogen peroxide or bicarbonate of soda. Each removes a different type of stain.

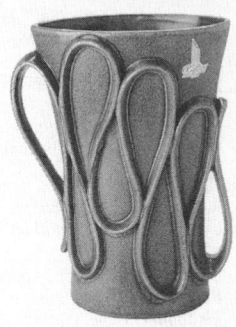

Red Wing,
Fleck Tan, Vase,
No. M1460,
Label, 9 1/4 In.

Art Pottery, Planter, Piano, Yellow Flecks	230.00
Art Pottery, Planter, Violin	80.00
Art Pottery, Vase, Elephant Head Handles, Cobalt Blue, 7 1/2 In.	195.00
Blue Band, Mixing Bowl, 7 In.	65.00
Bob White, Casserole, Cover, 13 In.	38.00
Bob White, Cup & Saucer	8.00
Bob White, Dinner Service, 64 Piece	200.00
Bob White, Hors D'Oeuvre Server	60.00 to 85.00
Bob White, Luncheon Set, 24 Piece	100.00
Bob White, Plate, 2 Sections, 14 In.	22.00
Bob White, Plate, 6 1/2 In.	4.00
Bob White, Salt & Pepper	35.00
Bob White, Tumbler	150.00
Cherry Band, Pitcher	175.00
Cherry Band, Pitcher, Milk, 6 Pt.	700.00
Clock, Black Mammy, Mursen, 10 In.	125.00 to 200.00
Cookie Jar, Carousel, 8 1/2 x 8 In.	375.00
Cookie Jar, Friar Tuck, Yellow, 10 1/2 In.	95.00 to 125.00
Cookie Jar, Katrina Dutch Girl, Yellow, 11 In.	145.00
Cookie Jar, Pierre, Chef, 11 In.	75.00 to 110.00
Fleck Tan, Vase, No. M1460, Label, 9 1/4 In.	*Illus* 60.00
Gray Line, Casserole, Cover, Blue & White, 7 In.	130.00 to 550.00
Gray Line, Pitcher, McHenry County Dry Cleaners, Medium	400.00
Grecian, Lamp, Mulberry, 21 In.	195.00
Hamm's Brewing Company, Salt & Pepper	200.00
Lanterns, Tray, Egg, Cover	195.00 to 235.00
Morning Glory, Cup & Saucer, Blue	6.00
Rose Garland, Basket, Oval	80.00
Stoneware, Ashtray, No. 825, 9 1/2 In.	35.00
Stoneware, Bank, Hamm's Bear, 1950s	550.00
Stoneware, Bean Pot, Emmons Merc. Co., Jack Sprat Store, Brown, White, 6 In.	220.00
Stoneware, Churn, Cover, Elephant Ear, 3 Gal.	275.00
Stoneware, Churn, Cover, Large Wing, 5 Gal.	150.00
Stoneware, Crock, Big Wing, 2 Gal.	90.00
Stoneware, Crock, Black Elephant Ear, 2 Gal.	65.00
Stoneware, Crock, Black Elephant Ear, No Oval, 2 Gal.	90.00
Stoneware, Crock, Butter, 20 Lb.	900.00
Stoneware, Crock, Cobalt Blue Leaf Design, Salt Glaze, Impressed R.W.S. Co., 5 Gal.	695.00
Stoneware, Crock, Elephant Ear, 2 Gal.	55.00
Stoneware, Crock, Wing & Oval, 50 Gal.	1350.00
Stoneware, Fruit Jar, Mason, Blue Lettering, Tin, Glass Lid, 8 In.	275.00
Stoneware, Jar, Packing, Bail Handle, 5 Gal.	300.00
Stoneware, Jardiniere, Green Leaves, 20 In.	135.00
Stoneware, Jug, Beehive, 3 Gal.	400.00
Stoneware, Jug, Beehive, Birch Leaves, 5 Gal.	425.00
Stoneware, Jug, Brown Top, 5 Gal.	450.00

Stoneware, Jug, Brown Top, Wing, 1 Gal. 110.00
Stoneware, Jug, Large Wing, 2 Gal. 650.00
Stoneware, Jug, No. 5, Cream, Cobalt & Red Transfer, 1890-1920, 17 3/4 In. 100.00
Stoneware, Jug, Williams Bros. & Charbonneau, Quebec Maple Syrup, 7 1/2 In. 135.00
Stoneware, North Star, Creamer, Star On Bottom 55.00
Stoneware, Refrigerator Jar, Blue & White, Bail Handle, No Cover, 5 Lb. 50.00
Stoneware, Vase, Allover Brown & Green Matte Glaze, Signed, 6 In. 330.00

REDWARE is a hard, red stoneware that originated in the late 1600s and
continues to be made. The term is also used to describe any common
clay pottery that is reddish in color.

Bank, Bee Hive, 3 1/2 In. 530.00
Bank, Crane, Molded, Applied Handle, Dark Brown Glaze, Paint Traces, 7 3/8 In. 125.00
Bank, Pig, Brown, Green & Yellow Glaze, 7 In. 575.00
Birdhouse, Hand Thrown, Applied Perch & Overhang Above Hole, Wire Hanger, 7 In. ... 120.00
Bowl, Green Circles, Black & White Lines On Sides, 3 x 8 1/4 In. 55.00
Bowl, Green Glaze, Brown Flecks & Amber Spots, White Slip Rim, 6 3/4 x 3 In. 275.00
Bowl, Interior White Slip Line Sgraffito, 11 1/2 x 12 1/4 x 4 In. 25.00
Bowl, Interior Yellow Bands, 2 x 6 In. 100.00
Bowl, Milk, Brown & Yellow Wavy & Straight Slip, 11 x 3 In. 385.00
Bowl, Yellow & Green Floral, 3 1/2 x 13 3/4 In. 175.00
Bowl, Yellow Glaze, 18 x 6 1/4 In. 140.00
Bowl, Yellow Slip, Red Design, Applied Finger Crimped Rim, 9 x 3 In. 330.00
Bowl, Yellow Wavy & Straight Slip, 8 5/8 In. 275.00
Bread Tray, Yellow Slip Abstract, Red Ground, Oblong Dish Shape, 11 x 18 In. 2070.00
Bust, Gentleman, Shirt, Bow-Tie, Jacket, 19th Century, 5 In. 290.00
Canister, Cover, Allover Yellow & Orange Glazed, 11 In. 275.00
Canteen, Side Cork, Pre-1800, 5 5/8 In. 240.00
Charger, Yellow Slip, 19th Century, 13 In. 168.00
Chicken Waterer, Manganese Glaze, Penna., 9 1/2 In. 120.00
Colander, Slip Design, John Nice, c.1830, 5 3/4 x 12 7/8 In. 4600.00
Custard Cup, Brown Design, 4 3/4 In. 60.00
Dish, 2 Sections, Divider, White Slip Design, 11 x 13 1/2 In. 138.00
Figurine, Dog, Seated, Brown, 3 3/4 In. 110.00
Figurine, Dog, Seated, Green Glaze, 6 3/4 In. 355.00
Figurine, Dog, Seated, Holding Basket, Oval Base, Mid-19th Century, 4 x 4 1/4 In. 2750.00
Figurine, Dog, Seated, Tooled Coat, Open Front Legs, 9 1/2 In. 412.00
Figurine, Lion, Mottled Tan & Cream, Unglazed, Label, 1931, 8 3/4 In. 385.00
Figurine, Spaniel, Glass Eyes, 20 In. 3520.00
Flask, 7 1/2 In. 135.00
Flask, Slip Design, Early 19th Century, 5 In. 1495.00
Flowerpot, John Bell, Glazed, 5 1/2 In. 850.00
Head, Lincoln With A Smile, c.1870, 8 1/2 In. 400.00
Inkwell, Heart Shape, Sand Shaker & Inkwell Insert, Adam-Awnhouse, 5 In. 690.00
Insert, Washboard, Dark Brown Splotches, 10 5/8 x 10 5/8 In. 220.00
Jar, Black Glaze, Applied Shoulder Handles, 11 3/4 In. 25.00
Jar, Black Splotches, Shoulder Handles, Egg Shape, 9 1/2 In. 220.00
Jar, Egg Shape, 8 1/8 In. 165.00
Jar, Impressed Snowflakes, Ring Handles, Safford & Allen, 1841 .... 770.00
Jar, John Bell, Waynesboro, 7 1/2 In. 135.00
Jardiniere, Floral, Reverse Bell Shaped Top, Speese Stamp, 29 In. 175.00
Jug, Black Glaze, Strap Handle, 7 3/4 In. 55.00
Jug, Clear Glaze, 19th Century, 9 5/8 In. 402.00
Jug, Glossy Glaze, Applied Handle, 5 1/4 In. 190.00
Jug, Green, Mid-19th Century, 12 1/2 In. 1500.00
Jug, Grotesque, Green Glaze, North Carolina, 7 3/4 In. 110.00
Jug, Mottled Green Glaze, Ribbed Strap Handle, Egg Shape, 8 1/2 In. 82.00
Jug, S.T. Suit Little Brown Jug, Whiskey Made 1869, Suitland, Md., Small 245.00
Jug, Strap Handle, Amber Glaze, Brown Flecks, 9 1/4 In. 138.00
Jug, Strap Handle, Fitted As Lamp, Egg Shape, 14 In. 275.00
Loaf Pan, 3 Line Yellow Slip, Coggled Rim, 17 In. 715.00
Loaf Pan, Slip Design, Squiggles, 11 x 7 1/2 In. 440.00

Mug, Mottled Glaze, Reeded Handle, 2 1/2 In.	190.00
Pie Plate, 3-Line Wavy Yellow Slip, 8 1/4 In.	275.00
Pie Plate, 3-Line Yellow Slip, Coggled Rim, 8 In.	195.00
Pie Plate, 3-Line Yellow Slip, Coggled Rim, 9 3/4 In.	385.00
Pie Plate, 3-Line Yellow Slip, Coggled Rim, 10 In.	55.00 to 465.00
Pie Plate, Brown Splotches, Salmon Ground, 8 1/8 In.	220.00
Pie Plate, Coggled Rim, Dots Of Yellow Slip, 9 In.	150.00
Pitcher, 9 In.	1485.00
Pitcher, Brushed Brown Slip, Wavy Lines, Initials B.B.C., 10 3/4 In.	55.00
Pitcher, Concentric White Lines, 7 In.	55.00
Pitcher, Cover, Clear Glaze, Brown Sponged, Ribbed Strap Handle, 9 In.	520.00
Pitcher, Incised American Eagle & Shield, Reeded Strap Handle, 7 In.	1760.00
Pitcher, Manganese Circle & Line Design, 19th Century, 11 1/2 In.	385.00
Pitcher, Yellow & Black Striped, Handle, 5 1/2 In.	630.00
Pitcher, Yellow Slip, Mottled Green Glaze, Ribbed Strap Handle, 10 3/4 In.	9900.00
Plate, 3 Yellow Slip Lines, Squiggles, Impressed Rim, 11 1/2 x 2 1/4 In.	245.00
Plate, Brown Daubs, Salmon Ground, 6 1/2 In.	82.00
Plate, Brushed Center Brown Design, 10 In., Pair	385.00
Plate, Made From Ohio River Flood Mud, March, 1936, Glazed, 7 1/2 In.	100.00
Plate, Manganese Splotching, Molded, 5 In.	110.00
Plate, Script Design, 19th Century, 12 1/8 In.	200.00
Plate, Sgraffito, Commemorative, Peafowl, 1792 & Eagle, 1809, 8 3/4 In., Pair	412.00
Plate, Slip Decorated, Crimped Rim, 19th Century, 11 1/2 In.	6900.00
Plate, Slip Design, 9 1/4 In.	465.00
Plate, Slip Design, Caleb, 10 1/2 In.	2500.00
Plate, Slip Design, Sam, 10 1/2 In.	2500.00
Plate, Yellow Slip Design, Crimped Rim, 9 1/2 x 7 1/2 In., 4 Piece	1265.00
Platter, John Written In Slip, 1840, 14 In.	1400.00
Pot, Applied Handle, Bulbous, 4 Yellow Slip Bands, 6 1/2 In.	460.00
Pot, Dark Brown Splotches, Strap Handle, Spout, 6 1/2 In.	140.00
Pot, Mismatched Cover, Dark Brown Sponged Glaze, Strap Handle, Spout, 5 In.	110.00
Stirrup Cup, Hound Shape, Glazed, Late 18th Century, 4 1/2 In.	287.00
Sugar, Cover, 4 In.	925.00
Teapot, 3 Mask & Paw Feet, Crab-Stock Handle & Spout, Fruiting Vine, 5 In.	632.00
Teapot, Dragon's Head Spout, Chinese, 19th Century, 8 In.	38.00
Tobacco Jar, Spit Glaze, Applied Ring Handles, Egg Shape, 10 1/2 In.	90.00
Umbrella Stand, Tree Trunk Shape, 9 x 20 In.	55.00
Umbrella Stand, Worn Floral Design, 21 3/4 In.	70.00
Vase, Incised Bands, Mottled Glaze, 2 Strap Handles, 11 In.	520.00
Wall Pocket, Orange Designs, Hanging, Drainage Hole, 8 1/4 x 10 1/4 In.	248.00
Washboard, Mottled Brown, Orange, Child's	695.00
Whistle, Bird, Glazed Head, Wings & Body, 2 x 1 1/2 In.	280.00

REGOUT, see Maastricht category.

RIDGWAY pottery has been made in the Staffordshire district in England since 1808 by a series of companies with the name Ridgway. The transfer-design dinner sets are the most widely known product. They are still being made. Other pieces of Ridgway are listed under Flow Blue.

Bowl, Asian Palace Scene, Low, 12 In.	575.00
Bowl, City Hall New York, Blue Transfer, Open Handle, Footed, 11 In.	4180.00
Bowl, Vegetable, Cover, Oriental, Undertray, Blue, White, 12 In.	185.00
Bowl, Willow, Blue, 9 1/2 In.	25.00
Charger, Coaching Days, In Snowstorm, Silver Luster Rim, 13 In.	57.00
Compote, Oriental, Handle, 9 3/4 In.	145.00
Dessert Service, Fruit On Marble Ledge, Gilt Border, Apple Green Ground, 28 Piece	7475.00
Dish, Sardine, Agra	375.00
Pitcher, Molded, Jousting Knights, Yellow Tan, Pewter Lift Lid, Rim, 8 1/4 In.	315.00
Pitcher, Seal Of United States, Beauties Of America, Dark Blue Transfer, 6 In.	575.00
Pitcher, Washington Independence, Beauties Of America, Dark Blue Transfer	990.00
Plate, Athenaeum, Boston, Beauties Of America, Dark Blue Transfer, 6 1/4 In.	99.00

Plate, Insane Hospital, Boston, Beauties Of America, Blue Transfer, 7 1/4 In.	110.00 to 405.00
Plate, LaGrange, Marquis Lafayette, Beauties Of America, Dark Blue Transfer	99.00
Plate, Library Philadelphia, Beauties Of America, Dark Blue Transfer, 8 1/4 In.	55.00
Plate, Library, Philadelphia, Blue, 8 1/4 In.	220.00
Plate, Willow, 10 In.	25.00
Platter, Chinoiserie Designs, Rectangular Form, Ironstone, Gilt, 21 1/4 In.	230.00
Platter, Columbus, Beauties Of America, Dark Blue Transfer, 14 5/8 In.	605.00
Platter, Court House, Boston, Beauties Of America, Dark Blue Transfer, 11 In.	605.00
Platter, Pennsylvania, Hospital, Philadelphia, Blue, Tree Well, 18 In.	1980.00
Soup, Dish, Octagon Church, Boston, Blue, 9 3/4 In.	660.00
Soup, Dish, Staughton's Church, Philadelphia, Beauties Of America, Blue Transfer	126.00

RIFLES that are firearms are not listed in this book. BB guns and air rifles are listed in the Toy category.

RIVIERA dinnerware was made by the Homer Laughlin Co. of Newell, West Virginia, from 1938 to 1950. The pattern was similar in coloring and in mood to Fiesta and Harlequin. The Riviera plates and cup handles were square. For more information, see *Kovels' Depression Glass & Dinnerware Price List.*

Blue, Cup	7.00
Dark Blue, Plate, 7 In.	75.00
Green, Bowl, Oatmeal	85.00 to 95.00
Green, Casserole, Cover	95.00
Green, Cup	7.00
Green, Plate, 6 In.	8.00
Green, Teapot	185.00
Green, Tumbler, Handle	650.00
Ivory, Bowl, Oatmeal	95.00 to 115.00
Ivory, Butter, 1/2 Lb.	155.00
Ivory, Cup & Saucer, After Dinner	115.00
Ivory, Plate, Deep	45.00
Mauve, Bowl, Oatmeal	60.00 to 95.00
Mauve, Casserole, Cover	110.00 to 185.00
Mauve, Pitcher, Juice	350.00
Mauve, Plate, 6 In.	12.00
Mauve, Plate, 7 In.	18.00
Mauve, Sauce Boat	45.00
Mauve, Sugar, Cover	25.00
Mauve, Tumbler, Handle	75.00
Mauve, Tumbler, Juice	95.00
Red, Bowl, Oatmeal	95.00
Red, Butter, Cover, 1/4 Lb.	85.00
Red, Casserole, Cover	165.00
Red, Nappy, 7 In.	25.00
Red, Oatmeal, Bowl	115.00
Red, Plate, 6 In.	18.00
Red, Plate, 7 In.	18.00
Red, Plate, 9 In.	45.00
Red, Salt & Pepper	15.00
Red, Syrup, Cover	90.00 to 115.00
Red, Syrup, Creamer	295.00
Yellow, Bowl, Oatmeal	85.00
Yellow, Cup	7.00
Yellow, Pitcher, Juice	130.00
Yellow, Platter, Handles, 11 In.	20.00

ROBLIN Art Pottery was founded in 1898 by Alexander W. Robertson and Linna Irelan in San Francisco, California. The pottery closed in 1906. The firm made faience with green, tan, dull blue, or gray glazes. Decorations were usually animal shapes. Some red clay pieces were made.

Plate, Frog, Chasing A Dragonfly, Hammer Mark, Linna Irelan, 7 In.	880.00

ROCKINGHAM, in the United States, is a pottery with a brown glaze that resembles tortoiseshell. It was made from 1840 to 1900 by many American potteries. Mottled brown Rockingham wares were first made in England at the Rockingham factory. Other types of ceramics were also made by the English firm. Related pieces may be listed in the Bennington category.

Bowl, Floral Cartouches, Floral Interior, Celeste Blue Ground, 10 In.	460.00
Bowl, Yellowware, 2 3/4 x 10 3/4 In.	60.00
Bowl, Yellowware, 3 1/4 x 9 1/2 In.	80.00
Butter, Floral Cover, Peacock & Park Scene, Embossed, 5 In.	45.00
Candlestick, Ringed Columnar Shape, Flared Foot, Flint Glaze	850.00
Figurine, Dog, Fancy Base, 10 1/2 In.	300.00
Figurine, Dog, Incised Eyes & Whiskers, Blue Glaze, 10 In.	1760.00
Figurine, Dog, Seated, Deer & Hound Design, 10 1/2 In.	440.00
Figurine, Dog, Seated, Freestanding Front Legs, 10 3/4 In.	365.00
Flask, Hunting Dogs, 7 1/4 In.	330.00
Jar, Cover, Molded Vintage, 9 1/2 In.	355.00
Jar, Fruit, Cover, Apple, Square	5000.00
Jug, Toby, 19th Century, 6 In.	22.00
Jug, Toby, 5 7/8 In.	125.00
Jug, Toby, Glazed, 19th Century, 4 1/8 In.	373.00
Loving Cup, Drinking Scenes, Dog Fight, Molded, 6 7/8 In.	248.00
Mixing Bowl, Molded, Gothic Arches, 13 In.	138.00
Mug, Yellowware, Ear Handle, 3 In.	55.00
Pitcher, Dog Shape, 8 7/8 In.	125.00
Pitcher, Eagle & Shield Both Sides, 8 1/2 In.	45.00
Pitcher, Embossed Corn, 11 In.	45.00
Pitcher, Embossed Medallion, Scroll, Yellowware, 8 1/2 In.	77.00
Pitcher, Embossed Rose Design, 9 3/4 In.	45.00
Pitcher, Hound, Handle, 9 5/8 In.	275.00
Teakettle, Rebecca At The Well Type, 8 1/2 In.	40.00

ROGERS, see John Rogers category.

ROOKWOOD pottery was made in Cincinnati, Ohio, from 1880 to 1960. All of this art pottery is marked, most with the famous flame mark. The R is reversed and placed back to back with the letter P. Flames surround the letters. After 1900, a Roman numeral was added to the mark to indicate the year. The name and some of the molds were purchased in 1984. A few new pieces were made, but these were glazed in colors not used by the original company.

Ashtray, Bird Form, White Matte, 1946, 4 1/8 In.	345.00
Ashtray, Crystalline Blue Matte Glaze, 1931, 4 In.	360.00
Ashtray, Magnolia, Green, 2 x 7 In.	82.00
Ashtray, Pinecone, Green, 1 1/8 x 4 5/8 In.	55.00
Ashtray, Rook, Green High Glaze	250.00
Basket, Gondola Shape, Yellow Daisies, Green Ground, 1888, 8 In.	660.00
Basket, Magnolia, Blue, 7 3/8 In.	82.00
Bookends, Egyptian Woman, Black Slip, 5 1/2 In.	1210.00
Bookends, Horse Heads, Green Glaze, 5 3/4 In.	375.00
Bookends, Indian, Mottled Rust Glaze, 5 1/4 In.	3300.00
Bookends, Kingfishers, Teal Matte Glaze, McDonald, 1937, 5 1/2 In., Pair	546.00
Bookends, Nude, Art Deco, Louise Abel, 1930, 7 In.	3410.00
Bookends, Owl, White, 6 In.	175.00
Bookends, Polychrome Flowers, 1928, 6 1/2 In.	605.00
Bookends, Rook & Flowering Branch Molded On Open Book, Yellow, 6 In.	350.00
Bookends, Rook, McDonald, 1931, 6 In.	195.00
Bookends, Rook, William McDonald, 1934, 5 3/8 In.	440.00
Bookends, Rooks Standing On Books, Matte Green Glaze, 6 1/2 x 6 1/2 In.	865.00
Bookends, Ship, Blue Glaze, William McDonald, 1927	365.00
Bookends, Squirrel, Holding Nut, Standing On Log, Gray, Green, Toohey, 4 In., Pair	747.00
Bookends, St. Francis, 1945, 7 1/4 In., Pair	605.00
Bookends, Union Terminal, 1933	4950.00

Bowl, Flowers Inside Triangles, Cecil Duell, 1907, 2 3/8 In.	1360.00
Bowl, Geometric Pattern, Matte Green Glaze, 1904, 3 In.	410.00
Bowl, Rose Rising To Tan, Inverted Rim, Circular, 1919, 5 1/2 In.	69.00
Bowl, Vine Design, Green Ground, Squat, 1920, 8 3/4 x 3 1/4 In.	315.00
Bowl, Windsor, Modern Designs Below Rim, No. 4, 3 1/2 x 10 5/8 In.	410.00
Candlestick, Dark Blue Matte, 3 In., Pair	259.00
Candy Dish, Boy In Knickers, Loop Handles, E. Foertmeyer, 1893, 4 7/8 In.	1320.00
Chocolate Pot, Bird In Flight, Oriental Grasses, Tan, Teal Glaze, 1885, 7 In.	345.00
Coffeepot, Red Clover Plants, 4 Bees, Carl Schmidt, 1900, 6 5/8 In.	330.00
Cornucopia, Pinecone, Brown, 8 1/4 In.	165.00
Creamer, Lily Of The Valley, Fred Rothenbusch, 1896, 2 In.	165.00
Creamer, Lily Of The Valley, Rose Fechheimer, 1901, 3 1/4 In.	880.00
Ewer, Branches Of White Cherry Blossoms, Gold, Laura A. Fry, 1883, 10 In.	1035.00
Ewer, Clover Blossoms, Yellow, Green & Brown Ground, 1894, 10 In.	715.00
Ewer, Dogwood Design, Charles J. Dibowski, 1895, 5 3/4 In.	410.00
Ewer, Drilled, Connie Baker, 8 1/8 In.	900.00
Ewer, Floral & Leaf Design, Brown & Yellow Glaze, Albert Valentien, 11 In.	550.00
Ewer, Holly, Berry Design, Tricornered Spout, Handle, Standard Glaze, Lincoln, 5 In.	431.00
Ewer, Honeysuckle Blossoms, Albert Valentien, 1889, 13 In.	650.00
Ewer, Painted Berries, Shaded Brown Ground, Standard Glaze, McDonald, 1892	715.00
Ewer, Red Poppy, Logo, Fred Rothenbusch, 8 3/4 In.	330.00
Ewer, Virginia Creeper Design, Standard Glaze, Fred Rothenbusch, 1900, 8 3/8 In.	400.00
Ewer, Yellow Blossoms, Silver Overlay, Harriette Strafer, 1892, 7 In. ....*Illus*	3850.00
Figurine, Antelope, Louise Abel, Paper Label, 6 1/4 In.	247.00
Figurine, Basset Hounds, Vellum Glaze, Signed, 1944, 5 x 5 In., Pair	385.00
Figurine, Elephant, No. 6488, 4 In.	180.00
Figurine, Tortoise, No. 1686, 1921	500.00
Flower Boat, Leaves, Vines, Standard Glaze, 1889, A.R. Valentien, 9 1/4 x 14 In.	805.00
Flower Frog, Teal Glaze	65.00
Humidor, Fish Encircling Lower Third, Logo, Green Glaze, 1929, 4 1/2 In.	2530.00
Humidor, Green Matte Glaze, Pink Glaze Interior, 4 1/2 In.	220.00
Humidor, Pipes, Matches, Cigars, Ocher, Orange, Green Ground, 1896	660.00
Inkwell, Woman's-Head Cover, Hair Swirls To Well & Tray, A. Valentien, 1903, 9 In.	1540.00
Jar, Cover, Incised Geometric Design, Red, Green Matte Glaze, 1908, 6 In.	412.00
Jar, Cover, Mauve, Green Matte Glaze, Squat, 1911, 3 1/2 In.	201.00
Jar, Potpourri, Apricot, Branching Apple Blossoms, Anna Bookprinter, 1887, 7 In.	1380.00
Jar, Potpourri, Band Of Pink Cherry Blossoms, Ivory Ground, McLaughlin, 6 In.	550.00
Jardiniere, Embossed Steer Skulls & Garlands, Green Glaze, 11 x 14 In.	715.00
Jardiniere, Pedestal, Bushberry, Blue, 24 3/8 In.	550.00
Jug, Brown & Gold, Carrie Steinle, c.1892	225.00
Jug, Cream, Berry, Leaf Design, Standard Glaze, Carrie Steinle, 1916, 3 1/4 In.	345.00
Jug, Desert Scene, Child Chasing Butterfly, Woman Arranging Flowers, Tan, 1884	2300.00
Jug, Green & Brown, 6 In.	115.00
Jug, Swallows, Oriental Grasses, Tan, Peach, Brown Ground, Handle, 1883, 9 In.	1380.00

Rookwood, Ewer,
Yellow Blossoms, Silver
Overlay,
Harriette Strafer, 1892,
7 In.

Rookwood, Plaque, Vellum Glaze, Birch
Landscape, E.T. Hurley, 1946, 12 x 14 In.

Jug, Water, Black, Blue, 2 Extending Spouts, Looped Handle At Top, 8 3/4 In. 1840.00
Jug, Whiskey, Crescent Moon, 2 Rooks, Kataro Shirayamadani, 1899, 10 1/4 In. 8500.00
Jug, Whiskey, Profile Of Lean Wolf, Adeliza Sehon, 1900, 9 3/8 In. 3300.00
Jug, Whiskey, Rounded Shoulders, Curved Handle From Neck To Lip, 10 1/4 In. 2560.00
Lamp, Cherry Blossom, Brown & Yellow, 8 5/8 In. 770.00
Lamp, Pink Poppies, Green Leaves, Light Green Ground, 18 In. 3575.00
Loving Cup, Portrait, 3 Handles, Laurence Sturgis, 1899, 6 1/2 In. 2500.00
Mug, Beer, Wiedemann Brewing Co., Pewter Lid, 1948, 5 1/2 In. ....495.00 to 550.00
Mug, Brownie, Perched On Mushroom Next To Stark Tree, Harriet Wilcox, 5 In. 1955.00
Mug, Indian Portrait, 5 x 3 1/2 In. 860.00
Mug, Indian Portrait, Sioux Chief Hollowhorn Bear, E. Brain, 5 In. 1610.00
Paperweight, Cat, Caramel High Glaze, 1958, 4 3/8 In. 520.00
Paperweight, Cat, Nubian Black Glaze, 1937, 2 5/8 In. 1100.00
Paperweight, Dog, Winking, Orange & Yellow Glaze, Showroom Label, 1930, 4 In. 360.00
Paperweight, Duck, Green Matte Glaze, 1964, 2 1/4 In. 165.00
Paperweight, Elephant, Oxblood Glaze, 1930, 3 1/4 In. 770.00
Paperweight, Elephant, Wine Madder Glaze, 1945, 3 3/4 In. 275.00
Paperweight, Fish, Blue-Green Glaze, Shirayamadani, c.1935, 2 1/4 In. 880.00
Paperweight, Ladybug, Ladybug, Nursery Rhyme, 1937 .... 1540.00
Paperweight, Lamb, White Matte Glaze, 1939, 2 3/4 In. 520.00
Paperweight, Monkey, Nubian Black Glaze, 1929, 3 3/4 In. 357.00
Paperweight, Monkey, Sitting On Book, Opening With Foot, 3 1/2 In. 825.00
Paperweight, Mouse, White Matte Glaze, Shirayamadani, 1937, 3 1/8 In. 1100.00
Paperweight, Mustard Seed Glaze, 1965, 3 7/8 In. 275.00
Paperweight, Nude, On Lily Pads, Looking At Frog, 1940, 4 1/2 In. 410.00
Paperweight, Oak Leaf, Acorns, Green Matte Glaze, 1904, 2 1/2 x 4 3/4 In. 374.00
Paperweight, Panther, Stalking, Caramel High Glaze, 1946, 3 In. 385.00
Paperweight, Puppy, Brown, Tan, 1926 .... 250.00
Paperweight, Rabbit, Cream, 1926 .... 170.00
Paperweight, Seal, Blue & Tan Glaze, 1928, 3 In. 715.00
Paperweight, Turtle, Mustard Seed Glaze, 1966, 2 1/4 In. 245.00
Pin Tray, Nude Figure, 1924, 3 In. 215.00
Pitcher, Cherry, Tricornered, 1901, 4 3/4 In. 375.00
Pitcher, Cider, Magnolia, 9 In. 250.00
Pitcher, Clouds, Spiders, Spider Webs, Hirschfeld, c.1882, 6 1/2 In. 805.00
Pitcher, Cover, White Narcissus, Salmon Pink Ground, A.M. Valentien, 8 x 6 In. 440.00
Pitcher, Irises, Peach, Cream Glaze, Flared Spout, 1887, 7 In. 345.00
Pitcher, Red Poppies, Lilies Of The Valley, Green Ground, M. Nourse, 1898, 10 1/4 In. .. 880.00
Planter, Cylindrical, Figures In A Garden, Blue & Tan, 19 In., Pair 3737.00
Plaque, Birch Trees By Lake, Dusk, Vellum Glaze, Ed Diers, 1921, 5 1/4 x 7 7/8 In. 2415.00
Plaque, Canal Scene, Boats & Skyline, Vellum, Frame, 6 x 10 In. 2300.00
Plaque, Harbor Scene, Fishing Boat In Small Bay, Frame, Vellum, S. Sax, 9 x 5 In. 2300.00
Plaque, Landscape, Blue, Green, Purple, Ed Diers, 1913, 8 5/8 In. 3450.00
Plaque, Mt. Rainier, Ed Diers, 1927, 12 x 9 In. 10450.00
Plaque, Mt. Ranier Scene, Vellum Glaze, Frame, Ed Diers, 1927, 12 x 9 In. 10450.00
Plaque, Swamp Scene, Uniformly Crazed, Louise Abel, 10 3/4 x 8 1/2 In. 5170.00
Plaque, Vellum Glaze, Birch Landscape, E.T. Hurley, 1946, 12 x 14 In. ....*Illus* 17600.00
Plate, Daisies, Sienna Ground, Harriet E. Wilcox, 1890, 12 In. 575.00
Sconce, Embossed Pair Of Owls, Green & Brown Glaze, 1910, 11 In. 660.00
Tea Set, Shipware, Porcelain, 12 Piece 1210.00
Tea Set, Wild Roses, Maroon Ground, Butterfly Finials, E. Lincoln, 1927, 3 Piece 1430.00
Tile, Geometric Design, Ocher Matte Glaze, Wood Box Frame, Square, 6 In. 110.00
Tile, Glasgow Rose, Pink, Green Leaves, Arts & Crafts Frame, 6 In. 1430.00
Tile, Landscape Design, Trees Along River Bank, Mountains, Oak Frame, 12 In. 2200.00
Tile, Landscape Scene, Brown, Green Trees, Grass, Arts & Crafts Oak Frame, 12 In. 2530.00
Tile, Parrot, 1925, 5 5/8 In. 385.00
Trivet, Allover Flowers & Stylized Birds, Square, 5 5/8 In. 110.00
Trivet, Duck, Flowers, 1917, 5 5/8 x 5 5/8 In. 330.00
Urn, Production, Mustard Crystalline Glaze, 1910, 12 x 9 1/2 In. 935.00
Vase, 1 Iris & 2 Buds On Front, Lenore Asbury, 1906, 10 1/4 In. 7150.00
Vase, 2 Doves On Myrtle Branch, Ivory, Brown, Cobalt Blue Ground, 5 x 5 In. 1760.00
Vase, 3 Lambs Grazing In A Field, Medium Blue, Cobalt, White, 1895, 7 1/2 In. 6325.00
Vase, 3 Stylized Dandelions, Green Matte Glaze, K. Shirayamadani, 5 In. 635.00

Vase, 4 Panels Of Flying Ducks, Forest Setting, 8 In. 450.00
Vase, 5 Fish, Shirayamadani, 1897, 10 In. 2850.00
Vase, Abstract Flowers, Blue, Green, Yellow Matte Glaze, Lincoln, 1930, 6 1/4 In. 460.00
Vase, Apple Blossom At Base, Lorinda Epply, 1909, 7 3/4 In. 630.00
Vase, Apple Blossoms, Silver Overlay, Standard Glaze, 1891, 5 3/4 In. 1725.00
Vase, Apple Blossoms, Vellum Glaze, Fred Rothenbusch, 1929, 5 3/8 In. 1980.00
Vase, Band Of Flowers, c.1921, 10 3/4 In. 287.00
Vase, Band Of Flowers, Leaves, Blue, Green Glaze, Taylor, 1920, 8 1/2 In. 2415.00
Vase, Berry Branch Design, Standard Glaze, Laura Lindeman, 1902, 5 1/4 In. 374.00
Vase, Berry Branch Design, Standard Glaze, Rose Fechheimer, 1898, 6 In. 172.00
Vase, Birch Trees By Lake, Vellum, McDermott, 1917, 7 In. 2420.00
Vase, Black Opal, Band Of Apple Blossoms On Shoulder, Harriet Wilcox, 1927, 7 In. 1430.00
Vase, Blue & Red Morning Glories, Green Leaves, Pumpkin Ground, 1924, 12 In. 1320.00
Vase, Blue Art Deco Design, Handles, 1930, 5 1/2 In. 125.00
Vase, Blue Bell-Shaped Flowers, Wax Matte Glaze, Lincoln, 1922, 10 x 3 In. 1210.00
Vase, Blue Berries, Gray Leaves, White Ground, Jens Jensen, 1944, 5 5/8 In. 550.00
Vase, Blue Crocuses, Green Leaves, Margaret McDonald, 1935, 6 1/8 In. 1100.00
Vase, Blue Crocuses, Lime Green To Cream Ground, Carl Schmidt, 1911, 9 3/8 In. 3740.00
Vase, Blue Flower, Leaf Design, 7 In. 495.00
Vase, Blue Flowers, Red Centers, Pink Ground, C. Klinger, 1925, 4 1/2 In. 660.00
Vase, Blue Iris, White Iris Glaze, Elizabeth Lincoln, 1906, 7 1/4 In. 1760.00
Vase, Blue Matte Glaze, 5 1/2 In. 110.00
Vase, Bottle Shape, Adam & Eve, With Flowers, Brown, Red, 8 In. 2860.00
Vase, Bottle Shape, Blue, Yellow Pansies, Standard Glaze, 1894, 6 x 3 In. 385.00
Vase, Brown Poppies, Green Stems, Amber Ground, Standard Glaze, J., Swing, 7 In. 605.00
Vase, Bud, Blue Flowers, Green Leaves, Burgundy Ground, 1922, 7 In. 715.00
Vase, Bulbous, Chevron Lines, Caramel Glaze, 7 In. 605.00
Vase, Butterflies, Raised Rim, Green Glossy Glaze, 1950, 4 3/4 In. 172.00
Vase, Butterfly Frieze Design, Turquoise, 1929, 7 In. 230.00
Vase, Cherry Blossoms, Shaded, Yellow Interior, Lenore Asbury, 1925, 6 1/4 In. 900.00
Vase, Chinese Junks, Blue, Brown & Green Ground, 1911, 8 1/2 In. 525.00
Vase, Clovers, Flared Rim, Standard Glaze, 1893, 2 1/4 In. 460.00
Vase, Coromandel Glaze, Dark Interior Glaze, 1932, 4 In., Pair 605.00
Vase, Curdled White Glossy Glaze, Black Matte Ground, 1953, 12 x 7 In. 495.00
Vase, Curling Fern Fronds, Rose, Green Matte Glaze, Shirayamadani, 1903, 8 In. 495.00
Vase, Cyclamen, Flared Rim, Standard Glaze, Lorinda Epply, 1898, 8 1/2 In. 862.00
Vase, Daisies, Iris Glaze, Irene Bishop, 1903, 6 1/8 In. 1320.00
Vase, Day Lilies, Green, Yellow, Orange, Standard Glaze, A.R. Valentien, 1889, 24 In. . . . 1725.00
Vase, Double-Leaf Form, Blue Matte Glaze, 1924, 12 In. 2420.00
Vase, Double-Leaf Form, Multitone Brown Matte Glaze, 1921, 12 In. 1870.00
Vase, Dragonfly, 4 In. 2500.00
Vase, Embossed Snowdrops, Glossy Turquoise Glaze, Bulbous, 1957, 4 x 4 In. 165.00
Vase, Eve In Eden, Flowers, Fish, Fowl, Brown, Blue, Ivory Butterfat Glaze, 8 In. 2090.00
Vase, Exotic Birds In Field Of Trees, Sepia, Cream Ground, A.R. Valentien, 12 In. 747.00
Vase, Flared Lip, Elongated Neck, Yellow Glaze, 1946, 9 3/4 In. 85.00
Vase, Flower Buds, Stems, Beaker Form, 1899, 6 1/4 In. 287.00
Vase, Flowers, Amphora Form, Elizabeth Neave Lincoln, 1903, 9 In. 1155.00
Vase, Flowers, Blue, Pink Ground, Vellum Glaze, K. Van Horne, 1913, 7 In. 345.00
Vase, Flowers, Howard Altman, 1903, 8 1/2 In. 400.00
Vase, Flowers, Iris Glaze, Fred Rothenbusch, 1903, 8 In. 1320.00
Vase, Flowers, Pastel Pink, Blue, Green & Yellow, Sallie Toohey, 1930, 6 1/4 In. 495.00
Vase, Flowers, Pink, White, Blue To Pink Ground, Edward Diers, 1926, 6 1/2 In. 747.00
Vase, Flowers, Pink, Yellow Ground, 6 1/4 In. 350.00
Vase, Fred Rothenbusch, 1926, 6 1/2 In. 600.00
Vase, Gazelles, Jumping, Lines, Dots, Green Matte Glaze, 1932, 4 1/2 In. 201.00
Vase, Geese, Flying, Perching, Swimming, Egg Shape, c.1920, 18 1/2 In. 5325.00
Vase, Geometric Band, Z-Line Design, Green, Matte Glaze, 5 In. 605.00
Vase, Geometric Design At Shoulder, Pink, Green Matte Glaze, 1912, 10 1/2 In. 440.00
Vase, Geometric Design, Brown, Cobalt Blue, Ivory Ground, W. Rehm, 1930, 7 In. 1320.00
Vase, Geometric Design, Green Matte Glaze, 1907, 14 In. 1100.00
Vase, Geometric Design, Green, Brown Matte Glaze, 3-Handled Form, 1910, 4 In. 467.00
Vase, Geometric Design, Light Green, Red Highlights, Navy Blue, 6 In. 1210.00

Vase, Goldenrod, Iris Glaze, Shaded Gray Ground, 1902, 10 In. 4400.00
Vase, Greek Key Design Top, Red & Brown Matte Glaze, 1911, 8 In. 715.00
Vase, Green & Deep Rose Matte Glaze, 2 Closed Handles, 1916, 9 In. 2310.00
Vase, Green Palm Fronds, Shaded Brown, Green Ground, 1900, 10 In. 935.00
Vase, Hazed Flowers, Red, Green Leaves, Speckled Brown Ground, Olga Reed, 5 In. 862.00
Vase, Holly, Standard Glaze, Clara Lindeman, c.1900, 6 1/2 In. 550.00
Vase, Hydrangea, White, Green, Brown, Sallie Toohey, 1896, 8 5/8 In. 855.00
Vase, Incised Geometric Design, Green, Blue Matte Glaze, 1905, 3 In. 440.00
Vase, Incised Geometric Design, Green, Blue Matte Glaze, 1910, 7 In. 187.00
Vase, Incised Geometric Design, Green, Rose Matte Glaze, 1914, 11 In. 660.00
Vase, Incised White & Yellow Irises, Blue-Gray Ground, McDonald, 1943, 11 In. 880.00
Vase, Indian Portrait, Artus Van Briggle, 13 1/2 In. 7150.00
Vase, Indian Portrait, Girl, Artus Van Briggle, 1898, 8 In. 7975.00
Vase, Indigo Irises, Green Leaves, Red, Green Ground, R. Fechheimer, 1906, 8 In. 6050.00
Vase, Iris Blossoms, Standard Glaze, Mary Nourse, 1902, 9 1/2 In. 690.00
Vase, Iris Glaze, Lavender Ground, John Dee Wareham, 1901, 11 7/8 In. 4400.00
Vase, Iris Glaze, Lavender, Carl Schmidt, 1903, 10 In. . . . . *Illus* 11000.00
Vase, Iris Glaze, Sara Sax, 1902, 7 7/8 In. 3180.00
Vase, Irises, Leaves, Soft Pink, Green, Teal, Lenore Asbury, 1907, 10 In. 3737.00
Vase, Jewel, Japanese Landscape, Mountains, Lake, 1922, 6 1/2 In. 3850.00
Vase, Jonquils, Edith Felten, 1899, 8 In. 880.00
Vase, Landscape, Woods, Snow, Vellum, Ed Diers, 1917, 9 1/4 x 3 In. 1320.00
Vase, Large Leaves, Green, Brown Matte Glaze, Spherical, 1913, 5 1/4 x 7 In. 880.00
Vase, Laurel, 2 Buttress Handles, Gold Foil Label, 9 1/2 In. 355.00
Vase, Laurel, Gold Foil Label, 6 1/8 In. 360.00
Vase, Lavender Magnolias, White To Blue Ground, Vellum, 1927, 11 In. 6050.00
Vase, Leopard, Growling, Standard Glaze, Urn Form, Horsfall, 1893, 9 In. 4887.00
Vase, Lilies Of The Valley, Howard Altman, 1901, 6 1/8 In. 660.00
Vase, Lilies Of The Valley, Vellum, Carl Schmidt, 1913, 8 3/4 In. 1495.00
Vase, Lotus, Yellow & Brown On Turquoise Ground, 1915, 10 3/4 In. 1100.00
Vase, Magnolia, Sallie Coyne, 1930, 7 1/2 In. 1760.00
Vase, Maple Leaves, Pods, Burgundy Ground, Olga Reed, 1907, 10 1/2 x 4 In. 6050.00
Vase, Maple Leaves, Raised Rim, Standard Glaze, 1905, 6 1/2 In. 489.00
Vase, Nasturtium, Squat Base, Flared Rim, Mary Nourse, 1896, 10 In. 517.00
Vase, Native American Girl, Artus Van Briggle, 1898, 8 In. 7975.00
Vase, Nature Scene, Autumn Trees At Sunset, Vellum, Edward Diers, 1921, 10 In. 1725.00
Vase, Oak Leaves, Brown, Green & Amber, Howard Altman, 6 3/4 In. 410.00
Vase, Ombroso, 2 Small Handles, C.S. Todd, 1914, 5 1/4 In. 660.00
Vase, Ombroso, Carved & Painted Flowers At Shoulder, C.S. Todd, 1918, 5 1/4 In. 605.00
Vase, Ombroso, Stylized Flowers, William Hentschel, 1915, 6 3/8 In. 2090.00
Vase, Oriental Flowers, Arthur Conant, 5 1/4 In. 2530.00
Vase, Orion, Turquoise & Tan, Black Lines Around Rim, Label, 10 3/8 In. 190.00
Vase, Painted & Incised Panels Under Rim, S.S. Todd, 1919, 4 3/8 In. 880.00
Vase, Pansies, 5 In. 550.00
Vase, Pansies, Standard Glaze, Canoe Shape, 5 1/2 In. 345.00
Vase, Pedestal, Morning Glory, Handles, 9 1/8 In. 660.00

Rookwood, Vase,
Iris Glaze, Lavender,
Carl Schmidt,
1903, 10 In.

Rookwood, Vase,
Yellow Clover, Silver
Overlay, 2 Handles,
C. Steinle, 1892, 4 In.

Vase, Pillow, Elk, Bellowing, Standard Glaze, Horsfall, 1896, 8 In. 2530.00
Vase, Pillow, Standard Glaze, 4 1/2 In. 210.00
Vase, Pink Flowers, Margaret McDonald, 6 In. 740.00
Vase, Pink Poppies, Gray Shaded Ground, Elizabeth Lincoln, 1907, 8 1/2 In. 475.00
Vase, Poppies, 2-Tone Blue Matte Glaze, 1912, 8 1/2 In. 605.00
Vase, Poppies, Pink & Green, Sara Sax, 1931, 9 In. 990.00
Vase, Poppy Pods, Blossoms, Brown, Red On Red Butterfat, Wax Matte, 10 In. 2640.00
Vase, Production, Flying Fish, Brown, Yellow, Burgundy Crystalline Glaze, 9 In. 715.00
Vase, Purple Bell-Shaped Flowers, Green Leaves, Wax Matte Glaze, Lincoln, 10 In. 1320.00
Vase, Purple Flowers, Green Leaves, Turquoise Butterfly, Wax Matte, 10 In. 1870.00
Vase, Purple Irises Band, Iris Glaze, Ivory Ground, 1909, 8 3/4 In. 1980.00
Vase, Purple Irises, Iris Glaze, Green Ground, 1903, 11 In. 5225.00
Vase, Purple Irises, Iris Glaze, Green Ground, 1906, 10 In. 4125.00
Vase, Purple Star Flowers, Kataro Shirayamadani, 1938, 5 7/8 In. 1540.00
Vase, Red & White Lotus, Wax Matte, K. Shirayamadani, 1941, 9 In. 2400.00
Vase, Red Flowers, Green Ground, Silver Overlay, 1915, 7 1/4 In. 1980.00
Vase, Red Flowers, Green Leaves, Orange Ground, Wax Matte, Lincoln, 1923, 9 In. 1540.00
Vase, Red Flowers, Green Leaves, Wax Matte Glaze, Lincoln, 1921, 9 x 4 In. 770.00
Vase, Red Flowers, Green Leaves, Yellow Matte Glaze, Elizabeth Barrett, 11 In. 575.00
Vase, Red Flowers, Pink Ground, Wax Matte, 1925, 7 In. 770.00
Vase, Red, Long Tapered Neck, 10 In. 395.00
Vase, Rose & Green Matte Glaze, 1915, 5 1/2 In. 230.00
Vase, Sailboats On Water, Vellum, E.T. Hurley, 1943, 7 x 3 In. 770.00
Vase, Sailboats, Trees, Green, 1911, 9 3/8 In. 800.00
Vase, Sailboats, Water, Aqua Sky, Vellum, Carl Schmidt, 7 In. 3300.00
Vase, Scenic, Flowers Dot Foreground, Fred Rothenbusch, 1929, 9 In. 1430.00
Vase, Scenic, Iris Glaze, Kataro Shirayamadani, 14 In. 13850.00
Vase, Small Sailboats Against Dusky Sky, Vellum, Schmidt, 10 In. 5225.00
Vase, Snow Scene, Small Houses, Stand Of Trees, Frozen Lake, H. Wilcox, 1894, 6 In. .. 2090.00
Vase, Spider Design, Dogwood Branch, Maria Storer, 16 In. 10305.00
Vase, Stylized Doves, Wispy, 10 1/2 In. 3585.00
Vase, Stylized Flowers & Leaves, Lavender To Blue, c.1935, 5 1/4 In. 95.00
Vase, Stylized Flowers, Brown Ground, C.S. Todd, 1916, 9 In. 900.00
Vase, Stylized Magnolia Blossoms, Soft Blue, Green, Pink, Sallie E. Coyne, 9 In. 920.00
Vase, Stylized Papyrus, C.S. Todd, 6 In. 2200.00
Vase, Sunflowers, Ivory Glaze, 5 1/2 In. 60.00
Vase, Swirling Leaves, Incised Ribs, Rose & Green Matte Glaze, 1915, 6 1/2 In. 715.00
Vase, Thorn Apple, Pink, 4 3/8 In. 110.00
Vase, Thorny Rose Branches, 2 Handles, Bulbous, K. Shirayamadani, 1890, 15 In. 2530.00
Vase, Tiger Eye, Amber Heron, Sparkling Brown Ground, K. Shirayamadani, 7 In. 1210.00
Vase, Tiger Eye, Goldstone Effect, Matt Daly, 1886, 8 1/8 In. 2860.00
Vase, Tree Scene, Green, Apricot, Vellum, Kataro Shirayamadani, 15 In. 4400.00
Vase, Venetian Harbor Scene, Carl Schmidt, 1923, 7 7/8 In. 5170.00
Vase, Violets, Leaves, Green, Purple, Everted Rim, Footed Base, 1938, 5 In. 345.00
Vase, Violets, Vellum Glaze, Ed Diers, 1930, 6 In. 975.00
Vase, White Bachelor's Buttons, Gray & Pink Ground, Irene Bishop, 1908, 5 In. 600.00
Vase, White Bachelor's Buttons, Iris Glaze, Gray Ground, 1908, 5 1/2 In. 660.00
Vase, White Birds, Magnolia Blossoms, Gray, Amber Ground, Spherical, 7 In. 1980.00
Vase, White Catalaya Orchids, Pink, Yellow, Silver Gray, Pale Pink, Reed, 15 In. 4887.00
Vase, White Hydrangea, Sea Green, Blue Green Ground, 1902, 6 In. 5225.00
Vase, White Roses, Ivory, Gray Ground, Vellum, M.H. McDonald, 1914, 7 x 4 In. 825.00
Vase, Woman, Wearing Hoop Skirt, Parasol, Blue, Brown, Gold, Cream, Pink, 6 In. 375.00
Vase, Wooded Landscape, Vellum Glaze, Sallie E. Coyne, 1922, 11 1/2 In. 2300.00
Vase, Woodland Scene, Ed Diers, 1921, 6 3/4 In. 2090.00
Vase, Woodland Scene, Sallie Coyne, 1915, 6 3/4 In. 880.00
Vase, Yellow Clover, Silver Overlay, 2 Handles, C. Steinle, 1892, 4 In. ....*Illus* 4950.00
Vase, Yellow Poppies, Yellow, Green, Brown, Leona Van Briggle, 1904, 7 In. 360.00
Vase, Yellow Roses & Stems, Egg Shape, Harriet Wilcox, c.1902, 8 1/4 In. 1380.00
Vase, Yellow Roses, Red Stems, Harriet Wilcox, 1902, 8 In. 2760.00
Vase, Yellow Tulips, Shaded Green, Red, Orange Ground, Standard Glaze, 10 In. 715.00
Vase, Yellow Water Lilies, Dark Gray Ground, Constance Baker, 1902, 9 x 5 In. 2310.00
Wall Pocket, Pink Tulips Form, Anna Valentien, 1903, 12 3/4 In. 2430.00
Window Box, Pinecone, Central Handle, 3 3/4 x 8 3/4 In. 190.00

RORSTRANDwas established near Stockholm, Sweden, in 1726. By the nineteenth century they were making English-style earthenware, bone china, porcelain, ironstone china, and majolica. The company is still working. The three crown mark has been used since 1884.

Vase, 2 Bands Of Spiky Fish & Mushrooms, Alf Wallander, 1914, 17 1/4 In. 3220.00

ROSALINE, see Steuben category.

ROSE BOWLS were popular during the 1880s. Rose petals were kept in the open bowl to add fragrance to a room, a popular idea in a time of limited personal hygiene. The glass bowls were made with crimped tops, which kept the petals inside. Many types of Victorian art glass were made into rose bowls.

Amber, Violin Player, Thick Enamel, Fluted Interior, Rossler, 1920, 5 In. 242.00
Cranberry, Gold Enamel, 19 1/2 In. 195.00
Cut Glass, Rayed Base, 6 In. 150.00
Gilt, Roses, Butterflies, Cornucopia, Polychrome Enamel, 10 x 4 In. 605.00
Sapphire Blue, Enamel Branch, Pink Flowers, Buds, 12-Crimp Top, 5 x 6 In. 210.00

ROSE CANTON china is similar to Rose Medallion, except no people or birds are pictured in the decoration. It was made in China during the nineteenth and twentieth centuries in greens, pinks, and other colors.

Bowl, Cut Corners, 19th Century, 10 1/2 In. 1090.00
Platter, Well & Tree, Early 20th Century, 18 7/8 In. 517.00
Punch Bowl, Alternating Floral & Butterfly Panels, Qing Dynasty, 15 1/2 In. 4025.00
Punch Bowl, Alternating Landscape, Flower, Butterfly, 18 In. 4675.00
Tazza, Fruit, Diamond Shape, 19th Century, 14 1/4 In. 745.00
Teapot, Fruit Finial, Turned Handle, 5 5/8 In. 425.00

ROSE MANDARIN china is similar to Rose Medallion. If the panels in the design picture only people and not birds, it is called Rose Mandarin.

Bowl, 6 x 14 3/4 In. 825.00
Bowl, Alternating Floral Panels, c.1850, 9 In. 330.00
Cake Stand, 8 5/8 In. 515.00
Charger, Floral Border, 13 1/2 In. 210.00
Cider Jug, Cover, Foo Dog Finial, Woven Double Strap Handle, 9 1/2 In. 2990.00
Dish, Butterfly & Floral Border, 9 7/8 In., 6 Piece 1430.00
Pitcher, Water, Handle, 19th Century, 9 1/2 In. 1955.00
Pitcher, Water, Scalloped Rim, Paneled, Handle, 7 3/4 In. 1380.00
Plate, Scalloped Edge, 15 Figures On Exterior, 8 3/8 In. 565.00
Platter, 6 Panels Alternating Figural & Figural, c.1840, 11 x 14 In. 402.00
Platter, Alternating Figural & Floral Panels, 16 3/4 In. 345.00
Platter, People & Floral Panels, 16 x 13 In. 345.00
Pot, Bough, Applied Squirrel, Berry, Vine Design, Hexagonal, 9 In. 1380.00
Punch Bowl, 19th Century, 14 3/4 In. 2645.00
Punch Bowl, Figural & Floral Reserves, 16 In. 990.00
Punch Bowl, Panels, People, Flowers, 15 1/2 x 6 1/2 In. 1035.00
Tazza, Fruit, Diamond Shape, 19th Century, 12 1/4 In. 750.00
Teapot, Dome Cover, Gilt Spout, Handle, 19th Century, 8 1/4 In. 1265.00
Vase, Alternating Mandarin & Floral Reserves, c.1835, 11 3/4 In., Pair 660.00
Vase, Cover, Long Neck, Globular, 19th Century, 18 1/2 In. 1320.00
Vase, Mounted As Lamp, 12 1/2 In. 357.00

ROSE MEDALLION china was made in China during the nineteenth and twentieth centuries. It is a distinctive design with four or more panels of decoration around a central medallion that includes a bird or a peony. The panels show birds and people. The background is a design of tree peonies and leaves. Pieces are colored in greens, pinks, and other colors. It is similar to Rose Canton.

Basket, Fruit, Undertray, Reticulated, 19th Century, 9 3/8 In. 920.00
Bonbon 995.00
Bottle, Water, Cover, Gilt, Enamel, 19th Century, 14 1/2 In. 431.00

Bottle, Water, Hardwood Stand, 15 In. 805.00
Bowl, Late 19th Century, 10 1/2 In. 440.00
Bowl, Oval, 11 In. 200.00
Bowl, Shaped, 9 3/4 x 8 1/2 x 2 3/4 In. 230.00
Bowl, Teak Stand, 5 x 10 3/4 In. 880.00
Brush Box, Divided Bottom Section, Rectangular, 7 x 3 1/2 x 2 3/4 In. ....315.00 to 545.00
Brush Pot, Cylindrical, 4 3/4 In. 520.00
Brush Pot, Cylindrical, 5 3/4 In. ....575.00 to 635.00
Candlestick, Late 19th Century, 6 1/2 In., Pair 770.00
Chamber Pot, 19th Century, 9 5/8 In. 632.00
Charger, Alternating Figural & Floral Panels, 11 3/4 In. 185.00
Charger, Circular, 19th Century, 21 1/2 In. Diam. 1100.00
Charger, Figural Panels, Bird & Flower Center, 14 In. 550.00
Compote, Reticulated, 19th Century, 3 5/8 x 7 5/8 In., Pair 632.00
Creamer, Curved Spout, 4 1/2 x 7 In. 260.00
Creamer & Sugar, Cover, Floral Reserves, Handles 358.00
Dish, Cover, 7 3/4 In., Pair 201.00
Dish, Cover, Pinecone Finial, Almond Shape, 9 In. 27.00
Dish, Cover, Vegetable, Famille Rose Palette Interior, Cut Corners, 9 1/2 In. 860.00
Dish, Leaf Form, 7 3/4 In. 230.00
Dish, Reticulated Border, 9 1/2 In. 70.00
Dish, Shrimp, 19th Century, 9 1/2 In. 345.00
Fruit Basket, Undertray, Reticulated, 19th Century 750.00
Garden Seat, 1890s 1725.00
Group, Butterfly Design, Floral Painted, 9 Piece 315.00
Jar, 4 1/4 x 3 1/2 In. 145.00
Jar, Cover, Signed, 12 1/2 In. 58.00
Mug, Twist Handle, 5 1/4 In. 880.00
Pitcher, Bowl, 19th Century, 13 1/2-In. Pitcher 1092.00
Pitcher, Octagonal, Late 19th Century, 5 1/2 In. 495.00
Plate, Reticulated, 1880-1885, 8 1/2 In. 65.00
Plate, Scalloped Edge, 9 1/2 In. 70.00
Platter, 11 1/4 x 9 In. ....155.00 to 200.00
Platter, 14 1/2 x 11 3/4 In. 290.00
Platter, 15 1/2 x 11 1/2 In. 405.00
Platter, 19th Century, 13 3/8 x 18 In., Pair 805.00
Platter, Cabbage Leaf Center, Oval, 16 1/2 x 13 1/4 In. 720.00
Platter, Oval, 10 x 8 In. 105.00
Platter, Oval, 18 x 14 1/2 In. 405.00
Platter, Round, Late 19th Century, 11 7/8 In. 220.00
Platter, Well & Tree, 2-Footed, Oval, 16 1/4 In. 260.00
Platter, Well & Tree, Late 19th Century, 16 1/4 In. 605.00
Platter, Well & Tree, Red Flowers, Butterflies, 18 3/4 x 13 1/4 In. 920.00
Pot, Bough, Applied Squirrel, Berries, Octagonal, 9 In., Pair 4887.00
Pot, Crocus, Cover, Octagonal, Handles, 19th Century, 9 1/2 In., Pair 3410.00
Punch Bowl, 1840, 11 1/2 In. 880.00
Punch Bowl, 19th Century, 12 1/2 In. ....1650.00 to 2070.00
Punch Bowl, Alternating Mandarin & Floral, Avian Reserves, 1840, 5 In. 1450.00
Punch Bowl, Gilt & Enamel, 5 1/4 x 13 1/4 In. 920.00
Punch Bowl, Gilt & Enamel, 6 x 14 7/8 In. 747.00
Punch Bowl, Louis XVI Style, Bronze Mounted, c.1825, 17 1/4 In. 3520.00
Punch Bowl, Panels, Floral, Birds, People, 15 3/4 x 6 1/2 In. 1208.00
Sauceboat, Figural Entwined Handle, 8 In. 242.00
Soap Dish, 3 Sections, 6 x 4 1/2 x 3 In. 315.00
Sugar, Cover, Strap Handle, 5 In. 230.00
Sugar & Creamer, Cover, 4 In. 200.00
Tazza, Gilt, Enamel, 19th Century, 3 1/2 x 14 1/8 In. 805.00
Teapot, 2 Cups In Wicker Caddy, 5 1/4 In. 247.00
Teapot, 4 In. 190.00
Teapot, Alternating Avian & Mandarin Reserves, Drum Form, 1825, 5 1/8 In. 137.00
Teapot, Cover, Tea Bowl, Box, Oval, Caned & Lined 468.00
Teapot, Dome Cover, Handle, 19th Century, 9 1/2 In. 1035.00
Teapot, Dome, Cover, Gold Rim, 8 1/2 In. 410.00

Teapot, Drum Shape, Figural Design, Fruit Finial, 5 1/2 In.	242.00
Teapot, Figural Design, Squat, 19th Century, 11 3/4 In.	595.00
Tray, Bun, Rectangular, 13 1/2 x 7 In.	920.00
Tray, Reticulated, Late 19th Century, 8 1/2 & 10 In., Pair	522.00
Tureen, Cover, Interlaced Strap Handles, Pedestal Base, 11 1/2 x 14 In.	1668.00
Tureen, Sauce, 8 In.	325.00
Umbrella Stand, 12 Panels, People, Birds, Butterflies, Flowers, 24 In.	1898.00
Umbrella Stand, Ribbed	2250.00
Vase, 12 1/2 In.	630.00
Vase, Alternating Mandarin, Floral, Avian Reserves, Gilt Handles, 25 In.	1815.00
Vase, Applied Kylins & Foo Dogs, Baluster, 19th Century, 9 In., Pair	630.00
Vase, Applied Kylins & Foo Dogs, Hardwood Stands, 24 In., Pair	2300.00
Vase, Bottle Form, Applied Kylins & Foo Dogs, 19th Century, 10 In.	373.00
Vase, Chih Lung Dragons, Foo Lion Handles, Mid-19th Century, 17 3/4 In.	880.00
Vase, Cover, Alternating Mandarin & Avian Reserves, 1830-1840, 13 1/4 In.	605.00
Vase, Ku-Form, Acanthus Leaf Ribbing, Gilt Dragon, Blue Ground, 12 3/8 In., Pair	3335.00
Washbowl, 16 In.	330.00
Washbowl, Hardwood Stand, 4 7/8 x 16 1/8 In.	1265.00

ROSE O'NEILL, see Kewpie category.

ROSE TAPESTRY porcelain was made by the Royal Bayreuth factory of Tettau, Germany, during the late nineteenth century. The surface of the porcelain was pressed against a coarse fabric while it was still damp, and the impressions remained on the finished porcelain. It looks and feels like a textured cloth. Very skillful reproductions are being made that even include a variation of the Royal Bayreuth mark, so be careful when buying.

Bowl, Dogs, Trees, Hunt Scene, Ruffled, Footed	275.00
Bowl, Figural Roses, Gold, 5 In.	375.00
Box, Dresser, Prince & His Lady, Signed, 3 1/2 x 6 In.	485.00
Charger, Bathers, 11 1/2 In.	250.00
Charger, Stag In Stream	950.00
Creamer, Cottage, Winter Scene, Signed	495.00
Hatpin Holder, Bathers, 4 1/2 In.	195.00
Hatpin Holder, Colonial Curtsy Scene, 4 1/2 In.	125.00
Hatpin Holder, White Rose, 4 1/2 In.	168.00
Humidor, Cavalier, Toaster	395.00
Pin Box	290.00
Pitcher, Gold, Pinched Spout, 3 1/2 In.	250.00
Pitcher, Highland Goats	60.00
Pitcher, Nudes In River	595.00
Planter, Pink, Liner	300.00
Rose Bowl, 6 In.	695.00
Sugar & Creamer, Cover, Bulbous, Low	325.00
Teapot, Textured, Ivory Band	325.00
Vase, Bathers, Ruffled & Sculptured Rim, Handles, Footed, 4 1/4 In.	140.00
Vase, Castle & Village By Lake, Mountains, Signed, 4 In.	275.00
Vase, Christmas Cactus, 4 1/2 In.	325.00
Vase, Pink & White Roses, Ruffled Rim, Handles, Yellow Ground, 7 x 8 In.	280.00
Vase, Portrait Lady, 4 5/8 x 4 In.	224.00

ROSEMEADE Pottery of Wahpeton, North Dakota, worked from 1940 to 1961. The pottery was operated by Laura A. Taylor and her husband, R.I. Hughes. The company was also known as the Wahpeton Pottery Company. Art pottery and commercial wares were made.

Ashtray, Duck	49.00
Creamer, Turkey	25.00
Figurine, Elephant, Pink	125.00
Figurine, Pheasant, Rooster, 14 1/2 In.	450.00
Flower Frog, Fish, Pink	40.00
Flower Frog, Heron	68.00
Flower Frog, Squirrel	50.00

Mug, Indian Head ....350.00 to 375.00
Plaque, God Of Peace, 9 1/2 In. 600.00
Salt & Pepper, Bears, Brown 75.00
Salt & Pepper, Bison 55.00
Salt & Pepper, Buffalo ....125.00 to 225.00
Salt & Pepper, Cat, Sitting 38.00
Salt & Pepper, Chihuahuas ....450.00 to 550.00
Salt & Pepper, Deer, Leaping 120.00
Salt & Pepper, Elephant 49.00
Salt & Pepper, Fish, Laying Down 249.00
Salt & Pepper, Fish, Tails Up ....38.00 to 75.00
Salt & Pepper, Gophers 95.00
Salt & Pepper, Greyhound 75.00
Salt & Pepper, Mallard Duck ....65.00 to 75.00
Salt & Pepper, Pheasant, Tail Up 40.00
Salt & Pepper, Quail 50.00
Salt & Pepper, Raccoons 245.00
Salt & Pepper, Skunks, Large 85.00
Salt & Pepper, Turkey ....50.00 to 65.00
Sugar & Creamer, Tulip 55.00
Tray, Hors D'Oeuvres, Standing Pheasant 150.00
Vase, Bird, 6 In. 45.00
Vase, Deer, 6 In. 50.00
Vase, Dog Head, 6 In. 40.00
Vase, Pink Flecks, 5 3/4 In. 152.00
Wall Pocket, Deer 45.00
Wall Pocket, Leaf 20.00

ROSENTHAL porcelain was made at the factory established in Selb, Bavaria, in 1880. The factory is still making fine-quality tablewares and figurines. A series of Christmas plates was made from 1910. Other limited edition plates have been made since 1971.

MARKE

Rosenthal

Bowl, Grape, Empress, Footed, 10 1/2 In. 375.00
Bowl, Moss Rose, Sterling Silver Base, c.1890, 4 1/4 x 9 1/2 In. 95.00
Candlestick, Tapered Cylinder, White, Gold Stripes, B. Wiinblad, 8 1/2 & 7 In., Pair 86.00
Chocolate Set, Blue & Gold, 13 Piece 467.00
Chocolate Set, Painted Roses, Signed, 13 Piece 465.00
Dessert Set, Burnt Umber, Sterling Overlay, c.1945, 22-Piece Set For 6 .... 2395.00
Dessert Set, Watteau, Figural Design, 7 Piece 275.00
Ewer, Lavender Floral, Handle, 6 In. 395.00
Figurine, 2 Angelfish, Blue, Gold Highlights, 15 1/4 In. 172.00
Figurine, Boy & Girl, Signed, 6 1/8 In., Pair 395.00
Figurine, Cat, Karner, 5 In. 150.00
Figurine, Dachshund, 7 In. ....235.00 to 250.00
Figurine, Deer & Fawn, Reclining, B. Butzke, 6 x 10 1/2 In. 295.00
Figurine, Frog, Green, 2 1/4 In. 78.00
Figurine, Horse, White, Gray, Oval Base, Otto Richter, 14 In. 400.00
Figurine, Pheasant, Light Green, Raised Plumed Tail, 12-In. Wingspan, 19 In. 525.00
Figurine, Rabbit, Laughing, White, Small ....70.00 to 75.00
Figurine, Seagulls, Meisel, 18 1/2 In. 2250.00
Figurine, Setter With Duck, 5 3/4 x 9 In. 140.00
Figurine, Tiger, T. Karner, 1924, 18 3/4 In. 2800.00
Gravy Boat, Moss Rose 50.00
Group, Child, With Monkey, Signed, Ferd Liebermann, 7 1/4 In. 120.00
Pitcher, Young Woman Portrait, Gold Floral & Scroll, White Handles, 12 1/2 In. ... 125.00
Plaque, Snow-Covered Mountain, Lake In Foreground, Original Frame, 10 x 12 In. 770.00
Plate, Dessert, Floral Design, 10 In., 12 Piece 300.00
Plate, Gold Leaf & Scroll Design, White & Navy Ground, 10 1/2 In., 4 Piece 100.00
Plate, Maria & Child, 1971 .... 275.00
Plate, Moss Rose, 8 1/2 In. 12.00
Salt & Pepper, Black Cat, Heidenreich 195.00
Tray, Light & Dark Rosebuds, Gilt Edge, 14 In. 40.00
Vase, Free-Form, Figural Line Design, Jean Cocteau, 1952, 9 1/2 In. 632.00

Vase, Tropical Fish In Seaweed, Wood Base, F. Heidenreich, 16 In. 230.00
Vase, Woman, Long Flowing Hair, Gypsy, Reverse, Signed, 9 1/2 In. . . . . .385.00 to 450.00

ROSEVILLE Pottery Company was organized in Roseville, Ohio, in 1890. Another plant was opened in Zanesville, Ohio, in 1898. Many types of pottery were made until 1954. Early wares include Sgraffito, Olympic, and Rozane. Later lines were often made with molded decorations, especially flowers and fruit. Most pieces are marked *Roseville*. Many reproductions made in China have been offered for sale the past few years.

Roseville U.S.A.

Apple Blossom, Basket, Blue, 8 In.	325.00
Apple Blossom, Basket, Blue, 10 In.	400.00
Apple Blossom, Basket, Green, 8 1/2 In.	190.00
Apple Blossom, Basket, Green, 10 In. . . . . .300.00 to 330.00	
Apple Blossom, Basket, Pink, 10 In.	300.00
Apple Blossom, Basket, Pink, 8 In.	77.00
Apple Blossom, Basket, Pink, Hanging	225.00
Apple Blossom, Bookends, Rose, Pair	260.00
Apple Blossom, Bowl, Flower Frog, Green, 10 In.	260.00
Apple Blossom, Bowl, Green, 6 In.	145.00
Apple Blossom, Bowl, Pink, Boat Form, 10 In.	55.00
Apple Blossom, Bowl, Pink, Low, 6 In.	44.00
Apple Blossom, Bowl, Pink, Spherical, 6 In.	55.00
Apple Blossom, Candlestick, Blue, 4 1/2 In., Pair . . . . .350.00 to 395.00	
Apple Blossom, Candlestick, Pink, 2 In., Pair	100.00
Apple Blossom, Console, Blue, 12 In.	195.00
Apple Blossom, Console, Blue, Low, 14 In.	55.00
Apple Blossom, Console, Green, 12 In.	140.00
Apple Blossom, Cornucopia, Green, 6 In.	75.00
Apple Blossom, Ewer, Pink, 8 In.	44.00
Apple Blossom, Ewer, Pink, 15 In.	475.00
Apple Blossom, Flowerpot, Blue, Saucer, 5 1/2 In.	165.00
Apple Blossom, Flowerpot, Green, Saucer, 6 In.	148.00
Apple Blossom, Jardiniere, Blue, Pedestal, 10 In.	2100.00
Apple Blossom, Jardiniere, Pink, 6 In.	99.00
Apple Blossom, Pedestal, Pink, 10 In.	425.00
Apple Blossom, Pitcher, Pink, 10 3/4 In.	115.00
Apple Blossom, Planter, Green, 12 In.	80.00
Apple Blossom, Planter, Pink, 12 In.	75.00
Apple Blossom, Tea Set, Pink	400.00
Apple Blossom, Teapot, Pink, 7 In.	330.00
Apple Blossom, Vase, Blue, 7 In.	225.00
Apple Blossom, Vase, Blue, Bud, 7 1/2 In.	105.00
Apple Blossom, Vase, Green, 7 In., Pair	300.00
Apple Blossom, Vase, Green, 8 In.	185.00
Apple Blossom, Vase, Green, 10 In.	225.00
Apple Blossom, Vase, Green, 2 Handles, 7 1/4 In.	137.00
Apple Blossom, Vase, Green, Branch Handles, 9 In.	80.00
Apple Blossom, Vase, Green, Bud, 7 1/2 In.	126.00
Apple Blossom, Vase, Pink, 6 In.	156.00
Apple Blossom, Vase, Pink, 10 In.	235.00
Apple Blossom, Vase, Pink, 12 In.	192.00
Apple Blossom, Vase, Pink, 18 In.	650.00
Apple Blossom, Vase, Pink, Brown Handles, 7 1/2 In., Pair	220.00
Apple Blossom, Wall Pocket, Blue, 9 In.	200.00
Apple Blossom, Wall Pocket, Green, 9 In.	190.00
Apple Blossom, Window Box	149.00
Baneda, Vase, Florals At Top, Shoulder Handles, 6 1/2 In.	880.00
Baneda, Vase, Green & Blue, 6 1/2 In.	440.00
Baneda, Vase, Green, 12 In.	1765.00
Baneda, Vase, Green, 2 Handles, 10 In.	1700.00
Baneda, Vase, Green, 2 Handles, 15 1/8 In.	3300.00
Baneda, Vase, Pink, 4 1/2 In.	285.00

Baneda, Vase, Red, 4 1/2 x 5 3/4 In. 500.00
Bittersweet, Basket, Orange Berries, Green Leaves, Branch Handle, 8 x 7 In. 187.00
Bittersweet, Bowl, Flower Frog, Green, 6 In. 150.00
Bittersweet, Bowl, Gray, 4 In. 60.00
Bittersweet, Candlestick, Light Green, Brown Handles, 5 In., Pair 220.00
Bittersweet, Vase, Gray, 5 In. 175.00
Bittersweet, Vase, Green, 16 In. 900.00
Blackberry, Console, 12 In. 700.00
Blackberry, Console, White Berries, 8 In. 598.00
Blackberry, Jardiniere, 4 In. 355.00
Blackberry, Planter, 13 In. 600.00
Blackberry, Vase, Gourd, 4 In. 605.00
Blackberry, Vase, Handles, 8 In. 835.00
Blackberry, Vase, Label, 5 In. ....*Illus* 440.00
Bleeding Heart, Bowl, Pink, Handle, 10 In. 198.00
Bleeding Heart, Candlestick, Pink, 2 3/8 In., Pair 165.00
Bleeding Heart, Console, Green, Scalloped Rim, 10 In. 137.00
Bleeding Heart, Jardiniere, Blue, 3 1/2 In. 135.00
Bleeding Heart, Pitcher, Pink, 8 In. 440.00
Bleeding Heart, Vase, Blue, Fan, Footed, 8 In. 110.00
Bleeding Heart, Vase, Pink, Scalloped Rim, Fan, 8 In. 165.00
Bleeding Heart, Vase, Pink, Triangular Buttressed Handles, 7 In., Pair 220.00
Bridge, Pitcher 55.00
Burmese, Wall Pocket, Green 385.00
Bushberry, Ashtray, Orange, 5 1/2 In. ....100.00 to 130.00
Bushberry, Basket, Green, 7 In. 160.00
Bushberry, Basket, Green, Hanging 255.00
Bushberry, Basket, Orange, 6 1/2 In. 180.00
Bushberry, Basket, Orange, Asymmetrical Handle, 8 In. 245.00
Bushberry, Bookends, Blue 165.00
Bushberry, Bookends, Orange 137.00
Bushberry, Candlestick, Orange, 2 In., Pair 100.00
Bushberry, Cider Set, Blue, 5 Piece 495.00
Bushberry, Cider Set, Orange, 7 Piece 440.00
Bushberry, Console Set, Blue, 3 Piece 205.00
Bushberry, Console, Blue, 10 In. 220.00
Bushberry, Cornucopia, 6 In. 105.00
Bushberry, Cornucopia, Orange, 6 1/4 In. 137.00
Bushberry, Jardiniere, Orange, 8 In. ....400.00 to 500.00
Bushberry, Jardiniere, Pedestal, Blue, 24 3/8 In. 550.00
Bushberry, Mug, Green, 3 1/2 In. 80.00
Bushberry, Pitcher, Orange, 8 1/2 In. 180.00
Bushberry, Sugar & Creamer, Blue, 2 In. 135.00
Bushberry, Tea Set, Orange 385.00
Bushberry, Umbrella Stand, Green, 21 In. 850.00
Bushberry, Umbrella Stand, Orange, 21 In. 550.00
Bushberry, Vase, Blue, 8 In. 240.00
Bushberry, Vase, Blue, 12 In. 265.00
Bushberry, Vase, Green, Handle, 14 1/2 In. 520.00
Bushberry, Vase, Orange, 2 Asymmetrical Handles, 15 In. 275.00
Bushberry, Vase, Orange, 4 In. 44.00
Bushberry, Vase, Orange, 6 In. 44.00
Bushberry, Vase, Orange, 8 In. 82.00
Bushberry, Vase, Orange, 10 In. 280.00
Bushberry, Vase, Orange, Bud, 4 1/2 In. 110.00
Bushberry, Vase, Orange, Flared, 2 Asymmetrical Handles, 12 In. 165.00
Bushberry, Vase, Orange, Pillow, 9 In. 82.00
Bushberry, Wall Pocket, Green 175.00
Carnelian I, Candlestick, 2-Tone Blue, Signed, 2 3/8 In., Pair 110.00
Carnelian I, Candlestick, Frog Form, Pink, Green 44.00
Carnelian I, Candlestick, Green, 3 In. 75.00
Carnelian I, Candlestick, Green, 3 In., Pair 200.00
Carnelian I, Vase, Blue Over Pink, Side Handles, 8 1/4 In. 225.00

Roseville, Blackberry,
Vase, Label, 5 In.

**Glue broken china with an
invisible mending cement
that is waterproof.**

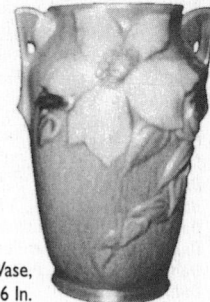

Roseville, Clematis, Vase,
Brown, 6 In.

Carnelian I, Wall Pocket, Blue, 8 1/4 In.	380.00
Carnelian II, Candlestick, Red, Green, 8 In.	250.00
Carnelian II, Jardiniere, Pink, 4 In.	475.00
Carnelian II, Vase, Lavender, Turquoise, 10 1/4 In.	495.00
Carnelian II, Vase, Mottled Pink Glaze, 15 1/8 In.	1540.00
Carnelian II, Vase, Pink, Purple, 8 In.	295.00
Cherry Blossom, Vase, Blue, 4 In.	425.00
Cherry Blossom, Vase, Blue, 8 In.	650.00
Cherry Blossom, Vase, Brown, 8 In.	495.00
Cherry Blossom, Wall Pocket, Brown	1200.00
Clematis, Basket, Blue, Hanging	250.00
Clematis, Basket, Brown, 7 In.	140.00
Clematis, Bowl, Green, 14 In.	145.00
Clematis, Console, 10 In.	225.00
Clematis, Cookie Jar, Blue, 10 In.	490.00
Clematis, Cookie Jar, No. 3, Brown, 10 In.	400.00
Clematis, Cornucopia, Blue, 6 In.	105.00
Clematis, Cornucopia, Brown, 8 In.	195.00
Clematis, Creamer, Green	33.00
Clematis, Ewer, Blue, 10 In.	225.00
Clematis, Ewer, Brown, 6 In.	175.00
Clematis, Urn, Brown, Faceted Rim, 10 In.	66.00
Clematis, Vase, Blue, 7 In.	120.00
Clematis, Vase, Blue, 15 In.	695.00
Clematis, Vase, Blue, 2 Handles, 8 In.	77.00
Clematis, Vase, Blue, Faceted Rim, 2 Handles, 10 In.	77.00
Clematis, Vase, Brown, 6 In. ....*Illus*	66.00
Clematis, Vase, Brown, 7 In.	95.00
Clematis, Vase, Brown, 8 In.	125.00
Clematis, Vase, Green, Double Bud, 5 In.	66.00
Clematis, Wall Pocket, Green	325.00
Colonial, Pitcher, 11 In.	200.00
Columbine, Ewer, Brown, Angular Neck, 7 3/4 In.	192.00
Columbine, Rose Bowl, Blue, 5 1/2 In.	88.00
Columbine, Vase, Blue, 3 In.	105.00
Columbine, Vase, Blue, 6 In.	165.00
Columbine, Vase, Brown, Squatty, 2 Handles, 4 In.	137.00
Columbine, Vase, Red, 12 1/2 In.	330.00
Columbine, Wall Pocket, Blue, 9 In.	285.00
Corinthian, Jardiniere, 9 In.	375.00
Corinthian, Vase, 8 In.	100.00
Cosmos, Basket, Green, 11 In.	230.00
Cosmos, Bowl, Green, Oval	165.00
Cosmos, Candlestick, Blue, 1 7/8 In.	220.00
Cosmos, Console, Blue, 11 1/2 In.	385.00
Cosmos, Cornucopia, Brown, Green Cone, 6 In., Pair	165.00
Cosmos, Flower Frog, Blue, 3 1/2 In.	220.00
Cosmos, Jardiniere, Green, 6 In.	125.00

Cosmos, Planter, Light Green, Floral Around Middle, 3 Handles 385.00
Cosmos, Vase, Blue, Double Bud, 5 In. 275.00
Cosmos, Vase, Green, 10 In. 235.00
Cosmos, Vase, Green, Handles, 4 In. 80.00
Cosmos, Vase, Tan, 8 In. 285.00
Cremona, Planter, Pink, 6 In. 275.00
Cremona, Vase, Green, 12 In. 300.00
Cremona, Vase, Green, Footed, Flared, 4 In. 88.00
Dahlrose, Bowl, Low, Circular, 10 In. 137.00
Dahlrose, Candlestick, 3 In., Pair 160.00
Dahlrose, Vase, 2 Buttressed Handles, Bud, 8 1/4 In. 105.00
Dahlrose, Vase, 2 Handles, 6 x 3 1/4 In., Pair ....165.00 to 247.00
Dahlrose, Vase, 2 Handles, 8 1/4 In. 137.00
Dahlrose, Vase, 8 1/2 In. 82.00
Dahlrose, Vase, Double Bud, 6 1/4 In. 105.00
Dahlrose, Vase, Handles, 1924, 6 In. ....175.00 to 200.00
Dahlrose, Vase, Triple Bud, 6 In. 300.00
Dahlrose, Vase, Triple Bud, 6 1/2 In. 82.00
Dawn, Vase, Pink, 6 In. 135.00
Dogwood I, Box, Cigarette, Cover, Green 175.00
Dogwood I, Jardiniere, Pedestal, Green, 12 In. 1700.00
Dogwood I, Jardiniere, Pedestal, Green, 35 In. 1495.00
Dogwood I, Vase, Bud, Green, 9 In. 165.00
Dogwood II, Jardiniere, Pedestal, Green, 12 In. 1700.00
Dogwood II, Vase, Asymmetrical, Green, 10 In. 330.00
Dogwood II, Vase, Bud, Green, 8 1/2 In. 165.00
Donatello, Basket, Hanging, 6 In. 150.00
Donatello, Basket, Hanging, 8 In. 430.00
Donatello, Bowl, Round, 6 In. 100.00
Donatello, Candlestick, 6 1/2 In. 265.00
Donatello, Jardiniere, 4 In. 82.00
Donatello, Jardiniere, 7 1/2 In. 245.00
Donatello, Jardiniere, Pedestal, 29 In. 635.00
Donatello, Vase, Double Bud, 5 In. 80.00
Elk Head, Mug, 4 1/2 In. 75.00
Elsie The Cow, Bowl, Plate & Mug 750.00
Falline, Vase, 2 Handles, 6 1/2 In. 770.00
Falline, Vase, 9 In. 1395.00
Falline, Vase, Flared, 2 Loop Handles, 8 1/4 In. 1430.00
Ferrella, Candlestick, Brown, 4 1/8 In., Pair 410.00
Ferrella, Vase, Red, Flared, 5 1/4 In. 192.00
Florane, Bowl, 8 1/2 In. 110.00
Florentine, Ashtray, Ivory, 3 In. 125.00
Florentine, Bowl, Brown, 4 In. 125.00
Florentine, Bowl, Brown, 8 1/2 In. 60.00
Florentine, Bowl, Flower Frog, 4 In. 125.00
Florentine, Jardiniere, Brown, 8 In. 465.00
Florentine, Jardiniere, Ivory, 6 In. ....90.00 to 135.00
Florentine, Jardiniere, Pedestal, Brown, 29 In. 440.00
Florentine, Vase, Brown, 6 In. 60.00
Florentine, Vase, Brown, 10 In. 125.00
Florentine, Vase, Brown, Footed, 4 1/2 In. 97.00
Florentine, Vase, Ivory, 8 In. 245.00
Florentine, Vase, Ivory, 10 In. 90.00
Florentine, Vase, Ivory, 12 3/8 In. 300.00
Foxglove, Bookends, Red, 5 5/8 In. 220.00
Foxglove, Bowl, Flower Frog, Green, 10 In. 245.00
Foxglove, Candlestick, Green, 4 In. 195.00
Foxglove, Console, Red, 10 In. 190.00
Foxglove, Cornucopia, Blue, 6 In. 165.00
Foxglove, Cornucopia, Blue, 7 3/4 In. 170.00
Foxglove, Cornucopia, Green, 6 In. ....175.00 to 195.00
Foxglove, Cornucopia, Red, 7 3/4 In. 170.00

Foxglove, Planter, Green, Conch Shell, 4 1/2 In. 190.00
Foxglove, Tray, Blue, 11 In. 105.00
Foxglove, Urn, Footed, Red, 8 In. 135.00
Foxglove, Vase, Blue, 8 In. 265.00
Foxglove, Vase, Blue, 14 In. 645.00
Foxglove, Vase, Blue, Double Bud, 5 In. 137.00
Foxglove, Vase, Green, 10 In. 235.00
Foxglove, Vase, Green, Double Bud 160.00
Foxglove, Vase, Red, 16 In. 750.00
Freesia, Basket, Blue, 7 In. 135.00
Freesia, Basket, Blue, 8 1/2 In. 110.00
Freesia, Basket, Brown, Hanging, 5 x 8 In. ....210.00 to 260.00
Freesia, Bookends, Brown, 5 In. 105.00
Freesia, Candlestick, Brown, 3 In. 55.00
Freesia, Cookie Jar, Brown 550.00
Freesia, Cookie Jar, Green 200.00
Freesia, Cornucopia, Blue, 6 1/2 In. 70.00
Freesia, Ewer, Blue, 6 1/2 In. 135.00
Freesia, Jardiniere, Blue, Bulbous, 6 In. ....88.00 to 110.00
Freesia, Jardiniere, Brown, 5 In. 82.00
Freesia, Jardiniere, Green, 5 In. 110.00
Freesia, Jardiniere, Pedestal, Blue, 24 In. 805.00
Freesia, Jardiniere, Pedestal, Green 1750.00
Freesia, Pitcher, Blue, 10 1/2 In. ....175.00 to 190.00
Freesia, Pitcher, Green, 10 1/2 In. 94.00
Freesia, Teapot, Brown, 7 In. 115.00
Freesia, Urn, Blue, 8 In. 80.00
Freesia, Urn, Brown, 6 In. 82.00
Freesia, Vase, Blue, 10 1/2 In. ....105.00 to 240.00
Freesia, Vase, Blue, Buttressed Handles, Trumpet Neck, 7 In. 192.00
Freesia, Vase, Brown, 2 Handles, 9 In. 69.00
Freesia, Window Box, Brown, 10 1/2 In. 80.00
Fuchsia, Jardiniere, Tan, 4 In. 145.00
Fuchsia, Vase, Blue, 6 In. 255.00
Fuchsia, Vase, Blue, 8 In. ....425.00 to 435.00
Fuchsia, Vase, Green, 4 In. 145.00
Fuchsia, Vase, Green, 6 In. 235.00
Fuchsia, Vase, Tan, Squat, 4 1/4 In. 165.00
Futura, Basket, Tan, Hanging 350.00
Futura, Bowl, Blue, 8 In. 325.00
Futura, Bowl, Flying Saucer, Flower Frog, Paper Label, 10 1/8 In. 1045.00
Futura, Jardiniere, Brown, Green, 10 In. 750.00
Futura, Vase, 3-Tone Blue, Stepped Disk Base, 9 In. 747.00
Futura, Vase, Blue, 3 Sides, Matte, 9 In. 245.00
Futura, Vase, Blue, 5 1/8 In. 300.00
Futura, Vase, Blue, 7 In. 1200.00
Futura, Vase, Blue, Triangle, 8 1/8 In. 440.00
Futura, Vase, Green, Blue, Yellow, Pink Disks, Angular Base, 8 1/4 In. 1265.00
Futura, Vase, Green, Globe On Legs, Paper Label, 8 1/4 In. 825.00
Futura, Vase, Mauve, Beige, Square Rim, 4-Footed, Matte, 1928, 9 In. 575.00
Futura, Vase, Orange, Gray, Cylindrical, 2 Handles, 6 1/4 In. 275.00
Futura, Vase, Pink, Embossed Vine, 6 Sides, Matte, Pillow, 4 1/2 In. 330.00
Futura, Vase, Pleated Star, Blue, 8 1/8 In. 190.00
Futura, Wall Pocket, Blue, 8 1/8 In. 550.00
Gardenia, Basket, Green, 8 In. 245.00
Gardenia, Ewer, Tan, 6 In. 78.00
Gardenia, Ewer, Tan, 10 In. 200.00
Gardenia, Jardiniere, Gray, 10 In. 400.00
Gardenia, Jardiniere, Green, 10 In. 390.00
Gardenia, Planter, Green, 3 In. 125.00
Gardenia, Vase, Tan, 8 In. 195.00
Gardenia, Wall Pocket, Gray 325.00
Holland, Pitcher, Tan, 12 In. 480.00

Imperial II, Bowl, Blue, 8 In. 425.00
Imperial II, Vase, Repeating Design Around Collar, Green Glaze, Label, 4 3/8 In. 410.00
Iris, Basket, Tan, 8 In. 295.00
Iris, Basket, Tan, Hanging 325.00
Iris, Bookends, Tan 325.00
Iris, Bowl, Blue, 6 In. 105.00
Iris, Console, Blue, 10 In. ....185.00 to 200.00
Iris, Jardiniere, Pedestal, Blue, 25 In. 770.00
Iris, Vase, Blue, 5 In. 120.00
Iris, Vase, Blue, Handles, 7 In. 95.00
Iris, Vase, Pink, 2 Handles, 6 In. 110.00
Iris, Vase, Pink, Silver Foil Label, 6 1/4 In. 137.00
Ixia, Bowl, Yellow, 8 In. 80.00
Ixia, Vase, Green, 6 In. 135.00
Ixia, Vase, Green, 8 In. 125.00
Ixia, Vase, Green, 12 1/2 In. 220.00
Jonquil, Basket 650.00
Jonquil, Jardiniere, 9 x 12 In. 725.00
Jonquil, Vase, 7 In. 270.00
Juvenile, Eggcup, Chick 250.00
Knights Of Pythias, Mug, 5 In., Pair 110.00
Landscape, Teapot, Brown, 7 1/2 x 7 3/4 In. 165.00
Laurel, Vase, Brown, Buttressed Handles, 7 In. 303.00
Laurel, Vase, Brown, Label, 6 In. 247.00
Laurel, Vase, Gold, 6 In. 220.00
Laurel, Vase, Gold, Buttressed Handles, 9 1/2 In. 355.00
Luffa, Vase, Brown, 6 3/4 In. 425.00
Luffa, Vase, Green, 8 1/4 In. 280.00
Luffa, Wall Pocket, Brown 1095.00
Magnolia, Ashtray, Green, 2 x 7 In. 82.00
Magnolia, Ashtray, Tan 110.00
Magnolia, Basket, Blue, 7 In. 175.00
Magnolia, Basket, Green, Hanging, 11 In. 135.00
Magnolia, Basket, Tan, 6 In. 99.00
Magnolia, Basket, Tan, Hanging 135.00
Magnolia, Bookends, Blue 250.00
Magnolia, Bowl, Tan, 3 In. 38.00
Magnolia, Cookie Jar, Tan 375.00
Magnolia, Cornucopia, Green, 5 In. 66.00
Magnolia, Ewer, Blue, 9 1/2 In. 165.00

Roseville, Magnolia, Teapot,
Tan, 8 x 10 In.;
Roseville, Magnolia, Pitcher,
Cider, Tan, 9 In.;
Roseville, Magnolia,
Sugar & Creamer, Tan,
1 1/2 x 3 In.

Magnolia, Ewer, Green, 15 In. 700.00
Magnolia, Ewer, Tan, 16 In. 137.00
Magnolia, Jardiniere, Blue, 3 In. 75.00
Magnolia, Jardiniere, Blue, 5 1/2 In. 80.00
Magnolia, Pitcher, Cider, Green, 9 In. . . . . *Illus* 250.00
Magnolia, Planter, Green, Conch Shell, 6 In. 99.00
Magnolia, Sugar & Creamer, Tan, 1 1/2 x 3 In. . . . . *Illus* 44.00
Magnolia, Teapot, Blue, 8 x 10 In. . . . . *Illus* 165.00
Magnolia, Vase, Blue, 6 In. 125.00
Magnolia, Vase, Blue, Flared Neck, 2 Handles, 9 In. 66.00
Magnolia, Vase, Blue, Footed, 6 In. 50.00
Magnolia, Vase, Green, 6 In. 110.00
Magnolia, Vase, Green, Bulbous, 2 Handles, 8 In. 77.00
Magnolia, Vase, Tan, 9 In. 77.00
Magnolia, Wall Pocket, Blue 360.00
Magnolia, Window Box, Tan, 6 In. 125.00
Mayfair, Pitcher, Lime, 8 In. 135.00
Mayfair, Tankard, Beige, 12 In. 135.00
Mayfair, Vase, Brown, 8 In. 80.00
Medallion, Dresser Set, 4 Piece 165.00
Ming Tree, Basket, Turquoise, Hanging, 8 In. 220.00
Ming Tree, Bowl, Turquoise, 9 In. 275.00
Ming Tree, Bowl, White . . . . .100.00 to 120.00
Ming Tree, Candlestick, Turquoise 90.00
Ming Tree, Candlestick, White, Pair 80.00
Ming Tree, Vase, White, 6 In. 75.00
Ming Tree, Vase, White, 10 In. 195.00
Mock Orange, Basket, Pink, Handle, 10 In. . . . . .190.00 to 235.00
Mock Orange, Bowl, Pink, 3-Footed, 6 In. 145.00
Mock Orange, Planter, Pink, 7 In. 110.00
Monticello, Vase, Aqua, 2 Handles, 9 1/8 In. 880.00
Monticello, Vase, Blue, 5 In. 495.00
Monticello, Vase, Blue, 9 1/8 In. 880.00
Monticello, Vase, Brown, 2 Buttressed Handles, 15 In. 550.00
Monticello, Vase, Brown, 4 In. 220.00
Morning Glory, Console, Green, 4 1/4 In. 290.00
Morning Glory, Vase, Green, 9 1/8 In. 660.00
Morning Glory, Vase, White, 6 In. 695.00
Morning Glory, Vase, White, 8 1/2 In. 148.00
Morning Glory, Vase, White, 12 In. 1200.00
Moss, Bowl, Pink & Blue, 3 x 7 1/2 In. 165.00
Moss, Candlestick, Pink & Green, 3 Sockets, 7 In., Pair 495.00
Moss, Flower Frog, Blue, 4 3/4 x 3 1/4 In. 75.00
Moss, Jardiniere, Blue, 5 In. 165.00
Moss, Rose Bowl, Tan & Blue, 4 1/2 In. 165.00
Moss, Vase, Blue & Pink, 2 Handles, 4 1/8 In. 248.00
Moss, Vase, Tan & Blue, Pillow, 8 1/2 In. 275.00
Mostique, Basket, Tan, Hanging, Heart-Shaped Holes For Rope, 6 x 7 In. 330.00
Mostique, Jardiniere, Pedestal, Tan, 28 In. 660.00
Mostique, Vase, Gray, With Spears, 8 In. 175.00
Mostique, Vase, Tan, 6 In. 80.00
Mostique, Vase, Tan, 8 In. 185.00
Mostique, Vase, Tan, Geometric Design, 2 Open Handles, 8 In. 1430.00
Mostique, Vase, Tan, Stylized Floral Design, 21 In. 1045.00
Orian, Vase, Rose, Double Ridge Waist, Beaded Long Handles, 7 In. 165.00
Orian, Vase, Turquoise, 8 In. 275.00
Orian, Vase, Yellow, 8 In. 275.00
Pasadena, Planter, Pink, Stylized Leaves Form Base & Flaring Top, 5 1/2 In. 242.00
Pauleo, Jar, Cover, Red, Blue Purple & Black Glaze, 6 3/4 In. 1320.00
Pauleo, Vase, Mottled Blue-Green Glaze, Black Streaks From Rim, 17 3/8 In. 1760.00
Pauleo, Vase, Mottled Rust & Black, 14 1/2 In. 1320.00
Peony, Basket, Brown, Hanging, 7 In. 105.00

Peony, Basket, Green, Hanging	150.00
Peony, Bowl, Brown, Handle, 4 In.	66.00
Peony, Candlestick, Brown, 1 In., Pair	80.00
Peony, Candlestick, Coral, 2 In., Pair	70.00
Peony, Ewer, Coral, 15 In.	600.00
Peony, Jardiniere, Green, 3 In.	60.00
Peony, Jardiniere, Pink, 7 In.	120.00
Peony, Mug, Brown, 3 1/2 In.	145.00
Peony, Mug, Green, 3 1/2 In.	115.00
Peony, Pitcher, Coral, 6 In.	44.00
Peony, Tray, Gold ....*Illus*	125.00
Peony, Vase, Brown, Footed, 6 In.	50.00
Peony, Vase, Pink, 4 In.	60.00
Peony, Window Box, Pink, 8 In.	110.00
Pine Cone, Ashtray, Green, 4 5/8 In.	55.00
Pine Cone, Ashtray, Pink, 4 x 5 In.	125.00
Pine Cone, Basket, Blue, Hanging, 6 In. ....375.00 to 550.00
Pine Cone, Basket, Brown, 11 In.	412.00
Pine Cone, Basket, Brown, Hanging, Original Chain, 6 In.	260.00
Pine Cone, Bookends, Brown	425.00
Pine Cone, Bowl, Brown, 7 In.	225.00
Pine Cone, Bowl, Brown, 11 In.	220.00
Pine Cone, Bowl, Brown, 4 x 6 In.	440.00
Pine Cone, Bowl, Green, Low, Handle, 2 1/2 x 9 1/2 In.	33.00
Pine Cone, Cigarette Holder, Cone At Bottom, 3 In.	248.00
Pine Cone, Console, Blue, Raised Vertical Panels, Oblong, 11 In.	220.00
Pine Cone, Console, Green, 12 In.	325.00
Pine Cone, Cornucopia, Brown	245.00
Pine Cone, Dish, Cone On Rim, Pink, 6 x 7 In.	125.00
Pine Cone, Flowerpot, Blue, 5 In.	355.00
Pine Cone, Flowerpot, Green, Flared, 5 In.	88.00
Pine Cone, Jardiniere, Blue, Applied Branches For Handles, 32 In.	4025.00
Pine Cone, Jardiniere, Brown, 5 In.	220.00
Pine Cone, Jardiniere, Brown, Buttressed Branch Handle, 7 In.	440.00
Pine Cone, Jardiniere, Flower At Side Top, Handles, 6 In.	220.00
Pine Cone, Jardiniere, Pedestal, Green, 28 3/4 In.	1670.00
Pine Cone, Lamp, Cone At Shoulder, Handles, 18 In.	633.00
Pine Cone, Pitcher, Green, 10 In.	1000.00
Pine Cone, Tumbler, Green, 5 In.	150.00
Pine Cone, Vase, Blue, 10 In.	750.00
Pine Cone, Vase, Blue, 12 In. ....350.00 to 680.00
Pine Cone, Vase, Blue, Double Bud	475.00
Pine Cone, Vase, Blue, Pillow, 8 In.	525.00
Pine Cone, Vase, Brown, 7 In.	235.00
Pine Cone, Vase, Brown, 9 In.	360.00

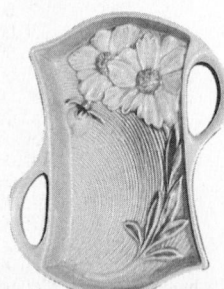

Roseville, Peony,
Tray, Gold

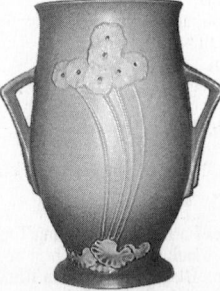

Roseville, Primrose,
Vase, Pink, 8 3/8 In.

Roseville, Sign, Dealer, Pink,
Molded Script, 7 1/2 In.

Pine Cone, Vase, Brown, 10 In. . . . . .439.00 to 500.00
Pine Cone, Vase, Green, 2 Branch Handles, 13 In. 330.00
Pine Cone, Vase, Green, 5 In. 230.00
Pine Cone, Vase, Green, 6 1/2 In. 255.00
Pine Cone, Vase, Green, 8 In. 175.00
Pine Cone, Vase, Green, Branch Handles, 12 1/2 In. 500.00
Pine Cone, Vase, Green, Fan, Reticulated Rim, 8 In. 275.00
Pine Cone, Vase, Green, Flared, 8 1/2 In. 368.00
Pine Cone, Vase, Green, Spherical, Squat, 4 In. 55.00
Pine Cone, Vase, Green, Trumpet Mouth, Bud, 9 In., 2 Piece 660.00
Pine Cone, Vase, Lavender, Square Base, 7 In. 495.00
Poppy, Flower Frog, Pink, Leaf Design, 3 1/2 In. 137.00
Primrose, Vase, Pink, 8 3/8 In. . . . . *Illus* 165.00
Raymor, Bean Pot, Cover, Brown, Individual 40.00
Raymor, Bean Pot, Cover, Gray 95.00
Raymor, Pitcher, Brown, 10 In. 175.00
Rosecraft, Bowl, Brown, Incised Circular Design, Burnt Orange Slip, 6 Sides, 4 In. 275.00
Rosecraft, Rose Bowl, Brown, 3 1/2 In. 110.00
Rosecraft, Vase, Brown Incised Circular Design, Burnt Orange Flow Drip, 5 1/4 In. 605.00
Rosecraft, Wall Pocket, Brown 325.00
Rosecraft Panel, Wall Pocket, Brown & Orange, Nude, 7 1/8 In. 825.00
Rosecraft Vintage, Planter, Light Brown, Leaf Veining, Jagged Leaf Edges, 5 3/4 In. 880.00
Rosecraft Vintage, Vase, Brown, Tan Vines, Grapes, Closed Mouth, 10 In. 550.00
Rozane, Bowl, Ivory, Footed, 9 In. 38.00
Rozane, Jardiniere, Ivory, 11 In. 82.00
Rozane, Letter Holder, Ocher, Mustard, Stylized Floral Design, 3 x 4 1/2 In. 165.00
Rozane, Urn, Ivory, Footed, 6 In. 50.00
Rozane, Vase, Floral, Signed, 7 1/8 In. 80.00
Rozane, Vase, Turquoise, 15 In. 330.00
Rozane Fudji, Vase, Art Nouveau Design, Tan Clay, 7 7/8 In. 1320.00
Rozane Royal, Vase, Charcoal To Pink, Wisteria, Pillow, Timberlake, 7 1/2 x 8 In. 765.00
Russco, Vase, Turquoise, Art Deco Form, Silver Foil Label, 6 1/8 In. 83.00
Russco, Vase, Yellow Over Green, Snowflake Crystalline, Silver Foil Label, 6 1/8 In. 220.00
Savona, Bowl, Fluted Design, Classical Shape, 2 Handles, 9 1/2 In. 100.00
Savona, Urn, Bulbous, 2 Scrolled Handles, 8 x 9 In. 66.00
Sign, Dealer, Mauve, Stylized Block Letters, 6 x 2 In. 1700.00
Sign, Dealer, Pink, Molded Script, 7 1/2 In. . . . . *Illus* 1925.00
Silhouette, Ashtray & Cigarette Box, Turquoise 285.00
Silhouette, Basket, Turquoise, 6 1/8 In. 82.00
Silhouette, Ewer, Turquoise 100.00
Silhouette, Ewer, White . . . . .60.00 to 100.00
Silhouette, Pitcher, Pink, Boy With Horn, 10 In. 385.00
Silhouette, Vase, Mauve, Leaf, Footed Base, 14 1/2 In. 460.00
Silhouette, Vase, Pink, Fan, 7 1/2 In. 410.00
Silhouette, Window Box, White, Blue Highlights, 8 1/2 In. 110.00
Snowberry, Ashtray, Blue . . . . .75.00 to 135.00
Snowberry, Ashtray, Green . . . . .38.00 to 69.00
Snowberry, Ashtray, Pink 100.00
Snowberry, Basket, Blue, 8 In. 150.00
Snowberry, Basket, Blue, 12 1/2 In. 245.00
Snowberry, Basket, Blue, Handle, 7 In. 175.00
Snowberry, Basket, Blue, Handle, 10 1/2 In. 165.00
Snowberry, Basket, Blue, Hanging . . . . .110.00 to 225.00
Snowberry, Basket, Green, 10 In. 235.00
Snowberry, Basket, Green, 12 In. 300.00
Snowberry, Basket, Pink, 7 In. 185.00
Snowberry, Basket, Pink, 10 In. . . . . .175.00 to 185.00
Snowberry, Candlestick, Blue, 4 1/2 In., Pair 132.00
Snowberry, Candy Dish, Pink, Cover, 6 In. 55.00
Snowberry, Console, Blue, 11 1/2 In. 165.00
Snowberry, Console, Blue, 16 1/2 In. 125.00
Snowberry, Console, Pink, 12 1/2 In. 66.00
Snowberry, Corncuopia, Blue, 6 In. . . . . .44.00 to 95.00

Snowberry, Cornucopia, Blue, 7 1/2 In. 110.00
Snowberry, Cornucopia, Blue, 8 1/2 In. 110.00
Snowberry, Ewer, Blue, 6 1/2 In. . . . . .110.00 to 145.00
Snowberry, Ewer, Blue, 10 1/2 In. 110.00
Snowberry, Ewer, Green, 5 In. 130.00
Snowberry, Jardiniere, Pedestal, Pink 950.00
Snowberry, Sugar & Creamer, Blue 33.00
Snowberry, Sugar & Creamer, Pink 95.00
Snowberry, Tea Set, Blue, 3 Piece 220.00
Snowberry, Tea Set, Pink, 3 Piece 450.00
Snowberry, Teapot, Pink 395.00
Snowberry, Vase, Blue, 6 1/2 In. 135.00
Snowberry, Vase, Blue, 7 1/2 In. . . . . .115.00 to 132.00
Snowberry, Vase, Blue, Bud, 7 1/2 In. 110.00
Snowberry, Vase, Blue, Handle, 8 1/2 In. 80.00
Snowberry, Vase, Blue, Handle, 12 1/2 In. 245.00
Snowberry, Vase, Blue, Pillow, 7 In. 110.00
Snowberry, Vase, Blue, Rim Handles, 8 In. 125.00
Snowberry, Vase, Green, 18 In. 350.00
Snowberry, Vase, Pink, 4 In. 110.00
Snowberry, Vase, Pink, Corseted, Fan, 9 In. 110.00
Snowberry, Vase, Pink, Flared Neck, 8 1/2 In. 175.00
Snowberry, Wall Pocket, Blue, 7 1/2 In. 165.00
Sunflower, Jardiniere, 7 x 9 1/2 In. 385.00
Sunflower, Umbrella Stand, 20 1/8 In. 7425.00
Sunflower, Vase, 2 V-Shaped Handles, 6 1/8 In. 632.00
Sunflower, Vase, 5 In. . . . . .350.00 to 650.00
Sunflower, Vase, 7 In. 1195.00
Sunflower, Vase, 8 1/2 In. . . . . .1595.00 to 1650.00
Sunflower, Vase, 9 In. . . . . .1870.00 to 1975.00
Sunflower, Vase, Buttressed Handles, 4 In. 467.00
Sunflower, Wall Pocket . . . . .1750.00 to 1850.00
Teasel, Candlestick, Blue, 2 In., Pair 160.00
Teasel, Vase, Ivory & Terra-Cotta, 9 1/4 In. 330.00
Thorn Apple, Bookends 150.00
Thorn Apple, Bowl, Brown, 7 In. . . . . , ... 115.00
Thorn Apple, Candlestick, Pink, 2 1/2 In., Pair 110.00
Thorn Apple, Rose Bowl, Blue, 6 1/2 In. 135.00
Thorn Apple, Vase, Blue, Footed, 4 1/2 x 6 In. 77.00
Thorn Apple, Vase, Brown, 6 In. . . . . .180.00 to 200.00
Thorn Apple, Vase, Brown, 8 In. 250.00
Thorn Apple, Vase, Footed, Pink, 6 In. 44.00
Thorn Apple, Vase, Pink, 4 3/8 In. 110.00
Topeo, Bowl, Blue, Green Glaze, Closed-In Shoulder, Low, 11 1/2 In. 99.00
Topeo, Vase, Red, 7 1/4 In. 425.00
Tourmaline, Candlestick, Blue, Label, 5 In., Pair 165.00
Tourmaline, Vase, Label, 6 In. 95.00
Tourmaline, Vase, Mottled Blue Matte Glaze, 10 1/8 In. 467.00
Tulip, Pitcher, 8 In. 165.00
Tuscany, Vase, Pink, 5 In. 125.00
Velmoss, Vase, Blue, Footed, Cylindrical, 7 1/4 x 5 1/2 In. 137.00
Velmoss, Vase, Red Matte Glaze, 2 Handles, Gold Foil Label, 12 1/4 In. 465.00
Venetian, Crock, Pudding, Stoneware, Blue, White 125.00
Vista, Jardiniere, 9 1/4 In. 605.00
Vista, Vase, 10 In. . . . . .575.00 to 655.00
Water Lily, Basket, Brown, 8 In. 115.00
Water Lily, Console Set, Tan, 3 Piece . . . .*Illus* 190.00
Water Lily, Cornucopia, Pink, 6 In. 44.00
Water Lily, Flowerpot, Blue, 5 In. 110.00
Water Lily, Pitcher, Blue, 10 In. 175.00
Water Lily, Vase, Blue, 24 In. 440.00
Water Lily, Vase, Blue, Handles, 8 In. 110.00

Roseville, Water
Lily, Console Set,
Tan, 3 Piece

Water Lily, Vase, Brown, 3 In. 60.00
Water Lily, Vase, Brown, 7 In. . . . . .90.00 to 105.00
Water Lily, Vase, Pink, 10 In. 250.00
Water Lily, Vase, Pink, Handle, 7 1/2 In. 135.00
White Rose, Basket, Pink 225.00
White Rose, Bowl, Blue, 6 In. 100.00
White Rose, Bowl, Blue, Embossed Mark, 7 1/2 In. 190.00
White Rose, Bowl, Brown & Green, 7 In. . . . . .66.00 to 110.00
White Rose, Cornucopia, Blue, 6 In. 110.00
White Rose, Cornucopia, Blue, Double, 8 1/2 In. 160.00
White Rose, Cornucopia, Brown & Green, 6 In. 110.00
White Rose, Cornucopia, Brown & Green, Double, 8 In. 145.00
White Rose, Ewer, Pink, 15 In. 370.00
White Rose, Flower Frog, Pink 110.00
White Rose, Flowerpot, Blue 185.00
White Rose, Saucer, Blue 40.00
White Rose, Teapot, Brown & Green 320.00
White Rose, Vase, Blue, 4 1/2 In. 75.00
White Rose, Vase, Blue, Handle, 7 In. 110.00
White Rose, Vase, Pink, 7 In. 180.00
Wincraft, Basket, Blue, Handle, Footed, 8 In. 55.00
Wincraft, Bookends, Chartreuse . . . . .115.00 to 120.00
Wincraft, Ewer, Chartreuse, Embossed Oak Leaves, 18 In.   303.00
Wincraft, Vase, Blue, 8 In. 130.00
Wincraft, Vase, Chartreuse, Angular, Fan, 6 In. 66.00
Wincraft, Vase, Chartreuse, Floriform, Footed, 8 In. 55.00
Wincraft, Window Box, Chartreuse, Begonia, 12 In. 88.00
Windsor, Bowl, Apricot, Modern Designs, 10 5/8 In. 410.00
Windsor, Vase, Apricot, Floral Sprays, Handles, Paper Label, 8 1/2 In. 660.00
Windsor, Vase, Apricot, Incised Ferns, Raised Leaves, Pumpkin Form, Handles, 7 In. 660.00
Wisteria, Bowl, Handles, Label, 4 In. 355.00
Wisteria, Urn, 5 In. . . . . .400.00 to 450.00
Wisteria, Vase, 2 Handles, Gold Foil Label, 6 1/8 In. 825.00
Wisteria, Vase, 2 Handles, Silver Foil Label, 4 In. 550.00
Zephyr Lily, Ashtray, Tan 75.00
Zephyr Lily, Basket, Blue, 7 In. 165.00
Zephyr Lily, Basket, Blue, 8 1/2 In. 220.00
Zephyr Lily, Basket, Blue, Handle, 10 In. 220.00
Zephyr Lily, Basket, Green, 10 In. 137.00
Zephyr Lily, Basket, Tan, 7 In. 140.00
Zephyr Lily, Cookie Jar, Blue, 10 In. 685.00
Zephyr Lily, Cornucopia, Blue, Double, 6 In. 190.00
Zephyr Lily, Cornucopia, Tan, Double, 6 In. 165.00
Zephyr Lily, Ewer, Blue, 6 1/2 In. . . . . .110.00 to 137.00
Zephyr Lily, Ewer, Blue, 10 1/2 In. 190.00
Zephyr Lily, Ewer, Green, 6 1/2 In. 115.00
Zephyr Lily, Jardiniere, Pedestal, Green, 24 3/4 In. 747.00
Zephyr Lily, Pitcher, Tan, 6 1/2 In. 75.00
Zephyr Lily, Rose Bowl, Tan, 14 In. 105.00
Zephyr Lily, Vase, Blue, 6 In. . . . . .110.00 to 120.00
Zephyr Lily, Vase, Blue, 7 1/2 In. 75.00

Zephyr Lily, Vase, Blue, 12 In. 300.00
Zephyr Lily, Vase, Blue, 15 1/2 In. 440.00
Zephyr Lily, Vase, Blue, Double Bud, 7 1/2 In. 165.00
Zephyr Lily, Vase, Blue, Handle, 8 In. 85.00
Zephyr Lily, Vase, Blue, Handle, 12 1/2 In. 185.00
Zephyr Lily, Vase, Brown, 9 In. 150.00
Zephyr Lily, Vase, Green, 2 Handles, 7 In. 110.00
Zephyr Lily, Vase, Green, 8 1/2 In. 137.00
Zephyr Lily, Vase, Green, Double Bud, 8 In. 165.00
Zephyr Lily, Vase, Tan, 8 In. 195.00
Zephyr Lily, Wall Pocket, Blue, 8 1/2 In. ....190.00 to 275.00

ROWLAND & MARSELLUS Company is part of a mark that appears on historical Staffordshire dating from the late nineteenth and early twentieth centuries. Rowland & Marsellus is the mark used by an American importing company in New York City. The company worked from 1893 to about 1937. Some of the pieces may have been made by the British Anchor Pottery Co. of Longton, England, for export to a New York firm. Many American views were made. Of special interest to collectors are the plates with rolled edges, usually blue and white.

Plate, American Poets, 10 In. 60.00
Plate, Block House, Signed, 10 In. 45.00
Plate, Charles Dickens Center, 1930s, 10 1/2 In. 62.00
Plate, Commemorate 1909 Alaska Yukon Pacific Exposition, 10 In. 62.00
Plate, New York, Statue Of Liberty, Rolled Edge, 10 1/2 In. 50.00
Plate, Panama Pacific Exposition, Horticulture Building, 1915, 10 1/2 In. .. 240.00
Plate, Pilgrims, Peace On Earth Good Will Towards Men, 9 1/4 In. 175.00
Plate, Theodore Roosevelt, Rough Rider, Scenes, 10 In. 50.00
Plate, Thousand Islands, Rolled Edge, 10 In. 105.00
Plate, Views Of Cincinnati, Ohio, Signed, 9 In. 75.00
Plate, Yale University, Old Brick Row Center, 9 In. 105.00
Plate, Zanesville, Rolled Edge, 10 1/2 In. 95.00

ROY ROGERS was born in 1911 in Cincinnati, Ohio. In the 1930s, he made a living as a singer; in 1935, his group started work at a Los Angeles radio station. He appeared in his first movie in 1937. From 1952 to 1957, he made 101 television shows. The other stars in the show were his wife, Dale Evans, his horse, Trigger, and his dog, Bullet. Roy Rogers memorabilia is collected, including items from the Roy Rogers restaurants.

Badge, Brass, Quaker Oats, Premium, 1950 .... 125.00
Badge, Deputy Sheriff, Stamped Brass, Pinback, Red, Green, 1950s 45.00
Bank, Boot Shape, Metal, Bronze Color, Image Of Roy & Trigger, 1960s ....75.00 to 98.00
Bank, Roy & Trigger Jumping, Pottery, No Closure, 6 x 3 x 7 In. 150.00
Book, Coloring, Dale Evans, Trigger, 64 Pages 125.00
Book, Little Golden Book, Dale Evans & The Lost Gold Mine, 1954 .... 20.00
Book, Outlaws Of Sundown Valley 100.00
Book, Rimrock Renegades 100.00
Boot, Leather, Red, Green & White 295.00
Box, Quaker Oats, Branding Iron Ring Offer 85.00
Button, Dale Evans, Multicolored, Grapenuts Flakes, Celluloid, Pinback, 1950s, 7/8 In. ... 20.00
Camera 110.00
Camera, Box 145.00
Cap Gun, Brown Grip 195.00
Chaps, 1950s, Large 120.00
Clock, Alarm, Animated, Riding Trigger Through A Canyon, Ingraham, 4 1/2 In. ..193.00 to 242.00
Comic Book, Dell, No. 88, 1955 .... 20.00
Figure, Bullet, Hartland, Mid-1950s, 6 1/2 In. 45.00
Flashlight, Whistle, Secret Code, Instructions, Box ....250.00 to 275.00
Guitar, Box, 1950s 130.00
Harmonica, King Of The Cowboys, Good Luck Emblem, Roy Rogers Face, 4 1/4 In. 50.00 to 52.00
Holster Set, 2 Guns 400.00
Holster Set, Leather, Embossed, Roy Rogers On Belt, RR Silver Nail Heads & Buckle .. 225.00

Jacket, Leather, Box, 1949 .... 1800.00
Knife, Pocket 60.00
Lunch Box, Saddlebag, With Thermos, Tan Vinyl, American Thermos, 1960 ..... 275.00 to 300.00
Lunch Box, Trigger, Steel, American Thermos Co., 1956, 8 1/2 x 6 1/2 x 3 1/2 In. 135.00
Neckerchief 45.00
Notebook, 11 1/2 x 10 In. 150.00
Pencil Case 150.00
Photograph, Dale Evans, In Hat, Holding Rope, Signed, Color, 8 x 10 In. 20.00
Play Set, Rodeo, Marx 170.00
Puzzle, Dale Evans Reading Good Manners For Dogs Book To Bullet, 4 x 5 In. 24.00
Puzzle, Serious-Looking Roy With Gun Drawn, 1956, 4 x 5 In. 24.00
Puzzle, Smiling Roy Holding 2 Collie Puppies, 1952, 4 x 5 In. 24.00
Puzzle, Smiling Roy Sitting On Back Of Trigger, 1952, 4 x 5 In. 24.00
Raincoat, Youth Size 235.00
Record, Child's Introduction To The West, Roy & Dale Illustrations, 33 1/3 LP 45.00
Saddle & Blanket, Pony 1550.00
Thermos 65.00
Toy, Truck, Roy Rogers, Trigger & Trigger Jr., Marx, 14 In. 425.00
Tray, 1950, 12 x 17 In. 35.00
Wristwatch, Dale Evans & Horse, Rectangular Case, Tan Leather Band, 1 1/4 In. 50.00
Yo-Yo, Photograph, Talking To Factory Owner 45.00
Yo-Yo, Roy Picture, 1950s .... 13.00 to 35.00
Yo-Yo, Trigger, Cellophane Wrap, Extra String, 1940s 13.00

ROYAL BAYREUTH is the name of a factory that was founded in Tettau, Bavaria, in 1794. It has continued to modern times. The marks have changed through the years. A stylized crest, the name *Royal Bayreuth*, and the word *Bavaria* appear in slightly different forms from 1870 to about 1919. Later dishes may include the words *U.S. Zone*, the year of the issue, or the word *Germany* instead of *Bavaria*. Related pieces may be found listed in the Rose Tapestry, Sand Babies, Snow Babies, and Sunbonnet Babies categories.

Ashtray, Devil Head, 2 1/2 x 5 1/2 In. 700.00
Ashtray, Eagle 495.00
Ashtray, Elk 175.00
Bowl, Peacock Scene, 10 In. 775.00
Bowl, Poppy, 8 In. 275.00
Bowl, Sugar, Purple Grape, 3 3/4 In. 85.00
Candleholder, Cow Scene 95.00
Candy Dish, Little Jack Horner 120.00
Celery Dish, Large Pink American Beauty Roses, Beaded Gold Rim, 13 x 5 In. 175.00
Coffeepot, Brittany Girl 250.00
Cracker Jar, Goose, Girl, Blue 50.00
Creamer, Alligator Mouth, Square Handle, 3 In. 425.00
Creamer, Bull, Gray, 4 In. 250.00
Creamer, Butterfly, Open Winged, Gray & Orange, 4 1/4 In. .... 225.00 to 350.00
Creamer, Coachman, 4 1/4 In. 250.00
Creamer, Corinthian, With Acanthus Leaf 40.00
Creamer, Crow, Brown Beak, 4 In. 160.00
Creamer, Devil & Cards, 4 In. 250.00
Creamer, Duck, 3 3/4 In. 200.00
Creamer, Eagle, Signed, 3 1/2 In. 400.00
Creamer, Elk, 4 1/2 In. 150.00
Creamer, Figural Roses, Gold 375.00
Creamer, Fish Head, Blue Mark .... 310.00 to 475.00
Creamer, Fox Hunt Scene 125.00
Creamer, Lemon, 3 3/4 In. 200.00
Creamer, Mountain Goat, Blue Mark, 4 In. .... 175.00 to 325.00
Creamer, Pansy, 4 In. .... 250.00 to 350.00
Creamer, Parakeet, 3 3/4 In. 415.00
Creamer, Pelican, 4 3/4 In. 275.00
Creamer, Perch 650.00
Creamer, Pig, Gray, Signed 750.00

Royal Bayreuth, Toothpick, Cavalier,
Musicians, 3 Handles

Royal Bayreuth, Toothpick, Corinthian,
Grecian Design On Red Ground

Creamer, Poodle, 4 1/2 In. . . . . .175.00 to 300.00
Creamer, Rabbit, Registered Mark, 4 In. 5000.00
Creamer, Red Coachman 225.00
Creamer, Robin 200.00
Creamer, Sheep, Landscape Scene 110.00
Creamer, Snake, Signed 1100.00
Creamer, St. Bernard, 3 1/2 In. . . . . .195.00 to 275.00
Creamer, Strawberry 200.00
Creamer, Water Buffalo, Green Mark, 3 3/4 In. 275.00
Dish, Arab Scene, Signed, 5 x 8 In. 115.00
Dresser Tray, Art Nouveau Lady, White, Satin Finish, 10 x 7 In. 700.00
Dresser Tray, Cottage By Waterfall, 8 x 11 In. 795.00
Figurine, Water Buffalo, Blue Mark, 5 In. 165.00
Hair Receiver, Woodland Scene, 3 Gilded Feet, Deer On Cover, 3 3/4 In. 135.00
Hatpin Holder, Cavalier, Musicians, Blue Mark, 4 1/2 In. 425.00
Hatpin Holder, Penguin, Red & Gray, 5 In. 1150.00
Hatpin Holder, Red Poppy, Blue Mark 595.00
Jug, Mud Men, Green Coat, 9 1/2 In. 355.00
Jug, Mud Men, Yellow Coat, 9 1/4 In. 295.00
Match Holder, Hanging, Conch Shell 325.00
Mug, Beer, Elk, Signed 475.00
Mug, Little Miss Muffet, Child's 175.00
Mustard Pot, Goose Girl Scene 130.00
Mustard Pot, Lobster, Signed . . . . .95.00 to 125.00
Mustard Pot, Tomato On Lettuce Leaf, 5 1/2 In. 65.00
Nappy, Little Bo-Peep, Rolled Edge, Handle, Signed, 6 In. 150.00
Pin Box, Heart Shape, Green & Yellow Ground, Brown & White Cows, 1 x 3 In. 65.00
Pitcher, Boy & Turkeys Scene, 5 In. 125.00
Pitcher, Coachman, Signed 1200.00

Royal Bayreuth,
Toothpick,
Elk Head

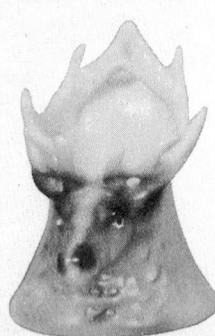

Royal Bayreuth, Toothpick, Goose Girl,
Tricornered

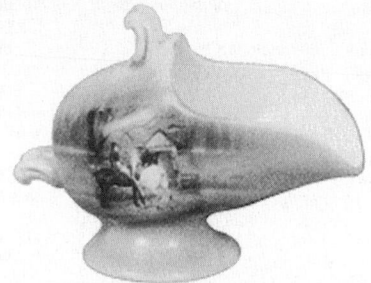

Royal Bayreuth, Toothpick,
Horses & Riders, 3 In.

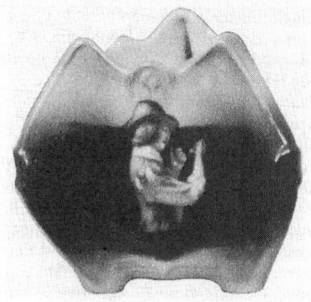

Royal Bayreuth, Toothpick,
Toaster Cavalier, Tricornered, Brown & Green

Pitcher, Eagle, Blue Mark, 5 In.	550.00
Pitcher, Elk, 7 In.	825.00
Pitcher, Little Jack Horner, 5 1/2 In.	200.00
Pitcher, Maple Leaf, Signed	1400.00
Pitcher, Pelican	1500.00
Pitcher, Seal, Signed	1400.00
Pitcher, Shell, Lobster Handle, 5 1/2 In.	295.00
Pitcher, Spiky Shell, Coral Handle, 5 1/2 In.	150.00
Pitcher, St. Bernard, Yellow Ears, Charcoal Ground, 5 In.	325.00
Pitcher, Turtle, Signed, 4 1/2 In.	750.00
Pitcher, Water Buffalo Scene, 5 In.	165.00
Plate, Donkey Boy, Farm Scene, 6 In.	45.00
Plate, Figural, Leaf, 6 Yellow Chicks Around Border, 9 1/2 In.	275.00
Plate, Girl, With Dog, 10 In.	325.00
Powder Jar, Peacock	200.00
Salt & Pepper, Grape, Purple	125.00
Salt & Pepper, Strawberry	120.00
Sugar, Pansy, Purple	225.00 to 310.00
Sugar & Creamer, Brittany Woman	265.00
Sugar & Creamer, Cover, Tomato, Leaf & Blossom Underplate	165.00
Tea Set, Tomato, Sugar, Creamer, Waste Bowl, Plate, 4 1/2 In. Teapot, 5 Piece	288.00
Tea Strainer, Anemone, Green, Brown & Yellow	395.00
Teapot, Child's, Jack & Beanstalk, Back Has Nursery Rhyme	125.00
Toothpick, Cavalier, Musicians, 3 Handles ....*Illus*	55.00
Toothpick, Corinthian, 3 Handles	110.00
Toothpick, Corinthian, Grecian Design On Red Ground ....*Illus*	66.00
Toothpick, Elk Head ....*Illus*	72.00
Toothpick, Goose Girl, Tricornered ....*Illus*	33.00
Toothpick, Horses & Riders, 3 In. ....*Illus*	105.00
Toothpick, Majesty Rose	150.00
Toothpick, Toaster Cavalier, Tricornered, Brown & Green ....*Illus*	72.00
Vase, Boy & Donkeys, Blue Mark, 4 In.	95.00
Vase, Cow Scene, 2 Handles, 3 In.	125.00
Vase, Cow Scene, Blue Mark, 8 In.	275.00
Vase, Girls With Witch, 4 In.	495.00
Vase, Goose Girl, 2 1/2 In.	90.00
Vase, Hunting Scene, Signed, 6 In.	125.00
Vase, Roses, Open Work Top, Scroll Work Bottom, Signed, 8 1/2 In.	200.00
Vase, Silver Rim Top, Handles, Signed, 3 1/4 In.	65.00

ROYAL BONN is the nineteenth- and twentieth-century trade name for the Bonn China Manufactory. It was established in 1755 in Bonn, Germany. A general line of porcelain was made. Many marks were used, most including the name *Bonn*, the initials *FM*, and a crown.

Charger, Irises, Embossed Mold, Signed, c.1890, 13 In.	190.00

Clock, Pink Floral Reserves, Pale Green Ground, 15 In. 805.00
Ewer, Yellow Flowers, Gold Trim, 7 In. 125.00
Ginger Jar, Cover, Blue, White Geometric Ground, Floral, Porcelain, 18 In. 95.00
Jug, 1885, 13 In. 500.00
Plate, Windmill, Seascape, Hand Painted, 8 In. 75.00
Stein, White, Blue Transfer, Pewter Lid, 2 Liter 460.00
Umbrella Stand, Irises & Color, 18 In. 325.00
Urn, Cover, Courting Couples, Late 19th Century, 20 1/2 In., Pair 1445.00
Urn, Floral Still Life, 2 Mask Form Handles, Paw Feet, 1900, 15 1/2 In. 316.00
Vase, Dresden Rose, Blue Ribbon Trellis Ground, 11 In., Pair 230.00
Vase, Floral Design, Gilt, Blue & Green, 9 1/2 In. 115.00
Vase, Gold & Green Orchids, Gold Encrusted, Pedestal, 11 In. 575.00
Vase, Large Roses, Italian Blue Shading To Blue, Pedestal, 10 In. 325.00
Vase, Orchids, Gold Border Around Flowers, Gourd Shape, 11 1/2 In. 155.00
Vase, Water Lilies, Applied Design Top, Bottom, 9 In. 300.00

ROYAL COPENHAGEN porcelain and pottery have been made in Denmark since 1772. The Christmas plate series started in 1908. The figurines with pale blue and gray glazes have remained popular in this century and are still being made. Many other old and new style porcelains are made today.

Basket, Fruit, Flora Danica, Brown Violet Plant, 8 & 8 1/4 In., Pair 2587.00
Basket, Fruit, Flora Danica, Purple Plums On Branch, Reticulated Rim 1840.00
Basket, Stand, Flora Danica, Reticulated Rim, Black Currant, Twig Handles 2587.00
Bottle, Green Glaze, Patina, Oval, Marked, Denmark/3208, 8 In. 58.00
Bowl, Flora Danica, Dog Violet Plant, Blue, Green, Brown, Square, 9 In. 1725.00
Bowl, Flora Danica, Green Vetch In Center, Pale Purple, 8 9/16 In. 1092.00
Bowl, Flora Danica, Sprig Of Everlasting Pea In Center, Square, 8 In. 747.00
Bowl, Flora Danica, Trailing Sprig Of Toadflax, Ogee Form, Circular, 9 In. 805.00
Bowl, Vegetable, Cover, Flora Danica, Botanical Specimen, Handle, 10 In. 1610.00
Bowl, Vegetable, Cover, Flora Danica, Cluster Of Blossoms, 15 In., Pair 4025.00
Bowl, Vegetable, Cover, Flora Danica, Veronica Specimen, Blue, Puce 2875.00
Box, Lid, Floral, Branch Handles, Circular 375.00
Centerpiece, Stand, Floral Border, Angular Handles, Gilt Rim, 16 In. 230.00
Cup, Cover, Stand, Flora Danica, Botanical Design, Triangular, 3 1/4 In. 862.00
Cup & Saucer, Flora Danica . . . . .375.00 to 395.00
Cup & Saucer, Flower, Blue & White 35.00
Cup & Saucer, Fluted, Lace, Blue 100.00
Dish, Figural, Gray Lobster, Pearl Ground, Stamped, 2 x 7 In. 220.00
Dish, Pickle, Flora Danica, Botanical Specimen, Leaf Shape, 8 In., 4 Piece 1840.00
Figurine, 2 Women, No. 1319, 11 1/2 In. 285.00
Figurine, Anne Marie, Nude, Wearing Powdered Floral Wig, Henning, 9 In. 1725.00
Figurine, Dog, Basset Hound, Sitting, 4 1/2 x 7 In. 195.00
Figurine, Dog, Fox Terrier, No. 3170 . . . . 250.00
Figurine, Dog, Scottie, No. 3162 . . . . 250.00
Figurine, Grief, Nude, Reclining, Satyr Seated At Her Feet, Henning, 10 In. 1725.00
Figurine, Madonna, Child, 9 In. 65.00
Figurine, Nude, Bathing, Henning, 13 1/2 In. 920.00
Figurine, Nude, Kneeling, With Hand Mirror, Henning, 7 x 4 In. 920.00
Figurine, Nude, Lying Down, No. 47039, 9 In. 265.00
Figurine, Nude, Reclining, Blue Glaze, Henning, 1957, 11 In. 1035.00
Figurine, Perch, No. 1138, 6 1/2 In. 195.00
Figurine, Princess & The Pea, Bewigged Princess, Blue, 17 In. 5462.00
Figurine, Susanna, Nude, Washing Her Hair, Henning, 7 In. 805.00
Figurine, Trout, No. 2676, 8 In. 155.00
Figurine, Venus, Nude, Reclining, Henning 920.00
Figurine, Weeping Faun, Boy, Seated With Head In Hands, Brown, 6 In. 690.00
Figurine, Whimsical Fox 225.00
Figurine, Young Boy With Pot 120.00
Fish Set, Different Game Fish, Double Lipped, c.1900, Service For 8 . . . . 2860.00
Group, Chinese Couple, Girl, With Flower In Each Hand, Henning, 13 In. 2185.00
Group, Fairy Tale I, Princess & Her Attendant, Embracing, Henning 1495.00
Group, Fairy Tale II, Young Nude Girl, Kneeling With Attendant, 9 In. 1495.00

Group, Fairy Tale III, Turban Man, Kissing A Nude, Henning, 8 x 9 x 5 In. 1380.00
Group, Fisherfolk Scene, Signed, Art Lecher, 12 1/2 In. 260.00
Group, Girl, Holding An Exotic Flower, Henning, 12 In. 1380.00
Group, Kiss On The Hand, Faun, Kneeling, Kissing Nude, Henning, 15 In. 1265.00
Group, Man & Woman, Kneeling Lovers, Henning, 9 In. 1495.00
Group, Nymph & Faun, Nude Kissing Faun, Henning 1150.00
Group, Scheherezade Scene, Ali & Pexi Danu, Henning, 1956, 9 In. 2645.00
Group, The Kiss After Rodin, 18 1/2 In. 650.00
Group, The Nightingale, Pair Of Lovers, Henning, 11 3/4 In. 1150.00
Humidor, Cover, Dogs On Cover, Allover Floral Design, Ornate, 5 1/2 In. 560.00
Plate, Armorial Design, White & Gilt Ground, Lion Form Mounts, 8 1/2 In. 460.00
Plate, Christmas, 1922, 3 Singing Angels 55.00
Plate, Christmas, 1951, Christmas Angel 305.00
Plate, Christmas, 1952, Christmas In The Forest 115.00
Plate, Christmas, 1953, Fredericksburg Castle 155.00
Plate, Christmas, 1956, Rosenborg Castle 150.00
Plate, Moon Landing, 1969 . . . . 85.00
Platter, Flora Danica, Botanical Specimen, Oval, 14 & 9 13/16 In., Pair 1840.00
Platter, Flora Danica, Botanical Specimen, Pink, Gold Border, 18 In. 1610.00
Platter, Flora Danica, Botanical Specimen, Serrated Rim, 16 In., Pair 2185.00
Platter, Flora Danica, Verbascum Plant, Yellow, Green, Brown, Oval, 14 In. . . . . 1265.00 to 1495.00
Platter, Serving, Blue Fluted, Oval, 15 In., Pair 515.00
Platter, Serving, Blue Fluted, Oval, 18 3/4 In., Pair 251.00
Platter, Serving, Blue Fluted, Oval, 21 1/2 In. 230.00
Tray, Flora Danica, Specimen Of Marsh Helleborine, Rectangular, 12 In. 977.00
Tureen, Soup, Cover, Flora Danica, Botanical Specimens, 13 x 15 In. 6900.00
Tureen, Soup, Cover, Flora Danica, Cluster Of Blossoms, Leaves, 13 In. 2589.00
Vase, Blue Floral Design, White Ground, 7 In. 70.00
Vase, Sage Green & Gray, 7 In. 100.00
Vase, Stylized Cornucopia, 2 Arabian Figures, Blue, Henning, 1957, 7 In. 1955.00
Wine Cooler, Flora Danica, Botanical Specimen, 2 Twig Handles, 5 In. 3737.00
Wine Cooler, Flora Danica, Floral Clusters 4025.00
Wine Cooler, Trailing Clover Plant, 2 Twig Handles, Green, Ocher, 10 In. 1840.00

ROYAL COPLEY china was made by the Spaulding China Company of
Sebring, Ohio, from 1939 to 1960. The figural planters and the small
figurines, especially those with Art Deco designs, are of great collector interest.

Bank, Pig, 7 In. 60.00
Figurine, Cat, Brown 70.00
Figurine, Cat, Pink Bow, Green Eyes, 8 In. 45.00
Figurine, Chicken, Royal Windsor, 7 In. 49.00
Figurine, Chicken, Stuffed 48.00
Figurine, Double Birds On Stump 49.00
Figurine, Parrot, Blue, 8 In. 48.00
Figurine, Peter Rabbit 43.00
Planter, Cat, With Cello, 7 1/2 In. 125.00
Planter, Rooster, 8 In. 46.00
Planter, Teddy Bear, With Basket On Back 69.00

ROYAL CROWN DERBY Company, Ltd., was established in England in
1890. There is a complex family tree that includes the Derby, Crown
Derby, and Royal Crown Derby porcelains. The Royal Crown Derby
mark includes the name and a crown. The words *Made in England*
were used after 1921. The company is now a part of Royal Doulton
Tableware Ltd.

Ewer, Cabinet, Gilt Cobalt Blue Ground, 1885, 7 1/8 In. 181.50
Figurine, Peacock, Multicolored Foliage On Base, Porcelain 230.00
Game Set, Birds, Native Landscape, Gilt Frame, 9 1/4 In., 12 Piece 2185.00
Pin Box, Napoleon Bust On Cover, Small 195.00
Plate, Birds In Landscape, Gilt Floral, Signed, 8 3/4 In., 12 Piece 3737.00
Plate, Vine, Grapevine Design, Pink Ground, 9 In., 8 Piece 170.00
Soup, Dish, Witch's Palette, c.1940, 9 1/4 In., 6 Piece 630.00

Tea Set, Japanese Imari Pattern, 1939, 6 Piece	225.00
Vase, Bulbous, Painted, Enameled, Floral Decoration, 4 In.	345.00

ROYAL DOULTON is the name used on Doulton and Company pottery made from 1902 to the present. Doulton and Company of England was founded in 1853. Pieces made before 1902 are listed in this book under Doulton. Royal Doulton collectors search for the out-of-production figurines, character jugs, vases, and series wares. Some vases and animal figurines were made with a special red glaze called flambe. Sung and Chang glazed pieces are rare. The multicolored glaze is very thick and looks as if it were dropped on the clay.

Animal, Dog, Airdale, HN 1023, 5 In.	250.00
Animal, Dog, Alsatian, HN 1117, 4 1/2 In.	165.00
Animal, Dog, Alsatian, K 13, 3 In.	100.00
Animal, Dog, Bulldog, K 1, 2 1/2 In.	85.00
Animal, Dog, Bulldog, K 2, 2 In.	125.00
Animal, Dog, Bulldog, Union Jack, HN 4607, 4 In.	295.00
Animal, Dog, Cocker Spaniel, HN 1001, 6 1/2 In.	300.00
Animal, Dog, Cocker Spaniel, HN 1002, 6 1/2 In.	550.00
Animal, Dog, Dachshund, Dahl Jenson, HN 1131	90.00
Animal, Dog, Dachshund, HN 1141, 3 In.	275.00
Animal, Dog, English Setter With Pheasant, HN 1028, 8 In.	595.00
Animal, Dog, English Setter, HN 1050, 5 In.	150.00
Animal, Dog, English Setter, HN 1051, 4 In.	195.00
Animal, Dog, English Setter, HN 2529, 8 1/2 x 10 1/2 In.	450.00
Animal, Dog, English Setter, Maesydd Mustard, HN 1049, 7 3/4 In.	290.00
Animal, Dog, Irish Setter, HN 1054, 7 1/2 In.	700.00
Animal, Dog, Irish Setter, HN 1055, 5 In.	145.00
Animal, Dog, Pekinese, HN 1011, 6 1/2 In.	750.00
Animal, Dog, Pekinese, HN 1012, 3 In.	135.00
Animal, Dog, Pekinese, K 6, 2 In.	110.00
Animal, Dog, Running, Character, HN 2510, 3 In.	425.00
Animal, Dog, Scottish Terrier, K 18, 2 In.	150.00
Animal, Dog, St. Bernard, K 19, 1 1/2 In.	120.00
Animal, Dog, Welsh Corgi, K 16	85.00
Animal, Elephant, Medium, Flambe	150.00
Animal, Fox, Lying Down, Flambe	110.00
Animal, Fox, Seated, Flambe	125.00
Animal, Hare, Lying Down, Flambe	125.00
Animal, Horse, Gray Mare & Foal, 1938-1960, Flambe	500.00
Animal, Horse, Gray Mare, HN 2570	325.00
Animal, Penguin, Pointed Nose, Flambe	125.00
Ash Pot, Old Charley	100.00
Ash Pot, Sairey Gamp	100.00
Bowl, Hunt Scene, Polychrome, Green Border, Gilt, 8 7/8 In.	140.00
Bowl, Oasis In Desert, 8 In.	110.00
Bunnykins, Bunnybank, D 6615, 8 1/2 In.	260.00
Candlestick, Old Moreton, Polychrome Transfer, No. 7277, 6 3/8 In.	83.00

Royal Doulton character jugs depict the head and shoulders of the subject. They are made in four sizes: large, 5 1/4 to 7 inches; small, 3 1/4 to 4 inches; miniature, 2 1/4 to 2 1/2 inches; and tiny, 1 1/4 inches. Toby jugs portray a seated, full figure.

Character Jug, 'Arriet, Green Hat, Large	300.00
Character Jug, 'Arry, Brown Hat, Small	155.00
Character Jug, Abraham Lincoln, Large	250.00
Character Jug, Airman, Small	50.00
Character Jug, Angel, Miniature	60.00
Character Jug, Anne Boleyn, Large .... .80.00 to	160.00
Character Jug, Apothecary, Miniature	70.00
Character Jug, Aramis, Large	125.00
Character Jug, Aramis, Small	45.00
Character Jug, Auld Mac, Large	120.00

Character Jug, Auld Mac, Small 70.00
Character Jug, Bacchus, Miniature . . . . .50.00 to 60.00
Character Jug, Beefeater, Large 100.00
Character Jug, Beefeater, Miniature 50.00
Character Jug, Benjamin Franklin, Small 110.00
Character Jug, Blacksmith, Miniature 75.00
Character Jug, Bootmaker, Large 135.00
Character Jug, Busker, Large 175.00
Character Jug, Cabinet Maker, Large 165.00
Character Jug, Captain Ahab, Small . . . . .50.00 to 80.00
Character Jug, Captain Hook, Large 750.00
Character Jug, Captain Hook, Miniature 500.00
Character Jug, Cardinal, Miniature 80.00
Character Jug, Catherine Of Aragon, Large 160.00
Character Jug, Cavalier, Small 85.00
Character Jug, Chelsea Pensioner, Large 180.00
Character Jug, Chopin, Large 175.00
Character Jug, Collector, Large 175.00
Character Jug, Cyrano De Bergerac, Large 130.00
Character Jug, Dick Turpin, Small 80.00
Character Jug, Don Quixote, Large 135.00
Character Jug, Don Quixote, Small 80.00
Character Jug, Drake, Hat, Large 190.00
Character Jug, Drake, Small 95.00
Character Jug, Elf, Miniature 55.00
Character Jug, Falconer, Large 140.00
Character Jug, Falconer, Miniature 45.00
Character Jug, Falstaff, Large 80.00
Character Jug, Falstaff, Miniature 45.00
Character Jug, Farmer John, Large 225.00
Character Jug, Fat Boy, Small 150.00
Character Jug, Field Marshall Montgomery, Large 180.00
Character Jug, Fireman, Large 180.00
Character Jug, Fortune Teller, Large 250.00
Character Jug, Gaoler, Large 135.00
Character Jug, Gardener, Large 240.00
Character Jug, Genie, Large 300.00
Character Jug, George Washington, 1982, Large 160.00
Character Jug, Golfer, Large . . . . .80.00 to 125.00
Character Jug, Golfer, Miniature 75.00
Character Jug, Golfer, Small 80.00
Character Jug, Gondolier, Miniature 450.00
Character Jug, Gone Away, Miniature 50.00
Character Jug, Gone Away, Small 100.00
Character Jug, Guardsman, Small 40.00
Character Jug, Gunsmith, Large 135.00
Character Jug, Hamlet, Large 155.00
Character Jug, Henry VIII, Miniature 75.00
Character Jug, Izaak Walton, Large 140.00
Character Jug, Jane Seymour, Large 125.00
Character Jug, Jockey, Large 425.00
Character Jug, John Peel, Miniature 70.00
Character Jug, John Peel, Small 95.00
Character Jug, Juggler, Large 240.00
Character Jug, Lawyer, Miniature . . . . .50.00 to 70.00
Character Jug, Leprechaun, Large 170.00
Character Jug, Lobster Man, Miniature 65.00
Character Jug, Lobster Man, Small . . . . .40.00 to 75.00
Character Jug, London Bobby, Large 175.00
Character Jug, Long John Silver, Large . . . . .90.00 to 135.00
Character Jug, Long John Silver, Miniature 45.00
Character Jug, Lord Nelson, Large 500.00
Character Jug, Lumberjack, Large 170.00

Character Jug, Mark Twain, Large ....72.00 to 180.00
Character Jug, Mark Twain, Small 140.00
Character Jug, Merlin, Large 145.00
Character Jug, Merlin, Miniature 50.00
Character Jug, Mine Host, Small 85.00
Character Jug, Montgomery Of Alamein, Large 175.00
Character Jug, Monty, Large 125.00
Character Jug, Mozart, Large 175.00
Character Jug, Mr. Micawber, Tiny ....75.00 to 95.00
Character Jug, Neptune, Large 175.00
Character Jug, Neptune, Miniature 50.00
Character Jug, Neptune, Small 75.00
Character Jug, Night Watchman, Large 150.00
Character Jug, North American Indian, Miniature 55.00
Character Jug, Old King Cole, Large 325.00
Character Jug, Old King Cole, Tiny 100.00
Character Jug, Old Salt, Large 125.00
Character Jug, Old Salt, Small 35.00
Character Jug, Paddy, Miniature 65.00
Character Jug, Parson Brown, Tiny 75.00
Character Jug, Pearly Queen, Large 95.00
Character Jug, Pied Piper, Large ....105.00 to 175.00
Character Jug, Poacher, Fish Handle, Large 125.00
Character Jug, Queen Victoria, Large 250.00
Character Jug, Red Queen, Large 300.00
Character Jug, Red Queen, Small 300.00
Character Jug, Ring Master, Large 200.00
Character Jug, Rip Van Winkle, Miniature 50.00
Character Jug, Robin Hood, Large 95.00
Character Jug, Robin Hood, Miniature 60.00
Character Jug, Robin Hood, Small 75.00
Character Jug, Robinson Crusoe, Small 75.00
Character Jug, Romeo, Large 150.00
Character Jug, Sam Weller, Tiny 75.00
Character Jug, Sancho Panca, Miniature 85.00
Character Jug, Santa Claus, Doll Handle, Large 275.00
Character Jug, Santa Claus, Holly Wreath Handle, Miniature 70.00
Character Jug, Santa Claus, Reindeer Handle, Large 300.00
Character Jug, Simon The Cellarer, Small ....80.00 to 90.00
Character Jug, Simple Simon, Large 330.00
Character Jug, Sir Thomas More, Large 275.00
Character Jug, Sleuth, Large 125.00
Character Jug, Sleuth, Miniature ....45.00 to 80.00
Character Jug, Smuggler, Small 100.00
Character Jug, Soldier, Small 75.00
Character Jug, St. George, Large 260.00
Character Jug, Tam O'Shanter, Miniature ....75.00 to 120.00
Character Jug, Thomas Jefferson, Large 225.00
Character Jug, Toby Philpots, Miniature 65.00
Character Jug, Vicar Of Bray, Large 300.00
Character Jug, Viking, Small 175.00
Character Jug, Walrus, Small 90.00
Character Jug, Winston Churchill, Large 325.00
Character Jug, Witch, Large 325.00
Character Jug, Yachtsman, Large 175.00
Character Jug, Yachtsman, Yellow Life Jacket, Large 175.00
Character Jug, Yeoman Of The Guard, Large 145.00
Chop Plate, Old Moreton, Polychrome, Black Transfer, D 3858, 12 3/4 In. 110.00
Cup & Saucer, Easter Morn 25.00
Figurine, Adrienne, HN 2152 .... 160.00
Figurine, Affection, HN 2236 .... 165.00
Figurine, Alison, HN 3264 .... 200.00

Figurine, Anna, HN 2802 . . . . .150.00 to 325.00
Figurine, Ariel, HN 3831 . . . . 495.00
Figurine, As Good As New, HN 2971 . . . . 220.00
Figurine, Ascot, HN 2356 . . . . .175.00 to 265.00
Figurine, At Ease, HN 2473 . . . . 95.00
Figurine, Automne, HN 3068 . . . . 1100.00
Figurine, Autumn Breezes, HN 1911 . . . . .80.00 to 175.00
Figurine, Autumn Breezes, HN 1913 . . . . 155.00
Figurine, Autumn Breezes, HN 1934 . . . . 280.00
Figurine, Autumn, HN 2087 . . . . 450.00
Figurine, Autumntime, HN 3231 . . . . 225.00
Figurine, Babie, HN 1679 . . . . 100.00
Figurine, Babie, HN 1842 . . . . 450.00
Figurine, Ballerina, HN 2116 . . . . 235.00
Figurine, Balloon Man, HN 1954 . . . . 250.00
Figurine, Balloons, HN 3187 . . . . 350.00
Figurine, Barbara, HN 2962 . . . . 275.00
Figurine, Bedtime, HN 1978 . . . . 40.00
Figurine, Belle O' The Ball, HN 1997 . . . . 275.00
Figurine, Belle, HN 3830 . . . . 495.00
Figurine, Biddy Penny Farthing, HN 1843 . . . . 137.00
Figurine, Blithe Morning, HN 2021 . . . . .77.00 to 225.00
Figurine, Blithe Morning, HN 2065 . . . . 250.00
Figurine, Bo-Peep, HN 1811 . . . . 125.00
Figurine, Boatman, HN 2417 . . . . 175.00
Figurine, Breton Dancer, HN 2383 . . . . 1000.00
Figurine, Bride, HN 2166 . . . . 140.00
Figurine, Bridesmaid, HN 2196 . . . . 125.00
Figurine, Broken Lance, HN 2041 . . . . 450.00
Figurine, Bunny's Bedtime, HN 3370 . . . . 165.00
Figurine, Bunnykins, Bathtime, SF 18 . . . . 32.00
Figurine, Bunnykins, Cooling Off 150.00
Figurine, Bunnykins, Drummer, DB 26 . . . . 650.00
Figurine, Bunnykins, Helping Mother, DB 2 . . . . .50.00 to 85.00
Figurine, Bunnykins, Jogging 110.00
Figurine, Bunnykins, Olympic Bunny, DB 28 . . . . 115.00
Figurine, Buttercup, HN 2309 . . . . 120.00
Figurine, Camellia, HN 2222 . . . . 260.00
Figurine, Carolyn, HN 2112 . . . . .210.00 to 350.00
Figurine, Carolyn, HN 2974 . . . . 265.00
Figurine, Carrie, HN 2800 . . . . 325.00
Figurine, Cherie, HN 2341 . . . . 185.00
Figurine, Chloe, HN 1479 . . . . 517.00
Figurine, Choice, HN 1959 . . . . 225.00
Figurine, Christine, HN 2792 . . . . 115.00
Figurine, Christmas Morn, HN 1992 . . . . 145.00
Figurine, Christmas Time, HN 2110 . . . . .287.00 to 425.00
Figurine, Cinderella, HN 3677 . . . . 595.00
Figurine, Cissie, HN 1809 . . . . 185.00
Figurine, Clare, HN 2793 . . . . 320.00
Figurine, Claribel, HN 1951 . . . . 625.00
Figurine, Clarinda, HN 2724 . . . . 190.00
Figurine, Cobbler, HN 1706 . . . . 225.00
Figurine, Congratulations, HN 3351 . . . . 220.00
Figurine, Cookie, HN 2218 . . . . 140.00
Figurine, Coppelia, HN 2115 . . . . 600.00
Figurine, Crinoline Lady, HN 655 . . . . 1300.00
Figurine, Daffy Down Dilly, HN 1712 . . . . 295.00
Figurine, Dainty May, HN 1639 . . . . 373.00
Figurine, Danielle, HN 3001 . . . . .200.00 to 220.00
Figurine, Darling, HN 1319 . . . . 120.00
Figurine, Darling, HN 1985 . . . . 35.00

Figurine, Debbie, HN 2385 .... 175.00
Figurine, Debbie, HN 2400 .... 165.00
Figurine, Diana, HN 1716 .... 350.00
Figurine, Diana, HN 1986 .... 175.00
Figurine, Dinky Doo, HN 1678 .... 145.00
Figurine, Discovery, HN 3428 .... 160.00
Figurine, Elaine, HN 2791 .... 406.25
Figurine, Elegance, HN 2264 ....77.00 to 130.00
Figurine, Eliza Farren, Countess Of Derby, HN 3442 .... 195.00
Figurine, Elyse, HN 2429 .... 275.00
Figurine, Emma, HN 2834 .... 225.00
Figurine, Enchantment, HN 2178 .... 110.00
Figurine, Ermine Coat, HN 1981 ....215.00 to 225.00
Figurine, Fair Lady, HN 2832 .... 265.00
Figurine, Fair Maiden, HN 2211 .... 185.00
Figurine, Faith, HN 3082 .... 275.00
Figurine, Fiona, HN 2694 .... 250.00
Figurine, Fleur, HN 2368 .... 100.00
Figurine, Flower Seller's Children, HN 1342 .... 355.00
Figurine, Francine, HN 2422 .... 44.00
Figurine, Friar Tuck, HN 2143 .... 450.00
Figurine, Genevieve, HN 1962 .... 250.00
Figurine, Geraldine, HN 2348 .... 220.00
Figurine, Giselle, Forest Glade, HN 2140 .... 176.00
Figurine, Giselle, HN 2139 .... 165.00
Figurine, Gollum, HN 2913 .... 140.00
Figurine, Goody Two Shoes, HN 1905 .... 255.00
Figurine, Grand Manner, HN 2723 .... 275.00
Figurine, Granny's Shawl, HN 1647 .... 750.00
Figurine, Greta, HN 1485 .... 550.00
Figurine, Happy Anniversary, HN 3097 .... 265.00
Figurine, Harmony, HN 2824 .... 275.00
Figurine, Heather, HN 2956 .... 188.00
Figurine, Huckleberry Finn, HN 2927 .... 135.00
Figurine, Indian Maiden, HN 3117 .... 365.00
Figurine, Innocence, HN 2842 .... 220.00
Figurine, Invitation, HN 2170 .... 120.00
Figurine, It Won't Hurt, HN 2963 .... 175.00
Figurine, Ivy, HN 1768 ....70.00 to 155.00
Figurine, Jack, HN 2060 .... 245.00
Figurine, Jane, HN 2806 .... 250.00
Figurine, Janet, HN 1537 .... 90.00
Figurine, Janine, HN 2461 ....275.00 to 290.00
Figurine, Jasmine, HN 1862 .... 770.00
Figurine, Jean, HN 2032 .... 200.00
Figurine, Jennifer, HN 2392 .... 300.00
Figurine, Jill, HN 2061 .... 245.00
Figurine, Judith, HN 2089 .... 295.00
Figurine, Julia, HN 2705 ....120.00 to 240.00
Figurine, Just One More, HN 2980 .... 190.00
Figurine, Karen, HN 2388 .... 490.00
Figurine, La Sylphide, HN 2138 .... 176.00
Figurine, Lady Anne Nevill, HN 2006 .... 550.00
Figurine, Lady Betty, HN 1967 .... 317.00
Figurine, Lady Charmian, HN 1948 .... 275.00
Figurine, Lady Charmian, HN 1949 ....110.00 to 210.00
Figurine, Laurianne, HN 2719 .... 265.00
Figurine, Leading Lady, HN 2269 .... 120.00
Figurine, Lily, HN 1798 ....150.00 to 220.00
Figurine, Linda, HN 2106 .... 255.00
Figurine, Little Boy Blue, HN 2062 .... 65.00
Figurine, Little Bridesmaid, HN 1433 .... 330.00

Figurine, Little Bridesmaid, HN 1434 .... 450.00
Figurine, Lizzie, HN 2749 .... 225.00
Figurine, Lorna, HN 2311 .... 77.00
Figurine, Lorraine, HN 3118 .... 330.00
Figurine, Love Letter, HN 2149 .... 495.00
Figurine, Lucy, HN 2863 .... 275.00
Figurine, Lydia, HN 1908 ....140.00 to 175.00
Figurine, Lynne, HN 2329 .... 225.00
Figurine, Make Believe, HN 2225 .... 175.00
Figurine, Mandy, HN 2476 .... 125.00
Figurine, Mantilla, HN 2712 .... 525.00
Figurine, Marie, HN 1370 .... 110.00
Figurine, Mary Had A Little Lamb, HN 2048 .... 180.00
Figurine, Mary, HN 2374 .... 420.00
Figurine, Mary, Mary, HN 2044 .... 115.00
Figurine, Matilda, HN 2011 .... 465.00
Figurine, Maureen, HN 1770 .... 272.00
Figurine, May, HN 2711 .... 188.00
Figurine, Maytime, HN 2113 .... 132.00
Figurine, Meg, HN 2743 .... 225.00
Figurine, Midinette, HN 2090 .... 250.00
Figurine, Miranda, HN 3037 .... 300.00
Figurine, Miss Muffet, HN 1936 ....150.00 to 170.00
Figurine, Monica, HN 1467 .... 125.00
Figurine, My Love, HN 2339 .... 95.00
Figurine, My Pet, HN 2238 .... 265.00
Figurine, Nancy, HN 2955 .... 175.00
Figurine, Nicola, HN 2839 .... 375.00
Figurine, Nicole, HN 3421 .... 168.00
Figurine, Nina, HN 2347 .... 220.00
Figurine, Norma, M 36 .... 812.00
Figurine, October, HN 2693 .... 220.00
Figurine, Old Balloon Seller, HN 1315 .... 250.00
Figurine, Olga, HN 2463 .... 325.00
Figurine, Orange Lady, HN 1759 .... 225.00
Figurine, Orange Lady, HN 1953 .... 185.00
Figurine, Owd Willum, HN 2042 .... 200.00
Figurine, Pantalettes, M 15 ....345.00 to 400.00
Figurine, Pantelettes, M 16 .... 275.00
Figurine, Parisian, HN 2445 .... 120.00
Figurine, Paula, HN 2906 .... 280.00
Figurine, Pauline, HN 1444 .... 488.00
Figurine, Peace, HN 2470 .... 66.00
Figurine, Pearly Boy, HN 2767 .... 150.00
Figurine, Pearly Girl, HN 2036 .... 255.00
Figurine, Peggy, HN 2038 .... 175.00
Figurine, Penelope, HN 1901 .... 295.00
Figurine, Penny, HN 2338 .... 110.00
Figurine, Pensive Moments, HN 2704 .... 275.00
Figurine, Potter, HN 1493 ....220.00 to 395.00
Figurine, Potter, HN 1522 .... 850.00
Figurine, Printemps, HN 3066 .... 1000.00
Figurine, Priscilla, HN 1340 .... 460.00
Figurine, Prized Possessions, HN 2942 ....373.00 to 400.00
Figurine, Professor, HN 2281 .... 175.00
Figurine, Rag Doll, HN 2142 ....80.00 to 165.00
Figurine, Rebecca, HN 2805 .... 575.00
Figurine, Regal Lady, HN 2709 .... 275.00
Figurine, Rest Awhile, HN 2728 .... 275.00
Figurine, Rhapsody, HN 2267 .... 260.00
Figurine, River Boy, HN 2128 .... 325.00
Figurine, Rosamund, M 32 .... 630.00

Figurine, Rosamund, M 33 . . . . 575.00
Figurine, Rose, HN 1368 . . . . 65.00
Figurine, Rose, HN 2123 . . . . 115.00
Figurine, Roseanna, HN 1926 . . . . .258.00 to 300.00
Figurine, Rosemary, HN 2091 . . . . 550.00
Figurine, Rosemary, HN 3143 . . . . 275.00
Figurine, Rowena, HN 2077 . . . . 475.00
Figurine, Royal Governor's Cook, HN 2233 . . . . 400.00
Figurine, Ruth, HN 2799 . . . . 425.00
Figurine, Salome, HN 3267 . . . . 850.00
Figurine, Samantha, HN 2954 . . . . 225.00
Figurine, Secret Thoughts, HN 2382 . . . . 325.00
Figurine, She Loves Me Not, HN 2045 . . . . 330.00
Figurine, Sheikh, HN 3083 . . . . 255.00
Figurine, Silks & Ribbons, HN 2017 . . . . 75.00
Figurine, Simone, HN 2378 . . . . 200.00
Figurine, Sleepy Darling, HN 2953 . . . . 275.00
Figurine, Snow White, HN 3678 . . . . 595.00
Figurine, Solitude, HN 2810 . . . . 375.00
Figurine, Sophie, HN 3257 . . . . 350.00
Figurine, Southern Belle, HN 2229 . . . . 370.00
Figurine, Spring Flowers, HN 1807 . . . . .230.00 to 385.00
Figurine, Springtime, HN 3033 . . . . 365.00
Figurine, Stop Press, HN 2683 . . . . 150.00
Figurine, Suitor, HN 2132 . . . . 385.00
Figurine, Summer Rose, HN 3309 . . . . 244.00
Figurine, Summer's Day, HN 2181 . . . . 175.00
Figurine, Sunday Best, HN 2698 . . . . 225.00
Figurine, Suzette, HN 2026 . . . . 350.00
Figurine, Sweet & Twenty, HN 1589 . . . . 201.00
Figurine, Sweet Dreams, HN 2380 . . . . 250.00
Figurine, Sweet Seventeen, HN 2734 . . . . 325.00
Figurine, Sweeting, HN 1935 . . . . 225.00
Figurine, Tess, HN 2865 . . . . 375.00
Figurine, This Little Pig, HN 1793 . . . . 100.00
Figurine, This Little Pig, HN 1994 . . . . 300.00
Figurine, Tinker Bell, HN 1677 . . . . .55.00 to 135.00
Figurine, Tom, HN 2864 . . . . 475.00
Figurine, Tootles, HN 1680 . . . . .100.00 to 135.00
Figurine, Top O' The Hill, HN 1833 . . . . 210.00
Figurine, Toymaker, HN 2250 . . . . 375.00
Figurine, Veneta, HN 2722 . . . . 225.00
Figurine, Victorian Lady, HN 728 . . . . 545.00
Figurine, Vivienne, HN 2073 . . . . 240.00
Figurine, West Indian Dancer, HN 2384 . . . . 1100.00
Figurine, Willy-Won't He, HN 2150 . . . . 550.00
Figurine, Windflower, HN 2029 . . . . 258.00
Figurine, Winter, HN 2088 . . . . 490.00
Figurine, Wistful, HN 2396 . . . . 375.00
Flask, Ben Jonson, Dewar's, Silver Plate Rim, 7 In. . . . . .125.00 to 195.00
Humidor, Flambe, Elephant Finial 2400.00
Humidor, Rhinoceros, Large 1300.00
Inkwell, Hinged Top, Hunting Dog, With Pheasant, Marble Base, 7 x 11 In. 495.00
Jug, Child's, Little Bo Peep 85.00
Jug, Old Curiosity Shop, 6 In. 27.00
Jug, Shakespeare, Black Transfer, Polychrome, D 2779 . . . . 72.00
Ladle, Soup, Egerton, c.1905 . . . . 495.00
Loving Cup, Geoffrey Chaucer, 2 Handles, Large 800.00
Loving Cup, Henry VIII, 2 Handles 1300.00
Loving Cup, Robin Hood, 2 Handles, Large 550.00
Loving Cup, Sir Henry Doulton, 2 Handles, Large 285.00
Loving Cup, William Shakespeare, 2 Handles 500.00
Match Holder, Floral, White 95.00

Matchbook Holder, Home Waters, Sailboats, 3 1/8 In. 55.00
Pitcher, Fisherman Form, Trout Handle, Multicolored, 1954, 7 In. 300.00
Pitcher, Pickwick Papers, 6 In. 175.00
Pitcher, Pickwick Papers, White Hart Inn, Southwark 225.00
Pitcher, Tavern & Hunting Scene, Spout, 3 1/2 In. 95.00
Plate, Bobbie Burns, Blue, White 75.00
Plate, Castle Scene, Blue, 9 In. 50.00
Plate, Charles Dickens, Blue, White 90.00
Plate, Deaf, D 2606, Stamped, 10 1/2 In. 255.00
Plate, Equestrian, Side Saddle, Flow Blue, c.1913, 9 1/2 In. 225.00
Plate, Evening Glow, Peace With Nature Series, Elizabeth Gray, 9 In. 30.00
Plate, Falconer, 10 In. 65.00
Plate, Flower Sellers Children, 10 In. 75.00
Plate, Gulliver's Travels, 10 In. 95.00
Plate, Hunting Scene, Cobalt, 11 In. 52.00
Plate, Juliet, 7 5/8 In. 175.00
Plate, Motoring, D 2406, Stamped, 10 1/2 In. 330.00
Plate, Musketeer, 7 1/2 In. 70.00
Plate, Parson, 10 In. 50.00
Plate, Poor Jo, 6 1/2 In. 100.00
Platter, Woman On Horse, c.1920, 14 In. 125.00
Tankard, Town & Landscape Scene, Brown, Green & Orange, 9 3/4 In. 58.00
Teapot, Trivet, Titanian Ware, Pink & Yellow Parrots, D 4031, 9 In. 115.00
Toby Jug, Falstaff, Large 175.00
Toby Jug, Happy John, Large 175.00
Toby Jug, Happy John, Small 110.00
Toby Jug, Honest Measure, Small 110.00
Toby Jug, Huntsman, Large 165.00
Toby Jug, Jester, Medium 250.00
Toby Jug, Jolly Toby, Large 125.00
Toby Jug, Jolly Toby, Variation 1 . . . . 90.00
Toby Jug, Sherlock Holmes, Large 225.00
Toby Jug, Sir Francis Drake, Large 175.00
Toby Jug, Tiny Explorers, With Stand, Set Of 6 . . . . 295.00
Toby Jug, Tonsil Town Crier, Medium 265.00
Toby Jug, Winston Churchill, Large 100.00
Toby Jug, Winston Churchill, Seated, Small 70.00
Tote & Water Basin, Blue Transfer, 1891 . . . . 1200.00
Umbrella Stand, Stoneware, Leaves In Green & Cream, c.1884, 24 1/2 In. 143.00
Vase, Alternating Colored Panels, Signed, 7 3/4 In. 467.00
Vase, Babes In The Woods, Picnic 895.00
Vase, Blue Persian Chintz, 6-Sided, 1900s, 7 3/4 x 25 In. 495.00
Vase, Flambe, Butterfish, Printed Mark, Signed, Sung, Noke, 7 1/4 In. . . . . *Illus* 800.00
Vase, White Daffodils, Blue Centers, Light Olive Ground, 1898, 6 3/4 In. 172.00
Vase, White Ground, England, 1910, 8 5/8 In. 920.00
Washbowl & Pitcher Set, Aubery, Blue, White, Gilt, Ironstone, 13 1/2 In. 550.00

Royal Doulton collectors can easily identify character jugs and figurines made before 1984. That year the words "hand made" and "hand decorated" were added above the lion and crown mark, in the shape of an arch.

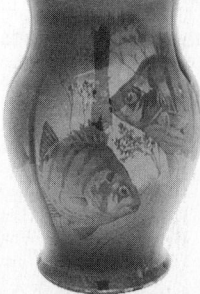

Royal Doulton,
Vase, Flambe, Butterfish,
Printed Mark, Signed,
Sung, Noke, 7 1/4 In.

ROYAL DUX is the more common name for the Duxer Porzellanmanu-faktur, which was founded by E. Eichler in Dux, Bohemia, in 1860. By the turn of the century, the firm specialized in porcelain statuary and busts of Art Nouveau–style maidens, large porcelain figures, and ornate vases with three-dimensional figures climbing on the sides. The firm is still in business.

Figurine, Boy, Playing Accordion	65.00
Figurine, Cockatoo	95.00
Figurine, Deer, 12 In.	170.00
Figurine, Elephant, White, 10 In.	88.00
Figurine, English Setter, Fowl In Mouth, Triangular Base, 12 In.	195.00
Figurine, Girl At Water Fountain Holding Jug, Boy, With Platter Of Fish, 20 In., Pair	350.00
Figurine, Harvester, Carrying Bundle Of Wheat, Green, Brown & Pink, 21 1/2 In.	345.00
Figurine, Polar Bear, Seated, Head Erect, 7 1/2 In.	126.00
Figurine, Tiger, 15 In.	165.00
Figurine, Victorian Lady, 12 In.	195.00
Figurine, Water Gatherer At A Well, Wearing Costume, Pink Patch Mark, Pair	460.00
Figurine, Woman, Blue Gown, Gold Shoes & Trim, 10 In.	240.00
Figurine, Youth & Water Sprite, Pastel Enameling, Hampel, 12 In.	715.00
Flower Frog, Nude	850.00
Group, 2 Dogs, One Standing, One Sitting, Soft Beige, Marked, 8 x 10 In.	375.00
Group, Diana The Huntress, Beige Tunic, Green Scarf, Signed, 26 1/2 In.	920.00
Vase, Bluebirds, White, Triangle With Acorn Mark, 12 In.	145.00
Vase, Draped Woman, 16 In.	110.00
Vase, Pair Of Mermaids, Lobster, Crab Within Ocean Spray, Porcelain, 11 In.	85.00
Vase, Winged Maiden, Pink, Triangle Mark, 16 In.	500.00

ROYAL FLEMISH glass was made during the late 1880s in New Bedford, Massachusetts, by the Mt. Washington Glass Works. It is a colored satin glass decorated with dark colors and raised gold designs. The glass was patented in 1894. It was supposed to resemble stained glass windows.

Biscuit Jar, 4 Roman Coins, Silver-Plated Cover, 9 In.	1150.00
Biscuit Jar, Concentric Circle Decoration, Deep Burgundy, Cover, 9 3/4 In.	1955.00
Biscuit Jar, Roman Coin Design, Emperor Nero, Gold Sections, 8 In.	1035.00
Bowl, Chrysanthemum, Colored Leaves, Pairpoint Cherub Holder, 11 1/2 In.	2300.00
Bowl, Ducks In Flight, Cover, 3 1/2 x 5 1/2 In.	1438.00
Ewer, Fairy With Wings, Front Figures, Reverse Floral Medallion, 17 In.	4620.00
Ewer, Heraldic, Gold Floral, Rope Handle, 9 In.	1380.00
Lamp, Interior Landscape Scene, 2-Socket Base, Silver Plated, 4 1/2 x 5 1/2 In.	2645.00
Mug, Band Of Leaves & Berries, Gold Rope Handle, 7 In.	3508.00
Vase, 5 Snow Geese In Flight, Blue & Green, Gold Stars, 14 In.	325.00
Vase, Pansy, Frosted Ground, Scrolled Top, 2 Gold-Leaf Handles, 6 x 6 In.	1150.00
Vase, Purple & Blue Violets, Leaf Handle, 6 1/4 In.	1150.00
Vase, Snow Geese, In Flight, Blue & Green Ground, Gold Stars, 14 1/2 In.	8050.00
Vase, Winged Serpent & Dragon, Bulbous, 10 x 8 In.	4025.00

ROYAL HAEGER, see Haeger category.

ROYAL IVY pieces are listed in the Pressed Glass category by that pattern name.

ROYAL NYMPHENBURG is the modern name for the Nymphenburg porcelain factory, which was established at Neudeck-ob-der-Au, Germany, in 1753 and moved to Nymphenburg in 1761. The company is still in existence. Marks include a checkered shield topped by a crown, a crowned *CT* with the year, and a contemporary shield mark on reproductions of eighteenth-century porcelain.

Figurine, Lion, 6 In.	90.00
Figurine, Male & Female, Frolicking Dancing Postures, 9 In., Pair	489.00
Figurine, Monkey, Marked, 5 1/2 In.	29.00
Figurine, Peacock, White, 7 In.	230.00
Figurine, Rabbit, White, 6 In.	145.00

ROYAL RUDOLSTADT, see Rudolstadt category.

ROYAL VIENNA, see Beehive category.

ROYAL WORCESTER is a name used by collectors. Worcester porcelains were made in Worcester, England, from about 1751. The firm went through many different periods and name changes. It became the Worcester Royal Porcelain Company, Ltd., in 1862. Today collectors call the porcelains made after 1862 *Royal Worcester*. In 1976, the firm merged with W. T. Copeland to become Royal Worcester Spode. Some early products of the factory are listed under Worcester.

Basket, Florals, Purples & Green, Basket Weave Handle, 4 1/2 x 5 In.	258.00
Biscuit Jar, Bamboo Molded Body & Handle, c.1887, 6 1/4 In.	460.00
Biscuit Jar, Fluted Sides, Flowers, 19th Century, 7 In.	550.00
Bowl, Leaf Design, Basket Weave, Pierced Rim, 4 x 8 1/2 In.	350.00
Cigarette Holder, Figure Of A Hand Holding Neoclassical Urn, Blue Enamel	52.00
Coffeepot, Purple & Pink Flowers, Beige Ground, Gold Trim, Marked, 9 In.	115.00
Compote, Butterfly & Floral, Gilt Edges, 1879, 9 3/4 In., Pair	100.00
Creamer, Polychrome Floral, Enameling & Gilt, Signed, 3 1/2 In.	110.00
Cup & Saucer, Imari, 1910	47.00
Dish, Leaf, Floral, 1880, 10 In.	135.00
Ewer, Bottle Shape, Metallic, Floral, Lizard Handle, 1886, 8 3/4 In.	230.00
Figurine, Bird, Blue Tit, No. 3199, 1937, 2 1/4 In.	55.00
Figurine, Bird, Robin, No. 3197, 1937, 2 3/4 In.	55.00
Figurine, Burmah, No. 3068, 1934, 5 In.	150.00 to 165.00
Figurine, Fisher Boy, Standing, With Basket In 1 Hand, Hadley, 1893, 17 In.	1380.00
Figurine, Grandmother's Dress, No. 3081, Doughty, 1935, 6 1/2 In.	100.00 to 175.00
Figurine, Turkish Man & Woman, 1899, 9 In., Pair	490.00
Figurine, Water Baby, No. 3151, 1936, 6 1/8 In.	38.00
Figurine, Woodland Dance, No. 3076, 1934, 4 In.	160.00
Flask, Pilgrim, Circular Panels, Figures, 1878, 10 In.	1380.00
Jar, Cover, Brown & Gray Rabbits, 2 Gold Handles, 15 In. ....*Illus*	5750.00
Jar, Reticulated Cover, Rabbits, Forest, Handles, Signed, 15 3/4 x 7 In.	5750.00
Jardiniere, Leaves Atop Basket Weave, c.1899, 6 1/2 In.	200.00
Jug, Flowers & Leaves, No. 1160, 1886, Signed, 6 In.	175.00
Jug, Gilt Dragon Handle, Ivory Ground, c.1889, 11 1/2 In.	345.00
Jug, Scrolled Handle, Leaf Molded Rim, Colored Floral, c.1889, 9 3/8 In.	258.00
Mug, Sailboat Scene	200.00
Pin Dish, Blue Flowers, Beige Ground, Scalloped, Purple Mark, 10 In.	60.00
Pitcher, Flat Back	85.00
Pitcher, Gilt & Floral Design, Ivory Ground, Late 19th Century, 10 In.	105.00
Pitcher, Milk, Polychrome Floral, Ivory, Signed, 5 In.	165.00
Pitcher, Multicolored Floral, Beige Ground, Leaf Handle, 8 x 6 In.	345.00
Pitcher, Pink Wild Rose, Purple Cyclamen, Lizard Handle, Signed, 9 In.	285.00
Pitcher, Yellow, Gold Handle, 10 1/2 In.	165.00

Never put a collector plate in a dishwasher or microwave oven. The glaze may be damaged. Never stack cups or bowls inside each other. Put foam or paper plates between the china plates stacked for storage.

Royal Worcester, Jar,
Cover, Brown & Gray Rabbits,
2 Gold Handles, 15 In.

Planter, Ram's Head, Aqua, Cobalt Blue 495.00
Plate, Canopic Jar, 9 1/4 In., 11 Piece 290.00
Plate, Elephant, Trunk Feet, Floral, 5 x 11 In. 770.00
Plate, Embassy, Chased Gold Edge, 12 Piece 355.00
Plate, Free-Form, Leaf & Cherry Design, Gold Trim, Cream Ground, 8 1/2 In. 145.00
Plate, Lillie, 12 Piece 460.00
Plate, Rose Mandarin Design, Enamel, 1865, 10 In. 230.00
Plate, Village Of Tewesbury, Natural Colors, Gold Trim, 1953, 10 3/4 In. 225.00
Platter, Well & Tree, White, Gilt Rim, c.1909, 22 In. 165.00
Tea Set, Hampton Court, Floral, 7 Piece 275.00
Teapot, Cover, Aesthetic, Young Man, Limp Wrist Forming Spout, 1882, 6 In. 6612.00
Teapot, Ivory Pumpkin, Trailing Vine, c.1890 .... 275.00
Teapot, Pumpkin Shape, Gold Leaf-Shaped Cover, Vine Handle, 1891, 6 In. 695.00
Urn, 2 Ravens In A Moonlit Landscape, 1880, 12 1/2 In. 172.00
Urn, Cover, Fruit Design, Raised Gilt Border, Cobalt Ground, 9 In., Pair 4830.00
Urn, Floral, Swag, Scroll & Mask Handles, Flared Neck, 1898 Mark, 15 In. 545.00
Vase, Cover, Raised Foliate Borders, Pierced Neck, 9 1/4 In. 402.00
Vase, Floral, Pierced Neck, 7 1/2 In. 110.00
Vase, Floral, Ribbed, Pedestal, 7 1/4 x 4 In. 245.00
Vase, Foliage At Base, Pierced Neck, Handles, c.1887, 10 1/4 In. 863.00
Vase, Nautilus Form, Lizards, 8 1/2 In., Pair 2640.00
Vase, Oriental, Blue, White Circular Geometric Design, Handles, 8 In., Pair 1955.00
Vase, Oriental, Leaf Design, Floral, Blue Enamel, Gilt, 2 Handles, 1879, 10 In. 175.00
Vase, Raised Leaves, Patent Metallic, Handles, c.1881, 12 1/2 In. 345.00
Vase, Spill, Stork & Vegetation Scene, Hexagonal, 1876, 6 In. 630.00
Vase, Spray Of Asters, Forget-Me-Nots, Gold Trim, Gold Footed, 1895, 10 x 5 In. 275.00

ROYCROFT products were made by the Roycrofter community of East
Aurora, New York, in the late nineteenth and early twentieth centuries.
The community was founded by Elbert Hubbard, famous philosopher,
writer, and artist. The workshops owned by the community made furniture, metalware, leatherwork, embroidery, and jewelry. A printshop
produced many signs, books, and the magazines that promoted the sayings of Elbert Hubbard. Furniture by the Roycroft community is listed
in the Furniture category.

Andirons, Pierced Scrolled Standards, Twist Finials, Wrought Iron, 1910, 35 In. 4025.00
Bookends, 2-Tone Brass, Copper, 4 1/2 In. 145.00
Bookends, Bands Forming Fleur-De-Lis, Copper, Hammered, Signed, 5 1/4 In., Pair 275.00
Bookends, Beaded Oval Center, Signed, 5 In. 220.00
Bookends, Copper, Hammered, Original Patina, 3 Legs, 5 In. 308.00
Bookends, Daisy Medallion, Tooled Leather, Embossed Mark, 5 1/4 In. 2090.00
Bookends, Poppy, Copper, Hammered, 5 1/4 x 5 1/2 In., Pair 1500.00
Bookends, Stylized Floral, Signed, 6 x 8 1/2 In., Pair 125.00
Bookends, Stylized Quatrefoil, Copper, Hammered, Signed, 8 1/4 x 5 3/4 In. 350.00
Bookrack, Little Journeys, 7 x 24 In. 275.00
Bowl, Copper, Hammered, Original Patina, 3-Footed, 7 x 4 In. 1100.00
Bowl, Copper, Hammered, Original Patina, 3-Footed, 10 x 4 In. 605.00
Box, Copper, Hammered, Stylized Floral Design On Front, Original Patina, 7 x 2 In. 1650.00
Calendar, Perpetual, Original Box 600.00
Candelabrum, Twisted Stems, 3 Branches, Brass Wash, Marked, 20 In. 1320.00
Candle Sconces, Spade Shape Back, Marked, 8 1/2 In. 500.00
Candleholder, Copper, Hammered, Brass Wash, Curly Feet, 20 1/2 In., Pair 1540.00
Candlestick, 4 Riveted Straps, Copper, Hammered, 13 In., Pair 1800.00
Candlestick, Copper, Bobeche, Attached 2 Supports, Square Base, 1915, 6 In., Pair 345.00
Candlestick, Copper, Karl Kipp Design, 1920s, 8 In., Pair 800.00
Candlestick, Princess, Wood Grain Pattern, 8 In., Pair 600.00
Candlestick, Secessionist Style, 4 Nickel-Silver Rods, Marked, Square Base, 8 In. 1980.00
Candlestick, Twisted Stem, Copper, Hammered, Signed, 12 1/2 In., Pair 1900.00
Cane, Walking Stick, Signed, July 7, 1903 .... 750.00
Footstool, Tacked On Leather Top, Tapered Feet, 9 x 15 x 9 3/4 In. 600.00
Holder, Poker Chip, Copper, Hammered, Brass Wash, 6 1/2 x 4 1/2 In. 522.50
Incense Burner 2860.00

Jug, Brown Matte Glaze, Pottery, Handle, 5 1/2 In., Pair 88.00
Lamp, Copper, Hammered, Domed Shade, Original Patina, 14 1/2 In. 2750.00
Lamp, Copper, Hammered, Karl Kipp, 16 In. 4500.00
Lamp, Copper, Hammered, Steuben Art Glass Shade, 15 1/2 In. 5000.00
Lamp, Copper, Hammered, Steuben Glass Shade, 14 In. 9900.00
Lamp, Helmet, Copper & Glass, Signed 3630.00
Lamp, Silver Wash, Acid Etched Finish, Signed, 23 In. 1100.00
Lamp, Table, Copper, Hammered, Opaque Light Green, Purple Glass Shade, Kipp 9900.00
Lamp, Table, Steuben Bell Shape Shade 9900.00
Lamp, Zigzag Design, Copper, Hammered, White, Butterscotch Dome Shade, 15 In. 4400.00
Letter Opener, Copper, Hammered, Enameled Geometric Design, 9 In. 275.00
Spoon, Nut, Signed, 6 1/2 In. 410.00
Tile, Is The World All Wrong, Reform Yourself, By Elbert Hubbard, 6 In. 130.00
Tray, Card, Copper, Hammered, Stylized Flowers, Blue Patina, 6 1/4 In. 110.00
Tray, Copper, Hammered, Impressed Geometric Design, Walter Jennings, 5 1/2 In. 605.00
Tray, Copper, Hammered, Original Brass Patina, 11 1/2 In. 240.00
Vase, Copper, Hammered, American Beauty, Brown Patina, Elongated Neck, 21 In. 2990.00
Vase, Copper, Hammered, American Beauty, Original Patina, 12 In. 1210.00
Vase, Copper, Hammered, Cylindrical, Incised Bell Flowers, Signed, 9 In. 1600.00
Vase, Copper, Hammered, Original Brass Patina, 4 1/2 In. 240.00
Vase, Copper, Hammered, Original Patina, Impressed Mark, 18 1/2 In. 5500.00
Vase, Copper, Hammered, Oval, Closed-In Rim, Signed, 4 3/4 In. 400.00
Vase, Copper, Hammered, Stylized Quatrefoils, Original Dark Patina, 7 x 2 In. 4070.00
Vase, Copper, Hammered, Stylized Quatrefoils, Verdigris Band, 4 3/4 x 2 1/4 In. 440.00
Vase, Copper, Hammered, Tooled Design, Trailing Floral Stems, 10 In. 1320.00
Vase, Hammered Body, Flared Rim, Signed, 8 1/2 In. 5956.00
Vase, Stylized Band, Nickel-Silver Overlay, Marked, 6 1/2 In. 1980.00

ROZANE, see Roseville category.

RRP is the mark used by the firm of Robinson-Ransbottom. It is not a
mark of the more famous Roseville Pottery. The Ransbottom brothers
started a pottery in 1900 in Ironspot, Ohio. In 1920, they merged with
the Robinson Clay Product Company of Akron, Ohio, to become
Robinson-Ransbottom. The factory is still working.

Cookie Jar, Oscar 60.00
Cookie Jar, Snowman 375.00
Cookie Jar, Whale 525.00

RS GERMANY is part of the wording in marks used by the Tillowitz,
Germany, factory of Reinhold Schlegelmilch from 1914 until about
1945. The porcelain was sold decorated and undecorated. The
Schlegelmilch families made porcelains marked in many ways. See
also ES Germany, RS Prussia, RS Suhl, and RS Tillowitz.

Berry Set, Acorn, Oakleaf Design, Gold Rim, 7 Piece 200.00
Biscuit Jar, White Flowers, Small 225.00
Bowl, Portrait, Handle, 10 In. 350.00
Bowl, Reflecting Water Lilies, 11 In. 445.00
Bowl, Serving, Pierced Handle 75.00
Bowl, White Dogwood Blossoms, Gold Rim, 10 In. 165.00
Candy Dish, Berry Leaves 150.00
Celery Vase, Open Handles, Roses & White Hydrangeas, 12 1/2 In. 125.00
Chocolate Set, Art Deco Mold, Pink Roses, Marked, 8 1/2-In. Pot, 5 Piece 75.00
Condiment Set, Tulips, Toothpick, Salt & Pepper, Mustard, 6-Sided Tray 145.00
Cup & Saucer, Roses, 4 Piece 120.00
Dish, 4-Footed, 7 1/4 x 5 1/2 In. 40.00
Dish, Cheese & Crackers, White Flowers, Green Background 120.00
Dish, Lobster, 2 Sections 85.00
Dish, Violets & Leaves, 2 Handles, Oval, Osborne, 8 3/4 In. 95.00
Mug, Puck 58.00
Mustard Pot, Ladle, Pink Roses, Green Leaves, White Background 115.00
Mustard Pot, Lilies 75.00

Nut Dish, Knight Scene, Handles 115.00
Pitcher, Lemonade, White Clematis 195.00
Plaque, Mill Scene, Steeple Mark, 14 1/2 x 10 3/4 In. 6000.00
Plate, Daffodil, 6 1/2 In. 20.00
Relish, Bird Design, 10 3/4 In. 65.00
Relish, Bird Of Paradise, Handle 250.00
Sugar & Creamer, Cover, Art Deco 95.00
Toothpick, Large Orange Flowers, Leaves 75.00
Tray, Bun, Woman With Oxen At Country House, Purple, Pink, Yellow, 12 In. 300.00
Vase, Poppies On Shaded Ground, Gold & Red Trim, Handles, 8 In. ....110.00 to 120.00

RS PRUSSIA appears in several marks used on porcelain before 1917. Reinhold Schlegelmilch started his porcelain works in Suhl, Germany, in 1869. See also ES Germany, RS Germany, RS Suhl, and RS Tillowitz.

Berry Set, Reflected Water Lilies, Icicle Mold, 6 Piece 375.00
Berry Set, Stag, Soft Yellow & Greens, Master Bowl, 6 Bowls, 7 Piece 4500.00
Biscuit Jar, Pink Roses On Green Ground, Scalloped Lid, Signed, 6 1/2 In. 335.00
Biscuit Jar, Sunflower Mold, Pink & Green, Satin Finish 325.00
Bowl, Farm Scene, Red Mark, 10 In. 750.00
Bowl, Icicle, Pink Roses, Red Mark, 11 In. 250.00
Bowl, Iris, Shaded Ground, Signed, 10 1/2 In. 250.00
Bowl, Lily Mold, Solid Gold Back, Scattered Roses, 10 In. 700.00
Bowl, Magnolias, Cream Divider, Gold Accents, Signed, 10 3/4 In. 190.00
Bowl, Peonies, Pink & Yellow, Footed, 4 1/4 x 9 In. 412.00
Bowl, Pink Poppies, Green Trim, Iris Mold, Gold & Bronze Highlights, 10 1/2 In. 700.00
Bowl, Red Mark, 10 1/2 In. 165.00
Bowl, Scalloped Edge, Blue & Ivory Flowers, 10 In. 95.00
Cake Plate, Border Of Roses & Daises, 10 In. 120.00
Cake Plate, Gold Laurel Leaves, Signed, 9 1/2 In. 75.00
Cake Plate, Pink & Yellow Roses, Green & White, Gold Trim, Red Mark, 10 In. .... *Illus* 160.00
Cake Plate, Portrait, Winter Season, Open Handled, Iris Mold, 10 1/4 In. 1750.00
Cake Plate, Ripple 275.00
Cake Plate, Snapdragons, 11 1/2 In. 300.00
Cake Plate, Snowbird Scene, Open Handled, 10 1/2 In. 1500.00
Cake Plate, Water Lilies, 10 1/2 In. 210.00
Celery Dish, Clover Mold, Open Handles, Roses 245.00
Celery Dish, Pink Roses, White Ground 255.00
Celery Plate, Portraits Of 4 Women, Pink & Yellow Interior, 12 x 6 In. 1380.00
Chocolate Set, Blue Flowers, Gold Trim, Pot, 4 Cups & Saucers 295.00
Coffeepot, Floral 150.00
Coffeepot, Roses, Satin Finish, 9 1/2 In. 395.00
Creamer, With Roses, 3 1/4 In. 55.00

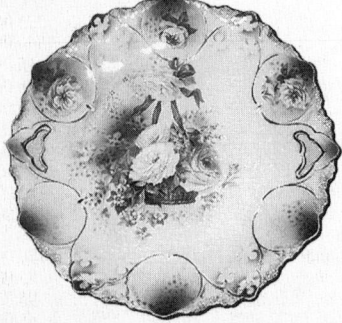

RS Prussia, Cake Plate, Pink & Yellow Roses,
Green & White, Gold Trim, Red Mark, 10 In.

Avoid burglaries. If you are painting your house, do not leave ladders leaning on the building or piled up near the house. Chain and lock the ladders so the casual burglar can't use them. Trim your trees to make access to the roof more difficult.

Cup, Jeweled, Small, Red Mark 50.00
Cup & Saucer, Deep Pink Flowers, Large 75.00
Dish, Dessert, Red Mark 35.00
Dresser Tray, Diana The Huntress, Molded Leaf Design, Green Ground, 12 x 9 In. 575.00
Dresser Tray, Portrait, Spring Season, Iris Mold, Tiffany, 11 In. 2100.00
Hair Receiver & Powder Jar, Flowers, Satinized Luster, Pair 475.00
Hatpin Holder, Swan In Evergreen, Mold 728 ....225.00 to 275.00
Mug, Swans On Lake, Satin Finish, Mold 577 .... 350.00
Nut Set, Rose Design, White, Pink, Green, Gilt, Bowl, 6 Dishes, 6 & 3 In., 7 Piece 385.00
Pitcher, Lemonade, Hidden Image, Girl, Pale Green Hair, Floral, 8 3/4 In. 2000.00
Pitcher, Scalloped Beaded Panels, Foliage, Scalloped Rim, Signed, 7 In. 315.00
Pitcher, Water, Open Roses, White, Red, Gilded Flowers, Reticulated Handle, 9 In. 375.00
Plate, Roses In Center, Gold Scalloped Rim, 8 1/2 In. 175.00
Plate, Roses, Pearl Finish, Blue Tints, 8 In. 125.00
Shaving Mug, Dogwood 125.00
Shaving Mug, Swan Scene 350.00
Sugar, Polychrome Roses, Shaded Ground, 6 1/2 In. 330.00
Sugar & Creamer, Allover Cobalt Blue & Gilt, Individual 130.00
Sugar & Creamer, Blue Floral, Red Mark 550.00
Sugar & Creamer, Dogwood 185.00
Sugar & Creamer, Mold 437 .... 300.00
Sugar & Creamer, Swan ....295.00 to 345.00
Tankard, Band With Scroll Design, Gold Handle, Teal Background, 13 1/2 In. 640.00
Tankard, Portrait, Melon Eaters, Ribbon & Jewel Mold, Green Tones, 11 1/2 In. 2200.00
Tankard, Ribbon & Jewel, Purple & Yellow Flowers, 11 In. 365.00
Tankard, White Flowers, Lavender, Pink, Green, 11 1/2 In. 600.00
Teapot, Bowl With Flowers Design, Mold 537, Gold 230.00
Teapot, Pink 400.00
Toothpick, Snowball, Floral, Red 125.00
Vase, Portrait, Fall Season, 3 Footed, 3 Handles, 6 3/4 In. 1900.00

RS SUHL is a mark used by the Erdmann Schlegelmilch factory in Suhl, Germany, between 1900 and 1917. The Schlegelmilch families made porcelains in many places. See also ES Germany, RS Germany, RS Prussia, and RS Tillowitz.

Suhl.

Box, Lift-Off Cover, Night Watch, Musketeers 45.00
Cup & Saucer, Night Watch, Musketeers 90.00
Sugar, Nightwatch, Scene Of 4 Men, Woman With Gun, Signed, 5 x 3 1/4 In. 75.00

RS TILLOWITZ was marked on porcelain by the Reinhold Schlegelmilch factory at Tillowitz from the 1920s to the 1940s. Table services and ornamental pieces were made. See also ES Germany, RS Germany, RS Prussia, and RS Suhl.

TILLOWITZ

Cake Plate, Fuchsias 46.00
Vase, 7 3/4 In. 160.00

RUBENA is a glassware that shades from red to clear. It was first made by George Duncan and Sons of Pittsburgh, Pennsylvania, about 1885. This coloring was used on many types of glassware. The pressed glass patterns of Royal Ivy and Royal Oak are listed under Pressed Glass.

Cruet, Thumbprint, Stopper, Bulbous 120.00
Pitcher, Opalescent Swirls, Ruffled Square Mouth, 8 1/2 In. 220.00
Sugar Shaker, Cut Glass, Silver Plated Cover, 19th Century 225.00
Vase, Drapery, Star Crimped Edge, 6 3/4 In. 93.00

RUBENA VERDE is a Victorian glassware that was shaded from red to green. It was first made by Hobbs, Brockunier and Company of Wheeling, West Virginia, about 1890.

Jug, Wine, Cylinder, Handle 365.00
Pitcher, Diamond-Quilted, Cranberry To Yellow, Yellow Handle, 9 In. 115.00
Vase, Calla Lily Shape, Enameled Flowers On Branch, 8 1/2 In. 175.00
Vase, Cylinder, Enameling In Pink & White, Deep Cranberry, 11 3/4 In., Pair 748.00

RUBY GLASS is the dark red color of the precious gemstone known as a *ruby*. It was a popular Victorian color that never went completely out of style. The glass was shaped by many different processes to make many different types of ruby glass. There was a revival of interest in the 1940s when modern-shaped ruby table glassware became fashionable. Sometimes the red color is added to clear glass by a process called flashing or staining. Flashed glass is clear glass dipped in a colored glass, then pressed or cut. Stained glass has color painted on a clear glass. Then it is refired so the stain fuses with the glass. Pieces of glass colored in this way are indicated by the word *stained* in the description. Related items may be found in other categories, such as Cranberry Glass, Pressed Glass, and Souvenir.

Battleship, Remember The Maine, 1900	175.00
Berry Set, Ruby Thumbprint, Boat Shape, 5 Piece	155.00
Bowl, Foliate Swag, Flared, Footed, Gilt Metal Mounted, 1900, 8 In., Pair	315.00
Ewer, Tricornered Rim, Elongated Handle, Stepped Disk Foot, 13 1/2 In.	374.00
Pitcher, Clear Handle, 9 1/2 In.	45.00

RUDOLSTADT was a faience factory in the Thuringia region of Germany from 1720 to about 1791. In 1854, Ernst Bohne began working in the area. From about 1887 to 1918, the New York and Rudolstadt Pottery made decorated porcelain marked with the RW and crown familiar to collectors. This porcelain was imported by Lewis Straus and Sons of New York, which later became Nathan Straus and Sons. The word *Royal* was included in their import mark. Collectors often call it *Royal Rudolstadt*. Most pieces found today were made in the late nineteenth or early twentieth century. Additional pieces may be listed in the Kewpie category.

Berry Bowl, Floral, Gold Border, 11 In.	55.00
Berry Bowl, Purple Violets, Marked, 9 1/2 In.	66.00
Bust, Bisque, Young Gentleman, Beige With Gold, 22 x 13 In., 2 Piece	460.00
Bust, Young Gentleman, Gold Lily Of The Valley, Signed, 22 In.	460.00
Butter Chip, Floral Petal Form, Gold & White	8.00
Figurine, Diana The Huntress, Bisque Body, Early 20th Century, 18 1/2 In.	750.00
Group, Hercules & Hebe, Standing On Naturally Molded Ground, Floral, 17 In.	201.00
Plate, 3 Roses, Gold Edge, 6 1/4 In.	25.00
Urn, Enameled Floral Decoration, Double Handle, 11 3/4 In.	156.00

RUGS have been used in the American home since the seventeenth century. The oriental rug of that time was often used on a table, not on the floor. Rag rugs, hooked rugs, and braided rugs were made by housewives from scraps of material.

Afghan, Mustard, Medallion & Floral, Floral & Geometric Borders, 3 Ft. 5 In. x 4 Ft. 8 In.	85.00
Afshar, Allover Stylized Vases Of Flowers, Ivory Field, 5 Ft. 10 In. x 5 Ft.	1955.00
Afshar, Alternating Cat Face Palmettes, Ivory Field, 5 Ft. 10 In. x 5 Ft.	1725.00
Afshar, Bagface, 2 Large Dark Red, Royal Blue Boteh, 1 Ft. 6 In. x 1 Ft.	1150.00
Afshar, Bagface, 2 Staggered Shield Rows, Red, Navy Blue, 2 Ft. 8 In. x 2 Ft.	805.00
Afshar, Bagface, Alternating Staggered Boteh Rows, Red, 3 Ft. 3 In. x 2 Ft. 2 In.	575.00
Afshar, Dark Red Ground, Medium Blue Borders, 3 Ft. 8 In. x 5 Ft. 6 In.	545.00
Afshar, Deep Coral, Powder Blue, Ivory, Camel, Teal, c.1900, 4 Ft. 2 In. x 5 Ft. 7 In.	2750.00
Afshar, Diamonds, Borders, Terra-Cotta, Brick, White, Black, 4 Ft. 5 In. x 6 Ft. 4 In.	660.00
Afshar, Staggered Boteh Rows, Midnight Blue Field, 5 Ft. 8 In. x 4 Ft. 2 In.	1725.00
Agra, Green, Pink & Burgundy, Ivory Ground, 10 Ft. 4 In. x 11 Ft. 8 In.	2750.00
Art Deco, Flower Head, Geometric Design, Maroon, Crimson, 11 Ft. 5 In. x 8 Ft. 2 In.	5750.00
Art Deco, Geometric Design, Cream, Beige & Gray, Wool, 6 Ft. 3 In. x 4 Ft. 8 In.	2875.00
Art Deco, Large Stylized Flower Heads, Yellow, 1930, 8 Ft. 11 In. x 5 Ft. 11 In.	6900.00
Aubusson, Allover Floral, Tan, Light Brown, Burgundy, 1900, 23 Ft. 6 In. x 14 Ft. 7 In.	25300.00
Aubusson, Floral Design, Floral Borders In Green, Blues & Off-White, 4 x 6 Ft.	143.00
Aubusson, Floral Design, Green Field, Floral Borders, 5 Ft. 9 In. x 7 Ft. 7 In.	290.00
Aubusson, Louis Philippe, Floral Design In Center, Brown, Tan, 19 Ft. 6 In. x 15 Ft.	17250.00
Aubusson, Napoleon III, Basket Of Flowers In Center, Gold, 10 Ft. 4 In. x 8 Ft.	8050.00
Bakhtiari, 2 Large Stepped Diamond Medallions, Red, Rose, 6 Ft. x 4 Ft. 4 In.	1150.00
Bakhtiari, Garden Design, c.1920, 12 Ft. 10 In. x 10 Ft. 7 In.	9900.00

Bakhtiari, Geometric, Dark Blue Ground, Multiple Borders, Fringe, 4 Ft. x 6 Ft. 5 In. . . . 605.00
Bakhtiari, Multicolored Panels, Garden & Floral, Burgundy Border, 10 Ft. x 12 Ft. 9 In. . 770.00
Bakhtiari, Pale Colors, Brown Border, Gray Spandrels, 5 x 8 Ft. 110.00
Bakhtiari, Silk, Multicolored Panels, Garden & Floral Designs, 8 Ft. x 11 Ft. 9 In. 2750.00
Bakhtiari, White Ground, Midnight Blue Border, 5 Ft. 4 In. x 7 Ft. 330.00
Baluchi, Square Medallion Surrounded By Large Rosettes, 2 Ft. 7 In. x 2 Ft. 7 In. 345.00
Baluchi, Staggered Rows Of Rectangular Medallions, 6 Ft. 3 In. x 3 Ft. 8 In. 1725.00
Bidjar, Allover Herati Design, Stepped Diamond Medallions, 12 Ft. x 7 Ft. 6 In. 3335.00
Bidjar, Allover Herati Design, Terra-Cotta Red Field, 11 Ft. 10 In. x 8 Ft. 6 In. 8625.00
Bidjar, Allover Mina Khani Floral Lattice, Red, Rose, 12 Ft. 8 In. x 8 Ft. 6 In. 12650.00
Bidjar, Allover Stylized Shield, Palmette Design, Wave Border, 4 Ft. 10 In. x 3 Ft. 4025.00
Bidjar, Center Medallion, Triangles At Corners, Deep Blues, Red, Wool, 10 x 14 Ft. 560.00
Bidjar, Floral & Scroll Design, 3 Borders, Dark Blue Ground, 6 Ft. x 4 Ft. 3 In. 2243.00
Bidjar, Lobed Circular Medallion, Red Spandrels, 12 Ft. 4 In. x 7 Ft. 6 In. 9200.00
Bidjar, Mauve Border, Spandrels, Midnight Blue Ground, 6 x 9 Ft. 330.00
Bidjar, Rust Red Spandrels, Camel Border, Black Ground, 3 Ft. 8 In. x 5 Ft. 1210.00
Bidjar, Rust, Slate, Blue, Brown Borders, Hexagonal, Geometric Designs, 7 x 4 Ft. 440.00
Bokhara, 6 Columns Of Symbols, Red Ground, 10 Ft. x 7 Ft. 11 In. 345.00
Bokhara, Guls, Red Field, Geometric Borders, Blue, Green, Ivory, 3 Ft. 8 In. x 5 Ft. 6 In. 430.00
Bokhara, Repeated Gul Design, Red Field, 4 Ft. 11 In. x 7 Ft. 605.00
Bokhara, Rust Field, 3 Ft. 9 In. x 6 Ft. 550.00
Braided, Crocheted & Embroidered Flowers, Beige, 49 x 70 In. 1200.00
Caucasian, 10 Medallions, Serrated Border, Rust Field, 5 Ft. 2 In. x 6 Ft. 7 In. 522.00
Caucasian, 2 Georgian Crosses, Sea Green Blossom Border, Cream Field, 5 Ft. 4 In. 5750.00
Caucasian, Allover Floral Design, Floral Borders, 4 Ft. 6 In. x 6 Ft. 7 In. 1445.00
Caucasian, Allover Geometric Medallion, Red, Blue, Brown Borders, 3 Ft. x 4 Ft. 4 In. . . 1955.00
Caucasian, Allover Palmette Design, Royal, Gold Field, 7 Ft. 4 In. x 2 Ft. 10 In. 2070.00
Caucasian, Animal Designs, Multiple Borders, Dark Blue, Tan, 3 Ft. x 12 Ft. 2 In. 990.00
Caucasian, Central Deep Blue Octagon, Tomato Red Field, 3 Ft. 7 In. x 2 Ft. 9 In. 2875.00
Caucasian, Prayer, Blue Mihrab, Floral, Geometric Borders, 3 Ft. 3 In. x 5 Ft. 2 In. 605.00
Chinese, Allover Ivory Cloud Design, Yellow, Pale Blue Roundel, 4 Ft. 10 In. x 2 Ft. 2070.00
Chinese, Beige, Gray Border, Flowers, Wool, 20th Century, 2 Ft. 3 In. x 10 Ft. 225.00
Chinese, Floral, Green Field, Floral Borders, Green, Tan, Brown, Red, 7 x 10 Ft. 230.00
Chinese, Floral, Red Field, Floral Borders, Red, Blue, Green, 3 Ft. 1 In. x 4 Ft. 11 In. 85.00
Chinese, Floral, Tan Ground, Floral Borders, Blue, Tan, 9 x 12 Ft. 405.00
Chinese, Pale Lemon Yellow Floral Roundel, Floral Sprays, 6 Ft. x 3 Ft. 9 In. 2875.00
Chinese, Vase, Vine & Floral Corners, Plum Field, Sand Border, 8 Ft. 9 In. x 11 Ft. 3 In. . 805.00
Derbend, Repeating Geometric, Brown, Beige, Blue, Brown Field, 4 Ft. 11 x 3 Ft. 6 In. . . 135.00
Ersari, 2 Columns Of 5 Concentric Diamonds, Rust Red Field, 6 Ft. 4 In. x 5 Ft. 4 In. . . . 1955.00
Ersari, Chuval, 3 Stepped Hexagonal Medallions, 6 Zigzag Stripes, 5 Ft. 4 In. x 3 Ft. 403.00
Ersari, Chuval, Allover Mina Khani Floral Lattice, Rust Field, 4 Ft. 9 In. x 2 Ft. 9 In. 920.00
Ersari, Chuval, Ikat Design, Indented Midnight, Royal Blue Diamonds, 5 Ft. x 3 Ft. 4 In. . 978.00
Ersari, Concentric Gabled Rectangular Medallion, Star Border, 4 Ft. 9 In. x 1 Ft. 8 In. . . . 460.00
Feraghan, Salmon Spandrels, Blue Border, Camel Ground, 4 Ft. 4 In. x 6 Ft. 3 In. 1265.00
Gabah, Stylized Animals, Black Border, Wool, 20th Century, 4 Ft. 10 In. x 7 Ft. 1 In. 815.00
Hamadan, 5 Stepped Diamond Medallion Columns, 13 Ft. 4 In. x 3 Ft. 9 In. 1380.00
Hamadan, Allover Herati Design, Geometric Borders, Blue Field, 3 x 6 Ft. 172.00
Hamadan, Boteh Design, Floral, Boteh Borders, Red Field, 4 Ft. 6 In. x 5 Ft. 8 In. 287.00
Hamadan, Floral Pattern, Floral & Vine Border, Navy, Wine, 11 Ft. 11 In. x 4 Ft. 7 In. . . . 2090.00
Hamadan, Floral, Floral Borders, Red, Blue, White, Blue Field, 3 Ft. 3 In. x 8 Ft. 7 In. . . . 175.00
Hamadan, Floral, Red Ground, Floral Borders, Blue, Green, 10 Ft. 4 In. x 6 Ft. 1 In. 460.00
Hamadan, Geometric Figures & Trees, Borders, Brown Ground, 6 Ft. x 3 Ft. 9 In. 220.00
Hamadan, Geometric Floral Design On Navy, Red Border, 10 Ft. 2 In. x 7 Ft. 11 In. 220.00
Hamadan, Herati Design, Dark Blue Ground, Red Border, Runner, 13 Ft. x 3 Ft. 6 In. 345.00
Hamadan, Ivory Field, Blue Border, 3 Ft. 5 In. x 5 Ft. 8 In. 165.00
Hamadan, Ivory Spandrels, Red Border, Dark Blue Ground, 4 Ft. 5 In. x 6 Ft. 7 In. 190.00
Hamadan, Persian, Brown Center, Undecorated Field, Red, Ivory Borders, 6 x 3 Ft. 6 In. . 220.00
Hamadan, Red Medallions, Dark Blue Ground, Borders, Runner, 3 Ft. 2 In. x 13 Ft. 3 In. . 990.00
Hamadan, Stepped Diamond Medallion, Herati, Deep Blue Ground, 9 Ft. 10 In. x 7 Ft. . . 1725.00
Hamadan, Stepped Hexagonal Medallion, Ivory Spandrels, 6 Ft. 3 In. x 4 Ft. 690.00
Heriz, 5 Serrated Hexagonal Medallions, Red, Gold, 11 Ft. 4 In. x 2 Ft. 10 In. 2415.00
Heriz, Allover Floral, Red Field, Geometric Floral Border, 9 x 12 Ft. 4600.00
Heriz, Allover Palmette Design, Large Serrated Leaves, 11 Ft. 6 In. x 9 Ft. 1150.00

Heriz, Black Border, Ivory Spandrels, Dark Red Ground, 5 x 6 Ft. 575.00
Heriz, Blue Border, Red Field, 9 Ft. x 11 Ft. 6 In. 1045.00
Heriz, Blue Central Medallion, Red Field, 11 Ft. 3 In. x 9 Ft. 1540.00
Heriz, Blue Medallion, Rust Field, Geometric Border, 9 x 11 Ft. 4400.00
Heriz, Center Geometric Medallion, Dark Blue, Orange Red, Ivory, 11 Ft. x 7 Ft. 9 In. . . . 920.00
Heriz, Central Floral Medallion, Floral Border, 20th Century, 9 x 12 Ft. 1150.00
Heriz, Central Geometric Medallion, Ivory, Blue, Red, 8 Ft. 6 In. x 6 Ft. 1 In. 575.00
Heriz, Diamond Medallions, White Ground, Multiple Borders, 12 Ft. x 16 Ft. 8 In. 9350.00
Heriz, Large Gabled Square Medallion, Serrated Leaves, 15 Ft. 6 In. x 10 Ft. 4 In. 4600.00
Heriz, Large Gabled Square Medallion, Terra-Cotta Field, 10 Ft. 8 In. x 8 Ft. 4312.50
Heriz, Red Field, Tan Border, 9 x 12 Ft. 1840.00
Heriz, Rust Red Ground, Midnight Blue Border, 7 Ft. 6 In. x 10 Ft. 6 In. 2200.00
Heriz, White Spandrels, Midnight Blue Borders, Burgundy Ground, 20 Ft. 3 In. x 18 Ft. . . . 5500.00
Hooked, 2 Black Horses, Green Ground, Concentric Rectangles, Rod Hanger, 27 x 49 In. . . 440.00
Hooked, 2 Circles, Primary Colors, 26 x 43 In. 495.00
Hooked, 2 Dogs On Picket Fence, 22 x 36 In. 165.00
Hooked, 2 Horse Heads, 36 x 23 In. 300.00
Hooked, 3 Bears Carrying Steaming Porridge, 20th Century, 30 x 45 In. 660.00
Hooked, 3 Horses, 19th Century, Mounted For Hanging, 26 x 39 In. 1250.00
Hooked, 3 White Swans, Swimming In Foreground, c.1870, 31 x 77 In. 1000.00
Hooked, Allover Block Design, Center Oak Leaves, 62 x 39 In. 1100.00
Hooked, Arts & Crafts, Stylized Vines, Pale Green With Burgundy, 60 x 96 In. 240.00
Hooked, Bicentennial, George Washington, On Horseback, Eagle On Crown, 50 x 34 In. . . 715.00
Hooked, Bird On Branch, Butterfly, 28 1/2 x 20 1/4 In. 1150.00
Hooked, Black Dog & Blackbirds, Multicolored Quarter Circles Corner, 31 x 41 In. 1980.00
Hooked, Black Galloping Horse, Green, Blue, Pink, Brown & White Ground, 22 x 40 In. . . 400.00
Hooked, Brown, Black Bear Strolling On Green Grass, Pink, Purple Flowers, 23 x 43 In. . . 805.00
Hooked, Cat & Kitten, Black, White, Green, Yellow, Blue, Brown, 29 1/2 x 24 In. 605.00
Hooked, Cat & Kittens, 52 x 27 In. 302.00
Hooked, Central Reserve, Seated Cat, Perched Bird, Late 19th Century, 24 1/2 x 43 In. . . 1265.00
Hooked, Collared Dog On Red Ground, 1820s, Mounted On Stretcher, 32 x 18 In. 1840.00
Hooked, Cornucopia With Fruit, 18 1/2 x 45 In. 495.00
Hooked, Cow, Odd Fellow Symbols, 1885, 38 x 63 In. 3190.00
Hooked, Eagle With Shield & Laurel, Red & Green Flowers, Frame, 38 x 51 In. 302.00
Hooked, Field Of Foliate & Hearts, Centering Hattie, Heart Border, 31 1/2 x 52 In. 1150.00
Hooked, Figure Of Ocean Liner Under Steam, Mounted On Stretcher, 1870s, 31 x 64 In. . . 4312.00
Hooked, Floral & Leaf, Blue, Salmon, Beige & Pale Green, Oval, 65 x 44 In. 55.00
Hooked, Floral & Leaf, Mauve, Ribbon Design, 50 x 30 In. 85.00
Hooked, Floral Cartouche, Braided Border, Leaves & Vines, 43 x 22 1/2 In. 1800.00
Hooked, Floral Center, Green Ground, Name & Date, Ingrid Quist, 1887, 39 x 25 In. 330.00
Hooked, Floral Design, Center Medallion, 144 x 108 In. 110.00
Hooked, Floral Design, Off-White Field, 36 x 60 In. 52.00
Hooked, Floral Design, Tan Ground, 141 1/2 x 103 In. 220.00
Hooked, Floral Medallion, Garlands, Purple, Black, Green, Blue, Red, 113 x 129 In. 2300.00
Hooked, Floral, Conch Shell Corners, Monogram, JFM, 45 x 28 In. 253.00
Hooked, Floral, Off-White Field, Floral Borders, Purple, Green, 96 x 120 In. 145.00
Hooked, Florals, 33 x 22 In. 225.00
Hooked, Fruit & Flowers Compote Center, Beige Ground, 22 x 29 In. 110.00
Hooked, House With Shed & Trees, Early 20th Century, 27 1/2 x 46 1/2 In. 230.00
Hooked, Hunter With Gun, 3 Rabbits Running, 1900s, 18 3/4 x 36 In. 252.00
Hooked, Jolly Old St. Nick, In Sleigh, Forest Heath, Half Moon Shape, 27 x 42 In. 315.00
Hooked, Lion, Standing, Green Shades, Gray, Brown, Mounted On Stretcher, 26 x 38 In. . . 1840.00
Hooked, Little Brown Church In The Vale, 24 x 36 In. 330.00
Hooked, Map Of Cape Cod, Jeanne M. McIver, 30 x 38 In. 990.00
Hooked, Mountain Lion Crouching On Branch, 1880s, 30 x 42 In. 4025.00
Hooked, Multicolored Stripes, Late 19th Century, 37 x 16 3/4 In. 1320.00
Hooked, Quail Family, Forest Ground, 27 x 25 In. 110.00
Hooked, Rabbit In Diamond, Black, Gray, Olive, Green Brown, 21 x 37 1/2 In. 140.00
Hooked, Rag & Yarn, Fishscale Design, Red, Green & Brown, Rebacked, 31 x 60 In. 220.00
Hooked, Rag & Yarn, Flowers, Beige, Embroidered L.B.M. Aug. 1, '39, 35 x 56 In. 40.00
Hooked, Rag, Black Dog On Gray Ground, 30 x 54 In. 770.00
Hooked, Rag, Black Rooster Center, Arabesque Of Stripes, 22 x 39 In. 138.00
Hooked, Rag, Geometric, Red, Blue, Beige, Gray & Maroon, 20th Century, 23 x 33 In. . . 135.00

Hooked, Rag, Leaping Deer, Gold, Brown, Blue, Green Shades, Tan & Black, 27 x 45 In.   220.00
Hooked, Rag, Lovebirds & Flowers, Black Ground, Mounted On Stretcher, 20 x 38 In. . . .   615.00
Hooked, Rag, Owl On Tree Branch, Silhouetted By Moon, Blue Border, 19 x 33 1/2 In. . .   248.00
Hooked, Rag, Winter Scene, Horse & Sleigh, Jeanne Broderer, 10 x 12 In. 220.00
Hooked, Roses, Petunias & Leaves, Border, 1920, 24 x 36 In. 395.00
Hooked, Round, Sailing Ship In Center, Zodiac Border, M. Anderson, '54, 72 In. 1100.00
Hooked, Running Horse, Black, Green & Peach, Mounted On Stretcher, 36 x 51 1/2 In. . .   1955.00
Hooked, Sailboats In Harbor, Church In Background, 17 1/2 x 33 1/2 In. 275.00
Hooked, Sailor's Homecoming, Ship, 2 Women, Mermaid, Forest Heath, 1879, 58 In. 1725.00
Hooked, Scotty, Off-White Oval, Flowers, Black Border, 20 x 32 1/2 In. 412.00
Hooked, Seated Cat With Ball Of Yarn Center, Oval, 29 x 18 In. 440.00
Hooked, Skunk, Reds, Blacks & Browns, 19th Century, 35 x 43 In. 3300.00
Hooked, Spotted Leopard, Brown, Green & Beige, Mounted On Stretcher, 26 x 46 In. . . .   1380.00
Hooked, Tan Ground, Flowers, Brown Border, 50 x 30 In. 55.00
Hooked, Tree Of Life, Doves, Green, Red, Blue, Orange, Vermont, c.1840, 39 x 78 In. . . .   8625.00
Hooked, Water Lily Center, Border, 26 x 37 In. 295.00
Hooked, Yellow, Gray Beavers Beneath Green Leaves, Yellow Stars, 21 x 37 1/2 In. 145.00
Indo-Persian, Floral, Green Field, Floral Borders, 5 Ft. 4 In. x 7 Ft. 115.00
Indo-Persian, Floral, Red Field, Floral Borders, Blue, Mustard, Black, 3 Ft. 6 In. x 6 Ft. . .   85.00
Indo-Tabriz, Floral, Blue Field, Floral Borders, 9 Ft. 1 In. x 12 Ft.   575.00
Isparta, Blue Field, Guls, Geometric Borders, Rose, Runner, 2 Ft. 4 In. x 10 Ft. 11 In. . . .   175.00
Isparta, Floral, Blue Field, Floral Borders, Red, Blue, Green, Brown, 9 x 12 Ft. 405.00
Isparta, Red Medallion Center, Blue Ground, Beige, Long Fringe, 9 x 12 Ft. 140.00
Joshogan, 3 Hooked Diamonds, Octagon, Deep Blue Ground, 5 Ft. 2 In. x 3 Ft. 10 In. . . .   290.00
Joshogan, Ivory Medallion, Repeating Floral Pattern, 15 Ft. 4 In. x 10 Ft. 11 In. 1100.00
Karabagh, 5 Large Diamond Medallions, Sky Blue, Red, Gold, 13 Ft. 9 In. x 3 Ft. 9 In. . .   1955.00
Karabagh, Allover Boteh Pattern, Signed, Early 1900s, 13 Ft. 10 In. x 4 Ft. 9 In. 4180.00
Karabagh, Chevrons, Midnight Blue, Red, Ivory Crab Border, 8 Ft. x 3 Ft. 7 In. 1150.00
Karabagh, Diagonal Boteh Rows, Red, Sky Blue, Gold, 12 Ft. 9 In. x 3 Ft. 4 In. 1265.00
Karabagh, Geometric, Borders, Brown, Light Green, Cream, 3 Ft. 1 In. x 10 Ft. 8 In. 220.00
Karabagh, Prayer, Terra-Cotta Medallion, Floral, Blue, 3 Ft. 9 In. x 2 Ft. 10 In. 165.00
Karabagh, White Border, Blue Ground, Runner, 3 Ft. 9 In. x 7 Ft. 6 In. 990.00
Karaja, 7 Medallions, Orange, Red, Green, Blue, Cream, Runner, 2 Ft. 6 In. x 9 Ft. 7 In. .   220.00
Karaja, Blue, Terra-Cotta, White, 3 Ft. 9 In. x 5 Ft. 8 In. 825.00
Karaja, Dark Blue Border, Red Ground, 3 Ft. 5 In. x 4 Ft. 4 In. 385.00
Kashan, Allover Palmette Design, Blossoming Vines, 18 Ft. 6 In. x 13 Ft. 6 In. 14950.00
Kashan, Boteh, White Field, Floral Borders, Red, Blue, 10 Ft. 2 In. x 13 Ft. 4 In. 575.00
Kashan, Central Medallion, Pendants, Blue Ground, Borders, 10 Ft. 7 In. x 12 Ft. 1 In. . . .   1035.00
Kashan, Floral, Light Blue Medallion, Ivory Ground, Borders, 11 Ft. 6 In. x 8 Ft. 8 In. . . .   2990.00
Kashan, Off-White Field, Allover Floral Borders, 4 Ft. 4 In. x 6 Ft. 6 In. 850.00
Kashan, Rust Red Ground, Dark Blue Border, Fringe, 10 Ft. 3 In. x 13 Ft. 10 In. 8525.00
Kashan, Spandrels, Red Ground, Dark Blue Border, 3 Ft. 4 In. x 5 Ft. 825.00
Kashan, Tan, Brown & Gray, Ivory Ground, 4 Ft. 5 In. x 6 Ft. 8 In. 880.00
Kazak, 2 Indented Cruciform Medallions, Red, Ivory, Gold, 6 Ft. 4 In. x 3 Ft. 9 In. 1725.00
Kazak, 3 Ivory, Madder Red Medallions, Forest Green Field, 7 Ft. 2 In. x 4 Ft. 1 In. 2530.00
Kazak, 3 Large Diamond Medallions, Navy, Sky Blue, Red Field, 7 Ft. 6 In. x 3 Ft. 9 In. .   2645.00
Kazak, 3 Octagonal Memling Guls, Red Field, 7 Ft. 4 In. x 4 Ft. 8 In. 2300.00
Kazak, 5 1/2 Memling Guls, Pale Madder Field, 6 Ft. 11 In. x 4 Ft. 3 In. 3737.00
Kazak, 6 Octagonal Memling Guls, Navy Blue Field, 7 Ft. x 3 Ft. 10 In. 1610.00
Kazak, 6 Rectangular Medallions, Stepped Zigzag Lines, 8 Ft. 4 In. x 5 Ft. 1495.00
Kazak, Blue Field, Brown, Green, Rust Geometric Design, 6 x 3 1/2 Ft. 303.00
Kazak, Geometric & Checkerboard, Double Prayer Rug Style, 7 Ft. 10 In. x 4 Ft. 6 In. . . .   2588.00
Kazak, Geometric Design, Multiple Borders, Tan, Slate, Terra-Cotta, 4 Ft. x 7 Ft. 9 In. . . .   330.00
Kazak, Geometric, Blue Ground, Borders, Ivory Diamond, 7 Ft. 1 In. x 3 Ft. 10 In. 520.00
Kazak, Ivory, Madder, Indigo Medallion, Madder Field, 1880, 8 Ft. 5 In. x 6 Ft. 5750.00
Kazak, Prayer, Pale Blue, Indigo, Ivory Polygons, Madder Field, 4 Ft. 7 In. x 3 Ft. 4312.00
Kazak, Sea Green Shield Medallion, Tomato Red Field, 7 Ft. 5 In. x 5 Ft. 2 In. 3162.00
Kerman, Allover Trailing Vine Design, Red Field, 7 Ft. 6 In. x 16 Ft. 8 In. 1045.00
Kerman, Center Medallion, Pink, Blue, Green, Cream Ground, 11 Ft. x 9 Ft. 9 In. 1440.00
Kerman, Elongated Floral Medallion, Royal Blue Tracery, Sky Blue Border, 22 x 10 Ft. . . .   2700.00
Kerman, Floral & Medallion Design, Tan Field, Floral Borders, 10 x 14 Ft. 865.00
Kerman, Floral, Pink Border, Ivory Ground, 9 Ft. 9 In. x 16 Ft. 8 In. 2090.00
Kerman, Maroon Spandrels & Borders, Ivory Ground, 3 Ft. 10 In. x 5 Ft. 8 In. 550.00

Kerman, Medallion Design, Blue & Green Ground, Floral Borders, 6 x 9 Ft. 290.00
Kerman, Scalloped Medallion, Floral Sprays, Ivory Ground, 13 Ft. 8 In. x 10 Ft. 2 In. . . . 1495.00
Khorasan, Burgundy Design, Multiple Borders, Olive, Ivory, 10 Ft. 9 In. x 16 Ft. 7 In. . . . 2530.00
Khorasan, Medallions, Herati Design, Midnight Blue Ground, 25 x 14 Ft. 6900.00
Kilim, Allover Floral Design, Mid-19th Century, 9 Ft. 8 In. x 7 Ft. 7 In. 18400.00
Kilim, Allover Geometric Design, 3 Ft. 9 In. x 9 Ft. 5 In. 460.00
Kilim, Geometric Floral, Black, Brown, Geometric Borders, 5 Ft. 10 In. x 11 Ft. 9 In. 175.00
Kilim, Geometric, Blue Ground, Red, Blue, Green, Brown, Off-White, 6 Ft. x 9 Ft. 6 In. . . . 1725.00
Kilim, Ivory Ground, Columns Of Polygons, 1830s, 15 Ft. 7 In. x 4 Ft. 11 In. 6900.00
Kilim, Maroon, Black, Cream & Blue, 8 Ft. 5 In. x 5 Ft. 10 In. 550.00
Konya, Prayer, Red, Blue, Gold, Selvage, Fringe, 3 Ft. 4 In. x 4 Ft. 330.00
Kuba, Allover Snowflakes, Ivory Slantleaf, Chalice Border, 5 Ft. 8 In. x 4 Ft. 6900.00
Kuba, Dark Abrash Blue Ground, Camel Border, 3 Ft. 8 In. x 5 Ft. 9 In. 1265.00
Kurd, 4 Gabled Square Medallions, Midnight Blue Field, 8 Ft. 8 In. x 5 Ft. 1265.00
Kurd, 5 Cruciform Medallions, 4 Serrated Leaves, 7 Ft. 6 In. x 3 Ft. 5 In. 1035.00
Kurd, Bagface, Geometric Palmette, Ivory Hexagon, Camel Field, 2 x 2 Ft. 1610.00
Kurd, Bagface, Hooked Diamond Lattice, Midnight Blue, Red, 2 Ft. x 1 Ft. 10 In. 518.00
Kurd, Bagface, Hooked Diamonds, Navy Blue, Red, Rose, 1 Ft. 10 In. x 1 Ft. 7 In. 288.00
Kurd, Bagface, Large Pale Blue, Madder Diamond, 1880, 1 Ft. 8 In. x 1 Ft. 8 In. 632.00
Kurd, Bagface, Rows Of Hooked Diamonds, Red, Coral, 1 Ft. 8 In. x 1 Ft. 6 In. 288.00
Kurd, Boteh & Animal Rows, Terra-Cotta Field, Boteh Border, 6 Ft. x 3 Ft. 8 In. 460.00
Kurd, Dark Blue Ground, Rust Orange Border, 3 Ft. 8 In. x 7 Ft. 3 In. 220.00
Kurd, Geometric Floral, Tan Ground, Floral & Geometric Border, 3 Ft. 5 In. x 5 Ft. 345.00
Kurd, Ivory Ground, Rosettes, Leaves, Dragon Border, c.1880, 8 Ft. 4 In. x 3 Ft. 9 In. . . . 2875.00
Kurd-Bidjar, Hexagonal Medallion, Sky Blue Spandrels, 11 Ft. 9 In. x 6 Ft. 4600.00
Lesghi, 4 Lesghi Stars, Surrounded By Animals, Deep Blue Field, 6 Ft. 3 In. x 3 Ft. 4025.00
Lillihan, c.1920, 4 Ft. 6 In. x 3 Ft. 6 In. 345.00
Lillihan, Center Medallion, Geometric, Multiple Borders, 4 Ft. 3 In. x 6 Ft. 4 In. 990.00
Lillihan, Floral Sprays, Slate Blue, Camel, Rose, Deep Red Field, 6 Ft. 6 In. x 5 Ft. 975.00
Lillihan, Geometric, Floral Borders, Red Ground, Blue, Green, 2 Ft. 6 In. x 3 Ft. 11 In. . . . 290.00
Lillihan, Mauve Ground, Midnight Blue Border, 9 Ft. 3 In. x 12 Ft. 550.00
Lillihan, Red Field, Floral, Floral Borders, Red, Blue, Green, White, 2 Ft. x 2 Ft. 8 In. . . . 140.00
Machine Woven, Abstract Design, Primary Colors, Kandinsky, 1980s, 6 x 9 Ft. 1870.00
Machine Woven, Black & White Geometric Squares, Art Deco, 4 Ft. 10 In. x 7 Ft. 5 In. . . 360.00
Machine Woven, Concentric Organics, Peach, Blue, Ivory, 1960s, 16 x 12 Ft. 935.00
Machine Woven, Geometric, Square, Black, Red, Gray & Yellow, 5 Ft. 2 In. x 7 Ft. 5 In. . . 330.00
Machine Woven, Mimos, Wool, Paper Cutouts, Henri Matisse, 1951, 4 Ft. 10 In. x 3 Ft. . . 3300.00
Machine Woven, Musical Notes, Pinks, Gray, Art Deco, 4 Ft. 11 In. x 8 Ft. 11 In. 1320.00
Mahal, Allover Herati Design, Red Palmette, Leafy Vine Border, 16 Ft. x 11 Ft. 8 In. 1725.00
Mahal, Dark Blue Center, Rust Red Border, 7 Ft. 2 In. x 10 Ft. 4 In. 1430.00
Mahal, Geometric, Blue Field, Brown Multiple Borders, 6 Ft. x 3 Ft. 6 In. 550.00
Mahal, Ivory Spandrels, Midnight Blue Ground, 7 Ft. x 11 Ft. 2 In. 1210.00
Mahal, Midnight Blue Ground, Rust & Ivory Borders, 4 Ft. 3 In. x 6 Ft. 10 In. 550.00
Mahal, Midnight Blue-Black Border, Multiple Borders, Red Ground, 9 Ft. x 1 Ft. 1320.00
Mahal, Stylized Floral Design, Terra-Cotta Field, Cream Borders, 6 Ft. x 8 Ft. 10 In. 770.00
Malayer, Red Ground, Slate Blue Spandrels, Blue Border, 8 Ft. 7 In. x 12 Ft. 3 In. 630.00
Needlepoint, Allover Fleur-De-Lis Diamonds, France, 19th C., 11 Ft. 5 In. x 8 Ft. 7 In. . . . 4600.00
Needlepoint, Allover Floral, Off-White Field, Floral Borders, 9 Ft. 10 In. x 16 Ft. 3 In. . . . 805.00
Needlepoint, Applied Cotton Band Borders, Blue, Brown, 11 Ft. 3 In. x 9 Ft. 8 In. 9775.00
Needlepoint, Figures, Animals, Flowering Branches, Greece, 4 Ft. 7 In. x 4 Ft. 2 In. 12650.00
Needlepoint, Floral, Gold, Tan, Light Brown, 11 Ft. 11 In. x 8 Ft. 7 In. 11500.00
Needlepoint, Floral, Light Blue, Pink, White, 1920, 12 Ft. 10 In. x 11 Ft. 5 In. 6325.00
Needlepoint, Floral, Pink, Rose, Tan, Black, 1920, 18 Ft. 2 In. x 13 Ft. 2 In. 13800.00
Needlepoint, Stylized Design, Silk, Cotton, France, 20th C., 11 Ft. 3 In. x 9 Ft. 8 In. 9775.00
Niris, Floral, 3 Borders, Red, Black, White, Gold, Runner, 3 Ft. 3 In. x 11 Ft. 4 In. 990.00
Northwest Persian, Blue & Red Borders, Tan Ground, 2 Ft. 10 In. x 13 Ft. 6 In. 3520.00
Northwest Persian, Floral Design, Red Field, Floral Borders, 3 Ft. 2 In. x 3 Ft. 10 In. . . . 375.00
Penny, Applied Stars, 3-Leaf Clovers, Felt, Wool, Gold Cotton Ground, 19 x 26 In. 245.00
Penny, Black, Red & Gray Wool, Olive Velvet, Embroidered, Scalloped Edge, 24 x 35 In. 195.00
Penny, Multicolored, Off-White Ground, Orange Border, Hexagonal, 41 x 52 In. 520.00
Persian, 3 Serrated Hexagonal Medallions, Camel Field, 14 Ft. 5 In. x 3 Ft. 8 In. 2530.00
Persian, Allover Flowering Vines, Palmettes, Serrated Leaves, Ivory Ground, 12 x 9 Ft. . . . 1955.00

Persian, Allover Herati, Navy Ground, Red Border, 5 Ft. 10 In. x 4 Ft. 8 In. 490.00
Persian, Allover Palmette Design, Deeply Notched Leaves, 5 Ft. 10 In. x 3 Ft. 9 In. 1610.00
Persian, Concentric Diamond Medallion, Red Border, 5 Ft. 3 In. x 3 Ft. 8 In. 402.00
Persian, Diamond Medallions, Brown Ground, Multiple Borders, 6 Ft. x 3 Ft. 11 In. 415.00
Persian, Floral & Medallion Design, Blue Ground, Floral Borders, 7 Ft. 1 In. x 10 Ft. 1610.00
Persian, Floral, Blue Field, Floral Borders, Red, Green, Rust, 6 Ft. 8 In. x 16 Ft. 8 Ft. . . . 865.00
Persian, Flowering Tree In A Navy Field, Maroon Border, 7 Ft. x 4 Ft. 7 1/2 In. 550.00
Persian, Geometric Medallion, Brown Field, Blue, Red, Runner, 3 Ft. 2 In. x 8 Ft. 11 In. . 460.00
Persian, Herati Design, Blue Field, Floral Borders, Red, Blue, Rust, Tan, 10 x 16 Ft. 1150.00
Persian, Medallion, Floral & Geometric Borders, Runner, 3 Ft. 6 In. x 20 Ft. 6 In. 2070.00
Persian, Navy Geometric Design, Diamond Medallions, Red Borders, 6 Ft. x 3 Ft. 6 In. . . 248.00
Persian, Round Medallion, Palmettes Surround, Blue Ground, 12 Ft. 9 In. x 1 Ft. 4025.00
Persian, Star-In-Rectangle Medallion, Serrated Leaves, 1 Ft. 8 In. x 1 Ft. 6 In. 403.00
Persian, Tribal, 3 Medallions, Geometric Patterns, Red Ground, Wool, 5 Ft. 6 In. x 6 Ft. . . 560.00
Persian Heriz, Ivory & Burgundy Spandrels, Midnight Blue Border, 9 Ft. 9 In. x 13 Ft. . . 685.00
Persian Heriz, Ivory Spandrels, Red Ground, Dark Blue Border, 6 Ft. 9 In. x 9 Ft. 9 In. . . 1210.00
Qashqai, Allover Herati, Rust Spandrels, 6 Ft. 8 In. x 4 Ft. 2645.00
Qashqai, Diagonal Rows Of Small Octagons, Ivory Border, 7 Ft. 6 In. x 4 Ft. 8 In. 1150.00
Qum, Tree Of Life, Birds, Deer, Flowers, Blue, Ivory Border, 8 Ft. 3 In. x 4 Ft. 3 In. 2645.00
Rag, Colorful Warp Stripes, Penna., 43 x 65 In. 165.00
Saraband, Boteh, Off-White Field, Geometric & Floral Borders, 3 Ft. 6 In. x 4 Ft. 10 In. . 145.00
Sarouk, 8 Leaf Floral Sprays, Red Ground, Midnight Blue Border, 6 Ft. 2 In. x 5 Ft. 2 In. 920.00
Sarouk, Allover Floral Design, Red Field, 7 Ft. 10 In. x 9 Ft. 10 In. 3960.00
Sarouk, Allover Floral Sprays, Midnight Blue, Camel, Ivory, 6 Ft. 5 In x 4 Ft. 3 In. 1840.00
Sarouk, Allover Floral, Blue Ground, Wide Red Border, 4 x 6 Ft. 550.00
Sarouk, Allover Floral, Multiple Borders, 7 Ft. 9 In. x 10 Ft. 1 In. 3190.00
Sarouk, Allover Mina Khani Variant Floral Lattice, 12 Ft. 2 In. x 8 Ft. 10 In. 10350.00
Sarouk, Allover Palmettes, Floral Sprays, Wine Red Field, 12 Ft. x 8 Ft. 10 In. 1725.00
Sarouk, Blue Ground, Red Border, Fringe 1 End, 3 Ft. 5 In. x 4 Ft. 11 In. 770.00
Sarouk, Blue Ground, Wide Red Border, 10 x 14 Ft. 1100.00
Sarouk, Blue Medallion, Red Field, Blue Border, 8 Ft. 11 In. x 11 Ft. 10 In. 920.00
Sarouk, Center Floral Medallion, Indigo Blue Field, 22 Ft. 2 In. x 4 Ft. 935.00
Sarouk, Floral Sprays, Blossoming Vines, Blue Border, 4 Ft. 10 In. x 3 Ft. 5 In. 373.00
Sarouk, Floral, Allover Red Field, Blue Border, 8 Ft. 9 In. x 11 Ft. 2 In. 2750.00
Sarouk, Floral, Deep Red Field, Floral Borders, 1 Ft. 11 In. x 2 Ft. 5 In. 287.00
Sarouk, Floral, Red Ground, Floral Borders, Blue, Tan, Red, Runner, 2 Ft. x 6 Ft. 6 In. . . . 805.00
Sarouk, Flowers, Blue Ground, Red Border, 11 Ft. x 9 Ft. 1 In. 4890.00
Sarouk, Garden, Blue Central Medallion, Floral Border, 5 Ft. x 3 Ft. 1 In. 220.00
Sarouk, Large Lobed Oval Medallion, Ivory Field, 11 Ft. 10 In. x 8 Ft. 5 In. 8050.00
Sarouk, Maroon Ground, Midnight Blue Border, 4 Ft. 7 In. x 6 Ft. 11 In. 1430.00
Sarouk, Midnight Blue Border, Burgundy Ground, 4 Ft. 2 In. x 6 Ft. 9 In. 1595.00
Sarouk, Navy, Sky Blue Floral Groups, Wine Red Field, 6 Ft. 8 In. x 4 Ft. 5 In. 2875.00
Sarouk, Stylized Floral & Vine, Multiple Borders, 1930s, 10 Ft. 3 In. x 17 Ft. 3 In. 8250.00
Savonnerie, Allover Rose Diamond Cartouche, Spain, 1805, 10 Ft. 3 In. x 9 Ft. 5 In. 4025.00
Seichour, Rose Design, Red, Dark Blue, Multiple Borders, 3 Ft. 4 In. x 5 Ft. 4 In. 2530.00
Seichour, Royal Blue, White, Rose, Black, Border, Fringe, 11 Ft. 8 In. x 4 Ft. 10 In. 10925.00
Sennah, Mother, Child Boteh Rows, Ivory Meander Border, 6 Ft. 6 In. x 3 Ft. 9 In. 3737.00
Shiraz, Burgundy Abrash Ground, 5 Ft. 2 In. x 7 Ft. 8 In. 275.00
Shiraz, Geometric Design, Red Ground, Geometric Floral Borders, 5 Ft. x 6 Ft. 3 In. 375.00
Shiraz, Multiple Borders, Red, Blue, Mauve, 3 Ft. x 5 Ft. 6 In. 330.00
Shirvan, 2 Groups Of Leaf Motifs, Hooked Vines, Ivory, Gold, 4 Ft. 2 In. x 3 Ft. 7 In. . . . 748.00
Shirvan, 3 Hooked Diamond Medallions, Green Blue Field, 5 Ft. 9 In. x 3 Ft. 10 In. 2070.00
Shirvan, 6 Stepped Diamond Medallions, Red, Sky Blue, Gold, 10 Ft. 4 In. x 4 Ft. 8 In. . . 4313.00
Shirvan, Allover Geometric, Blue Field, Red Border, 4 Ft. 6 In. x 9 Ft. 660.00
Shirvan, Blue, Red, Cream, Stepped Diamonds, Blue Border, 8 Ft. x 3 Ft. 9 In. 710.00
Shirvan, Ivory, Madder Medallions, Mustard Border, 4 Ft. 11 In. x 3 Ft. 8 In. 3450.00
Shirvan, Mustard Field, Stylized Floral Trellis Allover, 1880s, 3 Ft. 11 In. x 3 Ft. 1 In. . . . 2990.00
Shirvan, Prayer, Blue Mihrab & Field, Geometric Floral & Figural, 4 Ft. 11 In. x 6 Ft. 4890.00
Shirvan, Prayer, Blue Mihrab, Floral, Red, Blue, Brown, Floral Borders, 4 x 5 Ft. 2875.00
Shirvan, Prayer, Serrated Diamond Lattice, Navy Blue Field, 5 Ft. 6 In. x 3 Ft. 4 In. 4025.00
Shirvan, Serrated, Staggered Boteh Rows, Red, Ivory, Gold, 5 Ft. 2 In. x 3 Ft. 6 In. 1150.00
Shirvan, Stepped Diamond Medallions, Deep Blue Field, 9 Ft. 7 In. x 3 Ft. 9 In. 3162.00

Shirvan, Stepped Lattice Of Diamonds, Ivory Field, 5 Ft. 5 In. x 3 Ft. 7 In. 977.00
Soumak, 3 Stylized Pinwheel Medallions, Indigo, Brick Red Field, 6 Ft. 5 In. x 4 Ft. 3737.00
Soumak, 8 Medallions, Ivory Field, Red Border, 6 Ft. 6 In. x 6 Ft. 6 In. 880.00
Soumak, Bagface, 3 Boteh, Navy, Sky Blue, Red, 1 Ft. 10 In. x 1 Ft. 9 In. 633.00
Soumak, Geometric, Rose, Blue, Brown, 10 Ft. 5 In. x 8 Ft. 2 In. 5750.00
Soumak, Geometric, Rose, Light Blue, White, Brown, 9 Ft. 1 In. x 6 Ft. 9 In. 6325.00
Soumak, Medallions, Multiple Borders, Dark Blue, Red, Cream, c.1930, 9 x 12 Ft. 2530.00
Soumak, Octagons, Allover, Borders, White, Blue, Terra-Cotta, 3 Ft. x 5 Ft. 7 In. 1540.00
Stylized Blossoms, Red, Orange, Carpet, Oval, 1930, 8 Ft. 8 In. x 5 Ft. 7 In. 4600.00
Table, Appliqued & Patchwork, 13 Panel, Black Field, 50 3/4 x 30 3/4 In. 2645.00
Tabriz, Allover Herati Design, Navy, Light Blue, Light Red, Rust, Gold, 18 x 12 Ft. 2415.00
Tabriz, Central Medallion, Ivory Field, Floral Border, 10 Ft. 5 In. x 13 Ft. 5 In. 1100.00
Tabriz, Floral, Off-White Field, Floral Borders, Red, Blue, Green, Rust, 8 x 12 Ft. 575.00
Tabriz, Lobed Circular Medallion Surrounded By Vases, Bowls, 13 Ft. x 9 Ft. 1 In. 1265.00
Tabriz, Silk, Animal Designs, 1890-1910, 4 Ft. x 5 Ft. 8 In. 1540.00
Talish, Octagons, Gold, Blue, Green, Terra-Cotta Ground, Borders, 3 Ft. 8 In. x 6 Ft. 2 In. 4180.00
Tekke, 3 Salor Guls, Madder Ground, Narrow Border, 2 Ft. 9 In. x 4 Ft. 2 In. 1035.00
Tekke, 5 Large Flowering Plants, Gold, Plainweave Ivory Field, 5 Ft. x 2 Ft. 3 In. 1840.00
Tekke, 6 Chuval Guls, Midnight Blue, Red, Ivory, Blue Green, 3 Ft. 10 In. x 1 Ft. 56 In. . 460.00
Tekke, Engsi, Garden Plan Field, Rust, Apricot, Ivory, 5 Ft. 3 In. x 4 Ft. 6 In. 1150.00
Tekke, Engsi, Garden Plan Field, Rust, Midnight Blue Plants, 4 Ft. 9 In. x 4 Ft. 2 In. 920.00
Tekke, Engsi, Garden Plan Field, Rust, Midnight Blue, Red, Pole Tree Border, 5 x 4 Ft. . . 2645.00
Tekke, Ivory, Blue & Orange, Burgundy Ground, 3 Ft. 3 In. x 4 Ft. 3 In. 220.00
Tekke, Rows Of Guls, 8-Sided Symbols, Geometric Diamond, 10 Ft. x 5 Ft. 11 In. 1150.00
Tibetan, Floral, Blue Field, Geometric Borders, Blue, Red, Green, 11 Ft. x 14 Ft. 5 In. . . . 460.00
Turkish, Floral Design With Cartouche Main Border, 1920, 18 Ft. 3 In. x 20 Ft. 11 In. . . . 6160.00
Turkish, Floral, Burgundy Ground, Floral Borders, Red, Blue, Green, 9 x 12 Ft. 520.00
Turkish, Geometric Guls & Borders, Ivory Ground, Blue, Rose, 6 Ft. 5 In. x 8 Ft. 7 In. . . . 230.00
Turkish, Geometric Medallions On A Navy Field, Rust Border, 5 Ft. 11 In. x 2 Ft. 9 In. . . 275.00
Turkoman, Flatweave Ends, 3 Ft. 2 In. x 3 Ft. 7 In. 690.00
Ushak, Allover Large Herati, Midnight Blue Ground, Rose Border, 11 Ft. 8 In. x 11 Ft. . . 1380.00
Ushak, Early 20th Century, 9 Ft. 7 In. x 6 Ft. 11 In. 750.00
Ushak, Oval Medallion, Flowering Vines, Rose, Ivory Field, 13 Ft. 2 In. x 10 Ft. 4 In. . . . 11500.00
Ushak, Red Medallion & Script, Green Field, Red Border, 9 Ft. x 8 Ft. 2 In. 4675.00
Ushak, Small Diamond Medallion, Palmettes, Pale Rose Field, 14 Ft. x 7 Ft. 9 In. 575.00
Yarkand, Muted Orange, Brown & Pink, Border, 1930s, 11 Ft. 2 In. x 5 Ft. 9 In. 2200.00
Yomud, Ascending Branches, Ivory Field, Narrow Border, 1 Ft. 7 In. x 1 Ft. 4 In. 5175.00
Yomud, Ashik Lattice Guls, Dark Blue Green Serrated Border, 4 Ft. 6 In. x 3 Ft. 2990.00
Yomud, Serrated Zigzag Stripes, Midnight Blue, 1 Ft. 10 In. x 1 Ft. 4 In. 863.00
Yomud, Stylized Flowering Shrubs, 2 Camel Reserves, 1 Ft. 2 In. x 2 Ft. 8 In. 2645.00
Yomud, Stylized Kepse Guls, Walnut Field, Ivory Border, 6 Ft. 3 In. x 4 Ft. 6 In. 2530.00
Yomud, Torba, 2 Kepse Guls, Red, Midnight Blue, 1 Ft. 6 In. x 3 Ft. 5 In. 288.00

RUMRILL Pottery was designed by George Rumrill of Little Rock, Arkansas. From 1933 to 1938, it was produced by the Red Wing Pottery of Red Wing, Minnesota. In 1938, production was transferred to the Shawnee Pottery in Zanesville, Ohio. Production ceased in the 1940s.

RumRill

    Figurine, Athena, Nude, No. 576 . . . . 750.00
    Vase, Athena Nude, Suntan, No. 576 . . . . 1075.00
    Vase, Blue, 7 In. 35.00
    Vase, Pink & Aqua, Paper Label, 6 In. 35.00

RUSKIN is a British art pottery of the twentieth century. The Ruskin Pottery was started by William Howson Taylor, and his name was used as the mark until about 1899. The factory, at West Smethwick, Birmingham, England, stopped making new pieces in 1933 but continued to glaze and sell the remaining wares until 1935. The art pottery is noted for its exceptional glazes.

RUSKIN POTTERY WEST SMETHWICK

    Vase, Blue Iridescent, Marked, 1910, 8 3/4 In. 230.00
    Vase, Blue, Aubergine Glaze, Cylindrical, Marked, 1907, 8 3/4 In. 230.00
    Vase, Corseted, Medium Green Crystalline Glaze, Closed-In Rim, 8 x 4 1/4 In. 88.00
    Vase, Pale Blue Iridescent, Baluster, Impressed Mark, 1914, 9 1/4 In. 230.00

When restoring antiques or houses, take color pictures before and after for records of colors used, exact placement of decorative details, and insurance claims.

Russel Wright, Iroquois,
Plate, Advertising, 10 In.

RUSSEL WRIGHT designed dinnerwares in modern shapes for many companies. Iroquois China Company, Harker China Company, Steubenville Pottery, and Justin Tharaud and Sons made dishes marked *Russel Wright*. The Steubenville wares, first made in 1938, are the most common today. Wright was a designer of domestic and industrial wares, including furniture, aluminum, radios, interiors, and glassware. Dinnerwares and other pieces by Wright are listed here. For more information, see *Kovels' Depression Glass & Dinnerware Price List*.

American Modern, Celery Dish, Black, Chutney	30.00
American Modern, Celery Dish, Cantaloupe	35.00
American Modern, Chop Plate, Granite Gray	25.00
American Modern, Creamer, Coral	10.00
American Modern, Creamer, Seafoam	15.00
American Modern, Cup, Chartreuse, After Dinner	14.00
American Modern, Plate, Gray, 6 In.	3.00
American Modern, Plate, Gray, 10 In.	6.00
Casual, Bowl, Vegetable, Avocado, Yellow, 8 In.	25.00 to 35.00
Iroquois, Butter, Charcoal	145.00
Iroquois, Casserole, Cover, Avocado, Yellow, 4 Qt.	155.00
Iroquois, Casserole, Cover, Ice Blue, 4 Qt.	75.00
Iroquois, Plate, Advertising, 10 In.	*Illus* 85.00
Iroquois, Plate, Bread & Butter, Cantaloupe	25.00
Theme Formal, Cordial, 3 1/4 In., Pair	325.00
Theme Informal, Plate, Bread & Butter, Ember, 6 In.	85.00
Theme Informal, Plate, Dinner, Dune, 10 In.	195.00
Vase, Slanted Cylindrical Form, Textured Blue-Gray Glaze, c.1950, 10 1/4 In.	690.00

SABINO glass was made in the 1920s and 1930s in Paris, France. Founded by Marius-Ernest Sabino (1878–1961), the firm was noted for Art Deco lamps, vases, figurines, and animals in clear, colored, and opalescent glass. Production stopped during World War II but resumed in the 1960s with the manufacture of nude figurines and small opalescent glass animals. The new pieces are a slightly different color and can be recognized.

Bowl, Continuous Frieze Of Classical Maidens & Other Figures, Opalescent, 9 In.	1035.00
Dish, Cover, Band Of Molded Goldfish, Moths On Cover, Circular, 4 3/4 In.	115.00
Vase, Blue, White, 1969, 6 In.	595.00
Vase, Opalescent, Frosted, Signed, 6 3/4 In.	110.00
Vase, Overall Raised Flying Swallow, Bulbous Form, Signed, 15 1/2 In.	375.00
Vase, Smoky, Opalescent, Frosted, Signed, 5 3/4 In.	110.00

SALOPIAN ware was made by the Caughley factory of England during the eighteenth century. The early pieces were blue and white with some colored decorations. Another ware referred to as *Salopian* is a late nineteenth-century tableware decorated with color transfers.

Salopian

Creamer, Multicolored Floral & Foliate, 4 1/2 In.	440.00

Salopian, Cup & Saucer,
Milking Scene, Handleless

Salopian, Cup & Saucer, Robin,
Floral Vine, Handleless

Creamer, Multicolored Meadow Scene, Squat, 3 1/4 In. 440.00
Cup & Saucer, Milking Scene, Handleless . . . .*Illus* 358.00
Cup & Saucer, Multicolored Milking Scene, Handleless 355.00
Cup & Saucer, Robin, Floral Vine, Handleless . . . .*Illus* 248.00
Loving Cup, Allover Floral Design, 5 In. 143.00
Pitcher, Milk, Pearlware, Brown Oriental Transfer, 5 1/2 In. 300.00
Plate, Cottage & Castle Scene, Floral Border, 7 1/2 In. 300.00
Plate, Sheepherder, Scroll Border, 6 1/2 In. 355.00
Plate, Stag, Floral Border, Scalloped Edge, 7 1/4 In. 355.00
Waste Bowl, Milking Scene, Village, 6 In. 385.00

SALT AND PEPPER SHAKERS in matched sets were first used in the
nineteenth century. Collectors are primarily interested in figural examples made after World War I. *Huggers* are pairs of shakers that appear
to embrace each other. Many salt and pepper shakers are listed in other
categories and can be located through the index at the back of this
book.

Arizona, Indian Design, Gold Top, 3 In. 11.00
Art Deco, See Through, Celluloid, Red & Clear, Stand As 1 Unit, 1930s, 2 In. 20.00
Baseball Umpire, Angry Ball Player 48.00
Bear, Seated, Black & White, Composition, 1940s, 2 1/2 In. 15.00
Billiken 45.00
Black Boy & Dog, Huggers, Van Tellingen 90.00
Black Boy & Girl, Holding Ears Of Corn, Pottery, 3 In. 20.00
Black Clown Face 25.00
Blackamoor 78.00
Bonzo, White, Brown Paws, Pottery, Cork Stopper, Japan, 1930s, 3 In. 35.00
Boy & Girl, Folk Dress, Porcelain, Germany, 1930s, 3 In. 25.00
Boy & Girl, Yodeling, Ceramic, Gold Trim, 4 1/2 In. 22.00
Cactus In Pot, Porcelain, Golden Gate Expo., 1940 . . . . 35.00
Capt. John Smith & Pocahontas, Bust, Ceramic Masterpieces, 3 1/2 In. 25.00
Car, Model T, Box 35.00
Carmel, Fish Design, Vons, 1954, 2 1/2 In. 16.00
Cat In The Hat 75.00
Chalk Snakes, Souvenir Of Fargo, N.D., 2 1/8 In. 15.00
Chickens 75.00
Cities Service, 2 3/4 In. 110.00
Civil War Centennial, 1 With Shield, Other Confederate Flag, 1965, 2 1/2 In. 20.00
Cowboy, Vandor 10.00
Drum Set, Porcelain, Germany, 1920s 22.00
Empire State Building 30.00
Esso, Plastic, Katko's Service Station, New Brunswick, N.J., Box, 2 3/4 In. 72.00
Falstaff Beer, Paper Labels, 4 In. 20.00
Flying Saucer, 1950s 110.00
Golf Ball, White Plastic, Orange Tee, Box, 1940s 22.00
Greyhound Lines, Bus Shape, Metal, Die Cast, 1950s, 1 x 2 3/4 In. 58.00
Indian Couple, Bust, Costume, Ceramic, Japan, 1930s, 2 In. 22.00
Indian Man & Woman, Seated, Carved Wood, 1930s, 3 1/4 x 2 1/4 In. 35.00

Indian Mother With Child, Father, Carved Wood, Black Hills, S.D., 1947	30.00
Indian Squaw & Brave, Pottery, Jana, 1930s, 2 In.	22.00
Indian Squaw With Papoose, Brave Kneeling, 3 1/4 In.	25.00
Indian Squaw With Papoose On Back, Brave With Bow & Arrow, 4 In.	25.00
Joe, Camel, Plastic, c.1993	30.00
Kachina Doll, 1 Holding Real Feathers, 1940s, 4 In.	25.00
Kentucky Fried Chicken, Harland Sanders, Plastic, Canada, 4 1/4 In.	45.00
Kewpie, Thinker	45.00
Lady & Tramp	175.00
Leaping Deer, California	125.00
Letter S & P, Carved Wood, 1940s, 3 In.	9.00
Lord Nelson & His Lady, Bust Shape, Ceramic Masterpieces, 1940s, 3 1/2 In.	25.00
Monkey, Nodder	65.00
Mug Shape, State Of Michigan, Porcelain, 3 In.	8.00
Nipper, RCA, Porcelain, Lenox, 3 In.	33.00
Nude Woman, Bent Over Back, Rear Ends Form Top, 1951, 3 1/2 In.	25.00
Oriental Couple, Wooden, 4 1/4 In.	10.00
Penguin, Willie & Millie, Plastic, Kool Cigarettes, 3 1/2 In. . . . . .23.00 to 25.00
Phillips 66, Plastic, Box, 2 3/4 In.	45.00
Pillsbury Doughboy	15.00
Poodle	25.00
Potbelly Stove, Cast Iron, Square Base, 2 5/8 In.	22.00
Prayer Lady	20.00
Rabbit, Nodder	65.00
Raccoon, Holding Shakers, Flocked Plastic, DeeBeedbo Import, China, 5 3/4 In. . . . .*Illus*	10.00
RCA Victor, Nipper, Lenox	45.00
Robin Hood & Maid Marian, Bust, Don Winton, 1940s, 3 1/2 In.	20.00
Rooster, 1940s, 4 In.	9.00
Running Rabbit, California	25.00
Salty & Peppy	225.00
Sammy Seal, Metlox	75.00
Silver, Rose Pattern, Monogram On Base	143.00
Smokey Bear, Norcrest	45.00
Snail, Smiling, Porcelain, Red & Yellow, Bowties, 1 1/2 In.	11.00
Squirt, Glass, Box, 1950s	18.00
Teepee & Indian Figure, Pottery, 1940s, 4 & 2 1/2 In.	19.00
Totem Pole, 2 1/2 In.	7.00
Uncle Mose & Aunt Jemima, F & F	75.00
Vase, Porcelain, Hand Painted, Japan, 1920	22.00
Vase, Push Top, Mechanical, Maroon Bakelite, Art Deco, 1930s, 2 1/4 In.	35.00
Washboard, Tub With Suds	85.00
Wine Bottle, Raffia Cover, Pasticceria, A. Egidi & Figli, 3 1/2 In.	15.00
Wine Bottle, Straw Covering, Golden Gate Int. Expo, 1939, 3 1/8 In.	25.00
Yellow Bunny, Huggers, Van Tellingen	24.00
Ziggy	35.00

**Metal saltshaker tops can be kept from
rusting or oxidizing if they are cleaned
or sprayed with a silicone product.
Wax will also help. Add raw rice or a
few dried beans to the salt in an old
saltshaker. It will help absorb moisture
and keep the salt pouring.**

Salt & Pepper, Raccoon, Holding
Shakers, Flocked Plastic, DeeBeedbo
Import, China, 5 3/4 In.

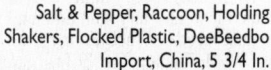

SALT GLAZE has a grayish white surface with a texture like an orange peel. It is a method of decoration that has been used since the eighteenth century. Salt-glazed pieces are still being made.

Canister, Lid, Diamond Point, Blue Maple Leaf, 7 1/4 x 8 In.	165.00
Cooler, Cobalt Blue Embossed Floral, Gray Glaze, 4 Gal.	135.00
Cooler, Dancing Elves & Vines, Female Goddess Opposite, 14 In.	825.00
Crock, Butterfly, 20 Gal.	270.00
Crock, Cobalt Blue Design, 11 In.	275.00
Crock, D. Roberts & Co. Utica., Cobalt Blue Flower, Tan & Gray Glaze, 8 In.	258.00
Crock, Pickle, Blue Bands Top & Bottom, H.J. Heinz Co., 5 1/2 In.	275.00
Figurine, Rat & Snake Around Egg, Tree, Pottery, No. 128, White, 1962, 3 3/4 In.	50.00
Jug, Batter, Cobalt Blue Design Around Spout, 9 In.	220.00
Jug, Bellarmine, Bearded Mask On Neck, Twisted Loop Handle, 11 1/2 In.	8625.00
Jug, Cobalt Lettering, Monmouth Pottery Co., Monmouth, Ills., Tan Glaze, 10 1/2 In.	45.00
Jug, Deep Rim, Strap Handle Over Shoulder, Bird On Branch, Number 5, 18 1/2 In.	1380.00
Jug, Molasses	30.00
Mug, Tooled Accent Lines, Rochester Brew Co., Barrel Shape, 5 In.	175.00
Pilsner, Tooled Lines, Blue, Haberle's Lager, 7 In.	385.00
Pitcher, Blue Shield Design, 9 In.	120.00
Pitcher, Cobalt Floral, 12 1/4 In., 1 1/2 Gal.	55.00
Pitcher, Dutch Boy & Girl, Kissing, Blue & White, c.1890, 6 3/4 In.	77.00
Pitcher, Molded, Cat-O'-Nine-Tails, England, 9 1/2 In.	105.00
Pitcher, Picture Around, Spout, Flared Lip, 1900, 3 1/2 In.	95.00
Pitcher, Tulips, 9 5/8 In.	75.00
Pot, Boston The Home Of The Bean Pot, Spirit Of 76 Bunker Hill, Blue & White, 7 In.	110.00
Salt, Lid, Hanging, Blue Swirl, c.1880, 6 In.	385.00
Sauceboat, Crabstock Handle, Star & Trellis Pattern	60.00
Sauceboat, Footed, Cobalt Highlights, Staffordshire	545.00
Sauceboat, Rococo	517.00
Stein, Pewter Lid, Female Profile One Side, Verse Opposite Side, 7 1/2 In.	330.00
Stein, Pewter Lid, Gargoyle Thumb Lift, Drinking Scene 1 Side, Verse Other, 13 1/2 In.	385.00
Teapot, Acorn Finial Cover, Floral, White Ground, Hanley, 8 1/2 In.	275.00
Teapot, Landskip	8050.00
Water Cooler, Single P, 4 Gal.	65.00

SAMPLERS were made in America from the early 1700s. The best examples were made from 1790 to 1840. Long, narrow samplers are usually older than square ones. Early samplers just had stitching or alphabets. The later examples had numerals, borders, and pictorial decorations. Those with mottoes are mid-Victorian. A revival of interest in the 1930s produced simpler samplers, usually with mottoes.

ABCDE

Adam & Eve Under Tree, Elizabeth Watson, 9th Year, 1815, 16 1/2 x 16 1/4 In.	2587.00
Alphabet, Birds, Bajamina Stroink, Aged 11, 1835, Frame, 17 1/2 x 15 3/4 In.	965.00
Alphabet, Flower Border, Ann Shaw Aged 12 Years 1833, Frame, 13 1/4 x 13 5/8 In.	522.00
Alphabet, Initials, Crowns, Agnes Douglas, Maple Frame, 19th Century, 9 x 8 In.	286.00
Alphabet, Maria W. Baldwin Shrewsbury, 1830, Frame, 9 x 13 In.	373.00
Alphabet, Mary W. Holmes, Walpole, N.H., August 8, 1802, Frame, 9 x 16 In.	1100.00
Alphabet, Numbers, 12 Herbs Listed, Plants, Red On White Ground, 1822, 10 x 16 In.	190.00
Alphabet, Numbers, Biblical Passages, Sary Love, July 3, 1734, 13 x 7 12 In.	287.00
Alphabet, Numbers, Mary Anne Wardeen Marcellus, 9 Years, September 5, 1817, 12 In.	230.00
Alphabet, Numbers, Multicolored, Appliqued N.J. Initials, Frame, 6 x 5 1/4 In.	275.00
Alphabet, Sarah Pales, 1783, Bristol, New England, 10 x 13 In. *Illus*	25300.00
Alphabets, 2 Groups Numbers, 16 1/2 x 10 In.	145.00
Alphabets, Ann Gibbs, Her Sampler, Silk On Linen Homespun, Frame, 15 x 15 In.	1100.00
Alphabets, Basket Of Flowers, Mariah Yates & Lisa B. Sherman, 1827, 17 x 16 In.	517.00
Alphabets, Bird, Fruit, Geometric Floral Border, Juliaett Ballad, Aged 11, 1833, Frame	1840.00
Alphabets, Birds, Blue, Salmon, Brown, Black, Frame, 9 3/8 x 22 3/4 In.	220.00
Alphabets, Birds, Ship, 1834, Silk On Linen, Frame, 19 x 20 1/4 In.	895.00
Alphabets, Catherine Farquaar, March 31st, 1836, Frame, 25 x 20 1/4 In.	550.00
Alphabets, Couple, Holding Hands, Flowers, Mary Ann Shaner, Frame, 13 x 23 In.	275.00
Alphabets, Deer, Flowers, F. Caymer, Aged 9, Wool, Frame, 14 x 13 In.	220.00
Alphabets, Elizabeth Kline, 1840, Wool, Frame, 17 x 17 In.	300.00

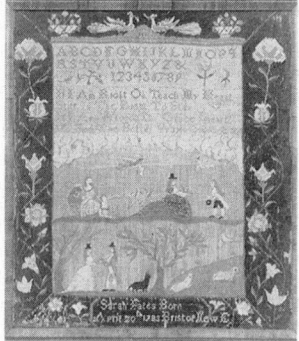

There are many old books about the care of antiques. These sometimes give false information because the products suggested have been changed. Ivory Snow was a pure soap recommended for washing vintage fabrics. It was reformulated in 1993 and is now a detergent, which is not safe for all fabrics.

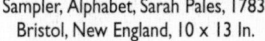

Sampler, Alphabet, Sarah Pales, 1783,
Bristol, New England, 10 x 13 In.

Alphabets, Flowers, Dog, Goose, Wool On Cotton Canvas, 1888, Gilt Frame 275.00
Alphabets, Flowers, Sarah Eliza Baker, 1840, Linen Homespun, Frame, 12 x 77 In. 415.00
Alphabets, Flowers, Susannah Fagan, 13 Years, 1833, Homespun, Frame, 16 x 25 In. 475.00
Alphabets, Flowers, Turkey, Dog, Multicolored, Petit Point, Maria Doltl, 1842 . . . . 440.00
Alphabets, Hannah Campaion Aged 10 Years, 1826, Linen, Frame, 18 x 18 In. 580.00
Alphabets, Huldah F. Hopkins, 8th Year Of Age, July, 1812, Frame, 18 x 13 In. 513.00
Alphabets, Jean Campbell, Aged 13, 1808, Silk On Linen, Frame, 20 x 12 In. 935.00
Alphabets, Marion Steele Aged 10, Silk On Linen, Frame, 17 3/4 x 15 5/8 In. 685.00
Alphabets, Minerva Root, Year Of Our Lord 1817, Silk On Linen, Frame, 15 x 23 In. 460.00
Alphabets, Numbers, Commandment, Rachel Park, Aged 8 Years, 1823, 16 x 13 In. 605.00
Alphabets, Numbers, Dog, Flowers, Josephine Guerdras, 1845, Silk On Linen, 7 x 18 In. . 310.00
Alphabets, Red House, Trees, Pious Verse, A. Heney, 1836, 17 3/4 x 18 In. 1150.00
Alphabets, Relief, Shumway/Hardwick, July 20, 1822, Aged 10, Mass., 16 x 16 In. 9775.00
Alphabets, Stars, Stag, Floral, Susanna Miller, 1814, Linen & Homespun, Frame, 20 In. . . 935.00
Alphabets, Trees, Dogs, Catherine Cruickshank, Needlepoint, Frame, 21 x 21 In. 577.00
Alphabets, Verse, Flowers, Jennie Lowes Loretto Convent, 1854, Frame, 22 x 22 In. 290.00
Alphabets, Verse, Mary Elizabeth Beary, Aged 8 Years, Silk On Linen, 20 x 20 In. 440.00
Ann Shaw Aged 12 Years, 1833, Silk On Linen, Frame, 13 1/4 x 13 5/8 In. 522.00
Basket Of Flowers, Mary Jane Va...., August 23rd, 1833, Silk On Linen, 17 x 18 In. 515.00
Baskets, Trailing Vines, Sloop, Margaret Aiken, 1837, Silk On Linen, 17 x 12 1/2 In. 770.00
Boy & Girl, Augusta Marsh, Wrought In 17th Year, 1822, 16 1/4 x 16 3/4 In. 4312.00
Caroline Galbraith's, Nov. 22nd, 1814, 9th Year, Silk On Linen, Frame, 15 x 13 In. 1595.00
Content Pickette Her Sampler, Frame, 1798, 8 1/4 x 8 1/4 In. 400.00
Duck & Rooster, Hannah Greenwood, Aged 12, May 1803, Frame, 12 1/4 x 10 In. 1450.00
Elizabeth Eldridge's, July 1837, Aged 12 Years, Frame, 16 1/2 x 16 1/2 In. 1155.00
Elizabeth Sherman, Aged 12, 1822, Floral, Verse, Silk On Linen, Frame, 9 x 17 In. 220.00
Eunice Eddy, Mrs. Simmons School In Providence, Aged 12, Frame, 7 x 17 In. 747.00
Family Register, Willow Tree, Urn, Hearts, Flowers, Scalloped Border, 16 x 16 1/4 In. . . . 1380.00
Flowers, Verse, Martha L. Larsons, 1825, Frame, 12 x 12 In. 748.00
Flowers & Church, Strawberry Border, Mary Miles, Silk On Linen, 25 x 9 In. 220.00
Fruit & Flower, Crewel, Hannah Ann Semans, 1822, Gilt Frame, 20 1/2 x 16 3/4 In. 4950.00
Geometric Plants, Birds, Deer, Berry, Vines, Ribbon Binding, England, 13 x 11 In. 350.00
Girl, Boat & Cabin, MAM 1838, Wool On Linen, Frame, 22 x 22 1/4 In. 245.00
Hannah Susannah Robenson, Born Sept. 11, 1826, 5 Births, Frame, 18 x 21 In. 4400.00
House, Mary Crosby, Born Year 1793, Silk On Linen Homespun, Frame, 15 x 14 In. 1925.00
I. Maks, 1817, Strawberry Border, Bird's-Eye Maple Frame, 19 1/4 x 20 1/4 In. 880.00
Mary Harrison, Age 13, 1818, Faith, Hope & Charity, Frame, 21 1/2 x 21 1/2 In. 2035.00
Orphan Asylum School Of Industry, Brown, Red, Green, Wrigglework Border, 5 In. 1725.00
Patterns & Verse, Henrietta Stevens, 1788, 18 x 15 In. 1485.00
Philadelphia Bold Letters, Christianna Barger, 18th Year, 1831, 21 x 21 In. 1380.00
Pious Verse, Adam & Eve, Trumpeting Angels, Geometric Floral Border, 13 x 9 In. 862.00
Pious Verse, Angels, Elizabeth Parker, April 19, Anno Domini, 1746, Frame, 16 x 12 In. . 1265.00
Pious Verse, Animal Scene, Geometric Floral Border, Martha James, Aged 11, Frame 517.00

Pious Verse, Rebecca Elizabeth Loomer, October 8, 1834, Married 1858, 21 x 19 In. 2300.00
Roses & Lyre, Elizabeth R. Thomas, November, 1829, 22 1/2 x 24 In. 675.00
Stylized Flowers, Birds, House, Vining Strawberry Border, 18 x 13 3/4 In. 300.00
Stylized Flowers, Mary White, Aged 9 Years, Silk On Homespun, Frame, 14 x 13 In. 495.00
Stylized Flowers, Tree, Verse, Margaret Evans, 1841, Linen, Frame, 21 x 17 In. 905.00
Stylized Flowers & Border, Jane Inglis 1817, 10 x 12 In. 522.00
Verse, 10 Commandments, John Field & Dianna Married June 1799, 19 x 22 In. 775.00
Verse, Gold Thread, Susannah Adams, Aged 14, Middlesex County, Frame, 17 x 16 In. .. 535.00
Verse, Hester Lewis Griffiths, 1825, Floral Border, Silk On Linen, 20 3/4 x 12 1/2 In. 1430.00
Verse, House, Catherine Elizabeth Allison, 13 Years, 1840, Silk, Frame, 17 3/8 In. 1412.00
Verse, Mary Ann Holmes Lincoln, 1819, Linen, 19 3/4 x 14 3/4 In. 605.00
Verses, Bowl Of Strawberries, Celestia Mary Combs, 1816, 21 x 16 In. 2090.00
View Of Grand Suspension Bridge, Wales, Anne Jones, 1839, 16 5/8 x 24 1/2 In. 920.00

SAMSON and Company, a French firm specializing in the reproduction of collectible wares of many countries and periods, was founded in Paris in the early nineteenth century. Chelsea, Meissen, Famille Verte, and Chinese Export porcelain are some of the wares that have been reproduced by the company. The firm uses a variety of marks on the reproductions. It is still in operation.

Basket, United States Eagle, Reticulated, Oval, 18th Century, 10 7/8 In. 550.00
Bowl, Armorial, Lobed, Chinese Export Style, 18th Century, 1890, 8 1/4 In., Pair 412.00
Bowl, Fruit, Armorial, Oval, 1895-1900, 3 1/8 x 10 1/4 In. 151.00
Charger, Heraldic Crest Design, Porcelain, 12 1/2 In. 65.00
Dish, Polychrome Ormolu Design, Scalloped Edge, Oval, 5 1/2 In. 240.00
Figurine, Shepherd & Shepherdess, 8 1/2 In., Pair 747.00
Flowerpot, Pink, Purple Hyacinth, Growing In Tall Vase, Exotic Birds, 10 In., Pair 690.00
Jar, Phoenix, Floral & Dragon, Famille Rose, Mounted As Lamp, 14 In. 575.00
Jug, Cover, Curved Stalk Handle, Molded Leaves, Green, Yellow Fruit, 5 In., Pair 3737.00
Plate, Figural Design, Ruby Back, Famille Rose, 19th Century, 9 1/2 In. 375.00
Urn, Colorful Peacocks, Campana Form, Blue Fish Scale Ground, 13 In., Pair 1840.00
Vase, Kakeimon Style, Signed, 9 1/2 In., Pair 1610.00

SAND BABIES were used as decorations on a line of children's dishes made by the Royal Bayreuth China Company. The children are playing at the seaside. Collectors use the names *Sand Babies* and *Beach Babies* interchangeably.

Creamer, Blue Mark, 3 x 4 1/2 In. 295.00

SANDWICH GLASS is any of the myriad types of glass made by the Boston and Sandwich Glass Works in Sandwich, Massachusetts, between 1825 and 1888. It is often very difficult to be sure whether a piece was really made at the Sandwich factory because so many types were made there and similar pieces were made at other glass factories. Additional pieces may be listed under Pressed Glass and in related categories.

Bowl, Geometric Design, Alternating Arms With Scrolls, 1830, 9 In. 440.00
Bowl, Gothic Arch, Inset Domed Cover, Opalescent, Octagonal, 1860, 5 In. 1210.00
Bowl, Peacock Feather & Diamond, Rectangular, 1845, 8 x 10 1/2 x 2 In. 880.00
Bowl, Tulip, Acanthus Leaf Base, 10 1/2 In. 198.00
Candlestick, Canary Yellow, 7 1/2 In. 100.00
Candlestick, Crucifix, Amethyst, 11 1/2 In. 220.00
Candlestick, Dolphin, Blue & White, 9 3/4 In. 690.00
Candlestick, Dolphin, Canary, Pair, 1 1/4 In. 1100.00
Candlestick, Loop, Canary, 7 In., Pair 330.00
Celery Vase, Chrysanthemum Leaf, Gold Trim 65.00
Compote, Roman Rosette, Scalloped Edge, Pedestal Base, 6 x 3 In. 523.00
Compote, Stylized Cornucopia, Circles & Diamonds, Foliate Base, 8 1/2 In. 880.00
Compote, Tulip, Flared, 7 1/2 x 4 3/4 In. 413.00
Creamer, Heart & Scale, 4 1/2 In. 40.00
Dish, Gothic Arch, Large Diamond In Center, Scalloped Edge, Cobalt Blue 5500.00
Dish, Sawtooth Edge, 4-Point Star Center, Amethyst, 1840, 9 3/8 In. 7425.00
Epergne, Applied Blue Glass Rim, 11 1/2 In. 144.00

Ewer, White Body, Ribbed Camphored Handle, Ruffled Edge, 10 1/2 In. 25.00
Lamp, Blackberry, Brilliant Blue, c.1895, 10 In. 475.00
Lamp, Diamond Point, 10 In. 121.00
Lamp, White Overlay Font, Blue Stem, Marble Base, c.1870 . . . . 1500.00
Perfume Bottle, Canary, 19th Century, 8 In. 340.00
Plate, Acorn & Oak, Opalescent, 6 In. 248.00
Plate, Eagle, Leafy Border, Octagonal, 1845, 6 In. 88.00
Plate, Pine Tree & Shield, Pointed Scalloped Edge, 6 In. 110.00
Plate, Roman Rosette, Golden Amber, Scalloped Edge, 5 5/8 In. 358.00
Salt, Boat Shape, Footed, Gold Amber 140.00
Salt, Lacy, Blue 935.00
Salt, Lafayette, Boat Shape, Blue 1650.00
Salt, Loop, 6-Sided, Amethyst, 1835-1865, 3 1/4 In. 100.00
Salt, Loop, 6-Sided, Cobalt Blue, 1835-1865, 3 1/8 In. 100.00
Smoke Bell, Milk Glass, Blue Rim Ruffle, Pontil, 4 1/2 In. 110.00
Smoke Bell, Milk Glass, Blue Rim, Ruffled, Pontil, 6 1/2 In. 220.00
Smoke Bell, Milk Glass, Brown Red Rim Ruffle, Pontil, 7 In. 45.00
Smoke Bell, Milk Glass, Floral Tooled Rim, 3 1/4 In. 230.00
Smoke Bell, Milk Glass, Red Rim Ruffle, 3 3/4 In. 90.00
Sugar, Cover, Opalescent, 4 1/4 In. 140.00
Syrup, Gooseberry, White 110.00
Vase, Tulip, Green, 9 1/2 In. 290.00

SARREGUEMINES is the name of a French town that is used as part of a china mark. Utzschneider and Company, a porcelain factory, made ceramics in Sarreguemines, Lorraine, France, from about 1775. Transfer-printed wares and majolica were made in the nineteenth century. The nineteenth-century pieces, most often found today, usually have colorful transfer-printed decorations showing peasants in local costumes.

Ewer, Striated Ground, Round Crystals, Signed, 11 7/8 In. 330.00
Jug, Scotsman, No. 3210 . . . .   165.00
Pitcher, Man With Toothache 225.00
Pitcher, Ugly Man's Head Shape, Blue Interior, 7 In. 275.00
Plate, Fruit, Majolica, 7 1/2 In. 375.00
Platter, Sarc Pattern, Rectangular, 14 1/2 In. 150.00
Vase, Lily Design, Yellow Stems, Brown Ground, Marked, 17 In. 275.00

SASCHA BRASTOFF made decorative accessories, ceramics, enamels on copper, and plastics of his own design. He headed a factory, Sascha Brastoff of California; Inc., in West Los Angeles, from 1953 until about 1973. He died in 1993. Pieces signed with the signature *Sascha Brastoff* were his work and are the most expensive. Other pieces marked *Sascha B.* or with a stamped mark were made by others in his company. Pieces made by Matt Adams after he left the factory are listed here with his name.

Ashtray, Alaska, 10 In. 45.00
Ashtray, Jewel Bird, Gray, Gold, Black, 7 In. . . . . .35.00 to 65.00
Ashtray, Roof Tops, Square, 7 1/2 In. 75.00
Ashtray, Star Steed, 6 In. 65.00
Ashtray, Star Steed, Horse, Gray Ground, Pink, White, Gold, Signed, 8 5/8 In. 80.00
Basket, Jewel Bird, Oval, 19 In. 195.00
Bowl, Americana, 5 1/2 In. 50.00
Charger, Fruit Still Life, Yellow Background, Signed, Sascha Brastoff, 22 In. 173.00
Cigarette Holder, Leaves, White Ground 32.00
Cigarette Lighter, Leaves, Table Style 60.00
Dish, Enameled Flowers, Footed 35.00
Figurine, Seal, Red 150.00
Plate, Blue Grapes, Pink Spatter On Brown, 10 In. 30.00
Teapot, Surf Ballet, Pink, Gold 140.00
Vase, Fish, Grays, 9 1/2 In. 185.00
Vase, Horse Painted Underglaze, Signed, 8 1/2 In. 250.00
Vase, Jewel Bird, 10 In. 75.00

SATIN GLASS is a late nineteenth-century art glass. It has a dull finish that is caused by hydrofluoric acid vapor treatment. Satin glass was made in many colors and sometimes has applied decorations. Satin glass is also listed by factory name, such as Webb, or in the Mother-of-Pearl category in this book.

Basket, Diamond-Quilted, Yellow, Pink Interior, Branch Handle, 10 x 8 1/2 In.	195.00
Basket, White, Pink Overlay, Applied Clear Glass Handle & Feet, c.1890, 12 In.	385.00
Bowl, Ruffled Edge, 6 In.	33.00
Cracker Jar, Enameled Orchids, Silver Plated Lid	195.00
Pitcher, Leaves & Roping, White Interior	275.00
Rose Bowl, Blue	135.00
Rose Bowl, Blue Stripes, Pinched Sides, Crimped Top, 3 5/8 In.	165.00
Rose Bowl, Pink, White Interior, 4 In.	45.00
Rose Bowl, Yellow	115.00
Tumbler, Diamond-Quilted, Pink	95.00
Vase, Bird, Perched On Branch, Pink To Amber Satin, Milk Glass Handles, 11 In.	345.00
Vase, Crimped Rim, Green & Amber Applied Floral Spray, 1885, 6 1/2 In.	220.00
Vase, Hobnail, Inverted Rim, White Liner, Mother-Of-Pearl, 1885, 5 1/2 In.	88.00

SATSUMA is a Japanese pottery with a distinctive creamy beige crackled glaze. Most of the pieces were decorated with blue, red, green, orange, or gold. Almost all Satsuma found today was made after 1860. During World War I, Americans could not buy undecorated European porcelains. Women who liked to make hand painted porcelains at home began to decorate plain Satsuma. These pieces are known today as *American Satsuma*.

Basket, Flower & Maple Leaf, Moon Shape, 4 In.	60.00
Basket, Samurai & Lohan, Signed, 3 1/4 In.	108.00
Bowl, Chrysanthemum & Floral, 3 x 8 In.	250.00
Bowl, Reserve Of Buddhist Saints, Foliate Shape, Brocade Borders, 5 1/2 In.	58.00
Bowl, Scenes From Life, Swirling Butterflies On Bottom Interior, Footed, 4 In.	1610.00
Box, Cover, People In A Garden On 1 Panel, Gold, Cobalt Blue Ground, 4 In.	1265.00
Box, Seven Happy Gods On Lid, Interior Symbols, Signed, 19th Century	185.00
Charger, Winter Scene, Gold, Meiji Period	675.00
Ewer, Black Dragon, Red Accents, Smoke Swirls, 10 1/2 x 13 In.	400.00
Incense Burner, Koro, Footed, Reticulated Cover	1900.00
Jar, Cover, Figures In Landscape, Juroku, 7 In.	173.00
Jar, Cover, Molded Phoenixes On Shoulder, Children Seated On Cover	345.00
Jar, Geese, Peony Flowers, Goldfish In Pond Under Wisteria Vine, Gilt, 10 x 9 In.	144.00
Jar, Potpourri, Enameled Scenes, Figures, 3 3/4 In.	192.00
Tea Caddy, Cover, Chrysanthemums, Butterflies Interior Cover, Hexagonal, 4 In.	980.00
Tea Dish, Cha-Ire, Brown, Ivory Cover, Loop Handles At Shoulder, 3 3/8 In.	755.00
Tea Set, Bamboo, Birds, Gilt Bamboo Handles, 7 Piece	60.00
Tea Set, Wisteria, Signed, Box, 21 Piece	515.00
Teapot, Garden Scene, Gold Flowers, Blue Ground, Diamond Shape, 4 In.	690.00
Urn, Cover, Pastel Enameled Scenes, Flowers & Butterflies, Dog Finial, 18 3/4 In.	82.00
Urn, Domed Cover, Lohan, Foo Lion Finial, 14 1/2 In.	540.00
Urn, Pagoda & Mountains Side, 8 Figures Other Side, Foo Dog Handles, 36 1/2 In.	1760.00
Vase, 1000 Face Design, Gilt Highlights, Multicolored Enamels, 7 3/8 In., Pair	690.00
Vase, 4 Figural Scenes, Gold Beading, Square, 9 1/2 In., Pair	575.00
Vase, Allover Gold Flowers, Leaves, Brocade, Cobalt Blue Ground, 9 1/2 In.	1610.00
Vase, Beauties & Attendant Young Girls Under Blooming Wisteria, 8 In.	230.00
Vase, Boating Scene, Baluster Form, Loop Handles, 3 1/2 In.	60.00
Vase, Butterflies & Dogwood Flowers, Meiji Period, 18 1/4 In.	120.00
Vase, Children, In A Landscape Scene, Raised Gold, 14 3/4 In.	175.00
Vase, Dragon, Green Ground, 2 Handles, 16 3/4 In.	275.00
Vase, Enameled & Gilt Flower & Figures, Meiji Period, 37 In.	2645.00
Vase, Enameled, Applied Bale, Tied String Design, Meiji Period, 34 1/2 In.	316.00
Vase, Feathers, Outlined In Gold Beads, c.1915, 15 In.	125.00
Vase, Figures In Coastal Village, 20th Century, 12 1/2 In., Pair	200.00
Vase, Figures, Gilt Design, Meiji Period, 9 1/2 In.	70.00
Vase, Floral, Reticulated Neck & Mouth, Dolphin Handles, 16 1/4 In.	290.00

Vase, Maiden Riding A Dragon, Gold, Green, Red Beading, 12 1/2 In., Pair 200.00
Vase, Ornate Banquet Scene, Fan Shape Medallions, Brocade Green Ground, 6 In. 2875.00
Vase, Portrait, Kwannon, 1915, 16 In. 300.00
Vase, Portrait, Rakans, Paradise, c.1915, 15 In. 300.00
Vase, Relief Dragon Spiraling Around Vase, Brocade Borders, Gold, 17 1/2 In. 1090.00
Vase, Shogun Warriors, Gilt Halos, Blue & Brown Ground, Pedestal, 11 3/4 x 9 In. 225.00
Vase, Tea Ceremony, Children, Brocades, Flared Neck, Foot, 5 3/4 In. 3795.00
Vase, Thousand Faces, Raised Gold Dragons, Handles, 6 3/4 & 5 1/2 In. 230.00
Vase, White Flowers, Textured Branches, Black Matte Ground, 16 In. 275.00
Vase, Woman, Allover Design, 10 In., Pair 625.00

SATURDAY EVENING GIRLS, see Paul Revere Pottery category.

SCALES have been made to weigh everything from babies to gold. Collectors search for all types. Most popular are small gold dust scales and special grocery scales.

  Analytic, Weight-Balance, Voland & Sons, Mahogany & Glass, 17 1/2 x 16 1/2 In. 203.00
  Apothecary, Henry Troemner, Mahogany & Glass Case 288.00
  Apothecary, Randolph Co., Dr. C.H. Fitch's, Richmond, Va., Case, 1885, 3 In. 185.00
  Balance, Brass Column, Drawer In Wooden Base, H. Kohibusch, 20 1/2 x 10 1/4 In. . .   65.00
  Balance, Cast Iron & Brass, Weighs To 7 Lbs., 32 In. 192.00
  Balance, Double, Stepped Marble Base, 22 In. 93.00
  Balance, H. Troemner, Philadelphia, Oak, Pink & Gray Marble Top, Brass Pans, 19 In. . . .   325.00
  Balance, Henry Troemner, Brass Pans, Cast Iron Base, 19 1/2 In. 165.00
  Balance, Henry Troemner, Weights, Bone Handle, Release Lever, Base Drawer, 9 1/4 In. .   192.00
  Balance, Oak Base, Set Of Weights, Brass, 10 3/4 In. 137.00
  Balance, Pelouze, 6 Brass Weights 65.00
  Balance, W. & T. Avery, Iron Balance Beam, Brass Pans, Oval Tin Box, 3 5/8 x 6 1/8 In. .   145.00
  Candy, IBM, Brass Trim, 5 Lb. 225.00
  Chicken, Iron, With Weight, 1900 . . . .   40.00
  Coin-Operated, Issues Tickets With Movie Star's Picture 1800.00
  Counter, White Daisies Around Porcelain Face, Iron 130.00
  Counterfeit Coin, Allender, Measures Weight & Thickness, Brass 300.00
  Double Pan, Brass, Marble Encased, c.1875, 8 1/2 x 24 1/2 In. 390.00
  Double Pan, White Marble & Brass, Fruitwood, Parcel Guilt, c.1875, 5 1/2 x 18 1/2 In. . .   300.00
  Drugstore, Watling, Set Of Keys, Mirrored Front, Enameled Red Base 700.00
  Fairbanks, Doctor's, Height Measure, Brass & Nickel Plated, 58 1/2 In. 412.00
  Medical, Traveling 300.00
  Micrometer, Dodge Mfg. Co., Yonkers, N.Y. 285.00
  Pocket, Daube & Hepken, Mahogany Case, 6 1/4 x 3 In. 93.00
  Postage, Rexall 14.00
  Postal, Brass, U.S. Scale, Patent 1877, North Brothers 190.00
  Postal, Pitney Bowes, To 16 Oz., 1957 . . . .   45.00
  Postal, Salter & Company, Iron, Brass 79.00
  Produce, Computing Scale Co., Dayton, Ohio, Cast Iron, Tin, Glass, c.1905, 18 x 31 In. . .   120.00
  Spring, Chatillons, Iron, Brass Front, 19 In. 16.00
  Steelyard, For Weighing Cotton, Solid Brass, Early 20th Century 350.00
  Traveling, Brass, Embossed Eagle On Leather-Bound Fitted Case, 6 7/8 x 3 1/8 In. 60.00
  Weighing, American Family, Metal, Black Paint, Gold Scroll Designs, Up To 24 Lbs. 20.00
  Weighing, Fairbank, Iron, Weights, Late 1800s 75.00
  Weighing, Turnbull's, Cast Iron, Pat. July 24th, 1877, 8 x 7 In. 250.00

SCHAFER & VATER, makers of small ceramic items, are best known for their amusing figurals. The factory was located in Volkstedt-Rudolstadt, Germany, from 1890 to 1962. Some pieces are marked with the crown and R mark, but many are unmarked.

  Ashtray, Googly-Eyed Dog 125.00
  Bottle, Bowling Man, 5 1/4 In. 150.00
  Bottle, Dr. Health, Pain Expeller, 4 1/4 In. 175.00
  Bottle, Drinkometer, Blue, 5 3/4 In. 150.00
  Bottle, Dutch Girl With Bottle, Green, Porcelain, Stopper, 8 In. 440.00
  Bottle, Gold-Water, Prospector, 6 1/2 In. 160.00
  Bottle, In The Bar, Brown, 8 In. 225.00

Bottle, Just A Little Nip, Bulldog Biting Woman's Leg, 4 3/4 In. 185.00
Bottle, Life Saver, Life Preserver, Blue ....250.00 to 385.00
Bottle, Man With Bowling Balls, Stopper, 6 1/4 In. 400.00
Bottle, Mr. Cocktail, Rooster, No. 2596, 8 1/4 In. 265.00
Bottle, Now You Pull One 350.00
Bottle, One Of The Boys, 6 3/4 In. 175.00
Bottle, Present For You, Hand Holding Woman, No. 9410, 6 In. 300.00
Bottle, Present From The Isle Of Man, 3-Legged Man, 7 1/2 In. 255.00
Bottle, Santa 238.00
Bottle, Scotch Boy, Never Drink Water ....85.00 to 90.00
Bottle, What A Night, 5 1/4 In. 160.00
Bottle, Whiskered Man, Drinkometer Motto On Back, Blue & White, 7 In. 145.00
Creamer, Figural, Dutch Girl, Basket On Back, Signed, 4 1/4 In. 165.00
Creamer, Pig 135.00
Creamer, Red Devil Riding Donkey, 4 1/2 In. 175.00
Cup & Saucer, Jeweled, Female Head Looking Right 145.00
Figurine, Baby In Chair, 3 1/2 In. 160.00
Figurine, Ballerina, 5 1/2 In. 205.00
Figurine, Black Cat With Red Bow, No. 7029, 5 3/4 In. 160.00
Figurine, Cassandra, Paul & Puppy, 3 3/4 In. 205.00
Figurine, Castle Walk, Couple Dancing, 5 1/2 In. 242.00
Figurine, Don't Tell Anyone, Boy Whispering To Girl, No. 8055, 3 7/8 In. 175.00
Figurine, Grizzly Bear, Cowboy & Woman Dancing, No. 9870, 6 In. 220.00
Figurine, Jester With Cymbals, 4 3/4 In. 115.00
Figurine, Lady With Fancy Hat, 4 1/2 In. 310.00
Figurine, Little Red Riding Hood With Wolf, 5 In. 125.00
Figurine, Man, Smoking Pipe 525.00
Figurine, Miss Proper Lady, No. 1094, 4 7/8 In. 160.00
Figurine, Mr. Adam, 7 1/2 In. 322.00
Figurine, Plantadge & Puppy, With Hat, 3 In. 140.00
Figurine, Plantadge & Puppy, Without Hat, 3 1/8 In. 205.00
Figurine, Tango, Couple Dancing, No. 9271, 6 In. 195.00
Hair Receiver, Cupids Playing Instruments, Bird Nest, White On Green 445.00
Match Holder, Gentleman Goose, No. 22, 6 1/4 In. 185.00
Match Holder, Gentleman With Flower, 5 In. 310.00
Match Holder, Hand It Over, Man With Oversized Hand, 3 1/2 In. 265.00
Match Holder, Nodder, Hookums, 4 1/4 In. 335.00
Match Holder, Nodder, Hungry Monk, No. 8080, 4 1/4 In. 460.00
Match Holder, Sailor & Woman, 3 In. 160.00
Match Holder, Smiling Boy With Happy Face Feet, No. 8198, 3 1/4 In. 185.00
Match Holder, Smiling Man, 3 1/4 In. 205.00
Match Holder, Strike, Cats, Don't Strike Me, Strike Mother, 3 3/4 In. 310.00
Match Holder, Strike, Rugby Player, 3 1/2 In. 265.00
Match Holder, Strike, Turkey, Don't Pull Too Hard, 3 3/4 In. 185.00
Match Holder, Woman With Dog, Holding Key, 4 In. 460.00
Mug, Elk 50.00
Pincushion, Dutch Girl, 4 1/2 In. 195.00
Pincushion, Nodder, Oriental Lady, No. 1357, 3 5/8 In. 405.00
Pitcher, Elf On Pig, 4 1/2 In. 322.00
Pitcher, Man Playing Mandolin, 3 1/4 In. ....140.00 to 155.00
Pitcher, Man, With Hat & Cane, Blue, White 125.00
Pitcher, Oriental Woman & Baby, No. 6821, 5 1/4 In. 185.00
Pitcher, Smiling Pear, Jasperware ....75.00 to 95.00
Sugar & Creamer, English Lady & Butler 2000.00

SCHNEIDER Glassworks was founded in 1913 at Epinay-sur-Seine, France, by Charles and Ernest Schneider. Art glass was made between 1913 and 1930. The company still produces clear crystal glass.   *Schneider*

Bowl, Etched 5 Beetles, Geometric Elements, Signed, 4 1/2 x 10 In. 690.00
Bowl, Yellow To Orange, Red, Maroon Streaks, 3 1/2 x 12 In. 374.00
Centerpiece, Mottled White, Violet, Broad Shallow Bowl, 12 In. 4660.00
Champagne, Pink, Straight Stem, Purple Circular Base, 5 1/2 In. 30.00
Compote, Blue, Green Mottled, Wrought-Iron Ivy & Scrolled-Footed Base, 10 In. 345.00

Compote, Short Purple Striped Knot, Disk Foot, Signed, 3 1/2 x 15 1/4 In. 345.00
Compote, Slender Purple Stems, Disk Foot, Signed, 7 1/2 x 6 1/4 In. 977.00
Compote, Striped Stem, 6-Point Tooled Rim, Disk Foot, 5 1/4 x 14 1/2 In. 460.00
Ewer, Arbutus Berries, Leaves, Lemon Yellow Mottled, Orange, Gray, 1924, 11 In. 5750.00
Vase, Faceted Scalloped Rim, 6 Repeating Units, Signed, 6 3/4 In. 230.00
Vase, Geometric Design, Amber, Green, White Mottled, Wrought Iron Base, 9 In. 1980.00
Vase, Layered Swirled Glass, Shoulder Stylized Blossoms, Signed, 15 1/2 In. 1035.00
Vase, Mottled Agate, Tapered, 1925, 11 In. 1210.00
Vase, Orange Poppy, With Stem, Red, Amethyst Mottled Base, Cameo, 1925, 15 In. 6325.00
Vase, Orange, Aubergine Splashes, White Ground, Flared Rim, 15 1/2 In. 2530.00
Vase, Pendant Seed Clusters, Spiked Leaves, Signed, 19 1/2 In. 862.00
Vase, Red, Orange Marble, Foliage, Berries, Black Handles, 3 Scrolled Feet, 15 In. 3220.00
Vase, Stylized Horseshoe Crabs, Signed, 11 1/2 In. 977.00
Vase, Stylized Palm Leaves, Pink, Yellow Applied Flowers, Smoky Topaz, 14 In. 2760.00
Vase, Swirled Pink, Red, White, Cluthra Type Bubbles, Flared, 12 In. 977.00
Vase, Yellow Flowers, Orange Centers, Pale Yellow Mottled, Cameo, 1925, 8 In. 7475.00

SCIENCE FICTION and fantasy collectibles included here are those
based on books, comics, movies, and TV shows. Early science fiction
and fantasy authors included Thomas More, who wrote of an ideal
society in *Utopia,* and Jonathan Swift, whose book *Gulliver's Travels*
was published in 1726. The father of modern science fiction was Jules
Verne, whose first book, *Five Weeks in a Balloon,* was published in
1863. Many of the items collected today are from the radio and TV
shows of the 40s and 50s. Other science fiction and fantasy collectibles
can be found under Batman, Buck Rogers, Captain Marvel, Flash Gordon, Superman, Movie, and Toy.

Bed Sheet, Star Wars, Scenes From Movie, Twin Size 27.00
Belt, Star Wars, Darth Vader, Black Vinyl, Leather, Metal Buckle, 28 In. 40.00
Belt Buckle, Star Wars, Empire Strikes Back, Silver Tone Brass, 1 3/4 x 2 3/4 In. 23.00
Book, Activity, Battlestar Galactica, Grosset & Dunlap, 1978, 64 Pages 10.00
Book, Activity, Planet Of The Apes, Artcraft, 1974, 26 Pages, 10 x 12 In. 8.00
Book, Activity, Planet Of The Apes, Saalfield, 1974, 24 Pages, 10 x 12 In. 18.00
Book, Activity, Planet Of The Apes, Saalfield, 1974, 80 Pages 15.00
Book, Doctor Who Technical Manual, Blueprints, Photos, 1983, 8 1/2 x 11 1/2 In. 13.00
Book, Lord Of The Rings, Fotonovel, Pictures From Movie, 1979, 400 Pages 10.00
Book, Star Wars, Iron-On Transfers, Ballantine Books, 1977 . . . . 30.00
Book Cover, Earth 2, 1994, 14 1/2 x 22 In. 18.00
Bottle, Shampoo, Star Wars, Darth Vader, Black, 8 3/4 In. 50.00
Box, Star Trek McDonald's Meal, Space Suit, Paramount Pictures, 1979, 9 x 11 In. 28.00
Calendar, J.R.R. Tolkien, 1977, Brothers Hildebrandt Illustrations 50.00
Card, Star Trek, Captain Kirk, Arm Moves, Have A Far-Out Birthday, 1976 . . . . 15.00
Clock Radio, Star Wars, Darth Vader Head, LCD, Battery Operated, Box, 5 x 6 In. 10.00
Coloring Book, Space Patrol, Buzz Corry, Ralston Purina Co., 1950s, 8 x 11 In. 55.00
Coloring Book, Star Trek Giant Story, Parks Run Publishing Co., 1978, 32 Pages 20.00
Coloring Book, Star Trek, Rescue At Raylo, Western Publishing, 1978, 60 Pages 8.00
Coloring Book, Star Trek, Whitman, Paramount Pictures Corp., 1978, 60 Pages 15.00
Comic Book, Star Trek, With Record, In Cellophane 18.00
Comic Book, Star Wars, No. 12, Marvel 12.00
Game, Battlestar Galactica, Parker Brothers, Board, Box, 1978, 9 x 18 In. . . . . .15.00 to 20.00
Game, Dragonriders Of Pern, Mayfair Games, Box, 1989 . . . . 66.00
Game, E.T., Elliot & E.T., Atari 2600, 1982 . . . . 3.00
Game, Planet Of The Apes, Milton Bradley, Board, 1974 . . . . 32.00
Game, Star Trek Star Fleet, McDonald's Star Trek Meal Premium, 1979, 5 x 10 In. 35.00
Game, Star Trek, Ideal, Board, 1974 . . . . 40.00
Game, Star Trek, Ideal, Paramount Pictures Corp., Box, 1967, 10 x 19 In. . . . . .58.00 to 125.00
Game, Star Trek, Super Phaser II Target Game, Battery Operated, Mego, Box, 1976 . . . . . 20.00
Game, Star Wars, Battle Of Sarlacc's Pit, Parker Brothers, 1983 . . . . 30.00
Game, Star Wars, Escape From Death Star, Kenner, Box, 1977 . . . . 10.00
Glass, Star Wars, C-3PO, R2-D2, Burger King, Coca-Cola, 1977, 5 3/4 In. 30.00
Jacket, Earth 2, VA-1587, Blue, Yellow, Roanoke Patch, 1994, Size Large 285.00
Jacket, Earth 2, VA-1587, Blue, Yellow, Roanoke Patch, 1994, Size Small 250.00
Jigsaw Puzzle, Alien, Creature, Cast Members, H.G. Toys, Box, 1979, 7 x 19 1/2 In. 65.00

Jigsaw Puzzle, Alien, Space Jockey, H.G. Toys, Fox, Box, 1979, 8 x 10 In. 15.00
Jigsaw Puzzle, Battlestar Galactica, Starbuck, Parker Bros., Box, 140 Piece 4.00
Jigsaw Puzzle, Planet Of The Apes, Tin Canister, H.G. Toys, 1967 . . . . 25.00
Jigsaw Puzzle, Space 1999, H.G. Toys, ATV Licensing, Box, 1975, 7 1/2 x 9 In. 18.00
Jigsaw Puzzle, Star Trek IV, Voyage Home, Cast Picture, Box, 18 x 24 In. 8.00
Jigsaw Puzzle, Star Trek, Beaming Down, Frame Tray, Whitman, 1979, 8 1/4 x 11 In. . . . 15.00
Jigsaw Puzzle, Star Trek, Captain Kirk Floating Freely In Space, 8 1/4 x 11 In. 10.00
Jigsaw Puzzle, Star Trek, Spock & Kirk, Eerie Outer Space Fog, 8 1/4 x 11 In. 10.00
Lobby Card, Day The Earth Stood Still, Title Card, 1951 . . . . 1185.00
Lobby Card, Forbidden Planet, Robot Carrying Lady, MGM, 1956 . . . . 1010.00
Mask, C-3PO, Black Latex, Gold Paint, Don Post, 177, Adult 28.00
Mug, Doctor Who, Tom Baker, Diamond Logo, Thermal, Plastic 10.00
Mug, Star Trek, Riker, Deanna Troi, Box 3.00
Mug, Star Wars, Obi-Wan Kenobi, Pottery, California Originals, 1977 . . . . 55.00
Postcard, Star Trek, Images From TV Show, Paramount Pictures, 1975, Set Of 4 . . . . 8.00
Poster, 20 Million Miles To Earth, 1957, Three Sheet 220.00
Poster, 2001: A Space Odyssey, Style A, 1968, One Sheet 350.00
Poster, Alien, 1979, One Sheet 450.00
Poster, Blade Runner, Harrison Ford, 1982, One Sheet 425.00
Poster, Day Of The Triffids, 1963, One Sheet 175.00
Poster, Earth vs. The Flying Saucers, 1956, One Sheet 450.00
Poster, Empire Strikes Back, 1980, Heavy Stock Silkscreen, 40 x 60 In. 635.00
Poster, Empire Strikes Back, Darth Vader's Head, 1980, Advance One Sheet 210.00
Poster, Forbidden Planet, MGM, 1956, One Sheet 3630.00
Poster, Invasion Of The Saucer Men, Steve Terrell, 1957, Three Sheet 2300.00
Poster, It Came From Outer Space, Richard Carlson, Barbara Rush, 1953, Insert 198.00
Poster, Star Wars, Luke, Leia, Darth Vader In Background, 1977, One Sheet 165.00
Poster, Star Wars, Mark Hamill, 1977, One Sheet 520.00
Poster, Star Wars, Style C, 1977, One Sheet 75.00
Press Kit, Battlestar Galactica, 9 Black & White Photos, Folder, 71 Pages, 1978 . . . . 30.00
Prop, Earth 2, Communications Gear, Headset, Lights Up, 1994 . . . . 500.00
Puzzle, Slide, Star Trek, Unscramble The Crew, Plastic, 2 7/8 x 3 1/2 In. 9.00
Record, Tom Corbett At The Space Academy, Rockhill, RCA Victor, 45 RPM, 1952 . . . . . 18.00
Record, Tom Corbett Space Cadet Song & March, Rockhill Prod., 78 RPM, 1951 . . . . 35.00
Robot, Lost In Space, B-9, Radio Control, Trendmasters, Box, 24 In. 93.00
T-Shirt, Star Trek IV, Starfleet On Front, Klingons On Back, Black, X-Large 10.00
Tea Tin, Doctor Who, Police Box, BBC Enterprises Ltd., 1980 . . . . 150.00
Tote Bag, Doctor Who, Jon Pertwee, Canvas, 16 In. 27.00
Towel, Star Trek, Mr. Spock, Alien City In Background, White, 29 x 48 In. 35.00
Toy, Battlestar Galactica, L.E.M. Lander, Plastic, On Card, 1978 . . . . 9.00
Toy, Kit, Battlestar Galactica, Viper Launch Station, Mattel, Box, 1978 . . . . 42.00
Toy, Model Kit, Space 1999, Eagle, MPC, Fundimensions, Box, 12 In. 35.00
Toy, Play Set, Space 1999, Eagle 1 Spaceship, Unassembled, Mattel, Box, 30 In. 455.00
Toy, Star Trek, Motion Picture, Enterprise, Die Cast, Dinky, On Card, 1979, 4 In. 22.00
Toy, Star Wars, Landspeeder, Spring-Loaded Wheels, Kenner, Box, 1978, 9 In. 55.00

SCIENTIFIC INSTRUMENTS of all kinds are included in this category.
Other categories such as Barometer, Binoculars, Dental, Nautical,
Medical, and Thermometer may also price scientific apparatus.

Alidade, W. & L.E. Gurley, Troy, N.Y., Leather Covered Case, 11 In. 440.00
Chronometer, A. Mager Brake, Silver Dial, Black Roman Numerals 2070.00
Chronometer, Fletcher, No. 2691, Brass Bound, Mahogany Case 1870.00
Colorimeter, J. Dubosco & P. Pellin, Brass, Steel Base, 15 1/2 In. 385.00
Compass, Brass, Cover, c.1820, 2 1/2 In. 175.00
Compass, Brass, England, 20th Century, 5 1/2 In. 70.00
Compass, Explorer's Sighting, G. Davis, Brass & Silvered Dial 950.00
Compass, Hunter Style, Brass Case, 1 3/4 In. 20.00
Compass, Sundial, Brass, Sunburst On Lid 275.00
Compass, Surveyor's, Richard Patten-New York, Walnut Case 990.00
Compass, Surveyor's, Wm. Davenport-Phila., Cherry Case, 14 In. 1155.00
Compass, USA Engineering Department, 1918, 1/4 x 1 3/4 In. 80.00
Compass, Vernier, Surveyor's, W.J. Young, Brass Dial Cover, 1830s 1250.00
Compass, W. & L.E. Fuelwy, World War I 60.00

Clean brass at least once or twice a year. Wear glasses and rubber gloves when cleaning with a commercial polish. The fumes can be irritating. Rinse, then dry. Water drops will make black spots that are hard to clean off.

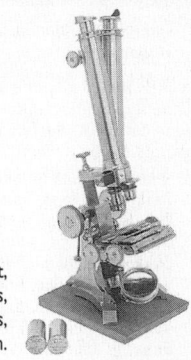

Scientific Instrument,
Microscope, C. Collins,
London, Binocular, Brass,
c.1875, 18 In.

Inclinometer, Mounted On Wooden Panel, 14 x 17 In.	247.00
Level, Surveyor's, Bausch, Lomb & Saegmuller, Brass, 8 3/8 x 21 In.	330.00
Magnifier, Mid-18th Century, 4 In.	150.00
Magnifying Glass, Ivory Handle, Fitted Case, Miniature	295.00
Microscope, 2 Power Revolving Lenses, Spencer, Case, 14 In.	110.00
Microscope, 3 Power Turret, Brass, Swivel Mirror, Crate, 12 In.	85.00
Microscope, 3 Power Turret, Extra Eye Piece, Brass & Steel, Case	192.00
Microscope, Bausch & Lomb, Case & Extra Lenses, Eye Pieces, Case	675.00
Microscope, Bausch & Lomb, Revolving 3 Power Turret, Case, 14 1/2 In.	385.00
Microscope, C. Collins, London, Binocular, Brass, c.1875, 18 In. ....*Illus*	1324.00
Microscope, Carl Zeiss, Model Jene #31195, Brass, Mahogany Case	336.00
Microscope, E. Leitz Wetzlar, 3 Power Turret, Brass, Leather Case, 11 In.	190.00
Microscope, E.H. & F.H. Tighe, 2 Pillar, Tripod Base, 15 In.	1050.00
Microscope, R. & J. Beck, Art Deco, 15 In.	325.00
Microscope, R. & J. Beck, Compound Monocular, 3 Power Turret	1450.00
Microscope, Rack & Pinion Movable Stage, 3 Wooden Slides, 1820s	1200.00
Microscope, Watson & Sons, London, 2 Power	110.00
Model, Steam Engine, Boiler, Flywheel, Dynamo Generator, 15 In.	220.00
Model, Steam Engine, Joy's Valve Gear, 4 Column, Brass, Steel, Painted	330.00
Model, Steam Engine, Pot Type Boiler, Flywheel Cylinder, Base, 12 In.	300.00
Model, Steam Engine, Power Plant, Horizontal Boiler, Flywheel, 16 In.	410.00
Model, Steam Engine, Vertical Boiler, Flywheel Cylinder, 13 3/4 In.	300.00
Model, Steam Engine, Vertical Boiler, Piston, Flywheel, Bavaria, 11 3/4 In.	300.00
Model, Steam Engine, Vertical Piston, 3 Speed Flywheel, 14 1/2 In.	355.00
Model, Steam Engine, Vertical Piston, Beam & Flywheel, 15 x 8 In.	495.00
Octant, F.W. Lincoln, Jr. & Co., Ebony, Ivory, Brass, Case, 13 x 11 1/2 In.	805.00
Octant, Matheson & Co., London, Case, 1860s	1250.00
Octant, Riggs & Bro. Philadelphia, Ebony, Ivory Inlaid Signature Panel	550.00
Quadrant, Ebony, Ivory & Brass, 18th Century	1250.00
Scale, Counter, Way Rite, Metal, Green, Dial Face, 25 Lbs., 5 x 9 In.	20.00
Sextant, Circular Case, 3 In.	70.00
Sextant, Ryland & Son, London, Brass	247.00
Telescope, 4 Section, Leather Covering, Mahogany Wall Mount, 20 3/4 In.	275.00
Telescope, Adie & Son, Edinburgh, Single Draw, Brass	1600.00
Telescope, Andrew J. Lloyd Co., Brass, Wood Stand, Boston, 32 In.	975.00
Telescope, B.D. Haggar & Son, Wooden, Brass, 21 In.	385.00
Telescope, Brass, Leather Celestial, Mahogany Case, England, 33 In.	575.00
Telescope, Brass, Leather Mounted, 1825-1830, 20 1/4 In.	363.00
Telescope, Brass, On Tripod, 19th Century, 53 In.	1320.00
Telescope, Brass, Spotting Scope, Adjusting Knob, London, Tripod	3300.00
Telescope, Brass, Table, 30 In.	690.00
Telescope, Fitted Wood Case, Tripod Stand, Germany, 17 In.	360.00
Telescope, J.H. Steward, 5 Section, Leather Sleeve & Shader, 34 3/4 In.	330.00
Telescope, T. Cooke & Sons, 2 Section, Leather Cover	110.00
Telescope, Table, William Harris & Co., Brass, Tripod Base, 38 In.	2200.00
Telescope, W. Ottway & Co., Ltd., Brass, Leather, Stand, 28 In.	975.00

Telescope, Walnut, Circular Leather, Victorian, 6 Ft. 6 In. 3740.00
Transit, Surveyor's, Brass, Mahogany Case, Tripod Stand, c.1900 . . . . 770.00

SCRIMSHAW is bone or ivory or whale's teeth carved by sailors and
others for entertainment during the sailing-ship days. Some scrimshaw
was carved as early as 1800. There are modern scrimshanders making
pieces today on bone, ivory, or plastic. Other pieces may be found in
the Ivory and Nautical categories.

Basket, Knitting, Splats, Whalebone, Mahogany Base, 12 x 6 In. 4070.00
Box, Shield Form, Mother-Of-Pearl Inlay, Plated Silver Frame, 2 3/4 x 2 1/4 In. 430.00
Box, Whalebone, Ditty, Brass Tack Design, Wooden Top, 8 1/4 x 6 x 4 In. 3105.00
Busk, Whalebone, 5 Panels, Geometric Shape, 19th Century, 12 1/2 In. 575.00
Busk, Whalebone, Engraved Compass, Stars, Hot Air Balloon, 11 1/4 In. 465.00
Busk, Whalebone, Engraved Floral, 11 3/4 In. 120.00
Busk, Whalebone, Floral Bouquet Design, Potted Plant, Ship At Sea, 13 In. 920.00
Busk, Whalebone, Whaling Scene, Whale Boat In Pursuit, 13 5/16 In. 2530.00
Busk, Whalebone, Whaling Vignettes, Vine Border, Scalloped End, 13 In. 515.00
Cane, Whalebone Handle, Fist Holds Snake, Swirled Shaft, 35 In. 8800.00
Cane, Whalebone Head, 2 Ebony Hands, Whalebone Tip, 36 In. 495.00
Cane, Whalebone, Carved Walrus Tusk, Lady's Leg Handle, 34 3/4 In. 90.00
Cane, Whalebone, Carved Whale Ivory, 2-Part Handle, Jockey Design, 38 In. 345.00
Cane, Whalebone, Carved Whale Ivory, Eagle's Head Handle, 34 3/4 In. 2530.00
Cane, Whalebone, Carved Whale Ivory, Horse's Hoof Handle, 36 In. 285.00
Cane, Whalebone, Whale Ivory, Carved Spiral Knob, Tapered Round Shaft, 37 In. 400.00
Caulking Tool, Whalebone, Boat Maker's, 4 1/2 In. 385.00
Cradle, Baby's, Whalebone, 5 In. 520.00
Crimper, Tusk, Walrus, Whalebone, 3-Tined, Double Jagging Wheel, 7 3/4 In. 1840.00
Doll, Whalebone, Painted, Carved Hair, Eyes & Mouth, 1830s, 4 3/4 In. 2750.00
Dominoes, Bone & Ebony, Cherry Box, 12 1/4 In. 330.00
Figurine, Dolphin, Whalebone, 19th Century, 3 3/4 In. 165.00
Figurine, Walrus Ivory, Mutt & Jeff, Cicero, St. Lawrence Is., 1920s, 5 1/2 In. 1850.00
Gavel, Whalebone, 19th Century, 9 1/2 In. 495.00
Jagging Wheel, Whalebone, Heart, Triangle & Foliate, 19th Century, 5 1/2 In. 330.00
Lamp Base, Tusk, Elephant, Engraved Whaling Ship, By Barcellus, 8 In., Pair 990.00
Match Holder, American Ships, Whale's Tooth, 1 On Each Side, 8 1/2 In. 1210.00
Page Turner, Walrus, Figure Of Liberty & Sailing Ship, Woman Bust Top, 19 In. 1035.00
Panel, Walrus, 3 Incised Flounders 1 Side, 1 On Reverse, 4 1/4 x 1 1/2 In. 220.00
Pie Crimper, Ebony & Mother-Of-Pearl Inlays, 19th Century, 7 1/4 In. 525.00
Pie Crimper, Tooth, Whale Ivory, Ebony Spacer, 7 1/2 In. 715.00
Pie Crimper, Whale Ivory, 3-Wheeled, Rose Blossom, Bud Stamp, 8 1/4 In. 5175.00
Pie Crimper, Whale Ivory, Abalone Shell & Fork, Lady's Leg Handle, 6 1/2 In. 3162.00
Pie Crimper, Whale Ivory, Ebony, Lady's Hand Shape, Oak Leaves, 8 3/4 In. 2300.00
Pie Crimper, Whale Ivory, Fruitwood, Gun Pistol Handle, Mid-19th Century, 9 In. 977.00
Pie Crimper, Whale Ivory, Sperm Whale's Tooth, Handle, Dark Wood, 5 1/4 In., Pair 4887.00
Pie Crimper, Whale Ivory, Stylized Seahorse, Black Mane, Mid-19th Century, 6 In. 7475.00
Pie Crimper, Whalebone & Baleen, Wheel, Fork At Other End, 9 In. 247.00
Pie Crimper, Whalebone, 19th Century, 6 1/2 In. 575.00
Pie Crimper, Whalebone, Baleen, Wheel, Fork, 9 In. 245.00
Porpoise Jaw, Shipping & Town Scenes, 15 In. 7475.00
Rolling Pin, Whalebone, South Sea Hardwood Core, 1860, 16 1/4 In. 550.00
Sailor's Horn, M. Pyne Of New Bedford, 1848, 8 1/4 In. 550.00
Sewing Bird, Whalebone, Mahogany, 1860, 3 x 4 1/8 x 4 In. 990.00
Shelf, Whalebone, 2 Engraved Teeth, Paw Footed 6035.00
Snuffbox, Cover, Whale's Tooth, Ship, Sailing, Full-Rigged, Brass, 5 In. 520.00
Snuffbox, Cover, Whalebone, Oval Medallion, Rectangular, 2 3/8 x 1 x 7/8 In. 285.00
Sperm Whale Tooth, Seated Woman, Bouquet, Reverse, Woman Braiding, 7 In. 2070.00
Spool Holder, Whalebone, 7 1/2 In. 8050.00
Spoon, Whalebone, Handle, Coconut Shell Bowl, 19th Century, 10 In. 110.00
Swift, Double, Whalebone, Scribed Staves, Cup, Ivory, 16 In. 1840.00
Swift, Inlaid Baleen, Abalone & Tortoiseshell 18400.00
Swift, Ivory & Whalebone 18400.00
Tooth, Sperm Whale, Whaleship Design, c.1950, Charles Morgan, 6 1/2 In. 330.00
Tooth, Whale, 2 Ships & Legend, Rescue, 5 3/4 In. 845.00

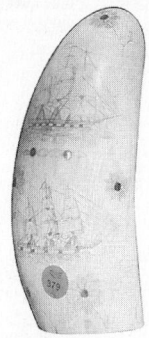

Don't wash ivory. The yellow color is preferred and white ivory has a much lower value. If you have a friend whose hands perspire profusely, have that person handle the ivory, as it will add to the patina and coloring.

Scrimshaw, Tooth, Whale,
Ships, Flowers, Mother-Of-
Pearl Centers, 7 & 8 In., Pair

Tooth, Whale, Allegorical Liberty, Ceres On Reverse, 4 1/4 In., Pair	345.00
Tooth, Whale, American Ships, Building, Flowers & Sperm Whales, 6 In.	1850.00
Tooth, Whale, Cupid Holding Vase, B.C. Blossom, 1880s, 4 1/4 In.	880.00
Tooth, Whale, Eagle In Oval Reserve, Geometric Border, 5 1/2 In.	1495.00
Tooth, Whale, Elegant Woman, 19th Century, 7 In.	920.00
Tooth, Whale, Elegant Woman, Seated Nude Woman, Initialed OM, 5 1/8 In.	862.00
Tooth, Whale, English Ship Of Line Under Sail, 19th Century, 4 1/2 In.	515.00
Tooth, Whale, Engraved, Whaling Ship, Spread-Winged Eagle, Flags, 9 In.	7475.00
Tooth, Whale, Figure Of Woman, Reverse With Heart, 5 In.	247.00
Tooth, Whale, Incised Fish, 19th Century, 4 1/4 In.	300.00
Tooth, Whale, Lady Liberty Holding American Flag & Eagle, 6 1/2 In.	1380.00
Tooth, Whale, Man On Horse, In Archway, 19th Century, 4 In.	330.00
Tooth, Whale, Naval Battle, Whaling Scene On Reverse, 6 In.	550.00
Tooth, Whale, Paperweight, 3 Teeth In Bone, Cetacean, Jan To Dec 1843, 6 In.	1155.00
Tooth, Whale, Sailing Ship, Polychrome	10925.00
Tooth, Whale, Sailor, Holding An American Flag, 4 1/2 In.	630.00
Tooth, Whale, Ships, Flowers, Mother-Of-Pearl Centers, 7 & 8 In., Pair ....*Illus*	9900.00
Tooth, Whale, Sperm Whale Spouting, 19th Century, 4 In.	880.00
Tooth, Whale, Spiraling Design, Various Ships Under Sail, Whaling Scene, 6 1/4 In.	1092.00
Tooth, Whale, Tree, C.B.M.S Curlew, Thomas Parker, 6 1/2 In.	1100.00
Tooth, Whale, Uncarved, 4 In., Set Of 4	220.00
Tooth, Whale, View Of Victorian Ladies, Wearing Elegant Dress, 3 3/4 In., Pair	490.00
Tooth, Whale, Warrior Wearing A Helmet, Lady, Seated, 5 1/2 In.	805.00
Tooth, Whale, Whaling Scene, 7 1/2 In.	330.00
Tooth, Whale, Whaling Scene, Boats In Pursuit, 19th Century, 9 In.	1725.00
Tooth, Whale, Whaling Scene, S. Eaton, Feb. 4th, 1831, 8 In.	9900.00
Tooth, Whale, Whaling Scene, Vessel Working On Pod Of Whales, 8 In.	2415.00
Tooth, Whale, Whaling Ship 1 Side, Graveyard & Monuments Other, 7 1/4 In.	605.00
Tooth, Whale, Whaling Ships, 19th Century, 6 In.	1375.00
Toothpick, Walrus Tusk, Anchor & American Eagle, 2 1/2 In.	1110.00
Tusk, Walrus, Carved, Swordfish & Tuna, 16 In.	355.00
Tusk, Walrus, Uncarved, 19th Century, 28 In., Pair	303.00
Watch Holder, Whalebone, Sunburst Shape, 8 1/4 In.	8625.00

SEBASTIAN MINIATURES were first made by Prescott W. Baston in 1938 in Marblehead, Massachusetts. More than 400 different designs have been made, and collectors search for the out-of-production models. The mark may say *Copr. P. W. Baston U.S.A.*, or *P. W. Baston, U.S.A.*, or *Prescott W. Baston.* Sometimes a paper label was used.

Blacksmith	20.00
Candy Store	80.00
Cottage, Base	78.00
Figurine, George Washington & Cannon	35.00
Old Woman Who Lived In Shoe, Jell-O	320.00
Shoemaker, Label	70.00
Songs At Cratchit's	30.00

The Doctor, Silver & Green Palette Label 75.00
William & Hannah Penn 200.00

SEG, see Paul Revere Pottery category.

SEVRES porcelain has been made in Sevres, France, since 1769. Many copies of the famous ware have been made. The name originally referred to the works of the Royal Porcelain factory. The name now includes any of the wares made in the town of Sevres, France. The entwined lines with a center letter used as the mark is one of the most forged marks in antiques. Be very careful to identify Sevres by quality, not just by mark.

Basin, Cover, Alternating Gilt Cartouches, Laurel Wreath Edge, Blue, Ground, 9 In. 4025.00
Bowl, Blue Feathered, Floral Spray, 3 Cabbage Leaves Interior, Gold, 1756, 9 In. 460.00
Bowl, Chateau De Tuileries, Gilt Metal Mount, 2 Handles, 1870, 7 x 9 In. 460.00
Bowl, Cover, Child, Seated, Landscape Scene, Blue Celeste Ground, 7 1/4 In., Pair 4025.00
Bowl, Exotic Bird, Flower Swags, Blue Mark, 18th Century, 3 1/4 x 8 3/4 In. 575.00
Bowl, Flowers, Cherubs Flanking Louis Philip Seal, Medium Blue, 11 1/4 x 4 1/4 In. 460.00
Bowl, Sugar, Cover, Panel Of Birds In Parkland, Blue Celeste Ground, Gilt Edge, 3 In. 517.00
Box, Oxblood Flambe Hinged, Ormolu Mounts, Porcelain, 3 1/2 x 4 1/2 In. 280.00
Bust, Young Napoleon, On Tapering Plinth, c.1850, 9 In. 440.00
Cachepot, Scenic River Landscape, 4 1/2 x 5 3/4 In. 258.00
Centerpiece, Courting Couple, Interior Rose Spray, Female Mask Handles, 13 1/2 In. 1510.00
Charger, Napoleon, On Horseback, Battlefront, Fire Surrounding, Signed, 1804, 12 In. .. 1195.00
Clock, White Enamel, Roman Numeral Dial, Pink, Blue C-Scroll Case, 15 3/4 In. 635.00
Coffee Cann & Saucer, Cabinet, Bare Breasted Maiden, Seated Amidst Flowers, 3 In. 8050.00
Coffee Cann & Saucer, Vase Of Roses On Marble Ledge, Roses, 1781, 3 In., Pair 8625.00
Compote, Cherub, Gilt Bronze, Tapered Pedestal, 9 1/2 In. 290.00
Cup, Ice, Panel Of Bird In Landscape, Gilt Edge, C-Scroll Handle, 1770, 2 In., 6 Piece ... 4887.00
Cup & Saucer, Cabinet, Basket Of Fruit & Flowers, Gilt Foliate Scroll, 1779, 3 In. 8050.00
Cup & Saucer, Cover, Pink Trailing Roses, Blue Bell Floral Border, Entwined Handle ... 4025.00
Cup & Saucer, Figure Of Shepherdess Sleeping Beneath Tree, Entwined Handle, 3 In. ... 5175.00
Cup & Saucer, Miter, Floral 45.00
Cup & Saucer, Tea, Child's, Panel Of Cherub, Berried Laurel Wreath Border, Blue, 2 In. . 3737.00
Cup & Saucer, Tea, Laurel, Pink Flower Swags, Gilt Border, 2 3/8 & 2 1/2 In. 5175.00
Dish, 6 Multicolored Flower Sprays, Sprigs, Gilt Rim, 1752, 8 5/8 In., Pair 920.00
Dish, Black Bird, Perched On Leafy Branch, Moss Green Border, Gilt, 1784, 8 1/2 In. 2300.00
Dish, Central Medallion Of Crossed Palmettes, Arrows, 4 Blue Panel, Square 1725.00
Dish, Courting Couple, Landscape, Metal Band & Feet, Foliate Handles, 13 3/4 In. 590.00
Dish, Floral Sprays, 1771, 8 1/2 In. 1380.00
Dish, Multicolored Flower Sprays, Sprigs, 1766, 8 7/8 In., Pair 2587.00
Dish, Multicolored Flower Sprays, Sprigs, Gilt Dentil Edged Rim, 1777, 7 In., Pair 1035.00
Dish, Multicolored Sprays, Gilt Blue Dash Line Border, Triangular, 1769, 8 5/8 In. 488.00
Dish, Peony Shape, 6 Multicolored Sprays, Floret Center, 1764, 8 15/16 In. 690.00
Dish, Scattered Flower Sprays, Sprigs, Gilt Dash Blue Line Border, Gilt Rim, 1760, Pair . 1380.00
Dish, Scattered Roses, Single Rose Blossom Border, 1777, 8 1/2 In. 1265.00
Dish, Shell Shape, Cluster Of Fruit & Flowers, Floral Garland Rim, Gilt, 1770, 8 3/4 In. .. 747.00
Dish, Shell Shape, Scattered Rose Blossoms, Buds, Red Berried Laurel Border, 9 In. 1380.00
Dish, Stylized Vine, Central Spray Of Flowers, Blue Fallot Border, Square, 9 In., Pair 1840.00
Dish, Yellow, Black Bird, Perched On Leafy Branch, Moss Green Border, 1786, 9 In. 2300.00
Figurine, Dancing Women, Gilt, 9 1/2 x 10 In., Pair 230.00
Handle, Magnifying Glass, Figural Cartouches, 14 1/2 In. 805.00
Inkwell, Gondola Shape, Green Painted Hull, Gilt Rim & Prow, 1 1/2 In. 285.00
Jar, Covered, Knop Finial, Cobalt Blue, Teal Glaze, 16 1/2 In. 980.00
Jardiniere, Neoclassical Figural Scene, Bouquets, Metal Bound, c.1880, 12 1/2 In. 2530.00
Jug, Hot Milk, Cover, Sprays Of Colorful Flowers, Gilt Rim, 1764, 5 1/8 In. 920.00
Plate, 3 People In Garden, Multicolored Flowers, Blue Border, 10 1/2 In. 550.00
Plate, Amorous Couple, Fishing On River, Cobalt Blue Rim, 9 1/2 In. 160.00
Plate, Blue Bird, Perched On Autumnal Branch, Moss Green Border, 1784, 9 1/4 In. 2300.00
Plate, Landscape Design, Courting Couple, Blue Ground, 9 3/8 In. 201.00
Plate, Putti In Center, Crowned, Rose, Gilt Foliate, Late 19th Century, 9 In. 140.00
Plate, Scattered Roses, Buds, 3 Oval Panels, 1771, 9 1/2 In. 1035.00

Punch Bowl, Imperial Crown Design, Porcelain, 1847, 4 1/4 x 11 1/4 In. 423.00
Salver, Central Cluster Of Fruit & Flowers, Apple Green, Gilt Edge, Circular, 9 In. 11500.00
Soup, Dish, Stylized Vine, Central Spray Of Flowers, Blue Border, Square, 9 In. 488.00
Soup, Dish, Stylized Vine, Central Spray Of Flowers, Pansy, Pink Rose Rim, 9 In. 690.00
Tazza, 3 Dolphins, Turquoise Center Sunken Ring, Gilt Bronze, 1865, 13 In. 1575.00
Teapot, Cover, Bands Of Laurel & Foliate, Roses, Flowers, Fruits, Gilt Border, 5 In. 4887.00
Teapot, Cover, Trophy Panel On 1 Side, Hat, Musical Instruments Other Side, Handle . . . 4312.00
Tray, Central Basket Of Roses, Orange, Red Ribbon, Berry, Leaf Border, Handles, Oval . . 5462.00
Tray, Central Scene Of Lovers In Arcadian River Landscape, Scalloped Edge, Oval, 12 In.   3162.00
Tray, Diamond Shape, 6 Multicolored Sprays, Gilt Blue Dash Line Border, 1769 . . . . 1035.00
Tray, Diamond Shape, Multicolored Flowers, Gilt Dentil Rim, 2 Handles, 1766, 15 In. . . . 3162.00
Urn, Art Nouveau, Woman With Decorated Cap, Flowers, Bronze Mounts, 25 1/2 In. 8050.00
Urn, Chinoiserie Scenes, Red Ground, Gilt Border, Bronze Handles, 23 1/2 In., Pair 5635.00
Urn, Cover, Classical Figures By Stream, Cobalt Blue, Gilt Floral Design, 63 In., Pair . . . 1265.00
Urn, Cover, Scene Of Couple At Play, Multicolored, Oval, 21 In.   545.00
Urn, Palace, Pastel Scene, Shield, French Blue, 32 1/2 x 15 In. 3735.00
Urn, Scene Of Lovers In A Landscape, Cobalt Blue, Ring Handles, 10 In., Pair 1150.00
Vase, Colorful Bird Perched On Small Tree, 5 3/8 In., Pair 1725.00
Vase, Cover, Deep Blue Background With Scenes, Bronze Mounts, Pair, 15 In. 2070.00
Vase, Floral, Raised Gilt Highlights, Green Panels, White Ground, 7 1/4 In. 170.00
Vase, Landscape Scene, Company In A Garden, Mask Ring Handles, Pink, 16 In. 2875.00
Vase, Landscape Scene, Courting Couple, Cobalt Blue Neck, Foliate Handles, 22 In. 1380.00
Vase, Lovers By A Waterfall, Cobalt Blue Ground, Porcelain, 16 In. 1840.00
Vase, Napoleonic Scene, Cobalt Blue, 3 Sections, 38 In. 5500.00
Vase, Quail, Blue, Red, 19th Century, 12 In. 290.00
Vase, Stylized Blue Foliage, Gilt Highlights, White, Porcelain, Cylindrical, 13 1/2 In. 1955.00

SEWER TILE figures were made by workers at the sewer tile and pipe
factories in the Ohio area during the late nineteenth and early twentieth centuries. Figurines, small vases, and cemetery vases were favored.
Often the finished vase was a piece of the original pipe with added decorations and markings. All types of sewer tile work are now considered
folk art by collectors.

Ashtray, Chimney, Tooled Stones, 10 In. 150.00
Bank, Basset Hound, Incised, 14 In. 1540.00
Bank, Pig, Incised, Green Amber Glaze, 9 In. 605.00
Birdhouse 165.00
Bust, General Grant, Full-Bodied, Mustache, Wearing Uniform, Pine, 7 In. 3450.00
Bust, Gentleman, Full-Bodied, Brown Hair, Mustache, Bowtie, 6 1/2 In. 290.00
Bust, Mustached Man, Unglazed Red, 19th Century 345.00
Dachshund 220.00
Dog, Seated, Molded, Free Standing Front Legs, 10 In. 275.00
Doll's Head, Young Girl, Short Wavy Hair, Black, White, Red, Pink, 11 In., 2 Piece 1035.00
Eagle, Molded R.O.E., Incised 1944 . . . .   55.00
Frog, 6 3/4 In. 160.00
Frog, Incised Bobby, 1924 . . . .   687.00
Keg, On Stand, Ice Cold 100% Cider 5 . . . .   550.00
Lamp Base, Tree & Bird 82.00
Lion, Lying Down, Yellow Clay, Molded Oval Base, 13 1/2 x 9 In., Pair 1725.00
Lion, Seated, Rectangular Base, Dark Glaze, 9 1/2 In. 340.00
Mannequin's Head, Almond-Shaped Eyes, Stepped Rectangular, Pine, 10 In. 1150.00
Owl, 17 In. 660.00
Paperweight, German Shepherd 302.00
Pig, Marked JD 110.00
Pig, Molded Flowers On Back, Incised 1917 . . . .   412.00

SEWING equipment of all types is collected, from sewing birds that
held the cloth to tape measures, needle books, and old wooden spools.
Sewing machines are included here. Needlework pictures are listed in
the Picture category.

Basket, Armadillo, Satin Lining, Tail Forms Handle 65.00
Basket, Wicker, Bags Of Thread, 14 In. 35.00

Bird, 1 Pincushion, Silver Plated Brass, Patent 1853 .... 335.00
Bird, 2 Brass Pincushions, Wing Edge, Patent 1853 .... 395.00
Bird, Brass, Pincushion, 1853 .... 95.00
Bird, Dog's Mouth Opens, Brass, 3 1/2 In. 795.00
Bird, Ratchet, Steel 95.00
Bobbin, Lace, Bone, Turned Design, Dyed Green & Red, England, 1850s 95.00
Box, Carved & Painted Pine, Late 19th Century, American, 8 1/4 x 13 1/4 In. 2587.00
Box, Chinese Export, Lacquer, Black & Gold, 10 1/2 x 13 1/2 In. 440.00
Box, Clarks Tartanware McDuff Clan 75.00
Box, Cottage, Pine, 2 Chimneys, Leaded Glass Dormer, Blue, Red Lined Interior, 6 In. 1380.00
Box, Domed Cover, Fitted Interior, Leather Covered, 3 x 6 In. 315.00
Box, Federal, Hinged Top, Interior Removable Shelf, Veneer & Inlay, 1800, 9 3/4 In. 9775.00
Box, Figure, Woman, Celluloid, Pink, Holds Sewing Items 22.00
Box, Fitted Interior, Ivory Items, Red, Chinese Lacquer, 5 1/2 x 13 In. 660.00
Box, Heart Shaped Crest, Spool Holder Shelf, Wall Pocket Type, 11 In. 55.00
Box, Inlaid Mahogany & Ivory, 3 Tier, Opens For Spools, 2 Drawers, 9 x 8 3/4 In. 690.00
Box, Inlaid, Inner Pincushion & Tray, Velvet Lined, 12 x 9 In. 550.00
Box, Mahogany, Lift Lid, Lift-Out Tray, 2 Secret Drawers, 9 1/8 x 11 In. 605.00
Box, Old Yellow Paint, Red, Green, Black, Round, 5 1/2 In. 605.00
Box, Pin, Porcelain, Black, White, Transfer Design, Iron Cross, 1914, 3 1/2 In. 160.00
Box, Pine, Whittled Conical Legs, 1 Nailed Drawer, Bentwood Handle, 8 3/4 x 10 In. 275.00
Box, Portrait Under Exterior Lid, S.J. North, New Britain, Ct., 3 1/2 x 4 3/4 In. 3500.00
Cabinet, Metal, 18 Shuttles, 73 Tubes With Needles, 47 Bobbins, Boye Needle Co., 1905 . 350.00
Cabinet, Spool, see Advertising category under Cabinet, Spool.
Caddy, Mahogany, Pincushion Top, 18th Century 200.00
Caddy, Thread, Pincushion Inside Lid, Spire Finial, Wooden, 8 1/2 x 8 3/4 In. 258.00
Clamp, Pincushion, Treenware, 19th Century, 9 In. 38.00
Clamp, Pincushion, Wooden, Carved Bone, Brass, 6 1/2 In. 75.00
Clamp, Queen Figure, Arrow Shape Thumbscrew, Carved Ivory, Pincushion 750.00
Clamp, Shaker Type, With Yarn Winder, Maple 200.00
Clamp, Tunbridge Ware, Wood, Ivory, England, 1850, 9 In. 265.00
Darner, Egg, Woman With Long Hair, Sterling Silver, Art Nouveau, 6 In. 110.00
Darner, Egg, Wooden 7.00
Darner, Glass, Aqua 50.00
Darner, Sterling Silver Handle 55.00
Dressmaker's Form, Brown Cloth, Papier-Mache Panels, Iron Stand, 1950s 25.00
Dressmaker's Form, Wire & Cloth Body 50.00
Flax Wheel, Chestnut, Bamboo Turned Legs, Early 19th Century 115.00
Frame, Quilting, Curly Maple, Turned Legs & Posts, Clamps, 36 x 111 In. 660.00
Kit, Egg Shape, Embossed, Tassel, Brass, Case, 1940s 48.00
Kit, Shoe Form, Wooden Models Of Dutch Clogs, 1930, Pair 45.00
Knitting Sheath, Treenware, Goose Wing, Carved, 18th Century, England 225.00
Machine, Hand Crank, Black Enamel & Gilding, 14 In. 165.00
Machine, Lemens Muller, Dresden, Germany 200.00
Machine, Singer, Featherlight, Attachments, Case 440.00
Machine, Singer, Featherweight, No. 221 ....300.00 to 395.00
Machine, Singer, No. 3, Portable, Hand Crank, Domed Case, 1898 .... 330.00
Machine, Wilcox & Gibbs, Manual, Box, c.1910 .... 410.00
Necessarie Case, 14 Original Items 395.00
Necessarie Case, Veneered, Inlaid, 4 Crystal Jars, Victorian 33.00
Needle Case, 1878 Paris Exhibition Scenes, Bone 145.00
Needle Case, Churn Shape, Improved Automatic, Mauchline 145.00
Needle Case, Ivory, Cylinder, England, 1860s 85.00
Needle Case, Ivory, Overall Dragon, China, 1840 .... 115.00
Needle Case, Lathe Turned Form, Bone, England, 1880s 50.00
Needle Case, Overall Beaded Design, Dark Blue, Red, White On Bone, 1840s 145.00
Needle Case, Parasol, Stanhope 72.00
Needle Case, Sterling Silver 8.00
Needle Case, Umbrella Form, Fist Handle, Bone, England, 1870s 165.00
Pattern, Simplicity, 2 White & 1 Black Young Girls Picture, 1970, Size 10, Used 5.00
Pincushion, Baby's Shoe 25.00
Pincushion, Beadwork, Velvet, Brown Chintz Backing, Victorian, 3 3/4 x 4 In. 55.00

Pincushion, Bellow Shape, Ivory, 1820 .... 235.00
Pincushion, Bisque, Rabbit, Pulling A Cart, 1900, 3 In. ....95.00 to 130.00
Pincushion, Bulldog, Glass Eyes 250.00
Pincushion, Car 65.00
Pincushion, Embroidered Flowers & Insects, Dated 1779, 6 x 7 1/2 In. 1500.00
Pincushion, Felix, Walking, 4 In. 132.00
Pincushion, Lion, On Branch 45.00
Pincushion, Pig, Porcelain 65.00
Pincushion, Shoe, Sterling Silver 85.00
Pincushion, Shoe, Yellow & Black, Green Velvet Insert, Victorian, 9 In. 525.00
Pincushion, Sterling Rim, Victorian, Large 165.00
Pincushion, Thimble Holding, Jockey Cap Form, 3 In. 220.00
Pincushion, Thread Holder, Wood, Velvet, Wax Strawberry 45.00
Pincushion Dolls are listed in their own category.
Prick Wheel, Brass & Leather, Thimble Head, Hidden Needle Case, England, 3 In. 250.00
Scissors, Jesus & Mary, Victorian 20.00
Scissors, Silver Sterling, Ornate Heart Shaped Handles 75.00
Sewing Set, Nancy & Sluggo, Original Box, 1949, 16 In. 100.00
Shuttle, Tatting, Celluloid, Pink, Green Pearlized, 1930s 65.00
Shuttle, Tatting, Sterling Silver, Floral Design, Art Nouveau, Early 20th Century 235.00
Shuttle, Tatting, Tortoiseshell, 1860 .... 65.00
Spool Cabinets are in the Advertising category under Cabinet, Spool.
Spool Holder, Wood, Drawer, 4 Tapered Feet, Pincushion On Top, 8 1/4 x 5 1/2 In. 145.00
Tape Loom, Boxed Tape, Box, 1830s, 20 In. 695.00
Tape Loom, Hand Held 770.00
Tape Loom, Mortise & Tenon Construction, Numbered Parts 1650.00
Tape Loom, Salesman's Sample, 6 Foot Pedals At Base, 12 x 10 In. 1750.00
Tape Loom, Weaving Tool, Rosehead Nails 1195.00
Tape Measure, Barrel Of Apples, Celluloid, Germany, 1920s, 1 1/2 In. 248.00
Tape Measure, Basket Form, Painted Flowers, Celluloid, Spring Wind, 1920s 145.00
Tape Measure, Bell Shape, Mauchline, Dartmouth University 75.00
Tape Measure, Bone, Barrel Form, Turned Design, England, 1850-1860 ....100.00 to 175.00
Tape Measure, Brass, Shoe Form, 3 Feet In 1 Shoe, 1900 .... 165.00
Tape Measure, Carstairs, Man Who Cares Says Carstairs, Steel 20.00
Tape Measure, Clam Form, A Clam With 3 Feet, White Metal, 1900 .... 195.00
Tape Measure, Clock, Alarm 65.00
Tape Measure, Egg, Box 45.00
Tape Measure, Fruit Basket, Celluloid, Germany, 2 In. 50.00
Tape Measure, General Electric Refrigerators, 1920s 40.00
Tape Measure, Hound Dog 20.00
Tape Measure, Ivory, Vegetable Form, Pierced, Manual Wind, England, 1860-1900 ..... 125.00
Tape Measure, Kimball's, Concord, N.H., Celluloid, Blue & White 24.00
Tape Measure, Lamp, Brass, Celluloid, Germany, 1930s, 2 1/2 In. 99.00
Tape Measure, Lion 55.00
Tape Measure, Lock, Nickel Plated Brass, Austria, c.1900, 1 3/4 In. 187.00
Tape Measure, Mandolin, Germany, 1930s, 4 In. 132.00
Tape Measure, Movie Star, Celluloid 125.00
Tape Measure, Owl, Metal, Glass Eyes, Germany, Pre-World War II, 1 1/2 In. 44.00
Tape Measure, Pig, Running, Celluloid, 2 In. 42.00
Tape Measure, Reddy Kilowatt, Metal Tape, Gold Tin Sides, 1 5/8 In. 27.00
Tape Measure, Rose Basket, Celluloid, Germany, 1 1/2 In. 50.00
Tape Measure, Sadiron 55.00
Tape Measure, Sailing Ship Form, Celluloid, Spring Wind, 1930s 155.00
Tape Measure, Scotty Dog, Celluloid 48.00
Tape Measure, Scotty Dogs 135.00
Tape Measure, Star Kist Tuna, Box 20.00
Tape Measure, Try Angelus Marshmallows 195.00
Tape Measure, Yours For Health, Lydia E. Pinkham, Celluloid, 1 1/2 In. 33.00
Thimble, Brass, Peeps, Gold, Fashion For Sportswomen, England 150.00
Thimble, Embossed Cherubs & Flowers, Sterling Silver 75.00
Thimble, Gold, Alternating Plain & Scroll Panels, Mt. Mongoram, Case 290.00
Thimble, Sterling Silver & Gold 60.00

Thimble, Sterling Silver Femme-Fleur-Swimmer, Stern Bros. 605.00
Thimble, Sterling Silver, 3 Views Of Washington, D.C., Simons Bros. Co. 405.00
Thimble, Sterling Silver, Amethyst Stone Top, Georg Jensen Type 230.00
Thimble, Sterling Silver, Birds In Foliage, Waite, Thresher Co. 230.00
Thimble, Sterling Silver, Cupids Holding Swags, Simons Bros., 1900 .... 275.00
Thimble, Sterling Silver, Enamel White Lilies, Moonstone Top, David Anderson, 1930 ... 260.00
Thimble, Sterling Silver, Florals On Band, Simons Bros., 1900 .... 45.00
Thimble, Sterling Silver, Marked Star & 11 .... 30.00
Thimble, Sterling Silver, Pale Blue Band Of Flowers, Enameled, Red Stone Top, 1900 ... 195.00
Thimble Holder, Acorn Shape 185.00
Thimble Holder, Mark Twain 30.00
Thimble Holder, Mother-Of-Pearl, Purse Form, Brass, England, 1860s 90.00
Thimble Holder, Queen Victoria Diamond Jubilee, 14K Gold Thimble 495.00
Thimble Holder, Tortoiseshell Case, England, 1860s 235.00
Thimble Holder, Velvet, Basket Shape, Red, White Arched Handle, England, 1860s 145.00
Thread Waxer, Acorn Shape, Sterling Top 145.00
Yarn Reel, Dark Natural Patina, Crooked Center Spindle, Primitive, 36 In. 50.00
Yarn Reel, Geared Counter, Hardwood, Turned & Chip Carved, Tabletop, 17 In. 192.00
Yarn Winder, 4 Carved Finials On Legs, Folk Art Type, Germany, 23 x 21 In. 950.00
Yarn Winder, Pine, Hardwood, 3 Footed, Turned Column, Revolving Reel, 32 In. 330.00
Yarn Winder, Pine, Maple, Turned, Counter Mechanism, 19th Century, 40 In. 80.00
Yarn Winder, Wooden, Expanding Slats, 19 In. 60.00

SHAKER items are characterized by simplicity, functionalism, and orderliness. There were many Shaker communities in America from the eighteenth century to the present day. The religious order made furniture, small wooden pieces, and packaged medicines, herbs, and jellies to sell to *outsiders*. Other useful objects were made for use by members of the community. Shaker furniture is listed in this book in the Furniture category.

Basket, 15 x 24 x 19 1/2 In. 200.00
Basket, 2 Handles, 4 x 11 1/2 In. 60.00
Basket, Berry, Slanted 65.00
Basket, Berry, Splint, Quart, 3 1/2 x 6 3/8 In. 242.00
Basket, Work, Rim Wrapping Red Satin Ribbon, Signed Mary L____N.Y., 5 x 15 In. ... 475.00
Bottle, Medicine, Shaker Cherry Pectoral Syrup, Canterbury, No. 1, 5 3/8 In. 220.00
Box, 1-Finger Base, 1-Finger On Lid, Oval, 2 1/2 x 5 x 3 1/4 In. 92.00
Box, 2-Finger Base, 1-Finger On Lid, Brown, Oval, 6 x 4 1/2 x 2 In. 173.00
Box, 2-Finger Base, 1-Finger On Lid, Chrome Yellow, 5 3/4 x 4 In. 3300.00
Box, 2-Finger Base, 1-Finger On Lid, Pincushion, Canterbury, Oval, 3 3/4 In. 1045.00
Box, 2-Finger Base, 1-Finger On Lid, Red Wash, 4 3/8 x 3 1/8 In. 825.00
Box, 3-Finger Base, 1-Finger On Lid, Blue Paint, Sabbathday Lake, 9 In. 2365.00
Box, 3-Finger Base, 1-Finger On Lid, Dark Mustard, 8 3/8 x 5 5/8 In. 2200.00
Box, 3-Finger Base, 1-Finger On Lid, Oval, 12 1/4 In. 1100.00
Box, 3-Finger Base, Bentwood, Oval, Inscribed J.W. Adams, Lid, 1862, 6 In. 920.00
Box, 3-Finger Base, Copper Tacks, 12 In. 205.00
Box, 3-Finger Base, Copper Tacks, Union Village, Ohio, 8 1/2 In. 192.00
Box, 3-Finger Base, Right Handed, Maple, c.1840, 5 x 13 1/4 In. 876.00
Box, 4-Finger Base, 1-Finger On Lid, Pumpkin, 11 3/8 x 8 In. 3850.00
Box, 4-Finger Base, Red Orange, Oval, Copper Tacks, Lid, 7 x 5 x 2 1/2 In. 978.00
Box, Bentwood, Copper Tacks, Harvard Style, Oval, 5 1/8 In. 510.00
Box, Bentwood, Green Paint, Harvard Style, Oval, 6 In. 455.00
Box, Blue Paint, Round, 6 3/4 In. 520.00
Box, Candle, Pine, Floral Design, White, Green, Yellow, Red Ground, 13 In. 245.00
Box, Cutlery, Bentwood, Lapped, Center Divider, Turned Handle 44.00
Box, Finger Construction, Steel Tacks, Presentation Inscription, 6 3/4 In. 165.00
Box, Gray Paint, Copper Tacks, Round, 6 3/4 In. 385.00
Box, Gray Paint, Copper Tacks, Round, 7 3/4 In. 135.00
Box, Gray, Blue Paint, Round, 5 3/8 In. 385.00
Box, Green Paint, Round, 7 1/2 In. 315.00
Box, Light Green Paint, White, Blue Highlights, Oval, 13 In. 715.00
Box, Natural Finish, Oval, 5 1/2 x 3 1/2 x 2 In. 405.00
Box, Sage Green Paint, Round, 15 x 6 3/8 In. 575.00

Box, Seed, Shakers Genuine Garden Seeds, Mt. Lebanon, 23 x 11 In. . . . . .770.00 to 1450.00
Box, Sewing, Cherry & Curly Maple, Tiered, Pincushion On Cover, 6 In. 247.00
Box, Sewing, Cover, Swing Handle, Pincushions, Copper Tacks, 6 3/4 In. 180.00
Box, Sewing, Sabbathday Lake Shakers Maine, Oval, Handle, 5 1/2 x 7 In. 175.00
Box, Sewing, White Silk Damask Lining, Swivel Handle, Copper Tacks, 7 3/4 In. 220.00
Box, White Pine & Maple, Mt. Lebanon, Oval, 1 3/4 x 4 1/4 In. 295.00
Broom, Cobweb, Union Village, Ohio, 94 In. 138.00
Brush, Hearth, Black Bristles, 21 1/2 In. 73.00
Bucket, Sugar, Interlaced Wooden Bands, Watervliet, 12 1/2 x 12 1/2 In. 605.00
Caddy, Thread, Hardwood, Bobbins, Velvet Pincushion, 6 In. 350.00
Canister, Spice, Bark, Wood, 3 Piece 200.00
Carrier, Egg, 2-Finger, Oval, 14 1/2 In. 880.00
Carrier, Egg, Bird's-Eye Maple, Wire Fasteners, Spring Clip, Enfield, 11 x 13 In. 1375.00
Carrier, Sewing, 4-Finger Construction, Copper Tacks, Cloth Lining, Handle, 9 In. 247.00
Cloak, Blue Wool, Child's, 25 In. 469.00
Coffeepot, Pewter Finial, Side Spout, 12 1/4 In. 100.00
Colander, Rim Handles, Tin, 22 In. 72.00
Darner, 6 In. 60.00
Dust Pan, Turned Wooden Handle, 34 1/2 In. 330.00
Foot Warmer, Tin, Wooden Base & Top, Punched Pinwheel Designs, Enfield, 11 In. 797.00
Hanger, Cloak, Pine & Poplar, Harvard, Mass., 36 1/2 In. 192.00
Lap Desk, Pine, Poplar & Walnut, Hinged Lid, Pull-Out Inkwell Drawer, Hancock, 11 In. . . 935.00
Mold, Box Maker's, Screw Clamp, 2 Sizes, 1 Oval, 1 Round, 14 3/4 In., Pair 412.00
Pail, Wooden, Blue, Diamond Shaped Metal Mount, Bail Handle, 3 1/2 x 4 1/2 In. 355.00
Peeler, Apple, Table Clamp, Canterbury, 17 In. 522.00
Poster, Shaker Fancy Goods, Painted, Frame, 8 1/2 x 5 1/2 In. 135.00
Rug, Hooked, Memorial, Myra V. Skinner, 40 x 63 In. 1250.00
Rug, Rag, Multicolored, Red & Olive Border, Canterbury, 23 x 38 In. 220.00
Sewing Kit, Folding Type, Pocket For Needle Packets, Silk, 1920 . . . . 60.00
Shawl, Shoulder Fitted, Wool, Fringe, Sister Mildred Barber, Sabbathday Lake, 24 In. . . . 93.00
Shovel, Grain, Wooden, 44 In. 385.00
Sieve, Cheese, Woven Splint, 9 In. 3357.00
Sieve, Horsehair, Sabbath Day Lake, 11 In. 105.00
Sieve, Woven Horsehair, Bentwood, Pleasant Hill, 9 In. 357.00
Stove, Cast Iron, 1 Door, Double Arched Panels Over Shelf, Cabriole Legs, 32 x 23 In. . . 415.00
Swift, Table Clamp, Hardwood, Yellow Varnish, 20 3/4 In. 440.00
Swift, Wooden, Yellow Varnish, 19 In. 55.00
Tool Chest, Cherry, Dovetailed Case, 9 Drawers, Union Village, 24 x 15 In. 1100.00

SHAVING MUGS were popular from 1860 to 1900. Many types were
made, including occupational mugs featuring pictures of men's jobs.
There were scuttle mugs, silver-plated mugs, glass-lined mugs, and
others.

2 Horse's Heads, Wm. Pohlman, Koken Barbers Supply, St. Louis, 4 In. 255.00
A Souvenir Of The Great Way, Pottery, 4 1/4 In. 55.00
Bust Of A Woman, A.J. Miller, Gold Trim, 1925, 3 1/2 In. 360.00
Crossed American Flags, Porcelain, 4 1/2 In. 151.00
Eagle & Crossed American Flags, C.T. Wilcox, 1925, 3 5/8 In. 155.00
Eagle & Crossed American Flags, H. Diven, 1895-1925, 4 In. 275.00
Floral, 3 1/2 In. 55.00
Fraternal, American Order Of United Workmen, Mark Greely, 4 In. 55.00
Fraternal, Brotherhood Of Railroad Trainmen, W.A. Crawshaw, 4 In. 145.00
Fraternal, Foresters Of America, John R. Martin, Limoges, 3 5/8 In. 575.00
Fraternal, G.A.R., Medal, Hollis Cook, Gold Trim, 3 3/8 In. 440.00
Fraternal, Odd Fellows, United Auto, Knights Templar, J. Smith, Limoges, 3 5/8 In. 1265.00
Fraternal, Order Of Eagles, C.J. Bonath, Gold Trim, 1885-1925, 3 3/4 In. 155.00
Fraternal, Woodsmen Of The World, Emil F. Rudert, Germany, 3 5/8 In. 155.00
Horses & Eagle, Virtue, Liberty & Independence, Pennsylvania 585.00
Hunter, 2 Hunting Dogs On Point, H.R. Rhorer, 1895-1925, 3 3/4 In. 165.00
Hunter Shooting Ducks, F.J. Mitschke, Limoges, 3 7/8 In. 205.00
Occupational, 2 Men Playing Billiards, L.C. Childress, 3 5/8 In. 330.00
Occupational, 2-Door Coupe, Full Blue Wrap, 1925, 3 1/2 In. 2100.00
Occupational, 3 Men Working In Bakery, J. Marisndki, Gold Trim, 3 7/8 In. 385.00

Occupational, Artist's Pallet, T.F. Wayne, c.1900, 3 1/2 In. 360.00
Occupational, Ax, John Deitrich, 1895-1925, 3 3/8 In. 175.00
Occupational, Baker, 1885-1925, 3 7/8 In. 1155.00
Occupational, Barroom Scene, Barney O'Bryan, 1885-1925, 3 7/8 In. 130.00
Occupational, Barroom Scene, Germany, 1885-1925, 3 3/4 In. 154.00
Occupational, Barroom Scene, Julius Mertz, c.1900 .... 305.00
Occupational, Barroom Scene, Thos. Wooley, Gold Trim, 3 1/2 In. 495.00
Occupational, Bartender, Haviland 55.00
Occupational, Baseball Player 3080.00
Occupational, Blacksmith, Shoeing Horse, J.W. Morrical, Limoges, 3 5/8 In. 525.00
Occupational, Blacksmith, Standing At Anvil, Wm. Johnson, Limoges, 3 5/8 In. 415.00
Occupational, Butcher Cutting Meat, Jos. Hiltz, 1890-1925, 3 5/8 In. 360.00
Occupational, Cabinet Maker, B.W. Riley, Limoges, 1885-1925, 3 5/8 In. 330.00
Occupational, Farmer Plowing Field, James Ford, 1885-1925, 3 1/2 In. 255.00
Occupational, Farmer Plowing His Field, K.E. Muenckow, c.1900, 3 3/4 In. 470.00
Occupational, Governor, Pennsylvania Coat Of Arms, W.C. Sproul, 1919-1923 .... 675.00
Occupational, Groceries, Enameled, Koken B.S. Co., St. Louis, Mo., 4 In. 495.00
Occupational, Grocery Scene, Clerk & Woman, Ed. Nye, c.1900, 3 3/4 In. 660.00
Occupational, Hand Operating Telegraph Key, J.A. Brownlee, 1925, 3 5/8 In. 415.00
Occupational, Hardware Store Scene, K. Raftshal, 1885-1925, 3 5/8 In. 260.00
Occupational, Horse Drawn Buggy, Aug. Kern Barber Supply Co., 3 3/4 In. 210.00
Occupational, Horse Drawn Dairy Wagon, 1885-1925, 3 1/2 In. 467.00
Occupational, Horse Drawn Lager Beer Wagon, Sig. Propst, Gold Trim, 3 3/4 In. 550.00
Occupational, Horse Drawn Milk Wagon & Driver, c.1900, 3 7/8 In. 525.00
Occupational, Horse Drawn Stake Wagon, Charley Cross, Gold Trim, 3 1/2 In. 550.00
Occupational, Horse Running In Field, Arthur Protzman, 1890-1925, 3 5/8 In. 110.00
Occupational, House Painter, 1885-1925, 3 5/8 In. 577.00
Occupational, Ice Block & Tongs, C.M. Mohler, Fire & Ice On Name, 3 5/8 In. 470.00
Occupational, Ice Man, Horse Drawn Wagon, Word Ice At Top, 3 3/4 In. 175.00
Occupational, Locomotive & Tender, Full Green Wrap, c.1900, 3 3/8 In. 305.00
Occupational, Locomotive On Trestle, Hans Gager, Gold Trim, 1925, 3 3/4 In. 110.00
Occupational, Mack Ice Truck, Stamped Germany, c.1900, 3 3/4 In. 1020.00
Occupational, Mail Man, Al Rowland, Stamped D & Co, c.1900, 3 5/8 In. 1075.00
Occupational, Man, Driving A Touring Car, Germany, 1885-1925, 3 3/4 In. 908.00
Occupational, Member Of Pennsylvania Legislature, State Logo 595.00
Occupational, Mortar & Pestle, C.W. Friedman, c.1900, 3 3/8 In. 220.00
Occupational, Mortar & Pestle, J.G. Scraggs, Gold Trim, 1925, 3 5/8 In. 275.00
Occupational, Mortar & Pestle, L.T. Hoy, Stamped H. & Co., c.1900, 3 7/8 In. 175.00
Occupational, Painter's Bucket, W.W. Stowe, c.1900, 3 5/8 In. 415.00
Occupational, Pipe & Musical Notes Bar, Albert Leon, 3 3/4 In. 495.00
Occupational, Pipe Wrench, Emil Flachsmann, Crossed Flags, 3 5/8 In. 190.00
Occupational, Portrait Painter, 3 Ladies, Diamond Medallions, Geo. S. Currant 295.00
Occupational, Railroad Caboose, F.M. Brallier, H. & B.T.R.R., c.1900, 3 7/8 In. 440.00
Occupational, Railroad Hand Car, Dan Tracy, c.1900, 3 1/2 In. 360.00
Occupational, Sea Captain, With Brush, Porcelain, E. Bohne Sohne, 4 In. 1035.00
Occupational, Shorn Sheep, C.H. Lord, 1890-1925, 3 3/4 In. 605.00
Occupational, Sportsman Fly Fishing 1815.00
Occupational, Stationary Engine, A.O. Beach, Regilt, 1885-1925, 4 In. 100.00
Occupational, Stationary Gasoline Engine, M. Binder, c.1900, 3 5/8 In. 230.00
Occupational, Stationary Machine, 1885-1925, 3 7/8 In. 467.00
Occupational, Steam Locomotive, Tender, Phillip Boyle, 3 7/8 In. 247.00
Occupational, Steer Standing, J.N. Farris, 1885-1925, 3 5/8 In. 265.00
Occupational, Steer's Head & Crossed Butcher's Tools, 3 7/8 In. 83.00
Occupational, Steer, Flowers, Hermann Giebisch, 1895-1925, 3 1/2 In. 230.00
Occupational, Stonecutter, With Pick, Gilt Trim 850.00
Occupational, Studio Camera & Tripod, Thos. McIntyre, c.1900, 4 In. 690.00
Occupational, Tinsmith, Math. Koob, 1885-1925, 3 3/4 In. 635.00
Occupational, Train Scene 295.00
Occupational, Violin & Guitar, Chas. Hughes, c.1900, 4 In. 360.00

SHAWNEE POTTERY was started in Zanesville, Ohio, in 1937. The company made vases, novelty ware, flowerpots, planters, lamps, and cookie jars. Three dinnerware lines were made: Corn, Lobster Ware, and Valencia (a solid color line). White Corn pattern utility pieces were made in 1945. Corn King was made from 1946 to 1954; Corn Queen, with darker green leaves and lighter colored corn, from 1954 to 1961. Shawnee produced pottery for George Rumrill during the late 1930s. The company closed in 1961.

Ashtray, Magnolia Blossom, 4 3/4 In.	15.00
Bank, Muggsy, Commemorative	195.00
Bank, Winnie Pig, Butterscotch	425.00
Casserole, Corn King, Cover, 11 In.	65.00 to 85.00
Coffeepot, Sunflower, 6 1/4 In.	80.00
Cookie Jar, Corn King, 9 3/4 In.	185.00 to 225.00
Cookie Jar, Drum Major, 10 In.	310.00 to 375.00
Cookie Jar, Drum Major, Gold Trim, 10 In.	650.00
Cookie Jar, Dutch Boy, Gold Decals	280.00
Cookie Jar, Dutch Girl, Gold Decals	305.00
Cookie Jar, Fern, Blue, Octagonal	85.00
Cookie Jar, Happy, Gold Trim, Patches	300.00
Cookie Jar, Jo Jo Clown	185.00 to 370.00
Cookie Jar, Lucky Elephant, Gold Trim, Flower Decals	575.00
Cookie Jar, Lucky Elephant, Gold, Decal	535.00
Cookie Jar, Owl, Gold Trim	125.00 to 185.00
Cookie Jar, Puss 'n Boots, Gold Trim, Decals	275.00
Cookie Jar, Puss 'n Boots, Long Tail	165.00 to 200.00
Cookie Jar, Smiley Pig, Bank Head, Gold	150.00
Cookie Jar, Smiley Pig, Chocolate	600.00
Cookie Jar, Smiley Pig, Chrysanthemum, Gold Trim	260.00 to 350.00
Cookie Jar, Smiley Pig, Poppy	800.00
Cookie Jar, Smiley Pig, Red Neckerchief	135.00
Cookie Jar, Smiley Pig, Tulip	350.00
Cookie Jar, Winnie Pig, Blue Neckerchief	300.00
Cookie Jar, Winnie Pig, Gold Trim	455.00
Cookie Jar, Winnie Pig, Shamrock	275.00 to 500.00
Creamer, Corn King	32.00
Creamer, Puss 'n Boots, Gold Trim	215.00
Figurine, Standing Bear, Sandy Rose	18.00
Figurine, Terrier, Sore Paw, 6 In.	39.00
Jug, Ball, Fern & Flower	48.00
Lamp, Bluebirds	100.00
Lamp, Mother Goose	125.00
Mug, Corn King, 8 Oz.	45.00
Pitcher, Bo Beep, 8 In.	90.00 to 110.00
Pitcher, Chanticleer	65.00 to 125.00
Pitcher, Smiley Pig, Blue, Red	165.00
Pitcher, Smiley Pig, Clover Blossom	220.00 to 300.00
Pitcher, Smiley Pig, Peach & Blue Flowers	120.00 to 185.00
Planter, Basket Weave	20.00
Planter, Boy & Chicken, Gold Trim	50.00
Planter, Deer	40.00
Planter, High Chair, Pink	28.00
Planter, Pony, Kenwood	60.00
Planter, Pony, Red	45.00
Planter, Ram	22.00
Planter, Squirrel With Stump	45.00
Planter, Tony Peddler	22.00
Planter, Water Can, Gold Decals, Blue	158.00
Salt & Pepper, Chanticleer, 5 1/2 In.	40.00
Salt & Pepper, Corn King, Large	30.00 to 35.00
Salt & Pepper, Dutch Boy & Girl, Gold Trim, Large	85.00
Salt & Pepper, Farmer Pig	55.00
Salt & Pepper, Flower & Fern	38.00
Salt & Pepper, Flowerpot, Gold Trim	22.00
Salt & Pepper, Muggsy	145.00 to 275.00

Salt & Pepper, Sailor & Girl, Gold Trim 50.00
Salt & Pepper, Winnie Pig & Smiley Pig, Blue Neckerchief 90.00
Salt & Pepper, Winnie Pig & Smiley Pig, Gold Decal, Green Neckerchief, Large 250.00
Sugar, Cottage 325.00
Teapot, Granny Anne, Peach Apron 90.00
Teapot, Granny Anne, Purple Apron 200.00

SHEARWATER pottery is a family business started by Mr. and Mrs. G. W. Anderson, Sr., and their three sons. The local Ocean Springs, Mississippi, clays were used to make the wares in the 1930s. The company is still in business.

Vase, Blue Glaze, Pottery, Early 20th Century, 7 In. 97.00
Vase, Blue, 6 In. 50.00
Vase, Fish, Birds, Pelican, Horse With Rider, Light Blue Glaze, 5 1/2 In. 495.00

SHEET MUSIC from the past centuries is now collected. The favorites are examples with covers featuring artistic or historic pictures. Early sheet music covers were lithographed, but by the 1900s photographic reproductions were used. The early music was larger than more recent sheets, and you must watch out for examples that were trimmed to fit in a twentieth-century piano bench.

3 Little Words, Amos & Andy 25.00
A Fellow On Furlough, B. Worth, Martin Block Pub Co., 1943 . . . .   6.00
Aba Daba Honeymoon, 2 Weeks With Love, Powell, Montalban, 1942 . . . .   15.00
Across The Field, Ohio State, Wm. Dougherty, 1915 . . . .   20.00
Admiral Dewey's Victory, Two Step March, Ernest L. Bolling 55.00
All Aboard For Home Sweet Home, A. Burkhart, A. Piantadosi & Co., 1918 . . . .   4.00
Always & Always, Movie Mannequin, Joan Crawford, 1937 . . . .   15.00
Amelia Earhart's Last Flight, 1939 . . . .   20.00
American Patrol, F.W. Meacham, Piano Solo, Moderne Pub., Chicago, 1941 . . . .   7.00
Anchors Aweigh, Frank Sinatra & Gene Kelly 15.00
Annie Get Your Gun 20.00
Any Bonds Today?, I. Berlin, GPO, 1941, 4 Pages 7.00
Baby Parade, Eddie Cantor 30.00
Basin Street Blues, Spencer Williams 15.00
Battle Of Fort Donelson, 1862, Multicolored Battle Scene 250.00
Be A Clown, From The Movie The Pirate, Judy Garland On Cover, 1948 . . . .   30.00
Book, 50 Popular Hawaiian Songs, 1936, 66 Pages 12.00
Book, Buffalo Bill's Wild West Song, 17 Songs, 1912, 10 x 14 In.   244.00
Book, Heathen Chinee Musical Album, Bret Harte Song, 1871, 8 x 11 In. 175.00
Book, Marines Hymn, Manhattan Publications, New York, 1941, 3 Pages 6.00
Born To Be Kissed, Jean Harlow & Howard Dietz On Cover, 1935 . . . .   70.00
Break The News To Mother Gently, N.Y., 1892 . . . .   5.00
Carry On, 316th Infantry Marching Song, K.S. Clark 12.00
Chiquita Banana, United Fruit Co., 1947 . . . .   75.00
Come On, Rally 'Round Our Flag Boys, Esene Pub. Co., New York, 1917, 2 Pages 7.00
Day After Forever, Going My Way, Bing Crosby, 1944 . . . .   8.00
Don't Fence Me In, C. Porter, Hollywood Canteen, 1944 . . . .   6.00
Don't Give Up The Ship, Shipmates Forever, Dick Powell & Ruby Keeler, 1935 . . . .   10.00
Dreaming Of Home Sweet Home, B. MacDonald, Shapiro, Bernstein & Co., 1918 . . . . . .   5.00
Eliza's Flight From Uncle Tom's Cabin, 1852, 13 x 10 1/4 In. 60.00
Everybody Two Step Rag, Black Dancers 25.00
Faithful Forever, Gulliver's Travels, Fleischer Studios, 1939 . . . .   18.00
Hand Of Fate, Shenandoah, 1925 . . . .   60.00
Have Yourself A Merry Little Christmas, Judy Garland Cover, 1944 . . . .   30.00
Here's To You, MacArthur, Picture, 1942 . . . .   40.00
I'll Be Home For Christmas, Melrose Music Corp., 1943, 2 Pages 6.00
I'm Always Chasing Rainbows, Dolly Sisters, Betty Grable, John Payne, 1945 . . . .   9.00
Intermezzo, Movie, Leslie Howard & Introducing Ingrid Bergman 12.00
Jerry Lewis, From The Movie The Caddy, 1950s 95.00
King Of The Air, Dedicated To Glenn Curtiss, Hudson Flyer, 1910 . . . .   65.00
Let The Rest Of The World Go By, Irish Eyes Are Smiling, D. Haynes, J. Haver, 1944 . . .   10.00

Life's Full Of Consequence, Cabin In The Sky, Lena Horne, 1943 .... 35.00
Loveliest Night Of The Year, Great Caruso, Mario Lanza & Anne Blyth, 1950 .... 8.00
Merry Widow Waltz, Maurice Chevalier, Jeannette MacDonald, 1935 .... 12.00
Moon Song, Hello Everybody, Kate Smith, 1932 .... 10.00
My Mammy, Al Jolson, 1931 .... 15.00
My Sweetheart Went Down With The Ship, Titanic On Cover, Roger, Lewis, 1912 ..... 35.00
New York & Coney Island Bicycle March Two-Step, E.T. Paull, 1898 .... 60.00
Oh What A Beautiful Morning, Oklahoma, 1943 .... 8.00
Oh! You Suffragettes, Parade Scene, Blue, Yellow & Black, 1912 .... 350.00
Old Apple Tree, Swing Your Lady, H. Bogart, 1938 .... 9.00
Ossian's Serenade, P.T. Barnum, Jenny Lind & Ossian Dodge, 1850 .... 100.00
Over There, World War I, By Geo. M. Cohan, Troops In Song, Rockwell, Cover, 1917 ... 45.00
Precious Little Thing Called Love, Shopworn Angel, G. Cooper, 1928 .... 90.00
Pullman Porter Blues, 1921 .... 20.00
Rag Doll, By Nacio Herb Brown, 1928 .... 20.00
Rainbow Round My Shoulder, Singing Fool, Al Jolson 10.00
Ramona, Dolores Del Rio, 1927 .... 8.00
Remember Pearl Harbor, D. Reid, Sammy Kaye, Republic Music Corp, 1942 .... 9.00
Rudolph The Red-Nosed Reindeer, St. Nicholas Music, 1949 .... 5.00
Sam, The Old Accordion Man, Fox Trot, 1927 .... 40.00
Say A Prayer For The Boys Over There, H. Magidson, Hers To Hold, 1943 .... 6.00
Shoo Fly, Don't Bother Me, Unbound, 4 Pages, 1869, 10 x 13 In. 148.00
Sonny Boy, Singing Fool, Al Jolson, 1928 .... 12.00
String Of Pearls, Glenn Miller Story, June Allyson, James Stewart On Cover, 1954 ..... 30.00
Sweet Dreams Sweetheart, Hollywood Canteen, 1944 .... 12.00
Temperance Battle Cry, Godey's Lady's, 1875, 2 Pages 10.00
There'll Always Be An England, G.V. Thompson Ltd., Toronto, 1939, 3 Pages 9.00
There'll Be A Hot Time In The Town Of Berlin, J. Bushkin, J. Devries, 1943 .... 8.00
There's A Star Spangled Banner Waving Somewhere, P. Roberts, S. Darnell, 1942 ..... 6.00
Thinking Of You, Three Little Words, Fred Astaire, Red Skelton, 1931 .... 15.00
Tramp, Tramp, Tramp, The Boys Are Marching, G.F. Root, 1864 .... 65.00
Vargas, Ziegfeld Follies, 1924 .... 45.00
Virginia Polka, Blind Negro Pianist, 1860, 10 1/2 x 14 In. 293.00
Washington Evening Star March, Stannard, Clifford Berryman Cover Art, 1924 .... 15.00
Wayward Wind, Gogi Grant Picture, 1956 .... 3.00
When The Boys Come Home, J. Hay & O. Speaks, 1917, 6 Pages 7.00
When The Lights Go On Again, All Over The World, E. Seiler, 1942 .... 6.00
Wreck Of Titanic, W. Baltzell, 1912 .... 110.00
Yankee Doodle Boy, G.M. Cohan, Movie, J. Cagney, 1933 .... 7.00

SHEFFIELD items are listed in the Silver-English and Silver Plate categories.

SHELLEY first appeared on English ceramics about 1912. The Foley China Works started in England in 1860. Joseph Ball Shelley joined the company in 1862 and became a partner in 1872. Percy Shelley joined the firm in 1881. The company went through a series of name changes, and in 1910 the then Foley China Company became Shelley China. In 1929 it became Shelley Potteries. The company was acquired in 1966 by Allied English Potteries, then merged with the Doulton group in 1971. The name *Shelley* was put into use again in 1980. A trio is the name for a cup, saucer, and cake plate set.

Bowl, Melody, 3 1/2 In. 125.00
Bowl, Melody, 5 In. 175.00
Butter, Cover, Gold Flowers, Square, 4 In. 55.00
Butter, Cover, Morning Glory 185.00
Butter, Cover, Regency 150.00
Butter, Cover, Stocks 180.00
Butter Chip, Primrose 25.00
Cake Plate, White, Dainty, Tab Handles, 8 x 9 1/2 In. 60.00
Coffeepot, Rock Garden 695.00
Coffeepot, Rose Red Daisy 295.00

Coffeepot, Turquoise, Polka Dot, 2 Cup 325.00
Cookie Jar, Orange With Green Accents, Chrome Handle, 6 1/2 In. 172.00
Creamer, Blue Rock 45.00
Cup, Rosebud, Dainty 95.00
Cup & Saucer, Begonia ....55.00 to 80.00
Cup & Saucer, Blue Rock ....45.00 to 110.00
Cup & Saucer, Blue Rock, 6 Flutes 65.00
Cup & Saucer, Blue Rock, Demitasse 48.00
Cup & Saucer, Bridal Rose, Demitasse 65.00
Cup & Saucer, Campanula 78.00
Cup & Saucer, Coronation 145.00
Cup & Saucer, Crochet 60.00
Cup & Saucer, Green, Gold Trim, Demitasse 50.00
Cup & Saucer, Harebell, Demitasse 245.00
Cup & Saucer, Maytime, Henley, Beige Trim 155.00
Cup & Saucer, Pink, Dainty 85.00
Cup & Saucer, Primrose 110.00
Cup & Saucer, Regency 40.00
Cup & Saucer, Rosebud 75.00
Cup & Saucer, Rosebud, Demitasse 50.00
Cup & Saucer, Shell Pink, 6 Flutes 65.00
Cup & Saucer, Sheraton 75.00
Cup & Saucer, Stocks 55.00
Cup & Saucer, White, Dainty 60.00
Cup & Saucer, Woodland 58.00
Eggcup, Blue Rock 25.00
Gravy Boat, Sheraton 200.00
Gravy Boat, Underplate, Blue, Dainty 395.00
Gravy Boat, White, Dainty 110.00
Jug, Cover, Evening Star, Dainty 150.00
Jug, Melody, 3 In. 175.00
Plate, Begonia, 9 1/4 In. 68.00
Plate, Blue Rock, 8 In. ....35.00 to 50.00
Plate, Blue, Dainty, 8 In. 90.00
Plate, Bridal Rose, Oleander, 10 1/2 In. 70.00
Plate, Dubarry, 6 In. 24.00
Plate, Melody, 9 In. 225.00
Plate, Rose Red Daisy, 6 1/4 In. 85.00
Plate, Rose Spray, 8 In. 40.00
Plate, Rosebud, 8 In. ....40.00 to 55.00
Plate, Server, Melody, 9 x 10 In. 275.00
Plate, Sheraton, 8 1/2 In. 45.00
Plate, Sheraton, Cobalt Blue, 9 3/4 In. 80.00
Saucer, Begonia 18.00
Snack Set, Regency, Tray & Cup 50.00
Sugar & Creamer, Blue, Dainty, Medium 150.00
Sugar & Creamer, Rose Red Daisy 95.00
Sugar & Creamer, Tray, Rosebud, 4 x 8 In. 185.00
Table Set, Rock Garden, 3 Piece 155.00
Tea Set, Thistle, 3 Piece 165.00
Teapot, Begonia 245.00
Teapot, Black Cat 85.00
Teapot, Blue Rock 200.00
Teapot, Chrysanthemum, 4 Cup 350.00
Teapot, Dainty, Blue 495.00
Teapot, Evening Star, Dainty, 6 In. 400.00
Teapot, Yellow Phlox, Large 350.00
Tray, Bridal Rose 185.00
Tray, Melody, Oval, 10 x 12 In. 375.00
Trio, Daffodil 110.00
Trio, Heather 110.00
Trio, Jonquil 110.00

Vase, Allover Circles, Lavender, Green, Blue, Orange, Baluster, 7 1/4 In. 210.00

SHIRLEY TEMPLE, the famous movie star, was born in 1928. She made her first movie in 1932. Thousands of items picturing Shirley have been and still are being made. Shirley Temple dolls were first made in 1934 by Ideal Toy Company. Millions of Shirley Temple cobalt blue glass dishes were made by Hazel Atlas Glass Company and U.S. Glass Company from 1934 to 1942. They were given away as premiums for Wheaties and Bisquick. A bowl, mug, and pitcher were made as a breakfast set. Some pieces were decorated with the picture of a very young Shirley, others used a picture of Shirley in her 1936 *Captain January* costume. Although collectors refer to a cobalt creamer, it is actually the 4 1/2-inch-high milk pitcher from the breakfast set. Many of these items are being reproduced today.

Book, How I Raised Shirley Temple, By Her Mother, 1935, 40 Pages	33.00
Carriage, Doll's, Shirley Hubcaps, Face On Sides, Canvas Hood, Wooden Base	575.00
Doll, Captain January, Vinyl, Ideal, 1982	60.00
Doll, Ideal, 13 In.	125.00
Doll, Ideal, Box, 12 In.	250.00
Doll, Ideal, Box, 15 In.	450.00
Doll, Ideal, Brown Composition, Painted Eyes, Hawaiian Outfit, c.1940, 13 In.	600.00
Doll, Ideal, Composition Head, Flower Print Dress, Underclothes, 18 In.	600.00
Doll, Stowaway, Vinyl, Ideal, 1982	60.00
Doll, Vinyl, 1984, 36 In.	650.00
Doll, Vinyl, Ideal, 1972	55.00
Figurine, Curly Top, Porcelain, Nostalgia Collectibles, Japan	60.00
Figurine, Flocked Red Dress, Plaster Soapstone, 1930s, 10 In.	90.00
Mirror, Pocket, 1935	35.00
Paper Doll, 1940	75.00
Paper Doll, 1976	30.00
Photograph, Child, 1981, 8 x 10 In.	40.00
Pitcher, Milk, Blue, 4 1/2 In. . . . .*Illus*	45.00
Plate, Baby Take A Bow, Porcelain, Nostalgia Collectibles, Japan, 1982	65.00
Program, Tournament Of Roses, Shirley Cover, Grand Marshall, 1939, 44 Pages . . . .38.00 to	50.00
Record, Shirley Temple Hits, On The Good Ship Lollipop, Other Hits, 45 RPM	10.00
Sheet Music, Simple Things In Life, Curly Top, 1935	30.00
Tea Set, 11 Piece	140.00
Tea Set, Plastic Pink, 1950s, 8 Piece	85.00
Window Card, Wee Willie Winkie, 1937	240.00

SHRINER, see Fraternal category.

Shirley Temple, Pitcher, Milk, Blue, 4 1/2 In.

Decorate with the neighborhood burglar in mind. Large windows can be made less attractive to intruders if you put shelves holding plants or collectibles across the window. Decorative shelves and grilles are made for this. Of course, be sure you can open the windows in case of fire.

SILVER DEPOSIT glass was first made during the late nineteenth century. Solid sterling silver is applied to the glass by a chemical method so that a cutout design of silver metal appears against a clear or colored glass. It is sometimes called silver overlay.

Candleholder, Vintage, 1-Light, Crystal, 4 In., Pair	145.00
Decanter, Ewer Shape, Scrolled Foliate Design, Stopper, 6 3/4 In.	745.00
Decanter, Scotch & Rye, Blown Glass, Pair	90.00
Decanter, Tapering Square Shape, Floral Faceted Stopper, 9 In.	690.00
Decanter, Teardrop Shape, Oak Leaf Design, Monogram, 9 1/2 In.	860.00
Perfume Bottle, Art Nouveau, Stopper, Alvin, 1920s, 6 1/2 In.	375.00
Perfume Bottle, John Scharling, Signed	225.00
Tea Set, Brown Pottery, Art Nouveau, 7 1/2 In. Teapot, 3 Piece	633.00

SILVER FLATFARE includes many of the current and out-of-production silver and silver-plated flatware patterns made in the past eighty years. Other silver is listed under Silver-American, Silver-English, etc. Most silver flatware sets that are missing a few pieces can be completed through the help of one of the many silver matching services that advertise in many of the national publications.

SILVER FLATWARE PLATED, Charter Oak, Carving Set, International, 3 Piece	285.00
Charter Oak, Food Pusher, International	65.00
Charter Oak, Salad Fork, International	38.00
Charter Oak, Seafood Fork, International	18.00
Fiddle Thread, Fish Slice, Pierced Blade, Wm. Hutton & Son, c.1870	66.00
LaVigne, Pastry Fork, Oneida	25.00
Vintage, Cheese Scoop, Hollow Handle, Rogers Bros.	125.00
SILVER FLATWARE STERLING, Alexander, Teaspoon, Lunt	15.00
Alhambra, Egg Spoon, Whiting	22.00
Avalon, Stuffing Spoon, International, 12 1/2 In.	375.00
Baronial, Punch Ladle, Frank Smith, Sons	165.00
Baronial, Punch Ladle, Tripartite Shape, Gorham, 1898, 12 In.	287.00
Bird Pattern, Child's Set, Knife, Fork, Spoon, Whiting	195.00
Botticelli, Cream Soup Spoon, Whiting	19.00
Bridal Bouquet, Citrus Spoon, Alvin	19.00
Bridal Bouquet, Cream Soup Spoon, Alvin	18.00
Bridal Rose, Ice Cream Slice, Alvin, 11 1/2 In.	450.00
Bridal Rose, Lettuce Fork, Alvin, 9 1/4 In.	185.00
Buckingham, Butter Knife, Stainless Blade, Gorham	12.00
Burgundy, Teaspoon, Gorham	25.00
Byzantine, Soup Ladle, Wood & Hughes	400.00
Cambridge, Dessert Spoon, Oval Bowl, Gorham	22.00
Camellia, Teaspoon, Gorham	10.00
Canterbury, Beef Fork, Towle	135.00
Canterbury, Berry Spoon, Towle	95.00
Canterbury, Fish Slice, Gilt, Towle	195.00
Canterbury, Lettuce Fork, Towle	95.00
Canterbury, Salad Serving Fork, Towle	100.00
Carthage, Bouillon Spoon, Wallace	12.00
Carthage, Cake Lifter, Royal Crest	19.00
Castle Rose, Stuffing Spoon, Wallace	49.00
Celestia, Berry Spoon, Wood & Hughes, 9 1/2 In.	350.00
Chambord, Sugar Spoon, Reed & Barton	18.00
Charles II, Pickle Fork, Lunt	35.00
Charles II, Sugar Spoon, Lunt	35.00
Chateau, Consomme Spoon, Lunt	22.00
Chateau Rose, Cream Sauce Ladle, Alvin	15.00
Cherub, Sugar Tongs, Watson, 4 1/2 In.	80.00
Chrysanthemum, Jelly Spoon, Durgin, 7 3/8 In.	200.00
Chrysanthemum, Luncheon Fork, Monogram, Durgin, 12 Piece	295.00
Cinderella, Iced Tea Spoon, Gorham	18.00
Classic Bouquet, Sugar Spoon, Gorham	25.00
Cluny, Tablespoon, Gorham, 6 Piece	350.00
Colonial, Cold Meat Fork, Lunt	40.00

Colonial, Gravy Ladle, Lunt 44.00
Colonial, Lettuce Fork, Whiting 75.00
Colonial, Sugar Spoon, Lunt 20.00
Colonial, Tomato Server, Engraved, Whiting 90.00
Columbia, Salad Fork, Lunt 21.00
Columbia, Teaspoon, Lunt 15.00
Corinthian, Jelly Server, Gold Wash, Gorham, c.1875, 7 1/2 In. 150.00
Damask Rose, Gravy Ladle, Oneida 30.00
Damask Rose, Lemon Fork, Oneida 14.00
Damask Rose, Teaspoon, Oneida 13.00
Dauphine, Soup Spoon, Oval, Wallace 14.00
Debussy, Iced Tea Spoon 26.00
Delicacy, Spoon, Lunt 23.00
Edward VII, Claret Ladle, Alvin, 13 1/2 In. 275.00
Eglantine, Berry Spoon, Gilt Bowl, Gorham, 9 3/8 In. 495.00
Eloquence, Cracker Scoop, Lunt 47.00
Eloquence, Salt Spoon, Lunt 11.00
Embassy Scroll, Tomato Server, Lunt 57.00
Engagement, Place Setting, Oneida, 4 Piece 48.00
Esplanade, Soup Spoon, Towle 24.00
Evening Rose, Cream Soup Spoon, Lunt 14.00
Evening Rose, Place Setting, Lunt, 4 Piece 52.00
Evening Rose, Salad Fork, Alvin 22.00
Fairfax, Baby Spoon, Pair 22.00
Fairfax, Baked Potato Server, Gorham 36.00
Fairfax, Cheese Scoop, Durgin 75.00
Fairfax, Grapefruit Spoon, Durgin, Monogram, 6 Piece 45.00
Fairfax, Iced Tea Spoon, Gorham 24.00
Festival, Bread Knife, Lunt 28.00
Festival, Butter Knife, Master, Lunt 16.00
Festival, Cream Soup Spoon, Lunt 16.00
Festival, Serving Spoon, Lunt 31.00
Fiancee, Bouillon Spoon, Weidlich 9.00
Fiancee, Teaspoon, Weidlich 14.00
Fiddle, Sugar Tongs, J. Stone, Exeter, England, c.1839 . . . . 77.00
Firelight, Butter Knife, Gorham 10.00
Firelight, Cold Meat Fork, Gorham 20.00
Firelight, Iced Tea Spoon, Gorham 18.00
Firelight, Pickle Fork, Gorham 17.00
First Frost, Baked Potato Server, Oneida 27.00
First Frost, Salad Fork, Oneida 22.00
First Frost, Teaspoon, Oneida 14.00
Fleetwood, Baby Fork, Manchester 16.00
Fleetwood, Cream Soup Spoon, Manchester 17.00
Fleetwood, Pie Server, Manchester 23.00
Fleetwood, Serving Spoon, Pierced, Manchester 37.00
Floral Lace, Sugar Spoon, Lunt 17.00
Florentine, Dessert Spoon, Alvin 32.00
Florentine, Olive Spoon, Alvin 35.00
Florentine Scroll, Baked Potato Server, Lunt 32.00
Fontainebleau, Serving Spoon, Bright Cut Floral, Gorham 125.00
Fontainebleau, Soup Ladle, Gorham 413.00
Fontana, Baked Potato Server, Towle 35.00
Fontana, Citrus Spoon, Towle 20.00
Formality, Baked Potato Server, State House 30.00
Formality, Cream Soup Spoon, State House 20.00
Formality, Grill Fork, State House 17.00
Francis I, Butter Knife, Reed & Barton 28.00
Francis I, Fruit Spoon, Reed & Barton 29.00
Francis I, Punch Ladle, Reed & Barton, 1907, 12 In. 370.00
Francis I, Serving Fork & Spoon, Reed & Barton, 1907 . . . . 201.00
Francis I, Serving Spoon, Long Handle, Reed & Barton, 14 In. 515.00
Francis I, Serving Spoon, Reed & Barton, 9 3/8 In. . . . . .154.00 to 260.00

French Provincial, Baby Fork, Towle	19.00
French Provincial, Butter Knife	12.00
French Provincial, Citrus Spoon, Towle	21.00
Frontenac, Cold Meat Fork, International, 8 7/8 In.	300.00
Frontenac, Serving Spoon, International Silver Co.	88.00
Georgian Shell, Carving Set, Whiting	35.00
Gladstone, Cold Meat Fork, Amston, 1890s	120.00
Grecian, Cake Knife, Whiting	295.00
Grecian, Mustard	95.00
Greenbrier, Teaspoon, Gorham	9.00
Hanover, Cracker Scoop, Gorham, 7 3/4 In.	250.00
Heiress, Butter Knife, Individual, Oneida	12.00
Heiress, Casserole Spoon, Oneida	30.00
Heiress, Cream Soup Spoon, Oneida	15.00
Heiress, Sugar Spoon, Oneida	13.00
Heraldic, Asparagus Fork, Gorham	475.00
Heraldic, Dessert Spoon, Gorham	42.00
Heraldic, Punch Ladle, Raised Foliage Handle, Whiting Mfg. Co., 13 In.	605.00
Heraldic, Salad Set, Gorham, 12 In.	550.00
Imperial Chrysanthemum, Cheese Scoop, Gorham, 8 1/4 In.	195.00
Imperial Queen, Beef Fork, Whiting	60.00
Imperial Queen, Berry Spoon, Whiting	125.00
Imperial Queen, Ice Cream Slice	245.00
Imperial Queen, Mustard Ladle	150.00
Irian, Gumbox Spoon, Wallace	75.00
Jenny Lind, Soup Ladle, Albert Coles	300.00
Kensington, Dessert Fork, Gold Wash, Gorham, 6 Piece	195.00
Keystone, Serving Spoon, Whiting	80.00
King, Sauce Ladle, Ribbed Bowl, R. & W. Wilson, Philadelphia	154.00
King Edward, Serving Spoon, Gorham, Whiting Division	99.00
King George, Butter Spreader, Gorham, 12 Piece	247.00
King Richard, Cocktail Fork, Towle	20.00
King Richard, Gravy Ladle, Towle	63.00
La Touraine, Punch Ladle, Reed & Barton, 12 In.	250.00
Lancaster, Macaroni Server, Gorham, 9 1/2 In.	450.00
Les Cinq Fleurs, Sardine Fork, Reed & Barton, 5 7/8 In.	145.00
Les Six Fleurs, Salad Set, Reed & Barton	172.00
Les Six Fleurs, Serving Spoon, Reed & Barton	88.00
Lily, Butter Knife, Whiting	47.00
Lily, Salad Serving Set, Gorham, 11 1/2 In.	200.00
Lily, Teaspoon, Whiting	22.00
Louis XV, Dessert Spoon, Monogram, Durgin, 6 Piece	295.00
Louis XV, Ladle, Monogram, Whiting	22.00
Louis XV, Sardine Tongs, Whiting	125.00
Love Disarmed, Fish Set, Reed & Barton, 2 Piece	770.00
Luxembourg, Butter Knife, Master	42.00
Luxembourg, Cheese Scoop, Gorham	90.00
Luxembourg, Cold Meat Fork, Gorham	90.00
Luxembourg, Cream Ladle	55.00
Lyric, Cream Soup Spoon, Gorham	13.00
Lyric, Sugar Spoon, Gorham	12.00
Lyric, Teaspoon, Gorham	9.00
Madam Jumel, Coffee Spoon	7.00
Madam Jumel, Serving Spoon	36.00
Madrigal, Pierced Tablespoon, Lunt	58.00
Madrigal, Sugar Spoon, Lunt	14.00
Majestic, Lettuce Fork, Alvin, 9 1/8 In.	150.00
Marguerite, Berry Spoon, Gorham, 8 3/4 In.	175.00
Marie Antoinette, Salad Fork, Dominick & Haff	45.00
Mazarin, Dessert Spoon, Monogram, Dominick & Haff	65.00
Meadow Song, Butter Knife, Master, Towle	17.00
Meadow Song, Dinner Fork, Towle, 7 5/8 In.	26.00
Meadow Song, Ice Cream Fork, Towle	22.00

Meadow Song, Serving Spoon, Pierced, Towle 45.00
Meadow Song, Sugar Spoon, Towle 21.00
Medallion, Soup Ladle, Gorham, 15 1/4 In. 1250.00
Medici, Dinner Fork, Gorham, 7 7/8 In. 38.00
Medici, Luncheon Fork, Gorham 16.00
Medici, Olive Fork, Gorham 17.00
Melbourne, Carving Set, Oneida 41.00
Melbourne, Cream Soup Spoon, Oneida 20.00
Melrose, Teaspoon, Alvin 12.00
Memory Lane, Gravy Ladle, Lunt 38.00
Michelangelo, Ice Cream Fork, Oneida 46.00
Michelangelo, Sugar Spoon, Oneida 22.00
Michelangelo, Teaspoon, Oneida 16.00
Michele, Knife, Wallace, 9 In. 14.00
Modern Classic, Berry Spoon, Lunt, 9 In. 56.00
Modern Classic, Bread Knife, Lunt 18.00
Modern Classic, Citrus Spoon, Lunt 20.00
Modern Classic, Cocktail Fork, Lunt 5.00
Modern Classic, Olive Fork, Lunt 19.00
Modern Classic, Vegetable Fork, Lunt, 8 3/4 In. 85.00
Modern Victorian, Asparagus Server, Lunt 60.00
Modern Victorian, Cream Soup Spoon, Lunt 27.00
Modern Victorian, Strawberry Fork, Lunt 18.00
Monte Cristo, Butter Knife, Master, Towle 8.00
Monte Cristo, Olive Fork, Towle 13.00
Moonbeam, Grapefruit Knife, International 15.00
Moonglow, Baked Potato Server, International 34.00
Moonglow, Citrus Spoon, International 19.00
Mothers, Bouillon Spoon, Gorham 9.00
Mothers, Cocktail Fork, Gorham 11.00
Mothers, Pastry Fork, Gorham 28.00
Mythologique, Preserve Spoon, Gorham, 8 In. 275.00
Navarre, Dinner Fork, Watson, 7 5/8 In. 31.00
Navarre, Salad Fork, Watson 26.00
Nocturne, Baked Potato Server, Gorham 30.00
Northern Lights, Cream Soup Spoon, International 26.00
Northern Lights, Sugar Spoon, International 23.00
Old Baronial, Butter Spreader, Gorham 25.00
Old Baronial, Fruit Spoon, Gorham 35.00
Old Baronial, Roast Meat Fork, Gorham 150.00
Old Colonial, Butter Knife, Towle 9.00
Old Colonial, Sugar Spoon, Towle 29.00
Old French, Knife, Hollow, Monogram, Towle 16.00
Old French, Tablespoon, Gorham 70.00
Old Mirror, Carving Set, Monogram, Towle, 2 Piece 55.00
Old Newbury, Butter Knife, Flat Handle, Towle, 5 3/4 In. 25.00
Old Newbury, Butter Knife, Master, Towle, 7 3/8 In. 35.00
Old Newbury, Butter Knife, Towle, 5 3/4 In. 25.00
Old Newbury, Casserole Spoon, Towle, 7 3/4 In. 95.00
Old Newbury, Cocktail Fork, Towle 19.00
Old Newbury, Cold Meat Fork, Towle, 8 1/2 In. 85.00
Old Newbury, Cream Ladle, Towle, 5 3/4 In. 45.00
Old Newbury, Fish Fork, Towle, 7 3/8 In. ....39.00 to 40.00
Old Newbury, Fish Knife, Towle, 8 3/8 In. ....38.00 to 40.00
Old Newbury, Fork, Monogram, Towle, 7 1/2 In. 35.00
Old Newbury, Fork, Monogram, Towle, 7 1/8 In. 25.00
Old Newbury, Fork, Towle, 7 1/8 In. 35.00
Old Newbury, Knife, Juvenile, 7 1/2 In. 30.00
Old Newbury, Lasagna Server, Stainless Blade, Towle, 9 5/8 In. 45.00
Old Newbury, Orange Knife, Silver Plate Blade, Towle, 7 3/8 In. ...35.00 to 38.00
Old Newbury, Soup Ladle, Towle 132.00
Old Newbury, Soup Spoon, Towle ....40.00 to 50.00
Old Newbury, Soup Spoon, Towle, 6 1/2 In. 42.00

Old Newbury, Soup Spoon, Towle, 6 3/4 In. 40.00
Old Newbury, Steak Knife, Individual, Towle 42.00
Old Newbury, Sugar Spoon, Towle, 5 1/2 In. ....25.00 to 27.00
Old Newbury, Sugar Tongs, Towle 55.00
Old Newbury, Tablespoon, Towle, 7 7/8 In. 70.00
Old Newbury, Teaspoon, Towle, 5 1/2 In. ....15.00 to 22.00
Old Newbury, Teaspoon, Towle, 6 In. 20.00
Old Newbury, Youth Spoon, Towle, 5 3/8 In. ....13.00 to 17.00
Old Orange Blossom, Bouillon Spoon, Alvin, 6 Piece 240.00
Olympian, Cake Slice, Tiffany, Monogram 605.00
Orange Blossom, Tomato Server, Alvin 375.00
Orchid, Pie Server, Watson, Newell, 9 3/4 In. 350.00
Pine Tree, Spoon, International 25.00
Plymouth, Fish Knife & Fork, Gorham, 12 Piece 545.00
Polhemus Corinthian, Fork, Monogram, 6 7/8 In. 28.00
Polhemus Corinthian, Tablespoon, Monogram 50.00
Pomona, Ice Cream Server, Towle 200.00
Portsmouth, Carving Set, Gorham 145.00
Princess Ingrid, Carving Set, Stainless Blade, Whiting, 2 Piece 108.00
Princess Ingrid, Fork, Frank Whiting 52.00
Princess Ingrid, Poultry Shears, Frank Whiting, 11 1/2 In. ....150.00 to 155.00
Princess Ingrid, Salad Fork, Whiting, 6 1/4 In. 35.00
Princess Ingrid, Teaspoon, Frank Whiting 24.00
Radiant, Ladle, Whiting, 1895, 10 1/2 In. 350.00
Raleigh, Gravy Ladle 85.00
Raleigh, Sardine Fork, Schofield 75.00
Rose, Bonbon Spoon, Stieff 45.00
Rose, Oyster Ladle, Knowles, 12 1/2 In. 375.00
Rose, Serving Spoon, Georg Jensen, 20th Century, 10 In. 259.00
Royal Windsor, Butter Knife, Towle 10.00
Royal Windsor, Cold Meat Fork, Towle 40.00
St. Cloud, Fish Slice, Gorham 200.00
Strasbourg, Punch Ladle, Gorham 297.00
Strasbourg, Punch Ladle, Gorham, 1897, 12 In. 165.00
Versailles, Sugar Tongs, Gorham, 5 In. 125.00
Versailles, Tablespoon, Gorham, 7 1/2 In. 100.00
Violet, Gravy Ladle, Wallace, 7 1/4 In. 75.00
Violet, Olive Spoon, 6 In., Whiting 95.00
Yankee Clipper, Dessert Serving Set, Concord, 3 Piece 45.00
Young Love, Sugar Spoon, Oneida 17.00

SILVER PLATE is not solid silver. It is a ware made of a metal, such as
nickel or copper, that is covered with a thin coating of silver. The letters *EPNS* are often found on American and English silver-plated
wares. Sheffield is a term with two meanings. Sometimes it refers to
sterling silver made in the town of Sheffield, England. In this section,
Sheffield refers to a type of silver plate, usually English.

Basket, 2 Handles, Cranberry Glass Insert, Pedestal, 9 x 6 1/2 x 5 In. 58.00
Basket, Applied Grape & Leaf Scrolling Border, Swing Handle, England 65.00
Basket, Bearded Man, Leaves On Stem, Fox Finial Handle, Reed & Barton, 8 1/4 In. 137.00
Basket, Chased Flowers & Foliage, Swing Handle, c.1870, 10 1/2 In. 70.00
Basket, Sweetmeat, Fenestrated, Swing Handle, 19th Century, 10 In. 132.00
Beaker, Osterreich Landesscheissen, St. Polten, Crest, Footed, 1882, 8 1/2 In. 240.00
Biscuit Box, Swan Finial, Lion Mask Handles, Mappin Bros., c.1900, 8 1/4 In. 360.00
Bowl, Centerpiece, Glass Bowl, Ram's Head & Key Fret Design, 13 1/4 In. 275.00
Bowl, Fruit, Thomas Crestwick, c.1900, 4 1/4 x 11 1/2 In. 85.00
Bowl, Leaf Form, Overlaid Grape Leaves, Cluster One End, c.1910, 13 1/4 In. 95.00
Bun Warmer, Reeded Rim, 4 Reeded & Paw Feet, England, 13 1/2 In. 230.00
Bun Warmer, Revolving Dome, Ivory Handle, Mappin Brothers, 8 x 12 In. 475.00
Butter, Cover, Insert, Embossed Floral, Signed, Tufts 150.00
Cake Basket, Flower & Scroll, Inner Ornament, Swing Handle, c.1880, 10 1/2 In. 240.00
Candelabrum is listed in its own category.

Candlesticks are listed in their own category.

Carafe, Wine, Bulbous Diamond, Foliage, Grapes, Tendrils, Vine Handle, 12 In.	150.00
Card Receiver, Full-Bodied Cupid, Mounted On Leaves & Vines, Handle	450.00
Card Receiver, Parrot, Embossed & Hammered, Tufts	150.00
Card Receiver, Racine Silverplate Co., 6 3/4 In., 7 5/8 In. Diam.	110.00
Casserole, Tripod Stand On Paw Feet, 9 1/2 In.	35.00
Centerpiece, 3 Dolphins On Standard, 12 In.	170.00
Centerpiece, Applied Cartouches, Foliate Ribbon Garlands, 2 Handles, 27 Oz.	1265.00
Coffee Set, Winthrop Shield, Reed & Barton, 12-In. Coffeepot, 3 Piece	375.00
Compote, Applied Figural Squirrel On Branch, 9 1/2 x 8 In.	150.00
Compote, Footed, Figural Base, Swing Handle, Parrot Figure, 19th Century, 6 In.	132.00
Compote, Swing Handle, Dog Finial, J.E. Caldwell & Co., Box, 8 1/2 In., Pair	400.00
Cookie Jar, Plated Head & Collar, Glass Eyes, Austrian, 20th Century, 9 7/8 In.	1092.00
Cup, Cover, Lions, Masks, Fruits, Bird Design, Continental, 36 In.	1610.00
Dish, Art Nouveau Style, Woman, Water Lilies, Quadruple Plate, Pairpoint, 8 x 13 In.	187.00
Dish, Art Nouveau, Wave Design, Child, Lizard, Floral Handle, W.M.F., 1900, 11 In.	440.00
Dish, Cover, Cushion Shape, Gadroon Borders, Sheffield Plate, 10 In., Pair	1610.00
Dish, Cover, Floral Design, Beaded Rim, Handle, Twig Monogram, Victorian, 16 In.	375.00
Dish, Cover, Floral Design, Beaded Rim, Handle, Victorian, 19 In.	375.00
Dish, Cover, Overall Floral Design, Beaded Handle, Rim, 14 In.	200.00
Dish, Entree, Leaf, Bead Border, Handles With Leaf, Ring Design, Christofle, 25 In.	230.00
Dish, Meat, Cover, Lobed Sides, Crest, Central Foliate Handle, Sheffield, 20 In.	400.00
Dish, Serving, Hinged Cover, Dolphin Finial, Shell Shape, 4 Paw Feet, Eton, 12 In.	47.00
Dish, Sweetmeat, Leaf Form, Leaf Handle, Porcelain Shell Liner, 6 x 7 In.	35.00
Dish, Warming, Revolving Top, Liner, Shell, Scroll, Floral Design, England, c.1880	1100.00
Epergne, 4-Arm, Oval Diamond Cut Glass Bowls, Center Bowl, c.1900, 15 x 16 In.	785.00
Epergne, Cut Glass, Lucius Hart, 1870, 23 In.	975.00
Figurine, Cock & A Hen, Hinged Wings, Detachable Heads, 20 In., Pair	1150.00
Flagon, Church Communion, Reed & Barton, c.1875, 14 1/2 In.	145.00
Flagon, Openwork Thumbpieces, Domed Bases, Sheffield Plate, 11 In., Pair	1150.00
Grape Scissors, Fox & Grapes On Handle	20.00
Grape Scissors, Leaves	140.00
Humidor, Glass Panels, Moonstone, 1880s	1698.00
Kettle, Hot Water, Urn Shape, 2 Handles, Quatrefoil Base, Heraldic Engraved	290.00
Kettle, Stand, 3 Branches Held Together With Rope, 3 Knife Feet, England, 15 In.	170.00
Kettle, Stand, Lamp, Scroll, Floral Chasing, Fluted Body, Wood Handle, Victorian	165.00
Knife Rest, Opposing Birds	95.00
Lamp, Hurricane, Etched Glass, Grapes & Leaves, Foliate Collar, 14 1/2 In., Pair	258.00
Meat Cover, Chased Floral, England, 14 x 9 x 8 In.	295.00
Meat Cover, Stepped Up, Gadrooned Mid Rib, Handles, Sheffield, 20 In.	550.00
Mirror Plateau, Round, Beveled Top, Concave Apron, Forbes Silver, 1910, 12 1/2 In.	110.00
Mirror Plateau, Round, Beveled, Cast Floral Feet, 1910-1920, 1 1/4 x 11 1/2 In.	270.00
Mustard Pot, Leaf Thumbpiece, Blue Glass Liner, 2 7/8 In.	145.00
Napkin Rings are listed in their own category.	
Nut Dish, Scalloped, Trans World Airlines, International Silver Co., 9 In.	40.00
Pepper Shaker, Pug In Boot, Glass Eyes, 2 3/4 x 2 3/4 In.	245.00
Pitcher, Bombe Cover, Floral, Leaf Design, Scroll Foliate Handle, 12 1/2 In.	75.00
Pitcher, Curved Lozenge Form, Angular Handle, Sue Et Mare, France, 7 In.	115.00
Pitcher, Fruits, Foliage Design, 2 Greek Key Bands, Monogram, 13 In.	50.00
Pitcher, Middle Wide Band Of Garlands & Festoons, Mulholland Bros., 13 1/2 In.	210.00
Pitcher, S-Curve Handle, Mounted With 3 Turquoise Stones, 11 1/4 In.	80.00
Pitcher, Water, Eagle Spout, Walrus Finial, Victorian, 12 1/2 In.	110.00
Place Card Holder, Coiled Snake Shape, Copper Eyes, 2 1/8 In., 14 Piece	805.00
Plate, Classical Floral Swags, 11 In.	192.00
Platter, Leaf, Bead Border, Oval, Christofle, 27 1/2 In.	170.00
Platter, Well & Tree, Scrolls, Shell Rim, Rectangular, 18 1/2 In.	57.00
Punch Bowl, Scrolling Foliage & Flowers, Floral Rim, Foliate Handles, 14 1/2 In.	690.00
Punch Bowl, Tray, Ladle, 12 Punch Cups, Vintage Pattern, International	715.00
Razor, Hone, Quadruple Plate, Embossed Floral, Stone Under Lid, Pairpoint, 8 In.	125.00
Saucepan, Octagonal Rosewood Handle, Engraved "dich Hate Dich...", 24 1/2 In.	412.00
Sconce, 3-Light, Amethyst Teardrop Prisms, 13 In., Pair	805.00
Server, Hors D'Oeuvres, Oval Form Cover, Warming Compartment, 10 x 7 In.	170.00

Server, Paneled Dome, Claw Feet, Mappin & Webb, 10 x 15 1/2 In. 545.00
Spoon, Souvenir, see Souvenir category.
Spoon Warmer, Nautilus Shell Form, Shell Form Handle, 5 1/4 x 6 In., Pair 430.00
Spoon Warmer, Victorian, 19th Century 115.00
Stand, Smoker's, Alcohol Lamp, Cylindrical Wells With Accessories, 7 1/2 In. 120.00
Stand, Warming, 3 Bowls, Cover, 3 Burners, Christofle, 10 1/2 x 30 1/2 x 9 In. 845.00
Sugar & Creamer, Hammered, Flat-Top Handles, Derby Silver Plate Co., 2 1/2 In. 135.00
Sugar & Creamer, Mappin & Webb, Sheffield, c.1930, 3 1/2 In. 75.00
Sugar & Creamer, Modern Form, Short Peg-Type Legs, WMF, 4 1/4 In. 125.00
Sugar Nips, England, c.1865 . . . . 275.00
Tantalus, 3 Decanters, Bun Footed, Handle, Grinsell's Patent, Late 19th Century 375.00
Tazza, Child On Large Wheel Bicycle Finial, Engraved, Victorian, 8 3/4 In. 275.00
Tazza, Grapes & Leaves Surrounded By Matching Edge, England, 13 1/4 In., Pair 575.00
Tea & Coffee Set, 25 In.-Tray, 5 Piece 115.00
Tea & Coffee Set, Baluster Shape, Fluted Corners, Foliate Handles, 11 1/4 In. 345.00
Tea & Coffee Set, Neo-Grecque, 1880, Reed & Barton, 7 Piece 665.00
Tea & Coffee Set, Reed & Barton, 11 1/2-In. Teapot, 5 Piece 460.00
Tea & Coffee Set, Royal Rose, Tray, Teapot, Coffeepot, Sugar & Creamer, Wallace 190.00
Tea & Coffee Set, Scroll & Foliate Cartouche, Loop Handles, 4 Piece 230.00
Tea Set, Chased Floral & Geometric, Monogram, 6 Piece 355.00
Tea Set, Countess, International, 5 Piece 108.00
Tea Set, Hexagonal Form, Monogram, English, 3 Piece 115.00
Tea Set, Holgate, 4 Piece 365.00
Tea Set, Kentshire, 6 Piece 240.00
Tea Set, Martin Hall & Co., Sheffield, 5 Piece 440.00
Tea Set, Meriden Britannia Co., Late 19th Century, 4 Piece 400.00
Tea Set, Rococo Style, Rockford, Homan & Ellis-Barker, c.1920, 4 Piece 70.00
Tea Strainer, Swivel 30.00
Tea Urn, Georgian Sheffield In The Adam Taste, 19th Century, 15 In. 330.00
Toast Rack, Ball & Claw Feet, 8 5/8 In. 165.00
Toast Rack, Figural, Skiff With Crossed Oars, 6 Slice, England, 1879 . . . . 265.00
Toothpick, Fish, 2 1/2 In. 245.00
Toothpick, Wishbone & Chick 60.00
Tray, Beaded Rim, Pierced Foliate Border, 2 Handles, England, 21 3/4 In. 375.00
Tray, Chased Flowers & Foliage Field, Repousse Floral Rim, 32 In. 60.00
Tray, China Insert, Courting Couple, Gold Washed, Signed, Pairpoint, 8 x 5 1/2 In. 285.00
Tray, Engraved Arms, Gadrooned Rim, Sheffield, c.1800, 29 1/2 In. 1725.00
Tray, Engraving & Cutout Work On Border, Handles, England, 24 x 17 In. 288.00
Tray, Flared Gadrooned Rim, Pierced Border, 2 Handles, England, 24 In. 325.00
Tray, Floral & Foliate Chased, Oval, Open Handles, England, 21 In. 170.00
Tray, Floral, Scroll Border, Bird & Floral, Monogram, J. Tufts, 26 In. 370.00
Tray, Gadrooned Rim, Field With Scrolling Foliage, Webster & Wilcox, 16 In. 210.00
Tray, Grape, Foliate Rim Design, Scrolls, Flowers, 2 Handles, England, 26 1/2 In. 80.00
Tray, Grapevine Edge, Round, 23 In. 250.00
Tray, Handles, Poole Silver Co., 26 1/2 In. 110.00
Tray, Heavy Cast Border, Animals & Figures, Embossed, Scroll Feet, 18 In. 280.00
Tray, Scroll, Shell Border, Oval, Matthew Boulton, Late 18th Century, 14 1/4 In. 201.00
Tray, Scrolled Acanthus Leaves, Flowers & Shells Edge, 33 1/4 In. 575.00
Tray, Service, 2 Handles, England, 24 1/2 In. 80.00
Tray, Serving, Rococo-Style, Scroll, Shell Border, Handles & Chasing, 30 In. 330.00
Tray, Winthrop Shield, Reed & Barton, 29 1/2 In. 275.00
Tureen, Dome Cover, Leaves Around Knob, Repousse Flower, France 200.00
Tureen, Domed Lid, Flower Form Finial, Christofle, 20th Century, 12 x 18 In. 546.00
Tureen, Soup, Cover, Engraved Crests, Shell-Capped Scroll Feet, 1820s, 15 In. 1955.00
Tureen, Soup, Notched Cover, Engraved Flowers, Barbour Bros. Co., 12 In. 35.00
Urn, Hot Water, Adams Style, Sheffield, England, 16 In. 440.00
Urn, Tea, Broad Foliate Rim, Scrolling Handles, 4 Scroll Feet, 21 In. 1090.00
Vase, Bowtie Floral Garlands, Egg, Dart Rim, Cobalt Glass Liner, 12 In., Pair 860.00
Vase, Garlands, Ribbon Border, Waist Centering Maiden, Rectangular, 12 In. 690.00
Water Cooler, Conical Cover, Acorn Finial, Swan Handles, 19th Century, 20 1/2 In. 517.00
Wine Cooler, Lion's Head, Loose Ring Handles, 7 3/4 In., Pair 440.00
Wine Cooler, Urn Shape, Neoclassical, Relief Floral Design, 11 1/2 In., Pair 520.00

SILVER, SHEFFIELD, see Silver Plate; Silver-English categories.

SILVER-AMERICAN. American silver is listed here. Coin and sterling silver are included. Most of the sterling silver listed in this book is subdivided by country. There are also other pieces of silver and silver plate listed under special categories, such as Candelabrum, Napkin Ring, Silver Flatware, Silver Plate, Silver-Sterling, and Tiffany Silver. For information about makers and marks, see *Kovels' American Silver Marks: 1650 to the Present.*

SILVER-AMERICAN, Almond Set, Reed & Barton, 12 Cups & Serving Dish	285.00
Ashtray, Floral & Scroll, Gorham, 1930-1940, 3 1/4 x 3 1/4 In., Pair	55.00
Basket, Bread, Reticulated Rim, Swing Handle, Black, Starr & Frost, 10 In.	260.00
Basket, Flower, Reed & Barton, 1942	975.00
Basket, Reticulated, Monogram, Footed, Howard Sterling Co., 8 1/2 In.	66.00
Basket, Rococo Style, Openwork Design, Raised Flared Foot, Howard & Co., 14 In.	345.00
Basket, Swing Handle, Marquand Co., Applied Grapevines, 11 In. Diam.	4510.00
Bell, Geometric Pierced Handle, Hammered Surface, Merrill Shops, 2 3/4 In.	225.00
Berry Server, Strawberry Vine, Shovel Form, R. & W. Wilson, c.1845, 8 1/2 In.	220.00
Berry Spoon, Coin, Gilded Bowl, Bright Cut Leaves, Floral Bowl, Knowles, 1880s	195.00
Berry Spoon, Fluted Bowl, Hotchkiss & Schreuder, 9 In.	137.00
Biscuit Box, Swan Finial, Lozenge Form, Engraved Design, N. Harding, 6 In.	1320.00
Bonbon Spoon, Pierced Scrolling Design, Putti, Gorham, 5 1/4 In.	230.00
Bowl, 3 Formed Lobes, Flared Flange At Rim, Cellini Craft, 10 In.	495.00
Bowl, Applied Border, Monogrammed, Mauser, 3 x 10 In.	120.00
Bowl, Applied Copper Bird, 3 Butterflies, Spot Hammered, Gorham	4830.00
Bowl, Applied Copper Bird, Butterfly, Rose Leaves, Spot Hammered, Gorham	5462.00
Bowl, Beaded Rim, Chased Floral Garland, Lincoln & Foss, 1850s, 3 1/8 In.	316.00
Bowl, Chased With Bird On Blackberry Branches, Shiebler, 1885, 8 In.	2530.00
Bowl, Chased With Blackberries, Foliage, 4 Scroll Feet, Gorham, 1900, 12 In.	8050.00
Bowl, Classical Profile Medallions, Drop Ring Handles, 1885, 8 In.	12650.00
Bowl, Classical Revival, Footed, Bailey, Banks & Biddle, 3 5/8 x 7 1/4 In.	345.00
Bowl, Cover, Oval, Frank M. Whiting, 11 x 8 In.	1115.00
Bowl, Dublin Pattern, Ribbed Form, Fisher, 20th Century, 11 1/8 In.	546.00
Bowl, Engraved Foliage & Flowers, Towle, 10 In.	75.00 to 80.00
Bowl, Engraved, Herbert, 19th Century, 5 In. Diam.	88.00
Bowl, Floral & Scroll Border, Dominick & Haff, 11 In. Diam.	370.00
Bowl, Floral Garlands, Seahorse Handles, Dolphin Feet, Reid & Son, 8 In.	2420.00
Bowl, Floral Repousse Border, James T. Wooley, Early 20th Century, 11 In.	440.00
Bowl, Floral Repousse, S. Kirk & Son, Baltimore, 9 In. Diam.	660.00
Bowl, Floral, Shaped Edge & Base, Shiebler, c.1900, 6 1/8 x 9 5/8 In.	1150.00
Bowl, Flower Form, Trailing Leaf & Blossom, Arthur J. Stone, 10 5/8 In.	6500.00
Bowl, Footed, Poole, 8 In.	115.00
Bowl, Francis I, Oval, Reed & Barton, 12 1/2 In.	630.00
Bowl, Francis I, Reed & Barton, 7 3/4 In.	290.00
Bowl, Inward & Outward Fluted Form, Hammered, Falick Novick, 8 In.	750.00
Bowl, Low Ring Foot, 2 Stylized Handles, G.C. Gebelein, 6 1/2 In.	250.00
Bowl, Nut, Boat Shape, Shell Handles, Stone, 5 In.	176.00
Bowl, Oval, Repousse & Engraved Border, Kirk, New York, 13 1/2 In.	1320.00
Bowl, Pedestal, Allover Floral, Whiting, 1895, 4 x 7 In.	695.00
Bowl, Raised Floral Design, Gorham, Footed	355.00
Bowl, Raised Flower 1 Side, Monogram, Art Nouveau, International, 7 In.	66.00
Bowl, Repousse, Allover Berry, Foliage, 4 Ball Feet, Dominick & Haff	805.00
Bowl, Repousse, Daisies, Chrysanthemums, Harris & Schafer, Pair	1035.00
Bowl, Repousse, Flowers & Leaves Rim, Gold Interior, Caldwell Co.	400.00
Bowl, Repousse, Handles, S. Kirk & Son, 1900, 5 1/4 In.	895.00
Bowl, Reticulated, Rococo Style Scrolls, Florals, J.E. Caldwell & Co., 2 1/2 In.	374.00
Bowl, Ribbed Body, 3-Footed, Monogram, Fasching In Venice, 1888, 5 In.	66.00
Bowl, Ribbed, Gadrooned Body, Wavy Edge, Ribbed, Ball Feet, Durgin, 8 In.	192.00
Bowl, Rolled Rim, Karl F. Leinonen, 9 In.	715.00
Bowl, Scalloped Rolled Rim, Woolley, 2 x 6 In.	360.00
Bowl, Stylized Flower, Everted Rim, Peter Muller-Munk, 1930, 10 3/4 In.	1150.00
Bowl, Vegetable, Finial Removable, Convert To 2 Open Dishes, Kirk, 1910, 9 In.	2095.00
Bowl, Waved Concentric Circles, Water Lilies, Whiting, 1880, 9 In.	3105.00
Box, Floral Repousse, Bigelow, Kennard & Co., 5 1/2 In.	220.00

Bread Basket, Repousse, Floral Border, Scroll Rim, Oval, Kirk & Son 489.00
Bread Plate, Oval, Rococo Design, Gorham, 5 1/2 In. 248.00
Bread Plate, Rose, Hand Chased, Stieff, 1929, 5 Piece 695.00
Bread Tray, Cased & Repousse Floral Rim, Oval, 1935, Kirk, 11 1/4 In. 270.00
Bread Tray, Oval, Chased Floral Design, Wallace, 11 1/2 In. 110.00
Bread Tray, Repousse, Round, Kirk, 1930, 6 3/4 x 12 In. 650.00
Butter, Repousse, Cover, Glass Insert, S. Kirk & Son, 1950, 8 1/2 In. 550.00
Butter Chip, Border Of Old Roses, Alvin, c.1920, 12 Piece 165.00
Cake Basket, Reticulated Edge & Handle, Foliate Feet, Reed & Barton, 12 In. 747.00
Cake Basket, Scrolls & Shells, Reticulate, Handle, Wm. B. Durgin, 12 x 8 In. 690.00
Cake Plate, Engraved Scrolls, Spreading Foot, Reed & Barton, 10 1/2 In. 170.00
Cake Slice, Scroll Design, Shiebler, Patent Date, 1915 . . . . 440.00
Candelabrum is listed in its own category.
Candlesticks are listed in their own category.
Candy Dish, Francis I, Fruit & Foliate Rim, Reed & Barton, 8 In., Pair 373.00
Cann, Bulbous Body, Handle, Elias Pelletreau, 1800s, 5 1/4 In. 3190.00
Cann, Cast Hollow Scroll Handle, William Swan, 1760s, 5 1/8 In. 1840.00
Castor, Baluster Form, Circular Foot, Reeded Rims, Knopped Finial, Stieff, 9 In. 460.00
Centerpiece, Shell, Swag Center Motifs, Lobster Handles, Whiting, 15 In. 2645.00
Chalice, S. Hoyt & Co., Engraved To T.C. Dudley, Purser Of Steamship, 8 In. 805.00
Chocolate Pot, Chantilly, Gorham, 1906 . . . . 1495.00
Chocolate Pot, Repousse, Footed, Kirk, 1880, 10 In. 2875.00
Cigarette Case, 14K Gold, 2 Colors, Elgin 50.00
Cigarette Case, Raised Caddy Carrying Bag Of Clubs, Unger Bros., 1900, 3 In. 775.00
Clothes Brush, Man's, Plastic Inlay, Bristles, International Sterling, 3 x 5 In. 25.00
Cocktail Set, Tray, Shaker, 8 Stemmed Cocktail Cups, Kalo Shop 8600.00
Cocktail Shaker, Deco Shape, Hammered Surfaces, Kalo Shop, 10 1/4 In. 1500.00
Coffee Set, Angled Spouts, Handles, Tapered, Dirk Van Erp, 1950, 3 Piece 9775.00
Coffee Set, Buttercup, Gorham, 1907-1909, 4 Piece 1100.00
Coffee Set, Ferns On Edge Of Tray, Jacobi & Jenkins, 1896, 4 Piece 2925.00
Coffee Set, M. Fred Hirsch, c.1930, 3 Piece 360.00
Coffee Set, Monogram, W. Duhme & Company, c.1893, 4 Piece 975.00
Coffee Set, Repousse, Ferns On Edge, Tray, Jacobi & Jenkins, 1896, 4 Piece 2925.00
Coffee Set, Stylized Foliage At Bases, Lona P. Schaffer, 3 Piece 3335.00
Coffeepot, Joseph Lownes, c.1815 . . . . 2750.00
Coffeepot, Rosebud Finial, Greek Key Banding, Ball & Black, c.1850, 12 3/8 In. 920.00
Compote, Cover, Bombe Stem, Incised Lines, Magnussen, Gorham Co. 6900.00
Compote, Cutouts On Base & Top, Bailey, Banks & Biddle, 8 1/8 x 7 In. 595.00
Compote, Pencil Thin Shaft, Fluted Shallow Dish, Kalo Shop, 6 x 7 In. 775.00
Compote, Reticulated, Circular, Floral Engraving, Wm. B. Durgin Co. 265.00
Compote, Shell, 3 Dolphin Footed, Howard & Co., 8 1/2 x 10 x 9 In. 6325.00
Cream Jug, Diagonal Ribbed Banding, Joseph Lownes, 5 1/2 In. 172.00
Creamer, Beaded Top Edge, Square Base, James Gough, 1780s, 6 In. 285.00
Creamer, Cover, Rosebud Finial, Greek Key Band, Ball, Black & Co., 9 1/4 In. 460.00
Creamer, Hammered, Applied Initials, Hand Beaten, Lebolt 77.00
Creamer, Helmet Form, John David, Engraved SML, Late 18th Century, 7 In. 770.00
Creamer, Long Handle, Spring Serenade, Lunt 40.00
Creamer, Overall Floral, Foliate Design, Jacobi & Jenkins, 1908, 6 In. 575.00
Creamer, Stylized Leaf Bands, Monogram, R. & W. Wilson, 1825, 7 In. 143.00
Creamer, Wheelright Arms, Samuel Minott, Boston, Footed, 3 3/4 In. 3080.00
Cup, Child's, Octagonal, John Morton Millar From John Morton, 1845 . . . . 275.00
Cup, Cover, Ruby Glass Liner, Domed Foot, Gorham, 1893, 13 1/2 In. 3910.00
Cup, Hammered, Kalo, Signed, 3 3/4 In. 230.00
Cup, Presentation, Loop Handle, Foliate Scroll Border, Gorham, 1890, 3 In. 120.00
Cup, Trophy, Bands Of Peonies, Scrolling Foliage, Gorham, 1902, 8 1/2 In. 1265.00
Cup, Wager, Reed & Barton, c.1970, 3 3/8 In. 125.00
Desk Pad Corners, Repousse, Kirk, 1940s 375.00
Dish, Chased With Chrysanthemums, Pin Oak Leaves, Gorham, 1908, 15 In. 4140.00
Dish, Flaring Sides, Flutes In Corners, Cellini Craft, 5 3/4 In. 225.00
Dish, Floral Design, Gorham, 7 1/4 In. 275.00
Dish, Footed, Reed & Barton, 1950, 4 x 8 In. 145.00
Dish, Fruit, Leaf Form, Hammered, Gilt Interior, Wood & Hughes, 1875, 11 In. 4140.00
Dish, Mayonnaise, Repousse, Footed, Kirk, 1915, 5 x 2 1/2 In. 225.00

Dish, Meat, Chippendale Design, Theodore Starr, NY, 13 3/4 In. 132.00
Dish, Raised Border, Wire Rim, Monogram, MEB, K.F. Leinonen, 9 1/4 In. 525.00
Dish, Serving, Floral & Scroll Design, Gorham, 10 3/4 In. 285.00
Dish, Serving, Floral Edge, Loop Handles, Paw Feet, Durgin, c.1890, 15 In. 845.00
Dish, Serving, Scroll Border, Whiting, c.1910, 8 1/2 x 11 1/2 In. 150.00
Dish, Sweetmeat, Reticulated Rim, Monogram, Gorham, 7 x 4 In. 165.00
Dish, Wide Floral Flange, 4 Lobed, Oval, Monogram, Gorham, 15 In. 385.00
Ewer, Chased With Arches, Floral Swags, Twig Handle, J.C. Moore, 14 In., Pair 3565.00
Ewer, Cover, Florals, Serpentine Handle, Domed Foot, Bailey & Co., 8 3/4 In. 632.00
Ewer, Engraved C-Scroll & Foliate Design, Lows, Ball & Co., 10 7/8 In. 546.00
Fish Knife, Stieff 220.00
Flask, Applied Bluebird Design, 4 Leaf Clover, Monogram, Howard, 5 1/2 In. 275.00
Flask, Crab Caught In A Fish Net, Screw Cap, Monogram, 7 3/4 In. 3335.00
Flask, Curved Outline, Screw Cap, Oblong, Cartier, N.Y., 7 1/4 In. 2415.00
Flask, Hibiscus Garland, Single Blossom On Cover, Reed & Barton, 11 In. 1380.00
Flask, Whiskey, Basket Weave, Glass Liner, Gorham, c.1910, 6 1/2 In. 1045.00
Flatware Set, Coin Silver, William Kendrick, Presentation Case, 32 Piece 400.00
Flower Arranger, Greek Key Border, Enameled Blossoms, Galt & Bro. 1950.00
Fork, Fiddle Terminal, Hayden & Whilden, 1855, 6 Piece 200.00
Frame, Reed & Barton, 10 x 8 In. 58.00
Ice Tongs, Coin, Mass., 1840 . . . . 75.00
Inkstand, Antelope Horn, Acanthus Scrolls, Redlich & Co., N.Y., 1900, 12 In. 1495.00
Julep Cup, E. & D. Kinsey, 4 In. 425.00
Kettle, On Stand, Classical Revival, Floral, Urn Shape Pot, Gorham, 1928 . . . . 920.00
Ladle, Coin, J. Peters, Philadelphia, 1830 . . . . 495.00
Ladle, Coin, Mumford, Newport, Rhode Island, c.1830, 11 1/2 In. 242.00
Ladle, Enameled, Pierced Handle, Mary P. Winlock, 5 In. 345.00
Ladle, Women & Children Musicians On Handle & Shaft, Gorham, 13 In. 300.00
Loving Cup, Vintage, Engraved View Of House, Gorham, 1899, 9 1/8 In. 4887.00
Mug, Allover Floral, Baluster Form, S. Kirk, 1846, 4 In. 517.00
Mug, Art Nouveau, Monogram, Marcus & Co., N.Y., 1905, 3 In. 345.00
Mug, Child's, Leslie Walker Millar From Leslie Millar, Gorham, 1872 . . . . 99.00
Mug, Coin, Baluster, Foliate Body, Scroll Handle, Robert Keyworth, 1830s 880.00
Mug, Coin, N.N. Weaver, Applied Loop Handle, Rolled Edge Rim, 3 1/4 In. 290.00
Mug, Presentation, c.1870, 4 In. 165.00
Napkin Rings are listed in their own category.
Nut Spoon, Green & White Enameled Chrysanthemum Design, 5 1/2 In. 248.00
Pencil Sharpener, Trumpet Foot, Key Twist Cover, 3 1/2 x 4 5/8 In. 745.00
Pitcher, Applied Copper Rose Branch, Tree Peony, Handle, Gorham, 7 In. 6900.00
Pitcher, Bombe Form, 8-Lobed, Rippled Rim, Scroll Handle, Gorham, 9 In. 8050.00
Pitcher, Chased Design, Paneled Baluster Form, Frank Smith, 10 In. 2645.00
Pitcher, Chased With Shell Motifs, Ferns, Primroses, Gorham, 1898, 12 In. 6900.00
Pitcher, Chased With Veined Leaves, Flowers, Scroll Handle, Gorham, 10 In. 9200.00
Pitcher, Coin, Chased Strawberries, Wood & Hughes, 11 In. . . . . *Illus* 1800.00
Pitcher, Engraved Colonial Revival Design, Reed & Barton, 10 3/8 In. 862.00
Pitcher, Exotic Flowers Under Moon, Spot Hammered, J.E. Caldwell, 1880 . . . . 4140.00
Pitcher, F.B. Rogers, 9 3/4 In. 275.00
Pitcher, Foliate Banding, Eagle's Head Handle, Fletcher & Gardiner, 9 1/4 In. 1495.00
Pitcher, Helmet Form, Swags, Shield, Serpent Handle, Bailey & Co., 1860 . . . . 1380.00
Pitcher, Leaf Capped Handle, Baluster, Reed & Barton, 20 Oz., 6 1/2 In. 315.00
Pitcher, Milk, S Monogram, Arthur Stone, 4 In. 445.00
Pitcher, Pear Shape, Pierced Panels Of Foliage, Scrolls, Gorham, 10 In. 5750.00
Pitcher, Pedestal, Handle, Bailey & Co., 1850, 13 5/8 In. 1950.00
Pitcher, Repousse, Chased Poppies, Leaf Handle, Redlich & Co., 9 In. 2300.00
Pitcher, Stag Heads Either Side, Masonic Royal Arch Chapter, Gorham, 7 3/4 In. 2875.00
Pitcher, Strap Handle, Tapering Body, Porter Blanchard, 7 1/2 In. 1900.00
Pitcher, Water, Arts & Crafts, Hammered, Shreve & Co., 7 1/4 In. 1195.00
Pitcher, Water, Buttercup By Gorham, Monogram, 1908 . . . . 935.00
Pitcher, Water, Chased With Pomegranates, Scroll Handle, Gorham 7475.00
Pitcher, Water, Chicago Silver Co. 500.00
Pitcher, Water, Flowers & Thistles, S. Kirk & Sons, 1880, 17 In. 2300.00
Pitcher, Water, Gorham, No. 6924, Monogram, 12 3/4 In. 495.00
Pitcher, Water, Lobed Body, Frank Whiting, 1904, 7 1/2 In. 330.00

Silver-American, Pitcher,
Coin, Chased Strawberries,
Wood & Hughes, 11 In.

**Toothpaste is a good
emergency silver polish.**

Silver-American, Rattle, Face, Bells
Hanging On Ears, Unger Bros.

Pitcher, Water, Manchester Silver Co.	475.00
Pitcher, Water, Repousse, Beaded Spout, Acanthus Leaf, Gorham, 1180, 10 In.	1850.00
Pitcher, Water, Repousse, Engraved Geese, Rococo, Dominick & Haff	1265.00
Pitcher, Water, Rococo, Scrolled Handle, T. B. Starr, 10 1/2 In.	1150.00
Pitcher, Water, Sprays Of Daffodils, Clover, Handle, Whiting, 1890, 8 3/8 In.	2875.00
Pitcher, Water, Threaded Border Shoulder, Spaulding & Co., 9 x 8 In.	805.00
Plate, Repousse, Floral Border, Stippled Ground, Jenkins & Jenkins	805.00
Platter, Fish, Boat Form, Clover, Lotus Border, Gorham, 1873, 28 In.	5462.00
Platter, Repousse, Flowers, Foliage On Border, Oval, Jenkins & Jenkins	975.00
Platter, Serving, Virginia Pattern, Dominick & Haff, Round, 1928, 12 In.	665.00
Porringer, Francis I, Reed & Barton, 4 3/4 In.	230.00
Porringer, Hammered, Reticulated Handle, Art Nouveau, 1 3/4 x 7 1/8 In.	805.00
Porringer, Monogram, Cast Handle, Samuel Casey, 1724, 5 In.	1150.00
Punch Bowl, Bombe, Grape Clusters, Leaves, Mauser Mfg. Co., 1901, 14 In.	6900.00
Punch Bowl, Die Rolled Band Of Classical Medallions, Whiting, 1890, 12 In.	3565.00
Punch Ladle, Coin, Engraved Frazer, S.H.M. & Co.	165.00
Punch Ladle, Down Turned Handle, William Grigg, 1700s, 13 1/2 In.	467.00
Punch Ladle, Gilded, Embossed Bowl, Monogram, Gorham	248.00
Punch Ladle, Monogram, Bailey & Co., 1850, 13 In.	225.00
Punch Ladle, Shell Bowl, Monogram, T.C. Garrett, 1829, 10 1/4 In.	363.00
Rattle, Face, Bells Hanging On Ears, Unger Bros. *Illus*	550.00
Salad Server, Love Disarmed Pattern, Reed & Barton, 10 In.	2530.00
Salt & Pepper, Lady Claire, Stieff, 1951	325.00
Salt & Pepper, Open, Hoofed Feet, Cobalt Liners, Redlich, 5 In. & 3 In.	230.00
Salt & Pepper, Pheasant, 7 In.	18.00
Salt & Pepper, Plain, 1948, Stieff, 5 1/4 In.	195.00
Salt & Pepper, Rose, Hand Chased, Stieff, 1940s	275.00
Salt & Pepper, Shaker, Wood & Hughes, Engraved, 19th Century, Pair	193.00
Salt Set, Curly Handles, Stamped, Georg Jensen, 6 Salts, 6 Spoons, 2 3/4 In.	440.00
Saltcellar, Saw-Pierced Keyhole Handles, Katherine Pratt, 1 x 3 1/4 In., Pair	335.00
Salver, Diapered Center, A.G. Schultz, Round, 1925, 12 In.	1295.00
Salver, Floral Edge, Machined Center, Cast Ball & Claw Feet, Kirk, 7 In.	220.00
Salver, Scalloped Rim, 3 Scrolled Feet, Gorham, 7 1/2 In.	95.00
Salver, Snowflake Center, Repousse, Footed, Kirk, 1905, 8 In.	595.00
Sauceboat, Allover Scrolls & Flowers, 2 Monogrammed Cartouches, Gorham	4140.00
Sauceboat, Deer Finial, S. Kirk & Son, 8 In.	825.00
Sauceboat, Tray, Monogram, Gorham, 2 Piece	120.00
Sauceboat, Wm. B. Kerr, 1900	350.00
Serving Fork, Vegetable, Sphinx-Head Handle, Gorham, 1900s, 10 In.	770.00
Serving Spoon, Beaded Border, William Gale & Sons, c.1858, 11 1/2 In.	100.00
Serving Spoon, Coin, Easton & Sanford, Nantucket, c.1830, 9 In.	412.00
Serving Spoon, Filigree Handle, Figure Of Putto, 5 Tines, Wood & Hughes	990.00
Serving Spoon, Fluted Bowl, Samuel Kirk, Baltimore, c.1827	412.00
Smoking Set, Aquatic Designs, Crabs & Fish, Gorham, 8 1/2-In. Tray, 3 Piece	770.00
Snuffer, Candle, Rose Pattern Handle, Stieff, Swivel Head	70.00
Soap Dish, Cover, Chased Design, Engraved, Gorham	132.00
Soup, Dish, Acorn, Oak Leaf Border Rim, S. Kirk & Son, 9 In., 10 Piece	2300.00
Soup Ladle, Coin, Fiddle Thread, H.P. Buckley, New Orleans	330.00

Soup Ladle, Devil's Head, Ram's Head Terminal, Giles & Bros. 373.00
Soup Ladle, Fiddle & Thread, Lincoln & Reed, 1835 . . . . 170.00
Soup Ladle, Fluted Bowl, J.W. Tucker, 12 5/8 In. 275.00
Soup Ladle, Hildeburn & Bros., Monogram, 1849 . . . . 400.00
Soup Ladle, Terminal Shell, Monogram, Charles A. Burnett, 1810, 13 In. 460.00
Spoon, Coin, J.B. Hill, Richmond, 1818-1850 . . . . 125.00
Spoon, Coin, N. Harding, Boston, 1796-1862 . . . . 125.00
Stand, Wine Bottle, Tooled Cord Design, Inscription, Shreve, Signed, 5 In. 220.00
Stretcher, Glove, Applied Floral Design On Stippled Ground, Gorham 115.00
Sugar, Beaded Rim, Foliate Design, Jones, Ball & Co., 1852, 4 1/2 In. 402.00
Sugar, Cover, Overall Floral & Scroll, Dominick & Haff, c.1900, 2 3/4 In. 165.00
Sugar, Swing Handle, Black, Starr & Frost, Cranberry Glass Insert, c.1880 . . . . 468.00
Sugar & Creamer, Coin, Inscribed Shields, Peter Krider, Phila., c.1850, 5 In. 303.00
Sugar & Creamer, Goat Finials, A.E. Warner, Jr., c.1880 . . . . 1245.00
Sugar & Creamer, Hammered, William W. Dodge 400.00
Sugar & Creamer, Rococo Floral Designs, Bigelow Kennard & Co., 3 In. 247.00
Sugar & Creamer, Rose, Stieff, 1928 . . . . 1150.00
Sugar & Creamer, Scalloped Rim, Swing Handle, Engraved, Gorham 132.00
Sugar & Creamer, Strap Handles, Wire Ring Feet, Marshall Field Craft Shop 325.00
Sugar & Creamer, Sugar Tongs, International 99.00
Sugar & Creamer, Swirled Rib Design, Durgin, 2 1/2 In. 132.00
Sugar & Creamer, Tapering Form, Fluted Corners, Monogram, Gorham 285.00
Sugar & Creamer, Thistle & Shell Band, William Thomson, 1830s, 8 3/4 In. 546.00
Sugar Basket, Micro Beaded Under Rim, Swing Handle, Gorham, c.1870, 3 In. 308.00
Sugar Shovel, Ebony Handle, Arthur Stone, 4 In. 425.00
Sugar Sifter, Pierced Shell Bowl, Mulford & Wendell, c.1842, 8 In. 165.00
Sugar Sifter, Repousse Top, Wilcox 250.00
Sugar Tongs, Coin, Engraved, Acorn Grips, 18th Century, I. Hostetter 880.00
Sugar Tongs, Coin, Shell Grips, J.C. Farr, 1824, 8 1/4 In. 110.00
Sugar Tongs, Lewis & Smith, c.1805, 7 In. 137.00
Tablespoon, Coin Silver, Upturned Fiddle End, Monogram, 9 In. 22.00
Tankard, Paul Revere, Revere Under Lid, c.1765, 28 Oz., 10 In. 8050.00
Tazza, Buffalo & Indian, Frosted Glass Liner, Reed & Barton, Pair, 8 1/2 In. 660.00
Tea & Coffee Set, 2 Handled Octagonal Tray, Black, Starr & Frost, 6 Piece 6325.00
Tea & Coffee Set, Acorn Finials, Floral Banding, Fisher & Grinnell, 1815, 6 Piece 6270.00
Tea & Coffee Set, Baluster Form, Monogrammed, Unger Bros., 5 Piece 488.00
Tea & Coffee Set, Berries & Leaves, Bud Finial, Thibault, 4 Piece 3735.00
Tea & Coffee Set, Bigelow & Kennard, 7 In. Teapot, 5 Piece 863.00
Tea & Coffee Set, Domed Lid, Baluster, Monogram, Gorham, 1947, 5 Piece 4310.00
Tea & Coffee Set, Draped Shoulder Garland, Goodnow & Jenks, 1897, 4 Piece 845.00
Tea & Coffee Set, Foliage, Reeded Rim, Reed & Barton, 6 Piece 2530.00
Tea & Coffee Set, Gorham, 10-In. Coffeepot, 7-In. Teapot, 4 Piece 690.00
Tea & Coffee Set, Hammered Surfaces, Lebolt & Company, 5 Piece 7800.00
Tea & Coffee Set, Inverted Pear Shapes, Hammered, Lebolt & Co., 5 Piece 6900.00
Tea & Coffee Set, Medallion, Wood & Hughes, 5 Piece, c.1865 . . . . 5500.00
Tea & Coffee Set, Octagonal Form, Ivory Insulators, Lebolt, 4 Piece 8000.00
Tea & Coffee Set, Repousse Floral, Foliage Design, S. Kirk & Son, 6 Piece 8337.00
Tea & Coffee Set, Royal Danish, International Sterling, 9 In., 4 Piece 880.00
Tea & Coffee Set, Squat, Circular, Bailey & Kitchen, c.1840 . . . . 2200.00
Tea Set, Coin, Panel Sides, J. & J. Cox, c.1820, 3 Piece, 10 1/2 In. 2970.00
Tea Set, Colonial Forms, Ivory Finial, Hammered Surfaces, Marshall Field, 3 Piece 1900.00
Tea Set, Floral & Leaf Repousse, Hand Chased, Sugar Tongs, Dunkirk, 6 Piece 1870.00
Tea Set, Floral Finial, Monogrammed, William Adams, c.1830, 3 Piece 1725.00
Tea Set, Fluted, Gallery Tray, Fluted Edge, Plated, Ball Feet, 5 Piece 1980.00
Tea Set, Plymouth, Gold Wash Interior, Gorham, 3 Piece 605.00
Tea Set, Plymouth, Monogram, Gorham, 1895, 5 Piece 1895.00
Tea Set, Repousse Flowers, Butterflies, Marcus & Co., N.Y., 4 Piece 2300.00
Tea Set, Repousse Flowers, Tree, Marcus & Co., N.Y., 6 Piece 5290.00
Tea Set, S. Kirk & Son, 5 Piece 4720.00
Tea Set, Scroll Cartouches Flanked Floral Design, Reed & Barton, 4 Piece 905.00
Tea Set, Scroll Finial, Monogram, Reed & Barton, 5 Piece 747.00
Tea Set, Swirled Rib Design, Gorham, Monogram, Nov. 17, 1904, 3 Piece 1210.00
Tea Set, Tray, Gadroon Rims, Chippendale Shape, Fisher, 6 Piece 880.00

Tea Strainer, Lily-Of-The-Valley, Whiting 120.00
Teapot, Domed Cover, Grapes, Foliage, Flame Finial, J.E. Caldwell, 5 1/2 In. 460.00
Teapot, Reeded Body, Spout & Lid, Whiting Division Of Gorham, 9 1/4 In. 75.00
Teapot, Repousse, Howard & Co., 1883, Individual 450.00
Teaspoon, Coin, Downturned Fiddle End, A. Miller 33.00
Tongs, Coin, Shell-Shape Tips, R. & A. Campbell, Baltimore, c.1840 . . . . 468.00
Tray, Art Nouveau, Chased Leaf Border, 12 x 18 In. 605.00
Tray, Chased With Flowers, Foliage, Monogrammed, Gorham, 31 In. 13800.00
Tray, Dresser, Man On Telephone, Chased Border, J. Fradley, NY, Late 1800s 132.00
Tray, Flared, Chased Corner Flutes, Hammered, Mulholland Bros., 12 1/2 In. 495.00
Tray, Hammered Oval, Chased Flutes Border, Arthur J. Stone, 20 1/2 x 15 In. 2400.00
Tray, Handles, Dominick & Haff, 1892, 24 x 19 1/2 In. 5500.00
Tray, Pastry, Floral Border, Towle, 13 In. 155.00
Tray, Repousse, Hand Chased, J.S. MacDonald, 28 In. 8250.00
Tray, Sandwich, Gorham, 10 In. 38.00
Tray, Scroll Border, Monogrammed Center, Black, Starr & Frost, 12 x 12 1/4 In. 230.00
Tureen, Cover, Bombe, Ram's Head Handles, Shreve, Stanwood & Co., 1869 . . . . 3910.00
Tureen, Finial Cover, Repousse, Handles, S. Kirk & Son, Oval 7920.00
Tureen, Lion Finial Cover, Acorns & Oak Leaves, Gorham, 15 x 11 In. 3300.00
Tureen, Soup, Cover, Beaded Edge, Fleur-De-Lis Rim, Ball, Black & Co., 17 In. 4255.00
Tureen, Soup, Cover, Gadroon Collar, On Pedestal Foot, E.C. Moore, 12 In. 6325.00
Tureen, Soup, Floral Band, Greek Key Border, Arc Handles, Gorham, 1873 . . . . 8625.00
Urn, Sugar, Urn Finial On Lid, Fenestrated Bowl Top, Square Base, 10 1/2 In. 1650.00
Vase, Chased With Swirled Lines, Poppies, Undulated Rim, Gorham, 19 In. 12650.00
Vase, Fish, Shells, Seagull Scene, Foliage 2-Tone, Gorham, 1878, 7 5/8 In. 3910.00
Vase, Hammered, Trumpet Form, Flaring Sides, Rolled Rim, Lebolt & Co., 9 In. 775.00
Vase, Repousse, Foliate Scrolls, Black, Starr & Frost, 14 In. 1090.00
Vase, Trumpet Flowers On Lower Body, George Shiebler & Co., 1900, 17 In. 3795.00
Vase, Trumpet Form, Chrysanthemum, Scroll, Bailey, Banks & Biddle, 16 In. 2530.00
Vase, Trumpet, Monogram, Kirk, 13 In. 700.00
Waiter, Chippendale, Circular, Reed & Barton, 14 In. Diam. 358.00
Waiter, Husk Border, Engraved Scrolls, Cartouche, Ivory Footed, N.Y., 8 In. 375.00
Wine, Flared Open Bowl, Wire Rim, Thin Pedestal, Kalo Shop, 4 5/8 In. 450.00
Wine Cooler, Die-Rolled Ornamental Band, 4 Footed Base, Gorham, 9 In. 5520.00
SILVER-AUSTRIAN, Bowl, Centerpiece, Oval, Glass Insert, Schopflick, 19th C., 12 1/2 In. . . . 365.00
  Fish Set, Scrolling Foliage, Leaf Capped & Spiral Handle, Marked 12 . . . . 170.00
  Sugar Box, Cover, Central Repousse Band, Scrolled Feet, 19 Troy Oz. 1092.00
  Tea & Coffee Set, Covered Sugar, Oval Tray, c.1900, 5 Piece 3300.00
  Tea & Coffee Set, Pear Shape, Ivory Handles & Finials, 6 Piece 1090.00
SILVER-BELGIAN, Centerpiece, Faceted Stem, Wolfers Freres, 20th C., 7 1/4 In. 2070.00
  Coffee Set, Chased With Circles, Handles, 1890, 3 Piece 12650.00
SILVER-CHINESE, Bowl, 6-Lobed Shape, Tree Branch Handles, Footed, 19th Century, 10 In. . . 1210.00
  Card Case, Applied Dragon Design, Curved Body, 19th Century, 3 1/2 x 5 In. 145.00
  Card Case, Filigree, Floral Design, 1840, 3 1/2 In. 230.00
  Cheroot Case, Signed Interior, 2 1/4 x 3 1/2 In. 240.00
  Cup, Figural & Dragon Design, Dragon Handle, Onnsing, 1840, 5 In. 1430.00
  Letter Opener, Floral Design, 10 1/4 In. 495.00
  Snuffbox, Domed Lid, Pseudo Georgian Marks, 1800, 3/4 x 3 In. 1320.00
  Snuffbox, Figures, Building & Boat, 1810, 3 1/4 x 2 1/2 In. 1650.00
  Snuffbox, Raised Figural Design, Wongshing, 1830-1835, 3/4 x 3 x 1 3/4 In. 700.00
  Tea Caddy, Hinged Cover, Repousse Dragon, 19th Century, 4 In. 130.00
  Tea Set, Art Deco Design, Floral Border, Lee Sung, 6 3/4-In. Teapot, 3 Piece 440.00
  Tea Set, Bamboo Design, Hoaching, 4 1/2-In. Teapot, 3 Piece 2090.00
  Tea Set, Landscape, Dragon Handles, Fitted Wooden Box, 4 Piece 3960.00
  Teapot, Hardstone & Jeweled Design, 9 1/2 In. 690.00
  Toast Rack, Ball Feet, Monogram, Wongshing, 1830-1835, 6 3/4 In. 1430.00
  Tray, Card, Ring-Footed, Wongshing, 7 In. Diam. 275.00
  Tray, Flower & Dragon Design, Pierced Border, Monogram, 17 1/2 In. 1320.00
  Vase, Repousse Dragon, Trumpet Form, Foliate Panels, Wooden Stand, 8 1/4 In. 258.00
SILVER-CONTINENTAL, Bowl, Geometric Pierced Design, Swing Handle, Glass Liner, 6 In. . . 200.00
  Bowl, Reticulated, Floral & Cherub Design, Pedestal, Glass Insert, 6 In. 155.00
  Bowl, Ribbed, Oval, 4 Scroll Footed, Monogram, 3 3/4 x 12 In. 345.00
  Box, Carved Ivory Renaissance Plaque Scene Cover, 3 1/8 x 2 3/8 In. 575.00

Box, Enameled Officer Oval Plaque Lid, R. Co., 3/4 x 1 7/8 x 1 1/2 In. 490.00
Box, Painted Genre Scene, Reticulated Surround, 3 5/8 x 2 3/8 In. 575.00
Box, Porcelain Plaque Neoclassical Women Lid, 1 1/8 x 1 7/8 x 2 In. 315.00
Box, Scrolls & Foliate, Cartouche Monogram, 2 1/2 x 6 7/8 In. 690.00
Box, Sugar, Locking, Dolphin Finial, Grapes & Leaves, 5 1/4 In. 230.00
Cake Plate, Central Cartouche Monogram, Flower Swag Border 90.00
Candy Dish, 3 Joined Scallop Shells, 7 In. 25.00
Cigarette Case, Gentleman, Partly Clad Maid On Cover, 1920s, 4 3/4 In. 2300.00
Cruet Stand, Paw Feet, 4 Cut Crystal Bottles, 2 Silver Lidded Jars, 11 In. 990.00
Cup Holder, Swan Finial, Animal Head & Scroll Handles, Ball Feet, 8 1/2 In. 165.00
Salt, Swan Form, Master, Smaller Pair, Silver Neck & Head, Glass Body 200.00
Snuffbox, Floral Design, Crimped Edge, Victorian, 2 1/2 In. 920.00
Tankard, Cover, Pomegranate Thumb Rest, Feet, 32 Oz., 7 3/4 In. 3680.00
Tazza, Fruit On Edge, Bands Of Grapes On Foot, 3 1/4 In., 4 Piece 315.00
Tea Caddy, Dome Top, Drape & Swag, Central Medallion, 1900s, 5 In. 1100.00
Tray, Relief Scroll & Cherub Design, 11 3/4 In. 230.00
SILVER-DANISH, Basket, Blossom, Georg Jensen, Post 1945, 3 1/2 In. 1092.00
Bottle Opener, Acorn, Georg Jensen 143.00
Bowl, Footed, Berries, Foliate Stem, Pattern 17a, Georg Jensen, 1925, 5 In. 690.00
Bowl, Openwork Berry & Foliate Stem, Flaring Cup, Georg Jensen, 1925, 4 1/16 In. 690.00
Bowl, Openwork Leaves, Flowers, Flared, 1932, Georg Jensen, 8 1/2 In. 6325.00
Bowl, Stylized Flower Center, Flared Ribbed Foot, Georg Jensen, 6 3/8 In. 575.00
Bowl, Vegetable, Cover, Acorn, Blossom Finial, Acorn Handles, Jensen, Pair 8050.00
Castor, Engraved Lid, Grape Cluster Finial, Georg Jensen, Post 1945, 6 In. 880.00
Cheese Knife, Acorn, Georg Jensen 274.00
Cheese Knife, Bernadotte, Georg Jensen 115.00
Compote, 10 Applied Beads, Leafy Stem, 1932, Georg Jensen, 3 In. 374.00
Compote, Overlapping Leaf Stem, Openwork Clusters, Georg Jensen, 8 In. 5462.00
Compote, Pedestal, Georg Jensen, 12 x 12 In. 7820.00
Creamer, Georg Jensen, 3 1/2 In. . . . . .275.00 to 286.00
Gravy Boat, Blossom, Carved Handle, Georg Jensen, Post 1945, 4 1/2 In. 2185.00
Pitcher, Elongated, Swept Handle, Georg Jensen, 1952, 11 1/2 In. 14375.00
Pitcher, Water, Hammered, Arts & Crafts, Georg Jensen, 7 1/2 In. 975.00
Plate, Hors D'Oeuvres, Shell Handles, Georg Jensen, Post 1945, 6 3/8 In., 5 Piece 1870.00
Salad Set, Pyramid, Georg Jensen 770.00
Salt & Pepper, Acorn, Georg Jensen, Post 1945, 3 1/2 In. 488.00
Serving Fork & Spoon, Argo, Georg Jensen, 6 1/4 In. 230.00
Serving Fork & Spoon, Cactus, Loop Handle, Georg Jensen, 1933, 7 3/4 In. 460.00
Sugar & Creamer, Wood Handles, Sterling, Cylindrical, 16 Oz. 201.00
Sugar Tongs, Angular Handle, Claw Tongs, Georg Jensen 258.00
Tea & Coffee Set, Blossom, 2 Handled Tray, Georg Jensen, 4 Piece 19550.00
Teapot, Blossom, Georg Jensen, c.1945 . . . .   5280.00
Tray, Blossom, Elliptical Form, George Jensen, Post 1945, 10 1/4 In. 1725.00
Vase, Garnet, Floral Body, Molded Border, 1910, Georg Jensen, 8 1/4 In. 4600.00
Water Pot, Bead Design, Ebony Handle, Georg Jensen, Post 1945, 7 In. 1495.00
SILVER-DUTCH, Bowl, Center Tavern Scene, Square Form, Late 19th Century, 8 1/2 In. 287.00
Castor, Urn Shape, Raised On 4 Ball Feet, Verschour, Marked, 5 3/8 In. 517.00
Figurine, Duck, Glass Eyes, Removable Head, 1913, 15 1/2 In. 4600.00
Fish Slice, 3 Different Fish, Scrolled Strapwork, Shell, Douwe Eysma, 1765 . . . .   3162.00
Salt, King, Horse-Drawn Chariot Shaped, Putto Holding Reins, 4 1/8 In. 460.00
Serving Dish, Geometric Handles, 4 Ball Feet, Schoonh Zilverfabr, 16 3/4 In. 265.00
Snuffbox, Recumbent Cherub On Lid, 1903, 3 1/ 2 x 2 1/2 In. 330.00
Soup Ladle, Beaded Rim 125.00
Tobacco Jar, Drum Form, Bright-Cut Borders, Jacob Van Nieuwcasteel, 6 In. 5175.00
Vase, Trumpet Shape, Etched Glass, Geometric Design, 19 3/4 In. 745.00

Some disciplined collectors have a rule:
Only add a new piece to your collection if you can get rid
of a less desirable old one. Most of us just keep adding.

SILVER-ENGLISH. English sterling silver is marked with a series of four or five small hallmarks. The standing lion mark is the most commonly seen sterling quality mark. The other marks indicate the city of origin, the maker, and the year of manufacture. These dates can be verified in many good books on silver.

SILVER-ENGLISH, Basket, Coat Of Arms, Swivel Handle, Edward Aldrige, 1764, 15 1/2 In. .	1598.00
Basket, Reticulated & Engraved, Swivel Handle, P. & A. Bateman, 14 3/4 In.	3510.00
Basket, Sugar, Engraved, Swing Handle, Boat Shape, 6 x 4 3/8 In.	605.00
Berry Spoon, Floral Design Handle, J. Lloyd, London, George III, 1807	55.00
Berry Spoon, Gilded Bowl, Fruit, Godbehere, Wigan, 1796, Pair	165.00
Berry Spoon, Gilt Repousse Bowls, Samuel Davenport, 1794, Pair	225.00
Bonbon, Fluted Pedestal, Fluted Plate, 5 x 8 1/2 In.	210.00
Book, Holy Bible, Silver Mounted Leather, c.1680, 5 1/2 x 3 In.	2530.00
Bottle, Scent, Bunch Of Fruit Shape, Bird Form Stopper, 3 In.	4310.00
Bowl, Bellflower & Shell Relief, Harrod's, 12 x 3 In.	715.00
Bowl, Gadrooned Edge, Paul Storr, 1809, 11 3/8 In.	2660.00
Bowl, Gadrooned Rim, Atkin Bros., 1904, 8 In.	110.00
Bowl, Monteith, Chased Laurel Swags, Gadroon Foot, C.S. Harris, 13 In.	17250.00
Bowl, Monteith, Scalloped Rim, Lion Mask Ring Handles, Lambert & Co., 9 In.	4312.00
Bowl, Reeded Rim, Swing Handle, Oval Foot, S. Adams, 1797, 6 In.	490.00
Bowl, Reticulated Sides, Pierced Floral Flange, W. Comyns, 1896, 9 x 7 In.	165.00
Bowl, Shell & Gadroon Rim, Coat Of Arms, Engraved, Paul Storr, 10 1/2 In.	2420.00
Bowl, Vegetable, Cover, Coat Of Arms In Center, Thomas Robins, 1806, 4 Piece	2875.00
Bowl, Vegetable, Cover, Gadrooned Shell, Foliate Rim, 1812, 12 In.	2875.00
Bowl, Vegetable, Gadrooned Rim, Oval, John Wakelin, Wm. Taylor, 13 In., Pair	3162.00
Bowl, Vegetable, Ring Handles, William Fountain, 1805, 9 In., Pair	1840.00
Box, Birmingham, Flowers & Vines, Engraved Date, 1896, 3 1/2 x 2 1/2 In.	235.00
Box, Cover, Peach Form, Enameled, Metal Mounts, Metal Leafs, 1800, 2 Piece	980.00
Box, Cylinder, London, M.T., 1805	66.00
Box, Engraved Diamond & Dot, Birmingham, 1802, 7/8 In.	85.00
Box, Patch, Cover, Spaniel On Cover, Pink, Floral Ground, 1 3/4 In.	2590.00
Box, Pepper, Coat Of Arms, William Darker, 1726, 4 1/8 In.	845.00
Box, Stamp, Hinged Lid, Floral & Foliate, Wood Interior, Birmingham, 2 1/2 In.	50.00
Box, Tobacco, Rectangular, Lined In Wood, Sterling, 1898	115.00
Box, Trinket, Art Nouveau, Bird & Butterfly, 5 3/4 In.	498.00
Bread Tray, Oval, Scrolled, Pierced Sides, Sheffield, 1907	330.00
Bun Warmer, Roll-Away Cover, Engraved Crest, Late 1900s, 13 In.	320.00
Caddy Spoon, Hallmark GW, 1829	145.00
Cake Basket, Beaded Border, Beaded Swing Handle, Crichton Bros., 13 In.	1265.00
Cake Basket, Gadroon Border, Square Handle, George III, 1807, 12 1/4 In.	1100.00
Cake Basket, Pierced, Hester Bateman, 1788, 15 1/4 x 10 x 13 In.	4800.00
Candelabrum is listed in its own category.	
Candle Snuffer, 1800-1801	80.00
Candlesticks are listed in their own category.	
Cann, London, 1770, 3 7/8 In.	520.00
Card Tray, 3 Claw & Ball Feet, Gadroon Border, Engraved Design, c.1770, 7 In.	440.00
Castor, Domed Cover, Scroll & Quatrefoil Design, MP, George II, 7 1/2 In.	2070.00
Castor, George III, London, 1794, 6 In.	175.00
Castor, London, 1788, 6 1/4 In.	145.00
Castor, Pear Shape, Molded Rib & Borders, Urn Finial, 1740-1750, 10 3/4 In.	1760.00
Centerpiece, Bowl, Cut Crystal, Sculptured Leaves, 1873, JB/EB, 15 In.	1980.00
Chocolate Pot, Swan Neck Spout, Cylindrical, George I, 22 Oz.	5750.00
Cigar Case, Holds 3, Gilt Lining, c.1884	695.00
Cigar Case, Holds 4, George Unite, c.1872	850.00
Coaster, Bombe Sides, Corded Rims, Turner & Fox, 1802, 6 In., 4 Piece	9775.00
Coffee Set, Flower Finial, Paneled, Leaves & Flowers, J. Angell, 1828, 4 Piece	2920.00
Coffee Set, With Tray, Angular Form, Wooden Handles, T.W., 5 Piece	690.00
Coffee Spoon, Bright Cut Design, Round End Handle, Hester Bateman, 6 Piece	460.00
Coffeepot, Baluster, Serpentine Spout, Wood Handle, Richard Gurney, 10 In.	1840.00
Coffeepot, Bird Head Spout, Fruitwood Handle, Richard Crossley, 1794, 10 In.	920.00
Coffeepot, Detachable Cover, Wooden Handle, 1796, 10 In.	2185.00
Coffeepot, Domed Cover, Pear Shape, Gadrooned Band, Handle, George III	980.00

Coffeepot, Domed Cover, Pear Shape, Gadrooned Rim, George III, 20 Oz. 1380.00
Coffeepot, Floral Finial, Chinoiserie Design, Pagodas, Cranes, 1840, 10 In. 1150.00
Coffeepot, Monogram, London, 1737 . . . . 805.00
Coffeepot, Oval Foot, Serpentine Spout, Peter, Ann, W. Bateman, 1805, 11 3/4 In. 1035.00
Coffeepot, Rampant Lion Cartouche, Thomas Mason, 1737, 9 1/4 In. 3737.00
Coffeepot, Robert Hennell, Pear Shape, Angular Ivory Handle, 1781, 8 In. 632.00
Coffeepot, Serpentine Spout, W. & J. Priest, Wooden Handle, 1770, 9 3/4 In. 1150.00
Creamer, Beaded Rim, Loop Handle, 1795 . . . . 250.00
Creamer, Bombe, Reeded Rim, Angular Reeded Handle, 1798, 4 x 2 In. 85.00
Creamer, Cut Floral Design, Reeded Loop Handle, George III, 8 In. 200.00
Creamer, Floral Capped Handle, Oval, Wm. Bateman, 1816, 6 In. 200.00
Creamer, Helmet Shape, Floral Garland, Peter & Ann Bateman, 5 7/8 In. 320.00
Creamer, Square Base, Bright-Cut Design, P. Bateman, 1799, 5 In. 358.00
Cruet Set, 6 Cut Glass Bottles, 2 Glass & Silver Casters, Tray, 1814 . . . . 2420.00
Cruet Stand, 4 Faceted Bottles, Rebecca Emes & Edward Barnard, 1812, 7 In. 2875.00
Cruet Stand, Reticulated, Handle, Ball, Claw Feet, 1759, 10 In. 575.00
Crumber, Ivory Handle, 1905, 13 In. 495.00
Cup, Caudle, Inverted Bell Form, Beaded Scroll Handles, W. Gamble, 5 In. 3162.00
Cup, Cover, Baroque Cartouches, Handles, A. Crichton, 1915, 12 1/2 In., Pair 10925.00
Cup, Cover, Domed, 2 Leaf Capped Scroll Handles, Comyns & Sons, 1912 . . . . 1380.00
Cup, Egg Shape, Chester, Marked 60.00
Cup, Flared Rim, Beaded Scroll Handles, P. Maingy, 1770, 2 5/8 In. 1610.00
Cup, Floral Design, Monogram, Ear Handle, E.J. & E.W. Barnard, 3 5/8 In. 513.00
Cup, Gilt Interior, Barrel, Scroll Handle, George III, 3 In. 375.00
Dish, Cover, Waisted Hemispherical Form, Coat Of Arms, 1810, 7 In., Pair 2300.00
Dish, Entree, Acanthus Leaves At Indented Corners, Coat Of Arms, 1781, Pair 3450.00
Dish, Entree, Contemporary Coat Of Arms, Gadroon Borders, George III, Pair 3220.00
Dish, Entree, Cover, Acanthus Leaves At Indented Corners, Paul Storr, Pair 7762.00
Dish, Entree, Cover, Cushion Shape, Twig Ring Handles, George III, 75 Oz., Pair 2875.00
Dish, Entree, Domed Cover, Contemporary Arms, Beaded Rims, 15 In., Pair 2760.00
Dish, Entree, Ribbon Bound Reeded Rim, Grape Clusters, 1810, 13 In., Pair 7475.00
Dish, Meat, Cover, Gadrooned Rims, Contemporary Coat Of Arms, 4 Piece 16100.00
Dish, Serving, Gadrooned Borders, Shells, Foliage, Wm. Stroud, 13 In., Pair 6900.00
Dish Cover, Center Handle, Lions, Leaf, Paul Storr, Round, 1814, 10 1/4 In. 460.00
Dish Cross, Pear Shape Lamp, Reeded Moldings, George III, 11 1/2 In. 3220.00
Dressing Spoon, Crested, Wm. Eley & Wm. Fearn, George III, 1802 . . . . 176.00
Epergne, 5 Oval Crystal Bowls, Lion Head, Paw Feet, Sheffield, c.1815, 13 In. 4675.00
Epergne, 5 Silver Dishes, 8 Cut Crystal Vases, Arkin Bros., Sheffield, 1907 . . . . 2750.00
Epergne, Trumpet Shape, Reticulated, 4 Scroll Arms, Sheffield, 12 x 14 In. 1610.00
Fish Server, Georgian, Pierced Blade, Thomas Daniel, London, 1779 . . . . 275.00
Fish Slice, Fiddle, Pierced Blade, Monogram, Wm. Kingdon, 1831 . . . . 220.00
Fish Slice, King, Mary Chawner, Engraved Crest, 1835 . . . . 465.00
Fish Slice, Solid Blade, Fiddle Handle, Crest, George III, 1805 . . . . 220.00
Flask, Fish Form, Tail Folded To 1 Side, Screw-On Cap, 1938, 5 3/4 In. 1840.00
Fork, Sucket, Rat-Tail Bowl, Francis Garthorne, c.1680, 4 1/4 In. 2990.00
Fork, Sucket, Rat-Tail Bowl, TH 6 May 86, 5 1/4 In. 1495.00
Fork, Toasting, 3-Pronged Rack, Mahogany Handle, J. Troby, 35 In. 690.00
Frame, 5 Oval Openings, Rococo, Easel, 9 3/4 x 10 1/2 In. 180.00
Frame, Neoclassical, Easel, Velvet Back, 8 x 10 In. 240.00
Frame, Repousse, Velvet Back, Japonesque, Easel, 13 x 11 In. 605.00
Fruit Set, Knives & Forks, Mother-Of-Pearl Handles, Box, 24 Piece 905.00
Fruit Set, Mother-Of-Pearl Handle, Wooden Box, Sheffield, 1927, 12 Piece 632.00
Funnel, Plain Conical Form, Molded Rim, Ring Handle, Marked, 3 1/2 In. 2070.00
Goblet, Inverted Bell Form, Unicorn Crest, Threaded Edge, Victorian, 4 Piece 1090.00
Goblet, Leaves On Circular Foot, Armorials, Chawner & Emes, 1796, 6 1/4 In., Pair 1380.00
Grape Scissors, Shell, London, 1904, 7 In. 80.00
Gravy Warmer, Argyll, Pineapple Finial, Wm. Turton, 1777, 7 1/2 In. 2200.00
Inkstand, Foliate Mantle, Urn Panels Flanked By Lions, Wm. Elliott, 12 In. 20700.00
Inkstand, Gadroon Rim, Boulton & Co., 1827, 11 In. 4600.00
Inkstand, Gadrooned Border, 2 Pen Wells, Langford & Schille, 1765, 12 In. 1380.00
Inkstand, Harvard, Tray, Engraved Name, Robert Garrard, 1812, 9 In. 575.00
Inkstand, Rocaille, Ball Footed, Marked F & S, 1906, 3 x 5 x 9 In. 375.00
Inkstand, Royal Presentation, Ebony, Wood Base, Rectangular, Robbins, 1806 . . . . 5175.00

Jug, Beer, Pear Shape, Capped Double Scroll Handle, 1743, 15 Oz. 3160.00
Jug, Cream, Molded Band, Reed Handle, William Hall, 1807, 4 1/4 In. 165.00
Jug, Hot Milk, Domed Lid, Reeded Rim & Foot, Wooden Handle, 1938 . . . . 390.00
Jug, Hot Water, Hinged Lid, Vase Shape, Wood Scroll Handle, 1791, 13 In. 2070.00
Jug, Water, Cover, Swirled Body-Scroll Wooden Handle, George III, 9 1/4 In. 1035.00
Kettle, Hot Water, On Stand, E.J. & W. Barnard Mark, 1849-1850, 15 In. 1725.00
Kettle, Paul Storr, London, 1837, 14 1/2 In. 6050.00
Kettle Lampstand, Pineapple Finial, Raffia Handle, J. Parker I & E. Wakelin, 10 In. 3162.00
Ladle, John Ziegler, Monogrammed Handle, 14 In. 165.00
Ladle, Monogrammed, 1785, 13 In. 431.00
Ladle, Stylized Flower, Rope Design, 1770, 4 Oz. 745.00
Marrow Spoon, William Reeve, 1731 . . . . 258.00
Meat Fork, Pierced & Engraved, William Hutton & Sons, 1884, 10 In. 330.00
Muffineer, Engraved Griffin, Pierced Top, Samuel Wood, 1745, 7 3/4 In. 847.00
Muffineer, John Corey, 1701, 5 7/8 In. 1575.00
Muffineer, Stylized Wheat Design, Comyns & Sons, 1901, 9 In. 805.00
Mug, Baluster Body, Gothic, Scroll Handle, W. & J. Deane, 1764 . . . . 715.00
Mug, Leaf Capped Double Scroll Handles, C. Wright, 4 In., Pair 3162.00
Mustard Pot, Crest, Reeded Rims, Blue Glass Insert, John Eames, 1803 . . . . 330.00
Mustard Pot, Swags, Hinged Cover, Glass Liner, Peter & Ann Bateman, 3 1/2 In. 425.00
Napkin Rings are listed in their own category.
Pail, Tub Form, Gadroon Rim, Gilt Interior, George IV, 1825, 5 In., Pair 2070.00
Pepper Pot, William Bond, 1781, 5 1/2 In., Pair 440.00
Picnic Set, Gilt Interior, Hinged Bail Handle, C. Reily, 1827, 9 In., 3 Piece 9200.00
Pitcher, Hammered, Spreading Circular Foot, 1935, 7 1/2 In. 690.00
Plate, Foliate Scrolls & Butterflies, George I Style, 9 5/8 In. 285.00
Plate, Gadrooned Edge, Monogrammed, 1777, 65 Troy Oz. 2070.00
Plate, Thomas Whipham, 1766, 9 1/2 In., 12 Piece 6900.00
Platter, Crest & Armorial Rim, Thomas Heming, 1770, 15 1/4 In. 1265.00
Platter, Meat, Contemporary Coat Of Arms, Crest, Gadrooned Rim, 1818 . . . . 6900.00
Platter, Meat, Contemporary Coat Of Arms, Gadrooned Rim, 16 In., Pair 5175.00
Platter, Meat, Gadrooned Rim, Coat Of Arms, Crest, Robert Sharp, 1796, 23 In. 5750.00
Platter, Meat, Trailing Grapevine, Contemporary Arms, Oval, 1801 . . . . 2587.00
Platter, Meat, Warming, Cover, Well & Tree, Handle, Sheffield, 26 x 19 In. 1955.00
Platter, Mottoed Crest In Gadrooned Rim, Robert Sharp, 1802, 20 In. 2587.00
Porringer, Gadrooned Base, Floral Medallion, 1766, 3 3/8 In. 275.00
Pot, Cream, Floral, Monogram, 3 Hoof Feet, Ear Handle, John Harvey, 3 7/8 In. 423.00
Punch Bowl, Tray, Pierced Undulating Rim, Oval Foot, Sheffield, 7 x 12 In. 1090.00
Punch Ladle, Fiddle, Rampant Lion Crest On Handle, 1829, 13 In. 453.00
Punch Ladle, Old English, Feathered, Shell Bowl, London, 13 1/2 In. 415.00
Punch Ladle, Old English, Monogram, Henry Nutting, 1798, 13 1/2 In. 230.00
Punch Ladle, Shell Bowl, Engraved Lion Head Handle, T. Chawner, 13 1/2 In. 605.00
Punch Ladle, Shell Bowl, Samuel Godbehere & Edward Wigan, 1796, 13 1/2 In. 485.00
Punch Ladle, Turned Wooden Handle, William Billings, 5 In. 330.00
Punch Ladle, Wooden Handle, George Bindon, 1750, 19 3/4 In. 365.00
Punch Set, Hand Chased, 19-In. Tray, Thomas Turner & Co., 14 Piece 950.00
Salt, 3 Hoof Feet, 1772, 2 1/2 In. 258.00
Salt, 3-Footed, Joseph Montgomery, c.1741, 1 1/2 In., Pair . . . . 165.00 to 285.00
Salt, Husk, Foliate, Gadroon Rims, Gilt Interior, Paul Storr, 1822, 4 In., Pair 2300.00
Salt, Open, Oval, Hoof Feet, London, 19th Century, Pair 110.00
Salt, Oval Shape, Raised On 4 Leaf, Scroll, Shell Feet, P. Storr, 5 In., 4 Piece 8050.00
Salver, Applied Rams' Heads, Gadrooned Rims, John Crouch II, 1810, 17 In. 3737.00
Salver, Armorial Over Mottoed Ribbon, S. Hougham, 1811, 12 1/4 In. 805.00
Salver, Chippendale Style, Piecrust Rim, C.S. Harris & Sons, 1909, 12 In. 550.00
Salver, Coat Of Arms, Edison, Shells Edge, John Hutson, 1787, 18 1/2 In. 2660.00
Salver, Contemporary Coat Of Arms In Center, Scroll Feet, 1840, 14 1/4 In. 2875.00
Salver, Engraved Crest & Motto, Gadrooned Rim, Border, William IV, 43 Oz. 5750.00
Salver, Field Of Scrolling Foliage, Vacant Cartouche, W. Bennett, 16 In. 1150.00
Salver, Gadrooned Border, Foliate Scrolled Feet, Wm. Bell, 8 1/2 In. 430.00
Salver, Later Coat Of Arms & Motto, Gadrooned Rim, 4 Feet, 10 In., Pair 5462.00
Salver, Leafy Scrolled Rim, Band Of Roses, Acorns, Peaston, George II, 20 In. 12650.00
Salver, Medallion, Beaded & Scalloped, Hester Bateman, 1780, 10 In. 1540.00

Salver, Pierced Border With Masks, Grape Foliage Panels, 3 Shell Feet, 16 In. 2875.00
Salver, Reeded George III, Ribbon-Tied Husk Cartouche, Richard Rugg, 1775, 11 In. 920.00
Salver, Reeded Rim, Border, Coat Of Arms In Center, 4 Feet, J. Hutson, 14 In. 2587.00
Salver, Robert Abercomby, 1735, 10 In. 2530.00
Salver, Shell & Floral Border, A. Bros., Ltd., 18 In. 1265.00
Salver, Shell, Scroll Rims, Contemporary Arms In Center, R. Rugg, 1765, 14 In. 5750.00
Salver, Swags Of Berried Laurel On Edge, Beaded Border, Carter, 15 In. 2760.00
Sauce Ladle, William Eaton, 1840 .... 143.00
Sauceboat, Beaded Rim, Leaf Capped 3-Scroll Handles, Jackson, 1786, Pair 4600.00
Sauceboat, Bombe, 3 Shell, Hoof Feet, E. Wakelin, George II, 9 In. 4025.00
Sauceboat, Daniel Smith & Robert Sharp, 8 1/2 In. 968.00
Sauceboat, Foliage, Gadroon Rim, Leaf Capped Scroll Handle, George II, 8 In. 515.00
Sauceboat, Leaf Scroll Handle, William Shaw & William Priest, 1740 .... 525.00
Sauceboat, Leaf-Capped Double Scroll Handles, George III, 16 Oz., Pair 2530.00
Sauceboat, Scroll Handle, Hoof Feet, Birmingham, 6 1/2 In. 315.00
Sauceboat, Scroll Mounts, Scroll Handle, Hoof Feet, London, 18th Century, 7 In. 330.00
Sauceboat, Scrolled Handle, Hoofed Feet, J. Priest, 1777, 8 Oz. 425.00
Sauceboat, Scrolled Rims, Scroll Handles, E. Wakelin, George II, 9 In., Pair 20700.00
Sauceboat, Thomas Heming, Georgian, 3 x 6 1/2 In., Pair 1125.00
Sauceboat, Wave Edge, Flying Scroll Handle, George II, 2 1/2 In. 230.00
Saucepan, Engraved Armorial, Turned Wooden Handle, Walter Brind, 5 Oz. 425.00
Serving Dish & Drainer, Coat Of Arms, Foliate Sprays, Ornamental Border, 1794 .... 2587.00
Serving Spoon, Fiddle Thread, Long Handle, 1828, 12 In. 393.00
Serving Spoon, London, Box, 8 1/2 In., Pair 175.00
Shaker, Bulbous Center, Domed Top, Hester Bateman, 1786-1787, 5 3/4 In. 375.00
Shaker, Pig Shape, 20th Century, 4 1/2 In. 330.00
Snuffbox, 4 Diamond Cover, Diamond Set Crown, Louis Willmott, 1908, 3 In. 5175.00
Snuffbox, Canary Shape, Enamel, Metal Mount, Late 18th Century, 2 In. 1035.00
Snuffbox & Grater, 1853, 1 3/8 x 1 1/2 In. 1200.00
Soup, Dish, Engraved Crest, London, 9 1/2 In. 248.00
Soup Ladle, Plain Fiddle Terminal, James Whiting, 1846 .... 460.00
Spoon, Monogram, Peter, Ann & William Bateman, London, 1800-1, 8 1/2 In. 115.00
Spoon, Strainer Bowl, Engraved Heraldic Device, Hester Bateman, George III 345.00
Spoon, Strainer Bowl, Walter Tweedie, 1774, 11 1/2 In. 363.00
Stuffing Spoon, Bright Cut Handle, Robert Cruickshank, 11 3/4 In. 210.00
Stuffing Spoon, English Stem, William Bateman, 1817, 12 In. 145.00
Stuffing Spoon, Hester Bateman, 1783 .... 315.00
Sugar & Cream Jug, Acorn & Oak Leaf Wreaths, John Emes, 1802, 4 In. 575.00
Sugar & Creamer, Floral & Leaf Design, Leaf Form Handle, W. Frisbee, 1810 .... 1265.00
Sugar & Creamer, Floral Shoulder Band, Rebecca Emes & Edward Barnard 230.00
Sugar & Creamer, H. Hayes, c.1899 .... 287.00
Sugar Basket, Swing Handle, R. & S. Hennel, 1818, 7 In. 345.00
Sugar Sifter, Gilt, Fiddle Thread, Shell, Order Of Garter Crest, London, 1781, Pair 1815.00
Sugar Tongs, Chased, Peter, Ann & William Bateman, London, c.1801, 5 1/2 In. 175.00
Sugar Tongs, James Beebe, 1821 .... 120.00
Sugar Tongs, Plain Terminals, 1813 .... 70.00
Sugar Tongs, Plain Terminals, James Beebe, 1821 .... 65.00
Sugar Tongs, Rattail Design, Plain Bowl, M.H. & Co., Sheffield, c.1912 .... 49.00
Sugar Tongs, Reeded Design On Handles 60.00
Sugar Tongs, Shell Terminals, 1850 .... 75.00
Sugar Tongs, Tapered Bowl, 3-Claw Terminals, Sheffield, c.1935 .... 44.00
Tablespoon, Feather Edge, Hester Bateman, 1777, 6 Piece 1035.00
Tablespoon, Folded Rim, Thomas Northcote, 1792, 12 Piece 1035.00
Tankard, Anthony Neime, 8 1/2 In. 5325.00
Tankard, Domed Lid, Scroll Handle, Peter & Ann Bateman, 1791, 7 5/8 In. 1100.00
Tankard, James Stamp, London, 1777, 8 1/2 In. 3630.00
Tazza, Armorial Surrounded By Fluted Sides, Edward Wakelin, 1758, 12 In., Pair 1955.00
Tea & Coffee Set, Floral Design, 1950s, 8 Piece 2013.00
Tea & Coffee Set, Gilt Interiors, Wood Finials, 1817-1820, 4 Piece 5462.00
Tea Caddy, Bright Cut Floral & Swags, Lion Head In Crown, S. Woods, 5 1/4 In. 1995.00
Tea Caddy, Cover, Engraved Borders, Foliate Finial, John Harvey, 1771, 4 In. 2760.00
Tea Caddy, Domed Cover, Wood Finial, 4 Ball Feet, Mappin Bros., 1892 .... 460.00

Tea Caddy, Engraved Crest, Stylized Bands, Hester Bateman, 1789, 5 5/8 In. 3450.00
Tea Caddy, Plain Oval, Reeded Borders, A & Co., Ltd., 1916 . . . . 260.00
Tea Set, Oval Teapot Stand, Henry Chawner, 1791, 4 Piece 2875.00
Tea Set, Pear Shape, Crochton, 4 Piece 1035.00
Tea Set, Regency, William Bateman, 1811, 5 1/2 In., 3 Piece 1955.00
Tea Set, Ribbing, Basket Weave Border, Ball Feet, C. Fuller, 1811, 4 Piece 1431.00
Tea Strainer, Double Pierced Handles, Thomas Allen, 1719, 6 7/8 In. 605.00
Teapot, Cover, Melon Shape, Shell Fluted Spout, Ivory Handle, George IV 1610.00
Teapot, Gadrooned Rim, Loop Handle, Peter, Ann & William Bateman, 1802 . . . . 960.00
Teapot, Gadrooned Rim, Wood Finial & Loop Handle, P. A. & W. Bateman 1090.00
Teapot, Oblong, Gadrooned Edge, Reeded Base, Hinged Lid, c.1813, 18 Oz. 275.00
Teapot, Oval Shape, Reeded Borders, Wooden Handle, 1787 . . . . 460.00
Teapot, Raised Floral & Foliate Design, Gourd Form, Ball Feet, Sheffield 140.00
Teapot, Serpentine Spout, Fruitwood Handle, Ball Feet, Bateman, 7 3/4 In. 630.00
Teapot, Stand, Crest, Gooseneck, Ivory Pineapple Finial, Simon Harris, 6 1/4 In. 1650.00
Teapot, Stand, Partially Reeded, Wooden Ear Handle, London, 1800, 9 1/2 In. 490.00
Toast Rack, Hester Bateman, Chased, Oval Base, 10 Wire Circles, Fluted Feet 405.00
Toast Rack, Scroll & Shell Handle & Feet, Wilkinson, 6 1/4 x 6 1/2 In. 345.00
Toddy Ladle, Coin Inset Bowl, Twisted Whalebone Handle, 1758, 13 7/8 In. 110.00
Toddy Ladle, Fluted, Baleen Handle, Edward Aldridge, 1741 . . . . 895.00
Toddy Ladle, Twist Handle, Crest, Unmarked 165.00
Tray, Armorial Within Scroll, Robert Abercromby, 1744, 8 1/4 In. 1495.00
Tray, Gadrooned Border, Chased Shell & Foliate, Foliate Handles, 29 In. 1955.00
Tray, Gadrooned Edge, Oval, Marked RS, 26 x 19 In. 2990.00
Tray, Pierced Gallery, Paw Feet, Lion's Head Medallions, 24 In. 800.00
Tray, Reeded Rim, Engraved With Contemporary Arms, Handles, 20 In. 5462.00
Tray, Serving, Asprey, Presentation Inscription, c.1947, 14 In. Diam. 550.00
Tray, Serving, Sheffield, Walker & Hall Mark, Handles, 1904-1905, 29 1/2 In. 1840.00
Tray, Sheffield, Oval, Pierced Border, Footed, Daniel Holy, 1800s, 14 In. 248.00
Tray, Shell Corner, Gadrooned Rim, 2 Loop Handles, Viner & Sons, 1931 . . . . 4025.00
Tray, Undulating Band, Bead, Reel Design, 2 Handles At Each End, 1894 . . . . 8050.00
Tureen, Sauce, 2 Contemporary Coats Of Arms, Ribbed Loop Handles, 3 Piece 3737.00
Tureen, Sauce, Cover, Raspberry Finial, Tiger Crest, Sheffield, c.1810, 8 In. 330.00
Tureen, Soup, Cover, Band Of Berries Laurel, Dart Rim, 2 Handles, 16 In. 13800.00
Urn, Cover, Angular Handles, Chrichton Bros., 1916, 11 1/2 In. 431.00
Vase, Hourglass, Blue, Green Oval Medallion, Enamel, Loop Handles, 1905, Pair 1265.00
Vinaigrette, Gilt, Chased Top, Joseph Taylor, Birmingham, 1815, 1 x 3/4 In. 175.00
Wine Cooler, Gadrooned Rim, Ring Handles, Burwash & Sibley, 7 In., Pair 20700.00
Wine Cooler, Pail Form, 4 Horizontal Bands, Hoop Handles, R. Garrard, 9 In. 7475.00
Wine Cooler, Reeded Body, Scroll Design, Original Liner, Handles, c.1810, 10 In. 825.00
SILVER-FRENCH, Basin, Swirled Lobed Body, Gadrooned Border, Roussel, 1880s, 17 1/2 In. 2185.00
Beaker, Awarded To Samuel Walker, Premium For Best Dahlias, 1843, 3 In. 192.00
Box, Enameled Woman & Children Scene, Scrolled, Geometrics, Oval, 3 x 2 In. 860.00
Card Tray, Reeded Edge, 7 1/4 x 6 In. 660.00
Cocktail Shaker, Hammered, LeBolt, 8 In. 770.00
Creamer, Hinged Cover, Monogram, 5 1/2 In. 110.00
Cruet, Altar, Hinged Lid, Stand, Cattails & Leaves, H. Puche, Pair 305.00
Dish, Caviar, Circular Cover, Rectangular Handles, Despres, 1925, 5 In. 10350.00
Dish, Reticulated Acanthus Leaf Border, Octagonal, 1880s, 9 5/8 In. 316.00
Ewer, Gold Edge, Simulated Straps, Bifurcated Handle, F. Boucheron, 6 In. 3450.00
Goblet, Engraved, Engine Turned Design, Mid 1800s, 5 3/4 In. 192.00
Jardiniere, Boat Shape, Floral Swags & Ivy, 2 Cartouches, Copper Liner, 14 In. 1380.00
Pepper Castor, Chased Design, Pair, 19th Century, 4 1/2 In., Pair 220.00
Punch Ladle, Long Scrolled Handle, 13 1/2 In. 210.00
Sugar Ladle, Stylized Knot Pattern, Pierced Shell Bowl, 8 In. 137.00
Sugar Shaker, Baluster Petal Molded Body, Circular Foot, 5 3/4 In. 460.00
Tea & Coffee Set, Stepped Bases, Rosewood Handles, Puiforcat, 4 Piece 3450.00
Tray, Hammered, Handled Form, Glass Bottom, Impressed Mark, 10 x 5 In. 357.00
Tray, Hammered, Impressed Mark, LeBolt, 11 In. 176.00
Vase, Fluted Hexagonal Base, Cylindrical, Puiforcat, 20th Century, 5 1/4 In. 5750.00
Vase, Silver Fillets, Removable Glass Liner, 2 Circular Handles, Puiforcat, 6 In. 6900.00
Wine Taster, Fluted & Dimpled Design, Deschamps A.M., 1838 . . . . 200.00

SILVER-GERMAN, Beaker, Cover, Chased, Classical Scene, 3 Ball Feet, G. Oberdieck, 1700 .   4312.00
Beaker, Deutsches Bundes-Scheissen, Munchen, Crest, Footed, 1881, 8 1/2 In. 490.00
Beaker, Tulip Shape, Chased Strapwork, Shells, Collet Foot, 1760, 4 3/8 In. 2300.00
Box, Chased & Floral Medallions, Rose Finial, 19th Century, 3 1/2 x 3 In. 275.00
Case, Theater, Lapis Lazuli Clasp, Interior Mirror, Comb, Money Clip, 3 x 4 In. 143.00
Chalice, Cover, Chased Design, Inscription, c.1897, 15 5/8 In. 1035.00
Creamer, Figural, Bird, Glass Eyes, Cobalt Blue Glass Liner 95.00
Creamer, Scroll, Floral Spray Design, Acanthus Handle, 4 Feet, 5 3/8 In. 145.00
Dish, Reticulated, Chased With 4 Putti In An Orchard, Rose Swags, 2 1/8 In. 287.00
Figurine, Parrot, Perched On Green Marble Pedestal, 1910, 10 In. 4025.00
Fruit Basket, Cherub & Scroll Design, Swing Handle, Glass Liner, c.1880, Pair 2970.00
Gravy Boat, Under Tray, Robert Anstead, 5 x 6 1/4 In. 180.00
Pokal, Cover, Foliage, Coins, Commemorative Medallions, Vollgold, 19 In. 6900.00
Snuffbox, Flying Bird Cover, White, Yellow Ground, Enamel, 1800, 2 1/2 In. 630.00
Soup Ladle, Leaf Tip Shaped Handle, Monogrammed, 13 1/2 In. 115.00
Tea & Coffee Set, Art Nouveau, Scrolling Foliage, Bud Finials, c.1900, 4 Piece 2070.00
Tea & Coffee Set, Colonial Style, Wooden Handles, Eichler, 20th Century, 4 Piece 546.00
Tea & Coffee Set, Ribbed Pear Form, E. Marcus, 1920s, 8 Piece 1150.00
Tea Set, Floral On Stipple Ground, A.D. Mark, 19th Century, 5 Piece 1955.00
Tea Set, Rococo Swirl Body, Late 19th Century, 4 Piece 920.00
Teapot, Scrolling Foliage, Center Putti & Birds In Landscape, Floral Finial, 8 In. 315.00
SILVER-IRISH, Card Tray, Gadroon Border, 3 Hoof Feet, Engraved Crest, 18th C., 7 In., Pair .   935.00
Curling Iron, Folding, Silver Handles, 19th Century 135.00
Fish Slice, Pierced, Fish & Foliate Border, Fiddle Handle, 1815, 12 In. 245.00
Ladle, Bright-Cut, Engraved Crest, Late 1700s 275.00
Salt, Open, Circular, Footed, Intertwined H's, 1800, Pair 220.00
Salver, Piecrust Border, Scroll Feet, Dublin, Late 18th Century, 7 In. Diam. 825.00
Stuffing Spoon, Engraved Crest, Charles Marsh, Dublin, 1831 ....   210.00
Stuffing Spoon, Engraved Crest, Marked WC, Dublin, 1826 ....   66.00
Sugar Scoop, SG, Dublin, 1833 ....   108.00
Teapot, Floral & Ribbon Design, Bird Head Spout, LeBass, 1870, 10 1/2 In. 575.00
Urn, Water, Grapes, Leaves On Neck, Leaf Tip Collar, Handle, William IV, 20 In. 6900.00
SILVER-ITALIAN, Basket, Fruit, Cover, Modeled Fruits, Twig Handle, 9 1/ 2 In. 7475.00
Tea & Coffee Set, Scrolls, Flowers & Foliage Ground, Floral Finial, 4 Piece 3735.00
Tureen, Cover, Bombe Oval Form, Spiral Fluting, Buccellati, 17 In. 8625.00
Tureen, Soup, Cover, Lobed, Fluted Bombe Sides, Openwork Foliate, Handles 4600.00
SILVER-JAPANESE, Spoon, Twig Handle, Twining Leaves, Blossoms, Chased Bowl, 7 1/2 In.   230.00
SILVER-MEXICAN, Ashtray, Coupe, 3 Ball Feet, Spratling, Stamped Hallmark, 2 1/4 In. 220.00
Basket, Woven, Square, 5 x 7 1/2 x 7 1/2 In. 517.00
Bowl, Mayonnaise, Underplate, Marked JR 145.00
Cheroot Case, Hinged Cover, Chased With Birds, Foliage, Gold, 1800, 3 In. 3740.00
Chocolate Pot, Wooden Handle & Finial, Stamped, William Spratling, 7 In. 990.00
Coffee Set, Vasiform Gadrooned Body, N.S. Co., c.1950, 4 Piece 480.00
Dish, Foliate Handles, Oval, 1940, 16 x 9 In. 120.00
Jewelry Tray, Sombrero Shape, Engraved Flowers, Eagle, Souvenir, 5 1/2 In. 25.00
Liqueur, Engraved Panels Below Floral Bands, 2 In., 8 Piece 60.00
Pitcher, Bar, Scroll Handle, Sanborns, 7 In. 650.00
Punch Bowl, Vermeil Interior, Fluted, Scrolled Rim, 94 Oz. 1495.00
Punch Ladle, Stylized Foliage On Handle 130.00
Sauceboat, Undertray, Fluted Body, Scroll Capped Handle, Beaded Rim 170.00
Sugar, Creamer & Undertray, Chased Band Of Flowers, 3 Piece 305.00
Tea & Coffee Set, Floral Finial, Sanborn's Dept. Store, 1940-1950, 6 Piece 1330.00
Tea & Coffee Set, Gonzalo Moreno, Waiter Tray, 2 Handles, 28 In., 6 Piece 1210.00
Tray, Grape Leaf & Vine Design, Wooden Handles, Oval, 23 In. 1840.00
Tray, Kidney Shape, 3 Ball Feet, 14 1/2 In. 230.00
Tray, Notched Border, Handles, Oval, Maker's Name, 16 1/4 In. 1560.00
Tumbler Set, Undecorated, Cylinder, 1950, 5 3/4 In., 4 Piece 270.00
SILVER-PERUVIAN, Dish, Scrolling Floral & Foliate Rim, Partly Fluted Body, 13 In. 373.00
Tea & Coffee Set, 7 Piece 1150.00
Vase, Native Design, Spherical, 7 1/2 In. 240.00
SILVER-POLISH, Teaspoon, Bright Cut Floral, Gilt Bowl, 6 Piece 138.00
SILVER-PORTUGUESE, Dish, Sideboard, Embossed Dragon In Center, Scalloped Rim, 11 In. .   2587.00

SILVER-RUSSIAN. Russian silver is marked with the Cyrillic, or Russian, alphabet. The numbers 84, 88, or 91 indicate the silver content. Russian silver may be higher or lower than sterling standard. Other marks indicate maker, assayer, or city of manufacture. Many pieces of silver made in Russia are decorated with enamel. Faberge pieces are listed in their own category.

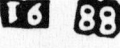

SILVER-RUSSIAN, Basket, Swing Handle, Gilt Interior, Pavel Sazikov, 1834, 6 1/2 In.	775.00
Beaker, Floral Sprays, Footed, Moscow, 1881, 2 1/8 In.	150.00
Beaker, Kostroma, 1885	90.00
Beaker, Niello, Gilt, 1865 Mark, Viktor Savinkov, 3 1/2 In.	430.00
Box, Cigarette, Sterling Silver, Blue Cabochon Thumbpiece, Rectangular, 10 In.	374.00
Box, Niello Inlay, 2 1/2 In.	110.00
Box, Sewing, Trompe L'oeil, Lace Handkerchief, Spool Of Cotton, 5 1/4 In.	6900.00
Bread Basket, Trompe L'oeil, Gold Wash Edge, 8 x 13 In.	8500.00
Bucket, Vodka, Circular Form, Bands Of Reeding, Foliate Carving, Swing Handle	517.00
Cake Basket, Scroll & Foliate Border, Swing Handle, Gilt, Sazikov, 1840, 14 In.	1955.00
Case, Elephant Family Repousse, Green Stone Latch Opener, 6 3/4 x 2 1/2 In.	460.00
Champagne, Woman's Head, Nouveau Design, Monogram, Marked, 6 1/4 In.	155.00
Cigarette Case, Enameled, Hinged, Told Wash Interior, 4 1/2 In.	740.00
Clasp, Cape, Man's, Double Eagle, Filigree, 2 Piece, 7 1/2 x 2 1/2 In.	235.00
Cup, Vodka, Bright Cut Floral, Fleur-De-Lis Band, 2 1/2 In., 6 Piece	315.00
Cup, Vodka, Enamel, Gilt, Melon Shape, Green Ground, 1958, 2 5/8 In.	72.00
Cup Holder, Floral Enamel Design, 84 Mark, 4 3/4 In.	775.00
Dish, Gilt, Floral Enamel, Plique-A-Jour Border, Open Foot, 6 3/4 In.	4312.00
Punch Bowl, Ladle, Kovsh, Cyrillic Inscription, Morozov, c.1912, 23 In.	3450.00
Purse, Double Lion Swag, Ribbon & Floral On Cover, Green Stone Clasp, 7 3/4 In.	182.00
Salt, Gold Washed, Enamel, Trigger Form Handle, 2 1/8 x 4 1/2 In.	920.00
Samovar, Lobed Section, C-Scroll Handles, Gustav Lindgren, 1827, 13 5/8 In.	5462.00
Samovar, Urn Form Body, Openwork Spigot, Geometric Border, 1887, 16 In.	8340.00
Snuffbox, Gold Washed Interior, 1 1/2 In.	330.00
Snuffbox, Stylized Design, A. Kuzmichev, 2 1/2 x 2 In.	80.00
Spoon, Blue & Red Enamel Design, 88 Mark, 1891, 5 1/8 In.	127.00
Spoon, Stylized Floral Enamel Design, 84 Mark, 6 7/8 In.	160.00
Sugar Tongs, Bright Cut, 2 Vacant Cartouches	115.00
Tea Strainer, Gilt, Scalloped Border, Blue Scrolling, Straight Handle, 5 1/2 In.	460.00
Tray, Raised Edge, Rays & Scrolls Corners, 19th Century, 10 1/2 x 9 In.	550.00
SILVER-SCOTTISH, Candlestick, Georgian, Square Base, Shell Corners, 1750s, 10 In., Pair	6325.00
Dish, Entree, Baron's Coronet On A Pillow Form, Gadrooned Border, 10 In., Pair	7187.00
Salt, Master, Floral Motif, C Scroll, Edinburgh, c.1844	220.00
Sugar Tongs, Beaded Rim, Shell Terminals, Monogram, 1876	80.00
Sugar Tongs, Shell Terminals, 1826	60.00
Tureen, Sauce, Stepped Dome Cover, Oval Body, Ring Handles, 8 1/2 In., Pair	920.00
SILVER-SIAMESE, Vase, Relief Figures, 6 1/4 In.	120.00
SILVER-SOUTH AMERICAN, Basin, Round, 16 3/4 x 2 3/4 In.	1495.00
Bowl, Vegetable, Cover, Footed, Hot Water Compartment, 14 x 10 In.	1150.00
Pitcher, Washbowl, P. Lino, Sequeiros, 12 1/2 & 16 In.	2415.00
SILVER-SPANISH, Jug, Claret, Owl Form, Chased Lip, Feathers, Green Glass Body, Handle	3737.00

SILVER-STERLING. Sterling silver is made with 925 parts silver out of 1,000 parts of metal. The word *sterling* is a quality guarantee used in the United States after about 1860. The word was used much earlier in England and Ireland. Pieces listed here are not identified by country. Other pieces of sterling quality silver are listed under Silver-American, Silver-English, etc.

SILVER-STERLING, Asparagus Tongs, Pierced Blades, Foliate Sprays, c.1850, 10 1/2 In.	1045.00
Berry Spoon, Georgian Style, Pair	345.00
Bottle Stopper, Horse Head, c.1930	125.00
Bottle Stopper, Ram's Head	102.00
Box, Cigarette, Lid, 4 Sections, Lucky Strike, Camel, Old Gold, Chesterfield	305.00
Box, Cigarette, Monogram, 5 7/8 In.	94.00
Candelabrum is listed in its own category.	
Candlesticks are listed in their own category.	
Card Case, Bright Cut Design, Monogram	88.00

Chalice, Repousse, Christ & Grapes On Bowl, Louis J. Hupfeld, 1960s, 8 1/2 In. 1500.00
Coffeepot, Rose Finial, Band Of Foliage, Scroll Cartouche, W.M., 1848, 10 In. 920.00
Compote, Art Nouveau, Openwork Foliate Stem, Arching Handle, 8 x 7 In. 1265.00
Cruet, Bulls, Head Rest, Other Poised To Charge, 5 In., Pair 575.00
Cup, Chased With Daisies, Foliage, Waved Rim, 3 Scrolled Handles, 11 In. 6900.00
Cup, Drinking, Squirrel Form, Holding Nut, Perched On Branch 2530.00
Cup, Presentation, 1907 Date, 3 Handles 575.00
Dish, 3 Sections, Linked By Interwoven Stems, Alfredo Sciarrotta, 9 In. 225.00
Dish, Grape, Fig Shape, Strawberry Finials, 1865-1870, 12 x 12 In. 3565.00
Flask, Trout, Landing On Rocky Bank, Spot Hammered Ground, Screw Cap 4830.00
Grape Scissors, Engraved Handles 140.00
Handle, Umbrella, Dated 1902, 9 1/2 In. 130.00
Ice Cream Set, Gold Washed Bowls, Serving Spoon, 1860s, 13 Piece 920.00
Inkwell, Tray, Square Repousse Tray, J.E. Caldwell & Co., 1890, 7 1/8 In. 795.00
Jar, Wire, Scroll & Ball Work, Light Hammered, William DeMatteo, 5 3/4 In. 975.00
Kettle, Rolled Border, Goose-Neck Spout, Foliate Body, Stand, 1850s, 15 In. 3740.00
Lipstick Holder, Engraved Swirls, Green Jewel, 2 In. 60.00
Loving Cup, Chased With Clover, Daisies, Leaves, 6-Lobed, 3 Handles, 14 In. 8050.00
Muffineer, Ribbed Bands, Baluster Form, Cartier, 20th Century, 7 1/4 In. 345.00
Napkin Rings are listed in their own category.
Oyster Fork, Dated 1898, 12 Piece 412.00
Pitcher, Grape & Leaf Border At Shoulder, Scroll Handle, 7 1/4 In. 345.00
Pitcher, Milk, No Monogram, Arthur Stone, 3 In. 415.00
Pitcher, Water, Serpent Shaped Handle, 9 1/2 In. 1900.00
Platter, Gadrooned Rim, Circular, 16 1/4 In. 201.00
Platter, Repousse Floral Garlands, Vacant Cartouches, Foliate Rim, 20 In. 1610.00
Porringer, Double Arched Keyhole Handle, Samuel Vernon, c.1730, 5 1/4 In. 4887.00
Porringer, Self Foot, Tab Handle, Volund Shop, c.1915, 6 1/4 In. 450.00
Punch Bowl, Chased With Panels Ancient Horsemen, Loop Handle, 1881 . . . . 3680.00
Punch Ladle, Double Lip, Applied Flowers On Handle 495.00
Punch Ladle, Prunus Blossoms Finial, Vine Wrapped Handle, 20th Century 402.00
Rattle, Humpty Dumpty Form, Victoria Hayes, Born, 3rd June, 1848 . . . . 475.00
Salt & Pepper, Barrel, 1940s, 1 1/2 In. 12.00
Scissors, Desk, Floral & Foliate Design, St. George Handle, 7 5/8 In. 247.00
Soup Ladle, Monogram, A.B. Lansert, 14 1/2 In. 745.00
Spoon, Fluted Pierced Bowl, A.B. Van Cott, Coin 165.00
Spoon, Souvenir, see Souvenir category.
Sugar, Acorn Finial, Gilded Interior, 3 3/4 In. 192.00
Sugar & Creamer, Classical Profile Medallions, Hammered, 1885, 14 Oz. 2875.00
Tea Ball, Teapot Shape, Chain 65.00
Tea Caddy, 4-Panels, 3 Children Playing Under Tree, European, 5 1/2 In. 495.00
Tea Infuser, Pierced Spherical Form, Hinged Lid, Link Chain, c.1925, 1 1/4 In. 66.00
Tea Set, Chase Decorated, 8 In. Teapot, 3 Piece 375.00
Tea Set, Floral & Panels Design, Rectangular Tray, 11 In. Teapot, 6 Piece 949.00
Tray, Border Of Grapes & Leaves, Vacant Cartouche, Foliate Handles, 29 1/2 In. 200.00
Tray, Center & Border Punchwork Designs, Mary Knight, 1905, 7 5/8 In. 2000.00
Tray, Chippendale Pattern, Cartier, 14 In. 275.00
Tray, Monogram, Raised Rim, Round, 16 In. 195.00
Tray, Raised Border, Oval, William L. DeMatteo, 9 In. 175.00
Tray, Repousse, Branch Shaped Handles, Twining Ivy, 21 Troy Oz. 517.00
Tureen, Soup, Cover, Gadroon Collar, Stiff Leaf Border, Loop Handles, 16 In. 6325.00
Tureen, Soup, Cover, Grape, Leaf Rim, 2 Classical Medallions, 1874, 17 In. 6612.00
Vase, Trumpet, Weighted, Monogram, 16 In. 80.00
Vegetable Stand, Open, Art Nouveau Poppy Repousse Border, Monogram, 13 In. 645.00
Water Set, C Scroll Handle, Bulbous Form Goblets, 10 1/4 In., 13 Piece 488.00

SINCLAIRE cut glass was made by H.P. Sinclaire and Company of
Corning, New York, between 1905 and 1929. He cut glass made at
other factories until 1920. Pieces were made of crystal as well as
amber, blue, green, or ruby glass. Only a small percentage of Sinclaire
glass is marked with the S in a wreath.

Bowl, Amber, 11 In. 100.00
Plate, Denver Pattern, 7 1/4 In. 250.00

SKIING, see Sports category.

SLAG GLASS resembles a marble cake. It can be streaked with different colors. There were many types made from about 1880. Caramel slag is the incorrect name for Chocolate glass. Pink slag was an American Victorian product made by Harry Barstow and Thomas E.A. Dugan at Indiana, Pennsylvania. Purple and blue slag were made in American and English factories. Red slag is a very late Victorian and twentieth-century glass. Other colors are known but are of less importance to the collector. New versions of chocolate glass and colored slag glass are being made.

Caramel slag is listed in the Chocolate Glass category.

Green, Mustard, Owl	45.00
Pink, Bowl, Inverted Fan & Scroll, Footed, 4 1/2 In.	137.00
Pink, Cruet, Inverted Fan & Scroll, Stopper, 5 1/4 In.	1100.00
Pink, Toothpick, Inverted Fan & Feather	600.00
Purple, Creamer, Owl	45.00
Purple, Tumbler, Sowerby, 8 Oz.	75.00
Red, Jar, Cover, Beaded	50.00

SLEEPY EYE collectors look for anything bearing the image of the nineteenth-century Indian chief with the drooping eyelid. The Sleepy Eye Milling Co., Sleepy Eye, Minnesota, used his portrait in advertising from 1883 to 1921. It offered many premiums, including stoneware and pottery steins, crocks, bowls, mugs, and pitchers, all decorated with the famous profile of the Indian. The popular pottery was made by Western Stoneware, Weir Pottery Company, and other companies long after the flour mill went out of business in 1921. Reproductions of the pitchers are being made today. The original pitchers came in only five sizes: 4 inches, 5 1/4 inches, 6 1/2 inches, 8 inches, and 9 inches. The Sleepy Eye image was also used by companies unrelated to the flour mill.

Apron, Clothespin	1100.00
Creamer, Blue & White, Indian, 4 In.	135.00
Crock, Butter, Blue & Gray, Stoneware, 5 In.	475.00
Hot Plate, Blue & White, 7 In. Diam.	3500.00 to 7000.00
Label, Flour Barrel, Frame, 16 In.	175.00
Mug, Blue & White, 4 1/4 In.	260.00
Mug, Brown & White, 4 1/4 In.	2300.00 to 3200.00
Mug, Handle, Blue & White, 4 3/4 In.	275.00
Mug, Yellow & Blue, 4 1/4 In.	750.00
Pillow Top, Trademark Head In A Circle	935.00
Pitcher, Blue & White, 4 In.	135.00 to 140.00
Pitcher, Blue, White, Reproduction, 2 1/4 In.	30.00
Pitcher, No. 1, Blue Rim, 4 In.	375.00
Pitcher, No. 1, Blue Rim, Maple Leaf Mark, 4in.	675.00

Sleepy Eye, Vase, Cattails,
Blue & White, 8 1/2 In.

In case of a major theft, keep careful records. You may be able to deduct part of the uninsured loss from your income tax.

In half of all burglaries, the thief came in through an unlocked window or door.

Pitcher, No. 2, Blue & Gray, 5 1/4 In. 325.00
Pitcher, No. 2, Blue & White, 5 3/8 In. 165.00
Pitcher, No. 2, Brown & White, 5 1/4 In. 3600.00
Pitcher, No. 3, Blue & White, 6 1/2 In. 275.00
Pitcher, No. 3, Yellow & Blue, 6 1/2 In. 6100.00
Pitcher, No. 4, Blue & White, 7 7/8 In. ....110.00 to 220.00
Pitcher, No. 4, Light Blue, 8 In. 1000.00
Pitcher, No. 5, Blue & White, 8 7/8 In. 165.00
Pitcher, No. 5, Blue Rim, Maple Leaf Mark, 9 In. 625.00
Pitcher, No. 5, Yellow & Blue, 9 In. 2900.00
Ruler, Wooden, 15 In. ....450.00 to 525.00
Sugar, Blue & White, 3 In. ....350.00 to 380.00
Sugar & Pitcher, No. 1, Yellow & Blue 2600.00
Vase, Cattails, Blue & Gray, 8 1/2 In. 360.00
Vase, Cattails, Blue & White, 8 1/2 In. ....*Illus* 550.00
Vase, Cattails, Blue & White, 9 In. ....165.00 to 295.00
Vase, Cattails, Green, 8 1/2 In. 950.00

SLOT MACHINES are included in the Coin-Operated Machine category.

SMITH BROTHERS glass was made after 1878. Alfred and Harry Smith had worked for the Mt. Washington Glass Company in New Bedford, Massachusetts, for seven years before going into their own shop. They made many pieces with enamel decoration.

Biscuit Jar, Enameled Pansies, Melon Ribbed, 7 1/2 In. 175.00
Sugar & Creamer, Floral, Demitasse 350.00
Sugar Shaker, Enameled Violets, Ribbed, White Shaded To Blue, 5 3/4 In. 385.00
Sugar Shaker, Owl, Tapering Cylinder 350.00
Sugar Shaker, Summer Blossoms, Ribbed, Opaque White Ground, 6 In. 575.00
Vase, Ball, White Daisies, Green Ferns, Peach Ground, White Dotted Rim, 4 In. 275.00
Vase, Blue Wisteria Pods, Leafy Vine, Melon Ribbed, Bulbous Neck, 8 1/2 In. 800.00
Vase, Enameled Cluster Of Wisteria Blossoms, Double Canteen Shape, 7 1/4 In. 1950.00

SNOW BABIES, made from bisque and spattered with glitter sand, were first manufactured in 1864 by Hertwig and Company of Thuringia. Other German and Japanese companies copied the Hertwig designs. Originally, Snow Babies were made of candy and used as Christmas decorations. There are also Snow Babies tablewares made by Royal Bayreuth. Copies of the small Snow Babies figurines are being made today and can easily confuse the collector.

Figurine, 2 Babies Dancing, Germany, 2 In. 250.00
Figurine, Baby On Tummy 70.00
Figurine, Girl On Sled, 1 1/2 In. 185.00
Figurine, Sitting On Polar Bear, 2 3/4 In. 175.00
Figurine, Skier, Standing With Flag, Germany, 4 1/2 In. 400.00
Pitcher, Milk 350.00
Tumbler, On Tummy, Germany, 3 1/2 In. 185.00
Tumbler, Seated, Germany, 2 1/4 In. 160.00

SNUFF BOTTLES are listed in the Bottle category.

SNUFFBOXES held snuff. Taking snuff was popular long before cigarettes became available. The gentleman or lady would take a small pinch of the ground tobacco or snuff in the fingers, then sniff it and sneeze. Snuffboxes were made of many materials, including gold, silver, enameled metal, and wood. Most snuffboxes date from the late eighteenth or early nineteenth centuries.

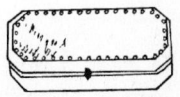

3/4 Portrait Of A Woman, Man & Musical Party, 3 In. 375.00
Bloodstone, Gilt Metal Mount, Rubies, Pearls, Continental, 19th Century, 3 1/4 In. 3335.00
Bone, Engraved House & Flowers, Inscription, 1 3/4 In. 70.00
Burl, Ebony Design On Cover, Blind Hinge, Tortoiseshell Interior, 1880s, 2 3/4 In. 375.00
Burl, Tin Hinge, 2 1/8 x 3 3/8 In. 140.00
Burl, Tortoiseshell Banding, Eglomise Reserve Of Benjamin Franklin, 3 3/8 In. 575.00
Burl & Tortoiseshell, Double Compartment, England, c.1820, 2 1/2 x 1 1/4 In. 895.00

Snuffbox, Horn, Leather, Cover, Wood Bottom,
2 1/2 x 1 1/4 In.

Snuffbox, Horn, Wood Top & Bottom, W
Scratched On Front, 3 x 1 3/4 In.

Carved Betel Nut, 5 Pieces Glued Together, Table, Late 18th Century, 4 In.	995.00
Copper, Enameled, Cherub Riding Large Cat, 2 1/4 In.	185.00
Cowrie Shell, Mounted In Silver, Initialed Top, c.1750	425.00
Enamel & Silver Gilt, Painted Classical Figures, 3 1/4 In.	1085.00
Gold, Enameled, Machine Turned, Turquoise Stones, Reymond, Geneva, 3 In.	4887.00
Gold, Mounted With Panels Of Lapis Lazuli, Gold & Enamel, Austrian, 1826, 3 In.	2587.00
Horn, Engraved Cover, Robert Lloyd, Flintlock Musket Engraved On Lid	195.00
Horn, Leather, Cover, Wood Bottom, 2 1/2 x 1 1/4 In. ....*Illus*	15.00
Horn, Needle Illustration On Lid, German Text, Mid 18th Century, 1 x 2 In.	895.00
Horn, Wood Top & Bottom, W Scratched On Front, 3 x 1 3/4 In. ....*Illus*	22.50
Ivory, Cover, Top Painted Elaborate Floral Still Life, 19th Century, 4 1/2 In.	200.00
Ivory, Top Painted With Lovers, Floral Design On Sides, 19th Century, 1 3/4 In.	230.00
Lacquer, Inlaid Mother-Of-Pearl, Bremen, 3 x 1 1/2 In. ....*Illus*	26.50
Lacquer, St. Peter With Skull, Crucifix In Background, 18th Century, 3 1/2 In.	450.00
Leather, Book, Brass Clasp, Paper Lining, 1870s, 2 1/2 x 3 3/4 In.	475.00
Paktong, Silvered, England, c.1780, 3 In.	195.00
Papier-Mache, Benjamin Franklin, Born, Boston, Jan. 17, 1706, In French	1850.00
Papier-Mache, France Receiving Ashes Of Napoleon Scene, Round	325.00
Papier-Mache, G.W. Gails Tobacco Works, 1830-1840, 4 1/2 x 1 1/2 In.	850.00
Papier-Mache, Napoleon & Marie Louise Portraits, Round, 1810	375.00
Papier-Mache, Naval Battle, Enterprise & Boxer, Black, Mustard, Round	750.00
Papier-Mache, Tomb Of Napoleon, Trees Form Silhouette	275.00
Papier-Mache, Treaty Of Ghent, Dec. 15, 1814, Allegorical Scene, Miss Liberty	700.00
Papier-Mache, Woman Portrait Lid, Rectangular	45.00
Pewter, Horse's Head Shape, England, Early 19th Century, 3 7/8 In.	150.00
Pewter, Shoe Shape, Simple Tooling, 3 1/2 In.	145.00
Porcelain, Floral In High Relief, Cream Ground, South Staffordshire, 1770	4025.00
Porcelain, Head Of Dog Form, Faceted Red Paste Eyes, London, 1882, 1 3/4 In.	287.00
Silver, Engraved, Oystershell On Top, Oystershell Shape, 2 1/2 In.	115.00
Silver, Gilt, Lavender Translucent Guilloche Enamel, c.1912, 2 1/2 In.	747.00
Silver, Hinged Lid, Engraved Courting Couple, Continental, 2 x 1 1/2 In.	200.00
Silver, Religious, Engraved Top & Sides, 2 3/4 In.	130.00
Silver, Stone Set In Top, England, Oval, 2 5/8 In.	265.00

To clean a veneered box or one made of porcupine quills or matchsticks, use a vacuum cleaner hose covered with a nylon stocking.

Snuffbox, Lacquer, Inlaid Mother-Of-Pearl,
Bremen, 3 x 1 1/2 In.

Silver, William & Mary, Lion Form, Glass Eyes, Hinged Door, 4 1/4 In. 7820.00
Tin, L.P. Roberts Scratched On Cover, Civil War, 1860, 2 x 3 In. 85.00
Tortoiseshell, Gold Inlay, Lozenge Shape, 3 3/4 In. 430.00
Tortoiseshell, Silver Lined, Border Of Flowers On Cover, c.1740, 3 1/2 In. 1255.00
Woman, Outside A Cottage & Battle Scene, Hand Painted, 3 1/4 In., Pair 230.00
Wood, Shoe Shape, 19th Century 265.00
Wood, Trick Lid, Coffin Form, 19th Century, 3 3/8 In. 190.00
Young Woman Holding Lamb, Lamb In Distress, 2 1/4 In. 200.00

SOAPSTONE is a mineral that was used for foot warmers or griddles because of its heat-retaining properties. Soapstone was carved into figurines and bowls in many countries in the nineteenth and twentieth centuries. Most of the soapstone seen today is from China or Japan. It is still being carved in the old styles.

Figurine, Enthroned Ming Emperor, 1900, 8 1/2 In. 45.00
Figurine, Priest Teaching Monkeys To Pray, Jade Color, 4 1/2 x 5 In. 120.00
Figurine, Sage, Standing, Holding Vase, 8 1/2 In. 88.00
Lamp, Foliate Arabesque, Bird, Wooden Base, 16 In. 115.00
Lamp, Table, Quanyin Form, Chinese, 9 In. 330.00
Seal, Yellow Landscape, Engraved Calligraphy, 3 3/4 In. 165.00

SOFT PASTE is a name for a type of pottery. Although it looks very much like porcelain, it is a chemically different material. Most of the soft-paste wares were made in the early nineteenth century. Other pieces may be listed under Gaudy Dutch or Leeds.

Bowl, Oriental Blue Transfer, 4 x 11 In. 495.00
Coffeepot, Adam Rose, 1820, 11 1/2 In. 330.00
Jug, Puzzle, Intricate Piercings, 8 1/4 In. 230.00
Mug, Castle Design, Porcelain, England, 4 3/4 In. 145.00
Mug, Elephant, Pagoda Design, Blue, White, England, 6 In. 130.00
Plate, Brush Stroke, 1840, 10 In. 100.00
Plate, Eagle & Nest, Red Transfer, 6 In. 145.00
Plate, King's Rose, Blue Flowers, 9 1/2 In. 540.00
Plate, Pink & Blue Floral Border, c.1880, 10 1/2 In. 127.00
Sugar, Cover, King's Rose, 5 3/4 In. 275.00
Sugar, Floral, 6 In. 110.00

SOUVENIRS of a trip—what could be more fun? Our ancestors enjoyed the same thing and souvenirs were made for almost every location. Most of the souvenir pottery and porcelain pieces of the nineteenth century were made in England or Germany, even if the picture showed a North American scene. In the twentieth century, the souvenir china business seems to have gone to the manufacturers in Japan, Taiwan, Hong Kong, England, and America. Another popular souvenir item is the souvenir spoon, made of sterling or silver plate. These are usually made in the country pictured on the spoon. Related pieces may be found in the Coronation and World's Fair categories.

Album, Berlin Olympics, Hardcover, 624 Pages, Olympic Rings, 1936 . . . . 255.00
Almanac, Olympic, Spalding's Official, 3rd Games, 1904 . . . . 3450.00
Ashtray, Indianapolis, Car Shape, Iridescent Pale Yellow, Late 1930s, 2 x 2 x 5 In. 45.00
Ashtray, Olympic, 1960 Squaw Valley, VIII Winter Games, Blue Ceramic, Ski Jumper . . . 115.00
Badge, Olympic, National Committee, 10th Games, 1932 . . . . 2070.00
Badge, Olympic, Official, 1936 Berlin, XI Summer Games, Gilt Bronze Color, Ribbon . . . 1230.00
Button, Hudson Fulton Celebration, Multicolored, Gold Rim, Pinback, 1 1/4 In. 75.00
Card, Omaha, 2 Gold Medals, Standard Sewing Machine Co., Cleveland, Oh., 1898 . . . . . 80.00
Card, Omaha, Stoughton Wagon Co., Gold Medal, Best Farm Wagons, 1898 . . . . 90.00
Cigarette Holder, 1939 Golden Gate International Exposition, 3 1/4 x 4 1/2 In. 51.00
Clothes Brush, Centennial 1776-1876, Leather, Gold Letters, 7 In. 125.00
Figurine, Dog, Seated, White, Dark Brown Glaze, Marked 1877, 7 1/4 In. 880.00
Figurine, Olympic, Amazon, Seated On Rearing Horse, Bronze, 1960, 11 2/3 In. 4025.00
Handkerchief, Buffalo Bill, Indian Designs, Blue Ground, Silk, 28 In. 775.00
Handkerchief, Melbourne Olympics, 1956, 4 Block Scenes, 13 In. 150.00
Handkerchief, Olympics, Frame, 1936, 16 x 17 In. 225.00

Souvenir, Matchbox, Merbein Park With Bridge,
Celluloid, 2 3/8 x 1 1/2 In.

Souvenir, Pillow Cover, Aloha From
Hawaii, Poem, Acetate, 17 In.

Handkerchief, Olympics, Olympic Rings, National Flags, Nazi Flag, 1936, 16 In.	40.00
Handkerchief, Remember The Maine, Red, White & Blue	65.00
Jogging Outfit, Olympics, Jacket, Pants, Blue Velour, Levi, 1984, Child's Size 7	22.00
Key Chain, Olympic, Alitalia Commemorative, 1960 Rome, XVII Summer, Bronze	40.00
Mascot, Olympic, Shuss/Jim, Plastic, 1968 Grenoble, X Winter Games, Looped	150.00
Matchbox, Merbein Park With Bridge, Celluloid, 2 3/8 x 1 1/2 In. . . . .*Illus*	3.00
Medal, Johnstown Flood, May 31, 1989	15.00
Medal, Olympic, 1912 Stockholm, V Summer Games, Tombac, Olympioska Spelen	150.00
Medal, Olympic, Bronze, V Winter Games, St. Moritz, 1948, Hand With Touch	5600.00
Medal, Olympic, Silver, II Winter Games, St. Moritz, 1928	1035.00
Medal, Participation, Olympic, 1904 St. Louis, III Summer, Nude Athlete On Back	15400.00
Medallion, U.S. Bicentennial, 1976, Bronze, Leather Case, France, 4 1/2 In.	48.00
Official Press Badge, Olympic, 1952 Oslo, VI Winter Games, Silver Bronze	505.00
Official Regulations, Olympic, 1948 XIV Summer Games, Black & White, 20 Pages	85.00
Official Report, Olympic, 1932 Los Angeles X Summer, Leather Cover, 815 Pages	1170.00
Pennant, Olympic, 1952 Helsinki, XV Summer, Stadium Tower, Blue, White Ground . . .	70.00
Pickle Fork, University Of Illinois	35.00
Pillow Cover, Aloha From Hawaii, Poem, Acetate, 17 In. . . . .*Illus*	62.00
Pillow Cover, Armored Force, Camp Campbell, Ky., Blue Satin, Yellow Fringe	12.00
Pillow Cover, Jefferson Barracks, No., 3 Airplanes, Winged Propeller	18.00
Pillow Cover, Ordnance Training Center, Aberdeen, Md., Blue, White Fringe	15.00
Pillow Cover, Souvenir Of The Tropics, Panama, Purple, White Fringe	15.00
Pillow Cover, U.S. Army, Fort Knox, Ky., Grant Tank & Marching Troops, Blue Fringe . .	18.00
Pin, Olympic, 1924 Paris, Gold Winner's, VIII Summer, Olympic Rings, Black Case	145.00
Pin, Olympic, Weightlifting, 1940 Helsinki, XII Summer Games	300.00
Pin, RAF, In Wreath, Crown, Wings, 1 1/8 In.	16.00
Pin, Senior Astronaut Wing, U.S. Sterling	27.00
Pin, U.S. Capitol, Washington, D.C., Sterling Silver, Turquoise Oval, Shield, 2 1/4 In. . . .	35.00
Pin, Wings, Col. Rosco Turner 57, Brass, 1934	16.00
Plate, Away To California, Gold Rush, Sailing Ship, 3 In.	325.00
Plate, Indianapolis Scenes, Staffordshire England, Acme Novelty Co., 8 In.	82.00
Plate, Mint, San Francisco, Sepia, Floral Border, Porcelain, 1890s, 7 3/4 In.	400.00
Plate, Seattle, 1909, Scenes, Scalloped, Japanese-Style, 5 In.	75.00
Plate, US Battleship Maine, Pink & Turquoise Border, 12 In.	175.00
Poster, Olympic, Javelin Thrower, Paris Skyline, Legend Below, 47 1/4 x 31 1/2 In.	3450.00
Program, Olympic, 1908 London, IV Summer Games, July 16, 4th Day, 56 Pages	380.00
Report, Olympic, 1920 Antwerp, VII Summer Games, Swedish, Hardcover, 160 Pages . . .	585.00
Ribbon, Admission Day, Yerba Buena Parlor, Silk, With Redwoods, 1890	85.00
Ribbon, Kansas Suffrage Ribbon, We Wage A Peaceful War, Yellow, 1894	45.00
Ribbon, Panama-Pacific International Exposition, Blue, Orange, Brown, 1915	29.00
Ring Box, Brandenburg Gate, Berlin, White Metal, Footed, Pre-World War II, 2 1/4 In. . . .	50.00
Ruler, Space Shuttle 3-D Space Picture, Kennedy Space Center, Florida, Late 1970s, 6 In.	4.00
Scarf, Golden Gate Exposition, Calif., Cotton, 1939, 20 x 20 In.	43.00

Scarf, Olympic, 1956 Melbourne, XVI Summer Games, Hand Rolled, Made In Japan	125.00
Silk, 1886, Minneapolis, Exposition Building, Red, White, Blue & Gold, 2 x 5 3/4 In.	17.00
Spoon, Admiral Dewey, Ear Of Corn, Kansas Corn Crop, 1899	50.00
Spoon, Civil War Soldier Handle, Marked, Gusky's, 1894	65.00
Spoon, Civil War Soldier Rifle Handle, 28th National Encampment, Pittsburgh, 1894	65.00
Spoon, Genesee Falls, Rochester	35.00
Spoon, New York State Fair Bowl, Schrafft's Chocolates, Floral Handle, Demitasse	4.00
Spoon, Signal Station Bowl, Manitou, Colorado, Pike's Peak Train Handle	6.00
Spoon, Silver Plate, Skyline Of New York City, Statue Of Liberty On End	45.00
Spoon, Sterling Silver, Brooklyn Bridge	55.00
Spoon, Sterling Silver, Chicago, Library, Water Tower, Ft. Dearborn, 1904	85.00
Spoon, Sterling Silver, Columbian Exposition, Columbus & Crew In Bowl	50.00
Spoon, Sterling Silver, Court House, Oklahoma City	35.00
Spoon, Sterling Silver, DeSota Hotel, Dalhart, Texas	35.00
Spoon, Sterling Silver, Duluth, Minnesota, On Stem, Skyline Scene Tip	23.00
Spoon, Sterling Silver, Figural, Moses Cleveland, Engraved Bowl	50.00
Spoon, Sterling Silver, Figural, New Orleans, Waterfront Skyline	55.00
Spoon, Sterling Silver, Figural, Stuyvesant, Flatiron Building In Bowl	50.00
Spoon, Sterling Silver, Hawaii, Enameled Hula Dancer, Demitasse	38.00
Spoon, Sterling Silver, Indiana Steel Company Mill, Gary, Indiana	40.00
Spoon, Sterling Silver, Jacksonville, Florida, Coconut Palm Tree Tip	23.00
Spoon, Sterling Silver, Last Dollar Mine, Cripple Creek, Colorado	150.00
Spoon, Sterling Silver, Michigan, Arch Rock On Mackinaw Island, State Seal, 5 1/2 In. . .	25.00
Spoon, Sterling Silver, Palm Beach, Down Stem, Palm Trees Cut Out Tip	22.00
Spoon, Sterling Silver, Public Library, Galesburg, Illinois	35.00
Spoon, Sterling Silver, Public Square, Watertown, New York	35.00
Spoon, Sterling Silver, Steer Head, Texas	35.00
Spoon, Sterling Silver, Sunny South, Black Boy, Floppy Hat, Jacksonville In Bowl	85.00
Spoon, Sterling Silver, Trinity Church, Tiffany	55.00
Spoon, Sterling Silver, Union Station, Fort Worth, Texas	40.00
Spoon, Victory Or Death, Texas One & Indivisible, Alamo, 1891	350.00
Tea Tin, Queen Elizabeth & Prince Edward, Opening Of St. Lawrence Seaway, 1959	30.00
Thimble, Washington, Capital & White House, Vermeil, Simon Bros. Co., 1981	115.00
Ticket, Olympic, 1928 Amsterdam IX Summer, U.S. Tryouts, June 16, L.A. Coliseum . . .	65.00
Ticket, Olympic, Bus, For Foreigners, 1964 Tokyo, XVIII Summer, Rt. 18, Opening Day .	105.00
Tray, Hearts, Estes Park, Colo., Cable Car, Big Thompson Cannon, Metal, 5 1/2 In.	30.00
Vase, Olympic, Winter & Summer Sports, Cloisonne, 9 In.	8050.00
Winner's Diploma, Olympic, 1932 Lake Placid, III Winter Games	865.00

SPANISH LACE is a type of Victorian glass that has a white lace design. Blue, yellow, cranberry, or clear glass was made with this distinctive white pattern. It was made in England and the United States after 1885. Copies are being made.

Bottle, Barber, Corset Shape	635.00
Butter, Cover, Blue	275.00
Celery Vase, Vaseline	135.00
Lamp, Miniature	2200.00
Pitcher, Cranberry	1800.00
Sugar Shaker	295.00

SPATTERWARE is the creamware or soft paste dinnerware decorated with colored spatter designs. The earliest pieces were made in the late eighteenth century, but most of the spatterware found today was made from about 1800 to 1850, or it is a form of kitchen crockery with added spatter designs, made in the late nineteenth and twentieth centuries. The early spatterware was made in the Staffordshire district of England for sale in America. The later kitchen type is an American product.

Bank, Pig, Blue Green, Tan, Cream Ground, 3 3/4 In.	330.00
Bank, Pig, Teal Green & Tan, Cream Ground, 6 In.	275.00
Creamer, 2 Eight-Sided Stars, Purple Border, 4 In.	605.00
Creamer, Black & Yellow Rainbow Allover, 4 In.	2310.00
Creamer, Blue & Purple Rainbow Allover, 4 3/4 In.	795.00

Creamer, Castle, Blue Border, Both Sides, 4 1/2 In. 1100.00
Creamer, Peafowl On Branch, Blue, Tan & Black, Green Border, 4 1/4 In. 1650.00
Creamer, Peafowl, Red Border, Paneled, 5 1/2 In. 1375.00
Creamer, Peafowl, Red, Yellow & Green, Blue Border, 3 5/8 In. 320.00
Cup & Saucer, Blue & Green Scalloped Border, Handleless 2640.00
Cup & Saucer, Blue, Purple & Green, Rainbow, Handleless 1705.00
Cup & Saucer, Buds, Red & Green, Rainbow Border, Handleless 3410.00
Cup & Saucer, Child's, Peafowl, Blue, Yellow & Red, Green Border 710.00
Cup & Saucer, Child's, Peafowl, Red, Yellow & Green, Blue Border 300.00
Cup & Saucer, Crisscross, Green & Blue, Red Bands, Handleless 3080.00
Cup & Saucer, Dahlia, Red Border, Handleless 715.00
Cup & Saucer, Dot Center, Red, Purple Border, Handleless 935.00
Cup & Saucer, Flower, Blue, Red Border, Handeless 467.00
Cup & Saucer, Fort, Blue Border, Handleless 185.00
Cup & Saucer, Lavender Border, Rose Design On Saucer 192.00
Cup & Saucer, Peafowl, Blue Border 605.00
Cup & Saucer, Peafowl, Blue, Yellow & Green, Red Border, Handleless 355.00
Cup & Saucer, Peafowl, Red Border 192.00
Cup & Saucer, Red & Green Allover, Handless 90.00
Cup & Saucer, Rose, Red Border, Handleless 330.00
Cup & Saucer, Schoolhouse, Brown & Green Trees, Red Border, Handleless 4400.00
Cup & Saucer, Schoolhouse, Red Border 4400.00
Cup & Saucer, Sprig, Green Border, Handleless 575.00
Cup & Saucer, Yellow Scalloped Border, Handleless 1650.00
Cup Plate, Peafowl, Blue, Red & Green, Blue & Green Border, 4 In. 990.00
Pitcher, Black & Purple Rainbow Allover, Paneled, 6 1/2 In. 3465.00
Pitcher, Blue Design, Bulbous, 10 In. 1390.00
Pitcher, Bowl, Red & Blue, Running Leaf Band, 9 In. 410.00
Pitcher, Castle, Blue Border, Paneled, 7 3/4 In. 1210.00
Pitcher, Olive Green & White Allover, Blue Rim Band, 6 1/2 In. 275.00
Pitcher, Pinwheel, Blue Sunburst Border, Both Sides, 10 1/4 In. 990.00
Pitcher, Pinwheel, Blue, Both Sides, Sunburst Border, 8 1/4 In. ....*Illus* 990.00
Pitcher, Red, Green, Yellow, Black & Blue Rainbow, Scrolled Handle, 11 1/4 In. 12100.00
Pitcher & Bowl, 4-Part Flower, Red, Blue Border, 10 3/4 x 12 5/8 In. 1375.00
Plate, Acorn, Double Yellow, Purple Border, Paneled, 5 In. 3190.00
Plate, Acorn, Triple Brown, Purple Border, Paneled, 9 1/4 In. 1320.00
Plate, Acorn, Triple Yellow, Blue Border, Paneled, 9 1/4 In. 3080.00
Plate, Blue Flying Eagle, Paneled, Impressed T. Walker, 8 1/2 In. 355.00
Plate, Bull's-Eye, Blue & Purple, Rainbow Border, 5 In. 190.00
Plate, Castle, Blue Border, Paneled, 9 3/4 In. ....*Illus* 1100.00
Plate, Dahlia, Red Border, Paneled, 9 1/4 In. ....*Illus* 1320.00
Plate, Flower, Yellow Border, 6 1/2 In. 3530.00
Plate, Flowers, Orange & Blue, Green Leaves, Blue & Green Rainbow Border, 8 In. 685.00
Plate, Morning Glory, Blue, Yellow, Black & Green Border, 9 3/4 In. 4070.00
Plate, Morning Glory, Yellow Border 400.00

Spatterware,
Pitcher, Pinwheel,
Blue, Both Sides,
Sunburst Border,
8 1/4 In.

Spatterware,
Plate, Castle, Blue
Border, Paneled,
9 3/4 In.

Coffee or tea stains can be removed from a cup by scrubbing with salt on a sponge.

Spatterware, Plate,
Dahlia, Red Border,
Paneled, 9 1/4 In.

Plate, Peafowl On Branch, Blue, Green & Red, Red Border, 8 5/8 In.	880.00
Plate, Peafowl, Blue, Adams, 8 7/8 In.	300.00
Plate, Peafowl, Blue, Yellow & Red, Blue Allover, 8 3/8 In.	795.00
Plate, Peafowl, Purple Border, 8 1/4 In.	484.00
Plate, Peafowl, Red Border, 7 3/4 In.	453.00
Plate, Primrose, Blue Border, 5 In.	440.00
Plate, Red Rose, Green Border, 8 1/8 In.	110.00
Plate, Rose, Blue Border, 9 1/4 In.	300.00
Plate, Schoolhouse, Red With Yellow Roof, Blue Border, Paneled, 8 1/2 In.	4070.00
Plate, Star, Red Sunburst Border, 8 1/2 In.	2310.00
Plate, Tulip, Purple Border, 10 1/2 In.	1705.00
Plate, Tulip, Yellow & Purple, Green Stem & Leaves, Red Border, 8 1/4 In.	2035.00
Platter, Red & Green Allover, Rectangular	2900.00
Platter, Red, Blue & Green Center, Yellow Border, 16 In.	410.00
Platter, Tulip, Blue & Red, Green & Red Rainbow Border, 14 1/2 x 18 In.	16500.00
Spoon Rest, Daffodil, Blue, Red & Green, Blue Border, 8 3/4 x 4 1/2 In.	1260.00
Sugar, Cover, Peafowl, Blue, Red Border, 6 In.	550.00
Sugar, Cover, Red & Blue Rainbow Allover, 5 1/8 In.	120.00
Sugar, Cover, Red & Green Rainbow Allover, 4 1/4 In.	220.00
Sugar, Green Allover, 5 1/4 In.	100.00
Sugar, Light Blue Allover, 5 1/2 In.	100.00
Tea Bowl, Acorn, Double Yellow, Blue Border, 5 x 3 In.	2200.00
Teapot, Adam's Rose, Blue Border	75.00
Tray, Maroon, 11 1/4 In.	190.00
Washbowl, Red, Green, Yellow, Blue & Black Rainbow, 13 1/2 In.	11550.00

SPELTER is a synonym for a zinc alloy. Figurines, candlesticks, and other pieces were made of spelter and given a bronze or painted finish. The metal has been used since about the 1860s to make statues, tablewares, and lamps that resemble bronze. Spelter is soft and breaks easily. To test for spelter, scratch the base of the piece. Bronze is solid; spelter will show a silvery scratch.

Bust, Atlas & Carmela, Art Nouveau, Pair	175.00
Clock, Figural, Lion At Top, Enameled Dial, Brass Hands, Arabic Numerals, 16 In.	430.00
Clock, Mantel, Black Slate, Female Figure In Renaissance Style, 1880, 22 3/4 In.	181.00
Figurine, Abraham Lincoln, Standing, Wearing Long Robe, Silver Patina, 20 In.	575.00
Figurine, Actress, Hardwood Base, Double Patinated, c.1880, 7 3/4 In.	60.00
Figurine, Army & Navy Soldier, In Uniform, Standing At The Ready, 13 In., Pair	920.00
Figurine, Can't You Talk, Figure Of Small Girl With Dog, c.1900, 8 In.	495.00
Figurine, Cavalier On Circular Wooden Base, Holding Poleax, 40 In., Pair	690.00
Figurine, Don Juan & Don Caesar, Stepped Base, Pair	220.00
Figurine, Fireman, Standing, Henry Weisse, Germany, 1900, 25 In.	375.00
Figurine, Gardeuse De Moutons, 20 In.	1650.00
Figurine, Horse & Man, 16 In.	495.00
Figurine, Irish Setter In Stride, Dark Brown, Green Patina, France, 31 x 14 In.	690.00
Figurine, Music & Dance On Cloudlike Surface, Socle Base, 1910, 26 In.	303.00
Figurine, Musical Nymphs, Mounted On Marble Base, Belle Epoque, 17 In., Pair	272.00
Figurine, Nude Salon Figure, Belle Epoque, 1920, 45 x 11 x 12 1/2 In.	1089.00

Figurine, Rembrandt Van Rijn, Peter Paul Rubens, Gilt, 1880, 18 1/2 In., Pair 333.00
Figurine, Romanesque Soldier In Full Attire, Posing On Pedestal, Gilt, 16 1/2 In. 390.00
Figurine, Warriors, Holding Sword & Shield, Dark Brown Patina, 19 x 20 In., Pair 660.00
Lamp, 4 Tulip Shades, Fairy On Base 900.00
Lamp, Caramel Slag Shade, 14 In. 385.00
Lamp, Hall, Art Nouveau, 3 Parrot Tulip Beaded Shades, c.1900, 22 1/2 In. 575.00
Lamp, Medieval Warriors Holding Flambeaux Aloft, 1890, 43 x 11 x 14 In., Pair 1573.00
Pitcher, Overshot, Square, 9 In. 239.00
Urn, Empire Style, Dolphin Form Handles, Lion Mask Collar, 13 1/2 In., Pair 247.00
Vase, Posy, Neoclassical, Reticulated, Oval, Holland, 1910, 7 x 10 3/4 x 6 In., Pair 212.00
Vase, Swallows Design, Marble, Belle Epoque, 1900, 17 x 7 In., Pair 272.00

SPINNING WHEELS in the corner have been symbols of earlier times for the past 100 years. Although spinning wheels date back to medieval days, the ones found today are rarely more than 200 years old. Because the style of the spinning wheel changed very little, it is often impossible to place an exact date on a wheel.

Bobbin & Distaff, Foot Pedal, 37 In. 137.00
Flax, Hardwood, Stamped Sr. Al., 1784-1848, 33 1/2 In. 330.00
Flax, Samuel Ring, Community Of Alfred, Maine 1250.00
Oak, Hardwood, Double Wheel, 2 Pedals, 39 In. 190.00
Oak, Hardwood, Turned Detail, 34 In. 105.00
Walnut & Oak, Carved Detail, Dark Brown Patina, Distaff & Bobbin, 36 In. 220.00

SPODE pottery, porcelain, and bone china were made by the Stoke-on-Trent factory of England founded by Josiah Spode about 1770. The firm became Copeland and Garrett from 1833 to 1847, then W.T. Copeland or W.T. Copeland and Sons until 1976. It then became Royal Worcester Spode Ltd. The word *Spode* appears on many pieces made by the factories. Most collectors include all the wares under the more familiar name of Spode. Porcelains are listed in this book by the name that appears on the piece. Related pieces are listed under Copeland and Copeland Spode.

Stone-China

Bowl, Botanical Scene, Dolphin, Foliate Border, Oval, 1875, 10 In., Pair 430.00
Bowl, Imari Style, Cut Corners, Square, c.1825, 9 3/4 In. 750.00
Box, Rose, Cover, Overlapping Pink Petals, Green 5-Leaf Base, Circular, 1820, 3 In. 920.00
Dish, Botanical, 3 Specimens, Small Flower Sprigs, Gilt Rim, 1820, 11 In. 3105.00
Pitcher, Assyrian, Cream Figures, c.1784, 10 In. 795.00
Plate, Flowers, Foliage, Blue Underglaze Rim, 1805, 8 5/8 In. 207.00
Plate, Production Hall, Cobalt, 10 In. 125.00
Plate, Service, Center Rosette, Gilt & Floral Edge, Foliate Swags, Signed, 9 3/4 In. 1150.00
Punch Bowl, Japan Pattern, Overglaze Gilding, 1815, 5 x 11 1/4 In. 1250.00
Sugar & Creamer, Tower, Blue 50.00
Teapot, Tower, Blue 75.00
Teapot, Underplate, Red Ribbon, Gilt, c.1810 .... 550.00
Tureen, Underplate, Oriental, Flowers & Birds, Lion's Head Handles, 14 1/2 In. 660.00
Urn, Florentine, Gray, Blue, Gold, Satyr's Head Handles, 9 In. 60.00

SPONGEWARE is very similar to spatterware in appearance. The designs were applied to the ceramics by daubing the color on with a sponge or cloth. Many collectors do not differentiate between spongeware and spatterware and use the names interchangeably. Modern pottery is being made to resemble the old spongeware, but careful examination will show it is new.

Bank, Pig 195.00
Bank, Shoe, Blue & White, 5 In. 22.00
Bean Pot, Blue & White, No Lid, 3 Qt., 6 1/2 In. 165.00
Bowl, Blue & White, 3 1/2 x 11 In. 95.00
Bowl, Blue & White, Bail Handle, 4 3/4 x 10 1/4 In. 190.00
Bowl, Blue & White, Fluted, 4 x 10 1/2 In. 245.00
Bowl, Blue & White, Stripes, 12 1/2 x 9 In. 275.00
Bowl, Blue, Wire Bale Handle, 4 x 9 In. 132.00
Bowl, Cover, Blue & White, 10 1/2 In. 140.00

Bowl, Cover, Blue, Geometric, Ohio Pottery, 2 1/4 x 3 1/4 In. 1070.00
Bowl, Rust, Blue, Tan Panels, 7 In. 75.00
Butter, Cover, Green & White, 5 1/2 In. 50.00
Cheese Dish, Slanted Cover, c.1860 .... 185.00
Cooler, Water, Cobalt Blue & White, Metal Spout, c.1900, 6 Gal., 13 1/4 In. 300.00
Creamer, Blue & White, 3 3/4 In. 220.00
Creamer, Blue & White, 4 1/4 In. 110.00
Crock, Butter, Blue & White, Wire Bail, Wooden Handle, 8 3/4 x 6 1/4 In. 275.00
Crock, Butter, Blue, White, 9 x 6 In. 300.00
Crock, Cobalt Blue & White, 2 Handles, Lid, c.1900, 5 Gal., 13 1/4 In. 130.00
Crock, Cover, Blue & White, Wire Bail Handle, 5 5/8 x 4 In. 245.00
Cup, Blue & White, Molded Scroll & Handle, 3 1/2 In. 55.00
Cup & Saucer, Blue & White, 3 In. ....75.00 to 125.00
Dish, Blue & White, Oval, 9 x 1 1/2 In. 315.00
Figurine, Dog, Dark Blue & White, 6 5/8 In. 165.00
Jar, Cover, Spaulding's Pure Fresh Cookies, Brown, Blue, Green & White, 9 1/4 In. 220.00
Jardiniere, Blue & White, Brown & Gold Trim, 6 1/2 In. 60.00
Jardiniere, Blue, White, Molded Foliage Scrolls, Gilt, 10 1/2 x 8 3/4 In. 190.00
Jug, Blue & White, 6 3/4 In. 82.00
Jug, Blue, F.H. Weeks, Akron, Oh., 5 1/2 In. 275.00
Jug, Grandmother's Maple Syrup, 1948, Small 650.00
Mixing Bowl, Blue & Green, Luster Highlights, Molded Scroll Border, 12 In. 93.00
Mixing Bowl, Blue & White, 9 1/2 In. 110.00
Mixing Bowl, Blue & White, 10 In. 220.00
Mixing Bowl, Blue & White, Stripes, 10 1/4 In. 275.00
Mixing Bowl, Blue & White, Stripes, 11 1/4 In. 275.00
Mixing Bowl, Blue, 6 3/4 In. 154.00
Mixing Bowl, Blue, Molded Border, 13 In. 190.00
Mug, Blue & White, Molded Handle, 3 5/8 In. 135.00
Mug, Light Blue & White, 5 1/4 In. 165.00
Pitcher, Blue & Brown, Cream Ground, 10 7/8 In. 105.00
Pitcher, Blue & White, 7 1/2 In. 195.00
Pitcher, Blue & White, 8 In. 465.00
Pitcher, Blue & White, Blue Stripes, 6 3/4 In. 605.00
Pitcher, Blue & White, Floral, Panel, 8 1/2 In. 135.00
Pitcher, Blue & White, Molded Swirled Ribs, 5 3/4 In. 55.00
Pitcher, Blue, Bands, No Spout, 7 1/4 In. 685.00
Pitcher, Blue, Embossed Rose, 9 In. 275.00
Pitcher, Green & Brown, R.V. Wright Oil & Gas, Raised Lettering, 4 1/2 In. 200.00
Pitcher, Milk, Blue & White, Gilt, 5 1/8 In. 245.00
Pitcher, Molded Floral Design, 9 1/2 In. 115.00
Pitcher, Olive Green & White, Blue Rim Band, 6 1/2 In. 275.00
Pitcher, Red & Blue, 10 3/4 In. 385.00
Pitcher, Tan & Blue, Raised Bands, 9 In. 145.00
Pitcher, Water, Blue & White, Paneled, 10 5/8 In. 220.00
Pitcher & Bowl, Blue & White, 12 1/2 In. 260.00
Plate, Blue & White, 8 1/4 In. 150.00
Plate, Blue & White, Scalloped, 9 1/4 In. ....70.00 to 220.00
Plate, Green, Red & White, 8 1/4 In. 25.00
Platter, Blue & White, 13 1/2 In. 355.00
Soap Dish, Blue & White, Red Trim, 4 x 6 1/2 In. 70.00
Soap Dish, Red & Blue, 3 1/2 x 4 5/8 In. 50.00
Teapot, Blue & Green, 6 1/2 In. 330.00
Teapot, Blue & White, Molded Ribs, 8 1/2 In. 320.00
Teapot, Blue & White, Paneled, 9 1/2 In. 340.00
Umbrella Stand, Blue & Brown, Tan Salt Glaze, 20 1/2 In. 330.00
Umbrella Stand, Blue & Red, Tan Salt Glaze, Red Wing, 17 1/2 In. 1320.00

SPORTS equipment, sporting goods, brochures, and related items are
listed here. Items are listed by sport. Other categories of interest are
Bicycle, Card, Fishing, Sword, Toy, and Trap.

    Archery, Arrow, Cedar, Colored Feathers, Ben Pearson, Box, 28 In., 9 Piece 35.00
    Auto Racing, Ashtray, Indianapolis 500, Lists Previous Winners, White, 1964, 7 x 7 In. .. 20.00

Auto Racing, Glass, Indianapolis Speedway, Tony Hulman Signature, 1964, 4 1/2 In. 14.00
Auto Racing, Goblet, Indianapolis 500, Mayor's Breakfast, 1970, 4 In. 15.00
Auto Racing, Lapel Pin, Race Car, NASCAR, 1957 .... 140.00
Auto Racing, Photograph, 1951 Supercharged Alfa Romeo, Valentine & Sons, England .. 50.00
Baseball, Ashtray, Cleveland Indians, Chief Wahoo, 1950s 85.00
Baseball, Ball, Autographed, Babe Ruth & Lou Gehrig 2090.00
Baseball, Ball, Autographed, Harrisburg Colored Giants, 1908 .... 3740.00
Baseball, Ball, Autographed, Joe Namath 30.00
Baseball, Ball, Autographed, Ken Griffey Jr., In Plastic Cube 75.00
Baseball, Ball, Autographed, Lou Gehrig, Signed, April 1, 1938 .... 3000.00
Baseball, Ball, Autographed, Mickey Mantle & Whitey Ford 285.00
Baseball, Ball, Autographed, Pete Rose, 3,000th Hit, 1978 .... 500.00
Baseball, Ball, Autographed, Pete Rose, Plastic Cube 45.00
Baseball, Ball, Autographed, Roger Maris, 1983 .... 450.00
Baseball, Ball, Autographed, Texas Rangers, In Plastic Cube, 1979 .... 50.00
Baseball, Ball, Mickey Mantle Autograph, Blue Ink, Sweet Spot 75.00
Baseball, Bank, Chief Wahoo, Gold Tooth 375.00
Baseball, Bank, National League Bats Stacked Around, Plastic, 1960s 95.00
Baseball, Bat, Autographed, Albert Belle 115.00
Baseball, Bat, Autographed, Joe DiMaggio, 1946 .... 2000.00
Baseball, Bat, Autographed, Ken Caminiti 100.00
Baseball, Bat, Autographed, Nolan Ryan 125.00
Baseball, Bat, Autographed, Ted Williams 600.00
Baseball, Bat, Fungo, Nellie Fox, Name Burned Into Barrel, Coaching, 1960s, 32 In. 575.00
Baseball, Bat, Hank Aaron Model 115.00
Baseball, Bat, Jimmie Fox Model, Hillerich & Bradsby, Printed Signature, 34 In. 70.00
Baseball, Bat, Lou Gehrig Model, Hillerich & Bradsby, Printed Signature, 34 In. 185.00
Baseball, Bat, Pete Rose, 1984 All Star Game, San Francisco 500.00
Baseball, Book, New York Yankees Sketch Book, Large Format, Soft Bound, 1950 ...... 50.00
Baseball, Book, Record, Jack Brickhouse, 1952 .... 25.00
Baseball, Button, Kansas City Royals, 2nd World Series, Gilt, Enamel, Case, 1985, 1 In. . 40.00
Baseball, Button, Roger Maris, 61st Home Run, Oversize 1175.00
Baseball, Cap, Mickey Mantle 250.00
Baseball, Cap, Ted Williams 200.00
Baseball, Comic Book, Larry Doby, Fawcett Publications, 1950 .... 125.00
Baseball, Doll, Babe Ruth, Cloth, Yankee Stadium & History On Box 75.00
Baseball, Exercise Kit, Mickey Mantle's Isometric Minute-A-Day Gym, 1960s, 14 In. ... 30.00
Baseball, Figure, Babe Ruth, Holding Bat, Pointing, Yankees, Hartland, 7 1/2 In. 165.00
Baseball, Figure, Don Drysdale, Pitcher, Dodgers, Hartland, 7 In. 165.00
Baseball, Figure, Hank Aaron At Bat, Atlanta Braves, Hartland, 7 In. 165.00
Baseball, Figure, Mickey Mantle, At Bat, Yankees, Hartland, 6 3/4 In. 195.00
Baseball, Figure, Yogi Berra, Catching, Removable Mask, Hartland, 6 1/2 In. 110.00
Baseball, Flip Book, Babe Ruth Hitting A Homer 100.00
Baseball, Game, Card, Dempsey's National-American, Box, 1910 .... 1355.00
Baseball, Game, Gaffney's Parlor Game Of Base Ball, 1885 .... 2420.00
Baseball, Game, Zimmer's Base Ball, McLoughlin Bros., 1893-1895 .... 25300.00
Baseball, Glass, Cubs, Wrigley Field, 1969 .... 20.00
Baseball, Glove, Billy Pierce Model, Higgins 20.00
Baseball, Glove, Bob Grim Model, Higgins 15.00
Baseball, Glove, Bobby Richardson Model, Macgregor 10.00
Baseball, Glove, Bubbles Hargrave, Faintly Autographed, 1930 .... 100.00
Baseball, Glove, Chuck Hiller Model, Sears 35.00
Baseball, Glove, Frank Robinson Model 40.00
Baseball, Glove, Harry Walker Model, Higgins 45.00
Baseball, Glove, Jim Davenport Model, Wilson 20.00
Baseball, Glove, Joe DiMaggio Model, Spalding 225.00
Baseball, Glove, Ken Williams Model, Marathon 75.00
Baseball, Glove, Leather, Dark Gray, Goldsmith, 1920s 105.00
Baseball, Glove, Roger Maris Model, Spalding 65.00
Baseball, Glove, Warren Spahn Model, Rawlings 40.00
Baseball, Jersey, Boston Red Sox, 1902 .... 7000.00
Baseball, Jersey, Boston Red Sox, 1908 .... 6000.00

Baseball, Jersey, Boston Red Sox, Road, 1930 .... 3500.00
Baseball, Jersey, Chicago White Sox, Home, 1917 .... 6000.00
Baseball, Jersey, Chicago White Sox, Home, 1928 .... 4000.00
Baseball, Jersey, Chicago White Sox, Road, 1907 .... 6000.00
Baseball, Jersey, Cleveland Indians, Home, 1928 .... 4000.00
Baseball, Jersey, Cleveland Indians, Road, 1903 .... 6000.00
Baseball, Jersey, Ted Williams, 500 Home Run Club 800.00
Baseball, Key Chain, Mickey Mantle, Pictures 1960 Topps Card 9.00
Baseball, Lapel Pin, Tris Speaker, Gold, All American Team, 1915 .... 1065.00
Baseball, Match Safe, Princeton Baseball, 1891 .... 699.00
Baseball, Matchbook Cover, Detroit Sports Park, Sports Figures, Stadium Design, 1939 .. 5.00
Baseball, Mirror, Philadelphia A's, Frank Baker, Celluloid, Round, 1911 .... 3850.00
Baseball, Nodder, Babe Ruth, Hang Tag, Facsimile Signature 75.00
Baseball, Nodder, Cincinnati Red, Baseball Head, Pottery, 7 3/4 In. 40.00
Baseball, Nodder, Cincinnati Red, Green Base, Papier-Mache, 1960s 298.00
Baseball, Nodder, Detroit Tiger, Box, 1960s 298.00
Baseball, Nodder, Houston Astro, Miniature 225.00
Baseball, Nodder, Kansas City Royal, Mascot, Pottery, Green Base, Decals, 8 In. 30.00
Baseball, Nodder, Lou Gehrig, Hang Tag, Facsimile Signature 65.00
Baseball, Nodder, Pittsburgh Pirates, Baseball Uniform, Pottery, 7 3/4 In. 50.00
Baseball, Nodder, Player, Detroit Lions, Box, 1960s 298.00
Baseball, Nodder, St. Louis Cardinal, Mascot, Pottery, Green Base, Decals, 8 In. 45.00
Baseball, Pencil, Mechanical, Louisville Slugger Souvenir, Gold Lettering, 1939 .... 25.00
Baseball, Pennant, Atlanta Braves, Screaming Brave, Stadium Graphic, 1966 .... 25.00
Baseball, Pennant, Boston Red Sox, Logo 12.00
Baseball, Pennant, Cleveland Indians World Series, 1948 .... 150.00
Baseball, Pennant, Cleveland Indians, Chief Wahoo Logo, Red, White & Blue 25.00
Baseball, Pennant, Cleveland Indians, Pre-1948 .... 85.00
Baseball, Pennant, Detroit Tigers, Logo Left Corner, Cap With Stars In Center, Felt 20.00
Baseball, Pennant, New York Yankees, 1950, Small 38.00
Baseball, Pennant, New York Yankees, American League Champs, Stadium, 1940s 485.00
Baseball, Pennant, New York Yankees, Blue & White, Mantle & Berra, 1950s 195.00
Baseball, Pennant, New York Yankees, Felt, 1940s 125.00
Baseball, Pennant, Pittsburgh Pirates, National League Champs, 1960 .... 95.00
Baseball, Photograph, Cincinnati Red Stockings, Carte De Visite, 1896 .... 550.00
Baseball, Photograph, Don Drysdale, Autographed, 8 x 10 In. 35.00
Baseball, Photograph, Ernie Banks, Autographed, 8 x 10 In. 22.00
Baseball, Photograph, George Brett, Autographed, 8 x 10 In. 25.00
Baseball, Photograph, Hank Aaron, Autographed, 8 x 10 In. 25.00
Baseball, Photograph, Homestead Grays, Front Of Bus, Mar. 23, 1946, 8 1/4 x 10 In. 395.00
Baseball, Photograph, Joe DiMaggio, Kneeling, With Bat, Autographed, Color, 8 x 10 In. . 70.00
Baseball, Photograph, John Montgomery Ward, Cabinet Card 1265.00
Baseball, Photograph, Mickey Mantle, Autographed, 8 x 10 In. 80.00
Baseball, Photograph, Wes Parker, Autographed, 8 x 10 In. 20.00
Baseball, Photograph, Willie Mays, Black & White, Autographed, 8 x 10 In. 40.00
Baseball, Postcard, Boston Red Sox, Photograph, Names Underneath, 1959 .... 280.00
Baseball, Postcard, N.Y. Giants, Wilson, McGraw, Murray, Mathewson Montage, 1912 ... 550.00
Baseball, Poster, Minnesota Twins, 25th Anniversary, 1986, 17 x 22 In. 25.00
Baseball, Program, Autographed, Lou Gehrig, Signed On 1st Page, Black Ink, 1935 ..... 1000.00
Baseball, Program, Old Timers Game, Cleveland, August 9, 1975 .... 8.00
Baseball, Program, Ticket, Pete Rose, 3,000th Hit, Seaver On Cover, 1978 .... 200.00
Baseball, Program, World Series, 1939, N.Y. Yankees vs. Cincinnati Reds 150.00
Baseball, Program, World Series, 1941, N.Y. Yankees vs. Brooklyn Dodgers 90.00
Baseball, Program, World Series, 1945, Detroit Tigers vs. Chicago Cubs 250.00
Baseball, Program, World Series, 1949, N.Y. Yankees vs. Brooklyn Dodgers .... .80.00 to 85.00
Baseball, Program, World Series, 1950, N.Y. Yankees vs. Philadelphia Phillies, 50 Pages . 85.00
Baseball, Program, World Series, 1951, N.Y. Giants vs. Yankees 180.00
Baseball, Program, World Series, 1951, N.Y. Yankees vs. N.Y. Giants, 50 Pages 85.00
Baseball, Program, World Series, 1958, N.Y. Yankees vs. Milwaukee Braves 90.00
Baseball, Program, World Series, Pittsburgh Pirates, 1960 .... 125.00
Baseball, Record, Stan The Man's Hit Record, Phillips 66 Promo, 1963, 33 1/3 RPM 20.00
Baseball, Record, Whitey Ford Interview, 33 1/3 RPM 25.00

Baseball, Ring, World Series, 1981, L.A. Dodgers, 10K Gold, Logo Between Garvey 2080.00
Baseball, Salt & Pepper, Umpire & Batter, Bisque 95.00
Baseball, Scorecard, Girl's Pro Team, Muskegon, Girl On Front, 1940s 98.00
Baseball, Ticket Stub, Tour Of Japan, 1917 .... 1265.00
Baseball, Toothpick Holder 1650.00
Baseball, Tray, Nellie Fox, Silver Plate, CBS Chicago Award, MVP, 1957 .... 480.00
Baseball, Uniform, Giants, Willie Mays, Road, Game-Worn 7700.00
Baseball, Uniform, Gray Wool Flannel, Blue Stripes, A On Chest, Medium Size 30.00
Baseball, Uniform, Mickey Mantle, Signed 7 .... 775.00
Baseball, Wristwatch, Bulova, Stephen Andreski, Brooklyn Dodgers, Ebbets Field, 1947 . 500.00
Baseball, Yearbook, Los Angeles Dodgers, 1958, 60 Pages 30.00
Baseball, Yearbook, Los Angeles Dodgers, 1980 .... 10.00
Basketball, Ball, Autographed, Julius Erving, Signed In Gold 170.00
Basketball, Ball, Autographed, Kareem Abdul-Jabbar, Leather 160.00
Basketball, Button, Minnesota Timberwolves, Opening Night, November 8, 1989, 3 In. .. 5.00
Basketball, Doll, Dennis Rodman, Vinyl, Extra Wig & Outfit, 12 In. 38.50
Basketball, Figure, New York Knicks, Black Dribbler, Japan, 1959 .... 35.00
Basketball, Jersey, Chicago Bulls, Michael Jordan, Game-Worn 1900.00
Basketball, Jersey, Golden State Warriors, Joe Smith, Game-Worn 195.00
Basketball, Postcard, Photograph, Ripon College, Team, Wisconsin, 1909 .... 50.00
Basketball, Shoes, Magic Johnson, Converse All-Star High-Tops, Signed, Size 14 1/2 ... 1290.00
Basketball, Sports Illustrated, Michael Jordan, Cover, Nov. 28, 1983 .... 65.00
Billiards, Cabinet, Cue Rack, Victorian 4950.00
Boxing, Bag, J.C. Higgins, Leather, Wooden, Metal, With Frame 125.00
Boxing, Clock, Joe Louis World Champ, Copper, Electric, United, 12 In. ....295.00 to 600.00
Boxing, Figure, Sugar Ray Leonard, Coors Beer, Life Size 85.00
Boxing, Gloves, Autographed, Cassius Clay, 1 Signed 450.00
Boxing, Gloves, Autographed, Mike Tyson, Both Gloves Signed 200.00
Boxing, Gloves, Benlee, Box, 2 Pairs 125.00
Boxing, Gloves, Jack Dempsey, Training, Leather, Signed Inside 1290.00
Boxing, Gloves, Muhammad Ali, Everlast, Leather 225.00
Boxing, Gloves, Primo Carnera, Training, Early 1930s 265.00
Boxing, Gloves, Sporting Marathon, 1940s 25.00
Boxing, Medal, Official, Daily News AA Golden Gloves, Metal, Ribbon, 1930, 1 1/2 In. .. 20.00
Boxing, Photograph, Autographed, Ingemar Johansson & Floyd Patterson, 8 x 10 In. 35.00
Boxing, Photograph, Autographed, Muhammad Ali & Chuck Wepner, 8 x 10 In. 45.00
Boxing, Photograph, Autographed, Muhammad Ali & Joe Frazier 225.00
Boxing, Photograph, Jack Dempsey, Heavyweight Champion, Inscription, 1926 .... 200.00
Boxing, Postcard, Jim Flynn-Jack Johnson Fight, Houses Near Las Vegas, Nev., 1912 ... 350.00
Boxing, Poster, Randy Turpin vs. Sugar Ray Robinson, Red, Black, 1952, 28 x 41 In. 250.00
Boxing, Program, Cassius Clay vs. Henry Cooper, Wembley Stadium, England, 6-18-63 .. 300.00
Boxing, Program, Muhammad Ali vs. Henry Cooper, London, 5-21-66 .... 300.00
Football, Ball, Autographed, Green Bay Packers, World Champions, Team, 1961 .... 500.00
Football, Bank, Mechanical, Football Player 525.00
Football, Button, Minnesota Vikings, NFC Champs, Player Roster, 1974, 6 In. 50.00
Football, Chair, Folding, Cleveland Browns, Metal, Helmet On Seat Cushion 535.00
Football, Helmet, A.J. Reach Co., Oversized Ears, Logo, 1920s 200.00
Football, Helmet, Hutch H-28, Leather 75.00
Football, Helmet, Wayne Millner, Padded Leather, Ear Flaps, Chin Strap, 1930s 1495.00
Football, Nodder, Green Bay Packer, Papier-Mache, Box, 1968 .... 250.00
Football, Pants, Canvas, Tan, Padded Hips, Hard Knee Protector Inserts, 1920s-1930s ... 20.00
Football, Photograph, Dan Marino, Autographed, 8 x 10 In. 170.00
Football, Photograph, Joe Montana, Autographed, 8 x 10 In. 165.00
Football, Photograph, Phil Simms & Lawrence Taylor, Autographed, 8 x 10 In. 30.00
Football, Photograph, Troy Aikman, Autographed, 8 x 10 In. 160.00
Football, Print, Cleveland Browns, Shell Oil, 1981, 11 x 13 3/4 In., Set Of 6 .... 25.00
Football, Program, Army-Navy, Howard Chandler Christy Cover, 1938 .... 125.00
Football, Program, Columbia vs. Yale, 1946, 60 Pages 34.00
Football, Program, Iowa vs. Notre Dame, 1946 .... 75.00
Football, Program, New York Giants vs. Cleveland Browns, Dec. 21, 1958 .... 20.00
Football, Program, Notre Dame vs. Illinois, Homecoming, 28 Pages, 8 x 10 1/2 In. 25.00
Football, Program, Rose Bowl, Alabama vs. Southern California 145.00
Football, Program, San Diego Chargers vs. Los Angeles Rams, August 29, 1970 .... 10.00

Football, Program, San Francisco 49ers vs. Chicago Rockets, Mascot On Cover, 9-1-46 .. 175.00
Football, Program, Southern California vs. Notre Dame, 1937 .... 125.00
Football, Ring, Super Bowl, New York Giants, World Champions, Gold, 1991 .... 800.00
Football, Schedule, Alabama, Follow The Pigskin To Birmingham, 1938, 3 1/2 In. 18.00
Football, Uniform, Jim Kelly, Buffalo Bills, White 12s On Both Sides, 1991 .... 400.00
Golf, Ball Marker, Tuname, Box, c.1940 .... 95.00
Golf, Ball, Chemico Triumph, Circular Mesh, c.1918 .... 80.00
Golf, Ball, Dimple, Original Wrapper, With Seal, 1938 .... 60.00
Golf, Ball, Dunlop Nimble, Mesh Pattern, c.1918 .... 195.00
Golf, Ball, Gene Sarazen, By Wilson, Cadwell-Geer Box Cover, c.1948, Unused 75.00
Golf, Ball, George Bush, State Department Seal, Facsimile Autograph 45.00
Golf, Ball, Gerald Ford, State Department Seal, Facsimile Autograph 45.00
Golf, Ball, Plus Colonel 31, Circular Mesh Pattern, By St. Mungo, c.1925 .... 85.00
Golf, Ball, Square Mesh, Spalding Kro-Flite, Crow On Seal 145.00
Golf, Ball, The Why Not Bramble, By Henley, c.1915 .... 250.00
Golf, Ball, Tommy Armour, Mesh, Signed, c.1930 .... 225.00
Golf, Ball, Zippo, RAM, Chemical Geological Laboratories, Yellow, Package, 12 Piece ... 125.00
Golf, Ball, Zippo, SDX, Ness Company Inc., White, Package, 3 Piece 25.00
Golf, Blotter, Brown & Bigelow, Golf Cartoon, 6 x 3 1/2 In. 17.00
Golf, Candy Dish, Raised Knickered Golfer In Center, Unger Bros., c.1900 .... 900.00
Golf, Cigarette Case, Knickered Golfer & Caddy On Cover, Silver Plate, 1935 .... 65.00
Golf, Decanter, Club Shape, George Dickel, Tennessee Sour Mash, 1965, 15 In. 17.00
Golf, Flipbook, Bobby Jones, Drive & Mashie, c.1935, No. 11a 345.00
Golf, Nail File, Golfer Finishing Swing, Flag Pin, Brass, c.1945 .... 45.00
Golf, Postcard, Desert Inn, Las Vegas, 2 Views On Front, 1960s 5.00
Golf, Postcard, Famous 16th Hole At Cypress Point Golf Course, Calif., Unused 3.00
Golf, Postcard, Golf Club, Cape May, N.J., Ocean City, 75th Anniversary, 1954 .... 5.00
Golf, Postcard, Woman Golfer, Photograph, Tinted, England 45.00
Golf, Poster, Harper's, Man Teeing Off Green Field, April 1898, 16 1/8 x 9 1/2 In. 2760.00
Golf, Putter, Spalding Cash-In, 1940 .... 400.00
Golf, Record, Album, Arnold Palmer, Easy Golf With Your Pro, 33 1/3 RPM, 1948 ...... 65.00
Golf, Scorekeeper, Pal, Worn On Wrist 75.00
Golf, Shoes, Ladies, Avon Duflex, By Goodyear, Sold By Abercrombie 125.00
Golf, Tee Holder, Pin To Lapel, Celluloid Tees, Leather 40.00
Golf, Tee, Double, Deep Side For Drivers, Shallow Die For Irons, Brass, c.1900 .... 1000.00
Golf, Watch Fob, Woman Golfer Finishes Her Swing, Caddie, Brass 65.00
Hiking, Backpack, Adirondack, Splint, Leather Hand Strap, Shoulder Straps, 12 1/4 In. 120.00
Hockey, Doll, Wayne Gretzky, Oiler Uniform, Mattel, 1980s, 12 In. 125.00
Hockey, Goalie's Mask, Lefty Wilson, Fiberglass, Leather Straps, 1960s 545.00
Hockey, Nodder, Boston Bruin, 1960s, Box 45.00
Hockey, Nodder, Chicago Blackhawk, 1960s, Box 45.00
Hockey, Nodder, Montreal Canadien, 1960s, Box 45.00
Hockey, Pennant, L.A. Kings, Logo, Purple Border, 1980s, 5 x 10 In. 15.00
Hockey, Photograph, Bobby Hull, Autographed, Black & White, Matted, 11 x 14 In. 20.00
Hockey, Puck, Autographed, Cam Neely 18.00
Hockey, Puck, Autographed, Chris Chelios 21.00
Hockey, Puck, Autographed, Eric Lindros 335.00
Hockey, Puck, Autographed, Steve Yzerman 28.00
Hockey, Puck, Autographed, Wayne Gretzky 40.00
Hockey, Puck, Stanley Cup, New York Rangers, Craig MacTavish, 1994 .... 30.00
Hockey, Sports Illustrated, Wayne Gretzky, Cover, Oct. 12, 1981 .... 35.00
Hockey, Stick, Autographed, Eric Lindros 100.00
Hockey, Stick, Autographed, Gordie Howe 1500.00
Hockey, Stick, Autographed, Paul Coffey 90.00
Hockey, Stick, Autographed, Wayne Gretzky, February 14, 1985 .... 1410.00
Hockey, Stick, Miniature, Autographed, Guy LaFleur, 10 In. 395.00
Horse Racing, Decanter, Kentucky Derby, 95th Running, Beam, 1969 .... 45.00
Horse Racing, Glass, Belmont, 1976 .... 55.00
Horse Racing, Glass, Belmont, 1986 .... 50.00
Horse Racing, Glass, Belmont, 1991 .... 20.00
Horse Racing, Glass, Kentucky Derby, 1945 .... 300.00
Horse Racing, Glass, Kentucky Derby, 1953 .... 45.00
Horse Racing, Glass, Kentucky Derby, 1955 .... 125.00

Horse Racing, Glass, Kentucky Derby, 1957 .... 90.00
Horse Racing, Glass, Kentucky Derby, 1958 .... 120.00
Horse Racing, Glass, Kentucky Derby, 1959 .... 85.00
Horse Racing, Glass, Kentucky Derby, 1961 ....75.00 to 80.00
Horse Racing, Glass, Kentucky Derby, 1963 .... 40.00
Horse Racing, Glass, Kentucky Derby, 1967 .... 40.00
Horse Racing, Glass, Kentucky Derby, 1968 .... 40.00
Horse Racing, Glass, Kentucky Derby, Aluminum, 1940 .... 455.00
Horse Racing, Glass, Preakness, 1974 .... 170.00
Horse Racing, Glass, Preakness, 1975 .... 55.00
Horse Racing, Glass, Preakness, 1978 .... 55.00
Horse Racing, Glass, Preakness, 1983 .... 30.00
Horse Racing, Glass, Preakness, 1991 .... 8.00
Horse Racing, Jockey's Chair, Oak, Attached Scale, Leather Seat, 19th Century 3737.00
Horse Racing, Plate, Kentucky Derby, Sterling Silver, 1964 .... 150.00
Hunting, Button, 1950 Ducks Unlimited, Celluloid, Multicolored 50.00
Hunting, Button, Shoot Peters Shells, Shot Shell Picture 80.00
Hunting, Crow Call, SR & C, Ranger, Walnut Barrel, Painted, Cardboard Tube, 5 1/4 In. . 95.00
Hunting, Horn, Carved From Steer's Horn, Man On Horse, 2 Men Carrying Deer, 14 In. . 130.00
Hunting, License, California, Printed Hunting Dog, Leather Cover, 1924-1925 .... 40.00
Hunting, Turkey Call, Wood, Metal, Leon's, Instruction Booklet, Box, 2 3/4 In. 30.00
Ice Skating, Nodder, Icey, Ice Capades Mascot, 1960s 190.00
Ice Skating, Rink Chair, 2 Opposing Seats, Iron, Oak, Curved Runners, 32 x 50 In. 690.00
Ice Skating, Runner, Brass, Acorn Tip, Leather, Brass Heel Cup, 1790 .... 295.00
Ice Skating, Skates, Metal Runners, Leather Straps, Wood 55.00
Ice Skating, Skates, Metal, Leather Heels, Straps, Winchester 30.00
Ice Skating, Skates, Wood, Iron, 1870, 14 1/2 In. 35.00
Medal, Weight Lifting World Championships, 1947 .... 15.00
Pool, Table, Converts To Breakfast Table, Slate Top, E.F. Riley, England, 64 x 30 In. 1150.00
Pool, Table, St. Bernard Mission, With Ivory Balls, Cues, Rack, 1905-1909 .... 7000.00
Pool, Table, Walnut, Billiards Practice, A.B.T. Manufacturing co., Chicago, 15 x 25 In. 660.00
Skiing, Western, Skier Going Downhill, Unused 3.50
Snooker, Table, 1 1/2-In. Slate, 6 Legs, 5 Ft. x 10 Ft. 5000.00
Soap Box Derby, Badge, Press, 8th Annual, Celluloid, Eagle & Shield, 1941, 3 1/2 In. 40.00
Soap Box Derby, Helmet, Composite Construction, Decal On Front, Adult Size 55.00
Tennis, Measure, Court, Leather & Brass 145.00
Tennis, Poster, Sporting Club De Lyon, Delaroche, Lyon, 1905, 29 1/2 x 19 1/4 In. 1495.00
Tennis, Trophy, Woman, City Of Westmount, Wm. A. Rogers, 1948, 8 3/4 In. 150.00

STAFFORDSHIRE, England, has been a district making pottery and porcelain since the 1700s. Hundreds of kilns are still working in the area. Thousands of types of pottery and porcelain have been made in the many factories that worked and still work in the area. Some of the most famous factories have been listed separately, such as Adams, Davenport, Ridgway, Rowland & Marsellus, Royal Doulton, Royal Worcester, Spode, Wedgwood, and others. Some Staffordshire pieces are listed under categories like Fairing, Flow Blue, Mulberry, Shaving Mug, etc.

Basket, Underplate, Gothic Ruins, Magenta & White, 11 In. ....*Illus* 522.00
Basket, White Lower Section, Flowerhead Upper Section, Reticulated, 6 In. 520.00
Bird Waterer, Multicolored Bird & Leaf Design, 5 1/2 In. 465.00
Bowl, Ben Franklin, Flying His Kite, Red Transfer, 11 x 3 1/4 In. 495.00
Bowl, Capital Scene, Dark Blue Transfer, 11 x 4 3/4 In. 575.00
Bowl, Center, Harbor Scenes, Ships Sailing, Figures Beside Stream, Bombe Shape 975.00
Bowl, City Hall, New York, Blue, Footed, 5 In. ....*Illus* 4180.00
Bowl, Cottage, Bridge, Dark Blue Transfer, 9 3/4 In. 245.00
Bowl, Ruin Scenes, Dark Blue, Shallow, 11 x 2 1/2 In. 165.00
Bowl, Ship & Sailors Hunting Polar Bears, Blue Transfer, 9 1/4 x 11 1/4 In. 300.00
Bowl, Underplate, Boston State House, Pierced Foot, Handle, Rogers, 10 1/4 In. 2310.00
Bowl, Vegetable, Cover, Floral & Ruins, Light Blue Transfer, 9 3/4 In. 245.00
Bowl, Vegetable, Cover, Rose Finial, Blue Transfer, Shell Border, 9 1/2 x 9 1/2 In. 275.00
Bowl, Vegetable, Cover, Yale College, New Haven, Light Blue Transfer, 12 1/2 In. 550.00
Bowl, Vegetable, Landing Of General Lafayette, Blue Transfer, 10 In. ....*Illus* 660.00

Staffordshire, Basket,
Underplate, Gothic Ruins,
Magenta & White, 11 In.

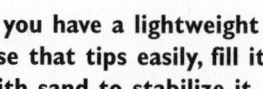

**If you have a lightweight
vase that tips easily, fill it
with sand to stabilize it.**

Bowl, Vegetable, States, Cover		5770.00
Bowl, Yellow, Red Brown Floral & Foliate, Green Highlights, 6 7/8 In.		440.00
Box, Cover, Central Floral Cartouches, 18th Century, 3 1/2 In.		1955.00
Box, Cover, Fruit & Flower Medallions, Shepherd Scene, 3 1/2 In.		665.00
Box, Cover, Gilt Latticework, Enamel Flowers, Rectangular, 18th Century, 2 In.		430.00
Box, Cover, Red Child Cartouches, Yellow Ground, 18th Century, 1 1/4 x 3 In.		490.00
Box, Cover, Riders On Horseback, Enamel, Late 18th Century, 3 In.		977.00
Box, Cover, Scrolled Floral Cartouches, Pink Ground, Clover Shape, 5 In.		920.00
Box, Cover, Stylized Flowers, Blue Ground, 18th Century, Round, 3 1/2 In.		545.00
Box, Cover, Venetian Scene, Aqua Ground, White Dots, Shell Shape, 3 5/8 In.		1725.00
Box, Cracked Ice Design, Pink Ground, Egg Shape, Grater Insert, 1 3/4 In.		630.00
Box, Gilt Scrolled Cartouches, Pink Ground, Oval, 18th Century, 2 In.		545.00
Box, Hen On Nest Cover, 8 1/2 x 9 x 6 In.		288.00
Box, Ink, Cover, Floral Cartouches, Blue Ground, Fitted, 18th Century, 4 In.		860.00
Bread Tray, Bird, Flowers & Bug, Gold Leaf Trim On Tab Handles, 12 x 9 In.		145.00
Bust, George Washington, Polychrome, 8 In.		165.00
Bust, John Locke, Pottery, 7 1/2 In.		175.00
Bust, Napoleon, Wearing Orange Coat, Blue Lapels, Green Border, 9 1/2 In.		750.00
Candleholder, Colonial Boy & Girl, 4 In., Pair		190.00
Candlestick, Floral Sprays, Enamel, Knopped Standard, 12 5/8 In., Pair		2300.00
Candlestick, Painted Flowers, White Ground, Domed Base, 10 In., Pair		1265.00
Candlestick, Scrolled Cartouches, Gilt Foliage, Blue Ground, 14 1/2 In., Pair		2300.00
Canister, Tea, Cover, Figure Of Apollo On Each Side, Brown Slip, 1780, 6 In.		2300.00
Chamber Set, Yesso Pattern, Brownfield & Sons, c.1880		350.00
Clock, Highland Lad & Lassie Scene, 1855-1870, 14 3/4 In.		333.00
Coffeepot, Baronial Halls, Blue & White, 19th Century, 12 In.		355.00
Coffeepot, Dome Top, Farmyard Scene, Blue Transfer, 11 1/4 In.		522.00
Coffeepot, Landscape, Blue & White, 11 In.	*Illus*	412.00
Coffeepot, Red & Light Green Sprig Design, Soft Paste, 1790s, 9 1/2 In.		650.00
Creamer, Cow, Blue, White, England		75.00
Creamer, Girl With Flower Basket, Floral Border, Dark Blue Transfer, 6 In.		175.00
Creamer, Horse Drawn Sleigh Scene, 6 In.		440.00
Creamer, Lafayette At Washington's Tomb		825.00
Creamer, Raised Hunting Design, Polychrome, 3 3/4 In.		55.00
Creamer, Seashell, Urn & Flower Design, Blue		70.00
Cup, 4 Square Panels, Geometric Borders, Reeded Strap Handle, 3 In.		805.00

Staffordshire, Bowl, City Hall,
New York, Blue, Footed, 5 In.

Staffordshire, Bowl,
Vegetable, Landing
Of General Lafayette,
Blue Transfer, 10 In.

Staffordshire,
Coffeepot, Landscape,
Blue & White, 11 In.

Staffordshire,
Cup Plate, Castle
Garden Battery,
Blue Transfer, Wood,
3 5/8 In.

Cup, Autumn, Industry Produceth Wealth, 3 Handles, Black Transfer, 6 In.	220.00
Cup, Boston Mails, Gentleman's Cabin, Brown, Handle, 3 3/8 In.	60.00
Cup & Saucer, Boy Fishing, English Country House, Blue Transfer, Handleless	165.00
Cup & Saucer, Castle, Brown Orange Transfer, Yellow, Handleless	385.00
Cup & Saucer, Fisherman Scene, Medium Blue Transfer, Handleless	137.00
Cup & Saucer, Floral, Birds, Shell, Dark Blue Transfer, Handleless, Pair	291.00
Cup & Saucer, Horse Drawn Sleigh Scene, Dark Blue, Handleless	275.00
Cup & Saucer, MacDonnough's Victory, Dark Blue Transfer, Handleless	192.00 to 330.00
Cup & Saucer, Mother & Children, Brown Transfer, Yellow, Handless	385.00
Cup & Saucer, Oriental Design, A Present From Morecambe, 19th Century	38.00
Cup & Saucer, Plate, Sporting Scenes, Brown Transfer, 1870-1890, 3 Piece	95.00
Cup & Saucer, Plate, Sporting, Brown Transfer, J.E. Wileman, 1890, 3 Piece	95.00
Cup & Saucer, River Scene, 2 Men By River, Dark Blue Transfer, Handleless	110.00
Cup & Saucer, Wadsworth Tower, Dark Blue Transfer, Shell Border, Handleless	165.00
Cup Plate, Anti-Slavery, Lovejoy-Tyrant's Foe, Light Blue, 4 In.	250.00
Cup Plate, Castle Garden Battery, Blue Transfer, Wood, 3 5/8 In. *Illus*	990.00
Cup Plate, General Andrew Jackson, Orange & Brown, Wood, 3 3/4 In.	880.00
Cup Plate, Holliday Street Theatre, Baltimore, 3 1/2 In.	850.00
Dish, 3 Florets, Peg Feet, Salt Glaze, White, Leaf Shape, 1760, 6 In., Pair	1380.00
Dish, Baronial Halls, Design On Inside & Outside, Octagonal, T. Mayer, 10 In.	200.00
Dish, Central Diaper Panel, White, Salt Glaze, Pierced Rim, 1760, 12 In.	1150.00
Dish, Cover, Underplate, Landing Of Lafayette, Blue Transfer, 5 1/2 In. *Illus*	1375.00
Dish, Domed Cover, Fruit, Floral Border, Foliate Handles, 5 x 11 In., Pair	920.00
Dish, Hen Cover, 1920s	250.00
Dish, Hen On Basket Cover, Yellow	330.00
Dish, Hen On Nest Cover, 11 1/4 In.	605.00
Dish, Herringbone Basketwork Center, Salt Glaze, Scalloped Rim, 12 In., Pair	1035.00
Dish, Sweetmeat, Enamel, Round, 1780-1795, 1 1/8 x 1 7/8 In.	242.00
Dish, Sweetmeat, Hound In Courtyard On Cover, Hound Head Shape, 2 In.	3565.00
Dish, Sweetmeat, Scene Of Boar Hunting On Cover, Boar Head Shape, 2 3/4 In.	2530.00
Dish, Sweetmeat, Toile De Jouy Cover, Shaded Rose, Enamel, 1795, 1 1/4 x 2 In.	242.00
Figurine, Abraham Lincoln, 15 1/2 In.	1300.00
Figurine, Benjamin Franklin, Holding Hat, 15 1/2 In.	1650.00
Figurine, Benjamin Franklin, Holding Paper Titled Freedom, 15 3/4 In.	1900.00
Figurine, Benjamin Franklin, Standing Wearing Cobalt Blue Coat, 14 In.	345.00
Figurine, Billy Water, Black Beggar Wearing A Blue Suit, 1925, 7 In., Pair	4025.00

Staffordshire, Dish, Cover,
Underplate, Landing Of Lafayette,
Blue Transfer, 5 1/2 In.

Figurine, Boy, With Dog, Standing, Barefoot, Before Bocage, 5 & 5 3/4 In., Pair 490.00
Figurine, Bull Baiting, Standing With Arms Raised, Pink, Black, 1830, 13 In. 8625.00
Figurine, Cat, Seated, Brown Marbling, Brown Slip, Blue, 1760, 3 1/4 In. 690.00
Figurine, Cat, Seated, Brown, White Marbling, White Face, Blue, 1760, 5 In. 2300.00
Figurine, Cat, Seated, Ears Erect, Brown, Green Mottled, Gray, Blue, 1770, 6 In. 1840.00
Figurine, Cat, Seated, Holding Small Brown Mouse In Its Mouth, Brown, 5 In. 1265.00
Figurine, Cat, Seated, Sponged, Black & Yellow, 4 1/4 In. 275.00
Figurine, Charles II, On Horseback, Gilt Highlights, 11 1/2 In. 120.00
Figurine, Cherub Standing Before Floral Bocage, 4 1/2 & 3 In., Pair 400.00
Figurine, Child With Cornucopia, Early 19th Century, 9 1/2 In. 200.00
Figurine, Cobbler & His Wife, 6 1/2 x 7 In., Pair 170.00
Figurine, Couple Exchanging Money, Hunter, Wearing Brown Coat, 8 x 7 In. 385.00
Figurine, Courting Couple, With Sheep, 6 In., Pair 275.00
Figurine, Courting Couple, With Sheep, 12 1/2 In. 220.00
Figurine, Cow & Calf, 5 x 6 In. 395.00
Figurine, Dog, Black & White, 7 In. 330.00
Figurine, Dog, Brown, White, Black, Gilt, Glass Eyes, 9 1/2 In. 305.00
Figurine, Dog, Copper Spots, Gold & Black Eyes, Numbered, 10 x 7 In. 225.00
Figurine, Dog, Greyhound, With Squirrel In Mouth, 6 In. 145.00
Figurine, Dog, Hounds, Reclining, 14 In. 145.00
Figurine, Dog, Poodle & Puppies, Clipped Dog & Pups, Reclining, 1840, 2 Piece 230.00
Figurine, Dog, Poodle, Clipped, Crouching On Yellow Cushion, 4 1/2 In., Pair 520.00
Figurine, Dog, Poodle, Nottingham Glaze, 19th Century, 5 1/2 In., Pair 110.00
Figurine, Dog, Pug, Glass Eyes, Gray Glaze, 12 In., Pair 690.00
Figurine, Dog, Pug, Sanded, 7 In., Pair 395.00
Figurine, Dog, Seated, Front Paws Spread, Teeth Bared, Blue Glaze, 1745, 6 In. 2185.00
Figurine, Dog, Spaniel, Black Glaze Eyes, Red Spots, 6 In. 145.00
Figurine, Dog, Spaniel, Black, White, Late 19 The Century, 9 In., Pair 385.00
Figurine, Dog, Spaniel, Glass Eyes, Black On Terra-Cotta Body, 11 In., Pair 450.00
Figurine, Dog, Spaniel, King Charles, Black Nose, White, 19th Century, 14 In., Pair 662.00
Figurine, Dog, Spaniel, On A Pillow, Yellow Glaze Eyes, Black, White, 5 In. 290.00
Figurine, Dog, Spaniel, Opposing, Brown & White, Gilt Collar, Chain, 12 1/2 In. 258.00
Figurine, Dog, Spaniel, Red, White, Painted Eyes, 19th Century, 12 In. 550.00
Figurine, Dog, Spaniel, Seated On Pillow Form Base, Brown & White, 12 1/2 In. 920.00
Figurine, Dog, Spaniel, Seated, Mid-19th Century, 14 3/4 In., Pair 325.00
Figurine, Dog, Spaniel, Seated, Pottery, 1845-1860, 11 x 9 x 4 1/2 In., Pair 423.00
Figurine, Dog, Spaniel, Seated, With Pink Roses, Mid-19th Century, 13 In., Pair 450.00
Figurine, Dog, Spaniel, Smoking A Pipe, Black, White, 8 1/2 In. 340.00
Figurine, Dog, Spaniel, White, 4 3/4 In., Pair 175.00
Figurine, Empress Eugenia, Seated, Holding Infant, Crown Prince, 8 In. 230.00
Figurine, Fisherwoman, 6 1/2 In. 115.00
Figurine, Fishmonger, 14 In. 345.00
Figurine, Four Seasons, Allegorical Figures, Spring & Winter, 5 In., 4 Piece 1725.00
Figurine, Gardener, Before Tree, Shovel In Hand, 6 In. 190.00
Figurine, Gardener, Standing Before Floral Molded Bocage, 5 1/4 In., Pair 575.00
Figurine, Gardener, Wearing White Hat, Cobalt Blue Coat, 6 1/4 In., Pair 345.00
Figurine, Girl With Goat, 19th Century, 6 3/4 In. 375.00
Figurine, Girl, On Dog, Luster Glaze, 5 3/4 In., Pair 200.00
Figurine, Girl, Sitting On Springer Spaniel, 5 1/2 In. 160.00
Figurine, Goat, Flat Back, 3 5/8 In. 220.00
Figurine, Hare, Crouching, About To Nibble A Leaf, White, Salt Glaze, 4 In. 6900.00
Figurine, Herder, Cow, Stream, 10 In. 1100.00
Figurine, Highlander, On Horse, Deer, 15 In. 395.00
Figurine, Horse, Flat Back, 4 In. 330.00
Figurine, Hunter, England, 19th Century, 7 1/8 In. 172.00
Figurine, Huntsman, 1845-1860, 17 x 9 1/2 x 4 In. 303.00
Figurine, Lady Wearing Light Purple Dress, 10 1/2 In. 430.00
Figurine, Lamb, Yellow, 2 In. 550.00
Figurine, Lass & Lassie, Holding Basket Of Fruit, Pottery, 13 1/2 In., Pair 275.00
Figurine, Lion, Early 20th Century, 10 3/4 In., Pair 420.00
Figurine, Lion, Glass Eyes, 9 1/2 In., Pair 575.00
Figurine, Lion, Standing With 1 Paw Resting On Globe, Pale Brown Coat, 10 In. 661.00
Figurine, Little Red Riding Hood & Wolf, 6 In. 100.00

Figurine, Little Red Riding Hood, Seated With Wolf, c.1835, 10 In. 275.00
Figurine, Lute Player, England, 19th Century, 5 1/8 In. 115.00
Figurine, Man & Woman, Wearing Scottish Clothes, 7 1/4 In., Pair 80.00
Figurine, Monkey, Seated, Erect On Domed Base, Green, Manganese, 6 In. 920.00
Figurine, Mounted Highland Warrior, 1855-1870, 15 x 9 x 3 In. 266.00
Figurine, Musician, Youth Holding A Horn, Seated On Grassy Mound, 6 1/2 In. 375.00
Figurine, New Marriage Act, Pew Group, 6 x 6 In. 1125.00
Figurine, Parson, Ralph Wood Style, Early 19th Century, 6 1/2 In. 440.00
Figurine, Prince Of Wales, Pottery, 7 1/4 In. 150.00
Figurine, Robert Burns & His Mary, 7 x 11 In. 95.00
Figurine, Samson & Lion, 1860, 10 In. 1275.00
Figurine, Scotsman, With Peacock, Pottery, 14 1/2 In. 550.00
Figurine, Sheep & Youth, With Black & White Spotted Dog, 5 & 4 In., Pair 230.00
Figurine, Shepherd & A Boy, Shepherd Standing, With Dog, 6 x 5 In. 430.00
Figurine, Spaniel, Standing, Dappled & Spattered Glazed Body, 11 1/2 In. 138.00
Figurine, Squirrel With Nut, 19th Century, 8 1/2 In. 1695.00
Figurine, Stag & Doe, Signed, 3 1/4 In., Pair 220.00
Figurine, Stag & Doe, Standing Before Bocage, Floral, Brown, Green Base, 6 In. 865.00
Figurine, Troubadour, Guitar, King Charles Spaniel, 13 1/4 In. 375.00
Figurine, Woman At Well, Gilt, 8 5/8 In. 165.00
Figurine, Woman Dancing, Tarantella, Tambourine & Goat, 19th Century, 10 1/4 In. 143.00
Figurine, Zebra, 1 Hoof Resting On Tree Stump, Oval Green Base, 4 & 5 In., Pair 980.00
Figurine, Zebra, Black & Green, 6 1/2 In. 225.00
Flask, Cucumber, Green Enameled, Porcelain, 7 1/2 In. 520.00
Group, Couple, Sitting On Rocky Base, 10 3/4 In. 270.00
Group, Courting Couple, 12 1/2 In. 330.00
Group, Dandies, Standing Arm-In-Arm, Carrying Umbrella, 6 x 6 3/4 In. 1495.00
Group, Highland Gardener Couple, Pottery, 1850-1860, 9 x 4 3/4 x 2 1/2 In. 273.00
Group, Lion & Lamb, Standing Over Recumbent White Lamb, 3 3/4 In., Pair 750.00
Group, Man, With 2 Rabbits, 9 1/4 In. 285.00
Group, Mothers & Children, Mother Wearing Blue, Yellow Bonnet, 9 x 8 In. 1495.00
Group, Scottish Couple, England, 19th Century, 8 In. 230.00
Group, Scottish Highland Dancers, 11 1/2 In. 290.00
Group, Sheep Standing, Two Lambs, Shepherdess, 1820, 6 In. 1840.00
Group, Village, Gentleman, Playing A Horn Above Lady, 19th Century, 7 1/2 In. 430.00
Group, Young Man & Woman, 14 In. 355.00
Incense Burner, Boy Sitting On Rooster, 4 3/4 In. 185.00
Jug, Cream, Cauliflower, Leaves Overlapping, White Florets, Green Glaze, 5 In. 1035.00
Jug, Spaniels In Begging Position Shape, Painted Facial Features, 10 In., Pair 805.00
Mug, Brown Flowers On Both Sides, Silver Luster Rim, Yellow, Orange, 5 In. 990.00
Mug, Child's, Alphabet, Fisherman Design, Early 20th Century, 2 3/4 In. 130.00
Mug, Child's, Blue & Orange Flowers, Yellow, 2 1/2 In. ....*Illus* 176.00
Mug, Child's, Orange Floral, Blue Leaves, 2 1/2 In. ....*Illus* 358.00
Mug, Child's, Woman Holding Rack Of Rabbits, Black Transfer, Yellow, 3 1/2 In. 355.00
Mug, Frog, 2 Handles, Pottery, 5 3/4 In. 260.00
Mug, Lafayette & Washington, Black Transfer, Yellow, 2 1/2 In. 2310.00

Staffordshire, Mug, Child's,
Blue & Orange Flowers,
Yellow, 2 1/2 In.

Staffordshire, Mug, Child's,
Orange Floral,
Blue Leaves, 2 1/2 In.

Staffordshire, Pitcher,
English Castle Scene, States,
Blue Transfer, 7 1/4 In.

Staffordshire,
Pitcher, Landing Of
General Lafayette,
Blue Transfer, 8 3/4 In.

Staffordshire, Plate,
Baltimore & Ohio
Railroad, Inclined, Blue,
Wood & Sons, 9 1/4 In.

Mug, Multicolored Band, Yellow, 2 1/2 In. 385.00
Mug, Sheep, Reclining, Brown Transfer, Silver Luster Rim, Yellow, 1 3/4 In. 330.00
Mug, Yellow, Frog Interior, Figures Both Sides, 5 1/2 In. 135.00
Pastille Burner, Castle, 7 In. 365.00
Pepper Shaker, Floral, English Scene Of Church & Fisherman, 4 5/8 In. 385.00
Pitcher, Adam's Rose, Gaudy, 7 In. 165.00
Pitcher, American Naval Heroes, Blue Transfer, 1830s, 7 1/4 In. 747.00
Pitcher, Blue Greek Key Design, Cream Ground, 9 3/4 In. 95.00
Pitcher, Boston State House, Dark Blue Transfer, Stubbs, 6 1/2 In. 920.00
Pitcher, Castle With Flag, Boats, Dark Blue, 9 3/4 In. 2783.00
Pitcher, English Castle Scene, States, Blue Transfer, 7 1/4 In. ....*Illus* 1320.00
Pitcher, Erie Canal, Dark Blue Transfer, 5 7/8 In. 115.00
Pitcher, Fairy Queen, Purple Transfer, 9 1/2 In. 275.00
Pitcher, General Lafayette & George Washington, Pottery, 5 1/4 In. 230.00
Pitcher, Insane Asylum, New York, Blue, 6 1/4 In. 550.00
Pitcher, Insane Asylum, New York, Handle, Dark Blue Transfer, 7 In. 385.00
Pitcher, Landing Of General Lafayette, At Castle Garden, Shield Shape, 8 In. 920.00
Pitcher, Landing Of General Lafayette, Blue Transfer, 8 3/4 In. ....*Illus* 852.00
Pitcher, Landscape, Light Blue Floral Transfer, 10 In. 220.00
Pitcher, Oriental, Blue Transfer, Bulbous, 10 3/4 In. 365.00
Pitcher, Prison, 3 Story Bldg., Dark Blue Transfer, 6 1/4 In. 935.00
Pitcher, Residence Of The Late Richard Jordan, New Jersey, J. H. & Co., 6 1/4 In. 290.00
Pitcher, Seal Of United States, With Eagle, Dark Blue Transfer, 7 3/8 In. 1320.00
Pitcher, Urns Issuing Flowers, Stylized Border, Transfer, 9 3/4 In. 258.00
Pitcher & Bowl, Arden, Blue & White, Burleigh, 1900, 2 Piece 500.00
Pitcher & Bowl, Castle, Purple Transfer, Leaf & Acorn Border, 14 x 13 In., 2 Piece 190.00
Plate, America & Independence, Dark Blue Transfer Border, 8 3/4 In. 275.00
Plate, America & Independence, Light Blue, 19th Century, 10 In. 100.00
Plate, Antelope, Halls Quadrupeds Series, Dark Blue Transfer, 8 In. 200.00
Plate, Arms Of New York, Thomas Mayer, 10 In. 880.00
Plate, Arms Of Rhode Island, Dark Blue Transfer, T. Mayer, 8 1/2 In. .... .220.00 to 690.00
Plate, Arms Of South Carolina, 7 1/2 In. 605.00
Plate, Athenaeum, Boston, Dark Blue, 6 1/4 In. 115.00
Plate, Baltimore & Ohio Railroad, Inclined, Blue, Wood & Sons, 9 1/4 In. ....*Illus* 330.00
Plate, Baltimore & Ohio Railroad, Level, Wood & Sons, Blue, 10 1/4 In. ....*Illus* 962.00
Plate, Baltimore Exchange, Fruit & Flower Series, Dark Blue Transfer, 10 In. 575.00
Plate, Battery, New York, Purple Transfer, 8 In. 82.00
Plate, Boston State House, Blue Transfer, 6 1/2 In. 55.00
Plate, Boston State House, Dark Blue Transfer, 8 1/2 In. 192.00
Plate, Building, Center Scene, Sheep On Lawn, Dark Blue, 8 3/4 In. 330.00
Plate, Chief Justice Marshall Troy, Dark Blue, Wood & Sons, 8 1/2 In. 545.00
Plate, City Hall, New York, Blue Transfer, Spread Eagle Border, Stubbs, 6 5/8 In. 110.00
Plate, City Hall, New York, Blue Transfer, Stubbs, 5 In. 220.00
Plate, City Hall, New York, Brown Transfer, Jackson's Warranted, 10 1/2 In. 70.00
Plate, City Hall, New York, Dark Blue Transfer, 9 3/4 In. 275.00
Plate, City Hall, New York, Medium Blue, Spread Eagle Border, Stubbs, 6 5/8 In. 345.00
Plate, City Hotel, New York, Blue Transfer, Acorn & Oak Leaves Border, 8 5/8 In. 220.00
Plate, City Of Albany, Shell Border, Dark Blue Transfer, 9 7/8 In. 518.00

Staffordshire,
Plate, Baltimore &
Ohio Railroad,
Level, Wood & Sons,
Blue, 10 1/4 In.

Staffordshire,
Plate, Commodore
MacDonnough's Victory,
Blue Transfer, 10 In.

Plate, City Of Albany, State Of New York, Blue, Wood & Sons, 10 In. 465.00
Plate, Columbia College, New York, Medium Blue, 6 3/8 In. 423.00
Plate, Commodore MacDonnough's Victory, Blue Transfer, 10 In. .... *Illus* 770.00
Plate, Commodore MacDonnough's Victory, Blue Transfer, Wood & Sons, 7 5/8 In. 260.00
Plate, Commodore MacDonnough's Victory, Dark Blue Transfer, 10 In. 385.00
Plate, Commodore MacDonnough's Victory, Shell Border, Wood & Sons, 6 In. 345.00
Plate, Constitution & The Guerierre, Blue Transfer, Wood & Sons, 10 In. 1380.00
Plate, Country Manor, Figures With Donkey, Dark Blue Transfer, 10 In. 155.00
Plate, Court House, Baltimore, Blue Transfer, 8 5/8 In. .... *Illus* 330.00
Plate, Court House, Baltimore, Blue Transfer, Fruit & Flower Border, 8 1/2 In. 412.00
Plate, Dam & Waterworks, Philadelphia, Dark Blue, 10 In. 440.00
Plate, Early Steamship Scene, Blue Transfer, Fruit & Flower Border, 8 In. 300.00
Plate, Erie Canal, Aqueduct Bridge At Rochester, Dark Blue Transfer, 8 1/2 In. 275.00
Plate, Exchange, Baltimore, Blue Transfer, Fruit & Flower Border, 10 In. 440.00
Plate, Fair Mount Near Philadelphia, Blue Transfer, Stubbs, 10 1/4 In. 230.00
Plate, Fall Of Montmorenci, Near Quebec, Dark Blue, Wood & Sons, 8 3/8 In. 165.00
Plate, Fisherman, Red Transfer, Enoch Wood & Sons, 10 1/2 In. 220.00
Plate, Floral, Yellow, Embossed Border, 8 1/4 In. .... *Illus* 1595.00
Plate, Fort Gansevoort, New York, Dark Blue Transfer, Vine Border, 6 7/8 In. 330.00
Plate, Franklin's Morals, Dark Blue, What Maintains One Vice, 7 5/8 In. 275.00
Plate, Gilpin's Mills On The Brandywine Creek, Blue, Wood & Sons, 9 1/4 In. ...355.00 to 545.00
Plate, Great Fire, New York City, Light Blue Transfer, 8 In. 385.00
Plate, Happy Couple At Tea, 7 In. 130.00
Plate, Harvard College, Blue Transfer, Stevenson & Williams, 10 In. 345.00
Plate, Harvard College, Blue, R. Stevens & Welles, 1810-1832, 7 In. 165.00
Plate, Harvard College, Dark Blue Transfer, Oak Leaf Border, 8 3/4 In. 200.00
Plate, Hobart Town, Dark Blue Transfer, 9 In. 55.00
Plate, Hoboken In New Jersey, Blue, Stubbs, 7 3/4 In. 175.00
Plate, Hudson River, Albany, New York, Blue Transfer, 10 1/4 In. 300.00
Plate, Iris, Flow Blue, 9 In. 55.00
Plate, Italian Scene, Red Transfer, 9 1/4 In., 6 Piece 165.00
Plate, Kansu, T. Walker, 10 1/2 In. 60.00
Plate, Lafayette At Washington's Tomb, Blue Transfer, 10 In. .... *Illus* 1017.00

Staffordshire,
Plate, Court House,
Baltimore, Blue
Transfer, 8 5/8 In.

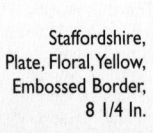

Staffordshire,
Plate, Floral, Yellow,
Embossed Border,
8 1/4 In.

Plate, Landing Of General Lafayette At Castle Garden, N.Y., Dark Blue, 7 In., Pair 460.00
Plate, Landing Of The Fathers At Plymouth, Blue, Enoch Wood & Sons, 10 In. ...290.00 to 550.00
Plate, Landing Of The Fathers At Plymouth, Blue, Mid-19th Century, 6 In............. 170.00
Plate, Landing Of The Fathers At Plymouth, Medium Blue Transfer, 8 5/8 In........... 137.00
Plate, London Institution, Regents Park Series, Dark Blue Transfer, 7 In. 55.00
Plate, Marine Hospital, Louisville, Kentucky, Dark Blue Transfer, Shell Border, 9 In. 165.00
Plate, Music Temple, New York, Blue Border, 7 1/2 In.......................... 575.00
Plate, Nahant Hotel, Near Boston, Blue, Acorn & Oak Leaves Border, 8 1/2 In. ...135.00 to 192.00
Plate, New York From Brooklyn Heights, Blue Transfer, 10 1/4 In. ....550.00 to 825.00
Plate, Orange Flowers, Green Foliage, 9 5/8 In. ...._Illus_ 990.00
Plate, Parisian Hateua, Brown, 10 In. 85.00
Plate, Park Theatre, New York, Dark Blue Transfer, 10 In. ....355.00 to 2200.00
Plate, Patrick Henry Addressing Virginia Assembly, St. Johns Church, 10 In. 75.00
Plate, Peace & Plenty, Dark Blue Transfer, 5 In. 247.00
Plate, Peace & Plenty, Dark Blue Transfer, 10 1/4 In. 495.00
Plate, Pekin, Flow Blue, 10 1/8 In. 120.00
Plate, Pittsburgh Steamship, Picturesque Views, Dark Brown Transfer, 10 3/4 In. 385.00
Plate, Playing At Draughts, Wilkie, Blue, 10 In. 300.00
Plate, President's House, Light Blue Transfer, 10 1/2 In. 300.00
Plate, Race Bridge, Philadelphia, Purple Transfer, 9 1/4 In. 110.00
Plate, Rhode Island, Blue, T. Mayer, 8 1/2 In. ....330.00 to 440.00
Plate, Scenes From Robinson Crusoe, Polychrome Enamel, 7 7/8 In, 4 Piece 330.00
Plate, Scudder's Museum, Dark Blue Transfer, Oak Leaf Border, 7 1/4 In. 550.00
Plate, Sheltered Peasants, R. Hall, Dark Blue Transfer, 7 1/2 In., Pair 460.00
Plate, Shepherd Boy With Flute, Blue, 7 1/2 In.............................. 65.00
Plate, Shepherd With Flute, Blue Transfer, 9 3/4 In. 110.00
Plate, St. Paul's Chapel, Dark Blue Transfer, Oak Leaf Border, 6 3/8 In. 660.00
Plate, Steamboat, Diorama Series, Dark Blue Transfer, 10 1/4 In. 165.00
Plate, Table Rock Niagara, Blue Transfer, Enoch Wood & Sons, 10 1/4 In. 600.00
Plate, The Capitol At Washington, Dark Blue Transfer, Shell Border, 7 1/2 In. 190.00
Plate, Transylvania University, Lexington, Dark Blue, Shell Border, 9 In. 363.00
Plate, Union Line, Dark Blue Transfer, Shell Border, 10 In......................... 495.00
Plate, Vermont State Capitol, Massachusetts State Capitol, Blue, 10 In., Pair 90.00
Plate, View In Central Park, Sunset On The Lake, Blue Border, 7 1/2 In. 585.00
Plate, View Of Liverpool, Dark Blue Transfer, Shell Border, 10 In. 330.00
Plate, View Of Trenton Falls, 3 People On Rock, Dark Blue Transfer, 7 1/2 In. 403.00
Plate, View Of Trenton Falls, Blue, Shell Border, Enoch Wood & Sons, 7 1/2 In. 245.00
Plate, Views Of New Orleans, c.1900, 10 In. 120.00
Plate, Washington Praying At Valley Forge, 10 In.............................. 150.00
Plate, Water Works, Philadelphia, Black Transfer, 7 3/4 In. 99.00
Plate, Water Works, Philadelphia, Dark Blue Transfer, Oak Leaf Border, 10 In.......... 495.00
Plate, Water Works, Philadelphia, Medium Blue, 10 In......................... 655.00
Plate, White Sulphur Springs, Delaware, Ohio, Blue & Black Transfer, 9 1/4 In. ..220.00 to 245.00
Plate, White Sulphur Springs, Delaware, Ohio, Light Blue Transfer, 8 In. 275.00
Plate, White Sulphur Springs, Delaware, Ohio, Purple Transfer, 8 In. 330.00
Plate, Woodlands Near Philadelphia, Blue, 6 3/4 In. 245.00
Plate, Yale College, Light Blue Transfer, Charles Meigh, 9 1/2 In. 115.00
Plate, Yellow, Embossed Floral Border, Allover Multicolored Floral, 8 1/4 In. 1595.00

Staffordshire, Plate,
Lafayette At Washington's
Tomb, Blue Transfer,
10 In.

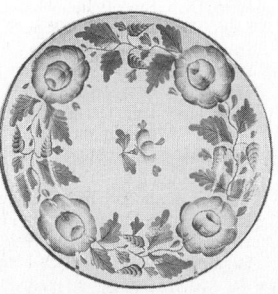

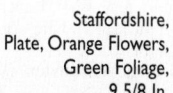

Staffordshire,
Plate, Orange Flowers,
Green Foliage,
9 5/8 In.

Platter, American Eagle Carrying Patriotic Banner In Flight, Teal Green, 19 In. 460.00
Platter, Boston Mails, Saloon, Blue Transfer, T. & T. Edwards, 17 1/2 x 13 1/2 In. 330.00
Platter, Boston State House, Dark Blue, Stubbs, 14 1/2 x 12 In. 1035.00
Platter, Castle Garden Battery, New York, Blue Transfer, 20 1/2 In. 3400.00
Platter, Castle Garden Battery, New York, Dark Blue Transfer, 18 1/2 In. 3000.00
Platter, Christianburg, Danish Settlement On The Gold Coast, Dark Blue, 18 1/2 In. 1265.00
Platter, Deaf & Dumb Asylum, Hartford, Conn., Dark Blue Transfer, 15 In. 110.00
Platter, Eddistone Lighthouse, Enoch Wood & Sons, 9 In. 770.00
Platter, Fairmount Park, Water Works, Philadelphia, c.1820, 16 3/4 x 20 1/2 In. 2415.00
Platter, Figures Before Tents Center, Pagoda In Landscape, 19 In. 2070.00
Platter, Floral, Lavender Transfer, 19 In. 355.00
Platter, Game Birds, Dark Blue Transfer, 16 1/2 In. 935.00
Platter, Gyrn, Flintshire Wales, Blue, R. Hall & Son, 17 x 13 1/2 In. 550.00
Platter, Hannibal Crossing The Alps, Blue Transfer, 19 1/2 x 15 3/4 In. 290.00
Platter, Hudson River View, Black Transfer, 17 3/4 In. 385.00
Platter, Kyoto, Brown Transfer Design, Off-White Ground, 19 1/2 In. 86.00
Platter, Lake George, New York, Shell Border, Blue, Enoch Wood & Sons, 16 1/2 In. . . .   385.00
Platter, Little Falls, Catskill Moss, New York, Black Transfer, 11 In. 220.00
Platter, Lumley Castle, Durham, Blue Transfer Design, Off-White Ground, 15 In. 345.00
Platter, Man, Being Tossed In A Blanket, Green, White, 12 3/4 In. 165.00
Platter, Mendenhall Ferry, Dark Blue Transfer, Spread Eagle Border, Stubbs, 17 In. 825.00
Platter, Multicolored Center, Flower, Butterfly Border, Blue, White, 17 x 14 In. 300.00
Platter, Oriental, Blue Transfer, Off-White Ground, 15 3/4 In. 126.00
Platter, Pastoral Ruins, Blue & White, Enoch Woods, 19th Century, 18 1/2 In. 412.00
Platter, Rhinoceros, Quadrupeds Series, 17 In. 2000.00
Platter, Rural Scene, Train Crossing An Aqueduct, Red Floral Border, Blue, 15 In. 375.00
Platter, Shipping Port On Ohio, Kentucky, Brown Transfer, 10 7/8 In. 550.00
Platter, States, America & Independence, Dark Blue Transfer, 14 3/4 In. 1210.00
Platter, Utica, New York, Brown Transfer, Lion, Unicorn Mark, 11 In. 220.00
Platter, Village Scene, Blue, 18 1/2 x 13 1/2 In. 355.00
Platter, Washington-Canova, Black Transfer, T. Mayer, 17 1/2 x 14 1/2 In. 345.00
Platter, Waverly, 12 x 15 1/2 In. 225.00
Platter, Wild Rose, Light Blue Transfer, 17 1/2 In. 275.00
Pot, Domed Cover, Roses, Floral, Dark Blue Transfer, 11 In. 825.00
Punch Bowl, Ancient Greece, Ruffled Edge, Blue, White, 12 x 5 1/2 In. 440.00
Punch Bowl, Architectural Design, Blue, White, 19th Century, 5 x 11 1/4 In. 550.00
Punch Pot, Cover, Birds, Floral Relief, Handle, Mid-18th Century, 8 In. 980.00
Rolling Pin, Cobalt Design, White, Wooden Handles, 1880-1920, 4 7/8 In. 385.00
Salt, Incised Zigzag, Yellow, Footed, Master, 2 In. 520.00
Saltceller, Gilt Scrolled Cartouches, Oval, 18th Century, 2 1/4 In. 290.00
Sauceboat, Boston State House, Blue, Rogers, 7 In. 300.00
Sauceboat, Fox & Swan, Band Of Stiff Leaves, Blue Feathered Border, 1815 . . . .   1380.00
Sauceboat, Fox & Swan, Watery Pale Brown Glaze, Swan Handle, 1790, 7 In. 1495.00
Sauceboat, Hoboken In New Jersey, Dark Blue, 7 3/4 In. 220.00
Snuffbox, Cover, Architectural Vignette Center, Enamel, 1800, 1 3/4 x 1 In. 303.00
Soap Dish, Black Transfer, Burford Bros., Oval, Blue, 5 1/4 In.   165.00
Soup, Dish, Arms Of New York, Dark Blue, T. Mayer, 9 3/4 In.   370.00
Soup, Dish, Baltimore & Ohio Railroad, Blue, Enoch Wood & Sons, 10 1/4 In. 880.00
Soup, Dish, Blue Transfer, Garden With Peacock 70.00
Soup, Dish, Boston State House, Blue, White, 10 In. 154.00
Soup, Dish, Harvard College, 9 7/8 In. 165.00
Soup, Dish, Historical, Guys Cliff, Warwickshire, Blue, White, 10 In. 130.00
Soup, Dish, Landing Of LaFayette, Blue, 19th Century, 8 1/2 In. 165.00
Soup, Dish, Octagon Church, Boston, Dark Blue, 9 3/4 In. 423.00
Soup, Dish, Park Theatre, New York, Medium Blue, 10 In. 423.00
Soup, Dish, United States Hotel Philadelphia, Blue, 10 1/4 In. 825.00
Spill Holder, Cow Shape, 19th Century, 11 1/2 In., Pair 575.00
Stirrup Cup, Dog's Head, Enamel, 4 1/2 In. 605.00
Sugar, Commodore MacDonough's Victory, Blue, Enoch Wood & Sons, 6 3/4 In. 690.00
Sugar, Cover, Mount Vernon, Floral Molded Handles, 6 In. 920.00
Sugar, Floral Design, Blue, White, 6 In. 165.00
Sugar, Mt. Vernon, Seat Of Late General Washington, Blue Transfer, 6 In. 825.00

Staffordshire, Tureen, Sauce, Cover, Underplate,
Savannah Bank, Blue Transfer, 7 In.

It is easy to glue pieces of broken china. Use a new fast-setting but not instant glue. Position the pieces correctly, then use tape to hold the parts together. If the piece needs special support, lean it in a suitable position in a box filled with sand.

Sugar, Stag Scene, Blue	33.00
Tea Bowl, Brown Orange Floral, Yellow, Scalloped Edge, 2 1/2 x 4 1/2 In.	605.00
Teapot, American Eagle On Urn, Dark Blue Transfer, 8 1/4 In.	688.00
Teapot, Commodore MacDonnough's Victory, Blue, 13 In.	431.00
Teapot, Floral, Lady With Urn In Medallion, Black Transfer, Yellow Glaze, 6 In.	920.00
Teapot, Flowers On Spout, Handle, Grapevine Border, Blue, White, 6 x 10 In.	170.00
Teapot, Girl & Dog, Landscape, Brown, White, 6 1/2 In.	145.00
Teapot, Lafayette At Franklin's Tomb, Floral Border	1035.00
Teapot, Landing Of Lafayette	2200.00
Teapot, Leaves, Overlapping, White Florets, Green Glaze, Greatbach, 5 In.	3220.00
Teapot, Oriental Design, Blue, White, 7 In.	190.00
Teapot, Scenic View, Black Transfer, Yellow Glaze, 7 In.	1150.00
Toby Jugs are listed in their own category.	
Tureen, Gravy, Columbia College, New York, Dark Blue Transfer, Vine Border, 9 In.	671.00
Tureen, Gravy, Dam & Waterworks, Philadelphia, Floral & Fruit Border, 9 In.	220.00
Tureen, Molded Geese Cover, 5 3/4 In.	373.00
Tureen, Nesting Dove, Pottery, 4 1/2 In.	201.00
Tureen, Nesting Hen, Pottery, 7 1/2 In.	170.00
Tureen, Sauce, Cover, Underplate, Boston Mails, Gentleman's Cabin, Brown, 3 Piece	520.00
Tureen, Sauce, Cover, Underplate, Savannah Bank, Blue Transfer, 7 In. ....*Illus*	1250.00
Tureen, Sauce, Underplate, Eastern Temple Scenes, Flowers, Ladle, 8 1/2 In.	330.00
Tureen, Soup, Cover, Castle Scenes, Bombe Shape, Branch Handles, Blue, White	1265.00
Tureen, Soup, Cover, Hector Retiring From Trenches, Blue & White, 1825	935.00
Tureen, Soup, Cover, Stylized Thistles, Exotic Figure & His Camel, Blue, White	1265.00
Tureen, Soup, Cover, Underplate, Birds Perched Amidst Floral Sprays, 10 In.	745.00
Tureen, Underplate, Boston State House, Enoch Wood & Sons, 8 3/8 In.	715.00
Tureen, Underplate, View Of Lancaster, John Rogers & Sons, 1830, 12 1/2 In.	1100.00
Tureen, Village Scenes, Printed Plinths & Flowers, Branch & Leaf Handles, 15 In.	546.00
Vase, 2 Green-Clad Huntsmen, Flanking A Large Seated Dog, 1860, 12 In.	333.00
Vase, Girl On Bridge, Fox Around Corner, Duck In Water, 6 x 9 In.	225.00
Vase, Robin Hood, 1850-1865, 15 x 9 1/2 x 4 In.	272.00
Vase, Spill, Couple Wearing Orange, Green, White Clothes, 7 & 5 In., Pair	635.00
Vase, Spill, Cow With Calf, 12 In.	315.00
Vase, Spill, Girl, Seated With A Sheep Beside Her, 19th Century, 6 In.	315.00
Vase, Spill, Lion & Lioness, Both With Cubs, 11 In., Pair	1380.00
Vase, Traveler's Rest, 2 Traveler's, 1840-1850, 11 x 8 x 2 1/2 In.	272.00
Vase, Winters Tale, Figural, Brown, Pink, Green, Black, Flesh Tones, 12 In.	400.00
Vase, Winters Tale, Flesh Tones, 12 In.	400.00
Wall Pocket, Flowers Issuing From Urn, Overlapping Acanthus Leaves, 9 In.	920.00
Wall Pocket, Grotesque Gargoyle Head, Waisted Shield Shape, 1765, 8 In.	1035.00
Wall Pocket, Women's Face Emerging From Foliage, Salt Glaze, White, 10 In.	920.00
Waste Bowl, Early Train, Red, Green Enamel, Black Transfer, 6 1/8 x 3 1/4 In.	55.00

STANGL Pottery traces its history back to the Fulper Pottery of New Jersey. In 1910, Johann Martin Stangl started working at Fulper. He bought into the firm in 1913, became president in 1926, and in 1929 changed the company name to Stangl Pottery. The pottery made dinnerwares and a line of limited-edition bird figurines. The company went out of business in 1978. The numbers used by Stangl for the bird figures indicate two birds in one figure by adding the letter *D,* for double.

Ashtray, Canada Goose	43.00
Ashtray, Iris, Square, 9 In.	45.00
Bird, Broadbill Hummingbird, No. 3629, 6 x 4 In.	145.00
Bird, Canary, Blue Flower, No. 3747	250.00
Bird, Cock Pheasant, No. 3492	225.00
Bird, Goldfinch, No. 3849	110.00
Bird, Hummingbird, Double, No. 3599D	400.00
Bird, Key West Quail Dove, No. 3454	250.00
Bird, Oriole, No. 3402	45.00
Bird, Paroquet, No. 3449	140.00
Bird, Passenger Pigeon, No. 3450	1200.00
Bird, Wren, Double, No. 3401D	115.00
Bird, Wren, No. 3401	70.00
Blueberry, Coffeepot	75.00
Blueberry, Salt & Pepper	22.00
Crying Baby, Mug	80.00
Floral Shape, Console Set	40.00
Fruit, Coffeepot	95.00
Fruit, Cookie Jar	125.00
Fruit & Flowers, Pitcher, 2 Qt.	28.00
Fruit & Flowers, Plate, 10 1/4 In.	22.00
Garden Flower, Charger, 11 1/4 In.	25.00
Golden Blossom, Pitcher, 6 In.	40.00
Goldfinch, Box, Cigarette	65.00
Kiddieware, Plate, Little Bo Peep	75.00
Lyric, Cigarette Box	145.00
Pheasants, Plate, Canada Geese, Quail, Ducks, 10 In., 4 Piece	325.00
Rooster, Plate, Yellow, 10 In., 6 Piece	15.00
Rooster, Salt & Pepper	195.00
Star Flower, Eggcup	15.00
Thistle, Butter, Cover	60.00
Thistle, Coffeepot	75.00
Town & Country, Plate, Blue, 6 In.	200.00
Town & Country, Plate, Blue, 8 In.	200.00
Town & Country, Plate, Blue, 10 In.	6.00
Town & Country, Spoon Holder, Blue	35.00
Tulip, Flowerpot, Yellow, 9 In.	28.00
Vase, Fulper Shape, 2 Blue Handles, 7 In.	35.00
Vase, Gold Trim, 10 In.	45.00
Vase, Tapered Cylinder, Multicolored, Brown & Blue Interior, 8 1/4 In.	60.00

STEINS have been used by beer and ale drinkers for over 500 years. They have been made of ivory, porcelain, stoneware, faience, silver, pewter, wood, or glass in sizes up to nine gallons. Although some were made by Mettlach, Meissen, Capo-di-Monte, and other famous factories, most were made by less important German potteries. The words *Geschutz* or *Musterschutz* on a stein are the German words for *patented* or *registered design,* not company names. Steins are still being made in the old styles. Lithophane steins may be found in the Lithophane category.

2 Dwarfs Drinking At Tree Stump, Etched, Pewter Lid, 1/2 Liter	345.00
3 Portraits Of Men, Etched, Pewter Lid, Hauber & Reuther, 1/2 Liter	341.00
4 Leaf Clover, Boch Head Spout, Stoneware, Pewter Lid, 1/4 Liter	121.00
50th Anniversary Of Schutzen Organization, Stoneware, Germany, 1909, 1/2 Liter	405.00
Anheuser-Busch, 1984 Olympics, Los Angeles, Flags, Ceramarte, 1/2 Liter	152.00 to 208.00
Anheuser-Busch, Bald Eagle, Germany, 1 Liter	1008.00

Anheuser-Busch, Bevo Fox, Lid, Thewalt, 1/2 Liter 196.00
Anheuser-Busch, Bud Man, Hollow Head, Ceramarte, 1/2 Liter .... .425.00 to 444.00
Anheuser-Busch, Endangered Species, Bald Eagle, Lid, Ceramarte, 1/2 Liter 425.00
Anheuser-Busch, General Ulysses S. Grant, Ceramarte, 1 Liter 115.00
Anheuser-Busch, Golden Retriever, Gerz, 1 Liter 98.00
Anheuser-Busch, Katakombe, Large Blue Ground, Ceramarte, 1/2 Liter 267.00
Anheuser-Busch, Owl, Germany, 1 Liter 108.00
Anheuser-Busch, Peregrine Falcon, Germany, 1 Liter 93.00
Anheuser-Busch, President Abraham Lincoln, Ceramarte, 1 Liter 128.00
Apple & Snake, Porcelain, E. Bohne Sohne, 1/3 Liter 1725.00
Art Nouveau, Stoneware, Pewter Lid, Marked Gerz 1328B, 3 1/2 Liter 430.00
Baking Scenes, Transfer & Enameled, Porcelain, Pewter Lid, 1/2 Liter 340.00
Bear, Pottery, 1/2 Liter 750.00
Beer Brewer, Porcelain, Pewter Lid, 1/2 Liter 545.00
Bell, Pottery, Wurzburger Glocklie, Merkelbach & Wick, c.1910, 1/2 Liter 1150.00
Bicycle Form, Man & Woman On Bicycle, Pewter Lid, Heinrich Krahmer, 1/2 Liter 275.00
Birds, Art Nouveau, Stoneware, Metal Lid, 1/2 Liter 150.00
Bismarck, Porcelain, Blue & White, Musterschutz, 1/2 Liter 430.00
Blue Floral, Blown Glass, Enamel, Pewter Lid, Zum Hochzeitstag, 1/2 Liter 82.00
Bowling Pin, Tan, Brown, Inlaid Lid, 1/2 Liter 144.00
Brauerei-Bachbrau, Weilheim, Stoneware, Pewter Lid, Impressed Design, 1/2 Liter 230.00
Budweiser, German Olympia, 1975 .... 45.00
Budweiser, Second Christmas, 1881 .... 195.00
Cabinet Maker, Transfer & Enameled, Porcelain, Pewter Lid, 1/2 Liter 415.00
Caroline, Chamois Thumblift, Porcelain Lid, Schierholz, 1/2 Liter 605.00
Cat, Dressed In Clothes, Stoneware, Multicolored Glaze, Inlaid Lid, 1/2 Liter 1045.00
Cherubs, Shooting Arrows At Doves, Porcelain Lid, Porcelain, 1 Liter 3300.00
Clown, Porcelain Lid, Schierholz, 1/2 Liter 289.00
Clown, Stoneware, Blue Salt Glaze, 1/2 Liter 775.00
Coin Spot Design, Glass, Amber, Blown, Pewter Lid, Base Rim, c.1890, 1/2 Liter 195.00
Couple In Relief, Stoneware, Barrel Shape, Pewter Lid, Whites Utica, 1 Liter 300.00
Couple On Horseback, Pottery, No. 846, J.W. Remy, Etched, Inlaid Lid, 1/2 Liter 375.00
Crests, Relief, Porcelain, Painted, Inlaid Lid, Wachtersbach, 1/2 Liter 240.00
Dancing Scene, Porcelain, Hauber & Reuther, Pewter Lid, 1/2 Liter 230.00
Dancing Scene, Pottery, Etched, Inlaid Lid, 1/2 Liter 105.00
Deep Amethyst, Olive Striation, Glass, 1830s, 5 1/2 In. 440.00
Double Headed Eagle On Front, Vines On Sides, Blue, Purple, Stoneware, 1/4 Liter 175.00
Dwarf Drinking Next To Barrel, Glass, Silver Plate Brass Lid, Amber, 1884, 1/2 Liter ... 550.00
Dwarf Filling Tankard For Second Dwarf, Etched, Pewter Lid, 1/2 Liter 346.00
Dwarf On Toadstool, Porcelain, Musterschutz, 1/2 Liter 1785.00
Eagle With Crown, Enameled, Pottery, Pewter Lid, 1/5 Liter 207.00
East Berlin Town Hall, Porcelain, 1/2 Liter 2990.00
Elephant, Seated, Pewter Lid, 1/2 Liter 660.00
Enameled Cherubs, Interior Fluted Body, Silver Plated Lid, c.1885, 6 1/2 Liter 392.00
Enameled Munich Child, Handworkers Convention, Pewter Lid, 1927, 1/2 Liter 190.00
Faience, Floral, Pewter Lid With Portrait Design, 18th Century, 1 Liter 1270.00
Faience, Floral, Pewter Lid, Erfurt, c.1750, 1 Liter 750.00
Faience, Floral, Sponge Design, Pewter Lid, 18th Century, 1 Liter 924.00
Faience, Grazing Stag, Pewter Lid, Footring, Thuringia, 1 Liter 635.00
Faience, Polychromed Continuous Deer Scene Frieze, Pewter, Germany, 7 In. 630.00
Farmer, Porcelain, Pewter Lid, 1/2 Liter 275.00
Farmer Scene, Pottery, Hinged Pewter, Tin Glazed, Germany, 18th Century, 7 1/4 In. 315.00
Festive Drinking Scenes, Etched, Pewter Lid, Hauber & Reuther, 1/2 Liter 365.00
Festive Outdoor Scene, Stoneware, Blue Salt Glaze, Pewter Lid, 2 Liter 115.00
Feurer Thurm, Bad Killingen, Pottery, 1/2 Liter 5750.00
Floral, Stoneware, Pewter Lid, 1/2 Liter 375.00
Floral Design, Silver, c.1900, 1 Liter 1095.00
Floral Enamel, Glass, Amber, Blown, Glass Inlaid Lid, 1/2 Liter 300.00
Geometric Design, Blue Handle, Stoneware, Pewter Lid, 1/2 Liter 266.00
Gnomes Drinking, Stoneware, Etched, Gnome On Lid, No. 170, Girmscheid, 2 Liter 490.00
Green Opaline, Matching Green Opaline Glass Inlaid Lid, 1/2 Liter 440.00
Hamms, St. Patrick's Day, 1974, Ceramarte 4.00
Happy Radish, Porcelain, Inlaid Lid, Schierholz, 1/2 Liter 240.00

Hops Lady, Porcelain, Musterschutz, Schierholz, 1/2 Liter ....360.00 to 635.00
Hunter & Elk In Forest, Horn Handle, Pottery, Horn Inlaid Lid With Elk, 1/2 Liter 137.00
Hunters Bidding Farewell, Etched, Inlaid Lid, Marzi & Remy, 1/2 Liter 330.00
Hunters Meeting Farmers In Forest, Tan, Green, Pottery, Pewter Lid, 1/4 Liter 88.00
Hunting Dog, Relief, Porcelain, Schierholz, 1/2 Liter 490.00
Knight, Pewter, Relief, c.1880, 1 1/2 Liter 405.00
Labrador, First Hunt Stein Series, Pottery, Gerz, 1 Liter 115.00
Leaf, Berry Design With Wheat, Pewter, Art Nouveau Lid, 1/2 Liter 139.00
Leaf Design, Stoneware, Plated Pewter Lid, White's, New York, 2 1/2 Liter 462.00
Line Design, Pressed Glass, Inlaid Porcelain Lid, Red Cross, 1/2 Liter 240.00
Lovers In Garden, Pottery, Pewter Lid, 1/2 Liter 141.00
Man, In Large Red Jacket, Stoneware, Enameled, Pewter Lid, Franz Ringer, 1/2 Liter 181.00
Man, In Large Yellow Coat, Enameled, Stoneware, Pewter Lid, Franz Ringer, 1/2 Liter ... 238.00
Man, Looking Into Empty Beer Stein, Stoneware, Pewter Lid, F. Ringer, 1/2 Liter 258.00
Man, On Barrel Flying Over Munchen, Etched, Inlaid Lid, Marzi & Remy, 1/2 Liter 425.00
Man, Riding Horse & Woman, Blue, Brown, Tan, Pottery, Pewter Lid, 1 Liter 77.00
Man & Woman, Etched, Inlaid Lid, Stoneware, Girmscheid, 1/2 Liter 324.00
Man & Woman Dancing, Etched, Inlaid Lid, Marzi & Remy, 1/2 Liter 382.00
Man & Woman Fishing, Inlaid Lid, Marzi & Remy, 1/2 Liter 128.00
Man & Woman Riding On Sled, Blown Glass, Pewter Lid, 1/4 Liter 390.00
Man At Table With King, Pottery, Inlaid Lid, Gerz, 1/2 Liter 340.00
Man Fishing, Blown Glass, Hobnail Design, Porcelain Inlaid Lid, 1/2 Liter 109.00
Man Who Constructs Floats, Sawmill On River, Porcelain, Pewter Lid, 1/2 Liter 1020.00
Mason Occupational, Glass, Facet Cut, Inlaid Porcelain Lid, Germany, c.1860, 1/2 Liter . 175.00
Men & Women Sitting On Logs, Pewter, Lid, Marzi & Remy, 1 Liter 254.00
Mettlach steins are listed in the Mettlach category.
Military, Relief Soldiers, Stoneware, 1914 Iron Crosses, Pewter Lid With Eagle, 1/2 Liter . 275.00
Military, Stoneware, Pewter Lid, Wachkommando Dillingen, Weihnachten 1915, 1 Liter .. 405.00
Military Monkey, Pottery, Tan, Blue, Brown, Inlaid Lid, 1/2 Liter 308.00
Mining Scene, Pottery, Pewter Lid, 1/2 Liter 550.00
Money Bag, Porcelain, E. Bohne Sohne, 1/2 Liter 1990.00
Monk, Pottery, Merkelbach & Wick, 1/2 Liter ....220.00 to 265.00
Monk, Wearing Red Robe, Lines In Lithophane, Inlaid Lid, 1/2 Liter 210.00
Monkey With Books, Quod Erat Demonstrandum, Monkey Handle, Inlaid Lid, 1/2 Liter . 230.00
Monks Testing Wine, Glass, Ribbed, Sea Shell Inlaid Lid, Amber, 1/2 Liter 360.00
Mountain Scene, Transfer & Enameled, Pewter Lid, 1907, 1 Liter 1650.00
Munich Child, Pottery, Full Color Face, J. Rheinemann, 1/4 Liter 195.00
Munich Child, Pottery, Tan, Black, Yellow, Green, Inlaid Lid, J. Reinemann, 1 Liter 341.00
Munich Child On Barrel, Porcelain, Fish Handle, Musterschutz, 1/2 Liter 920.00
Musical Scene With Several People, Etched, Pewter Lid, Hauber & Reuther, 1/2 Liter ... 82.00
Musicians, Stoneware, Blue & Brown Salt Glaze, Pewter Lid, Whites Utica, 2 Liter 575.00
Nun, Pottery, 1/2 Liter 160.00
Nun, Wearing Black Robe, Lines In Lithophane, Inlaid Lid, 1/2 Liter 176.00
Nurnberg Funnel, Leaves, Hops, Wheat, Porcelain Lid, Schierholz, 1/2 Liter 560.00
Nurnberg Tower, Pewter, F. & M.N. Mark, 1/2 Liter 405.00
Nurnberg Tower, Pottery, 6019 F. & M.N. Mark, 1/4 Liter 160.00
Old Woman Carrying Radishes, Porcelain Lid, Schierholz, 1/2 Liter 289.00
Olympia Brewing, Factory Scene, 1980s, 6 In. 18.00
Orange, Purple Swirl Design On Body, Glass, White Interior Layer, Pewter Lid, 1 Liter .. 1980.00
Owl, Porcelain, E. Bohne Sohne, 1/2 Liter 1785.00
Owl, Stoneware, Multicolored Glaze, Inlaid Lid, 1/2 Liter 385.00
Owl, Tan, Green, Cream, Inlaid Lid, 1/2 Liter 176.00
People In Rowboats, Etched, Pewter Lid, Hauber & Reuther, 1/2 Liter 364.00
Pig With Pipe, Porcelain, White & Blue, Musterschutz, 1/2 Liter 2415.00
Pink Opaline, Blown, Pink Inlaid Lid, 1/3 Liter 405.00
Pointer, First Hunt Stein Series, Pottery, Gerz, 1 Liter 115.00
Poodle With Top Hat, Porcelain Lid, Schierholz, 1/2 Liter 319.00
Porcelain, Hand Painted, Pewter Lid, Hauber & Reuther, 1/2 Liter 375.00
Post Coach, Transfer & Enameled, Pewter Lid, 1915, 1/2 Liter 1070.00
Regimental, 2-Sided Scene, 126th Infantry, Strassburg, Porcelain, 1/2 Liter 185.00
Regimental, 2-Sided Scene, 13th Infantry Munster, 1900, Porcelain, 1/2 Liter 185.00
Regimental, 2-Sided Scene, Eagle Thumblift, Pottery, 1908-1911, 1 Liter ....865.00 to 950.00
Regimental, 2-Sided Scene, No. 6 Dragoon, Diedenhofen, Porcelain, 1/2 Liter 227.00

Regimental, 4-Sided Scene, 6th Field Artillery, Lion Thumblift, Porcelain, 1/2 Liter 205.00
Regimental, 4-Sided Scene, Machine Gun Company, Eagle Thumblift, 1/2 Liter 635.00
Regimental, 4-Sided Scene, Wren Thumblift, Porcelain, 1899-1901, 1/2 Liter 405.00
Regimental, Navy Ship Scene, Stoneware, Lion Thumblift, 1 Liter 525.00
Regimental, Ship Scene, Thick Enameled Waves, 7 1/2 In. 525.00
Regimental, Skull, Horse & Rider Thumblift, Porcelain, 1/2 Liter 3300.00
Rizzi-Brau, Kulmbach, Pottery, Pewter Lid, 1/2 Liter 265.00
Roly Poly Bar Maid, Pottery, Inlaid Lid, 1/2 Liter 470.00
Rook, Stoneware, J. Reinemann, 1/2 Liter 1555.00
Saturday Evening Post, All I Want For Christmas, Gerz, 1/2 Liter 137.00
Saturday Evening Post, Triple Self-Portrait, Gerz, 1 Liter 148.00
Skull On Book, Porcelain, E. Bohne Sohne, 1/2 Liter 605.00
Springer Spaniel, First Hunt Stein Series, Pottery, Gerz, 1 Liter 100.00
Student, Blown Glass, Hobnail, Relief, Pewter Lid, Germany, c.1875, 1/2 Liter 195.00
Student Crest, Glass, Green, Blown, Enamel, Pewter Lid, Egermann, c.1890, 1/2 Liter .. 605.00
Swirled Design, Porcelain, Verse In Front, Hauber & Reuther, Pewter Lid, 1 Liter 174.00
Tower, Pewter, Copper & Brass Trim, 1 Liter 2415.00
Tower, Pewter, Copper & Brass Trim, 1/2 Liter 1440.00
Tower, Vines Growing On Sides, Stoneware, Pewter Lid, 1/2 Liter 990.00
Truck & Brewery Scenes, Transfer & Enameled, Porcelain, Pewter Lid, 1/2 Liter 910.00
Turner Design, Blown Glass, Applied Amber Prunts Around Base, Pewter Lid, 1/2 Liter .. 231.00
U.S. Military, Crossed Anchors, Shield, Eagle, Porcelain, Inlaid Lid, 1/2 Liter 185.00
Utica Club Schultz, West Germany, 1959, 12 In. 30.00
Warriors On Horseback, Etched, Inlaid Lid, Marzi & Remy, 1 Liter 577.00
Warriors Returning From Battle, Pewter, Lid, Marzi & Remy, 1 Liter 462.00
Wedding, Blown Glass, Floral Enamel, Pewter Lid, 1846, 1 Liter 575.00
Wedding, Blown Glass, Floral Enamel, Pewter Lid, 1854, 1 Liter 720.00
Wendelstein Mountain, Stoneware, Martin Pauson, 1/2 Liter 720.00
Wheel Cut Family Crest, Glass, Pewter Lid, Base Rim, Germany, c.1750, 1 Liter 3910.00
Yellow, Floral & Dragonfly, Glass, Enamel, Pewter Lid, Theresienthal, c.1890, 1/2 Liter .. 115.00

STEREO CARDS that were made for stereoscope viewers became popular after 1840. Two almost identical pictures were mounted on a stiff cardboard backing so that, when viewed through a stereoscope, a three-dimensional picture could be seen. Value is determined by maker and by subject. These cards were made in quantity through the 1930s.

10th Cavalary, Black Soldiers, Gambling, Spanish-American War, Griffith & Griffith 152.00
Alcatraz Island, From Meigg's Wharf, No. 325, Lawrence & Houseworth, 1866 .... 90.00
American Army Of Occupation, Rhine, Near Ehrenbreitstein 8.00
Anti-Aircraft Gun Being Worked In A Trench, Underwood & Underwood 8.00
Army Blacksmith, Antietam, Working With Anvil, Horses, Wagons, 1862 .... 100.00
Army Medical Museum Skull, American Indians, 200, Viewer 8250.00
Beauty Of Niagara, View From Museum Grounds, Canada, E. Anthony 25.00
Billiard Room, 4 Men, 1 Woman, Gun Rack, Pool Cue Rack 247.00
Black Cotton Press, Aiken, S.C., J.A. Palmer 35.00
Blackfoot, Grass Dance Of Blackfoot, Pipe Of Peace, N.A. Forsyth 150.00
Blackfoot, Painted Lodges Of Blackfoot Children, N.A. Forsyth 90.00
Buffalo Bill, Horse, Rifle, American Scenery Series, No. 1392, C.W. Woodward 122.00
Buffalo Bill, On Horse & Firing Rifle 112.00
Calcutta Town Hall, People In Courtyard, Sasne & Westfield 60.00
Chief Sitting Bull, Squaw & Twins, Sitting Outside Tent, Bailey, Dix, Mead 550.00
Chinese Visitors, Woodward's Gardens, 3 Views 75.00
Chippewa, Chief Of Rabbit Lake, Nan-Gun-E-Gahbow, C.A. Zimmerman 200.00
Croquet Party, 2 Hold Flags, Julius Hall, Berkshire 40.00
Custer & Colonel Ludlow, Grizzly Bear, August, 1874 .... 700.00
Erie Canal Locks, Lockport, New York, Canal Boat, F.B. Clench 35.00
Flatheads, Duncan McDonald & Wife, On Horses, Flag, N.A. Forsyth 55.00
Ford TriMotor Airplane, Leaving Chicago For Minneapolis 25.00
General Burnside's Headquarters, Brady, Anthony 1100.00
General George Armstrong Custer, War For The Union, Taylor & Huntington, 1864 .... 770.00
General George McClellan, Little Mac, War For Union Series, 1862 .... 50.00
General Grant, Chief Of Staff General Rawlins, Cold Harbor, Va., Anthony 450.00
German Submarines, U139 & U159, Cherbourg Harbour, W.E. Troutman, 1910s 10.00

Hot Springs Park, Santa Clara County, 3 Views 65.00
Indians, Armed, Holding Revolver, Gun Belt, Winchester, Other Guns 545.00
Japanese Performers At Woodwar's Gardens, Yellow Mount, 1869 .... 75.00
Klamath Mine & Mill, Fort Jones, Louis Heller, 1866-1872 .... 60.00
Large Parlor Ship Model, Navada, Capt. Barter 40.00
Leadville Mine, Pub In Colorado Springs, L.K. Oldroyd 222.00
Medicine Woman, Praying To Sun, Sepia, N.A. Forsyth 75.00
Mill View, Pacific Coast, From The Point, No. 230, C.E. Watkins 400.00
Minnesota Ice Harvest, Blocks Of Ice, Chas. A. Zimmerman 75.00
Minnesota Logging, Winter In Pine Forests, Cookboat, Dinner Table Set, 1860s 48.00
Our Cook, E.J. Hayward, Santa Barbara, Ca., Chinese Man Holding Opium Pipe 160.00
Penn Central Series, Altoona Factory, Workers, No. 504 .... 56.00
Pocahontas Saving John Smith, Keystone View Co., Norfolk, 1905 .... 17.00
President Wilson & Brand Whitlock, At Neuport, Belfium 8.00
Pullman Palace Car, Interior, No. 20, O.C. Smith 157.00
Santa Fe, Main Street, Mud, Distant Wagon, Gurnsey's Rocky Mt. Views, No. 220 ...... 55.00
Sing Sing Prison Series, Workers, Marble Quarry, No. 4298, E. & H.T. Anthony 39.00
Sioux, Tepees Of Sioux Indians, Zimmerman 125.00
Socorro, New Mexico, Aztec Ruins, Cliff Sides, W.H. Williscraft 175.00
St. Louis World's Fair, Plow, Daniel Webster, 1904 .... 12.00
St. Maurice, Lumber Camp, Work Crew Eating, Tents, No. 26, R.W. Anderson 42.00
Suffragette Parade, Woodrow Wilson's Inauguration, Inez Milholland, 1913 .... 135.00
Surf, Pacific Coast View, No. 260, C.E. Watkins 150.00
Tangled Ruins Of Marne Bridge, Blown Up, Underwood & Underwood 8.00
They Shall Not Pass, Entrance To Verdun, World War I, W.E. Troutman Inc. 8.00
Through Sickly Shrapnel, Sown Meadows Reaped By Death Alone 12.00
U.S. Battleship Transports, Bringing Home Troops, Louisiana At Dock In New York 10.00
U.S. Transport, Leviathan, Largest Ship Afloat 8.00
Verde Valley, Ruins On Oak Creek, Williscraft 45.00
Vigilantes, 6 Men On Horseback, Tinted 350.00
Vineyard Haven Harbor, New England, No. 334, C.H. Shute 50.00
White Pastor, Father Gresin, Black Children, Tree Scene, Charleston, S.C., Anderson ... 135.00
Whitehall St., Atlanta, War For The Union, Soldiers, Horses 45.00
Woman & 4 Men Playing Billards 247.00
Woman's Rights, Off To Lecture Room, Littleton, N.H., Weller, 1871 .... 45.00
World War I, Ruins Of Village Of Belleau, W.E. Troutman Inc. 8.00
Wounded Soldier About To Undergo Operation, New York 8.00

STEREOSCOPES were used for viewing stereo cards. The hand viewer was invented by Oliver Wendell Holmes, although more complicated table models were used before his was produced in 1859. Do not confuse the stereoscope with the stereopticon, a magic lantern that used glass slides.

Brewster Style, Ivory Label, c.1860, 15 In. 1210.00
Collapsible, Opens To Functional Viewer, France, 1880s, 7 x 4 In., Flat 220.00
Keystone Telebinocular, Adjustable Metal Stand 242.00
Viewbox, Watkins, 429 Montgomery St., Holds 25 Views 50.00
Viewer, Wooden, With 70 Photographs, 1900 .... 95.00

STERLING SILVER, see Silver-Sterling category.

STEUBEN glass was made at the Steuben Glass Works of Corning, New York. The factory, founded by Frederick Carder and T.G. Hawkes, Sr., was purchased by the Corning Glass Company. They continued to make glass called *Steuben*. Many types of art glass were made at Steuben. The firm is still making exceptional quality glass but it is clear, modern-style glass. Additional pieces may be found in the Aurene, Cluthra, and perfume bottle categories.

Basket, Verre De Soie, Berry Prunt At Applied Handle, Carder, 14 1/4 In. 805.00
Beaker, Ruby Over Clear, Pulled Feather Design, Clear Foot, 5 1/2 In. 310.00
Bowl, Calcite, Flared, Scalloped Rim, Interior Gold Iridescent, 2 In. 172.00
Bowl, Celeste Blue, 12 In. 135.00
Bowl, Celeste Blue, Flared, 4 1/2 x 11 In. 230.00

Bowl, Crimped Edge, Light Jade Blue, Multiple Glass Threads, 13 In. 275.00
Bowl, Diamond-Quilted, Reeded, Black, 12 In. 175.00
Bowl, Flared, Blue, Circular Foot, 12 In. 315.00
Bowl, Grotesque, 3-Lined Pillar Floriform Body, Ruffled Rim, 6 3/4 In. 230.00
Bowl, Grotesque, Ivory, 12 3/8 In. 350.00
Bowl, Matzu, Jade Green, 6 3/4 In. 825.00
Bowl, Oblong, Amber, Signed, 7 In. 125.00
Bowl, Oval, George Thompson, 1964, 21 1/2 In. 460.00
Bowl, Pedestal Base, Signed, 3 x 2 1/2 In. 80.00
Bowl, Pedestal, George Thompson, 1940, 10 1/8 In. 375.00
Bowl, Pomona Green, Signed, 14 1/2 In. 150.00
Bowl, Steep Sides, 6 Scroll Feet, John Dreves, 1942, 9 1/4 In. 632.00
Bowl, Undulating Base, Donald Pollard, 1960, 9 x 6 1/4 In. 260.00
Candelabrum, 3-Light, Floral Finial, Brass Connector, 19 In. 2115.00
Candlestick, Floret, No. 8081, Donald Pollard, 1956, 5 1/2 In., Pair 275.00
Candlestick, Pomona Green, 4 In. 82.00
Candlestick, Rosaline, Alabaster Foot, 8 1/2 In. 247.00
Candlestick, Teardrop, David Hills, 1949, 4 3/8 In., Pair 330.00
Champagne, Trumpet, Signed, 5 In., 12 Piece 605.00
Cocktail Set, Reeded, Applied Mirror Black Threads, Stopper, 6 Cups 410.00
Compote, Bristol Yellow, Footed, No. 5194 .... 170.00
Compote, Jade Green, Applied Alabaster Stems, Disk Feet, 3 In., Pair 489.00
Console, Pomona Green, Rolled Edge, No. 6108, 11 In. 100.00
Cup & Saucer, Rose, Alabaster Handle, 2 1/4 In. 190.00
Decanter, No. 8043, Donald Pollard, 1953, 12 In. 115.00
Dish, Amethyst, Footed, 6 1/2 In. 60.00
Dish, Cover, Alabaster, Rosaline 260.00
Dish, George Thompson, 1955, 7 1/4 In. 144.00
Figurine, Cat, Tall, No. 8102, Donald Pollard, 1960, 8 3/4 In. 385.00
Figurine, Duckling, Signed, 8 In. 517.00
Figurine, Eagle, Signed 2315.00
Figurine, Fox, Seated, Tail Wrapped, Signed, 8 3/4 In. 1455.00
Figurine, Koala, Signed, 1976, 5 3/4 In. 1155.00
Figurine, Leaping Dolphin, Signed, 5 3/4 In. 258.00
Figurine, Phoenix, Signed, 13 In. 1500.00
Figurine, Rooster, No. 8074, 1955, 9 1/2 In. 990.00
Figurine, Songbird, No. 8112, George Thompson, 1963, 4 1/2 In. 247.00
Figurine, Squirrel, Upright, Tail Extended, Signed, 6 In. 925.00
Figurine, Whale, Signed, 5 In. 403.00
Goblet, Celeste Blue, Clear Stem 59.00
Goblet, Oriental Poppy, Swirled Optic Rib Design, Carder, 5 3/4 In., Pair 575.00
Goblet, Trumpet, Signed, 7 In., 12 Piece 1200.00
Hand Cooler, Frog, Signed, 2 1/2 In. 115.00
Jar, Cover, Amethyst, Applied Polychrome Fruits, F. Carder, 11 1/2 In. 440.00
Lamp, Moss Agate, Purple, Red, Blue, Classic Urn Form, Acanthus Leaf, Carder, 10 In. .. 2645.00
Lamp Base, Oriental Jade, Applied Red Threading, Elongated Neck, Carder, 10 In. 862.00
Lampshade, Calcite, Dome, Mushroom, Engraved Urn & Swag Design, No. 2730, 18 In. . . 460.00
Lampshade, Pulled Green Feather Design, Gold, White Ground, Signed, 5 In. 145.00
Light Globe, Calcite, Vine & Leaf Decorated Banding, No. 5200, 16 1/2 In. 405.00
Light Globe, Garland Etched, Brass Fixture 575.00
Paperweight, Crystal, Ornamental, George Thompson, 1952, 3 1/8 In. 230.00
Perfume Bottle, Applied Polychrome Fruit, Stopper, F. Carder, 7 1/2 In. 231.00
Plaque, Relief, Bust Of Thomas Edison, Frederick Carder, Signed, 1929, 8 5/8 x 6 5/8 In. 110.00
Plate, White Pelican, Audubon, Signed, c.1940, 10 In. 550.00
Platter, Green, Controlled Bubbles, 13 In. 125.00
Pokal, Indian, Wheel Cut, Controlled Bubble Pattern On Base, Signed, 6 1/4 In. 575.00
Pokal, Woodsman, Wheel Cut, Controlled Bubble Pattern On Base, Signed, 6 1/4 In. 575.00
Sherbet, Crystal Flared Bowl, Twisted Green Stem, Signed, 12 Piece 660.00
Torchere, Oriental Poppy, Interior Striped Shade, Twisted Metal Shaft, 9 In. 3300.00
Tumbler, Cintra, Cranberry, Crystal Foot, Black Rim, Cone Shape, 4 In. 150.00
Urn, Ivrene, Flared, Stepped Square Foot, 12 In., Pair 2070.00
Vase, 2 Applied Scrolls On Base, Conical Shape, Signed, 6 In., Pair 247.00
Vase, Celeste Blue, Blue Rib Form, Flared, Disk Foot, Fleur-De-Lis Mark, 7 In. 316.00

Vase, Cintra, Geese In Flight, Black, Double Handles, 13 In.	3300.00
Vase, Fan, Green, Bubbles, 8 1/2 In.	135.00
Vase, Fluted Swirl, Cylindrical, 10 In.	515.00
Vase, Green Jade, Spherical Body, High Relief Acid-Etched Chrysanthemums, 8 In.	1265.00
Vase, Grotesque, White, Opalescent, 11 3/4 In.	630.00
Vase, Ivory, Black Handles, 10 In.	1610.00
Vase, Ivrene, Ribbed, 3 Applied Aqua Cintra Handles, Carder, 11 In.	1380.00
Vase, Jack-In-The-Pulpit, Signed, 8 In.	1995.00
Vase, Jade Green, Floral Design, Globular, 7 1/4 In.	575.00
Vase, John Dreves, 1939, 12 1/4 In.	288.00
Vase, Olive Green, Heart-Shape Leaf, Vines, Millefiori Blossoms, 2 1/4 In.	1495.00
Vase, Oriental Poppy, 16 Integrated Opal Stripes, Pink, Oval, Carder, 6 In.	690.00
Vase, Oriental Poppy, Opalescent Swirls, 6 In.	385.00
Vase, Phoenix Birds, Scrolls, Mounted As Lamp, Bronze Metal Base, 17 In.	1150.00
Vase, Pomona Green, Etched, 7 In.	235.00
Vase, Rosaline, Alabaster Foot, 6 In.	275.00
Vase, Rose, Flared Rim, Oval, Fleur-De-Lis Mark, 10 1/2 In.	1380.00
Vase, Silverina, Jack-In-The-Pulpit, Blue, Carder, 1910, 8 3/8 In.	4310.00
Vase, Stylized Floral Design, Blue Cut, 11 3/8 In.	1150.00
Vase, Twisted Knot Knop, Raised Circular Base, Signed, 10 3/4 In.	690.00
Vase, Verre De Soie, Cerise Ruby Threading, Diamond Quilted, 6 1/4 x 4 In.	60.00
Vase, Verre De Soie, Flared, Scalloped Rim, 8 3/8 In.	230.00

STEVENGRAPHS are woven pictures made like fancy ribbons. They were manufactured by Thomas Stevens of Coventry, England, and became popular in 1862. Most are marked *Woven in silk by Thomas Stevens* or were mounted on a cardboard that tells the story of the Stevengraph. Other similar ribbon pictures have been made in England and Germany.

Bookmark, George Washington, Silk, Philadelphia, 1876, 1 9/16 x 8 3/8 In.	82.00
Bookmark, To My Dear Sister	59.00
Bookmark, U.S. Centennial, Philadelphia, George Washington Image, 1876	140.00
Picture, Called To The Rescue, 19th Century, 2 x 6 In.	57.00
Picture, For Life Or Death, 19th Century, 2 x 6 In.	57.00
Picture, Japanese Baseball Game, Black Silk Threads, Red, Yellow, Blue, 2 x 5 3/4 In.	1725.00
Ribbon, General U.S. Grant, Labeled, Tassel, 5 1/4 In.	110.00

STEVENS & WILLIAMS of Stourbridge, England, made many types of glass, including layered, etched, cameo, and art glass, between the 1830s and 1930s. Some pieces are signed *S & W*. Many pieces are decorated with flowers, leaves, and other designs based on nature.

Epergne, Triple Case, Blue, 9 x 12 In.	695.00
Ewer, Gold Fern & Flower, Swirled, Mother-Of-Pearl, 11 In.	3450.00
Finger Bowl, Matching Plate, Cut Grapes & Leaves, Green, 4 3/4 In.	295.00
Finger Bowl, Underplate, Blue Zipper	22.00
Finger Bowl, Underplate, Ruffled Borders, Amber Threading	165.00
Finger Bowl, Underplate, Ruffled Borders, Green Threading	132.00
Goblet, Green Over Clear, Wheel Cut, c.1900, 6 In.	362.00
Lamp, Cranberry Over Yellow Cut, Daisy Pattern, 3 x 6 In.	975.00
Perfume Bottle, Mother-Of-Pearl Satin Glass, Matching Stopper, 5 1/2 In.	345.00
Plate, Beehive, Dark Blue, 6 1/8 In.	160.00
Rose Bowl, Blue, Crimped Edge, 3 x 3 1/2 In.	135.00
Rose Bowl, Flowering Branch, Inverted Ruffled Rim, 5 1/2 x 6 In.	115.00
Rose Bowl, Flowering Branch, Marbled & Flecked, 5 1/2 x 6 In.	95.00
Rose Bowl, Vaseline Base, Shell Feet, 4 3/4 x 5 1/2 In.	350.00
Tazza, Blue, Footed, 3 1/4 x 7 In.	44.00
Tazza, Pink, Diamond, Threaded Glass, 2 3/4 x 6 In.	60.00
Vase, Applied Plums, Vines, Flowers, Amber Feet, 9 In.	412.00
Vase, Cream, Strawberries, Leaves, Applied Handle, Feet, 12 1/2 In.	1093.00
Vase, Floral, Ruffled Rim, Wheel Cut, 1900, 7 In.	110.00
Vase, Green Trailing, Silver Ground, Shadings Of Blue Green, Signed, 6 In.	1435.00
Vase, Intaglio Cut, Ferns On Inside Layer, Stripes On Feet, 3 5/8 In.	225.00
Vase, Lacy Intaglio Designs, Cut To White Lining, 4 1/4 In.	195.00

Vase, Pink Outside, Yellow Interior, Cut Intaglio Designs, 4 In. 225.00
Vase, Pompeian Swirl, Pink Lining, 8 /14 In. 230.00
Vase, Pompeian Swirl, Satin Glass, Amberina, 8 1/4 In. 230.00
Vase, White Flowers, Cranberry Ground, 5 In. 770.00
Vase, White Fuchsia On Royal Blue Ground, 3 3/4 In. 990.00

STIEGEL TYPE glass is listed here. It is almost impossible to be sure a piece was actually made by Stiegel, so the knowing collector refers to this glass as *Stiegel type*. Henry William Stiegel, a colorful immigrant to the colonies, started his first factory in Pennsylvania in 1763. He remained in business until 1774. Glassware was made in a style popular in Europe at that time and was similar to the glass of many other makers. It was made of clear or colored glass and was decorated with enamel colors, mold blown designs, or etching.

Bottle, Floral & Foliage, Pewter Cap, 7 In. 355.00
Bottle, Sapphire Blue, Multicolored Enamel Figure & Flowers, Pewter Mount, 6 In. 1650.00
Creamer, Sapphire Blue, Applied Handle, Foot, 4 In. 550.00
Flask, Daisy & Hexagon, Amethyst, Globular, Open Pontil, 5 x 4 In. 7475.00
Salt, Master, Sapphire Blue, Expanded Diamond Pattern, Footed, 3 x 2 1/2 In. 575.00
Salt, Master, Sapphire Blue, Fluted, 3 In. 220.00
Tumbler, Connected Hearts, Clasped Hands, Enamel, German Words, 1708, 3 1/2 In. 690.00
Tumbler, Flip, Cover With Finial, Engraved Basket, Flowers, 9 3/4 In. 1320.00
Tumbler, Flip, Fluted Base, Engraved Band, 6 In. 275.00

STONEWARE is a coarse, glazed, and fired potter's ceramic that is used to make crocks, jugs, bowls, etc. It is often decorated with cobalt blue decorations. In the nineteenth and early twentieth centuries, potters often decorated crocks with blue numbers indicating the size of the container. A "2" meant 2 gallons. Stoneware is still being made.

Bank, Cobalt Blue Foliage, Bird Finial, Parnude Dennis, 8 3/8 In. 880.00
Batter Jug, Bird, Frank B. Norton, Worcester 1980.00
Batter Jug, Blue Gray, Embossed Flowers, 5 1/2 In. 60.00
Batter Pail, Lid, Bale Handle, Tin Spout, Havana, c.1870, 8 In. 77.00
Beaker, 100th Anniversary, 1813-1913, Enameled, 1/4 Liter 88.00
Bottle, City Beer, Blue Accent At Name, W.W. Wright, 11 In. 100.00
Bottle, Pig, Tan, Gray Salt Glaze, 8 1/2 In. 467.00
Bottle, Root Beer, Durfee's Nicker-Bocker Root-Beer, Gray & Brown Salt Glaze, 10 In. .. 315.00
Bottle, Taft's Sugar Ale, Blue Accents At Name, Signed, 10 1/2 In. 275.00
Bowl, Blue & White Spatter, Ring, 13 x 6 1/2 In. 90.00
Bowl, Blue, 3 Applied Shoulder Handles, 8 x 5 1/2 In. 55.00
Bowl, Cobalt Blue Lines, 3 3/4 In. 165.00
Bowl, Cobalt Blue Stenciled Label, A.P. Donagho, 6 1/2 x 12 3/4 In. 308.00
Bowl, Dome Cover, Cobalt Blue Design, Rim Spout, 9 3/4 In. 740.00
Cake Pan, Angel Food, Brown Salt Glaze, 4 x 11 In. 45.00
Canister, Cover, Beans, Blue & White 258.00
Canister, Cover, Rice, Blue & White 258.00
Chamber Pot, Lid, Green Sponge, Wire Bail, Wooden Handle, 12 In. 95.00
Churn, Blue Quill Work, 3 Applied Shoulder Handles, Oval, 13 3/4 In. 80.00
Churn, Cobalt Blue 2 & Foliage, John Burger, 2 Gal. 275.00
Churn, Cobalt Blue Bird, New York Stoneware Co. Fort Edward, N.Y., Handles, 4 Gal. .. 550.00
Churn, Cobalt Blue Floral, Brown Albany Slip, Shoulder Handles, 3 In. 2310.00
Churn, Cobalt Blue Floral, Haxstun Ottman & Co., N.Y., Handles, 2 Gal. 355.00
Churn, Cobalt Blue Flower & 6, Replaced Lid & Dasher, Oval, 18 1/4 In. 110.00
Churn, Cobalt Blue Flower, Applied Shoulder Handles, 17 3/4 In. 220.00
Churn, Cobalt Blue Flower, Harrington & Burger, Rochester, Handles, 2 Gal. 415.00
Churn, Cobalt Blue Flower, Shoulder Handles, Wooden Lid, 19 In. 195.00
Churn, Cobalt Blue Flowers, 19th Century, 5 Gal. 460.00
Churn, Cobalt Blue Flowers, Lyons, Ear Handles, 1850, 2 Gal., 10 In. 190.00
Churn, Cobalt Blue Freehand Lettering, S.R. Glenn & Co., 6 Gal. 350.00
Churn, Cobalt Blue Quill & 3, Bubbly Glaze, Applied Shoulder Handles, 15 1/2 In. 110.00
Churn, Cobalt Blue Quill & 3, Replaced Wooden Lid & Rod, 14 In. 190.00
Churn, Cobalt Blue Stencil, Applied Handles, A.P. Donagho, W. Va., 17 1/2 In. 300.00
Churn, Cobalt Blue Stenciled Eagle, E Pluribus Unum, 4, 15 1/2 In. 220.00

Churn, Cobalt Blue Stenciled Eagle, Handle, Lid, Tan Salt Glaze, 3 Gal. 195.00
Churn, Cobalt Blue Tulips & 6, Ovoid, Shoulder Handles, 18 In. 220.00
Churn, Double Flower Top To Bottom, A.O. Wittemore, c.1870, 18 In., 6 Gal. 990.00
Churn, J. Lambright, Newport, Ohio, Double Ear Handles, 21 In. 1375.00
Churn, Lambright, 4 Gal. 475.00
Churn, Norton, Worcester, Mass., Blue Bird, 4 Gal. 1320.00
Crock, 3 Cobalt Blue Floral Bands, Handles, 3 Gal. 990.00
Crock, A.K. Ballard, 3 Gal. 295.00
Crock, Applied Handles, Blue Design, A.P. Donagho, 13 1/4 In. 375.00
Crock, Bird On Triple Flower, Roberts, c.1860, 13 1/2 In., 5 Gal. 550.00
Crock, Bird, F.T. Wright 445.00
Crock, Blue Bird, Signed Roberts, Binghampton, 3 Gal. 310.00
Crock, Blue Chicken Pecking Corn, Brady & Ryan, c.1885, 9 In., 2 Gal. 577.00
Crock, Blue Dotted Bird On Plume, Seymour & Bosworth, 1880, 8 1/2 In. 247.00
Crock, Blue Floral & 5, Frank B. Norton, Worcester, Mass., 12 1/4 In. 220.00
Crock, Blue Floral, G.S. Grey & Co., Fort Edward, N.Y., Applied Handles, 11 1/4 In. 80.00
Crock, Blue Flowers & 2, M. Woodruff, Cortland, Applied Handles, 10 In. 275.00
Crock, Blue, White Sponge, 11 x 6 In. 70.00
Crock, Bull's-Eye Floral Spray, O.L. & A.K. Ballard, c.1875, 9 In., 2 Gal. 120.00
Crock, Butter, Blue, White, Marked, Village Farm Dairy, 4 5/8 In. 330.00
Crock, Butter, Cover, 7 1/4 x 5 1/8 In. 385.00
Crock, Butter, Cover, Blue & White Floral, Wire Handle, 5 In. 80.00
Crock, Butter, Cover, Cobalt Blue Designs, 7 1/2 In. 30.00
Crock, Butter, Cover, Cobalt Blue Foliage, 10 In. 245.00
Crock, Butter, Cover, Cobalt Blue Tulips, Foliage, Handles, 10 In. 495.00
Crock, Butter, Shield Logo, Producers Creamery, Benton Harbor, Mich., 5 Lb. 195.00
Crock, Cake, Cobalt Blue Floral, 3 Gal. 330.00
Crock, Clover Blossom Cottage Cheese 38.00
Crock, Cobalt Blue 2 Over Flower, Handles, Connelly & Palmer, 2 Gal. 100.00
Crock, Cobalt Blue 2, Daubed Design, Applied Handles, 9 In. 110.00
Crock, Cobalt Blue 3, Applied Handles, 10 1/2 In. 135.00
Crock, Cobalt Blue Bird Perched On Branch, W. Roberts, Binghamton, N.Y., 2 Gal. 1300.00
Crock, Cobalt Blue Bird, Impressed 6, Tan & Gray Salt Glaze, Handles, 8 1/2 In. 300.00
Crock, Cobalt Blue Bird, New York Stoneware Co., Fort Edward, N.Y., 2 Handles, 2 Gal. . 110.00
Crock, Cobalt Blue Bird, Salt Glaze, Edinger & Caire, 11 In. 357.00
Crock, Cobalt Blue Bird, Seymour Bosworth, 9 3/4 In., 2 Gal. 330.00
Crock, Cobalt Blue Bird, West Troy Pottery, N.Y., Tan Salt Glaze, Handles, 2 Gal. 330.00
Crock, Cobalt Blue Chicken, Impressed 4, Tan Salt Glaze, Handles, 4 Gal. 150.00
Crock, Cobalt Blue Coggle Wheel Design, Dove, South Amboy, N.J., 1 Gal. 336.00
Crock, Cobalt Blue Design, A. Conrad, Shinnston, W.Va., 2 Gal. 95.00
Crock, Cobalt Blue Design, Ear Handles, 12 In., 4 Gal. 155.00
Crock, Cobalt Blue Dropped Target, Gray Salt Glaze, Handles, 4 Gal. 90.00
Crock, Cobalt Blue Dropped Target, Tan Salt Glaze, Handles, 10 1/2 In. 125.00
Crock, Cobalt Blue Floral & 2, New York Stoneware Co., 9 1/2 In. 165.00
Crock, Cobalt Blue Floral & 5, Applied Handles, 13 In. 110.00
Crock, Cobalt Blue Floral & 5, Shoulder Handles, 13 1/4 In. 110.00
Crock, Cobalt Blue Floral Design, Tan Salt Glaze, Edmands & Co., Handles, 3 Gal. 95.00
Crock, Cobalt Blue Floral, 6, Applied Handles, 13 1/2 In. 150.00
Crock, Cobalt Blue Floral, Applied Handle, 11 3/4 In. 165.00
Crock, Cobalt Blue Floral, Applied Handles, 9 In. 255.00
Crock, Cobalt Blue Floral, E. & L.P. Norton, Bennington, Vt., 2 Gal. 440.00
Crock, Cobalt Blue Flower & 2, Burger, Applied Handles, 9 In. 85.00
Crock, Cobalt Blue Flower, 4, Polka Dots, Handles, 12 1/4 In. 148.00
Crock, Cobalt Blue Flower, C.F. Worthen, Peabody, Mass., Handles, 3 Gal. 100.00
Crock, Cobalt Blue Flower, Ottman Bros. & Co., Fort Edward, N.Y., Handles, 4 Gal. 275.00
Crock, Cobalt Blue Flower, Stamped 2, 2 Gal. 66.00
Crock, Cobalt Blue Flower, Tan Salt Glaze, Handles, Impressed 3, 3 Gal. 90.00
Crock, Cobalt Blue Flowers & 6, Ribbed Strap Handle, 13 1/2 In. 110.00
Crock, Cobalt Blue Flowers, Applied Handles, 9 1/2 In. 165.00
Crock, Cobalt Blue Foliage, Applied Handles, 19 3/4 In. 110.00
Crock, Cobalt Blue Houseboat, A.O. Whittemore, Havana, N.Y., 3 Gal. 465.00
Crock, Cobalt Blue Ladybug, Hubbell & Chesebro, Geddes, N.Y., Handles, 3 Gal. 85.00
Crock, Cobalt Blue Leaf Design, Impressed 2, Brown & Tan Salt Glaze, Handles, 2 Gal. . 95.00

Crock, Cobalt Blue Leaves, F.B. Norton & Co., c.1870, 11 1/2 In. . . . . *Illus*   180.00
Crock, Cobalt Blue Lettering, Knights' Oregon Pickles, Portland, Or., Handles, 13 In. 265.00
Crock, Cobalt Blue Man In The Moon, Cowden & Wilcox, Blue Handle, 2 Gal. 3400.00
Crock, Cobalt Blue Parrot On Branch, 2, White's, Utica, Handles, 10 1/2 In. 385.00
Crock, Cobalt Blue Plumes, Morse & Bigelow, c.1870, 11 In. . . . . *Illus*   440.00
Crock, Cobalt Blue Quill Bird, Applied Handles, 7 1/2 In. 275.00
Crock, Cobalt Blue Quill Flower, Applied Handles, 13 In. 220.00
Crock, Cobalt Blue Quill Polka-Dot Bird, Flying, With Shield, Medallion, 12 In. 467.00
Crock, Cobalt Blue Quill Tulip, Foliage, Polka Dots, Handle, 5 In. 440.00
Crock, Cobalt Blue Squiggle Design, 4 Gal. 45.00
Crock, Cobalt Blue Stencil, Pure Apple Cider, Jones Bros. & Co. Inc., Handle, 18 In. 150.00
Crock, Cobalt Blue Target Design, Gray Glaze, F.T. Warren & Son, Taunton, Ma., 3 Gal. . .   110.00
Crock, Cobalt Blue Tulip Design, Gray Glaze, Handles, 4 3/4 In.   240.00
Crock, Cobalt Blue Tulip Design, Handle, Pa., 3 Gal. 275.00
Crock, Cobalt Blue Tulip, 1/2 Gal. 165.00
Crock, Cobalt Blue Tulip, Cowden & Wilcox, Applied Handles, 5 Gal. 990.00
Crock, Cobalt Blue Wreath, Burger & Lang, 2 Handles, c.1870, 14 In. . . . . *Illus*   632.00
Crock, Cobalt Line & Lettering, R.T. Williams, Gray Ground, 2 Gal. 90.00
Crock, Cover, Cobalt Floral, Incised Banding, Cowden & Wilcox, 12 In. 485.00
Crock, Crimped Rim, Mottled Glaze, S. Bell & Son, 9 In. 1540.00
Crock, Daisy & Trellis, 5 3/4 In. 100.00
Crock, Dark Cobalt Blue Bird On Branch, H.A. White & Son, Utica, N.Y., 4 Gal. 770.00
Crock, Dark Floral & Foliage, White & Wood, Handles, 5 Gal. 190.00
Crock, Double Bird Design, Ovoid, Holmes & Purdee, c.1850, 9 In., 1 Gal. 495.00
Crock, Electroplating Chemicals, Acids, Hanson & Van Winkle Co., 10 Gal. 200.00
Crock, Floral, 2, New York Stoneware Co., Fort Edwards, N.Y., Handles, 9 1/2 In. 165.00
Crock, Floral, J. & E. Norton, Bennington, Vermont, 4 Gal. 287.00
Crock, Floral, J. Remmey, c.1795, 8 3/4 In., 1 Gal. 3410.00
Crock, Flower John Stewart, Jr., Great Falls, N.H., 6 Gal. 440.00
Crock, Flower, P. Mugler & Co., c.1850, 3 Gal. 330.00
Crock, Gray, A.P. Donagho, Parkersburg, W.V., 19th Century, 11 1/2 In. 286.00
Crock, H.C. Ward, Stoneware Depot, Zanesville, Oh., Applied Handles, 16 1/2 In. 385.00
Crock, Impressed Letters, Dark Gray Brown, I. Thomas, 1850-1880, 8 3/8 In. 130.00
Crock, Incised Swan, Medford, McFeat & Swan Ship Grocers, c.1850, 7 1/2 In. 132.00
Crock, Jelly, C.W. Rodefer Co., Shadyside, Ohio, Cobalt Lettering, 1 Qt. 160.00
Crock, Overall Swag & Floral, Blue, 14 In. 245.00
Crock, Raised Letters, A.P. Donagho, Black Inside & Out, 2 Gal., 12 In. 175.00
Crock, Salt Glaze, Blue, J.H. Dipple, Lewistown, 4 Gal. 515.00
Crock, Salt Glaze, Dark Gray Brown, Cooper & Power, Maysville, Ky., 8 In. 100.00
Crock, Salt Glaze, Impressed Letters, 1, Dark Gray, I. Thomas, 10 In. 130.00
Crock, Salt Glaze, Stenciled, W.M. Albert, Bardolph, Ill., 5 Gal.   2250.00
Crock, Standing Dog Amid Ground Cover, West Troy Pottery, c.1880, 5 Gal. 2750.00
Crock, Stenciled & Freehand Label, Thomas Medford, Queensware, 6 3/4 In. 440.00
Crock, Stenciled Leaf, E. & L.P. Norton, Bennington, Vt., Ear Handles, 1865, 7 In. 70.00

Stoneware, Crock, Cobalt Blue Leaves,
F.B. Norton & Co., c.1870, 11 1/2 In.

Stoneware, Crock, Cobalt Blue Plumes,
Morse & Bigelow, c.1870, 11 In.

If you have an alarm system, set it each
time you leave the house, not just at
night. Most home burglaries occur
during the day or early evening.

Stoneware, Crock, Cobalt Blue
Wreath, Burger & Lang,
2 Handles, c.1870, 14 In.

Crock, Stenciled Name, Stripes, Coyers Knotts, Ovoid, c.1880, 8 In., 1 Gal. 198.00
Crock, Stenciled Tiger, F.F. Wright & Son, 4 Gal. 445.00
Crock, Thick Blue Bird, Stylized 3, c.1877, 10 1/2 In., 3 Gal. 577.00
Crock, Tulips, Leaves & Flourishes, Ear Handles, 1 Gal. 675.00
Crock, Western Butter, Sam Lerner & Son Dairy, Chicago, Ill., 10 Lb. 225.00
Cuspidor, Cobalt Blue Floral, 7 1/2 x 3 1/2 In. 400.00
Ewer, Incised Floral, Birds, Pewter Lid, 10 3/4 In. 77.00
Figurine, Cupid With Arrow, Salt Glaze, Blue Stripes, Erwin Frey, 1938, 10 1/2 In. 495.00
Figurine, Rabbit, Cobalt Blue, 4 3/4 In. 190.00
Figurine, Robin, Nicodemus, 4 1/2 In. 140.00
Flask, Cobalt Blue Design, Salt Glaze, Remmey, New York, 1789, 6 In. 12650.00
Flowerpot, Attached Saucer, Cobalt Sponge, Gray, Ovoid 250.00
Flowerpot, Cobalt Blue Design, Red Clay, 7 3/4 In. 135.00
Flowerpot, Cream Glaze, 5 In. 30.00
Inkwell, Incised Blue Floral Designs, 4 1/2 In. 1430.00
Jar, Bird On Leaf, Cobalt Blue Slip, Impressed 4, Applied Shoulder Handles, 14 In. 330.00
Jar, Blue 3, Hamilton & Jones, Greensboro, Pa., Applied Shoulder Handles, 14 3/4 In. ... 220.00
Jar, Blue Floral & 4, Hamilton, Greensboro, Pa., Applied Shoulder Handles, 15 In. 550.00
Jar, Blue Highlights, James Green & Co., Worcester, Mass., 3 3/4 In. 275.00
Jar, Blue, White Sponge, 4 1/4 In. 780.00
Jar, Blue-Gray Floral, Shoulder Handles, 11 1/2 In. 220.00
Jar, Blue-Gray Flower, Amber Highlights, 5 In. 275.00
Jar, Canning, Blue Flower, Penn Yan, c.1860, 9 1/2 In., 1 Gal. 195.00
Jar, Canning, Cobalt Blue Bands, Tulip, 6 7/8 In. 632.00
Jar, Canning, Cobalt Blue Eagle, A.P. Donagho, 9 1/2 In. 935.00
Jar, Canning, Cobalt Blue Floral, 9 In. 80.00
Jar, Canning, Cobalt Blue Floral, Strap Handle, 14 In. 110.00
Jar, Canning, Cobalt Blue Flowers, Stripes, 10 In. 440.00
Jar, Canning, Cobalt Blue Foliage, 9 1/2 In. 140.00
Jar, Canning, Cobalt Blue Freehand Stencil, Hamilton & Co., 10 In. 165.00
Jar, Canning, Cobalt Blue Stencil, D.W. Rhodes, West Virginia, 10 1/4 In. 412.00
Jar, Canning, Cobalt Blue Stencil, Jacob Roemer, Dry Goods, 8 3/4 In. 412.00
Jar, Canning, Cobalt Blue Stenciled Apple, Leaf, 7 In. 740.00
Jar, Canning, Cobalt Blue Stenciled Peaches, 8 In. 330.00
Jar, Canning, Cobalt Blue Stenciled Pears, 8 3/8 In. 797.00
Jar, Canning, Cover, Cobalt Blue Stenciled Cherries, 6 5/8 In. 220.00
Jar, Canning, Curlicue Design, O.L. & A.K. Ballard, c.1880, 12 1/2 In., 3 Gal. 143.00
Jar, Canning, Gray Salt Glaze, Frerly & Bro., Strasburg, Va., Impressed Label 55.00
Jar, Canning, Stenciled Handshake, Friendship, Somerset Potters, c.1880, 14 1/2 In. 412.00
Jar, Canning, Tin Hinged Lid, Cobalt Blue Stenciled Eagle, 6 1/8 In. 770.00
Jar, Cheap, Cash, Grocery, 5, John R. Rottinghams, Portsmouth, Ohio, 15 3/4 In. 1375.00
Jar, Cobalt Blue 10, Donagho Co., Parkersburg, Applied Shoulder Handles, 19 1/2 In. ... 110.00
Jar, Cobalt Blue Band, White Salt Glaze, Dodson & Braun's Fine Pickles, 14 In. 150.00
Jar, Cobalt Blue Brushed Star, Oval, Bennett & Chollar, Shoulder Handles, 8 In. 412.00
Jar, Cobalt Blue Design, A.P. Donagho, Shoulder Handles, 16 3/4 In. 220.00
Jar, Cobalt Blue Design, Applied Shoulder Handles, 12 1/2 In. 135.00
Jar, Cobalt Blue Design, Ear Handles, 9 1/2 x 10 In. 385.00
Jar, Cobalt Blue Design, Peoria Pottery, Salt Glaze, 3 Gal. 545.00

Jar, Cobalt Blue Floral & 3, Applied Handle, 16 In. 245.00
Jar, Cobalt Blue Floral & 12, James Hamilton, 21 1/2 In. 990.00
Jar, Cobalt Blue Floral, Bulbous, Handle, 9 1/2 x 10 In. 385.00
Jar, Cobalt Blue Floral, Nichols & Boynton, Burlington, Vt. 2, 10 1/2 In. 330.00
Jar, Cobalt Blue Flower & 2, L. Eberhardt, Shoulder Handles, 13 In. 357.00
Jar, Cobalt Blue Flower Band, Salt Glaze, Molded Shoulder, 2 1/2 Gal. 325.00
Jar, Cobalt Blue Flower, 4, Applied Handles, 15 3/4 In. 330.00
Jar, Cobalt Blue Flower, 10 1/2 In. 137.00
Jar, Cobalt Blue Flower, Cowden & Wilcox Harrisburg, Pa., Oval, 1 1/2 Gal. 110.00
Jar, Cobalt Blue Flower, J. Fisher & Co., Lyons, N.Y., Applied Handle, 16 In. 220.00
Jar, Cobalt Blue Flower, L. Eberhardt, 2 Gal. 357.00
Jar, Cobalt Blue Flowers, 1/2 Gal. 145.00
Jar, Cobalt Blue Freehand & Stencil, Williams & Reppert, Greensboro, Pa., 14 In. 250.00
Jar, Cobalt Blue Fruit & 2, L. Norton & Son, Bennington, Oval, 10 3/4 In. 220.00
Jar, Cobalt Blue Lettering, Brown & Gray, A.P. Donagho, Parkersburg, W.V., 8 In. 55.00
Jar, Cobalt Blue Polka Dots, Applied Handles, 11 1/4 In. 412.00
Jar, Cobalt Blue Stencil & 2, F.H. Cowden, Harrisburg, Oval, 10 In. 205.00
Jar, Cobalt Blue Stencil, Hamilton & Jones, Greensboro, Pa., 8 1/2 In. 190.00
Jar, Cover, Cabbage Style Flower, N. Clark & Co., c.1850, 12 In., 2 Gal. 797.00
Jar, Cover, Embossed Design, Sichel's Mixture Tobacco, 7 1/2 In.   415.00
Jar, Domed Cover, Cobalt Blue Flowers, Polka Dots, 8 1/2 In. 1210.00
Jar, Graham & Stone, General Merchandise, 11 3/4 In., 2 Gal. 275.00
Jar, Gray Stencil, Hamilton & Jones, Greensboro, Pa., 9 1/2 In. 165.00
Jar, Hamilton & Jones, 14 In., 3 Gal. 1295.00
Jar, Lid, Oval, I.M. Mead, Blue At Label & Handles, 15 1/2 In. 55.00
Jar, Ribbed Design, France, 1880, 29 In. 484.00
Jar, Ribbed Design, France, 1880, 33 1/2 In. . . . . .363.00 to 545.00
Jar, Ribbed Design, France, 1880, 39 In. 514.00
Jar, Shoulder Handles, 3, I.M. Mead, Cobalt Blue At Handles & Label, 13 In. 138.00
Jar, Shoulder Handles, Impressed 3, J. Bennage, 188-, 13 1/2 In. 110.00
Jar, Stencil, H.P. Behrens, 2 Gal. 143.00
Jar, Stenciled & Freehand Design, Knox, Haught, Shoulder Handles, 12 3/4 In. 1017.00
Jar, Stylized Leaf Design, Edmands & Co., c.1870, 15 In., 4 Gal. 110.00
Jar, Tan Paint, Brown Sponge, Incised Flower & 2, Oval, 11 3/4 In. 245.00
Jar, Wine, Ocher Glaze, Spout, Handle, France, 15 In. 242.00
Jar, Yellow Glaze, Brown Dot Bands, 3 Squiggle, Swag 385.00
Jug, Bird On Branch, Blue Slip, Cowden & Wilcox, 15 1/2 In. 3025.00
Jug, Bird, Hart, 2 Gal. 850.00
Jug, Blue Accents, I. Seymour, 1 Gal. 44.00
Jug, Blue Basket Of Flowers, Satterlee & Morey, c.1865, 17 1/2 In., 4 Gal. 1760.00
Jug, Blue Bird, F.B. Norton, Worcester, Ma., 1 Gal. 625.00
Jug, Blue Design, Biedinger Caire, 2 Gal. 165.00
Jug, Blue Design, I.M. Mead & Co., Ortage Co., Ohio, Oval, Blue Handle, 15 In. 165.00
Jug, Blue Floral & Leaf Design, Cowden & Wilcox, 13 In. 330.00
Jug, Blue Floral Design, Strap Handle, 11 In. 137.00
Jug, Blue Flower Design, S. Blair, Oval, c.1830, 13 In., 2 Gal. 175.00
Jug, Blue Flowers, Norton & Fenton, Bennington, Vt., Strap Handle, Oval, 13 In. 330.00
Jug, Blue Leaf & Vine Top To Bottom, Carved Wooden Stopper, c.1870, 15 In. 220.00
Jug, Blue Male Profile Amid Vines, Jordan, c.1850, 12 In., 1 Gal.   1320.00
Jug, Blue Man In The Moon, Cowden & Wilcox, 15 In. 2640.00
Jug, Blue Quill Work, Frank B. Norton, Worcester, Mass., Strap Handle, 14 In. 300.00
Jug, Blue Script, S.F. Eagan, J. Fisher, c.1880, 10 1/2 In., 1 Gal. 132.00
Jug, Blue Transfer, Shaker Brand Ketchup, E.D. Pettengill Co., 14 In. 880.00
Jug, Blue Tree Design, I. Seymour, Oval, c.1810, 4 Gal. 715.00
Jug, Blue, Salt Glaze, 19th Century, 9 1/4 In. 145.00
Jug, Blue, White Sponge, 3 1/4 In. 1045.00
Jug, Brown Albany Slip, Scratch, J.E. Wallace Co., 8th Ave., Altoona, Pa., 3 1/8 In. 130.00
Jug, Brown Glaze, 2 Circles, Germany, 17th Century, 14 In. 450.00
Jug, Cobalt Blue 2, Scalloped, Conical Spout, Filler Hole, Applied Handle, 8 1/2 In. 305.00
Jug, Cobalt Blue 3, H.C. Smith, Alexa, D.C., 15 3/4 In. 2530.00
Jug, Cobalt Blue Design & 3, Oval, 15 1/2 In. 190.00
Jug, Cobalt Blue Design, Impressed N.B. Pearse & 3, Oval, Handle, 17 In. 240.00
Jug, Cobalt Blue Design, Strap Handle, 11 1/4 In. 190.00

Jug, Cobalt Blue Design, Strap Handle, 14 1/2 In. 110.00
Jug, Cobalt Blue Design, Strap Handle, 1877, 8 3/8 In. 440.00
Jug, Cobalt Blue Design, Strap Handle, C. Kamper's Sons, Buffalo, N.Y., 10 In. 110.00
Jug, Cobalt Blue Design, Strap Handle, Impressed Label, Chelsea 2, 14 In. 160.00
Jug, Cobalt Blue Floral & 2, Cowden & Wilcox, Strap Handle, 13 3/8 In. 220.00
Jug, Cobalt Blue Floral & 2, F.B. Norton & Co., Worcester, Mass., Strap Handle, 14 In. ... 275.00
Jug, Cobalt Blue Floral Design, L. Norton & Co., Bennington, Oval, 13 In. 330.00
Jug, Cobalt Blue Floral Design, Strap Handle, Impressed 2, 13 1/2 In. 160.00
Jug, Cobalt Blue Floral Spray, Salt Glaze, 19th Century, 13 In. 210.00
Jug, Cobalt Blue Floral Sunburst, Cowden & Wilcox, Harrisburg, Pa., 3 Gal. 5050.00
Jug, Cobalt Blue Floral, Cowden & Wilcox, No Handle, 4 Gal. 135.00
Jug, Cobalt Blue Floral, Fort Edward Pottery Co., Strap Handle, 15 In. 475.00
Jug, Cobalt Blue Floral, Gray Ground, T. Harrington, 15 In. 270.00
Jug, Cobalt Blue Floral, Hastings & Belding, Ashfield, Mass., Strap Handle, 11 In. 220.00
Jug, Cobalt Blue Floral, S. Risley, Norwich, Strap Handle, 13 3/4 In. 220.00
Jug, Cobalt Blue Floral, Strap Handle, 13 1/4 In. 632.00
Jug, Cobalt Blue Floral, Tan Glaze, New York Stoneware Co., Handles, 1 1/2 Gal. 110.00
Jug, Cobalt Blue Flower & 2, Strap Handle, Oval, 15 3/4 In. 275.00
Jug, Cobalt Blue Flower, 1 Gal. 130.00
Jug, Cobalt Blue Flower, E & L.P. Norton, Bennington, Vt., Handles, 10 3/4 In. 85.00
Jug, Cobalt Blue Flower, Gray Glaze, Impressed White's Utica, 2 Gal. 110.00
Jug, Cobalt Blue Flower, Impressed Albany, N.Y., Strap Handle, 13 In. 250.00
Jug, Cobalt Blue Flower, Strap Handle, 12 3/4 In. 550.00
Jug, Cobalt Blue Flower, Strap Handle, 15 1/2 In. 80.00
Jug, Cobalt Blue Flower, Strap Handle, Oval, 11 1/2 In. 100.00
Jug, Cobalt Blue Flowering Plant & 5, White's Utica, Double Ear Handles, 17 1/2 In. 2090.00
Jug, Cobalt Blue Leafy Scroll, Strap Handle, 11 1/2 In. 100.00
Jug, Cobalt Blue Lettering, Jos. Hirschfield & Son, Long Branch, N.J., 2 Gal. 300.00
Jug, Cobalt Blue Lettering, Tan Glaze, Est. D. McAteer Patterson N.J., 1 Gal. 300.00
Jug, Cobalt Blue Lion, Salt Glaze, 14 1/2 In., Pair 3450.00
Jug, Cobalt Blue Quill Work, Feathery Foliage, Edmands & Co., Strap Handle, 2, 14 In. ... 250.00
Jug, Cobalt Blue Quill Work, Strap Handle, 13 1/2 In. 105.00
Jug, Cobalt Blue Quill, Strap Handle, 17 1/2 In. 135.00
Jug, Cobalt Blue Scroll & Flowers, Oval, 19th Century, 13 In. 245.00
Jug, Cobalt Blue Tulip & Leaves, 16 In., 3 Gal. 165.00
Jug, Cobalt Blue, Incised Scallop Design, Gray, Salt Glaze, 1790-1820, 14 1/2 In. 800.00
Jug, Cobalt Blue, N. White, Utica, Strap Handle, 3, Oval, 15 1/2 In. 960.00
Jug, Cobalt Blue, N. White, Utica, Strap Handle, Oval, 13 1/2 In. 335.00
Jug, Con Keefe, 8 & 10, Cambridge, Boston, Mass., Strap Handle, 4 3/4 In. 110.00
Jug, Cream, Brown, Compliments Of The Keystone Grocery, Colorado Springs, 3 In. 415.00
Jug, Cushman & Co., Importers Of Wines, Haxstun & Co., c.1880, 15 1/2 In., 3 Gal. 385.00
Jug, Dark Blue Design, Gray, A.B. Taft & Co., 1 Gal. 235.00
Jug, Deodorizer, Pullman Company, Cobalt Blue, 9 In., 1/2 Gal. 40.00
Jug, Double Flower Design, Squat Form, Riedinger & Caire, c.1870, 14 In., 3 Gal. 143.00
Jug, Double Flower Sprig, Wines & Liquors, Teron Johnstone, 15 In., 3 Gal. 240.00
Jug, F.H. Weeks, Akron, Oh., Wire Bale, Wooden Handle, 8 In. 1375.00
Jug, Face, Applied Stone Teeth, Down-Turned Horns, Lanier Meaders, 10 3/4 In. 2530.00
Jug, Floral, J. Shepard Jr., Geddes, N.Y., Strap Handle, 15 3/4 In. 355.00
Jug, Flowers, Double Snake Design, H. & G. Nash, c.1835, 11 In., 1 Gal. 1100.00
Jug, Franke S. Harvey, Cooperative Pottery Co., c.1880, 11 In., 1 Gal. 185.00
Jug, Impressed Letters, Dark Brown Glaze, E. Lambden, New Rochelle, N.Y., 6 1/4 In. ... 55.00
Jug, Incised Blue Bird Design, R.W. Weaver, c.1810, 4 Gal. 2415.00
Jug, Incised Blue Flower, P. Cross, c.1805, 16 In., 2 Gal. 990.00
Jug, Incised Cobalt Blue Bird, Salt Glaze, Pulled Handle, 16 In. 2070.00
Jug, Incised Man & Flower, L. Norton, Bennington, 16 In. 4888.00
Jug, Leaf Design, Cobalt Blue Polka Dots, Quill Work, 11 In. 115.00
Jug, Light Gray, Cobalt Transfer, City Wine Store, Montpelier, Vermont, 3 7/8 In. 230.00
Jug, N & A Seymour, c.1840, 9 In. 475.00
Jug, Ocher Glaze, 2 Handles, c.1895, 11 1/4 In. 151.00
Jug, Ocher Glaze, 2 Handles, c.1895, 12 1/4 In. 151.00
Jug, Ocher Glaze, 2 Handles, c.1895, 13 1/2 In. 180.00
Jug, Ocher Glaze, 2 Handles, c.1895, 14 In. 266.00
Jug, Ocher Glaze, 2 Handles, France, 1895, 8 3/4 In. 121.00

Jug, Peacock Design, J. & E. Norton, 4 Gal. 9750.00
Jug, Pewter Lid, Cobalt Blue Glaze, Inscribed CG 1754, 8 In. 495.00
Jug, Ribbed & Dotted Flower, E. Selby & Co., c.1850, 2 Gal. 275.00
Jug, Tooled Neck, Gray Salt Glaze, Charlestown, Strap Handle, 10 1/4 In. 220.00
Jug, Variegated Glaze, Handle, 19th Century, 9 1/2 In. 143.00
Jug, Whiskey, Tan, Brown, Compliments Of The Klondyke, W. Weingarth, 5 3/8 In. 200.00
Jug, Woman & Flowers, Rope Twist Handle, 2 Spouts, 11 1/2 In. 357.00
Muff Warmer, Queen's Screw Cap, England, 5 1/2 In. 165.00
Muff Warmer, Tan, Brown Glaze, Bourne Denby, Screw Top, England, 2 1/4 In. 85.00
Mug, Cobalt Blue Band At Base & Rim, Floral Design Center, White Glaze, 4 1/2 In. 100.00
Mug, Gezsundeit Beer, Black Pictorial Transfer 43.00
Pedestal, Stump Form, Branches, Leaves & Birds, Blue & White, 19 1/2 In. 1073.00
Pie Rack, Arched Handle, Pierced Platform, Hanson & Van Winkle, 9 x 11 In. 515.00
Pitcher, Avenue Of Trees, Blue, White, 8 In. 265.00
Pitcher, Blue, White Sponge, 7 3/8 In. 110.00
Pitcher, Brown Slip Interior, Handle, 6 In. 330.00
Pitcher, Brushed Floral, Cobalt Blue, 16 In. 495.00
Pitcher, Bulbous, Cowden, Pinched Spout, 2 Gal. 110.00
Pitcher, Cabin, Teepee, Gray, White, Blue, 3 In. 300.00
Pitcher, Cobalt Blue & White, Windmill, 8 1/4 In. 40.00
Pitcher, Cobalt Blue Design, 10 1/2 In., 1 Gal. 1200.00
Pitcher, Cobalt Blue Floral Design, Strap Handle, 13 1/4 In. 880.00
Pitcher, Cobalt Blue Floral, Remmy, Strap Handle, 8 7/8 In. 300.00
Pitcher, Cobalt Blue Leaf Design & No. 2, Strap Handle, 13 In. 170.00
Pitcher, Colonial Man, Woman, Child, Man Drinking, 9 1/4 In. 225.00
Pitcher, Cow, Blue, White, 7 1/4 In. 435.00
Pitcher, Cow, Green, 7 1/2 In. 270.00
Pitcher, Dutch Boy & Girl, Blue, White, 7 In. 135.00
Pitcher, Dutch Children, Windmill, Blue & White, 7 In. 180.00
Pitcher, Embossed Sheep On Both Sides, 10 1/2 In. 350.00
Pitcher, Flatiron Building, 7 In. 175.00
Pitcher, Fox Hunt Scene, Verse, Peter Gertz Factory, c.1880, 9 In. 175.00
Pitcher, Incised Cobalt Blue Floral, Westerwald, 8 In. 110.00
Pitcher, Indian Boy & Girl, Blue, White, 8 In. 320.00
Pitcher, Indian Head Medallion, Blue, White, 2 7/8 In. 110.00
Pitcher, Man's Bust, Molded Roses, Blue & White, 8 In. 135.00
Pitcher, Molded Dog's Head, Man, Woman, Blue, White, German Inscription, 11 In. 220.00
Pitcher, Molded Rose, 9 In. 495.00
Pitcher, Old Man With Beard, Molded Leaves, Blue & White, 8 In. 135.00
Pitcher, Stag & Pine Trees, Blue & Tan, 8 1/4 In. 200.00
Pitcher, Windmill, Blue On Raised Portion, 7 1/2 In. 22.00
Rolling Pin, Blue Stripes, Parret & Co., Normal, Illinois 150.00
Sugar, Cobalt Freehand Lettering, Bristol Glaze, Mrs. J.R. Fulkerson, Jerseyville, Ill. 725.00
Tankard, Incised Cobalt Diamond, Pewter Lid, Westerwald, 1 Liter 27.00
Tenderizer, 1877, 9 In. 110.00
Vase, Circular Panel Form, Brown & Buff Glaze, Daniel Rhodes, 7 1/4 In. 230.00
Vase, Mulberry & White, Wandering Scholar, Japanese, c.1870, 13 In. 270.00
Vessel, Abstract Rectangular Shape, Buff, Tan, Daniel Rhodes, 9 1/2 x 15 1/4 In. 635.00
Water Cooler, Barrel Form, Incised Winged Eagle, Shield Body, E. White, 1841, 20 In. ... 4400.00
Water Cooler, Barrel-Form, Inscribed E. White, July 20th AD 1841, Pennsylvania 4000.00
Water Cooler, Blue Sponge 3, Lid, 10 1/2 In. 110.00
Water Cooler, Brick & Flower Design, Spigot, Bristol Glaze, 11 In. 357.00
Water Cooler, Cobalt Blue Embossed Leaf, Sponge, Monmouth Filter, 16 In. 145.00
Water Cooler, Cobalt Blue Incised Floral, N. Clark & Co., Lyons, Oval, 14 In. 825.00
Water Cooler, Cobalt Blue, Grape & Foliate, Footed, 18 1/2 In. 862.00
Water Cooler, Cover, Flying Bird & Flower, Blue At Bunghole, Charlestown, c.1850, 5 Gal. 715.00
Water Cooler, Incised & Cobalt Design, c.1860 .... 2800.00

STORE fixtures, cases, cutters, and other items that have no advertising
as part of the decoration are listed here. Most items found in an old
store are listed in the Advertising category in this book.

Bag Sorter, Poplar, Black Stencil, Red Trim, 16 In. 550.00
Bin, Bolt, Revolving, Pine, 32 Wedge-Shaped Drawers, Refinished, 32 x 22 In. 440.00

Cabinet, Hardware, Revolving, 8 Sides, 77 Drawers, Porcelain Knobs, 1920s, 36 x 21 In. . 1900.00
Cabinet, Hardware, Rotating, 80 Drawers 1700.00
Cabinet, Ribbon Display, Oak, 4 Glass Swing-Down Doors, A.N. Russell & Sons, 28 In. . 275.00
Case, Display, Cigar Store, Oak, Glass, Sliding Vent, Oak Doors, 50 x 96 In. 1000.00
Cigar Cutter, Hoar's Tusk 245.00
Coffee Grinders are listed in their own category.
Counter, Seed, 8 Ft. 1900.00
Display, Ice Cream Cone, Papier-Mache, 1920-1930, 18 In. 490.00
Display, Stand, Marble, Revolving, 1960-1970, 16 x 11 In. 185.00
Dolly, R.A. Merrow Inventor & Patentee, Railroad Track Wheels, Repainted, 11 x 24 In. . 135.00
Foot Locker, 2 Tiers, 9 Sections, 3 Ft. x 2 Ft. x 20 In. 1150.00
Head, Milliner's Model, Black, Wadleigh's Fashionable Millinary & Cap Rooms 750.00
Holder, Ice Cream Cone, Jar, Glass, Metal Lid, 14 1/4 In. 465.00
Humidor, Calamander, Ivory Mounted, Inset Compass On Top, 9 1/4 In. 1150.00
Mailbox, From Santa Claus, Indiana, 1950s 325.00
Mannequin, Man, 1850, Life Size 2400.00
Mannequin, Man, Wearing Fireman's Outfit & Hat, Liberty J.C.W., 80-In. Hat 415.00
Salesman's Sample, Colorings, Flavors, Perfumes, 30 Vials, Brown Co., Elmira, N.Y. 110.00
Salesman's Sample, Oil Kit, 18 Vials, Solar Products Co., Cleveland 125.00
Sign, Boot Shape, Wooden, Tin Weather Cap, Gold Repaint, Ohio, 1857, 27 3/4 In. 2200.00
Sign, Penknife Shape, Wood Carved, Silver Leaf Traces On Blade, 33 x 22 In. 2090.00
Spice Chest, Grange Store, 8 Drawers, Stenciled Titles, 19th Century, 18 In. 315.00
Stand, Blu-J Brooms, Country Store, Tin Lithograph Both Sides, 16 Brooms, 34 x 23 In. . 260.00
Strawholder, Glass, 3 Pointed Ribs, Surround Holder, 12 3/4 x 4 1/2 In. 440.00
Strawholder, Glass, Colonial Open Petal, Contains Paper Straws, 9 1/2 x 5 1/4 In. 175.00
Strawholder, Glass, Metal Lid, Florence, 1916, 12 x 3 1/2 In. 355.00
Tobacco Cutter, Chip-Carved Wooden Base, Iron Horse-Shaped Blade, 14 In. 220.00

STOVES have been used in America for heating since the eighteenth century and for cooking since the nineteenth century. Most types of wood, coal, gas, kerosene, and even some electric stoves are collected.

Brazier, Wrought Iron, Turned Wooden Handle, 9 x 10 In. 220.00
Camp, Wood & Iron, 18th Century 138.00
Cook, Alcazar, 4 Burners, Gas, Tan 250.00
Cook, Bellaire Stove Co., Bellaire, O. Scout No. 8, Cast Iron, 22 In. 55.00
Cook, Chambers, Flamingo Red, 1948 .... 5000.00
Cook, Copper Clad, Black & White, Warmer & Water Jacket, 1930s 650.00
Cook, Crescent, With Accessories 30.00
Cook, Detroit Jewel, White, 4 Burners, Gas 250.00
Cook, Green & Black Enamel, 4 Brass Burners, 44 x 48 x 18 In. 165.00
Cook, Home Comfort Kitchen, Wood Burning, White Porcelain 375.00
Cook, Magic Chef, Cream Colored Porcelain, 4 Burners 1700.00
Cook, Painted Putti, Birds & Foliage, Urn Finial, F. Kuppersbusch, 51 In. 1610.00
Cook, Quickmeal, Speckled Enamel 2000.00
Cook, Universal Electric, 1930s 450.00
Counter, Seed & Bean, Oak, 28 Drawers, Walker, 6 Ft. 900.00
Heating, Kerosene, Ivanhoe No. 110, Graniteware, Black & Gray Canister 11.00
Heating, Parlor, Figural, Woman, Cast Iron, 19th Century 8750.00
Heating, Pine Grove Furnace, Michael Ege, Ironmaster, Plate, Iron, 29 x 22 In. 452.00
Railroad Station, Agent, No. 22, Ring Around Center To Rest Feet, 49 In. 600.00

SULPHIDES are cameos of unglazed white porcelain encased in transparent glass. The technique was patented in 1819 in France and has been used ever since for paperweights, decanters, tumblers, marbles, and other type of glassware. Paperweights and marbles are listed in their own categories.

Decanter, White Putti, Cut Glass, Stepped Shoulder, Fluted Base, Stopper, 10 1/2 In. 145.00

SUMIDA, or Sumida Gawa, is a Japanese pottery. The pieces collected by that name today were made about 1895 to 1970. There has been much confusion about the name of this ware, and it is often called *Korean Pottery*. Most pieces have a very heavy orange-red, blue, or green glaze, with raised three-dimensional figures as decorations.

Coffee Set, 3-Dimensional Elephant, 6 Piece 330.00

Pitcher, Monkeys, Blue Jar Form, Signed, 12 1/4 In. 630.00
Teapot, Applied Male Figure & House, Squat Compressed Form, c.1920, 5 1/2 In. 250.00
Teapot, Applied Sea Dragon, Wicker Handle, Squat Compressed Form, c.1920, 7 1/2 In. . 400.00
Teapot, Lions 700.00
Vase, Inlaid Mother-Of-Pearl, Black Lacquer, 11 In. 85.00
Vase, Lotus Blossom Form, Japanese Gentleman, c.1920, 7 In. 300.00
Vase, Man & Dog, 9 3/4 In. 270.00

SUNBONNET BABIES were first introduced in 1900 in the book *The Sunbonnet Babies*. The stories were by Eulalie Osgood Grover, illustrated by Bertha Corbett. The children's faces were completely hidden by the sunbonnets. The children had been pictured in black and white before this time, but the color pictures in the book were immediately successful. The Royal Bayreuth China Company made a full line of children's dishes decorated with the Sunbonnet Babies. Some Sunbonnet Babies plates have been reproduced, but are clearly marked.

Book, Grover, 1905 .... 125.00
Book, Sunbonnet Babies In Holland, Rand McNally, 1929 .... 37.00
Candlestick, Ironing 295.00
Hair Receiver, Sewing, 3-Footed 550.00
Pitcher, Sweeping 175.00
Plate, Fishing, 7 In. 189.00
Plate, Monday, Washing 70.00
Plate, Sweeping, 6 In. 345.00
Seashell, Painted, Says Pan American, 1901 .... 40.00
Tea Set, Different Scene Each Piece, Child's 675.00
Tray, Tin Lithograph 95.00
Vase, Girl With Doll, 4 In. 475.00

SUNDERLAND luster is a name given to a special type of pink luster made by Leeds, Newcastle, and other English firms during the nineteenth century. The luster glaze is metallic and glossy and appears to have bubbles in it. Other pieces of luster are listed in the Luster category.

Bowl, Ship Caroline, Black Transfer, 10 5/8 In. 305.00
Creamer, Cover, Cow, Pink Luster, Red, Green Enamel, 5 In. 490.00
Creamer, Luster, Black Mariner's Compass Transfer, 4 3/8 In. 160.00
Jug, Pink Luster, Lifesaving, 10 In. 1595.00
Jug, Puzzle, House & Landscape Design, England, 1820, 6 1/2 In. 290.00
Pitcher, Polychrome Enamel Ship, Maiden & Seaman, Verses, 7 1/8 In. 785.00
Plaque, Locomotive, Luster, Frame, 9 3/4 x 7 3/4 In. 250.00
Plaque, Ship, May Peace & Plenty On Our Nation Smile, Frame, 7 x 8 1/2 In. 201.00

SUPERMAN was created by two seventeen-year-olds in 1938. The first issue of *Action* comics had the strip. Superman remains popular and became the hero of a radio show in 1940, cartoons in the 1940s, a television series, and several major movies.

Book, The Adventures Of Superman, George Lowther, 1942, 9 1/2 x 6 In. 192.00
Cookie Jar, Warner Brothers, Box 75.00
Costume, Cape, Pants, Shirt, Ben Cooper, Box, Size 12-14 .... 260.00
Figure, Flicker Ring, Ideal 225.00
Figure, Wood, Jointed, Red, Blue, Cape, Ideal Novelty Co., 1940s, 12 1/2 In. 275.00
Game, Superman II, Milton Bradley, Box, 1981 .... 20.00
Game, Superman III, Parker Bros., 1982 .... 20.00
Gun, Squirt, 1950s 140.00
Hairbrush, Figural, Avon, Blue Plastic, Nylon Bristles, Box, 8 1/2 In. 28.00
Lunch Box, Christopher Reeve, Aladdin, 1978 .... 50.00
Lunch Box, Plastic, 1986 .... 20.00
Mug, Rumph, 1978 .... 125.00
Radio 120.00
Record Player, Graphics 165.00
Ring, Crusader, 1940s 192.00
Ring, Good Luck, Tin 1980.00

Ring, Prize, 1940s 7150.00
Ring, Secret Compartment, 1940 .... 1100.00
Toy, Lifts Tank, Tin Lithograph, Battery Operated, Linemar, Japan, 1959, 11 In. 1495.00
Toy, Super Powers, On Card, 1983 .... 35.00
Toy, Tank, Rollover, Windup, Chrome, Tin Lithograph, Marx, 1940, 4 In. 415.00
Toy, Tank, Superman Lifts Tank, Windup, Tin, Linemar, 4 In. 357.00
Van, Die Cast, Silver Paint, Corgi Junior, On Card, 1976, 2 1/2 In. 20.00
Wallet, 1966 ....40.00 to 45.00
Wallet, Brown Leather, Embossed Image Of Flying Superman, c.1940 .... 95.00

SWANKYSWIGS are small drinking glasses. In 1933, the Kraft Food Company began to market cheese spreads in these decorated, reusable glass tumblers. They were discontinued from 1941 to 1946, then made again from 1947 to 1958. Then plain glasses were used for most of the cheese, although a few special decorated Swankyswigs have been made since that time. A complete list of prices can be found in *Kovels' Depression Glass & Dinnerware Price List.*

Antique, Blue, 3 3/4 In. 5.00
Bustlin' Betsy, Blue, 3 3/4 In. .... .3.00 to 5.00
Bustlin' Betsy, Brown, 3 3/4 In. .... .3.00 to 5.00
Bustlin' Betsy, Green, 3 3/4 In. 3.00
Bustlin' Betsy, Yellow, 3 3/4 In. 3.00
Cornflower, No. 1, Light Blue, 3 1/2 In. 2.50
Cornflower, No. 2, Dark Blue, 3 1/2 In. .... .2.50 to 4.25
Cornflower, No. 2, Yellow, 3 1/2 In. .... .2.50 to 3.50
Cornflower, Red, 3 1/2 In. 4.00
Forget-Me-Not, Dark Blue, 3 1/2 In. 3.50
Forget-Me-Not, Red, 3 1/2 In. 4.00
Forget-Me-Not, Yellow, 3 1/2 In. 4.00
Kiddie Kup, Bird & Elephant, Red, 3 3/4 In. 4.00
Kiddie Kup, Piglet & Bear, Blue, 3 3/4 In. 4.00
Posy Tulip, Green, No. 1, 3 1/2 In. 4.00
Tulip, No. 2, Dark Blue, 3 3/4 In. 4.00

SWORDS of all types that are of interest to collectors are listed here. The military dress sword with elaborate handle is probably the most wanted. Be sure to display swords in a safe way, out of reach of children.

Alexander Coppel-Solingen Marked Blade, Waffen Marks, Wire Grip, 31 1/2 In. 175.00
Bayonet, Austria, Black Leather Grips, Steel Frame, 18 1/2 -In. Blade 143.00
Bayonet, Belgium, Brass Grip, Hallmarked, 1874, 38 Saw Teeth, 19 1/8-In. Blade 200.00
Bayonet, Combat, With Frog .... .34.00 to 38.00
Bayonet, Combat, Without Scabbard 35.00
Bayonet, Sawtooth, Fireman's Dress, Imperial .... .65.00 to 207.00
Bayonet, Wehrmacht Dress .... .51.00 to 61.00
Bayonet, Wehrmacht Dress, Single Engraved 200.00
Cavalry, Iron Pommel Cap, 3 Branch Guard, Civil War, 35 7/8 In. 860.00
Cutlass, Germany, Hunting, Gilt Bow & Pommel, Staghorn Grip, 30 1/2 In. 165.00
Dagger, Naval Cadet, Imperial, 1919 .... 330.00
Dagger, Whalebone, Steel, Hand Shape, 19 In. 330.00
Dirk, Scotland, Brass Mounted Wooden Grip, Basket Weave Panels, 1830, 13 In. 1250.00
Dirk, Scotland, Regimental, Basket Weave Wooden Grip, 19th Century, 12 In. 950.00
Double Edged Blade, 2-Hand, Wooden Grip, 2 Oval Ring Guards, 5 3/4 In. 4025.00
German, Scabbard, Brass Handguard, Eagle, Swastika, Inscribed, 1930s, 34 1/2 In. 980.00
Germany, Marked Solingen, Sheath, 20th Century, 36 In. 38.00
Green Cloth-Wrapped Handle, Scabbard, Bronze Design, 20th Century, 25 In. 230.00
Hunting, England, Brass Hilt, Rococo Foliage Pommel Cap, Scabbard, 1680, 12 3/8 In. .. 575.00
Japanese, Cloth-Wrapped Black Sharkskin Handle, Scabbard, Bronze Hilt, 26 In. 525.00
Japanese Military, Damascus Blade, Etched Stag Next To Tree, 8 1/4 In. 405.00
Knight's Cross Of The War, Merit 1500.00
Luftwaffe Officer's, Plated Hilt Mounts, Blue Leather Grip, Scabbard, 1940s, 28 In. 460.00
Mace, Ceremonial India, Head Of Horned Bull On Shaft, 21 3/4 In. 143.00
Military, Dress, Leather & Gilt Metal, Matching Mounts, 26 1/4 In. 95.00

Noncommissioned Officer's, Germany, 1834 .... 108.00
Noncommissioned Officer's, Japan, Aluminum Grip 155.00
Officer's, Etched U.S. Foliage, J.J. Garven Name, Scabbard, 1902 .... 295.00
Officer's, Marked, Eickhorn, Imperial Naval Dress 288.00
Officer's, Scotland, Engraved Steel Blade, Brass Hilt, Leather Grip, 37 1/2 In. 1850.00
Pioneer, Russia, Crimean War, Ordnance Marks On Both Sides Of Blade, 1854 .... 575.00
Pioneer, Russia, Sawback Blade, Brass Hilt, 1838, 19 In. 395.00
Saber, Cavalry Officer's, W. Walschel, Solingen, Scabbard, Civil War 1045.00
Saber, Cavalry, Model 1840, Tiffany, 3 Branch Guard Leather Grip, Civilian, 35 1/2 In. .. 575.00
Saber, Dress Artillery, Imperial, Bakelite Grips, Plated Scabbard, Germany, 1913 .... 110.00
Saber, England, Naval Officer's Black Dress, Lion's Head, Pommel, Gold Bullion 120.00
Saber, Indian War, Officer's, Nickel Plated Scabbard, 1896, 30 1/8 In. 175.00
Saber, U.S. Cavalry, Leather Grip, German Blade, Scabbard 440.00
Saber, U.S. Cavalry, Leather Grip, Scabbard 330.00
Saber, U.S. Cavalry, W.O. Codey, Leather Grip, Scabbard 385.00
Saber, U.S. Model 1913 Patton, Bronze Paint On Guard, 1918, 35 In. 150.00
Sapper, Short, 1838 .... 94.00
Spanish-American War, May 9, 1898, M.C. Lilley & Co., Bronze Hilt, Gilt Wire Wrap .. 1375.00
Staff & Field Officer's, Eagle & Vines, Fishskin Wrap, 32 In. 175.00
U.S. Foot Officer's, Arms & Floral, Brass Pommel, Guard & Bow, Scabbard, 1861 ...... 1320.00
U.S. Musician's, Angels Camp Mickey Pulliam, Leather Scabbard, 1961 .... 330.00

TAPESTRY, PORCELAIN, see Rose Tapestry category.

TEA CADDY is the name for a small box made to hold tea leaves. In the
eighteenth century, tea was very expensive and it was stored under
lock and key. The first tea caddies were made with locks. By the nineteenth century, tea was more plentiful and the tea caddy was larger.
Often there were two sections, one for green tea, one for black tea.

Allover Figures, Pagodas, Trees & Flowers, Pewter Boxes, China, 11 In. 977.00
Apple Form, Iron Escutcheon, Georgian, 5 In. 2530.00
Bird's-Eye Maple, Fitted Interior, c.1800, 5 x 5 In. 715.00
Bird's-Eye Maple, String Inlay, Bail Handle, George III, 6 x 12 x 6 In. 690.00
Black Lacquer, Liner, Chinese, 1880s, 5 x 10 x 6 In. 150.00
Black Lacquer, Nacre Inlay, Painted Lily Of The Valley, Gilding, 6 1/2 In. 385.00
Brass, Hammered Panels, Celtic Knot, Ceramic Cabochon, Arts & Crafts, 5 In. 600.00
Brass & Tortoiseshell, Serpentine Front, Scrolled Inlay, Rosewood Interior, 9 In. 1150.00
Brass Ball Feet, 2 Covered Ivory Compartments, Regency, 5 x 8 x 4 1/2 In. 290.00
Bronze, Bullfighting Scenes On Cover, 6 1/4 In. 440.00
Burl, Oval Inlaid Top, Ivory Inlaid Escutcheon, Late 18th Century, 4 1/2 x 5 In. 978.00
Burl, Sarcophagus Form, c.1790, 10 x 18 1/2 In. 880.00
Conch Shell Finial, Fan Inlaid Front, Ivory Handles, Regency, c.1790, 7 1/2 In. 2310.00
Cover, Gilt Black, Figures Seated Beneath Tree, China, 7 x 15 x 13 In. 980.00
Eagle & Arms Of Rhode Island, Restored Cover, China, 5 In. 2200.00
Figural Gilt Design, c.1820, China, 3 3/4 In. 358.00
Figured Mahogany Veneer, Diamond Escutcheon, 2 Canisters, Mixing Bowl, 12 In. 240.00
Flower Head Finial, Fluted Cover, Flowers & Leaves On Body, Scandinavian, 7 In. 402.00
Fruitwood, Apple Form, George III, 5 In. ....2530.00 to 3450.00
Fruitwood, Apple Form, Wooden Stem, George III, Early 19th Century, 4 3/4 In. 4600.00
Fruitwood, Melon Form, George III, 6 1/4 In. ....5175.00 to 8050.00
Fruitwood, Melon Form, Original Stem, Lock, Green, George III, 6 In. 10925.00
Fruitwood, Melon Form, Regency, 6 In. 4887.00
Fruitwood, Melon Form, Triangular, George III, Early 19th Century, 5 1/2 In. 4887.00
Fruitwood, Pear Form, 6 In. 8050.00
Fruitwood, Pear Form, England, 7 In. 2587.00
Fruitwood, Pear Form, Original Lock, Regency, 8 In. 6900.00
Greek Key Border, Interior Compartments, George III, 6 x 12 In. 550.00
Hepplewhite, Floral, 8 Sided, 1810, 7 1/2 In. 925.00
Lacquer, Chinoiserie, Lozenge Shape, Animal Claw Footed, Pewter Interior, 8 1/2 In. 420.00
Lacquer, Mother-Of-Pearl Flower & Bird Design, 2 Boxes, Lids, 5 x 9 x 4 1/2 In. 85.00
Lacquer, Paddlewheel Steamboat Shape, Wheels, Chinese Export, 19 1/2 In. 2875.00
Lacquer, Red, Gold & Black Landscape, Chinoiserie, 6 In. 192.00

Leaf Design, Copper, George Prentiss Kendrick, c.1892, 3 1/4 In. 2300.00
Mahogany, Bombe Form, Brass Handle, Ogee Feet, Georgian, c.1760, 11 1/2 In. 660.00
Mahogany, Canted Sides, Button Feet, 2 Interior Lids, 19th Century 303.00
Mahogany, Chinese Bowl Inside, 2 Compartments, Mid-19th Century, 6 x 12 In. 345.00
Mahogany, Color Inlay, 2 Interior Compartments, 6 In. 440.00
Mahogany, Dovetailed Case, Brass Bale Handle, Divided Interior, 11 3/4 In. 1650.00
Mahogany, Inlaid Conch Shell Front, Fan Inlay On Cover, George III 1000.00
Mahogany, Inlaid Square Section, Bale Handle, Lead Lined, 18th Century, 7 3/4 In. 230.00
Mahogany, Inlay, Dentil Band At Base, George III, 1880s, 5 In. 1035.00
Mahogany, Ivory Escutcheon, 3 Interior Compartments, Brass, Georgian, c.1770 .... 198.00
Mahogany, Satinwood, Shell Patera, Ivory Keyhold, Birds, Foliage, Regency, 5 In. 430.00
Mahogany & Satinwood, Original Key 373.00
Mahogany Veneer Over Dovetailed Line, Inlay, Silver Lining, Mixing Bowl 395.00
Marquetry Castle & Roses On Sides, Tunbridge Wells, Kent, 1860, 6 x 10 In. 1995.00
Oak, Silver, Samuel Taylor, London, Georgian, 1765 .... 7750.00
Papier-Mache, Mother-Of-Pearl, Castle Landscape, Bouquet Front, 6 x 8 In. 132.00
Pewter, Engraved Bird & Flower, Rectangular, Chinese Export 45.00
Rosewood, Brass Knob Handles, 6 1/2 In. 220.00
Rosewood, Cover, Interior Glass Cylinder, Foil Lined, Ring Turned Handles, 8 In. 690.00
Rosewood, Dome Top, 2 Lift-Lid Domed Boxes Interior, 8 x 14 In. 330.00
Rosewood, Triple Compartment, Mixing Bowl Center, c.1830, 7 x 11 1/2 In. 240.00
Rosewood, Tulip & Crossbanded Satinwood, George III, Late 18th Century, 6 In. 2070.00
Rosewood Veneer, Inlaid Ivory Diamond Escutcheons, England, 12 1/4 In. 360.00
Satinwood, Octagonal, Pear Wood Inlays, Fitted Interior, Georgian, 5 x 6 3/4 In. 495.00
Shell Inlay, Regency 2310.00
Silver, Chippendale Style With Pineapple Finial, Theodore B. Starr, 5 In. 412.00
Silver, Engraved Design Front, With Key, Sheffield 355.00
Silver Plate, Pineapple Finial, Bright Cut Stylized Foliate Rim, 6 1/4 In. 230.00
Sterling Silver, Arts & Crafts, Franz J.R. Gyllenberg, 20th Century, 5 In. 495.00
Sterling Silver, Nesmiths From Morses, Hand Hammered, Woolley, 1916, 5 In. 595.00
Tortoiseshell, Domed Lid, Carved Fan Front, Silver Mounts, 4 1/2 x 3 1/4 In. 1870.00
Tortoiseshell, Ivory Edging, Interior Lids Veneered With Tortoiseshell, 7 3/4 In. 1695.00
Tortoiseshell, Monogrammed Silver Medallion On Lid, 4 3/4 x 5 In. 575.00
Tortoiseshell, Mother-Of-Pearl Inlaid Flowers, Ivory Feet, England, 5 In. 1540.00
Tortoiseshell, Serpentine Front, 2 Interior Jars, Ball Feet, Regency, c.1830, 7 1/4 In. 747.00
Tortoiseshell Banded, Ivory, Divided Interior, Paktong Lining, c.1820, 4 3/4 In. 1870.00
Tortoiseshell Veneer, Columns At Corners, Silvered Feet, Regency, c.1810 .... 6400.00
Walnut, Dome Cover, Ivory, Gilt Metal Mounted, Victorian 575.00
Walnut, Inlaid Satinwood, Carved Panels, Hinged Cover, H-D & O.C.T. 1905, 9 In. 125.00

TEA LEAF IRONSTONE dishes are named for their decorations. There
was a superstition that it was lucky if a whole tea leaf unfolded at the
bottom of your cup. This idea was translated into the pattern of dishes
known as *tea leaf*. By 1850, at least twelve English factories were
making this pattern, and by the 1870s, it was a popular pattern in many
countries. The tea leaf was always a luster glaze on early wares,
although now some pieces are made with a brown tea leaf.

Bowl, 5 3/8 In. 24.00
Bowl, 6 5/8 In. 26.00
Bowl, Copper Trim, Adams, 5 3/8 In. ....20.00 to 27.00
Bowl, Copper Trim, Adams, 6 5/8 In. ....28.00 to 29.00
Bowl, Copper Trim, Oval, 9 3/4 In. ....45.00 to 89.00
Bowl, Empress, Copper Trim, Adams, 6 5/8 In. ....27.00 to 30.00
Bowl, Fruit, Empress, Copper Trim, Adams, 5 3/8 In. 20.00
Bowl, Oval, 9 3/4 In. ....38.00 to 140.00
Bowl, Vegetable, Cover, Oval 300.00
Bowl, Vegetable, Cover, Rectangular 300.00
Bowl, Vegetable, Cover, Shaw 220.00
Bowl & Pitcher, Copper Lustre, Alfred Meakin, 13 In. 125.00
Bread Plate, Bamboo Handle, Square, Alfred Meakin, 9 In. 11.00
Cake Plate, Empress, Handle, Copper Trim, Adams, 11 3/4 In. 120.00
Casserole, Cover, Lustre, Alfred Meakin, 9 In. 75.00
Chamber Pot, Lid, Meakin 200.00

Coffeepot, Cover, Empress, Copper Trim, Adams 180.00
Coffeepot, Cover, Empress, Lid Only, Copper Trim, Adams 55.00
Coffeepot, Cover, Red Cliff 180.00
Coffeepot, Gold Leaf Center, Red Cliff Chine 180.00
Compote, Burgess, 9 In. 350.00
Creamer ....56.00 to 59.00
Creamer, Copper Trim, Adams 58.00
Creamer, Empress, Copper Trim, Adams 60.00
Creamer, Shaw, 6 In. 275.00
Cup & Saucer, Clementson 95.00
Cup & Saucer, Copper Trim, Adams, 2 1/2 In. ....48.00 to 49.00
Cup & Saucer, Empress, Copper Trim, Adams, 2 1/2 In. 50.00
Cup & Saucer, Gold Trim, Flintridge, 2 1/4 In. 52.00
Cup & Saucer, Meakin 65.00
Cup & Saucer, Red Cliff 35.00
Cup & Saucer, Shaw 60.00
Gravy Boat, Attached Underplate, Flintridge 129.00
Gravy Boat, Empress, Underplate, Copper Trim, Adams 150.00
Gravy Boat, Mellor Taylor 50.00
Gravy Boat, Shaw 70.00
Gravy Boat, Stand, Adams 150.00
Gravy Boat, Underplate, Daisy & Chain 85.00
Gravy Boat, Underplate, Red Cliff 160.00
Gravy Boat, Undertray ....98.00 to 101.00
Jug, Meakin, 6 In. 70.00
Mixing Bowl, 3 Piece 60.00
Pitcher, 6 3/4 In. 91.00
Pitcher, Empress, Copper Trim, Adams, 6 3/4 In. ....80.00 to 140.00
Pitcher, Meakin, 8 In. 225.00
Pitcher, Milk, Bridgwood 30.00
Pitcher, Walley, 5 1/2 In. 250.00
Plate, 6 1/4 In. 13.00
Plate, 10 1/8 In. 46.00
Plate, Copper Trim, 10 1/8 In. 25.00
Plate, Copper Trim, Adams, 6 1/4 In. 17.00
Plate, Copper Trim, Adams, 7 3/4 In. ....7.00 to 25.00
Plate, Copper Trim, Adams, 10 1/8 In. 48.00
Plate, Copper Trim, Tea Leaf Center, Wedgwood, 9 7/8 In. ....30.00 to 32.00
Plate, Empress, Copper Trim, Adams, 6 1/4 In. 5.00
Plate, Empress, Copper Trim, Adams, 7 3/4 In. 25.00
Plate, Empress, Copper Trim, Adams, 8 7/8 In. ....25.00 to 42.00
Plate, Empress, Copper Trim, Adams, 10 1/8 In. 50.00
Plate, Gold Design, Meakin, 6 3/4 In. 23.00
Plate, Gold Leaf Center, Red Cliff China, 6 1/2 In. 16.00
Plate, Gold Leaf Center, Red Cliff China, 8 3/8 In. 25.00
Plate, Gold Leaf Center, Red Cliff China, 10 In. 44.00
Plate, Gold Trim, Flintridge, 6 3/8 In. 20.00
Plate, Red Cliff, 6 1/2 In. 25.00
Plate, Red Cliff, 8 3/4 In. 30.00
Plate, Red Cliff, 10 In. 50.00
Plate, Shaw, 9 1/2 In. 100.00
Plate, Toddy, Clementson, 5 In. 165.00
Platter, 13 1/2 In. 105.00
Platter, Clementson, 14 In. 200.00
Platter, Copper Trim, Oval, Adams, 11 1/2 In. 130.00
Platter, Copper Trim, Tea Leaf Center, 13 In. 110.00
Platter, Copper Trim, Tea Leaf Center, 14 In. ....135.00 to 150.00
Platter, Copper Trim, Tea Leaf Center, Wedgwood, 12 1/4 In. 100.00
Platter, Empress, Serving, Oval, Adams, 11 1/2 In. 140.00
Platter, Gold Design, Meakin, 12 3/8 In. 117.00
Platter, Gold Design, Meakin, 15 3/4 In. 135.00
Platter, Oval, 11 1/2 In. ....90.00 to 130.00
Platter, Oval, 13 1/2 In. 105.00

Platter, Oval, 15 3/4 In. 200.00
Platter, Oval, E & F, 13 In. 240.00
Platter, Rectangular, 12 1/4 In. . . . . .95.00 to 140.00
Platter, Rectangular, 14 In. 234.00
Platter, Rectangular, Copper Trim, Tea Leaf Center, 12 1/4 In. 100.00
Platter, Rectangular, Copper Trim, Tea Leaf Center, 14 In. 150.00
Platter, Red Cliff, Rectangular, 11 3/8 In. 140.00
Platter, Serving, Empress, Copper Trim, Oval, Adams, 11 1/2 In. 98.00
Platter, Serving, Empress, Copper Trim, Oval, Adams, 13 1/2 In. 120.00
Relish, Meakin 11.00
Salt & Pepper, Empress, Copper Trim, Adams 90.00
Saltshaker 30.00
Saucer, Empress, Copper Trim, Adams . . . . .8.00 to 16.00
Shaving Mug, Lily-Of-The-Valley Mold, Anthony Shaw, 3 1/2 In. 190.00
Shaving Mug, Shaw 110.00
Soap Dish, Liner, Shaw 100.00
Soup, Dish, Empress, Copper Trim, Adams, 8 In. . . . . .38.00 to 50.00
Sugar, Cover 80.00
Sugar, Cover, Copper Trim, Adams . . . . .78.00 to 79.00
Sugar, Cover, Flintridge 79.00
Sugar, Lid, Gold Luster, Powell & Bishop 75.00
Sugar, Mayer 45.00
Sugar, Meakin 75.00
Teapot, Copper Trim 180.00
Teapot, Cover, Empress, Copper Trim, Adams 180.00
Teapot, Shaw 250.00
Tureen, Sauce, Red Cliff, 4 Piece 170.00
Tureen, Soup, Shaw, 4 Piece 1900.00
Waste Bowl, Shaw 40.00

TECO is the mark used on the art pottery line made by the American Terra Cotta and Ceramic Company of Terra Cotta and Chicago, Illinois. The company was an offshoot of the firm founded by William D. Gates in 1881. The Teco line was first made in 1885 but was not sold commercially until 1902. It continued in production until 1922. Over 500 designs were made in a variety of colors, shapes, and glazes. The company closed in 1930.

T E C O

Bookends, Indian Maiden At Well, Signed, 7 In. 200.00
Bowl, Green Matte Glaze, Closed Form, 9 x 2 In. 605.00
Bowl, Molded Floral Design, Green Matte Glaze, Heavy Charcoaling, 8 1/2 x 2 1/2 In. . . . 385.00
Candlestick, Green Matte Glaze, Wax Covered, Handled Form, 6 1/2 In. 121.00
Jardiniere, Green Matte Glaze, 3 Footed, Signed, 6 3/4 In. 375.00
Jardiniere, Green Matte Glaze, Closed-In Rim, Charcoal, Impressed Mark, 4 x 7 In. 660.00
Pitcher, Brown Matte Glaze, 4 In. 154.00
Vase, 2 Buttressed Handles, Dripping Blue Gray Over Brown Matte Glaze, 7 x 4 In. 660.00
Vase, 2 Buttressed Handles, Green Matte Glaze, Die Stamp, 8 x 5 3/4 In. 2530.00
Vase, 2 Buttresses, Closed, Green Matte Glaze, Impressed Mark, Paper Label, 11 In. 1210.00
Vase, 2 Buttresses, Green Matte Glaze, 5 1/2 In. 385.00
Vase, 2 Buttresses, Open, Green Matte Glaze, Impressed Mark, 9 In. 1650.00
Vase, 2 Closed Handles, Green Matte Glaze, Heavy Charcoaling, 9 In. 770.00
Vase, 2 Handles, Green Matte Glaze, Heavy Charcoaling, 11 In. 935.00
Vase, 4 Buttressed Handles, Gray Matte Glaze, 5 1/2 In. 495.00
Vase, Amphora, 2 Handles, Green Matte Glaze, Die Stamp, 9 x 5 In. 990.00
Vase, Beige Matte Glaze, Shouldered Form, Impressed Mark, 11 In. 495.00
Vase, Bulbous, Green Matte Glaze, Charcoal, Impressed Mark, 4 x 3 3/4 In. 470.00
Vase, Buttresses, Double Gourd, Green Matte Glaze, 6 1/2 In. 3190.00
Vase, Flared Rim, Leaves, Green Matte Glaze, 11 1/2 x 4 3/4 In. 7700.00
Vase, Flared, Scalloped Rim, Green Matte Glaze, Charcoal, Impressed Mark, 5 x 4 In. . . . 440.00
Vase, Globular Form, Green Matte Glaze, 4 3/4 In. 460.00
Vase, Green Glaze, Impressed Mark, 13 In. 1100.00
Vase, Green Matte Glaze, 4 Footed, 18 1/2 In. 4400.00
Vase, Green Matte Glaze, Charcoal, Impressed Mark, 6 1/4 x 3 1/4 In. 415.00
Vase, Green Matte Glaze, Impressed Mark, 4 1/4 x 3 1/2 In. 330.00

Vase, Green Matte Glaze, Ribbed, Cylindrical, 5 x 4 In. 495.00
Vase, Green Matte Glaze, Signed, 5 x 6 1/4 In. 275.00
Vase, Horizontally Ribbed Side, Green Matte Glaze, Signed, 4 3/4 In. 495.00
Vase, Ribbed, Squat, Green Matte Glaze, Impressed Marked, 4 x 4 In. 385.00
Vase, Tulip Shape, Cobalt Matte Glaze, Fernand Moreau, 11 1/2 x 5 In. 3575.00
Vase, Tulip Shape, Green & Charcoal Glaze, Fernand Moreau, 11 1/2 In. 2400.00
Vessel, Green Matte Glaze, Handle, Impressed Marks, 9 In. 1100.00
Wall Pocket, Fritz Albert, 17 x 6 3/4 In., Pair 5500.00

TEDDY BEARS were named for a president of the United States. The
first teddy bear was a cuddly toy said to be inspired by a hunting trip
made by Teddy Roosevelt in 1902. Morris and Rose Michtom started
selling their stuffed bears as *teddy bears* and the name stayed. The
Michtoms founded the Ideal Novelty and Toy Company. The German
version of the teddy bear was made about the same time by the Steiff
Company. There are many types of teddy bears and all are collected.
The old ones are being reproduced. Other bears are listed in the Toy
section.

Ideal, Mohair, Blond, Fully Jointed, Rust Embroidered Features, c.1919, 34 In. 2530.00
Ideal, Mohair, Ginger, Fully Jointed, Embroidered Features, 1919, 20 In. 460.00
Ideal, Mohair, Yellow Plush, Embroidered Features, Fully Jointed, 1920s, 15 In. 230.00
Kareem Abdul Ja-Bear, Tag & Basketball 595.00
Light Tan, Large Round Ears, Glass Eyes, Turning Head, 32 x 14 In. 1610.00
Mohair, Gold, Articulated Front Legs, Felt Paw Pads 220.00
Mohair, Gold, Articulated Limbs, Bead Eyes, Paw Pads, 10 In. 1045.00
Mohair, Gold, Articulated Limbs, Hump, Straw Stuffing, 2 Recovered Pads, 22 In. 410.00
Mohair, Gold, Articulated Limbs, Hump, Straw Stuffing, Missing Eyes, 22 In. 110.00
Mohair, Gold, Articulated Limbs, Leatherized Cloth Foot Pads, Open Mouth, 31 In. 275.00
Mohair, Gold, Button Eyes, Replaced Paw Pads, 19 In. 220.00
Mohair, Gold, Excelsior Stuffed, Swivel Head, Glass Eyes, Jointed, 16 In. 305.00
Mohair, Gold, Girl, Polka Dot Dress, Articulated Limbs, Glass Eyes, 28 In. 80.00
Mohair, Gold, Glass Eyes, Felt Paw Pads, 23 1/2 In. 220.00
Mohair, Gold, Glass Eyes, Jointed, Ivory Felt Paws, 25 In. 525.00
Mohair, Gold, Glass Eyes, Vinyl Paw Pads, Jointed, Blue Ribbon Toys, 22 In. 55.00
Mohair, Gold, Hand Warmer, Glass Eyes, 11 1/2 In. 465.00
Mohair, Gold, Jointed, Pink Felt Paws, Glass Eyes, 26 1/2 In. 550.00
Mohair, Gold, Pointed Nose, Button Eyes, Homemade Sweater, 13 1/2 In. 95.00
Mohair, Light Gold, Jointed, Glass Eyes, Ivory Felt Paws, Squeak Voice Box, 27 In. 358.00
Mohair, Pointed Nose, Hump, Embroidered Mouth & Toes, Jointed, 9 In. 410.00
Mohair, Stuffed, Jointed, Swivel Head, Upturned Snout, Hump Back, 24 In. 1100.00
Mohair, White, Hand Warmer, Glass Eyes, 6 In. 25.00
Mohair, Yellow, Glass Eyes, Ivory Felt Paws, Jointed, 23 In. 195.00
Plush, Seated, Gold, Black Shoe Button Eyes, Stitched-On Ears, Felt Paws, 18 In. 950.00
Schuco, Mohair, Light Brown, Rounded Head, Stitched-On Ears, Felt Paws, 22 In. 3100.00
Schuco, On Wheels, 15 In. 375.00
Steiff, Bears In Tub, Rub-A-Dub-Dub, Gold, Yellow, Brown, Accessories, Box, 10 In. ... 330.00
Steiff, Beige Mohair, Fully Jointed Body, c.1905, 3 1/2 In. 805.00
Steiff, Black, Voice Box, Label, Box, 16 In. 205.00
Steiff, Brown Cub, Light Brown Mohair, Standing, Amber Eyes, 1950, 8 In. 425.00
Steiff, Cream Color, Ear Button, 10 In. 85.00
Steiff, Dicky, Golden, Label, Box, 13 In. 170.00

**If you buy an old teddy bear at a garage sale, bring it home
and put it in a plastic bag with some mothballs for a few
weeks. Don't let the mothballs touch the bear. The fur and
stuffing of old bears attracts many types of hungry insects.**

Steiff, Excelsior, Swivel Neck, Jointed, Wears Photo Of Dickens, c.1910, 10 In. 2700.00
Steiff, Fireman 275.00
Steiff, Golden, Baby In Wooden Crib, Label, Box, 12 In. 220.00
Steiff, Golden, With Baby, Margarite Steiff Ltd. Edition, Label, Box, 14 In. 195.00
Steiff, Growler, Beige, Button In Ear, 24 In. 1500.00
Steiff, Growler, Gold Color, Felt Mouth, Tongue Sticking Out, 17 In. 475.00
Steiff, Harod's Victorian Bear 450.00
Steiff, Koala, Mohair, Brown Glass Eyes, Articulated Limbs, c.1955, 8 In. 700.00
Steiff, Medium Tan, Button & Tag, 20 In. 600.00
Steiff, Mohair, Amber, Black Bead Eyes, Swivel Head, Jointed, c.1950, 3 1/2 In. 200.00
Steiff, Mohair, Blond, Fully Jointed, Pointed Nose, c.1907, 12 In. 287.00
Steiff, Mohair, Brown, Glass Eyes, Ear Button, Voice Box, On Wheels, 31 In. 2090.00
Steiff, Mohair, Brown, Seated, Amber Eyes, Jointed Arms, Legs, Suede Paws, 7 In. 350.00
Steiff, Mohair, Brown, Swivel Neck, Black Bead Eyes, Stitched-On Ears, 1950, 3 In. 325.00
Steiff, Mohair, Caramel, Inset Eyes, Jointed Shoulders & Hips, 38 In. 700.00
Steiff, Mohair, Champagne, Swivel Head, Jointed, Tag, Button, c.1950, 6 In. 275.00
Steiff, Mohair, Gold, Steel Eyes, Fully Jointed, Embroidered Features, 1905, 16 In. 1955.00
Steiff, Mohair, Gold, Steel Eyes, Fully Jointed, Excelsior Stuffing, 1905, 14 In. 1380.00
Steiff, Mohair, Golden Plush, Swivel Neck, Black Shoe-Button Eyes, 1910, 16 In. 2400.00
Steiff, Mohair, Gray, Glass Eyes, Leather Collar, On Wheels, 22 In. 825.00
Steiff, Mohair, Leather Paws, 1909, 14 In. 175.00
Steiff, Mohair, Light Brown, Swivel Head, Pointy Snout, Felt Paws, 10 In. 2100.00
Steiff, Mohair, Swivel Head, Jointed Limbs, Glass Eyes, Germany, c.1950, 8 In. 250.00
Steiff, Mohair, White, Seated, Swivel Neck, Black Shoebutton Eyes, 13 In. 3600.00
Steiff, Mohair, Yellow, Fully Jointed, Embroidered Features, 24 In. 2760.00
Steiff, Onga, West Germany, 27 x 33 In. 428.00
Steiff, Petsey, Blond Dralon, Button 95.00
Steiff, Teddy Clown, Yellow, Ruff, Clown Hat, Label, Box, 16 In. 205.00
Steiff, Zotty, Mohair, Long Brown, Swivel Neck, Stitched Ears, Bead Eyes, 1969, 8 In. .. 325.00
Steiff, Zotty, Mohair, Silver Brown, Amber Mohair Chest, Jointed, c.1950, 9 In. 200.00
Straw Stuffed, Jointed, Swivel Head, Button Eyes, Hump Back, 10 1/2 In. 305.00

TELEPHONES are wanted by collectors if the phones are old enough or unusual enough. The first telephone may have been made in Havana, Cuba, in 1849, but it was not patented. The first publicly demonstrated phone was used in Frankfurt, Germany, in 1860. The phone made by Alexander Graham Bell was shown at the Centennial Exhibition in Philadelphia in 1876, but it was not until 1877 that the first private phones were installed. Collectors today want all types of old phones, phone parts, and advertising. Even recent figural phones are popular.

Airplane, Orange, Yellow, Dial 145.00
American Bell Telephone Co., Candlestick, Potbelly, Adjustable Mouthpiece 7763.00
American Bell Telephone Co., Candlestick, Tapered, Crystal Mouthpiece 2300.00
American Electric Co., Wall, Oak Stand At Bottom, Folds Down, Quartersawn Oak 155.00
American Telephone Co., Candlestick, Dialer 201.00
American Telephone Co., Candlestick, Porcelain Mouthpiece 403.00
Automatic Electric Co., Desk, Red, Chrome 2300.00
Beetle Bailey 85.00
Bell Telephone Co., Shade, Bell System 1035.00
Bell Telephone Co., Shade, Hanging, Paneled, Public Telephone 805.00
Bell Telephone Co., Shade, Local & Long Distance Telephone 2185.00
Booth, Oak, Paneled, 36 1/4 x 42 3/4 x 85 In. 250.00
Booth, Walnut, Seat, Light, Fan, Folding Glass 1200.00
Bugs Bunny, Figural 70.00
Buzz Lightyear, Canada 85.00
Cabbage Patch Doll, Figural 95.00
Century, Candlestick, Tapered 863.00
Charlie Tuna, Figural 75.00
Chas. Williams, Jr., Wall, Walnut, 3 Box, Key 2473.00
Connecticut, Telephone, Wall, Oak Case, 15 Line 288.00
Couch & Seeley, Wall, Oak, Watchcase Receiver, Single Bell 148.00
Darth Vader, Speakerphone, Chest Lights, LucasFilm, 1983, 15 In. 65.00
DeVeau, Candlestick, Tapered, Crystal Mouthpiece, 6 Line 2530.00

Ericophon, Rotary Dial, Abstract Sculpture Style, Brown 55.00
Ericophon, Rotary Dial, Abstract Sculpture Style, Pink 30.00
Ericophone, 1 Piece, 1960s 95.00
Ericsson, Cradle, Side Crank, Black Metal, Fabric Cord, 5 x 8 x 10 1/2 In. 45.00
Farr Telephone Co., Wall, Oak, Side Bell, Signal Button 431.00
Federal Telephone Co., Wall 81.00
Garfield 35.00
Gray Automatic Pay Station, Candlestick, Coin Box, Restored, 1898-1919 .... 795.00
Gray, Pay, Unusual Mouthpiece 1265.00
Holtzer & Cabot Electric Co., Candlestick, Oak Case, Fluted, Potbelly 4313.00
Holtzer & Cabot Electric Co., Ness Automatic, Oak, Potbelly, 16 Lines 719.00
Kellogg, Candlestick, Pay, Porcelain Mouthpiece 2300.00
Kellogg, Desk, Mahogany 144.00
Kermit The Frog, Touch Tone, 1970s ....135.00 to 150.00
Loeffler, Candlestick, 3 Line 431.00
Manhattan Elec. Co., Wall, Dry Battery Box 575.00
Motorcycle, Harley-Davidson, Figural, On Stand 75.00
North Electric Co., Desk, Butterscotch 288.00
Oak, Wall Mounted, Early 20th Century 115.00
Oak, Wall, 2 Bell, Porcelain & Crystal Battery 575.00
Paperweight, Telephone Pioneers Of America, Bell Shape, Blue Glass, 3 In. 25.00
Penna. Keating, Wall, Cast Iron 2185.00
PH & R, Candlestick, Potbelly 3105.00
Pizza Inn, Figural, Vinyl, Red, Black Outfit, 1970s, 10 In. 30.00
Pooh-Lamp Type, Figural 300.00
Reliable Electric, Candlestick, Potbelly 4600.00
Reliance, Wall, Oak, Watchcase Receiver 201.00
Ronald McDonald 450.00
Sampson, Wall, Walnut, Watchcase Receiver 150.00
Shyver, Jukebox Style, Multi 1380.00
Sign, Bell Telephone, Underground Cable, Do Not Disturb, Porcelain, 7 x 3 1/2 In. 68.00
Sign, Candlestick, Public Telephone 1783.00
Sign, Marble Bell Telephone Co. 58.00
Sign, N.Y. Telephone Co., Enamel ....259.00 to 374.00
Sign, N.Y. Telephone, American Telephone & Telegraph, Porcelain, 12 x 11 In. 225.00
Sign, Public Independent Telephone, Flange, 1940-1950, Square, 18 In. 140.00
Sign, Public Telephone, Bell System, Black, White, Flange, Porcelain, 11 x 11 In. 90.00
Sign, Public Telephone, Black Lettering, Black Ground, 18 x 16 In. 135.00
Sign, Sorry, Temporarily Out Of Service, Bell System, Aluminum, 5 x 3 In. 30.00
Sign, Western Union & AT&T 575.00
Snoopy, 1976 .... 150.00
Space Saver, Rotary Dial, Wall 35.00
Sterling Co., Wall, 10 Line, Walnut, Watchcase Receiver 345.00
Stockholm, Desk, Double Bell, Swivel Mouthpiece, Open Works 4255.00
Stromberg-Carlson, Black, Rotary Dial, 1940s 25.00
Tabletop, Dial, White Metal, Black Enamel, Bakelite Receiver, Fabric Cord, 5 x 8 In. ... 25.00

Telephone, Utica Fire
Alarm, Candlestick,
Potbelly

Telephone, Wilhelm,
Oak & Metal, Wall Phone

Tabletop, No Dial, Black Bakelite, 9 x 5 x 6 In. 65.00
Test Set, Wooden 65.00
The Orator, Rawson Electric Co., Wall, Crank, Lower Double Bell, Oak 1035.00
The Ray, Wall, Transmitter Crank, Double Bell, Extended Mouthpiece 748.00
Tillman & Euler Telephone Co., Candlestick, Bulbous Mouthpiece, Signal Button 4600.00
Utica Fire Alarm, Candlestick, Potbelly ....*Illus* 5175.00
Wall, Black Metal, Bakelite Receiver, Cradle On Top, Rectangular, Late 1940s, 13 In. ... 80.00
Western Electric, Candlestick, 2 Receivers, 1 Watchcase, Crystal Mouthpiece 748.00
Western Electric, Candlestick, Advertising, North Hampton Bank 920.00
Western Electric, Candlestick, Brass Plated, Bakelite Mouthpiece, 1910s, 12 1/2 In. 70.00
Western Electric, Candlestick, Microphone Mouthpiece 230.00
Western Electric, Desk, Cinnamon 201.00
Western Electric, Desk, Gold, 5 Line 1150.00
Western Electric, Desk, Green 403.00
Western Electric, Desk, Ivory 173.00
Western Electric, Mod Dial, Yellow, 1970s 90.00
Western Electric, Wall Box, 250W, Oak, 20 1/2 x 9 1/2 In. 425.00
Wilhelm, Candlestick, Pencil Shaft, Double Diaphragm 6900.00
Wilhelm, Oak & Metal, Wall Phone ....*Illus* 1208.00
Wilhelm, Wall, Cast Iron, Bulbous Mouthpiece Handset 4888.00
Wilhelm, Wall, Oak, Cast Iron, Double Diaphragm Transmitter 1035.00
Wilhelm, Wall, Oak, Metal, Double Diaphragm Transmitter, 6 Line, Single Bell 1208.00
Wilhelm, Wall, Small Tiger Maple Case 805.00
Wilhelm, Wall, Walnut, Extended Mouthpiece 4313.00
William & Norton, Wall, Oak, Wood Receiver 1380.00

TEPLITZ refers to art pottery manufactured by a number of companies in the Teplitz-Turn area of Bohemia during the late nineteenth and early twentieth centuries. The Amphora Porcelain Works and the Alexandra Works were two of these companies.

Basket, Green Applied Hops Blossoms, Basket Weave 50000.00
Candlestand, Fall Colors & Leaves, 3-Footed, Amphora, 10 In. 385.00
Centerpiece, Venus Rising From Sea, Pastel Enamel, Gilt, E. Stellmacher, 28 In. 1240.00
Chamberstick, Amphora 239.00
Ewer, Green Grass, Leaves, Iridescent, Amphora, 5 1/2 In. 95.00
Ewer, Lavender Iris, Cobalt Blue Top, Gold Trim, Signed, Bohemia, 7 1/2 In. ......*Illus* 250.00
Ewer, Poppies, Green Leaves, Gold Outline, Ornate Handle, 10 1/2 In. ....125.00 to 165.00
Sugar, Pebbled Beige, Incised Bands Of Flowers, Amphora 95.00
Vase, 2 Exotic Birds, Amphora, Marked, 10 1/2 In. 275.00
Vase, 4 Dragonflies Around Rim, 8 Dragonflies Below, Open Handles, Amphora, 6 In. 1320.00
Vase, Applied Floral Design, Red Underglaze, Baluster, 7 In. 34.00
Vase, Applied Flowers, Winged Creature At Neck, Gold, Ivory Reticulated Top, 15 In. ... 319.00
Vase, Blue Butterfly, Gold Outline, Gold Flowers, 2 Handles, 8 In. 715.00
Vase, Blue, Purple Circular Design, 4 Handles, Bulbous, Marked, Amphora, 9 1/2 In. 520.00
Vase, Bold Trees, Impressed Mark, Amphora, 17 1/2 In. 1320.00
Vase, Butterflies Amongst Dangling Moths, Flared Rim, Green, Amphora, 9 In. 2645.00
Vase, Capped Gentleman, Stellmacher, 7 In. 95.00
Vase, Cherries & Leaves, Marked, Amphora, 15 In. 750.00
Vase, Corseted, Stylized White Roses, Gilt Leaves, Embossed, Blue Gray, 14 x 6 In. 660.00
Vase, Dragon Around Neck, Marked, c.1920, 13 1/4 In. 2875.00
Vase, Dragon Around Neck, Orange, Green, Brown, Amphora, 13 In. 2875.00
Vase, Dragon, Around Shaped Vessel, Closed-In Rim, Signed, 20 In. 5750.00
Vase, Dragon, Bronze Gunmetal Glaze, Green, Red, Black, Amphora, 17 In. 5500.00
Vase, Etruscan, Figures In Daily Pursuits, Handles, Raised On Circular Foot, 24 In. 495.00
Vase, Gilt Sea Horse, Head Forms Handle, Mottled Ground, Marked, c.1900, 9 1/2 In. 1380.00
Vase, Grapes & Fruit, Applied Handles, Green Iridescent, Amphora, 8 1/2 In. 345.00
Vase, Green Matte Glaze, Marked, Tydell, 12 1/2 In. 495.00
Vase, Inlay Of Cavalier, Gun & Sword, Double Handled, 15 In. 450.00
Vase, Large Moth In Center, Applied Branch-Like Handles, Amphora, 11 In. 1840.00
Vase, Lion In Desert Oasis, Marked, Amphora, 11 In. 440.00
Vase, Maiden In Profile, Setting Sun, Aquamarine Ground, 11 In. 3200.00
Vase, Molded Eagles On Sides, Blue, Gold Geometric Design, 13 In. 880.00
Vase, Molded Floral Design, Red, Green, Yellow, 2 Cutout Handles, Amphora, 16 In. 2750.00

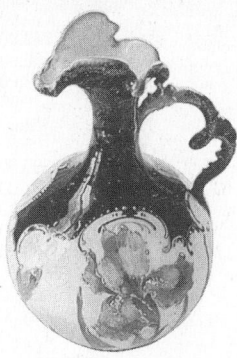

Never burn Christmas greens in the fireplace. The wood will send sparks up the chimney and some evergreens burn so "hot" they could cause a fire in the flue or a buildup of creosote in the chimney.

Teplitz, Ewer, Lavender
Iris, Cobalt Blue Top,
Gold Trim, Signed,
Bohemia, 7 1/2 In.

Vase, Mother-Of-Pearl Iris, Gold Ground, 4 Handles, 9 In.	550.00
Vase, Mottled Blue & Mauve Ground, 4 Handles, Gilt Outlining, Signed, 10 1/4 In.	345.00
Vase, Mushroom Form, Female Figures, Whirling, Amphora, 1920, 6 1/2 In.	690.00
Vase, Poppies & Buds, Blue Matte Finish, 6 1/2 In.	175.00
Vase, Poppies & Grapes, Cream, Green, 18 In.	635.00
Vase, Portrait, Multicolored, Gold Outlines, Impressed Mark, Amphora, 7 In.	935.00
Vase, Stylized Birds, Blue, Red, Gray, Swollen Cylinder, Amphora, c.1900, 13 1/2 In.	172.00
Vase, Stylized Blown Out Design At Top, Gold Accents, Pink Centers, P. Daschel, 8 In.	770.00
Vase, Vertical Ribs, Textured, Gunmetal To Black Glaze, 2 Handles, Amphora, 13 In.	4840.00
Vase, White Flowers, Jeweled Opaline Centers, 11 In.	500.00
Vase, Woman's Head, Flowing Hair, Blossoms, 2 Asymmetrical Handles, 13 In.	495.00
Vase, Woman, Stellmacher, 7 In.	175.00

TERRA-COTTA is a special type of pottery. It ranges from pale orange to dark reddish-brown in color. The color comes from the clay, which is fired but not always glazed in the finished piece.

Bust, Officer, Ceremonial Headdress, Continental, 21 1/2 In.	400.00
Bust, Roman Emperor Type, Circular Stepped Pedestal, Continental, 32 x 26 In.	4600.00
Bust, Woman, Carpeaux, 1876, 25 1/2 In.	2990.00
Cup, Etruscan, Black Slip Glaze, Stemmed	23.00
Figurine, Bull Dog, Seated, 12 1/2 In.	374.00
Figurine, Bullfighter, Period Costume, 19th Century, 11 In.	11500.00
Figurine, Cherub & Bacchante, Seated, Cherub With Grapes, 16 In.	920.00
Figurine, Christ Child, Standing, Hands Raised, Glass Eyes, 27 1/2 In.	2530.00
Figurine, Duck, Squawking, Standing, Wings Outspread, Beak Open, 20 In.	805.00
Figurine, Fancy Boy, Holding Dog, Fancy Girl, Holding Cat, 17 In., Pair	2070.00
Figurine, Hunter & Huntress, Polychrome, France, 11 1/2 In., Pair	920.00
Figurine, Joseph, Wearing Heavy Robes, Sitting, Northern Italy, 13 In.	8050.00
Figurine, Lion, Recumbent, Mossy Patina, Wooden Plinths, 19 In., Pair	5175.00
Figurine, Male & Female, Green Robes, Raised On Plinth Base, 17 & 18 In., Pair	805.00
Figurine, Muse, Representing The Arts, Paint Traces, Italy, 19th Century, 12 1/2 In.	1495.00
Figurine, Mythological Being, 4 In.	115.00
Figurine, Rooster, 9 1/2 In.	290.00
Figurine, Rooster, Crouching, 9 1/2 In., Pair	145.00
Figurine, Woman, Reclining With Wheat, D.H. Chiparus, 29 1/2 In.	10350.00
Fountain, Wall, Lion, Snarling Mask Backplate, Scallop Shell, 25 In., 2 Piece	240.00
Group, Virgin & Child, St. Joseph, 2 Shepherds, Cow, Mule, 8 1/2 In.	1150.00
Humidor, Tobacco, Boy, Holding Watermelon, 12 In.	825.00
Jam Jar, Handles, c.1890, 15 1/2 In.	135.00
Jar, French Provincial, 2 Handles, c.1890, 11 1/4 In.	220.00
Jar, Interior Glazed Yellow, 2 Handles, c.1900, 10 1/4 In.	192.00
Jardiniere, Pedestal, Putti, Cherubs, Playing, Clawed Feet, 19th Century, 43 In.	2012.00
Oil Jar, Rigaree Band At Neck, France, 23 x 17 In.	151.00
Pedestal, Faux Marble, Charcoal, Ecru, 1820, 47 1/2 In., Pair	3146.00
Planter, Garden Wall, River God Mask Form, England, 17 x 16 1/2 In.	150.00
Planter, Leaf Design, 4 Griffins On Base, 19th Century, 23 In.	140.00

Planter, Wall, Head Form, Of King Arthur, England, 12 x 10 1/4 x 5 In., Pair 270.00
Planter, Wall, Louis XVI, England, 11 1/2 x 18 1/2 x 7 1/4 In., Pair 242.00
Planter, Wall, River God Mask Form, England, 17 x 16 1/2 x 8 1/2 In. 150.00
Plaque, Classical Goddess Among Putti, Foliate & Floral Band, 25 In. 212.00
Storage Jar, 2 Ring Handles, Flat Bottom, 19th Century, 22 In. 240.00
Storage Jar, French Provincial, Incised Line Design, 1890, 34 In. 303.00
Storage Jar, French Provincial, Ribbed Design, France, 1890, 42 In. 303.00
Tobacco Jar, Skull, JM 3386 Mark, 4 1/2 In. 300.00
Urn, Cover, Grapevine Swags, 2 Acanthine Handles, On Fluted Stand, 63 In., Pair 1331.00
Urn, Horned Masks, Floral, Foliate Swags, On Fluted Stand, 18 x 19 In., Pair 303.00
Urn, Neoclassical, Campana Shape, Mask Handles, Square Base, Italy, 20 In., Pair 3160.00
Urn, Neoclassical, Greek Style, Satyrs & Garlands, Square Base, 41 x 17 1/2 In. 3160.00
Urn, Relief Wreaths & Faces A Handles, 20 3/4 In. 467.00
Urn, Wrought Iron, Meandering Floral Border Rim, Glazed, Art Deco, 43 In., Pair 920.00
Vase, Burgundy, Cylinder, 8 1/2 In. 145.00
Vase, Foliate Scrolls, Black Glaze, 12 In., Pair 172.00

TEXTILES listed here include many types of printed fabrics and table
and household linens. Some other textiles will be found under Clothing, Coverlet, Quilt, Rug, etc.

Altar Cloth, Beaded Floral, Silk Chamois, Metal Fringe, 59 x 28 In. 1250.00
Banner, Welcome Centennial US Of A, Eagle & Military Pattern, 1876, 12 x 18 In. 45.00
Bed Cloth, Silk, Embroidered, Classical Women, Armorials, Border, Italy, 100 x 67 In. ... 400.00
Bedspread, Chenille, Peach, Double 50.00
Bedspread, Crocheted, 7-In. Fringe, 75 x 103 In. 33.00
Bedspread, Crocheted, White Floral Design, Knotted Fringe, 90 x 100 In. 110.00
Bedspread, Crocheted, White, Yellow Rosettes & Bands, 3-In. Fringe, 70 x 80 In. 50.00
Bedspread, Glazed Chintz, Quilted Top, Gathered Skirt, 70 x 64 In. 605.00
Bedspread, Rayon, Reversible, Pink, Bates, 88 x 112 In. 35.00
Bedspread, Woven, White, 80 x 84 In. 55.00
Blanket, Pendleton, 1930, 55 x 80 In. 355.00
Blanket, Wool, Blue Star & Borders, Hand Woven, 72 x 106 In. 440.00
Blanket, Wool, Hand Woven, 2 Panel, Orange & Blue Checkerboard, 1850, 85 x 81 In. .. 90.00
Bolt Of Fabric, Jagged Design, Yellow & Green, Girard, Herman Miller, 1961, 48 In. 520.00
Comforter, Patchwork, Log Cabin, Sunshine & Shadow, Multicolored, Cotton, 87 In. 110.00
Curtain, Ivory Floral, Peach, Caramel & Olive, Arts & Crafts, 33 x 33 In., 3 Piece 230.00
Curtain, Linen, Flowers, Peach & Caramel Ground, Arts & Crafts, 33 x 55 In., 3 Piece .. 210.00
Flag, 38 Stars, Glazed Cotton, 12 x 16 In. 150.00
Flag, 38 Stars, Original Pole, In Frame 245.00
Flag, 717 Coast Artillery Battalion, Embroidered, Red, Yellow Fringe, 36 x 48 In. 375.00
Flag, American, 45 Stars, 48 1/2 x 69 In. 440.00
Flag, American, World War II 35.00
Flag, Deed Of Pen, Map Of Louisiana Purchase, Woman, Silk, 8 1/2 x 12 In. 225.00
Handkerchief, Child's, Margy, Scrappy, Yippy, Orange, 9 In. ....*Illus* 12.00
Handkerchief, Child's, Scrappy, Playing Football, Yellow, 9 In. ....*Illus* 18.00
Handkerchief, Silk, Printed Design, Red, Yellow & Green, 13 x 15 In. 125.00
Handkerchief, Washington Leaning On Horse With Letter, Stars, Frame, 13 x 10 In. 30.00
Homespun, Blue, White, 67 x 80 In. 300.00
Lambrequin, Applied, Velvet, Embroidered, Silk, Maroon Velvet, Victorian, 106 x 53 In. . 630.00
Napkin, White Linen Damask, 12 Piece 120.00
Needlepoint, Parrots & Flowerpot, Scrolled Border, Frame, 20th Century, 23 x 17 In. ... 385.00
Panel, Aubusson, Floral & Neoclassical Design, Off-White Field, 48 x 138 In., Pair 4890.00
Panel, Embroidered Silk, Red Fox, Stevengraph Style, England, Frame, 2 3/4 x 6 In. 55.00
Panel, Needlework, Moses In Bulrushes, Wool On Silk, Old Frame, 21 x 24 In. 630.00
Panel & Valance, Royal Blue Satin, Napoleonic Design, France, 19th Century, 120 In. ... 2800.00
Pillow, Embroidered, 15 x 18 In. 390.00
Pillow, Painted Indian, Victorian, 13 x 13 In. 325.00
Pillow, Painted Lady, Victorian, 13 x 13 In. 325.00
Pillow, Snoopy, Figural, Black & White, 1963, 14 1/2 In. 20.00
Pillow Sham, Appliqued, Center Medallion, Blue Tulips In Corners, Pair 130.00
Pillow Sham, Appliqued, Floral, Red & Green, White Ground, Pair 165.00
Pillow Sham, Patchwork, Embroidered, Cats & Rabbits, 16 x 30 In., Pair 330.00
Pillow Sham, White, Embroidered, 17 x 40 In. 40.00

Textile, Handkerchief, Child's, Margy,
Scrappy, Yippy, Orange, 9 In.

Textile, Handkerchief, Child's, Scrappy,
Playing Football, Yellow, 9 In.

Place Mat, Crocheted, White, Diamond & Square, 1930s, 14 x 17 In., 6 Piece 60.00
Place Mat, Hemstitched, Linen, Lithographed Storage Box, c.1930, 13 Piece 85.00
Robe, Sleigh, Horsehair, Red Roses, Center Leaves, Tan & Brown Border, 7 x 9 In. 110.00
Runner, Homespun, 12-In. Crocheted Edge, 21 x 44 In. 24.00
Shawl, Piano, Embroidered Silk, Floral Design, Ivory Ground, 70 x 70 In. 230.00
Tablecloth, Banquet, Hand Embroidered, Linen & Lace, 12 Napkins 900.00
Tablecloth, Brussels Ecru Lace, Linen, 12 Napkins, 67 x 100 In. 330.00
Tablecloth, Ecru, Lace Border, Linen, 12 Napkins, 68 x 120 In. 165.00
Tablecloth, Hand Crocheted, Ecru, 89 x 52 In. 125.00
Tablecloth, Lace Panels, Cutwork & Embroidery, 12 Napkins, 68 x 106 In. 192.00
Tablecloth, Point De Venise, Central Medallion, Trailing Flowers, c.1920, 64 x 118 In. ... 220.00
Tablecloth, White, Gray Embroidery, Scalloped, Linen, 12 Napkins, 81 x 62 In. 135.00
Tapestry, 2 Swans, Swimming In Pond, Towns In Distance, 1670s, 98 1/2 x 100 In. 8050.00
Tapestry, After The Hunt, Figures In A Landscape, 17th Century, 96 x 63 In. 4890.00
Tapestry, Aubusson Style, Child At Play With Archer, 59 1/4 x 74 In. 2345.00
Tapestry, Aubusson, Floral, Bird & Figural Design, Floral Borders, 57 x 66 In. 3450.00
Tapestry, Aubusson, Multicolored Flower Filled Border, Green, Brown, 100 x 40 In. 3335.00
Tapestry, Aubusson, Peonies, Roses & Dahlias, Earth Tones, 126 x 52 In. 6037.00
Tapestry, Crane At Left, Flowering Bush At Right, Castle, 1680s, 100 1/2 x 84 1/2 In. ... 6325.00
Tapestry, Falconing Party, France, 19th Century, 79 x 91 In. 6325.00
Tapestry, Hunt Scene, Men & Women On Horseback, Dogs, 55 x 78 In. 412.00
Tapestry, Ladies & Gentleman Picking Apples In Landscape, 56 x 56 In. 1265.00
Tapestry, Lady & The Unicorn, 20th Century, 45 x 62 In. 690.00
Tapestry, Needlepoint, Couple In Garden, Frame, France, 1920, 59 x 40 1/2 In. 270.00
Tapestry, Outdoor Tavern Scene, Framed, 19 x 19 In. 138.00
Tapestry, Pastoral Scene, Brussels, 19th Century, 61 x 82 In. 2185.00
Tapestry, Petit Point, Children Dancing Around Fountain, 46 x 64 In. 1320.00
Tapestry, Sailing Ships, Trees, Birds, Hand Woven, Mounted On Metal Rod, 66 x 77 In. . 1540.00
Tapestry, Village Scene In Earth Tones, Early 20th Century, 51 x 42 In. 165.00
Tapestry, Wall Hanging, Peasant Woman With Cows In Pasture, 49 x 49 In. 110.00
Tea Cozy, Blue Beaded, Double-Sided 698.00
Tick Cover, Blue & White Check, Homespun, 1 Panel, 1 Long Side Open, 85 x 33 In. ... 130.00
Tobacco Pouch, Brocade, Buddha's Hand Fruit Shape, Gilt, 19th Century 110.00
Tobacco Pouch, Needlework, Dragon, Pearl, Tiger Form, Japan 135.00
Tobacco Pouch, Needlework, Floral Design, Metal, Japan, 19th Century 110.00
Weaving, Silk, On The Town, Contemporary, 48 x 84 In. 1320.00

THERMOMETER is a name that comes from the Greek word for heat.
The thermometer was invented in 1731 to measure the temperature of
either water or air. All kinds of thermometers are collected, but those
with advertising messages are the most popular.

7-Up, Porcelain, Bottle 120.00
7-Up, Round, 9 In. 175.00
7-Up, Round, 12 In. 100.00
Akron Farmers Co-Op, Young Boy With Telephone Picture, 13 x 5 In. 30.00

Alka-Seltzer, Glass & Aluminum, T.W.O. Connell & Co., Chicago, Round, 12 In. 415.00
Alka-Seltzer, Round, Pam, 1950s, 12 In. 345.00
Arden Dairy Products, Pictures Vanilla Ice Cream 1/2 Gal., 36 In. 198.00
Arden Flavor Fresh Milk, Your Best Buy, Red Lettering, 8 x 36 In. 198.00
Becht Laundry Co., Desk Top, Porcelain, White Enamel Paint, 6 In. 30.00
Best Feeds, Porcelain 950.00
Bisque, Lovely Girl, Standing By Climbing Vine, 7 x 4 In. 100.00
Borden Smith Douglass Fertilizer 40.00
Briggs & Stratton Gas Engines, Glass, Plastic, 1940-1950, 14 In. 255.00
Calendar, Baby Boy With His Dog, Signed, Charlott Becker, 1941 .... 45.00
Calumet Baking Powder, Painted Wood 950.00
Campbell's Tomato Soup Can, Porcelain, Round Center Thermometer, 12 In. 4195.00
Canong's Chocolates, Porcelain, 38 3/4 In. 220.00
Castrol, Porcelain, Self-Framed, Emaille Belg.T.P., Bruxeles, 1959, 30 x 9 In. 190.00
Chew Mail Pouch Tobacco, 1920-1930, 19 x 74 In. 605.00
Clark Bar, Wooden, 1930s, 5 x 19 In. 175.00
Colburn's Mustard, Yellow, Wood, 30 In. 193.00
Dr Pepper, Frosty Man, Tin, 1950-1960, 6 x 16 In. 920.00
Dr Pepper, Hot Or Cold, Round, 1950-1960, 12 In. 775.00
Dr Pepper, Hot Or Cold, Tin, 1960s, 16 In. 260.00
Dr Pepper, Light-Up, Chevron 275.00
Dr Pepper, Plastic, 1950-1960, 11 In. 92.00
Dr. Scholl's, Metal, 37 In. 50.00
Drink Moxie, It's Always A Pleasure To Serve You, 1952, 10 x 26 In. 1380.00
Duffy's Malt Whiskey, Medicine For All Mankind, Wooden, 21 x 5 In. 175.00
Eat More Lowney's Chocolate Bars & Cracker Jack, 8 x 30 In. 220.00
Ex-Lax, Metal, 37 In. 49.00
Ex-Lax, Porcelain, 5 Colors, 8 x 36 In. 175.00
Ex-Lax, We Recommend Ex-Lax For Constipation, Black Ground, 8 x 38 In. 231.00
Famous Royal Scarlet Brand, Pure Food Products, 7 x 2 In. 303.00
Florida Fruit & Vegetable Assoc., 11 In. 60.00
Frostie Root Beer, Bottle Form 275.00
Frostie Root Beer, Tin, 36 x 8 In. 230.00
Ganong's Chocolates, The Gift Of Gladness, Dark Brown Ground, 8 x 38 In. 231.00
Grads Cigarettes, Porcelain, Graphic 275.00
Grant's Dairy, Round, 10 In. 65.00
Hill's Bros. Man In Turban, Logo, Porcelain, c.1915, 21 x 9 In. 120.00
Hill's Bros. Red Can Coffee, Indian Man, Drinking Coffee, 8 3/4 x 21 In. 660.00
Hires Root Beer, Bottle Shape, Tin, Die Cut, 28 1/2 In. 145.00
Land O'Lakes, When The Flavor Really Counts, Indian Maiden 55.00
Lash's Bitters 365.00
Leaders Laundry Co., Baby Boy With Dog, Charlott Becker, Calendar, 1941 .... 45.00
Lincoln Cab Co., Wood, Glass Tube, Metal Holders, 15 x 4 In. 88.00
Mail Pouch Tobacco, 36 In. 225.00
Mail Pouch Tobacco, Treat Yourself To The Best, Chew Mail Pouch, 8 x 39 In. .... 82.00 to 231.00
Mail Pouch Tobacco, Treat Yourself To The Best, Porcelain, Frame, 72 x 18 In. 285.00
Mail Pouch Tobacco, White Lettering, Blue With Yellow, Wooden, June, 1947 .... 75.00
Mobil, Tin, Glass, Pam Clock Co. Inc., New Rochelle, N.Y., Copyright 1957, 12 In. 440.00
Moxie, 1930-1940, 10 x 26 In. 4145.00
Moxie, Drink Moxie Take Home A Case Tonight, Green, Black, Box, 25 x 9 In. 1265.00
Moxie, It's Always A Pleasure To Serve You, Tin, 1950s, 10 x 25 1/2 In. 240.00
Nash 4-Door Coupe, Wooden, 3-Digit Phone Number, 21 x 9 In. 275.00
Nesbitt's, Bottle, Orange Sipping Through Straw, Tin, 16 In. 130.00
None Such Mincemeat, Tin Body, Stone Lithograph Under Glass, Tin Case, 1888 ...... 80.00
NuGrape, Bottle Shape, Tin, Die Cut, Embossed, 5 x 17 In. 270.00
Orange Crush, Bottle Cap Logo, Pam, Glass, 1940-1950, Round 275.00
Orange Crush, Bottle Shape, Tin, Die Cut, 28 1/2 In. 205.00
Orange Crush, Die Cut Bottle, 1950s, 29 In. 65.00
Orange Crush, With Bottle, Tin, 1930-1940, 6 x 15 In. 235.00
Orange Kist, 36 In. 125.00
Penn Fishing Tackle Mfg. Co. 100.00
Phillips 66, Round Float Top 115.00
Piels Real Draft Beer 75.00

Potato Sales Company, Wooden, 15 x 4 In. 27.00
Prestone Anti-Freeze, Porcelain, 36 In. 120.00
Prestone Anti-Freeze, Set, Safe, Sure 220.00
Ramon's Brownie Pills, Ramon's Pink Pills, Tin, 21 x 8 1/2 In. 220.00
Ramon's Brownie Pills, Ramon's Pink Pills, Wooden, 21 x 8 1/2 In. ....205.00 to 240.00
Risolene, c.1949, 25 1/2 x 10 In. 120.00
Royal Scarlet Pure Food Products, Porcelain, 27 In. 300.00
Salem Cigarettes 40.00
Salem Tobacco, Pack Of Salems On Front, Yellow, Metal, 9 1/4 In. 20.00
Shell Gasoline, Porcelain, Pat. Mar. 16, 1915, 27 x 7 1/4 In. 1980.00
Squirt, Embossed Tin, 1963, 13 1/2 x 6 In. 190.00
Stephen's Inks, Porcelain & Wood, 61 x 12 In. 385.00
Stephenson Union Suits, 2 Men In Underwear 1250.00
Storz, Bitter Free Beer, Bubble Glass, 12 1/2 In. 100.00
Suer's The National Extract, Wooden, 1910, 6 x 24 In. 575.00
Sun Drop, Round, 12 In. 125.00
Suncrest Soda, Bottle Form, 1940s 350.00
Thirsty? Just Whistle, Remounted Aluminum Frame, Pam, 1940s, 12 In. 375.00
Trico Wiper Blades, Stamped Metal, Plastic Cover, Dial Type, 15 In. 45.00
Tru Ade, Tin Lithograph, 6 x 15 In. 175.00
Tums, For The Tummy, Blue, Green, Tin, 4 x 9 In. 23.00
Vernor's Ginger Ale, Dome, Round, 1950, 12 In. 75.00
Ward's Vitovim Bread, 1920s, 9 x 21 In. 720.00
Waterman Pen Co., Fountain Pen Shape 1495.00
Winchester Ammunition, Tin, 26 1/2 In. 304.00
Winchester Western, Sporting Ammunition Sold Here, Red Ground, 7 x 26 In. 308.00
Ya Gotta Have Moxie, Moxie Man, Tin, 12 x 6 1/2 In. 193.00

TIFFANY is a name that appears on items made by Louis Comfort Tiffany, the American glass designer who worked from about 1879 to 1933. His work included iridescent glass, Art Nouveau styles of design, and original contemporary styles. He was also noted for stained glass windows, unusual lamps, bronze ware, pottery, and silver. Other types of Tiffany are listed under Tiffany Glass, Tiffany Pottery, or Tiffany Silver. The famous Tiffany lamps are listed in this section. Tiffany jewelry is listed in the jewelry and wristwatch categories. Reproductions of some types of Tiffany are being made.

Louis C. Tiffany

Ash Receiver, Hinged Case, Bronze, Gold Dore, 26 1/2 In. 690.00
Ashstand, Ashtray Insert, Signed, 31 In. 2300.00
Ashtray, Removable Center Insert, Bronze, Signed, 3 1/4 In. 400.00
Ashtray Set, Nested, Bronze, Gold Dore, Ruffled, 2 3/4 To 5 In., 4 Piece 325.00
Blotter Ends, Adam, 19 x 2 1/4 In., Pair 175.00
Blotter Ends, American Indian, Bronze, Gold Dore, 12 x 2 In., Pair 300.00
Blotter Ends, Nautical, Dark Patina, 19 1/2 x 2 1/4 In., Pair 750.00
Blotter Ends, Pine Needle, Pair 295.00
Blotter Ends, Rocker, Adam, Raised Handle, 5 x 3 In. 150.00
Blotter Ends, Rocker, Zodiac 120.00
Bonbon, Bronze, Gold Dore, Scalloped, Pedestal, 1 1/2 x 3 3/4 In. 150.00
Bookends, Bookmark, Bronze, Gold Dore, 4 3/4 x 6 In. 750.00
Bookends, Buddha, Bronze, Gold Dore, 6 In., Pair 750.00
Bookends, Venetian, Bronze, Gold Dore, 5 x 6 In., Pair 950.00
Bookends, Zodiac, Bronze, Patina, 5 x 6 In. 1045.00
Bookrack, Grapevine, Green Slag Glass, Bronze, Signed, 14 In. 1800.00
Bowl, Bronze, Gold Dore, Monogram, 9 In. 83.00
Bowl, Cover, Berry Branches, Green Mottled Interior, Bronze, 5 1/2 x 4 In. 5462.00
Box, Antique Gold Finish, Chest Type, Bronze, 8 x 3 3/4 x 3 In. 1200.00
Box, Card, Hinged Cover, Pine Needle, Green Slag Glass, Bronze, 3 x 2 x 4 1/2 In. 1500.00
Box, Cover, Blue, Green Enameled, Cedar Liner, Bronze, Gold Dore, 3 1/2 In. 460.00
Box, Cover, Zodiac, Gold Dore, 6 3/4 In. 865.00
Box, Dresser, Acid Etched Bands, 1907, 2 3/4 x 3 7/8 In. 430.00
Box, Glove, Pine Needle, Green Slag Glass, Bronze, 13 1/4 x 4 1/4 In. 2700.00
Box, Grapevine, Beige & White Glass, Bronze, Beaded Edge, Signed, 4 3/8 In. 430.00
Box, Handkerchief, Grapevine, Slag Glass, Bronze, Beaded Edge, 1928, 7 In. 1265.00

Box, Hinged Cover, Enameled Geometric, Bronze, Signed, 2 3/4 In. 450.00
Box, Hinged Cover, Zodiac, Bronze, Signed, 4 1/2 x 3 1/2 x 2 In. 550.00
Box, Jewelry, Pine Needle, Slag Glass, Bronze, Beaded Edge, 9 1/2 In. 2000.00
Box, Pine Needle, Slag Glass, Bronze, Gold Dore, Ball Footed, Signed, 6 1/2 x 4 x 2 In. ... 650.00
Box, Stamp, Hinged Cover, Abalone, Bronze, 3 Sections, Signed 550.00
Box, Stamp, Venetian, Bronze, Tiffany Studios, c.1899, 2 1/4 x 5 1/2 In. 488.00
Box, Stamp, Venetian, Gold Dore, Chainlink Hinged Closure, Signed, 2 x 4 In. 450.00
Box, Utility, Adam, Bronze, Green Enameled, Tiffany Studios, 2 x 4 3/8 In. 431.00
Brush Holder, Bronze, Patina, Brush, Tiffany Studios, N.Y., Early 1900s, 2 1/4 In. 225.00
Calendar, American Indian, Frog Heads, Bronze, Brown Patina, 6 x 7 In. 345.00
Calendar, Zodiac, Bronze, Gold Dore, Impressed Mark, 4 1/2 In. 121.00
Calendar, Zodiac, Bronze, Tiffany Studios, c.1899, 4 In. 488.00
Candleholder, Pastel Pink, Mushroom Cap Candle Cups, 3 1/2 In., Pair 1610.00
Candlestick, Bronze, 3 Raised Arms, Circular Foot, Brown Patina, 1918, 17 3/4 In. 1380.00
Candlestick, Bronze, Bamboo, Bottom As 8 Spreading Tree Trunks, Signed, 10 1/2 In. ... 2000.00
Candlestick, Bronze, Cantilevered Arm, Irregular Lily Pad Base, 1918, 6 1/4 In. 1725.00
Candlestick, Bronze, Channeled Supports, Paw Foot, Square Base, 11 In., Pair 1725.00
Candlestick, Bronze, Tripod With Bud Holder, 14 In., Pair 1955.00
Candlestick, Favrile, Bronze, Wide Gadrooned Base, Red, Brown Patina, 17 In. 3450.00
Candlestick, Favrile, Green, 3 Splayed Legs, 1918, 8 In., Pair 3220.00
Candlestick, Gilt Bronze, Sinuous Vine Stem, 7 1/4 In. 1150.00
Candlestick, Gilt Bronze, Stylized Lily Pad Base, 10 In., Pair 517.00
Candlestick, Green Slag Glass, Bronze, Flared Rim, Ribbed Circular Foot, 15 In. 2300.00
Canister, Bronze Cover, Dark Patina, Signed, 3 1/2 x 3 In. 225.00
Card Tray, Footed, Engraved Crest, 20th Century 132.00
Chamberstick, 2-Light, Bronze, Blown Green Glass, Signed, 9 In. 2000.00
Chatelaine, Perfume Bottle, Signed, Copper Butterflies & Dragonflies, c.1880 .... 4830.00
Cigarette Holder, Bronze, Green Patina, Tiffany Studios, c.1899, 4 1/2 In. 460.00
Clock, Bronze, Cresting Wave, Various Marine Life, Circular Face, 22 1/2 In. 2990.00
Clock, Desk, Zodiac, Bronze, Tiffany Studios, c.1899, 3 1/4 In. 805.00
Clock, Mantel, Black Marble, Malachite Inlay, Incised Gold, 8 1/4 x 14 In. 545.00
Clock, Mantel, Brass, Reeded Pillars, Glass Front, Cherubs, 1900, 13 x 10 1/2 In. 805.00
Clock, Mantel, Pagoda, Enamel, Brass Columns, Finials, 10 1/2 In. 1320.00
Clock, Shelf, Bronze, 4 In. 355.00
Coaster, Wine Bottle, c.1890, 3 1/2 In. 1200.00
Compact, Art Deco, Sunburst Design, Ruby & Gold Accents, Gold Interior 345.00
Compact, Engine Turned Design, Mirrored Compartment 316.00
Compote, Adam, Bronze, Gold Dore, 3 Curved-Footed Pedestal, 4 x 7 In. 350.00
Compote, Bronze, Gold Dore, Peacock Eyes, 8 In. 400.00
Compote, Double Shaped Ribbed Body, Scalloped, Signed, 3 3/4 In. 750.00
Compote, Greek Key, Bronze, Staggered Line Design, Circular Foot, 3 3/4 x 6 1/4 In. ... 259.00
Compote, Green Enameled, Classical Border, Bronze, Gold Dore 977.00
Desk Set, Favrile, Spider Web Pen Rest, Grapevine Blotter Ends, 6 Piece 1380.00
Desk Set, Zodiac, Bronze, Amber, Brown Patina, 1918, 9 Piece 920.00
Desk Set, Zodiac, Bronze, Gold Dore, 3 Piece 632.00
Desk Set, Zodiac, Green & Brown Finish, 4 Piece 690.00
Easter Egg, Lilies, Ram's Heads, Rubies On Body, Gem Set, Signed, 2 1/2 In. 8050.00
Fernery, Arrowroot Mosaic, Bronze, 11 1/2 In. 1200.00
Flower Holder, Bronze, Gold Dore, Heart Base, 10 Tubes, 9 In. 1200.00
Frame, Double, Grapevine, Bronze, Easel Back, Signed, 10 x 7 1/2 In. 3000.00
Frame, Glass & Bronze, Signed, 8 5/8 x 7 1/8 In. 4370.00
Frame, Venetian, Gold Dore, Mink Rows Base, 9 x 12 In. 2000.00
Frame, Zodiac, Bronze, Easel Back, Signed, 8 x 7 In. 1200.00
Humidor, Double Cover, Pine Needle, Slag Glass, Bronze, Signed 3200.00
Inkstand, Hinged Cover, Blue, Silver Plate, 2 x 2 3/4 x 2 2/3 In. 287.00
Inkstand, Hinged Cover, Zodiac, Bronze, Gold Dore 431.00
Inkstand, Turtleback, Jeweled, Green, Bronze, Tiffany Studios, c.1902, 4 In. 2300.00
Inkwell, Bronze, Gold Iridescent Brickwork Favrile Tiles, Blue, Cylindrical, 3 1/2 In. 13800.00
Inkwell, Bronze, Green Favrile Blown Glass, Abstract Design On Cover, 4 In. 1610.00
Inkwell, Favrile, Blue, Green Tiles, Bronze, Gold Liner, Dark Brown Patina, 2 In. 4600.00
Inkwell, Favrile, Cracquelure, Green Opalescent, Bronze, 1918, 3 1/2 In. 2875.00
Inkwell, Gold Iridescent Favrile Mosaic Tiles, Domed Cover, 4 1/2 x 3 In. 13800.00
Inkwell, Hinged Cover, Adam, Bronze, Gold Dore, Oval, 4 x 3 x 2 1/2 In. 350.00

Inkwell, Hinged Cover, American Indian, Bronze, Glass Insert, 5 1/2 x 3 In. 650.00
Inkwell, Hinged Cover, Chinese, Octagonal, Glass Insert, 4 3/4 In. 750.00
Inkwell, Hinged Cover, Grapevine, Embossed Columns, Signed, 2 1/2 x 2 3/8 In. 168.00
Inkwell, Hinged Cover, Grapevine, Green Slag Glass, Bronze, Signed, 7 In. 1500.00
Inkwell, Hinged Cover, Nautical, Dolphin Footed, 5 1/4 x 3 1/2 In. 1200.00
Inkwell, Hinged Cover, Zodiac, Brown Mottled Patina, 3 5/8 In.   3450.00
Inkwell, Pine Needle, Caramel Slag Glass, Bronze, Square 345.00
Inkwell, Reticulated Bronze, Favrile Glass, Circular Form, Tiffany Studios, c.1899, 4 In. . .   1840.00
Inkwell, Scarab, Signed, Bronze, 4 In. 5175.00
Inkwell, Stylized Foliate, Bronze, Enameled, Signed, Round, 7 x 4 In. 1200.00
Lamp, Acorn Border, Green, Rippled Favrile, Bronze Urn Base, Signed, 20 In. 8050.00
Lamp, Acorn, Amber, Green, Bronze Bridge Base, Tiffany Studios, 58 In. 21275.00
Lamp, Acorn, Favrile, Amber & Green Striated Shade, Rectangular Tiles, 21 In. 13800.00
Lamp, Acorn, Favrile, Bronze, Rectangular Amber & White Striated Shade 11500.00
Lamp, Acorn, Favrile, Rectangular Green & White Striated Shade, 17 x 10 In. 6325.00
Lamp, Amber Pleated Glass Panels, Bronze, Gold Dore, Square Foot, 18 3/4 In. 5225.00
Lamp, Bronze, Brown, Raised Square Relief, Green Patina, 1920, 28 1/2 In. 4600.00
Lamp, Bronze, Columnar Standard, Curl Cushion Form Base, 4-Footed, 18 In. 2760.00
Lamp, Bronze, Columnar Standard, Scrolling Lappets, 4-Footed, 28 In. 3737.00
Lamp, Bronze, Single Standard, 3 Scrolling Arms, Paw Feet, 1928, 58 In. 5462.00
Lamp, Candlestick, Green Pulled Feather Design, Amber Iridescent Shade, Favrile 1150.00
Lamp, Cherry & Cherry Blossom, Cat's Paw Base, 22 5/8 In. 93500.00
Lamp, Chinese Pattern, Octagon Amber & Slag Glass, Bronze, Signed, 17 In. 6000.00
Lamp, Crocus, Bronze, 19 In. . . . . 14300.00 to 15730.00
Lamp, Daffodil, Favrile, Bronze, Trumpet Base, 25 In. . . . . *Illus* 60375.00
Lamp, Damascene Shade, Adjustable Harp, Favrile, Bronze, Signed, 18 1/4 In. 1760.00
Lamp, Dogwood, Blue Background, Bronze, Pumpkin Base . . . . *Illus* 44850.00
Lamp, Dogwood, Favrile Domed Shade, Bronze, 1928, 32 In. 5174.00
Lamp, Domed Shade, Acorn Border, Yellow Mottled, Dark Brown Patina, 22 In. 6325.00
Lamp, Double Arm, Gold Dore, Hexagon Shades, Signed, 13 x 12 In. 3000.00
Lamp, Dragonfly, Dome Shade, Bronze, 30 x 22 In. 425.00
Lamp, Favrile Domed Orange Shade, Bronze, Gold Dore, Scalloped, 12 In. 4370.00
Lamp, Favrile, Gold, Rose Iridescent, 3 Bronze Arms, Signed, 7 x 15 In. 5500.00
Lamp, Favrile, Swirled Silver Blue Waves, White, Green Shade, Bronze, 19 In. 5750.00
Lamp, Geometric Tiles, Bronze, Brown, Green Patina, Favrile, 21 In. 8050.00
Lamp, Geometric, Yellow Amber Mottled, Favrile, Bronze, 1920, 21 1/2 In. 9775.00
Lamp, Gold Iridescent Favrile Glass Shade, Bronze, 3 Tripod Feet, 55 x 10 In. 7762.00
Lamp, Iridescent Abalone Discs, Curved Arm, Signed, 9 In. 3500.00
Lamp, Lily, 3-Light, 12 3/4 In. 3105.00
Lamp, Lily, 3-Light, Pulled Green Leaves, Opalescent, Bronze, Favrile, 13 In. 5750.00
Lamp, Linenfold, 16 Panels Favrile Glass Shade, Bronze, Brown Patina, 20 1/2 In. 5750.00
Lamp, Linenfold, Favrile, Overlapping Leaves, Bronze, Brown Patina, 16 In. 9200.00
Lamp, Mosque, Green Pulled Feathers Shade, Bronze, Gold Dore Top, Signed, 8 1/2 In. . .   2800.00
Lamp, Mosque, Opalescent Bottom, Gold Dore, Wooden Base, 8 1/2 In. 2800.00

Tiffany, Lamp, Daffodil,
Favrile, Bronze, Trumpet Base,
25 In.

Tiffany, Lamp, Dogwood,
Blue Background, Bronze,
Pumpkin Base

Tiffany, Lamp, Pond Lily,
Favrile, Bronze, Cushion Base,
25 In.

Lamp, Nautilus, Mother-Of-Pearl, Bronze, Bronze, Signed, 13 1/2 In. 9775.00
Lamp, Oil, Favrile Ribbed Opal Shade, Gold Pulled, Coiled Feathers, 15 In. 5750.00
Lamp, Paneled Shade, Favrile, Bronze, Green, Brown Finish, 17 In. 4312.00
Lamp, Piano, Green Leaves & Grass, 3 Lily Shades, 8 1/2 In. 2990.00
Lamp, Pivoting Shade In Amber, Silvery Blue Favrile, Bronze, 55 In. 2875.00
Lamp, Pond Lily, Favrile, Bronze, Cushion Base, 25 In. . . . . *Illus* 44850.00
Lamp, Poppies, Leaves, Bronze, Base With Birds, 20 1/2 In. 825.00
Lamp, Pulled Feathers, Favrile, Mint & Emerald Green Tiles, Bronze, Brown Patina 9200.00
Lamp, Scarab, Favrile, Blue Glass Pivoting Shade, Bronze, Brown Patina, 8 In. 9775.00
Lamp, Scarab, Green, Purple, Gold Iridescent, Bronze, 8 In. 6600.00
Lamp, Swirling Leaves, Favrile, Domed Shade, Green & White Opalescent, 26 In. 12650.00
Lamp, Swirling Leaves, Signed Shade & Base, 24 x 18 In. 7150.00
Lamp, Turtleback, Arms, Bronze Shade, Adjustable, Signed, 7 1/2 In. 3800.00
Lamp, Turtleback, Domed Green, Amber Shade, Bronze, Knob Feet, 15 In. 5175.00
Lamp, Turtleback, Favrile, 2 Blue Iridescent Tiles, Brown Patina, 14 In. 8625.00
Lamp, Weight-Balance, Desk, Shade Signed, Favrile, 12 1/2 In. 8050.00
Lamp, Weight-Balance, Glass & Bronze, Signed, 14 5/8 In. 9200.00
Lamp, Weight-Balance, Glass & Bronze, Signed, 15 3/4 In. 8050.00
Lamp, Zodiac, Favrile Domed Shade, Harp Arms, Bronze, Gilt, 13 In. 3220.00
Letter Clip, Abalone, Bronze, Gold Dore, Signed, 2 x 2 3/4 In. 550.00
Letter Holder, Grapevine, Green Slag Glass, Bronze, 4 1/2 x 6 1/4 x 2 3/4 In. 950.00
Letter Holder, Pine Needle, Caramel Slag Glass, Bronze, 2 Sections, 6 x 10 In. 295.00
Letter Holder, Pine Needle, Green Slag Glass, Bronze, 2 Sections, 4 1/2 x 6 1/4 In. 950.00
Letter Holder, Zodiac, Bronze, Green Patina, Marked 120.00
Letter Opener, Adam, Gold Dore, Curved Handle, 10 In. 250.00
Letter Opener, American Indian, Bronze, Gold Dore, 10 1/2 In. 200.00
Letter Opener, Graduate, Bronze, Gold Dore, Signed, 9 In. 200.00
Letter Opener, Grapevine, Amber Slag Glass, Bronze, Gold Dore, Signed, 9 In. 275.00
Letter Opener, Heraldic, Enameled, Silver Shield, 9 1/2 In. 250.00
Letter Opener, Louis XVI, Bronze, Gold Dore, Wreath Handle, 10 In. 250.00
Letter Opener, Venetian, Bronze, Gold Dore, Signed, 9 1/2 In. 225.00
Letter Rack, Abalone, Bronze, Gold Dore, 2 Sections, Signed 900.00
Letter Rack, Adam, Bronze, Gold Dore, 2 Sections, 9 1/4 x 2 1/4 x 6 In. 450.00
Letter Rack, American Indian, Bronze, 2 Sections, 11 x 5 3/4 x 2 3/4 In. 900.00
Letter Rack, Grapevine, Amber Slag Glass, Bronze, 2 Sections, Signed, 6 1/4 In. 750.00
Magnifying Glass, Venetian, Bronze, Gold Dore, Signed, 9 In. 1200.00
Match Stand, Ashtray, Nautical, Bronze, Signed, 6 1/2 x 5 1/2 In. 650.00
Medal, Major Gen. George H. Thomas, Nov. 2, 1865, Bronze, 3 In. 1200.00
Paperweight, Abalone, Bronze, Gold Dore, Pyramid Shape, Signed, 1 3/4 In. 800.00
Paperweight, Dog, Reclining, Holding A Top, Bronze, 1 1/2 x 2 1/2 In. . . . . .230.00 to 475.00
Paperweight, Glass & Bronze, Favrile, Signed, 4 In. 2300.00
Paperweight, Lion, Bronze, Original Patina, Impressed Mark, 5 In. 440.00
Paperweight, Lion, Reclining, Bronze, Gold Dore, 1 3/4 x 4 3/4 In. 460.00
Paperweight, Lioness, Reclining, Bronze, Gold Dore, Signed, 5 In. 700.00
Paperweight, Ninth Century, Jeweled, Bronze, Gold Dore, Signed, 4 1/4 In. 550.00
Paperweight, Owl, Bronze, 3 In. 850.00
Pen Brush, Zodiac, Bronze 175.00
Pen Tray, Adam, Bronze 195.00
Pen Tray, Adam, Bronze, Handles, 3 Sections, 9 1/2 x 2 3/4 In. 200.00
Pen Tray, American Indian, Bronze 230.00
Pen Tray, American Indian, Bronze, Gold Dore, 2 Sections, Signed, 11 x 4 In. 300.00
Pen Tray, Nautical, Bronze, Brown Patina, 9 In. 1092.00
Pen Tray, Zodiac, Bronze, 3 x 10 In. 325.00
Pen Wipe, Favrile, Mosaic Glass Tiles, Green, Blue Amber, Orange, Copper, 9 In. 8625.00
Pencil, Mechanical, Chrome 50.00
Planter, Geometric Design, Silver Finish, Removable Copper Liner, Squat, 3 x 10 In. 575.00
Plaque, Glass Mosaic Goldfish, Blue Ground, Handles, Signed, 14 In. 825.00
Plate, Bronze, Gold Dore, Marked, 9 In. 135.00
Postage Scale, Grapevine, Slag Glass, Bronze, Signed, 6 1/2 In. 3500.00
Postage Scale, Pine Needle, Green Slag Glass, Bronze, Signed 750.00
Postage Scale, Zodiac, Bronze 395.00
Screen, Tea, 3-Panel, Green Slag Glass, Bronze, 4 1/2 x 7 1/2 In. 3500.00
Seal, Scarab, Gold, Monogrammed, 1 1/4 In. 515.00

Shade, 12-Sided Amber Panels, Bronze, 1927, 7 1/4 x 19 1/4 In. 8625.00
Shade, Favrile, Cream Opalescent Shade, Ruffled Edge, Bronze, 24 In. 5750.00
Thermometer, Bookmark, Easel, Bronze, Brown, Green Patina, 9 In. 862.00
Thermometer, Zodiac, Easel, Bronze, Signed, 4 1/4 x 8 In. 1500.00
Tobacco Jar, Pine Needle, Slag Glass, Bronze, Signed, 6 1/2 In. 2185.00
Tray, Abalone, Dot, Dash, Curlicue Border, Bronze, 7 1/2 In. 144.00
Tray, Abalone, Geometric Design, Bronze, Gold Dore, 9 In. 172.00
Tray, Abalone, Raised Border, Bronze, Gold Dore, 12 In. 288.00
Tray, Art Nouveau, Bronze, Gold Dore, Round, Signed, 10 In. 250.00
Tray, Central Medallion Surrounded By Cabochons, 8 Sections, Bronze, 13 In. 5520.00
Tray, Geometric Border, Bronze, Gold Dore, 12 In. 300.00
Tray, Geometric Design, Bronze, Gold Dore, Short Pedestal, 9 3/4 In. 225.00
Trivet, Favrile, Dragonfly, Gold Iridescent Wings, Bronze, Dark Brown Patina, 7 In. 10350.00
Vase, Bronze, Gold Dore, Bulbous, Flared Rim, Signed, 6 1/2 In. 450.00
Vase, Bud, Bronze, Allover Diagonal Ribs, 3 1/2 x 1 3/4 In. 225.00
Vase, Bud, Copper, Hammered, Bird Of Prey On A Branch, Peach, Blue, 1905, 6 In. 9200.00
Vase, Favrile, 18 Ribs, Cobalt Blue, Blue Enameled Metal, 17 In. 2990.00
Vase, Knop, Cover, Berried Foliage, Earth Tone Finish, 9 1/2 In., Pair 2300.00
Vase, Trumpet, Bronze Base, 18 In. 1200.00
Vase, Trumpet, Bronze, Gold Dore, Green Pulled Leaves, 12 In. 316.00
Vase, Trumpet, Pulled Feathers, Bronze Holder, Signed, 12 In. 4200.00
TIFFANY GLASS, Bottle, Favrile, Gray, Silver, Gold Iridescent, Stopper, c.1892, 12 1/2 In. . . 920.00
Bowl, 8 Ribs, Blue, Scalloped Edge, Favrile, 3 3/4 In. 345.00
Bowl, 10 Ribs, Blue Iridescent, Favrile, 2 In. 690.00
Bowl, Gold Iridescent, Favrile, Ruffled Edge, Footed, 4 x 2 In. 450.00
Bowl, Gold Iridescent, Pulled Chain, Signed, Louis C. Tiffany, 7 1/2 x 3 In. 104.00
Bowl, Gold Iridescent, Wide Pinched Rim, Signed, 3 x 4 1/4 In. 385.00
Bowl, Gold Spotted Opal, Emerald Green, Blue Rim, Favrile, 3 Shell Feet 920.00
Bowl, Green Trailing Hearts & Vines, Gold Iridescent, Favrile, L.C.T. Favrile, 12 In. 550.00
Bowl, Iridescent Yellow, Signed, Paper Label, 1 1/2 x 4 1/4 In. 425.00
Bowl, Ruffled, Gold Iridescent, Ribbed Body, Signed, 2 x 4 In. 400.00
Bowl, Underplate, Gold Iridescent, Favrile, Ruffled Edge, 4 1/2 x 2 In., 2 Piece 750.00
Bowl, Underplate, Yellow, Amber Exterior To Opalescent Interior, Favrile, 7 In. 1092.00
Box, Cover, Pulled Feathers, Green, Yellow, Blue, Favrile, 5 In. 3105.00
Candlestick, Amber, Ribbed Body, Flared Rim, Favrile, c.1900, 12 1/4 In., Pair 2587.00
Candlestick, Blue, Purple Iridescent, Signed, Favrile, 5 1/4 x 4 In., Pair 1950.00
Candlestick, Champagne, Bronze, Amber, Favrile, 22 1/2 In. 1840.00
Candlestick, Domed Shades, Amber Linenfold, 3 Leg Base, 14 3/4 In. 2875.00
Candlestick, Gold Ruffled Shade, Swirled Rib Gold Holder, Favrile, 12 In. 1150.00
Candlestick, Green Pulled Feathers, Amber Iridescent, Favrile, 1918, 9 1/2 In. 4025.00
Chalice, Gold Iridescent, Square Knop, Raised Circular Foot, 10 1/2 In. 1725.00
Compote, 5 Pulled Green Feathers, Gold Iridescent Interior, Gold Luster Rim 1495.00
Compote, Blue, White Edge, Clear, Gold, Footed, Signed, L.C.T. Favrile, 5 1/2 In. 440.00
Compote, Chinese Gold Top, Ribs On Underside, Favrile, Signed 900.00
Compote, Deep Amber Iridescent, Scalloped Edge, Ribbed Body, 1928, 3 3/4 In. 345.00
Compote, Etched Leaf & Vine, Foliate Bronze Base, Signed, 11 1/2 In. 1650.00
Compote, Favrile, Amber Iridescent, Ruffled Edge, Circular Foot, 1920, 4 In., Pair 517.00
Compote, Favrile, Iridescent Pink, Diamond Optic Center, 8 x 2 1/2 In. 1500.00
Compote, Gold Iridescent, Purple Highlights, Signed, 6 In. 485.00
Compote, Green Opalescent, Favrile, Signed, 6 In. 630.00
Compote, Inverted Stem, Domed Foot, Ruffled Edge Tray, Signed, 1920, 6 In. 977.00
Compote, Opalescent Diamond Optic Center, Short Pedestal, Signed, 6 1/4 In. 900.00
Cordial, Gold Highlights, Signed, L.C.T. Favrile, 5 1/2 In. 275.00
Decanter Set, Diamond, Gold, Green Swirling Design, Spherical Stopper, 11 In. 4600.00
Ewer, Favrile, Amber, Applied Scroll, Silver Blue Iridescent, 1920, 9 In. . . . . .862.00 to 1092.00
Flask, Sterling Silver, Leather Covering 165.00
Goblet, Amber, Tapering Bowl, Inverted Rim, 1899, 10 In. 1035.00
Goblet, Optic Ribbed, Glossy Exterior, Signed, 6 1/2 In. 395.00
Pitcher, Gold Iridescent, Green Leaf Design, Signed, L.C. Tiffany, Favrile, 4 1/4 In. 173.00
Pitcher, Lava, Amber Iridescent Trailings, Favrile, Cobalt, 1918, 5 In. 7475.00
Salt, Favrile, Gold Iridescent, Ruffled Edge, Ribbed, 2 x 4 In. 400.00
Salt, Gold Iridescent, Ruffled Edge, Crimped Rim, Signed, 1 x 2 1/2 In. 200.00
Salt, Lily Pad, Blue Opalescent, 4 In., Pair 440.00

Salt, Twisted Stump Design, 1 1/4 In. 320.00
Scent Bottle, Diamond, Scrolled Leafage, Blossoms, Favrile, 1900, 5 In. 13800.00
Shade, Favrile, Acorn, Rectangular Green Glass Tiles, Heart Shape Leaves, 16 In. 8625.00
Shade, Gold Iridescent, Feather Line & Swirl, Hanging, 6 x 13 In. 2900.00
Shade, Pomegranate, Yellow Fruit, Segmented 2-Tone Green, 6 3/4 x 16 In. 9625.00
Tile, Blue Iridescent, Textured Design Across Top, Square, 4 In. 400.00
Tumbler, Whiskey, Favrile, Gold Iridescent, Blue Iridescent Interior, 1 3/4 x 1 In. 300.00
Tumbler, Whiskey, Pinched All Around, Gold Iridescent, Signed 235.00
Vase, 6 Pulled Gold Leaves, Black Satin, Favrile, 7 In. 7475.00
Vase, 18-Ribs Urn, Ambergris To Peacock Blue, 5 In. 2875.00
Vase, Agate, Ocher, Lime Green, Olive Green, Amber Iridescent, 1895, 8 In. 11500.00
Vase, Amber Iridescent Raised Swirls, Favrile, 1928, 4 1/4 In. 3737.00
Vase, Amber Iridescent, Favrile, Vertical Ribbing, Tapered, 1928, 7 1/2 In. 143.00
Vase, Amber, Pink, Green Iridescent Trailings, Blue, Black Sides, 1899, 5 In. 4600.00
Vase, Amber, Ribbed Flared Form, Favrile, Ribbed Circular Foot, 1928, 14 In. 690.00
Vase, Blue Trailing Hearts & Vines, Favrile, Black Iridescent, 1902, 7 In. 6325.00
Vase, Blue Trailing Hearts & Vines, Favrile, Rainbow Iridescent, 6 3/4 In. 1035.00
Vase, Blue, Baluster, Favrile, 10 In. 1095.00
Vase, Blue, Gold, Rose Iridescent, Flared Neck, Signed, L.C.T. Favrile, 6 In. 550.00
Vase, Blue, Purple Iridescent, Ribbed Neck, Signed, L.C.T. Favrile, 9 In. 880.00
Vase, Bud, Peacock Blue Base, Gold Iridescent Top, Signed, 11 In. 1800.00
Vase, Cabinet, Dimpled, Favrile, Signed, 1 7/8 In. 332.00
Vase, Cobalt Blue Rows Of Tendrils, Amber Iridescent, 1902, 6 1/8 In. 17250.00
Vase, Crimson Lobed Lappets At Top, Yellow Below, 1908, 5 1/8 In. 2875.00
Vase, Crimson Red, 1919, 2 In. 1955.00
Vase, Crimson Red, Iridescent Gold Trailings, Flared Rim, 1906, 3 1/2 In. 4312.00
Vase, Crimson, Black Pulled Feathers, Silver Blue Trailings, 1903, 5 1/4 In. 4312.00
Vase, Cypriote, Brown Mottled, Textured Ground, Tangerine Interior, 7 1/2 In. 6325.00
Vase, Cypriote, Deep Blue Black, Amber Iridescent, 1896, 5 In. 7475.00
Vase, Cypriote, Favrile, Bronze Rim, Stylized Petaled Foot, 1928, 10 1/4 In. 4025.00
Vase, Cypriote, Green Opaque, Abstract Petal Vine, Yellow, Gold, Red, 1902, 6 In. 3737.00
Vase, Damascene, Allover Gold Design, Ruffled Rim, Favrile, 12 1/2 In. 1725.00
Vase, Deep Amber, White, Pink Flower Heads, Gourd Shape, 1913, 8 In. 4025.00
Vase, Deep Blue, Gold, Blue Iridescent, Favrile, Footed, 1920, 10 In. 977.00
Vase, Deep Eggplant Scrolls, Teal Green Ground, Flared Rim, 11 1/4 In. 7475.00
Vase, Emerald Green Ribs, Cream Opalescent, 1902, 7 1/4 In. 3737.00
Vase, Emerald Green, Electric Blue Waves, Cream Ground, 9 1/2 In. 2070.00
Vase, Favrile, Blue, 9 3/4 In. 275.00
Vase, Favrile, Gunmetal Gray Matte, 1910, 14 1/2 In. 2990.00
Vase, Favrile, Opalescent Amber, Egg Shape, c.1892, 3 1/4 In. 920.00
Vase, Flower-Form, Amber Iridescent, Ribbed Dome Foot, 1918, 14 1/2 In. 1495.00
Vase, Flower-Form, Amber, Green Pulled Feathers, 15 In. 6325.00
Vase, Flower-Form, Deep Cobalt Blue, Green Trailings, Leaves, Favrile, 1918, 9 In. 3450.00
Vase, Flower-Form, Deep Green Trailings, Orange Iridescent, Favrile, 1900, 10 In. 5175.00
Vase, Flower-Form, Favrile, Signed, 15 1/2 In. ....*Illus* 4830.00
Vase, Flower-Form, Green & Opalescent Exterior, Gold Interior, Signed, 13 In. 5400.00
Vase, Flower-Form, Pulled Green Leaves, White Opalescent Interior, 15 In. 4887.00
Vase, Flower-Form, Signed, c.1905, 15 3/8 In. 6900.00
Vase, Flower-Form, White, Orange Pulled Feathers, Favrile, 1918, 5 1/2 In. 3737.00
Vase, Gold Band Iridescent Trailings, Favrile, Coiled Side Handles, Amber, 6 In. 5175.00
Vase, Gold Damascene, Applied Leaf, Vine Design, Favrile, Medium Relief, 4 In. 4600.00
Vase, Gold Dimpled Form, Signed, L.C.T. Favrile, 3 In. 330.00
Vase, Gold Iridescent, Green Leaves, Favrile, 5 3/4 x 3 1/2 In. 1800.00
Vase, Gold Iridescent, Green Vines, Bulbous Top, Signed, Favrile, 6 1/2 In. 1800.00
Vase, Gold Iridescent, Squat Ribbed Body, Circular Foot, Favrile, 6 3/4 In. 1150.00
Vase, Gold Pulled Feather At Bottom, Blue, Purple Iridescent, Favrile, 20 In. 2860.00
Vase, Gold Pulled Leaves, Satin, Cylinder, Bronze Holder, Signed, 14 In. 1720.00
Vase, Gold Rainbow Iridescent, Flared Rim, Circular Foot, Favrile, 12 In. 1150.00
Vase, Gold, 8-Ribs Body, Scalloped Rim, Favrile, 3 In. 315.00
Vase, Grapes, Vine, Leafage, Gray, Green Grass Overlay, 1908, 11 In. 9200.00
Vase, Gray, Overall Silver Blue, Gold Iridescent, 1900, 8 In. 575.00
Vase, Green Iridescent Trailing Hearts & Vines, Gold Ground, Favrile, 6 In. 1035.00
Vase, Green Lobed Leaf, Vine, Gold Iridescent, Circular, 4 In. 1265.00

When you go away on a driving trip, be sure to cover the window in your garage door so the missing car won't be noticed. New garage doors usually have no window at all, for security reasons.

Tiffany Glass, Vase, Flower-Form, Favrile, Signed, 15 1/2 In.

Vase, Green Trailing Hearts & Vines, Amber, Signed, c.1915, 10 3/8 In. 690.00
Vase, Green Trailing Hearts & Vines, Flared Rim, Deep Blue Iridescent, 3 In. 1955.00
Vase, Green Trailing Ivy, 3 Loop Handles, Amber, c.1908, 5 1/8 In. 1495.00
Vase, Green, Blue Mottled, Double Gourd, 5 1/2 In. 1495.00
Vase, Intaglio Flowers, Leaves, Amber Iridescent, Favrile, 1915, 10 In. 3737.00
Vase, Jack-In-The-Pulpit, Amber Base, Signed, c.1905, 8 1/4 In. 2645.00
Vase, Jack-In-The-Pulpit, Amber Iridescent, Pink, Purple, 1905, 14 1/2 In. 11500.00
Vase, Jack-In-The-Pulpit, Signed, 15 In. 6250.00
Vase, Leaf, Applied Band, Rainbow Iridescent, Favrile, 10 In. 1150.00
Vase, Leaves, Gold Iridescent, Flared Rim, Pad Foot, Favrile, 12 1/2 In. 2990.00
Vase, Leaves, Vine, Green, Gold Iridescent, Pale Yellow, Favrile, 16 In. 4500.00
Vase, Light Amber Trailings, Leaves, Pale Yellow, Favrile, 7 1/2 In. 3169.00
Vase, Millefiori, Signed, 9 7/8 In. 5175.00
Vase, Overall Gold Luster, Applied Scrolled Shell Handles, Favrile, 4 1/2 In. 1265.00
Vase, Overall Gold Luster, Applied Scrolled Shell Handles, Favrile, 6 1/2 In. 1265.00
Vase, Overlapping Arrowroot Leaves, Emerald Green, 1907, 14 In. 18400.00
Vase, Pale Yellow, Green Pulled Feathers, Silver Blue Iridescent, 11 In. 2070.00
Vase, Paperweight, Amber, Pink Iridescent Trails, Deep Green, Favrile, 4 In. 4600.00
Vase, Paperweight, Brick Red, Ocher Leaf Trailings, Pale Amber, 5 In. 6325.00
Vase, Paperweight, Emerald Green, White, Silver Blue Trailings, 1912, 5 In. 2587.00
Vase, Paperweight, Layered Floral, 5 3/4 In. 3630.00
Vase, Paperweight, Nasturtium Blossoms, Leafage, Amber, 1907, 7 In. 7475.00
Vase, Paperweight, Ocher, Green Trailing Hearts & Vines, Red, Green, 9 In. 3162.00
Vase, Paperweight, Pale Amber Trailings, Leaves, Emerald Green, 12 In. 4025.00
Vase, Paperweight, Trailing Blossoms, Violet, Amber, Favrile, 5 1/2 In. 16100.00
Vase, Pastel Yellow, White, Tapered, Circular Foot, 9 1/2 In. 690.00
Vase, Peacock Blue Iridescent, Open Handles, Signed, 3 1/4 In. 850.00
Vase, Peacock Feather, Gold Pulled Feathers, Purple, Green, 1908, 24 In. 18400.00
Vase, Pearlescent Amber, Amber Lappets, Mauve Ground, Favrile, 1899, 8 In. 2300.00
Vase, Pink, Green Hooked Swirls, Light Amber Glass, Oval, 1 3/4 In. 1380.00
Vase, Pulled Feather, Green, Gold, Brown, Pink, Purple Iridescent, Favrile, 3 In. 770.00
Vase, Pulled Feathers, Dash, Pale Amber Iridescent, Favrile, 1894, 5 In. 3450.00
Vase, Pulled Feathers, Pale Green, Yellow, Favrile, 14 1/4 In. 1150.00
Vase, Pulled Trailings, Pink, Green, Baluster, Favrile, Signed, 5 1/4 In. 2530.00
Vase, Pulled Vertical Trailings, Golden Amber, Bottle Form, Favrile, 1906, 12 In. 2587.00
Vase, Pulled Waves, Light Green Ground, Favrile, Paper Label, 4 1/2 In. 412.00
Vase, Red Color, Black, Green Applied Rim, Shouldered, 11 In. 345.00
Vase, Red Iridescent, Silver Swirls, Wide Top, 2 1/2 x 1 3/4 In. 2500.00
Vase, Ribbed Body, Flared Top, Uneven Rim, Platinum Iridescent, Favrile, 3 In. 495.00
Vase, Ribbed Body, Uneven Rim, Platinum Iridescent, Favrile, 4 1/2 In. 495.00
Vase, Ribbed Emerald Green, Gold Iridescent Trailings, Favrile, 1901, 7 3/8 In. 2587.00
Vase, Scroll, Salmon Iridescent, Gold Ground, Flared Rim, Favrile, 8 1/2 In. 2875.00
Vase, Silver Blue Lozenges, Dotted Rib, Black, 6 In. 2875.00
Vase, Silver Blue Pulled Feathers, Deep Red, 1902, 4 1/2 In. 6900.00
Vase, Silver Blue Trailing Hearts & Vines, Favrile, 1902, 4 1/8 In. 7475.00
Vase, Silver Blue, Amber Iridescent Lappets, Blue, Amber Accents, 1899, 8 In. 1840.00
Vase, Silver, Gray, Ocher Iridescent Pulled Trailings, Favrile, 1918, 9 3/8 In. 2300.00
Vase, Striated Pale Ocher, Yellow Cased, Stylized Blossoms, Favrile, 4 In. 4600.00

Vase, Striated Pulled Feathers, Zipper, Amber, Ocher, Favrile, 1896, 11 3/4 In. 4025.00
Vase, Stylized Amber, Rust Leaves, Tendrils, Teal Blue, Favrile, 1896, 5 1/4 In. 7475.00
Vase, Tel El Amarna, Aqua Blue, Gold Iridescent, Black Rim, Favrile, 16 In. 8625.00
Vase, Tel El Amarna, Chain, Golden Amber Rim, Foot, Deep Amber, 1913, 11 In........ 4312.00
Vase, Tel El Amarna, Crimson Red Iridescent, Black Foot, 1904, 4 5/8 In. 6900.00
Vase, Tel El Amarna, Deep Green, Amber Iridescence, Bronze, Favrile, 1918, 6 In. 2587.00
Vase, Tel El Amarna, Emerald Green Sides, Silver Blue Bands, 1918, 9 In. 3680.00
Vase, Tel El Amarna, Fire Engine Red Sides, Tomato Red Ground, Favrile, 6 In. 10350.00
Vase, Tel El Amarna, Zigzag, Lime Green, Straited Amber, Silver Blue, 1912, 4 In. 3450.00
Vase, Tel El Amarna, Zigzag, Striated Silver Blue, Red, Pale Amber Ground, 8 In. 8050.00
Vase, Tomato Red Iridescent, Striated Caramel Pulled Feathers, 1904, 6 In. 3737.00
Vase, Tricorn, Allover Luster Iridescent, Gold Oval Body, Favrile, 4 1/2 In............. 690.00
Vase, Trumpet, Amber Trailing Hearts & Vines, Domed Circular Foot, 16 In. 6900.00
Vase, Trumpet, Cobalt Blue, Green, Lobed Base, Flared Rim, 11 In. 975.00
Vase, Trumpet, Electric Blue Iridescent, Green Trailings, 10 1/2 In. 2760.00
Vase, Trumpet, Green & Pale Yellow, Bronze, Signed, 13 1/2 In. 1430.00
Vase, Yellow, Amber Swirls, Red Orange Leaves, Favrile, 1906, 5 1/2 In. 3162.00
TIFFANY POTTERY, Ginger Jar, Branch On Cover, Raised Leaves & Vines, Signed, 9 In. 3500.00
   Lamp Base, Stylized Lion, Raised Paws, Amber, Blue, Pink, Cream, 15 In. 5175.00
   Vase, 4 Lobes, Rippling Rim, Metallic Black & Green Finish, 9 1/2 In. 7000.00
   Vase, Embossed Jonquil & Leaves, Shellac & Moss Finish, Signed, 12 In. 5000.00
   Vase, Fern Tendrils To Top, Scalloped Edge, Green To Yellow Interior, 10 In. 33500.00
   Vase, Gray Mottled Over Green, Ocher Interior, Bulbous, 12 1/2 In. 3162.00
   Vase, Leaves Raised From Branches, Glazed Inside & Out, Signed, 8 In. 2000.00
   Vase, Molded Leaves On Neck, Caramel, Beige Mottled, 5 In....................... 920.00
   Vase, Narcissus, Brown, Dark Blue, Khaki Matte Glaze, Cylindrical Neck, 14 In. 1389.00
   Vase, Overlapping Tulips, Leaves, Green Glaze Interior, Bulbous, 5 In. 2875.00
   Vase, Poppies, Leaves, Green Mottled Interior, Bisque, 1914, 9 In. 2300.00
   Vase, Purple, Green & Black, Glazed Inside & Out, Signed, 4 1/2 In. 1500.00
   Vase, Spatters Of Red-Brown & Dripping Of Green All Around, Signed, 6 In. 1500.00
   Vase, Urn Form, Floral Medallions, Geometric, Green, Cobalt Blue, 9 In. 4370.00
TIFFANY SILVER, Bookweight, Men Playing Lacrosse Scene, Rectangular, 1875, 11 x 2 In. ... 460.00
   Bowl, 3 Foliate & Dolphin Feet, 5 1/2 In., Pair.................................... 1380.00
   Bowl, Circular, Swirled Fluted, Floral & Foliate Border, Sterling, 1875, 9 1/4 In. 925.00
   Bowl, Cut Border, Scalloped Edge, 10 1/4 In...................................... 805.00
   Bowl, Flared Rim, Circular Base, 7 3/4 In. 545.00
   Bowl, Floral Border, Reticulated Sides, 11 x 8 In. 650.00
   Bowl, Fruit, Ribbed Rim & Base Bands, Paneled, 1907, 8 7/8 In. 575.00
   Bowl, Incised Bands To Center, Flared Rim, Spreading Foot, 3 x 5 5/8 In. 170.00
   Bowl, Inlaid Copper, Lotus Design, 8 In. 880.00
   Bowl, Scalloped Edge, 10 1/4 In. 715.00
   Bowl, Swirled & Fluted, Floral & Leaf Border, 1875, 9 1/4 In. 925.00
   Box, Jewelry, Plum Colored Velvet Pincushion Top & Interior, 1920s, 6 In. 498.00
   Bread Tray, Pierced Border, 10 1/2 In. 305.00
   Cake Plate, Pierced Floral Border, Footed, Signed, 4 x 9 In., Pair 2300.00
   Candelabra, 3-Light, Monogram, 16 In., Pair 2530.00
   Cane, Ivory Swirls & Lines Top, Art Nouveau, Inscribed Name, 1900 .... 4400.00
   Coffeepot, Domed Cover, Foliate Border, Fruit Finial, After Dinner, Signed, 9 In. 1150.00
   Compact, Silver Radiating Ribs, Gold Geometric Thumbpiece, 1940................. 315.00
   Creamer, Scroll Edge, 4 1/8 In. 495.00
   Crumber 350.00
   Cup, Sunburst Headers, Indian River Scene, 3 Scroll Handles, 1905, 9 In. 9487.00
   Dish, Floral Garlands, Molded Rim, Circular Foot, 1938, 10 1/4 In. 575.00
   Dish, Serving, Oval, 2 Sections 345.00
   Dresser Tray, Plain, 5 1/2 x 9 In. 242.00
   Fish Slice, Winthrop, 1909, 11 3/4 In. 120.00
   Flask, 3 Frogs, Carousing, Screw Cap, Monogrammed, 1885, 7 1/4 In. 4255.00
   Flask, Cockerel, Crowing, On Branch, Screw Cap, Monogrammed, 1885, 8 In. 1840.00
   Flask, Hip, Arabesque Etch, Monogrammed, 1907, 6 1/4 In. 545.00
   Flask, Woman, Riding Horse, Jumping Fence, Screw Cap, 1895, 7 1/4 In. 1840.00
   Fork, Olympian, 1878, 8 3/4 In. 400.00
   Frame, 2 Hearts, Crossed Quiver & Torch, Sterling, 1875, 11 x 8 1/2 In. 920.00
   Frame, Red & Gray Geometric & Swirl Enameled, 9 5/8 x 11 1/4 In. 690.00

Gravy Ladle, Chrysanthemum, Scalloped Bowl 295.00
Ice Pail, Wooden Tub Shape, 2 Hoop Handles, 1874, 7 In. 6037.00
Jar, Talcum, Plain, Cylinder, 6 1/2 In. 195.00
Jug, Diagonal Ribbing, Ear Shaped Handle, Scrolled Leaf Border, 11 In. 517.00
Jug, Water, Ivy Leaves & Scrolls, Band Of Ivy Leaves, Bud Finial, 8 1/4 In. 1380.00
Kettle, Engraved Greek Key Band, Serpentine Spout, Corn Finial, 9 1/2 In. 1380.00
Key Ring, Ball Design, Box & Carrying Case 20.00
Lemon Fork, 4 3/8 In. 135.00
Loving Cup, Vermeil Finish, Marked 325.00
Meat Serving Fork, Faneuil, Pierced 195.00
Mug, Geometric, Bird Design On Lower Part, Beaded Rim, 1891, 3 3/4 In. 700.00
Penholder, Shell Form, Ball Feet, Signed, 3 x 2 3/4 In. 60.00
Pie Server, Palm 350.00
Pitcher, 10-Sided Cylindrical Body, 4 1/2 Pts. 4900.00
Pitcher, Compressed Bulging Form, Floral Handle, 1873, 6 3/4 In. 1870.00
Pitcher, Leaves, Loop Handle, Reeded Rim, Monogrammed, 10 1/2 In. 2070.00
Pitcher, Paneled, Floral Clusters, Scroll Handle, Leafy Feet, c.1902, 10 In. 2180.00
Pitcher, Plume Bands, Monogrammed, 7 3/4 In. 1045.00
Pitcher, Repousse Flowers Top, Ribbed Base, 1878, 3 Qt., 8 1/2 In. 4000.00
Pitcher, Water, Bombe, Butterflies, Maple Leaves, Spot Hammered, 8 In. 6325.00
Pitcher, Water, Gourd Form, 4 Silver Turtles, Crawling, 1879, 7 5/8 In. 16100.00
Pitcher, Yachting, Acanthus Leaf Handle, 1875, 9 1/2 In. 4600.00
Platter, Twined Laurel Leaf Border, Monogrammed, 14 & 18 In., Pair 1840.00
Punch Ladle, Wood Handle 330.00
Salad Set, Broom Corn, Monogram 465.00
Salver, Molded Rim, 27 Oz., 12 1/4 In. 630.00
Sandwich Tongs, Broom Corn, Monogrammed, 1890, 7 3/4 In. 690.00
Sauceboat, Chrysanthemum, Foliage, Gilt Interior, Rectangular, 6 In. 4600.00
Sauceboat, Scroll & Leaf Handle, Shell Feet 160.00
Soup Ladle, Beekman, Gilt Bowl, 14 1/4 In. 550.00
Sugar & Creamer, Swing Handle, Pedestal Base, Monogram 198.00
Sugar Sifter, Chrysanthemum, Floral & Foliate Handle, 1880, 5 1/2 In. 550.00
Sugar Sifter, Vine, 6 3/8 In. 365.00
Tape Measure, Square 138.00
Tazza, Beaded Foot, Flat Leaf Border, Monogram, 1907-1938 .... 230.00
Tazza, Gallery, Pierced Geometric Design, Monogrammed, 8 1/2 In. 690.00
Tazza, Intertwined Copper Inlay, Cypress Tree, Ridged Border, 1912, 4 In. 2530.00
Tea & Coffee Set, Cartouches, Gadroon, Ovolo Borders, 1920, 7 Piece 6900.00
Tea Set, Monogrammed LLC, Signed, 4 Piece 1650.00
Teapot, Hinged Cover, Bombe, Floral, Wooden Handle, Tapered, 8 3/4 In. 520.00
Tongs, Bird Claw & Shell, Monogrammed, 5 5/8 In. 522.00
Toothpaste Key, Sterling 40.00
Tray, Beveled Edge, 1910, 9 5/8 x 12 5/8 In. 1175.00
Tray, Divided Stepped Gallery Rail, Oval, 82 Oz., 19 In. 2760.00
Tray, Flower-Form, Petal Border, c.1935, 9 1/2 In. 330.00
Tray, Oval, 2 Open Handles, Monogram, 1923, 26 x 18 In. 4313.00
Tray, Stylized Trumpet Flowers Rim, Lappet Border, 1900, 14 In. 4312.00
Tureen, Domed Cover, Flat Leaf Feet, 1875, 11 1/4 x 8 1/2 In. 5175.00
Tureen, Soup, Cover, Chased With Pomegranates, Ring Handle, Footed, 13 In. 6612.00
Vase, Band Of Cranes, Foliage, Prunus Branch, 4 Bamboo Legs, 1874, 7 1/2 In. 3220.00
Vase, Horn Shape, Front Raised On 2 Splayed Legs, Paw Feet, 1891, 7 x 11 In. 1725.00
Waste Bowl, Decorative Band On Base, c.1860, 3 5/8 x 5 1/2 In. 198.00
Wine Cooler, 3 Handles, 1900 .... 5750.00
Wine Cooler, Raised On Square Foot, Molded Rim, Signed, 10 5/8 In. 1092.00

TIFFIN Glass Company of Tiffin, Ohio, was a subsidiary of the United
States Glass Co. of Pittsburgh, Pennsylvania, in 1892. The U.S. Glass
Co. went bankrupt in 1963, and the Tiffin plant employees purchased
the building and the inventory. They continued running it from 1963 to
1966, when it was sold to Continental Can Company. In 1969, it was
sold to Interpace, and in 1980, it was closed. The black satin glass,
made from 1923 to 1926, and the stemware of the last twenty years are
the best-known products.

Black Satin, Vase, Bud, Enameled Floral, 10 In., Pair 33.00

Black Satin, Vase, Poppy, 8 1/2 In.	95.00
Byzantine, Cocktail, 3 1/2 Oz.	12.00
Cherokee Rose, Bowl, 10 In.	55.00
Cherokee Rose, Candlestick, Pair	95.00
Cherokee Rose, Champagne, 5 1/2 Oz.	16.00
Cherokee Rose, Champagne, Fuchsia, 5 1/2 Oz.	12.00
Cherokee Rose, Claret, 4 Oz.	55.00
Cherokee Rose, Cocktail, 3 1/2 Oz.	16.00 to 25.00
Cherokee Rose, Cocktail, Fuchsia, 3 1/2 Oz.	14.00
Cherokee Rose, Compote, Beaded Stem, Blown Bowl	145.00
Cherokee Rose, Cordial, 1 Oz.	50.00
Cherokee Rose, Creamer	22.00
Cherokee Rose, Goblet, 9 Oz.	22.00 to 55.00
Cherokee Rose, Iced Tea, Footed, 10 1/2 Oz.	35.00
Cherokee Rose, Pitcher, Footed	695.00
Cherokee Rose, Plate, 7 7/8 In.	12.00
Cherokee Rose, Sugar & Creamer	27.00
Cherokee Rose, Sugar & Creamer, Beaded Handle	60.00
Cherokee Rose, Vase, Bud, 6 In.	25.00
Cherokee Rose, Vase, Bud, 8 In.	45.00
Cherokee Rose, Vase, Bud, 10 1/2 In.	38.00
Cherokee Rose, Vase, Bud, 11 In.	46.00
Classic, Cocktail, 3 1/2 Oz.	32.00
Classic, Plate, 10 1/2 In.	125.00
Classic, Tumbler, 8 Oz.	45.00
Classic, Tumbler, Whiskey, Footed, 2 Oz.	75.00
Empire, Champagne, Pink, 5 1/2 Oz.	22.00
Flanders, Bowl, Pink	795.00
Flanders, Bowl, Rolled Rim, Pink, 13 In.	345.00
Flanders, Cocktail, Pink, 3 1/2 Oz.	45.00
Flanders, Cordial, 1 Oz.	55.00
Flanders, Cup & Saucer, Yellow	100.00
Flanders, Iced Tea, Footed, Pink	75.00
Flanders, Parfait, Pink	85.00
Flanders, Parfait, With Handle, Pink	150.00
Flanders, Pitcher, Pink	350.00
Flanders, Wine, 3 1/2 Oz.	30.00
Flanders, Wine, Yellow, 3 1/2 Oz.	40.00
Inverted Diamond, Jar, Cover, Ice Blue, 11 In.	22.00
June, Ice Bucket, Yellow	140.00
June, Salt & Pepper, Yellow	185.00
June Night, Champagne, 5 1/2 Oz.	14.00
June Night, Sherry, 2 Oz.	30.00
June Night, Vase, Bud, Footed, 8 In.	30.00
Persian Pheasant, Champagne, 5 1/2 Oz.	24.00 to 50.00
Persian Pheasant, Claret, 4 Oz.	45.00
Persian Pheasant, Cocktail, 3 1/2 Oz.	18.00 to 20.00
Persian Pheasant, Cordial, 1 Oz.	37.00 to 40.00
Trophy, Vase, Fuchsia, Handles, 11 In.	250.00

TILES have been used in most countries of the world as a sturdy building material for floors, roofs, fireplace surrounds, and surface toppings. Many of the American tiles are listed in this book under the factory name.

Blue Crab, Green & Brown Ground, Faience, Arts & Crafts Frame, Hartford, 6 In.	1100.00
Boy, Girl, Yellow Background, Harris Strong, 18 x 12 In., 12 Piece	465.00
Cave Animal, Green, Dark Brown Outline, Frame, Harris Strong, 6 In.	85.00
Cherub, Under Blue Glaze, Trent, 6 x 6 In.	230.00
Cubist Head, 12 Piece, Blue & Green Glaze, Wooden Frame, Harris Strong, 12 x 36 In.	715.00
Fishing Scene, Walnut Board, Harris Strong, 18 x 60 In.	550.00
Flower, Encircled By Twisted Rope, Gray, Green, Cranberry, Faience, 4 In.	225.00
Horse, Erica & Kjeld Deichmann	170.00
Lion & Shield, Buff Clay, Marked, Square, 4 1/4 In.	245.00

MacArthur, Old Soldiers Never Die, American Flag, Square, 6 In. 75.00
Madonna & Child, Iron Mounted Surround, Faience, 12 Piece, 8 1/8 x 24 3/8 In. 745.00
Molded Flowers, 2-Tone Blue, Medium Green Ground, Arts & Crafts Oak Frame, 6 In. . . 467.00
Pastoral Landscape, Farmer, Cow, Frame, Harris Strong, 6 x 36 In., 6 Piece 165.00
Rialto Bridge, Venice, Frame, Harris Strong, 6 x 30 In., 6 Piece 110.00
Sailing Ship At Sea, C. Pardee Works, 4 1/4 x 4 1/4 In. 330.00
Ships In An Inlet With Peasants On Shore, Faience, Signed, Frame, Square, 6 In. 40.00
Solon, Ship At Sea, Blue, Camel Ground, Arts & Crafts Oak Frame, Square, 5 1/2 In. 550.00
Souvenir, Provincetown Monument 75.00
Stylized, Flower, Light Green, Aqua Ground, Arts & Crafts Oak Frame, 6 x 12 In. 660.00
Stylized English Rose, Blue, Purple Center, Caramel, Arts & Crafts, Oak Frame, 6 In. . . . 330.00
Tree Scene, Bungalow & Boat, Multicolored, Oak Frame, Claycraft, 4 x 7 In. 1540.00
Trees, Curved Road, Mountainside, Arts & Crafts Oak Frame, Claycraft, 4 x 12 In. 1870.00
Warrior Scene, Green Ground, 13 x 10 In. 695.00
Women In Garden, Black Painted Wood Frame, Porcelain, Japan, 10 x 10 In., Pair 83.00
Yellow & Green Tulip, Blue Ground, C. Pardee Works, 4 1/4 x 4 1/4 In. 220.00

TINWARE containers for household use have been made in America
since the seventeenth century. The first tin utensils were brought from
Europe, but by 1798, tin plate was imported and local tinsmiths made
the wares. Painted tin is called tole and is listed separately. Some tin
kitchen items may be found listed under Kitchen. The lithographed tin
containers used to hold food and tobacco are listed in the Advertising
category under Tin.

Basket, Bread, Bautler Shop, Early 19th Century, 13 1/2 In. 475.00
Bed Warmer, Pierced, Hickory Frame, Bail Handle, 9 In. 165.00
Coffeepot, 9 x 11 In. 92.00
Coffeepot, Gooseneck, Ribbed Design, Strap Handle, 10 1/2 In. 745.00
Coffeepot, Punch, Gothic Arch, Leaf & Flower, 11 1/2 In. 330.00
Comb Case, Eagle On Back, Stars At Ends, Hanging Holes, Stamped Combcase, 6 1/4 In. 68.00
Flint Box, Green Paint, Striker, Oval, 5 3/8 x 3 7/8 In. 475.00
Foot Warmer, Circle Design, Poplar Frame, Turned Corner Posts, Red, 7 3/4 x 8 3/4 In. . . 80.00
Foot Warmer, Pierced Hearts, Pegged Wood Frame, 9 1/8 x 7 7/8 x 5 3/4 In. 240.00
Foot Warmer, Punched Heart & Circle, Mortised Hardwood Frame, 8 x 9 x 5 3/4 In. 195.00
Foot Warmer, Punched Heart & Circles, Mortised Wooden Frame, 7 1/2 x 9 x 6 In. 195.00
Lantern, Candle, Cone Top, Early 19th Century, 17 In. 165.00
Lantern, Candle, Pyramid Top, 4 Glass Sides, Pierced Star, Parker's Patent 1859, 7 In. . . . 358.00
Lantern, Star & Diamond Cutouts, Black Paint, 17 In. 445.00
Mold, Candle, 2 Tube, Strap Handle 90.00
Mold, Candle, 4 Tube, 19th Century, 10 1/2 In. 55.00
Mold, Candle, 4 Tube, Ear Handle, 5 1/2 In. 495.00
Mold, Candle, 6 Tube, Original Wicks, 10 3/8 x 4 In. 115.00
Mold, Candle, 10 Tube, Poplar Frame, 5 1/2 x 17 1/2 x 15 3/4 In. 770.00
Mold, Candle, 12 Tube 22.00
Mold, Candle, 12 Tube, Strap Handle 310.00
Mold, Candle, 24 Tube, 8 1/2 In. 140.00
Mold, Candle, 36 Tube, 12 5/8 x 10 In. 490.00
Mold, Candle, 36 Tube, Dovetailed Cherry Case, 15 x 18 1/4 In. 1210.00
Mold, Candle, 48 Tube, 19th Century, Top Holes For Wicks, 10 5/8 x 11 3/4 In. 475.00
Ornament, Pierced & Punched Floral, Tubular Easel Back, 20 In., Pair 80.00
Snuffbox, Domed Cover, Portrait, Of General Scott, 19th Century, 1 1/8 x 1 3/4 In. 1035.00
Tinderbox, Candle Socket On Lid, Flint & Damper, 4 1/2 In. 330.00
Wastebasket, Laugh-In, Show Characters 75.00

TOBACCO CUTTERS may be listed in either the Advertising or Store categories.

TOBACCO JAR collectors search for those made in odd shapes and colors. Because tobacco needs special conditions of humidity and air, it
has been stored in special containers since the eighteenth century.

Arab Man, Porcelain, 4 1/2 In. 60.00
Barrel Man, Terra-Cotta, JM 3538 Mark, 7 1/2 In. . . . . 460.00 to 520.00
Bear With Pipe, Majolica, 5 3/4 In. 545.00
Black Boy, Porcelain, 4 1/2 In. 160.00

Black Elk, Scenery, Orange Ground, Pipe Finial, Noritake, 4 In. 95.00
Black Man, Stoneware, 5 1/4 In. 460.00
Bowler, Terra-Cotta, 9 1/4 In. 865.00
Devil, Terra-Cotta, 5 1/4 In. 405.00
Drunken Monkey, Porcelain, Musterschutz, Schierholz, 7 In. 290.00
Dwarf In Bag, Terra-Cotta, Marked, 2 In. 275.00
Elephant, Majolica, 6 1/2 In. 240.00
Englishman's Head, Top Hat, No. 3865, 6 In. 225.00
Field Marshal Von Hindenburg, Terra-Cotta, 13 In. 385.00
Fisherman, Porcelain, 4 1/2 In. 185.00
Fisherman In Barrel, Terra-Cotta, Ceramique D'Art, 6 3/4 In. 300.00
Floral Cartouche On Name Straasburger, Brass Lid, Delft, 1850 .... 1650.00
Frog, Majolica, 6 1/2 In. 375.00
Hand Painted American Indian, 5 1/2 In. 137.00
Hunter, Terra-Cotta, BB 8351 Mark, 11 5/8 In. 1380.00
Hunter & Fox, Majolica, 5 In. 300.00
Huntsman, Doulton, 1910 .... 350.00
Indian Head, Smoking Pipe, 4 1/2 x 7 In. 170.00
Lady Smoking, Porcelain, 10 1/2 In. 633.00
Lignum Vitae, 4 7/8 x 3 7/8 In. 130.00
Man, On Stump, Terra-Cotta, BB 194 Mark, 10 1/4 In. 1093.00
Man, On Wall, Terra-Cotta, 9 1/2 In. 920.00
Monkey With Pipe, Porcelain, 5 1/2 In. 375.00
Munich Child, Majolica, 6 1/2 In. 160.00
Munich Child Leaning On Barrel, Terra-Cotta, Marked, 10 In. 880.00
Pig With Pipe, Porcelain, Musterschutz, Schierholz, 6 1/8 In. 460.00
Pipe Design, Man, Playing Cards On Each Side, Chalkware, 10 In. 880.00
Porcelain, Figures, Silhouette Heads Of Smokers, Lavender, White, 6 x 4 In. . 425.00
Scottish Man, Majolica, 5 3/4 In. 195.00
Scottish Man, Terra-Cotta, 5 3/4 In. 300.00
Smiling Black Boy, Porcelain, Germany 175.00
Soldier & Woman, Terra-Cotta, JM 3295 Mark, 11 1/2 In. 1725.00
Student Dog, Terra-Cotta, FGW 507 Mark, 8 In. 805.00
Tapering Barrel Form, Parquetry Inlay, Ironbound, Hardwood, c.1785, 6 3/8 In. 99.00
White Reliefs & Lion Heads, Cobalt Blue, Wedgwood, Late 19th Century, 5 In. 200.00
Young Boy, Majolica, 5 In. 105.00
Young Girl, Terra-Cotta, BB 8047, 5 3/4 In. 265.00

TOBY JUG is the name of a very special form of pitcher. It is shaped like the full figure of a man or woman. A pitcher that shows just the top half of a person is not correctly called a toby. More examples of toby jugs can be found under Royal Doulton and other factory names.

Cavalier, Seated In Chair, Late 19th Century, 10 In. 135.00
Cover, Man, Seated, Green Coat, Yellow Hat, 10 In. 130.00
Cover, Woman, Standing, Elaborate Bonnet, Staffordshire, 11 In. 2310.00
Gentleman, Pink Pants, Seated On Keg, Home Brewed Ale, Staffordshire, 11 In. 192.00
Gentleman, Seated With Pitcher, Staffordshire, 8 In. 412.00
Gentleman, Seated, Hearty Good Fellow, Staffordshire, 11 In. 192.00
Man, Seated & Smoking Cigar, Blue Suit, Polka-Dot Necktie, 9 1/4 In. 172.00
Man, With Mug Of Beer, Staffordshire, 11 1/2 In. 230.00
Nelson, Polychrome Enamel, Staffordshire, 11 3/4 In. 55.00
Portly Gentleman, Seated, Blue Glaze, Staffordshire, Mid-19th Century, 5 1/2 In. 82.00

TOLE is painted tin. It is sometimes called *japanned ware*, *pontypool*, or *toleware*. Most nineteenth-century tole is painted with an orange-red or black background and multicolored decorations. Many recent versions of toleware are made and sold. Related items may be listed in the Tinware category.

Bin, Peacock Design, Green, Black Ground, 10 x 8 In. 175.00
Box, Bread, Stenciled Floral, Blue, Silver, Gold & Black, 14 In. 50.00
Box, Comb, 8 1/2 In. 165.00
Box, Deed, Dome Top, Floral, Black, Yellow Striping, 9 In. 66.00
Box, Deed, Dome Top, Stenciled Bowl Of Fruit & Foliage, Band On Lid, 9 1/4 In. 495.00

Box, Deed, White Band, Red, Yellow, Dark Brown Japanning, 4 1/4 In. 55.00
Box, Document, Black, Herbert C. Wright, 19th Century, 6 1/4 x 14 x 10 1/4 In. 55.00
Box, Document, Red, Green & Pink Floral, 8 In. 880.00
Box, Document, Red, Green Leaf Design, Yellow Swag, 4 x 7 1/2 In. 385.00
Box, Dome Top, Floral, Brown Japanning, Yellow, Red, Green Stripes, 7 In. 220.00
Box, Dome Top, Floral, White Band, Yellow, Red, Brown Japanning, 7 In. 330.00
Box, Floral, Gold, Orange, Dark Brown Japanning, 6 3/8 In. 55.00
Box, Lock, Black & Red, 4 1/2 In. 225.00
Bread Basket, Flowers & Fruit, Black Ground, 19th Century, 4 x 10 1/2 In. 305.00
Bread Basket, Gilt, Green, 14 x 7 1/2 In. 145.00
Bread Tray, 14 Stylized Apples 935.00
Bucket, Faux Mahogany Border, Lion's Mask & Rim Handles, 11 3/4 In., Pair 1380.00
Cachepot, Liner, Trophies Border, Red Ground, Mask & Paw Feet, 7 3/4 In., Pair 1840.00
Canister, Hinged Lid, Red Daubed, Black Paint, Cylindrical, 6 1/2 In. 27.00
Canister, Tea, Calligraphic Design, Black Ground, Round, 17 1/2 In. 120.00
Canister, Tea, Soldered, Green Lacquer, Large Number, 19th Century, 18 In., Pair 3500.00
Canteen, Painted Encampment Scene, 6 3/8 In. 2750.00
Coffeepot, Brown Japanning, Floral, 10 1/2 In. . . . . .370.00 to 605.00
Coffeepot, Design In Ovals, 19th Century 840.00
Coffeepot, Domed Lid, Lid Guard, Brown, Apples & Leaves, 10 1/2 In. 1090.00
Coffeepot, Domed Lid, Painted, Marked Uebele 5500.00
Coffeepot, Floral, Black Ground, 10 1/2 In. 220.00
Coffeepot, Fruit & Tulip Design, 19th Century, 9 In. 220.00
Coffeepot, Hinged Lid, Floral, Red, Green, Blue, Yellow, Dark Brown Japanning, 10 In. .   495.00
Coffeepot, Hinged Lid, Floral, Red, Green, Yellow, White, 9 1/2 In. 852.00
Coffeepot, Lighthouse Form, Gooseneck, Floral, Black Ground, 19th Century, 10 In. 990.00
Cookie Cutter, Heart Shape, Graduated, Nest, Fitted Box, 6 Piece 220.00
Creamer, Hinged Lid, Floral, Yellow, Green, Red, White, Dark Brown Japanning 522.00
Jardiniere, Faux Porphyry, Greek Key, Rectangular Waisted Body, 12 x 7 In., Pair 1475.00
Jardiniere, Landscape Scene, Green Ground, Late 19th Century, 7 In. 172.00
Jardiniere, Neoclassical, Gilt Metal, Rope Lip, Lion Feet, Baltic, 12 x 26 x 15 In. 4600.00
Jardiniere, Neoclassical, Urn Form, 3 Tulip Stem Candle Branches, Green, Gold, 18 In. . .   1380.00
Jardiniere, Rectangular Outscrolled Lip, Chinoiserie Design On 4 Sides, 11 x 9 3/4 In. . . .   5060.00
Jardiniere, Rectangular Tapered Body, Chinoiserie Design On 3 Sides, 11 In., Pair 2070.00
Jardiniere, Rectangular Tapered Body, Chinoiserie Design On 4 Sides, 11 In., Pair 5290.00
Jardiniere, Rectangular Waisted Body, Greek Key Design, Paw Feet, 12 1/4 x 7 In., Pair .   1495.00
Jardiniere, Ribbed Band, Tapered Cylindrical Body, Paw Feet, 28 x 26 In., Pair 3737.00
Jardiniere, Ribbed Band, Tapering Cylindrical, Lion Head Masks, 28 x 27 In., Pair 3735.00
Lamp, 2-Light, Allover Floral Garlands, Tole Shades 460.00
Lamp, Bouillette, Gilt Foliate Design, Dark Red Ground, Continental, 20 In. 300.00
Lamp, Bouillotte, Greek Key, Leaves & Berries, 3 Nozzles, Tole Shade, 21 3/4 In. 1840.00
Lamp, Palm Tree Form, Square Yellow Shade, 19 In. 575.00
Lamp, Rumford Type, Early 19th Century, 14 In. 330.00
Lamp, Table, Urn Shape, Classical Maidens, Swan Handles, Oatmeal Ground 520.00
Lunch Box, Painted, 17 x 26 x 12 In. 398.00
Planter, Entwined Lovers, Floral, Red, 10 1/2 In. 770.00
Spice Box, Yellow Border, Center Medallion, Black Ground, 19th Century, 8 1/2 In. 220.00
Tea Caddy, Red Field, Yellow Bird, Leaves & Flowers, 19th Century, 8 In. 2255.00
Tea Caddy, Regency Style, Hinged Lid, Painted Gilt Border, Heart Shape Lock, 3 1/2 In. . .   185.00
Tray, 18th-Century Style Genre Scene, Oval, 19th Century, 30 1/4 In. 1495.00
Tray, Basket Of Fruit & Flowers, 3 Exotic Birds, Chippendale Form, 22 x 29 In. 3520.00
Tray, Birds, Floral, Black & Gold, 2 Closed Handles, 26 x 19 In. 55.00
Tray, Floral & Bird, 28 1/2 x 20 1/2 In. 176.00
Tray, Floral & Birds, Gold & Polychrome, Black Ground, 22 1/2 x 30 1/4 In. 302.00
Tray, Floral & Fruit, Faux Bamboo Stand, Regency, 1830, 21 x 26 x 21 In. 1089.00
Tray, Floral & Fruit, Handles, Faux Bamboo Stand, Regency, 1820, 21 x 28 In. 1010.00
Tray, Floral, c.1875, 21 1/2 x 9 1/2 In. 145.00
Tray, Floral, Early 20th Century, 22 x 17 In. 120.00
Tray, Floral, Early 20th Century, 26 x 19 In. 154.00
Tray, Floral, Yellow Scalloped Band, Octagonal, 12 x 14 In. 100.00
Tray, Landscape, Figural Medallions, Mahogany Stand, Oval, 19th Century, 30 In. 1955.00
Tray, Peacock In Landscape, Faux Bamboo Stand, c.1850, 21 1/2 In. 362.00
Tray, Pheasants & Pavilion, 22 x 17 In. 120.00

Tray, Red, Yellow, Green Flowers, Fruit, Black Ground, Mid-19th Century, 12 In. 1725.00
Tray, Riverscape, Chinoiserie, Painted Red, Gilded, Mid-19th Century, 26 In. 345.00
Tray, Seascape, Red Reserve, Gilt Vine & Grape Border, c.1800, 25 1/2 x 20 1/2 In. 935.00
Tray, Spaniel & Pug, Ebonized Faux Stand, c.1860, 21 1/2 x 30 In. 1090.00
Tray, Swans & Church, Early 20th Century, 15 x 20 1/2 In. 120.00
Tray, Wood Cutter, Smoking Pipe, Wolfhound, Thatched Cottage, 30 1/8 In. 805.00
Urn, Chestnut, Cover, Foliage, Gilt, Black Ground, Handles, 12 x 9 x 5 In., Pair 2300.00
Urn, Chestnut, Cover, Gilt Flowers, Lion's Mask & Ring Handles, 1830s, 13 In., Pair 3680.00
Urn, Figural & Floral Design, Flared Square, Green Ground, Brass Knees, 11 In., Pair . . . 1380.00
Water Cooler, Red Paint, Stylized Floral Transfer, Black, Gold, 23 In. 280.00

TOM MIX was born in 1880 and died in 1940. He was the hero of over 100 silent movies from 1910 to 1929, and 25 sound films from 1929 to 1935. There was a Ralston Tom Mix radio show from 1933 to 1950, but the original Tom Mix was not in the show. Tom Mix comics were published from 1942 to 1953.

Badge, Dobie County Sheriff, Dated 1946 . . . . 60.00
Belt Buckle, Tom Mix Ralston Straight Shooter, Gold Finish, 1 1/2 x 2 1/2 In. 135.00
Bowl, Tom, Riding Horseback, White, 1982, 2 1/2 x 5 1/2 In. 28.00
Key Chain, Magnifying Glass & Compass 40.00
Knife, Pocket 50.00
Photograph, Tom, Smiling With Tony, Silver Frame, 1937, 1 1/2 x 2 1/2 In. 135.00
Poster, Green Cross For Safety, Late 1940s, 17 x 22 In. 58.00
Ring, Look-In Mystery 115.00
Ring, Magnet, 1940s 150.00
Sheet Music, 1919 . . . . 75.00
Watch Fob, Gold Ore, Brass, Box, 1940 . . . . 90.00

TOOLS of all sorts are listed here, but most are related to industry. Other tools may be found listed under Iron, Kitchen, Tinware, and Wooden.

Adze, Blacksmith Made, Iron, Stamped With Touchmark, A. Good, 18th Century 250.00
Adze, Cooper's, Flat Blade, 8-In. Handle 55.00
Angle Divider, Stanley, No. 30, Pat. Oct. 27, 1903, Original Box, 8 In. 165.00
Anvil, Gem City Elevator Works, Nickel Plated, 3 1/2 In. 125.00
Anvil, Jewelry Store 30.00
Auger, Bung, Wooden, Iron, 14 In., Pair 5.00
Auger, Cast Iron, Hollow With Pivoting Head 115.00
Auger Bit, Keen Kutter, Adjustable, To 3 In. 35.00
Ax, Cooper's, T. Kirkland, Ohio City, Stamp 75.00
Ax, Kelley-How-Thomson Co., Duluth, Minn., Marked With Hickory Logo, 36 In. 245.00
Ax, Lee, Colt & Anderson Hardware, Omaha, c.1900, 20 In. 125.00
Ax, Lumberjack's, Center Embossed Bust Of Lincoln, Kretschmer-Tredway Company . . . 267.00
Ax, Plumb, Fayette R., Embossed Logos, 15 In. 675.00
Ax, Tin Head, Black Wooden Handle, 38 In. 40.00
Battery Tester, Dry Cell, Signal Corps, 1950 . . . . 85.00
Beader, Hand, Stanley, No. 66, Guides, 8 Cutters 175.00
Beader, Hand, Stanley, No. 66, Nickel Plate, Box, 11 In. 22.00
Beam Compass, B. & J. Mfg. Co., Detroit, Mich., 4 1/2 In. 45.00
Bee Smoker 20.00
Bellows, Turn Adjustable Wheel To Operate, Iron & Brass, 21 5/8 In. 230.00
Belt, Sanding, Garnet, Resin Bond Cloth, Open Coat 150 Grit, 5 x 200 In., 10 Piece 35.00
Belt, Sanding, Resinall, Metalite Cloth, Aluminum Oxide, 36 Grit, 10 x 111 In., 5 Piece . . 25.00
Bench Hook, Millers Falls Co., No. 56, Screw Adjust, Japan, 2 1/2 In. 45.00
Bevel, Craftsman Wood Service Co., Chicago, Original Card, 6 In. 45.00
Bevel, Hall & Knapp, New Britain, Conn., Rosewood, 8 In. 295.00
Bevel, St. Johnsbury Tool Co., Rosewood & Steel, Pat. June 14, 1870, 15 In. 895.00
Bevel, Standard Tool Co., Athol, Mass., Stephen Bellows Square, Pat. 3-11-1884, 9 In. . . . 550.00
Blow Torch, Hot Blast, Wooden Box, Instruction Card 55.00
Box, Cabinet Maker's, Quartersawn Oak, Raised Panel 125.00
Box, Chestnut, Original Hardware, Key, Compartments, 19th Century, 21 x 22 x 43 In. 280.00
Box, Dovetailed, Brass Band, Iron Handles, Brass Tack Design, Large 135.00
Box, Farrier's, Pink, Handled Basket, Compartment, Legs, 19th Century, 15 x 9 x 22 In. . . . 56.00
Box, Keen Kutter 300.00

Brace, Corner, Millers Falls, No. 502 .... 23.00
Brace, Corner, Millers Falls, Pat. 6-29-1897 .... 250.00
Brace, Ebony, Brass-Framed, Holtzapffel 1310.00
Brace, Morrison, The Challenge, Pat. Feb. 1, 1898, 19 In. 745.00
Cabinetmaker's Mortise Scribe, Tiger Maple, New England, 18th Century 160.00
Caliper, Gear Tooth, Starrett, No. 456-B, Box 873.00
Caliper, Inside, Starrett, 4 In. 15.00
Caliper, Lady's Leg, 19th Century, 4 1/2 In. 165.00
Caliper, Lady's Leg, Heavy Gauge Steel, 8 1/4 x 3 3/4 In. 85.00
Caliper, Rope, Rebone, No. 1206, Belfast Ropework Co., Ltd. 85.00
Caliper Rule, Carpenter's, Stanley, No. 36 1/2L 30.00
Carryall, Blacksmith's, Pine Drawer, 22 x 28 1/4 In. 275.00
Chest, Cabinet Maker's, Mahogany, Drawers, Secret Compartments, Tools, 25 x 40 In. ... 8406.00
Chest, Carpenter's, Inlaid Clover Leaf On Diamond On Lid, 2 Drawers, 18 1/2 In. 165.00
Chest, Carpenter's, Pine, Dovetailed, Fitted Interior, Rope Handles, 38 In. 330.00
Chest, Carpenter's, Pine, Rabbet Joints, Hinged Lid, Iron Handles, 40 x 21 x 21 In. ... 110.00
Chest, Dovetailed, Black Paint, Striping, Phillip Hoffman, 10 x 29 x 43 In. 385.00
Chest, Laminated Walnut, Maple, Brass Plate Marked Belding, 36 x 23 x 22 In. 275.00
Chest, Marquetry Animals, Birds, Flowers, 19th Century, America, 26 x 40 x 27 In. 8500.00
Chest, Oak, Wall Hanging, Signed 245.00
Chisel, Butt, Keen Kutter, 1 1/2 In. 20.00
Clamp, Cabinet Maker's, Wooden Bar 20.00
Cobbler's Bench, Pine, Drawer, Leather Seat, 48 In. 55.00
Cobbler's Bench, Pine, Stepped Shape, Drawers, Leather Work Area, 28 x 45 x 22 In. ... 3680.00
Cobbler's Bench, Wooden, Traces Of Leather Seat, 20 x 50 x 14 In. 55.00
Comb, Weaver's, Dryad Handicrafts, Leicester, 1 Piece, 19th Century, 7 3/8 In., Pair 95.00
Compressor, Cork, Cutter, Pharmacist's, Patent January 6, 1863 .... 215.00
Cornering Tool, Stanley, No. 29 .... 25.00
Cutter, Dowel, Stanley, No. 77, 3/8 In. 65.00
Digger, Weed, Blacksmith Made, Iron, 18h Century 150.00
Dividers, Face Of Man-In-The-Moon Both Sides Of Hinge, German Silver 1127.00
Drafting Set, Brass, Steel, Mahogany Case, England, Mid-19th Century 185.00
Drill, Hand, Jeweler's 47.00
Flashlight, Wards, Copper 18.00
Flashlight, Winchester, Metal, Trademark, 7 1/2 x 1 3/4 In. 45.00
Gauge, Ebony & Brass, Alex Mathieson, Glasgow 85.00
Gauge, Marking, Mortise, A.H. Blaisdell, Patent 1868 .... 400.00
Gauge, Marking, Stanley, No. 0, Beech, Sweetheart Trademark 45.00
Gauge, Rule Finger Lumber, Lufkin, 3 In. 125.00
Grain Trough, Lift Lid, Oak, Lead Interior, Casters, England, Country, 1880, 98 x 39 In. . 545.00
Gunpowder Measure, BGI Co. 23.00
Hackle, 2 Round Medallions, Compass Scribed Design, 30 1/2 In. 660.00
Hacksaw, Keen Kutter 35.00
Hacksaw, Millers Falls, No. 300, Nickel Plated, Plastic Handle 30.00
Halberd, Iron, 1740-1760, 19 x 7 1/2 In. 650.00
Harness Collar, Bentwood, Heart Design Iron Overlay, Marked M.D.P., Norway, 13 In. ... 55.00
Hat Form, Woman's, Basswood, Wide Brim, 1930, 14 In., 2 Piece 55.00
Hatchet, Hand Forged, Hickory Handle, Marked AH, 10 3/4 In. 247.00
Hatchet, Knapsack, Butchering Small Game, American Revolutionary War 235.00
Hay Fork, Oak, 3 Forged Iron Tines, 19th Century, 67 In. 145.00
Haystack Measure, Copper, Dovetailed, Stamped Gallon, England, 12 In. 220.00
Hide Scraper, Bone, Removable Knife Blade, Late 19th Century, 10 In. 225.00
Hone, Razor, Keen Kutter, Box 70.00
Incubator, Pine Wainscot, 4 Legs, 1 Door, 2 Glass Panes, 27 x 24 x 23 In. 90.00
Jeweler's Bench, Oak, 11 Drawers, 2 Doors, Late 19th Century, 50 x 44 In. 385.00
Knapper, Iron, Flint Sharpener For Musket, American, 18th Century, 6 In. 185.00
Knife, Folding, Wrought Iron, Steel, Continental, 1860, 6 In. 60.00
Lathe, Jeweler's, 14 Collets, American Watch & Tool Company 280.00
Leather Working, Burl, Natural Root Growth, 5 In. 30.00
Level, Carpenter's, Stanley, No. 0, Cherry, 24 In. 30.00
Level, Davis Level & Tool Co., No. 2, Cast Iron 695.00
Level, Goodell Pratt Company, No. 509, Open End Style, 18 In. 65.00
Level, Machinist's, Stanley, No. 38 1/2, 4 In. 40.00

Level, Pocket, Stanley, No. 41, Brass Top, Pat. June 23, 1896, 3 In. 65.00
Level, Standard Tool Company, Athol, Mass., Bellows Pat. Square, March 11, 1884 . . . . . 550.00
Level, Stratton Brothers, Greenfield, Mass., No. 10, Rosewood, Brass Bound, 10 In. 950.00
Level, Surveyor's, Keuffel & Esser Co., 6 1/2 x 11 In. 192.00
Level, Transit, Surveyor's, W. & L.E. Gurley, Brass, Mahogany Case, 12 1/2 In. 825.00
Machine, Broom Making 1000.00
Marker, Clapboard Siding, Stanley, No. 88 . . . . 28.00
Maul, Saddler's, Maple, Seth Kiddy, 12 1/2 In. 235.00
Meat Hook, Butcher's, Cast Iron, Wall Mount, Gloeklers Patent May 28, 1888, 60 In. . . . 495.00
Model, Lawnmower, Push Scissors Type, Oak Handle, 6 In. 395.00
Mold, Bullet, Colts Patent, Brass, 2 Hole, 31 Cal. 90.00
Mold, Bullet, Winchester, Walnut Handles, 40-82 Cal. 63.00
Mold, For Pewter Spoon, Bronze, Dark Patina, 8 3/4 In. 110.00
Mold, Military Hat, Shako, Pine, 1830s 95.00
Monkey Wrench, Iron, Pocket, Jaw Beam Graduated mm 25.00
Monkey Wrench, Winchester, 10 In. 75.00
Nippers, Sugar, Wrought Iron, Whalebone & Wood, Whalebone Handle, 12 In. 575.00
Nippers, Sugar, Wrought Steel & Brass, Wooden Handle, 11 In. 165.00
Oilcan, Teapot-Shape, Spout Cap 235.00
Opener-Hammer, Burgharts Cigar 75.00
Paddle, Lard, Wooden, Weathered, 19th Century, 38 In. 5.00
Permanent Wave Unitemp Machine, Electric, Frederics, Inc., New York, 1930s 275.00
Pipe Tongs, Wrought Iron, Rivets, 11 1/2 In. 140.00
Plane, Block, Davis, No. 18, Some Japanning 285.00
Plane, Block, Double End, Stanley, No. 130 . . . . 335.00
Plane, Block, Double, Sargent, No. 227, Japanned, Original Knob 95.00
Plane, Block, Stanley, No. 120, Box 38.00
Plane, Bull-Nose, Stanley, 4 x 1 In. 35.00
Plane, Cabinet Scraper, Stanley, No. 83 . . . . 100.00
Plane, Circular, Stanley, No. 20, Nickel Finish 175.00
Plane, Circular, Victor, Stanley, No. 20, Cast Iron, Nickel Plated 350.00
Plane, Combination, Stanley, No. 45, Set Of 20 Cutters, Wooden Box 325.00
Plane, Fulton, New York, No. 5320, Block Style, Pat. March 21, 1893, 7 In. 125.00
Plane, Gutter, Lignum Vitae, Beech Handle, Replaced Wedge, 11 3/4 In. 55.00
Plane, Horn, H. Chapin Union Factory 75.00
Plane, Jack, Millers Falls, No. 714, Buck Rogers 125.00
Plane, Jack, Stanley, No. 5 1/2C, Cast Iron, Rosewood Handle & Knob, 14 3/4 In. 50.00
Plane, Jack, Winchester, No. 3010 . . . . 85.00
Plane, Jointer, Millers Falls, No. 7, Patent, 1931, 21 3/4 In. 65.00
Plane, Millers Falls Company, No. 56, Screw Adjust, 3 In. 55.00
Plane, Miter, Heathcott, Sheffield, Boxwood Vertical Mouth Adjuster 200.00
Plane, Molding, Casey & Co., Adjustable Gate, Rosewood, Boxwood, Brass, 11 In. 412.00
Plane, Musical Instrument Maker's, Iron, 17th Century, 6 In. 2423.00
Plane, Musical Instrument Maker's, Wrought Iron, 6 3/4 In. 4302.00
Plane, Plow, Miller's Patent Adjustable, Stanley, No. 43, 1 Blade 450.00
Plane, Plow, Stanley, No. 41, Miller's Patent Adjustable, Extra Fence, 9 Of 10 Cutters . . . 950.00
Plane, Plow, Yount & Master, Wood Screws 85.00
Plane, Rabbet, Bull-Nose, Stanley, No. 75 . . . . 35.00
Plane, Rabbet, Carriage Maker's, Stanley, No. 10 1/4, Tilt Handle 550.00
Plane, Router, Stanley, No. 71, Pat. 1884 . . . . 50.00
Plane, Sargent, No. 1085, 51 Cutters, Case 280.00
Plane, Scraper, Cabinet Maker's, Stanley, No. 85, Patented 4/11/1905 . . . . 600.00
Plane, Smooth, Bed Rock, Stanley, No. 602, 1936 . . . . 700.00
Plane, Smooth, Jenny, Stanley, No. 37 . . . . 185.00
Plane, Smooth, Liberty Bell, Stanley, No. 104, 1895 . . . . 165.00
Plane, Smooth, Shipfitter's, Marine Bronze 175.00
Plane, Toothing, 18th Century 225.00
Plane, Violin Maker, Brass, Wood Pusher, Brass, 1 5/8 In. 125.00
Plane, Wedge Arm Plow, Young & McMaster, 1 Cutter 175.00
Plane, Wood Jointer, Keen Kutter, Sawtooth Logo 40.00
Pliers, Bent Nose 110.00
Pliers, Ford, Herbrand, Fremont, Ohio 17.00
Pliers, Hammer, Spike & Lever, Upholsterer's 98.00

Plumb Bob, Bergen Tool Co., Batavia, Ill., Original Fitted Spindle, 4 3/4 In. 395.00
Plumb Bob, Stanley, No. 1, Marked With Patent 235.00
Pump, Bilge, Femyers & Bros., Brass & Cast Iron, Ashland, Ohio, 1895 .... 75.00
Radio Receiver, Signal Corps, 1945 .... 50.00
Rake, Blueberry, Wooden Handle, 2 1/4-In. Teeth, 11 1/2 In. 85.00
Rake, Cranberry, Hand Forged Teeth, Hand Cut Nails & Rivets, Walnut Shaft, 7 x 13 In. . 215.00
Rake, Potato, Hinged, Hand Wrought 450.00
Rake, Wooden, 4 Tines, 64 1/2 In. 275.00
Repair Kit, Shoe & Harness, Vise, Awls, Instructions, Dovetailed Box, 14 In. 16.00
Router, Millers Falls Company, No. 77, Coated-Throat, Original Irons, 9 In. 145.00
Router, No. 71, Stanley, Pat. 1884 .... 50.00
Rule, 3 Sides, Darling, Brown, 7 Sharp, No. 73, Metal, 1879 .... 110.00
Rule, Carpenter's, Stanley, No. 61, Folding 20.00
Rule, Carpenter's, Stanley, No. 62 1/2, Folding, Brass Bound, 24 In. 60.00
Rule, Folding, Biddle & Co., No. 54, 4-Fold, Brass Bound, Arch Joint 125.00
Rule, Folding, John Rodgers Baltr., Brass, 24 In. 165.00
Rule, Shipmast Maker's, Samson Aston, Boxwood, 2-Fold, Brass Slide, 1833-1870, 24 In. 2459.00
Rule, Stanley, No. 32, Sweetheart Mark, Left Hand 65.00
Ruler, Peanuts Gang, Characters At School Desks, Hallmark, United Features, 12 In. 4.00
Saddle Form, Wooden, Weathered, Western, Worming, 19 In. 90.00
Saw, Armorer's, Ram's Horn, Locking Nut, Original Blade, 18th Century 692.00
Saw, Butcher, Keystone Disston, 24 In. 12.00
Saw, Fret, Buck, Rosewood & Boxwood, 1838-61, 17 x 15 In. 205.00
Saw, Hand, Winchester, No. 13 .... 110.00
Saw, Keyhole, Keen Kutter 65.00
Saw, Scroll, Sutton, Rochester, N.Y., Flywheel, Tag Marked March 30, 1880, 9 In. 3650.00
Saw, Stair, Disston 65.00
Saw Blade, Clemson Brothers In., Middletown, No. 1218, The Star Hack Saw, 12 In. 25.00
Scoop, Cranberry, Steel Tines & Spring, Brass Screws, Marked T.P. 185.00
Screwdriver, Brown & Co., R.H. Westville, Conn., Original Bits, Hardwood Box, 8 In. .. 295.00
Screwdriver, Millers Falls Co., No. 29X, Spiral Ratchet Type, 10 1/2 In. 45.00
Screwdriver, Millers Falls Co., No. 850, No. 4 Size, Phillips Head, 8-In. Blade, 14 In. ... 45.00
Screwdriver, Spiral, Greenlee, Patent 1935, 17 In. 65.00
Shaper, Stroke Metal, Ammco, Motor & Light, 7 In. 475.00
Shovel, Scoop, Ash, Carved, 36 In. 75.00
Slide Rule, Bamboo, Box, Instructions 15.00
Slide Rule, Tavella Sales Co., New York, Circular, Original Pouch, Copyright 1936, 4 In. . 45.00
Spokeshave, Barton Cooper, Wooden Handles 30.00
Spokeshave, Fenton & Marsden, Brass Adjusting Thumbscrew 30.00
Spokeshave, Herbert, Detroit, Mich., Pattern Maker's, Solid Bronze, 1920s, 4 In. 195.00
Spokeshave, Razor Edge, Stanley, No. 84, Sweetheart Trademark, 11 1/2 In. 195.00
Sprayer, Flit, Theodore Geisel (Dr. Seuss) Drawings, Stanco, Inc., N.J., 18 1/2 In. . . . *Illus* 25.00
Square, Carpenter's Take Down, Stanley, No. 100N, Nickel Plate 95.00
Square, Lufkin Rule Co., Saginaw, Mich., No. 166, Machined Steel, 4 1/2 In. 45.00
Steam Engine, Jensen Mfg. Co., Jeannette, Pa., 110 Volts AC Or DC 375.00
Striker, Flint, Figural, Sea Monster, Curved Tail, 17th Century, 4 In. 395.00
Sundial, Surveyor's, Mahogany, Brass, Octagonal, 19th Century, 3 3/4 In. 330.00
Surveyor's Instrument, Brass, Walnut, T.F. Randolph, Cincinnati, O., '78, 17 In. 1155.00

**Clean metal with a back-and-forth
motion, not a circular motion.
Use a soft, clean, lint-free cloth
and turn it often to avoid reusing
a soiled part.**

Tool, Sprayer, Flit, Theodore Geisel
(Dr. Seuss) Drawings, Stanco, Inc., N.J., 18 1/2 In.

Swift, Maple, Copper Rivets, 25 1/2 In. 285.00
Tack Puller, Buffum Tool Co., Louisana, Missouri, Forged Steel, Swastika Logo, 7 In. ... 115.00
Tack Puller, McGillis, Brown & Pratt Co., Original Handbill, 6 In. 55.00
Tape Measure, DeFiance, No. 1262, Nickel 30.00
Tape Measure, Stanley, No. 6386, Marked Direct Reading, 72 In. 65.00
Tinderbox, Brass Panel 1 Side, Striker & Flint, Sheet Iron, c.1750 .... 250.00
Tomahawk, Spiked, 13 1/4 In. 350.00
Trammel, Cast Brass, Marked JBO, 4 1/2 In. 115.00
Transit, Brass, Mahogany Tripod, E. Brown & Sons, 1823-1840 .... 880.00
Transit, Craftsman, Tripod, Case, Instruction Book 66.00
Transit, Surveyor's, Brass, Mahogany, Silver Dial, Tripod, Wm. H. Plister, 12 In. 1320.00
Trowel, Mason's, Wrought Iron, 12 3/4 In. 130.00
Tube Tester, Hickock, Signal Corps 75.00
Tweezers, Woman's Leg Shape, Stockings, Ribbon Garter, Pat. Mar. 1, 1910, Marked 128.00
Vise, Bench, Stanley, No. 741, Black Japanned, 1 1/2-In. Jaws 52.00
Vise, Hand, 6 Small Tools In Handle, Early 1900s, 1 1/4 In. 40.00
Vise, Leather Worker's, Chestnut, Union Village, Ohio, 28 In. 115.00
Vise, Millers Falls, Iron, Box, 2 1/2 In. 80.00
Wagon Jack, Conestoga, Iron, Adjustable Arm, Wood, Initials C.G., 1758, 20 In. 75.00
Warmer, Mitten, Attached B Strap To Stovepipe, Cast Iron, Patent 1862, 17 1/2 In. 135.00
Workbench, Chestnut, Made To Disassemble & Fold, Drawer, Backstop, 19 x 51 In. 240.00
Wrench, Alligator, ADJ 90.00
Wrench, Alligator, No. 30, Keen Kutter 30.00
Wrench, Atwater's Tiger Wrench, Brazilian Rosewood Handle, Pat. Aug. 18, 1878, 5 In. .. 545.00
Wrench, Bemis & Call Co., Springfield, Mass., No. 75, Crescent Style, 6 In. 55.00
Wrench, Billings & Spencer Co., Nut Wrench, Pat. Feb. 18, 1879, 6 In. 55.00
Wrench, Buggy, Joys, Patent Feb. 1, '98, Nickel Plated, 10 In. 75.00
Wrench, Cellman Wrench Corp., No. 91, Quick Adjust, Pat. April 17, 1923, 9 In. 55.00
Wrench, Chas. E. Hall Co., Buffalo, N.Y., No. 15, 7 In. 110.00
Wrench, Elgin, Pat. June 8, 1897, 7 In. 25.00
Wrench, Ellis, Nickel Plated, Pat. Nov. 3, 1903, 6 In. 365.00
Wrench, Fruit Jar, Hoffman Hinge & Foundry, Cleveland, Cast Iron 125.00
Wrench, Key Lock, Coe's, Patent 1903, 31 In. 275.00
Wrench, Motorcycle, Indian, Adjustable, 7 In. 95.00
Wrench, Pipe, Schick, Aluminum, 10 In. 55.00
Wringer, Horseshoe, No. 2 Gem American Wringer Co., Salesman's Sample 210.00

TOOTHPICK HOLDERS are sometimes called *toothpicks* by collectors.
The variously shaped containers used to hold small wooden toothpicks
are made of glass, china, or metal. Most of the toothpick holders are
Victorian. Additional items may be found in other categories, such as
Bisque, Silver Plate, Slag Glass, etc.

   Bulging Loops, Pink Cased 110.00
   Caramel Color, Joe St. Clair 70.00
   Cat, Bronze, Enamel, France, 3 x 5 In. 500.00
   Chrysanthemum, Base Swirl, White Opalescent 90.00
   Codova, Green 30.00
   Colorado, Footed, Green, 3 In. 25.00
   Daisy & Button, Square, Blue 30.00
   Daisy & Button With Ornament, Vaseline 55.00
   Draped Beads, Milk Glass 45.00
   Fern Heart, Milk Glass 20.00
   Flute, Amethyst, Carnival Glass 85.00
   Indian Head, Figural, Porcelain, 3 1/4 In. 45.00
   Iris With Meander, White, Opalescent 55.00
   Ladder To The Stars 55.00
   New Jersey, Gold Trim 65.00
   Peerless, Heisey 55.00
   Spearpoint Band, Gold Trim 50.00
   Spread Winged Bird Beneath Holder, Pressed Glass, Canary Yellow, 2 3/4 In. 65.00
   Stars & Stripes, McKee 45.00
   Sunbeam, Green 50.00
   Thousand Eye, Blue 50.00

TORQUAY is the name given to ceramics by several potteries working near Torquay, England, from 1870 until 1962. Until about 1900, the potteries used local red clay to make classical-style art pottery vases and figurines. Then they turned to making souvenir wares. Items were dipped in colored slip and decorated with painted slip and sgraffito designs. They often had mottoes or proverbs, and scenes of cottages, ships, birds, or flowers. The *Scandy* design was a symmetrical arrangement of brushstrokes and spots done in colored slips. Potteries included Watcombe Pottery (1870–1962); Torquay Terra-Cotta Company (1875–1905); Aller Vale (1881–1924); Torquay Pottery (1908–1940); and Longpark (1883–1957).

TORQUAY

Bowl, Black Cockerel, Be Aisy With That Sugar, 5 1/4 In.	110.00
Bowl, Kingfisher, 4 In.	45.00
Candlestick, Motto Ware, Allervale, 4 1/2 In., Pair	110.00
Creamer, Brixsham Boat Scene, Straight From The Cow	40.00
Creamer, Seagull, Blue, 1 3/4 x 2 In.	55.00
Cup & Saucer, Cottage, Motto Ware, Cup That Cheers	60.00
Cup & Saucer, Motto Ware, Make Hay While The Sun Shines, 2 1/2 In.	55.00
Eggcup, Motto Ware, Just Laid, 1 3/4 x 1 1/2 In.	45.00
Jam Pot, Cover, Motto Ware, Watcombe	22.00
Match Holder, Striker, I'll Help Console Ye, Scandy	65.00
Mug, Motto Ware, None Are So Good As They Should Be, 5 x 4 In.	75.00
Perfume Bottle, Devon Violets	45.00
Pitcher, Applied Roses, 7 In.	200.00
Pitcher, Karswell Daisy, Motto Ware, 6 In.	140.00
Plate, Cottage, Motto Ware, 5 1/2 In.	55.00
Teapot, Buckfast Cottage Scene, 4 3/4 In.	100.00

TORTOISESHELL is the shell of the tortoise. It has been used as inlay and to make small decorative objects since the seventeenth century. Some species of tortoise are now on the endangered species list, and old and new objects made from these shells cannot be sold legally.

Box, Desk, Jewel Casket Shape, Ivory, 1875, 4 3/4 x 13 x 9 7/8 In.	2904.00
Box, Desk, Silver Inlaid, Blond, Emerald Baize Interior, Ivory Bun Feet, 2 x 6 In.	847.00
Box, Mother-Of-Pearl, Fluted, Midnight Blue Velvet Interior, 1825, 1 5/8 x 2 In.	800.00
Box, Overall Figural Landscape, 3 3/4 x 4 x 4 In.	145.00
Box, Painted Scene Of Man & 2 Women On Cover, Oval, 1880s, 3 x 3 x 6 In.	820.00
Box, Patch, Male & Female, Fingers To Lips, Regency Attire, 3 1/2 In., Pair	345.00
Box, Sewing, Double Hinged Lid, Mother-Of-Pearl, Victorian, 8 x 9 3/4 In.	1035.00
Case, Bone Cheroot, England, 1865, 5 1/8 x 2 3/4 x 1 In.	363.00
Ox, Overall Carved Figures & Landscape, 19th Century, 5 In.	460.00
Pin Box, Rectangular, Ivory Ball Feet, 19th Century	165.00
Snuffbox, Silver Inlaid, White Opaline Glass Bun Feet, 1810-1820, 1 1/4 In.	303.00
Tea Caddy, Ivory, 2 Lidded Compartments, Bun Feet, Regency, 6 1/4 x 7 In.	1955.00
Tea Caddy, Ivory, Serpentine Front, 2 Lidded Compartments, Regency, 6 In.	2590.00

TORTOISESHELL GLASS was made during the 1800s and after by the Sandwich Glass Works of Massachusetts and some firms in Germany. Tortoiseshell glass is, of course, named for its resemblance to real shell from a tortoise. It has been reproduced.

Pitcher, Brown & Amber, Applied Amber Handle, 3 1/2 In.	87.00
Vase, Elongated Neck, Flask Form, Banding At Neck, c.1890, 11 In.	83.00

TOY collectors have special clubs, magazines, and shows. Toys are designed to entice children, and today they have attracted new interest among adults who are still children at heart. All types of toys are collected. Tin toys, iron toys, battery-operated toys, and many others are collected by specialists. Dolls, Games, Teddy Bears, and Bicycles are listed in their own categories. Other toys may be found under company or celebrity names.

Acrobat, Clown, Polka Dot Cloth Top, Yellow Pants, Lehmann, 1920, 10 In.	1265.00
Acrobat, Gripping Gymnast's Bar Connected To Tinplate Box, Clockwork, 1883, 13 In.	3740.00
Acrobat, Windup, Wyandotte, 1920s	175.00

Aircraft Carrier, Coral Sea, Tin Lithograph, Friction, Bandai, Box, 15 In. 210.00
Aircraft Carrier, Super Flat Top, 6 Airplanes, Paper, Die Cut, Box, 1942, 20 In. 175.00
Airplane, Air France, Battery Operated, Red, Beige, Red Lettering, 21-In. Wingspan 880.00
Airplane, Air Mail, Yellow Fuselage, Brown Wings, Disc Wheels, Keystone, 23 In. 468.00
Airplane, Air Mail, Yellow, Embossed Airmail On Wing, 7 3/4-In. Wingspan 110.00
Airplane, American Airlines, DC Flagship, Linemar, 19 1/2 In. 250.00
Airplane, American Airlines, Jetliner, Battery Operated, Remote Control, Tin, 20 In. 195.00
Airplane, American Flagship, 4 Propellers, Marx, 1940, 27 3/4-In. Wingspan 450.00
Airplane, Animal Jet, Yogi, Huckleberry Hound, Woody, Tin, Marubishi, 1960, 8 In. 265.00
Airplane, Army Air Corps, P-39 Style, Die Cast, Red Paint, 5 1/4-In. Wingspan 27.00
Airplane, Army Scout, Tri-Motor, Decals, Steelcraft, USA, 23-In. Wingspan 468.00
Airplane, B17, Bomber, U.S. Air Force, Friction, Marked BK2250, 17 1/2-In. Wingspan . .   358.00
Airplane, Biplane, TWA Mail, Tin Lithograph, 4 Motors, Marx 302.00
Airplane, Biplane, Wood Cylinders & Wheels, Propellers Turn, Tin, Pull Toy, Schieble . . .   105.00
Airplane, BOAC Comet, Friction, Tin Lithograph, Blue, Silver, Japan, Box, 7 In. 140.00
Airplane, Boeing 747, Pan-Am. Airways, Stop & Go, See-Through Cockpit, Box, 7 In. . . .   225.00
Airplane, Boeing, 2 Motors, Cast Iron, 4 3/4 In. 195.00
Airplane, Boeing, AMC 361, Die Cast, Green Paint, 3 1/2 x 4 1/2 In. 120.00
Airplane, Bomber, Olive Green Body, Pilot Seated In Cockpit, 14 1/2-In. Wingspan 770.00
Airplane, Boycraft, NX 107, Army Scout, Steelcraft 950.00
Airplane, Bremen, Cast Iron, Green, Hubley, 6 1/2-In. Wingspan 1075.00
Airplane, China Clipper, Triple Tail, Wyandotte 390.00
Airplane, Corvair Inter Continental Jet, Friction, Box, 14 In. 145.00
Airplane, Dagwood's Flight, Tin Lithograph, Clockwork, Marx, 1935, 9 In. 1540.00
Airplane, Fighter, Spitfire, Gas Powered, Plastic, Green, Thimbledrome, 23-In. Wingspan .   35.00
Airplane, Fighter, U.S. Navy Demon F3H-2, Friction, Tin Lithograph, Japan, 6 1/2 In. . . .   80.00
Airplane, Fighter, Windup, Ikarus No. 653, Lehmann, Germany, 11 In. 440.00
Airplane, Fokker, Silver, Embossed Lettering, Cast Iron, Vindex, 9 3/4-In. Wingspan 5060.00
Airplane, Jet Fighter, General Dynamics Grumman F111A, Battery Operated, 16 In. 170.00
Airplane, Junkuer, Windup, T.T.C., 22-In. Wingspan 1365.00
Airplane, KLM Corvair Jet, Royal Dutch Airlines, Friction, 14 In. 95.00
Airplane, Lindy, Gray Body, Red Embossed Lettering, Cast Iron, 14 1/2-In. Wingspan . . .   1320.00
Airplane, Lockheed Sirius, Twin Cockpit, Battery Operated, Steelcraft, 21-In. Wingspan . .   468.00
Airplane, Looping, Mechanical, Marx 200.00
Airplane, Lucky Boy, 1 Motor, Cast Iron, 4 In. 175.00
Airplane, Mail Plane, Tri Motor, Pressed Steel, Wheel-Driven Propellers, 18-In. Wingspan   175.00
Airplane, Military, Windup, Tin, Marx, 18 1/2-In. Wingspan, Box 725.00
Airplane, Monoplane, Cast Iron, Red, Arcade, 5-In. Wingspan 385.00
Airplane, Monoplane, Indian Arrow Ford Tri-Motor Decal, Tin, 26 In. 2070.00
Airplane, Pan-American Airways, Propeller, 4 Motors, 27-In. Wingspan. 187.00
Airplane, Pan-American Airways, Tin, American Flag, Japan, Box, 6 x 7 1/2 In. 385.00
Airplane, Pedal, Silver Line, Pressed Steel, Steelcraft, 1940, 44 x 30-In. Wingspan 1100.00
Airplane, Pilot At The Tiller, Red, Yellow, Paper Wings, Tin, Lehmann, 1920, 11 In. 4430.00
Airplane, Pure Oil, White, Black Decals, Metalcraft, 17 1/2 In. 425.00
Airplane, Radiant 5600 KLM, Battery Operated, Schuco 700.00
Airplane, Radio Controlled, Telemaster 40, Gas Engine 300.00
Airplane, Red, Blue-Edged Wings, 4 Working Propellers, Marx, 18-In. Wingspan 495.00
Airplane, Ride-On, Keystone 750.00
Airplane, Rollover, Seated Pilot, Blue Body, Tin, Box, 6-In. Wingspan 385.00
Airplane, Single Engine, Tin, Passengers & Pilot Decals, Schieble, 26 3/4-In. Wingspan . .   440.00
Airplane, Single Propeller, 2 Seats, Steelcraft, 21 1/2-In. Wingspan 430.00
Airplane, Sit & Ride, Marx, 31 In. 195.00
Airplane, Sky Cruiser, Marx, Box 495.00
Airplane, Spirit Of St. Louis, Circles Tower, Electric Motor, Tin, 20 x 39 In. 192.00
Airplane, Spirit Of St. Louis, Circles Tower, Gold Plane, United Electrical Mfg. Co. 2025.00
Airplane, Spirit Of St. Louis, Swing Arms On Tower, 2 Airplanes At Ends, 20 In. 880.00
Airplane, Spirit Of St. Louis, Tin, Marked NX211, Strauss, 9-In. Wingspan 550.00
Airplane, Tail Gunner, Hot Wheels, No. 29 . . . .   75.00
Airplane, Trans Canada, Tin Lithograph, Retractable Landing Gear, Box 495.00
Airplane, Transport, Blue, White, Buddy L, 1946, 27-In. Wingspan 190.00
Airplane, Transport, Tri-Motor, Tin, 3 Spinning Propellers, Schieble, 27-In. Wingspan . . .   633.00
Airplane, Tri-Motor, Cast Iron, 4 In. 195.00

Airplane, Vickers Viscount, Battery Operated, Box 995.00
Alabama Coon Jigger, Tin Lithograph, Lehmann, c.1911, 10 In. 405.00
Alabama Coon Jigger, Windup, Jointed Man Dances, Strauss Mfg., 5 x 8 3/4 In. 440.00
Alabama Coon Jigger, Windup, Tin, Lehmann, Germany, 10 In. 440.00
Alligator, Wood, Jointed, Painted Eyes, Leather Feet, Schoenhut, 12 In. 230.00
Ambulance, City, White, Red Crosses, Cast Iron, Arcade, 1930s, 5 3/4 In. 660.00
Ambulance, Red Cross, Pressed Steel, Sturditoy, 1920s 12650.00
Ambulance, Windup, Composition Driver, Attendant, 2 Patients, Camouflage, Tin 1380.00
Amusement Park, Kiddy Whip Ride, Mangels 4400.00
Aquaplane, American Flyer Style, La Rosa, 20-In. Wingspan 1295.00
Aquaplane, Windup, Bing, c.1920, 16 In. 5000.00
Arab, Chief, Standing, Wearing Turban, Black Beard, Schoenhut, 1912, 8 In. 7475.00
Arab, Sulky Driver, Windup, Western Germany, Box 155.00
Autograph Book, Barbie, Black, Vinyl, 1962, 6 x 4 1/2 In. 100.00
B.O. Plenty, Windup, Walker, Tin, By Marx, 8 1/2 In. 110.00
Baby Snookums, Windup, Hand Painted, Germany, 6 1/2 In. 440.00
Badge, Captain Kangaroo, Metal 20.00
Badge, Gang Busters, 1937 .... 35.00
Bakery Wagon, White, Red Lettering, Red Wheels, Cast Iron, 13 In. 248.00
Ballerina, Windup, Tiptoes On Ball As It Rolls, Tin, 8 In. 360.00
Balloon, Hot Air, Gondola & Passenger, Lehmann, 1920, 6 In. 2755.00
Balloon, Hot Air, Windup, Tin, Clown, Wicker Gondola, G & K, Germany, 10 1/2 In. 1320.00
Balloon, Luna, Suspended From Ceiling, Red, White, Gold, Lehmann, 1930, 5 1/2 In. ... 3670.00
Bamm Bamm, White Tunic, Label, Dakin, Hanna-Barbera, 1970, 6 3/4 In. 60.00
Barney Rubble, Friction Car, Tin, 3 1/2 In. 60.00
Barney Rubble, On Dino, Windup, Marx, Japan, 8 In. 225.00
Bartender, Charley Weaver, Battery Operated 95.00
Bartender, Rosko, Shakes Mixer, Pours & Drinks, Ears Smoke, Box 75.00
Baseball Player & Bat, Celluloid, 6 In. 60.00
Battleship, Clockwork, 3 Stacks, Dual-Barrel Gun Turrets, Gold, Red, Carette, 18 In. 2875.00
Battleship, St. Vincent, Windup, Tin, Lehmann, 13 3/4 In. 440.00
Bears are also listed in the Teddy Bears category.
Bear, Blond, On Wheels, Pull Toy, c.1935, 20 x 28 In. ....*Illus* 2415.00
Bear, Climbing, White Fur, Climbs Up A Pole, Martin, 1910, 20 In. 690.00
Bear, Hopping, Windup, Tin, Red Striped Shirt, Blue Pants, Marx, 1960s, 4 In. 34.00
Bear, Licking Jam, Windup, Tongue & Arm Move, Linemar, Box 185.00
Bear, Mama Feeds Hungry Baby, Battery Operated, Tin, Plush, Japan, Box, 9 1/2 In. 220.00
Bear, Maxwell House Coffee, Battery Operated, 11 In. 275.00
Bear, Moves Head From Side To Side, Clockwork, Dark Brown Fur, Ives, 1890, 10 In. .. 980.00
Bear, On Wheels, Blond Plush, Pull Toy, Steiff, 1935, 20 In. 2415.00
Bear, On Wheels, Brown Mohair, Steel Frame & Wheels, Embroidered Nose, 9 1/4 In. ... 200.00
Bear, Performing, Clockwork, Stands On Hind Legs, Front Paws Claw Air, Ives, 9 In. ... 920.00
Bear, Picks Up Telephone, Battery Operated, Tin, Japan, Box 145.00
Bear, Polar Bear, Clockwork, Off-White Mohair, Glass Eyes, Composition Nose, 12 In. .. 975.00
Bear, Smokey Bear, Shovel, Inflatable, Jennie G., Taiwan, c.1970, 24 In. 45.00
Bear, Smokey Bear, Shovel, Vinyl, Cloth, Rubber Hat, Japan, 1970s, 8 In. 58.00
Bear, Smokey Bear, Sitting, Inflatable, Vinyl, Ideal Toy Co., 1970s, 14 In. 20.00
Bear, With Trainer, Clockwork, Tin, Painted, Gunthermann, 6 In. & 8 1/2 In. 1375.00
Beauty Salon, Sue & Her, Original Store Display Box, 1960s 295.00
Bed, Chest & Chairs, Doll's, Wood, Wicker & Upholstered, 1950 .... 85.00
Bed, Doll's, Cast Iron, Sculpted Designs, Scrolled Feet, Paisley Cushions, c.1863, 20 In. . 1400.00
Bed, Doll's, Mahogany, Inlaid Fruitwood Band, Blanket, Pillow, France, c.1880, 19 In. 350.00
Bed, Doll's, Pine, Painted, Scalloped, Mattress, Pillow, 1893 On Side, 8 x 15 x 9 In. 165.00
Bed, Doll's, Tester, Oak, Metal Posts, Valance & Curtains, Dutch, 23 3/4 In. 315.00
Bed, Doll's, Wood, Scrubbed, Pencil Post, Primitive, 7 1/2 x 11 1/2 x 8 In. 85.00
Bedroom Set, Doll's, Renaissance Revival, Walnut, Burl Veneer, 1870, 4 Piece 862.00
Bee-Bop Jigger, Windup, Tin, Plastic, Marx, 1950s, 9 In. 80.00
Beetle, Clockwork, Tin, Painted, Germany 265.00
Bell Ringer, 2 Cast Iron Figures, Saluting Flag, Push Handle, Cast Iron & Steel, 1930s ... 275.00
Bell Ringer, 2 Men, Cast Iron, Chrome & Pressed Steel Frame, Wheels, Pull Toy, 14 1/2 In. 330.00
Bell Ringer, Boys Sawing Watermelon, Waltrous Mfg. Co., c.1900, 9 In. 6325.00
Bell Ringer, Circus Dog, Pull Toy 50.00

Toy, Bear, Blond,
On Wheels, Pull Toy,
c.1935, 20 x 28 In.

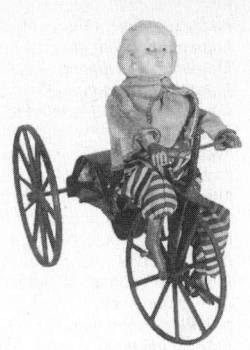

Toy, Bicycle,
Velocipede, Clockwork,
Stevens & Brown, 1870

Bell Ringer, Clapper Is Double Faced Man, Cast Iron, Nickel Finish, 6 3/4 In.	160.00
Bell Ringer, Clown & Dog, Cast Iron	9775.00
Bell Ringer, Clown On Donkey, N.N. Hill Brass Co., c.1905, 7 In.	632.00
Bell Ringer, Horse Drawn, Painted Tin, 1870s, 9 In.	315.00
Bell Ringer, Man Ringing A Bell Suspended From Lamppost, Martin, 1888, 7 In.	690.00
Bell Ringer, Monkey & Coconut, Wheeled Log, Raises & Lowers Arm, 6 In.	805.00
Bell Ringer, Monkey & Dog, Tinplate Wheels, Monkey Bobs Up & Down, c.1900	460.00
Bell Ringer, Rabbit Hunter, Man With Gun, Wheeled Base, N.N. Hill, c.1900, 6 1/2 In.	1495.00
Bellhop, Billy Boy, Windup, Celluloid Boy, Tin Suitcase, Japan, 7 In.	110.00
Bench, Doll's, Rectangular Backrest, Hinged Seat, Breton, 8 1/4 In.	110.00
Bicycle, Boy On Bicycle, Windup, Does Figure 8, Strauss, 1920s	595.00
Bicycle, Clockwork Girl On Bicycle, Speeds Around Circle, Tinplate, 8 1/2 x 19 In.	14950.00
Bicycle, Musical, Hand-Painted Cyclist, White Cap, Jersey, Blue Stripes, 1898, 4 In.	1660.00
Bicycle, Racing, Clockwork, Pair Of Cyclists Riding High-Wheeled Bikes, 1890, 12 In.	5110.00
Bicycle, Tandem, Clockwork, Hand-Painted Racers, 1890, 6 In.	3195.00
Bicycle, Tricycle, Ignatz Mouse, Wood, Tinplate, Chein, 7 In.	1150.00
Bicycle, Velocipede, Clockwork, Stevens & Brown, 1870 .... *Illus*	3025.00
Bicycle, Zigzag Cycle, Windup, 3 Wheels, Tin Driver, Landau Top, Germany, 10 In.	3960.00
Bicycles that are large enough to ride are listed in their own category.	
Bionic Woman, Mission Purse, Box	165.00
Bird, Pecking, Windup, Tin Lithograph, Green Felt Feathers, CS In Diamond, Japan, 4 In.	25.00
Bird, Pecking, Windup, Tin, Scurries About, Feeding, German, 5 In.	25.00
Birdhouse, Singing Bird, Mechanical	120.00
Black Boy, Steering Velocipede, Red Jacket, Iron, Stevens & Brown, 11 In.	3162.00
Black Dancer, Push Down Hat To Activate, Tin Lithograph, Lehmann, 7 3/4 In.	660.00
Black Man, Trumpet Player, Windup, Japan, Box	250.00
Black Woman, Sweeping, Windup, Hand Painted, German, 7 In.	350.00
Blocks, Bozo The Clown, Paper-Covered Wood, Capital Records	75.00
Blocks, Crandall's Building Blocks, Box, c.1880	275.00
Blocks, Fire Dept. Pictures, ABCs, Wood, McLoughlin Bros., Box, 1893, 8 1/2 x 13 In.	605.00
Blocks, Hollow, Paper Lithograph, Box, c.1880, 12 x 18 In.	495.00
Blocks, Little Playmates Picture Cubes, McLoughlin Bros., 9 Blocks, Box, 1890s	165.00
Blocks, Nesting, Nursery Rhymes On Face, McLoughlin, 7 Piece	1500.00
Blocks, Nesting, Paper Lithograph, ABC	275.00
Blocks, Nesting, Paper Lithograph, Cock Robin	121.00
Blocks, Nursery Rhymes, Red, White & Black, 2 1/8 In.	220.00
Blocks, Wood, Animals & ABC's, 1 3/4 x 1 3/4 In., 29 Piece	110.00
Boat, Baby Wee Speed, Windup, Tin Lithograph, Painted, USA, 10 1/4 In.	55.00
Boat, Bliss Boston Boat, Crashing Waves, 4 Wood Cannons, Cream Sides, 1900, 20 In.	3165.00
Boat, Cabin Cruiser, Clockwork, Arnold, U.S. Zone, 5 3/4 In.	650.00
Boat, Cabin Cruiser, Friction, Germany, Box, 1960s, 10 In.	450.00
Boat, Cabin Cruiser, On-Off Switch, Princess Pat., Chein, Box, 1940s, 4 In.	275.00
Boat, Cabin Cruiser, Orkin, Red, Green Cabin, Cream Color, Chrome, 1930, 29 In.	2025.00
Boat, Cabin Cruiser, Windup, Tin, Box	185.00
Boat, Canoe, Li'l Abner Dogpatch Speshul, Windup, Plastic, 11 1/2 In.	130.00
Boat, Canoe, Woman Canoeist, Wood, Tin, Clockwork, France, c.1927, 27 1/2 In.	4180.00

Boat, Climber, Friction, Cannon Each End, 10 In. 165.00
Boat, Ferry, Lackawanna Railroad, Lifeboats On Upper Deck, Red Body, 10 In. 275.00
Boat, King, Brown, Black, Yellow Deck, Mast & Stack, Tin, Ives, 10 1/2 In. 605.00
Boat, Monitor, Scenes Of Firing Cannons, Sailors, Wood, Marble Slots, 1885, 25 1/2 In. . 2405.00
Boat, Motor Boat, Cabin Cruiser, Peggy Jane, Tin, Chein, Box, 1930s, 14 x 3 In. 225.00
Boat, Motor Boat, Cabin Cruiser, Princess Pat, Tin, Chein, Box, 1940s, 15 x 4 In. 275.00
Boat, Motor, Outboard, Wood, Adjustable Centerboard, c.1930, 23 1/4 In. 210.00
Boat, Ocean Liner, 2 Masts, Portholes, Fleischmann, Box, 19 In. 1955.00
Boat, Ocean Liner, Blue, White, Red, Tin, Germany, 12 1/2 In. 990.00
Boat, Ocean Liner, Fleischmann, Box 1250.00
Boat, Ocean Liner, Red, White, Blue, 2 Stacks, Flags, Tin, Germany, 4 1/2 In. 193.00
Boat, Ocean Liner, White, 4 Lifeboats, Twin Masts, Fleischmann, 1950, 20 In. 2530.00
Boat, Ocean Liner, Windup, 3 Stacks, Painted Steel, Arnold, 13 3/8 In. 430.00
Boat, PT 512 Torpedo, Friction, Sparking, Tin Lithograph, Japan, Box, 6 1/4 In. 120.00
Boat, Racing, Flying Fish, Seated Driver, Green Body, Yellow Trim, Tin, 12 In. 187.00
Boat, Racing, White Rubber Tires, Headlight, Wyandotte, 8 1/2 In. 132.00
Boat, River, Clockwork, Schoenner, c.1900 .... 2500.00
Boat, Riverboat, Great Swanee, Friction, Paddlewheels Turn, Tin Lithograph, 11 In. 22.00
Boat, Rowboat, Oarsman Pulls At Oars, Tinplate, Ives, 1875, 11 In. 3740.00
Boat, Rowboat, Windup, Tin Lithograph, Japan, Box 193.00
Boat, Rowers & Rowboat, Blue Tinplate Boat, 2 Wood Rowers, 1900, 8 In. 1840.00
Boat, Runabout, Clockwork, Arnold, 11 In. 450.00
Boat, Schooner, Jib, Foresail, Mainsail, Black, Gold Hull, Schoenhut, 1910, 19 In. 1265.00
Boat, Scull, Windup, Tin, 8 Crewmen, Coxswain, Germany, 1910-1930, 29 x 2 In. 4400.00
Boat, Shark 35, Battery Operated, Tin Lithograph, Japan, Box 495.00
Boat, Side-Wheeler, City Of New York, Cast Iron, 15 1/2 In. 330.00
Boat, Speedboat, Battery Operated, Wood, Japan, 1950s, 9 1/2 In. 40.00
Boat, Speedboat, JoJoan, Jr., Battery Operated, Tin, Rex Electric Motor, 1930s 193.00
Boat, Speedboat, Tin, Lindstrom, 1930s 125.00
Boat, Speedboat, Windup, Tin Lithograph, Plastic, T. Cohen Inc., 7 1/2 In. 16.00
Boat, Speedboat, Yogi Bear, Plastic, Yogi Driver, 1960s, 17 1/2 In. 165.00
Boat, Steamboat, George Washington, Steam Driven, Painted Steel, Marklin, 9 1/2 In. ... 1092.00
Boat, Steamboat, Windup, Motorized, Kingsbury, 9 1/2 In. 275.00
Boat, Steamship, Clockwork, 2 Stacks, Lifeboat Holder, Ives, 13 1/2 In. ... 373.00
Boat, Tugboat, Harrisburg, Penna. Railroad, Marketing Corp. Of America, 36 In. 2420.00
Boat, Tugboat, Neptune, Battery Operated, Black, Red Trim, Tin, Modern Toys, 14 In. ... 77.00
Boat, Windup, Tin, Fleischmann, 20 In. 880.00
Boob McNutt, Windup, Tin Lithograph, Strauss, 8 1/2 In. ....193.00 to 495.00
Boomerang, Pearson's Rocket, Plastic, Jolly Weaver Toy, On Cardboard, 1950s, 6 x 8 In. . 4.00
Bowler, Man, Brown Coat, Gray Pants, Swinging Arm Forward, Martin, 1905, 7 In. 2555.00
Bowling Set, Standing Guards Tenpins, With Ball, Ives, Box 4180.00
Box, Green Hornet Gun, Professionally Restored Lid, 1966 .... 50.00
Boxers, Ring & Tap, Windup, Tin, Boxers In Ring, 5 x 6 In., Box 550.00
Boy, Fishing, Windup, Tin Lithograph 95.00
Boy, Jockey, Helping Horse Roll Forward, Wheeled Base, Martin, 1911, 7 In. 4600.00
Boy, Pulling Dog With Nodding Head, Windup, Celluloid, Japan, 6 1/2 In. 908.00
Boy, Roller Skating, Sailor Outfit, Martin, 1912, 8 In. 1495.00
Bride, Anxious Bride, Windup, Chauffeur On Cycle, Lehmann, Germany, 8 1/2 In. 1155.00
Building Set, Plastic, Illustrations, Dupage, Wood Box, 13 In. 16.00
Bull, Matador, Bull Chases Cape-Waving Matador, Martin, 1894, 9 In. 1534.00
Bunny, Pulling Cart, Fisher-Price 95.00
Bus, Black & Red Paint, New York-Chicago On Side, Cast Iron, Dent, 10 In. 550.00
Bus, Blue, Arcade, 5 In. 80.00
Bus, Blue, Nickel-Plated Wheels & Driver, Cast Iron, Arcade, c.1930, 9 1/4 In. 303.00
Bus, Bright Blue, Pressed Steel, Cor-Cor, 24 In. 715.00
Bus, Bus Line, Cast Iron, Orange, Dent, c.1920, 8 1/2 In. 330.00
Bus, Double-Decker, Green, Gold Trim, Rear Stairway, Cast Iron, Arcade, 1929, 8 In. ... 605.00
Bus, Double-Decker, Green, Red Band, White Rubber Tires, Arcade, 10 1/2 In. 1375.00
Bus, Double-Decker, Inter-State, Windup, Driver, Rear Staircase, Strauss, 10 In. 635.00
Bus, Double-Decker, London, Mobil & Shell, Tin, Friction, Rubber Wheels, Box, 7 In. ... 175.00
Bus, Double-Decker, Penny Toy 1045.00
Bus, Double-Decker, Routemaster, Die Cast Metal, Budgie Toy, 1950-1970, 1/43 Scale .. 22.00
Bus, Flivver, Stamped Prototype, Cowdery, 15 1/2 In. 1320.00

Bus, Greyhound, Blue, White, Rubber Tires, Cast Iron, Arcade, 1937, 8 3/4 In. 352.00
Bus, Greyhound, Century Of Progress, Chicago, Iron, Arcade, 1933, 10 1/2 In. . . . .295.00 to 375.00
Bus, Greyhound, Friction, Tin Lithograph, Cragstan, Japan, Box, 11 1/4 In. 230.00
Bus, Greyhound, Keystone, Windup, Metal, Front Wheels Move, 18 In. 358.00
Bus, Greyhound, Scenic Cruiser, Box, 15 In. 295.00
Bus, Greyhound, Scenic Cruiser, Friction, Tin, Blue, White, SSS, Japan, 6 In. 25.00
Bus, Greyhound, Scenic Cruiser, Tootsietoy 50.00
Bus, Inter-State, Windup, Driver On Right Side, Tin Lithograph, Strauss, 10 1/8 In. 488.00
Bus, Orange, Iron, Dent, 1920s, 8 1/2 In. 450.00
Bus, Passenger, Green, Gray Roof, Green Disc Wheels, Pressed Steel, Buddy L, 28 In. . . . 3960.00
Bus, Radicon, Remote Control, Red, Modern Toys, Japan, Box, 13 1/2 In. 275.00
Bus, Red, Gold Accents, Nickel-Plated Driver, Cast Iron, c.1930, 9 1/4 In. 578.00
Bus, School, Driver & 3 Children, Buddy L 17.00
Bus, School, Hubley, Box, 1960 . . . . 50.00
Butler, Civil War General, Dressed In Blue Top, Red Pants, Walker, Ives, 1885, 9 In. 2415.00
Buttercup, Windup, Tin, Crawling Baby, Original Tag, J. Murphy, Germany, 7 1/2 In. . . . 770.00
Buttercup & Spare Ribs, Tin, Buttercup Holds Tail, Pull Toy, Nifty, 7 1/2 In. 687.00
Buzzy Bee, Fisher-Price, No. 325 . . . . 25.00
Cable Car, Yellow, Blue, White, 2 Passengers, Green Crank Pulley, Lehmann, 1935 . . . . . 460.00
Camel, 2 Humps, Leather Ears, Rope Tail, Carved & Painted Wood, 23 1/2 In. 287.00
Camel, Arabian, Painted Eyes, Schoenhut 358.00
Camel, Bactrian, Glass Eyes, Schoenhut 688.00
Camel, Dark Brown, Plush Burlap, 4-Wheeled Cast Iron Stand, Pull Toy, 12 x 6 In. 130.00
Camera, Pathe, Tin, Marx, Prewar, 6 In. 130.00
Camper, Bump & Go, Battery Operated, Flashing Red Light, Taiyo, Japan 74.00
Camper, Raggedy Ann & Raggedy Andy, Buddy L . . . . .195.00 to 350.00
Candombero Boys, Black Man Plays Drums, Dances, Windup, Tin Lithograph 210.00
Cannon, Civil War, Johnny Reb, Plunger, 2 Balls, Remco 135.00
Cannon, Red Wheels, Nickel Barrel, Cast Iron, 6 1/2 In. 20.00
Cap Gun, All Action T-Diamond 7, Battery Operated, Plastic, Metal, 21 In. 80.00
Cap Gun, Automatic Shape, Patent June 29, 1909, 4 In. 66.00
Cap Gun, Big Chief, Cast Iron, 1930, 3 1/2 In. 50.00
Cap Gun, Big Scout, Cast Iron 65.00
Cap Gun, Buffalo Bill, Cast Iron, Single Shot, Kenton, 1931 . . . . 475.00
Cap Gun, Bullock Long Range Anti-Tank, Die Cast, Green Paint, Britains, Box, 11 In. . . . 95.00
Cap Gun, Cheyenne Shooter, Hamilton . . . . .65.00 to 70.00
Cap Gun, Colt 45, Revolving Cylinder, Die Cast, 1959 . . . . 120.00
Cap Gun, Cowboy, Cast Iron 140.00
Cap Gun, Cowboy, Iron, White Plastic Grips, Maverick Holster Belt, Hubley 145.00
Cap Gun, Cowboy, White Plastic Steer's-Head Grips, Firing Action, Hake's 385.00
Cap Gun, Derringer, Metal, Checkered Grips, DRGM, Germany, 4 1/4 In. 35.00
Cap Gun, Hamilton Cheyenne Shooter 70.00
Cap Gun, Kit Carson 75.00
Cap Gun, Long Boy, Cast Iron, 12 In. 150.00
Cap Gun, Mounties, Lever Release Pop-Up Magazine, Kilgore, Box 45.00
Cap Gun, Musket, Daniel Boone Style, Wood Stock, Metal Barrel, Decals, 1960s, 52 In. . 30.00
Cap Gun, Paladin, Pot Metal, Plastic Grips, 9 In. 100.00
Cap Gun, Peace Maker, Cast Iron 175.00
Cap Gun, Pig On Stick 1200.00
Cap Gun, Pirate Style, Die Cast, Wood Stock, Parris, 1950s, 11 In. 25.00
Cap Gun, Ranger, Cast Iron, Nickel Finish, Plastic Grips, Kilgore, c.1940, 8 1/2 In. 375.00
Cap Gun, Scout, Brass, Pat'd June 17, 1890, Stevens 100.00
Cap Gun, Sheriff, Plastic Insert Grips, Top Loading, Box, c.1940 . . . . 155.00
Cap Gun, Shoo Fly, Cast Iron 300.00
Cap Gun, Stallion .45, Mark II, Gold & Silver Plated, Blue Handles, Nichols, Box, 12 In. . 745.00
Cap Gun, Texan Jr., Gold Finish, Hubley, Pair 120.00
Cap Gun, Texas Junior, Hubley 80.00
Cap Gun, Wild Bill Hickok, Henry 165.00
Cap Gun, Wyatt Earp, Box 150.00
Cap Gun, Wyatt Earp, Buntline Special, Long Barrel, Hubley, 1955 . . . . 160.00
Cap Gun Set, .45 Stallion Mark 11, Gold, Silver Plated, Plastic Handle, Nichols, 12 In. . . 675.00
Captain Action, Aquaman, Accessories, Ideal, Box, 1966 . . . . 500.00
Captain America, Windup, Vinyl Super Hero, Marx, Japan, Box, 1967, 5 1/2 In. 110.00

Car, Adams Probe 16, Die Cast, Metallic Lime, Blue Canopy, Corgi, 1970, 1/43 Scale . . . 30.00
Car, Archie's Jalopy, Windup, Tin, Spanish Phrases On Car, Marx, 7 In. 39.00
Car, Atom Racer, Friction, Rubber-Skinned Tires, Yonezawa, Japan, 1950s, 15 1/2 In. 1045.00
Car, Austin Healy, Barbie, Orange & Aqua, Plastic, Convertible, Irwin, 1962 . . . . 130.00
Car, Betty Rubble, Friction, Tin, Marx, Japan, 3 1/2 In. 175.00
Car, BMW, 3.5 CSL Turbo, Battery Operated, Tin, Dunlop & Bosch Electric, Box 120.00
Car, Bugatti, Windup, Bow Tail, Tin, Meccano, England, c.1935, 11 1/2 In. 745.00
Car, Buick, 1952 Model, Battery Operated, 8 1/2 In. 460.00
Car, Buick, Green, Black, Rubber Tires, Spoked Wheels, 1927, 8 1/2 In. 3300.00
Car, Bumper Car, Pop-Up Clown, Friction, W. Toys, Japan, 6 1/2 In. 175.00
Car, Bumper Car, Windup, Driver & Passenger, Tin 120.00
Car, Cadillac, 1953 Model, G-Man Patrol, Remote Control, Linemar, Box 525.00
Car, Cadillac, Convertible, Friction, Rag Top, Bandai, Japan, Box, 1959, 11 1/2 In. 230.00
Car, Cadillac, Friction, 1952 Model, Gray, Marusan, Japan, 11 1/2 In. 1395.00
Car, Car, Model T, Windup, Tin Lithograph, Styrofoam Ball, KO, Japan, 5 In. 75.00
Car, Chevrolet, Arcade, 7 In. 605.00
Car, Chevrolet, Camaro, 1967 Model, 7 Spokes, Hot Wheels, No. 399 . . . . 25.00
Car, Chevrolet, Camaro, Bucket Seats, Late 1960s, 13 1/2 In. 250.00
Car, Chevrolet, Camaro, Z28, Red, Chrome Base, Hot Wheels, No. 33 . . . . 46.00
Car, Chevrolet, Coupe, Harrisville, N.Y. Dealership, Cast Iron, Arcade, c.1930, 8 1/2 In. . . 7700.00
Car, Chevrolet, Coupe, Windup, Forward & Reverse Action, c.1948, Japan, Box, 4 In. . . . 110.00
Car, Chevrolet, Impala, 1963 Model, Friction, Tin, Red, Haji, Japan, Box, 8 In. 225.00
Car, Chevrolet, Linemar, Black Roof, Gray, White Stripes, Chrome, Tin, 1954, 11 In. 1320.00
Car, Chrysler, Airflow, Cast Iron, Lavender Paint, White Rubber Tires, Hubley, 8 In. 3190.00
Car, Chrysler, Airflow, Pink, Hubley, 4 1/2 In. 285.00
Car, Chrysler, Airflow, Red, Chrome Accents, Cast Iron Limousine, 1934, 6 1/4 In. 413.00
Car, Chrysler, Airflow, Windup, Tin, Chrome Grill, Kingsbury, 1934, 14 In. 770.00
Car, Citroen, Coupe, Battery Operated, 2-Tone Red, Driver's Door Opens, 12 In. 1725.00
Car, Citroen, Open, Butter Cream, Black, Brown Interior, 1925, 14 1/2 In. 1610.00
Car, Citroen, Roadster, Clockwork Motor, Boat Tail, Red, Black Finish, 1928, 12 In. 2025.00
Car, Convertible, Driver At Wheel Of Open Auto, Red, Tin, Schuco, 9 3/4 In. 495.00
Car, Convertible, Driver, Battery Operated, Tin, Blue Enamel Paint, KO, Japan, 9 In. 340.00
Car, Convertible, Ford, T-Bird, 1964, Tin Flip Top, White, Maroon, Ichiko, 16 1/2 In. 475.00
Car, Convertible, Mercedes, Barbie, Green & Cream, Plastic, Irwin, 1960s 70.00
Car, Coupe, 1930 Model, Cast Iron, Dent, 5 In. 88.00
Car, Coupe, 2-Door, Rumble Seat, Driver, Cast Iron, Arcade, 6 3/4 In. 550.00
Car, Coupe, Black, Schieble, 1920s, 17 In. 750.00
Car, Coupe, Black, Spoked Wheels, Cast Iron, Dent, 1930, 5 In. 33.00
Car, Coupe, Cast Iron, Dark Blue, 1920-1940, 3 1/2 In. 45.00
Car, Coupe, Dayton/Republic, Friction, Hand Painted Driver, 1920s, 18 In. 330.00
Car, Coupe, Red, Black Running Boards, Disc Wheels, Cast Iron, Kenton, 8 In. 2420.00
Car, Coupe, Red, Slant Windshield, Cast Iron, Nickel Plated Driver, Kenton, 6 1/2 In. 578.00
Car, Coupe, Windup, Steel, Yellow, Folding Luggage Rack, Girard, 1930s 220.00
Car, Crazy, Komikal Kop, Windup, Tin, Marx, Prewar, 7 In. 215.00
Car, Crazy, Krazy Kar, Windup, Clown Driver, Balloons, Tin, Strauss, 1920, 11 In. 470.00
Car, Crazy, Krazy Kar, Windup, Clown Driver, Tin Lithograph, Unique Art, Prewar, 7 In. . 220.00
Car, Crazy, Mortimer Snerd, Windup, Tin, Marx, 1939, 7 In. 358.00
Car, Crazy, Rodeo Joe, Unique Art Mfg., Co., 1930s, 11 1/2 In. 230.00
Car, Crazy, Rodeo Joe, Windup, Tin Lithograph, Unique Art, 9 In. 245.00
Car, Dagwood, Tin, Marx, Box, 8 In. 1430.00
Car, DeSoto, Green, Rubber Tires, Cast Iron, Arcade, 6 1/8 In. 165.00
Car, Dodge, Battery Operated, Tin, Light Blue, Japan, Box, 1959, 9 1/2 In. 525.00
Car, Facing Seats, Windup, Tin, Bicycle Wheels, Driver, Gunthermann, 1920s, 10 In. 2860.00
Car, Fire Chief, Battery Operated, Friction, Tin, Roof Light Revolves, Box, 1959, 9 In. . . . 77.00
Car, Fire Chief, Bell, Tin, T. Cohen, Box 295.00
Car, Fire Chief, Metal, Clanging Bell, Pull Toy, T. Cohen, 1940s 275.00
Car, Fix-It Of Tomorrow, X-600, Ideal, Box 150.00
Car, Flintstone Flivver, Fred, Friction, Marx, Japan, 7 In. 305.00
Car, Ford, 4-Door, 6 Windows, Cast Iron, Painted, Arcade, c.1923, 6 1/2 In. 385.00
Car, Ford, Brewster, Open Chauffeur Area, Cast Iron, 6 1/2 In. 800.00
Car, Ford, Bronco, White, Hot Wheels, No. 56 . . . . 45.00
Car, Ford, Coupe, 1927 Model, Cast Iron, Arcade, 6 3/4 In. 475.00
Car, Ford, Coupe, Black Body, Red Spokes, Silvered Wheels, Buddy L, 7 1/4 In. 350.00

Car, Ford, Falcon, Friction, Tin, Green & Cream Paint, Bandai, Japan, 8 In. 155.00
Car, Ford, Falcon, Friction, Tin, Plastic Canopy, Ragtop, Marx, 20 In. 258.00
Car, Ford, Friction, Japan, 10 1/2 In. 295.00
Car, Fred Flintstone, Friction, Marx, Japan, 3 1/2 In. 100.00
Car, Green Hornet Secret Service, Battery Operated, Vinyl Half Figure, 11 In. 590.00
Car, Hi-Way Henry, Jalopy, Bearded Driver With Wife, Doghouse Front End, 1920 . . . . . . 2875.00
Car, Hill Climber, Red & Black, Passengers, Clark, 1904, 6 In. 660.00
Car, Horseless Carriage, Windup, Tin, Lehmann, 4 In. 360.00
Car, House Trailer, Friction, Tin, Japan, 12 In. 145.00
Car, Jaguar, Friction, Tin, White, Red Flames, Cragstan, Japan, Box, 8 1/2 In. 135.00
Car, Krazy, Clown, Windup, Super Action, Japan, Box 175.00
Car, Lamborghini, Countach, Battery Operated, Red, Black, Box 120.00
Car, LaSalle, Coupe, Chrome, Tin Lithograph Balloon Tires, 1937, 11 In. 220.00
Car, Leaping Lena, Jalopy, Strauss, 1920s 695.00
Car, Limousine, 6 Doors, Red Paint, Cast Iron, Hubley, c.1920, 7 In. . . . . .230.00 to 250.00
Car, Limousine, Carrette, Tin Lithograph, Clockwork, Germany 5445.00
Car, Limousine, Chauffeur Area Open, Rear Doors Open, Windup, Tin, Karl Bub, 14 In. . . . 1155.00
Car, Limousine, Clockwork, Hand Brake, Driver, Key, Carette, c.1911, 16 In. 5462.00
Car, Limousine, Mercedes, Windup, Fold-Down Luggage Rack, Driver, Karl Bub, 12 In. . . 1035.00
Car, Limousine, Seated Driver, Brown, Blue Trim, Spoked Wheels, Tin, Germany, 4 In. . . 165.00
Car, Limousine, Uniformed Chauffeur Jumps Out & Opens Door, 1930, 10 In. 3335.00
Car, Limousine, Windup, Driver, Mounted Spare Tire, Yellow, Black, 1930, 13 In. 1520.00
Car, Limousine, Windup, Tin, Silver, Acetylene Type, Lights, Karl Bub, Germany, 14 In. . 1760.00
Car, Lincoln, Zephyr, Chrome Accents, Late 1930s, Hubley, 7 In. 770.00
Car, Mercedes-Benz, Blue, Bandai, Early-Mid 1960s, 8 1/2 In. 95.00
Car, Mercedes-Benz, Gull Wing, Friction, Tin, Orange, Yonezawa, Japan, 8 In. 85.00
Car, MG, Die Cast, Pressed Steel, Detailed Interior, Model Toys, 15 In. 205.00
Car, Model T Ford, Jalopy, Windup, Zany Sayings On Car, Marx, Box, 1930s 390.00
Car, Mr. Magoo, Sitting At The Wheel, Battery Operated, Yellow, Hubley, Box, 9 1/2 In. . 385.00
Car, Nash, Friction, Lupor, USA, Box, 7 In. 65.00
Car, Oldsmobile, Super 88, Friction, Tin, Plaid Interior, Japan, 13 In. 330.00
Car, Open, Orange & Yellow, Spoked Wheels, Windup, Tin, Ferdinand Strauss, 8 In. 99.00
Car, Oscar Mayer, Friction, Box, 10 x 5 In. 12.00
Car, Packard, Caribbean, 1956 Model, White, Blue, Marty Martino, 1986, 14 In. 525.00
Car, Packard, Coupe, 1914 Model, Friction, Clicking Motor, 4 1/2 x 7 1/2 In. 22.00
Car, Phaeton, Clockwork, Tin Lithograph, Rubber Wheels, Gunthermann, 10 In. 25300.00
Car, Police, Buick Riviera, Battery Operated, Tin, Bandai, Japan, 1960s, 10 In. 85.00
Car, Police, Dodge Dart, State Police, Light & Siren, 1969, 12 In. 250.00
Car, Police, Ford, Sedan, Friction, No. 7, Taiyo, Japan, Box, 1959, 9 In. 55.00
Car, Police, Mystery, Battery Operated, Japan 225.00
Car, Police, Tin Lights, 1st Precinct Siren Patrol, Battery Operated, 1930s, 15 In. 132.00
Car, Police, Tin Lithograph, Lupor, USA, Box, 7 In. 45.00
Car, Pontiac, Salsa, Chrome Base, Hot Wheels, No. 596 . . . . 22.00
Car, Pontiac, Sedan K, 4-Door, Black, Steerable, Japan, 1936, 12 In. 3300.00
Car, Porsche 356, Battery Operated, Remote Control, Box 135.00
Car, Porsche 930, Green, Hot Wheels, No. 148 . . . . 52.00
Car, Racing Set, Electric, Track, Brass, Composition, Lionel, c.1915, 8-In. Car 1375.00
Car, Racing Set, Shutdown Plymouth Super Stock, Electric, Plastic Drag Strip, Box, 1968 . 20.00
Car, Racing Set, Tru-Action, Model 5301, Electric, Tudor Metal Products, 1959 . . . . 55.00
Car, Racing, Alfa Romeo, Die Cast, Rubber Wheels, Red, Dinky Toy, 1954, 1/43 Scale . . . 50.00
Car, Racing, Andy Gump, Cast Iron, Red Paint, Arcade, 7 In. 1980.00
Car, Racing, ASC, Friction, Tin Lithograph, 11 In. 190.00
Car, Racing, Auburn, Rubber 65.00
Car, Racing, Battery Operated, Tin Lithograph, Adjustable Steering, Japan, 6 1/2 In. 95.00
Car, Racing, Bullet Shape, Die Cast, Silver Paint, Dinky Toy, England, 3 1/2 In. 40.00
Car, Racing, Burd Piston Ring Special, 1940 Ignition Engine Power, Red, 20 In. 3410.00
Car, Racing, Champion 98, Troy Ruttman Autograph, Yonezawa, 8 1/2 In. 825.00
Car, Racing, Champion's Racer, Beige, Red Flames, Chrome Pipe, 1950, 18 In. 1895.00
Car, Racing, Cleveland, Prewar Boat Tail, Cast Aluminum, Rubber & Steel Wheels, 12 In. . 185.00
Car, Racing, Duesenberg, Red, 1939 . . . . 2640.00
Car, Racing, England Special No. 8, Gas Engine, Sheet Aluminum, Leather Seats 825.00
Car, Racing, Ford Lotus, Vinyl Driver, Steerable Front End, Yonezawa, 1960s, 15 In. 121.00
Car, Racing, Gas Powered, Super 60 Engine, Tank, Rear-End Housing, 1930s, 20 In. 550.00

Car, Racing, Golden Arrow, Dunlop Cord Racing Tires, Kingsbury, 1930s, 19 In. 530.00
Car, Racing, Golden Arrow, Windup, Metallic Blue, Red Racing Stripes, 1929, 21 In. 1075.00
Car, Racing, Indianapolis, Sears, Box, 16 In. 1650.00
Car, Racing, Indy 500, Battery Operated, Gunthermann, 1929, 21 In. 1075.00
Car, Racing, Indy 500, Firebird, Friction, Cragstan, 14 In. 33.00
Car, Racing, Indy 500, Friction, Gray, Red, Japan, 1960s, 14 1/2 In. 770.00
Car, Racing, Indy 500, La Motta, Prestone, 85, Bardahl, Die Cast, Hand Brake, 11 In. 1100.00
Car, Racing, Indy 500, Roadster, Windup, 1st Place 1948, Tin Lithograph, Box, 11 In. ... 415.00
Car, Racing, Mercedes Grand Prix, Windup, Aluminum, Boat Tail, 9 1/2 In. 110.00
Car, Racing, Mercedes Grand Prix, Windup, Boat Tail, Steers, Marklin, Germany, 11 In. .. 143.00
Car, Racing, Mercedes, Battery Operated, Tin Lithograph, Box, 10 In. 160.00
Car, Racing, Mercedes, Grand Prix Style, Windup, Tin, Blue, 8 1/2 In. 330.00
Car, Racing, No. 1, Green, Hubley, 8 In. 350.00
Car, Racing, No. 5, Cast Iron, Yellow, White Tires, Hubley, 9 In. 2640.00
Car, Racing, Penny Toy, Black, Driver, 5 1/2 In. 743.00
Car, Racing, Penny Toy, Silver, Driver, 5 1/2 In. 330.00
Car, Racing, Rocket No. 5, Friction, Tin, Green, Yellow, Hadson, Japan, 6 1/2 In. 190.00
Car, Racing, Rocket, Friction, Sparking, Tin, Japan, Box, 1950s 285.00
Car, Racing, Silver Bullet, Windup, 12 Cylinder Exhaust, 1920s-1930s, Buffalo, 12 In. ... 275.00
Car, Racing, Spring Power, Tin Lithograph, Eleanee Toys, 1930s, 10 In. 105.00
Car, Racing, Starfire, Friction, Tin Lithograph, Marusan Toys, 11 1/2 In. 245.00
Car, Racing, Thimble Drome, Red, Roy Cox, 9 1/2 In. 121.00
Car, Racing, V-Rroom Guide Whip Racer, Control Rod, Motor Roars, Mattel, Box 125.00
Car, Racing, Whee-Whiz, Windup, Cars Race On Track, Tin Litho, Marx, Box, 13 In. 1075.00
Car, Racing, Windup, Midget, Steerable Front End, Original Key, Schuco, Box, 3 In. 83.00
Car, Racing, Windup, Sparking, Tin Lithograph, 8 1/4 In. 275.00
Car, Racing, Windup, Tin, Walter Bing, Germany, 6 In. 580.00
Car, Roadster, Battery-Operated Lights, Painted Steel, Kingsbury, 1920s, 12 3/4 In. 460.00
Car, Roadster, Flivver, Buddy L, 10 1/2 In. 550.00
Car, Roadster, G.M., Futuristic, Friction, Tin, Cragstan, Japan, Box, c.1953, 13 1/2 In. ... 240.00
Car, Roadster, Metal, Rubber Tires, Tonka, c.1930, 5 1/2 x 4 x 14 1/2 In. 120.00
Car, Rolls-Royce, Convertible, Friction, Green, Bandai, Japan, Box, 1960, 11 1/2 In. 580.00
Car, Rumble Seat, Driver, Red, Cast Iron, Nickel Wheels, Kilgore Co., 6 In. 143.00
Car, Run-About, Windup, Bing, 6 In. 350.00
Car, Saloon, Penny Toy, Driver & Passengers, Meier Co. 853.00
Car, Sedan, A.C. Williams, Cast Iron, Dark Blue, Yellow Wheels, 6 1/2 In. 305.00
Car, Sedan, Electric Lights, France, Late 1920s, 15 In. 1800.00
Car, Sedan, Flivver, No. 49, Center Door, With Hat Pin, Cowdery Toy Works, Box 1430.00
Car, Sedan, Friction, Maroon, Tinted Glass, Bandai, Japan, Box, 1961, 11 1/2 In. 330.00
Car, Sedan, Pathe News, Marx, 1920s 2875.00
Car, Sedan, Streamline Slush Mold, Brown, White Rubber Tires, Barclay, 1930s, 5 3/4 In. 40.00
Car, Station Wagon, Ford, Tin, Bandai, 1955, 12 In. 150.00
Car, Station Wagon, Rambler, Die Cast, Green, Cream, HO Series, Tootsietoy, 2 1/2 In. .. 20.00
Car, Station Wagon, Woody, Paper Over Wood, Buddy L, 1940s, 18 1/2 In. 415.00
Car, Steam, Flywheel Friction, Germany, 7 1/2 In. 295.00
Car, Studebaker, Red, Nickel Grill, Rubber Tires, Cast Iron, Hubley, 6 5/8 In. 528.00
Car, Tin, Structo, 1920s, 15 1/2 x 7 In. 995.00
Car, Touring, Berolina, Windup, Tin, Folding Cloth Top, Jump Seat, Lehmann, 6 1/2 In. ... 1155.00
Car, Touring, Clockwork, Painted Tin, Wood Headlights & Lamps, 15 In. 1725.00
Car, Touring, Driver, Seated, Green, Yellow Interior, Spoked Wheels, Tin, Germany, 4 In. .. 220.00
Car, Touring, Driver, Windup, Tin Lithograph, 5 In. 160.00
Car, Touring, Driver, Windup, Tin Lithograph, c.1915, 10 In. 308.00
Car, Touring, Penny Toy, Tin Lithograph, Cutout Passenger Silhouettes, Meier, 4 1/2 In. .. 853.00
Car, Touring, Penny Toy, With Passengers, Meier 523.00
Car, Touring, Windup, Articulated Tin Driver, Bing, Germany, 12 1/2 In. 800.00
Car, Touring, Windup, Tin, Dunlop Tires, Terrier Radiator Mascot, Tipp & Co., 16 In. 908.00
Car, Trailer, Pressed Steel, Wyandotte, 1930s, 23 In. 495.00
Car, Turbo Jet, Ideal, 1955 .... 250.00
Car, TWA Airlines Airport Service, Tin, Friction, 11 In. 120.00
Car, UHU Amphibious, Zeppelin Shape, Driver, c.1920, 9 1/2 In. .... 977.00 to 1100.00
Car, Van, TV Service, Die Cast, Tan, Red Ladder, Lesney Matchbox, 2 1/2 In. 25.00
Car, Vis-A-Vis, Penny Toy, Driver, Meier, 3 In. 198.00
Car, Volkswagen, Beetle, Battery Operated, Tin, Red, Blue, Bandai, 1960s, 10 In. 145.00

Car, Volkswagen, Beetle, Battery Operated, Tin, White, Robot Logo, Taiyo, 9 In. 145.00
Car, Volkswagen, Red, Tonka, No. 52680, 8 3/4 x 3 5/8 x 3 1/4 In. 62.00
Car, What's-It, Part Zeppelin, Car & Boat, Windup, Clown Spins, Tin, Strauss, 9 1/2 In. . . .   495.00
Car, Whoopee Car, Cowboy, Windup, Tin, Cows On Wheels, Marx, 8 In. . . . . .205.00 to 325.00
Car, Whoopee Car, Milton Berle, Windup, Tin, Marx 525.00
Car, Whoopee Car, Rodeo Joe, Unique Art 285.00
Car, Whoopee Car, Spinning-Head Driver, 2 Flappers Sitting On Trunk, Marx, 1930, 8 In.   1035.00
Car, Wilma Flintstone, Friction, Blue, 3 1/2 In. 275.00
Car, Windup, Cloth Folding Top, Fisher, 8 1/4 In. 1150.00
Car, Zigzag, 1 White Figure, 1 Black Figure, 2 Oversized Wheels, Lehmann 6960.00
Carousel, 3 Children In Boats, Musical, Unique Art 395.00
Carousel, Horse, Yellow Platform Fitted With 4 Horses, Tinplate, Key Wind, 1900, 15 In. .   3450.00
Carousel, Spinning Airplanes, Jockeys & Horses, Tin, Wolverine, 12 x 13 In. 495.00
Carousel, Spring Activated, Tin Lithograph, Wyandotte 132.00
Carpenter, Dressed In Cloth Attire, Painted Tie, Standing At Tinplate Workbench, 6 In. . .   5175.00
Carriage, 2 Seats, Metal, 1905, 13 x 11 1/2 In. 75.00
Carriage, 2 Wheels, Fold-Out Roof, Upholstered Interior, Horse, Platform, Tin, 21 In. . . .   2760.00
Carriage, Doll's, Victorian, Bentwood & Wicker, Wire Spoke Wheels 285.00
Carriage, Doll's, Wood, Blue Paint, Wood Wheel, Fringed, 26 x 29 In. 165.00
Carriage, Doll's, Wood, Curved Sides, Stenciled, Joel Ellis Style, c.1880, 28 In. 500.00
Carriage, Doll's, Wood, Steel Frame, Leatherized Cloth Top, Fringe, 36 x 33 In. 385.00
Carriage, Doll's, Yellow & White, Leatherette Upholstery, Sun Shade, 1870s, 31 1/8 In. . .   230.00
Carriage, Horse Drawn, Driver Seated On Open Bench, Blue Carriage, Tin, Germany 154.00
Carriage & Doll, Bisque Head, Stenciled Wood, Clockwork Carriage, 11 x 11 In. 2035.00
Carrying Case, Barbie, Vinyl, Suburban Shopper, Standard Plastic Products, 1961 . . . .   100.00
Carrying Case, Ken, Campus Hero, Teal, Vinyl, Saturday Date Outfit, 1964, 10 x 12 In. . .   30.00
Carrying Case, Miss Barbie, White, Vinyl, Standard Plastic Products, 1963, 11 x 12 In. . .   200.00
Cart, Chinaman, Windup, Cast Iron, Creation Toys, France, Box, 6 1/2 In. 275.00
Cart, Dog Pulling Woman, Windup, Germany, 1900-1920, 8 In.   358.00
Cart, Donkey, Driver, Cast Iron, 10 In. 110.00
Cart, Dump Flivver, Black, Red Spoked Wheels, Pressed Steel, Buddy L, 12 1/2 In. 935.00
Cart, Farm, Pulled By Ox, Cast Iron, Spoked Wheels, Dent, 5 1/4 In. 44.00
Cart, Horse Drawn, Tin, Standing Figure, Whirligig Attached To Hat, Germany, 7 1/2 In. .   143.00
Cart, Horse Drawn, Wood, Tin, Wire, Cast Iron, Pull Toy, 13 1/2 In. 275.00
Cart, Monkey Steering Cart, 4 Wood Wheels, Steiff, 1838, 9 In.   345.00
Cart, Plantation, Seated Black Driver, Pulled By Ox, Red Cart, Cast Iron, Kenton, 11 In. .   330.00
Cart, Porter, Windup, Blue, Tin, Checkered Jacket, Strauss, 6 x 5 1/2 In. 143.00
Cart, Wicker, Doll Moves Head Side To Side, Whip Moves Up & Down 3800.00
Casey The Cop, Swings Billy Club, Windup, Tin, Unique Art, Prewar, 8 1/2 In. 440.00
Cash Register, Benjamin Franklin, Tin, Vanguard Industries, 6 1/4 x 7 1/4 In. 90.00
Cash Register, Play Money, Pressed Steel, Decals, Buddy L, 9 In. 99.00
Cash Register, Tom Thumb, 1950s 65.00
Cat, Bead Eyes, Pink Ribbon, Brass Bell, Pull Toy, Steiff, 7 1/2 In. 410.00
Cat, Beige Velvet, Black Paint, Red Ribbon, Pink Paw Warmer, Steiff, 7 In. 550.00
Cat, Chases Mouse In Cage, Windup, Tin, Germany, 10 1/4 In. 660.00
Cat, Dr. Seuss, Cat In The Hat, Talking, Stuffed, Plastic Head, Mattel, 10 In. 35.00
Cat, Drummer, Windup, Tin, 6 1/4 In. 165.00
Cat, Felix, Delivery Wagon, Pull Toy, 1936, 10 In. 275.00
Cat, Felix, On Scooter, Tin, Chein, 7 1/2 In. 660.00
Cat, Felix, Speedy, Red Roadster, Felix Moves Up & Down As Auto Pulled, 11 3/4 In. . . .   315.00
Cat, Felix, Stencil Set, Light Blue Ground, Red Trim, Spear's Games, 8 x 8 In. 120.00
Cat, Felix, Walking, Windup, Tin, Gunthermann, 7 In. 550.00
Cat, Felix, Windup, Stuffed Felt, Metal, Glass Eyes, c.1922 . . . .   358.00
Cat, Felix, Wood, Jointed, Pat Sullivan, 1925, 4 In. 130.00
Cat, Felix, Wood, Jointed, Pat Sullivan, 1925, 8 In. 360.00
Cat, Felix, Wood, Jointed, Schoenhut, 1924, 4 In. 143.00
Cat, Felix, Wood, Jointed, Schoenhut, 1924, 7 1/2 In. 220.00
Cat, Gray Mohair, Glass Eyes, Steiff, 18 1/2 In. 330.00
Cat, Kitten In Can, Clockwork, White Angora, Tongue Out, Ives, 8 1/2 In. 8340.00
Cat, Nina, Calico Cat, Turns Head From Side To Side, Lehmann, 1935 . . . .   2150.00
Cat, Pip-Squeak, Black, White, Orange, Green, Gray Stripes, Papier-Mache, 6 1/4 In. 275.00
Cat, Pip-Squeak, Gray, Black Stripes, Papier-Mache, 11 In. 190.00
Cat, Pip-Squeak, Red, Yellow, Black, Gray Stripes, Papier-Mache, 5 In. 440.00

Cat, Pip-Squeak, With 2 Kittens, Black, Red, White, Green, Yellow, Gray, 3 3/4 In. 275.00
Cat, Pip-Squeak, With Kitten, Black, Green, Yellow, Red, White, Gray Stripes, 3 In. 65.00
Cat, Pip-Squeak, With Mouse, Black, Green, Gray Stripes, Papier-Mache, 4 1/2 In. 110.00
Cat, Pip-Squeak, With Mouse, Gray, Green, Yellow, 5 1/4 In. 65.00
Cat, Pip-Squeak, With White Kitten, Black, Red, Green, Yellow, Gray, 5 3/4 In. 330.00
Cat, Puss 'n' Boots, Wood, Jointed, 4 In. 39.00
Cat, Seated, Gray Velvet, Black Stripes, Bead Eyes, 4 In. 245.00
Cat, Seated, Gray, White, Glass Eyes, Papier-Mache, 7 In. 110.00
Cat, Seated, Pale Gray Mohair, Black Stripes, Glass Eyes, Steiff, 7 In. ....125.00 to 165.00
Cat, Swivel Neck, Holding Mouse, White, Steiff, Large 850.00
Cat, White Mohair Coat With Gray Stripes, Glass Eyes, Bell, Pull Toy, 14 In. 1980.00
Cat, Wood Ball Between Paws, Windup, Tin Lithograph, U.S. Zone Germany, 4 In. 35.00
Cement Mixer, Kenton Hardware, Kenton, Ohio, Cast Iron, c.1930, 7 In. 375.00
Chalkboard, Kayo, 1950 .... 150.00
Chariot, With Doll, Whimsical, Tinplate, Bisque Doll Driver, 1890, 9 In. 1150.00
Charlie Brown, In Baseball Cap, Vinyl, Pocket Pal 55.00
Charlie Brown, Peanuts, Plastic, Painted, United Features, Hungerford, 1950s, 9 In. 115.00
Charlie Brown, World's Greatest Paratrooper, Hasbro, On Card, 1971, 3 In. 30.00
Chef, Celluloid, Googly Eyes, Japan, Prewar, 7 1/2 In. 120.00
Chemistry Set, Chemistry Lab, Skil Craft, No. 505P, Box, 1962 .... 75.00
Chest, Doll's, 4 Drawers, Blue Paint, 1860s, 8 1/2 x 9 x 3 3/4 In. 635.00
Chicken, Pip-Squeak, In Cage, Bellows, 7 In. 135.00
Child, Russian Peasant, Bisque Head, Wood, Jointed, Germany, 8 In. 135.00
China Cabinet, Doll's, Oak, Pressed Back, 10 x 7 In. 38.00
Chinese Warrior, Man Dressed In Tunic, Raising His Left Hand, Martin, 1900, 8 In. 920.00
Church, Tinplate, Red Roof, Gothic Window, 5 In. 6875.00
Circus, Bandwagon, Overland Circus, Horse Drawn, Kenton, 17 In. 575.00
Circus, Horses, Overland Circus, Outriders, Cast Iron, Kenton, Box, 14 In., 4 Piece 605.00
Circus, Humpty Dumpty, Tent, Ring & Flexible Cage, 36 x 35 3/4 x 24 In. 660.00
Circus, Ring-A-Ling Circus, Scenes, Ringmaster On Floor, Marx, 1925, 8 In. 1150.00
Circus, Ring-A-Ling, Windup, Ringmaster, Elephant, Lion, Tin, Marx, 7 x 7 1/4 In. 577.00
Circus, Ringling, Animals On Circus Wagon, Pull Toy, Box, c.1925, 12 x 10 x 5 In. 295.00
Circus, Wonder Circus, Plastic, Sterling, Box, 1950s, 12 x 16 In. 110.00
Circus Chariot, Clown, Wood, Paper, Glass-Eyed Horse, Schoenhut, c.1900, 17 In. 2090.00
Circus Performers, Woman Acrobat, Lion Tamer, 1910, Schoenhut, 8 In. 2645.00
Circus Set, Horse, Donkey, Elephant, Hobo, 3 Clowns, Painted Eyes, Props, c.1910 ..... 176.00
Circus Set, Ladder, Performing Ring, Trapeze, Clowns, Red Trim, Wood, 12 In. 495.00
Circus Tent, Red, White Striped Canvas Roof, Schoenhut, 1928, 30 x 17 In. 17250.00
Circus Tent & Ring, Schoenhut, Tie-Down Inserts, Box 798.00
Circus Wagon, Lion, Arcade 895.00
Circus Wagon, Overland Circus, Band, 6 Musicians, Red, Gold Trim, Cast Iron, 15 In. ... 605.00
Circus Wagon, Overland Circus, Bear Cage, Red, White, Yellow Spoked Wheels, Iron ... 248.00
Circus Wagon, Paul's Soap Circus, Wood, Animal-Shaped Castile Soap, c.1900, 12 In. ... 500.00
Circus Wagon, Polar Bear, Driver, Horses Pull Cage, Wood, 1890, 26 In. 115.00
Circus Wagon Driver, Red Jacket, Schoenhut 1980.00
Clicker, Ray Gun, Blue Plastic, Scope Top, Planets & Rocket On Handle, 5 In. 75.00
Clock, Hickory Dickory Dock, Mattel 40.00
Clocks, Painted, Alphabet, Numbers, Animals, Simple Words, 10 Piece 88.00
Clown, 2 Connected By Metal Rods, Composition, 1910, 16 In. 747.00
Clown, Acrobat, Swings In Hoop, Bell, Windup, Linemar, Japan, 7 In. 550.00
Clown, Balancing On Hands, Inching Forward Trying To Maintain Balance, 9 In. 1495.00
Clown, Balancing Spinning Monkey In Chair, Windup, Tin, Japan, 9 In. 360.00
Clown, Bozo, Plastic, Soft Vinyl, Larry Harmon Pictures, R. Dakin, 1974, 7 1/2 In. 55.00
Clown, Cirko The Clown, Riding Tricycle, Marx, Box, 1935, 8 In. 1495.00
Clown, Clockwork, Tin Lithograph, Strauss, 4 1/2 In. 66.00
Clown, Does Handstands, Windup, Tin Lithograph, Chein 66.00
Clown, Driving Smiley-Faced Car, Tin Lithograph, Unique Art Mfg. Co., 7 x 9 x 3 In. ... 200.00
Clown, Go-Go The Clown, Tightrope Cyclist, Celluloid, Cloth, Box, 18 In. 65.00
Clown, Juggling, Windup, Japan 250.00
Clown, Magician, Raising Fan To Cover Face, Windup, 1910, 9 In. 2185.00
Clown, Musician, Parading Forward, Beating Wheeled Drum, 1900, 10 In. 1150.00
Clown, On High Wheeler, Windup, Gay '90s, Tin 150.00
Clown, On Stilts, Playing Violin, TPS, Japan, 10 1/2 In. 143.00

Clown, Pip-Squeak, Papier-Mache 465.00
Clown, Standing, Directing Horse & Rider, Rotate Around Center, Girl Rider, Tokyo, 7 In.   920.00
Clown, Stretches Eyes, Rolls Eyes, Windup, Tin, U.S. Zone Germany, 6 In. 95.00
Clown, Swings On Acrobat's Bar, Windup, Tin, Cloth, Modern Toys, Japan, Box, 6 In. . . . 195.00
Clown, Tin, Holding Ball, Windup, TPS, Japan, 5 In. 240.00
Clown, Tumbling Pete, Does Somersaults, Windup, Celluloid, Painted, Japan, 6 In. 45.00
Clown, With Violin, Smiling, Seated On Upended Drum, Drawing Bow, 1910, 9 In. 1015.00
Clown, With Violin, Windup, Cone Hat, Felt, Tin, Schuco, Prewar, 4 1/2 In. 330.00
Clown, With Violin, Windup, Feathered Hat, Felt, Tin, Schuco, Prewar, 4 1/2 In. 248.00
Coach, 8 Horses, Napoleonic, Pre-1945 . . . . 9775.00
Coal Wagon, Cast-Iron Horse, Black Driver, Painted, Hubley, 15 In. 385.00
Coal Wagon, Driver, Seated, Red Body, 4 Yellow Spoked Wheels, Iron, Hubley, 15 In. . . . 248.00
Coffee Grinder, Daisy, A.C. Williams 88.00
Comical Tap Dancer, Bakelite, Articulated Arms, Legs, Wood Dowel Control, 9 1/2 In. . . 145.00
Compass, Satellite Finder, Plastic, Blue Vinyl Strap, On Card, 1 1/2 x 2 In. 18.00
Construction Set, Men Working On Road, Cast Iron, Arcade, 5 Piece 220.00
Covered Wagon, 2 Horses & Driver, Cast Iron, Kenton, Box, 14 3/4 In. 220.00
Cow, Collar, Bell, Glass Eyes, Schoenhut 1018.00
Cow, Milky The Marvelous Cow, Drinks Water, Plastic, Kenner, 14 1/2 x 10 1/2 x 4 In. . . 30.00
Cow, Molly The Moo Cow, Moos, Pull Toy, Fisher-Price, 1972, 9 In. 27.00
Cow, On Wheels, Papier-Mache, Pull Toy, c.1915 . . . . 135.00
Cowboy, Horse, Windup, Composition, Fabric, Plush, Tail Spins, 8 In. 65.00
Cowboy, On Horse, Tin, Haji, Japan, Box, 1950s, 7 x 9 In. 110.00
Cowboy, Rider, Windup, Tin, Cowboy, Lasso, Rearing Horse, Marx, 1930 . . . . 430.00
Cradle, Doll's, Blue Paint, 5 1/2 x 11 In. . . . . .195.00 to 225.00
Cradle, Doll's, Pine, Dovetailed, Heart Cutout In Footboard, 26 In. 165.00
Cradle, Doll's, Pine, Dovetailed, Pennsylvania, 19 In. 295.00
Cradle, Doll's, Pine, Hand-Carved Spindles, 18 In. 45.00
Cradle, Doll's, Pine, Painted Design, 19th Century, 20 In. 88.00
Cradle, Doll's, Poplar, Green Paint, Yellow Striping, Design, 13 In. 135.00
Cradle, Doll's, Walnut, 10 1/4 In. 190.00
Crane, Electro-Magnet To Pick Items Up, Electro 95.00
Crane, Sliding Boom, Nylint, 18 In. 16.00
Crawling Baby, Windup, Celluloid, Cloth, Japan, 4 In. 85.00
Crib, Doll's, Folding, Wood, Lithograph Of Children, Lamb, c.1900, 8 1/2 In. 75.00
Cup, Captain Kangaroo, Figural, Plastic, Flicker Eyes, 1960s 55.00
Cupboard, Doll's, 2 Glass Doors, Enamel Knobs, Folk Art, Made From Dynamite Boxes . 495.00
Cupboard, Doll's, Step Back, Red Paint, 16 x 30 x 10 In. 225.00
Dancer, Black Man, Yellow Cap, Red Plaid Pants, Oh My, Lehmann, 1920, 10 In. 690.00
Dancer, Celluloid, Windup, Schuco 650.00
Dancer, Clown, Dandy-Jim, Windup, Tin, Dances, Claps Cymbals, Strauss, 1921, 10 In. . . 275.00
Dancer, Do The Twist, On Tin Pedestal, Box 75.00
Dancing Couple, Windup, Tin, Germany, 8 In. 660.00
Dancing Dan, Front Of Lamppost, Jointed Figure Dances, Box, 13 In. 375.00
Dancing Dan, Lamppost On Stage, Microphone, Remote Control, 13 In. 375.00
Dancing Sam, Tin, Windup, S. & E., Japan, 9 In. 205.00
Dare Devil, Tin, Lehmann, 1881 . . . . 295.00
Deep Sea Diver, 10 In. 395.00
Desk, Doll's, Kneehole, 5 Drawers, 6 1/4 x 11 3/8 In. 65.00
Desk, Doll's, Roll Top, 5 1/2 x 7 In. 85.00
Dino, Fred Flintstone Riding, Battery Operated, Marx, 22 In. 400.00
Dish, Little Abner, Cap Enterprises, 1968, 7 x 7 In. 68.00
Doctor Doolittle, Pushme-Pullyu, Box, Set Of 2 . . . . 125.00
Dog, Begging, Movable Head & Tail Work Together, White Mohair, 9 In. 185.00
Dog, Boxer, Mohair, Black Trim, Glass Eyes, Collar, Head Turns, Steiff, 16 1/2 In. 165.00
Dog, Bulldog, Blond Plush, c.1958, 24 x 35 In. . . . .*Illus*   632.00
Dog, Bulldog, Plays Piano, Battery Operated, Tin, Plush, Marusan Toys, Box, 9 x 10 In. . . 420.00
Dog, Bulldog, Plush, Brown & Black Spots, Head Turns, Wood, Steiff, 1958, 24 In. 635.00
Dog, Bulldog, Schoenhut 895.00
Dog, Button Eyes, Plush, On Iron Frame & Wheels, Pull Toy, Steiff, 25 In. 2875.00
Dog, Cocker Spaniel, Windup, Tin Lithograph, Tail Spins, Yanoman, Japan, 5 1/4 In. 35.00
Dog, Dachshund, Walks Forward, Swivel Head, Clockwork, 8 In., Pair 1035.00
Dog, Dalmatian, Brown, Cream, Button, Steiff, 25 In., Pair 1150.00

Dog, Excelsior-Filled, Mohair, Swivel Head, Embroidered Nose, Steiff, 1910, 11 In. 425.00
Dog, Nodder, Pull Toy, Glass Eyes, Papier-Mache, England, 19th Century, 11 x 18 In. 920.00
Dog, On Wheels, Shepherd, Glass Eyes, Ear Button, Embroidered Features, 1910, 8 In. .. 172.00
Dog, Orange & White Mohair, Glass Eyes, Voice Box, Pull Toy, Steiff, 15 1/2 In. 280.00
Dog, Poor Pete, Nipping At Boy, Windup, Celluloid, Japan, 6 In. 305.00
Dog, Sandy, Crouching, Rolls Forward When Tail Is Pushed Down, Box, 7 In. 1210.00
Dog, Sandy, Wood, Jointed, 4 In. 83.00
Dog, Seated, Glass Eyes, Embroidered Features, Steiff, 1913, 5 1/2 In. 172.00
Dog, Silver Mohair, Button Eyes, 12 In. 95.00
Dog, Sitting, Yellow Mohair, Embroidered Nose & Claws, 1913, 5 1/2 In. 170.00
Dog, Sitting, Yellow Mohair, Glass Eyes, Embroidered, Steiff, c.1913, 5 1/2 In. 220.00
Dog, St. Bernard, Rocking, Ear Button, Synthetic Fur, Steiff, 23 x 50 In. 172.00
Dog, Terrier, Long Orange & Brown Mohair, Button, Steiff, 1950s, 15 x 13 In. 325.00
Dog, Terrier, Windup, Alps, Japan, 1960s 50.00
Dog, Windup, Plaid Coat, Tin, Felt, Mohair, Schuco, Germany, Prewar, 5 1/4 In. 248.00
Dog, Windup, White Fur Over Composition, Glass Eyes, Metal Legs, 8 x 6 In. 83.00
Dog Sled, Dumpster Bed, Wood, Worn Varnish & Red Paint, Stencil, 29 In. 190.00
Dolls are listed in their own category.
Doll Case, Midge, Black, Vinyl, Wearing Lunch-Date Outfit, 1964, 10 In. 90.00
Doll Case, Skooter, Turquoise, Vinyl, Pictures, Country Picnic, 1965, 7 x 10 In. 150.00
Dollhouse, Bliss, Wood & Paper Lithograph 1295.00
Dollhouse, Log Cabin, Wood, Furniture, Folk Art, Textured Wood Base, 20 x 13 In. 2400.00
Dollhouse, Schoenhut, 1 Room, Pressed Paper Bricks, Furniture, c.1920, 17 In. 550.00
Dollhouse, Schoenhut, Bungalow, Raising Roof, 2 Exterior Walls Swing Open 1050.00
Dollhouse, Schoenhut, Cardboard Roof, Wood, Square, 24 In. 850.00
Dollhouse, Schoenhut, Cottage, White, 2-Story, Trellis, Red Barn Roof, 16 x 10 In. 575.00
Dollhouse, Schoenhut, Daggle, 2 Story, Wood, 8 Rooms Plus Attic, 1923, 27 5/8 In. 2415.00
Dollhouse Furniture, 2 Chairs, Table, Ginny, 1950s 130.00
Dollhouse Furniture, Bed, Canopy, Floral Painting, Linens, c.1890, 12 x 25 In. 650.00
Dollhouse Furniture, China Closet, Oak, Glass Doors, 3 Shelves, 1930s, 20 x 12 3/4 In. .. 165.00
Dollhouse Furniture, Hoosier Cupboard, 1920s, 24 In. 195.00
Dollhouse Furniture, Kitchen Accessories, Cast, Arcade, 1920s, 7 Piece 1150.00
Dollhouse Furniture, Piano, 2 1/2 Octaves, Jaymar 50.00
Dollhouse Furniture, Settee, Windsor, 17 In. 70.00
Dollhouse Furniture, Victorian, Cast Iron, Painted, Germany, c.1890, 6 Piece 210.00
Donkey, Na-Ob, Pulling Man On Cart, Tin, Solid Wheels, Lehmann, 6 x 3 In. ....138.00 to 230.00
Donkey, Wood, Sitting, Schoenhut, 12 In. 4070.00
Drawing Set, Electric, Skipper, Lights, Traces Outfits, Lakeside Toys, 1964, 9 x 14 In. ... 60.00
Dredge, Pulleys, Shovel, Brake, Levers, Boiler, Steel, Buddy L, 1920s, 12 x 32 In. 100.00
Dresser, Doll's, Pine, 2 Drawers, Painted, Mirror, 17 x 12 In. 38.00
Drum, Farmer Chasing Man, Ohio Art, 6 1/4 In. 25.00
Drum, Mutt & Jeff, At Carnival, Bud Fisher, Converse, Prewar, 8 In. 360.00
Drum, Tin Lithograph, Animals In Parade, 6 In. 33.00
Drum, Town Of Granville, Mass., Red Label 25.00
Drum Major, Full Parade Dress, Carrying Marching Drum, Tin, 13 1/4 In. 220.00
Drum Major, Windup, Celluloid, Wood Stand, Nifty, Japan, Box, Prewar, 10 1/2 In. 440.00

Keep front hedges and fences under two feet in height so prowlers or break-ins can be seen from the street. See-through fences are best.

Toy, Dog, Bulldog,
Blond Plush,
c.1958, 24 x 35 In.

Drummer, Arthur A Go-Go, Long-Haired Man Playing Drums, Cloth & Metal, Battery .. 145.00
Drummer, Black Man, Standing, Large Orange Drum, Schoenhut, 7 In. 5750.00
Drummer, George The Drummer Boy, Windup, Tin, Marx, Box, 1950s, 9 In. 248.00
Drummer, Windup, Tin Lithograph, Chein, 8 1/2 In. 22.00
Drummer Boy, Windup, Chein, 1930s 180.00
Drummer Boy, Windup, Marx, 1930s 180.00
Drunkard, Man, Dressed In Cotton Top, Hat Resting At Jaunty Angle, 8 In. 690.00
Duck, Family, Quacking, Pull Toy, Fisher-Price, No. 777, 1960s 40.00
Duck, Paak-Paak, Pulling Basket Of Ducklings, Windup, Tin, Lehmann, 7 1/2 In. 385.00
Duck, Standing On Base, 4 Wheels, Green, Brown, Orange, Pull Toy, 5 In., 2 Piece 805.00
Duck, Waggles, Friction, Germany 125.00
Duck, Windup, Metal, Red Vest, J. Chein & Co., 4 3/4 In. 125.00
Earthmover, Nylint, 26 In. 16.00
Elephant, Circus, Wood, Jointed, Painted Eyes, Leather Ears, Schoenhut, 10 In. 645.00
Elephant, Jumbo, Blows Bubbles 160.00
Elephant, Kid, Clockwork, Papier-Mache, Walks, France, c.1900, 15 In. 1000.00
Elephant, Pull Toy, Nodder, Flocked Coat, Papier-Mache, Germany, 8 1/2 In. 192.00
Elephant, Sitting, Wood, Crease In Ears, Schoenhut, 12 In. 4070.00
Elephant, Smoking, Battery Operated 110.00
Elephant, Tan Plush, Gray Toenails, Wood Tusks, Smiling Face, Steiff, 1960, 25 In. 805.00
Elephant, Wood, Leather Ears, Rubber Trunk, Schoenhut U.S.A., 1950s, 6 In. 88.00
Elf, Windup, Walker, Tin Lithograph, Chein, 5 1/2 In. 360.00
Engine, Live Steam, No. 43, Weeden 450.00
Erector Set, Gilbert, No. 7, Manual, Wood Box, 8 x 21 In. 330.00
Erector Set, Gilbert, No. 8 1/2, Locomotive & Tender, Wood Chest, 6 1/2 x 29 In. 1322.00
Erector Set, Gilbert, Rocket Launcher 150.00
Erector Set, Marklin, Box 450.00
Erector Set, White, Truck, Construction Equipment In Box, 1920s, 28 In. 398.00
Espresso Cafe Snack Bar, Open View, Yellow, Schuco, Box, 8 In. 165.00
Express Wagon, Horse Drawn, Red Body, White Horse, Tin, Merriam, 1870s, 11 In. 690.00
Farm Figures, Farmer With Rake, Milkmaid With Pail, 1910, Schoenhut 1150.00
Fashion Shop, Barbie, Cardboard, Mirrored, Stage, Folding Furniture, 1962 .... 300.00
Felix The Cat, Glass Eyes, Neck Ribbons, Continental, 13 In. 125.00
Ferris Wheel, Mechanical, Buffalo Toys 450.00
Ferris Wheel, Mechanical, Tin, Chein, 17 In. 550.00
Ferris Wheel, Realistic Colorful Seats, Ohio Art 295.00
Ferris Wheel, Sand Toy, Tin Lithograph, Buffalo Toy, 9 In. 395.00
Ferris Wheel, Steam Powdered, 6 Enclosed Cars, Germany, 10 In. 695.00
Ferris Wheel, Windup, Tin Lithograph, Plastic Seats, Bell, 10 3/4 x 16 x 5 In. 210.00
Ferris Wheel, Windup, Tin Lithograph, Stop Lever, 9 x 8 1/2 x 8 In. 50.00
Fiddler, Dressed In Blue Velveteen, Rocking Back & Forth, Checked Pants, 1880, 9 In. .. 3740.00
Fire Pumper, 1929 Model, Triple Team, Black & White Horses, Kenton, 15 In. 402.00
Fire Pumper, 2 Horses, 2 Firemen, Bell, Dent, 1905, 18 In. 1095.00
Fire Pumper, 2 Horses, White Wagon, Wheels, Ives, c.1910, 19 3/4 In. 402.00
Fire Pumper, Atlantic, Painted & Stenciled Tin, Cast Iron Wheels 3850.00
Fire Pumper, Horse Drawn, 3 Horses Pull Steam Pumper, Bell, Iron, Wilkins, 21 In. 330.00
Fire Pumper, Hose & Nozzle, Hand-Cranked Indicator, Arcade, 6 1/4 In. 275.00
Fire Pumper, Live Steam, Red, 2 Hand Levers, Open Bench, Tin, Germany, 1900 ...... 1320.00
Fire Pumper, No. 7, American LaFrance Replica, Sturditoy, 25 1/2 In. 578.00
Fire Pumper, Red, Yellow Piping, Cast Iron, Marklin, 1902 .... 7475.00
Fire Pumper, Seated Driver, Red, Rubber Tires, Cast Iron, Kenton, 7 1/4 In. 110.00
Fire Pumper, Sheet Metal, 25 3/4 In. 385.00
Fire Pumper, Striking Bell, 2 Horses, George Brown, 1870s, 14 1/4 In. 3520.00
Fire Pumper, Suburban, Pressed Steel, Hydrant, Connector Hose, Tonka, Box, 17 In. 440.00
Fire Pumper, Windup, Tin, Cast Iron, Bell, Wilkins, 11 In. 330.00
Fire Station, 2 Trucks, Wood, Pressed Cardboard, Buddy L, 15 In. 200.00
Fire Truck, 2 Extension Ladders, Hose Reel, Bell, Keystone, 1929, 28 1/4 In. 517.00
Fire Truck, 3 Ladders, 2 Firemen, Cast Iron, Kenton, 17 In. 950.00
Fire Truck, Aerial Ladder, Decals, 29 In. 745.00
Fire Truck, Aerial Ladder, Pressed Steel, Decals, Buddy L, 40 In. 935.00
Fire Truck, Aerial Ladder, Steerable Front, Doepke, Model Toys, Box, 32 In. 470.00
Fire Truck, Clockwork, Tin, Painted, George Brown, 1870, 15 In. 8800.00
Fire Truck, Friction, Metal, Wood Back Fender, Bell, 11 In. 285.00

If your battery-operated toy stops
working, try sanding the terminals and
the ends of the batteries. There may
be slight corrosion that interferes with
the battery connections.

Toy, Frog, Footrest, Green & Tan Plush,
Steiff, 12 x 22 In.

Fire Truck, Hook & Ladder, 2 Firemen, 2 Horses, 3 Ladders, Carpenter, 1884, 26 In. 2395.00
Fire Truck, Hook & Ladder, 3 Horses, Driver, Cast Iron, Wood Ladders, Painted, 30 In. .. 665.00
Fire Truck, Hook & Ladder, 5 Wood Ladders, Bell, 3 Horses, Wilkins, 1910, 25 1/4 In. 1050.00
Fire Truck, Hook & Ladder, Driver & 4 Ladders, Friction, Metal, 17 In. 40.00
Fire Truck, Hook & Ladder, Hydraulic, Red Pressed Steel, Structo, 3 In. 173.00
Fire Truck, Hook & Ladder, Open Cab, Ladder Lift, Buddy L, 1929, 27 5/8 In. ...776.00 to 1500.00
Fire Truck, Hook & Ladder, Windup, Courtland 195.00
Fire Truck, Hook & Ladder, Wyandotte, 25 In. 80.00
Fire Truck, Hose Reel, Bell, Cast Iron, Painted, Pratt & Letchworth 5170.00
Fire Truck, Hubley, 7 In. 150.00
Fire Truck, Hydraulic, Tonka, 1957 .... 225.00
Fire Truck, Ladder, 3 Horses, Cast Iron, Bell, Water Pail, White, Red Wheels, 25 1/2 In. ... 220.00
Fire Truck, Ladder, American LaFrance, Marked Rossmoyne, Doepke, Box, 33 In. 495.00
Fire Truck, Ladder, Big Boy, Steel, Wood Ladders, Steerable Front, Kelmet, 27 In. 990.00
Fire Truck, Ladder, Cast Iron, White Rubber Tires, Ahrens-Fox Pumper, Hubley, 11 In. 3630.00
Fire Truck, Ladder, Pressed Steel, 2 Tin Ladders, Bell, Structo, 21 In. 185.00
Fire Truck, Ladders & Firemen, Die Cast, Cast Iron, A.C. Williams Co., 7 1/2 In. 93.00
Fire Truck, No. 1941, Ladders, 3 Riders, Cast Iron, Arcade, 16 In. 358.00
Fire Truck, Ride-On, Stamped Steel, Steering Wheel, Rubber Tires, Structo, 26 In. 85.00
Fire Truck, Snoopy Gus, Hook & Ladder, Windup, Tin, Marx, Prewar, 9 In. 990.00
Fire Truck, Snorkel, Tonka, 17 In. 65.00
Fire Truck, Sound Machine Water Cannon, Nylint, Box, 28 In. 44.00
Fire Truck, Suburban Pumper, Nylint 17.00
Fire Truck, Tin Lithograph, Ladder Flips Up, Penny Toy, 4 In. 410.00
Fire Truck, Water Tower, Adjustable, Rear Steering, Lift-Front Hood, Keystone, 31 In. ... 578.00
Fire Truck, Water Tower, Adjustable, Rear Steering, Pressed Steel, Sturditoy, 33 In. 578.00
Firehouse, Clockwork, Cast Iron & Wood, Bell, Pumper Shoots Out, Ives, 19th Century .. 7150.00
Firehouse, Clockwork, Hinged Doors, 8 Windows, Bell, Door Opens, Ives, 12 x 8 In. 4312.00
Fireman, Climbing Tinplate Ladder Step By Step, Martin, 1904, 9 In. 1495.00
Fireman, Climbing, Windup, Tin Lithograph, Plastic, Marx, Box, 24 In. 135.00
Fisherman, Seated, Broad-Brimmed Hat, Kicks Up Legs, Martin, 1908, 8 In. 1725.00
Flying Saucer, Battery Operated, Japan, Box 195.00
Flying Saucer, Space Pilot, Revolving Antenna, Tin, Orange 395.00
Fox, Rooster, Windup, Hand Painted, c.1899 .... 750.00
Foxy Grandpa, Horse-Drawn Cart, Cast Iron, 1910, 11 In. 305.00
Frankenstein, Blushing, Battery Operated, 1960s ....120.00 to 295.00
Frankenstein, Inflatable, Universal, 6 Ft. 95.00
Fred Flintstone, Bedrock Band, Beats Drum, Cymbal, Alps, Japan, Box, 9 1/2 In. 94.00
Fred Flintstone, Hopper, Windup, Marx, Japan, 3 1/2 In. 210.00
Fred Flintstone, On Dino, Battery Operated, Marx ....395.00 to 425.00
Fred Flintstone, On Dino, Tin Lithograph, Windup, Linemar, Box, 8 In. 735.00
Fred Flintstone, On Dino, Windup, Marx, Japan, 8 In. 295.00
Fred Flintstone, On Dino, Windup, Vinyl Head, 1962 .... 550.00
Frog, Footrest, Green & Tan Plush, Steiff, 12 x 22 In. ....*Illus* 1380.00
Frog, Vest, Tan Trousers, Bongo Drum, Cloth, Felt, Dakin Dream Pets, 1960s, 8 In. 18.00
Furniture Set, Doll's, Victorian, Cast Iron, Painted Orange, c.1890, 4 In., 6 Piece 210.00
G.I. Joe, Australian Jungle Fighter, Shirt, Shorts, 12 In. 88.00

G.I. Joe, Captain Zargon, Space Pilot, Box 395.00
G.I. Joe, Danger Of Depth 450.00
G.I. Joe, Green Beret 450.00
G.I. Joe, Hidden Missile Discovery, Contents, Box, 1969 . . . . 850.00
G.I. Joe, Jeep, Combat, Battery Operated, Plastic, Box, 1965 . . . . 450.00
G.I. Joe, Jeep, Desert Patrol, Machine Gun, Portable Radio, Hasbro, Box, 20 In. 650.00
G.I. Joe, Jouncing Jeep, Windup, Tin Lithograph, Unique Art, 1941 . . . . .120.00 to 325.00
G.I. Joe, Jungle Survival 325.00
G.I. Joe, K-9 Pups, Windup, Tin Lithograph, Unique Art 120.00
G.I. Joe, Marine, 30th Anniversary, 12 In. 75.00
G.I. Joe, Mouth Of Doom, Contents, Box, 1969 . . . . 1295.00
G.I. Joe, Mysterious Explosion, Contents, Box, 1969 . . . . 850.00
G.I. Joe, Race Car Driver, Blond Hair, Racing Suit, 1964, 12 In. 255.00
G.I. Joe, Sailor, Work Shirt, Jeans, Scuba Tank, Face Mask, 12 In. 55.00
G.I. Joe, Secret Mission To Spy Island, Contents, Box, 1969 . . . . 995.00
G.I. Joe, Sky Dive To Danger . . . . : 395.00
G.I. Joe, Soldier, 30th Anniversary, 12 In. 75.00
G.I. Joe, Soldier, Field Shirt, German Helmet, Luger In Case, 12 In. 88.00
G.I. Joe, Space Ranger, Talking, Commander, Box 395.00
G.I. Joe, Windup, Tin, Military Garb, Holding K-9 Pups, 1940s, 9 In. . . . . .121.00 to 154.00
Games are listed in their own category.
Garage, Car, Children, Red Roof, Lehmann, 1935, 5 1/4 x 6 1/4 In. 885.00
Garage, Front Doors Open, Red Sedan, Tin, Schuco, 6 In. 193.00
Garage, Tin, Bing, 3 1/4 x 6 1/4 In. 135.00
Garage, White Wood, Gray Asphalt Shingles, Swinging Doors, Large 145.00
Gardener, Walking, Clockwork, Black Face, Lehmann 440.00
Gas Pump, Early Style, Actual Working Model, Rubber Bladder, Pressed Steel, 9 In. 330.00
Gas Pump, Gilmore Gas, Red Lion, Brass Nozzle, Chrome, Wood Base, 1920s, 17 In. . . . 210.00
Gas Station, Front Doors Open, Beige, Red Trim, Schuco, 6 In. 303.00
Gas Station, Standard & Esso, Electric Switch, Tin Lithograph, Kibri, 7 x 3 1/2 In. 550.00
Gas Station, Sunnyside, Electrical Lid, Marx 1265.00
Gazelle, Painted Eyes, Schoenhut 1320.00
Gazelle, Tan, Cream, Jointed Legs, Leather Ears, Schoenhut, 1910, 6 In. . . . . . . .1760.00 to 2645.00
Giraffe, Painted Eyes, Schoenhut 358.00
Giraffe, Plush, Glass Eyes, Articulated Neck, Steiff, Postwar, 59 In. 1495.00
Girl, Jumping Rope, Clockwork, Automatic Toy Co., 8 In. 2640.00
Girl, Riding Velocipede, Cloth Dress, Pivoting Wheel, Stevens & Brown, 11 In. 1840.00
Go-Kart, Tom & Jerry, Plastic, Friction Drive, Copyright 1973 Hong Kong, 6 In. 200.00
Going To The Fair, Windup, Tin, Lehmann, 6 1/4 In. 1430.00
Goose, Golden, Lays Golden Eggs, Windup, Tin Lithograph, Marx, Box, 1924, 9 In. 198.00
Goose & Beetle, White Body, Orange Beak, Webbed Feet, Penny Toy, Germany 55.00
Gorilla, Magilla, Holding Cane, Squeeze Toy, Vinyl, Screen Gems, Spain, 1967, 8 In. . . . 305.00
Gorilla, Standing With Arms Apart, Roaring Mouth, 1912, Schoenhut, 8 In. 3737.00
Grasshopper, Green, Articulated Legs, Cast Iron, Pull Toy, Hubley, Box, 9 In. 3080.00
Grinder, Flasho, Mechanical, Girard Model Works, Box, c.1920 . . . . 72.00
Guitar, Bass, Monkees, Box 960.00
Guitar, Bugs Bunny, Mattel 35.00
Guitar, Cowboy, Model 601, Chord Maker, Songbook, Emenee, Box, 1955, 31 In. 300.00
Guitar, Tin Lithograph, 1950s, Box 95.00
Gun, Air Pistol, Air Arms Pro Elite, .177 Caliber, Barrel Cocker 375.00
Gun, Air Pistol, Beeman P-2, M-25 Scope, Combat Grips 300.00
Gun, Air Pistol, Daisy Powerline, No. 45 . . . . 35.00
Gun, Air Pistol, Daisy Powerline, No. 790, .77 Caliber, Box 85.00
Gun, Air Rifle, Crosman No. 100 Pneumatic, .22 Caliber 125.00
Gun, Air Rifle, Smith & Wesson, No. 77a, .22 Caliber, Pneumatic 120.00
Gun, Air Rifle, Walther LGV, .177 Caliber, Match Sights 475.00
Gun, Anti-Aircraft, Pompom, Friction, Tin, Rubber Tires, Japan, 1950s, 7 1/2 In. 55.00
Gun, Anti-Aircraft, Unit 5, Plastic, Pressed Steel, Hand Crank, Olive Green, Marx, 22 In. . . 55.00
Gun, BB, Crosman No 781, .177 Caliber, Pump Pneumatic 25.00
Gun, BB, Daisy Powerline, No. 850, .177 Caliber, Beeman Scope 70.00
Gun, BB, Daisy Red Ryder, Model 40, No. 11 . . . . 45.00
Gun, BB, Daisy, Model 99, Champion, Wood Stock, Lever Action, Canvas Sling 40.00
Gun, Cowboy, Tin Lithograph, Wyandote, 7 In. 40.00

Gun, Dart, Cast Iron, 1903, 7 In. 150.00
Gun, Flying Saucer Shape, Launches Tops, U.S. Plastic Co., Box, 1950s, 7 1/2 x 8 1/2 In. 65.00
Gun, Green Hornet, Metal, Box 200.00
Gun, Howitzer, Tin Plate, Rubber Tires, Olive Drab, Spring Mechanism, Japan, 10 In. ... 25.00
Gun, Johnny Eagle, Skeet Shooter 275.00
Gun, Jr. Police Chief, Cast Iron 90.00
Gun, Machine Gun, Mac, Shoots Paper, McDowell, 1920s 44.00
Gun, Machine Gun, Rapid Fire, Cast Iron 375.00
Gun, Ray, Friction, Sparking, Plastic, Green Tinted, 1950-1970, 6 1/2 In. 20.00
Gun, Ray, Friction, Whirring Sound, Plastic, Cream, Translucent Red, China, 9 In. 70.00
Gun, Repeating, Gold Plated, Black Plastic Handle, Hubley, 11 1/2 In. 425.00
Gun, Shore, German Style, Tin Lithograph, Orange, Green & Brown Camouflage, 5 In. ... 50.00
Gun, Space, Battery Operated, 3 Colors 95.00
Gun, Space, Clicker, Hard Plastic, Silver Color 25.00
Gun, Squirt, Jolly Jumbo, On Card 49.00
Gun, Squirt, Rocket Jet, Rocket Shaped, Tail Fin, Plastic, U.S. Plastics Co., 1950s, 5 In. ... 24.00
Gun, Squirt, Tin, ABC 20.00
Gun & Holster Set, Cap Gun, Marshall, Hubley 90.00
Gun & Holster Set, Cap Gun, Spittin' Image, Double Holster, Daisy Western, Box 125.00
Ham & Sam, Banjo Player Jigs, Friend Plays Piano, Tin, Windup, Strauss, 8 In. 495.00
Handcar, Moon Mullins, Tin Lithograph, Marx, Box, c.1930, 6 In. 632.00
Handcar, Windup, Jiggs & Friend With Box Of Dynamite, Tin Lithograph, 6 In. 470.00
Handcuffs, G-Men Deluxe Training Outfit, Gun, Badge, New York Toy Co., 1936 .... 135.00
Hansom Cab, Blue, Seated Driver, White Horse, Yellow Spoked Wheels, Iron, 11 In. 358.00
Hansom Cab, Cast Iron, Pratt & Letchworth, 1890s, 13 In. 1375.00
Hansom Cab, Horse, Driver & Passenger, Kenton, Cast Iron, 15 3/4 In. 220.00
Hansom Cab, Horse, Driver, Woman Passenger, Kenton, Cast Iron, 15 1/2 In. 535.00
Hansom Cab, Li La, Dark Blue, Woman With Raised Arm, Dog, Lehmann, 1910, 6 In. 2150.00
Happy Hooligan, Driving Donkey Cart, Windup, Ingap 1275.00
Happy Hooligan, Iron Wagon, Pulled By Donkey, Nodder 700.00
Happy Hooligan, Windup, Walker, Tin Lithograph, Chein, USA, 6 In. 190.00
Happy Hooligan, Wood, Pull Toy, c.1920, 4 1/2 x 6 In. 132.00
Happy Life, Windup, Child Rocks, Goose, Parasol Spins, Celluloid, Tin, C.K., Japan, 9 In. 200.00
Happy Times, Drunk, Lamppost, Moves Head, Musical, Windup, TKR, Japan, Box 90.00
Harvester, Cast Iron, Arcade, 11 1/2 In. 495.00
Hat Box, Barbie, Vinyl, Zipper, Standard Plastic Products, 1961, 12 x 10 1/2 In. 125.00
Hatchet, Shingling, Iron & Wood, 6 In. 5.00
Hedgehog, Micki Girl, Steiff 175.00
Helicopter, Chein 150.00
Helicopter, Evacuation, Windup, Tin, Marx, Box 225.00
Helicopter, Fire Department, Friction, Rotating Blades, Tin, Cragstan, 11 In. 145.00
Helicopter, Rescue Battalion, Windup, Japan, 10 In. 2145.00
Helmet, Doughboy, Stamped Metal, Olive Drab, Cotton Strap, 10 In. 27.00
Helmet, German WWII Style, Plastic, Gray, Brown Vinyl Strap, 1960s 60.00
Helmet, Space Patrol, Cardboard, Die Cut, Premium, Unused, 1953, 10 x 16 In. 85.00
Helmet, Texaco Fire Chief, With Microphone 125.00
Helmet, World War I Style, Cloth Chinstrap, Argo-Mazola Premium, Child's Small 40.00
Hen, Cackling, Fisher-Price, No. 120 .... 30.00 to 60.00
Hen House, Pip-Squeak, Hen & Rooster, Wood, Germany, 6 1/2 x 4 x 6 In. 45.00
Henry, Eating Candy, Clockwork, Tin Lithograph, Linemar, 1950s, 5 1/2 In. 415.00
Henry, Mahout, On Tricycle, Cargo Bed, Windup, Tin, Celluloid, Japan, Prewar, 5 In. 800.00
Henry, On Elephant, Windup, Celluloid, Japan 550.00
Henry, Towing Nodding Little Brother, Windup, Celluloid, Anderson, Box, 6 1/2 In. 1100.00
Hey Hey Chicken Snatcher, Windup, Marx, Box 3000.00
High Chair, Doll's, Brown, Stenciled Crest, Alligatored, 1880s, 26 In. 300.00
Honeymoon Express, Windup, Tin, Marx, 1950s, 9 In. .... 66.00 to 176.00
Hooligan's Hack, Windup, Tin Lithograph, Strauss, 8 In. 358.00
Hoop Toy, With Ram, Tin, Painted, Altof Bergman, 6 1/8 In. 1210.00
Hopper, Casper The Ghost, Windup, Tin, Linemar, Japan, 4 1/2 In. 385.00
Hopper, Flintstones, Barney Rubble, Windup, Marx, Japan, 3 1/2 In. 230.00
Horse, Bucking Bronco, Windup, Painted, Lehmann, Germany, 7 1/2 In. 360.00
Horse, Bucking Palomino, Hard Plastic, Pull Toy, 16 In. 85.00
Horse, Hobbyhorse, Black Cloth Head, Brown Fur Mane, Button Eyes, 47 In. 110.00

Horse, Leaping, Brown, Black & White, Wood, 8 1/2 In. 55.00
Horse, Leather Saddle, White, Schoenhut, 8 In. 325.00
Horse, Mr. Ed, Talking Horse, Box 125.00
Horse, No. 17, Marx, 1973 . . . . 35.00
Horse, On Platform, Tin Wheels, Papier-Mache & Wood, Pull Toy, 10 In. 192.00
Horse, On Wheels, Hide Covered, Horsehair Tail, Wood Base, 1910s, 10 x 10 5/8 In. 345.00
Horse, Planet Of The Apes, Battery, Plastic, Mego, Box, 1974, 8 1/2 x 10 1/2 In. 38.00
Horse, Rocking, Carved, Painted Dapple Gray, Horsehair Mane, Marked Caledonia 1955.00
Horse, Rocking, English Saddle, Victorian . . . . .332.00 to 445.00
Horse, Rocking, Hide Cover, Horsehair Mane & Tail, Nikolaus Klein, 1950, 30 x 46 In. . . 545.00
Horse, Rocking, Horsehide Saddle, Wood Hoofs, Stirrups, Platform, 30 1/2 x 33 In. 180.00
Horse, Rocking, Laminated Wood, Dapple Gray Paint, Glass Eyes, 36 In. 495.00
Horse, Rocking, Oak, 2 Panels, Red Plank Seat, Hand-Painted Design 55.00
Horse, Rocking, Oak, Maple, Dark Varnish, 1800, 47 x 12 1/2 In. 975.00
Horse, Rocking, Padded Seat, Black & Gray Paint, Carved Legs, 19th Century, Child's . . 1610.00
Horse, Rocking, Pine, Black Paint, Red Striping, White Mane, Seat With Arms, 39 In. . . . 220.00
Horse, Rocking, Plush, Red Saddle, Reins, Button In Ear, Steiff, 36 x 48 In. 1610.00
Horse, Rocking, Rearing, Dapple Gray, Leather Saddle, England, 47 In. 3450.00
Horse, Rocking, Red, Orange Saddle, Papier-Mache, Wood, Germany, 5 1/4 In. 220.00
Horse, Rocking, Serpent Rockers, 45 In. 4125.00
Horse, Rocking, Stand, Gray, Yarn Mane, Glass Eyes, Leather Bridle, Saddle, 35 In. 1092.00
Horse, Rocking, Wood, Black & White Paint, 7 1/4 In. 140.00
Horse, Rocking, Wood, Composition, Glass Eyes, 39 In. 385.00
Horse, Rocking, Wood, Crossbars, Gray, Wood Platform, 45 In. 495.00
Horse, Rocking, Wood, Dapple Gray, Trestle Platform, 40 In. 480.00
Horse, Swing, Painted, 19th Century, Victorian, 34 x 26 In. 695.00
Horse, Thunderbolt, 10 In. 43.00
Horse, Walking, Black Stallion, Red Straps Around Middle Of Body, 1880, 9 In. 3450.00
Horse, Wood, Carved, White & Brown Paint, Glass Eyes, Leather Ears, 24 x 23 In. 1320.00
Horse, Wood, Composition, Mohair, Saddle, Cast Iron Wheels, Pull Toy, 11 x 12 In. 355.00
Horse, Wood, Jointed, Schoenhut U.S.A., 1950s, 7 In. 44.00
Horse, Wood, Leather Saddle, Cast Iron Wheels, Pull Toy, Germany, Stearn & Co., 24 In. 990.00
Horse, Wood, Papier-Mache, Dapple Paint, Stub Tail, Wheels, Pull Toy, 12 3/4 x 14 In. . . 165.00
Horse & Buckboard, Green, Yellow & Black, Black Chauffeur, Cast Iron, 10 1/2 In. 105.00
House, Barbie, New Dream House, Fold Up, Furniture, 1965, 21 x 15 In. 500.00
Huckleberry Hound, Plush, Vinyl Face, 17 In. 20.00
Hula Dancer, Windup, Celluloid, Japan, Prewar, 9 In. 90.00
Hutch, Doll's, Pine, 2 Base Doors, Green & Cream Paint, 12 x 15 In. 40.00
Hyena, Standing, Glass Eyes, Open Mouth, Laughing, Schoenhut, 1912, 6 In. 5750.00
Indian, Brave Eagle, Beats Drum & Raises War Hoop, Battery Operated, Box 145.00
Iron, Baby Betsey Ross 50.00
Jack-In-The-Box, Bugs Bunny, Rubber Ears 95.00
Jack-In-The-Box, Casper The Friendly Ghost, Tin Lithograph, Mattel, 1959 . . . . .35.00 to 92.00
Jack-In-The-Box, Clown 45.00
Jack-In-The-Box, House, Wood, Paper Lithograph, Papier-Mache, Cloth, Germany 468.00
Jack-In-The-Box, Polychrome Painted Papier-Mache & Cloth Figure, 8 In. 200.00
Jack-In-The-Box, Porky Pig 45.00
Jack-In-The-Box, Romper Room Clown 85.00
Jack-In-The-Box, Snoopy, Musical, Plastic, Fabric, Mattel, 1976, 5 1/2 In. 45.00
Jackie Coogan, The Kid, Eyes Move Side To Side, Walker, Tin Lithograph, 7 1/4 In. 440.00
Jane West, Plastic, Rubber & Plastic Accessories, Best Of The West, Marx, 11 In. 20.00
Jazzbo Jim, Dancer On Roof, Tin Lithograph, Clockwork, Unique Art, 1920s, 10 In. 525.00
Jazzbo Jim, Strauss, Box 595.00
Jazzbo Jim, Violin Player, Dancer, On Cabin, Windup, Unique Art, 1921, 10 In. 580.00
Jeep, Army, Radio, Aerial, Fold-Down Windshield, Yellow Seats, Friction 70.00
Jeep, Driver, Wood, Jointed, Hand Painted, Composition Head, K.F.S., 1935, 6 1/2 In. . . . 40.00
Jeep, Jolly Joe, Windup, Tin, Marx, 5 1/2 In. 130.00
Jeep, Jumping, Tin, 4 Soldiers With Machine Guns, Tin, Marx, 1930s 390.00
Jeep, Jumping, Windup, Tin, 4 Figures Shooting Machine Guns, Marx, 6 x 4 1/2 In. 77.00
Jeep, U.S. Army, White Star On Hood, 3 Metal Soldiers, Friction, Japan 90.00
Jeep, White Top, Blue, Tonka 17.00
Jester, Clockwork, Performing On Cloth-Covered Stage, Wood, Jointed, 9 In. 2070.00
Jigger, Clockwork, Fisher-Price, 6 1/2 In. 1200.00

Toy, Jump Rope, Painted Figural Handles,
Children In Knickers, 5 3/4 In.

Toy, Merrymakers, Piano, Mice, Windup, Tin,
Marx, Box, 1935, 9 1/2 In.

Jigger, Strutting Sam, Black Tap Dancer On Pedestal, Tin, Box, 11 In. 475.00
Jigger, Strutting Sam, Exaggerated Facial Features, Dances, Japan, 1950s, 10 In. 120.00
Jiggs, Squinting, Smoking Cigar, Cloth, Hat, 1930, 19 In. 1150.00
Jiggs, Wood, Jointed, 5 In. 40.00
Joe Penner & Coo Coo Duck, Windup, Tin, Hat Moves, 1930s, Marx, Box, 8 In. 880.00
Judge, Standing At Podium, Reading Legal Brief, Red Robe, Martin, 1905, 9 In. 1495.00
Jump Rope, Painted Figural Handles, Children In Knickers, 5 3/4 In. . . . . *Illus* 42.00
Jungle Trip, Monkey & Elephant Band, Battery Operated, Linemar, Box, c.1950 . . . . 660.00
Kangaroo, With Baby, Windup, Tin, TPS, Japan, 1950s, 6 In. 44.00
Katerina, Shako, Tin, Lindstrom, 1930s 175.00
Keymonica, Blow Accordion, Finger Keys, Plastic, Song Sheet, Magnus, Box, 1949 . . . . 20.00
Kitchen Set, Stove & Icebox, Metal, Enamel, Green, Red & Yellow Flowers, c.1910 . . . . 155.00
Kitchen Set, Stove & Sink, Wolverine 75.00
Kite, Spaceships, Astronauts, Planets, Paper, Wood, Max, 1950s 15.00
Ko-Ko, Sandwich Man, Mechanical, Box, TK, Japan 55.00
Krazy Kat Express, Train, Pull Toy, Chein, 1932, 9 In. 1650.00
Lamb, On Wood Wheels, Wool, Pull Toy, Button, Steiff, 7 In. 725.00
Laurel & Hardy, Windup, Vinyl, 1960s, 5 1/2 In. 80.00
Leopard, Spotted Plush, Real Whiskers, Plush Tail, Steiff, 37 In. 345.00
Li'l Abner Dogpatch Band, Characters, Piano, Tin, Unique Art, 1945, 5 3/4 x 9 In. 715.00
Limousine, Windup, Tin Lithograph, Open, 2 Passengers, Chauffeur, Caret, 8 1/2 In. 825.00
Lincoln Logs, Building Set, Design Book, Set 3-L, Box, 1944 . . . . 125.00
Lion, Gold Mohair, Glass Eyes, Steel Frame, Ring Pull Voice Box, Pull Toy, Steiff, 21 In. 495.00
Lion, Green Platform, Tin, Pull Toy, 4 1/2 In. 120.00
Lion, King Of The Jungle, Reclining, Glass Eyes, Wood Teeth, Steiff, Postwar 1380.00
Lion, Leo, Yellow Mohair, Gold Mohair, 3 Claws, Steiff, 22 In. 300.00
Lion, Standing, Regal Bearing, Ferocious Wood Teeth, Steiff, Postwar, 39 In. 2185.00
Little King, Animated, Pull Toy, Jaymar, Box, 3 7/8 In. 60.00
Little Lulu's Tubbydoll Maker Kit, Whitman, 1973 . . . . 95.00
Little Theatre Gift Set, Barbie & Ken, Arabian Nights Outfit, 1964 . . . . 7500.00
Lucy, Peanuts, Molded Plastic, Painted, United Features, Hungerford, 1950s, 9 In. 115.00
Maggie & Jiggs, Rolling Pin, Cigar, Cloth Clothes, Box 1100.00
Maggie & Jiggs, Windup, Tin, Red Wheels, I.F.S., Germany, 1924, 7 In. 800.00
Magic Set, Hocus Pocus, Adams, Box 125.00
Mama Katzenjammer In Cart, Horse Bobs, Painted Wood, Pull Toy, 12 x 5 x 7 1/2 In. . . 165.00
Man, Butter & Eggs, With Duck, Windup, Eggs Laid To Order, Tin, 8 1/2 In. 470.00
Man, Climbing On Windmill, Windmill Spins, Hand Painted, 20 In. 70.00
Man, Dancing, Hinged Waging Jaw, Black Velvet Jacket, 11 In. 2300.00
Man, Dancing, On Drum, Wood, Jointed, Ives Washington, 1874, 9 1/2 In. 4025.00
Man, Dancing, Sheet Metal, Articulated, Riveted Joins, Wire Hanger, 12 In. 165.00
Man, Gourd Head, Papier-Mache, Vegetable, 7 1/2 In. 1155.00
Man, Herding 2 Pigs To Market, Martin, 1910, 7 1/2 In. 2530.00
Man, Playing Pool, Kellerman 121.00
Man, Pumping Water Into A Fountain, Rubber-Band Mechanism, Martin, 1897, 6 In. 1150.00
Man, Pushing Wheelbarrow, 3 In. 44.00
Man, Pushing Wheelbarrow, Smoking Pipe, Tin, Germany, 2 3/4 In. 143.00

Man, Walks Sideways, Windup, Tin Plate, Painted, Germany, 7 1/2 In. 360.00
Man & Woman, Walking Down Broadway, Walking Dog, Lehmann, 1895, 6 In. 6325.00
Mandarin, Windup, Tin Lithograph, Lehmann, 7 1/2 In. 2200.00
Mary & Lamb, Windup, Jointed Mary, Nodding Lamb, Celluloid, Japan, Box, 6 1/2 In. . . . 303.00
Mary & Lamb, Windup, Mary Pulling Lamb, Celluloid, Japan, Box, 4 In. 248.00
McGregor, Smoking Cigar Scotsman, Battery Operated, Box 195.00
Megaphone, Snoopy, Chein 35.00
Melody Train, Xylophone Tracks, Battery Operated, Matsuzo Kosuge, 1966, 6 In. 30.00
Merry-Go-Round, 4 Tin Flags & Airplanes, Wolverine 595.00
Merry-Go-Round, Bears Sitting In Teacup, On Saucer, Japan, Box, 1950s 275.00
Merry-Go-Round, Buster Brown & Dog Pictured, 6 Horses, 6 In. 2200.00
Merry-Go-Round, Clockwork, 4 Bisque-Headed Dolls Whirl Around, 1910, 20 In. 2415.00
Merry-Go-Round, Cyclists Racing, Red Canopy, Green Base, 1910, Meier, 2 1/2 In. 3835.00
Merrymakers, Piano, Mice, Windup, Tin, Marx, Box, 1935, 9 1/2 In. . . . . *Illus* 1610.00
Microscope, Gold Medal Premium, Transogram, Box, 1950s 40.00
Microscope, Space Patrol, Metal, Green, Black, J.V.Z. Co., 1950s, 3 1/2 In. 78.00
Microscope, Tasco Deluxe, Japan, Box, 1960s 40.00
Microscope Set, Contents, A.C. Gilbert, Box, 10 x 18 In. 210.00
Mighty Mouse, Pip-Squeak 45.00
Mirror, Barbie, Pink, Plastic, Ponytail Barbie, Let's Dance, 1962 . . . . 40.00
Mirror, Doll's, Walnut, Fruitwood Inlay, Hinged Frame, France, 1875, 13 In. 300.00
Missile Set, Cape Canaveral, Marx 200.00
Model, Airplane, Grumman Gulfstream II, Plastic, Base, Early 1970s, 12 In. 95.00
Model Kit, Airplane, Bomber, Convair B-24 Liberator, Plastic, Revell, Box, 1/72 Scale . . 20.00
Model Kit, Airplane, Eastern Airlines DC-3, Monogram, Box, 1/48 Scale 30.00
Model Kit, Airplane, Lockheed Lightning, 40-In. Wingspan 50.00
Model Kit, Airplane, WWII Hungarian Stuka Bomber, Plastic, Revell, 1971, 1/32 Scale . . 25.00
Model Kit, Babe Ruth, Sealed Box, Aurora 395.00
Model Kit, Blimp, U.S. Navy, Lighter-Than-Aircraft, Plastic, Ringo, Box, 11 In. 30.00
Model Kit, Car, 1961 Compact Car Customizing Kit, Plastic, AMT Corp., 1/25 Scale 70.00
Model Kit, Car, Lotus Elan, Friction, Bandai, Box, 8 In. 105.00
Model Kit, Frankenstein, Aurora, Box 1895.00
Model Kit, Gladiator With Lion, Box, 1964 . . . . 175.00
Model Kit, Gold Knight Of Nice, Aurora, Box, 1957 . . . . 295.00
Model Kit, Hercules & Lion, Aurora, Box 295.00
Model Kit, Missile, Vought Regulas II U.S. Navy Test Missile, Plastic, Revell, 1958 . . . . . 50.00
Model Kit, Missiles, U.S. Space, Monogram, Mattel, Box, 1969 . . . . 75.00
Model Kit, Phantom Of The Opera, Sealed Box, Aurora 450.00
Model Kit, Robot, Lost In Space, Aurora, Box 795.00
Model Kit, Rocket Launcher, Amphibious, Soviet, Electric Motor, ITC Model Craft, Box . 50.00
Model Kit, Silver Knight Of Augsburg 1560, Plastic, Aurora, 1956, 9 In. 85.00
Model Kit, Spacecraft, Apollo, LEM, Columbia, Box, 1969, 5 x 7 In. 12.00
Model Kit, Upright, Steam Engine, Weeden, Box 100.00
Monkey, Acrobatic Marvel, Windup, Tin Lithograph, Marx, 10 In. 85.00
Monkey, Banjo Playing, Windup, Occupied Japan 100.00
Monkey, Blowing Bubbles, Raises Hand, Battery Operated, Box 195.00
Monkey, Bongo Drums, Battery Operated, Apls, Japan, 9 1/2 In. 150.00
Monkey, Climbing, Tin, Lehmann, Box 130.00
Monkey, Consul The Educated Monkey, Instructions, 5 1/2 x 6 In. 60.00
Monkey, Drummer, Felt, Mohair, Tin, Schuco, Germany, Prewar, 4 1/2 In. 220.00
Monkey, Flipping, Windup, Tin, Linemar, Japan, 4 In. 70.00
Monkey, Frankie, Remote Control, Roller Skates, Rubber, Plush, Japan, Box, 13 In. 170.00
Monkey, Jacko, Does Handstands, Windup, Tin Lithograph, Porter's Outfit, Marx, 5 In. . . 100.00
Monkey, Jolly Jacko, Windup, Combs Hair, Tin, Cloth, C.K., Japan, Box, Prewar, 5 In. . . . 90.00
Monkey, Playing Trumpet, Battery Operated, Cragstan, Box 375.00
Monkey, Playing Violin, Felt, Mohair, Tin, Schuco, Germany, Prewar, 4 1/2 In. 220.00
Monkey, Red Mohair, Metal Face, Felt Ears, Hands & Feet, Schuco, 1930s, 2 1/2 In. 150.00
Monkey, Seated, Clockwork, Red Coat, Blue Pants, Ives, 8 In. 3450.00
Monkey, Swinging, Long-Tailed Monkey Balancing On Pole, Martin, 1908, 9 In. 690.00
Monkey, Walking, Plays Cymbals, Mechanical, Plush, 1920-1930, Japan 175.00
Monkey, With Yo-Yo, Windup, Tin, Brown Plush, Japan, 6 1/2 In. 100.00
Moon Mullins, Wood, Jointed, 5 1/2 In. 44.00
Mortimer Snerd, Windup, Walker, Tin Lithograph, Marc, 1939, 8 1/2 In. 200.00

Mother Goose, Windup, Tin Lithograph, Marx, Box, 1930 .... 1925.00
Motor Scooter, Italian Shape, Luggage Rack, Rubber Tires, Painted Metal, 36 In. 405.00
Motorcycle, Battery Operated, Hasbro, 1971 .... 120.00
Motorcycle, Champion, Rubber Tires, Blue Paint, Hubley, 7 1/4 In. 345.00
Motorcycle, Crash Car, Indian Decal, Fire Hose, Hatchet, 3 Tanks, Hubley, 11 1/2 In. 2970.00
Motorcycle, Curvo 1000, Red Shirt, Brown Pants, Schuco, Box 680.00
Motorcycle, Harley-Davidson, Orange, Twin-Cylinder Engine, Gold Trim, Hubley, 9 In. ... 990.00
Motorcycle, Indian, Civilian Driver, Green, Hubley, 9 In. 6270.00
Motorcycle, Military Police, Friction, Tin Lithograph, Japan, 3 1/2 In. 20.00
Motorcycle, Mirakomat, Windup, 1950, Schuco, No. 1012, Box, 5 1/2 In. 859.00
Motorcycle, Patrol, Cast Iron, Black Rubber Wheels, 6 3/8 In. 90.00
Motorcycle, Policeman Dismounts, Battery, Tin, Modern Toys, Japan, 11 1/2 In. 470.00
Motorcycle, Policeman, Battery Operated, Japan, 12 In. 385.00
Motorcycle, Policeman, Mounts & Dismounts, Battery, Modern Toys, 12 In. 260.00
Motorcycle, Policeman, Red, Aluminum Handlebars, Rubber Tires, Globe, 1930 .... 1320.00
Motorcycle, Rider, Cast Iron, Champion 125.00
Motorcycle, Rider, Curvo 1000, Tin, Schuco, Box, 5 In. 550.00
Motorcycle, Rider, Hill Climber, Blue, Black Gas Tank, Cast Iron, Hubley, 6 1/2 In. 462.00
Motorcycle, Rider, Kilgore, 4 1/4 In. 400.00
Motorcycle, Rider, Orange, Rubber Tires, Cast Iron, Hubley, 6 In. 352.00
Motorcycle, Rrrumblers, Die Cast Metal, Hot Wheels, Mattel, On Card, 1971, 2 3/4 In. .. 30.00
Motorcycle, Sidecar, Battery Operated, Electric Headlight, Red Paint, Hubley, 8 1/2 In. .. 4950.00
Motorcycle, Sidecar, Policeman, Red, 2-Cylinder Engine, Cast Iron, Hubley, 8 In. 935.00
Motorcycle, Sidecar, Policeman, Red, Blue, Rubber Tires, Cast Iron, Champion, 5 In. 440.00
Motorcycle, Sidecar, Policeman, Red, Spoked Wheels, Rubber Tires, Globe, 1930, 9 In. .. 880.00
Motorcycle, Sidecar, Windup, Black Driver, Tonneau Cover, Red Paint, Hubley, 8 1/2 In. . 7700.00
Motorcycle, Windup, Tin Lithograph, Technofix, 7 In. 220.00
Mountain Climber, Mechanical, Lithograph, Box, Marx, Japan, 12 In. 60.00
Movie Theatre, Home Town, Knobs Turn, Bobby & Betty's Trip, Marx, 5 In. 45.00
Mr. Dan Coffee Drinking Man, Raises Coffeepot, Pours, Drinks, Japan, Box 95.00
Mr. Magoo, In Old Car, Box 395.00
Mr. Potato Head, 2nd Version, Box 25.00
Mule, Balky Mule, Pulling Rocking Clown, Lehmann, 7 1/2 In. 132.00
Mule, Balky Mule, Wagon, 2 Mules & Driver, Marx, 1930s 450.00
Mule, Balky Mule, Windup, Tin, Lehmann, Box 550.00
Music Box, Dancing Dude, Mattel 70.00
My Fair Dancer, Battery Operated, Naval Clothes, Tin, Pedestal, Box, 11 In. 225.00
Noah's Ark, 19 Carved Wood Animals, 4 People, 10 In. 375.00
Noah's Ark, 21 Animals, 4 People, Shingled Roof, Wood, 16 In. 1300.00
Noah's Ark, 27 Carved Wood Animals, Noah, Wife & Son, Germany, 9 In. 900.00
Noah's Ark, 38 Carved Wood Animals, Hinged Roof, Noah, Germany, 14 In. 575.00
Noah's Ark, 43 Animals, Noah & Wife, Blue, Orange Striping, Gray Base, 15 In. 700.00
Noah's Ark, 46 Animals & Birds, 3-Story Interior, Stalls & Stairways, England, 1850s ... 9500.00
Noah's Ark, 67 Carved Wood Animals, Shingled Roof, 2 People, Germany, 12 In. 750.00
Noah's Ark, 72 Carved Wood Animals, Hinged Roof, Original Finish, Germany 1100.00
Noah's Ark, Polychrome, Germany, 15 Piece 220.00
Old Woman In A Shoe, Cast Iron, 5 Clothed Bisque Children In Lap, Pull Toy 4400.00
Old Woman In A Shoe, Tin, Pull Toy 2970.00
Organ, Crank, Harmonica Music Box Mechanism, Tin Litho, Wolverine, Box, 10 1/2 In. . 105.00
Organ Grinder, Cranks Organ, Monkey Dances, Windup, Distler, Germany, Prewar, 9 In. . 935.00
Oswald The Rabbit, Ideal, 1930s 295.00
Owl, Woodsy Owl, Hard Vinyl, Movable Head, Arms, Legs, Dakin, Late 1960s, 7 1/2 In. . 45.00
Paddy & Pig, Windup, Tin, Man Riding Pig Covered With Blanket, Lehmann, 6 x 6 In. .. 715.00
Pail, 3 Little Pigs, Chein 295.00
Pail, Black Native Musicians, Tin, France, 1920s 125.00
Pail, Children On Beach, Chein, 1950s, 1 Gal. 30.00
Pail, Spaceman In Cockpit, Shooting Stars, Blue Ground, Ohio Art, 6 1/4 x 6 In. 90.00
Paint Set, Blondie, Tin Lithograph Lid, 1952 .... 50.00
Paint Set, Oil, Frankenstein, Hasbro 2266.00
Panda, Yes-No, Mohair, Amber Crystal Eyes, Jointed Limbs, Schuco, 1950s, 13 In. 2300.00
Parachute Pack, Canvas, Brown, World War II Era, 10 x 14 In. 35.00
Parrot, Repeats Recorded Message, Beak Moves, Battery Operated, Plush, Marx, 18 In. . 155.00
Patrol Wagon, 2 Horses, Red Base With Bell, 3 Riders, Kenton, Cast Iron, 17 In. 165.00

Peacock, Windup, Tin, With Bellows, Germany, 10 x 7 In. 358.00
Pedal Car, American Boy, Wood, Cast-Iron Steering Wheel, Red Paint, Pre-1920, 42 In. .. 1045.00
Pedal Car, American Racer No. 23, 1915 .... 770.00
Pedal Car, Austin J40, Battery Operated Lights & Horn, 1954 .... 4025.00
Pedal Car, Blue Paint, Rubber Wheels, Gendron Wheel Co., 41 In. 1210.00
Pedal Car, BMC, 1960s 375.00
Pedal Car, Buick, Torpedo, Black, Brown Interior, Chrome Trim, Pressed Steel, 39 In. ... 1650.00
Pedal Car, Cadillac, Orange, Black & Silver, Steelcraft, 1928 .... 1980.00
Pedal Car, Champion, Murray, 1955 .... 495.00
Pedal Car, Dump Truck, Ford, 1935 .... 1210.00
Pedal Car, Dump Truck, Mack, 1937 .... 1900.00
Pedal Car, Dump Truck, Mack, Bullnose, License Plate, Horn, Steelcraft, 1926, 63 In. ... 5720.00
Pedal Car, Dump Truck, Sand & Gravel, No. 7, Steel, Rubber Tires, Murray, 23 x 49 In. . 1320.00
Pedal Car, Fire Truck, Ladder, White Walls, Bell, Seagrave, American National, 1920s ... 3600.00
Pedal Car, Fire Truck, Murray 795.00
Pedal Car, Fire Truck, Red, Hinged Hood, Headlights, Electric Horn, Steel Plate, 60 In. .. 2645.00
Pedal Car, Ford, 6000 Commander 1700.00
Pedal Car, Ford, Diesel 5250.00
Pedal Car, Kidillac, Pink & Silver, Spare Tire On Trunk, Decal Dashboard, 34 x 18 In. ... 440.00
Pedal Car, Racing, Fire Ball 450.00
Pedal Car, Roadster, Buick, Spoked Wheels, Sidway-Topliff Co., 1929, 52 In. 3960.00
Pedal Car, Steelcraft, 1924 .... 4750.00
Pedal Car, Steelcraft, 1936 .... 2600.00
Pedal Car, Tandem, Sheet Metal & Wood, Nash, Gendron, Toledo, Ohio, 64 In. 2090.00
Pedal Car, Torpedo, Streamlined Convertible, Maroon, Chrome Trim, 38 In. ..... 690.00 to 1265.00
Pedal Car, Tractor, AMF, Motor Trac, Red, Worn Seat ....*Illus* 100.00
Pedal Car, Tractor, Ford, White 6000.00
Pedal Car, Tractor, John Deere 25000.00
Pedal Car, Tractor, Oliver 4400.00
Pedal Car, Tractor, Tru-Matic 475.00
Pedal Car, Train, Casey Jones, Cannonball Express No. 9, Bell, 42 x 24 In. 440.00
Pencil Case, Barbie, Zippered Opening, Ponytail Barbie, 1963, 8 x 4 In. 200.00
Penguin, Waddles, Windup, Tin, Chein, USA, 4 1/2 In. ....50.00 to 65.00
Pep Rally Gift Set, Barbie, Midge, Ken, Drum Major, Majorette, Cheerleader, 1964 ..... 800.00
Peter Rabbit, Chick-Mobile, Windup, Pumps Handcar On Track, Lionel, 8 1/2 In. 375.00
Phantom Of The Opera, Windup, Universal Monsters, Box, 1967 .... 175.00
Phonograph, Barbie, Vinyl, Plays 16 78-RPM Records, Vanity Fair, 1963, 12 x 5 In. 150.00
Phonograph, Bing Pigmy Phone, Tin, Painted, With Record, Germany, 6 x 6 In. 120.00
Phonograph, Bozo The Clown, Capitol Records, Early 1950s, 10 x 12 In. 55.00
Phonograph, Electric, No. 276, Lindstrom, Box 55.00
Phonograph, Standing, Tootsietoy 250.00
Phonograph Dancers, Boxers Move When Placed On Pin, Record Plays, 1915, 6 x 8 In. . 280.00
Piano, Schoenhut, 32 In. ....155.00 to 200.00
Piano, Upright, 15 Keys, Wood, Lithograph, Flowers, Cherubs, Bliss, c.1900, 16 In. 425.00
Piano, With Stool, 20 x 24 x 11 In. 44.00
Piano Player, Coifed Musician At Keyboard, Tinplate, Martin, 1910, 5 In. 2300.00
Piano Player, Head Turns, Mechanical, Secor, 9 In. 10637.00

Toy, Pedal Car, Tractor, AMF, Motor Trac,
Red, Worn Seat

**Never unplug an electrical cord
by pulling the cord. Always hold
the plastic part of the plug.
Weak cords cause fires.**

Pigs, Wolf, Windup, Tin, Pigs Hold Flute, Violin, Trowel, Linemar, 4 In., 4 Piece 853.00
Pile Driver, Crank Handle Raises Pile-Driver, Cast Iron, Arcade, c.1905, 12 In. 154.00
Playset, Adventure City, Incredible Hulk & Amazing Spider Man 125.00
Playset, Fire Department, No. 5211, Tootsietoy, Box, 10 x 13, 12 Piece 495.00
Playset, Main Street No. 400, Cardboard Village, Skyline Mfg. Co., Box, 1940s 55.00
Playset, Steve Zodiac's Fireball XL5 Space City, Box, 21-In. Spaceship 460.00
Playset, Triple Thingmaker For Girls, Picadoos, Fun Flowers, Zoofie Goofies, Box 145.00
Playset, Waltons, House, Family, Truck, Porch Swing, Milton Bradley, Box, 1974 ...... 65.00
Playset, Western Ranch Set, Trees, Livestock, Fencing, Plastic, Marx, Box 80.00
Playset, Zeroid, Commander Action, Zogg Zeroid, Box 425.00
Policeman, Gendarme Shuffling Forward, Waving Hand, Martin, 1903, 8 In. 1380.00
Polly Ann Knitting Knob, Wood, Box, 1939 .... 50.00
Pool Player, Tin, Clockwork, Gunthermann, 11 In. 440.00
Pool Players, Windup, Tin, Holding Cue Sticks, Ranger USA, 14 In. 150.00
Poor Pete, Dog Nips At Boy With Watermelon, Celluloid, Windup, Japan, 6 1/2 In. 440.00
Porky Pig, Umbrella, Windup, Tin, Marx, Box, 8 1/2 In. 715.00
Porter, Cart, Windup, Tap-Tap, Tin, Lehmann, 7 x 5 1/2 In. ....175.00 to 230.00
Porter, Pushing Cart, Dog In Trunk, Windup, Strauss, 7 1/2 In. 495.00
Porter, Pushing Cart, Windup, Tin, Strauss, 6 In. 205.00
Porter, Shuffling Forward Using Cane, Carrying Large Canvas Sack, 1902, 8 In. 1265.00
Power Shovel, Steel, Marx, Box 250.00
Powerful Katrina, Pushing Cart, Windup, Nifty Co., Germany, 1923, 5 1/2 In. ....825.00 to 880.00
Preacher, Clockwork, Black Man At Podium With Bible, Ives, 9 In. 6040.00
Printing Press, Box, 1960s 30.00
Projector, Viewmaster Jr. 55.00
Pull, Airplane, Keystone Motor, Airmail, Mailbag, 1930s, 24-In. Wingspan 1760.00
Punching Bag, Tony The Tiger, Plastic, 36 In. 75.00
Puppet Stage, Proscenium, Wood, Helen Joseph's Marionettes, 27 In., Box 715.00
Purse, Little Red Riding Hood, c.1930 .... 325.00
Rabbit, Holding Basket, Clockwork, Composition, Metal, Cloth, Germany, 8 In. 675.00
Rabbit, In Hoop, Painted Tin, 1870s, 4 3/4 In. 2530.00
Rabbit, Nicki, Gray & White Mohair, Steiff, 1950s Button, 11 In. 350.00
Rabbit, Seesaw, Sand Toy, Tin Lithograph, Chein, 9 x 8 In. 80.00
Rabbit, Standing, Tawny, Cream Coat, Painted Eyes, 1920, Schoenhut, 4 In. 460.00
Rabbit, Telephone, Battery Operated, Tin, Plush, Masutoko Toys, Japan, Box, 10 In. 150.00
Rabbit, Walking, Windup, Tin Feet, Wood & Felt, 9 In. 800.00
Ramp Walker, Benny The Ball & Top Cat 60.00
Ramp Walker, Chilly Willy 25.00
Ramp Walker, Cowboy On Horse 25.00
Ramp Walker, Kangaroo, With Baby 45.00
Ramp Walker, Nanny Pushing Carriage 20.00
Range, Kitchen, Tin Lithograph, Pink, 4 Burners, Wizard Toy, Wolverine, 11 x 7 x 12 In. . 30.00
Rattle, Baby's, 4 Nickel-Plated Bells, Leatherized Cloth Strap, Turned Handle, 6 In. 150.00
Rattle, Baby's, Bone, 4 Bells, Whistle Handle, 4 In. 165.00
Rattle, Baby's, Molded Rubber, White, Bell Embedded In End, 5 1/8 In. 83.00
Rattle, Baby's, Tin, Boy & Girl, Cat & Dog, Lithograph, 4 1/2 In. 165.00
Rattle, Baby's, Twisted Wire, 4 Bells, Turned Wood Handle, 8 1/4 In. 165.00
Rattle, Bells & Whistles, Coral Teether, 18th Century 895.00
Rattle, Eagle, For A Good Child, Tin, 7 In. 110.00
Record Tote, Barbie, Black, Vinyl, Holds 10 45-RPM Records, Ponytail Tune Tote, 1961 . 30.00
Reindeer, Die Cast Metal, Germany, Prewar, 4 In., 3 Piece 33.00
Rescue Wagon, American La France, Corgi, 11 In. 40.00
Rescue Wagon, Auburn Fire Department, Rubber, Yellow Tires, 1940s, 7 1/2 x 2 1/2 In. .. 20.00
Rickshaw, Masuyama, Windup, Woman Passenger, Lehmann, 7 1/2 In. 632.00
Rickshaw, Woman Passenger, Man In Turban, Windup, 1900, 8 In. 805.00
Ring, Buffalo Bill Jr. 30.00
Ring, Captain Video, Flying Saucer 600.00
Ring, Flasher, 3 Stooges, I'm Moe, Silver Plastic, Vari-Vue, 1960 .... 45.00
Ring, Flicker, Green Hornet 25.00
Ring, Sky King Navaho Treasure, Metal, Simulated Turquoise, 1950s 66.00
Ring Binder, Barbie, White, Vinyl, 3-Ring Notebook, Standard Plastic Products, 1964 ... 300.00
Road Grader, Red, Structo, Box, 18 1/2 In. 305.00
Road Roller, Cast Iron, Wood Roller, 3 1/2 In. 65.00

Toy, Robot, Gear,
Windup, Yoshiya,
10 In.

Toy, Robot, High
Wheel, Windup,
Yoshiya, 10 In.

Toy, Robot, Mr. Robot,
Mechanical Brain, Battery
Operated, Yonezawa, Alps, 12 In.

Toy, Robot, Robby,
Battery Operated,
Mechanized, Box, 13 1/2 In.

Road Scraper, Yellow, Silver Scraper, Rubber Tires, Hubley, Box, 10 In. 165.00
Robot, Answer Game Machine, Battery Operated, Green Body, Tin, 14 1/2 In. 550.00
Robot, Astronaut, Gold Cover, Swivel-O-Matic 450.00
Robot, Astronaut, Windup, Rolls Along, Propeller On Top Of Head Spins, Box, 6 In. 22.00
Robot, Frankenstein, Battery Operated, Marx 1595.00
Robot, Gear Chest, Silver, Gray, 2 Antennas On Shoulders, Red Shoes, Tin, Japan, 11 In. . 165.00
Robot, Gear, Windup, Yoshiya, 10 In. . . . . *Illus* 137.00
Robot, High Wheel, Windup, Yoshiya, 10 In. . . . . *Illus* 302.00
Robot, Lost In Space, Aurora, Box 795.00
Robot, Machine Guns In Chest, Battery Operated, Tin Lithograph, Japan, 1950s, 11 In. . . 335.00
Robot, Missile, Windup, Plastic, Japan, 5 In. 60.00
Robot, Mr. Atom, Walking, Red, Gray Plastic, Advance Doll & Toy Co., Box, 18 In. 495.00
Robot, Mr. Robot, Mechanical Brain, Battery Operated, Yonezawa, Alps, 12 In. . . . . *Illus* 17600.00
Robot, Remo-Con, Battery Operated, Box 95.00
Robot, Robby, Battery Operated, Mechanized, Box, 13 1/2 In. . . . . *Illus* 605.00
Robot, Rock-Em Sock-Em, Marx, Box, 1966 . . . . 110.00
Robot, Silver, 2 Gun Barrels, Large Red Shoes, Tin, Japan, 16 In. 605.00
Robot, Smoking Engine, See-Through Piston Action, Japan, Box 175.00
Robot, Space Scout, Secret Weapon . . . . .475.00 to 550.00
Robot, Spaceman, Tin Lithograph, Space Rifle, Japan, Early 1950s 800.00
Robot, Super Astronaut, Battery Operated, Tin, Box 265.00
Robot, Super, Battery Operated, Dark Gray, Large Red Shoes, Tin, Japan, 11 1/2 In. 138.00
Robot, Tomy Omnibot 130.00
Robot, Video, Walking, Tin, Japan 175.00
Rocket Gun, Star Trek, Desilu, Remco, 1967 . . . . 1495.00
Rocket Ship, Indian Army Supersonic Jet, Windup, Tin, Rubber Tip, India, 1950s, 9 In. . . 44.00
Rocket Ship, Space Frontier, Battery, Tin, Plastic Nose Cone, Japan, Box, 18 In. 155.00
Rocket Ship, X-9 Rocket, Friction, Tin Lithograph, Tail Fins, Modern Toys, Japan, 4 In. . . 275.00
Roller, Chimes To Tinkle, Push Toy c.1870 . . . . 950.00
Roller Coaster, 2 Cars, Chein, Box 590.00
Roller Coaster, Coney Island, Technofix, Germany, Box, 22 x 15 In. 395.00
Roller Coaster, Tin, With Track, Wolverine, 1930s, 21 In. 275.00
Roller Coaster, Windup, Tin Lithograph, Chein, 1950s 145.00
Roller Skates, Case, 1950s 50.00
Rollo-Chair, Atlantic City, Windup, Black Man, Pushing 3-Wheeled Cart, 1910, 6 In. . . . 920.00
Roly Poly, Clown, 8 In. 745.00
Roly Poly, Worker, Running Punch Machine, Tin, 4 1/4 x 3 1/4 x 4 1/2 In. 100.00
Rooster, Pip-Squeak, In Cage, Felt, Wood, 10 1/4 In. 190.00
Rooster, Pip-Squeak, Papier-Mache With Gesso, 9 1/2 In. 165.00
Rooster, Pulling Egg Cart, Rabbit On Top, Windup, Tin, Lehmann, Duo, 7 In. 578.00
Rooster, Windup, Mohair White Coat, Red Felt Comb, Glass Eyes, Tin, 6 3/4 In. 275.00
Rooster & Hen, In Cage, Pip-Squeak, Wood, Papier-Mache, Tin Wheels, Germany, 8 In. . 110.00
Sadiron, Trivet, Removable Handle 38.00

Sailor, Dancing, Blue Cloth Uniform, Swaying, Staggering, Lehmann, 1930 . . . . 1075.00
Sailor, Dancing, Windup, Hat Says S.M.S. Brandenburg, Tin, Lehmann, Box, 7 1/2 In. . . . 1045.00
Sand Sifter, Ohio Art 200.00
Satellite, Space Patrol, Battery, Tin, Green, Amico, Modern Toys, Japan, Box, 8 In. 180.00
Satellite Jumping Shoes, Rapaport Bros., Box, 1950s 150.00
School Slate, Paperboard Covers, Blue & Black Design, Birch Frame, 1800s, 11 x 8 In. . . 70.00
Schoolbag, Barbie, Blue, Black Plastic Trim, Standard Plastic Products, 1963, 11 x 9 In. . . 350.00
Schoolboy, Calculator, Standing In Front Of Blackboard, Tinplate, Tipp & Co., 8 In. 4600.00
Schoolhouse, Barbie & Skipper, Fold Up, 6-Sided Carrying Case, 1965, Mattel 300.00
Scissors Grinder, Windup, Tin Litho, Articulated Figure, Germany, 1920s, 5 1/2 In. 115.00
Scooter, 2 Pedals, 3 Wheels, Red Paint, Gold Trim, 1930s 175.00
Scooter, Zephyr, Red, Silver Highlights, Nickel Handlebars, Cast Iron, Williams, 4 In. . . . 770.00
Seal, With Ball On Stand, Steiff 85.00
Searchlight, Army, Mobile, Marx, 12 In. 55.00
Seesaw, On Housetop, Tinplate Roof Swinging Back & Forth, Wood, Ives, 1875, 10 In. . . 6900.00
Sewing Machine, Baby, Cast Iron, Chrome, Handle, Patent 1894 . . . . 165.00
Sewing Machine, Clamp On, Soezy, 1901 . . . . 2100.00
Sewing Machine, Holly Hobby 40.00
Sewing Machine, Jaymar 60.00
Sewing Machine, Little Comfort Automatic Hand Sewing Machine, 1897 . . . . 520.00
Sewing Machine, Miller, Germany 190.00
Sewing Machine, Necchi, Supermova, Plastic 45.00
Sewing Machine, Red Riding Hood, Germany 140.00
Sewing Machine, Sears Zigzag 100.00
Sewing Machine, Singer, No. 20, Box, Instructions, 1948 . . . . 190.00
Sewing Machine, Singer, Sew Handy, Box, 1955 . . . . 115.00
Sewing Machine, Stitch Mistress 76.00
Sewing Machine, Stitchwell, Cast Iron, Instructions, Wood Box 550.00
Sewing Machine, Tin, Germany, 8 In. 55.00
Sheep, Leather Ears, Glass Eyes, Schoenhut, 8 In. 495.00
Sheik, On Camel, Trudging Forward, Neck Sways Side To Side, Martin, 1895, 8 In. 1150.00
Sheriff Sam, Windup, Marx 150.00
Shoeshine Boy, Brushing A Shoe On Blacking Box, Martin, 1898, 5 1/4 In. 2300.00
Shooting Gallery, Carnival, Windup, Tin, Box 121.00
Shooting Gallery, Steel Lithograph, Windup, Wyandotte, 11 In. 66.00
Shooting Gallery, Windup, Wyandotte 295.00
Shovel, Yogi Bear, Red, Yellow, Hard Vinyl, 1960s-1970s, 26 In. 25.00
Signalscope, Sky King 50.00
Ski Jump, Sun Valley, Paper On Wood, Wood Skier, Wolverine, 26 In. 110.00
Ski Jumper, U.S.A., Wolverine, Tin, 26 In. 175.00
Skier, 2-Piece Blue Suit, Lehmann, 1936, 7 1/2 In. 3740.00
Skittles Set, Animals, Steiff, c.1913 . . . . *Illus* 17250.00
Skunk, Pepe Le Pew, You're A Real Stinker, Plastic, Vinyl, Dakin, Late 1960s, 7 In. 30.00
Sky Rangers, Airship & Airplane Rotate Around Tower, Tin Litho, Unique Art, 1930 . . . . 390.00

Toy, Skittles Set, Animals, Steiff, c.1913

Slave Family Set, Hubley 650.00
Sled, Central Lake Landscape, Black Borders, Iron Rungs, Early 19th Century 190.00
Sled, Chestnut, Iron, 40 In. 110.00
Sled, Child's, Built Up Sides, Wood, Handle 325.00
Sled, Child's, Red, Gilt & Black Seat Section, 19th Century, 30 In. 248.00
Sled, Child's, White Star, Paris, 19th Century, 40 In. 330.00
Sled, Floral Bouquet, Salmon Platform, 36 In. 600.00
Sled, Marked Christmas, 1898 .... 595.00
Sled, Sno-Plane, 3 Rudders, Patent Documentation 225.00
Sled, Wood Slats, Metal Edged Runners, 1920-1930 .... 110.00
Sled, Wood, Bentwood Runners, Lake & Mountain Landscape Stencil, 40 In. 385.00
Sled, Wood, Metal Runners, Red, Green, Floral Design, Hand Painted, 33 x 12 In. 575.00
Sled, Wood, Metal-Tipped Runners, Francis P. Drake, 37 In. 55.00
Sled, Yellow Striping, Black Stenciled Lion, Spider Web, Wood, 36 In. 247.00
Sleigh, Doll's, Red Paint, Yellow Striping, Design 275.00
Sleigh, Push, Doll's, Red & Black Paint, Upholstered Seat, Victorian, 36 In. 395.00
Sleigh, Upward Curved Seat Both Ends, Serpents'-Head Legs, 49 1/4 In. 1725.00
Sleigh, Wood, Black & Yellow Paint, Pinstripes, Late 1800s, 32 In. 1430.00
Sleigh, Wood, Iron, Green Paint, Red Interior, 32 In. 220.00
Slinky, Pop-Up, James Ind., Box, 1960s 50.00
Smitty, On Scooter, 3-Wheeled Scooter, Marx, 1930, 8 In. 2300.00
Smoking Grandpa, Battery Operated, Marusan, 7 1/2 In. 45.00
Snoopy, Astronaut, Domed Space Helmet, Flight Safety Kit, Orange Scarf, Plastic, 9 In. .. 250.00
Snoopy, In Tuxedo, Vinyl 50.00
Snoopy, On Skateboard, Plastic, Aviva, 1966, 2 1/2 x 1 1/2 x 4 In. 30.00
Snoopy, Peanuts, Vinyl, Painted, Hungerford, 1950s, 7 1/2 In. 165.00
Snoopy, Plush Ears, Poseable, Molded Plastic, Determined Productions, 1966, 8 In. 22.00
Snoopy, White Sweater, Blue Jeans, Tennis Shoes, Soft Rubber, 3 3/4 In. 20.00
Snoopy, Woodstock On Lap, Ears Rotate, Plastic, Pull Toy, Hasbro, 8 In. 25.00
Snoopy, WWI Flying Ace, Brown Helmet, Blue Scarf, 1966, Molded Plastic, 7 1/4 In. ... 70.00
Snoopy, WWI Flying Ace, Brown Helmet, Goggles, Molded Plastic, Hong Kong, 7 In. ... 40.00
Soldier, 9 Wood Soldiers, Cannon, Turned Parts, Polychrome Paint, 6 In., 10 Piece 127.00
Soldier, Artillery Observer, Kneeling, German Outfit, Lineol, 2 3/4 In. 20.00
Soldier, Bicycle Dispatch Rider, Die Cast Metal, Manoil, U.S.A., 1950s, 3 In. 44.00
Soldier, Boer War, Soldier With Raised Rifle, Brown Outfit, Hat, Martin, 8 In. 1150.00
Soldier, Cavalry & Infantry, U.S., Rifles, Tent With Flag, Heyde, Box, 1880s, 53 Piece ... 517.00
Soldier, Cavalry & Infantry, U.S., Spanish-American War, Heyde, Box, c.1890, 12 Piece . 373.00
Soldier, Civil War, Lead, Johillco, 26 Piece 95.00
Soldier, Coldstream Guards, Britains, 21 Piece 550.00
Soldier, Drummer, Windup, Wolverine, 1930s 190.00
Soldier, German Infantry, Backpack, 3 In. 15.00
Soldier, Highlanders, Bagpipes, Die Cast Metal, England, 1950s, 1 1/2 In., 7 Piece 33.00
Soldier, Infantry, American, Heyde, Box, c.1900, 21 Piece 373.00
Soldier, Infantry, WWI, Gas Mask, Throwing Grenade, Die Cast Metal, Manoil, 3 1/4 In. . 30.00
Soldier, New York 7th Regiment, Cannon, Ives, Box 110.00
Soldier, On Base, Legs Move, Wood, Tin, Pull Toy, Ted Toy, Mass., 4 x 8 x 10 In. 45.00
Soldier, Russian, 2 Officers, 2 Standing, Drummer, 13 Infantry, Heyde, Box, 1870s 315.00
Soldier, Stony Smith, Action Figure, Marx, Box 225.00
Soldier, Tenpins, Paper Soldiers, Wood Cannon, McLoughlin Bros., N.Y., Box 90.00
Soldier, Tommy Gunner, WWI, Die Cast Metal, Manoil, 3 In. 25.00
Soldier, Vehicle Pulling Bomb, Die Cast Metal, Manoil, U.S.A., 1950s 55.00
Space Capsule, Friendship 7, Allen Shephard Seated Inside, Tin, 9 In. 110.00
Space Capsule, Friendship 7, Friction, Tin, Early 1960s, SH, Japan, 10 In. 150.00
Space Port, Captain Video, Tin Lithograph, Superior, 1950s 250.00
Spaceman Equipment, Moon McDare, Binoculars, Compass, Gilbert, 1965, 6 x 8 In. 18.00
Spaceship, Mystery Spaceship, Marx, Box, Instructions 125.00
Spaceship, Solar-X7, Battery Operated, Tin Lithograph, Plastic Nose Cone, Japan, 16 In. . 130.00
Spark Plug, Moon Mullins, Wood, Jointed, Horse, Twine Tail, Schoenhut, 1922 .... 413.00
Spark Plug, Windup, Rears Back & Forth, Rocking, Tin, Nifty, Germany, 1922, 7 In. 825.00
Sparkler, Amos & Andy, Glass Eyes, 1930, 6 1/2 In. 500.00
Sparkler, Amos & Andy, Tin, 1930, 6 1/2 In. 880.00
Spic & Span The Hams What Am, Windup, Tin Lithograph, Marx, 9 3/4 In. 1815.00
Sprite, Talking, Battery Operated, Vinyl, Box 35.00

Stable, Painted Wood, 47 x 32 In. 578.00
Steam Engine, Corliss, Scale Model, 22 1/4 In. 3850.00
Steam Shovel, 220, Black With Red Corrugated Roof, Buddy L, 14 In. 115.00
Sticker Book, Barbie & Ken, Whitman, 1962 .... 20.00
Stork, On Platform, Red Beak, Legs, Tin, Germany, 2 3/4 In. 358.00
Stove, Buck's Stove & Range Co., Buck's Junior, 19 In. 1155.00
Stove, Cast Iron, Tin, Kenton Royal, 6 x 3 1/2 In. 40.00
Stove, Crescent On Door, Cast Iron, Accessories 110.00
Stove, Doll's, Roxbury, 1867, 4 Burners & Oven, Bella Gibby, Cast Iron, 8 In. 115.00
Stove, Eagle, Cast Iron, Tin, Coal Pail, Pan, Shovel, Hubley, 3 1/2 x 4 1/2 In. 33.00
Stove, Electric, 1930s, 8 x 8 In. 145.00
Stove, Electric, 4 Burner Knobs, Lionel 825.00
Stove, Empire, Electric, 15 x 15 In. 795.00
Stove, Gas, 2 Burners, A.C. Williams, 4 1/2 In. 40.00
Stove, Gas, Superior 22.00
Stove, Heating, Salesman's Sample, Anodized Sheet Metal, Iron, 1920s-1930s, 11 x 8 In. . 360.00
Stove, Libertas, Cast Iron, 6 x 7 x 11 In. 365.00
Stove, Novelty, Sheet Metal, Cast Iron, Kenton, Utensils, 12 x 14 In. 550.00
Stove, Queen, Pots 35.00
Stove, Royal, Red, Cast Iron, 4 In. 65.00
Stove, Salesman's Sample, Marked Rival S, Pat. July 5, 1895, Reservoir, 12 x 14 In. 125.00
Stove, Suzy Homemaker, Topper Toys, 1960s, 19 x 12 x 10 In. 30.00
Street Sweeper, Battery Operated, Tin, Nylint, 8 In. 75.00
Street Vendor, Windup, Cast Figure Pushing Cart, Tin, Creation Toys, Paris, Box, 6 In. .. 360.00
Street Vendor, Windup, Woman Pushing Cart, Cast Iron, Painted, Martin, 6 In. 580.00
Streetcar, Elec-Traction, Birney Type, Plastic, General Models, Box, 6 In. 50.00
Streetcar, Horse Drawn, 12 In. 330.00
Streetcar, Horse Drawn, Cast Iron, Broadway Car Line, Wilkins 2200.00
Streetcar, Horse Drawn, Cast Iron, Consolidated Street R.R., Wilkins 4620.00
Strongman, Lifting Barbells, Weights, Martin, 1905, 7 In. 9490.00
Strutting Sam, Black Tap Dancer, Tin, Battery Operated, 11 In. 350.00
Submarine, Electro Submarino, Battery Operated, Tin, Schuco, Instructions, Box, 12 In. . 325.00
Sulky, Driver, Green, Yellow & Blue Paint, Cast Iron, Dent, 5 1/4 In. 88.00
Swan, Seated, Wheeled Platform, White Body, Red Beak, Tin, Germany 825.00
Sweeping, Woman, Windup, Tin Lithograph & Paint, 6 1/2 In. 550.00
Sweeping Betty, Windup, Tin Lithograph, Lindstrom, 7 In. 155.00
Sweeping Woman, Swaying Left & Right With Broom, Windup, 1895, 7 In. 3325.00
Swinging Doll, Bisque, Cloth Dress, Seated, Lehmann, Box, 1895, 7 In. 6960.00
Table, Doll's, Bronze, Marble Top, Floral Medallion, Cherubs, France, c.1875, 6 In. 800.00
Table, Doll's, Drop Leaf, Sheraton, 19th Century, 2 6-In. Leaves, 18 x 19 x 11 1/2 In. 467.00
Table & Chairs, Doll's, Mahogany, Dark Red, Gilt, Schoenhut, 8 3/4 x 6 1/2 In. 135.00
Tailor, Living Picture, 3 Men Hard At Work, Shadowbox Frame, Schoenhut, 1895, 13 In. . 1265.00
Tam Tam, Space Vehicle Feeds Down Spiral Metal Rod, Tin, Lehmann, 3 x 10 In. 132.00
Tank, Bulldog, Remco, Box 125.00
Tank, Combat, Battery Operated, Box, 1970s 185.00
Tank, Doughboy, Windup, Animated Sharpshooter & Flag, Tin, Marx, 9 1/2 In. 140.00
Tank, Japan, Prewar 325.00
Tank, M-105, Battery Operated, Tin Lithograph, WACO, Japan, Box, 4 1/2 In. 95.00
Tank, M-15, Tin Lithograph, Olive Drab Green Paint, Japan, 3 1/4 In. 20.00
Tank, Rollover, Super-X, X-81, Windup, Tin Litho, Khaki, Hero Toys, Japan, 3 1/2 In. ... 70.00
Tank, Turnover, Jetsons, Tin, China, 1960s, 4 3/4 x 3 1/2 In. 165.00
Tank, Windup, Doughboy Inside, Marx, 1930, 10 In. 175.00
Tank, Windup, Metal, U.S. Zone Germany, 3 In. 95.00
Target, Dragnet, Knickerbocker, 1955, 11 x 13 In. 55.00
Target Board, U.S. Air Force, Airplanes, N.Y. Toy & Game Mfg. Co., 1940s, 17 1/2 In. .. 18.00
Target Set, Happy Hooligan, Cardboard Lithograph, Wood Gun, Milton Bradley, 1925 ... 305.00
Taxi, Andy Gard, Yellow, Remote Control, Box, 1940s, 10 In. 250.00
Taxi, Businessman's Cab, Cast Iron, Black, White, Arcade, 8 In. 1155.00
Taxi, Hansom, Clockwork, Tin Lithograph, 8 In. 575.00
Taxi, Seated Driver, Yellow Body, Black Roof, Tin, Germany, 7 In. 1760.00
Taxi, Sedan, 4-Door, Yellow, Black, Cast Iron, Driver, Spare Tire, Arcade, 9 In. ...345.00 to 440.00
Taxi, Yellow Cab, Arcade, 5 In. 580.00
Taxi, Yellow Cab, Black, Disc Wheels, Cast Iron, Arcade, 5 1/4 In. ....308.00 to 580.00

Taxi, Yellow Cab, Limousine, Nickel-Plated Wheels, Decal, Arcade, 8 1/2 In. 690.00
Taxi, Yellow Cab, Orange & Black, Driver, Iron, Arcade, 9 x 4 1/2 In. 743.00
Taxi, Yellow Cab, Sedan, 4-Door, Cast Iron, Arcade, 8 In. 303.00
Taxi, Yellow Cab, Windup, Maine License 6525, Tin, 6 In. 100.00
Taxi, Yellow Cab, Windup, Steerable Front End, Chein, 6 In. 187.00
Tea Set, Doll's, Porcelain, Floral Design, Carmen, Germany, c.1890, 10 Piece 125.00
Teddy Bears are also listed in the Teddy Bear category.
Teddy Roosevelt, Schoenhut 1595.00
Tenpins, Cannon & Artillery Set, Ives, Box 355.00
Tent, Soldier's, Company C, Crossed Rifles, White Fabric, World War II Era, 7 x 6 In. 30.00
Thresher, McCormick Deering, Cast Iron 795.00
Tidy Tim, Man Pushing Wheel Barrel, Tin Lithograph, Marx, 8 1/2 x 7 1/2 In. 995.00
Tiger, Molly Jungtiger, Steiff, 19 In. 165.00
Tiger, Windup, Tin Lithograph, Rubber Tail, Wheels, Marx, Japan, 6 In. 55.00
Tip-Top, Windup, Strauss 110.00
Toaster, Sunnie Miss, Ohio Art 30.00
Tool Box, Wood, Gilbert Toys, 1940s, 21 x 8 1/2 In. 98.00
Tool Box, Wood, Handles, Buddy L, 23 In. 40.00
Top, Sleepy Teddy, Ohio Art 55.00
Top, Snoopy, Peanuts Characters, Tin Lithograph, Plunger Action, Ohio Art, 5 1/2 In. 20.00
Top, Wood & Metal, Des Moines Jobbers & Mfg. 5.00
Tractor, & Dump Trailer, Allis Chalmers, Arcade, 1937, 12 3/4 In. 220.00
Tractor, & Dump Trailer, Arcade, Box 2200.00
Tractor, & Earth Hauler, Ford, Arcade 1100.00
Tractor, Boy & Dog, Bell, Fisher-Price, No. 240 .... 70.00
Tractor, Bulldozer, Marx, Box 3225.00
Tractor, Cast Iron, Green Paint, 4 In. 85.00
Tractor, Caterpillar, Windup, Rubber Track, 1930s 150.00
Tractor, Climbing, Windup, Marx, 1930s, 8 1/2 In. 175.00
Tractor, Climbing, Windup, Red, Yellow, Tin Lithograph, Rubber Track, Marx, Box, 8 In. 88.00
Tractor, Corn Planter, Windup, Orange Plastic, Silver Grill, Tin Plate, Max 50.00
Tractor, Diesel, Reversible, Metal Wheels, Driver, Plastic Body, 1950s, 10 In. 90.00
Tractor, Driver, Clockwork, Black Rubber Tires, Pot Metal, 5 In. 55.00
Tractor, Farm, Blue, Cast Iron, Arcade, 4 In. 66.00
Tractor, Farm, Red, Rubber Tires, Yellow Hubs, Hubley, Box, 7 In. ....110.00 to 165.00
Tractor, Farm, Red, Silver Grill, Rubber Tires, Die Cast, Hubley, Box, 9 1/2 In. 110.00
Tractor, Farm, Red, Steerable, Rubber Spoke Wheels, Hubley, Box, 9 In. 220.00
Tractor, Farmall, Green Rubber Wheels, Lincoln Toys 125.00
Tractor, Flatbed, Carrying Small Green Farm Tractor, Die Cast, Hubley, Box, 10 In. 275.00
Tractor, Fordson, Man, Arcade, 1920s 375.00
Tractor, Friction, Wide Front, 3 x 5 In. 20.00
Tractor, Front Bucket, Orange, Hubley 150.00
Tractor, Green Acres, Eddie Albert & Eva Gabor On Box, 1965 .... 75.00
Tractor, Hubley, 1950s 190.00
Tractor, Lawn, John Deere, Orange & White, Box 300.00
Tractor, Loader, Orange, Silver Scoop Does Up & Down, Rubber Tires, Hubley 165.00
Tractor, Rider, Cast Iron, Arcade, 1940s, 4 In. 95.00
Tractor, Tin, Nickel Finish, Lindstrom, 12 In. 125.00
Tractor, Woodhaven, Windup, Blade On Front, 1916, 8 In. 175.00
Trail Wagon, Seated Driver, Blue, Yellow Cast-Iron Spoked Wheels, Pressed Steel, 11 In. . 110.00
Trailer, Farm & Horse, Blue, Tonka 250.00
Trailer, Red, Silver Grill, Fenders, Die Cast, Hubley, Box, 14 In. 248.00
Train, American Flag & Post, Die Cast, Blue With Gold Shield, Old Glory 660.00
Train, American Flyer, No. 977, Caboose, Brakeman Moves 35.00
Train, Bassett-Lowe, No. 513, Locomotive, Tender, 2 Gauge 4620.00
Train, Boxcar, Erie, Steel, Corrugated Sides & End, 12 In. 33.00
Train, Buddy L, Cattle Car, Pressed Steel, 21 In. ....360.00 to 410.00
Train, Buddy L, No. 3017, Caboose, Red, Pressed Steel, 18 1/2 In. 495.00
Train, Buddy L, No. 35407, Boxcar, Red, Pressed Steel, Doors Slide Open, 21 In. 385.00
Train, Buddy L, Tank Car, Pressed Steel, 21 In. 385.00
Train, Express, Technofix Mountain, Windup, Tin, Cable Car, Box, U.S. Zone Germany .. 75.00
Train, Gunthermann, Locomotive, Floor Model, 1890s 2000.00
Train, Hubley, Locomotive, Windup, Cast Iron 2500.00

Train, Huffy Puffy, Fisher-Price, No. 999 . . . . 50.00
Train, Lionel, Electric Engine, O Gauge, Box, 6 3/4 In. 70.00
Train, Lionel, Engine, Santa Fe, Electric, Gray & Red, Gold Striping 660.00
Train, Lionel, No. X2454, Boxcar, Baby Ruth, Orange 30.00
Train, Marklin, No. E921, Clockwork 2365.00
Train, Maxwell Hemmens, Locomobile, Steam Engine 53441.00
Train, No. 4010, Tank Car, AF Lines Air Service, Yellow, Railing, Platform, Box . . . 1540.00
Train, No. 4019, Locomotive, 0-4-0, Tin Lithograph, Maroon, Box 1430.00
Train, No. 4696, Locomotive, Die Cast, Black, Electric, Light On Front, Box 1320.00
Train, Reed, Hercules Atlantic & Pacific, Wood, Stencil, 46 In., 3 Piece 1320.00
Train, Reed, Mother Goose, Jack & Jill Wood Locomotive, Children, Playing, 1890 . . . . . 1380.00
Train, Reed, Palace Car & American Locomotive, Wood, Stenciled, Pat. 1877, 32 In. 440.00
Train, Ride-On, Erie, Steerable Front, Pressed Steel, Steelcraft, 30 In. 155.00
Train Accessories, Derrick, Standard Gauge, Lionel, 1926 . . . . 300.00
Train Accessories, Gate Man, Automatic, Lionel 33.00
Train Accessories, Hellgate Bridge, Lionel, 28 In. 3960.00
Train Accessories, Lamppost, Metal, Lionel, 6 1/2 In. 20.00
Train Accessories, Railroad Station, Glass Dome, Ives 1694.00
Train Accessories, Railroad Station, Grand Central Station, Ives 8800.00
Train Accessories, Railroad Station, Lionel, Box, 4 Piece 750.00
Train Accessories, Railroad Station, Lithograph Roof, Ives 978.00
Train Case, Skipper & Skooter, Vinyl, Zipper, Standard Plastic Product, 1965, 10 In. 20.00
Train Set, American Flyer, Locomotive, 3 Coaches, Maroon, Brass Trim Windows, Tin . . 715.00
Train Set, American Flyer, Locomotive, 3 Passenger Cars, O Gauge, 1932 . . . . 450.00
Train Set, American Flyer, No. 2, Engine, 2 Coaches, c.1907 . . . . 4620.00
Train Set, American Flyer, No. 4687, President's Special, Box, 1927 . . . . .3190.00 to 7700.00
Train Set, American Flyer, Orange Locomotive, 3 Coaches, Tin 660.00
Train Set, American Flyer, Tender, 3 Passenger Cars, O Gauge 425.00
Train Set, Battery Operated, Japan, Box, 1950s, 10 1/2 In. 95.00
Train Set, Bing, Freight & Locomotive, Tin Lithograph, 5 Piece 320.00
Train Set, Buddy L, Engine, Tender, Black Paint, 29-In. Engine, 17-In. Tender 910.00
Train Set, Buddy L, Industrial, Pressed Steel, Tracks, 5 Piece 523.00
Train Set, Chicago Limited, 2 Pullman Cars, Children's Faces At Window, 48 In. 4600.00
Train Set, Engine, First, Second & Third Class Cars, Japan, Box, c.1920, 10 1/2 In. 240.00
Train Set, Flintstones, Battery Operated, Plastic, Empire Toys, Box, 1979 . . . . 100.00
Train Set, Flying Colonel, No. 4686, Locomotive, 2 Passenger Cars, Observation Car . . . 2420.00
Train Set, Hubley, Pennsylvania Lines, Locomotive, 3 Passenger Cars, Cast Iron, 35 In. . . . 231.00
Train Set, Ives, Locomotive, Chair Car, Windup, Tin Lithograph 230.00
Train Set, Ives, Major Seagraves Special, Copper Flash, Nickel-Plated Roofs, O Gauge . . 6270.00
Train Set, Ives, No. 1, Harvard, Yale, Baggage Car, Box 9900.00
Train Set, Ives, No. 6, Locomotive, Tender, 3 Cars, Tin, Track 275.00
Train Set, Ives, No. 11, Locomotive, Tender, Tin Lithograph 1072.00
Train Set, Ives, No. 1694, Engine, 3 Passenger Cars, Beige & Red 6820.00
Train Set, Kingsbury, Tin Tender, 3 Passenger Cars 225.00
Train Set, Lionel, Blue Comet, Standard Gauge 6500.00
Train Set, Lionel, Locomotive, 2 Pullman Cars, Observatory, 4 Piece 66.00
Train Set, Lionel, Locomotive, 3 Passenger Cars, Standard Gauge, 1924 . . . . 375.00
Train Set, Lionel, No. 148, Engine, 3 Cars, Track, Box, 13 In. 715.00
Train Set, Lionel, No. 224E, Engine, Coal Car, Metal, Plastic, O Gauge 105.00
Train Set, Lionel, No. 294, Engine, Pullmans, Observation Car, Coal Car, Box 385.00
Train Set, Lionel, No. 318E, Engine No. 309, Passenger Car, Mail Car, Observation Car . 825.00
Train Set, Lionel, No. 400E, Locomotive, Tender, Crackle Blue & Dark Blue, 1930s 1100.00
Train Set, Lionel, No. 2025, Locomotive, Transformer, 50 Pieces Of Track, Switches 155.00
Train Set, Lionel, Yellow Diesel Engine, 4 Cars, Transformer, Track 95.00
Train Set, Marx, Locomotive, Tender, 4 Cars, Box 374.00
Train Set, Milton Bradley, Hercules Locomotive, Brown, Green Tender, Wood Coaches . . 3220.00
Train Set, No. 4678, Eagle, Locomotive, Passenger Car, Tin Lithograph, Box 1980.00
Train Set, No. 4678, Hamiltonian, Locomotive 4340, Club 4341, Pullman 4342 . . . . 1650.00
Train Set, No. 4696, Die Cast, Black Locomotive, Tender, Yellow Tank Car, Box 1870.00
Train Set, TN, Cable, Electric, Japan, Box, 1950s 125.00
Train Set, W.T. Fey, Portland Terminal, Steam Engine, Tender 825.00
Transport, Army, With Cannon, Buddy L, Box 325.00
Travel Case, Barbie & Midge, Black, Vinyl, Silhouettes, 1963, 10 x 6 In. 35.00

Some repairs make the sale of an
antique very difficult, if not impossible.
Don't buff pewter. Don't wash ivory.
Don't repaint old toys. Don't tape old
paper. Don't wash oil paintings.

Toy, Trolley, Toonerville,
Fontaine Fox, Windup,
Tin Lithograph, 1922

Travel Case, Barbie, Black, Vinyl, Round, Standard Plastic Products, 1962, 10 x 11 In. 60.00
Travel Trunk, Barbie & Skipper, Vinyl, Double, Pictures, Barbie, Ken, Skipper, 1965 . . . . 175.00
Tree, Spooky Kooky, Brown, Eyes & Limbs Move, Battery Operated, Whistling, 14 In. . . 770.00
Tricycle, Child Riding, Clockwork, France, 1890, 9 In. 3835.00
Tricycle, Child Riding, Clockwork, Stevens & Brown, 1870 . . . . 2750.00
Tricycle, Cyclist, Kiddy, Windup, Unique 395.00
Tricycle, Cyclist, Windup, Tin, Jointed, Saalheimer & Strauss, Germany, c.1930, 8 1/2 In. . 3410.00
Tricycle, Kiddie Cyclist, Windup, Boy, Sailor Suit, Tin Lithograph, 8 3/4 In. 165.00
Tricycle, Man Riding, Clockwork, Hand Painted Features, Goatee, 10 In. 5110.00
Tricycle, Wilma Flintstone, Celluloid, Linemar, Japan, 1962, 4 1/2 In. . . . . .200.00 to 355.00
Troll, Devil, 1960s, 7 In. 100.00
Trolley, Broadway 270, Tin Lithograph, J. Chein & Co., 8 1/4 In. 100.00
Trolley, Broadway Line, Horse Drawn, Iron, Wilkins, 1890s, 14 In. 715.00
Trolley, Hand-Painted Yellow Body, Black Roof, 2 Gauge 3025.00
Trolley, Horse Drawn, Painted Tin, Wm. Darker Jr., West Phila., Penna. 6050.00
Trolley, Suburban, No. 810, Ives, Box 7920.00
Trolley, Toonerville, Cast Iron, Red, Box, 5 1/2 In. 605.00
Trolley, Toonerville, Fontaine Fox, Windup, Tin Lithograph, 1922 . . . . *Illus* 660.00
Trolley, Windup, Standing Conductor, Tin, Germany, 6 In. 565.00
Trombone Player, Windup, Tin Lithograph, Linemar, Japan, 4 1/2 In. 150.00
Truck, Airmail, Black Cab, Red Body, Pressed Steel, Buddy L, 23 In. 1870.00
Truck, Camper, Friction, Tin, Box, 8 In. 175.00
Truck, Camper, Striped Cloth Cover, Stub Nosed, Plastic, Whitewall Tires, 11 1/2 In. 60.00
Truck, Cannon, Mack Truck Bullnose-Style Front, Chein USA, 7 1/2 In. 200.00
Truck, Car Carrier, 2-Door Sedans, Marked Austin, Arcade, USA, 12 In. 725.00
Truck, Car Carrier, Double Transport, 4 Cars, Metal, Barclay, c.1960, 4 1/2 In. 105.00
Truck, Carrier, Boat, Structo, 1951 . . . . 3350.00
Truck, Cement Mixer, Decal On Side, Buddy L, 1929, 23 1/2 In. 460.00
Truck, Cement Mixer, Jaeger, Orange, Metal Wheels, Kenton, c.1930, 7 In. 375.00
Truck, Cement Mixer, Rotating Bucket, Die Cast Metal, Lesney, England, 1 5/8 In. 20.00
Truck, Cement Mixer, Tin Lithograph, Lime Green, Yellow, Gray, Japan, 4 In. 35.00
Truck, Circus, Arcade, 9 1/2 In. 350.00
Truck, Circus, Overland, Driver, Cast Iron, Kenton, 8 In. 1250.00
Truck, Communication, Structo, 1950 . . . . 495.00
Truck, Construction, Open-Hood Design, Structo, 1940s, 21 In. 220.00
Truck, Cracker Jar, Tin, Reads Marshmallows On Side, 1 x 1 In. 125.00
Truck, Crane, Magirus-Deutz, Die Cast, Silver, Orange Boom, Lesney, 2 1/2 In. 25.00
Truck, Curtiss Candy, Plastic, Marx, 1950s, Box, 9 In. 315.00
Truck, Delivery, Bunte Candies, Goodrich Rubber Tires, Lights, Metalcraft, 12 In. 210.00
Truck, Delivery, Curtiss Candies, Baby Ruth, Rich In Dextrose, Red, Buddy L, 33 In. 413.00
Truck, Delivery, Dairy, Cream Enclosed Cab, Pressed Steel, 34 In. 3410.00
Truck, Delivery, Flivver Huckster, Black Cab, Pressed Steel, Buddy L, 14 In. 2970.00
Truck, Delivery, Ford, Flowers For Gracious Living, Blue, Green, Tin, Japan, 12 In. 2090.00
Truck, Delivery, Fruit & Vegetable, Windup, Tin Lithograph, Great Britain, 7 1/2 In. 75.00
Truck, Delivery, Heinz, B.F. Goodrich Tires, Headlight, Metalcraft USA, 12 In. 1300.00

Truck, Delivery, Ice Cream, Arctic Ice Cream, Cast Iron, Blue, Orange, Kilgore, 8 In. 1265.00
Truck, Delivery, Ice Cream, Decals, Buddy L 275.00
Truck, Delivery, Ice, 1 Rear Wheel, Canvas Top, Buddy L, 1926, 25 In. . . . . . . .2645.00 to 2980.00
Truck, Delivery, Ice, Wyandotte, Metal, Red Cab, White Bed, Stenciled, 12 In. 121.00
Truck, Delivery, Kilo DBS 550, Windup, Tin, Germany, 15 In. 175.00
Truck, Delivery, Milk & Cream, Hubley, 3 1/2 In. 355.00
Truck, Delivery, Milk, Toy Town Milk Co., Wyandotte, 12 In. 61.00
Truck, Delivery, Milk, Windup, Kingsbury, 9 In. 61.00
Truck, Delivery, Minute Maid, Tonka, Box 405.00
Truck, Delivery, Plee-Zing Quality Products, Metalcraft, 11 In. 415.00
Truck, Delivery, Pure Food Products 57 Varieties, Battery Operated, 12 In. 330.00
Truck, Delivery, Stake, Chrome Wheels, Arcade Decal On Driver Door, 7 In. 330.00
Truck, Delivery, Stake, Meadow Brook Dairy, Wood Tires, Wyandotte, 1830s 110.00
Truck, Delivery, Walgreen's Ice Cream, Metal, Tin Lithograph, Marx, 20 In. 330.00
Truck, Delivery, Windup, Tin, Fischer, 1920s, 8 1/2 In. 485.00
Truck, Delivery, Wrigley's Spearmint Gum, Green, Pressed Steel, Buddy L, 14 1/2 In. . . . 83.00
Truck, Dump & Plow, State Highway Department, Tonka, 16 In. 325.00
Truck, Dump, Blue, Orange, Disc Wheels, Rubber Tires, Pressed Steel, Kingsbury, 10 In. . 248.00
Truck, Dump, Cast Iron, Orange, Green, Hubley, 3 1/2 In. 110.00
Truck, Dump, Chain, Black, Red Chassis, Aluminum Disc Wheels, Buddy L, 25 In. 495.00
Truck, Dump, Chrome Spoked Wheels, Cast Iron, Decal, Arcade, c.1930, 5 3/4 In. 440.00
Truck, Dump, Flivver, Black, Aluminum Wheels, Pressed Steel, Buddy L, 11 In. 825.00
Truck, Dump, Highway Maintenance, Buddy L, 14 In. 110.00
Truck, Dump, Hydraulic, Black Driver's Seat, Red Chassis Body, 24 In. 1760.00
Truck, Dump, Hydraulic, Structo, Sealed Box, 13 In. 250.00
Truck, Dump, International Harvester, Decals, Red, Cast Iron, Arcade, 10 1/2 In. 413.00
Truck, Dump, Keystone, 17 In. 308.00
Truck, Dump, Muir Hill, Die Cast, Red Enamel Paint, Lesney Matchbox, 3 In. 30.00
Truck, Dump, Plastic Grill Guard, Painted, Buddy L, 15 In. 11.00
Truck, Dump, Pressed Steel, Buddy L, 1927, 11 In. 2090.00
Truck, Dump, Pressed Steel, Chain Drive, Black Paint, Buddy L, 24 1/2 In. 1100.00
Truck, Dump, Red, Green & Yellow Wheels, Wyandotte, 1930 . . . . 150.00
Truck, Dump, Red, Green Body, Silver Highlights, Die Cast Cab, Hubley, Box, 16 1/4 In. . 413.00
Truck, Dump, Sand & Gravel, Metal Wheels, Black Cab, Red Bed, Metalcraft, 11 In. 715.00
Truck, Dump, Sand & Gravel, Metal Wheels, Radiator White, Metalcraft, 11 In. . . .175.00 to 248.00
Truck, Dump, Sand & Gravel, Plastic & Tin, Marx 125.00
Truck, Dump, State Highway Department, Tonka, 16 In. 325.00
Truck, Dump, Steel Bed, Hot Wheels, No. 38 . . . . 7.00
Truck, Dump, Windup, Tin, Nifty, Germany, 9 1/2 In. 605.00
Truck, Dump, Wyandotte Construction, Red, Green, All Metal Products, 24 x 10 In. 143.00
Truck, Earthmover, Goodyear Tires, Decals, Pressed Steel, Doepke, Box, 31 In. . . .358.00 to 825.00
Truck, Excavating, Mack, Side Dump Carts, Spoked Wheels, Tootsietoy, 11 In., 4 Piece . . 88.00
Truck, Express Line, Yellow, Red, Red Spoked Wheels, Pressed Steel, Buddy L, 34 In. . . . 825.00
Truck, Farm, Battery Operated, Alps 195.00
Truck, Farm, Tonka, 1959 . . . . 225.00
Truck, Flatbed, Dinky Toy 50.00
Truck, Flatbed, John Deere, Ertl, 17 In. 44.00
Truck, Flatbed, Windup, Tin, Red, Yellow Trim, England, 9 In. 60.00
Truck, Flywheel Motion, Penny Toy, 4 In. 375.00
Truck, Ford, Ranchero, Friction, Tin Lithograph, Orange, Blue, France, 1958, 11 In. 130.00
Truck, Friction, Tin Lithograph, Enamel, Aqua, Tailgate Lowers, Bandai, 9 3/4 In. 345.00
Truck, Front Loader, Sand & Gravel, Marx, 15 In. 27.00
Truck, Gasoline, Mach, Cast Iron, 7 In. 295.00
Truck, Gasoline, Mobil, Die Cast, Pressed Steel, Red, Smith-Miller, 23 In. . . . . . . .275.00 to 675.00
Truck, Gasoline, Mobil, Die Cast, Tootsietoy 45.00
Truck, Gasoline, Mobil, Tin Lithograph, Friction, Japan, 11 1/4 In. 100.00
Truck, Gasoline, No. 6, Bulldog, 1925 . . . . 95.00
Truck, Gasoline, Pure Oil, Battery Operated, Pressed Steel, Box, 1930s, 15 In. 358.00
Truck, Gasoline, Pure Oil, Metalcraft 850.00
Truck, Gasoline, Shell Motor Oil, Metalcraft, USA, 11 1/2 In. 210.00
Truck, Gasoline, Sinclair, Die Cast, Tootsietoy 66.00
Truck, Gasoline, Standard Oil, Metalcraft, USA, 11 1/2 In. 400.00
Truck, Gasoline, Texaco, Battery Operated, Metal, Smoke Stack, 1970s, 19 In. 2530.00

Truck, Gasoline, Texaco, Buddy L, 23 In. 190.00
Truck, Grain Hauler, Friction, Metal, Japan, 1950s, 13 In. 245.00
Truck, Grain Hauler, International Grain, Orange & White, Tru-Scale, 15 In. 110.00
Truck, Heavy Duty Express, 10-Wheeled Plastic Cab, Steel Bed, Marx, Box, 1952, 19 In. 110.00
Truck, Heinz 57, Battery Operated, Steel, Decals, Metalcraft, 13 1/2 In. 330.00
Truck, Heinz, Battery Operated, Headlights, Spare Tire, Metalcraft, Box, 12 In. 1430.00
Truck, Hi-Way Express, Marx, 16 In. . . . . .165.00 to 300.00
Truck, Horse Drawn, National Biscuit Co., Wood, Tin, 1931, 19 In. 715.00
Truck, Huckster, Buddy L 7370.00
Truck, Lazy Day Farms, Marx, 18 In. . . . . .22.00 to 65.00
Truck, Livestock Van, Tonka, 1954, 24 In. 125.00
Truck, Logging, Red, 5 Logs, Structo, Box, 18 In. 210.00
Truck, Logging, With Trailer, Logs, Smith-Miller, 36 In. 635.00
Truck, Lumber, Contractors, Red & Yellow Steel, Marx, 20 In. 115.00
Truck, Merry-Go-Round, Japan, Friction 195.00
Truck, Merry-Go-Round, Remote Control, TN, Japan, 1950s, 8 1/2 In. 550.00
Truck, Moving Van, Allied, Tonka, Orange, 1956, 24 In. 105.00
Truck, Moving Van, Bekins, White Body, Pressed Steel, 34 In. 660.00
Truck, Moving Van, Lincoln Transfer & Storage, Windup, Lithograph, Driver, 12 3/4 In. . . 460.00
Truck, Moving Van, Mayflower Transit, Yellow, Black, Plastic, 10-Wheeler, 1950s, 19 In. 132.00
Truck, Moving Van, Wood, Orange & Black, Buddy L, 1940s . . . .*Illus* 275.00
Truck, Oil, Black Cab, Opening Doors, Dark Green Tank, Pressed Steel, Buddy L, 24 In. . 1980.00
Truck, Panel, White Rubber Tires, Decals, Arcade, 9 1/2 In. 3630.00
Truck, Panel, Wyman's, Cast Iron, Nickel-Plated Driver, Wheels, Arcade, 8 In. 9020.00
Truck, Pickup, Buddy L, 1960s, 12 In. 40.00
Truck, Pickup, Friction, Tin, Blue, Cream, Japan, 1958, 6 In. 45.00
Truck, Plee-Zing, Metalcraft, USA, 11 In. 375.00
Truck, Railway Express Agency, Green & Yellow, Marx, 1950s, 20 In. 374.00
Truck, Railway Express, Box Van, Platform Lift Mechanism, Marx, 1950s, 19 1/2 In. 231.00
Truck, Railway Express, Keystone, 25 In. 300.00
Truck, Railway Express, Rear Gate, Screened Top, 1930s 800.00
Truck, Railway Express, Steelcraft 1150.00
Truck, RCA Television Service, Plastic, Marx, Box, 1950s, 8 In. 290.00
Truck, Repair-It, Buddy L 150.00
Truck, Rescue Squad, Tonka, 1956, 12 In. 72.00
Truck, Ride-On, Saddle Speedster, Battery Operated Lights, Buddy L, 18 3/4 In. 135.00
Truck, Sand Loader, Buddy L 198.00
Truck, Satellite Launching, Box 700.00
Truck, Scoop-A-Dunk, Complete, Buddy L 85.00
Truck, Sprinkler, Buddy L 1500.00
Truck, Sprite Boy On Sides, Yellow, 1940s, 20 In. 250.00
Truck, Stake, 5-Ton, Windup, Red & Gold Highlights, Cast Iron, Tin, Hubley, 17 In. 825.00
Truck, Stake, Cast Iron, Red, White Rubber Tires, Barclay, 5 1/2 In. 165.00
Truck, Stake, Express, Battery Operated, Body Lights, Metalcraft, 12 In. 358.00
Truck, Stake, Green, Red, Wyandotte, 1940, 16 In. 44.00
Truck, Stake, International, Nickel Plated Driver, Cast Iron, Arcade, 9 1/2 In. 1540.00
Truck, Stake, Pressed Steel, Spoke Wheels, Buddy L, 25 In. 1595.00
Truck, Stake, Pressed Steel, Wood Wheels, 1920s Style, Wyandotte 110.00
Truck, Stake, Pressed Steel, Wyandotte, 13 1/2 In. 70.00

Left: Toy, Truck, Tow, Cities Service, Pressed Steel, Box

Above: Toy, Truck, Moving Van, Wood,
Orange & Black, Buddy L, 1940s

Truck, Stake, Red, Green, Pressed Steel, Germany, 16 In. 1320.00
Truck, Stake, Rotating Crank Start, Tiller Steering, Cast Iron, Kenton, 6 1/2 In. 176.00
Truck, Stake, Tin, Red, White, Gray Chassis, Plastic Tires, Marx, 14 In. 45.00
Truck, Stake, Whiteking Express, Pressed Steel, White Grill, Metalcraft, 1930s 214.00
Truck, Stake, Wood Wheels, Pressed Steel, Wyandotte, c.1935, 16 1/2 In. 132.00
Truck, Stake, Wyandotte, 21 In. 70.00
Truck, Stockyard, Red, Silver Bumper & Grill, Die Cast, Hubley, Box, 10 1/4 In. 220.00
Truck, Tanker, Pure Oil Co., Electric Headlights, Grille, Bumpers, Metalcraft, 14 1/2 In. .. 600.00
Truck, Telephone, Auburn, 7 In. 20.00
Truck, Telephone, Bell Telephone, Pole Wagon & Wench, Cast Iron, Hubley, 10 In. 750.00
Truck, Telephone, Hubley, 18 In. 287.00
Truck, Tow, 2-Tone Blue, Red, Nickel Bumper, Cast Iron, Champion, 7 1/2 In. 198.00
Truck, Tow, Battery Operated, Emergency Light, Buddy L, 15 In. 50.00
Truck, Tow, Champion, Cast Iron, Rubber Tires, Red Paint, 7 1/2 In. 300.00
Truck, Tow, Cities Service, Pressed Steel, Box .... *Illus* 300.00
Truck, Tow, Ford, Iron Red Cab, Green Weaver Crane, Spoked Wheels, Cast Iron, 8 In. ... 352.00
Truck, Tow, Goodrich Silvertown, Battery, 3 Goodrich Tires In Rack, 12 In. 660.00
Truck, Tow, Hercules, Mack Logo, Bullnose, Tin Plate, Black, Red, Chein, 19 1/2 In. 1155.00
Truck, Tow, Hubley, 5 In. 390.00
Truck, Tow, International Harvester, Driver, Hand Crank Winch, Arcade, c.1930, 10 In. .. 805.00
Truck, Tow, Mack, Red, Bullnose Front End, Cast Iron, Arcade, 10 1/2 In. 1980.00
Truck, Tow, Metal Wheels, Marked Towing-Repairs, Metalcraft, St. Louis, 11 In. 660.00
Truck, Tow, Official AAA Service, Wyandotte, 13 In. 577.00
Truck, Tow, Power Wrench, Adjustable Crane, Minic, Box, 5 1/2 In. 185.00
Truck, Tow, Wrecker, Wyandotte, 1930s, 18 In. 365.00
Truck, Trailer, Allis Chalmers, Structo, Box 65.00
Truck, Trailer, Wyandotte Truck Lines, Construction, 24 In. 155.00
Truck, Transport, Auto, Mack Bullnose, 3 Cars, Tootsietoy, Box, 1930s, 8 1/2 In. 470.00
Truck, Transport, Auto, Wyandotte, 22 In. 45.00
Truck, Transport, Cattle, Structo, Box, 1953 .... 250.00
Truck, Trolley, Century Of Progress, 4 Trucks Carrying People, Arcade, 14 In. 1895.00
Truck, U-Haul Pickup &, Trailer, Nylint, 21 In. 72.00
Truck, U-Haul, Chevrolet Cab, Roll-Up Rear Gate, Nylint, 1970s, 19 In. 88.00
Truck, U-Haul, Metal, 7 x 18 In. 22.00
Truck, U.S. Army, Packard, Khaki Body, Green Disc Wheels, Pressed Steel, 26 In. 605.00
Truck, U.S. Army, Pressed Steel, USA Stenciled On Flatbed Side, Sturditoy, 26 In. 303.00
Truck, U.S. Army, Searchlight, Buddy L 150.00
Truck, U.S. Army, Searchlight, Marx, 12 In. 55.00
Truck, U.S. Army, Supply, Cover, Chein, USA, 8 In. 175.00
Truck, U.S. Army, Transport, Friction, Tin, Painted, Linemar, Japan, Box, 9 1/2 In. 110.00
Truck, U.S. Army, Troop Carrier, Marx, 18 In. 165.00
Truck, U.S. Army, Troop Carrier, Olive Green, Chein, 8 In. 240.00
Truck, U.S. Mail, Junior Mail Express, Pressed Steel, Split Windshield, Buddy L, 22 In. .. 4950.00
Truck, U.S. Mail, Packard Style, Pressed Steel, Buddy L, 25 1/2 In. 1540.00
Truck, Utility Service, Orange, Blue Trim, Pressed Steel, Marx, Box, 16 1/2 In. 660.00
Truck, Windup, Tin, Pulling 4 Carts, Barrels, U.B. & C., France, 24 In. 413.00
Trumpet Player, Louis Armstrong, Old Satchmo, Windup, Tin Lithograph 485.00
Trunk, Francie & Skipper, Blue, Vinyl, Triple, 1966, 10 x 13 In. 90.00
Tunnel, Lincoln, Windup, Unique, 1930s .... 350.00 to 395.00
Typewriter, Marx 40.00
Typewriter, Orga Privat, Patent 1925, Bing 295.00
Typist, Miss Friday, Battery Operated, Tin Lithograph, Vinyl, Box, 7 In. 160.00
Van, Delivery, Green Body, Black Cab, Metalcraft, St. Louis, 11 In. 100.00
Vehicle, New Century, 3 Wheels, Man Steering, Tiller, Umbrella Spins, Lehmann, 5 In. .. 523.00
View-Master, Barbie, Trip Around The World, 3 Reels, Booklet, Itinerary, 1965 .... 80.00
View-Master, Charlotte's Web, 3 Reels, 1973 .... 14.00
View-Master, Honolulu, Waikiki & Oahu, 1958, Set Of 3 .... 20.00
View-Master, Honolulu, Waikiki, Oahu, Envelope, 1958, 3 Piece 20.00
View-Master, Huckleberry Hound, Huck With Fireworks, Yogi, 3 Reels, Booklet, 1960 ... 25.00
View-Master, Mighty Mouse, 3 Reels, Envelope, 1958, 4 1/2 In. 18.00
View-Master, Wild Animals Of North America, No. 2, 1958 .... 3.00
Violinist, Wearing Top Hat, Tinplate, Black, White Checkered Pants, 1897, 8 In. 1380.00

Toy, Wagon, Blocks, Wood, Holgate,
150th Anniversary, 1939, 15 x 8 In.

For your health and the well-being of your collection, do not smoke. The nicotine will stain fabrics, pictures, and wood.

Violinist, Windup, Tin, Linemar, Japan, 5 1/2 In.	110.00
Waffle Iron, Wagner Mfg. Co., 7 1/2 In.	165.00
Wagon, ABC Wheel, 2 Boys, Driver, Large Drum, 1890, 23 In.	3795.00
Wagon, Auto-Wheel-Coaster, Wood, Stenciling, 41 In.	250.00
Wagon, Blocks, Wood, Holgate, 150th Anniversary, 1939, 15 x 8 In. *Illus*	65.00
Wagon, Drawn By 3 Horses, Wilkins Aerial Water Tower, 1890s, 43 In.	5500.00
Wagon, Dray, Driver, Seated, Green, Red Spoked Wheels, Cast Iron, Kenton, 14 In.	165.00
Wagon, Dray, Open, Black Center-Mounted Wheels, Black Horse, Cast Iron, 1882, 10 In.	248.00
Wagon, Farm, Gray Horse, Red Wagon, Green Chassis, Arcade, 1939, 10 3/4 In.	330.00
Wagon, Farm, Seated Driver, Green Body, Red Spoked Wheels, Cast Iron, Kenton, 14 In.	138.00
Wagon, Fire Patrol, Horse Drawn, Red Open Seat, 3 Riders, Driver, Cast Iron, 12 In.	660.00
Wagon, Fire Patrol, Water Cans, Driver, Carpenter, 1885, 16 1/2 In.	1295.00
Wagon, Fire Patrol, Wood, Iron Strap, Red, Black, Paris Mfg. Co., 1895, 80 In.	2785.00
Wagon, Horse Drawn, American Milk Co., Carved Horse, Cloth Over Wood, Hair, 26 In.	468.00
Wagon, Horse Drawn, Cast Iron, Chrome, Bell, Pull Toy, 8 1/2 In.	61.00
Wagon, Horse Drawn, Ice, Black Horses, Burnt Orange, Cast Iron, Hubley, 12 1/2 In.	330.00
Wagon, Horse Drawn, Ice, Red, Tan, Tin, 13 x 6 In.	412.00
Wagon, Horse Drawn, Milk, Borden's, Cart & Horse	1750.00
Wagon, Horse Drawn, Milk, Red, Tan, Tin, 14 x 6 In.	385.00
Wagon, Horse Drawn, Sand & Gravel, Dark Green Wagon, Red Wheels, Kenton, 1940	303.00
Wagon, Horse Drawn, Stake, Cast Iron, Nickel Plated Driver, 2 Horses, 10 In.	130.00
Wagon, Horse Drawn, Wood, Painted, Branded, Pull Toy, S.A. Smith Mfg. Co., 20 1/2 In.	275.00
Wagon, Horse Drawn, Yankee Notions, Painted Tin, 2 Horses, George Brown	3960.00
Wagon, Log, 2 Oxen, Hubley, 1900s	1695.00
Wagon, Mt. Joy, Wood, Green, Orange Chassis	330.00
Wagon, My Pal, Metal, Pines Winterfront Co., Chicago, Ill., 8 x 9 x 23 1/2 In.	1210.00
Wagon, Swan, Young Girls, Hand Painted, Skittles, 1900, 20 In.	1035.00
Wagon, Tin Lithograph, Scenes Of Children, 9 1/2 In.	135.00
Wagon, Wood, High Spoked Wheels, Removable Seat & Handle, Express On Side, 28 In.	203.00
Wagon, Wood, Spoked Wheels, Hand Brake, Steel, 34 In.	330.00
Wagon, Wood, Spoked Wheels, Steel Axle Rods, 24 1/2 In.	522.00
Wallet, Barbie, Blue, Vinyl, Bubble-Cut Barbie, Comb, Change Holder, 4 x 4 In.	40.00
Wardrobe, Doll's, Paneled Door, Over 1 Full Drawer, Brown & Yellow, 17 x 11 x 6 In.	1045.00
Washboard, Doll's, Tin, Wood, 6 In.	22.00
Washer, 3 Little Pigs, Chein, Box	650.00
Water Tower, Suction Hose, Sturditoy, 1920s	2150.00
Watering Can, Baby In Bonnet, Duck, Red Stripe, Ohio Art, 7 In.	45.00
Watering Can, Wolverine	175.00
Wheel, Gaming, Red & Yellow, 25 In.	395.00
Wheelbarrow, Poplar, Brown Finish, 23 1/2 In.	85.00
Whistle, Clown, Figural, Wood, Papier-Mache, Lace Collar, White Gesso, 11 1/2 In.	165.00
Whistle, Space Gun Shape, Plastic, Gold, Brown, 1950s, 3 In.	25.00
Woman, Dancing, Lassie, Windup, Lindstrom, 1940s	125.00
Woman In Wide-Brimmed Hat, Windup, Walker, Light Blue Felt Dress, 1910, 8 In.	2810.00
Xylophone, Portable, T.T., Japan, Box	40.00
Yeti, Abominable Snowman, Battery Operated, Marx, 13 In.	600.00
Yo-Yo, Superb Chico Junior, Wood, Black, 1940s, 2 In.	22.00
Zebra, Pulling Bouncing Cowboy, Windup, Tin, Lehmann, 6 3/4 In.	330.00
Zebra, Schoenhut, Painted Eyes	413.00

Zebu, Standing, Hump On Shoulders, Brown Patina, 1912, Schoenhut, 7 In. 1725.00
Zeppelin, Cast Iron, Marked Zep, Painted Silver, c.1930, 4 3/4 In. 85.00
Zeppelin, Cast Iron, Pull Toy, Painted, 6 In. 140.00
Zeppelin, Die Cut Passengers, Propellers Spin, Meier, Germany, 4 1/2 In. 255.00
Zeppelin, Gold, Red Gondolas, Red Propeller, Lehmann, 1930, 8 In. 1520.00
Zeppelin, Goodyear, Gray, Pressed Steel, Decals, 31 In. 935.00
Zeppelin, Shenandoah, Windup, Tin, Flies In Circles, Lehmann, 1907, 7 1/2 In. 578.00
Zeppelin, Tippco, 11 In. 1100.00
Zirka, Windup, Tin, Lehmann, Box, 7 In. 990.00
Zulu, Tin Lithograph, Slot In Buggy Rear, No Whip, Windup, Lehmann, 5 1/2 x 7 In. 1540.00
Zulu, Windup, Tin, Lehmann, 6 3/4 In. 880.00

TRAMP ART is a form of folk art made since the Civil War. It is usually made from chip-carved cigar boxes. Examples range from small boxes and picture frames to full-sized pieces of furniture.

Box, Chip-Carved Pedestal 250.00
Box, Comb, Watch Safe At Peak, Over Mirror, 1 Drawer Over 2 Drawers, 26 1/2 In. 815.00
Box, Footed, 12 x 7 1/2 x 7 3/4 In. 220.00
Box, Geometric Inlay, 10 x 6 1/4 x 7 In. 375.00
Box, Hinged Cover, 4 Stepped Tiers, Crenelated Rim, c.1930, 8 In. 402.00
Box, Hinged Lid, Lining, Brass Button Design, Victorian, 10 x 6 1/2 In. 110.00
Box, Jewelry, 3 Drawers, 10 1/4 x 5 3/4 x 9 1/2 In. 250.00
Box, Lid & All Sides, Notched Panels In Descending Steps, 7 x 10 1/4 x 8 In. 220.00
Box, Lift-Off Lid, Interlocking Pieces, 1930s, 2 x 2 1/2 In. 95.00
Box, Sewing, Needlepoint Lift-Off Lid 195.00
Box, Spice 395.00
Chest, Floral Style Crest, 4 Drawers 1900.00
Clock, Cigar Box Base, Hinged Back Door, Initials A.W., 10 1/2 x 10 x 6 1/2 In. 330.00
Comb Case, Octagonal Mirror Frame, Diamond Layered Wood, 24 x 16 In. 825.00
Cross, Painted White, 12 In. 75.00
Frame, Rosette Pediment, Foliage Trailing From Top Corner, 19 x 12 In. 195.00
Frame, Walnut Stain, Stacked Layers Of Wood, 24 x 20 In. 85.00
Match Holder, Carved Birds, Hanging, 7 x 14 In. 250.00
Mirror, Crossed Corners, 21 x 18 1/2 In. 140.00
Mirror, Shaving, White Paint 325.00
Shelves, Green Repaint, 3 Tiers, 29 x 12 1/2 x 39 In. 220.00

TRAPS for animals may be handmade. One of the most unusual is the mousetrap made so that when the mouse entered the trap, it was hit on the head with a mallet. Other traps were commercially manufactured and often are marked with the name of the manufacturer. Many traps were designed to be as humane as possible, and they would trap the live animal so it could be released in the woods.

Bear, 2-Spring, Hand Forged 350.00
Flytrap, Glass, Blown, Cobalt Blue, Hanging, French Provincial, Bottle Shape, 1860, 7 In. 150.00
Flytrap, Glass, Blown, Green, French Provincial, Tripodal, Clear Stopper, 1880, 8 In. 270.00
Flytrap, Glass, Green, 3-Footed, Open Base, Applied Neck Ring, 5 1/8 In. 385.00
Flytrap, Glass, Tooled Funnel Lip, Spout, Nostetangen, Norway, 1780, 3 x 2 3/4 In. 770.00
Flytrap, Glass, Turquoise, Thumbprint Pattern, String Lip, 1910, 6 1/4 In. 1155.00
Lobster, Maine 100.00
Mouse, Square Lead-Filled Drop Weight, Sloped Bait Ramp, Oak, 7 1/2 In. 2760.00
Mouse, Wooden, 19th Century, 14 In. 425.00
Spring, Throws Practice Shooting Disks, Duvrock, Peters Cartridge Co., 1930 . . . . 120.00

TREEN, see Wooden category.

TRENCH ART is a form of folk art made by soldiers. Metal casings from bullets and mortar shells were cut and decorated to form useful objects, such as vases.

Ashtray, Rendova Munda, Brass, Japanese Shell, Palm Trees, 5 x 3 1/2 In. 45.00
Cigar Cutter, Made From 75mm Warhead 70.00
Lighter, Bullet From Machine Gun Cartridge, Partial Box, 1943 . . . . 20.00
Magnifying Glass, Bullet Handle 20.00

Napkin Ring, Made From Brass Bullet Case 30.00

TRIVETS are now used to hold hot dishes. Most trivets of the late nineteenth and early twentieth centuries were made to hold hot irons. Iron or brass reproductions are being made of many of the old styles.

Bell Metal, Grape & Vine Design, Baltimore, Marked W B R	45.00
Brass, Bird Design, Claw & Ball Feet, 4 x 6 x 11 In.	77.00
Brass, Fender, Tea Cup, c.1880	215.00
Brass, Gadrooned, Openwork Design, 20 1/2 x 4 In.	160.00
Brass, Ornate, 10 x 4 x 1 In.	15.00
Brass, Square, 19th Century, 10 1/2 x 8 In.	55.00
Brass, Victorian, Star Motif, Handle, Cabriole Legs, Paw Feet, 1840, 11 1/2 x 22 x 16 In. .	180.00
Brass Over Iron, Royal Coat Of Arms On Top, Bold Cabriole Legs, 19th Century, 17 In. .	2587.00
Brass Over Iron, Royal Coat Of Arms On Top, Serpentine, Cabriole Legs, 17 In.	4025.00
Cast Iron, Revolving, 19th Century, 24 In....................................	66.00
Dutch Oven, No. 10	60.00
Griswold, No. 1725, Cast Iron	25.00
Iron, Colebrookdale Iron Co., Pottstown, Pa., 6 x 4 1/2 In.	30.00
Iron, Hex Type, Handle, Baltimore, 1841	975.00
Iron, Star	23.00
Steel, Penny Feet, 18th Century, 9 1/2 In.	250.00
Wrought Iron, Round Ring, New England, Early 19th Century	185.00

TRUNKS of many types were made. The nineteenth-century sea chest was often handmade of unpainted wood. Brass-fitted camphorwood chests were brought back from the Orient. Leather-covered trunks were popular from the late eighteenth to mid-nineteenth centuries. By 1895, trunks were covered with canvas or decorated sheet metal. Embossed metal coverings were used from 1870 to 1910. By 1925, trunks were covered with vulcanized fiber or undecorated metal.

Brass & Leather Bound, On Stand, c.1820, 17 1/2 x 29 In.	770.00
Bride's, Pyrography, 15 1/2 x 27 x 16 1/2 In.	600.00
Campaign, Dovetailed, Brass Mounts, Handles, England, 19th Century, 18 x 38 x 19 In. ...	330.00
Camphor, Dovetailed, Brass Hardware, Late 19th Century, 19 x 37 x 21 In.	225.00
Camphor, Leather & Brass Bound, Floral Design, 20 1/2 x 24 1/2 In.	770.00
Carved Scrolling Foliate Design, Hinged Lid, Iron Hinges, Polychrome Paint, 44 In.	1840.00
Cosmetics, Case, Louis Vuitton	1495.00
Dome Top, Baroque Tooled Leather, Spanish, 1729, 16 1/2 x 33 1/2 In.	3500.00
Dome Top, Cotter-Pin Hinged Top, Yellow Interior, Black, Pink, Yellow Sides, Front ...	1840.00
Dome Top, Leather Covered, Brass Bound, Nail Heads, 1845-1860, 25 x 48 x 23 In.	2904.00
Dome Top, Oak, Brass, Embossed, 1755-1770, 33 x 47 x 20 1/4 In..................	2662.00
Dome Top, Parcel Gilt, Mahogany Stand, Wrought Iron, 33 1/2 x 25 In.	240.00
Dome Top, Pine, Allover Grained, Medallion On Lid, New Eng., 1830, 15 x 36 x 17 In. ..	330.00
Dome Top, Pine, Green Repaint, Reeded Top, Brass Bail Handles, On Stand, 27 In.	190.00
Dome Top, Poplar, Floral & Leaf Design, White Ground, 9 1/2 x 13 1/2 In.	3205.00
Dome Top, Tooled Leather Covering, 2 Trays, 19 1/2 x 30 3/4 In.	220.00
Dome Top, Wood Trim, Stamped Tin Acorn & Oakleaf Design, 36 x 22 x 31 In.	125.00
Flat Top, Child's, 21 x 13 1/2 In.	55.00
Hinged Lift Top, Bracket Feet, 18 1/2 x 30 1/4 In.	115.00
Hinged Lift Top, Metal Carrying Handles, Pigskin Cover, 13 x 31 1/4 In.	170.00
Leather Covered, Brass Fittings, Tooled Design, Red & Gold, Oriental, 10 In.	55.00
Leather Covered, Brass Stud Trim, Paper Lining, 25 1/2 In.	40.00
Leather Covered, Brass Tacking, c.1800, 15 1/2 In. x 19 1/2 In.	20.00
Leather Covered, Painted Scenes & Figures, Brass Hardware, Oriental, 15 In.	275.00
Louis Vuitton, 29 1/2 x 17 In.	500.00
Louis Vuitton, Canvas Over Wood, Leather Trim, Lift-Out Tray, 1930s, 23 x 40 1/2 In....	2195.00
Louis Vuitton, Steamer, c.1900	2475.00
Louis Vuitton, Steamer, Cover, Black Lacquer, 13 1/4 x 43 1/4 x 21 1/2 In.............	1725.00
Louis Vuitton, Steamer, Leather, Lift-Out Trays, Quilted Lid, Locks, 28 x 44 x 24 In.	1650.00
Louis Vuitton, Striped Canvas, Removable Trays, 1887, 44 x 27 x 24 In.	1725.00
Louis Vuitton, Valet	1155.00
Storage, Leather Covered, Early 20th Century, 6 Ft. 2 In.	175.00

Storage, Wicker, Brass Bindings & Lock, Oriental Design, 36 x 20 x 20 In. 115.00
Suitcase, Brown Leatherette, Brass Plated Hinges, Decals, 1950s, 21 x 7 x 14 In. 40.00

TUTHILL Cut Glass Company of Middletown, New York, worked from 1902 to 1923. Of special interest are the finely cut pieces of stemware and tableware.

Bowl, Rex, Flat Base, 10 x 2 3/4 In. 1200.00
Bowl, Vintage, Flared, Marked, 12 x 3 In. 805.00
Compote, Intaglio Floral, 9 In. 190.00
Compote, Jelly, Intaglio Cherries & Leaves, Signed 150.00
Holder, Lemon, Intaglio Primrose Floral & Geometrics, Sawtooth Edge, 7 1/2 In. 295.00
Platter, Fan & Star, 9 1/2 In. 375.00
Sugar & Creamer, Intaglio Floral 110.00
Vase, Trumpet, Floral, Reeded Shaft, Cut Base, Signed, 12 In. 300.00
Water Set, Intaglio Floral, Brilliant, 9 In.-Pitcher, 5 Piece 450.00

TYPEWRITER collectors divide typewriters into two main classifications: the index machine, which has a pointer and a dial for letter selection, and the keyboard machine, most commonly seen today. The first successful typewriter was made by Sholes and Glidden in 1874.

Edison Mimeograph, No. 1, 1894 .... 13940.00
North's, No. 2382, London, 1892 ....*Illus* 8713.00
Oliver, Model No. 9, Box, Patented 1912 .... 350.00
Olivetti, Lettera 22, Tan Enamel Casing, No Carrying Case, Marked, 1950, 12 x 4 In. 330.00
Portable, Continental Case 350.00
Portable, Field Typewriter, Groma Case 385.00
Royal, Upright, Uses 2-Color Ribbons 20.00
Sampo, Sweden, 1894 .... 9758.00

TYPEWRITER RIBBON TINS are now being collected. The lithographed tin containers have been used since the 1870s. Most popular with collectors are tins with pictorial graphics.

Addison, Green, Yellow, Round 89.00
American Brand, Indian With Headdress, Red, Round 152.00
Amesco Brand 44.00
Apollo, Yellow, Round 67.00
Beaver, Duroc, Contents, Colored Lithograph 160.00
Benjamin Franklin Brand 50.00
Carter's Ambassador 18.00
Carter's Stylewriter 10.00
Challenge 55.00
Coco Pure Silk 255.00
Continental 137.00
Crowfoot 84.00
Degan Typewriter Ribbon, Woman Typing, Bag Over Head 185.00
Elk Brand 155.00
Excalibur, Knight On Horseback, Stripes, Round 169.00

Typewriter, North's, No. 2382, London, 1892

Remove small rust spots from old metal with an ink-removing eraser or an old typewriter eraser.

Globe Brand	30.00 to 40.00
Handy, Learning Is Light, Aladdin-Type Lantern, Round	86.00
IBM, International, Electric Machine Division	260.00
Invincible	111.00
Keelox Brand	90.00
Keelox-Geischa	210.00
Lily Brand, Nelson-Eismann Co., Chicago, Ill., Square	85.00
Longhorn, American Carbon Paper Mfg. Company	38.00
Marvello, Sold Only By Sears Roebuck	88.00
Non-Smut	48.00
Panama	120.00
Pigeon Brand, Corona Typewriter Co., 1 5/8 In.	35.00 to 40.00
Pilot Brand	105.00
Princess Brand	131.00
Quality, The Peak Of Perfection, Blue, Soldier, Square	101.00
Ramar Brand	382.00
Red Feather Brand	36.00
Remington	90.00
Rex	35.00
Siltex, Egyptian Fibre	139.00
Standard Adding Machine	20.00
Starlight, Skyline Scene, Round	125.00
Swallow Brand	22.00
Texas Brand	255.00
Texas Pride	104.00
True-Mark	27.00
Vertex Roytype	30.00

UHL pottery was made in Evansville, Indiana, in 1854. The pottery moved to Huntingburg, Indiana, in 1908. Stoneware and glazed pottery were made until the mid-1940s.

Uhl Pottery
Hand Turned
Since 1849
Huntingburg Ind.

Basket, Light Green, Stamped, 5 1/2 In.	185.00
Bowl, Picket Fence, Blue, 6 In.	25.00
Bowl, Tulip	50.00
Ewer, Handle, Iridescent Black, Signed, 10 1/2 In.	66.00
Ewer, Iridescent Black, Handle, 10 1/2 In.	65.00
Jug, Acorn, Miniature, 3 1/8 In.	315.00
Jug, Baseball	34.00
Jug, Brown Glaze On Top Half, 1 1/4 In.	75.00
Jug, Cudjo's Cave, Cumberland Gap, Brown, White, Blue Letters, Miniature, 3 1/2 In.	230.00
Jug, Football, Meier's Paper Label, Cork	30.00
Jug, Meier's Ohio Port Wine, Gold Foil Label, Miniature, 5 In.	55.00
Mug, Brown, White Interior, 2 1/2 In.	75.00
Mug, Tan, White Interior, 4 1/2 In.	15.00
Mug, White Interior, Tan Exterior, Signed, No. 16	15.00
Pitcher, Barrel, Brown, White Interior, Stamped, 8 3/4 In.	45.00
Pitcher, Blue, 9 In.	120.00
Pitcher, Brown Glaze, Mold No. 183, 5 3/4 In.	50.00
Pitcher, Grape, 5 1/2 In.	250.00
Planter, Baby Shoe, Blue, 5 x 3 In.	50.00
Sugar, Dark Green, Stamped, 3 1/4 In.	35.00
Vase, Bud, Black, Stamped, 5 In.	90.00
Vase, Yellow, 8 In.	35.00

UMBRELLA collectors like rain or shine. The first known umbrella was owned by King Louis XIII of France in 1637. The earliest umbrellas were sunshades, not designed to be used in the rain. The umbrella was embellished and redesigned many times. In 1852, the fluted steel rib style was developed, and it has remained the most useful style.

Handle, Gold Plated, Repousse, Monogram, Tattered Cloth	105.00
Handle, Sterling Silver, Repousse, Tattered Cloth	105.00
Parasol, Folding Carved Whalebone Handle	33.00
Parasol, Victorian, Turned Bone Handle, Silk Webbing	120.00

UNION PORCELAIN WORKS was established at Greenpoint, New York, in 1848 by Charles Cartlidge. The company went through a series of ownership changes and finally closed in the early 1900s. The company made a fine quality white porcelain that was often decorated in clear, bright colors.

Oyster Plate, 7 Wells, 12 Piece 4500.00
Oyster Plate, Shells, Seaweed Design, 1881, 8 In., 4 Piece 980.00

UNIVERSITY OF NORTH DAKOTA, see North Dakota School of Mines category.

VAL ST. LAMBERT Cristalleries of Belgium was founded by Messieurs Kemlin and Lelievre in 1825. The company is still in operation. All types of table glassware and decorative glassware have been made. Pieces are often decorated with cut designs.

Val St Lambert

Beaker, Cobalt Over Clear, Acid Cut Building Scene, c.1930, 4 3/4 In. 150.00
Bowl, Blue Milk Glass, Underplate, Signed, 7 In. 38.00
Candy Dish, Stem, 3-Footed, 6 1/4 In. 125.00
Tumbler, Water, Scenic Landscape, Lemon Yellow, Crimson, 5 1/2 In., 4 Piece 575.00
Vase, Bud, Green, 9 1/2 In. 50.00
Vase, Emerald Green, Cut To Clear Crystal, Signed, 6 In. 57.00
Vase, Geometric, 3-Dimensional Diamond, Signed, 6 1/2 In. 188.00
Vase, Multicolored Design At Top, Pink, Original Label, 14 In. 660.00
Vase, Stylized Leaves, Flared Rim, Cylindrical, 7 3/4 In. 80.00

VALLERYSTHAL Glassworks was founded in 1836 in Lorraine, France. In 1854, the firm became Klenglin et Cie. It made table and decorative glass, opaline, cameo, and art glass. A line of covered, pressed glass animal dishes was made in the nineteenth century. The firm is still working.

Jar, Grape Leaf, Footed, Cover, Blue Milk Glass 75.00

VAN BRIGGLE pottery was made by Artus Van Briggle in Colorado Springs, Colorado, after 1901. Van Briggle had been a decorator at Rookwood Pottery of Cincinnati, Ohio. He died in 1904. His wares usually had modeled relief decorations and a soft, dull glaze. The pottery is still working and still making some of the original designs.

Bookends, Peacock, Rose, c.1920 .... 215.00
Bookends, Peacock, Turquoise, c.1920 .... 195.00
Bowl, Brown Gloss, 10 x 15 In. 85.00
Bowl, Dark Blue Over Light Blue At Top, 4 1/4 In. 60.00
Bowl, Embossed Holly, Green Matte Glaze, Signed, 1906, 5 1/2 In. ....800.00 to 900.00
Bowl, Oak Leaf, Mulberry Brown, Signed, c.1920, 5 1/2 In. 55.00
Candlestick, Floral Design, Purple, Maroon Matte Glaze, 1913-1920, 7 In., Pair 264.00
Ewer, Turquoise, Incised With Logo, 1930s, 6 1/2 In. 65.00
Figurine, Brave & Squaw, Turquoise, 12 1/4 In., Pair 400.00
Figurine, Nude On Rock, Rose, 10 1/4 In. ....235.00 to 275.00
Figurine, Shell Girl, Moonglo 75.00
Flower Frog, 3 Frogs, Blue, 5 In. ....125.00 to 250.00
Lamp, Girl Wearing Dress & Cape, Seated On Rocks, Shade, Nellie Walker 165.00
Lamp, Lovebird On Tree Stem, Blue, Butterflies On Shade, Signed 150.00
Lamp, Raised Leaf, Bulb Design, Blue Matte Glaze, 1940, 8 1/2 In. 172.00
Lamp, Swan, Early Shade, Blue, Aqua 275.00
Mug, Green Matte Glaze, Incised Aza/Colo Springs/1907/28b, 4 x 5 In. 355.00
Mug, Green Matte Glaze, Signed, 1907, 5 x 4 1/2 In. 325.00
Paperweight, Elephant, Turquoise Matte Glaze 50.00
Paperweight, Rabbit, Maroon, Blue Matte Glaze, Pair 150.00
Plate, Grape Cluster, Embossed Purple, Aqua Ground, 1907, 8 In. 605.00
Plate, Grapes & Leaves, Deep Burgundy, Blue Matte Glaze, 1907-1912, 8 1/2 In. 230.00
Plate, Poppies, Bright Green Glaze, 1902, Incised, 8 1/2 In. 1540.00
Tile, Calla Lily, Turquoise, 10 In. 85.00
Tile, Scenic, Cream, Mustard, Green, Blue Matte Glaze, 6 1/8 x 6 In. ....1380.00 to 1495.00
Tile, Swirled Leaf, Turquoise, 5 In. 45.00
Vase, 2 Female Heads On Each Side, Charcoal, Brown, Green, 1912, 13 x 7 In. 7150.00

Vase, 3 Carved Dragonflies, Mustard Matte Glaze, 1912, 3 x 1 1/2 In. 880.00
Vase, Crocuses, Embossed, Bulbous, Green Glaze, Impressed, 1907, 7 In. 770.00
Vase, Daffodils, Embossed, Turquoise & Blue Glaze, 1920s, 13 In. 700.00
Vase, Daffodils, Embossed, Turquoise & Blue Glaze, Incised, 1920s, 13 In. 770.00
Vase, Daffodils, Molded, 2-Tone Blue Glaze, Marked, c.1919, 9 1/2 In. 605.00
Vase, Dogwood Blossoms, Dark Green Glaze, 1906, 8 1/4 x 5 In. 2420.00
Vase, Dogwood Blossoms, Embossed, Ovoid, Green Glaze, 1906, 9 1/2 In. 2420.00
Vase, Embossed, Blossoms & Leaves, Cylindrical, Burgundy, Incised, 1903, 10 In. 2750.00
Vase, Feather, Stylized, Embossed, Dark Green Matte Glaze, 1912, 7 In. 1210.00
Vase, Feathers, Stylized, Bulbous, Embossed, Dark Green Matte, 1907, 12 In. 1210.00
Vase, Floral Design, Green, Purple Matte Glaze Tulips, 1905, 4 1/2 In. 880.00
Vase, Floral, 2-Tone Blue Matte Glaze, Signed, 1930s, 5 In. 45.00
Vase, Floral, Embossed, Bulbous, Green, Mustard, 1915, 7 In. 525.00
Vase, Floral, Molded, Green, Rose Matte Glaze, Signed, 1905, 10 1/2 In. 1210.00
Vase, Floral, Stylized, Embossed, Green, Brown, Blue Glaze, 1903, 4 In. 1650.00
Vase, Floral, Stylized, Glaze, Signed, 1907-1912 . . . . 190.00
Vase, Floral, Stylized, Mustard Ground, 1915, 4 x 4 In. 475.00
Vase, Flowers On Stems, Molded, 2-Tone Green, Blue Matte Glaze, 1912, 9 In. 770.00
Vase, Gooseberries, Embossed, Green, Raspberry Ground, 2-Handle, 1905, 7 In. 2750.00
Vase, Gooseberries, Embossed, Purple, Green Leaves, Raspberry Ground, 1905, 8 In. . . . 2700.00
Vase, Gooseberry Leaves, Fruit, Green Glaze, Raspberry Ground, 2 Handles, 9 In. 2750.00
Vase, Holly, Embossed, Green Glaze, Brown Ground, 1906, 2 x 5 In. 880.00
Vase, Leaf & Berry, Ivory, Maroon Highlights, Signed, 5 x 10 1/2 In. 2645.00
Vase, Leaf, Stylized, Blue Over Aqua, Signed, 6 1/8 In. 165.00
Vase, Leaves, Embossed, Amber Clap, Gun Metal Brown Glaze, 1913, 5 In. 1210.00
Vase, Leaves, Embossed, Bulbous, Gunmetal Brown Glaze, 1915, 4 In. 1200.00
Vase, Leaves, Embossed, Green Glaze, Incised, 1906, 4 In. 2200.00
Vase, Leaves, Embossed, Mauve Glaze, c.1910, 8 In. 1320.00
Vase, Leaves, Mauve, Bulbous, 1908-1911, Signed, 8 In. 1200.00
Vase, Light Blue Matte Glaze, 1915, 4 In. 275.00
Vase, Lilies, Embossed, Purple Glaze, 1903, 14 In. 5225.00
Vase, Maroon Matte Glaze, 1914, 7 In. 330.00
Vase, Midnight Blue, Twisted Handle, 9 In. 350.00
Vase, Morning Glories, Embossed Yellow Glaze, 1903, 10 1/4 In. 4400.00
Vase, Mulberry & Blue Glaze, Poppies, Raised, 1922-1929, 8 In. 165.00
Vase, Peacock Feathers, Embossed, Green Glaze, Blue Ground, 1904, 11 x 4 In. 3850.00
Vase, Persian Rose, Incised With Logo, 1930s, 3 1/2 In. 80.00
Vase, Poppies, Embossed & Molded, Light Green Matte Glaze, 1902, 4 In. 1210.00
Vase, Poppies, Embossed, Brown Matte Glaze, 1902, 4 In. 1650.00
Vase, Poppies, Embossed, Green Matte Glaze, 1904, 4 In. 2200.00
Vase, Poppies, Embossed, Turquoise Matte Glaze, 1916, 7 1/2 x 4 In. 935.00
Vase, Poppies, Molded, Green, Blue Matte Glaze, 1912, 6 1/2 In. 1540.00
Vase, Poppies, Molded, Green, Brown Matte Glaze, 1920, 3 1/2 In. 330.00
Vase, Poppies, Oval, Embossed, Turquoise Matte Glaze, 1916, 7 1/2 In. 935.00
Vase, Poppies, Stylized, Spherical, Dark Blue Matte Glaze, c.1910, 5 x 6 In. 990.00
Vase, Poppy Pods, Dark Brown, Ivory Matte Glaze, 1907, 6 In. 247.50
Vase, Poppy Pods, Maroon Glaze, Signed, 6 7/8 In. 1210.00
Vase, Poppy Pods, Swirling, Brown Glaze, 1904, 3 3/4 In. 600.00
Vase, Sunflowers, Molded, Maroon & Blue Glaze, Incised Mark, c.1916, 9 1/2 In. 1210.00
Vase, Three-Headed Indian, 11 In. 550.00
Vase, Trefoils, Embossed, Bulbous, Feathered Black & Green Matte Glaze, 7 In. 2970.00
Vase, Trefoils, Embossed, Green Matte Glaze, 1904, 7 1/4 In. 1200.00
Vase, Trefoils, Stylized, Long Stems, Blue Matte Glaze, 5 1/2 In. 517.00
Vase, Trumpet Form, Blue Matte Glaze, Old Mark, 7 In. 195.00
Vase, Tulip, Green, Ivory Matte Glaze, 6 1/2 In. 357.00
Vase, Vertical Ribs, Dark Brown, Light Blue Glaze, 5 In. 1045.00
Vase, Vertical Ribs, Tapered, Pale Blue Glaze, Incised, 5 1/2 In. 1045.00
Vase, Yucca Leaves, Stylized, Purple Glaze, Green Ground, 1915, 15 1/2 In. 5225.00

Remove stains from old ceramic vases by scrubbing with salt.

VASA MURRHINA is the name of a glassware made by the Vasa Murrhina Art Glass Company of Sandwich, Massachusetts, about 1884. The glassware was transparent and was embedded with small pieces of colored glass and metallic flakes. The mica flakes were coated with silver, gold, copper, or nickel. Some of the pieces were cased. The same type of glass was made in England. Collectors often confuse Vasa Murrhina glass with aventurine, spatter, or spangle glass. There is uncertainty about what actually was made by the Vasa Murrhina factory.

Basket, Rose Bowl, Mica Flakes, White Lining, Blue, 9 1/4 In.	295.00
Ewer, Gold Mica, Clear Handles, 8 /34 In., Pair	165.00
Pitcher, Swirled Ribs, Spangled Glass, Metallic Flakes, 9 In.	110.00
Rose Bowl, 6 Crimp Top, Mica Flakes Outside, White Lining, 3 3/4 In.	95.00
Rose Bowl, 8 Crimp Top, Mica Flakes In Coral Design, 3 3/4 x 3 3/8 In.	115.00
Rose Bowl, Double Cased, White & Clear Over Blue & Mica, 7 1/2 In.	325.00
Rose Bowl, Egg Shape, Red, White, 4 In.	88.00
Vase, Blue, Rigaree, 10 In.	325.00
Vase, Rainbow, White Cased, 7 1/2 In.	192.00

VASART is the signature used on a late type of art glass made by the Streathearn Glass Company of Scotland. Pieces are marked with an engraved signature on the bottom. Most of the glass is mottled or shaded.

Bowl, Gold Stone, Blue & Gray Cluthra, 3 x 8 In.	28.00

VASELINE GLASS is a greenish-yellow glassware resembling petroleum jelly. Some vaseline glass is still being made in old and new styles. Pressed glass of the 1870s was often made of vaseline-colored glass. Additional pieces of vaseline glass may also be listed under Pressed Glass in this book.

Compote, Clark's Teaberry Gum, Rectangular, 7 x 5 x 3/4 In.	39.00
Dish, Rabbit Shape, Summit Art Glass Co., c.1980	50.00
Epergne	300.00
Mustard Pot, Bird At Stump, Leaf Lid	80.00
Paperweight, Owl, c.1969, 4 1/2 In.	60.00
Paperweight, Rabbit, c.1975, 6 x 5 In.	75.00
Pin Box, Sunburst Design, Victorian, 3 x 2 In.	20.00
Tray, Card, Argonaut Shell	90.00
Vase, Pinched Sides, Square Bottom, 4 3/4 In.	110.00

VENETIAN GLASS, see Glass-Venetian category.

VENINI GLASS, see Glass-Venetian category.

VERLYS glass was made in France after 1931. It was made in the United States from 1935 to 1951. The glass is either blown or molded. The American glass is signed with a diamond-point-scratched name, but the French pieces are marked with a molded signature. The designs resemble those used by Lalique.

Bowl, Birds & Cherry, Signed, 8 In.	345.00
Bowl, Thistle, 8 1/2 In.	110.00 to 135.00
Candlestick, Water Lily, Directoire, Blue, Pair	350.00
Platter, Iris, Signed, 14 In.	115.00
Vase, Alpine Thistle, Frosted, Signed, 8 3/4 In.	265.00
Vase, Alpine Thistle, Opalescent, 9 In.	765.00
Vase, Mandarin, Frosted, 9 1/4 In.	395.00 to 400.00

VERNON KILNS was the name used after 1958 by Vernon Potteries, Ltd. The company, which started in 1931 in Vernon, California, made dinnerware and figurines until it was bought by Metlox in 1958. Collectors search for the brightly colored dinnerware and the pieces designed by Rockwell Kent, Walt Disney, and Don Blanding. For more information, see *Kovels' Depression Glass & Dinnerware Price List.*

Brown-Eyed Susan, Platter, 12 In.	25.00

Carlsbad Cavern, Cup & Saucer, Demitasse 25.00
Casualware, Casserole, Cover, Pink, 2 1/2 x 9 In. 35.00
Chatelaine, Cup & Saucer, Topaz 40.00
Chatelaine, Plate, 10 In. 30.00
Coral Reef, Cup & Saucer, Blue, Jumbo 50.00
Fantasia, Plate, 9 In. 225.00
Flowers, Chop Plate, 14 In. 100.00
Gingham, Pitcher, 11 In. 80.00
Harvest, Tumbler, 13 Oz. 35.00
Hawaii, Plate, Pineapples & Scenes Border, 10 1/2 In. 50.00
Hawaiian Flowers, Plate, Maroon, 9 In. ....25.00 to 50.00
Hawaiian Flowers, Salt & Pepper, Blue 65.00
Homespun, Carafe 80.00
Homespun, Pitcher, 2 Qt. 47.00
Lei Lani, Chop Plate, 14 In. 110.00
Lei Lani, Gravy Boat 165.00
Lei Lani, Nappy, 9 In. 165.00
Lei Lani, Plate, 9 In. 50.00
Moby Dick, Chop Plate, Brown, 14 In. 195.00
Moby Dick, Pitcher, 1 Pt. 160.00
Moby Dick, Tumbler, Brown 195.00
Modern California, Pitcher, 5 In. 20.00
Perfume Bottle, Round Stopper, 8-Footed Base, 6 1/2 In. 130.00
Plate, State Of Colorado, 10 In. 20.00
Raffia, Pitcher, 2 Qt. 40.00
Tapping For Sugar, Plate, 8 1/2 In. 32.00
Tam O'Shanter, Plate, 9 1/2 In. 12.00

VERRE DE SOIE glass was first made by Frederick Carder at the
Steuben Glass Works from about 1905 to 1930. It is an iridescent glass
of soft white or very, very pale green. The name means *glass of silk*,
and it does resemble silk. Other factories have made verre de soie, and
some of the English examples were made of different colors. Verre de
soie is an art glass and is not related to the iridescent, pressed, white
carnival glass mistakenly called by its name. Related pieces may be
found in the Steuben category.

  Basket, Berry Print, Applied Handles, Iridized, 10 3/4 In. 920.00
  Vase, Floral Design, Flared Rim, Cylindrical, 12 In. 305.00
  Vase, Ruffled, 5 In. 200.00
  Water Set, Hawkes Engraved & Cut Design, 8 3/4-In. Pitcher, 6 Piece 745.00

VIENNA, see Beehive category.

VIENNA ART plates are round metal serving trays produced at the turn
of the century. The designs, copied from Royal Vienna porcelain
plates, usually featured a portrait of a woman encircled by a wide,
ornate border. Many were used as advertising or promotional items and
were produced in Coshocton, Ohio, by J.F. Meeks Tuscarora Advertising Co. and H.D. Beach's Standard Advertising Co.

  Plate, Marguerite, 1905 .... 155.00
  Plate, Woman, Gold Shadowbox Frame, 1908-1912, Square 1035.00
  Tray, Apple Blossom, Compliments Of John Pritzlaff Hardware, 1909, 10 In. 155.00
  Tray, Claire, Signed, 1905, 10 In. 130.00
  Tray, Jill, Compliments Of John Pritzlaff Hardware, 1908, 10 In. 155.00
  Tray, Tin, Henry Irving, John Merriam Havana Cigars, 3 Acting Scenes, Round 250.00

VILLEROY & BOCH Pottery of Mettlach was founded in 1841. The firm
made many types of wares, including the famous Mettlach steins. Collectors can be confused because although Villeroy & Boch made most
of its pieces in the city of Mettlach, Germany, they also had factories
in other locations. The dating code impressed on the bottom of most
pieces makes it possible to determine the age of the piece. Additional
items, including steins and earthenware pieces marked with the

famous castle mark or the word *Mettlach,* may be found in the Mettlach category.

Bowl, Cover, Onion, 1910, 10 In.	80.00
Candlestick, Fruit & Flower Design, 4 1/2 In., Pair	50.00
Candlestick, Fruit Design, White, Gold Trim, 4 1/2 In, Pair	95.00
Charger, Village Landscape, Title Hannover On Reverse, c.1900, 17 3/8 In.	252.00
Jardiniere, Karyatida Pattern, Yellow, Turquoise & Rust	115.00
Tray, Coasters, Pierced Brass, Secessionist Brown & White Pottery, 5 Piece	350.00
Vase, Organic Geometric Design, Celadon Ground, 4 Handles, 9 1/4 In.	325.00

VOLKMAR pottery was made by Charles Volkmar of New York from 1879 to about 1911. He was associated with several firms, including the Volkmar Ceramic Company, Volkmar and Cory, and Charles Volkmar and Son. Volkmar had been a painter, and his designs often look like oil paintings drawn on pottery.

VOLKMAR
Corona N.Y

Bowl, Broad Leaves Under Green Glaze, Organic Shape, Signed, 9 1/4 In.	450.00
Bowl, Centerpiece, Turquoise Interior, Blue Exterior, 1928, 6 1/2 x 13 1/2 In.	770.00

VOLKSTEDT was a soft-paste porcelain factory started in 1760 by Georg Heinrich Macheleid at Volkstedt, Thuringia. Volkstedt-Rudolstadt was a porcelain factory started at Volkstedt-Rudolstadt by Beyer and Bock in 1890. Most pieces seen in shops today are from the later factory.

Figurine, Allegorical Female, Holding Musical Instrument, 7 3/4 In.	115.00
Figurine, Ballerina, Standing On Point, Maiden, Sitting Under Tree, 8 1/2 In.	69.00
Group, 3 Maidens, Elaborately Costumed, Dancing Around Pedestal, 1925, 11 In.	212.00
Group, Courting Couple, Spanish Dress, 9 3/4 In.	145.00
Vase, Cherubs Perched On Calla Lily Blossoms, c.1895, 7 1/2 In.	110.00

WADE pottery is made by the Wade Group of Potteries started in 1810 near Burslem, England. Several potteries merged to become George Wade & Son, Ltd. early in the twentieth century, and other potteries have been added through the years. The best-known Wade pieces are the small figurines given away with Red Rose Tea and other promotional items. The Disney figures are listed in this book in the Disneyana category.

WADE
figures

c. 1936+

Dish, Dog, Spaniel	36.00
Eggcup, Swan	50.00
Figurine, Elephant, Whimsey, 1971-1974	12.00
Figuriere, Fawn, Whimsey, 1953-1959	45.00
Figurine, Fox Cub, Whimsey, 1953-1959	70.00
Figurine, Gingerbread Bread Boy	45.00
Figurine, Hippo, Whoppas, 1976-1981	15.00
Figurine, Humpty Dumpty, Red Rose Tea Premium, Canada	4.00
Figurine, Mr. Plod	150.00
Figurine, Nursery Set, Red Rose Tea Premium, Canada, Miniature, 24 Piece	150.00
Figurine, Pied Piper, Red Rose Tea Premium, Canada	4.00
Figurine, Rabbit, Sitting, Red Rose Tea Premium, U.S.A.	5.00
Figurine, Raccoon, Whoppas, 1976-1981	20.00
Figurine, Snow White & 7 Dwarfs	875.00
Figurine, Squirrel, Gray	40.00
Figurine, Squirrel, Red Rose Tea Premium, U.S.A.	5.00
Figurine, Tortoise, No. 4, Box, Jumbo	60.00
Figurine, Whoppas, 15 Piece	250.00
Mug, Cider, Taunton, Mill Scene, Double Handles, 3 1/4 In.	65.00
Pin Dish, Pekingese	25.00
Tankard, Car, Veteran, Cadillac, 1/2 Pt.	15.00

WAHPETON POTTERY, see Rosemeade category.

WALLACE NUTTING photographs are listed under Print, Nutting. His reproduction furniture is listed under Furniture.

WALRATH was a potter who worked in New York City; Rochester, New York; and at the Newcomb Pottery in New Orleans, Louisiana. Frederick Walrath died in 1920. Pieces listed here are from his Rochester period.

Walrath
Pottery

Flower Frog, Nude, Green Matte Glaze, Signed, 6 x 8 1/2 In.	1300.00
Flower Frog, Scarab, Signed, 3 1/5 In.	165.00
Mug, Silhouette Of Cherries On Trellis, Arts & Crafts, Signed, 5 In.	467.00

WALT DISNEY, see Disneyana category.

WALTER, see A. Walter category.

WATCH pockets held the pocket watch that was important in Victorian times because it was not until World War I that the wristwatch was used. All types of watches are collected: silver, gold, or plated. Watches are arranged by company name or by style. Pocket watches are listed here; wristwatches are a separate category.

Agassiz, Hunting Case, Chronograph, Split Second, Porcelain Dial, 14K Gold	1495.00
Agassiz, Hunting Case, Double Chronograph, Porcelain Dial, Size 18	1650.00
Albus, Lapel, Silvertone Dial, 15 Jewel, Sailboats, Suspended From Fish Brooch	517.00
B.K. Company, Lever Set, Stem Wind, Nickel Movement, 14K Gold Case	220.00
Besancon, Gilt Brass, White Enamel, Gold Arrow Hands, 1809	2530.00
Borel Fils & Cie., Hunting Case, Nickel Lever Movement, Gilt Dial, Arabic Numerals . . .	2645.00
Breguet, Gilt Brass, 3 Automaton Jacks, Numerals, Blue Steel Hands, 1820	9545.00
Breguet, Gilt Brass, Our Sailor King, George V, Silver, Roman Numerals, 1910	1265.00
Breiting Bros., Hunting Case, Jeweled Patent Lever, Key Wind, 18K Gold	330.00
C.L. Guinand, Porcelain Dial, Minutes & Seconds Dials	805.00
Conrail, Fob & Chain, Display Case	180.00
Cornell University, Key & Fob, Gold On Ribbon, 14K Gold	25.00
Corum, Spartacus, 21 Jewel, Textured Champagne Dial, Baton Numerals, Case, 1970	2875.00
Dunand, Repeater, 15 Jewel, 14K Yellow Gold Case	1800.00
Elgin, 17 Jewel, Farmhouse Engraving On Back, Yellow Gold Case	65.00
Elgin, Coin Silver, 19th Century, 3 x 2 In.	120.00
Elgin, Enameled Face, Floral & Leaves Case	48.00
Elgin, Hunting Case, Enamel Dial, Roman Numerals, 5 Diamonds, Ruby, 14K Gold	224.00
Elgin, Hunting Case, National Movement, 14K Yellow Gold, 1884	290.00
Elgin, Hunting Case, National Movement, Gold Filled, 1908	85.00
Elgin, Hunting Case, National, 14K Yellow Gold, 1890	230.00
Elgin, Hunting Case, Porcelain Dial, Fahys Montauk, 1 3/8 In.	67.00
Elgin, Hunting Case, Porcelain Face, 20 Years, Warranted B&B, Gold, 1 1/2 In.	56.00
Elgin, Porcelain Dial, Seconds Dial, Stem Wind, Hunter Case, 1 3/8 In.	95.00
Elgin, Presentation Inscription, Monogrammed, Chain, 18K Yellow Gold, 1886, 2 In. . . .	220.00
Fob, San Francisco Mine Rescue Contest, 3 1/2-In. Leather, 1 1/2-In. Brass, 1915	67.00
Gambler, Pale Green Enamel, Gilt Brass, Polished Steel Hands, 1900	1725.00
Gilt Brass, White Enamel, Roman Numerals, Outer Silver Revolving Ring, 1900	1955.00
Hamilton, 17 Jewel, White Enamel Dial, Black, Gold Arabic Numerals	1150.00
Hamilton, Bridge, Open Face, 19 Jewel, 14K Gold, 5 Positions, c.1921	275.00
Hamilton, Electric Railway Special, 17 Jewel, Gold Filled Open Face	145.00
Hamilton, Open Face, Swing Out Movement, 21 Jewel, 14K Gold	345.00
Hamilton, Railroad, 21 Jewel, Gold Filled, 1920, 3 x 2 1/8 In.	212.00
Hamilton, Regulus, Stainless Steel Case	300.00
Hampden, Hunting Case, Coin Silver, 19th Century, 3 1/8 x 2 1/8 In.	120.00
Hampden, Hunting Case, Gladiator, Engraved Gold Filled, Chain & Fob	75.00
Hampden, Molly Stark, Hunting Case, Engraved, Enameled Dial, Gold Filled	145.00
Howard, 14K Yellow Gold, 1920, 2 1/4 x 1 7/8 In.	85.00
Howard, Open Face, 25-Year Case, Gold Filled	230.00
Howard, Series 7, Open Face, 14K Gold, 17 Jewel, Presentation, Keystone Case, 1917 . . .	345.00
Howard Watch Co., Open Face, Chain, Gold Filled, Pocket, 1915	85.00
Huguenin & Greget, Hunting Case, Split Second Chronograph, 2 Train, Gold	1375.00
Hunting Case, Chronograph, Calendar, Moon Phases, White Enamel Dial, 18K Gold	2300.00
Hunting Case, Chronograph, Nickel Lever Movement, White Enamel Dial, 18K Gold . . .	19550.00
Hunting Case, Chronograph, Nickel Pivoted Movement, White Enamel Dial	1610.00

Hunting Case, Coin Silver, George V, Key Wind, White Enamel Dial 85.00
Hunting Case, Gilt Cylinder Movement, Blue Enamel, Foliate, 18K Gold, 1863 .... 2587.00
Hunting Case, Gilt Lever Movement, Gold Cuvette White Enamel Dial, 1920 .... 3162.00
Hunting Case, Key Wind, Yellow Gold Filled, 1880 .... 260.00
Hunting Case, Open Face, 18K Gold, White Enamel Dial, Arabic Numerals, 1900 ...... 1840.00
Hunting Case, Repeating, Double Sunk White Enamel Dial, Roman Numerals, Gold 3105.00
Hunting Case, Repeating, Gilt Lever Movement, 18K Gold & Enamel Case, 1910 ...... 40205.00
Hunting Case, White Enamel Dial, Calendar & Moon Phases, Roman Numerals 10350.00
Illinois, 19 Jewel, Foliate Design, Roman Numerals, Second Hand, Chain, 14K Gold 125.00
Illinois, Open Face, Gold Filled, Pocket, 1902 .... 575.00
Illinois, Porcelain Railroad Dial, 17 Jewel, 2 In. 112.00
Ingersoll, Tom Mix, Pocket, Round Face, Tom On Horse, Pocket, c.1933 .... 450.00
James Narden, Hunting Case, 21 Jewel, Floral Engraving, Seconds Dial, 18K Gold 460.00
John Norton, Coin Silver Fusee, Porcelain Dial, Pocket 230.00
LeCoultre, Hunting Case, Silver Dial, Gold Floral, Repeating, Swiss, 32 Jewel 5390.00
LeCoultre, Woman's, 18K Pink Gold, Silvered Matte Dial, Arabic Baton Numerals 2300.00
Niello, Key Wind, Diamond Chips, 18K Gold, France, Paris Expo Box 550.00
Open Face, 2 Train, Independent Seconds, White Enamel Dial, Blue, 18K Gold, 1900 ... 2585.00
Open Face, 23 Jewel, Gilt Lever Movement, White Enamel Dial, Arabic Numerals, 1910 . 7187.00
Open Face, 32 Jewel, Champagne Matte Dial, Arabic Numerals, 18K Gold 9775.00
Open Face, Chronograph, Gold Cuvette White Enamel Dial, Arabic Numerals, 1912 ..... 3450.00
Open Face, Decorated Dial, Colored Gold Leaves, Second Hand, 18K Gold, 1830s 1150.00
Open Face, Engine Turned Dial, Arabic Numerals, Wavy Engine Ground, 14K Gold 2875.00
Open Face, England, 18K Gold, 19th Century 385.00
Open Face, Nickel Lever Movement, Black Matte Dial, Arabic Numerals, Case 920.00
Open Face, Nickel Lever Movement, White Enamel Dial, 18K Gold, 1925 .... 2185.00
Open Face, Nickel Lever Movement, White Enamel Dial, Roman Numerals, 1895 ...... 9200.00
Open Face, Silver Matte Dial, Jump Hour, With Minutes, 18K White Gold, 1940 .... 9200.00
Open Face, White Porcelain Dial, Black Arabic Numerals, 18K Yellow Gold Case 1725.00
Patek Philippe, 18 Jewel, Blue Matte Dial, Baton Numerals, 18K White Gold, 1975 .... 5405.00
Patek Philippe, Bracelet, 18K Pink Gold, Silver Matte Dial, Square, 1945 .... 3450.00
Patek Philippe, Open Face, 18 Jewel, Nickel Lever Movement, Silver Matte Dial 3737.00
Patek Philippe, Open Face, White Enamel Dial, Roman Numerals, 1915 .... 3737.00
Patek Philippe, Woman's, 18 Jewel, Black Enamel Geometric, 8 Adjustments, 1925 .... 8050.00
Patek Philippe, Woman's, 20 Jewel, 18K Gold, Champagne Matte Dial, Case, 1959 ... 2300.00
Patek Philippe, Woman's, Pendant, White Enamel Dial, Arabic Numerals, 1900 .... 2875.00
Pavel Buhre, Hunting Case, Presentation, Imperial Eagle On Cover, c.1900, 2 In. 3162.00
Pendant, 18 Jewel, Gilt Lever Movement, Engine Turned Dial, 1915 .... 4025.00
Pendant, 18K Gold, Scarab Form, White Enamel Dial, Seed Pearl Links 7475.00
Pendant, Helmet Suspended From Wings, Allied Flags, 1942, 2 1/2 In. 75.00
Perret & Co., Scenes On Both Sides Of Case, Paddle Wheeler, Gentleman On Deck 140.00
Piaget, Woman's, 17 Jewel, Silvered Matte Dial, Baton Numerals, Circular Case, 1970 .. 1725.00
Piaget, Woman's, 18 Jewel, Circular Nickel Lever Movement, Baton Numerals, Case 4600.00
Piguet, Hunting Case, Chronograph, White Enamel Dial, Arabic Numerals, 1890 .... 12650.00
Railroad, Conrail, Fob & Chain, Display Case 180.00
Railroad, Fusee Movement, England 275.00
Railroad, Nickel Movement, 19 Jewel, Dated December 8, 1800, Gold Filled Case 385.00
Railroad, Santa Fe Railroad, Fob & Chain, Display Case 180.00
Railroad, Southern Railroad, Fob & Chain, Display Case 180.00
Repeating, Chronograph, Nickel Lever Movement, White Enamel Dial, France, 1890 .... 3162.00
Repeating, Gilt Lever Movement, Silver Dial, Roman Numerals, 18K Gold, 1899 ...... 5175.00
Rockford, 17 Jewel, Gold Filled, Pocket 60.00
Rockford, Key Wind, Open Face, White Enamel Seconds Dial 75.00
Rolex, Cellini, Open Face, Silver Matte Dial, Baton Numerals, 18K Gold, 1960 .... 1725.00
South Bend, 7 Jewel, Chrome Case 45.00
Southern Railroad, Fob & Chain 180.00
Touchon & Co., 24 Jewel, Open Face, Minute Repeating, 18K Gold 2530.00
Ulysse Nardin, Hunting Case, Chronograph, White Enamel Dial, 1900, 18K Gold 3737.00
Ulysse Nardin, Hunting Case, Chronograph, White Enamel Dial, Arabic Numerals 3165.00
Vacheron & Constantin, Breguet Numerals, White Enamel Dial, Gilt Brass, 1823 ...... 1265.00
Vacheron & Constantin, Open Face, Signed Geneve Dial, 18K Gold Case 1725.00
Waltham, 15 Jewel, Chrome Case 50.00

Waltham, 19 Jewel, 14K Yellow Gold, Pocket, Yellow Gold Watch Fob 302.00
Waltham, Hunting Case, Bird In Tree, 12 Diamonds, 7 Jewel, Gold, Pocket 250.00
Waltham, Hunting Case, Engraved, White Enamel Dial, Second Hand 55.00
Waltham, Hunting Case, Motto, 17 Jewel, Chain & Fob 520.00
Waltham, Textured Gold Wreath, Seed Pearls, Black Arabic Numerals, 14K Gold, 1900 . . 1495.00
Woman's, Repeating Feather & Star, Gilt Metal Dust Cover, 14K Yellow Gold Case 143.00
Woman's, Silver, Roman Numerals, Open Face, On Chain, Pocket 45.00

WATCH FOBS were worn on watch chains. They were popular during
Victorian times and after. Many styles, especially advertising designs,
are still made today.

Advertising, International Harvester Co., Tractor, Ehrbar, 1950s, 1 7/8 In. 65.00
Anheuser-Busch Beer, Brass & Leather, 1880s, 1 x 3 1/2 In. 93.00
Arrowhead, Mystic Workers 36.00
Avery Steam Tractor 45.00
Baseball Mitt, Brass 55.00
Black & Tan Shoe Polish, Black & Tan Dog, Herriott Bros. & Co., St. Louis, Mo. 105.00
Buffalo Bill, Pawnee Bill, Names Around Bottom, Metal, 1 3/4 In. 220.00
Buffalo Bill, Wild West Show, 1916 . . . . 175.00
Buffalo Head 110.00
Buster Brown Shoes, Celluloid, 1930s 125.00
Constitution Sesqui, Commission, Busts, Independence Hall, 1937, 1 3/4 In. 22.00
Dead Shot Powder, American Powder Mills, Falling Duck, Bronze, 1 1/4 In. 50.00
Dr Pepper, Silver Metal, Waco, Texas, Reverse 300.00
Euclid Earth Moving Equipment, Dump Truck, Silver Metal, 1 1/2 In. 22.00
Florida, Land Of Sunshine & Flowers, Alligator On Bottom, Gold Finish, 40 x 45 In. 49.00
Gardeau Denver Drill, Figural 15.00
Hamlight Lantern, Lantern Shape 95.00
Kansas City, Eagle, With Outstretched Wings, Red Enamel 79.00
Maxwell House Coffee, Red Enamel, Embossed Package Of Coffee 125.00
Medal, Brown vs. Amherst Dual Meet 1916, Running High Jump, Silver, 1 1/4 In. 20.00
Napoleon Flour 90.00
National Sportsman 50.00
Old Dutch Cleanser, Brass 65.00
OVB Sporting Goods 60.00
State Fair School, Boy's, Ears Of Corn Center, Black Lettering, 1 3/4 x 1 1/8 In. 39.00
United States Steel Corporation, 25 Years Of Service At Top, Sterling 49.00
Washington State, 4 Leaf Clover Shape, Bust & State Name, 1 1/4 In. 11.00

WATERFORD type glass resembles the famous glass made from 1783 to
1851 in the Waterford Glass Works in Ireland. It is a clear glass that
was often decorated by cutting. Modern glass is being made again in
Waterford, Ireland, and is marketed under the name *Waterford*.

Bell, Christmas, 1989 . . . . 80.00
Biscuit Jar, Colleen 130.00
Bowl, Aran Isles, 10 In. 115.00
Bucket, Champagne, Large 300.00
Clock, 6-Sided, Box 110.00
Compote, Diamond Point, Foliate Band, Reeded Rim, 8 x 10 In., Pair 690.00
Decanter, Ship's, 10 3/4 In. . . . . .105.00 to 127.00
Figurine, Labrador Retriever, 5 In. 75.00
Goblet, Colleen, 4 3/4 In. . . . . .130.00 to 140.00
Jar, Cover, Pineapple, 8 1/2 In. 129.00
Paperweight, Capital 70.00
Punch Bowl, 9 1/4 x 11 1/4 In. 385.00
Tumbler, Brandy, Lismore, 6 Piece 115.00
Tumbler, Diamond Cut, Beveled, 5 Oz. 23.00
Tumbler, Donegal, Footed, 5 1/4 In., 12 Piece 600.00
Vase, Footed, 7 In. 75.00
Wine, Maeve, 8 Piece 385.00
Wine, Tyrone, Diamond Cutting 42.00
Wine Set, Decanter, 8 Stemmed Glasses, Rayed Bottom, Signed, 10 x 7 1/2 In. 500.00

WATT family members bought the Globe pottery of Crooksville, Ohio, in 1922. They made pottery mixing bowls and tableware of the type made by Globe. In 1935 they changed the production and made the pieces with the freehand decorations that are popular with collectors today. Apple, Starflower, Rooster, Tulip, and Autumn Foliage are the best-known patterns. Pansy, also called Rio Rose, was the earliest pattern. Apple, the most popular pattern, can be dated from the leaves. Originally, the apples had three leaves; after 1958 two leaves were used. The plant closed in 1965. For more information, see *Kovels' Depression Glass & Dinnerware Price List.*

Apple, Bowl, 2-Leaf, Spaghetti, No. 39	200.00
Apple, Bowl, Cereal, No. 94	85.00
Apple, Bowl, Spaghetti, No. 39	125.00 to 185.00
Apple, Grease Jar, No. 01	500.00
Apple, Mixing Bowl, Ribbed, No. 04	65.00
Apple, Pitcher, No. 15	85.00
Apple, Salt & Pepper, Hourglass, Advertising, 4 1/2 In.	250.00
Brownstone, Pitcher, Green, No. 16	35.00
Butterfly, Creamer, No. 62	3200.00
Cherry, Bowl, No. 55	190.00
Cookie Jar, Policeman, 11 In.	700.00
Crocus, Pitcher, No. 15	1000.00
Double Apple, Baker, No. 96	135.00
Double Apple, Mixing Bowl, No. 04	195.00
Dutch Tulip, Bean Pot, 2 Handles, No. 76	275.00
Dutch Tulip, Cheese Crock, Cover, No. 80	700.00
Dutch Tulip, Creamer, No. 62	25.00
Dutch Tulip, Pitcher, No. 15	250.00
Esmond, Cookie Jar, Happy, Sad Face, No. 34	120.00
Kitch-N-Queen, Ice Bucket, No. 59	200.00
Kitch-N-Queen, Pie Plate, No. 33	100.00
Orchard Ware, Pitcher, Greenbriar, Plain Lip, No. 17	145.00
Pansy, Bull's-Eye, Bowl, Spaghetti, No. 39	195.00
Pansy, Cross Hatch, Cookie Jar, No. 21	120.00
Pansy, Cut-Leaf, Bowl, Spaghetti, No. 39	125.00
Pansy, Cut-Leaf, Cookie Jar	88.00
Pansy, Cut-Leaf, Pie Plate, No. 33	165.00
Pansy, Cut-Leaf, Pitcher, No. 15	210.00
Pansy, Cut-Leaf, Pitcher, No. 16	100.00
Pansy, Cut-Leaf, Pitcher, No. 17	110.00
Par-T-Que, Creamer, No. 62	650.00
Par-T-Que, Plate, Dinner, No. 101	95.00
Rooster, Creamer, No. 62	275.00
Rooster, Dutch Oven, No. 70	395.00
Rooster, Pitcher, No. 15	94.00
Rooster, Pitcher, Porter's Gas Miller, S.D., 4 In.	65.00
Rooster, Pitcher, Refrigerator, No. 69	325.00 to 850.00
Rooster, Salt & Pepper, Barrel	500.00
Starflower, 4-Petal, Creamer, No. 62	275.00 to 425.00
Starflower, 4-Petal, Jar, Grease, No. 47	375.00
Starflower, 4-Petal, Mug, No. 501	70.00
Starflower, Bowl, Spaghetti, Slant Side, No. 39	140.00
Starflower, Pitcher, Green-On-Brown, No. 17	175.00
Starflower, Pitcher, No. 62	50.00
Starflower, Pitcher, Refrigerator, No. 69	850.00
Tear Drop, Creamer, No. 62	160.00 to 450.00
Tear Drop, Pitcher, Refrigerator, No. 69	230.00
Tulip, Cookie Jar, No. 503	400.00
Tulip, Creamer, No. 62	158.00 to 250.00
Tulip, Pitcher, Ice Lip, No. 17	400.00
Tulip, Pitcher, No. 16	140.00

WAVE CREST glass is an opaque white glassware manufactured by the Pairpoint Manufacturing Company of New Bedford, Massachusetts, and some French factories. It was decorated by the C.F. Monroe Company of Meriden, Connecticut. The glass was painted in pastel colors and decorated with flowers. The name *Wave Crest* was used after 1898.

WAVE CREST WARE

Biscuit Jar, Hand Painted Floral, Raised Ribs, Silver Plated Lid & Handle, 7 1/2 In.	188.00
Biscuit Jar, Pink Flowers On White, Silver Plate Top & Handle	250.00
Bowl, Floral, Blue, England, 7 1/2 In.	350.00
Bowl, Monkey On Side, Ormolu Rim	300.00
Box, Baroque Shell, Enameled Florals & Scrolls, Brass Fittings, Satin Lining, 7 In.	1000.00
Box, Cigar Band, Blue Lining, 2 1/2 x 3 3/4 In.	1250.00
Box, Cover, Baroque Shell, Allover Design, Satin Lining, 5 1/2 In.	460.00
Box, Cover, Helmschmied Swirl, Pink Flowers, On Yellow, Satin Lining, 5 1/2 In.	430.00
Box, Cover, Mill Scene, New Liner, 4 In.	440.00
Box, Dresser, Yellow Centered Stylized Flowers, Hinged Rim, 3 3/4 x 6 3/4 In.	488.00
Box, Floral, Pink Lined, 6 In.	650.00
Box, Floral, Pink, Soft Blue Ground, New Liner, 7 In.	495.00
Box, Flowers & Heart Design, Keys, 7 In.	900.00
Box, Helmschmied Swirl, Enameled Flowers, White Silk Lining, Round, 8 In.	850.00
Box, Helmschmied Swirl, Floral, 3 In.	192.00
Box, Helmschmied Swirl, Floral, Blue, Cream, 6 1/2 In.	467.00
Box, Helmschmied Swirl, Lily Of The Valley, Pale Blue, 3 In.	205.00
Box, Helmschmied Swirl, New Liner, 6 1/2 In.	522.00
Box, Helmschmied Swirl, Yellow & Green, Pink Floral, Signed, 3 3/4 x 5 1/2 In.	530.00
Box, Pink, Burgundy Etching, Octagonal, Signed, 8 1/2 In.	1150.00
Box, Pink, Metal Feet, Signed, 4 x 6 In.	350.00
Ewer, Melon Ribbed Shape, Wild Rose, Metal Mounted, 15 1/4 x 5 In., Pair	200.00
Fernery, Egg Crate Shape, Original Liner	395.00
Jar, Silver Cover, Opal Ware, Pink Shadow Traceries, Apple Blossom, 6 1/2 In.	490.00
Jardiniere, Flowers, Scrolled Border, Signed, 8 1/2 In.	250.00
Planter, Light Blue, Embossed Rococo, Original Liner, 4 1/2 In.	425.00
Salt & Pepper, Cats In Green Wreath Design, Rib Base	145.00
Salt & Pepper, Helmschmied Swirl, Puffy Shape	135.00
Sugar, Cherub, Floral, Yellow	60.00
Tobacco Jar, Clover Design, Blue Ground, 5 In.	880.00
Tray, Mirror, Swivel, Floral, Ormolu Mounts, 9 1/2 x 9 1/2 x 6 In.	1035.00
Vase, Blue & Pink Flowers, White Enamel Beads, 6 3/4 In.	475.00
Vase, Blue Flowers, Metal Handles & Base, 5 In.	475.00

WEAPONS listed here include instruments of combat other than guns, knives, rifles, or swords. Firearms are not listed in this book. Knives and swords are listed in their own categories.

Billy Club, Hardwood, Legend Sailor's Rights, Reverse Greasey Luck, 28 In.	1035.00
Nightstick, Police, Blond Hardwood, 23 1/2 In.	20.00

WEATHER VANES were used in seventeenth-century Boston. The direction of the wind was an indication of coming weather, important to the seafaring and farming communities. By the mid-nineteenth century, commercial weather vanes were made of metal. Today's collectors often consider weather vanes to be examples of folk art, even though they may not have been handmade.

Alligator, Chasing Boy, Tin, Wood, Wrought-Iron Base, 57 x 49 In.	715.00
Arrow, Fish Center, Green Paint, Pine Base, 20th Century, 37 x 29 In.	225.00
Arrow, Steel, 20 Pierced Feathers, Scrolls, Directionals, 74 In.	2185.00
Arrow & Banner, Gilding, Late 19th Century, 22 1/2 x 47 In.	1840.00
Arrow & Directional, Copper, American, 19th Century, 51 In.	1092.00
Banner, Arrow, Pointing Hand, Openwork, Cast Zinc Head, Yellow, 14 In.	4600.00
Banner, Arrow, Pointing, Sheet Metal, Pierced Stars, Cast Zinc Head, 13 In.	9200.00
Banner, Copper, Rope Edge Square, Trefoil Mounts, 1860, 23 x 25 1/2 In.	935.00
Blackhawk, Copper, Allover Verdigris, Late 19th Century, 17 x 25 In.	3105.00
Bull, Standing, Copper, Allover Verdigris, Late 19th Century, 30 x 42 In.	34500.00
Bull, Tin, 6 1/2 x 9 1/4 In.	120.00
Calf, Stand, Tin, 19th Century, 15 x 21 In.	3630.00

Cow, Cast Zinc Head, Copper Ears, Gilt, Tassel Tail, 27 In. 6325.00
Cow, Copper, 19th Century, 16 3/4 x 28 1/4 In. 2464.00
Cow, Copper, Cushing & White, Boston, Mass., On Stand, Bullet Hole, 17 x 28 In. 2465.00
Cow, Copper, Gilt, Zinc Head, 19 x 27 In. 6325.00
Cow, Molded Gilt, Copper, Verdigris Surface, 19th Century, 21 x 33 x 8 In. 23000.00
Cow, Molded Gilt, Copper, Verdigris Surface, Late 19th Century, 28 In. 2185.00
Cow, Swell-Bodied, Cast Zinc Head, Copper, 19th Century, 33 In. 9200.00
Cupid, Standing, Perched On Arrow, Sheet Iron 290.00
Dove, 3-Dimensional, Arched Wings, Gilt, On Ball Over Arrow, 21 x 25 In. 4950.00
Dragon, Copper, Ball Finial, Post, 1890-1910, 45 x 37 In. 660.00
Eagle, Copper, Allover Verdigris, On Contemporary Stand, 9 x 17 1/4 In. 230.00
Eagle, Copper, Outstretched Wings, Perched On Belted Ball Directional, 29 In. 345.00
Eagle, Full-Bodied, Copper, Perched On Ball With An Arrow, 21 x 25 In. 375.00
Eagle, On Ball On Arrow, 26-In. Wingspan 2850.00
Eagle, On Globe, Blue Hawkeye Globe, NEWS, Painted, Tin & Metal, 29 x 17 In. 330.00
Eagle, On Globe, Tin, Painted, 17 x 27 In. 355.00
Eagle, Raised Wings, Yellow Gold, Sheet Iron, 12 x 22 In. 1035.00
Elephant, Sheet Steel, Blue Paint, Directionals, 28 1/2 In. 55.00
Ewe, Late 19th Century 2860.00
Fish, Codfish, Molded Copper & Zinc, American, 19th Century, 10 In. 8625.00
Fish, Copper, Iron Shaft With Iron Flange, 25 x 43 In. 300.00
Fox, Running, Cast & Gilded Zinc, American, 19th Century, 14 1/2 In. 4887.00
Goose, Verdigris, 20 In. 450.00
Horse, Arabian Prancer, Full-Bodied, c.1870, 14 x 20 In. 2800.00
Horse, Copper, Iron Directionals, 50 In. 165.00
Horse, Flying, Sheet Iron, Silhouetted Figure, Black, Red, 19 1/2 In. 2587.00
Horse, Jumping, Copper, Gilt, Old Painted Surface, Late 19th Century, 18 In. 2300.00
Horse, Running, Copper, Hollow Body, Zinc Head, Iron Directionals, 65 1/4 In. 1100.00
Horse, Running, Copper, Mane, Tail Flowing, Mounted On Rod Standard, 26 In. 345.00
Horse, Running, Copper, Zinc, Counted On Rod & Base, J. Howard & Co., 36 In. 9775.00
Horse, Running, Molded Copper, Late 19th Century, 15 1/2 x 26 In. 430.00
Horse, Running, Wrought Iron, Yellow, Black Painted Surface, 1870, 18 In. 2640.00
Horse, Running, Zinc, Late 19th Century, 19 x 31 In. 2760.00
Horse, Sheet Iron, Old Green Paint, Late 19th Century, 29 1/2 x 30 In. 430.00
Horse, Trotting, Copper, Gilt, Late 19th Century, 17 1/4 x 32 1/2 In. 1035.00
Horse, Trotting, Driver, Copper, 25 1/2 In. 1035.00
Horse, Trotting, Driver, Copper, Painted Gray, Iron Finders, Pole, 32 In. 550.00
Horse & Rider, Copper, Zinc, Gilt, 1870-1890, 24 1/2 In. 11550.00
Horse & Rider, Sheet Iron, Old Green Paint, 19 1/2 x 20 In. 575.00
Horse & Sulky, Copper, 3-Dimensional, Directionals, 1890-1910, 44 x 25 In. 6050.00
Horse & Sulky, Molded & Gilded Copper, 19th Century, 21 1/4 In. 9775.00
Indian, Aiming Arrow, Copper, 24 In. 935.00
Indian, Holding Bow & Arrow, Copper, Molded, 24 In. 12650.00
Leaping Stag, On Rod In Metal, Base, Copper & Zinc, 23 1/2 In. 8050.00
Lightning Rod, Tin, Embossed Car & Driver, Arrows, Cobalt Glass Ball, 23 x 66 In. 385.00
Lightning Rod, Tin, Wrought Iron Arrows, Embossed, Cobalt Glass Ball, 48 In. 155.00
Lion, Rampant, Holding Chalice, Heart Cutouts, Wrought Iron, 32 In. 1045.00
Locomotive, Silhouetted Steam Engine, Dark Green, 20 x 15 In. 920.00
Man & Woman Riding Tandem Bike On Arrow, Cap Cod Weathervane Co., 1960s 160.00
Marlin, Full-Bodied, Copper, c.1920, 16 x 45 In. 825.00
Painter's Palette & Paint, Copper, Wooden Base, Early 20th Century, 42 1/2 In. 2875.00
Peacock, Sheet Iron, On Stand With Directionals, Green Paint, 64 In. 2300.00
Pig, With Insulating Ball, Pressed Stars & Arrow, Copper, Zinc & Steel, 72 In. 355.00
Pony, Full-Bodied, Copper, Fiske, Late 19th Century, 16 1/2 x 23 In. 1265.00
Rattlesnake, Slithering, Carved, Curled Serpent, Red, Yellow, 35 In. 6612.00
Rooster, Cast Zinc & Sheet Steel, 24 x 51 In. 1127.00
Rooster, Iron, Sheet Metal, Directional, Black Paint, 20th Century, 13 In. 85.00
Rooster, Molded, Copper & Gilt, 28 In. 10350.00
Rooster, On Full Arrow, Gilt Copper, 16 In. 1510.00
Rooster, On Stand, Zinc, 19th Century, 18 1/2 In. 785.00
Rooster, Painted White, Sheet Iron, 26 In. 975.00
Rooster, Robust, 3 Thickness Of Wood, Red Cox Comb, Sheet Metal Plate, 20 In. 3450.00
Rooster, Sheet Metal, With Finder, 13 1/2 In. 605.00

Rooster, Silhouette, Galvanized Sheet Metal, Traces Of Paint, 24 In. 275.00
Rooster, Silhouette, Sheet Steel, White Repaint, 24 1/2 In. 605.00
Rooster, Tin, Red Paint, Painted Wooden Stand, 20 In. 345.00
Rooster, Verdigris Patina, In Flight, Late 19th Century, 22 In. 1090.00
Sailing Vessel, Metal Masts, Sail & Rigging, Wooden, 34 In. 2875.00
Schooner, 2-Masted, Gilt, Display Stand, 64 x 59 In. 5175.00
Schooner, Golden Gilt & Copper, 2 Masted Vessel, Full-Bodied, Flags, 64 x 59 In. 5195.00
Ship, Wood & Tin, Original Paint, c.1940, 30 In. 985.00
Snake, Slithering, Carved, Round, Incised Scales, Pine, 36 In. 460.00
St. Julian With Sulky, Hollow Copper, Iron Horse Head, J.W. Fiske, 1887, 38 In. 2530.00
Steam Engine, Belching Smoke, Sheet Iron, 24 In. 325.00
Sulky Rider, Full-Bodied Horse, Sheet Sulky & Rider, c.1890, 24 x 46 In. 5225.00
Trumpet Figure, Sheet Metal, Pine, Angel Gabriel, 15 x 45 1/4 In. 4600.00
Whale, Wood, Hinged Tail, Late 19th Century, 30 In. 1650.00
Young Man Chasing Dog, Chasing Bird, Copper, 24 In. 977.00

WEBB glass is made by Thomas Webb & Sons of Ambelcot, England.
Many types of art and cameo glass were made by them during the Victorian era. Production ceased by 1991, and the factory was demolished
in 1995. Webb Burmese and Webb Peachblow are special colored
glasswares of the Victorian era. They are listed at the end of this section. Glassware that is not Burmese or Peachblow is included here.

Webb

Biscuit Jar, Flower & Acorn, Gold Prunus Blossom, Pinched Sides, Plated Lid, 9 3/4 In. . 1320.00
Bowl, Butterflies, Gold Vines, 7 In. 200.00
Creamer, Gold Prunus Blossoms, Gold At Rim & Base, 3 1/4 In. 385.00
Dish, Gold Prunus Blossoms & Butterfly, Silver Plated Holder, 3 x 5 1/2 In. 265.00
Ewer, Cranberry, White, Applied Cranberry Handle, 11 1/4 In. 173.00
Jar, Sweetmeat, Gold Prunus, White Mother-Of-Pearl, Silver Plated Fittings, 3 1/4 In. 770.00
Mug, Alexandrite, Applied Handle, Citron To Rose To Blue, 2 3/4 In. 805.00
Perfume Bottle, Citron, White, Lily-Of-The-Valley Decoration, Case 2645.00
Perfume Bottle, Floral, Overlay, Conforming Stopper, 5 In. 5950.00
Rose Bowl, Apricot To Pink To Lavender, Gold Encrusted Blossoms, 2 1/4 In. 825.00
Rose Jar, Ruby Overlay, Wild Roses, Cameo, Silver Plated Cover, 9 In. 3735.00
Vase, Basket Weave, Blue To White, 12 In. 205.00
Vase, Diamond-Quilted, Blue, Gold Design, 10 1/2 In. 285.00
Vase, Etched Grape & Vine Design, Faceted Body, Hexagonal Stem, Footed, 11 1/2 In. .. 210.00
Vase, Floral, Ruby Red, Opal White Narcissus, Ornamental Grasses On Reverse, 7 In. ... 2760.00
Vase, Gold Bird With Leaves & Berries, Oriental Base, 9 3/4 In. 345.00
Vase, Hawthorn Blossoms & Birds, Jewel Eyes, 10 1/2 In. 1000.00
Vase, Iris, Wild Flowers, Diamond-Quilted, Red On Opaque White, 8 In. 575.00
Vase, Mythological Bird Serpent Design, Floral Grounds, Old Ivory, 8 1/2 In. . . .3737.00 to 5175.00
Vase, Orchid, Red, Opal White, Daisies On Reverse, Amber Body, Gold Ground, 5 3/4 In. . 5175.00
Vase, Raindrop, Butterscotch Mother-Of-Pearl, Signed, 6 In. 145.00
Vase, Watermelon Color, Enamel Beaded Design, 7 In. 175.00
Vase, White Flowers, Red Ground, Cameo, 7 3/4 In. 345.00
Vase, White Morning Glories, Citron Ground, 5 1/8 In. 1650.00
Vase, White, Blue, Cameo, 4 3/8 In. 247.00
Vase, White, Leafy Vines, Floral Clusters, Cranberry Ground, 9 3/4 In. 7700.00

WEBB BURMESE is a colored Victorian glass made by Thomas Webb
& Sons of Stourbridge, England, from 1886.

Bowl, Pink Shading To Yellow, Ruffled Edge, Rolled Rim, 6 x 6 x 2 In. 288.00
Bowl, Salmon Shading To Yellow, Ruffled Edge, 2 1/2 x 4 In. 235.00
Epergne, Queen's, 3 Burmese Lilies, Signed, 15 In. 3740.00
Jam Jar, Grapes & Leaves, Silver Plated, 7 x 4 In. 285.00
Lamp, Fairy, Double, Clarke Base, Signed, 11 1/2 In. 4600.00
Lamp, Fairy, Skirt Base 950.00
Nut Dish, Salmon To Yellow, Petal Top, 2 1/4 x 3 1/2 In. 145.00
Rose Bowl, Green & Brown Leaves, Blue Berries, Beaded Top, 2 3/4 x 2 1/4 In. 170.00
Rose Bowl, Prunus Blossom, Footed, Satin, 3 3/4 x 2 1/2 In. ....290.00 to 375.00
Rose Bowl, Prunus Blossom, Satin, 2 1/2 x 2 3/4 In. ....285.00 to 315.00
Rose Bowl, Prunus Design, Matte Finish, 3 3/4 x 2 1/2 In. 285.00
Rose Bowl, Star Top, 2 5/8 In. 247.00

Sugar & Creamer, Currants & Leaves, 2 3/4 In. 460.00
Sugar & Creamer, Pinecone, Satin, 2 1/2 In. 630.00
Toothpick, Hat, Blue Threading, 2 1/4 x 3 In. 200.00
Tumbler, Grape & Vine, Leaves, Satin, 3 3/4 In. 200.00
Vase, Curio, Fuchsia, Petal Top, Satin, Marked, 3 1/2 x 3 In. 230.00
Vase, Curio, Green & Teal Design, Bulbous, Petal Top, 3 3/4 x 3 In. 260.00
Vase, Curio, Green Ivy, Ruffled Edge, 4 1/2 In. 59.00
Vase, Curio, Leaves & Vines, Satin, 4 In. 345.00
Vase, Curio, Prunus Blossom, Petal Top, 3 3/4 x 3 In. 230.00
Vase, Curio, Prunus Blossom, Ruffled Edge, 4 1/2 x 2 In. 260.00
Vase, Curio, Prunus Blossom, Satin, 3 1/2 x 3 In. 290.00
Vase, Curio, Red Flowers, Green Leaves, Petal Top, 3 3/4 In. 230.00
Vase, Wild Rose, Brown Leaves, Bulbous, Signed, 2 3/4 x 3 1/2 In. 290.00

WEBB PEACHBLOW is a colored Victorian glass made by Thomas
Webb & Sons of Stourbridge, England, from 1885.

Biscuit Jar, Gold Enamel Floral, Butterfly, Plated Top, Brass Handle, 7 In. 630.00
Finger Bowl, Underplate, Floral, Gold Enamel, Insect 522.00
Rose Bowl, 3 1/8 In. 412.00
Vase, Gold Design, c.1890, 12 In. 1700.00
Vase, Gold, Enameled, Floral, 2 Applied White Handles, 6 1/2 In. 170.00

WEDGWOOD, one of the world's most successful potteries, was
founded by Josiah Wedgwood, who was considered a cripple by his
brother and was forbidden to work at the family business. The pottery
was established in England in 1759. A large variety of wares has been
made, including the well-known jasperware, basalt, creamware, and
even a limited amount of porcelain. There are two kinds of jasperware.
One is made from two colors of clay, the other is made from one color
of clay with a color dip to create the contrast in design. The firm is still
in business. Other Wedgwood pieces may be listed under Flow Blue,
Majolica, or in other porcelain categories.

WEDGWOOD

Basket, Undertray, Creamware, Basket Weave Centers, 10 In. 485.00
Biscuit Jar, Blue Jasper, Maidens With Cherubs, Silver Plate Mounted, 1900, 6 In. 135.00
Biscuit Jar, Cover, Dip, Jasperware, Lilac, Hunting Scene, White Relief, 5 1/2 In. 600.00
Biscuit Jar, Cover, Jasperware, Blue, Sacrifice To Cupid, Handle, Ball Feet, 6 In. 250.00
Biscuit Jar, Cover, Jasperware, Cobalt Blue, Dip, Maternal Affection, Handle, 5 In. 225.00
Biscuit Jar, Cover, Jasperware, Cobalt, Sacrifice To Cupid, Handle, 5 1/4 In. 250.00
Biscuit Jar, Cover, Jasperware, Light Blue, Hunting Scene, Handles, 5 1/4 In. 425.00
Biscuit Jar, Cover, Jasperware, Lilac, Sacrifice To Cupid, Handle, 5 1/4 In. 375.00
Biscuit Jar, Cover, Jasperware, Sage Green, White Grapevine Border, Handle 500.00
Biscuit Jar, Cover, Tricolor, Dark Blue Panel, Light Blue Ground, Handle, 5 In. 500.00
Biscuit Jar, Dip, Jasperware, Lilac, Handle With Ivory Knob, 5 1/2 In. 475.00
Biscuit Jar, Jasperware, Tricolor, Yellow Banding On Both Sides Of Black Frieze 850.00
Biscuit Jar, Yellow Ground, Black Swag, Silver Mounts, 4 3/4 In. 320.00
Bottle, Coachman, Moonstone, Etruria 65.00
Bough Pot, Cover, Classical Figures, Floral Urns, White Relief, Light Blue, 9 In. 3335.00
Bowl, Black Basalt, Cover, Black Classical Relief, 19th Century, 4 In. 230.00
Bowl, Commemorative, Vignettes Of Presidents & Monuments, 12 In. 90.00
Bowl, Domestic Scenes, Foliate Frame, Signed, Early 20th Century, 6 1/8 In. 200.00
Bowl, Dragon Luster, Blue & Gold Exterior, Green Interior, 2 1/4 x 4 In. 95.00
Bowl, Dragon Luster, Green Exterior, Mother-Of-Pearl Interior, 1920, 9 In. 635.00
Bowl, Dragon Luster, Iridescent Green & Gold, Octagonal, 5 x 9 In. 350.00
Bowl, Dragon Luster, Mottled Orange Exterior, Blue Interior, 5 1/2 In. 175.00
Bowl, Dragon Luster, Ruby Exterior, Mother-Of-Pearl Interior, 1920, 8 In. 635.00
Bowl, Fairyland Luster, Birds On Exterior, Octagonal, 4 3/4 In. 495.00
Bowl, Fairyland Luster, Blue Exterior, Mother-Of-Pearl Interior, 1920, 6 In. 375.00
Bowl, Fairyland Luster, Boxing Match Interior, Octagonal, 1920, 10 In. 5460.00
Bowl, Fairyland Luster, Castle On A Road, Fairy In Cage Interior, c.1920, 9 In. 3737.00
Bowl, Fairyland Luster, Geisha, Octagonal, 6 In. 2530.00
Bowl, Fairyland Luster, Gold Butterflies & Bug, Maroon Exterior, 10 1/2 In. 715.00
Bowl, Fairyland Luster, Nizami Interior, Wolf, Stag Border, 1920, 8 In. 5460.00
Bowl, Fairyland Luster, Phoenix & Dragon Design, Octagonal, 7 In. 920.00

Bowl, Jasperware, Cobalt Blue, White Relief, Domestic Scenes, Footed, 6 In.	175.00
Bowl, Jasperware, Dancing Hours, Black, White Relief, England, 1965, 9 In.	375.00
Bowl, Jasperware, Light Blue, White Oak Leaf Border, Footed, Ball Feet, 7 1/4 In.	225.00
Bowl, Jasperware, Tricolor, White, Green Acanthus Leaves, Lilac Bell Flowers, 6 In.	450.00
Bowl, Majolica, Band Of Leaf, Berry Design, Scalloped Rim, 1874, 9 5/8 In.	690.00
Bowl, Sugar, Cover, Jasperware, Blue, White Classical Relief, Rim, 4 1/4 In.	150.00
Box, Cover, Jasperware, Dark Blue, Heart Shape, Floral Border, 6 In.	200.00
Box, Cover, Jasperware, Yellow, White Prunus, Late 19th Century, 3 1/4 In.	80.00
Bulb Pot, Jasperware, Dark Blue, Footed, Liner, 5 x 8 1/4 In., Pair	305.00
Bust, Byron, Black Basalt, Waisted Circular Base, Mid-19th Century, 8 In.	635.00
Bust, John Wesley, Black Basalt, Waisted Circular Base, 1883, 8 In.	400.00
Bust, Joseph Addison, Black Basalt, On Raised Square Plinth, 10 In.	690.00
Bust, Mercury, Black Basalt, Waisted Circular Base, 9 In.	980.00
Bust, Mercury, Black Basalt, Winged Cap, 1875, 19 1/2 In.	6900.00
Bust, Mercury, Waisted Circular Base, England, 1850, 17 In.	2300.00
Bust, Milton, Black Basalt, Waisted Circular Base, England, 13 In.	750.00
Bust, Paul Bunyan, Waisted Circular Base, England, 1860, 14 In.	460.00
Bust, Plato & Homer, Black Basalt, 12 & 10 1/2 In., Pair	1150.00
Bust, Shakespeare, Black Basalt, England, 1964, 10 In.	375.00
Bust, Sir Isaac Newton, Black Basalt, Waisted Circular Base, 9 In.	490.00
Bust, Stephenson, Waisted Circular Base, England, 1858, 14 In. . . . . .345.00 to 635.00
Bust, Virgil, Waisted Circular Base, England, 12 In.	520.00
Butter, Jasper Dip, Blue, White Floral, Foliate, Classical Figures, 6 In.	300.00
Butter, Tub, Cover, Jasperware, Dark Blue, White Classical Figures, 4 1/4 In.	175.00
Cachepot, Blue & White, Floral, Basalt, 4 7/8 x 4 1/4 In., Pair	58.00
Cachepot, Jasper Dip, Olive Green, Sacrifice To Cupid, 6 In.	225.00
Cachepot, Jasperware, Black, White Relief Of Muses, Floral Border, 5 1/4 In.	325.00
Cachepot, Jasperware, Cobalt, White Classical Figures, Stylized Floral Border	125.00
Cachepot, Jasperware, Cobalt, White Relief Of Maidens, Floral Border, 9 In.	200.00
Cachepot, Jasperware, Olive Green, White Floral Border, 7 x 10 In.	300.00
Cachepot, Jasperware, Sage Green, White Relief Of Muses, White Floral Festoons	225.00
Candlestick, Bell Flower Border, Signed, Early 20th Century, 7 1/4 In., Pair	345.00
Candlestick, Black Basalt, Dolphin, 1790s, Pair	5900.00
Candlestick, Black Basalt, Dolphin, Shell Border, Rectangular, 9 In., Pair	1495.00
Candlestick, Jasperware, Light Green, White Bell Flower Border, 7 1/2 In., Pair	300.00
Candlestick, Jasperware, Olive Green, Bell Flower Border, Handle, 7 In., Pair	300.00
Candlestick, Jasperware, Tricolor, Yellow Body, Black Foliate Border, 6 In., Pair	850.00
Candlestick, Muses, 19th Century, Pair	400.00
Charger, Earthenware, Landscape Scene, Pont Tyntur, North Wales, 1883, 16 In.	520.00
Chocolate Set, Acanthus & Bellflowers, Oak Leaf Boarder, Signed, 3 Piece	2855.00
Clock, Jasperware, Classical, Dark Blue & White, 6 x 5 In.	750.00
Coffeepot, Cover, Black Basalt, Inverted Beehive Form, Engine Turned, 8 In.	430.00
Coffeepot, Cover, Drabware, Arabesque Design, Orange Peel Ground, 9 In.	230.00
Coffeepot, Cover, Queensware, Pear Shape, Tea Party, Black Transfer, 1770, 7 In.	400.00
Crane, Glass Eyes, Rocky Base, Ernest Light, 1915, 6 In.	430.00
Demitasse Set, Green, Gilt Banded Border, 24 Piece	320.00
Dish, Cheese, Cover, Lilac Jasper Dip, White Classical Relief, 1875, 7 In.	1265.00
Dish, Dog Finial On Cover, Smear Ware, c.1820, 4 1/2 In.	275.00
Dish, Queensware, French Soldier Counting Money, Scalloped Rim, 1860, 11 In.	405.00
Dish, Shell Form, Bone China, Enamel Shell, Seaweed, England, 12 3/8 In.	85.00
Dish, Smearware, Potpourri, Blue Fruiting Grapevine, Handles, 9 In.	600.00
Ewer, Jasperware, Cobalt Blue, White Floral Festoon, Handle, 1888, 8 In.	475.00
Figurine, Apollo & Mercury, Black Basalt, Oval Base, 11 In., Pair	3220.00
Figurine, Boy, Black Basalt, Sleeping, Five Boys Of Fiammingo, 5 In. . . . . .520.00 to 805.00
Figurine, Boy, Black Basalt, Sleeping, Mid-19th Century, 4 5/8 In.	520.00
Figurine, Cockatoo, Black Basalt, Ernest Light, England, 1915, 4 In.	430.00
Figurine, Cupid & Psyche, Seated On Rock Circular Base, Black Basalt, 8 In., Pair	2185.00
Figurine, Dragon, Fairyland Luster, 8 In.	1100.00
Figurine, Duiker, Lying, Moonstone, Cream, John Skeaping, England, 20th Century, 5 In. . .	85.00
Figurine, Duiker, Standing, Moonstone, Black Basalt, J. Skeaping, England, 20th Cent., 8 In.	200.00
Figurine, Egret, Black Basalt, Glass Eyes, Rocky Base, Ernest Light, 1915, 7 In.	320.00
Figurine, Fallow Deer, Moonstone, Cream Glaze, John Skeaping, 20th Century, 7 In.	115.00
Figurine, Hercules, Black Basalt, c.1975, 11 3/8 In.	220.00

Figurine, Hope, Black Basalt, Partially Nude Figure, Oval Base, 9 3/8 In. 980.00
Figurine, Raven, Black Basalt, Glass Eyes, Ernest Light, 1915, 4 In. 375.00
Figurine, Sea Lion, Moonstone, John Skeaping, England, 20th Century, 8 In. 200.00
Figurine, Seal, Moonstone, Buff Colored, John Skeaping, 20th Century, 7 In. 115.00
Figurine, Tiger & Buck, Moonstone, Black Basalt, John Skeaping, 20th Century, 6 In. . . . 750.00
Figurine, Tiger & Buck, Moonstone, Buff Colored, John Skeaping, 20th Century, 7 1/2 In. 145.00
Figurine, Tiger & Buck, Moonstone, John Skeaping, England, 20th Century, 8 In. 260.00
Figurine, Toucans, 2 Birds Perched On Rocky Base, Ernest Light, 1915, 5 In. 805.00
Game Dish, Cover, Majolica, 2-Bird Finial, Ducks, Griffin Handles, 6 1/2 x 11 In. 920.00
Humidor, Jasperware, Blue, White, Lion's Head Ring Handles, 19th Century, 5 In. 193.00
Incense Burner, Cover, Jasperware, Light Blue Foliate Festoons, 5 In., Pair 2415.00
Inkstand, Drabware, Bird Head Handles, 1820, 8 In. 1090.00
Inkstand, Jasperware, Light Blue Medallions, White Classical Relief, Wood, 13 In. 290.00
Jam Jar, Black Grapevine Festoons, Lion Heads, Silver Plate Cover, Signed, 3 1/4 In. 170.00
Jam Jar, Cobalt Blue, c.1870 . . . . 225.00
Jam Jar, Cover, Black Basalt, Floral, Enamel, Mid-19th Century, 4 In. 865.00
Jam Jar, Jasperware, Dark Blue, White Classical Relief, Border, 20th Century, 3 In. 100.00
Jam Jar, Jasperware, Tricolor, Yellow Body, White Border, Lion Heads, 3 1/4 In. 150.00
Jardiniere, Jasperware, Band Of Male & Female Figures, Grape & Leaf Swag, 9 In. 200.00
Jardiniere, Majolica, Stand, Pink, Yellow Glaze, 1887, 16 x 24 In. 2300.00
Jardiniere, Majolica, Stand, Scrolled Flowers, Brown, Green Glaze, 1864, 25 In. 4890.00
Jug, Blue & White Classical Figures, 7 In. 275.00
Jug, Dip, Jasperware, Cobalt, Fruiting Vine Border, Sacrifice To Cupid, 5 1/4 In. 125.00
Jug, Dip, Jasperware, Yellow, Floral Festoon Border, Early 20th Century, 4 In. 550.00
Jug, Etruscan, Jasperware, Cobalt Blue, Greco Roman Key Border, 6 In. 300.00
Jug, Etruscan, Jasperware, Tricolor, Stylized Floral Bands, White Border, 7 In. 1000.00
Jug, Jasperware, Black & White, Classical, Dutch, 5 x 6 In. 425.00
Jug, Jasperware, Cobalt Blue, Floral Festoons, Sacrifice To Cupid, 4 1/4 In. 200.00
Jug, Jasperware, Crimson, White, Fruiting Vine Border, Tapered, 5 1/4 In. 950.00
Jug, Jasperware, White, Buff, Fruiting Vine Border, Sacrifice To Cupid, 7 1/2 In. 475.00
Lamp, Reading, Black Basalt, Female Figure Seated, 1875, 9 In. 2185.00
Loving Cup, Jasperware, Light Green, White Classical Relief, 3 Handles, 4 1/4 In. 400.00
Majolica, Jug, Berries, Leaf, Blossoms, Bark Mold, England, 1870, 6 3/8 In. 375.00
Matchbox, Modeled As Fly, Wings Lift To Reveal Striker, 5 1/2 In. 2990.00
Mug, Black Basalt, Silver Mounted, Molded Oak Leaf Body, 3 In. 635.00
Pin Tray, Jasperware, Light Blue, 6 x 3 1/2 In. 25.00
Pitcher, Jasper Dip, Black, Fruiting Vine Border, Rope Handle, 3 1/4 In. 200.00
Pitcher, Jasperware, Grecian Ladies & Cupids Around Body, 6 1/4 In. 175.00
Pitcher, Majolica, Black Berries, Flowers, 7 1/2 In. 85.00
Pitcher, Memorial To Lord Alfred Tennyson, Grisaille, Porcelain, 8 In. 144.00
Pitcher, Multicolored, Pearlware 975.00
Pitcher, Washington, 9 In. 330.00
Plant Pot, Figural Landscape, Medallions, Signed, Emile Lessore, 1863, 8 In. 865.00
Planter, Classical, Dark Blue & White, 3 Legs, 5 In. 495.00
Plaque, Bacchanalian Boys, White Classical Relief, 1900, 5 x 13 In. 1092.00
Plaque, Black Basalt, Gladiators, Gilt Wood Frame, 10 x 12 In. 10925.00
Plaque, Classical Figures, Green, White, Gilt Box Frame, 5 x 9 In., Pair 200.00
Plaque, Dancing Hours, Applied White Relief, Light Blue, Wood Frame, 18 In. 1150.00
Plaque, Jasperware, Tricolor, Dancing Hours, Light Blue, Green Border, 4 x 11 In. 1725.00
Plaque, Queensware, Figural Landscape, Enamel, Oval, 1860, 6 x 8 In. 1035.00
Plate, American Clipper Ships, Brown Transfer, 9 1/4 In., 12 Piece 165.00
Plate, Fairyland Luster, Blue Roc Bird, Black Border, Orange, 10 1/2 In. 4180.00
Plate, Fairyland Luster, Daisy Makeig-Jones, c.1920, 9 3/4 In. 4180.00
Plate, Fairyland Luster, Imps On Bridge, c.1920, 10 1/2 In. 5750.00
Plate, Fairyland Luster, Imps On Bridge, Roc Center, Floral Rim, c.1920, 10 1/2 In. 5750.00
Plate, Little Girl, Anticipation If Rather Dangerous, Seated By Boiling Pot, 1863 . . . . 395.00
Plate, Old London Views, 1941, Set Of 12 . . . . 225.00
Plate, Old London, First Edition, 1941 . . . . 100.00
Plate, Trophy, Jasper Dip, Lilac, Applied White Classical Relief, 8 In. 1265.00
Plate, Wellesley College Chapel, 1948, 10 1/2 In. 32.00
Platter, Atlanta, Flow Blue, 20 1/4 In. 275.00
Potpourri, Cover, Applied Acanthus, Bellflower, Green Lilac, 1840, 10 In. 1265.00
Potpourri, Cover, Black Basalt, Leaf, Berry Festoons, 19th Century, 15 In. 8050.00

Potpourri, Cover, Queensware, Floral, Foliate, 2 Handles, Gilt, 9 In. 345.00
Salt, Jasperware, Dark Blue 130.00
Stirrup Cup, Black Basalt, Fox Head Shape, Wedgwood & Bentley, 1775, 5 In. 3000.00
Sugar & Creamer, Jasperware, Light Blue 98.00
Sugar Sifter, Dark Blue & White, Classical, Silver Plated Top, 6 In. 295.00
Tea & Coffee Service, Queensware, Pear Shape, Rococo Border, Red, 7 In. 1725.00
Tea Caddy, Light Blue Jasperware Medallions, White Classical Relief, Wood, 9 In. 635.00
Teabowl, Saucer, Light Blue Jasperware, Children, White Classical Relief, 5 In. 805.00
Teacup, Fairyland Luster 35.00
Teacup & Saucer, Jasperware, Green, White Foliate Relief, England, 5 In. 690.00
Teapot, Bamboo Style, Yellow, Green Leaves, Impressed Mark, 6 x 7 In. 405.00
Teapot, Black Basalt, Black Widow Finial, 6 1/2 In. 660.00
Teapot, Cover, Black Basalt, Birch, Widow Finial, Cylindrical, England, 6 In. 635.00
Teapot, Cover, Black Basalt, Floral Sprays, 7 In. 500.00
Teapot, Cover, Drabware, Arabesque Design, Scrolled Vinework, 9 In. 345.00
Teapot, Cover, Majolica, Argenta, Floral Relief, England, 1878, 4 In. 460.00
Teapot, Cover, Queensware, Tea Party, Leaf Molded, Handle, Black Transfer, 4 In. 460.00
Teapot, Creamware, Cabaret, Japanned Design 95.00
Teapot, Grisaille, Leaves, Porcelain, 1878, 8 1/4 In. 172.00
Teapot, Jasperware, Light Green, Maternal Affection, Early 20th Century, 7 In. 450.00
Teapot, Lavender, Large 125.00
Teapot, Redware, Egyptian Designs, Alligator Finial, Impressed Mark, 5 x 10 In. 460.00
Teapot, Terra-Cotta, Polychrome & Enamel Flowers, 9 In. 63.00
Tile, Bellflower, Blue & White, Square, 6 In. 45.00
Tile, Calendar, 1911 . . . . 125.00
Tile, Calendar, 1915 . . . . 125.00
Tile, Calendar, 1923 . . . . 125.00
Tile, Majolica, Ribbon & Floral Swag, Brown Glaze, Pair 200.00
Tobacco Jar, Jasperware, Cobalt Blue, White Classical Relief, Lion Heads, 5 In. 175.00
Tray, Ice Cream, Majolica, Sea Lions On Interior, Sea Weed, England, 16 In. 2300.00
Tray, Majolica, Green, Yellow, Brown Glaze, Oval, England, 1888, 17 In. 260.00
Tureen, Pearlware, Nautilus Shell Form, Blue Floral Designs, 1820, 5 In. 175.00
Urn, Cover, Jasperware, Black, Dancing Hour, Foliate Relief, Bacchus Heads, 9 In. 475.00
Urn, Cover, Jasperware, Black, White Dancing Ours, Ram Head Handles, 7 In. 1500.00
Urn, Cover, Jasperware, Blue, 7 1/2 In., Pair 275.00
Urn, Cover, Jasperware, Blue, White Classical Figures, 2 Handles, 15 In. 575.00
Urn, Cover, Tricolor, Ram's Horn Handles, Oval Medallions, 19th Century, 10 In. 1950.00
Urn, Cover, Tricolor, White Classical Figures, Light Blue, Ram Horn Handles, 10 In. 1700.00
Urn, Jasperware, Cobalt, White Medallions, Floral Swags, Open Handle, 6 In. 700.00
Urn, Jasperware, Light Green, White Foliate Relief Border, 20th Century, 12 In. 425.00
Urn, Jasperware, Tricolor, Yellow, Black Acanthus Leaves, Bellflowers, 8 1/4 In. 1400.00
Urn, Maternal Affection, Fruiting Border, Rope Handle, Signed, 1948, 3 3/4 In. 225.00
Urn, Wedding Of Prince Andrew & Sarah Ferguson, Box, 1966, 11 3/4 In. 275.00
Vase, Agate Surface, Brown, Blue, Ocher Glaze, Black Basalt Plinth, 1775, 6 In. 690.00
Vase, Alternating Brown Slip, Green Glaze Hoops, White Terra-Cotta, 9 In. 1610.00
Vase, Applied White Drapery Swags, White Terra-Cotta, 5 In. 980.00
Vase, Bacchanalian Boys In Relief, Black Basalt, Mid-19th Century, 5 In., Pair 865.00
Vase, Black Basalt, Dragons In Relief, Gilt, Mid-19th Century, 8 In. 4315.00
Vase, Black Basalt, Engine Turned Banding, England, 1940, 7 In. 520.00
Vase, Black Basalt, Laurel, Berry Swags, Horned Bacchus Head Handles, 10 In. 690.00
Vase, Black Basalt, Leaf Molded Handles, Wedgwood & Bentley, 1775, 9 In. 1150.00
Vase, Black Basalt, Relief Of Oval Medallion Of Classical Subject, 5 In. 520.00
Vase, Bone China, Stylized Gilt Foliate Design, 2 Handles, Ivory, 8 In. 635.00
Vase, Cover, Black Basalt, Canopic, Hieroglyphic Relief, 1978, 9 In. 3105.00
Vase, Cover, Black Basalt, Canopic, Terra-Cotta Hieroglyphic Bands, 9 3/8 In. 1380.00
Vase, Cover, Black Basalt, Drapery Swags Centering Palmettes, 2 Handles, 6 In. 1495.00
Vase, Cover, Black Basalt, Drapery Swags, Wedgwood & Bentley, 1775, 7 In. 2070.00
Vase, Cover, Black Basalt, Floral Festoons, Acanthus Leaves, 9 In. 5175.00
Vase, Cover, Black Basalt, Foliate & Beadwork Borders, Scrolled Handles, 10 In. 1725.00
Vase, Cover, Bone China, Enamel Floral, Foliate Design, 2 Handles, 10 In., Pair 345.00
Vase, Cover, Canopic, Primrose Jasperware, Terra-Cotta Hieroglyphic Bands, 9 In. 920.00
Vase, Cover, Jasperware, Tricolor, Green, Lilac Classical Medallions, 7 In., Pair 690.00
Vase, Cover, Queensware, Lizard In Relief, Bamboo Leaves, Ivory, 9 In. 260.00

Vase, Dragon Luster, Blue Exterior, Mother-Of-Pearl Interior, 1920, 9 In. 690.00
Vase, Dragon Luster, Blue Exterior, Mother-Of-Pearl Interior, 1920, 11 In. 805.00
Vase, Etruscan, Green Cock & Goat, Foliage, Flared, 1920, 7 3/4 In., Pair 85.00
Vase, Fairyland Luster, Castle On A Road, 10 In. 3105.00
Vase, Fairyland Luster, Mother-Of-Pearl Luster, Drake Neck Green, 1920, 8 In. 1840.00
Vase, Golcondaware, Raised Slip Floral, Foliate, Gilt, 1885, 16 In. 690.00
Vase, Golcondaware, Raised Slip Floral, Foliate, Gold, Blue, Iron Red, 1885, 9 In. 375.00
Vase, Grecian Figures, 5 In. 145.00
Vase, Green Glaze, Vertical Ribs, Cylindrical, Keith Murray, 1930, 7 3/4 In. 805.00
Vase, Green Jasper Dip, Bacchus Mask Handles, Laurel, Berry Swags, 17 In. 690.00
Vase, Hound Design, Powder Blue, Bone China, 1920, 7 In. 290.00
Vase, Hummingbird Luster, Blue Exterior, Orange Interior, 1920, 7 In. 520.00
Vase, Jasper Dip, Chocolate Brown, White Satyr Handle, England, 7 In. 460.00
Vase, Jasper Dip, Crimson, White Classical Relief, 1920, 5 In. 980.00
Vase, Jasperware, Black, Sacrifice To Cupid, Flared, 20th Century, 7 In. 175.00
Vase, Jasperware, Classical, Light Blue & White, 6 1/4 In. 550.00
Vase, Jasperware, Dark Blue, White Classical Relief, Lion, Ring Handles, 6 In., Pair 750.00
Vase, Jasperware, Dark Blue, White Figural Reliefs, Floral Border, 5 In. 100.00
Vase, Jasperware, Tricolor, Green, Lilac Classical Relief, White Ground, 5 In., Pair 1840.00
Vase, Jasperware, Tricolor, Green, Lilac Classical Relief, White, 2 Handles, 7 In. 490.00
Vase, Jasperware, Tricolor, Ram Heads, Light Green Ground, 7 1/4 In. 1300.00
Vase, Jasperware, Yellow, Pear Shape, Black Foliate Border, 7 In., Pair 1200.00
Vase, Overall Cream Yellow Glaze, Horizontal Bands On Neck, Keith Murray, 6 In. 345.00
Vase, Potpourri, Cover, Black Basalt, Oval Classical Medallions, Floral, 14 In. 2875.00
Vase, Queensware, Birds, Flowers, Cream, Gilt Trim, 2 Handles, 1876, 7 In. 260.00
Vase, Queensware, Figural, Single Side Handle, Globular, 1862, 3 1/4 In. 550.00
Vase, Queensware, Floor, Defeat Of Porus, 2 Handles, Emile Lessore, 60 In. 16100.00
Vase, Shell Form, Coral Branches To A Shell, Seaweed, Bone China, 1895, 7 In. 175.00
Vase, Spill, Jasper Dip, Black, White & Black Vertical Bands, Foliage, 3 In. 1300.00
Vase, Spill, Jasperware, Chocolate, Acanthus Border, 1850, 4 1/2 In. 850.00
Vase, Spill, Jasperware, Cobalt, White Frieze Of Muses, Foliate Border, 4 In. 150.00
Vase, White Glaze, Horizontal Bands, Short Neck, Spherical, Keith Murray, 7 In. 546.00
Vase, White, Gray Glaze, Horizontal Bands, Keith Murray, 1930, 7 In. 632.00
Vase, White, Gray Horizontal Bands, Spherical, Keith Murray, 1930, 9 3/4 In. 632.00

WELLER pottery was first made in 1872 in Fultonham, Ohio. The firm
moved to Zanesville, Ohio, in 1882. Art wares were introduced in
1893. Hundreds of lines of pottery were produced, including
Louwelsa, Eocean, Dickens Ware, and Sicardo, before the pottery
closed in 1948.

LOUWELSA
WELLER

Ardsley, Console Set, Water Lily, 3 Piece 330.00
Ardsley, Flower Frog, Kingfisher, Natural Colors, 9 In. 195.00
Ardsley, Jardiniere, Kingfisher, Ivory Vertical Columns, 8 1/2 In. 65.00
Aurelian, Jardiniere, Signed, 9 In. 1000.00
Aurelian, Lamp, Brown Glossy Glaze, Apple Blossom Branches, Brass Shade, 26 In. 230.00
Aurelian, Vase, Grapevine, 23 1/2 In. 745.00
Aurelian, Vase, Signed, 5 1/2 In. 375.00
Baldin, Vase, Red Apples, Blue Background, Signed, 9 5/8 In. 247.00
Barcelona, Ewer, 9 1/2 In. 275.00
Barcelona, Vase, 2 Handles, 7 In. 145.00
Blue Ware, Jardiniere, Foliage, Grotesque Heads, Signed, 21 In. 192.00
Bonito, Vase, Floral Design, Brown Slip, 11 1/4 In. 165.00
Brighton, Figurine, Kingfisher, Signed, 8 1/2 In. 247.00
Brighton, Figurine, Mad Parrot, 7 5/8 In. 715.00
Brighton, Flower Frog, Kingfisher, 9 In. 195.00
Bronze Ware, Vase, Golden Brown Glaze, Maroon, Red Iridescent, Flared, 15 In. 495.00
Burntwood, Bowl, Lions, With Wings, 8 In. 125.00
Burntwood, Urn, 6 In. 225.00
Burntwood, Vase, Birds, 12 In. 225.00
Camelot, Vase, Geometric Designs, Olive & Ivory Glaze, 6 1/2 In. 120.00
Chase, Vase, Blue, White, 6 In. 350.00
Chase, Vase, Fox Hunt Scene, Blue, 9 3/4 x 7 1/2 In. 450.00
Chengtu, Vase, Chinese Red, Semimatte Glaze, Signed, 6 In. 100.00

Cicada, Wall Pocket, Sicard 385.00
Coppertone, Ashtray, Frog & Lotus Blossom 1 End, Signed, 2 1/8 x 6 In. 330.00
Coppertone, Birdbath 3000.00
Coppertone, Figurine, Turtle, With Lily Pad, Ink Stamp Mark, Half Kiln, 5 In. 165.00
Coppertone, Flower Frog, Lily 325.00
Coppertone, Garden Ornament, 2 Dancing Frogs, 13 7/8 In. 1450.00
Coppertone, Jardiniere, 2 Closed Handles, Drill Hole, 13 x 11 In. 715.00
Coppertone, Lamp, Pillow Vase Body, 2 Buttressed Handles, Green Glaze, 20 1/2 In. ... 412.00
Coppertone, Ornament, Banjo Frog, 12 1/4 In. 10450.00
Coppertone, Vase, Green Matte Glaze, Broad Mouth, Tapered Base, 6 1/2 In. 247.00
Coppertone, Vase, Green, Brown Mottled Glaze, Flared Rim, 12 1/2 In. 604.00
Coppertone, Vase, Green, Rust Matte Glaze, 2 Closed Handles, 8 1/2 x 7 In. 660.00
Cornish, Bowl, Beige, 8 In. 85.00
Delsa, Vase, Floral, Green Matte Ground, 13 In. 120.00
Dickens Ware, Jug, Fish Swimming, Waves, Second Line, Tan To Green, 5 1/2 In. 355.00
Dickens Ware, Jug, Monk, Raised Floral Design, Teal Green, Brown, Tan, 5 1/2 x 5 In. .. 440.00
Dickens Ware, Jug, Whiskey, Steel Bridge Spanning River, 6 In. 605.00
Dickens Ware, Mug, Indian Full Headdress, Second Line, Anna Daugherty, 5 1/2 In. 695.00
Dickens Ware, Tobacco Jar, Turk, Terra-Cotta, Second Line, 7 3/8 In. 410.00
Dickens Ware, Vase, Fish & Seaweed, Dark Blue, Second Line, 9 1/4 In. 935.00
Dickens Ware, Vase, Incised & Painted Monk Portrait, Second Line, 16 1/2 In. 265.00
Dickens Ware, Vase, Incised Portrait Of White Swan, Second Line, A. Daugherty, 9 In. .. 880.00
Dickens Ware, Vase, Man In Hat, Handles, Second Line, 3 3/4 x 6 In. 285.00
Dickens Ware, Vase, Portrait Of Indian, Crimped Mouth, Pink, White, Aqua, 9 x 4 In. ... 935.00
Dickens Ware, Vase, Scene From Chaucer's Canterbury Tales, 15 Characters, 17 1/2 In. .. 7425.00
Dresden, Vase, Windmills, Sailboats On Lake, Signed, 6 5/8 In. 605.00
Eocean, Vase, Tan & Brown, 5 In. 250.00
Eocean, Vase, Tan & Brown, 7 1/2 In. 275.00
Eocean Rose, Tankard, Monk, Group, Signed, 12 In. 3100.00
Eocean Rose, Vase, Burgundy Roses, 14 In. 2300.00
Etna, Jug, Smoky Black Grapes Protruding At Mid-Sections, 6 x 5 In. 137.00
Etna, Mug, 5 1/2 In. 200.00
Etna, Tankard, Gray Grapes, 14 In. 295.00
Etna, Vase, Chrysanthemums, Pale Green Foliage, 15 In. 770.00
Etna, Vase, Floral, Signed, 9 In. 77.00
Etna, Vase, Pink Floral, Off-White & Gray Ground, c.1906, Impressed Mark, 5 3/4 In. ... 90.00
Etna, Vase, Red & Lavender Flowers, Yellow Centers, 5 1/2 In. 275.00
Flemish, Flower Box, Cows In Pasture, Signed, 6 3/4 x 12 In. 1320.00
Flemish, Jardiniere, Floral, 7 1/2 In. 150.00
Flemish, Jardiniere, Pedestal, Incised Birds, Leaves, Branches, Pedestal, 31 1/2 In. 350.00
Flemish, Jardiniere, Trees & Birds In Repeating Pattern, 7 1/2 In. 165.00
Flemish, Umbrella Stand, Raised Apple Design, 22 1/2 In. 795.00
Fleron, Vase, Ear Handles, 7 In. 72.00
Florenzo, Vase, Flower Holder Lid, Signed, 7 1/2 In. 270.00
Forest, Jardiniere, 3 1/4 x 7 In. 55.00
Forest, Jardiniere, Marked, 7 In. ....*Illus* 275.00
Forest, Jardiniere, Pedestal, Landscape In Earth Tones, Blue Sky, R. Lorber, 28 In. 1430.00
Forest, Vase, 12 x 6 1/4 In. 500.00
Forest, Vase, 8 In. 200.00
Forest, Vase, Raised Design, Signed, 12 In. 725.00
Forest, Vase, Textured Landscape Scene, 8 1/2 In. 165.00
Glendale, Vase, Bird Design, Blue & Brown, Signed, 4 x 4 In. 65.00
Glendale, Vase, Bird In Brown Wetlands Ground, 6 1/2 In. 495.00
Glendale, Vase, Bird Nest, Brown & Green, 9 x 8 In. 1100.00
Glendale, Vase, Bird With Nest Of Eggs, Brown & Green, c.1920, 8 In. 385.00
Glendale, Vase, Forest Scene, 2 Parakeets On Branch, Blue & Brown, Signed, 9 In. 550.00
Glendale, Wall Pocket, Double Bud, Brown & Green 460.00
Greenbriar, Vase, Art Deco Shape, 7 3/8 In. 110.00
Greora, Vase, Bottle Shape, Signed, 8 3/4 In. 180.00
Hobart, Flower Frog, Seated Nude, On Base, Blue, 7 In. 185.00
Hudson, Bowl, Clover In Red & Green, Lavender Ground, Claude Leffler, 5 1/2 In. 357.00
Hudson, Bowl, Lily Of The Valley, Dorothy England, Signed, 2 7/8 x 5 3/4 In. 522.00
Hudson, Floral Design, Ivory Ground, 11 1/2 In. 230.00

Hudson, Vase, Blue Forget-Me-Nots, Cream, 7 In. 425.00
Hudson, Vase, Blue Paneled, Floral Edge, 9 3/8 In. 137.00
Hudson, Vase, Bud, Stylized Masses Of Flowers Atop One Another, Pastels, 10 In. 303.00
Hudson, Vase, Buff To Blue Flowers, 7 In. 500.00
Hudson, Vase, Female Nude Bather, Rocky Seaside Cliff, Blue Ground, Signed, 12 In. 5060.00
Hudson, Vase, Floral, 8 1/2 In. 228.00
Hudson, Vase, Iris, Blue Ground, Hester W. Pillsbury, 27 In. 3100.00
Hudson, Vase, White Flowers, 8 1/2 In. 400.00
Kenova, Vase, Raised Fiddle Head Fern, Signed, 8 1/2 In. 440.00
Klyro, Vase, Hanging Flowers, 22 Cutout Windows, 6 1/2 In. 65.00
Knifewood, Bowl, Swans, Hi-Glaze, 5 1/2 In. 155.00
Knifewood, Vase, Goldfinches & Wisteria, Signed, 4 5/8 In. 770.00
LaSa, Lamp Base, Evergreen, Mountain View At Sunset, 9 In. 275.00
LaSa, Vase, Evergreen Tree On Shore Of Lake, Mountains, 5 In. 155.00
LaSa, Vase, Iridized Scenic, 7 1/2 In. ....375.00 to 440.00
LaSa, Vase, Palm Trees, Gold, Red, Purple Iridescent, 16 In. ....*Illus* 2070.00
LaSa, Vase, Pine Trees & Water Scene, Gold, 10 x 5 In. 465.00
LaSa, Vase, Scenic, Signed, 9 In. 350.00
LaSa, Vase, Twisted Trees On Shoreline, Signed, 12 In. 200.00
Lavonia, Basket, 8 In. 325.00
Lavonia, Vase, Embossed Wheat, 12 In. 770.00
LeMar, Vase, Castle Scene Amongst Striking Landscape, With Trees, Baluster, 15 In. 715.00
LeMar, Vessel, Black Tall Pines, Closed-Mouth, Deep Maroon Ground, 8 1/2 In. 220.00
Louwelsa, Ewer, Grapes, 4 In. 350.00
Louwelsa, Jardiniere, Pansies, Signed 250.00
Louwelsa, Lamp, Oil, Orange & Brown Iris, Green Leaves, Signed, Electrified, 13 In. ... 495.00
Louwelsa, Umbrella Stand, Iris 495.00
Louwelsa, Vase, Bust Of Ram, Brown, Cream Glaze, Urn Form, 1910, 14 1/4 In. 431.00
Louwelsa, Vase, Flowers, Brown, 4 In. 235.00
Louwelsa, Vase, Jonquil, Floral Design, Vivid Yellow, Pale Sage Green Glaze, 14 In. 715.00
Louwelsa, Vase, Large Double Pansy, Crimped Mouth, Teal Green Ground, Hall, 5 In. ... 192.00
Louwelsa, Vase, Long-Beaked Bird, Amid Palm Leaves, Ed Able, 14 1/2 In. 3300.00
Louwelsa, Vase, Pillow, Portrait Of Dog, Olive Brown High Glaze, Blake, 7 1/2 In. 1100.00
Louwelsa, Vase, Portrait, Beethoven, Levi J. Burgess, Signed, 15 1/4 In. 5060.00
Malverne, Vase, 7 In. 45.00
Marvo, Jardiniere, Light Green, Pedestal, 26 In. 2300.00
Marvo, Pitcher, Green, 7 3/4 In. 82.00
Marvo, Vase, Hourglass, Butterscotch, Green Matte Glaze, Foliate, 1930, 9 In. ....172.00 to 265.00
Muskota, Figure, Fisher Boy, 20 1/2 In. 7975.00
Muskota, Figurine, Fishing Boy, 7 In. 155.00
Muskota, Flower Frog, Frog Emerging From Lotus Blossom, 4 1/2 In. 220.00
Muskota, Flower Frog, Lobster, Signed, 5 1/2 In. 175.00
Nasturtium, Bowl, Buff & Grass Green, Signed, c.1905, 5 x 7 In. 50.00
Neiska, Vase, Blue, 10 In. 75.00
Novelty, Dachshund, Tan, 4 1/2 x 8 1/2 In. 110.00
Novelty, Terrier, Matte Glaze, Light Brown, 10 3/4 In. 2420.00
Oak Leaf, Vase, Cream, Brown, 9 In. 110.00
Patricia, Lamp, Pelicans, Green & White, Brass Base 160.00

Weller, Forest, Jardiniere,
Marked, 7 In.

Weller, LaSa, Vase,
Palm Trees, Gold, Red,
Purple Iridescent, 16 In.

Perfecto, Jardiniere, Pedestal, Standing Crane, Palm Fronds, Albert Haubrich, 32 In. 4950.00
Perfecto, Vase, Pink & Purple Peonies, Green Leaves, Dorothy England, 9 x 9 In. 935.00
Plaque, Abe Lincoln, World's Fair, Pale Green 100.00
Pumila, Vase, Green & Butterscotch Glaze, Signed, 10 1/4 In. 279.00
Rochelle, Vase, Multicolored Flowers, Gray, 5 x 2 In. 155.00
Roma, Bowl, Swags Of Flowers, Cream, 14 In. 120.00
Roma, Jardiniere, 5 1/2 In. 245.00
Scandia, Vase, Incised Black Vertical Stripes, 9 1/4 In. 310.00
Sicardo, Jardiniere, Stylized Jonquils, At Different Stages Of Life, Drip Glaze, 10 In. 2200.00
Sicardo, Vase, Floral, Signed, 5 1/2 In. 500.00
Sicardo, Vase, Freeform Floral, Blue & Green Iridescent, 4 In. 446.00
Sicardo, Vase, Landscape, Blue, Gold, Red Iridescent, Cylindrical, 1920, 7 1/2 In. 287.00
Sicardo, Vase, Leaves, Berries In Flowing Lines, Bell Shape, Blue, Green, Purple, 4 In. .. 1386.00
Sicardo, Vase, Mottled, Twist Form, 5 In. 465.00
Silvertone, Basket, Gnarly Handle, Cranberry Colored Flowers, Signed, 8 1/2 In. 300.00
Silvertone, Flower Frog, Pastels 100.00
Silvertone, Vase, White Basket, Grapes & Red Flowers, 9 5/8 In. 412.00
Souevo, Basket, Hanging, Brown Matte, Chains, 9 1/2 In. 200.00
Souevo, Vase, Native American Designs, Cranberry Matte Glaze, Signed, 6 7/8 In. 410.00
Squirrel, Wall Pocket 250.00
Sunflower, Jardiniere, Pedestal, Brown, Green & Ivory, Signed, 38 1/2 In. 460.00
Turada, Jar, Cover, Open Work On Cover, 5 In. 450.00
Turada, Jardiniere, Brown & Yellow Hi-Glaze, 7 1/2 In. 175.00
Tutone, Vase, Green & Red, Signed, 5 7/8 In. 82.00
Warwick, Vase, Tree Trunk Handles, Signed, 4 5/8 In. 135.00
Woodcraft, Bowl, Squirrel, Signed, 4 x 8 In. 295.00
Woodcraft, Planter, Log, Signed, 4 1/4 x 11 In. 110.00
Woodcraft, Vase, Bud, Double 175.00
Woodcraft, Vase, Bud, Tree Trunk Form, 8 1/4 In. 110.00
Woodcraft, Vase, Fan, 7 In. 45.00
Woodcraft, Vase, Nature Scene, Owl, Peering From A Knot Hole, Handles, 18 In. 920.00
Woodcraft, Vase, Owl Design, Signed, 15 1/2 In. 1585.00
Woodcraft, Vase, Trees, 9 1/2 In. 150.00
Woodcraft, Vase, Wall, Tree Trunk, 9 In. 150.00
Woodcraft, Wall Pocket, Owl, 11 3/8 In. 522.00
Woodcraft, Wall Pocket, Owl, 12 In. 390.00
Woodcraft, Wall Pocket, Owl, Bulging, Peering Through Knot Hold, Rolled Rim, 10 In. . 467.00
Woodcraft, Wall Pocket, Owl, Green, Brown & Ivory, 11 x 5 3/4 In. 560.00
Woodcraft, Wall Pocket, Pink Flowers 225.00
Woodcraft, Wall Pocket, Squirrel, 9 In. ....250.00 to 350.00
Woodrose, Jardiniere, Panels Of Leaves & Pink Roses, 7 1/2 x 9 In. 130.00
Zona, Pitcher, Kingfisher, Blue 165.00

WESTMORELAND GLASS was made by the Westmoreland Glass Company of Grapeville, Pennsylvania, from 1890 to 1984. They made clear and colored glass of many varieties, such as milk glass, pressed glass, and slag glass.

Beaded Grape, Cup & Saucer 12.00
Beaded Grape, Honey, Cover 20.00
Beaded Grape, Plate, 7 In. 7.00
Beaded Grape, Plate, Blueberry Decoration, 7 In. 12.00
Beaded Grape, Tumbler, Apple Decoration, Footed 20.00
Beaded Grape, Tumbler, Daisy Decoration, Footed 20.00
Beaded Grape, Tumbler, Footed 16.00
Beaded Grape, Tumbler, Peach Decoration, Footed 20.00
Block Optic, Sherbet, Cone Shape, Green 4.00
Dolphin Cover, Sauceboat, Blue Slag, 7 1/2 In. 65.00
English Hobnail, Bowl, 6 1/2 In. 24.00
English Hobnail, Console Set, 3 Piece 155.00
English Hobnail, Cup & Saucer 10.00
English Hobnail, Cup, Demitasse, ... 20.00
English Hobnail, Goblet, Cocktail, Square Base 12.00
English Hobnail, Goblet, Water, Round Base 11.00

English Hobnail, Ice Tub, Handles 50.00
English Hobnail, Ivy Ball 10.00
English Hobnail, Sugar & Creamer 27.00
English Hobnail, Wine, Vase 13.00
Figurine, Eagle, Glass Eyes, Signed, 6 x 7 In. ....
Floral Bouquet, Vase, Red Roses Decoration 25.00
Hen On Nest Cover, Dish, Blue Slag, 2 11/16 In. 55.00
Old Quilt, Bowl, Footed, 6 In. 18.00
Old Quilt, Candlestick, 4 In., Pair 20.00
Old Quilt, Cheese Dish, Cover 45.00
Old Quilt, Cruet 25.00
Old Quilt, Tumbler, Footed, 4 1/4 In. 10.00
Paneled Grape, Appetizer Set 60.00
Paneled Grape, Banana Boat, 12 In. 125.00
Paneled Grape, Basket, Handle, Oval, 6 In. 20.00
Paneled Grape, Basket, Skirt Base, Milk Glass, 8 In. 55.00
Paneled Grape, Bowl, Crimped Edge, 6 In. 17.00
Paneled Grape, Bowl, Crimped Edge, 10 In. 77.00
Paneled Grape, Bowl, Footed, 11 In. ....53.00 to 65.00
Paneled Grape, Bowl, Fruit Cocktail 6.00
Paneled Grape, Bowl, Gold Grapes, 10 1/2 In. 95.00
Paneled Grape, Bowl, Milk Glass, 10 In. 50.00
Paneled Grape, Bowl, Oval, Crimped Edge, Footed, 12 In. 95.00
Paneled Grape, Bread Plate, 5 1/2 In. ....4.00 to 8.00
Paneled Grape, Butter, Cover, 1/4 Lb. 30.00
Paneled Grape, Cake Stand, 11 In. ....60.00 to 85.00
Paneled Grape, Cake Stand, Milk Glass, 11 In. 50.00
Paneled Grape, Candlestick, 3-Light, Pair 500.00
Paneled Grape, Cologne Bottle 45.00
Paneled Grape, Compote, Cover, 7 In. 45.00
Paneled Grape, Cup & Saucer 15.00
Paneled Grape, Dresser Set, 4 Piece ....175.00 to 250.00
Paneled Grape, Dresser Set, Rose & Bows Decoration, 4 Piece 325.00
Paneled Grape, Goblet, Water, 9 Oz. 18.00
Paneled Grape, Gravy Boat, Underplate 70.00
Paneled Grape, Iced Tea, 12 Oz. 25.00
Paneled Grape, Jug, 1 Qt. 22.00
Paneled Grape, Pitcher, 1 Pt. 48.00
Paneled Grape, Pitcher, 1 Qt. 40.00
Paneled Grape, Planter, 6 x 9 In. ....35.00 to 38.00
Paneled Grape, Plate, Dinner, 10 1/2 In. 45.00
Paneled Grape, Plate, Salad, 8 1/2 In. 18.00
Paneled Grape, Punch Set, 15 Piece ....325.00 to 375.00
Paneled Grape, Salt & Pepper, Footed ....23.00 to 25.00
Paneled Grape, Sugar & Creamer 9.00
Paneled Grape, Sugar, Cover, Footed 40.00
Paneled Grape, Torte Plate, Milk Glass, 15 In. 125.00
Paneled Grape, Tumbler, 12 Oz. 22.00
Paneled Grape, Vase, Rosebud Decoration, 18 In. 50.00
Paneled Grape, Wine, 3 Oz. 20.00
Patrician, Plate, Amber, 10 In. 5.00
Robin On Nest Cover, Bowl, Amber, 6 3/4 In. 78.00
Sapphire Blue, Bowl Set, Nested, 3 Piece 60.00

WHEATLEY Pottery was established in 1880. Thomas J. Wheatley had
worked in Cincinnati, Ohio, with the founders of the art pottery movement, including M. Louise McLaughlin of the Rookwood Pottery.
Wheatley Pottery was purchased by the Cambridge Tile Manufacturing Company in 1927.

Chamberstick, Embossed Leaves, Scroll Handle, Green Matte Glaze, 4 x 6 In. 467.00
Jardiniere, Molded Vertical Leaves, Green Matte Glaze, Impressed Mark, 11 1/2 In. 1760.00
Mug, Shield Design, Pretzel Handle, Green Matte Glaze, Signed, 7 In. 130.00
Planter, Raised Woven Design, Buff Terra-Cotta, 8 Sides, 24 x 14 In. 770.00

Tile, 4 Ornaments, Ribbon Top, Multicolored High Glazes, 4 In.	175.00
Tile, Geometric Circles, Flower In Center, Pink, Yellow, Orange Matte Glaze, 6 In.	325.00
Vase, Rib Shoulder, Green Glaze, 9 In.	1320.00
Vase, Wave Design, Striated Green Glaze, Signed, 8 1/2 In.	2115.00

WHIELDON was an English potter who worked alone and with Josiah Wedgwood in eighteenth-century England. Whieldon made many pieces in natural shapes, like cauliflowers or cabbages.

Jug, Cream, Splash Design, Wood, c.1760, 3 3/16 In.	875.00
Plate, Molded Border, Birds, Dark Green, Brown, 7 1/2 In.	245.00
Plate, Scroll Diaper Panels, Basket Weave Border, Gray, c.1760, 9 In., 6 Piece	3105.00
Strainer, Emerald Green Glaze, 1760	300.00

WILLETS Manufacturing Company of Trenton, New Jersey, began work in 1879. The company made Belleek in the late 1880s and 1890s in shapes similar to those used by the Irish Belleek factory. They stopped working about 1912. A variety of marks were used, all including the name Willets.

Clock Case, Belleek, c.1880, 13 1/2 In.	1150.00
Mug, Men In Period Clothing, Smoking Pipes, Dragon Handle, Gold Rim, Belleek	91.00
Mug, Pink Roses, Dragon Handle, Gold Rim, Belleek, Signed, R.O. Smith	197.00
Salt, Crimped Rim, Cream, 1 1/2 In.	15.00
Salt, Crimped Ruffled Edge, Flowers & Leaves, Pink, Green, Gold, 1 3/4 In.	104.00
Vase, Rose Design, Belleek, 5 1/2 In.	377.00

WILLOW pattern has been made in England since 1780. The pattern has been copied by factories in many countries, including Germany, Japan, and the United States. It is still being made. Willow was named for a pattern that pictures a bridge, birds, willow trees, and a Chinese landscape. Most pieces are blue and white.

Bouillon	35.00
Bowl, Allerton Scalloped Edge, Crown Mark, 5 In.	10.00
Bowl, Cranberry, Homer Laughlin, 5 In.	37.00
Bowl, Rectangular Cover	465.00
Bowl, Rice, Japan, 4 1/4 In.	13.00
Bowl, Vegetable, Round, Homer Laughlin, 8 3/4 In.	22.00
Bread Plate, Homer Laughlin, 6 1/4 In.	6.00
Canister, Ringtons, Limited Tea Merchants, England, 7 3/4 In.	170.00
Chop Plate, Shenango, 11 In.	27.00
Creamer, Footed, Japan	29.00
Creamer, Homer Laughlin, 3 1/2 In.	25.00
Cup & Saucer, 1916, 2 3/8 In.	81.00
Cup & Saucer, Homer Laughlin	20.00
Cup & Saucer, Japan, 2 1/4 In.	16.00
Footbath, Late 19th Century, 10 x 21 x 14 In.	1430.00
Gravy Boat, Homer Laughlin	46.00
Grill Plate, Japan, 10 1/2 In.	15.00 to 20.00
Mug, Handle, Japan, 3 1/2 In.	14.00
Pitcher, Blue, White, Ashworth Bros., 6 1/2 In.	175.00
Plate, 1913, 6 3/8 In.	30.00
Plate, 1917, 8 3/8 In.	143.00
Plate, Homer Laughlin, 6 1/4 In.	8.00
Plate, Homer Laughlin, 9 1/8 In.	3.00 to 10.00
Plate, Homer Laughlin, 10 In.	18.00
Plate, Japan, 6 1/4 In.	6.00
Plate, Japan, 7 5/8 In.	12.00
Plate, Japan, 9 In.	9.00 to 12.00
Plate, Occupied Japan, 6 1/4 In.	710.00
Plate, Occupied Japan, 9 1/4 In.	13.00
Platter, 19th Century, 15 1/2 In.	121.00
Platter, 19th Century, 17 1/2 In.	145.00
Platter, Cartwright & Edwards, 1850, 19 x 18 1/2 x 14 In.	363.00
Platter, England, 1850, 13 In.	150.00

Platter, Oval, Homer Laughlin, 9 1/2 In. 14.00
Platter, Oval, Homer Laughlin, 11 3/4 In. 25.00
Platter, Oval, Japan, 12 1/2 In. 33.00
Platter, Staffordshire, 18 In. 220.00
Saucer, Dessert, Japan, 5 3/4 In. 2.00
Saucer, Fruit, Japan, 5 3/8 In. 10.00
Snack Set, Box, 8 Piece 145.00
Soup, Dish, 7 In. 15.00
Soup, Dish, 9 In. 20.00
Soup, Dish, Allerton 8.00
Soup, Dish, Homer Laughlin, 8 1/4 In. ....5.00 to 19.00
Sugar, Cover, Handle, Homer Laughlin 29.00
Tea Set, Tin, Child's, 11 Piece 60.00
Toby Jug, 19th Century, 4 1/2 In. 121.00
Water Set, Pitcher, 6 Tumblers, 5 1/2 In. 395.00

WINDOW glass that was stained and beveled was popular for houses during the late nineteenth and early twentieth centuries. The old windows became popular with collectors in the 1970s; today, old and new examples are seen.

Diamond Panels, Casement, Leaded, 18 1/2 x 75 In., 9 Piece 265.00
Leaded, Amber Border, Diamond Pattern, Center Medallion, Frame, 84 x 86 In. 275.00
Leaded, Flower Center, Steel Frame, 23 1/2 x 27 In. 110.00
Leaded, Flower Garland, Ribbon, Jewels, Frame, 29 3/4 x 69 1/2 In. 3220.00
Leaded, Jeweled, Urn, Palm Fronds, Ribbon Swag, Victorian, 60 x 27 In., Pair 2760.00
Leaded, Nature Scene, Boy & Girl In Peasant Clothing, Mountains, 62 x 42 In. 2990.00
Leaded, Owl On Brown Tree, Curtains, Books, Candle, 31 1/2 x 18 1/2 In. 3968.00
Leaded, Panel, Enameled Knight & Maiden, Germany, c.1875, 13 1/2 x 17 In. 775.00
Leaded, Peacock Shape, Colored Glass On Clear Ground, 48 x 42 1/2 In. 4295.00
Leaded, Prairie School, Chevron, Green, 3 Panels, Beveled Glass Border, 21 x 40 In. 2860.00
Leaded, Scrolled Leaves, Glass Jewel Accents, Wooden Frame, 52 x 33 In., Pair 2415.00
Leaded, Stained, Procession Before Gate Of Avignon, 17th Century, 19 1/2 In. 850.00
Leaded, Vase, Red Flowers, Opalescent Jewels, Frame, 30 x 45 In. 515.00
Leaded, Woman, Picking Pink Dogwood Flowers, Birds, Frame, 33 x 16 In. 690.00
Leaded, Woman, Wearing Winter Cape, Floral Border, Frame, 33 x 16 In. 460.00
Mullions, Oval, Victorian, 17 3/4 x 36 In. 330.00
Stained, Blue & Amber, 30 x 84 In. 395.00
Stained, Center Opens As Vent, 10 1/2 x 2 1/2 In. 2900.00
Stained, Coat Of Arms, Narrow Border, 22 1/2 x 39 1/2 In. 425.00
Stained, Jewels, Victorian, 1890, 32 x 64 In. 1925.00
Stained, Multicolored Panels, Stenciled Boar's Head, Horse's Head, 40 x 25 In. 430.00
Stained, Saint Christoper & Christ Child, Saint Margaret, 1527, 48 x 19 In., Pair 7475.00
Transom, Ruby Flash, Wheel Etched Floral, Demilune 430.00

WOOD CARVINGS and wooden pieces are listed separately in this book. Many of the wood carvings are figurines or statues. There are also wooden pieces found in other categories, such as Kitchen.

Angel, 1 Log, Mahogany, 19th Century, 7 1/2 x 12 3/8 In. 235.00
Angel, Kneeling, Painted, Arms Out, On Base, Continental, 21 In., Pair 1670.00
Bear, Ashtray Form, Glass Eyes, 1910, 1/4 In. 375.00
Bear, Penholder, Glass Eyes, Canada, 3 1/2 x 6 1/2 x 3 1/2 In. 346.00
Bear, Seated On Inkwell, Glass Eyes, Hinged Head, 1910, 4 1/2 In. 318.00
Bear, Squatting With Extended Arms To Hold Bowl, 1920, 6 1/2 In. 185.00
Bear, Walking, Glass Eyes, 1910, 4 x 7 1/2 In. 318.00
Bird, Kingfishers, On Tree Branch, Blue Base, Primitive, 16 In. 220.00
Bowl, Recessed Handles, Figured Grain, 19th Century, 16 1/2 x 12 1/2 In. 1800.00
Bust, Woman, Walnut, Erwin Frey, 20 In. 495.00
Canada Goose Swimmer, Clem Wilding, 31 In. 165.00
Cigarette Case, Carved Man, Derby Hat 42.00
Cow, Bell On Neck, 18 1/2 x 15 1/2 In. 935.00
Cow, Dressed In Blue Coat, Ascot, Riffled Shirt, France, 15 In. 1265.00
Deer Head, Glass Eyes, Real Horns, Plaque, 16 x 15 x 13 In. 385.00
Deer Head, Shelf Form, Glass Eyes, 1910, 8 x 7 In. 330.00

Wood Carving,
Madonna & Child,
Painted, 30 In.

Wood Carving,
Saint, Woman,
Holding Sword, Paint,
Gilt, Italy, 64 In.

Always dust from the top down. Dust falls.

Deer Head, Trophy Style, Real Antlers, 13 In.	1100.00
Dog, Resting, Head Up, Glass Inset Eyes, Black, Brown, 3 In.	1035.00
Eagle, American, Pine, Red, White, Blue & Gold Painted Shield, 30 1/2 In.	5225.00
Eagle, Black Paint, Traces Of Colors On Shield, 42 1/2 In.	605.00
Eagle, Federal, Painted, Gilt, 1880, 9 x 19 x 4 In., Pair	425.00
Eagle, For Flag Pole, Signed D.M. Ludwig, 19 In.	825.00
Eagle, Gilt, 23-In. Wingspan, 12 1/2 In.	275.00
Eagle, Pine, Upraised Wings, Painted, Speckled Feathers, Stand, 10 1/4 x 13 In.	5175.00
Eagle, Polychrome Paint, 4 1/2 x 25 1/4 In.	1725.00
Eagle, Red, Black, Yellow & Green, Schimmel Style, D. Ludwig, 11 x 23 In.	295.00
Eagle, Spread Wing, Gilt Traces, Small Block Mount, 19th Century, 8 In.	355.00
Eagle, Yellow Pine, Wrought Iron Legs, 18th Century, 49-In. Wingspan	3920.00
Eagle In Branches, Spread Wings, Gilt, White Head, 69 x 23 In.	1840.00
Female Torso, Wide Base, William Zorach, 1914, 19 1/4 In.	10175.00
Fish, Double-Sided, 31 x 80 In.	1430.00
Flapper Woman, On Stand, Bertrand Card, 1939	3000.00
Fox, Holding 2 Trays Of Grapes, Linden Wood, Round Base, 1910, 38 x 24 In.	6050.00
Fox, Standing On Hind Legs, Holding Grapes, Germany	6050.00
Goat, Resting, Painted Horns, Hooves, 24 In., 3 Pieces	1610.00
Guanyin, Seated With Foo Dog, Holding Peach, 9 1/2 In.	345.00
Horse, Standing On Sphere, From 1 Piece, 36 In.	2500.00
Indian Holy Cow, Saddle, Beaded Neckpiece, 10 x 12 3/4 In.	805.00
Indian Man & Woman, Sitting, Dark Red Tone, 1930s, 3 1/4 x 2 1/4 In.	35.00
Kangaroo, With Joey, Tropical Wood, Weathered Gray Paint, Oak Base, 19 In.	50.00
Lion, French Shield, Spear, Inscription, Helvetiorum Fidei Ac Virtuti, 8 1/2 In.	105.00
Lion, Resting, Polychrome Design, 19th Century, 9 1/2 x 12 In.	650.00
Madonna & Child, Painted, 30 In. ....*Illus*	5060.00
Man, Monkey Head, West Africa, 31 In.	155.00
Mask, African, Carved, Angular Stylized Face, 14 1/4 In.	100.00
Mask, Aztec Warrior, Feathered Headdress, Painted, Wall Mount, 27 In.	115.00
Mask, Bamora, Rawhide & Animal Hair Tips On Horns, 18 In.	100.00
Mask, Helmet, African, Bird On Back, Horns Curving To Front, 15 x 18 In.	288.00
Mask, Helmet, Kuba Tribe, Zaire, Curved Knot On Top Of Head, Band, 17 x 12 In.	230.00
Mask, Japan, Noh, Demon, Open Mouth, Flaring Nose, Gold Paint, 8 1/2 In.	132.00
Mask, Japan, Noh, Man, White, Black Goatee, 11 In.	138.00
Mask, Mexican, Bald Man With Beard & Mustache, Hand Painted, 18 In.	115.00
Mask, Mexican, Man's Face, Chicken Head, Neck, Wings, Feathers On Top, 14 In.	144.00
Mask, Senufo, Horns, Head Finial, 13 1/2 In.	132.00
Mask, Senufo, String & Bead Tassels, Africa, 29 1/2 In.	110.00
Mask, Winged Putto, Spanish Colonial, Baroque, 16 x 54 x 7 1/2 In.	425.00
Mask, Yaka Tribe, Zaire, Lizard On Head, Grass Hair, Cloth Hat, Mounted, 40 In.	288.00
Monk, Holding Book, Gilt Black Robe, 19th Century, 23 1/2 In.	805.00
Monk, Kneeling, Hands In Praying Position, 27 1/2 In., Pair	1380.00
Mortar & Pestle, Carved Handle, Female Captive, Erotic Pose, 1882, 8 3/4 In.	2600.00
Mourning Virgin, Seated, Embellished Veil & Cloak, Mexican, 25 1/3 In.	5750.00
Nandi Bull, Saddle Blanket, Rectangular Base With Leaf Trim, 20 In.	6325.00

Noah's Ark, Noah & Wife, With 48 Animals, 3/4 To 2 In. 2400.00
Owl, White, Pi's Tooth Beak, Frank Finney, Va. 900.00
Panel, Relief, Man On Horseback, Continental, 18th Century 5720.00
Parrot, Perched, Wire Legs, Painted, Made From 1 Piece, 1900, 11 x 13 In. 685.00
Pedestal, Gilt, Polychromed, Ornate Bow & Garland Shape, 48 In., Pair 4400.00
Plaque, American Eagle, Glass Eye, Walnut, 14 x 12 1/2 In. 90.00
Plaque, Neoclassical Woman Mask, Putto Bracket, Continental, 9 x 15 In., Pair 690.00
Rooster, Polychromed, Signed D & BX '74, 10 In. 240.00
Saint, Hollow Back, 24 In. 575.00
Saint, Woman, Holding Sword, Paint, Gilt, Italy, 64 In. . . . . *Illus* 6037.00
Saint Joseph, Cradling Jesus, Spanish, 30 1/2 In. 2875.00
Santos, Pine, Colonial 170.00
Ship, Shenandoah, Pine, Four Masts, American, 20th Century, 28 1/4 In. 1035.00
Snake, Twisted Root, Wire Nail Eyes, c.1900, 6 x 39 In. 95.00
Sperm Whale, Robert Innis, Shell Base, 13 In. 605.00
St. Roc & His Dog, Polychrome, Wooden Base, 19th Century 920.00
Totem Pole, Tropical Bird Head At Top, Signed, Jamaica, 1950s, 21 In. 300.00
Tyrolean Man, Smoking Pipe, Carrying Umbrella, 5 1/4 In. 33.00
Virgin Mary, Polychrome, Mexican, c.1840, 10 In. 185.00
Wall Mount, Eagle, Perched On Scroll, Giltwood, 24 x 20 In., Pair 920.00
Watch Holder, Wall, Blue & Gray Polychrome, 19th Century, 10 x 12 In. 1265.00
Woman, Attached Arms, Painted, On Carved Base, 18th Century, 35 In. 2128.00
Woman, Seated, Wearing A Diadem & Blue Gown, Painted, 41 In. 3450.00
Woman Holding Fan, Standing, Feather & Bird, Japan, 15 In. 288.00

WOODEN wares were used in all parts of the home. Wood was used for
many containers and tools. Small wooden pieces are called *treenware*
in England, but the term woodenware is more common in the United
States. Additional pieces may be found in the Advertising, Kitchen,
and Tool categories.

Barrel, Coffee, Lid, 55 Lb. 25.00
Barrel, Water, Oak, Mustard Pain Traces, Replaced Bands, 26 x 18 In. 90.00
Bed Rest, Hardwood, Adjustable, Canvas Back 11.00
Bowl, Ash Burl, 12 x 5 1/4 In. 330.00
Bowl, Ash Burl, Oval, 14 1/4 x 19 x 8 In. 1100.00
Bowl, Ash Burl, Red Traces, Worn Interior, 15 x 16 x 6 In. 880.00
Bowl, Ash Burl, Refinished, 11 x 5 In. 550.00
Bowl, Ash Burl, Soft Varnish, 13 1/2 x 6 In. 660.00
Bowl, Ash Burl, Worn Finish, 14 x 6 In. 1540.00
Bowl, Ash, Footed, 10 1/4 In. 825.00
Bowl, Ash, Footed, Molded Edge, Thin Wall, 6 1/4 In. 765.00
Bowl, Blue Paint Remnants On Exterior, 19 1/2 In. 975.00
Bowl, Burl, 6 1/2 In. 2970.00
Bowl, Burl, Soft Finished, Carved Foot, 3 3/4 x 1 1/2 In. 220.00
Bowl, Light Blue Exterior, Turned, 16 3/4 x 17 1/2 x 5 3/4 In. 465.00
Bowl, Natural Patina, Hand Work, 10 x 17 1/2 x 4 In. 110.00
Bowl, Old Blue, Green Exterior, Round, 16 x 5 1/2 In. 245.00
Bowl, Old Gray Exterior, Turned, 19 x 19 1/4 x 5 3/4 In. 415.00
Bowl, Old Gray Paint Exterior, Turned, 18 1/2 x 19 1/2 In. 300.00
Bowl, Old Red Exterior, Turned, 15 3/4 x 16 1/2 x 5 In., Pair 630.00
Bowl, Old Red Exterior, Turned, 19 1/2 x 20 1/2 x 6 1/2 In. 520.00
Bowl, Pine, Scallops & Leaf Design On Outside, Painted, 19th Century, 7 x 22 In. 1265.00
Bowl, Poplar, Red Brown Stain Exterior, Turned, 27 x 8 1/2 In. 495.00
Bowl, Poplar, Worn Finish, Turned, 15 1/2 x 16 1/2 In. 140.00
Bowl, Red, Interior Old Patina, Turned, 7 1/2 x 2 1/4 In. 385.00
Bowl, Turned Maple, Honey Colored Patina, 19th Century, 17 In. 50.00
Bowl, Walnut, Turned, James Prestini, 11 x 3 In. 660.00
Box, Cigarette Dispenser, Pop-Up Lady, Japan 65.00
Box, Pantry, Long Fingers, Reddish Brown Paint, New England, c.1900, 7 In. 310.00
Box, Patch, Interior Mirror, 18th Century 195.00
Box, Sweetheart, For Trinkets, Chestnut Wood, Heart Shape Treen, 18th Century, 3 In. . . . 295.00
Bracket, Neoclassical, Black Walnut, Stained, Leaves, Russia, 1840, 19 In., Pair 4025.00
Bucket, Bail, Brass Hoops, Some Blue Paint, 19th Century, 5 In. 95.00

Bucket, Duck Form, Woven Splint Binders, 19th Century, 8 1/2 x 10 In. 180.00
Bucket, Pine, Sheet Metal Bands, Freehand Painted Pussy Willows, 1880, 8 x 8 In. 4600.00
Bucket, Stave Construction, Hinged Lid, Wooden Handle, Wire Bail, Worn Paint, 10 In. . . 82.00
Bucket, Stave Construction, Stenciled Birds, Metal Bands, Wooden Handle, 3 1/2 In. 165.00
Bucket, Stave Construction, Swivel Handle, Stamped Label, 11 In. 300.00
Bucket, Stave Construction, Wooden Handle, Wire Bands & Bail, Red, 6 x 4 1/2 In. 300.00
Bucket, Sugar, Branded Label, F. Lane & Co., 11 3/4 In. 165.00
Bucket, Sugar, Fitted Cover, Pine, Bail, 11 In. 85.00
Bucket, Sugar, Stave Construction, Blue Paint, Ephram Murdock, 12 x 12 In. 745.00
Bucket, Sugar, Stave Construction, Brown Paint, Wire Bail, Wooden Handle, Lid, 6 In. . . 250.00
Bucket, Sugar, Stave Construction, Copper Tacks, Brown Patina, Branded Label, 10 In. . . 275.00
Bucket, Sugar, Stave Construction, Gray Repaint, Bentwood Handle, 12 In. 220.00
Bucket, Sugar, Stave Construction, Gray Repaint, Wire & Wooden Bail Handle, 6 In. 275.00
Bucket, Sugar, Stave Construction, Green Paint, Lid, 12 In. 195.00
Bucket, Sugar, Stave Construction, Green Paint, Wire & Wooden Bail Handle, 8 In. 355.00
Bucket, Sugar, Stave Construction, Red Paint, Copper Tacks, 11 3/4 x 11 1/2 In. 495.00
Bucket, Sugar, Stave Construction, Red, Copper Tacks, Bentwood Handle, 5 In. 440.00
Buddha, Standing, On Square Wood Plinth, Japan, 11 In. 520.00
Canteen, Buttonhole Bands, Corncob Stopper, Wooden Bung, 18th Century, 9 In. 295.00
Canteen, Circular, Wooden Stopper, Red, Blue, Leather Strap Holders, 7 x 2 1/2 In. 1380.00
Canteen, Sapling Bands, Iron Bail Handle, Pewter Spout, 18th Century, 7 In. 195.00
Carrier, Cover, Bentwood, Wooden Handle, Wire Bail, Round, 11 3/4 In. 190.00
Cheese Trolley, Mahogany, 2 Brass Wheels, 19th Century, 8 x 16 In. 700.00
Chest, Dome Top, Grain Painted, Handwrought Hardware, 30 x 13 3/4 In. 1150.00
Cigar Holder, Silver Ferrule, Bakelite Tip, Case 90.00
Cigarette Case, Karelian, Birch, Oblong, Russia, 1987, 6 3/4 In. 150.00
Coffer, Jacobean, Planked Construction, 17th Century, 12 x 20 1/2 In. 385.00
Comb Case, Abstract Carvings, Brass Ends, Norwegian, 18th Century, 5 3/4 In. 525.00
Comb Case, Pine, Mirror, Primitive, 9 x 3 3/4 x 11 1/2 In. 110.00
Comb Case, Walnut, Wall Mount, Round Mirror, Victorian, 21 In. 125.00
Compote, Ash Burl, Shellac Finish, 9 x 4 1/4 In. 790.00
Compote, Footed, Continental, 13 x 7 In. 330.00
Cup, Bird's-Eye Burl, Natural Shape, Handle, 5 1/4 In. 385.00
Cup, Maple, Brown Amber Finish, Carved Handle, Chip Carved, 6 1/4 In. 135.00
Cup & Saucer, Lehnware, Strawberry Design, Gray Pink Ground, 3-In. Saucer 900.00
Desk Set, Pen, Letter Opener, Pencil, Quill Knife, Dog Top, Stand, 19th Century 385.00
Dish, Bread & Salt, Sheaf Of Wheat, Cyrillic Inscription, 11 In., Pair 1725.00
Dish, Burl, Carved Animal Handle, 4 3/8 x 1 1/2 In. 745.00
Dish, Laminated Birch, Tapio Wirkkala, Incised Monogram, 10 x 8 x 1 In. 2750.00
Eggcup, Lehnware, Floral, Pink Ground, Green, Red, Blue Base, 2 1/2 In. 1155.00
Goblet, Treen, Incised Animal & Crest Panels, Between Verse, England, 8 In. 9200.00
Grinder, Curly Maple Frame, Damaged Teeth, 20 In. 190.00
Humidor, Bird, Glass Eyes, Hinged Lid, Side Pockets . . . . *Illus* 1200.00
Humidor, Mahogany, Cedar Lined, Monogrammed AW, 1920s, 11 x 17 In. 620.00
Humidor, Skull, Ivory Snake Crawling In & Out, Frog On Head, 6 In. 500.00
Ice Bucket, Cover, Teak, Tapering Staves, Bridge Handle, Marked, Quistgaard, 19 In. . . . 173.00
Ice Bucket, Cover, Teak, Tapering Staves, Recessed Handles, Signed, Jensen, 11 In. 173.00
Jar, Cover, Treen, Mustard Paint 575.00
Jar, Maple, Ring Turned Base, Finial, 4 1/4 In. 110.00
Jar, Worn Varnish, Wire Bail, Wooden Handle, Pease, 9 1/2 In. 960.00
Jardiniere, Rootwood, Bamboo, Rustic Type, Continental, 33 1/2 In., Pair 5175.00
Keg, Rum, American, 18th Century, 5 1/4 In. 160.00
Keg, Stave Construction, Laced Wooden Bands, Blue Repaint, 15 In. 70.00
Measure, Grain, Steel Bands, Cast-Iron Handles, 8 x 14 1/2 In. 82.00
Measures, Nesting, Cast Iron Handles, Daniel Cragin, 5 3/4 To 14 1/2 In., 4 Piece 137.00
Mold, Cigar, Durex, 10 Cigars, 12 In. 22.00
Paddle, Curly Maple, Bird's-Head Handle, Refinished, 10 In. 250.00
Plate, Cherry, New England, c.1750, 9 1/4 In. 395.00
Plate, Curly Poplar, Inscription Made 1880 By Wm. Ashton, 8 3/8 In. 110.00
Porringer, Burnt Sienna Patina, 4 3/4 x 7 In. 495.00
Rack, Drying, Mortised, Arched Footed, 1820-1840 . . . . 245.00
Rack, Towel, Walnut, 5 Turned Bars Over Lower Shelf, Victorian, 35 x 24 x 11 In. 85.00
Salt, Master, Lehnware, Strawberry, Vine, Red Band, Pink Base, 2 1/2 x 2 1/4 In. 465.00

Ivory, bone, horn, wood, and
mother-of-pearl handled tableware
should never be washed in a
dishwasher. The heat and soaking
will crack these materials.

Wooden,
Humidor, Bird,
Glass Eyes,
Hinged Lid,
Side Pockets

Salt, Treen, Pedestal 125.00
Shovel, Grain, 32 1/4 x 11 1/4 In. 185.00
Splint & Rush, Holder, Wrought Iron, Wooden Base, 19th Century, 19 In. 50.00
Stand, Crock, Right-Angle Shelves, 7 Stepped Tiers, 41 x 57 In.   522.00
Tankard, Burl, Detailed Carving, Thumb Tap & Cover, Treen, Mid-18th Century 950.00
Tankard, Burl, Silver Mounts, Trinity College, England, 1740 . . . .   9950.00
Tantalus, Nickel-Plated Trim, 3 Cut Glass Decanters, Key, 13 3/4 x 11 1/2 In. 280.00
Tazza, Irregular Edge, Red Brown Patina, 6 x 10 In. 675.00
Tray, Mahogany, Marquetry, Brass Basket Weave Border, 1879, 1 1/2 x 21 x 12 In. 120.00
Tray, Pen, Mahogany, Scrimshaw Whales' Teeth, Center Tooth Inkwell, 1860 . . . .   950.00
Tray, Pen, Regency, Rosewood, Spindled Supports, Brass Finials, 8 x 6 3/4 x 1 1/2 In. . . .   115.00
Tray, Scalloped, Burl Walnut, Faux Bamboo Stand, c.1860, 21 1/2 In. 725.00
Tray, Yellow Pine, Trace Of Red Wash, Square Nail Construction 275.00
Trencher, Poplar, Handles, 20 1/2 x 11 In. 210.00
Tub, Poplar, Red, Yellow Sponging, 10 3/4 x 6 In. 245.00
Tumbler, Curly Maple, Old Finish, 3 1/8 In. 55.00
Urn, Cover, Faux Bois, Neoclassical, Satinwood, Mahogany, Greek Key, 27 In., Pair 4025.00
Urn, Lion's-Mask Handle, Medallion, Classical Landscape, Chestnut, 13 In., Pair 2300.00
Vase, Bear, Standing On Hind Legs, Glass Eyes, 1910, 6 3/4 In. 185.00
Wall Pocket, Softwood, Flaking Gray Paint, Country, 13 1/2 In. 100.00
Watch Safe, Mahogany, Form Of Grandfather Clock, Ebonized, 15 1/4 In. 300.00

WORCESTER porcelains were made in Worcester, England, from 1751.
The firm went through many name changes and eventually, in 1862,
became The Royal Worcester Porcelain Company Ltd. Collectors
often refer to *Dr. Wall*, Barr, *Flight*, and other names that indicate time
periods or artists at the factory. It became part of Royal Worcester
Spode Ltd. in 1976. Related pieces may be found in the Royal Worcester category.

Basket, Chestnut, Blue, White, Open Lattice Exterior, Diaper Rim, Handles, 9 x 8 In. 980.00
Basket, Interlinking Circles, Red, Yellow Flower Heads, Puce Rim, 1770, 6 In., Pair 3737.00
Basket, Pinecone, Blue, White, Entwined Loop Handles, 1770, 8 1/4 In., Pair . . .1035.00 to 1955.00
Basket, Pinecone, Interlinking Circles, Blue Interior, C-Scroll Rim, 3 x 7 In., Pair 1955.00
Bowl, Armorial, Red, Gold, Blue, Green, Gray Center, Flight Barr & Barr, 11 In. 13800.00
Bowl, Fruit, Dr. Wall, Blue Crescent Mark, 1775, 3 x 10 In. 786.00
Bowl, Lozenge Form, Pinecone Interior Transfer, Floral, Blue Glaze, 4 x 12 In. 980.00
Bowl, Pinecone, Flowers, Foliage, Blue Glaze, Scalloped Rim, 9 In., Pair 980.00
Cake Plate, Tea Party, Leopard, Mandolin, Flute, Dark Gray Transfer, Hancock, 7 In. 635.00
Charger, Pinecone, Cluster Of Flowers, Fruit, Moth, Blue Glaze, 15 In. 865.00
Coffeepot, Rock & Strata Island, Dr. Wall, c.1770, 7 1/2 In. 1093.00
Creamer, Cabbage Leaves, Blue Floral, Mask Spout, Signed, 5 7/8 In. 695.00
Creamer, Tea Party, Garden Statuary On Other Side, Wishbone Handle, 3 In. 400.00
Creamer, Tea Party, Manservant, Standing, Loop Handle, Black Transfer, 4 In. 290.00
Crock, Cobalt Blue Parrot, Egg Shape 995.00
Cup & Saucer, Dr. Wall, Handleless 180.00
Cup & Saucer, Tea Party, Dark Gray Transfer, Hancock, 1757, 4 x 2 In. 750.00

Dish, Blind Earl, Leaf, Molding, Green, Yellow Enamel, Scalloped Rim, Blue, 8 In. 3335.00
Dish, Exotic Birds In Parkland In Center, Lozenge Shape, Gilt, Notched Rim, Pair 2070.00
Dish, Fig Leaf, Scattered Insects, Pale Puce Veins, 1765, 7 In., Pair 3740.00
Dish, Leaf Form, Veined Interior Transfer, Blue, Floral Sprays, Moths, 13 In., Pair 1090.00
Dish, Scattered Flower Sprigs, Petal Rim, Gadroon Border, Scroll Handle, 9 In., Pair 310.00
Dish, Sweetmeat, Blind Ear, 1770-1775, 7 3/4 In., Pair 3872.00
Dish, Sweetmeat, Blue & White, Dr. Wall, 1765, 2 1/2 x 6 1/2 In. 665.00
Dish, Sweetmeat, Blue & White, Dr. Wall, 1775, 6 x 1 1/2 In. 605.00
Dish, Sweetmeat, Dr. Wall, Blue, White, Blue Crescent Mark, 1760, 2 1/2 x 6 In. 393.00
Dish, Vine Leaf, 2 Overlapping Leaves, Green, Black Veining, 1765, 7 5/8 In., Pair 4025.00
Jug, Pearlware, Sparrow Beak, Dr. Wall, 4 1/2 In. 190.00
Jug, White Cabbage Leaf, 19th Century, 9 In. 200.00
Jug, White Cabbage Leaf, Floral Sprays, Moths, Blue Glaze, C-Scroll Handle, 11 In. 1035.00
Plate, Armorial, Flight Barr & Barr, 10 1/2 In. 145.00
Plate, Exotic Birds, G. Davis, Barr, Flight & Barr, 1807-1813, 8 In. 403.00
Plate, Imari Brocade, Blue Glaze, Red, Salmon, Green Turquoise, Gilt Rim, 9 In. 2530.00
Plate, Scattered Roses, Small Blue Flowers, Barr, Flight & Barr, 1813, 9 3/8 In., Pair 437.00
Platter, Pinecone, Floral Sprays, Moths, Blue Floral Spray Rim, 11 In. 635.00
Platter, Rose, Tulip Blue Transfer, Cell Diaper Border, Twig Handles, 8 In., Pair 400.00
Sauceboat, Floral Sprigs, Blue Glaze, Floral Sprig Interior, 7 1/2 In., Pair 460.00
Sauceboat, Silver Shape, Chinese Lady, Holding Fan, Leaf Sprig Panels, 9 In. 1265.00
Sauceboat, Silver Shape, Chinese Lady, Holding Fan, Pine Tree, 1755, 8 In. 1955.00
Tea Canister, Tea Party, Black Transfer, Globular, 1765, 4 7/8 In. 230.00
Teapot, Cover, Blue, White, Flower Finial, 6 In. 247.00
Teapot, Cover, Tea Party, Turned Finial, Loop Handle, Black Transfer, 5 5/8 In. 1150.00
Teapot, Pearlware, Applied Flower & Leaves Finial Lid, Marked, Dr. Wall, 5 1/4 In. 275.00
Teapot, Polychrome, Gold Design, Signed, c.1760 .... 795.00
Teapot, Three Flowers, c.1770 .... 875.00
Tray, Spoon, Tea Party, Black Transfer, Oval, 1760, 5 7/8 In. 490.00
Tureen, Cover, Butterflies, Insects, Cauliflower, Black & Green Leaves, 1760, 4 In. 3450.00
Tureen, Cover, Flower Sprigs, Garlands, Twig Handles, Blue Scale, 7 In., Pair 4025.00
Tureen, Cover, Paneled Floral, Vine Design, Red Rim Cover, Dr. Wall, 5 In. 201.00
Tureen, Cover, Rich Queen, Loop Handles, Gilt Frame, Chamberlain, 1807, 14 In. 19550.00
Tureen, Cover, Stand, Pinecone, Floral Sprays, Insects At Rim, c.1775, 10 3/4 In. 3162.00
Tureen, Cover, Undertray, Floral Finial, Branch & Leaf Handles, Dr. Wall, c.1751 ...... 2520.00
Waste Bowl, Tea Party, Man, In Gardener's Hat, Presenting Pot To Seated Lady, 4 In. ... 520.00

WORLD WAR I and World War II souvenirs are collected today. Be careful not to store anything that includes live ammunition. Your local police will tell you how to dispose of the explosives. See also Sword and Trench Art.

WORLD WAR I, Badge, Army, U.S., Wound, Black, Iron, 1914 .... 28.00
Badge, Army, U.S., Wound, Gold, 1914 .... 80.00
Badge, Pilot, Prussia, Hollow Back 400.00
Badge, Submarine, Anchor, Austria 505.00
Badge, Wound, 3-Piece Screw Back, Silver, 1914 .... 126.00
Badge, Wound, Black, 1914 .... 20.00
Badge, Wound, Silver, 1914 .... 40.00
Belt Buckle, Enlisted Man, Austria 50.00
Belt Buckle, Gott Mit Uns, Steel, Germany 23.00
Binoculars, Military, Leather Case, Instructions, Germany 100.00
Book, Defending The Flag, Aviation & Naval Scenes, Gabriel Sons, 12 Pages 18.00
Book, Diary Of A Rainbow Veteran 50.00
Boots, Cavalry, German Officer 425.00
Bust, Remembrance Of Service Time Memorial 60.00
Cap, U.S. Reserve Torpedo Flotilla, Checkered Lining 115.00
Card, P.O.W., French Comite De Secours Aux Prisonniers De Guerre, 3 5/8 In. 10.00
Case, Artillery Level Quadrant, Leather, 1918 .... 35.00
Coat, 78th Division Patch, 1917 .... 66.00
Coat, Army Service, 26th Division 50.00
Coat, Army Service, 36th Division 34.00
Coffeepot, Patriotic, Small 40.00
Compass, U.S. Engineer Corps, Strap 55.00

Flare Gun, U.S. Navy, 1917 .... 225.00
Flight Pants, Leather Sheepskin Lining, Pair 80.00
Flight Suit, U.S. Air Service, Dog Hair Lining 295.00
Hat, Cavalry, U.S. 165.00
Helmet, Army Officer, Green Felt 295.00
Helmet, Army, Double Decal, M 35 .... 180.00
Helmet, Army, M 17 .... 195.00
Helmet, Brass Trimmed, Spiked, Prussia 325.00
Helmet, Combat, 1916 .... 335.00
Helmet, Doughboy, 36 Infantry Div. Patch Design, Strap 55.00
Helmet, Ersatz Felt, Bavaria 600.00
Helmet, Ersatz Felt, Prussia 299.00
Helmet, Foot Artillery, Bavaria, 1915 .... 995.00
Helmet, Garde Infantry, Spiked, Prussia 425.00
Helmet, Luftwaffe Cameo Paratrooper 720.00
Helmet, Luftwaffe Flight, Complete 320.00
Helmet, Luftwaffe M 35, Camouflaged With Chickenwire 1000.00
Helmet, Luftwaffe Single Decal, M 40 .... 250.00
Helmet, Officer's, Anhalt, Spiked, Carry Case 1925.00
Helmet, Officer's, Wurttemberg, 26th Dragoon Regiment, Carry Case 3855.00
Helmet, Parade 465.00
Helmet, Spiked, Prussia 227.00
Jacket, Flight, Winter, Luftwaffe Eastern Front 300.00
Letter Opener, Patriotic, Allied 268.00
Medal, Imperial 50.00
Medal, Iron Cross, 1st Class, Case, Box 280.00
Medal, Iron Cross, 2nd Class, Germany .... 35.00 to 44.00
Medal, Maria Theresa Bust, 2 Wounded Soldiers, Reverse, 1914-1917, 4 In. 170.00
Medal, Red Cross Merit, Prussia 50.00
Medal, Service 25.00
Photograph, Sgt. Alvin C. York, Medals, Inscription, Black & White, 8 x 10 In. 375.00
Pillow, Love & Remembrance, Verse, Solider & Lover, Silk, 13 1/2 x 9 1/4 In. ...... *Illus* 50.00
Pin, Bundles For Blue Jackets, Celluloid, Blue, White, Pinback, 7/8 In. 25.00
Pin, Lapel, 6th Div. Expeditionary 12.00
Plaque, Memorial, Wreathed Cross, Flowers Growing, 41 x 72 mm. 110.00
Postcard, New Zealand Red Cross, Ambulance, 2 Soldiers, Photograph, 1915 .... 35.00
Postcard, Statue Of Liberty, To Our American Friends, France, 1917 .... 40.00
Poster, Billy Maine As Private Goldbrick, Overseas Revue Scenes In France 40.00
Poster, Happy Jack Thrift Club, Cardboard, T.W. Burgess, 1918, 7 x 11 In. 60.00
Poster, Have You A Red Cross Flag, Jessie Wilcox Smith Artwork, 1918, 21 x 28 In. 120.00
Poster, Jewish War Sufferers, Our Boys Freed Them, 1917, 27 x 19 In. 5750.00
Poster, Red Cross, Christmas, Jessie Wilcox Smith 250.00
Poster, Uncle Sam, Flyswatter, War Savings Thrift Stamp, Kaiser, Frame, 35 In. 1100.00
Poster, War Bonds, Boy Scout & Statue Of Liberty, J.C. Leyendecker 250.00
Poster, War Knows No Justice, German Infantry Fieldpost, 1915 .... 45.00
Poster, We Protect You, First National Bank, Soldier, With Gun, Tin, 13 x 20 In. 350.00
Print, Somewhere In France, Matted, Frame, F. Marion Dyer, 1918, 10 x 14 In. 105.00
Range Finder Scope, U.S.M.C. 210.00
Saber, Blucher 161.00
Shovel, Trench, Carrier, Germany 150.00
Trousers, Flight, Luftwaffe, Leather 660.00
Tunic, Dress, Army Colonel, Summer Weight 520.00
Tunic, Dress, Artillery 450.00
Tunic, Dress, Luftwaffe Officer's, Summer Weight, White 415.00
Tunic, USMC, 2 Pockets 110.00
Uniform, 3rd Army Medical Officer, U.S. 140.00
Uniform, World War I 2nd Corps School 250.00
Uniform, World War I Tank Corps 99.00
WORLD WAR II, Aircraft Warning Service, Volunteer Observer, Plane, 1 1/4 In. 13.00
Armband, SS, Germany 44.00
Badge, Army, 50 General Assault, Marked RK, Germany, 2 Piece 55.00
Badge, Cap, U.S. Navy Officer, Eagle, Shield, Anchors, Sterling Silver 85.00
Badge, Minesweepers, Germany 66.00

World War I, Pillow, Love & Remembrance, Verse, Solider & Lover, Silk, 13 1/2 x 9 1/4 In.

World War II, Figure, Hitler Skunk, Pottery, Painted, 5 x 5 1/2 In.

Badge, Naval, Cherry Blossom Center, Anchor, Crossed Shells, Box, Japan	198.00
Banner, Son In Service	30.00
Bayonet, With Frog, Japan	70.00
Belt Buckle, Hitler Youth, With RZM Rag	50.00
Belt Buckle, Luftschutz	75.00 to 85.00
Belt Buckle, Police, U.S.A.	50.00
Belt Buckle, Pro-Nazi, Lithuanian	330.00
Belt Buckle, Waffen SS Em/Nco, Steel, Gray Paint, Germany	80.00
Binoculars, Case, 6 x 30 In.	135.00
Binoculars, Navy Style	250.00
Bobby Pins, Vicky Victory, Save Steel, Full Box, 1940s, 2 1/2 In.	25.00
Booklet, Know Your Enemies: The Jap Army, Infantry Journal Inc., 1942	75.00
Boots, Black, Leather, Tall	150.00
Boots, Cavalry Officer, Germany	120.00
Boots, Combat	68.00
Boots, Hobnail, Germany	185.00
Boots, Hobnail, Mountain, Ankle Lace-Up, Germany	155.00
Boots, Officer's	220.00
Boots, RAF Pilot, 1939	325.00
Boots, Riding, Officer's	140.00 to 200.00
Boots, Sentry, Russian Front, Germany	95.00
Boots, U.S. Army	121.00
Button, Be Calm But Alert And You Won't Get Hurt, Red, White, Blue, 1 1/4 In.	18.00
Button, Keep 'Em Afloat, Warship	13.00
Button, Keep 'Em Flying, V, Plane, White, 1 1/4 In.	15.00
Button, Let's Blast The Japs Clean Off The Map	20.00
Button, Wanted For Murder, Picture Of Hitler, 1 1/4 In.	30.00
Camera, Looks Like Machine Gun, Lens Barrel, Japan, Box, 38 In.	440.00
Canteen, Medical	80.00
Cap, Admiral's, Blue Wool, Chin Strap, Japan	275.00
Cap, Field, Black Panzer Wool, Cotton Lining, Germany, Size 56	245.00
Cap, SS Officer's, Visor, Gabardine, Satin Lining, Germany	45.00
Coat, Deck	170.00
Compass, Wehrmacht	30.00
Dagger, Army, Tiger-Solingen, Plastic Grip, Scabbard & Hangers, Germany	330.00
Dagger, SA, RZM M7/10, 1938, Zwillengen, Germany	240.00
Dagger & Sheath, Naval, Japanese	395.00
Figure, Hitler Skunk, Pottery, Painted, 5 x 5 1/2 In.	*Illus* 175.00
Flag, Alten Garde, NSDAP, Swastika Center, Oak Leaf Around, 3 x 7 1/2 Ft.	385.00
Flag, Ball, White Ground, Silk, Japanese Symbols, Japan	80.00
Flag, Lead Weights Sewn In Edge, Germany, 3 x 2 Ft.	80.00
Flashlight, Field, Daimon Maker	50.00
Flask, Field, Wool Felt Cover, No Cup Or Straps, Germany, Dated 1940	5.00
Flight Jacket, B-15	295.00
Gas Mask, 2nd Model, 1943	57.00
Gas Mask, Civilian, Auer Luftschutz	60.00

Goggles, Flak, AAF Gunner's 205.00
Goggles, Flight Pilot, Third Reich 160.00
Handbook, Pilot's, TBM-3 Avenger III Airplane, U.S. Navy, 1944 . . . . 125.00
Headset, Radio Communications, Germany 135.00
Helmet, Luftschutz 95.00
Helmet, Luftschutz, Decal, Germany, Size 58 . . . . 175.00
Helmet, Luftwaffe, M35, Double Decal 445.00
Helmet, Nazi Police, Civil 70.00
Helmet, Paratrooper, 1st Type, U.S. 310.00
Helmet, Pith, Tropical, Tan Cloth, Red Cotton Lining, Germany 45.00
Jacket, Flight 268.00
Jacket, Flight, Leather, Fur Collar 100.00
Jacket, Flight, Type B-10 . . . . 550.00
Jacket, Flight, Type B-3 . . . . 246.00
Jacket, U.S. Marine Corps Camouflage 231.00
Lantern, Field, Bakelite 120.00
Lighter, Vulcan, Cloisonne, 13 Fighter Interceptor Squadron Insignia 27.00
Manual, Enemy Air-Borne Forces, Military Intelligence Service 75.00
Map, Esso, Invasion Edition, General Drafting Corp. 12.00
Map, Global War & Global Peace, Alcoa Aluminum 20.00
Map, Lowell Thomas' War Map Of The World, Sunoco, Rand McNally 12.00
Map, U.S. Army Aerial Grid, Camp Hood, Texas, 18 1/2 x 21 In. 9.00
Map Case, Wehrmacht 50.00
Medal, Iron Cross, 2nd Class Ribbon, Germany 38.00
Medal, Mother's Cross, Marked '16 Dez 1938, Hitler Picture, Germany 90.00
Mirror, Remember Pearl Harbor, Celluloid, Red, White & Blue 45.00
Painting, B-25 Mitchell Landing On Back Of Period Packing Crate 395.00
Painting, Reverse On Glass, American Flag, Pearl Harbor, Frame, 9 x 11 In. 65.00
Pamphlet, Second War Loan, Describes War Bonds Available, April 1943, 9 x 4 In. 20.00
Picture, Remember Pearl Harbor, Pledge Of Allegiance, Glass, Metal, 11 x 14 In. 70.00
Pillow Case, Embroidered USA-Chine-Burma-India, O Sister With Love, 1945 . . . . 85.00
Pincushion, Hitler, Figural 75.00
Postcard, Map Of Germany, Hitler Photograph, Nazi, 1938 . . . . 25.00
Poster, Buy Your Extra Bonds Here, 7th War Loan, Iwo Jima, 1945, 20 x 29 In. 100.00
Poster, Catastrophe, Moscow, Green Man, Red Woman, On Black, 1926, 29 x 27 In. 3680.00
Poster, Food Is A Weapon, Don't Waste It!, 1943, 22 1/2 x 16 1/8 In. 79.00
Poster, Hitler, For Book Mein Kampf, 1930s, 14 x 22 In. 200.00
Poster, I Want You For The Navy, WAC, H.C. Christy, Frame, 25 x 38 In. 375.00
Poster, I'll Carry Mine Too!, Office Of War, 1943, 27 7/8 x 22 In. 49.00
Poster, Ours...To Fight For Freedom From Fear, Norman Rockwell, 1943, 56 x 40 In. . . . 73.00
Poster, Pvt. Joe Louis Says, Soldier Clothes, With Gun, 1942, 7 x 10 In. 200.00
Poster, Their Fight Is Our Fight, United Jewish Appeal, 14 x 22 In. 396.00
Poster, This Is What God Gave Us, U.S. Food Administration, A. Hendee, 32 In. 200.00
Poster, We Have Just Begun To Fight, Office Of War, 1943, 40 x 28 1/4 In. 73.00
Poster, Young Soldiers, Military Costume, Marching, Riding, France, 1900, 51 In. 1380.00
Pouch, Flare, Germany 180.00
Range Finder, Pocket, Folding Metal Frame, Germany 44.00
Shirt, Fatigue, Camouflage, Army 560.00
Shovel, Trench, Germany 210.00
Sword, Cane Cutter, Palm Leaf Sheath, 24 3/4 In. 6.00
Sword, Nazi Officer's, Army, Lion Head Pommel, Ruby Eyes, Scabbard 185.00
Sword, Nazi Officer's, Army, Oakleaf, Acorn Pommel, Scabbard 145.00
Sword, Shaska, Cast Pommel, No Scabbard, Russia, 1938 . . . . 220.00
Sword, Short Sword, English Home Guard 125.00
Sword, SS Officer's, Dress, Scabbard 2185.00
Telephone, Field, Germany 45.00
Token, Campaign, Adolf Hitler Nazi Party, Aluminum, Sept. 14, 1930 . . . . 50.00
Trousers, Combat, U.S. 100.00
Trousers, Summer Weight, Khaki . . . . .45.00 to 60.00
Tunic, Army, Reed Green, Bevor Eagle & Collar Tabs, 4 Pockets, Germany 330.00
Tunic, British RAF Officer, Embroidered Wings Over Breast Pocket, 10/5/40 . . . . 190.00
Uniform, Jacket, Skirt, Army Nurse Officer . . . . .95.00 to 126.00
USMC Winter Service 30.00

USS Maine, Sailor, Lest We Forget, Red, White, Blue, E. Herrick Co., 12 x 18 In.	175.00
Vest, Emergency, Type C-1, AAF	58.00
Visor Cap, Army General's	140.00
Visor Cap, Diplomatic	125.00
Wall Hanger, I Helped Save His Life Today, G.I., Hitler & Tojo Cartoons, 9 x 6 In.	40.00

WORLD'S FAIR souvenirs from all of the fairs are collected. The first fair was the Great Exhibition of 1851 in London. Other important exhibitions and fairs include Philadelphia, 1876 (Centennial); Chicago, 1893 (World's Columbian); Buffalo, 1901 (Pan-American); St. Louis, 1904 (Louisiana Purchase); San Francisco, 1915 (Panama-Pacific); Philadelphia, 1926 (Sesquicentennial); Chicago, 1933 (Century of Progress); Cleveland, 1936 (Great Lakes); San Francisco, 1939 (Golden Gate International); New York, 1939 (World of Tomorrow); Seattle, 1962; New York, 1964; Montreal, 1967; New Orleans, 1984; Tsukuba, Japan, 1985; Vancouver, B.C., 1986; Brisbane, Australia, 1988; Seville, Spain, 1992; and Genoa, Italy, 1992; Seoul, Korea, 1993; and Lisbon, Portugal, 1998. Memorabilia of fairs include directories, pictures, fabrics, ceramics, etc. Memorabilia from other similar celebrations may be listed in the Souvenir category.

Album, 1876, Philadelphia, Centennial, Pocket	25.00
Ashtray, 1933, Chicago, Chrysler Exhibit, Box	22.00
Ashtray, 1939, Chicago, Syroco Wood	15.00
Ashtray, 1939, New York, Blue, White, Trylon & Perisphere, 2 1/2 x 3 1/4 In.	25.00
Ashtray, 1964, New York, Yellow, Brown City Design, Blue Sky Ground, 5 x 7 In.	18.00
Badge, 1893, Chicago, Signing Of Declaration, Pin	25.00
Badge, 1904, St. Louis, 12K Gold, Handmade, Engraved, Mary Coleman, 2 7/8 In.	600.00
Badge, 1933, Chicago, Century Of Progress Polish Week, Ribbon, 3 In.	26.00
Badge, 1933, Chicago, Lapel, Silver	33.00
Bank, 1893, Chicago, Columbian Exposition, Kenton, 7 x 5 3/8 In.	385.00
Bank, 1893, Chicago, Columbian Exposition, Mechanical, J. & E. Stevens	3200.00
Bank, 1893, Chicago, Columbian Exposition, Metal, Administration Bldg., 5 x 5 In.	88.00
Bank, 1893, Chicago, Metal, Domed Building, Columbia Bank, 5 1/2 x 7 In.	190.00
Bank, 1933, Chicago, Mickey & Minnie Mouse, At Fair	250.00
Bank, 1939, New York, Unisphere, Ceramic, Gold Letters	75.00
Bank, 1939, New York, Unisphere, Plastic, Blue Globe, Astronauts Orbit, Box	95.00
Bank, 1964, New York, Boy & Girl With Balloons, Orange, Blue, Beige, 2 x 4 In.	58.00
Bank, 1964, New York, Globe, On Base, Metal	95.00
Basket, 1904, St. Louis, Ceramic, B&W Palace Of Mines, Raised Floral, Handles	85.00
Bone Dish, 1893, Chicago, Center Scene, Blue Decorative Border, 6 3/4 In.	44.00
Book, 1904, St. Louis, Louisiana Purchase Exposition, Sight, Scenes & Wonders	20.00
Book, 1915, San Francisco, Panama-Pacific, Exposition Palaces, Courts, 151 Pages	25.00
Book, 1939, New York, Kraft Cheese	10.00
Book, 1939, New York, New York Advancing, La Guardia Foreword, 170 Pages, 8 In. ...	25.00
Booklet, 1893, Chicago, Cardboard Cover, 4 Pages, Dried Flowers, 3 1/2 x 5 1/2 In.	110.00
Booklet, 1893, Chicago, Columbian Exposition, Thatcher's Baking Powder	25.00
Booklet, 1933, Chicago, Chevrolet-Fisher, Making Of A Motor Car, 16 Pages	28.00
Booklet, 1933, Chicago, Firestone Factory, How Gum Dipped Tires Are Made	22.00
Booklet, 1933, Chicago, Morton Salt The Story Of Salt, 8 1/2 x 11 In.	10.00
Bookmark, 1893, Chicago, Silk, Flag, Star Spangled Banner Lyrics, 12 1/2 In.	120.00
Bookmark, 1901, Pan-American, Silk, Electric Tower, 2 3/4 x 11 In.	75.00
Bookmark, 1904, St. Louis, Silk, B&W, Teddy Roosevelt, Fair Name, 3 x 8 In.	113.00
Bookmark, 1905, Portland, Lewis & Clark Exposition	79.00
Bookmark, 1915, San Francisco, Celluloid, Pacific Coast Condensed Milk, 2 x 5 In.	45.00
Bookmark, 1933, Chicago, Emblem, Carillon Tower, 4 3/4 In.	30.00
Bookmark, 1939, New York, Trylon & Perisphere, 4 In.	20.00
Bowl, 1939, New York, Silver Plate, Logo In Bottom, Hammercraft, 11 In.	63.00
Box, Jewelry, 1893, Chicago, Lid, Floral Design, 3 In.	27.00
Box, Jewelry, 1904, St. Louis, Reverse Glass, Cascades, 3 In.	150.00
Button, 1901, Buffalo, Pan-American, Blue Ground, Celluloid, Pinback	75.00
Calendar, 1939, New York, Advertising, J. Marcinkowski Groceries, 15 x 23 In.	400.00
Calling Card, 1893, Chicago, Columbian, Fair Building, 2 1/4 x 4 In.	18.00
Camera, 1939, New York, Kodak, Baby Brownie, Trylon & Perisphere, 2 x 3 In.	170.00

World's Fair, License Plate, 1967, Montreal,
Quebec, Child's, Karen, Aluminum, 2 1/4 x 4 In.

Camera, 1964, New York, Kodak, Flash, 127 Film, AGI Bulbs, 5 In.	28.00
Cane, 1893, Chicago, Man's Head, Metal, Large	100.00
Cane, 1893, Chicago, Metal, Head Of Columbus	165.00
Cane, 1933, Chicago, Wooden, Hall Of Science, Curved Handle	25.00
Card, 1876, Philadelphia, Agricultural Hall, Black & White, 3 x 5 In.	22.00
Card, 1926, Philadelphia, Liberty Bell, Colored Flags, 5 3/4 x 8 1/4 In.	16.00
Card, Courtesy, 1939, New York, Westinghouse Hall Of Electrical Living, 4 In.	33.00
Carpet Sweeper, 1939, New York, Bissell's, Trylon & Perisphere, Blue, White	133.00
Charm, 1939, New York, Mobil Gas, Trylon & Perisphere, Red Hard Rubber, 1 In.	30.00
Coaster, 1939, New York, Everlast Metal, Trylon & Perisphere, 3 3/4 In.	7.00
Coaster, 1939, New York, Trylon & Perisphere, Blue & Orange, 3 In.	15.00
Coaster, 1939, San Francisco Golden Gate International Exposition, 3 3/8 In.	25.00 to 28.00
Coin, 1939, New York, Bust, George Washington, 150th Anniversary Inauguration	28.00
Coin, 1939, New York, George Washington, Oath Of Office, Trylon & Perisphere	28.00
Coin Holder, 1893, Chicago, Columbian Exposition, 2, 5, 10 & 25 Cent	175.00
Compact, 1933, Chicago, Geometric Design Base, Silver Logo, 1 3/4 x 2 In.	22.00
Cup, 1904, St. Louis, Building Views, Copper, National Novelty Co., 3 1/2 In.	25.00
Cup, Collapsible, 1904, St. Louis, Aluminum, Border On Lid, 2 1/2 In.	33.00
Cup & Saucer, 1893, Chicago, Porcelain, Oriental, White Flowers, Gilt	475.00
Dairy, 1939, New York, Hotel Chesterfield, Radio City, Times Square, 6 x 8 In.	28.00
Dollar, 1893, Chicago, Saint-Gaudens, Columbian Exposition	36.00
Fan, 1876, Philadelphia Centennial, 1776-1876, U.S. Flag, 30 Sticks, Opens To 20 In.	150.00
Fan, 1876, Philadelphia, Lady's, Independence Hall, Eagle, Flags, 20 In.	100.00
Figurine, 1915, San Francisco, Porcelain, Bear, Oakland, San Francisco Scenes, 4 In.	150.00
Figurine, 1939, New York, Statue Of Liberty, Logo, Bronzed White Metal, 6 In.	25.00
Flier, 1904, St. Louis, Ferris Wheel, History Of Wheel, 3 x 6 In.	88.00
Fob, 1893, Chicago, 3 Square Medalets, Patriotic Designs, Eagle, 4 1/2 In.	25.00
Fob, 1904, St. Louis, Palace Of Liberal Arts, Eagle, Nickel, 3 Piece	60.00
Glass, 1901, Buffalo, Manufacturers, Liberal Arts Buildings, Gold Trim, 3 3/4 In.	22.00
Glass, 1964, New York, Schafer Beer, Red Transfer, 6 In.	22.00
Guide Book, 1934, Chicago, Red, 192 Pages, 5 1/2 x 8 1/2 In.	28.00
Guide Book, 1939, New York, Second Edition, 256 Pages, 5 x 8 In.	28.00
Handkerchief, 1876, Philadelphia, Centennial, Memorial Hall, Eagle, Linen, 25 In.	.95.00 to 183.00
Handkerchief, 1893, Chicago, Columbian, Silk, Embroidered, 12 In.	40.00
Handkerchief, 1893, Chicago, Set Of 3	60.00
Handkerchief, 1893, Chicago, Silk, Embroidered Design, Shield, Branches, 12 In.	25.00
Handkerchief, 1904, St. Louis, White, Linen, French Flag, Embroidered, 12 x 12 In.	25.00
Handkerchief, 1909, Yukon, Pacific Exposition, Silk, Eagles, Seattle Skyline, 12 In.	25.00
Handkerchief, 1939, New York, Trylon & Perisphere In Corner, Linen, Pink, 12 In.	20.00
Hot Pad, 1933, Chicago, A Century Of Progress, Tan Suede, Cardboard, 6 x 8 In.	18.00
Ice Pick, 1939, San Francisco, Steel, Wooden Handle, 8 In.	16.00 to 18.00
Invitation, 1905, Portland, Lithograph, Bridge Of All Nations, Raised Floral	20.00
Invitation, 1905, Portland, Lt. Governor & Mrs. Bruce, Card, Envelopes	60.00
Invitation, 1939, New York, N.Y. Firemen's Convention, Tournament, 9 x 12 In.	33.00
Lamp, 1901, Buffalo, Oil, Green Glass, Pan-Am Logo, 5 In.	90.00
Letter Opener, 1901, Buffalo, Pan American Exposition, Bronze	45.00
License Plate, 1967, Montreal, Quebec, Child's, Karen, Aluminum, 2 1/4 x 4 In. ....*Illus*	20.00

Map, 1933, Chicago, Brochure, Showing Trolleys, Bus Lines, Color, 16 Pages, 9 In. 35.00
Map, 1933, Chicago, Century Of Progress, Fair Scene, 8 x 9 In. 35.00
Map, 1933, Chicago, Century Of Progress, PRR, Photographs, 8 x 9 In. 35.00
Map, 1939, Chicago, Greyhound, Where To Go What To See 30.00
Map, 1939, Greater New York, Street Railways Adv. Co., Color 30.00
Map, 1939, New York, Fold-Out 10.00
Marble Bag, 1933, Chicago 145.00
Match Holder, 1933, Century Of Progress, Burlington Zephyr Train, Chrome 75.00
Match Safe, 1893, Chicago, Columbus Bust, Striker Bottom, 1 1/2 x 2 1/2 In. 170.00
Match Safe, 1893, Chicago, Columbus Head, Columbian, Plated Brass, 2 5/8 In. 265.00
Match Safe, 1901, Buffalo, Pan-American, Celluloid, 1 1/2 x 2 1/4 In. 220.00
Match Safe, 1904, St. Louis, Metal, Pearl, Striker Edge, Push-Button Top 45.00
Medal, 1893, Chicago, Columbian, Columbus Bust, 1492-1892, 1 In. 25.00
Medal, 1893, Chicago, Columbian, Saint-Gaudens, Columbus, Unbronzed 165.00
Medal, 1893, Chicago, Columbus Bust, Beard, Ruffled Collar, 1 In. 13.00
Medal, 1893, Chicago, Republican Candidates, White House, Landing Scene Reverse 36.00
Medal, 1893, Chicago, Saint-Gaudens, Columbus, Ship 80.00
Medal, 1926, Philadelphia, Eagle In Nest, Independence Hall, Award 230.00
Medal, 1933, Chicago, Official, Commemorative, Youth, Map 37.00
Medal, 1933, Chicago, Wooden, Lincoln Bust 37.00
Mug, 1893, Chicago, Quadruple Plate, Floral Border, 3 1/2 In. 25.00
Mug, 1901, Buffalo, Pan-American Exposition, Beer, Embossed Scene, 5 In. 138.00
Mug, 1904, St. Louis, B & W Cascade Gardens, Gilt Trim, 4 In. 68.00
Napkin, Cocktail, 1893, Chicago, Red, Beige, Embroidery, 6 x 6 In. 25.00
Napkin Ring, 1904, St. Louis, Heavy Tin, 1 3/4 In. 25.00
Needle Folder, 1933, Chicago, Century Of Progress, Photos, Fair Buildings 12.00
Pamphlet, 1905, Portland, Lewis & Clark, Map, Fairgrounds, 3 1/8 x 5 In. 22.00
Paperweight, 1876, Philadelphia, Buildings, Lithograph, Felt Bottom, 2 1/2 x 5 In. 130.00
Paperweight, 1876, Philadelphia, Centennial, Inset, Memorial Hall, 4 x 5 1/2 In. 36.00
Paperweight, 1901, Buffalo, Pan-Am, Electric Tower, Sepia Picture 23.00
Paperweight, 1904, St. Louis, Advertising, Cascade View On Bottom, 2 1/2 x 4 In. 85.00
Paperweight, 1907, Norfolk, Jamestown, Glass, Star Center, Gilt Trim, 5 1/4 In. 28.00
Paperweight, 1939, New York, Brass Plated, 2 Suitcases & Golf Bag, 2 1/2 In. 97.00
Paperweight, 1964, New York, Unisphere, Silver, Gold Lettering, Plastic, 2 3/4 In. 18.00
Pen, 1898, Omaha, Pythian Jubilee, Oct. 10 To 15, 1898, Trans-Mississippi Expo 90.00
Pencil, 1939, San Francisco, Trylon & Perisphere, Giant Eagle Pencil, 10 1/2 In. 20.00
Pennant, 1936, Cleveland, Great Lakes Exposition, 17 In. 25.00
Pennant, 1940, New York, Showing Visitor On Final Fair Day, Yellow, 4 x 9 In. 70.00
Pillow, 1933, Chicago, Red Felt, Electrical Building, Square, 11 1/4 In. 37.00
Pin, 1901, Buffalo, Pan American, Logo, Celluloid, 1 1/4 In. 28.00
Pin, 1904, St. Louis, Celluloid, Alameda County, California, 2 In. 40.00
Pin, 1909, Seattle, Sterling Silver, Enameled, Flower Center, 2 1/8 In. 38.00
Pin, 1939, New York, Trylon & Perisphere, Blue, Orange, White, 1 1/4 In. 25.00
Pin Box, 1893, Chicago, Columbian, Building, Metal Filigree, Glass, 2 3/4 In. 165.00
Pin Tray, 1904, St. Louis, Palace Of Electricity, Aluminum, 3 x 4 3/8 In. 30.00
Pin Tray, 1904, St. Louis, Uncle Sam & France, Metal, 2 7/8 x 3 5/8 In. 35.00
Pin Tray, 1915, San Francisco, Panama Pacific, Silver Plated, Van Bergh, 4 In. 28.00
Pinball Machine, 1933, San Francisco, Aerial View, Rock-Ola Mfg., 38 x 42 In. 1200.00
Pitcher, 1893, Chicago, Columbian, Ribbed, Handle, Peachblow, 3 1/2 In. 345.00
Pitcher, 1893, Chicago, Fisheries Bldg., Pottery, Brown, White, Bridgewood, 5 In. 280.00
Plaque, 1893, Chicago, Center Raised Scene, Landing Of Columbus, 12 In. 80.00
Plaque, 1893, Chicago, Landing, Border With Crops, Gilt On Cast, 7 x 9 In. 25.00
Plaque, 1904, St. Louis, Eagle 200.00
Plate, 1876, Philadelphia, Child's, Alphabet, Independence Hall 55.00
Plate, 1893, Chicago, Columbian, U.S. Government Building, Wedgwood 28.00
Plate, 1904, St. Louis, 3 Men, Horseback, Gen. Fred Grant & Friends, Grant Hill 200.00
Plate, 1904, St. Louis, B & W Festival Hall, Cascades, Copeland Spode, England 150.00
Plate, 1904, St. Louis, Festival Hall & Cascade Gardens In Center, Gold, White, 7 In. ... 18.00
Plate, 1904, St. Louis, Jefferson Center Scenes, Blue, Rolled Edge, 10 In. 165.00
Plate, 1909, Seattle, Oregon State Building, Fair Name, City In Gilt, 8 In. 33.00
Plate, 1915, San Francisco, Milk Glass, Electricity Building, 5 3/8 In. 35.00
Plate, 1939, New York, Deco Fair Building, Charles Murphy, Homer Laughlin 180.00
Plate, 1939, New York, Turquoise, Potter At Wheel ....20.00 to 55.00

Plate, 1964, New York, Orange, Blue Bicycle, Gold, White, 2 x 4 In. 28.00
Plate, 1964, New York, Unisphere Center, 6 Fair Scenes, 10 In. 14.00
Platter, 1964, New York, Texas Pavilion, Frontier Palace, Oval, 9 1/4 x 12 In. 28.00
Pocket Knife, 1939, New York, Celluloid Grip, 2 Blade, Colonial, Prov., R.I. 20.00
Portrait, 1904, St. Louis, Indian Smoking Unglazed Pipe, Weller, 4 5/8 In. 160.00
Portrait, 1904, St. Louis, President Grant, Weller, 4 1/2 In. 160.00
Postcard, 1901, Buffalo, Pan American, Electric Tower, Sparkles, 6 x 9 In. 200.00
Postcard, 1901, Buffalo, Pan American, Manufacturers & Liberal Arts Building 7.00
Postcard, 1904, St. Louis, Exhibit Building Views, English Text, Germany, Set 600.00
Postcard, 1904, St. Louis, Hold-To-Light, Cascade Gardens & Grand Basin, 6 x 9 In. 280.00
Postcard, 1904, St. Louis, Wooden, Painted Gold Dollar, 3 1/2 x 5 1/2 In. 27.00
Postcard, 1909, Seattle, Alaska Yukon Pacific 15.00
Postcard, 1915, San Francisco, Panama Pacific, Underwood Typewriter, Buildings 22.00
Postcard, 1933, Chicago, Montage, Statue, Native American & USA Map 250.00
Postcard, 1934, Chicago, Ripley Auditorium 3.00
Postcard, 1939, San Francisco, Golden Gate International Expo, Pilsener Beer 60.00
Poster, 1876, Philadelphia, Art Gallery & Main Bldg., Harrison Brothers, 26 In. 40.00
Poster, 1876, Philadelphia, Seated Liberty, Wreath, Battle, 21 3/4 x 27 1/2 In. 113.00
Potlid, 1853, New York, Crystal Palace, Prattware, Multicolored, 5 In. 350.00
Potlid, 1876, Philadelphia, Centennial, Ceramic, Fair Building, Visitors 103.00
Print, 1853, New York, Crystal Palace, Flags, Visitors, Oil Color, 8 x 11 In. 250.00
Program, 1915, San Francisco, Panama-Pacific International Exposition 26.00
Purse, Coin, 1904, St. Louis, Hall Of Festivals & Cascades, Chain Handle, 2 3/4 In. 50.00
Puzzle, 1933, Chicago, Century Of Progress, Preview, Box, 300 Piece 165.00
Quilt, 1893, Chicago, Cotton, Top, White, Red Embroidery, 12 Squares, 6 x 8 Ft. 495.00
Ribbon, 1893, Chicago, Silk, Eagles, Flags, Shield, Star-Spangled Banner Verse 35.00
Ribbon, 1901, Buffalo, Great Pan-American Emancipation, Brass Hanger, 4 1/2 In. 55.00
Salad Set, 1939, New York, Trylon & Perisphere, Wooden, 10 In. 40.00
Saltshaker, 1904, St. Louis, Cascades, Fair Name, Pewter, 2 1/4 In. 30.00
Saucer, 1893, Chicago, Transportation Building, Brown Transfer, Bridgewood, 6 In. 40.00
Scarf, 1933, Chicago, Century Of Progress, Made Of Japanese Silk Sticker, Folded 28.00
Scarf, 1939, New York, Squares, Fair Name, Couples, Ethnic Costumes, 17 x 20 In. 35.00
Scarf, Dresser, 1876, Philadelphia, Eagle On Shield, Flags, Fringe, 20 1/2 In. 100.00
Scarf, Dresser, 1893, Chicago, Eagle, Shield, Columbus Bust, 23 x 38 In. 25.00
Scarf, Dresser, 1901, Buffalo, White, Red Trim, Pan-American Expo, 18 x 28 In. 46.00
Sheet Music, 1876, Philadelphia, Centennial March, E. Mack 25.00
Snowdome, 1939, San Francisco, Trylon & Perisphere, Bakelite Base, 4 In. 165.00
Spoon, 1876, Philadelphia, Centennial, Bust On Handle, Ship In Bowl, Silver 30.00
Spoon, 1892, Chicago, Bust Of Columbus, Sterling Silver, Gold Toned, 4 In. 20.00
Spoon, 1893, Chicago, Aluminum Eagle & Flag, Ship & Columbus Bust Handle 50.00
Spoon, 1893, Chicago, Columbus Bust On Handle Top 25.00
Spoon, 1893, Chicago, Court Scene In Bowl, Ship, Columbus Bust On Handle 10.00
Spoon, 1893, Chicago, Demitasse, Sterling, Eagle On Globe, Name, City In Bowl 37.00
Spoon, 1904, St. Louis, Demitasse, Administration Building, Decorative Handle 25.00
Spoon, 1904, St. Louis, Demitasse, Industries In Bowl 14.00
Spoon, 1904, St. Louis, Railroad, Cascade Gardens, Lake Shore Michigan S. Railway . . . 16.00
Spoon, 1904, St. Louis, Sterling, Cascade Gardens, Court House, Jefferson Bust 37.00
Spoon, 1904, St. Louis, Sterling, Demitasse, Festival Hall & Cascades, Seal, Teepee 28.00
Spoon, 1904, St. Louis, Sterling, Demitasse, Mines & Metallurgy Building In Bowl 28.00
Spoon, 1904, St. Louis, Sterling, Demitasse, U.S. Government Building In Bowl 21.00
Spoon, 1904, St. Louis, Sterling, Industrial Palace, Eagle, Jefferson, Napoleon 39.00
Spoon, 1909, Seattle, Sterling, Alaska Building In Bowl, Totem Pole Handle, Huskies . . . 36.00
Spoon, 1915, San Francisco, Plain Bowl, Tower Of Jewels On Handle 25.00
Spoon, 1939, New York, Trylon & Perisphere On Handle, Blue Enamel Ground 25.00
Spoon, 1967, Montreal, Fair Logo, Name On Handle, Oneida, Box, 1 1/2 In. 2.00
Stamp Case, 1904, St. Louis, Aluminum, Hinge, Embossed 35.00
Stein, 1904, St. Louis, 3 Scenes, Pewter Lid, Germany, 2 Liter 1625.00
Stein, 1904, St. Louis, O'Hara Watch Dial Co., Pottery, Palace Of Mines, 5 In. 225.00
Stein, 1904, St. Louis, Woman Opening Machine, Pewter Lid, 1/2 Liter 660.00
Sticker, 1939, New York, Air Mail, Fly Braniff To The N.Y. World's Fair, 19 Piece 25.00
Tapestry, 1939, New York, Woven, Maroon, 9 x 13 In. 40.00
Taxi, 1933, Chicago, Ford, Sedan, Century Of Progress On Roof, Cast Iron, 6 1/2 In. 688.00
Textile, 1893, Chicago, U.S. Capitol, George Washington, Chintz, 22 x 60 In. 187.00

Thermometer, 1939, New York, Trylon & Perisphere, Bakelite, 4 In. 65.00
Thermometer, 1939, San Francisco, Trylon & Perisphere, Box, 3 3/4 In. 72.00
Thermometer Paperweight, 1939, San Francisco, Trylon, Perisphere, Steel, 8 1/2 In. 25.00
Thimble, 1904, St. Louis, Sterling Silver, Golden Spike, Simons Bros. Co. 745.00
Ticket, 1853, New York, Crystal Palace, Northern Railway, Canada, 2 x 2 3/4 In. 90.00
Ticket, 1901, Buffalo, Pan-American, Goddess, Triumphal Bridge Picture, 2 In. 44.00
Ticket, Admission, 1893, Chicago, Columbian, Indian, Other Columbus Bust 55.00
Ticket & Pack, 1934, New York 25.00
Ticket Book, 1939, New York, Washington Statue, Fair Buildings, 2 1/4 x 6 In. 18.00
Token, 1876, Philadelphia, Eagle On Bell, Fair Name, Date, Flag On Reverse 25.00
Token, 1876, Philadelphia, Independence Hall & 1776, Liberty Bell 10.00
Token, 1898, Omaha, Building & Lagoon 37.00
Toothpick, 1893, Chicago, Ruby Glass 35.00
Toothpick, 1904, St. Louis, RWB, Enameled, Fleur-De-Lis, Gilt Tin, 1 3/4 In. 30.00
Toy, 1933, Chicago, Tumbling Mice, Decal On Back, Germany, Box 965.00
Tray, 1964, New York, Gold Accents, 5 x 6 1/4 x 3/4 In., 4 Piece . . . . .22.00 to 24.00
Tumbler, 1904, St. Louis, Ceramic, Pylonic Gateway, Tyrolian Village, 3 7/8 In. 120.00
Umbrella, 1936, Cleveland Great Lakes Exposition, Floral, Paper, Bamboo Handle 40.00
Uniform, 1939, New York, Jacket, Employee, Khaki, Blue Collar, Epaulettes, Orange 90.00
Unisphere, 1964, New York, Building, Metal, 3 In. 7.00
Vase, 1904, St. Louis, Art Glass, Iridescent Blue, Green, Violet, Apollo Silver, 6 In. 795.00
Vase, 1904, St. Louis, Ceramic, Palace Of Electricity, Floral Spray, 4 7/8 In. 113.00
Vase, 1939, New York, Crystal, Bulb Design, Pink Center, Gold Lettering, 3 3/4 In. 28.00
Vase, 1939, New York, Trylon & Perisphere, Glass, Ruby Flashed, 3 3/4 In. 40.00
Vase, 1939, New York, Trylon & Perisphere, Japan, 3 In. 75.00
Viewer, 1964, New York, Television Shape, Orange & Blue Plastic, 2 1/4 In. 35.00
Wagon, 1933, Chicago, Radio Flyer, Tin, Blue, 4 1/2 In. 65.00
Wine, 1893, Columbian Exposition, Ruby Thumbprint, 4 1/2 In. 30.00

WPA is the abbreviation for Works Progress Administration, a program created by executive order in 1935 to provide jobs for millions of unemployed Americans. Artists were hired to create murals, paintings, drawings, and sculptures for public buildings. Pieces are marked WPA and may have the artist's name on them.

Badge, Employee, Celluloid, Black & White, N.Y. 60.00
Card, Membership, Pinback Button, 1930s 30.00
Doll, Greek Woman, Clay Legs, Cloth Arms & Body, Human Hair, Chemise, 1930s 40.00
House, Brick Model, Wood Painted Base, District 15 . . . . 158.00
National Road In Song & Story, 1940, 48 Pages, 5 1/2 x 8 1/2 In. 32.00
Painting, Oil On Canvas, Industrial Scene, Bessie Rigrodsky, 1939, 25 x 20 In. 1224.00
Picture, Watercolor, Beachcomber's Return, Karl Knaths, 8 1/4 x 6 1/2 In. 234.00
Poster, Golden Gate Exposition, Pomo Basket, Louis Siegriest, 1939, 25 x 36 In. 820.00
Poster, Safety, First Law Of Camping, Penn. Dept. Of Forests & Water, 14 1/4 x 11 In. . . 183.00
Puppet, Fire King, Papier-Mache Head, Wooden Arms & Legs, Cloth Body, 1930s 37.00
Puppet, Mama Pig, Papier-Mache Head, Wooden Arms & Legs, Cloth Body, 13 In. 88.00
Tumbler, North Dakota, Blue, Pottery, 3 1/2 In. 105.00
Vase, Indented Top Rim, WPA Ceramics, No. Dak., 7 1/4 In. 157.00
Woodcut, Backyard, Urban Tenement Scene, Isaac Friedlander, 9 1/8 x 7 In. 415.00

WRISTWATCHES came into use during World War I. Wristwatches are listed here by manufacturer or as advertising or character watches. Pocket watches are listed in the Watch category.

1861 Silver Dollar Coin, Stainless Steel Back, 17 Jewel, Swank 140.00
Abra Watch Co., Diamond Bezel, Link Bracelet, 17 Jewel, Platinum 2070.00
Advertising, Goodyear, Windup 55.00
Advertising, Helbros, Buy U.S. War Bonds, Gold Front 65.00
Advertising, Mercedes-Benz Radiator, Silver Matte Dial, B. Girod, 18K Gold, 1970 . . . . . 4025.00
Advertising, Oster-Man Flying, Windup, 1960s 55.00
Advertising, Ritz Crackers 895.00
Airian, Military, 17 Jewel, Black Arabic Numerals, Auxiliary Dial, 1960 . . . . 690.00
Altanus, Sea Diver, Automatic, Stainless, Date, Rotating Bezel, Swiss 325.00
Aviator's, Breitling, Black, Silver Matte, Arabic Numerals, Slide Rule 1265.00
Aviator's, Cyma, 15 Jewel, Black, Arabic Numerals, Baton Hands, 1940 . . . . 437.00

Baume & Mercier, 15 Jewel, Black Arabic Numerals, Gilt Brass, 1950, 11 In. 405.00
Bracelet, 17 Jewel, 18K Gold, Silver Matte Dial, Baton Numerals, 1945 . . . .   3450.00
Bracelet, 18K Gold, Gilt Dial, Textured Brickwork Links, Square Case, 1960 . . . .   1495.00
Bracelet, 18K Pink Gold, Silver Matte Dial, Rectangular Case, 1950 . . . .   3737.00
Bracelet, Pearls & Sapphires, 14K Gold 900.00
Breguet, Aviator's, 17 Jewel, Black Arabic Numerals, Lever Escapement, 1970 . . . .   4370.00
Breguet, Chronograph, 18K Gold, Black Matte Dial, 1935 . . . .   2990.00
Breitling, 17 Jewel, Breguet Numerals, Silver, Gold, 1930, 12 1/4 In. 1955.00
Bulgari, 18K 3-Tone Gold, Black Matte Dial, Arabic Numerals, 1980 . . . .   4890.00
Bulova, 17 Jewel, Day, Date, Automatic, Stainless Case & Band 50.00
Bulova, Accutron, Quartz, Diamond Set Bezel, 14K Gold Mesh Strap 230.00
Bulova, Accutron, Spaceview 275.00
Cartier, 15 Jewel, 18K Gold, Backwind Set, Silver Matte Dial, Rectangular, 1945 . . . . . .   2875.00
Cartier, 17 Jewel, 18K Gold, Silver Engine Dial, Roman Numerals, Case, 1975 . . . .   2587.00
Cartier, 17 Jewel, 18K Gold, Silver Matte Dial, Hinged Cover, 1950 . . . .   3162.00
Cartier, 17 Jewel, 18K Gold, White Matte Dial, Roman Numerals, 1985 . . . .   3875.00
Cartier, 17 Jewel, 18K Gold, White Matte Dial, Roman Numerals, Case, 1970 . . . .   4600.00
Cartier, 17 Jewel, 18K Gold, White Matte Dial, Roman Numerals, Case, 1985 . . . .   4887.00
Cartier, 17 Jewel, 18K Gold, White Matte Dial, Roman Numerals, Self-Winding 3450.00
Cartier, 17 Jewel, White Dial, Roman Numerals, Baron Hands, 18K Yellow Gold 745.00
Cartier, 18K Gold, Bell Form, Silver Matte Dial, Roman Numerals, 1988 . . . .   2300.00
Cartier, 18K Gold, Circular Nickel Lever Movement, Silver Matte Dial, 1948 . . . .   4310.00
Cartier, 18K Gold, White Matte Dial, Roman Numerals, Square Case, 1970 . . . .   11500.00
Cartier, 19 Jewel, 8 Adjustments, Eggshell White Matte Dial, Roman Numerals 13800.00
Cartier, White Matte Dial, Roman Numerals, Circular Case, 14K Gold, 1970 . . . .   1725.00
Character, Barbie, 3 Bands, Original Red Plastic Display Box, 1971 . . . .   65.00
Character, Barbie, Peppermint Princess, Fossil 70.00
Character, Cat In The Hat, Red Vinyl Band 125.00
Character, Cinderella 35.00
Character, Cinderella, 3 Bands, Box, Bradley, 1967 . . . .   165.00
Character, Diver's, Hollywood Polo Club, Stainless Steel, Date, Automatic 150.00
Character, Dukes Of Hazard, Digital, Plastic Band, Unopened Box, 1981 . . . .   15.00
Character, Dukes Of Hazard, Quartz, Digital, Melody Alarm, Steel Band, Box 25.00
Character, E.T., Metal Case, Blue Vinyl Strap, Nelsonic, 1982, 1 1/8 In. 85.00
Character, Jerry Lewis, Caricature 75.00
Character, Lord Nelson, Triangular, Thermometer Inside, White Face, 1950s 65.00
Character, Lucy, Peanuts, Sweep Second Hand, Leather Band, Flower Design 50.00
Character, Smokey Bear, Shovel Hands, Blue Band, Chrome Case, Bradley, 1979 . . . . . .   78.00
Character, Snoopy 25.00
Character, Snoopy, In Flying Helmet, Clear Acrylic, Vinyl Band, Armitron, Box 22.00
Character, Space Patrol, Metal Band . . . . .50.00 to 75.00
Character, Strawberry Shortcake 45.00
Character, Tom Corbett, Space Graphic, Leather Band, 1950s 225.00
Chronograph, 18K Gold, Silver Matte Dial, Triangular Baton Numerals, 1940 . . . .   2415.00
Chronograph, Stainless Steel Case, Lizard Band, Continental 230.00
Concord, Woman's, Quartz, Brushed Stainless Steel Band 45.00
Corum, Gold Coin, U.S. Dollar Liberty Head, Leather Strap, Box, 1906 . . . .   1840.00
Cravelle, 17 Jewel, Skeleton 40.00
Croton, 14K Gold, Dial Inlaid With 5 Diamonds 375.00
Eberhard & Co., Silver Matte Dial, Breguet Numerals, Baton Hands, 1930 . . . .   1380.00
Gerald, Genta, 18K Gold, Overall Scrolls, Perpetual Calendar, Self-Winding, 1990 . . . . . .   12650.00
Gerald Genta, 18K Gold, Gold Skeleton Lever Movement, Scrolls, 1985 . . . .   5750.00
Gruen, Curvex, Diamond Dial, 14K Gold 1000.00
Gruen, Yellow Gold Filled Bezel 50.00
Gucci, 17 Jewel, 18K Yellow Gold, White Dial, Gold Strap, Black Roman Numerals 690.00
Hamilton, Diamond Dial, Hooded Lugs, 14K Gold 1100.00
Hamilton, Gold Filled, Silver Tone, Metal Band, Plastic Case 30.00
Hamilton, Le Baron, Abalone Face, Gilt Frame, Battery, Leather Band, Case 35.00
Helbros, Invincible, Flexible Steel Band, Stem Wind, Jewelry Style Case 35.00
International Watch Co., 14K Gold, Cushion Gold Case, Gold Arabic Numerals 660.00
Juvenia, 17 Jewel, 18K Gold, Stick Chapters, Mesh Band 860.00
LeCoultre, 18K Gold, White Matte Dial, Arabic Numerals, Rectangular Case, 1983 . . . . .   4600.00
LeCoultre, Alarm, 18K Pink Gold, Silver Matte Dial, Circular Case, 1950 . . . .   1955.00

Lemania, Black, Arabic Numerals, Chronograph, Baton Hands, 1960 .... 863.00
Locle & Geneve, 18K Gold, Nickel Lever Movement, Black Matte Dial, 1945 .... 3450.00
Longines, 14K Gold, Chronograph, White Enamel Dial, Circular Case, 1925 .... 2300.00
Longines, 15 Jewel, Champagne Dial, Black Roman Numerals, Circular Case, 1940 ..... 690.00
Longines, White Metal Expandable Band, White Face, Second Hand 45.00
Lucerne, Woman's, Diamond Set Flowerhead Cover, 17 Jewel, 14K Gold 460.00
Lucien Piccard, 14K Gold, Face & Back Like $20 U.S. Gold Piece 165.00
Lucien Piccard, Woman's, 17 Jewel, 14K Gold, Oval Case, Nugget-Type Band 145.00
Mappin & Webb, 18K Gold, Register, White Enamel Dial, 1930 .... 2530.00
Movado, 15 Jewel, 14K Gold, Silver Dial, Tiffany & Co., Spandex Band 120.00
Movado, Black Abstract Indicators, Platinum Band, Gold Clasp 690.00
Movado, Black Matte Dial, Arabic Numerals, 1945 .... 2070.00
Omega, 17 Jewel, 18K Pink Gold, Silver Matte Dial, Arabic Numerals, 1945 ...... 2587.00
Omega, 18K Gold 400.00
Omega, 18K Gold, Silver Matte Dial, Square Baton Numerals, Signed, 1945 .... 1840.00
Omega, 18K Gold, Square, Cloth Band 115.00
Omega, 18K Yellow Gold, Quartz, Stick Chapters, Mesh Band 865.00
Omega, Gold Plated, Date Window, Alligator Band 70.00
Omega, Military, 15 Jewel, Black, Arabic Numerals, Baton Hands, 1940 .... 265.00
Omega, Silver Dial, Gold Baton Markers, Gold Link Strap, 1960 .... 375.00
Omega, Woman's, Quartz, Mesh Band, Cut Diamond On Dial, 18K Gold 805.00
Patek Philippe, 18 Jewel, 18K Gold, Free-Sprung Regulator, Baton Numerals 2875.00
Patek Philippe, 18 Jewel, 18K Gold, White Matte Dial, Baton Numerals, 1980 .... 4312.00
Patek Philippe, 18 Jewel, 18K Pink Gold, Pink Matte Dial, Rectangular Case 8050.00
Patek Philippe, 18 Jewel, 18K White Gold, Silver Matte Dial, Arabic Numerals 2875.00
Patek Philippe, 18 Jewel, Circular Nickel Lever Movement, Black Matte Dial 3737.00
Patek Philippe, 18 Jewel, Off-White Matte Dial, Single Cut Diamond Numerals 7475.00
Patek Philippe, 18 Jewel, Silver Matte Dial, Arabic, Disc Numerals, 1940 .... 4025.00
Patek Philippe, 18 Jewel, Silver Matte Dial, Silver Baton Numerals 8050.00
Patek Philippe, 18K Gold, Champagne Matte Dial, Oval Case, 1980 .... 3910.00
Patek Philippe, 18K Gold, Gilt Lever Movement, White Enamel Dial, 1912 .... 5750.00
Patek Philippe, 18K Gold, Gilt Matte Dial, Arabic Numerals, Octagonal Case 5750.00
Patek Philippe, 18K Gold, Nickel Lever Movement, Ivory Matte Dial, 1986 .... 3450.00
Patek Philippe, 18K Gold, Nickel Lever Movement, Silver Matte Dial, 1950 .... 4310.00
Patek Philippe, 18K Gold, Nickel Lever Movement, Silver Matte Dial, Case 4887.00
Patek Philippe, 18K Gold, Silver Matte Dial, 5 Adjustments, Case, 1965 .... 6325.00
Patek Philippe, 18K Gold, Silver Matte Dial, Baton Numerals, 1960 .... 6325.00
Patek Philippe, 18K Gold, Silver Matte Dial, Nickel Lever Movement, Case 2990.00
Patek Philippe, 18K Gold, Silver Matte Dial, Rectangular Case, 1954 .... 4025.00
Patek Philippe, 18K Pink Gold, Nickel Lever Movement, Silver Matte Dial 6900.00
Patek Philippe, 18K Pink Gold, Pink Matte Dial, Arabic, Baton Numerals 4310.00
Patek Philippe, 18K White Gold, Blue Matte Dial, Baton Numerals, 1985 .... 7475.00
Patek Philippe, 18K White Gold, Silver Matte Dial, Baton Numerals, 1965 .... 6325.00
Patek Philippe, 18K Yellow Gold, Herringbone Bracelet, 1958 .... 1265.00
Patek Philippe, 29 Jewel, 18K Gold, Nickel Lever Movement, White Matte Dial 6990.00
Patek Philippe, 29 Jewel, 18K Gold, White Matte Dial, Roman Numerals, 1981 .... 7475.00
Patek Philippe, 29 Jewel, 18K White Gold, Silver Matte Dial, Platinum 6327.00
Patek Philippe, 36 Jewel, 18K Gold, 5 Adjustments, Champagne Matte Dial 5175.00
Patek Philippe, 37 Jewel, 18K Gold, Nickel Lever Movement, Self-Winding 5635.00
Patek Philippe, 37 Jewel, 18K Pink Gold, Silver Matte Dial, Circular Case 6900.00
Patek Philippe, Nickel Lever Movement, Gold Textured Dial, Baton Numerals 5060.00
Piaget, 17 Jewel, 18K Gold, Champagne Matte Dial, Roman, Baton Numerals 1725.00
Piaget, 18 Jewel, 18K Gold, Black Onyx Dial, Diamond Set Numerals, 1975 .... 3162.00
Piaget, 18K Gold, Black Onyx Dial, Circular Case, 1975 .... 1725.00
Piaget, Asymmetrical Bracelet, 18K Gold, Lapis Lazuli Dial, 1970 .... 2587.00
Piaget, Cushion, 18K White Gold, Textured Dial, Bracelet, 1970 .... 2300.00
Piguet, 18K Gold, 7 Adjustments, Silver Matte Dial, Arabic Numerals, 1925 .... 4025.00
Piguet, 18K Gold, Gold Skeleton Lever Movement, Scrolls, 1970 .... 5175.00
Piguet, 18K Gold, Silver Matte Dial, Nickel Lever Movement, Case, 1925 .... 6900.00
Piguet, 33 Jewel, 18K Gold, Silver Matte Dial, Arabic Numerals, 1985 .... 3450.00
Rolex, 17 Jewel, Brown Dial, White Baton Hands, Arabic Numerals, 1950, 15 In. 6325.00
Rolex, 2-Tone Gold, Circular Nickel Lever Movement, 1924 .... 2587.00
Rolex, Cellini, 19 Jewel, Red Enamel Dial, Gold Roman Numerals, 1985 .... 2530.00

Rolex, Explorer, Screw-Down Crown, Silver Matte Dial, Baton Numerals, 1965 .... 1495.00
Rolex, Oyster Perpetual, 25 Jewel, 18K Pink Gold, Silver Matte Dial, 1960 .... 2990.00
Rolex, Oyster Perpetual, Champagne Matte Dial, Gold Textured Bezel, Case, 1970 ...... 2587.00
Rolex, Oyster, 18K Gold, Champagne Matte Dial, Baton Numerals, 1980 .... 4600.00
Rolex, Oyster, 18K Gold, Screw-Down Crown, Champagne Matte Dial, 1975 .... 4600.00
Rolex, Oyster, 18K Gold, Screw-Down Crown, Champagne Matte Dial, 1980 .... 3450.00
Rolex, Oyster, 18K Gold, Silver Textured Dial, Baton Numerals, 1955 .... 4025.00
Rolex, Oyster, 18K Pink Gold, Silver Matte Dial, Engine-Turned Bezel, 1955 .... 4600.00
Rolex, Oyster, 18K White Gold, Screw-Down Crown, Baton Numerals, 1975 .... 9200.00
Rolex, Oyster, 26 Jewel, 14K Gold, Screw-Down Crown, Silver Matte Dial, 1975 ...... 2185.00
Rolex, Oyster, 26 Jewel, 18K Gold, Silver Matte Dial, Baton Numerals, 1955 .... 3450.00
Rolex, Oyster, 26 Jewel, Black Matte Dial, Self-Winding, 1970 .... 3737.00
Rolex, Oyster, 26 Jewel, Champagne Matte Dial, Baton Numerals, 1980 .... 2300.00
Rolex, Oyster, 26 Jewel, Nickel Lever Movement, Champagne Matte Dial, 1980 ...... 2300.00
Rolex, Oyster, 26 Jewel, Pink Matte Dial, Baton Numerals, Self-Winding, 1970 .... 3450.00
Rolex, Oyster, 26 Jewel, Screw-Down Crown, Brown Matte Dial, 1988 .... 2185.00
Rolex, Oyster, 26 Jewel, Screw-Down Crown, Champagne Matte Dial, 1985 .... 8625.00
Rolex, Oyster, 26 Jewel, Screw-Down Crown, White Matte Dial, 1975 .... 4600.00
Rolex, Oyster, 27 Jewel, Screw-Down Crown, Blue Matte Dial, 1988 .... 2300.00
Rolex, Oyster, 27 Jewel, Screw-Down Crown, Champagne Matte Dial, 1986 .... 2070.00
Rolex, Oyster, 29 Jewel, Screw-Down Crown, White Matte Dial, 1988 .... 2875.00
Rolex, Oyster, Screw-Down Crown, Black Matte Dial, Triangular Numerals, 1945 ...... 8050.00
Rolex, Oyster, Screw-Down Crown, Black Matte Dial, Triangular Numerals, 1983 ...... 2875.00
Rolex, Oyster, Screw-Down Crown, Champagne Matte Dial, 1945 .... 1610.00
Rolex, Oyster, Screw-Down Crown, Pink Matte Dial, Baton Numerals, 1960 .... 3162.00
Rolex, Oyster, Screw-Down Crown, Silver Matte Dial, Mappin, 1940 .... 5175.00
Rolex, Oyster, Silver Matte Dial, Triangular Baton Numerals, 1955 .... 9200.00
Rolex, Precision, 10 Jewel, 18K Pink Gold, Ball Form, Silver Matte Dial 3160.00
Rolex, Woman's, Ball-Form Bracelet, 18K Pink Gold, 10 Jewel, 1945 .... 3160.00
Sarcar Geneve, Silver Dial, Brown Leather Strap, 18K White Gold 251.00
Tissot, 17 Jewel, Black Arabic Numerals, Lozenge Hands, 1940 .... 863.00
Universal, 18K Pink Gold, Gilt Lever Movement, Arabic Numerals 3450.00
Universal, Day, Date, Month, Moon Phase, 18K Gold 1350.00
Universal, Woman's, 18K Gold, 18K Gold Strap 470.00
Vacheron & Constantin, 17 Jewel, 18K Gold, Black Textured Dial, Square, 1945 ...... 3162.00
Vacheron & Constantin, 17 Jewel, 18K Gold, Seconds Dial, Box, c.1953 .... 2310.00
Vacheron & Constantin, 17 Jewel, 18K Gold, Silver Matte Dial, Baton Numeral 2300.00
Vacheron & Constantin, 17 Jewel, Silver Matte Dial, Platinum, Curved Lugs 5520.00
Vacheron & Constantin, 18 Jewel, 18K Pink Gold, Champagne Matte Dial, 1950 ...... 2587.00
Vacheron & Constantin, 18K Gold, Silver Matte Dial, Roman Numerals, 1945 .... 2300.00
Vacheron & Constantin, 18K Gold, Silver Matte Dial, Roman Numerals, 1960 .... 3450.00
Vacheron & Constantin, 18K Pink Gold, Champagne Matte Dial, 1945 .... 9200.00
Vacheron & Constantin, 18K Pink Gold, Silver Matte Dial, Square Case, 1950 .... 3220.00
Vacheron & Constantin, Silvertone Dial, Leather Strap, 14K Gold 4025.00
Vixa, 17 Jewel, Anti-Magnetic, Black Arabic Numerals, Auxiliary Dial, 1950 .... 863.00
Waltham, 25 Jewel, Round Case, Automatic, Stainless Steel 50.00
Waltham, Riverside Movement, 21 Jewel, 14K Gold, Silver Dial 155.00
Westfield, Slimline, Gold Filled, White Face, Leather & Metal Band, 1930s 65.00
Woman's, 14K Gold, Diamonds, Rubies, Retro Design 575.00
Woman's, 14K White Gold, Florentine Finish, Case 230.00
Woman's, 17 Jewel, 14K Yellow Gold, Silvertone Dial, Black Arabic Numerals 489.00
Woman's, 18K Gold, White Matte Dial, Baton Numerals, Circular Case, 1990 .... 2875.00
Woman's, 18K Yellow Gold, Black Dial, Onyx Crown, Leather Band 315.00
Woman's, 18K Yellow Gold, Black Onyx Dial, Bark Finish Band 1380.00
Woman's, Silver Matte Dial, 18K 2-Tone Gold, Baton Numerals, Case, 1950 .... 2875.00

YELLOWWARE is a heavy earthenware made of a yellowish clay. It varies in color from light yellow to orange-yellow. Many nineteenth- and twentieth-century kitchen bowls and jugs were made of yellowware. It was made in England and in the United States. Another form of pottery that is sometimes classed as yellowware is listed in this book in the Mocha category.

    Ashtray, Panama Hats For Horses, Transfer Of Horse Wearing Hat 95.00

Bank, Pear Form, 4 In. 55.00
Bowl, Blue Sponging, Spout, Wooden Handle, Wire Bail, 9 x 5 In. 55.00
Bowl, Spongeware Band, Blue, White, Crow's Foot, 13 1/2 In. 175.00
Butter, Cover, Blue Sponging, Gold Trim, Insert, 5 1/4 In. 55.00
Butter Tub, Cover, Brown & White Stripes, c.1880, 4 1/2 In. 132.00
Butter Tub, Cover, Brown Sponging 44.00
Butter Tub, White Sanded Exterior, Blue Bands 385.00
Casserole, Cover, Blue Band 380.00
Chamber Pot, No Decoration 75.00
Chamber Pot, White Band, Miniature 22.00
Crock, Salt, Brown & Gray Sponging, Hinged Wooden Lid, Gilt Word Salt, 6 In. 137.00
Cup & Saucer, Brushed Design 450.00
Ewer, Pewter Cover, Molded Battle Scenes, Nov. 1st, 1839, 7 3/8 In. 165.00
Figurine, Cat, Seated, Dark Amber Brown Glaze, 12 In. 1265.00
Figurine, Dog, Seated, 9 3/8 In. 1870.00
Figurine, Dog, Seated, Brown Glaze, 10 3/4 In. 330.00
Figurine, Girl Holding Ducks, Sitting By Box & Bucket, Gilt Trim, 9 x 6 x 5 In. 230.00
Humidor, Deer Heads, Branches, Nesting Eagle On Lid, Signed K&E 66, 9 1/4 In. 200.00
Mixing Bowl, 2 White Bands, 2 Brownish Orange Bands, 5 1/4 x 11 1/2 In. 80.00
Mixing Bowl, 3 White Bands, 2 Brown & Orange Bands, 7 1/2 x 16 1/2 In. 198.00
Mixing Bowl, Green & Brown Sponge Decoration, 3 x 7 In. 80.00
Mixing Bowl, Paneled Sides & Rim, Late 19th Century, 4 x 8 In. 12.00
Mixing Bowl, Pink & Blue Stripes, 12 1/4 In. 40.00
Mug, Applied Classical Design, England, 1825, Large 925.00
Mug, Barrel Shape, Tan & Blue Sponging, 4 1/2 In. 60.00
Mug, Brown, White Bands, 3 1/4 & 3 3/4 In., Pair 240.00
Mug, Farming & Hunting Design, Strap Handle, H. & P. Pennell, 1825, 5 1/8 In. 850.00
Pie Plate, Blue & Brown, Raised Pointed Arrow Design, 1 3/4 x 9 1/2 In. 95.00
Pitcher, Blue & White Stripes, Ribbed Handle With Leaf, 5 1/4 In. 357.00
Pitcher, Green & Brown Mottled Design, 5 1/2 In. 160.00
Pitcher, Indian Chief, Waffled Ground, Green & Buff, 8 3/8 In. 325.00
Pitcher, Sponging, Brown, Green & Black, 6 7/8 In. 165.00
Plate, Scalloped Rim, Brown Sponging, England, 9 In., Pair 440.00
Tray, Country Scene Transfer, Floral, Reticulated Border, 9 In. 300.00
Vase, Pilgrim & Island Scenes, c.1900, 8 In. 145.00

ZANE Pottery was founded in 1921 by Adam Reed and Harry McClelland in South Zanesville, Ohio, at the old Peters and Reed Building. Zane pottery is very similar to Peters and Reed pottery, but it is usually marked. The factory was sold in 1941 to Lawton Gonder.

Vase, Leaf Design, 4 3/4 In., Pair 175.00

ZSOLNAY pottery was made in Hungary after 1862 and was characterized by Persian, Art Nouveau, or Hungarian motifs. A series of new Zsolnay figurines with green-gold luster finish is available in many shops today. Early Zsolnay was not marked, but by 1878 the tower trademark was used.

Basket, Egg Shape, Reticulated, Yellow, Blue & Pink, 6 1/2 x 8 1/2 In. 795.00
Bowl, Gold, Blue Iridescent, Squat Circular Form, 3 In. 69.00
Bowl, White Reserves Of Garden Party, Boat Shape, Signed, 21 1/2 In. 440.00
Dish, 3 Molded Crows & Pond, 6 3/4 In. 45.00
Dish, Figural, Dove Form With Snail, Signed, 5 x 11 In. 715.00
Figurine, Fish, 7 1/2 In., Pair 100.00
Figurine, Monk, Sitting On Bench, 6 x 6 In. 750.00
Figurine, Partially Clad Female, Reclining, Green, Gold, Pink Luster Glaze, 10 In. 990.00
Inkwell, Iridescent Green Glaze, Orange Eyes, 7 1/4 x 9 In. 395.00
Pitcher, Cover, Flowers & Leaves, 20th Century, 12 1/4 In. 402.00
Pitcher, Molded Maidens On Sides, 8 In. 50.00
Vase, Caravan Of Men On Camels, Carrying Guns & Spears, c.1910, 8 In. 2300.00
Vase, Draped Woman At Shoulder Of Vase, Green, Blue Metallic Glaze, 9 In. 660.00
Vase, Floral Design, Overall Red, Tan, Gold Iridescent, Signed, 8 In. 1210.00
Vase, Ruffled Rim, 2 Irregular Handles, Green Iridescent, 8 1/2 In. 57.00

INDEX

This index is computer-generated, making it as complete as possible. References in uppercase type are category listings. Those in lowercase letters refer to additional pages where the piece can be found. There is also an internal cross-referencing system used in the main part of the book, so if you look for a Kewpie doll in the Doll category, you will be told it is in its own category. There is additional information at the end of many paragraphs about where to find prices of pieces similar to yours.

THE LABEL MADE ME BUY IT:
FROM AUNT JEMIMA TO ZONKERS —
THE BEST-DRESSED BOXES, BOTTLES, AND
CANS FROM THE PAST

Visually stunning and in full color, *The Label Made Me Buy It* is filled with photos of advertising labels, one of today's most popular paper collectibles. Discover the history of the food companies that used the labels and the printers who made them. Learn the clues you need to date your labels, and why food companies used buildings, airplanes, or long-dead politicians to sell their products. **0-609-6168-7 224 pages/$40.00 hardcover**

KOVELS' AMERICAN ART POTTERY
Hundreds of superb color photographs of pottery, rare historical photos of artists and factories, 1,000 illustrations of artist and factory marks. Art pottery firms listed with detailed history, makers, marks, dates, lines of pottery. Included are Rookwood, Roseville, Weller, Grueby, Ohr, Fulper, and many less well-known pottery and tile factories. Extensive bibliography, complete index. **0-517-8012-8 336 pages/$60.00 hardcover**

KOVELS' NEW DICTIONARY OF MARKS —
POTTERY AND PORCELAIN: 1850 TO THE PRESENT

More than 3,500 marks for 19th- and 20th-century American, European, and Oriental pottery and porcelain illustrated. Factory dates, locations, other needed information listed. Marks sorted by shape. Special section on date letter codes and factory "family trees."
0-517-55914-5
304 pages/$19.00 hardcover

KOVELS' DICTIONARY OF MARKS —
POTTERY AND PORCELAIN: 1650 — 1850
The best-selling guide to 5,000 marks on American and European pottery and porcelain made from 1580 to 1880. Marks are sorted by shape to make this an easy book for beginners. **0-517-70137-5 288 pages/$17.00 hardcover**

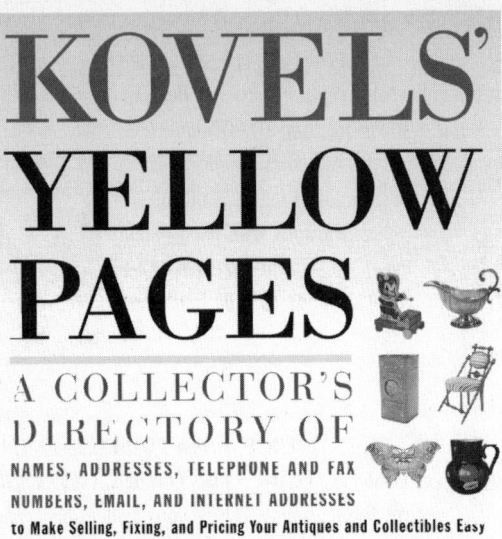

KOVELS' YELLOW PAGES

A COLLECTOR'S DIRECTORY OF

NAMES, ADDRESSES, TELEPHONE AND FAX NUMBERS, EMAIL, AND INTERNET ADDRESSES

to Make Selling, Fixing, and Pricing Your Antiques and Collectibles Easy

What, When, Where & How to Sell or Fix Your Collectibles • Buying & Selling by Mail, Phone, or Internet • Pricing Repair Services • Sources for Parts • Matching Services • Conservation & Restoration Supplies • Clubs & Publications • Price Guides • Reference Books • Appraisers • Auction Houses • Displaying Collectibles

KOVELS' YELLOW PAGES:
A COLLECTOR'S DIRECTORY OF NAMES, ADDRESSES, TELEPHONE AND FAX NUMBERS, E-MAIL, AND INTERNET ADDRESSES TO MAKE SELLING, FIXING, AND PRICING YOUR ANTIQUES AND COLLECTIBLES EASY

Kovels' Yellow Pages guides collectors to the help they need—whether they want to sell Grandma's desk, fix its sticky drawers, or refinish its water-stained surface. *Kovels' Yellow Pages* points collectors to the people who repair or restore antiques and collectibles, who sell hard-to-find parts and supplies, who appraise antiques, who sell at auctions, and who provide matching services for china, crystal, and silver. Entries include addresses, telephone and fax numbers, e-mail addresses, and Internet sites. This edition of one of the Kovels' favorite books is an A-to-Z directory of more than 100 categories of antiques and collectibles, from advertising and dishes to furniture and fountain pens. Every category is chock-full of expert advice and insider tips on selling and fixing antiques and collectibles, including lists of useful books and current collector publications that can be of even more help. *Kovels' Yellow Pages* provides coast-to-coast coverage, bringing collectors into contact with experts they might not find in their area. It's a practical and essential resource for experienced and rookie collectors, no matter where they live.

0-609-80417-0   304 pages/$18.00 paperback

KOVELS' DEPRESSION GLASS AND DINNERWARE
PRICE LIST, 6TH EDITION

Two books in one. Identifies hundreds of patterns, and prices more than 8,000 pieces of Depression glass and dinnerware made from the 1920s to the 1980s. More than 400 photographs and drawings in color and black and white. Includes histories of manufacturers, factory marks, cross-references, information on reproductions, bibliographies for both glass and dinnerware, and lists of clubs and publications. Plus tips on buying, repairing, storing, and insuring your treasures, and a 16-page color insert on the history of glass and ceramic dinnerware.

0-609-80310-7   240 pages/$16.00 paperback

KOVELS' BOTTLES
PRICE LIST, 11TH EDITION

Prices of more than 12,000 old and modern bottles and hundreds of photographs. The most comprehensive book of its kind. More than 80 categories of bottles, including figurals, bitters, flasks, ink, beer, milk, soda, perfume, medicine, Avon, Jim Beam, Ezra Brooks, and others. Company histories; lists of bottle clubs, publications, and auction houses; extensive bibliography. Special 16-page full-color insert on recent bottle sales and a helpful picture dictionary of bottle shapes.

0-609-80312-3   288 pages/$16 paperback

K O V E L S

SEND ORDERS & INQUIRIES TO: **CROWN PUBLISHERS**
c/o RANDOM HOUSE, 400 HAHN ROAD, WESTMINSTER, MD 21157
    ATTN: ORDER DEPARTMENT
WEB SITE: www.randomhouse.com

Sales & Title Information:
1-800-733-3000
For order entry:
FAX# 1-800-659-2436

NAME_____

ADDRESS _____

CITY & STATE _____ ZIP_____

Please send me the following books:

ITEM NO.	QTY.	TITLE	PRICE	TOTAL
0-609-80471-5	___	Kovels' Antiques & Collectibles Price List — 32nd Edition	PAPER $15.95	_____
0-517-58012-8	___	Kovels' American Art Pottery: The Collector's Guide to Makers, Marks, and Factory Histories	HARDCOVER $60.00	_____
0-517-54668-X	___	American Country Furniture 1780 –1875	PAPER $16.95	_____
0-517-70137-5	___	Dictionary of Marks—Pottery and Porcelain	HARDCOVER $17.00	_____
0-517-55914-5	___	Kovels' New Dictionary of Marks	HARDCOVER $19.00	_____
0-517-56882-9	___	Kovels' American Silver Marks	HARDCOVER $40.00	_____
0-609-80312-3	___	Kovels' Bottles Price List—11th Edition	PAPER $16.00	_____
0-609-80310-7	___	Kovels' Depression Glass & Dinnerware Price List — 6th Edition	PAPER $16.00	_____
0-517-57806-9	___	Kovels' Know Your Antiques, Revised and Updated	PAPER $16.00	_____
0-517-58840-4	___	Kovels' Know Your Collectibles Updated	PAPER $16.00	_____
0-517-88381-3	___	Kovels' Quick Tips: 799 Helpful Hints on How to Care for Your Collectibles	PAPER $12.00	_____
0-609-60168-7	___	The Label Made Me Buy It: From Aunt Jemima to Zonkers	HARDCOVER $40.00	_____
0-609-80417-0	___	Kovels' Yellow Pages: A Collector's Directory of Names, Addresses, Telephone and Fax Numbers, E-Mail, and Internet Addresses to Make Selling, Fixing, and Pricing Your Antiques and Collectibles Easy	PAPER $18.00	_____
	___	TOTAL ITEMS	TOTAL RETAIL VALUE	_____

CHECK OR MONEY ORDER ENCLOSED
MADE PAYABLE TO CROWN PUBLISHERS, INC.
or telephone 1-800-733-3000
(No cash or stamps, please)

Shipping & Handling Charge
$2.00 for one book;
50¢ for each additional book.
Please add applicable sales tax._____

CHARGE: ☐ Master Card ☐ Visa ☐ American Express
Account Number (include all digits) Expires: MO.____ YR.____

TOTAL AMOUNT DUE   _____

_____

PRICES SUBJECT TO CHANGE WITHOUT
NOTICE. If a more recent edition of a price
list has been published at the same price, it
will be sent instead of the old edition.

Thank you for your order

_____
Signature